CIVIL PROCEDURE

CASES AND MATERIALS

Eighth Edition

By

John J. Cound
Professor of Law
University of Minnesota

Jack H. Friedenthal
Freda H. Alverson Professor of Law
The George Washington University Law School

Arthur R. Miller
Bruce Bromley Professor of Law
Harvard University

John E. Sexton
Dean and Professor of Law
New York University

AMERICAN CASEBOOK SERIES®

WEST GROUP

A THOMSON COMPANY

ST. PAUL, MINN., 2001

American Casebook Series, and the West Group symbol
are registered trademarks used herein under license.

COPYRIGHT © 1968, 1974, 1980, 1985, 1989 COUND, FRIEDENTHAL, MILLER & SEXTON

COPYRIGHT © 1993 WEST PUBLISHING CO.

COPYRIGHT © 1997 WEST GROUP

COPYRIGHT © 2001 By WEST GROUP
     610 Opperman Drive
     P.O. Box 64526
     St. Paul, MN 55164–0526
     1–800–328–9352

All rights reserved
Printed in the United States of America

ISBN 0–314–25329–7

*TEXT IS PRINTED ON 10% POST
CONSUMER RECYCLED PAPER*

Preface

This Eighth Edition, which has been prepared by Jack H. Friedenthal, Arthur R. Miller, and John E. Sexton, has had the benefit of many comments of colleagues from the large number of schools in which the first seven editions have been used. These responses have been gratifying in confirming our own conclusion that the book continues to be a highly successful teaching tool, regardless of the precise form of the civil procedure course being taught or of the specific material covered. As a result, the Eighth Edition preserves the same basic format and much of the material included in the earlier editions.

A new edition cannot be justified merely to reflect minor changes in the law or to substitute newer material of the same substance as the old. There have, however, been some significant developments in a number of areas of procedure that give rise to intellectually stimulating questions and policy considerations that require inclusion in a contemporary casebook. The effect of emerging technological changes—particularly the Internet—on the processes of litigation is both fascinating and important knowledge for future attorneys. Supreme Court pronouncements as to the advancement and limitations of the *Erie* doctrine are excellent topics for classroom discussions. Refinements of the Federal Rules regarding pretrial discovery are significant and thought-provoking. Cases governing the direction and future of class actions are, to say the least, fascinating topics for analysis. The areas of the book covering these and other matters that have been affected by new rules, cases, and statutes have been carefully reworked. New sections have been added where appropriate and, of course, introductory material, case notes, and citations to treatises, law review articles, and cases have been revised and updated.

We have looked for modern cases in which the facts are interesting, the conflicting policies seem to be in equipoise, or in which the context has extrinsic fascination, rather than for cases whose opinions offer tight little monographs on various aspects of procedure. There can be no question that a student's preparation and participation in class discussion frequently are in direct proportion to the extent to which the materials are interesting and involving. We believe that the study of civil procedure can and should be one of the most enjoyable courses taught in law school and that is true for the instructor as well as the students.

The notes and questions that follow nearly every principal case have been designed primarily to encourage deeper analysis of the problems raised in the principal cases rather than to fill the student with additional detail. At the same time, we have provided sufficient and selective references to secondary sources for the student who wishes to look deeper into a subject.

We have not attempted to construct a "hard" book, but rather an enlightening and enjoyable one. Civil procedure is sufficiently mysterious, especially to beginning law students, that its ability to challenge operates best when presented in a clear and simple environment. The danger is not in patronizing students, but of losing them. In the textual survey at the beginning of Chapter One, in the long note on the operation of the class-action device in Chapter Ten, as well as in the briefer introductions to other sections of the book, we have tried to tell students where they are going. Through extensive cross-referencing and questions we have tried to require them to review where they have been and constantly to gain greater prospective on the ways in which the various aspect of procedure fit together.

We have not concentrated on the law of any one jurisdiction, although there is substantial emphasis on the operation of the Federal Rules of Civil Procedure, which serve as a model and focal point for serious discussion and implementation of procedural reform in a large majority of state courts. In general the book operates on a comparative basis, except in contexts in which an in-depth exploration of a single system has greater utility.

We have attempted to strike a balance between exploring underlying philosophical problems and analyzing day-to-day matters that arise frequently in office practice or in the courts. Our theory is that a mixture of both is necessary to give students a comprehensive understanding of procedure and its significance in the development of the law. Thus they must learn why, even today, after so many years of study, revision, and reform, major proposals for alteration of adjective law are still being made, and, undoubtedly, will continue to be made in the years to come. In addition, significant use has been made of historical material, not only when it is directly relevant to today's system, as in the study of the right to jury trial, but also in contexts in which it is necessary for a true grasp of the basic problems.

Because courses in civil procedure vary greatly as to the hours allotted, the extent to which they are mandatory or optional, and the law school year or years when students are expected to enroll in them, the materials in this edition are designed for maximum flexibility. The cases and subjects covered have been selected primarily for a comprehensive, year-long course beginning in the first term of the law student's first year; yet the book may easily be divided into two or more quite distinct subjects to be taught as preliminary or advanced courses.

The first chapter of this casebook sets forth a basic, textual statement of a procedural system's framework, without which an understanding of any particular part of the system is difficult, if not impossible. This initial discussion defines those procedural terms necessary for comprehending legal opinions, whether they deal with procedural or substantive matters. This is an important function of a procedure course, especially when it forms part of the curriculum in a student's first year of law school. The textual analysis can be assigned for study with little or no classroom discussion. It is followed by a series of illustrative cases designed to raise the basic problems of a procedural system, to illustrate the interplay among its various aspects, and to highlight many of the points made in the initial text. An effort has been made to select cases that can be handled with relative dispatch so that the introduction does not become a de facto study of the entire course. In general, Chapter One is intended to let students form some idea as to the nature of the litigation "forest" before asking them to master any of its "trees." Teachers of short or advanced courses may choose to omit it.

After the first chapter, the structure of the book proceeds in a chronological fashion. The authors believe that this is the most logical way to teach civil procedure because it permits students to understand how cases begin, develop, and mature. Furthermore, by studying personal and subject-matter jurisdiction and the materials dealing with the history of civil procedure before subjects such as pleading, joinder, and discovery, first year students are given "breathing time" in which to absorb enough substantive law in courses such as torts, contracts, and property to enable them to comprehend such matters as "pleading a cause of action," "alleging contributory negligence," and "establishing the existence of joint and several interests." Finally, we believe that despite its conceptual difficulty, personal jurisdiction is a much more teachable and exhilarating introduction to civil procedure than would be pleading and joinder.

The chapters on jurisdiction include an extensive treatment of the federal courts. An investigation of a single system seems to be the best way to impress students with the significance attached by courts to the concept of jurisdiction over the subject matter. The length of this material is greater than is customary in a civil procedure book, but parts of it may readily be treated at the end of the course or left for consideration in an advanced course. We believe, however, that without a working knowledge of such concepts as diversity of citizenship and supplemental jurisdiction, the procedural ramifications of the *Erie* doctrine and such indisputably procedural problems as joinder cannot properly be understood.

We have determined that it is important to include a section on common-law pleading, the forms of action, equity, and the nineteenth century reforms (although many procedure casebooks do not do so). The background provided is important, if for no other reason, in order for students to understand the right to jury trial and the concept of a claim. Nevertheless we are cognizant of time constraints that may require the chapter to be skipped and its basic substance to be provided by lecture. Therefore the chapter on modern pleading that follows has been planned as a choate whole, and does not require coverage of the earlier background material.

As has been the case with all of the past editions, the materials in this volume refer to and are augmented by a Supplement, which contains not only the federal statutes and rules governing procedure, as is traditional, but also comparative state provisions. A number of other materials, such as Advisory Committee notes, proposed rule alterations, and local court rules, are also included. Thus at a glance students are able to see different solutions put forth for particular procedural problems and are induced to explore reasons why one rule has not been universally acclaimed as "superior" and adopted by all jurisdictions. Use of the Supplement has the added advantage of permitting teachers and students to keep abreast of interesting amendments to oft-changing procedural statutes and rules without constant revision of the casebook itself.

All teachers of civil procedure are well aware of how difficult it is for students to grapple with problems in the abstract; for example they may have only a vague notion of just how a case proceeds and what a pleading or motion looks like. The Supplement therefore also contains a litigation timechart and an illustrative problem, showing how a case develops in practice and samples of the documents that actually might have formed a portion of the record, It is important to note that these samples are not designed as models to be emulated. To the contrary, they often contain defects intended to induce students to criticize them in light of knowledge they have obtained from the cases and classroom discussion.

The cases and excerpts from other materials obviously have been carefully and extensively edited in order to shorten them and clarify issues for discussion. With a few exceptions, the materials from the Seventh Edition have not been significantly shortened in preparing the Eighth Edition; we see no reason to alter what has been working well. With regard to footnotes, the same numbering appears in the casebook as appears in the original sources; our footnotes are indicated by letters.

———————

The authors are deeply grateful to a host of people who have assisted us in the preparation of this volume, the earlier editions, and the Supplements. Among our students deserving special mention for the aid they have provided in preparing one or more editions of the book are Prudence Beatty Abram, Sam L. Abram, Kim Barry, Richard B. Bernstein, (Professor) Barry B. Boyer, (Professor) Michael Broyde, William M. Burns, Bertram Carp, (Professor) Sanford Caust-Ellenbogen, Jeffrey J. Chapman, Daniel Chazin, Tan Yee Cheung, Adam S. Cohen, Stephanie Cohen, Steven Cohen, Diane Costa, David Drueding, Gary Eisenberg, Lisa Fair, (Judge) Raymond Fisher, Grant H. Franks, Stacy Gershwind, Lisa E. Goldberg, Robert H. Goldman, Steven F. Goldman, Ashley K. Goodale, Kevin A. Griffin, Edward Hartnett, Wendy B. Jacobs, (Professor) Joe J. Kalo, (Dean) Mary Kay Kane, Lonnie Keene, Daniel Laguardia, Fredrick W. Lambert, Judyann M. Lee, Christopher Mahon, Shirin Malkani, Maureen P. Manning, (Professor) John J. McGonagle, Matthew McGrath, Kiran H. Mehta, Franklin N. Meyer, Gary Meyerhoff, Jennifer Nevins, Marcy Oppenheimer, Jennifer Pariser, Dawn A. Pederson, Kate Elizabeth Phillips, Norman A. Platt, Martin C. Recchuite, Christopher Reich, James E. Rossman, Beth A. Rotman, Gregory S. Schmolka, Marc Schuback, (Professor) Linda J. Silberman, Donna Silverberg, (Professor) William Slomanson, Roger D. Smith, David A. Stein, Brian A. Stern, Mara E. Trager, Jacqueline Veit, (Professor) Michael Vitiello, and Gail Zweig. A special thanks to Jo Anne Friedenthal, Dan Evans, and Stephen Wagner for their invaluable work on this volume and prior editions.

Finally, we sincerely thank our many colleagues across the legal community for the countless excellent suggestions they have offered. Their contributions have been instrumental in the preparation of this Eighth Edition.

J.H.F
A.R.M.
J.E.S.

June, 2001

Summary of Contents

*

Table of Contents

*

Table of Cases

The principal cases are in bold type. Cases cited or discussed in the text are roman type. References are to pages. Cases cited in principal cases and within other quoted materials are not included.

Vevelstad v. Flynn, 16 Alaska 83, 230 F.2d 695 (9th Cir.1956), 566

Vicom, Inc. v. Harbridge Merchant Services, Inc., 20 F.3d 771 (7th Cir.1994), 531

Victor Talking Mach. Co. v. George, 105 F.2d 697 (3rd Cir.1939), 1186

Virginia, Commonwealth of v. Westinghouse Elec. Corp., 542 F.2d 214 (4th Cir.1976), 687

Vitale v. Elliott, 120 R.I. 328, 387 A.2d 1379 (R.I.1978), 951

Vizzini v. Ford Motor Co., 569 F.2d 754 (3rd Cir.1977), 1107

Volkswagenwerk Aktiengesellschaft v. Schlunk, 486 U.S. 694, 108 S.Ct. 2104, 100 L.Ed.2d 722 (1988), 204

Von Dunser v. Aronoff, 915 F.2d 1071 (6th Cir.1990), 334

Vons Companies, Inc. v. Seabest Foods, Inc., 58 Cal.Rptr.2d 899, 926 P.2d 1085 (Cal.1996), 140

Wainwright v. Kraftco Corp., 54 F.R.D. 532 (N.D.Ga.1972), 710

Waldon v. Marshall, Y.B.Mich. 43 Ed. 3, f. 33, pl. 38, p. 486

Walgrave v. Ogden, 74 Eng.Rep. 205 (K.B. 1590), 485

Walker v. Armco Steel Corp., 446 U.S. 740, 100 S.Ct. 1978, 64 L.Ed.2d 659 (1980), 221, **402,** 406, 407, 411

Walker v. City of Hutchinson, Kan., 352 U.S. 112, 77 S.Ct. 200, 1 L.Ed.2d 178 (1956), 198

Walker v. Holiday Lanes, Inc., 196 Kan. 513, 413 P.2d 63 (Kan.1966), 1083

Walker v. Liggett Group, Inc., 175 F.R.D. 226 (S.D.W.Va.1997), 578, 760

Walker v. Sauvinet, 92 U.S. 90, 2 Otto 90, 23 L.Ed. 678 (1875), 956

Wallace v. Hanover Ins. Co. of New York, 164 So.2d 111 (La.App. 1 Cir.1964), 580

Wallace Hardware Co., Inc. v. Abrams, 223 F.3d 382 (6th Cir.2000), 574

Wallis v. Pan Am. Petroleum Corp., 384 U.S. 63, 86 S.Ct. 1301, 16 L.Ed.2d 369 (1966), 452

Walters v. Shari Music Pub. Corp., 193 F.Supp. 307 (S.D.N.Y.1961), 303

Ward v. Board of County Com'rs of Love County, Okl., 253 U.S. 17, 40 S.Ct. 419, 64 L.Ed. 751 (1920), 455

Ward v. Taggart, 51 Cal.2d 736, 336 P.2d 534 (Cal.1959), 1198

Warner v. Pacific Tel. & Tel. Co., 121 Cal. App.2d 497, 263 P.2d 465 (Cal.App. 2 Dist. 1953), 636

Washburn v. Moorman Mfg. Co., 25 F.Supp. 546 (S.D.Cal.1938), 518

Washington County v. Gunther, 452 U.S. 161, 101 S.Ct. 2242, 68 L.Ed.2d 751 (1981), 549

Washington Hosp. Center Nat. Rehabilitation Hosp. v. Collier, 947 F.2d 1498, 292 U.S.App.D.C. 129 (D.C.Cir.1991), 655

Washington Hospital Center v. Cheeks, 394 F.2d 964, 129 U.S.App.D.C. 339 (D.C.Cir. 1968), 846

Washington Nat. Trust Co. v. W.M. Dary Co., 116 Ariz. 171, 568 P.2d 1069 (Ariz.1977), 560

Waterman S.S. Corp. v. Ranis, 141 Misc.2d 772, 534 N.Y.S.2d 321 (N.Y.Sup.1988), 226

Watts v. Smith, 375 Mich. 120, 134 N.W.2d 194 (Mich.1965), 629

Webb v. Webb, 32 F.R.D. 615 (W.D.Mo.1963), 522

Weinstein, State ex rel. Smith v., 398 S.W.2d 41 (Mo.App.1965), 629

Wells v. Simonds Abrasive Co., 345 U.S. 514, 73 S.Ct. 856, 97 L.Ed. 1211 (1953), 258

Weng v. United States, 137 F.3d 709 (2nd Cir.1998), 201

West v. Conrail, 481 U.S. 35, 107 S.Ct. 1538, 95 L.Ed.2d 32 (1987), 221

Western Union Tel. Co. v. Commonwealth of Pa., by Gottlieb, 368 U.S. 71, 82 S.Ct. 199, 7 L.Ed.2d 139 (1961), 665

West Mifflin, Borough of v. Lancaster, 45 F.3d 780 (3rd Cir.1995), 318, 324, **325,** 331

Wetzel v. Liberty Mut. Ins. Co., 508 F.2d 239 (3rd Cir.1975), **725,** 731, 732, 734

Wharff v. Wharff, 244 Iowa 496, 56 N.W.2d 1 (Iowa 1952), 681, 682

White v. Halstead Industries, Inc., 750 F.Supp. 395 (E.D.Ark.1990), 268

Whitehead v. American Sec. & Trust Co., 285 F.2d 282, 109 U.S.App.D.C. 202 (D.C.Cir. 1960), 1198

Whitlock v. Salmon, 104 Nev. 24, 752 P.2d 210 (Nev.1988), 1027

Wichita and Affiliated Tribes of Oklahoma v. Hodel, 788 F.2d 765, 252 U.S.App.D.C. 140 (D.C.Cir.1986), 647

Wilko v. Swan, 346 U.S. 427, 74 S.Ct. 182, 98 L.Ed. 168 (1953), 1367

Will v. United States, 389 U.S. 90, 88 S.Ct. 269, 19 L.Ed.2d 305 (1967), 1172

Williams v. Board of County Com'rs of Unified Government of Wyandotte County and Kansas City, Kan., 192 F.R.D. 698 (D.Kan. 2000), 826

Williams v. Capital Transit Co., 215 F.2d 487, 94 U.S.App.D.C. 221 (D.C.Cir.1954), 212

Williams v. Florida, 399 U.S. 78, 90 S.Ct. 1893, 26 L.Ed.2d 446 (1970), 1015

Williams v. Holland, 131 Eng.Rep. 848 (C.P. 1833), 483

Williams v. Lane, 129 F.R.D. 636 (N.D.Ill. 1990), 747

Williams v. Thomas Jefferson University, 343 F.Supp. 1131 (E.D.Pa.1972), 811

Willy v. Coastal Corp., 503 U.S. 131, 112 S.Ct. 1076, 117 L.Ed.2d 280 (1992), 334

Wilmington Chemical Corp. v. Celebrezze, 229 F.Supp. 168 (N.D.Ill.1964), 1216

Wilson v. Moore & Associates, Inc., 564 F.2d 366 (9th Cir.1977), 950

Wilson v. Smith, 1833 WL 3080 (N.Y.Sup. 1833), 478

Wilver v. Fisher, 387 F.2d 66 (10th Cir.1967), 951

Wingerter v. Maryland Cas. Co., 313 F.2d 754 (5th Cir.1963), 1087

*

CIVIL PROCEDURE

CASES AND MATERIALS

*

Chapter 1

A SURVEY OF THE CIVIL ACTION

SECTION A. THE CONCERN AND CHARACTER OF CIVIL PROCEDURE

In our Anglo–American legal tradition, courts have been established to provide a decision "by an agent of state power, [of] a controversy existing between two individuals (or the State and an individual), by rational (not merely personal) considerations, purporting to rest on justice and law (i.e. the community's general sense of order)."[a] Although this definition is terribly inadequate and contains question-begging elements that need definition themselves, it provides a starting point for understanding our judicial system. It will suffice at this point if it helps you understand the following points: (1) The judicial process deals not with abstract questions or hypothetical situations but with actual controversies between real parties. (2) The community will direct its collective force to the resolution of these controversies. (3) This resolution proceeds not arbitrarily but according to some standards of general application. (4) These standards are applied in a proceeding that follows some fixed lines set out by a system of rules known as procedure.

In resolving the legal disputes they are presented, the courts will apply two types of law—*substantive* and *procedural*. Your other courses (such as Torts and Contracts) will deal with the substantive rights and duties that regulate the everyday relationships among individuals and between individuals and institutions. The substantive law also defines the standard of liability in a particular case. This course, by contrast, will explore the procedures used by the courts to resolve the disputes that are brought before them. Our focus will be on how attorneys frame their cases in order to bring them properly before a particular court, and how the case proceeds from its institution until a judgment is reached and enforced. We also will study the availability of appellate review and the scope and effect of any judgment that is entered.

You should not be fooled into thinking, however, that the line separating the substantive law from the procedural law is clear in every instance. Certainly a requirement that all papers filed with a particular court be on 8½″ 14″ paper is a procedural rule. Equally certain is that the elements of the law of assault and battery are substantive. But not every legal rule can be so easily classified. For example, a statute of limitations (which determines the

a. Wigmore, *The Judicial Function*, in *Science of Legal Method xxvi, xxviii (1917)*.

1

length of time a party has to sue on a claim) may appear at first glance to be purely procedural. But upon closer examination, it becomes clear that the length of a jurisdiction's statute of limitations is as much a product of public policy, and will affect the plaintiff's ability to recover as much as any purely "substantive" provision of the jurisdiction's law. As a student of civil procedure, you always should be aware of the substance-procedure dichotomy, but you also should remain wary of its rigid and unquestioned application.

This course deals with the procedural questions presented in *civil* suits; the aspects of *criminal* suits will not concern us. In analyzing questions of civil procedure, however, you should bear in mind the societal goals of civil suits as compared with those of criminal suits. The principal difference, of course, is that civil suits generally are initiated and litigated by private parties attempting to vindicate their legal rights vis-a-vis other private parties. The community thus is seeking to provide a method for resolving the disputes that arise out of the everyday interactions of private parties. Criminal suits, by contrast, are instituted and prosecuted by the government (on behalf of "the People") in an effort to punish those individuals whose conduct has violated the community's moral judgments as expressed in its penal law. Government involvement, however, is not always an indicator of a criminal suit since the government often is a party to civil suits, and can be either a plaintiff or a defendant.

The most distinctive element of our procedure for resolving legal controversies is the *adversary system*. The central feature of this system is the almost total responsibility placed on the parties to the controversy for beginning suit, for shaping the issues, and for producing evidence; the court takes almost no active part in these facets of the process; it does not do its own investigating, it rarely even asks a question. By contrast, the judicial systems in civil law countries employ the *inquisitorial system*. Under the inquisitorial model, the court conducts an active and independent inquiry into the merits of each case, which may include having the judge question and examine witnesses, as well as specifically ordering certain fact-finding.

In recent times, the trend in this country has been toward increasing the affirmative or active functions of the court. This is evidenced by the participation of judges in the settlement process, during the pretrial conference stage, and in the various management techniques by which courts are responding to complex modern litigation, such as massive class actions or suits involving the reorganization of entire industries, schools, or prison systems. Nonetheless, it cannot be doubted that in the United States the primary responsibility and control over almost all phases of the judicial process continue to reside in the parties.

The reasons for the prevalence of our adversary system are manifold, but four postulates are certainly among the most important: (1) A truer decision is reached as the result of a contest directed by interested parties. (2) The parties, who after all are the ones principally interested in the controversy's resolution, should bear the major burden of the time and energy required. (3) Although impartial investigation may be better when no final decision need be reached, setting up sides makes easier the type of yes-or-no decision that is thought to be necessary in a lawsuit. (4) Since resort to law has replaced the resort to force that characterized primitive ages, the atavistic instinct to do battle is better satisfied by a means of settling disputes that is very much in the hands of the parties.

When one reflects on the fact that the adversary system often means that victory will turn on considerations other than the justice or true merits of the cause, there is reason to believe that we have permitted it to assume an exaggerated place in our civil dispute resolution scheme. But the system remains and its presence will color every facet of this course. Full understanding of the materials in this book will require your constant attention to its existence as well as critical analysis of its shortcomings.

There is but one test of a good system of procedure: *Does it tend to lead to the just and efficient determination of legal controversies?* In this connection you must understand one thing: despite the fact that this course is only an introduction to procedure, you are not to assume that your function simply is to digest uncritically the law you read. Instead, this course will play an integral part in your process of learning to examine, to question, "to wash in cynical acid," each rule, each form, each principle you learn. But while doing so keep in mind that many, diverse, and complex are the aspects of both justice and efficiency.

SECTION B. AN OUTLINE OF THE PROCEDURE IN A CIVIL ACTION

The first step in a lawsuit strictly speaking is not a matter of law, certainly not a matter of the law of civil procedure. As already suggested, lawsuits do not begin themselves. Someone must first decide to sue someone else. If this decision is made intelligently, the person choosing to sue must have weighed several matters, among which at least three are basic.

A potential litigant obviously feels aggrieved or would not be thinking of a lawsuit. But he or she must further consider whether the grievance is one for which the law furnishes relief. There are a great many hurts a person may feel that the law will not redress. She is offended by the paint on her neighbor's house; he has worked for weeks to persuade a grocer to buy his brand of peas, and sees the sale go to a competitor; she has been holding a plot of ground for speculation expecting industry to move in and the area is zoned for residential use; he slips on a spot of grease in the county courthouse but the county is immune from suit. If the injury is among those not redressable by a court of law, litigation would be a fruitless and wasteful exercise.

Even if she concludes that the grievance is one for which the courts will grant relief, a potential litigant must consider the probability of winning a lawsuit. She must ask whether the person who has caused the injury can be found and brought into court; whether witnesses and documents will be available to support the claims being sued on; whether this proof will be believed; whether the potential adversary can justify its conduct or establish any defenses to the action; and whether an accurate assessment of the law can be made ahead of time.

Then, and perhaps most important of all, a potential litigant must consider whether what is won will be worth the time, the effort, and the expense it will cost, and must weigh against this the alternatives to suit, among them settlement, arbitration, self-help, and letting matters rest. What form will the relief take? Most frequently it will be restricted to a judgment for damages. If this is true, the potential litigant must decide whether the injury is one for which a monetary payment will be satisfactory. Assuming it is, will defendant be rich enough to pay? How difficult will a judgment be to collect? How expensive? Will the recovery be enough to pay the lawyer's fees and the other litigation expenses that undoubtedly will be incurred? Even in a context in which the court may grant specific relief—for example, an order directing the opposing party to do something or to stop doing something—will compliance by defendant be possible? Worthwhile? Sufficient? In the same vein, a potential litigant also must consider whether there are risks not directly tied to the suit: Will she acquire the reputation of a crank? Will he antagonize people whose goodwill he needs? Will the action publicize an error of judgment on her part or open her private affairs to public gaze?

Only after considerable thought has resolved these and similar questions will the prospective plaintiff be ready for the steps that follow. Let us now consider those steps in the light of a relatively uncluttered hypothetical case:

> Aikins, while crossing the street in front of her private home, was struck and seriously injured by an automobile driven by Beasley. On inquiry, Aikins found that the automobile was owned by Cecil and that Beasley apparently had been in Cecil's employ. Beasley was predictably without substantial assets and a judgment against him for Aikins' injuries promised little material compensation. But Cecil was wealthy, and Aikins was advised that if she could establish that Beasley had indeed been working for Cecil and had been negligent, she then could recover from Cecil. Aikins decided to sue Cecil for $80,000.

1. SELECTING A PROPER COURT

Aikins initially must determine in which court to bring the action. She probably will have some choice, but it will be a limited one. This is true because the court selected must have *jurisdiction over the subject matter* (that is, the constitution and statutes under which the court operates must have conferred upon it power to decide this type of case) and must also have *jurisdiction over the person* of Cecil (that is, Cecil must be subject or amenable to suit in the state in which the court is located).

Aikins probably will bring suit in a state court, for as we shall shortly see the subject-matter jurisdiction of the federal courts is severely limited. If the court organization of Aikins' state is typical, there will be courts of *original jurisdiction* in which cases are brought and tried, and one court of *appellate jurisdiction* that sits, with rare exceptions, only to review the decisions of lower courts. (In most states there will also be a group of intermediate courts of appellate jurisdiction.) The courts of original jurisdiction probably consist of one set of courts of *general jurisdiction* and several sets of courts of *inferior jurisdiction*. The courts of general jurisdiction are organized into districts comprising for the most part several counties, although the largest or most populous counties each may constitute single districts. These district courts hear cases of many kinds and are competent to grant every kind of relief, but in order to bring a case in one of them plaintiff must have a claim for more than a specific amount, perhaps five or ten thousand dollars. The courts of inferior jurisdiction will include municipal courts, whose jurisdiction resembles that of the district courts except that the claims they hear are of less importance; justice-of-the-peace courts, which hear very minor matters; and specialized tribunals such as the traffic courts. Since Aikins' injuries are quite serious and her claim correspondingly large, she will, if she sues in a state court, bring the action in one of the district courts.

The federal government of course also operates a system of courts. The principal federal courts are the United States District Courts, courts of original jurisdiction of which there is at least one in every state; the thirteen United States Courts of Appeals, each of which reviews the decisions of federal district courts in the several states within its circuit (with the exception of the Courts of Appeals for the District of Columbia Circuit and the Federal Circuit); and the Supreme Court of the United States, which not only reviews the decisions of federal courts but also reviews decisions of state courts that turn on an issue of federal law.

The jurisdiction over the subject-matter of the United States District Courts extends to many, but by no means all, cases involving federal law, and also to many cases, similar to Aikins', that do not involve federal law; the latter are cases in which there is *diversity of citizenship* (the parties are citizens of different states or one of them is a citizen of a foreign country) and the required *amount in controversy* (more than $75,000) is at stake. Diversity jurisdiction, in common with most of the federal courts' jurisdiction, is not *exclusive;* the state courts also are competent to hear these cases. But if Cecil is not a citizen of Aikins' state, Aikins may bring an action for $80,000 in a federal court. Indeed, in these circumstances, if Aikins sued Cecil in a state court in Aikins' home state Cecil could *remove* the action from the state court in which it was commenced to the federal district court in that state.[b]

It is not enough that the court selected by Aikins has jurisdiction over the subject-matter, however. That court, whether state or federal, must be one in which Cecil can be required to appear. This generally means that Cecil must reside or be found in the state in which the court sits. But the restrictions on a court's jurisdiction over the person have diminished in recent decades, and if Cecil is not present in Aikins' state but he directed Beasley to drive there, Aikins probably will be able to bring the action in that state. (Even in the event that these facts cannot be established, and Cecil cannot be found in Aikins' state, it may be possible to sue him there, if he owns property in that state, but the judgment will be limited to the value of that property.)

Not every court that has jurisdiction over the subject-matter and jurisdiction over the person of defendant will hear a case. It also is necessary that an action be brought in a court having proper *venue.* Thus, although every court in Aikins' state could assert personal jurisdiction over Cecil if he was within its boundaries, that state's statutes typically will provide that the case should be brought in a court whose district includes the county in which either Aikins or Cecil lives. Similarly, if Aikins decides to sue in federal court based

b. If Cecil is not a citizen of Aikins' state and Beasley is, then one of the considerations Aikins will have in deciding to join Beasley as a defendant is the effect on the availability of subject-matter jurisdiction in the federal courts. If Aikins wants to be in the federal court, she should not join Beasley; if Aikins wants to begin and stay in a state court, she should join him. In the latter case, there will not be complete diversity between plaintiff on the one side and defendants on the other.

on diversity of citizenship, she must bring suit in a district in which Cecil resides, or in a district where a substantial part of the events giving rise to the claim occurred, or in a district where Cecil is subject to personal jurisdiction, if there is no district in which the action otherwise may be brought.

Jurisdiction over the subject-matter is jealously guarded, and cannot be waived. If Aikins and Cecil are both citizens of the same state, a federal court will refuse to hear the action even though both are anxious that it do so. Jurisdiction over the person and venue, on the other hand, essentially are protections for defendant, who may waive them if he wishes.

2. COMMENCING THE ACTION

After the court has been selected, Aikins must give notice to Cecil by *service of process*. The process typically consists of a *summons*, which directs defendant to appear and defend under penalty of *default;* that is, unless defendant answers the summons, a judgment will be entered against him. Service of process generally is achieved by *personal service;* the summons is physically delivered to defendant or is left at his home, sometimes by plaintiff or her attorney, sometimes by a public official such as a sheriff or a United States marshal. If Cecil lives in another state, but the circumstances are such that a court in Aikins' state may assert jurisdiction over Cecil, the summons may be personally delivered to him, or some form of *substituted service,* such as sending the papers by registered mail or delivering the summons to his agent within Aikins' state, may be employed. Even if Cecil cannot be located, service in yet another form, usually by *publication* in a newspaper for a certain length of time, may be allowed, although the validity of this kind of service in the type of case Aikins is bringing against Cecil is unlikely to be upheld. The United States Supreme Court repeatedly has emphasized that service must be of a kind reasonably calculated to bring the action to defendant's notice, and from this perspective service by publication is rarely sufficient.

3. PLEADING AND PARTIES

With the summons, Aikins usually will serve on Cecil the first of the *pleadings,* commonly called the *complaint*. This is a written statement that will contain Aikins' claim against Cecil. What should be required of such a statement? Obviously it may vary from a simple assertion that Cecil owes her $80,000, to a second-by-second narration of the accident, closely describing the scene and the conduct of each party, followed by a gruesome recital of Aikins' medical treatment and her prognosis for recovery. No procedural system insists upon either of these extremes, but systems do vary greatly in the detail required in the pleadings. The degree of detail required largely reflects the purposes that the pleadings are expected to serve. These purposes are many, but three objectives are particularly relevant and to the extent that a procedural system regards one rather than another as crucial, we may expect to find differing amounts of detail required.

First, the system may desire the pleadings to furnish a basis for identifying and separating the legal and factual contentions involved so that the legal issues—and hopefully through them the entire case—may be disposed of at an early stage. Thus, suppose that Cecil's liability for Beasley's driving depends upon the degree of independence with which Beasley was working at the time of the accident. A dispute on this issue might exist on either or both of two elements. The parties might disagree as to what Beasley's duties were, and they might disagree as to whether those duties put Beasley so much under the control of Cecil that the law will impose liability on Cecil for Beasley's actions. The first disagreement would be a question of fact, and there would be no alternative to trying the suit and letting the finder of fact (usually the jury) decide the truth. But if there was agreement on that first element, a question of law would be presented by the second issue, which could be determined by the judge without a trial. The objective of which we are speaking would be fully served in such a case only if the pleadings set forth exactly what Beasley's job required him to do. It would be very inadequately served if the complaint stated only that "Beasley was driving the car on Cecil's business."

Second, the pleadings may be intended to establish in advance what a party proposes to prove at trial so that his opponent will know what contentions he must prepare to meet. If this objective is regarded as very important it will not be enough for the complaint to state that Beasley was negligent, or that Aikins suffered serious bodily injuries. It must say that Beasley was speeding, or was not keeping a proper look-out, or had inadequate brakes, or describe some other act of negligence and say that Aikins suffered a concussion, or a broken neck, or fractures of three ribs, or other injuries.

Third, the pleadings may be intended to give each party only a general notice of his opponent's contentions, in which event the system would rely upon subsequent stages of the lawsuit to identify the legal and factual contentions of the parties and to enable each to prepare to meet the opponent's case. In such a case a complaint similar to that in Form 9 of the Federal Rules of Civil Procedure would be sufficient.

Obviously each of the first two objectives is desirable. It is a waste of everybody's time to try lawsuits when the underlying legal claim is inadequate to support a judgment, and it is only fair that a person called upon to defend a judicial proceeding should know what he is alleged to have done. But to achieve the first objective fully may require pleading after pleading in order to expose and sharpen the issues; if detail is insisted upon, a long time may be consumed in producing it. Moreover, a single pleading oversight may eliminate a contention necessary to one party's case that easily could have been proven, but that will be held to have been waived. To achieve the second objective through the pleadings will mean that the parties must take rigid positions as to their factual contentions at the very beginning when they do not know what they will learn about their cases by the time trial begins. Either the first or second objective, if fully pursued, requires that the parties adhere to the positions taken in the pleadings. They could not be permitted to introduce evidence in conflict with the pleadings or to change them. For to the extent that *variances* between pleading and proof or *amendments* to the pleadings are permitted, the objectives will be lost. The court frequently will find itself forced either to depart from these objectives or to tolerate cases turning on the skill of the lawyers rather than on the merits of the controversy.

The third objective, insofar as it allows the parties to use the later stages of the lawsuit to identify and flesh out the issues in the case, avoids the delays and potential injustices created by trying to decide the case based simply on the pleadings. However, simple notice pleading may be used to harass defendant when plaintiff has no real claim. More often, though, plaintiff will use notice pleading to subject defendant to pretrial discovery (discussed more fully below), and in the process to reveal information so that plaintiff can determine whether a bona fide claim actually exists. Lawyers often refer to such use of the pleadings as a "fishing expedition," or alternatively as a "springboard into litigation." One way that courts have dealt with these problems is to sanction parties and lawyers who bring baseless claims.

4.   THE RESPONSE

Following the service of Aikins' complaint, Cecil must respond. He may challenge the complaint by a *motion to dismiss*. This motion may challenge the court's jurisdiction over the subject-matter or Cecil's person, the service of process, or venue. It also may be a *motion to dismiss for failure to state a claim or cause of action* (or a *demurrer*). For the purpose of this motion, the facts alleged in the complaint are accepted as true, and the court considers whether, on this assumption, plaintiff has shown that the pleader is entitled to legal relief.

There are three general situations in which such a motion might be granted. First, the complaint may clearly show that the injury is one for which the law furnishes no redress; for example, when plaintiff simply alleges that "defendant has made faces at me." Second, plaintiff may have failed to include an allegation on a necessary part of the case; for example, Aikins might have alleged the accident, her injuries, and Beasley's negligence, and have forgotten to allege that Beasley was Cecil's servant. Third, the complaint may be so general or so confused that the court finds that it does not give adequate notice of what plaintiff's claim is; this would be true, for example, of a complaint in which Aikins merely said, "Cecil injured me and owes me $80,000," although complaints far more specific have fallen on this ground. Obviously, the extent to which motions to dismiss will be granted on the second and third grounds will vary with the degree of detail that the particular system requires of its pleadings.

If the motion to dismiss is denied, or if none is made, Cecil must file an *answer*. In this pleading, he must admit or deny the allegations made by Aikins in the complaint. Moreover if Cecil wishes to rely on certain contentions called *affirmative defenses,* he must plead them in the answer. Thus, if he wishes to contend that Aikins was negligent in the manner in which she tried to cross the street and that this negligence was also a cause of the accident, he must in many states plead this in the answer; if the answer only denied the allegations in Aikins' complaint, Cecil may not advance at trial the contention that Aikins' negligence caused the accident.

There may be further pleadings, particularly a *reply* by Aikins. But the tendency today is to close the pleadings after the answer, and if Cecil has raised new matters in his answer, they automatically are taken as denied by Aikins. There is one major exception: if Cecil has a claim against Aikins, particularly one that arises out of the same occurrence being sued upon by Aikins, Cecil may plead this claim as a *counterclaim* as part of the answer.

This is in essence a complaint by Cecil, and Aikins will have to respond to it just as Cecil had to respond to the original complaint.

The original action between Aikins and Cecil may expand in terms of the number of parties, and this frequently will occur at the pleading stage. For example, although Aikins decided not to sue Beasley, Cecil might *implead* Beasley, asking that Beasley be held liable to him for whatever amount he may be found liable to Aikins, since his liability depends upon Beasley having been at fault. Cecil will decide whether to do this in light of a number of practical concerns, including the effect Beasley's presence will have on the Aikins v. Cecil suit.

5. OBTAINING INFORMATION PRIOR TO TRIAL

In our discussion of the objectives of pleading, it was noted that some procedural systems do not regard the pleadings as the appropriate vehicle for enabling the parties to prepare for trial. The procedure viewed as primarily charged with this function is pretrial *discovery*. This is a generic term for several methods of obtaining information from an opposing party or from witnesses.

The chief method is to take *depositions* of parties and witnesses. In this procedure, the person whose deposition is to be taken is questioned by lawyers for each side through direct and cross-examination; the *deponent's* statements are taken down and transcribed. The device is useful in finding information that is relevant to the case, including unearthing leads as to other witnesses or documents; it also is useful in laying a basis for impeaching a witness who attempts to change his story at trial. The two parties almost certainly will want depositions taken of each other, as well as of Beasley; the depositions of Aikins and Cecil will be particularly important because they are treated as admissions, and can be used by their adversaries as evidence at trial. In some circumstances, even the deposition of a nonparty witness who is unavailable at trial may be used in place of live testimony.

Another device especially adapted to probing the content of an opponent's case is *written interrogatories,* which usually may be addressed only to a party to the suit. (The availability of interrogatories may be one reason why Aikins might join Beasley as a defendant with Cecil or why Cecil might implead Beasley.) These interrogatories are answered by the party with counsel's aid, and the answers will not be as spontaneous as they would be on a deposition; on the other hand, interrogatories will require him to supply some information that he does not carry in his head but can get, and may be even more valuable than the deposition in finding out what he will try to prove. Thus, information regarding Beasley's employment that Cecil cannot be expected to have in his mind may best be exposed in this way.

Other discovery devices include *the production of documents,* such as the service record of Cecil's automobile, and *requests for admissions,* which will remove uncontested issues from the case. A particularly useful device for Cecil will be a court order directing Aikins to submit to a *physical examination* by a physician of Cecil's choice to determine the real extent of Aikins' alleged injuries.

The availability of discovery, which is now common throughout the country, has had its effect on the philosophy of pleadings. This is not simply because it enables parties to prepare for trial better than pleadings ever did. Of more significance perhaps is the fact that if broad discovery is allowed, it is senseless to make parties take rigid positions with respect to the issues at the very beginning of the lawsuit before they have had the chance to utilize these very useful devices for obtaining information. In addition, the availability of discovery does much to make summary judgment, which is discussed below, a viable and fair procedure, since it enables a party to ascertain those issues on which the opposing party has no evidence, and it also gives the opponent a real chance to develop such evidence.

Amendments to the Federal Rules of Civil Procedure were promulgated in recent years that, in time, may revolutionize the way in which litigants conduct pretrial discovery. They require both parties—automatically in most cases—to identify individuals and provide copies of documents "that the disclosing party may use to support its claims or defenses." This mandatory self-disclosure procedure theoretically should decrease considerably the amount of time and the amount of resources that the judicial system expends in overseeing the discovery process, but it is still too early to know how well they actually will work.

6. SUMMARY JUDGMENT

One of the basic difficulties with attempting to resolve cases at the pleading stage is that the allegations of the parties must be accepted as true for the purpose of ruling on a motion to dismiss. Thus, if the plaintiff tells a highly unlikely but possible story in the complaint, the court cannot dismiss the complaint even though it does not believe the allegations or think that the plaintiff will be able to prove the tale. The judge is not the person and the pleading stage is not the time to resolve questions of fact.

But in some cases it will be possible to supplement the pleadings with additional documents to show that an apparent issue that is decisive of the case is spurious. This is done by a motion for *summary judgment*. This motion can be supported by demonstrating that the crucial issue will have to be resolved in the mover's favor at trial, because the opposing party will be unable to produce any admissible evidence in support of her position on the issue. For example, suppose that it is Cecil's position that prior to the accident he had fired Beasley, but that Beasley had secreted keys to Cecil's automobile and had taken Cecil's car without permission shortly before the accident. On the face of the pleadings, we have only an allegation that Beasley was Cecil's employee and a denial of that allegation; thus, the pleadings seem to present a question of credibility that cannot be resolved at this stage. Cecil now moves for summary judgment, alleging that this issue is not a genuine one; he accompanies his motion with affidavits of his own and two other witnesses that he had fired Beasley; a deposition of the garage attendant indicating that he had been instructed not to allow Beasley to have the car, and that it was taken without Cecil's knowledge; and a deposition of Beasley to the effect that he had been fired, but wanted to use the car once more for his own purposes. It is now incumbent upon Aikins to show that the issue is genuine; Aikins cannot rely simply upon her own assertion that all this is not so; after all, she has no personal knowledge of the facts. Aikins must convince the court that she has admissible evidence that Beasley still was acting as Cecil's employee in driving the car at the time of the accident. If Aikins fails to do so, judgment will be entered against her.

It should be noted that in ruling on a motion for summary judgment the judge does not decide which side is telling the truth. If Aikins presents an affidavit of a witness who claims to have been present when Cecil allegedly fired Beasley, and says that Cecil told Beasley that this was only a subterfuge and that he wanted him to continue to work for him but to pretend to steal the car, summary judgment will not be appropriate even though the judge is firmly convinced that Aikins' affiant is lying.

7. SETTING THE CASE FOR TRIAL

After discovery is completed, and if the case has not been terminated by dismissal, summary judgment, or settlement, it must be set for *trial*. Typically either party may file a *note of issue,* at which time the case will be given a number and placed on a *trial calendar*. These calendars have become extremely long in many courts, and the case may have to wait a year, three years, or more before it is called for trial, especially if a jury trial has been requested.

8. THE JURY AND ITS SELECTION

In most actions for damages, the parties have a right to have the facts tried by a *jury*. This right is assured in the federal courts by the Seventh Amendment to the Constitution, and is protected in the courts of most states by similar constitutional provisions. If there is a right to a trial by jury, either party may assert it, but if neither wishes to do so, a judge will try the facts as well as the law. Largely for historical reasons growing out of a division of authority in the English court structure, there are many civil actions in which neither party has a right to a jury trial; these include most cases in which plaintiff wants an order directing or prohibiting specified action by defendant rather than a judgment for damages—a so-called *equitable* remedy.

If a jury has been demanded, the first order of business at trial will be to impanel the jurors. A large number of people, selected in an impartial manner from various lists, tax rolls, or street directories, will have been ordered to report to the courthouse for jury duty at a given term of court. The prospective jurors will be questioned—usually by the judge but sometimes by the lawyers—as to their possible biases. If one of the persons called has prior knowledge of the case or is a personal friend of one of the parties, he or she probably will be successfully *challenged for cause* and excused. But suppose Aikins is an architect and her lawyer finds that one of the jury panel has recently constructed a house and believes that he was greatly overcharged for its design and construction; this will likely not be enough to persuade the judge to excuse him, but fearing the juror may be prejudiced against her client, Aikins' lawyer will probably exercise one of the small number of *peremptory challenges* allowed for which no reason need be given. Ultimately, a panel of between six and twelve hopefully unbiased jurors will be selected.

9. THE TRIAL

After the jurors have been sworn, plaintiff's lawyer will make an *opening statement,* in which she will describe for the jury what the case is about, what contentions she will make, and how she will prove them. Defendant's lawyer also may make an opening statement at this time, but he may reserve the right to do so until he is ready to present his own case. Following the opening statement, plaintiff's lawyer calls her witnesses one by one. Each witness is first questioned by the lawyer who has called that witness—this is the *direct examination;* then the lawyer for the other side has the opportunity to *cross-examine* the same witness; this may be followed by *re-direct* and *re-cross* examination, and even further stages. The judge maintains some control over the length and tenor of the examination, and in particular will see to it that the stages beyond cross-examination are not prolonged.

Just as the primary responsibility for introducing evidence is on the lawyers, so too is the responsibility for objecting to evidence that is thought to be inadmissible under the rules of evidence. Suppose that Aikins' lawyer asks: "What happened while you were lying on the ground after the accident?" To which Aikins replies: "The driver of the car came over and said that he had been going too fast and he was sorry." Aikins' answer is objectionable because it contains *hearsay evidence;* that is, it repeats what someone else has said for the purpose of proving the truth of what was said. The judge will not raise this issue herself, however; it is up to Cecil's counsel to object, and then the judge must rule on the objection. This particular issue is not an easy one, for Aikins' answer may well come within one of the exceptions to the rule excluding hearsay evidence. This kind of issue will recur continually throughout the trial and the judge must be prepared to make instantaneous rulings if the trial is to proceed with dispatch. Small wonder that evidentiary rulings form a major source of the errors raised on appeal, but at the same time appellate courts are very reluctant to disturb the trial judge's determination. What happens if the judge rules that Aikins' answer is inadmissible? She will instruct the jury to disregard it. Can a juror who has heard such an important confession totally drive it from his or her mind?

Documents, pictures, and other tangible items may be put into evidence, but unless their admissibility has been stipulated in advance, they will be introduced through witnesses. For example, if Aikins' lawyer has had pictures taken of the accident scene and wishes to get them to the jury, she will call the photographer as a witness, have him testify that he took pictures of the scene, and then show them to the photographer who will identify them as the pictures he took. At this point they may be formally introduced into evidence.

When plaintiff's lawyer has called all of her witnesses, and their examinations are over, plaintiff will *rest*. At this point, defendant's lawyer may ask for a *directed verdict* (now called a judgment as a matter of law in federal practice) for defendant on the ground that plaintiff has not established a prima facie case; the thrust of the motion is that plaintiff has not introduced enough evidence to permit the jury to find in her favor. If the motion is denied, defendant may rest and choose to rely on the jury's agreeing with him, but in almost all cases he will proceed to present witnesses of his own and these witnesses will be exposed to the same process of direct and cross-examination. When defendant has rested, plaintiff may present additional evidence to meet any new matter raised by defendant's witnesses. In turn, defendant, after plaintiff rests, may meet any new matter presented by plaintiff. This procedure will continue until both parties rest. Again, the trial judge will maintain considerable control to prevent the protraction of these latter stages.

When both parties have rested, either or both may move for a directed verdict. Again, this motion asks the trial judge to rule that under the evidence presented, viewed most favorably to the nonmoving party, the jury cannot find in his or her favor. If these motions are denied, the case must be submitted to the jury.

10. SUBMITTING THE CASE TO THE JURY

At this stage the judge and the lawyers will confer out of the jury's hearing with regard to the content of the judge's *instructions* or *charge* to the jury. Each lawyer may submit proposed instructions, which the trial judge will grant or deny, but the judge is under a duty to charge the jury on the basic aspects of the case in any event. If a party's lawyer has neither requested a particular instruction nor objected to the judge's charge, however, a claim that the charge was erroneous generally will not be upheld on appeal.

Ordinarily the lawyers will make their final arguments to the jury before the judge delivers the charge. The lawyers will review the evidence from their own points of view, and may suggest how the jury should weigh certain items and resolve specific issues, but it is improper for the lawyers to discuss a matter that has been excluded or has never been introduced. In other words, they are arguing, not testifying.

In the instructions the judge will summarize the facts and issues, tell the jury about the substantive law to be applied on each issue, give general information on determining the credibility of witnesses, and state who has the *burden of persuasion* on each issue of fact. The burden of persuasion in a civil case ordinarily requires that one party prove her contention on a given issue by a preponderance of the evidence. On most issues Aikins will carry this burden but on an affirmative defense such as contributory negligence the burden probably will be on Cecil. What the burden means is that if a juror is unable to resolve an issue in his mind, he should find on that issue against the party who has the burden. In the federal courts and in some states, the judge may comment on the evidence, as long as she emphasizes that her comments represent her own opinion and that the jurors should not feel bound by it; judicial comment is rare, however, and in many states it is not permitted at all.

Following the charge, the jury retires to reach its *verdict*. The verdict, the jury's decision, will be of a type chosen by the judge. There are three types, of which by far the most common is the *general verdict*. This verdict permits the jurors to determine the facts and apply the law on which they have been charged to those facts; it is simple in form in that only the conclusion as to who prevails, and the amount of the damages, if that party is a claimant, is stated. A second type is the *general verdict with interrogatories,* which combines the form of the general verdict with several key questions that are designed to test the jury's understanding of the issues. Suppose that the accident occurred five miles away from Beasley's appointed route. Aikins' evidence is that Beasley detoured to have the vehicle's brakes fixed; Cecil's is that Beasley was going to visit his friend. The judge might charge the jury that in the former event, but not in the latter, Beasley was acting within the scope of his employment and Cecil would be liable for his negligence, and she might direct the jury, in addition to rendering a verdict for Aikins or for Cecil, to answer the question, "Why did Beasley depart from his route?" If the general verdict was for Aikins, but the jury's answer was that Beasley was driving to his friend's home, the judge would order judgment for Cecil, for if the answer is inconsistent with the verdict, the answer controls. The third type of verdict is the *special verdict,* in which all of the factual issues in the case are submitted to the jury as questions without instructions as to their legal effect; the judge applies the law to the jury's answers and determines which party prevails.

Traditionally, only a unanimous jury verdict has been effective. In many states, and by consent of the parties in the federal courts, a nonunanimous verdict by the jurors may stand in a civil action. If the minimum number of jurors required for a verdict are unable to reach agreement, the jury is said to be *hung,* and a new trial before a different jury is necessary.

11. POST-TRIAL MOTIONS

After the jury has returned its verdict, judgment will be entered thereon, but the losing party will have an opportunity to make certain post-trial motions. There may be a motion for a *judgment notwithstanding the verdict* (commonly called a motion for a *judgment n.o.v.,* from the Latin non obstante veredicto, but now called a renewed motion for judgment as a matter of law in federal practice); this motion raises the same question as a motion for a directed verdict. The losing party also may move for a *new trial;* the grounds for this motion are many, and may include assertions that the judge erred in admitting certain evidence, that the charge was defective, that attorneys, parties, or jurors have been guilty of misconduct, that the damages awarded are excessive, or that the jury's verdict is against the clear weight of the evidence. Should these motions fail, it is sometimes possible to reopen a judgment, even several months after the trial, on the grounds of clerical mistake, newly discovered evidence, or fraud, but the occasions on which relief is granted are very rare.

12. THE JUDGMENT AND ITS ENFORCEMENT

The *judgment* is the final determination of the lawsuit, absent an appeal. Judgment may be rendered on default when the defendant does not appear; or following the granting of a demurrer, a motion to dismiss, or a motion for summary judgment; or upon the jury's verdict, or the findings of fact and conclusions of law of the trial judge in a nonjury case. The judgment may be in the form of an award of money to plaintiff, a declaration of rights between the parties, specific recovery of property, or an order requiring or prohibiting some future activity. When defendant has prevailed, the judgment generally will not be "for" anything nor will it order anything; it simply will provide that plaintiff takes nothing by her complaint.

In most cases a judgment for plaintiff will not order defendant to do anything; typically it will simply state that plaintiff shall recover a sum of money from defendant. This does not necessarily mean that defendant will pay. It is up to plaintiff to collect the money. *Execution* is the common method of forcing the losing party to satisfy a money judgment, if the loser does not do so voluntarily. A *writ of execution* is issued by the court commanding an officer—usually the sheriff—to seize property of the losing party and, if necessary, to sell it at public sale and use the proceeds to satisfy plaintiff's judgment.

When plaintiff's recovery takes the form of an *injunction* requiring defendant to do something or to stop doing something, the judgment (in this context typically called the *decree*) is said to operate against defendant's person (in personam). Its sanction is direct, and if defendant fails to obey, he may be held in *contempt of court* and punished by fine or imprisonment.

Costs provided by statute and certain out-of-pocket disbursements are awarded the prevailing party and included in the judgment. Usually these costs are nominal in relation to the total expense of litigation and include only such items as the clerk's fee and witnesses' mileage. In the United States, in contrast to England, attorney's fees are not recoverable as costs in ordinary litigation.

13. APPEAL

Every judicial system provides for review by an appellate court of the decisions of the trial court. Generally a party has the right to appeal any judgment to at least one higher court. When the system contains two levels of appellate courts, appeal usually lies initially to one of the intermediate courts; review at the highest level is only at the discretion of that court except in certain classes of cases. Thus, in the federal courts, district-court decisions are reviewed by the courts of appeals, but review in the United States Supreme Court must be sought in most cases by a *petition for a writ of certiorari,* which that Court may deny as a matter of discretion without reaching any conclusion as to the merits of the case.[c] The discretion of a higher-level appellate court generally is exercised so that only cases whose legal issues are of broad importance are taken.

The *record* on appeal will contain the pleadings, at least a portion of the *transcript of the trial* (the court reporter's verbatim record of the trial), and the orders and rulings relevant to the appeal. The parties present their contentions to the appellate court by written *briefs* and in addition, in most cases, by *oral argument.* The appellate court may review any ruling of law by the trial judge, although frequently it will limit the scope of its review by holding that particular matters were within the trial judge's discretion or that the error if any was not prejudicial, that is, it did not substantially affect the outcome of the case. There are constitutional limits to the review of a jury's verdict, but even when these limits do not apply—for example, when the judge has sat without a jury—an appellate court rarely will re-examine a question of fact, for a cold record does not convey the nuances of what the trier observed, notably the demeanor of the witnesses.

The appellate court has the power to *affirm, reverse,* or *modify* the judgment of the trial court. If it reverses, it may order that judgment be entered or it may *remand* the case to the trial court for a new trial or other proceedings not inconsistent with its decision. The decision of an appellate court usually is accompanied by a written *opinion,* signed by one of the judges

    c. In a few cases, a direct appeal lies from the district court to the Supreme Court.

hearing the appeal, there always being more than one judge deciding an appeal. Concurring and dissenting opinions also may be filed. The opinions of a court are designed to set forth the reasons for a decision and to furnish guidance to lower courts, lawyers, and the public. You will spend much of your time in law school—and afterwards—reading the opinions of appellate courts. Although trial courts frequently deliver opinions when ruling on motions or sitting without a jury, except in federal courts these usually are not published.

There is an important distinction between the *reviewability* of a particular ruling of a trial judge and its *appealability*. For example, a trial judge's ruling excluding certain evidence at trial as hearsay is reviewable; that is, when the judgment is appealed, that ruling may be assigned as error and the appellate court will consider whether it was correct. But trial would be impossible if an appeal could be taken from every ruling. Thus, appeals lie only from judgments and from certain orders made in the course of litigation when immediate review is deemed so important that a delay in the action during appeal can be tolerated. Judicial systems differ in the extent to which *interlocutory orders* can be appealed. In the federal system, very little other than a final judgment can be taken to the courts of appeals; in some states, on the other hand, many kinds of orders can be appealed.

A good example of the contrast between the two approaches can be seen by looking at the consequences of an order denying a motion to dismiss. Suppose that Cecil moves to dismiss Aikins' complaint on the grounds that even on Aikins' view of the facts Cecil is not responsible for the conduct of Beasley, and this motion is denied. In the federal courts such an order would not be appealable, since it does not terminate the lawsuit. Indeed, the disposition of the motion means that the action will continue. In some states, however, this question could be taken immediately to a higher court for a ruling, while the other stages of the litigation wait.

The question as to which system is better is not easy to answer. One may argue in favor of the federal practice that everything should be done at one level before going to the next, that too much time is taken in waiting for appellate courts to decide these questions serially, and that no appeal may ever be necessary, since Cecil may prevail anyway. But on the other hand, if the appellate court holds at this early stage that Aikins has no claim against Cecil we will save the time necessary for discovery and trial.

One point worth noting is that the resolution of the question of the appealability of interlocutory orders has an important bearing on the procedural developments within a given system. In the case of motions to dismiss, for example, if denials are not appealable, the law on this subject will be made largely in the trial courts. The trial judge who is in doubt may tend to deny such motions rather than to grant them, and her decision generally will not be disturbed; even though the ruling theoretically is reviewable after final judgment, by that time the significance of the ruling on the pleadings may have been displaced by more substantive questions. If the denial is appealable, a tactical consideration is added and such motions will be resorted to more frequently, inasmuch as they will afford defendant an additional opportunity to delay trial and thus to wear down his opponent. With respect to other procedural rulings—as in the discovery area—the absence of an interlocutory appeal will strengthen the hand of the trial judge; she will in fact, if not in theory, be given a wider discretion because fewer of her rulings will come before the appellate courts and when they do they will be enmeshed in a final judgment, which will make it easy to conclude that any error was not prejudicial.

14. THE CONCLUSIVENESS OF JUDGMENTS

After the appeal and whatever further proceedings may take place, or, if no appeal is taken, when the time for appeal expires, the judgment is final. It cannot be challenged in another proceeding. It is *res judicata*, a thing decided, and now at rest. Defining the scope and effect of this finality is one of the most complex tasks in the entire law of procedure.

SECTION C. A NOTE ON MOTION PRACTICE

Throughout the previous Section the term "motion" is used frequently, and for good reason. What a motion is, how one makes a motion, and when one should make a motion are all questions of "motion practice." A motion is the procedural device by which a litigant asks a court for an order. For example, a request for an order to dismiss a complaint for failure to state a claim, a request for an order granting a summary judgment, and a request for an order granting a new trial all are formally made to a court through a motion.

A litigant generally must make a motion in writing. Two exceptions to this rule are when the court is recording a hearing verbatim or when a trial is taking place. A motion generally must state with particularity the reasons or grounds supporting the motion and the relief sought. The written motion also must appear in a proper form, which usually is determined by local court rules.

The litigant also must serve the motion on her adversary. In addition, a notice of hearing regarding the motion, a brief or memorandum of law in support of the motion, a proposed order, and affidavits, if necessary, generally accompany a motion. Briefs usually have a maximum page limit (and quite often are not brief). Not all courts require the movant to submit a proposed order. Only certain motions require affidavits.

All motions in federal court require the signature of the litigant's attorney or the litigant. The signature attests that the attorney or litigant has read the motion papers and that the motion has sufficient grounds and is made in good faith. If a court decides that any of these are not true, the court may sanction the attorney or the litigant. Sanctions have been imposed more frequently in recent years.

A party served with a motion may answer and usually must do so within a time period specified by the rules. A party also may move for an extension of time, either to make a cross-motion, to extend the time to respond to the motion, or both. In addition, making a motion may defer the next stage of litigation. Finally, making a particular motion may preserve other legal rights.

It is the interrelationship between motions, their intended effects, their secondary effects, and their effects on the other side that determine how a party utilizes motion practice. A motion such as summary judgment is usually designed to win the lawsuit. A successful motion to exclude certain material from discovery may convince an adversary that he cannot obtain the information necessary to establish his case and thus may induce him to end the lawsuit early without an unfavorable judgment. A motion to bring a third party into the lawsuit may help convince an adversary that the lawsuit will be more time consuming and costly than expected. A lawyer deciding to make a motion must consider carefully what benefits will accrue to the movant and what obstacles will be imposed on her adversary as a result of the motion.

But a motion may have negative aspects. One of the drawbacks may be the time and expense of making the motion, including drafting and serving multiple copies of papers, spending hours preparing the brief in support of the motion, and taking resources from other more fruitful pursuits. Repeated, unsuccessful motions will result in expense and delay that may reduce client satisfaction.

In addition, poor motion practice may leave the judge with the impression that the lawyer is sloppy, shoddy, and disorganized. Arguing motions at a hearing that the attorneys could have settled without a hearing may convince the judge that the movant is contentious by nature. In short, an unwise use of a motion may do more harm in the long run than not making the motion at all, even if the motion is granted.

In sum, motion practice is a central part of a litigator's arsenal. When a particular motion can be made, how it must be made, and what its effect will be are questions that can be answered by studying the applicable procedural rules. When a motion *should* be made and how it can affect the course of the lawsuit are matters of judgment and experience.

SECTION D. A NOTE ON REMEDIES

The remedies that may be obtained in a modern civil action should principally be viewed as a part of the substantive law: contract law, tort law, commercial law, labor law, and so forth. Yet because the goal of a lawsuit is the remedy and the means of securing it is procedural, there necessarily is a close relationship between them. For example, the range of available remedies in a case may be limited by the manner in which plaintiff has pleaded, and on the other hand certain procedural aspects of the case, such as whether it is tried to a judge or a jury, may be determined by the remedy that is being sought; again, whether a person may be joined as a party may depend on the relief that is being sought, and conversely certain remedies may be available only if all interested persons can be joined.

Without question, the most important relationship between procedure and remedies grows out of the existence in English law of two great branches of jurisprudence administered in different courts: common law and equity; the latter was envisioned as complementary to the former. There are two special facts about equity that are important for our purpose. First, already alluded to, it had no jury. Second, the injunction was a creature of equity and remained in its sole custody so long as the two branches remained distinct.

From this heritage, two consequences of immense significance for the law of procedure result. One, the right of a trial by jury in the United States today, especially in the federal courts, is determined by inquiring whether the matter in question was a subject of a legal or equitable cognizance in 1791—the date of the Seventh Amendment—and to some extent this question depends on the remedy sought, since the availability of injunctive relief was one font of equity's jurisdiction. Two, just as equity was regarded as a special kind of law to be resorted to only when the common law was inadequate, so too the injunction—and most forms of specific relief, even in those limited circumstances in which it is available at law—has been and still is regarded as a form of exceptional relief, to be allowed only when the ordinary remedy of damages is inadequate.

The most important types of relief that a court may award in a civil action fall into three categories: *declarative, specific,* and *compensatory.* Declarative relief consists simply in a court's defining the rights and duties of the parties in a particular legal context. Suppose a person believes that an agreement she has entered into is not a valid contract and that she is under no obligation to perform it; however, she is afraid to act on this belief in the face of another's insistence that she perform, because if the contract is enforceable the damages for the nonperformance will be great. In these circumstances she may seek a declaratory judgment asking the court to determine whether she is under a duty to perform. This type of relief is not as common as those discussed below and its availability often is limited by statute. In numerous situations, however, it is invaluable.

Specific relief consists generally of an order directing conduct. Defendant may be commanded to return a jewel he has taken from plaintiff, to stop operating a pig farm in a residential neighborhood, to deliver a car he has contracted to sell, or to refrain from opening a barbershop next door to a person to whom he has just sold his former barbershop. Obviously, specific relief is not possible in all cases. For example, no kind of specific relief will compensate or cure Aikins in our hypothetical case; Beasley cannot retroactively be ordered not to run into her. On the other hand, in some kinds of cases specific relief is available almost as a matter of course. A person who has contracted to sell a house or a piece of land ordinarily will be ordered to perform the agreement, for the law regards each bit of real property as unique. But beyond the real-property context, specific relief will be given only if damages would be completely inadequate. Thus, if you order a tuxedo from a tailor who fails to perform his promise to deliver it, it is unlikely that any remedy except damages will be forthcoming. The reasons for this are not purely historical. There is a burden on the court in ordering and supervising performance of a decree of specific performance that is avoided if a simple judgment for money damages is entered; moreover, specific performance might impose a hardship or at least an indignity on the tailor not commensurate with the advantage to be gained by your receiving this tailor's garment rather than one from another tailor. But it may well be asked whether our courts today are not being too reluctant to grant that form of relief that will most adequately redress plaintiff's grievance.

Compensatory relief calls for a judgment that defendant pay plaintiff a certain sum of money. But you should recognize that when we speak of compensation—of the remedy of damages—although we are speaking of one form of relief, it can be computed in accordance with many measures. In your action against the tailor, for example, if you had struck a good bargain, you might claim the difference between the price you agreed to pay and the value the tuxedo would have had if the tailor had performed the promise; or you might claim only the money you had advanced as a down payment; or you might claim the amount you paid for opera tickets you were unable to use without the tuxedo. The difference in amount that could be collected under these theories might be very substantial.

There is a final point to be considered in evaluating the adequacy of any judicial remedy: how much of it will be consumed by the cost of litigation? As we have noted, the costs awarded to a successful plaintiff will not, in most cases, reimburse her for the fees of her lawyer or for many other substantial costs of a suit, such as the expense of investigation or the fees of expert witnesses. It is not possible to give any meaningful figure for the cost of an average trial, but it can be assumed that as the stakes rise the fees will be correspondingly higher and indeed, some top attorneys charge upward of $400 an hour for their services.

In most personal-injury actions plaintiff's cost of recovery must be computed differently because the attorney will be litigating the case under a contingent-fee agreement; that is, the attorney will receive a percentage—one-third is common—of plaintiff's judgment. Thus, in a real sense, an adequate legal remedy is not one that simply compensates plaintiff for a loss but is one that covers both the loss and the cost of recovering it. This distinction has not been ignored by many triers of fact. Indeed, it has been suggested that if damages for pain and suffering ever are abolished, defendants should be required explicitly to pay plaintiffs' legal fees. O'Connell, *A Proposal to Abolish Defendants' Payment for Pain and Suffering in Return for Payment of Claimants' Attorneys' Fees*, 1981 U.Ill.L.Rev. 333.

SECTION E. ILLUSTRATIVE CASES

The cases that follow have been selected to illustrate many of the basic concepts, doctrines, and devices about which you have just read. This group of cases is designed to furnish examples of a broad spectrum of procedural problems, and it has been arranged for the most part to present these problems in the order in which they were discussed in the preceding text. Three factors have dominated the choice of the cases: First, each focuses on a specific issue that is typical of a range of problems involving a particular principle and at the same time throws some light on the policies that underlie the principle itself. Second, none of the cases is a "sitting duck"; in each instance strong reasons can be advanced for and against the court's result. Third, each case arises in a context that you can understand and presents an issue about which you should be able to form an opinion, however hesitant it may be. Another purpose of these cases is to help you develop a familiarity with procedural language and a feeling for procedural problems. You must, of course, consider the cases from the perspective of the courts that decided them, seeking to understand not only their rulings but why they were made, asking what other options were before them, and thinking through the consequences of those possibilities. But if the full pedagogical objectives of these cases are to be achieved, you also must regard each of them as a practical lawyer's problem—or rather a problem presenting difficulties and opportunities to the lawyers on the opposite sides. You must inquire why they acted as they did and what else they might have done; finally, you must ask in what position the decision has left them and what if anything they should do next.

1. THE AUTHORITY OF THE COURT TO PROCEED WITH THE ACTION

Plaintiff, having decided to sue, must determine in what court to bring the action. A court must be chosen that has jurisdiction over the subject matter of the suit and in which jurisdiction over the person of the defendant may be obtained. In the following case, the word "jurisdiction" is used without either of these modifiers. But from the context and from the information you have been given above you should be able to identify the kind of jurisdiction involved.

CAPRON v. VAN NOORDEN

Supreme Court of the United States, 1804.
6 U.S. (2 Cranch) 126, 2 L.Ed. 229.

Error to the [United States] circuit court of North Carolina. The proceedings stated Van Noorden to be late of Pitt county [North Carolina], but did not allege Capron, the plaintiff, to be an alien, nor a citizen of any state, nor the place of his residence.

Upon the general issue, in an action of trespass on the case, a verdict was found for the defendant, Van Noorden, upon which judgment was rendered.

The writ of error was sued out by Capron, the plaintiff below, who assigned for error, among other things, first, "that the circuit court aforesaid is a court of limited jurisdiction, and that by the record aforesaid it doth not appear, as it ought to have done, that either the said George Capron, or the said Hadrianus Van Noorden, was an alien at the time of the commencement of said suit, or at any other time, or that one of the said parties was at that or any other time, a citizen of the state of North Carolina where the suit was brought, and the other a citizen of another state; or that they the said George and Hadrianus were, for any cause whatever, persons within the jurisdiction of the said court, and capable of suing and being sued there." And, secondly, "that by the record aforesaid it manifestly appeareth that the said circuit court had not any jurisdiction of the cause aforesaid, nor ought to have held plea thereof or given judgment therein, but ought to have dismissed the same, whereas the said court hath proceeded to final judgment therein."

Harper, for the plaintiff in error, stated the only question to be whether the plaintiff had a right to assign for error the want of jurisdiction in that court to which he had chosen to resort. * * *

The defendant in error did not appear, but the citation having been duly served, the judgment was reversed.

Notes and Questions

1. The Supreme Court obviously regarded the defect in this case as extremely serious. Does the fact that it was the plaintiff who brought the case to the Supreme Court make this particularly clear? Why? Why is such significance attached to an error of this kind?

2. Read Article III, Section 2, of the United States Constitution, which is set out in the Supplement. What specific language in that Section is pertinent to the Supreme Court's opinion in *Capron?*

3. The Supreme Court reversed the judgment of the lower court. What was the effect of this reversal? Does it mean that Capron wins the lawsuit? If not, why had he sought review in the appellate court?

4. Those of you who have studied American government or political science may recall that one year before *Capron* was decided by the Supreme Court, the broad issue of the case had been involved in MARBURY v. MADISON, 5 U.S. (1 Cranch) 137, 2 L.Ed. 60 (1803), the case that is the cornerstone of judicial review in the United States.

———

Unlike the federal courts, which only exercise the limited subject-matter jurisdiction bestowed by the Constitution, as further restricted by acts of Congress, state courts of general jurisdiction have jurisdiction over the subject matter of a very broad spectrum of lawsuits. Indeed, questions of the competence of those courts to decide a particular kind of case rarely arise. But before any court may proceed, it also must have the power to require the appearance of defendant. In the next case, the court must decide whether it has that power, and whether it will exercise it.

TICKLE v. BARTON

Supreme Court of Appeals of West Virginia, 1956.
142 W.Va. 188, 95 S.E.2d 427.

HAYMOND, JUDGE. The plaintiff, Richard Tickle, an infant, who sues by his next friend, instituted this action of trespass on the case in the Circuit Court of McDowell County in March, 1955, to recover damages from the defendants, Raymond Barton, a resident of Austinville, Virginia, and Lawrence Coleman, for personal injuries inflicted upon him by a motor vehicle, owned by the defendant Raymond Barton and operated by his agent the defendant Lawrence Coleman, * * * in that county which the plaintiff alleges were caused by the negligence of the defendants.

* * * [A first attempt to serve Barton had been made and the validity of this service was still undecided at the time the instant decision was rendered.]

On December 5, 1955, one of the attorneys for the plaintiff caused an alias process to be issued against the defendants * * * and delivered it to a deputy sheriff for service upon the defendant Barton in McDowell County; and in the evening of December 6, 1955, that process was served by the deputy upon the defendant Barton in person at the War Junior High School in the town of War in that county where he appeared to attend a banquet which was held there at that time.

By his amended plea in abatement No. 2, the defendant Barton challenged the validity of the service of the alias process upon him on the ground that he had been induced to come to that place in McDowell County by trickery, artifice and deceit practiced upon him by the attorney for the plaintiff.

The circuit court overruled the demurrer of the plaintiff to the amended plea in abatement and * * * certified its ruling upon the demurrer to this Court on the joint application of the plaintiff and the defendant Barton.

After reciting the prior proceedings in this case, the amended plea in abatement alleges in substance that after procuring alias process for the purpose of causing it to be served upon the defendant Barton in McDowell County, and inducing him to come to the Junior High School in the town of War in that county, an attorney representing the plaintiff in this action, in the evening of December 5, 1955, called by telephone the defendant Barton at his home in Austinville, Virginia, and wrongfully and deceitfully represented that, in behalf of the sponsors of a banquet honoring a championship high school football team to be held at the Junior High School in the town of War, * * * he extended an invitation to the defendant Barton, whose son had been a member of an earlier football team of that school, to attend the banquet; that during that telephone conversation between them the attorney, though requested to do so by the defendant Barton, did not disclose his identity except to say that he called him in behalf of the sponsors to extend the defendant Barton a special invitation to attend the banquet; that the defendant Barton before being so invited did not know that the banquet would be held and did not intend to attend it; that he did not know or suspect the identity of the attorney, or realize that the telephone call was a trick or device to entice, induce and inveigle him to come into McDowell County to be served with process in this action; that the attorney was not connected with any of the sponsors of the banquet and was not authorized by them to invite the defendant Barton to attend it; that the attorney called the defendant Barton and invited him to the banquet solely for the purpose of tricking, deceiving and inveigling him to come to the town of War in order to obtain personal service * * * upon him * * *; that the defendant Barton, believing that the invitation was extended in good faith, by a person authorized to extend it, and not suspecting the real purpose of the telephone call, accepted the invitation and informed the attorney that he would be present at the banquet and on December 6, 1955, left Austinville, Virginia, and went to the town of War with the intention of attending it; that, when he entered the high school where the banquet was held * * * he was served by the deputy sheriff with the alias process * * *; that the service of the alias process upon the defendant Barton, having been procured by trickery, deceit and subterfuge which was not realized or suspected by him, is, for that reason, null and void and of no force or effect and does not confer upon the Circuit Court of McDowell County jurisdiction of the person of the defendant Barton in this action.

The amended plea in abatement also alleges, on information and belief, that after the defendant Barton had left his home * * * the attorney for the plaintiff * * * made a telephone call to the residence of the defendant Barton, or caused some other person to make such call, and inquired of the wife of the defendant Barton if he intended to attend the banquet and was informed by her that he had left his home to attend it * * *.

The amended plea in abatement further avers that * * * the attorney for the plaintiff denied that he had made, or procured any person to make, either of the foregoing telephone calls, and denied that he had any knowledge whatsoever of either of them.

The question certified to this Court for decision is whether the allegations of the amended plea in abatement, which insofar as they are material and are well pleaded must be considered as true upon demurrer, are sufficient to render invalid the personal service of process upon the defendant Barton * * *.

* * * In 42 Am.Jur., Process, Section 35, the general principle is stated thus:

* * * "[I]f a person resident outside the jurisdiction of the court and the reach of its process is inveigled, enticed, or induced, by any false representation, deceitful contrivance, or wrongful device for which the plaintiff is responsible, to come within the jurisdiction of the court for the purpose of obtaining service of process on him in an action brought against him in such court, process served upon him through such improper means is invalid, and upon proof of such fact the court will, on motion, set it aside." * * *

The foregoing principle applies to the party when such service is procured by his agent or by someone acting for and in his behalf. * * *

In Economy Electric Company v. Automatic Electric Power and Light Plant, 185 N.C. 534, 118 S.E. 3, the court, discussing service of process by fraudulent means, used this language: "Where service of process is procured by fraud, that fact may be shown, and, if shown seasonably, the court will refuse to exercise its jurisdiction and turn the plaintiff out of court. The law will not lend its sanction or support to an act, otherwise lawful, which is accomplished by unlawful means. * * * Such a fraud is one affecting the court itself and the integrity of its process. * * * The objection, strictly, is not that the court is without jurisdiction, but that it ought not, by reason of the alleged fraud, to take or to hold jurisdiction of the action. * * * "

Under the material allegations of the amended plea in abatement which, as already indicated, must be considered as true upon demurrer, the defendant Barton was induced or enticed to come into McDowell County by the unauthorized invitation extended to him by the attorney for the plaintiff whose purpose at the time was to obtain personal service upon the defendant Barton * * *; the defendant Barton knew that the present action against him was pending in the circuit court by reason of the service of the original process upon him * * * but he did not suspect or realize that he would be served with process while present in McDowell County to attend the banquet; he was induced to come into that county by the invitation to the banquet; and he would not have come into that jurisdiction if the attorney for the plaintiff had disclosed his identity and his real purpose in extending the invitation, all of which he concealed from the defendant Barton.

* * *

The amended plea in abatement is sufficient on demurrer and the action of the circuit court in overruling the demurrer was correct.

It should perhaps be emphasized that, as the factual allegations of the amended plea in abatement have not been denied at this stage of this action by any pleading filed by the plaintiff, the question of the truth or the falsity of those allegations is not before this Court * * *.

Ruling affirmed.

GIVEN, JUDGE (dissenting).

My disagreement with the majority is not as to the rule of law laid down. I think the rule a salutary one, and masterfully stated. I do not believe, however, that the facts properly pleaded, and the inferences which may be rationally drawn therefrom, bring the facts of this case within the influence of the rule.

Stripped of all explanatory language, and of many allegations of conclusions of fact, * * * the plea in abatement charges no more than that the attorney, by telephone, inquired at defendant's home whether defendant intended to attend a certain social function to be held in McDowell County, to which defendant was then invited by the attorney; that the attorney, though requested to give his name, did not do so; that the attorney later, or someone for him, again by telephone, inquired whether defendant had decided to attend the social function, and was advised that defendant had made arrangements to attend; and that the attorney caused process to be served on defendant while attending the social function. * * * The principal, if not only, fact of wrongdoing, if wrongdoing, alleged against the attorney was his failure to inform defendant of the identity of the telephone caller. * * * It seems to me that the facts properly alleged can not be held to establish fraud or wrongdoing. At most, they would simply show that the attorney took advantage of an opportunity, the holding of the social function in McDowell County and the interest of defendant's son in the holding of the function, to try to obtain proper service of process, which was no more than a duty owed his client. In considering the questions arising, it should be kept in mind that defendant had full knowledge of the institution of the action against him in McDowell County, of the fact that he had questioned the validity of the service of other process issued in that action, and of the fact that the alleged cause of action arose in McDowell County, where ordinarily it would have been triable.

* * *

Notes and Questions

1. Did the court in this case decide that West Virginia courts did not have jurisdiction over the person of defendant (assuming his story were true), or that those courts should not exercise jurisdiction in these circumstances even though they had it?

2. When should a court be able to demand that a person appear before it and defend an action? In what circumstances should this demand be permitted against a nonresident? Why should a nonresident be subject to suit if he is served with process within the state? Insofar as these reasons are concerned, should it make any difference why he is present in the state?

3. In thinking about the cases you read, you should consider how the court might approach the problem presented by a particular case with certain facts changed. For example, should service in West Virginia in the following situations be treated in the same way as it was under the facts alleged in the principal case? (a) Tickle had asked Barton to appear as a witness in a suit against a third party involved in the accident; (b) Tickle had asked Barton to come to West Virginia to discuss settling the case; (c) Tickle had telephoned Barton and falsely told him

that his son lay critically injured in a West Virginia hospital; (d) Tickle (like the Sheriff of Nottingham) had scheduled a football banquet in West Virginia that he knew Barton (like Robin Hood) would be unable to resist attending, although he did not personally invite him.

4. When the case is reconsidered by the West Virginia Circuit Court on remand, Barton's lawyer must prove his allegations if Barton is to avoid trial in West Virginia. What problems do you foresee in his being able to prove them, and how should he proceed to do so?

5. You will later become familiar with state statutes that confer upon their courts power to summon out-of-state motorists to defend actions arising out of their operating automobiles within the state. Tickle had first sought to serve Barton under a statute of this type, but because the accident had occurred on private property rather than a West Virginia public highway, a serious question as to the statute's application existed; this uncertainty prompted the second attempt at service discussed in the case.

2. DEFINING AND DETERMINING THE CASE BEFORE TRIAL

At this point, you should re-read the part of the Outline of a Civil Action that deals with pleading, especially the portion that discusses the "three general situations" in which a motion to dismiss for failure to state a claim might be granted. Is the court in the following case saying that plaintiff has not properly pleaded its case or that it has no case at all?

CASE v. STATE FARM MUTUAL AUTOMOBILE INSURANCE CO.

United States Court of Appeals, Fifth Circuit, 1961.
294 F.2d 676.

CAMERON, CIRCUIT JUDGE. Appellant Case filed this action against the three insurance companies named as appellees for damages growing out of the termination of his representation of the three Companies as local agent. He charged in his complaint that he was appointed agent by a written contract attached as an exhibit to his complaint, which he charged, and the parties agree, constituted him an independent contractor for all purposes and provided that he was not required to "devote all of his working time to any one of the Companies;" that he represented the three Companies "through the years 1954, 1955, 1956, 1957 and 1958, and up until March 28, 1959," on which date the appellees "began to and did meddle and interfere with the plaintiff's work as agent of [the three Companies] in disregard of the agreement between the defendants and the plaintiff."[1]

1. The meddling and interference upon which appellant lays so much stress before us is stated in the complaint in these words:

"That on or about March 1, 1959, that he, the Plaintiff, publicly announced his candidacy for the office of Supervisor of District Five (5) of Adams County, Mississippi, and Plaintiff shows further that on or about March 28, 1959, the Defendants, * * * began to and did meddle and interfere with the Plaintiff's work as agent of the State Farm

Insurance Companies in disregard of the agreement between the Defendants and the Plaintiff. The Plaintiff was informed orally and by letter by representatives of his principals that his agency would have to be handled in a particular manner and he was directed as to when, how and why his work should be done in a certain manner and was orally informed as well as by letter that he would have to submit his decision as to whether he would be a candidate for the

Properly construed in connection with the remaining allegations of the complaint,[2] appellant stated nothing in his pleading except an action based upon what he conceived to be the malicious and wrongful cancellation of the written contract between him and appellees, and on that alone. So construed, every word in the complaint related to the alleged wrongful termination of the written contract between the parties. That writing gave either party the right to terminate it with or without cause, and the charges in the complaint relating to meddling and interference make sense only when construed in the light of the allegations that the appellees expressed the purpose not to continue the contractual relationship with appellant unless he would agree to abjure the seeking and holding of the public office of county supervisor. Their efforts to induce him to follow the course which alone would permit the continuation of that contractual relationship related manifestly to the termination which finally took place. The contract gave the appellees the right to cancellation "with or without cause," and in terminating it the appellees acted entirely within their rights.

Appellant argues the case as if it were one in tort for interference with his civil rights. The allegations of the pleadings do not support such an argument. * * *

It is clear also that the complaint does not set forth an independent claim for damages based upon meddling and interference by appellees with appellant's performance of the contract. Appellant invokes the oft repeated statement of the courts that a complaint should not be dismissed if it charges facts upon which a court could possibly grant relief. * * * What the courts have said does not mean that it is the duty of the trial court or the appellate court to create a claim which appellant has not spelled out in his pleading.

The court below was faced with a complaint and a motion to dismiss. Its duty was to judge the complaint by the language used in it. The only damages

office of supervisor or have his contract or appointment with State Farm Insurance Companies terminated as of May 1, 1959, all of which was done wrongfully in malicious and wanton disregard of the Plaintiff's rights according to his appointment as agent of the Defendants, State Farm Insurance Companies, with the intention of coercing the Plaintiff into withdrawing from the political race and devoting his full time as an employee in the master and servant relationship to the performance of his service for said Defendants.

* * *

"Plaintiff charges and avers that the malicious intentional and wrongful direction as to his activities as agent of the Defendants was such a breach and repudiation of his contract or agreement with him as set out in Exhibit I as to entitle him, the Plaintiff to damages for the loss due to the breach or repudiation of the said agreement listed as Exhibit I."

2. E.g., immediately following the language quoted in Footnote 1, supra, the complaint charges the following:

"Plaintiff further shows unto the Court that at the time of the said repudiation or breach of contract by the Defendants, that the Plaintiff's income from the Defendants for the previous year was nine thousand seventy-three ($9,073.00) dollars and that the Plaintiff's life expectancy at his present age of 45 was 25.21 years according to the C.S.O. Mortality table, and that but for the wrongful breach, repudiation and termination of the Plaintiff's contract of agency with the Defendants, the Plaintiff would have been entitled to continued remuneration from the Defendants for the sum of two hundred twenty-six thousand, seven hundred twenty-five ($226,725.00) dollars and that but for the malicious, wanton meddling and interfering and wrongful breach, repudiation and cancellation of the Plaintiff's contract the Plaintiff is entitled to punitive damages in the sum of two hundred thousand ($200,000) dollars."

* * *

claimed by the appellant were those based entirely upon his claim that the written contract was wrongfully terminated, and the language concerning the meddling and interference is reasonably construed as referring to appellees' indication to appellant that he would have to give up his quest of public office if he desired to retain his contractual relationship with appellees. We are called upon here merely to test whether the court below erred in interpreting the meaning of language which was, viewed as a whole, clear and unambiguous. We do not think that it did.

If appellant had desired to pursue a charge that appellees had wrongfully interfered with the running of his business in violation of the terms of the written contract, it would have been quite simple for him to file an amended complaint. Doubtless the court below would have permitted this even after the order of dismissal had been granted. But aside from that, appellant had an absolute right to amend his complaint once, no responsive pleading having been filed. * * *

It is apparent that the complaint charged that appellees did nothing more than to exercise the right of termination given them by the explicit terms of the contract exhibited with appellant's complaint. * * * This being true, and since appellant claims no damages whatever except such as would flow from the wrongful termination of the contract, we think the court below correctly granted the motion to dismiss. Its judgment is

Affirmed.

Notes and Questions

1. Which of the three objectives of pleading discussed in the Outline of a Civil Action, in connection with the content of a complaint, was most significantly involved in this case?

2. Suppose a valid legal theory did exist that would have entitled Case to some relief, but that Case neglected to invoke it in his pleading. Would the court have been justified in dismissing the complaint on the principle that "it is [not] the duty of the trial court or the appellate court to create a claim which appellant has not spelled out in his pleading"? Wouldn't that simply punish Case for his lawyer's sloppy pleading?

3. In ROSEN v. TEXAS CO., 161 F.Supp. 55 (S.D.N.Y.1958), on a motion to dismiss under Federal Rule of Civil Procedure 12(b)(6), Judge Dimock said:

Even after a score of years of experience it is still doubtful just how much a complaint must state to avoid dismissal. * * * The principle is now expressed by many courts by the statement that a complaint will not be dismissed for failure to state a claim on which relief can be granted "unless it appears to a certainty that plaintiff is entitled to no relief under any state of facts which could be proved in support of the claim." * * *

This would seem to mean that all a plaintiff need state is what he wants from the court, but the Advisory Committee on the Rules seems to cling to the words of Rule 8(a) that the pleader must show that he is entitled to relief. In the Advisory Committee's Report * * * the Committee stated its opinion that Rule 8(a) "requires the pleader to disclose adequate information as to the basis of his claim for relief as distinguished from a bare averment that he wants relief and is entitled to it".

* * *

These motions have, all to no purpose, consumed a large amount of time of counsel for defendant in making them, of counsel for plaintiff in opposing them and of the court in considering and determining them and the progress of the litigation has been correspondingly delayed. It is my personal belief that the profession would do well to accept the fact that little can be accomplished by motions on the pleadings. The very uncertainty as to what constitutes a statement of a "claim upon which relief can be granted" demonstrates the unimportance of the question. We all should realize that the place of pleadings and motions thereon has been taken by interrogatories, depositions and discovery.

Id. at 57, 59.

4. In deciding the motion to dismiss in *Case,* should any significance have been given to the availability of discovery procedures to the parties? Of what relevance is the availability or nonavailability of other pretrial motions, such as summary judgment, that also might terminate the litigation before trial?

5. What was the effect of the dismissal in *Case?* Should plaintiff have been permitted to amend the complaint and start again? Could plaintiff interpose a new and slightly altered complaint that would survive another motion to dismiss?

6. Suppose that after the motion to dismiss had been granted Case discovered a letter agreement dated after the contract and signed by all of the parties stipulating that the insurance agency agreement could be terminated only for "good cause." Should he be able to amend his complaint and sue again in federal court? In state court?

———

Disputes often involve more than two people. The following case explores whether all those who are interested in a controversy always must be made parties to a single lawsuit.

TEMPLE v. SYNTHES CORP.

Supreme Court of the United States, 1990.
498 U.S. 5, 111 S.Ct. 315, 112 L.Ed.2d 263.

Certiorari to the United States Court of Appeals for the Fifth Circuit.

PER CURIAM. Petitioner Temple, a Mississippi resident, underwent surgery in October 1986 in which a "plate and screw device" was implanted in his lower spine. The device was manufactured by respondent Synthes, Ltd. (U.S.A.) (Synthes), a Pennsylvania corporation. Dr. S. Henry LaRocca performed the surgery at St. Charles General Hospital in New Orleans, Louisiana. Following surgery, the device's screws broke off inside Temple's back.

Temple filed suit against Synthes in the United States District Court for the Eastern District of Louisiana. The suit, which rested on diversity jurisdiction, alleged defective design and manufacture of the device. At the same time, Temple filed a state administrative proceeding against Dr. LaRocca and the hospital for malpractice and negligence. At the conclusion of the administrative proceeding, Temple filed suit against the doctor and the hospital in Louisiana state court.

Synthes did not attempt to bring the doctor and the hospital into the federal action by means of a third-party complaint, as provided in Federal

Rule * * * 14(a). Instead, Synthes filed a motion to dismiss Temple's federal suit for failure to join necessary parties pursuant to Federal Rule of Civil Procedure 19. Following a hearing, the District Court ordered Temple to join the doctor and the hospital as defendants within twenty days or risk dismissal of the lawsuit. According to the court, the most significant reason for requiring joinder was the interest of judicial economy. The court relied on this Court's decision in Provident Tradesmens Bank & Trust Co. v. Patterson, 390 U.S. 102, 88 S.Ct. 733, 19 L.Ed.2d 936 (1968), wherein we recognized that one focus of Rule 19 is "the interest of the courts and the public in complete, consistent, and efficient settlement of controversies." When Temple failed to join the doctor and the hospital, the court dismissed the suit with prejudice.

Temple appealed, and the United States Court of Appeals for the Fifth Circuit affirmed. The court deemed it "obviously prejudicial to the defendants to have the separate litigations being carried on," because Synthes' defense might be that the plate was not defective but that the doctor and the hospital were negligent, while the doctor and hospital, on the other hand, might claim that they were not negligent but that the plate was defective. The Court of Appeals found that the claims overlapped and that the District Court therefore had not abused its discretion in ordering joinder under Rule 19. * * *

* * * Temple contends that it was error to label joint tortfeasors as indispensable parties under Rule 19(b) and to dismiss the lawsuit with prejudice for failure to join those parties. We agree. Synthes does not deny that it, the doctor, and the hospital are potential joint tortfeasors. It has long been the rule that it is not necessary for all joint tortfeasors to be named as defendants in a single lawsuit. * * * The Advisory Committee Notes to Rule 19(a) explicitly state that "a tortfeasor with the usual 'joint-and-several' liability is merely a permissive party to an action against another with like liability." * * * There is nothing in Louisiana tort law to the contrary. * * *

The opinion in *Provident Bank* does speak of the public interest in limiting multiple litigation, but that case is not controlling here. There, the estate of a tort victim brought a declaratory judgment action against an insurance company [for the alleged tortfeasor. The total claims of the persons harmed in the accident exceeded the insurance policy monetary limits, and the purpose of the suit was to determine to which persons the insurance proceeds would be paid]. We assumed that the policyholder was a person "who, under [Rule 19] (a), should be joined if 'feasible' " * * *, and went on to discuss the appropriate analysis under Rule 19(b), because the policyholder could not be joined without destroying diversity. After examining the factors set forth in Rule 19(b), we determined that the action could proceed without the policyholder; he therefore was not an indispensable party whose absence required dismissal of the suit.

Here, no inquiry under Rule 19(b) is necessary, because the threshold requirements of Rule 19(a) have not been satisfied. As potential joint tortfeasors with Synthes, Dr. LaRocca and the hospital were merely permissive parties. The Court of Appeals erred by failing to hold that the District Court abused its discretion in ordering them joined as defendants and in dismissing the action when Temple failed to comply with the court's order. For these reasons, we grant the petition for certiorari, reverse the judgment of the

Court of Appeals for the Fifth Circuit, and remand for further proceedings consistent with this opinion.

It is so ordered.

Notes and Questions

1. Why do you think Temple didn't name Dr. LaRocca and the hospital as defendants in his federal suit? Why would Temple seek to duplicate his time and effort by litigating a suit in federal court at the same time that he is litigating one in state court with respect to precisely the same injury?

2. Although the Supreme Court failed to specify the citizenship of Dr. LaRocca and the hospital, they were in fact citizens of Louisiana, meaning that complete diversity existed between Temple and the three defendants. See Temple v. Synthes Corp., 130 F.R.D. 68, 69 n. 1 (E.D.La.1989). Does this information change your answers to the questions in Note 1, supra?

3. What do you make of the Fifth Circuit's concern with the potential for inconsistent judgments? Does the Supreme Court find that this concern is not warranted? Or does it find that there are other more important considerations? If so, what are they?

4. When this case returns to the district court, could the court order Synthes to file a third-party complaint against the doctor and the hospital under Federal Rule of Civil Procedure 14(a)? Should a court ever have the power to order parties added to a lawsuit? Why?

5. Suppose that both Temple and Synthes do not want the doctor and the hospital to be added as parties and the court doesn't order that they be added. Could the doctor and the hospital join the federal suit of their own accord? See Federal Rule of Civil Procedure 24. Should Temple and/or Synthes be able to stop them from intervening?

————

The purposes of discovery are many. The most important are obtaining evidence for one's own case and identifying weaknesses in the opposition's. The party seeking discovery usually is asking about something of which he is ignorant or uncertain, but sometimes he seeks information about a matter within his own knowledge. In reading the next case, consider why plaintiff is so determined to obtain the evidence and why defendant is equally determined that he shall not have it.

DiMICHEL v. SOUTH BUFFALO RY. CO.[d]

Court of Appeals of New York, 1992.
80 N.Y.2d 184, 590 N.Y.S.2d 1, 604 N.E.2d 63.

WACHTLER, CHIEF JUDGE. * * * [W]e consider whether surveillance films prepared by a defendant in a personal injury action are discoverable by the plaintiff before trial. * * * The Appellate Division held * * * that the defen-

d. The court's treatment of the companion case, Poole v. Consolidated Rail Corp., has been omitted.

dants would be obligated to disclose only those tapes which they planned to use at trial. Under the facts present here, we find this balance to be an appropriate one. Accordingly, * * * we affirm. * * *

Plaintiff Anthony DiMichel commenced this action against South Buffalo Railway Company (South Buffalo) in Supreme Court, Erie County, by service of summons and complaint dated January 16, 1986. Plaintiff alleged that on June 6, 1984, while employed by South Buffalo, he sustained injuries in a fall. DiMichel charged South Buffalo with violations of the Federal Employees' Liability Act, the Safety Appliance Act and the Boiler Inspection Act and asked for $500,000 in damages.

In the course of pre-trial discovery, plaintiff asked for disclosure of all videotapes or surveillance films that defendant may have taken of plaintiff. Without conceding that it in fact possessed surveillance materials, South Buffalo contended that any such material was not discoverable. Plaintiff then moved to compel disclosure. * * * [T]he motion to compel disclosure was granted and defendant was ordered "to turn over to plaintiff for inspection and copying any and all videotapes and/or surveillance films of the plaintiff," but stayed this order pending appeal to the Appellate Division. The Appellate Division modified, * * * holding that the defendant was obligated to turn over those surveillance materials it intended to use at trial, and that the defendant would be precluded from using any surveillance material it did not supply to plaintiff within 60 days of its order. * * *

* * *

* * * [W]e now turn to the unique problems posed by surveillance films. Personal injury defendants secure surveillance materials in order to verify the extent of a plaintiff's purported injuries and introduce them because they are powerful and immediate images that cast doubt upon the plaintiff's claims. And indeed, if accurate and authentic, a surveillance film that undercuts a plaintiff's claims of injury may be devastatingly probative. At the same time, however, film and videotape are extraordinarily manipulable media. Artful splicing and deceptive lighting are but two ways that an image can be skewed and perception altered. As one court has noted, "[t]he camera may be an instrument of deception. It can be misused. Distances may be minimized or exaggerated. Lighting, focal lengths, and camera angles all make a difference. Action may be slowed down or speeded up. The editing and splicing of films may change the chronology of events. An emergency situation may be made to appear commonplace. That which has occurred once, can be described as an example of an event which recurs frequently. * * * Thus, that which purports to be a means to reach the truth may be distorted, misleading and false." Snead v. American Export–Isbrandtsen Lines, 59 F.R.D. 148, 150 [(E.D.Pa. 1973)].

Thus, while an accurate surveillance film may indeed prove to be a bombshell, the possibility of inaccuracy, given the nature of the medium, is very real. In resolving the question now before us, then, it is important to note that New York has long favored open and far-reaching pre-trial discovery. To a large extent, New York's open disclosure policy was intended to mark an end to the presentation of totally unexpected evidence and to substitute honesty and forthrightness for gamesmanship. * * *

* * *

This is clearly an issue that has fragmented the four departments of the Appellate Division. * * * [T]he First Department would treat surveillance films as discoverable in their entirety * * * [as] party statements. The Second Department followed the lead of the Fourth Department in [this case] by treating surveillance films as material prepared for litigation and by holding that substantial need and undue hardship inhered in the nature of the films themselves. Finally, the Third Department, while also treating these films as material prepared for litigation, held that such films were discoverable only upon a showing of substantial need and undue hardship.

Having considered the different approaches, we agree with the Second, Third and Fourth Departments that surveillance films should be treated as material prepared in anticipation of litigation, and as such, are subject to a qualified privilege that can be overcome only by a factual showing of substantial need and undue hardship.

That the plaintiffs * * * have a substantial need to view surveillance films before trial is manifest. Because films are so easily altered, there is a very real danger that deceptive tapes, inadequately authenticated, could contaminate the trial process. The question that remains, therefore, is whether plaintiffs confronted with surveillance films for the first time at trial would have an adequate opportunity to ascertain the films' accuracy and authenticity. * * * Authentication of surveillance films can be a slow and painstaking process, and because of the potentially devastating effects of such evidence, it would be improper to curtail a plaintiff's efforts to do so. Thus, a plaintiff, confronted with a surveillance film at trial, would certainly be entitled to a continuance to examine the video evidence. Indeed, it would appear to be well within the discretion of a Trial Judge, under certain circumstances, to give plaintiff an extended continuance in order to retain an expert who could ascertain the authenticity of proffered video evidence. Thus, if defendants were allowed to withhold surveillance evidence until trial, personal injury trials could be routinely disrupted and delayed.

Further, a plaintiff confronted with altered video evidence for the first time at trial would likely be prejudiced by the apparent weight and authority of such evidence. Even if after careful examination plaintiff was able to demonstrate that the evidence had indeed been distorted, it would be difficult to undo its initial impact and to erase the impression left in the minds of the jury members.

Defendants dispute plaintiffs' claims of substantial need, arguing that the real reason they seek to obtain the tapes prior to trial is to learn what evidence the defendants intend to produce at trial so that they may tailor their trial testimony accordingly. This, defendants argue, would greatly impair the truth-finding function of cross-examination. This argument, however, is flawed for at least two reasons. First, it runs counter to New York's open pre-trial disclosure policy, as discussed earlier. Clearly, to permit defendants to withhold this evidence until trial, even for the ostensible purpose of promoting vigorous cross-examination, would be to return to an earlier time, when subterfuge and surprise were common trial strategies. Second, it is persuasive only if we assume that surveillance tapes are always accurate and plaintiffs always dishonest. As noted above, however, surveillance films are extraordinarily susceptible to manipulation, and, once altered, are peculiarly dangerous. Thus, we cannot fashion a rule that is premised upon their authenticity, as defendants urge. However, the danger identified by defendants is a real one. We believe that it can be largely eliminated by providing that surveillance films should be turned over only after a plaintiff has been deposed.

We further find that plaintiffs have established that they cannot without undue hardship obtain the substantial equivalent of surveillance materials by other means. Although plaintiffs are aware of their own physical ailments and the nature of their disabilities, this is no substitute for viewing the surveillance materials taken by the defendants. It is only by viewing the surveillance film that plaintiffs can determine when it was made and whether the activities depicted were typical of that time or were the product of an emergency situation. Visual evidence of this kind is unique because it memorializes a particular set of conditions that can likely never be replicated. Only by observing the conditions as they appear on film can the plaintiffs respond to possible distortions or prepare to explain seeming inconsistencies to the jury. * * *

* * * Having concluded that the plaintiff was entitled to view those tapes that the defendant intended to use at trial, if indeed any such tapes exist, our analysis * * * is at an end. Accordingly, the order of the Appellate Division should be affirmed * * *.

* * *

Notes and Questions

1. * * * [T]he common law * * * *recognized no rule requiring prior notice* of intended evidence to be given to the opponent or furnishing legal process for obtaining such information * * *.

It might be supposed that, in the court of Chancery, a bill for discovery served as a means of evading the strict common-law rule, and that thereby a notice could be compulsorily obtained of the evidence intended to be produced by the opponent. But there was here no radical departure from the established doctrine of the common law; it was a policy, not of one Court rather than another Court, but of the whole legal system * * * [of England].

* * * It is true that, to a limited extent * * * the result of a bill of discovery would usually be the revelation of some portion of information not before known to the applicant. But the general theory remained, and the rule was strictly enforced, that the adversary's own evidence was not to be revealed on a bill for discovery.

In short, equitable discovery involved no more than the negation of the party's privilege at common-law trials not to testify *against* his own cause, and was not intended to give relief against the common-law principle which refused to exact before trial a disclosure of the tenor of the evidence intended to be given *for* his cause.

6 Wigmore, *Evidence* §§ 1845, 1846, at 378, 380 (3d ed. 1940).

2. The court in *DiMichel* held that materials prepared in anticipation of trial normally are exempt from discovery, unless a party can show a substantial need and an undue hardship. Do you agree that surveillance videotapes present such a situation? In general, why are materials prepared for trial exempt from discovery at all?

3. Is the holding in *DiMichel* limited to videotaped evidence or does it apply to other types of impeachment evidence as well? Suppose plaintiff is deposed and testifies that prior to the accident being sued on she had never suffered a disabling injury. Plaintiff then attempts to have defendant answer an interrogatory as to what information defendant has regarding plaintiff's prior medical history. What result? See Boldt v. Sanders, 261 Minn. 160, 111 N.W.2d 225 (1961).

4. Is the court in *DiMichel* correct in not allowing videotapes to be disclosed until after plaintiff has been deposed? If the court is truly following a policy of open discovery, why does it matter when the videotapes are disclosed?

———

In ruling on a motion to dismiss for failure to state a claim as in Case v. State Farm Mutual Automobile Ins. Co., p. 26, supra, the judge must accept as true the allegations in the complaint. If defendant files an answer denying those allegations, the denials are only assertions of defendant and do not demonstrate whose story is correct. The motion for summary judgment enables a party to show that there is admissible evidence to support the allegations made and to call for a similar showing by the opposing party. The judge will not try to decide a factual dispute when each party has presented evidence on an issue. But if it becomes clear that one party cannot possibly prove his allegations, there is no "genuine issue" and a futile trial may be avoided by granting the motion.

ALDERMAN v. BALTIMORE & OHIO R. CO.

United States District Court, Southern District of West Virginia, 1953.
113 F.Supp. 881.

MOORE, CHIEF JUDGE. Plaintiff * * * brings this action against defendant, * * * to recover for personal injuries sustained by her as a result of the derailment of one of defendant's trains near Adrian, West Virginia, on February 14, 1952.

Plaintiff was not a fare-paying passenger. She was traveling on a trip pass, which afforded her free transportation * * *. The following conditions were printed on the pass: "In consideration of the issuance of this free pass, I hereby assume all risk of personal injury and loss of or of damage to property from whatever causes arising, and release the company from liability therefor, and I hereby declare that I am not prohibited by law from receiving free transportation and that this pass will be lawfully used."

Plaintiff in her original complaint charged defendant with negligence in the maintenance of its tracks and the operation of its train. After a pre-trial conference, at which the legal effect of the release from liability contained in the pass was discussed, plaintiff filed an amended complaint charging defendant with wilful or wanton conduct.

On the basis of the amended pleadings and supporting affidavits filed by defendant, defendant moved for summary judgment under Rule 56 * * *.

It is undisputed that the derailment was caused by a break in one of the rails as the train was passing over the track. It is also shown by defendant's affidavits, and not denied, that the break in the rail was due to a transverse fissure inside the cap of the rail, which broke vertically under the weight of the train; that such a fissure is not visible upon inspection; that such defects occur in both new and old rails; and that a visual inspection was in fact made of this particular rail the day preceding the accident and the defect was not discovered.

Since plaintiff was an intrastate passenger, and since the accident occurred in West Virginia, the law of West Virginia governs both the effect to be given to the release and the degree of care which defendant owed plaintiff. * * *

However, counsel have been unable to direct the Court's attention to, and the Court has not found, any West Virginia decision which has determined the effect which a release from liability contained in a pass has upon the carrier's duty to the holder of such a pass. * * *

Since the Federal statute and the West Virginia statute authorizing the issuance of free passes are similar, 49 U.S.C.A. § 1(7), and W.Va.Code, Ch. 24, Art. 3, § 4, it is pertinent to examine the United States Supreme Court decisions construing the Federal statute. The Supreme Court has held that a carrier may contract against liability for negligent injury to one who accepts a free pass * * *; but that for reasons of public policy it cannot relieve itself of liability for wilful or wanton acts. * * *

I am therefore of [the] opinion that the sole duty imposed upon defendant under the facts of this case was to refrain from wilfully or wantonly injuring plaintiff.

In Kelly v. Checker White Cab, Inc., 131 W.Va. 816 at page 822; 50 S.E.2d 888 at page 892, the West Virginia court, quoting from 29 Cyc. 510 said:

In order that one may be held guilty of wilful or wanton conduct, it must be shown that he was conscious of his conduct, and conscious, from his knowledge of existing conditions, that injury would likely or probably result from his conduct, and that with reckless indifference to consequences he consciously and intentionally did some wrongful act or omitted some known duty which produced the injurious result. * * *

The substance of plaintiff's contention that defendant wilfully injured her is that defendant used old and obsolescent rails in its tracks, knowing that the use of these rails made derailments reasonably probable. It is charged that defendant used old rails because the cost of derailments was less than the cost of replacing the old rails, and that for this reason defendant was willing to take the risk of derailments.

I am of opinion that the complaint fails to state sufficient facts to substantiate a charge of wilfulness, as that term is defined by the West Virginia court. It is clear that plaintiff has stated a charge of negligence; but that is not the test in this case. To establish wilfulness it would be necessary to charge that defendant knew of this particular defect in the rail; that the defect would probably result in a break in the rail if the train were run over it, causing a derailment of the train; and that defendant, with this knowledge of existing conditions, and the likelihood or probability of an injury resulting from its conduct, intentionally drove its train over the defective rail with an indifference to the consequences. The undenied affidavits of defendant show clearly that plaintiff cannot establish these facts.

At the hearing of this motion, counsel for plaintiff moved for a continuance of the hearing to enable him to substantiate a newspaper report to the effect that defendant was using old and obsolescent rails in its tracks because the cost of derailments was cheaper than the cost of replacing the rails. The motion was denied since this contention, even if it were true, merely has a bearing on an issue of negligence, and not upon the question of wilful conduct. Plaintiff does not contend that she can establish that defendant knew of the particular defect in the rail that caused the derailment.

For the reasons stated above, defendant's motion for summary judgment will be sustained. * * *

Notes and Questions

1. If very specific allegations of all of the facts giving rise to plaintiff's cause of action were required to be set forth in the complaint, would it have been possible to handle the *Alderman* case by a motion to dismiss or a demurrer? To the extent that this would have been possible, does the case present a strong argument for more specific pleading of facts? Consider whether the court should have ruled as it did if the motion for summary judgment had been made immediately upon the service of the complaint and before plaintiff had an opportunity to utilize the discovery process. What provision does Federal Rule of Civil Procedure 56 make for this contingency? Analytically, the motion for summary judgment can be thought of as a demurrer-plus. You should not forget, however, that if summary judgment is to be a fair and effective device, it must frequently be preceded by discovery, so that each party will have an opportunity to disclose the gaps in her opponent's case and to cure any defects in her own.

2. What advantage did defendant gain in *Alderman* by moving for summary judgment, rather than moving to dismiss? Reread the third paragraph of the case. Should plaintiff be able to amend a complaint in this situation? Was her amendment made merely to prolong litigation in the hope of forcing a settlement?

3. Should a court always grant a motion for summary judgment if the requirements of Rule 56 are met? In KENNEDY v. SILAS MASON CO., 334 U.S. 249, 256–57, 68 S.Ct. 1031, 1034, 92 L.Ed. 1347, 1350–51 (1948), Justice Jackson, speaking for the Court, said:

> * * * [S]ummary procedures, however salutary where issues are clear-cut and simple, present a treacherous record for deciding issues of far-flung import, on which this Court should draw inferences with caution from complicated courses of legislation, contracting and practice.

> We consider it the part of good judicial administration to withhold decision of the ultimate questions involved in this case until this or another record shall present a more solid basis of findings based on litigation or on a comprehensive statement of agreed facts. While we might be able, on the present record, to reach a conclusion that would decide the case, it might well be found later to be lacking in the thoroughness that should precede judg-

ment of this importance and which it is the purpose of the judicial process to provide.

4. A motion for summary judgment may be useful even though the moving party believes it will be unsuccessful. For what reasons, other than a hope of obtaining judgment, might defendant in a case like *Alderman* make such a motion?

3. JUDGE AND JURY

You probably will be surprised (and perhaps dismayed) by the comparatively small part of a Civil Procedure course devoted to the actual process of trial. It is true that the trial, if one occurs, is the most important and most interesting stage of a lawsuit. But most of the "law" about trials is the subject-matter of a course in Evidence. The most important aspect of trial with which this course is concerned is the division of functions between judge and jury and the various ways in which the judge acts to insure that the jury performs its proper function. In this section, we look at four of those ways: the instruction of the jury as to the law it shall apply, the form that the verdict takes, judicial control over the matters the jury may consider, and the taking from the jury of its power to decide a case when the evidence is inadequate.

a. *Instructing the Jury*

Broadly stated, it is a function of the judge to decide questions of law and a function of the jury to decide questions of fact. But in most cases the jury's final decision will be that one or the other party is entitled to judgment and the jury must apply the law to the facts to reach this decision. Therefore the jury must be told what the law is. The vehicle for this is the judge's charge to the jury, which comes at the end of the trial, immediately before the jury retires to consider its verdict.

An important issue concerning these instructions is how far the adversary system should extend to this stage of the lawsuit. Counsel for both parties may request that particular instructions be given to the jury, and when there is a dispute between them as to the law, they ordinarily will submit conflicting requests. The judge must resolve such conflicts, and it is the court's duty in any event to instruct the jury whether or not the parties make specific requests. The judge, even though an expert on the law, may err. To what extent is it the responsibility of counsel to attempt to correct the trial judge? The next case involves not only this question, but it also introduces you to the question of allocating the burden of proof (or burden of persuasion). Why is there any rule that says one party or the other has this burden?

ALEXANDER v. KRAMER BROS. FREIGHT LINES, INC.

United States Court of Appeals, Second Circuit, 1959.
273 F.2d 373.

Swan, Circuit Judge. The present action is a sequel to a collision between two tractor-trailer trucks on the Pennsylvania Turnpike in or near Somerset, Pennsylvania. It occurred * * * about six o'clock in the morning, when there was spotty fog on the Turnpike. The corporate plaintiff owned one of the trucks. It was badly damaged and its operator, the plaintiff Alexander, sustained serious injuries. The other truck was owned by the defendant corporation. Its answer to the complaint denied any negligence on its part and set up the defense of contributory negligence on the part of the plaintiffs. The jury found a verdict for the plaintiffs. * * *

Because of the character of the questions raised, a very brief statement concerning the testimony will suffice. The only eye witnesses to the accident were drivers of the two trucks. The drivers' stories were contradictory and raised issues as to the exact location of the accident and the manner in which it occurred. Both trucks were proceeding westerly. Alexander testified that the collision occurred where there was an entrance to the Turnpike from the right, that defendant's truck cut in ahead of him, and that the fog was such that he could not see the entering truck in time to avoid hitting it. Holman, defendant's driver, denied that he entered from the right and claimed that plaintiff's truck had been following for some time before it ran into the rear end of his truck. Thus the issues of negligence and contributory negligence raised questions of credibility for the jury.

The first question for consideration is whether the judgment should be reversed because of the court's erroneous charge as to the burden of proof of contributory negligence, despite defendant's failure to request a charge on that subject or to object or take exception to the charge given, as required by Rule 51 * * *. Appellant contends that he is excused from complying with the Rule by what occurred in colloquy with the court near the close of the plaintiffs' case. In the colloquy, the court stated that "the burden of proof of contributory negligence is on the defendant." Counsel for plaintiffs expressed agreement with the statement, and counsel for defendant said, "I take an exception," to which the court replied, "Yes, I give you that exception." The plaintiff then rested, and defendant proceeded to put in its case.

* * * Under the [applicable law] the plaintiffs in an action where death has not resulted * * * carry the burden of proving freedom from contributory negligence. The cases now relied upon by appellant to prove the charge wrong were never brought to the trial court's attention either in the colloquy or at the time when counsel submitted numerous requests to charge on other matters. Had they been, it seems probable that Judge Inch would have changed the view he expressed in colloquy. The obvious purpose of the requirement in Rule 51 that objection must be made to matters in the charge in order to assign them as error, is to permit the trial judge to evaluate the objection and correct his charge if further thought persuades him of its error. This purpose is not fulfilled by taking an exception to a statement made by the judge several days prior to the time for charging the jury when nothing was before the judge requiring a ruling in respect to the statement made in colloquy. Certainly an exception under such circumstances does not meet the literal requirement of Rule 51 and, in our opinion, it is an insufficient excuse for failure to object or except to the charge.

The cases relied upon by the appellant deal either with situations where an exception was taken at the time of the charge and the question is whether the exception was sufficiently explicit, or to cases involving evidentiary rulings where exception was taken at the time of the ruling but no further exception was taken at the time of the charge. * * * Nor do we think the instant case of the exceptional character in which an appellate court will sometimes correct an error in the charge in the absence of objection or exception. See Troupe v. Chicago, D. & G. Bay Transit Co., 2 Cir., 234 F.2d 253, 260.

* * *

Judgment affirmed.

Notes and Questions

1. The opinion in this case speaks of the "burden of proof of contributory negligence." In this book, we use the term "burden of persuasion" when we are referring to the kind of burden involved in *Alexander*. There is another kind of burden—the burden of initially putting in evidence on an issue, without which the issue is not in the case at all. This kind of burden we call the "burden of production." The two burdens are distinct, but the term "burden of proof" often is used to mean either of them. For this reason we avoid it. Ordinarily the burden of production and the burden of persuasion on an issue are placed on the same party. But not always. For example, when a defense is one that is seldom raised, it might be a waste of time to require plaintiff in every case to introduce evidence refuting it; the burden of production would be placed on defendant. But once there is enough evidence on the issue to go to the jury, the court might rule that plaintiff should have the burden of persuasion—that is, establishing that the defense is not valid—as plaintiff does on most issues.

2. What factors should be considered in determining whether the burden of persuasion on the issue of contributory negligence should be placed on plaintiff or defendant? Are these the same factors that should be involved in deciding who shall be required to plead on the issue of contributory negligence? Why might the two burdens be placed differently?

3. In the *Troupe* case, cited at the end of the principal case, Judge Frank, in a concurring opinion, said, at 234 F.2d at 260–61:

On the negligence issue, the judge, at defendant's request, charged, "It is enough if the steps and paint are commonly used and accepted in the industry at the time." This was as obvious an error, on a material matter, as one can imagine. For the Supreme Court, this court and others have often held that usual practices, by others in the same industry or trade, similar to a defendant's practices, do not constitute a defense in a negligence action.

My colleagues indicate that, were it not for our reversal on the unseaworthiness issue, they would probably have disregarded this error. I cannot agree. My colleagues refer to Rule 51 and the fact that, before the jury retired, plaintiffs' counsel did not state distinctly that he objected and the grounds of the objection. My colleagues concede that, in an exceptional case, we may review errors not "saved" by a proper objection. They suggest this is not an exceptional case, relying on a statement in United States v. Atkinson, 297 U.S. 157, 160, 56 S.Ct. 391, 392, 80 L.Ed. 555. There the Supreme Court, set forth, in the disjunctive, two grounds for reviewing such errors:

(1) "the errors are obvious

or

(2) they otherwise seriously affect the fairness, integrity, or public reputation of judicial proceedings."

My colleagues stress the second ground. But the first ground alone suffices, as the cases make clear. And here, as observed above, the error was magnificently obvious. A litigant surely has the right to assume that a federal trial judge knows the elementary substantive legal rules, long established by the precedents, and that therefore the judge will act accordingly, without prompting by the litigant's lawyer.

Was the trial judge's error in *Alexander* "obvious"? What factors are relevant to this question?

b. *The Form of the Verdict*

In most cases, the jury is asked to return a "general verdict." In substance, the jury simply says, "We find for plaintiff and fix damages at *x* dollars" or "We find for defendant." But as previously discussed in the Outline, pp. 13–14, supra, there are two variations on the general verdict. One is the special verdict, in which the jury is asked to answer questions as to the facts; the judge then applies the law to the facts as found by the jury. The other is the general verdict with interrogatories; the jury is told to return a verdict in the same form as a general verdict, but in addition it is told to answer certain questions about the facts of the case. If those answers are not consistent with the general verdict, the answers control. There are a number of reasons for using the special verdict or the general verdict with interrogatories. For example, in a complicated case, the special verdict obviates the necessity of instructing the jury about the law and permits it to concentrate on determining the facts. But you should bear in mind that both of these verdict forms also are devices for controlling the jury—for preventing the jury from ignoring the law and simply deciding the case for the party the jurors want to win.

DINIERO v. UNITED STATES LINES CO.

United States Court of Appeals, Second Circuit, 1961.
288 F.2d 595, certiorari denied 368 U.S. 831, 82 S.Ct. 54, 7 L.Ed.2d 34.

MEDINA, CIRCUIT JUDGE. * * * Julio Diniero, a Junior Third Assistant Engineer aboard the S.S. Pioneer Land, owned by United States Lines Company, claimed to have suffered such repeated strains in his back in the performance of his duties as to cause a ruptured disc with resultant pain and suffering, culminating some years later in a fusion operation and the removal of the disc. According to Diniero's testimony, there was a blow-down valve located below a floor plate * * *. There was a slot in the floor plate and normally the valve could be opened or closed as circumstances required by using a reach rod. For a variety of reasons * * * which include the absence of a reach rod and defects in the valve, Diniero said the only way he could operate the valve was by removing the deck plate, crouching down and moving the wheel of the valve by the use of a wrench. He claimed the injuries to his back were the effect of repeatedly operating the valve under these difficult conditions. The shipowner * * * claimed there was nothing wrong with the valve, nor any necessity to remove the floor plate or to use a wrench. The eight day trial was devoted to * * * the controverted issue of liability, and there was also considerable medical proof on the general subject of whether Diniero's trouble was due to a long continued condition caused by a degenerative disc disease and having no relation whatever to the operation of the blow-down valve * * *.

At the close of the evidence the trial judge submitted the case to the jury in a wholly unexceptionable charge. In an endeavor to assist the jury in its deliberations, however, * * * he submitted eight questions to be signed and returned as the verdict of the jury. The last two were in the form of a general verdict for plaintiff or defendant, questions 2 to 6 [related] * * * to unseaworthiness, negligence, contributory negligence and proximate cause. The trouble was caused by question number 1, as follows:

> Did the plaintiff injure himself aboard the Pioneer Land because in operating the blow-down valve he had to remove the floor plates, then crouch and exert physical effort with a wrench and not his hand to stop it from leaking?
>
> Answer yes or no.

After some hours of deliberation and the receipt of a number of communications from the jury, the trial judge withdrew all the questions, told the jury to disregard them and bring in a general verdict in the usual form; and, after further deliberations the jury brought in a verdict in favor of the seaman for $46,150. * * *

The position of the shipowner is that * * * Rule 49(b) authorizes the submission of written interrogatories but does not authorize the withdrawal of such interrogatories, after they have once been submitted and the jury has commenced its deliberations thereon. The shipowner further argues that question number 1 related to "one or more issues of fact the decision of which is necessary to a verdict," and that * * * it was a clear abuse of discretion to withdraw a proper and material interrogatory, relating to an issue that must necessarily be decided in plaintiff's favor, if plaintiff was to recover any damages whatever. To permit such withdrawal, the shipowner claims, would defeat the very purpose of * * * Rule 49(b), and smooth the way for a reluctant jury, unable to agree on the facts basic to recovery, to do "popular justice" through the medium of "an old-fashioned verdict."

* * *

The jury commenced their deliberations at 2:45 p.m. At 5:40 p.m. the trial judge received a note from the jury reading: "Your Honor, could we ask for your interpretation of the word 'had' in the second line, first question? Did the plaintiff injure himself?"

Appellant's counsel assures us that the question and the explanation given by the trial judge is just as simple as * * * whether he was injured in the manner described by him in his testimony. What the trial judge said, however, is as follows:

> What I was trying to find out by the first question was whether or not plaintiff injured himself on board this ship, assuming that he had to remove the plates, assuming that he had to crouch down, and assuming he exerted this pressure with the wrench instead of his hand?
>
> So in answer to your specific question as to the interpretation of the word "had" it means that I assumed that he had to remove the plates, and he had to do this, and he had to do that. I didn't mean to take away

from you the question as to whether he did in fact have to do that. In other words, the purpose of the question is to find out whether the plaintiff injured himself on board the ship in the manner that he described. The defendant claims that he did not. So the first question that I wanted answered was did he injure himself aboard the ship by doing what he said he did?

If you find that he didn't remove the plates or he didn't bend down, or he didn't crouch, or he didn't have to, or he didn't do it, those questions will be answered as you go on further down by your answers to the other questions.

But in my first question I assumed as a fact, accepted the plaintiff's testimony, that he had to bend down, that he had to crouch, that he had to remove the plates.

What I wanted to find out was, assuming all of that, did he injure himself on board the Pioneer Land.

Now I hope that is clear. If it isn't you can write me another note.

The jury retired again at 5:50 p.m. and returned with another note at 6:40 p.m. * * * as follows: "Your Honor, we cannot agree on question one. It appears there is no chance for agreement." Thereupon the trial judge withdrew all the questions from the consideration of the jury and asked them to see if they could not agree on a general verdict.

* * * [T]he jury still could not soon reach agreement. At 9:22 p.m. the jury informed the trial judge that "it finds it impossible to arrive at a unanimous agreement in this case." The trial judge thereupon read a quotation from Allen v. United States, 1896, 164 U.S. 492, 501, 17 S.Ct. 154, 41 L.Ed. 528, and returned the jury for further deliberations at 9:30 p.m. * * * At 10:30 p.m. the verdict was announced and the jury polled.

There was an inherent ambiguity in question one, and it is plain enough that the explanation failed to remove the ambiguity. Under these circumstances we think it was not an abuse of discretion to withdraw the questions and give the jury an opportunity to agree upon a general verdict. * * * It was a matter of judgment whether to attempt some further elucidation of the question, or to declare a mistrial, or to withdraw all the questions and authorize a general verdict. We cannot say the decision made here under the circumstances of this case was wrong, particularly as the jury continued its deliberations from about 6:45 p.m. until 10:30 p.m., after the withdrawal of the questions.

* * *

Other cases present the problem in its simplest form. After the submission of material and proper interrogatories, there is a delay of a few hours and the trial judge of his own motion, or on the application of plaintiff's counsel, calls in the jury, withdraws the questions, tells the jury to bring in a general verdict over the objection of defendant's counsel, and shortly thereafter the jury returns a verdict for the plaintiff. This has been held to be an abuse of discretion and ground for reversal. * * * The reason is that the action of the trial judge would probably be prejudicial to defendant. * * * This is a good general rule, and we agree with it. But it has no application to the case before us now, as the interrogatory causing all the difficulty here was unclear and ambiguous. The withdrawal of all the questions was for the purpose of eliminating the confusion caused by the formulation of an improper question. And it is to be noted that a confusing and improperly worded interrogatory cannot fairly be considered a "material" question, or one the answer to which "is necessary to a verdict." Under the circumstances it was, we think, good judgment to withdraw all the questions. Certainly we cannot say to do so was an abuse of discretion.

Affirmed.

Notes and Questions

1. Do you believe the interrogatory as first given to the jury was ambiguous? What are the possible meanings of the question? Could the jury answer the question "No" under any of these meanings and still find for plaintiff? If the jury had answered the interrogatory "No," and a reviewing court found that there was no evidence at all to support a finding that Diniero was *not* required to remove the plate, crouch down, and turn the valve with a wrench, but that a genuine issue existed on the question whether his condition was caused by this work, would the reviewing court be required to reverse a verdict for defendant that was based on the answer to the first interrogatory?

2. Could the judge simply have rewritten the interrogatory in clearer language and resubmitted it? What reasons mitigate against allowing that practice?

3. Could the jury have properly reached a decision for plaintiff without resolving the issue that the judge said in his explanation he intended the interrogatory to present? If it could not, was it proper to withdraw the interrogatory altogether and say to the jury: "What I am going to do, in an effort to see whether you can agree, I am going to ask you to forget all of the questions I gave you and see whether you can't agree on a general verdict. * * * I think that might relieve the situation some. I hope you can come to some agreement." (Judge's Instruction, quoted from the Petition for a Writ of Certiorari, p. 11.)

4. Do you think the judge's explanation of the interrogatory was clear? Read it again very carefully before you decide. Then reflect upon the fact that it was delivered orally to the jurors, even though the interrogatories themselves were in writing. When the jury is asked to return a general verdict, the charge, frequently including very complex instructions on the law, is given orally, and although the jurors may ask to have parts of it repeated, they usually are not given a copy. From the experience in this case do you think written instructions would be a better idea?

5. The use of special verdicts and general verdicts with interrogatories is sometimes criticized as atomizing the jury's deliberations and making a unanimous result more difficult to reach. Assume that in an ordinary automobile accident case, three members of the jury believe that defendant was going too fast but the other three believe that he was not; moreover, the latter group of jurors believes that defendant was not looking where he was going, but the first group believes that defendant was. Could the jury return a unanimous verdict for plaintiff? For defendant? Would the problem be aggravated by the use of a special verdict or a general verdict with interrogatories? For a perceptive discussion of the general problem, see Ginsburg, *Special Findings and Jury Unanimity in the Federal Courts*, 65 Colum.L.Rev. 256 (1965). See also Trubitt, *Patchwork Verdicts*,

Different–Juror Verdicts, and American Jury Theory: Whether Verdicts Are Invalidated by Juror Disagreement on Issues, 36 Okla.L.Rev. 473 (1983).

6. ALLEN v. UNITED STATES, 164 U.S. 492, 17 S.Ct. 154, 41 L.Ed. 528 (1896), which the trial court in *Diniero* quoted to the jury, involved a variation on what has come to be called the "dynamite charge," an instruction that is sometimes given in the principal charge but more frequently is given only to a jury that has been unable to reach a unanimous verdict for either party after a substantial period of time. In *Allen* this charge was given some time after the main charge. Its content was,

> in substance, that in a large proportion of cases absolute certainty could not be expected; that, although the verdict must be the verdict of each individual juror, and not a mere acquiescence in the conclusion of his fellows, yet they should examine the question submitted with candor, and with a proper regard and deference to the opinions of each other; that it was their duty to decide the case if they could conscientiously do so; that they should listen, with a disposition to be convinced, to each other's arguments; that, if much the larger number were for conviction, a dissenting juror should consider whether his doubt was a reasonable one which made no impression upon the minds of so many men, equally honest, equally intelligent with himself. If, upon the other hand, the majority were for acquittal, the minority ought to ask themselves whether they might not reasonably doubt the correctness of a judgment which was not concurred in by the majority.

Id. at 501, 17 S.Ct. at 157, 41 L.Ed. at 530–31. The United States Supreme Court said:

> While, undoubtedly, the verdict of the jury should represent the opinion of each individual juror, it by no means follows that opinions may not be changed by conference in the jury room. The very object of the jury system is to secure unanimity by a comparison of views, and by arguments among the jurors themselves. It certainly cannot be the law that each juror should not listen with deference to the arguments, and with a distrust of his own judgment, if he finds a large majority of the jury taking a different view of the case from what he does himself. It cannot be that each juror should go to the jury room with a blind determination that the verdict shall represent his opinion of the case at that moment, or that he should close his ears to the arguments of men who are equally honest and intelligent as himself.

Id. at 501, 17 S.Ct. at 157, 41 L.Ed. at 530. Does this opinion adequately answer the objections that may be made to such a charge?

c. *The Jury's Deliberation*

After the judge completes the charge, the jury retires to deliberate in private. Extensive precautions are taken to insure that the jury is undisturbed and unheard during this period. The jury will have been instructed to decide the case in accordance with the law as explained by the judge and only on the basis of the evidence that has been brought forward in the trial. It is improper for the jury to ignore what the judge has said about the law or to speculate about what evidence that was not introduced might have proved. It also is improper for the jurors to decide the case on the basis of their own personal knowledge of the facts of the case. Indeed, if a juror has specific knowledge of the facts, it should be disclosed at the beginning of the trial, and that person probably will be excused from serving. But a more difficult question is presented by a juror's more general knowledge and experience as it relates to the case. A strength of the jury system is thought to be that it brings together a cross-section of community standards and experienced judgments. At the same time, the parties are not able to meet the special knowledge of jurors of which they are unaware. How should the line between general experience and special knowledge be drawn?

TEXAS EMPLOYERS' INSURANCE ASSOCIATION v. PRICE

Court of Civil Appeals of Texas, Eastland, 1960.
336 S.W.2d 304.

COLLINGS, JUSTICE. Loyal Grant Price brought suit * * * to set aside an award of the Industrial Accident Board * * *. The defendant Texas Employers' Insurance Association answered by general denial and specifically pleaded that plaintiff's alleged injury did not result in total or permanent incapacity, but that any injury plaintiff may have received resulted only in partial and temporary incapacity, or resulted from other injuries and diseases or a combination thereof. * * *

The case was tried before a jury which found that plaintiff received an accidental injury while working for the Port Houston Iron Works, Inc.; * * * that such injury was the producing cause of total disability; that total disability began November 27, 1957; that such disability was permanent and was not partial * * *. Judgment was entered for the plaintiff for $13,415.96 in a lump sum with interest thereon at the legal rate. * * *

In appellant's first four points it is contended that there was no evidence, and in the alternative that the evidence was insufficient to support the findings that any total incapacity sustained by appellee was permanent and the finding that appellee sustained total and permanent incapacity was so against the great weight and preponderance of the evidence as to be clearly wrong and unjust. * * *

In support of its contention in this respect, appellant further urges that appellee's own doctor testified that his back had been improved by the operation and stated that he "would estimate his (appellee's) partial permanent disability as approximately twenty percent as applied to general deficiency." This testimony is not consistent with the finding of the jury and the testimony of appellee to the effect that he has sustained total and permanent incapacity. It is the province of the jury, however, to determine the weight to be given evidence and to reconcile conflicts or inconsistencies therein. * * * The matter under consideration was not one for experts and skilled witnesses alone. Appellee testified that he could not work without pain, that his back was getting worse, that he was having to wear a brace with which he had previously been fitted by Dr. Brelsford. Dr. Brelsford testified that appellee had sustained permanent incapacity although not total, but that he would not pass him to follow his trade. The fact that appellee's testimony was in conflict with expert opinion testimony concerning the extent of his disability did not, under the circumstances, render it insufficient to support the verdict. * * *

Appellant further urges that the court erred in refusing to grant a new trial on the ground of jury misconduct. The evidence concerning some of the alleged jury misconduct was conflicting and would support a finding that such misconduct did not occur. The implied findings of the court in support of the order overruling appellant's motion for a new trial, which findings have support in the evidence, are binding on us. * * *

The existence of one of the alleged acts of jury misconduct is shown conclusively and in our opinion constitutes reversible error. The question whether the incapacity of appellee was total and permanent or only permanent partial was close, as already indicated. It is our opinion that the evidence supports the finding of total permanent incapacity and that such finding is not against the great weight and preponderance of the evidence. But it is further noted that appellee's own doctor testified, in effect, that his disability was approximately twenty percent partial. It is undisputed that one of the jurors related his personal experiences to persuade the jury that appellee was totally and permanently incapacitated. The witness stated to the jury as follows:

I said it has been my experience that in employment that if a man has an injury and it is obvious, such as, a scar on his back if he is being examined by a doctor for employment that he would want a statement from that man concerning that injury, and if he mentioned a back injury I doubted very much if he would get employment. The reason that came out was we were discussing whether or not the injury was partial or total.

The juror testified that he got this experience in union work; that he had read a letter from his company concerning back injuries showing that the company wanted to be more careful in hiring people with such injuries and that he told the jury about this experience. He testified that, in making the above statements to the jury, he was attempting to persuade a juror to come over to his side of the case; that he felt it was proper to give the jury the benefit of his personal knowledge and experience; and that was what he did. He further stated that he knew from experience that appellee could not get a job with Rohm and Haas, Shell Oil Company, Sinclair, or any other company that has a union contract or employee benefits and so advised the jury. He stated his opinion to the jury that appellee should receive total and permanent disability because he could not pass the physical examination he would be required to take; that it had been his experience that companies were very strict about whom they hire and that prospective employees were required to pass a most rigid physical examination. In this connection the juror testified that he also stated to the jury that there might be some jobs that appellee could handle but that he had a doubt whether appellee "could compete favorably on the labor market." The above evidence is undisputed. It shows that a juror related his personal experiences to the jury concerning the practice of company employers in hiring and employing workmen, and that the purpose and effect of such statements was to show that appellee was totally incapacitated. It was misconduct for the juror to relate to the other jurors his own personal experience as original evidence of material facts to be considered in their deliberation. * * * Considered in connection with the entire record, we are of the opinion that the misconduct shown was material and that it reasonably appears that injury probably resulted to appellant. * * *

For the reasons stated the judgment of the trial court is reversed and the cause is remanded.

Notes and Questions

1. Why is it misconduct for a juror "to relate to the other jurors his own personal experience as original evidence of material facts to be considered in their deliberation"? In HEAD v. HARGRAVE, 105 U.S. (15 Otto) 45, 49–50, 26 L.Ed. 1028, 1030 (1881), a case involving the value of legal services, Justice Field said:

> It was the province of the jury to weigh the testimony of the attorneys as to the value of the services, by reference to their nature, the time occupied in their performance, and other attending circumstances, and by applying to it their own experience and knowledge of the character of such services. To direct them to find the value of the services from the testimony of the experts alone, was to say to them that the issue should be determined by the opinions of the attorneys, and not by the exercise of their own judgment of the facts on which those opinions were given. * * * So far from laying aside their own general knowledge and ideas, the jury should have applied that knowledge and those ideas to the matters of fact in evidence in determining the weight to be given to the opinions expressed * * *. While they cannot act in any case upon particular facts material to its disposition resting in their private knowledge, but should be governed by the evidence adduced, they may, and to act intelligently they must, judge of the weight and force of that evidence by their own general knowledge of the subject of inquiry. If, for example, the question were as to the damages sustained by a plaintiff from a fracture of his leg by the carelessness of a defendant, the jury would ill perform their duty and probably come to a wrong conclusion, if, controlled by the testimony of the surgeons, not merely as to the injury inflicted, but as to the damages sustained, they should ignore their own knowledge and experience of the value of a sound limb. Other persons besides professional men have knowledge of the value of professional services; and, while great weight should always be given to the opinions of those familiar with the subject, they are not to be blindly received * * *.

Can the principal case be reconciled with this language?

2. The issue of jury misconduct is complicated by the doctrine, recognized in most jurisdictions but enforced with varying strictness, that a jury verdict may not be impeached by evidence that comes from the jurors themselves. In KILGORE v. GREYHOUND CORP., 30 F.R.D. 385, 388 (E.D.Tenn.1962), in which a juror conducted an unsupervised and unauthorized study of the accident scene and reported thereon to his fellow jurors, it was said:

> Any time a new trial is sought on the basis of the misconduct of a juror, or the receipt and consideration by a jury of improper evidence which may have had prejudicial effect on the jurors, the Court is forced to choose between the possibility that a party litigant may have been done an injustice, and, on the other hand, the possibility that the Court will inflict a public injury which will result if jurors are permitted to testify regarding what happened in the jury room.

What is the possible "public injury" of which this court speaks? Why are jurors generally prohibited from impeaching their verdict?

3. The question of the extent to which jurors may rely on their own experience and knowledge may arise in contexts other than jury misconduct. In Head v. Hargrave, Note 1, supra, the issue was whether or not the jury was bound by the expert testimony. The issue also may be raised in terms of whether or not there is sufficient evidence to sustain a particular verdict. Compare Holt v. Pariser, 161 Pa.Super. 315, 54 A.2d 89 (1947) (holding that a jury could properly find reasonable a very long delay in the repair of a truck in light of a wartime shortage of parts, although no evidence of the reason for the delay had been introduced), with Harris v. Pounds, 185 Miss. 688, 187 So. 891 (1939) (holding that a jury in a timber-growing county could not properly find that a hardwood log 15 feet in length and 12 inches in diameter was too heavy to be safely carried by six men over rough, uneven ground in the absence of evidence as to its weight).

d. Taking the Case From the Jury

The most direct and drastic example of jury control occurs in those cases in which it is held that there is no evidence on which a reasonable jury could find for a particular party (usually plaintiff, but sometimes defendant). If the judge makes this determination at the close of the evidence, she will direct the jury to return a verdict for the other party. Even after the jury has returned a verdict for one party, the judge in most systems may order that judgment be entered for the other party "notwithstanding the verdict," if she decides that the case should not have been submitted to the jury. The judge also has the power to set aside the verdict and order a new trial on the ground that the verdict is against the great weight of the evidence or because of mistakes or erroneous rulings during trial.

So also, an appellate court may determine, even in the face of a jury verdict, that no reasonable jury could have reached the result announced. Clearly when these devices are used, the jury is more than "controlled"; it is eliminated from the process. If such devices were not available, the jury could decide a case any way it wanted without respect to the evidence or the law. But if the devices are not very severely restricted, the right to a jury trial can be negated.

LAVENDER v. KURN

Supreme Court of the United States, 1946.
327 U.S. 645, 66 S.Ct. 740, 90 L.Ed. 916.

On Writ of Certiorari to the Supreme Court of the State of Missouri.

MR. JUSTICE MURPHY delivered the opinion of the Court.

* * *

Petitioner, the administrator of the estate of L.E. Haney, brought this suit under the [Federal Employers' Liability] Act against the respondent trustees of the St. Louis–San Francisco Railway Company (Frisco) and the respondent Illinois Central Railroad Company. It was charged that Haney, while employed as a switch-tender by the respondents in the switchyard of the Grand Central Station in Memphis, Tennessee, was killed as a result of respondents' negligence. Following a trial * * *, the jury returned a verdict in favor of petitioner and awarded damages in the amount of $30,000. * * * On appeal, however, the Supreme Court of Missouri reversed the judgment, holding that there was no substantial evidence of negligence to support the submission of the case to the jury. * * *

[Haney was employed by the Illinois Central which owned the yards; Frisco's trains used the yards, and part of Haney's wages were paid by Frisco.]

The Illinois Central tracks run north and south directly past and into the Grand Central Station. About 2700 feet south of the station the Frisco tracks cross at right angles to the Illinois Central tracks. A westbound Frisco train wishing to use the station must stop some 250 feet or more west of this crossing and back into the station over a switchline curving east and north. The events in issue center about the switch several feet north of the main Frisco tracks at the point where the switch line branches off. This switch controls the tracks at this point.

It was very dark on the evening of December 21, 1939. At about 7:30 p.m. a westbound interstate Frisco passenger train stopped on the Frisco main line, its rear some 20 or 30 feet west of the switch. Haney, in the performance of his duties, threw or opened the switch to permit the train to back into the station. The respondents claimed that Haney was then required to cross to the south side of the track before the train passed the switch; and the conductor of the train testified that he saw Haney so cross. But there was also evidence that Haney's duties required him to wait at the switch north of the track until the train had cleared, close the switch, return to his shanty near the crossing and change the signals from red to green to permit trains on the Illinois Central tracks to use the crossing. The Frisco train cleared the switch, backing at the rate of 8 or 10 miles per hour. But the switch remained open and the signals still were red. Upon investigation Haney was found north of the track near the switch lying face down on the ground, unconscious. An ambulance was called, but he was dead upon arrival at the hospital.

Haney had been struck in the back of the head, causing a fractured skull from which he died. There were no known eye-witnesses to the fatal blow. Although it is not clear there is evidence that his body was extended north and south, the head to the south. Apparently he had fallen forward to the south; his face was bruised on the left side from hitting the ground and there were marks indicating that his toes had dragged a few inches southward as he fell. His head was about 5½ feet north of the Frisco tracks. Estimates ranged from 2 feet to 14 feet as to how far west of the switch he lay.

The injury to Haney's head was evidenced by a gash about two inches long from which blood flowed. The back of Haney's white cap had a corresponding black mark about an inch and a half long and an inch wide, running at an angle downward to the right of the center of the back of the head. A spot of blood was later found at a point 3 or 4 feet north of the tracks. The conclusion following an autopsy was that Haney's skull was fractured by "some fast moving small round object." One of the examining doctors testified that such an object might have been attached to a train backing at the rate of 8 or 10 miles per hour. But he also admitted that the fracture might have resulted from a blow from a pipe or club or some similar round object in the hands of an individual.

Petitioner's theory is that Haney was struck by the curled end or tip of a mail hook hanging down loosely on the outside of the mail car of the backing train. This curled end was 73 inches above the top of the rail, which was 7 inches high. The overhang of the mail car in relation to the rails was about 2 to 2½ feet. The evidence indicated that when the mail car swayed or moved around a curve the mail hook might pivot, its curled end swinging out as much as 12 to 14 inches. The curled end could thus be swung out to a point 3 to 3½ feet from the rail and about 73 inches above the top of the rail. Both east and west of the switch, however, was an uneven mound of cinders and dirt rising at its highest points 18 to 24 inches above the top of the rails. Witnesses differed as to how close the mound approached the rails, the estimates varying from 3 to 15 feet. But taking the figures most favorable to the petitioner, the mound extended to a point 6 to 12 inches north of the overhanging side of the mail car. If the mail hook end swung out 12 to 14 inches it would be 49 to 55 inches above the highest parts of the mound. Haney was 67½ inches tall. If he had been standing on the mound about a foot from the side of the mail car he could have been hit by the end of the mail hook, the exact point of contact depending upon the height of the mound at the particular point. His wound was about 4 inches below the top of his head, or 63½ inches above the point where he stood on the mound—well within the possible range of the mail hook end.

Respondents' theory is that Haney was murdered. They point to the estimates that the mound was 10 to 15 feet north of the rail, making it impossible for the mail hook end to reach a point of contact with Haney's head. Photographs were placed in the record to support the claim that the ground was level north of the rail for at least 10 feet. * * * It also appears that many hoboes and tramps frequented the area at night in order to get rides on freight trains. Haney carried a pistol to protect himself. This pistol was found loose under his body by those who came to his rescue. It was testified, however that the pistol had apparently slipped out of his pocket or scabbard as he fell. Haney's clothes were not disarranged and there was no evidence of a struggle or fight. No rods, pipes or weapons of any kind, except Haney's own pistol, were found near the scene. Moreover, his gold watch and diamond ring were still on him after he was struck. Six days later his unsoiled billfold was found on a high board fence about a block from the place where Haney was struck and near the point where he had been placed in an ambulance. It contained his social security card and other effects, but no money. His wife testified that he "never carried much money, not very much more than $10." Such were the facts in relation to respondents' theory of murder.

Finally, one of the Frisco foremen testified that he arrived at the scene shortly after Haney was found injured. He later examined the fireman's side of the train very carefully and found nothing sticking out or in disorder. In explaining why he examined this side of the train so carefully he stated that while he was at the scene of the accident "someone said they thought that train No. 106 backing in to Grand Central Station is what struck this man" and that Haney "was supposed to have been struck by something protruding on the side of the train." The foreman testified that these statements were made by an unknown Illinois Central switchman standing near the fallen body of Haney. The foreman admitted that the switchman "didn't see the accident." This testimony was admitted by the trial court over the strenuous objections of respondents' counsel that it was mere hearsay falling outside the *res gestae* rule.

The jury was instructed that Frisco's trustees were liable if it was found that they negligently permitted a rod or other object to extend out from the side of the train as it backed past Haney and that Haney was killed as the direct result of such negligence, if any. The jury was further told that Illinois Central was liable if it was found that the company negligently maintained an unsafe and dangerous place for Haney to work, in that the ground was high and uneven and the light insufficient and inadequate, and that Haney was injured and killed as a direct result of the said place being unsafe and dangerous. This latter instruction as to Illinois Central did not require the jury to find that Haney was killed by something protruding from the train.

The Supreme Court, in upsetting the jury's verdict against both the Frisco trustees and the Illinois Central, admitted that "It could be inferred from the facts that Haney could have been struck by the mail hook knob *if* he were standing on the south side of the mound and the mail hook extended out as far as 12 or 14 inches." * * * But it held that "all reasonable minds would agree that it would be mere speculation and conjecture to say that Haney was struck by the mail hook" and that "plaintiff failed to make a submissible case on that question." It also ruled that there "was no substantial evidence that the uneven ground and insufficient light were causes or contributing causes of the death of Haney." Finally, the Supreme Court held that the testimony of the foreman as to the statement made to him by the unknown switchman was inadmissible under the *res gestae* rule since the switchman spoke from what he had heard rather than from his own knowledge.

* * *

The evidence we have already detailed demonstrates that there was evidence from which it might be inferred that the end of the mail hook struck Haney in the back of the head, an inference that the Supreme Court admitted could be drawn. That inference is not rendered unreasonable by the fact that Haney apparently fell forward toward the main Frisco track so that his head was 5½ feet north of the rail. He may well have been struck and then wandered in a daze to the point where he fell forward. The testimony as to blood marks some distance away from his head lends credence to that possibility, indicating that he did not fall immediately upon being hit. When that is added to the evidence most favorable to the petitioner as to the height and swing-out of the hook, the height and location of the mound and the nature of Haney's duties, the inference that Haney was killed by the hook cannot be said to be unsupported by probative facts or to be so unreasonable as to warrant taking the case from the jury.

It is true that there is evidence tending to show that it was physically and mathematically impossible for the hook to strike Haney. And there are facts from which it might reasonably be inferred that Haney was murdered. But such evidence has become irrelevant upon appeal, there being a reasonable basis in the record for inferring that the hook struck Haney. The jury having made that inference, the respondents were not free to relitigate the factual dispute in a reviewing court. Under these circumstances it would be an undue invasion of the jury's historic function for an appellate court to weigh the conflicting evidence, judge the credibility of witnesses and arrive at a conclusion opposite from the one reached by the jury. * * *

It is no answer to say that the jury's verdict involved speculation and conjecture. Whenever facts are in dispute or the evidence is such that fair-minded men may draw different inferences, a measure of speculation and conjecture is required on the part of those whose duty it is to settle the dispute by choosing what seems to them to be the most reasonable inference. Only when there is a complete absence of probative facts to support the conclusion reached does a reversible error appear. But where, as here, there is an evidentiary basis for the jury's verdict, the jury is free to discard or disbelieve whatever facts are inconsistent with its conclusion. And the appellate court's function is exhausted when that evidentiary basis becomes apparent. * * *

We are unable, therefore, to sanction a reversal of the jury's verdict against Frisco's trustees. Nor can we approve any disturbance in the verdict as to Illinois Central. The evidence was uncontradicted that it was very dark at the place where Haney was working and the surrounding ground was high and uneven. The evidence also showed that this area was entirely within the domination and control of Illinois Central * * *. It was not unreasonable to conclude that these conditions constituted an unsafe and dangerous working place * * *.

In view of the foregoing disposition of the case, it is unnecessary to decide whether the allegedly hearsay testimony was admissible under the *res gestae* rule. Rulings on the admissibility of evidence must normally be left to the sound discretion of the trial judge in actions under the Federal Employers' Liability Act. But inasmuch as there is adequate support in the record for the jury's verdict apart from the hearsay testimony, we need not determine whether that discretion was abused in this instance.

The judgment of the Supreme Court of Missouri is reversed and the case is remanded for whatever further proceedings may be necessary not inconsistent with this opinion.

THE CHIEF JUSTICE and MR. JUSTICE FRANKFURTER concur in the result.

MR. JUSTICE REED dissents.

Notes and Questions

1. Why does a trial judge or an appellate court have the power to take a case away from the jury or to set aside its verdict? Does the existence of this power necessarily mean that a jury cannot properly refer to its members own knowledge (see Texas Employers' Ins. Ass'n v. Price, p. 46, supra)? Why?

2. In PENNSYLVANIA R. CO. v. CHAMBERLAIN, 288 U.S. 333, 339, 53 S.Ct. 391, 393, 77 L.Ed. 819, 822–23 (1933), the Supreme Court, in approving a directed verdict for defendant, said:

* * * At most there was an inference to that effect drawn from observed facts which gave equal support to the opposite inference * * *.

We, therefore, have a case belonging to that class of cases where proven facts give equal support to each of two inconsistent inferences; in which event, neither of them being established, judgment, as a matter of law, must go against the party upon whom rests the necessity of sustaining one of these inferences as against the other, before he is entitled to recover.

Is this language consistent with the opinion of the Court in the principal case? Is there a difference between cases in which the evidence simply fails to point one way or the other, and cases in which the evidence on one side is overwhelming, in terms of taking a case away from the jury? Would *Lavender* have been decided the same way if stronger evidence was presented that Haney had been murdered?

3. When the *Lavender* case is remanded to the Missouri Supreme Court, what should that court do? In this connection, do you agree with the United States Supreme Court that it was unnecessary to determine whether evidence of the statement of the unknown switchman was improperly admitted?

4. APPEAL

The grounds for appeal are chiefly mistakes of law—for example, an erroneous ruling that the court had jurisdiction, an improper admission of evidence, or an incorrect instruction to the jury. Even if an error of law has been committed, the appellate court must be convinced that the error was prejudicial, and that the case probably would not have come out the same if the error had not occurred. In the event of an erroneous ruling on jurisdiction the prejudice is obvious. But appellate courts are reluctant to reverse merely because an error has been committed during the trial.

An appellate court rarely will reverse a decision on the ground that a question of fact was decided improperly. If there has been a jury, the constitutional right to jury trial itself is involved in such a ruling by an appellate court. See Amendment VII to the United States Constitution, which is set out in the Supplement. When there has been no jury, no constitutional problem is involved, but it may be asked whether a broad scope of review of the trial judge's findings of fact will not encourage needless appeals and denigrate the function of the trial judge.

HICKS v. UNITED STATES

United States Court of Appeals, Fourth Circuit, 1966.
368 F.2d 626.

SOBELOFF, CIRCUIT JUDGE. This action was brought under the Federal Tort Claims Act, 28 U.S.C. § 1346, to recover damages for the death of Carol Greitens. The plaintiff, administrator of her estate, alleges that death was due to the negligence of the doctor on duty at the dispensary of the United States Naval Amphibious Base, Little Creek, Virginia, in diagnosing and treating her illness. The District Court, concluding that the evidence was insufficient to establish that the doctor was negligent, or that his concededly erroneous diagnosis and treatment was the proximate cause of her death, dismissed the complaint. * * *

The decedent, 25 years of age, had been a diabetic since the age of 13, although the condition was under control. * * * Mrs. Greitens' husband brought her to the dispensary at about 4 a.m. on August 25, 1963, suffering from intense abdominal pain and continual vomiting which had begun suddenly an hour before. The corpsman on duty in the examining room procured her medical records, obtained a brief history, took her blood pressure, pulse, temperature, and respiration and summoned the doctor on duty, then asleep in his room at the dispensary. The doctor arrived 15 or 20 minutes later and after questioning the patient concerning her symptoms, felt her abdomen and listened to her bowel sounds with the aid of a stethoscope. Recording his diagnosis on the chart as gastroenteritis, he told Mrs. Greitens that she had a "bug" in her stomach, prescribed some drugs for the relief of pain, and released her with instructions to return in eight hours. The examination took approximately ten minutes.

The patient returned to her home, and after another episode of vomiting, took the prescribed medicine and lay down. At about noon, she arose and drank a glass of water, vomited immediately thereafter and fell to the floor unconscious. She was rushed to the dispensary, but efforts to revive her were unsuccessful. She was pronounced dead at 12:48 p.m. and an autopsy revealed that she had a high obstruction, diagnosed formally as an abnormal congenital peritoneal hiatus with internal herniation into this malformation of some of the loops of the small intestine. Death was due to a massive hemorrhagic infarction of the intestine resulting from its strangulation.

I

The plaintiff contends that the doctor at the dispensary did not meet the requisite standard of care and skill demanded of him by the law of Virginia. Compliance with this standard, the plaintiff maintains, would have required a more extended examination and immediate hospitalization. More specifically, plaintiff's expert witnesses, two general practitioners in the Norfolk–Virginia Beach area, testified that, according to prevailing practice in the community, the doctor should have inquired whether the patient had had diarrhea and should have made a rectal examination to determine whether the patient was suffering from an obstruction rather than from gastroenteritis. While the latter condition does not ordinarily require immediate radical treatment, a high obstruction is almost invariably lethal unless promptly operated upon. Plaintiff's experts further testified that on observing the symptoms manifested by Mrs. Greitens, the procedure of general practitioners in the community would have been to order immediate hospitalization. * * *

The standard of care which Virginia law exacts from a physician, in this case a general practitioner, is * * * [such that] if he uses ordinary care in reaching his diagnosis, and thereafter acts upon it, he incurs no liability, even if the diagnosis proves to be a mistake in judgment.

It is undisputed that the symptoms of high obstruction and of gastroenteritis are quite similar. The District Court placed great emphasis on this fact as an indication that the doctor's erroneous diagnosis was not negligent, but was merely an error of judgment. It would seem, however, that where the symptoms are consistent with either of two possible conditions, one lethal if not attended to promptly, due care demands that a doctor do more than make a cursory examination and then release the patient. * * * The fact that an intestinal obstruction is a rare occurrence, and that some form of gastroenteritis is the more likely of the two conditions, does not excuse the failure to make inquiries and perform recognized additional tests that might have served to distinguish the one condition from the other. The dispensary doctor himself, as well as the experts for both sides, agreed that an inquiry as to diarrhea and a rectal examination were the "proper procedure" and "the accepted standard" in order to be able to rule out gastroenteritis and to make a definite diagnosis of high intestinal obstruction. If he had made the inquiry which he admits was the accepted standard, he would at least have been alerted to the fact that the case was one calling for close observation with a view to immediate surgical intervention if the graver diagnosis were confirmed. In these circumstances, failure to make this investigation constitutes a lack of due care on the part of the physician. * * * Only if a patient is adequately examined, is there no liability for an erroneous diagnosis.

Our conclusion that the physician was negligent in his diagnosis and treatment of the patient is not inconsistent with * * * [Rule] 52(a), which declares that the trial judge's findings of fact are not to be disturbed unless clearly erroneous. This Rule comes into play primarily where the trial judge as fact finder has had to reconcile conflicting testimony. Where the veracity of witnesses is in issue, the decision is for the judge who has had the opportunity to see and evaluate the witnesses' demeanor. * * * But we are dealing here with the testimony of expert witnesses who are not in controversy as to the basic facts; thus, the opportunity of the trial court to observe the witnesses is of limited significance. It has often been held that where the trial court's conclusions are based on undisputed facts, they are not entitled to the finality customarily accorded basic factual findings under Rule 52(a). * * *

The question before us is not one of fact in the usual sense, but rather whether the undisputed facts manifest negligence. Although the absence of a factual dispute does not *always* mean that the conclusion is a question of law, it becomes so *here* since the ultimate conclusion to be drawn from the basic facts, i.e., the existence or absence of negligence, is actually a question of law. For this reason, the general rule has been that when a judge sitting without a jury makes a determination of negligence his conclusion, as distinguished from the evidentiary findings leading to it, is freely reviewable on appeal. * * * The determination of negligence involves not only the formulation of the legal standard, but more particularly in this case, its application to the evidentiary facts as established; and since these are uncontested, there is no basis for applying the "clearly erroneous" rule. * * *

The government's expert opined that the dispensary physician exercised "average judgment," but analysis of his entire testimony points unavoidably to the opposite conclusion. Revealing are his statements that it was wrong not to inquire about diarrhea, conceding that "that is one question that one usually asks," and that given a patient with abdominal pain of one hour's duration, it is too soon "to expect anybody to come up with a proper diagnosis." Furthermore, his opinion was predicated upon a factual assumption not permissible in this case. His assumption was that the dispensary physician had made only a "working" or "tentative" diagnosis * * *. However, the uncontradicted evidence indicates that this was not a "tentative" diagnosis.

The examining doctor himself testified that he had already considered and ruled out at the beginning of his examination the possibility of an obstruction without making the additional differentiating diagnostic tests. He said that his only reason for asking the patient to return eight hours later was because her diabetic condition could become complicated by a case of gastroenteritis. * * * By releasing the patient, the dispensary physician made his diagnosis final, allowing no further opportunity for revision * * *.

On careful scrutiny, therefore, the government's expert is seen to have demonstrated that the examiner did *not* conform to the required standard of care. Coupled with the explicit testimony of the plaintiff's experts, the government's testimony leads us inevitably to the conclusion that the doctor was negligent as a matter of law. We think that the District Court gave undue weight to the purely conclusory opinion of the government witness. The District Court is not bound by his statement that "average judgment" had been exercised, nor are we bound by it. Only the standard of care is to be established by the testimony of experts. If under the undisputed facts the defendant failed to meet that standard it is not for the expert but for the court to decide whether there was negligence.

* * *

Judgment reversed and cause remanded for the determination of damages.

Notes and Questions

1. Would the Court of Appeals have reached the same result if the judgment appealed from had been based on the verdict of a jury rather than the findings of a judge? Why is there any difference between the standard enunciated in Lavender v. Kurn and that in Federal Rule 52(a)?

2. Is the question whether certain conduct is negligent one of law or of fact? Legal scholars have long debated the issue without resolution. In any event, the issue ordinarily is left to the jury. Why? Are the reasons for giving the issue to the jury any less persuasive when the finder of fact is a judge sitting without a jury? Is there a difference if the standard of care to be applied by the judge sitting without a jury must be derived from the testimony of experts? Why?

3. In ANDERSON v. CITY OF BESSEMER CITY, 470 U.S. 564, 105 S.Ct. 1504, 84 L.Ed.2d 518 (1985), the Supreme Court, in interpreting Rule 52(a), said: "Where there are two permissible views of the evidence, the factfinder's choice between them cannot be clearly erroneous." The Court added:

> This is so even when the district court's findings do not rest on credibility determinations, but are based instead on physical or documentary evidence or inferences from other facts. To be sure, various Courts of Appeals have on occasion asserted the theory that an appellate court may exercise *de novo* review over findings not based on credibility determinations * * *.
>
> The rationale for deference to the original finder of fact is not limited to the superiority of the trial judge's position to make determinations of credibility. The trial judge's major role is the determination of fact, and with experience in fulfilling that role comes expertise. Duplication of the trial judge's efforts in the court of appeals would very likely contribute only negligibly to the accuracy of fact determination at a huge cost in diversion of judicial resources * * *. As the Court has stated in a different context, the trial on the merits should be "the 'main event' * * * rather than a 'tryout on the road.'"

Id. at 574, 105 S.Ct. at 1511–12, 84 L.Ed.2d at 528–29. Does *Anderson* undermine the basis of the Fourth Circuit's holding in *Hicks*? Does *Anderson* overrule *Hicks*?

5. CONCLUSIVENESS OF JUDGMENTS

Lawsuits are designed to settle disputes. An idealist might argue that nothing should be considered settled until it is settled *correctly*. A pragmatist could counter that nothing is settled at all unless it is settled *finally*. Cosmic questions may be debated endlessly, but controversies between individuals that are expected to result in enforceable judgments for damages or orders that must be obeyed under penalty of contempt must come to an end if the judicial process is to work at all. Res judicata requires that occasionally we let a judgment stand even when we become convinced that it was wrongly decided. A doctrine that only correct decisions have res judicata effect would furnish no finality at all.

The following case decided almost 300 years ago raises the same doubts that the res judicata doctrine raises today: Is the decision fair to plaintiff? Would an opposite decision be fair to defendant?

FETTER v. BEALE, 1 Ld.Raym. 339, 91 Eng.Rep. 1122 (King's Bench 1697). Plaintiff had brought an action for battery against defendant and recovered £11. Subsequently "part of his skull by reason of the said battery came out of his head," and plaintiff brought another action. Plaintiff's counsel argued that "this action differed from the nature of the former * * * because the recovery in the former action was only for the bruise and battery, but here there is a maihem by the loss of the skull."

And per totam Curiam, the jury in the former action considered the nature of the wound, and gave damages for all the damages that it had done to the plaintiff; and therefore a recovery in the said action is good here. And it is the plaintiff's fault, for if he had not been so hasty, he might have been satisfied for this loss of the skull also. Judgment for the defendant * * *.

A particularly difficult question of res judicata is presented when it is alleged that the first decision—now advanced as conclusive—was rendered by a court that lacked jurisdiction over the subject matter. This group of Illustrative Cases began with a decision that demonstrated the grave concern of the United States Supreme Court to keep the federal courts from deciding cases outside their constitutional and statutory jurisdiction. Res judicata was not involved in Capron v. Van Noorden, p. 21, supra; the trial court's decision was reversed in the ordinary course of appellate review. What if plaintiff in that case had not sought a writ of error but had permitted the decision to become final and then instituted another action?

DES MOINES NAVIGATION & R. CO.
v. IOWA HOMESTEAD CO.

Supreme Court of the United States, 1887.
123 U.S. 552, 8 S.Ct. 217, 31 L.Ed. 202.

Error to the Supreme Court of the State of Iowa.

MR. CHIEF JUSTICE WAITE delivered the opinion of the court.

This suit was brought by the Iowa Homestead Company against the Des Moines Navigation and Railroad Company to recover the same taxes for the years 1864 to 1871, both inclusive, which formed part of the subject matter of the litigation between the same parties in Homestead Co. v. Valley Railroad, 17 Wall. 153 * * *. The Railroad Company set up the decree in its favor in that suit as a bar to the present action, and to this the Homestead Company replied "that the decree or judgment referred to is null and void, for the reason that the courts of the United States had no jurisdiction of said suit, and no legal power or authority to render said decree or judgment."

* * * It must be conceded that the Homestead Company and the Navigation and Railroad Company were both Iowa corporations, and, therefore, in law, citizens of the same State; but the defendants * * * who caused the removal to be made [from the Iowa state court to the United States Circuit Court], were citizens of the State of New York. After the removal was effected, all the above named defendants, as well as * * * the Navigation and Railroad Company, appeared, filed answers, and defended the action. The Homestead Company took issue on all the answers, and actually contested the matters in dispute with the Navigation and Railroad Company, as well as the other defendants, in the Circuit Court, and in this court on appeal, without taking any objection to the jurisdiction.

The precise question we have now to determine is whether the adjudication by this court, under such circumstances, of the matters then and now at issue between the Homestead Company and the Navigation and Railroad Company was absolutely void for want of jurisdiction. The point is not whether it was error in the Circuit Court to take jurisdiction of the suit, or of so much of it as related to the Navigation and Railroad Company, originally, but as to the binding effect of the decree of this court so long as it remains in force, and is not judicially annulled, vacated, or set aside.

* * *

It was settled by this court at a very early day, that, although the judgments and decrees of the Circuit Courts might be erroneous, if the records failed to show the facts on which the jurisdiction of the court rested, such as that the plaintiffs were citizens of different States from the defendants, yet that they were not nullities, and would bind the parties until reversed or otherwise set aside. * * * In * * * McCormick v. Sullivant, 10 Wheat. 192 [(1825)] * * * this court held on appeal that "the courts of the United States are courts of *limited*, but not of *inferior*, jurisdiction. If the jurisdiction be not alleged in the proceedings, their judgments and decrees may be reversed for that cause on a writ of error or appeal; but until reversed they are conclusive between the parties and their privies." "But they are not nullities." There has never been any departure from this rule.

It is said, however, that these decisions apply only to cases where the record simply fails to show jurisdiction. Here it is claimed that the record shows there could be no jurisdiction, because it appears affirmatively that the Navigation and Railroad Company, one of the defendants, was a citizen of the same State with the plaintiff. But the record shows, with equal distinctness, that all the parties were actually before the court, and made no objection to its jurisdiction. The act of 1867, under which the removal was had, provided that when a suit was pending in a state court "in which there is a controversy between a citizen of the State in which the suit is brought and a citizen of another State, * * * such citizen of another State, * * * if he will make and file an affidavit stating that he has reason to and does believe that, from prejudice or local influence, he will not be able to obtain justice in such state court, may * * * file a petition in such state court for the removal of the suit" into the Circuit Court of the United States, and, when all things have been done that the act requires, "it shall be * * * the duty of the state court to * * * proceed no further with the suit," and, after the record is entered in the Circuit Court, "the suit shall then proceed in the same manner as if it had been brought there by original process."[e]

In the suit now under consideration there was a separate and distinct controversy between the plaintiff, a citizen of Iowa, and each of the citizens of New York, who were defendants. Each controversy related to the several tracts of land claimed by each defendant individually, and not as joint owner with the other defendants. Three of the citizens of New York caused to be made and filed the necessary affidavit and petition for removal, and thereupon, by common consent apparently, the suit as an entirety was transferred to the Circuit Court for final adjudication as to all the parties. * * * Whether in such a case the suit could be removed was a question for the Circuit Court to decide when it was called on to take jurisdiction. If it kept the case when it ought to have been remanded, or if it proceeded to adjudicate upon matters in dispute between two citizens of Iowa, when it ought to have confined itself to those between the citizens of Iowa and the citizens of New York, its final decree in the suit could have been reversed, on appeal, as erroneous, but the decree would not have been a nullity. To determine whether the suit was removable in whole or in part or not, was certainly within the power of the Circuit Court. The decision of that question was the exercise and the rightful exercise of jurisdiction, no matter whether in favor of or against taking the cause. Whether its decision was right, in this or any other respect, was to be finally determined by this court on appeal. As the Circuit Court entertained the suit, and this court, on appeal, impliedly recognized its right to do so, and proceeded to dispose of the case finally on its merits, certainly our decree cannot, in the light of prior adjudications on the same general question, be deemed a nullity. It was, at the time of the trial in the present case in the court below, a valid and subsisting prior adjudication of the matters in controversy, binding on these parties, and a bar to this action. In refusing so to decide, the court failed to give full faith and credit to the decree of this court * * * and this was error.

* * *

e. The Judiciary Act of 1789 had been interpreted by the Supreme Court to require complete diversity of citizenship (all the plaintiffs being of a citizenship different from that of any defendant) for removal. It was widely argued that the 1867 statute referred to in the *Des Moines* case, because of a difference in language, did not have the same requirement. The Supreme Court held that the 1867 statute did require complete diversity, Case of the Sewing Machine Cos., 85 U.S. (18 Wall.) 553, 21 L.Ed. 914 (1874), but this decision came a year *after* the Court's decision in the Homestead Company's first suit in which the issue had not been raised.

Notes and Questions

1. When a court has rendered a judgment in a contested action, the judgment precludes the parties from litigating the question of the court's subject-matter jurisdiction in subsequent litigation except if:

(1) The subject matter of the action was so plainly beyond the court's jurisdiction that its entertaining the action was a manifest abuse of authority; or

(2) Allowing the judgment to stand would substantially infringe upon the authority of another tribunal or agency of government; or

(3) The judgment was rendered by a court lacking capability to make an adequately informed determination of a question concerning its own jurisdiction and as a matter of procedural fairness the party seeking to avoid the judgment should have opportunity belatedly to attack the court's subject matter jurisdiction.

Restatement (Second), Judgments § 12 (1982). What factors should a court regard as important in deciding such questions as what is "a manifest abuse of authority," or when a judgment "substantially" infringes a tribunal's authority, or when a court lacks "capability to make an adequately informed determination"?

2. Was it critical to the Supreme Court's opinion in this case that the first case had been heard and determined by the Supreme Court itself? Would the case have been decided differently if no review had been sought in the first case at all?

3. Was the fact that the question of jurisdiction was a doubtful one at the time the first *Homestead Company* case arose relevant to the Supreme Court's decision in the second case?

4. Suppose that the issue of jurisdiction is raised in a case and erroneously decided. Is this a factor arguing for or against the application of res judicata in a second action?

5. Since it is clear in the principal case that in the suit before the Court there was no diversity of citizenship and the writ of error was to the Supreme Court of Iowa, what was the basis for appellate jurisdiction in the United States Supreme Court?

Chapter 2

JURISDICTION OVER THE PARTIES OR THEIR PROPERTY

SECTION A. THE TRADITIONAL BASES FOR JURISDICTION

PENNOYER v. NEFF

Supreme Court of the United States, 1877.
95 U.S. (5 Otto) 714, 24 L.Ed. 565.

Error to the Circuit Court of the United States for the District of Oregon.

MR. JUSTICE FIELD delivered the opinion of the court.

This is an action to recover the possession of a tract of land, of the alleged value of $15,000, situated in the State of Oregon. The plaintiff asserts title to the premises by a patent of the United States issued to him in [March] 1866, under the Act of Congress of September 27th, 1850, 9 Stat. at L., 496, usually known as the Donation Law of Oregon. The defendant claims to have acquired the premises under a sheriff's deed, made upon a sale of the property on execution issued upon a judgment recovered against the plaintiff in one of the circuit courts of the State. The case turns upon the validity of this judgment.

It appears from the record that the judgment was rendered in February, 1866, in favor of J.H. Mitchell, for less than $300, including costs, in an action brought by him upon a demand for services as an attorney; that, at the time the action was commenced and the judgment rendered, the defendant therein, the plaintiff here, was a non-resident of the State; that he was not personally served with process, and did not appear therein; and that the judgment was entered upon his default in not answering the complaint, upon a constructive service of summons by publication.

The Code of Oregon provides for such service when an action is brought against a non-resident and absent defendant, who has property within the State. It also provides, where the action is for the recovery of money or damages, for the attachment of the property of the non-resident. And it also declares that no natural person is subject to the jurisdiction of a court of the State, "unless he appear in the court, or be found within the State, or be a resident thereof, or have property therein; and in the last case, only to the extent of such property at the time the jurisdiction attached." Construing this latter provision to mean that, in an action for money or damages where a defendant does not appear in the court, and is not found within the State, and is not a resident thereof, but has property therein, the jurisdiction of the court extends only over such property, the declaration expresses a principle of general, if not universal, law. The authority of every tribunal is necessarily restricted by the territorial limits of the State in which it is established. Any attempt to exercise authority beyond those limits would be deemed in every other forum, as has been said by this court, an illegitimate assumption of power, and be resisted as mere abuse. * * * In the case against the plaintiff, the property here in controversy sold under the judgment rendered was not attached, nor in any way brought under the jurisdiction of the court. Its first connection with the case was caused by a levy of the execution. It was not, therefore, disposed of pursuant to any adjudication, but only in enforcement of a personal judgment, having no relation to the property, rendered against a non-resident without service of process upon him in the action, or his appearance therein. The court below did not consider that an attachment of the property was essential to its jurisdiction or to the validity of the sale, but held that the judgment was invalid from defects in the affidavit upon which the order of publication was obtained, and in the affidavit by which the publication was proved.

There is some difference of opinion among the members of this court as to the rulings upon these alleged defects. The majority are of opinion that, inasmuch as the statute requires, for an order of publication, that certain facts shall appear by affidavit *to the satisfaction of the court or judge,* defects in such affidavit can only be taken advantage of on appeal, or by some other direct proceeding, and cannot be urged to impeach the judgment collaterally. The majority of the court are also of opinion that the provision of the statute requiring proof of the publication in a newspaper to be made by the "affidavit of the printer, or his foreman, or his principal clerk," is satisfied when the affidavit is made by the editor of the paper. * * *

If, therefore, we were confined to the rulings of the court below upon the defects in the affidavits mentioned, we should be unable to uphold its decision. But it was also contended in that court, and is insisted upon here, that the judgment in the State Court against the plaintiff was void for want of personal service of process on him, or of his appearance in the action in which it was rendered, and that the premises in controversy could not be subjected to the payment of the demand of a resident creditor except by a proceeding *in rem;* that is, by a direct proceeding against the property for that purpose. If these positions are sound, the ruling of the Circuit Court as to the invalidity of that judgment must be sustained, notwithstanding our dissent from the reasons upon which it was made. And that they are sound would seem to follow from two well established principles of public law respecting the jurisdiction of an independent State over persons and property. The several States of the Union are not, it is true, in every respect independent, many of the rights and powers which originally belonged to them being now vested in the government created by the Constitution. But, except as restrained and limited by that instrument, they possess and exercise the authority of independent States, and the principles of public law to which we have referred are applicable to them. One of these principles is, that every State possesses exclusive jurisdiction and sovereignty over persons and property within its territory. As a consequence, every State has the power to determine for itself the civil *status* and capacities of its inhabitants; to prescribe the subjects upon which they may contract, the forms and solemnities with which their contracts shall be executed, the rights and obligations arising from them, and the mode in which their validity shall be determined and their obligations enforced; and also to regulate the manner and conditions upon which property situated within such territory, both personal and real, may be acquired, enjoyed and transferred. The other principle of public law referred to follows from the one mentioned; that is, that no State can exercise direct jurisdiction and authority over persons or property without its territory. * * * The several States are of equal dignity and authority, and the independence of one implies the exclusion of power from all others. And so it is laid down by jurists, as an elementary principle, that the laws of one State have no operation outside of its territory, except so far as is allowed by comity; and that no tribunal established by it can extend its process beyond that territory so as to subject either persons or property to its decisions. * * *

But as contracts made in one State may be enforceable only in another State, and property may be held by non-residents, the exercise of the jurisdiction which every State is admitted to possess over persons and property within its own territory will often affect persons and property without it. To any influence exerted in this way by a State affecting persons resident or property situated elsewhere, no objection can be justly taken; whilst any direct exertion of authority upon them, in an attempt to give ex-territorial operation to its laws, or to enforce an ex-territorial jurisdiction by its tribunals, would be deemed an encroachment upon the independence of the State in which the persons are domiciled or the property is situated, and be resisted as usurpation.

Thus the State, through its tribunals, may compel persons domiciled within its limits to execute, in pursuance of their contracts respecting property elsewhere situated, instruments in such form and with such solemnities as to transfer the title, so far as such formalities can be complied with; and the exercise of this jurisdiction in no manner interferes with the supreme control over the property by the State within which it is situated. * * *

So the State, through its tribunals, may subject property situated within its limits owned by non-residents to the payment of the demand of its own citizens against them; and the exercise of this jurisdiction in no respect infringes upon the sovereignty of the State where the owners are domiciled. Every State owes protection to its own citizens; and, when non-residents deal with them, it is a legitimate and just exercise of authority to hold and appropriate any property owned by such non-residents to satisfy the claims of its citizens. It is in virtue of the State's jurisdiction over the property of the non-resident situated within its limits that its tribunals can inquire into that non-resident's obligations to its own citizens, and the inquiry can then be carried only to the extent necessary to control the disposition of the property. If the non-resident have no property in the State, there is nothing upon which the tribunals can adjudicate.

* * * If, without personal service, judgments *in personam*, obtained *ex parte* against non-residents and absent parties, upon mere publication of process, which, in the great majority of cases, would never be seen by the

parties interested, could be upheld and enforced, they would be the constant instruments of fraud and oppression. Judgments for all sorts of claims upon contracts and for torts, real or pretended, would be thus obtained, under which property would be seized, when the evidence of the transactions upon which they were founded, if they ever had any existence, had perished.

Substituted service by publication, or in any other authorized form, may be sufficient to inform parties of the object of proceedings taken where property is once brought under the control of the court by seizure or some equivalent act. The law assumes that property is always in the possession of its owner, in person or by agent; and it proceeds upon the theory that its seizure will inform him, not only that it is taken into the custody of the court, but that he must look to any proceedings authorized by law upon such seizure for its condemnation and sale. * * * In other words, such service may answer in all actions which are substantially proceedings *in rem*. But where the entire object of the action is to determine the personal rights and obligations of the defendants, that is, where the suit is merely *in personam*, constructive service in this form upon a non-resident is ineffectual for any purpose. Process from the tribunals of one State cannot run into another State, and summon parties there domiciled to leave its territory and respond to proceedings against them. Publication of process or notice within the State where the tribunal sits cannot create any greater obligation upon the non-resident to appear. Process sent to him out of the State, and process published within it, are equally unavailing in proceedings to establish his personal liability.

The want of authority of the tribunals of a State to adjudicate upon the obligations of non-residents, where they have no property within its limits, is not denied by the court below; but the position is assumed that, where they have property within the State, it is immaterial whether the property is in the first instance brought under the control of the court by attachment or some other equivalent act, and afterwards applied by its judgment to the satisfaction of demands against its owner; or such demands be first established in a personal action, and the property of the non-resident be afterwards seized and sold on execution. But the answer to this position has already been given in the statement, that the jurisdiction of the court to inquire into and determine his obligations at all is only incidental to its jurisdiction over the property. Its jurisdiction in that respect cannot be made to depend upon facts to be ascertained after it has tried the cause and rendered the judgment. If the judgment be previously void, it will not become valid by the subsequent discovery of property of the defendant, or by his subsequent acquisition of it. The judgment, if void when rendered, will always remain void; it cannot occupy the doubtful position of being valid if property be found, and void if there be none. Even if the position assumed were confined to cases where the non-resident defendant possessed property in the State at the commencement of the action, it would still make the validity of the proceedings and judgment depend upon the question whether, before the levy of the execution, the defendant had or had not disposed of the property. If, before the levy, the property should be sold, then, according to this position, the judgment would not be binding. This doctrine would introduce a new element of uncertainty in judicial proceedings. The contrary is the law; the validity of every judgment depends upon the jurisdiction of the court before it is rendered, not upon what may occur subsequently. * * *

The force and effect of judgments rendered against non-residents without personal service of process upon them, or their voluntary appearance, have been the subject of frequent consideration in the courts of the United States and of the several States, as attempts have been made to enforce such judgments in States other than those in which they were rendered, under the provision of the Constitution requiring that "Full faith and credit shall be given in each State to the public Acts, records and judicial proceedings of every other State;" and the Act of Congress providing for the mode of authenticating such Acts, records and proceedings, and declaring that, when thus authenticated, "They shall have such faith and credit given to them in every court within the United States as they have by law or usage in the courts of the State from which they are or shall be taken." In the earlier cases, it was supposed that the Act gave to all judgments the same effect in other States which they had by law in the State where rendered. But this view was afterwards qualified so as to make the Act applicable only when the court rendering the judgment had jurisdiction of the parties and of the subject-matter, and not to preclude an inquiry into the jurisdiction of the court in which the judgment was rendered, or the right of the State itself to exercise authority over the person or the subject-matter. * * *

Since the adoption of the 14th Amendment to the Federal Constitution, the validity of such judgments may be directly questioned, and their enforcement in the State resisted, on the ground that proceedings in a court of justice to determine the personal rights and obligations of parties over whom that court has no jurisdiction do not constitute due process of law. Whatever difficulty may be experienced in giving to those terms a definition which will embrace every permissible exertion of power affecting private rights, and exclude such as is forbidden, there can be no doubt of their meaning when applied to judicial proceedings. They then mean a course of legal proceedings according to those rules and principles which have been established in our systems of jurisprudence for the protection and enforcement of private rights. To give such proceedings any validity, there must be a tribunal competent by its constitution—that is, by the law of its creation—to pass upon the subject-matter of the suit; and, if that involves merely a determination of the personal liability of the defendant, he must be brought within its jurisdiction by service of process within the State, or his voluntary appearance.

Except in cases affecting the personal *status* of the plaintiff, and cases in which that mode of service may be considered to have been assented to in advance as hereinafter mentioned, the substituted service of process by publication allowed by the law of Oregon and by similar laws in other States, where actions are brought against non-residents, is effectual only where, in connection with process against the person for commencing the action, property in the State is brought under the control of the court, and subjected to its disposition by process adapted to that purpose, or where the judgment is sought as a means of reaching such property or affecting some interest therein; in other words, where the action is in the nature of a proceeding *in rem*. * * *

It is true that, in a strict sense, a proceeding *in rem* is one taken directly against property, and has for its object the disposition of the property, without reference to the title of individual claimants; but, in a larger and more general sense, the terms are applied to actions between parties, where the direct object is to reach and dispose of property owned by them, or of some interest therein. Such are cases commenced by attachment against the property of debtors, or instituted to partition real estate, foreclose a mortgage, or enforce a lien. So far as they affect property in the State, they are substantially proceedings *in rem* in the broader sense which we have mentioned.

* * *

It follows from the views expressed that the personal judgment recovered in the State Court of Oregon against the plaintiff herein, then a non-resident of the State, was without any validity, and did not authorize a sale of the property in controversy.

To prevent any misapplication of the views expressed in this opinion, it is proper to observe that we do not mean to assert, by anything we have said, that a State may not authorize proceedings to determine the *status* of one of its citizens towards a non-resident, which would be binding within the State, though made without service of process or personal notice to the non-resident. The jurisdiction which every State possesses to determine the civil *status* and capacities of all its inhabitants involves authority to prescribe the conditions on which proceedings affecting them may be commenced and carried on within its territory. The State, for example, has absolute right to prescribe the conditions upon which the marriage relation between its own citizens shall be created, and the causes for which it may be dissolved. One of the parties guilty of acts for which, by the law of the State, a dissolution may be granted, may have removed to a State where no dissolution is permitted. The complaining party would, therefore, fail if a divorce were sought in the State of the defendant; and if application could not be made to the tribunals of the complainant's domicil in such case, and proceedings be there instituted without personal service of process or personal notice to the offending party, the injured citizen would be without redress. * * *

Neither do we mean to assert that a State may not require a non-resident entering into a partnership or association within its limits, or making contracts enforceable there, to appoint an agent or representative in the State to receive service of process and notice in legal proceedings instituted with respect to such partnership, association or contracts, or to designate a place where such service may be made and notice given, and provide, upon their failure, to make such appointment or to designate such place that service may be made upon a public officer designated for that purpose, or in some other prescribed way, and that judgments rendered upon such service may not be binding upon the non-residents both within and without the State. * * * Nor do we doubt that a State, on creating corporations or other institutions for pecuniary or charitable purposes, may provide a mode in which their conduct may be investigated, their obligations enforced, or their charters revoked, which shall require other than personal service upon their officers or members. * * *

In the present case, there is no feature of this kind and, consequently, no consideration of what would be the effect of such legislation in enforcing the contract of a non-resident can arise. * * *

Judgment affirmed.

[The dissenting opinion of JUSTICE HUNT is omitted.]

Notes and Questions

1. The colorful characters and scandalous facts surrounding Pennoyer v. Neff have been chronicled by Professor Perdue:

> Our story begins with a young man, Marcus Neff, heading across the country by covered wagon train, presumably to seek his fortune. Neff left Iowa in early 1848 * * * [and] was one of the earliest settlers to claim land under the Oregon Donation Act. * * *

> Early in 1862 Neff made the unfortunate decision to consult a local Portland attorney, J.H. Mitchell. * * * Neff may have consulted Mitchell in an attempt to expedite the paperwork concerning his land patent. * * * "J.H. Mitchell" was actually the Oregon alias of one John Hipple. Hipple had been a teacher in Pennsylvania who, after being forced to marry the 15–year–old student whom he seduced, left teaching and took up law. * * * [I]n 1860 Hipple headed west taking with him four thousand dollars of client money and his then current paramour, a local school teacher. They made their way to California where Hipple abandoned the teacher, * * * and moved on to Portland, Oregon. There, using the name John H. Mitchell, he quickly established himself as a successful lawyer, specializing in land litigation and railroad right-of-way cases. He also remarried without bothering to divorce his first wife. * * *

> On November 3, 1865, Mitchell filed suit against Neff in Oregon state court [seeking payment for the legal services that had been rendered.] * * * A default judgment * * * was entered against Neff on February 19, 1866. Although Mitchell had an immediate right to execute on the judgment, he waited until early June 1866 to seek a writ of execution, possibly waiting for the arrival of Neff's land patent. * * * On August 7, 1866, the property was sold at a sheriff's auction * * *. Notably, the buyer was not Sylvester Pennoyer, as the Supreme Court opinion and commentators have implied. The property was purchased by none other than J.H. Mitchell, who three days later assigned the property to Sylvester Pennoyer. * * *

> Following the litigation, Neff disappeared into obscurity; not so Pennoyer and Mitchell. Pennoyer went on to be Governor of Oregon * * *. Mitchell * * * was elected to the United States Senate in 1872, [but] lost his senate seat in 1879 * * *. * * * Shortly before the 1885 election, Judge Deady, the lower court judge in *Pennoyer v. Neff,* came into possession of a set of love letters which Mitchell had written to Mitchell's second wife's younger sister during the five years that he carried on an affair with her. Deady turned the love letters over to a newspaper, the *Oregonian* * * *. [However, in spite of] the scandal, Mitchell was [re]elected four days later * * *. In July of 1905, while still serving in the United States Senate, Mitchell was convicted [of land fraud] and sentenced to six months in jail, a $1,000 fine, and complete disbarment from public office.

Perdue, *Sin, Scandal and Substantive Due Process: Personal Jurisdiction and Pennoyer Reconsidered,* 62 Wash.L.Rev. 479, 481–90 (1987).

2. Traditional analysis distinguishes three types of jurisdiction. In a proceeding in personam, the court exercises its power to render a judgment for or against a person by virtue of his presence within the state's territory or his citizenship there. In a proceeding in rem, the court exercises its power to determine the

status of property located within its territory, and the determination of the court is binding with respect to all possible interest holders in that property. In a proceeding quasi-in-rem, the court renders a judgment for or against a person but recovery is limited to the value of property that is within the jurisdiction and thus subject to the court's authority. The dispute that gives rise to an action quasi-in-rem may be related to the property or unrelated to it. In an action quasi-in-rem, the property may be used to satisfy any judgment assessed in the action.

3.   The concepts of jurisdiction found in the *Pennoyer* opinion were derived from nineteenth-century international law. In the traditional international model, a citizen of Country A might have been injured by a citizen of Country B in Country A. The citizen of Country A seeking relief had three options: proceed against the citizen of Country B in personam in Country A (with the likelihood that the paper called a judgment would be worthless because the courts of Country B would not enforce it against citizens of Country B); proceed against the citizen of Country B quasi-in-rem in Country A (with the advantage that the property of the citizen of Country B in Country A would be available to satisfy at least part of the judgment); or proceed against the citizen of Country B in the courts of Country B (in the hope of winning a judgment enforceable in Country B). Given these choices, it is understandable that the citizen of Country A would probably prefer the courts of Country A to the courts of Country B, the latter being farther away and possibly more disposed to find in favor of the citizen of Country B, or to sue quasi-in-rem in Country A, so at least partial payment would be assured.

Do the same factors warrant applying these distinctions in jurisdiction in the context of the American federal system? Does not the Full Faith and Credit Clause of the Constitution require states to recognize and enforce valid judgments by other states? Do the states have the same kind of interest in adjudicating claims brought by their citizens when the stake is state sovereignty rather than national sovereignty?

4.   Does the length of time the defendant is in the jurisdiction matter in an in personam action? Does the reason why the person is in the jurisdiction make a difference? In Grace v. MacArthur, 170 F.Supp. 442 (E.D.Ark.1959), service of the complaint was made on the defendant while he was a passenger on a commercial flight from Tennessee to Texas when the plane was over Arkansas. The court upheld the exercise of jurisdiction by the federal district court sitting in Arkansas. For further discussion of "transient" jurisdiction, see pp. 167–77, infra.

5.   Can a court assert jurisdiction over a citizen who is absent from the jurisdiction? In BLACKMER v. UNITED STATES, 284 U.S. 421, 438–39, 52 S.Ct. 252, 255, 76 L.Ed. 375, 383 (1932), petitioner, an American citizen, sought reversal of a contempt conviction resulting from his refusal to comply with a subpoena issued by an American court and served upon him in France in connection with a proceeding that grew out of the Teapot Dome Scandal. Service was authorized by federal statute. The Supreme Court concluded that no violation of due process had taken place because

> the jurisdiction of the United States over its absent citizen, so far as the binding effect of its legislation is concerned, is a jurisdiction in personam, as he is personally bound to take notice of the laws that are applicable to him and to obey them. * * * The question of the validity of the provision for actual service of the subpoena in a foreign country is one that arises solely between the * * * United States and the citizen. The mere giving of such a notice to the citizen in the foreign country of the requirement of his

government that he shall return is in no sense an invasion of any right of the foreign government and the citizen has no standing to invoke any such supposed right.

The *Blackmer* principle was applied to state-court litigation in MILLIKEN v. MEYER, 311 U.S. 457, 462–63, 61 S.Ct. 339, 342–43, 85 L.Ed. 278, 283 (1940). Milliken sued Meyer, a Wyoming resident, in a Wyoming state court. Personal service was effected in Colorado under a Wyoming statute that permitted such service, in lieu of service by publication, on absent residents. Meyer did not appear and an in personam judgment was entered against him. Four years later Meyer asked a Colorado court to restrain Milliken's enforcement of the Wyoming judgment. The United States Supreme Court held the Wyoming judgment valid and entitled to full faith and credit. According to the Court:

> * * * Domicile in the state is alone sufficient to bring an absent defendant within the reach of the state's jurisdiction for purposes of a personal judgment by means of appropriate substituted service. * * * [T]he authority of a state over one of its citizens is not terminated by the mere fact of his absence from the state. The state which accords him privileges and affords protection to him and his property by virtue of his domicile may also exact reciprocal duties.

The Court's opinion made no attempt to distinguish among "resident," "domicile," and "citizen." What factors are relevant in deciding whether defendant's relationship with the forum state is sufficient to invoke the *Milliken* doctrine? Does Section 1 of the Fourteenth Amendment help answer the question by defining what it means to be a citizen of a state? Do *Blackmer* and *Milliken* fall within the scope of the statement in *Pennoyer* that "every State has the power to determine for itself the civil *status* and capacities of its inhabitants," or do they involve a different basis of jurisdiction?

6.   Suppose a plaintiff brings suit in a forum with which she has no other connection. Should that forum be able to entertain a suit *against* the plaintiff? Consider ADAM v. SAENGER, 303 U.S. 59, 67–68, 58 S.Ct. 454, 458, 82 L.Ed. 649, 654–55 (1938). The Beaumont Export & Import Co., a Texas corporation, brought suit against Montes in a California state court. In accordance with California procedure, Montes filed a cross-action against the corporation. The corporation then defaulted, its suit was dismissed, and Montes obtained a default judgment on his cross-action. Montes later assigned his judgment to Adam, who sought to enforce it in a Texas court. The Texas court refused to recognize the California judgment, holding that California law did not permit service of the complaint in the cross-action on the corporation's attorney, and that the corporation had not been otherwise "present" in California for purposes of jurisdiction. The United States Supreme Court reversed, holding that the method of service in the cross-action was authorized by California law and the judgment was entitled to full faith and credit:

> There is nothing in the Fourteenth Amendment to prevent a state from adopting a procedure by which a judgment *in personam* may be rendered in a cross-action against a plaintiff in its courts, upon service of process or of appropriate pleading upon his attorney of record. The plaintiff having, by his voluntary act in demanding justice from the defendant, submitted himself to the jurisdiction of the court, there is nothing arbitrary or unreasonable in treating him as being there for all purposes for which justice to the defendant requires his presence. It is the price which the state may exact as the condition of opening its courts to the plaintiff.

Would it matter whether or not the action is between the same two parties? Suppose a third party had instituted suit in California against Beaumont in an action unrelated to the suit with Montes. Would the California court have had jurisdiction? If there was jurisdiction, would it be based on Beaumont's presence in the state or on some other notion? In this regard, what is the significance of the Court's reference to the fact that Beaumont voluntarily acted to invoke the authority of the California courts? Should a state be permitted to condition the use of its courts on consent to the jurisdiction of those courts for purposes unrelated to the initial lawsuit?

7. The civil-law tradition with regard to personal jurisdiction is somewhat different from our own. Whereas the cornerstone of the common-law's concept of jurisdiction historically has been defendant's presence, domicile has been the key in The Netherlands and Switzerland, plaintiff's nationality has been of great importance in France, and domicile and the situs of property have been of major significance in Germany. "In this area of law, differences among civil-law countries are as great as differences between given civil-law and common-law countries." de Vries & Lowenfeld, *Jurisdiction in Personal Actions—A Comparison of Civil Law Views,* 44 Iowa L.Rev. 306, 344 (1959). See also Juenger, *Judicial Jurisdiction in the United States and in the European Communities: A Comparison,* 82 Mich.L.Rev. 1195 (1984).

SECTION B. EXPANDING THE BASES OF PERSONAL JURISDICTION

Increased interstate travel in the early twentieth century, particularly as a result of the growing popularity of the automobile, brought with it increased interstate litigation. In order to ensure that transient drivers not be beyond jurisdiction when they drove into another state, some states came to condition the use of their roads by out-of-state drivers on consent to the jurisdiction of the state's courts over matters arising from a party's activity within the state. In Kane v. New Jersey, 242 U.S. 160, 37 S.Ct. 30, 61 L.Ed. 222 (1916), the Supreme Court held that New Jersey could require an out-of-state motorist to file a formal instrument appointing a New Jersey agent to receive process prior to using the state's highways. Eventually, some states moved beyond express consent as a basis for asserting jurisdiction.

 HESS v. PAWLOSKI

Supreme Court of the United States, 1927.
274 U.S. 352, 47 S.Ct. 632, 71 L.Ed. 1091.

In Error to the Superior Court of Worcester County, Massachusetts.

MR. JUSTICE BUTLER delivered the opinion of the Court.

This action was brought by defendant in error to recover damages for personal injuries. The declaration alleged that plaintiff in error negligently and wantonly drove a motor vehicle on a public highway in Massachusetts, and that by reason thereof the vehicle struck and injured defendant in error. Plaintiff in error is a resident of Pennsylvania. No personal service was made on him, and no property belonging to him was attached. The service of process was made in compliance with chapter 90, General Laws of Massachusetts, as amended by Stat.1923, c. 431, § 2, the material parts of which follow:

The acceptance by a nonresident of the rights and privileges conferred by section three or four, as evidenced by his operating a motor vehicle thereunder, or the operation by a nonresident of a motor vehicle on a public way in the commonwealth other than under said sections, shall be deemed equivalent to an appointment by such nonresident of the registrar or his successor in office, to be his true and lawful attorney upon whom may be served all lawful processes in any action or proceeding against him, growing out of any accident or collision in which said nonresident may be involved while operating a motor vehicle on such a way, and said acceptance or operation shall be a signification of his agreement that any such process against him which is so served shall be of the same legal force and validity as if served on him personally. Service of such process shall be made by leaving a copy of the process with a fee of two dollars in the hands of the registrar, or in his office, and such service shall be sufficient service upon the said nonresident: Provided, that notice of such service and a copy of the process are forthwith sent by registered mail by the plaintiff to the defendant, and the defendant's return receipt and the plaintiff's affidavit of compliance herewith are appended to the writ and entered with the declaration. * * *

Plaintiff in error appeared specially for the purpose of contesting jurisdiction, and filed an answer in abatement and moved to dismiss on the ground that the service of process, if sustained, would deprive him of his property without due process of law, in violation of the Fourteenth Amendment. The court overruled the answer in abatement and denied the motion. The Supreme Judicial Court held the statute to be a valid exercise of the police power, and affirmed the order. * * * At the trial the contention was renewed and again denied. Plaintiff in error excepted. The jury returned a verdict for defendant in error. The exceptions were overruled by the Supreme Judicial Court. * * * Thereupon the superior court entered judgment. The writ of error was allowed by the Chief Justice of that court.

The question is whether the Massachusetts enactment contravenes the due process clause of the Fourteenth Amendment.

The process of a court of one state cannot run into another and summon a party there domiciled to respond to proceedings against him. Notice sent outside the state to a nonresident is unavailing to give jurisdiction in an action against him personally for money recovery. Pennoyer v. Neff * * *. There must be actual service within the state of notice upon him or upon some one authorized to accept service for him. * * * A personal judgment rendered against a nonresident, who has neither been served with process nor appeared in the suit, is without validity. McDonald v. Mabee, 243 U.S. 90, 37 S.Ct. 343, 61 L.Ed. 608, L.R.A.1917F, 458. The mere transaction of business in a state by nonresident natural persons does not imply consent to be bound by the process of its courts. Flexner v. Farson, 248 U.S. 289, 39 S.Ct. 97, 63 L.Ed. 250. The power of a state to exclude foreign corporations, although not absolute, but qualified, is the ground on which such an implication is supported as to them. * * * But a state may not withhold from nonresident individuals the right of doing business therein. The privileges and immunities clause of the Constitution (section 2, art. 4), safeguards to the citizens of one state the right "to pass through, or to reside in any other state for purposes of trade, agriculture, professional pursuits, or otherwise." And it prohibits state legislation discriminating against citizens of other states. * * *

Motor vehicles are dangerous machines, and, even when skillfully and carefully operated, their use is attended by serious dangers to persons and property. In the public interest the state may make and enforce regulations reasonably calculated to promote care on the part of all, residents and nonresidents alike, who use its highways. The measure in question operates to require a nonresident to answer for his conduct in the state where arise causes of action alleged against him, as well as to provide for a claimant a convenient method by which he may sue to enforce his rights. Under the statute the implied consent is limited to proceedings growing out of accidents or collisions on a highway in which the nonresident may be involved. It is required that he shall actually receive and receipt for notice of the service and a copy of the process. And it contemplates such continuances as may be found necessary to give reasonable time and opportunity for defense. It makes no hostile discrimination against nonresidents, but tends to put them on the same footing as residents. Literal and precise equality in respect of this matter is not attainable; it is not required. * * * The state's power to regulate the use of its highways extends to their use by nonresidents as well as by residents. * * * And, in advance of the operation of a motor vehicle on its highway by a nonresident, the state may require him to appoint one of its officials as his agent on whom process may be served in proceedings growing out of such use. Kane v. New Jersey * * *. That case recognizes power of the state to exclude a nonresident until the formal appointment is made. And, having the power so to exclude, the state may declare that the use of the highway by the nonresident is the equivalent of the appointment of the registrar as agent on whom process may be served. * * * The difference between the formal and implied appointment is not substantial, so far as concerns the application of the due process clause of the Fourteenth Amendment.

Judgment affirmed.

Notes and Questions

1. Would a nonresident-motorist statute that purported to assert jurisdiction over any cause of action that arises out of the presence of defendant's vehicle within the state, or over people other than the driver of the vehicle, be constitutional? Would it be wise? Could the implied consent to jurisdiction created by driving within a state be employed to support jurisdiction over a nonresident in a matter unrelated to her conduct within the state?

2. The idea of implied consent has been used in other contexts as well. In HENRY L. DOHERTY & CO. v. GOODMAN, 294 U.S. 623, 55 S.Ct. 553, 79 L.Ed. 1097 (1935), the Supreme Court upheld Iowa's right to apply a similar concept to assert jurisdiction over a nonresident who was selling securities in Iowa regarding controversies arising out of those sales.

SECTION C.   A NEW THEORY OF JURISDICTION

The jurisdictional bases developed in *Pennoyer*—presence and citizenship—were not easily applied to corporations. A corporation, after all, is a fiction. It exists on paper and acts through its employees, directors, and shareholders. It generally was accepted well into the nineteenth century that a "corporation can have no legal existence out of the boundaries of the sovereignty by which it is created." Bank of Augusta v. Earle, 38 U.S. (13 Pet.) 519, 588, 10 L.Ed. 274, 308 (1839) (Taney, J.). Nonetheless, as corporations grew beyond those boundaries, courts were forced to develop ways to apply the jurisdictional principles of *Pennoyer* to them.

The courts first developed the "consent" theory, which presupposed that a foreign corporation could transact business in a state only with that state's consent. Under this theory, a foreign corporation could be required to consent to service of process in the state by appointing an agent to receive process within the state, as a condition of obtaining permission to do business there. The courts soon began to apply this principle both when the corporation actually designated an agent to receive process and when it did not appoint an agent and, thus, could be said only to have granted implied consent.

As the courts became increasingly disenchanted with the unrealistic nature of the "consent" theory, they developed the "presence" theory premised on the notion that: "A foreign corporation is amenable to process * * * if it is doing business within the State in such manner and to such extent as to warrant the inference that it is present there." Philadelphia & Reading Ry. Co. v. McKibbin, 243 U.S. 264, 265, 37 S.Ct. 280, 61 L.Ed. 710, 711–12 (1917) (Brandeis, J.). This doctrine measured the propriety of a state's assertion of jurisdiction over a foreign corporation in terms of the actual activities of the corporation in the state. Under the presence theory, however, a court lost its adjudicatory authority over a corporation once it ceased doing business in the state. In addition, "presence" is a conclusory term, and all too often it was used by the courts without any meaningful analysis.

Under both the presence theory and the implied consent theory, the first question to be asked was whether the corporation was "doing business" within the state. As the number of cases making this factual inquiry multiplied, "doing business" gradually came to be a test in and of itself. The cases became cluttered with refined and often senseless distinctions that sought to measure the quantity of defendant's activities within the state but paid little or no attention to the burden imposed on the corporation of asserting jurisdiction over it or the overall desirability of litigating in the particular forum.

> With doctrine in so bad a state of disrepair, the time had long since passed for the Supreme Court to acknowledge the truth of Holmes' dictum that "[t]he Constitution is not to be satisfied with a fiction." International Shoe Co. v. Washington afforded the Court an opportunity to begin to set its house in order in this field.

Kurland, *The Supreme Court, the Due Process Clause and the In Personam Jurisdiction of State Courts—From Pennoyer to Denckla: A Review*, 25 U.Chi. L.Rev. 569, 586 (1958).

INTERNATIONAL SHOE CO. v. WASHINGTON

Supreme Court of the United States, 1945.
326 U.S. 310, 66 S.Ct. 154, 90 L.Ed. 95.

Appeal from the Supreme Court of the State of Washington.

MR. CHIEF JUSTICE STONE delivered the opinion of the Court.

The questions for decision are (1) whether, within the limitations of the due process clause of the Fourteenth Amendment, appellant, a Delaware corporation, has by its activities in the State of Washington rendered itself amenable to proceedings in the courts of that state to recover unpaid contributions to the state unemployment compensation fund exacted by state statutes, * * * and (2) whether the state can exact those contributions consistently with the due process clause of the Fourteenth Amendment.

The statutes in question set up a comprehensive scheme of unemployment compensation, the costs of which are defrayed by contributions required to be made by employers to a state unemployment compensation fund. The contributions are a specified percentage of the wages payable annually by each employer for his employees' services in the state. The assessment and collection of the contributions and the fund are administered by respondents. Section 14(c) of the Act, Wash.Rev.Stat.1941 Supp., § 9998—114c, authorizes respondent Commissioner to issue an order and notice of assessment of delinquent contributions upon prescribed personal service of the notice upon the employer if found within the state, or, if not so found, by mailing the notice to the employer by registered mail at his last known address. That section also authorizes the Commissioner to collect the assessment by distraint if it is not paid within ten days after service of the notice. * * *

In this case notice of assessment for the years in question was personally served upon a sales solicitor employed by appellant in the State of Washington, and a copy of the notice was mailed by registered mail to appellant at its address in St. Louis, Missouri. Appellant appeared specially before the office of unemployment and moved to set aside the order and notice of assessment on the ground that the service upon appellant's salesman was not proper service upon appellant; that appellant was not a corporation of the State of Washington and was not doing business within the state; that it had no agent within the state upon whom service could be made; and that appellant is not an employer and does not furnish employment within the meaning of the statute.

The motion was heard on evidence and a stipulation of facts by the appeal tribunal which denied the motion and ruled that respondent Commissioner was entitled to recover the unpaid contributions. That action was affirmed by the Commissioner; both the Superior Court and the Supreme Court affirmed. * * * Appellant in each of these courts assailed the statute as applied, as a violation of the due process clause of the Fourteenth Amendment, and as imposing a constitutionally prohibited burden on interstate commerce.

* * * Appellant is a Delaware corporation, having its principal place of business in St. Louis, Missouri, and is engaged in the manufacture and sale of shoes and other footwear. It maintains places of business in several states, other than Washington, at which its manufacturing is carried on and from

which its merchandise is distributed interstate through several sales units or branches located outside the State of Washington.

Appellant has no office in Washington and makes no contracts either for sale or purchase of merchandise there. It maintains no stock of merchandise in that state and makes there no deliveries of goods in intrastate commerce. During the years from 1937 to 1940, now in question, appellant employed eleven to thirteen salesmen under direct supervision and control of sales managers located in St. Louis. These salesmen resided in Washington; their principal activities were confined to that state; and they were compensated by commissions based upon the amount of their sales. The commissions for each year totaled more than $31,000. Appellant supplies its salesmen with a line of samples, each consisting of one shoe of a pair, which they display to prospective purchasers. On occasion they rent permanent sample rooms, for exhibiting samples, in business buildings, or rent rooms in hotels or business buildings temporarily for that purpose. The cost of such rentals is reimbursed by appellant.

The authority of the salesmen is limited to exhibiting their samples and soliciting orders from prospective buyers, at prices and on terms fixed by appellant. The salesmen transmit the orders to appellant's office in St. Louis for acceptance or rejection, and when accepted the merchandise for filling the orders is shipped f.o.b. from points outside Washington to the purchasers within the state. All the merchandise shipped into Washington is invoiced at the place of shipment from which collections are made. No salesman has authority to enter into contracts or to make collections.

The Supreme Court of Washington was of opinion that the regular and systematic solicitation of orders in the state by appellant's salesmen, resulting in a continuous flow of appellant's product into the state, was sufficient to constitute doing business in the state so as to make appellant amenable to suit in its courts. But it was also of opinion that there were sufficient additional activities shown to bring the case within the rule frequently stated, that solicitation within a state by the agents of a foreign corporation plus some additional activities there are sufficient to render the corporation amenable to suit brought in the courts of the state to enforce an obligation arising out of its activities there. * * * The court found such additional activities in the salesmen's display of samples sometimes in permanent display rooms, and the salesmen's residence within the state, continued over a period of years, all resulting in a substantial volume of merchandise regularly shipped by appellant to purchasers within the state. The court also held that the statute as applied did not invade the constitutional power of Congress to regulate interstate commerce and did not impose a prohibited burden on such commerce.

Appellant's argument, renewed here, that the statute imposes an unconstitutional burden on interstate commerce need not detain us. * * *

Appellant also insists that its activities within the state were not sufficient to manifest its "presence" there and that in its absence the state courts were without jurisdiction, that consequently it was a denial of due process for the state to subject appellant to suit. It refers to those cases in which it was said that the mere solicitation of orders for the purchase of goods within a state, to be accepted without the state and filled by shipment of the purchased goods interstate, does not render the corporation seller amenable to suit within the state. * * * And appellant further argues that since it was not present within the state, it is a denial of due process to subject it to taxation or other money exaction. It thus denies the power of the state to lay the tax or to subject appellant to a suit for its collection.

Penn. v. Neff Historically the jurisdiction of courts to render judgment in personam is grounded on their de facto power over the defendant's person. Hence his presence within the territorial jurisdiction of a court was prerequisite to its rendition of a judgment personally binding him. Pennoyer v. Neff * * *. But now that the capias ad respondendum has given way to personal service of summons or other form of notice, due process requires only that in order to subject a defendant to a judgment in personam, if he be not present within the territory of the forum, he have certain minimum contacts with it such that the maintenance of the suit does not offend "traditional notions of fair play and substantial justice." Milliken v. Meyer * * *. See Holmes, J., in McDonald v. Mabee, 243 U.S. 90, 91, 37 S.Ct. 343, 61 L.Ed. 608, L.R.A.1917F, 458. * * *

Since the corporate personality is a fiction, although a fiction intended to be acted upon as though it were a fact * * *, it is clear that unlike an individual its "presence" without, as well as within, the state of its origin can be manifested only by activities carried on in its behalf by those who are authorized to act for it. To say that the corporation is so far "present" there as to satisfy due process requirements, for purposes of taxation or the maintenance of suits against it in the courts of the state, is to beg the question to be decided. For the terms "present" or "presence" are used merely to symbolize those activities of the corporation's agent within the state which courts will deem to be sufficient to satisfy the demands of due process. L. Hand, J., in Hutchinson v. Chase & Gilbert * * *. Those demands may be met by such contacts of the corporation with the state of the forum as make it reasonable, in the context of our federal system of government, to require the corporation to defend the particular suit which is brought there. An "estimate of the inconveniences" which would result to the corporation from a trial away from its "home" or principal place of business is relevant in this connection. * * *

"Presence" in the state in this sense has never been doubted when the activities of the corporation there have not only been continuous and systematic, but also give rise to the liabilities sued on, even though no consent to be sued or authorization to an agent to accept service of process has been given. * * * Conversely it has been generally recognized that the casual presence of the corporate agent or even his conduct of single or isolated items of activities in a state in the corporation's behalf are not enough to subject it to suit on causes of action unconnected with the activities there. * * * To require the corporation in such circumstances to defend the suit away from its home or other jurisdiction where it carries on more substantial activities has been thought to lay too great and unreasonable a burden on the corporation to comport with due process.

While it has been held in cases on which appellant relies that continuous activity of some sorts within a state is not enough to support the demand that the corporation be amenable to suits unrelated to that activity * * *, there have been instances in which the continuous corporate operations within a state were thought so substantial and of such a nature as to justify suit against it on causes of action arising from dealings entirely distinct from those activities. * * *

Finally, although the commission of some single or occasional acts of the corporate agent in a state sufficient to impose an obligation or liability on the corporation has not been thought to confer upon the state authority to enforce it, Rosenberg Bros. & Co. v. Curtis Brown Co., 260 U.S. 516, 43 S.Ct. 170, 67 L.Ed. 372, other such acts, because of their nature and quality and the circumstances of their commission, may be deemed sufficient to render the corporation liable to suit. Cf. Kane v. New Jersey * * *; Hess v. Pawloski * * *. True, some of the decisions holding the corporation amenable to suit have been supported by resort to the legal fiction that it has given its consent to service and suit, consent being implied from its presence in the state through the acts of its authorized agents. * * * But more realistically it may be said that those authorized acts were of such a nature as to justify the fiction. * * *

It is evident that the criteria by which we mark the boundary line between those activities which justify the subjection of a corporation to suit, and those which do not, cannot be simply mechanical or quantitative. The test is not merely, as has sometimes been suggested, whether the activity, which the corporation has seen fit to procure through its agents in another state, is a little more or a little less. * * * Whether due process is satisfied must depend rather upon the quality and nature of the activity in relation to the fair and orderly administration of the laws which it was the purpose of the due process clause to insure. That clause does not contemplate that a state may make binding a judgment in personam against an individual or corporate defendant with which the state has no contacts, ties, or relations. * * *

But to the extent that a corporation exercises the privilege of conducting activities within a state, it enjoys the benefits and protection of the laws of that state. The exercise of that privilege may give rise to obligations; and, so far as those obligations arise out of or are connected with the activities within the state, a procedure which requires the corporation to respond to a suit brought to enforce them can, in most instances, hardly be said to be undue. * * *

Applying these standards, the activities carried on in behalf of appellant in the State of Washington were neither irregular nor casual. They were systematic and continuous throughout the years in question. They resulted in a large volume of interstate business, in the course of which appellant received the benefits and protection of the laws of the state, including the right to resort to the courts for the enforcement of its rights. The obligation which is here sued upon arose out of those very activities. It is evident that these operations establish sufficient contacts or ties with the state of the forum to make it reasonable and just according to our traditional conception of fair play and substantial justice to permit the state to enforce the obligations which appellant has incurred there. Hence we cannot say that the maintenance of the present suit in the State of Washington involves an unreasonable or undue procedure.

We are likewise unable to conclude that the service of the process within the state upon an agent whose activities establish appellant's "presence" there was not sufficient notice of the suit, or that the suit was so unrelated to those activities as to make the agent an inappropriate vehicle for communicating the notice. It is enough that appellant has established such contacts with the state that the particular form of substituted service adopted there gives reasonable assurance that the notice will be actual. * * *

Appellant having rendered itself amenable to suit upon obligations arising out of the activities of its salesmen in Washington, the state may maintain the present suit in personam to collect the tax laid upon the exercise of the privilege of employing appellant's salesmen within the state. For Washington has made one of those activities, which taken together establish appellant's "presence" there for purposes of suit, the taxable event by which the state brings appellant within the reach of its taxing power. The state thus has constitutional power to lay the tax and to subject appellant to a suit to recover it. The activities which establish its "presence" subject it alike to taxation by the state and to suit to recover the tax. * * *

Affirmed.

MR. JUSTICE JACKSON took no part in the consideration or decision of this case.

MR. JUSTICE BLACK delivered the following opinion.

* * *

I believe that the Federal Constitution leaves to each State, without any "ifs" or "buts," a power to tax and to open the doors of its courts for its citizens to sue corporations whose agents do business in those States. Believing that the Constitution gave the States that power, I think it a judicial deprivation to condition its exercise upon this Court's notion of "fair play," however appealing that term may be. Nor can I stretch the meaning of due process so far as to authorize this Court to deprive a State of the right to afford judicial protection to its citizens on the ground that it would be more "convenient" for the corporation to be sued somewhere else.

There is a strong emotional appeal in the words "fair play," "justice," and "reasonableness." But they were not chosen by those who wrote the original Constitution or the Fourteenth Amendment as a measuring rod for this Court to use in invalidating State or Federal laws passed by elected legislative representatives. No one, not even those who most feared a democratic government, ever formally proposed that courts should be given power to invalidate legislation under any such elastic standards. Express prohibitions against certain types of legislation are found in the Constitution, and under the long settled practice, courts invalidate laws found to conflict with them. This requires interpretation, and interpretation, it is true, may result in extension of the Constitution's purpose. But that is no reason for reading the due process clause so as to restrict a State's power to tax and sue those whose activities affect persons and businesses within the State, provided proper service can be had. * * *

Notes and Questions

1. For more of the facts of *International Shoe,* see Cameron & Johnson, *Death of a Salesman?: Forum Shopping and Outcome Determination Under International Shoe,* 28 U.C.Davis L.Rev. 769 (1995).

2. *International Shoe* has been described as part of a "dual trend in jurisdictional decisions: in defining the court with jurisdiction, a trend from the court with immediate power over the defendant to the court where the parties may most conveniently settle their dispute; and in defining due process of law, a trend from the emphasis on territorial limitations of courts to emphasis on providing notice and an opportunity to be heard." SMYTH v. TWIN STATE IMPROVEMENT CORP., 116 Vt. 569, 80 A.2d 664 (1951). Do you agree?

3. Did the subject matter of the dispute in *International Shoe* provide a reason to find jurisdiction over the corporation? After all, Washington was suing to collect state taxes. Doesn't every state have an especially strong interest in enforcing its tax laws? It is probable that wherever the action was brought the substantive law to be applied would be Washington law. What interest would another state, such as Delaware, International Shoe's state of incorporation, have in adjudicating this dispute?

4. *International Shoe* uses contacts with the forum in two different ways. First, a defendant may have sufficient contact with the forum to warrant asserting jurisdiction over it for all matters. This is termed "general jurisdiction," and we will return to study it in more detail later in this Chapter. Second, a defendant may have sufficient contact with the forum to warrant asserting jurisdiction over it for matters related to its activity with the forum without having sufficient contact with the forum to warrant general jurisdiction. In such a case, the jurisdiction is termed "specific jurisdiction." Whether a corporation is subject to specific or general jurisdiction, however, depends on the nature and number of contacts it has with the forum. Determining what constitutes sufficient business within the state, or what matters are related to activity within it, often are uncertain questions that may blur the distinction between general and specific jurisdiction. See Brilmayer, *Related Contacts and Personal Jurisdiction,* 101 Harv.L.Rev. 1444 (1988).

SECTION D.   SPECIFIC JURISDICTION AND STATE LONG–ARM LAWS

1.   THE DEVELOPMENT OF LONG-ARM LAWS

The Supreme Court's decision in Hess v. Pawloski, p. 71, supra, encouraged states to utilize their police powers to enact a number of statutes asserting jurisdiction based not only on the operation of automobiles within a state but also on engaging in a variety of other hazardous activities or enterprises. As time progressed and liberal judicial construction and emboldened state legislatures gave broader scope to these statutes, the usefulness of the technique suggested by the nonresident motorist statutes became even more apparent.

The Court's decision in *International Shoe*—with its emphasis on contacts with the forum state—further encouraged states to expand their jurisdictional reach and led to efforts on the part of many state legislatures to conform their statutory pattern to the Supreme Court's latest view as to when personal jurisdiction could be asserted consistently with the Constitution. This spate of legislative activity came largely in the form of "long-arm" or "single-act" statutes, which seek to provide personal jurisdiction over nonresidents who cannot be found and served in the forum. These statutes predicate jurisdiction over nonresidents upon the defendant's general activity in the state, or the commission of any one of a series of enumerated acts within the jurisdiction, or, in some cases, the commission of a certain act outside the jurisdiction causing consequences within it. The theory supporting the assertion of jurisdiction in these circumstances flows naturally from the Court's decision in *International Shoe* and its emphasis on the quantum and quality of the defendant's activity in the forum state.

The first truly comprehensive long-arm statute was enacted in Illinois and it was used as a model by a number of states. According to the Illinois Supreme Court, the statute was an attempt to assert jurisdiction to the fullest permissible constitutional limits. Under the Illinois act an individual or a corporation, whether a citizen or noncitizen of Illinois, is said to be amenable to the jurisdiction of the state's courts if he transacts any business within the state; commits a tort within the state; owns, uses, or possesses any real estate within the state; or contracts to insure any person, property, or risk located within the state. Several years after its enactment, the Illinois statute was amended to include jurisdiction over claims involving alimony, support, and property division against former residents. Other states soon followed Illinois' lead in expanding the jurisdictional reach of their courts.

Contemporary long-arm statutes run the gamut from very broad ones that permit states to assert jurisdiction up to the limits allowed by the Constitution, to narrow ones that only carve out small parts of their constitutionally permitted authority. The Rhode Island long-arm statute, R.I. Gen.L. § 9–5–33, which is set out in the Supplement, is an example of a broad long-arm statute. It permits Rhode Island courts to assert jurisdiction over any foreign corporations, nonresident individuals (or their executors or administrators), and partnerships or associations amenable to suit within the state and having the necessary minimum contacts required by the Constitution.

Other state long-arm statutes are more limited in application, requiring the doing of business or an act or omission within the state. Many long-arm statutes apply only to corporate defendants, and some states have enacted separate statutes for individuals and corporations. Several long-arm statutes are available only to resident plaintiffs. One limitation that generally is placed on the use of long-arm statutes is that they apply only to suits brought in the courts of the state in which the jurisdictional act occurs or in the federal courts sitting in that state. Despite the textual similarities of many of these statutes, judicial construction of them often differs.

———

Read the selected state jurisdiction statutes in the Supplement.

———

GRAY v. AMERICAN RADIATOR & STANDARD SANITARY CORP.

Supreme Court of Illinois, 1961.
22 Ill.2d 432, 176 N.E.2d 761.

KLINGBIEL, JUSTICE. Phyllis Gray appeals from a judgment of the circuit court of Cook County dismissing her action for damages. The issues are concerned with the construction and validity of our statute providing for substituted service of process on nonresidents. Since a constitutional question is involved, the appeal is direct to this court.

The suit was brought against the Titan Valve Manufacturing Company and others, on the ground that a certain water heater had exploded and injured the plaintiff. The complaint charges, *inter alia,* that the Titan company, a foreign corporation, had negligently constructed the safety valve; and that the injuries were suffered as a proximate result thereof. Summons issued and was duly served on Titan's registered agent in Cleveland, Ohio. The corporation appeared specially, filing a motion to quash on the ground that it had not committed a tortious act in Illinois. Its affidavit stated that it does no business here; that it has no agent physically present in Illinois; and that it sells the completed valves to defendant, American Radiator & Standard Sanitary Corporation, outside Illinois. The American Radiator & Standard Sanitary Corporation (also made a defendant) filed an answer in which it set up a cross claim against Titan, alleging that Titan made certain warranties to American Radiator, and that if the latter is held liable to the plaintiff it should be indemnified and held harmless by Titan. The court granted Titan's motion, dismissing both the complaint and the cross claim.

Section 16 of the Civil Practice Act provides that summons may be personally served upon any party outside the State; and that as to nonresidents who have submitted to the jurisdiction of our courts, such service has the force and effect of personal service within Illinois. (Ill.Rev.Stat.1959, chap. 110, par. 16.) Under section 17(1)(b) a nonresident who, either in person or through an agent, commits a tortious act within this State submits to jurisdiction. * * * The questions in this case are (1) whether a tortious act was committed here, within the meaning of the statute, despite the fact that the Titan corporation had no agent in Illinois; and (2) whether the statute, if so construed, violates due process of law.

The first aspect to which we must direct our attention is one of statutory construction. Under section 17(1)(b) jurisdiction is predicated on the committing of a tortious act in this State. It is not disputed, for the purpose of this appeal, that a tortious act was committed. The issue depends on whether it was committed in Illinois, so as to warrant the assertion of personal jurisdiction by service of summons in Ohio.

The wrong in the case at bar did not originate in the conduct of a servant physically present here, but arose instead from acts performed at the place of manufacture. Only the consequences occurred in Illinois. It is well established, however, that in law the place of a wrong is where the last event takes place which is necessary to render the actor liable. Restatement, Conflict of Laws, sec. 377. A second indication that the place of injury is the determining factor is found in rules governing the time within which an action must be brought. In applying statutes of limitation our court has computed the period from the time when the injury is done. * * * We think it is clear that the alleged negligence in manufacturing the valve cannot be separated from the resulting injury; and that for present purposes, like those of liability and limitations, the tort was committed in Illinois.

Titan seeks to avoid this result by arguing that instead of using the word "tort," the legislature employed the term "tortious act"; and that the latter refers only to the act or conduct, separate and apart from any consequences thereof. We cannot accept the argument. To be tortious an act must cause injury. The concept of injury is an inseparable part of the phrase. In determining legislative intention courts will read words in their ordinary and popularly understood sense. * * * We think the intent should be determined less from technicalities of definition than from considerations of general purpose and effect. To adopt the criteria urged by defendant would tend to promote litigation over extraneous issues concerning the elements of a tort and the territorial incidence of each, whereas the test should be concerned more with those substantial elements of convenience and justice presumably contemplated by the legislature. As we observed in Nelson v. Miller, 11 Ill.2d 378, 143 N.E.2d 673, the statute contemplates the exertion of jurisdiction over nonresident defendants to the extent permitted by the due-process clause.

The Titan company contends that if the statute is applied so as to confer jurisdiction in this case it violates the requirement of due process of law. The precise constitutional question thus presented has not heretofore been considered by this court. * * *

Under modern doctrine the power of a State court to enter a binding judgment against one not served with process within the State depends upon two questions: first, whether he has certain minimum contacts with the State * * * and second, whether there has been a reasonable method of notification. See International Shoe Co. v. State of Washington * * *. In the case at bar there is no contention that section 16 provides for inadequate notice or that its provisions were not followed. Defendant's argument on constitutionality is confined to the proposition that applying section 17(1)(b), where the injury is defendant's only contact with the State, would exceed the limits of due process.

A proper determination of the question presented requires analysis of those cases which have dealt with the quantum of contact sufficient to warrant jurisdiction. Since the decision in Pennoyer v. Neff * * * the power of a State to exert jurisdiction over nonresidents has been greatly expanded, particularly with respect to foreign corporations. * * * [In International Shoe Co. v. Washington,] the court pointed out that the activities of the corporation in Washington were not only continuous and systematic but also gave rise to the liability sued on. It was observed that such operations, which resulted in a large volume of business, established "sufficient contacts or ties with the state of the forum to make it reasonable and just according to our traditional conception of fair play and substantial justice to permit the state to enforce the obligations which appellant has incurred there." * * *

Where the business done by a foreign corporation in the State of the forum is of a sufficiently substantial nature, it has been held permissible for the State to entertain a suit against it even though the cause of action arose from activities entirely distinct from its conduct within the State. Perkins v. Benguet Consolidated Mining Co. * * *. But where such business or other activity is not substantial, the particular act or transaction having no connection with the State of the forum, the requirement of "contact" is not satisfied. * * *

In the case at bar the defendant's only contact with this State is found in the fact that a product manufactured in Ohio was incorporated in Pennsylvania, into a hot water heater which in the course of commerce was sold to an Illinois consumer. The record fails to disclose whether defendant has done any other business in Illinois, either directly or indirectly; and it is argued, in reliance on the International Shoe test, that since a course of business here has not been shown there are no "minimum contacts" sufficient to support jurisdiction. We do not think, however, that doing a given volume of business is the only way in which a nonresident can form the required connection with this State. Since the International Shoe case was decided the requirements for jurisdiction have been further relaxed, so that at the present time it is sufficient if the act or transaction itself has a substantial connection with the State of the forum.

In McGee v. International Life Insurance Co., 355 U.S. 220, 78 S.Ct. 199, 201, 2 L.Ed.2d 223 (1957), suit was brought in California against a foreign insurance company on a policy issued to a resident of California. The defendant was not served with process in that State but was notified by registered mail at its place of business in Texas, pursuant to a statute permitting such service in suits on insurance contracts. The contract in question was delivered in California, the premiums were mailed from there and the insured was a resident of that State when he died, but defendant had no office or agent in California nor did it solicit any business there apart from the policy sued on. After referring briefly to the International Shoe case the court held that "it is sufficient for purposes of due process that the suit was based on *a contract* which had substantial connection" with California. (Emphasis supplied.)

In Smyth v. Twin State Improvement Corp. * * * the court discussed the principal authorities on the question and concluded, *inter alia,* that "continuous activity within the state is not necessary as a prerequisite to jurisdiction."

In Nelson v. Miller * * * the commission of a single tort within this State was held sufficient to sustain jurisdiction under the present statute. The defendant in that case, a resident of Wisconsin, was engaged in the business of selling appliances. It was alleged that in the process of delivering a stove in Illinois, an employee of the defendant negligently caused injury to the plaintiff. In holding that the defendant was not denied due process by being required to defend in Illinois, this court observed * * *: "The defendant sent his employee into Illinois in the advancement of his own interests. While he was here, the employee and the defendant enjoyed the benefit and protection of the laws of Illinois, including the right to resort to our courts. In the course of his stay here the employee performed acts that gave rise to an injury. The law of Illinois will govern the substantive rights and duties stemming from the incident. Witnesses, other than the defendant's employee, are likely to be found here, and not in Wisconsin. In such circumstances, it is not unreasonable to require the defendant to make his defense here."

Whether the type of activity conducted within the State is adequate to satisfy the requirement depends upon the facts in the particular case. * * * The question cannot be answered by applying a mechanical formula or rule of thumb but by ascertaining what is fair and reasonable in the circumstances. In the application of this flexible test the relevant inquiry is whether defendant engaged in some act or conduct by which he may be said to have invoked the benefits and protections of the law of the forum. * * * The relevant decisions since Pennoyer v. Neff show a development of the concept of personal jurisdiction from one which requires service of process within the State to one which is satisfied either if the act or transaction sued on occurs there or if defendant has engaged in a sufficiently substantial course of activity in the State, provided always that reasonable notice and opportunity to be heard are afforded. * * * [T]he trend in defining due process of law is away from the emphasis on territorial limitations and toward emphasis on providing adequate notice and opportunity to be heard: from the court with immediate power over the defendant, toward the court in which both parties can most conveniently settle their dispute.

In the McGee case the court commented on the trend toward expanding State jurisdiction over nonresidents, observing that: "In part this is attributable to the fundamental transformation of our national economy over the years. Today many commercial transactions touch two or more States and may involve parties separated by the full continent. With this increasing nationalization of commerce has come a great increase in the amount of business conducted by mail across state lines. At the same time modern transportation and communication have made it much less burdensome for a party sued to defend himself in a State where he engages in economic activity."

It is true that courts cannot "assume that this trend heralds the eventual demise of all restrictions on the personal jurisdiction of state courts." Hanson v. Denckla * * *. An orderly and fair administration of the law throughout the nation requires protection against being compelled to answer claims brought in distant States with which the defendant has little or no association and in which he would be faced with an undue burden or disadvantage in making his defense. It must be remembered that lawsuits can be brought on frivolous demands or groundless claims as well as on legitimate ones, and that procedural rules must be designed and appraised in the light of what is fair and just to both sides in the dispute. * * *

In the case at bar defendant does not claim that the present use of its product in Illinois is an isolated instance. While the record does not disclose the volume of Titan's business or the territory in which appliances incorporating its valves are marketed, it is a reasonable inference that its commercial transactions, like those of other manufacturers, result in substantial use and consumption in this State. To the extent that its business may be directly affected by transactions occurring here it enjoys benefits from the laws of this State, and it has undoubtedly benefited, to a degree, from the protection which our law has given to the marketing of hot water heaters containing its valves. Where the alleged liability arises, as in this case, from the manufacture of products presumably sold in contemplation of use here, it should not matter that the purchase was made from an independent middleman or that someone other than the defendant shipped the product into this State.

With the increasing specialization of commercial activity and the growing interdependence of business enterprises it is seldom that a manufacturer deals directly with consumers in other States. The fact that the benefit he derives from its laws is an indirect one, however, does not make it any the less essential to the conduct of his business; and it is not unreasonable, where a cause of action arises from alleged defects in his product, to say that the use of such products in the ordinary course of commerce is sufficient contact with this State to justify a requirement that he defend here.

As a general proposition, if a corporation elects to sell its products for ultimate use in another State, it is not unjust to hold it answerable there for any damage caused by defects in those products. Advanced means of distribution and other commercial activity have made possible these modern methods of doing business, and have largely effaced the economic significance of State lines. By the same token, today's facilities for transportation and communication have removed much of the difficulty and inconvenience formerly encountered in defending lawsuits brought in other States.

* * *

The principles of due process relevant to the issue in this case support jurisdiction in the court where both parties can most conveniently settle their dispute. The facts show that the plaintiff, an Illinois resident, was injured in Illinois. The law of Illinois will govern the substantive questions, and witnesses on the issues of injury, damages and other elements relating to the occurrence are most likely to be found here. Under such circumstances the courts of the place of injury usually provide the most convenient forum for trial. * * * In Travelers Health Association v. Commonwealth of Virginia, 339 U.S. 643, 70 S.Ct. 927, 94 L.Ed. 1154, a Nebraska insurance corporation was held subject to the jurisdiction of a Virginia regulatory commission although it had no paid agents within the State and its only contact there was a mail-order business operated from its Omaha office. The court observed, by way of *dictum,* that "suits on alleged losses can be more conveniently tried in Virginia where witnesses would most likely live and where claims for losses would presumably be investigated. Such factors have been given great weight in applying the doctrine of *forum non conveniens.* * * * And prior decisions of this Court have referred to the unwisdom, unfairness and injustice of permitting policyholders to seek redress only in some distant state where the insurer is incorporated. The Due Process Clause does not forbid a state to protect its citizens from such injustice." 339 U.S. at page 649, 70 S.Ct. at page 930, 94 L.Ed. at 1161–1162. * * *

* * * We conclude accordingly that defendant's association with this State is sufficient to support the exercise of jurisdiction.

* * *

Reversed and remanded, with directions.

Notes and Questions

1. As *Gray* illustrates, the application of long-arm statutes often entails difficult questions of statutory construction. In FEATHERS v. McLUCAS, 15 N.Y.2d 443, 463–64, 261 N.Y.S.2d 8, 23–24, 209 N.E.2d 68, 79–80, certiorari

denied 382 U.S. 905, 86 S.Ct. 241, 15 L.Ed.2d 158 (1965), the New York court was asked to construe a New York statute which, like the Illinois statute involved in *Gray*, authorized jurisdiction over a non-domiciliary "if, in person or through an agent, he * * * commits a tortious act within the state." In the New York case, plaintiffs were injured by the explosion of a tractor-drawn tank of liquid propane gas on a highway near their home in New York. The tank had been manufactured in Kansas and sold to a Missouri corporation, "presumably with knowledge that the latter would mount the tank on a wheelbase and then sell it to * * * a Pennsylvania corporation, which operated as a licensed interstate carrier." The New York court refused to assert jurisdiction over the Kansas manufacturer. In reaching this result, it criticized the conclusion in *Gray* that a tort had been committed in Illinois for purposes of that state's jurisdiction statute:

> * * * It certainly does not follow that, if the "place of wrong" for purposes of conflict of laws is a particular state, the "place of the commission of a tortious act" is also that same state for purposes of interpreting a statute conferring jurisdiction, on that basis, over nonresidents. * * * Moreover, the place of the "tort" is not necessarily the same as the place of the defendant's commission of the "tortious act." * * *

> In sum, then, it is our conclusion, based not only on the plain language of the statute but on its legislative history, that * * * [the New York statute] covers only a tortious act committed (by a nondomiciliary) in this State. * * *

In 1966, the New York legislature amended its jurisdictional statute (C.P.L.R. § 302) to reach defendants in cases like *Feathers*. Is the text of the current New York provision, which is set out in the Supplement, broader or narrower than the Illinois act? In what ways?

2. In GREEN v. ADVANCE ROSS ELECTRONICS CORP., 86 Ill.2d 431, 437–38, 439–40, 56 Ill.Dec. 657, 660–62, 427 N.E.2d 1203, 1206–08 (1981), the issue was whether Advance Ross, a Delaware corporation with headquarters in Illinois, in an action claiming breaches of fiduciary duty, could assert jurisdiction over Green, a Texas resident, who once served as president of two of its affiliates. All of Green's corporate responsibilities, including the acts that allegedly injured the corporation, were performed outside Illinois. Nonetheless, Advance Ross argued that, under Section 17(1)(b) of Illinois' long-arm statute, an out-of-state resident submits to the jurisdiction of the Illinois courts when he commits a tort that causes a diminution of the funds of a corporation organized or headquartered in Illinois. The Illinois Supreme Court, distinguishing *Gray*, refused to read Section 17(1)(b) to establish jurisdiction:

> As in *Gray* * * *, for the purpose of disposing of the propriety of long-arm jurisdiction there is no dispute that tortious acts were committed. To be resolved is whether their commission was "within this State" as those words are used in section 17(1)(b).

> * * * [Advance Ross'] theory is that although the misconduct of Green, Sr., took place outside Illinois, the consequences of his misconduct were felt in Illinois. They * * * contend that the misconduct alleged resulted in a drain upon those assets in Illinois. But the consequences upon which [Advance Ross relies] are too remote from the misconduct of Green, Sr., to support the conclusion that the tortious acts complained of were committed in Illinois. The situs of the last event whose happening was necessary to hold Green, Sr., liable was in Texas.

In support of its conclusion, the Illinois court noted:

[A]cceptance of the theory of long-arm jurisdiction advanced by [Advance Ross] would be tantamount to permitting a corporation operating nationwide to sue employees, suppliers, customers and perhaps others, at the company's State of incorporation or at its headquarters no matter how far away they lived and worked or their contact with the corporation was. Any interpretation of the Illinois long-arm statute which would permit that result is neither fair nor wise as a matter of policy. The meaning [which Advance Ross] ask[s] us to give the words "within this State" takes us too easily out of this State to be acceptable. Dealing by a Texas resident with an Illinois corporation only in Texas is too remote from Illinois to regard any part of the action as occurring in Illinois.

3. Illinois' long-arm statute (Ill.Rev.Stat. ch. 110, ¶ 2–209(a)) was amended in 1989 to give the Illinois state courts jurisdiction over any cause of action arising out of:

* * *

(7) The making or performance of any contract or promise substantially connected with this State; * * *

(11) The breach of any fiduciary duty within this State;

(12) The performance of duties as a director or officer of a corporation organized under the laws of this State or having its principal place of business within this State; * * *.

If these provisions had been in effect, would the Illinois Supreme Court have decided *Advance Ross* the same way? In this regard, consider whether *Gray* and *Advance Ross* are applicable only to cases asserting jurisdiction based on a "tortious act within this State," or whether they apply equally to all assertions of jurisdiction under Illinois' long-arm statute.

4. Section 3(c) of Massachusetts' long-arm statute, M.G.L.A., ch. 223A, gives to that state's courts jurisdiction over parties who cause "tortious injury by an act or omission in this commonwealth." This language is derived from the Uniform Interstate and International Procedure Act, which is set out in the Supplement, and represents an effort to resolve, legislatively, the type of conflict over the meaning of the term "tortious act within this state" that developed between the Illinois (*Gray*) and the New York (*Feathers*) courts. The courts have read Section 3(c) to apply only when the tortious conduct causing the injury occurs within the Commonwealth. See, e.g., Kolikof v. Samuelson, 488 F.Supp. 881, 883 (D.Mass. 1980).

5. The words "within the state" have been interpreted more liberally when the relevant act is an intentional tort. Thus, for example, in MURPHY v. ERWIN–WASEY, INC., 460 F.2d 661, 664 (1st Cir.1972), an action for fraud, deceit, and breach of contract, Murphy alleged that the defendant had misrepresented the true amount of its billings, thereby depriving him of commissions. Murphy sought to base jurisdiction on Massachusetts' Section 3(c), arguing that when the defendant, in New York, communicated by mail or telephone false statements to him in Massachusetts, the act causing the injury occurred within the Commonwealth. The First Circuit agreed, in part on the basis of a distinction between intentional and unintentional tort cases:

[W]hile sending a defective tool to a dealer * * * merely creates the condition from which damage might later arise, sending a libel into a state is indistinguishable from "the frequently hypothesized but rarely encountered gunman firing across a state line."

We believe that the same is true of the mailing of a fraudulent misrepresentation into a state. We would be closing our eyes to the realities of modern business practices were we to hold that a corporation subjects itself to the jurisdiction of another state by sending a personal messenger into that state bearing a fraudulent misrepresentation but not when it follows the more ordinary course of employing the United States Postal Service as its messenger. Where a defendant knowingly sends into a state a false statement, intending that it should there be relied upon to the injury of a resident of that state, he has, for jurisdictional purposes, acted within that state.

But see McIlwee v. ADM Industries, Inc., 17 F.3d 222 (7th Cir.1994), in which the court held that an alleged failure to disclose information defendants had a duty to disclose during telephone calls to Illinois that were initiated in other states was not the commission of a tortious act in Illinois for jurisdiction purposes.

6. It also is possible to assert jurisdiction over a defendant in a tort case on the authority of a long-arm provision not designed expressly to cover tort claims. For example, in GRIMANDI v. BEECH AIRCRAFT CORP., 512 F.Supp. 764 (D.Kan.1981), French plaintiffs brought a product liability suit in Kansas for damages resulting from an airplane crash in France. They named as one of the defendants a Canadian corporation that regularly sold airplane engines (up to 30 million dollars in sales annually) to the Kansas-based manufacturer of the ill-fated plane. The plaintiffs asserted jurisdiction under a provision of Kansas' statute authorizing jurisdiction over a defendant when the cause of action arises from the transaction of any business within the state.

Because the engine in the plane that crashed was a replacement engine that had been installed in Canada and that never had been sold to the Kansas manufacturer or sent to Kansas, there was some doubt whether the claim "arose from" the defendant's transaction of business in Kansas as required by the statute. The court, however, found jurisdiction. It ruled that the "arising from" requirement could be met by "but for" causation and that if it had not been for the Canadian manufacturer's business with the Kansas company, it would not have had the occasion to install the replacement engine in Canada.

The Seventh and Ninth Circuits also have adopted the "but for" standard for determining whether a cause of action "arises from" the business transacted in the state by the defendant. See In re Oil Spill by Amoco Cadiz off Coast of France, 699 F.2d 909 (7th Cir.) (but for negotiation and signing of contract in Illinois for the building of the oil tanker, it would not have broken up off the coast of France, spilled oil, and caused damages), certiorari denied 464 U.S. 864, 104 S.Ct. 196, 78 L.Ed.2d 172 (1983); Shute v. Carnival Cruise Lines, 897 F.2d 377 (9th Cir.1990) (but for defendant's solicitation of business in Washington, plaintiff would not have taken the cruise and would not have been injured), reversed on other grounds 499 U.S. 585, 111 S.Ct. 1522, 113 L.Ed.2d 622 (1991). However, other courts have held that "whether a cause of action arises out of or relates to a defendant's forum contact is analogous to the issue of proximate cause in tort law." Russo v. Sea World of Florida, Inc., 709 F.Supp. 39, 42 (D.R.I.1989) (plaintiff's slip-and-fall in Florida did not "arise out of or relate" to defendant's national advertisement or plaintiff's purchase of theme park ticket from travel agent in Rhode Island). For a general discussion of the requirement that a cause of action "arise from or relate to" the defendant's contact with the forum state, see Maloney, *Specific Jurisdiction and the "Arise From or Related to" Require-ment ... What Does It Mean?*, 50 Wash. & Lee L.Rev. 1265 (1993).

7.   Long-arm provisions authorizing jurisdiction over a defendant on the basis of the defendant's business within the forum often require that the plaintiff's cause of action "be related to" or "arise from" the business transacted within the state. Under these provisions, jurisdiction will not exist when the cause of action is unrelated to the defendant's contacts with the forum.

For example, in JIM FOX ENTERPRISES, INC. v. AIR FRANCE, 664 F.2d 63 (5th Cir.1981), a Texas corporation brought a breach-of-warranty action against Air France, a foreign corporation, to recover the costs of repairing a defective navigation system as well as consequential damages. The plaintiff sought to establish jurisdiction under the then existing Texas long-arm statute, which provided that jurisdiction would exist when a foreign corporation has engaged in business in Texas and the action is one "arising out of such business." Air France's considerable business in Texas notwithstanding, the District Court dismissed the action for want of personal jurisdiction, and the Fifth Circuit affirmed. Judge Brown, writing for the Court of Appeals, pointed to Air France's "thriving business in Texas" (and to the fact that at least one member of the court had flown the airline to Paris), but concluded:

> [T]he Texas long-arm statute requires some nexus between the cause of action and the defendant's contacts with Texas. This requirement means that Texas does not reach nearly as far as Due Process would permit. Fox conceded that its claim does not relate to Air France's business in Texas. As a result of this anachronistic but made-in-Texas statutory provision, Air France, a foreign corporation that undoubtedly did substantial business in Texas and has "minimum contacts" galore, * * * nonetheless, under the Texas statute, slips through the fingers at the end of the Long-arm.

Id. at 63–64.

8.   In the *Jim Fox Enterprises* case, a federal court was construing Texas' long-arm statute. Subsequently, the Supreme Court of Texas had occasion to examine the same provision in HALL v. HELICOPTEROS NACIONALES DE COLOMBIA, S.A., 638 S.W.2d 870 (Tex.1982), reversed 466 U.S. 408, 104 S.Ct. 1868, 80 L.Ed.2d 404 (1984).

The defendant Helicol did not maintain an office in Texas, was not authorized to do business, performed no helicopter operations, and did not recruit workers there. The contract between Helicol and the joint venture was negotiated in Houston, however; and, Helicol did purchase substantially all of its helicopters in Texas, spent an average of $50,000 a month there for parts, sent pilots to Texas to pick up helicopters, sent pilots and maintenance personnel there for training, had employees there on a year-round rotation basis, and maintained a New York bank account that received roughly $5,000,000 in payments in the form of checks drawn upon the joint venture's Texas account.

On these facts, the Texas Supreme Court concluded that jurisdiction was authorized by Texas' transacting-business provision. Indeed, it held that the Texas provision reaches as far as the constitutional requirements of the Due Process Clause will permit. In examining the statutory requirement that the cause of action arise out of the contacts of the defendant with Texas, the court said:

> * * * [The "arising out of" test] is useful in any fact situation in which a jurisdiction question exists; and is a necessary requirement where the nonres-ident defendant only maintained single or few contacts with the forum.

However, the [test] is unnecessary when the nonresident defendants presence in the forum through numerous contacts is of such a nature, as in this case, so as to satisfy the demands of the ultimate test of due process. * * *

638 S.W.2d at 872. The court went on to hold that the Due Process Clause did not bar the assertion of jurisdiction in the case before it. The United States Supreme Court subsequently disagreed, see pp. 133–42, infra.

After the Texas Supreme Court rendered its decision in the *Helicopteros* case, the Fifth Circuit, on a petition for rehearing in the *Jim Fox Enterprises* case, Note 7, above, indicated that the interpretation of Texas' long-arm statute offered in its initial opinion in *Jim Fox Enterprises* was no longer in accord with Texas authority. It therefore approved the assertion of jurisdiction over Air France. Jim Fox Enterprises, Inc. v. Air France, 705 F.2d 738 (5th Cir.1983).

9.   Many state courts have adopted the view, articulated in *Gray* and echoed in the Texas Supreme Court's decision in *Helicopteros,* that a seemingly limited long-arm provision was intended to extend to the limits of the Due Process Clause. Does this effectively transform statutes of the Illinois, New York, or Texas type into statutes of the California or Rhode Island type? Is it desirable to make every decision on jurisdiction a constitutional one? This approach to enumerated-act statutes has been criticized in Taylor v. Portland Paramount Corp., 383 F.2d 634, 640 (9th Cir.1967): "In effect, what these courts have done is to abdicate their duty to construe the statutes of their own states and to turn it over to the Supreme Court of the United States, which is the ultimate interpreter of the Constitution * * *."

2.   DUE PROCESS AND LONG–ARM STATUTES

As is illustrated by the decision of the Illinois Supreme Court in *Gray,* interpreting the relevant long-arm statute is only half of the job. Once the meaning of the statute has been determined, it must be asked whether the statute, as interpreted, is consistent with the Due Process Clause of the Constitution.

———

McGEE v. INTERNATIONAL LIFE INSURANCE CO., 355 U.S. 220, 222–24, 78 S.Ct. 199, 200–01, 2 L.Ed.2d 223, 225–26 (1957). The plaintiff, McGee, was the beneficiary of a life insurance policy issued by the Empire Mutual Insurance Co., an Arizona corporation, to one Lowell Franklin, a resident of California. In 1948, the defendant, International Life Insurance Co., assumed Empire Mutual's insurance obligations. Franklin and International Life transacted business by mail until Franklin's death in 1950. Neither Empire Mutual nor International Life ever had any office or agent in California, and, as far as the record disclosed, International Life had never solicited or done any insurance business in California other than the policy with Franklin.

When International Life refused to pay McGee upon Franklin's death, she sued in a California state court, basing jurisdiction on the California Unauthorized Insurer's Process Act. The Act subjects foreign corporations to suit on insurance contracts with in-state residents. After recovering a judgment in California, McGee sought to enforce the judgment in Texas. The Texas court refused to enforce the judgment, holding it to be void under the Fourteenth Amendment on the ground that the California courts could not assume jurisdiction over International Life without service of process within its boundaries. The Supreme Court held that the exercise of jurisdiction by California was proper.

The Court noted that, with increased "nationalization of commerce," the tremendous growth "in the amount of business conducted by mail across state lines" and the frequency with which "commercial transactions touch two or more States," there had developed "a trend * * * clearly discernible toward expanding the permissible scope of state jurisdiction over foreign corporations and other nonresidents."

> * * * [W]e think it apparent that the Due Process Clause did not preclude the California court from entering a judgment binding on respondent. It is sufficient * * * that the suit was based on a contract which had substantial connection with that State. * * * The contract was delivered in California, the premiums were mailed from there and the insured was a resident of that State when he died. * * * California has a manifest interest in providing effective means of redress for its residents when their insurers refuse to pay claims. These residents would be at a severe disadvantage if they were forced to follow the insurance company to a distant State in order to hold it legally accountable. When claims were small or moderate individual claimants frequently could not afford the cost of bringing an action in a foreign forum—thus in effect making the company judgment proof. Often the crucial witnesses—as here on the company's defense of suicide—will be found in the insured's locality. Of course there may be inconvenience to the insurer if it is held amenable to suit in California * * * but certainly nothing which amounts to a denial of due process. * * * There is no contention that respondent did not have adequate notice of the suit or sufficient time to prepare its defenses and appear.

Notes and Questions

1. Did the *McGee* Court modify the *International Shoe* test? Is *McGee* consistent with *International Shoe*?

2. The *McGee* opinion seems to focus on the interests of California and the plaintiff in having the suit heard in California. But isn't the issue to be determined whether the defendant's due process rights have been violated? That question appears to be independent of countervailing factors supporting the exercise of jurisdiction in California. Is it fair to characterize the *McGee* Court as using a two-step approach? The first is to determine whether sufficient minimum contacts exist so as to make the exercise of personal jurisdiction permissible. The second is to balance the interests of the plaintiff, defendant, and the forum to determine if exercising jurisdiction is desirable. Or is the thrust of *McGee* that the number of contacts between the defendant and the forum that normally would be required for jurisdiction are reduced when the interests of the forum state and plaintiff strongly support jurisdiction?

3. The Court said in *McGee* that improvements in transportation and communication make it less burdensome for out-of-state litigants to defend suits. Does this observation sufficiently justify making the defendant travel to the forum

chosen by the plaintiff? Don't advances in transportation and communication also make it easier for plaintiffs to sue out of state? For an extremely useful discussion of the influence of social attitudes and developments on judicial principles, see Kalo, *Jurisdiction as an Evolutionary Process: The Development of Quasi In Rem and In Personam Principles,* 1978 Duke L.J. 1147.

———

HANSON v. DENCKLA, 357 U.S. 235, 78 S.Ct. 1228, 2 L.Ed.2d 1283 (1958). Dora Donner, a resident of Pennsylvania, established a trust in Delaware, naming a Delaware bank as trustee. By the terms of the trust, during her lifetime the income from the trust would go to her and, upon her death, the remainder would pass to whomever she had appointed as beneficiaries. Mrs. Donner retained the power to change the appointed beneficiaries at any time.

Later, Mrs. Donner moved to Florida, and, several years before her death, she executed her last will and testament, leaving most of her estate to two of her daughters. On the same day, she executed (for the last time) her power to change the appointed beneficiaries under the trust—this time, she designated two of her grandchildren (the children of a third daughter) beneficiaries of a significant portion of the trust's assets, with the remainder going to her estate.

After Mrs. Donner's death, the two daughters named in the will brought an action in Florida claiming that the appointment of their sister's children as beneficiaries of the trust had been ineffective. If that were true, the assets of the trust would pass under the will to the two daughters, as legatees.

The defendants argued that the suit could not go forward because the Florida court could not assert jurisdiction over the Delaware trustee, an indispensable party under Florida law.

The Florida court found that it had jurisdiction over the trustee for the purpose of the action, concluded that the trust was invalid and that the exercise of the power of appointment was ineffective to pass title, and held that the trust property therefore passed under the will. Before the Florida judgment was rendered, an action was commenced in Delaware to determine who was entitled to share the trust assets, which were situated in Delaware. With minor exceptions, the parties were the same as in the Florida action. When the Florida judgment was rendered, the legatees under the will unsuccessfully urged it as res judicata of the Delaware action. The Delaware court ultimately held the trust and the exercise of the power of appointment valid under Delaware law.

Accepting both cases for review, a divided Supreme Court found that because the trustee's contacts with Florida had been less than minimal, that state could not assert personal jurisdiction over it. Since Florida had not obtained personal jurisdiction over an indispensable party to the action, the trustee, Delaware was justified in refusing full faith and credit to the Florida decree. Writing for a majority of five, Chief Justice Warren explained that:

> * * * [T]he requirements for personal jurisdiction over nonresidents have evolved from the rigid rule of Pennoyer v. Neff * * * to the flexible standard of International Shoe Co. v. State of Washington * * *. But it is

a mistake to assume that this trend heralds the eventual demise of all restrictions on the personal jurisdiction of state courts. * * * Those restrictions are more than a guarantee of immunity from inconvenient or distant litigation. They are a consequence of territorial limitations on the power of the respective States. However minimal the burden of defending in a foreign tribunal, a defendant may not be called upon to do so unless he has had the "minimal contacts" with that State that are a prerequisite to its exercise of power over him. * * *

We fail to find such contacts in the circumstances of this case. The defendant trust company has no office in Florida, and transacts no business there. None of the trust assets has ever been held or administered in Florida, and the record discloses no solicitation of business in that State either in person or by mail. * * *

The cause of action in this case is not one that arises out of an act done or transaction consummated in the forum State. * * * From Florida Mrs. Donner carried on several bits of trust administration that may be compared to the mailing of premiums in *McGee*. But the record discloses no instance in which the trustee performed any acts in Florida that bear the same relationship to the agreement as the solicitation in *McGee*. Consequently, this suit cannot be said to be one to enforce an obligation that arose from a privilege the defendant exercised in Florida. * * *

* * * The unilateral activity of those who claim some relationship with a nonresident defendant cannot satisfy the requirement of contact with the forum State. The application of that rule will vary with the quality and nature of the defendant's activity, but it is essential in each case that there be some act by which the defendant purposefully avails itself of the privilege of conducting activities within the forum State, thus invoking the benefits and protections of its laws. * * *

* * * As we understand [Florida's] law, the trustee is an indispensable party over whom the court must acquire jurisdiction before it is empowered to enter judgment in a proceeding affecting the validity of a trust. It does not acquire that jurisdiction by being the "center of gravity" of the controversy, or the most convenient location for litigation. The issue is personal jurisdiction, not choice of law. * * *

Id. at 251–54, 78 S.Ct. at 1238–40, 2 L.Ed.2d at 1296–98.

Justice Black's dissent stands in sharp contrast to the Chief Justice's perception of personal jurisdiction.

In light of the * * * circumstances it seems quite clear to me that there is nothing in the Due Process Clause which denies Florida the right to determine whether [the] appointment was valid as against its statute of wills. * * * Not only was the appointment made in Florida by a domiciliary of Florida, but the primary beneficiaries also lived in that State. In my view it could hardly be denied that Florida had sufficient interest so that a court with jurisdiction might properly apply Florida law, if it chose, to determine whether the appointment was effectual. * * * True, the question whether the law of a State can be applied to a transaction is different from the question whether the courts of that State have jurisdiction to enter a judgment, but the two are often closely related and to a substantial degree depend upon similar considerations. It seems to me that where a transaction has as much relationship to a State as * * * [this] appointment had to Florida its courts ought to have power to adjudicate controversies arising out of that transaction, unless litigation there would impose such a heavy and disproportionate burden on a nonresident defendant that it would offend what this Court has referred to as "traditional notions of fair play and substantial justice." * * * Florida, the home of the principal contenders * * *, was a reasonably convenient forum for all. Certainly there is nothing fundamentally unfair in subjecting the corporate trustee to the jurisdiction of the Florida courts. It chose to maintain business relations with [the settlor] in that State for eight years, regularly communicating with her with respect to the business of the trust including the very appointment in question.

Florida's interest in the validity of [the] appointment is made more emphatic by the fact that her will is being administered in that State. It has traditionally been the rule that the State where a person is domiciled at the time of his death is the proper place to determine the validity of his will, to construe its provisions and to marshal and distribute his personal property. Here Florida was seriously concerned with winding up [this] estate and with finally determining what property was to be distributed under her will. * * *

Id. at 258–59, 78 S.Ct. at 1242–43, 2 L.Ed.2d at 1300–01.

Notes and Questions

1. Under the last appointment of the trust, the children of Mrs. Donner's daughter Elizabeth would have received about $400,000 from the trust. Mrs. Donner's other two daughters, the residual legatees under the will, would have received over $1,000,000 from the estate. The Florida decision would have invalidated the last appointment over the trust, defeated Mrs. Donner's estate plan, and added $400,000 to the amount received by Elizabeth's sisters at the expense of Elizabeth's family.

2. In EMPIRE ABRASIVE EQUIP. CORP. v. H.H. WATSON, INC., 567 F.2d 554, 557 (3d Cir.1977), Judge Gibbons described the concerns for state sovereignty that underlie limits on the exercise of in personam jurisdiction:

[O]ut of respect for values of federalism, the due process clause [forbids] a state to exercise its adjudicatory authority in a manner that would encroach upon the sovereignty of a sister state. A state must have some palpable interest—rationally connected with public policy—in adjudicating a dispute within its borders for jurisdiction to be lawfully acquired. * * * Although some other sovereign state may have a superior interest in having the controversy finally adjudged in its courts, our system of federalism has recognized that such conflicts between states will often arise, and has concluded that as long as the forum's interest in opening its courts to the litigants is of due process dimensions, the sovereign rights of a sister state are not unconstitutionally abridged.

How much of an interest must the forum state have to justify its exercise of sovereign authority to decide a dispute to the exclusion of other potentially interested states? Does the Due Process Clause define a rather low level of state interest? Or does due process require the forum state's interests to outweigh the interests of other states? Compare California's interests in *McGee,* in which jurisdiction was upheld, with Florida's interests in *Hanson,* in which jurisdiction was denied.

3. Could the *Hanson* decision be justified on the ground that Delaware, as the state where the trust was validly established (at least under Delaware law), had a stronger interest in the disposition of the trust's funds than Florida? Delaware's interest certainly is sufficient to support jurisdiction in Delaware. Is Delaware's interest sufficient to preclude jurisdiction in Florida? Could it be that the result in this case is a function of the fact that the Court had before it two conflicting judgments and that it could not accord full faith and credit to both? For a discussion of federalism and the due process clause, see Trangsrud, *The Federal Common Law of Personal Jurisdiction,* 57 Geo.Wash.L.Rev. 849 (1989). See also Brussack, *Political Legitimacy and State Court Jurisdiction: A Critique of the Public Law Paradigm,* 72 Neb.L.Rev. 1082 (1993).

4. What defines a state "interest" sufficient to support jurisdiction? Is a legislative desire to provide a forum enough? Every long-arm statute manifests a legislative desire to extend jurisdiction in a given class of cases, yet we subject these statutes to scrutiny under the Due Process Clause and sometimes invalidate them. Does a state's desire to provide a forum for its residents constitute an interest? Surely, the residence of the plaintiff is not sufficient by itself to provide a basis for depriving a defendant of her property. Does the fact that a state has contacts with the events giving rise to the litigation, regardless of whether those contacts are attributable to the defendant, create an "interest" sufficient to support jurisdiction? In *Hanson,* Florida had contacts with the litigation, and the Court denied its courts jurisdiction. Should state substantive regulation of a particular class of cases influence the decision on personal jurisdiction? In *McGee,* jurisdiction over the nonresident insurance company may have been justified by California's regulation of the insurance industry. Is a state's substantive regulation of an area the only interest relevant to jurisdiction? See generally Brilmayer, *How Contacts Count: Due Process Limitations on State Court Jurisdiction,* 1980 Sup.Ct.Rev. 77; Carrington & Martin, *Substantive Interests and the Jurisdiction of State Courts,* 66 Mich.L.Rev. 227 (1967); Drobak, *The Federalism Theme in Personal Jurisdiction,* 68 Iowa L.Rev. 1015 (1983); Lewis, *The "Forum State Interest" Factor in Personal Jurisdiction: Home Court Horses Hauling Constitutional Carts,* 33 Mercer L.Rev. 769 (1982).

5. In their opinions in *Hanson,* the Chief Justice and Justice Black agree that the question whether a court may apply its own law to a controversy is to be decided by a standard that differs from that used to decide the question whether the court can adjudicate the controversy at all. That is, the constitutional power to apply local law is of a different dimension from the constitutional power to assert jurisdiction. Can this difference be justified?

6. Consider the following argument:

The *Hanson* Court's implication * * * is that more contacts with the forum state are needed for jurisdiction than for choice of law. I suggest that this implication is counterintuitive. The impact of a conflict of laws decision more seriously affects the rights of the parties than a decision on jurisdiction, which merely directs the parties to an appropriate forum in which to litigate their case. * * * I am confident that, given the choice, the Florida plaintiffs would rather have litigated in a Delaware Court applying Florida law than in a Florida court applying Delaware law.

Silberman, *Shaffer v. Heitner: The End of an Era,* 53 N.Y.U.L.Rev. 33, 82–83 (1978). Given a choice of fora with different substantive rules, it is obvious that the plaintiff would prefer one and the defendant another. But, should jurisdiction turn on the interests of the parties? Is it the state's interest that should be relevant? Is the state's interest the only relevant interest?

7. Might it be appropriate to allow a court to adjudicate any controversy to which it might apply local law under the applicable choice-of-law rule? In ALL-STATE INS. CO. v. HAGUE, 449 U.S. 302, 312–13, 101 S.Ct. 633, 640, 66 L.Ed.2d 521, 531 (1981), the plurality opinion held that "for a State's substantive law to be selected in a constitutionally permissible manner, that State must have a significant contact or significant aggregation of contacts, creating state interests, such that choice of its law is neither arbitrary nor fundamentally unfair." Under this test, the plurality upheld Minnesota's decision to apply its own law in an action by a former Wisconsin resident who moved to Minnesota just prior to filing suit to collect proceeds under an automobile insurance policy made in Wisconsin covering vehicles owned by a Wisconsin resident who had been killed in an accident in Wisconsin. After *Hague* it seems clear that the Due Process Clause allows states extraordinary latitude in developing choice-of-law rules. The due process restrictions on state jurisdiction are considerably greater than those on choice of law.

WORLD–WIDE VOLKSWAGEN CORP. v. WOODSON

Supreme Court of the United States, 1980.
444 U.S. 286, 100 S.Ct. 559, 62 L.Ed.2d 490.

Certiorari to the Supreme Court of Oklahoma.

MR. JUSTICE WHITE delivered the opinion of the Court.

The issue before us is whether, consistently with the Due Process Clause of the Fourteenth Amendment, an Oklahoma court may exercise *in personam* jurisdiction over a nonresident automobile retailer and its wholesale distributor in a products liability action, when the defendants' only connection with Oklahoma is the fact that an automobile sold in New York to New York residents became involved in an accident in Oklahoma.

I

Respondents Harry and Kay Robinson purchased a new Audi automobile from petitioner Seaway Volkswagen, Inc. (Seaway) in Massena, N.Y., in 1976. The following year the Robinson family, who resided in New York, left that State for a new home in Arizona. As they passed through the State of Oklahoma, another car struck their Audi in the rear, causing a fire which severely burned Kay Robinson and her two children.

The Robinsons subsequently brought a products liability action in the District Court for Creek County, Okla., claiming that their injuries resulted from defective design and placement of the Audi's gas tank and fuel system. They joined as defendants the automobile's manufacturer, Audi NSU Auto Union Aktiengesellschaft (Audi); its importer, Volkswagen of America, Inc. (Volkswagen); its regional distributor, petitioner World–Wide Volkswagen Corporation (World–Wide); and its retail dealer, petitioner Seaway. Seaway and World–Wide entered special appearances, claiming that Oklahoma's exercise of jurisdiction over them would offend the limitations on the State's jurisdiction imposed by the Due Process Clause of the Fourteenth Amendment.

The facts presented to the District Court showed that World–Wide is incorporated and has its business office in New York. It distributes vehicles, parts, and accessories, under contract with Volkswagen, to retail dealers in New York, New Jersey, and Connecticut. Seaway, one of these retail dealers, is incorporated and has its place of business in New York. Insofar as the record reveals, Seaway and World–Wide are fully independent corporations whose relations with each other and with Volkswagen and Audi are contractual only. Respondents adduced no evidence that either World–Wide or Seaway does any business in Oklahoma, ships or sells any products to or in that State, has an agent to receive process there, or purchases advertisements in any media calculated to reach Oklahoma. In fact, * * * there was no showing that any automobile sold by World–Wide or Seaway has ever entered Oklahoma with the single exception of the vehicle involved in the present case.

Despite the apparent paucity of contacts between petitioners and Oklahoma, the District Court rejected their constitutional claim and reaffirmed that ruling in denying petitioners' motion for reconsideration. Petitioners then sought a writ of prohibition in the Supreme Court of Oklahoma to restrain the District Judge, respondent Charles S. Woodson, from exercising *in personam* jurisdiction over them. They renewed their contention that, because they had no "minimal contacts" * * * with the State of Oklahoma, the actions of the District Judge were in violation of their rights under the Due Process Clause.

The Supreme Court of Oklahoma denied the writ, * * * holding that personal jurisdiction over petitioners was authorized by Oklahoma's "long-arm" statute, Okla.Stat., Tit. 12, § 1701.03(a)(4) (1971).[7] Although the court noted that the proper approach was to test jurisdiction against both statutory and constitutional standards, its analysis did not distinguish these questions, probably because § 1701.03(a)(4) has been interpreted as conferring jurisdiction to the limits permitted by the United States Constitution. The court's rationale was contained in the following paragraph * * *:

> In the case before us, the product being sold and distributed by the petitioners is by its very design and purpose so mobile that petitioners can foresee its possible use in Oklahoma. This is especially true of the distributor, who has the exclusive right to distribute such automobile in New York, New Jersey and Connecticut. The evidence presented below demonstrated that goods sold and distributed by the petitioners were used in the State of Oklahoma, and under the facts we believe it reasonable to infer, given the retail value of the automobile, that the petitioners derive substantial income from automobiles which from time to time are used in the State of Oklahoma. This being the case, we hold that under the facts presented, the trial court was justified in concluding

---

7. This subsection provides:

"A court may exercise personal jurisdiction over a person, who acts directly or by an agent, as to a cause of action or claim for relief arising from the person's * * * causing tortious injury in this state by an act or omission outside this state if he regularly does or solicits business or engages in any other persistent course of conduct, or derives substantial revenue from goods used or consumed or services rendered, in this state * * *." * * *

that the petitioners derive substantial revenue from goods used or consumed in this State.

H

We granted certiorari * * * to consider an important constitutional question with respect to state-court jurisdiction and to resolve a conflict between the Supreme Court of Oklahoma and the highest courts of at least four other States. We reverse.

II

* * *

As has long been settled, and as we reaffirm today, a state court may exercise personal jurisdiction over a nonresident defendant only so long as there exist "minimum contacts" between the defendant and the forum State. International Shoe Co. v. Washington * * *. The concept of minimum contacts, in turn, can be seen to perform two related, but distinguishable, functions. It protects the defendant against the burdens of litigating in a distant or inconvenient forum. And it acts to ensure that the States, through their courts, do not reach out beyond the limits imposed on them by their status as coequal sovereigns in a federal system.

The protection against inconvenient litigation is typically described in terms of "reasonableness" or "fairness." We have said that the defendant's contacts with the forum State must be such that maintenance of the suit "does not offend 'traditional notions of fair play and substantial justice.'" * * * The relationship between the defendant and the forum must be such that it is "reasonable * * * to require the corporation to defend the particular suit which is brought there." * * * Implicit in this emphasis on reasonableness is the understanding that the burden on the defendant, while always a primary concern, will in an appropriate case be considered in light of other relevant factors, including the forum State's interest in adjudicating the dispute * * *; the plaintiff's interest in obtaining convenient and effective relief, * * * at least when that interest is not adequately protected by the plaintiff's power to choose the forum * * *; the interstate judicial system's interest in obtaining the most efficient resolution of controversies; and the shared interest of the several States in furthering fundamental substantive social policies * * *.

The limits imposed on state jurisdiction by the Due Process Clause, in its role as a guarantor against inconvenient litigation, have been substantially relaxed over the years. As we noted in McGee v. International Life Ins. Co., * * * this trend is largely attributable to a fundamental transformation in the American economy:

> Today many commercial transactions touch two or more States and may involve parties separated by the full continent. With this increasing nationalization of commerce has come a great increase in the amount of business conducted by mail across state lines. At the same time modern transportation and communication have made it much less burdensome for a party sued to defend himself in a State where he engages in economic activity.

The historical developments noted in *McGee,* of course, have only accelerated in the generation since that case was decided.

Nevertheless, we have never accepted the proposition that state lines are irrelevant for jurisdictional purposes, nor could we, and remain faithful to the principles of interstate federalism embodied in the Constitution. * * * [T]he Framers * * * intended that the States retain many essential attributes of sovereignty, including, in particular, the sovereign power to try causes in their courts. The sovereignty of each State, in turn, implied a limitation on the sovereignty of all of its sister States—a limitation express or implicit in both the original scheme of the Constitution and the Fourteenth Amendment.

Hence, even while abandoning the shibboleth that "[t]he authority of every tribunal is necessarily restricted by the territorial limits of the State in which it is established," Pennoyer v. Neff, * * * we emphasized that the reasonableness of asserting jurisdiction over the defendant must be assessed "in the context of our federal system of government," International Shoe Co. v. Washington, * * * and stressed that the Due Process Clause ensures not only fairness, but also the "orderly administration of the laws," id. As we noted in Hanson v. Denckla * * *:

> As technological progress has increased the flow of commerce between the States, the need for jurisdiction over nonresidents has undergone a similar increase. At the same time, progress in communications and transportation has made the defense of a suit in a foreign tribunal less burdensome. In response to these changes, the requirements for personal jurisdiction over nonresidents have evolved from the rigid rule of Pennoyer v. Neff * * * to the flexible standard of International Shoe Co. v. Washington. * * * But it is a mistake to assume that this trend heralds the eventual demise of all restrictions on the personal jurisdiction of state courts. * * * Those restrictions are more than a guarantee of immunity from inconvenient or distant litigation. They are a consequence of territorial limitations on the power of the respective States.

Thus, the Due Process Clause "does not contemplate that a state may make binding a judgment *in personam* against an individual or corporate defendant with which the state has no contacts, ties, or relations." International Shoe Co. v. Washington * * *. Even if the defendant would suffer minimal or no inconvenience from being forced to litigate before the tribunals of another State; even if the forum State has a strong interest in applying its law to the controversy; even if the forum State is the most convenient location for litigation, the Due Process Clause, acting as an instrument of interstate federalism, may sometimes act to divest the State of its power to render a valid judgment. Hanson v. Denckla * * *.

III

Applying these principles to the case at hand, we find in the record before us a total absence of those affiliating circumstances that are a necessary predicate to any exercise of state-court jurisdiction. Petitioners carry on no activity whatsoever in Oklahoma. They close no sales and perform no services there. They avail themselves of none of the privileges and benefits of Oklahoma law. They solicit no business there either through salespersons or through advertising reasonably calculated to reach the State. Nor does the record show that they regularly sell cars at wholesale or retail to Oklahoma customers or residents or that they indirectly, through others, serve or seek to serve the Oklahoma market. In short, respondents seek to base jurisdiction on one, isolated occurrence and whatever inferences can be drawn therefrom: the fortuitous circumstance that a single Audi automobile, sold in New York to New York residents, happened to suffer an accident while passing through Oklahoma.

It is argued, however, that because an automobile is mobile by its very design and purpose it was "foreseeable" that the Robinsons' Audi would cause injury in Oklahoma. Yet "foreseeability" alone has never been a sufficient benchmark for personal jurisdiction under the Due Process Clause. In Hanson v. Denckla * * * it was no doubt foreseeable that the settlor of a Delaware trust would subsequently move to Florida and seek to exercise a power of appointment there; yet we held that Florida courts could not constitutionally exercise jurisdiction over a Delaware trustee that had no other contacts with the forum State. * * *

If foreseeability were the criterion, a local California tire retailer could be forced to defend in Pennsylvania when a blowout occurs there, * * * a Wisconsin seller of a defective automobile jack could be haled before a distant court for damage caused in New Jersey, * * * or a Florida soft-drink concessionaire could be summoned to Alaska to account for injuries happening there * * *. Every seller of chattels would in effect appoint the chattel his agent for service of process. His amenability to suit would travel with the chattel. * * *

This is not to say, of course, that foreseeability is wholly irrelevant. But the foreseeability that is critical to due process analysis is not the mere likelihood that a product will find its way into the forum State. Rather, it is that the defendant's conduct and connection with the forum State are such that he should reasonably anticipate being haled into court there. * * * The Due Process Clause, by ensuring the "orderly administration of the laws," * * * gives a degree of predictability to the legal system that allows potential defendants to structure their primary conduct with some minimum assurance as to where that conduct will and will not render them liable to suit.

When a corporation "purposefully avails itself of the privilege of conducting activities within the forum State," * * * it has clear notice that it is subject to suit there, and can act to alleviate the risk of burdensome litigation by procuring insurance, passing the expected costs on to customers, or, if the risks are too great, severing its connection with the State. Hence if the sale of a product of a manufacturer or distributor such as Audi or Volkswagen is not simply an isolated occurrence, but arises from the efforts of the manufacturer or distributor to serve, directly or indirectly, the market for its product in other States, it is not unreasonable to subject it to suit in one of those States if its allegedly defective merchandise has there been the source of injury to its owner or to others. The forum State does not exceed its powers under the Due Process Clause if it asserts personal jurisdiction over a corporation that delivers its products into the stream of commerce with the expectation that they will be purchased by consumers in the forum State. Cf. Gray v. American Radiator & Standard Sanitary Corp. * * *.

But there is no such or similar basis for Oklahoma jurisdiction over World–Wide or Seaway in this case. Seaway's sales are made in Massena, N.Y. World–Wide's market, although substantially larger, is limited to dealers in New York, New Jersey, and Connecticut. There is no evidence of record that any automobiles distributed by World–Wide are sold to retail customers outside this tristate area. It is foreseeable that the purchasers of automobiles sold by World–Wide and Seaway may take them to Oklahoma. But the mere "unilateral activity of those who claim some relationship with a nonresident defendant cannot satisfy the requirement of contact with the forum State." Hanson v. Denckla * * *.

In a variant on the previous argument, it is contended that jurisdiction can be supported by the fact that petitioners earn substantial revenue from goods used in Oklahoma. * * * While this inference seems less than compelling on the facts of the instant case, we need not question the court's factual findings in order to reject its reasoning.

This argument seems to make the point that the purchase of automobiles in New York, from which the petitioners earn substantial revenue, would not occur *but for* the fact that the automobiles are capable of use in distant States like Oklahoma. Respondents observe that the very purpose of an automobile is to travel, and that travel of automobiles sold by petitioners is facilitated by an extensive chain of Volkswagen service centers throughout the country, including some in Oklahoma. However, financial benefits accruing to the defendant from a collateral relation to the forum State will not support jurisdiction if they do not stem from a constitutionally cognizable contact with that State. * * * In our view, whatever marginal revenues petitioners may receive by virtue of the fact that their products are capable of use in Oklahoma is far too attenuated a contact to justify that State's exercise of *in personam* jurisdiction over them.

Because we find that petitioners have no "contacts, ties, or relations" with the State of Oklahoma, International Shoe Co. v. Washington, * * * the judgment of the Supreme Court of Oklahoma is

Reversed.

[The dissenting opinions of JUSTICE MARSHALL and JUSTICE BLACKMUN are omitted.]

MR. JUSTICE BRENNAN, dissenting.

* * *

I

The Court's opinions focus tightly on the existence of contacts between the forum and the defendant. In so doing, they accord too little weight to the strength of the forum State's interest in the case and fail to explore whether there would be any actual inconvenience to the defendant. The essential inquiry in locating the constitutional limits on state-court jurisdiction over absent defendants is whether the particular exercise of jurisdiction offends " 'traditional notions of fair play and substantial justice.' " * * * The clear focus in *International Shoe* was on fairness and reasonableness. * * * The Court specifically declined to establish a mechanical test based on the quantum of contacts between a State and the defendant * * *. The existence of contacts, so long as there were some, was merely one way of giving content to the determination of fairness and reasonableness.

Surely *International Shoe* contemplated that the significance of the contacts necessary to support jurisdiction would diminish if some other consideration helped establish that jurisdiction would be fair and reasonable. The interests of the State and other parties in proceeding with the case in a particular forum are such considerations. McGee v. International Life Ins. Co., * * * for instance, accorded great importance to a State's "manifest interest in providing effective means of redress" for its citizens. * * *

Another consideration is the actual burden a defendant must bear in defending the suit in the forum. * * * Because lesser burdens reduce the unfairness to the defendant, jurisdiction may be justified despite less significant contacts. The burden, of course, must be of constitutional dimension. Due process limits on jurisdiction do not protect a defendant from all inconvenience of travel * * *. Instead, the constitutionally significant "burden" to be analyzed relates to the mobility of the defendant's defense. For instance, if having to travel to a foreign forum would hamper the defense because witnesses or evidence or the defendant himself were immobile, or if there were a disproportionately large number of witnesses or amount of evidence that would have to be transported at the defendant's expense, or if being away from home for the duration of the trial would work some special hardship on the defendant, then the Constitution would require special consideration for the defendant's interests.

That considerations other than contacts between the forum and the defendant are relevant necessarily means that the Constitution does not require that trial be held in the State which has the "best contacts" with the defendant. * * * The defendant has no constitutional entitlement to the best forum or, for that matter, to any particular forum. Under even the most restrictive view of *International Shoe,* several States could have jurisdiction over a particular cause of action. We need only determine whether the forum States in these cases satisfy the constitutional minimum.

II

* * * I would find that the forum State has an interest in permitting the litigation to go forward, the litigation is connected to the forum, the defendant is linked to the forum, and the burden of defending is not unreasonable. Accordingly, I would hold that it is neither unfair nor unreasonable to require these defendants to defend in the forum State.

* * *

* * * [T]he interest of the forum State and its connection to the litigation is strong. The automobile accident underlying the litigation occurred in Oklahoma. The plaintiffs were hospitalized in Oklahoma when they brought suit. Essential witnesses and evidence were in Oklahoma. * * * The State has a legitimate interest in enforcing its laws designed to keep its highway system safe, and the trial can proceed at least as efficiently in Oklahoma as anywhere else.

The petitioners are not unconnected with the forum. Although both sell automobiles within limited sales territories, each sold the automobile which in fact was driven to Oklahoma where it was involved in an accident. It may be true, as the Court suggests, that each sincerely intended to limit its commercial impact to the limited territory, and that each intended to accept the benefits and protection of the laws only of those States within the territory.

But obviously these were unrealistic hopes that cannot be treated as an automatic constitutional shield.

An automobile simply is not a stationary item or one designed to be used in one place. An automobile is *intended* to be moved around. Someone in the business of selling large numbers of automobiles can hardly plead ignorance of their mobility or pretend that the automobiles stay put after they are sold. It is not merely that a dealer in automobiles foresees that they will move. * * * The dealer actually intends that the purchasers will use the automobiles to travel to distant States where the dealer does not directly "do business." The sale of an automobile does *purposefully* inject the vehicle into the stream of interstate commerce so that it can travel to distant States. * * *

The Court accepts that a State may exercise jurisdiction over a distributor which "serves" that State "indirectly" by "deliver[ing] its products into the stream of commerce with the expectation that they will be purchased by consumers in the forum State." * * * It is difficult to see why the Constitution should distinguish between a case involving goods which reach a distant State through a chain of distribution and a case involving goods which reach the same State because a consumer, using them as the dealer knew the customer would, took them there. In each case the seller purposefully injects the goods into the stream of commerce and those goods predictably are used in the forum State. The manufacturer in the case cited by the Court, *Gray v. American Radiator & Standard Sanitary Corp.* [p. 82, supra] * * *, had no more control over which States its goods would reach than did the petitioners in this case.

* * *

III

It may be that affirmance of the judgments in these cases would approach the outer limits of *International Shoe*'s jurisdictional principle. But that principle, with its almost exclusive focus on the rights of defendants, may be outdated. * * *

International Shoe inherited its defendant focus from Pennoyer v. Neff * * * and represented the last major step this Court has taken in the long process of liberalizing the doctrine of personal jurisdiction. Though its flexible approach represented a major advance, the structure of our society has changed in many significant ways since *International Shoe* was decided in 1945. * * * As the Court acknowledges, * * * both the nationalization of commerce and the ease of transportation and communication have accelerated in the generation since 1957. The model of society on which the *International Shoe* Court based its opinion is no longer accurate. Business people, no matter how local their businesses, cannot assume that goods remain in the business' locality. Customers and goods can be anywhere else in the country usually in a matter of hours and always in a matter of a very few days.

In answering the question whether or not it is fair and reasonable to allow a particular forum to hold a trial binding on a particular defendant, the interests of the forum State and other parties loom large in today's world and surely are entitled to as much weight as are the interests of the defendant. The "orderly administration of the laws" provides a firm basis for according some protection to the interests of plaintiffs and States as well as of defendants. Certainly, I cannot see how a defendant's right to due process is violated if the defendant suffers no inconvenience. * * *

The conclusion I draw is that constitutional concepts of fairness no longer require the extreme concern for defendants that was once necessary. Rather, * * * minimum contacts must exist "among the *parties,* the contested transaction, and the forum State."[15] The contacts between any two of these should not be determinative. * * *

In effect the Court is allowing defendants to assert the sovereign rights of their home States. The expressed fear is that otherwise all limits on personal jurisdiction would disappear. But the argument's premise is wrong. I would not abolish limits on jurisdiction or strip state boundaries of all significance * * *; I would still require the plaintiff to demonstrate sufficient contacts among the parties, the forum, and the litigation to make the forum a reasonable State in which to hold the trial.

I would also, however, strip the defendant of an unjustified veto power over certain very appropriate fora—a power the defendant justifiably enjoyed long ago when communication and travel over long distances were slow and unpredictable and when notions of state sovereignty were impractical and exaggerated. * * *

The plaintiffs * * * brought suit in a forum with which they had significant contacts and which had significant contacts with the litigation. I am not convinced that the defendants would suffer any "heavy and disproportionate burden" in defending the suits. Accordingly, I would hold that the Constitution should not shield the defendants from appearing and defending in the plaintiffs' chosen fora.

Notes and Questions

1. Neither Audi nor Volkswagen of America objected to jurisdiction. How would they have fared had they contested it? Is it likely that specific jurisdiction would exist with regard to them? General jurisdiction? See pp. 131–42, infra. Both?

Considering the deep pockets of Audi and Volkswagen, why were the plaintiffs so interested in gaining jurisdiction over Seaway and World–Wide? To answer the question, you must consider trial tactics as well as the rules of personal jurisdiction. Both Seaway and World–Wide were incorporated and had their places of business in New York. For diversity purposes, the Robinsons were New York citizens at the time the action was commenced. With Seaway and World–Wide as defendants, there would be incomplete diversity jurisdiction, and the Robinsons would not have to worry about removal to federal court. Is it possible that the fight really was about whether the case would be tried in state court or federal court in Oklahoma? Would it help you answer the question if you knew that, at the time, federal juries in Oklahoma were often finding for defendant or awarding smaller damages on claims like the Robinsons' than were their state counterparts? Professor Lowenfeld reports:

---

15. In some cases, the inquiry will resemble the inquiry commonly undertaken in determining which State's law to apply. That it is fair to apply a State's law to a nonresident defendant is clearly relevant in determining whether it is fair to subject the defendant to jurisdiction in that State. * * *

In the end, the forum shopping calculations of both sides proved accurate. Once the Supreme Court decided that World–Wide and Seaway could not be sued in Oklahoma, the principal defendants * * * removed the case to the U.S. Court for the Northern District of Oklahoma. Following discovery under the federal rules, the case was tried to a jury, which in January 1982 returned a verdict for defendants.

Lowenfeld, *Conflict of Laws* 565 (1986).

For more details of what happened to the Robinsons, see Adams, *Worldwide Volkswagen v. Woodson—The Rest of the Story,* 72 Neb.L.Rev. 1122 (1993).

2. In the course of its *World-Wide Volkswagen* opinion, the Court employs both notions of sovereignty (like those emphasized in *Hanson*) and of convenience (like those emphasized in *McGee*). Is there a tension between these two notions? Is the Court promulgating a two-part test with a "sovereignty branch" and a "convenience branch"? Is this a new test or a refinement of the "minimum contacts" test announced in *International Shoe*?

In INSURANCE CORP. OF IRELAND v. COMPAGNIE DES BAUXITES DE GUINEE, 456 U.S. 694, 102 S.Ct. 2099, 72 L.Ed.2d 492 (1982), Justice White, the author of *World-Wide Volkswagen,* wrote for eight Justices. He described the personal jurisdiction requirement imposed by the Due Process Clause as one that "recognizes and protects an individual liberty interest." His opinion further elaborated this thought in a footnote that expressly addressed his opinion in *World-Wide Volkswagen:*

It is true that we have stated that the requirement of personal jurisdiction, as applied to state courts, reflects an element of federalism and the character of state sovereignty vis-a-vis other states. [Justice White then quoted from *World-Wide Volkswagen*] * * *. The restriction on state sovereign power described in *World-Wide Volkswagen Corp.,* however, must be seen as ultimately a function of the individual liberty interest preserved by the Due Process Clause. That clause is the only source of the personal jurisdiction requirement and the clause itself makes no mention of federalism concerns. Furthermore, if the federalism concept operated as an independent restriction on the sovereign power of the court, it would not be possible to waive the personal jurisdiction requirement: Individual actions cannot change the powers of sovereignty, although the individual can subject himself to powers from which he may otherwise be protected.

Id. at 702 n.10, 102 S.Ct. at 2104–05 n.10, 72 L.Ed.2d at 501 n.10. Does this footnote transform the "sovereignty branch" of the *World-Wide Volkswagen* test? Do the Due Process Clause limitations on personal jurisdiction serve state sovereignty merely as a by-product of the protection of litigants' rights? Certainly the "minimum contacts" requirement assures that only those states sufficiently connected with the defendant may litigate the dispute. Is it possible to say that the Court's opinion in *World-Wide Volkswagen* demonstrates that protection of interstate federalism is a reason for including in the test for personal jurisdiction a requirement of pre-litigation contact with the forum, but that the Court's use of its test shows that the protection of federalism is not an independent component of the test? How could a defendant waive the requirement of minimum contacts (as he can) if the protection of federalism created an independent restriction on the power of a court? For thoughtful discussions of this issue, see Stein, *Styles of Argument and Interstate Federalism in the Law of Personal Jurisdiction,* 65 Texas

L.Rev. 689, 725 (1987), and Knudson, *Keeton, Calder, Helicopteros and Burger King—International Shoe's Most Recent Progeny,* 39 U.Miami L.Rev. 309 (1985).

3. How would *Volkswagen* have been decided if the Robinsons had been Oklahoma residents and had bought the ill-fated car while in New York on vacation? What if the driver of the other car sued World–Wide and Seaway for injuries resulting from the exploding gas tank? What if that driver never had been outside the state of Oklahoma?

4. Does *World-Wide Volkswagen* invalidate assertions of jurisdiction such as Gray v. American Radiator & Standard Sanitary Corp., p. 82, supra? In BO-DINE'S INC. v. SUNNY–O, INC., 494 F.Supp. 1279, 1283 (N.D.Ill.1980), the same long-arm statute that was interpreted in *Gray* was at issue. Bodine's sued Sunny–O for breach of warranty and fraud in connection with a delivery by Sunny–O of orange juice concentrate to Bodine's in Illinois. Personal jurisdiction was based upon the Illinois long-arm statute providing for jurisdiction over causes of action arising from the commission of a tortious act within the state. Sunny–O contested jurisdiction, arguing that the exercise of jurisdiction would be inappropriate under *World-Wide Volkswagen.* The District Court upheld jurisdiction:

> Rather than suggesting the invalidity of the exercise of personal jurisdiction under Section 17(1)(b) herein, the decision in *World-Wide Volkswagen* only supports further the Court's view that such jurisdiction is proper. Unlike *World-Wide Volkswagen,* this case does not involve the sale of a product by a foreign corporation to a foreign resident. Nor can the presence of defendant's product in Illinois be termed a "fortuitous circumstance." Rather, the sale of the orange juice concentrate to plaintiff arose from defendant's effort to serve, directly or indirectly, the market for its products in various states, including Illinois.

Does the passage quoted completely dispose of the due process issue? What of *World-Wide Volkswagen's* "convenience branch"?

5. In KEETON v. HUSTLER MAGAZINE, INC., 465 U.S. 770, 104 S.Ct. 1473, 79 L.Ed.2d 790 (1984), Kathy Keeton, a resident of New York, brought a libel suit against Hustler Magazine, an Ohio corporation, in federal court in New Hampshire. Keeton chose the New Hampshire court because New Hampshire was the only state where the action was not time-barred when it was filed. She argued that jurisdiction existed under New Hampshire's long-arm statute because Hustler sold 10,000 to 15,000 magazines a month in the state. Keeton herself had only one connection to New Hampshire: a magazine that she helped to produce was circulated there.

The District Court dismissed Keeton's suit for lack of jurisdiction, and the First Circuit affirmed, holding that Keeton's lack of contacts with New Hampshire rendered the state's interest in redressing the libel to the plaintiff too attenuated to support jurisdiction over a suit necessarily involving nationwide damages. In the Circuit Court's words, "the New Hampshire tail is too small to wag so large an out-of-state dog."

The Supreme Court unanimously reversed, saying:

> [R]egular monthly sales of thousands of magazines cannot by any stretch of the imagination be characterized as random, isolated, or fortuitous. It is, therefore, unquestionable that New Hampshire jurisdiction over a complaint based on those contacts could ordinarily satisfy the requirement of the Due Process Clause that a State's assertion of personal jurisdiction over a nonresident defendant be predicated on "minimum contacts" between the defendant

and the State. And, as the Court of Appeals acknowledged, New Hampshire
has adopted a "long-arm" statute authorizing service of process on nonresident corporations whenever permitted by the Due Process Clause. Thus, all
the requisites for personal jurisdiction over Hustler Magazine, Inc., in New
Hampshire are present.

Id. at 774–75, 104 S.Ct. at 1478, 79 L.Ed.2d at 797. Is the key to the Court's
decision in *Keeton* that the defendants intentionally acted in the forum? Does the
Keeton Court apply both the "sovereignty branch" and the "convenience branch"
of *World-Wide Volkswagen*?

What of Hustler's argument that the plaintiff's contacts with New Hampshire
were minimal? Is that argument relevant to the sovereignty branch? Or the
convenience branch? In discussing the argument, the Supreme Court said:

> * * * [I]mplicit in the Court of Appeals' analysis of New Hampshire's
> interest is an emphasis on the extremely limited contacts of the *plaintiff* with
> New Hampshire. But we have not to date required a plaintiff to have
> "minimum contacts" with the forum State before permitting that State to
> assert personal jurisdiction over a nonresident defendant. On the contrary, we
> have upheld the assertion of jurisdiction where such contacts were entirely
> lacking. * * *

Id. at 779, 104 S.Ct. at 1480–81, 79 L.Ed.2d at 800. The Court went on to say,
however, that "[t]he plaintiff's residence is not, of course, completely irrelevant to
the jurisdiction inquiry." The Court noted, for example, that a plaintiff's residence
in the forum, because of the defendant's relationship with the plaintiff, may
enhance the defendant's contacts with the forum.

What of the argument that it was unfair to allow suit to be brought in the
only state where it was not time-barred? Is that relevant to the jurisdictional
inquiry? The Court did not believe that it was:

> * * * [A]ny potential unfairness in applying New Hampshire's statute of
> limitations to all aspects of this nationwide suit has nothing to do with the
> jurisdiction of the Court to adjudicate the claims. "The issue is personal
> jurisdiction, not choice of law." Hanson v. Denckla * * *. The question of the
> applicability of New Hampshire's statute of limitations to claims for out-of-
> state damages presents itself in the course of litigation only after jurisdiction
> over respondent is established, and we do not think that such choice of law
> concerns should complicate or distort the jurisdictional inquiry.

Id. at 778, 104 S.Ct. at 1480, 79 L.Ed.2d at 800.

6. A defendant may have contacts with the forum state that are related or
unrelated to the controversy that has come to court. In applying *World-Wide
Volkswagen*, it is important to keep this distinction between related and unrelated
contacts in mind. Related contacts are weighed more heavily in favor of jurisdiction than unrelated ones. Unrelated contacts—if continuous and substantial—may
support general jurisdiction, but even a single contact may support jurisdiction
when the cause of action arises out of the contact.

Suppose that World–Wide Volkswagen had maintained an agent in Oklahoma
and had advertised there. These contacts with Oklahoma would have been
unrelated to the Robinsons' accident in that state, since they had bought their car
in New York. Suppose also that World–Wide's contacts with the state were
insufficient to support general jurisdiction. What, if any, weight should be given to
World–Wide's unrelated contacts with Oklahoma in assessing, under the Due

Process Clause, the propriety of Oklahoma's attempt to assert jurisdiction over World–Wide in *Robinson v. World–Wide Volkswagen*? See the discussion of general jurisdiction, pp. 131–42, infra.

———

KULKO v. SUPERIOR COURT, 436 U.S. 84, 98 S.Ct. 1690, 56 L.Ed.2d 132 (1978), was a suit for modification of a child support agreement by a California citizen against her ex-husband, a New Yorker. The couple's two children lived with their father in New York under the original separation agreement. However, when the daughter told defendant that she wanted to live with her mother, he assented and bought her a one-way plane ticket to California. The other child also joined his mother in California, after receiving a one-way ticket from her, without defendant's knowledge.

The California Supreme Court upheld jurisdiction over the defendant husband under the California long-arm statute, which authorized the exercise of jurisdiction "on any basis not inconsistent with the Constitution." The court concluded that it was "fair and reasonable" for the New York defendant to be subject to personal jurisdiction in California because by purchasing his daughter's airline ticket, he had committed a "purposeful act" outside the state that caused an effect within the state. The United States Supreme Court reversed:

> * * * We cannot accept the proposition that appellant's acquiescence in Ilsa's desire to live with her mother conferred jurisdiction over appellant in the California courts in this action. A father who agrees, in the interests of family harmony and his children's preferences, to allow them to spend more time in California than was required under a separation agreement can hardly be said to have "purposefully availed himself" of the "benefits and protections" of California's laws. * * *

> Nor can we agree with the assertion of the court below that the exercise of *in personam* jurisdiction here was warranted by the financial benefit appellant derived from his daughter's presence in California for nine months of the year. * * * [T]his circumstance, even if true, does not support California's assertion of jurisdiction here. Any diminution in appellant's household costs resulted, not from the child's presence in California, but rather from her absence from appellant's home.

Id. at 94–95, 98 S.Ct. at 1698, 56 L.Ed.2d at 142–43.

The Court also noted that the California court's reliance on the "effects" test was misplaced because that approach applies only to wrongful activity without the state causing injury within it or to commercial activity affecting state residents, when that application would not be "unreasonable." Merely causing an effect within the forum state without purposeful availment will not support jurisdiction.

> The circumstances in this case clearly render "unreasonable" California's assertion of personal jurisdiction. There is no claim that appellant has visited physical injury on either property or persons within the State of California. The cause of action herein asserted arises, not from the defendant's commercial transactions in interstate commerce, but

rather from his personal, domestic relations. * * * Furthermore, the controversy between the parties arises from a separation that occurred in the State of New York * * *.

Finally, basic considerations of fairness point decisively in favor of appellant's State of domicile as the proper forum for adjudication of this case, whatever the merits of appellee's underlying claim. It is appellant who has remained in the State of the marital domicile, whereas it is appellee who has moved across the continent. * * * [Exercising jurisdiction] would impose an unreasonable burden on family relations, and one wholly unjustified by the "quality and nature" of appellant's activities in or relating to the State of California. * * *

Id. at 96–98, 98 S.Ct. at 1699–1700, 56 L.Ed.2d at 144–45.

Notes and Questions

1. Why is the Court emphasizing "the" proper forum as opposed to "a" proper forum. Do not the cases from *International Shoe* to *World-Wide Volkswagen* admit that jurisdiction can be proper in more than one forum? Does the switch in emphasis have to do with the type of action involved?

2. Before 1984, some cases suggested that the First Amendment imposed a significant limitation upon the exercise of jurisdiction over defendants whose rights of expression might thereby be compromised. See, e.g., New York Times Co. v. Connor, 365 F.2d 567 (5th Cir.1966). In 1984, however, the Supreme Court rejected this line of cases. In CALDER v. JONES, 465 U.S. 783, 790–91, 104 S.Ct. 1482, 1487–88, 79 L.Ed.2d 804, 813 (1984), a professional entertainer who lived and worked in California brought suit in California Superior Court, claiming that she had been libeled in an article published in the National Enquirer, a national magazine having its largest circulation in California. The plaintiff sued the writer and editor of the article, both residents of Florida, as well as the magazine. The writer and the editor moved to quash service of process for lack of personal jurisdiction, and the Superior Court granted the motion on the ground that First Amendment concerns weighed against an assertion of jurisdiction otherwise proper under the Due Process Clause. Ultimately, the United States Supreme Court disagreed, saying: "We also reject the suggestion that First Amendment concerns enter into jurisdictional analysis. The infusion of such concerns would needlessly complicate an already imprecise inquiry." Given that the writer and editor had acted intentionally to produce an article for dissemination in California, the Court had no trouble finding that they could foresee being haled into court there. See also Keeton v. Hustler Magazine, Inc., 465 U.S. 770, 780 n. 12, 104 S.Ct. 1473, 1481 n. 12, 79 L.Ed.2d 790, 801 n. 12 (1984), Note 5, p. 107, supra ("[W]e reject categorically the suggestion that invisible radiations from the First Amendment may defeat jurisdiction otherwise proper under the Due Process Clause."). For a more in-depth discussion of *Calder, Keeton,* and the relationship between the First Amendment and personal jurisdiction, see Matheson, *Procedure in Public Person Defamation Cases: The Impact of the First Amendment,* 66 Texas L.Rev. 215, 257–71 (1987).

3. In addition to the limitations on jurisdiction derived from the Due Process Clause, other limitations derived from other parts of the Constitution may exist. For example, in DAVIS v. FARMERS' CO–OP. EQUITY CO., 262 U.S. 312, 43 S.Ct. 556, 67 L.Ed. 996 (1923), the Supreme Court ruled that a Minnesota court

was barred by the Commerce Clause from asserting jurisdiction over a Kansas railroad in a suit brought by a Kansas corporation for damages resulting from the loss of grain shipped from one point in Kansas to another. Since the potential burden on interstate commerce is a factor that can be considered under the "minimum contacts" test, however, Commerce Clause objections to jurisdiction are rare today. But see Bendix Autolite Corp. v. Midwesco Enterprises, Inc., 486 U.S. 888, 108 S.Ct. 2218, 100 L.Ed.2d 896 (1988) (Ohio law permanently tolling the state's statute of limitations as to foreign corporations that do not consent to the general jurisdiction of the Ohio courts violates the Commerce Clause).

BURGER KING CORP. v. RUDZEWICZ

Supreme Court of the United States, 1985.
471 U.S. 462, 105 S.Ct. 2174, 85 L.Ed.2d 528.

[Burger King is a Florida corporation whose principal offices are in Miami. Franchisees are licensed to use its trademarks and service marks in leased standardized restaurant facilities for a period of twenty years. The governing contracts provide that the franchise relationship is established in Miami and governed by Florida law, and call for payment of all required monthly fees and forwarding of all relevant notices to the Miami headquarters. The Miami headquarters sets policy and works directly with the franchisees in attempting to resolve major problems. Day-to-day monitoring of franchisees, however, is conducted through district offices that in turn report to the Miami headquarters. John Rudzewicz is a Michigan resident who, along with another Michigan resident (Brian MacShara), entered into a twenty-year franchise contract with Burger King to operate a restaurant in Michigan. Subsequently, when the restaurant's patronage declined, the franchisees fell behind in their monthly payments. Burger King then brought a diversity action in Federal District Court in Florida, alleging that the franchisees had breached their franchise obligations and requesting damages and injunctive relief. The franchisees claimed that, because they were Michigan residents and because Burger King's claim did not "arise" within Florida, the District Court lacked personal jurisdiction over them. But the court held that the franchisees were subject to personal jurisdiction pursuant to Florida's long-arm statute, which extends jurisdiction to any person, whether or not a citizen or resident of the State, who breaches a contract in the State by failing to perform acts that the contract requires to be performed there. Thereafter, the court entered judgment against the franchisees on the merits. The Court of Appeals reversed, holding that "[j]urisdiction under these circumstances would offend the fundamental fairness which is the touchstone of due process," but the Supreme Court disagreed.]

Appeal from the United States Court of Appeals for the Eleventh Circuit.

JUSTICE BRENNAN delivered the opinion of the Court.

[After a lengthy presentation of the facts, Justice Brennan began Part II of his opinion by rehearsing the basic jurisdictional rules. In that context, he turned to the requirement that the defendant "purposefully direct" his activity toward the forum state.]

* * *

We have noted several reasons why a forum legitimately may exercise personal jurisdiction over a nonresident who "purposefully directs" his activities toward forum residents. A State generally has a "manifest interest" in providing its residents with a convenient forum for redressing injuries inflicted by out-of-state actors. * * * Moreover, where individuals "purposefully derive benefit" from their interstate activities, * * * it may well be unfair to allow them to escape having to account in other States for consequences that arise proximately from such activities; the Due Process Clause may not readily be wielded as a territorial shield to avoid interstate obligations that have been voluntarily assumed. And because "modern transportation and communications have made it much less burdensome for a party sued to defend himself in a State where he engages in economic activity," it usually will not be unfair to subject him to the burdens of litigating in another forum for disputes relating to such activity. McGee v. International Life Insurance Co. * * *.

Notwithstanding these considerations, the constitutional touchstone remains whether the defendant purposefully established "minimum contacts" in the forum State. * * * Although it has been argued that foreseeability of causing *injury* in another State should be sufficient to establish such contacts there when policy considerations so require, the Court has consistently held that this kind of foreseeability is not a "sufficient benchmark" for exercising personal jurisdiction. * * * Instead, "the foreseeability that is critical to due process analysis * * * is that the defendant's conduct and connection with the forum State are such that he should reasonably anticipate being haled into court there." * * *

This "purposeful availment" requirement ensures that a defendant will not be haled into a jurisdiction solely as a result of "random," "fortuitous," or "attenuated" contacts, * * * or of the "unilateral activity of another party or a third person" * * *. Jurisdiction is proper, however, where the contacts proximately result from actions by the defendant *himself* that create a "substantial connection" with the forum State. * * * Thus where the defendant "deliberately" has engaged in significant activities within a State, * * * or has created "continuing obligations" between himself and residents of the forum, * * * he manifestly has availed himself of the privilege of conducting business there, and because his activities are shielded by "the benefits and protections" of the forum's laws it is presumptively not unreasonable to require him to submit to the burdens of litigation in that forum as well. * * *

Once it has been decided that a defendant purposefully established minimum contacts within the forum State, these contacts may be considered in light of other factors to determine whether the assertion of personal jurisdiction would comport with "fair play and substantial justice." * * * Thus courts in "appropriate case[s]" may evaluate "the burden on the defendant," "the forum State's interest in adjudicating the dispute," "the plaintiff's interest in obtaining convenient and effective relief," "the interstate judicial system's interest in obtaining the most efficient resolution of controversies," and the "shared interest of the several States in furthering fundamental substantive social policies." * * * These considerations sometimes serve to establish the reasonableness of jurisdiction upon a lesser showing of minimum contacts than would otherwise be required. * * * On the other hand, where a defendant who purposefully has directed his activities at forum residents seeks to defeat jurisdiction, he must present a compelling case that the presence of some other considerations would render jurisdiction unreasonable. Most such considerations usually may be accommodated through means short of finding jurisdiction unconstitutional. For example, the potential clash of the forum's law with the "fundamental substantive social policies" of another State may be accommodated through application of the forum's choice-of-law rules. Similarly, a defendant claiming substantial inconvenience may seek a change of venue. Nevertheless, minimum requirements inherent in the concept of "fair play and substantial justice" may defeat the reasonableness of jurisdiction even if the defendant has purposefully engaged in forum activities. * * * As we previously have noted, jurisdictional rules may not be employed in such a way as to make litigation "so gravely difficult and inconvenient" that a party unfairly is at a "severe disadvantage" in comparison to his opponent. * * *

B

(1)

Applying these principles to the case at hand, we believe there is substantial record evidence supporting the District Court's conclusion that the assertion of personal jurisdiction over Rudzewicz in Florida for the alleged breach of his franchise agreement did not offend due process. At the outset, we note a continued division among lower courts respecting whether and to what extent a contract can constitute a "contact" for purposes of due process analysis. If the question is whether an individual's contract with an out-of-state party *alone* can automatically establish sufficient minimum contacts in the other party's home forum, we believe the answer clearly is that it cannot. The Court long ago rejected the notion that personal jurisdiction might turn on "mechanical" tests, or on "conceptualistic * * * theories of the place of contracting or of performance" * * *. Instead, we have emphasized the need for a "highly realistic" approach that recognizes that a "contract" is "ordinarily but an intermediate step serving to tie up prior business negotiations with future consequences which themselves are the real object of the business transaction." * * * It is these factors—prior negotiations and contemplated future consequences, along with the terms of the contract and the parties' actual course of dealing—that must be evaluated in determining whether the defendant purposefully established minimum contacts within the forum.

In this case, no physical ties to Florida can be attributed to Rudzewicz other than MacShara's brief training course in Miami.[22] Rudzewicz did not maintain offices in Florida and, for all that appears from the record, has never even visited there. Yet this franchise dispute grew directly out of "a contract which had a *substantial* connection with that State." McGee v. International Life Insurance Co. * * *. Eschewing the option of operating an independent

---

22. The Eleventh Circuit held that MacShara's presence in Florida was irrelevant to the question of Rudzewicz's minimum contacts with that forum, reasoning that "Rudzewicz and MacShara never formed a partnership" and "signed the agreements in their individual capacities." * * * The two did jointly form a corporation through which they were seeking to conduct the franchise, however. * * * They were required to decide which one of them would travel to Florida to satisfy the training requirements so that they could commence business, and Rudzewicz participated in the decision that MacShara would go there. We have previously noted that when commercial activities are "carried on in behalf of" an out-of-state party those activities may sometimes be ascribed to the party, * * * at least where he is a "primary participan[t]" in the enterprise and has acted purposefully in directing those activities. * * * Because MacShara's matriculation at Burger King University is not pivotal to the disposition of this case, we need not resolve the permissible bounds of such attribution.

local enterprise, Rudzewicz deliberately "reach[ed] out beyond" Michigan and negotiated with a Florida corporation for the purchase of a long-term franchise and the manifold benefits that would derive from affiliation with a nationwide organization. * * * Upon approval, he entered into a carefully structured 20–year relationship that envisioned continuing and wide-reaching contacts with Burger King in Florida. In light of Rudzewicz's voluntary acceptance of the long-term and exacting regulation of his business from Burger King's Miami headquarters, the "quality and nature" of his relationship to the company in Florida can in no sense be viewed as "random," "fortuitous," or "attenuated." * * * Rudzewicz's refusal to make the contractually required payments in Miami, and his continued use of Burger King's trademarks and confidential business information after his termination, caused foreseeable injuries to the corporation in Florida. For these reasons it was, at the very least, presumptively reasonable for Rudzewicz to be called to account there for such injuries.

The Court of Appeals concluded, however, that in light of the supervision emanating from Burger King's district office in Birmingham [Michigan], Rudzewicz reasonably believed that "the Michigan office was for all intents and purposes the embodiment of Burger King" and that he therefore had no "reason to anticipate a Burger King suit outside of Michigan." * * * This reasoning overlooks substantial record evidence indicating that Rudzewicz most certainly knew that he was affiliating himself with an enterprise based primarily in Florida. The contract documents themselves emphasize that Burger King's operations are conducted and supervised from the Miami headquarters, that all relevant notices and payments must be sent there, and that the agreements were made in and enforced from Miami. * * * Moreover, the parties' actual course of dealing repeatedly confirmed that decisionmaking authority was vested in the Miami headquarters and that the district office served largely as an intermediate link between the headquarters and the franchisees. When problems arose over building design, site development fees, rent computation, and the defaulted payments, Rudzewicz and MacShara learned that the Michigan office was powerless to resolve their disputes and could only channel their communications to Miami. Throughout these disputes, the Miami headquarters and the Michigan franchisees carried on a continuous course of direct communications by mail and by telephone, and it was the Miami headquarters that made the key negotiating decisions out of which the instant litigation arose.

Moreover, we believe the Court of Appeals gave insufficient weight to provisions in the various franchise documents providing that all disputes would be governed by Florida law. The franchise agreement, for example, stated:

> This Agreement shall become valid when executed and accepted by BKC at Miami, Florida; it shall be deemed made and entered into in the State of Florida and shall be governed and construed under and in accordance with the laws of the State of Florida. The choice of law designation does not require that all suits concerning this Agreement be filed in Florida.

* * * The Court of Appeals reasoned that choice-of-law provisions are irrelevant to the question of personal jurisdiction, relying on Hanson v. Denckla for the proposition that "the center of gravity for choice-of-law purposes does not

necessarily confer the sovereign prerogative to assert jurisdiction." * * * This reasoning misperceives the import of the quoted proposition. The Court in *Hanson* and subsequent cases has emphasized that choice-of-law *analysis*—which focuses on all elements of a transaction, and not simply on the defendant's conduct—is distinct from minimum-contacts jurisdictional analysis—which focuses at the threshold solely on the defendant's purposeful connection to the forum. Nothing in our cases, however, suggests that a choice-of-law *provision* should be ignored in considering whether a defendant has "purposefully invoked the benefits and protections of a State's laws" for jurisdictional purposes. Although such a provision standing alone would be insufficient to confer jurisdiction, we believe that, when combined with the 20–year interdependent relationship Rudzewicz established with Burger King's Miami headquarters, it reinforced his deliberate affiliation with the forum State and the reasonable foreseeability of possible litigation there. * * * Rudzewicz "purposefully availed himself of the benefits and protections of Florida's laws" by entering into contracts expressly providing that those laws would govern franchise disputes. * * *

(2)

Nor has Rudzewicz pointed to other factors that can be said persuasively to outweigh the considerations discussed above and to establish the *unconstitutionality* of Florida's assertion of jurisdiction. We cannot conclude that Florida had no "legitimate interest in holding [Rudzewicz] answerable on a claim related to" the contacts he had established in that State. [See] McGee v. International Life Insurance Co. * * * (noting that State frequently will have a "manifest interest in providing effective means of redress for its residents").[25] Moreover, although Rudzewicz has argued at some length that Michigan's Franchise Investment Law * * * governs many aspects of this franchise relationship, he has not demonstrated how Michigan's acknowledged interest might possibly render jurisdiction in Florida *unconstitutional*.[26] Finally, the Court of Appeals' assertion that the Florida litigation "severely impaired [Rudzewicz's] ability to call Michigan witnesses who might be essential to his defense and counterclaim" * * * is wholly without support in the record. And even to the extent that it is inconvenient for a party who has minimum contacts with a forum to litigate there, such considerations most frequently can be accommodated through a change of venue. * * * Although the Court has suggested that inconvenience may at some point become so substantial as to achieve *constitutional* magnitude, McGee v. International Life Insurance Co., * * * this is not such a case.

---

25. Complaining that "when Burger King is the plaintiff, you won't 'have it your way' because it sues all franchisees in Miami," * * * Rudzewicz contends that Florida's interest in providing a convenient forum is negligible given the company's size and ability to conduct litigation anywhere in the country. We disagree. Absent compelling considerations, cf. McGee v. International Life Insurance Co., * * * a defendant who has purposefully derived commercial benefit from his affiliations in a forum may not defeat jurisdiction there simply because of his adversary's greater net wealth.

26. Rudzewicz has failed to show how the District Court's exercise of jurisdiction in this case might have been at all inconsistent with Michigan's interests. * * * In any event, minimum-contacts analysis presupposes that two or more States may be interested in the outcome of a dispute, and the process of resolving potentially conflicting "fundamental substantive social policies" * * * can usually be accommodated through choice-of-law rules rather than through outright preclusion of jurisdiction in one forum. * * *

The Court of Appeals also concluded, however, that the parties' dealings involved "a characteristic disparity of bargaining power" and "elements of surprise," and that Rudzewicz "lacked fair notice" of the potential for litigation in Florida because the contractual provisions suggesting to the contrary were merely "boilerplate declarations in a lengthy printed contract." * * * Rudzewicz presented many of these arguments to the District Court, contending that Burger King was guilty of misrepresentation, fraud, and duress; that it gave insufficient notice in its dealings with him; and that the contract was one of adhesion. * * * After a 3–day bench trial, the District Court found that Burger King had made no misrepresentations, that Rudzewicz and MacShara "were and are experienced and sophisticated businessmen," and that "at no time" did they "ac[t] under economic duress or disadvantage imposed by" Burger King. * * * Federal Rule of Civil Procedure 52(a) requires that "[f]indings of fact shall not be set aside unless clearly erroneous," and neither Rudzewicz nor the Court of Appeals have pointed to record evidence that would support a "definite and firm conviction" that the District Court's findings are mistaken. * * *

III

Notwithstanding these considerations, the Court of Appeals apparently believed that it was necessary to reject jurisdiction in this case as a prophylactic measure, reasoning that an affirmance of the District Court's judgment would result in the exercise of jurisdiction over "out-of-state consumers to collect payments due on modest personal purchases" and would "sow the seeds of default judgments against franchisees owing smaller debts." * * * We share the Court of Appeals' broader concerns and therefore reject any talismanic jurisdictional formulas; "the facts of each case must [always] be weighed" in determining whether personal jurisdiction would comport with "fair play and substantial justice." * * * The "quality and nature" of an interstate transaction may sometimes be so "random," "fortuitous," or "attenuated" that it cannot fairly be said that the potential defendant "should reasonably anticipate being haled into court" in another jurisdiction. * * * We also have emphasized that jurisdiction may not be grounded on a contract whose terms have been obtained through "fraud, undue influence, or overweening bargaining power" and whose application would render litigation "so gravely difficult and inconvenient that [a party] will for all practical purposes be deprived of his day in court." * * * Just as the Due Process Clause allows flexibility in ensuring that commercial actors are not effectively "judgment proof" for the consequences of obligations they voluntarily assume in other States, McGee v. International Life Insurance Co., * * * so too does it prevent rules that would unfairly enable them to obtain default judgments against unwitting customers. * * *

For the reasons set forth above, however, these dangers are not present in the instant case. Because Rudzewicz established a substantial and continuing relationship with Burger King's Miami headquarters, received fair notice from the contract documents and the course of dealing that he might be subject to suit in Florida, and has failed to demonstrate how jurisdiction in that forum would otherwise be fundamentally unfair, we conclude that the District Court's exercise of jurisdiction * * * did not offend due process. The judgment of the Court of Appeals is accordingly reversed, and the case is remanded for further proceedings consistent with this opinion.

JUSTICE POWELL took no part in the consideration or decision of this case.

JUSTICE STEVENS, with whom JUSTICE WHITE joins, dissenting.

In my opinion there is a significant element of unfairness in requiring a franchisee to defend a case of this kind in the forum chosen by the franchisor. It is undisputed that respondent maintained no place of business in Florida, that he had no employees in that State, and that he was not licensed to do business there. Respondent did not prepare his french fries, shakes, and hamburgers in Michigan, and then deliver them into the stream of commerce "with the expectation that they [would] be purchased by consumers in" Florida. * * * To the contrary, respondent did business only in Michigan, his business, property, and payroll taxes were payable in that State, and he sold all of his products there.

Throughout the business relationship, respondent's principal contacts with petitioner were with its Michigan office. Notwithstanding its disclaimer, * * * the Court seems ultimately to rely on nothing more than standard boilerplate language contained in various documents * * * to establish that respondent " 'purposefully availed himself of the benefits and protections of Florida's laws.' " * * * Such superficial analysis creates a potential for unfairness not only in negotiations between franchisors and their franchisees but, more significantly, in the resolution of the disputes that inevitably arise from time to time in such relationships.

Judge Vance's opinion for the Court of Appeals for the Eleventh Circuit adequately explains why I would affirm the judgment of that court. I particularly find the following more persuasive than what this Court has written today:

> Nothing in the course of negotiations gave Rudzewicz reason to anticipate a Burger King suit outside of Michigan. The only face-to-face or even oral contact Rudzewicz had with Burger King throughout months of protracted negotiations was with representatives of the Michigan office. Burger King had the Michigan office interview Rudzewicz and MacShara, appraise their application, discuss price terms, recommend the site which the defendants finally agreed to, and attend the final closing ceremony. There is no evidence that Rudzewicz ever negotiated with anyone in Miami or even sent mail there during negotiations. He maintained no staff in the state of Florida, and as far as the record reveals, he has never even visited the state.

> The contracts contemplated the startup of a local Michigan restaurant whose profits would derive solely from food sales made to customers in Drayton Plains. The sale, which involved the use of an intangible trademark in Michigan and occupancy of a Burger King facility there, required no performance in the state of Florida. Under the contract, the local Michigan district office was responsible for providing all of the services due Rudzewicz, including advertising and management consultation. Supervision, moreover, emanated from that office alone. To Rudzewicz, the Michigan office was for all intents and purposes the embodiment of Burger King. He had reason to believe that his working relationship

with Burger King began and ended in Michigan, not at the distant and anonymous Florida headquarters. * * *

Given that the office in Rudzewicz' home state conducted all of the negotiations and wholly supervised the contract, we believe that he had reason to assume that the state of the supervisory office would be the same state in which Burger King would file suit. Rudzewicz lacked fair notice that the distant corporate headquarters which insulated itself from direct dealings with him would later seek to assert jurisdiction over him in the courts of its own home state. * * *

Just as Rudzewicz lacked notice of the possibility of suit in Florida, he was financially unprepared to meet its added costs. The franchise relationship in particular is fraught with potential for financial surprise. The device of the franchise gives local retailers the access to national trademark recognition which enables them to compete with better-financed, more efficient chain stores. This national affiliation, however, does not alter the fact that the typical franchise store is a local concern serving at best a neighborhood or community. Neither the revenues of a local business nor the geographical range of its market prepares the average franchise owner for the cost of distant litigation. * * *

The particular distribution of bargaining power in the franchise relationship further impairs the franchisee's financial preparedness. In a franchise contract, "the franchisor normally occupies [the] dominant role". * * *

We discern a characteristic disparity of bargaining power in the facts of this case. There is no indication that Rudzewicz had any latitude to negotiate a reduced rent or franchise fee in exchange for the added risk of suit in Florida. He signed a standard form contract whose terms were non-negotiable and which appeared in some respects to vary from the more favorable terms agreed to in earlier discussions. In fact, the final contract required a minimum monthly rent computed on a base far in excess of that discussed in oral negotiations. Burger King resisted price concessions, only to sue Rudzewicz far from home. In doing so, it severely impaired his ability to call Michigan witnesses who might be essential to his defense and counterclaim.

In sum, we hold that the circumstances of the Drayton Plains franchise and the negotiations which led to it left Rudzewicz bereft of reasonable notice and financially unprepared for the prospect of franchise litigation in Florida. Jurisdiction under these circumstances would offend the fundamental fairness which is the touchstone of due process. * * *

Accordingly, I respectfully dissent.

Notes and Questions

1. Is the Supreme Court's decision in *Burger King* consistent with its decision in *World-Wide Volkswagen?* In what way were Rudzewicz's contacts with Florida quantitatively or qualitatively different from Seaway's contacts with Oklahoma? Which measuring rod should be more important?

2. The First Circuit has described the Supreme Court's decision in *Burger King* as mandating a "contract-plus" analysis:

> [A] court is to look at all of the communications and transactions between the parties, before, during and after the consummation of the contract, to determine the degree and type of contacts the defendant has with the forum, apart from the contract alone.

Ganis Corp. of California v. Jackson, 822 F.2d 194, 197–98 (1st Cir.1987). What purpose is served by this "plus" analysis? Is it constitutionally compelled? Does this type of analysis allow defendants to structure their business dealings so as to avoid personal jurisdiction in certain states? Should a contract standing alone ever be enough to subject a defendant to jurisdiction? Has *McGee* been overruled by *Burger King?*

3. How important to the decision in *Burger King* was the inclusion of the choice-of-law provision in the franchise agreement? Is that type of provision appropriately considered a "contact" with the chosen forum? Does the relative bargaining position of the parties affect your answer to this question?

4. In *Burger King,* Justice Brennan mentioned MacShara's attendance at Burger King University in Florida as a possible contact between Rudzewicz and the forum, but found other contacts sufficient to sustain jurisdiction so that he "need not resolve the permissible bounds of such attribution." Under what circumstances should the contacts of one individual or entity be considered the contacts of another legally related individual or entity? Should the contacts of a subsidiary corporation be attributed to its parent? Should the contacts of an agent be attributed to her principal? Consider the following case.

In HASENFUS v. CORPORATE AIR SERVS., 700 F.Supp. 58 (D.D.C.1988), the plaintiffs, Eugene and Sally Hasenfus, brought suit against Corporate Air Services, Southern Air Transport, Richard Secord, and Albert Hakim for breach of a written employment contract connected with the Iran–Contra affair. None of the defendants were residents of the District of Columbia and none of them transacted any business there. All of the conversations and activities related to the employment contract occurred in Florida, Central America, and (perhaps) in Wisconsin, where plaintiffs resided. Plaintiffs failed to allege that the employment contract was performed or breached in the District of Columbia or that any injuries were suffered there. Instead, the plaintiffs attempted to assert personal jurisdiction over the defendants based upon their affiliation with "the Enterprise"—the Contra resupply operation directed by Lieutenant Colonel Oliver North from its "nerve center" in Washington, D.C. However, the court found that the plaintiffs' allegations of a conspiracy were unsubstantiated and granted defendants' motion to dismiss for lack of personal jurisdiction. The court stated: "Bald speculations that defendants are alleged co-conspirators do not constitute the threshold showing necessary to carry the burden of establishing personal jurisdiction." Id. at 62. Would it have been proper for the court to assert jurisdiction over these defendants if plaintiffs had presented evidence sufficient to demonstrate that a conspiracy existed? For a thoughtful analysis of the circumstances under which the contacts of one individual or entity should be considered the contacts of another legally related individual or entity, see Brilmayer & Paisley, *Personal Jurisdiction and Substantive Legal Relations: Corporations, Conspiracies and Agency,* 74 Calif.L.Rev. 1 (1986).

5. Some courts have concluded that a single sale contract may be sufficient to support long-arm jurisdiction (usually under a "transaction of business" provision) over a nonresident seller. For example, in ALCHEMIE INTERNATIONAL, INC. v. METAL WORLD, INC., 523 F.Supp. 1039, 1050 (D.N.J.1981), the court upheld jurisdiction over the defendant, Metal World, a non-resident

seller, even though Metal World maintained no office in New Jersey and had sent no personnel into the state; it was enough that Metal World, by numerous mail and telephone contacts with Alchemie, a New Jersey corporation, had solicited, executed, and allegedly breached a substantial commercial contract. The goods never entered New Jersey; and there was no evidence indicating the parties anticipated that the goods were to be taken into New Jersey. Nor was there any evidence of other contacts with the forum, unrelated to the contract at issue. Nonetheless, the district judge ruled that the assertion of jurisdiction was consistent with due process. He stated:

> I see little to distinguish a corporation's using the telephone and mail to solicit or negotiate a contract the size of that at issue here from that same corporation sending an agent into the state in pursuit of the identical contract from the identical buyer. * * * Indeed, a refusal to acknowledge the fashion in which modern business is conducted and the increasingly dominant role played in that conduct by mail and telephone communications is as much a return to the shibboleths of Pennoyer v. Neff, * * * long abandoned by the Court, * * * and the "magical and medieval concepts of presence and power" that typified that era as would resurrection of the notion that a defendant must be present within the territorial jurisdiction of a court before its judgment will bind him. I therefore count defendant's calls and mail communications to plaintiff as significant contacts with the State of New Jersey.

On the other hand, some courts have been reluctant to assert personal jurisdiction over a non-resident buyer having the same type of contacts with the forum state. See, e.g., CPC–Rexcell, Inc. v. La Corona Foods, Inc., 912 F.2d 241 (8th Cir.1990); Borg–Warner Acceptance Corp. v. Lovett & Tharpe, Inc., 786 F.2d 1055 (11th Cir.1986).

6. Doesn't *World-Wide Volkswagen* teach that the key question—at least for the "sovereignty branch"—is whether the defendant purposefully availed herself of the protection and benefits of the forum? The buyer-seller distinction is usually linked to stereotypical notions of the profiting, actively involved seller and the passive, unknowing buyer. But there are many cases in which the parties are of relatively even bargaining strength—and in which the buyer plays the more active role in creating the deal. In such cases, would it not be consistent with *Volkswagen* to permit a state to assert jurisdiction over the nonresident buyer? Is *Burger King* such a case?

Some of the cases that have found jurisdiction over nonresident buyers have placed weight on the fact that the purchaser physically came to the forum to negotiate or finalize the deal. Is the judge in *Alchemie International* correct that giving weight to such presence is a throwback to *Pennoyer*? Or is the purchaser's presence in the forum an indication that she is playing an active rather than a passive role in the transaction and that she is thus more likely to be purposefully availing herself of the protection and benefits of the forum? For a general discussion, see Note, *Minimum Contacts in Contract Cases: A Forward Looking Evaluation*, 58 Notre Dame L.Rev. 635 (1983).

7. For further discussions of the application of "minimum contacts" analysis to contract cases, see Louis, *Jurisdiction Over Those Who Breach Their Contracts: The Lessons of Burger King*, 72 N.C.L.Rev. 55 (1993); Stephens, *The Single Contract as Minimum Contacts: Justice Brennan "Has It His Way,"* 28 Wm. & Mary L.Rev. 89 (1986); Note, *Minimum Contacts in Single Contract Cases: Burger King Has Its Way*, 1986 B.Y.U.L.Rev. 505; Note, *Quest for a Bright Line Personal*

Jurisdiction Rule in Contract Disputes—Burger King Corp. v. Rudzewicz, 61 Wash.L.Rev. 703 (1986).

_____

ASAHI METAL INDUSTRY CO. v. SUPERIOR COURT

Supreme Court of the United States, 1987.
480 U.S. 102, 107 S.Ct. 1026, 94 L.Ed.2d 92.

Certiorari to the Supreme Court of California.

JUSTICE O'CONNOR announced the judgment of the Court and delivered the unanimous opinion of the Court with respect to Part I, the opinion of the Court with respect to Part II–B, in which THE CHIEF JUSTICE, JUSTICE BRENNAN, JUSTICE WHITE, JUSTICE MARSHALL, JUSTICE BLACKMUN, JUSTICE POWELL, and JUSTICE STEVENS join, and an opinion with respect to Parts II–A and III, in which THE CHIEF JUSTICE, JUSTICE POWELL, and JUSTICE SCALIA join.

This case presents the question whether the mere awareness on the part of a foreign defendant that the component it manufactured, sold, and delivered outside the United States would reach the forum state in the stream of commerce constitutes "minimum contacts" between the defendant and the forum state such that the exercise of jurisdiction "does not offend 'traditional notions of fair play and substantial justice.'" * * *

I

On September 23, 1978, on Interstate Highway 80 in Solano County, California, Gary Zurcher lost control of his Honda motorcycle and collided with a tractor. Zurcher was severely injured, and his passenger and wife, Ruth Ann Moreno, was killed. In September 1979, Zurcher filed a product liability action in the Superior Court of the State of California in and for the County of Solano. Zurcher alleged that the 1978 accident was caused by a sudden loss of air and an explosion in the rear tire of the motorcycle, and alleged that the motorcycle tire, tube, and sealant were defective. Zurcher's complaint named, *inter alia,* Cheng Shin Rubber Industrial Co., Ltd. (Cheng Shin), the Taiwanese manufacturer of the tube. Cheng Shin in turn filed a cross-complaint seeking indemnification from its codefendants and from petitioner, Asahi Metal Industry Co., Ltd. (Asahi), the manufacturer of the tube's valve assembly. Zurcher's claims against Cheng Shin and the other defendants were eventually settled and dismissed, leaving only Cheng Shin's indemnity action against Asahi.

California's long-arm statute authorizes the exercise of jurisdiction "on any basis not inconsistent with the Constitution of this state or of the United States." * * * Asahi moved to quash Cheng Shin's service of summons arguing the State could not exert jurisdiction over it consistent with the Due Process Clause of the Fourteenth Amendment.

In relation to the motion, the following information was submitted by Asahi and Cheng Shin. Asahi is a Japanese corporation. It manufactures tire valve assemblies in Japan and sells the assemblies to Cheng Shin, and to several other tire manufacturers, for use as components in finished tire tubes. Asahi's sales to Cheng Shin took place in Taiwan. The shipments from Asahi to Cheng Shin were sent from Japan to Taiwan. Cheng Shin bought and incorporated into its tire tubes 150,000 Asahi valve assemblies in 1978; 500,000 in 1979; 500,000 in 1980; 100,000 in 1981; and 100,000 in 1982. Sales to Cheng Shin accounted for 1.24 percent of Asahi's income in 1981 and 0.44 percent in 1982. Cheng Shin alleged that approximately 20 percent of its sales in the United States are in California. Cheng Shin purchases valve assemblies from other suppliers as well, and sells finished tubes throughout the world.

In 1983 an attorney for Cheng Shin conducted an informal examination of the valve stems of the tire tubes sold in one cyclery in Solano County. The attorney declared that of the approximately 115 tire tubes in the store, 97 were purportedly manufactured in Japan or Taiwan, and of those 97, 21 valve stems were marked with the circled letter "A", apparently Asahi's trademark. Of the 21 Asahi valve stems, 12 were incorporated into Cheng Shin tire tubes. The store contained 41 other Cheng Shin tubes that incorporated the valve assemblies of other manufacturers. * * * An affidavit of a manager of Cheng Shin whose duties included the purchasing of component parts stated: " 'In discussions with Asahi regarding the purchase of valve stem assemblies the fact that my Company sells tubes throughout the world and specifically the United States has been discussed. I am informed and believe that Asahi was fully aware that valve stem assemblies sold to my Company and to others would end up throughout the United States and in California.' " * * * An affidavit of the president of Asahi, on the other hand, declared that Asahi " 'has never contemplated that its limited sales of tire valves to Cheng Shin in Taiwan would subject it to lawsuits in California.' " * * * The record does not include any contract between Cheng Shin and Asahi. * * *

Primarily on the basis of the above information, the Superior Court denied the motion to quash summons, stating that "Asahi obviously does business on an international scale. It is not unreasonable that they defend claims of defect in their product on an international scale." Order Denying Motion to Quash Summons * * *.

The Court of Appeal of the State of California issued a peremptory writ of mandate commanding the Superior Court to quash service of summons. The court concluded that "it would be unreasonable to require Asahi to respond in California solely on the basis of ultimately realized foreseeability that the product into which its component was embodied would be sold all over the world including California." * * *

The Supreme Court of the State of California reversed and discharged the writ issued by the Court of Appeal. * * * The court observed that "Asahi has no offices, property or agents in California. It solicits no business in California and has made no direct sales [in California]." * * * Moreover, "Asahi did not design or control the system of distribution that carried its valve assemblies into California." * * * Nevertheless, the court found the exercise of jurisdiction over Asahi to be consistent with the Due Process Clause. It concluded that Asahi knew that some of the valve assemblies sold to Cheng Shin would be incorporated into tire tubes sold in California, and that Asahi benefited indirectly from the sale in California of products incorporating its components. The court considered Asahi's intentional act of placing its components into the stream of commerce—that is, by delivering the components to Cheng Shin in Taiwan—coupled with Asahi's awareness that some of the components would eventually find their way into California, sufficient to form the basis for state court jurisdiction under the Due Process Clause.

We granted certiorari * * * and now reverse.

II

A

* * * Most recently we have reaffirmed the oft-quoted reasoning of Hanson v. Denckla * * * that minimum contacts must have a basis in "some act by which the defendant purposefully avails itself of the privilege of conducting activities within the forum State, thus invoking the benefits and protections of its laws." *Burger King* * * *. "Jurisdiction is proper * * * where the contacts proximately result from actions by the defendant *himself* that create a 'substantial connection' with the forum State." Ibid., quoting McGee v. International Life Insurance Co. * * * (emphasis in original).

Applying the principle that minimum contacts must be based on an act of the defendant, the Court in World–Wide Volkswagen Corp. v. Woodson * * * rejected the assertion that a *consumer's* unilateral act of bringing the defendant's product into the forum State was a sufficient constitutional basis for personal jurisdiction over the defendant. It had been argued in *World-Wide Volkswagen* that because an automobile retailer and its wholesale distributor sold a product mobile by design and purpose, they could foresee being haled into court in the distant States into which their customers might drive. The Court rejected this concept of foreseeability as an insufficient basis for jurisdiction under the Due Process Clause. * * * The Court disclaimed, however, the idea that "foreseeability is wholly irrelevant" to personal jurisdiction, concluding that "[t]he forum State does not exceed its powers under the Due Process Clause if it asserts personal jurisdiction over a corporation that delivers its products into the stream of commerce with the expectation that they will be purchased by consumers in the forum State." * * *.

* * *

In *World-Wide Volkswagen* itself, the state court sought to base jurisdiction not on any act of the defendant, but on the foreseeable unilateral actions of the consumer. Since *World-Wide Volkswagen,* lower courts have been confronted with cases in which the defendant acted by placing a product in the stream of commerce, and the stream eventually swept defendant's product into the forum State, but the defendant did nothing else to purposefully avail itself of the market in the forum state. Some courts have understood the Due Process Clause, as interpreted in *World-Wide Volkswagen,* to allow an exercise of personal jurisdiction to be based on no more than the defendant's act of placing the product in the stream of commerce. Other courts have understood the Due Process Clause and the above-quoted language in *World-Wide Volkswagen* to require the action of the defendant to be more purposefully directed at the forum State than the mere act of placing a product in the stream of commerce.

The reasoning of the Supreme Court of California in the present case illustrates the former interpretation of *World-Wide Volkswagen.* The Supreme Court of California held that, because the stream of commerce eventually brought some valves Asahi sold Cheng Shin into California, Asahi's awareness that its valves would be sold in California was sufficient to permit California to exercise jurisdiction over Asahi consistent with the requirements of the Due Process Clause. The Supreme Court of California's position was consistent with those courts that have held that mere foreseeability or awareness was a constitutionally sufficient basis for personal jurisdiction if the defendant's product made its way into the forum State while still in the stream of commerce. * * *

Other courts, however, have understood the Due Process Clause to require something more than that the defendant was aware of its product's entry into the forum State through the stream of commerce in order for the state to exert jurisdiction over the defendant. In the present case, for example, the State Court of Appeal did not read the Due Process Clause, as interpreted by *World-Wide Volkswagen,* to allow "mere foreseeability that the product will enter the forum state [to] be enough by itself to establish jurisdiction over the distributor and retailer." * * *

We now find this latter position to be consonant with the requirements of due process. The "substantial connection" * * * between the defendant and the forum State necessary for a finding of minimum contacts must come about by *an action of the defendant purposefully directed toward the forum State.* * * * The placement of a product into the stream of commerce, without more, is not an act of the defendant purposefully directed toward the forum State. Additional conduct of the defendant may indicate an intent or purpose to serve the market in the forum State, for example, designing the product for the market in the forum State, advertising in the forum State, establishing channels for providing regular advice to customers in the forum State, or marketing the product through a distributor who has agreed to serve as the sales agent in the forum State. But a defendant's awareness that the stream of commerce may or will sweep the product into the forum State does not convert the mere act of placing the product into the stream into an act purposefully directed toward the forum State.

Assuming, *arguendo,* that respondents have established Asahi's awareness that some of the valves sold to Cheng Shin would be incorporated into tire tubes sold in California, respondents have not demonstrated any action by Asahi to purposefully avail itself of the California market. Asahi does not do business in California. It has no office, agents, employees, or property in California. It does not advertise or otherwise solicit business in California. It did not create, control, or employ the distribution system that brought its valves to California. * * * There is no evidence that Asahi designed its product in anticipation of sales in California. * * * On the basis of these facts, the exertion of personal jurisdiction over Asahi by the Superior Court of California exceeds the limits of due process.

B

* * *

We have previously explained that the determination of the reasonableness of the exercise of jurisdiction in each case will depend on an evaluation of several factors. A court must consider the burden on the defendant, the interests of the forum state, and the plaintiff's interest in obtaining relief. It must also weigh in its determination "the interstate judicial system's interest in obtaining the most efficient resolution of controversies; and the shared interest of the several States in furthering fundamental substantive social policies." * * *

A consideration of these factors in the present case clearly reveals the unreasonableness of the assertion of jurisdiction over Asahi, even apart from the question of the placement of goods in the stream of commerce.

Certainly the burden on the defendant in this case is severe. Asahi has been commanded by the Supreme Court of California not only to traverse the distance between Asahi's headquarters in Japan and the Superior Court of California in and for the County of Solano, but also to submit its dispute with Cheng Shin to a foreign nation's judicial system. The unique burdens placed upon one who must defend oneself in a foreign legal system should have significant weight in assessing the reasonableness of stretching the long arm of personal jurisdiction over national borders.

When minimum contacts have been established, often the interests of the plaintiff and the forum in the exercise of jurisdiction will justify even the serious burdens placed on the alien defendant. In the present case, however, the interests of the plaintiff and the forum in California's assertion of jurisdiction over Asahi are slight. All that remains is a claim for indemnification asserted by Cheng Shin, a Taiwanese corporation, against Asahi. The transaction on which the indemnification claim is based took place in Taiwan; Asahi's components were shipped from Japan to Taiwan. Cheng Shin has not demonstrated that it is more convenient for it to litigate its indemnification claim against Asahi in California rather than in Taiwan or Japan.

Because the plaintiff is not a California resident, California's legitimate interests in the dispute have considerably diminished. The Supreme Court of California argued that the State had an interest in "protecting its consumers by ensuring that foreign manufacturers comply with the state's safety standards." * * * The State Supreme Court's definition of California's interest, however, was overly broad. The dispute between Cheng Shin and Asahi is primarily about indemnification rather than safety standards. Moreover, it is not at all clear at this point that California law should govern the question whether a Japanese corporation should indemnify a Taiwanese corporation on the basis of a sale made in Taiwan and a shipment of goods from Japan to Taiwan. * * * The possibility of being haled into a California court as a result of an accident involving Asahi's components undoubtedly creates an additional deterrent to the manufacture of unsafe components; however, similar pressures will be placed on Asahi by the purchasers of its components as long as those who use Asahi components in their final products, and sell those products in California, are subject to the application of California tort law.

World-Wide Volkswagen also admonished courts to take into consideration the interests of the "several States," in addition to the forum state, in the efficient judicial resolution of the dispute and the advancement of substantive policies. In the present case, this advice calls for a court to consider the procedural and substantive policies of other *nations* whose interests are affected by the assertion of jurisdiction by the California court. The procedural and substantive interests of other nations in a state court's assertion of jurisdiction over an alien defendant will differ from case to case. In every case, however, those interests, as well as the Federal interest in its foreign relations policies, will be best served by a careful inquiry into the reasonableness of the assertion of jurisdiction in the particular case, and an unwillingness to find the serious burdens on an alien defendant outweighed by minimal interests on the part of the plaintiff or the forum State. "Great care and reserve should be exercised when extending our notions of personal jurisdiction into the international field." * * *

Considering the international context, the heavy burden on the alien defendant, and the slight interests of the plaintiff and the forum State, the exercise of personal jurisdiction by a California court over Asahi in this instance would be unreasonable and unfair.

III

Because the facts of this case do not establish minimum contacts such that the exercise of personal jurisdiction is consistent with fair play and substantial justice, the judgment of Supreme Court of California is reversed, and the case is remanded for further proceedings not inconsistent with this opinion.

It is so ordered.

JUSTICE BRENNAN, with whom JUSTICE WHITE, JUSTICE MARSHALL, and JUSTICE BLACKMUN join, concurring in part and concurring in the judgment.

I do not agree with the interpretation in Part II–A of the stream-of-commerce theory, nor with the conclusion that Asahi did not "purposely avail itself of the California market." * * * I do agree, however, with the Court's conclusion in Part II–B that the exercise of personal jurisdiction over Asahi in this case would not comport with "fair play and substantial justice" * * *. This is one of those rare cases in which "minimum requirements inherent in the concept of 'fair play and substantial justice' . . . defeat the reasonableness of jurisdiction even [though] the defendant has purposefully engaged in forum activities." * * * I therefore join Parts I and II–B of the Court's opinion, and write separately to explain my disagreement with Part II–A.

Part II–A states that "a defendant's awareness that the stream of commerce may or will sweep the product into the forum State does not convert the mere act of placing the product into the stream into an act purposefully directed toward the forum State." * * * Under this view, a plaintiff would be required to show "[a]dditional conduct" directed toward the forum before finding the exercise of jurisdiction over the defendant to be consistent with the Due Process Clause. * * * I see no need for such a showing, however. The stream of commerce refers not to unpredictable currents or eddies, but to the regular and anticipated flow of products from manufacture to distribution to retail sale. As long as a participant in this process is aware that the final product is being marketed in the forum State, the possibility of a lawsuit there cannot come as a surprise. Nor will the litigation present a burden for which there is no corresponding benefit. A defendant who has placed goods in the stream of commerce benefits economically from the retail sale of the final product in the forum State, and indirectly benefits from the State's laws that regulate and facilitate commercial activity. These benefits accrue regardless of whether that participant directly conducts business in the forum State, or engages in additional conduct directed toward that State. Accordingly, most courts and commentators have found that jurisdiction premised on the placement of a product into the stream of commerce is consistent with the Due Process Clause, and have not required a showing of additional conduct.

* * *

JUSTICE STEVENS, with whom JUSTICE WHITE and JUSTICE BLACKMUN join, concurring in part and concurring in the judgment.

The judgment of the Supreme Court of California should be reversed for the reasons stated in Part II–B of the Court's opinion. While I join Parts I and II–B, I do not join Part II–A for two reasons. First, it is not necessary to the Court's decision. An examination of minimum contacts is not always necessary to determine whether a state court's assertion of personal jurisdiction is constitutional. See Burger King Corp. v. Rudzewicz * * *. Part II–B establishes, after considering the factors set forth in World–Wide Volkswagen Corp. v. Woodson, * * * that California's exercise of jurisdiction over Asahi in this case would be "unreasonable and unfair." * * *. This finding alone requires reversal; this case fits within the rule that "minimum requirements inherent in the concept of 'fair play and substantial justice' may defeat the reasonableness of jurisdiction even if the defendant has purposefully engaged in forum activities." *Burger King* * * *. Accordingly, I see no reason in this case for the plurality to articulate "purposeful direction" or any other test as the nexus between an act of a defendant and the forum State that is necessary to establish minimum contacts.

Second, even assuming that the test ought to be formulated here, Part II–A misapplies it to the facts of this case. The plurality seems to assume that an unwavering line can be drawn between "mere awareness" that a component will find its way into the forum State and "purposeful availment" of the forum's market. * * *. Over the course of its dealings with Cheng Shin, Asahi has arguably engaged in a higher quantum of conduct than "[t]he placement of a product into the stream of commerce, without more.* * * " * * * Whether or not this conduct rises to the level of purposeful availment requires a constitutional determination that is affected by the volume, the value, and the hazardous character of the components. In most circumstances I would be inclined to conclude that a regular course of dealing that results in deliveries of over 100,000 units annually over a period of several years would constitute "purposeful availment" even though the item delivered to the forum State was a standard product marketed throughout the world.

Notes and Questions

1. Given the division among the Justices, which opinion states the law as it now stands?

2. The Supreme Court did not disturb the California court's finding that "Asahi knew that some of the valve assemblies sold to Cheng Shin would be incorporated into tire tubes sold in California." Under Part II–A of Justice O'Connor's opinion, this knowledge alone could not serve as a basis for jurisdiction unless Asahi had taken some further action "purposefully directed toward the forum state."

In PARRY v. ERNST HOME CENTER CORP., 779 P.2d 659 (Utah 1989), plaintiff was injured in Utah while splitting logs with a maul manufactured by

Hirota, a Japanese manufacturer. The maul had been sold by Hirota to Okada Hardware in Japan for export to the United States. Okada sold it to Mansour, a California corporation, who then sold it to Pacific Marine Schwabacher, its regional distributor. Schwabacher distributed and sold the mauls to retailers throughout the western portion of the United States, including defendant Ernst Home Center Corp. The Ernst Home Center in Twin Falls, Idaho, sold the maul to Linda Thayne in 1979. She then gave it to her father in Utah. Plaintiff borrowed it from him and was injured while using it.

Both Hirota and Okada had been informed that the maul would be sold in the United States, but there was no evidence that either company directly sold or advertised any of their products in Utah. Plaintiff contended that Utah had personal jurisdiction over Hirota and Okada under the stream-of-commerce theory. In analyzing whether the assertion of jurisdiction over the foreign defendants would violate the Due Process Clause, the Utah Supreme Court relied on *Asahi* and reasoned that:

> * * * Hirota and Okada had not taken active steps to sell its product in Utah or Idaho * * *. They were informed of potential sales to the western United States, but they neither came to Utah nor sent sales representatives to Utah to facilitate the marketing and purchase of their product. Further, the record does not provide the number or percentage of mauls manufactured which were actually sold in Utah. Finally, * * * although plaintiff was injured and resides in Utah, an advertising effort in Utah had not occurred sufficient to link the Japanese defendants to this forum.

> Of the following examples of "additional conduct" outlined in *Asahi*, Hirota and Okada had not engaged in even one. The record does not show special designing for Utah's market, advertising in Utah, establishing channels for providing regular advice to customers in Utah, or marketing the product through a distributor who has agreed to act as a sales agent in Utah. * * *.

> The record does not reveal any further knowledge or intent by Hirota and Okada to specifically sell the product in Utah or in any other given state. True, the Japanese defendants have not placed any restrictions upon the sale of their products in any particular section of the United States. But an intentional and knowing distribution of the product in the western United States is not necessarily sufficient to satisfy the "minimum contacts" requirement. Further, Hirota and Okada have their principal place of business in Japan; neither has an office in Utah. They have no sales representatives or other agents, no bank account, and no personal property in Utah. They do not own, lease, or rent real property in Utah. Hirota and Okada have not solicited, directly or indirectly, the sale of any of its products in Utah. They have not provided brochures or sent any sales representatives to Utah. They do not render services in Utah and do not give advice to anyone in Utah with regard to the * * * maul. Without a showing of "additional conduct," we are unable to find that the eventual sale of a product in Utah justifies personal jurisdiction.

Id. at 666–67. Was it proper for the Utah Supreme Court to apply the "additional conduct" test? Did the court apply the test correctly? What is the rationale for requiring "additional conduct"? Will the effect be to allow manufacturers to organize their operations so as to avoid the safety standards of a particular state? By organizing their business as they have, are Hirota and Okada effectively immune from suit in the United States? See Note, *Parry v. Ernst Home Center Corp.: The "Mauling" of Personal Jurisdiction Theory*, 1990 Utah L.Rev. 479.

3. In NELSON BY CARSON v. PARK INDUS., INC., 717 F.2d 1120, 1125–26 (7th Cir.1983), cited in *Asahi*, a minor, who had suffered severe burns when the cotton flannel shirt she was wearing ignited, sued the retailer (F.W. Woolworth) and its insurance company as well as the purchasing agent for the flannel shirt and the manufacturer of the shirt in a federal court in Wisconsin. Interpreting *World-Wide Volkswagen* as limiting the reach of Wisconsin's long-arm statute, the District Court granted the motions of the purchasing agent and the manufacturer, both Hong Kong corporations, to dismiss the complaints against them for lack of personal jurisdiction. The manufacturer produced 100% of the cotton flannel shirts purchased by Woolworth for sale in the United States, but it had no direct commercial relationship with Woolworth. All contacts between the two companies were made through the purchasing agent. The agent had a relationship with Woolworth dating back to World War II. The Seventh Circuit reversed the District Court and found that jurisdiction might properly be asserted:

> The *World-Wide Volkswagen* Court's recognition of a distinction among the various entities that might compose a distribution system of a product is pivotal to the decision in this case. The two defendants in *World-Wide Volkswagen* who were not amenable to Oklahoma jurisdiction were at the end of the automobile's distribution system. The scope of the foreseeable market served by those defendants and of the benefits those defendants derived from the sale of the product was narrow. In contrast, the relevant scope is generally broader with respect to manufacturers and primary distributors of products who are at the start of a distribution system and who thereby serve, directly or indirectly, and derive economic benefit from a wider market. Such manufacturers and distributors purposely conduct their activities to make their product available for purchase in as many forums as possible. For this reason, a manufacturer or primary distributor may be subject to a particular forum's jurisdiction when a secondary distributor and retailer are not, because the manufacturer and primary distributor have intended to serve a broader market and they derive direct benefits from serving that market.

Did the Seventh Circuit correctly apply *World-Wide Volkswagen*? If it did, is it possible to argue that the Hong Kong manufacturer had any more control over the whereabouts of the flannel shirt than Seaway had over the whereabouts of the Robinsons' car in *World–Wide*? Would the case be decided the same way after *Asahi*?

4. Lower courts have been divided in their interpretations of *Asahi*. In LESNICK v. HOLLINGSWORTH, 35 F.3d 939, 945 (4th Cir.1994), the Fourth Circuit adopted Justice O'Connor's "purposeful availment" test, stating that "our reading of *World-Wide Volkswagen* and *Asahi* is that the Supreme Court has not abandoned the *International Shoe* two-pronged test. The touchstone of the minimum contacts analysis remains that an out-of-state person have engaged in some activity purposefully directed toward the forum state." The First Circuit did likewise in BOIT v. GAR–TEC PRODUCTS, INC., 967 F.2d 671, 683 (1st Cir. 1992), holding that "[b]ecause 'mere awareness' that a product may end up in the forum state does not constitute 'purposeful availment', the district court could not have constitutionally exercised personal jurisdiction over [the defendant]." For cases following Justice Brennan's "stream of commerce" test, see State ex rel. CSR Ltd. v. MacQueen, 190 W.Va. 695, 441 S.E.2d 658 (1994); Ruston Gas

Turbines, Inc. v. Corchran, Inc., 9 F.3d 415 (5th Cir.1993); and Dehmlow v. Austin Fireworks, 963 F.2d 941, 947 (7th Cir.1992).

5. What did Justice O'Connor mean by suggesting that "designing the product for the market in the forum State" is an example of "additional conduct"? In SOO LINE R.R. CO. v. HAWKER SIDDELEY CANADA, INC., 950 F.2d 526 (8th Cir.1991), the defendant manufactured railroad cars in Canada in compliance with standards set by the Association of American Railroads ("AAR"). AAR is not a governmental entity, but almost all railroads in Mexico, Canada, and the forty-eight contiguous United States are either members of AAR, or signatories to the AAR agreement. The Eighth Circuit, however, held that since defendant "did not design its railcars for use in Minnesota *per se*," that "[t]he relationship between [defendant] and the State of Minnesota is too remote to qualify as 'purposeful availment.' " Do you agree?

6. Some courts have chosen to disregard both stream-of-commerce tests in *Asahi* and have chosen, instead, to rely on *World-Wide Volkswagen*. For example, in IRVING v. OWENS–CORNING FIBERGLAS CORP., 864 F.2d 383, 385–86 (5th Cir.), certiorari denied 493 U.S. 823, 110 S.Ct. 83, 107 L.Ed.2d 49 (1989), Judge Davis reasoned that:

> Because the Court's splintered view of minimum contacts in *Asahi* provides no clear guidance on this issue, we continue to gauge [defendant's] contacts with Texas by the stream of commerce standard as described in *World-Wide Volkswagen* and embraced in this circuit. * * *. To borrow *World-Wide Volkswagen*'s phrase, [defendant] reasonably should have anticipated being haled into a Texas court given its contacts with that forum.

Isn't the Fifth Circuit really applying Justice Brennan's view of the stream-of-commerce theory as articulated in *Asahi*? See also DeMoss v. City Market, Inc., 762 F.Supp. 913 (D.Utah 1991).

7. Is *Asahi* limited in its application to assertions of jurisdiction over foreign defendants? The Supreme Court made clear that: "The unique burdens placed upon one who must defend oneself in a foreign legal system should have significant weight in assessing the reasonableness of stretching the long arm of personal jurisdiction over national borders." Does the importance of this factor decrease the less the distance is that the defendants must travel and the more familiar they are with the American legal system? See Theunissen v. Matthews, 935 F.2d 1454, 1462 (6th Cir.1991) (burdens on defendant are "slight" since Windsor, Ontario is only ten miles from Detroit and "Canada and the United States are rooted in the same common law tradition").

8. In IN RE DES CASES, 789 F.Supp. 552, 587 (E.D.N.Y.1992), Judge Weinstein, attempting to reconcile the Supreme Court personal jurisdiction precedents and apply them in a mass tort case, developed the following pair of principles as the appropriate due process standard for asserting personal jurisdiction over defendants in mass tort cases:

> I. The court must first determine if the forum state has an appreciable interest in the litigation, i.e., whether the litigation raises issues whose resolution would be affected by, or have a probable impact on the vindication of, policies expressed in the substantive, procedural or remedial laws of the forum. If there is an appreciable state interest, the assertion of jurisdiction is *prima facie* constitutional.

> II. Once a *prima facie* case is made, the assertion of jurisdiction will be considered constitutional unless, given the actual circumstances of the case,

the defendant is unable to mount a defense in the forum state without suffering relatively substantial hardship.

Evidence to be considered in determining the defendant's relative hardship includes, *inter alia*, (1) the defendant's available assets; (2) whether the defendant has or is engaged in substantial interstate commerce; (3) whether the defendant is being represented by an indemnitor or is sharing the cost of the defense with an indemnitor or co-defendant; (4) the comparative hardship defendant will incur in defending the suit in another forum; and (5) the comparative hardship to the plaintiff if the case were dismissed or transferred for lack of jurisdiction.

Are these principles consistent with the "minimum contacts" test? Are deviations from this standard justified by the unique circumstances of a mass tort case?

9. For further discussions, see Stephens, *Sovereignty and Personal Jurisdiction Doctrine: Up the Stream of Commerce Without a Paddle,* 19 Fla.St.L.Rev. 105 (1991); Stravitz, *Sayonara to Minimum Contacts: Asahi Metal Industry Co. v. Superior Ct.,* 39 S.Car.L.Rev. 729 (1988); Maltz, *Unraveling the Conundrum of the Law of Personal Jurisdiction: A Comment on Asahi Metal Industry Co. v. Superior Ct. of California,* 1987 Duke L.Rev. 669; Dessem, *Personal Jurisdiction After Asahi: The Other (International) Shoe Drops,* 55 Tenn.L.Rev. 41 (1987).

SECTION E.   GENERAL JURISDICTION AND STATE LONG–ARM LAWS

PERKINS v. BENGUET CONSOLIDATED MINING CO., 342 U.S. 437, 445–48, 72 S.Ct. 413, 418–20, 96 L.Ed. 485, 492–94 (1952). The defendant, a Philippine corporation, was sued by a nonresident of Ohio in an Ohio state court on two causes of action arising from activities conducted by defendant outside of Ohio. Plaintiff claimed $68,400 in dividends due her as a stockholder, and $2,500,000 in damages due to defendant's failure to issue to her certificates for 120,000 shares of its stock. The Ohio state courts granted defendant's motion to quash the service of summons. The Supreme Court addressed the issue of whether or not the Due Process Clause of the Fourteenth Amendment prohibited Ohio from exercising jurisdiction:

* * * The corporate activities of a foreign corporation which, under state statute, make it necessary for it to secure a license and to designate a statutory agent upon whom process may be served provide a helpful but not a conclusive test. * * * [I]f the same corporation carries on, in that state, other continuous and systematic corporate activities as it did here—consisting of directors' meetings, business correspondence, banking, stock transfers, payment of salaries, purchasing of machinery, etc.— those activities are enough to make it fair and reasonable to subject that corporation to proceedings *in personam* in that state, at least insofar as the proceedings *in personam* seek to enforce causes of action relating to those very activities or to other activities of the corporation within the state.

The instant case takes us one step further to a proceeding *in personam* to enforce a cause of action not arising out of the corporation's activities in the state of the forum. * * * [W]e find no requirement of federal due process that either *prohibits* Ohio from opening its courts to the cause of action here presented or *compels* Ohio to do so. * * *

It remains only to consider * * * whether, as a matter of federal due process, the business done in Ohio by the respondent mining company was sufficiently substantial and of such a nature to *permit* Ohio to entertain a cause of action against a foreign corporation, where the cause of action arose from activities entirely distinct from its activities in Ohio. * * *.

Issue

* * * [T]he following facts are substantially beyond controversy: The company's mining properties were in the Philippine Islands. Its operations there were completely halted during the occupation of the Islands by the Japanese. During that interim the president, who was also the general manager and principal stockholder of the company, returned to his home in Clermont County, Ohio. There he maintained an office in which he conducted his personal affairs and did many things on behalf of the company. He kept there office files of the company. He carried on there correspondence relating to the business of the company and to its employees. He drew and distributed there salary checks on behalf of the company, both in his own favor as president and in favor of two company secretaries who worked there with him. He used and maintained in Clermont County, Ohio, two active bank accounts carrying substantial balances of company funds. A bank in Hamilton County, Ohio, acted as transfer agent for the stock of the company. Several directors' meetings were held at his office or home in Clermont County. From that office he supervised policies dealing with the rehabilitation of the corporation's properties in the Philippines and he dispatched funds to cover purchases of machinery for such rehabilitation. Thus he carried on in Ohio a continuous and systematic supervision of the necessarily limited wartime activities of the company. * * * While no mining properties in Ohio were owned or operated by the company, many of its wartime activities were directed from Ohio and were being given the personal attention of its president in that State at the time he was served with summons. * * * [W]e conclude that, under the circumstances above recited, it would not violate federal due process for Ohio either to take or decline jurisdiction of the corporation in this proceeding.

Reasoning

On remand the Ohio courts refused to quash the summons. 158 Ohio St. 145, 107 N.E.2d 203 (1952).

Notes and Questions

1. Consider the following cases in light of the Supreme Court's decision in *Perkins*. In FISHER GOVERNOR CO. v. SUPERIOR COURT, 53 Cal.2d 222, 225, 1 Cal.Rptr. 1, 3, 347 P.2d 1, 3 (1959), a wrongful death action growing out of an explosion in Idaho, plaintiffs served defendant, an Iowa corporation, by delivering the papers to a California manufacturers' agent who sold defendant's products. The California Supreme Court ordered the process quashed. In his opinion for the court, Justice Traynor said:

Although a foreign corporation may have sufficient contacts with a state to justify an assumption of jurisdiction over it to enforce causes of action having no relation to its activities in that state * * *, more contacts are required for the assumption of such extensive jurisdiction than sales and sales promotion within the state by independent nonexclusive sales representatives. * * * To hold otherwise would subject any corporation that promotes the sales of its goods on a nationwide basis to suit anywhere in the United States without regard to other considerations bearing on "the fair and orderly administration of the laws which it was the purpose of the due process clause to insure." * * * Accordingly, we must look beyond defendant's sales activities in this state to determine whether jurisdiction may constitutionally be assumed.

2. In FRUMMER v. HILTON HOTELS INT'L, INC., 19 N.Y.2d 533, 281 N.Y.S.2d 41, 227 N.E.2d 851, certiorari denied 389 U.S. 923, 88 S.Ct. 241, 19 L.Ed.2d 266 (1967), a New York tourist who fell and injured himself while taking a shower in the London Hilton brought a personal injury action against the hotel (an English corporation) in New York. Jurisdiction was upheld on the basis of the activities of the Hilton Reservation Service, a separate corporation. Although separate, the interlocking ownership of the two corporations and other facts persuaded New York's highest court that an agency relationship existed between them. It thus held that London Hilton did business in New York by "do[ing] all the business which [the principal] could do were it [in New York] by its own officials."

3. In RATLIFF v. COOPER LABORATORIES, INC., 444 F.2d 745 (4th Cir.), certiorari denied 404 U.S. 948, 92 S.Ct. 271, 30 L.Ed.2d 265 (1971), the court held that South Carolina could not assert personal jurisdiction over the defendants, two drug manufacturing companies incorporated in Delaware with principal places of business in Connecticut and New York, because their contacts with South Carolina were insufficient to satisfy due process requirements. The court placed great significance on the facts that the plaintiffs were nonresidents of South Carolina who chose the forum for its long statute of limitations, that the allegedly defective drugs were both manufactured and consumed outside the forum, and that the cause of action was unrelated to defendants' activities in the forum.

HELICOPTEROS NACIONALES DE COLOMBIA, S.A. v. HALL

Supreme Court of the United States, 1984.
466 U.S. 408, 104 S.Ct. 1868, 80 L.Ed.2d 404.

Certiorari to the Supreme Court of Texas.

Justice Blackmun delivered the opinion of the Court.

We granted certiorari in this case * * * to decide whether the Supreme Court of Texas correctly ruled that the contacts of a foreign corporation with the State of Texas were sufficient to allow a Texas state court to assert jurisdiction over the corporation in a cause of action not arising out of or related to the corporation's activities within the State.

I

Petitioner Helicopteros Nacionales de Colombia, S.A., (Helicol) is a Colombian corporation with its principal place of business in the city of Bogota in that country. It is engaged in the business of providing helicopter transportation for oil and construction companies in South America. On January 26, 1976, a helicopter owned by Helicol crashed in Peru. Four United States citizens were among those who lost their lives in the accident. Respondents are the survivors and representatives of the four decedents.

At the time of the crash, respondents' decedents were employed by Consorcio, a Peruvian consortium, and were working on a pipeline in Peru. Consorcio is the alter-ego of a joint venture named Williams–Sedco–Horn (WSH). The venture had its headquarters in Houston, Texas. Consorcio had been formed to enable the venturers to enter into a contract with Petro Peru, the Peruvian state-owned oil company. Consorcio was to construct a pipeline for Petro Peru running from the interior of Peru westward to the Pacific Ocean. Peruvian law forbade construction of the pipeline by any non-Peruvian entity.

Consorcio/WSH needed helicopters to move personnel, materials, and equipment into and out of the construction area. In 1974, upon request of Consorcio/WSH, the chief executive officer of Helicol, Francisco Restrepo, flew to the United States and conferred in Houston with representatives of the three joint venturers. At that meeting, there was a discussion of prices, availability, working conditions, fuel, supplies, and housing. Restrepo represented that Helicol could have the first helicopter on the job in 15 days. The Consorcio/WSH representatives decided to accept the contract proposed by Restrepo. Helicol began performing before the agreement was formally signed in Peru on November 11, 1974. The contract was written in Spanish on official government stationery and provided that the residence of all the parties would be Lima, Peru. It further stated that controversies arising out of the contract would be submitted to the jurisdiction of Peruvian courts. In addition, it provided that Consorcio/WSH would make payments to Helicol's account with the Bank of America in New York City. * * *.

Aside from the negotiation session in Houston between Restrepo and the representatives of Consorcio/WSH, Helicol had other contacts with Texas. During the years 1970–1977, it purchased helicopters (approximately 80% of its fleet), spare parts, and accessories for more than $4 million from Bell Helicopter Company in Fort Worth. In that period, Helicol sent prospective pilots to Fort Worth for training and to ferry the aircraft to South America. It also sent management and maintenance personnel to visit Bell Helicopter in Fort Worth during the same period in order to receive "plant familiarization" and for technical consultation. Helicol received into its New York City and Panama City, Florida, bank accounts over $5 million in payments from Consorcio/WSH drawn upon First City National Bank of Houston.

Beyond the foregoing, there have been no other business contacts between Helicol and the State of Texas. Helicol never has been authorized to do business in Texas and never has had an agent for the service of process within the State. It never has performed helicopter operations in Texas or sold any product that reached Texas, never solicited business in Texas, never signed any contract in Texas, never had any employee based there, and never recruited an employee in Texas. In addition, Helicol never has owned real or personal property in Texas and never has maintained an office or establishment there. Helicol has maintained no records in Texas and has no shareholders in that State. None of the respondents or their decedents were domiciled in Texas, * * *[5] but all of the decedents were hired in Houston by Consorcio/WSH to work on the Petro Peru pipeline project.

Respondents instituted wrongful-death actions in the District Court of Harris County, Texas, against Consorcio/WSH, Bell Helicopter Company, and Helicol. Helicol filed special appearances and moved to dismiss the actions for lack of *in personam* jurisdiction over it. The motion was denied. After a consolidated jury trial, judgment was entered against Helicol on a jury verdict of $1,141,200 in favor of respondents.[6] * * *.

The Texas Court of Civil Appeals, Houston, First District, reversed the judgment of the District Court, holding that *in personam* jurisdiction over Helicol was lacking. * * *. The Supreme Court of Texas * * * reversed the judgment of the intermediate court. * * *. In ruling that the Texas courts had *in personam* jurisdiction, the Texas Supreme Court first held that the State's long-arm statute reaches as far as the Due Process Clause of the Fourteenth Amendment permits. * * *.[7] Thus, the only question remaining for the court to decide was whether it was consistent with the Due Process Clause for Texas courts to assert *in personam* jurisdiction over Helicol. * * *.

II

* * *. Due process requirements are satisfied when *in personam* jurisdiction is asserted over a nonresident corporate defendant that has "certain minimum contacts with [the forum] such that the maintenance of the suit does not offend 'traditional notions of fair play and substantial justice.'" * * *. When a controversy is related to or "arises out of" a defendant's contacts with the forum, the Court has said that a "relationship among the defendant, the forum, and the litigation" is the essential foundation of *in personam* jurisdiction. * * *.

Even when the cause of action does not arise out of or relate to the foreign corporation's activities in the forum State, due process is not offended by a State's subjecting the corporation to its *in personam* jurisdiction when there are sufficient contacts between the State and the foreign corporation. * * *

Rules

All parties to the present case concede that respondents' claims against Helicol did not "arise out of," and are not related to, Helicol's activities within Texas.[10] We thus must explore the nature of Helicol's contacts with the

5. Respondents' lack of residential or other contacts with Texas of itself does not defeat otherwise proper jurisdiction. * * *. We mention respondents' lack of contacts merely to show that nothing in the nature of the relationship between respondents and Helicol could possibly enhance Helicol's contacts with Texas. The harm suffered by respondents did not occur in Texas. Nor is it alleged that any negligence on the part of Helicol took place in Texas.

6. Defendants Consorcio/WSH and Bell Helicopter Company were granted directed verdicts with respect to respondents' claims against them. Bell Helicopter was granted a directed verdict on Helicol's cross-claim against it. * * *. Consorcio/WSH, as cross-plaintiff in a

claim against Helicol, obtained a judgment in the amount of $70,000. * * *.

7. * * * It is not within our province, of course, to determine whether the Texas Supreme Court correctly interpreted the State's long-arm statute. We therefore accept that court's holding that the limits of the Texas statute are coextensive with those of the Due Process Clause.

10. * * * Because the parties have not argued any relationship between the cause of action and Helicol's contacts with the State of Texas, we, contrary to the dissent's implication, * * * assert no "view" with respect to that issue.

State of Texas to determine whether they constitute the kind of continuous and systematic general business contacts the Court found to exist in *Perkins*. We hold that they do not.

It is undisputed that Helicol does not have a place of business in Texas and never has been licensed to do business in the State. Basically, Helicol's contacts with Texas consisted of sending its chief executive officer to Houston for a contract-negotiation session; accepting into its New York bank account checks drawn on a Houston bank; purchasing helicopters, equipment, and training services from Bell Helicopter for substantial sums; and sending personnel to Bell's facilities in Fort Worth for training.

The one trip to Houston by Helicol's chief executive officer for the purpose of negotiating the transportation-services contract with Consorcio/WSH cannot be described or regarded as a contact of a "continuous and systematic" nature, as *Perkins* described it, * * * and thus cannot support an assertion of *in personam* jurisdiction over Helicol by a Texas court. Similarly, Helicol's acceptance from Consorcio/WSH of checks drawn on a Texas bank is of negligible significance for purposes of determining whether Helicol had sufficient contacts in Texas. There is no indication that Helicol ever requested that the checks be drawn on a Texas bank or that there was any negotiation between Helicol and Consorcio/WSH with respect to the location or identity of the bank on which checks would be drawn. Common sense and everyday experience suggest that, absent unusual circumstances, the bank on which a check is drawn is generally of little consequence to the payee and is a matter left to the discretion of the drawer. Such unilateral activity of another party or a third person is not an appropriate consideration when determining whether a defendant has sufficient contacts with a forum State to justify an assertion of jurisdiction. * * *.

The Texas Supreme Court focused on the purchases and the related training trips in finding contacts sufficient to support an assertion of jurisdiction. We do not agree with that assessment, for the Court's opinion in Rosenberg Bros. & Co. v. Curtis Brown Co., 260 U.S. 516 (1923) (Brandeis, J., for a unanimous tribunal), makes clear that purchases and related trips, standing alone, are not a sufficient basis for a State's assertion of jurisdiction.

* * *

* * * In accordance with *Rosenberg,* we hold that mere purchases, even if occurring at regular intervals, are not enough to warrant a State's assertion

The dissent suggests that we have erred in drawing no distinction between controversies that "relate to" a defendant's contacts with a forum and those that "arise out of" such contacts. * * *. This criticism is somewhat puzzling, for the dissent goes on to urge that, for purposes of determining the constitutional validity of an assertion of specific jurisdiction, there really should be no distinction between the two. * * *

We do not address the validity or consequences of such a distinction because the issue has not been presented in this case. Respondents have made no argument that their cause of action either arose out of or is related to Helicol's contacts with the State of Texas. Ab-

sent any briefing on the issue, we decline to reach the questions (1) whether the terms "arising out of" and "related to" describe different connections between a cause of action and a defendant's contacts with a forum, and (2) what sort of tie between a cause of action and a defendant's contacts with a forum is necessary to a determination that either connection exists. Nor do we reach the question whether, if the two types of relationship differ, a forum's exercise of personal jurisdiction in a situation where the cause of action "relates to," but does not "arise out of," the defendant's contacts with the forum should be analyzed as an assertion of specific jurisdiction.

of *in personam* jurisdiction over a nonresident corporation in a cause of action not related to those purchase transactions. Nor can we conclude that the fact that Helicol sent personnel into Texas for training in connection with the purchase of helicopters and equipment in that State in any way enhanced the nature of Helicol's contacts with Texas. The training was a part of the package of goods and services purchased by Helicol from Bell Helicopter. The brief presence of Helicol employees in Texas for the purpose of attending the training sessions is no more a significant contact than were the trips to New York made by the buyer for the [Oklahoma] retail store in *Rosenberg*. * * *.

III

We hold that Helicol's contacts with the State of Texas were insufficient to satisfy the requirements of the Due Process Clause of the Fourteenth Amendment. Accordingly, we reverse the judgment of the Supreme Court of Texas.

It is so ordered.

JUSTICE BRENNAN, dissenting.

* * * Based on essentially undisputed facts, the Court concludes that petitioner Helicol's contacts with the State of Texas were insufficient to allow the Texas state courts constitutionally to assert "general jurisdiction" over all claims filed against this foreign corporation. Although my independent weighing of the facts leads me to a different conclusion, * * * the Court's holding on this issue is neither implausible nor unexpected.

What is troubling about the Court's opinion, however, are the implications that might be drawn from the way in which the Court approaches the constitutional issue it addresses. * * * I believe that the undisputed contacts in this case between petitioner Helicol and the State of Texas are sufficiently important, and sufficiently related to the underlying cause of action, to make it fair and reasonable for the State to assert personal jurisdiction over Helicol for the wrongful-death actions filed by the respondents. Given that Helicol has purposefully availed itself of the benefits and obligations of the forum, and given the direct relationship between the underlying cause of action and Helicol's contacts with the forum, maintenance of this suit in the Texas courts "does not offend [the] 'traditional notions of fair play and substantial justice,'" * * * that are the touchstone of jurisdictional analysis under the Due Process Clause. I therefore dissent.

I

* * * As active participants in interstate and foreign commerce take advantage of the economic benefits and opportunities offered by the various States, it is only fair and reasonable to subject them to the obligations that may be imposed by those jurisdictions. And chief among the obligations that a nonresident corporation should expect to fulfill is amenability to suit in any forum that is significantly affected by the corporation's commercial activities.

As a foreign corporation that has actively and purposefully engaged in numerous and frequent commercial transactions in the State of Texas, Helicol clearly falls within the category of nonresident defendants that may be subject to the forum's general jurisdiction. Helicol not only purchased helicopters and other equipment in the State for many years, but also sent pilots and management personnel into Texas to be trained in the use of this equipment and to consult with the seller on technical matters. Moreover, negotiations for the contract under which Helicol provided transportation services to the joint venture that employed the respondents' decedents also took place in the State of Texas. Taken together, these contacts demonstrate that Helicol obtained numerous benefits from its transaction of business in Texas. In turn, it is eminently fair and reasonable to expect Helicol to face the obligations that attach to its participation in such commercial transactions. Accordingly, on the basis of continuous commercial contacts with the forum, I would conclude that the Due Process Clause allows the State of Texas to assert general jurisdiction over petitioner Helicol.

II

The Court also fails to distinguish the legal principles that controlled our prior decisions in *Perkins* and *Rosenberg*. In particular, the contacts between petitioner Helicol and the State of Texas, unlike the contacts between the defendant and the forum in each of those cases, are significantly related to the cause of action alleged in the original suit filed by the respondents. Accordingly, in my view, it is both fair and reasonable for the Texas courts to assert specific jurisdiction over Helicol in this case.

By asserting that the present case does not implicate the specific jurisdiction of the Texas courts, * * * the Court necessarily removes its decision from the reality of the actual facts presented for our consideration. Moreover, the Court refuses to consider any distinction between contacts that are "related to" the underlying cause of action and contacts that "give rise" to the underlying cause of action. In my view, however, there is a substantial difference between these two standards for asserting specific jurisdiction. Thus, although I agree that the respondents' cause of action did not formally "arise out of" specific activities initiated by Helicol in the State of Texas, I believe that the wrongful-death claim filed by the respondents is significantly related to the undisputed contacts between Helicol and the forum. On that basis, I would conclude that the Due Process Clause allows the Texas courts to assert specific jurisdiction over this particular action.

The wrongful-death actions filed by the respondents were premised on a fatal helicopter crash that occurred in Peru. Helicol was joined as a defendant in the lawsuits because it provided transportation services, including the particular helicopter and pilot involved in the crash, to the joint venture that employed the decedents. Specifically, the respondents claimed in their original complaint that "Helicol is * * * legally responsible for its own negligence through its pilot employee." * * *. Viewed in light of these allegations, the contacts between Helicol and the State of Texas are directly and significantly related to the underlying claim filed by the respondents. The negotiations that took place in Texas led to the contract in which Helicol agreed to provide the precise transportation services that were being used at the time of the crash. Moreover, the helicopter involved in the crash was purchased by Helicol in Texas, and the pilot whose negligence was alleged to have caused the crash was actually trained in Texas. * * *. This is simply not a case, therefore, in which a state court has asserted jurisdiction over a nonresident defendant on the basis of wholly unrelated contacts with the forum. Rather, the contacts between Helicol and the forum are directly related to the negligence that was alleged in the respondent Hall's original complaint.[4] * * * *

Despite this substantial relationship between the contacts and the cause of action, the Court declines to consider whether the courts of Texas may assert specific jurisdiction over this suit. Apparently, this simply reflects a narrow interpretation of the question presented for review. * * *. It is nonetheless possible that the Court's opinion may be read to imply that the specific jurisdiction of the Texas courts is inapplicable because the cause of action did not formally "arise out of" the contacts between Helicol and the forum. In my view, however, such a rule would place unjustifiable limits on the bases under which Texas may assert its jurisdictional power.

Limiting the specific jurisdiction of a forum to cases in which the cause of action formally arose out of the defendant's contacts with the State would subject constitutional standards under the Due Process Clause to the vagaries of the substantive law or pleading requirements of each State. For example, the complaint filed against Helicol in this case alleged negligence based on pilot error. Even though the pilot was trained in Texas, the Court assumes that the Texas courts may not assert jurisdiction over the suit because the cause of action "did not 'arise out of,' and [is] not related to," that training. * * *. If, however, the applicable substantive law required that negligent training of the pilot was a necessary element of a cause of action for pilot error, or if the respondents had simply added an allegation of negligence in the training provided for the Helicol pilot, then presumably the Court would concede that the specific jurisdiction of the Texas courts was applicable.

Our interpretation of the Due Process Clause has never been so dependent upon the applicable substantive law or the State's formal pleading requirements. * * * [T]he principal focus when determining whether a forum may constitutionally assert jurisdiction over a nonresident defendant has been on fairness and reasonableness to the defendant. To this extent, a court's specific jurisdiction should be applicable whenever the cause of action arises out of *or* relates to the contacts between the defendant and the forum. It is eminently fair and reasonable, in my view, to subject a defendant to suit in a forum with which it has significant contacts directly related to the underlying cause of action. Because Helicol's contacts with the State of Texas meet this standard, I would affirm the judgment of the Supreme Court of Texas.

Notes and Questions

1. *Helicopteros* was the first case in which the Supreme Court acknowledged and adopted the distinction between "general jurisdiction" and "specific jurisdiction," although it first was articulated almost twenty years earlier. See von Mehren & Trautman, *Jurisdiction to Adjudicate: A Suggested Analysis*, 79 Harv. L.Rev. 1121, 1136–63 (1966). Is such a distinction artificial? Is it constitutionally compelled? What purpose is it meant to serve?

2. General jurisdiction encompasses all assertions of jurisdiction that do not qualify as assertions of specific jurisdiction. Given the higher "minimum contacts"

---

4. The jury specifically found that "the pilot failed to keep the helicopter under proper control," that "the helicopter was flown into a treetop fog condition, whereby the vision of the pilot was impaired," that "such flying was negligence," and that "such negligence * * * was a proximate cause of the crash." * * *

threshold for general jurisdiction, it is not surprising that Justice Brennan attempted to establish as broad a definition of "specific jurisdiction" as possible. As a result, he argued that specific jurisdiction is implicated whenever the defendant's contacts with the forum "relate to" the cause of action. He was concerned, however, that the Court had defined specific jurisdiction to require the cause of action to "arise out of" the defendant's forum contacts and, as such, to entangle personal jurisdiction with the substantive law of the case.

Professor Brilmayer has proposed just such a "substantive relevance" standard:

> Substantive relevance provides a natural test. A contact is related to the controversy if it is the geographical qualification of a fact relevant to the merits. A forum occurrence which would ordinarily be alleged as part of a comparable domestic complaint is a related contact. In contrast, an occurrence in the forum State of no relevance to a totally domestic cause of action is an unrelated contact, a purely jurisdictional allegation with no substantive purpose. If a fact is irrelevant in a purely domestic dispute, it does not suddenly become related to the controversy simply because there are multi-state elements.

Brilmayer, *How Contacts Count: Due Process Limitations on State Court Jurisdiction*, 1980 Sup.Ct.Rev. 77, 82–83. Is Justice Brennan correct in asserting that such an approach would "subject constitutional standards under the Due Process Clause to the vagaries of the substantive law or pleading requirements of each State"? See Vons Cos., Inc. v. Seabest Foods, Inc., 14 Cal.4th 434, 58 Cal.Rptr.2d 899, 926 P.2d 1085 (1996) for a court's detailed analysis and rejection of the substantive relevance test.

Should a state be allowed to assert specific jurisdiction over a defendant when its forum conduct is "similar to," but not causally related to, the conduct that forms the basis for the plaintiff's cause of action? For instance, in *World-Wide Volkswagen*, consider whether Audi's sales of automobiles in Oklahoma should have subjected the company to specific jurisdiction in Oklahoma over a cause of action technically "arising from" the sale of an automobile in New York. See Twitchell, *The Myth of General Jurisdiction*, 101 Harv.L.Rev. 610, 660 (1988). Professor Twitchell argues that a court should consider *all* ties between the claim and the defendant's forum contacts in order to make a proper assessment of the question of fairness to the defendant.

Professor Brilmayer, in response, has criticized Professor Twitchell's approach for failing to provide the courts with adequate guidance and for simply adding the question of what constitutes adequate "similarity." Brilmayer, *Related Contacts and Personal Jurisdiction*, 101 Harv.L.Rev. 1444, 1460 (1988). Professor Brilmayer's approach is rooted in a conception of the political legitimacy of a state exercising jurisdiction over a particular defendant. Is that the proper constitutional question? If not, what is?

3.   Are notions of general jurisdiction obsolete? See Nichols v. G.D. Searle & Co., 991 F.2d 1195, 1200 (4th Cir.1993) (noting that expansion of specific jurisdiction has enabled plaintiffs to bring suit in fora in which claims arise and concluding that "broad constructions of general jurisdiction should be generally disfavored"). Are general and specific jurisdiction two separate categories or are they two ends of a continuum? For an interesting discussion, see Richman, *Review Essay, Part II: A Sliding Scale to Supplement the Distinction Between General and Specific Jurisdiction*, 72 Calif.L.Rev. 1328 (1984).

4. The *Helicopteros* decision provided the lower courts with little guidance in applying general jurisdiction in the individual case and left many questions unanswered. For example, are assertions of general jurisdiction subject to the same "minimum contacts" test developed by *International Shoe* and its progeny in the context of specific jurisdiction?

In de REYES v. MARINE MANAGEMENT & CONSULTING, LTD., 586 So.2d 103 (La.1991), the Louisiana Supreme Court held that the two-part (minimum contacts/convenience) test adopted by the Supreme Court in *International Shoe* and the later specific jurisdiction cases should also be applied to determine the existence of general jurisdiction. *de Reyes* involved a wrongful-death action arising out of the death of a Honduran seaman in an accident off the coast of Oregon. The principal defendant was Wallem Shipmanagement, Ltd., a Hong Kong ship management corporation with a regional office in New Orleans. Wallem challenged Louisiana's assertion of *in personam* jurisdiction. The Louisiana Supreme Court first found that sufficient continuous and systematic contacts existed between Wallem and the forum: (1) Wallem had maintained a corporate office in New Orleans from which it conducted operations for five years; (2) Wallem's employees in New Orleans performed substantial ship management services; and (3) the New Orleans office was staffed with two management level employees responsible for implementing instructions from the Hong Kong office. The court then determined that the burden placed on Wallem in having to defend itself in Louisiana did not violate due process, saying that

> the mere fact that defendant's principal corporate office is located a great distance from the forum does not necessarily establish that it will suffer a hardship or inconvenience rising to the level of a denial of due process; indeed, for a global ship management enterprise such as Wallem accustomed to constantly handling a multitude of transactions of great magnitude and variety thousands of miles from its principal office, it should not be any more inconvenient to defend this lawsuit in New Orleans, than in Honduras, Hong Kong or any other nation where its vessels may call.

Id. at 112. Is the test developed in the context of specific jurisdiction properly applicable to cases asserting general jurisdiction? Or can it be said that a showing of continuous and systematic contacts by the defendant with the forum state renders the exercise of jurisdiction fair *per se*? See Behagen v. Amateur Basketball Ass'n, 744 F.2d 731 (10th Cir.1984).

5. In CRESSWELL v. WALT DISNEY PRODUCTIONS, 677 F.Supp. 284 (M.D.Pa.1987), plaintiffs brought suit in Pennsylvania for injuries suffered in connection with a monorail fire at Walt Disney World in Florida. Named as defendants were Walt Disney Company, a California corporation, which was the corporate successor of Walt Disney Productions, also a California corporation, and Walt Disney World, a Delaware corporation with its principal place of business in Florida. The court denied defendants' motion to dismiss, finding that sufficient "substantial and continuous" contacts existed with the forum based on the defendants'

> advertising on Pennsylvania radio stations and in Pennsylvania newspapers; sending representatives to Philadelphia to encourage Pennsylvania citizens to visit Walt Disney World; conveying Honorary Disney World Citizenship on the Mayor of Philadelphia; selling Walt Disney Company products and services in Pennsylvania; broadcasting the Walt Disney Channel in Pennsylvania; providing a toll-free telephone number for Pennsylvania residents to call; and regularly visiting Keystone Junior College to recruit employees.

Id. at 285. Was the court correct in finding general jurisdiction in this case? Do the economic benefits that defendants have received from their operations in Pennsylvania justify their being burdened with defending this suit? Is the assertion of jurisdiction legitimate even though the cause of action arguably did not "arise out of" the forum contacts?

SECTION F. NEW BASES OF JURISDICTION- TECHNOLOGICAL CONTACTS

In recent years technological advances such as the cell phone, fax machine, e-mail, and the Internet have made it possible for businesses, as well as individuals, to communicate and carry on commercial relationships over great distances. The Internet in particular, as the Supreme Court has recognized, is "a unique and wholly new medium of worldwide human communication," and as such raises unique questions about traditional personal jurisdiction doctrine. Reno v. A.C.L.U., 521 U.S. 844, 850 n. 4, 117 S.Ct. 2329, 2334 n. 4, 138 L.Ed.2d 874, 884 n. 4 (1997). As you read this portion of the Chapter ask yourself how courts should weigh these forms of contact when deciding whether to exercise personal jurisdiction.

BELLINO v. SIMON
United States District Court, Eastern District of Louisiana, 1999.
1999 WL 1059753.

VANCE, J.

Before the Court is the motion of defendants, Richard Simon and James Spence, Jr., to dismiss this action for lack of personal jurisdiction. For the following reasons, defendants' motion is granted as to Mr. Spence and denied as to Mr. Simon.

Plaintiffs, Forensic Document Services and its President, James Bellino, filed this action alleging defamation, fraud and deceptive trade practices by defendants Richard Simon and James Spence, Jr. None of the parties is a resident of Louisiana. FDS is a sole proprietorship with its principal place of business in California. Mr. Bellino also resides in California.

Mr. Simon, a New York resident, is the president of Richard Simon Sports, Inc., a New York corporation. Mr. Spence, a Pennsylvania resident, is the Managing Member of James Spence III Vintage Autographs, L.L.C., a limited liability company formed in Pennsylvania. Both defendants are engaged in the business of buying, selling, and authenticating sports memorabilia and autographs.

In their complaint, plaintiffs assert that defamatory statements made by Mr. Simon to the New York City Department of Consumer Affairs caused the suspension of plaintiffs' business from the on-line Internet service, eBay. Plaintiffs allegedly suffered lost eBay sales in excess of $500,000, and a loss of business reputation in Louisiana and throughout the country. Plaintiffs further contend that defendants' defamatory statements to Christopher J. Aubert, a Louisiana resident, caused Mr. Aubert to return two baseballs he had purchased from plaintiffs. As a result, plaintiffs allegedly suffered injuries in Louisiana, including a lost sale in the amount of $25,000 and the loss of future business with Mr. Aubert.

Plaintiffs assert that this Court has general jurisdiction over Mr. Simon by virtue of his extensive Internet website solicitations and over Mr. Spence because of his website in conjunction with his advertising in a national sports memorabilia trade magazine. Further, plaintiffs maintain that specific jurisdiction exists over defendants because they reached out to Louisiana to commit the intentional torts alleged in the complaint. At issue are e-mail and telephone conversation[s] [sic] between Mr. Aubert and Mr. Spence, regarding the authenticity of two baseballs autographed by Babe Ruth and Lou Gehrig that Mr. Aubert had purchased on approval from FDS.

In an effort to learn more about baseballs Mr. Aubert located the Richard Simon Sports website on the Internet. In early June 1999, Mr. Aubert initiated contact with Mr. Simon by completing a visitor form on the website that allows readers to e-mail Mr. Simon directly. * * * Mr. Simon responded, and the two men apparently exchanged several casual e-mails discussing an authentication debate underway in the sports memorabilia field. * * * Mr. Aubert then invited Mr. Simon to call him to discuss this topic further. * * * Mr. Simon accepted the invitation and, during their subsequent telephone conversation, Mr. Simon allegedly made defamatory remarks about FDS and Mr. Bellino. * * * In addition to the telephone call, Mr. Simon e-mailed Mr. Aubert approximately seven times between June 7 and June 9, 1999. * * * Three of these e-mails contained allegedly defamatory comments about plaintiffs. * * * The other e-mails included invitations for Mr. Aubert to call Mr. Simon at home in New York and a solicitation to purchase a signed photograph of Babe Ruth. * * *

On June 8, 1999, Mr. Aubert asked Mr. Simon if he could forward to him the scans of the two baseballs he had purchased. * * * After reviewing the scans, Mr. Simon responded that "he would not buy either ball" because they were "very good forgeries" and invited Mr. Aubert to call him at home that night if he wished to discuss the matter further. * * * Mr. Aubert did so, and plaintiffs allege that Mr. Simon made additional defamatory statements about FDS during that telephone call. * * * Defendants point out that Mr. Simon never charged Mr. Aubert for his opinion regarding the baseballs' authenticity. * * *

On Mr. Simon's recommendation, Mr. Aubert also called Mr. Spence during the first week of June 1999 to request that he authenticate the two baseballs. * * * Mr. Spence allegedly defamed plaintiffs during that call. * * * Thereafter, Mr. Spence sent written examination reports to Mr. Aubert, indicating that he could not authenticate the baseballs. * * *

In his deposition, Mr. Aubert states that, although independent examination revealed that the baseballs were indeed authentic, he subsequently returned the baseballs to plaintiffs based on the allegedly defamatory comments of Mr. Simon and Mr. Spence. * * * Mr. Aubert further states that he considered the customer/seller relationship between himself and plaintiffs to be "unsalvageable." * * * Nevertheless, the law firm of Aubert & Pajares, in which Mr. Aubert is a partner, currently represents plaintiffs in this matter. * * * Furthermore, on September 14, 1999, one week after he gave his deposition, Mr. Aubert listed the two baseballs for sale on eBay and they sold for $25,000 on September 19, 1999. * * * At oral argument, counsel for plaintiffs conceded that Mr. Aubert may have used the $25,000 towards defraying plaintiffs' legal bills.

Defendants Simon and Spence now move to dismiss this action on the grounds that the Court lacks personal jurisdiction over them. * * * Defendants assert that they do not have minimum contacts with Louisiana, either through specific or general jurisdiction. Finally, defendants argue that plaintiffs did not actually suffer any injury in Louisiana because Mr. Aubert's law firm represents plaintiffs and he used the proceeds of the sales of the baseballs to defray plaintiffs' legal expenses.

In a diversity action, personal jurisdiction may be exercised over a nonresident defendant if (1) the long-arm statute of the forum state confers personal jurisdiction over that defendant; and (2) exercise of such jurisdiction by the forum state comports with the Fourteenth Amendment's due process clause. Because Louisiana's long-arm statute extends to the full limits of due process, the Court must determine whether the exercise of jurisdiction satisfies the due process clause.

The exercise of personal jurisdiction over a nonresident defendant satisfies due process when (1) the defendant has purposefully availed himself of the benefits and protections of the forum state by establishing "minimum contacts" with that state; and (2) the exercise of jurisdiction over the defendant comports with "traditional notions of fair play and substantial justice."

* * *

Defendants argue that the fiduciary shield doctrine precludes the exercise of personal jurisdiction over them because they were at all times acting in their capacities as officers of their respective companies. The fiduciary shield doctrine is a "thorny jurisdictional issue" that continues to evolve. See Saktides v. Cooper, 742 F.Supp. 382, 385 (W.D.Tex.1990) (quoting Schubert v. Gay & Taylor, Inc., 716 F.Supp. 1129, 1131 (N.D.Ill.1989)). The doctrine protects corporate officers and employees from personal jurisdiction based on contacts with the forum state made solely in their corporate capacity. * * * However, because it is an equitable, not a constitutional, doctrine, "[s]ome Courts have ... stated that the fiduciary shield doctrine is unnecessary where the State's long-arm statute has been held to extend to the limits of due process." Saktides, 742 F.Supp. at 385 * * *. Moreover, the Fifth Circuit has recognized a fraud exception to the fiduciary shield doctrine, and district courts have extended it to other intentional torts. * * * Because plaintiffs allege that defendants committed fraud and defamation in Louisiana, the fiduciary shield doctrine does not preclude jurisdiction.

Plaintiffs argue that this Court has personal jurisdiction over Mr. Simon and Mr. Spence because they reached out to Louisiana by means of telephone and e-mail to defame and injure plaintiffs here. To determine whether specific jurisdiction exists over a nonresident defendant, the Court must examine whether the defendant purposefully directed his activities toward the forum state or purposefully availed himself of the privilege of conducting activities therein and whether the cause of action arises out of or relates to those activities. * * * When these conditions exist, the defendant should reasonably anticipate being haled into court in the forum state. * * * The <u>Supreme Court</u> has <u>held</u> that <u>minimum contacts may exist</u> not only when a nonresident defendant defames a plaintiff within the state, but <u>also when</u> the <u>defendant</u> <u>acts outside</u> of the <u>state</u> and the "<u>effects</u>" of the <u>defamation</u> are <u>felt within</u> <u>the state.</u> * * *

    * * * The crucial inquiry involves whether the contacts suggest that the nonresident defendant purposefully availed himself "of the privilege of conducting activities within the forum State, thus invoking the benefits and protections of its laws." [quoting *Hanson* citing *International Shoe*] * * * "Considerations such as the quality, nature, and extent of the activity in the forum, the foreseeability of consequences within the forum from activities outside it, and the relationship between the cause of action and the contacts, relate to whether it can be said that the defendant's actions constitute 'purposeful availment.' " D.J. Investments [Inc. v. Metzeler Motorcycle Tire Agent Gregg, Inc., 754 F.2d 542, 545 n.1 (5th Cir. 1985)] * * *

    Plaintiff cites Brown [v. Flowers Indus., Inc., 688 F.2d 328 (5th Cir.1982)] in support of his argument that specific jurisdiction exists over Mr. Simon and Mr. Spence as a result of defamatory phone calls and e-mails made to Mr. Aubert in Louisiana. In Brown, the Fifth Circuit reversed the district court and found that personal jurisdiction existed in Mississippi over three nonresident defendants as a result of a single long-distance telephone call initiated by one defendant to a third party residing in Mississippi. The defendant allegedly defamed the plaintiffs, a Mississippi resident and corporation, during that phone call. Accordingly, the Fifth Circuit found that the defendants could have easily foreseen that the injurious effect of the tort would be felt by plaintiffs in Mississippi.

    In D.J. Investments the Fifth Circuit also found sufficient minimum contacts to justify personal jurisdiction when the nonresident defendants allegedly committed fraudulent misrepresentations during the course of several telephone calls between defendants and plaintiffs residing in the forum state. Although the plaintiffs initiated the contact with the defendants, the court noted that some of the subsequent calls may have originated with defendants. Moreover, one of the defendants made further intentional misrepresentations to plaintiffs during a visit to the forum.

    In contrast to Brown and D.J. Investments, the Fifth Circuit upheld a finding of no personal jurisdiction on the grounds of one unsolicited and allegedly defamatory telephone call in Wilson [v. Belin, 20 F.3d at 644 (5th Cir.1994)]. The plaintiff there, a Pennsylvania resident, filed suit against an Indiana resident and an Iowa resident in a Texas district court. Plaintiff alleged defamation arising from remarks made by defendants when contacted in Indiana and Iowa by a Dallas newspaper reporter and asked to comment on a speech given by plaintiff in Texas. The court distinguished Brown, emphasizing that the Wilson defendants merely answered one uninitiated and unsolicited phone call.

    With regard to Mr. Spence, the Court finds that plaintiff has not established specific contacts sufficient to support personal jurisdiction over this Pennsylvania resident in Louisiana. Plaintiff concedes that Mr. Aubert initiated the telephone call in which Mr. Spence allegedly defamed plaintiffs. This telephone call was the only contact between Mr. Spence and Mr. Aubert related to plaintiffs' defamation claim. Based on Wilson, this Court will not exercise personal jurisdiction based on one unsolicited telephone call from the forum state to a nonresident defendant.

The Court now addresses whether specific jurisdiction exists over Mr. Simon. It is uncontested that allegedly defamatory comments made by Mr. Simon first occurred during a telephone call made by Mr. Aubert. However, this telephone call resulted from several e-mail communications which began when Mr. Aubert took advantage of a visitor form on Mr. Simon's company website allowing readers to contact Mr. Simon directly. In a broad sense, Mr. Simon solicited this communication. Moreover, it is undisputed that Mr. Simon initiated several subsequent e-mails relating to plaintiffs' defamation charge. For instance, in a June 7, 1999 e-mail message from Mr. Simon to Mr. Aubert, Mr. Simon stated that FDS was removed from eBay when eBay was "presented with incontrovertible evidence that [an FDS document examiner] authenticated a forgery." On June 8, 1999, Mr. Simon added that "I hate to badmouth people, but the things I told you last night were fact, not opinions." In addition, Mr. Simon remarked in a June 9, 1999 e-mail to Mr. Aubert that the two baseballs Mr. Aubert had purchased from FDS were "very good forgeries" and stated further "[i]f you want to discuss it, call me tonite [sic]." When Mr. Aubert called Mr. Simon again, plaintiffs allege that Mr. Simon made additional defamatory statements about FDS. The Court finds that the foregoing facts more closely resemble D.J. Investments and Brown than Wilson. Even assuming that Mr. Aubert, a third party, initiated the two telephone calls, Mr. Simon affirmatively directed the allegedly tortious e-mails to Louisiana. That allegedly defamatory comments are made over the Internet does not alter the jurisdictional analysis. Accordingly, the Court concludes that plaintiffs have met their prima facie burden of showing that Mr. Simon purposefully established minimum contacts with Louisiana such that he could reasonably anticipate being haled into court here.

At oral argument, defendants asserted that this Court cannot assert personal jurisdiction over Mr. Simon because plaintiffs did not suffer any injury in Louisiana. Specifically, defendants assert that Mr. Aubert's deposition testimony that he will not do anymore business with plaintiffs as a result of Mr. Simon's defamatory statements conflicts with his actions in selling the baseballs on eBay and representing plaintiffs' as legal counsel in this matter. At this initial stage in the litigation, however, the Court must resolve any factual conflicts in plaintiffs' favor. * * *

Finally, the Court addresses Mr. Simon's argument that any purposeful contacts between him and Louisiana related to this action were manufactured by plaintiffs in order to establish personal jurisdiction here. Mr. Simon asserts that the law firm of Aubert & Pajares, in which Mr. Aubert is a member, was retained to represent plaintiffs with regard to another matter on June 14, 1999. The allegedly defamatory statements were made to Mr. Aubert during the first week of June 1999. Mr. Simon cites Millennium Enterprises, Inc. v. Millennium Music, LP, 33 F.Supp.2d 907 (D.Or.1999), in which the district court declined to exercise specific jurisdiction over a nonresident defendant based on the sale of one compact disc into the forum because the record demonstrated that an acquaintance of plaintiff's counsel instructed a third party to purchase the disc from the defendants. The Court finds Millennium Enterprises distinguishable from this case because defendants have provided no evidence that plaintiffs instructed Mr. Aubert to contact defendants. Moreover, even if plaintiffs had done so, plaintiffs could not have predicted that defendants would respond by defaming them. Finally, as noted above, although Mr. Aubert arguably initiated the first telephone call, Mr. Simon sent allegedly defamatory e-mails to Mr. Aubert thereafter. Accordingly, the Court rejects Mr. Simon's "jurisdictional entrapment" defense and concludes that sufficient contacts exist to exercise personal jurisdiction over Mr. Simon.

When a cause of action does not arise out of a nonresident defendant's purposeful contacts with the forum state, due process requires continuous and systematic contacts between the defendant and the forum before jurisdiction over the defendant can be exercised. Accordingly, the Court must analyze Mr. Spence's contacts with Louisiana to determine if they are sufficient to justify the exercise of general personal jurisdiction. Plaintiffs argue that this Court has general personal jurisdiction over Mr. Spence because of his extensive Internet website and his advertising in a national trade magazine. However, plaintiffs offer no evidence to contradict defendant's assertion that the website at issue is maintained by Spence Vintage Autographs, and not by Mr. Spence individually. In addition, plaintiffs have provided a copy of the advertisement on which they rely to assert general jurisdiction over Mr. Spence. The advertisement is clearly for Spence Vintage Autographs. Accordingly, the Court rejects plaintiffs' argument that general personal jurisdiction exists over Mr. Spence based on the website and national advertising of his company. The Court further agrees with Mr. Spence that two sales to Louisiana residents in 1995 and a personal visit to Louisiana for one night in 1991 do not constitute "continuous and systematic" contacts with the forum. Mr. Spence has never owned, leased, rented or controlled any real or personal property in Louisiana; maintained a bank account or paid taxes in Louisiana; maintained a business or an office in Louisiana; or had a mailing address, employees or an agent for service of process in Louisiana.

[margin note: Why Spence not P.J.]

Under the second prong of the due process analysis, the Court must determine whether the exercise of personal jurisdiction over a nonresident defendant comports with "traditional notions of fair play and substantial justice." The fairness factors considered by the court include: (1) the defendant's burden; (2) the forum state's interest; (3) the plaintiff's interest in convenient and effective relief; (4) the judicial system's interest in efficient resolution of controversies; and (5) the state's shared interest in furthering fundamental social policies. "When minimum contacts have been established, often the interests of the plaintiff and the forum in the exercise of jurisdiction will justify even the serious burdens placed on the alien defendant." Asahi * * *. The defendant must present a compelling case that conducting the litigation in this court would be so gravely difficult and inconvenient that he would be at a severe disadvantage in comparison to plaintiffs.

[margin note: Fairness Factors]

Here, the Court has found that sufficient minimum contacts exist to exercise personal jurisdiction over Mr. Simon in Louisiana. Mr. Simon asserts that it would nevertheless offend traditional notions of fair play and substantial justice to compel him to defend this suit in Louisiana because plaintiffs, the injured parties, do not live in Louisiana. Defendant also maintains that forcing him to litigate this action in Louisiana would be overly burdensome to him and any witnesses as, with the exception of Mr. Aubert, all of the witnesses, parties, and documents related to this case are located in Califor-

[margin note: Simon Argument of unfairness]

nia, New York, and Pennsylvania. The Court recognizes that Louisiana's interest in this dispute is considerably diminished by the fact that plaintiffs are not Louisiana residents. Nevertheless, the effect of the tortious activity was felt here, and Louisiana law applies. Moreover, the Supreme Court has held in the context of a libel action that "plaintiff's residence in the forum State is not a separate requirement, and lack of residence will not defeat jurisdiction established on the basis of defendant's contacts.... There is no justification for restricting libel actions to the plaintiff's home forum." Finally, although other witnesses may be located outside the forum state, the principal witness in this litigation is Mr. Aubert, a Louisiana resident. Mr. Simon has not shown that he would suffer a great burden by litigating this case in Louisiana. Weighing all of these factors, the Court is not persuaded that exercising jurisdiction over Mr. Simon would violate due process.

For the foregoing reasons, the Court grants defendants' motion to dismiss Mr. Spence from this action but denies the motion to dismiss with regard to Mr. Simon.

THE INTERNET

The size of the Internet is difficult to estimate accurately, but it is indisputable that it has grown exponentially in the past ten years. In 1989, approximately 90,000 computers were connected to the Internet; by 1996, over 9,400,000 computers worldwide were estimated to be connected, and that number has grown. The number is now estimated to be over 200 million Internet users, and these numbers do not include personal computers used to access the Internet through modems. Perhaps the most far-reaching aspect of this development is the growth of e-commerce, or businesses operating on the Internet. Unlike newspaper, mail, radio, television, and other media containing advertisements and solicitations, most Internet businesses are not directed at a specific geographic area or market; to the contrary, they target all users of the Internet. At times the courts have found that attempting to apply established notions of personal jurisdiction in the fast-developing world of the Internet is "somewhat like trying to board a moving bus." See Millennium Enterprises, Inc. v. Millennium Music, LP, 33 F.Supp.2d 907, 916 (D.Or. 1999).

One of the first cases to deal with the question of personal jurisdiction and the Internet was INSET SYSTEMS, INC. v. INSTRUCTION SET, INC., 937 F.Supp. 161 (D.Conn.1996), in which the court found that an Internet website advertisement operated by a nonresident, although not directed at any state in particular, was sufficient to establish personal jurisdiction in Connecticut under the purposeful availment test. Since that time courts have been reluctant to find jurisdiction based solely on the existence of website advertisements. In CYBERSELL, INC. v. CYBERSELL, INC., 130 F.3d 414, 418 (9th Cir.1997), the court held that "something more" than the mere maintenance of a website is required to show that the defendant purposefully directed its activities at the forum. See also Bensusan Restaurant Corp. v. King, 937 F.Supp. 295 (S.D.N.Y.1996), affirmed 126 F.3d 25 (2d Cir.1997). In ZIPPO MFG. CO. v. ZIPPO DOT COM, INC., 952 F.Supp. 1119, 1124 (W.D.Pa.1997) the court articulated what has become known as the "sliding scale" test, under which "the likelihood that personal jurisdiction can be constitutionally exercised is directly proportionate to the nature and quality of commercial activity that an entity conducts over the Internet." At one end of this scale are defendants that conduct business over the Internet with residents of a particular forum through what are called "active" websites; in those situations the assertion of jurisdiction is almost always proper. At the other end are websites that do little more than make information available to those who are interested. These "passive" sites rarely are grounds for the assertion of personal jurisdiction. The debate is over the middle ground, so-called "interactive" websites, that permit a user to exchange information with a host computer. It is in these cases that the sliding scale becomes relevant.

Courts have reached differing conclusions in cases that fall into this middle "interactive" category. One commentator noted that, "the current hodgepodge of case law is inconsistent, irrational, and irreconcilable." Stravitz, *Personal Jurisdiction in Cyberspace: Something More is Required on the Electronic Stream of Commerce*, 49 S.C.L.Rev. 925, 939 (1998). Some courts find that an interactive website alone is sufficient to establish minimum contacts; others require additional non-Internet activity in the forum, regardless of whether the activity is related to the underlying claim. Millenium Enterprises, Inc. v. Millenium Music, LP, 33 F.Supp.2d at 917. Finally, some courts have required additional conduct in the forum that is related to the plaintiff's cause of action. Id. The Supreme Court has yet to consider the issue of personal jurisdiction based upon Internet contacts. The confusion on this subject likely will continue until the Court does so.

Many commentators believe that the "sliding scale" approach adopted in *Zippo* best addresses the unique questions raised by Internet contacts. The *Zippo* court's approach has been followed or cited with approval by at least three federal courts of appeal. See Soma Medical Int'l v. Standard Chartered Bank, 196 F.3d 1292, 1296 (10th Cir.1999); Mink v. AAAA Dev. LLC, 190 F.3d 333, 336 (5th Cir.1999); Cybersell, Inc. v. Cybersell, Inc., 130 F.3d 414, 419 (9th Cir.1997). Numerous federal district courts also have accepted this approach. See, e.g., Roche v. Worldwide Media, Inc., 90 F.Supp.2d 714 (E.D.Va.2000).

Other commentators suggest that ordinary principles of real-space jurisdiction can and should be applied to cyberspace, advocating a narrow application of the traditional purposeful-availment test to the Internet. See Burk, *Jurisdiction in a World Without Borders*, 1 Va. J.L. & Tech. 3, 44–53, 61 (1997); Case Note, 113 Harv.L.Rev. 2128 (2000). Others suggest courts should abandon both the traditional purposeful-availment test, as well as the recently developed "sliding scale" approach, for methods that specifically are tailored to address the unique personal jurisdiction problems created by the rise of the Internet. See Johnson & Post, *Law and Borders: The Rise of Law in Cyberspace*, 48 Stan.L.Rev. 1367, 1367 (1996) (arguing that the Internet is a self regulating community in which the users should decide on the laws that will apply to them); Perritt, *Jurisdiction in Cyberspace*, 41 Villa.L.Rev. 1, 100–03 (1996) (proposing creation of a new federal court with jurisdiction over cyberspace activities).

Notes and Questions

1. Which approach seems best suited for the jurisdictional challenges raised by the continuing expansion of the Internet? Is it clear that the Internet presents questions that cannot be solved within the existing doctrinal framework of *International Shoe* and its progeny?

2. Critics of the "sliding scale" approach adopted by the *Zippo* court suggest that it requires a case-by-case determination of interactivity, and accordingly cannot establish meaningful precedent. See Case Note, 113 Harv.L.Rev. 2128 (2000). They fear that, "a website operator whose site falls into this potentially vast middle ground would have difficulty knowing in advance of a lawsuit whether a court would define its site as 'interactive' and thereby subject to jurisdiction." Id. at 2133. Do these fears seem justified? Is this kind of fact-specific inquiry substantially different from the inquiry already being made using the purposeful availment test in deciding traditional personal jurisdiction questions?

3. In *Millenium*, which is discussed in *Bellino*, the court suggested that the category of Internet contacts described as "interactive" in *Zippo* needed to be refined to include a fundamental requirement of personal jurisdiction: "deliberate action" directed at the residents of the forum. Would this combination of the traditional jurisdictional test with the "sliding scale" approach address the concerns of those who fear the *Zippo* approach is too inclusive? Is it possible that the *Zippo* court had assumed that the traditional personal jurisdiction inquiries would be made in addition to the use of the "sliding scale"? Is that what the court meant in GTE NEW MEDIA SERV., INC. v. BELLSOUTH CORP., 199 F.3d 1343, 1350 (D.C.Cir.2000) by stating: "We do not believe that the advent of advanced technology * * * should vitiate long-held and inviolate principles of federal court jurisdiction," or is it suggesting that the sliding scale is unnecessary?

4. How do e-mail, facsimile transmissions, and telephone calls fit into this discussion? Should they be governed by the same standard as Internet websites? Is this what the court was saying in *GTE* when it suggested that the use of the Internet in that case was no different than making a telephone call or looking something up in the yellow pages?

5. Could an e-mail, fax, or telephone call directed at a resident within a forum state be sufficient to establish personal jurisdiction over a nonresident sender? Should a court approach each of these communications with the same jurisdictional standard? What about foreign websites that can be reached from the United States? What standard should be used in determining whether their operators are subject to personal jurisdiction within the United States?

6. How should courts treat noncommercial Internet uses for purposes of determining whether to exercise personal jurisdiction? See Barrett v. Catacombs Press, 44 F.Supp.2d 717 (E.D.Pa.1999), for an interesting discussion of this topic.

SECTION G. JURISDICTION BASED UPON POWER OVER PROPERTY

Reread Pennoyer v. Neff, p. 62, supra.

TYLER v. JUDGES OF THE COURT OF REGISTRATION, 175 Mass. 71, 55 N.E. 812 (1900), writ of error dismissed 179 U.S. 405, 21 S.Ct. 206, 45

L.Ed. 252 (1900). Petitioner sought a writ of prohibition against the judges of the Court of Registration to prevent their passing upon an application to register title to a parcel of land in which petitioner claimed an interest. The basis of the petition was that the act establishing the court violated due process because it deprived all persons except the registered owner of any interest in the land, and it provided for insufficient notice to persons having adverse claims.

The statute in question established a procedure and court for registering and confirming titles to land. It provided that the decree of registration "shall bind the land and quiet the title thereto," and "shall be conclusive upon and against all persons" whether named in the proceedings or not. It further required that notice of the proposed registration be published in a newspaper, posted on the land, and mailed to adjoining owners and all persons known to have an adverse interest. Chief Justice Holmes, writing for the majority, denied the petition and upheld the act as constitutional, but cautioned that it ought to be amended to insure actual notice:

> If it does not satisfy the constitution, a judicial proceeding to clear titles against all the world hardly is possible; for the very meaning of such a proceeding is to get rid of unknown as well as known claims,—indeed, certainty against the unknown may be said to be its chief end,—and unknown claims cannot be dealt with by personal service upon the claimant. * * *

> Looked at either from the point of view of history or of the necessary requirements of justice, a proceeding in rem, dealing with a tangible res, may be instituted and carried to judgment without personal service upon claimants within the state, or notice by name to those outside of it, and not encounter any provision of either constitution. Jurisdiction is secured by the power of the court over the res. * * *

> But it is said that this is not a proceeding "in rem." It is certain that no phrase has been more misused. * * * If the technical object of the suit is to establish a claim against some particular person, with a judgment which generally in theory, at least, binds his body, or to bar some individual claim or objection, so that only certain persons are entitled to be heard in defense, the action is in personam, although it may concern the right to, or possession of, a tangible thing. * * * If, on the other hand, the object is to bar indifferently all who might be minded to make an objection of any sort against the right sought to be established, and if any one in the world has a right to be heard on the strength of alleging facts which, if true, show an inconsistent interest, the proceeding is in rem. * * * All proceedings, like all rights, are really against persons. Whether they are proceedings or rights in rem depends on the number of persons affected. Hence the res need not be personified, and made a party defendant * * *. It need not even be a tangible thing at all * * *. Personification and naming the res as defendant are mere symbols, not the essential matter. They are fictions, conveniently expressing the nature of the process and the result; nothing more. * * *

Id. at 73, 75–76, 55 N.E. at 813–14.

———

PENNINGTON v. FOURTH NATIONAL BANK, 243 U.S. 269, 271–72, 37 S.Ct. 282, 282–83, 61 L.Ed. 713 (1917):

The 14th Amendment did not, in guarantying due process of law, abridge the jurisdiction which a state possessed over property within its borders, regardless of the residence or presence of the owner. That jurisdiction extends alike to tangible and to intangible property. Indebtedness due from a resident to a nonresident—of which bank deposits are an example—is property within the state. * * * It is, indeed, the species of property which courts of the several states have most frequently applied in satisfaction of the obligations of absent debtors. * * * Substituted service on a nonresident by publication furnishes no legal basis for a judgment in personam. * * * But garnishment or foreign attachment is a proceeding quasi in rem. * * * The thing belonging to the absent defendant is seized and applied to the satisfaction of his obligation. The Federal Constitution presents no obstacle to the full exercise of this power.

* * * The power of the state to proceed against the property of an absent defendant is the same whether the obligation sought to be enforced is an admitted indebtedness or a contested claim. * * * It is likewise immaterial that the claim is, at the commencement of the suit, inchoate, to be perfected only by time or the action of the court. The only essentials to the exercise of the state's power are presence of the res within its borders, its seizure at the commencement of proceedings, and the opportunity of the owner to be heard.

Notes and Questions

1. What is the situs of corporate stock for purposes of attachment—the corporation's place of incorporation, the domicile of the shareholder, or the state in which the stock certificates actually are located? See generally Note, *Attachment of Corporate Stock: The Conflicting Approaches of Delaware and the Uniform Stock Transfer Act*, 73 Harv.L.Rev. 1579 (1960).

2. Prior to 1963, the federal courts had no general original quasi-in-rem jurisdiction. This was a curious limitation since the federal courts permitted the removal of actions initially commenced in a state court by attachment. See Rorick v. Devon Syndicate, Ltd., 307 U.S. 299, 59 S.Ct. 877, 83 L.Ed. 1303 (1939). In 1963 this inconsistency was eliminated by the amendment of Federal Rule 4. Full discussions of this topic are found in Carrington, *The Modern Utility of Quasi in Rem Jurisdiction*, 76 Harv.L.Rev. 303 (1962); Currie, *Attachment and Garnishment in the Federal Courts*, 59 Mich.L.Rev. 337 (1961). See also 4A Wright & Miller, *Federal Practice and Procedure: Civil 3d* §§ 1119–23 (1987) (2001).

Quasi-in-rem jurisdiction in the federal courts also is specifically provided for in 28 U.S.C. § 1655 in connection with certain types of claims to land when defendant cannot be served personally within the state. See Blume, *Actions Quasi in Rem Under Section 1655, Title 28, U.S.C.*, 50 Mich.L.Rev. 1 (1951).

———

HARRIS v. BALK, 198 U.S. 215, 25 S.Ct. 625, 49 L.Ed. 1023 (1905). Harris, a citizen of North Carolina, owed Balk, also of North Carolina, $180. Epstein, a Maryland citizen, claimed that Balk owed him $344. On August 6, 1896, while Harris was visiting Baltimore, Epstein instituted a garnishee proceeding in a Maryland court, attaching the debt due Balk from Harris. Harris was personally served with the writ of attachment and summons, and notice of the suit was posted at the courthouse door, as required by Maryland law. Harris consented to the entry of judgment against him and paid the $180 to Epstein. On August 11, 1896, Balk commenced an action against Harris in a North Carolina court to recover the $180. Harris asserted that he no longer owed Balk the $180, having paid that sum to Epstein in partial satisfaction of Balk's debt to Epstein, since the Maryland judgment and his payment thereof was valid in Maryland, and was therefore entitled to full faith and credit in the courts of North Carolina. The trial court ruled in favor of Balk and the North Carolina Supreme Court affirmed on the ground that the Maryland court had no jurisdiction over Harris to attach the debt because Harris was only temporarily in the state, and the situs of the debt was in North Carolina. The Supreme Court reversed:

> * * * We do not see how the question of jurisdiction *vel non* can properly be made to depend upon the so-called original situs of the debt, or upon the character of the stay of the garnishee, whether temporary or permanent, in the state where the attachment is issued. Power over the person of the garnishee confers jurisdiction on the courts of the state where the writ issues. * * * If, while temporarily there, his creditor might sue him there and recover the debt, then he is liable to process of garnishment, no matter where the situs of the debt was originally. We do not see the materiality of the expression "situs of the debt," when used in connection with attachment proceedings. If by situs is meant the place of the creation of the debt, that fact is immaterial. If it be meant that the obligation to pay the debt can only be enforced at the situs thus fixed, we think it plainly untrue. The obligation of the debtor to pay his debt clings to and accompanies him wherever he goes. He is as much bound to pay his debt in a foreign state when therein sued upon his obligation by his creditor, as he was in the state where the debt was contracted. * * * It would be no defense to such suit for the debtor to plead that he was only in the foreign state casually or temporarily. * * * It is nothing but the obligation to pay which is garnished or attached. This obligation can be enforced by the courts of the foreign state after personal service of process therein, just as well as by the courts of the domicil of the debtor. * * *

Id. at 222, 25 S.Ct. at 626, 49 L.Ed. at 1026. The Court indicated in dictum that the result might have been different if Balk had not been given notice of the attachment and an opportunity to defend in the Maryland action.

Notes and Questions

1. Professor Lowenfeld provides the following interesting information concerning Harris, Balk, and Epstein. Epstein was an importer of goods who regularly did business with Balk, a retailer. The $344 debt was for money owed on shipments of goods by Epstein to Balk. Harris was a dry goods merchant from the same town as Balk, and had borrowed money from Balk on several occasions, including a $10 loan just before the fateful trip to Baltimore. Harris carried with him on that trip a message from Balk to Epstein saying that Balk would be coming to Baltimore soon. Lowenfeld, *In Search of the Intangible: A Comment on Shaffer v. Heitner*, 53 N.Y.U.L.Rev. 102, 104–06 (1978).

If this case were to occur today, could Epstein have sued Balk in personam, assuming a long-arm statute similar to Rhode Island's? Could Epstein have served Harris as Balk's agent?

2. For purposes of determining whether or not quasi-in-rem jurisdiction may be asserted, does it matter why Harris was in Baltimore? Consider the following variations on what actually happened:

(a) Balk sends Harris into Maryland to conduct some business for him.

(b) Harris goes into Maryland with Balk's knowledge, but to do business unrelated to Balk.

(c) Harris goes into Maryland without Balk's knowledge.

(d) Harris goes to Maryland at Epstein's request who promised Harris "it'll be worth your while."

SHAFFER v. HEITNER

Supreme Court of the United States, 1977.
433 U.S. 186, 97 S.Ct. 2569, 53 L.Ed.2d 683.

On Appeal from the Supreme Court of Delaware.

MR. JUSTICE MARSHALL delivered the opinion of the Court.

* * *

I

Appellee Heitner, a nonresident of Delaware, is the owner of one share of stock in the Greyhound Corp., a business incorporated under the laws of Delaware with its principal place of business in Phoenix, Ariz. On May 22, 1974, he filed a shareholder's derivative suit in the Court of Chancery for New Castle County, Del., in which he named as defendants Greyhound, its wholly owned subsidiary Greyhound Lines, Inc.,[1] and 28 present or former officers or directors of one or both of the corporations. In essence, Heitner alleged that the individual defendants had violated their duties to Greyhound by causing it and its subsidiary to engage in actions that resulted in the corporations being held liable for substantial damages in a private antitrust suit and a large fine in a criminal contempt action. The activities which led to these penalties took place in Oregon.

Simultaneously with his complaint, Heitner filed a motion for an order of sequestration of the Delaware property of the individual defendants pursuant to Del.Code Ann., Tit. 10, § 366 (1975). This motion was accompanied by a supporting affidavit of counsel which stated that the individual defendants were nonresidents of Delaware. The affidavit identified the property to be sequestered as [shares of Greyhound Corporation stock and stock options] * * *. The requested sequestration order was signed the day the motion was filed. Pursuant to that order, the sequestrator "seized" approximately 82,000 shares of Greyhound common stock belonging to 19 of the defendants, and options belonging to another 2 defendants. These seizures were accomplished by placing "stop transfer" orders or their equivalents on the books of the

1. Greyhound Lines, Inc., is incorporated in California and has its principal place of business in Phoenix, Ariz.

Greyhound Corp. So far as the record shows, none of the certificates representing the seized property was physically present in Delaware. The stock was considered to be in Delaware, and so subject to seizure, by virtue of Del.Code Ann., Tit. 8, § 169 (1975), which makes Delaware the situs of ownership of all stock in Delaware corporations.

All 28 defendants were notified of the initiation of the suit by certified mail directed to their last known addresses and by publication in a New Castle County newspaper. The 21 defendants whose property was seized (hereafter referred to as appellants) responded by entering a special appearance for the purpose of moving to quash service of process and to vacate the sequestration order. They contended that the *ex parte* sequestration procedure did not accord them due process of law and that the property seized was not capable of attachment in Delaware. In addition, appellants asserted that under the rule of International Shoe Co. v. Washington * * *, they did not have sufficient contacts with Delaware to sustain the jurisdiction of that State's courts.

The Court of Chancery rejected these arguments * * *.

On appeal, the Delaware Supreme Court affirmed the judgment of the Court of Chancery. * * * Most of the Supreme Court's opinion was devoted to rejecting appellants' contention that the sequestration procedure is inconsistent with the due process analysis developed in the *Sniadach* [v. Family Finance Corp., 395 U.S. 337, 89 S.Ct. 1820, 23 L.Ed.2d 349 (1969), Note 1, p. 237, infra] line of cases. The court based its rejection of that argument in part on its agreement with the Court of Chancery that the purpose of the sequestration procedure is to compel the appearance of the defendant, a purpose not involved in the *Sniadach* cases. The court also relied on what it considered the ancient origins of the sequestration procedure and approval of that procedure in the opinions of this Court,[10] Delaware's interest in asserting jurisdiction to adjudicate claims of mismanagement of a Delaware corporation, and the safeguards for defendants that it found in the Delaware statute. * * *

* * *

Appellants' claim that the Delaware courts did not have jurisdiction to adjudicate this action received much more cursory treatment. * * *[12] We reverse.

II

The Delaware courts rejected appellants' jurisdictional challenge by noting that this suit was brought as a *quasi in rem* proceeding. Since *quasi in rem* jurisdiction is traditionally based on attachment or seizure of property present in the jurisdiction, not on contacts between the defendant and the State, the courts considered appellants' claimed lack of contacts with Dela-

---

10. The court relied * * * on our decision in Ownbey v. Morgan, 256 U.S. 94, 41 S.Ct. 433, 65 L.Ed. 837 (1921) * * *. The only question before the Court in *Ownbey* was the constitutionality of a requirement that a defendant whose property has been attached file a bond before entering an appearance. We do not read the recent references to *Ownbey* as necessarily suggesting that *Ownbey* is consistent with more recent decisions interpreting the Due Process Clause.

12. Under Delaware law, defendants whose property has been sequestered must enter a general appearance, thus subjecting themselves to *in personam* liability, before they can defend on the merits. * * *

ware to be unimportant. This categorical analysis assumes the continued soundness of the conceptual structure founded on the century-old case of Pennoyer v. Neff * * *.

[The Court's description of *Pennoyer* is omitted.] * * *

From our perspective, the importance of *Pennoyer* is not its result, but the fact that its principles and corollaries derived from them became the basic elements of the constitutional doctrine governing state-court jurisdiction. * * * As we have noted, under *Pennoyer* state authority to adjudicate was based on the jurisdiction's power over either persons or property. This fundamental concept is embodied in the very vocabulary which we use to describe judgments. If a court's jurisdiction is based on its authority over the defendant's person, the action and judgment are denominated *"in personam"* and can impose a personal obligation on the defendant in favor of the plaintiff. If jurisdiction is based on the court's power over property within its territory, the action is called *"in rem"* or *"quasi in rem."* The effect of a judgment in such a case is limited to the property that supports jurisdiction and does not impose a personal liability on the property owner, since he is not before the court.[17] In *Pennoyer*'s terms, the owner is affected only "indirectly" by an *in rem* judgment adverse to his interest in the property subject to the court's disposition.

[Justice Marshall's historical analysis of the expansion of in personam jurisdiction is omitted.] * * *

No equally dramatic change has occurred in the law governing jurisdiction *in rem*. There have, however, been intimations that the collapse of the *in personam* wing of *Pennoyer* has not left that decision unweakened as a foundation for *in rem* jurisdiction. Well-reasoned lower court opinions have questioned the proposition that the presence of property in a State gives that State jurisdiction to adjudicate rights to the property regardless of the relationship of the underlying dispute and the property owner to the forum. * * * The overwhelming majority of commentators have also rejected *Pennoyer*'s premise that a proceeding "against" property is not a proceeding against the owners of that property. Accordingly, they urge that the "traditional notions of fair play and substantial justice" that govern a State's power to adjudicate *in personam* should also govern its power to adjudicate personal rights to property located in the State. * * *

Although this Court has not addressed this argument directly, we have held that property cannot be subjected to a court's judgment unless reasonable and appropriate efforts have been made to give the property owners actual notice of the action. * * * Mullane v. Central Hanover Bank & Trust Co., 339 U.S. 306 (1950) [p. 191, infra]. This conclusion recognizes, contrary to *Pennoyer,* that an adverse judgment *in rem* directly affects the property

---

17. "A judgment *in rem* affects the interest of all persons in designated property. A judgment *quasi in rem* affects the interests of particular persons in designated property. The latter is of two types. In one the plaintiff is seeking to secure a pre-existing claim in the subject property and to extinguish or establish the non-existence of similar interests of particular persons. In the other the plaintiff seeks to apply what he concedes to be the property of the defendant to the satisfaction of a claim against him. Restatement, Judgments, 5–9." Hanson v. Denckla, 357 U.S. 235, 246 n. 12, 78 S.Ct. 1228, 1235, 2 L.Ed.2d 1283 (1958).

As did the Court in *Hanson,* we will for convenience generally use the term *"in rem"* in place of *"in rem* and *quasi in rem."*

owner by divesting him of his rights in the property before the court. * * * Moreover, in *Mullane* we held that Fourteenth Amendment rights cannot depend on the classification of an action as *in rem* or *in personam* * * *.

It is clear, therefore, that the law of state-court jurisdiction no longer stands securely on the foundation established in *Pennoyer*. We think that the time is ripe to consider whether the standard of fairness and substantial justice set forth in *International Shoe* should be held to govern actions *in rem* as well as *in personam*.

III

The case for applying to jurisdiction *in rem* the same test of "fair play and substantial justice" as governs assertions of jurisdiction *in personam* is simple and straightforward. It is premised on recognition that "[t]he phrase, 'judicial jurisdiction over a thing', is a customary elliptical way of referring to jurisdiction over the interests of persons in a thing." Restatement (Second) of Conflict of Laws § 56, Introductory Note * * *. This recognition leads to the conclusion that in order to justify an exercise of jurisdiction *in rem*, the basis for jurisdiction must be sufficient to justify exercising "jurisdiction over the interests of persons in a thing." The standard for determining whether an exercise of jurisdiction over the interests of persons is consistent with the Due Process Clause is the minimum-contacts standard elucidated in *International Shoe*.

This argument, of course, does not ignore the fact that the presence of property in a State may bear on the existence of jurisdiction by providing contacts among the forum State, the defendant, and the litigation. For example, when claims to the property itself are the source of the underlying controversy between the plaintiff and the defendant, it would be unusual for the State where the property is located not to have jurisdiction. In such cases, the defendant's claim to property located in the State would normally indicate that he expected to benefit from the State's protection of his interest. The State's strong interests in assuring the marketability of property within its borders and in providing a procedure for peaceful resolution of disputes about the possession of that property would also support jurisdiction, as would the likelihood that important records and witnesses will be found in the State. The presence of property may also favor jurisdiction in cases, such as suits for injury suffered on the land of an absentee owner, where the defendant's ownership of the property is conceded but the cause of action is otherwise related to rights and duties growing out of that ownership.

It appears, therefore, that jurisdiction over many types of actions which now are or might be brought *in rem* would not be affected by a holding that any assertion of state-court jurisdiction must satisfy the *International Shoe* standard. For the type of *quasi in rem* action typified by Harris v. Balk and the present case, however, accepting the proposed analysis would result in significant change. These are cases where the property which now serves as the basis for state-court jurisdiction is completely unrelated to the plaintiff's cause of action. Thus, although the presence of the defendant's property in a State might suggest the existence of other ties among the defendant, the State, and the litigation, the presence of the property alone would not support the State's jurisdiction. If those other ties did not exist, cases over which the State is now thought to have jurisdiction could not be brought in that forum.

Since acceptance of the *International Shoe* test would most affect this class of cases, we examine the arguments against adopting that standard as they relate to this category of litigation. Before doing so, however, we note that this type of case also presents the clearest illustration of the argument in favor of assessing assertions of jurisdiction by a single standard. For in cases such as *Harris* and this one, the only role played by the property is to provide the basis for bringing the defendant into court. Indeed, the express purpose of the Delaware sequestration procedure is to compel the defendant to enter a personal appearance. In such cases, if a direct assertion of personal jurisdiction over the defendant would violate the Constitution, it would seem that an indirect assertion of that jurisdiction should be equally impermissible.

The primary rationale for treating the presence of property as a sufficient basis for jurisdiction to adjudicate claims over which the State would not have jurisdiction if *International Shoe* applied is that a wrongdoer

> should not be able to avoid payment of his obligations by the expedient of removing his assets to a place where he is not subject to an in personam suit. Restatement [(Second) of Conflicts] § 66, Comment a.

* * * This justification, however, does not explain why jurisdiction should be recognized without regard to whether the property is present in the State because of an effort to avoid the owner's obligations. Nor does it support jurisdiction to adjudicate the underlying claim. At most, it suggests that a State in which property is located should have jurisdiction to attach that property, by use of proper procedures, as security for a judgment being sought in a forum where the litigation can be maintained consistently with *International Shoe*. * * * Moreover, we know of nothing to justify the assumption that a debtor can avoid paying his obligations by removing his property to a State in which his creditor cannot obtain personal jurisdiction over him. The Full Faith and Credit Clause, after all, makes the valid *in personam* judgment of one State enforceable in all other States.

It might also be suggested that allowing *in rem* jurisdiction avoids the uncertainty inherent in the *International Shoe* standard and assures a plaintiff of a forum.[37] * * * We believe, however, that the fairness standard of *International Shoe* can be easily applied in the vast majority of cases. Moreover, when the existence of jurisdiction in a particular forum under *International Shoe* is unclear, the cost of simplifying the litigation by avoiding the jurisdictional question may be the sacrifice of "fair play and substantial justice." That cost is too high.

We are left, then, to consider the significance of the long history of jurisdiction based solely on the presence of property in a State. Although the theory that territorial power is both essential to and sufficient for jurisdiction has been undermined, we have never held that the presence of property in a State does not automatically confer jurisdiction over the owner's interest in that property. This history must be considered as supporting the proposition

37. This case does not raise, and we therefore do not consider, the question whether the presence of a defendant's property in a State is   a sufficient basis for jurisdiction when no other forum is available to the plaintiff.

that jurisdiction based solely on the presence of property satisfies the demands of due process * * *, but it is not decisive. * * * The fiction that an assertion of jurisdiction over property is anything but an assertion of jurisdiction over the owner of the property supports an ancient form without substantial modern justification. Its continued acceptance would serve only to allow state-court jurisdiction that is fundamentally unfair to the defendant.

We therefore conclude that all assertions of state-court jurisdiction must be evaluated according to the standards set forth in *International Shoe* and its progeny.

IV

The Delaware courts based their assertion of jurisdiction in this case solely on the statutory presence of appellants' property in Delaware. Yet that property is not the subject matter of this litigation, nor is the underlying cause of action related to the property. Appellants' holdings in Greyhound do not, therefore, provide contacts with Delaware sufficient to support the jurisdiction of that State's courts over appellants. If it exists, that jurisdiction must have some other foundation.[40]

Appellee Heitner did not allege and does not now claim that appellants have ever set foot in Delaware. Nor does he identify any act related to his cause of action as having taken place in Delaware. Nevertheless, he contends that appellants' positions as directors and officers of a corporation chartered in Delaware provide sufficient "contacts, ties, or relations" * * * with that State to give its courts jurisdiction over appellants in this stockholder's derivative action. This argument is based primarily on what Heitner asserts to be the strong interest of Delaware in supervising the management of a Delaware corporation. That interest is said to derive from the role of Delaware law in establishing the corporation and defining the obligations owed to it by its officers and directors. In order to protect this interest, appellee concludes, Delaware's courts must have jurisdiction over corporate fiduciaries such as appellants.

This argument is undercut by the failure of the Delaware Legislature to assert the state interest appellee finds so compelling. Delaware law bases jurisdiction, not on appellants' status as corporate fiduciaries, but rather on the presence of their property in the State. Although the sequestration procedure used here may be most frequently used in derivative suits against officers and directors, * * * the authorizing statute evinces no specific concern with such actions. Sequestration can be used in any suit against a nonresident * * * and reaches corporate fiduciaries only if they happen to

---

40. Appellants argue that our determination that the minimum contacts standard of *International Shoe* governs jurisdiction here makes unnecessary any consideration of the existence of such contacts. * * * They point out that they were never personally served with a summons, that Delaware has no long-arm statute which would authorize such service, and that the Delaware Supreme Court has authoritatively held that the existence of contacts is irrelevant to jurisdiction under Del. Code Ann., Tit. 10, § 366 (1975). As part of its sequestration order, however, the Court of

Chancery directed its clerk to send each appellant a copy of the summons and complaint by certified mail. The record indicates that those mailings were made and contains return receipts from at least 19 of the appellants. None of the appellants has suggested that he did not actually receive the summons which was directed to him in compliance with a Delaware statute designed to provide jurisdiction over non-residents. In these circumstances, we will assume that the procedures followed would be sufficient to bring appellants before the Delaware courts, if minimum contacts existed.

own interests in a Delaware corporation, or other property in the State. But as Heitner's failure to secure jurisdiction over seven of the defendants named in his complaint demonstrates, there is no necessary relationship between holding a position as a corporate fiduciary and owning stock or other interests in the corporation. If Delaware perceived its interest in securing jurisdiction over corporate fiduciaries to be as great as Heitner suggests, we would expect it to have enacted a statute more clearly designed to protect that interest.

Moreover, even if Heitner's assessment of the importance of Delaware's interest is accepted, his argument fails to demonstrate that Delaware is a fair forum for this litigation. The interest appellee has identified may support the application of Delaware law to resolve any controversy over appellants' actions in their capacities as officers and directors. But we have rejected the argument that if a State's law can properly be applied to a dispute, its courts necessarily have jurisdiction over the parties to that dispute. * * *

Appellee suggests that by accepting positions as officers or directors of a Delaware corporation, appellants performed the acts [sufficient to justify the assertion of jurisdiction by Delaware courts under] Hanson v. Denckla. He notes that Delaware law provides substantial benefits to corporate officers and directors, and that these benefits were at least in part the incentive for appellants to assume their positions. It is, he says, "only fair and just" to require appellants, in return for these benefits, to respond in the State of Delaware when they are accused of misusing their power. * * *

But like Heitner's first argument, this line of reasoning establishes only that it is appropriate for Delaware law to govern the obligations of appellants to Greyhound and its stockholders. It does not demonstrate that appellants have "purposefully avail[ed themselves] of the privilege of conducting activities within the forum State," Hanson v. Denckla * * *, in a way that would justify bringing them before a Delaware tribunal. Appellants have simply had nothing to do with the State of Delaware. Moreover, appellants had no reason to expect to be haled before a Delaware court. Delaware, unlike some States, has not enacted a statute that treats acceptance of a directorship as consent to jurisdiction in the State. And "[i]t strains reason * * * to suggest that anyone buying securities in a corporation formed in Delaware 'impliedly consents' to subject himself to Delaware's * * * jurisdiction on any cause of action." Folk & Moyer, [*Sequestration in Delaware: A Constitutional Analysis,* 73 Colum.L.Rev. 749, 785 (1973)] * * *. Appellants, who were not required to acquire interests in Greyhound in order to hold their positions, did not by acquiring those interests surrender their right to be brought to judgment only in States with which they had had "minimum contacts."

* * * Delaware's assertion of jurisdiction over appellants in this case is inconsistent with that constitutional limitation on state power. The judgment of the Delaware Supreme Court must, therefore, be reversed.

It is so ordered.

MR. JUSTICE REHNQUIST took no part in the consideration or decision of this case.

MR. JUSTICE POWELL, concurring.

* * *

I would explicitly reserve judgment * * * on whether the ownership of some forms of property whose situs is indisputably and permanently located within a State may, without more, provide the contacts necessary to subject a defendant to jurisdiction within the State to the extent of the value of the property. In the case of real property, in particular, preservation of the common law concept of *quasi in rem* jurisdiction arguably would avoid the uncertainty of the general *International Shoe* standard without significant cost to " 'traditional notions of fair play and substantial justice.' " * * *

Subject to the foregoing reservation, I join the opinion of the Court.

MR. JUSTICE STEVENS, concurring in the judgment.

* * *

One who purchases shares of stock on the open market can hardly be expected to know that he has thereby become subject to suit in a forum remote from his residence and unrelated to the transaction. As a practical matter, the Delaware sequestration statute creates an unacceptable risk of judgment without notice. Unlike the 49 other States, Delaware treats the place of incorporation as the situs of the stock, even though both the owner and the custodian of the shares are elsewhere. Moreover, Delaware denies the defendant the opportunity to defend the merits of the suit unless he subjects himself to the unlimited jurisdiction of the court. Thus, it coerces a defendant either to submit to personal jurisdiction in a forum which could not otherwise obtain such jurisdiction or to lose the securities which have been attached. If its procedure were upheld, Delaware would, in effect, impose a duty of inquiry on every purchaser of securities in the national market. For unless the purchaser ascertains both the State of incorporation of the company whose shares he is buying, and also the idiosyncrasies of its law, he may be assuming an unknown risk of litigation. I therefore agree with the Court that on the record before us no adequate basis for jurisdiction exists and that the Delaware statute is unconstitutional on its face.

How the Court's opinion may be applied in other contexts is not entirely clear to me. I agree with MR. JUSTICE POWELL that it should not be read to invalidate *in rem* jurisdiction where real estate is involved. I would also not read it as invalidating other long-accepted methods of acquiring jurisdiction over persons with adequate notice of both the particular controversy and the fact that their local activities might subject them to suit. My uncertainty as to the reach of the opinion, and my fear that it purports to decide a great deal more than is necessary to dispose of this case, persuade me merely to concur in the judgment.

MR. JUSTICE BRENNAN, concurring in part and dissenting in part.

I join Parts I–III of the Court's opinion. I fully agree that the minimum-contacts analysis * * * represents a far more sensible construct for the exercise of state-court jurisdiction than the patchwork of legal and factual fictions that has been generated from the decision in Pennoyer v. Neff * * *. It is precisely because the inquiry into minimum contacts is now of such overriding importance, however, that I must respectfully dissent from Part IV of the Court's opinion.

I

The primary teaching of Parts I–III of today's decision is that a State, in seeking to assert jurisdiction over a person located outside its borders, may only do so on the basis of minimum contacts among the parties, the contested transaction, and the forum state. The Delaware Supreme Court could not have made plainer, however, that its sequestration statute * * * does not operate on this basis, but instead is strictly an embodiment of *quasi in rem* jurisdiction, a jurisdictional predicate no longer constitutionally viable * * *. This state-court ruling obviously comports with the understanding of the parties, for the issue of the existence of minimum contacts was never pleaded by appellee, made the subject of discovery, or ruled upon by the Delaware courts. These facts notwithstanding, the Court in Part IV reaches the minimum-contacts question and finds such contacts lacking as applied to appellants. Succinctly stated, once having properly and persuasively decided that the *quasi in rem* statute that Delaware admits to having enacted is invalid, the Court then proceeds to find that a minimum-contacts law that Delaware expressly *denies* having enacted also could not be constitutionally applied in this case.

In my view, a purer example of an advisory opinion is not to be found. True, appellants do not deny having received actual notice of the action in question. * * * But notice is but one ingredient of a proper assertion of state-court jurisdiction. The other is a statute authorizing the exercise of the State's judicial power along constitutionally permissible grounds—which henceforth means minimum contacts. As of today, § 366 is not such a law.[1] Recognizing that today's decision fundamentally alters the relevant jurisdictional ground rules, I certainly would not want to rule out the possibility that Delaware's courts might decide that the legislature's overriding purpose of securing the personal appearance in state courts of defendants would best be served by reinterpreting its statute to permit state jurisdiction of the basis of constitutionally permissible contacts rather than stock ownership. Were the state courts to take this step, it would then become necessary to address the question of whether minimum contacts exist here. But in the present posture of this case, the Court's decision of this important issue is purely an abstract ruling.

My concern with the inappropriateness of the Court's action is highlighted by two other considerations. First, an inquiry into minimum contacts inevitably is highly dependent on creating a proper factual foundation detailing the contacts between the forum state and the controversy in question. Because neither the plaintiff-appellee nor the state courts viewed such an inquiry as germane in this instance, the Court today is unable to draw upon a proper factual record in reaching its conclusion; moreover, its disposition denies appellee the normal opportunity to seek discovery on the contacts issue. Second, it must be remembered that the Court's ruling is a constitutional one and necessarily will affect the reach of the jurisdictional laws of all 50 States. Ordinarily this would counsel restraint in constitutional pronounce-

---

1. Indeed, the Court's decision to proceed to the minimum-contacts issue treats Delaware's sequestration statute as if it were the equivalent of Rhode Island's long-arm law, which specifically authorizes its courts to assume jurisdiction to the limit permitted by the Constitution, R.I.Gen.Laws Ann. § 9–5–33 (1970), thereby necessitating judicial consideration of the frontiers of minimum contacts in every case arising under that statute.

ments. * * * Certainly it should have cautioned the Court against reaching out to decide a question that, as here, has yet to emerge from the state courts ripened for review on the federal issue.

II

Nonetheless, because the Court rules on the minimum-contacts question, I feel impelled to express my view. While evidence derived through discovery might satisfy me that minimum contacts are lacking in a given case, I am convinced that as a general rule a state forum has jurisdiction to adjudicate a shareholder derivative action centering on the conduct and policies of the directors and officers of a corporation chartered by that State. Unlike the Court, I therefore would not foreclose Delaware from asserting jurisdiction over appellants were it persuaded to do so on the basis of minimum contacts.

It is well settled that a derivative lawsuit as presented here does not inure primarily to the benefit of the named plaintiff. Rather, the primary beneficiaries are the corporation and its owners, the shareholders. * * *

Viewed in this light, the chartering State has an unusually powerful interest in insuring the availability of a convenient forum for litigating claims involving a possible multiplicity of defendant fiduciaries and for vindicating the State's substantive policies regarding the management of its domestic corporations. I believe that our cases fairly establish that the State's valid substantive interests are important considerations in assessing whether it constitutionally may claim jurisdiction over a given cause of action.

In this instance, Delaware can point to at least three interrelated public policies that are furthered by its assertion of jurisdiction. First, the State has a substantial interest in providing restitution for its local corporations that allegedly have been victimized by fiduciary misconduct, even if the managerial decisions occurred outside the State. The importance of this general state interest in assuring restitution for its own residents previously found expression in cases that went outside the then-prevailing due process framework to authorize state-court jurisdiction over nonresident motorists who injure others within the State. * * * More recently, it has led States to seek and to acquire jurisdiction over nonresident tortfeasors whose purely out-of-state activities produce domestic consequences. * * * Second, state courts have legitimately read their jurisdiction expansively when a cause of action centers in an area in which the forum State possesses a manifest regulatory interest. * * * Only this Term we reiterated that the conduct of corporate fiduciaries is just such a matter in which the policies and interests of a domestic forum are paramount. * * * Finally, a State like Delaware has a recognized interest in affording a convenient forum for supervising and overseeing the affairs of an entity that is purely the creation of that State's law. For example, even following our decision in *International Shoe,* New York courts were permitted to exercise complete judicial authority over nonresident beneficiaries of a trust created under state law, even though, unlike appellants here, the beneficiaries personally entered into no association whatsoever with New York. Mullane v. Central Hanover Bank & Trust Co. [p. 191, infra] * * * .

To be sure, the Court is not blind to these considerations. It notes that the State's interests "may support the application of Delaware law to resolve any controversy over appellants' actions in their capacities as officers and directors." * * * But this, the Court argues, pertains to choice of law, not jurisdiction. I recognize that the jurisdictional and choice-of-law inquiries are not identical. * * * But I would not compartmentalize thinking in this area quite so rigidly as it seems to me the Court does today, for both inquiries "are often closely related and to a substantial degree depend upon similar considerations." [Hanson v. Denckla, 357 U.S.] at 258, 78 S.Ct. at 1242 (Black, J., dissenting). * * * At the minimum, the decision that it is fair to bind a defendant by a State's laws and rules should prove to be highly relevant to the fairness of permitting that same State to accept jurisdiction for adjudicating the controversy.

Furthermore, I believe that practical considerations argue in favor of seeking to bridge the distance between the choice-of-law and jurisdictional inquiries. Even when a court would apply the law of a different forum, as a general rule it will feel less knowledgeable and comfortable in interpretation, and less interested in fostering the policies of that foreign jurisdiction, than would the courts established by the State that provides the applicable law. * * * Obviously, such choice-of-law problems cannot entirely be avoided in a diverse legal system such as our own. Nonetheless, when a suitor seeks to lodge a suit in a State with a substantial interest in seeing its own law applied to the transaction in question, we could wisely act to minimize conflicts, confusion, and uncertainty by adopting a liberal view of jurisdiction, unless considerations of fairness or efficiency strongly point in the opposite direction.

This case is not one where, in my judgment, this preference for jurisdiction is adequately answered. Certainly nothing said by the Court persuades me that it would be unfair to subject appellants to suit in Delaware. The fact that the record does not reveal whether they "set foot" or committed "acts related to [the] cause of action" in Delaware * * * is not decisive, for jurisdiction can be based strictly on out-of-state acts having foreseeable effects in the forum State. * * * I have little difficulty in applying this principle to nonresident fiduciaries whose alleged breaches of trust are said to have substantial damaging effect on the financial posture of a resident corporation. Further, I cannot understand how the existence of minimum contacts in a constitutional sense is at all affected by Delaware's failure statutorily to express an interest in controlling corporate fiduciaries. * * * To me this simply demonstrates that Delaware did not elect to assert jurisdiction to the extent the Constitution would allow. Nor would I view as controlling or even especially meaningful Delaware's failure to exact from appellants their consent to be sued. * * * Once we have rejected the jurisdictional framework created in Pennoyer v. Neff, I see no reason to rest jurisdiction on a fictional outgrowth of that system such as the existence of a consent statute, expressed or implied.

I, therefore, would approach the minimum-contacts analysis differently than does the Court. Crucial to me is the fact that appellants voluntarily associated themselves with the State of Delaware, "invoking the benefits and protections of its laws," * * * by entering into a long-term and fragile relationship with one of its domestic corporations. They thereby elected to assume powers and to undertake responsibilities wholly derived from that State's rules and regulations, and to become eligible for those benefits that Delaware law makes available to its corporations' officials. E.g., Del.Code Ann., Tit. 8, § 143 (1975) (interest-free loans); § 145 (1975 ed. and Supp.

1976) (indemnification). While it is possible that countervailing issues of judicial efficiency and the like might clearly favor a different forum, they do not appear on the meager record before us; and, of course, we are concerned solely with "minimum" contacts, not the "best" contacts. * * *

Notes and Questions

1. Within thirteen days after the decision in *Shaffer*, the Delaware legislature amended its laws to provide that every nonresident who is elected or appointed a director of a Delaware corporation after September 1, 1977, shall "be deemed" to have consented to the appointment of the corporation's registered agent in Delaware, or, if there is no registered agent, of the Secretary of State of Delaware, as his agent for service of process in any Delaware action based on violation of the director's duties as director after September 1, 1977. 10 Del.Code § 3114. The constitutionality of the section was upheld by the Supreme Court of Delaware in Armstrong v. Pomerance, 423 A.2d 174 (Del.1980), a suit against nonresidents whose sole contact with Delaware was their status as directors of a Delaware corporation. See also Stearn v. Malloy, 89 F.R.D. 421 (E.D.Wis.1981) (reaching the same conclusion under a similar Wisconsin statute). See Comment, *Constitutional Analysis of the New Delaware Director–Consent-to-Service Statute,* 70 Geo.L.J. 1209 (1983).

Greyhound Corporation, shortly after the enactment of the Delaware directors-consent-to-service statute, sought and obtained the approval of its shareholders to reincorporate in Arizona, where Greyhound also has its principal headquarters. A stated reason was that "it would be an unreasonable burden upon directors, not resident in Delaware, several of whom reside in Arizona and California, to be required to journey to Delaware to defend a case there when they have no contact with that state." Ratner & Schwartz, *The Impact of Shaffer v. Heitner on the Substantive Law of Corporations,* 45 Brooklyn L.Rev. 641, 653–54 (1979).

2. Does *Shaffer* preclude a state from rendering a judgment in a pure in rem action that is binding against the world? In this regard, is footnote 37 of Justice Marshall's opinion relevant?

3. In RHOADES v. WRIGHT, 622 P.2d 343 (Utah 1980), certiorari denied 454 U.S. 897, 102 S.Ct. 397, 70 L.Ed.2d 212 (1981), the court upheld the attachment for jurisdictional purposes of farm land in Utah owned by the defendant, a resident of Colorado, who was being sued for the wrongful death of a Utah resident killed outside Utah. The court considered the presence of the land (as distinguished from the kind of intangible and movable property involved in *Shaffer*), together with the fact that the Colorado defendant actively used the land, sufficient contacts with Utah to satisfy due process requirements for the exercise of quasi-in-rem jurisdiction.

4. Does *Shaffer* overturn Harris v. Balk? In FEDER v. TURKISH AIRLINES, 441 F.Supp. 1273 (S.D.N.Y.1977), decided after *Shaffer*, the court upheld quasi-in-rem jurisdiction based on the attachment of the defendant's New York bank account. The bank account, established by the airline to pay for aircraft parts and components, was the airline's only contact with the forum. The action was a wrongful-death suit stemming from an accident that occurred in Turkey. The plaintiffs were New York residents. Is the result in *Feder* consistent with *Shaffer*?

5. Can an insurance obligation be attached? In SEIDER v. ROTH, 17 N.Y.2d 111, 269 N.Y.S.2d 99, 216 N.E.2d 312 (1966), the plaintiffs attached the obligation of an automobile insurance company to indemnify an out-of-state policy holder, and jurisdiction was upheld. New York's highest court held that the contractual obligation constituted a debt that was subject to attachment.

After *Shaffer*, the Second Circuit concluded that "[t]he fall of Harris v. Balk * * * does not necessarily topple *Seider*." O'CONNOR v. LEE–HY PAVING CORP., 579 F.2d 194, 199 (2d Cir.), certiorari denied 439 U.S. 1034, 99 S.Ct. 639, 58 L.Ed.2d 696 (1978). The court distinguished *Shaffer* and *Harris* as cases in which the property that furnished the basis for quasi-in-rem jurisdiction was completely unrelated to the plaintiff's claim, but that in *O'Connor* the attached property was an insurance policy that was purchased to protect against the type of liability that was the subject of the lawsuit.

The United States Supreme Court laid the *Seider* doctrine to rest in RUSH v. SAVCHUK, 444 U.S. 320, 100 S.Ct. 571, 62 L.Ed.2d 516 (1980). In finding the attachment of an insurance policy to effect quasi-in-rem jurisdiction unconstitutional, the Court separated the contacts between the defendant and the forum from the contacts between the insurer and the forum. Having done so, the Court held that sufficient contacts between the defendant and the forum did not exist and that the Due Process Clause forbade assertion of jurisdiction.

6. Can a federal admiralty court after *Shaffer* exercise jurisdiction based on an attachment of property in the district when the defendant otherwise lacks contacts with the forum? In AMOCO OVERSEAS OIL CO. v. COMPAGNIE NATIONALE ALGERIENNE DE NAVIGATION, 605 F.2d 648, 655 (2d Cir.1979), the court upheld jurisdiction based on the attachment of a foreign corporation's bank account in New York. The court distinguished *Shaffer* stressing, in part, the special history of admiralty jurisdiction:

> * * * *Shaffer* did not consider assertion of jurisdiction over property in the admiralty context. Because the perpetrators of maritime injury are likely to be peripatetic, Ex Parte Louisville Underwriters, 134 U.S. 488, 493, 10 S.Ct. 587, 33 L.Ed. 991 (1890), and since the constitutional power of the federal courts is separately derived in admiralty, U.S. Constitution Art. III § 2, suits under admiralty jurisdiction involve separate policies to some extent. This tradition suggests not only that jurisdiction by attachment of property should be accorded special deference in the admiralty context, but also that maritime actors must reasonably expect to be sued where their property may be found.

The court also considered it relevant to the jurisdictional issue that the property attached was related to the matter in controversy and that, if jurisdiction was not exercised, the defendant might not be amenable to suit anywhere in the United States. Is this a satisfactory explanation for possibly depriving an absentee of its due process rights?

7. Some state long-arm statutes may be less inclusive than the constitutional grant of jurisdiction under the Due Process Clause. In BANCO AMBROSIANO, S.P.A. v. ARTOC BANK & TRUST LTD., 62 N.Y.2d 65, 476 N.Y.S.2d 64, 464 N.E.2d 432 (1984), a New York court found sufficient minimum contacts to support the exercise of quasi-in-rem jurisdiction over the defendant, a bank organized under the laws of the Bahamas, with respect to an account it kept in a New York bank that was reasonably related to the dispute brought before it. The

court noted that in personam jurisdiction could not be obtained because the state long-arm statute did not authorize it.

8. For an excellent discussion of *Shaffer*, see Silberman, *Shaffer v. Heitner: The End of an Era*, 53 N.Y.U.L.Rev. 33 (1978). Further commentary is found in symposia on the impact of *Shaffer* in 45 Brooklyn L.Rev. 493 (1979); 1978 Wash.U.L.Q. 273. See also Maltz, *Reflections on a Landmark: Shaffer v. Heitner Viewed From a Distance*, 1986 B.Y.U.L.Rev. 1043; Nordenberg, *State Courts, Personal Jurisdiction and the Evolutionary Process*, 54 Notre Dame Law. 587 (1979); Riesenfeld, *Shaffer v. Heitner: Holding, Implications, Forebodings*, 30 Hastings L.J. 1183 (1979); Smit, *The Enduring Utility of In Rem Rules: A Lasting Legacy of Pennoyer v. Neff*, 43 Brooklyn L.Rev. 600 (1977).

SECTION H. A REFRAIN: JURISDICTION BASED UPON PHYSICAL PRESENCE

BURNHAM v. SUPERIOR COURT

Supreme Court of the United States, 1990.
495 U.S. 604, 110 S.Ct. 2105, 109 L.Ed.2d 631.

Certiorari to the Court of Appeal of California, First Appellate District.

JUSTICE SCALIA announced the judgment of the Court and delivered an opinion in which THE CHIEF JUSTICE and JUSTICE KENNEDY join, and in which JUSTICE WHITE joins with respect to Parts I, II–A, II–B, and II–C.

The question presented is whether the Due Process Clause of the Fourteenth Amendment denies California courts jurisdiction over a nonresident, who was personally served with process while temporarily in that State, in a suit unrelated to his activities in the State.

I

Petitioner Dennis Burnham married Francie Burnham in 1976 in West Virginia. In 1977 the couple moved to New Jersey, where their two children were born. In July 1987 the Burnhams decided to separate. They agreed that Mrs. Burnham, who intended to move to California, would take custody of the children. Shortly before Mrs. Burnham departed for California that same month, she and petitioner agreed that she would file for divorce on grounds of "irreconcilable differences."

In October 1987, petitioner filed for divorce in New Jersey state court on grounds of "desertion." Petitioner did not, however, obtain an issuance of summons against his wife and did not attempt to serve her with process. Mrs. Burnham, after unsuccessfully demanding that petitioner adhere to their prior agreement to submit to an "irreconcilable differences" divorce, brought suit for divorce in California state court in early January 1988.

In late January, petitioner visited southern California on business, after which he went north to visit his children in the San Francisco Bay area, where his wife resided. He took the older child to San Francisco for the weekend. Upon returning the child to Mrs. Burnham's home on January 24, 1988, petitioner was served with a California court summons and a copy of Mrs. Burnham's divorce petition. He then returned to New Jersey.

proc. H.

Later that year, petitioner made a special appearance in the California Superior Court, moving to quash the service of process on the ground that the court lacked personal jurisdiction over him because his only contacts with California were a few short visits to the State for the purposes of conducting business and visiting his children. The Superior Court denied the motion, and the California Court of Appeal denied mandamus relief, rejecting petitioner's contention that the Due Process Clause prohibited California courts from asserting jurisdiction over him because he lacked "minimum contacts" with the State. The court held it to be "a valid jurisdictional predicate for *in personam* jurisdiction" that the "defendant [was] present in the forum state and personally served with process." * * *. We granted certiorari. * * *.

II

A

The proposition that the judgment of a court lacking jurisdiction is void traces back to the English Year Books, see Bowser v. Collins, Y.B.Mich. 22 Edw. IV, f. 30, pl. 11, 145 Eng.Rep. 97 (Ex. Ch. 1482), and was made settled law by Lord Coke in *Case of the Marshalsea,* 10 Coke Rep. 68b, 77a, 77 Eng.Rep. 1027, 1041 (K.B. 1612). Traditionally that proposition was embodied in the phrase *coram non judice,* "before a person not a judge"—meaning, in effect, that the proceeding in question was not a *judicial* proceeding because lawful judicial authority was not present, and could therefore not yield a *judgment.* American courts invalidated, or denied recognition to, judgments that violated this common-law principle long before the Fourteenth Amendment was adopted. * * *. In Pennoyer v. Neff, * * * we announced that the judgment of a court lacking personal jurisdiction violated the Due Process Clause of the Fourteenth Amendment as well.

To determine whether the assertion of personal jurisdiction is consistent with due process, we have long relied on the principles traditionally followed by American courts in marking out the territorial limits of each State's authority. That criterion was first announced in Pennoyer v. Neff, * * * in which we stated that due process "mean[s] a course of legal proceedings according to those rules and principles which have been established in our systems of jurisprudence for the protection and enforcement of private rights," * * * including the "well-established principles of public law respecting the jurisdiction of an independent State over persons and property" * * *. In what has become the classic expression of the criterion, we said in International Shoe Co. v. Washington, * * * that a state court's assertion of personal jurisdiction satisfies the Due Process Clause if it does not violate " 'traditional notions of fair play and substantial justice.' " * * * Since *International Shoe,* we have only been called upon to decide whether these "traditional notions" permit States to exercise jurisdiction over absent defendants in a manner that deviates from the rules of jurisdiction applied in the 19th century. We have held such deviations permissible, but only with respect to suits arising out of the absent defendant's contacts with the State. * * *. The question we must decide today is whether due process requires a similar connection between the litigation and the defendant's contacts with the State in cases where the defendant is physically present in the State at the time process is served upon him.

B

Among the most firmly established principles of personal jurisdiction in American tradition is that the courts of a State have jurisdiction over nonresidents who are physically present in the State. The view developed early that each State had the power to hale before its courts any individual who could be found within its borders, and that once having acquired jurisdiction over such a person by properly serving him with process, the State could retain jurisdiction to enter judgment against him, no matter how fleeting his visit. * * *. That view had antecedents in English common-law practice, which sometimes allowed "transitory" actions, arising out of events outside the country, to be maintained against seemingly nonresident defendants who were present in England. * * *. Justice Story believed the principle, which he traced to Roman origins, to be firmly grounded in English tradition: "[B]y the common law[,] personal actions, being transitory, may be brought in any place, where the party defendant may be found," for "every nation may * * * rightfully exercise jurisdiction over all persons within its domains." J. Story, Commentaries on the Conflict of Laws §§ 554, 543 (1846). * * *.

Recent scholarship has suggested that English tradition was not as clear as Story thought * * *. Accurate or not, however, judging by the evidence of contemporaneous or near-contemporaneous decisions, one must conclude that Story's understanding was shared by American courts at the crucial time for present purposes: 1868, when the Fourteenth Amendment was adopted. * * *

Decisions in the courts of many States in the 19th and early 20th centuries held that personal service upon a physically present defendant sufficed to confer jurisdiction, without regard to whether the defendant was only briefly in the State or whether the cause of action was related to his activities there. * * *. Although research has not revealed a case deciding the issue in every State's courts, that appears to be because the issue was so well settled that it went unlitigated. * * * Particularly striking is the fact that, as far as we have been able to determine, *not one* American case from the period (or, for that matter, not one American case until 1978) held, or even suggested, that in-state personal service on an individual was insufficient to confer personal jurisdiction. Commentators were also seemingly unanimous on the rule. * * *.

This American jurisdictional practice is, moreover, not merely old; it is continuing. It remains the practice of, not only a substantial number of the States, but as far as we are aware *all* the States and the Federal Government—if one disregards (as one must for this purpose) the few opinions since 1978 that have erroneously said, on grounds similar to those that petitioner presses here, that this Court's due process decisions render the practice unconstitutional. * * *. We do not know of a single state or federal statute, or a single judicial decision resting upon state law, that has abandoned in-state service as a basis of jurisdiction. Many recent cases reaffirm it. * * *.

C

Despite this formidable body of precedent, petitioner contends, in reliance on our decisions applying the *International Shoe* standard, that in the absence of "continuous and systematic" contacts with the forum, * * * a nonresident defendant can be subjected to judgment only as to matters that arise out of or relate to his contacts with the forum. This argument rests on a thorough misunderstanding of our cases.

The view of most courts in the 19th century was that a court simply could not exercise *in personam* jurisdiction over a nonresident who had not been personally served with process in the forum. * * *. Pennoyer v. Neff, while renowned for its statement of the principle that the Fourteenth Amendment prohibits such an exercise of jurisdiction, in fact set that forth only as dictum and decided the case (which involved a judgment rendered more than two years before the Fourteenth Amendment's ratification) under "well-established principles of public law." * * *. Those principles, embodied in the Due Process Clause, required (we said) that when proceedings "involv[e] merely a determination of the personal liability of the defendant, he must be brought within [the court's] jurisdiction by service of process within the State, or his voluntary appearance." * * *

Later years, however, saw the weakening of the *Pennoyer* rule. In the late 19th and early 20th centuries, changes in the technology of transportation and communication, and the tremendous growth of interstate business activity, led to an "inevitable relaxation of the strict limits on state jurisdiction" over nonresident individuals and corporations. * * *. States required, for example, that nonresident corporations appoint an in-state agent upon whom process could be served as a condition of transacting business within their borders, * * * and provided in-state "substituted service" for nonresident motorists who caused injury in the State and left before personal service could be accomplished * * *. We initially upheld these laws under the Due Process Clause on grounds that they complied with *Pennoyer*'s rigid requirement of either "consent," * * * or "presence" * * *. As many observed, however, the consent and presence were purely fictional. * * *. Our opinion in *International Shoe* cast those fictions aside and made explicit the underlying basis of these decisions: Due process does not necessarily *require* the States to adhere to the unbending territorial limits on jurisdiction set forth in *Pennoyer*. The validity of assertion of jurisdiction over a nonconsenting defendant who is not present in the forum depends upon whether "the quality and nature of [his] activity" in relation to the forum * * * renders such jurisdiction consistent with " 'traditional notions of fair play and substantial justice.' " * * *. Subsequent cases have derived from the *International Shoe* standard the general rule that a State may dispense with in-forum personal service on nonresident defendants in suits arising out of their activities in the State. * * *

Nothing in *International Shoe* or the cases that have followed it, however, offers support for the very different proposition petitioner seeks to establish today: that a defendant's presence in the forum is not only unnecessary to validate novel, nontraditional assertions of jurisdiction, but is itself no longer sufficient to establish jurisdiction. That proposition is unfaithful to both elementary logic and the foundations of our due process jurisprudence. The distinction between what is needed to support novel procedures and what is needed to sustain traditional ones is fundamental * * *. The short of the matter is that jurisdiction based on physical presence alone constitutes due process because it is one of the continuing traditions of our legal system that define the due process standard of "traditional notions of fair play and substantial justice." That standard was developed by *analogy* to "physical presence," and it would be perverse to say it could now be turned against that touchstone of jurisdiction.

D

Petitioner's strongest argument, though we ultimately reject it, relies upon our decision in Shaffer v. Heitner * * *.

It goes too far to say, as petitioner contends, that *Shaffer* compels the conclusion that a State lacks jurisdiction over an individual unless the litigation arises out of his activities in the State. *Shaffer,* like *International Shoe,* involved jurisdiction over an *absent defendant,* and it stands for nothing more than the proposition that when the "minimum contact" that is a substitute for physical presence consists of property ownership it must, like other minimum contacts, be related to the litigation. Petitioner wrenches out of its context our statement in *Shaffer* that "all assertions of state-court jurisdiction must be evaluated according to the standards set forth in *International Shoe* and its progeny" * * *. When read together with the two sentences that preceded it, the meaning of this statement becomes clear * * *. *Shaffer* was saying * * * not that all bases for the assertion of *in personam* jurisdiction (including, presumably, in-state service) must be treated alike and subjected to the "minimum contacts" analysis of *International Shoe;* but rather that *quasi in rem* jurisdiction, that fictional "ancient form," and *in personam* jurisdiction, are really one and the same and must be treated alike—leading to the conclusion that *quasi in rem* jurisdiction, *i.e.,* that form of *in personam* jurisdiction based upon a "property ownership" contact and by definition unaccompanied by personal, in-state service, must satisfy the litigation-relatedness requirement of *International Shoe.* The logic of *Shaffer*'s holding—which places all suits against absent nonresidents on the same constitutional footing, regardless of whether a separate Latin label is attached to one particular basis of contact—does not compel the conclusion that physically present defendants must be treated identically to absent ones. As we have demonstrated at length, our tradition has treated the two classes of defendants quite differently, and it is unreasonable to read *Shaffer* as casually obliterating that distinction. *International Shoe* confined its "minimum contacts" requirement to situations in which the defendant "be not present within the territory of the forum," * * * and nothing in *Shaffer* expands that requirement beyond that.

It is fair to say, however, that while our holding today does not contradict *Shaffer,* our basic approach to the due process question is different. We have conducted no independent inquiry into the desirability or fairness of the prevailing in-state service rule, leaving that judgment to the legislatures that are free to amend it; for our purposes, its validation is its pedigree, as the phrase "*traditional notions* of fair play and substantial justice" makes clear. *Shaffer* did conduct such an independent inquiry, asserting that " 'traditional notions of fair play and substantial justice' can be as readily offended by the perpetuation of ancient forms that are no longer justified as by the adoption of new procedures that are inconsistent with the basic values of our constitutional heritage." * * *. Perhaps that assertion can be sustained when the "perpetuation of ancient forms" is engaged in by only a very small minority of the States. Where, however, as in the present case, a jurisdictional principle is both firmly approved by tradition and still favored, it is impossible to imagine what standard we could appeal to for the judgment that it is "no longer justified." * * * For new procedures, hitherto unknown, the Due Process Clause requires analysis to determine whether "traditional notions of fair play and substantial justice" have been offended. * * *. But a doctrine of personal jurisdiction that dates back to the adoption of the Fourteenth Amendment and is still generally observed unquestionably meets that standard.

III

A few words in response to Justice Brennan's opinion concurring in the judgment: It insists that we apply "contemporary notions of due process" to determine the constitutionality of California's assertion of jurisdiction. * * * The "contemporary notions of due process" applicable to personal jurisdiction are the enduring "*traditional* notions of fair play and substantial justice" established as the test by *International Shoe*. By its very language, that test is satisfied if a state court adheres to jurisdictional rules that are generally applied and have always been applied in the United States.

But the concurrence's proposed standard of "contemporary notions of due process" requires more: It measures state-court jurisdiction not only against traditional doctrines in this country, including current state-court practice, but also against each Justice's subjective assessment of what is fair and just. Authority for that seductive standard is not to be found in any of our personal jurisdiction cases. It is, indeed, an outright break with the test of "traditional notions of fair play and substantial justice," which would have to be reformulated "*our* notions of fair play and substantial justice."

The subjectivity, and hence inadequacy, of this approach becomes apparent when the concurrence tries to explain *why* the assertion of jurisdiction in the present case meets its standard of continuing-American-tradition-*plus*-innate-fairness. Justice Brennan lists the "benefits" Mr. Burnham derived from the State of California—the fact that, during the few days he was there, "[h]is health and safety [were] guaranteed by the State's police, fire, and emergency medical services; he [was] free to travel on the State's roads and waterways; he likely enjoy[ed] the fruits of the State's economy." * * *. Three days' worth of these benefits strike us as powerfully inadequate to establish, as an abstract matter, that it is "fair" for California to decree the ownership of all Mr. Burnham's worldly goods acquired during the 10 years of his marriage, and the custody over his children. * * * It would create "an asymmetry," we are told, if Burnham were *permitted* (as he is) to appear in California courts as a plaintiff, but were not *compelled* to appear in California courts as defendant; and travel being as easy as it is nowadays, and modern procedural devices being so convenient, it is no great hardship to appear in California courts. * * *. The problem with these assertions is that they justify the exercise of jurisdiction over *everyone, whether or not* he ever comes to California. The only "fairness" elements setting Mr. Burnham apart from the rest of the world are the three days' "benefits" referred to above—and even those do not set him apart from many other people who have enjoyed three days in the Golden State * * * but who were fortunate enough not to be served with process while they were there and thus are not (simply by reason of that savoring) subject to the general jurisdiction of California's courts. * * *. In other words, even if one agreed with Justice Brennan's conception of an equitable bargain, the "benefits" we have been discussing would explain why it is "fair" to assert general jurisdiction over Burnham-returned-to-New-Jersey-after-service only at the expense of proving that it is also "fair" to assert general jurisdiction over Burnham-returned-to-New–Jersey-*without*-service—which we *know* does not conform with "contemporary notions of due process."

There is, we must acknowledge, one factor mentioned by Justice Brennan that *both* relates distinctively to the assertion of jurisdiction on the basis of personal in-state service *and* is fully persuasive—namely, the fact that a defendant voluntarily present in a particular State has a "reasonable expecta-tio[n]" that he is subject to suit there. * * *. By formulating it as a "reasonable expectation" Justice Brennan makes that seem like a "fairness" factor; but in reality, of course, it is just tradition masquerading as "fairness." The only reason for charging Mr. Burnham with the reasonable expectation of being subject to suit is that the States of the Union assert adjudicatory jurisdiction over the person, and have always asserted adjudicatory jurisdiction over the person, by serving him with process during his temporary physical presence in their territory. That continuing tradition, which anyone entering California should have known about, renders it "fair" for Mr. Burnham, who voluntarily entered California, to be sued there for divorce—at least "fair" in the limited sense that he has no one but himself to blame. Justice Brennan's long journey is a circular one, leaving him, at the end of the day, in complete reliance upon the very factor he sought to avoid: The existence of a continuing tradition is not enough, fairness also must be considered; fairness exists here because there is a continuing tradition.

* * * Suppose, for example, that a defendant in Mr. Burnham's situation enjoys not three days' worth of California's "benefits," but 15 minutes' worth. Or suppose we remove one of those "benefits"—"enjoy[ment of] the fruits of the State's economy"—by positing that Mr. Burnham had not come to California on business, but only to visit his children. Or suppose that Mr. Burnham were demonstrably so impecunious as to be unable to take advantage of the modern means of transportation and communication that Justice Brennan finds so relevant. Or suppose, finally, that the California courts lacked the "variety of procedural devices" * * * that Justice Brennan says can reduce the burden upon out-of-state litigants. One may also make additional suppositions, relating not to the absence of the factors that Justice Brennan discusses, but to the presence of additional factors bearing upon the ultimate criterion of "fairness." What if, for example, Mr. Burnham were visiting a sick child? Or a dying child? * * *. Since, so far as one can tell, Justice Brennan's approval of applying the in-state service rule in the present case rests on the presence of *all* the factors he lists, and on the absence of any others, every different case will present a different litigable issue. Thus, despite the fact that he manages to work the word "rule" into his formulation, Justice Brennan's approach does not establish a rule of law at all, but only a "totality of the circumstances" test, guaranteeing what traditional territorial rules of jurisdiction were designed precisely to avoid: uncertainty and litigation over the preliminary issue of the forum's competence. It may be that those evils, necessarily accompanying a freestanding "reasonableness" inquiry, must be accepted at the margins, when we evaluate *non*traditional forms of jurisdiction newly adopted by the States * * *. But that is no reason

for injecting them into the core of our American practice, exposing to such a "reasonableness" inquiry the ground of jurisdiction that has hitherto been considered the very *baseline* of reasonableness, physical presence.

The difference between us and Justice Brennan has nothing to do with whether "further progress [is] to be made" in the "evolution of our legal system." * * *. It has to do with whether changes are to be adopted as progressive by the American people or decreed as progressive by the Justices of this Court. Nothing we say today prevents individual States from limiting or entirely abandoning the in-state-service basis of jurisdiction. And nothing prevents an overwhelming majority of them from doing so, with the consequence that the "traditional notions of fairness" that this Court applies may change. But the States have overwhelmingly declined to adopt such limitation or abandonment, evidently not considering it to be progress. The question is whether, armed with no authority other than individual Justices' perceptions of fairness that conflict with both past and current practice, this Court can compel the States to make such a change on the ground that "due process" requires it. We hold that it cannot.

Because the Due Process Clause does not prohibit the California courts from exercising jurisdiction over petitioner based on the fact of in-state service of process, the judgment is

Affirmed.

JUSTICE WHITE, concurring in part and concurring in the judgment.

I join Parts I, II–A, II–B, and II–C of Justice Scalia's opinion and concur in the judgment of affirmance. The rule allowing jurisdiction to be obtained over a nonresident by personal service in the forum State, without more, has been and is so widely accepted throughout this country that I could not possibly strike it down, either on its face or as applied in this case, on the ground that it denies due process of law guaranteed by the Fourteenth Amendment. * * *

JUSTICE BRENNAN, with whom JUSTICE MARSHALL, JUSTICE BLACKMUN, and JUSTICE O'CONNOR join, concurring in the judgment.

I agree with Justice Scalia that the Due Process Clause of the Fourteenth Amendment generally permits a state court to exercise jurisdiction over a defendant if he is served with process while voluntarily present in the forum State. I do not perceive the need, however, to decide that a jurisdictional rule that " 'has been immemorially the actual law of the land,' " * * * automatically comports with due process simply by virtue of its "pedigree." * * * Unlike Justice Scalia, I would undertake an "independent inquiry into the * * * fairness of the prevailing in-state service rule." * * *. I therefore concur only in the judgment.

I

I believe that the approach adopted by Justice Scalia's opinion today—reliance solely on historical pedigree—is foreclosed by our decisions in International Shoe Co. v. Washington * * * and Shaffer v. Heitner * * *. * * * The critical insight of *Shaffer* is that all rules of jurisdiction, even ancient ones, must satisfy contemporary notions of due process. * * * I agree with this approach and continue to believe that "the minimum-contacts analysis developed in *International Shoe* * * * represents a far more sensible construct for the exercise of state-court jurisdiction than the patchwork of legal and factual fictions that has been generated from the decision in Pennoyer v. Neff." * * *

While our *holding* in *Shaffer* may have been limited to *quasi in rem* jurisdiction, our mode of analysis was not. Indeed, that we were willing in *Shaffer* to examine anew the appropriateness of the *quasi in rem* rule—until that time dutifully accepted by American courts for at least a century—demonstrates that we did not believe that the "pedigree" of a jurisdictional practice was dispositive in deciding whether it was consistent with due process. * * * If we could discard an "ancient form without substantial modern justification" in *Shaffer,* * * * we can do so again. Lower courts, commentators, and the American Law Institute all have interpreted *International Shoe* and *Shaffer* to mean that *every* assertion of state-court jurisdiction, even one pursuant to a "traditional" rule such as transient jurisdiction, must comport with contemporary notions of due process. Notwithstanding the nimble gymnastics of JUSTICE SCALIA's opinion today, it is not faithful to our decision in *Shaffer.*

II

Tradition, though alone not dispositive, is of course *relevant* to the question whether the rule of transient jurisdiction is consistent with due process.[7] Tradition is salient not in the sense that practices of the past are automatically reasonable today; indeed, under such a standard, the legitimacy of transient jurisdiction would be called into question because the rule's historical "pedigree" is a matter of intense debate. The rule was a stranger to the common law and was rather weakly implanted in American jurisprudence "at the crucial time for present purposes: 1868, when the Fourteenth Amendment was adopted." * * * For much of the 19th century, American courts did not uniformly recognize the concept of transient jurisdiction, and it appears that the transient rule did not receive wide currency until well after our decision in Pennoyer v. Neff * * *.

Rather, I find the historical background relevant because, however murky the jurisprudential origins of transient jurisdiction, the fact that American courts have announced the rule for perhaps a century * * * provides a defendant voluntarily present in a particular State *today* "clear notice that [he] is subject to suit" in the forum. * * * [Thus, t]he transient rule is consistent with reasonable expectations and is entitled to a strong presumption that it comports with due process. * * *

By visiting the forum State, a transient defendant actually "avail[s]" himself * * * of significant benefits provided by the State. His health and safety are guaranteed by the State's police, fire, and emergency medical

---

7. I do not propose that the "contemporary notions of due process" to be applied are no more than "each Justice's subjective assessment of what is fair and just." * * * Rather, the inquiry is guided by our decisions beginning with International Shoe Co. v. Washington, * * * and the specific factors that we have developed to ascertain whether a jurisdictional rule comports with "traditional notions of fair play and substantial justice." * * *. This analysis may not be "mechanical or quantitative," * * * but neither is it "freestanding," * * * or dependent on personal whim. Our experience with this approach demonstrates that it is well within our competence to employ.

services; he is free to travel on the State's roads and waterways; he likely enjoys the fruits of the State's economy as well. Moreover, the Privileges and Immunities Clause of Article IV prevents a state government from discriminating against a transient defendant by denying him the protections of its law or the right of access to its courts. * * * Without transient jurisdiction, an asymmetry would arise: A transient would have the full benefit of the power of the forum State's courts as a plaintiff while retaining immunity from their authority as a defendant. * * *

The potential burdens on a transient defendant are slight. " '[M]odern transportation and communications have made it much less burdensome for a party sued to defend himself' " in a State outside his place of residence. * * * That the defendant has already journeyed at least once before to the forum— as evidenced by the fact that he was served with process there—is an indication that suit in the forum likely would not be prohibitively inconvenient. Finally, any burdens that do arise can be ameliorated by a variety of procedural devices. For these reasons, as a rule the exercise of personal jurisdiction over a defendant based on his voluntary presence in the forum will satisfy the requirements of due process. * * *

In this case, it is undisputed that petitioner was served with process while voluntarily and knowingly in the State of California. I therefore concur in the judgment.

JUSTICE STEVENS, concurring in the judgment.

As I explained in my separate writing, I did not join the Court's opinion in Shaffer v. Heitner * * * because I was concerned by its unnecessarily broad reach. * * *. The same concern prevents me from joining either Justice Scalia's or Justice Brennan's opinion in this case. For me, it is sufficient to note that the historical evidence and consensus identified by Justice Scalia, the considerations of fairness identified by Justice Brennan, and the common sense displayed by Justice White, all combine to demonstrate that this is, indeed, a very easy case.* Accordingly, I agree that the judgment should be affirmed.

Notes and Questions

1.   The Justices agreed on the result in *Burnham,* but could not agree on its theoretical underpinnings. Which opinion states the law of transient personal jurisdiction as it now stands? Which approach do you find to be more persuasive? Is the intense debate in *Burnham* evidence of a deeper disagreement between Justice Scalia and Justice Brennan? If so, what is it?

2.   Has Justice Scalia correctly interpreted the word "traditional" in the phrase "traditional notions of fair play and substantial justice"? If he has not, what was its intended meaning? Similarly, what is the correct interpretation of the language in Shaffer v. Heitner to the effect that: "all assertions of state-court jurisdiction must be evaluated according to the standards set forth in *International Shoe* and its progeny"? What effect, if any, do you think the failure to answer this question will have on the continued viability of transient jurisdiction?

---

* Perhaps the adage about hard cases making bad law should be revised to cover easy cases.

3. What effect does the decision in *Burnham* have on cases like Grace v. MacArthur, Note 4, p. 69, supra, in which the defendant is served while passing over the state in an airplane? Could an astronaut orbiting the earth be similarly served?

4. Does *Burnham* signal a retreat from the flexible notions of due process developed in *International Shoe* and its progeny, and a return to a strictly territorial approach to personal jurisdiction? Would such a retreat be desirable? See Borchers, *The Death of the Constitutional Law of Personal Jurisdiction: From Pennoyer to Burnham and Back Again,* 24 U.C. Davis L.Rev. 19 (1990).

5. Are there special factors in a case brought against a foreign defendant that would argue in favor of adopting Justice Brennan's, rather than Justice Scalia's, approach? See Hay, *Transient Jurisdiction Especially Over International Defendants: Critical Comments on Burnham v. Superior Court of California,* 1990 U.Ill.L.Rev. 593.

6. In QUILL CORP. v. NORTH DAKOTA, 504 U.S. 298, 112 S.Ct. 1904, 119 L.Ed.2d 91 (1992), the Supreme Court held that the Due Process Clause does not prohibit a North Dakota state court from asserting personal jurisdiction in a suit brought by the State to enforce its use tax against an out-of-state mail-order house with neither outlets nor sales representatives in the State. The Court found that the company's contacts with in-state customers through the mails were sufficient to support jurisdiction with respect to goods purchased for use in the State. In so doing, the Court made clear that:

> to the extent that [prior] decisions have indicated that the Due Process Clause *requires* physical presence in a State for the imposition of a duty to collect a use tax, we overrule those holdings as superseded by developments in the law of due process.

Id. at 308, 112 S.Ct. at 1911, 119 L.Ed.2d at 104 (emphasis added). The Court, however, proceeded to strike down the tax as unconstitutional on the ground that it unduly burdened interstate commerce.

7. For further discussions, see *The Future of Personal Jurisdiction: A Symposium on Burnham v. Superior Court,* 22 Rutgers L.J. 559 (1991). See also Note, *Burnham v. Superior Court: The Supreme Court Agrees on Transient Jurisdiction in Practice, But Not in Theory,* 69 N.C.L.Rev. 1271 (1991); Note, *An Easy Case Makes Bad Law—Burnham v. Superior Court,* 66 Wash.L.Rev. 623 (1991); Note, *A Pedigree for Due Process?,* 56 Mo.L.Rev. 353 (1991).

SECTION I.   ANOTHER BASIS OF JURISDICTION: CONSENT

Earlier we saw that even under the regime of Pennoyer v. Neff, p. 62, supra, a defendant could consent to personal jurisdiction. In the simplest case, a defendant consents to personal jurisdiction either by expressly agreeing to submit to the court or by performing certain acts that constitute a waiver of objections to personal jurisdiction or by failing to assert a defense of lack of jurisdiction. For example, Rule 12(h)(1) of the Federal Rules provides that a defendant who fails to raise an objection to personal jurisdiction in the answer or in an initial motion under Rule 12 is subsequently precluded from raising the issue. Not all consent cases are "simple," however. As you read the following case, note that it seems that a defendant can consent to varying levels of involvement in a lawsuit.

———

F →

INSURANCE CORP. OF IRELAND v. COMPAGNIE DES BAUXITES DE GUINEE, 456 U.S. 694, 102 S.Ct. 2099, 72 L.Ed.2d 492 (1982). The plaintiff, Compagnie des Bauxites de Guinee (CBG), a bauxite producer incorporated in Delaware but doing business only in the Republic of Guinea, had purchased business-interruption insurance from a domestic insurer in Pennsylvania and from a group of foreign insurance companies through a London brokerage house. When a mechanical failure forced a halt in production, CBG filed a multi-million dollar claim, which the insurers refused to pay. CBG then sued in federal court in Pennsylvania, but most of the foreign insurance companies contested personal jurisdiction. CBG attempted to use discovery to establish the essential jurisdictional facts. After the companies failed to comply with the court's orders for production of the requested information and after repeated warnings, the District Court, pursuant to Rule 37(b)(2)(A), imposed a sanction consisting of a presumptive finding that the insurers were subject to the jurisdiction of the court because of their business contacts in Pennsylvania. The Supreme Court upheld the sanction.

* * * The requirement that a court have personal jurisdiction flows not from Art. III, but from the Due Process Clause. * * *

Because the requirement of personal jurisdiction represents first of all an individual right, it can, like other such rights, be waived. * * *

* * * By submitting to the jurisdiction of the court for the limited purpose of challenging jurisdiction, the defendant agrees to abide by that court's determination on the issue of jurisdiction * * *, [and] the manner in which the court determines whether it has personal jurisdiction may include a variety of legal rules and presumptions, as well as straightforward factfinding. * * *

CBG was seeking through discovery to respond to [the insurers'] contention that the District Court did not have personal jurisdiction. Having put the issue in question, [the insurers] did not have the option of blocking the reasonable attempt of CBG to meet its burden of proof. * * * [They] surely did not have this option once the court had overruled [their] objections. Because of [the insurers'] failure to comply with the discovery orders, CBG was unable to establish the full extent of the contacts between [the insurers] and Pennsylvania, the critical issue in proving personal jurisdiction. * * * [Their] failure to supply the requested information as to [their] contacts with Pennsylvania supports "the presumption that the refusal to produce evidence * * * was but an admission of the want of merit in the asserted defense." * * * The sanction took as established the facts—contacts with Pennsylvania—that CBG was seeking to establish through discovery.

Id. at 702–09, 102 S.Ct. at 2104–08, 72 L.Ed.2d at 501–05.

Notes and Questions

1. In *Ireland*, the defendants appeared to contest jurisdiction. Is it not clear that by making the special appearance they at least consented to the adjudication of that issue by the district court? Does that obligate them to abide by the rules—including the discovery rules—laid down by the court to govern determination of the issue? Was it necessary to base the holding in *Ireland* on concepts of waiver and consent? Isn't the authority of a federal court to determine its jurisdiction implicit in the grant of limited jurisdiction? And, if a court always has jurisdiction to determine whether it has jurisdiction, doesn't that mean that it has authority to force the parties, including the defendant, to cooperate in helping it to resolve that question?

2. Is the imposition of burdens of production in a distant place one of the core elements of unfairness that the due process cases from *International Shoe* to *World-Wide Volkswagen* sought to avoid? It is small comfort to the defendant that the cost is being imposed only for the purpose of determining whether or not the court has the authority to impose it. Does the Due Process Clause require the plaintiff to make a showing of any kind before the defendant can be forced to produce documents and witnesses for discovery in a distant forum? What if the defendant could make a prima facie showing of both the absence of minimum contacts related to the claim and the absence of continuous and substantial forum presence?

3. We have seen earlier that consent to personal jurisdiction often will be implied from the defendant's conduct preceding the lawsuit. See pp. 71–73, supra. In most states a foreign corporation that registers as a condition of doing business in a state is regarded as having consented to suit in the courts of that state even as to actions unconnected with the corporation's activities in the forum. See, e.g., N.Y. Bus. Corp. Law §§ 304–06; Knowlton v. Allied Van Lines, Inc., 900 F.2d 1196 (8th Cir.1990); Rykoff–Sexton, Inc. v. American Appraisal Assocs., Inc., 469 N.W.2d 88 (Minn.1991). But is it true that the consent extracted from a foreign corporation as a condition of doing business in a state, as Justice Holmes observed, is a "mere fiction," Flexner v. Farson, 248 U.S. 289, 39 S.Ct. 97, 63 L.Ed. 250 (1919), and that under general due process principles the fiction should not be invoked unless the requisite "minimum contacts" exist? In RATLIFF v. COOPER LABS., INC., 444 F.2d 745 (4th Cir.), certiorari denied 404 U.S. 948, 92 S.Ct. 271, 30 L.Ed.2d 265 (1971), the Court of Appeals held that a foreign corporation that had qualified to do business in South Carolina and regularly sent salesmen into the state could not be sued in South Carolina by plaintiffs from Florida and Indiana who purchased and consumed in their home states drugs manufactured by the defendant, and who sued in South Carolina because of that state's relatively long statute of limitations: "Applying for the privilege of doing business is one thing, but the actual exercise of that privilege is quite another. * * * The principles of due process require a firmer foundation than mere compliance with state domestication statutes." See also In re Mid–Atlantic Toyota Antitrust Litigation, 525 F.Supp. 1265, modified 541 F.Supp. 62 (D.Md.1981), affirmed 704 F.2d 125 (4th Cir.1983).

4. If a foreign corporation, not authorized, and not doing business in a state, represents to the plaintiff that it is so authorized, may the corporation be estopped from denying jurisdiction over it in a subsequent lawsuit? In FARMING-DALE STEER–INN, INC. v. STEER INN REALTY CORP., 51 Misc.2d 986, 274

N.Y.S.2d 379 (Sup.Ct.1966), the New York court concluded that it would be unfair to permit a defendant, which had represented that it was authorized to do business in New York, to assert later on that it was not subject to jurisdiction. The facts in the *Steer Inn* case were particularly egregious, since the corporation represented not merely that it was doing business in New York, but that it was in fact authorized by the Secretary of State to do business.

How far can this notion of estoppel be pushed? Suppose that the National Widget Corporation bills itself in its advertising as "a manufacturer servicing the nation's need for widgets." In fact, National Widget, a Montana Corporation, never has sold a widget to anyone outside of the northwestern United States. Can National Widget be sued in New York on the ground that it has consented to jurisdiction anywhere in the United States by virtue of its advertisement? Can it be prevented from contesting jurisdiction by virtue of its prior statement? Would it matter if it could be shown that a market for widgets only exists west of the Mississippi?

———

The possibility of jurisdiction by consent is not limited to situations in which a defendant, in one form or another, consents to jurisdiction in an ongoing action. Frequently, in forming a contract, the parties will draft an express agreement to submit to personal jurisdiction. Sometimes they will agree to submit to the jurisdiction of a designated court for any action arising out of the transaction. Sometimes they will agree to submit to the jurisdiction of a designated court—to the exclusion of all others—for any action arising out of the transaction. And, sometimes they will agree to submit to the jurisdiction of *any* court for any action arising out of the transaction. Consider the agreements and resulting disputes in the cases that follow.

M/S BREMEN v. ZAPATA OFF–SHORE CO., 407 U.S. 1, 92 S.Ct. 1907, 32 L.Ed.2d 513 (1972). Plaintiff Zapata, a Houston-based American corporation, contracted with Unterweser, a German corporation, to tow Zapata's drilling rig from Louisiana to Italy. The contract contained a provision that all disputes were to be litigated before the "London Court of Justice." The Bremen was the ship Unterweser used to tow the drilling rig. In the course of the towing, the rig was damaged in a storm off Florida, and was towed to Tampa. Zapata commenced suit against Unterweser in a federal court in Florida. Unterweser, citing the forum-selection clause in the contract, moved to dismiss, or, alternatively, to stay the action pending the submission of the dispute to the High Court of Justice in London. Simultaneously, Unterweser sued Zapata for breach of contract in the English court.

The District Court refused to dismiss or stay the American action, and the Court of Appeals affirmed. But the Supreme Court reversed:

> We hold * * * that far too little weight and effect were given to the forum clause in resolving this controversy. * * * The expansion of American business and industry will hardly be encouraged if, notwithstanding solemn contracts, we insist on a parochial concept that all disputes must be resolved under our laws and in our courts. * * * We cannot have trade and commerce in world markets and international waters exclusively on our terms, governed by our laws, and resolved in our courts.

Id. at 8–9, 92 S.Ct. at 1912–13, 32 L.Ed.2d at 519–20.

CARNIVAL CRUISE LINES, INC. v. SHUTE, 499 U.S. 585, 111 S.Ct. 1522, 113 L.Ed.2d 622 (1991). Plaintiffs, Eulala and Russel Shute, purchased passage for a seven-day cruise on defendant's ship, the Tropicale, through a Washington State travel agent. Plaintiff paid the fare to the agent who forwarded the payment to defendant's headquarters in Florida. Defendant then prepared the tickets and sent them to plaintiffs in Washington. The ticket included a provision stating that:

> 8. It is agreed by and between the passenger and the Carrier that all disputes and matters whatsoever arising under, in connection with or incident to this Contract shall be litigated, if at all, in and before a Court located in the State of Florida, U.S.A., to the exclusion of the Courts of any other state or country.

Plaintiffs boarded the Tropicale in Los Angeles, California and sailed for Puerto Vallarta, Mexico. Off the coast of Mexico, Mrs. Shute slipped on a deck mat and was injured. Plaintiffs filed suit in federal District Court in Washington, claiming that the negligence of defendant and its employees had caused Mrs. Shute's injuries. The District Court held that defendant's contacts with Washington were constitutionally insufficient to exercise personal jurisdiction. Reasoning that "but for" defendant's solicitation of business in Washington plaintiffs would not have taken the cruise and Mrs. Shute would not have been injured, the Ninth Circuit Court of Appeals concluded that defendant did have sufficient contacts with Washington, and reversed the lower court.

The Supreme Court, however, did not consider defendant's "minimum contacts" argument; instead, it addressed the enforceability of the forum-selection clause. Rejecting the argument that *Zapata* was limited to contracts between two business corporations, the Court held that:

Reversed

> * * * Including a reasonable forum clause in a form contract of this kind well may be permissible for several reasons: First, a cruise line has a special interest in limiting the fora in which it potentially could be subject to suit. Because a cruise ship typically carries passengers from many locales, it is not unlikely that a mishap on a cruise could subject the cruise line to litigation in several different fora. * * * Additionally, a clause establishing *ex ante* the forum for dispute resolution has the salutary effect of dispelling any confusion about where suits arising from the contract must be brought and defended, sparing litigants the time and expense of pretrial motions to determine the correct forum, and conserving judicial resources that otherwise would be devoted to deciding those motions. * * * Finally, it stands to reason that passengers who purchase tickets containing a forum clause like that at issue in this case benefit in the form of reduced fares reflecting the savings that the cruise line enjoys by limiting the fora in which it may be sued. * * *

Id. at 593, 111 S.Ct. at 1527, 113 L.Ed.2d at 632.

Notes and Questions

1. The *Zapata* Court indicated that forum-selection clauses will be honored "unless enforcement is shown by the resisting parties to be 'unreasonable' under the circumstances." Likewise, the *Shute* Court emphasized that forum-selection clauses contained in "form passage contracts are subject to judicial scrutiny for fundamental fairness." What factors should enter a trial court's assessment of the reasonableness or fairness of the stipulated forum? The bargaining power of the parties to the contract? The identity of the party who drafted the contract? The relative convenience of litigating the case where it was brought as opposed to the stipulated forum? The substantive law that would apply? Are you satisfied with the Supreme Court's assessment of these factors in *Shute*?

2. In evaluating whether to give force to a forum-selection clause, to what extent should the court consider its interest in adjudicating the dispute? For example, in *Zapata*, did the district court have an interest in regulating activity in the territorial waters of the United States? What about the sovereign's interest in providing a forum for its citizens? To what extent does the Supreme Court balance these interests against the interests of contracting parties who want to know that provisions will be enforced?

3. Suppose a plaintiff sues a defendant for breach of contract, choosing a forum other than the one required by a forum-selection clause in the contract. The defendant, invoking the forum-selection clause, objects to jurisdiction. Is *Zapata* dispositive in all cases? Cf. Stewart Organization, Inc. v. Ricoh Corp., 487 U.S. 22, 108 S.Ct. 2239, 101 L.Ed.2d 22 (1988), p. 408, infra.

4. Suppose that the Shutes purchased tickets for a pleasure cruise in the Mediterranean Sea from a company based in Greece, and that their ticket contained a forum-selection clause specifying that all litigation was to take place before the courts in Athens. Would the result have been different? See Mullenix, *Another Easy Case, Some More Bad Law: Carnival Cruise Lines and Contractual Personal Jurisdiction*, 27 Texas Int'l L.J. 323 (1992).

SECTION J. JURISDICTIONAL REACH OF THE FEDERAL DISTRICT COURTS

———

Read Federal Rule of Civil Procedure 4 and the accompanying materials in the Supplement.

———

The United States has by statute or rule imposed a number of territorial limits upon the exercise of personal jurisdiction by federal courts. In 1993, Rule 4 was amended to broaden substantially the reach of federal judicial process. Rule 4(k)(1)(A), which embodies the former Rule 4(e), provides that, in actions other than federal question and interpleader cases, the federal court may assert jurisdiction over a defendant in a state when a court of that state would be empowered to do so. In addition, Rule 4(k)(1)(B) permits service outside the forum state (but within 100 miles of the court where the action is commenced or is to be tried) if such service is necessary to add a third party under Rule 14, or to join, under Rule 19, an indispensable party to an action or a counterclaim or cross-claim. Moreover, Rule 4(k)(1)(C) permits service on a defendant who is subject to federal interpleader jurisdiction under 28 U.S.C. § 1335. Finally, Rule 4(k)(1)(D) recognizes that Congress in some instances expressly has authorized nationwide, or even worldwide service of process.

Another exception, set out in Rule 4(k)(2) is in the nature of a limited federal long-arm provision. The rule allows federal courts to exercise jurisdiction over a defendant against whom federal law claims are asserted in a case in which the defendant is not subject to the jurisdiction of any single state but the Constitution of the United States would permit jurisdiction.

What are the constitutional limitations on the exercise of adjudicatory authority by a federal court? Clearly, they are not to be found in the Fourteenth Amendment, which applies only to the states; the logical source is the Due Process Clause in the Fifth Amendment. To what extent if any, does the Fifth Amendment require the application of the "minimum contacts" standard developed in *International Shoe?* Is there a difference between the concept of due process as applied to the states and that concept as applied to the federal government?

Notes and Questions

1. Rule 4(k)(2) was promulgated partly in response to the Supreme Court's decision in OMNI CAPITAL INTERNATIONAL v. RUDOLF WOLFF & CO., 484 U.S. 97, 108 S.Ct. 404, 98 L.Ed.2d 415 (1987). In that case, an investor brought a private action in a Louisiana federal District Court against Omni Capital International, Ltd. and Omni Capital Corporation (collectively "Omni") under the Commodity Exchange Act. Omni was a New York corporation that marketed a commodities futures investment program. Omni impleaded Rudolf Wolff & Co., a British corporation employed by Omni to handle trades in London, and James Gourlay, a British citizen, who, as Wolff's representative, solicited Omni's business. Wolff and Gourlay were not present in Louisiana, and the Louisiana long-arm statute did not reach them. They moved to dismiss for lack of personal jurisdiction. The Supreme Court upheld both lower federal courts' findings that jurisdiction was unobtainable over the foreign defendants. Essentially this meant that foreign defendants doing business in the United States might not be amenable to service of process in any particular state and thus would be unaccountable in the United States for alleged violations of federal law. The Court was well aware of the consequences of its ruling, but insisted that it was for the legislature, not the courts, to fashion a rule authorizing service of process in this situation.

2. When the alleged basis for jurisdiction is Rule 4(k)(2), which party has the burden of proving the amenability or lack of amenability of the defendant to suit in any single state? Would the party with the burden have to canvas the jurisdictional provisions of all fifty states, demonstrating whether each would or would not support jurisdiction over the defendant? Remember that the availability of personal jurisdiction under any state's law makes jurisdiction unavailable under Rule 4(k)(2).

3. For a discussion of the 1993 amendments to Rule 4, see Newman & Burrows, *Changes to the Federal Rules of Civil Procedure,* 211 New York Law Journal 3 (1994).

4. Does Congress have the constitutional authority to provide for nationwide in personam jurisdiction? In STAFFORD v. BRIGGS, 444 U.S. 527, 100 S.Ct. 774,

63 L.Ed.2d 1 (1980), Justice Stewart in dissent, expressed approval of a theory of "national contacts" under the Due Process Clause of the Fifth Amendment.

The petitioners concede that previous cases in this area have involved the Fourteenth Amendment requirement that a state court may acquire personal jurisdiction only if there exist "minimum contacts" between the defendant and the forum State. Reasoning by analogy, however, the petitioners argue that traditional notions of fair play and substantial justice inherent in the Due Process Clause of the Fifth Amendment similarly limit the exercise of congressional power to provide for nationwide *in personam* jurisdiction.

The short answer to this argument is that due process requires only certain minimum contacts between the defendant and the sovereign that has created the court. * * * The issue is not whether it is unfair to require a defendant to assume the burden of litigating in an inconvenient forum, but rather whether the court of a particular sovereign has power to exercise personal jurisdiction over a named defendant. The cases before us involve suits against residents of the United States in the courts of the United States. No due process problem exists.

Id. at 553–54, 100 S.Ct. at 789, 63 L.Ed.2d at 21. Has Justice Stewart simply disregarded the fairness concerns developed in *International Shoe* and its progeny? Or is fairness simply irrelevant when the defendant is found within the boundaries of the sovereign asserting jurisdiction? Would fairness to a foreign defendant be a concern if worldwide service of process were involved? In the *Oxford First* case discussed below, consider what due process limitations should be placed on federal courts hearing federal question cases.

5. In a thoughtful opinion by Judge Becker in OXFORD FIRST CORP. v. PNC LIQUIDATING CORP., 372 F.Supp. 191 (E.D.Pa.1974), the court concluded that, although federal statutes authorizing extra-district service of process are not constrained by the constitutional strictures defined in *International Shoe*, their application is limited by fundamental notions of "fairness" derived from the Due Process Clause of the Fifth Amendment. Among the factors identified as being relevant to the "fairness" inquiry were: (1) the extent of the defendant's contacts with the place where the action was brought, (2) the inconvenience of defending in a distant forum, (3) judicial economy, (4) the probable locus of discovery, and (5) the interstate character and impact of defendant's activities. Applying these standards to the case, the court upheld the exercise of jurisdiction. See also Duckworth v. Medical Electro–Therapeutics, Inc., 768 F.Supp. 822 (S.D.Ga.1991) (applying a national contacts test consisting of the *Oxford* factors).

Most courts that have considered the question, however, have refused to adopt the *Oxford* factors as a test of whether an assertion of personal jurisdiction by a federal court complies with due process. "The 'fairness' measured by these factors does not relate to the fairness of the exercise of power by a particular sovereign * * * but instead to the fairness of imposing the burdens of litigation in a particular forum. As such, these factors are more appropriately used [in determining whether venue is properly laid in a particular district], and we decline to import them into determination of the constitutionality of exercise of personal jurisdiction." Fitzsimmons v. Barton, 589 F.2d 330 (7th Cir.1979). See also United Rope Distributors, Inc. v. Seatriumph Marine Corp., 930 F.2d 532 (7th Cir.1991); Go–Video, Inc. v. Akai Electric Co., 885 F.2d 1406 (9th Cir.1989).

6. The "minimum contacts" standard of *International Shoe* does apply when a federal court, pursuant to Rule 4(k)(1) resorts to the law of the forum state to serve process on an out-of-state defendant. The rule authorizes service to establish in personam jurisdiction over "a defendant who could be subjected to the jurisdiction of a court of general jurisdiction in the state in which the district court is located." This means that a federal court can use the forum state's long-arm statute only to reach those parties whom a court of the state also could reach. The apparent intent of the drafters of Rule 4(k) was to use state provisions for service in order to permit the federal courts in a state to hear those cases that could be brought in the state's own courts when a basis for asserting federal subject-matter jurisdiction exists.

7. The growth of international commerce has resulted in an increased number of claims against alien defendants brought in American courts. If a federal statute expressly or impliedly authorizes worldwide service of process, a federal court apparently may exercise in personam jurisdiction based on the alien's aggregate contacts with the United States. See Texas Trading & Milling Corp. v. Federal Republic of Nigeria, 647 F.2d 300, 314 (2d Cir.1981), certiorari denied 454 U.S. 1148, 102 S.Ct. 1012, 71 L.Ed.2d 301 (1982). But if a federal court must rely on a state long-arm statute, it can exercise in personam jurisdiction based only on the alien's contacts with the forum state, even if the alien's aggregate contacts with the United States as a whole would satisfy due process requirements mandated by the Fifth Amendment. See DeJames v. Magnificence Carriers, Inc., 491 F.Supp. 1276 (D.N.J.1980), affirmed 654 F.2d 280 (3d Cir.), certiorari denied 454 U.S. 1085, 102 S.Ct. 642, 70 L.Ed.2d 620 (1981). This apparent anomaly is discussed in Lilly, *Jurisdiction Over Domestic Alien Defendants,* 69 Va.L.Rev. 85 (1983); Note, *Alien Corporations and Aggregate Contacts: A Genuinely Federal Jurisdictional Standard,* 95 Harv.L.Rev. 470 (1981). A critique of the current law and a suggestion of an alternative approach are found in Degnan & Kane, *The Exercise of Jurisdiction Over and Enforcement of Judgments Against Alien Defendants,* 39 Hastings L.J. 799 (1988).

8. The amenability of a party to service in the federal courts when federal law governs is discussed in Lusardi, *Nationwide Service of Process: Due Process Limitations on the Power of the Sovereign,* 33 Villa.L.Rev. 1 (1988); Fullerton, *Constitutional Limits on Nationwide Personal Jurisdiction in the Federal Courts,* 79 Nw.U.L.Rev. 1 (1984); Note, *Nationwide Personal Jurisdiction in All Federal Question Cases: A New Rule 4,* 64 N.Y.U.L.Rev. 1117 (1989). The question whether state or federal law governs amenability in diversity of citizenship cases is an aspect of the general choice-of-law problem discussed in Chapter Six, infra.

SECTION K.   CHALLENGING A COURT'S EXERCISE OF JURISDICTION OVER THE PERSON OR PROPERTY

1.   RAISING THE JURISDICTIONAL ISSUE DIRECTLY

Read Federal Rules of Civil Procedure 12(b), (g), and (h) and the accompanying material in the Supplement.

———

The term "special appearance" refers to the procedure at common law by which a defendant presented a challenge to the court's exercise of personal jurisdiction without submitting to the court's jurisdiction for any other purpose. The rules varied from state to state on the technical requirements for making a special appearance. A defendant generally had to designate the appearance "special" and limit himself to raising the jurisdictional defense. If he did anything else, such as argue the merits in any way, the defendant would be deemed to have made a "general appearance," constituting a voluntary submission to the court's jurisdiction and a waiver of any defects in the court's jurisdiction. Although substantial variation still may be encountered among different systems of state procedure, the general rules regarding objections to personal jurisdiction are illustrated by the federal scheme.

Assuming that the jurisdictional issue is timely raised, what procedures should a trial court follow to resolve the issue when the relevant facts are sharply disputed by the parties? Consider the discussion in DATA DISC, INC. v. SYSTEMS TECHNOLOGY ASSOCIATES, INC., 557 F.2d 1280, 1285–86 and n. 2 (9th Cir.1977):

A defendant may move, prior to trial, to dismiss the complaint for lack of personal jurisdiction. Fed.R.Civ.P. 12(b)(2). Because there is no statutory method for resolving this issue, the mode of its determination is left to the trial court. * * * The limits which the district judge imposes on the pre-trial proceedings will affect the burden which the plaintiff is required to meet.

If the court determines that it will receive only affidavits or affidavits plus discovery materials, these very limitations dictate that a plaintiff must make only a prima facie showing of jurisdictional facts through the submitted materials in order to avoid a defendant's motion to dismiss. Any greater burden—such as proof by a preponderance of the evidence— would permit a defendant to obtain a dismissal simply by controverting the facts established by a plaintiff through his own affidavits and supporting materials. Thus a plaintiff could not meet a burden of proof requiring a preponderance of the evidence without going beyond the written materials. Accordingly, if a plaintiff's proof is limited to written materials, it is necessary only for these materials to demonstrate facts which support a finding of jurisdiction in order to avoid a motion to dismiss. * * *

If a plaintiff make [sic] such a showing, however, it does not necessarily mean that he may then go to trial on the merits. If the pleadings and other submitted materials raise issues of credibility or disputed questions of fact with regard to jurisdiction, the district court has the discretion to take evidence at a preliminary hearing in order to resolve the contested issues. * * * In this situation, where plaintiff is put to his full proof, plaintiff must establish the jurisdictional facts by a preponderance of the evidence, just as he would have to do at trial. * * *

In a footnote, the court observed:

Where the jurisdictional facts are intertwined with the merits, a decision on the jurisdictional issues is dependent on a decision of the merits. In such a case, the district court could determine its jurisdiction in a plenary pretrial proceeding. * * * However, it is preferable that this determination be made at trial, where a plaintiff may present his case in a coherent, orderly fashion and without the risk of prejudicing his case on the merits. * * * Accordingly, where the jurisdictional facts are enmeshed with the merits, the district court may decide that the plaintiff should not be required in a Rule 12(d) preliminary proceeding to meet the higher burden of proof which is associated with the presentation of evidence at a hearing, but rather should be required only to establish a prima facie showing of jurisdictional facts with affidavits and perhaps discovery materials. * * * Of course, at any time when the plaintiff avoids a preliminary motion to dismiss by making a prima facie showing of jurisdictional facts, he must still prove the jurisdictional facts at trial by a preponderance of the evidence.

Notes and Questions

1. *Data Disc* suggests that trial courts have broad leeway in determining the procedures they will follow in resolving the jurisdictional issue. Is this degree of discretion consistent with due process considerations? Should a court have to determine the jurisdictional issue at the earliest possible stage of the proceeding by the most expeditious means? Is early resolution of the jurisdictional issue required to protect the defendant's constitutional right not to have to defend in a forum that does not have jurisdiction over her?

2. Occasionally the issue upon which jurisdiction depends is also an issue related to the merits of the claim. For example, in H.V. ALLEN CO. v. QUIP-MATIC, INC., 47 N.C.App. 40, 266 S.E.2d 768, review denied 301 N.C. 85, 273 S.E.2d 298 (1980), the plaintiff brought an action against a nonresident defendant alleging a breach of an oral contract. The plaintiff argued that jurisdiction was proper under North Carolina's long-arm statute, which authorized jurisdiction over defendants who had entered into contracts to be performed in the state. The defendant moved to dismiss for lack of personal jurisdiction and simultaneously sought summary judgment on the ground that there was no contract. In a case like *Quip-Matic*, what standard of proof must the plaintiff meet to establish jurisdiction? Would requiring proof by a preponderance of the evidence effectively create a trial on the merits? Would it be better to require the plaintiff to prove only a reasonable likelihood of success on the merits in order to establish jurisdiction and, if that standard is met, to put the jurisdictional issue to rest? A "reasonable likelihood" standard would avoid the anomalous result produced by a dismissal for lack of jurisdiction (an action that has no res judicata effect) after the merits have been fully litigated and decided by a jury in favor of defendant.

In *Quip-Matic*, the trial court denied the motion to dismiss for lack of jurisdiction, but granted the motion for summary judgment. When both parties appealed, the court of appeals ruled that the trial court should have dismissed for want of jurisdiction. Does this favor the plaintiff, since it can reinstitute the action in another forum as if there had been no ruling that no contract existed?

2. COLLATERAL ATTACK ON PERSONAL JURISDICTION

If a defendant contests a court's exercise of personal jurisdiction and loses, may he challenge jurisdiction again in a later action to enforce the judgment? Consider BALDWIN v. IOWA STATE TRAVELING MEN'S ASS'N, 283 U.S. 522, 51 S.Ct. 517, 75 L.Ed. 1244 (1931), in which respondent attempted to attack a judgment rendered against it in a Missouri federal District Court. The company had made a special appearance in the prior suit and had moved to set aside service and dismiss the case for a lack of personal jurisdiction, alleging that (1) it was an Iowa corporation, (2) it had never been present in Missouri, and (3) the person who had been served was not a proper agent for receiving process. The motion was overruled after a full hearing on affidavits and briefs. The company failed to plead on the merits, and judgment was entered against it. No appeal was taken. Suit then was brought in Iowa to enforce the judgment. In rejecting the respondent's attempt to attack the first judgment collaterally, the Supreme Court stated:

> * * * It is of no moment that the appearance was a special one expressly saving any submission to such jurisdiction. That fact would be important upon appeal from the judgment, and would save the question of the propriety of the court's decision on the matter, even though, after the motion had been overruled, the respondent had proceeded, subject to a reserved objection and exception, to a trial on the merits. * * * The special appearance gives point to the fact that the respondent entered the Missouri court for the very purpose of litigating the question of jurisdiction over its person. It had the election not to appear at all. * * * It had also the right to appeal from the decision of the Missouri District Court. * * *

> Public policy dictates that there be an end of litigation; that those who have contested an issue shall be bound by the result of the contest; and that matters once tried shall be considered forever settled as between parties. We see no reason why this doctrine should not apply in every case where one voluntarily appears, presents his case and is fully heard, and why he should not, in the absence of fraud, be thereafter concluded by the judgment of the tribunal to which he has submitted his cause.

Id. at 524–26, 51 S.Ct. at 517–18, 75 L.Ed. at 1245.

The *Baldwin* opinion repeats the established rule that a defendant who makes no appearance whatsoever remains free to challenge a default judgment for want of personal jurisdiction. The principle that a court has power to determine its own personal jurisdiction is limited to defendants who submit the question for resolution in that court. Would it be unthinkable to require a defendant to raise the jurisdictional objection in the initial forum or lose the opportunity to contest personal jurisdiction?

3. THE LIMITED–APPEARANCE PROBLEM

Can a defendant in an action commenced on a quasi-in-rem basis appear for the limited purpose of defending his interest in the attached property without submitting to the full in personam jurisdiction of the court? Is it fair to force a defendant in such an action to choose between appearing, and thereby risking the possibility of an in personam judgment in excess of the value of the attached property, or not appearing, thereby, as a practical matter, suffering the forfeiture of his property? Is it a violation of due process because it imposes an unconstitutional condition on a defendant's ability to protect his property? See *Developments in the Law—State Court Jurisdiction,* 73 Harv.L.Rev. 909, 954 (1960). How satisfactory is the answer given in U.S. INDUSTRIES, INC. v. GREGG, 58 F.R.D. 469, 479–80 (D.Del.1973), a case in which a Florida resident whose property had been sequestered in Delaware was refused the right to make a limited appearance and told that any judgment the court might enter in favor of the plaintiff would be an in personam one?

> There is * * * a legitimate public interest behind the general appearance rule. If a state or federal court is required by a defendant's response to a complaint to try and determine all of the issues upon which an *in personam* claim turns, there is a public interest in having that expenditure of judicial resources settle the rights of the parties with respect to that claim and in not leaving open the possibility of subsequent, duplicative litigation in the same court or another. This interest is similar to, though stronger, than, the one reflected in compulsory counterclaim rules.

> One must still ask, however, whether the price which a general appearance rule extracts from a defendant is excessive despite the countervailing public interest. Gregg suggests that it is because the forum, by definition, is one with which his only contact is the presence of his property within its jurisdiction. Requiring him to litigate in such a forum, he says, imposes an unconscionable burden. This Court has already held, however, that the acquisition of quasi-in-rem jurisdiction by sequestration is constitutional. Given the right of a court to require that a defendant whose property is seized defend on the merits or default, it is difficult to see what additional litigation burden a general appearance rule imposes upon a defendant. If he defaults recovery will be limited to the property seized. If he defends on the merits the trouble and expense of litigation will be no different whether a general or limited appearance rule is applied.

> Also unpersuasive is Gregg's argument that a general appearance rule gives a plaintiff an unfair advantage by allowing him to bring suit on a large claim in a jurisdiction where the original basis for jurisdiction is the presence of property having a comparatively small value. Any such unfairness does not rise to constitutional proportions. A similar phenomenon frequently occurs under compulsory counterclaim rules.

> Put in Gregg's "contact" terminology, if he defends upon the merits he has created an additional relationship with the forum jurisdiction; he is present in the forum court to litigate the factual and legal issues upon which a claim turns. This is sufficient contact to permit the court to adjudicate that very claim once and for all. * * *

Notes and Questions

1. Does the limited appearance have a constitutional basis after Shaffer v. Heitner, p. 154, supra? Of course, limited appearances still may be desirable as a matter of state law. For example, suppose that the state long-arm statute does not permit the exercise of personal jurisdiction to the full extent of the Due Process Clause, but that the statute for quasi-in-rem jurisdiction does. Without a limited-

appearance provision, defendants would be forced either to forego litigation on the merits or to accept full in personam liability—this, even when the long-arm statute would not allow in personam litigation. The trend has been toward permitting defendants the right of a "limited appearance." See, e.g., Dry Clime Lamp Corp. v. Edwards, 389 F.2d 590 (5th Cir.1968); Harvard Trust Co. v. Bray, 138 Vt. 199, 413 A.2d 1213 (1980).

2.   In SALMON FALLS MFG. CO. v. MIDLAND TIRE & RUBBER CO., 285 Fed. 214, 217 (6th Cir.1922), a case originally commenced in an Ohio state court and then removed to a federal court, the court permitted a limited appearance with the following caveat: "[H]ad defendant, while protesting against the court's jurisdiction to render personal judgment without reference to the value of the attached property, yet asked relief on the merits beyond that value, whether before or in connection with the making of its protest, [he] would be deemed to have appeared generally, and so to have waived lack of personal jurisdiction." But see Norris, Inc. v. M.H. Reed & Co., 278 Fed. 19 (5th Cir.1922); Grant v. Kellogg Co., 3 F.R.D. 229 (S.D.N.Y.1943), affirmed on other grounds 154 F.2d 59 (2d Cir.1946). Should a federal court exercising original quasi-in-rem jurisdiction under Rule 4(k) permit a limited appearance or should it follow the practice of the state in which it is sitting?

Chapter 3

PROVIDING NOTICE AND AN OPPORTUNITY TO BE HEARD

SECTION A. THE REQUIREMENT OF REASONABLE NOTICE

We have seen that the Due Process Clause limits the power of courts to assume adjudicatory authority over the parties to an action. In this section of the Chapter we focus on another requirement imposed by the Due Process Clause: the requirement that the parties be given reasonable notice of the lawsuit. This section will emphasize the constitutional dimension of the notice requirement. Sections B and C will treat some of the more mechanical issues raised by service of process.

As you think about notice, ask whether the definition of adequate notice should take into account the distinctions between and among in personam, quasi-in-rem, and in rem actions. Should there be more stringent requirements when jurisdiction is asserted pursuant to a long-arm statute? What if jurisdiction is based upon implied consent, as in *Hess*? Do the improvements in transportation and communication highlighted in *McGee* suggest that we need to worry less about notice?

 ## MULLANE v. CENTRAL HANOVER BANK & TRUST CO.

Supreme Court of the United States, 1950.
339 U.S. 306, 70 S.Ct. 652, 94 L.Ed. 865.

Appeal from the Court of Appeals of New York.

MR. JUSTICE JACKSON delivered the opinion of the Court.

This controversy questions the constitutional sufficiency of notice to beneficiaries on judicial settlement of accounts by the trustee of a common trust fund established under the New York Banking Law * * *. The New York Court of Appeals considered and overruled objections that the statutory notice contravenes requirements of the Fourteenth Amendment * * *. The case is here on appeal * * *.

Common trust fund legislation is addressed to a problem appropriate for state action. Mounting overheads have made administration of small trusts undesirable to corporate trustees. In order that donors and testators of moderately sized trusts may not be denied the service of corporate fiduciaries, the District of Columbia and some thirty states other than New York have permitted pooling small trust estates into one fund for investment administration. The income, capital gains, losses and expenses of the collective trust are shared by the constituent trusts in proportion to their contribution. By this plan, diversification of risk and economy of management can be extended to those whose capital standing alone would not obtain such advantage.

Statutory authorization for the establishment of such common trust funds is provided in the New York Banking Law, § 100–c * * *. Under this Act a trust company may, with approval of the State Banking Board, establish a common fund and, within prescribed limits, invest therein the assets of an unlimited number of estates, trusts or other funds of which it is trustee. Each participating trust shares ratably in the common fund, but exclusive management and control is in the trust company as trustee, and neither a fiduciary nor any beneficiary of a participating trust is deemed to have ownership in any particular asset or investment of this common fund. The trust company must keep fund assets separate from its own, and in its fiduciary capacity may not deal with itself or any affiliate. Provisions are made for accountings twelve to fifteen months after the establishment of a fund and triennially thereafter. The decree in each such judicial settlement of accounts is made binding and conclusive as to any matter set forth in the account upon everyone having any interest in the common fund or in any participating estate, trust or fund.

In January, 1946, Central Hanover Bank and Trust Company established a common trust fund in accordance with these provisions, and in March, 1947, it petitioned the Surrogate's Court for settlement of its first account as common trustee. During the accounting period a total of 113 trusts, approximately half *inter vivos* and half testamentary, participated in the common trust fund, the gross capital of which was nearly three million dollars. The record does not show the number or residence of the beneficiaries, but they were many and it is clear that some of them were not residents of the State of New York.

The only notice given beneficiaries of this specific application [for judicial settlement of the account] was by publication in a local newspaper [for four successive weeks] in strict compliance with the minimum requirements of N.Y. Banking Law § 100–c(12) * * *. Thus the only notice required, and the only one given, was by newspaper publication setting forth merely the name and address of the trust company, the name and the date of establishment of the common trust fund, and a list of all participating estates, trusts or funds.

At the time the first investment in the common fund was made on behalf of each participating estate, however, the trust company, pursuant to the requirements of § 100–c(9), had notified by mail each person of full age and sound mind whose name and address was then known to it and who was "entitled to share in the income therefrom * * * [or] * * * who would be entitled to share in the principal if the event upon which such estate, trust or fund will become distributable should have occurred at the time of sending such notice." Included in the notice was a copy of those provisions of the Act relating to the sending of the notice itself and to the judicial settlement of common trust fund accounts.

Upon the filing of the petition for the settlement of accounts, appellant was, by order of the court pursuant to § 100–c(12), appointed special guardian and attorney for all persons known or unknown not otherwise appearing who had or might thereafter have any interest in the income of the common trust fund; and appellee Vaughan was appointed to represent those similarly interested in the principal. There were no other appearances on behalf of any one interested in either interest or principal.

Appellant appeared specially, objecting that notice and the statutory provisions for notice to beneficiaries were inadequate to afford due process under the Fourteenth Amendment, and therefore that the court was without jurisdiction to render a final and binding decree. Appellant's objections were entertained and overruled [by] the Surrogate * * *. A final decree accepting the accounts has been entered, affirmed by the Appellate Division of the Supreme Court * * * and by the Court of Appeals of the State of New York * * *.

The effect of this decree, as held below, is to settle "all questions respecting the management of the common fund." We understand that every right which beneficiaries would otherwise have against the trust company, either as trustee of the common fund or as trustee of any individual trust, for improper management of the common trust fund during the period covered by the accounting is sealed and wholly terminated by the decree. * * *

We are met at the outset with a challenge to the power of the State—the right of its courts to adjudicate at all as against those beneficiaries who reside without the State of New York. It is contended that the proceeding is one *in personam* in that the decree affects neither title to nor possession of any *res,* but adjudges only personal rights of the beneficiaries to surcharge their trustee for negligence or breach of trust. Accordingly, it is said, under the strict doctrine of Pennoyer v. Neff * * * the Surrogate is without jurisdiction as to nonresidents upon whom personal service of process was not made.

Distinctions between actions *in rem* and those *in personam* are ancient and originally expressed in procedural terms what seems really to have been a distinction in the substantive law of property under a system quite unlike our own. * * * The legal recognition and rise in economic importance of incorporeal or intangible forms of property have upset the ancient simplicity of property law and the clarity of its distinctions, while new forms of proceedings have confused the old procedural classification. American courts have sometimes classed certain actions as *in rem* because personal service of process was not required, and at other times have held personal service of process not required because the action was *in rem.* * * *

Judicial proceedings to settle fiduciary accounts have been sometime termed *in rem,* or more indefinitely *quasi in rem,* or more vaguely still, "in the nature of a proceeding *in rem.*" It is not readily apparent how the courts of New York did or would classify the present proceeding, which has some characteristics and is wanting in some features of proceedings both *in rem* and *in personam.* But in any event we think that the requirements of the Fourteenth Amendment to the Federal Constitution do not depend upon a classification for which the standards are so elusive and confused generally and which, being primarily for state courts to define, may and do vary from state to state. Without disparaging the usefulness of distinctions between actions *in rem* and those *in personam* in many branches of law, or on other issues, or the reasoning which underlies them, we do not rest the power of the State to resort to constructive service in this proceeding upon how its courts or this Court may regard this historic antithesis. It is sufficient to observe that, whatever the technical definition of its chosen procedure, the interest of each state in providing means to close trusts that exist by the grace of its laws and are administered under the supervision of its courts is so insistent and rooted in custom as to establish beyond doubt the right of its courts to determine the interests of all claimants, resident or nonresident, provided its procedure accords full opportunity to appear and be heard.

Quite different from the question of a state's power to discharge trustees is that of the opportunity it must give beneficiaries to contest. Many controversies have raged about the cryptic and abstract words of the Due Process Clause but there can be no doubt that at a minimum they require that deprivation of life, liberty or property by adjudication be preceded by notice and opportunity for hearing appropriate to the nature of the case.

In two ways this proceeding does or may deprive beneficiaries of property. It may cut off their rights to have the trustee answer for negligent or illegal impairments of their interests. Also, their interests are presumably subject to diminution in the proceeding by allowance of fees and expenses to one who, in their names but without their knowledge, may conduct a fruitless or uncompensatory contest. Certainly the proceeding is one in which they may be deprived of property rights and hence notice and hearing must measure up to the standards of due process.

Personal service of written notice within the jurisdiction is the classic form of notice always adequate in any type of proceeding. But the vital interest of the State in bringing any issues as to its fiduciaries to a final settlement can be served only if interests or claims of individuals who are outside of the State can somehow be determined. A construction of the Due Process Clause which would place impossible or impractical obstacles in the way could not be justified.

Against this interest of the State we must balance the individual interest sought to be protected by the Fourteenth Amendment. This is defined by our holding that "The fundamental requisite of due process of law is the opportunity to be heard." Grannis v. Ordean, 234 U.S. 385, 394, 34 S.Ct. 779, 783, 58 L.Ed. 1363. This right to be heard has little reality or worth unless one is informed that the matter is pending and can choose for himself whether to appear or default, acquiesce or contest.

The Court has not committed itself to any formula achieving a balance between these interests in a particular proceeding or determining when constructive notice may be utilized or what test it must meet. Personal service has not in all circumstances been regarded as indispensable to the process due to residents, and it has more often been held unnecessary as to nonresidents.
* * *

An elementary and fundamental requirement of due process in any proceeding which is to be accorded finality is notice reasonably calculated, under all the circumstances, to apprise interested parties of the pendency of the action and afford them an opportunity to present their objections. * * * The notice must be of such nature as reasonably to convey the required information * * * and it must afford a reasonable time for those interested to make their appearance * * *. But if with due regard for the practicalities and peculiarities of the case these conditions are reasonably met the constitutional requirements are satisfied. * * *

But when notice is a person's due, process which is a mere gesture is not due process. The means employed must be such as one desirous of actually informing the absentee might reasonably adopt to accomplish it. The reasonableness and hence the constitutional validity of any chosen method may be defended on the ground that it is in itself reasonably certain to inform those affected * * *, or, where conditions do not reasonably permit such notice, that the form chosen is not substantially less likely to bring home notice than other of the feasible and customary substitutes.

It would be idle to pretend that publication alone, as prescribed here, is a reliable means of acquainting interested parties of the fact that their rights are before the courts. It is not an accident that the greater number of cases reaching this Court on the question of adequacy of notice have been concerned with actions founded on process constructively served through local newspapers. Chance alone brings to the attention of even a local resident an advertisement in small type inserted in the back pages of a newspaper, and if he makes his home outside the area of the newspaper's normal circulation the odds that the information will never reach him are large indeed. The chance of actual notice is further reduced when as here the notice required does not even name those whose attention it is supposed to attract, and does not inform acquaintances who might call it to attention. In weighing its sufficiency on the basis of equivalence with actual notice we are unable to regard this as more than a feint.

Nor is publication here reinforced by steps likely to attract the parties' attention to the proceeding. It is true that publication traditionally has been acceptable as notification supplemental to other action which in itself may reasonably be expected to convey a warning. The ways of an owner with tangible property are such that he usually arranges means to learn of any direct attack upon his possessory or proprietary rights. Hence, libel of a ship, attachment of a chattel or entry upon real estate in the name of law may reasonably be expected to come promptly to the owner's attention. When the state within which the owner has located such property seizes it for some reason, publication or posting affords an additional measure of notification. A state may indulge the assumption that one who has left tangible property in the state either has abandoned it, in which case proceedings against it deprive him of nothing * * *, or that he has left some caretaker under a duty to let him know that it is being jeopardized. * * *

In the case before us there is, of course, no abandonment. On the other hand these beneficiaries do have a resident fiduciary as caretaker of their interest in this property. But it is their caretaker who in the accounting becomes their adversary. Their trustee is released from giving notice of jeopardy, and no one else is expected to do so. Not even the special guardian is required or apparently expected to communicate with his ward and client, and, of course, if such a duty were merely transferred from the trustee to the guardian, economy would not be served and more likely the cost would be increased.

This Court has not hesitated to approve of resort to publication as a customary substitute in another class of cases where it is not reasonably possible or practicable to give more adequate warning. Thus it has been recognized that, in the case of persons missing or unknown, employment of an indirect and even a probably futile means of notification is all that the situation permits and creates no constitutional bar to a final decree foreclosing their rights. * * *

Those beneficiaries represented by appellant whose interests or whereabouts could not with due diligence be ascertained come clearly within this category. As to them the statutory notice is sufficient. However great the odds that publication will never reach the eyes of such unknown parties, it is not in the typical case much more likely to fail than any of the choices open to legislators endeavoring to prescribe the best notice practicable.

Nor do we consider it unreasonable for the State to dispense with more certain notice to those beneficiaries whose interests are either conjectural or future or, although they could be discovered upon investigation, do not in due course of business come to knowledge of the common trustee. Whatever searches might be required in another situation under ordinary standards of diligence, in view of the character of the proceedings and the nature of the interests here involved we think them unnecessary. We recognize the practical difficulties and costs that would be attendant on frequent investigations into the status of great numbers of beneficiaries, many of whose interests in the common fund are so remote as to be ephemeral; and we have no doubt that such impracticable and extended searches are not required in the name of due process. The expense of keeping informed from day to day of substitutions among even current income beneficiaries and presumptive remaindermen, to say nothing of the far greater number of contingent beneficiaries, would impose a severe burden on the plan, and would likely dissipate its advantages. These are practical matters in which we should be reluctant to disturb the judgment of the state authorities.

Accordingly we overrule appellant's constitutional objections to published notice insofar as they are urged on behalf of any beneficiaries whose interests or addresses are unknown to the trustee.

As to known present beneficiaries of known place of residence, however, notice by publication stands on a different footing. Exceptions in the name of necessity do not sweep away the rule that within the limits of practicability notice must be such as is reasonably calculated to reach interested parties. Where the names and post office addresses of those affected by a proceeding are at hand, the reasons disappear for resort to means less likely than the mails to apprise them of its pendency.

The trustee has on its books the names and addresses of the income beneficiaries represented by appellant, and we find no tenable ground for dispensing with a serious effort to inform them personally of the accounting, at least by ordinary mail to the record addresses. * * * Certainly sending them a copy of the statute months and perhaps years in advance does not answer this purpose. The trustee periodically remits their income to them, and we think that they might reasonably expect that with or apart from their remittances word might come to them personally that steps were being taken affecting their interests.

We need not weigh contentions that a requirement of personal service of citation on even the large number of known resident or nonresident beneficiaries would, by reasons of delay if not of expense, seriously interfere with the proper administration of the fund. Of course personal service even without the jurisdiction of the issuing authority serves the end of actual and personal notice, whatever power of compulsion it might lack. However, no such service is required under the circumstances. This type of trust presupposes a large number of small interests. The individual interest does not stand alone but is identical with that of a class. The rights of each in the integrity of the fund and the fidelity of the trustee are shared by many other beneficiaries. Therefore notice reasonably certain to reach most of those interested in objecting is likely to safeguard the interests of all, since any objections sustained would inure to the benefit of all. We think that under such circumstances reasonable risks that notice might not actually reach every beneficiary are justifiable. * * *

The statutory notice to known beneficiaries is inadequate, not because in fact it fails to reach everyone, but because under the circumstances it is not reasonably calculated to reach those who could easily be informed by other means at hand. However it may have been in former times, the mails today are recognized as an efficient and inexpensive means of communication. Moreover, the fact that the trust company has been able to give mailed notice to known beneficiaries at the time the common trust fund was established is persuasive that postal notification at the time of accounting would not seriously burden the plan.

We hold the notice of judicial settlement of accounts required by the New York Banking Law § 100–c(12) is incompatible with the requirements of the Fourteenth Amendment as a basis for adjudication depriving known persons whose whereabouts are also known of substantial property rights. * * *

Reversed.

MR. JUSTICE DOUGLAS took no part in the consideration or decision of this case.

[The dissenting opinion of JUSTICE BURTON is omitted.]

Notes and Questions

1. *Mullane* seems to require notice that is reasonably calculated to succeed. Does this mean that the method *most likely* to succeed is not required? How does *Mullane* justify this? What role should cost play in determining what is reasonable? Does *Mullane* justify applying different notice requirements for small claims than for large claims?

2. In McDONALD v. MABEE, 243 U.S. 90, 92, 37 S.Ct. 343, 344, 61 L.Ed. 608, 609–10 (1917), suit was brought against Mabee, a domiciliary of Texas, upon a promissory note. Although his family was residing in the state, he had left Texas to establish a domicile elsewhere. Service was attempted through publication in a local newspaper once a week for four successive weeks after Mabee's departure from the state. Mabee never appeared in the action.

The United States Supreme Court, reversing the Texas Supreme Court, held that the Texas judgment was void under the Fourteenth Amendment:

> There is no dispute that service by publication does not warrant a personal judgment against a nonresident. * * * When the former suit was begun, Mabee, although technically domiciled in Texas, had left the state intending to establish his home elsewhere. Perhaps in view of his technical position and the actual presence of his family in the state a summons left at his last and usual place of abode would have been enough. But it appears to us that an advertisement in a local newspaper is not sufficient notice to bind a person who has left a state intending not to return. To dispense with personal service the substitute that is most likely to reach the defendant is the least that ought to be required if substantial justice is to be done.

How does *Mullane* affect *Mabee*? Would service at the last and usual place of abode be reasonably calculated to succeed? Would publication in a local newspaper be sufficient if Mabee were still in Texas? What if Mabee had moved to a different part of Texas?

3. In WUCHTER v. PIZZUTTI, 276 U.S. 13, 48 S.Ct. 259, 72 L.Ed. 446 (1928), the Supreme Court invalidated a New Jersey nonresident-motorist statute similar to the one involved in Hess v. Pawloski, p. 71, supra, because it did not expressly require the Secretary of State to communicate notice of the commencement of the action to the nonresident. In fact, notice actually was given by the Secretary of State. According to the Supreme Court: "Every statute of this kind * * * should require the plaintiff bringing the suit to show in the summons to be served the post office address or residence of the defendant being sued, and should impose either on the plaintiff himself or upon the official receiving service or some other, the duty of communication by mail or otherwise with the defendant."

Why would the Supreme Court have invalidated service even though the defendant received actual notice of the action? One commentator has suggested the following explanation: "Apart from the defendant's personal constitutional right to notice, the due process clause also imposes restrictions on how a state must act when it imposes unique burdens on persons. One such restriction, *Wuchter* seems to say, is that the steps that can lead to the imposition of such a burden must be formally and officially predetermined and declared rather than determined ad hoc." Casad, Book Review, 80 Mich.L.Rev. 664, 670 (1982). Does this explanation convince you? Would the result of *Wuchter* be the same after *Mullane*?

4. *Mullane* states that attachment of a chattel or real estate, together with publication, may provide adequate notice, under the theory that property owners usually are aware of and concerned about the status of their property. Is this consistent with Justice Jackson's insistence that jurisdiction labels, such as in personam and in rem, should not be considered significant? In later cases, the Court held that the manner of notice used in state condemnation proceedings did not meet due process requirements when the only notice to the property owners was by publication in a local newspaper, Walker v. City of Hutchinson, 352 U.S. 112, 77 S.Ct. 200, 1 L.Ed.2d 178 (1956), or by publication coupled with signs posted on trees, Schroeder v. City of New York, 371 U.S. 208, 83 S.Ct. 279, 9 L.Ed.2d 255 (1962). In both cases the names and addresses of the owners were known or ascertainable from public records.

In MENNONITE BOARD OF MISSIONS v. ADAMS, 462 U.S. 791, 103 S.Ct. 2706, 77 L.Ed.2d 180 (1983), the Court held that notice by publication and posting did not provide a mortgagee of real property with adequate notice of a proceeding to sell the mortgaged property for nonpayment of taxes. "When the mortgagee is identified in a mortgage that is publicly recorded, constructive notice by publication must be supplemented by notice mailed to the mortgagee's last known available address, or by personal service. But unless the mortgagee is not reasonably identifiable, constructive notice alone does not satisfy the mandate of *Mullane*." Id. at 798, 103 S.Ct. at 2711, 77 L.Ed.2d at 187. The Court observed that personal service or mailed notice is required even though the mortgagee may have known of the delinquency in the payment of taxes, or as a sophisticated creditor had the means to discover that the taxes had not been paid and that a tax sale proceeding was therefore likely to be initiated.

In light of these Supreme Court decisions are there any instances in which it is safe to say that attachment plus publication is a sufficient procedure to establish jurisdiction?

5. Consider TULSA PROFESSIONAL COLLECTION SERVICES, INC. v. POPE, 485 U.S. 478, 108 S.Ct. 1340, 99 L.Ed.2d 565 (1988). Under the nonclaim provision of Oklahoma's probate code, creditors' claims against an estate generally are barred unless presented to the executor or executrix within two months of the publication of notice of the commencement of probate proceedings. Jeanne Pope, an executrix, published the required notice in compliance with the terms of the nonclaim statute and a probate court order, but Tulsa Professional Collection Services, Inc., failed to file a timely claim. For this reason, the probate court denied appellant's application for payment, and both the Oklahoma Court of Appeals and Supreme Court affirmed, rejecting appellant's contention that, in failing to require more than publication notice, the nonclaim statute violated due process.

The United States Supreme Court reversed, holding that if Tulsa Professional's identity as a creditor was known or "reasonably ascertainable" by Pope (a fact the Court said could not be determined from the record before it), the Due Process Clause of the Fourteenth Amendment required that the collection agency be given notice by mail or such other means as is certain to ensure actual notice.

The Court rejected Pope's argument that the nonclaim statute was simply a self-executing statute of limitations. Rather, it reasoned, the probate court's intimate involvement throughout the probate proceedings—particularly the court's activation of the statute's time bar by the appointment of an executor—constituted state action adversely affecting protected property interests, since untimely claims, such as that of Tulsa Professional's, were completely extinguished.

Given this view of the nonclaim provision, the Court went on to say that, on balance, satisfying creditors' substantial practical need for actual notice in the probate setting is not so cumbersome or impracticable as to burden unduly the state's undeniably legitimate interest in the expeditious resolution of the proceedings, since mail service (which already is routinely provided at several points in the probate process) is inexpensive, efficient, and reasonably calculated to provide actual notice, and since publication notice will suffice for creditors whose identities are not ascertainable by reasonably diligent efforts or whose claims merely are conjectural. For further discussions of *Pope,* see Waterbury, *Notice to Decedents' Creditors,* 73 Minn.L.Rev. 763 (1989); Note, *New Requirements of Creditor Notice in Probate Proceedings,* 54 Mo.L.Rev. 189 (1989).

6. In GREENE v. LINDSEY, 456 U.S. 444, 102 S.Ct. 1874, 72 L.Ed.2d 249 (1982), the Supreme Court considered a Kentucky statute that provided, in forcible entry and detainer actions, for service of process by posting a summons on the door of a tenant's apartment. A group of tenants in a public housing project, each of whom faced eviction, sought a declaration from a federal court that the notice procedure employed as a predicate to the eviction proceedings did not satisfy the *Mullane* standard. They claimed never to have seen the posted summonses, and that they did not learn of the eviction proceedings until they were served with writs of possession, executed after default judgments had been entered against them, and after their opportunity for appeal had lapsed. The Supreme Court, in an opinion by Justice Brennan, found the notice insufficient to satisfy the Due Process Clause.

> The empirical basis of the presumption that notice posted upon property is adequate to alert the owner or occupant of property of the pendency of legal proceedings would appear to make the presumption particularly well-founded where notice is posted at a residence. With respect to claims affecting the continued possession of that residence, the application of this presumption seems particularly apt: If the tenant has a continuing interest in maintaining possession of the property for his use and occupancy, he might reasonably be expected to frequent the premises; if he no longer occupies the premises, then the injury that might result from his not having received actual notice as a consequence of the posted notice is reduced. Short of providing personal service, then, posting notice on the door of a person's home would, in many or perhaps most instances, constitute not only a constitutionally acceptable means of service, but indeed a singularly appropriate and effective way of ensuring that a person who cannot conveniently be served personally is actually apprised of proceedings against him.

> But whatever the efficacy of posting in many cases, it is clear that, in the circumstances of this case, merely posting notice on an apartment door does not satisfy minimum standards of due process. In a significant number of instances, reliance on posting pursuant to the provisions of * * * [the statute] results in a failure to provide actual notice to the tenant concerned. Indeed, appellees claim to have suffered precisely such a failure of actual notice. As the process servers were well aware, notices posted on apartment doors in the area where these tenants lived were "not infrequently" removed by children or other tenants before they could have their intended effect. Under these conditions, notice by posting on the apartment door cannot be considered a "reliable means of acquainting interested parties of the fact that their rights are before the courts."

Id. at 452–54, 102 S.Ct. at 1879–80, 72 L.Ed.2d at 257–58. Justice Brennan conceded that the reasonableness of the notice provided must be tested with reference to the existence of feasible alternatives and supplements to the form of notice chosen, but he concluded that, given the danger that posted notice alone would not succeed in the circumstances before the Court, the Due Process Clause required that the posting be supplemented by notice through the mails.

Justice O'Connor, joined by Chief Justice Burger and Justice Rehnquist, dissented.

> The Court * * * holds that notice via the mails is so far superior to posted notice that the difference is of constitutional dimension. How the Court reaches this judgment remains a mystery, especially since the Court is unable, on the present record, to evaluate the risks that notice mailed to

public housing projects might fail due to loss, misdelivery, lengthy delay, or theft. Furthermore, the advantages of the mails over posting, if any, are far from obvious. It is no secret, after all, that unattended mailboxes are subject to plunder by thieves. Moreover, unlike the use of the mails, posting notices at least gives assurance that the notice has gotten as far as the tenant's door.

Id. at 459–60, 102 S.Ct. at 1883, 72 L.Ed.2d at 261. Did Justice Brennan find that notice by mail was, as a matter of constitutional law, superior to notice posted upon the apartment door? See Greenbaum, *The Postman Never Rings Twice: The Constitutionality of Service of Process by Posting After Greene v. Lindsey,* 33 Am.U.L.Rev. 601 (1984).

In *Greene,* did Justice Brennan use the *Mullane* standard or did he employ a higher standard? Upon whom did he impose the burden of proof on the issue of reasonableness? How can that burden be carried? Remember, the method of notice challenged in *Greene* had been approved by the Kentucky state legislature.

Should the constitutional standard used to judge the reasonableness of notice vary according to the type of action or the nature of issue at stake? In her dissent, Justice O'Connor suggested that the need for swift action in eviction proceedings might justify a lower standard for notice. Shouldn't the issue at stake, however, be phrased as the tenants' right to possess their apartments?

7. If personal service is impossible or impractical, what methods of service become reasonable? In DOBKIN v. CHAPMAN, 21 N.Y.2d 490, 289 N.Y.S.2d 161, 236 N.E.2d 451 (1968), the New York Court of Appeals upheld court-ordered substituted service in three automobile accident cases (by ordinary mail to the defendant's last known address and publication in a local newspaper), when the whereabouts of the defendants were unknown and service in the manner attempted was the best the plaintiffs could do in these "situations in which insistence on actual notice, or even on the high probability of actual notice, would be both unfair to plaintiffs and harmful to the public interest." The court stressed that if the defendants failed to get notice it was their fault since they either had failed to furnish the plaintiff a correct address at the scene of the accident, as required by New York law, or had failed to leave a forwarding address.

8. What if circumstances exist that would affect the particular notice's effectiveness and the defendant's ability to respond to the complaint? In COVEY v. TOWN OF SOMERS, 351 U.S. 141, 146–47, 76 S.Ct. 724, 727, 100 L.Ed. 1021, 1026 (1956), the Court held that notice by mail of a proceeding to foreclose a lien for delinquent taxes on real property, although ordinarily sufficient, would not satisfy due process requirements when it was mailed to someone known to have been adjudged insane and committed to a hospital, and who is without the protection of a guardian. Would notice by mail have been sufficient if the town authorities were unaware of the defendant's disability?

Should there be a heightened notice requirement when the federal government is the plaintiff and the defendant is incarcerated in a federal prison? In WENG v. United States, 137 F.3d 709 (2d Cir.1998), the court held that actual notice is required in those circumstances. In UNITED STATES v. CLARK, 84 F.3d 378 (10th Cir.1996), however, the Tenth Circuit ruled that notice mailed to the detention facility in which the defendant was being held was sufficient. More recently, the Third Circuit in UNITED STATES v. ONE TOSHIBA COLOR TELEVISION, 213 F.3d 147 (3d Cir.2000), took the intermediate position that the government need only prove either actual notice or a notice-giving procedure reasonably calculated to provide notice. Should it matter if the defendant is incarcerated in a state prison? In DONOVAN v. UNITED STATES, 172 F.3d 53 (7th Cir.1999) (opinion in Westlaw), the court held that a heightened notice requirement would be too burdensome when the prisoner is in state rather than federal prison. Does this distinction make sense?

9. The question of what methods for communicating notice are acceptable is different from the question of what the content of the notice should be. Is the Due Process Clause also concerned with the content of the notice given? In AGUCHAK v. MONTGOMERY WARD CO., 520 P.2d 1352 (Alaska 1974), Montgomery Ward, the plaintiff, sold a snowmobile and freezer to the Aguchaks, which they took to a remote area where they lived. When the Aguchaks allegedly did not pay, Montgomery Ward sent a summons to which the Aguchaks did not respond and a default judgment of $988.22 plus costs was entered against them. The summons did not inform the Aguchaks that they could appear by a written pleading, nor did it inform them that they had a right to request a change of venue. In order to appear in person at the court, the defendants would have had to fly at a cost of $186 with at least one night stopover. On appeal, the Supreme Court of Alaska held that the summons in small claims cases had to include this information, and set aside the default judgment.

The federal rules also reflect some concern regarding the content of the summons: Rule 4(a) generally prescribes the contents of the summons to be used in federal actions, and the Supreme Court has approved an illustrative form of summons, Official Form 1, which is reproduced in the Supplement. See generally 4A Wright & Miller, *Federal Practice and Procedure: Civil 3d* §§ 1088, 1131 (2001).

The content of the notice is also prescribed in California's Code of Civil Procedure § 412.20, which requires a bold-faced warning in Spanish and English that the recipient is being sued. Counties may designate additional languages.

SECTION B. THE MECHANICS OF GIVING NOTICE

————

Read Federal Rule of Civil Procedure 4 and the comparable state statutes set out in the Supplement.

————

1. INTRODUCTION

Notice of a suit is given by the service of process upon the defendant. Each jurisdiction has a set of rules governing the correct methods of making service. Traditionally, process consists of a copy of the plaintiff's complaint, together with a summons directing the defendant to answer. Service of process is made by personal delivery of the summons and complaint to the defendant. Other methods of service, such as delivery by mail, have assumed greater importance since the advent of long-arm statutes.

The procedure governing service of process in federal actions was changed significantly in 1983, and again in 1993. In 1982, the Supreme Court proposed but Congress rejected an amendment to the Rules that would have permitted service by registered or certified mail, return receipt, with delivery restricted to the addressee. It was asserted that the use of certified mail causes problems when, for example, the signature on the return receipt is illegible or the name signed differs somewhat from that of the defendant, or when it is difficult to determine whether mail has been "refused" or "unclaimed." It also was claimed that the result of relying on the mail for service of process would be the entry of many more unnecessary and unfair default judgments, which would have to be reopened when challenged. Other objections were directed to the provision restricting delivery: mail carriers could easily deliver process to the wrong person or fail to make the necessary inquiries to find the proper person. See Cong. Record, December 15, 1982, at H9848–H9856, reproduced in 96 F.R.D. at 116–35.

In 1983, Congress instead chose a system of service by mail modeled after the one used in California. See Cal.Code Civ.Pro. § 415.30. The summons and complaint could be sent by ordinary first class mail, together with a form for acknowledging receipt of service. If the acknowledgment form was not returned, plaintiff had to effect service through some other means authorized by the Rules. In order to encourage defendants to execute and return the form, the Rule directed the court to order a defendant who did not cooperate to pay the costs incurred by the plaintiff in making personal service, unless the defendant could show good cause for failing to return the acknowledgment form.

This system was not always successful because it relied on the defendant's cooperation in returning the acknowledgment form. Thus, after a decade of use, Rule 4 was revised again in 1993. The most significant change was that the "service by mail" provision was replaced by Rule 4(d), which strongly encourages waiver of formal service. Under this modification, an action commences when the plaintiff sends a form (Form 1A) entitled "Notice of Lawsuit and Request for Waiver of Service of Summons," or similar document, by mail or some other "reliable" means. Domestic defendants have thirty days from the date on which the waiver was sent to return the waiver; otherwise they will be charged with the costs associated with providing formal service. Along with the threat of paying for the costs of service, defendants receive a positive incentive in that they are allowed sixty days after the date on which the waiver was sent to answer the complaint if the waiver is returned in a timely fashion. Note that even under the new rule, if a plaintiff is confronting a statute of limitations deadline in a state in which the statute continues to run until a defendant is served, see pp. 220–22, infra, formal service sometimes may still be the wisest course of action, because the defendant may refuse to waive service.

The specific means of making personal service on, among others, individuals, corporations, partnerships, and other associations subject to suit under a common name are set out in several subdivisions of Rule 4. In addition, Rule 4(e)(1) provides an alternative to these methods by broadly authorizing the use in federal courts of the procedures governing the manner of service prescribed by the law of the state in which the District Court is sitting. And Rule 4(e) specifically provides that state procedures to serve a party "may be effected in any judicial district in the United States," thus enabling federal courts to take advantage of the reach of state long-arm statutes. See 4A Wright & Miller, *Federal Practice and Procedure: Civil 3d* §§ 1112–16, 1119–23 (2001); Foster, *Long-Arm Jurisdiction in Federal Courts,* 1969 Wis.

L.Rev. 9; Foster, *Judicial Economy; Fairness and Convenience of Place of Trial: Long–Arm Jurisdiction in District Courts,* 47 F.R.D. 73 (1969).

Note should be made of the elaborate provision for service of process in a foreign country in Federal Rule 4(f). A comparable provision is found in § 2.01 of the Uniform Interstate and International Procedure Act. 13 Uniform Laws Ann. 355, 382–84 (1986). The intention of these provisions is to provide American attorneys with an extremely flexible framework to permit accommodation to the widely divergent procedures for service of process employed by the various nations of the world. This accommodation is necessary in order to avoid violating the sovereignty of other countries by committing acts within their borders that they may consider to be "official" and to maximize the likelihood that the judgment rendered in the action in this country will be recognized and enforced abroad. Service of process in a foreign country and other procedural aspects of civil litigation having multi-national incidents are discussed in Miller, *International Cooperation in Litigation Between the United States and Switzerland: Unilateral Procedural Accommodation in a Test Tube,* 49 Minn.L.Rev. 1069, 1075–86 (1965); Comment, *Revitalization of the International Judicial Assistance Procedures of the United States: Service of Documents and Taking of Testimony,* 62 Mich.L.Rev. 1375, 1377–86 (1964). See also 4A Wright & Miller, *Federal Practice and Procedure: Civil 3d* §§ 1133–36 (2001).

The 1993 revision of the Federal Rules expressly provides in Rule 4(f) that "any internationally agreed means reasonably calculated to give notice" may be used to effect service on persons outside the United States. The most important internationally agreed means concerning the service of process are contained in the Hague Service Convention, which has been adopted by over thirty-five countries. (Convention on the Service Abroad of Judicial and Extrajudicial Documents in Civil or Commercial Matters, The Hague, 1965, 20 U.S.T. 361, T.I.A.S. No. 6638, 658 U.N.T.S. 163, reproduced (with declarations by the contracting states) in 28 U.S.C.A. following Fed.R.Civ.P. 4.) The heart of the Convention is a requirement that each Contracting State establish a Central Authority, which will receive and execute requests for service from judicial authorities in other Contracting States, and will see that a certification that service has been effected is returned to the court of origin. Service may be made either in accordance with the law of the nation in which service is to be made or (unless incompatible with that law) by a particular method requested by the applicant. 1 B. Ristau, *International Judicial Assistance (Civil and Commercial)* § 4–3–1 (rev. ed. 1990).

There are, however, several circumstances involving foreign defendants not governed by the Hague Convention. To begin with, the Convention does not govern in those countries that are not Contracting States. Furthermore, the United States Supreme Court held in VOLKSWAGENWERK AKTIENGESELLSCHAFT v. SCHLUNK, 486 U.S. 694, 108 S.Ct. 2104, 100 L.Ed.2d 722 (1988) that the Convention applies only if service actually is made *abroad,* rather than on the domestic subsidiary of a foreign corporation deemed to be the corporation's involuntary agent for service of process. Moreover, as a result of the 1993 change in Rule 4(d) described above from "service by agreement" to "waiver of service," the Hague Convention appears to be inapplicable when the defendant takes advantage of the waiver procedure. Because the Convention is only invoked by "service" abroad, an agreement to waive service, if voluntary and private, may be regarded as not implicating the Convention, although some other nations might well take a contrary position. Foreign defendants, like domestic defendants, are given incentives by Rule 4(d) to waive service in the form of longer times to respond, but they are not to be charged with the costs for formal service should they refuse to return the waiver, since otherwise the waiver could be deemed compulsory and thus might violate the Convention. See Born & Vollmer, *The Effect of the Revised Federal Rules of Civil Procedure on Personal Jurisdiction, Service and Discovery in International Cases,* 150 F.R.D. 221, 230–41 (1994).

2. SPECIFIC APPLICATIONS OF THE SERVICE PROVISIONS

a. *"Waiver of Service"*

MARYLAND STATE FIREMEN'S ASSOCIATION v. CHAVES

United States District Court, District of Maryland, 1996.
166 F.R.D. 353.

MESSITTE, DISTRICT JUDGE.

I.

The Maryland State Firemen's Association ("MSFA") has sued John Chaves, President of the FireFighters Association of America ("FFA"), alleging that Chaves illegally solicited charitable contributions that MSFA has the right to recover. The Complaint was filed on January 2, 1996. On March 4, MSFA filed a Motion for Judgment by Default. On March 11, based on MSFA's attorney's affidavit of service, the Clerk entered default against Chaves for failure to plead.

On April 9, the Court sent a letter to MSFA's counsel questioning the validity of the service and requesting a more detailed affidavit describing the type of service employed and a brief legal memorandum indicating why counsel believed service was effective. The Court has now received and considered MSFA's submission. Because the Court judges service of process invalid in this case, the Court will SET ASIDE the Clerk's Entry of Default and DENY MSFA's Motion for Default Judgment.

II.

It is axiomatic that service of process must be effective under the Federal Rules of Civil Procedure before a default or a default judgment may be entered against a defendant. See Fed.R.Civ.P. 55(a) (requiring entry of default when a defendant "has failed to plead or otherwise defend as provided by these rules"); Dahl v. Kanawha Inv. Holding Co., 161 F.R.D. 673, 685 (N.D.Iowa 1995) (where it appears that plaintiffs "have never properly served the defendants, neither entry of default nor entry of default judgment would be proper").

III.

The affidavits submitted by MSFA's counsel posit these facts: MSFA served Chaves with the summons and complaint by first class mail on or about January 3, 1996. These were sent to the address on Chaves's letterhead, which MSFA's attorney was in possession of by reason of prior correspondence with Chaves. Between January 9 and January 15, MSFA's attorney received three phone calls from one Mitchell Gold, purportedly speaking on behalf of FFA. According to Gold, the defense of the instant action was being referred to an attorney in New York named Seth Pearlman. Since the three phone calls, however, MSFA's attorney has not heard from anyone on behalf of Chaves or FFA.

IV.

MSFA contends that service was effective under Federal Rule * * * 4(c)(2)(C)(ii). That rule, however, has been superseded by Rule 4(d) via the 1993 Amendments. Nonetheless, under either the old rule or the new rule, service was invalid. Alternatively, MSFA may be contending that service was effective under Maryland Rules of Procedure 2–121 or 2–122. This argument would also be unavailing.

A.   The Old Rule 4(c)(2)(C)(ii)

Prior to the 1993 Amendments, Rule 4(c)(2)(C)(ii) allowed service of process by mailing a copy of the summons and of the complaint (by first-class mail, postage prepaid) to the person to be served, together with two copies of a notice and acknowledgment and a return envelope, postage prepaid, addressed to the sender. If no acknowledgment of service under this subdivision of this rule is received by the sender within 20 days after the date of mailing, service of such summons and complaint shall be made under other provisions of this rule.

The United States Court of Appeals for the Fourth Circuit explained that the effectiveness of Rule 4(c)(2)(C)(ii) was "dependent upon an appropriate response by the defendant on the Notice and Acknowledgment for Service by Mail form." Armco, Inc. v. Penrod–Stauffer Bldg. Sys., Inc., 733 F.2d 1087, 1088 (4th Cir.1984). Even if a defendant had actual notice that an action had commenced by the filing of a complaint, as in Armco, "the rules [were] there to be followed, and plain requirements for the means of effecting service of process [could] not be ignored." * * *

MSFA argues that the U.S. Court of Appeals for the Second Circuit in Morse v. Elmira Country Club, 752 F.2d 35 (2d Cir.1984), held that service pursuant to Rule 4(c)(2)(C)(ii) was effective so long as it could be shown that the defendant actually received the mail. This argument is misplaced. Second Circuit law regarding compliance with the terms of Rule 4(c)(2)(C)(ii) was never applicable; the Fourth Circuit's rule of strict compliance was. See Armco, supra. Moreover, the Fourth Circuit rule was the majority rule. * * *[3]

---

3. In any event, Morse is distinguishable from this case. In Morse, plaintiff effected personal service after defendant failed to return the acknowledgment of service contemplated under Rule 4(c)(2)(C)(ii). In the meantime, the statute of limitations had run. The court held that service by mail was effective. While the Morse plaintiff went on to serve defendant personally, MSFA has not done so in the present case. Even the Morse court acknowledged that Rule 4(c)(2)(C)(ii) called "for a second (personal) service should defendant ignore the rule by refusing to return the acknowledgment." Id. at 39.

B. The New Rule 4(d)

For cases pending on or after December 1, 1993, including the present case, Rule 4(d) replaces the old Rule 4(c)(2)(C)(ii). * * * A plaintiff is authorized to send a defendant notice of the action and a request for waiver of service. Fed.R.Civ.P. 4(d). If a plaintiff chooses this path, the defendant has a duty to avoid unnecessary costs of serving the summons. Id. If a defendant in the United States refuses to waive service, "the court shall impose the costs subsequently incurred in effecting service on the defendant unless good cause for the failure be shown." Rule 4(d)(2). The Committee Notes to Rule 4(d) state: "Unless the addressee consents, receipt of the request under the revised rule does not give rise to any obligation to answer the lawsuit [and] does not provide a basis for default judgment." * * * While the Fourth Circuit has yet to interpret this aspect of Rule 4(d), its requirement of strict compliance with old Rule 4(c)(2)(C)(ii) strongly suggests that Rule 4(d) will also be strictly enforced, even where a defendant has actual notice of the pendency of a lawsuit.

C. Maryland Rules

Under the federal rules, a plaintiff may serve process "pursuant to the law of the state in which the district court is located, or in which service is effected." Fed.R.Civ.P. 4(e). The closest fit to the facts of the present case is Maryland Rule of Procedure 2–121, which allows service of process by certified mail. MSFA, however, sent the complaint and summons to Chaves by first class, not certified, mail. Thus it did not meet the requirements of Rule 2–121. MSFA also cites Maryland Rule 2–122, which allows service by posting or publication, but only in in rem or quasi in rem proceedings and then only upon court order. The rule has no bearing. The present proceeding is neither in rem nor quasi in rem, and this Court has never authorized any form of service.

V.

Since service of process was invalid, the Clerk's Entry of Default was improper and the Court will set it aside. See Fed.R.Civ.P. 55(c). MSFA's Motion for Default Judgment will be denied.

Notes and Questions

1. It is apparent that the defendant in *Chaves* received actual notice since the MSFA attorney spoke to Chaves' attorney three times before a default judgment was entered. Does it make sense that service nonetheless was held invalid? Why should defendants who have actual notice be able to claim that they were not served properly?

2. In AUDIO ENTERPRISES v. B & W LOUDSPEAKERS, 957 F.2d 406, 409 (7th Cir.1992), the court rejected service by private delivery reasoning that "rule 4(c)(2)(C)(ii) [now Rule 4(d)] specifies first class mail, postage prepaid. Federal Express is not first class mail." Most other circuits have agreed. See Magnuson v. Video Yesteryear, 85 F.3d 1424 (9th Cir.1996). Does this make any sense?

Consider service by facsimile transmission or e-mail. Although the Advisory Committee that drafted the 1993 revisions to Rule 4 emphasized that facsimile may be the most efficient and economical means of serving process, especially in certain foreign countries, the commentaries of the drafters do not address the apparently irreconcilable requirement that the defendants be provided with a "prepaid means of compliance in writing."

b. *Personal Delivery on Natural Persons*

McKELWAY, PROFILES—PLACE AND LEAVE WITH, New Yorker, August 24, 1935, at 23–26:

* * * In a little frame house near the intersection of Rogers and Flatbush Avenues in Brooklyn there lived until a few years ago an old lady named Mrs. Katherina Schnible. She was seventy-two and a little lame. She owned the house and rented out the first two floors as apartments, but there were mortgages and she had not met the payments. She knew the bank that held the mortgages was about to foreclose * * *. Her son, who lived with her, went out to work at eight in the morning and did not return until six, so from eight till six every day, except Sunday, Mrs. Schnible stayed in her room on the third floor and refused to open the door, no matter who knocked. Came a day when she heard a heavy footfall on the first landing, heard somebody running frantically up the first flight of stairs, heard a man's voice shouting something. Then the footsteps came closer, up the second flight of stairs, and right outside her door she heard yelled the word "Fire!" Mrs. Schnible opened her door and hobbled hurriedly into the hall. "Hello, Mrs. Schnible," said a man standing there. "Here's a summons for you." He handed her the papers, and the proceedings were begun which eventually put Mrs. Schnible out of her house.

Harry Grossman, who was the man in the hall, is regarded by those who employ him as the champion process-server of the day. He is an instrument of justice and his profession is a corner-stone of civil law, but not many of the people he serves appreciate that. * * * Grossman has been cursed by hundreds of defendants, many of them distinguished citizens. Defendants have thrown him down flights of stairs and shoved him off porches. He has been pinched, slapped, punched, and kicked by scores of individuals, and he was beaten up one time by a family of seven.

* * *

"Place and leave with" is the legal phrase for what a process-server must do with a summons when he goes out to serve papers on a defendant, but the courts never have explained precisely what that means. Where the process-server must place the papers is still a nice legal question. A process-server once threw a summons-and-complaint at James Gordon Bennett and hit him in the chest with it, but the courts held that this was not a proper service. Another famous case in the lawbooks tells of a defendant named Martin, who in 1893 hid himself under his wife's petticoats and refused to receive the papers. The process-server saw him crouching there, so he put the papers on what seemed to be the defendant's shoulder, and went away. The Supreme Court rendered a decision which held that "where a person, to avoid service of summons, shelters himself in his wife's petticoats, the laying of the papers on his shoulder will be a sufficient service." * * *

Grossman has never bothered to look up legal precedents for his actions; he simply places the papers in the hands of the defendant and leaves them there. On innumerable occasions he has had to use ingenuity in order to get close enough to the defendant to do this, and only once has he been forced to depart from a literal interpretation of the legal phrase. That was in the case of an elderly lady, who, like Mrs. Schnible, was trying to hide from him. This lady, whose name was Mrs. Mahoney, refused to leave her apartment in the East Side tenement she owned, and Grossman's routine tricks * * * failed to budge her. He knew she was there, because he had wheedled his way into a flat across the court from her and had seen her sitting at her kitchen table in front of an open window, peeling potatoes. Grossman went home to his own apartment in Brooklyn and thought for a while, and then began to practice throwing the summons. He put rubber bands around the paper to make it compact, placed a salad bowl on the dining-room table, and practiced all that afternoon, throwing the subpoena into the bowl from the middle of the living-room. He went back next morning to the flat across the court from Mrs. Mahoney's kitchen. She came into the kitchen a little before noon, puttered around for a while, and then sat down at the table with a bowl of potatoes in front of her and began placidly to peel them. Grossman leaned out of his window and tossed the subpoena. The papers landed in the bowl just as the old lady reached into it. "There you are, Mrs. Mahoney!" Grossman shouted. "There's a foreclosure paper for you!" The courts never questioned his method of placing these papers, and Mrs. Mahoney lost her property.

Tens of thousands of papers have to be served in the course of a year in this city, and the majority of them are handled for the law firms by process-serving agencies, which rely for their profits on quantity and a quick turn-over. * * * Cases involving expert dodgers or stubborn hug-the-hearths usually are turned over to private detective agencies, and the detective agencies usually hire Grossman to serve the papers. When the Electrical Research Product Institute sued the Fox Film Corporation for $15,000,000 in 1930, the lawyers for the plaintiff, naturally, surmised that it would be difficult to "place and leave with" William Fox, Winfield Sheehan, and other defendants, the papers summoning them to come to court. Grossman received the assignment through a detective agency. He got in to see Fox by having a telegram sent from Boston saying that Mr. Grossman had "closed the theatre deal" and would call on Fox at eleven o'clock the next morning. When Grossman reached Fox's office, the film executive's secretary told him Mr. Fox had received the wire but was not sure what deal it was that had been closed. "My God," said Grossman, "the theatre deal—that's what deal! If this is the way I am to be received, never mind—to hell with it!" He started out, and the secretary called him back. "Just wait one moment," she said. "I'll tell Mr. Fox." She opened a door marked "Private" and went into an inner office. Grossman followed her and handed Fox the subpoena. Fox started up from his desk indignantly, but Grossman's indignation expressed itself first. "You, a multi-millionaire!" Grossman shouted. "Is it decent, is it nice, for a multi-millionaire who can be sued for fifteen million dollars to hide from me? Why don't you take the papers like a man?" This so flabbergasted Fox that he sank back in his chair, and Grossman went through the corporation's offices unimpeded and served papers on Sheehan, two vice-presidents, the secretary, and the treasurer.

* * * Harry established a reputation as an adroit private detective before he was old enough to serve subpoenas. * * * But after he had passed his

eighteenth birthday and had begun to serve summonses and subpoenas, it was evident to his employer, and to everybody else who knew him, that he had found a vocation in which he might expect to excel. During his first year he served Maude Adams by posing as a youthful adorer. When she came out of the stage entrance at the Empire Theatre after a performance one evening, Grossman stepped in front of her holding in his left hand a bouquet of jonquils. "Are you Maude Adams?" he asked. "Oh, are those really for me?" she exclaimed, reaching for the flowers, "No, but this is," said Grossman, jerking back the bouquet. With his right hand he served her with a summons. He still remembers that he had paid fifty cents for the jonquils and that he was able to sell them back to the florist for twenty.

His ability to become more indignant at the attitude of defendants than defendants are at his actions has saved Grossman from bodily injury on many occasions. One of his early triumphs involved Gutzon Borglum. The sculptor was at that time modelling life-size figures in a studio in the Gramercy Park section. Grossman entered by means of what he calls the rush act. A maid opened the door and Grossman rushed past her, saying perfunctorily "Is Mr. Borglum in?" Borglum was chipping stone on a nearly completed nude. "Here's a summons for you, Mr. Borglum," said Grossman. "Of all the effrontery," began the sculptor. "You * * * you * * * you ought to be * * *." Then Grossman began to shout. "How about you?" he asked. "Shouldn't you maybe be ashamed of yourself? You and your naked women!" He went out spluttering with indignation, leaving Borglum speechless, clutching the summons in his hand.

c. Service on a Person Residing in Defendant's Dwelling House or Usual Place of Abode

As an alternative to personal delivery, Rule 4(e)(2) permits service of process to be made upon an individual by leaving a copy of the summons and complaint at his "dwelling house or usual place of abode with some person of suitable age and discretion then residing therein." Despite the length of time these words have been a part of federal practice, the decisions do not make clear precisely what they mean, and the facts of a particular case often prove to be crucial.

ROVINSKI v. ROWE, 131 F.2d 687, 689 (6th Cir.1942). Rowe brought suit against Rovinski in a Michigan state court, service of process being effected under the state's nonresident motorist statute. Rovinski moved to dismiss on the ground that he was a resident of Michigan, and hence not amenable to service under the statute. After the action was dismissed, Rowe commenced a diversity action against Rovinski in a federal court. Service of process was made under what is now Federal Rule of Civil Procedure 4(e)(2) by leaving a copy of the summons and complaint with Rovinski's mother at the address that he had given as his residence in an affidavit supporting his motion to dismiss in the prior state action. Rovinski again challenged the propriety of service, contending that his "dwelling place and usual place of abode" had been in Minnesota for the past two years, and that he had returned to his mother's house only to visit, even though he considered it his legal residence. The District Court held the service of process valid, and the Sixth Circuit affirmed:

In construing * * * Rule * * * [4(e)(2)] liberally, the district court effectuated the declared purpose of the Supreme Court Advisory Committee in submitting a service of process rule, which would provide "a good deal of freedom and flexibility in service." * * * That the rule should be liberally construed seems logical, when consideration is given to the fact that uncertainty of its applicability to varying situations would be increased by strict construction. This is apparent from the irreconcilable conflict among state courts upon the meaning and interpretation of the expression "usual place of abode." * * *

The wide diversity of opinion may be illustrated by two examples. On the one hand, delivery of process to defendant's wife at an apartment in Miami Beach, Florida, where his family had been living for about two months and where he had previously visited them, but from which he had departed to his permanent home in another state, was held *sufficient* under a Florida statute * * *. On the other hand, delivery of service of process to the father of a minor defendant at the family home where the defendant had lived up to the time of his enlistment in the United States Army less than one month previously was held *insufficient* under a New Jersey statute * * *.

The only pertinent reported Federal decision is Skidmore v. Green, D.C.N.Y., 33 F.Supp. 529, 530, wherein service was upheld under Rule * * * [4(e)(2)] against a peregrinating policeman, who, after retiring from the New York force, spent most of his time traveling about the country in an automobile and trailer. Process had been delivered at the home of defendant's brother which, in the application for his New York automobile license, defendant had given as his address. In his application for his South Carolina automobile license, he had stated that he was a resident of New York. The district judge commented that "so far as the migratory nature of his life" permitted of any place of abode or dwelling house, that place was his brother's home.

Notes and Questions

1. In FIRST NAT. BANK & TRUST CO. OF TULSA v. INGERTON, 207 F.2d 793, 795 (10th Cir.1953), defendants, who were horse owners, appeared to change their residence whenever their horses moved to a new race track. Their furniture was stored in a warehouse in Raton, New Mexico, and some of their possessions were left at a hotel there, at which they continued to receive mail. Process was served on defendants' daughter at a furnished home that they had rented for one month in Denver, Colorado. The trial court later quashed the service on the ground that defendants' usual place of abode was Raton. The appellate court affirmed but Judge Murrah dissented, noting that "the record clearly shows that as race horse owners, the Ingertons' usual place of abode was wherever their horses happened to be running." See also National Development Co. v. Triad Holding Corp., 930 F.2d 253, 258 (2d Cir.), certiorari denied 502 U.S. 968, 112 S.Ct. 440, 116 L.Ed.2d 459 (1991) (the defendant was a wealthy, globe-trotting Saudi businessman who testified that the $20–25 million apartment in New York where papers were delivered on his housekeeper was one of twelve residences around the world in which he spent his time; service was upheld because "Khashoggi [the defendant] was actually living in [the apartment when

service was effected], service there on that day was, if not the most likely method of ensuring that he received the summons and complaint, reasonably calculated to provide actual notice"). But see Northbrook Indem. Co. v. Westgate, Ltd., 769 So.2d 890 (Ala.2000) (defendant corporation's former office was not a usual place of business despite the fact that that address was the one used on the contract sued upon).

2. To what extent should it be relevant that a defendant actually received the summons and complaint at the particular place where it was served? In KARLSSON v. RABINOWITZ, 318 F.2d 666, 668 (4th Cir.1963), the Fourth Circuit validated service that was left with the defendant's wife in Maryland even though the family was in the process of moving and the defendant already had left for Arizona, with no intent ever to return. On facts similar to *Karlsson,* the District of Columbia Circuit held that service was invalid because the papers were left with defendant's estranged wife and he did not receive the summons and complaint until three years after default judgment was entered against him. Williams v. Capital Transit Co., 215 F.2d 487 (D.C.Cir.1954). Does this insistence on actual receipt of service create a "double" standard for construing the language of Rule 4(e)(2)? Does this make sense? Under what circumstances should actual notice not be required? See Blackhawk Heating & Plumbing Co. v. Turner, 50 F.R.D. 144 (D.Ariz.1970) (service of process on a defendant who had actual notice was upheld when service was left with the defendant's daughter in an apartment where the defendant had lived until shortly before service was made, rent was paid by the defendant, no forwarding address was left, and the defendant left all furniture in the apartment and automobiles in the state).

d. *Delivery to an Agent Authorized by Appointment*

A third method of effecting personal service on an individual under Rule 4(e)(2) is by delivering a copy of the summons and complaint to an agent of the defendant who is "authorized by appointment or by law" to receive process. The cases dealing with agency by appointment indicate that an actual appointment for the specific purpose of receiving process normally is expected. Consistent with this judicial construction of "appointment," the courts have held that claims by an agent that he has authority to receive process or the fact that an agent actually accepts process is not enough to bind defendant; there must be evidence that defendant himself intended to confer such authority upon the agent.

NATIONAL EQUIPMENT RENTAL, LTD. v. SZUKHENT

Supreme Court of the United States, 1964.
375 U.S. 311, 84 S.Ct. 411, 11 L.Ed.2d 354.

Certiorari to the United States Court of Appeals for the Second Circuit.

MR. JUSTICE STEWART delivered the opinion of the Court.

* * * The petitioner is a corporation with its principal place of business in New York. It sued the respondents, residents of Michigan, in a New York federal court, claiming that the respondents had defaulted under a farm equipment lease. The only question now before us is whether the person upon whom the summons and complaint were served was "an agent authorized by appointment" to receive the same, so as to subject the respondents to the jurisdiction of the federal court in New York.

The respondents obtained certain farm equipment from the petitioner under a lease executed in 1961. The lease was on a printed form less than a page and a half in length, and consisted of 18 numbered paragraphs. The last numbered paragraph, appearing just above the respondents' signatures and printed in the same type used in the remainder of the instrument, provided that "the Lessee hereby designates Florence Weinberg, 47–21 Forty-first Street, Long Island City, N.Y., as agent for the purpose of accepting service of any process within the State of New York." The respondents were not acquainted with Florence Weinberg.

In 1962 the petitioner commenced the present action by filing in the federal court in New York a complaint which alleged that the respondents had failed to make any of the periodic payments specified by the lease. The Marshal delivered two copies of the summons and complaint to Florence Weinberg. That same day she mailed the summons and complaint to the respondents, together with a letter stating that the documents had been served upon her as the respondents' agent for the purpose of accepting service of process in New York, in accordance with the agreement contained in the lease. The petitioner itself also notified the respondents by certified mail of the service of process upon Florence Weinberg.

Upon motion of the respondents, the District Court quashed service of the summons and complaint, holding that, although Florence Weinberg had promptly notified the respondents of the service of process and mailed copies of the summons and complaint to them, the lease agreement itself had not explicitly required her to do so, and there was therefore a "failure of the agency arrangement to achieve intrinsic and continuing reality." * * * The Court of Appeals affirmed * * * and we granted certiorari * * *.

We need not and do not in this case reach the situation where no personal notice has been given to the defendant. Since the respondents did in fact receive complete and timely notice of the lawsuit pending against them, no due process claim has been made. The case before us is therefore quite different from cases where there was no actual notice * * *. Similarly, as the Court of Appeals recognized, this Court's decision in Wuchter v. Pizzutti * * * is inapposite here. * * * *Wuchter* dealt with the limitations imposed by the Fourteenth Amendment upon a statutory scheme by which a State attempts to subject nonresident individuals to the jurisdiction of its courts. The question presented here, on the other hand, is whether a party to a private contract may appoint an agent to receive service of process within the meaning of Federal Rule * * * [4(e)(2)], where the agent is not personally known to the party, and where the agent has not expressly undertaken to transmit notice to the party.

The purpose underlying the contractual provision here at issue seems clear. The clause was inserted by the petitioner and agreed to by the respondents in order to assure that any litigation under the lease should be conducted in the State of New York. The contract specifically provided that "This agreement shall be deemed to have been made in Nassau County, New York, regardless of the order in which the signatures of the parties shall be affixed hereto, and shall be interpreted, and the rights and liabilities of the parties here determined, in accordance with the laws of the State of New York." And it is settled, as the courts below recognized, that parties to a contract may agree in advance to submit to the jurisdiction of a given court, to permit notice to be served by the opposing party, or even to waive notice altogether. * * *

Under well-settled general principles of the law of agency, Florence Weinberg's prompt acceptance and transmittal to the respondents of the summons and complaint pursuant to the authorization was itself sufficient to validate the agency, even though there was no explicit previous promise on her part to do so. * * *

We deal here with a Federal Rule, applicable to federal courts in all 50 States. But even if we were to assume that this uniform federal standard should give way to contrary local policies, there is no relevant concept of state law which would invalidate the agency here at issue. In Michigan, where the respondents reside, the statute which validates service of process under the circumstances present in this case contains no provision requiring that the appointed agent expressly undertake to notify the principal of the service of process. Similarly, New York law, which it was agreed should be applicable to the lease provisions, does not require any such express promise by the agent in order to create a valid agency for receipt of process. * * *

It is argued, finally, that the agency sought to be created in this case was invalid because Florence Weinberg may have had a conflict of interest. This argument is based upon the fact that she was not personally known to the respondents at the time of her appointment and upon a suggestion in the record that she may be related to an officer of the petitioner corporation. But such a contention ignores the narrowly limited nature of the agency here involved. Florence Weinberg was appointed the respondents' agent for the single purpose of receiving service of process. An agent with authority so limited can in no meaningful sense be deemed to have had an interest antagonistic to the respondents, since both the petitioner and the respondents had an equal interest in assuring that, in the event of litigation, the latter be given that adequate and timely notice which is a prerequisite to a valid judgment.

A different case would be presented if Florence Weinberg had not given prompt notice to the respondents, for then the claim might well be made that her failure to do so had operated to invalidate the agency. We hold only that, prompt notice to the respondents having been given, Florence Weinberg was their "agent authorized by appointment" to receive process within the meaning of Federal Rule * * * [4(e)(2)].

* * *

Judgment of Court of Appeals reversed and case remanded.

Mr. Justice Black, dissenting.

* * * I disagree with * * * [the Court's] holding, believing that (1) whether Mrs. Weinberg was a valid agent upon whom service could validly be effected under Rule * * * [4(e)(2)] should be determined under New York law and that we should accept the holdings of the federal district judge and the Court of Appeals sitting in New York that under that State's law the purported appointment of Mrs. Weinberg was invalid and ineffective; (2) if however, Rule * * * [4(e)(2)] is to be read as calling upon us to formulate a new federal definition of agency for purposes of service of process, I think our

formulation should exclude Mrs. Weinberg from the category of an "agent authorized by appointment * * * to receive service of process"; and (3) upholding service of process in this case raises serious questions as to whether these Michigan farmers have been denied due process of law in violation of the Fifth and Fourteenth Amendments.

* * *

The end result of today's holding is not difficult to foresee. Clauses like the one used against the Szukhents—clauses which companies have not inserted, I suspect, because they never dreamed a court would uphold them— will soon find their way into the "boilerplate" of everything from an equipment lease to a conditional sales contract. Today's holding gives a green light to every large company in this country to contrive contracts which declare with force of law that when such a company wants to sue someone with whom it does business, that individual must go and try to defend himself in some place, no matter how distant, where big business enterprises are concentrated, like, for example, New York, Connecticut, or Illinois, or else suffer a default judgment. In this very case the Court holds that by this company's carefully prepared contractual clause the Szukhents must, to avoid a judgment rendered without a fair and full hearing, travel hundreds of miles across the continent, probably crippling their defense and certainly depleting what savings they may have, to try to defend themselves in a court sitting in New York City. I simply cannot believe that Congress, when by its silence it let Rule * * * [4(e)(2)] go into effect, meant for that rule to be used as a means to achieve such a far-reaching, burdensome, and unjust result. Heretofore judicial good common sense has, on one ground or another, disregarded contractual provisions like this one, not encouraged them. It is a long trip from San Francisco—or from Honolulu or Anchorage—to New York, Boston, or Wilmington. And the trip can be very expensive, often costing more than it would simply to pay what is demanded. The very threat of such a suit can be used to force payment of alleged claims, even though they be wholly without merit. This fact will not be news to companies exerting their economic power to wangle such contracts. * * *

MR. JUSTICE BRENNAN, with whom THE CHIEF JUSTICE and MR. JUSTICE GOLDBERG join, dissenting.

I would affirm. In my view, federal standards and not state law must define who is "an agent authorized by appointment" within the meaning of Rule * * * [4(e)(2)]. * * * In formulating these standards I would, *first,* construe Rule * * * [4(e)(2)] to deny validity to the appointment of a purported agent whose interests conflict with those of his supposed principal * * *. *Second,* I would require that the appointment include an explicit condition that the agent after service transmit the process forthwith to the principal. Although our decision in Wuchter v. Pizzutti * * * dealt with the constitutionality of a state statute, the reasoning of that case is persuasive that, in fashioning a federal agency rule, we should engraft the same requirement upon Rule * * * [4(e)(2)]. *Third,* since the corporate plaintiff prepared the printed form contract, I would not hold the individual purchaser bound by the appointment without proof, in addition to his mere signature on the form, that the individual understandingly consented to be sued in a State not that of his residence. * * * It offends common sense to treat a printed form which closes an installment sale as embodying terms to all of which the individual knowingly assented. The sales pitch aims solely at getting the signature on the form and wastes no time explaining or even mentioning the print. * * *

Notes and Questions

1. In BUDGET MARKETING, INC. v. TOBACK, 88 F.R.D. 705 (S.D.Iowa 1981), a franchisee successfully moved to dismiss a franchisor's suit against him on the ground that he never was served in a manner permitted by law. The District Court held that service was improper when pursuant to a provision in a loan agreement, the franchisor caused a copy of the summons and complaint to be delivered to its own vice-president (the designated agent of the franchisee for service of process) and the vice-president mailed (certified mail, return receipt requested) a copy of the summons and complaint to the franchisee at its last known address. The court ruled that the agency for receiving service of process was invalid per se and could not be validated by forwarding the papers. Is the result in *Toback* consistent with *Szukhent?* Does *Toback* turn on the fact that the plaintiff itself was the agent? Would it have made a difference if, instead of appointing the plaintiff's vice-president as its agent, the defendant had appointed the vice-president's husband? After all, in *Szukhent,* Florence Weinberg was possibly "related to an officer of the [plaintiff] corporation." If *Szukhent* and *Toback* are inconsistent, which of the two makes more sense?

2. Like jurisdiction, notice and service of process requirements may be waived by a party at trial or even in advance of litigation. For example, under the provisions of a cognovit note, a debtor may agree to submit to the jurisdiction of any court chosen by the creditor for an action to collect the debt and even may empower the creditor or any attorney to appear in the suit and confess judgment. Typically, by a cognovit note, the debtor waives objection to jurisdiction, notice, and service of process. In D.H. OVERMYER CO. v. FRICK CO., 405 U.S. 174, 92 S.Ct. 775, 31 L.Ed.2d 124 (1972), the Supreme Court considered the constitutionality of cognovit provisions and ruled that they were not per se violative of the Due Process Clause. Such agreements must be judged on a case-by-case basis, with particular sensitivity to whether there was inequality of bargaining power or lack of consideration. See, e.g., Atlantic Leasing & Financial, Inc. v. IPM Technology, Inc., 885 F.2d 188 (4th Cir.1989) (holding that guarantor's assent to confessed-judgment provision was voluntarily, knowingly, and intelligently made). If cognovit notes are constitutionally acceptable, could the appointment in *Toback* be unconstitutional per se? Shouldn't the question in *Toback* have been whether the negotiation leading to the appointment was between parties with equal power? Or, is *Overmyer* wrongly decided?

Many state courts have invalidated cognovit notes and other "consent to judgment" provisions. See, e.g., Isbell v. County of Sonoma, 21 Cal.3d 61, 145 Cal.Rptr. 368, 577 P.2d 188, certiorari denied 439 U.S. 996, 99 S.Ct. 597, 58 L.Ed.2d 669 (1978). They rarely are employed outside of Pennsylvania, Delaware, Ohio, and Illinois.

e. Service on Artificial Entities: Corporations, Partnerships, and Unincorporated Associations

Rule 4(h) authorizes service upon corporations, partnerships, and unincorporated associations that are subject to suit under a common name. The most frequently invoked portion of the rule is the part permitting service by delivery of process to an officer, a managing agent, or a general agent.

In INSURANCE CO. OF NORTH AMERICA v. S/S "HELLENIC CHAL-LENGER," 88 F.R.D. 545 (S.D.N.Y.1980), a United States Marshal deposited the summons and complaint with a claims adjuster at the office of defendant. The complaint stated an admiralty and maritime claim for nondelivery, shortage, loss, and damage relating to pickled sheepskins shipped to New York aboard defendant's vessel.

The adjuster who had accepted service of the summons and complaint was not expressly authorized by defendant to accept process; the only employees endowed with express authority to do so on behalf of defendant were all titled officers and the claims manager. At the time of service of the summons and complaint, the claims manager was absent due to illness and the adjuster, an assistant to the claims manager, accepted service.

Since the adjuster misplaced the summons and complaint, defendant remained unaware of the pendency of the lawsuit until its bank informed it that its account had been attached by the plaintiff. Only then did the defendant learn that the plaintiff's counsel had filed a default judgment and that a writ of execution had been issued. The court denied the defendant's motion to set aside the judgment on the basis of improper service of process:

> Rule * * * [4(h)] has been liberally construed by the courts and, as interpreted, does not require rigid formalism. To be valid, service of process is not limited solely to officially designated officers, managing agents or agents appointed by law for the receipt of process. Rather, "[r]ules governing service of process [are] to be construed in a manner reasonably calculated to effectuate their primary purpose: to give the defendant adequate notice that an action is pending. * * * [T]he rule does not require that service be made solely on a restricted class of formally titled officials, but rather permits it to be made 'upon a representative so integrated with the organization that he will know what to do with the papers. Generally, service is sufficient when made upon an individual who stands in such a position as to render it fair, reasonable and just to imply the authority on his part to receive services.' " * * *

Plaintiff's method of service of the summons and complaint was indeed "reasonably calculated" to alert defendants to the initiation of the suit. * * * [T]he adjuster served with the summons and complaint, can be categorized as a representative of defendant "well-integrated" into the organization and quite familiar with the formalities associated with the receipt of service of summonses and complaints. He had accepted service of summonses and complaints on behalf of defendant on at least two previous occasions * * * in connection with his ordinary duties of receiving and investigating new claims against defendant. Furthermore, it may be inferred from the facts presented on this motion that [the adjuster] had easy access to * * * the claims manager officially authorized to accept service of process, since the two men are separated from each other only by [the claims manager's] glass-walled office. [The adjuster's] familiarity with service of process negates any and all suspicion that the U.S. Marshal delivered the summons and complaint to a representative of defendant who had infrequent contact with summonses and complaints and whose unfamiliarity with service of process increased the risk of careless or improper handling. * * *

In the case at hand, the * * * adjuster's loss of the summons and complaint is a mistake in the ordinary course of the internal operations of defendant's business and thus does not merit remedial relief * * *.

Id. at 547–48.

Notes and Questions

1. Is the court's willingness to disregard labels and conclusory terms such as "general" and "managing" agent consistent with the clear requirements of Rule 4(h)(1)? Should the court simply have held that the claims adjuster could be regarded as a "managing" agent of the defendant? See also Direct Mail Specialists, Inc. v. Eclat Computerized Technologies, Inc., 840 F.2d 685, 688 (9th Cir.1988) (service of process on receptionist of shared office of defendant corporation and another corporation was sufficient to create personal jurisdiction under the circumstances). But see American Institute of Certified Public Accountants v. Affinity Card, Inc., 8 F.Supp.2d 372 (S.D.N.Y.1998) (service on vice president of one corporation sharing office with defendant corporation insufficient to create personal jurisdiction despite fact that both corporations were owned by the same individual and he received actual notice). Does the distinction make sense?

2. Could the court reasonably have reached the same result by finding that the claims adjuster was an agent authorized by appointment to receive process? In FASHION PAGE, LTD. v. ZURICH INS. CO., 50 N.Y.2d 265, 270–73, 428 N.Y.S.2d 890, 892–94, 406 N.E.2d 747, 749–51 (1980), the process-server went to the defendant's office where he was greeted by a receptionist. The receptionist told him to proceed down a certain corridor and to "see the girl sitting down there." Following instructions, the process-server went to the executive secretary of the vice president in charge of the New York office. She asked to see the papers and after perusing them said: "Okay, leave it with me. * * * I'll take it." When the process-server questioned her authority, she responded: "I can take it."

There was doubt that the executive secretary possessed sufficient discretionary authority to be a "managing agent" for purposes of service. The New York Court of Appeals, however, refused to be drawn into that issue, finding instead that the executive secretary was an "agent authorized by appointment * * * to receive service." The executive secretary testified that she had regularly accepted summonses for at least five years whenever the vice president was not in the office. During that period about half of the summonses brought to his office had been accepted by her.

> Thus a corporation may assign the task of accepting process and may establish procedures for insuring that the papers are directed to those ultimately responsible for defending its interests. * * * The corporation however cannot escape the consequences of establishing alternative procedures which it may prefer. * * * Reliance may be based on the corporate employees to identify the proper person to accept service. * * *

See also M. Prusman, Ltd. v. Ariel Maritime Group, Inc., 719 F.Supp. 214, 220 (S.D.N.Y.1989).

3. RETURN OF SERVICE

After the process-server has delivered the papers, she must file a return, which should disclose enough facts to demonstrate that defendant actually has been served and given notice that he is required to appear in court. Thus, although the actual service of process and not the proof of that act is a prerequisite to the court assuming jurisdiction, it has been held that a proper return ordinarily is necessary to enable the trial court to conclude it has jurisdiction. The specific form that proof of service must take varies from state to state, as well as according to the method of service used. An affidavit executed by the person who performed the acts constituting service, or the sworn statement of the officer—the marshal, sheriff, or deputy—who made the service, is the usual proof.

Should the process-server's return of service be considered conclusive or merely presumptive evidence that service has been effected? Consider the rationale advanced by the Supreme Court in MIEDREICH v. LAUENSTEIN, 232 U.S. 236, 34 S.Ct. 309, 58 L.Ed. 584 (1914), in which plaintiff sought to vacate a mortgage foreclosure judgment rendered in a prior suit. She was not a resident of the county in which the action was brought, was not served with process, and had no knowledge of the prior proceeding; the sheriff had made a false return of summons. The Supreme Court upheld the prior judgment:

> In the present case the * * * original party in the foreclosure proceeding did all that the law required in the issue of and attempt to serve process; and, without fraud or collusion, the sheriff made a return to the court that service had been duly made. * * * [A]lthough contrary to the fact, in the absence of any attack upon it, the court was justified in acting upon such return as upon a true return. If the return is false the law of the State * * * permitted a recovery against the sheriff upon his bond. We are of the opinion that this system of jurisprudence, with its provisions for safeguarding the rights of litigants, is due process of law. It may result, unfortunately, * * * that the recovery upon the sheriff's bond will not be an adequate remedy, but statutes must be framed and laws administered so as to protect * * * all litigants and other persons who derive rights from the judgments of courts. * * * [T]he purchaser at the sheriff's sale had a right to rely upon the record * * *.

Id. at 246, 34 S.Ct. at 312, 58 L.Ed. at 591. Is it significant that *Miedreich* involved a collateral attack on the sheriff's return? Would the result have been the same if a direct attack in the original proceeding had been involved?

In most American jurisdictions, the return of service is considered strong evidence of the facts stated, but it is not conclusive and may be controverted by proof that the return is inaccurate. However, the defendant's own testimony generally will not be sufficient to impeach the return unless it is corroborated by other evidence. See, e.g., Trustees of Local Union No. 727 Pension Fund v. Perfect Parking, Inc., 126 F.R.D. 48 (N.D.Ill.1989) (retaining "strong and convincing evidence" standard to overcome return of a private process server); FROF, Inc. v. Harris, 695 F.Supp. 827 (E.D.Pa.1988) (suggesting, but not holding, that the creation of a rebuttable presumption as to the facts of service might be appropriate for the return of a private process server). See generally 4A Wright & Miller, *Federal Practice and Procedure: Civil 3d* § 1130 (2001).

"Sewer" Service

In UNITED STATES v. BRAND JEWELERS, INC., 318 F.Supp. 1293 (S.D.N.Y.1970), noted in 37 Brooklyn L.Rev. 426, 84 Harv.L.Rev. 1930, 46 N.Y.U.L.Rev. 367, 20 J.Pub.L. 337, 24 Vand.L.Rev. 829, 17 Wayne L.Rev. 1287, 1971 Wis.L.Rev. 665, it was held that the United States had standing to seek an injunction preventing defendant from systematically obtaining default judgments against economically disadvantaged people by utilizing so-called "sewer" service techniques, by which the process-server simply disposes of the papers and makes a false affidavit of service. The actions were for the purchase price of consumer goods sold on "easy credit terms" by door-to-door salesmen. The court reasoned that continuously failing to make proper service of process or preparing false affidavits of service imposed "a burden on interstate commerce." Moreover, defendants' alleged conduct was held to be "state action" so that the United States had standing to sue to end a widespread unconstitutional deprivation of property without due process of law.

In 1972, the case was settled, and a consent decree issued. It vacated the default judgments obtained by Brand Jewelers from 1969 to 1971, established procedures to notify those who were not properly served that they could proceed to a trial on the merits, and placed upon Brand Jewelers' attorney the duty of ensuring that future service of process would be fair and in good faith. What are the advantages and disadvantages of placing that duty on an attorney? See Federal Rule 11 for an example of relying on an attorney's good faith in a different context.

Responding to the mounting criticism of "sewer service," in 1970 New York radically changed the requirements of personal service. Until then, delivery of a summons to a person other than the defendant was not permitted unless the process-server had first exercised due diligence to locate the defendant. The burden of this requirement was viewed as the single most important cause of "sewer service." The revision adopted by the legislature allows service by leaving one copy of the summons with a person of suitable age and discretion at the place where the defendant actually works, dwells, or usually abides and by mailing a second copy to defendant's last known address. N.Y.C.P.L.R. § 308(2). In 1973, the legislature took the additional step of requiring process-servers to make more detailed statements relating to how the process was served; and, in 1991, the legislature mandated that a copy of the summons be filed with the return of service. N.Y.C.P.L.R. §§ 306, 306–a.

4. SERVICE OF PROCESS AND STATUTES OF LIMITATIONS

All states have statutes of limitations that fix specific time limits within which various categories of actions must be brought. They are supplemented by bodies of law that define when various causes of action are said to "accrue," the point when the limitations clock begins to run on an action, and the circumstances in which the running of the clock is suspended or "tolled" because a plaintiff for some reason has been prevented from timely asserting her rights. See generally *Developments in the Law—Statutes of Limitations*, 63

Harv.L.Rev. 1177 (1950). Although statutes of limitations generally are deemed "procedural," their impact decidedly is "substantive"—a plaintiff loses the opportunity to invoke the assistance of the courts to obtain relief for an otherwise valid claim. Almost the first duty of a lawyer for a potential plaintiff is to determine, by the most conservative estimates, the latest possible day for commencing an action.

When is a suit "commenced" for purposes of a statute of limitations? In some states, an action is not deemed "commenced" until process is served on the defendant. In these states, a defect in service can be fatal to the plaintiff's claim, because the statute of limitations may have run before the plaintiff has a chance to correct his error.

Consider MARKOFF v. SOUTH NASSAU COMMUNITY HOSP., 61 N.Y.2d 283, 473 N.Y.S.2d 766, 461 N.E.2d 1253 (1984), a medical malpractice action by decedent's executrix against a hospital and three physicians. The plaintiff experienced difficulty in personally serving the physicians, and just before the limitations period was to expire obtained an ex parte order permitting her to leave the summonses at the defendant hospital, where they were apparently received by the physicians. However, the physicians were successful in having the action dismissed on the ground that the service was improper. Plaintiff later succeeded in personally delivering a summons to each of the doctors, effectively starting a new action against them on the same claim. Defendants moved to dismiss the second action as well, this time asserting the bar of the statute of limitations. And the action clearly was barred unless plaintiff could invoke the New York "saving" statute, which permits a party six months to reinstitute an action that was timely when originally commenced and was terminated other than on the merits. The Court of Appeals held that an action dismissed for a defect of service has not been "commenced" for the purposes of the "saving" statute, and therefore cannot make timely a second action brought on the same claim. Markoff has since been superseded by N.Y.C.P.L.R. 306(b), which gives the plaintiff 120 days to refile after an action is dismissed because of a defect in service.

In other states, an action is deemed "commenced" for purposes of the statute of limitations merely by filing the complaint with the court. In California, an action is "commenced" once the plaintiff files the complaint—though, after filing, the plaintiff may take up to three years to serve process, Cal.Code Civ.Proc. §§ 411.10, 583.210, and the California courts have suggested that they even have discretion to extend the time further.

In federal court, when the underlying cause of action is based on federal law, Rule 3 governs when the action is commenced. Thus, the suit is commenced when a copy of the complaint is filed with the district court. West v. Conrail, 481 U.S. 35, 107 S.Ct. 1538, 95 L.Ed.2d 32 (1987). However, when the underlying cause of action is based on state law, state law will govern when the action is commenced. See Walker v. Armco Steel Corp., 446 U.S. 740, 100 S.Ct. 1978, 64 L.Ed.2d 659 (1980), p. 402, infra.

As a separate matter, it is noteworthy that Rule 4(m), adopted in 1983, requires a federal court to dismiss without prejudice an action when the defendant has not been served within 120 days of the filing of the complaint, if the plaintiff fails to show "good cause" for not completing service within that time. If the statute of limitations expires during that period, and if the plaintiff's action is dismissed, can the plaintiff refile the complaint and thus still maintain the action? See Burks v. Griffith, 100 F.R.D. 491 (N.D.N.Y. 1984) (attempt at refiling civil rights action met with a successful statute of limitations challenge; court observed that the problem could have been avoided had plaintiff utilized Rule 6(b) and requested an extension of time to serve her summons and complaint).

If service is promptly attempted but improperly made, should a federal court dismiss the action without prejudice, or should it merely quash service and order the plaintiff to re-serve? The general view has been that the court has discretion in this matter—discretion that is exercised with an eye toward the circumstances of the case. Courts dismiss when the plaintiff has little likelihood of effecting proper service. In cases in which the plaintiff cannot hope to acquire jurisdiction over the defendant through proper service, keeping the action alive unnecessarily burdens the courts. On the other hand, when the plaintiff can make proper service quickly, courts generally quash the faulty service without prejudice to the plaintiff to serve again. See, e.g., Romandette v. Weetabix Co., 807 F.2d 309, 311 (2d Cir.1986) ("[A] case in which proper service could be yet obtained.").

SECTION C.   IMMUNITY FROM PROCESS AND ETIQUETTE OF SERVICE

1.   IMMUNITY FROM PROCESS

A court sometimes will immunize a party from service of process, despite the fact that the constitutional and statutory conditions governing personal jurisdiction and service of process have been met. In such cases, the grant of immunity usually is justified as promoting the administration of justice. Thus, although the doctrine may help a party avoid suit, it does so not for the benefit of the party, but for the benefit of the court. For example, witnesses, parties, and attorneys who come to a state to participate in a lawsuit often are granted immunity from service of process in other suits.

STATE ex rel. SIVNKSTY v. DUFFIELD

Supreme Court of Appeals of West Virginia, 1952.
137 W.Va. 112, 71 S.E.2d 113.

[On June 30, 1951, while vacationing in Gilmer County, West Virginia, petitioner Sivnksty's automobile struck and injured two children who were walking along the highway. He was arrested on charges of reckless driving, and, being unable to post bond, was incarcerated in the county jail until his trial on July 2. While he was in jail awaiting trial, Sivnksty was served with process in a tort action brought by one of the children in the Circuit Court of Gilmer County. Sivnksty was found guilty of the criminal charge and his appeals from that conviction failed.

Sivnksty made a special appearance in the civil action and filed a plea in abatement, alleging that the court was without jurisdiction because at the time of service he was a nonresident of the county and a prisoner in the county jail. The court sustained a demurrer to the plea in abatement, whereupon Sivnksty petitioned the Supreme Court of Appeals of West Virginia for a writ of prohibition against the judge of the trial court. A stipulation was filed with the appellate court stating that Sivnksty had entered Gilmer County on June 30, 1951, with the intention of remaining there through the Fourth of July holiday and that he left the county immediately upon his release on appeal bond following his conviction on July 2, 1951.]

RILEY, PRESIDENT. * * *

The sole question presented by this record is: In the circumstances of this case was the petitioner immune from civil process at the time he was served with process in the civil action? Petitioner asserts here that the mere fact that he intended, when he came into Gilmer County, to remain for a period of a few days could not render his continuing presence in Gilmer County, after he was arrested, one of a voluntary status, when he was, in fact, incarcerated in the county jail there against his will.

The original and prime purpose for which the privilege of immunity from civil process on nonresidents of a county or state charged with crime therein was the protection of the court itself from interference with its judicial processes. Thus, originally the rule was asserted as the privilege of the court to secure the administration of justice free from outside interference or influence. Later the rule was enlarged for the protection of suitors, witnesses, jurors, and court officials from process, both in civil and criminal cases. Whited v. Phillips, 98 W.Va. 204, 205, 206, 126 S.E. 916, 917, 40 A.L.R. 83. In the Whited case the Court said: "It is well said that, if there is ever a time when a man should be relieved of all other concerns, and when he should be permitted to use unhampered his every faculty, it is when he is on trial under charge of a crime. Judicial reasoning also recognizes the right of a man, ordinarily, to be tried by a jury in the vicinity in which he resides, so that he may have such advantage and safeguard there as his conduct and character shall merit."

In addition the privilege of immunity from civil process of a nonresident of a county or state, charged with crime therein, has underlying it the public policy that a person charged with crime in a county of which he is a nonresident will not be deterred from appearing before the courts of that county or state by the threat of civil or other process; and thus a person so charged with crime because of the immunity extended will be encouraged to return to the county or state in which he is charged with crime to respond to the criminal process.

* * *

In the syllabus to Whited v. Phillips, supra, perhaps the leading case in this jurisdiction, bearing on the instant subject matter, this Court held: "A non-resident of West Virginia, who voluntarily and without compulsion of law, submits himself to the jurisdiction of a state court, in answer to an indictment therein against him, and who is not at the time a fugitive from justice, is privileged while attending court from service of process in a civil suit." In this jurisdiction the immunity rule has been applied to a case in which a defendant in a civil action was served with process while he was in a county, of which he was not a resident, in obedience to a citation from a member of the Department of Public Safety to answer a criminal charge. Morris v. Calhoun, 119

W.Va. 603, pt. 3 syl., 195 S.E. 341. It has also been applied to a case in which a person charged with a criminal offense in a county of which he was a nonresident, was arrested therefor in that county and later released on bond on his own recognizance, and who, in pursuance of such recognizance, returned to the county to answer the charge on the day set for trial. Lang v. Shaw, 113 W.Va. 628, syl., 169 S.E. 444. But in the case of State ex rel. Godby v. Chambers, 130 W.Va. 115, pt. 2 syl., 42 S.E.2d 255, 256, * * * the Court refused the writ of prohibition on the ground that after petitioner's conviction, sentence, and incarceration on a misdemeanor charge, the reason for the application of the immunity rule was not present, and that in that case there was no criminal process within the meaning of the immunity rule. * * *

In the instant case the petitioner went to Gilmer County of his own volition: he did not enter the county in response to a criminal process, because at the time of his entry therein he had committed no crime, and there was pending against him no criminal case. * * * In Crusco v. Strunk Steel Co., 365 Pa. 326, 74 A.2d 142, 20 A.L.R.2d 160, the Pennsylvania Supreme Court held that a defendant residing outside of a county in which a civil action had been commenced, and who was arrested on a warrant issued on an information of the plaintiff in the civil action and brought within the county, was not immune from civil process merely because of his status as a criminal defendant. * * * In 72 C.J.S., Process, § 82, the rule is well stated as follows: "A person confined in jail on a criminal charge or imprisoned on conviction for such charge is subject to service of civil process, irrespective of the question of residence, at least if he was voluntarily in the jurisdiction at the time of the arrest and confinement." * * *

As the petitioner did not come and was not brought into Gilmer County under criminal process, the reason for the application of the immunity rule is not present, and he is not entitled to the writ of prohibition prayed for.

Writ denied.

LOVINS, JUDGE (dissenting).

* * * This court in the Whited case used the following language: "Judicial reasoning also recognizes the right of a man, ordinarily, to be tried by a jury in the vicinity in which he resides, so that he may have such advantage and safeguard there as his conduct and character shall merit. An additional argument for the extension of the rule is that a person should not ordinarily be drawn into a foreign jurisdiction 'and there be exposed to entanglements in litigation far from home, which means he shall be attended with augmented expense.' " * * *

The specific question here considered is: May a defendant in a criminal charge, confined in jail on such charge and unable to furnish bail bond, be served with process commencing a civil action based on the same facts as those involved in the criminal prosecution?

An examination of the various authorities will disclose that the courts of last resort which have considered this question are not in accord and that the authorities are in confusion with respect to the same. * * *

In the instant case, Sivnksty came into Gilmer County voluntarily for the purpose of fishing. While there, he had an accident and thereafter was incarcerated in the jail. His presence in Gilmer County, originally voluntary, became involuntary. * * * I think whether Sivnksty came into Gilmer County voluntarily or otherwise has no pertinency to the question here presented.

Sivnksty will be forced to trial in a county far from his residence, among strangers. Even though he may have led an exemplary life and may have had a good reputation in the county of his residence, he would derive little or no benefit from those factors. In addition, he was harassed in his defense of the criminal charge by the institution of the civil suit against him while the criminal charge was still pending. This case is dissimilar from State ex rel. Godby v. Chambers, supra. In that case, the defendant had already been convicted.

Another element enters into this case. It is a matter of common knowledge that in this day and age there is much travel by motor vehicles. Under the rule laid down in the majority opinion, the luckless motorist, who has the misfortune to have an accident injuring persons or property in a county or state far from his residence, may be arrested and incarcerated in jail on a criminal charge, based on a real or fancied violation of an ordinance or statute having no connection with the accident, and while so incarcerated, the person suffering the injury would immediately commence an action in his own home county for the recovery of alleged damages. This could and may lead to widespread abuse of judicial process.

* * *

Notes and Questions

1. Although immunity from process serves legitimate goals, when carried to extremes it ignores the resident plaintiff's desire to litigate in a local forum. What limitations could be imposed on a witness' immunity from process in order to reach some form of balance between the competing interests? Should immunity be denied when the witness furthers some personal goal by entering the state to testify, or would such a test be too evanescent to enforce? See St. John v. Superior Court, 178 Cal.App.2d 794, 3 Cal.Rptr. 535 (2d Dist.1960) (motion to quash service of summons on nonresident president of corporation in California, to attend a hearing before a commission was properly denied, when the president was present in the jurisdiction to testify on a related action that the president's company had instigated); Franklin v. Superior Court, 98 Cal.App.2d 292, 220 P.2d 8 (1st Dist.1950) (holding that, when petitioner came into state to litigate custody of his son with maternal grandmother, but spent eight days in the state before commencing a habeas corpus proceeding to secure child, reasonable inference was that petitioner's controlling purpose in filing this action was to avoid litigation in another action, and therefore petitioner was not exempt from service of process in that other action). Should a nonresident attorney be exempt from process while in a state representing a client on a matter unrelated to the suit in which he is served? What if it is related? Should immunity depend upon whether the forum is a "convenient" one for defendant? What would be the ingredients of such a standard? See Note, *Immunity of Non–Resident Participants in a Judicial Proceeding from Service of Process—A Proposal for Renovation,* 26 Ind.L.J. 459 (1951). Under what circumstances should a court deny immunity to a witness or governmental official as a matter of discretion? See Lamb v. Schmitt, 285 U.S. 222, 52 S.Ct. 317, 76 L.Ed. 720 (1932); Keefe & Roscia, *Immunity and Sentimen-*

tality, 47 Cornell L.Q. 471 (1947). See generally 4 Wright & Miller, *Federal Practice and Procedure: Civil 3d* §§ 1076–81 (2001).

2. In many instances immunity from process is governed by statute. For example, 22 U.S.C. §§ 254a–d and 288d(b) grant immunity to certain representatives of foreign governments, their families, and members of their households. What justification is there for giving these people immunity?

3. Does it make any sense to grant a defendant who can be reached outside the state under a long-arm statute immunity from process when she is within the state for a purpose that otherwise would qualify for immunity? California and New York have abrogated immunity in these cases. See, e.g., Silverman v. Superior Court, 203 Cal.App.3d 145, 249 Cal.Rptr. 724 (2d Dist.1988); Waterman S.S. Corp. v. Ranis, 141 Misc.2d 772, 534 N.Y.S.2d 321 (Sup.Ct.1988).

2. ETIQUETTE OF SERVICE

WYMAN v. NEWHOUSE

United States Court of Appeals, Second Circuit, 1937.
93 F.2d 313, certiorari denied 303 U.S. 664, 58 S.Ct. 831, 82 L.Ed. 1122 (1938).

MANTON, CIRCUIT JUDGE. This appeal is from a judgment entered dismissing the complaint on motion before trial. The action is on a judgment entered by default in a Florida state court, a jury having assessed the damages. The recovery there was for money loaned, money advanced for appellee, and for seduction under promise of marriage.

* * *

Appellant and appellee were both married, but before this suit appellant's husband died. They had known each other for some years and had engaged in meretricious relations.

The affidavits submitted by the appellee * * * established that he was a resident of New York and never lived in Florida. On October 25, 1935, while appellee was in Salt Lake City, Utah, he received a telegram from the appellant, which read: "Account illness home planning leaving. Please come on way back. Must see you." Upon appellee's return to New York he received a letter from appellant stating that her mother was dying in Ireland; that she was leaving the United States for good to go to her mother; that she could not go without seeing the appellee once more; and that she wanted to discuss her affairs with him before she left. Shortly after the receipt of this letter, they spoke to each other on the telephone, whereupon the appellant repeated, in a hysterical and distressed voice, the substance of her letter. Appellee promised to go to Florida in a week or ten days and agreed to notify her when he would arrive. This he did, but before leaving New York by plane he received a letter couched in endearing terms and expressing love and affection for him, as well as her delight at his coming. Before leaving New York, appellee telegraphed appellant, suggesting arrangements for their accommodations together while in Miami, Fla. She telegraphed him at a hotel in Washington, D.C., where he was to stop en route, advising him that the arrangements requested had been made. Appellee arrived at 6 o'clock in the morning at the Miami Airport and saw the appellant standing with her sister some 75 feet distant. He was met by a deputy sheriff who, upon identifying appellee, served him with process in a suit for $500,000. A photographer was present who attempted to take his picture. Thereupon a stranger introduced himself and offered to take appellee to his home, stating that he knew a lawyer who was acquainted with the appellant's attorney. The attorney whom appellee was advised to consult came to the stranger's home and seemed to know about the case. The attorney invited appellee to his office, and upon his arrival he found one of the lawyers for the appellant there. Appellee did not retain the Florida attorney to represent him. He returned to New York by plane that evening and consulted his New York counsel, who advised him to ignore the summons served in Florida. He did so, and judgment was entered by default. * * *

These facts and reasonable deductions therefrom convincingly establish that the appellee was induced to enter the jurisdiction of the state of Florida by a fraud perpetrated upon him by the appellant in falsely representing her mother's illness, her intention to leave the United States, and her love and affection for him, when her sole purpose and apparent thought was to induce him to come within the Florida jurisdiction so as to serve him in an action for damages. * * *

This judgment is attacked for fraud perpetrated upon the appellee which goes to the jurisdiction of the Florida court over his person. A judgment procured fraudulently, as here, lacks jurisdiction and is null and void. * * * A fraud affecting the jurisdiction is equivalent to a lack of jurisdiction. * * * The appellee was not required to proceed against the judgment in Florida. His equitable defense in answer to a suit on the judgment is sufficient. A judgment recovered in a sister state, through the fraud of the party procuring the appearance of another, is not binding on the latter when an attempt is made to enforce such judgment in another state. * * *

The appellee was not required to make out a defense on the merits to the suit in Florida. * * * An error made in entering judgment against a party over whom the court had no jurisdiction permits a consideration of the jurisdictional question collaterally. The complaint was properly dismissed.

Judgment affirmed.

Notes and Questions

1. Reread Tickle v. Barton, p. 22, supra. Which case presents a stronger case for quashing service—*Wyman* or *Tickle?* Why? Would the result have been the same in *Wyman* if Mr. Newhouse had been in Florida and the trickery had been used to "flush him out of hiding"? In GUMPERZ v. HOFMANN, 245 App.Div. 622, 283 N.Y.S. 823 (1st Dep't 1935), affirmed 271 N.Y. 544, 2 N.E.2d 687 (1936), the court distinguished between actions designed to induce a party into a jurisdiction and actions calculated to facilitate service on a party already in the jurisdiction. In upholding service obtained by using trickery on a party who voluntarily was in New York, the court found a duty on the part of the party to accept service of process. The trickery, although reprehensible, did not lead to a quashing of service, since it merely was used to enforce a duty.

2. Instances in which a plaintiff will resort to tactics such as fraud, force, and artifice surely must be rare in an age when legitimate means of obtaining jurisdiction and serving process readily are available under long-arm statutes. Are the doctrines just examined obsolete? Are these rules justified simply because,

even in the rare case, they will deter plaintiffs from doing such things? See, e.g., Shaw v. Hughes, 303 S.C. 337, 400 S.E.2d 501 (Ct.App.1991) (court did not have jurisdiction since service of process was procured by fraud and trickery); Terlizzi v. Brodie, 38 A.D.2d 762, 329 N.Y.S.2d 589 (2d Dep't 1972) (when New Jersey defendants were told that they had been chosen to receive two tickets to Broadway show in New York as a promotion to get their opinion as to new curtain time, service of process after show was invalid).

SECTION D.   OPPORTUNITY TO BE HEARD

The Due Process Clause defines several conditions that must exist before a court may render a valid judgment. We already have seen that the court must have jurisdiction over the parties and issues before it. And we have seen that the parties must have adequate notice of the action. Yet another condition is imposed by the Due Process Clause: the parties must have an adequate opportunity to present their side of the case to the court.

In simple terms, a defendant has an adequate opportunity to be heard when—in light of the interests at stake in the litigation—she is able to develop the facts and legal issues in the case. Depending on the interests involved, a proper hearing may suffice, or a full trial may be required, or something in between may pass muster. One common requirement is that the defendant must be informed of the action (that is, must receive notice) long enough in advance of the time when she is required to respond so as to allow her to obtain counsel and prepare a defense. Thus, when, in ROLLER v. HOLLY, 176 U.S. 398, 20 S.Ct. 410, 44 L.Ed. 520 (1900), the defendant had been served in Virginia with process requiring him to defend an action in Texas only five days after the service was made, the Supreme Court held that the Due Process Clause had been violated. Consequently, Federal Rule 12(a) and state statutes generally allow defendants twenty days or more after service in which to respond.

The so-called "provisional remedies"—temporary restraining orders, preliminary injunctions, pre-action attachments and the like—represent important exceptions to the ordinary requirements associated with the constitutionally required opportunity to be heard. See Chapter Fifteen, infra. For that reason, they present the most difficult problems in this area. The following cases examine the extent to which the Due Process Clause imposes limitations on the use of provisional remedies because they do not provide an adequate opportunity to be heard.

FUENTES v. SHEVIN

Supreme Court of the United States, 1972.
407 U.S. 67, 92 S.Ct. 1983, 32 L.Ed.2d 556, rehearing denied
409 U.S. 902, 93 S.Ct. 177, 34 L.Ed.2d 165.

Appeal from the United States District Court for the Southern District of Florida.

Mr. Justice Stewart delivered the opinion of the Court.

* * *

I

The appellant in No. 5039, Margarita Fuentes, is a resident of Florida. She purchased a gas stove and service policy from the Firestone Tire and Rubber Company (Firestone) under a conditional sales contract calling for monthly payments over a period of time. A few months later, she purchased a stereophonic phonograph from the same company under the same sort of contract. The total cost of the stove and stereo was about $500, plus an additional financing charge of over $100. Under the contracts, Firestone retained title to the merchandise, but Mrs. Fuentes was entitled to possession unless and until she should default on her installment payments.

For more than a year, Mrs. Fuentes made her installment payments. But then, with only about $200 remaining to be paid, a dispute developed between her and Firestone over the servicing of the stove. Firestone instituted an action in a small claims court for repossession of both the stove and the stereo, claiming that Mrs. Fuentes had refused to make her remaining payments. Simultaneously with the filing of that action and before Mrs. Fuentes had even received a summons to answer its complaint, Firestone obtained a writ of replevin ordering a sheriff to seize the disputed goods at once.

* * *

Shortly thereafter, Mrs. Fuentes instituted the present action in a federal district court, challenging the constitutionality of the Florida prejudgment replevin procedures under the Due Process Clause of the Fourteenth Amendment. She sought declaratory and injunctive relief against continued enforcement of the procedural provisions of the state statutes that authorize prejudgment replevin.

The appellants in No. 5138 filed a very similar action in a federal district court in Pennsylvania, challenging the constitutionality of that State's prejudgment replevin process. Like Mrs. Fuentes, they had had possessions seized under writs of replevin. Three of the appellants had purchased personal property—a bed, a table, and other household goods—under installment sales contracts like the one signed by Mrs. Fuentes; and the sellers of the property had obtained and executed summary writs of replevin, claiming that the appellants had fallen behind in their installment payments. The experience of the fourth appellant, Rosa Washington, had been more bizarre. She had been divorced from a local deputy sheriff and was engaged in a dispute with him over the custody of their son. Her former husband, being familiar with the routine forms used in the replevin process, had obtained a writ that ordered the seizure of the boy's clothes, furniture, and toys.

In both No. 5039 and No. 5138, three-judge district courts were convened to consider the appellants' challenges to the constitutional validity of the Florida and Pennsylvania statutes. The courts in both cases upheld the constitutionality of the statutes. * * *

II

Under the Florida statute challenged here, "[a]ny person whose goods or chattels are wrongfully detained by any other person * * * may have a writ of replevin to recover them * * *." Fla.Stats. § 78.01, F.S.A. There is no requirement that the applicant make a convincing showing before the seizure that the goods are, in fact, "wrongfully detained." Rather, Florida law * * * requires only that the applicant file a complaint, initiating a court action for repossession and reciting in conclusory fashion that he is "lawfully entitled to the possession" of the property, and that he file a security bond * * *. On the sole basis of the complaint and bond, a writ is issued "command[ing] the officer to whom it may be directed to replevy the goods and chattels in possession of defendant * * * and to summon the defendant to answer the complaint." Fla.Stats. § 78.08. If the goods are "in any dwelling house or other building or enclosure," the officer is required to demand their delivery; but if they are not delivered, "he shall cause such house, building or enclosure to be broken open and shall make replevin according to the writ * * *." Fla.Stats. § 78.10, F.S.A.

Thus, at the same moment that the defendant receives the complaint seeking repossession of property through court action, the property is seized from him. He is provided no prior notice and allowed no opportunity whatever to challenge the issuance of the writ. *After* the property has been seized, he will eventually have an opportunity for a hearing, as the defendant in the trial of the court action for repossession, which the plaintiff is required to pursue. And he is also not wholly without recourse in the meantime. For under the Florida statute, the officer who seizes the property must keep it for three days, and during that period the defendant may reclaim possession of the property by posting his own security bond in double its value. But if he does not post such a bond, the property is transferred to the party who sought the writ, pending a final judgment in the underlying action for repossession. * * *

The Pennsylvania law differs, though not in its essential nature, from that of Florida. As in Florida, a private party may obtain a prejudgment writ of replevin through a summary process of *ex parte* application, although a prothonotary rather than a court clerk issues the writ. As in Florida, the party seeking the writ may simply post with his application a bond in double the value of the property to be seized. * * * There is no opportunity for a prior hearing and no prior notice to the other party. On this basis, a sheriff is required to execute the writ by seizing the specified property. Unlike the Florida statute, however, the Pennsylvania law does not require that there *ever* be opportunity for a hearing on the merits of the conflicting claims to possession of the replevied property. The party seeking the writ is not obliged to initiate a court action for repossession. Indeed, he need not even formally allege that he is lawfully entitled to the property. * * * If the party who loses property through replevin seizure is to get even a postseizure hearing, he must initiate a lawsuit himself. He may also, as under Florida law, post his own counterbond within three days after the seizure to regain possession. * * *

III

* * * [Prejudgment replevin statutes] are most commonly used by creditors to seize goods allegedly wrongfully detained—not wrongfully taken—by debtors. At common law, if a creditor wished to invoke state power to recover goods wrongfully detained, he had to proceed through the action of debt or detinue. These actions, however, did not provide for a return of property before final judgment. And, more importantly, on the occasions when the

common law did allow prejudgment seizure by state power, it provided some kind of notice and opportunity to be heard to the party then in possession of the property, and a state official made at least a summary determination of the relative rights of the disputing parties before stepping into the dispute and taking goods from one of them.

IV

For more than a century the central meaning of procedural due process has been clear: "Parties whose rights are to be affected are entitled to be heard; and in order that they may enjoy that right they must be notified." Baldwin v. Hale, 68 U.S. 223, 1 Wall. 223, 17 L.Ed. 531. * * * It is equally fundamental that the right to notice and an opportunity to be heard "must be granted at a meaningful time and in a meaningful manner." Armstrong v. Manzo, 380 U.S. 545, 552, 85 S.Ct. 1187, 1191, 14 L.Ed.2d 62.

The primary question in the present cases is whether these state statutes are constitutionally defective in failing to provide for hearings "at a meaningful time." The Florida replevin process guarantees an opportunity for a hearing after the seizure of goods, and the Pennsylvania process allows a post-seizure hearing if the aggrieved party shoulders the burden of initiating one. But neither the Florida nor Pennsylvania statute provides for notice or an opportunity to be heard *before* the seizure. * * *

The constitutional right to be heard is a basic aspect of the duty of government to follow a fair process of decisionmaking when it acts to deprive a person of his possessions. The purpose of this requirement is not only to ensure abstract fair play to the individual. Its purpose, more particularly, is to protect his use and possession of property from arbitrary encroachment—to minimize substantively unfair or mistaken deprivations of property, a danger that is especially great when the State seizes goods simply upon the application of and for the benefit of a private party. So viewed, the prohibition against the deprivation of property without due process of law reflects the high value, embedded in our constitutional and political history, that we place on a person's right to enjoy what is his, free of governmental interference. * * *

The requirement of notice and an opportunity to be heard raises no impenetrable barrier to the taking of a person's possessions. But the fair process of decision-making that it guarantees works, by itself, to protect against arbitrary deprivation of property. For when a person has an opportunity to speak up in his own defense, and when the State must listen to what he has to say, substantively unfair and simply mistaken deprivations of property interests can be prevented. It has long been recognized that "fairness can rarely be obtained by secret, one-sided determination of facts decisive of rights. * * * [And n]o better instrument has been devised for arriving at truth than to give a person in jeopardy of serious loss notice of the case against him and opportunity to meet it." Joint Anti–Fascist Refugee Committee v. McGrath, 341 U.S. 123, 170–172, 71 S.Ct. 624, 647, 95 L.Ed. 817 (Frankfurter, J., concurring).

If the right to notice and a hearing is to serve its full purpose, then, it is clear that it must be granted at a time when the deprivation can still be prevented. At a later hearing, an individual's possessions can be returned to him if they were unfairly or mistakenly taken in the first place. Damages may even be awarded to him for the wrongful deprivation. But no later hearing and no damage award can undo the fact that the arbitrary taking that was subject to the right of procedural due process has already occurred. "This Court has not * * * embraced the general proposition that a wrong may be done if it can be undone." Stanley v. Illinois, 405 U.S. 645, 647, 92 S.Ct. 1208, 1210, 31 L.Ed.2d 551.

This is no new principle of constitutional law. The right to a prior hearing has long been recognized by this Court under the Fourteenth and Fifth Amendments. Although the Court has held that due process tolerates variances in the *form* of a hearing "appropriate to the nature of the case," Mullane v. Central Hanover Tr. Co., * * * and "depending upon the importance of the interests involved and the nature of the subsequent proceedings [if any]," Boddie v. Connecticut, 401 U.S. 371, 378, 91 S.Ct. 780, 786, 28 L.Ed.2d 113, the Court has traditionally insisted that, whatever its form, opportunity for that hearing must be provided before the deprivation at issue takes effect. * * * "That the hearing required by due process is subject to waiver, and is not fixed in form does not affect its root requirement that an individual be given an opportunity for a hearing *before* he is deprived of any significant property interest, except for extraordinary situations where some valid governmental interest is at stake that justifies postponing the hearing until after the event." Boddie v. Connecticut, supra, 401 U.S., at 378–379, 91 S.Ct., at 786 (emphasis in original).

The Florida and Pennsylvania prejudgment replevin statutes fly in the face of this principle. To be sure, the requirements that a party seeking a writ must first post a bond, allege conclusorily that he is entitled to specific goods, and open himself to possible liability in damages if he is wrong, serve to deter wholly unfounded applications for a writ. But those requirements are hardly a substitute for a prior hearing, for they test no more than the strength of the applicant's own belief in his rights.[13] Since his private gain is at stake, the danger is all too great that his confidence in his cause will be misplaced. Lawyers and judges are familiar with the phenomenon of a party mistakenly but firmly convinced that his view of the facts and law will prevail, and therefore quite willing to risk the costs of litigation. Because of the understandable, self-interested fallibility of litigants, a court does not decide a dispute until it has had an opportunity to hear both sides—and does not generally take even tentative action until it has itself examined the support for the plaintiff's position. The Florida and Pennsylvania statutes do not even require the official issuing a writ of replevin to do that much.

The minimal deterrent effect of a bond requirement is, in a practical sense, no substitute for an informed evaluation by a neutral official. More specifically, as a matter of constitutional principle, it is no replacement for the right to a prior hearing that is the only truly effective safeguard against arbitrary deprivation of property. While the existence of these other, less effective, safeguards may be among the considerations that affect the form of

---

13. They may not even test that much. For if an applicant for the writ knows that he is dealing with an uneducated, uninformed consumer with little access to legal help and little familiarity with legal procedures, there may be a substantial possibility that a summary seizure of property—however unwarranted—may go unchallenged, and the applicant may feel that he can act with impunity.

hearing demanded by due process, they are far from enough by themselves to obviate the right to a prior hearing of some kind.

V

The right to a prior hearing, of course, attaches only to the deprivation of an interest encompassed within the Fourteenth Amendment's protection. In the present cases, the Florida and Pennsylvania statutes were applied to replevy chattels in the appellants' possession. The replevin was not cast as a final judgment; most, if not all, of the appellants lacked full title to the chattels; and their claim even to continued possession was a matter in dispute. Moreover, the chattels at stake were nothing more than an assortment of household goods. Nonetheless, it is clear that the appellants were deprived of possessory interests in those chattels that were within the protection of the Fourteenth Amendment.

A

* * * The Florida and Pennsylvania statutes do not require a person to wait until a post-seizure hearing and final judgment to recover what has been replevied. Within three days after the seizure, the statutes allow him to recover the goods if he, in return, surrenders other property—a payment necessary to secure a bond in double the value of the goods seized from him.[14] But it is now well settled that a temporary, nonfinal deprivation of property is nonetheless a "deprivation" in the terms of the Fourteenth Amendment.
* * *

* * * The Fourteenth Amendment draws no bright lines around three-day, 10–day or 50–day deprivations of property. Any significant taking of property by the State is within the purview of the Due Process Clause. While the length and consequent severity of a deprivation may be another factor to weigh in determining the appropriate form of hearing, it is not decisive of the basic right to a prior hearing of some kind.

B

The appellants who signed conditional sales contracts lacked full legal title to the replevied goods. The Fourteenth Amendment's protection of "property," however, has never been interpreted to safeguard only the rights of undisputed ownership. Rather, it has been read broadly to extend protection to "any significant property interest" * * *.

The appellants were deprived of such an interest in the replevied goods— the interest in continued possession and use of the goods. * * * They had acquired this interest under the conditional sales contracts that entitled them to possession and use of the chattels before transfer of title. In exchange for immediate possession, the appellants had agreed to pay a major financing

---

14. The appellants argue that this opportunity for quick recovery exists only in theory. They allege that very few people in their position are able to obtain a recovery bond, even if they know of the possibility. Appellant Fuentes says that in her case she was never told that she could recover the stove and stereo and that the deputy sheriff seizing them gave them at once to the Firestone agent, rather than holding them for three days. She further asserts that of 442 cases of prejudgment replevin in small claims courts in Dade County, Florida, in 1969, there was not one case in which the defendant took advantage of the recovery provision.

charge beyond the basic price of the merchandise. Moreover, by the time the goods were summarily repossessed, they had made substantial installment payments. Clearly, their possessory interest in the goods, dearly bought and protected by contract, was sufficient to invoke the protection of the Due Process Clause.

Their ultimate right to continued possession was, of course, in dispute. If it were shown at a hearing that the appellants had defaulted on their contractual obligations, it might well be that the sellers of the goods would be entitled to repossession. But even assuming that the appellants had fallen behind in their installment payments, and that they had no other valid defenses, that is immaterial here. The right to be heard does not depend upon an advance showing that one will surely prevail at the hearing. * * *

C

Nevertheless, the district courts rejected the appellants' constitutional claim on the ground that the goods seized from them—a stove, a stereo, a table, a bed, and so forth—were not deserving of due process protection, since they were not absolute necessities of life. The courts based this holding on a very narrow reading of Sniadach v. Family Finance Corp., [395 U.S. 337, 89 S.Ct. 1820, 23 L.Ed.2d 349 (1969), p. 237, infra] * * * and Goldberg v. Kelly, * * * [397 U.S. 254, 90 S.Ct. 1011, 25 L.Ed.2d 287 (1970)], in which this Court held that the Constitution requires a hearing before prejudgment wage garnishment and before the termination of certain welfare benefits. They reasoned that Sniadach and Goldberg, as a matter of constitutional principle, established no more than that a prior hearing is required with respect to the deprivation of such basically "necessary" items as wages and welfare benefits.

This reading of Sniadach and Goldberg reflects the premise that those cases marked a radical departure from established principles of procedural due process. They did not. Both decisions were in the mainstream of past cases, having little or nothing to do with the absolute "necessities" of life but establishing that due process requires an opportunity for a hearing before a deprivation of property takes effect. * * * While Sniadach and Goldberg emphasized the special importance of wages and welfare benefits, they did not convert that emphasis into a new and more limited constitutional doctrine.

* * *

VI

There are "extraordinary situations" that justify postponing notice and opportunity for a hearing. Boddie v. Connecticut, supra, 401 U.S., at 379, 91 S.Ct., at 786. These situations, however, must be truly unusual. Only in a few limited situations has this Court allowed outright seizure[23] without opportuni-

---

23. * * * In three cases, the Court has allowed the attachment of property without a prior hearing. In one, the attachment was necessary to protect the public against the same sort of immediate harm involved in the seizure cases—a bank failure. Coffin Bros. & Co. v. Bennett, 277 U.S. 29, 48 S.Ct. 422, 72 L.Ed. 768. Another case involved attachment necessary to secure jurisdiction in state court—

clearly a most basic and important public interest. Ownbey v. Morgan, 256 U.S. 94, 41 S.Ct. 433, 65 L.Ed. 837. It is much less clear what interests were involved in the third case, decided with an unexplicated per curiam opinion simply citing Coffin Bros. and Ownbey. McKay v. McInnes, 279 U.S. 820, 49 S.Ct. 344, 73 L.Ed. 975. As far as essential procedural due process doctrine goes, McKay cannot stand ty for a prior hearing. First, in each case, the seizure has been directly necessary to secure an important governmental or general public interest. Second, there has been a special need for very prompt action. Third, the State has kept strict control over its monopoly of legitimate force; the person initiating the seizure has been a government official responsible for determining, under the standards of a narrowly drawn statute, that it was necessary and justified in the particular instance. Thus, the Court has allowed summary seizure of property to collect the internal revenue of the United States, to meet the needs of a national war effort, to protect against the economic disaster of a bank failure, and to protect the public from misbranded drugs and contaminated food.

The Florida and Pennsylvania prejudgment replevin statutes serve no such important governmental or general public interest. They allow summary seizure of a person's possessions when no more than private gain is directly at stake.[29] * * *

Nor do the broadly drawn Florida and Pennsylvania statutes limit the summary seizure of goods to special situations demanding prompt action. There may be cases in which a creditor could make a showing of immediate danger that a debtor will destroy or conceal disputed goods. But the statutes before us are not "narrowly drawn to meet any such unusual condition." Sniadach v. Family Finance Corp., supra, 395 U.S. at 339, 89 S.Ct. at 1821. And no such unusual situation is presented by the facts of these cases.

The statutes, moreover, abdicate effective state control over state power. Private parties, serving their own private advantage, may unilaterally invoke state power to replevy goods from another. No state official participates in the decision to seek a writ; no state official reviews the basis for the claim to repossession; and no state official evaluates the need for immediate seizure. There is not even a requirement that the plaintiff provide any information to the court on these matters. The State acts largely in the dark.

VII

Finally, we must consider the contention that the appellants who signed conditional sales contracts thereby waived their basic procedural due process rights. The contract signed by Mrs. Fuentes provided that "in the event of default of any payment or payments, Seller at its option may take back the merchandise * * *." The contracts signed by the Pennsylvania appellants similarly provided that the seller "may retake" or "repossess" the merchan-

---

for any more than was established in the *Coffin Bros.* and *Ownbey* cases on which it relied completely. * * *

29. By allowing repossession without an opportunity for a prior hearing, the Florida and Pennsylvania statutes may be intended specifically to reduce the costs for the private party seeking to seize goods in another party's possession. Even if the private gain at stake in repossession actions were equal to the great public interests recognized in this Court's past decisions, * * * the Court has made clear that the avoidance of the ordinary costs imposed by the opportunity for a hearing is not sufficient to override the constitutional right. * * *

[The] * * * cost of an opportunity to be heard before repossession should not be exaggerated. For we deal here only with the right to an *opportunity* to be heard. Since the issues and facts decisive of rights in repossession suits may very often be quite simple, there is a likelihood that many defendants would forgo their opportunity, sensing the futility of the exercise in the particular case. And, of course, no hearing need be held unless the defendant, having received notice of his opportunity, takes advantage of it.

dise in the event of a "default in any payment." These terms were parts of printed form contracts, appearing in relatively small type and unaccompanied by any explanations clarifying their meaning.

* * * For a waiver of constitutional rights in any context must, at the very least, be clear. The contractual language relied upon must, on its face, amount to a waiver.

The conditional sales contracts here simply provided that upon a default the seller "may take back," "may retake" or "may repossess" merchandise. The contracts included nothing about the waiver of a prior hearing. They did not indicate *how* or *through what process*—a final judgment, self-help, prejudgment replevin with a prior hearing, or prejudgment replevin without a prior hearing—the seller could take back the goods. Rather, the purported waiver provisions here are no more than a statement of the seller's right to repossession upon occurrence of certain events. * * *

VIII

We hold that the Florida and Pennsylvania prejudgment replevin provisions work a deprivation of property without due process of law insofar as they deny the right to a prior opportunity to be heard before chattels are taken from their possessor. Our holding, however, is a narrow one. We do not question the power of a State to seize goods before a final judgment in order to protect the security interests of creditors so long as those creditors have tested their claim to the goods through the process of a fair prior hearing. The nature and form of such prior hearings, moreover, are legitimately open to many potential variations and are a subject, at this point, for legislation—not adjudication. * * *

Vacated and remanded.

Mr. Justice Powell and Mr. Justice Rehnquist did not participate in the consideration or decision of these cases.

Mr. Justice White, with whom The Chief Justice and Mr. Justice Blackmun join, dissenting.

* * * [The dissenters first noted that state proceedings were in progress when these actions were commenced so that jurisdiction should have been refused because there was an adequate remedy at law.]

Second: * * *.

* * * The Court holds it constitutionally essential to afford opportunity for a probable cause hearing prior to repossession. Its stated purpose is "to prevent unfair and mistaken deprivations of the property." But in these typical situations, the buyer-debtor has either defaulted or he has not. If there is a default, it would seem not only "fair," but essential, that the creditor be allowed to repossess; and I cannot say that the likelihood of a mistaken claim of default is sufficiently real or recurring to justify a broad constitutional requirement that a creditor do more than the typical state law requires and permits him to do. Sellers are normally in the business of selling and collecting the price for their merchandise. I could be quite wrong, but it would not seem in the creditor's interest for a default occasioning repossession to occur; as a practical matter it would much better serve his interests if the transaction goes forward and is completed as planned. Dollar and cents considerations weigh heavily against false claims of default as well as against precipitate action that would allow no opportunity for mistakes to surface and be corrected. Nor does it seem to me that creditors would lightly undertake the expense of instituting replevin actions and putting up bonds.

* * * Viewing the issue before us in this light, I would not construe the Due Process Clause to require the creditors to do more than they have done in these cases to secure possession pending final hearing. Certainly, I would not ignore, as the Court does, the creditor's interest in preventing further use and deterioration of the property in which he has substantial interest. Surely under the Court's own definition, the creditor has a "property" interest as deserving of protection as that of the debtor. At least the debtor, who is very likely uninterested in a speedy resolution that could terminate his use of the property, should be required to make those payments, into court or otherwise, upon which his right to possession is conditioned. * * *

Third: The Court's rhetoric is seductive, but in end analysis, the result it reaches will have little impact and represents no more than ideological tinkering with state law. It would appear that creditors could withstand attack under today's opinion simply by making clear in the controlling credit instruments that they may retake possession without a hearing, or, for that matter, without resort to judicial process at all. Alternatively, they need only give a few days' notice of a hearing, take possession if hearing is waived or if there is default; and if hearing is necessary merely establish probable cause for asserting that default has occurred. It is very doubtful in my mind that such a hearing would in fact result in protections for the debtor substantially different from those the present laws provide. On the contrary, the availability of credit may well be diminished or, in any event, the expense of securing it increased.

None of this seems worth the candle to me. The procedure which the Court strikes down is not some barbaric hangover from bygone days. The respective rights of the parties in secured transactions have undergone the most intensive analysis in recent years. * * *

Notes and Questions

1. As the Court in *Fuentes* noted, its holding as to replevin statutes was an application of its earlier decision in SNIADACH v. FAMILY FINANCE CORP., 395 U.S. 337, 89 S.Ct. 1820, 23 L.Ed.2d 349 (1969), which struck down a Wisconsin prejudgment wage garnishment procedure as violative of due process guarantees:

A prejudgment garnishment of the Wisconsin type is a taking which may impose tremendous hardship on wage earners with families to support. Until a recent act of Congress, * * * which forbids discharge of employees on the ground that their wages have been garnished, garnishment often meant the loss of a job. Over and beyond that was the great drain on family income.

* * * [P]rejudgment garnishment of the Wisconsin type may as a practical matter drive a wage-earning family to the wall. Where the taking of one's property is so obvious, it needs no extended argument to conclude that absent notice and a prior hearing * * * this prejudgment garnishment procedure violates the fundamental principles of due process.

Id. at 340–42, 89 S.Ct. at 1822–23, 23 L.Ed.2d at 353–54.

2. How sound is the dissent's argument that creditors can avoid the restrictions of *Fuentes* by providing in their financing contracts that they may retake possession of property without a hearing? Reconsider D.H. Overmyer Co. v. Frick Co., Note 2, p. 216, supra, in which the Court held that a clause authorizing a creditor upon default to use a confession-of-judgment procedure and secure the entry of judgment against a debtor without service of process or notice was not per se violative of the Fourteenth Amendment requirements of prejudgment notice and a hearing. Then, consider KOSCHES v. NICHOLS, 68 Misc.2d 795, 327 N.Y.S.2d 968 (N.Y.City Civ.Ct.1971), in which the court stated:

> * * * The court also recognizes that, in these adhesion agreements where the buyer has no alternative but to purchase on credit, the parties are not in equal bargaining position. The era of the company store where the purchaser had no place else to go may not be dead. * * * Needless to say, the clauses giving the seller the right to enter a debtor's residence and seize the goods without a court order are unconscionable.

Id. at 797, 327 N.Y.S.2d at 970. See also Hopson, *Cognovit Judgments: An Ignored Problem of Due Process and Full Faith and Credit,* 29 U.Chi.L.Rev. 111 (1961).

MITCHELL v. W.T. GRANT CO., 416 U.S. 600, 601, 604–07, 611, 614–15, 617–20, 94 S.Ct. 1895, 1897–1900, 1902, 1904–06, 40 L.Ed.2d 406, 410, 412–13, 415, 418–20 (1974) (White, J.):

In this case, a state trial judge in Louisiana ordered the sequestration of personal property on the application of a creditor who had made an installment sale of the goods to petitioner and whose affidavit asserted delinquency and prayed for sequestration to enforce a vendor's lien under state law. The issue is whether the sequestration violated the Due Process Clause of the Fourteenth Amendment because it was ordered *ex parte,* without prior notice or opportunity for a hearing. * * *

Plainly enough, this is not a case where the property sequestered by the court is exclusively the property of the defendant debtor. The question is not whether a debtor's property may be seized by his creditors, *pendente lite,* where they hold no present interest in the property sought to be seized. The reality is that both seller and buyer had current, real interests in the property, and the definition of property rights is a matter of state law. Resolution of the due process question must take account not only of the interests of the buyer of the property but those of the seller as well.

* * *

Louisiana statutes provide for sequestration where "one claims the ownership or right to possession of property, or a mortgage, lien, or privilege thereon * * * if it is within the power of the defendant to conceal, dispose of, or waste the property or the revenues therefrom, or remove the property from the parish, during the pendency of the action." Art. 3571. The writ, however, will not issue on the conclusory allegation of ownership or possessory rights. Article 3501 provides that the writ of sequestration shall issue "only when the nature of the claim and the amount thereof, if any, and the grounds relied upon for the issuance of the writ clearly appear from specific facts" shown by a verified petition or affidavit. In the parish where this case arose, the clear showing required must be made to a judge, and the writ will issue only upon his authorization and only after the creditor seeking the writ has filed a sufficient bond to protect the vendee against all damages in the event the sequestration is shown to have been improvident. Arts. 3501 and 3574.

The writ is obtainable on the creditor's *ex parte* application, without notice to the debtor or opportunity for a hearing, but the statute entitles the debtor immediately to seek dissolution of the writ, which must be ordered unless the creditor "proves the grounds upon which the writ was issued," Art. 3506, the existence of the debt, lien, and delinquency, failing which the court may order return of the property and assess damages in favor of the debtor, including attorney's fees.

The debtor, with or without moving to dissolve the sequestration, may also regain possession by filing his own bond to protect the creditor against interim damage to him should he ultimately win his case and have judgment against the debtor for the unpaid balance of the purchase price which was the object of the suit and of the sequestration. Arts. 3507 and 3508.

* * *

Petitioner asserts that his right to a hearing before his possession is in any way disturbed is nonetheless mandated by a long line of cases in this Court * * *.

* * * The suing creditor in *Sniadach* had no prior interest in the property attached, and the opinion did not purport to govern the typical case of the installment seller who brings a suit to collect an unpaid balance and who does not seek to attach wages pending the outcome of the suit but to repossess the sold property on which he had retained a lien to secure the purchase price. * * * [The *Fuentes*] holding is the mainstay of petitioner's submission here. But we are convinced that *Fuentes* was decided against a factual and legal background sufficiently different from that now before us and that it does not require the invalidation of the Louisiana sequestration statute, either on its face or as applied in this case.

* * * In Florida and Pennsylvania property was only to be replevied in accord with state policy if it had been "wrongfully detained." This broad "fault" standard is inherently subject to factual determination and adversarial input. * * * [I]n *Fuentes* this fault standard for replevin was thought ill-suited for preliminary *ex parte* determination. In Louisiana, on the other hand, the facts relevant to obtaining a writ of sequestration are narrowly confined. As we have indicated, documentary proof is particularly suited for questions of the existence of a vendor's lien and the issue of default. There is thus far less danger here that the seizure will be mistaken and a corresponding decrease in the utility of an adversary hearing which will be immediately available in any event.

* * * Our conclusion is that the Louisiana standards regulating the use of the writ of sequestration are constitutional. * * *

Notes and Questions

1. Justice Powell joined the majority opinion, but would have decided the case on narrower grounds. Justices Stewart, Douglas, and Marshall dissented arguing that (1) the Louisiana affidavit requirement was little more than a standardized form that only tested the creditor-applicant's own belief in his rights, (2) replacing the court clerk with a judge would have no effect on the assessment of the affidavit or the issuance of the writ, (3) the factual issues in *Mitchell* were no different from those in *Fuentes,* and (4) the majority had unjustifiably disregarded *stare decisis* in overruling *Fuentes.* Justice Brennan agreed with the other dissenters that *Fuentes* required the reversal of the judgment of the Supreme Court of Louisiana.

2. Are you, as was the majority, "convinced that *Fuentes* was decided against a factual and legal background sufficiently different" to justify the result in *Mitchell?* Can *Fuentes* and *Mitchell* be reconciled or was Justice Stewart's dissenting opinion correct in its assessment that *Mitchell*

> has unmistakably overruled a considered decision of this Court that is barely two years old, without pointing to any change in either societal perceptions or basic constitutional understandings that might justify this total disregard of *stare decisis.*

Id. at 635, 94 S.Ct. at 1913, 40 L.Ed.2d at 429.

3. In the majority opinion, Justice White wrote: "In our view, this statutory procedure effects a constitutional accommodation of the conflicting interests of the parties." Although the Louisiana statute required the creditor to make more specific allegations than did the Florida and Pennsylvania statutes, can this requirement adequately replace the debtor's opportunity for a prior hearing? Is it of constitutional significance that the official who signs the writ after the ex parte application is a judge rather than a court clerk?

NORTH GEORGIA FINISHING, INC. v. DI–CHEM, INC., 419 U.S. 601, 601–08, 95 S.Ct. 719, 720–23, 42 L.Ed.2d 751, 754–58 (1975) (White, J.):

Under the statutes of the State of Georgia, plaintiffs in pending suits are "entitled to the process of garnishment." Ga.Code Ann. § 46–101. To employ the process, plaintiff or his attorney must make an affidavit before "some officer authorized to issue an attachment, or the clerk of any court of record in which the said garnishment is being filed or in which the main case is filed, stating the amount claimed to be due in such action * * * and that he has reason to apprehend the loss of the same or some part thereof unless process of garnishment shall issue." § 46–102. To protect defendant against loss or damage in the event plaintiff fails to recover, that section also requires plaintiff to file a bond in a sum double the amount sworn to be due. Section 46–401 permits the defendant to dissolve the garnishment by filing a bond "conditioned for the payment of any judgment that shall be rendered on said garnishment." Whether these provisions satisfy the Due Process Clause of the Fourteenth Amendment is the issue before us in this case.

* * * [The Court proceeded to explain the background of the case. Respondent had filed suit against petitioner, alleging that petitioner owed it $51,279 for goods sold and delivered. Before petitioner received service of the complaint, respondent filed an affidavit and bond for garnishing petitioner's bank account. Petitioner responded first by filing its own bond to discharge the bank as garnishee and then by filing a motion to discharge its bond on the ground that the statute unconstitutionally failed to provide notice and hearing prior to the garnishment. The Georgia Supreme Court upheld the constitutionality of the statute.]

The Georgia court recognized that Sniadach v. Family Finance Corp. * * * had invalidated a statute permitting the garnishment of wages without notice and opportunity for hearing, but considered that case to have done nothing more than to carve out an exception, in favor of wage earners, "to the general rule of legality of garnishment statutes." * * * The garnishment of other assets or properties pending the outcome of the main action * * * was apparently thought not to implicate the Due Process Clause.

This approach failed to take account of Fuentes v. Shevin * * *. Because the official seizures had been carried out without notice and without opportunity for a hearing or other safeguard against mistaken repossession, they were held to be in violation of the Fourteenth Amendment.

The Georgia statute is vulnerable for the same reasons. Here, a bank account, surely a form of property, was impounded and, absent a bond, put totally beyond use during the pendency of the litigation on the alleged debt, all by a writ of garnishment issued by a court clerk without notice or opportunity for an early hearing and without participation by a judicial officer.

Nor is the statute saved by the more recent decision in Mitchell v. W.T. Grant Co. * * *.

The Georgia garnishment statute has none of the saving characteristics of the Louisiana statute. The writ of garnishment is issuable on the affidavit of the creditor or his attorney, and the latter need not have personal knowledge of the facts. § 46–103. The affidavit, like the one filed in this case, need contain only conclusory allegations. The writ is issuable, as this one was, by the court clerk, without participation by a judge. Upon service of the writ, the debtor is deprived of the use of the property in the hands of the garnishee. Here a sizable bank account was frozen, and the only method discernible on the face of the statute to dissolve the garnishment was to file a bond to protect the plaintiff creditor. There is no provision for an early hearing at which the creditor would be required to demonstrate at least probable cause for the garnishment. Indeed, it would appear that without the filing of a bond the defendant debtor's challenge to the garnishment will not be entertained, whatever the grounds may be.

Respondent also argues that neither *Fuentes* nor *Mitchell* is apposite here because each of those cases dealt with the application of due process protections to consumers who are victims of contracts of adhesion and who might be irreparably damaged by temporary deprivation of household necessities, whereas this case deals with its application in the commercial setting to a case involving parties of equal bargaining power. * * * It is asserted in addition that the double bond posted here gives assurance to petitioner that it will be made whole in the event the garnishment turns out to be unjustified. It may be that consumers deprived of household appliances will more likely suffer irreparably than corporations deprived of bank accounts, but the probability of irreparable injury in the latter case is sufficiently great so that some procedures are necessary to guard against the risk of initial error. We are no more inclined now than we have been in the past to distinguish among different kinds of property in applying the Due Process Clause. * * *

Enough has been said, we think, to require the reversal of the judgment of the Georgia Supreme Court. * * *

Notes and Questions

1. Although the Court in *Di-Chem* claimed to have relied on *Fuentes* in declaring the Georgia garnishment statute unconstitutional, did the Court actually insist that the Georgia statute provide an opportunity for a pre-seizure hearing? Would the Georgia statute have been acceptable if it had provided for an immediate post-seizure hearing, as did the Louisiana statute in *Mitchell?* What did the Court in *Di-Chem* mean by the words "or other safeguard against mistaken repossession" on page 241, supra?

2. Has the *Di-Chem* Court reconciled its earlier decisions in *Sniadach, Fuentes,* and *Mitchell?* What is left of *Fuentes* after *Di-Chem?* Of *Mitchell?* Has *Mitchell* become an exception to the *Fuentes* case or has *Mitchell* become the new standard? See Catz & Robinson, *Due Process and Creditor's Remedies: From Sniadach and Fuentes to Mitchell, North Georgia and Beyond,* 28 Rutgers L.Rev. 541 (1975).

3. Might the result in *Di-Chem* have been different if the creditor had a pre-existing interest in the garnished bank account, as did the creditor in *Mitchell?*

4. For a discussion of these four cases, see generally Kay & Lubin, *Making Sense of the Prejudgment Seizure Cases,* 64 Ky.L.J. 705 (1976); Comment, *A Confusing Course Made More Confusing: The Supreme Court, Due Process, and Summary Creditor Remedies,* 70 Nw.U.L.Rev. 331 (1975).

CONNECTICUT v. DOEHR

Supreme Court of the United States, 1991.
501 U.S. 1, 111 S.Ct. 2105, 115 L.Ed.2d 1.

Certiorari to the United States Court of Appeals for the Second Circuit.

JUSTICE WHITE delivered an opinion, Parts I, II, and III of which are the opinion of the Court.*

This case requires us to determine whether a state statute that authorizes prejudgment attachment of real estate without prior notice or hearing, without a showing of extraordinary circumstances, and without a requirement that the person seeking the attachment post a bond, satisfies the Due Process Clause of the Fourteenth Amendment. We hold that, as applied to this case, it does not.

---

* The Chief Justice, Justice Blackmun, Justice Kennedy, and Justice Souter join Parts I,   II, and III of this opinion, and Justice Scalia joins Parts I and III.

I

On March 15, 1988, Petitioner John F. DiGiovanni submitted an application to the Connecticut Superior Court for an attachment in the amount of $75,000 on respondent Brian K. Doehr's home in Meridan, Connecticut. DiGiovanni took this step in conjunction with a civil action for assault and battery that he was seeking to institute against Doehr in the same court. The suit did not involve Doehr's real estate nor did DiGiovanni have any pre-existing interest either in Doehr's home or any of his other property.

Connecticut law authorizes prejudgment attachment of real estate without affording prior notice or the opportunity for a prior hearing to the individual whose property is subject to the attachment. The State's prejudgment remedy statute provides, in relevant part:

"The court or a judge of the court may allow the prejudgment remedy to be issued by an attorney without hearing * * * upon verification by oath of the plaintiff or of some competent affiant, that there is probable cause to sustain the validity of the plaintiff's claims and (1) that the prejudgment remedy requested is for an attachment of real property * * *." Conn.Gen.Stat. § 52–278e (1991).

The statute does not require the plaintiff to post a bond to insure the payment of damages that the defendant may suffer should the attachment prove wrongfully issued or the claim prove unsuccessful.

As required, DiGiovanni submitted an affidavit in support of his application. In five one-sentence paragraphs, DiGiovanni stated that the facts set forth in his previously submitted complaint were true; that "I was willfully, wantonly and maliciously assaulted by the defendant, Brian K. Doehr"; that "[s]aid assault and battery broke my left wrist and further caused an ecchymosis to my right eye, as well as other injuries"; and that "I have further expended sums of money for medical care and treatment." The affidavit concluded with the statement, "In my opinion, the foregoing facts are sufficient to show that there is probable cause that judgment will be rendered for the plaintiff."

On the strength of these submissions the Superior Court judge * * * found "probable cause to sustain the validity of the plaintiff's claim" and ordered the attachment on Doehr's home "to the value of $75,000." The sheriff attached the property four days later * * *. Only after this did Doehr receive notice of the attachment. He also had yet to be served with the complaint * * *. As the statute further required, the attachment notice informed Doehr that he had the right to a hearing: (1) to claim that no probable cause existed to sustain the claim; (2) to request that the attachment be vacated, modified, or that a bond be substituted; or (3) to claim that some portion of the property was exempt from execution. * * *

Rather than pursue these options, Doehr filed suit against DiGiovanni in Federal District Court, claiming that [the statute] was unconstitutional under the Due Process Clause of the Fourteenth Amendment. The District Court upheld the statute and granted summary judgment in favor of DiGiovanni. * * * On appeal, a divided panel of the United States Court of Appeals for the Second Circuit reversed. * * * Judge Pratt, who wrote the opinion for the court, concluded that the Connecticut statute violated due process in permitting *ex parte* attachment absent a showing of extraordinary circumstances. "The rule to be derived from Sniadach v. Family Finance Corp. * * * and its progeny, therefore, is not that postattachment hearings are generally acceptable provided that the plaintiff files a factual affidavit and that a judicial officer supervises the process, but that a prior hearing may be postponed where exceptional circumstances justify such a delay, *and where* sufficient additional safeguards are present." * * *

A further reason to invalidate the statute, the court ruled, was the highly factual nature of the issues in this case. In [Mitchell v. W.T. Grant Co.] there were "uncomplicated matters that len[t] themselves to documentary proof" and "[t]he nature of the issues at stake minimize[d] the risk that the writ [would] be wrongfully issued by a judge." * * * Judge Pratt observed that in contrast the present case involved the fact-specific event of a fist fight and the issue of assault. He doubted that the judge could reliably determine probable cause when presented with only the plaintiff's version of the altercation. * * * Judge Pratt went on to conclude that in his view, the statute was also constitutionally infirm for its failure to require the plaintiff to post a bond for the protection of the defendant in the event the attachment was ultimately found to have been improvident.

* * *

II

With this case we return to the question of what process must be afforded by a state statute enabling an individual to enlist the aid of the State to deprive another of his or her property by means of the prejudgment attachment or similar procedure. Our cases reflect the numerous variations this type of remedy can entail. [See, e.g., *Sniadach, Fuentes, Mitchell,* and *Di-Chem.*] * * * In [Mathews v. Eldridge, 424 U.S. 319, 96 S.Ct. 893, 47 L.Ed.2d 18 (1976)], we drew upon * * * [these] decisions to determine what process is due when the government itself seeks to effect a deprivation on its own initiative. * * * That analysis resulted in * * * [a] threefold inquiry requiring consideration of "the private interest that will be affected by the official action"; "the risk of an erroneous deprivation of such interest through the procedures used, and the probable value, if any, of additional or substitute safeguards"; and lastly "the Government's interest, including the function involved and the fiscal and administrative burdens that the additional or substitute procedural requirement would entail." Id. at 335, 96 S.Ct. at 903.

Here the inquiry is similar but the focus is different. Prejudgment remedy statutes ordinarily apply to disputes between private parties rather than between an individual and the government. * * * For this type of case, therefore, the relevant inquiry requires, as in *Mathews,* first, consideration of the private interest that will be affected by the prejudgment measure; second, an examination of the risk of erroneous deprivation through the procedures under attack and the probable value of additional or alternative safeguards; and third, in contrast to *Mathews,* principal attention to the interest of the party seeking the prejudgment remedy, with, nonetheless, due regard for any ancillary interest the government may have in providing the procedure or forgoing the added burden of providing greater protections.

We now consider the *Mathews* factors in determining the adequacy of the procedures before us, first with regard to the safeguards of notice and a prior hearing, and then in relation to the protection of a bond.

III

We agree with the Court of Appeals that the property interests that attachment affects are significant. For a property owner like Doehr, attachment ordinarily clouds title; impairs the ability to sell or otherwise alienate the property; taints any credit rating; reduces the chance of obtaining a home equity loan or additional mortgage; and can even place an existing mortgage in technical default where there is an insecurity clause. * * *

* * * [Connecticut] correctly points out that these effects do not amount to a complete, physical, or permanent deprivation of real property; their impact is less than the perhaps temporary total deprivation of household goods or wages. * * * But the Court has never held that only such extreme deprivations trigger due process concern. * * * To the contrary, our cases show that even the temporary or partial impairments to property rights that attachments, liens, and similar encumbrances entail are sufficient to merit due process protection. * * *

We also agree with the Court of Appeals that the risk of erroneous deprivation that the State permits here is substantial. By definition, attachment statutes premise a deprivation of property on one ultimate factual contingency—the award of damages to the plaintiff which the defendant may not be able to satisfy. * * * For attachments before judgment, Connecticut mandates that this determination be made by means of a procedural inquiry that asks whether "there is probable cause to sustain the validity of the plaintiff's claim." Conn.Gen.Stat. § 52–278e(a). * * * What probable cause means in this context, however, remains obscure. The State initially took the position * * * that the statute requires a plaintiff to show the objective likelihood of the suit's success. * * * DiGiovanni * * * reads the provision as requiring no more than that a plaintiff demonstrate a subjective good faith belief that the suit will succeed. * * * At oral argument, the State shifted its position to argue that the statute requires something akin to the plaintiff stating a claim with sufficient facts to survive a motion to dismiss.

We need not resolve this confusion since the statute presents too great a risk of erroneous deprivation under any of these interpretations. If the statute demands inquiry into the sufficiency of the complaint, or, still less, the plaintiff's good-faith belief that the complaint is sufficient, requirement of a complaint and a factual affidavit would permit a court to make these minimal determinations. But neither inquiry adequately reduces the risk of erroneous deprivation. Permitting a court to authorize attachment merely because the plaintiff believes the defendant is liable, or because the plaintiff can make out a facially valid complaint, would permit the deprivation of the defendant's property when the claim would fail to convince a jury, when it rested on factual allegations that were sufficient to state a cause of action but which the defendant would dispute, or in the case of a mere good-faith standard, even when the complaint failed to state a claim upon which relief could be granted. The potential for unwarranted attachment in these situations is self-evident and too great to satisfy the requirements of due process absent any counter-vailing consideration.

Even if the provision requires the plaintiff to demonstrate, and the judge to find, probable cause to believe that judgment will be rendered in favor of the plaintiff, the risk of error was substantial in this case. As the record shows, and as the State concedes, only a skeletal affidavit need be and was filed. The State urges that the reviewing judge normally reviews the complaint as well, but concedes that the complaint may also be conclusory. It is self-evident that the judge could make no realistic assessment concerning the likelihood of an action's success based upon these one-sided, self-serving, and conclusory submissions. And as the Court of Appeals said, in a case like this involving an alleged assault, even a detailed affidavit would give only the plaintiff's version of the confrontation. Unlike determining the existence of a debt or delinquent payments, the issue does not concern "ordinarily uncomplicated matters that lend themselves to documentary proof." * * *

What safeguards the State does afford do not adequately reduce this risk. Connecticut points out that the statute also provides an "expeditiou[s]" postattachment adversary hearing * * *; notice for such a hearing * * *; judicial review of an adverse decision * * *; and a double damages action if the original suit is commenced without probable cause * * *. Similar considerations were present in *Mitchell* * * *. But in *Mitchell,* the plaintiff had a vendor's lien to protect, the risk of error was minimal because the likelihood of recovery involved uncomplicated matters that lent themselves to documentary proof, * * * and plaintiff was required to put up a bond. None of these factors diminishing the need for a predeprivation hearing is present in this case. It is true that a later hearing might negate the presence of probable cause, but this would not cure the temporary deprivation that an earlier hearing might have prevented. * * *

Finally, we conclude that the interests in favor of an *ex parte* attachment, particularly the interests of the plaintiff, are too minimal to supply such a consideration here. Plaintiff had no existing interest in Doehr's real estate when he sought the attachment. His only interest in attaching the property was to ensure the availability of assets to satisfy his judgment if he prevailed on the merits of his action. Yet there was no allegation that Doehr was about to transfer or encumber his real estate or take any other action during the pendency of the action that would render his real estate unavailable to satisfy a judgment. Our cases have recognized such a properly supported claim would be an exigent circumstance permitting postponing any notice or hearing until after the attachment is effected. * * * Absent such allegations, however, the plaintiff's interest in attaching the property does not justify the burdening of Doehr's ownership rights without a hearing to determine the likelihood of recovery.

No interest the government may have affects the analysis. The State's substantive interest in protecting any rights of the plaintiff cannot be any more weighty than those rights themselves. Here the plaintiff's interest is *de minimis.* Moreover, the State cannot seriously plead additional financial or administrative burdens involving predeprivation hearings when it already claims to provide an immediate post-deprivation hearing. * * *

* * *

IV

A

Although a majority of the Court does not reach the issue, Justices Marshall, Stevens, O'Connor, and I deem it appropriate to consider whether due process also requires the plaintiff to post a bond or other security in addition to requiring a hearing or showing of some exigency.

As noted, the impairments to property rights that attachments affect merit due process protection. Several consequences can be severe, such as the default of a homeowner's mortgage. In the present context, it need only be added that we have repeatedly recognized the utility of a bond in protecting property rights affected by the mistaken award of prejudgment remedies. * * *

Without a bond, at the time of attachment, the danger that these property rights may be wrongfully deprived remains unacceptably high even with such safeguards as a hearing or exigency requirement. The need for a bond is especially apparent where extraordinary circumstances justify an attachment with no more than the plaintiff's *ex parte* assertion of a claim. * * * Until a postattachment hearing * * *, a defendant has no protection against damages sustained where no extraordinary circumstance in fact existed or the plaintiff's likelihood of recovery was nil. Such protection is what a bond can supply. Both the Court and its individual members have repeatedly found the requirement of a bond to play an essential role in reducing what would have been too great a degree of risk in precisely this type of circumstance. * * *

But the need for a bond does not end here. A defendant's property rights remain at undue risk even when there has been an adversarial hearing to determine the plaintiff's likelihood of recovery. At best, a court's initial assessment of each party's case cannot produce more than an educated prediction as to who will win. This is especially true when, as here, the nature of the claim makes any accurate prediction elusive. * * * In consequence, even a full hearing under a proper probable-cause standard would not prevent many defendants from having title to their homes impaired during the pendency of suits that never result in the contingency that ultimately justifies such impairment, namely, an award to the plaintiff. Attachment measures currently on the books reflect this concern. All but a handful of States require a plaintiff's bond despite also affording a hearing either before, or (for the vast majority, only under extraordinary circumstances) soon after, an attachment takes place. * * *

The State stresses its double damages remedy for suits that are commenced without probable cause. * * * This remedy, however, fails to make up for the lack of a bond. As an initial matter, the meaning of "probable cause" in this provision is no more clear here than it was in the attachment provision itself. Should the term mean the plaintiff's good faith or the facial adequacy of the complaint, the remedy is clearly insufficient. A defendant who was deprived where there was little or no likelihood that the plaintiff would obtain a judgment could nonetheless recover only by proving some type of fraud or malice or by showing that the plaintiff had failed to state a claim. * * *

Nor is there any appreciable interest against a bond requirement. * * * [A] plaintiff [is not required] to show exigent circumstances nor any pre-existing interest in the property facing attachment. A party must show more than the mere existence of a claim before subjecting an opponent to prejudgment proceedings that carry a significant risk of erroneous deprivation. * * *

B

Our foregoing discussion compels the four of us to consider whether a bond excuses the need for a hearing or other safeguards altogether. If a bond is needed to augment the protections afforded by preattachment and postattachment hearings, it arguably follows that a bond renders these safeguards unnecessary. That conclusion is unconvincing, however, for it ignores certain harms that bonds could not undo but that hearings would prevent. The law concerning attachments has rarely, if ever, required defendants to suffer an encumbered title until the case is concluded without any prior opportunity to show that the attachment was unwarranted. Our cases have repeatedly emphasized the importance of providing a prompt postdeprivation hearing at the very least. * * *

The necessity for at least a prompt postattachment hearing is self-evident because the right to be compensated at the end of the case, if the plaintiff loses, for all provable injuries caused by the attachment is inadequate to redress the harm inflicted, harm that could have been avoided had an early hearing been held. An individual with an immediate need or opportunity to sell a property can neither do so, nor otherwise satisfy that need or recreate the opportunity. The same applies to a parent in need of a home equity loan for a child's education, an entrepreneur seeking to start a business on the strength of an otherwise strong credit rating, or simply a homeowner who might face the disruption of having a mortgage placed in technical default. * * * [It should be clear that r]eliance on a bond does not sufficiently account for the harms that flow from an erroneous attachment to excuse a State from reducing that risk by means of a timely hearing.

If a bond cannot serve to dispense with a hearing immediately after attachment, neither is it sufficient basis for not providing a preattachment hearing in the absence of exigent circumstances even if in any event a hearing would be provided a few days later. The reasons are the same: a wrongful attachment can inflict injury that will not fully be redressed by recovery on the bond after a prompt postattachment hearing determines that the attachment was invalid.

* * *

V

Because Connecticut's prejudgment remedy provision * * * violates the requirements of due process by authorizing prejudgment attachment without prior notice or a hearing, the judgment of the Court of Appeals is affirmed, and the case is remanded to that court for further proceedings consistent with this opinion.

It is so ordered.

CHIEF JUSTICE REHNQUIST with whom JUSTICE BLACKMUN joins, concurring.

I agree with the Court that the Connecticut attachment statute, "as applied in this case," * * * fails to satisfy the Due Process Clause of the Fourteenth Amendment. I therefore join Parts I, II and III of its opinion. Unfortunately, the remainder of the Court's opinion does not confine itself to the facts of this case, but enters upon a lengthy disquisition as to what combination of safeguards are required to satisfy Due Process in hypothetical cases not before the Court. I therefore do not join Part IV.

* * * The Court's opinion is, in my view, ultimately correct when it bases its holding of unconstitutionality of the Connecticut statute as applied here on [*Sniadach, Fuentes, Mitchell,* and *Di–Chem*] * * *. But I do not believe that the result follows so inexorably as the Court's opinion suggests. All of the cited cases dealt with personalty—bank deposits or chattels—and each involved the physical seizure of the property itself, so that the defendant was deprived of its use. * * * [I]n all of them the debtor was deprived of the use and possession of the property. In the present case, on the other hand, Connecticut's prejudgment attachment on real property statute, which secures an incipient lien for the plaintiff, does not deprive the defendant of the use or possession of the property.

The Court's opinion therefore breaks new ground * * *. * * * I agree with the Court, however, that upon analysis the deprivation here is a significant one, even though the owner remains in undisturbed possession. * * *

* * *

It is both unwise and unnecessary, I believe, for the Court to proceed, as it does in Part IV, from its decision of the case before it to discuss abstract and hypothetical situations not before it. * * * The two elements of due process with which the Court concerns itself in Part IV—the requirement of a bond, and of "exigent circumstances"—prove to be upon analysis so vague that the discussion is not only unnecessary, but not particularly useful. Unless one knows what the terms and conditions of a bond are to be, the requirement of a "bond" in the abstract means little. The amount to be secured by the bond and the conditions of the bond are left unaddressed—is there to be liability on the part of a plaintiff if he is ultimately unsuccessful in the underlying lawsuit, or is it instead to be conditioned on some sort of good faith test? The "exigent circumstances" referred to by the Court are admittedly equally vague; non-residency appears to be enough in some states, an attempt to conceal assets is required in others, an effort to flee the jurisdiction in still others. We should await concrete cases which present questions involving bonds and exigent circumstances before we attempt to decide when and if the Due Process Clause of the Fourteenth Amendment requires them as prerequisites for a lawful attachment.

[The concurring opinion of JUSTICE SCALIA is omitted.]

Notes and Questions

1. Is the Supreme Court's decision in *Doehr* consistent with its prior decisions in *Sniadach, Fuentes, Mitchell,* and *Di–Chem*? Or has the Court announced a new test for determining whether a defendant has been accorded his constitutionally required opportunity to be heard? Consider whether application of

the "*Mathews* factors" would have changed the outcome in *Mitchell*. Are you convinced by the *Doehr* Court's attempt to distinguish its decision from *Mitchell*? By not overruling *Mitchell*, has the Court effectively made the constitutionally required opportunity to be heard depend on the underlying substantive law claim? On whether the plaintiff has a pre-existing interest in the attached property?

2. Mr. Doehr continued to possess, and in fact reside in, his home, yet the Court found that he had been constitutionally deprived of his property. Do you agree? See Note, *Lis Pendens and Procedural Due Process: A Closer Look After Connecticut v. Doehr*, 51 Md.L.Rev. 1054 (1992).

3. In *Doehr*, the Supreme Court applies the *Mathews* factors (used to "determine what process was due when the government itself seeks to effect a deprivation on its own initiative") to a dispute between two private parties. Is this importation appropriate? Can one test be effectively used to deal with the two types of cases? Consider RICHMOND TENANTS ORGANIZATION, INC. v. KEMP, 956 F.2d 1300 (4th Cir.1992), in which the plaintiff, a public housing tenants' organization, challenged the National Public Housing Asset Forfeiture Project on behalf of a nationwide class of tenants. The Forfeiture Project was designed to encourage United States Attorneys to utilize forfeiture procedures to evict drug offenders from public housing immediately without notice and without a hearing. The court concluded that, in the absence of exigent circumstances, the Due Process Clause of the Fifth Amendment requires the federal government to provide notice and an opportunity to be heard before a tenant may be evicted. The government argued that drug activity "constitutes in every case an extraordinary situation which requires prompt governmental action to protect other innocent tenants from dangerous drug activities in their buildings." The court, however, disagreed and held that:

> While the level and type of drug trafficking in a particular location might amount to exigent circumstances warranting a summary eviction, the mere use or possession of narcotics would not in every case constitute an extraordinary situation permitting federal law enforcement officers to summarily remove all persons occupying the housing unit where the activity had occurred.

Id. at 1308. Do you agree? Should a case involving a national policy, such as the "War on Drugs," be decided according to the same due process standard as the run-of-the-mill vendors' lien case? See also United States v. James Daniel Good Real Property, 510 U.S. 43, 114 S.Ct. 492, 126 L.Ed.2d 490 (1993) (the seizure of claimant Good's house violated the Fifth Amendment Due Process Clause when the United States, after it had obtained an ex parte writ of arrest in rem from a magistrate judge on the basis that it had made a prima facie showing that the claimant's house had been used in drug trafficking (more than four years earlier) and was thus subject to forfeiture under 21 U.S.C. § 881, ordered rent payments from tenants living in the house to be paid to the government rather than to the claimant).

4. As noted in *Doehr*, the process that is constitutionally mandated in a given situation, in part, turns on the interests at stake. Consider the interests involved, and the process that is due someone who has their car immobilized, or towed and destroyed. In PATTERSON v. CRONIN, 650 P.2d 531 (Colo.1982), plaintiff's car had been illegally parked on seven separate occasions before the city of Denver ordered it to be immobilized with a "Denver boot." (The boot is a huge clamp applied to a car's wheel.) Plaintiff argued that the city's failure to provide a hearing before immobilizing his auto violated due process. Applying the *Mathews*

factors, the court found that the governmental interest in enforcing parking ordinances was important enough that a hearing prior to immobilization was not constitutionally mandated—provided that a hearing procedure was available after the immobilization. However, Denver failed to provide such a post-deprivation hearing and, as a result, the court concluded that the immobilization of plaintiff's vehicle violated his due process rights. Is the city's interest in parking ordinances really that strong?

In PROPERT v. DISTRICT OF COLUMBIA, 948 F.2d 1327 (D.C.Cir.1991), plaintiff's automobile was towed and destroyed pursuant to the district's policy covering "junk" vehicles. Plaintiff's 1969 Volkswagen Karmann Ghia was parked four doors away from his residence, and was not blocking traffic or otherwise creating a safety hazard. The car also was properly registered and displayed current license plates, a current inspection sticker, and a valid parking permit. Based solely on the vehicle's physical appearance and the fact that it had been parked in the same spot for quite some time, it was determined to be "junk." The court held that since no formal hearing was afforded before the plaintiff's car was destroyed, his due process rights had been violated. Do these cases stand for the proposition that a plaintiff who has violated the law is entitled to less of an opportunity to be heard? Or are they distinguishable on another ground?

5. To what other types of situations might the *Sniadach* line of cases apply? Consider, for example, the provisions of Federal Rule 65(b) authorizing issuance of temporary restraining orders without notice or a hearing. Note that Rule 65(b) provides that a TRO is effective only for a period of ten days. During that time, a hearing may be held to determine whether or not a preliminary injunction should issue. If a preliminary injunction is granted, it remains in effect until a final judgment is rendered. Do the procedures outlined in Rule 65(b) satisfy the Due Process Clause as interpreted in *Sniadach* and its progeny? Which of those procedures are constitutionally required?

6. The preceding cases dealt with pre-action attachment to secure property pending litigation. Of course, attachment often is effected for reasons other than security—for example, to create quasi-in-rem jurisdiction. In light of the cases you have just read (especially *Fuentes*), what is the status of pre-action attachment to effect quasi-in-rem jurisdiction? Is the availability of in personam jurisdiction relevant to your answer? At least one court has held that the quasi-in-rem attachment procedure cannot be used if the defendant is subject to in personam jurisdiction. McQueeny v. J.W. Fergusson & Sons, Inc., 527 F.Supp. 728 (D.N.J. 1981). Is this decision correct? If quasi-in-rem is the only way to assert jurisdiction over the defendant, would jurisdictional attachment be one of those "extraordinary situations," referred to by the Court in *Fuentes*, that "justify postponing notice and opportunity for a hearing"? See generally Jonnet v. Dollar Sav. Bank, 530 F.2d 1123 (3d Cir.1976); Bourne, *The Demise of Foreign Attachment*, 21 Creighton L.Rev. 141 (1987); Silberman, *Shaffer v. Heitner: The End of an Era*, 53 N.Y.U.L.Rev. 33, 53–62 (1978). Does it make any difference, in answering the previous question, if quasi-in-rem is the only available jurisdictional basis solely because the state's long-arm statute, which might have provided in personam jurisdiction, is a restrictive one?

Suppose that property is attached to effect quasi-in-rem jurisdiction. Can the defendant consent to in personam jurisdiction and demand that the attachment be lifted? In UNITECH USA, INC. v. PONSOLDT, 91 A.D.2d 903, 457 N.Y.S.2d 526 (1st Dep't 1983), a New York court read that state's quasi-in-rem statute to say that the mere fact that an unlicensed foreign corporation whose assets have been attached appears in an action and submits to in personam jurisdiction does not mean the attachment automatically must be vacated. The New York court found that the state's attachment provision was designed to provide security for collecting the judgment as well as jurisdiction. Was the court correct in introducing the security interest while examining a jurisdiction statute?

In BRASTEX CORP. v. ALLEN INTERNATIONAL, INC., 702 F.2d 326 (2d Cir.1983), the Second Circuit examined the same statute, but required that the attachment be lifted once the defendant had submitted to in personam jurisdiction. An order of attachment was signed against a foreign corporation that had no license to do business in New York. Two weeks before the oral argument of the motion to confirm the attachment order, the defendant qualified to do business in New York. Denying the plaintiff's motion to confirm the order of attachment, the Second Circuit held that whether an order of attachment is proper must be decided as of the date an attack is made on it. The plaintiff argued that denying its motion would give defendants the power to pull the attachment rug from under a plaintiff at any time. The court refused to hold that the attachment could continue in force because the corporation did not file its qualification papers "in the normal course of business."

In ELTON LEATHER CORP. v. FIRST GENERAL RESOURCES CO., 138 A.D.2d 132, 529 N.Y.S.2d 769 (1st Dep't 1988), the New York Appellate Division rejected the *Brastex* court's conclusion that a foreign corporation's post-attachment, pre-confirmation application to do business in New York removes the statutory basis for attachment. Instead, it cited favorably the Second Circuit's subsequent decision in ITC Entertainment, Ltd. v. Nelson Film Partners, 714 F.2d 217 (2d Cir.1983). In this latter opinion, the Second Circuit construed the New York statute more broadly:

> New York's nonresident attachment statute is designed to serve two independent purposes: obtaining jurisdiction over and securing judgments against nondomiciliaries residing without the state. New York courts have long recognized that provisions for attachment against nonresidents are based on the assumption that "[t]here is much more propriety in requiring a debtor, whose domicile is without the state, to give security for the debt than one whose domicile is within."

Id. at 220. See also Giorgio Morandi, Inc. v. Texport Corp., 697 F.Supp. 777 (S.D.N.Y.1988) (foreign corporation's post-attachment application to do business in New York did not require court to vacate prejudgment attachment). Does the Due Process Clause permit New York to take this approach to attachment?

7. In PERALTA v. HEIGHTS MEDICAL CENTER, INC., 485 U.S. 80, 108 S.Ct. 896, 99 L.Ed.2d 75 (1988), the Supreme Court considered attachment in another context. In *Peralta,* a default judgment was entered in a suit by a hospital against Peralta to recover a medical bill owed by one of Peralta's employees and guaranteed by him. A writ of attachment was issued and Peralta's property was sold to satisfy the judgment.

Later, Peralta brought an action to set aside the default judgment and void the sale. In this later action, he alleged that the return of service in the first action showed that it was not timely, and that he in fact had not been served personally. The Texas courts denied his requests, holding that in order to have a default judgment reversed there must be a showing of a meritorious defense. But the United States Supreme Court held that requiring a party seeking to vacate a judgment to show a meritorious defense violated the Due Process Clause. Justice White wrote:

> The Texas courts * * * held, as appellee urged them to do, that to have the judgment set aside, appellant was required to show that he had a meritorious defense, apparently on the ground that without a defense, the same judgment would again be entered on retrial and hence appellant had suffered no harm from the judgment entered without notice. But this reasoning is untenable. As appellant asserts, had he had notice of the suit, he might have impleaded the employee whose debt had been guaranteed, worked out a settlement, or paid the debt. He would also have preferred to sell his property himself in order to raise funds rather than to suffer it sold at a constable's auction.

> Nor is there any doubt that the entry of the judgment itself had serious consequences. It is not denied that the judgment was entered on the county records, became a lien on appellant's property, and was the basis for issuance of a writ of execution under which appellant's property was promptly sold, without notice. Even if no execution sale had yet occurred, the lien encumbered the property and impaired appellant's ability to mortgage or alienate it; and state procedures for creating and enforcing such liens are subject to the strictures of due process. * * * Here, we assume that the judgment against him and the ensuing consequences occurred without notice to appellant, notice at a meaningful time and in a meaningful manner that would have given him an opportunity to be heard.

Id. at 85–86, 108 S.Ct. at 899, 99 L.Ed.2d at 81.

8. In FINBERG v. SULLIVAN, 634 F.2d 50 (3d Cir.1980), the court, sitting en banc, held that Pennsylvania's post-judgment garnishment procedure violated the Due Process Clause. Beatrice Finberg was a sixty-eight year old widow entirely dependent on social security for her income. A discount company obtained a default judgment against her and sought to execute the judgment pursuant to Pennsylvania practice permitting the seizure of assets, without notice or opportunity for a hearing, upon a judgment creditor's petition (to a clerk or magistrate) for a writ of execution. Under this procedure, the plaintiff garnished Finberg's bank accounts, which contained the proceeds of her social security benefits. The critical fact was that all of the garnished money was exempt from seizure because federal law proscribes the seizure of social security benefits and Pennsylvania law provides a $300 cash exemption to debtors in Mrs. Finberg's position. The *Finberg* court held the Pennsylvania practice unconstitutional because it failed to require the creditor to inform the debtor of existing exemptions and because it did not provide prompt post-seizure adjudication of claims to exemption. Is the Third Circuit's decision correct? Does the proceeding underlying the judgment satisfy the requirements of due process? In *Finberg,* the underlying proceeding produced a default judgment. Would it make a difference if there had been a full trial? Or, is something beyond liability at stake? See also Kirby v. Sprouls, 722 F.Supp. 516, 522 (C.D.Ill.1989) ("Due process requires the existence and notice of procedures by which a judgment debtor may assert exemptions to which he may be entitled.").

9. When, as in *Mitchell,* a pre-action attachment is sought to secure property pending a disposition, what should the focus of the inquiry be? Should the party seeking attachment be required to show a likelihood that the property to be attached will be removed from the jurisdiction or destroyed? Should she be required to show a likelihood that she will prevail on the merits? If the party

seeking attachment is not required to demonstrate a need to secure the property and a likelihood of success on the merits, wouldn't there be a serious danger that the pre-action attachment procedure would be used to harass?

When an attachment is sought, not for security purposes, but to establish quasi-in-rem jurisdiction, should the substantive focus of the inquiry be the same as for security attachments? When a jurisdictional attachment is sought, is there any reason why the need for security should militate for or against an attachment? Aren't the only relevant concerns in assessing the propriety of a jurisdictional attachment the likelihood that the plaintiff will prevail on the merits and the existence or non-existence of minimum contacts sufficient to satisfy *Shaffer*?

When, as in *Finberg*, a post-action attachment is sought to enforce a judgment, should the substantive focus of the inquiry be the same as for other types of attachments? Surely, the plaintiff should not have to demonstrate that the property is in danger. And, since a judgment has been obtained, the likelihood that the plaintiff will prevail on the merits has been demonstrated. Is the only issue the existence or non-existence of exempted property, as in *Finberg*?

Chapter 4

JURISDICTION OVER THE SUBJECT MATTER OF THE ACTION— THE COURT'S COMPETENCY

As was described briefly in Chapter One, pp. 4–6, supra, most Anglo–American jurisdictions have distributed judicial power to hear disputes among a variety of courts. In many instances this is accomplished by segregating certain types of controversies from the mainstream of litigation and giving special courts subject-matter jurisdiction over them, as usually is done with domestic relations and probate matters, and formerly was true of "actions at law" and "suits in equity." As described by one commentator:

> * * * In practically all states * * * there are separate courts for large and small cases with an arbitrary line of division between them. There are usually separate courts of first instance and of review. Separate courts of probate, criminal courts, courts of equity, and courts for causes arising in certain localities are common. Jurisdiction of the same kind is often apportioned among several different courts, each exercising only a designated and restricted part of it, as where certain appeals must be taken to one reviewing court and other appeals to another. Sometimes different courts with concurrent jurisdiction in certain classes of cases and exclusive jurisdiction in others are established. It is not uncommon to find a large number of municipal courts in the various cities of the same state, no two of which exercise the same jurisdiction. And as a final complication, the legislature is constantly shifting and changing the jurisdiction of the various courts, practically every change involving litigation to construe the meaning and ascertain the effect of the legislative act.

Sunderland, *Problems Connected with the Operation of a State Court System,* 1950 Wis.L.Rev. 585, 585–86. As you gain familiarity with the materials in this Chapter, give some thought to the extent to which historical allocations of subject-matter jurisdiction over matters such as probate, divorce, disputes involving land, and patents continue to make sense.

Probably the most common method of limiting judicial power is by providing that the court only can adjudicate controversies involving more than a certain minimum or less than a stated maximum amount of money, or its equivalent. These rules often are designed to direct the quantitative and qualitative flow of litigation into the various courts within a jurisdiction. Thus, for example, it is provided by statute, 28 U.S.C. § 1332, that cases in the federal courts based solely on diversity of citizenship must involve more than $75,000. If a dispute does not, it must be brought in a state court. Amount-in-controversy restrictions also are common in state systems. These often provide that a plaintiff cannot bring his action in a particular court— typically called a court of inferior, limited, or special jurisdiction—if the amount involved exceeds a statutorily established jurisdictional maximum. What factors are relevant in choosing appropriate jurisdictional amount figures? Are the same factors relevant for both the state and federal courts?

SECTION A.   SUBJECT–MATTER JURISDICTION IN STATE COURTS

LACKS v. LACKS

New York Court of Appeals, 1976.
41 N.Y.2d 71, 390 N.Y.S.2d 875, 359 N.E.2d 384.

BREITEL, CHIEF JUDGE. * * * The parties were married in New York in 1938. After an apparently turbulent marriage, marked since 1953 by a series of bitter litigations, the husband, on August 10, 1965, began this action for a separation on the ground of cruelty. After nonjury trial, Supreme Court, on June 28, 1967, dismissed the complaint, but, on March 26, 1968, the Appellate Division reversed, and ordered a new trial. At the second trial, plaintiff husband, in reliance upon the then recent liberalizing changes in the divorce law, added a prayer for a judgment of absolute divorce, on the same allegations and proof as the earlier cause for separation. The husband was granted a judgment of divorce on March 16, 1970, and, after modifications not now relevant, the judgment was affirmed by the Appellate Division on October 26, 1972. Leave to appeal to the Court of Appeals was denied by both the Appellate Division and this court. The final judgment was thus beyond further review.

Then, nearly two years later, defendant, through her most recently retained lawyer, moved to vacate the judgment, contending that the court had been without subject matter jurisdiction to entertain the divorce action. She argued that the husband had not been a resident of New York for a full year preceding the commencement of the original action, and that the court had thus erroneously granted a divorce judgment in violation of the provisions of section 230. * * *

The confusion [in this case], if there be confusion, starts with a line of decisions dating back to the last century and continuing into the present in which this court has said with less than perfect meticulousness that "jurisdiction" of New York courts in matrimonial cases is limited to the powers conferred by statute * * *. Jurisdiction is a word of elastic, diverse, and disparate meanings * * *.

A statement that a court lacks "jurisdiction" to decide a case may, in reality, mean that elements of a cause of action are absent * * *. Similarly, questions of mootness and standing of parties may be characterized as raising questions of subject matter jurisdiction * * *. But these are not the kinds of judicial infirmities to which CPLR 5015 * * * is addressed. That provision is designed to preserve objections so fundamental to the power of adjudication of a court that they survive even a final judgment or order * * *.

In Thrasher v. United States Liab. Ins. Co., * * * this court, in discussing subject matter jurisdiction, drew a clear distinction between a court's competence to entertain an action and its power to render a judgment on the merits * * *. Absence of competence to entertain an action deprives the court of "subject matter jurisdiction"; absence of power to reach the merits does not.

* * * [I]t has often been said: "the Supreme Court is a court of original, unlimited and unqualified jurisdiction" and "competent to entertain all causes of action unless its jurisdiction has been specifically proscribed" * * *.

Against the State Constitution's broad grant of jurisdiction to the Supreme Court, defendant offers the language of section 230 of the Domestic Relations Law. It provides merely that "[a]n action * * * for divorce on separation may be maintained only when" the residence requirements are met. Not even the catchall word "jurisdiction" appears in the statute, much less an explicit limitation on the court's competence to entertain the action. In no way do these limitations on the cause of action circumscribe the power of the court in the sense of competence to adjudicate causes in the matrimonial categories. That a court has no "right" to adjudicate erroneously is no circumscription of its power to decide, rightly or wrongly.

* * *

The court has never before considered the unlikely question, until this case, whether the judicial error on an essential element of the cause of action was so fundamental as to permit vacatur of a final judgment, collaterally or after final judgment beyond ordinary appellate review. Had that ever been the problem unlikely until this case, perhaps the need for a less elastic and encompassing term than the word "jurisdiction" would have been apparent.

* * *

Hence, any error of law or fact which might have been committed in the divorce action did not deprive the court of jurisdiction to adjudicate the case, CPLR 5015 * * * is inapplicable, and Special Term erroneously vacated the final judgment.

In sum, the overly stated principle that lack of subject matter jurisdiction makes a final judgment absolutely void is not applicable to cases which, upon analysis, do not involve jurisdiction, but merely substantive elements of a cause for relief. To do so would be to undermine significantly the doctrine of *res judicata,* and to eliminate the certainty and finality in the law and in litigation which the doctrine is designed to protect.

In concluding the jurisdiction-competence issue it is not assumed that the courts in the action made any error of law or fact in determining the durational or initial residence requirements to maintain an action for a separation or a divorce. Nor is it assumed that the same courts did not consider and determine the issues of residence, whether or not raised by the wife. On the contrary, there was considerable evidence of residence by the husband, and the court obviously determined that the husband had some residence even if not of the duration to satisfy the matrimonial statutes. The point is that the litigation having gone to final judgment, the right to review by appeal having been exhausted, that is and should be the end of the matter.

On the foregoing analysis it has been unnecessary to dissect the elements of subject matter jurisdiction, because it turns out that the contentions of the wife are not addressed to bases for subject matter jurisdiction. Rather, despite her characterization of subject matter jurisdiction in order to invoke CPLR 5015 * * * to undo a final judgment of four years' standing, the defects to which she points relate only to substantive elements in a cause of action adjudicable by the Supreme Court, a court competent to decide all the substantive issues.

Accordingly, the order of the Appellate Division should be affirmed, without costs.

Notes and Questions

1. A state court of general jurisdiction is presumably permitted and may be under a constitutional duty to hear a cause of action arising under the laws of another state. In HUGHES v. FETTER, 341 U.S. 609, 71 S.Ct. 980, 95 L.Ed. 1212 (1951), the Supreme Court held that the Full Faith and Credit Clause, U.S. Const. Art. IV, § 1, precluded Wisconsin from closing its courts to a suit under the Illinois wrongful-death act in the absence of a valid Wisconsin policy to weigh against the national interest favoring the availability of a Wisconsin forum. "[A state] * * * cannot escape [its] constitutional obligation to enforce the rights and duties validly created under the laws of other states by the simple device of removing jurisdiction from courts otherwise competent." *Hughes* has not been construed as a bar to a state applying its own law to vindicate policies related to the conduct of litigation in its courts. For example, a state may apply its own statute of limitations even though the claim would be timely under the law of the state under which the cause of action arose. See Wells v. Simonds Abrasive Co., 345 U.S. 514, 73 S.Ct. 856, 97 L.Ed. 1211 (1953). Conversely, a state may apply its own longer statute of limitations even though the claim would have been time-barred under the law of the state under which the cause of action arose. See Sun Oil Co. v. Wortman, 486 U.S. 717, 108 S.Ct. 2117, 100 L.Ed.2d 743 (1988).

2. Unless Congress has made federal jurisdiction exclusive, a state court may entertain an action even though it is based entirely on federal law.

> * * * [U]nder our federal system, the States possess sovereignty concurrent with that of the Federal Government, subject only to limitations imposed by the Supremacy Clause. Under this system of dual sovereignty, we have consistently held that state courts have inherent authority, and are thus presumptively competent, to adjudicate claims arising under the laws of the United States. * * *

> This deeply rooted presumption in favor of concurrent state court jurisdiction is, of course, rebutted if Congress affirmatively ousts the state courts of jurisdiction over a particular claim. * * * "Thus, the presumption of concurrent jurisdiction can be rebutted by an explicit statutory directive, by

unmistakable implication from legislative history, or by a clear incompatibility between state-court jurisdiction and federal interests." * * *

TAFFLIN v. LEVITT, 493 U.S. 455, 458–59, 110 S.Ct. 792, 795, 107 L.Ed.2d 887, 894 (1990).

3. If a state court can hear a case arising under federal law, must it do so? In HOWLETT v. ROSE, 496 U.S. 356, 110 S.Ct. 2430, 110 L.Ed.2d 332 (1990), plaintiff, a former high school student, brought suit pursuant to 42 U.S.C. § 1983 in a Florida state court against the local school board alleging that his federal constitutional rights had been violated when his car was searched and when he was suspended from classes without due process. The Florida court dismissed the complaint holding that Florida's statutory waiver of sovereign immunity applied only to state court tort actions, but remained in full effect with respect to federal civil rights actions brought in state court. Noting that the Florida court's holding "raises the concern that the state court may be evading federal law and discriminating against federal causes of action," a unanimous Supreme Court found that:

> Respondent has offered no neutral or valid excuse for the [Florida] Circuit Court's refusal to hear § 1983 actions against state entities. The Circuit Court would have had jurisdiction if the defendant were an individual officer and the action was based on § 1983. It would also have had jurisdiction over the defendant school board if the action were based on established state common law or statutory law. A state policy that permits actions against state agencies for the failure of their officials to adequately police a parking lot and for the negligence of such officers in arresting a person on a roadside, but yet declines jurisdiction over federal actions for constitutional violations by the same persons can be based only on the rationale that such persons should not be liable for § 1983 violations in the courts of the State. That reason, whether presented in terms of direct disagreement with substantive federal law or simple refusal to take cognizance of the federal cause of action, flatly violates the Supremacy Clause.

Id. at 380–81, 110 S.Ct. at 2445, 110 L.Ed.2d at 356.

SECTION B. THE SUBJECT–MATTER JURISDICTION OF THE FEDERAL COURTS— DIVERSITY OF CITIZENSHIP

Read Art. III, § 2 and 28 U.S.C. §§ 1332, 1359 in the Supplement.

Article III, Section 2 of the United States Constitution extends the judicial power of the United States to controversies "between Citizens of different States * * * and between a State, or the Citizens thereof, and Foreign States, Citizens or Subjects."[a] The current scope of the diversity jurisdiction granted to the federal courts by Congress is set out in 28 U.S.C. § 1332. One of the most important limitations on federal diversity jurisdiction

---

a. Controversies between a citizen of a state and an alien technically are denominated "alienage cases," but may be considered as diversity cases for purposes of this Section.

is the rule of "complete diversity" announced by Chief Justice Marshall in STRAWBRIDGE v. CURTISS, 7 U.S. (3 Cranch) 267, 2 L.Ed. 435 (1806). The rule provides in effect that there is no diversity jurisdiction if any plaintiff is a citizen of the same state as any defendant, no matter how many parties are involved in the litigation. The precise status of the complete diversity doctrine has been a subject of considerable debate because until quite recently it was not clear that the *Strawbridge* decision was intended by Chief Justice Marshall as simply a construction of the diversity statute then in force rather than as a constitutional limitation on federal-court jurisdiction. See pp. 671–76, infra.

The origin and purposes of diversity-of-citizenship jurisdiction have long been the subject of vigorous debate. The most widely accepted rationale was offered by Chief Justice Marshall in BANK OF THE UNITED STATES v. DEVEAUX, 9 U.S. (5 Cranch) 61, 87, 3 L.Ed. 38, 45 (1809):

> However true the fact may be, that the tribunals of the states will administer justice as impartially as those of the nation, * * * it is not less true that the constitution itself either entertains apprehensions on this subject, or views with such indulgence the possible fears and apprehensions of suitors, that it has established national tribunals for the decision of controversies * * * between citizens of different states.

Another argument that has been advanced to justify diversity jurisdiction is that the availability of a federal tribunal during our nation's formative period afforded some measure of security to investors developing the southern and western portions of the country. Analyses of the historical origins of diversity jurisdiction can be found in Frank, *Historical Bases of the Federal Judicial System*, 13 Law & Contemp.Prob. 1 (1948); Friendly, *The Historic Basis of the Diversity Jurisdiction*, 41 Harv.L.Rev. 483 (1928); and Phillips & Christenson, *The Historical and Legal Background of the Diversity Jurisdiction*, 46 A.B.A.J. 959 (1960).

Assuming that diversity jurisdiction was created to protect out-of-state litigants against local prejudice and that it has helped speed the economic growth of the country, are these realistic or meaningful bases for continuing diversity jurisdiction today? Statistical data on the actual existence of local prejudice against out-of-state parties, or whether an attorney's belief in the existence of such prejudice is a factor influencing forum choice, is sparse and inconclusive. See Miller, *An Empirical Study of Forum Choices in Removal Cases Under Diversity and Federal Question Jurisdiction*, 41 Am.U.L.Rev. 369 (1992); see also Flango, Litigant Choice Between State and Federal Courts, 46 S. Car. L.Rev. 961 (1995). Are there other reasons that are more persuasive for retaining or even enlarging the scope of diversity jurisdiction? In what ways should the existing diversity scheme be modified to make it more rational and responsive to current conditions?

More than 55,000 diversity cases were filed in the federal district courts in 1997. This figure represents approximately 20.3% of the total number of federal civil cases filed during that year. In view of the amount of federal judicial time and energy devoted to diversity cases, it is not surprising that the utility of diversity jurisdiction has been the subject of sharp debate. Proposals to curtail or abolish diversity jurisdiction have been made in Congress since the 1920's.

The Terms of the Debate

The arguments against the continued existence of any diversity jurisdiction concentrate primarily on five problems resulting from the creation of that jurisdiction. The first, often noted by Justice Frankfurter, is the congestion diversity cases allegedly cause in the federal courts. Second, the rule of Erie Railroad Co. v. Tompkins, p. 374, infra, which requires the application of state law to substantive issues in diversity cases, has been thought by many to make the handling of diversity cases by federal judges unnecessary, wasteful, and inappropriate. The reasoning behind this argument is that only the state courts are considered to be authoritative on matters of substantive law and the federal courts therefore are unable to exercise their creative function and are performing an unneeded service in avowedly aiming to follow state-court decisions. Third, it is argued that judicial and legislative authority should be coextensive, and that for federal courts to decide cases arising under state law is an undesirable interference with state autonomy. A fourth and related problem is the effect that the diversion of litigation to federal courts may have in retarding the development of state law. Fifth, and finally, it is said that the continuation of diversity jurisdiction diminishes the incentives for state court reform by those influential professional groups who, by virtue of diversity jurisdiction, are able to avoid litigation in the state courts.

Although each of these arguments has some merit, they do not make a case for the total abolition of diversity jurisdiction if it can be shown that diversity jurisdiction in fact serves some useful purpose in the federal system. Thus we are left with the ultimate question. Of what utility is diversity jurisdiction today?

It is remarkable how little justification is offered in the literature, even by those who are friendly to diversity jurisdiction. Since this jurisdiction "is at least as traditionally federal as the Flag and the 4th of July," many of the writers who support diversity content themselves with asserting that the burden of proof is on those who would limit or abolish it. This approach, of course, avoids, if indeed it does not beg, the question. Other defenders of diversity do undertake to justify its present value, but their arguments rarely rise beyond the level of mere assertion.

The most common explanation for the creation of diversity jurisdiction was a fear that state courts would be prejudiced against out-of-state parties. Those who favor the retention of diversity jurisdiction contend that this prejudice still exists. But in a society infinitely more mobile than the one that existed at the time the Constitution was framed, it is difficult to believe that prejudice against a litigant based upon his being a citizen of a different state is a significant factor. Regrettably, prejudice may take a number of different forms, but diversity jurisdiction has no bearing on most of them.

Another argument, with respectable historical antecedents, is that diversity jurisdiction is necessary in order to implement the constitutional guarantee that the citizens of each state shall be entitled to all the privileges and immunities of citizens of the several states. This argument has been characterized as specious, on the ground that abridgment of the Privileges and Immunities Clause is in itself sufficient for federal-question jurisdiction, and that diversity jurisdiction is not needed for this purpose. In this connection, it is worth noting that other federal systems have flourished without anything comparable to diversity jurisdiction, although meaningful comparison of federal systems is very difficult.

A further argument, again going back to Hamilton, is that the federal courts qualitatively are so superior to the state courts that it is desirable to channel as many cases as possible to the federal courts, or at least that out-of-state litigants, who have no opportunity to work for the improvement of the state courts, should be spared exposure to them. There may be merit to this argument. Federal judges enjoy life tenure, they are free to comment on the evidence, and they sit with juries selected from a broader geographical area than most state tribunals. Most importantly, federal judges are appointed; since many state judges are elected, state judges are thought to be more susceptible to political pressure and local biases than federal judges. Not all lawyers would agree, however, that these differences lead to better justice, and even though the prestige of the federal courts generally has been high, there have been long periods when procedural differences have led to suspicion that the federal courts are rich people's courts or defendants' courts. Furthermore, arguments stemming from a supposed inferiority of state justice are not susceptible of proof and hardly politic to advance.

There is, however, a somewhat related argument to the effect that the existence of concurrent state and federal jurisdiction creates a competition between the two that acts as a spur to higher standards of justice in each court system. It is hard to believe that already crowded state courts will feel a strong incentive in order to keep the comparative handful of cases in which diversity exists and in which, therefore, the litigants have a choice of forum. In any event, concurrent jurisdiction exists over many federal-question cases, and whatever benefits concurrent judicial power may be thought to confer can be had from that phase of jurisdiction.

In addition, regardless of the supposed inferiority of the state courts, as long as diversity exists the choice of forum undoubtedly will be utilized for tactical purposes by particular litigants in particular cases, who think they may obtain an advantage from one forum or the other. To the extent this type of forum shopping exists, as it surely does, it seems more an abuse of concurrent jurisdiction than an argument for the retention of diversity jurisdiction.

Proponents of diversity jurisdiction also contend that the interaction between state and federal courts that results from the existence of concurrent jurisdiction in areas of substantive law practiced by substantial segments of the bar has resulted in improvements in the procedures followed by both state and federal courts. According to this theory, the large number and variety of cases litigated in federal courts because of diversity jurisdiction are essential to maintain this flow of ideas. However, even if diversity jurisdiction were restricted or abolished, a substantial number of cases involving significant state matters still would be adjudicated in federal courts, and the exchange of ideas would not come to an end.

Finally, it has been argued that a fear on the part of investors that local prejudice may exist provides a justification for diversity jurisdiction. This argument at one time was endorsed by the Judicial Conference of the United States.

If it is true that diversity jurisdiction is an indispensable condition to the free flow of capital from one part of the nation to another, then it should be retained. At first glance it might seem that the merit of this argument is dependent on the other arguments for diversity, which we have seen are of doubtful validity. If local prejudice will not be a significant factor and if state courts are as competent as federal courts, then there is no apparent reason why the decisions of entrepreneurs to invest their funds in other parts of the country should be affected by the availability of recourse to the federal courts. On reflection, however, this response is insufficient, as most of those who have put forward the flow-of-capital argument point out. The key question is not whether out-of-state investors in fact will receive fair treatment from state courts, but whether they think they will. If the abolition, or significant curtailment, of diversity jurisdiction would give rise to fears by investors, and inhibit their willingness to invest in different parts of the country, then diversity serves a useful purpose and should be retained. It may be that investors are now sufficiently national-minded, and accustomed enough to investing abroad where they enjoy no protection from the federal courts, that they no longer have fears of state courts. But it is hard to know how this can be proved short of the heroic experiment of abolishing diversity jurisdiction.

It is unfortunate that the future of diversity jurisdiction is not likely to be resolved by an objective consideration of the arguments for and against it. Any proposal to modify diversity meets immediate organized opposition from those who believe that they have a vested interest in preserving, for their own advantage, the widest possible choice of forum.

Notes and Questions

1. Various views on the diversity jurisdiction debate can be found in Frankfurter, *Distribution of Judicial Power Between United States and State Courts,* 13 Cornell L.Q. 499 (1928); Marbury, *Why Should We Limit Federal Diversity Jurisdiction?,* 36 A.B.A.J. 379 (1960); Moore & Weckstein, *Diversity Jurisdiction: Past, Present and Future,* 43 Texas L.Rev. 1 (1964); Shapiro, *Federal Diversity Jurisdiction: A Survey and Proposal,* 91 Harv.L.Rev. 317 (1977); Rowe, *Abolishing Diversity Jurisdiction: Positive Side Effects and Potential for Further Reforms,* 92 Harv.L.Rev. 963 (1979); Miner, *The Tensions of a Dual Court System and Some Prescriptions for Relief,* 51 Albany L.Rev. 151, 153–58 (1987).

2. There are two important areas, probate matters and domestic relations cases, in which judicially created exceptions to the statute provide that the federal courts will not act even though diversity is present. These exceptions were first developed at a time when the diversity statute granted jurisdiction of "suits of a civil nature in law or in equity," and it was thought that probate and domestic relations cases, being matters that would have been heard in the ecclesiastical courts, did not fit this description. The 1948 Judicial Code substituted the term "civil action" for the phrase used in the older statutes, but the exceptions have persisted. Today the exceptions may more rationally be defended on the ground that these are areas of the law in which the states have an especially strong interest and a well-developed competence for dealing with them.

The probate matters exception is far from absolute. It turns, instead, on unclear distinctions of the utmost subtlety. For example, a federal court may not probate a will nor undertake the administration of an estate, but if diversity or some other basis for jurisdiction is present, the federal court can entertain actions against administrators, executors, and other claimants in which plaintiffs seek to establish their claims against an estate so long as the federal court does not interfere with the probate proceedings or assume general jurisdiction of the probate or control of the property in the custody of the state court. The federal action in such a case will establish the claimant's right in a fashion that will be binding in the state proceedings, but the federal court cannot order actual distribution of property in the custody of the state court nor give execution on its judgment.

The domestic-relations exception was addressed by the Supreme Court for the first time in ANKENBRANDT v. RICHARDS, 504 U.S. 689, 112 S.Ct. 2206, 119 L.Ed.2d 468 (1992), in which plaintiff brought suit on behalf of her daughters in federal court based on diversity of citizenship against the children's father and his female companion alleging physical and sexual abuse of the children. The Court found that a domestic relations exception does exist as a matter of statutory construction, but that it is not mandated by the Constitution. The Court, however, limited the exception to cases involving the issuance of a divorce, alimony, or child custody decree. As a result, the Supreme Court upheld the District Court's jurisdiction over this tort action and ordered it to proceed. Is this distinction reasonable? Appropriate?

The *Ankenbrandt* Court also stated: "As a matter of judicial economy, state courts are eminently more suited to work of this type than are federal courts, which lack the close association with the state and local government organizations dedicated to handling issues that arise out of conflict over divorce, alimony, and child custody decrees." Id. at 704, 112 S.Ct. at 2215, 119 L.Ed.2d at 482. Does this rationale apply to all issues on which a state agency represents the primarily responsible government institution, as is true of subjects such as education, fire safety, water management, public transportation, and recreation? If so, what justification is there for having federal courts hear these cases? Should state courts resolve cases when a "close association" is desirable? Consider another argument by the *Ankenbrandt* Court in favor of the domestic relations exception: "Moreover, as a matter of judicial expertise, it makes far more sense to retain the rule that federal courts lack power to issue these types of decrees because of the special proficiency developed by state tribunals over the past century and a half in handling issues that arise in the granting of such decrees." Id. at 704, 112 S.Ct. at 2215, 119 L.Ed.2d at 482–83. Does this prove too much? What about tort law, an area that is predominantly and traditionally state law? How far do the domestic relations and probate exceptions extend? See 13B Wright, Miller & Cooper, *Federal Practice and Procedure: Jurisdiction and Related Matters 2d* §§ 3609, 3610 (1984).

1. DETERMINING CITIZENSHIP

MAS v. PERRY
United States Court of Appeals, Fifth Circuit, 1974.
489 F.2d 1396, certiorari denied 419 U.S. 842, 95 S.Ct. 74, 42 L.Ed.2d 70.

AINSWORTH, CIRCUIT JUDGE.

* * *

Appellees Jean Paul Mas, a citizen of France, and Judy Mas were married at her home in Jackson, Mississippi. Prior to their marriage, Mr. and Mrs. Mas were graduate assistants, pursuing coursework as well as performing teaching duties, for approximately nine months and one year, respectively, at Louisiana State University in Baton Rouge, Louisiana. Shortly after their marriage, they returned to Baton Rouge to resume their duties as graduate assistants at LSU. They remained in Baton Rouge for approximately two more years, after which they moved to Park Ridge, Illinois. At the time of the trial in this case, it was their intention to return to Baton Rouge while Mr. Mas finished his studies for the degree of Doctor of Philosophy. Mr. and Mrs. Mas were undecided as to where they would reside after that.

Upon their return to Baton Rouge after their marriage, appellees rented an apartment from appellant Oliver H. Perry, a citizen of Louisiana. This appeal arises from a final judgment entered on a jury verdict awarding $5,000 to Mr. Mas and $15,000 to Mrs. Mas for damages incurred by them as a result of the discovery that their bedroom and bathroom contained "two-way" mirrors and that they had been watched through them by the appellant during three of the first four months of their marriage.

At the close of the appellees' case at trial, appellant made an oral motion to dismiss for lack of jurisdiction. The motion was denied by the district court. Before this Court, appellant challenges the final judgment below solely on jurisdictional grounds, contending that appellees failed to prove diversity of citizenship among the parties and that the requisite jurisdictional amount is lacking with respect to Mr. Mas. Finding no merit to these contentions, we affirm. Under section 1332(a)(2), the federal judicial power extends to the claim of Mr. Mas, a citizen of France, against the appellant, a citizen of Louisiana. Since we conclude that Mrs. Mas is a citizen of Mississippi for diversity purposes, the district court also properly had jurisdiction under section 1332(a)(1) of her claim.

It has long been the general rule that complete diversity of parties is required in order that diversity jurisdiction obtain; that is, no party on one side may be a citizen of the same State as any party on the other side. Strawbridge v. Curtiss * * *. This determination of one's State citizenship for diversity purposes is controlled by federal law, not by the law of any State. * * * As is the case in other areas of federal jurisdiction, the diverse citizenship among adverse parties must be present at the time the complaint is filed. * * * Jurisdiction is unaffected by subsequent changes in the citizenship of the parties. * * * The burden of pleading the diverse citizenship is upon the party invoking federal jurisdiction * * * and if the diversity jurisdiction is properly challenged, that party also bears the burden of proof.

To be a citizen of a State within the meaning of section 1332, a natural person must be both a citizen of the United States * * * and a domiciliary of that State. * * * For diversity purposes, citizenship means domicile; mere residence in the State is not sufficient. * * *

A person's domicile is the place of "his true, fixed, and permanent home and principal establishment, and to which he has the intention of returning whenever he is absent therefrom * * *." * * * A change of domicile may be effected only by a combination of two elements: (a) taking up residence in a different domicile with (b) the intention to remain there. * * *

It is clear that at the time of her marriage, Mrs. Mas was a domiciliary of the State of Mississippi. While it is generally the case that the domicile of the wife—and, consequently, her State citizenship for purposes of diversity jurisdiction—is deemed to be that of her husband, * * * we find no precedent for extending this concept to the situation here, in which the husband is a citizen of a foreign state but resides in the United States. Indeed, such a fiction would work absurd results on the facts before us. If Mr. Mas were considered a domiciliary of France—as he would be since he had lived in Louisiana as a student-teaching assistant prior to filing this suit * * *—then Mrs. Mas would also be deemed a domiciliary, and thus, fictionally at least, a citizen of France. She would not be a citizen of any State and could not sue in a federal court on that basis; nor could she invoke the alienage jurisdiction to bring her claim in federal court, since she is not an alien. * * * On the other hand, if Mrs. Mas's domicile were Louisiana, she would become a Louisiana citizen for diversity purposes and could not bring suit with her husband against appellant, also a Louisiana citizen, on the basis of diversity jurisdiction. These are curious results under a rule arising from the theoretical identity of person and interest of the married couple. * * *

An American woman is not deemed to have lost her United States citizenship solely by reason of her marriage to an alien. 8 U.S.C. § 1489. Similarly, we conclude that for diversity purposes a woman does not have her domicile or State citizenship changed solely by reason of her marriage to an alien.

Mrs. Mas's Mississippi domicile was disturbed neither by her year in Louisiana prior to her marriage nor as a result of the time she and her husband spent at LSU after their marriage, since for both periods she was a graduate assistant at LSU. * * * Though she testified that after her marriage she had no intention of returning to her parents' home in Mississippi, Mrs. Mas did not effect a change of domicile since she and Mr. Mas were in Louisiana only as students and lacked the requisite intention to remain there. Until she acquires a new domicile, she remains a domiciliary, and thus a citizen of Mississippi. * * *

[The court's discussion of the jurisdictional amount is omitted.]

Thus the power of the federal district court to entertain the claims of appellees in this case stands on two separate legs of diversity jurisdiction: a claim by an alien against a State citizen; and an action between citizens of different States. We also note, however, the propriety of having the federal district court entertain a spouse's action against a defendant, where the district court already has jurisdiction over a claim, arising from the same transaction, by the other spouse against the same defendant. * * * In the case before us, such a result is particularly desirable. The claims of Mr. and Mrs. Mas arise from the same operative facts, and there was almost complete interdependence between their claims with respect to the proof required and the issues raised at trial. Thus, since the district court had jurisdiction of Mr. Mas's action, sound judicial administration militates strongly in favor of federal jurisdiction of Mrs. Mas's claim.

Affirmed.

Notes and Questions

1. The court equates citizenship with domicile for purposes of diversity jurisdiction but distinguishes domicile from residence. If the goal of diversity jurisdiction is to protect out-of-staters from bias in suits against in-staters, does it make sense to disregard residence in defining citizenship for diversity purposes?

2. The party asserting the existence of diversity jurisdiction has the burden of proving its existence. How could a party prove citizenship for diversity purposes? Would it make sense for Perry to bear the burden of proof in this case, or are Mr. and Mrs. Mas in a superior position to come forward with evidence?

3. In 1988, Congress amended Section 1332(a) to provide that for the purpose of diversity jurisdiction "an alien admitted to the United States for permanent residence shall be deemed a citizen of the State in which such alien is domiciled." Would this provision have changed the outcome in Mas v. Perry? In what way?

Courts disagree on whether Section 1332(a) authorizes jurisdiction over a suit between an alien plaintiff and an alien defendant. In CHINA NUCLEAR ENERGY INDUS. CORP. v. ANDERSEN, LLP, 11 F.Supp.2d 1256 (D.Colo.1998), the District Court held that Section 1332(a) does not permit an alien corporation to sue a partnership made up of both United States citizens and permanent resident aliens. China Nuclear, a foreign corporation, sued Andersen, an accounting partnership, alleging that Andersen had issued a false and misleading report on the net worth of one of China Nuclear's clients, upon which China Nuclear relied and ultimately suffered damages. The court noted that a partnership's citizenship is determined by the citizenship of each of its individual partners, so that Andersen is a citizen or subject of every state or nation that its partners are citizens. The court interpreted Section 1332(a) to adhere to the longstanding rule that there must be complete diversity between each plaintiff and each defendant, even in alienage cases. Although the plain meaning of Section 1332(a) seems to provide for jurisdiction over China Nuclear's claim, the district court argued that giving effect to the plain meaning clearly would contravene both Article III's grant of constitutional authority to the courts and the complete diversity rule. The court held that Congress could not have intended to expand the scope of diversity jurisdiction beyond its constitutional and historical limits, and dismissed plaintiff's case for want of jurisdiction. Similar cases include Saadeh v. Farouki, 323 U.S.App.D.C. 239, 107 F.3d 52 (D.C.Cir.1997) (federal jurisdiction under § 1332 does not extend to cases involving alien plaintiffs and alien defendants); Arai v. Tachibana, 778 F.Supp. 1535 (D.Haw.1991); Lloyds Bank v. Norkin, 817 F.Supp. 414, 416 (S.D.N.Y.1993) ("[I]t is clear that Article III of the Constitution does not give Congress the power to grant federal courts jurisdiction over an action between two aliens."). But see Singh v. Daimler-Benz, 9 F.3d 303 (3d Cir. 1993). The controversy may have been ended by dictum in a footnote by the Supreme Court in Ruhrgas AG v. Marathon Oil Co., 526 U.S. 574, 580 n.2, 119 S.Ct. 1563,

1568 n.2, 143 L.Ed.2d 760, 768 n.2 (1999) to the effect that aliens on both sides of the action "rendered diversity incomplete."

Should a court construe a statute to avoid it being held unconstitutional, no matter how unreasonable that interpretation? In *Singh*, the court felt that there was no constitutional problem because there was minimal diversity, with a citizen and an alien on opposing sides. See pp. 671–77, infra. Should courts narrowly construe the statute or narrowly construe the Constitution? The court in *Saadeh* stated that the language of the statute is always the starting point for statutory interpretation. When should a court look beyond the plain meaning of the text to favor policy rationales or constitutional principles? See generally Johnson, *Why Alienage Jurisdiction? Historical Foundations and Modern Justifications for Federal Over Disputes Involving Noncitizens*, 21 Yale J. Int'l L. 1 (1996).

4. Is an alien, who also is a stateless person, a citizen or subject of a foreign state under the diversity statute? In BLAIR HOLDINGS CORP. v. RUBINSTEIN, 133 F.Supp. 496 (S.D.N.Y.1955), the defendant was described in the complaint as "not [being] a citizen of the United States." The plaintiff argued that it was not incumbent upon it to establish that the defendant was a citizen or subject of a particular foreign state. The court disagreed, and interpreted 28 U.S.C. § 1332(a)(2) to require a showing that the defendant was a citizen of a foreign state. Since that showing had not been made, suit could not be maintained in federal court. One reason that the plaintiff had not made the required showing was that the defendant, Serge Rubinstein, had been issued a so-called "Nansen" passport (a passport given to stateless persons) by the League of Nations and had registered as a stateless person with the United States Department of Justice.

5. Under Section 1332, a corporation, unlike a natural person, can be a citizen of more than one state. A corporation is a citizen of (1) the state(s) in which it is incorporated and (2) of the state in which it has its principal place of business. It generally is accepted that a corporation can have only one principal place of business for purposes of Section 1332. How should a court determine where that is? What factors might be relevant?

The Circuit Courts of Appeals use three different tests to determine a corporation's principal place of business. The first test is the "nerve center" test. * * * Under this test, "the locus of corporate decision-making authority and overall control constitutes a corporation's principal place of business for diversity purposes." * * *

The second test is referred to as the "corporate activities" or "operating assets" test. Greater weight is attached to the location of a corporation's production or service activities in determining the principal place of business under this test. * * *

The third test is known as the "total activity" test. This test is a hybrid of the "nerve center" and "corporate activities" tests and considers all the circumstances surrounding a corporation's business to discern its principal place of business. "The 'total activity' test provides a realistic, flexible and nonformalistic approach to determining a corporation's principal place of business through a balancing of all relevant factors." * * *

WHITE v. HALSTEAD INDUSTRIES, INC., 750 F.Supp. 395, 397 (E.D.Ark. 1990). Is any one of these tests significantly more reasonable than the others? Or should the circumstances of the individual case dictate which test is applied?

6. In general, courts have held that an unincorporated association is not treated as a citizen for purposes of federal diversity jurisdiction, but instead courts consider the citizenship of each of its members. See United Steelworkers of America v. R.H. Bouligny, Inc., 382 U.S. 145, 86 S.Ct. 272, 15 L.Ed.2d 217 (1965).

A limited partnership is also not a citizen of the state under whose laws it was created for purposes of diversity jurisdiction. The Supreme Court has held that the citizenship of a limited partnership is determined by the citizenship of each of its partners. See CARDEN v. ARKOMA ASSOCIATES, 494 U.S. 185, 110 S.Ct. 1015, 108 L.Ed.2d 157 (1990). Does it make sense that a limited partnership is treated any differently than a corporation? Should Congress amend Section 1332 to make a limited partnership a citizen of its state of organization and its principal place of business? See Note, *"Incorporating" Limited Partnerships into Federal Diversity Jurisdiction: Correcting Carden v. Arkoma Associates,* 65 Notre Dame L.Rev. 287 (1990).

7. Plaintiffs often will prefer to have certain claims heard in federal court as opposed to state court and will attempt to create diversity of citizenship to accomplish their goal. In KRAMER v. CARIBBEAN MILLS, INC., 394 U.S. 823, 89 S.Ct. 1487, 23 L.Ed.2d 9 (1969), a Panamanian corporation assigned its interest under a contract with a Haitian corporation to Kramer, a Texas attorney, for $1. By a separate agreement, Kramer reassigned 95% of any net recovery on the assigned cause of action to the Panamanian company. Kramer then commenced suit against the Haitian company on the basis of diversity of citizenship. The District Court denied defendant's motion to dismiss for want of jurisdiction. The Court of Appeals reversed, holding that the assignment was "improperly or collusively made" within the meaning of 28 U.S.C. § 1359. The Supreme Court affirmed, holding that:

> If federal jurisdiction could be created by assignments of this kind, which are easy to arrange and involve few disadvantages for the assignor, then a vast quantity of ordinary contract and tort litigation could be channeled into the federal courts at the will of one of the parties. Such "manufacture of Federal jurisdiction" was the very thing which Congress intended to prevent when it enacted § 1359 and its predecessors.

Id. at 828–29, 89 S.Ct. at 1490, 23 L.Ed.2d at 14. Would it have made a difference if the assignment had been made for a valid business reason? Note that Section 1359 prohibits only the creation of diversity jurisdiction and says nothing about its destruction. Is such a "one-way street" consistent with the purposes that diversity jurisdiction is intended to serve? See Grassi v. Ciba-Geigy, Ltd., 894 F.2d 181 (5th Cir.1990) (assignments that destroy diversity and those that create diversity should be analyzed under the same standard).

8. In 1988, Congress added to Section 1332(c) a provision that "the legal representative of the estate of a decedent shall be deemed to be a citizen only of the same State as the decedent, and the legal representative of an infant or incompetent shall be deemed to be a citizen only of the same State as the infant or incompetent." In so doing, Congress articulated a rule that prevented the appointment of administrators to create (or destroy) diversity. See, e.g., Mecom v. Fitzsimmons Drilling Co., 284 U.S. 183, 52 S.Ct. 84, 76 L.Ed. 233 (1931); Vaughan v. Southern Ry. Co., 542 F.2d 641 (4th Cir.1976). See generally Mullenix, *Creative Manipulation of Federal Jurisdiction: Is There Diversity After Death?,* 70 Cornell L.Rev. 1011 (1985). Could the courts have used Section 1359 to solve the problem? Why wasn't it used?

9. Plaintiffs also may attempt to destroy diversity of citizenship to make removal to federal court impossible for the defendant. In ROSE v. GIAMATTI, 721 F.Supp. 906 (S.D.Ohio 1989), plaintiff, Peter Edward Rose, was the field manager of the Cincinnati Reds baseball team. The Commissioner of Baseball, A. Bartlett Giamatti, was conducting an investigation into allegations that Rose had wagered on major league baseball games in violation of the Rules of Major League Baseball. Rose filed suit in an Ohio state court seeking a temporary restraining order and preliminary injunction against pending disciplinary proceedings on the ground that he was being denied his right to a fair hearing because Giamatti was a biased decisionmaker. Rose named Giamatti, Major League Baseball, and the Cincinnati Reds as defendants. Giamatti removed the action to federal district court in Ohio. Rose, a citizen of Ohio, sought to have the case remanded to the Ohio state court arguing that diversity was lacking between himself, and both the Cincinnati Reds and Major League Baseball (an unincorporated association), who he alleged were also citizens of Ohio. Giamatti, a citizen of New York, argued that the citizenship of the other defendants should be ignored. The District Court noted that:

* * * [I]t is * * * a long-established doctrine that a federal court in its determination of whether there is diversity of citizenship between the parties, must disregard nominal or formal parties to the action, and determine jurisdiction based solely upon the citizenship of the real parties to the controversy. * * * A real party in interest defendant is one who, by the substantive law, has the duty sought to be enforced or enjoined. * * * [A] formal or nominal party is one who, in a genuine legal sense, has no interest in the result of the suit, * * * or no actual interest or control over the subject matter of the litigation. * * *

The court then concluded that:

the controversy in this case is between plaintiff Rose and defendant Giamatti; that they are the real parties in interest in this case; that the Cincinnati Reds and Major League Baseball, are, at best, nominal parties in this controversy; and that, consequently, the citizenship of the Cincinnati Reds and Major League Baseball may be disregarded for diversity of citizenship purposes. The Court determines that diversity of citizenship exists between Rose, * * * and Commissioner Giamatti, * * * and that the Court has diversity subject matter jurisdiction over this action.

Id. at 914, 923–24. Is it right for a court to disregard parties it determines to be "formal or nominal"? Do you agree that the Cincinnati Reds and Major League Baseball were "nominal" parties? Why was Rose so anxious to keep the case in state court? Is *Rose* the prototypical case in which diversity jurisdiction serves to protect an out-of-state defendant against local prejudice? See Case Note, *"Root, Root, Root for the Home Team": Pete Rose, Nominal Parties and Diversity Jurisdiction,* 66 N.Y.U.L.Rev. 148 (1991).

10. Another method used by plaintiffs to destroy diversity jurisdiction was the naming of fictitious defendants. For example, in ABELS v. STATE FARM FIRE & CAS. CO., 770 F.2d 26 (3d Cir.1985), plaintiffs brought suit against State Farm over the company's failure to pay on their fire insurance claim on the belief that the fire had been caused by the insureds. Plaintiffs, citizens of California, also named as defendants "Does 1 through 10," who they identified as "employees of [State Farm] who were responsible for processing plaintiffs claim for benefits under the fire insurance policy * * *," and who plaintiffs alleged were also citizens of California. The Third Circuit held that the "Doe allegations" were

sufficient to defeat diversity jurisdiction since the employees had been specifically identified. See also Bryant v. Ford Motor Co., 832 F.2d 1080 (9th Cir.1987) (en banc), certiorari denied 488 U.S. 986, 109 S.Ct. 542, 102 L.Ed.2d 572 (1988). This practice, however, was curtailed by a 1988 amendment to 28 U.S.C. § 1441(a) providing that for purposes of removal, "the citizenship of defendants sued under fictitious names shall be disregarded." Is this provision consistent with the notion that the federal courts are courts of limited jurisdiction?

11. In 1990, the Federal Courts Study Committee recommended to Congress that diversity jurisdiction be eliminated except in complex multi-state litigation and suits involving aliens. In the alternative, the Committee suggested a number of other measures, including: (1) prohibiting plaintiffs from invoking diversity jurisdiction in their home states; (2) treating corporations as citizens of every state in which they are licensed to do business; (3) excluding non-economic damages, such as punitive damages from the amount in controversy; and (4) raising the amount in controversy to $75,000 and indexing to inflation thereafter. *Report of the Federal Courts Study Commission* 38–43 (April 2, 1990). See also Kramer, *Diversity Jurisdiction,* 1990 B.Y.U.L.Rev. 97. Are these proposals sensible? The first and fourth recommendations were incorporated into the initial version of the Federal Courts Improvement Act of 1996. However, Congress ultimately approved only the raising of the amount in controversy to $75,000.

Statistics indicate that 31% of all new diversity cases are filed by in-state plaintiffs, suggesting that the Federal Courts Study Committee recommendation to eliminate in-state plaintiff diversity jurisdiction could decrease the federal courts' caseload significantly. *Federal Courts Improvement Act, 1995: Hearings on H.R. 1989 Before the Subcomm. on Administrative Oversight and the Courts of the Senate Comm. on the Judiciary,* 104th Cong., 1st Sess. (1995) (statement of Judge Stephen H. Anderson, Chair, Judicial Conference Committee on Federal–State Jurisdiction). Is that assumption correct, or might many plaintiffs opt to file cases in the federal courts of neighboring states? What are the likely consequences of such a provision on the caseload of the state courts?

2. AMOUNT IN CONTROVERSY

A.F.A. TOURS, INC. v. WHITCHURCH

United States Court of Appeals, Second Circuit, 1991.
937 F.2d 82.

KEARSE, CIRCUIT JUDGE. Plaintiff A.F.A. Tours, Inc., doing business as Alumni Flights Abroad ("AFA"), appeals from a final judgment of the United States District Court for the Southern District of New York * * * dismissing for lack of subject matter jurisdiction this diversity action against defendant Desmond Whitchurch for misappropriation of trade secrets. The district court summarily dismissed the complaint on the ground that it would not be possible for AFA to prove damages amounting to more than $50,000. For the reasons below, we vacate and remand for further proceedings.

* * * AFA operates a travel and tour business, specializing in deluxe tours for United States residents to overseas destinations including Australia, New Zealand, and New Guinea. It expended large sums of money and invested significant time and labor to develop, *inter alia,* a client and customer list, marketing information, and tour information. It regarded this information as confidential trade secrets.

From 1972 through 1989, Whitchurch was employed by AFA as its exclusive tour escort in the above areas. In that position, Whitchurch was privy to certain of the above confidential information. The complaint alleged that in or about October 1989, Whitchurch resigned from AFA, misappropriated the confidential information known to him, and organized his own tour business. Since that time, he has offered or intends to offer tours that compete with those offered by AFA; in connection with his own tours, he has solicited or intends to solicit participants from AFA's customer list.

AFA commenced the present diversity action in the district court for misappropriation of its trade secrets, seeking an injunction against any use by Whitchurch of confidential AFA information, and damages "in an amount which is not presently ascertainable, but which is believed to exceed the sum of $50,000.00." It also sought punitive damages of "no less than $250,000.00."

Whitchurch denied all of the material allegations of the complaint and quickly moved for summary judgment on the ground that the AFA information possessed by Whitchurch was not confidential. * * *

Whitchurch stated that from February to May 1990, he had attempted to organize a tour on his own. In this effort he had, *inter alia,* written to former AFA tour participants he had escorted, informed them of his separation from AFA, and solicited their participation. Only two people reserved space on the planned tour, however, and it was canceled. He opposed the present lawsuit because he remained interested in conducting tours in the future.

AFA opposed Whitchurch's summary judgment motion, contending that there were genuine issues of fact as to, *inter alia,* the confidential nature of the AFA information and Whitchurch's knowledge of that confidentiality. It submitted affidavits describing its own operations and detailing steps it had taken to maintain the confidentiality of its customer list * * *.

* * *

At the oral argument of Whitchurch's motion, Whitchurch's attorney began by characterizing the motion as "turn[ing] on a very narrow issue" of whether the AFA information constituted trade secrets * * *, and stating that the case was important to Whitchurch because "he may one day in the future wish to organize a tour, and write letters to individuals again" * * *. The court, however, asked whether it even had to reach the question of trade secrets, raising sua sponte the question of whether the value of AFA's claims exceeded $50,000, a jurisdictional prerequisite for a diversity action. In response to the court's jurisdictional question, Whitchurch's attorney stated that Whitchurch, in soliciting for his planned tour, had written to 100–200 former AFA tour participants but had received favorable responses from only two. * * *

AFA's attorney argued that Whitchurch's lack of success on his first effort was hardly dispositive of the issue of the amount of damages AFA might suffer, in light of Whitchurch's desire to conduct other tours in the future. * * * AFA's attorney, noting that over the years Whitchurch had escorted some 1,500 AFA clients on tours and had indicated that he would conduct a number of tours, argued that AFA's damages would be substantial. He stated that a single 10-customer tour to the area in question would easily generate more than $50,000 * * *. * * *

At the close of this hearing, the court granted summary judgment in favor of Whitchurch * * *. * * * On appeal, AFA contends that the dismissal for lack of jurisdiction was improper because the court (1) failed to give AFA an appropriate opportunity to show that it satisfied the jurisdictional amount, and (2) failed to apply the proper standard to AFA's requests for (a) damages and (b) injunctive relief. * * * For the reasons below, we conclude that the dismissal on the jurisdictional ground was improper. * * *

The district courts have jurisdiction over civil diversity suits "where the matter in controversy exceeds the sum or value of $50,000, exclusive of interest and costs." 28 U.S.C. § 1332 (1988). The test for determining whether a plaintiff meets the jurisdictional amount, established by the Supreme Court in St. Paul Mercury Indemnity Co. v. Red Cab Co., 303 U.S. 283, 58 S.Ct. 586, 82 L.Ed. 845 (1938), is as follows:

> The rule governing dismissal for want of jurisdiction in cases brought in the federal court is that, unless the law gives a different rule, the sum claimed by the plaintiff controls if the claim is apparently made in good faith. It must appear *to a legal certainty* that the claim is really for less than the jurisdictional amount to justify a dismissal.

303 U.S. at 288–89, 58 S.Ct. at 590 (emphasis added).

The amount of damages recoverable in an action for misappropriation of trade secrets may be measured either by the plaintiff's losses, * * * or by the profits unjustly received by the defendant * * *. In addition, if punitive damages are permitted under the controlling law, the demand for such damages may be included in determining whether the jurisdictional amount is satisfied. * * *. New York law apparently allows the recovery of punitive damages in a trade secrets case if the defendant's conduct has been sufficiently "gross and wanton." * * *.

Further, in appropriate circumstances, the owner of trade secrets may obtain an injunction against their use or disclosure by another in breach of his confidential relationship with the owner. * * *. Where the plaintiff seeks injunctive relief, the value of his claim is generally assessed with reference to the right he seeks to protect and measured by the extent of the impairment to be prevented by the injunction. * * *. In calculating that impairment, the court may look not only at past losses but also at potential harm. * * *.

Before making a determination that the plaintiff's claim does not meet the jurisdictional minimum, the court must afford the plaintiff an "appropriate and reasonable opportunity to show good faith in believing that a recovery in excess of [the jurisdictional amount] is reasonably possible." * * *. Under these substantive and procedural principles, although the record indicates that AFA has not yet suffered actual damages even approaching $50,000, we have difficulty with the district court's decision.

First, though AFA did not make an evidentiary showing in support of its contention that the value of its claims exceeded $50,000, it was not afforded a proper opportunity to do so. The issue of the jurisdictional amount was first raised by the district court sua sponte at the argument on the summary judgment motion, and the court rendered its decision at the end of that argument. To the extent that the court thought AFA could not meet the jurisdictional minimum, it should not have dismissed without giving AFA an opportunity to present substantiation directed toward that issue.

Second, despite AFA's lack of an opportunity to present evidence addressed directly to the jurisdictional question, there was evidence in the record to suggest that the matter could not be conclusively resolved against it, for the oral arguments made by AFA's attorney to show that its claims were worth more than $50,000 had some support from documents already before the court. For example, he said Whitchurch had the names of some 1,500 AFA customers; this was consistent with (a) Whitchurch's own statement that in the 17 years he was employed by AFA he had led approximately seven tours each year (thus totaling some 119 tours) and (b) his attorney's statement that there were usually 10–15 people per tour. * * * As to AFA's attorney's estimate that a single tour of this type "[i]s about seven to ten thousand dollars per customer," the evidence in the record as to the destination and deluxe nature of the tours, including evidence that some participants traveled first class and reserved preferred hotel accommodations, supports an inference that a 28–day tour could well cost $10,000 per person.

What this means in terms of loss of earnings to a tour operator, however, is not revealed by the present record. AFA's suggestion that the tour operator himself would earn $10,000 per tourist * * * does not have the same record support and seems questionable. The district court was also undoubtedly correct in its assumption that many of the persons who traveled to the South Pacific with Whitchurch during the 17 years he was with AFA are not likely to travel to that area again. But it could not be said to a legal certainty that no one would return to that area. There was ample support in the record for the proposition that AFA has the prospects for repeat customers. For example, AFA had submitted from one of its brochures two pages excerpting comments from participants in a recent AFA tour * * *; nearly one-third of those quoted indicated that they either had been on other AFA tours or would hope to go on future AFA tours. * * * If a tour operator could earn 17% of the price of a tour, and if Whitchurch were eventually successful in soliciting even 30 of the approximately 1,500 AFA participants he has escorted (i.e., 2%, which may reflect the ratio of his success on his first attempt), the profit he could siphon from AFA would total $51,000. Thus, on the present record, the court could not conclude to a legal certainty that the value of AFA's claims did not exceed the jurisdictional minimum.

Further, AFA requested injunctive relief not just against Whitchurch's solicitation of its customers but also against any use of the information. Presumably such an injunction would include a prohibition against Whitchurch's sale or disclosure of the names and addresses of AFA's customers to other tour operators who might be better equipped than Whitchurch to exploit the information and attract more than 2% of the persons whose names Whitchurch could provide them. In addition, AFA's request for punitive damages in the amount of $250,000 might provide a basis for satisfaction of the jurisdictional amount. Whether or not AFA will be able to prove that Whitchurch's conduct was "gross and wanton" and warrants the recovery of such damages under New York law is an open question. But the present record does not foreclose that possibility.

In all the circumstances, we conclude that the record as it existed in the district court did not permit the court to find with legal certainty that the value of AFA's claims did not exceed $50,000.

* * *

Notes and Questions

1. Until 1980, 28 U.S.C. § 1331 contained an amount-in-controversy requirement for federal-question cases. In that year, the requirement was deleted. Jurisdictional amount is now an issue only in diversity cases and in some rare federal-question cases (actions brought under the Consumer Product Safety Act, for example) when a statute expressly requires that the federal question present a given amount in controversy.

2. When Congress raised the jurisdictional amount in diversity cases to $75,000 in 1996, it was a compromise between those who wished to abolish diversity jurisdiction and those who wished to maintain the rights of litigants to choose between the state and federal courts. Is it possible that plaintiffs simply increase the amount of damages sought and undermine the purpose of the amendment? See generally Baker, *The History and Tradition of the Amount in Controversy Requirement: A Proposal to "Up the Ante" in Diversity Jurisdiction*, 102 F.R.D. 299 (1984).

In ARNOLD v. TROCCOLI, 344 F.2d 842 (2d Cir.1965), plaintiff's personal-injury action for $15,000, which originally had been brought for $6,000 in a state court, was dismissed as a colorable claim asserted for the sole purpose of conferring federal jurisdiction. There appeared to be no justification for the increase in claimed damages, and plaintiff's counsel admitted that the switch from state to federal court was made because of the congested condition of the state courts. In the course of its opinion, the Second Circuit examined statistics prepared by New York's Judicial Conference showing that 97% of all accident claims in New York result in settlements or judgments of less than $10,000. Of what relevance is this statistic in determining whether plaintiff's claim is "in excess of $10,000," the then applicable required amount in controversy? What if plaintiff discovers new facts during pretrial proceedings that show that any possible recovery cannot reach the jurisdictional amount, and his attorney files a written stipulation to that effect? Must the action be dismissed or is it saved by the fact that the original claim was made in "good faith"? See National Sur. Corp. v. City of Excelsior Springs, 123 F.2d 573 (8th Cir.1941).

3. The liberal joinder provisions of the Federal Rules raise a number of questions as to whether "aggregation" can be used to meet the jurisdictional amount. See Wright, *Federal Courts* § 36 (5th ed. 1994); 14B Wright, Miller & Cooper, *Federal Practice and Procedure: Jurisdiction and Related Matters 3d* §§ 3704–06 (1998). In ZAHN v. INTERNATIONAL PAPER CO., 414 U.S. 291, 94 S.Ct. 505, 38 L.Ed.2d 511 (1973), four owners of Vermont lakefront property brought a diversity action on behalf of a class consisting of themselves and 200 other lakefront property owners seeking damages from a New York corporation alleged to have polluted the waters of Lake Champlain and, as a result, to have damaged the value and utility of the surrounding property. The Supreme Court held that only those plaintiffs who individually met the then applicable $10,000 jurisdictional amount requirement could be members of the class. The holding in Zahn has been called into doubt, however. See Note 3, p. 319, infra.

Consider whether a federal court can assert jurisdiction in the following situations:

(a) One plaintiff sues one defendant claiming $40,000 in property damage and $45,000 for personal injury resulting from the same accident. *yes*

(b) One plaintiff sues one defendant on two unrelated claims, one for $40,000 and the other for $45,000. *yes*

(c) Two plaintiffs sue one defendant each seeking $40,000 in damages. *No.*

(d) Two plaintiffs sue one defendant jointly seeking $80,000 in damages.

(e) One plaintiff sues seeking $40,000 from each of two defendants. *No.*

(f) Two plaintiffs sue one defendant on the same issue. One plaintiff seeks $45,000 in damages; the other seeks $35,000. *No.*

In general, single plaintiffs can aggregate claims against single defendants. Two plaintiffs may not aggregate if they have separate and distinct claims. If there is a single indivisible harm, plaintiffs may aggregate. Does this distinction make any sense? To what extent do these rules follow from a plain reading of Section 1332 and to what extent are they motivated by concerns of judicial economy? Why should the rules distinguish between cases with single plaintiffs and defendants and those with multiple parties?

4. Determining the amount in controversy, for jurisdictional purposes, in diversity cases seeking injunctive relief poses a difficult problem for federal courts. In McCARTY v. AMOCO PIPELINE CO., 595 F.2d 389, 391–93 (7th Cir.1979), Judge Swygert described this task as follows:

Valuation of the matter in controversy in suits for declaratory or injunctive relief is a complex task. The court must not only undertake to evaluate intangible rights as opposed to objects commonly found in the marketplace, but it must decide what rights are involved in the controversy and from whose viewpoint their value is to be measured. * * *

Some courts have resolved the difficulty by adopting the rule that only the value to the plaintiff may be used to determine the jurisdictional amount. Support for this interpretation is principally garnered from the Supreme Court's opinion in Glenwood Light & Water Co. v. Mutual Light, Heat & Power Co., 239 U.S. 121, 36 S.Ct. 30, 60 L.Ed. 174 (1915) * * *.

Although supportive of the "plaintiff viewpoint" rule, the holding in *Glenwood* is only that jurisdiction is present if the value to the plaintiff exceeds the required amount regardless of the value to the defendant. The *Glenwood* case does not exclude the possibility that jurisdiction would be present in a case where the value required was present from the defendant's viewpoint but not from the plaintiff's. * * *

Another approach taken by some courts is to view the amount in controversy from the point of view of the party seeking to invoke federal jurisdiction. Under this rule, the court would look to the plaintiff's viewpoint in a case brought originally in federal court and to the defendant's viewpoint in a case removed to federal court from a state court.

Although this rule has certain attractive features such as tying the controlling viewpoint to the burden of proof as to jurisdiction, two problems with it arise. The first is the possibility of anomalous results. Under the rule, if a case originally brought in federal court were dismissed for failure to meet the jurisdictional amount from the plaintiff's viewpoint, it could yet end up in federal court if the plaintiff reinstituted the case in state court and the defendant—from whose point of view the required amount was present—then removed it. * * *

There is yet a third rule which a number of courts have adopted and which may be termed the "either viewpoint" rule. Under this rule, as the court stated it in Ronzio v. Denver & R.G.W.R. Co., 116 F.2d 604, 606 (10th Cir.1940) * * *:

> In determining the matter in controversy, we may look to the object sought to be accomplished by the plaintiffs' complaint; the test for determining the amount in controversy is the pecuniary result to either party which the judgment would directly produce.

* * *

SECTION C. THE SUBJECT–MATTER JURISDICTION OF THE FEDERAL COURTS—FEDERAL QUESTIONS

MISHKIN, THE FEDERAL "QUESTION" IN THE DISTRICT COURTS, 53 Colum.L.Rev. 157, 157–59 (1953):

Although the framers of our Constitution could not agree upon whether there should be any federal trial courts at all, it was generally conceded at the Convention that the national judicial power should, in some form, extend to cases arising under the laws of the new government. However, though the first Congress did exercise its option to establish a system of "inferior" national tribunals, it did not assign to them general jurisdiction over cases of that type. With the exception of an extremely shortlived statute enacted just after the end of the eighteenth century, it was not until 1875 that the federal courts were given initial cognizance of all types of federal question cases. * * *

Whatever may have been the circumstances and needs during the first century of our country's history, there seems to be little doubt that today, with the expanding scope of federal legislation, the exercise of power over cases of this sort constitutes one of the major purposes of a full independent system of national trial courts. The alternative would be to rely entirely upon United States Supreme Court review of state court decisions. But, at least in our present judicial system, Supreme Court pronouncements as to any particular segment of national law are comparatively few. Consequently, sympathetic handling of the available Supreme Court rulings assumes a role of substantial importance in achieving widespread, uniform effectuation of federal law. Presumably judges selected and paid by the central government, with tenure during good behavior—and that determined by the Congress—and probably even somewhat insulated by a separate building, are more likely to give full scope to any given Supreme Court decision, and particularly ones unpopular locally, than are their state counterparts. By the same token, should a district judge fail, or err, a more sympathetic treatment of Supreme Court precedents can be expected from federal circuit judges than from state appellate courts.

Thus, the exercise of federal question jurisdiction by lower federal tribunals presumably permits the Supreme Court to confine itself (insofar as any such distinction can be drawn) to the solving of new problems rather than the policing of old solutions, without the loss that might otherwise be entailed in the effectuation of national rights. Further, the fact that the lower federal bench is chosen by officials of the national government under the same procedure as the members of the high Court suggests a greater similarity in the interpretation of national law, even on first impression, among the several parts of the national system than between the Supreme Court and any state system, or among the various state tribunals themselves. Insofar as this is true, it also promotes a more uniform, correct application of federal law in that significant group of cases where, either because of the novelty of the question, disproportionate expense or for other reasons, recourse to the Supreme Court has previously either not been attempted or been precluded. Finally, it might even be argued that the very existence of an alternative forum stimulates state courts to give a more attentive treatment to claims of federal right.

These factors suggest that it is desirable that Congress be competent to bring to an initial national forum all cases in which the vindication of federal policy may be at stake. However, it does not follow from this that at any given time all such cases should in fact be brought before the federal courts. There are other considerations which must enter into any decision as to the actual use of the national judiciary. For example, there are limits on the volume of litigation which they can handle without an expansion which might not be warranted by the advantages to be gained; the hardships which the geographic location of these courts may impose on the litigants and a willingness to trust that a party's self-interest will lead him to bring or remove an appropriate case to the federal courts might well justify the current rule that federal question jurisdiction is, for the most part, shared by the local courts; in some circumstances, such as where the validity of state action may be at issue, it may avoid friction and wasted effort, without sacrificing national authority, to allow the initial adjudication to be made by the state's tribunals subject to ultimate review by the United States Supreme Court. Other factors could easily be added. * * *

———

OSBORN v. BANK OF THE UNITED STATES, 22 U.S. (9 Wheat.) 738, 6 L.Ed. 204 (1824). The Bank of the United States brought suit in federal court to enjoin the state auditor of Ohio from collecting from it a tax alleged to be unconstitutional. The court granted a temporary injunction restraining the state auditor from collecting the tax. The state auditor, however, forcibly entered the bank and took the money he claimed the state was owed. The court ordered the state officials to return the money that had been taken from the bank. The officials appealed on the grounds that the federal court lacked subject-matter jurisdiction over the case.

The congressional act chartering the bank authorized it "to sue and be sued * * * in any Circuit Court of the United States." First, Chief Justice Marshall held that this authorization was a grant by Congress to the federal courts of jurisdiction in all cases to which the bank was a party. He then considered whether Congress had the constitutional power to confer jurisdiction over these cases pursuant to the "arising under" language of Article III, § 2. That power clearly existed in the actual case, since the bank was alleging that Ohio's attempt to tax it violated the federal Constitution. The Chief Justice, however, undertook to support the validity of the jurisdictional grant in all cases to which the bank was a party. In particular, he discussed the situation presented if the bank asserted a claim under state law arising out of a contract:

> When [the] Bank sues, the first question which presents itself, and which lies at the foundation of the cause, is, has this legal entity a right to sue? Has it a right to come, not into this Court particularly, but into any Court? This depends on a law of the United States. The next question is, has this being a right to make this particular contract? If this question be decided in the negative, the cause is determined against the plaintiff; and this question, too, depends entirely on a law of the United States. These are important questions, and they exist in every possible case. The right to sue, if decided once, is decided for ever; but the power of Congress was exercised antecedently to the first decision on that right, and if it was constitutional then, it cannot cease to be so, because the particular question is decided. It may be revived at the will of the party, and most probably would be renewed, were the tribunal to be changed. But the question respecting the right to make a particular contract, or to acquire a particular property, or to sue on account of a particular injury, belongs to every particular case, and may be renewed in every case. The question forms an original ingredient in every cause. Whether it be in fact relied on or not, in the defence, it is still a part of the cause, and may be relied on. The right of the plaintiff to sue, cannot depend on the defence which the defendant may choose to set up. His right to sue is anterior to that defence, and must depend on the state of things when the action is brought. The questions which the case involves, then, must determine its character, whether those questions be made in the cause or not.

> The appellants say, that the case arises on the contract; but the validity of the contract depends on a law of the United States, and the plaintiff is compelled, in every case, to show its validity. The case arises emphatically under the law. The act of Congress is its foundation. The contract could never have been made, but under the authority of that act. The act itself is the first ingredient in the case, is its origin, is that from which every other part arises. That other questions may also arise, as the execution of the contract, or its performance, cannot change the case, or give it any other origin than the charter of incorporation. The action still originates in, and is sustained by, that charter.

Id. at 823–25, 6 L.Ed. at 224–25.

Notes and Questions

1. The contract case discussed in *Osborn* in fact was presented by the companion case of BANK OF THE UNITED STATES v. PLANTERS' BANK OF GEORGIA, 22 U.S. (9 Wheat.) 904, 6 L.Ed. 244 (1824). The Bank of the United States had purchased notes issued by a state bank, which refused to honor them. The Bank of the United States sued for payment, and the state bank contested the federal court's jurisdiction. The Supreme Court held that the question had been "fully considered" in *Osborn*, and that it was "unnecessary to repeat the reasoning used in that case."

2.   The *Osborn* decision has been said to allow Congress to confer jurisdiction "whenever there exists in the background some federal proposition that might be challenged, despite the remoteness of the likelihood of actual presentation of such a federal question." Textile Workers Union v. Lincoln Mills, 353 U.S. 448, 471, 77 S.Ct. 912, 928–29, 1 L.Ed.2d 972, 989 (1957) (Frankfurter, J., dissenting). Is this statement of the holding in *Osborn* accurate? Under this formulation, are there any cases that do not colorably "arise under" federal law?

3.   The *Osborn* decision took on added importance after an 1875 statute (the predecessor to 28 U.S.C. § 1331) gave the federal courts general jurisdiction over federal question cases. Given the virtual similarity of the "arising under" language in the Constitution and in this statute, the intended scope of the statute was not immediately clear. In reading the cases that follow, consider the relationship of these provisions.

Read 28 U.S.C. §§ 1331, 1334, 1337, 1338, 1343, 1345, and 1346, which are in the Supplement.

LOUISVILLE & NASHVILLE R. CO. v. MOTTLEY

Supreme Court of the United States, 1908.
211 U.S. 149, 29 S.Ct. 42, 53 L.Ed. 126.

Appeal from the Circuit Court of the United States for the Western District of Kentucky * * *.

The appellees (husband and wife), being residents and citizens of Kentucky, brought this suit in equity in the circuit court of the United States for the western district of Kentucky against the appellant, a railroad company and a citizen of the same state. * * *

The bill alleged that in September, 1871, plaintiffs, while passengers upon the defendant railroad, were injured by the defendant's negligence, and released their respective claims for damages in consideration of the agreement for transportation during their lives, expressed in the contract. It is alleged that the contract was performed by the defendant up to January 1, 1907, when the defendant declined to renew the passes. The bill then alleges that the refusal to comply with the contract was based solely upon that part of the act of Congress of June 29, 1906 (34 Stat. at L. 584, chap. 3591, U.S.Comp. Stat.Supp.1907, p. 892), which forbids the giving of free passes or free transportation. The bill further alleges: First, that the act of Congress referred to does not prohibit the giving of passes under the circumstances of this case; and, second, that, if the law is to be construed as prohibiting such passes, it is in conflict with the 5th Amendment of the Constitution, because it deprives the plaintiffs of their property without due process of law. The defendant demurred to the bill. The judge of the circuit court overruled the demurrer, entered a decree for the relief prayed for, and the defendant appealed directly to this court.

MR. JUSTICE MOODY, after making the foregoing statement, delivered the opinion of the court:

Two questions of law were raised by the demurrer to the bill, were brought here by appeal, and have been argued before us. They are, first, whether * * */(the act of Congress of June 29, 1906 * * * makes it unlawful to perform a contract for transportation of persons who, in good faith, before the passage of the act, had accepted such contract in satisfaction of a valid cause of action against the railroad;)and, second, whether the statute, if it should be construed to render such a contract unlawful, is in violation of the 5th Amendment of the Constitution of the United States. We do not deem it necessary, however, to consider either of these questions, because, in our opinion, the court below was without jurisdiction of the cause. Neither party has questioned that jurisdiction, but it is the duty of this court to see to it that the jurisdiction of the circuit court, which is defined and limited by statute, is not exceeded. * * *

There was no diversity of citizenship, and it is not and cannot be suggested that there was any ground of jurisdiction, except that the case was a "suit * * * arising under the Constitution or laws of the United States." 25 Stat. at L. 434, chap. 866, U.S.Comp.Stat.1901, p. 509. It is the settled interpretation of these words, as used in this statute, conferring jurisdiction, that a suit arises under the Constitution and laws of the United States only when the plaintiff's statement of his own cause of action shows that it is based upon those laws or that Constitution. It is not enough that the plaintiff alleges some anticipated defense to his cause of action, and asserts that the defense is invalidated by some provision of the Constitution of the United States. Although such allegations show that very likely, in the course of the litigation, a question under the Constitution would arise, they do not show that the suit, that is, the plaintiff's original cause of action, arises under the Constitution. In Tennessee v. Union & Planters' Bank, 152 U.S. 454, 38 L.Ed. 511, 14 S.Ct.Rep. 654, the plaintiff, the state of Tennessee, brought suit in the circuit court of the United States to recover from the defendant certain taxes alleged to be due under the laws of the state. The plaintiff alleged that the defendant claimed an immunity from the taxation by virtue of its charter, and that therefore the tax was void, because in violation of the provision of the Constitution of the United States, which forbids any state from passing a law impairing the obligation of contracts. The cause was held to be beyond the jurisdiction of the circuit court, the court saying, by Mr. Justice Gray (p. 464): "A suggestion of one party, that the other will or may set up a claim under the Constitution or laws of the United States, does not make the suit one arising under that Constitution or those laws." Again, in Boston & M. Consol. Copper & S. Min. Co. v. Montana Ore Purchasing Co., 188 U.S. 632, 47 L.Ed. 626, 23 S.Ct.Rep. 434, the plaintiff brought suit in the circuit court of the United States for the conversion of copper ore and for an injunction against its continuance. The plaintiff then alleged, for the purpose of showing jurisdiction, in substance, that the defendant would set up in defense certain laws of the United States. The cause was held to be beyond the jurisdiction of the circuit court, the court saying, by Mr. Justice Peckham (pp. 638, 639):

It would be wholly unnecessary and improper, in order to prove complainant's cause of action, to go into any matters of defense which the defendants might possibly set up, and then attempt to reply to such defense, and thus, if possible, to show that a Federal question might or probably would arise in the course of the trial of the case. To allege such defense and then make an answer to it before the defendant has the opportunity to itself plead or prove its own defense is inconsistent with any known rule of pleading, so far as we are aware, and is improper.

The rule is a reasonable and just one that the complainant in the first instance shall be confined to a statement of its cause of action, leaving to the defendant to set up in his answer what his defense is, and, if anything more than a denial of complainant's cause of action, imposing upon the defendant the burden of proving such defense.

Conforming itself to that rule, the complainant would not, in the assertion or proof of its cause of action, bring up a single Federal question. The presentation of its cause of action would not show that it was one arising under the Constitution or laws of the United States.

* * *

* * * The application of this rule to the case at bar is decisive against the jurisdiction of the circuit court.

It is ordered that the judgment be reversed and the case remitted to the circuit court with instructions to dismiss the suit for want of jurisdiction.

Notes and Questions

1. To what extent is the *Mottley* decision a reaction to *Osborn*'s broad reading of the "arising under" language in the Constitution? Would the "well-pleaded complaint" rule of *Mottley* have changed the outcome of *Planters' Bank*?

2. What justifications are there for the Supreme Court's disposition of *Mottley*? Why should subject-matter jurisdiction depend on technical pleading rules and the content of the complaint? Following the Court's decision, the Mottleys commenced an action in a Kentucky state court. The case ultimately was brought to the United States Supreme Court by appeal from the highest court in Kentucky on the question of the validity and construction of the 1906 Act; three years after the Supreme Court dismissed the federal action it examined the merits of the Mottleys' contentions and decided in favor of the railroad. In light of this history, what was gained by the original dismissal? Consider the proposal of the American Law Institute, *Study of the Division of Jurisdiction Between State and Federal Courts* § 1312(d) (1969), which provides that a federal court may retain subject-matter jurisdiction even when the complaint does not present a claim within its original jurisdiction if defendant introduces a federal defense or counterclaim. See also Doernberg, *There's No Reason for It; It's Just Our Policy: Why the Well–Pleaded Complaint Rule Sabotages the Purposes of Federal Question Jurisdiction*, 38 Hastings L.J. 597 (1987).

3. Would there have been jurisdiction in the principal case if the railroad had sought, as it can today, a judicial declaration, see pp. 18–20, supra, under the Declaratory Judgment Act, 28 U.S.C. §§ 2201–02, to the effect that the 1906 Act had rendered the passes invalid? See SKELLY OIL CO. v. PHILLIPS PETROLE-UM CO., 339 U.S. 667, 673–74, 70 S.Ct. 876, 880, 94 L.Ed. 1194, 1200–01 (1950), in which suit was brought under the Declaratory Judgment Act for a declaration that certain contracts had not been terminated. Had the plaintiff (who also was the party who initiated the declaratory action) simply sued to enforce the contract, the complaint would not have raised a federal question; in defending against the breach of contract complaint, however, the defendant would have argued termi-

nation, and the effectiveness of an attempted termination turned on a federal question. The Court denied jurisdiction, writing, "[t]o sanction suits for declaratory relief as within the jurisdiction of the District Courts merely because, as in this case, artful pleading anticipates a defense based on federal law would contravene the whole trend of jurisdictional legislation by Congress, disregard the effective functioning of the federal judicial system and distort the limited procedural purposes of the Declaratory Judgment Act." How would the assertion of jurisdiction in *Skelly* have done all of these things?

4. In FRANCHISE TAX BOARD v. CONSTRUCTION LABORERS VACATION TRUST, 463 U.S. 1, 103 S.Ct. 2841, 77 L.Ed.2d 420 (1983), a state tax board sued a trust in state court, claiming that the trust had "failed to comply with three tax levies issued under [California law]." The trust answered that it was regulated under the Employee Retirement Income Security Act of 1974 (ERISA), and that, under ERISA, it did not have to comply with the state regulations. The trust sought to remove the action to federal court. The Supreme Court eventually held that the district court lacked subject-matter jurisdiction over the case because, under the well-pleaded complaint rule articulated in *Mottley*, the federal question did not appear in the tax board's complaint.

The tax board also sought a declaration under a state declaratory judgment statute that the trust was "legally obligated to honor all future levies by the Board." The Court reasoned that:

> If federal district courts could take jurisdiction, either originally or by removal, of state declaratory judgment claims raising questions of federal law, without regard to the doctrine of *Skelly Oil*, the federal Declaratory Judgment Act—with the limitations of *Skelly Oil* read into it—would become a dead letter.

Id. at 18, 103 S.Ct. at 2851, 77 L.Ed.2d at 436. The Court also rejected an argument that since the trust had been granted the right to seek injunctive relief in federal court when its rights and duties under ERISA are at issue, the tax board's declaratory judgment suit arose under federal law. According to the Court:

> States are not significantly prejudiced by an inability to come to federal court for a declaratory judgment in advance of a possible injunctive suit by a person subject to federal regulation. They have a variety of means by which they can enforce their own laws in their own courts, and they do not suffer if the preemption questions such enforcement may raise are tested there. The express grant of federal jurisdiction in ERISA is limited to suits brought by certain parties * * * as to whom Congress presumably determined that a right to enter federal court was necessary to further the statute's purposes. It did not go so far as to provide that any suit *against* such parties must also be brought in federal court when they themselves did not choose to sue.

Id. at 21, 103 S.Ct. at 2852, 77 L.Ed.2d at 438. See Twitchell, *Characterizing Federal Claims: Preemption, Removal, and the Arising–Under Jurisdiction of the Federal Courts*, 54 Geo.Wash.L.Rev. 812 (1986); Comment, *Federal Preemption, Removal Jurisdiction, and the Well–Pleaded Complaint Rule*, 51 U.Chi.L.Rev. 634 (1984).

5. In BRIGHT v. BECHTEL PETROLEUM, INC., 780 F.2d 766 (9th Cir. 1986), plaintiff brought suit against his employer in state court alleging that the employer had breached his employment contract by paying him less than the contract required because the employer withheld state and federal income taxes. The employer removed the case to federal court arguing that plaintiff had artfully

pleaded what really was a challenge to the employer's compliance with federal law. The Ninth Circuit, allowing an exception to the "well-pleaded complaint" rule, found that federal-question jurisdiction existed.

> Although the plaintiff is generally considered the "master of his complaint" and is free to choose the forum for his action, this principle is not without limitation. * * * A plaintiff will not be allowed to conceal the true nature of a complaint through "artful pleading." * * *

Id. at 769.

T.B. HARMS CO. v. ELISCU

United States Court of Appeals, Second Circuit, 1964.
339 F.2d 823, certiorari denied 381 U.S. 915, 85 S.Ct. 1534, 14 L.Ed.2d 435 (1965).

FRIENDLY, CIRCUIT JUDGE. A layman would doubtless be surprised to learn that an action wherein the purported sole owner of a copyright alleged that persons claiming partial ownership had recorded their claim in the Copyright Office and had warned his licensees against disregarding their interests was not one "arising under any Act of Congress relating to * * * copyrights" over which 28 U.S.C. § 1338 gives the federal courts exclusive jurisdiction. Yet precedents going back for more than a century teach that lesson and lead us to affirm Judge Weinfeld's dismissal of the complaint.

The litigation concerns four copyrighted songs. * * * The music for the songs was composed by Vincent Youmans for use in a motion picture, "Flying Down to Rio," pursuant to a contract made in 1933 with RKO Studios, Inc. He agreed to assign to RKO the recordation and certain other rights relating to the picture during the existence of the copyrights and any renewals. RKO was to employ a writer of the lyrics and to procure the publishing rights in these for Youmans, who was "to pay said lyric writer the usual and customary royalties on sheet music and mechanical records." Subject to this, Youmans could assign the publication and small performing rights to the music and lyrics as he saw fit. In fact RKO employed two lyric writers, Gus Kahn and the defendant Edward Eliscu, who agreed to assign to RKO certain rights described in a contract dated as of May 25, 1933. Max Dreyfus, principal stockholder of the plaintiff Harms, which has succeeded to his rights, acquired Youmans' reserved rights to the music and was his designee for the assignment with respect to the lyrics. Allegedly—and his denial of this is a prime subject of dispute—Eliscu then entered into an agreement dated June 30, 1933, assigning his rights to the existing and renewal copyrights to Dreyfus in return for certain royalties.

When the copyrights were about to expire, proper renewal applications were made by the children of Youmans, by the widow and children of Kahn, and by Eliscu. The two former groups executed assignments of their rights in the renewal copyrights to Harms. But Eliscu, by an instrument dated February 19, 1962, recorded in the Copyright Office, assigned his rights in the renewal copyrights to defendant Ross Jungnickel, Inc., subject to a judicial determination of his ownership. Thereafter Eliscu's lawyer advised ASCAP and one Harry Fox—respectively the agents for the small performing rights and the mechanical recording license fees—that Eliscu had become vested with a half interest in the renewal copyrights and that any future payments which failed to reflect his interest would be made at their own risk; at the same time he demanded an accounting from Harms. Finally, Eliscu brought an action in the New York Supreme Court for a declaration that he owned a one-third interest in the renewal copyrights and for an accounting.

Harms then began the instant action in the District Court for the Southern District of New York for equitable and declaratory relief against Eliscu and Jungnickel. Jurisdiction was predicated on 28 U.S.C. § 1338; plaintiff alleged its own New York incorporation and did not allege the citizenship of the defendants, which concededly is in New York. Defendants moved to dismiss the complaint for failure to state a claim on which relief can be granted and for lack of federal jurisdiction; voluminous affidavits were submitted. The district court dismissed the complaint for want of federal jurisdiction * * *.

In line with what apparently were the arguments of the parties, Judge Weinfeld treated the jurisdictional issue as turning solely on whether the complaint alleged any act or threat of copyright infringement. He was right in concluding it did not. Infringement, as used in copyright law, does not include everything that may impair the value of the copyright; it is doing one or more of those things which * * * the Act * * * reserves exclusively to the copyright owner. * * *

Although Chief Justice Marshall, construing the "arising under" language in the context of Article III of the Constitution, indicated in Osborn v. Bank of the United States * * * that the grant extended to every case in which federal law furnished a necessary ingredient of the claim even though this was antecedent and uncontested, the Supreme Court has long given a narrower meaning to the "arising under" language in statutes defining the jurisdiction of the lower federal courts. * * * If the ingredient theory of Article III had been carried over to the general grant of federal question jurisdiction now contained in 28 U.S.C. § 1331, there would have been no basis—to take a well-known example—why federal courts should not have jurisdiction as to all disputes over the many western land titles originating in a federal patent, even though the controverted questions normally are of fact or of local land law. Quite sensibly, such extensive jurisdiction has been denied. * * *

The cases dealing with statutory jurisdiction over patents and copyrights have taken the same conservative line. * * * Just as with western land titles, the federal grant of a patent or copyright has not been thought to infuse with any national interest a dispute as to ownership or contractual enforcement turning on the facts or on ordinary principles of contract law. Indeed, the case for an unexpansive reading of the provision conferring exclusive jurisdiction with respect to patents and copyrights has been especially strong since expansion would entail depriving the state courts of any jurisdiction over matters having so little federal significance.

In an endeavor to explain precisely what suits arose under the patent and copyright laws, Mr. Justice Holmes stated that "[a] suit arises under the law that creates the cause of action"; in the case *sub judice,* injury to a business involving slander of a patent, he said, "whether it is a wrong or not depends upon the law of the State where the act is done" so that the suit did not arise under the patent laws. American Well Works Co. v. Layne & Bowler Co. * * *

The Holmes "creation" test explains the taking of federal jurisdiction in a great many cases, notably copyright and patent infringement actions, both clearly authorized by the respective federal acts, * * * and thus unquestionably within the scope of 28 U.S.C. § 1338; indeed, in the many infringement suits that depend only on some point of fact and require no construction of federal law, no other explanation may exist.

Harms' claim is not within Holmes' definition. The relevant statutes create no explicit right of action to enforce or rescind assignments of copyrights, nor does any copyright statute specify a cause of action to fix the locus of ownership. To be sure, not every federal cause of action springs from an express mandate of Congress; federal civil claims have been "inferred" from federal statutes making behavior criminal or otherwise regulating it. * * * Such statutes invariably impose a federal duty and usually create some express remedy as well, while the relevant copyright provision merely authorizes an assignment by written instrument, 17 U.S.C. § 28. * * *

It has come to be realized that Mr. Justice Holmes' formula is more useful for inclusion than for the exclusion for which it was intended. Even though the claim is created by state law, a case may "arise under" a law of the United States if the complaint discloses a need for determining the meaning or application of such a law. * * * But Harms likewise does not meet this test. The crucial issue is whether or not Eliscu executed the assignment to Dreyfus; possibly the interpretation of the initial May, 1933, contract is also relevant, but if any aspect of the suit requires an interpretation of the Copyright Act, the complaint does not reveal it.

* * *

Mindful of the hazards of formulation in this treacherous area, we think that an action "arises under" the Copyright Act if and only if the complaint is for a remedy expressly granted by the Act, e.g., a suit for infringement or for the statutory royalties for record reproduction, * * * or asserts a claim requiring construction of the Act, * * * or, at the very least and perhaps more doubtfully, presents a case where a distinctive policy of the Act requires that federal principles control the disposition of the claim. The general interest that copyrights, like all other forms of property, should be enjoyed by their true owner is not enough to meet this last test.

* * *

Affirmed.

Notes and Questions

1. Would a congressional statute conferring federal-question jurisdiction over a case like *Harms* be constitutional? In this regard, consider Chief Justice Marshall's opinion in *Osborn*.

2. SMITH v. KANSAS CITY TITLE & TRUST CO., 255 U.S. 180, 41 S.Ct. 243, 65 L.Ed. 577 (1921), provides an example of a claim that, although created by state law, "arises under" a law of the United States by virtue of requiring a determination of the meaning or application of such law. In *Kansas City Title*, a shareholder sued to enjoin the Trust Company, a Missouri corporation, from

investing in certain federal bonds on the ground that the Act of Congress authorizing their issuance was unconstitutional. The plaintiff claimed that under Missouri law an investment in securities the issuance of which had not been authorized by a valid law was *ultra vires* and enjoinable. The cause of action was thus state-created. Nonetheless, the Supreme Court held that the action "arose under" federal law.

> The general rule is that where it appears from the bill or statement of the plaintiff that the right to relief depends upon the construction or application of the Constitution or laws of the United States, and that such federal claim is not merely colorable, and rests upon a reasonable foundation, the District Court has jurisdiction. * * *

Id. at 199, 41 S.Ct. at 245, 65 L.Ed. at 585. Justice Holmes dissented on the ground that the cause of action had been created by state law and not by federal law, and, therefore, did not "arise under" federal law.

The holding of *Smith*, however, appears to be contradicted by the Court's later decision in MOORE v. CHESAPEAKE & OHIO RY. CO., 291 U.S. 205, 54 S.Ct. 402, 78 L.Ed. 755 (1934). In *Moore*, plaintiff brought an action under Kentucky's Employer Liability Act, which provided that a plaintiff could not be held responsible for contributory negligence or assumption of risk where his injury resulted from the violation of any state or federal statute enacted for the safety of employees. Plaintiff alleged that his injury was due to the defendant's failure to comply with the Federal Safety Appliance Act. As a result, although the cause of action was state created, an important issue was whether the terms of the federal statute had been violated. The Supreme Court found that federal-question jurisdiction did not exist, holding that:

> a suit brought under the state statute which defines liability to employees who are injured while engaged in intrastate commerce, and brings within the purview of the statute a breach of the duty imposed by the federal statute, should [not] be regarded as a suit arising under the laws of the United States and cognizable in the federal court in the absence of diversity of citizenship.

Id. at 214–15, 54 S.Ct. at 406, 78 L.Ed. at 762. Can the Court's decisions in *Smith* and *Moore* be reconciled?

3. Should all causes of action created by federal law confer federal-question jurisdiction? The Supreme Court addressed this question in SHOSHONE MINING CO. v. RUTTER, 177 U.S. 505, 20 S.Ct. 726, 44 L.Ed. 864 (1900). Congress had established a system which allowed miners to file patents on their claims, and which set up a scheme for settling the conflicting claims of miners. The federal statute provided that the right to possession was to be determined by the "local customs or rules of miners in the several mining districts, so far as the same are applicable and not inconsistent with the laws of the United States." The Court determined:

> Inasmuch * * * as the "adverse suit" to determine the right of possession may not involve any question as to the construction or effect of the Constitution or laws of the United States, but may present simply a question of fact as to the time of the discovery of mineral, the location of the claim on the ground, or a determination of the meaning and effect of certain local rules and customs prescribed by the miners of the district, or the effect of state statutes, it would seem to follow that it is not one which necessarily arises under the Constitution and laws of the United States.

Id. at 509, 20 S.Ct. at 727, 44 L.Ed. at 866. The situation in *Shoshone* is the reverse of *Smith: Smith* arose from a state-created cause of action that turned on issues of federal law, *Shoshone* arose from a federally created cause of action that turned on issues of state law.

4. What types of cases should be heard in the federal courts? In formulating your thoughts on the subject, keep in mind that the character of federal litigation has changed dramatically in the past few decades. To a large degree this stems from fundamental rethinking of the role of the federal government in assuring justice, proper resource allocation, and individual rights. Often these changes are reflected in legislation that provides for public or private rights of actions to vindicate statutory policies. For example, the Civil Rights Act of 1964 and the Voting Rights Act of 1965 have spawned a multitude of cases challenging racial and sex-based discrimination; similarly, the Truth in Lending and Fair Credit Reporting Acts exemplify the federal statutes that have led to the growth of consumer protection litigation. Other incentives to sue have been generated by the federal courts recognizing private rights of action under federal statutes, particularly in the securities and antitrust fields, as well as by showing an increasing sensitivity to due process concerns. What effect should these changes in federal litigation have on the distribution of federal judicial resources?

5. Legislation creating an enforceable private right of action may do so either expressly or by implication. In CORT v. ASH, 422 U.S. 66, 95 S.Ct. 2080, 45 L.Ed.2d 26 (1975), the Supreme Court announced a four-part test for determining whether a private right of action should be implied from a federal statute that does not expressly provide for a private remedy.

> * * * First, is the plaintiff "one of the class for whose *especial* benefit the statute was enacted," * * *—that is, does the statute create a federal right in favor of the plaintiff? Second, is there any indication of legislative intent, explicit or implicit, either to create such a remedy or to deny one? * * * Third, is it consistent with the underlying purposes of the legislative scheme to imply a remedy for the plaintiff? * * * And finally, is the cause of action one traditionally relegated to state law, in an area basically the concern of the States, so that it would be inappropriate to infer a cause of action based solely on federal law? * * *

Id. at 78, 95 S.Ct. at 2088, 45 L.Ed.2d at 36–37. In subsequent cases, however, the Court has stressed that the central inquiry is solely whether Congress intended to create a private right of action and that the four factors discussed in *Cort* merely highlight the evidence relevant to making that determination. See Transamerica Mortgage Advisors, Inc. v. Lewis, 444 U.S. 11, 100 S.Ct. 242, 62 L.Ed.2d 146 (1979).

Implied private rights of action also may arise under the Constitution itself. For example, in BIVENS v. SIX UNKNOWN NAMED AGENTS OF THE FEDERAL BUREAU OF NARCOTICS, 403 U.S. 388, 91 S.Ct. 1999, 29 L.Ed.2d 619 (1971), the Supreme Court held that the Fourth Amendment provides a private cause of action against a federal agent for damages resulting from unreasonable searches and seizures. The Court directed the Court of Appeals to develop the details of the implied remedy on remand. Should the standards for determining whether an implied private right of action exists be different in a case in which the action is based upon the Constitution as contrasted with a case in which it is based upon a statute?

6. Areas in which Congress has given the federal courts exclusive jurisdiction include, *inter alia,* bankruptcy, 28 U.S.C. § 1334, patents and copyrights, 28 U.S.C. § 1338(a), actions against foreign consuls and vice-consuls, 28 U.S.C. § 1351, actions to recover a fine, penalty, or forfeiture under federal law, 28 U.S.C. § 1355, and actions involving certain seizures, 28 U.S.C. § 1356. What factors should motivate Congress in choosing between a grant of concurrent or exclusive jurisdiction? See Note, *Exclusive Jurisdiction of the Federal Courts in Private Civil Actions,* 70 Harv.L.Rev. 509 (1957).

7. As suggested in *Harms,* the notion that a federal court has exclusive jurisdiction often means less than it seems to say. Consider disputes involving patents. In LUCKETT v. DELPARK, INC., 270 U.S. 496, 510–11, 46 S.Ct. 397, 402, 70 L.Ed. 703, 708–09 (1926), the patentee apparently could have sued for infringement of his patent but chose instead to sue for breach of contract. The District Court dismissed for want of jurisdiction, and the Supreme Court affirmed.

> [W]here a patentee complainant makes his suit one for recovery of royalties under a contract of license or assignment, or for damages for a breach of its covenants, or for a specific performance thereof, or asks the aid of the Court in declaring a forfeiture of the license or in restoring an unclouded title to the patent, he does not give the federal district court jurisdiction of the cause as one arising under the patent laws.

What is the point of the grant of exclusive jurisdiction if a plaintiff by artful pleading can choose whether the claim is to be heard in state or federal court?

8. The Supreme Court first promulgated the "artful pleading doctrine" as a challenge to the well-pleaded complaint and master-of-the-complaint rules in Avco Corp. v. Aero Lodge No. 735, 390 U.S. 557, 88 S.Ct. 1235, 20 L.Ed.2d 126 (1968). In that case, the Supreme Court held that a claim pled under state law is deemed to arise under federal law when the state law on which the plaintiff purports to rely is preempted by federal law, and the only possible relief is federal. In these circumstances, the plaintiff may not defeat the defendant's right to removal by failing to plead federal law.

The lower courts attempted to reconcile *Avco* with accepted law by distinguishing between cases in which federal law completely preempts state claims and replaces them with parallel federal claims and cases in which federal preemption extinguishes any state right to relief. The lower courts tended to allow removal only in the former category, see, e.g., Calhoon v. Bonnabel, 560 F.Supp. 101, 107–08 & n. 14 (S.D.N.Y.1982); Neiger v. Sheet Metal Workers Int'l Ass'n, 470 F.Supp. 622, 625–27 (W.D.Mo.1979), a result approved by the Supreme Court in Metropolitan Life Ins. Co. v. Taylor, 481 U.S. 58, 107 S.Ct. 1542, 95 L.Ed.2d 55 (1987). In recent years some federal courts have enlarged the scope of the artful pleading doctrine. However, Professor Robert A. Ragazzo has concluded, "that the artful pleading doctrine is an ill-advised departure from more than a century of established law and should be recanted or limited to the narrowest possible extent." Ragazzo, *Reconsidering the Artful Pleading Doctrine,* 44 Hastings L.J. 273 (1993).

9. A federal court must dismiss a claim arising under federal law for want of subject-matter jurisdiction if the claim is "so attenuated and unsubstantial as to be absolutely devoid of merit." Hagans v. Lavine, 415 U.S. 528, 536, 94 S.Ct. 1372, 1379, 39 L.Ed.2d 577, 587 (1974). It similarly must dismiss for want of jurisdiction if the claim clearly is foreclosed by prior decisions of the Supreme Court. Levering & Garrigues Co. v. Morrin, 289 U.S. 103, 105, 53 S.Ct. 549, 550, 77 L.Ed. 1062,

1064 (1933). The test for dismissal is a rigorous one and, if there is any foundation of plausibility to the claim, federal jurisdiction exists.

MERRELL DOW PHARMACEUTICALS INC. v. THOMPSON

Supreme Court of the United States, 1986.
478 U.S. 804, 106 S.Ct. 3229, 92 L.Ed.2d 650.

Certiorari to the United States Court of Appeals for the Sixth Circuit.

JUSTICE STEVENS delivered the opinion of the Court.

The question presented is whether the incorporation of a federal standard in a state-law private action, when Congress has intended that there not be a federal private action for violations of that federal standard, makes the action one "arising under the Constitution, laws, or treaties of the United States," 28 U.S.C. § 1331.

I

The Thompson respondents are residents of Canada and the MacTavishes reside in Scotland. They filed virtually identical complaints against petitioner, a corporation, that manufactures and distributes the drug Bendectin. The complaints were filed in the Court of Common Pleas in Hamilton County, Ohio. Each complaint alleged that a child was born with multiple deformities as a result of the mother's ingestion of Bendectin during pregnancy. In five of the six counts, the recovery of substantial damages was requested on common-law theories of negligence, breach of warranty, strict liability, fraud, and gross negligence. In Count IV, respondents alleged that the drug Bendectin was "misbranded" in violation of the Federal Food, Drug, and Cosmetic Act (FDCA), * * * because its labeling did not provide adequate warning that its use was potentially dangerous. Paragraph 26 alleged that the violation of the FDCA "in the promotion" of Bendectin "constitutes a rebuttable presumption of negligence." Paragraph 27 alleged that the "violation of said federal statutes directly and proximately caused the injuries suffered" by the two infants. * * *.

Petitioner filed a timely petition for removal from the state court to the Federal District Court alleging that the action was "founded, in part, on an alleged claim arising under the laws of the United States." After removal, the two cases were consolidated. Respondents filed a motion to remand to the state forum on the ground that the federal court lacked subject-matter jurisdiction. Relying on our decision in Smith v. Kansas City Title & Trust Co., * * * the District Court held that Count IV of the complaint alleged a cause of action arising under federal law and denied the motion to remand. It then granted petitioner's motion to dismiss on *forum non conveniens* grounds.

The Court of Appeals for the Sixth Circuit reversed. * * * [N]oting "that the FDCA does not create or imply a private right of action for individuals injured as a result of violations of the Act," it explained:

"Federal question jurisdiction would, thus, exist only if plaintiffs' right to relief *depended necessarily* on a substantial question of federal law. Plaintiffs' causes of action referred to the FDCA merely as one available criterion for determining whether Merrell Dow was negligent. Because the jury could find negligence on the part of Merrell Dow without finding a violation of the FDCA, the plaintiffs' causes of action did not depend necessarily upon a question of federal law. Consequently, the causes of action did not arise under federal law and, therefore, were improperly removed to federal court." * * *.

We granted certiorari, * * * and we now affirm.

II

* * *

* * * [T]he propriety of the removal in this case * * * turns on whether the case falls within the original "federal question" jurisdiction of the federal courts. There is no "single, precise definition" of that concept * * *. * * * This much, however, is clear. The "vast majority" of cases that come within this grant of jurisdiction are covered by Justice Holmes' statement that a " 'suit arises under the law that creates the cause of action.' " * * * American Well Works Co. v. Layne & Bowler Co. * * *. Thus, the vast majority of cases brought under the general federal-question jurisdiction of the federal courts are those in which federal law creates the cause of action. * * * We have, however, also noted that a case may arise under federal law "where the vindication of a right under state law necessarily turned on some construction of federal law." [See, e.g., Smith v. Kansas City Title & Trust Co., Note 2, p. 286, supra.]

This case does not pose a federal question of the first kind; respondents do not allege that federal law creates any of the causes of action that they have asserted. This case thus poses what Justice Frankfurter called the "litigation-provoking problem," * * *—the presence of a federal issue in a state-created cause of action.

* * *

In this case, both parties agree with the Court of Appeals' conclusion that there is no federal cause of action for FDCA violations. For purposes of our decision, we assume that this is a correct interpretation of the FDCA. Thus, as the case comes to us, it is appropriate to assume that, under the settled framework for evaluating whether a federal cause of action lies, some combination of the following factors is present: (1) the plaintiffs are not part of the class for whose special benefit the statute was passed; (2) the indicia of legislative intent reveal no congressional purpose to provide a private cause of action; (3) a federal cause of action would not further the underlying purposes of the legislative scheme; and (4) the respondents' cause of action is a subject traditionally relegated to state law. [See Cort v. Ash, Note 5, p. 288, supra.] In short, Congress did not intend a private federal remedy for violations of the statute that it enacted.

This is the first case in which we have reviewed this type of jurisdictional claim in light of these factors. * * * The recent * * * development [of this framework] does not, however, diminish its importance. Indeed, the very reasons for the development of the modern implied remedy doctrine—the "increased complexity of federal legislation and the increased volume of federal litigation," as well as "the desirability of a more careful scrutiny of legislative intent" * * *—are precisely the kind of considerations that should inform the concern for "practicality and necessity" * * * when jurisdiction is asserted because of the presence of a federal issue in a state cause of action.

The significance of the necessary assumption that there is no federal private cause of action thus cannot be overstated. For the ultimate import of such a conclusion, as we have repeatedly emphasized, is that it would flout congressional intent to provide a private federal remedy for the violation of the federal statute. We think it would similarly flout, or at least undermine, congressional intent to conclude that the federal courts might nevertheless exercise federal-question jurisdiction and provide remedies for violations of that federal statute solely because the violation of the federal statute is said to be a "rebuttable presumption" or a "proximate cause" under state law, rather than a federal action under federal law.

III

Petitioner advances three arguments to support its position that, even in the face of this congressional preclusion of a federal cause of action for a violation of the federal statute, federal-question jurisdiction may lie for the violation of the federal statute as an element of a state cause of action.

First, petitioner contends that the case represents a straightforward application of the statement * * * that federal-question jurisdiction is appropriate when "it appears that some substantial, disputed question of federal law is a necessary element of one of the well-pleaded state claims." * * * [H]owever, * * * the long-settled understanding [has been] that the mere presence of a federal issue in a state cause of action does not automatically confer federal-question jurisdiction. * * *

* * * Given the significance of the assumed congressional determination to preclude federal private remedies, the presence of the federal issue as an element of the state tort is not the kind of adjudication for which jurisdiction would serve congressional purposes and the federal system. * * *. We simply conclude that the congressional determination that there should be no federal remedy for the violation of this federal statute is tantamount to a congressional conclusion that the presence of a claimed violation of the statute as an element of a state cause of action is insufficiently "substantial" to confer federal-question jurisdiction.[12]

Second, petitioner contends that there is a powerful federal interest in seeing that the federal statute is given uniform interpretations, and that

---

12. Several commentators have suggested that our § 1331 decisions can best be understood as an evaluation of the *nature* of the federal interest at stake. * * *

Focusing on the nature of the federal interest, moreover, suggests that the widely perceived "irreconcilable" conflict between the finding of federal jurisdiction in Smith v. Kansas City Title & Trust Co., * * * and the finding of no jurisdiction in Moore v. Chesapeake & Ohio R. Co. [Note 2, p. 287, supra], * * * is far from clear. For the difference in result can be seen as manifestations of the differences in the nature of the federal issues at stake. In *Smith,* as the Court emphasized,

the issue was the constitutionality of an important federal statute. * * *. In *Moore,* in contrast, the Court emphasized that the violation of the federal standard as an element of state tort recovery did not fundamentally change the state tort nature of the action. * * *.

The importance of the nature of the federal issue in federal-question jurisdiction is highlighted by the fact that, despite the usual reliability of the Holmes test as an inclusionary principle, this Court has sometimes found that formally federal causes of action were not properly brought under federal-question jurisdiction because of the overwhelming predominance of state-law issues. See * * * Shoshone federal review is the best way of insuring such uniformity. * * * To the extent that petitioner is arguing that state use and interpretation of the FDCA pose a threat to the order and stability of the FDCA regime, petitioner should be arguing, not that federal courts should be able to review and enforce state FDCA-based causes of action as an aspect of federal-question jurisdiction, but that the FDCA pre-empts state-court jurisdiction over the issue in dispute. Petitioner's concern about the uniformity of interpretation, moreover, is considerably mitigated by the fact that, even if there is no original district court jurisdiction for these kinds of action, this Court retains power to review the decision of a federal issue in a state cause of action.

Finally, petitioner argues that, whatever the general rule, there are special circumstances that justify federal-question jurisdiction in this case. Petitioner emphasizes that it is unclear whether the FDCA applies to sales in Canada and Scotland; there is, therefore, a special reason for having a federal court answer the novel federal question relating to the extraterritorial meaning of the Act. We reject this argument. We do not believe the question whether a particular claim arises under federal law depends on the novelty of the federal issue. * * * The novelty of an FDCA issue is not sufficient to give it status as a federal cause of action; nor should it be sufficient to give a state-based FDCA claim status as a jurisdiction-triggering federal question.

IV

We conclude that a complaint alleging a violation of a federal statute as an element of a state cause of action, when Congress has determined that there should be no private, federal cause of action for the violation, does not state a claim "arising under the Constitution, laws, or treaties of the United States." 28 U.S.C. § 1331.

The judgment of the Court of Appeals is affirmed.

It is so ordered.

JUSTICE BRENNAN, with whom JUSTICE WHITE, JUSTICE MARSHALL, and JUSTICE BLACKMUN join, dissenting.

* * *

I

While the majority of cases covered by § 1331 may well be described by Justice Holmes' adage that "[a] suit arises under the law that creates the cause of action," * * * it is firmly settled that there may be federal-question jurisdiction even though both the right asserted and the remedy sought by the plaintiff are state created. [See, e.g., Smith v. Kansas City Title & Trust Co.] * * *

The continuing vitality of *Smith* is beyond challenge. We have cited it approvingly on numerous occasions, and reaffirmed its holding several times * * *. Moreover, in addition to Judge Friendly's authoritative opinion in T.B. Harms Co. v. Eliscu, * * * *Smith* has been widely cited and followed in the lower federal courts. * * *. Furthermore, the principle of the *Smith* case has been recognized and endorsed by most commentators as well. * * *.[1]

Mining Co. v. Rutter [Note 3, p. 287, supra] * * *.

1. * * * In one sense, the Court is correct in asserting that we can reconcile *Smith* and

Moore on the ground that the "nature" of the federal interest was more significant in *Smith* than in *Moore*. Indeed, as the Court appears to believe, * * * we could reconcile many of the

There is, to my mind, no question that there is federal jurisdiction over the respondents' fourth cause of action under the rule set forth in *Smith* * * *. Respondents pleaded that petitioner's labeling of the drug Bendectin constituted "misbranding" in violation of * * * the Federal Food, Drug, and Cosmetic Act (FDCA), * * * and that this violation "directly and proximately caused" their injuries. * * *. Respondents asserted in the complaint that this violation established petitioner's negligence *per se* and entitled them to recover damages without more. * * *. No other basis for finding petitioner negligent was asserted in connection with this claim. As pleaded, then, respondents' "right to relief depend[ed] upon the construction or application of the Constitution or laws of the United States." *Smith* * * *. * * * [Furthermore, p]etitioner's principal defense is that the Act does not govern the branding of drugs that are sold in foreign countries. It is certainly not immediately obvious whether this argument is correct. Thus, the statutory question is one which "discloses a need for determining the meaning or application of [the FDCA]," T.B. Harms Co. v. Eliscu, * * * and the claim raised by the fourth cause of action is one "arising under" federal law within the meaning of § 1331.

II

* * * According to the Court, if we assume that Congress did not intend that there be a private federal cause of action under a particular federal law (and, presumably, *a fortiori* if Congress' decision not to create a private remedy is express), we must also assume that Congress did not intend that there be federal jurisdiction over a state cause of action that is determined by that federal law. Therefore, assuming—only because the parties have made a similar assumption—that there is no private cause of action under the FDCA, the Court holds that there is no federal jurisdiction over the plaintiffs' claim * * * * * *.

The Court nowhere explains the basis for this conclusion. Yet it is hardly self-evident. Why should the fact that Congress chose not to create a private federal *remedy* mean that Congress would not want there to be federal *jurisdiction* to adjudicate a state claim that imposes liability for violating the federal law? Clearly, the decision not to provide a private federal remedy should not affect federal jurisdiction unless the reasons Congress withholds a federal remedy are also reasons for withholding federal jurisdiction. Thus, it is necessary to examine the reasons for Congress' decisions to grant or withhold

seemingly inconsistent results that have been reached under § 1331 with such a test. But this is so only because a test based upon an ad hoc evaluation of the importance of the federal issue is infinitely malleable: at what point does a federal interest become strong enough to create jurisdiction? What principles guide the determination whether a statute is "important" or not? * * * The point is that if one makes the test sufficiently vague and general, virtually any set of results can be "reconciled." * * *

My own view is in accord with those commentators who view the results in *Smith* and

Moore as irreconcilable. * * *. That fact does not trouble me greatly, however, for I view *Moore* as having been a "sport" at the time it was decided and having long been in a state of innocuous desuetude. Unlike the jurisdictional holding in *Smith*, the jurisdictional holding in *Moore* has never been relied upon or even cited by this Court. * * * *Moore* simply has not survived the test of time; it is presently moribund, and, to the extent that it is inconsistent with the well-established rule of the *Smith* case, it ought to be overruled.

both federal jurisdiction and private remedies, something the Court has not done.

A

In the early days of our Republic, Congress was content to leave the task of interpreting and applying federal laws in the first instance to the state courts; with one short-lived exception, Congress did not grant the inferior federal courts original jurisdiction over cases arising under federal law until 1875. * * *. The reasons Congress found it necessary to add this jurisdiction to the district courts are well known. First, Congress recognized "the importance, and even necessity of *uniformity* of decisions throughout the whole United States, upon all subjects within the purview of the constitution." Martin v. Hunter's Lessee, [1 Wheat. 304, 347–48 (1816)] (Story, J.) (emphasis in original). * * *. Concededly, because federal jurisdiction is not always exclusive and because federal courts may disagree with one another, absolute uniformity has not been obtained even under § 1331. However, while perfect uniformity may not have been achieved, experience indicates that the availability of a federal forum in federal-question cases has done much to advance that goal. * * *

In addition, § 1331 has provided for adjudication in a forum that specializes in federal law and that is therefore more likely to apply that law correctly. Because federal-question cases constitute the basic grist for federal tribunals, "[t]he federal courts have acquired a considerable expertness in the interpretation and application of federal law." * * * As a result, the federal courts are comparatively more skilled at interpreting and applying federal law, and are much more likely correctly to divine Congress' intent in enacting legislation.[6] * * *

These reasons for having original federal-question jurisdiction explain why cases like this one and *Smith*—*i.e.*, cases where the cause of action is a creature of state law, but an essential element of the claim is federal—"arise under" federal law within the meaning of § 1331. Congress passes laws in order to shape behavior; a federal law expresses Congress' determination that there is a federal interest in having individuals or other entities conform their actions to a particular norm established by that law. Because all laws are imprecise to some degree, disputes inevitably arise over what specifically Congress intended to require or permit. It is the duty of courts to interpret these laws and apply them in such a way that the congressional purpose is realized. * * *

B

The only remaining question is whether the assumption that Congress decided not to create a private cause of action alters this analysis in a way that makes it inappropriate to exercise original federal jurisdiction. According to the Court, "the very reasons for the development of the modern implied

---

6. * * * One might argue that this Court's appellate jurisdiction over state-court judgments in cases arising under federal law can be depended upon to correct erroneous state-court decisions and to insure that federal law is interpreted and applied uniformly. However, * * * having served on this Court for 30 years, it is clear to me that, realistically, it cannot even come close to "doing the whole job" and that § 1331 is essential if federal rights are to be adequately protected.

remedy doctrine" support the conclusion that, where the legislative history of a particular law shows (whether expressly or by inference) that Congress intended that there be no private federal remedy, it must also mean that Congress would not want federal courts to exercise jurisdiction over a state-law claim making violations of that federal law actionable. * * *. These reasons are " 'the increased complexity of federal legislation,' " " 'the increased volume of federal litigation,' " and " 'the desirability of a more careful scrutiny of legislative intent.' " * * *.

These reasons simply do not justify the Court's holding. Given the relative expertise of the federal courts in interpreting federal law, * * * the increased complexity of federal legislation argues rather strongly in *favor* of recognizing federal jurisdiction. And, while the increased volume of litigation may appropriately be considered in connection with reasoned arguments that justify limiting the reach of § 1331, I do not believe that the day has yet arrived when this Court may trim a statute solely because it thinks that Congress made it too broad.

This leaves only the third reason: " 'the desirability of a more careful scrutiny of legislative intent.' " * * * I certainly subscribe to the proposition that the Court should consider legislative intent in determining whether or not there is jurisdiction under § 1331. But the Court has not examined the purposes underlying either the FDCA or § 1331 in reaching its conclusion that Congress' presumed decision not to provide a private federal remedy under the FDCA must be taken to withdraw federal jurisdiction over a private state remedy that imposes liability for violating the FDCA. Moreover, such an examination demonstrates not only that it is consistent with legislative intent to find that there is federal jurisdiction over such a claim, but, indeed, that it is the Court's contrary conclusion that is inconsistent with congressional intent.

* * * Congress has provided the [Food and Drug Administration (FDA)] with a wide-ranging arsenal of weapons to combat violations of the FDCA * * *. Significantly, [however,] the FDA has no independent enforcement authority; final enforcement must come from the federal courts, which have exclusive jurisdiction over actions under the FDCA. * * *. Thus, while the initial interpretive function has been delegated to an expert administrative body whose interpretations are entitled to considerable deference, final responsibility for interpreting the statute in order to carry out the legislative mandate belongs to the federal courts. * * *.

Given that Congress structured the FDCA so that all express remedies are provided by the federal courts, it seems rather strange to conclude that it either "flout[s]" or "undermine[s]" congressional intent for the federal courts to adjudicate a private state-law remedy that is based upon violating the FDCA. * * *

It may be that a decision by Congress not to create a private remedy is intended to preclude all private enforcement. If that is so, then a state cause of action that makes relief available to private individuals for violations of the FDCA is pre-empted. But if Congress' decision not to provide a private federal remedy does *not* pre-empt such a state remedy, then, in light of the FDCA's clear policy of relying on the federal courts for enforcement, it also should not foreclose federal jurisdiction over that state remedy. * * *

The Court's contrary conclusion requires inferring from Congress' decision not to create a private federal remedy that, while some private enforcement is permissible in state courts, it is "bad" if that enforcement comes from the *federal* courts. But that is simply illogical. * * * [I]f anything, Congress' decision not to create a private remedy *strengthens* the argument in favor of finding federal jurisdiction over a state remedy that is not pre-empted.

Notes and Questions

1. Both Justice Stevens and Justice Brennan attempt to "fit" their *Merrell Dow* opinions within the Court's earlier decisions in *Smith* and *Moore*. Does either succeed? How would you have decided *Merrell Dow* in light of these earlier decisions? In this regard, also consider Justice Stevens' attempt to harmonize the *Shoshone* decision with *Smith, Moore,* and *Merrell Dow*.

2. Is *Smith* still good law after *Merrell Dow*? Is *Moore*? *Shoshone*? Or have all three cases been overruled to the extent that they express categorical rules, and affirmed to the extent that they turn on a weighing of the federal interests involved? See Smith v. Industrial Valley Title Ins. Co., 957 F.2d 90 (3d Cir.) (following *Merrell Dow* and holding that the incorporation of a federal law into a state-created cause of action does not present a federal question), certiorari denied 505 U.S. 1221, 112 S.Ct. 3034, 120 L.Ed.2d 903 (1992); Clark v. Velsicol Chem. Corp., 944 F.2d 196 (4th Cir.1991) (same), certiorari denied 502 U.S. 1096, 112 S.Ct. 1173, 117 L.Ed.2d 418 (1992).

3. Justice Stevens argues that it would be inconsistent for the Court to find that Congress did not intend for an implied private right of action to exist and, at the same time, to allow the federal court to hear a state-created cause of action addressing the same issue. On this view, the only way the federal court in *Merrell Dow* would have had jurisdiction would have been if Congress had created an express cause of action. How does this differ, if at all, from Justice Holmes' test?

4. Justice Brennan argues that *Merrell Dow* is a case in which federal jurisdiction should exist even though the cause of action is state-created. Consider anew whether a state-created claim ever can be said to "arise under" federal law in light of Justice Holmes' dissent in *Smith*.

It is evident that the cause of action arises not under any law of the United States but wholly under Missouri law. The defendant is a Missouri corporation and the right claimed is that of a stockholder to prevent the directors from doing an act, that is, making an investment, alleged to be contrary to their duty. But the scope of their duty depends upon the charter of their corporation and other laws of Missouri. If those laws had authorized the investment in terms the plaintiff would have no case, and this seems to me to make manifest what I am unable to deem even debatable, that, as I have said, the cause of action arises wholly under Missouri law. If the Missouri law authorizes or forbids the investment according to the determination of this Court upon a point under the Constitution or acts of Congress, still that point is material only because the Missouri law saw fit to make it so. The whole foundation of the duty is Missouri law, which at its sole will incorporated the other law as it might incorporate a document. The other law or document depends for its relevance and effect not on its own force but upon the law that took it up, so I repeat once more the cause of action arises wholly from the law of the State.

Smith v. Kansas City Title & Trust Co., 255 U.S. at 214, 41 S.Ct. at 250, 65 L.Ed. at 591 (Holmes, J., dissenting). Compare Justice Holmes' statutory interpretation of the words "arising under" with Justice Marshall's constitutional interpretation of the same words.

5. Professor Cohen has argued that the search for "a single, all-purpose, neutral analytical concept which marks out federal question jurisdiction" is futile. He suggests a "pragmatic" test that would include consideration of the extent of the effect of the court's caseload if jurisdiction is recognized, the extent to which a class of cases is likely to turn on issues of state or federal law, the extent to which the federal courts would have expertise in the area, and the extent to which a sympathetic tribunal is necessary. Cohen, *The Broken Compass: The Requirement that a Case Arise "Directly" Under Federal Law*, 115 U.Pa.L.Rev. 890 (1967). See also Shapiro, *Jurisdiction and Discretion*, 60 N.Y.U.L.Rev. 543 (1985). How does this approach differ from Justice Stevens' approach in *Merrell Dow?*

SECTION D. THE SUBJECT–MATTER JURISDICTION OF THE FEDERAL COURTS— SUPPLEMENTAL CLAIMS AND PARTIES

Sometimes a federal court may decide matters that, if presented independently, would not provide a basis for federal subject-matter jurisdiction. The judicially created doctrines of pendent and ancillary jurisdiction describe two such situations. The term "pendent jurisdiction" has been used when the plaintiff, in her complaint, appends a claim lacking an independent basis for federal subject-matter jurisdiction to a claim possessing such a basis. The term "ancillary jurisdiction" has been used when either a plaintiff or a defendant injects a claim lacking an independent basis for jurisdiction by way of a counterclaim, cross-claim, or third-party complaint. Although these doctrines were spawned from two separate lines of authorities, they became two species of the same generic phenomenon. In 1990, when Congress undertook to codify these doctrines in statutory form, it gave them the collective name of "supplemental jurisdiction." In analyzing these doctrines, consider what constitutional barriers there are to the assertion of jurisdiction over such claims, as well as what nonconstitutional factors should be considered in determining whether jurisdiction should be asserted over them. Finally, consider the way these doctrines have and have not been codified by 28 U.S.C. § 1367.

UNITED MINE WORKERS OF AMERICA v. GIBBS

Supreme Court of the United States, 1966.
383 U.S. 715, 86 S.Ct. 1130, 16 L.Ed.2d 218.

Certiorari to the United States Court of Appeals for the Sixth Circuit.

MR. JUSTICE BRENNAN delivered the opinion of the Court.

Respondent Paul Gibbs was awarded compensatory and punitive damages in this action against petitioner United Mine Workers of America (UMW) for alleged violations of § 303 of the Labor Management Relations Act, 1947, and of the common law of Tennessee. The case grew out of the rivalry between the

United Mine Workers and the Southern Labor Union over representation of workers in the southern Appalachian coal fields. Tennessee Consolidated Coal Company, not a party here, laid off 100 miners of the UMW's Local 5881 when it closed one of its mines in southern Tennessee during the spring of 1960. Late that summer, Grundy Company, a wholly owned subsidiary of Consolidated, hired respondent as mine superintendent to attempt to open a new mine on Consolidated's property at nearby Gray's Creek through use of members of the Southern Labor Union. As part of the arrangement, Grundy also gave respondent a contract to haul the mine's coal to the nearest railroad loading point.

On August 15 and 16, 1960, armed members of Local 5881 forcibly prevented the opening of the mine, threatening respondent and beating an organizer for the rival union. The members of the local believed Consolidated had promised them the jobs at the new mine; they insisted that if anyone would do the work, they would. * * * George Gilbert, the UMW's field representative for the area including Local 5881, * * * [had] explicit instructions from his international union superiors to establish a limited picket line, to prevent any further violence, and to see to it that the strike did not spread to neighboring mines. There was no further violence at the mine site * * *.

Respondent lost his job as superintendent, and never entered into performance of his haulage contract. He testified that he soon began to lose other trucking contracts and mine leases he held in nearby areas. Claiming these effects to be the result of a concerted union plan against him, he sought recovery not against Local 5881 or its members, but only against petitioner, the International. The suit was brought in the United States District Court for the Eastern District of Tennessee, and jurisdiction was premised on allegations of secondary boycotts under § 303. The state law claim, for which jurisdiction was based upon the doctrine of pendent jurisdiction, asserted "an unlawful conspiracy and an unlawful boycott aimed at him and [Grundy] to maliciously, wantonly and willfully interfere with his contract of employment and with his contract of haulage."

* * * The jury's verdict was that the UMW had violated both § 303 and state law. Gibbs was awarded $60,000 as damages under the employment contract and $14,500 under the haulage contract; he was also awarded $100,000 punitive damages. On motion, the trial court set aside the award of damages with respect to the haulage contract on the ground that damage was unproved. It also held that union pressure on Grundy to discharge respondent as supervisor would constitute only a primary dispute with Grundy, as respondent's employer, and hence was not cognizable under § 303. Interference with employment was cognizable as a state claim, however, and a remitted award was sustained on the state law claim. * * * The Court of Appeals for the Sixth Circuit affirmed. * * * We granted certiorari. * * *

I.

A threshold question is whether the District Court properly entertained jurisdiction of the claim based on Tennessee law. * * *

* * * The Court held in Hurn v. Oursler, 289 U.S. 238, 53 S.Ct. 586, 77 L.Ed. 1148, that state law claims are appropriate for federal court determination if they form a separate but parallel ground for relief also sought in a

substantial claim based on federal law. The Court distinguished permissible from non-permissible exercises of federal judicial power over state law claims by contrasting "a case where two distinct grounds in support of a single cause of action are alleged, one only of which presents a federal question, and a case where two separate and distinct causes of action are alleged, one only of which is federal in character. In the former, where the federal question averred is not plainly wanting in substance, the federal court, even though the federal ground be not established, may nevertheless retain and dispose of the case upon the nonfederal *ground;* in the latter it may not do so upon the nonfederal *cause of action.*" 289 U.S., at 246, 53 S.Ct., at 589. The question is into which category the present action fell.

Hurn was decided in 1933, before the unification of law and equity by the Federal Rules of Civil Procedure. At the time, the meaning of "cause of action" was a subject of serious dispute * * *. The Court in *Hurn* identified what it meant by the term by citation of Baltimore S.S. Co. v. Phillips, 274 U.S. 316, 47 S.Ct. 600, 71 L.Ed. 1069, a case in which "cause of action" had been used to identify the operative scope of the doctrine of *res judicata*. In that case the Court had noted that " 'the whole tendency of our decisions is to require a plaintiff to try his whole cause of action and his whole case at one time,' " 274 U.S., at 320, 47 S.Ct., at 602, and stated its holding in the following language, quoted in part in the *Hurn* opinion:

> Upon principle, it is perfectly plain that the respondent [a seaman suing for an injury sustained while working aboard ship] suffered but one actionable wrong, and was entitled to but one recovery, whether his injury was due to one or the other of several distinct acts of alleged negligence, or to a combination of some or all of them. In either view, there would be but a single wrongful invasion of a single primary right of the plaintiff, namely, the right of bodily safety, whether the acts constituting such invasion were one or many, simple or complex.

> A cause of action does not consist of facts, but of the unlawful violation of a right which the facts show. The number and variety of the facts alleged do not establish more than one cause of action so long as their result, whether they be considered severally or in combination, is the violation of but one right by a single legal wrong. The mere multiplication of grounds of negligence alleged as causing the same injury does not result in multiplying the causes of action. "The facts are merely the means, and not the end. They do not constitute the cause of action, but they show its existence by making the wrong appear." Id., at 321, 47 S.Ct. at 602.

Had the Court found a jurisdictional bar to reaching the state claim in *Hurn,* we assume that the doctrine of *res judicata* would not have been applicable in any subsequent state suit. But the citation of *Baltimore S.S. Co.* shows that the Court found that the weighty policies of judicial economy and fairness to parties reflected in *res judicata* doctrine were in themselves strong counsel for the adoption of a rule which would permit federal courts to dispose of the state as well as the federal claims.

With the adoption of the Federal Rules of Civil Procedure and the unified form of action * * * much of the controversy over "cause of action" abated. The phrase remained as the keystone of the *Hurn* test, however, and * * *

[handwritten margin note: issue has been definitively settled by judicial decision, barring same parties from litigating 2nd suit on same claim.]

has been the source of considerable confusion. Under the Rules, the impulse is toward entertaining the broadest possible scope of action consistent with fairness to the parties; joinder of claims, parties and remedies are strongly encouraged. Yet because the *Hurn* question involves issues of jurisdiction as well as convenience, there has been some tendency to limit its application to cases in which the state and federal claims are, as in *Hurn,* "little more than the equivalent of different epithets to characterize the same group of circumstances." 289 U.S., at 246, 53 S.Ct. at 590.

This limited approach is unnecessarily grudging. Pendent jurisdiction, in the sense of judicial *power,* exists whenever there is a claim "arising under [the] Constitution, the Laws of the United States, and Treaties made, or which shall be made, under their Authority * * *," U.S. Const., Art. III, § 2, and the relationship between that claim and the state claims made in the complaint permits the conclusion that the entire action before the court comprises but one constitutional "case." The federal claim must have substance sufficient to confer subject matter jurisdiction on the court. Levering & Garrigues Co. v. Morrin, 289 U.S. 103, 53 S.Ct. 549, 77 L.Ed. 1062. The state and federal claims must derive from a common nucleus of operative fact. But if, considered without regard for their federal or state character, a plaintiff's claims are such that he would ordinarily be expected to try them all in one judicial proceeding, then, assuming substantiality of the federal issues, there is *power* in federal courts to hear the whole.

That power need not be exercised in every case in which it is found to exist. It has consistently been recognized that pendent jurisdiction is a doctrine of discretion, not of plaintiff's right. Its justification lies in considerations of judicial economy, convenience and fairness to litigants; if these are not present a federal court should hesitate to exercise jurisdiction over state claims, even though bound to apply state law to them, Erie R. Co. v. Tompkins * * * [p. 374, infra]. Needless decisions of state law should be avoided both as a matter of comity and to promote justice between the parties, by procuring for them a surer-footed reading of applicable law. Certainly, if the federal claims are dismissed before trial, even though not insubstantial in a jurisdictional sense, the state claims should be dismissed as well. Similarly, if it appears that the state issues substantially predominate, whether in terms of proof, of the scope of the issues raised, or of the comprehensiveness of the remedy sought, the state claims may be dismissed without prejudice and left for resolution to state tribunals. There may, on the other hand, be situations in which the state claim is so closely tied to questions of federal policy that the argument for exercise of pendent jurisdiction is particularly strong. In the present case, for example, the allowable scope of the state claim implicates the federal doctrine of pre-emption; while this interrelationship does not create statutory federal question jurisdiction, Louisville & N.R. Co. v. Mottley, * * * its existence is relevant to the exercise of discretion. Finally, there may be reasons independent of jurisdictional considerations, such as the likelihood of jury confusion in treating divergent legal theories of relief, that would justify separating state and federal claims for trial, Fed.Rule Civ.Proc. 42(b). If so, jurisdiction should ordinarily be refused.

The question of power will ordinarily be resolved on the pleadings. But the issue whether pendent jurisdiction has been properly assumed is one which remains open throughout the litigation. Pretrial procedures or even the trial may reveal a substantial hegemony of state law claims, or likelihood of jury confusion, which could not have been anticipated at the pleading stage. Although it will of course be appropriate to take account in this circumstance of the already completed course of the litigation, dismissal of the state claim might even then be merited. For example, it may appear that the plaintiff was well aware of the nature of his proofs and the relative importance of his claims; recognition of a federal court's wide latitude to decide ancillary questions of state law does not imply that it must tolerate a litigant's effort to impose upon it what is in effect only a state law case. Once it appears that a state claim constitutes the real body of a case, to which the federal claim is only an appendage, the state claim may fairly be dismissed.

We are not prepared to say that in the present case the District Court exceeded its discretion in proceeding to judgment on the state claim. * * *

It is true that the § 303 claims ultimately failed and that the only recovery allowed respondent was on the state claim. We cannot confidently say, however, that the federal issues were so remote or played such a minor role at the trial that in effect the state claim only was tried. Although the District Court dismissed as unproved the claims that petitioner's secondary activities included attempts to induce coal operators other than Grundy to cease doing business with respondent, the court submitted the § 303 claims relating to Grundy to the jury. The jury returned verdicts against petitioner on those § 303 claims, and it was only on petitioner's motion for a directed verdict and a judgment *n.o.v.* that the verdicts on those claims were set aside. * * * Although there was some risk of confusing the jury in joining the state and federal claims—especially since, as will be developed, differing standards of proof of UMW involvement applied—the possibility of confusion could be lessened by employing a special verdict form, as the District Court did. * * *

[The Court went on to hold that the plaintiff could not recover damages for conspiracy under Tennessee common law on the basis of the record.]

Reversed.

THE CHIEF JUSTICE took no part in the decision of this case.

[A concurring opinion by JUSTICE HARLAN, joined by JUSTICE CLARK, is omitted.]

Notes and Questions

1. To what extent are Hurn v. Oursler and United Mine Workers of America v. Gibbs inconsistent with the notion that the subject-matter jurisdiction of the federal courts is limited by Article III of the Constitution and whatever enabling legislation Congress chooses to enact? Surely convenience and judicial administration, although admirable goals, cannot always be used to override basic tenets regarding the distribution of judicial business in a federal system. In this connection, consider the following passage:

> * * * [T]he exercise of pendent jurisdiction must be judged by whether it furthers some federal policy. Measured by that test pendent jurisdiction serves two purposes. First, it ensures that litigants will not be dissuaded from maintaining their federal rights in a federal court solely because they can dispose of all claims by one litigation in the state but not the federal forum. When jurisdiction over the federal claim is exclusive in the federal judiciary,

only pendent jurisdiction makes possible a complete remedy for vindication of the plaintiff's rights. Second, assuming that the litigants are in a federal forum, pendent jurisdiction serves the interest of avoiding piecemeal litigation, thus promoting judicial economy and greater expedition for the litigants. In respect to judicial economy, one must reject the idea * * * of a dichotomy between the state and federal judicial systems; rather they are copartners in the judicial endeavor to effectuate justice throughout the nation with the least burden on national and individual resources.

Note, *The Evolution and Scope of the Doctrine of Pendent Jurisdiction in the Federal Courts,* 62 Colum.L.Rev. 1018, 1044 (1962). For a general discussion of pendent jurisdiction, see 13B Wright, Miller & Cooper, *Federal Practice and Procedure: Jurisdiction and Related Matters 2d* § 3567 (1984). See also McManamon, *Dispelling the Myths of Pendent and Ancillary Jurisdiction: The Ramifications of a Revised History,* 46 Wash. & Lee L.Rev. 863 (1989).

2.   The aspect of *Hurn* that caused the most interpretive difficulties was the requirement that the state and federal claims merely be two distinct grounds of a "single cause of action" rather than "two separate and distinct causes of action." What considerations are relevant to the question whether two claims are but aspects of a "single cause of action"? See Armstrong Paint & Varnish Works v. Nu–Enamel Corp., 305 U.S. 315, 59 S.Ct. 191, 83 L.Ed. 195 (1938); Kleinman v. Betty Dain Creations, Inc., 189 F.2d 546 (2d Cir.1951). See generally Comment, *Discretionary Federal Jurisdiction Over the Pendent Cause,* 46 Ill.L.Rev. 646 (1951). What is the test for pendency that emerges from *Gibbs*? Is it any easier to apply than the *Hurn* test?

3.   Should the considerations of judicial economy and party convenience underlying pendent subject-matter jurisdiction also allow the court to assert "pendent" personal jurisdiction over the defendant for the purposes of adjudicating a nonfederal claim in circumstances in which the court would not have adjudicative authority over the defendant on that claim standing alone? For example, if jurisdiction over the defendant has been effected pursuant to a federal statute providing for nationwide service of process, but the defendant would not be subject to process in the forum state for purposes of the joined state claim, must the court dismiss the latter? See Rice v. Nova Biomedical Corp., 763 F.Supp. 961 (N.D.Ill.1991). See also Note, *Pendent Personal Jurisdiction and Nationwide Service of Process,* 64 N.Y.U.L.Rev. 113 (1989).

4.   When is the federal question that forms the basis for a claim of pendent jurisdiction "plainly wanting in substance"? Is an adequate answer provided by the "sufficient substance" test for federal claims in general articulated in Levering & Garrigues Co. v. Morrin, 289 U.S. 103, 53 S.Ct. 549, 77 L.Ed. 1062 (1933), see Note 9, p. 289, supra, which was decided shortly before *Hurn* and is cited in *Gibbs*? The Court in *Levering* noted that a federal question may be plainly insubstantial either because it is "obviously without merit" or because "its unsoundness so clearly results from previous decisions of this court." A number of federal courts have applied a somewhat different test and denied pendent jurisdiction when the federal claim was dismissed on the pleadings. See, e.g., Strachman v. Palmer, 177 F.2d 427 (1st Cir.1949); Walters v. Shari Music Publishing Corp., 193 F.Supp. 307 (S.D.N.Y.1961). What are the advantages, if any, of this test? Is it more or less permissive than the one suggested in *Levering*?

In *Gibbs,* the plaintiff joined federal and state claims against a single defendant. What if a federal claim is asserted against one defendant and a closely related state claim is asserted against another, whose presence in the action would destroy complete diversity of citizenship? In the years following *Gibbs,* many lower federal courts recognized "pendent party" jurisdiction in such situations.

However, in ALDINGER v. HOWARD, 427 U.S. 1, 96 S.Ct. 2413, 49 L.Ed.2d 276 (1976), the Supreme Court refused to apply pendent jurisdiction to an additional party with respect to whom no independent basis of federal jurisdiction existed. The suit was brought by a citizen of Washington against several officers of Spokane County, Washington, and alleged violations of the Civil Rights Act (42 U.S.C. § 1983). Plaintiff sought to join the county itself as an additional defendant, but under the construction given the federal statute at the time, counties were not considered to be subject to it.[b] Therefore, plaintiff was forced to sue the county under state law, and argue that a federal court could hear her claim under its pendent jurisdiction, despite the absence of diversity, since her two claims met the *Gibbs* "common nucleus of operative fact" test. The Supreme Court rejected the argument and distinguished *Gibbs* on two grounds:

> * * * From a purely factual point of view, it is one thing to authorize two parties, already present in federal court by virtue of a case over which the court has jurisdiction, to litigate in addition to their federal claim a state-law claim over which there is no independent basis of federal jurisdiction. But it is quite another thing to permit a plaintiff, who has asserted a claim against one defendant with respect to which there is federal jurisdiction, to join an entirely different defendant on the basis of a state-law claim over which there is no independent basis of federal jurisdiction, simply because his claim against the first defendant and his claim against the second defendant "derive from a common nucleus of operative fact." * * * True, the same considerations of judicial economy would be served * * *. But the addition of a completely new party would run counter to the well-established principle that federal courts, as opposed to state trial courts of general jurisdiction, are courts of limited jurisdiction marked out by Congress. * * *
>
> There is also a significant legal difference. In * * * *Gibbs* Congress was silent on the extent to which the defendant, already properly in federal court under a statute, might be called upon to answer nonfederal questions or claims; the way was thus left open for the Court to fashion its own rules under the general language of Art. III. But the extension of *Gibbs* to this kind of "pendent party" jurisdiction—bringing in an additional defendant at the behest of the plaintiff—presents rather different statutory jurisdictional considerations. Petitioner's contention that she should be entitled to sue Spokane County as a new third party, and then to try a wholly state-law claim against the county, all of which would be "pendent" to her federal claim against respondent county treasurer, must be decided, not in the context of congressional silence or tacit encouragement, but in quite the opposite context. The question here, which it was not necessary to address in *Gibbs* * * *, is whether by virtue of the statutory grant of subject-matter jurisdiction, upon which petitioner's principal claim against the treasurer rests, Congress has

b. Municipalities and other governmental units since have been held to be amenable to suit under the Civil Rights Act. See Monell v. Department of Social Servs. of City of New York, 436 U.S. 658, 98 S.Ct. 2018, 56 L.Ed.2d 611 (1978).

addressed itself to the *party* as to whom jurisdiction pendent to the principal claim is sought. And it undoubtedly has done so.

* * *

Resolution of a claim of pendent-party jurisdiction, therefore, calls for careful attention to the relevant statutory language. As we have indicated, we think a fair reading of the language used in [the relevant statutes] * * * requires a holding that the joinder of a municipal corporation, like the county here, for purposes of asserting a state-law claim not within federal diversity jurisdiction, is without the statutory jurisdiction of the district court.

Id. at 14–18, 96 S.Ct. at 2420–22, 49 L.Ed.2d at 286–88.

However, the Court carefully refused to lay down any "sweeping pronouncement upon the existence or exercise of [pendent party] jurisdiction":

* * * Other statutory grants and other alignments of parties and claims might call for a different result. When the grant of jurisdiction to a federal court is exclusive, for example, as in the prosecution of tort claims against the United States * * *, the argument of judicial economy and convenience can be coupled with the additional argument that *only* in a federal court may all of the claims be tried together. * * *

Id. at 18, 96 S.Ct. at 2422, 49 L.Ed.2d at 288. District courts also were instructed that before they could conclude that pendent-party jurisdiction existed, they must ask if "Congress in the statutes conferring jurisdiction has not expressly or by implication negated its existence."

Two years later, the Supreme Court addressed the propriety of pendent-party jurisdiction in the context of diversity-of-citizenship jurisdiction. In OWEN EQUIPMENT & ERECTION CO. v. KROGER, 437 U.S. 365, 98 S.Ct. 2396, 57 L.Ed.2d 274 (1978), Mrs. Kroger, a citizen of Iowa, sued Omaha Public Power District (OPPD), a Nebraska corporation, for the wrongful death of her husband. Her husband had been electrocuted when the beam of a steel crane, next to which he was walking, came too close to a high-tension electric line. Mrs. Kroger brought the action in federal district court in Nebraska based on diversity of citizenship, alleging that OPPD's negligent operation of the power line had caused her husband's death. OPPD, in turn, filed a third-party complaint pursuant to Federal Rule 14(a) against Owen Equipment and Erection Company alleging that the crane was owned and operated by Owen, and that it was Owen's negligence that had been the proximate cause of the decedent's death.

Plaintiff was then allowed to amend her complaint to name Owen as a defendant, who she alleged was a Nebraska corporation with its principal place of business in Nebraska. OPPD then requested, and was granted, summary judgment, leaving Owen as the sole defendant. During the course of the trial, it was discovered that Owen's principal place of business actually was in Iowa. As a result, Owen moved to dismiss the case based on a lack of subject-matter jurisdiction. The District Court denied the motion and the Court of Appeals affirmed. The Supreme Court, however, reversed in an opinion by Justice Stewart:

It is apparent that *Gibbs* delineated the constitutional limits of judicial power. * * * Constitutional power[, however,] is merely the first hurdle that must be overcome in determining that a federal court has jurisdiction over a particular controversy. For the jurisdiction of the federal courts is limited not only by the provisions of Art. III of the Constitution, but by Acts of Congress.
* * *

That statutory law as well as the Constitution may limit a federal court's jurisdiction over nonfederal claims is well illustrated by * * * Aldinger v. Howard * * *. * * * The *Aldinger* * * * [case] make[s] clear that a finding that federal and nonfederal claims arise from a "common nucleus of operative fact," the test of *Gibbs,* does not end the inquiry into whether a federal court has power to hear the nonfederal claims along with the federal ones. Beyond this constitutional minimum, there must be an examination of the posture in which the nonfederal claim is asserted and of the specific statute that confers jurisdiction over the federal claim, in order to determine whether "Congress in [that statute] has * * * expressly or by implication negated" the exercise of jurisdiction over the particular nonfederal claim. * * *

The relevant statute in this case, 28 U.S.C. § 1332(a)(1), * * * and its predecessors have consistently been held to require complete diversity of citizenship. * * * Over the years Congress has repeatedly re-enacted or amended the statute conferring diversity jurisdiction, leaving intact this rule of complete diversity. Whatever may have been the original purposes of diversity-of-citizenship jurisdiction, this subsequent history clearly demonstrates a congressional mandate that diversity jurisdiction is not to be available when any plaintiff is a citizen of the same State as any defendant. * * *.

Thus it is clear that the respondent could not originally have brought suit in federal court naming Owen and OPPD as codefendants, since citizens of Iowa would have been on both sides of the litigation. Yet the identical lawsuit resulted when she amended her complaint. Complete diversity was destroyed just as surely as if she had sued Owen initially. * * * [U]nder the reasoning of the Court of Appeals in this case, a plaintiff could defeat the statutory requirement of complete diversity by the simple expedient of suing only those defendants who were of diverse citizenship and waiting for them to implead nondiverse defendants. * * *

* * *

It is not unreasonable to assume that, in generally requiring complete diversity, Congress did not intend to confine the jurisdiction of federal courts so inflexibly that they are unable to protect legal rights or effectively to resolve an entire, logically entwined lawsuit. Those practical needs are the basis of the doctrine of ancillary jurisdiction. But neither the convenience of litigants nor considerations of judicial economy can suffice to justify extension of the doctrine of ancillary jurisdiction to a plaintiff's cause of action against a citizen of the same State in a diversity case. Congress has established the basic rule that diversity jurisdiction exists * * * only when there is complete diversity of citizenship. * * * To allow the requirement of complete diversity to be circumvented as it was in this case would simply flout the congressional command.

Id. at 371–74, 377, 98 S.Ct. at 2401–03, 2404, 57 L.Ed.2d at 280–82, 284.

The Supreme Court's approach to determining whether an exercise of pendent-party jurisdiction was proper in a particular case (articulated in *Aldinger* and *Kroger*) was transformed radically by the Court's decision in FINLEY v. UNITED STATES, 490 U.S. 545, 109 S.Ct. 2003, 104 L.Ed.2d 593 (1989). In *Finley,* the plaintiff's husband and two of her children were killed when their plane struck electric power lines on its approach to a city-run airfield in San Diego, California. Suit was filed in federal district court against the United States under the Federal

Tort Claims Act (FTCA), 28 U.S.C. § 1346(b), alleging that the Federal Aviation Administration had been negligent in its operation and maintenance of the runway lights and in its performance of air traffic control functions.

The plaintiff later was allowed to amend her complaint to include state-law tort claims against both the city of San Diego and the utility company that maintained the power lines. The Court of Appeals reversed the District Court's decision to allow the amendment, and the Supreme Court affirmed, with Justice Scalia writing for a majority of five Justices:

> * * * It remains rudimentary law that "[a]s regards all courts of the United States inferior to this tribunal, two things are necessary to create jurisdiction, whether original or appellate. The Constitution must have given to the court the capacity to take it, *and an act of Congress must have supplied it* * * *. To the extent that such action is not taken, the power lies dormant." The Mayor v. Cooper, 73 U.S. (6 Wall.) 247, 252, 18 L.Ed. 851 (1868) (emphasis added) * * *.

> Despite this principle, in a line of cases by now no less well established we have held, without specific examination of jurisdictional statutes, that federal courts have "pendent" claim jurisdiction * * * to the full extent permitted by the Constitution. Mine Workers v. Gibbs * * *. * * * Analytically, petitioner's case is fundamentally different from *Gibbs* in that it brings into question what has become known as pendent-*party* jurisdiction, that is, jurisdiction over parties not named in any claim that is independently cognizable by the federal court. We may assume, without deciding, that the constitutional criterion for pendent-party jurisdiction is analogous to the constitutional criterion for pendent-claim jurisdiction, and that petitioner's state-law claims pass that test. Our cases show, however, that with respect to the addition of parties, as opposed to the addition of only claims, we will not assume that the full constitutional power has been congressionally authorized, and will not read jurisdictional statutes broadly. * * *

> * * *

> * * * The FTCA, § 1346(b), confers jurisdiction over "civil actions on claims against the United States." It does not say "civil action on claims that include requested relief against the United States," nor "civil actions in which there is a claim against the United States"—formulations one might expect if the presence of a claim against the United States constituted merely a minimum jurisdiction requirement, rather than a definition of the permissible scope of FTCA actions. Just as the statutory provision "between * * * citizens of different States" has been held to mean citizens of different States and no one else, * * * so also here we conclude that "against the United States" means against the United States and no one else. * * *

> * * *

> As we noted at the outset, our cases do not display an entirely consistent approach with respect to the necessity that jurisdiction be explicitly conferred. The *Gibbs* line of cases was a departure from prior practice, and a departure that we have no intent to limit or impair. But *Aldinger* indicated that the *Gibbs* approach would not be extended to the pendent-party field, and we decide today to retain that line. Whatever we say regarding the scope of jurisdiction conferred by a particular statute can of course be changed by Congress. What is of paramount importance is that Congress be able to legislate against a background of clear interpretive rules, so that it may know

the effect of the language it adopts. All our cases * * * have held that a grant of jurisdiction over claims involving particular parties does not itself confer jurisdiction over additional claims by or against different parties. Our decision today reaffirms that interpretive rule; the opposite would sow confusion.

Id. at 547–49, 552, 556, 109 S.Ct. at 2005–07, 2008, 2010, 104 L.Ed.2d at 600–01, 603–04, 606.

In dissent, Justice Stevens noted the Court's radical departure from its earlier decision in Aldinger v. Howard:

> In *Aldinger*, we adopted a rule of construction that assumed the existence of pendent jurisdiction unless "Congress in the statutes conferring jurisdiction has * * * expressly or by implication negated its existence" * * *. We rejected the assertion of pendent-party jurisdiction there because it arose "not in the context of congressional silence or tacit encouragement, but in quite the opposite context." * * * Congress' exclusion of municipal corporations from the definition of persons under § 1983, we concluded, evinced an intent to preclude the exercise of federal-court jurisdiction over them. If congressional silence were sufficient to defeat pendent jurisdiction, the careful reasoning in our *Aldinger* opinion was wholly unnecessary, for obviously the civil rights statutes do not affirmatively authorize the joinder of any state-law claims.

>   * * *

> The Court today adopts a sharply different approach. Without even so much as acknowledging our statement in *Aldinger* that before a federal court may exercise pendent party jurisdiction it must satisfy itself that Congress "has not expressly or by implication negated its existence," * * * it now instructs that "a grant of jurisdiction over claims involving particular parties does not itself confer jurisdiction over additional claims by or against different parties." * * *

Id. at 573, 574–75, 109 S.Ct. at 2019–20, 2020, 104 L.Ed.2d at 617, 618 (Stevens, J., dissenting).

———

Read 28 U.S.C. § 1367 in the Supplement.

———

MENGLER, BURBANK & ROWE, CONGRESS ACCEPTS SUPREME COURT'S INVITATION TO CODIFY SUPPLEMENTAL JURISDICTION, 74 Judicature 213 (December/January, 1991):

Just before it recessed last October, Congress filled a widening chasm in the jurisdictional authority of the federal courts. That gap, opened by the Supreme Court a little over a year earlier in Finley v. United States, was threatening to subvert the federal courts' power to deal with related matters efficiently, in single rather than in multiple litigation. At risk were the doctrines of pendent and ancillary jurisdiction, which permit parties in many circumstances to litigate an entire controversy, typically all transactionally-related claims, as long as the district court has a statutory basis for asserting subject-matter jurisdiction over a claim raised in plaintiff's complaint. * * *

* * *

A fair reading of *Finley* suggests that the majority was not oblivious to the possible need for a legislative response. Indeed, Justice Scalia's opinion for the Court virtually invited Congress to fill the jurisdictional gaps its decision had created. * * * Congress through 28 U.S.C. § 1367 has accepted the Court's invitation. * * *

With a few exceptions discussed below, section 1367 codifies supplemental jurisdiction as it existed before the *Finley* decision. Theoretical arguments can be made for broadening supplemental jurisdiction even as it existed prior to *Finley*. But expanding supplemental jurisdiction would require relaxing the requirements for diversity jurisdiction and would cut against the dominant perception, shared by the Federal Courts Study Committee, that federal courts should focus more of their resources on federal question cases and fewer (or none at all) on diversity cases. In order to repair *Finley*'s damage in a noncontroversial manner without expanding the scope of diversity jurisdiction, the statutory measure was therefore framed to restore and regularize supplemental jurisdiction, not to revamp it.

Section 1367(a), for example, generally authorizes the district courts to exercise jurisdiction over a supplemental claim whenever it forms part of the same constitutional case or controversy as the claim that provides the basis of the district court's original jurisdiction. In reaching to the limits of Article III, subsection (a) codifies supplemental jurisdiction at the outer constitutional boundary that existed before *Finley*'s statutory revisionism. [See United Mine Workers of America v. Gibbs, p. 298, supra.] * * *

The second sentence of subsection (a), making explicit the federal courts' authority to hear supplemental claims "that involve the joinder or intervention of additional parties," in part simply reinstates the prior settled law. Thus, for example, as under pre-*Finley* practice, impleader claims against nondiverse third-party defendants are authorized, as are compulsory counterclaims and cross-claims involving additional parties. The second sentence, however, modifies current law by overruling *Finley*. Congress thus has resolved the controversy over pendent party jurisdiction by providing the explicit statutory authorization found lacking and regarded as necessary by the *Finley* majority.

Subsection (b) restricts the federal courts' exercise of supplemental jurisdiction in diversity cases by, in effect, codifying the principal rationale of Owen Equipment & Erection Co. v. Kroger * * * by naming initially only defendants of diverse citizenship and waiting for them to implead nondiverse defendants. Subsection (b) fully implements the *Kroger* rationale by prohibiting the district courts, in actions founded solely on the diversity statute, from exercising supplemental jurisdiction over claims by plaintiffs against persons made parties through any of several of the joinder devices of the Federal Rules * * * when doing so would be inconsistent with the jurisdictional requirements of section 1332.

In the same vein, the subsection also prohibits the exercise of supplemental jurisdiction in connection with the joinder or intervention of persons as plaintiffs when it would be inconsistent with section 1332. Class actions * * * are not included in the diversity cases to which the restrictions in subsection (b) apply, and the legislative history makes clear that section 1367 is not intended to affect their jurisdictional requirements as previously determined. Thus, the Supreme Court's holdings that not only the named class representatives must satisfy the citizenship requirement of section 1332, but that all class members must satisfy the amount in controversy requirement, remain good decisional law.

Subsection (b) alters prior law in one modest but significant way, we think in a manner consistent with the spirit of *Kroger*. Anomalously, cases predating section 1367 held that a person might intervene as of right under Federal Rule of Civil Procedure 24(a) on a supplemental basis, but the same person would not come within supplemental jurisdiction if the person was sought to be joined under Federal Rule 19. This disparity, which may have had the effect of encouraging certain nondiverse plaintiffs to evade the diversity requirements by intervening in an action shortly after it was filed by diverse plaintiffs, has been abolished in subsection (b). Now, that person can neither intervene as a plaintiff under Rule 24(a) nor be joined as a plaintiff under Rule 19 if intervention or joinder would be inconsistent with the diversity requirements. * * *

Subsection (c) provides federal courts with discretion in some circumstances to decline to exercise supplemental jurisdiction. It codifies those factors that the Supreme Court in United Mine Workers v. Gibbs recognized as providing a sound basis for a lower court's discretionary decision to decline supplemental jurisdiction. * * * Additionally, the subsection accommodates exceptional circumstances, not defined, in which grounds for dismissal of the supplemental claim may be compelling. In each of these circumstances, * * * the district court in exercising its discretion must undertake a case-specific analysis. * * *

The possibility that a district court may dismiss supplemental claims brought by one or more parties raises a variety of concerns. * * * One concern is that a party, in refiling a claim in state court after the federal court has dismissed it, may face a limitations problem. Congress has explicitly addressed this problem in subsection (d) by providing a period of tolling of statutes of limitations for any supplemental claim that is dismissed and for any other claims voluntarily dismissed at the same time or thereafter. * * * [T]he purpose of subsection (d) is to prevent the loss of claims to statutes of limitations where state law fails to toll the running of its limitations period while a supplemental claim is pending in federal court. Moreover, subsection (d) eliminates any disincentive to parties who wish to litigate their entire action in state court after their supplemental claims have been dismissed, by providing a tolling period of at least 30 days (more if state law allows) for the nonsupplemental claims voluntarily dismissed in federal court and refiled in state court.

In effect, section 1367(d) contemplates, without specifically addressing the procedural means for doing so, that some parties will desire to take their entire action to state court if they are prohibited from raising some or all of their supplemental claims in federal court. * * *

Not all parties, of course, will choose or be able to refile their entire action in state court after their supplemental claims are dismissed. Some will continue to litigate what is left of their federal action in federal court, while choosing to refile their supplemental claims in state court. When the district court has exercised its discretion to dismiss a supplemental claim pursuant to subsection (c), a party is forced by court order to split a single "constitutional case" between the federal and state court systems, if that party wishes both to retain its right to a federal forum and to pursue the supplemental claim in a forum that will adjudicate it. * * *

Notes and Questions

1. Professors Mengler, Burbank, and Rowe participated in the drafting of Section 1367. Their work has been criticized by Professor Freer, who, in commenting on the new statute and the "Trio's" article (excerpted above), argued that:

The supplemental jurisdiction statute has been heralded, at least by its drafters, as a "model of successful dialogue between the judicial and legislative branches." It is no such thing. This statute does the judiciary no favors. It throws back to the courts at least as many problems as they had before, problems that should have been anticipated easily and addressed in the statute. Had the supplemental jurisdiction statute not been drafted in such haste, had the legislation been reviewed meaningfully, the product could have been ameliorative. Instead, we get confusion from an effort that should have made things clear. While the courts ultimately may work around the problems, there is no guarantee that they will do so consistently, quickly, or easily. The process of making sense out of this statute may be every bit as painful and time-consuming as interpreting *Finley*.

Freer, *Compounding Confusion and Hampering Diversity: Life After Finley and the Supplemental Jurisdiction Statute,* 40 Emory L.J. 445, 486 (1991).

2. The debate continues within the academic community over the efficacy of Section 1367. Many commentators argue that the statute has created confusion. Their questions include: Does the statute allow a party to circumvent the complete diversity requirement? Does the statute restrict the plaintiff's ability to join parties to the suit? Others defend the statute, noting that it clarified the inconsistent case law, and that this benefit outweighs whatever faults the statute might have. For a discussion of these criticisms, see Symposium, *A Reappraisal of The Supplemental–Jurisdiction Statute: Title 28 U.S.C. § 1367,* 74 Ind.L.J. 1 (1998); Arthur & Freer, *Close Enough for Government Work: What Happens When Congress Doesn't Do Its Job,* 40 Emory L.J. 1007 (1991); Arthur & Freer, *Grasping at Burnt Straws: The Disaster of the Supplemental Jurisdiction Statute,* 40 Emory L.J. 963 (1991); Dreyfuss, *Colloquy: Perspectives on Supplemental Jurisdiction—The Debate Over Section 1367: Defining the Power to Define Federal Judicial Power,* 41 Emory L.J. 13 (1992); Mengler, Burbank & Rowe, *A Coda on Supplemental Jurisdiction,* 40 Emory L.J. 993 (1991); Rowe, Burbank & Mengler, *Compounding or Creating Confusion About Supplemental Jurisdiction? A Reply to Professor Freer,* 40 Emory L.J. 943 (1991).

3. Section 1367(a) defines supplemental jurisdiction as going to the limits of the constitutional definition of a "case or controversy." It generally is accepted that Congress intended the *Gibbs* test to define what constitutes a "case or controversy" for purposes of supplemental jurisdiction. Was it wise to force the

courts to interpret the Constitution every time they decide whether or not a supplemental claim or party is properly before them? Would it have been possible to draft a more narrow statutory definition of supplemental jurisdiction? Or should Congress simply have tracked the language of Article III, as it did in Sections 1331 and 1332, and allow the courts to refine the statutory scope of supplemental jurisdiction? See McLaughlin, *The Federal Supplemental Jurisdiction Statute—Constitutional and Statutory Analysis*, 24 Ariz.St.L.J. 849 (1992).

4. How do you explain the codification of *Kroger?* Is there an argument for requiring complete diversity only between the plaintiffs and the defendants named in the initial complaint? Did *Kroger* have to be codified for Congress to accomplish its goal of overriding *Finley?*

5. Section 1367(b) places significant restrictions on a plaintiff's ability to assert claims against nondiverse parties. These limitations are supposed to prevent circumvention of the complete diversity requirement. Do these limitations make sense, however, when the action has been removed to a federal court from a state court? Similarly, what if the plaintiff has been placed in a defensive posture by a counterclaim or cross-claim? In GUARANTEED SYSTEMS, INC. v. AMERICAN NATIONAL CAN CO., 842 F.Supp. 855 (M.D.N.C.1994), the defendant, after removing the action on the ground of diversity, asserted a counterclaim against the plaintiff. The plaintiff's motion to implead a nondiverse third-party in defense against the counterclaim was denied by the court, although with some reluctance. Such seemingly anomalous results have led Professor Freer, long a critic of Section 1367, to write:

> It is one thing to tell the diversity plaintiff—as *Kroger* did—that she will not be able to file a Rule 14(a) claim against a nondiverse third-party defendant impleaded by the defendant. It is quite another to tell the diversity plaintiff what § 1367(b) tells her: (1) that if a claim is asserted against her, she cannot implead a nondiverse third-party defendant who may owe her indemnity or contribution; (2) that if a claim is asserted against her, she cannot assert a cross-claim against a nondiverse co-plaintiff; (3) that a nondiverse third-party defendant may assert a claim against her, but that she cannot assert a compulsory counterclaim in response; and (4) that she cannot assert a claim against a nondiverse intervenor or necessary party, even though their claims against her will invoke supplemental jurisdiction. This is a formidable set of roadblocks, unknown to pre-*Finley* law and unnecessary to protect the complete diversity rule.

Freer, *Toward a Principled Statutory Approach to Supplemental Jurisdiction in Diversity of Citizenship Cases*, 74 Ind.L.J. 5, 14–15 (1998). Do you agree?

6. Does the enactment of Section 1367 mean that there no longer can be any judicially created jurisdiction not provided for by statute? In KOKKONEN v. GUARDIAN LIFE INS. CO. OF AMERICA, 511 U.S. 375, 114 S.Ct. 1673, 128 L.Ed.2d 391 (1994), the plaintiff sued in federal court to enforce a settlement agreement that resolved a prior federal action. The defendant challenged jurisdiction on the ground that the District Court lost jurisdiction after it entered an order dismissing the prior litigation. The Supreme Court, without citing Section 1367, held that federal courts have "ancillary jurisdiction" to enforce their decrees and orders; however, in this particular case the Court agreed with the defendant because the District Court had not made compliance with the settlement agreement a condition of dismissal. A number of lower courts have followed *Kokkonen* in locating an equitable, common-law ancillary enforcement jurisdiction. See Alexandria Resident Council, Inc. v. Alexandria Redevelopment & Housing Au-

thority, 218 F.3d 307 (4th Cir.2000) (discussing the distinction between statutory supplemental jurisdiction and equitable ancillary jurisdiction); United States v. Alpine Land & Reservoir Co., 174 F.3d 1007 (9th Cir.1999). For a discussion of *Kokkonen*, see Green, *Justice Scalia and Ancillary Jurisdiction: Teaching a Lame Duck New Tricks in Kokkonen v. Guardian Life Insurance Company of America*, 81 Va.L.Rev. 631 (1995).

EXECUTIVE SOFTWARE NORTH AMERICA, INC. v. UNITED STATES DISTRICT COURT FOR THE CENTRAL DISTRICT OF CALIFORNIA

United States Court of Appeals, Ninth Circuit, 1994.
24 F.3d 1545.

D.W. NELSON, CIRCUIT JUDGE.

Executive Software North America, Inc., Craig Jensen, and Sally Jensen ("Petitioners") petition this court for a writ of mandamus to compel the United States District Court for the Central District of California to retain jurisdiction over certain pendent state law claims filed in an employment discrimination suit against them by the plaintiff-real-party-in-interest, Donna Page. Petitioners contend that, in remanding the plaintiff's pendent state law claims, the district court misapprehended the scope of the supplemental jurisdiction statute * * * and failed to undertake the case-specific analysis required by that statute. In addition, Petitioners contend that, on a proper application of section 1367, a remand of their state law claims cannot be justified. * * * For the reasons stated below, we grant the writ, but on narrower grounds than urged by the parties.

FACTUAL AND PROCEDURAL BACKGROUND

On April 8, 1993, Donna Page filed a complaint in state court against the petitioners. She claimed to have experienced several acts of discrimination during her employment with Executive Software. Specifically, Page, a black female, alleged that the company required all of its employees to study the teachings of the Church of Scientology written by L. Ron Hubbard. Page contends that when she refused to comply, she was charged with having made a number of errors in her work, and that when she attempted to contest the charges she was denied an opportunity to do so and was terminated. Page further asserts that the charges and subsequent termination were a mere "subterfuge for illegal discrimination against non believers in the Church of Scientology, women and racial minorities."

In her complaint, Page alleged two federal causes of action, (1) a claim under Title VII, 42 U.S.C. § 2000(e) *et seq.* (1988), and (2) a claim under 42 U.S.C. § 1983 (1988), as well as three state-law causes of action, including (1) a claim for unlawful religious and racial discrimination under the California Fair Employment and Housing Act ("FEHA"), * * * (2) a claim of wrongful termination in violation of the California Constitution, Art. I § 7(a), and (3) a claim for negligent supervision.

Based on the two federal claims, the defendants removed the action to federal court. Subsequently, on May 20, 1993, the district court issued an order *sua sponte* to show cause why the three state-law claims should not be remanded to state court. The court stated that "jurisdiction over the state claims depends upon whether this Court exercises its discretion to retain [them]," and admonished the parties to consider that "the Supreme Court defined the parameters of a federal court's supplemental jurisdiction in *United Mine Workers v. Gibbs* * * *." After noting the requirements set forth in *Gibbs* for exercising supplemental jurisdiction, the Court added:

> Even if [the *Gibbs* test is] met, however, a federal court has discretion to decline jurisdiction over state law claims if, for instance, the state claims substantially predominate, the state claims involve novel or complex issues of state law, trial of the state and federal claims together is likely to result in jury confusion, or retention of the state claims requires the expenditure of substantial additional judicial time and effort. * * *

> The Removing Party(ies) should also be aware that this Court does not interpret the 1990 enactment of Section 1367 as restricting the discretionary factors set forth in *Gibbs*. Rather, this Court interprets Section 1367 as merely allowing this Court, at its discretion, to exercise jurisdiction over supplemental parties, which was previously foreclosed by *Finley v. United States* * * *.

The district court thereafter remanded the three state law claims, but provided no reasons.

* * *

A. Did the District Court Commit Clear Error?

The district court provided no reasons for its remand. However, in its Show Cause Order, the court stated that it did not "interpret Section 1367 as restricting the discretionary factors set forth in *Gibbs*. * * *."

We find this interpretation of section 1367 erroneous. It is clear that, once it is determined that the assertion of supplemental jurisdiction is permissible under sections 1367(a) and (b), section 1367(c) provides the only valid basis upon which the district court may decline jurisdiction and remand pendent claims. Moreover, we conclude that although subsections (c)(1)–(3) appear to codify most preexisting applications of the *Gibbs* doctrine, subsection (c)(4), which also permits a court to decline jurisdiction when, "in exceptional circumstances, there are other compelling reasons," channels the district court's discretion to identify new grounds for declining jurisdiction more particularly than did preexisting doctrine. Accordingly, we conclude the district court erred to the extent that it relied on a basis for remanding pendent claims not permitted under section 1367(c). Finally, we conclude that, because the district court failed to articulate reasons for its remand of the pendent claims, we cannot determine whether the district court relied on a statutory ground and exercised its discretion in a permissible manner. Consequently, we conclude that the district court clearly erred.

* * *

[The court's historical discussion is omitted.]

2. The Relationship of Section 1367(c) to Gibbs

Initially, we must determine whether, as Petitioners contend, the section 1367(c) factors are the exclusive means by which supplemental jurisdiction, if permitted by sections 1367(a) and (b), can be declined. In addition, we must ascertain whether the scope of the section 1367(c) categories is coextensive with the *Gibbs* regime, or if, as Petitioners contend, section 1367 has altered the analysis.

a.

Section 1367 retains the basic division, reflected in *Gibbs,* between the power of a court to entertain a pendent claim and the authority of a court, in its discretion, to decline to exercise that power. However, Congress, in codifying supplemental jurisdiction, has chosen to codify as well the discretionary factors that warrant declining jurisdiction. Section 1367(a), * * * confers power to entertain supplemental jurisdiction in mandatory terms. By use of the word "shall," the statute makes clear that if power is conferred under section 1367(a), and its exercise is not prohibited by section 1367(b), a court can decline to assert supplemental jurisdiction over a pendent claim only if one of the four categories specifically enumerated in section 1367(c) applies. * * *

By selecting this statutory structure, it is clear that Congress intended section 1367(c) to provide the exclusive means by which supplemental jurisdiction can be declined by a court. Not only is this conclusion supported by the legislative history, * * * but a contrary reading of the statute would appear to render section 1367(c) superfluous. Accordingly, unless a court properly invokes a section 1367(c) category in exercising its discretion to decline to entertain pendent claims, supplemental jurisdiction must be asserted. * * *

b.

A consequence of the statutory structure chosen by Congress is that section 1367(c) somewhat changes the nature of the *Gibbs* discretionary inquiry. Although * * * *Gibbs* and its progeny identified a number of concrete instances in which declining pendent jurisdiction normally would be appropriate, the ultimate inquiry for the courts remained whether the assertion of pendent jurisdiction "best accomodate[s] (sic) the values of economy convenience, fairness and comity." * * * Application of these underlying values to circumstances not identified in prior cases was not only contemplated, but demanded. * * *

The statute, however, channels the application of the underlying values to a greater degree than the *Gibbs* regime, although section 1367(c) continues to recognize the doctrine's dynamic aspects. Subsections (c)(1)–(c)(3) appear to codify concrete applications of the underlying *Gibbs* values recognized in preexisting case law. Subsection (c)(2) (state law claim "substantially predominates") and (c)(3) (district court has dismissed all claims over which it had original jurisdiction), are derived directly from *Gibbs* itself, * * * while subsection (c)(1), permitting a remand when "the claim raises a novel or complex issue of State law," implicates the subsequently developed line of cases tacitly approved of in *Pennhurst* [*State School & Hosp. v. Halderman,* 465 U.S. 89, 104 S.Ct. 900, 79 L.Ed.2d 67 (1984)] * * *.

By codifying preexisting applications of *Gibbs* in subsections (c)(1)–(3), however, it is clear that Congress intended the exercise of discretion to be triggered by the court's identification of a factual predicate that corresponds to one of the section 1367(c) categories. Once that factual predicate is identified, the exercise of discretion, of course, still is informed by whether remanding the pendent state claims comports with the underlying objective of "most sensibly accommodat[ing]" the values of "economy, convenience, fairness, and comity." * * *

We believe that the "catchall * * * provided by subsection (c)(4) should be interpreted in a similar manner. Subsection (c)(4) permits a discretionary remand of pendent claims when "*in exceptional circumstances, there are other compelling reasons* for declining jurisdiction." * * * Congress's use of the word "other" to modify "compelling reasons" indicates that what ought to qualify as "compelling reasons" for declining jurisdiction under subsection (c)(4) should be of the same nature as the reasons that gave rise to the categories listed in subsections (c)(1)–(3). Because, as discussed above, the subsection (c)(1)–(3) fact patterns constitute situations in which the underlying *Gibbs* values ordinarily will "point toward" declining jurisdiction, * * * we believe that "compelling reasons" for the purposes of subsection (c)(4) similarly should be those that lead a court to conclude that declining jurisdiction "best accommodate[s] the values of economy, convenience, fairness, and comity." * * *

By providing that an exercise of discretion under subsection 1367(c)(4) ought to be made only in "exceptional circumstances" Congress has sounded a note of caution that the bases for declining jurisdiction should be extended beyond the circumstances identified in subsections (c)(1)–(3) only if the circumstances are quite unusual. In short, although we find that "other compelling reasons" clearly refers the district court back to the subsection (c)(1)–(3) categories, and thus requires the court to balance the underlying values that they embody, we think "exceptional circumstances" requires an additional inquiry.

Of course, when the balance of the *Gibbs* values indicates that there are "compelling reasons" to decline jurisdiction, the underlying circumstances that inform this calculus usually will demonstrate how the circumstances confronted are "exceptional." We do not believe, however, this always will be the case. Even when a court's balancing of the *Gibbs* values provides, in its judgment, "compelling reasons" for declining jurisdiction, it might still be the case that the differences between the case it is confronting and the case in which supplemental jurisdiction is appropriate are not sufficient to justify the conclusion that the court would, in fact, be applying subsection (c)(4) properly. We think that it [is] clear from the language chosen by Congress, however, that declining jurisdiction outside of subsection (c)(1)–(3) should be the exception, rather than the rule. Courts therefore must ensure that the reasons identified as "compelling" are not deployed in circumstances that threaten this principle. The inquiry is not particularly burdensome. A court simply must articulate why the circumstances of the case are exceptional in addition to inquiring whether the balance of the *Gibbs* values provide compelling reasons for declining jurisdiction in such circumstances.

We think this interpretation is compelled not only by our understanding of the meaning of the term "other" in subsection (c)(4) and a common-sense understanding of "exceptional," but also by the statutory structure of section 1367(c). As discussed above, the subsection (c)(1)–(3) categories require both the presence of a factual predicate that triggers the exercise of discretion and a case-specific analysis of whether the *Gibbs* values would be best served by declining jurisdiction. Our interpretation of subsection (c)(4) carries forward this structure into that subsection: the court must identify the predicate that triggers the applicability of the category (the exceptional circumstances), and then determine whether, in its judgment, the underlying *Gibbs* values are best served by declining jurisdiction in the particular case (the compelling reasons).

We also think this result is mandated by the plain language of the statute—that "*in* exceptional circumstances, there are other compelling reasons for declining jurisdiction." * * * To deprive "in exceptional circumstances" of all meaning would unnecessarily conflate distinct statutory terms, a result that we are reluctant to embrace. * * *

Therefore, to the extent that *Gibbs* and [its progeny] were interpreted as permitting courts to extend the doctrine's underlying values beyond previously recognized applications *whenever* doing so was consistent with those values, * * * we believe that section 1367(c)(4) more carefully channels courts' discretion by requiring the court to identify how the circumstances that it confronts, and in which it believes the balance of the *Gibbs* values provides "compelling reasons" for declining jurisdiction, are "exceptional."

* * *

c.

With the above analysis providing the necessary conceptual foundation, we conclude that the district court clearly erred. The court, although acknowledging section 1367(c), stated that it did not rely on the statute, but *Gibbs*. Although this might be insignificant if the Show Cause Order indicated that the court considered only the codified applications of *Gibbs* enumerated therein, the court further intimated that *Gibbs* permitted it to decline jurisdiction when "retention of the state claims [would] require[ ] the expenditure of substantial judicial time and effort." If this statement was intended to go beyond preexisting applications of *Gibbs* by invoking its underlying values, it was an impermissible attempt. More fundamentally, as discussed above, subsection (c)(4) requires the district court not only to determine if consideration of the *Gibbs* values provides compelling reasons for a remand, but also to articulate how the circumstances that warrant declining jurisdiction are exceptional. Even if we were confident that the district court balanced the *Gibbs* values, there is no indication that it undertook this latter inquiry. Therefore, the district court clearly erred by articulating a basis for declining jurisdiction that is unauthorized by statute.

* * *

For the above reasons, the writ of mandamus is **GRANTED,** and the remand order entered by the district court shall be **VACATED.**

Leavy, Circuit Judge, dissenting:

I dissent.

* * * I cannot agree with the majority that this court should conclude that the district court clearly erred because we cannot determine the exact ground upon which the court relied.

* * *

The record does not suggest that the court relied on any ground or factor not mentioned in its order to show cause. Because the court made no findings, we do not know which one or more of the grounds it relied on. On that basis alone, however, the majority concludes that the district court may have relied on a ground not enumerated in section 1367(c); that this was in error, and not only error, but *clear error* for the purpose of mandamus. I cannot join the majority's reasoning to the effect that our inability to find that the court did not err puts it in *clear error*.

Grounds one and two, suggested in the order to show cause, are mentioned in section 1367(c)(1) and (2). Ground three, jury confusion, in my view would be a sufficiently compelling reason for remand, as would the fourth ground, "the expenditure of substantial additional judicial time and effort."

The district court committed no error unless it relied on an unauthorized ground in exercising its discretion to remand. The court did not say that it relied on an unauthorized ground nor does the record tell us that it did, unless the majority means to hold that likely jury confusion or the expenditure of substantial additional judicial time are not exceptional circumstances in which compelling reasons for declining jurisdiction can be found. The fact that the district court does not interpret the 1990 enactment of section 1367 as restricting the discretionary factors set forth in *Gibbs* is of no moment unless we can say that the trial court exceeded its lawful authority wherever it may be found.

* * *

According to *Gibbs*, the justification for pendent jurisdiction lies in considerations of judicial economy, convenience, and fairness to litigants. Congress chose to except from section 1367(a) those cases that were to be remanded under section 1367(c). In (a) it said, "Except as provided in subsection (b) and (c) ... in any civil action in which the district courts have original jurisdiction, the district courts shall have supplemental jurisdiction over all other claims.... " The sentence that Congress used to confer jurisdiction excepts from its scope those claims over which the district court may decline to exercise jurisdiction. The statute does not say that the court shall "exercise" jurisdiction. * * *

Just as the doctrine of supplemental jurisdiction itself is justified by considerations of judicial economy, convenience, and fairness to litigants, * * * so should a federal court "consider and weigh in each case, and at every stage of the litigation, the values of judicial economy, convenience, fairness, and comity in order to decide whether to exercise jurisdiction over a case brought in that court involving pendent state-law claims." * * *

Notes and Questions

1. Does Section 1367 expand or limit the instances in which a federal court should exercise supplemental jurisdiction? Do you agree with the statement in *Executive Software* that "section 1367(c) provides the only valid basis upon which a district court may decline jurisdiction and remand pendent claims"? The federal courts have not spoken consistently on this point. Compare this approach, for example, with that of the Third Circuit in Borough of West Mifflin v. Lancaster, 45 F.3d 780 (3d Cir.1995), p. 325, infra.

2. Section 1367 allows a federal court discretion to retain or dismiss state law claims when the federal basis for an action drops away. Does that discretion also apply to diversity cases in which the amount in controversy drops below the jurisdictional requirement? In SHANAGHAN v. CAHILL, 58 F.3d 106 (4th Cir.1995), the plaintiff brought a diversity action to recover from the defendant three separate debts, in the amounts of $40,000, $23,696, and $14,700. The district court granted summary judgment for the defendant on the $40,000 claim and dismissed the remaining claims, noting that the amount in controversy had fallen below $50,000, the then applicable requirement. On appeal, the Fourth Circuit ruled that, when the federal basis for an action disappears, a district court is free to decide whether to assert jurisdiction over the remaining claims, in accordance with Section 1367; it went on to hold that similar discretion exists when the amount in controversy falls below the statutory minimum. How does this ruling compare to that in St. Paul Mercury Indemnity Co. v. Red Cab Co., 303 U.S. 283, 58 S.Ct. 586, 82 L.Ed. 845 (1938). See Wolde–Meskel v. Vocational Instruction Project Community Servs., Inc., 166 F.3d 59, 64–65 (2d Cir.1999) (rejecting *Shanaghan* for confusing "(i) state-law claims that are supplemental to claims within the court's original jurisdiction (which are covered by 28 U.S.C. § 1367 and heard at the court's discretion) with (ii) state-law claims that are aggregated to satisfy the amount in controversy requirement for diversity (which are within the court's original jurisdiction)").

3. Section 1367 raises an additional question for federal courts: was the Supreme Court's decision in Zahn v. International Paper Co., Note 3, p. 275, supra, which held that only those plaintiffs who individually met the jurisdictional amount requirement of Section 1332(b) could be members of a class action suit, effectively overruled by the statute? In STROMBERG METAL WORKS, INC. v. PRESS MECHANICAL, INC., 77 F.3d 928 (7th Cir.1996), two Maryland subcontractors filed suit against an Illinois contractor for nonpayment of debts. Press hired Stromberg to install a heating, ventilation, and air-conditioning system, and Comfort Control was contracted to test that system. The agreement required Press to pay the subcontractors periodically as the work was completed. Press, however, was unable to make those payments and the subcontractors filed suit in the District Court for the Eastern District of Illinois to recover the outstanding balances. Stromberg claimed it was owed $407,430 and Comfort Control alleged $27,090 in unpaid invoices. The District Court dismissed the Comfort Control claim, holding that *Zahn* would not allow a party to be joined under Section 1367 if that party's claim did not meet the jurisdictional requirement. The Court of Appeals disagreed. It held that Comfort Control's claim could be heard pursuant to Section 1367. The court found support for its decision in a Fifth Circuit case, In re Abbott Laboratories, 51 F.3d 524 (5th Cir.1995). The *Stromberg* opinion noted,

> Abbott Laboratories concluded that under § 1367 only the named representatives [of a class must meet the jurisdictional amount]. Our case, by contrast, has just two plaintiffs. But § 1367 does not distinguish class actions from other cases; neither did *Zahn*. Indeed, the point of *Zahn* was that the class device made no difference. * * * *Zahn* added only that the status of pendent parties as class members (rather that as named representatives) does not make a difference. Section 1367(a) has changed the basic rule by authorizing pendent-party jurisdiction [over claims without an independent basis of jurisdiction], and that change effects * * * *Zahn* * * *.

77 F.3d at 931.

Courts disagree about the effect of Section 1367 on *Zahn*. Some read the statute literally to overrule *Zahn*. See In re Abbott Laboratories, 51 F.3d at 528 ("We cannot search legislative history for congressional intent unless we find the statute unclear or ambiguous. Here it is neither. The statute's first section vests federal courts with the power to hear supplemental claims generally, subject to limited exceptions set forth in the statute's second section. Class actions are not among the enumerated exceptions."). On the other hand, if a court relies on legislative intent in its interpretation of Section 1367, it might conclude that *Zahn* is not overruled. Both the Third and the Tenth Circuits have so concluded. In LEONHARDT v. WESTERN SUGAR CO., 160 F.3d 631 (10th Cir.1998), the Tenth Circuit disagreed with the Fifth and Seventh Circuits and argued that a literal reading of Section 1367 preserves *Zahn*. However, recognizing the existence of ambiguity in light of *Abbott Laboratories* and *Stromberg*, the *Leonhardt* court also relied on the statute's legislative history to support its holding. According to the Court of Appeals:

> The House Report that accompanies the Judicial Improvements Act * * * expressly states that § 1367 "is not intended to affect the jurisdictional requirements of 28 U.S.C. § 1332 in diversity-only class actions, as those requirements were interpreted prior to [*Finley* * * *]." H.Rep. No. 101–734, at 29 (1990), *reprinted in* 1990 U.S.C.C.A.N. 6860, 6875. The House Report then cites *Zahn* as an example of the pre-*Finley* interpretation of the jurisdictional requirements of § 1332 that is not to be disturbed. Id. & n.17. * * *

Id. at 640. See also Meritcare Inc. v. St. Paul Mercury Ins. Co., 166 F.3d 214, 222 (3d Cir.1999) ("We conclude that there is sufficient ambiguity in the statute to make resort to the legislative history appropriate. As noted earlier, the House Report leaves no doubt that Congress intended *Zahn*'s restrictions to remain in effect. * * * Even were we to conclude that Section 1367 is unambiguous, * * * we would nevertheless turn to the legislative history because this is one of those 'rare cases [in which] the literal application of a statute will produce a result demonstrably at odds with the intentions of its drafters.' "). For a discussion of different approaches to interpreting Section 1367, see Pfander, *Supplemental Jurisdiction and Section 1367: The Case for a Sympathetic Textualism*, 148 U.Pa.L.Rev. 109 (1999).

There was some hope that the ambiguity over *Zahn* would be resolved when the Supreme Court granted certiorari to review *Abbott Laboratories*. An equally divided Court, however, left undisturbed the result reached by the Fifth Circuit in a one-line affirmance. Free v. Abbott Laboratories, 528 U.S. 1018, 120 S.Ct. 525, 145 L.Ed.2d 406 (1999). Lower courts, therefore, continue to operate in an uncertain environment, and the current division among the circuits awaits a final resolution.

For a general discussion of the issue, see Hirshfeld, *The $50,000 Question; Does Supplemental Jurisdiction Extend to Claims Between Diverse Parties Which Do Not Meet 1332's Amount in Controversy Requirement*, 68 Temple L.Rev. 107 (1995); Rensberger, *The Amount in Controversy: Understanding the Rules of Aggregation*, 26 Ariz.St.L.J. 925 (1994); Comment, *Judicial Interpretation of the Effect of the Supplemental Jurisdiction Statute on the Complete Amount in Controversy Rule: A Case for Plain Meaning Statutory Construction*, 46 Emory L.J. 435 (1997); Case Comment, 110 Harv.L.Rev. 1173 (1997); Case Comment, 109 Harv.L.Rev. 858 (1996).

SECTION E. THE SUBJECT–MATTER JURISDICTION OF THE FEDERAL COURTS—REMOVAL

Read 28 U.S.C. § 1441 in the Supplement.

Removal is an anomalous form of jurisdiction. It gives a defendant who has been sued in a state court of competent jurisdiction the right to substitute a forum of his or her own choosing for that originally selected by the plaintiff, although the defendant's choice is limited. Removal jurisdiction is not mentioned in the Constitution. Nevertheless, the removal of cases from state to federal courts has been provided for ever since the original Judiciary Act of 1789.

SHAMROCK OIL & GAS CORP. v. SHEETS, 313 U.S. 100, 105–09, 61 S.Ct. 868, 871–72, 85 L.Ed. 1214, 1217–19 (1941), presented the question whether a plaintiff could remove a state-court action to the federal courts because defendant had interposed a counterclaim. Justice Stone, writing for a unanimous Court, held no:

Section 12 of the Judiciary Act of 1789 * * * declared that "if a suit be commenced in any state court against an alien * * * or * * * against a citizen of another state, and the matter in dispute exceeds" the jurisdictional amount "and the defendant shall, at the time of entering his appearance in such state court, file a petition for the removal of the cause," it shall be removable to the circuit court. In West v. Aurora City, 6 Wall. 139, 18 L.Ed. 819, this Court held that removal of a cause from a state to a federal court could be effected under § 12 only by a defendant against whom the suit is brought by process served upon him. Consequently a non-citizen plaintiff in the state court, against whom the citizen-defendant had asserted in the suit a claim by way of counterclaim which, under state law, had the character of an original suit, was not entitled to remove the cause. The Court ruled that the plaintiff, having submitted himself to the jurisdiction of the state court, was not entitled to avail himself of a right of removal conferred only on a defendant who has not submitted himself to the jurisdiction.

By § 3 of the Act of 1875 * * * the practice on removal was greatly liberalized. It authorized "either party, or any one or more of the plaintiffs or defendants entitled to remove any suit" from the state court to do so upon petition in such suit to the state court "before or at the term at which said cause could be first tried and before the trial thereof." These provisions were continued until the adoption of the provisions of the present statute so far as now material by the Act of 1887 * * *.

We cannot assume that Congress, in thus revising the statute, was unaware of the history which we have just detailed, or certainly that it regarded as without significance the omission from the earlier act of the phrase "either party," and the substitution for it of the phrase authorizing removal by the "defendant or defendants" in the suit, or the like omission of the provision for removal at any time before the trial, and the substitution for it of the requirement that the removal petition be filed by the "defendant" at or before the time he is required to plead in the state court.

* * *

Not only does the language of the Act of 1887 evidence the Congressional purpose to restrict the jurisdiction of the federal courts on removal, but the policy of the successive acts of Congress regulating the jurisdiction of federal courts is one calling for the strict construction of such legislation. * * *

Notes and Questions

1. Why should Section 1441(b) permit a defendant to remove a federal-question action when plaintiff has commenced it in a state court of competent jurisdiction and presumably is content to have it adjudicated in a local forum? Is defendant's right of removal consistent with the denial of original or removal jurisdiction when plaintiff anticipates or defendant raises a federal defense, as in the *Mottley* case? See Wechsler, *Federal Jurisdiction and the Revision of the Judicial Code,* 13 Law & Contemp.Prob. 216, 233–34 (1948).

2. After defendant removes, can plaintiff amend her complaint to ask for less than the jurisdictional amount in an attempt to destroy the federal court's jurisdiction? See St. Paul Mercury Indem. Co. v. Red Cab Co., 303 U.S. 283, 58 S.Ct. 586, 82 L.Ed. 845 (1938). Is it permissible for plaintiff to seek recovery for "no more than $75,000" in order to defeat defendant's right of removal? See Capps v. New Jellico Coal Co., 87 F.Supp. 369 (E.D.Tenn.1950). Is removal precluded if the amount in controversy is not apparent from the face of the plaintiff's complaint? For a discussion of the jurisdictional amount in the context of removal, see 14C Wright, Miller & Cooper, *Federal Practice and Procedure: Jurisdiction and Related Matters 3d* § 3725 (1998). May plaintiff prevent an out-of-state defendant from removing by joining an in-state defendant? Section 1304(b) of the American Law Institute, *Study of the Division of Jurisdiction Between State and Federal Courts* 141–47 (1969), suggests that an out-of-state defendant may remove the entire action if she could have done so had she been sued alone. However, courts have not followed the Institute. See 14B Wright, Miller & Cooper, *Federal Practice and Procedure: Jurisdiction and Related Matters 3d* § 3723 (1998).

3. To what extent should the determination of jurisdiction be different in the initial and removal contexts? In the initial context, the plaintiff is seeking to invoke the jurisdiction of the court. She controls the selection of the court and the selection of the parties to the suit. In the removal context, though, it is the defendant who seeks to invoke the court's jurisdiction. To what extent should we require him to be governed by the plaintiff's choices of court and parties?

4. The removal procedure is set out in 28 U.S.C. § 1446, which is in the Supplement.

5. If a case is removed erroneously, a federal court must remand it to the state court. See 28 U.S.C. § 1447(c). Section 1447(d) states that a remand order is not reviewable, except in civil rights cases pursuant to Section 1443. In THERM-TRON PRODS., INC. v. HERMANSDORFER, 423 U.S. 336, 96 S.Ct. 584, 46 L.Ed.2d 542 (1976), the Supreme Court stated that Section 1447(d) should not be read alone, suggesting that a class of remand orders could be reviewed. The district court judge had remanded a properly removed action because his docket was overcrowded, reasoning that the litigants would receive speedier adjudication of the case in the state courts. Review was sought by a writ of mandamus. The Court of Appeals for the Sixth Circuit held that it had no jurisdiction to review the order or to issue the writ because of Section 1447(d). The Supreme Court, dividing five to three, reversed, holding that Section 1447(c) and (d) should be read together so that remand may be directed only if it is based on the grounds specified in subsection (c)—removal was improvident and without jurisdiction—and only an order invoking these reasons is immune from review under subsection (d). *Cf.* Quackenbush v. Allstate Ins. Co., 517 U.S. 706, 116 S.Ct. 1712, 135 L.Ed.2d 1 (1996) (orders for remand can be reviewed as final decisions).

What if a district court erroneously denies remand of an action when grounds for federal jurisdiction do not exist and later the defect is remedied —for example, by dropping a nondiverse party— prior to the time a final judgment is rendered? In Caterpillar Inc. v. Lewis, 519 U.S. 61, 117 S.Ct. 467, 136 L.Ed.2d 437 (1996), a unanimous Supreme Court, citing practical grounds, reversed the decision of the Sixth Circuit and upheld the trial court judgment. Could the Supreme Court ruling result in game playing by litigants?

6. In CARNEGIE–MELLON UNIVERSITY v. COHILL, 484 U.S. 343, 108 S.Ct. 614, 98 L.Ed.2d 720 (1988), a former employee and his wife brought an action in state court against his former employer and supervisor for violation of federal and state age discrimination laws, wrongful discharge, breach of contract, intentional infliction of emotional distress, defamation, and misrepresentation. Defendants removed the case to federal court. Plaintiffs moved to amend their complaint to delete the federal claims, and for remand to state court. The District Court granted the motion, and remanded the case to state court. Defendants then sought a writ of mandamus.

The Supreme Court affirmed the Court of Appeals' denial of the writ, holding that a district court has discretion to remand a case to state court after determining that retaining jurisdiction over the case would be inappropriate. Remand "generally will be preferable to a dismissal when the statute of limitations on plaintiff's state-law claims has expired before the federal court has determined that it should relinquish jurisdiction over the case. * * * Even when the applicable statute of limitations has not expired, a remand may best promote the values of economy, convenience, fairness and comity." Id. at 351–53, 108 S.Ct. at 619–20, 98 L.Ed.2d at 731. The Court rejected an argument that giving district courts discretion to remand cases involving pendent state-law claims might permit plaintiffs to obtain a state forum by use of manipulative tactics:

> A district court can consider whether the plaintiff has engaged in any manipulative tactics when it decides whether to remand a case. If the plaintiff has attempted to manipulate the forum, the court should take this behavior into account in determining whether the balance of factors to be considered under the pendent jurisdiction doctrine support a remand in the case. The district courts thus can guard against forum manipulation without a blanket

rule that would prohibit the remand of all cases involving pendent state-law claims.

Id. at 357, 108 S.Ct. at 622, 98 L.Ed.2d at 734. What effect, if any, does *Cohill* have on the Court's decision in *Thermtron?* See Foster v. Chesapeake Ins. Co., 933 F.2d 1207 (3d Cir.), certiorari denied 502 U.S. 908, 112 S.Ct. 302, 116 L.Ed.2d 245 (1991).

Compare *Cohill* to In re Mobile, Alabama, 75 F.3d 605 (11th Cir.1996) (holding that once a federal claim has properly been removed, the court may not decline to exert supplemental jurisdiction and remand state claim). See also Borough of West Mifflin v. Lancaster, 45 F.3d 780 (3d Cir.1995), p. 325, infra (stating "nothing in § 1367(c) authorizes a district court to decline to entertain a claim over which it has original jurisdiction and, accordingly, that section clearly does not sanction the district court's remand of this entire case * * * to the state court").

7.   Section 1446(b) requires the notice of removal to be filed by the defendant within thirty days of receipt of the initial pleading or service of summons. Prior to the Supreme Court's ruling in Murphy Bros., Inc. v. Michetti Pipe Stringing, Inc., 526 U.S. 344, 119 S.Ct. 1322, 143 L.Ed.2d 448 (1999), many courts allowed informal service of process or courtesy copies of the complaint to activate the removal period. However, the Supreme Court in *Murphy Bros.* ruled that only formal service of process initiates the removal period. If multiple defendants are involved in a case, should the removal period begin to run when the first defendant is served with process, or should service on each defendant begin a new removal period? See Sentry Marketing, Inc. v. Unisource Worldwide, Inc., 42 F.Supp.2d 188 (N.D.N.Y.1999). Cf. Brierly v. Alusuisse Flexible Packaging, Inc., 184 F.3d 527 (6th Cir.1999), certiorari denied 528 U.S. 1076, 120 S.Ct. 790, 145 L.Ed.2d 667 (2000).

8.   The plaintiff generally is considered the master of his complaint. There-fore, a plaintiff may choose to avoid federal jurisdiction by pleading only state law claims or joining parties who will destroy diversity jurisdiction. However, there are three notable exceptions to this rule. First, a plaintiff may not defeat diversity jurisdiction by fraudulently joining a defendant against whom the plaintiff has no cause of action. Second, the plaintiff may not disguise federal causes of action that would make the case removable. See 14B Wright, Miller & Cooper, *Federal Practice and Procedure: Jurisdiction and Related Matters 3d* § 3722 (1998). As previously discussed, Note 8, p. 289, supra, this device is appropriately called artful pleading. Third, a version of artful pleading mandates that certain causes of action are so exclusively federal in character that even if the plaintiff does not plead them, they will completely preempt any state cause of action and make any cause of action the plaintiff attempts to plead federal, and, therefore, removable. See Rivet v. Regions Bank of Louisiana, 522 U.S. 470, 118 S.Ct. 921, 139 L.Ed.2d 912 (1998). See generally Miller, *Artful Pleading: A Doctrine in Search of Defini-tion*, 76 Texas L. Rev. 1781 (1998).

———

Read 28 U.S.C. § 1441(c) in the Supplement.

———

Section 1441(c) has provoked considerable discussion among courts and commentators. In AMERICAN FIRE & CAS. CO. v. FINN, 341 U.S. 6, 71 S.Ct. 534, 95 L.Ed. 702 (1951), the Supreme Court rendered what is still the most important interpretation of Section 1441(c). Finn, a Texan, sued two foreign insurance companies and their local agent, also a Texan, in a Texas state court. The complaint contained alternative claims for recovery for a fire loss suffered by plaintiff alleging that one or the other insurer had issued policies that covered the loss or that the local agent was liable for having failed to keep plaintiff's property insured. The foreign insurance companies removed the entire case to the appropriate federal court, relying on Section 1441(c). A jury trial was held and ultimately a judgment was entered for the amount of the plaintiff's loss against one of the insurers and in favor of the other company and the agent. The company against which judgment had been entered then sought to vacate the judgment on the ground that the action had been improperly removed and that the federal court lacked jurisdiction. The Supreme Court agreed, reading the Reviser's Notes to the 1948 amendments to the Judicial Code as evidencing a congressional objective to restrict removal.

The Court then attempted to define the elusive concept of "cause of action," using the passage from Baltimore S.S. Co. v. Phillips, discussed and quoted in *Gibbs,* which appears at p. 300, supra. Id. at 13, 71 S.Ct. at 539–40, 95 L.Ed. at 708. The *Finn* Court concluded that "where there is a single wrong to plaintiffs, for which relief is sought, arising from an interlocked series of transactions, there is no separate and independent claim or cause of action under § 1441(c)." Id. at 14, 71 S.Ct. at 540, 95 L.Ed. at 708–09. This statement has been applied by many courts to determine whether Section 1441(c) is applicable.

BOROUGH OF WEST MIFFLIN v. LANCASTER
United States Court of Appeals, Third Circuit, 1995.
45 F.3d 780.

[Allan D. Lindsey and Randall Coughanour alleged that security guards at a mall in West Mifflin Borough "harassed, threatened, and assaulted" them. When they requested help from the West Mifflin Police Department, Officer Evan responded to the call. However, he refused to admonish the guards, and told Lindsey and Coughanour that if they ever returned to the mall, he would arrest them. For three weeks Lindsey unsuccessfully attempted to contact somebody from the DeBartolo organization, which owned the mall, to find out why Coughanour and he had been accosted and banned from the mall. On September 27, 1991, Lindsey and Coughanour returned to the mall and were accosted by security guards and arrested by Officer Evan. They subsequently were convicted on charges stemming from the incidents on the mall; however, a three judge panel of the Superior Court of Pennsylvania vacated the convictions and discharged them.

Lindsey and Coughanour then filed a seven-count complaint in the Court of Common Pleas of Allegheny County alleging that they had been maliciously abused and prosecuted. Among other claims, they alleged that 42 U.S.C. § 1983 had been violated because the municipal defendants (the Borough of West Mifflin and Officer Evan) and the DeBartolo defendants (the mall owners, supervisors, and security officers) had conspired to deprive Lindsey and Coughanour of their civil rights.

The municipal defendants relied on the Section 1983 claim to remove the case to the United States District Court for the Western District of Pennsylvania. Lindsey and Coughanour moved to remand. The Magistrate Judge recommended a remand of the entire case, including the Section 1983 claim. He found that, "[t]he issues of state law clearly predominate in this matter." District Judge Lancaster adopted the recommendation and granted the motion to remand the entire case.

The municipal defendants sought a writ of mandamus claiming the District Judge had exceeded his authority when he remanded the entire case under Section 1441(c).]

PRATT, CIRCUIT JUDGE

* * *

DISCUSSION

Preliminarily, it is clear that we have jurisdiction to review the district court's remand order. While appellate review of remands is somewhat restricted * * *, this case, which was removed because it included a § 1983 civil rights claim brought under 28 U.S.C. §§ 1331 and 1343, falls within the specific exception to § 1447(d), which states that

> an order remanding a case to the State court from which it was removed pursuant to section 1443 ["civil rights cases"] of this title shall be reviewable by appeal or otherwise.

* * * Thus, Congress has demonstrated a special concern to preserve our power to review remand orders in civil rights cases.

* * *

C. *Application of § 1441(c).*

The dispute on this mandamus application focuses on the effect of subdivision (c) of § 1441. That provision, prior to 1990, read:

> Whenever a separate and independent claim or cause of action, which would have been removable if sued upon alone, is joined with one or more otherwise nonremovable claims or causes of action, the entire case may be removed and the district court may determine all issues therein, or, in its discretion, remand all matters not otherwise within its original jurisdiction.

In 1990, Congress amended § 1441(c) in a manner which the parties contend affects our decision in this case. See Judicial Improvements Act of 1990, Pub.L. No. 101–650 § 312, 104 Stat. 5089, 5114 (1990). Section 1441(c) now reads:

> Whenever a separate and independent claim or cause of action within the jurisdiction of [Section] 1331 of this title is joined with one or more otherwise non-removable claims or causes of action, the entire case may be removed and the district court may determine all issues therein, or, in its discretion, may remand all matters in which State law predominates.

In enacting the amendment to § 1441(c), Congress altered two provisions of the statute. First, it replaced the phrase "a separate and independent claim or cause of action, *which would have been removable if sued upon alone*" with "a separate and independent claim or cause of action *within the jurisdiction of 1331 of this title*". Second, it replaced the phrase "the district court may ... remand all matters not otherwise in its original jurisdiction" with "the district court may ... remand all matters *in which State law predominates.*"

A fair reading of the Congressional intent in enacting the amendment to § 1441(c) is that it was designed to restrict removal to only those cases falling within the court's federal question jurisdiction and to bring the remand provisions into harmony with 28 U.S.C. § 1367, thereby possibly avoiding piecemeal litigation. * * *

In the present case, the district court relied upon the addition which reads "the district court may ... remand all matters in which State law predominates" to remand the entire case, including the § 1983 claim, to state court. It did so without regard for the requirement, which the Congress left unchanged when it amended § 1441(c), that the federal cause of action removed by the municipal defendants had to be "separate and independent" from the state causes of action.

Thus, § 1441(c) provides for removal or remand only where the federal question claims are "separate and independent" from the state law claims with which they are joined in the complaint. However, where there is a single injury to plaintiff for which relief is sought, arising from an interrelated series of events or transactions, there is no separate or independent claim or cause of action under § 1441(c). American Fire & Casualty Co. v. Finn * * *. Suits involving pendent (now "supplemental") state claims that "derive from a common nucleus of operative fact", see United Mine Workers v. Gibbs, * * * do not fall within the scope of § 1441(c), since pendent claims are not "separate and independent". * * *

It is apparent, then, that "§ 1441(c) grants the district court only a limited authority to remand a case." Kabealo v. Davis, 829 F.Supp. 923, 926 (S.D.Ohio 1993) (citing to Buchner v. F.D.I.C., 981 F.2d 816 (5th Cir.1993)). * * *

* * *

* * * Other district courts have apparently read the 1990 amendments as broadening rather than narrowing the scope of their discretion to remand. We cannot agree.

For instance, in Moore v. DeBiase, 766 F.Supp. 1311 (D.N.J.1991), the complaint presented allegations similar to the allegations found in the present case. Moore had accused DeBiase, a police supervisor, of malicious abuse of authority, abuse of police procedure, a conspiracy to terminate Moore, defamation, and violation of § 1983 by depriving him of his "rights, privileges, and immunities secured by the United States Constitution and New Jersey Law." Id. at 1314. Moore also sought damages against the Borough of Dunnellen and the Dunnellen Police Department under conspiracy and respondeat superior theories. Id.

Without determining that Moore's § 1983 claim was "separate and independent" from his state law claims, the district court remanded all of Moore's claims, including his § 1983 claim. It did so in the belief that the phrase "all matters in which State law predominates" in § 1441(c) permits the remand of even federal claims within the district court's original federal jurisdiction if, in the discretion of the district court, state law predominated in the action as a whole.

As we have pointed out, however, unless the federal question claims removed by the defendant were "separate and independent" from the state law claims, § 1441(c) cannot apply and the district court must retain the federal claim. Hence, the district court's discretion to remand under § 1441(c) can pertain only to those *state law claims* which the district court could decline to hear under 28 U.S.C. § 1367. * * * Thus, we reject the reasoning of Moore v. DeBiase and those courts which have adopted its rationale. * * *

Similarly in the present case, Lindsey and Coughanour rely on the same series of events for all counts of their complaint, including the federal § 1983 count; therefore, the federal claim is not separate and independent under § 1441(c), and the district court had no authority to remand the case under that section.

D. *Application of § 1367(c).*

The plaintiffs insist that, even if the district court was not authorized to remand this entire case under § 1441(c), its action should be sustained under the authority of 28 U.S.C. § 1367(c) which gives a district court discretion to decline to hear certain state claims it would have supplemental jurisdiction to entertain under § 1367(a). We disagree for two reasons. First, nothing in § 1367(c) authorizes a district court to decline to entertain a claim over which is has original jurisdiction and, accordingly, that section clearly does not sanction the district court's remand of this entire case, including the civil rights claims, to the state court.

Further, § 1367(c) cannot legitimately be invoked to affirm even the district court's remand of the state claims to the state court. While we agree with plaintiffs that the discretion bestowed by § 1367(c) exists with respect to removed claims as well as claims filed initially in the district court, it is apparent that the district court has not exercised that discretion in this case. The magistrate judge's opinion, adopted by the district court, refers only to § 1441(c) and it is apparent from that opinion that the court remanded the entire case based solely on the authority of that section. Moreover, the result of an exercise of discretion under § 1367(c) in circumstances like those before the district court would have been two parallel proceedings, one in federal court and one in the state system, and a district court cannot properly exercise its discretion under § 1367(c) without taking that fact into account. The district court's § 1441(c) analysis accordingly cannot serve as a surrogate for a § 1367(c) analysis that was not conducted.

As we have indicated, § 1367(c) is potentially applicable in a removed case involving federal claims and state claims over which the district court has supplemental jurisdiction. A district court may thus be called upon to exercise its discretion at any time during the course of such a proceeding in light of the circumstances that then exist. Gibbs * * *. Because the district court in this case may hereafter be called upon to exercise its discretion under § 1367(c), we offer the following guidance.

* * *

While § 1367(c) does not specify what disposition the district court is to make of state claims it decides not to hear, based on the teachings of Carnegie–Mellon, [Note 6, p. 323, supra,] * * * we believe that in a case that has been removed from a state court, a remand to that court is a viable alternative to a dismissal without prejudice. * * *

Section 1367(a)'s grant of "supplemental" jurisdiction was intended to broaden the preexisting scope of what had previously been termed "pendent" jurisdiction to include claims involving the addition of parties. * * *

Under Gibbs jurisprudence, where the claim over which the district court has original jurisdiction is dismissed before trial, the district court must decline to decide the pendent state claims unless considerations of judicial economy, convenience, and fairness to the parties provide an affirmative justification for doing so. * * * Where the original federal jurisdiction claim is proceeding to trial, however, such considerations will normally counsel an exercise of district court jurisdiction over state claims based on the same nucleus of operative facts unless the district court can point to some substantial countervailing consideration. * * *

Plaintiffs do not suggest that subparagraphs (1), (3), or (4) of § 1367(c) are applicable here. They do maintain that their state claims substantially predominate over their federal claims and, accordingly, that this case falls within subparagraph (2). The district court is in a better position than we to pass upon this contention. Moreover, even if § 1367(c) does not authorize a refusal to hear the state claims based on the current record, it might provide that authority at some later stage in the proceeding. Accordingly, the following observations concerning § 1367(c)(2) are offered solely by way of guidance and are not intended to foreclose the district court from hereafter exercising its discretion under § 1367(c) upon appropriate application.

As we have noted, the "substantially predominates" standard of § 1367(c)(2) comes from Gibbs. It is important to recognize that this standard was fashioned as a limited exception to the operation of the doctrine of pendent jurisdiction—a doctrine that seeks to promote judicial economy, convenience, and fairness to litigants by litigating in one case all claims that arise out of the same nucleus of operative fact. When a district court exercises its discretion not to hear state claims under § 1367(c)(2), the advantages of a single suit are lost. For that reason, § 1367(c)(2)'s authority should be invoked only where there is an important countervailing interest to be served by relegating state claims to the state court. This will normally be the case only where "a state claim constitutes the real body of a case, to which the federal claim is only an appendage," Gibbs, * * *—only where permitting litigation of all claims in the district court can accurately be described as allowing a federal tail to wag what is in substance a state dog.

Given the origin of the "substantially predominate" standard, a district court's analysis under § 1367(c)(2) should track the Supreme Court's explication of that standard in Gibbs. We do not understand plaintiffs to suggest that there is a substantial quantity of evidence supporting their state claims that would not be relevant to the federal claims that the defendants, acting under color of state law, conspired to violate plaintiffs' constitutional rights by assaulting, wrongfully arresting, and maliciously prosecuting them. Thus, in the terminology of Gibbs, the state issues would not appear to "substantially predominate ... in terms of proof." * * *. Nor would they appear to "substantially predominate ... in terms of ... the comprehensiveness of the remedy sought." Id. The remedy sought based on the state claims is the same remedy sought based on the federal claims—damages for the same set of injuries to the plaintiffs. As we observed in Sparks [v. Hershey, 661 F.2d 30 (3d Cir.1981)], * * * the difficulty of avoiding duplicative recoveries is a factor tending to weigh against litigating related federal and state claims in different fora.

This leaves the issue of whether the state claims can be said to "substantially predominate ... in terms of ... the scope of the issues raised." Id. It is true that the state claims here outnumber the federal claims. The "substantially predominate" standard, however, is not satisfied simply by a numerical count of the state and federal claims the plaintiff has chosen to assert on the basis of the same set of facts. An analysis more sensitive to the relevant interests is required.

While federal constitutional tort law under § 1983 derives much of its content from the general common law of torts, plaintiffs' civil rights claims based on the alleged assault, arrest, and prosecution are nevertheless governed exclusively by federal law. * * * While the claims based upon the arrest and the prosecution may require an inquiry into whether the defendants had probable cause to believe a crime had been committed and this may in part require some reference to the state criminal law, the probable cause issue and the other issues raised by these claims are nevertheless issues of federal law and concern. * * *

There are, to be sure, a complementary set of state law issues arising out of the state claims based on the alleged assault, arrest, and prosecution. But these state issues do not appear from our vantage point to substantially predominate over the comparable but distinct federal issues. Plaintiffs do not suggest that these state issues are more important, more complex, more time consuming to resolve, or in any other way more significant than their federal counterparts.

The only other state issues are those which may arise from the plaintiffs' negligence claims against the municipal defendants and the DeBartolo defendants. The dimensions of those claims are not clear at this stage of the case, but it seems unlikely to us that they will cause the state issues to "substantially predominate" within the meaning of § 1367(c)(2). If the factual allegations of the complaint are accepted at face value, as we are required to do at this point, this case involves several substantial claims that the plaintiffs' constitutional rights have been infringed. In such circumstances, we believe it will be the rare case, at least, where the addition of straightforward negligence claims based on the same facts as the constitutional claims will cause the state issues to substantially predominate.

In short, while we do not foreclose the parties from hereafter arguing, and the district court from hereafter considering, the issue posed by § 1367(c)(2), we think it unlikely that either will be able to point to a countervailing interest that would justify bifurcating this case into a federal and a state suit that will essentially duplicate each other.

* * *

Accordingly, the petition for a writ of mandamus is granted.

Notes and Questions

1. The 1990 amendment of Section 1441(c) eliminated the use of diversity of citizenship jurisdiction as a basis for removal under Section 1441(c). However, even before this change, many commentators argued that diversity cases could not be brought under Section 1441(c). See 14C Wright, Miller & Cooper, *Federal Practice and Procedure: Jurisdiction and Related Matters 3d* § 3724 (1998). One obvious effect of the 1990 amendment was to limit the number of diversity cases that can be brought in federal court. In addition to prohibiting removal of diversity cases, the 1990 amendment was interpreted to bar the defendant in ROE v. LITTLE COMPANY OF MARY HOSPITAL, 800 F.Supp. 620 (N.D.Ill.1992), from removing because claims asserted against one of the defendants, the Red Cross, came within federal question jurisdiction based upon 36 U.S.C. § 2, rather than Section 1331, thereby making it ineligible for removal under Section 1441(c) given the language of that provision. Do the policy reasons for limiting the ability to remove under Section 1441(c) on the basis of diversity jurisdiction apply to cases such as *Roe*?

2. When Section 1367 was first enacted, there were some doubts as to its applicability to cases removed from state courts to federal courts. In CITY OF CHICAGO v. INTERNATIONAL COLLEGE OF SURGEONS, 522 U.S. 156, 118 S.Ct. 523, 139 L.Ed.2d 525 (1997), the Supreme Court laid these doubts to rest and held that Section 1367 applies equally to state claims in removed cases. In addition, the Court held that supplemental jurisdiction exists over state law claims for (deferential, on-the-record) judicial review of decisions by a local administrative agency. The interplay between Section 1367 and Section 1441 (the general removal statute) of Title 28 has been a source of much confusion. In particular, the "separate and independent claim" requirement of Section 1441(c) seems either redundant in light of Section 1367 or simply unconstitutional in light of *Gibbs*. For a full discussion of the problems, see Steinman, *Crosscurrents: Supplemental Jurisdiction, Removal and the ALI Revision Project*, 74 Ind.L.J. 75 (1998).

3. In order to qualify for removal under Section 1441(c), a claim must be "separate and independent;" in order to qualify for supplemental jurisdiction under Section 1367, a claim must "form part of the same case or controversy." As *Borough of West Mifflin* makes clear, a claim cannot simultaneously satisfy both of these standards. However, are there any claims that are too interconnected to qualify as separate and independent, but not adequately connected to qualify as part of the same case or controversy? Courts have been silent on this topic.

4. What policies underlie the removability of (a) "a separate and independent claim or cause of action" and (b) "the entire case," including "otherwise non-removable claims or causes of action," when a removable separate and independent claim is present? See generally 14C Wright, Miller & Cooper, *Federal Practice and Procedure: Jurisdiction and Related Matters 3d* § 3724 (1998).

5. In Hurn v. Oursler, quoted at length in United Mine Workers v. Gibbs, pp. 299–301, supra, the Supreme Court limited pendent jurisdiction by saying that "the rule does not go so far as to permit a federal court to assume jurisdiction of a separate and distinct non-federal cause of action because it is joined in the same complaint with a federal cause of action." How is this consistent with the

requirement in Section 1441(c) that a federal claim must be "separate and independent" before the otherwise nonremovable claims can be heard in a federal court? See generally Cohen, *Problems in the Removal of a "Separate and Independent Claim or Cause of Action,"* 46 Minn.L.Rev. 1 (1961); Lewin, *The Federal Courts' Hospitable Back Door—Removal of "Separate and Independent" Non–Federal Causes of Action*, 66 Harv.L.Rev. 423 (1953); Moore & Van Dercreek, *Multi-Party, Multi–Claim Removal Problems: The Separate and Independent Claim Under Section 1441(c)*, 46 Iowa L.Rev. 489 (1961); Comment, *Diversity Removal Where the Federal Court Would Not Have Original Jurisdiction: A Suggested Reform*, 114 U.Pa.L.Rev. 709 (1966).

6. A suit is brought in state court. The defendant properly removes the action and impleads a third-party defendant. The original plaintiff now wishes to assert a transactionally related claim against the third-party defendant, but there is no independent basis for federal jurisdiction over the claim. Does Section 1367(b) prevent a federal district court from exercising supplemental jurisdiction over the claim? See Steinman, *Removal, Remand, and Review in Pendent Claim and Pendent Party Cases*, 41 Vand.L.Rev. 923 (1988).

7. Is 28 U.S.C. § 1441(c) constitutional? Consider the following:

If the state claims are sufficiently related to the federal claims to be within supplemental jurisdiction, then the case is removable under § 1441(a) and § 1441(c) does not apply, while if the state claims are sufficiently unrelated to the federal claims to be beyond the constitutional scope of supplemental jurisdiction, then § 1441(c)'s apparent attempt to bring them within federal jurisdiction is unconstitutional.

Hartnett, *A New Trick From An Old and Abused Dog: Section 1441(c) Lives and Now Permits the Remand of Federal Question Cases*, 63 Fordham L.Rev. 1099, 1149 (1995). Professor Hartnett, however, argues that it is constitutional to remove a case that includes claims beyond the common nucleus of operative fact, and thus not within the court's supplemental jurisdiction. He does not argue that it is constitutional to adjudicate the entire case, but that the district court must remand those claims outside the scope of Article III. Compare McFarland, *The Unconstitutional Stub of Section 1441(c)*, 54 Ohio St.L.J. 1059 (1993) ("The correct, broad definition of claim for purposes of supplemental jurisdiction leaves no constitutional room for section 1441(c), as amended in 1990, to operate. Separate claim removal jurisdiction today can apply only to a theory of recovery completely factually unrelated to the federal question. Such a factually discrete theory is beyond the Osborn constitutional case, as the limits were defined in Gibbs. Consequently, that operation is beyond the limited authority of the federal courts granted by the Constitution.").

8. Can a state action be removed to federal court on the basis of supplemental jurisdiction because of its relationship to a prior or pending federal action? The court in AHEARN v. CHARTER TOWNSHIP OF BLOOMFIELD, 100 F.3d 451 (6th Cir.1996), answered in the negative, holding that supplemental jurisdiction is not a source of original jurisdiction and that removal is proper only when the district court has original jurisdiction over the action. What if the state action can be consolidated with a related action already in federal court? See Keene v. Auto Owners Ins. Co., 78 F.Supp.2d 1270 (S.D.Ala.1999) (holding removal improper).

SECTION F. CHALLENGING THE SUBJECT–MATTER JURISDICTION OF THE COURT

1. DIRECT ATTACK ON A COURT'S LACK OF SUBJECT–MATTER JURISDICTION

———

Read Federal Rules of Civil Procedure 8(a)(1), 12(b)(1), and (h)(3), 60(b)(4), and Official Form 2, and 28 U.S.C. § 1653 in the Supplement.

———

As we repeatedly have seen, in the federal courts a lack of subject-matter jurisdiction may be asserted at any time by any interested party, either in the answer, or in the form of a suggestion to the court prior to final judgment or on appeal. And it is axiomatic that the parties may not create the jurisdiction of a federal court by agreement or by consent. See, e.g., Mansfield, C. & L. M. R. Co. v. Swan, 111 U.S. 379, 4 S.Ct. 510, 28 L.Ed. 462 (1884). To what extent is this required because the objection arguably goes to the power of a court of limited jurisdiction to hear and decide a case?

Notes and Questions

1. Generally, a court should decide subject-matter jurisdiction issues before anything else, because if it is lacking the court must dismiss and other matters need not be determined. But since personal jurisdiction also is a threshold issue that deals with the court's power to decide a case, must it decide a subject-matter jurisdiction issue before deciding personal jurisdiction?

In RUHRGAS AG v. MARATHON OIL CO., 526 U.S. 574, 119 S.Ct. 1563, 143 L.Ed.2d 760 (1999), the defendant removed the case to federal court, and the plaintiff moved to remand for lack of subject-matter jurisdiction. The defendant then moved to dismiss for lack of personal jurisdiction, and the District Court dismissed for lack of personal jurisdiction without deciding the subject-matter jurisdiction question. A panel of the Fifth Circuit reversed, holding that the trial court had to determine subject-matter jurisdiction prior to deciding other matters. The Fifth Circuit sitting en banc agreed with the panel. The Supreme Court unanimously reversed, holding that since both subject-matter and personal juris-diction are required by the Constitution and affect a federal court's power to adjudicate a case, there is no reason to require a district court to decide subject-matter jurisdiction first:

> Where * * * a district court has before it a straightforward personal jurisdic-tion issue presenting no complex question of state law, and the alleged defect in subject-matter jurisdiction raises a difficult and novel question, the court does not abuse its discretion by turning directly to personal jurisdiction.

Id. at 588, 119 S.Ct. at 1572, 143 L.Ed.2d at 773. How far does the Supreme Court's approach go? May a court decide a statute of limitations issue or some aspect of the merits when the case may be more efficiently disposed of on one of those grounds than by grappling with a difficult question of jurisdiction? See Friedenthal, *The Crack in the Steel Case*, 68 Geo. Wash. L. Rev. 258 (2000).

2. Are there situations in which defects in subject-matter jurisdiction should be immune from direct attack? In Di FRISCHIA v. NEW YORK CENTRAL R. CO., 279 F.2d 141, 144 (3d Cir.1960), the defendants initially objected to the jurisdiction of the court, asserting lack of diversity, but then filed a stipulation withdrawing the objection. After extensive pretrial preparations, and after the statute of limitations had run on any state-court action, the defendant reasserted its jurisdictional objection. The District Court dismissed the action, but the Third Circuit reversed, refusing to permit defendant to "play fast and loose with the judicial machinery and deceive the courts." Accord, American Law Institute, *Study of the Division of Jurisdiction Between State and Federal Courts* § 1386, at 64–66, 366–74 (1969). See Dobbs, *Beyond Bootstrap: Foreclosing the Issue of Subject–Matter Jurisdiction Before Final Judgment*, 51 Minn.L.Rev. 491 (1967). *Di Frischia* has since been criticized and distinguished as limited to its facts. See, e.g., Von Dunser v. Aronoff, 915 F.2d 1071, 1074–75 (6th Cir.1990); Rubin v. Buckman, 727 F.2d 71, 72 (3d Cir.1984). And it was at least implicitly disapproved by the Supreme Court in Owen Equipment & Erection Co. v. Kroger, p. 305, supra. See also Martineau, *Subject–Matter Jurisdiction as a New Issue on Appeal: Reining in an Unruly Horse*, 1988 B.Y.U.L.Rev. 1.

3. In UNITED STATES v. UNITED MINE WORKERS, 330 U.S. 258, 67 S.Ct. 677, 91 L.Ed. 884 (1947), the District Court issued a temporary restraining order to prevent a strike in mines that earlier had been seized by the government. The union and its officers disobeyed the order, and subsequently were held in contempt of court, notwithstanding the defendants' contention that under the Norris–LaGuardia Act the District Court lacked jurisdiction to issue injunctions in labor disputes. A divided Supreme Court held that the order had to be obeyed until set aside, and that the defendants could not raise the asserted lack of jurisdiction as a defense to the contempt charges. Justice Frankfurter, concurring in the result only, emphasized the power of a federal court to determine its jurisdiction:

> Only when a court is so obviously traveling outside its orbit as to be merely usurping judicial forms and facilities, may an order issued by a court be disobeyed and treated as though it were a letter to a newspaper. Short of an indisputable want of authority on the part of a court, the very existence of a court presupposes its power to entertain a controversy, if only to decide, after deliberation, that it has no power over the particular controversy.

Id. at 309–10, 67 S.Ct. at 704, 91 L.Ed. at 921. Subsequent decisions suggest a general principle that obedience to a temporary restraining order is required, even though the issuing court may lack subject-matter jurisdiction or otherwise may have based its decision on an incorrect view of the law, unless there is no opportunity for effective appellate review of the decree. See Hampton Tree Farms, Inc. v. Yeutter, 956 F.2d 869, 871 (9th Cir.), certiorari denied 506 U.S. 816, 113 S.Ct. 56, 121 L.Ed.2d 25 (1992); 11A Wright, Miller & Kane, *Federal Practice and Procedure: Civil 2d* § 2960 (1995).

4. In WILLY v. COASTAL CORP., 503 U.S. 131, 112 S.Ct. 1076, 117 L.Ed.2d 280 (1992), plaintiff brought a wrongful discharge action against his former employer, who removed the action to federal court. The District Court dismissed the case for failure to state a claim, and imposed sanctions on the plaintiff pursuant to Federal Rule 11. Plaintiff appealed, arguing that the District Court had no authority to impose sanctions since it lacked subject-matter jurisdiction. The Supreme Court upheld the ability of the District Court to impose sanctions:

The District Court order which the petitioner seeks to upset is one that is collateral to the merits. * * * Such an order implicates no constitutional concern because it "does not signify a district court's assessment of the legal merits of the complaint." * * * It therefore does not raise the issue of a district court adjudicating the merits of a "case or controversy" over which it lacks jurisdiction.

Id. at 137, 112 S.Ct. at 1080, 117 L.Ed.2d at 289.

2. COLLATERAL ATTACK ON A JUDGMENT FOR LACK OF SUBJECT–MATTER JURISDICTION

If neither the parties nor the court notice the absence of subject-matter jurisdiction at any time during the original proceeding, can defendant successfully raise the lack of jurisdiction as a defense to a subsequent proceeding by plaintiff to enforce the decree? Would it make any difference for purposes of collateral attack if the issue of jurisdiction had been raised and litigated in the original action and it had been decided that the court did have power to proceed? In grappling with this problem, reconsider Capron v. Van Noorden, p. 21, supra, and Des Moines Navigation & R. Co. v. Iowa Homestead Co., p. 58, supra, and recall that one of the oldest pieces of jurisdiction dogma is the maxim that a judgment rendered by a court that lacked jurisdiction over the subject matter (or the "cause," to use the older terminology) is void and a nullity. See, e. g., The Case of the Marshalsea, 10 Co.Rep. 68b, 77 Eng.Rep. 1027 (K.B. 1613); Elliott v. Peirsol, 26 U.S. (1 Pet.) 328, 7 L.Ed. 164 (1828). Of course, the subject is considerably more complex than the dogma would indicate, and *Des Moines* demonstrates that collateral attack is not always an available technique for challenging a judgment on the ground that the rendering court lacked subject-matter jurisdiction.

Section 10 of the first *Restatement of Judgments* analyzed the question of the availability of collateral attack in terms of balancing the policies underlying res judicata and finality of judgments, which are treated in detail in Chapter Fourteen, against the policy of prohibiting a court from exceeding the powers conferred upon it by the legislature or the jurisdiction's organic law. It stated that if the court in the original action determined that it had subject-matter jurisdiction, the permissibility of collateral attack depended on weighing a non-exclusive list of factors:

(a) the lack of jurisdiction over the subject matter was clear;

(b) the determination as to jurisdiction depended upon a question of law rather than of fact;

(c) the court was one of limited and not of general jurisdiction;

(d) the question of jurisdiction was not actually litigated;

(e) the policy against the court's acting beyond its jurisdiction is strong.

The *Restatement (Second), Judgments* §§ 12, 69 (1982) takes the approach that the judgment in a contested action, whether or not the question of subject-matter jurisdiction actually was litigated, is beyond collateral attack unless there are no justifiable interests of reliance that must be protected, and:

(1) The subject matter of the action was so plainly beyond the court's jurisdiction that its entertaining the action was a manifest abuse of authority; or

(2) Allowing the judgment to stand would substantially infringe the authority of another tribunal or agency of government; or

(3) The judgment was rendered by a court lacking capability to make an adequately informed determination of a question concerning its own jurisdiction and as a matter of procedural fairness the party seeking to avoid the judgment should have opportunity belatedly to attack the court's subject-matter jurisdiction.

In addition, the *Restatement (Second) of Judgments* generally permits collateral attack on the original court's subject-matter jurisdiction, as well as on personal jurisdiction and inadequate notice, in default judgment situations. Id. § 65. Does this approach go far enough, or too far, toward giving preclusive effect to the original court's judgment? See generally Moore, *Collateral Attack on Subject–Matter Jurisdiction: A Critique of the Restatement (Second) of Judgments*, 66 Cornell L.Rev. 534 (1981).

The Supreme Court has had to deal with problems of collateral attack on numerous occasions. In CHICOT COUNTY DRAINAGE DIST. v. BAXTER STATE BANK, 308 U.S. 371, 60 S.Ct. 317, 84 L.Ed. 329 (1940), parties who had notice but chose not to appear in the original action attempted to attack collaterally a judgment rendered by a district court sitting as a court of bankruptcy under a statute that was later declared unconstitutional. The Supreme Court refused to allow the attack:

> * * * If the general principles governing the defense of *res judicata* are applicable, [respondents], having the opportunity to raise the question of invalidity, were not the less bound by the decree because they failed to raise it. * * *

> * * * The lower federal courts are all courts of limited jurisdiction, that is, with only the jurisdiction which Congress has prescribed. But none the less they are courts with authority * * * to determine whether or not they have jurisdiction to entertain the cause and for this purpose to construe and apply the statute under which they are asked to act. Their determinations of such questions, while open to direct review, may not be assailed collaterally.

Id. at 375–76, 60 S.Ct. at 319, 84 L.Ed. at 333.

But collateral attack was allowed by the Court in KALB v. FEUER-STEIN, 308 U.S. 433, 60 S.Ct. 343, 84 L.Ed. 370 (1940), decided the same day as *Chicot*. The questions for decision in *Kalb* were whether a state court had jurisdiction to render a judgment confirming a foreclosure sale while the mortgagor's petition under the Bankruptcy Act was pending in a bankruptcy court, and, if not, whether the mortgagor was prohibited from attacking the state-court judgment collaterally. The Court answered both questions in the negative:

> It is generally true that a judgment by a court of competent jurisdiction bears a presumption of regularity and is not thereafter subject to collateral attack. But Congress, because its power over the subject of

bankruptcy is plenary, may by specific bankruptcy legislation create an exception to that principle and render judicial acts taken with respect to the person or property of a debtor whom the bankruptcy law protects nullities and vulnerable collaterally. * * *

We think the language and broad policy of the * * * Act conclusively demonstrate that Congress intended to, and did deprive the Wisconsin County Court of the power and jurisdiction to continue or maintain in any manner the foreclosure proceedings against appellants without the consent * * * of the bankruptcy court * * *.

Id. at 438–40, 60 S.Ct. at 346, 84 L.Ed. at 374–75.

Which of the categories in the two *Restatements* seems determinative of the *Kalb* case? Are *Chicot* and *Kalb* reconcilable? A fuller discussion of *Chicot* and *Kalb* can be found in Boskey & Braucher, *Jurisdiction and Collateral Attack: October Term, 1939,* 40 Colum.L.Rev. 1006 (1940).

DURFEE v. DUKE, 375 U.S. 106, 84 S.Ct. 242, 11 L.Ed.2d 186 (1963), involved a dispute over title to a tract of bottom land on the Missouri River, which forms the boundary between Nebraska and Missouri. A Missouri federal District Court allowed collateral attack on a Nebraska judgment quieting title, on the ground that considerations of territorial sovereignty outweighed the policies of res judicata. The Nebraska court's subject-matter jurisdiction depended on whether the land was within Nebraska, which "depended entirely upon a factual question—whether a shift in the river's course had been caused by avulsion or accretion." The question had been fully litigated in the Nebraska action. The Supreme Court reversed:

> * * * [W]hile it is established that a court in one State, when asked to give effect to the judgment of a court in another State, may constitutionally inquire into the foreign court's jurisdiction to render that judgment, the modern decisions of this Court have carefully delineated the permissible scope of such an inquiry. From these decisions there emerges the general rule that a judgment is entitled to full faith and credit—even as to questions of jurisdiction—when the second court's inquiry discloses that those questions have been fully and fairly litigated and finally decided in the court which rendered the original judgment. * * *
>
> To be sure, the general rule of finality of jurisdictional determinations is not without exceptions. Doctrines of federal preemption or sovereign immunity may in some contexts be controlling. Kalb v. Feuerstein * * *. But no such overriding considerations are present here.

Id. at 111–14, 84 S.Ct. at 245–47, 11 L.Ed.2d at 191–93. The decision in *Durfee* was followed in Underwriters Nat. Assurance Co. v. North Carolina Life, Acc. & Health Ins. Guar. Ass'n, 455 U.S. 691, 102 S.Ct. 1357, 71 L.Ed.2d 558 (1982).

A more recent example of the Supreme Court's attitude toward collateral attack can be found in UNITED STATES CATHOLIC CONFERENCE v. ABORTION RIGHTS MOBILIZATION, INC., 487 U.S. 72, 108 S.Ct. 2268, 101 L.Ed.2d 69 (1988). In the underlying action, Abortion Rights Mobilization (ARM) sued to revoke the tax-exempt status of the Roman Catholic Church because of the church's intervention in favor of political candidates who supported the church's position on abortion. ARM served the Conference with a subpoena seeking extensive documentary evidence to support its claims. The Conference refused to comply with the subpoena and was held in civil contempt with a fine of $50,000 per day for further noncompliance. The Supreme Court held that a nonparty witness, the Conference, could challenge the court's lack of subject-matter jurisdiction in defense of a civil contempt citation. The Court reasoned:

> * * * The distinction between subject-matter jurisdiction and waivable defenses is not a mere nicety of legal metaphysics. It rests instead on the central principle of a free society that courts have finite bounds of authority, some of constitutional origin, which exist to protect citizens from the very wrong asserted here, the excessive use of judicial power. The courts, no less than the political branches of the government, must respect the limits of their authority.

Id. at 77, 108 S.Ct. at 2271, 101 L.Ed.2d at 77.

See generally 18 Wright, Miller & Cooper, *Federal Practice and Procedure: Jurisdiction and Related Matters* § 4428 (1981) (2001 Pocket Part); Dobbs, *The Validation of Void Judgments: The Bootstrap Principle, Part I*, 53 Va.L.Rev. 1003 (1967); Note, *Filling the Void: Judicial Power and Jurisdictional Attacks on Judgments*, 87 Yale L.J. 164 (1977).

Chapter 5

VENUE, TRANSFER, AND FORUM NON CONVENIENS

SECTION A. VENUE

1. GENERAL PRINCIPLES

STEVENS, VENUE STATUTES: DIAGNOSIS AND PROPOSED CURE, 49 Mich.L.Rev. 307, 307–15 (1951):

Venue * * * means the place of trial in an action within a state. Given a cause of action, and having decided what court has jurisdiction over the subject matter, the lawyer must lay the venue, that is, select the place of trial. In making this decision, the lawyer in every state of the United States turns in the first instance, not to common law, but to statute, constitutional provision or rule of court. And he finds that the "proper" venue of his action depends upon the theory of his claim, the subject matter of his claim, the parties involved, or a combination of these factors.

Most codes make provision for the place of trial in local actions, and all codes provide in one way or another for venue in transitory actions arising both within and without the state. Many states make special provision for divorce actions, actions against executors, and actions for the specific recovery of personal property. Most states also provide for venue in actions against residents, against nonresidents, against corporations, domestic and foreign, against partnerships, associations and individuals doing business in the state, and against the state, or a county, or a city or public officers generally or specifically. The nature of the plaintiff, as a resident or nonresident, corporation, domestic or foreign, or political entity, is another factor frequently considered and provided for. * * *

A comparative study of contemporary venue provisions reveals some thirteen different fact situations upon which venue statutes are predicated.

A. *Where the subject of action or part thereof is situated.* The common law concept of actions which were local because the facts could have occurred only in a particular place still persists. As might well be expected, the proper venue for such actions is the county where the subject of the action is situated. There is, however, considerable variation from state to state as to what types of cases are local and fall into this category. * * *

This type of venue * * * is based upon the idea that the court of the county in which the res, which is the subject matter of the suit, is located is best able to deal with the problem. The local sheriff can attach, deliver or execute upon the property. The local clerk can make the necessary entries with a minimum of red tape where title to land is affected. Trial convenience is served where "a view" is necessary or of value in reaching a determination. Third parties can readily ascertain, at a logical point of inquiry, the status of a res in which they may be interested.

It is submitted that these factors are of sufficient importance in this type of case to outweigh other considerations such as convenience of parties or witnesses in the selection of place of trial. * * *

B. *Where the cause of action, or part thereof, arose or accrued.* Convenience of witnesses is the most logical reason for venue provisions allowing the action to be brought in the county where the cause of action, or part thereof, arose or accrued. And since convenience of witnesses is a very practical problem in the trial of a law suit, one would expect to find venue based upon the place where the cause of action arose or accrued a rather common, and general, provision. * * *

The idea behind this type of venue provision * * * is sound and popular. * * * However, its usefulness has been somewhat impaired by difficulties arising out of problems of statutory interpretation. First, what do the words "arose" and "accrued" mean? Second, what is the difference, if any, between "arose" and "accrued"? And, third, what is the meaning of the phrase "or part thereof"? * * *

C. *Where some fact is present or happened.* There is a sizeable group of statutes which provide for trial of the action in the county where some particular fact or fact situation related to, but no part of, the cause of action is present or happened. * * *

If the purpose of venue is trial convenience, either of parties, or witnesses, or the court or court officials, then it is hard to find any real justification for this group of venue provisions. Most if not all of them are examples of singling out certain specific types of actions for special treatment where a need for special treatment is not or at least no longer [is] apparent. * * *

D. *Where the defendant resides.* Convenience of the defendant is the reason usually given for venue statutes which provide for the place of trial in the county where the defendant resides—the theory probably being, as suggested by Professor E.R. Sunderland, "that since the plaintiff controls the institution of the suit he might behave oppressively toward the defendant unless restrained." * * *

E. *Where the defendant is doing business.* * * * Convenience of the defendant, and of witnesses, appears to be the reason behind such provisions where they are tied to causes of action arising out of the doing of business in the state. Convenience of the defendant, and even more clearly, convenience of the plaintiff, by providing a county in which to lay the venue against a nonresident individual, partnership, company or corporation without undue inconvenience to defendant, is served by the broader type of provision— against certain classes of defendants generally. * * *

F. *Where defendant has an office or place of business, or an agent, or representative, or where an agent or officer of defendant resides.* [These venue statutes] * * * are quite common where a corporation, company or some other type of business organization is the defendant. Convenience of the plaintiff, rather than the defendant, is the moving consideration behind such statutes in most instances. * * *

G. *Where the plaintiff resides.* * * *

Convenience of the plaintiff is the obvious reason behind venue statutes of this nature. Convenience of plaintiff's witnesses may or may not be served, depending upon the nature of the action. * * * In certain types of cases against certain classes of defendants—such as an action on a foreign cause of action against a nonresident—this type of provision is both logical and practical. * * *

H. *Where the plaintiff is doing business.* * * * Obviously the convenience of the plaintiff is the sole consideration behind such a provision. It is submitted that other factors of trial convenience such as convenience of witnesses and of the defendant are more important, and that in view of the number of adherents to this ground of venue, it would be wise to advocate its abandonment. * * *

I. *Where the defendant may be found.* Venue based upon the county where the defendant may be found is in accord with the common law doctrine that the right of action follows the person. * * *

It is difficult to find any sound reason for venue based upon where the defendant may be found. It serves no useful purpose—no trial convenience of either witnesses or parties. It is a good example of a historical hang-over—a type of provision which has long since outlived its usefulness. The problem which this type of provision was designed to solve was and is not one of venue but of service of process. * * *

J. *Where the defendant may be summoned or served.* Another group of statutes, also based upon the common law doctrine that the right of action follows the person, provides that venue may be laid in the county where the defendant may be summoned, or served with process. * * *

The comments which were made with respect to venue based upon where the defendant may be found apply with equal force to this type of provision. * * *

K. *In the county designated in the plaintiff's complaint.* * * *

Venue provisions of this type give the plaintiff an unnecessary economic advantage not warranted by convenience of parties or witnesses. In the interests of justice and trial convenience they should be eliminated.

L. *In any county.* The broadest venue provision on the books is that which provides that the plaintiff may lay the venue in any county. * * *

M. *Where the seat of government is located.* * * *

Statutes of this sort have a sound and practical reason behind them. With one exception, this type of provision is reserved for actions by or against governmental units or agencies. Convenience of the government appears to be the controlling factor. * * *

Notes and Questions

1. What should be the underlying goals of a venue system? Is it really necessary to superimpose notions of venue on a soundly conceived jurisdictional system, especially one with a long-arm statute? What statistics and empirical data do you think are relevant to deciding where contract, tort, and property actions should be brought? One author has suggested that juries in some regions or cities give higher damage awards in comparable tort cases than in other regions or cities. See Zeisel, *Social Research on the Law: The Ideal and the Practical*, in Law and Sociology 130–32 (Evan ed. 1962) (stating general rule derived from empirical data: "add 10 percent to the average if the trial takes place on the East or West coast; add another 10 percent if it is conducted in a large metropolitan city; subtract 10 percent if it is conducted in the South or the Midwest; and another 10 percent if it takes place in a rural area"). In what ways should the venue system for the federal courts differ from the ways in which the states allocate judicial business among their courts?

2. In BURLINGTON NORTHERN R.R. CO. v. FORD, 504 U.S. 648, 112 S.Ct. 2184, 119 L.Ed.2d 432 (1992), two railroad employees sued their employer under the Federal Employers' Liability Act in a state court in Yellowstone County, Montana. Defendant moved for a change of venue to Hill County, where it claimed to have its principal place of business in Montana. The court denied the motion and defendant challenged the state's venue rules on the ground that they violated the Equal Protection Clause of the Fourteenth Amendment. Montana's venue rules permit a plaintiff to sue a corporation incorporated in Montana only in the county of its principal place of business, but permit suit in any county against a corporation, like the defendant, that is incorporated elsewhere. The Supreme Court upheld the constitutionality of the state's venue rules in a unanimous opinion by Justice Souter:

> Venue rules generally reflect equity or expediency in resolving disparate interests of parties to a lawsuit in the place of trial. * * * The forum preferable to one party may be undesirable to another, and the adjustment of such warring interests is a valid state concern. * * * In striking the balance between them, a State may have a number of choices, any of which would survive scrutiny, each of them passable under the standard tolerating some play in the joints of governmental machinery. * * * Thus, we have no doubt that a State would act within its constitutional prerogatives if it were to give so much weight to the interest of plaintiffs as to allow them to sue in the counties of their choice under all circumstances. It is equally clear that a State might temper such an "any county" rule to the extent a reasonable assessment of defendants' interest so justified.

> Here, Montana has decided that the any-county rule should give way to a single-county rule where a defendant resides in Montana, arguably on the reasonable ground that a defendant should not be subjected to a plaintiff's tactical advantage of forcing a trial far from the defendant's residence. At the same time, Montana has weighed the interest of a defendant who does not reside in Montana differently, arguably on the equally reasonable ground that for most nonresident defendants the inconvenience will be great whether they have to defend in, say, Billings or Havre. * * * Montana could thus have decided that a nonresident defendant's interest in convenience is too slight to outweigh the plaintiff's interest in suing in the forum of his choice.

Id. at 651–52, 112 S.Ct. at 2186–87, 119 L.Ed.2d at 438.

2. LOCAL AND TRANSITORY ACTIONS

REASOR–HILL CORP. v. HARRISON

Supreme Court of Arkansas, 1952.
220 Ark. 521, 249 S.W.2d 994.

GEORGE ROSE SMITH, JUSTICE. Petitioner asks us to prohibit the circuit court of Mississippi County from taking jurisdiction of a cross-complaint filed by D.M. Barton. In the court below the petitioner moved to dismiss the cross-complaint for the reason that it stated a cause of action for injury to real property in the state of Missouri. When the motion to dismiss was overruled the present application for prohibition was filed in this court.

The suit below was brought by the Planters Flying Service to collect an account for having sprayed insecticide upon Barton's cotton crop in Missouri. In his answer Barton charged that the flying service had damaged his growing crop by using an adulterated insecticide, and by cross-complaint he sought damages from the petitioner for its negligence in putting on the market a chemical unsuited to spraying cotton. The petitioner is an Arkansas corporation engaged in manufacturing insecticides and is not authorized to do business in Missouri.

The question presented is one of first impression: May the Arkansas courts entertain a suit for injuries to real property situated in another State? For the respondent it is rightly pointed out that if the suit is not maintainable Barton has no remedy whatever. The petitioner cannot be served with summons in Missouri; so unless it is subject to suit in Arkansas it can escape liability entirely by staying out of Missouri until the statute of limitations has run. * * * The petitioner answers this argument by showing that with the exception of the Supreme Court of Minnesota every American court that has passed upon the question (and there have been about twenty) has held that jurisdiction does not exist.

We agree that the weight of authority is almost unanimously against the respondent, although in some States the rule has been changed by statute and in others it has been criticized by the courts and restricted as narrowly as possible. But before mechanically following the majority view we think it worthwhile to examine the origin of the rule and the reasons for its existence.

The distinction between local and transitory actions was recognized at the beginning of the fourteenth century in the common law of England. Before then all actions had to be brought where the cause of action arose, because the members of the jury were required to be neighbors who would know something of the litigants and of the dispute as well. But when cases were presented that involved separate incidents occurring in different communities the reason for localizing the action disappeared, for it was then impossible to obtain a jury who knew all the facts. Consequently the courts developed the distinction between a case that might have arisen anywhere, which was held to be transitory, and one that involved a particular piece of land, which was held to be local. * * *

As between judicial districts under the same sovereign the rule has many advantages and has been followed in America. As between counties our statutes in Arkansas require that actions for injury to real estate be brought where the land lies. * * * But we permit the defendant to be served anywhere in the State * * *; so that plaintiff is not denied a remedy even though the defendant is a resident of another county.

The English courts, in developing the law of local and transitory actions, applied it also to suits for injuries to real property lying outside England. If, for example, there had been a trespass upon land in France, the courts would not permit the plaintiff to bring suit in England, even though the defendant lived in England and could not be subjected to liability in France. The American courts, treating the separate States as independent sovereigns, have followed the English decisions.

In the United States the leading case is unquestionably Livingston v. Jefferson * * *. That suit was a part of the famous litigation between Edward Livingston and Thomas Jefferson * * *. The case was heard by Marshall as circuit justice and Tyler as district judge. Both agreed that the suit, which was for a wrongful entry upon land in Louisiana, could not be maintained in Virginia. In Marshall's concurring opinion he examined the English precedents and concluded that the law was so firmly established that the court was bound to follow it, though Marshall expressed his dissatisfaction with a rule which produced "the inconvenience of a clear right without a remedy."

Since then the American courts have relied almost uniformly upon the Livingston case in applying the rule to interstate litigation in this country. At least three reasons have been offered to justify the rule, but it is easy to show that each reason is more applicable to international controversies than to interstate disputes.

First, the ground most frequently relied upon is that the courts are not in a position to pass upon the title to land outside the jurisdiction. As between nations this reasoning may be sound. The members of this court have neither the training nor the facilities to investigate questions involving the ownership of land in France, in Russia, or in China. But the same difficulties do not exist with respect to land in another State. In our library we have the statutes and decisions of every other State, and it seldom takes more than a few hours to find the answer to a particular question. Furthermore, the American courts do not hesitate to pass upon an out-of-state title when the issue arises in a transitory action. If, for example, Barton had charged that this petitioner converted a mature crop in Missouri and carried it to Arkansas, our courts would decide the case even though it became necessary to pass upon conflicting claims of title to the land in Missouri. Again, a suit for damages for nonperformance of a contract to purchase land is transitory and may be maintained in another State, even though the sole issue is the validity of the seller's title. To put an extreme example, suppose that two companion suits, one local and one transitory, were presented to the same court together. In those States where the courts disclaim the ability to pass upon questions of title in local actions it might be necessary for the court to dismiss the local action for that reason and yet to decide the identical question in the allied transitory case.

Second, it has been argued that since the tort must take place where the land is situated the plaintiff should pursue his remedy before the defendant leaves the jurisdiction. This argument, too, has merit when nations are concerned. A sovereign, by its control of passports and ports of entry, may detain those who wish to cross its borders. But the citizens of the various States have a constitutional right to pass freely from one jurisdiction to another. * * * In the case at bar * * * Barton could hardly be expected to discover the damage and file an attachment suit before the pilot returned to his landing field in Arkansas.

Third, there is an understandable reluctance to subject one's own citizens to suits by aliens, especially if the other jurisdiction would provide no redress if the situation were reversed. * * * One may have some sympathy for this position in international disputes, but it has no persuasive effect when the States are involved. We do not feel compelled to provide a sanctuary in Arkansas for those who have willfully and wrongfully destroyed property, torn down houses, uprooted crops, polluted streams, and inflicted other injuries upon innocent landowners in our sister States. Yet every jurisdiction which follows the rule of the Livingston case affords that refuge to any person—whether one of its citizens or not—who is successful in fleeing from the scene of such misdeeds.

The truth is that the majority rule has no basis in logic or equity and rests solely upon English cases that were decided before America was discovered and in circumstances that are not even comparable to those existing in our Union. Basic principles of justice demand that wrongs should not go unredressed. * * * Under the majority rule we should have to tell Barton that he would have been much better off had the petitioner stolen his cotton outright instead of merely damaging it. And the only reason we could give for this unfortunate situation would be that English juries in the thirteenth century were expected to have personal knowledge of the disputes presented to them. We prefer to afford this litigant his day in court.

Writ denied.

GRIFFIN SMITH, C.J., concurs.

McFADDIN and WARD, JJ., dissent.

McFADDIN, JUSTICE (dissenting).

* * *

In the first place, the majority says that we have ample facilities to determine the land laws of other States in the United States. * * * This statement about the size of the law library seems rather weak, because land actions are tried in lower courts and not in the Supreme Court library. Just because we have a fine law library does not mean that we are prepared to determine the title to lands in Texas,[4] Missouri, Vermont, or any other State. But if we have the jurisdiction which the majority claims, then we could determine ejectment actions involving ownership of lands in other States. We might undertake to do this, but the Full Faith and Credit clause of the U.S.

---

4. The writer knows by experience that only one skilled in Texas Land Law can suc- cessfully handle an action of Trespass to Try Title in the State of Texas.

Constitution would not require the Sister State to recognize our judgment. * * *

Secondly, the majority says that the rule, requiring that an action be brought in the jurisdiction in which the land is situated, is a good rule between Nations, but is not good as between States in the American Union. For answer to this, I say: I have always understood that each of the American States is Sovereign; that the Federal Government is a government of delegated powers; and that all powers not delegated to the Federal Government are retained by the States and the People. Surely the majority is not attempting to reduce our American States to the level of mere local administrative units. Yet such, unfortunately, is the natural conclusion to which the majority opinion would carry us, when it concedes one rule for Nations and another for States.

Thirdly, the majority says that it does not desire to afford Arkansas Citizens a sanctuary from damage actions by citizens of other States. This is an argument that should be made—if at all—in the Legislative branch of Government, rather than in a judicial opinion. It is for the Legislative Department to determine when and where actions may be prosecuted. * * *

* * * [M]any, many cases * * * have considered the question here involved; and each Court—with the sole exception of Minnesota—has seen fit to follow the great weight of authority which has come down to us from the common law. In matters affecting real property particularly, we should leave undisturbed the ancient landmarks. * * *

Questions

In those jurisdictions following the "majority" or "local action" rule, can the parties consent to a waiver of the venue objection to actions involving foreign land? See, e.g., Taylor v. Sommers Bros. Match Co., 35 Idaho 30, 204 P. 472 (1922). If not, doesn't the local-transitory action distinction really raise a more serious problem than simply a defect in venue? Why does the dissenting opinion in *Reasor-Hill* say that a judgment in ejectment rendered by the Arkansas courts involving lands in other states would not be entitled to full faith and credit?

3. VENUE IN THE FEDERAL COURTS

Read 28 U.S.C. § 1391 in the Supplement.

BATES v. C & S ADJUSTERS, INC.
United States Court of Appeals, Second Circuit, 1992.
980 F.2d 865.

NEWMAN, CIRCUIT JUDGE. This appeal concerns venue in an action brought under the Fair Debt Collection Practices Act * * *. Specifically, the issue is whether venue exists in a district in which the debtor resides and to which a bill collector's demand for payment was forwarded. The issue arises on an appeal by Phillip E. Bates from the May 21, 1992, judgment of the District Court for the Western District of New York, dismissing his complaint because of improper venue. We conclude that venue was proper under 28 U.S.C. § 1391(b)(2) and therefore reverse and remand.

Bates commenced this action in the Western District of New York upon receipt of a collection notice from C & S Adjusters, Inc. ("C & S"). Bates alleged violations of the Fair Debt Collection Practices Act, and demanded statutory damages, costs, and attorney's fees. The facts relevant to venue are not in dispute. Bates incurred the debt in question while he was a resident of the Western District of Pennsylvania. The creditor, a corporation with its principal place of business in that District, referred the account to C & S, a local collection agency which transacts no regular business in New York. Bates had meanwhile moved to the Western District of New York. When C & S mailed a collection notice to Bates at his Pennsylvania address, the Postal Service forwarded the notice to Bates' new address in New York.

In its answer, C & S asserted two affirmative defenses and also counterclaimed for costs, alleging that the action was instituted in bad faith and for purposes of harassment. C & S subsequently filed a motion to dismiss for improper venue, which the District Court granted.

Bates concedes that the only plausible venue provision for this action is 28 U.S.C. § 1391(b)(2), which allows an action to be brought in "a judicial district in which a substantial part of the events or omissions giving rise to the claim occurred." Prior to 1990, section 1391 allowed for venue in "the judicial district * * * in which the claim arose." * * * This case represents our first opportunity to consider the significance of the 1990 amendments.

Prior to 1966, venue was proper in federal question cases, absent a special venue statute, only in the defendant's state of citizenship. If a plaintiff sought to sue multiple defendants who were citizens of different states, there might be no district where the entire action could be brought. * * * Congress closed this "venue gap" by adding a provision allowing suit in the district "in which the claim arose." This phrase gave rise to a variety of conflicting interpretations. Some courts thought it meant that there could be only one such district; others believed there could be several. Different tests developed, with courts looking for "substantial contacts," the "weight of contacts," the place of injury or performance, or even to the boundaries of personal jurisdiction under state law. * * *

The Supreme Court gave detailed attention to section 1391(b) in Leroy v. Great Western United Corp., 443 U.S. 173, 99 S.Ct. 2710, 61 L.Ed.2d 464 (1979). The specific holding of *Leroy* was that Great Western, a Texas corporation, which had attempted to take over an Idaho corporation, could not bring suit in Texas against Idaho officials who sought to enforce a state anti-takeover law. Although the effect of the Idaho officials' action might be felt in Texas, the Court rejected this factor as a basis for venue, since it would allow the Idaho officials to be sued anywhere a shareholder of the target corporation could allege that he wanted to accept Great Western's tender offer. * * *. The Court made several further observations: (1) the purpose of the 1966 statute was to close venue gaps and should not be read more broadly than necessary to close those gaps * * *; (2) the general purpose of the venue statute was to protect defendants against an unfair or inconvenient trial location * * *; (3)

location of evidence and witnesses was a relevant factor * * *; (4) familiarity of the Idaho federal judges with the Idaho anti-takeover statute was a relevant factor * * *; (5) plaintiff's convenience was not a relevant factor * * *; and (6) in only rare cases should there be more than one district in which a claim can be said to arise * * *.

Subsequent to *Leroy* and prior to the 1990 amendment to section 1391(b), most courts have applied at least a form of the "weight of contacts" test * * *. Courts continued to have difficulty in determining whether more than one district could be proper. * * *

Against this background, we understand Congress' 1990 amendment to be at most a marginal expansion of the venue provision. The House Report indicates that the new language was first proposed by the American Law Institute in a 1969 Study, and observes:

The great advantage of referring to the place where things happened * * * is that it avoids the litigation breeding phrase "in which the claim arose." It also avoids the problem created by the frequent cases in which substantial parts of the underlying events have occurred in several districts.

H.R.Rep. No. 734, 101st Cong., 2d Sess. 23, reprinted in 1990 U.S.C.C.A.N. 6860, 6869. Thus it seems clear that *Leroy*'s strong admonition against recognizing multiple venues has been disapproved. Many of the factors in *Leroy*—for instance, the convenience of defendants and the location of evidence and witnesses—are most useful in distinguishing between two or more plausible venues. Since the new statute does not, as a general matter, require the District Court to determine the best venue, these factors will be of less significance. * * * Apart from this point, however, *Leroy* and other precedents remain important sources of guidance. * * *

Under the version of the venue statute in force from 1966 to 1990, at least three District Courts held that venue was proper under the Fair Debt Collection Practices Act in the plaintiff's home district if a collection agency had mailed a collection notice to an address in that district or placed a phone call to a number in that district. * * * None of these cases involved the unusual fact, present in this case, that the defendant did not deliberately direct a communication to the plaintiff's district.

We conclude, however, that this difference is inconsequential, at least under the current venue statute. The statutory standard for venue focuses not on whether a defendant has made a deliberate contact—a factor relevant in the analysis of personal jurisdiction—but on the location where events occurred. Under the new version of section 1391(b)(2), we must determine only whether a "substantial part of the events * * * giving rise to the claim" occurred in the Western District of New York.

In adopting this statute, Congress was concerned about the harmful effect of abusive debt practices on consumers. See 15 U.S.C. § 1692(a) ("Abusive debt collection practices contribute to the number of personal bankruptcies, to marital instability, to the loss of jobs, and to invasions of individual privacy."). This harm does not occur until receipt of the collection notice. Indeed, if the notice were lost in the mail, it is unlikely that a violation of the Act would have occurred. Moreover, a debt collection agency sends its dunning letters so that they will be received. Forwarding such letters to the district to which a debtor has moved is an important step in the collection process. If the bill collector prefers not to be challenged for its collection practices outside the district of a debtor's original residence, the envelope can be marked "do not forward." We conclude that receipt of a collection notice is a substantial part of the events giving rise to a claim under the Fair Debt Collection Practices Act.

The relevant factors identified in *Leroy* add support to our conclusion. Although "bona fide error" can be a defense to liability under the Act, * * * the alleged violations of the Act turn largely not on the collection agency's intent, but on the content of the collection notice. The most relevant evidence—the collection notice—is located in the Western District of New York. Because the collection agency appears not to have marked the notice with instructions not to forward, and has not objected to the assertion of personal jurisdiction, trial in the Western District of New York would not be unfair.

* * *

Notes and Questions

1. Changes in the statute governing venue in the federal courts, 28 U.S.C. § 1391, reflect the need to conform venue to the expanding notions of jurisdiction. In 1939, when the Supreme Court decided NEIRBO CO. v. BETHLEHEM SHIPBUILDING CORP., 308 U.S. 165, 60 S.Ct. 153, 84 L.Ed. 167 (1939), the general venue statute required that diversity actions be brought "in the district of the residence of either the plaintiff or the defendant." In *Neirbo*, defendant Bethlehem objected to venue in New York on the ground that it was not incorporated under the laws of that state. Prior cases had held that "residence" meant "state of incorporation" in the case of corporations. The Supreme Court held that Bethlehem's appointment of an agent to receive service of process in New York, an act required by the laws of that state as a condition of doing business there, was a "voluntary act" that gave "actual consent by Bethlehem to be sued in the courts of New York, federal as well as state."

A similar argument was advanced by plaintiff in OLBERDING v. ILLINOIS CENT. R. CO., 346 U.S. 338, 74 S.Ct. 83, 98 L.Ed. 39 (1953). The railroad, an Illinois corporation, brought suit in a Kentucky District Court against Olberding, a citizen of Indiana and owner of a truck that had caused the derailment of an Illinois Central train by striking a railroad overpass in Kentucky. Jurisdiction over Olberding was asserted under a nonresident-motorist statute similar to the one upheld in Hess v. Pawloski, p. 71, supra. The venue statute enacted in 1948 required that a diversity action be brought "only in the judicial district where all plaintiffs or all defendants reside." Plaintiff argued, on the basis of *Hess* and *Neirbo*, that Olberding had impliedly consented to a waiver of his federal venue objection by driving into Kentucky. This contention was rejected by Justice Frankfurter:

> * * * In point of fact * * *, jurisdiction in these cases does not rest on consent at all. * * * The potentialities of damage by a motorist, in a population as mobile as ours, are such that those whom he injures must have opportunities of redress against him provided only that he is afforded an opportunity to defend himself. We have held that this is a fair rule of law * * * and that the requirements of due process are therefore met. Hess v. Pawloski * * *. But to conclude from this holding that the motorist, who never consented to anything and whose consent is altogether immaterial, has

actually agreed to be sued and has thus waived his federal venue rights is surely to move in the world of Alice in Wonderland.

Id. at 341, 74 S.Ct. at 85–86, 98 L.Ed. at 43. *Neirbo* was distinguished as involving "actual consent." Justice Reed dissented, saying: "I see no difference of substance between the signing of a paper under the New York statute upon which *Neirbo* is based and the acceptance, by action in driving a motor car, of the privilege of using state highways under the Kentucky statute." Id. at 345, 74 S.Ct. at 87, 98 L.Ed. at 45.

2. *Olberding* was legislatively overruled in 1963 by the addition of a new Section 1391(f), providing for venue in tort claims "arising out of the manufacture, assembly, repair, ownership, maintenance, use or operation of an automobile * * * in the judicial district wherein the act or omission complained of occurred." This provision was repealed in 1966, and the phrase "where the claim for relief arose" was added to subsections (a) and (b). As discussed in *Bates,* this phrase led to protracted litigation over where a claim arises, with one of the major unanswered questions being whether or not a claim could arise in more than one district. See Leroy v. Great Western United Corp., 443 U.S. 173, 99 S.Ct. 2710, 61 L.Ed.2d 464 (1979). See generally Comment, *Federal Venue: Locating the Place Where the Claim Arose,* 54 Texas L.Rev. 392 (1976). As the *Bates* court points out, the 1990 amendments were an effort to alleviate the burden of unnecessary litigation and to solve the unanswered questions by providing for venue in "a judicial district in which a substantial part of the events or omissions giving rise to the claim occurred, or a substantial part of the property that is the subject matter of the action is situated." But see Alcoholics Anonymous World Servs., Inc. v. Friedman, 1992 WL 150633 (S.D.N.Y.) (discussing what constitutes "substantial" activity). See generally Oakley, *Recent Statutory Changes in the Law of Federal Jurisdiction and Venue: The Judicial Improvements Acts of 1988 and 1990,* 24 U.C.Davis L.Rev. 735, 769–82 (1991).

3. In 1988, Congress amended Section 1391(c) to make a corporation a citizen, for venue purposes, of any judicial district in which it is subject to personal jurisdiction at the time the action is commenced. In a state with more than one judicial district, a corporation is deemed to reside in any district within which its contacts would be sufficient to subject it to personal jurisdiction if that district were a separate state. Do the considerations that justify the "minimum contacts" test for personal jurisdiction apply with equal force for venue?

The interrelationship between venue and personal jurisdiction also has been recognized in Section 1391(e), which is a broad venue provision for suits against federal officials and agencies, allowing nationwide service of process by registered mail. The Supreme Court has narrowed the reach of Section 1391(e) in holding that Congress intended it to apply only in actions that "are nominally against an individual officer but are in reality against the Government." Stafford v. Briggs, 444 U.S. 527, 542, 100 S.Ct. 774, 783, 63 L.Ed.2d 1, 14 (1980). In an action for damages against a government official in her individual capacity, the venue rules in suits against private individuals normally will apply. Therefore, if the claim arose in a district in a state without a long-arm statute, the District Court might not be able to secure jurisdiction over the defendant.

4. For diversity jurisdiction, a natural person is a citizen of only one state. Should the term "residence" in the venue statute be restricted in the same way? See 15 Wright, Miller & Cooper, *Federal Practice and Procedure: Jurisdiction and Related Matters 2d* § 3805 (1986).

5. For venue purposes, should an unincorporated association be held to "reside" in any state in which one of its members resides, only in the state in which all of its members reside, in any state in which the association is doing business, or only in the state in which the association has its principal place of business? This question was resolved by the Supreme Court in DENVER & R.G.W.R. CO. v. BROTHERHOOD OF RAILROAD TRAINMEN, 387 U.S. 556, 559–62, 87 S.Ct. 1746, 1748–50, 18 L.Ed.2d 954, 958–59 (1967):

> * * * [W]e think that the question of the proper venue for such a defendant * * * should be determined by looking to the residence of the association itself rather than that of its individual members. Otherwise, § 1391(b) would seem to require either holding the association not suable at all where its members are residents of different States, or holding that the association "resides" in any State in which any of its members resides. The first alternative * * * removes federal-question litigation from the federal courts unnecessarily; the second is patently unfair to the association when it is remembered that venue is primarily a matter of convenience of litigants and witnesses.

> * * *

> We think it most nearly approximates the intent of Congress to recognize the reality of the multi-state, unincorporated association such as a labor union and to permit suit against that entity, like the analogous corporate entity, wherever it is "doing business."

6. Various questions arise in applying the venue requirements when an action involves multiple claims or multiple parties. For example, can a properly impleaded third-party defendant secure a dismissal of the third-party claim for lack of venue if the venue in the principal action is proper? Would it make any difference if the subject-matter jurisdiction over the third-party claim is merely ancillary to the jurisdiction over the principal action? See Bredberg v. Long, 778 F.2d 1285, 1288 (8th Cir.1985). See also Note, *Ancillary Process and Venue in the Federal Courts,* 73 Harv.L.Rev. 1164 (1960).

7. Can the parties contractually agree on a forum for litigating any action arising out of their contract? Can they designate a place other than those provided in the general venue statutes? See National Equipment Rental, Ltd. v. Szukhent, p. 212, supra. What are some of the factors the court should consider in deciding whether to uphold the stipulation? Compare M/S Bremen v. Zapata Off–Shore Co., p. 180, supra, and Carnival Cruise Lines v. Shute, p. 181, supra, with Leasewell, Ltd. v. Jake Shelton Ford, Inc., 423 F.Supp. 1011 (S.D.W.Va.1976).

8. Do we need venue provisions at all, given the kind of convenience analysis that *World-Wide Volkswagen* constitutionally requires for making personal jurisdiction decisions? See Clermont, *Refuting Territorial Jurisdiction and Venue for State and Federal Courts,* 66 Cornell L.Rev. 411 (1981).

SECTION B.   TRANSFER OF VENUE
IN FEDERAL COURTS

HOFFMAN v. BLASKI

Supreme Court of the United States, 1960.
363 U.S. 335, 80 S.Ct. 1084, 4 L.Ed.2d 1254.

Certiorari to the United States Court of Appeals for the Seventh Circuit.

MR. JUSTICE WHITTAKER delivered the opinion of the Court.

* * *

The instant cases present the question whether a District Court, in which a civil action has been properly brought, is empowered by § 1404(a) to transfer the action, on the motion of the defendant, to a district in which the plaintiff did not have a *right* to bring it.

Respondents, Blaski and others, residents of Illinois, brought this patent infringement action in the United States District Court for the Northern District of Texas against one Howell and a Texas corporation controlled by him, alleging that the defendants are residents of, and maintain their only place of business in, the City of Dallas, in the Northern District of Texas, where they are infringing respondents' patents. After being served with process and filing their answer, the defendants moved, under § 1404(a), to transfer the action to the United States District Court for the Northern District of Illinois. Respondents objected to the transfer on the ground that, inasmuch as the defendants did not reside, maintain a place of business, or infringe the patents in, and could not have been served with process in, the Illinois district, the courts of that district lacked venue over the action and ability to command jurisdiction over the defendants; that therefore that district was not a forum in which the respondents had a right to bring the action, and, hence, the court was without power to transfer it to that district. Without mentioning that objection or the question it raised, the District Court found that "the motion should be granted for the convenience of the parties and witnesses in the interest of justice," and ordered the case transferred to the Illinois district. Thereupon, respondents moved in the Fifth Circuit for leave to file a petition for a writ of mandamus directing the vacation of that order. That court, holding that "[t]he purposes for which § 1404(a) was enacted would be unduly circumscribed if a transfer could not be made 'in the interest of justice' to a district where the defendants not only waive venue but to which they seek the transfer," denied the motion. * * *

Upon receipt of a certified copy of the pleadings and record, the Illinois District Court assigned the action to Judge Hoffman's calendar. Respondents promptly moved for an order remanding the action on the ground that the Texas District Court did not have power to make the transfer order and, hence, the Illinois District Court was not thereby vested with jurisdiction of the action. After expressing his view that the "weight of reason and logic" favored "retransfer of this case to Texas," Judge Hoffman, with misgivings, denied the motion. Respondents then filed in the Seventh Circuit a petition for a writ of mandamus directing Judge Hoffman to reverse his order. After hearing and rehearing, the Seventh Circuit, holding that "[w]hen Congress provided [in § 1404(a)] for transfer [of a civil action] to a district 'where it might have been brought,' it is hardly open to doubt but that it referred to a district where the plaintiff * * * had a right to bring the case," and that respondents did not have a *right* to bring this action in the Illinois district, granted the writ, one judge dissenting. * * *

Petitioners' "thesis" and sole claim is that § 1404(a), being remedial, * * * should be broadly construed, and, when so construed, the phrase "where it might have been brought" should be held to relate not only to the time of the bringing of the action but also to the time of the transfer; and that "if at such time the transferee forum has the power to adjudicate the issues of the action, it is a forum in which the action might *then* have been brought." (Emphasis added.) They argue that in the interim between the bringing of the action and the filing of a motion to transfer it, the defendants may move their residence to, or, if corporations, may begin the transaction of business in, some other district, and, if such is done, the phrase "where it might have been brought" should be construed to empower the District Court to transfer the action, on motion of the defendants, to such other district; and that, similarly, if, as here, the defendants move to transfer the action to some other district and consent to submit to the jurisdiction of such other district, the latter district should be held one "in which the action might *then* have been brought." (Emphasis added.)

We do not agree. * * *

It is not to be doubted that the transferee courts, like every District Court, had jurisdiction to entertain actions of the character involved, but it is obvious that they did not acquire jurisdiction over these particular actions when they were brought in the transferor courts. The transferee courts could have acquired jurisdiction over these actions only if properly brought in those courts, or if validly transferred thereto under § 1404(a). Of course, venue, like jurisdiction over the person, may be waived. A defendant, properly served with process by a court having subject matter jurisdiction, waives venue by failing seasonably to assert it, or even simply by making default. * * * But the power of a District Court under § 1404(a) to transfer an action to another district is made to depend not upon the wish or waiver of the defendant but, rather, upon whether the transferee district was one in which the action "might have been brought" by the plaintiff.

The thesis urged by petitioners would not only do violence to the plain words of § 1404(a), but would also inject gross discrimination. That thesis, if adopted, would empower a District Court, upon a finding of convenience, to transfer an action to any district desired by the *defendants* and in which they were willing to waive their statutory defenses as to venue and jurisdiction over their persons, regardless of the fact that such transferee district was not one in which the action "might have been brought" by the plaintiff. Conversely, that thesis would not permit the court, upon motion of the *plaintiffs* and a like showing of convenience, to transfer the action to the same district, without the consent and waiver of venue and personal jurisdiction defenses by the defendants. Nothing in § 1404(a), or in its legislative history, suggests such a unilateral objective and we should not, under the guise of interpretation, ascribe to Congress any such discriminatory purpose.

* * *

Inasmuch as the respondents (plaintiffs) did not have a right to bring these actions in the respective transferee districts, it follows that the judgments of the Court of Appeals were correct and must be affirmed.

Affirmed.

[A concurring opinion by JUSTICE STEWART and a dissenting opinion by JUSTICES FRANKFURTER, HARLAN, and BRENNAN have been omitted. Both of these opinions pertained only to Hoffman v. Blaski.]

MR. JUSTICE FRANKFURTER, whom MR. JUSTICE HARLAN and MR. JUSTICE BRENNAN join, dissenting.*

* * *

The part of § 1404(a) the meaning of which is at issue here is its last phrase * * *. The significance of this phrase is this: even though a place be found to be an overwhelmingly more appropriate forum from the standpoint of "convenience" and "justice," the litigation may not be sent to go forward there unless it is a place where the action "might have been brought." Upon the scope to be given this phrase thus depends almost entirely the effectiveness of § 1404(a) to insure an appropriate place of trial, when the action is begun in an oppressive forum.

One would have to be singularly unmindful of the treachery and versatility of our language to deny that as a mere matter of English the words "where it might have been brought" may carry more than one meaning. * * * On the face of its words alone, the phrase may refer to * * * venue, amenability to service, or period of limitations, to all of them or to none of them, or to others as well. * * *

Surely, the Court creates its own verbal prison in holding that "the plain words" of § 1404(a) dictate that transfer may not be made in this case although transfer concededly was in the interest of "convenience" and "justice." Moreover, the Court, while finding the statutory words "plain," decides the case by applying, not the statutory language, but a formula of words found nowhere in the statute, namely, whether plaintiffs had "a right to bring these actions in the respective transferee districts." This is the Court's language, not that of Congress. * * * There can be expected to be very few, if any, alternative forums in a given case where the plaintiff has a "right" to sue, considering that that means places of unobjectionable venue where the defendant is amenable to service of process and where there are no other impediments such as a statute of limitations which the defendant can rely on to defeat the action.

* * * At the crux of the business, as I see it, is the realization that we are concerned here not with a question of a limitation upon the power of a federal court but with the place in which that court may exercise its power. We are dealing, that is, not with the jurisdiction of the federal courts, which is beyond

---

* This opinion applies only to [the companion case of] Sullivan v. Behimer [which raised the same question as Hoffman v. Blaski]. [Footnote by the Court.]

the power of litigants to confer, but with the locality of a lawsuit, the rules regulating which are designed mainly for the convenience of the litigants. * * *

In light of the nature of rules governing the place of trial in the federal system * * *, what are the competing considerations here? The transferee court in this case plainly had and has jurisdiction to adjudicate this action with the defendant's acquiescence. As the defendant, whose privilege it is to object to the place of trial, has moved for transfer, and has acquiesced to going forward with the litigation in the transferee court, it would appear presumptively, unless there are strong considerations otherwise, that there is no impediment to effecting the transfer so long as "convenience" and "justice" dictate that it be made. It does not counsel otherwise that here the plaintiff is to be sent to a venue to which he objects, whereas ordinarily, when the defendant waives his privilege to object to the place of trial, it is to acquiesce in the plaintiff's choice of forum. This would be a powerful argument if, under § 1404(a), a transfer were to be made whenever requested by the defendant. Such is not the case, and this bears emphasis. A transfer can be made under § 1404(a) to a place where the action "might have been brought" only when "convenience" and "justice" so dictate, not whenever the defendant so moves. A legitimate objection by the plaintiff to proceeding in the transferee forum will presumably be reflected in a decision that the interest of justice does not require the transfer, and so it becomes irrelevant that the proposed place of transfer is deemed one where the action "might have been brought." * * *

On the other hand, the Court's view restricts transfer, when concededly warranted in the interest of justice, to protect no legitimate interest on the part of the plaintiff. And by making transfer turn on whether the defendant could have been served with process in the transferee district on the day the action was brought, the Court's view may create difficult problems in ascertaining that fact, especially in the case of non-corporate defendants. These are problems which have no conceivable relation to the proper administration of a provision meant to assure the most convenient and just place for trial.

* * *

The relevant legislative history of § 1404(a) is found in the statement in the Reviser's Notes, accompanying the 1948 Judicial Code, that § 1404(a) "was drafted in accordance with the doctrine of forum non conveniens." Under that doctrine, the remedy for an inconvenient forum was not to transfer the action, but to dismiss it. In Gulf Oil Corp. v. Gilbert [p. 359, infra] * * * we held that "[i]n all cases in which the doctrine of *forum non conveniens* comes into play, it presupposes at least two forums in which the defendant is amenable to process; the doctrine furnishes criteria for choice between them." It is entirely "in accordance" with this view of the doctrine of *forum non conveniens* to hold that transfer may be made at the instance of the defendant regardless of the plaintiff's right as an original matter to sue him in the transferee court, so long as the defendant stipulates to going forward with the litigation there. Indeed, to hold otherwise as the Court does is to limit § 1404(a) to a much narrower operation than the nonstatutory doctrine of *forum non conveniens.* * * *

The only consideration of the Court not resting on the "plain meaning" of § 1404(a) is that it would constitute "gross discrimination" to permit transfer to be made with the defendant's consent and over the plaintiff's objection to a district to which the plaintiff could not similarly obtain transfer over the defendant's objection. * * * Transfer cannot be made under this statute unless it is found to be in the interest of "convenience" and in the interest of "justice." Whether a party is in any sense being "discriminated" against through a transfer is certainly relevant to whether the interest of justice is being served. If the interest of justice is being served, as it must be for a transfer to be made, how can it be said that there is "discrimination" in any meaningful sense? Moreover, the transfer provision cannot be viewed in isolation in finding "discrimination." It, after all, operates to temper only to a slight degree the enormous "discrimination" inherent in our system of litigation, whereby the sole choice of forum, from among those where service is possible and venue unobjectionable, is placed with the plaintiff. * * *

Notes and Questions

1. To what extent does the decision in *Blaski* favor plaintiffs at the expense of defendants? How does the transferor court determine whether defendant is amenable to service in the transferee district? Does *Blaski* require the movant to demonstrate conclusively that defendant was amenable to process in the transferee district court at the time the action was commenced, or should a lesser showing be sufficient? See Dill v. Scuka, 198 F.Supp. 808 (E.D.Pa.1961); Comment, *The Requirement of Personal Jurisdiction When Transferring an Action Under Section 1404(a)*, 57 Nw.U.L.Rev. 456 (1962).

2. The Ninth Circuit has upheld a transfer from California to Delaware on the ground that the action could have been brought as a permissive counterclaim in an action between the parties already underway in Delaware. A.J. INDUSTRIES, INC. v. UNITED STATES DISTRICT COURT, 503 F.2d 384 (9th Cir. 1974). The court stated that Hoffman v. Blaski has been widely criticized, and that there was no reason to "extend it unnecessarily."

3. Is the fact that an action would be barred by the statute of limitations in the transferee district relevant to the decision of a motion under Section 1404(a)? To what extent should the transferee court attempt to reach the same result on the merits that would have been reached by the transferor court? Must the transferee court apply the law of the transferor court? In VAN DUSEN v. BARRACK, 376 U.S. 612, 639, 84 S.Ct. 805, 821, 11 L.Ed.2d 945, 962–63 (1964), the Supreme Court held that, in diversity cases, the law applicable in the transferor forum follows the transfer.

However, a consensus appears to be developing against applying the *Van Dusen* rule to transferred federal claims. The District of Columbia Circuit has held that the law of the transferor forum on federal questions merits close consideration but does not have *stare decisis* effect in a transferee forum situated in another circuit. See In re Korean Air Lines Disaster of Sept. 1, 1983, 829 F.2d 1171 (D.C.Cir.1987), affirmed on other grounds sub nom. Chan v. Korean Air Lines, Ltd., 490 U.S. 122, 109 S.Ct. 1676, 104 L.Ed.2d 113 (1989). Accord In re Pan American Corp., 950 F.2d 839, 847 (2d Cir.1991). But see In re Dow Co. "Sarabond" Products Liability Litigation, 666 F.Supp. 1466, 1468 (D.Colo.1987) (applying law of transferor fora). See also Marcus, *Conflict Among Circuits and Transfers Within the Federal Judicial System*, 93 Yale L.J. 677, 721 (1984); Steinman, *Law of the Case: A Judicial Puzzle in Consolidated and Transferred Cases and in Multidistrict Litigation*, 135 U.Pa.L.Rev. 595, 662–706 (1987).

4. What circumstances might motivate a plaintiff to request a transfer of venue? Must a transferee court apply the law of the transferor court when the plaintiff initiates the transfer? In FERENS v. JOHN DEERE CO., 494 U.S. 516, 110 S.Ct. 1274, 108 L.Ed.2d 443 (1990), plaintiff, a citizen of Pennsylvania, lost a hand when it allegedly became caught in a harvester manufactured by defendant, a Delaware corporation. Plaintiff failed to file suit within Pennsylvania's two–year tort limitations period. But, in the third year, plaintiff filed one suit in federal court in Pennsylvania raising contract and warranty claims, which were not yet time-barred, and a second suit in federal court in Mississippi alleging tort claims. Mississippi had a six–year tort statute of limitations which the federal court was required to apply. The federal court in Mississippi then granted plaintiff's motion to transfer the tort action to the Pennsylvania court under Section 1404(a). The Pennsylvania court, however, refused to apply Mississippi's statute of limitations and dismissed the tort claims as time-barred under Pennsylvania's statute of limitations, and the Court of Appeals affirmed. Relying on *Van Dusen,* the Supreme Court reversed, holding that, in a diversity suit, the transferee forum is required to apply the law of the transferor court, regardless of who initiates the transfer. Is this a sound result? See Note, *Confusion and Dissension Surrounding the Venue Transfer Statutes,* 53 Ohio St.L.J. 319 (1992); Note, *Is 28 U.S.C. § 1404(a) a Federal Forum–Shopping Statute?,* 66 Wash.L.Rev. 851 (1991). See generally Steinberg, *The Motion to Transfer and the Interests of Justice,* 66 Notre Dame L.Rev. 443 (1990). Can a clever plaintiff intentionally bring suit in an inconvenient forum with favorable law and then move for transfer under Section 1404(a), ending up with both the forum and law of her choice?

5. Should the defendant be able to obtain a transfer under Section 1404(a) of a quasi-in-rem action? If transfer is permitted, what should happen to the property that was attached? To what degree does the availability of transfer under 28 U.S.C. § 1404(a) mitigate the inconvenience to defendants that might be caused by the assertion of quasi-in-rem jurisdiction? Is this relevant to the application of Shaffer v. Heitner, p. 154, supra, in federal-court actions? See Note, *Transfer of Quasi in Rem Actions Under 28 U.S.C. § 1404(a): A Study in the Interpretation of "Civil Action,"* 31 U.Chi.L.Rev. 373 (1964).

6. Section 1406(a) permits the district court to dismiss "or if it be in the interest of justice" to transfer a case to any district in which it could have been brought when it was brought initially in a court in which venue was improper. This provision should be distinguished from Section 1404(a), which presupposes that venue in the district of commencement is proper. Should the *Ferens* doctrine apply if a case is transferred pursuant to Section 1406(a)?

One of the more interesting cases involving Section 1406(a) is GOLDLAWR, INC. v. HEIMAN, 369 U.S. 463, 82 S.Ct. 913, 8 L.Ed.2d 39 (1962), a treble-damage action under the antitrust laws commenced in the Eastern District of Pennsylvania against a number of defendants. On motion, the District Court found both a lack of personal jurisdiction and improper venue and transferred the case to the Southern District of New York, where venue was proper and defendants could be reached by process. The New York federal court, however, dismissed the case on the ground that the Pennsylvania court could not transfer the action because it lacked personal jurisdiction. The Supreme Court reversed.

> * * * The problem which gave rise to the enactment of the section was that of avoiding the injustice which had often resulted to plaintiffs from dismissal of their actions merely because they had made an erroneous guess with regard to the existence of some elusive fact of the kind upon which

venue provisions often turn. Indeed, this case is itself a typical example of the problem sought to be avoided, for dismissal here would have resulted in plaintiff's losing a substantial part of its cause of action under the statute of limitations merely because it made a mistake in thinking that the respondent corporations could be "found" or that they "transact * * * business" in the Eastern District of Pennsylvania. The language and history of § 1406(a) * * * show a congressional purpose to provide as effective a remedy as possible to avoid precisely this sort of injustice.

The language of § 1406(a) is amply broad enough to authorize the transfer of cases, however wrong the plaintiff may have been in filing his case as to venue, whether the court in which it was filed had personal jurisdiction over the defendants or not. The section is thus in accord with the general purpose which has prompted many of the procedural changes of the past few years—that of removing whatever obstacles may impede an expeditious and orderly adjudication of cases and controversies on their merits. When a lawsuit is filed, that filing shows a desire on the part of the plaintiff to begin his case and thereby toll whatever statutes of limitation would otherwise apply. The filing itself shows the proper diligence on the part of the plaintiff which such statutes of limitation were intended to insure. If by reason of the uncertainties of proper venue a mistake is made, Congress, by the enactment of § 1406(a), recognized that "the interest of justice" may require that the complaint not be dismissed but rather that it be transferred in order that the plaintiff not be penalized * * *.

Id. at 466–67, 82 S.Ct. at 915–16, 8 L.Ed.2d at 42. Justice Harlan and Justice Stewart dissented for the following reasons:

The notion that a District Court may deal with an *in personam* action in such a way as possibly to affect a defendant's substantive rights without first acquiring jurisdiction over him is not a familiar one in federal jurisprudence. No one suggests that Congress was aware that * * * § 1406(a) might be so used when it enacted that statute. The "interest of justice" of which the statute speaks * * * is assuredly not a one-way street. And it is incongruous to consider, as the Court's holding would seem to imply, that in the "interest of justice" Congress sought in § 1406(a) to deal with the transfer of cases where *both* venue and jurisdiction are lacking in the district where the action is commenced, while neglecting to provide any comparable alleviative measures for the plaintiff who selects a district where venue is proper but where personal jurisdiction cannot be obtained.

Id. at 467–68, 82 S.Ct. at 916, 8 L.Ed.2d at 43.

The *Goldlawr* decision leaves open a number of questions that raise doubts as to its soundness. Suppose that plaintiff commences an action in a district court that patently lacks personal jurisdiction one day before the expiration of the applicable statute of limitations and ten days later moves to transfer the action to a district in which venue and jurisdiction are proper. If plaintiff is permitted to transfer, hasn't defendant lost the benefit of the statute of limitations? Put another way, shouldn't plaintiff be required to institute an action in a district having personal jurisdiction over defendant prior to the end of the limitations period? Furthermore, shouldn't defendant be guaranteed an opportunity to contest the transfer motion? If the court lacks personal jurisdiction over her, how will defendant know that the action has been instituted and a transfer motion made? An even broader question is to what extent *Goldlawr* results in plaintiff abdicating the obligation to choose an appropriate forum in which defendant is amenable to suit and foisting that task upon the federal courts.

The ramifications of the *Goldlawr* case are discussed in Note, *Change of Venue in Absence of Personal Jurisdiction Under 28 U.S.C. §§ 1404(a) and 1406(a),* 30 U.Chi.L.Rev. 735 (1963); Comment, *Personal Jurisdiction Requirements Under Federal Change of Venue Statutes,* 1962 Wis.L.Rev. 342.

7. One significant development in federal venue procedure has been the enactment of 28 U.S.C. § 1407, which provides for the temporary transfer to one district of related complex cases such as multidistrict antitrust actions. Transfer is appropriate when the cases involve common questions of fact and law and when it would be for the convenience of the parties and witnesses and in the interests of justice. This provision frequently has been used to take advantage of coordinated pretrial discovery, for example. A Panel on Multidistrict Litigation, composed of seven Court of Appeals and District Court judges appointed by the Chief Justice, makes decisions on whether or not cases should be transferred. The statute authorizes consolidation of cases for pretrial purposes only. In LEXECON, INC. v. MILBERG WEISS BERSHAD HYNES & LERACH, 523 U.S. 26, 118 S.Ct. 956, 140 L.Ed.2d 62 (1998), the Supreme Court held that the language of Section 1407 requires the panel on multidistrict litigation to remand cases consolidated under Section 1407 to their original courts for trial. Prior to this ruling, it was common practice for transferee courts to transfer cases to themselves for trial under Section 1404(a). Given that the intent of Section 1407 is to allow federal courts to handle complex cases more efficiently, what purposes are served by returning cases to their original districts for trial? Should the parties to the litigation be allowed to consent to having the case tried in the transferee court? Does the Court's reading of the statute properly balance efficiency concerns with traditional deference for the plaintiff's choice of forum? Should Congress amend Section 1407 and overrule *Lexecon?* See 15 Wright, Miller & Cooper, *Federal Practice and Procedure: Jurisdiction and Related Matters 2d* § 3862 (1986).

SECTION C. FORUM NON CONVENIENS

GULF OIL CORP. v. GILBERT, 330 U.S. 501, 67 S.Ct. 839, 91 L.Ed. 1055 (1947), delineated the factors to be considered in deciding a motion based upon the principle of forum non conveniens:

> The principle of *forum non conveniens* is simply that a court may resist imposition upon its jurisdiction even when jurisdiction is authorized by the letter of a general venue statute. These statutes are drawn with a necessary generality and usually give a plaintiff a choice of courts, so that he may be quite sure of some place in which to pursue his remedy. But the open door may admit those who seek not simply justice but perhaps justice blended with some harassment. A plaintiff sometimes is under temptation to resort to a strategy of forcing the trial at a most inconvenient place for an adversary, even at some inconvenience to himself.
>
> Many of the states have met misuse of venue by investing courts with a discretion to change the place of trial on various grounds, such as the convenience of witnesses and the ends of justice. The federal law contains no such express criteria to guide the district court in exercising its power. But the problem is a very old one affecting the administration of the

courts as well as the rights of litigants, and both in England and in this country the common law worked out techniques and criteria for dealing with it.

* * *

If the combination and weight of factors requisite to given results are difficult to forecast or state, those to be considered are not difficult to name. An interest to be considered, and the one likely to be most pressed, is the private interest of the litigant. Important considerations are the relative ease of access to sources of proof; availability of compulsory process for attendance of unwilling, and the cost of obtaining attendance of willing witnesses; possibility of view of premises, if view would be appropriate to the action; and all other practical problems that make trial of a case easy, expeditious and inexpensive. There may also be questions as to the enforcibility [sic] of a judgment if one is obtained. The court will weigh relative advantages and obstacles to fair trial. It is often said that the plaintiff may not, by choice of an inconvenient forum, "vex," "harass," or "oppress" the defendant by inflicting upon him expense or trouble not necessary to his own right to pursue his remedy. But unless the balance is strongly in favor of the defendant, the plaintiff's choice of forum should rarely be disturbed.

Factors of public interest also have place in applying the doctrine. Administrative difficulties follow for courts when litigation is piled up in congested centers instead of being handled at its origin. Jury duty is a burden that ought not to be imposed upon the people of a community which has no relation to the litigation. In cases which touch the affairs of many persons, there is reason for holding the trial in their view and reach rather than in remote parts of the country where they can learn of it by report only. There is a local interest in having localized controversies decided at home. There is an appropriateness, too, in having the trial of a diversity case in a forum that is at home with the state law that must govern the case, rather than having a court in some other forum untangle problems in conflict of laws, and in law foreign to itself.

Id. at 507–09, 67 S.Ct. at 842–43, 91 L.Ed. at 1062–63.

PIPER AIRCRAFT CO. v. REYNO

Supreme Court of the United States, 1981.
454 U.S. 235, 102 S.Ct. 252, 70 L.Ed.2d 419.

Certiorari to the United States Court of Appeals for the Third Circuit.

JUSTICE MARSHALL delivered the opinion of the Court.

* * *

I

A

In July 1976, a small commercial aircraft crashed in the Scottish highlands during the course of a charter flight from Blackpool to Perth. The pilot and five passengers were killed instantly. The decedents were all Scottish subjects and residents, as are their heirs and next of kin. There were no eyewitnesses to the accident. At the time of the crash the plane was subject to Scottish air traffic control.

The aircraft, a twin-engine Piper Aztec, was manufactured in Pennsylvania by petitioner Piper Aircraft Co. (Piper). The propellers were manufactured in Ohio by petitioner Hartzell Propeller, Inc. (Hartzell). At the time of the crash the aircraft was registered in Great Britain and was owned and maintained by Air Navigation and Trading Co., Ltd. (Air Navigation). It was operated by McDonald Aviation, Ltd. (McDonald), a Scottish air taxi service. Both Air Navigation and McDonald were organized in the United Kingdom. The wreckage of the plane is now in a hangar in Farnsborough, England.

The British Department of Trade investigated the accident several months after it occurred. A preliminary report found that the plane crashed after developing a spin, and suggested that mechanical failure in the plane or the propeller was responsible. At Hartzell's request, this report was reviewed by a three-member Review Board, which held a 9–day adversary hearing attended by all interested parties. The Review Board found no evidence of defective equipment and indicated that pilot error may have contributed to the accident. The pilot, who had obtained his commercial pilot's license only three months earlier, was flying over high ground at an altitude considerably lower than the minimum height required by his company's operations manual.

In July 1977, a California probate court appointed respondent Gaynell Reyno administratrix of the estates of the five passengers. Reyno is not related to and does not know any of the decedents or their survivors; she was a legal secretary to the attorney who filed this lawsuit. Several days after her appointment, Reyno commenced separate wrongful death actions against Piper and Hartzell in the Superior Court of California, claiming negligence and strict liability. Air Navigation, McDonald, and the estate of the pilot are not parties to this litigation. The survivors of the five passengers whose estates are represented by Reyno filed a separate action in the United Kingdom against Air Navigation, McDonald, and the pilot's estate. Reyno candidly admits that the action against Piper and Hartzell was filed in the United States because its laws regarding liability, capacity to sue, and damages are more favorable to her position than are those of Scotland. Scottish law does not recognize strict liability in tort. Moreover, it permits wrongful death actions only when brought by a decedent's relatives. The relatives may sue only for "loss of support and society."

On petitioners' motion, the suit was removed to the United States District Court for the Central District of California. Piper then moved for transfer to the United States District Court for the Middle District of Pennsylvania, pursuant to 28 U.S.C. § 1404(a). Hartzell moved to dismiss for lack of personal jurisdiction, or in the alternative, to transfer.[5] In December 1977, the District Court quashed service on Hartzell and transferred the case to the Middle District of Pennsylvania. Respondent then properly served process on Hartzell.

---

5. The District Court concluded that it could not assert personal jurisdiction over Hartzell consistent with due process. However, it decided not to dismiss Hartzell because the corporation would be amenable to process in Pennsylvania.

B

In May 1978, after the suit had been transferred, both Hartzell and Piper moved to dismiss the action on the ground of *forum non conveniens.* The District Court granted these motions in October 1979. It relied on the balancing test set forth by this Court in Gulf Oil Corp. v. Gilbert [p. 359, supra] * * *.

* * * [T]he District Court analyzed the facts of [this case]. It began by observing that an alternative forum existed in Scotland; Piper and Hartzell had agreed to submit to the jurisdiction of the Scottish courts and to waive any statute of limitations defense that might be available. It then stated that plaintiff's choice of forum was entitled to little weight. The court recognized that a plaintiff's choice ordinarily deserves substantial deference. It noted, however, that Reyno "is a representative of foreign citizens and residents seeking a forum in the United States because of the more liberal rules concerning products liability law," and that "the courts have been less solicitous when the plaintiff is not an American citizen or resident, and particularly when the foreign citizens seek to benefit from the more liberal tort rules provided for the protection of citizens and residents of the United States." * * *

The District Court next examined several factors relating to the private interests of the litigants, and determined that these factors strongly pointed towards Scotland as the appropriate forum. Although evidence concerning the design, manufacture, and testing of the plane and propeller is located in the United States, the connections with Scotland are otherwise "overwhelming." * * * The real parties in interest are citizens of Scotland, as were all the decedents. Witnesses who could testify regarding the maintenance of the aircraft, the training of the pilot, and the investigation of the accident—all essential to the defense—are in Great Britain. Moreover, all witnesses to damages are located in Scotland. Trial would be aided by familiarity with Scottish topography, and by easy access to the wreckage.

The District Court reasoned that because crucial witnesses and evidence were beyond the reach of compulsory process, and because the defendants would not be able to implead potential Scottish third-party defendants, it would be "unfair to make Piper and Hartzell proceed to trial in this forum." * * * The survivors had brought separate actions in Scotland against the pilot, McDonald, and Air Navigation. "[I]t would be fairer to all parties and less costly if the entire case was presented to one jury with available testimony from all relevant witnesses." * * * Although the court recognized that if trial were held in the United States, Piper and Hartzell could file indemnity or contribution actions against the Scottish defendants, it believed that there was a significant risk of inconsistent verdicts.

The District Court concluded that the relevant public interests also pointed strongly towards dismissal. The court determined that Pennsylvania law would apply to Piper and Scottish law to Hartzell if the case were tried in the Middle District of Pennsylvania.[8] As a result, "trial in this forum would be

---

8. Under Klaxon v. Stentor Electric Mfg. Co., 313 U.S. 487, 61 S.Ct. 1020, 85 L.Ed. 1477 (1941), [p. 423, infra] a court ordinarily must apply the choice-of-law rules of the State in which it sits. However, where a case is transferred pursuant to 28 U.S.C. § 1404(a), it must apply the choice-of-law rules of the State from which the case was transferred. Van Dusen v.

hopelessly complex and confusing for a jury." * * * In addition, the court noted that it was unfamiliar with Scottish law and thus would have to rely upon experts from that country. The court also found that the trial would be enormously costly and time-consuming; that it would be unfair to burden citizens with jury duty when the Middle District of Pennsylvania has little connection with the controversy; and that Scotland has a substantial interest in the outcome of the litigation.

In opposing the motions to dismiss, respondent contended that dismissal would be unfair because Scottish law was less favorable. The District Court explicitly rejected this claim. * * *

C

On appeal, the * * * Third Circuit reversed and remanded for trial. The decision to reverse appears to be based on two alternative grounds. First, the Court held that the District Court abused its discretion in conducting the *Gilbert* analysis. Second, the Court held that dismissal is never appropriate where the law of the alternative forum is less favorable to the plaintiff.

The Court of Appeals began its review of the District Court's *Gilbert* analysis by noting that the plaintiff's choice of forum deserved substantial weight, even though the real parties in interest are nonresidents. It then rejected the District Court's balancing of the private interests. It found that Piper and Hartzell had failed adequately to support their claim that key witnesses would be unavailable if trial were held in the United States: they had never specified the witnesses they would call and the testimony these witnesses would provide. The Court of Appeals gave little weight to the fact that Piper and Hartzell would not be able to implead potential Scottish third-party defendants, reasoning that this difficulty would be "burdensome" but not "unfair" * * *. Finally, the court stated that resolution of the suit would not be significantly aided by familiarity with Scottish topography, or by viewing the wreckage.

The Court of Appeals also rejected the District Court's analysis of the public interest factors. It found that the District Court gave undue emphasis to the application of Scottish law: "the fact that the court is called upon to determine and apply foreign law does not present a legal problem of the sort which would justify the dismissal of a case otherwise properly before the court." * * * In any event, it believed that Scottish law need not be applied. After conducting its own choice-of-law analysis, the Court of Appeals determined that American law would govern the actions against both Piper and Hartzell. The same choice-of-law analysis apparently led it to conclude that Pennsylvania and Ohio, rather than Scotland, are the jurisdictions with the greatest policy interests in the dispute, and that all other public interest factors favored trial in the United States.

Barrack [Note 3, p. 356, supra] * * *. Relying on these two cases, the District Court concluded that California choice-of-law rules would apply to Piper, and Pennsylvania choice-of-law rules would apply to Hartzell. It further concluded that California applied a "governmental interests" analysis in resolving choice-of-law problems, and that Pennsylvania employed a "significant contacts" analysis. The court used the "governmental interests" analysis to determine that Pennsylvania liability rules would apply to Piper, and the "significant contacts" analysis to determine that Scottish liability rules would apply to Hartzell.

In any event, it appears that the Court of Appeals would have reversed even if the District Court had properly balanced the public and private interests. The court stated:

"[I]t is apparent that the dismissal would work a change in the applicable law so that the plaintiff's strict liability claim would be eliminated from the case. But * * * a dismissal for forum non conveniens, like a statutory transfer, 'should not, despite its convenience, result in a change in the applicable law.' Only when American law is not applicable, or when the foreign jurisdiction would, as a matter of its own choice of law, give the plaintiff the benefit of the claim to which she is entitled here, would dismissal be justified." 630 F.2d at 163–164 * * * .

In other words, the court decided that dismissal is automatically barred if it would lead to a change in the applicable law unfavorable to the plaintiff.

We granted certiorari * * * .

II

The Court of Appeals erred in holding that plaintiffs may defeat a motion to dismiss on the ground of *forum non conveniens* merely by showing that the substantive law that would be applied in the alternative forum is less favorable to the plaintiffs than that of the present forum. The possibility of a change in substantive law should ordinarily not be given conclusive or even substantial weight in the *forum non conveniens* inquiry.

* * *

In fact, if conclusive or substantial weight were given to the possibility of a change in law, the *forum non conveniens* doctrine would become virtually useless. Jurisdiction and venue requirements are often easily satisfied. As a result, many plaintiffs are able to choose from among several forums. Ordinarily, these plaintiffs will select that forum whose choice-of-law rules are most advantageous. Thus, if the possibility of an unfavorable change in substantive law is given substantial weight in the *forum non conveniens* inquiry, dismissal would rarely be proper.

* * *

The Court of Appeals' approach is not only inconsistent with the purpose of the *forum non conveniens* doctrine, but also poses substantial practical problems. If the possibility of a change in law were given substantial weight, deciding motions to dismiss on the ground of *forum non conveniens* would become quite difficult. Choice-of-law analysis would become extremely important, and the courts would frequently be required to interpret the law of foreign jurisdictions. First, the trial court would have to determine what law would apply if the case were tried in the chosen forum, and what law would apply if the case were tried in the alternative forum. It would then have to compare the rights, remedies, and procedures available under the law that would be applied in each forum. Dismissal would be appropriate only if the court concluded that the law applied by the alternative forum is as favorable to the plaintiff as that of the chosen forum. The doctrine of *forum non conveniens,* however, is designed in part to help courts avoid conducting complex exercises in comparative law. As we stated in *Gilbert,* the public interest factors point towards dismissal where the court would be required to "untangle problems in conflict of laws, and in law foreign to itself." * * *

Upholding the decision of the Court of Appeals would result in other practical problems. At least where the foreign plaintiff named an American manufacturer as defendant, a court could not dismiss the case on grounds of *forum non conveniens* where dismissal might lead to an unfavorable change in law. The American courts, which are already extremely attractive to foreign plaintiffs, would become even more attractive. The flow of litigation into the United States would increase and further congest already crowded courts.

* * *

We do not hold that the possibility of an unfavorable change in law should *never* be a relevant consideration in a *forum non conveniens* inquiry. Of course, if the remedy provided by the alternative forum is so clearly inadequate or unsatisfactory that it is no remedy at all, the unfavorable change in law may be given substantial weight; the district court may conclude that dismissal would not be in the interests of justice.[22] In these cases, however, the remedies that would be provided by the Scottish courts do not fall within this category. Although the relatives of the decedents may not be able to rely on a strict liability theory, and although their potential damages award may be smaller, there is no danger that they will be deprived of any remedy or treated unfairly.

III

The Court of Appeals also erred in rejecting the District Court's *Gilbert* analysis. The Court of Appeals stated that more weight should have been given to the plaintiff's choice of forum, and criticized the District Court's analysis of the private and public interests. However, the District Court's decision regarding the deference due plaintiff's choice of forum was appropriate. Furthermore, we do not believe that the District Court abused its discretion in weighing the private and public interests.

A

The District Court acknowledged that there is ordinarily a strong presumption in favor of the plaintiff's choice of forum, which may be overcome only when the private and public interest factors clearly point towards trial in the alternative forum. It held, however, that the presumption applies with less force when the plaintiff or real parties in interest are foreign.

The District Court's distinction between resident or citizen plaintiffs and foreign plaintiffs is fully justified. * * * When the home forum has been chosen, it is reasonable to assume that this choice is convenient. When the plaintiff is foreign, however, this assumption is much less reasonable. Because

---

22. At the outset of any *forum non conveniens* inquiry, the court must determine whether there exists an alternative forum. Ordinarily, this requirement will be satisfied when the defendant is "amenable to process" in the other jurisdiction. *Gilbert* * * *. In rare circumstances, however, where the remedy offered by the other forum is clearly unsatisfactory, the other forum may not be an adequate alternative, and the initial requirement may not be satisfied. Thus, for example, dismissal would not be appropriate where the alternative forum does not permit litigation of the subject matter of the dispute. * * *

the central purpose of any *forum non conveniens* inquiry is to ensure that the trial is convenient, a foreign plaintiff's choice deserves less deference.

B

The *forum non conveniens* determination is committed to the sound discretion of the trial court. It may be reversed only when there has been a clear abuse of discretion; where the court has considered all relevant public and private interest factors, and where its balancing of these factors is reasonable, its decision deserves substantial deference. * * * Here, the Court of Appeals expressly acknowledged that the standard of review was one of abuse of discretion. In examining the District Court's analysis of the public and private interests, however, the Court of Appeals seems to have lost sight of this rule, and substituted its own judgment for that of the District Court.

(1)

In analyzing the private interest factors, the District Court stated that the connections with Scotland are "overwhelming." * * * This characterization may be somewhat exaggerated. Particularly with respect to the question of relative ease of access to sources of proof, the private interests point in both directions. As respondent emphasizes, records concerning the design, manufacture, and testing of the propeller and plane are located in the United States. She would have greater access to sources of proof relevant to her strict liability and negligence theories if trial were held here. However, the District Court did not act unreasonably in concluding that fewer evidentiary problems would be posed if the trial were held in Scotland. A large proportion of the relevant evidence is located in Great Britain.

The Court of Appeals found that the problems of proof could not be given any weight because Piper and Hartzell failed to describe with specificity the evidence they would not be able to obtain if trial were held in the United States. It suggested that defendants seeking *forum non conveniens* dismissal must submit affidavits identifying the witnesses they would call and the testimony these witnesses would provide if the trial were held in the alternative forum. Such detail is not necessary. Piper and Hartzell have moved for dismissal precisely because many crucial witnesses are located beyond the reach of compulsory process, and thus are difficult to identify or interview. Requiring extensive investigation would defeat the purpose of their motion. Of course, defendants must provide enough information to enable the District Court to balance the parties' interests. Our examination of the record convinces us that sufficient information was provided here. Both Piper and Hartzell submitted affidavits describing the evidentiary problems they would face if the trial were held in the United States.

The District Court correctly concluded that the problems posed by the inability to implead potential third party defendants clearly supported holding the trial in Scotland. Joinder of the pilot's estate, Air Navigation, and McDonald is crucial to the presentation of petitioners' defense. If Piper and Hartzell can show that the accident was caused not by a design defect, but rather by the negligence of the pilot, the plane's owners, or the charter company, they will be relieved of all liability. It is true, of course, that if Hartzell and Piper were found liable after a trial in the United States, they could institute an action for indemnity or contribution against these parties in Scotland. It would be far more convenient, however, to resolve all claims in one trial. The Court of Appeals rejected this argument. Forcing petitioners to rely on actions for indemnity or contributions would be "burdensome" but not "unfair." * * * Finding that trial in the plaintiff's chosen forum would be burdensome, however, is sufficient to support dismissal on grounds of *forum non conveniens.*

(2)

The District Court's review of the factors relating to the public interest was also reasonable. On the basis of its choice-of-law analysis, it concluded that if the case were tried in the Middle District of Pennsylvania, Pennsylvania law would apply to Piper and Scottish law to Hartzell. It stated that a trial involving two sets of laws would be confusing to the jury. It also noted its own lack of familiarity with Scottish law. Consideration of these problems was clearly appropriate under *Gilbert;* in that case we explicitly held that the need to apply foreign law pointed towards dismissal. The Court of Appeals found that the District Court's choice-of-law analysis was incorrect, and that American law would apply to both Hartzell and Piper. Thus, lack of familiarity with foreign law would not be a problem. Even if the Court of Appeals' conclusion is correct, however, all other public interest factors favored trial in Scotland.

Scotland has a very strong interest in this litigation. The accident occurred in its airspace. All of the decedents were Scottish. Apart from Piper and Hartzell, all potential plaintiffs and defendants are either Scottish or English. As we stated in *Gilbert,* there is "a local interest in having localized controversies decided at home." * * * Respondent argues that American citizens have an interest in ensuring that American manufacturers are deterred from producing defective products, and that additional deterrence might be obtained if Piper and Hartzell were tried in the United States, where they could be sued on the basis of both negligence and strict liability. However, the incremental deterrence that would be gained if this trial were held in an American court is likely to be insignificant. The American interest in this accident is simply not sufficient to justify the enormous commitment of judicial time and resources that would inevitably be required if the case were to be tried here.

* * *

Reversed.

[JUSTICE POWELL and JUSTICE O'CONNOR took no part in the decision of this case. JUSTICE WHITE concurred in part and dissented in part. JUSTICE STEVENS, with whom JUSTICE BRENNAN joined, dissented.]

Notes and Questions

1. Does *Piper Aircraft* convert forum non conveniens into forum conveniens? Justice Marshall seems to be evaluating whether Scotland is a better forum than the United States. Is the relevant inquiry whether the United States is an inconvenient forum? As Justice Marshall points out, there are some reasons for having a trial in the United States. The aircraft, for example, was manufactured in the United States and records pertaining to manufacture are contained here.

See generally Hoffman & Rowley, *Forum Non Conveniens in Federal Statutory Cases*, 49 Emory L.J. 1137 (2000); Stein, *Forum Non Conveniens and the Redundancy of Court–Access Doctrine*, 133 U.Pa.L.Rev. 781 (1985).

2. What if the injured parties in *Piper Aircraft* had been American? Would the United States still be an inappropriate forum? If the answer is no, what does this say about the doctrine of forum non conveniens? Is it a doctrine aimed at protecting the courts from suits they have no interest in adjudicating? Is forum non conveniens being used in this case as an excuse to protect a domestic corporation from the application of a harsh law? Should we evaluate a plaintiff's interest in litigating in a particular forum differently depending on whether that plaintiff is a citizen of the jurisdiction or not? See Note, *One–Way Ticket Home: The Federal Doctrine of Forum Non Conveniens and the International Plaintiff*, 77 Cornell L.Rev. 650 (1992); Note, *Foreign Plaintiffs and Forum Non Conveniens: Going Beyond Reyno*, 64 Texas L.Rev. 193 (1985); Note, *Singapore Accident, Singapore Plaintiff, Singapore Law, Where Else But Texas? Texas Courts Will Apply State Forum Non Conveniens Law in Admiralty Actions Involving Foreign Nationals*, 37 S. Texas L.Rev. 231 (1996).

3. In part, the doctrine of forum non conveniens operates to ameliorate the burden imposed upon a defendant when jurisdictional rules would permit a plaintiff to force her to litigate in an especially inconvenient forum. However, the doctrine does not relieve the court of the burden of deciding whether it has jurisdiction to hear the lawsuit. For example, in DE CEDENO v. AROSA MERCANTILE, S.A., 91 Misc.2d 577, 398 N.Y.S.2d 250 (Sup.Ct.1977), the defendants urged the court to decide their forum non conveniens motion before their challenges to personal and subject-matter jurisdiction, arguing that discovery on the jurisdictional issues should be avoided when it is abundantly clear that the forum is an inconvenient one. The trial judge disagreed and held that the jurisdictional issues *must* be decided first: "A motion to dismiss [on the basis of forum non conveniens] is addressed to the court's discretion to refuse to retain and entertain an action, *otherwise properly before it*, [and] * * * therefore, 'presupposes the existence of a valid jurisdiction.' " Id. at 579, 398 N.Y.S.2d at 252 (emphasis in original). See also Allstate Life Ins. Co. v. Linter Group, Ltd., 782 F.Supp. 215, 219 (S.D.N.Y.1992).

4. Inconvenience to the defendant is, of course, one of the factors considered in determining whether an exercise of jurisdiction over a defendant violates due process. But inconvenience to the defendant of less magnitude than that required to invoke due process may be sufficient to justify granting a motion to dismiss under the doctrine of forum non conveniens. There are important conditions precedent to the application of the doctrine in such situations, however.

One important requirement is that there must exist another more convenient forum where the plaintiff can obtain adequate relief. See Annot., 57 A.L.R.4th 973 (1987). Need this forum have been available to the plaintiff when she commenced the action? Should the court grant a forum non conveniens motion if personal jurisdiction could not have been obtained over the defendant in any other jurisdiction at the start of the lawsuit but the defendant is now willing to waive his objection to personal jurisdiction in a more convenient forum? What if the statute of limitations has run in the more convenient forum (but not in the forum where the motion is made) but the defendant is willing to stipulate that he will waive the defense? Courts often have based their willingness to grant motions to dismiss for forum non conveniens on a stipulation from the defendant accepting these conditions. Thus, for example, even though a state court does not have the authority to transfer a suit to another state, it may use its ability to shape the form of the dismissal to obtain the same result. See, e.g., In re Union Carbide Corp. Gas Plant Disaster at Bhopal, India in Dec., 1984, 809 F.2d 195 (2d Cir.), certiorari denied 484 U.S. 871, 108 S.Ct. 199, 98 L.Ed.2d 150 (1987).

Notwithstanding the considerable latitude available to courts to grant forum non conveniens motions, however, it remains the case that courts are loathe to cede jurisdiction once obtained and that motions based upon forum non conveniens arguments are not granted with great frequency. See Stewart, *Forum Non Conveniens: A Doctrine in Search of a Role,* 74 Calif.L.Rev. 1259 (1986).

5. In ISLAMIC REPUBLIC OF IRAN v. PAHLAVI, 62 N.Y.2d 474, 478 N.Y.S.2d 597, 467 N.E.2d 245 (1984), certiorari denied 469 U.S. 1108, 105 S.Ct. 783, 83 L.Ed.2d 778 (1985), the Islamic Republic of Iran sued the Shah and his wife to recover $35 billion dollars in Iranian funds, which they allegedly had misappropriated. Iran asked the New York court to impress a constructive trust on the defendants' assets located throughout the world. The Shah was served at New York Hospital where he was undergoing cancer therapy, and the Empress was served at the same time at the New York home of the Shah's sister. The trial court granted the defendants' motion to dismiss the action on forum non conveniens grounds, concluding that the parties had no connection with New York other than a claim that the Shah had deposited some funds in a New York bank. The intermediate appellate court affirmed, even though it appeared from the record that no alternative forum was available to the plaintiff, because of the political situation in Iran.

The New York Court of Appeals affirmed, finding that the application of the doctrine of forum non conveniens is a matter of discretion for the lower courts and that those courts had not abused that discretion. The Court of Appeals concluded that New York's courts were not required to entertain litigation that had no connection with the state—especially when, as in this case, the burden on the state's courts would be tremendous. The court noted the plaintiff's argument that the availability of an alternative forum was a precondition to dismissal on forum non conveniens grounds, and acknowledged the language in *Gulf Oil* (quoted in *Piper Aircraft*) supporting the plaintiff's view. But it dismissed the passage in *Gulf Oil* as dicta (because there was an alternative forum in that case) and found that the availability of another forum was just a "most important" factor to be considered.

Is this decision correct? Is it relevant that the plaintiff asked the New York court to provide sweeping review of the political and financial management of the Iranian government during the Shah's regime?

6. A forum non conveniens motion is not the only remedy available to a defendant who objects to plaintiff's choice of forum. Defendant also may institute a suit in another court to enjoin plaintiff from proceeding in the objectionable forum. See generally Comment, *Injunctions Against Suits In Foreign Jurisdictions,* 10 La.L.Rev. 302, 302–12 (1950). However, defendant usually must demonstrate that plaintiff chose the forum to gain some form of advantage or to harass defendant. See Christensen v. Integrity Ins. Co., 719 S.W.2d 161 (Tex.1986).

      * * * This requirement, which is not part of the doctrine of forum non conveniens, may have arisen from judicial concern about the disruptive effect of injunctions against suit on interstate relations. * * *

Occasionally, injunctions are issued without regard either for the criteria of trial convenience or the propriety of plaintiff's motive, but rather to promote interests local to the enjoining forum. Some courts, for example, have sought to prevent the "exportation" of particular classes of claims arising within the state; others have issued injunctions in order to guarantee the application of local law to controversies based on domestic incidents.

* * *

But a choice between the two remedies is not always available. * * * Many states reject the doctrine [of forum non conveniens] entirely;[a] and of those in which it is applied, relief is unlikely if either party is a resident of the forum state.

Comment, *Forum Non Conveniens, Injunctions Against Suit and Full Faith and Credit*, 29 U.Chi.L.Rev. 740, 747–50 (1962).

The principal defect of injunctions to restrain parties from proceeding in another court is the fact that frequently they are unenforceable; if the enjoining court cannot subject plaintiff or his property to its control, the threat of contempt proceedings may be ineffective. Moreover the original forum occasionally will issue a counter-injunction to restrain defendant from enforcing the injunction purporting to direct the parties to refrain from proceeding in the original action. See, e.g., James v. Grand Trunk W.R. Co., 14 Ill.2d 356, 152 N.E.2d 858, certiorari denied 358 U.S. 915, 79 S.Ct. 288, 3 L.Ed.2d 239 (1958). This procedure obviously may have a detrimental effect on the relations among state courts or between federal and state courts. See generally Note, *State Injunction of Proceedings in Federal Courts*, 75 Yale L.J. 150 (1965).

Another approach to the problem of the inconvenient forum already has been mentioned—the court may grant a motion by defendant to stay the proceedings on the condition that defendant make himself available in the alternative forum. How does this procedure differ from the forum non conveniens practice? What are the respective merits of dealing with the inconvenient-forum problem by dismissal, injunction, or stay? To what extent must the court investigate the availability of jurisdiction in the alternative forum when it employs each of these techniques? See, e.g., Mercier v. Sheraton Int'l, Inc., 981 F.2d 1345 (1st Cir.1992), certiorari denied 508 U.S. 912, 113 S.Ct. 2346, 124 L.Ed.2d 255 (1993).

---

a. E.g., State of Missouri ex rel. Southern Ry. v. Mayfield, 362 Mo. 101, 240 S.W.2d 106, certiorari denied 342 U.S. 871, 72 S.Ct. 107, 96 L.Ed. 655 (1951).

Chapter 6

ASCERTAINING THE APPLICABLE LAW

Civil actions involving citizens of a single state and a transaction that occurred entirely within the boundaries of that state do not present any problems of choosing the proper body of substantive law to be applied in determining the rights and liabilities of the parties. However, as soon as the litigation touches two or more states, one is likely to be confronted with the serious question of choosing between two or more sources of law. For example, suppose plaintiff and defendant, both citizens of State X, are involved in an automobile accident or agree to perform a contract or engage in a transfer of property in State Y. Should questions pertaining to defendant's alleged negligence or failure to perform the contract or the ownership of the property be decided under the law of State X or the law of State Y? Should the choice be made in the same way in tort, contract, and property actions? The complexity of these questions increases if plaintiff and defendant are citizens of different states and the event, relationship, or property that forms the predicate of the controversy can be traced to a third, and perhaps a fourth or fifth, state. You will be exposed to problems of this type on numerous occasions during the Civil Procedure course and therefore must learn to recognize them. However, formal education in the philosophy of choosing among the laws of two or more states must be postponed until the course in Conflict of Laws.

This Chapter is devoted to choice-of-law problems of a somewhat different dimension. Let us suppose that plaintiff is a citizen of State X and defendant is a citizen of State Y and that plaintiff has decided to litigate a tort or contract claim against defendant in a federal district court in State Y. What law should the federal court apply to adjudicate this action? The law of State X? Of State Y? Federal law? Would the answer be different if, assuming personal jurisdiction could be acquired, the action was commenced in a federal district court in State X? The problem of choosing between federal and state law also is present when a state court is called upon to decide cases arising under federal statutes or cases in which federal rights and liabilities are in issue. As one might surmise, the process of choosing between the law of two states and that of choosing between federal and state law are analogous. In some situations, particularly diversity cases, they are intertwined. This Chapter will explore some of the problems created by the application of state law in the federal courts and the role of federal law in the state courts.

A final observation before beginning: If the law applied by one court differs materially from that applied by another, an attorney interested in achieving a particular result for a client obviously may wish to steer the lawsuit, if the jurisdiction and venue rules permit, to a particular tribunal. To what extent should a court take account of this type of forum manipulation in choosing the law to be applied?

SECTION A. STATE LAW IN THE FEDERAL COURTS

1. THE RULE OF SWIFT v. TYSON

Although Article III of the Constitution sets limits on the jurisdiction of the federal court system, it does not establish any lower federal courts. The power to establish those "inferior" courts was left to Congress, which quickly used it. The Judiciary Act of 1789 established a lower federal court system and promulgated rules governing its jurisdiction and operation. Among those rules, in Section 34 of the Judiciary Act, was the so-called Rules of Decision Act. The modern version of this Act is found in 28 U.S.C. § 1652 and reads:

> The laws of the several states, except where the Constitution or treaties of the United States or Acts of Congress otherwise require or provide, shall be regarded as rules of decision in civil actions in the courts of the United States, in cases where they apply.

For nearly one hundred years, the Supreme Court's decision in SWIFT v. TYSON, 41 U.S. (16 Pet.) 1, 10 L.Ed. 865 (1842), provided the basic interpretation of the language of the Rules of Decision Act. In *Swift,* some Maine land speculators sold land that they did not own to some New Yorkers. Although the speculators planned to use the New Yorkers' money to purchase the land, the New Yorkers thought that the speculators already owned the land. Some New Yorkers, including George W. Tyson, gave the speculators negotiable instruments instead of money to pay for their investments. Tyson "accepted" a bill of exchange in return for a six-month postponement in his payments on the land contract.

One of the speculators gave Tyson's note to Joseph Swift, a Maine banker, in satisfaction of a preexisting debt. When Swift sought payment from Tyson, Tyson refused to pay on the ground that his obligation was unenforceable since he had been induced to "accept" the bill by the speculator's fraud. Swift sued Tyson in federal court in New York based upon diversity jurisdiction. The principal question before the court was whether the case should be governed by New York contract law, under which the fraud tainting the transaction provided a defense for Tyson, or by the new law of negotiable instruments that was developing in recent English decisions, under which Tyson would have to pay Swift if Swift had accepted the instrument without notice of the fraud.

Whether New York law applied or not turned upon the meaning of the phrase "laws of the several states" in the Rules of Decision Act. If the phrase encompassed both the statutory and the decisional law of the states (that is, if the Act commanded federal courts to follow both state statutes and state court decisions in cases in which they covered the controversy), then the New York rule (which was judge-made, not part of a statute) had to be applied. If, on the other hand, the phrase encompassed only statutory law (that is, if the Act commanded federal courts to follow the state rule *only* if it was in a state statute), then the federal court in *Swift* was free to use the emerging rule or any other it felt was best. Justice Story, writing for a unanimous Court, concluded that the Act commanded federal courts to follow simply the statutory law of the states.

It is observable that the Courts of New York do not found their decisions upon this point upon any local statute, or positive, fixed, or ancient local usage: but they deduce the doctrine from the general principles of commercial law. It is, however, contended, that the thirty-fourth section of the judiciary act of 1789, ch. 20, furnishes a rule obligatory upon this Court to follow the decisions of the state tribunals in all cases to which they apply. * * * In order to maintain the argument, it is essential, therefore, to hold, that the word "laws," in this section, includes within the scope of its meaning the decisions of the local tribunals. In the ordinary use of language it will hardly be contended that the decisions of Courts constitute laws. They are, at most, only evidence of what the laws are, and are not of themselves laws. They are often reexamined, reversed, and qualified by the Courts themselves, whenever they are found to be either defective, or ill-founded, or otherwise incorrect. The laws of a state are more usually understood to mean the rules and enactments promulgated by the legislative authority thereof, or long established local customs having the force of laws. In all the various cases, which have hitherto come before us for decision, this Court have uniformly supposed, that the true interpretation of the thirty-fourth section limited its application to state laws strictly local, that is to say, to the positive statutes of the state, and the construction thereof adopted by the local tribunals, and to rights and titles to things having a permanent locality, such as the rights and titles to real estate, and other matters immovable and intraterritorial in their nature and character. It never has been supposed by us, that the section did apply, or was designed to apply, to questions of a more general nature, not at all dependent upon local statutes or local usages of a fixed and permanent operation, as, for example, to the construction of ordinary contracts or other written instruments and especially to questions of general commercial law, where the state tribunals are called upon to perform the like functions as ourselves, that is, to ascertain upon general reasoning and legal analogies, what is the true exposition of the contract or instrument, or what is the just rule furnished by the principles of commercial law to govern the case. And we have not now the slightest difficulty in holding, that this section, upon its true intendment and construction, is strictly limited to local statutes and local usages of the character before stated, and does not extend to contracts and other instruments of a commercial nature, the true interpretation and effect whereof are to be sought, not in the decisions of the local tribunals, but in the general principles and doctrines of commercial jurisprudence. * * *

Id. at 18–19, 10 L.Ed. at 871.

Is Justice Story correct when he asserts that "[i]n the ordinary use of language it will hardly be contended that the decisions of Courts constitute laws"? Does it make sense to have the federal courts promulgate general, uniformly applied commercial laws? Why should a person suing in federal court in Oklahoma not receive the same remedy as a person suing in federal court in Vermont? On the other hand, if a federal court sitting in diversity is forced to apply the forum state's court decisions, what advantage would a party have in going to federal court?

The *Swift* decision must be evaluated in the context in which it was decided. First, *Swift* was decided in the heyday of "the common law." Justice Story believed that judges were responsible for finding "the truth" by examining all of the available authorities. In commercial matters, such as contracts, Story saw no need to adhere to the decisions of a single jurisdiction: Since the nature of commercial contracts is universal, the principles that should guide them are universal and are to be found by tapping the wisdom and experience of humankind.

Second, the federal government, including the judiciary, were seeking greater uniformity and stability in interstate commerce and, in this specific context, wanted to encourage businessmen to trust out-of-state negotiable instruments. On the other hand, the states' attitudes were guided by provincial concerns, such as trying to protect local debtors from foreign creditors. Thus, the *Swift* decision helped simplify commercial law and simultaneously encouraged the nationalist goals of the federal government.

2. THE *ERIE* DOCTRINE: THE RULES OF DECISION ACT AND THE RULES ENABLING ACT

ERIE R. CO. v. TOMPKINS

Supreme Court of the United States, 1938.
304 U.S. 64, 58 S.Ct. 817, 82 L.Ed. 1188.

[Slightly after midnight on July 27, 1934, Harry James Tompkins was walking home along a well-trodden footpath running parallel to the Erie Railroad tracks in Hughestown, Pennsylvania, when he was struck by "a black object that looked like a door" protruding from a passing train. Tompkins' right arm was severed.

Under Pennsylvania law, a traveler like Tompkins on a parallel (or "longitudinal") path was regarded as a trespasser to whom the railroad merely owes a duty to avoid wanton negligence. The majority rule in most states, however, was that a railroad owes a duty of ordinary care to a traveler on a parallel footpath.

Tompkins' lawyers were well aware of the rule in *Swift* that, absent state statutory law, federal courts apply "general law," and thus they tried to avoid the harsh Pennsylvania rule by suing the New York-based railroad in federal court. As anticipated, the District Court applied "general law," the majority rule, and the jury awarded Tompkins $30,000 in damages.

The Court of Appeals affirmed, holding that

upon questions of general law the federal courts are free, in absence of a local statute, to exercise their independent judgment as to what the law is; and it is well settled that the question of the responsibility of a railroad for injuries caused by its servants is one of general law. * * * Where the public has made open and notorious use of a railroad right of way for a long period of time and without objection, the company owes to persons on such permissive pathway a duty of care in the operation of its trains. * * * It is likewise generally recognized law that a jury may find that negligence exists toward a pedestrian using a permissive path on the railroad right of way if he is hit by some object projecting from the side of the train.

The Supreme Court granted certiorari. After hearing the opening arguments, Chief Justice Hughes declared: "If we wish to overrule Swift v. Tyson, here is our opportunity."]

Certiorari to the Circuit Court of Appeals for the Second Circuit.

MR. JUSTICE BRANDEIS delivered the opinion of the Court.

* * *

First. Swift v. Tyson * * * held that federal courts exercising jurisdiction on the ground of diversity of citizenship need not, in matters of general jurisprudence, apply the unwritten law of the state as declared by its highest court; that they are free to exercise an independent judgment as to what the common law of the state is—or should be * * *.

* * * The federal courts assumed, in the broad field of "general law," the power to declare rules of decision which Congress was confessedly without power to enact as statutes. Doubt was repeatedly expressed as to the correctness of the construction given section 34, and as to the soundness of the rule which it introduced. But it was the more recent research of a competent scholar, who examined the original document, which established that the construction given to it by the Court was erroneous; and that the purpose of the section was merely to make certain that, in all matters except those in which some federal law is controlling, the federal courts exercising jurisdiction in diversity of citizenship cases would apply as their rules of decision the law of the state, unwritten as well as written.[5]

Criticism of the doctrine became widespread after the decision of Black & White Taxicab & Transfer Co. v. Brown & Yellow Taxicab & Transfer Co., 276 U.S. 518, 48 S.Ct. 404, 72 L.Ed. 681, 57 A.L.R. 426. There, Brown & Yellow, a Kentucky corporation owned by Kentuckians, and the Louisville & Nashville Railroad, also a Kentucky corporation, wished that the former should have the exclusive privilege of soliciting passenger and baggage transportation at the Bowling Green, Ky., railroad station; and that the Black & White, a competing Kentucky corporation, should be prevented from interfering with that privilege. Knowing that such a contract would be void under the common law of Kentucky, it was arranged that the Brown & Yellow reincorporate under the law of Tennessee, and that the contract with the railroad should be executed there. The suit was then brought by the Tennessee corporation in the federal court for Western Kentucky to enjoin competition by the Black & White; an injunction issued by the District Court was sustained by the Court of Appeals;

5. Charles Warren, New Light on the History of the Federal Judiciary Act of 1789   (1923) 37 Harv.L.Rev. 49, 51–52, 81–88, 108.

and this Court, citing many decisions in which the doctrine of Swift v. Tyson had been applied, affirmed the decree.

Second. Experience in applying the doctrine of Swift v. Tyson, had revealed its defects, political and social; and the benefits expected to flow from the rule did not accrue. Persistence of state courts in their own opinions on questions of common law prevented uniformity; and the impossibility of discovering a satisfactory line of demarcation between the province of general law and that of local law developed a new well of uncertainties.

On the other hand, the mischievous results of the doctrine had become apparent. Diversity of citizenship jurisdiction was conferred in order to prevent apprehended discrimination in state courts against those not citizens of the state. Swift v. Tyson introduced grave discrimination by noncitizens against citizens. It made rights enjoyed under the unwritten "general law" vary according to whether enforcement was sought in the state or in the federal court; and the privilege of selecting the court in which the right should be determined was conferred upon the noncitizen. Thus, the doctrine rendered impossible equal protection of the law. In attempting to promote uniformity of law throughout the United States, the doctrine had prevented uniformity in the administration of the law of the state.

The discrimination resulting became in practice far-reaching. This resulted in part from the broad province accorded to the so-called "general law" as to which federal courts exercised an independent judgment. In addition to questions of purely commercial law, "general law" was held to include the obligations under contracts entered into and to be performed within the state, the extent to which a carrier operating within a state may stipulate for exemption from liability for his own negligence or that of his employee; the liability for torts committed within the state upon persons resident or property located there, even where the question of liability depended upon the scope of a property right conferred by the state; and the right to exemplary or punitive damages. Furthermore, state decisions construing local deeds, mineral conveyances, and even devises of real estate, were disregarded.

In part the discrimination resulted from the wide range of persons held entitled to avail themselves of the federal rule by resort to the diversity of citizenship jurisdiction. Through this jurisdiction individual citizens willing to remove from their own state and become citizens of another might avail themselves of the federal rule. And, without even change of residence, a corporate citizen of the state could avail itself of the federal rule by reincorporating under the laws of another state, as was done in the Taxicab Case.

The injustice and confusion incident to the doctrine of Swift v. Tyson have been repeatedly urged as reasons for abolishing or limiting diversity of citizenship jurisdiction. Other legislative relief has been proposed. If only a question of statutory construction were involved, we should not be prepared to abandon a doctrine so widely applied throughout nearly a century. But the unconstitutionality of the course pursued has now been made clear, and compels us to do so.

Third. Except in matters governed by the Federal Constitution or by acts of Congress, the law to be applied in any case is the law of the state. And whether the law of the state shall be declared by its Legislature in a statute or by its highest court in a decision is not a matter of federal concern. There is no federal general common law. Congress has no power to declare substantive rules of common law applicable in a state whether they be local in their nature or "general," be they commercial law or a part of the law of torts. And no clause in the Constitution purports to confer such a power upon the federal courts. As stated by Mr. Justice Field when protesting in Baltimore & Ohio R.R. Co. v. Baugh, 149 U.S. 368, 401, 13 S.Ct. 914, 927, 37 L.Ed. 772, against ignoring the Ohio common law of fellow-servant liability: "I am aware that what has been termed the general law of the country—which is often little less than what the judge advancing the doctrine thinks at the time should be the general law on a particular subject—has been often advanced in judicial opinions of this court to control a conflicting law of a state. I admit that learned judges have fallen into the habit of repeating this doctrine as a convenient mode of brushing aside the law of a state in conflict with their views. And I confess that, moved and governed by the authority of the great names of those judges, I have, myself, in many instances, unhesitatingly and confidently, but I think now erroneously, repeated the same doctrine. But, notwithstanding the great names which may be cited in favor of the doctrine, and notwithstanding the frequency with which the doctrine has been reiterated, there stands, as a perpetual protest against its repetition, the constitution of the United States, which recognizes and preserves the autonomy and independence of the states,—independence in their legislative and independence in their judicial departments. Supervision over either the legislative or the judicial action of the states is in no case permissible except as to matters by the constitution specifically authorized or delegated to the United States. Any interference with either, except as thus permitted, is an invasion of the authority of the state, and, to that extent, a denial of its independence."

The fallacy underlying the rule declared in Swift v. Tyson is made clear by Mr. Justice Holmes.[23] The doctrine rests upon the assumption that there is "a transcendental body of law outside of any particular State but obligatory within it unless and until changed by statute," that federal courts have the power to use their judgment as to what the rules of common law are; and that in the federal courts "the parties are entitled to an independent judgment on matters of general law":

> But law in the sense in which courts speak of it today does not exist without some definite authority behind it. The common law so far as it is enforced in a State, whether called common law or not, is not the common law generally but the law of that State existing by the authority of that State without regard to what it may have been in England or anywhere else. * * *

> The authority and only authority is the State, and if that be so, the voice adopted by the State as its own [whether it be of its Legislature or of its Supreme Court] should utter the last word.

Thus the doctrine of Swift v. Tyson is, as Mr. Justice Holmes said, "an unconstitutional assumption of powers by the Courts of the United States which no lapse of time or respectable array of opinion should make us hesitate to correct." In disapproving that doctrine we do not hold unconstitutional

---

23. Kuhn v. Fairmont Coal Co., 215 U.S. 349, 370–372, 30 S.Ct. 140, 54 L.Ed. 228; Black & White Taxicab, etc., Co. v. Brown & Yellow Taxicab, etc., Co., 276 U.S. 518, 532–536, 48 S.Ct. 404, 408, 409, 72 L.Ed. 681, 57 A.L.R. 426.

section 34 of the Federal Judiciary Act of 1789 or any other act of Congress. We merely declare that in applying the doctrine this Court and the lower courts have invaded rights which in our opinion are reserved by the Constitution to the several states.

Fourth. The defendant contended that by the common law of Pennsylvania * * * the only duty owed to the plaintiff was to refrain from willful or wanton injury. The plaintiff denied that such is the Pennsylvania law. In support of their respective contentions the parties discussed and cited many decisions of the Supreme Court of the State. The Circuit Court of Appeals ruled that the question of liability is one of general law; and on that ground declined to decide the issue of state law. As we hold this was error, the judgment is reversed and the case remanded to it for further proceedings in conformity with our opinion.

Reversed.

Mr. Justice Cardozo took no part in the consideration or decision of this case.

Mr. Justice Butler (dissenting).

* * *

Defendant's petition for writ of certiorari presented two questions: Whether its duty toward plaintiff should have been determined in accordance with the law as found by the highest court of Pennsylvania, and whether the evidence conclusively showed plaintiff guilty of contributory negligence. Plaintiff contends that, as always heretofore held by this Court, the issues of negligence and contributory negligence are to be determined by general law against which local decisions may not be held conclusive * * *.

No constitutional question was suggested or argued below or here. And as a general rule, this Court will not consider any question not raised below and presented by the petition. * * * Here it does not decide either of the questions presented, but, changing the rule of decision in force since the foundation of the government, remands the case to be adjudged according to a standard never before deemed permissible.

* * *

The doctrine of * * * [Swift v. Tyson] has been followed by this Court in an unbroken line of decisions. So far as appears, it was not questioned until more than 50 years later, and then by a single judge.[1] Baltimore & O. Railroad Co. v. Baugh * * *.

And since that decision, the division of opinion in this Court has been of the same character as it was before. In 1910, Mr. Justice Holmes, speaking for himself and two other Justices, dissented from the holding that a court of the United States was bound to exercise its own independent judgment in the construction of a conveyance made before the state courts had rendered an authoritative decision as to its meaning and effect. Kuhn v. Fairmont Coal Co. * * *. But that dissent accepted * * * as "settled" the doctrine of Swift v.

1. Mr. Justice Field filed a dissenting opinion.

Tyson, and insisted * * * merely that the case under consideration was by nature and necessity peculiarly local.

* * *

So far as appears, no litigant has ever challenged the power of Congress to establish the rule as construed. It has so long endured that its destruction now without appropriate deliberation cannot be justified. There is nothing in the opinion to suggest that consideration of any constitutional question is necessary to a decision of the case. * * * Against the protest of those joining in this opinion, the Court declines to assign the case for reargument. It may not justly be assumed that the labor and argument of counsel for the parties would not disclose the right conclusion and aid the Court in the statement of reasons to support it. Indeed, it would have been appropriate to give Congress opportunity to be heard before divesting it of power to prescribe rules of decision to be followed in the courts of the United States. * * *

The course pursued by the Court in this case is repugnant to the Act of Congress of August 24, 1937, 50 Stat. 751, 28 U.S.C.A. §§ 17 and note, 349a, 380a and note, 401. It declares that: "Whenever the constitutionality of any Act of Congress affecting the public interest is drawn in question in any court of the United States in any suit or proceeding to which the United States, or any agency thereof, or any officer or employee thereof, as such officer or employee, is not a party, the court having jurisdiction of the suit or proceeding shall certify such fact to the Attorney General. In any such case the court shall permit the United States to intervene and become a party for presentation of evidence * * * and argument upon the question of the constitutionality of such Act. * * * " If defendant had applied for and obtained the writ of certiorari upon the claim that, as now held, Congress has no power to prescribe the rule of decision, section 34 as construed, it would have been the duty of this Court to issue the prescribed certificate to the Attorney General in order that the United States might intervene and be heard on the constitutional question. * * * Congress intended to give the United States the right to be heard in every case involving constitutionality of an act affecting the public interest. In view of the rule that, in the absence of challenge of constitutionality, statutes will not here be invalidated on that ground, the Act of August 24, 1937 extends to cases where constitutionality is first "drawn in question" by the Court. * * *

I am of opinion that the constitutional validity of the rule need not be considered, because under the law, as found by the courts of Pennsylvania and generally throughout the country, it is plain that the evidence required a finding that plaintiff was guilty of negligence that contributed to cause his injuries, and that the judgment below should be reversed upon that ground.

MR. JUSTICE MCREYNOLDS concurs in this opinion.

MR. JUSTICE REED (concurring in part).

I concur in the conclusion reached in this case, in the disapproval of the doctrine of Swift v. Tyson, and in the reasoning of the majority opinion, except in so far as it relies upon the unconstitutionality of the "course pursued" by the federal courts.

The "doctrine of Swift v. Tyson," as I understand it, is that the words "the laws," as used in section 34 of the Federal Judiciary Act of September

24, 1789, do not include in their meaning "the decisions of the local tribunals." * * *

To decide the case now before us and to "disapprove" the doctrine of Swift v. Tyson requires only that we say that the words "the laws" include in their meaning the decisions of the local tribunals. As the majority opinion shows, by its reference to Mr. Warren's researches and the first quotation from Mr. Justice Holmes, that this Court is now of the view that "laws" includes "decisions," it is unnecessary to go further and declare that the "course pursued" was "unconstitutional," instead of merely erroneous.

The "unconstitutional" course referred to in the majority opinion is apparently the ruling in Swift v. Tyson that the supposed omission of Congress to legislate as to the effect of decisions leaves federal courts free to interpret general law for themselves. I am not at all sure whether, in the absence of federal statutory direction, federal courts would be compelled to follow state decisions. There was sufficient doubt about the matter in 1789 to induce the first Congress to legislate. No former opinions of this Court have passed upon it. * * * If the opinion commits this Court to the position that the Congress is without power to declare what rules of substantive law shall govern the federal courts, that conclusion also seems questionable. The line between procedural and substantive law is hazy, but no one doubts federal power over procedure. * * * The Judiciary Article, 3, and the "necessary and proper" clause of article 1, § 8, may fully authorize legislation, such as this section of the Judiciary Act.

* * *

Notes and Questions

1. Is *Erie* a constitutional decision or does it rest on other grounds? What constitutional provision could provide the basis for Justice Brandeis' opinion? Is he claiming that the result in *Swift* was unconstitutional because a regime of federal common law making is not authorized by any constitutional provision? Or is he claiming that federal courts cannot make common law for traditionally state causes of action, such as contracts, torts, and property? The Commerce Clause of the Constitution, Article I, Section 8, certainly allows Congress to regulate interstate railroads. If Congress can legislate in this area, why can't the courts act as well?

The constitutional discussion in *Erie* is sometimes referred to as "dicta." Is Justice Brandeis' reference to the Constitution merely a way of bolstering his interpretation of the Rules of Decision Act? See Clark, *State Law in the Federal Courts: The Brooding Omnipresence of Erie v. Tompkins*, 55 Yale L.J. 267, 278 (1946).

2. If discrimination against in-state defendants really is a problem, could it not be solved by allowing in-state defendants to remove to federal court? Does it make sense to require federal courts to apply state law in diversity cases simply out of a desire for parity between in-state defendants who cannot remove and out-of-state defendants who can?

Justice Brandeis uses the *Black & White Taxicab* case to illustrate the evils resulting from *Swift*. But could not the problem presented in that case be handled without overruling *Swift* by preventing reincorporation solely to assert diversity jurisdiction? Reread 28 U.S.C. § 1359, set out in the Supplement. Would application of Section 1359 have alleviated the problem?

3. In the article referred to at footnote 5 of the Court's opinion, Professor Charles Warren revealed a previously unknown draft of what became the Rules of Decision Act of 1789. The draft read:

> And be it further enacted, That the Statute law of the several States in force for the time being and their unwritten or common law now in use, whether by adoption from the common law of England, the ancient statutes of the same or otherwise, except where the Constitution, treaties or statutes of the United States shall otherwise require or provide, shall be regarded as rules of decision in the trials at common law in the courts of the United States in cases where they apply.

Did Justice Brandeis properly interpret the Rules of Decision Act given this legislative history? Or, did the shorter final version reflect congressional intent to limit the definition of "laws of the several states" to statutory laws, thus expanding the federal common law making power of the federal courts in diversity cases?

4. Reactions to the *Erie* decision voiced shortly after it was handed down include Shulman, *The Demise of Swift v. Tyson*, 47 Yale L.J. 1336 (1938); Tunks, *Categorization and Federalism: "Substance" and "Procedure" After Erie Railroad v. Tompkins*, 34 Ill.L.Rev. 271 (1939). More recent treatments of the subject are found in Corr, *Thoughts on the Vitality of Erie*, 41 Am. U.L.Rev. 1087 (1992) (advocating a repudiation of *Erie* and a return to the approach taken in *Swift*); Friendly, *In Praise of Erie—And of the New Federal Common Law*, 39 N.Y.U.L.Rev. 383 (1964); Gelfand & Abrams, *Putting Erie on the Right Track*, 49 U.Pitt.L.Rev. 937 (1988); Hill, *The Erie Doctrine and the Constitution*, 53 Nw. U.L.Rev. 427, 541 (1958); Kurland, *Mr. Justice Frankfurter, the Supreme Court and the Erie Doctrine in Diversity Cases*, 67 Yale L.J. 187 (1957); Note, *The Law Applied in Diversity Cases: The Rules of Decision Act and the Erie Doctrine*, 85 Yale L.J. 678 (1976). Perhaps the strongest attack on the *Erie* doctrine in the literature is found in Keeffe, Gilhooley, Bailey & Day, *Weary Erie*, 34 Cornell L.Q. 494 (1949). For an interesting debate on the meaning of *Erie*, see Redish & Phillips, *Erie and the Rules of Decision Act: In Search of the Appropriate Dilemma*, 91 Harv.L.Rev. 356 (1977); Westen & Lehman, *Is There Life for Erie After the Death of Diversity?*, 78 Mich.L.Rev. 311 (1981); Redish, *Continuing the Erie Debate: A Response to Westen and Lehman*, 78 Mich.L.Rev. 959 (1982); Westen, *After "Life for Erie"—A Reply*, 78 Mich.L.Rev. 971 (1982).

GUARANTY TRUST CO. v. YORK

Supreme Court of the United States, 1945.
326 U.S. 99, 65 S.Ct. 1464, 89 L.Ed. 2079.

[The Guaranty Trust Company served as trustee for some of the note-holders of Van Sweringen Corporation. In October 1930, Guaranty loaned money to corporations affiliated with and controlled by Van Sweringen. By October 1931, it was evident that the corporation was having trouble meeting its financial obligations. Guaranty and several other banks worked out a plan by which Guaranty would offer to purchase the notes by paying $500 and twenty shares of Van Sweringen stock for each $1,000 note.

Respondent York received $6,000 of the notes from a donor who had not accepted Guaranty's offer. York brought a diversity suit alleging that Guaranty had breached its fiduciary duties. York's complaint involved allegations of fraud and misrepresentation, relief for which was governed by equitable principles. On appeal, the Circuit Court of Appeals, one judge dissenting, found that in a suit brought on the equity side of a federal district court the court was not required to apply the state statute of limitations that would govern similar suits in state courts, even though the exclusive basis of federal jurisdiction was diversity of citizenship. The Supreme Court granted review in order to decide whether federal courts should apply state statutes of limitations in such cases.]

Certiorari to the Circuit Court of Appeals for the Second Circuit.

MR. JUSTICE FRANKFURTER delivered the opinion of the Court.

* * *

Our starting point must be the policy of federal jurisdiction which Erie R. Co. v. Tompkins * * * embodies. In overruling Swift v. Tyson * * * Erie R. Co. v. Tompkins did not merely overrule a venerable case. It overruled a particular way of looking at law which dominated the judicial process long after its inadequacies had been laid bare. * * * Law was conceived as a "brooding omnipresence" of Reason, of which decisions were merely evidence and not themselves the controlling formulations. Accordingly, federal courts deemed themselves free to ascertain what Reason, and therefore Law, required wholly independent of authoritatively declared State law, even in cases where a legal right as the basis for relief was created by State authority and could not be created by federal authority and the case got into a federal court merely because it was "between Citizens of different States" under Art. III, § 2 of the Constitution * * *.

In exercising their jurisdiction on the ground of diversity of citizenship, the federal courts, in the long course of their history, have not differentiated in their regard for State law between actions at law and suits in equity. Although § 34 of the Judiciary Act of 1789 * * * directed that the "laws of the several states * * * shall be regarded as rules of decision in trials of common law * * *," this was deemed, consistently for over a hundred years, to be merely declaratory of what would in any event have governed the federal courts and therefore was equally applicable to equity suits. * * * Indeed, it may fairly be said that the federal courts gave greater respect to State-created "substantive rights," Pusey & Jones Co. v. Hanssen, 261 U.S. 491, 498, 43 S.Ct. 454, 456, 67 L.Ed. 763, in equity than they gave them on the law side, because rights at law were usually declared by State courts and as such increasingly flouted by extension of the doctrine of Swift v. Tyson, while rights in equity were frequently defined by legislative enactment and as such known and respected by the federal courts. * * *

Partly because the States in the early days varied greatly in the manner in which equitable relief was afforded and in the extent to which it was available, * * * Congress provided that "the forms and modes of proceeding in suits * * * of equity" would conform to the settled uses of courts of equity. * * * But this enactment gave the federal courts no power that they would not have had in any event when courts were given "cognizance," by the first

Judiciary Act, of suits "in equity." From the beginning there has been a good deal of talk in the cases that federal equity is a separate legal system. And so it is, properly understood. The suits in equity of which the federal courts have had "cognizance" ever since 1789 constituted the body of law which had been transplanted to this country from the English Court of Chancery. * * * In giving federal courts "cognizance" of equity suits in cases of diversity jurisdiction, Congress never gave, nor did the federal courts ever claim, the power to deny substantive rights created by State law or to create substantive rights denied by State law.

This does not mean that whatever equitable remedy is available in a State court must be available in a diversity suit in a federal court, or conversely, that a federal court may not afford an equitable remedy not available in a State court. * * * State law cannot define the remedies which a federal court must give simply because a federal court in diversity jurisdiction is available as an alternative tribunal to the State's courts. Contrariwise, a federal court may afford an equitable remedy for a substantive right recognized by a State even though a State court cannot give it. Whatever contradiction or confusion may be produced by a medley of judicial phrases severed from their environment, the body of adjudications concerning equitable relief in diversity cases leaves no doubt that the federal courts enforced State-created substantive rights if the mode of proceeding and remedy were consonant with the traditional body of equitable remedies, practice and procedure, and in so doing they were enforcing rights created by the States and not arising under any inherent or statutory federal law.

* * *

And so this case reduces itself to the narrow question whether, when no recovery could be had in a State court because the action is barred by the statute of limitations, a federal court in equity can take cognizance of the suit because there is diversity of citizenship between the parties. Is the outlawry, according to State law, of a claim created by the States a matter of "substantive rights" to be respected by a federal court of equity when that court's jurisdiction is dependent on the fact that there is a State-created right, or is such statute of "a mere remedial character," * * * which a federal court may disregard?

Matters of "substance" and matters of "procedure" are much talked about in the books as though they defined a great divide cutting across the whole domain of law. But, of course, "substance" and "procedure" are the same keywords to very different problems. Neither "substance" nor "procedure" represents the same invariants. Each implies different variables depending upon the particular problem for which it is used. * * * And the different problems are only distantly related at best, for the terms are in common use in connection with situations turning on such different considerations as those that are relevant to questions pertaining to *ex post facto* legislation, the impairment of the obligations of contract, the enforcement of federal rights in the State courts and the multitudinous phases of the conflict of laws. * * *

Here we are dealing with a right to recover derived not from the United States but from one of the States. When, because the plaintiff happens to be a non-resident, such a right is enforceable in a federal as well as in a State court, the forms and mode of enforcing the right may at times, naturally enough, vary because the two judicial systems are not identic. But since a federal court adjudicating a State-created right solely because of the diversity of citizenship of the parties is for that purpose, in effect, only another court of the State, it cannot afford recovery if the right to recover is made unavailable by the State nor can it substantially affect the enforcement of the right as given by the State.

And so the question is not whether a statute of limitations is deemed a matter of "procedure" in some sense. The question is whether such a statute concerns merely the manner and the means by which a right to recover, as recognized by the State, is enforced, or whether such statutory limitation is a matter of substance in the aspect that alone is relevant to our problem, namely, does it significantly affect the result of a litigation for a federal court to disregard a law of a State that would be controlling in an action upon the same claim by the same parties in a State court?

It is therefore immaterial whether statutes of limitation are characterized either as "substantive" or "procedural" in State court opinions in any use of those terms unrelated to the specific issue before us. Erie R. Co. v. Tompkins was not an endeavor to formulate scientific legal terminology. It expressed a policy that touches vitally the proper distribution of judicial power between State and federal courts. In essence, the intent of that decision was to insure that, in all cases where a federal court is exercising jurisdiction solely because of the diversity of citizenship of the parties, the outcome of the litigation in the federal court should be substantially the same, so far as legal rules determine the outcome of a litigation, as it would be if tried in a State court. The nub of the policy that underlies Erie R. Co. v. Tompkins is that for the same transaction the accident of a suit by a non-resident litigant in a federal court instead of in a State court a block away should not lead to a substantially different result. * * * A policy so important to our federalism must be kept free from entanglements with analytical or terminological niceties.

Plainly enough, a statute that would completely bar recovery in a suit if brought in a State court bears on a State-created right vitally and not merely formally or negligibly. As to consequences that so intimately affect recovery or non-recovery a federal court in a diversity case should follow State law. * * *

Diversity jurisdiction is founded on assurance to non-resident litigants of courts free from susceptibility to potential local bias. The Framers of the Constitution, according to Marshall, entertained "apprehensions" lest distant suitors be subjected to local bias in State courts, or, at least, viewed with "indulgence the possible fears and apprehensions" of such suitors. Bank of the United States v. Deveaux, 5 Cranch 61, 87, 3 L.Ed. 38. And so Congress afforded out-of-State litigants another tribunal, not another body of law. The operation of a double system of conflicting laws in the same State is plainly hostile to the reign of law. Certainly, the fortuitous circumstance of residence out of a State of one of the parties to a litigation ought not to give rise to a discrimination against others equally concerned but locally resident. The source of substantive rights enforced by a federal court under diversity jurisdiction, it cannot be said too often, is the law of the States. * * *

The judgment is reversed and the case is remanded for proceedings not inconsistent with this opinion.

So ordered.

MR. JUSTICE ROBERTS and MR. JUSTICE DOUGLAS took no part in the consideration or decision of this case.

[JUSTICE RUTLEDGE dissented in an opinion in which JUSTICE MURPHY joined.]

Notes and Questions

1. Does the Rules of Decision Act apply to a federal court sitting as an equity court in the same way that it does to a federal court sitting as a court of law? If a New York State equity court would not have granted a remedy to York for whatever reason, should a federal court sitting in diversity nevertheless grant a remedy? In answering this question, consider Justice Frankfurter's discussion of the difference between recognizing a state-created right and providing a remedy for infringement of that right. Could it not be argued that available remedies actually define the scope of the underlying rights?

2. Almost any legal rule, whether labelled as procedural or substantive, has the potential to affect the outcome of litigation. Does this mean that, after *York,* a federal court in a diversity case must apply every state legal rule that, if enforced, would affect the outcome of litigation? Does this include housekeeping rules like rules about the size of briefs or the color of paper used? Did Justice Frankfurter mean any rule that could affect the outcome, or would he say that only rules that influence a lawyer's choice of forum at the time she is choosing a forum are "outcome determinative"?

3. To what extent does *York* require the displacement of a Federal Rule of Civil Procedure in favor of a contrary state practice? Consider the following cases:

Shortly after *York,* the Supreme Court considered a trio of cases all decided by the Court on the same day. RAGAN v. MERCHANTS TRANSFER & WAREHOUSE CO., 337 U.S. 530, 69 S.Ct. 1233, 93 L.Ed. 1520 (1949), grew out of a highway accident that occurred on October 1, 1943. On September 4, 1945, Ragan filed a diversity action in a federal court in Kansas. However, service was not made on the defendant until December 28. Kansas had a two-year statute of limitations on tort claims. Ragan claimed that according to Rule 3 of the Federal Rules, the suit was commenced (and hence the statute tolled) by the filing of the complaint. The defendant countered that Kansas law dictated that service had to have been made within the two-year period. The Supreme Court held that Rule 3 was not intended to govern questions concerning the tolling of statutes of limitations, and, therefore, state law would determine in diversity when the statute was tolled.

In COHEN v. BENEFICIAL INDUSTRIAL LOAN CORP., 337 U.S. 541, 69 S.Ct. 1221, 93 L.Ed. 1528 (1949), the Court held that a federal court must apply a New Jersey statute requiring a plaintiff in a shareholder derivative suit to post a security-for-expenses bond—even though what is now Federal Rule 23.1, which ostensibly governs such cases, did not require a bond. The Court found that whether the New Jersey statute was classified as procedural or substantive, it created substantive liabilities for expenses. In the Court's view, Rule 23.1 did not contradict the New Jersey statute, but was addressed to independent concerns.

And, finally, in WOODS v. INTERSTATE REALTY CO., 337 U.S. 535, 69 S.Ct. 1235, 93 L.Ed. 1524 (1949), the Court held that a Tennessee corporation that had not qualified to do business in Mississippi could not maintain a diversity action in a federal court in that state if, by virtue of its failure to qualify, the Mississippi state courts were closed to it.

Strong dissents were filed in all three cases. Justice Rutledge, dissenting in *Cohen,* argued that these cases were a perversion of the *Erie* doctrine. To him, *Erie* involved an issue that clearly was substantive, while these cases presented issues that were at least arguably procedural. What do you think? See 19 Wright, Miller & Cooper, *Federal Practice and Procedure: Jurisdiction and Related Matters 2d* § 4510 (1996).

4. Evaluate the following passage:

The *York* case, of necessity, spelled death to the hope for a completely uniform federal procedure. When its doctrine is logically applied, each important step in a diversity action must be examined in the light of two systems of law—first, under the Federal Rules, and then under the law of the state in which the federal court sits. In one state, a particular Rule might not clash with a local law or decision which significantly bears upon the outcome of a litigation. Under such circumstances, the Rule should prevail, although the determination as to its applicability is actually made under state law. In another state, the same Rule might conflict in some substantial way with that state's policy or law. In such instances, state law, and not the Rule, will govern a federal court's decision.

Merrigan, *Erie to York to Ragan—A Triple Play on the Federal Rules,* 3 Vand. L.Rev. 711, 717 (1950).

BYRD v. BLUE RIDGE RURAL ELECTRIC COOPERATIVE, INC.

Supreme Court of the United States, 1958.
356 U.S. 525, 78 S.Ct. 893, 2 L.Ed.2d 953.

Certiorari to the United States Court of Appeals for the Fourth Circuit.

MR. JUSTICE BRENNAN delivered the opinion of the Court.

This case was brought in the District Court for the Western District of South Carolina. Jurisdiction was based on diversity of citizenship. * * * The petitioner, a resident of North Carolina, sued respondent, a South Carolina corporation, for damages for injuries allegedly caused by the respondent's negligence. He had judgment on a jury verdict. The Court of Appeals for the Fourth Circuit reversed and directed the entry of judgment for the respondent. * * *

The respondent is in the business of selling electric power to subscribers in rural sections of South Carolina. The petitioner was employed as a lineman in the construction crew of a construction contractor. The contractor, R.H. Bouligny, Inc., held a contract with the respondent * * * for the building of some * * * power lines, the reconversion to higher capacities of * * * existing lines, and the construction of 2 new substations and a breaker station. The petitioner was injured while connecting power lines to one of the new substations.

One of respondent's affirmative defenses was that under the South Carolina Workmen's Compensation Act, the petitioner—because the work contracted to be done by his employer was work of the kind also done by the respondent's own construction and maintenance crews—had the status of a statutory employee of the respondent and was therefore barred from suing the respondent at law because obliged to accept statutory compensation benefits as the exclusive remedy for his injuries. Two questions concerning this defense are before us: (1) whether the Court of Appeals erred in directing judgment for respondent without a remand to give petitioner an opportunity to introduce further evidence; and (2) whether petitioner, state practice notwithstanding, is entitled to a jury determination of the factual issues raised by this defense.

* * *

[The Supreme Court initially decided to remand the case to the trial court to provide the petitioner an opportunity to introduce evidence on the question of whether the respondent was a statutory employer.]

A question is also presented as to whether on remand the factual issue is to be decided by the judge or by the jury. The respondent argues on the basis of the decision of the Supreme Court of South Carolina in Adams v. Davison–Paxon Co., 230 S.C. 532, 96 S.E.2d 566, that the issue of immunity should be decided by the judge and not by the jury. That was a negligence action brought in the state trial court against a store owner by an employee of an independent contractor who operated the store's millinery department. The trial judge denied the store owner's motion for a directed verdict made upon the ground that [South Carolina Code, 1952] § 72–111 barred the plaintiff's action. The jury returned a verdict for the plaintiff. The South Carolina Supreme Court reversed, holding that it was for the judge and not the jury to decide on the evidence whether the owner was a statutory employer, and that the store owner had sustained his defense. * * *

The respondent argues that this state-court decision governs the present diversity case and "divests the jury of its normal function" to decide the disputed fact question of the respondent's immunity under § 72–111. This is to contend that the federal court is bound under Erie R. Co. v. Tompkins * * * to follow the state court's holding to secure uniform enforcement of the immunity created by the State.

First. It was decided in Erie R. Co. v. Tompkins that the federal courts in diversity cases must respect the definition of state-created rights and obligations by the state courts. We must, therefore, first examine the rule in Adams v. Davison–Paxon Co. to determine whether it is bound up with these rights and obligations in such a way that its application in the federal court is required. * * *

The Workmen's Compensation Act is administered in South Carolina by its Industrial Commission. The South Carolina courts hold that, on judicial review of actions of the Commission under § 72–111, the question whether the claim of an injured workman is within the Commission's jurisdiction is a matter of law for decision by the court, which makes its own findings of fact relating to that jurisdiction. The South Carolina Supreme Court states no reasons in Adams v. Davison–Paxon Co. why, although the jury decides all other factual issues raised by the cause of action and defenses, the jury is displaced as to the factual issue raised by the affirmative defense under § 72–111. * * * A State may, of course, distribute the functions of its judicial machinery as it sees fit. The decisions relied upon, however, furnish no reason for selecting the judge rather than the jury to decide this single affirmative defense in the negligence action. They simply reflect a policy * * * that administrative determination of "jurisdictional facts" should not be final but subject to judicial review. The conclusion is inescapable that the Adams holding is grounded in the practical consideration that the question had theretofore come before the South Carolina courts from the Industrial Commission and the courts had become accustomed to deciding the factual issue of immunity without the aid of juries. We find nothing to suggest that this rule was announced as an integral part of the special relationship created by the statute. Thus the requirement appears to be merely a form and mode of enforcing the immunity * * * and not a rule intended to be bound up with the definition of the rights and obligations of the parties. * * *

Second. But cases following *Erie* have evinced a broader policy to the effect that the federal courts should conform as near as may be—in the absence of other considerations—to state rules even of form and mode where the state rules may bear substantially on the question whether the litigation would come out one way in the federal court and another way in the state court if the federal court failed to apply a particular local rule. E.g., Guaranty Trust Co. of New York v. York, supra; Bernhardt v. Polygraphic Co., 350 U.S. 198, 76 S.Ct. 273, 100 L.Ed. 199. Concededly the nature of the tribunal which tries issues may be important in the enforcement of the parcel of rights making up a cause of action or defense, and bear significantly upon achievement of uniform enforcement of the right. It may well be that in the instant personal-injury case the outcome would be substantially affected by whether the issue of immunity is decided by a judge or a jury. Therefore, were "outcome" the only consideration, a strong case might appear for saying that the federal court should follow the state practice.

But there are affirmative countervailing considerations at work here. The federal system is an independent system for administering justice to litigants who properly invoke its jurisdiction. An essential characteristic of that system is the manner in which, in civil common-law actions, it distributes trial functions between judge and jury and, under the influence—if not the command—of the Seventh Amendment, assigns the decisions of disputed questions of fact to the jury. * * * The policy of uniform enforcement of state-created rights and obligations * * * cannot in every case exact compliance with a state rule—not bound up with rights and obligations—which disrupts the federal system of allocating functions between judge and jury. * * * Thus the inquiry here is whether the federal policy favoring jury decisions of disputed fact questions should yield to the state rule in the interest of furthering the objective that the litigation should not come out one way in the federal court and another way in the state court.

We think that in the circumstances of this case the federal court should not follow the state rule. It cannot be gainsaid that there is a strong federal policy against allowing state rules to disrupt the judge-jury relationship in the federal courts. In Herron v. Southern Pacific Co., [283 U.S. 91, 51 S.Ct. 383, 75 L.Ed. 857 (1931),] * * * the trial judge in a personal-injury negligence action brought in the District Court for Arizona on diversity grounds directed a verdict for the defendant when it appeared as a matter of law that the plaintiff was guilty of contributory negligence. The federal judge refused to be bound by a provision of the Arizona Constitution which made the jury the sole arbiter of the question of contributory negligence. This Court sustained the action of the trial judge, holding that "state laws cannot alter the essential character or function of a federal court" because that function "is not in any sense a local matter, and state statutes which would interfere with the appropriate performance of that function are not binding upon the federal court under either the Conformity Act or the 'Rules of Decision' Act." * * * Perhaps even more clearly in light of the influence of the Seventh Amendment, the function assigned to the jury "is an essential factor in the process for which the Federal Constitution provides." * * * Concededly the *Herron* case was decided before Erie R. Co. v. Tompkins, but even when Swift v. Tyson * * * was governing law and allowed federal courts sitting in diversity cases to disregard state decisional law, it was never thought that state statutes or constitutions were similarly to be disregarded. * * * Yet *Herron* held that state statutes and constitutional provisions could not disrupt or alter the essential character or function of a federal court.[14]

Third. We have discussed the problem upon the assumption that the outcome of the litigation may be substantially affected by whether the issue of immunity is decided by a judge or a jury. But clearly there is not present here the certainty that a different result would follow * * * or even the strong possibility that this would be the case * * *. There are factors present here which might reduce that possibility. The trial judge in the federal system has powers denied the judges of many States to comment on the weight of evidence and credibility of witnesses, and discretion to grant a new trial if the verdict appears to him to be against the weight of the evidence. We do not think the likelihood of a different result is so strong as to require the federal practice of jury determination of disputed factual issues to yield to the state rule in the interest of uniformity of outcome.[15]

* * *

Reversed and remanded.

* * *

[JUSTICE WHITTAKER concurred in Part I of the Court's opinion but dissented from Part II on the ground that the South Carolina rule requiring "its courts—not juries—to determine whether jurisdiction over the subject matter of cases like this is vested in its Industrial Commission" should be honored by a federal court. JUSTICE FRANKFURTER and JUSTICE HARLAN dissented on the ground that the evidence required the district court to direct a verdict for the respondent.]

14. Diederich v. American News Co., 10 Cir., 128 F.2d 144, decided after Erie R. Co. v. Tompkins, held that an almost identical provision of the Oklahoma Constitution, art. 23, § 6, O.S.1951 was not binding on a federal judge in a diversity case.

15. Stoner v. New York Life Ins. Co., 311 U.S. 464, 61 S.Ct. 336, 85 L.Ed. 284, is not contrary. It was there held that the federal court should follow the state rule defining the evidence sufficient to raise a jury question whether the state-created right was established. But the state rule did not have the effect of nullifying the function of the federal judge to control a jury submission as did the Arizona constitutional provision which was denied effect in *Herron*. The South Carolina rule here involved affects the jury function as the Arizona provision affected the function of the judge: The rule entirely displaces the jury without regard to the sufficiency of the evidence to support a jury finding of immunity.

Notes and Questions

1. What does Justice Brennan mean when he writes that "the influence—if not the command—of the Seventh Amendment" determined the result in *Byrd*? If the Seventh Amendment provides a rule of decision for *Byrd*, isn't the Rules of Decision Act inapplicable by its own terms? Indeed, if the Seventh Amendment "commands" that a federal court utilize a jury to decide who is a statutory employee, could the Rules of Decision Act dictate a contrary result? On the other hand, if the Seventh Amendment does not "command" the result in *Byrd*, why should it "influence" the result?

In this light, consider the following excerpt from SIMLER v. CONNER, 372 U.S. 221, 222, 83 S.Ct. 609, 610–11, 9 L.Ed.2d 691, 693 (1963):

> The federal policy favoring jury trials is of historic continuing strength. * * * Only through a holding that the jury-trial right is to be determined according to federal law can the uniformity in its exercise which is demanded by the Seventh Amendment be achieved. In diversity cases, of course, the substantive dimension of the claim asserted finds its source in state law, * * * but the characterization of that state-created claim as legal or equitable for purposes of whether a right to jury trial is indicated must be made by recourse to federal law.

2. Is Justice Brennan correct in asserting that the South Carolina rule at issue in *Byrd* is "merely a form and mode of enforcing the immunity * * * and not a rule intended to be bound up with the definition of the rights and obligations of the parties"? Most states have adopted their worker compensation schemes only after carefully balancing the equities involved in the typical workplace accident. These statutes are complex and detailed and often are the result of a political compromise. Does it seem likely, then, that South Carolina randomly would have appropriated to the judge the function of defining a statutory employee?

3. In *Byrd*, Justice Brennan proposes what appears to be a balancing test for determining *Erie* questions. Does the balancing test in *Byrd* replace the outcome-determinative test of *York*? Whether it replaces the outcome-determinative test or not, how does Justice Brennan's balancing test work? If a state rule is "bound up with the definition of the rights and obligations of the parties," does a federal court still engage in balancing? How does a court determine whether a state rule is "bound up with the definition of the rights and obligations of the parties"?

4. Once it begins to engage in the balancing process dictated in *Byrd*, how does a federal court identify and then weigh the competing state and federal policies? What sources should it examine in pursuing this inquiry? In ALLSTATE INS. CO. v. CHARNESKI, 286 F.2d 238 (7th Cir.1960), the court dismissed an action for a judgment declaring an insurance company's nonliability. The court, after reviewing the major *Erie*-doctrine cases and concluding that a Wisconsin court would dismiss the declaratory-judgment action before it, employed the following reasoning:

> First, as to the State of Wisconsin. This is not a case where a federal declaratory judgment action is filed in a state which has no statute providing for such relief. Wisconsin has passed a general statute providing declaratory relief. However, this statute was held not applicable * * * [by the Wisconsin Supreme Court] because it conflicted with the Wisconsin state policy of

providing direct actions against insurance companies. This is a declaration of the *substantive* law of Wisconsin. The Wisconsin Supreme Court held that to allow declaratory relief in such circumstances would undercut its policy of direct actions against an insurance company and thereby concluding the action—defining the rights of the insurer, the insured, and the injured party—in a single suit. This holding represents a legitimate and proper implementation of Wisconsin policy. * * *

The federal interest to be served here is slight. There is the general interest of a court controlling its own procedure. There is the general policy evidenced by the federal Declaratory Judgments Act. However, no right to jury trial, guaranteed by the Seventh Amendment, is involved here, as in Byrd. The cause of action arising from the accident, the issue of coverage of the policy, and the rights of the insured, the insurer and the injured parties are intimately connected with Wisconsin law and have no connection with the federal government except that the latter provides a fair and orderly forum in which to try the diversity case. Finally, relief under the Federal act is expressly discretionary. Such relief is permissive and not absolute. Declaratory relief "may" be granted, and need not be when it would create an unnecessary federal-state conflict.

286 F.2d at 244. Is the court's analysis of the Wisconsin and federal policies adequate? Is it persuasive?

5. In BERNHARDT v. POLYGRAPHIC CO. OF AMERICA, INC., 350 U.S. 198, 203, 76 S.Ct. 273, 276, 100 L.Ed. 199, 205 (1956), plaintiff brought an action in a Vermont state court for damages resulting from his discharge by defendant. Defendant removed the action to a federal district court and moved for a stay pending arbitration in New York pursuant to the contract. The District Court denied the stay, ruling that under *Erie* the arbitration provision was governed by Vermont law, which permitted revocation of an agreement to arbitrate any time before an award was made. The Second Circuit reversed on the ground that arbitration merely relates to the form of the trial. The Supreme Court disagreed and reversed and remanded, stating:

> * * * If the federal court allows arbitration where the state court would disallow it, the outcome of litigation might depend on the courthouse where suit is brought. For the remedy by arbitration, whatever its merits or shortcomings, substantially affects the cause of action created by the State. The nature of the tribunal where suits are tried is an important part of the parcel of rights behind a cause of action. The change from a court of law to an arbitration panel may make a radical difference in ultimate result. Arbitration carries no right to trial by jury that is guaranteed both by the Seventh Amendment and by Ch. 1, Art. 12th, of the Vermont Constitution. Arbitrators do not have the benefit of judicial instruction on the law; they need not give their reasons for their results; the record of their proceedings is not as complete as it is in a court trial; and judicial review of an award is more limited than judicial review of a trial * * *.

After *Byrd,* would *Bernhardt* be decided the same way? Is state law governing arbitration bound up with the definition of the parties' rights and obligations?

6. Between 1960 and 1965, one of the most debated subjects in procedural circles was whether a federal court in a diversity action should employ a federal or state standard to determine the existence or nonexistence of in personam jurisdiction over a foreign corporation. Over the years, the post-*Byrd* cases appear to have

opted for the state standard. E.g., Arrowsmith v. United Press Int'l, 320 F.2d 219 (2d Cir.1963) (en banc), apparently overruling a contrary two-to-one decision in Jaftex Corp. v. Randolph Mills, Inc., 282 F.2d 508 (2d Cir.1960). See 4 Wright & Miller, *Federal Practice and Procedure: Civil 3d* § 1075 (2001); 19 Wright, Miller & Cooper, *Federal Practice and Procedure: Jurisdiction and Related Matters* 2d § 4510 (1996).

If *Erie* is constitutionally based, does Congress or do the federal courts have the power to establish jurisdictional standards for diversity actions? Putting the question another way, are jurisdictional rules substantive or procedural within the meaning of *Erie* and *York* or don't they fall entirely within either category? Would a federal test for personal jurisdiction promote or discourage forum-shopping? Assuming federal power, have either Congress or the federal courts established a clear test for amenability to suit in a federal court? Is the standard in International Shoe Co. v. Washington, p. 75, supra, relevant? What about Federal Rule of Civil Procedure 4 or 28 U.S.C. §§ 1391, 1693? A lengthy dialogue on these questions is offered by the late Judges Clark and Friendly in the *Jaftex* and *Arrowsmith* cases.

In 1934, Congress passed 28 U.S.C. § 2072, commonly known as the Rules Enabling Act. Read the current version of this Act, which is in the Supplement.

HANNA v. PLUMER

Supreme Court of the United States, 1965.
380 U.S. 460, 85 S.Ct. 1136, 14 L.Ed.2d 8.

Certiorari to the United States Court of Appeals for the First Circuit.

MR. CHIEF JUSTICE WARREN delivered the opinion of the Court.

The question to be decided is whether, in a civil action where the jurisdiction of the United States District Court is based upon diversity of citizenship between the parties, service of process shall be made in the manner prescribed by state law or that set forth in Rule 4(d)(1) of the Federal Rules of Civil Procedure.

On February 6, 1963, petitioner, a citizen of Ohio, filed her complaint in the District Court for the District of Massachusetts, claiming damages in excess of $10,000 for personal injuries resulting from an automobile accident in South Carolina, allegedly caused by the negligence of one Louise Plumer Osgood, a Massachusetts citizen deceased at the time of the filing of the complaint. Respondent, Mrs. Osgood's executor and also a Massachusetts citizen, was named as defendant. On February 8, service was made by leaving copies of the summons and the complaint with respondent's wife at his residence, concededly in compliance with Rule 4(d)(1) [Rule 4, particularly Rule 4(d)(1), has been amended in several respects since 1965.] * * *. Respondent filed his answer on February 26, alleging, *inter alia,* that the action could not be maintained because it had been brought "contrary to and in violation of the provisions of Massachusetts General Laws (Ter.Ed.) Chapter 197, Section 9." That section provides:

Except as provided in this chapter, an executor or administrator shall not be held to answer to an action by a creditor of the deceased which is not commenced within one year from the time of his giving bond for the performance of his trust, or to such an action which is commenced within said year unless before the expiration thereof the writ in such action has been served by delivery in hand upon such executor or administrator or service thereof accepted by him or a notice stating the name of the estate, the name and address of the creditor, the amount of the claim and the court in which the action has been brought has been filed in the proper registry of probate. * * *

On October 17, 1963, the District Court granted respondent's motion for summary judgment, citing Ragan v. Merchants Transfer & Warehouse Co. * * * and Guaranty Trust Co. of New York v. York * * * in support of its conclusion that the adequacy of the service was to be measured by § 9, with which, the court held, petitioner had not complied. On appeal, petitioner * * * argued that Rule 4(d)(1) defines the method by which service of process is to be effected in diversity actions. The Court of Appeals for the First Circuit, finding that "[r]elatively recent amendments [to § 9] evince a clear legislative purpose to require personal notification within the year,"[1] concluded that the conflict of state and federal rules was over "a substantive rather than a procedural matter," and unanimously affirmed. * * *

We conclude that the adoption of Rule 4(d)(1), designed to control service of process in diversity actions, neither exceeded the congressional mandate embodied in the Rules Enabling Act nor transgressed constitutional bounds, and that the Rule is therefore the standard against which the District Court should have measured the adequacy of the service. Accordingly, we reverse the decision of the Court of Appeals.

* * * Under the cases construing the scope of the Enabling Act, Rule 4(d)(1) clearly passes muster. Prescribing the manner in which a defendant is to be notified that a suit has been instituted against him, it relates to the "practice and procedure of the district courts." * * *

The test must be whether a rule really regulates procedure,—the judicial process for enforcing rights and duties recognized by substantive law and for justly administering remedy and redress for disregard or infraction of them. Sibbach v. Wilson & Co., [p. 399, infra] * * *.

In Mississippi Pub. Corp. v. Murphree, 326 U.S. 438, 66 S.Ct. 242, 90 L.Ed. 185, this Court upheld Rule 4(f) [now Rule 4(e)], which permits service of a

1. Section 9 is in part a statute of limitations, providing that an executor need not "answer to an action * * * which is not commenced within one year from the time of his giving bond * * *." This part of the statute, the purpose of which is to speed the settlement of estates, * * * is not involved in this case, since the action clearly was timely commenced. (Respondent filed bond on March 1, 1962; the complaint was filed February 6, 1963; and the service—the propriety of which is in dispute—was made on February 8, 1963.) * * *.

Section 9 also provides for the manner of service. Generally, service of process must be made by "delivery in hand." * * * The purpose of this part of the statute, which *is* involved here, is, as the court below noted, to insure that executors will receive actual notice of claims. * * * Actual notice is of course also the goal of Rule 4(d)(1); however, the Federal Rule reflects a determination that this goal can be achieved by a method less cumbersome than that prescribed in § 9. In this case the goal seems to have been achieved; although the affidavit filed by respondent in the District Court asserts that he had neither been served in hand nor accepted service, it does not allege lack of actual notice.

summons anywhere within the State (and not merely the district) in which a district court sits:

> We think that Rule 4(f) is in harmony with the Enabling Act * * *. Undoubtedly most alterations of the rules of practice and procedure may and often do affect the rights of litigants. Congress' prohibition of any alteration of substantive rights of litigants was obviously not addressed to such incidental effects as necessarily attend the adoption of the pre-scribed new rules of procedure upon the rights of litigants who, agreeably to rules of practice and procedure, have been brought before a court authorized to determine their rights. * * * The fact that the application of Rule 4(f) will operate to subject petitioner's rights to adjudication by the district court for northern Mississippi will undoubtedly affect those rights. But it does not operate to abridge, enlarge or modify the rules of decision by which that court will adjudicate its rights. Id., at 445–446, 66 S.Ct. at 246.

Thus were there no conflicting state procedure, Rule 4(d)(1) would clearly control. National Equipment Rental, Ltd. v. Szukhent * * * [p. 212, supra]. However, respondent, focusing on the contrary Massachusetts rule, calls to the Court's attention another line of cases, a line which—like the Enabling Act—had its birth in 1938. Erie R. Co. v. Tompkins, * * * overruling Swift v. Tyson, * * * held that federal courts sitting in diversity cases, when deciding questions of "substantive" law, are bound by state court decisions as well as state statutes. The broad command of *Erie* was therefore identical to that of the Enabling Act: federal courts are to apply state substantive law and federal procedural law. However, as subsequent cases sharpened the distinction between substance and procedure, the line of cases following *Erie* diverged markedly from the line construing the Enabling Act. * * *

Respondent, by placing primary reliance on *York* and *Ragan*, suggests that the *Erie* doctrine acts as a check on the Federal Rules of Civil Procedure, that despite the clear command of Rule 4(d)(1), *Erie* and its progeny demand the application of the Massachusetts rule. Reduced to essentials, the argu-ment is: (1) *Erie*, as refined in *York*, demands that federal courts apply state law whenever application of federal law in its stead will alter the outcome of the case. (2) In this case, a determination that the Massachusetts service requirements obtain will result in immediate victory for respondent. If, on the other hand, it should be held that Rule 4(d)(1) is applicable, the litigation will continue, with possible victory for petitioner. (3) Therefore, *Erie* demands application of the Massachusetts rule. The syllogism possesses an appealing simplicity, but is for several reasons invalid.

In the first place, it is doubtful that, even if there were no Federal Rule making it clear that in hand service is not required in diversity actions, the *Erie* rule would have obligated the District Court to follow the Massachusetts procedure. "Outcome determination" analysis was never intended to serve as a talisman. Byrd v. Blue Ridge Rural Elec. Cooperative * * *. Indeed, the message of *York* itself is that choices between state and federal law are to be made not by application of any automatic, "litmus paper" criterion, but rather by reference to the policies underlying the *Erie* rule. Guaranty Trust Co. of New York v. York * * *.

The *Erie* rule is rooted in part in a realization that it would be unfair for the character or result of a litigation materially to differ because the suit had been brought in a federal court. * * * The decision was also in part a reaction to the practice of "forum-shopping" which had grown up in response to the rule of Swift v. Tyson. * * * That the *York* test was an attempt to effectuate these policies is demonstrated by the fact that the opinion framed the inquiry in terms of "substantial" variations between state and federal litigation. * * * Not only are nonsubstantial, or trivial, variations not likely to raise the sort of equal protection problems which troubled the Court in *Erie*; they are also unlikely to influence the choice of a forum. The "outcome-determination" test therefore cannot be read without reference to the twin aims of the *Erie* rule: discouragement of forum-shopping and avoidance of inequitable administration of the laws.[9]

The difference between the conclusion that the Massachusetts rule is applicable, and the conclusion that it is not, is of course at this point "outcome-determinative" in the sense that if we hold the state rule to apply, respondent prevails, whereas if we hold that Rule 4(d)(1) governs, the litigation will continue. But in this sense *every* procedural variation is "outcome-determinative." For example, having brought suit in a federal court, a plaintiff cannot then insist on the right to file subsequent pleadings in accord with the time limits applicable in state courts, even though enforcement of the federal timetable will, if he continues to insist that he must meet only the state time limit, result in determination of the controversy against him. So it is here. Though choice of the federal or state rule will at this point have a marked effect upon the outcome of the litigation, the difference between the two rules would be of scant, if any, relevance to the choice of a forum. Petitioner, in choosing her forum, was not presented with a situation where application of the state rule would wholly bar recovery; rather, adherence to the state rule would have resulted only in altering the way in which process was served.[11] Moreover, it is difficult to argue that permitting service of defendant's wife to take the place of in hand service of defendant himself alters the mode of enforcement of state-created rights in a fashion sufficiently "substantial" to raise the sort of equal protection problems to which the *Erie* opinion alluded.

9. The Court of Appeals seemed to frame the inquiry in terms of how "important" Section 9 is to the State. In support of its suggestion that Section 9 serves some interest the State regards as vital to its citizens, the court noted that something like Section 9 has been on the books in Massachusetts a long time, that Section 9 has been amended a number of times, and that Section 9 is designed to make sure that executors receive actual notice. * * * The apparent lack of relation among these three observations is not surprising, because it is not clear to what sort of question the Court of Appeals was addressing itself. One cannot meaningfully ask how important something is without first asking "important for what purpose?" *Erie* and its progeny make clear that when a federal court sitting in a diversity case is faced with a question of whether or not to apply state law, the importance of a state rule is indeed relevant, but only in the context of asking whether application of the rule would make so important a difference to the character or result of the litigation that failure to enforce it would unfairly discriminate against citizens of the forum State, or whether application of the rule would have so important an effect upon the fortunes of one or both of the litigants that failure to enforce it would be likely to cause a plaintiff to choose the federal court.

11. * * * We cannot seriously entertain the thought that one suing an estate would be led to choose the federal court because of a belief that adherence to Rule 4(d)(1) is less likely to give the executor actual notice than Section 9, and therefore more likely to produce a default judgment. Rule 4(d)(1) is well designed to give actual notice, as it did in this case. * * *

There is, however, a more fundamental flaw in respondent's syllogism: the incorrect assumption that the rule of Erie R. Co. v. Tompkins constitutes the appropriate test of the validity and therefore the applicability of a Federal Rule of Civil Procedure. The *Erie* rule has never been invoked to void a Federal Rule. It is true that there have been cases where this Court has held applicable a state rule in the face of an argument that the situation was governed by one of the Federal Rules. But the holding of each such case was not that *Erie* commanded displacement of a Federal Rule by an inconsistent state rule, but rather that the scope of the Federal Rule was not as broad as the losing party urged, and therefore, there being no Federal Rule which covered the point in dispute, *Erie* commanded the enforcement of state law. * * * (Here, of course, the clash is unavoidable; Rule 4(d)(1) says—implicitly, but with unmistakable clarity—that in hand service is not required in federal courts.) At the same time, in cases adjudicating the validity of Federal Rules, we have not applied the *York* rule or other refinements of *Erie*, but have to this day continued to decide questions concerning the scope of the Enabling Act and the constitutionality of specific Federal Rules in light of the distinction set forth in *Sibbach*. * * *

Nor has the development of two separate lines of cases been inadvertent. The line between "substance" and "procedure" shifts as the legal context changes. * * * It is true that both the Enabling Act and the *Erie* rule say, roughly, that federal courts are to apply state "substantive" law and federal "procedural" law, but from that it need not follow that the tests are identical. For they were designed to control very different sorts of decisions. When a situation is covered by one of the Federal Rules, the question facing the court is a far cry from the typical, relatively unguided *Erie* choice: the court has been instructed to apply the Federal Rule, and can refuse to do so only if the Advisory Committee, this Court, and Congress erred in their prima facie judgment that the Rule in question transgresses neither the terms of the Enabling Act nor constitutional restrictions.

We are reminded by the *Erie* opinion that neither Congress nor the federal courts can, under the guise of formulating rules of decision for federal courts, fashion rules which are not supported by a grant of federal authority contained in Article I or some other section of the Constitution; in such areas state law must govern because there can be no other law. But the opinion in *Erie*, which involved no Federal Rule and dealt with a question which was "substantive" in every traditional sense * * *, surely neither said nor implied that measures like Rule 4(d)(1) are unconstitutional. For the constitutional provision for a federal court system (augmented by the Necessary and Proper Clause) carries with it congressional power to make rules governing the practice and pleading in those courts, which in turn includes a power to regulate matters which, though falling within the uncertain area between substance and procedure, are rationally capable of classification as either. * * * Neither *York* nor the cases following it ever suggested that the rule there laid down for coping with situations where no Federal Rule applies is coextensive with the limitation on Congress to which *Erie* had adverted. Although this Court has never before been confronted with a case where the applicable Federal Rule is in direct collision with the law of the relevant State, courts of appeals faced with such clashes have rightly discerned the implications of our decisions.

"One of the shaping purposes of the Federal Rules is to bring about uniformity in the federal courts by getting away from local rules. This is especially true of matters which relate to the administration of legal proceedings, an area in which federal courts have traditionally exerted strong inherent power, completely aside from the powers Congress expressly conferred in the Rules. The purpose of the *Erie* doctrine, even as extended in *York* and *Ragan*, was never to bottle up federal courts with 'outcome-determinative' and 'integral-relations' stoppers—when there are 'affirmative countervailing [federal] considerations' and when there is a Congressional mandate (the Rules) supported by constitutional authority." Lumbermen's Mutual Casualty Co. v. Wright, 322 F.2d 759, 764 (C.A.5th Cir. 1963).

Erie and its offspring cast no doubt on the long-recognized power of Congress to prescribe housekeeping rules for federal courts even though some of those rules will inevitably differ from comparable state rules. * * * Thus, though a court, in measuring a Federal Rule against the standards contained in the Enabling Act and the Constitution, need not wholly blind itself to the degree to which the Rule makes the character and result of the federal litigation stray from the course it would follow in state courts, * * * it cannot be forgotten that the *Erie* rule, and the guidelines suggested in *York*, were created to serve another purpose altogether. To hold that a Federal Rule of Civil Procedure must cease to function whenever it alters the mode of enforcing state-created rights would be to disembowel either the Constitution's grant of power over federal procedure or Congress' attempt to exercise that power in the Enabling Act. Rule 4(d)(1) is valid and controls the instant case.

Reversed.

Mr. Justice Black concurs in the result.

Mr. Justice Harlan, concurring.

* * *

Erie was something more than an opinion which worried about "forum-shopping and avoidance of inequitable administration of the laws," * * * although to be sure these were important elements of the decision. I have always regarded that decision as one of the modern cornerstones of our federalism, expressing policies that profoundly touch the allocation of judicial power between the state and federal systems. *Erie* recognized that there should not be two conflicting systems of law controlling the primary activity of citizens, for such alternative governing authority must necessarily give rise to a debilitating uncertainty in the planning of everyday affairs. And it recognized that the scheme of our Constitution envisions an allocation of law-making functions between state and federal legislative processes which is undercut if the federal judiciary can make substantive law affecting state affairs beyond the bounds of congressional legislative powers in this regard. * * *

The shorthand formulations which have appeared in some past decisions are prone to carry untoward results that frequently arise from oversimplification. The Court is quite right in stating that the "outcome-determinative" test of Guaranty Trust Co. of New York v. York * * * if taken literally, proves too much, for any rule, no matter how clearly "procedural," can affect the outcome of litigation if it is not obeyed. In turning from the "outcome" test of *Guaranty* back to the unadorned forum-shopping rationale of *Erie*, however, the Court falls prey to like oversimplification, for a simple forum-shopping rule also proves too much; litigants often choose a federal forum merely to obtain what they consider the advantages of the Federal Rules of Civil Procedure or to try their cases before a supposedly more favorable judge. To my mind the proper line of approach in determining whether to apply a state or a federal rule, whether "substantive" or "procedural," is to stay close to basic principles by inquiring if the choice of rule would substantially affect those primary decisions respecting human conduct which our constitutional system leaves to state regulation. If so, *Erie* and the Constitution require that the state rule prevail, even in the face of a conflicting federal rule.

The Court weakens, if indeed it does not submerge, this basic principle by finding, in effect, a grant of substantive legislative power in the constitutional provision for a federal court system * * *, and through it, setting up the Federal Rules as a body of law inviolate. * * * So long as a reasonable man could characterize any duly adopted federal rule as "procedural," the Court, unless I misapprehend what is said, would have it apply no matter how seriously it frustrated a State's substantive regulation of the primary conduct and affairs of its citizens. Since the members of the Advisory Committee, the Judicial Conference, and this Court who formulated the Federal Rules are presumably reasonable men, it follows that the integrity of the Federal Rules is absolute. Whereas the unadulterated outcome and forum-shopping tests may err too far towards honoring state rules, I submit that the Court's "arguably procedural, *ergo* constitutional" test moves too fast and far in the other direction.

The courts below relied upon this Court's decisions in Ragan v. Merchants Transfer & Warehouse Co. * * * and Cohen v. Beneficial Indus. Loan Corp. * * *. Those cases deserve more attention than this Court has given them, particularly *Ragan* which, if still good law, would in my opinion call for affirmance of the result reached by the Court of Appeals. * * *

* * * I think that the [*Ragan*] decision was wrong. At most, application of the Federal Rule would have meant that potential Kansas tort defendants would have to defer for a few days the satisfaction of knowing that they had not been sued within the limitations period. The choice of the Federal Rule would have had no effect on the primary stages of private activity from which torts arise, and only the most minimal effect on behavior following the commission of the tort. In such circumstances the interest of the federal system in proceeding under its own rules should have prevailed.

* * * [A statute like the one in *Cohen*] is not "outcome determinative"; the plaintiff can win with or without it. The Court now rationalizes the case on the ground that the statute might affect the plaintiff's choice of forum * * * but as has been pointed out, a simple forum-shopping test proves too much. The proper view of *Cohen* is in my opinion, that the statute was meant to inhibit small stockholders from instituting "strike suits," and thus it was designed and could be expected to have a substantial impact on private primary activity. Anyone who was at the trial bar during the period when *Cohen* arose can appreciate the strong state policy reflected in the statute. I

think it wholly legitimate to view Federal Rule 23 as not purporting to deal with the problem. But even had the Federal Rules purported to do so, and in so doing provided a substantially less effective deterrent to strike suits, I think the state rule should still have prevailed. * * *

It remains to apply what has been said to the present case. * * * The evident intent of [the Massachusetts] statute is to permit an executor to distribute the estate which he is administering without fear that further liabilities may be outstanding for which he could be held personally liable. If the Federal District Court in Massachusetts applies Rule 4(d)(1) of the Federal Rules of Civil Procedure instead of the Massachusetts service rule, what effect would that have on the speed and assurance with which estates are distributed? As I see it, the effect would not be substantial. It would mean simply that an executor would have to check at his own house or the federal courthouse as well as the registry of probate before he could distribute the estate with impunity. As this does not seem enough to give rise to any real impingement on the vitality of the state policy which the Massachusetts rule is intended to serve, I concur in the judgment of the Court.

Notes and Questions

1. How are procedural rules formally included in the Federal Rules of Civil Procedure different from procedural rules adopted by a court on its own? Chief Justice Warren seems to give the Federal Rules special status. Why? Reread the Rules Enabling Act and the Rules of Decision Act. How do these statutes interact? Are they consistent? If not, how can the inconsistencies be resolved? Upon which of these two statutes is the holding in *Hanna* based?

2. The distinction between substance and procedure is important in both the Rules Enabling Act and the Rules of Decision Act. The second sentence of the Rules Enabling Act says that no Federal Rule may "abridge, enlarge, or modify any substantive right," and of course the distinction between substance and procedure is at the core of the line of cases interpreting the Rules of Decision Act. How does Chief Justice Warren treat the distinction between substance and procedure in *Hanna*? How does he define that distinction for purposes of the Rules Enabling Act? For purposes of the Rules of Decision Act? Are the definitions the same?

In SIBBACH v. WILSON & CO., 312 U.S. 1, 61 S.Ct. 422, 85 L.Ed. 479 (1941), plaintiff sued defendant in an Illinois federal district court for damages inflicted in Indiana. The Supreme Court affirmed the District Court's order that plaintiff undergo a physical examination pursuant to Federal Rule 35, despite an Illinois policy forbidding compulsory physical examinations. The Court concluded that the promulgation of Rule 35 was within the ambit of congressional power, since Rule 35 does not "abridge, enlarge, [or] modify substantive rights, in the guise of regulating procedure." Moreover, the Court rejected plaintiff's argument that a rule regulating procedure still could so affect a substantial personal right as to violate the Rules Enabling Act. In an opinion written by Justice Roberts, the Court held:

> * * * If we were to adopt the suggested criterion of the importance of the alleged right we should invite endless litigation and confusion * * *. The test must be whether a rule really regulates procedure—the judicial process for enforcing rights and duties recognized by substantive law and for justly

administering remedy and redress for disregard or infraction of them. That the rules in question are such is admitted.

In dissent, Justice Frankfurter maintained that Rule 35, which provides for "the invasion of the person," is quite different from other rules of procedure. He noted, furthermore, that the Rules are effective automatically absent a veto by Congress.

> * * * [T]o draw any inference of tacit approval from non-action by Congress is to appeal to unreality. And so I conclude that to make the drastic change that Rule 35 sought to introduce would require explicit legislation.

Is the distinction in *Sibbach* usable to interpret the distinction between substance and procedure as that distinction is embodied in the Rules of Decision Act?

3. After *Hanna,* what consideration should be given to *York*'s "outcome determinative" and *Byrd*'s "bound up with the rights and obligations" tests? Has the test enunciated in *Hanna* rendered the earlier tests obsolete, or is the entire discussion of the *Erie* question in *Hanna* merely dictum?

4. In his concurrence, Justice Harlan advocates an approach that "inquir[es] if the choice of rule would substantially affect those primary decisions respecting human conduct which our constitutional system leaves to state regulation." What does he mean by "primary" decisions or conduct? As Justice Harlan understands the majority opinion in *Hanna,* any "arguably procedural" rule would apply "no matter how seriously it frustrated a State's substantive regulation of the primary conduct and affairs of its citizens." Although Justice Harlan thinks the "outcome determinative" test in *York* "may err too far in honoring state rules," he criticizes the *Hanna* majority as not giving enough weight to state interests. Do you think Justice Harlan has succeeded in finding a middle ground?

5. Chief Justice Warren asserts that "the *Erie* rule is rooted in part in a realization that it would be unfair for the character or result of a litigation materially to differ because the suit had been brought in federal court [and] in part a reaction to the practice of forum-shopping." Has he abandoned part of Justice Brandeis' argument in *Erie*? Was not *Erie* based in important part on notions of state and federal relations?

6. What is the effect of *Hanna* on state statutes that close the doors of the state courts to suits by foreign corporations that have not registered to do business in the state? Can the Diversity Clause in Article III of the Constitution be said to exude a federal policy that there be a forum in every state for the protection of foreign corporations? Does anything turn on the nature of the policies underlying the state statute? See Szantay v. Beech Aircraft Corp., 349 F.2d 60 (4th Cir.1965). Compare the earlier decisions in Angel v. Bullington, 330 U.S. 183, 67 S.Ct. 657, 91 L.Ed. 832 (1947), and Woods v. Interstate Realty Co., p. 385, supra.

7. In MARSHALL v. MULRENIN, 508 F.2d 39 (1st Cir.1974), the First Circuit challenged the Supreme Court's interpretation of the Massachusetts statute applied in *Hanna* and held the Massachusetts rule for amendments changing the party against whom a claim is asserted to be controlling over Federal Rule 15(c). The decision meant that the plaintiff could maintain the action against the substituted defendants even though these defendants had not received actual notice of the institution of the action within the applicable statute of limitations as required by Rule 15(c)(1) and (2) because the Massachusetts rule allows any amendment "which may enable the plaintiff to sustain the action for the cause for

which it was intended to be brought." Given *Hanna*, is the *Marshall* decision correct? Can these two cases be explained by the fact that both permitted an adjudication on the merits? For an analysis of *Marshall* and its relationship to *Hanna*, see Comment, *Federal Rules of Civil Procedure—The Erie Doctrine—State Relation–Back Provision Found Controlling Over Rule 15(c)—Marshall v. Mulrenin*, 50 N.Y.U.L.Rev. 952 (1975). In 1991, Rule 15(c) was amended in an attempt to deal with the problem. See pp. 575–76, 578, infra.

———

Since *Hanna*, commentators have been attempting to define precisely the test to be used to answer *Erie* questions. Consider the following:

> * * * [T]he indiscriminate mixture of all questions respecting choices between federal and state law in diversity cases, under the single rubric of "the Erie doctrine" or "the Erie problem," has served to make a major mystery out of what are really three distinct and rather ordinary problems of statutory and constitutional interpretation. Of course there will be occasions with respect to all three on which reasonable persons will differ, but that does not make the problems mysterious or even very unusual. The United States Constitution, I shall argue, constitutes the relevant text only where Congress has passed a statute creating law for diversity actions, and it is in this situation alone that *Hanna*'s "arguably procedural" test controls. Where a nonstatutory rule is involved, the Constitution necessarily remains in the background, but it is functionally irrelevant because the applicable statutes are significantly more protective of the prerogatives of state law. Thus, where there is no relevant Federal Rule of Civil Procedure or other Rule promulgated pursuant to the Enabling Act and the federal rule in issue is therefore wholly judge-made, whether state or federal law should be applied is controlled by the Rules of Decision Act, the statute construed in *Erie* and *York*. Where the matter in issue is covered by a Federal Rule, however, the Enabling Act—and not the Rules of Decision Act itself or the line of cases construing it—constitutes the relevant standard. To say that, however, and that is one of the things *Hanna* said, is by no means to concede the validity of all Federal Rules, for the Enabling Act contains significant limiting language of its own. The Court has correctly sensed that that language cannot be construed to protect state prerogatives as strenuously as the Rules of Decision Act protects them in the absence of a Federal Rule. However, the Court's recent appreciation that the Enabling Act constitutes the only check on the Rules—that "Erie" does not stand there as a backstop—should lead it in an appropriate case to take the Act's limiting language more seriously than it has in the past.

Ely, *The Irrepressible Myth of Erie*, 87 Harv.L.Rev. 693, 697–98 (1974).

Compare Professor Ely's analysis with the following:

> If a valid and pertinent federal rule exists, then of course it applies, notwithstanding any state rule to the contrary. The supremacy clause says so. The real task under *Erie*, therefore, is not to choose between federal law and state law, but rather to decide if there really is a valid federal rule on the issue. * * * [T]he Rules of Decision Act is an explicit

grant of authority: It directs the federal courts to apply state law with regard to any issue that is not governed by a pertinent and valid federal rule. It reminds the federal courts that if a valid federal rule exists—whether constitutional, statutory, or judge-made—the federal rule shall govern. * * *

To understand how *Erie* operates in diversity cases, it is important to distinguish between the *pertinence* of federal rules and their *validity*. To say a federal rule is "pertinent" means that it was intended or designed to govern the issue at hand—that the rule's purposes would be served by applying it. To say a rule is "valid" means that it has been adopted in conformity with the legal norms controlling the creation of federal law—that it is consistent with the Constitution and other organic statutes regulating the formation of federal law. These combined qualities of pertinence and validity are necessary and sufficient for the proper application of a federal rule: If either quality is absent, a federal rule cannot be lawfully applied; if both are present, the federal rule must be applied.

* * *

Federal rules of civil procedure should be analyzed in the same way as federal statutes, except the rules must satisfy an additional standard of validity. The pertinence analysis is precisely the same for rules as it is for other laws. The court must determine whether the framers of a rule intended that it govern the issue at hand; if so (and if the rule is valid), the rule applies; if not, state law applies.

Westen & Lehman, *Is There Life for Erie After the Death of Diversity?*, 78 Mich.L.Rev. 311, 314–15, 342, 359 (1980).

WALKER v. ARMCO STEEL CORP.

Supreme Court of the United States, 1980.
446 U.S. 740, 100 S.Ct. 1978, 64 L.Ed.2d 659.

Certiorari to the United States Court of Appeals for the Tenth Circuit.

JUSTICE MARSHALL delivered the opinion for a unanimous Court.

This case presents the issue whether in a diversity action the federal court should follow state law or, alternatively, Rule 3 of the Federal Rules of Civil Procedure in determining when an action is commenced for the purpose of tolling the state statute of limitations.

I

According to the allegations of the complaint, petitioner, a carpenter, was injured on August 22, 1975, in Oklahoma City, Okla., while pounding a Sheffield nail into a cement wall. Respondent was the manufacturer of the nail. Petitioner claimed that the nail contained a defect which caused its head to shatter and strike him in the right eye, resulting in permanent injuries. The defect was allegedly caused by respondent's negligence in manufacture and design.

Petitioner is a resident of Oklahoma, and respondent is a foreign corporation having its principal place of business in a State other than Oklahoma. Since there was diversity of citizenship, petitioner brought suit in the United

States District Court for the Western District of Oklahoma. The complaint was filed on August 19, 1977. Although summons was issued that same day, service of process was not made on respondent's authorized service agent until December 1, 1977. On January 5, 1978, respondent filed a motion to dismiss the complaint on the ground that the action was barred by the applicable Oklahoma statute of limitations. Although the complaint had been filed within the 2–year statute of limitations, * * * state law does not deem the action "commenced" for purposes of the statute of limitations until service of the summons on the defendant, Okla.Stat., Tit. 12, § 97 (1971). If the complaint is filed within the limitations period, however, the action is deemed to have commenced from that date of filing if the plaintiff serves the defendant within 60 days, even though that service may occur outside the limitations period. * * * In this case, service was not effectuated until long after this 60–day period had expired. Petitioner in his reply brief to the motion to dismiss admitted that his case would be foreclosed in state court, but he argued that Rule 3 of the Federal Rules of Civil Procedure governs the manner in which an action is commenced in federal court for all purposes, including the tolling of the state statute of limitations.

The District Court dismissed the complaint as barred by the Oklahoma statute of limitations. * * * The court concluded that Okla.Stat., Tit. 12, § 97 (1971) was "an integral part of the Oklahoma statute of limitations," and therefore under Ragan v. Merchants Transfer & Warehouse Co. [p. 385, supra.] * * * state law applied. The court rejected the argument that *Ragan* had been implicitly overruled in Hanna v. Plumer * * *.

The United States Court of Appeals for the Tenth Circuit affirmed. * * * That court concluded that Okla.Stat., Tit. 12, § 97 (1971), was in "direct conflict" with Rule 3. * * * However, the Oklahoma statute was "indistinguishable" from the statute involved in *Ragan,* and the court felt itself "constrained" to follow *Ragan.* * * *.

We granted certiorari * * * because of a conflict among the Courts of Appeals. We now affirm.

II

The question whether state or federal law should apply on various issues arising in an action based on state law which has been brought in federal court under diversity of citizenship jurisdiction has troubled this Court for many years. [The Court discussed Guaranty Trust Co. v. York, p. 381, supra, emphasizing its focus on whether or not applying state law could substantially affect the outcome.]

The decision in *York* led logically to our holding in Ragan v. Merchants Transfer & Warehouse Co. * * *. In *Ragan,* the plaintiff had filed his complaint in federal court on September 4, 1945, pursuant to Rule 3 of the Federal Rules of Civil Procedure. The accident from which the claim arose had occurred on October 1, 1943. Service was made on the defendant on December 28, 1945. The applicable statute of limitations supplied by Kansas law was two years. Kansas had an additional statute [regarding tolling that was essentially identical to the Oklahoma statute at issue in this case]. The defendant moved for summary judgment on the ground that the Kansas statute of limitations barred the action since service had not been made within either the 2–year period or the 60–day period. It was conceded that had the case been brought in Kansas state court it would have been barred. Nonetheless, the District Court held that the statute had been tolled by the filing of the complaint. The Court of Appeals reversed * * *.

We affirmed, relying on *Erie* and *York*. "We cannot give [the cause of action] longer life in the federal court than it would have had in the state court without adding something to the cause of action. We may not do that consistently with Erie R. Co. v. Tompkins." * * *. We rejected the argument that Rule 3 of the Federal Rules of Civil Procedure governed the manner in which an action was commenced in federal court for purposes of tolling the state statute of limitations. Instead, we held that the service of summons statute controlled because it was an integral part of the state statute of limitations, and under *York,* that statute of limitations was part of the state-law cause of action.

Ragan was not our last pronouncement in this difficult area, however. In 1965 we decided Hanna v. Plumer * * *, holding that in a civil action where federal jurisdiction was based upon diversity of citizenship, Rule 4(d)(1) * * *, rather than state law, governed the manner in which process was served. * * *

The Court in *Hanna* * * * concluded that the *Erie* doctrine was simply not the appropriate test of the validity and applicability of one of the Federal Rules of Civil Procedure:

> "The *Erie* rule has never been invoked to void a Federal Rule. It is true that there have been cases where this Court had held applicable a state rule in the face of an argument that the situation was governed by one of the Federal Rules. But the holding of each such case was not that *Erie* commanded displacement of a Federal Rule by an inconsistent state rule, but rather that the scope of the Federal Rule was not as broad as the losing party urged, and therefore, there being no Federal Rule which covered the point in dispute, *Erie* commanded the enforcement of state law." * * *

The Court cited *Ragan* as one of the examples of this proposition * * *. The Court explained that where the Federal Rule was clearly applicable, as in *Hanna,* the test was whether the Rule was within the scope of the Rules Enabling Act, 28 U.S.C. § 2072, and if so, within a constitutional grant of power such as the Necessary and Proper Clause of Art. I. * * *

III

The present case is indistinguishable from *Ragan*. The statutes in both cases require service of process to toll the statute of limitations, and in fact the predecessor to the Oklahoma statute in this case was derived from the predecessor to the Kansas statute in *Ragan*. * * * Here, as in *Ragan,* the complaint was filed in federal court under diversity jurisdiction within the 2–year statute of limitations, but service of process did not occur until after the 2–year period and the 60–day service period had run. In both cases the suit would concededly have been barred in the applicable state court, and in both instances the state service statute was held to be an integral part of the statute of limitations by the lower court more familiar than we with state law.

Accordingly, as the Court of Appeals held below, the instant action is barred by the statute of limitations unless *Ragan* is no longer good law.

Petitioner argues that the analysis and holding of *Ragan* did not survive our decision in *Hanna*.[8] Petitioner's position is that Okla.Stat., Tit. 12, § 97 (1971), is in direct conflict with the Federal Rule. Under *Hanna,* petitioner contends, the appropriate question is whether Rule 3 is within the scope of the Rules Enabling Act and, if so, within the constitutional power of Congress. In petitioner's view, the Federal Rule is to be applied unless it violates one of those two restrictions. * * *   *tradition*

We note at the outset that the doctrine of *stare decisis* weighs heavily against petitioner in this case. Petitioner seeks to have us overrule our decision in *Ragan.* * * *

This Court in *Hanna* distinguished *Ragan* rather than overruled it, and for good reason. Application of the *Hanna* analysis is premised on a "direct collision" between the Federal Rule and the state law. * * * In *Hanna* itself the "clash" between Rule 4(d)(1) and the state in-hand service requirement was "unavoidable." * * * The first question must therefore be whether the scope of the Federal Rule in fact is sufficiently broad to control the issue before the Court. It is only if that question is answered affirmatively that the *Hanna* analysis applies.[9]

As has already been noted, we recognized in *Hanna* that the present case is an instance where "the scope of the Federal Rule [is] not as broad as the losing party urge[s], and therefore, there being no Federal Rule which cover[s] the point in dispute, *Erie* command[s] the enforcement of state law." * * * Rule 3 simply states that "[a] civil action is commenced by filing a complaint with the court." There is no indication that the Rule was intended to toll a state statute of limitations,[10] much less that it purported to displace state tolling rules for purposes of state statutes of limitations. In our view, in diversity actions[11] Rule 3 governs the date from which various timing require-

8. Mr. Justice Harlan in his concurring opinion in *Hanna* concluded that *Ragan* was no longer good law. * * *

9. This is not to suggest that the Federal Rules of Civil Procedure are to be narrowly construed in order to avoid a "direct collision" with state law. The Federal Rules should be given their plain meaning. If a direct collision with state law arises from that plain meaning, then the analysis developed in Hanna v. Plumer applies.

10. "Rule 3 simply provides that an action is commenced by filing the complaint and has as its primary purpose the measuring of time periods that begin running from the date of commencement; the rule does not state that filing tolls the statute of limitations." 4 C. Wright & A. Miller, Federal Practice and Procedure § 1057, p. 191 (1969) (footnote omitted).

The Note of the Advisory Committee on the Rules states:

"When a Federal or State statute of limitations is pleaded as a defense, a question may arise under this rule whether the mere filing of the complaint stops the running of the statute, or whether any further step is required, such as, service of the summons and complaint or their delivery to the marshal for service. The answer to this question may depend on whether it is competent for the Supreme Court, exercising the power to make rules of procedure without affecting substantive rights, to vary the operation of statutes of limitations. The requirement of Rule 4(a) that the clerk shall forthwith issue the summons and deliver it to the marshal for service will reduce the chances of such a question arising." * * *

This Note establishes that the Advisory Committee predicted the problem which arose in *Ragan* and arises again in the instant case. It does not indicate, however, that Rule 3 was *intended* to serve as a tolling provision for statute of limitations purposes; it only suggests that the Advisory Committee thought the Rule *might* have that effect.

11. The Court suggested in *Ragan* that in suits to enforce rights under a federal statute Rule 3 means that filing of the complaint tolls the applicable statute of limitations. * * * We ments of the Federal Rules begin to run, but does not affect state statutes of limitations. * * *

In contrast to Rule 3, the Oklahoma statute is a statement of a substantive decision by that State that actual service on, and accordingly actual notice by, the defendant is an integral part of the several policies served by the statute of limitations. * * * The statute of limitations establishes a deadline after which the defendant may legitimately have peace of mind; it also recognizes that after a certain period of time it is unfair to require the defendant to attempt to piece together his defense to an old claim. A requirement of actual service promotes both of those functions of the statute. * * * As such, the service rule must be considered part and parcel of the statute of limitations. Rule 3 does not replace such policy determinations found in state law. Rule 3 and Okla.Stat., Tit. 12, § 97 (1971), can exist side by side, therefore, each controlling its own intended sphere of coverage without conflict.

Since there is no direct conflict between the Federal Rule and the state law, the *Hanna* analysis does not apply. Instead, the policies behind *Erie* and *Ragan* control the issue. * * * [A]lthough in this case failure to apply the state service law might not create any problem of forum shopping, the result would be an "inequitable administration" of the law. Hanna v. Plumer * * *. There is simply no reason why, in the absence of a controlling federal rule, an action based on state law which concededly would be barred in the state courts by the state statute of limitations should proceed through litigation to judgment in federal court solely because of the fortuity that there is diversity of citizenship between the litigants. The policies underlying diversity jurisdiction do not support such a distinction between state and federal plaintiffs, and *Erie* and its progeny do not permit it.

The judgment of the Court of Appeals is affirmed.

Notes and Questions

1. Rule 3 states that "[a] civil action is commenced by filing a complaint with the court," but does not specify for what purposes. Two arguments were thus available for the Court in *Walker* to find that Rule 3 did not operate to toll the Oklahoma statute of limitations. First, the Court could have held that Rule 3 applies only to time requirements in other Federal Rules of Civil Procedure, tolling neither state nor federal statutes of limitations. Alternatively, the Court could have found that Rule 3 tolls federal but not state statutes of limitations.

Which argument is more persuasive? Which does the Court make in *Walker*? Note that there was abundant authority, cited in footnote 11 of the Court's opinion (including a dictum in *Ragan*), suggesting that Rule 3 does operate to toll federal statutes of limitations. *Walker* reserves this question, holding that, even if Rule 3 governs federal statutes of limitations, it does not apply to state statutes. But if Rule 3 does not toll federal statutes of limitations, what does?

2. Can you reconcile the Court's interpretation of Rule 3 in *Walker* with its interpretation of Rule 4 in *Hanna*? Rule 4 says simply that service may be made

do not here address the role of Rule 3 as a tolling provision for a statute of limitations, whether set by federal law or borrowed from state law, if the cause of action is based on federal law.

by leaving a copy of the summons and complaint at the defendant's home; it does not qualify this permission in any way or say anything about federal-question cases or diversity cases. Therefore, the *Hanna* Court concluded, Rule 4 says "implicitly, but with unmistakable clarity" that in-hand service is not required in either type of case. Rule 3 is equally plain: it says simply that an action is commenced in federal court by filing the complaint. Yet the *Walker* Court assumes, contrary to the apparent intent of the Advisory Note (quoted in footnote 10), that Rule 3 may toll federal but not state statutes of limitations. Why is Rule 4 read broadly, making a clash with state law "unavoidable," while Rule 3 is read to incorporate an implied exception for state statutes? Is the difference that Oklahoma's tolling provision serves a substantive purpose while the Massachusetts service rule in *Hanna* is purely procedural in nature? And what do you make of the statement in footnote 9 that Federal Rules are not "to be narrowly construed in order to avoid a 'direct collision' with state law"? Isn't that exactly what the Court does in *Walker?*

3.   In BURLINGTON NORTHERN R. CO. v. WOODS, 480 U.S. 1, 107 S.Ct. 967, 94 L.Ed.2d 1 (1987), Woods had obtained a jury verdict against Burlington Northern in a personal injury action prosecuted in an Alabama federal district court. After the verdict had been affirmed on appeal without modification, the Court of Appeals assessed the penalty (10% of the damages) prescribed by Alabama law for all unsuccessful appeals of money judgments. Burlington Northern objected, arguing that Rule 38 of the Federal Rules of Appellate Procedure controlled the case—and that, under Rule 38, penalties were appropriate only if, in the judgment of the appellate court, the appeal was frivolous.

The Supreme Court held that Rule 38 controlled. Justice Marshall, writing for the Court, reasoned:

> In *Hanna* * * * we set forth the appropriate test for resolving conflicts between state law and Federal Rules. The initial step is to determine whether, when fairly construed, the scope of Federal Rule 38 is "sufficiently broad" to cause a "direct collision" with the state law or, implicitly, to "control the issue" before the court, thereby leaving no room for the operation of that law. * * * The Rule must then be applied if it represents a valid exercise of Congress' rulemaking authority, which originates in the Constitution and has been bestowed on this Court by the Rules Enabling Act * * *.

> * * * Rule 38 affords a court of appeals plenary discretion to assess "just damages" in order to penalize an appellant who takes a frivolous appeal and to compensate the injured appellee for the delay and added expense of defending the district court's judgment. Thus, the Rule's discretionary mode of operation unmistakably conflicts with the mandatory provision of Alabama's affirmance penalty statute. Moreover, the purposes underlying the Rule are sufficiently coextensive with the asserted purposes of the Alabama statute to indicate that the Rule occupies the statute's field of operation so as to preclude its application in federal diversity actions.

> Respondents argue that, because Alabama has a similar Appellate Rule which may be applied in state court alongside the affirmance penalty statute, * * * a federal court sitting in diversity could impose the mandatory penalty and likewise remain free to exercise its discretionary authority under Federal Rule 38. This argument, however, ignores the significant possibility that a court of appeals may, in any given case, find a limited justification for imposing penalties in an amount *less than* 10% of the lower court's judgment. Federal Rule 38 adopts a case-by-case approach to identifying and deterring

frivolous appeals; the Alabama statute precludes any exercise of discretion within its scope of operation. Whatever circumscriptive effect the mandatory affirmance penalty statute may have on the state court's exercise of discretion under Alabama's Rule 38, that Rule provides no authority for defining the scope of discretion allowed under Federal Rule 38.

Federal Rule 38 regulates matters which can reasonably be classified as procedural, thereby satisfying the constitutional standard for validity. Its displacement of the Alabama statute also satisfies the statutory constraints of the Rules Enabling Act. The choice made by the drafters of the Federal Rules in favor of a discretionary procedure affects only the process of enforcing litigants' rights and not the rights themselves.

480 U.S. at 4–8, 107 S.Ct. at 969–71, 94 L.Ed.2d at 7–9. Is the Alabama penalty substantive or procedural law? What purpose is served by interpreting Rule 38 to displace this Alabama rule in a diversity case?

STEWART ORGANIZATION, INC. v. RICOH CORP.

Supreme Court of the United States, 1988.
487 U.S. 22, 108 S.Ct. 2239, 101 L.Ed.2d 22.

Certiorari to the United States Court of Appeals for the Eleventh Circuit.

JUSTICE MARSHALL delivered the opinion of the Court.

This case presents the issue whether a federal court sitting in diversity should apply state or federal law in adjudicating a motion to transfer a case to a venue provided in a contractual forum-selection clause.

I

The dispute underlying this case grew out of a dealership agreement that obligated petitioner company, an Alabama corporation, to market copier products of respondent, a nationwide manufacturer with its principal place of business in New Jersey. The agreement contained a forum-selection clause providing that any dispute arising out of the contract could be brought only in a court located in Manhattan. Business relations between the parties soured under circumstances that are not relevant here. In September 1984, petitioner brought a complaint in the United States District Court for the Northern District of Alabama. The core of the complaint was an allegation that respondent had breached the dealership agreement, but petitioner also included claims for breach of warranty, fraud, and antitrust violations.

Relying on the contractual forum-selection clause, respondent moved the District Court either to transfer the case to the Southern District of New York under 28 U.S.C. § 1404(a) or to dismiss the case for improper venue under 28 U.S.C. § 1406. The District Court denied the motion. * * * It reasoned that the transfer motion was controlled by Alabama law and that Alabama looks unfavorably upon contractual forum-selection clauses. The court certified its ruling for interlocutory appeal, * * * and the Court of Appeals for the Eleventh Circuit accepted jurisdiction.

On appeal, a divided panel of the Eleventh Circuit reversed the District Court. The panel concluded that questions of venue in diversity actions are governed by federal law, and that the parties' forum-selection clause was enforceable as a matter of federal law. * * * The panel therefore reversed the order of the District Court and remanded with instructions to transfer the case to a Manhattan court. After petitioner successfully moved for rehearing en banc, * * * the full Court of Appeals proceeded to adopt the result, and much of the reasoning, of the panel opinion. * * * We now affirm under somewhat different reasoning.

II

Both the panel opinion and the opinion of the full Court of Appeals referred to the difficulties that often attend "the sticky question of which law, state or federal, will govern various aspects of the decisions of federal courts sitting in diversity." * * * A district court's decision whether to apply a federal statute such as § 1404(a) in a diversity action, however, involves a considerably less intricate analysis than that which governs the "relatively unguided *Erie* choice." * * * Our cases indicate that when the federal law sought to be applied is a congressional statute, the first and chief question for the district court's determination is whether the statute is "sufficiently broad to control the issue before the Court." * * * This question involves a straight-forward exercise in statutory interpretation to determine if the statute covers the point in dispute.[4]

If the district court determines that a federal statute covers the point in dispute, it proceeds to inquire whether the statute represents a valid exercise of Congress' authority under the Constitution. * * * If Congress intended to reach the issue before the district court, and if it enacted its intention into law in a manner that abides with the Constitution, that is the end of the matter; "[f]ederal courts are bound to apply rules enacted by Congress with respect to matters * * * over which it has legislative power" * * *.[6] Thus, a district court sitting in diversity must apply a federal statute that controls the issue before the court and that represents a valid exercise of Congress' constitutional powers.

III

Applying the above analysis to this case persuades us that federal law, specifically 28 U.S.C. § 1404(a), governs the parties' venue dispute.

* * *

B

* * * Under the analysis outlined above, we first consider whether [§ 1404(a)] is sufficiently broad to control the issue before the court. That

4. Our cases at times have referred to the question at this stage of the analysis as an inquiry into whether there is a "direct collision" between state and federal law. * * * Logic indicates, however, and a careful reading of the relevant passages confirms, that this language is not meant to mandate that federal law and state law be perfectly coextensive and equally applicable to the issue at hand; rather, the "direct collision" language, at least where the applicability of a federal statute is at issue, expresses the requirement that the federal statute be sufficiently broad to cover the point in dispute. * * * It would make no sense for

the supremacy of federal law to wane precisely because there is no state law directly on point.

6. If no federal statute or Rule covers the point in dispute, the district court then proceeds to evaluate whether application of federal judge-made law would disserve the so-called "twin aims of the *Erie* rule: discouragement of forum-shopping and avoidance of inequitable administration of the laws." * * * If application of federal judge-made law would disserve these two policies, the district court should apply state law. * * *

issue is whether to transfer the case to a court in Manhattan in accordance with the forum-selection clause. We believe that the statute, fairly construed, does cover the point in dispute.

Section 1404(a) is intended to place discretion in the district court to adjudicate motions for transfer according to an "individualized, case-by-case consideration of convenience and fairness." * * * A motion to transfer under § 1404(a) thus calls on the district court to weigh in the balance a number of case-specific factors. The presence of a forum-selection clause such as the parties entered into in this case will be a significant factor that figures centrally in the district court's calculus. In its resolution of the § 1404(a) motion in this case, for example, the District Court will be called on to address such issues as the convenience of a Manhattan forum given the parties' expressed preference for that venue, and the fairness of transfer in light of the forum-selection clause and the parties' relative bargaining power. The flexible and individualized analysis Congress prescribed in § 1404(a) thus encompasses consideration of the parties' private expression of their venue preferences.

Section 1404(a) may not be the only potential source of guidance for the District Court to consult in weighing the parties' private designation of a suitable forum. The premise of the dispute between the parties is that Alabama law may refuse to enforce forum-selection clauses providing for out-of-state venues as a matter of state public policy. If that is so, the District Court will have either to integrate the factor of the forum-selection clause into its weighing of considerations as prescribed by Congress, or else to apply, as it did in this case, Alabama's categorical policy disfavoring forum-selection clauses. Our cases make clear that, as between these two choices in a single "field of operation," * * * the instructions of Congress are supreme. * * *

It is true that § 1404(a) and Alabama's putative policy regarding forum-selection clauses are not perfectly coextensive. Section 1404(a) directs a district court to take account of factors other than those that bear solely on the parties' private ordering of their affairs. The district court also must weigh in the balance the convenience of the witnesses and those public-interest factors of systemic integrity and fairness that, in addition to private concerns, come under the heading of "the interest of justice." It is conceivable in a particular case, for example, that because of these factors a district court acting under § 1404(a) would refuse to transfer a case notwithstanding the counterweight of a forum-selection clause, whereas the coordinate state rule might dictate the opposite result. * * * But this potential conflict in fact frames an additional argument for the supremacy of federal law. Congress has directed that multiple considerations govern transfer within the federal court system, and a state policy focusing on a single concern or a subset of the factors identified in § 1404(a) would defeat that command. Its application would impoverish the flexible and multifaceted analysis that Congress intended to govern motions to transfer within the federal system. The forum-selection clause, which represents the parties' agreement as to the most proper forum, should receive neither dispositive consideration (as respondent might have it) nor no consideration (as Alabama law might have it), but rather the consideration for which Congress provided in § 1404(a). * * * This is thus not a case in which state and federal rules "can exist side by side * * * each controlling its own intended sphere of coverage without conflict." * * *

Because § 1404(a) controls the issue before the District Court, it must be applied if it represents a valid exercise of Congress' authority under the Constitution. The constitutional authority of Congress to enact § 1404(a) is not subject to serious question. As the Court made plain in *Hanna,* "the constitutional provision for a federal court system * * * carries with it congressional power to make rules governing the practice and pleading in those courts, which in turn includes a power to regulate matters which, though falling within the uncertain area between substance and procedure, are rationally capable of classification as either." * * * Section 1404(a) is doubtless capable of classification as a procedural rule, and indeed, we have so classified it in holding that a transfer pursuant to § 1404(a) does not carry with it a change in the applicable law. * * * It therefore falls comfortably within Congress' powers under Article III as augmented by the Necessary and Proper Clause. * * *

We hold that federal law, specifically 28 U.S.C. § 1404(a), governs the District Court's decision whether to give effect to the parties' forum-selection clause and transfer this case to a court in Manhattan. * * * The case is remanded so that the District Court may determine in the first instance the appropriate effect under federal law of the parties' forum-selection clause on respondent's § 1404(a) motion.

It is so ordered.

Notes and Questions

1. The opinions in both *Stewart* and *Walker* were written by Justice Marshall for a unanimous Court. Which approach to interpreting the relevant provision of federal law makes more sense? Do these opinions conflict or are they consistent?

2. For a discussion of *Stewart* and its implications as to whether a federal court can ground its refusal to hear a case on the doctrine of forum non conveniens, if sitting in a state that would not apply the doctrine, see Stein, *Erie and Court Access,* 100 Yale L.J. 1935 (1991).

GASPERINI v. CENTER FOR HUMANITIES, INC.

Supreme Court of the United States, 1996.
518 U.S. 415, 116 S.Ct. 2211, 135 L.Ed.2d 659.

Certiorari to the United States Court of Appeals for the Second Circuit
JUSTICE GINSBURG delivered the opinion of the Court.

Under the law of New York, appellate courts are empowered to review the size of jury verdicts and to order new trials when the jury's award "deviates materially from what would be reasonable compensation." N. Y. Civ. Prac. Law and Rules (CPLR) § 5501(c) * * *. Under the Seventh Amendment, which governs proceedings in federal court, but not in state court, "the right of trial by jury shall be preserved, and no fact tried by a jury, shall be otherwise re-examined in any Court of the United States, than according to the rules of the common law." The compatibility of these provisions, in an action based on New York law but tried in federal court by reason of the parties' diverse citizenship, is the issue we confront in this case. * * *

We hold that New York's law controlling compensation awards for excessiveness or inadequacy can be given effect, without detriment to the Seventh Amendment, if the review standard set out in CPLR § 5501(c) is applied by the federal trial court judge, with appellate control of the trial court's ruling limited to review for "abuse of discretion."

I

Petitioner William Gasperini, a journalist for CBS News and the Christian Science Monitor, began reporting on events in Central America in 1984. * * * During the course of his seven-year stint in Central America, Gasperini took over 5,000 slide transparencies, depicting active war zones, political leaders, and scenes from daily life. In 1990, Gasperini agreed to supply his original color transparencies to The Center for Humanities, Inc. (Center) for use in an educational videotape, Conflict in Central America. Gasperini selected 300 of his slides for the Center; its videotape included 110 of them. The Center agreed to return the original transparencies, but upon the completion of the project, it could not find them.

Gasperini commenced suit in the United States District Court for the Southern District of New York, invoking the court's diversity jurisdiction * * *. The Center conceded liability for the lost transparencies and the issue of damages was tried before a jury.

At trial, Gasperini's expert witness testified that the "industry standard" within the photographic publishing community valued a lost transparency at $1,500. * * *

After a three-day trial, the jury awarded Gasperini $450,000 in compensatory damages. This sum, the jury foreperson announced, "is [$] 1500 each, for 300 slides." Moving for a new trial under Federal Rule of Civil Procedure 59, the Center attacked the verdict on various grounds, including excessiveness. Without comment, the District Court denied the motion. * * *

The Court of Appeals for the Second Circuit vacated the judgment entered on the jury's verdict. * * * Mindful that New York law governed the controversy, the Court of Appeals endeavored to apply CPLR § 5501(c), which instructs that, when a jury returns an itemized verdict, as the jury did in this case, the New York Appellate Division "shall determine that an award is excessive or inadequate if it deviates materially from what would be reasonable compensation." The Second Circuit's application of § 5501(c) as a check on the size of the jury's verdict followed Circuit precedent elaborated two weeks earlier * * *. Surveying Appellate Division decisions that reviewed damage awards for lost transparencies, the Second Circuit concluded that testimony on industry standard alone was insufficient to justify a verdict; prime among other factors warranting consideration were the uniqueness of the slides' subject matter and the photographer's earning level.

Guided by Appellate Division rulings, the Second Circuit held that the $450,000 verdict "materially deviates from what is reasonable compensation." * * * [T]he Second Circuit set aside the $450,000 verdict and ordered a new trial, unless Gasperini agreed to an award of $100,000.

* * *

II

Before 1986, state and federal courts in New York generally invoked the same judge-made formulation in responding to excessiveness attacks on jury verdicts: courts would not disturb an award unless the amount was so exorbitant that it "shocked the conscience of the court." * * *

In both state and federal courts, trial judges made the excessiveness assessment in the first instance, and appellate judges ordinarily deferred to the trial court's judgment. * * *

In 1986, as part of a series of tort reform measures, New York codified a standard for judicial review of the size of jury awards. Placed in CPLR § 5501(c), the prescription reads:

"In reviewing a money judgment ... in which it is contended that the award is excessive or inadequate and that a new trial should have been granted unless a stipulation is entered to a different award, the appellate division shall determine that an award is excessive or inadequate if it deviates materially from what would be reasonable compensation." * * *

* * * New York state-court opinions confirm that § 5501(c)'s "deviates materially" standard calls for closer surveillance than "shock the conscience" oversight. * * *

Although phrased as a direction to New York's intermediate appellate courts, § 5501(c)'s "deviates materially" standard, as construed by New York's courts, instructs state trial judges as well. * * *Application of § 5501(c) at the trial level is key to this case.

To determine whether an award "deviates materially from what would be reasonable compensation," New York state courts look to awards approved in similar cases. * * *

III

In cases like Gasperini's, in which New York law governs the claims for relief, does New York law also supply the test for federal-court review of the size of the verdict? The Center answers yes. The "deviates materially" standard, it argues, is a substantive standard that must be applied by federal appellate courts in diversity cases. The Second Circuit agreed. * * * Gasperini, emphasizing that § 5501(c) trains on the New York Appellate Division, characterizes the provision as procedural, an allocation of decisionmaking authority regarding damages, not a hard cap on the amount recoverable. Correctly comprehended, Gasperini urges, § 5501(c)'s direction to the Appellate Division cannot be given effect by federal appellate courts without violating the Seventh Amendment's Reexamination Clause.

As the parties' arguments suggest, CPLR § 5501(c), appraised under *Erie R. Co. v. Tompkins* * * * and decisions in *Erie*'s path, is both "substantive" and "procedural": "substantive" in that § 5501(c)'s "deviates materially" standard controls how much a plaintiff can be awarded; "procedural" in that § 5501(c) assigns decisionmaking authority to New York's Appellate Division. Parallel application of § 5501(c) at the federal appellate level would be out of sync with the federal system's division of trial and appellate court functions, an allocation weighted by the Seventh Amendment. The dispositive question, therefore, is whether federal courts can give effect to the substantive thrust of

§ 5501(c) without untoward alteration of the federal scheme for the trial and decision of civil cases.

A

* * *

Classification of a law as "substantive" or "procedural" for *Erie* purposes is sometimes a challenging endeavor.[7] *Guaranty Trust Co. v. York*, * * * an early interpretation of *Erie*, propounded an "outcome-determination" test: "[D]oes it significantly affect the result of a litigation for a federal court to disregard a law of a State that would be controlling in an action upon the same claim by the same parties in a State court?" * * * Ordering application of a state statute of limitations to an equity proceeding in federal court, the Court said in *Guaranty Trust*: "Where a federal court is exercising jurisdiction solely because of the diversity of citizenship of the parties, the outcome of the litigation in the federal court should be substantially the same, so far as legal rules determine the outcome of a litigation, as it would be if tried in a State court." * * * A later pathmarking case, qualifying *Guaranty Trust*, explained that the "outcome-determination" test must not be applied mechanically to sweep in all manner of variations; instead, its application must be guided by "the twin aims of the *Erie* rule: discouragement of forum shopping and avoidance of inequitable administration of the laws." *Hanna v. Plumer* * * *.

* * * [W]e address the question whether New York's "deviates materially" standard, codified in CPLR § 5501(c), is outcome affective in this sense: Would "application of the [standard] ... have so important an effect upon the fortunes of one or both of the litigants that failure to [apply] it would [unfairly discriminate against citizens of the forum State, or] be likely to cause a plaintiff to choose the federal court"? * * *[8]

We start from a point the parties do not debate. Gasperini acknowledges that a statutory cap on damages would supply substantive law for *Erie* purposes. * * * Although CPLR § 5501(c) is less readily classified, it was designed to provide an analogous control.

* * *

It thus appears that if federal courts ignore the change in the New York standard and persist in applying the "shock the conscience" test to damage awards on claims governed by New York law, " 'substantial' variations between state and federal [money judgments]" may be expected. * * * We therefore agree with the Second Circuit that New York's check on excessive damages implicates what we have called "twin aims." * * * Just as the *Erie* principle precludes a federal court from giving a state-created claim "longer life ... than [the claim] would have had in the state court," * * * so *Erie* precludes a recovery in federal court significantly larger than the recovery that would have been tolerated in state court.

7. Concerning matters covered by the Federal Rules of Civil Procedure, the characterization question is usually unproblematic: It is settled that if the Rule in point is consonant with the Rules Enabling Act, 28 U.S.C. § 2072, and the Constitution, the Federal Rule applies regardless of contrary state law. See *Hanna v.* *Plumer* * * *; *Burlington Northern R. Co. v. Woods* * * *. Federal courts have interpreted the Federal Rules, however, with sensitivity to important state interests and regulatory policies. * * *

8. *Hanna* keyed the question to *Erie*'s "twin aims" * * *.

B

CPLR § 5501(c) * * * is phrased as a direction to the New York Appellate Division. Acting essentially as a surrogate for a New York appellate forum, the Court of Appeals reviewed Gasperini's award to determine if it "deviate[d] materially" from damage awards the Appellate Division permitted in similar circumstances. The Court of Appeals performed this task without benefit of an opinion from the District Court, which had denied "without comment" the Center's Rule 59 motion. Concentrating on the authority § 5501(c) gives to the Appellate Division, Gasperini urges that the provision shifts fact finding responsibility from the jury and the trial judge to the appellate court. Assigning such responsibility to an appellate court, he maintains, is incompatible with the Seventh Amendment's Reexamination Clause, and therefore, Gasperini concludes, § 5501(c) cannot be given effect in federal court. Although we reach a different conclusion than Gasperini, we agree that the Second Circuit did not attend to "an essential characteristic of [the federal-court] system," * * * when it used § 5501(c) as "the standard for [federal] appellate review." * * *

* * *

The Seventh Amendment, which governs proceedings in federal court, but not in state court, bears not only on the allocation of trial functions between judge and jury, the issue in *Byrd*; it also controls the allocation of authority to review verdicts, the issue of concern here. * * *

Byrd involved the first Clause of the Amendment, the "trial by jury" Clause. This case involves the second, the "re-examination" Clause. In keeping with the historic understanding, the Reexamination Clause does not inhibit the authority of trial judges to grant new trials "for any of the reasons for which new trials have heretofore been granted in actions at law in the courts of the United States." That authority is large. * * * "The trial judge in the federal system," we have reaffirmed, "has ... discretion to grant a new trial if the verdict appears to [the judge] to be against the weight of the evidence." This discretion includes overturning verdicts for excessiveness and ordering a new trial without qualification, or conditioned on the verdict winner's refusal to agree to a reduction (remittitur). * * *

In contrast, appellate review of a federal trial court's denial of a motion to set aside a jury's verdict as excessive is a relatively late, and less secure, development. Such review was once deemed inconsonant with the Seventh Amendment's Reexamination Clause. * * *

As the Second Circuit explained, appellate review for abuse of discretion is reconcilable with the Seventh Amendment as a control necessary and proper to the fair administration of justice: "We must give the benefit of every doubt to the judgment of the trial judge; but surely there must be an upper limit, and whether that has been surpassed is not a question of fact with respect to which reasonable men may differ, but a question of law." [citations omitted] * * * We now approve this line of decisions, and thus make explicit what Justice Stewart thought implicit in our * * * disposition [in an earlier case]: "[N]othing in the Seventh Amendment ... precludes appellate review of the trial judge's denial of a motion to set aside [a jury verdict] as excessive." * * *

C

In *Byrd*, the Court faced a one-or-the-other choice: trial by judge as in state court, or trial by jury according to the federal practice. In the case before us, a choice of that order is not required, for the principal state and federal interests can be accommodated. The Second Circuit correctly recognized that when New York substantive law governs a claim for relief, New York law and decisions guide the allowable damages. * * *

New York's dominant interest can be respected, without disrupting the federal system, once it is recognized that the federal district court is capable of * * * apply[ing]the State's "deviates materially" standard in line with New York case law evolving under CPLR § 5501(c).[22] * * *

Within the federal system, practical reasons combine with Seventh Amendment constraints to lodge in the district court, not the court of appeals, primary responsibility for application of § 5501(c)'s "deviates materially" check. Trial judges have the "unique opportunity to consider the evidence in the living courtroom context," * * * while appellate judges see only the "cold paper record."

District court applications of the "deviates materially" standard would be subject to appellate review under the standard the Circuits now employ when inadequacy or excessiveness is asserted on appeal: abuse of discretion. * * * In light of *Erie*'s doctrine, the federal appeals court must be guided by the damage-control standard state law supplies, but as the Second Circuit itself has said: "If we reverse, it must be because of an abuse of discretion.... The very nature of the problem counsels restraint.... We must give the benefit of every doubt to the judgment of the trial judge."

IV

It does not appear that the District Court checked the jury's verdict against the relevant New York decisions demanding more than "industry standard" testimony to support an award of the size the jury returned in this case. As the Court of Appeals recognized, * * * the uniqueness of the photographs and the plaintiff's earnings as photographer—past and reasonably projected—are factors relevant to appraisal of the award. * * * Accordingly, we vacate the judgment of the Court of Appeals and instruct that court to remand the case to the District Court so that the trial judge, revisiting his ruling on the new trial motion, may test the jury's verdict against CPLR § 5501(c)'s "deviates materially" standard.

It is so ordered.

22. JUSTICE SCALIA finds in Federal Rule of Civil Procedure 59 a "federal standard" for new trial motions in " 'direct collision' " with, and " 'leaving no room for the operation of,' " a state law like CPLR § 5501(c). * * * The relevant prescription, Rule 59(a), has remained unchanged since the adoption of the Federal Rules by this Court in 1937. Rule 59(a) is as encompassing as it is uncontroversial. It is indeed "Hornbook" law that a most usual ground for a Rule 59 motion is that "the damages are excessive." See C. Wright, Law of Federal Courts 676–677 (5th ed. 1994). Whether damages are excessive for the claim-in-suit must be governed by some law. And there is no candidate for that governance other than the law that gives rise to the claim for relief—here, the law of New York. * * *

JUSTICE STEVENS, dissenting.

* * *

I

* * *

The District Court had its opportunity to consider the propriety of the jury's award, and it erred. The Court of Appeals has now corrected that error after "drawing all reasonable inferences in favor of" petitioner. * * * As there is no reason to suppose that the Court of Appeals has reached a conclusion with which the District Court could permissibly disagree on remand, I would not require the District Court to repeat a task that has already been well performed by the reviewing court. I therefore would affirm the judgment of the Court of Appeals.

* * *

III

* * * I agree with the majority that the Reexamination Clause does not bar federal appellate courts from reviewing jury awards for excessiveness. I confess to some surprise, however, at its conclusion that " 'the influence—if not the command—of the Seventh Amendment,' " * * * requires federal courts of appeals to review district court applications of state-law excessiveness standards for an "abuse of discretion." * * *

Certainly, our decision in *Byrd* does not make the Clause relevant. There, we considered only whether the Seventh Amendment's first clause should influence our decision to give effect to a state-law rule denying the right to a jury altogether. * * * That holding in no way requires us to consult the Amendment's second clause to determine the standard of review for a district court's application of state substantive law.

My disagreement is tempered, however, because the majority carefully avoids defining too strictly the abuse-of-discretion standard it announces. To the extent that the majority relies only on "practical reasons" for its conclusion that the Court of Appeals should give some weight to the District Court's assessment in determining whether state substantive law has been properly applied, * * * I do not disagree with its analysis.

* * *

In the end, therefore, my disagreement with the label that the majority attaches to the standard of appellate review should not obscure the far more fundamental point on which we agree. Whatever influence the Seventh Amendment may be said to exert, Erie requires federal appellate courts sitting in diversity to apply "the damage-control standard state law supplies." * * *

IV

Because I would affirm the judgment of the Court of Appeals, and because I do not agree that the Seventh Amendment in any respect influences the proper analysis of the question presented, I respectfully dissent.

JUSTICE SCALIA, with whom the CHIEF JUSTICE and JUSTICE THOMAS join, dissenting.

* * *

I

* * *

A

* * * [T]he practice of *federal* appellate reexamination of facts found by a jury is precisely what the People of the several States considered *not* to be good legal policy in 1791. Indeed, so fearful were they of such a practice that they constitutionally prohibited it by means of the Seventh Amendment.

* * *

* * * The Reexamination Clause put to rest "apprehensions" of "new trials by the appellate courts," by adopting, in broad fashion, "the rules of the common law" to govern federal-court interference with jury determinations. The content of that law was familiar and fixed. * * * It quite plainly barred reviewing courts from entertaining claims that the jury's verdict was contrary to the evidence.

At common law, review of judgments was had only on writ of error, limited to questions of law. * * *

Nor was the common-law proscription on reexamination limited to review of the correctness of the jury's determination of liability on the facts. No less than the existence of liability, the proper measure of damages "involves only a question of fact," * * * as does a "motion for a new trial based on the ground that the damages ... are excessive." * * * As appeals from denial of such motions necessarily pose a factual question, courts of the United States are constitutionally forbidden to entertain them.

* * *

This view was for long years not only unquestioned in our cases, but repeatedly affirmed.

B

Respondent's principal response to these cases, which is endorsed by JUSTICE STEVENS, is that our forebears were simply wrong about the English common law. The rules of the common-law practice incorporated in the Seventh Amendment, it is claimed, did *not* prevent judges sitting in an appellate capacity from granting a new trial on the ground that an award was contrary to the weight of the evidence. This claim simply does not withstand examination of the actual practices of the courts at common law. The weight of the historical record strongly supports the view of the common law taken in our early cases.

* * *

I am persuaded that our prior cases were correct that, at common law, "reexamination" of the facts found by a jury could be undertaken only by the trial court, and that appellate review was restricted to writ of error which could challenge the judgment only upon matters of law. Even if there were some doubt on the point, we should be hesitant to advance our view of the common law over that of our forebears, who were far better acquainted with the subject than we are. But in any event, the question of how to apply the "rules of the common law" to federal appellate consideration of motions for new trials is one that has already been clearly and categorically answered, by our precedents. * * * Cases of this Court reaching back into the early 19th century establish that the Constitution forbids federal appellate courts to "reexamine" a fact found by the jury at trial; and that this prohibition encompasses review of a district court's refusal to set aside a verdict as contrary to the weight of the evidence.

C

* * *

* * * The cases upon which the Court relies neither affirmed nor rejected the practice of appellate weight-of-the-evidence review that has been adopted by the courts of appeals—a development that, in light of our past cases, amounts to studied waywardness by the intermediate appellate bench. * * *

In any event, it is not *this* Court's statements that the Court puts forward as the basis for dispensing with our prior cases. Rather, it is the Courts of Appeals' unanimous "agree[ment]" that they may review trial-court refusals to set aside jury awards claimed to be against the weight of the evidence. * * * This current unanimity is deemed controlling, notwithstanding the "relatively late" origin of the practice, * * * and without any inquiry into the reasoning set forth in those Court of Appeals decisions. * * *

The Court's only suggestion as to what rationale might underlie approval of abuse-of-discretion review is to be found in a quotation * * * to the effect that review of denial of a new trial motion, if conducted under a sufficiently deferential standard, poses only " 'a question of law.' " * * * But that is not the test that the Seventh Amendment sets forth. Whether or not it is possible to characterize an appeal of a denial of new trial as raising a "legal question," it is not possible to review such a claim without engaging in a "reexamin[ation]" of the "facts tried by the jury" in a manner "otherwise" than allowed at common law. Determining whether a particular award is excessive requires that one first determine the nature and extent of the harm—which undeniably requires reviewing the facts of the case. That the court's review also entails application of a legal standard (whether "shocks the conscience," "deviates materially," or some other) makes no difference, for what is necessarily *also* required is *reexamination of facts* found by the jury.

* * *

II

The Court's holding that federal courts of appeals may review district court denials of motions for new trials for error of fact is not the only novel aspect of today's decision. The Court also directs that the case be remanded to the District Court, so that it may "test the jury's verdict against CPLR § 5501(c)'s 'deviates materially' standard." * * * This disposition contradicts the principle that "the proper role of the trial and appellate courts in the federal system in reviewing the size of jury verdicts is . . . a matter of federal law." * * *

* * * The Court approves the "accommodat[ion]" achieved by having district courts review jury verdicts under the "deviates materially" standard, because it regards that as a means of giving effect to the State's purposes "without disrupting the federal system." * * * But changing the standard by which trial judges review jury verdicts *does* disrupt the federal system, and is plainly inconsistent with the "strong federal policy against allowing state rules to disrupt the judge-jury relationship in the federal court." * * *

We discussed precisely the point at issue here in *Browning-Ferris Industries of Vt., Inc. v. Kelco Disposal, Inc.*, 492 U.S. 257, 109 S.Ct. 2909, 106 L.Ed.2d 219 (1989), and gave an answer altogether contrary to the one provided today. *Browning-Ferris* rejected a request to fashion a federal common-law rule limiting the size of punitive damages awards in federal courts * * *. * * * "In reviewing an award of punitive damages," it said, "the role of the district court is to determine whether the jury's verdict is within the confines set by state law, and to determine, by reference to federal standards developed under Rule 59, whether a new trial or remittitur should be ordered." Id., at 279, 109 S.Ct. at 2922, 106 L.Ed.2d at 240. The same distinction necessarily applies where the judgment under review is for compensatory damages: State substantive law controls what injuries are compensable and in what amount; but federal standards determine whether the award exceeds what is lawful to such degree that it may be set aside by order for new trial or remittitur.

The Court does not disavow those statements in *Browning-Ferris* (indeed, it does not even discuss them), but it presumably overrules them, at least where the state rule that governs "whether a new trial or remittitur should be ordered" is characterized as "substantive" in nature. * * *

* * * It seems to me quite wrong to regard [§ 5501(c)] as a "substantive" rule for *Erie* purposes. The "analog[y]" to "a statutory cap on damages" * * * fails utterly. There is an absolutely fundamental distinction between a *rule of law* such as that, which would ordinarily be imposed upon the jury in the trial court's instructions, and a *rule of review*, which simply determines how closely the jury verdict will be scrutinized for compliance with the instructions. A tighter standard for reviewing jury determinations can no more plausibly be called a "substantive" disposition than can a tighter appellate standard for reviewing trial-court determinations. The one, like the other, provides additional assurance *that the law has been complied with*; but the other, like the one, *leaves the law unchanged*.

The Court commits the classic *Erie* mistake of regarding whatever changes the outcome as substantive * * *. * * * Outcome-determination "was never intended to serve as a talisman," and * * * does not have the power to convert the most classic elements of the process of assuring that the law is observed into the substantive law itself. The right to have a jury make the findings of fact, for example, is generally thought to favor plaintiffs, and that advantage is often thought significant enough to be the basis for forum selection. But no one would argue that *Erie* confers a right to a jury in federal court wherever state courts would provide it; or that, were it not for the

Seventh Amendment, *Erie* would require federal courts to dispense with the jury whenever state courts do so.

In any event, the Court exaggerates the difference that the state standard will make. It concludes that different outcomes are likely to ensue depending on whether the law being applied is the state "deviates materially" standard of § 5501(c) or the "shocks the conscience" standard. * * * Of course, it is not the federal *appellate* standard but the federal *district-court* standard for granting new trials that must be compared with the New York standard to determine whether substantially different results will obtain—and it is far from clear that the district-court standard *ought* to be "shocks the conscience." * * * What seems to me far more likely to produce forum shopping is the consistent difference between the state and federal *appellate* standards, which the Court leaves untouched. Under the Court's disposition, the Second Circuit reviews only for abuse of discretion, whereas New York's appellate courts engage in a *de novo* review for material deviation, giving the defendant a double shot at getting the damages award set aside. The only result that would produce the conformity the Court erroneously believes *Erie* requires is the one adopted by the Second Circuit and rejected by the Court: *de novo* federal appellate review under the § 5501(c) standard.

To say that application of § 5501(c) in place of the federal standard will not consistently produce disparate results is not to suggest that the decision the Court has made today is not a momentous one. The *principle* that the state standard governs is of great importance, since it bears the potential to destroy the uniformity of federal practice and the integrity of the federal court system. Under the Court's view, a state rule that directed courts "to determine that an award is excessive or inadequate if it deviates *in any degree* from *the proper measure of compensation*" would have to be applied in federal courts, effectively requiring federal judges to determine the amount of damages de novo, and effectively taking the matter away from the jury entirely. * * * Or consider a state rule that allowed the defendant a second trial on damages, with judgment ultimately in the amount of the lesser of two jury awards. * * * Under the reasoning of the Court's opinion, even such a rule as that would have to be applied in the federal courts.

The foregoing describes why I think the Court's *Erie* analysis is flawed. But in my view, one does not even reach the *Erie* question in this case. The standard to be applied by a district court in ruling on a motion for a new trial is set forth in Rule 59 of the Federal Rules of Civil Procedure, which provides that "[a] new trial may be granted . . . for any of the reasons for which new trials have heretofore been granted in actions at law *in the courts of the United States*" (emphasis added). That is undeniably a federal standard.[12] Federal district courts in the Second Circuit have interpreted that standard to permit the granting of new trials where " 'it is quite clear that the jury has reached a seriously erroneous result' " and letting the verdict stand would result in a " 'miscarriage of justice.' " * * * Assuming (as we have no reason to question) that this is a correct interpretation of what Rule 59 requires, it is

---

12. I agree with the Court's entire progression of reasoning in its footnote * * *, leading to the conclusion that state law must determine "whether damages are excessive." But the question whether damages are excessive is quite separate from the question of when a jury award may be set aside for excessiveness. * * * It is the latter that is governed by Rule 59 * * *.

undeniable that the Federal Rule is " 'sufficiently broad' to cause a 'direct collision' with the state law or, implicitly, to 'control the issue' before the court, thereby leaving no room for the operation of that law." * * * It is simply not possible to give controlling effect both to the federal standard and the state standard in reviewing the jury's award. That being so, the court has no choice but to apply the Federal Rule, which is an exercise of what we have called Congress's "power to regulate matters which, though falling within the uncertain area between substance and procedure, are rationally capable of classification as either * * *."

* * * I respectfully dissent.

Notes and Questions

1. The first part of the Court's decision in *Gasperini* revives a *York*-style outcome-determinative approach to determining the applicable law. Although *York* had not been overruled, its influence had waned after *Byrd* and *Hanna*, and the Court surprised many observers in *Gasperini* by abandoning the balancing approach established by these later cases. What role do the "twin aims" of *Erie* continue to play in determining the applicable law? It remains unclear how courts should determine the applicable law in diversity cases that do not involve a Federal Rule or some other element of federal law.

2. The *Gasperini* opinion does not discuss *Byrd* until it already has determined the applicable law. Why not? Like *Byrd*, *Gasperini* involved the division of trial functions between judge and jury. Although in *Byrd* the Court ultimately declined to apply state law, one commentator has suggested it need not have reached the same result in *Gasperini*:

> [T]he state practice in *Byrd* allocated responsibilities based only on a "practical consideration" that was not "bound up with the definition of the rights and obligations of the parties." In contrast, the New York legislature wanted to enact a substantive damage limitation when it enacted 5501(c). The *Gasperini* Court could easily have found the state interest to outweigh the federal interest under *Byrd*, then performed an identical Seventh Amendment analysis, and reached the same result. It simply chose not to do so.

Leading Cases, 110 Harv.L.Rev. 135, 265 (1996). What is the status and range of application of *Byrd* after *Gasperini*? In *Byrd*, the Court held that South Carolina's division between judge and jury was not "bound up" with the substantive rights of the parties. In *Gasperini*, however, the Court finds that New York's damage award rule is substantive. Does *Gasperini* provide a new approach that replaces *Byrd*, or can the two decisions be reconciled?

3. The majority in *Gasperini* claims that Federal Rule 59(a)(1) does not apply. Is this correct? In Atlas Food Sys. & Servs. v. Crane Nat. Vendors, Inc., 99 F.3d 587 (4th Cir.1996), the court held that although state law supplies the framework for damage awards, the judgment a jury makes as to the damage amount is reviewed by federal courts under the Rule less deferentially than are factual findings. If the Federal Rules should be "interpreted with sensitivity to important state interests and regulatory policies," as the Court suggests in footnote 7, then perhaps Rule 59 should be interpreted narrowly to avoid a conflict with the substantive purposes of New York's Legislature. See Freer, *Some Thoughts on the State of Erie After Gasperini*, 76 Texas L.Rev. 1637 (1998).

4. For further discussion of *Gasperini*, See Floyd, *Erie Awry: A Comment on Gasperini v. Center for Humanities, Inc.*, 1997 B.Y.U.L.Rev. 267; Perdue, *The Sources and Scope of Federal Procedural Common Law: Some Reflections on Erie and Gasperini*, 46 U.Kan.L.Rev. 751 (1998); Rowe, *Not Bad for Government Work: Does Anyone Else Think the Supreme Court is Doing a Halfway Decent Job in its Erie–Hanna Jurisprudence?*, 73 Notre Dame L.Rev. 963 (1998).

SECTION B.   THE PROBLEM OF ASCERTAINING STATE LAW

1.   DETERMINING WHICH STATE'S LAW GOVERNS

In *Erie*, the parties—and the courts—appear to have assumed that if state law applied, Pennsylvania tort law would govern—even though the action was being tried in a federal court in New York. Why did they make this assumption? Was the federal court free to choose the most appropriate state law to govern the dispute? Or was it that New York's choice-of-law rules pointed to an application of Pennsylvania law?

———

KLAXON CO. v. STENTOR ELECTRIC MFG. CO., 313 U.S. 487, 61 S.Ct. 1020, 85 L.Ed. 1477 (1941). The Supreme Court held that in order to promote the desired uniform application of substantive law within a state, federal courts must apply the conflicts-of-laws rules of the states in which they sit. The Court explained:

> * * * Whatever lack of uniformity this may produce between federal courts in different states is attributable to our federal system, which leaves to a state, within the limits permitted by the Constitution, the right to pursue local policies diverging from those of its neighbors. It is not for the federal courts to thwart such local policies by enforcing an independent "general law" of conflict of laws. * * * [T]he proper function of [a] federal court is to ascertain what the state law is, not what it ought to be.

Id. at 496–97, 61 S.Ct. at 1022, 85 L.Ed. at 1480–81.

Notes and Questions

1.   Could Congress enact a statute specifying choice-of-law rules for federal courts in diversity cases? In answering this question, remember that, although it is true today that every state contains at least one federal judicial district, there is no constitutional provision that compels this. What if Congress had established only regional courts? Under such a scheme, would Congress or the courts have been forced to establish their own choice-of-law rules?

2.   The states have been allowed great leeway in establishing choice-of-law rules. In ALLSTATE INS. CO. v. HAGUE, Note 7, p. 97, supra, the Supreme Court held that a state could apply its substantive law in a case, so long as the state had significant contacts or a significant aggregation of contacts with the parties and the transaction. See also Phillips Petroleum Co. v. Shutts, 472 U.S.

797, 105 S.Ct. 2965, 86 L.Ed.2d 628 (1985), p. 738, infra. Doesn't *Hague* encourage plaintiffs to forum shop and *Klaxon* seal the defendant's fate?

3. If a diversity case is transferred under 28 U.S.C. § 1404(a), what law should the transferee court apply? Does it matter whether the plaintiff or the defendant moved to transfer? In VAN DUSEN v. BARRACK, 376 U.S. 612, 639, 84 S.Ct. 805, 820, 821, 11 L.Ed.2d 945, 962–63 (1964), defendants sought to transfer the action from federal court in Pennsylvania to federal court in Massachusetts, where the state law was more favorable to their case. The Supreme Court rejected a wooden reading of *Erie*, which would require the transferee court to apply the law of the state in which it sits—that is, Massachusetts law. Rather, the Court determined that the "critical identity" is between the federal court that decides the case and the courts of the state in which the action was filed. According to the Court: "A change of venue under § 1404(a) generally should be, with respect to state law, but a change of courtrooms."

The Court speaks of not letting the "accident" of federal diversity jurisdiction affect the outcome of the lawsuit. Yet, it appears that *Van Dusen* makes it possible for a suit to be filed in federal court in one state and then transferred to a different state with the result that the law applied will differ from the law that would have applied if the suit had been filed initially in the transferee court. Isn't the real policy behind *Van Dusen* simply to prevent the defendant from forum shopping?

2. ASCERTAINING THE STATE LAW

MASON v. AMERICAN EMERY WHEEL WORKS
United States Court of Appeals, First Circuit, 1957.
241 F.2d 906.

MAGRUDER, CHIEF JUDGE. Whit Mason, a citizen of Mississippi, filed his complaint in the United States District Court for the District of Rhode Island against The American Emery Wheel Works, a Rhode Island corporation. The case was one in tort for personal injuries alleged to have been suffered by the plaintiff in Mississippi as a result of negligent misfeasance by the defendant in putting out in commerce without adequate care and inspection, a dangerously defective emery wheel. According to the allegations of the complaint, at some time prior to the date of the accident defendant negligently manufactured, inspected and tested a certain emery wheel designed for attachment to a bench grinder; that due to such negligence the emery wheel was not reasonably fit for the use for which it was intended, but on the contrary subjected to a risk of personal injury all persons lawfully using a bench grinder with the emery wheel attached * * *.

On the face of the complaint it did not specifically appear that plaintiff was not in privity of contract with defendant. The answer of defendant, in addition to denying negligence, and denying that it had manufactured the particular emery wheel which had caused plaintiff's injuries, also set forth as a "First Defense" that the complaint failed to state a claim upon which relief might be granted, and as a "Fourth Defense" that defendant "owed no duty to the said plaintiff as there is no privity of contract between the plaintiff and the defendant."

* * * Plaintiff's evidence tended to show that a certain emery wheel * * * was purchased by the Hoover Company, a New Jersey corporation, from

the defendant for attachment to a bench grinding machine made by the Hoover Company; that the Hoover Company affixed to the said bench grinding machine, with emery wheel attached, a label indicating that the bench grinder had been manufactured by Miller Falls Company, a Massachusetts corporation; that said bench grinder * * * was successively sold by the Hoover Company to Miller Falls Company, by the latter to Komp Equipment Company, and finally by Komp Equipment Company to T.H. Pearce Company, the plaintiff's employer; * * * that while plaintiff was using it in the ordinary and proper manner the emery wheel disintegrated and exploded in plaintiff's face, causing the injuries complained of.

At the conclusion of the plaintiff's case defendant made an oral motion to dismiss the complaint under Rule 41(b) * * *. This motion to dismiss was granted by the district court, and an order was entered dismissing the complaint, from which the present appeal was taken.

Since the injury was inflicted in Mississippi, the district court, no doubt correctly under now familiar authorities, deemed itself to be obliged to apply the Mississippi local law to determine the tort liability, if any, of a manufacturer to one not in privity of contract with him. * * * The district court came to the conclusion "reluctantly" that it was bound by the Mississippi law as declared in Ford Motor Co. v. Myers, 1928, 151 Miss. 73, 117 So. 362; that the "harsh rule" of Mississippi as so declared, "contrary to the great weight of authority" elsewhere, was that a manufacturer was not liable for negligence in the manufacture of appliances which could and would become highly *Rule* dangerous when put to the uses for which they are intended, where there is no privity of contract between the user and the manufacturer.

Ford Motor Co. v. Myers, supra, was the only Mississippi case relied upon, or even referred to, by the district court. In that case the Supreme Court of Mississippi, in a half-page opinion, did in fact apply what was at one time the prevailing rule, in holding that Ford Motor Company as the manufacturer of a truck owed no duty of care to a remote subvendee of the truck who was injured when the truck collapsed and plunged into a ditch because of a defect which could have been detected by reasonable inspection by the manufacturer before the vehicle left the factory.

* * *

MacPherson v. Buick Motor Co., [217 N.Y. 382, 111 N.E. 1050 (1916)] * * * started a new trend in this particular field of the law, and its substantive result has found favor in § 395 of the * * * Restatement of Torts. If the Supreme Court of Mississippi had recently reconsidered the rule it applied in Ford Motor Co. v. Myers, supra, and had decided to adhere to it on the ground of stare decisis, no doubt the federal courts would have had to accept the local law as so declared. But it would be gratuitous and unwarranted to assume that the Supreme Court of Mississippi would now so hold, when we bear in mind the readiness of other courts, in conservative jurisdictions at that, to overrule their earlier holdings and to bring their jurisprudence into accord with what is now the overwhelming weight of authority. * * * In Anderson v. Linton, 7 Cir., 1949, 178 F.2d 304, the court of appeals declined to accept as the local law of Iowa what it narrowly construed to be a dictum of the Supreme Court of Iowa enunciating the old ruling of nonliability in Larrabee v. Des Moines Tent & Awning Co., 1920, 189 Iowa 319, 178 N.W. 373. * * *

Of course it is not necessary that a case be explicitly overruled in order to lose its persuasive force as an indication of what the law is. A decision may become so overloaded with illogical exceptions that by erosion of time it may lose its persuasive or binding force even in the inferior courts of the same jurisdiction. And where, as in Ford Motor Co. v. Myers, the Supreme Court of Mississippi, twenty or thirty years ago, applied an old rule which has since been generally discredited elsewhere, it is relevant to consider what the Supreme Court of Mississippi has subsequently said on the point. * * * We think that appellant herein rightly stresses the importance of E.I. Du Pont De Nemours & Co. v. Ladner, 1954, 221 Miss. 378, 73 So.2d 249. In that very recent case, the Supreme Court of Mississippi was able to dispose of the particular issue on another ground without the necessity of expressly overruling its earlier decision in Ford Motor Co. v. Myers. But the court did take occasion, in a long and careful opinion, to indicate its awareness of the modern trend in the area * * *. And it quoted, with apparent approval, many more recent authorities in support of the "modern doctrine." * * * We think it is fair to infer from this latest expression by the Supreme Court of Mississippi that it is prepared to reconsider and revise the rule it applied in Ford Motor Co. v. Myers whenever it may have before it a case that squarely presents the issue. We have no doubt that when this occasion does come to pass, the Supreme Court of Mississippi will declare itself in agreement with the more enlightened and generally accepted modern doctrine.

A judgment will be entered vacating the order of the District Court, dismissing the complaint and remanding the case to the District Court for further proceedings not inconsistent with this opinion.

HARTIGAN, CIRCUIT JUDGE (concurring).

I concur in the opinion of the court but I am constrained to comment briefly. We were informed in oral argument by counsel for the appellee that the district court in deciding this case had before it both the Ford and the Du Pont decisions. Moreover, the district court knew from the official Mississippi report that the MacPherson case, then approximately twelve years old, had been considered and rejected by the Mississippi Supreme Court sitting in the Ford case. Therefore, "reluctantly" Judge Day adopted the Ford holding since it, as the only binding and conclusive statement of Mississippi law on the issue, had not been expressly modified or overruled. * * *

We, however, have inferred from pure dicta in the Du Pont case and from the status of the law elsewhere on this issue that Mississippi is prepared to discard the Ford rule and adopt the modern rule. I believe this is a sound inference since the dicta in the Du Pont case though not expressly mentioning Ford, is sufficiently clear and the Ford rule is sufficiently outdated. Yet, in doing so I realize that we present a difficult problem for district judges when they must apply the Erie doctrine to situations wherein the considerations as between conflicting holdings and dicta are not as clearly defined as they are here. The question of how clear dicta must be to prevail over a prior controlling decision does not lend itself to easy solution.

Notes and Questions

1. The history of the privity rule in Mississippi following *Mason* is interesting. Relying heavily on Judge Magruder's opinion, the Fifth Circuit held in Grey v. Hayes-Sammons Chem. Co., 310 F.2d 291 (5th Cir.1962), that under Mississippi law a lack of privity was not a bar to a claim by a Mississippi consumer against a manufacturer of a cotton spray. The Fifth Circuit reached similar conclusions in Necaise v. Chrysler Corp., 335 F.2d 562 (5th Cir.1964), and Putman v. Erie City Mfg. Co., 338 F.2d 911 (5th Cir.1964). Finally, the Mississippi Supreme Court, in State Stove Mfg. Co. v. Hodges, 189 So.2d 113 (Miss.1966), certiorari denied sub nom. Yates v. Hodges, 386 U.S. 912, 87 S.Ct. 860, 17 L.Ed.2d 784 (1967), reconsidered the privity question and overruled its decision in Ford Motor Co. v. Myers. In doing so, however, the court did not cite either the First Circuit's decision in *Mason* or the series of decisions in the Fifth Circuit.

2. What is the basis for Judge Magruder's statement in *Mason:* "Since the injury was inflicted in Mississippi, the district court, no doubt correctly under now familiar authorities, deemed itself to be obliged to apply the Mississippi local law"?

3. In McKENNA v. ORTHO PHARMACEUTICAL CORP., 622 F.2d 657 (3d Cir.), certiorari denied 449 U.S. 976, 101 S.Ct. 387, 66 L.Ed.2d 237 (1980), the plaintiffs brought suit against Ortho Pharmaceutical Corp. (Ortho) for negligence, misrepresentation and products liability. The plaintiff charged that she suffered severe personal injury and permanent disability as a result of ingesting Ortho–Novum, an oral contraceptive manufactured and marketed by Ortho. The action was commenced in a Pennsylvania state court and was removed to the federal district court in Pittsburgh on the defendant's motion. All of the significant events pertinent to the action occurred in Ohio and it was not disputed that the cause of action arose in Ohio and that under Pennsylvania law the substantive law of Ohio governed this action.

Although Pennsylvania courts ordinarily apply the statute of limitations of the forum state, the Pennsylvania "borrowing statute" in effect when the case was tried provided a statutory exception to this rule. It declared:

When a cause of action has been fully barred by the law of the state in which it arose, such bar shall be a complete defense to an action thereon in any of the courts of this Commonwealth.

The district court granted Ortho's motion for a directed verdict on the ground that the action was barred under the statute of limitations. The court, in granting Ortho's motion, reasoned that the Pennsylvania statute borrowed not only Ohio's two year limitation period, but also Ohio's law governing the determination when a cause of action arises. On this basis, it concluded that the statute began to run when the plaintiff developed symptoms and that the cause of action was barred because it was filed more than two years after that time.

On appeal, the plaintiffs argued that this was error because even though the Pennsylvania statute "borrows" the law of Ohio regarding the length of the applicable limitations period, when that limitations period begins must be determined not by Ohio but by Pennsylvania law. In reviewing the district court's conclusion, the Third Circuit stated:

We are persuaded, rather, that the apparent purpose of the Pennsylvania "borrowing statute" requires us to look to the law of the state where the cause of action arose to determine not only the prescribed period of limitations but also the point at which the statute begins to run. In our view, the essential question posed under the "borrowing statute" is whether the action in question is precluded by the laws of the state in which it accrued, and the answer to that question also must be based on the law of the state in which the claim arose. * * * The problem of ascertainment arises when, as here, the highest state court has not yet authoritatively addressed the critical issue. Recent opinions of this court make clear that our disposition of such cases must be governed by a prediction of how the state's highest court would decide were it confronted with the problem. Although some have characterized this assignment as speculative crystal-ball gazing, nonetheless it is a task which we may not decline.

An accurate forecast of Ohio's law, as it would be expressed by its highest court, requires an examination of all relevant sources of that state's law in order to isolate those factors that would inform its decision. * * * In the absence of authority directly on point, decisions by that court in analogous cases provide useful indications of the court's probable disposition of a particular question of law. * * * Considered dicta by the state's highest court may also provide a federal court with reliable indicia of how the state tribunal might rule on a particular question.

Id. at 660–62.

The federal court went on to determine that based on "[a] fair scrutiny of the relevant Ohio precedents with an eye toward the principles and policies underlying them," the Ohio Supreme Court would decide that the applicable statutes of limitation in this case were tolled until the plaintiff knew, or by the exercise of reasonable diligence should have discovered, the cause of her injuries.

4.   It has been suggested that the Supreme Court decision in Commissioner v. Bosch's Estate, 387 U.S. 456, 87 S.Ct. 1776, 18 L.Ed.2d 886 (1967), stands for the proposition that decisions of lower state courts, although entitled to some weight, do not control a federal diversity court's reading of state law. Does such a rule invite a federal judge to circumvent the rule in *Erie?* If intermediate state courts consistently reach the same conclusion on a matter of state law and the state's highest court has not addressed the issue, should not a federal court be obligated to find that the intermediate state courts have determined accurately what the state law is?

Many states' highest courts, like the United States Supreme Court, have considerable discretion in deciding which cases to hear. Should not a federal court view the state's highest court's refusal to hear those cases as an implicit acknowledgement that the lower courts have articulated the state law accurately?

5.   Should a federal court sitting in diversity jurisdiction accord an *unreported* state decision any weight? Would a federal court be bound by a state statute that provided: "Only such cases as are hereafter reported in accordance with the provisions of this section shall be recognized by and receive the official sanction of any court within the state"? See Gustin v. Sun Life Assur. Co., 154 F.2d 961 (6th Cir.), certiorari denied 328 U.S. 866, 66 S.Ct. 1374, 90 L.Ed. 1636 (1946).

6.   What should a federal court do when the courts of the state in which it is sitting have not considered the particular problem before the federal court? Should it stay its own proceeding and allow the litigants to seek a declaratory judgment from a state court? See United Servs. Life Ins. Co. v. Delaney, 328 F.2d 483 (5th Cir.1964). What problems are created by such a procedure? See Agata,

Delaney, Diversity and Delay: Abstention or Abdication?, 4 Houston L.Rev. 422 (1966). May a federal diversity court refuse to accept jurisdiction over such a case? See Meredith v. City of Winter Haven, 320 U.S. 228, 64 S.Ct. 7, 88 L.Ed. 9 (1943); Daily v. Parker, 152 F.2d 174 (7th Cir.1945).

7.   Several states have adopted certification procedures that permit federal courts to petition a state's highest court to rule on an issue of state law upon which the state's highest court has not spoken. Illinois Supreme Court Rule 20, which is set forth in the Supplement, is representative of these statutes. Under what circumstances should a federal court certify a question to the highest court in the state in which it is located? See Arizonans for Official English v. Arizona, 520 U.S. 43, 117 S.Ct. 1055, 137 L.Ed.2d 170 (1997). See also Tunick v. Safir, 209 F.3d 67 (2d Cir.2000). What is the interrelationship between the *Erie* doctrine and such a rule? Consider the following:

> When state law is clear, the task of applying "the law of the State" is relatively straightforward. When state law is unsettled or indeterminate, however, *Erie*'s dual command–that federal courts apply and not declare state law–places federal courts in a precarious position. * * *

> * * * [L]ower federal courts confronted with this dilemma generally attempt to "predict" what rule the highest court of the state would adopt if the question were before it * * *. * * * [T]he federal courts use of the predictive approach is in tension with the principles of judicial federalism adopted in Erie to implement the constitutional structure.

> * * *

> If agents of the state have not adopted rules of decision that provide determinate answers to [legal issues] * * * then arguably there is simply no law to apply * * * and federal courts should rule against the party who bears the burden of persuasion on the question at issue. If a rule of decision applied in federal court does not constitute a command of the state sovereign, then by default the rule in question is * * * a command issued by agents of the federal sovereign. * * *

> * * * [F]ederal courts [could also] simply "apply the forum as [they] infer it presently to be, not as it might come to be." * * * This static approach alleviates the judicial federalism concerns * * * because federal courts cannot be charged with usurping the lawmaking power of the states. * * *

> A potential difficulty * * * with this approach, however, is that it undermin[es] the so-called "twin aims of the *Erie* rule"—to discourage forum shopping and to avoid inequitable administration of the law. * * *

> * * * [F]ederal courts can largely avoid the * * * defects associated with prediction, abstention, and the static approach by employing a presumption in favor of certifying unsettled questions of state law to highest court of the state whenever state law authorizes this procedure.

Clark, *Ascertaining the Laws of the Several States: Positivism and Judicial Federalism After Erie*, 145 U.Pa.L.Rev. 1459, 1461–64 (1997).

8.   In POMERANTZ v. CLARK, 101 F.Supp. 341, 345–46 (D.Mass.1951), a diversity action by policyholders against directors of an insurance company to retrieve for the company certain sums allegedly improvidently and illegally loaned, Judge Wyzanski held that no action was maintainable under Massachusetts law and stated:

In considering whether * * * [to create] an exception to the Massachusetts rule that before bringing a derivative suit a member must first lay his case before the body of members, the never-to-be-forgotten caution is that this Court is not free to render such decision as seems to it equitable, just and in accordance with public policy and responsive to all those jurisprudential criteria which so often enter into what Justice Cardozo called "The Nature of the Judicial Process." A federal judge sitting in a diversity jurisdiction case has not a roving commission to do justice or to develop the law according to his, or what he believes to be the sounder, views. His problem is less philosophical and more psychological. His task is to divine the views of the state court judges. * * *

The eminence of the Massachusetts Supreme Judicial Court, an eminence not surpassed by any American tribunal, is in large measure due to its steadiness, learning and understanding of the durable values long prized in this community. Subtle variations and blurred lines are not characteristic of that court. Principles are announced and adhered to in broad magisterial terms. The emphasis is on precedent and adherence to the older ways, not on creating new causes of action or encouraging the use of novel judicial remedies that have sprung up in less conservative communities. Here abides the ancient faith in the right of men to choose their own associates, make their own arrangements, govern themselves and thus grow in responsibility without much in the way of either hindrance or help from the state. This basic philosophy permeates the Massachusetts rules governing derivative suits * * *.

Compare Judge Friendly's observation in Nolan v. Transocean Air Lines, 276 F.2d 280, 281 (2d Cir.1960): "Our principal task, in this diversity of citizenship case, is to determine what the New York courts would think the California courts would think on an issue about which neither has thought." See generally 19 Wright, Miller & Cooper, *Federal Practice and Procedure: Jurisdiction and Related Matters 2d* § 4507 (1996).

9. Judge Adams wrote in *McKenna* that, when a state's highest court has not directly addressed a particular legal question, a federal court may analyze that state court's decisions in analogous areas to determine the state court's "probable disposition" of the legal question at issue. Suppose, however that recent personnel changes in the state court give a federal court strong reason to believe that older, yet still valid, decisions from analogous areas no longer are adequate indicators. Suppose further that the federal judge believes nonetheless that the best rule is provided by the law previously announced in the analogous areas. How should the federal judge interpret the state law?

10. In FACTORS ETC., INC. v. PRO ARTS, INC., 652 F.2d 278 (2d Cir.1981), certiorari denied 456 U.S. 927, 102 S.Ct. 1973, 72 L.Ed.2d 442 (1982), a federal court sitting in New York was required to apply Tennessee law to the question of whether Elvis Presley's right of publicity survived his death. Tennessee state courts had never addressed that issue, but the Sixth Circuit (the circuit encompassing Tennessee) had decided a similar case. The Second Circuit held that the District Court, in such a circumstance, was bound by the Sixth Circuit's view of Tennessee law. The court reasoned that the Sixth Circuit was more familiar with Tennessee law since it frequently was required to interpret Tennessee law.

The dissent argued that there was no reason to follow the Sixth Circuit's views when they were not derived from the laws or decisions of the state. Since the Sixth Circuit was only espousing what it considered the preferable common-law rule, its decision should be accorded no greater deference than that given to any circuit court's views. The dissent also pointed out that, considering the physical size of the circuit and the relatively small number of diversity cases appealed to the court, the Sixth Circuit was unlikely to have any special familiarity with Tennessee law.

Which position is correct? Or are both incorrect in that the relevant question is not what Tennessee's law is, but, rather, what would a New York state court think that Tennessee's law is? If the relevant view is that of a New York state court, is it not likely that, in the absence of a Tennessee precedent, New York would find a way to justify using New York's rule on the issue? See Note, *Circuit Court of Appeals Must Accord Conclusive Deference to Another Circuit: Factors Etc., Inc. v. Pro Arts, Inc.,* 67 Cornell L.Rev. 415 (1982).

By the time the District Court heard the case on remand from the Second Circuit, a Tennessee court had addressed the issue. Accordingly, the District Court applied the Tennessee court's holding to the facts of the case. See 562 F.Supp. 304 (S.D.N.Y.1983).

11. Does the sometimes erroneous interpretation of state law by federal diversity courts suggest an argument for abolishing diversity jurisdiction? Consider the following:

> Until corrected by the state supreme court, such incorrect predictions inevitably skew the decisions of persons and businesses who rely on them and inequitably affect the losing federal litigant who cannot appeal the decision to the state supreme court; they may even mislead lower state courts that may be inclined to accept federal predictions as applicable precedent. Indeed, some evidence suggests that federal courts have shown a preference for citing federal decisions on state law instead of state decisions at rates approaching pre-Erie levels. * * *

> Consider then the anomalous position of federal judges who are required to render an opinion on uncertain state law when they sit in diversity but must abstain on questions of uncertain state law in federal question cases. * * *

> When federal judges make state law—and we do, by whatever euphemism one chooses to call it—judges who are not selected under the state's system and who are not answerable to its constituency are undertaking an inherent state court function. * * * [T]here is no longer any valid basis to justify the fundamental incompatibility of diversity jurisdiction with the most basic principles of federalism.

Sloviter, *A Federal Judge Views Diversity Jurisdiction Through the Lens of Federalism,* 78 Va.L.Rev. 1671, 1681–82, 1684, 1687 (1992).

SECTION C. FEDERAL "COMMON LAW"

1. THE TRADITIONAL BASES OF FEDERAL COMMON LAW

MELTZER, STATE COURT FORFEITURES OF FEDERAL RIGHTS, 99 Harv.L.Rev. 1128, 1167–71 (1986):

Despite *Erie*'s declaration that "[t]here is no federal general common law," courts have fashioned what Judge Friendly has termed "specialized federal common law" to govern a broad range of areas. Unlike the "spurious" federal common law of the era of Swift v. Tyson, this new federal common law is binding under the supremacy clause in the state courts.

The proper scope of federal common lawmaking is a matter of considerable uncertainty. If *Erie* held that federal court jurisdiction does not in itself provide the power to fashion common law, then some more specialized source must be found for each example of judicial lawmaking. The lawmaking power of federal courts has been viewed as far more limited than that of Congress, for two reasons extrapolated from the constitutional structure. The first is the idea of separation of powers and the supremacy (in matters not governed by the Constitution) of Congress. But perhaps more important is the view that federal law is and should be interstitial, operating against a background of existing bodies of state law. Restricted federal common lawmaking reduces the number of agencies broadly fashioning federal rules of decision, and preserves the primary role for Congress, in which the interests of the states are more strongly represented—and in which inertia is more powerful. Hence, state law is presumptively operative, and if it is to be displaced, ordinarily it must be Congress that does so.

But these structural concerns do not indicate whether federal common law should be considered altogether illegitimate or simply restricted in scope. And important countervailing arguments support the existence of some common law power in the federal courts. Numerous cases raise issues implicating important federal interests that are not specifically governed by a statutory or constitutional rule. Congress could have enacted a rule governing the issue, but may not have done so, because it lacked time, foresight, or a political consensus. The Court has, accordingly, recognized that federal common law may be a " 'necessary expedient.' " Nor does Congress's failure to specify a view on a particular subject indicate that Congress preferred that state rules be followed. Here, as elsewhere, congressional inaction is hardly a clear-cut guide for determining congressional intent, and a failure by a court to make law is itself an important and controversial decision.

Thus, legislative inertia and the political safeguards of federalism are ultimately a double-edged sword. They help explain why the authority to make federal common law is nowhere near so broad as congressional authority to legislate, but also argue that federal common lawmaking may be necessary to fill in the interstices of congressional and constitutional mandates or otherwise to deal with matters of important national concern. Despite extensive discussion in the cases and commentary, no clear standard for judging the appropriateness of federal common law has emerged. [Nonetheless, some general points are] * * * accepted by most cases and commentators.

To begin with, there must be a strong need for the formulation of federal common law in order to justify displacing otherwise operative state rules. Moreover, federal common law, perhaps even more than federal law generally, should be interstitial, building upon the total "corpus juris" of the states. Federal common law fits most easily when it supplements federal constitutional or statutory provisions, providing rules of decision that implement or safeguard the norms embodied in such provisions.

Even where federal interests are implicated, it is often possible, and desirable, to rely upon extant state law for the rule of decision. Such reliance eliminates the need for (and possible difficulties in) fashioning a new rule from scratch, and also promotes intrastate uniformity, which may be of great value. Thus, the decision to formulate federal common law is one of judicial policy, in which a court must find that the advantages of borrowing state law are outweighed by either the need for national uniformity or the inconsistency of state law (either of states generally or of the particular state involved) with federal interests.

Regardless of how the balance is struck in particular states, it is clear that there is a distinctive body of federal common law, and recognized and defensible authority for its creation. * * *

Federal common law has developed in several broad situations. For example, federal common law is used to resolve cases involving important federal interests. These strong federal interests have emerged in several contexts. When interstate disputes have erupted, federal common law has been adopted where it would be unfair to apply the statutes or decisional law from either state. See, e.g., Hinderlider v. La Plata River & Cherry Creek Ditch Co., 304 U.S. 92, 58 S.Ct. 803, 82 L.Ed. 1202 (1938) (dispute over the apportionment of the water of an interstate stream). Similarly, federal common law has become firmly established in the admiralty and maritime contexts, because the desire for a uniform body of substantive law has long been considered of primary importance. See, e.g., Kossick v. United Fruit Co., 365 U.S. 731, 81 S.Ct. 886, 6 L.Ed.2d 56 (1961). And, cases implicating the international relations of the United States have provided another occasion for resort to federal common law, including cases involving commercial disputes between United States citizens and foreign parties. See, e.g., Banco Nacional de Cuba v. Sabbatino, 376 U.S. 398, 84 S.Ct. 923, 11 L.Ed.2d 804 (1964). The various facets of federal common law are discussed in 19 Wright, Miller & Cooper, *Federal Practice and Procedure: Jurisdiction and Related Matters 2d* §§ 4514–4519 (1996).

Another interesting but sometimes confusing use of federal common law occurs in cases involving the legal activities of the United States. These cases often invoke issues concerning the federal government's contract rights, tort liabilities, rights to collect loans and proceeds due to it, or the management of United States bonds and securities.

CLEARFIELD TRUST CO. v. UNITED STATES

Supreme Court of the United States, 1943.
318 U.S. 363, 63 S.Ct. 573, 87 L.Ed. 838.

[A check issued by the United States had been mailed, but was not received by its intended recipient. An unknown person, who presumably had stolen the check, cashed the check at a J.C. Penney store, endorsing it by signing the name of the intended recipient. J.C. Penney in turn endorsed the check to Clearfield Trust, which accepted it. Clearfield then endorsed the check with a guaranty of all prior endorsements, collected the amount of the check from the Federal Reserve and paid it to J.C. Penney. Neither Penney nor Clearfield had suspected forgery. Federal officials did not inform any of the interested parties of the forgery until eight months after they had learned that the intended recipient had not received the check.

The United States sued Clearfield on Clearfield's express guaranty of prior endorsements. The District Court held that the rights of the parties were to be determined by the law of Pennsylvania. Since the United States had unreasonably delayed giving notice of the forgery, it was barred from recovery under Pennsylvania law and the District Court dismissed the complaint. The Court of Appeals for the Third Circuit reversed.]

Certiorari to the Circuit Court of Appeals for the Third Circuit.

Mr. Justice Douglas delivered the opinion of the Court.

* * *

We agree with the Circuit Court of Appeals that the rule of Erie R. Co. v. Tompkins * * * does not apply to this action. The rights and duties of the United States on commercial paper which it issues are governed by federal rather than local law. When the United States disburses its funds or pays its debts, it is exercising a constitutional function or power. This check was issued for services performed under the Federal Emergency Relief Act of 1935 * * *. The authority to issue the check had its origin in the Constitution and the statutes of the United States and was in no way dependent on the laws of Pennsylvania or of any other state. * * * The duties imposed upon the United States and the rights acquired by it as a result of the issuance find their roots in the same federal sources.[2] * * * In absence of an applicable Act of Congress it is for the federal courts to fashion the governing rule of law according to their own standards. * * *

In our choice of the applicable federal rule we have occasionally selected state law. * * * But reasons which may make state law at times the appropriate federal rule are singularly inappropriate here. The issuance of commercial paper by the United States is on a vast scale and transactions in that paper from issuance to payment will commonly occur in several states. The application of state law, even without the conflict of laws rules of the forum, would subject the rights and duties of the United States to exceptional uncertainty. It would lead to great diversity in results by making identical transactions subject to the vagaries of the laws of the several states. The desirability of a uniform rule is plain. And while the federal law merchant developed for about a century under the regime of Swift v. Tyson * * * represented general commercial law rather than a choice of a federal rule designed to protect a federal right, it nevertheless stands as a convenient source of reference for fashioning federal rules applicable to these federal questions.

United States v. National Exchange Bank, 214 U.S. 302, 29 S.Ct. 665, 53 L.Ed. 1006 * * * falls in that category. The Court held that the United States could recover as drawee from one who presented for payment a pension check

2. Various Treasury Regulations govern the payment and endorsement of government checks and warrants and the reimbursement of the Treasurer of the United States by Federal Reserve banks and member bank depositories on payment of checks or warrants bearing a forged endorsement. * * * Forgery of the check was an offense against the United States. * * *

on which the name of the payee had been forged, in spite of a protracted delay on the part of the United States in giving notice of the forgery. * * *

The *National Exchange Bank* case went no further than to hold that prompt notice of the discovery of the forgery was not a condition precedent to suit. It did not reach the question whether lack of prompt notice might be a defense. We think it may. If it is shown that the drawee on learning of the forgery did not give prompt notice of it and that damage resulted, recovery by the drawee is barred. * * * The fact that the drawee is the United States and the laches those of its employees are not material. * * * The United States as drawee of commercial paper stands in no different light than any other drawee. As stated in United States v. National Exchange Bank * * *, "The United States does business on business terms." It is not excepted from the general rules governing the rights and duties of drawees "by the largeness of its dealings and its having to employ agents to do what if done by a principal in person would leave no room for doubt." * * * But the damage occasioned by the delay must be established and not left to conjecture. Cases * * * place the burden on the drawee of giving prompt notice of the forgery—injury to the defendant being presumed by the mere fact of delay. * * * But we do not think that he who accepts a forged signature of a payee deserves that preferred treatment. It is his neglect or error in accepting the forger's signature which occasions the loss. * * * He should be allowed to shift that loss to the drawee only on a clear showing that the drawee's delay in notifying him of the forgery caused him damage. * * * No such damage has been shown by Clearfield Trust Co. who so far as appears can still recover from J.C. Penney Co. The only showing on the part of the latter is contained in the stipulation to the effect that if a check cashed for a customer is returned unpaid or for reclamation a short time after the date on which it is cashed, the employees can often locate the person who cashed it. It is further stipulated that when J.C. Penney Co. was notified of the forgery in the present case none of its employees was able to remember anything about the transaction or check in question. The inference is that the more prompt the notice the more likely the detection of the forger. But that falls short of a showing that the delay caused a manifest loss. * * * It is but another way of saying that mere delay is enough.

Affirmed.

Mr. Justice Murphy and Mr. Justice Rutledge did not participate in the consideration or decision of this case.

Notes and Questions

1. Why doesn't the *Clearfield* Court mention the Rules of Decision Act?

2. Once a court has decided to use federal common law, how does the court determine what the appropriate federal law should be? In UNITED STATES v. KIMBELL FOODS, INC., 440 U.S. 715, 99 S.Ct. 1448, 59 L.Ed.2d 711 (1979), the question arose whether federal or state rules should be used for Small Business Administration and Farmers Home Administration loans in order to determine whether the federal government or a private creditor would be able to collect first on a loan. In addressing this issue, the Court embarked upon a two-step analysis. First, the Court interpreted *Clearfield* broadly as permitting federal courts to

develop federal law for "questions involving the rights of the United States arising under nationwide federal programs." Thus, the Court held that "the priority of liens stemming from federal lending programs must be determined with reference to federal law" and that the "SBA and FHA unquestionably perform federal functions within the meaning of *Clearfield*."

Having decided that federal law controlled, the Court turned to the second and more challenging task of determining the content of the federal law.

> Controversies directly affecting the operations of federal programs, although governed by federal law, do not inevitably require resort to uniform federal rules. * * * Whether to adopt state law or to fashion a nationwide federal rule is a matter of judicial policy "dependent upon a variety of considerations always relevant to the nature of the specific governmental interests and to the effects upon them of applying state law." * * *

> Undoubtedly, federal programs that "by their nature are and must be uniform in character throughout the Nation" necessitate formulation of controlling federal rules. * * * Conversely, when there is little need for a nationally uniform body of law, state law may be incorporated as the federal rule of decision. Apart from considerations of uniformity, we must also determine whether application of state law would frustrate specific objectives of the federal programs. If so, we must fashion special rules solicitous of those federal interests. Finally, our choice-of-law inquiry must consider the extent to which application of a federal rule would disrupt commercial relationships predicated on state law. * * *

Id. at 727–30, 99 S.Ct. at 1458–59, 59 L.Ed.2d at 723–25.

After weighing these factors with respect to priority rules for the SBA and FHA loans, the Court held that there was no need for an independent federal rule. Thus, the Court chose to adopt the state rule as federal law rather than to develop a separate federal rule.

If a federal court chooses to adopt state law as the federal law in a given situation, should the method for determining state law differ from the process outlined in *Ortho Pharmaceutical*, Note 3, p. 427, supra?

3. The *Clearfield* decision has been criticized for adopting federal common law in a situation in which there were insufficient considerations to justify a uniform federal rule. As one commentator explains, the presence of a federal function, the issuance of commercial paper, merely signals that federal law may be appropriate. A federal interest in uniformity does not follow automatically:

> * * * [T]his interest in uniformity [in the law of commercial paper] is open to serious question. The Government cannot be overly inconvenienced in issuing commercial paper when dozens of major corporations issue it on a nationwide scale, apparently without varying state law causing undue difficulties. The Treasury has never broached the subject of facilitating its operations with uniform national rules. And the work of the Treasury is left unchanged by *Clearfield* since it is only through negligence that it will fail to give warning of a known forgery.

> The attainability of uniform rules is often ignored just as the importance of them is overstated. The Supreme Court lacks the time to erect common law principles governing everything from the construction of government contracts to the issuance of United States commercial paper. The barriers to uniformity resulting from divergence of opinion among courts of appeals may

be intensified when state courts exercise their concurrent jurisdiction over these cases. Some state courts treat lower federal court rulings as binding and may follow its interpretation of the federal common law, but some do not. Nor is a state court bound by the interpretation of its local circuit; thus a general lack of uniformity may be complicated by a situation conflicting with the policy of *Erie* in which the federal common law applicable depends upon the forum in which suit was brought.

[Another] interest in uniformity which generally cuts against the creation of federal common law is that of individuals who would prefer to look to but one source of law to govern the same or similar transactions. The failure to consider this interest is a further problem with the *Clearfield* decision. As Judge Friendly has noted, it is far from clear why the convenience uniform rules afforded the Treasury should be placed ahead of the inconvenience to Pennsylvanians of having two systems of law govern similar commercial paper moving through identical channels.

Note, *Federal Common Law*, 82 Harv.L.Rev. 1512, 1530–31 (1969).

4. Courts have not perceived a need for federal common law in every case involving commercial paper. In BANK OF AMERICA NATIONAL TRUST & SAVINGS ASSOCIATION v. PARNELL, 352 U.S. 29, 77 S.Ct. 119, 1 L.Ed.2d 93 (1956), the Bank of America brought a diversity action alleging that two individual defendants (Parnell and Rocco) and two corporate defendants (First National Bank of Indiana and Federal Reserve Bank of Cleveland) had converted 73 Home Owners' Loan Corporation bonds which belonged to Bank of America. The bonds were bearer bonds with payment guaranteed by the United States. They carried interest coupons calling for semi-annual payment. They were due to mature May 1, 1952, but pursuant to their terms, had been called on or about May 1, 1944. On May 2, 1944, the bonds disappeared while petitioner was getting them ready for presentation to the Federal Reserve Bank for payment. In 1948 they were presented to the First National Bank for payment by Parnell on behalf of Rocco. The First National Bank forwarded them to the Federal Reserve Bank of Cleveland. It cashed them and paid the First National Bank, which issued cashier's checks to Parnell. Parnell then turned the proceeds over to Rocco less a fee—there was conflicting testimony as to whether the fee was nominal or substantial.

The principal issue at the trial was whether the defendants took the bonds in good faith, without knowledge or notice of the defect in title. On this issue the trial judge charged the jury based on state law. The jury brought in verdicts for Bank of America against the defendants.

On appeal, the Court of Appeals for the Third Circuit, sitting *en banc,* reversed. It held that the District Court had erred in treating the case as an ordinary diversity case and in regarding state law as governing the rights of the parties and the burden of proof. It considered *Clearfield Trust* controlling and held that federal law placed the burden of proof on Bank of America to show notice and lack of good faith on the part of the defendants. As the Third Circuit saw it, there was no evidence of bad faith by the First National Bank since the bonds were not "overdue" as a matter of federal law when presented to it; the court therefore directed entry of judgment for First National. On the other hand, the Circuit Court concluded that there was evidence of bad faith on the part of Parnell; thus, it ordered a new trial because of the erroneous instructions.

The Supreme Court reversed, saying:

Securities issued by the Government generate immediate interests of the Government. * * * But they also radiate interests in transactions between private parties. The present litigation is purely between private parties and does not touch the rights and duties of the United States. The only possible interest of the United States in a situation like the one here, exclusively involving the transfer of Government paper between private persons, is that the floating of securities of the United States might somehow or other be adversely affected by the local rule of a particular State regarding the liability of a converter. This is far too speculative, far too remote a possibility to justify the application of federal law to transactions essentially of local concern.

We do not mean to imply that litigation with respect to Government paper necessarily precludes the presence of a federal interest, to be governed by federal law, in all situations merely because it is a suit between private parties, or that it is beyond the range of federal legislation to deal comprehensively with Government paper. We do not of course foreclose such judicial or legislative action in appropriate situations by concluding that this controversy over burden of proof and good faith represents too essentially a private transaction not to be dealt with by the local law of Pennsylvania where the transactions took place. Federal law of course governs the interpretation of the nature of the rights and obligations created by the Government bonds themselves. A decision with respect to the "overdueness" of the bonds is therefore a matter of federal law, which, in view of our holding, we need not elucidate.

Id. at 33–34, 77 S.Ct. at 121–22, 1 L.Ed.2d at 96–97.

The majority view did not go unchallenged. Justices Black and Douglas dissented:

We believe that the "federal law merchant," which Clearfield Trust Co. v. United States * * * held applicable to transactions in the commercial paper of the United States, should be applicable to all transactions in that paper. * * * Not until today has a distinction been drawn between suits by the United States on that paper and suits by other parties to it. But the Court does not stop there. Because this is "essentially a private transaction," it is to be governed by local law. Yet the nature of the rights and obligations created by commercial paper of the United States Government is said to be controlled by federal law. Thus, federal law is to govern some portion of a dispute between private parties, while that portion of the dispute which is "essentially of local concern" is to be governed by local law. The uncertainties which inhere in such a dichotomy are obvious. * * *

The virtue of a uniform law governing bonds, notes, and other paper issued by the United States is that it provides a certain and definite guide to the rights of all parties rather than subjecting them to the vagaries of the laws of many States. The business of the United States will go on without that uniformity. But the policy surrounding our choice of laws is concerned with the convenience, certainty, and definiteness in having one set of rules governing the rights of all parties to government paper, as contrasted to multiple rules. If the rule of the *Clearfield Trust* case is to be abandoned as to some parties, it should be abandoned as to all and we should start afresh on this problem.

Id. at 34, 77 S.Ct. at 122, 1 L.Ed.2d at 97–98.

MIREE v. DEKALB COUNTY

Supreme Court of the United States, 1977.
433 U.S. 25, 97 S.Ct. 2490, 53 L.Ed.2d 557.

Certiorari to the United States Court of Appeals for the Fifth Circuit.

Mr. Justice Rehnquist delivered the opinion of the Court.

These consolidated cases arise out of the 1973 crash of a Lear Jet shortly after takeoff from the DeKalb–Peachtree Airport. The United States Court of Appeals for the Fifth Circuit, en banc, affirmed the dismissal of petitioners' complaint against respondent DeKalb County (hereafter respondent), holding that principles of federal common law were applicable to the resolution of petitioners' breach-of-contract claim. We granted certiorari to consider whether federal or state law should have been applied to that claim; we conclude that the latter should govern.

I

Petitioners are, respectively, the survivors of deceased passengers, the assignee of the jet aircraft owner, and a burn victim. They brought separate lawsuits, later consolidated, against respondent in the United States District Court for the Northern District of Georgia. The basis for federal jurisdiction was diversity of citizenship, 28 U.S.C. § 1332, and the complaints asserted that respondent was liable on three independent theories: negligence, nuisance, and breach of contract. The District Court granted respondent's motion to dismiss each of these claims. The courts below have unanimously agreed that the negligence and nuisance theories are without merit; only the propriety of the dismissal of the contract claims remains in the cases.

Petitioners seek to impose liability on respondent as third-party beneficiaries of contracts between it and the Federal Aviation Administration (FAA). Their complaints allege that respondent entered into six grant agreements with the FAA. * * * Under the terms of the contracts respondent agreed to

> take action to restrict the use of land adjacent to or in the immediate vicinity of the Airport to activities and purposes compatible with normal airport operations including landing and takeoff of aircraft. * * *

Petitioners assert that respondent breached the FAA contracts by owning and maintaining a garbage dump adjacent to the airport, and that the cause of the crash was the ingestion of birds swarming from the dump into the jet engines of the aircraft.

Applying Georgia law, the District Court found that petitioners' claims as third-party beneficiaries under the FAA contracts were barred by the county's governmental immunity, and dismissed the complaints under Fed.Rule Civ. Proc. 12(b)(6). A divided panel of the Court of Appeals decided that under state law petitioners could sue as third-party beneficiaries and that governmental immunity would not bar the suit. * * * The dissenting judge argued that the court should have applied federal rather than state law; he concluded that under the principles of federal common law the petitioners in this case did not have standing to sue as third-party beneficiaries of the contracts. Sitting en banc, the Court of Appeals reversed the panel on the breach-of-contract issue and adopted the panel dissent on this point as its opinion. * * * Judge Morgan, who had written the panel opinion, argued for five dissenters that there was no identifiable federal interest in the outcome of this diversity case, and thus that federal common law had no applicability.

II

Since the only basis of federal jurisdiction alleged for petitioners' claim against respondent is diversity of citizenship, the case would unquestionably be governed by Georgia law, Erie R. Co. v. Tompkins, * * * but for the fact that the United States is a party to the contracts in question, entered into pursuant to federal statute. * * * The en banc majority of the Court of Appeals adopted, by reference, the view that, given these factors, application of federal common law was required * * *.

We do not agree with the conclusion of the Court of Appeals. The litigation before us raises no question regarding the liability of the United States or the responsibilities of the United States under the contracts. The relevant inquiry is a narrow one: whether petitioners as third-party beneficiaries of the contracts have standing to sue respondent. While federal common law may govern even in diversity cases where a uniform national rule is necessary to further the interests of the Federal Government, Clearfield Trust Co. v. United States * * *, the application of federal common law to resolve the issue presented here would promote no federal interests even approaching the magnitude of those found in *Clearfield Trust*. * * *

* * * [I]n this case, the resolution of petitioners' breach-of-contract claim against respondent will have no direct effect upon the United States or its Treasury. The Solicitor General, waiving his right to respond in these cases, advised us [that the United States' "interests would not be directly affected" by the resolution of these issues] * * * . The operations of the United States in connection with FAA grants such as these are undoubtedly of considerable magnitude. However, we see no reason for concluding that these operations would be burdened or subjected to uncertainty by variant state-law interpretations regarding whether those with whom the United States contracts might be sued by third-party beneficiaries to the contracts. Since only the rights of private litigants are at issue here, we find the *Clearfield Trust* rationale inapplicable.

We think our conclusion that these cases do not fit within the *Clearfield Trust* rule follows from the Court's later decision in Bank of America Nat. Trust & Sav. Assn. v. Parnell, * * * in which the Court declined to apply that rule in a fact situation analogous to this one. * * *

* * *

The parallel between *Parnell* and these cases is obvious. The question of whether petitioners may sue respondent does not require decision under federal common law since the litigation is among private parties and no substantial rights or duties of the United States hinge on its outcome. On the other hand, nothing we say here forecloses the applicability of federal common law in interpreting the rights and duties of the United States under federal contracts.

Nor is the fact that the United States has a substantial interest in regulating aircraft travel and promoting air travel safety sufficient, given the narrow question before us, to call into play the rule of *Clearfield Trust.* * * * The question of whether private parties may, as third-party beneficiaries, sue a municipality for breach of the FAA contracts involves this federal interest only insofar as such lawsuits might be thought to advance federal aviation policy by inducing compliance with FAA safety provisions. However, even assuming the correctness of this notion, we adhere to the [view] that the issue of whether to displace state law on an issue such as this is primarily a decision for Congress. Congress has chosen not to do so in this case.[5] Actually the application of federal common law, as interpreted by the Court of Appeals here would frustrate this federal interest *pro tanto*, since that court held that this breach-of-contract lawsuit would not lie under federal law. On the other hand, at least in the opinion of the majority of the panel below, Georgia law would countenance the action. * * * We conclude that any federal interest in the outcome of the question before us "is far too speculative, far too remote a possibility to justify the application of federal law to transactions essentially of local concern." Parnell, 352 U.S., at 33–34, 77 S.Ct., at 121.

Although we have determined that Georgia law should be applied to the question raised by respondent's motion to dismiss, we shall not undertake to decide the correct outcome under Georgia law. * * * We therefore vacate the judgment and remand to the Court of Appeals for consideration of the claim under applicable Georgia law.

* * *

[CHIEF JUSTICE BURGER concurred in the judgment.]

Notes and Questions

1. In KOHR v. ALLEGHENY AIRLINES, INC., 504 F.2d 400 (7th Cir.1974), certiorari denied sub nom. Forth Corp. v. Allegheny Airlines, Inc., 421 U.S. 978, 95 S.Ct. 1980, 44 L.Ed.2d 470 (1975), an Allegheny Airlines jet and an aircraft owned by a corporation and operated by a student pilot were involved in a mid-air collision. The crash took place over Indiana. The collision totally destroyed both aircraft and killed all 83 occupants. The United States was involved because at the time of the crash the Allegheny jet was adhering to air traffic control radar directions from an employee of the Federal Aviation Administration.

Separate actions were filed in various federal district courts on behalf of the estates of almost all of the passengers against the corporation, the estate of the student pilot, Allegheny Airlines, and the United States. Although not all of the suits had been commenced in Indiana, the Judicial Panel on Multidistrict Litigation consolidated the suits in the Indiana district court. The United States and Allegheny filed cross claims seeking indemnity and contribution from the corporation and the estate of the student pilot.

The District Court held that Indiana law governed the indemnity and contribution claims, and that this law precluded recovery. The court arrived at this holding by the standard practice of applying the choice-of-law rule of the state in

---

5. The Congress has considered, but not passed, a bill to provide for a federal cause of action arising out of aircraft disasters. * * *

which it sat (Indiana, in this case). That rule in turn referred the court to Indiana substantive law. The Court of Appeals reversed in part and remanded the case, holding that federal law governed:

> The basis for imposing a federal law of contribution and indemnity is what we perceive to be the predominant, indeed almost exclusive, interest of the federal government in regulating the affairs of the nation's airways. Moreover, the imposition of a federal rule of contribution and indemnity serves a second purpose of eliminating inconsistency of result in similar collision occurrences as well as within the same occurrence due to the application of differing state laws on contribution and indemnity. Given the prevailing federal interest in uniform air law regulation, we deem it desirable that a federal rule of contribution and indemnity be applied.

> * * * With the passage of the Federal Aviation Act of 1958, 49 U.S.C. § 1301 et seq., Congress expressed the view that the control of aviation should rest exclusively in the hands of the federal government. * * * The explicit objective of the Act is to foster the development of air commerce. 49 U.S.C. § 1346. To that end, it has been recognized that the principal purpose of the Act is to create one unified system of flight rules and to centralize in the Administrator of the Federal Aviation Administration the power to promulgate rules for the safe and efficient use of the country's airspace. * * * When the notion of federal preemption over aviation is viewed in combination with the fact that this litigation ensues from a mid-air collision occurring in national airspace, the Government is a party to the action pursuant to the Federal Tort Claims Act (28 U.S.C. § 1346(b) et seq.) and that this litigation has since its inception been subject to the supervision of the Judicial Panel created by the Multidistrict Litigation Act (28 U.S.C. § 1407 et seq.), there is no perceptible reason why federal law should not be applied to determine the rights and liabilities of the parties involved. The interest of the state wherein the fortuitous event of the collision occurred is slight as compared to the dominant federal interest. Accordingly, the rights and liabilities of Allegheny and the United States are peculiarly federal in nature and are to be governed by a federal rule of contribution and indemnity.

Id. at 403–04. How might *Kohr* and *Miree* be reconciled? Does *Miree* overrule *Kohr*?

2. What factors persuaded the court in *Kohr* to apply federal common law? Suppose the case had involved the crash of a non-commercial plane on an intrastate flight that resulted in the deaths of four people. Would the federal interest in regulating air space demand the application of federal common law in this situation? See Smith v. Cessna Aircraft Corp., 428 F.Supp. 1285 (N.D.Ill. 1977).

3. Mass tort disasters easily can become unmanageable for a federal court sitting in diversity jurisdiction. Should a federal court, in the interest of judicial economy, develop one general law to cover the situation? Would it have the authority under either Article III or statute to do so?

In IN RE "AGENT ORANGE" PRODUCT LIABILITY LITIGATION, 580 F.Supp. 690 (E.D.N.Y.1984), the court considered the problem of a nationwide class action involving veterans from all over the country who alleged injury resulting from the use of toxic defoliants in Viet Nam. It concluded that every state court that would have adjudicated an Agent Orange class action involving plaintiffs from many states would have decided that a national rule of decision would have been adopted by all other state courts adjudicating this type of case. The need for a uniform rule of decision, the unique relationship between the United States and its servicemen, and the special relationship between the United States and its defense would have compelled such adoption.

* * * [A] state court passing on the claims of an individual or a group of veterans might well recognize the unfairness in treating differently legally identical claims involving servicemen who fought a difficult foreign war shoulder-to-shoulder and were exposed to virtually identical risks. As the Supreme Court stated in a related context, because "the Armed Services perform a unique, nationwide function in protecting the security of the United States," it makes "little sense for the Government's liability to members of the Armed Services [to be] dependent on the fortuity of where the soldier happened to be stationed at the time of his injury." * * *

It quickly becomes apparent that it is impossible through sensible application of Restatement (Second) choice of law doctrine or analysis to identify the interest of any one state as being sufficiently greater than that of any others to a degree sufficient to justify the application of that state's law in resolving the issues in this litigation. Any narrow and mechanical state choice of law system simply collapses under the weight of the multiplicity of contacts, policies and unarticulated or conflicting state interests in this unique case. A state court, therefore, because of its inability to identify and select any other state's law to be applied as the rule of decision and because of the need for uniformity across the country, would seek to divine what the national rule of decision with regard to product liability law would be so that such law would appropriately reflect the national and international characteristics of this case. By contrast, the application of an individual state's law rather than a federal law or a national consensus law would be irrational and unfair.

* * *

The policies of the United States, broadly speaking, parallel the states': on the one hand, it has a policy of compensating servicemen who are injured in the course of military service. On the other hand, there is the policy expressed by the government contract defense of insulating defense contractors who merely produced military equipment according to the specifications set forth by the government. * * * How the balance should be struck in this case between those two conflicting policies need not be decided at this point. What is important is that these federal policies are far more specific than those of the states and the national interest in this litigation is far greater than that of any individual state. * * *

Id. at 703.

4. Why doesn't the Court in *Miree* use the two-step technique outlined in *Kimbell Foods*, Note 2, p. 435, supra?

5. *Miree* raises the question whether plaintiffs have standing to sue as third-party beneficiaries of a federal government contract. This question implicates both general contract law (does a third-party beneficiary of a contract have a right to sue for breach of contract?) and the interpretation of the particular contract at issue. Is the Court in *Miree* holding that state law governs both of these issues? Should it?

2. INTERSTITIAL FEDERAL COMMON LAW

One of the most challenging contexts of federal common lawmaking involves statutes that express national policy in a particular area but leave one or more of the specifics to be developed by the federal courts. Two questions typically arise in these cases. First, is the particular statutory gap at issue one that the federal courts should fill? If the answer is yes, on what sources should a federal court rely in order to derive the law? The answers to these questions can be crucial in shaping the overall national policy involved in the statute.

LAMPF, PLEVA, LIPKIND, PRUPIS & PETIGROW v. GILBERTSON

Supreme Court of the United States, 1991.
501 U.S. 350, 111 S.Ct. 2773, 115 L.Ed.2d 321.

Certiorari to the United States Court of Appeals for the Ninth Circuit.

JUSTICE BLACKMUN delivered the opinion of the Court, except as to Part II–A.

In this litigation we must determine which statute of limitations is applicable to a private suit brought pursuant to § 10(b) of the Securities Exchange Act of 1934 * * * and to Securities and Exchange Commission Rule 10b–5 * * * promulgated thereunder.

I

The controversy arises from the sale of seven Connecticut limited partnerships formed for the purpose of purchasing and leasing computer hardware and software. Petitioner Lampf, Pleva, Lipkind, Prupis & Petigrow is a West Orange, N.J., law firm that aided in organizing the partnerships and that provided additional legal services, including the preparation of opinion letters addressing the tax consequences of investing in the partnerships. The several plaintiff-respondents purchased units in one or more of the partnerships during the years 1979 through 1981 with the expectation of realizing federal income tax benefits therefrom.

The partnerships failed, due in part to the technological obsolescence of their wares. In late 1982 and early 1983, plaintiff-respondents received notice that the United States Internal Revenue Service was investigating the partnerships. The IRS subsequently disallowed the claimed tax benefits because of overvaluation of partnership assets and lack of profit motive.

On November 3, 1986, and June 4, 1987, plaintiff-respondents filed their respective complaints in the United States District Court for the District of Oregon, naming as defendants petitioner and others involved in the preparation of offering memoranda for the partnerships. The complaints alleged that plaintiff-respondents were induced to invest in the partnerships by misrepresentations in the offering memoranda, in violation of, among other things, § 10(b) of the 1934 Act and Rule 10b–5. * * * Plaintiff-respondents asserted that they became aware of the alleged misrepresentations only in 1985 following the disallowance by the IRS of the tax benefits claimed.

After consolidating the actions for discovery and pretrial proceedings, the District Court granted summary judgment for the defendants on the ground that the complaints were not timely filed. * * * Following precedent of its controlling court, * * * the District Court ruled that the securities claims were governed by the state statute of limitations for the most analogous forum-state cause of action. The court determined this to be Oregon's 2-year limitations period for fraud claims. * * * The court found that reports to plaintiff-respondents detailing the declining financial status of each partnership and allegations of misconduct made known to the general partners put plaintiff-respondents on "inquiry notice" of the possibility of fraud as early as October 1982. * * * The court also ruled that the distribution of certain fiscal reports and the installation of a general partner previously associated with the defendants did not constitute fraudulent concealment sufficient to toll the statute of limitations. Applying the Oregon statute to the facts underlying plaintiff-respondents' claims, the District Court determined that each complaint was time barred.

The Court of Appeals for the Ninth Circuit reversed and remanded the cases. * * * In its unpublished opinion, the Court of Appeals found that unresolved factual issues as to when plaintiff-respondents discovered or should have discovered the alleged fraud precluded summary judgment. Then, as did the District Court, it selected the 2-year Oregon limitations period. In so doing, it implicitly rejected petitioner's argument that a federal limitations period should apply to Rule 10b–5 claims. * * * In view of the divergence of opinion among the Circuits regarding the proper limitations period for Rule 10b–5 claims, we granted certiorari to address this important issue. * * *

II

Plaintiff-respondents maintain that the Court of Appeals correctly identified common-law fraud as the source from which § 10(b) limitations should be derived. They submit that the underlying policies and practicalities of § 10(b) litigation do not justify a departure from the traditional practice of "borrowing" analogous state-law statutes of limitations. Petitioner, on the other hand, argues that a federal period is appropriate, contending that we must look to the "1–and–3–year" structure applicable to the express causes of action in § 13 of the Securities Act of 1933 * * * and to certain of the express actions in the 1934 Act.[2] * * * The Solicitor General, appearing on behalf of the Securities and Exchange Commission, agrees that use of a federal period is indicated, but urges the application of the 5-year statute of repose specified in § 20A of the 1934 Act. * * * The 5-year period, it is said, accords with "Congress's most recent views on the accommodation of competing interests, provides the closest federal analogy, and promises to yield the best practical and policy results in Rule 10b–5 litigation." * * * For the reasons discussed below, we agree that a uniform federal period is indicated, but we hold that the express causes of action contained in the 1933 and 1934 Acts provide the source.

---

2. Although not identical in language, all these relate to one year after discovery and to three years after violation.

A

It is the usual rule that when Congress has failed to provide a statute of limitations for a federal cause of action, a court "borrows" or "absorbs" the local time limitation most analogous to the case at hand. * * * This practice, derived from the Rules of Decision Act * * *, has enjoyed sufficient longevity that we may assume that, in enacting remedial legislation, Congress ordinarily "intends by its silence that we borrow state law." Agency Holding Corp. v. Malley–Duff & Associates, Inc., 483 U.S. 143, 147, 107 S.Ct. 2759, 2762, 97 L.Ed.2d 121 (1987).

The rule, however, is not without exception. We have recognized that a state legislature rarely enacts a limitations period with federal interests in mind, * * * and when the operation of a state limitations period would frustrate the policies embraced by the federal enactment, this Court has looked to federal law for a suitable period. * * * These departures from the state-borrowing doctrine have been motivated by this Court's conclusion that it would be "inappropriate to conclude that Congress would choose to adopt state rules at odds with the purpose or operation of federal substantive law." * * *

Rooted as it is in the expectations of Congress, the "state-borrowing doctrine" may not be lightly abandoned. We have described federal borrowing as "a closely circumscribed exception," to be made "only 'when a rule from elsewhere in federal law clearly provides a closer analogy than available state statutes, and when the federal policies at stake and the practicalities of litigation make that rule a significantly more appropriate vehicle for interstitial lawmaking.' " * * *

Predictably, this determination is a delicate one. Recognizing, however, that a period must be selected, our cases do provide some guidance as to whether state or federal borrowing is appropriate and as to the period best suited to the cause of action under consideration. From these cases we are able to distill a hierarchical inquiry for ascertaining the appropriate limitations period for a federal cause of action where Congress has not set the time within which such an action must be brought.

First, the court must determine whether a uniform statute of limitations is to be selected. Where a federal cause of action tends in practice to "encompass numerous and diverse topics and subtopics," * * * such that a single state limitations period may not be consistently applied within a jurisdiction, we have concluded that the federal interests in predictability and judicial economy counsel the adoption of one source, or class of sources, for borrowing purposes. * * * This conclusion ultimately may result in the selection of a single federal provision, * * * or of a single variety of state actions. * * *

Second, assuming a uniform limitations period is appropriate, the court must decide whether this period should be derived from a state or a federal source. In making this judgment, the court should accord particular weight to the geographic character of the claim:

"The multistate nature of [the federal cause of action at issue] indicates the desirability of a uniform federal statute of limitations. With the possibility of multiple state limitations, the use of state statutes would present the danger of forum shopping and, at the very least, would 'virtually guarante[e] ... complex and expensive litigation over what should be a straightforward matter.' " Agency Holding Corp. 483 U.S., at 154, 107 S.Ct., at 2766 * * *.

Finally, even where geographic considerations counsel federal borrowing, the aforementioned presumption of state borrowing requires that a court determine that an analogous federal source truly affords a "closer fit" with the cause of action at issue than does any available state-law source. Although considerations pertinent to this determination will necessarily vary depending upon the federal cause of action and the available state and federal analogues, such factors as commonality of purpose and similarity of elements will be relevant.

B

In the present litigation, our task is complicated by the nontraditional origins of the § 10(b) cause of action. The text of § 10(b) does not provide for private claims. Such claims are of judicial creation, having been implied under the statute for nearly half a century. * * * Although this Court repeatedly has recognized the validity of such claims, * * * we have made no pretense that it was Congress' design to provide the remedy afforded. * * * It is therefore no surprise that the provision contains no statute of limitations.

In a case such as this, we are faced with the awkward task of discerning the limitations period that Congress intended courts to apply to a cause of action it really never knew existed. Fortunately, however, the drafters of § 10(b) have provided guidance.

We conclude that where, as here, the claim asserted is one implied under a statute that also contains an express cause of action with its own time limitation, a court should look first to the statute of origin to ascertain the proper limitations period. We can imagine no clearer indication of how Congress would have balanced the policy considerations implicit in any limitations provision than the balance struck by the same Congress in limiting similar and related protections. * * * When the statute of origin contains comparable express remedial provisions, the inquiry usually should be at an end. Only where no analogous counterpart is available should a court then proceed to apply state-borrowing principles.

In the present litigation, there can be no doubt that the contemporaneously enacted express remedial provisions represent "a federal statute of limitations actually designed to accommodate a balance of interests very similar to that at stake here—a statute that is, in fact, an analogy to the present lawsuit more apt than any of the suggested state-law parallels." * * * The 1934 Act contained a number of express causes of action, each with an explicit limitations period. With only one more restrictive exception, each of these includes some variation of a 1-year period after discovery combined with a 3-year period of repose. In adopting the 1934 Act, the 73d Congress also amended the limitations provision of the 1933 Act, adopting the 1-and 3-year structure for each cause of action contained therein. * * *

C

We therefore conclude that we must reject the Commission's contention that the 5-year period contained in § 20A, added to the 1934 Act in 1988, is more appropriate for § 10(b) actions than is the 1–and–3–year structure in the Act's original remedial provisions. * * * There is no indication that the drafters of § 20A sought to extend [its] enhanced protection to [anything but the insider trading] provisions of the 1934 Act. * * *

Finally, the Commission contends that the adoption of a 3–year period of repose would frustrate the policies underlying § 10(b). The inclusion, however, of the 1–and–3–year structure in the broad range of express securities actions contained in the 1933 and 1934 Acts suggests a congressional determination that a 3–year period is sufficient. * * *

Thus, we agree with every Court of Appeals that has been called upon to apply a federal statute of limitations to a § 10(b) claim that the express causes of action contained in the 1933 and 1934 Acts provide a more appropriate statute of limitations than does § 20A. * * *

Necessarily, we also reject plaintiff-respondents' assertion that state-law fraud provides the closest analogy to § 10(b). The analytical framework we adopt above makes consideration of state-law alternatives unnecessary where Congress has provided an express limitations period for correlative remedies within the same enactment. * * *

IV

Litigation instituted pursuant to § 10(b) and Rule 10b–5 therefore must be commenced within one year after the discovery of the facts constituting the violation and within three years after such violation. As there is no dispute that the earliest of plaintiff-respondents' complaints was filed more than three years after petitioner's alleged misrepresentations, plaintiff-respondents' claims were untimely.

The judgment of the Court of Appeals is reversed.

It is so ordered.

[JUSTICE SCALIA concurred in part and concurred in the judgment. JUSTICE STEVENS dissented in an opinion in which JUSTICE SOUTER joined.]

JUSTICE O'CONNOR, with whom JUSTICE KENNEDY joins, dissenting.

I agree that predictability and judicial economy counsel the adoption of a uniform federal statute of limitations for actions brought under § 10(b) and Rule 10b–5. For the reasons stated by Justice Kennedy, however, I believe we should adopt the 1–year–from–discovery–rule, but not the 3–year period of repose. I write separately only to express my disagreement with the Court's decision in Part IV to apply the new limitations period *in this case.* In holding that respondents' suit is time barred under a limitations period that did not exist before today, the Court departs drastically from our established practice and inflicts an injustice on the respondents. The Court declines to explain its unprecedented decision, or even to acknowledge its unusual character.

Respondents, plaintiffs below, filed this action in Federal District Court in 1986. Everyone agrees that, at that time, their claims were governed by the *state* statute of limitations for the most analogous state cause of action. This was mandated by a solid wall of binding Ninth Circuit authority dating back more than 30 years. * * * The case proceeded in the District Court and the Court of Appeals for almost four years. During that time, the law never changed; the governing limitations period remained the analogous *state* statute of limitations. Notwithstanding respondents' entirely proper reliance on this limitations period, the Court now holds that their suit must be dismissed as untimely because respondents did not comply with a *federal* limitations period announced for the first time today—4½ years after the suit was filed. Quite simply, the Court shuts the courthouse door on respondents because they were unable to predict the future.

* * *

JUSTICE KENNEDY, with whom JUSTICE O'CONNOR joins, dissenting.

I am in full agreement with the Court's determination that, under our precedents, a uniform federal statute of limitations is appropriate for private actions brought under § 10(b) of the Securities Exchange Act of 1934 and that we should adopt as a limitations period the 1–year-from-discovery rule Congress employed in various provisions of the 1934 Act. I must note my disagreement, however, with the Court's simultaneous adoption of the 3–year period of repose Congress also employed in a number of the 1934 Act's provisions. This absolute time bar on private § 10(b) suits conflicts with traditional limitations periods for fraud-based actions, frustrates the usefulness of § 10(b) in protecting defrauded investors, and imposes severe practical limitations on a federal implied cause of action that has become an essential component of the protection the law gives to investors who have been injured by unlawful practices. * * *

Section 10(b) provides investors with significant protections from fraudulent practices in the securities markets. Intended as a comprehensive anti-fraud provision operating even when more specific laws have no application, § 10(b) makes it unlawful to employ in connection with the purchase or sale of any security "any manipulative or deceptive device or contrivance" in violation of the Securities and Exchange Commission's rules. * * * Although Congress gave the Commission the primary role in enforcing this section, private § 10(b) suits constitute "an essential tool for enforcement of the 1934 Act's requirements," * * * and are " 'a necessary supplement to Commission action.' " * * * We have made it clear that rules facilitating § 10(b) litigation "suppor[t] the congressional policy embodied in the 1934 Act" of combating all forms of securities fraud. * * *

The practical and legal obstacles to bringing a private § 10(b) action are significant. Once federal jurisdiction is established, a § 10(b) plaintiff must prove elements that are similar to those in actions for common-law fraud. Given the complexity of modern securities markets, these facts may be difficult to prove.

The real burden on most investors, however, is the initial matter of discovering whether a violation of the securities laws occurred at all. This is particularly the case for victims of the classic fraudlike case that often arises under § 10(b). * * * The most extensive and corrupt schemes may not be discovered within the time allowed for bringing an express cause of action under the 1934 Act. * * *

The practicalities of litigation, indeed the simple facts of business life, are such that the rule adopted today will "thwart the legislative purpose of creating an effective remedy" for victims of securities fraud. * * * By adopting a 3–year period of repose, the Court makes a § 10(b) action all but a dead letter for injured investors who by no conceivable standard of fairness or practicality can be expected to file suit within three years after the violation occurred. In so doing, the Court also turns its back on the almost uniform rule rejecting short periods of repose for fraud-based actions. In the vast majority of States, the only limitations periods on fraud actions run from the time of a victim's discovery of the fraud. * * * Congress itself has recognized the importance of granting victims of fraud a reasonable time to discover the facts underlying the fraud and to prepare a case against its perpetrators. * * * The Court, however, does not.

A reasonable statute of repose, even as applied against fraud-based actions, is not without its merits. It may sometimes be easier to determine when a fraud occurred than when it should have been discovered. But more important, limitations periods in general promote important considerations of fairness. "Just determinations of fact cannot be made when, because of the passage of time, the memories of witnesses have faded or evidence is lost." * * * Notwithstanding these considerations, my view is that a 3–year absolute time bar is inconsistent with the practical realities of § 10(b) litigation and the congressional policies underlying that remedy. The 1–year-from-discovery rule is sufficient to ensure a fair balance between protecting the legitimate interests of aggrieved investors, yet preventing stale claims. In the extreme case, moreover, when the period between the alleged fraud and its discovery is of extraordinary length, courts may apply equitable principles such as laches should it be unfair to permit the claim. * * * A 3–year absolute bar on § 10(b) actions simply tips the scale too far in favor of wrongdoers.

The Court's decision today forecloses any means of recovery for a defrauded investor whose only mistake was not discovering a concealed fraud within an unforgiving period of repose. As fraud in the securities markets remains a serious national concern, Congress may decide that the rule announced by the Court today should be corrected. But even if prompt congressional action is taken, it will not avail defrauded investors caught by the Court's new and unforgiving rule, here applied on a retroactive basis to a pending action.

* * *

Notes and Questions

1. In response to criticism surrounding the Court's retroactive application of the statute of limitations announced in *Lampf,* Congress added Section 27A to the Securities and Exchange Act of 1934. See the Federal Deposit Insurance Corporation Improvement Act of 1991, P.L. No. 102–242, 105 Stat. 2234, 15 U.S.C.A. § 78aa–1(a). Section 27A(a) required the courts to apply forum state limitations periods to Section 10(b) actions that were commenced before the *Lampf* decision and were still pending. Section 27A(b) directed the courts to reinstate any actions that had been brought before the *Lampf* decision and then dismissed as a result of that decision. However, in Plaut v. Spendthrift Farm, Inc., 514 U.S. 211, 115 S.Ct. 1447, 131 L.Ed.2d 328 (1995), the Supreme Court found Section 27A(b) to be an unconstitutional infringement upon the Article III powers of the federal judiciary. Section 27A(a) remains valid, and *Lampf* still requires that the federal limitations period be applied in all subsequent actions. See 19 Wright, Miller & Cooper,

Federal Practice and Procedure: Jurisdiction and Related Matters 2d § 4519 (1996). See also Mikva & Pfander, *On the Meaning of Congressional Silence: Using Federal Common Law to Fill the Gap in Congress's Residual Statute of Limitations*, 107 Yale L.J. 393 (1997).

2. In TEXTILE WORKERS UNION v. LINCOLN MILLS, 353 U.S. 448, 77 S.Ct. 912, 1 L.Ed.2d 972 (1957), the union brought suit to compel arbitration of various grievances. The collective bargaining agreement provided for arbitration after the other grievance procedures had been exhausted. Justice Douglas, writing for the majority, held that federal common law would govern the decision of whether the court had jurisdiction to enforce the collective bargaining agreement under § 301 of the Labor Management Relations Act of 1947. After examining the legislative history, Justice Douglas explained:

> * * * Both the Senate Report and the House Report indicate a primary concern that unions as well as employees should be bound to collective bargaining contracts. But there was also a broader concern—a concern with a procedure for making such agreements enforceable in the courts by either party. * * *

Justice Douglas added that federal common law dictated that the agreement to arbitrate would be specifically enforced:

> It seems, therefore, clear to us that Congress adopted a policy which placed sanctions behind agreements to arbitrate grievance disputes, by implication rejecting the common-law rule * * * against enforcement of executory agreements to arbitrate. We would undercut the Act and defeat its policy if we read § 301 narrowly as only conferring jurisdiction over labor organizations.
>
> The question then is, what is the substantive law to be applied in suits under § 301(a)? We conclude that the substantive law to apply in suits under § 301(a) is federal law, which the courts must fashion from the policy of our national labor laws. * * * The Labor Management Relations Act expressly furnishes some substantive law. It points out what the parties may or may not do in certain situations. Other problems will lie in the penumbra of express statutory mandates. Some will lack express statutory sanction but will be solved by looking at the policy of the legislation and fashioning a remedy that will effectuate that policy. The range of judicial inventiveness will be determined by the nature of the problem. * * * Federal interpretation of the federal law will govern, not state law. * * * But state law, if compatible with the purpose of § 301, may be resorted to in order to find the rule that will best effectuate the federal policy. * * * Any state law applied, however, will be absorbed as federal law and will not be an independent source of private rights.

Id. at 453, 456–57, 77 S.Ct. at 916–18, 1 L.Ed.2d at 978, 980–81. In the absence of a federal statutory scheme governing labor relations in the United States, would federal courts be able to fashion common law in this area?

3. Even if a statutory scheme is silent as to a particular procedure or remedy, the federal courts will not necessarily fashion federal common law to fill the gaps. In TEXAS INDUSTRIES, INC. v. RADCLIFF MATERIALS, INC., 451 U.S. 630, 101 S.Ct. 2061, 68 L.Ed.2d 500 (1981), the Court held that it could not fashion federal common law in order to permit contribution among joint antitrust violators:

> In contrast to the sweeping language of §§ 1 and 2 of the Sherman Act, the remedial provisions defined in the antitrust laws are detailed and specific:

(1) violations of §§ 1 and 2 are crimes; (2) Congress has expressly authorized a private right of action for treble damages, costs, and reasonable attorney's fees; (3) other remedial sections also provide for suits by the United States to enjoin violations or for injury to its "business or property," and *parens patriae* suits by state attorneys general; (4) Congress has provided that a final judgment or decree of an antitrust violation in one proceeding will serve as prima facie evidence in any subsequent action or proceeding; and (5) the remedial provisions in the antimerger field, not at issue here, are also quite detailed.

> The presumption that a remedy was deliberately omitted from a statute is strongest when Congress has enacted a comprehensive legislative scheme including an integrated system of procedures for enforcement. * * *

That presumption is strong indeed in the context of antitrust violations; the continuing existence of this statutory scheme for 90 years without amendments authorizing contribution is not without significance. There is nothing in the statute itself, in its legislative history, or in the overall regulatory scheme to suggest that Congress intended courts to have the power to alter or supplement the remedies enacted.

Id. at 644–45, 101 S.Ct. at 2069, 68 L.Ed.2d at 511–12.

Many states today allow contribution among joint tortfeasors, and antitrust violators frequently are analogized to tortfeasors. Is the Court's decision not to allow contribution actually a decision to fashion federal common law to reach a result different from what state law would yield? Consider that in Wallis v. Pan American Petroleum Corp., 384 U.S. 63, 86 S.Ct. 1301, 16 L.Ed.2d 369 (1966), the Court intimated that Congress enacts legislation against a background of the total corpus juris of the states. If the Court could not develop federal common law in *Texas Industries,* should the prevailing state remedy have applied?

4. What law should govern state law claims by federal agencies acting pursuant to a federal statutory scheme on behalf of private creditors? In O'MELVENY & MYERS v. FDIC, 512 U.S. 79, 114 S.Ct. 2048, 129 L.Ed.2d 67 (1994), the Supreme Court addressed whether federal common law or state law fills gaps in suits involving the Resolution Trust Corporation (RTC) and its successor, the Federal Deposit Insurance Corporation (FDIC). In *O'Melveny*, the FDIC was acting as a receiver for an insolvent California savings and loan (S & L). The FDIC required the S & L to make refunds to its investors because of its fraudulent real estate transactions. The FDIC sued O'Melveny & Myers, a law firm, alleging state causes of action for professional negligence and breach of fiduciary duty arising from its representation of the S & L in real estate transactions. O'Melveny & Myers moved for summary judgment, claiming that because the FDIC was acting as a receiver, and hence "standing in the shoes" of the S & L, the S & L's knowledge of its own fraud should be imputed to the FDIC. Therefore, O'Melveny & Myers asserted that the FDIC should be estopped from asserting fraud claims on behalf of the very institution that created the fraud. The District Court granted summary judgment for O'Melveny & Myers, and the Ninth Circuit reversed. The Supreme Court reversed the Ninth Circuit and remanded, finding that state law, not federal common law, governs the imputation of a corporate officer's knowledge to a corporation generally, and the FDIC specifically, when it is asserting causes of action under state law. Justice Scalia, writing for a unanimous Court, concluded that the Financial Institutions Reform, Recovery and Enforcement Act of 1989 (FIRREA), the statute that establishes the FDIC's receivership role, does not

authorize federal courts to develop a federal common law rule of decision for the tort liability of attorneys who provided services to a failed bank:

> Section 1821(d)(2)(A)(i) [of FIRREA] * * * indicate[s] that the FDIC as receiver "steps into the shoes" of the failed S & L, obtaining the rights of the insured depository institution that existed prior to receivership. Thereafter, in litigation by the FDIC asserting the claims of the S & L * * * " 'any defense good against the original party is good against the receiver.' " (quoting Allen v. Ramsay, 179 Cal.App.2d, 843, 854 (1960)).

> Respondent argues that § 1821(d)(2)(A)(i) should be read as a nonexclusive grant of rights to the FDIC receiver * * *. * * * This argument is demolished by those provisions of FIRREA which specifically create special federal rules of decision regarding claims by, and defenses against, the FDIC as receiver. * * * It is hard to avoid the conclusion that § 1821(d)(2)(A)(i) places the FDIC in the shoes of the insolvent S & L, to work out its claims under state law, except where provision in the extensive framework of the FIRREA provides otherwise. To create additional "federal common law" exceptions is not to "supplement" this scheme, but to alter it.

* * *

> * * *[The use of federal common law is] limited to situations where there is a "significant conflict between some federal policy or interest and the use of state law." Wallis v. Pan American Petroleum Corp., 384 U.S. 63, 68 (1966) * * *. * * * What is fatal to respondent's position in the present case is that it has identified *no* significant conflict with an identifiable federal policy or interest. There is not even at stake that most generic (and lightly invoked) of alleged federal interests, the interest in uniformity. * * *

Id. at 86–88, 114 S.Ct. at 2054–55, 129 L.Ed.2d at 75–76. Note that in *O'Melveny*, the FDIC was not acting on behalf of the federal government; it acted only as the receiver of failed institutions and it did not pursue the government's interest as a bank insurer. However, the FDIC is a federal agency created under federal law. Should federal law likewise govern that agency's rights and duties? Does it undermine the supremacy of federal law to subject a federal agency to state law? What effect will a presumption in favor of applying state law instead of federal common law have on federal policies and interests? See Lund, *The Decline of Federal Common Law*, 76 B.U.L.Rev. 895 (1996).

In ATHERTON v. FDIC, 519 U.S. 213, 117 S.Ct. 666, 136 L.Ed.2d 656 (1997), the RTC was acting as receiver for City Federal Savings Bank, a federally chartered, federally insured savings association. The RTC sued several of the officers and directors of City Federal, claiming that they had violated the standard of care they owed to a federally chartered and insured institution. The RTC alleged gross negligence on the part of the officers that caused the bank to make bad loans, leading it into receivership. Petitioner FDIC, acting as successor to the RTC, alleged that federal common law provides the standard of care that the officer and directors owe federally insured savings associations. The District Court held that federal common law did provide the standard of care, but the Third Circuit reversed. A unanimous Supreme Court upheld that decision and ruled that federal common law does not provide the standard of care. *Atherton* mirrored *O'Melveny* by requiring that a federal court resort to federal common law only when there is a specific showing that the use of state law would create a significant conflict with, or threat to, some federal policy or interest. Justice

Breyer, writing for the Court, found that applying state law standards of care to federal savings institutions did not threaten any federal policy or interest. The Court then went on to apply federal statutory negligence standards under FIR-REA as a "floor" for officers and directors to meet, but allowed states to impose stricter standards on officers.

In both *O'Melveny* and *Atherton*, the Court rejected the FDIC's concerns about depletion of the government insurance fund to bail out insolvent, federally insured institutions. Was the Court correct in these instances? Isn't the solvency of that insurance pool of great importance to the entire program of federal deposit insurance?

O'Melveny and *Atherton* are significant because they establish a strong presumption in favor or applying state law to fill gaps in federal programs rather than creating new federal common law. What constitutional principles does the Court implicitly invoke to justify this unwillingness to resort to federal common law in *O'Melveny* and *Atherton*? Is the Court concerned about the separation of powers between Congress and the Judiciary, the balance between federal and state law, or both? Remember, in both *O'Melveny* and *Atherton*, the Court accepts Congress' power to enable the FDIC to act as a receiver and to provide the FDIC with special federal rights when acting as the receiver of a failed bank. Presumably, this power originates from the Constitution's Interstate Commerce Clause and the Banking Clause. With that in mind, is the Court really centering its decision on federalism grounds? Is there a unique concern about what should be the scope of power of Article III courts? How do *O'Melveny* and *Atherton* alter (if at all) the balance of judicial federalism between state and federal courts?

From a practical standpoint, it is very difficult for Congress to fill in all the potential gaps in its regulatory programs; legislators are not omniscient, and they cannot foresee all effects and problems that may arise under a statute. Legislatures, however, also are notoriously slow to respond when problems arise. Wouldn't it be far easier to allow federal courts to employ the common law method to repair statutes when problems arise, as many state courts do? Do you agree with Justices Scalia and Breyer that federal courts are ill-equipped to perform this type of interstitial lawmaking?

5.   State law is borrowed in many areas of law. In DE SYLVA v. BALLEN-TINE, 351 U.S. 570, 76 S.Ct. 974, 100 L.Ed. 1415 (1956), for example, the Court looked to state law in determining who is a "child" for purposes of the Copyright Act. Justice Harlan, writing for the majority, noted that in questions of domestic relations, when there is no federal law and when the subject is largely a matter of state concern, it was reasonable to borrow the state standards. Justices Douglas and Black disagreed, arguing that a federal standard was needed in order to ensure uniformity.

Assuming that the Court were to apply a federal standard to the question of who is a child, how would it derive that standard? Most likely, there is no federal legislative history on the point. Isn't it true that the Court would have before it only the various state definitions and its own notion of the "better view"? In that case, why not simply use the state law on the point?

6.   For discussions of federal common law and the *Erie* doctrine, see Bourne, *Federal Common Law and the Erie–Byrd Rule,* 12 U.Balt.L.Rev. 426 (1983); Johnson, *Bridging the Gap: Some Thoughts About Interstitial Lawmaking and the*

Federal Securities Laws, 48 Wash. & Lee L.Rev. 879 (1991); Perdue, *The Sources and Scope of Federal Procedural Common Law: Some Reflections on Erie and Gasperini*, 46 U.Kan.L.Rev. 751 (1998). See generally Lund, *The Decline of Federal Common Law*, 76 B.U.L.Rev. 895 (1996).

SECTION D. FEDERAL LAW IN THE STATE COURTS

State courts often are called upon to construe and apply federal law. Indeed, Congress has created a number of statutory causes of action, such as actions under the Federal Employers' Liability Act, that can be asserted by plaintiff in either a state or federal court but which defendant cannot remove from a state court. When a state attempts to adjudicate such a right, the Supremacy Clause, U.S. Const. Art. VI, requires the application of federal law. Ward v. Love County, 253 U.S. 17, 40 S.Ct. 419, 64 L.Ed. 751 (1920). A federally created right also may become germane to a state-court action when it is interposed as a defense to a claim based on state law. For example, in an action for royalties due under a contract licensing the use of a copyright or patent, defendant commonly will assert that the copyright or patent is invalid under the substantive tests established by the Copyright or Patent Act or that the copyright or patent has been used in violation of the federal antitrust laws. See, e.g., Sola Elec. Co. v. Jefferson Elec. Co., 317 U.S. 173, 63 S.Ct. 172, 87 L.Ed. 165 (1942). By way of further example, federal law may become relevant to a state lawsuit because of the presence of some federal interest or policy, which often springs out of its proprietary or governmental activities, or because one of the parties asserts a right protected by the United States Constitution. Finally, federal decisional law may come into play because it provides precedents bearing on issues being litigated before the state court in a nonfederal action. See generally Oakley & Coon, *The Federal Rules in State Courts: A Survey of State Court Systems of Civil Procedure*, 61 Wis.L.Rev. 1367 (1986).

TESTA v. KATT, 330 U.S. 386, 67 S.Ct. 810, 91 L.Ed. 967 (1947). Petitioner bought an automobile from respondent for $1100. The Emergency Price Control Act of 1942 set a ceiling price for such a purchase at $890. Petitioner then sued respondent under Section 205(e) of the Act in Rhode Island state court, seeking treble damages plus attorney's fees. The Act specifically provided, in Section 205(c), that the federal courts had concurrent jurisdiction with the state courts over matters arising under the Act. On appeal, the Rhode Island Supreme Court refused to enforce the statute and dismissed the action, interpreting Section 205(e) to be "a penal statute in the international sense." It reasoned that since, under widely recognized principles, state courts need not enforce the penal laws of other states or nations, they do not have to enforce the penal laws of the federal government.

The Supreme Court reversed, holding that:

 * * * [W]e cannot accept the basic premise on which the Rhode Island Supreme Court held that it has no more obligation to enforce a

valid penal law of the United States than it has to enforce a penal law of another state or a foreign country. Such a broad assumption flies in the face of the fact that the States of the Union constitute a nation. It disregards the purpose and effect of Article VI, § 2 of the Constitution * * *.

It cannot be assumed, the supremacy clause considered, that the responsibilities of a state to enforce the laws of a sister state are identical with its responsibilities to enforce federal laws. Such an assumption represents an erroneous evaluation of the statutes of Congress and the prior decisions of this Court in their historic setting. Those decisions establish that state courts do not bear the same relation to the United States that they do to foreign countries. * * *

* * * [W]hen in Mondou v. New York, N.H. & H.R. Co., * * * this Court was presented with a case testing the power and duty of states to enforce federal laws, it found the solution in the broad principles announced in the *Claflin* opinion.

* * * The contention that enforcement of the congressionally created right was contrary to Connecticut policy was answered as follows:

> The suggestion that the act of Congress is not in harmony with the policy of the State, and therefore that the courts of the state are free to decline jurisdiction, is quite inadmissible, because it presupposes what in legal contemplation does not exist. When Congress, in the exertion of the power confided to it by the Constitution, adopted that act, it spoke for all the people and all the states, and thereby established a policy for all. That policy is as much the policy of Connecticut as if the act had emanated from its own legislature, and should be respected accordingly in the courts of the State. * * *

The Rhode Island court in its *Robinson* decision on which it relies cites cases of this Court which have held that states are not required by the full faith and credit clause of the Constitution to enforce judgments of the courts of other states based on claims arising out of penal statutes. But those holdings have no relevance here, for this case raises no full faith and credit question. Nor need we consider in this case prior decisions to the effect that federal courts are not required to enforce state penal laws. * * * For whatever consideration they may be entitled in the field in which they are relevant, those decisions did not bring before us our instant problem of the effect of the supremacy clause on the relation of federal laws to state courts. Our question concerns only the right of a state to deny enforcement to claims growing out of a valid federal law.

It is conceded that this same type of claim arising under Rhode Island law would be enforced by that State's courts. Its courts have enforced claims for double damages growing out of the Fair Labor Standards Act * * *. Thus the Rhode Island courts have jurisdiction adequate and appropriate under established local law to adjudicate this action. Under these circumstances the State courts are not free to refuse enforcement of petitioners' claim. * * *

Id. at 389–94, 67 S.Ct. at 812–15, 91 L.Ed. at 970–72.

Questions

What are the limits on the rule announced in *Testa*? Suppose that a state does not allow suits brought by corporations not registered to do business in that state. Could they be compelled under *Testa* to hear a federal claim brought by such a corporation in its court system?

DICE v. AKRON, CANTON & YOUNGSTOWN R. CO.

Supreme Court of the United States, 1952.
342 U.S. 359, 72 S.Ct. 312, 96 L.Ed. 398.

Certiorari to the Supreme Court of Ohio.

Opinion of the Court by MR. JUSTICE BLACK, announced by MR. JUSTICE DOUGLAS.

Petitioner, a railroad fireman, was seriously injured when an engine in which he was riding jumped the track. Alleging that his injuries were due to respondent's negligence, he brought this action for damages under the Federal Employers' Liability Act, 35 Stat. 65, 45 U.S.C. § 51 et seq., in an Ohio court of common pleas. Respondent's defenses were (1) a denial of negligence and (2) a written document signed by petitioner purporting to release respondent in full for $924.63. Petitioner admitted that he had signed several receipts for payments made him in connection with his injuries but denied that he had made a full and complete settlement of all his claims. He alleged that the purported release was void because he had signed it relying on respondent's deliberately false statement that the document was nothing more than a mere receipt for back wages.

After both parties had introduced considerable evidence the jury found in favor of petitioner and awarded him a $25,000 verdict. The trial judge later entered judgment notwithstanding the verdict. In doing so he reappraised the evidence as to fraud, found that petitioner had been "guilty of supine negligence" in failing to read the release, and accordingly held that the facts did not "sustain either in law or equity the allegations of fraud by clear, unequivocal and convincing evidence." This judgment notwithstanding the verdict was reversed by the Court of Appeals of Summit County, Ohio, on the ground that under federal law, which controlled, the jury's verdict must stand because there was ample evidence to support its finding of fraud. The Ohio Supreme Court, one judge dissenting, reversed the Court of Appeals' judgment and sustained the trial court's action, holding that: (1) Ohio, not federal, law governed; (2) under that law petitioner, a man of ordinary intelligence who could read, was bound by the release even though he had been induced to sign it by the deliberately false statement that it was only a receipt for back wages; and (3) under controlling Ohio law factual issues as to fraud in the execution of this release were properly decided by the judge rather than by the jury. * * *

First. We agree with the Court of Appeals of Summit County, Ohio, and the dissenting judge in the Ohio Supreme Court and hold that validity of releases under the Federal Employers' Liability Act raises a federal question to be determined by federal rather than state law. Congress in § 1 of the Act granted petitioner a right to recover against his employer for damages negligently inflicted. State laws are not controlling in determining what the incidents of this federal right shall be. * * * Manifestly the federal rights affording relief to injured railroad employees under a federally declared standard could be defeated if states were permitted to have the final say as to what defenses could and could not be properly interposed to suits under the Act. Moreover, only if federal law controls can the federal Act be given that uniform application throughout the country essential to effectuate its purposes. * * * Releases and other devices designed to liquidate or defeat injured employees' claims play an important part in the federal Act's administration. * * * Their validity is but one of the many interrelated questions that must constantly be determined in these cases according to a uniform federal law.

Second. In effect the Supreme Court of Ohio held that * * * the negligence of an innocent worker is sufficient to enable his employer to benefit by its deliberate fraud. Application of so harsh a rule to defeat a railroad employee's claim is wholly incongruous with the general policy of the Act to give railroad employees a right to recover just compensation for injuries negligently inflicted by their employers. And this Ohio rule is out of harmony with modern judicial and legislative practice to relieve injured persons from the effect of releases fraudulently obtained. * * * We hold that the correct federal rule is that * * * a release of rights under the Act is void when the employee is induced to sign it by the deliberately false and material statements of the railroad's authorized representatives made to deceive the employee as to the contents of the release. The trial court's charge to the jury correctly stated this rule of law.

Third. Ohio provides and has here accorded petitioner the usual jury trial of factual issues relating to negligence. But Ohio treats factual questions of fraudulent releases differently. It permits the judge trying a negligence case to resolve all factual questions of fraud "other than fraud in the factum." The factual issue of fraud is thus split into fragments, some to be determined by the judge, others by the jury.

It is contended that since a state may consistently with the Federal Constitution provide for trial of cases under the Act by a nonunanimous verdict, Minneapolis & St. Louis R. Co. v. Bombolis, 241 U.S. 211, 36 S.Ct. 595, 60 L.Ed. 961, Ohio may lawfully eliminate trial by jury as to one phase of fraud while allowing jury trial as to all other issues raised. The *Bombolis* case might be more in point had Ohio abolished trial by jury in all negligence cases including those arising under the federal Act. But Ohio has not done this. It has provided jury trials for cases arising under the federal Act but seeks to single out one phase of the question of fraudulent releases for determination by a judge rather than by a jury. * * *

We have previously held that "The right to trial by jury is 'a basic and fundamental feature of our system of federal jurisprudence'" and that it is "part and parcel of the remedy afforded railroad workers under the Employers' Liability Act." Bailey v. Central Vermont R. Co., 319 U.S. 350, 354, 63 S.Ct. 1062, 1064, 87 L.Ed. 1444. We also recognized in that case that to deprive railroad workers of the benefit of a jury trial where there is evidence to support negligence "is to take away a goodly portion of the relief which Congress has afforded them." It follows that the right to trial by jury is too substantial a part of the rights accorded by the Act to permit it to be classified as a mere "local rule of procedure" for denial in the manner that Ohio has here used. * * *

Reversed and remanded with directions.

MR. JUSTICE FRANKFURTER, whom MR. JUSTICE REED, MR. JUSTICE JACKSON and MR. JUSTICE BURTON join, concurring for reversal but dissenting from the Court's opinion.

Ohio, as do many other States, maintains the old division between law and equity as to the mode of trying issues, even though the same judge administers both. * * * [I]n all cases in Ohio, the judge is the trier of fact on this issue of fraud, rather than the jury. It is contended that the Federal Employers' Liability Act requires that Ohio courts send the fraud issue to a jury in the cases founded on that Act. To require Ohio to try a particular issue before a different fact-finder in negligence actions brought under the Employers' Liability Act from the fact-finder on the identical issue in every other negligence case disregards the settled distribution of judicial power between Federal and State courts where Congress authorizes concurrent enforcement of federally-created rights.

* * *

In 1916 the Court decided without dissent that States in entertaining actions under the Federal Employers' Liability Act need not provide a jury system other than that established for local negligence actions. States are not compelled to provide the jury required of Federal courts by the Seventh Amendment. Minneapolis & St. L.R. Co. v. Bombolis * * *. In the thirty-six years since this early decision after the enactment of the Federal Employers' Liability Act * * *, the *Bombolis* case has often been cited by this Court but never questioned. Until today its significance has been to leave to States the choice of the fact-finding tribunal in all negligence actions, including those arising under the Federal Act. * * *

Although a State must entertain negligence suits brought under the Federal Employers' Liability Act if it entertains ordinary actions for negligence, it need conduct them only in the way in which it conducts the run of negligence litigation. The *Bombolis* case directly establishes that the Employers' Liability Act does not impose the jury requirements of the Seventh Amendment on the States *pro tanto* for Employers' Liability litigation. If its reasoning means anything, the *Bombolis* decision means that, if a State chooses not to have a jury at all, but to leave questions of fact in all negligence actions to a court, certainly the Employers' Liability Act does not require a State to have juries for negligence actions brought under the Federal Act in its courts. Or, if a State chooses to retain the old double system of courts, common law and equity * * *, surely there is nothing in the Employers' Liability Act that requires traditional distribution of authority for disposing of legal issues as between common law and chancery courts to go by the board. * * * So long as all negligence suits in a State are treated in the same way, by the same mode of disposing equitable, non-jury, and common law, jury issues, the State does not discriminate against Employers' Liability suits nor does it make any inroad upon substance.

Ohio and her sister States with a similar division of functions between law and equity are not trying to evade their duty under the Federal Employers' Liability Act * * *. The States merely exercise a preference in adhering to historic ways of dealing with a claim of fraud; they prefer the traditional way of making unavailable through equity an otherwise valid defense. The State judges and local lawyers who must administer the Federal Employers' Liability Act in State courts are trained in the ways of local practice; it multiplies the difficulties and confuses the administration of justice to require, on purely theoretical grounds, a hybrid of State and Federal practice in the State courts as to a single class of cases. Nothing in the Employers' Liability Act or in the judicial enforcement of the Act for over forty years forces such judicial hybridization upon the States. The fact that Congress authorized actions under the Federal Employers' Liability Act to be brought in State as well as in Federal courts seems a strange basis for the inference that Congress overrode State procedural arrangements controlling all other negligence suits in a State * * *. Such an inference is admissible, so it seems to me, only on the theory that Congress included as part of the right created by the Employers' Liability Act an assumed likelihood that trying all issues to juries is more favorable to plaintiffs. * * *

Even though the method of trying the equitable issue of fraud which the State applies in all other negligence cases governs Employers' Liability cases, two questions remain for decision: Should the validity of the release be tested by a Federal or a State standard? And if by a Federal one, did the Ohio courts in the present case correctly administer the standard? If the States afford courts for enforcing the Federal Act, they must enforce the substance of the right given by Congress. They cannot depreciate the legislative currency issued by Congress—either expressly or by local methods of enforcement that accomplish the same result. * * * In order to prevent diminution of railroad workers' nationally-uniform right to recover, the standard for the validity of a release of contested liability must be Federal. * * *

Notes and Questions

1. In what ways is the question of what law governs the right to jury trial in *Dice* the same or distinguishable from the question of the governing law in *Byrd*? Under what circumstances might a state court ignore federal law when it deems it to be inconsistent with its own law or policy? By what method is uniform construction and application of federal law by state courts assured?

2. Under what circumstances might a state court or legislature voluntarily incorporate or apply federal law to a state-created right? Would such an incorporation or application present a federal question for purposes of original jurisdiction in the federal district courts or appellate jurisdiction in the United States Supreme Court? See generally Hart, *The Relations Between State and Federal Law*, 54 Colum.L.Rev. 489, 536–38 (1954); Note, *Supreme Court Review of State Interpretations of Federal Law Incorporated by Reference*, 66 Harv.L.Rev. 1498 (1953). Are the federal courts bound by the state construction of the incorporated federal law?

3. In BROWN v. WESTERN RY. OF ALABAMA, 338 U.S. 294, 70 S.Ct. 105, 94 L.Ed. 100 (1949), respondent demurred to petitioner's complaint in an action brought in a Georgia state court under the Federal Employers' Liability Act. The

theory of the demurrer was that the complaint failed to "set forth a cause of action and is otherwise insufficient in law." The Georgia courts sustained the demurrer on the basis of a state practice rule requiring pleading allegations to be construed "most strongly against the pleader." The Supreme Court reversed, stating in part:

> It is contended that this construction of the complaint is binding on us. The argument is that while state courts are without power to detract from "substantive rights" granted by Congress in FELA cases, they are free to follow their own rules of "practice" and "procedure." To what extent rules of practice and procedure may themselves dig into "substantive rights" is a troublesome question at best * * *. [C]ases in this Court point up the impossibility of laying down a precise rule to distinguish "substance" from "procedure." Fortunately, we need not attempt to do so. A long series of cases previously decided, from which we see no reason to depart, makes it our duty to construe the allegations of this complaint ourselves in order to determine whether petitioner has been denied a right of trial granted him by Congress. This federal right cannot be defeated by the forms of local practice. * * *

> Strict local rules of pleading cannot be used to impose unnecessary burdens upon rights of recovery authorized by federal laws. * * * Should this Court fail to protect federally created rights from dismissal because of over-exacting local requirements for meticulous pleadings, desirable uniformity in adjudication of federally created rights could not be achieved.

Id. at 296, 298–99, 70 S.Ct. at 106, 108, 94 L.Ed. at 102–04. Of what relevance is the presence or absence under Georgia practice of a right to replead following a demurrer?

4. Is the process of applying federal law in a state court identical to the process of applying state law in a federal court under the *Erie* doctrine? How does a state court ascertain federal law? Suppose, for example, that there is a conflict between the federal courts of appeals over what a statute means, or over an issue of federal common law. Is the state court free to adopt any position it wishes? What if the federal courts never have ruled on the issue? Should the state court try to figure out how the federal courts might rule? Which federal court? How does a state court determine which aspects of federal law it must apply?

5. May the federal government require state courts to apply the Federal Rules in order to ensure that a federally created right is enforced with procedures which the federal government approves? Should the federal government do so? In FEDERAL ENERGY REGULATORY COMMISSION v. MISSISSIPPI, 456 U.S. 742, 102 S.Ct. 2126, 72 L.Ed.2d 532 (1982), the Supreme Court upheld provisions of the Public Utilities Regulatory Policies Act of 1978 (PURPA) which required state public utility commissions to observe certain federal procedures in regulating energy usage. Justice Powell, concurring in part of the judgment and dissenting in part, wrote:

> "The general rule, bottomed deeply in belief in the importance of state control of state judicial procedure, is that federal law takes the state courts as it finds them." Hart, The Relations Between State and Federal Law, 54 Colum.L.Rev. 489, 508 (1954). I believe the same principle must apply to other organs of state government. It may be true that the procedural provisions of the PURPA may not effect dramatic changes in the laws and procedures of some States. But I know of no other attempt by the Federal Government to supplant state-prescribed procedures that in part define the

nature of their administrative agencies. If Congress may do this, presumably it has the power to pre-empt state-court rules of civil procedure and judicial review in classes of cases found to affect commerce.

Id. at 774, 102 S.Ct. at 2145, 72 L.Ed.2d at 556–57.

6. The question of federal control over state procedures when a state court is adjudicating a federal cause of action is discussed in Meltzer, *State Court Forfeitures of Federal Rights,* 99 Harv.L.Rev. 1130 (1986); Neuborne, *Toward Procedural Parity in Constitutional Litigation,* 22 Wm. & Mary L.Rev. 725 (1981); Redish & Muench, *Adjudication of Federal Causes of Action in State Court,* 75 Mich. L.Rev. 311 (1976). See also Steinglass, *The Emerging State Court § 1983 Action: A Procedural Review,* 38 U.Miami L.Rev. 381 (1984).

Chapter 7

THE DEVELOPMENT OF MODERN PROCEDURE

SECTION A. COMMON–LAW PLEADING

STEPHEN, THE PRINCIPLES OF PLEADING IN CIVIL ACTIONS 37, 147–50 (Tyler ed. 1882):[a]

In the course of administering justice between litigating parties there are two successive objects: to ascertain the subject for decision, and to decide. It is evident that, towards the attainment of the first of these results, there is, in a *general* point of view, only one satisfactory mode of proceeding; and that this consists in making each of the parties state his own case, and collecting, from the opposition of their statements, the points of the legal controversy. Thus far, therefore, the course of every system of judicature is the same. It is common to them all to require, on behalf of each contending party, before the decision of the cause, a statement of his case. But from this point the coincidence naturally ceases. * * *

The manner of allegation in our courts may be said to have been first methodically formed and cultivated as a science in the reign of Edward I [1272–1307]. From this time the judges began systematically to prescribe and enforce certain *rules of statement* * * *. None of them seem to have been originally of legislative enactment, or to have had any authority except usage or judicial regulation; but, from the general perception of their wisdom and utility, they acquired the character of fixed and positive institutions, and grew up into an entire and connected *system of pleading*. * * *

As the object of all pleading or judicial allegation is to ascertain the subject for decision, so the main object of that system of pleading established in the common law of England is to ascertain it by the production of an *issue;* and this appears to be peculiar to that system. * * *

The author is of opinion that this peculiarity of coming to issue took its rise in the practice of *oral* pleading. It seems a natural incident of that practice, to compel the pleaders to short and terse allegations, applying to each other by way of answer, in somewhat of a logical form, and at length reducing the controversy to a precise point. For while the pleading was *merely*

---

a. This edition is based upon Stephen's own second edition of 1827, which is the last of his editions before the reform of common-law pleading in England in 1834.

oral, * * * the court and the pleaders would have to rely exclusively on their memory for retaining the tenor of the discussion; and the development of some precise question or issue would then be a very convenient practice, because it would prevent the necessity of reviewing the different statements, and leave no burden on the memory but that of retaining the question itself so developed. And even after the practice of recording was introduced, the same brief and logical forms of allegation would naturally continue to be acceptable, while the pleadings were still *viva voce* * * *.

A co-operative reason for coming to issue was the variety of the modes of decision which the law assigned to different kinds of question. * * * As questions of law were decided by the *court,* and matters of fact referred to other kinds of investigation, it was, in the first place, necessary to settle whether the question in the cause or issue was a matter of *law* or *fact*. Again, if it happened to be a matter of fact, it required to be developed in a form sufficiently specific to show what was the method of trial appropriate to the case. And, unless the state of the question were thus adjusted between the parties, it is evident that they would not have known whether they were to put themselves on the judgment of the court or to go to trial; nor, in the latter case, whether they were to prepare themselves for trial by jury or for one of the other various modes of deciding [the] matter of fact.

Notes

1. The change from oral to written pleadings cannot be dated precisely. The shift began in the late fourteenth century and extended into the second half of the sixteenth. Predictably the change increased the rigor and technicality of the pleading rules.

> * * * [T]his system of oral pleading had one great advantage over the later system of written pleadings. It made for far greater freedom in the statement of the case. * * * [W]hen all objections to the writ and process had been disposed of * * * the debate between the opposing counsel, carried on subject to the advice or the rulings of the judge, allowed the parties considerable latitude in pleading to the issue. Suggested pleas will, after a little discussion, be seen to be untenable; a proposition to demur will, after a few remarks by the judge, be obviously the wrong move. The counsel feel their way towards an issue which each can accept and allow to be enrolled. * * *

3 Holdsworth, *A History of English Law* 635 (4th ed. 1935). Milsom, *Historical Foundations of the Common Law* 28–37, 39–40 (1969), contains a good description of oral pleadings as well as an excellent explanation of the Yearbooks, from which most of our knowledge of early pleading is derived; this book is a particularly valuable reference for most of the matters covered in this Chapter.

2. In this discussion we are concerned with pleading in the royal courts. It should be noted that at the time of the Norman Conquest (1066) and for a century or more afterward the ordinary recourse of suitors was not to the royal courts but to local, or communal, courts and to feudal courts in which a lord heard cases involving his tenants. The royal courts existed primarily to try offenses against the king's laws and to hear cases involving his tenants-in-chief, which came before the king in his capacity as a feudal lord. Gradually, however, these royal courts began to absorb business from the communal and feudal courts.

A person with a grievance against another sought justice from the king, and the king issued a *writ*, ordering the sheriff to bring the other person before the king's judges to answer the complaint. In the course of the twelfth century this pattern became standardized. When it became established that the king's courts would hear a particular kind of case—for example, an action for assault, an action for debt, an action for the possession of land—the complainant in such a case could obtain a writ from the king's chief minister, the chancellor, as a matter of course. See Milsom, *Historical Foundations of the Common Law* 22–25 (1969).

The writ, strictly speaking, was simply the document that commenced the action, similar in function to the modern summons; but each writ came to embody a *form of action*, a concept that governed the method of commencing the suit, the substantive requirements of the case, the manner of trial, and the type of sanction that would attend the eventual judgment. See pp. 474–78, infra. For the present it is enough to say that there was a writ for each type of case—or form of action— that the royal courts would hear; thus, for example, there was a writ of trespass, a writ of debt, and a writ of nuisance. If plaintiff selected a writ that did not fit the case, the action would fail. If there was no writ that fit the case, and the chancellor would not draw up a new one, plaintiff could obtain no relief in the royal courts.

3. The "modes of decision" for issues of fact, referred to in the extract from Stephen, were, at an early date, "trial" by ordeal, by combat, and by oath. These were not trials in the sense in which we now understand and use that term; rather they were proofs undertaken by one of the parties (or both in the case of combat) at the direction of the court. Ordeal—proof by carrying a red-hot iron unscathed or by sinking when thrown into a pool of water[b]—disappeared in England after it was proscribed by the Lateran Council in 1215. Combat—waged by champions of the parties—was resisted as a Norman importation, and during the reign of Henry II (1154–1189) an early form of jury began to supplant it, although it was not formally abolished until 1819.

For our purpose the most important of these early methods of proof was that by oath, or as more generally known, *wager of law* or *compurgation*. It required one of the parties to swear to his case with strict and elaborate formalities, accompanied by a number of "oath-helpers," usually twelve, who swore to the truthfulness of the party's oath, or in later periods to their belief in its truth. If all went as prescribed, he prevailed; but if the party or any of the "helpers" made an error by using a wrong word, that party lost.

It is hard for us to say how this ancient procedure worked in practice, hard to tell how easy it was to get oath-helpers who would swear falsely, hard to tell how much risk there was in an ordeal. The rational element of law must, it would seem, have asserted itself in the judgment which decided how and by whom the proof should be given; the jurisprudence of the old courts must have been largely composed of the answers to this question; * * * for example, we can see that even before the Norman Conquest the man who has been often accused has to go to the ordeal instead of being allowed to purge himself with oath-helpers.

Maitland, *Equity, Also the Forms of Action at Common Law* 310 (1909).

b. See Lea, *Superstition and Force* 252, 279 (3d ed. 1878). In ordeal by water, it was thought that the water would reject the evildoer; a rope was tied to the person making the proof in the hope that if proved innocent he could be kept from drowning.

The importance of this procedure in legal history lies in the fact that a right to wage one's law was firmly established in certain classes of cases by the last half of the twelfth century, long before the jury began to emerge as an instrument for fact-determination. In its original form the jury, developed as a body for valuing property for taxes, decided cases on its own knowledge rather than after hearing witnesses. Even in this form suitors saw in the jury a more rational mode of trial, and sought to use forms of action such as trespass, which having developed at a relatively late period did not provide a right to wager of law.[c] Thus, as we shall see in Section B of this Chapter, judicial development of the law for four-and-a-half centuries was channeled and motivated to a substantial degree by increasingly successful attempts to avoid the older modes of trial.[d]

1. A BRIEF OVERVIEW OF COMMON-LAW PLEADING

The basic structure of common-law pleading was simple and well-calculated to bring the parties to an issue of law or of fact. It was based on the following analysis. A substantive response to a claim—other than an expression of total agreement—will fall into one of three categories: (1) A party can deny that the alleged facts, even if true, give the claimant any legal right; (2) a party can deny that the alleged facts are true; or (3) a party can say that even if the alleged facts are true and taken alone would establish a right, additional facts not mentioned by the claimant negate that right. Responses (1) and (2) raise issues of law and of fact respectively. Response (3) does not itself raise a contested issue; there is as yet no necessary disagreement between the parties. To raise the necessary issue the claimant must respond to the response, and this response also may fall into any of the three categories. If this response is again of type (3) no issue will have been raised and the process must continue. (How do the Federal Rules avoid the necessity for further pleading after a type (3) response? See Federal Rules 7(a) and 8(d).)

Of course the real process was more complex than this. Plaintiff's claim was set forth in the *declaration*. This document had to meet many formal requirements that might differ from one type of case to another. But stripped of much verbiage, and stated in modern English, it might have said: "Defendant promised to deliver a horse to plaintiff and plaintiff promised to pay 100 dollars for it, but defendant has refused to deliver the horse."

At this point, defendant had to *demur* or *plead*. A demurrer would challenge the legal sufficiency of the declaration. Thus prior to STRANGBOROUGH & WARNERS CASE, 4 Leon. 3, 74 Eng.Rep. 686 (K.B. 1589), the modern language declaration set out above would have failed on demurrer, because a promise was not regarded as good consideration for a promise until

---

c. A similar desire to avoid trial by combat was among the causes for the desuetude of the writ of right, once the most important action. Preference for jury trial also encouraged the expanding jurisdiction of royal courts at the expense of the feudal courts since the jury was found only in the former.

d. For a time in the fourteenth century it seemed that wager of law might be denied when the facts were well known to witnesses,

but this development aborted. Fifoot, *History and Sources of the Common Law—Tort and Contract* 28–29 (1949). By the last quarter of the sixteenth century, however, "a defendant proposing to wage his law was somehow examined and admonished." Milsom, *Historical Foundations of the Common Law* 292–93 (1969).

that decision. A demurrer also would succeed if plaintiff had chosen the wrong writ (or form of action). There were also a great many technical sins that the declaration might commit, but by statute, 27 Eliz. 1, c. 5, § 1 (1585) and 4 Anne, c. 16, § 1 (1705), unless these defects were raised by a *special demurrer,* which precisely spelled out the faults, they were waived. If a demurrer was sustained, plaintiff was out of court, although he generally was free to begin again if he could correct the mistake, as by suing in another form of action if the original form was incorrect. If the demurrer was quashed, judgment was entered for plaintiff.

If defendant did not demur, he responded to the declaration in a *plea.* Pleas were of two types, *dilatory* and *peremptory.* Dilatory pleas did not deny the merits of plaintiff's claim, but challenged plaintiff's right to have the court hear the case; they included pleas to the jurisdiction of the court, pleas of a variance between the declaration and the writ, and pleas that the case must be suspended (when, for example, one of the parties was under age at the time of suit). A peremptory plea, or *plea in bar,* was on the merits. If defendant denied that he had promised to sell the horse, the plea was a *traverse;* a traverse terminated the pleadings and the case would go to trial to dispose of the issue raised by plaintiff's allegation and defendant's denial. But suppose defendant wanted to allege that at the time of the purported contract he was a minor; defendant would then plead by *confession and avoidance,* that is, admit the allegations of the declaration and seek to avoid them by pleading minority. If defendant followed this course, no issue would have been reached, and plaintiff would have to respond.

Plaintiff's response might be a demurrer to defendant's plea, which would raise the question whether minority was a defense to the agreement he had pleaded and defendant had confessed.[e] Or plaintiff might plead in a *replication,* either traversing defendant's allegation of his age, or confessing it, and alleging that defendant had lied about his age when making the contract. If plaintiff pleaded in confession and avoidance, defendant would again have to respond, by demurrer or by *rejoinder.* The pleas in confession and avoidance theoretically might go on indefinitely, and in some of the cases we read of a *surrejoinder,* a *rebutter,* and a *surrebutter.* Lack of formal names beyond that point suggests that even the ingenuity of the common-law pleader may have had its limits.

The common-law pleading system may seem ornate to you, even after only the brief description on the preceding pages. Yet bear in mind that this is only a skeletal outline. When the outline is filled in with special instances, inexplicable exceptions, arbitrary rules, and untraversable fictions, the result is one of the most complex and snare-ridden creations ever devised by man. Let us look at a common-law record and decision. (The reporter of the case, it should be noted, is the victorious lawyer, Saunders.)

VEALE v. WARNER
Court of King's Bench, 1670.
1 Wms. Saund. 323, 326, 85 Eng.Rep. 463, 468.

Be it remembered that * * * before our lord the King at Westminster came Thomas Veale Esquire * * * and brought here * * * his certain bill

---

e. After a successful demurrer to a dilatory plea, judgment was not entered for plaintiff, but by an order *respondeat ouster,* defendant was directed to plead over.

against William Warner, * * * in the custody of the marshal, & c. of a plea of
debt: and there are pledges of prosecution, to wit, John Doe and Richard Roe;
which said bill follows in these words, * * * [Veale] complains of [Warner]
* * * that he render to him 2000l., of lawful money of England, which he
owes to, and unjustly detains from him; for that whereas the said William,
* * * at London aforesaid, to wit, in the parish of St. Mary-le Bow in the ward
of Cheap, by his certain writing obligatory, sealed * * * and to the Court of
our said lord the King now here shewn, * * * acknowledged himself to be
held and firmly bound to * * * [Veale] in the said 2000l. to be paid to the said
Thomas when he should be thereunto requested. Nevertheless, the said
William (although often requested) hath not yet paid the said 2000l. to the
said Thomas, but to pay the same to him hath hitherto altogether refused,
and yet refuses, to the damage of him the said Thomas of 100l.: and therefore
he brings suit, & c.

And [Warner] * * * comes and defends the wrong and injury when, & c.
and prays oyer of the said writing obligatory, and it is read to him, & c. He
also prays oyer of the condition of the said writing, & c. and it is read to him
in these words, to wit: "The condition of this obligation is such, that if * * *
[Warner] shall and do in all things well and truly stand to, obey, abide,
perform, fulfil, and keep the award * * * of John Coggs, gent. and John
Foxwell, arbitrators * * * to arbitrate * * * and determine of and concerning
all and all manner of action and actions, cause and causes of actions, suits,
bills, bonds, specialties, judgments, executions, extents, quarrels, controversies, trespasses, damages, and demands whatsoever, at any time heretofore
had, made, moved, brought, commenced, sued, prosecuted, done, suffered,
committed, or depending by or between the said parties, * * * then this
obligation to be void and of none effect, or else to remain in full force and
virtue." Which being read and heard, the said William saith, that * * *
[Veale] ought not to have his aforesaid action against him, because he saith
that * * * the arbitrators in the said condition named, * * * made their
award * * * that [Warner] * * * should satisfy, content, and pay to [Veale]
* * * the full sum of 3169l. 16s. and 3d. of lawful money of England. And they
further awarded that [Warner] * * * should seal, and as his deed deliver to
[Veale] * * * a full and general release and discharge of all and all manner of
actions, and causes of actions, suits, bills, bonds, specialties, judgments,
executions, extents, quarrels, controversies, trespasses, damages, and demands whatsoever, at any time before the date of the bond brought here into
Court had, made, moved, commenced, sued, prosecuted, committed, or depending by or between the said parties. And * * * [Warner] further saith,
that he the said William * * * paid to * * * [Veale] the said sum * * * and
also, then and there did seal, and as his deed deliver to * * * [Veale] the said
full release * * * and this he is ready to verify: wherefore he prays judgment
if the said Thomas ought to have or maintain his said action thereof against
him & c.

And * * * [Veale] saith, that he by any thing by * * * [Warner] above in
pleading alleged, ought not to be barred from having his said action thereof
against the said William, because he saith that * * * [Warner] did not pay the

said sum * * * as the said William hath above thereof in pleading alleged; and this he prays may be inquired of by the country, & c.

And * * * [Warner] saith that * * * [Veale] ought not to be admitted to say that he the said William hath not paid the said sum * * * because he saith that he the said Thomas, * * * by his certain writing acknowledged that he the said William had paid the said sum to the said Thomas * * * and this he is ready to verify: wherefore he prays judgment if the said Thomas ought to be admitted, against his own acknowledgment, to say, that he the said William hath not paid the said sum of money, & c.

Demurrer and joinder in demurrer.

* * *

And now in this term the plaintiff moved to have judgment. And Saunders for the defendant objected that the plaintiff could not have judgment, because it appeared by the record that the award was void, being all to be performed by the defendant and nothing by the plaintiff: and, therefore, if the award is void, it is not material whether the defendant has performed it or not, although he has pleaded a performance of it. And now he has acknowledged the contrary by his waiver of the issue offered by the plaintiff and pleading a bad rejoinder. And the plaintiff and defendant have both agreed, that the award pleaded by the defendant was the true award made by the arbitrators, which is altogether vicious. But if the plaintiff would have helped himself, he ought to have shewn the other part of the award before he assigned the breach, which he has not done here; and therefore he cannot have judgment.

And of such opinion was the whole Court clearly. But they would not give judgment for the defendant, because they conceived it was a trick in pleading; but they gave the plaintiff leave to discontinue on payment of costs. And Kelynge Chief Justice, reprehended Saunders for pleading so subtly on purpose to trick the plaintiff by the omission of the other part of the award. But it was a case of the greatest hardship on the defendant; for the bond of submission was only in the penalty of 2000l., and the arbitrators had awarded him to pay 3100l., being 1100l. more than the real penalty of the bond; when in truth there was nothing at all due to the plaintiff, but he was indebted to the defendant. And afterwards the defendant exhibited an English bill in the Exchequer, disclosing bad practice of the plaintiff with the arbitrators, and had relief against the bond: and so this matter was at rest. * * *

Notes and Questions

1. "[B]efore our lord the King at Westminster." Veale v. Warner was brought in the Court of King's Bench, one of the three royal common-law courts, maintaining separate existence until merged in the High Court of Justice in 1873. The others were the Court of Common Pleas and the Court of Exchequer. All three developed out of the *Curia Regis* (the King's Court), which at the time of the Norman Conquest and for a period thereafter performed administrative and judicial functions in conjunction with the king. The first offshoot was Exchequer, which originally was charged with the collection and administration of the king's finances, but by 1250 had acquired full judicial jurisdiction. Next to develop separate status was Common Pleas, established by Henry II as the primary

tribunal to hear cases not involving the crown. The remaining part of the King's Court supervised Common Pleas through the writ of error, and heard matters particularly touching the king's interests, such as criminal actions and cases involving his tenants in chief; it developed into King's Bench, but the fiction was maintained that hearings before that tribunal were before the king himself. See Plucknett, *A Concise History of the Common Law* 143–51 (5th ed. 1956).

2. "[H]is * * * bill against William Warner, * * * in the custody of the marshal, & c." Common Pleas was supposed to have exclusive jurisdiction over actions of debt, such as Veale v. Warner. But the judges and lawyers of each common-law court zealously sought to expand the jurisdiction of their tribunal, and Veale v. Warner illustrates one method by which King's Bench accomplished this. Not all common-law proceedings were commenced by writ; to an undefined extent each court could proceed on a *bill*, which was a complaint addressed directly to the court. See 2 Holdsworth, *A History of English Law* 339 (3d ed. 1923). One instance in which a court clearly could proceed on a bill was an action against one of the court's officers or a person within its custody, and such a bill might be brought on a cause of action that ordinarily was not within the jurisdiction of the court. Thus, a plaintiff who desired to bring an action of debt in King's Bench would first charge defendant with trespass, and by a "bill of Middlesex" that court would order the sheriff of Middlesex to arrest defendant and deliver him to the custody of the marshal of the Marshalsea—the court's prison; once defendant was within the custody of King's Bench, plaintiff could proceed against him by bill in the action of debt. Predictably, the arrest and commitment eventually became wholly fictitious, but defendant was not permitted to challenge the allegation that they had occurred. A similar device used to expand the jurisdiction of Exchequer was the writ of *quo minus,* by which a debtor to the crown could bring suit in that court on the theory that anyone withholding money from the debtor was rendering him unable to pay what was owed the king; in time, the allegation of plaintiff's debt to the king also became untraversable. See Plucknett, op. cit. supra at 161, 387; Milsom, *Historical Foundations of the Common Law* 53–59 (1969).

3. "[P]ledges of prosecution." The original writ in a lawsuit directed the sheriff, to whom it was addressed, to take some action, conditioned on plaintiff's "mak[ing] you secure of prosecuting his claim." Thus plaintiff had to furnish sureties, who would be liable to pay a fine that was imposed upon unsuccessful claimants. As the names of the pledges in the case suggest, the requirement became a sham.

4. "[I]n the parish of St. Mary-le Bow in the ward of Cheap." As the jury originally decided cases on its own knowledge, it was necessary that jurors be drawn from the vicinity in which a transaction had occurred; the action therefore had to be brought near the place at which it arose, and the declaration had to show this. Since an English court could not summon jurors from abroad, technically it would have been impossible to bring an action on a contract made outside England. In such cases, however, plaintiff made an untraversable allegation that the contract had been made in the aforesaid parish and ward of the city of London. See Sack, *Conflict of Laws in the History of English Law,* in *3 Law: A Century of Progress* 342, 370 (1937). Some cases actually must have arisen there, but you cannot tell from the records which they are.

5. "[T]o the Court * * * now here shewn"; "prays oyer." A plaintiff suing upon a deed or a bond made profert of the document—that is, the plaintiff formally tendered it to the court, although it was strictly speaking not a part of

the pleading. If defendant wanted to get the document in the pleadings in order to raise a question of law about it, she had to demand oyer of it, which meant that defendant was entitled to read it and copy as much of it as she chose into the plea. At this point you might conclude that if defendant demurred, she would be demurring to her own pleading, but even though the document was set out in the plea, it was treated as if it were a part of the declaration. See Sutton, *Personal Actions at Common Law* 103 (1929), which is a particularly valuable introduction to common-law pleading. In what way does this process resemble the modern motion for summary judgment? See pp. 10–11, supra.

6. "[W]herefore he prays judgment if the said Thomas ought to have or maintain his said action." This is the standard conclusion of a pleading in confession and avoidance. Compare the conclusion of plaintiff's replication in the next paragraph of the report of the case. Why was defendant's allegation that he had performed the bond treated as a matter of confession and avoidance?

7. "[W]herefore he prays judgment if the said Thomas ought to be admitted, against his own acknowledgment, to say." Plaintiff in his replication had traversed defendant's claim of payment. Thus the replication already had created an issue, and defendant's rejoinder could not be one of the three responses described in the Overview of Common–Law Pleading, pp. 466–67, supra; it is a plea of estoppel, and as stated in Saunders' argument waives the issue created by the traverse in plaintiff's replication. Why was this rejoinder "bad"? Did it allege that the award had been paid?

8. Why did Saunders, a thoroughly capable lawyer, file what he knew was an inadequate rejoinder? The answer lies in a peculiar facet of the demurrer:

> * * * [O]n demurrer the court will consider the whole record, and give judgment for the party, who on the whole, appears to be entitled to it. Thus, on demurrer to the replication, if the court think the replication bad, but perceive a substantial fault in the *plea,* they will give judgment, not for the defendant, but the plaintiff, provided the *declaration* be good; but if the declaration also be bad in substance, then, upon the same principle, judgment would be given for the defendant.

Stephen, *The Principles of Pleading in Civil Actions* 160 (Tyler ed. 1882). Thus, by making a rejoinder that he knew plaintiff would demur to, Saunders baited the trap he had set in his plea.

9. "[A]n English bill in the Exchequer." That part of the report of Veale v. Warner beginning, "But it was a case of the greatest hardship * * * "is not a part of the record, but is simply the reporter's justification of his own tactics. An English bill was a bill in equity, so-called because it was written in English rather than in the Latin of the common-law courts. As we will see, many instances of fraud and overreaching did not constitute defenses at law, but when such factors were established equity would enjoin a victorious plaintiff from enforcing the judgment at law. See p. 498, infra. But how could such relief be obtained in Exchequer, which was a common-law court? The answer is that Exchequer had an equity side.

2. THE QUEST FOR A SINGLE ISSUE: PATHS AND PITFALLS

The principal aim of common-law pleading was the production of a single issue; in many ways, the most serious problems in common-law pleading grew out of this persistent drive. To achieve the goal of singleness of issue, it was necessary to prohibit *duplicity* in pleading. That term did not connote fraud, but simply meant raising more than one issue in a pleading. Thus, in our example concerning the sale of the horse, defendant might wish to deny that he had made any promise *and* to assert that he was a minor at the time *and* to contend that a promise was not good consideration for another promise. There would be nothing devious or inconsistent in claiming all three defenses, but he was not permitted to do so. The traverse, the plea in confession and avoidance, and the demurrer were mutually exclusive.

A procedure was available that, in effect, permitted a party to delay the "demurrer." After trial and verdict for plaintiff, defendant could *move to arrest the judgment*, thereby raising the question whether the pleadings could support the judgment. In the case of a verdict for defendant, plaintiff's equivalent motion was for *judgment notwithstanding the verdict*—a term that has now come to identify a motion on a quite different theory. See p. 14, supra. By following this procedure, however, a party could not escape the expense of trial (costs not being awarded to the prevailing party on such a motion), and that party assumed the risk that the defect in a pleading might be cured by a later pleading or aided by the verdict; in any event, a fault that required the use of a special demurrer would not support such a delayed motion. Nonetheless, the practice became very popular.

No such procedure was available to the party who wanted to deny his adversary's allegations and at the same time advance affirmative allegations of his own. For the plea in confession and avoidance had to give *color*. "As a term of pleading, * * * ["color"] signifies an apparent or prima facie right; and the meaning of the rule, that every pleading in confession and avoidance must give color, is, that it must admit an apparent right in the opposite party, and rely, therefore, on some new matter by which that apparent right is defeated." Stephen, *The Principles of Pleading in Civil Actions* 206–07 (Tyler ed. 1882). A plea in confession and avoidance that failed to give color was doomed, even though it revealed a defense that could have been raised by traverse. In GIBBONS v. PEPPER, 1 Ld.Raym. 38, 91 Eng.Rep. 922 (K.B. 1695), an action for running down plaintiff, defendant admitted the trespass but pleaded that his horse had become so frightened he could not control it; on demurrer the court ordered judgment for plaintiff, holding that if defendant's facts were true there had been no battery at all and the plea should have been a traverse.

Out of this rule that a party could not plead new matter without confessing the opposing party's prima-facie right grew one of the weirder formulae of common-law pleading—the giving of *express color*. Today, we mercifully are spared the necessity of learning the hoary details that surrounded this device, but a brief look at it will illustrate the complexities of the system that lay beneath the surface of our original simple outline.

Suppose that plaintiff had brought an action of trespass against defendant for entering on plaintiff's land, and that the only genuine issue in the case was the title to the land, defendant contending that although plaintiff had been in possession of the land, defendant was the true owner. If defendant denied the trespass by a traverse, she would be permitted to establish her own title as a defense. However, even if the only issue concerning her title was a question of law, there would have to be a full trial and the case would be decided by a jury under the guidance of the judge. Trial could not be avoided unless defendant somehow could introduce the new matter—her claim of title—into the pleadings and thereby permit it to be made the subject of a demurrer. Yet under the rule that required a plea in confession and avoidance to give color to plaintiff's claim, defendant could not assert new matter without confessing plaintiff's apparent right. The solution of express color was for defendant to confess the existence of a plausible, but imperfect, title in plaintiff, and then to assert her own title by way of avoidance. Having done this, plaintiff could not traverse the confession—even though it was the sheerest fiction—for that would leave two issues in the case; he had to respond to the matter pleaded in avoidance, and when the validity of defendant's claim turned on a question of law, the appropriate response would be a demurrer. You should note, however, that although giving express color enabled defendant to introduce her claim of title into the case, defendant was not able at the same time to deny that she had entered the land at all.

The insistence on arriving at a single issue also prohibited raising more than one issue of fact in a pleading. The fault could be challenged only by a special demurrer, and over a long period the strictness of the prohibition against multiple issues was relaxed, but it never ceased to pose a problem for the pleader. Originally a declaration could not state more than one cause of action; at an early date, however, plaintiffs were permitted to join causes of action arising under the same writ, and, as long as they were stated in separate counts, different versions of the same cause of action could be pleaded.[f] Defendant was permitted to plead separately to each count, and indeed might demur to one, traverse a second, and confess and avoid a third. But defendant could not plead two or more defenses to a single count and the ability to deny more than one of its allegations was severely restricted. By a statute, 4 Anne, c. 16, § 4 (1705), this was changed to allow more than one plea to a count with the court's permission, but as long as common-law pleading survived there could be no more than one replication to a plea.

As a consequence of these rules, a defendant who did not demur was safest if he could make a defense under a plea of the *general issue,* which challenged plaintiff's whole case.[g] This plea spared defendant the necessity of spelling out his defense, which meant that he did not have to divulge it to plaintiff or run the risk of misstating it. More importantly, the general issue in effect permitted defendant to traverse a number of plaintiff's allegations and, in addition, to raise defenses that ordinarily would be matters of confession and avoidance. Of course not all defenses could be raised under the general issue, and knowing which defenses had to be specially pleaded in particular forms of action was a matter of subtle learning. Although the whole theoretical structure of common-law pleading and its quest for a single issue

---

f. This privilege was widely used because of the strictness of the rule against *variances* between pleading and proof. A good example of the prohibition on variances is Latham v. Rutley, 2 B. & C. 20, 107 Eng.Rep. 290 (K.B. 1823). Plaintiff who had pleaded breach of a contract to carry and deliver goods safely was nonsuited because he proved a contract to carry and deliver goods safely, fire and robbery excepted, even though the verdict established that the loss was not caused by either fire or robbery.

g. Plaintiff's equivalent to the plea of the general issue, the replication *de injuria,* was less frequently available, and in most cases plaintiff was permitted to seize on only one facet of the plea. The most famous illustration is Crogate's Case, 8 Coke 66b, 77 Eng.Rep. 574 (K.B. 1608), which forms the basis for a brilliant satire on the common-law system. Hayes, *Crogate's Case: A Dialogue in Ye Shades on Special Pleading,* in 9 Holdsworth, *A History of English Law* 417 (2d ed. 1938).

was threatened by the general issue, inexorable pressures—particularly in the eighteenth century—gradually expanded its scope and availability. In conjunction with the common counts—a particularly cryptic form of declaration in contract, see pp. 489–90, infra—the plea of the general issue permitted some cases to come to trial with the issues not only unnarrowed, but indeed undisclosed. A good example of the problem was stated by Henry Brougham in a seminal speech to Parliament on law reform:

> * * * The plaintiff declares, that the defendant, being indebted to him for so much money had and received to the use of the said plaintiff * * * undertook and faithfully promised to pay it, but broke his engagement; and the count is thus framed, the self-same terms being invariably used, whatever be the cause of action which can be brought into Court under this head. * * * In the first place, such is the declaration for money paid by one individual to another, for the use and benefit of the plaintiff; this is what alone the words of the count imply, but to express this they are rarely, indeed, made use of. 2dly, The self-same terms are used on suing for money received on a consideration that fails, and used in the same way to describe all the endless variety of cases which can occur of such failure * * *. 3dly, The same words are used * * * to recover money paid under mistake of fact. 4thly, To recover money paid by one person to a stakeholder, in consideration of an illegal contract made with another person. 5thly, Money paid to revenue officers for releasing the goods illegally detained, of the person paying. 6thly, To try the right to any office, instead of bringing an assize. 7thly, To try the liability of the landlord for rates levied on his tenant. What information, then, does such a declaration give?

> * * *

> In the [form of action of] *indebitatus assumpsit,* from which I took my first example, * * * under [a plea of the general issue] no less than eight different defences may be set up; as, for instance, a denial of the contract, payment, usury, gaming, infancy, coverture, accord and satisfaction, release.

Brougham, *Present State of the Law* 70–71, 73 (1828).

Thus the pleadings in the English common-law courts immediately preceding the period of reform that began in 1825 presented a strange potpourri of ornate and sinuous paths toward an elusive single issue, side by side with a series of pleading rules that fostered abstract and unilluminating statements of dispute.

SECTION B.   THE FORMS OF ACTION

1. THE DEVELOPMENT OF THE FORMS—CHIEFLY OF TRESPASS

MAITLAND, EQUITY, ALSO THE FORMS OF ACTION AT COMMON LAW 296, 298–99, 304–05, 314–15, 332, 335, 342–47, 359–61 (1909):

Let it be granted that one man has been wronged by another; the first thing that he or his advisers have to consider is what form of action he shall bring. * * * This choice is not merely a choice between a number of queer technical terms, it is a choice between methods of procedure adapted to cases of different kinds.

* * * '[A] form of action' has implied a particular original process, a particular mesne process, a particular final process, a particular mode of pleading, of trial, of judgment. But further to a very considerable degree the substantive law administered in a given form of action has grown up independently of the law administered in other forms. Each procedural pigeon-hole contains its own rules of substantive law, and it is with great caution that we may argue from what is found in one to what will probably be found in another; each has its own precedents. It is quite possible that a litigant will find that his case will fit some two or three of these pigeon-holes. If that be so he will have a choice, which will often be a choice between the old, cumbrous, costly, on the one hand, the modern, rapid, cheap, on the other. Or again he may make a bad choice, fail in his action, and take such comfort as he can from the hints of the judges that another form of action might have been more successful. * * * Lastly he may find that, plausible as his case may seem, it just will not fit any one of the receptacles provided by the courts and he may take to himself the lesson that where there is no remedy there is no wrong.

* * * So long as the forms of action were still in use, it was difficult to tell the truth about their history. * * * But now, * * * the truth might be discovered and be told, and one part of the truth is assuredly this that throughout the early history of the forms of action there is an element of struggle, of struggle for jurisdiction. In order to understand them we must not presuppose a centralized system of justice * * *; rather we must think that the forms of action, the original writs, are the means whereby justice is becoming centralized, whereby the king's court is drawing away business from other courts.

* * * I shall attempt a sketch in brief outline of the order in which the different forms of action are developed. * * *

I.   1066–1154. The first [period] * * * would end with the great reforms of Henry II. Litigation of an ordinary kind still takes place chiefly in the communal and feudal courts; even the king's court may be considered as a feudal court, a court of and for the king's tenants in chief. * * * His court is concerned chiefly with (1) the pleas of the crown, i.e. cases in which royal rights are concerned, (2) litigation between the king's tenants in chief—for such tenants it is the proper feudal court, (3) complaints of default of justice in lower courts. * * *

II.   1154–1189. The legislative activity of Henry II's reign marks a second period. Under Henry II the exceptional becomes normal. He places royal justice at the disposal of anyone who can bring his case within a certain formula. From the end of his reign we have Glanvill's book, and we see already a considerable apparatus of writs * * *; they have assumed distinct forms, forms which they will preserve until the nineteenth century * * *; each writ is the beginning of a particular form of action. * * *

As regards those claims which in after days give rise to the personal actions, those actions which, as we say, are founded on contract or founded on tort, Glanvill has but little to tell us; they are seldom prosecuted in the king's court. But the action of Debt is known there. * * *

III. 1189–1272. This, our third period, extending from the death of Henry II to the accession of Edward I, is a period of rapid growth * * *. New writs are freely invented, though towards the end of Henry III's reign this gives rise to murmurs * * *. There is now a large store of original writs which are writs of course (*brevia de cursu*), that is to say, they may be obtained from the subordinate officers of the royal chancery * * *.

Meanwhile the actions which came to be known as personal make their appearance. The oldest seems to be 'Debt–Detinue' * * *. Gradually this action divides itself into two, Detinue for a specific chattel, Debt for a sum of money—this differentiation takes place early in the thirteenth century. As in Detinue the judgment given for the plaintiff awards him either the chattel itself, or its value; and, as the defendant thus has the option of giving back the chattel or paying its value, Bracton is led to make the important remark that there is no real action for chattels—an important remark, for it is the foundation of all our talk about real and personal property. To Debt and Detinue we must now add Replevin, the action for goods unlawfully taken in distress. * * * Covenant also has appeared * * *. Gradually the judges came to the opinion that the only acceptable evidence of a covenant is a sealed writing, and one of the foundations of our law of contract is thus laid. * * *

But the most important phenomenon is the appearance of Trespass—that fertile mother of actions. Instances of what we can not but call actions of trespass are found even in John's reign, but I think it clear that the writ of trespass did not become a writ of course until very late in Henry III's reign. Now trespass * * * has its roots in criminal law * * *. The old criminal action (yes, action) was the Appeal of Felony * * *. It was but slowly supplanted by indictment—the procedure of the common accuser set going by Henry II, the appeal on the other hand being an action brought by a person aggrieved by the crime.

* * * The new phenomenon appears about the year 1250, it is an action which might be called an attenuated appeal based on an act of violence. * * * The action of trespass is founded on a breach of the king's peace:—with force and arms the defendant has assaulted and beaten the plaintiff, broken the plaintiff's close, or carried off the plaintiff's goods; he is sued for damages. The plaintiff seeks not violence but compensation, but the unsuccessful defendant will also be punished and pretty severely. In other actions the unsuccessful party has to pay an amercement for making an unjust, or resisting a just claim; the defendant found guilty of trespass is fined and imprisoned. What is more, the action for trespass shows its semi-criminal nature in the process that can be used against a defendant who will not appear—if he will not appear, his body can be seized and imprisoned; if he can not be found, he may be outlawed. We thus can see that the action of trespass is one that will become very popular with plaintiffs because of the stringent process against defendants. I very much doubt whether in Henry III's day the action could as yet be used save where there really had been what we might fairly call violence and breach of the peace; but gradually the convenience of this new action showed itself. In order to constitute a case for 'Trespass *vi et armis*,' it was to the last necessary that there should be some wrongful

application of physical force to the defendant's lands or goods or person—but a wrongful step on his land, a wrongful touch to his person or chattels was held to be force enough and an adequate breach of the king's peace. This action then has the future before it.

* * *

IV. 1272–1307. The reign of 'the English Justinian' may be treated as a period by itself—a period of statutory activity. Statutes made by king and parliament now interfere with many details both of substantive law and of procedure. * * * The whole system stiffens. Men have learnt that a power to invent new remedies is a power to create new rights and duties, and it is no longer to be suffered that the chancellor or the judges should wield this power. How far the process of crystallisation had gone, how rigid the system was becoming, we learn from a section of the Statute of Westminster II, 13 Edw. I c. 24 (1285). Men have been obliged to depart from the Chancery without getting writs, because there are none which will exactly fit their cases, although these cases fall within admitted principles. It is not to be so for the future * * *. 'And whensoever from henceforth it shall fortune in the Chancery, that in one case a writ is found, and in a like case falling under like law, and requiring like remedy, is found none, the clerks of the Chancery shall agree in making the writ; or * * * let the cases be written in which they can not agree, and let them refer them until the next Parliament, and by consent of men learned in the law, a writ shall be made, lest it might happen after that the court should long time fail to minister justice unto complainants.' * * * [W]hen we say that but little use was made of this Statute there is one great exception. It is regarded as the statutory warrant for the variation of the writs of trespass so as to suit special cases, until at length—about the end of the Middle Ages—lawyers perceive that they have a new form 'Trespass upon the special case' or 'Case.' * * * It is worth noting that a writ issued by the Chancery is not necessarily a good writ. The justices may quash it as contrary to law, and in the later Middle Ages the judges are conservative * * *. At any rate the tale of common law (*i.e.* non-statutory) actions was now regarded as complete. The king's courts had come to be regarded as omnicompetent courts, they had to do all the important civil justice of the realm and to do it with the limited supply of forms of action which had been gradually accumulated in the days when feudal justice and ecclesiastical justice were serious competitors with royal justice.

V. 1307–1833. * * *

From Edward I's day onwards trespass *vi et armis* is a common action. We may notice three main varieties—unlawful force has been used against the body, the goods, the land of the plaintiff; so we have trespass in assault and battery, trespass *de bonis asportatis, trespass quare clausum fregit.* * * *

I have already said that the writ-making power wielded by the king and his Chancellor was gradually curbed by our parliamentary constitution, and in Edward I's day it has become necessary to tell the Chancery that it is not to be too pedantic, but may make variations in the old formulas when a new case falls under an old rule. * * * [T]he most important use made of this liberty consisted in some extensions of the action of trespass. Gradually during Edward III's reign we find a few writs occurring which in form are extremely like writs of trespass—and they are actually called writs of trespass—but the wrong complained of does not always consist of a direct application of unlawful physical force * * *; sometimes the words *vi et armis* do not appear. Sometimes there is no mention of the king's peace. Still they are spoken of as writs of trespass * * *. The plaintiff is said to bring an action upon his case, or upon the special case, and gradually it becomes apparent that really a new and a very elastic form of action has thus been created. I think that lawyers were becoming conscious of this about the end of the fourteenth century. Certain procedural differences have made their appearance—when there is *vi et armis* in the writ, then the defendant if he will not appear may be taken by *capias ad respondendum* or may be outlawed—this can not be if there is no talk of force and arms or the king's peace. Thus Case falls apart from Trespass—during the fifteenth century the line between them becomes always better marked. * * *

Case becomes a sort of general residuary action; much, particularly, of the modern law of negligence developed within it. Sometimes it is difficult to mark off case from trespass.

Notes and Questions

1. Case developed into a remedy not only for wrongs that were similar to those governed by trespass, but for wrongs that were much more similar to those for which the action of debt was appropriate. Yet case never lost its roots in trespass. Why didn't actions of debt on the case develop? See Kiralfy, *The Action on the Case* 3, 44 (1951).

2. Maitland's conclusions that trespass grew out of the appeal of felony and that case drew its authority from the Statute of Westminster II are debatable. Others have found the root of trespass in the assize of novel disseisin, in the proceedings of local courts, and in *queralae* ("innominate" actions without writ frequently found in the records of royal courts throughout the thirteenth century). The diversity of opinion is comprehensively reported in Fifoot, *History and Sources of the Common Law—Tort and Contract* 44–56, 66–74 (1949), a book of very great value in the study of the forms. See also Milsom, *Historical Foundations of the Common Law* 244–70 (1969).

3. In England's American colonies, the distinctions between the forms of action, although recognized, were not enforced with the rigor that characterized the procedure of the mother country. For example, there are instances of the use of both trespass and case for the specific recovery of chattels and real property, and trover and assumpsit frequently were not distinguished from case. Ejectment, when it was still regarded as a modern improvement in England, was unused in New England because of its technicalities. See Morris, *Studies in the History of American Law* 46–59 (2d ed. 1959). Since law books were scarce in the colonies, and many of the judges were laymen, these developments were to be expected. The most technical applications of the forms of action in this country came during the first half of the nineteenth century after the bar had grown in influence, and texts such as Blackstone had become available. See, e.g., Adams v. Hemmenway, 1 Mass. 145 (1804); Wilson v. Smith, 10 Wend. 324 (N.Y.1833).

2. THE LINES BLUR

a. *Trespass or Case?*

SCOTT, AN INFANT, BY HIS NEXT FRIEND v. SHEPHERD, AN INFANT, BY GUARDIAN

Court of Common Pleas, 1773.
2 Wm.Bl. 892, 96 Eng.Rep. 525.

Trespass and assault * * *. On not guilty pleaded, the cause came on to be tried before Nares, J., * * * when the jury found a verdict for the plaintiff with 100£. damages, subject to the opinion of the Court on this case: * * * [D]efendant threw a lighted squib, made of gunpowder, & c. from the street into the market-house, * * * where a large concourse of people were assembled; which lighted squib, * * * fell upon the standing of one Yates, who sold gingerbread, & c. That one Willis instantly, and to prevent injury to himself and the said wares of the said Yates, took up the said lighted squib from off the said standing, and then threw it across the said market-house, when it fell upon another standing there of one Ryal, * * * who instantly, and to save his own goods from being injured, took up the said lighted squib from off the said standing, and then threw it to another part of the said market-house, and, in so throwing it, struck the plaintiff * * * in the face therewith, and the combustible matter then bursting, put out one of the plaintiff's eyes. Qu. If this action be maintainable?

* * *

NARES, J., was of opinion, that trespass would well lie in the present case. That the natural and probable consequence of the act done by the defendant was injury to somebody, and therefore the act was illegal at common law. * * * Being therefore unlawful, the defendant was liable to answer for the consequences, be the injury mediate or immediate. * * * The principle I go upon is what is laid down in *Reynolds and Clark,* Stra. 634, that if the act in the first instance be unlawful, trespass will lie. Wherever therefore an act is unlawful at first, trespass will lie for the consequences of it. * * * [Defendant] * * * is the person, who, in the present case, gave the mischievous faculty to the squib. That mischievous faculty remained in it till the explosion. No new power of doing mischief was communicated to it by Willis or Ryal. It is like the case of a mad ox turned loose in a crowd. The person who turns him loose is answerable in trespass for whatever mischief he may do. The intermediate acts of Willis and Ryal will not purge the original tort in the defendant. * * *

BLACKSTONE, J., was of opinion, that an action of trespass did not lie for Scott against Shepherd upon this case. He took the settled distinction to be, that where the injury is immediate, an action of trespass will lie; where it is only consequential, it must be an action on the case: *Reynolds and Clarke,* Lord Raym. 1401. * * * The lawfulness or unlawfulness of the original act is not the criterion; though something of that sort is put into Lord Raymond's mouth in Stra. 635 * * *. But this cannot be the general rule; for it is held by the Court in the same case, that if I throw a log of timber into the highway, (which is an unlawful act), and another man tumbles over it, and is hurt, an action on the case only lies, it being a consequential damage; but if in throwing it I hit another man, he may bring trespass, because it is an immediate wrong. Trespass may sometimes lie for the consequences of a lawful act. If in lopping my own trees a bough accidentally falls on my neighbour's ground, and I go thereon to fetch it, trespass lies. * * * But then the entry is of itself an immediate wrong. And case will sometimes lie for the consequence of an unlawful act. If by false imprisonment I have a special damage, as if I forfeit my recognizance thereby, I shall have an action on the case. * * * Yet here the original act was unlawful, and in the nature of trespass. So that lawful or unlawful is quite out of the case; the solid distinction is between direct or immediate injuries on the one hand, and mediate or consequential on the other. And trespass never lay for the latter. If this be so, the only question will be, whether the injury which the plaintiff suffered was immediate, or consequential only; and I hold it to be the latter. The original act was, as against Yates, a trespass; not as against Ryal, or Scott. The tortious act was complete when the squib lay at rest upon Yates's stall. He, or any bystander, had, I allow, a right to protect themselves by removing the squib, but should have taken care to do it in such a manner as not to endamage others. But Shepherd, I think, is not answerable in an action of trespass and assault for the mischief done by the squib in the new motion impressed upon it, and the new direction given it, by either Willis or Ryal; who both were free agents, and acted upon their own judgment. This differs it from the cases put of turning loose a wild beast or a madman. They are only instruments in the hand of the first agent. Nor is it like diverting the course of an enraged ox, or of a stone thrown, or an arrow glancing against a tree; because there the original motion, the vis impressa, is continued, though diverted. Here the instrument of mischief was at rest, till a new impetus and a new direction are given it, not once only, but by two successive rational agents. But it is said that the act is not complete, nor the squib at rest, till after it is spent or exploded. It certainly has a power of doing fresh mischief, and so has a stone that has been thrown against my windows, and now lies still. Yet if any person gives that stone a new motion, and does farther mischief with it, trespass will not lie for that against the original thrower. No doubt but Yates may maintain trespass against Shepherd. And, according to the doctrine contended for, so may Ryal and Scott. Three actions for one single act! nay, it may be extended in infinitum. If a man tosses a football into the street, and after being kicked about by one hundred people, it at last breaks a tradesman's windows; shall he have trespass against the man who first produced it? Surely only against the man who gave it that mischievous direction. But it is said, if Scott has no action against Shepherd, against whom must he seek his remedy? I give no opinion whether case would lie against Shepherd for the consequential damage; though, as at present advised, I think, upon the circumstances, it would. But I think, in strictness of law, trespass would lie against Ryal, the immediate actor in this unhappy business. * * * The throwing it across the market-house, instead of brushing it down, or throwing [it] out of the open sides into the street, (if it was not meant to continue the sport, as it is called), was at least an unnecessary and incautious act. * * * And I admit that the defendant is answerable in trespass for all the direct and inevitable effects caused by his own immediate act. * * * But he is not responsible for the acts of other men. * * * In our case the verdict is suspended till the determination of the Court. And though after verdict the Court will not look with eagle's eyes to spy out a variance, yet, when a question is put by the jury upon such a variance, and it is made the very point of the cause, the Court will not wink against the light, and say that evidence, which at most is only applicable to an action on the case, will maintain an action of trespass. * * * The same evidence that will maintain trespass, may also frequently maintain case, but not e converso. Every action of trespass with a "per quod" includes an action on the case. I may bring trespass for the immediate injury, and subjoin a "per quod" for the consequential damages;— or may bring case for the consequential damages, and pass over the immediate injury * * *. But if I bring trespass for an immediate injury, and prove at most only a consequential damage, judgment must be for the defendant * * *.

GOULD, J., was of the same opinion with Nares, J., that this action was well maintainable.—The whole difficulty lies in the form of the action, and not in the substance of the remedy. The line is very nice between case and trespass upon these occasions: I am persuaded there are many instances wherein both or either will lie. I agree with brother Nares, that wherever a man does an unlawful act, he is answerable for all the consequences; and trespass will lie against him, if the consequence be in nature of trespass. But, exclusive of this, I think the defendant may be considered in the same view as if he himself had personally thrown the squib in the plaintiff's face. The terror impressed upon Willis and Ryal excited self-defence, and deprived them of the power of recollection. * * *

DE GREY, C.J. * * * I agree with my brother Blackstone as to the principles he has laid down, but not in his application of those principles to the present case. The real question certainly does not turn upon the lawfulness or unlawfulness of the original act; for actions of trespass will lie for legal acts when they become trespasses by accident * * *. They may also not lie for the consequences even of illegal acts, as that of casting a log in the highway, & c.—But the true question is, whether the injury is the direct and immediate act of the defendant; and I am of opinion, that in this case it is. The throwing the squib was an act unlawful and tending to affright the bystanders. So far, mischief was originally intended; not any particular mischief, but mischief indiscriminate and wanton. Whatever mischief therefore follows, he is the author of it * * *. Every one who does an unlawful act is considered as the doer of all that follows. * * * I look upon all that was done subsequent to the original throwing as a continuation of the first force and first act, which will continue till the squib was spent by bursting. And I think that any innocent person removing the danger from himself to another is justifiable; the blame lights upon the first thrower. * * * It has been urged, that the intervention of a free agent will make a difference: but I do not consider Willis and Ryal as free agents in the present case, but acting under a compulsive necessity for their own safety and self-preservation. * * *

Postea to the plaintiff.

Notes and Questions

1. In what ways does Justice Blackstone differ from Chief Justice De Grey? From Justice Nares? On what facts might Chief Justice De Grey and Justice Nares reach a different result? Chief Justice De Grey and Justice Gould? Since Justice Blackstone believes an action in case would lie against Shepherd, is there really any substantive difference between him and his brethren? Would they have agreed with him that Scott could have maintained an action against Ryal? What would have been the nature of that action? In light of Gibbons v. Pepper, p. 472, supra, would actions of trespass lie against both Shepherd and Ryal?

2. Trials ordinarily were held at common law before a single judge and a jury. After verdict, if the losing party wanted the judgment of the entire court on a question of law that was involved in the case, that party asked for a rule *nisi*. A hearing before the court *en banc* was then held, and if that court sustained the rulings of the trial judge it denied the rule; otherwise, it made the rule *absolute*. When a verdict was taken subject to the opinion of the court *en banc,* as in Scott v. Shepherd, the ordinary procedure of applying for a rule *nisi* was unnecessary. Therefore, instead of denying a rule or making it absolute, the order of the court *en banc* was in the form of a *postea* to the prevailing party, which authorized the entry of judgment.

b. *Case Captures Negligence*

The close of the eighteenth century brought before the judges a great number of cases of a kind theretofore little known but which ever since have glutted our courts: running-down accidents and vehicular collisions. Echoes of Lord Raymond's distinction in Reynolds v. Clarke were less frequently heard, but the categories of direct and indirect injuries became mixed with those of wilful and negligent conduct, often in a context complicated by the involvement of servants. Matters would not stay within the simple confines that Justice Blackstone envisioned.

DAY v. EDWARDS, 5 T.R. 648, 101 Eng.Rep. 361 (K.B.1794), was an action in case against a defendant who had driven his cart "so furiously, negligently and improperly" that it "struck with great force and violence * * * against plaintiff's carriage." Plaintiff's lawyer touched on all the elements that had been or would become significant—legality, indirectness, negligence; the "act of driving * * * in consequence of which the injury arose, was a legal one in itself, although negligently exercised," he said. But Lord Kenyon merely repeated the immediate injury-consequential injury distinction, found that plaintiff "complains of the immediate act," and gave judgment for defendant.

One year later in MORLEY v. GAISFORD, 2 H.Bl. 441, 126 Eng.Rep. 639 (C.P.1795), Common Pleas held case was proper when defendant's servant was alleged to have "badly, ignorantly, and negligently" driven a cart against plaintiff's chaise, saying "it was difficult to put a case where the master could be considered as a trespasser for an act of his servant, which was not done at his command."

The *Morley* holding clearly turned on the issue of a master's liability in trespass, but when plaintiffs brought an action of case against defendants for having "so incautiously, carelessly, negligently, and inexpertly managed, steered and directed" their ship that it collided with plaintiffs' vessel, their counsel relied upon *Morley* solely for the proposition that trespass lay for wilful conduct and case for negligence, and two of the three judges accepted it. OGLE v. BARNES, 8 T.R. 188, 101 Eng.Rep. 1338 (K.B.1799). Lord Kenyon continued to insist upon the distinction between an immediate and a consequential injury, but he agreed that case was proper, since the charge was that by reason of defendants' negligence, their ship sailed against plaintiffs' vessel.

By 1803, we find defendant in LEAME v. BRAY, 3 East 593, 102 Eng.Rep. 724 (K.B.), challenging an action of trespass for a highway collision on the ground that the evidence showed his conduct to be negligent only, and that the action should therefore have been case. The court, however, reaffirmed its position in Day v. Edwards, that trespass lay for an immediate injury. Justice Lawrence, who had sat in *Ogle,* explained now that "what I principally relied on there was, that it did not appear that the mischief happened from the personal acts of the defendants: it might have happened from the operation of the wind and tide counteracting their personal efforts at the time: or indeed they might not even have been on board."

Common Pleas, which now clearly favored case for these actions, twice suggested that *Leame* be reconsidered, but King's Bench under Lord Ellenborough stood fast. In HALL v. PICKARD, 3 Camp. 187, 170 Eng.Rep. 1350 (K.B.1812), however, he raised the question whether it "may * * * be worthy of consideration, whether, in those instances where trespass may be maintained, the party may not waive the trespass, and proceed for the tort?" Later cases built on this suggestion until at last WILLIAMS v. HOLLAND, 10 Bing. 112, 131 Eng.Rep. 848 (C.P.1833), was accepted as settling the matter:

> The declaration * * * states the ground of action to be an injury occasioned by the carelessness and negligence of the Defendant in driving his own gig; * * * and the jury have found in the very terms of the declaration, that the jury [sic] was so occasioned. Under such a form of action, therefore, and with such a finding by the jury, the present objection ought not to prevail, unless some positive and inflexible rule of law, or some authority too strong to be overcome, is brought forward in its support. * * *

> But upon examining the cases cited in argument, both in support of, and in answer to, the objection, we cannot find one in which it is distinctly held, that the present form of action is not maintainable under the circumstances of this case.

> * * * [T]he late case of Moreton v. Hardern [4 B. & C. 223, 107 Eng.Rep. 1042 (K.B.1825)], appears to us to go the full length of deciding, that * * * where the injury is occasioned by the carelessness and negligence of the Defendant, the Plaintiff is at liberty to bring an action on the case, notwithstanding the act is immediate, so long as it is not a wilful act * * *.

3.   THE LOSS AND DETENTION OF PERSONAL PROPERTY

The writ of detinue lay when defendant had possession of plaintiff's personal property and refused to relinquish it. The writ would lie, for example, against a bailee who refused to redeliver bailed goods or an executor who withheld the title-deed to an heir's real property. Although the gist of the action was wrongful detention, rather than wrongful taking, detinue would lie against a thief. But in this type of case trespass *de bonis asportatis* was preferred because detinue had several drawbacks: Defendant had a right to wage his law, and could deliver up the property in lieu of paying damages, even though it was damaged, for detinue did not lie for mere harm to goods.

Not surprisingly, plaintiffs began to try to substitute an action on the case in circumstances that seemed to call for detinue. They succeeded, first in the situation in which detinue was clearly inadequate—when the goods had spoiled—and then in situations in which its remedy might be appropriate but its mode of trial was unsatisfactory. See Fifoot, *History and Sources of the Common Law—Tort and Contract* 102–04 (1949). By 1500, case was essentially an alternative to detinue, and in the course of the sixteenth century a distinct species of case developed—the action of trover. The form of this new action was predicated upon a fiction—plaintiff alleged that he had lost goods, that they had been found by defendant and were now in that party's possession, and that defendant refused to deliver them upon request. Loss and finding soon became recognized as formal allegations only, but the allegations concerning the request for return of the goods and defendant's refusal to deliver retained some significance; after all, your bailee cannot be considered to have committed a tort if you have not asked for your goods back. What might constitute a legitimate, conditional refusal to deliver—as in the case of a finder who wished to check the credentials of a claimant—became an important issue. Apart from the fact that defendant was not entitled to wage his law, trover differed from detinue in this respect: Plaintiff was under no obligation to take back the goods, and in an action against a thief was under no obligation to demand them. The essence of trover was the conversion of the goods.

What is a conversion? The term has troubled the courts for several hundred years, but the most famous definition is that of Chief Justice Holt, in BALDWIN v. COLE, 6 Mod. 212, 87 Eng.Rep. 964 (K.B.1705): "[W]hat is a conversion, but an assuming upon one's self the property and right of disposing another's goods; and he that takes upon himself to detain another man's goods from him without cause, takes upon himself the right of disposing of them * * *." Is this really helpful? Consider the following case.

BUSHEL v. MILLER

Court of King's Bench, 1718.
1 Strange 128, 93 Eng.Rep. 428.

Upon the Custom–House quay there is a hut, where particular porters put in small parcels of goods, if the ship is not ready to receive them when they are brought upon the quay. The porters, who have a right in this hut, have each particular boxes or cupboards, and as such the defendant had one. The plaintiff being one of the porters puts in goods belonging to A and lays them so that the defendant could not get to his chest without removing them. He accordingly does remove them about a yard from the place where they lay, towards the door, and without returning them into their place goes away, and the goods are lost. The plaintiff satisfies A of the value of the goods, and brings trover against the defendant. And upon the trial two points were ruled by the C.J.

1. That the plaintiff having made satisfaction to A for the goods, had thereby acquired a sufficient property in them to maintain trover.

2. That there was no conversion in the defendant. The plaintiff by laying his goods where they obstructed the defendant from going to his chest, was in that respect a wrong-doer. The defendant had a right to remove the goods, so that thus far he was in no fault. Then as to the not returning the goods to the place where he found them; if this were an action of trespass, perhaps it might be a doubt; but he was clear it could not amount to a conversion.

Notes and Questions

1. Plaintiff's goods were delivered by a ship's captain to defendant wharfingers to be held for plaintiff. The goods were then lost or stolen from defendants. Could defendants be said to have converted them? In ROSS v. JOHNSON, 5 Burrow 2825, 98 Eng.Rep. 483 (K.B.1772), Lord Mansfield said case, not trover, was the only remedy: "[I]n order to maintain trover, there must be an injurious conversion. This is not to be deemed a refusal to deliver the goods. They can't deliver them: it is not in their power to do it. It is a bare omission."

2. If defendant so negligently kept twenty barrels of plaintiff's butter that "they were become of little value," would trover lie? See Walgrave v. Ogden, 1 Leon. 224, 74 Eng.Rep. 205 (K.B.1590).

GORDON v. HARPER

Court of King's Bench, 1796.
7 T.R. 9, 101 Eng.Rep. 828.

In trover for certain goods, being household furniture * * *. [Plaintiff leased a house with the goods in question to A for a term still extant at the time of trial. While A was in possession under the lease, defendant sheriff seized the goods in execution of a judgment against B, who had sold the furniture to plaintiff sometime before the lease. Defendant after the seizure sold the goods.]

Lord Kenyon, Ch. J. The only point for the consideration of the Court in the case of Ward v. Macauley [4 T.R. 489, 100 Eng.Rep. 1135 (K.B.1791)] was, whether in a case like the present, the landlord could maintain an action of trespass against the sheriff for seizing goods, let with a house, under an execution against the tenant; and it was properly decided that no such action could be maintained. What was said further by me in that case, that trover was the proper remedy, was an extrajudicial opinion, to which upon further consideration I cannot subscribe. The true question is, whether when a person has leased goods in a house to another for a certain time, whereby he parts with the right of possession during the term to the tenant, and has only a reversionary interest, he can notwithstanding recover the value of the whole property pending the existence of the term in an action of trover. The very statement of the proposition affords an answer to it. If, instead of household goods, the goods here taken had been machines used in manufacture, which had been leased to a tenant, no doubt could have been made but that the sheriff might have seized them under an execution against the tenant, and the creditor would have been entitled to the beneficial use of the property during the term: the difference of the goods then cannot vary the law. * * * I forbear to deliver any opinion as to what remedy the landlord has in this case, not being at present called upon so to do: but it is clear that he cannot maintain trover.

Ashhurst, J. I have always understood the rule of law to be, that in order to maintain trover the plaintiff must have a right of property in the thing, and a right of possession, and that unless both these rights concur, the action will not lie. * * *

Grose, J. The only question is whether trover will lie where the plaintiff had neither the actual possession of the goods taken at the time, nor the right of possession. * * * Where goods are delivered to a carrier, the owner has still a right of possession as against a tort-feasor, and the carrier is no more than his servant. But here it is clear that the plaintiff had no right of possession; and he would be a trespasser if he took the goods from the tenant: then by what authority can he recover them from any other person during the term? * * *

LAWRENCE, J. * * *. Now here if the taking of the goods by the sheriff determined the interest of the tenant in them, and revested it in the landlord, I admit that the latter might maintain trover for them * * *: but it is clearly otherwise; for here the tenant's property and interest did not determine by the sheriff's trespass, and the tenant might maintain trespass against the wrong-doer, and recover damages. * * *

Postea to the defendant.

Notes and Questions

1. Plaintiff pawned a jeweled hatband to X for 25 pounds with no certain time fixed for redemption. X delivered it to defendant, and then died. Plaintiff tendered 25 pounds to the executrix, who refused it, and then demanded the hatband of defendant. Would trover lie? See Ratcliff v. Davies, Croke Jac. 244, 79 Eng.Rep. 210 (K.B.1611).

2. Plaintiff leased a farm with cattle to Y for one year. After a few months, Y sold the cattle to defendant and absconded. What theory might be used to allow plaintiff to bring trover against defendant? See Swift v. Moseley, 10 Vt. 208 (1838).

4.   THE CREATION OF CONTRACT LAW

a.   *Special Assumpsit*

Glanvill said, shortly before 1200: "[I]t is not the custom of the court of the lord king to protect private agreements, nor does it concern itself with such contracts as can be considered to be like private agreements." *The treatise on the laws and customs of the realm of England commonly called Glanvill*, Bk. X [18] (Hall ed. 1965). By the middle of the fourteenth century, there remained a good deal of truth in this. Two forms of action, each with significant shortcomings, lay for breach of contract—the writs of covenant and debt. Covenant required a sealed instrument and did not lie when debt was available. Debt lay only when an agreement had been fully performed by one party and he was entitled to a sum certain, and as in the case of detinue, defendant was entitled to wage his law, unless the agreement was sealed. Again, plaintiffs resorted to case as a safety valve for the deficiencies of covenant and debt, but progress was slower than it had been in the evasion of detinue, perhaps because the effort was not so much to avoid a particular writ as to create a new area of substantive law.

By 1400, plaintiff could maintain case against a defendant who had carried out his promise so badly that plaintiff was in a worse position than before defendant made his promise. Thus in 1370 case was held to lie against a defendant who having undertaken to cure plaintiff's horse, treated it so negligently that it died. WALDON v. MARSHALL, Y.B.Mich. 43 Ed. 3, f. 33, pl. 38. Chief Justice Cavendish, in an action against a surgeon for maiming plaintiff while trying to cure him, said "this action of covenant of necessity is maintained without specialty, since for every little thing a man cannot always have a Clerk to make a specialty for him." THE SURGEON'S CASE, Y.B.Hil. 48 Ed. 3, f. 6, pl. 11 (K.B.1375). But case did not lie for nonfeasance. Through the fifteenth century there were occasional departures, but the courts seemed always to return to this rule. Then suddenly it was abandoned for good, and a new form of action developed from case and received judicial acceptance—special assumpsit. No single case seems to have established assumpsit as a remedy for nonperformance of a promise, but shortly after 1500 it had become the accepted view.

b. General Assumpsit

Special assumpsit filled a major gap left by the action of debt, but it did not take the place of debt, as trover substantially had taken the place of detinue. For another century, argument flared on the question whether assumpsit would lie for a debt. Gradually it was established that if a person, who already was indebted to another, made a fresh promise to pay the debt, assumpsit would lie for a breach of that promise, even though it would not have lain for the debt itself. The question then arose whether the fresh promise actually had to be made, or assumpsit would lie even when the promise was a fiction. In part, the answer lay in the desires of two courts to draw business to themselves; debt was the exclusive province of Common Pleas, while assumpsit with its background in trespass could be brought there or in King's Bench. For thirty years they squabbled over the matter.

SLADE'S CASE

Court of Exchequer Chamber, 1602.
4 Co.Rep. 92b, 76 Eng.Rep. 1074.

John Slade brought an action on the case in the King's Bench against Humphrey Morley * * * and declared, that whereas the plaintiff * * * was possessed of a close of land * * * and being so possessed, the plaintiff * * * the said close had sowed with wheat and rye, which wheat and rye * * * were grown into blades, the defendant, in consideration that the plaintiff, at the special instance and request of the said Humphrey, had bargained and sold to him the said blades of wheat and rye growing upon the said close, * * * assumed and promised the plaintiff to pay him 16l. * * *: and for non-payment thereof * * * the plaintiff brought the said action: the defendant pleaded *non assumpsit modo et forma;* and on the trial of this issue the jurors gave a special verdict, *sc.* that the defendant bought of the plaintiff the wheat and rye in blades growing upon the said close * * * and further found, that between the plaintiff and the defendant there was no other promise or assumption but only the said bargain * * *. And for the honour of the law, and for the quiet of the subject in the appeasing of such diversity of opinions * * * the case was openly argued before all the Justices of England, and Barons of the Exchequer, * * * and after many conferences between the justices and Barons, it was resolved, that the action was maintainable, and that the plaintiff should have judgment. And in this case these points were resolved:—1. That although an action of debt lies upon the contract, yet the bargainor may have an action on the case, or an action of debt at his election * * *. 3. It was resolved, that every contract executory imports in itself an *assumpsit,* for when one agrees to pay money, or to deliver anything, thereby he assumes or promises to pay, or deliver it, and therefore when one sells any goods to another, and agrees to deliver them at a day to come, and the other in consideration thereof agrees to pay so much money as such a day, in that case both parties may have an action of debt, or an action on the case on *assumpsit,* for the mutual executory agreement of both parties imports in itself reciprocal actions upon the case, as well as actions of debt * * *. 4. It was resolved, that the plaintiff in this action on the case on assumpsit should not recover only damages for the special loss (if any be) which he had, but also for the whole debt, so that a recovery or bar in this action would be a good bar in an action of debt brought upon the same contract * * *. And as to the objection which has been made, that it would be mischievous to the defendant that he should not wage his law, forasmuch as he might pay it in secret: to that it was answered, that it should be accounted his folly that he did not take sufficient witnesses with him to prove the payment he made: but the mischief would be rather on the other party, for now experience proves that men's consciences grow so large that the respect of their private advantage rather induces men (and chiefly those who have declining estates) to perjury * * *.

Note

You should remember in considering the demise of wager of law that at this time, and for two centuries more, parties were incompetent to testify at a trial. The enactment of the Statute of Frauds, 29 Charles 2, c. 3 (1677), which required several kinds of contracts to be in writing, is attributed by many to the problem of proof posed by the result in Slade's Case. See, e.g., Plucknett, *A Concise History of the Common Law* 648 (5th ed. 1956).

––––––––––

The recognition of *indebitatus assumpsit* (literally, "being indebted, he promised"), or *general assumpsit,* did more than deliver the quietus to debt. The contract-like sanction it imposed upon an obligation that did not really arise out of an actual promise provided the structure for wholly new developments. When A has delivered goods to B or has performed services for the latter, it may be presumed that A expects payment and B expects to pay; but the common law had furnished no remedy in the absence of an actual agreement. Now a new action of quantum meruit developed based upon an implied promise to pay the reasonable value of the goods or services, not unlike the imputed promise to pay the debt that furnished the basis for Slade's Case. Even more significant was the extension of this same formula into circumstances in which a promise to pay was the last thing in defendant's mind.

LAMINE v. DORRELL

Court of Queen's Bench, 1705.
2 Ld.Raym. 1216, 92 Eng.Rep. 303.

In an indebitatus assumpsit for money received by the defendant to the use of the plaintiff as administrator of J.S. on non assumpsit pleaded, upon evidence the case appeared to be, that J.S. died intestate possessed of certain Irish debentures; and the defendant pretending to a right to be administrator, got administration granted to him, and by that means got these debentures into his hands, and disposed of them: then the defendant's administration was repealed, and administration granted to the plaintiff, and he brought this action against the defendant for the money he sold the debentures for. And it being objected upon the evidence, that this action would not lie, because the defendant sold the debentures as one that claimed a title and interest in them, and therefore could not be said to receive the money for the use of the plaintiff, which indeed he received to his own use; but the plaintiff ought to have brought trover or detinue for the debentures: the point was saved to the defendant, and now the Court was moved, and the same objection made.

POWELL JUSTICE. It is clear the plaintiff might have maintained detinue or trover for the debentures * * *. But the plaintiff may dispense with the wrong, and suppose the sale made by his consent, and bring an action for the money they were sold for, as money received to his use. * * *

HOLT CHIEF JUSTICE. These actions have crept in by degrees. * * * So the defendant in this case pretending to receive the money the debentures were sold for in the right of the intestate, why should he not be answerable for it to the intestate's administrator? If an action of trover should be brought by the plaintiff for these debentures after judgment in this indebitatus assumpsit, he may plead this recovery in bar of the action of trover, in the same manner as it would have been a good plea in bar for the defendant to have pleaded to the action of trover, that he sold the debentures, and paid to the plaintiff in satisfaction. * * * This recovery may be given in evidence upon not guilty in the action of trover, because by this action the plaintiff makes and affirms the act of the defendant in the sale of the debentures to be lawful, and consequently the sale of them is no conversion.

* * *

MOSES v. MACFERLAN, 2 Burrow 1005, 97 Eng.Rep. 676 (K.B.1760). Plaintiff had endorsed four promissory notes to defendant under a written agreement that he should not be liable thereon; in defendant's suit in a Court of Conscience (a small claims court), however, the agreement was not recognized, and plaintiff was found liable for six pounds, which he paid. (On these facts, would Lamine v. Dorrell support an action for money had and received?) Lord Mansfield said:

2d objection.—"That no assumpsit lies, except upon an express or implied contract: but here it is impossible to presume any contract to refund money, which the defendant recovered by an adverse suit."

Answer. If the defendant be under an obligation, from the ties of natural justice, to refund; the law implies a debt, and gives this action, founded in the equity of the plaintiff's case, as it were upon a contract ("quasi ex contractu," as the Roman law expresses it).

* * *

Money may be recovered by a right and legal judgment; and yet the iniquity of keeping that money may be manifest, upon grounds which could not be used by way of defence against the judgment.

* * *

Suppose a man recovers upon a policy for a ship presumed to be lost, which afterwards comes home;—or upon the life of a man presumed to be dead, who afterwards appears;—or upon a representation of a risque deemed to be fair, which comes out afterwards to be grossly fraudulent.

* * *

One great benefit, which arises to suitors from the nature of this action, is, that the plaintiff needs not state the special circumstances from which he concludes "that, ex aequo & bono, the money received by the defendant, ought to be deemed as belonging to him:" he may declare generally, "that the money was received to his use;" and make out his case, at the trial.

* * *

This kind of equitable action to recover back money, which ought not in justice to be kept, is very beneficial, and therefore much encouraged. It lies only for money which, ex aequo et bono, the defendant ought to refund: it does not lie for money paid by the plaintiff, which is claimed of him as payable in point of honor and honesty, although it could not have been recovered from him by any course of law; as in payment of a debt barred by the Statute of Limitations, or contracted during his infancy, or to the extent of principal and legal interest upon an usurious contract, or, for money fairly lost at play: because in all these cases, the defendant may retain it with a safe conscience, though by positive law he was barred from recovering.

An important procedural result of the development of indebitatus assumpsit was a new manner of pleading contract actions. The declaration in money had and received, as Lord Mansfield noted in his opinion in Moses v. MacFerlan, was broad in the extreme. The declarations in other actions derived from indebitatus assumpsit were equally broad. Pleaders seized upon this liberality to develop what became known as the "common counts," standardized allegations concealing virtually all of the particulars of an action. The principal common counts were for money had and received, for goods sold and delivered, for work done, for money lent, for money paid by plaintiff to the use of defendant, and for money due on an account stated. See Fifoot, *History and Sources of the Common Law—Tort and Contract* 369–70, 393–94 (1949).

SECTION C. THE OTHER SYSTEM: EQUITY

1. THE RISE OF CHANCERY

MAITLAND, EQUITY, ALSO THE FORMS OF ACTION AT COMMON LAW 2–10 (1909):

In Edward I's day, at the end of the thirteenth century, three great courts have come into existence * * *.

One of the three courts, namely, the Exchequer, is more than a court of law. From our modern point of view it is not only a court of law but a 'government office'. * * * What we should call the 'civil service' of the country is transacted by two great offices or 'departments'; there is the Exchequer which is the fiscal department, there is the Chancery which is the secretarial department, while above these there rises the king's permanent Council. At the head of the Chancery stands the Chancellor, usually a bishop; he is we may say the king's secretary of state for all departments, he keeps the king's great seal and all the already great mass of writing that has to be done in the king's name has to be done under his supervision.

He is not as yet a judge, but already he by himself or his subordinates has a great deal of work to do which brings him into a close connexion with the administration of justice. One of the duties of that great staff of clerks over which he presides is to draw up and issue those writs whereby actions are begun in the courts of law—such writs are sealed with the king's seal. * * *

But by another route the Chancellor is brought into still closer contact with the administration of justice. Though these great courts of law have been established there is still a reserve of justice in the king. Those who can not get relief elsewhere present their petitions to the king and his council praying for some remedy. * * * In practice a great share of this labour falls on the Chancellor. He is the king's prime minister, he is a member of the council, and the specially learned member of the council. It is in dealing with these petitions that the Chancellor begins to develop his judicial powers.

* * * Very often the petitioner requires some relief at the expense of some other person. He complains that for some reason or another he can not get a remedy in the ordinary course of justice and yet he is entitled to a remedy. He is poor, he is old, he is sick, his adversary is rich and powerful, will bribe or will intimidate jurors, or has by some trick or some accident acquired an advantage of which the ordinary courts with their formal procedure will not deprive him. The petition is often couched in piteous terms, the king is asked to find a remedy for the love of God and in the way of charity. Such petitions are referred by the king to the Chancellor. Gradually in the course of the fourteenth century petitioners, instead of going to the king, will go straight to the Chancellor * * *. Now one thing that the Chancellor may do in such a case is to invent a new writ and so provide the complainant with a means of bringing an action in a court of law. But in the fourteenth century the courts of law have become very conservative and are given to quashing writs which differ in material points from those already in use. But another thing that the Chancellor can do is to send for the complainant's adversary and examine him concerning the charge that has been made against him.

Gradually a procedure is established. The Chancellor having considered the petition, or 'bill' as it is called, orders the adversary to come before him and answer the complaint. The writ whereby he does this is called a subpoena—because it orders the man to appear upon pain of forfeiting a sum of money * * *. It is very different from the old writs whereby actions are begun in the courts of law. They tell the defendant what is the cause of action against him * * *. The subpoena, on the other hand, will tell him merely that he has got to come before the Chancellor and answer complaints made against him by A.B. Then when he comes before the Chancellor he will have to answer on oath, and sentence by sentence, the bill of the plaintiff. * * *

I do not think that in the fourteenth century the Chancellors considered that they had to administer any body of substantive rules that differed from the ordinary law of the land. * * * The complaints that come before them are in general complaints of indubitable legal wrongs * * * of which the ordinary courts take cognizance, wrongs which they ought to redress. * * * However this sort of thing can not well be permitted. * * * And so the Chancellor is warned off the field of common law—he is not to hear cases which might go to the ordinary courts, he is not to make himself a judge of torts and contracts, of property in lands and goods.

But then just at this time it is becoming plain that the Chancellor is doing some convenient and useful works that could not be done, or could not easily be done by the courts of common law. He has taken to enforcing uses or trusts. * * * No doubt they were troublesome things, things that might be used for fraudulent purposes, and statutes were passed against those who employed them for the purpose of cheating their creditors or evading the law of mortmain. But I have not a doubt that they were very popular, and I think we may say that had there been no Chancery, the old courts would have discovered some method of enforcing these fiduciary obligations. That method however must have been a clumsy one. A system of law which will never compel, which will never even allow, the defendant to give evidence, a system which sends every question of fact to a jury, is not competent to deal adequately with fiduciary relationships. On the other hand the Chancellor had a procedure which was very well adapted to this end.

* * * And then there were some other matters that were considered to be fairly within his jurisdiction. An old rhyme allows him 'fraud, accident, and breach of confidence'—there were many frauds which the stiff old procedure of the courts of law could not adequately meet, and 'accident,' in particular the accidental loss of a document, was a proper occasion for the Chancellor's interference.

* * * In James I's day occurred the great quarrel between Lord Chancellor Ellesmere and Chief Justice Coke which finally decided that the Court of Chancery was to have the upper hand over the courts of law. If the Chancery was to carry out its maxims about trust and fraud it was essential that it should have a power to prevent men from going into the courts of law and to prevent men from putting in execution the judgments that they had obtained in courts of law. In fraud or in breach of trust you obtain a judgment against me in a court of law; I complain to the Chancellor, and he after hearing what you have to say enjoins you not to put in force your judgment, says in effect that if you do put your judgment in force you will be sent to prison.

Understand well that the Court of Chancery never asserted that it was superior to the courts of law; it never presumed to send to them such mandates as the Court of King's Bench habitually sent to the inferior courts, telling them that they must do this or must not do that or quashing their proceedings * * *. It was addressed not to the judges, but to the party. * * * For all this, however, it was natural that the judges should take umbrage at this treatment of their judgments. Coke declared that the man who obtained such an injunction was guilty of the offence denounced by the Statutes of Praemunire, that of calling in question the judgments of the king's courts in other courts (these statutes had been aimed at the Papal curia). King James had now a wished-for opportunity of appearing as supreme over all his judges, and all his courts * * *.

ARGUMENTS PROVING FROM ANTIQUITY THE DIGNITY, POWER, AND JURISDICTION OF THE COURT OF CHANCERY

1 Chan.Rep. (App.) 1, 20, 23–24, 49–50, 21 Eng.Rep. 576, 581–82, 588 (1616).

* * *

His said Majesty being informed of this Difference between his two Courts of Chancery and King's Bench, * * * directed, That his Attorney General, calling to him the Rest of his Learned Counsel, should peruse the * * * Precedents, and certify his Majesty the Truth thereof with their Opinions.

* * *

And afterwards a Case was presented to his Majesty as followeth.

THE CASE.

A.   hath a Judgment and Execution in the King's Bench or Common Pleas against B. in an Action of Debt of £1000, and in an *Ejectione Firmae* of the Manor of D. B. complains in the Chancery to be relieved against these Judgments according to Equity and Conscience, allowing the Judgment to be lawful and good by the Rigour and strict Rules of the Law, and the Matter in Equity to be such, as the Judges of the Common Law being no Judges of Equity, but bound by their Oaths to do the Law, cannot give any Remedy or Relief for the same, either by Error or Attaint, or by any other Means.

QUESTION.

Whether the Chancery may relieve B. in this or such like Cases, or else leave him utterly remediless and undone? And if the Chancery be restrained herein by any Statute of Praemunire, then by what Statute, and by what Words in any Statute is the Chancery so restrained, and Conscience and Equity excluded, banished and damned?

Which Case his Majesty referred again to his said Attorney and Learned Counsel * * *.

* * *

Upon which Certificate the King gave his Judgment as followeth.

Forasmuch as Mercy and Justice be the true Supporters of our Royal Throne, and that it properly belongeth unto us in our Princely Office to take Care and provide, that our Subjects have equal and indifferent Justice ministered unto them: And that where their Case deserveth to be relieved in Course of Equity by Suit in our Court of Chancery, they should not be abandoned and exposed to perish under the Rigor and Extremity of our Laws, We in our Princely Judgment * * * do approve, ratify and confirm, * * * the Practice of our Court of Chancery * * *. And do will and command that our Chancellor, or Keeper of the Great Seal for the Time being, shall not hereafter desist to give unto our Subjects, * * * such Relief in Equity (notwithstanding any Proceedings at the Common Law against them) as shall stand with the Merit and Justice of their Cause, and with the former, ancient and continued Practice and Presidency of our Chancery have done. * * *

BEALE, EQUITY IN AMERICA, 1 Cambridge L.J. 21, 22–23 (1921):

At about the time of the English Revolution colonies came to be more rigorously governed. Most of the old charters were forfeited, and a new provincial form of government was established; and from that time the Judges were appointed, through the royal governors, by the Crown, and they came to be regarded, naturally, as the enemies of popular rights and as creatures of the Crown. The situation at about the time of the American Revolution was that Judges in the North were still regarded as tools of the King and as enemies of the popular will. * * *

In the South conditions were very different. The ruling class was well satisfied with the condition of affairs in England, and, although there were popular uprisings in some parts of the South, notably in Virginia and Maryland, the power of the aristocracy on the whole was never shaken. They determined the laws, they had no distrust of Judges, and in those States there was no desire to hamper a Judge or to exalt the jury at his expense. * * *

We should not be surprised, therefore, to find that in the North at least the people were very jealous of giving any jurisdiction to the Court of Equity, there being no jury in that Court. Equity seemed to the people of America, a hundred years ago even, as a non-popular method of applying law, which it was the duty of the people alone to deal with. The Courts administering equity were, so to speak, royalist persons administering the law of an effete monarchy which had never taken foothold in the democratic part of America. The consequence was that in New England there was no equity jurisdiction and very little admixture of equity in the law. The law administered was the strictly legal portion of the law; and the books cited, when they came to cite books, were the reports of the common law Courts. In New York there was a Chancellor from the time of the original constitution; but that Chancellor was not supposed to be a Judge who administered the English system of equity. * * *

Pennsylvania never had any Court of equity. The law, however, had more of what they regarded as equitable doctrines in it than the law of Massachusetts * * *. In New Jersey and Delaware, however, and throughout the South, there was set up at the time of our Revolution a separate Court of Chancery, sitting beside the Common Law Court and administering the principles of English equity.

2. PROCEDURE IN EQUITY

BOWEN, PROGRESS IN THE ADMINISTRATION OF JUSTICE DURING THE VICTORIAN PERIOD, 1 Select Essays in Anglo–American Legal History 516, 524–27 (1907):

* * * A bill in a Chancery suit was a marvellous document, which stated the plaintiff's case at full length and three times over. There was first the part in which the story was circumstantially set forth. Then came the part which "charged" its truth against the defendant—or, in other words, which set it forth all over again in an aggrieved tone. Lastly came the interrogating part, which converted the original allegations into a chain of subtly framed inquiries addressed to the defendant, minutely dovetailed and circuitously arranged so as to surround a slippery conscience and to stop up every earth. No layman, however intelligent, could compose the "answer" without professional aid. It was inevitably so elaborate and so long, that the responsibility for the accuracy of the story shifted, during its telling, from the conscience of the defendant to that of his solicitor and counsel, and truth found no difficulty in disappearing during the operation. * * * [The form of the answer] often rendered necessary a re-statement of the plaintiff's whole position, in which case an amended bill was drawn requiring another answer, until at last the voluminous pleadings were completed and the cause was at issue. By a system which to lawyers in 1887 appears to savour of the Middle Ages, the evidence for the hearing was thereupon taken by interrogatories written down beforehand upon paper and administered to the witnesses in private before an examiner or commissioner. At this meeting none of the parties were allowed to be present, either by themselves or their agents, and the examiner himself was sworn to secrecy. If cross-examined at all (for cross-examination under such conditions was of necessity somewhat of a farce), the witnesses could only be cross-examined upon written inquiries prepared equally in advance by a counsel who had never had the opportunity of knowing what had been said during the examination-in-chief. * * * On the day of the publication of the depositions copies were furnished to the parties at their own expense; but, from that moment, no further evidence was admissible, nor could any slip in the proofs be repaired, except by special permission of the court, when, if such leave was granted, a fresh commission was executed with the same formalities and in the same secret manner as before. The expense of the pleadings, of the preparation for the hearing, and of the other stages of the litigation may be imagined, when we recollect that it was a necessary maxim of the Court of Chancery that all parties interested in the result must be parties to the suit. If, for example, relief was sought against a breach of trust, all who were interested in the trust estate had to be joined, as well as all who had been privy to the breach of trust itself. During the winding journey of the cause towards its termination, whenever any death occurred, bills of review or supplemental suits became necessary to reconstitute the charmed circle of litigants which had been broken. On every such catastrophe the plaintiff had again to begin wearily to weave his web, liable on any new death to find it unravelled and undone. It was satirically observed that a suit to which fifty defendants were necessary parties (a perfectly possible contingency) could

never hope to end at all, since the yearly average of deaths in England was one in fifty, and a death, as a rule, threw over the plaintiff's bill for at least a year. The hearing in many cases could not terminate the cause. Often inquiries or accounts were necessary, and had still to be taken under the supervision of a master. Possibly some issue upon the disputed facts required to be sent for trial at the assizes, or a point of law submitted to a common law court. In such cases, the verdict of the jury, or the opinions of the court so taken, in no way concluded the conscience of the Court of Chancery. It resumed charge of the cause again, when the intermediate expedition to the common law was over, and had the power, if it saw fit, to send the same issue to a new trial, or to disregard altogether what had been the result. * * * When a cause had reached its final stage—when all inquiries had been made, all parties represented, all accounts taken, all issues tried—justice was done with vigour and exactitude. Few frauds ever in the end successfully ran the gauntlet of the Court of Chancery. But the honest suitor emerged from the ordeal victorious rather than triumphant, for too often he had been ruined by the way.

Notes and Questions

1. What differences do you find between procedure at common law and procedure in equity as it is described by Bowen? What are the differences in pleading, the manner of receiving evidence, the attitude toward singleness of issue, and the determination of questions of fact? The rules of evidence, which are chiefly concerned with the exclusion of testimony of doubtful value, were developed in the common-law courts and were never strictly applied in equity. How is this fact related to the differences in equity and common-law procedures?

2. Although the division between law and equity in the federal courts never took the form of separate courts or judges of law and equity, the two were separately administered in the federal system until 1938. From the beginning, procedure at law was conformed to that of the state in which the court was held, but—due in part to the fact that some states had no system of equity in 1789—equity procedure in the federal courts was governed by statutes of Congress and rules promulgated by the Supreme Court. In 1915, Congress provided that when "a suit at law should have been brought in equity or a suit in equity should have been brought at law, the court shall order any amendments to the pleadings which may be necessary to conform them to the proper practice," and that in "all actions at law equitable defenses may be interposed by answer, plea, or replication without the necessity of filing a bill on the equity side of the court." 38 Stat. 956.

———

The elements of procedure in equity discussed in the foregoing materials are significant because of their impact on the substantive and remedial doctrines of equity. Together with the method of enforcing equity decrees, which is discussed below, these elements largely determined the type of case that equity would hear and the disposition it would order. As you read the materials that follow, ask yourself how these differences between law and equity may explain the particular equitable approach in question.

3. THE UNIQUE CHARACTER OF EQUITABLE RELIEF

a. *Specific Relief*

The ordinary judgment of a common-law court consisted of a declaration of a legal relationship. When plaintiff prevailed in the action, this declaration in all but rare instances was that plaintiff was entitled to a sum of money from defendant. Even this declaration was not an order that defendant pay the sum; if defendant did not pay, plaintiff had to take further steps to execute the judgment. The decree in equity, on the other hand, was an order directed at defendant; imprisonment and fines were used not only to coerce compliance, but to punish disobedience. This difference between the remedies in the two systems of courts was summed up in the maxim that equity acts in personam and not in rem. The primary means by which equity acted in personam was the injunction—an order directing defendant to perform or to stop performing an act.

The injunction and other forms of specific relief shaped the substantive doctrines of equity. But it affected the common law as well in at least three important ways. First, the availability of specific relief through the injunction or specific performance when compensatory relief through a judgment for damages would be inadequate was the chief basis for drawing common-law causes into equity. As a result equity now dominates many areas of controversy originally governed by the common law, because damages are an impotent remedy in such cases; a good example is nuisance. Similarly the enforcement of contracts for the sale of real property has become principally a concern of equity, because specific performance is ordered as a matter of course. Second, the availability of specific relief in equity has effectively dampened pressures to develop common-law remedies in that direction. Third, the injunction was the means by which equity imposed its substantive doctrines on the common-law courts. As noted in the extract from Maitland, if the chancellor found that a common-law judgment had been obtained by fraud, the equity court did not purport to negate it; the chancellor simply took the equally effective step of threatening the judgment creditor with jail if the latter sought to enforce it. In similar fashion equity enjoined the bringing of suits in inconvenient fora and compelled interpleader and class actions in multiparty suits.

A plaintiff who sought specific relief also might have sustained an injury that an injunction could not cure. But there was no necessity for choosing between equitable relief and compensatory damages. A "clean-up" doctrine gave Chancery authority to accord full relief in any case of which it had cognizance even though giving such relief might mean redressing injuries for which there was an adequate remedy at law. See pp. 958–59, infra.

b. *Availability of Relief*

You must not think that the doctrine of the adequate remedy at law was the only restriction on the use of equitable remedies. Equity carefully husbanded its power. It was reluctant to issue orders that it might not be able to enforce or that might involve it in detailed supervision of a transaction. Traditionally, equity would not direct a party to take action outside its territorial jurisdiction or order specific performance of a building or personal services contract. For other reasons, activity that might be criminal ordinarily would not be enjoined. While the Court of Star Chamber flourished there was no call for criminal jurisdiction in equity, and after that court was abolished in 1642, Chancery, perhaps for fear of meeting a similar fate, refrained from encroaching on this particular domain of the common-law courts. What aspects of Chancery procedure might have seemed particularly odious in criminal cases to people who celebrated the common law as the palladium of their liberty?

The availability of equitable relief also was hedged by doctrines of fairness and justice. Thus the opinions of the chancellor continually repeat that he who seeks equity must do equity, that he must come into equity with "clean hands," that equity abhors a forfeiture, and that equity will not protect one who sleeps on his rights. Is there any reason why these ideas should have been applied only in equity?

c. Fraud

Fraud often is spoken of as a fount of equitable jurisdiction. Yet the common law also permitted actions for fraud, and defenses as well. Why was protection against fraud thought to be a peculiarly equitable concern? For at least two reasons. For one thing, it was a function of equity's getting there first and going further. The common law would not recognize fraud as a defense to an action on a sealed instrument. Thus, before the rise of assumpsit, at a time when most of the agreements that were enforced by the courts were under seal, equity furnished the only remedy for fraud in the great bulk of cases. When simple contracts—to which fraud was a common-law defense—became enforceable, Chancery sustained its lead by developing the doctrine of constructive fraud, a doctrine in which the rigid technicalities of the common-law fraud concept played little part.

The second reason lay in equity's procedure. Equity implemented its concern with fraud in two ways. First, by denying its own relief to fraudulent complainants, and second, by enjoining legal suitors from pressing their claims or enforcing their judgments. The fraud concept in the latter case has come to be known as an "equitable defense," together with such doctrines as accident, undue influence, and estoppel. Of course, the term "equitable defense" does not indicate a defense in an equity suit, but connotes an effective—if not technical—defense to an action at law.

d. Discovery

Equity and the common law should not be thought of as conflicting systems. In many respects the relationship was one of cooperation, especially after the confrontation of 1616. The most important aspect of this mutual assistance, for our purposes, was discovery, by which a party at law might obtain through equity information for his case. The procedure and the limitations are set forth by Lord Chief Baron Abinger:

> * * * A party has a right to compel the production of a document in which he has an equal interest, though not equal in degree, yet to a certain extent equal, with the party who detains it from him. In that case he may file a bill of discovery, in order to have the possession of it, and the inspection of it. A party has also a right to file a bill of discovery for

the purpose of obtaining such facts as may tend to prove his case; and if those facts are either in possession of the other party, or, if they consist of documents in possession of the other party, in which he either has an interest, or which tend to prove his case, and have no relation to the case of the other party, he has a right to have them produced, and he may file a bill of discovery, in order to aid him in law or in equity, to exhibit those documents in evidence, or compel a statement of those facts. * * * Has he a right, as against the defendant, to discover the defendant's case? * * * The ground on which he files his bill, is to make the defendant discover what is material to his (the plaintiff's) case; but he has no right to say to the defendant, "Tell me what your title is—tell me what your case is—tell me how you mean to prove it—tell me the evidence you have to support it—disclose the documents you mean to make use of in support of it—tell me all these things, that I may find a flaw in your title." Surely that is not the principle of a bill of discovery.

COMBE v. CITY OF LONDON, 4 Y. & C.Ex. 139, 154, 160 Eng.Rep. 953, 959 (Exch.1840). What aspects of equitable procedure explain the availability of discovery in equity? In this connection, reread those portions of Maitland and Bowen in this Section dealing with the pleadings and the taking of evidence in equity.

SECTION D. REFORM: NEW PLEADING, ABOLITION OF THE FORMS, AND THE MERGER OF LAW AND EQUITY

1. THE EMERGENCE OF CODE PROCEDURE

The first significant reform in procedure occurred in England in the period between 1825 and 1834. Chancery practice was substantially reformed during these years. One form of writ was adopted for all three common-law courts. All but three real actions were abolished. Debt and detinue were reshaped. Wager of law was ended.

The capstone of the reform was a body of new rules of pleading, drafted by a committee that included Henry Stephen, author of the treatise cited earlier in this Chapter, and Sir James Parke, who, as a judge of the Court of Exchequer, was to become the foremost expositor of the new rules. Many of their recommendations were distinct improvements on existing practice; one—not accepted—would have permitted the joinder of counts in trespass and case, and amendments from the one form of action to the other. The principal defect the commissioners found in the existing system of pleading, however, was the ubiquitous availability of the general issue. The commissioners attributed to pleas of the general issue "the unnecessary accumulation of proof," the failure to raise questions of law by demurrer, the imposition of the duty to separate law and fact upon the busy *nisi prius* judge, and the proliferation of new trials. This position was reflected by the new rules announced under the authority of an Act of Parliament by the judges of all three common-law courts at Hilary Term, 1834, and known as the Hilary Rules; the defenses that could be proved under a plea of the general issue were greatly reduced, and special pleading was substantially restored. 2 C. & M. 1–30, 149 Eng.Rep. 651–63 (1834).

The result was a disaster. "Under the common-law system the matter was bad enough with a pleading question decided in every sixth case. But under the Hilary Rules it was worse. Every fourth case decided a question on the pleadings. Pleading ran riot." Whittier, *Notice Pleading,* 31 Harv.L.Rev. 501, 507 (1918). Fortunately, corrective action was not long in coming. The Common Law Procedure Acts of 1852, 1854, and 1860 weakened the forms of action, expanded joinder, and liberalized pleading. Finally, the Judicature Acts of 1873 and 1875 combined Chancery and the common-law courts into one Supreme Court of Judicature, fused law and equity, and abolished the forms of action. See 15 Holdsworth, *A History of English Law* 104–38 (Goodhart & Hanbury ed. 1965).

Meanwhile in the United States,[h] a new constitution in New York in 1846 abolished the Court of Chancery and directed the legislature to provide for the appointment of commissioners to "revise, reform, simplify, and abridge" the civil procedure of the state. N.Y. Const. 1846 Art. VI, § 24. The legislature implemented this directive in 1847 and expressly charged the newly appointed commissioners to "provide for the abolition of the present forms of actions and pleadings in cases at common law; for a uniform course of proceeding in all cases whether of legal or equitable cognizance, and for the abandonment * * * of any form and proceeding not necessary to ascertain or preserve the rights of the parties." N.Y.Laws 1847, c. 59, § 8.

FIRST REPORT OF THE COMMISSIONERS ON PRACTICE AND PLEADINGS (New York) 73–74, 87, 123–24, 137–38, 140–41, 144 (1848):

The history of jurisprudence, both in this state and in England, * * * affords a most convincing proof of the wisdom of the measure adopted by the people of this state, in abolishing the distinction between law and equity tribunals. Notwithstanding their separate existence, they had, under the institutions of this state, but one common object, the administration of justice—depending not upon the mere discretion of the court, but ascertained by fixed and certain rules of law. And yet, while they were kept distinct, though their jurisdictions continually encroached upon each other, there were certain rules, not well defined, but yet existing, by which their powers were distinguished. It is, therefore, no matter of surprise, that the books are filled with cases, in which the injustice has been imposed upon parties, of suffering the loss of a substantial right, because of a mistake in the choice of a forum, before which its enforcement was sought. * * *

From the period [in which the forms of action developed] * * *—a period comparatively benighted and ignorant, in all that is valuable in science—to the present, these forms have been adhered to with a sort of bigoted devotion. While the principles of legal science have expanded and adapted themselves to the exigencies of each successive age, through which they have passed, we find ourselves met with the standing argument against improvement, that the time-honored institutions of ages must be held sacred, and that these forms,

---

h. The textual discussion is limited to states with a common-law heritage. Louisiana had adopted a system based on Spanish law with only one form of action by 1812, the year it was admitted to the Union. Texas experimented briefly with separate systems but by 1845 had a unitary system based on Spanish–Mexican jurisprudence.

which may have been well suited to the age in which they originated, must be left untouched.

* * * It seems to us, clear, that neither the forms of remedies, nor the mode in which they are stated, require the complexity, in which both are now enveloped. The embarrassments, to which they have given rise, have resulted from no difficulty in determining the real rights of parties, but simply in the means of enforcing them; and in this respect, we feel no hesitation in recommending, that the retention of forms, which serve no valuable purpose, should no longer constitute a portion of the remedial law of this state. * * *

The rules respecting parties in the courts of law, differ from those in the courts of equity. The blending of the jurisdictions makes it necessary to revise these rules, to some extent. In doing so, we have had a three-fold purpose in view: first, to do away with the artificial distinctions existing in the courts of law, and to require the real party in interest to appear in court as such: second, to require the presence of such parties as are necessary to make an end of the controversy: and third, to allow otherwise great latitude in respect to the number of parties who may be brought in.

* * *

The courts of law generally administer justice betweee [sic] those parties only who stand in the same relation to * * * [each] other; while courts of equity bring before them various parties, standing in different relations, that the whole controversy may be settled, if possible, in one suit, and others avoided. This reasonable and just rule, we would adopt for all actions. * * *

As has been already remarked, the change in the mode of pleading is the key of the reform which we propose. Without this, we should despair of any substantial and permanent improvement in our modes of legal controversy. * * *

The pleadings, we have said, are the written allegations of the parties of the cause of action on one side, and the defence on the other. Their object is three-fold: to present the facts on which the court is to pronounce the law; to present them in such a manner, as that the precise points in dispute shall be perceived, to which the proofs may be directed; and to preserve the record of the rights determined. Not one of these objects is gained by the law of pleading as it now exists in this state.

* * *

There are many treatises and books of forms, indispensable to the lawyer, on the mode of pleading and the forms of the allegations. The rules and the commentaries upon them, form one of the most technical and abstruse branches of the law * * *. We are * * * disposed to pronounce it a system of dialectics, very fit for the schoolmen with whom it originated, but unfit for the practical business of life.

So unfit has it been found, that in instances almost numberless, the legislature and the courts have departed from it and gone to the other extreme. * * * A form of plea was devised which in many cases would virtually deny every material allegation of the declaration without disclosing any particular defence. The courts from time to time have admitted new defences under these general issues, and still further to encourage them, a statute has been passed allowing the defendant to plead the general issue, and with it give notice of any defence, which he could not otherwise introduce under such issue. * * *

Besides the general issues, we have general declarations, or in technical language, common counts. These have been so contrived as to give no information of the particular demand. They also have been encouraged by the courts and numberless demands allowed to be proven under them. * * *

In truth the arguments of those who defend the present system destroy each other. One is the advantage of having the question of fact drawn out so precisely, that the court and jury may see what they have to try, and the parties be prepared with their proofs; the other is the advantage of having the facts stated in so general a form, that the allegations shall cover any state of facts that may appear on the trial, or in other words, the advantage of having no question of fact drawn out by the pleadings at all.

* * *

Disentangling the questions and separating those of fact and of law, is rarely effected by the present system of pleading at common law. * * * This is necessarily so, so long as the pleadings state the conclusions of fact, instead of the facts themselves. * * *

———

Following the report of the commissioners, the New York legislature enacted a Code of Civil Procedure, commonly called the Field Code after David Dudley Field, the most influential of the commissioners. N.Y.Laws 1848, c. 379. This Code proved to be the prototype for numerous state codes— at one time more than one-half the states had codes patterned to some degree after the Field Code—and the precursor of the Federal Rules. Among its most important provisions were the following:

§ 69. [§ 62][i] The distinction between actions at law and suits in equity, and the forms of all such actions and suits, heretofore existing, are abolished; and, there shall be in this state, hereafter, but one form of action, for the enforcement or protection of private rights and the redress of private wrongs, which shall be denominated a civil action.

§ 140. [§ 118] All the forms of pleading heretofore existing, inconsistent with the provisions of this act, are abolished * * *.

§ 142. [§ 120] The complaint shall contain:

1. * * *

2. A statement of the facts constituting the cause of action, in ordinary and concise language, without repetition, and in such a manner as to enable a person of common understanding to know what is intended;

i. The New York legislature added several sections to the Code in 1849, and renumbered the provisions first enacted in 1848 with some very slight changes in language. N.Y.Laws 1849, c. 438. Because the 1849 version became the best known, it is used here. Section numbers in brackets refer to the sections of the 1848 Code.

3. A demand of the relief, to which the plaintiff supposes himself entitled. If the recovery of money be demanded, the amount thereof shall be stated.

§ 156. [§ 132] No other pleading shall be allowed than the complaint, answer, reply and demurrers.

§ 159. [§ 136] In the construction of a pleading, for the purpose of determining its effect, its allegations shall be liberally construed, with a view to substantial justice between the parties.

§ 176. [§ 151] The court shall, in every stage of an action, disregard any error, or defect in the pleadings or proceedings, which shall not affect the substantial rights of the adverse party; and no judgment shall be reversed or affected by reason of such error or defect.

Note

In 1851 the New York legislature amended Section 142(2) to read: "A plain and concise statement of the facts constituting a cause of action without unnecessary repetition." N.Y.Laws 1851, c. 479, § 1.

2. SOME OLD PROBLEMS PERSIST

Could it have been reasonably expected that the transition from the common-law system of procedure to the code system would represent a clean break with the past? Consider the following factors:

(a) The substantive law was supposed to remain unaltered, yet the substantive law had been intimately tied to the older mode of procedure. Moreover, certain procedural institutions—notably trial by jury—had acquired the character of substantive rights.

(b) The most fundamental aspects of procedure—such as the necessity of striking a balance between the function of pleading as setting the limits of the controversy and the function of trial as determining the true merits of the case—are not created by a particular system of procedure but are an integral part of an adjudicative process based upon a theory of party-presentation. Indeed it is rare that any system of procedure attempts by rigid rule to settle these issues definitively. Much will depend on the attitudes, experiences, and predispositions of those who are called upon to apply the rules.

(c) The problems presented by the change in procedure confronted a profession that had traditionally chosen precedent as its polestar, a profession comprised of people who might feel they had an interest in their established ways of proceeding and who in any event were trained in analysis under the older system. The judges who were called upon to interpret the new provisions were of course established members of this profession; indeed, if the methods of judicial selection were effective, they were lawyers who had performed quite competently under the older procedure and they understandably may have been a little impatient with complaints that this procedure was replete with snares and absurdities.

Whatever the reasons, it is clear that many courts did not view the new codes as having been written on a clean slate. Even today concepts of the common-law system occasionally seem to assume a significant role in the decision of pleading and procedure questions. We will see more of this in the next Chapter. For the present we will look at one aspect of the perseverance of common-law notions—the "theory of the pleading" doctrine and related questions.

JONES v. WINSOR

Supreme Court of South Dakota, 1908.
22 S.D. 480, 118 N.W. 716.

CORSON, J. This is an appeal by the defendant from an order overruling his demurrer to the complaint.

It is alleged in the complaint, in substance: That on or about the 1st of April, 1907, the plaintiffs, being desirous of securing a franchise for a city railway system in the city of Sioux Falls, employed the defendant to act as an attorney for them in securing or attempting to secure an ordinance from the city council granting the plaintiffs such license; that carrying out their purpose, * * * it became necessary for the plaintiffs to make a deposit with the city treasurer, and on said day the plaintiffs delivered to the defendant the sum of $2,500 to be by him deposited with the said treasurer of the city, and which money was so deposited * * *; that on or about the 4th day of April the defendant received a further sum of $130, which was to be used by the defendant for these plaintiffs in securing or attempting to secure the said franchise; that the said franchise which plaintiffs were attempting to secure from said city was not granted to these plaintiffs, and thereupon, about the 17th day of April, the city treasurer returned to the defendant the said sum of $2,500 "as money belonging to these plaintiffs and for their use and benefit"; that on or about the same day the said defendant rendered to these plaintiffs an account of all moneys received by him for and on account of these plaintiffs, with an itemized statement of all disbursements, and in connection therewith a pretended charge for his services or fee of $1,250, and with said account was a draft drawn in favor of the plaintiffs for $1,012.25; that the pretended charge of the defendant of the sum of $1,250 as shown upon said account and alleged to be for services rendered by him is unjust, unlawful, and fraudulent, and the reasonable value of the services rendered by the defendant was not and is not of the value of more than $250; that of the moneys so received by the defendant for and on behalf of these plaintiffs and for their use and benefit there remains in his hands the sum of $1,000, which he has refused and still refuses to pay over to these plaintiffs, although frequently requested so to do, and "he has wrongfully and fraudulently converted to his own use the said sum of $1,000"; that on or about the 10th day of September, 1907, the plaintiffs demanded of the said defendant payment * * * "but the said defendant then and there refused and still refuses to pay the same or any part thereof to the plaintiffs and has wrongfully converted the same to his own use." Wherefore "plaintiffs demand judgment against the said defendant for the sum of $1,000 and interest thereon from the 17th day of April, 1907, for the wrongful conversion of said property and for the costs of this action." * * *

It is contended by the appellant that the complaint does not state facts sufficient to constitute a cause of action in trover or conversion, for the reason that the complaint nowhere alleges ownership by the plaintiffs of the property alleged to have been converted at the time the action was brought; nor does it allege ownership or possession of the property in the plaintiffs at the time it is alleged to have been converted which is absolutely essential in the form of action. Assuming that the complaint in this case was intended to state an action for the conversion of this money by the defendant, it is clearly insufficient in not alleging that the plaintiffs, at the time the defendant is charged with having converted it, were the owners or in possession of the money so alleged to have been converted. * * * But it is somewhat difficult to determine from the complaint whether the plaintiffs intended that their action should be for a tort or one ex contractu, as the complaint seems to have been framed with a double aspect. Taking a general view of the allegations of the complaint, it would seem that the pleaders intended to state a cause of action as for money had and received; but looking at the complaint in another aspect, and giving effect to some of the allegations therein, it would seem that the pleaders intended it as an action in conversion, in the nature of the old action of trover.

It is contended by the respondent, in support of the ruling of the court below upon the demurrer, that the action is to recover money had and received by the plaintiffs, and that the allegations contained in the complaint alleged [sic] the fraudulent conversion of the property, etc., may be treated as surplusage. Such a complaint, framed with a double aspect or to unite distinct and incongruous causes of actions, cannot be sustained on demurrer. While our Code has abolished forms of pleading, and only requires that the facts shall be stated in a plain and concise manner without unnecessary repetition, still the distinctions between actions as they formerly existed cannot be entirely ignored. In Pierce v. Carey, 37 Wis. 232, * * * Chief Justice Ryan, quotes with approval * * * Supervisors of Kewaunee County v. Decker, 30 Wis. 624, as follows: "Dixon, C.J. It would certainly be a most anomalous and hitherto unknown condition of the laws of pleading, were it established that the plaintiff in a civil action could file and serve a complaint, the particular nature and object of which no one could tell, but which might and should be held good, as a statement of two or three or more different and inconsistent causes of action, as one in tort, one upon money demand on contract, and one in equity, all combined or fused and moulded into one count or declaration, so that the defendant must await the accidents and events of trial, and until the plaintiff's proofs are all in, before being informed with any certainty or definiteness, what he was called upon to meet. The proposition that a complaint, or any single count of it, may be so framed with a double, treble, or any number of aspects looking to so many distinct and incongruous causes of action, in order to hit the exigencies of the plaintiff's case or any possible demands of his proofs at the trial, we must say, strikes us as something exceedingly novel in the rules of pleading. We do not think it is the law * * *."

As before stated, it is contended by the respondents that these allegations for conversion, etc., may be treated as surplusage, and the complaint held good as an action in assumpsit for money had and received; but in our opinion we would not be justified in holding that these allegations constitute mere surplusage and might be disregarded by the court. To so hold would introduce into the law too much uncertainty and ambiguity in pleading which would have a tendency to mislead the courts and the opposing party. A complaint should be framed upon the theory that it is either a complaint in tort or one ex contractu, and the two theories cannot be combined in one action; neither can an action at law and an action in equity be combined in one count in the same action. As was stated in the headnote in the case of Supervisors of Kewaunee County v. Decker, supra: " * * * On demurrer to a complaint, or any count thereof, the court must determine what cause of action such complaint or count is designed to state, and then whether it states facts sufficient to constitute such a cause of action; and, if not, the demurrer must be sustained, though facts may be stated sufficient to show that plaintiff has a cause of action of a different character."

* * *

The order of the circuit court overruling the demurrer is reversed.

Notes and Questions

1. Reread the provision of the Field Code, pp. 502–03, supra, that tells what a complaint shall contain. Is there language in that provision that lends support to the decision in the principal case?

2. Is it appropriate for a court to insist that plaintiff's complaint is based on a theory that is not supported by the alleged facts, as in Jones v. Winsor, especially when the facts are adequate to support a different theory? Would your answer be different if the facts in the complaint were adequate to sustain either theory but the less apparent theory was the only one proved at trial? Is the result in *Jones* consistent with Section 159 of the Field Code, which is set out on p. 486, supra?

———

CONAUGHTY v. NICHOLS, 42 N.Y. 83 (1870). Plaintiff alleged that he had consigned goods to defendants for sale, that they had been sold for $690.82, and that after deducting the expenses of the sale there was due to plaintiff $618.43, that defendants had refused to pay this amount over to plaintiff and "have converted the same to their own use." After trial, plaintiff moved to amend the complaint by striking the allegation of conversion, but this motion was denied by the referee who then nonsuited plaintiff "on the ground that the cause of action stated in the complaint was for a tort, and the proof established a cause of action upon contract." The General Term reversed the judgment, and the Court of Appeals affirmed:

* * * If the words "and have converted the same to their own use" had been omitted in the complaint, it could not reasonably be contended, that the same was not adapted to the cause of action established by the evidence. The case, therefore, seems to be reduced to the proposition, whether the plaintiff, having alleged facts constituting a cause of action, and having sustained them by proof upon the trial, should have been nonsuited, because the pleading contained an allegation adapted to a complaint in an action *ex delicto,* and which was unnecessary to be stated or proved, to justify a recovery on contract. We are of opinion that no such rigid rule of construction in regard to pleading should prevail under the liberal system introduced by the Code.

* * * If the complaint in question had merely stated facts sufficient to authorize a recovery for a wrongful detention of the money, and upon the trial, the plaintiff had applied to amend by inserting facts appropriate to a cause of action on contract, and thereby changing the form and character of the action, the application should have been denied. That, however, was not the case, as the facts were fully stated, and the defendants apprized of what they were to meet upon the trial, and there was no pretense that they were surprised. If they chose to accept the complaint without moving to strike out any portion of it, or to compel the plaintiff to make it more definite, or to elect in regard to the form of action, they should not, upon the trial, have been allowed to prevent a recovery by the plaintiff of a judgment for the amount of his demand. * * * It is quite probable that the plaintiff intended, down to the trial, to recover against the defendants for a wrongful conversion of the proceeds of the sale of the property consigned to them, and doubtless the mistake should have been fatal but for the ample statement of facts contained in the complaint, which justified a recovery on contract for the amount of his demand. It does not follow that, because the parties go down to the trial upon a particular theory, which is not supported by the proof, the cause is to be dismissed, when there are facts alleged in the complaint, and sustained by the evidence, sufficient to justify a recovery upon a different theory or form of action. * * *

Questions

Is *Conaughty* consistent with Jones v. Winsor? "The reasoning of the Court in Conaughty v. Nichols that where the pleading is misleading the defendant should move to make it definite or to have the pleader elect between the possible theories, and that if he proceeds without doing so he is to be taken as fully understanding the pleading, seems very weak." Whittier, *The Theory of a Pleading*, 8 Colum.L.Rev. 523, 534 (1908). Why? If you were preparing a complaint in New York after *Conaughty*, what moral would you draw from the opinion in that case?

GARRITY v. STATE BOARD OF ADMINISTRATION

Supreme Court of Kansas, 1917.
99 Kan. 695, 162 P. 1167.

PORTER, J. * * * A demurrer to the petition was sustained; plaintiff elected to stand upon the petition and appeals.

The petition charges that in July, 1911, the board of regents of the state university, by its assistant curator of mammals, wrongfully and without plaintiff's knowledge or consent, entered upon his farm in Wallace county and removed therefrom a large and valuable fossil, the property of plaintiff, and wrongfully converted it to the use and benefit of the board of regents and its successors, depositing the fossil in the museum of the university for exhibition and scientific purposes; that the fossil was of the value of $2,500, and plaintiff had received no compensation therefor. It is alleged that the board of administration is a board created by law for the government, management, and control of the university of Kansas, * * * and is the successor of the board of regents, subrogated to the rights, duties, and responsibilities of the board of regents, and subject to its obligations and liable for its debts and contracts. * * *

1. It is the defendants' contention that both the original and the amended petition were subject to demurrer because, if they stated a cause of action at all, it was barred by the statute of limitations; that the action is one sounding in tort, and therefore barred by the two-year statute * * *. On the other hand the plaintiff claims the right to waive the tort and recover upon an implied promise to pay what the fossil is worth. We think, if [the] petition stated a cause of action against defendants, it must be held that sufficient facts were stated to authorize plaintiff to waive the tort and rely upon an implied promise to pay the value of the property converted. * * *

The two-year statute of limitations was therefore no bar to the action.

* * *

3. The principal question raised by the appeal is whether the action can be maintained against the board of administration, the original defendant. Prior to 1913 the state university was managed and controlled by a board of regents which was a body corporate created by the Legislature. It went out of existence when the act of 1913 placed the state educational institutions in control of the state board of administration, which was not made a body corporate. The act * * * provided that the board shall manage and control the property of the educational institutions named, including the state university, and conferred upon the board power "to execute trusts or other obligations now or hereafter committed to any of the said institutions * * *." The power "to execute trusts or other obligations now or hereafter committed to any of * * * said institutions" cannot be construed so as to make either the board of administration or its members liable for a tort committed by the board of regents; and the plaintiff cannot, by waiving the tort, make either the board or its members liable upon the theory of an implied promise.

* * *

The judgment is affirmed. All the Justices concurring.

Notes and Questions

1. Is *Garrity*, in either its statute-of-limitations aspect or its liability aspect, concerned with the theory of the pleading? In what way, if any, is the problem in *Garrity* different?

2. Why did the court hold that the action was in contract for purposes of the statute of limitations but in tort for purposes of deciding whether the Board was liable for the Regents' action?

3. Governments generally are immune from suit except as their immunity has been expressly waived by statute. Suits in contract are more commonly consented to than suits in tort. See 3 Davis, *Administrative Law Treatise* § 25.01 (1958). Under a statute consenting to suit in contract only, should a plaintiff be permitted to "waive" a tort and sue in "assumpsit"?

4. In a contract action, may a claim for money had and received based upon a conversion be brought as a counterclaim under a statute that provides that "in an action on contract, any other cause of action on contract" may be brought as a

counterclaim? See Manhattan Egg Co. v. Seaboard Terminal & Refrig. Co., 137 Misc. 14, 242 N.Y.S. 189 (N.Y.City Ct.1929).

3. THE ARRIVAL OF MODERN PROCEDURE

Modern procedure arrived on September 16, 1938, when the Federal Rules of Civil Procedure came into effect. The adoption of the Federal Rules followed an extended period of agitation for uniform procedural rules in the federal district courts and for uniting the procedure of law and equity under one form of action. In 1934, Congress passed the Rules Enabling Act, 28 U.S.C. § 2077, authorizing the United States Supreme Court to promulgate rules of procedure for the district courts. On June 3, 1935, the Supreme Court appointed an Advisory Committee of distinguished lawyers and law professors to prepare and submit a draft of unified rules. The Committee prepared and received public comments on two published drafts. It submitted its final report to the Supreme Court in November 1937. The Supreme Court carefully reviewed and made a number of changes in the rules recommended by the Committee. The rules as adopted by the Court on December 20, 1937, were transmitted to the Attorney General and were submitted by him to the 75th Congress on January 3, 1938. Pursuant to the terms of the Rules Enabling Act, the rules came into effect when the Congress adjourned without taking action to postpone their effective date. See generally Burbank, *The Rules Enabling Act of 1934*, 130 U.Pa.L.Rev. 1015 (1982).

The chief characteristics of the Federal Rules are common sense, simplicity, and flexibility of procedure. Rule 1 states the purpose of the rules is "to secure the just, speedy and inexpensive determination of every action." Some of the major aspects in which the Rules advanced federal practice were the union of law and equity as one form of action, the simplification of pleadings and issues, pretrial procedure, discovery, and trial reforms. All of these subjects are developed in the succeeding Chapters of this book.

Note

The Federal Rules of Civil Procedure have had a strong impact on court procedures in most of the states. Nonetheless, state rules of civil procedure still vary greatly. Some states had adopted code systems similar to New York's Field Code, others modeled their rules after the Federal Rules, and others maintained common-law rules. Most states have been influenced by two or more of these models and have adopted elements of each. For example, some states, such as Delaware and New Jersey, have maintained separate court systems for law and for equity, yet they have abandoned common-law pleading. For a state-by-state discussion, see Oakley & Coon, *The Federal Rules in State Courts: A Survey of State Court Systems of Civil Procedure,* 61 Wash.L.Rev. 1367 (1986).

Chapter 8

MODERN PLEADING

Chapter Seven discussed the history of the pleading rules. Those rules served four functions: (1) providing notice of the nature of a claim or defense; (2) identifying baseless claims; (3) setting each party's view of the facts; and (4) narrowing the issues. Modern pleading rules generally are not calculated to perform the last three of these functions. Thus, Federal Rule of Civil Procedure 8(a) requires only a short and plain statement of the claim showing that the plaintiff is entitled to relief. The shift in emphasis embodied in the Federal Rules on pleading in part reflects a view of the place of litigation in the dispute-resolution process.

At the outset of a lawsuit, one of the court's objectives is to deter baseless claims that may clog its calendar. The framers of the Federal Rules were satisfied that this limited objective could be achieved by requiring a short and plain statement of the claim and a certification that the pleadings were truthful (Rule 11) and by establishing other provisions designed expressly to screen baseless claims (most notably, the motion to dismiss under Rule 12 and the motion for summary judgment under Rule 56).

As the presence of Rules 12 and 56 makes clear, the shift in emphasis embodied in the federal pleading rules also reflects the rulemakers' intention to relegate to procedural devices other than the pleading rules the primary responsibility for serving several of the functions performed by pleading rules under earlier systems of procedure. As noted, Rules 11, 12, and 56 are designed to serve the function of screening baseless claims. Other rules are designed to serve the other functions of detailed pleadings. For example, the Federal Rules create a wide array of discovery devices that make it unnecessary for the parties to provide a detailed statement of the facts at the pleading stage. By shifting from the pleading stage to the discovery stage the attempt to establish each party's view of the facts, the Rules implement their framers' conviction that parties should not be forced to take positions before they have access to facts and documents, some of which may be obtainable only from the other party.

However, some contend that the current rules allow too many baseless suits that require costly discovery and waste valuable court time. Although there is very little empirical evidence of a need, in recent years there have been legislative proposals and enactments purporting to "reform" tort law, extending sanctions under Federal Rule 11, and imposing procedural restrictions on securities litigation—all ostensibly in the interest of eliminating "frivolous" litigation. As you work through this Chapter, consider whether the pleading rules should be revised to make it more difficult to bring suit, and whether each of those rules should be applicable to all lawsuits or whether particular issues or claims require specific rules of pleading or procedure.

SECTION A. THE COMPLAINT

1. DETAIL REQUIRED UNDER THE CODES

Read Nebraska Revised Statutes §§ 25–804, 25–806, which appear in the Supplement in conjunction with Federal Rules of Civil Procedure 8 and 12, respectively.

Although a majority of states have adopted the federal pleading rules, a number still follow all or part of the codes. Some continue to require a "statement of facts" constituting a "cause of action"; others specify a "statement of facts" demonstrating a "right to relief." Is there an important difference between these formulations? Some state provisions specifically call for a statement of "ultimate facts." A number of these code states soften any harsh results of technical enforcement by stating that a pleading is satisfactory if it gives "fair notice" to the opposing party.

GILLISPIE v. GOODYEAR SERVICE STORES, 258 N.C. 487, 128 S.E.2d 762 (1963). Plaintiff alleged:

> [T]he defendants, without cause or just excuse and maliciously came upon and trespassed upon the premises occupied by the plaintiff as a residence, and by the use of harsh and threatening language and physical force directed against the plaintiff assaulted the plaintiff and placed her in great fear, and humiliated and embarrassed her by subjecting her to public scorn and ridicule, and caused her to be seized and exhibited to the public as a prisoner, and to be confined in a public jail, all to her great humiliation, embarrassment and harm.

Under the North Carolina code then in force, plaintiff was required to make a "plain and concise statement of the facts constituting a cause of action." North Carolina cases interpreting the pleading standard had stated that the complaint must "disclose the issuable facts" and allege "the material, essential and ultimate facts upon which plaintiff's right of action is based." The court held that the allegations were insufficient, noting that the pleading was necessary not only to enable the opposing party to respond but also to enable the court to declare the law upon the facts stated. The court could not do so if "a mere legal conclusion" such as "assault" or "trespass" is stated. The court concluded:

The complaint states no facts upon which * * * legal conclusions may be predicated. Plaintiff's allegations do not disclose *what* occurred, *when* it occurred, *where* it occurred, *who* did *what*, the relationships between defendants and plaintiff or of defendants *inter se*, or any other factual data that might identify the occasion or describe the circumstances of the alleged wrongful conduct of defendants.

Id. at 490, 128 S.E.2d at 766.

The court also discussed the sufficiency of pleadings in other types of case:

> When a complaint alleges defendant is indebted to plaintiff in a certain amount and such debt is due, but does not allege in what manner or for what cause defendant became indebted to plaintiff, it is demurrable for failure to state facts sufficient to constitute a cause of action. * * *

> "In an action or defense based upon negligence, it is not sufficient to allege the mere happening of an event of an injurious nature and call it negligence on the part of the party sought to be charged. This is necessarily so because negligence is not a fact in itself, but is the legal result of certain facts. Therefore, the facts which constitute the negligence charged and also the facts which establish such negligence as the proximate cause, or as one of the proximate causes, of the injury must be alleged." Shives v. Sample, 238 N.C. 724, 79 S.E.2d 193.

Id. at 489–90, 128 S.E.2d at 765.

Notes and Questions

1. Is the court in *Gillispie* legitimately concerned with the inability of defendants to ascertain the claims against them in order that they might answer and prepare their defenses? Can it be said that the pleading in *Gillispie* is unsatisfactory because the trial judge will not know what evidence is or is not relevant?

2. To what extent might the court in *Gillispie* have been motivated by the notion that a detailed account of the facts might well show that plaintiff did not have a valid claim for relief? Is it significant that at the time of the *Gillispie* decision North Carolina did not have a provision for summary judgment? Has the North Carolina court simply followed a hard and fast line concerning the "fact" pleading requirement, thereby undermining its basic purpose as a device for pretrial communication?

3. Plaintiff was given leave to amend the complaint after the *Gillispie* decision. Suppose that plaintiff's amended complaint also is deficient. Will she be given leave to amend again? How should the right to amend affect the question of whether or not a pleading is or is not satisfactory?

4. In ROBINSON v. BOARD OF COUNTY COMMISSIONERS, 262 Md. 342, 278 A.2d 71 (1971), plaintiff alleged that defendants "did then and there falsely, maliciously, and without just cause * * * arrest [plaintiff] * * * on charge[s] of disorderly conduct and resisting arrest, * * * [they took him] to the police station where he was forceably imprisoned, kept, detained and restrained of his liberty * * * [but upon trial he] was acquitted * * *. [Defendants] well knew that the prosecution was false, groundless, and without probable cause * * *." The court held that this passage stated facts sufficient to constitute a cause of

action. Compare this pleading with that in *Gillispie.* Is one of the pleadings more informative than the other? See also D'Auria v. Niemiec, 15 Misc.2d 449, 450, 182 N.Y.S.2d 378, 379 (Sup.Ct.1959), upholding as sufficient an allegation "That on or about July 1, 1956, on Amherst Street in the City of Buffalo, New York, the defendant assaulted, battered and beat plaintiff without any provocation or just cause." On the other hand, consider VAN DEKERKHOV v. CITY OF HERRIN, 51 Ill.2d 374, 282 N.E.2d 723 (1972), holding that an allegation that defendant "had charge of" certain construction work was a conclusion of law, which resulted in the dismissal of the action based on a statute that imposed liability on any "person having charge of" the work in question.

COOK, STATEMENTS OF FACT IN PLEADING UNDER THE CODES, 21 Colum.L.Rev. 416, 416–19, 422 (1921):

In a recent case in New York [California Packing Corp. v. Kelly Storage & Distributing Co., 228 N.Y. 49, 126 N.E. 269 (1920)] the plaintiff alleged in his complaint that the promise for the breach of which he was suing was made in exchange for "a valuable consideration." The case went to the Court of Appeals upon the question whether this allegation is a "statement of fact" or a "conclusion of law." [The court held it was the former.] * * * An examination of the authorities in [New York and] other code jurisdictions reveals a conflict of authority. * * *

The movement for "simplified procedure" began in this country about the middle of the last century. How comes it that after more than seventy years of discussion and judicial decision, a question of this kind can still be an open one? Why is it that eminent judges and lawyers took and still take opposite views upon this and similar questions? * * *

These [code] provisions at first sight seem simple, and probably the men who first drew them so believed. That the simplicity is not real, however, becomes clear when one reads the hundreds, not to say thousands, of decisions which have passed upon the question whether in a given case the pleader has "stated the facts" in an acceptable manner. In many cases he is told that he has pleaded "evidentiary facts" instead of the "facts constituting the cause of action"; in many others he is held to have stated merely "conclusions of law."

[Upon careful analysis] * * * it will appear at once that there is no logical distinction between statements which are grouped by the courts under the phrases "statements of fact" and "conclusions of law." It will also be found that many, although by no means all, pleadings held bad because they are said to plead "evidence" rather than "the facts constituting the cause of action" or defense really do nevertheless "state" the operative facts which the pleader will have to prove at the trial, but in a form different from that to which courts and lawyers are accustomed to recognize as a proper method of pleading.

* * *

The facts of life which compose the group of "operative facts" to which the law attaches legal consequences are always *specific* and not *generic.* * * * [I]n an action on the case for, let us say, negligently injuring the plaintiff by the operation of an automobile, the "operative" or "ultimate" facts proved at the trial will always be specific. It will appear that the defendant was driving a particular kind of automobile at some particular rate of speed, *etc., etc.* If now a plaintiff were to state the facts thus specifically in his complaint he would doubtless be told by the average court that he had "pleaded his evidence" and not the "facts constituting the cause of action." This would of course be erroneous. What is according to accepted notions the proper way to plead is merely a mode of stating the facts generically rather than specifically.

It must of course be recognized that at times a pleader really does err by "pleading evidence," i.e., by stating, generically or specifically, facts which do not form part of the group of operative facts, but are merely facts from which by some process of logical inference the existence of the operative facts can be inferred. More often, however, the "error" consists merely in pleading the operative facts more specifically than is usual.

So much for the cases involving the distinction between pleading "evidence" and "ultimate facts." Let us now examine "conclusions of law." The first thing noticed upon analysis is that a so-called "conclusion of law" is a generic statement which can be made only after some legal rule has been applied to some specific group of operative facts. Consider, for example, a statement in a pleading that "defendant owes plaintiff $500." Standing by itself in a pleading this is usually treated as a mere "conclusion of law." It can, however, be made only when one knows certain facts and also the applicable legal rule. It is, in fact, the conclusion of a logical argument: Whenever certain facts, a, b, c, *etc.,* exist, B (defendant) owes A (plaintiff) $500; facts a, b, c, *etc.,* exist; therefore B owes A $500. This being so, when the bare statement is made that "B owes A $500" we may, if we wish, regard it as a statement in generic form that all the facts necessary to create the legal duty to pay money described by the word "owe" are true as between A and B. In dealing, for example, with misrepresentation, such statements are more often than otherwise regarded in exactly this way. The same statement may, however, under proper circumstances be merely a statement as to the law applicable to facts given or known, and so be purely a statement of a "conclusion of law."

* * * How specific or how generic statements in a pleading may and must be can obviously not be settled by mere logic, but according to notions of fairness and convenience. The pleading should give the adversary and the court reasonable notice of the real nature of the claim or defense; nothing more should be required.

Notes and Questions

1. "Quite commonly an allegation has been held bad as a statement of law only. The stating of evidence, while subject to criticism, is not so often held to render the pleading bad, since the court itself will draw the ultimate conclusion where it is the one necessarily following from the allegations made." Clark, *Code Pleading* § 38, at 228 (2d ed. 1947). When does the ultimate conclusion "necessarily follow"? Compare Robinson v. Meyer, 135 Conn. 691, 693–94, 68 A.2d 142, 143 (1949), in which the court inferred title by adverse possession on the basis of allegations of "all the facts necessary to establish ouster," with O'Regan v. Schermerhorn, 25 N.J.Misc. 1, 50 A.2d 10 (Sup.Ct.1946), in which the court

refused to infer the defense of truth in a defamation suit when defendant alleged he believed the statement to be true and further alleged the facts on which that belief was based.

    2.   Should a party be able to plead an essential fact merely by referring to an exhibit in which the fact is stated? Consider ANDERSON v. CHAMBLISS, 199 Or. 400, 409, 262 P.2d 298, 302 (1953), in which the court refused to permit a lien notice attached to and referred to in the complaint to supply the necessary allegation that the notice was filed within sixty days of completion of construction. The court said: "[A]nnexing an exhibit to a pleading does not amount to an allegation that the statements contained therein are true. * * * [Hence it] cannot serve the purpose of supplying necessary and material averments." See also Lion Secor Real Estate Co. v. Westgate Village Shopping Center, Inc., 117 Ohio App. 96, 191 N.E.2d 179 (1962). But see Standard Register Co. v. Greenberg, 120 Vt. 112, 116, 132 A.2d 174, 177 (1957), holding that a reference to a writing in the pleading, coupled with its annexation, is sufficient to allege its contents. Note that Federal Rule 10(c) makes a written instrument that is attached to a pleading as an exhibit "a part thereof for all purposes."

---

2. DETAIL REQUIRED UNDER THE FEDERAL RULES

Read Federal Rules of Civil Procedure 8(a) and 12(b) in the Supplement.

DIOGUARDI v. DURNING

United States Circuit Court of Appeals, Second Circuit, 1944.
139 F.2d 774.

Clark, Circuit Judge. In his complaint, obviously home drawn, plaintiff attempts to assert a series of grievances against the Collector of Customs at the Port of New York growing out of his endeavors to import merchandise from Italy "of great value," consisting of bottles of "tonics." We may pass certain of his claims as either inadequate or inadequately stated and consider only these two: (1) that on the auction day, October 9, 1940, when defendant sold the merchandise at "public custom," "he sold my merchandise to another bidder with my price of $110, and not of his price of $120," and (2) "that three weeks before the sale, two cases, of 19 bottles each case, disappeared." Plaintiff does not make wholly clear how these goods came into the collector's hands, since he alleges compliance with the revenue laws; but he does say he made a claim for "refund of merchandise which was two-thirds paid in Milano, Italy," and that the collector denied the claim. These and other circumstances alleged indicate (what, indeed, plaintiff's brief asserts) that his original dispute was with his consignor as to whether anything more was due upon the merchandise, and that the collector, having held it for a year (presumably as unclaimed merchandise under 19 U.S.C.A. § 1491), then sold it, or such part of it as was left, at public auction. For his asserted injuries plaintiff claimed $5,000 damages, together with interest and costs, against the defendant individually and as collector. This complaint was dismissed by the District Court, with leave, however, to plaintiff to amend, on motion of the United States Attorney, appearing for the defendant, on the ground that it "fails to state facts sufficient to constitute a cause of action."

Thereupon plaintiff filed an amended complaint, wherein, with an obviously heightened conviction that he was being unjustly treated, he vigorously reiterates his claims, including those quoted above and now stated as that his "medicinal extracts" were given to the Springdale Distilling Company "with my betting [bidding?] price of $110: and not their price of $120," and "It isn't so easy to do away with two cases with 37 bottles of one quart. Being protected, they can take this chance." An earlier paragraph suggests that defendant had explained the loss of the two cases by "saying that they had leaked, which could never be true in the manner they were bottled." On defendant's motion for dismissal on the same ground as before, the court made a final judgment dismissing the complaint, and plaintiff now comes to us with increased volubility, if not clarity.

It would seem, however, that he has stated enough to withstand a mere formal motion, directed only to the face of the complaint, and that here is another instance of judicial haste which in the long run makes waste. Under the new rules of civil procedure, there is no pleading requirement of stating "facts sufficient to constitute a cause of action," but only that there be "a short and plain statement of the claim showing that the pleader is entitled to relief," * * * rule 8(a) * * *; and the motion for dismissal under Rule 12(b) is for failure to state "a claim upon which relief can be granted." The District Court does not state why it concluded that the complaints showed no claim upon which relief could be granted; and the United States Attorney's brief before us does not help us, for it is limited to the prognostication—unfortunately ill founded so far as we are concerned—that "the most cursory examination" of them will show the correctness of the District Court's action.

We think that, however inartistically they may be stated, the plaintiff has disclosed his claims that the collector has converted or otherwise done away with two of his cases of medicinal tonics and has sold the rest in a manner incompatible with the public auction he had announced—and, indeed, required by 19 U.S.C.A. § 1491, above cited, and the Treasury Regulations promulgated under it * * *. As to this latter claim, it may be that the collector's only error is a failure to collect an additional ten dollars from the Springdale Distilling Company; but giving the plaintiff the benefit of reasonable intendments in his allegations (as we must on this motion), the claim appears to be in effect that he was actually the first bidder at the price for which they were sold, and hence was entitled to the merchandise. Of course, defendant did not need to move on the complaint alone; he could have disclosed the facts from his point of view, in advance of a trial if he chose, by asking for a pre-trial hearing or by moving for a summary judgment with supporting affidavits. But, as it stands, we do not see how the plaintiff may properly be deprived of his day in court to show what he obviously so firmly believes and what for present purposes defendant must be taken as admitting. * * *

On remand, the District Court may find substance in other claims asserted by plaintiff, which include a failure properly to catalogue the items (as the cited Regulations provide), or to allow plaintiff to buy at a discount from the catalogue price just before the auction sale (a claim whose basis is not apparent), and a violation of an agreement to deliver the merchandise to the plaintiff as soon as he paid for it, by stopping the payments. In view of plaintiff's limited ability to write and speak English, it will be difficult for the District Court to arrive at justice unless he consents to receive legal assistance in the presentation of his case. The record indicates that he refused further help from a lawyer suggested by the court, and his brief (which was a recital of facts, rather than an argument of law) shows distrust of a lawyer of standing at this bar. It is the plaintiff's privilege to decline all legal help * * *; but we fear that he will be indeed ill advised to attempt to meet a motion for summary judgment or other similar presentation of the merits without competent advice and assistance.

Judgment is reversed and the action is remanded for further proceedings not inconsistent with this opinion.

Notes and Questions

1. Dioguardi's amended complaint read as follows:

UNITED STATES DISTRICT COURT

SOUTHERN DISTRICT OF NEW YORK

JOHN DIOGUARDI

Plaintiff,

-against-

HARRY M. DURNING
Individually and as Collector of Customs
at the Port of New York

Defendant

Plaintiff, as and for his bill of amended complaint the defendant, respectfully alleges:

FIRST: I want justice done on the basis of my medicinal extracts which have disappeared saying that they had leaked, which could never be true in the manner they were bottled.

SECOND: Mr. E.G. Collord Clerk in Charge, promised to give me my merchandise as soon as I paid for it. Then all of a sudden payments were stopped.

THIRD: Then, he didn't want to sell me my merchandise at catalogue price with the 5% off, which was very important to me, after I had already paid $5,000 for them, beside a few other expenses.

FOURTH: Why was the medicinaly given to the Springdale Distilling Co. with my betting price of $110; and not their price of $120.

FIFTH: It isn't so easy to do away with two cases with 37 bottles of one quart. Being protected, they can take this chance.

SIXTH: No one can stop my rights upon my merchandise, because of both the duly and the entry.

WHEREFORE: Plaintiff demands judgment against the defendant, individually and as Collector of Customs at the Port of New York, in the sum of Five Thousand Dollars

($5,000) together with interest from the respective dates of payment as set forth herein, together with the costs and disbursements of this action.

2.   The *Dioguardi* decision was sharply criticized in McCaskill, *The Modern Philosophy of Pleading: A Dialogue Outside the Shades*, 38 A.B.A.J. 123 (1952), and became a focal point of opposition to the so-called liberal "notice-pleading" of the Federal Rules. How would the *Dioguardi* case have been decided in a jurisdiction that requires a statement of "facts constituting a cause of action"?

3.   Does Federal Rule 8(a) have the effect of completely eliminating the requirement of detailed fact pleadings? Is *Dioguardi* typical or atypical? The Supreme Court in CONLEY v. GIBSON, 355 U.S. 41, 47–48, 78 S.Ct. 99, 103, 2 L.Ed.2d 80, 85 (1957), cited *Dioguardi* and expressed its views as follows:

> * * * [T]he Federal Rules of Civil Procedure do not require a claimant to set out in detail the facts upon which he bases his claim. To the contrary, all the Rules require is "a short and plain statement of the claim" that will give the defendant fair notice of what the plaintiff's claim is and the grounds upon which it rests. The illustrative forms appended to the Rules plainly demonstrate this. Such simplified "notice pleading" is made possible by the liberal opportunity for discovery and the other pretrial procedures established by the Rules to disclose more precisely the basis of both claim and defense and to define more narrowly the disputed facts and issues.

See also Leatherman v. Tarrant County Narcotics Intelligence & Coordination Unit, 507 U.S. 163, 168, 113 S.Ct. 1160, 122 L.Ed.2d 517 (1993), discussed at Notes 1 and 2, pp. 532–33, infra, in which the Court quoted from *Conley* in holding that federal judges were not authorized to require more detailed pleading in civil rights actions than in other cases.

Shortly after the *Conley* decision Judge Clark made the following comment:

> * * * Some people love to say that all the rules require is fair notice, that pleading under the rules is only notice pleading. * * * . I don't use that expression—not that I object to it as such. I think it is something like the Golden Rule, which is a nice hopeful thing; but I can't find that it means much of anything and it isn't anything that we can use with any precision. What we require is a general statement of the case, and our best precedents are those that have been honored over the years, which show that we haven't done anything really violent. We do not require detail. We require a general statement. How much? Well, the answer is made in what I think is probably the most important part of the rules so far as this particular topic is concerned, namely, the Forms. These are important because when you can't define you can at least draw pictures to show your meaning.

Clark, *Pleading Under the Federal Rules*, 12 Wyo.L.J. 177, 181 (1958).

4.   Examples of the simplicity of pleading under Rule 8(a) are found in the Appendix of Forms, which are set out in the Supplement following the Federal Rules of Civil Procedure; in particular see Forms 9 and 11. Note that in 1946, Rule 84 was amended to state that the Forms were not mere guides but were themselves "sufficient under the rules." This change was intended to overcome the effect of WASHBURN v. MOORMAN MFG. CO., 25 F.Supp. 546 (S.D.Cal. 1938), in which it was held that a complaint failed to state a claim for relief despite the fact that it followed one of the forms.

5. Lest one get the impression that there no longer exists any controversy over the requirements of Rule 8(a)(2), consider BAUTISTA v. LOS ANGELES COUNTY, 216 F.3d 837 (9th Cir.2000), a federal civil rights action, in which the trial court had dismissed plaintiffs' second amended complaint with prejudice. Each of the three distinguished Court of Appeals judges wrote a separate opinion. Judge Schwarzer, writing for the court, summarized the complaint as follows:

> The first claim, on behalf of twenty of the named plaintiffs, alleges that they were over the age of forty [which brings them within the scope of the federal statute prohibiting discrimination on the basis of age] and were denied employment by defendant in favor of younger employees. The second claim, on behalf of fifty-one named plaintiffs, alleges that defendant discriminated against them on account of their race, national origin and ancestry by denying them employment while employing less qualified Anglo employees. The third claim, on behalf of three named plaintiffs, alleges that plaintiff discriminated against them on the basis of their physical disabilities while employing less qualified employees.

Id. at 840. Judge Schwarzer found these allegations to be insufficient under Rule 8 because each individual plaintiff did not set out a claim that "he or she is a member of a particular protected class, was qualified and applied for the position he or she sought, and was rejected on a prohibited ground." Id. However, Judge Schwarzer voted to reverse the trial court on the ground that the latter abused its discretion by failing to give plaintiffs guidance as to how the defects in the complaint could have been cured and a chance to cure them.

Judge Reinhardt concurred but on the entirely different ground that the existing complaint met the requirements of Rule 8: "True, the complaint states the relevant facts at a high level of generality. But that is the point of notice pleading * * *. * * * [T]o the extent that a complaint lacks detail that the defendants believe they need * * * they can obtain such detail readily through interrogatories or early depositions. Surely Judge Schwarzer does not intend to say that each plaintiff in a multi-plaintiff action must plead separately each element of his or her claim in repetitious separate paragraphs." Id. at 843.

Judge O'Scannlain dissented. He agreed with Judge Schwarzer that the complaint was deficient, but he rejected the notion that the trial judge abused his discretion by not giving plaintiffs and their "experienced counsel" guidance on how to plead their case. Id. at 844.

Which of these positions makes the most sense? Compare Sparrow v. United Air Lines, Inc., 216 F.3d 1111, 1115 (D.C.Cir.2000) (complaint is sufficient if it alleges "I was turned down for a job because of my race"). And see Marcus, *The Puzzling Persistence of Pleading Practice*, 76 Texas L.Rev. 1749 (1998) for a discussion of the extent to which pleading requirements continue to be of significance in the federal courts.

6. Under the Federal Rules, can a pleading be rejected for including too much information? See McHENRY v. RENNE, 84 F.3d 1172 (9th Cir.1996) in which the court affirmed the dismissal of plaintiffs' complaint with prejudice. The court noted:

> [T]he complaint in the case at bar is argumentative, prolix, replete with redundancy, and largely irrelevant. * * * Prolix, confusing complaints such as the ones filed in this case impose unfair burdens on litigants and judges. As a practical matter, the judge and opposing counsel, in order to perform their responsibilities, cannot use [such] a complaint * * * and must prepare

outlines to determine who is being sued for what. * * * The judge wastes half a day in chambers preparing the "short and plain statement" which Rule 8 obligated plaintiffs to submit. He must then manage the litigation without knowing what claims are made against whom. This leads to discovery disputes and lengthy trials, prejudicing litigants in other case[s] who follow the rules, as well as defendants in the case in which the prolix pleading is filed. * * * "The forms of action we have buried, but they still rule us from their graves [quoting F.W. Maitland, in Forms of Action at Common Law]." * * * As Maitland explains, there are good reasons why the forms of action still shape pleadings, though the rules no longer require pleadings to conform to the ancient forms. Pleadings of the kind shaped by the traditional forms enable determination of * * * the appropriate procedures for the particular type of adjudication, the type of trial, and the remedies available.

Id. at 1177, 1179–80.

Compare MIRSHAK v. JOYCE, 652 F.Supp. 359, 370 (N.D.Ill.1987) in which the defendants asked the court to strike from plaintiff's complaint paragraphs that defendants characterized as "a confusing melange of irrelevant, immaterial, repetitive, incompetent, conclusory and self-serving evidentiary recitations." The court denied relief because the complaint gave fair notice to the defendants of the claims against them regardless of the unnecessary allegations.

7. Consider which, if any, of the following pleadings would, in itself, be sufficient to state a claim under Federal Rule 8(a)(2).

(a) D is legally liable to P for damages.

(b) D negligently caused P's injury.

(c) D negligently caused P's injuries on July 4, 2000, at Dreamworld Amusement Park.

(d) D negligently operated a roller coaster ride on which P was a passenger on July 4, 2000, at Dreamworld Amusement Park. As a result of this negligence, P suffered a broken arm and was otherwise injured, and P incurred hospital and other medical expenses, and was prevented from transacting business, resulting in damages of $80,000.

(e) D negligently operated a roller coaster ride on which P was a passenger on July 4, 2000, at Dreamworld Amusement Park. D was negligent because it was operating the roller coaster at excessive speed and the ride was improperly maintained. As a result of this negligence, P suffered a broken arm and was otherwise injured, and P incurred hospital and other medical expenses, and was prevented from transacting business, resulting in damages of $80,000.

(f) D negligently operated a roller coaster ride on which P was a passenger on July 4, 2000, at Dreamworld Amusement Park. D was negligent because it was operating the roller coaster at excessive speed (the roller coaster was travelling at a speed of 32 mph, exceeding the safe speed by 5 mph) and the ride was improperly maintained. As a result of this negligence, P suffered a broken arm and was otherwise injured and P incurred hospital and other medical expenses, and was prevented from transacting business, resulting in damages of $80,000.

(g) D negligently operated a roller coaster ride on which P was a passenger on July 4, 2000, at Dreamworld Amusement Park. D was negligent because it was operating the roller coaster at excessive speed (the roller coaster was travelling at a speed of 32 mph, exceeding the safe speed by 5 mph), and the ride was improperly maintained. P was not contributorily negligent. As a result of this negligence, P suffered a broken arm and was otherwise injured and P incurred hospital and other medical expenses, and was prevented from transacting business, resulting in damages of $80,000.

Does Official Form 9 provide a benchmark for judging any of these? Which satisfy Federal Form 9? Which are too vague? Which of these forms are too specific?

———

LODGE 743, INTERNATIONAL ASS'N OF MACHINISTS v. UNITED AIRCRAFT CORP., 30 F.R.D. 142 (D.Conn.1962). Plaintiff brought suit under the Labor Management Relations Act, 29 U.S.C. § 185, alleging a violation of a strike settlement contract in that defendant-employer had failed to recall strikers to work as jobs for which they were qualified became available. Defendant moved for a more definite statement under Federal Rule 12(e), demanding that plaintiff identify by name the strikers involved and specify the jobs for which they were qualified. Defendant claimed that some 2,000 registered strikers were covered by the contract and it had no knowledge of any violation.

Plaintiff contended that if the court granted the motion, it would be tantamount to a dismissal of its action because the agreement imposed the obligation to keep proper hiring lists on the defendant and thus the information sought was obtainable only from the latter's own personnel files. As the court stated:

> The overwhelming weight of authority is to the effect that a motion for a bill of particulars or a motion for more definite statement of the claim should not be granted if the complaint sets forth a cause of action with sufficient definiteness to enable the defendant to frame an answer. Additional details that the defendant needs in order to prepare for trial shall be obtained by discovery after issue is joined. * * * [see Federal Rules 26–37] * * *.

> In the present case, however, the [union's] allegations might be applicable to a few or as many as 2,000 registered strikers. It is the company's claim that it has no information within its possession of any instance where those allegations are applicable and is at a loss to prepare a proper defense.

> The plaintiff-union contends that while it has substantial reason to believe the allegations of the complaint are true, it is not presently in a position to name the union members to whom the allegations apply nor the jobs which they claim have been unjustly and illegally filled and their members discriminated against. Under such circumstances, no good purpose could be accomplished at this time by the defendant-corporation resorting to the use of interrogatories, in order to procure more definite specifications in this regard.

* * *

The motion of the defendant for more definite statement is granted * * *. However, the plaintiff shall not be required to answer any part of said motion until its own discovery proceedings are completed. This order is without prejudice to the defendant to move for a modification of this ruling during the course of the discovery proceedings by the plaintiff, if good cause appears.

Notes and Questions

1. In WEBB v. WEBB, 32 F.R.D. 615 (W.D.Mo.1963), defendant was charged with negligence in extracting a tooth and rendering postoperative care. He moved for a more definite statement to require plaintiff to specify the acts of negligence. The court denied the motion, pointing out that the complaint clearly was sufficient under Form 9. Does the *Webb* decision in any way subvert the policy of Federal Rule 12(e)? Is *Webb* consistent with *United Aircraft*? Why shouldn't a plaintiff be required to specify the elements of defendant's alleged negligence?

2. The proper function of the Federal Rule 12(e) motion for a more definite statement is better understood in light of its history. Read the commentary accompanying the Rule in the Supplement and consider the amendments that have been made in the Rule since its original promulgation. What was the purpose of these changes? Is the decision in the principal case consistent with the policies underlying the amendments? Why shouldn't the Federal Rules contain a provision for a bill of particulars as an additional method of discovery? See 5A Wright & Miller, *Federal Practice and Procedure: Civil 2d* §§ 1374–75 (1990) (2001 Pocket Part).

3. In current practice, Rule 12(e) motions are disfavored because of the liberal notice-pleading standard of Rule 8 and the availability of extensive discovery. Because Rule 12(e) should not be a substitute for discovery, a motion under it will be denied when the information sought by the moving party is available through discovery. See generally 5A Wright & Miller, *Federal Practice and Procedure: Civil 2d* §§ 1376–77 (1990) (2001 Pocket Part). "[A] motion for more definite statement is generally disfavored and is used to provide a remedy only for an unintelligible pleading rather than a correction for lack of detail." Its use is confined to situations when a party cannot reasonable be required to frame a responsive pleading. Nebout v. City of Hitchcock, 71 F. Supp.2d 702, 706 (S.D.Tex. 1999). See Frederick v. Koziol, 727 F.Supp. 1019, 1021 (E.D.Va.1990).

3. PLEADING THE RIGHT TO RELIEF

———

Read Federal Rule of Civil Procedure 8(a)(2) in the Supplement.

———

GARCIA v. HILTON HOTELS INTERNATIONAL, INC.

United States District Court, District of Puerto Rico, 1951.
97 F.Supp. 5.

ROBERTS, DISTRICT JUDGE. The action here is for damages for defamation brought by plaintiff, a citizen and resident of Puerto Rico, against defendant, a Delaware corporation, in the District Court of Puerto Rico and removed to this Court by defendant corporation. The complaint sets forth two causes of action and the paragraphs considered herein are identical in each cause. Defendant has moved to dismiss the complaint for failure to state a claim upon which relief can be granted and, in the alternative, to strike Paragraphs 5, 6, 7 and 8 and for a more definite statement.

In supoprt [sic] of its motion to dismiss, defendant contends that no publication of the alleged slanderous statement is alleged and that the complaint, therefore, fails to state a cause of action. This contention will be considered first with respect to Paragraph 4 of the complaint, which reads as follows: "4. On August 22, 1950, the plaintiff was violently discharged by the defendant, being falsely and slanderously accused of being engaged in bringing women from outside the Hotel and introducing them into the rooms thereof for the purpose of developing prostitution in the Hotel and that such women brought by him from outside the Hotel and introduced therein carried on acts of prostitution in said Hotel."

* * *

The controlling question here, with respect to the motion to dismiss, is whether the allegations of Paragraph 4 of the complaint, state a claim upon which relief can be granted. An examination of the authorities is persuasive that is [sic] does. It is settled, with respect to motions to dismiss for insufficiency of statement, that the complaint is to be construed in the light most favorable to the plaintiff with all doubts resolved in his favor and the allegations accepted as true. If, when a complaint is so considered, it reasonably may be anticipated that plaintiff, on the basis of what has been alleged, could make out a case at trial entitling him to some relief, the complaint should not be dismissed. * * *

In the instant case, it is true that Paragraph 4, of the complaint, fails to state, in so many words, that there was a publication of the alleged slanderous utterance and, to that extent, the cause of action is defectively stated. However, it does not follow that the allegations do not state a claim upon which relief can be granted. It is alleged that plaintiff was "violently discharged" and was "falsely and slanderously accused" of procuring for prostitution. While in a technical sense, this language states a conclusion, it is clear that plaintiff used it intending to charge publication of the slanderous utterance and it would be unrealistic for defendant to claim that it does not so understand the allegations. * * * Clearly, under such allegations it reasonably may be conceived that plaintiff, upon trial, could adduce evidence tending to prove a publication. * * *

In further support of its motion to dismiss, defendant contends that the alleged slanderous utterance was conditionally privileged. Conceding that to be so does not require that a different conclusion be reached with respect to the motion to dismiss. Rule 12(b) requires that every defense in law or fact be asserted in a responsive pleading when one is required or permitted under the rules. The rule, however, enumerates certain defenses which may be asserted by motion to dismiss, all of which go to the jurisdiction except that of failure to state a claim upon which relief can be granted, rule 12(b)(6). And this latter defense may be asserted successfully by a motion prior to responsive pleading only when it appears to a certainty that plaintiff would be entitled to no relief under any state of fact which could be proved in support of the claim asserted by him. * * *

The conclusiveness of privilege as a defense depends upon whether the privilege involved in [sic] absolute or conditional. When the privilege involved is absolute, it constitutes a finally determinative or conclusive defense to an action based on the utterance. Consequently, when it appears from a complaint that absolute privilege exists, the defense of failure to state a claim properly may be asserted to accomplish a dismissal on motion under rule 12(b). It is for the court to determine the existence of privilege and when absolute privilege is found, it constitutes an unassailable defense and, clearly, in such a case, the claim stated is one upon which relief cannot be granted.

But conditional privilege is not a conclusive defense to an action based on a slanderous utterance. It is but a qualified defense which may be lost to the defendant if plaintiff can prove abuse of the privilege or actual malice. * * * When from the allegations contained therein, a complaint indicates the availability of the defense of conditional privilege, it cannot be held therefrom as a matter of law, that there has been a failure to state a claim upon which relief can be granted, such as will warrant dismissal of the complaint on motion under rule 12(b)(6), for the factual question remains whether defendant abused the privilege or made the communication maliciously. * * *

As has been noted, on motion to dismiss for failure to state a claim, complaint must be construed in the light most favorable to plaintiff with all doubts resolved in his favor and the allegation taken as true. That being so, when allegations are sufficient to sustain the defense of conditional privilege they will be, generally, sufficient to permit the introduction of evidence tending to prove abuse of the privilege or actual malice. Save in some extraordinary situation, allegations which are adequate for the admission of evidence to prove the defense of qualified privilege are adequate for the admission of evidence to negative that defense. It appears from the complaint in the instant case that defendant is entitled to raise the defense of conditional privilege. But this defense may be lost to it if plaintiff proves abuse of the privilege or actual malice. And, clearly, plaintiff may introduce evidence under the allegations for the purpose of proving abuse of the privilege or actual malice. Therefore, it is concluded that defendant's motion to dismiss the complaint for failure to state a claim upon which relief can be granted should be denied.

The conclusion to deny defendant's motion to dismiss requires that consideration be given its alternative motion to strike Paragraphs 5, 6, 7 and 8 of the complaint. It is alleged in these paragraphs, in substance, that upon being discharged, plaintiff made claim with the Labor Department of Puerto Rico for severance pay and overtime as is provided for by law (Section 20, Organic Act of Labor Department of Puerto Rico, approved April 14, 1931); that during a hearing on such claim held by the Labor Department, defendant, falsely and slanderously, repeated its charge that plaintiff had been engaged in procuring for prostitution; and, that, after said hearing defendant had compromised plaintiff's claim for severance pay and overtime. As respects defendant's motion to strike, the controlling allegations are contained in Paragraph 7 of this complaint.

Section 4 of "An Act Authorizing Civil Actions to recover Damages for Libel and Slander," enacted by the Legislature of Puerto Rico and approved on February 19, 1902, (Code of Civil Procedure of Puerto Rico, Ed. 1933, page 309) provides in part as follows: "Section 4. A publication or communication shall not be held or deemed malicious when made in any legislative or judicial proceeding or in any other proceeding authorized by law. * * * "

The effect of the above quoted portions of the statute is to confer absolute privilege upon any communication made in any of the proceedings contemplated therein. If the hearing held by the Labor Department on plaintiff's claim for severance pay and overtime, referred to in Paragraph 7 of the complaint, is a proceeding within the meaning of the phrase "or any other proceeding authorized by law" as used in said Section 4 of the Act of February 19, 1902, the utterance was absolutely privileged and such privilege constitutes a conclusive defense in an action based on that utterance.

It appears that the hearing on plaintiff's claim by the Labor Department, referred to in Paragraph 7 of the complaint, is a proceeding "authorized by law" within the meaning of Section 4 of the Act of February 19, 1902. The Labor Department is authorized to hold such a hearing by Act No. 122 of the Legislature of Puerto Rico, approved April 27, 1949, which statute requires the Commissioner of Labor to enforce labor protecting laws. * * *

It appears, upon examination, that this Statute (Act No. 122) has for its purpose the protection of the welfare of the workman and the furtherance of the public good, and that when hearings are held pursuant to its terms it is necessary, if those purposes are to be effectuated, that those called upon to give evidence therein must be protected against liability, civil or criminal, for communications given in evidence at such hearings. And this without regard for the motives of the witness or the truth or falsity of his statements. For otherwise, the giving of full, free and honest testimony, essential to the enforcement of such laws, will be discouraged. Therefore, communications made by witnesses in the course of such hearings, should be absolutely privileged in the same manner and to like extent as those made in the course of a judicial proceeding.

* * *

Clearly, then, the utterance of the defendant made during the Labor Department hearing referred to in Paragraph 7 of the complaint was absolutely privileged and that Paragraph 7 is, therefore, redundant in that it fails to state a claim upon which relief can be granted. It appears then, that defendant's motion to strike Paragraphs 5, 6, 7 and 8 should be granted.

The parties have agreed on hearing in open court that Paragraph 9 of the complaint should be stricken. And this Court being of the opinion that Paragraphs 5, 6, 7 and 8 should be stricken as redundant, defendant's motion for a more definite statement need be considered only with respect to the allegations of Paragraph 4 of the complaint.

As has been noted herein, conditional privilege is an affirmative defense which properly should be raised by its assertion in a responsive pleading. Consequently, when it appears from a complaint that the defense of conditional privilege may be available to a defendant, the allegations thereof should be reasonably adequate to permit the preparation of a responsive pleading asserting such defense. But when, in an action for slander, the complaint fails to set out substantially the utterance alleged to have been slanderously made or the facts relied upon to establish a publication of such utterance, such omission constitutes vagueness such as is a ground for granting a motion for more definite statement within the contemplation of rule 12(e). Obviously, when such material allegations are insufficient, it would be unreasonable to require the defendant to prepare a responsive pleading without a more definite statement of the pertinent facts.

Considering the allegations of Paragraph 4 of the complaint, the defense of conditional privilege is indicated. However, the allegations suffer from vagueness with respect to the utterance alleged to have been slanderously made and the facts relied upon to establish a publication of the utterance. It is concluded that the defendant here is entitled to a more definite statement setting forth substantially the words alleged to have been slanderously uttered and the facts relied upon to establish a publication thereof.

Defendant's motion to dismiss the complaint for failure to state a claim upon which relief can be granted is denied. Defendant's motion to strike Paragraphs 5, 6, 7 and 8 of the complaint is granted. Defendant's motion for a more definite statement with respect to the matters prescribed in this opinion, is granted. Paragraph 9 of the complaint is ordered stricken. The decisions herein reached are hereby made applicable to the second cause of action set out in the complaint.

Notes and Questions

1. To what extent could plaintiff in *Garcia* have phrased the complaint to avoid the granting of defendant's motions? How should plaintiff alter the complaint to satisfy the court's order for a more definite statement? Can he merely eliminate some of the allegations that gave rise to the conditional privilege?

2. Suppose defendant's motion under Federal Rule 12(e) had been denied by the court. What other means might it have used to learn the details of the alleged defamatory publication? What advantage, if any, is there to a motion under Federal Rule 12(e) as opposed to these other means?

3. Assume plaintiff in *Garcia* had not included any facts in the complaint indicating either a conditional or absolute privilege. How could defendant have raised these issues? See Federal Rule 8(c). Since privilege is obviously a matter of defense, why should it be significant whether plaintiff raises it in the complaint? Shouldn't these matters simply be ignored unless defendant pursues them in the answer? Consider ELLIS v. BLACK DIAMOND COAL MINING CO., 265 Ala. 264, 267, 90 So.2d 770, 773 (1956): "Even though a complaint at law shows on its face that the cause of action is barred by the statute of limitations the defense of the statute cannot be taken by demurrer." But see Davis v. A.G. Edwards & Sons, Inc., 823 F.2d 105 (5th Cir.1987) (plaintiffs held bound by allegations as to when cause arose for purpose of applying the statute of limitations). Compare BAGGETT v. CHAVOUS, 107 Ga.App. 642, 642–43, 131 S.E.2d 109, 110 (1963) (involving the anticipated defense of accord and satisfaction in a contract action): " 'Ordinarily the plaintiff, in his petition, need not anticipate or negative a possible defense. Where, however, such defense is anticipated, it must be effectively avoided, or the complaint is bad.' " On what basis, if any, can *Ellis* and *Baggett*

be reconciled? Would it be fair to say that the decision in *Garcia* is consistent with *Ellis* and inconsistent with *Baggett*?

―――――

The Burden of Pleading and the Burden of Production

The burden of pleading an issue usually is assigned to the party who has the burden of producing evidence on that issue at trial. Plaintiff has the burden of production on two types of issues. First, plaintiff must put forth evidence on certain matters basic to the claim for relief or he cannot prevail. In a slander action, for example, plaintiff must introduce evidence that the remarks were made, that they were published, and that he was injured thereby. If plaintiff rests his case without producing evidence on any one of these issues, the court will dismiss the action and enter judgment for defendant. Second, if, but only if, defendant establishes a defense, plaintiff will then have a second burden of production, this time to introduce evidence as to facts that will avoid defendant's defense. For example, if defendant proves that allegedly slanderous statements were made to plaintiff's prospective employer under conditions that rendered the statements privileged, plaintiff then must carry the burden of producing evidence showing that the statements were made maliciously and solely with intent to injure plaintiff, thereby vitiating the defense.

Plaintiff has the burden of pleading all matters of the first type in the complaint; that is, he is required to plead those matters on which he must introduce evidence at trial. The rationale for the rule is simple. If plaintiff cannot legitimately allege the existence of each of the basic elements of his claim, it may be assumed that he could not introduce evidence on them at trial. Since the action would have to be dismissed as soon as plaintiff rested his case, it would be an idle act to permit the trial to begin, and the action might as well be terminated at the pleading stage.

On the other hand, plaintiff normally does not have to plead matters on which defendant must introduce proof. If plaintiff were required to plead the nonexistence of every defense, not only would the pleading be long, complex, and fraught with danger for a plaintiff who omitted a remote possibility, but the pleadings would not reveal, in any direct way, precisely upon which defenses defendant actually intended to rely. By placing the burden of pleading defenses on defendant, the court and parties know exactly on which of the many possible defenses he intends to introduce evidence, thus making preparation for trial and the actual work at trial more manageable. Obviously, plaintiff is not required to plead, in the original complaint, matters to avoid defenses, since he cannot tell which defenses will be raised until the answer is filed. In some jurisdictions plaintiff is required to set forth matters that avoid the defendant's defenses in a second pleading, which serves as a reply to the answer; in other jurisdictions the decision whether to require a reply is left to the trial court's discretion.

―――――

Other Considerations in Allocating
the Burden of Pleading

Aside from those matters upon which he must initially introduce evidence if he is to prevail, plaintiff, in the complaint, is sometimes required to plead the nonexistence of certain defenses upon which defendant has the burden of proof, although as we have seen, such a requirement is technically illogical. The reason for these special rules is sometimes historical and sometimes practical. Consider, for example, a case in which plaintiff sues defendant on an overdue note. Payment of a note traditionally has been considered a defense to be proved by defendant, who by virtue of having a receipt usually is in a better position to put in evidence on the issue. Nevertheless, plaintiff, as part of the claim, must allege nonpayment. Without such an allegation the complaint would really say nothing justifying legal action; it simply would set forth the existence of the note without mentioning the nature of the breach of its terms. To inform the court and defendant as to the basis of the complaint, an allegation of nonpayment is essential. It is only when a defense, such as payment, goes to the very heart of the action, so that plaintiff should, in order to state a claim, be required to face the issue and allege in good faith that such defense does not exist, that the burden of pleading and the burden of producing evidence need not coincide. Another example occurs in the slander context in which some courts consider the truth of the remarks an absolute defense. In some of these jurisdictions, although not all, falsity is thought to be so much a part of the basic action, that plaintiff must plead it, even though defendant has the burden of introducing evidence of truth.

Because of the technical imbalance in cases in which plaintiff must plead the nonexistence of a defense in order to state a claim, some courts require defendant to raise the defense specially in the answer, rather than by simply denying plaintiff's allegation, if defendant really intends to pursue it; otherwise the defense will be waived. Thus before such an issue actually is tried, it will be pleaded both in the complaint and in the answer.

Allocation of the pleading burden sometimes is complicated by rules or statutes that specifically set forth matters that are to be considered defenses and contained in the answer. See, e.g., Federal Rule of Civil Procedure 8(c). The enumerated matters usually are those that traditionally have been treated as defenses both as to the burden of pleading and the burden of proof. Not all jurisdictions have adhered to these traditional views, however. For example, contributory negligence historically was treated as a defense, but today, in a number of jurisdictions, plaintiff, in order to prevail in a negligence case, must prove his own due care. If the pleading rule in these jurisdictions deems the issue of plaintiff's negligence to be a defense, it creates a serious anomaly, since defendant must raise the issue even though plaintiff is required to prove it. Furthermore, since a defense is waived if defendant does not plead it, the failure of defendant to raise the matter in the answer seems to obviate any need for plaintiff to prove the matter, thus thwarting the express policy of the jurisdiction requiring plaintiff to prove his own due care.

Fortunately those situations in which the burden of proof and burden of pleading do not coincide are few in number and usually are well known. By following approved pleading forms and precedents covering these odd cases, most attorneys handle these instances without incident.

4. PLEADING SPECIAL MATTERS

Read Federal Rule of Civil Procedure 9 and the related materials in the Supplement.

 DENNY v. CAREY

United States District Court, Eastern District of Pennsylvania, 1976.
72 F.R.D. 574.

JOSEPH S. LORD, III, CHIEF JUDGE.

Plaintiff brings this proposed class action on behalf of himself and other purchasers of First Pennsylvania Corporation ("First Penn") securities alleging violation of federal and state securities laws. * * * Defendants have not answered the complaint, but have moved to dismiss pursuant to Fed.R.Civ.P. 12(b)(6) on the ground that plaintiff's allegations fail to state the circumstances constituting the alleged fraud with sufficient particularity as required by Fed.R.Civ.P. 9(b). * * *

On information and belief, plaintiff alleges that from January 1, 1974 to January 28, 1976 defendants conspired to conceal the true picture of First Penn's financial condition by issuing false and fraudulent statements which unreasonably avoided recognition and accrual of losses and inadequately provided for loan losses and total reserves, thereby inflating First Penn's equity and net income. * * *

Specifically, plaintiff alleges, *inter alia,* that First Penn: (1) improperly included as income accruals of interest where the borrower had already defaulted; (2) engaged in sales of foreclosed properties on terms which would not have been made in good faith with arm's length bargaining ("paper sales") to avoid showing substantial losses; (3) inadequately provided for loan losses by not accounting for expected uncollectibles in real estate loans where the mortgage loans constituted a high percentage of the total cost of projects undertaken by borrowers; and (4) concealed the default of loans by entering into extensions, modifications and other arrangements with defaulting borrowers. * * *

Defendants contend that these allegations fail to state the circumstances constituting fraud with sufficient particularity to comply with Fed.R.Civ.P. 9(b), and hence, do not state a claim upon which relief can be granted. Defendants also assert that plaintiff's allegations are "conclusory"—that they are "neutral," simply track the statutory language and fail to delineate the underlying acts and transactions. * * * Defendants state that plaintiff's deficiency is exacerbated by the fact that all of the operative allegations are made on information and belief without a statement of the facts upon which plaintiff's belief is founded. * * *

Defendants believe that plaintiff's burden of pleading fraud with particularity is a "rigorous" one. They point to several rationales given for Rule 9(b) which they believe support this position. Defendants state that since fraud is easily charged and such allegations of moral turpitude may at times be advanced only for their nuisance or settlement value, Rule 9(b) serves to protect defendants. * * * Defendants also argue that Rule 9(b) shields defendants, especially accountants and other professional defendants, from lawsuits which wrongfully damage their reputations. * * *

Defendants are incorrect when they argue that Rule 9(b) places a "rigorous" burden of pleading on plaintiff. A court may become too demanding if it unduly focuses on potential harm to defendants' reputations or the possibility of a "strike" or nuisance suit. "[R]ule 9(b) does not insulate professionals from claims of fraud where a complaint alleges the fraudulent acts with particularity * * *." Felton v. Walston and Co., [508 F.2d 577, 581–82 (2d Cir.1974)] * * *. "A strict application of Rule 9(b) in class action securities fraud cases could result in substantial unfairness to persons who are the victims of fraudulent conduct." In re Caesars Palace Securities Litigation, 360 F.Supp. 366, 388 (S.D.N.Y.1973). This is especially true where many of the matters are peculiarly within the knowledge of defendants. * * * Certainly in such cases, once plaintiff has satisfied the minimum burden of Rule 9(b), plaintiff should be allowed to flesh out the allegations in the complaint through discovery. * * *

Fed.R.Civ.P. 8 requires a short and plain statement of the claim which is simple, concise and direct. Rule 9(b) must be harmonized with the notice pleading mandate of Rule 8. * * * "Rule 9(b) does not require nor make legitimate the pleading of detailed evidentiary matter." *Moore* ¶ 9.03 at 1930 * * *.

Since fraud embraces a wide variety of potential misconduct, *Wright & Miller* § 1296 at 400, Rule 9(b) requires slightly more notice than would be forthcoming under Rule 8.[5] * * * But the requirement of Rule 9(b) is met when there is sufficient identification of the circumstances constituting fraud so that the defendant can prepare an adequate answer to the allegations. * * *

We find that the complaint [though not a model of perfect pleading] satisfies the requirement of Rule 9(b). * * * Before discovery, any stricter application of Rule 9(b) is especially inappropriate in a case such as this where the matters alleged are peculiarly within the knowledge of defendants. * * *

Notes and Questions

1. DENNY v. BARBER, 576 F.2d 465 (2d Cir.1978), was a case remarkably similar to Denny v. Carey. Both were brought by the same plaintiff, represented by the same counsel, and the same public accounting firm was one of the defendants in each case. The complaint, couched only in general terms, alleged, inter alia, that defendants had fraudulently concealed defendant Chase Manhattan Corporation's true financial picture by not revealing that the corporation had

---

5. *Wright & Miller* § 1300 at 425 points out: "the notion that Rule 9(b) does not actually require significantly more particularity than Rule 8 seems to be supported by the text of Official Form 13, which contains little more than a general allegation of fraud."

made "risky and speculative" investments without providing adequate reserves for losses and had delayed in writing off uncollectible loans. The court held that Rule 9(b) had not been satisfied:

> Plaintiff's counsel has called our attention to a number of district court decisions * * * [including Denny v. Carey] which are alleged to have sustained complaints no more specific than this. We see no profit in attempting to analyze these decisions, which may or may not be consistent and each of which necessarily rests on its particular facts. * * * [There] must be more than vague allegations that, as shown by subsequent developments, the corporation's true financial picture was not so bright in some respects as its annual reports had painted and that the defendants knew, or were reckless in failing to know, this. The admission in [plaintiff's] counsel's * * * statement [that he could provide no further facts] * * * in the absence of discovery is significant. The Supreme Court has admonished that to the extent that such discovery "permits a plaintiff with a largely groundless claim to simply take up the time of a number of other people, with the right to do so representing an *in terrorem* increment of the settlement value, rather than a reasonably founded hope that the process will reveal relevant evidence, it is a social cost rather than a benefit." Blue Chip Stamps v. Manor Drug Stores * * * 421 U.S. at 741. * * *

See also Romani v. Shearson Lehman Hutton, Inc., 929 F.2d 875, 878–80 (1st Cir.1991).

2. What are the policies underlying Rule 9(b), requiring particularity in pleading fraud? Is it designed to discourage nuisance suits? If so, why doesn't Rule 11, which requires truthful pleadings, handle this problem? And in any event, why would concern about nuisance suits be more acute with regard to fraud than with regard to other causes of action? Is it because a defendant who is accused of fraud often might be harmed even if subsequently he prevails on the merits? Requiring particularity in these cases has the effect of screening out such cases early on, instead of relying on other devices, such as summary judgment. Is the special Rule 9(b) requirement necessary because without it the defendant would not receive adequate notice of the particulars of the circumstances constituting the fraud?

Over the years, concern over a perceived increase in the amount of frivolous litigation led some courts to enforce Rule 9(b) more rigorously. See, e.g., Vicom, Inc. v. Harbridge Merchant Services, Inc., 20 F.3d 771 (7th Cir.1994). See generally 5 Wright & Miller, *Federal Practice and Procedure:* Civil 2d § 1298, at pp. 626–27 (1990). Partly in response to this perception, Congress passed the Private Securities Litigation Reform Act of 1995, see Notes 4 and 5, pp. 534–35, infra, which significantly heightens the pleading requirements in securities cases.

Is the particularity requirement of Rule 9(b) justified as a means of shielding defendants from the heavy expense of complying with burdensome discovery requests in lawsuits that appear on the face of the complaint to be marginal? Would a better solution be to shift the expense of discovery in fraud cases? See Sovern, *Reconsidering Federal Civil Rule 9(b): Do We Need Particularized Pleading Requirements in Fraud Cases?*, 104 F.R.D. 143 (1985); Richman, Lively & Mell, *The Pleading of Fraud: Rhymes Without Reason*, 60 S.Cal.L.Rev. 959 (1987). Note, *Pleading Securities Fraud Claims with Particularity Under Rule 9(b)*, 97 Harv.L.Rev. 1432 (1984); Note, *Using Rule 9(b) To Reduce Nuisance Securities Litigation*, 99 Yale L.J. 1591 (1990).

Not only with respect to cases involving securities fraud, but in certain types of cases not covered by Federal Rule 9(b), for example, complex litigation involving such matters as antitrust violations, and civil rights claims, which weigh heavily on federal court dockets, some courts have imposed more rigorous pleading requirements than in other types of cases. As noted in Marcus, *The Revival of Fact Pleading Under the Federal Rules of Civil Procedure,* 86 Colum.L.Rev. 433, 445–50 (1986):

> Undoubtedly, lax pleading has * * * benefitted plaintiffs. Plaintiffs have an incentive to plead vaguely in hopes that discovery will turn up material on which to base a more specific charge. Indeed, it has even been suggested that specificity inherently favors defendants. Moreover, under *Conley v. Gibson* [p. 518, supra] courts may be inclined to deny motions to dismiss precisely because they cannot tell enough about a plaintiff's claim from the pleadings to decide whether the plaintiff has a chance of prevailing at trial. * * * [P]laintiffs with weak claims have good reason to want to stave off dismissal in hopes of a settlement.

> A natural antidote to pro-plaintiff biases and the impulse toward vagueness is to promote pleadings decisions, and the courts have adopted this solution in areas that were viewed as particularly troubling. The Supreme Court itself, while approaching pleading issues with what has been called "appalling casualness" and continuing outwardly to adhere to *Conley*, has nevertheless provided some support for such creativity. It has suggested that "insubstantial" cases can be dismissed despite "artful pleading" and appeared receptive to using pleading motions to weed out meritless cases. In a 1983 decision reversing dismissal of an antitrust case, for example, it exhorted the district court to require plaintiff to plead with particularity, concluding that "in a case of this magnitude, a district court must retain the power to insist upon some specificity in pleading before allowing a potentially massive factual controversy to proceed."

As the Notes that follow indicate, however, because these matters are not covered by special rule, the Supreme Court has held that heightened pleading requirements in civil rights cases are improper and federal courts generally have increasingly reached the same conclusion as to complex cases. On the other hand, Congress, unhappy with the undemanding interpretation of Rule 9(b) by some courts in securities litigation, such as Denny v. Carey, above, has decreed that a higher standard is required in those cases.

Notes and Questions

1. As noted, cases brought under the Civil Rights Acts had been singled out for special pleading treatment by some federal courts. In LEATHERMAN v. TARRANT COUNTY NARCOTICS INTELLIGENCE & COORDINATION UNIT, 507 U.S. 163, 113 S.Ct. 1160, 122 L.Ed.2d 517 (1993), a unanimous Supreme Court held that a federal court may not apply a more stringent pleading standard in civil rights cases alleging municipal liability under 42 U.S.C. § 1983.

We think that it is impossible to square the "heightened pleading standard" applied by the Fifth Circuit in this case with the liberal system of "notice pleading" set up by the Federal Rules. Rule 8(a)(2) requires that a complaint include only "a short and plain statement of the claim showing that the pleader is entitled to relief." In *Conley v. Gibson*, 355 U.S. 41, 78 S.Ct. 99, 2 L.Ed.2d 80 (1957) [p. 518, supra], we said in effect that the Rule meant what it said:

> "[T]he Federal Rules of Civil Procedure do not require a claimant to set out in detail the facts upon which he bases his claim. To the contrary, all the Rules require is 'a short and plain statement of the claim' that will give the defendant fair notice of what the plaintiff's claim is and the grounds upon which it rests." Id., at 47, 78 S.Ct., at 103 (footnote omitted).

Rule 9(b) does impose a particularity requirement in two specific instances. It provides that "[i]n all averments of fraud or mistake, the circumstances constituting fraud or mistake shall be stated with particularity." Thus, the Federal Rules do address in Rule 9(b) the question of the need for greater particularity in pleading certain actions, but do not include among the enumerated actions any reference to complaints alleging municipal liability under § 1983. *Expressio unius est exclusio alterius.*

The phenomenon of litigation against municipal corporations based on claimed constitutional violations by their employees dates from our decision in [Monell v. New York City Dep't of Social Services, 436 U.S. 658, 98 S.Ct. 2018, 56 L.Ed.2d 611 (1978)], where we for the first time construed § 1983 to allow such municipal liability. Perhaps if Rules 8 and 9 were rewritten today, claims against municipalities under § 1983 might be subjected to the added specificity requirement of Rule 9(b). But that is a result which must be obtained by the process of amending the Federal Rules, and not by judicial interpretation. In the absence of such an amendment, federal courts and litigants must rely on summary judgment and control of discovery to weed out unmeritorious claims sooner rather than later.

Id. at 168, 113 S.Ct. at 1162, 122 L.Ed.2d at 524.

2. *Leatherman* has been applied almost universally to disallow court-created heightened pleading requirements in civil rights cases. However, since *Leatherman* left the question open, lower courts sometimes have upheld heightened pleading requirements for plaintiffs bringing actions against government officials who claim qualified immunity. See, e.g., Schultea v. Wood, 47 F.3d 1427 (5th Cir.1995). Should Congress enact heightened pleadings requirements in these and other cases? For an analysis of the application of the *Leatherman* holding in lower courts, see Blum, *Heightened Pleading: Is There Life After Leatherman?*, 44 Cath.U.L.Rev. 59 (1994). How far can courts go in requiring detailed pleadings so as to provide "fair notice" to the opposing party? See Loftus v. Southeastern Pennsylvania Transportation Authority, 843 F.Supp. 981 (E.D.Pa.1994) (detailed allegations required when alleging a conspiracy between defendants).

3. An area of special concern has been the role of pleading in cases containing numerous complex factual issues, a prime example being antitrust suits in the federal courts. From time to time some federal judges have urged that a separate, more rigorous standard of pleading should apply in those cases. See, e.g., Baim & Blank, Inc. v. Warren–Connelly Co., 19 F.R.D. 108, 109–10 (S.D.N.Y.1956). Numerous courts, however, have specifically held that the so-called "big case" cannot

receive special treatment since the Federal Rules do not provide for it. See, e.g., Baxley–DeLamar Monuments, Inc. v. American Cemetery Ass'n, 843 F.2d 1154 (8th Cir.1988); Quality Foods de Centro America, S.A. v. Latin American Agribusiness Development Corp., 711 F.2d 989 (11th Cir.1983); Nagler v. Admiral Corp., 248 F.2d 319 (2d Cir.1957). But see Associated Gen. Contractors of California, Inc. v. California State Council of Carpenters, 459 U.S. 519, 528 n. 17, 103 S.Ct. 897, 903 n. 17, 74 L.Ed.2d 723, 732 n. 17 (1983) (suggesting in dictum that courts may require some minimal and reasonable particularity in pleading before they allow an antitrust action to proceed); Sutliff, Inc. v. Donovan Cos., 727 F.2d 648, 654 (7th Cir.1984) ("The heavy costs of modern federal litigation, especially antitrust litigation, and the mounting caseload pressures on the federal courts, counsel against launching the parties into pretrial discovery if there is no reasonable prospect that the plaintiff can make out a cause of action from the events narrated in the complaint."); General Acquisition, Inc. v. GenCorp., 766 F.Supp. 1460, 1465 (D.Ohio 1990).

For various views of the problem, see Report to the Judicial Conference of the United States, *Procedure in Antitrust and Other Protracted Cases,* 13 F.R.D. 62, 66–68 (1953); Clark, *Special Pleading in the "Big Case,"* 21 F.R.D. 45 (1958); Freund, *The Pleading and Pre–Trial of an Antitrust Claim,* 46 Cornell L.Q. 555 (1961). See generally 5 Wright & Miller, *Federal Practice and Procedure: Civil 2d* § 1228 (1990) (2001 Pocket Part).

4. The Private Securities Litigation Reform Act of 1995, Pub.L. 104–67, was enacted, over President Clinton's veto, in December 1995. With respect to pleading requirements, the history of the Act and its proper interpretation are ably discussed by a number of courts, including Novak v. Kasaks, 216 F.3d 300 (2d Cir.), certiorari denied __ U.S. __, 121 S.Ct. 567, 148 L.Ed.2d 486 (2000), and Malin v. Ivax Corp., 17 F.Supp.2d 1345 (S.D.Fla.1998). The Act was designed to discourage abusive securities litigation. Among other things its intent is to create a heightened pleading standard for securities fraud cases. Under the Act, plaintiffs are required to plead with particularity "facts that give rise to the strong inference that defendants operated with the required state of mind." In the case of fraud this means that defendants must have acted with "scienter." Prior to the Act a disagreement had developed as to the level of detail that had to be set out to plead scienter satisfactorily under Rule 9(b). The Ninth Circuit had permitted plaintiffs to allege the necessary mental state without providing any facts to support the allegation. The Second Circuit had employed a stricter standard by requiring either (1) facts constituting strong circumstantial evidence of recklessness or intentional conduct, or (2) facts showing that defendant had both motive and opportunity to commit fraud. Neither the Act nor its history made clear whether Congress intended to codify the Second Circuit position or create an even stricter standard. A majority of courts have followed the Second Circuit standard. See, e.g., Marksman Partners, L.P. v. Chantal Pharmaceutical Corp., 927 F.Supp. 1297 (C.D.Cal.1996). Others, however, have held that the Act eliminated recklessness as a basis for substantive liability and require more than a pleading of motive and opportunity to commit fraud to set forth a sufficient allegation of scienter. The latter courts thus require plaintiff to allege facts showing intentional behavior on the part of defendant. In re Silicon Graphics Inc. Securities Litigation, 183 F.3d 970 (9th Cir.), rehearing and rehearing en banc denied, 195 F.3d 521 (9th Cir.1999).

The *Malin* court took an intermediate view, shared by a number of other cases. It agreed that a pleading of facts showing motive and opportunity was, by itself, insufficient to state a claim. On the other hand, it held that the Act did not eliminate liability for reckless behavior. Therefore a plaintiff could continue to use the Second Circuit method of stating a claim by alleging reckless as well as intentional behavior. The court in the *Novak* case struggled with the same issue and reached a similar conclusion.

5.   Although everybody is against "abusive litigation," many, including President Clinton, felt that the Private Securities Litigation Reform Act would do more harm than good by creating a pleading burden so onerous that it would prevent the bringing of legitimate securities fraud cases. What problems might flow from creating this kind of substance-based procedural rule? Should the requirements of a procedural system be uniform regardless of the character of the claim? These are the questions addressed in discussions of the merits of "trans-substantive procedure." While considering them, remember that the ease of bringing cases to court has been an engine of social justice as well as an opportunity for abuse by an allegedly "litigious society." For discussions of trans-substantive procedure, see Stemple, *Halting Devolution or Bleak to the Future: Subrin's New–Old Procedure as a Possible Antidote to Dreyfuss's "Tolstoy Problem,"* 46 Fla.L.Rev. 57 (1994); Dreyfuss, *The What and Why of the New Discovery Rules,* 46 Fla.L.Rev. 9, 11–15 (1994); Subrin, *Fudge Points and Thin Ice in Discovery Reform and the Case for Selective Substance–Specific Procedure,* 46 Fla.L.Rev. 27, 28 (1994).

5.   ALTERNATIVE AND INCONSISTENT ALLEGATIONS

Read Federal Rule of Civil Procedure 8(e)(2) and the related materials in the Supplement.

In the past, some courts have held pleadings that contain inconsistent allegations defective, at least if the inconsistency appeared in a single cause of action or defense. See, e.g., Pavalon v. Thomas Holmes Corp., 25 Wis.2d 540, 131 N.W.2d 331 (1964). Many of these same courts approved these allegations so long as they were contained in separately stated causes or defenses. See Bischoff v. Hustisford State Bank, 195 Wis. 312, 218 N.W. 353 (1928).

Despite occasional statements indicating that inconsistent allegations are improper, see, e.g., Katz v. Feldman, 23 Cal.App.3d 500, 504, 100 Cal.Rptr. 367, 369 (1972), virtually all courts today permit inconsistent allegations, whether separately pleaded or not, if they are made in good faith, for example, in a situation in which the pleader has been unable to ascertain all the facts prior to filing the complaint or answer. See, e.g., McCormick v. Kopmann, 23 Ill.App.2d 189, 161 N.E.2d 720 (1959). A number of states specifically have altered their pleading rules to permit inconsistent pleadings. See, e.g., Mo. R.Civ.P. 55.10 (revised in 1973). Compare Ga.Code Ann. § 9–11–8(e)(2), with Republic Mortgage Co. v. Beasley, 117 Ga.App. 303, 160 S.E.2d 429 (1968) (decided under prior Georgia law).

As previously noted, see pp. 471–74, supra, under the original common-law rules, pleadings were designed to reduce every controversy to a single issue of law or fact. Alternative and hypothetical allegations would have made the search for the single issue impossible and therefore they were forbidden.

See generally McDonald, *Alternative Pleading: I,* 48 Mich.L.Rev. 311 (1950). Is there any justification today for a rule prohibiting alternative allegations? To what extent does the availability of discovery, pretrial conference, and summary judgment affect your answer?

The Separate–Statement Requirement

Rules permitting parties to plead in the alternative usually are coupled with provisions requiring each separate cause of action or defense to be separately stated. See the state provisions set out in connection with Federal Rule 10(b) in the Supplement.

Federal Rule 10(b) does not contain a formal separate-statement requirement, although the Rule does express the hope that "as far as practicable" each paragraph will be limited "to a statement of a single set of circumstances." The Rule also requires separation of claims founded on different transactions "whenever separation facilitates the clear presentation of the matters set forth." One commentator argues that this type of discretionary rule coupled with Rule 8(e), which permits inconsistent allegations in a single count, may be too liberal and may encourage confusion in pleading. He goes on to state:

> * * * If consistency promotes clarity, it is no great burden upon the plaintiff for him to state his separate grounds of recovery consistently. But if his position is clear, and it is obvious that the inconsistencies arise from an attempt to press alternative interpretations of the facts, little is to be gained by striking the pleading only to have it reformed in multiple counts asserting the same grounds of recovery.

McDonald, *Alternative Pleading in the United States: I,* 52 Colum.L.Rev. 443, 464 (1952). See also O'Donnell v. Elgin, J. & E. Ry. Co., 338 U.S. 384, 70 S.Ct. 200, 94 L.Ed. 187 (1949). Is the code-system requirement of separate counts, each of which is consistent within itself, preferable to Federal Rule 10(b)?

When a party violates the separate-statement requirement, the appropriate corrective procedure may be a motion to compel separate statements, see Aetna Cas. & Sur. Co. v. Merchants Mut. Ins. Co., 84 A.D.2d 736, 444 N.Y.S.2d 79 (1st Dep't 1981), or a motion to strike, see Ledesma v. Cannonball, Inc., 182 Ill.App.3d 718, 131 Ill.Dec. 280, 538 N.E.2d 655 (1989), or a special preliminary objection, see Duquesne Light Co. v. United States Industrial Fabricators, Inc., 334 Pa.Super. 444, 483 A.2d 534 (1984). In any case the party will be allowed to amend his pleading to conform to the rules. If a plaintiff refuses to amend, should the case be dismissed? See Bautista v. Los Angeles, Note 5, p. 519, supra (federal courts have power to order separate statements and to dismiss if party fails to comply); Souper Spud, Inc. v. Aetna Cas. & Sur. Co., 5 Conn.App. 579, 501 A.2d 1214 (1985) (default judgment or judgment of nonsuit proper).

6. PLEADING DAMAGES

Reread Federal Rule of Civil Procedure 9(g) in the Supplement.

 ## ZIERVOGEL v. ROYAL PACKING CO.

St. Louis Court of Appeals, Missouri, 1949.
225 S.W.2d 798.

McCULLEN, JUDGE. This action was brought by respondent as plaintiff against appellant as defendant to recover damages for injuries plaintiff alleged she sustained as a result of a collision between an automobile driven by her and a motor vehicle (tractor-trailer, also referred to as truck) operated by defendant's employee. A trial before the court and a jury resulted in a verdict and judgment in favor of plaintiff against defendant in the sum of $2000.00. After an unavailing motion for a new trial defendant appealed.

* * * Describing her injuries plaintiff alleged in her petition that "Plaintiff sustained injuries to her neck, back, spine and nervous system and was otherwise injured and her earning capacity has been permanently impaired."

* * *

For its first point defendant contends that the trial court erred in permitting plaintiff's counsel in his opening statement, over defendant's objection, to state to the jury that plaintiff's blood pressure had increased by the accident and in refusing to declare a mistrial on defendant's motion because of such statement and in permitting plaintiff to introduce evidence over defendant's objection of plaintiff's increased blood pressure and in refusing to declare a mistrial on defendant's motion because of the introduction of such evidence and also in permitting [plaintiff] over defendant's objection to present evidence of an injury to her shoulder. Defendant points out that plaintiff's petition does not allege that she was caused to develop high blood pressure or that such an existing condition was aggravated by the accident. Defendant further contends that the evidence does not establish that a continuing elevation in blood pressure is an inevitable or necessary result of the injuries averred and that the evidence of such condition was, therefore, inadmissible. In support of these contentions defendant cites a number of cases which apply the principle of law that before a plaintiff can recover for a physical condition claimed to have resulted from the negligence of another, such condition must be pleaded or the evidence must establish the condition as being the inevitable or necessary result of injuries which are particularly set out in the petition. The reason underlying such decisions is that it would be unjust to permit a plaintiff to take advantage of a defendant at the trial by presenting evidence of injuries of which the defendant did not have the kind of notice required by law, namely, through allegations in plaintiff's petition.

It is true the evidence in this case does show, as plaintiff contends, that defendant had actual notice before trial of plaintiff's increased blood pressure, which she claimed was a result of the collision, through a statement made by plaintiff to that effect to the Claim Agent of defendant's insurer and through an examination of plaintiff made by defendant's doctor, Dr. Leo A. Will, and reported by him to said Claim Agent as well as through plaintiff's deposition which was taken by defendant. However, we are of the opinion that although it cannot be said that defendant was "surprised" when plaintiff presented evidence at the trial relating to the condition of her blood pressure, defendant nevertheless had the right to object to such evidence on the ground that it related to "special damages" which were not pleaded in plaintiff's petition. Although defendant could not have claimed "surprise" upon the introduction of such evidence, it was not required to do so and its objections at the trial to such evidence in the absence of proper allegations thereon in plaintiff's petition should have been sustained. No such special damages were pleaded by plaintiff, nor did plaintiff ask leave to amend her petition to include such special damages which she could have done on such terms, at that stage of the proceedings, as the court should order. However, plaintiff did not amend her petition, nor ask leave to amend, and defendant had the right to object to the evidence in question.

* * * [Missouri Rule of Civil Procedure 55.19] expressly provides: "When items of special damage are claimed, they shall be specifically stated." * * *

It has been held by our Supreme Court that a specific personal injury which is not the necessary or inevitable result of an injury alleged in the petition constitutes an element of "special damage" which must be specifically pleaded before evidence thereof is admissible. See State ex rel. Grisham v. Allen, 344 Mo. 66, 124 S.W.2d 1080. * * *

In the case at bar the only allegations in plaintiff's petition with respect to the injuries she suffered as the result of the collision were as follows: "Plaintiff sustained injuries to her neck, back, spine and nervous system and was otherwise injured and her earning capacity has been permanently impaired." It will be observed that not only is there no mention of increased blood pressure but no injuries are alleged from which it can reasonably be said that an increase in blood pressure was an inevitable or necessary result. Nor was there any evidence to show that the increased blood pressure was the necessary or inevitable result of the injuries alleged in the petition.

* * *

What we have said herein with respect to the evidence of plaintiff's increase of blood pressure applies with equal force to the evidence of the injury to plaintiff's shoulder. In the absence of any allegation in plaintiff's petition relating to that injury, it was error for the court to admit such evidence.

* * *

On Motion for Rehearing or, in the Alternative, to Transfer to Supreme Court.

McCULLEN, JUDGE. Plaintiff has filed an extended motion for rehearing in which she earnestly argues that this court committed error in holding that the trial court erred in permitting plaintiff to introduce evidence of her high blood pressure when no such damage was pleaded in plaintiff's petition. * * *

It is contended by plaintiff that [the Missouri rule] * * *, which provides that when "items of special damage" are claimed "they shall be specifically stated," having been copied verbatim from Rule 9(g) of the Federal Rules

* * *, the "construction" given said Rule 9(g) by the Federal Courts must be given to [the Missouri rule as well] * * *.

* * *

In the lengthy argument of plaintiff she repeatedly refers to the "construction" given to Federal Rule 9(g) but nowhere is there cited any authority showing what such "construction" was in any kind of a case. * * * Plaintiff evidently has found no case in point on the facts of this case (just as we have found none) because, as we see it, the words of both Federal Rule 9(g) and the state [rule] * * *, are so simple, plain and unambiguous that no one has even heretofore contended in a court of last resort that a party could plead only "general" damages and recover for "special" damages.

* * *

[Motion denied.]

Notes and Questions

1. In EPHREM v. PHILLIPS, 99 So.2d 257, 260–61 (Fla.App. 1st Dist.1957), a case arising out of an auto accident, plaintiff, who alleged only that she was "painfully, seriously and permanently injured, bruised and lacerated in and throughout her head, body and limbs," sought and was permitted to collect damages for a required abortion. The court held:

> Within the allegations of the complaint it is clear that plaintiff might show any change in her physical condition due to the injuries sustained, and such was the abortion. Where only such damages as may be reasonably expected to follow an injury are claimed, no allegation of special damages is required. In personal injury actions proof that the plaintiff's pain and suffering resulted in and were aggravated by an abortion is clearly admissible. So far as the abortion augments the physical injury, pain or suffering, then so far is it proper to be considered on the question of damages.

> For the foregoing reasons we hold that a claim based upon pain and anguish, suffered as a consequence of injuries sustained from the negligent act of another, is not an item of special damages merely because such pain and anguish resulted in and was aggravated by an abortion.

Can *Ziervogel* and *Ephrem* be reconciled? Did plaintiff's lawyer in *Ziervogel* hurt his client's case by pleading too much? See THACKER v. WARD, 263 N.C. 594, 140 S.E.2d 23, certiorari denied 382 U.S. 865, 86 S.Ct. 134, 15 L.Ed.2d 104 (1965), in which the court refused to permit a plaintiff who had alleged physical injuries to his body and nervous system to collect damages for unpleaded psychological disturbances that resulted from the physical injuries but had an emotional, rather than a physical, basis.

2. Should medical bills incurred as a result of personal injuries be considered special damages requiring special pleading or should they be provable as a logical and necessary result of the injuries themselves? See Sossamon v. Nationwide Mut. Ins. Co., 243 S.C. 552, 135 S.E.2d 87 (1964), which held a general allegation of damages sufficient to permit proof of doctor and hospital bills. See also Newman v. Aluminum Co. of America, 643 S.W.2d 109 (Tenn.App.1982) (unnecessary to plead medical expenses specially when injury is alleged to be serious). There are many cases that take a contrary view.

Elements of special damages that must be pleaded if proof of them is to be allowed at trial also may appear in other types of actions. In contract actions, for example, special damages are those that normally would not be foreseen as the consequence of defendant's breach. See Sheek v. Lee, 289 S.C. 327, 345 S.E.2d 496 (1986). Special damages can be recovered in contract actions from a defaulting party who was informed that they might result from a breach. See Bumann v. Maurer, 203 N.W.2d 434, 440–41 (N.D.1972).

3. Must punitive damages be demanded under Rule 9(g) to be recoverable? See Anheuser–Busch, Inc. v. John Labatt, Ltd., 89 F.3d 1339, 1349 (8th Cir.1996), Note 4, p. 544, infra.

4. Although the normal consequence of failing to plead special damages is being barred from proving them at trial, it is important to note that with regard to a few types of cases the existence of special damages is an integral part of the claim, and the failure to plead them renders the complaint subject to a demurrer or motion to dismiss. See, e.g., Paine–Erie Hospital Supply, Inc. v. Lincoln First Bank, 82 Misc.2d 432, 370 N.Y.S.2d 370 (Sup.Ct.1975). Should the degree of specificity required in pleading special damages be the same in all cases or should it depend on whether the special damages are simply added elements of injury or are an integral part of the claim? Does the fact that a distinction along these lines is drawn by the courts of the state in which the federal court is sitting have any relevance to a federal court's construction of Federal Rule 9(g)?

7. THE PRAYER FOR RELIEF

Read Federal Rules of Civil Procedure 8(a)(3) and 54(c) in the Supplement.

BAIL v. CUNNINGHAM BROTHERS, INC.

United States Court of Appeals, Seventh Circuit, 1971.
452 F.2d 182.

PELL, CIRCUIT JUDGE. * * * The final contention raised by defendant on this appeal is that the judgment against defendant should be remitted from $135,000 to $85,000.

Plaintiff's original complaint sought damages in the amount of $100,000. On the morning the trial was to begin, plaintiff presented a motion to amend the complaint requesting that the ad damnum clause in the complaint against defendant be increased from $100,000 to $250,000. The district judge denied this motion " * * * for the reason that the case is at issue, it is set for trial this date, and the defendant was not given notice of the filing of the motion."

The jury notwithstanding the complaint-contained limitation of $100,000 returned a verdict for the higher figure of $150,000. In a post-trial motion Bail sought and was granted leave to amend the complaint by increasing the ad damnum clause to $150,000. Bail had received $15,000 from another defendant originally named in the complaint in return for "a covenant not to pursue." This payment had been set off, leaving the final judgment of

$135,000. It has been said that the office of the ad damnum in a pleading is to fix the amount beyond which a party may not recover on the trial of his action. Gable v. Pathfinder Irrigation District, 159 Neb. 778, 68 N.W.2d 500, 506 (1955). However, an examination of the cases reveals that the rule thus enunciated, if indeed it still be a rule, has flexibility to the virtual point of nonexistence. Thus, in *Gable* the court pointed out that there was also a general rule that amendment may be made to a pleading which did not change the issues or affect the quantum of proof as to a material fact and that no good reason was apparent for not applying this privilege of amendment to the ad damnum clause. Id. at 506.

In the case before us, even though it is a diversity case, a matter of procedure is involved and governed, therefore, entirely by the federal rules. Riggs, Ferris & Geer v. Lillibridge, 316 F.2d 60, 62 (2d Cir.1963).

* * *

There is substantial authority for the proposition that pursuant to Rule 54(c) a claimant may be awarded damages in excess of those demanded in his pleadings. * * *

Cunningham, however, contends that the authority is not all one way * * * [citing, inter alia,] the case of Wyman v. Morone, 33 A.D.2d 168, 306 N.Y.S.2d 115 (1969), to the effect that under New York law the granting of the motion to increase the amount sued for, after a jury has rendered its verdict, is an abuse of discretion. We, of course, in view of Rule 54(c) are not in any way bound by the interpretation of this lower court of New York as to the law of that state but do observe that there apparently was some significance attached to the extended delay in moving to amend and in any event feel that the dissenting opinion in *Wyman* swims with the main current of judicial thinking in this particular area as opposed to the contrary movement of the majority opinion.

The difficulty, if any there be, posed here, however, lies in the fact that Bail attempted to amend the ad damnum clause in advance of trial and the right of amendment was denied by the court. In this respect the case would seem to be one of first impression as no case involving this exact factual situation has been brought to our attention. It appears to us that the motion to amend, even though on the morning of the trial, should have been granted. It not having been granted, our inquiry must be as to whether the normal rule prevailing under 54(c) should be varied. In our opinion, it should not be.

On oral argument, inquiry was directed to counsel for Cunningham as to how the conduct of the trial would have differed if the pretrial motion to amend had been granted. The thought was ventured that the attorneys might have tried the case differently, that they might have argued damages to the jury (which subject they conspicuously avoided in final argument) or they might have cross-examined more extensively. With hindsight, they may well think that they should have argued damages even if no post-trial amendment were to be permitted and the limitation on recovery were left at $100,000. In essence, however, we cannot see that the quantum of proof as to any material fact varied or that any change of issues resulted, or would have resulted, from an amendment of the ad damnum clause. Counsel competently and vigorously defended on the theory of no liability whatsoever, and we can find no basis for an assumption that $100,000 is such an insignificant amount that counsel somehow would try harder if they knew that the exposure might be $250,000.

No doubt if the ad damnum had sought some insignificant amount such as $1,000, the case would not have received the attention from trial counsel that it did. In the case before us, however, defense counsel were never confronted with an insignificant amount.

It perhaps is unfortunate that the district court did not permit the amendment as requested in advance of trial so as to eliminate the claim that the defendant somehow was prejudiced in relying on this. Finding, however, no real prejudice we will follow the rule generally prevailing to the effect that even though the party was not successful in demanding such relief in his pleadings, he was entitled thereto under the evidence. At least the jury thought that he was so entitled, and we find no basis for upsetting their determination irrespective of whether we would have reached this exact amount in assessing damages. Further, the district court who heard the evidence on a front line basis was satisfied that the amendment should be allowed on a post-trial motion.

Although Bail's counsel under the constraint of the court's ruling did confine his final argument to an amount within the unamended ad damnum clause, it is not entirely unreasonable to assume that he and his client would have been well satisfied with a verdict of $100,000 and, indeed, it does not stretch the imagination too far to conceive that a settlement could have been arrived at for less than that figure if the general practical pattern of settlements in personal injury cases had had any application here. Nevertheless, the case was not settled and inasmuch as the damages cannot be shown to be excessive, nor to have been dictated by passion and prejudice, the verdict will stand. While Cunningham finds some source of complaint in the fact that plaintiff's counsel himself argued less than $100,000 and while it may not now be much solace to Cunningham, nevertheless there was the trial advantage to the defense that plaintiff was precluded from arguing a larger sum.

What we have had to say with regard to the ad damnum clause is indicative of the anachronistic character of the clause. Indeed, there is a well publicized school of thought that it should be done away with altogether. * * * It is true that in some suits it is necessary to allege a jurisdictional amount, but ordinarily this is far less than the ad damnum prayer and can be gleaned in most instances from the pleadings and discovery procedures.

As a matter of fact in the case before us it appears from the record that the jury was in no way aware of the amount of the ad damnum in the complaint and, therefore, clearly their verdict did not reflect a conscious arrival at a figure in excess of the ad damnum.

* * *

Affirmed.

Notes and Questions

1. Is the damage prayer anachronistic as the court in *Bail* suggests? Should it be abolished? What problems would that create? Would elimination of the ad damnum clause have avoided the uncertainty upon which defendant in *Bail* based

the claim of prejudice? Suppose the court had found defendant to have been unduly prejudiced by the trial court's refusal to grant plaintiff's pretrial amendment. In that case should the jury award have been reduced? What other remedy is available? See pp. 1081–84, 1101–08, infra.

In many states the prayer for relief has been eliminated in medical malpractice cases, except that the complaint generally must allege that the amount in controversy meets the jurisdictional requirements of the court. See, e.g., Ga.Code Ann. § 9–11–8(a)(2) (1980 amendment); N.Y.C.P.L.R. 3017(c) (1980 amendment). Some courts have extended this policy to all major personal injury cases. See, e.g., Cal.Code Civ.Proc. § 425.10(b) (1979 amendment); Ill.Comp.Stat. ch. 735,5/2–604 (1983 amendment). Michigan has extended it to every action seeking monetary relief, unless the amount is less than $25,000, is a sum certain, or can be computed. MCR 2.111(B)(2) (1985 amendment). What purpose, if any, do these provisions serve? Consider Hughes v. Children's Clinic, P.A., 269 S.C. 389, 404, 237 S.E.2d 753, 760 (1977), upholding the practice of permitting the jury to see the pleadings and allowing plaintiff's counsel to call the jurors' attention to the size of the demand.

2. Note that under Federal Rule 54(c) relief is limited by the ad damnum clause in default cases. Why? See 10 Wright, Miller & Kane, *Federal Practice and Procedure: Civil 3d* § 2663 (1998). Why should courts permit relief to be granted that is different from or in excess of plaintiff's demand? Why should a defendant who defaults be protected by a cap on damages, but a defendant who participates be exposed to damages greater than those pleaded by the plaintiff? Although the vast majority of state courts have followed Federal Rule 54(c), a few apparently did not, even in litigated cases. See Stromberg v. Crowl, 257 Iowa 348, 353, 132 N.W.2d 462, 465 (1965). However, more recently, in state cases in which the plaintiff does not allege the specific amount of damages, see Note 1, supra, there cannot be any limit, even in default cases. Should some limit be imposed, perhaps by allowing pretrial discovery of the amount claimed? See Iowa R.Civ.Pr.70(a).

3. How far does the mandate found in Federal Rule 54(c) go? Suppose a party claims a certain element of damage on the basis of proof at trial despite the fact that the pleadings contained no claim or indication of a claim that would permit such recovery? In CONVERTIBLE TOP REPLACEMENT CO. v. ARO MFG. CO., 312 F.2d 52, 58 (1st Cir.1962), modified on other grounds 377 U.S. 476, 84 S.Ct. 1526, 12 L.Ed.2d 457 (1964), a suit for patent infringement, defendant not only answered, alleging, *inter alia,* the defense of patent misuse, but also counterclaimed for a declaratory judgment that plaintiff had misused the patent. The trial court's finding against defendant on the issue of misuse was not challenged on appeal. Defendant argued, however, that having asserted a counterclaim it could recover, under Rule 54(c), any relief to which it was entitled, and that the record in the case showed that plaintiff had violated the federal antitrust laws, which permitted defendant to recover treble damages. The court denied the claim as follows:

> * * * The short answer to this contention is that Aro has never pleaded a cause of action under the antitrust laws.

> * * * [Rule 54(c)] does not authorize a grant of the relief requested. That Rule should be liberally construed to grant a prevailing party substantial justice. But it is not to be so liberally construed as to conflict with the requirement of Rule 8(a) * * *. There is no merit whatever in this appeal.

Is this decision sound? Is it merely a return to the generally discarded theory-of-the-pleadings doctrine? See pp. 503–09, supra.

4.   In ANHEUSER–BUSCH, INC. v. JOHN LABATT LTD., 89 F.3d 1339, 1349 (8th Cir.1996), plaintiff failed to mention punitive damages in its pleadings or answers to interrogatories. Plaintiff did plead a valid claim for injurious falsehood under state law and requested instructions on punitive damages a week prior to the trial. Over defendant's objection the matter was presented to the jury, which awarded punitive damages in the amount of $5 million. The trial court struck the punitive damage award on the ground that plaintiff had not given sufficient notice of its intent to seek punitive damages. The appellate court affirmed. It did not cite Federal Rules 8(a)(3), 9(g), or 54(c). Should it have been unnecessary for plaintiff to specify punitive damages in its demand for relief so long as the alleged facts would justify such an award?

5.   In HANEY v. BURGIN, 106 N.H. 213, 208 A.2d 448 (1965), plaintiff originally brought suit for $15,000. After the first day of trial plaintiff was permitted to amend the complaint to request $25,000. Two days later, when defendant's sole witness strongly supported plaintiff's case, plaintiff was allowed to amend to pray for $50,000 damages. Subsequently the jury returned a verdict of $87,345. Plaintiff, in order to receive the full amount of the verdict, once again was permitted to amend the prayer, this time to $100,000. The New Hampshire Supreme Court held that since defendant had not requested a continuance as a condition of granting any of the motions to amend, he could not have been prejudiced and therefore there was no error. Does the use of amendment to permit full recovery in a jurisdiction that does not allow relief in excess of that requested in the pleadings make more sense than the adoption of a provision like Federal Rule 54(c)?

6.   The jurisdiction of inferior state tribunals often is limited as to the type and amount of relief that can be awarded. See p. 256, supra. What if plaintiff obtains a verdict for an amount in excess of the court's jurisdictional maximum? Should plaintiff be held to have waived any excess by bringing suit in such a court? If not, may a plaintiff waive the excess amount should he choose to do so? See Cal.Code Civ.Proc. § 396, which specifically provides that if plaintiff's *demand* exceeds the jurisdictional maximum of the inferior court "the excess may be *remitted* and the action may continue in the court where it is pending." [Emphasis added.] Should a waiver, if allowed, require the consent of defendant as well as of plaintiff? See Azzopardi v. St. Vincent's Medical Center of Richmond, 132 Misc.2d 412, 503 N.Y.S.2d 700 (N.Y.City Civ.Ct.1986). For a general discussion of jurisdictional amount problems, reread pp. 271–77, supra.

SECTION B.   RESPONDING TO THE COMPLAINT

1.   THE TIME PERMITTED FOR A RESPONSE

Read Rule 12(a) and the accompanying materials in the Supplement.

Rule 12(a) gives most defendants twenty days from the service of the complaint to respond either by a motion pursuant to Rule 12 or by answering the complaint. In reality, defense counsel routinely requests, and plaintiff's counsel routinely consents to, an extension of the defendant's time to answer. These agreements generally are considered a matter of courtesy among counsel, and Rule 6(a) authorizes the court to grant these extensions. Although practices vary, most judges will order an extension based upon a written stipulation of the attorneys.

2. MOTIONS TO DISMISS

Read Federal Rules of Civil Procedure 12(b), 12(c), and 12(f) and the materials accompanying them in the Supplement.

———

a. *Historical Antecedents*

The origins of the motion to dismiss can be traced to the common-law demurrer. As described in Chapter Seven, under common-law pleading rules, a party who faced a complaint could either answer, responding to each of the claims, or demur. If the defendant demurred, he was not allowed to contest the complaint's facts if the demurrer was overruled. On the other hand, if the demurrer was sustained, the plaintiff had no right to replead or amend her complaint. Later, these harsh rules were modified to allow a party to proceed to the merits if the demurrer was overruled and to allow the plaintiff to amend her complaint if the demurrer was sustained.

The common-law demurrer was incorporated into code pleading. In most code states, a complaint could be dismissed on the pleadings for failure to state facts sufficient to constitute a cause of action, absence of subject-matter jurisdiction, and deficiencies in the form of the pleading. The demurrer and its code equivalents elevated the importance of technicalities and produced considerable delay. Dissatisfaction frequently was expressed:

> * * * In an earlier period, when the ruling on the demurrer terminated the action, it was strategic to demur only for clear defects of form or substance. But since the ruling no longer serves to end the litigation but merely postpones the trial, the demurrer is used as a convenient means of delay by counsel with too much business or too little ambition. And where further delay is desired counsel may invoke separately the several motions which exist concurrently with the demurrer: motions to strike, expunge, elect or separate; motions to make more definite and certain or for a bill of particulars. This multiplicity of weapons has inevitably led to a host of tenuous distinctions: whether demurrer or motion is proper, what kind of demurrer, what kind of motion. By the use of successive demurrers and motions, it is possible, then, not only to delay but also to discourage altogether the party whose pleading is subjected to this barrage of objections.

Pike, *Objections to Pleadings Under the New Federal Rules of Civil Procedure,* 47 Yale L.J. 50, 51 (1937).

b. The Motion to Dismiss for Failure to State a Claim

Rule 12(b)(6), the federal system's counterpart to the common-law demurrer, must be viewed in conjunction with other federal pleading rules. For example, because Rule 8 requires only "a short and plain statement of the claim showing that the pleader is entitled to relief," few pleadings are likely to fail under Rule 12(b)(6). This does not mean, however, that the motion is useless. Pure questions of law can be tested by using the motion. The availability under the Federal Rules of summary judgment and partial summary judgment, directed verdict, and judgment notwithstanding the verdict (all of which are discussed later), also diminishes the importance of using Rule 12(b)(6) to screen frivolous cases.

> * * * The salvaged minutes that may accrue from circumventing these procedures can turn to wasted hours if the appellate court feels constrained to reverse the dismissal of an action. That is one of the reasons why a motion to dismiss is viewed with disfavor in the federal courts. Another is the basic precept that the primary objective of the law is to obtain a determination of the merits of any claim; and that a case should be tried on the proofs rather than the pleadings. * * * This is not to say or imply that a motion to dismiss should never be granted. It is obvious that there are cases which justify and indeed compel the granting of such motion. The line between the totally unmeritorious claims and the others cannot be drawn by scientific instruments but must be carved out case by case by the sound judgment of trial judges. That judgment should be exercised cautiously on such a motion.

RENNIE & LAUGHLIN, INC. v. CHRYSLER CORP., 242 F.2d 208, 213 (9th Cir.1957).

AMERICAN NURSES' ASSOCIATION v. ILLINOIS

United States Court of Appeals, Seventh Circuit, 1986.
783 F.2d 716.

POSNER, CIRCUIT JUDGE.

The class action charges the State of Illinois with sex discrimination in employment, in violation of Title VII of the Civil Rights Act of 1964, 42 U.S.C. § 2000e, and the equal protection clause of the Fourteenth Amendment. * * * The precise allegations of the complaint will require our careful attention later, but for now it is enough to note that they include as an essential element the charge that the state pays workers in predominantly male job classifications a higher wage not justified by any difference in the relative worth of the predominantly male and the predominantly female jobs in the state's roster.

* * * [T]he district judge dismissed the complaint under Fed.R.Civ.P. 12(b)(6) * * * [on the ground] that the complaint pleaded a comparable worth case and that a failure to pay employees in accordance with comparable worth does not violate federal antidiscrimination law. The plaintiffs appeal. They argue that their case is not (or perhaps not just) a comparable worth case and that in characterizing the complaint as he did the district judge terminated the lawsuit by a semantic manipulation. * * *

* * * [A]s we understand the plaintiffs' position it is not that a mere failure to rectify traditional wage disparities between predominantly male and

predominantly female jobs violates federal law. The circuits that have considered this contention have rejected it. * * *

The * * * question is whether a failure to achieve comparable worth—granted that it would not itself be a violation of law—might permit an inference of deliberate and therefore unlawful discrimination, as distinct from passive acceptance of a market-determined disparity in wages. * * *

* * *

* * * Knowledge of a disparity is not the same thing as an intent to cause or maintain it; if for example the state's intention was to pay market wages, its knowledge that the consequence would be that men got higher wages on average than women and that the difference might exceed any premium attributable to a difference in relative worth would not make it guilty of intentionally discriminating against women. Similarly, even if the failure to act on the comparable worth study could be regarded as "reaffirming" the state's commitment to pay market wages, this would not be enough to demonstrate discriminatory purpose. To demonstrate such a purpose the failure to act would have to be motivated at least in part by a desire to benefit men at the expense of women.

* * *

So if all that the plaintiffs in this case are complaining about is the State of Illinois' failure to implement a comparable worth study, they have no case and it was properly dismissed. We must therefore consider what precisely they are complaining about. Our task would be easier if the complaint had been drafted with the brevity that the Federal Rules of Civil Procedure envisage though do not require. * * *

[But t]he idea of "a plain and short statement of the claim" has not caught on. Few complaints follow the models in the Appendix of Forms. Plaintiffs' lawyers, knowing that some judges read a complaint as soon as it is filed in order to get a sense of the suit, hope by pleading facts to "educate" (that is to say, influence) the judge with regard to the nature and probable merits of the case, and also hope to set the stage for an advantageous settlement by showing the defendant what a powerful case they intend to prove. The pleading of facts is well illustrated by the present case. The complaint is twenty pages long and has a hundred page appendix (the comparable worth study).

A plaintiff who files a long and detailed complaint may plead himself out of court by including factual allegations which if true show that his legal rights were not invaded. * * * The district judge thought the plaintiffs had done that here. Let us see.

The key paragraph of the complaint is paragraph 9:

Defendants State of Illinois, its Departments and other Agencies subject to the State Personnel Code, and State Officials, have intentionally discriminated and continue to intentionally discriminate against female state employees in the terms and conditions of their employment because of their sex and because of their employment in historically female-dominated sex-segregated job classifications. Defendants have intentionally discriminated and continue to discriminate against male state employees because of their employment in historically female-dominated sex-segregated job classifications. The acts, practices and policies of discrimination for which defendants are responsible include, but are not limited to, the following:

(a) Use of a sex-biased system of pay and classification which results in and perpetuates discrimination in compensation against women employed in historically female-dominated sex-segregated job classifications;

(b) Use of a sex-biased system of pay and classification which, because it results in and perpetuates discrimination in compensation against women employed in historically female-dominated sex-segregated job classifications, adversely affects males employed in such historically female-dominated sex-segregated job classifications;

(c) Compensation at lower rates of pay of female employees in historically female-dominated sex-segregated job classifications which are or have been evaluated as being of comparable, equal, or greater worth than historically male-dominated sex-segregated job classifications which receive higher rates of pay;

(d) Compensation at lower rates of pay of male employees in historically female-dominated sex-segregated job classifications which are or have been evaluated as being of comparable, equal, or greater worth than historically male sex-segregated job classifications which receive higher rates of pay;

(e) Compensation at lower rates of pay of female employees than male employees performing work of equal skill, effort and responsibility under similar working conditions;

(f) More favorable treatment in compensation of male state employees than of similarly situated female employees;

(g) Discrimination in classification.

If this were the entire charging part of the complaint, there would be no question of dismissing it for failure to state a claim.

The paragraph initially charges the state with intentional discrimination against its female employees, because of their sex; and this, standing alone, would be quite enough to state a claim under Title VII. It continues, "and because of their employment in historically female-dominated sex-segregated job classifications," and then adds a claim on behalf of male employees in those classifications. The continuation could be interpreted as an allegation that the state's failure to adopt a wage scale based on the principle of comparable worth violates Title VII, and if so fails to state a claim. But the mention of "sex-segregated" blurs the picture. If the state has deliberately segregated jobs by sex, it has violated Title VII. Anyway a complaint cannot be dismissed merely because it includes invalid claims along with a valid one. Nothing is more common.

Subparagraphs (a) through (g) present a list of particular discriminatory practices; and since they are merely illustrative ("not limited to"), the complaint would not fail even if none of them were actionable. Some are, some aren't. * * * [If subparagraph (a)] means to allege that the state has departed from the market measure on grounds of sex—not only paying higher than market wages in predominantly male job classifications and only market wages in predominantly female classifications, but keeping women from entering the predominantly male jobs ("sex-segregated")—it states a claim. Subparagraph (b) adds nothing. If the state is discriminating against women by maintaining unwarranted wage differentials between predominantly male and predominantly female jobs, any men who happen to find themselves in predominantly female jobs will be, as it were, dragged down with the women—will be incidental victims of a discrimination targeted against others.

Subparagraph (c) is an effort to fit the case to the mold of * * * [County of Washington v. Gunther, 452 U.S. 161, 101 S.Ct. 2242, 68 L.Ed.2d 751 (1981)]. * * * But as we said earlier, the failure to accept the recommendations in a comparable worth study is not actionable. Paragraph 9(c) thus fails to state a claim—as does (d), which is the same as (c) except that it, like subparagraph (b), complains on behalf of male occupants of predominantly female jobs.

Subparagraphs (e) and (f) are inscrutable. If they complained about payment of unequal pay for the same work they would state a claim under the Equal Pay Act. But that Act is not cited in the complaint, perhaps deliberately, and the substitution of "work of equal skill" etc. for "equal work * * * of equal skill" etc. may also be deliberate. The intention may be to claim that different pay for different *but comparable* work violates Title VII—and if so this is a comparable worth claim by a different name, and fails. However, when a defendant is unclear about the meaning of a particular allegation in the complaint, the proper course is not to move to dismiss but to move for a more definite statement. * * *

That leaves subparagraph (g)—"Discrimination in classification." This could be a reprise of the comparable worth allegations or it could mean that in classifying jobs for pay purposes the responsible state officials had used the fraction of men in each job as a factor in deciding how high a wage to pay—which would be intentional discrimination.

Maybe the allegations in paragraph 9 are illuminated by subsequent paragraphs of the complaint. Paragraph 10, after summarizing the comparable worth study, says, "Defendants knew or should have known of the historical and continuing existence of patterns and practices of discrimination in compensation and classification, as documented at least in part by the State of Illinois Study." All that the study "documents," however, is that 28 percent of the employees subject to the state's personnel code are employed in 24 job classifications, in each of which at least 80 percent of the employees are of the same sex, and that based on the principles of comparable worth the 12 predominantly female job classifications are underpaid by between 29 and 56 percent. * * * These disparities are consistent, however, with the state's paying market wages, and of course the fact that the state knew that market wages do not always comport with the principles of comparable worth would not make a refusal to abandon the market actionable under Title VII. But at the very end of paragraph 10 we read, "Moreover, defendants have knowingly and *willfully* failed to take any action to correct such discrimination" (emphasis added), and in the word "willfully" can perhaps be seen the glimmerings of another theory of violation that could survive a motion to dismiss. Suppose the state has declined to act on the results of the comparable worth study not because it prefers to pay (perhaps is forced by labor-market or fiscal constraints to pay) market wages but because it thinks men deserve to be paid more than women. * * * This would be the kind of deliberate sex discrimination that Title VII forbids, once the statute is understood to allow wage disparities between dissimilar jobs to be challenged * * *.

"Willfully" is, however, a classic legal weasel word. Sometimes it means with wrongful intent but often it just means with knowledge of something or other. Willful evasion of taxes means not paying when you know you owe tax. After reading the comparable worth study the responsible state officials knew that the state's compensation system might not be consistent with the principles of comparable worth ("might" because there has been no determination that the comparable worth study is valid even on its own terms—maybe it's a lousy comparable worth study). But it would not follow that their failure to implement the study was willful in a sense relevant to liability under Title VII. They may have decided not to implement it because implementation would cost too much or lead to excess demand for some jobs and insufficient demand for others. The only thing that would make the failure a form of intentional and therefore actionable sex discrimination would be if the motivation for not implementing the study was the sex of the employees—if for example the officials thought that men ought to be paid more than women even if there is no difference in skill or effort or in the conditions of work. * * *

We have said that a plaintiff can plead himself right out of court. But the court is not to pounce on the plaintiff and by a crabbed and literal reading of the complaint strain to find that he has pleaded facts which show that his claim is not actionable, and then dismiss the complaint on the merits so that the plaintiff cannot replead. (The dismissal would preclude another suit based on any theory that the plaintiff could have advanced on the basis of the facts giving rise to the first suit.) * * * The district judge did not quite do that here, because this complaint can easily be read to allege a departure from the principles of comparable worth, and no more. But that reading is not inevitable, and the fact that it is logical and unstrained is not enough to warrant dismissal. In the system created by the Federal Rules of Civil Procedure a complaint "should not be dismissed for failure to state a claim unless it appears beyond doubt that the plaintiff can prove no set of facts in support of his claim which would entitle him to relief." Conley v. Gibson [Note 3, p. 518, supra] * * *. This language, repeated though it has been in countless later cases * * *, should not be taken literally; for taken literally it would permit dismissal only in frivolous cases. As we said earlier, if the plaintiff, though not required to do so, pleads facts, and the facts show that he is entitled to no relief, the complaint should be dismissed. There would be no point in allowing such a lawsuit to go any further; its doom is foretold. But this is not such a case. * * * A complaint that alleges intentional sex discrimination * * * cannot be dismissed just because one of the practices, indeed the principal practice, instanced as intentional sex discrimination—the employer's failure to implement comparable worth—is lawful.

Furthermore, a complaint is not required to allege all, or any, of the facts logically entailed by the claim. If Illinois is overpaying men relative to women, this must mean—unless the market model is entirely inapplicable to labor markets—that it is paying women at least their market wage (and therefore men more), for women wouldn't work for less than they could get in the market; and if so the state must also be refusing to hire women in the men's jobs, for above-market wages in those jobs would be a magnet drawing the women from their lower-paying jobs. Maybe the references in the complaint to the segregation of jobs by sex are meant to allege such refusals but if not this pleading omission would not be critical. A plaintiff does not have to plead evidence. If these plaintiffs admitted or the defendants proved that there was no steering or other method of segregating jobs by sex, the plaintiffs' theory of discrimination might be incoherent, and fail. But a complaint does not fail to state a claim merely because it does not set forth a complete and convincing picture of the alleged wrongdoing. So the plaintiffs do not have to allege steering even if it is in some sense implicit in their claim.

* * * We do not want to arouse false hopes; the plaintiffs have a tough row to hoe. They may lose eventually on summary judgment if discovery yields no more evidence than is contained in the unsupported assertions and stale and seemingly isolated incidents in the plaintiffs' exhibits. But the plaintiffs are entitled to make additional efforts to prove a case of intentional discrimination within the boundaries sketched in this opinion.

Reversed and Remanded.

Notes and Questions

1.   How should a court resolve mixed questions of fact and law when deciding Rule 12(b)(6) motions? In HARTFORD ACCIDENT & INDEMNITY CO. v. MERRILL LYNCH, PIERCE, FENNER & SMITH, INC., 74 F.R.D. 357 (W.D.Okl. 1976), plaintiff sued defendant for negligently failing to inform a bank that its employee was investing with defendant in margin accounts. The employee had forged signatures on certain certificates of deposit drawn from that bank that he had used as collateral to procure personal loans from other banks. When the employee defaulted, the lending banks recovered their losses from plaintiff under plaintiff's blanket fidelity bond. Plaintiff alleged that defendant's failure to inform was the proximate cause of its loss. The court dismissed plaintiff's claim:

> A Complaint should not be dismissed for failure to state a claim unless it appears beyond doubt that the plaintiff can prove no set of facts in support of his claim which would entitle him to relief. * * * However, the legal effect ascribed by the pleader is not to be admitted, but is to be determined by its terms, as a matter of law. * * *

> The Oklahoma cases indicate that under proper circumstances the existence of probable cause becomes a question of law for the Court. * * * In considering the allegations of the Complaint, the Court finds that the facts contained therein are insufficient to show any causal connection between the alleged negligent acts of Merrill Lynch in failing to advise Conine's employer and obtaining said employer's permission for him to engage in trading on margin accounts and the loss sustained by Plaintiff on its banker's fidelity bond. The Complaint fails to show the required proximate cause between the negligence alleged and the injuries complained of as a matter of law.

> The facts as set out in the Complaint indicate the alleged forgeries or obtaining forged documents by the bank officer were the efficient cause which set in motion the chain of circumstances leading to the loss sustained by Plaintiff Hartford on its banker's fidelity bond. The allegation that negligent acts of Defendant Merrill Lynch permitted the continued employment of the

alleged defalcating bank officer only appears to indicate a condition which permitted the acts to go undetected and possibly allowed subsequent wrongful acts to be committed by the bank officer after the first had been committed. Such condition is not any more related to the proximate cause of the loss sustained by Plaintiff than the acts of the directors of the Oklahoma State Bank who initially placed Conine in the position of employment as an officer of the bank and retained him in said position while the wrongful acts were committed.

Id. at 358.

Under the standards expressed in *American Nurses' Ass'n,* did the District Court in *Hartford* err in granting the Rule 12(b)(6) motion? Was the District Court justified in concluding that plaintiff could prove no set of facts in support of its contention as a matter of law? Does the *Erie* doctrine require the court to follow the Oklahoma courts' declaration that under proper circumstances the existence of proximate cause is a question of law?

2. The Supreme Court, in SCHEUER v. RHODES, 416 U.S. 232, 236, 94 S.Ct. 1683, 1686, 40 L.Ed.2d 90, 96 (1974), said that "[w]hen a federal court reviews the sufficiency of a complaint, * * * the issue is * * * whether the claimant is entitled to offer evidence to support the claims." Under that standard, did the District Court in *Hartford* err in granting the Rule 12(b)(6) motion?

3. If a plaintiff's complaint filed *in forma pauperis* fails to state a claim under Federal Rule 12(b)(6), is it automatically frivolous under 28 U.S.C. § 1915(d), which authorizes courts to dismiss a claim *in forma pauperis* if "the action is malicious or frivolous." The Supreme Court held in NEITZKE v. WILLIAMS, 490 U.S. 319, 328, 109 S.Ct. 1827, 1833, 104 L.Ed.2d 338, 349 (1989), that although there is "considerable common ground between these standards," Section 1915(d) and Rule 12(b)(6) do not "encompass" each other. Section 1915(d) is meant to discourage *in forma pauperis* plaintiffs from bringing baseless claims that paying plaintiffs ordinarily would not. Therefore, "[w]hen a complaint raises an arguable question of law which the district court ultimately finds is correctly resolved against the plaintiff, dismissal on Rule 12(b)(6) grounds is appropriate, but dismissal on the basis of frivolousness is not."

4. Should a Rule 12(b)(6) motion be granted in a case in which the "claim" exists but the desired remedy is not available? In DOPICO v. GOLDSCHMIDT, 687 F.2d 644 (2d Cir.1982), plaintiffs, wheelchair-bound handicapped people, sued local and federal transit officials, claiming violations of federal statutes and regulations relating to making transit facilities accessible to the handicapped. The District Court dismissed the plaintiffs' complaint against the local officials for failure to state a claim upon which relief could be granted. It based its decision on a finding that the plaintiffs could not obtain the "massive relief involving extraordinary expenditures" that they sought. The Court of Appeals did not disagree, but reversed, saying that "[t]he extreme result of dismissing the claim would be proper only if plaintiffs would not be entitled to any relief, even if they were to prevail on the merits. We do not believe that conclusion can be reached at this preliminary stage of the law suit." Id. at 649.

5. What is the effect of a successful Rule 12(b)(6) motion? Can the plaintiff modify the complaint and re-serve the complaint, or do principles of res judicata bar that? In SHAW v. MERRITT–CHAPMAN & SCOTT CORP., 554 F.2d 786 (6th Cir.1977), certiorari denied 434 U.S. 852, 98 S.Ct. 167, 54 L.Ed.2d 122 (1977), the court held that absent specific language to the contrary by the district court, a

Rule 12(b)(6) motion constitutes an adjudication on the merits, and so further actions on the same claim are barred. Is this result too harsh? Does it provide the plaintiff with adequate notice of preclusion? Would it be better to convert the motion to dismiss into a motion for summary judgment? See 5A Wright & Miller, *Federal Practice and Procedure: Civil 2d* § 1357, at 360–74 (1990) (2001 Pocket Part). See also Udom v. Fonseca, 846 F.2d 1236, 1238 (9th Cir.1988) (dismissing claims barred by statute of limitations but granting party leave to amend in order to state claims that are not time barred).

6. Consider the following assessment:

[R]ule 12(b)(6), the vaunted motion to dismiss for failure to state a claim upon which relief can be granted * * *, is a wonderful tool on paper, but * * * it was last effectively used during the McKinley Administration.

Miller, *The August 1983 Amendments to the Federal Rules of Civil Procedure: Promoting Effective Case Management and Lawyer Responsibility* 7–8 (1984). In light of the cases you have read, and putting aside that the reference to McKinley is hyperbole since he was President before the adoption of the Federal Rules, is Professor Miller's observation valid today?

7. In the federal system, a motion to strike, pursuant to Rule 12(f), is the mechanism for challenging the substantive sufficiency of defenses raised in an adversary's answer or other responsive pleading. A motion for judgment on the pleadings, pursuant to Rule 12(c), is a method of attacking the substantive sufficiency of an opposing party's pleading after all the pleadings have been completed. Both motions raise the same issues raised by a motion under Rule 12(b), and are dealt with by the courts in the same manner.

At common law and under the codes, the "speaking demurrer," a demurrer that attempted to introduce material outside the pleadings, was not permitted. Technically this is still the rule even in most modern jurisdictions. However, in most courts today a motion for summary judgment is available to challenge the factual basis of a pleading that on its face is sufficient to state a claim or defense. Under the Federal Rules and comparable state rules, the distinction between a pleading challenge and a motion for summary judgment is blurred, since a pleading challenge simply is treated as a motion for summary judgment if outside matter is introduced. The Rules were amended in 1948 to provide an express basis for courts to treat motions under Rules 12(b)(6) and 12(c) as motions for summary judgment when matters outside the pleadings are considered.

8. In addition to a Rule 12(b)(6) motion to dismiss for failure to state a claim, Rule 12(b) provides the pleader with the option of raising six other defenses by motion prior to service of a responsive pleading. The defenses in Rules 12(b)(1) through 12(b)(5) and 12(b)(7) are essentially modern counterparts to the common-law pleas of abatement. There never was any doubt as to the court's considering extra-pleading material on these motions, and so, although Rule 12(b) as amended in 1948 expressly permits the use of extraneous matters on a Rule 12(b)(6) motion only, the practice before (and since) the amendment allows "speaking motions" in connection with these other defenses. Their validity rarely is apparent on the face of the pleadings, and motions raising them generally require referral to matters outside the pleadings.

Of the six defenses, which, if any, may a party who makes a motion to dismiss under Rule 12(b) waive by not raising it in the motion? Which may a party waive by failing to raise it either by motion under Rule 12(b) or by the party's answer?

When, if ever, is it too late to challenge a pleading for failure to state a claim or defense?

9. Although the seven motions specifically enumerated in Rule 12(b) theoretically are the only motions that can be made prior to a responsive pleading, in fact the preliminary motion practice in the federal courts has a much broader compass. For example, although affirmative defenses under Rule 8(c) probably were intended to be raised only by responsive pleading, it is now common to allow an affirmative defense to be asserted by a motion under Rule 12(b)(6) when the validity of that defense is apparent from the face of the pleading. A complaint showing that the statute of limitations has run on the claim is the most common situation in which the affirmative defense appears on the face of the pleading. Moreover, the procedure in Rule 12(b) for converting the motion into a Rule 56 motion for summary judgment by presenting matters outside the pleadings, and the possibility of defendant moving for summary judgment prior to serving his responsive pleading, have the effect of allowing the early assertion of defenses other than those specifically enumerated in Rule 12(b).

3. OTHER MOTIONS ATTACKING PLEADINGS

One problem regarding challenges to the form of the pleadings already has been considered in connection with the *United Aircraft* and *Garcia* cases, which dealt with motions for a more definite statement. See pp. 521–26, supra. A somewhat different challenge to the form arises when a party has included "scandalous," "impertinent," or "irrelevant" matter in a pleading. Traditionally, the remedy afforded is a motion to strike. See, e.g., Federal Rule 12(f); N.Y.C.P.L.R. 3024(b). On occasion some parties have attempted to utilize this motion to destroy or undercut their opponents' statements of valid claims or defenses. As held in GATEWAY BOTTLING, INC. v. DAD'S ROOTBEER CO., 53 F.R.D. 585, 588 (W.D.Pa.1971):

> With respect to the complaint that the material is scandalous, the question is again whether it asserts a valid and good faith defense to plaintiff's claim. To strike material as scandalous it must be obviously false and unrelated to the subject matter of the action. * * * The facts here may be unpleasant for plaintiff to have on the record and they certainly contain charges of reprehensible conduct but the same is true of many facts of life which are entitled to be pleaded as relevant to a cause of action or defense. Such, for example, are the facts concerning a divorce for adultery. These may be scandalous and annoying and prejudicial to the accused party but plaintiff or defendant is certainly entitled to plead them.

Both because striking a portion of a pleading is a drastic remedy and because it often is sought by the movant simply as a dilatory tactic, motions under Rule 12(f) are viewed with disfavor and are infrequently granted. See 5A Wright & Miller, *Federal Practice and Procedure: Civil 2d* §§ 1380–83 (1990) (2001 Pocket Part). See also Stabilisierungsfonds Fur Wein v. Kaiser Stuhl Wine Distrib. Pty. Ltd., 647 F.2d 200, 201 (D.C.Cir.1981); Colaprico v. Sun Microsystems, Inc., 758 F.Supp. 1335, 1339 (N.D.Cal.1991). Even when allegations are not related to the subject matter of the case, the general rule is that they will not be stricken from a complaint unless their presence will prejudice the adverse party. See Abrams v. Lightolier, Inc., 702 F.Supp. 509,

511 (D.N.J.1988). The common-law and code motions to strike allegations because they were "sham," "frivolous," "irrelevant," "redundant," "repetitious," "unnecessary," "immaterial," or "impertinent" have been eliminated, which "reflects a basic judgment that nothing is gained in the way of speedy and accurate disposition of litigation by disputes over the formal propriety of the allegations in the pleadings." 3 Weinstein, Korn & Miller, *New York Civil Practice* ¶ 3024.01.

The question whether allegations really are prejudicial seems to turn on whether the contents of the pleadings will be disclosed to the jury. In some instances pleadings themselves can become part of the evidence in the case and then, of course, the jury will be able to see and use them. However, such usage is strictly limited by the rules of evidence and irrelevant or prejudicial matters in the pleadings will be excluded. See Razorback Cab of Fort Smith, Inc. v. Lingo, 304 Ark. 323, 802 S.W.2d 444 (1991); Emery–Waterhouse, Co. v. Rhode Island Hosp. Trust Nat'l Bank, 757 F.2d 399 (1st Cir.1985). Courts are divided on whether and to what extent such disclosure is proper when the pleadings are not introduced as part of the evidence in the case. What circumstances, if any, would justify a motion to strike redundant, impertinent, or scandalous material in a case tried before a judge or before a jury in a jurisdiction that does not permit the jury to see the pleadings? See Fantasy, Inc. v. Fogerty, 664 F.Supp. 1345 (N.D.Cal.1987).

There also is another group of cases in which an entire pleading is challenged, either because it was filed too late, or necessary court approval had not been obtained, or other rules or orders have not been satisfied. Traditionally, this type of defect is reached by a motion to strike the pleading or to dismiss the claims that it contains. See Salahuddin v. Cuomo, 861 F.2d 40 (2d Cir.1988); Mutuelle Generale Francaise Vie v. Life Assur. Co. of Pennsylvania, 688 F.Supp. 386 (N.D.Ill.1988).

4. ANSWERING THE COMPLAINT

a. *Denials*

Rule 8 requires a defendant to make one of three responses to the contents of plaintiff's complaint. Defendant may admit, deny, or plead insufficient information in response to each allegation. Rule 8(d) provides that all averments to which defendant does not specifically respond are deemed admitted. To avoid an unintended admission, defendants often add an all-inclusive paragraph in their answers denying each and every averment of the complaint unless otherwise admitted.

A defendant under Rule 8 and most state rules also may deny generally the entire complaint, but general denials tend to defeat the purpose of pleading as a means of narrowing and focusing the issues in controversy. For this reason, the Federal Rules discourage the use of the general denial, which must be made in good faith and only in situations in which everything in the complaint can be denied legitimately. Using a general denial can be risky. If a court decides that a general denial does not "fairly meet the substance of the averments denied," it may deem defendant to have admitted plaintiff's specific averments. In addition, a general denial does not put in issue such matters as capacity or conditions precedent, which under Rule 9 must be specifically challenged by defendant.

ZIELINSKI v. PHILADELPHIA PIERS, INC.

United States District Court, Eastern District of Pennsylvania, 1956.
139 F.Supp. 408.

VAN DUSEN, DISTRICT JUDGE. Plaintiff requests a ruling that, for the purposes of this case, the motor-driven fork lift operated by Sandy Johnson on February 9, 1953, was owned by defendant and that Sandy Johnson was its agent acting in the course of his employment on that date. The following facts are established by the pleadings, interrogatories, depositions and uncontradicted portions of affidavits:

1. Plaintiff filed his complaint on April 28, 1953, for personal injuries received on February 9, 1953, while working on Pier 96, Philadelphia, for J.A. McCarthy, as a result of a collision of two motor-driven fork lifts.

2. Paragraph 5 of this complaint stated that "a motor-driven vehicle known as a fork lift or chisel, owned, operated and controlled by the defendant, its agents, servants and employees, was so negligently and carelessly managed * * * that the same * * * did come into contact with the plaintiff causing him to sustain the injuries more fully hereinafter set forth."

3. The "First Defense" of the Answer stated "Defendant * * * (c) denies the averments of paragraph 5 * * *."

4. The motor-driven vehicle known as a fork lift or chisel, which collided with the McCarthy fork lift on which plaintiff was riding, had on it the initials "P.P.I."

5. On February 10, 1953, Carload Contractors, Inc. made a report of this accident to its insurance company, whose policy No. CL 3964 insured Carload Contractors, Inc. against potential liability for the negligence of its employees contributing to a collision of the type described in paragraph 2 above.

6. By letter of April 29, 1953, the complaint served on defendant was forwarded to the above-mentioned insurance company. This letter read as follows:

Gentlemen:

* * *

We find that a fork lift truck operated by an employee of Carload Contractors, Inc. also insured by yourselves was involved in an accident with another chisel truck, which, was alleged, did cause injury to Frank Zielinski, and same was reported to you by Carload Contractors, Inc. at the time, and you assigned Claim Number OL 0153–94 to this claim.

Should not this Complaint in Trespass be issued against Carload Contractors, Inc. and not Philadelphia Piers, Inc.?

We forward for your handling.

7. Interrogatories * * * and the answers thereto, which were sworn to by defendant's General Manager on June 12, 1953, and filed on June 22, 1953, read as follows:

1. State whether you have received any information of an injury sustained by the plaintiff on February 9, 1953, South Wharves. If so, state when and from whom you first received notice of such injury. A. We were first notified of this accident on or about February 9, 1953 by Thomas Wilson.

2. State whether you caused an investigation to be made of the circumstances of said injury and if so, state who made such investigation and when it was made. A. We made a very brief investigation on February 9, 1953 and turned the matter over to (our insurance company) for further investigation.

* * *

8. At a deposition taken August 18, 1953, Sandy Johnson testified that he was the employee of defendant on February 9, 1953, and had been their employee for approximately fifteen years.

9. At a pre-trial conference held on September 27, 1955,[3] plaintiff first learned that over a year before February 9, 1953, the business of moving freight on piers in Philadelphia, formerly conducted by defendant, had been sold by it to Carload Contractors, Inc. and Sandy Johnson had been transferred to the payroll of this corporation without apparently realizing it, since the nature or location of his work had not changed.

* * *

11. Defendant now admits that on February 9, 1953, it owned the fork lift in the custody of Sandy Johnson and that this fork lift was leased to Carload Contractors, Inc. It is also admitted that the pier on which the accident occurred was leased by defendant.

12. There is no indication of action by either party in bad faith and there is no proof of inaccurate statements being made with intent to deceive. Because defendant made a prompt investigation of the accident (see answers to Interrogatories 1, 2, * * *), its insurance company has been representing the defendant since suit was brought, and this company insures Carload Contractors, Inc. also, requiring defendant to defend this suit, will not prejudice it.

Under these circumstances, and for the purposes of this action, it is ordered that the following shall be stated to the jury at the trial:

It is admitted that, on February 9, 1953, the towmotor or fork lift bearing the initials "P.P.I." was owned by defendant and that Sandy Johnson was a servant in the employ of defendant and doing its work on that date.

This ruling is based on the following principles:

1. Under the circumstances of this case, the answer contains an ineffective denial of that part of paragraph 5 of the complaint which alleges that "a motor driven vehicle known as a fork lift or chisel (was) owned, operated and

---

3. The applicable statute of limitations prevented any suit against Carload Contractors, Inc. after February 9, 1955, 12 P.S. § 34.

controlled by the defendant, its agents, servants and employees." [See] F.R.Civ.P. 8(b) * * *.

For example, it is quite clear that defendant does not deny the averment in paragraph 5 that the fork lift came into contact with plaintiff, since it admits * * * that an investigation of an occurrence of the accident had been made and that a report dated February 10, 1953, was sent to its insurance company stating "While Frank Zielinski was riding on bumper of chisel and holding rope to secure cargo, the chisel truck collided with another chisel truck operated by Sandy Johnson causing injuries to Frank Zielinski's legs and hurt head of Sandy Johnson." Compliance with the above-mentioned rule required that defendant file a more specific answer than a general denial. A specific denial of parts of this paragraph and specific admission of other parts would have warned plaintiff that he had sued the wrong defendant.

* * *

Under circumstances where an improper and ineffective answer has been filed, the Pennsylvania courts have consistently held that an allegation of agency in the complaint requires a statement to the jury that agency is admitted where an attempt to amend the answer is made after the expiration of the period of limitation. * * * Although the undersigned has been able to find no federal court decisions on this point, he believes the principle of these Pennsylvania appellate court decisions may be considered in view of all the facts of this case, where jurisdiction is based on diversity of citizenship, the accident occurred in Pennsylvania, and the federal district court is sitting in Pennsylvania. * * *

2. Under the circumstances of this case, principles of equity require that defendant be estopped from denying agency because, otherwise, its inaccurate statements and statements in the record, which it knew (or had the means of knowing within its control) were inaccurate, will have deprived plaintiff of his right of action.

If Interrogatory 2 had been answered accurately by saying that employees of Carload Contractors, Inc. had turned the matter over to the insurance company, it seems clear that plaintiff would have realized his mistake. The fact that if Sandy Johnson had testified accurately, the plaintiff could have brought its action against the proper party defendant within the statutory period of limitations is also a factor to be considered, since defendant was represented at the deposition and received knowledge of the inaccurate testimony.

At least one appellate court has stated that the doctrine of equitable estoppel will be applied to prevent a party from taking advantage of the statute of limitations where the plaintiff has been misled by conduct of such party. See, Peters v. Public Service Corporation, 132 N.J.Eq. 500, 29 A.2d 189, 195 (1942). In that case, the court said, 29 A.2d at page 196:

> Of course, defendants were under no duty to advise complainants' attorney of his error, other than by appropriate pleadings, but neither did defendants have a right, knowing of the mistake, to foster it by its acts of omission.

* * *

Since this is a pre-trial order, it may be modified at the trial if the trial judge determines from the facts which then appear that justice so requires. * * *

Notes and Questions

1. In BIGGS v. PUBLIC SERV. COORDINATED TRANSP., 280 F.2d 311, 313–14 (3d Cir.1960), a diversity-of-citizenship case, the defendant generally denied plaintiff's jurisdictional allegations, including an express claim that defendant was a New Jersey corporation. The court stated:

> We cannot for a moment believe that defendant's counsel was denying in good faith that his client was a New Jersey corporation. We think the only fair interpretation of the pleading in this case is that the denial does not run to the allegation of defendant's citizenship. Therefore, that allegation must be deemed to be admitted. Fed.R.Civ.P. 8(d).

See also Moore v. Greater Cleveland Regional Transit Auth., 44 Ohio Misc.2d 25, 542 N.E.2d 359 (Mun.Ct.1987) (striking general denial made in bad faith).

2. In the *Biggs* case defendant, in addition to the general denial, had specifically denied the allegation that the amount in controversy exceeded the minimum jurisdictional amount required in diversity cases. Does this help to explain the decision? Should a defendant who joins general and special denials in the answer be permitted to rely upon a general denial to put in issue those allegations by plaintiff that have not been specially denied? See Fawcett v. Miller, 85 Ohio L.Abs. 443, 172 N.E.2d 328 (Ct.App.1961) (failure of defendant to elect to rely on a general denial results in admissions of all facts not specially denied). Suppose a defendant's answer couples a general denial with specific admissions of facts alleged in the complaint. Should defendant be permitted to elect to stand on the denial at trial, thus forcing plaintiff to prove even those facts admitted? See Johnson v. School Dist. No. 3, 168 Neb. 547, 96 N.W.2d 623 (1959) (admissions take precedence over a general denial even though admissions were made in connection with an affirmative defense).

3. To what extent should defendant be permitted to respond that "he neither admits nor denies" plaintiff's allegations? Should it make any difference whether or not a general denial is allowed? See Rahal v. Titus, 107 Ga.App. 844, 131 S.E.2d 659 (1963). In many jurisdictions statutes specifically prohibit "evasive denials." E.g., Ill.Comp.Stat. ch. 535, 5/2–610(c). Compare the language of Federal Rule 8(b).

4. In California, if a complaint is verified, the answer cannot contain a general denial. See Cal.Code Civ.Proc. § 431.30(d) (1986 amendment). What justification is there for this provision?

IMPROPER FORMS OF DENIAL

1. Denials for Lack of Information–Under Federal Rule 8(b) a party may deny an allegation on the ground that it "is without knowledge and information sufficient to form a belief as to the truth" of the allegation. Similar provisions exist under state codes. But there are limits on the use of this form of denial. In OLIVER v. SWISS CLUB TELL, 222 Cal.App.2d 528, 35

Cal.Rptr. 324 (1963), defendant denied for lack of information its existence as an unincorporated association. This was held to be an admission of defendant's status, since the matter was "presumptively within defendant's knowledge." The consequences of the admission were ameliorated, however, because the issue apparently was subsequently inserted, perhaps inadvertently, in a pretrial order.

What facts are "presumptively within the knowledge" of a defendant? To what extent should defendant be obligated to ascertain facts that are easily obtainable? For example, should a corporate enterprise be charged with knowledge of representations to customers made by several of its salesmen? Does the answer depend on the size and nature of the business? See Kayser v. Railway Express Agency, 54 N.Y.S.2d 623 (Sup.Ct.1945); Commonwealth, by Preate v. Rainbow Associates, 138 Pa.Cmwlth. 56, 587 A.2d 357 (1991). Suppose plaintiff's complaint alleges facts that can be ascertained only by a detailed and costly search of defendant's records? Should defendant be required to discharge this burden prior to its answer? See Olin v. Town of North Hempstead, 194 N.Y.S.2d 979 (Sup.Ct.1959). See also Mellon Bank, N.A. v. Joseph, 267 Pa.Super. 307, 406 A.2d 1055 (1979). To what extent is the response affected by the fact that under state rules defendant usually has—at most—30 days in which to file an answer? See, e.g., Mo.R.Civ.P. 55.25(a) (30 days); cf. Fed.R.Civ.P. 12(a) (20 days). See Washington Nat. Trust Co. v. W.M. Dary Co., 116 Ariz. 171, 568 P.2d 1069 (1977) (ample opportunity to investigate exists when answer delayed until six months after complaint); State Farm Mut. Auto. Ins. Co. v. Krohn, 24 Ohio Misc.2d 3, 492 N.E.2d 1262 (Mun.Ct.1985).

2. Negative Pregnant Denials–Suppose plaintiff alleges that defendant owes her $89,000 under a contract. Defendant denies "that he owes plaintiff $89,000." In some state courts this type of denial has been referred to as a "negative pregnant," and it results in an admission that defendant owes plaintiff one cent less than the specified $89,000. See, e.g., Wingfoot California Homes Co. v. Valley Nat. Bank, 80 Ariz. 133, 294 P.2d 370 (1956). These technical decisions are not very common today, or at least they can be cured easily by amending the denial to add words such as "or any other sum." See Frank v. Solomon, 94 Ariz. 55, 381 P.2d 591 (1963).

3. Conjunctive Denials–In JANEWAY & CARPENDER v. LONG BEACH PAPER & PAINT CO., 190 Cal. 150, 211 P. 6 (1922), plaintiff alleged that defendant "made, executed, and delivered its contract for goods to the plaintiff." Defendant denied the allegation specifically, using the identical words of the complaint. The court held that this denial was evasive and therefore admitted the existence of a contract. What arguments can be made in support of the decision? What arguments against? This type of pleading defect is termed a "conjunctive denial." To what extent does it differ from a "negative pregnant"?

———

b. Affirmative Defenses

———

Read Federal Rule of Civil Procedure 8(c) in the Supplement.

———

Rule 8(c) lists nineteen affirmative defenses that must be raised specifically. This list is not exhaustive, however. In determining whether a particular defense must be raised affirmatively, courts look to statutes in federal question cases, and to state practice in diversity cases. In general, defendants must raise affirmatively defenses that do not flow logically from the plaintiff's complaint. For example, a defense of the statute of frauds may not flow logically from a plaintiff's contract claim, and so it must be raised affirmatively. The function of the Rule, then, is to provide notice to plaintiff of the possible existence of the defenses and defendant's intention to advance them.

INGRAHAM v. UNITED STATES

United States Court of Appeals, Fifth Circuit, 1987.
808 F.2d 1075.

POLITZ, CIRCUIT JUDGE:

The appellees in these consolidated cases sued the United States, under the Federal Tort Claims Act, for severe injuries caused by the negligence of government physicians. In each case, after entry of adverse judgment the government moved for relief from the judgment to the extent that the damages exceeded the limit imposed on medical malpractice awards by the Medical Liability and Insurance Improvement Act of Texas * * *. The respective district courts denied these post-trial motions. Concluding that the government did not raise the issue timely before the trial courts, [and] that the issues were not preserved for appeal, * * * we affirm both judgments.

BACKGROUND

In 1977, in response to what was perceived to be a medical malpractice crisis, the Legislature of Texas, like several other state legislatures, adopted certain limitations on damages to be awarded in actions against health care providers, for injuries caused by negligence in the rendering of medical care and treatment. Of particular significance to these appeals is the $500,000 cap placed on the *ex delicto* recovery, not applicable to past and future medical expenses.

On February 12, 1979, Dwight L. Ingraham was operated on by an Air Force surgeon. During the back surgery a drill was negligently used and Ingraham's spinal cord was damaged, causing severe and permanent injuries. The court awarded Ingraham judgment for $1,264,000. This total included $364,000 for lost wages and $900,000 for pain, suffering, and disability. There is no reference to the Medical Liability and Insurance Improvement Act of Texas in the pleadings, nor was any reference made to the Act during the trial. After entry of judgment, the United States filed a notice of appeal. Thereafter, urging the Act's limitations, the government sought relief from judgment under Fed.R.Civ.P. 60(b). The district court denied that motion.
* * *

Similarly, in March of 1979, Jocelyn and David Bonds, and their infant daughter Stephanie, were victims of the negligent performance by an Air Force physician. Because of the mismanagement of the 43rd week of Jocelyn Bonds's first pregnancy, and the negligent failure to perform timely a caesarian section delivery, Stephanie suffered asphyxiation *in utero*. The loss of oxygen caused extensive brain damage, resulting in spastic quadriparesis, cortical blindness, seizures, and mental retardation. In their FTCA action the court awarded Stephanie $1,814,959.70 for medical expenses and $1,675,595.90 for the other losses. Jocelyn Bonds was awarded $750,000 for her losses, including loss of the society of her daughter. As in the Ingraham case, the government did not invoke the Texas malpractice limitation in pleading or at trial. Post judgment the government filed a motion to amend the judgment under Fed.R.Civ.P. 59, but, again, there was no mention of the limitations Act. Subsequently, three months after entry of the judgment, the government filed a pleading entitled "Motion for Reconsideration," in which it advanced the malpractice Act. That motion was denied. * * *

These appeals do not challenge the courts' findings of liability, but object only to quantum, contending that damages are limited by the Medical Liability and Insurance Improvement Act * * *.

ANALYSIS

Appellees maintain that we should not consider the statutory limitation of liability invoked on appeal because it is an affirmative defense under Rule 8(c) of the Federal Rules of Civil Procedure, and the failure to raise it timely constitutes a waiver. We find this argument persuasive.

Rule 8(c) first lists 19 specific affirmative defenses, and concludes with the residuary clause "any other matter constituting an avoidance or affirmative defense." In the years since adoption of the rule, the residuary clause has provided the authority for a substantial number of additional defenses which must be timely and affirmatively pleaded. These include: exclusions from a policy of liability insurance; breach of warranty; concealment of an alleged prior undissolved marriage; voidable preference in bankruptcy; noncooperation of an insured; statutory limitation on liability; the claim that a written contract was incomplete; judgment against a defendant's joint tortfeasor; circuity of action; discharge of a contract obligation through novation or extension; re[s]cission or mutual abandonment of a contract; failure to mitigate damages; adhesion contract; statutory exemption; failure to exhaust state remedies; immunity from suit; good faith belief in lawfulness of action; the claim that a lender's sale of collateral was not commercially reasonable; a settlement agreement or release barring an action; and custom of trade or business. * * *

Determining whether a given defense is "affirmative" within the ambit of Rule 8(c) is not without some difficulty. We find the salient comments of Judge Charles E. Clark, Dean of the Yale Law School, later Chief Judge of the United States Second Circuit Court of Appeals, and the principal author of the Federal Rules to be instructive:

> [J]ust as certain disfavored allegations made by the plaintiff * * * must be set forth with the greatest particularity, so like disfavored defenses must be particularly alleged by the defendant. These may

include such matters as fraud, statute of frauds * * *, statute of limitations, truth in slander and libel * * * and so on. In other cases the mere question of convenience may seem prominent, as in the case of payment, where the defendant can more easily show the affirmative payment at a certain time than the plaintiff can the negative of nonpayment over a period of time. Again it may be an issue which may be generally used for dilatory tactics, such as the question of the plaintiff's right to sue * * * a vital question, but one usually raised by the defendant on technical grounds. These have been thought of as issues "likely to take the opposite party by surprise," which perhaps conveys the general idea of fairness or the lack thereof, though there is little real surprise where the case is well prepared in advance.

Clark, *Code Pleading*, 2d ed. 1947, § 96, at 609–10 * * *.

Also pertinent to the analysis is the logical relationship between the defense and the cause of action asserted by the plaintiff. This inquiry requires a determination (1) whether the matter at issue fairly may be said to constitute a necessary or extrinsic element in the plaintiff's cause of action; (2) which party, if either, has better access to relevant evidence; and (3) policy considerations: should the matter be indulged or disfavored? * * *

Central to requiring the pleading of affirmative defenses is the prevention of unfair surprise. A defendant should not be permitted to "lie behind a log" and ambush a plaintiff with an unexpected defense. * * * The instant cases illustrate this consideration. Plaintiffs submit that, had they known the statute would be applied, they would have made greater efforts to prove medical damages which were not subject to the statutory limit. In addition, plaintiffs maintain that they would have had an opportunity and the incentive to introduce evidence to support their constitutional attacks on the statute.

This distinction separates the present cases from our recent decision in Lucas v. United States, 807 F.2d 414 (5th Cir.1986). In *Lucas,* although the limitation of recovery issue was not pleaded, it was raised at trial. We held that the trial court was within its discretion to permit the defendant to effectively amend its pleadings and advance the defense. The treatment we accorded this issue in *Lucas* is consistent with long-standing precedent of this and other circuits that " 'where [an affirmative defense] is raised in the trial court in a manner that does not result in unfair surprise, * * * technical failure to comply with Rule 8(c) is not fatal.' " * * *

We view the limitation on damages as an "avoidance" within the intendment of the residuary clause of 8(c). Black's Law Dictionary * * * defines an avoidance in pleadings as "the allegation or statement of new matter, in opposition to a former pleading, which, admitting the facts alleged in such former pleading, shows cause why they should not have their ordinary legal effect." Applied to the present discussion, a plaintiff pleads the traditional tort theory of malpractice and seeks full damages. The defendant responds that assuming recovery is in order under the ordinary tort principles, because of the new statutory limitation, the traditional precedents "should not have their ordinary legal effect."

Considering these factors, against the backdrop and with the illumination provided by other applications of Rule 8(c), we conclude that the Texas statutory limit on medical malpractice damages is an affirmative defense which must be pleaded timely and that in the cases at bar the defense has been waived.

* * *

TAYLOR v. UNITED STATES, 821 F.2d 1428 (9th Cir.1987), certiorari denied 485 U.S. 992, 108 S.Ct. 1300, 99 L.Ed.2d 510 (1988). The United States appealed from a decision of the United States District Court, Northern District of California, awarding a patient's wife $500,000 in damages for loss of consortium and emotional distress, after the patient sustained permanent brain damage while receiving medical treatment at an army hospital. After the District Court awarded the damages, the government moved, pursuant to Federal Rules 59(a), 59(e), and 60(b), for a reduction in damages to $250,000 under California Civil Code § 3333.2, as incorporated by the Federal Tort Claims Act. Section 3333.2 limits recovery for noneconomic injuries in actions based on professional negligence to $250,000. The Ninth Circuit reversed the lower court's decision over objections that the government had waived the protection afforded by Section 3333.2 by failing to raise the issue before judgment.

Section 3333.2 is a limitation of liability, not an affirmative defense. Unlike affirmative defenses listed in Fed.R.Civ.Proc. 8(c), § 3333.2 limits, but does not bar recovery for noneconomic damages. If the Federal Rules do not require plaintiffs to plead the extent of damages sought, defendants should not be required to plead the limitation of damages prescribed by § 3333.2. A contrary characterization of § 3333.2 would require defendants to anticipate an award of noneconomic damages in excess of $250,000—a requirement which is unrealistic and inconsistent with the practical notions underlying notice pleading. * * *

Furthermore, Rule 8(d) specifies that averments as to the amount of damage which defendant does not deny in his answer are not deemed admitted. This provision indicates that the Federal Rules do not consider limitations of damages affirmative defenses, which, by contrast, must be pleaded. Accordingly, the government was not required to raise § 3333.2 in its answer.

We recognize, however, that application of § 3333.2 may in some instances require resolution of factual issues. In such cases, plaintiffs may be prejudiced if defendants do not raise § 3333.2 prior to judgment. We need not decide the question in this case because application of § 3333.2 here requires no additional factual inquiry on our part. * * *

Id. at 1433. How can *Taylor* be reconciled with the holding in *Ingraham* that a limitation of damages is an affirmative defense under the residuary clause in Rule 8(c)? Which court makes the better argument? Should it matter that the limitation of damages was not raised until the appeal? Is it relevant that, under California state law, Section 3333.2 is an affirmative defense? See Justice White's dissent from the denial of certiorari in *Taylor* and Simon v. United States, 891 F.2d 1154, 1156 (5th Cir.1990).

* * *

Notes and Questions

1. Consider PYCA INDUSTRIES, INC. v. HARRISON COUNTY, 177 F.3d 351, 362–63 (5th Cir.1999), in which the complaint alleged damages for breach of contract. The responding party sought to rely on a clause in the contract that provided a defense to the claim. The party who brought the action argued that the responding party could not rely on the clause because it had not been pleaded in the responsive pleading and therefore was waived. Should reliance on the clause have been considered an affirmative defense?

2. At what point does defendant's failure to plead an affirmative defense constitute a waiver? In SANDERSON–CRUZ v. UNITED STATES, 88 F.Supp.2d 388 (E.D.Pa.2000), defendant requested a partial summary judgment to bar plaintiff from recovering non-economic damages on the basis of an applicable state statute barring such relief in certain cases. Plaintiff objected on the ground that defendant had failed to plead the statutory bar either originally or by an amended answer. The court, citing Kleinknecht v. Gettysburg College, 989 F.2d 1360, 1373 (3d Cir.1993), held that the bar was an affirmative defense but that it had not been waived because the court determined that plaintiff was not prejudiced in her ability to respond to the summary judgment motion.

3. Suppose defendant fails to raise an affirmative defense in the response. When, if ever, should the court do so *sua sponte*? In Acosta v. Artuz, 221 F.3d 117, 122–23 (2d Cir.2000), the court stated that such action is appropriate only when "the defense implicates values beyond the interests of the parties." Plaintiff was but one of the many prisoners who seek release from incarceration through a writ of habeas corpus. The petition was filed well beyond the applicable one-year limitations period. The court found it appropriate to raise that defense on its own because of the large volume of those petitions that clog the federal courts and are rarely successful. Why shouldn't a court be free to raise an unpleaded issue whenever it believes the interests of justice so demand?

SECTION C.   THE REPLY

––––––

Read Federal Rule of Civil Procedure 7(a) and the accompanying materials in the Supplement. Pay particular attention to Section 25–820 of the Nebraska Revised Statutes.

––––––

Notes and Questions

1. The two prevailing types of provisions governing use of the reply are represented by Federal Rule 7(a) and the Nebraska statute. In Nebraska all allegations of an affirmative defense are admitted unless they are denied in a reply. Neb.Rev.Stat. § 25–842. Even the Nebraska statute, by cutting off or severely restricting pleadings at the reply stage, see Neb.Rev.Stat. § 25–803, departs significantly from the common-law practice, which required pleadings to continue back and forth between plaintiff and defendant until disputed issues were isolated.

Is Federal Rule 7(a), when read in conjunction with Rule 8(d), consistent with Federal Rule 8(b), which requires a defendant to answer plaintiff's allegations specifically?

2.   Although the text of Federal Rule 7(a) expressly provides that a court may order plaintiff to reply to allegations other than counterclaims, judges have been reluctant to do so, at least in the absence of "a clear and convincing factual showing of necessity or other extraordinary circumstances of a compelling nature." MOVIECOLOR LTD. v. EASTMAN KODAK CO., 24 F.R.D. 325, 326 (S.D.N.Y.1959). Why, given liberal discovery rules, should it ever be necessary to order a reply? Cf. Reynolds v. Needle, 132 F.2d 161 (D.C.Cir.1942) (granting summary judgment when plaintiff's complaint revealed affirmative defense and plaintiff failed to request leave to reply or otherwise attempt to avoid the defense).

BECKSTROM v. COASTWISE LINE, 14 Alaska 190, 13 F.R.D. 480, 482–83 (D.Alaska 1953), provides an interesting illustration of a tactical use of the reply. Under the terms of Federal Rule 38(b), a party who wishes a trial by jury of any issue must make a demand therefor not later than 10 days after the service of the *last pleading directed to such issue.* Defendants had answered plaintiff's complaint on August 22, alleging several affirmative defenses: on October 6 plaintiff moved for leave to reply and, at the same time, made his first demand for trial by jury.

> * * * Plaintiff has not shown a substantial reason for seeking permission to file a reply or for being *ordered* to do so. Accordingly, plaintiff's motion * * * must be denied.

> * * * [I]n the absence of a reply now denied, [defendant's answer] was the last pleading directed to the issues between the plaintiff and the defendants in this action. The demand for jury trial as of right must therefore be denied.

What would you have done to improve plaintiff's strategy in this case? Do you consider this a proper or ethical use of the pleadings? Demand for trial by jury is discussed further at pp. 1010–15, infra.

3.   Allegations to which a reply is not permitted or required are considered avoided or denied and plaintiff may controvert them at trial. See Federal Rule 8(d); N.Y.C.P.L.R. 3018(a). Conversely, matters requiring a responsive pleading are taken as admitted if not denied in the reply or if a reply is not filed. See Federal Rule 8(d); Neb.Rev.Stat. § 25–842.

Suppose defendant's answer contains an allegation denominated a "counterclaim," but plaintiff believes it is properly an affirmative defense. Or suppose in a "new matter" jurisdiction, such as Nebraska, plaintiff thinks defendant's "affirmative defense" could have been raised by a simple denial. See Vevelstad v. Flynn, 230 F.2d 695, 703 (9th Cir.), certiorari denied 352 U.S. 827, 77 S.Ct. 40, 1 L.Ed.2d 49 (1956) ("a counterclaim" held to be really a denial not requiring reply); Sais v. City Elec. Co., 26 N.M. 66, 188 P. 1110 (1920) ("affirmative defense" that could have been raised by denial does not require responsive pleading). What if plaintiff does not reply and the court believes that the material in fact was a counterclaim? See Dyotherm Corp. v. Turbo Mach. Co., 39 F.R.D. 370 (E.D.Pa.1966) (plaintiff granted 10 days to file reply after court ruled against its contention that defendant's answer was not a properly denominated counterclaim). Should the court always grant plaintiff some relief? See Federal Rule 8(c).

SECTION D. AMENDMENTS

———

Read Federal Rule of Civil Procedure 15 and the accompanying materials in the Supplement.

———

Parties may amend their complaints before trial and during trial. Rule 15(a) says a party may amend its pleading any time before a response has been served, or within twenty days of the service of the original pleading if no response is required. After that, an amending party must obtain the leave of the court or the consent of the opposing party. During the trial, parties may amend their pleadings, with leave of the court, to conform to issues raised by unexpected evidence (Rule 15(b)). They also may add supplemental pleadings to their original pleadings to cover events that occur after the original pleading (Rule 15(d)). Rule 15(c) mandates that, when an original pleading is amended, the new pleadings "relate back" to the original pleadings. They are considered by the court as if they had been pled in the initial pleading. If the statute of limitations expired between the original pleading and the amendment, the party still may be allowed to raise the claim.

———

MOORE v. MOORE

District of Columbia Court of Appeals, 1978.
391 A.2d 762.

FERREN, ASSOCIATE JUDGE:

Reuben and Sidney Moore, plaintiff-appellant and defendant-appellee, respectively, were married on October 19, 1968, in the District of Columbia. Their only child, Jessica Moore, was born on August 4, 1973. The marriage deteriorated [and in December, 1975] * * * Sidney Moore moved with Jessica to her parents' home in Schenectady, New York.

Reuben Moore soon initiated a custody action in New York. The court orally granted temporary custody of Jessica to Mrs. Moore, with visitation rights for Mr. Moore. On February 22, 1976, pursuant to a plan aided by a detective he had hired, Reuben Moore took Jessica from the physical custody of her maternal grandfather and brought her to Washington, D.C.

* * * [W]hile leaving a hospital where he had been visiting his ill father on March 17, 1976, Reuben Moore was confronted and grabbed by his wife and her parents. They wrested control of the child from him and returned, with Jessica, to Schenectady.

On April 2, 1976, Reuben Moore * * * filed the present action: a complaint for custody. Sidney Moore * * * answered the complaint * * * [and] the matter came to trial on October 20–21, 1976, in the Family Division of the Superior Court.

* * *

On October 27, 1976, Sidney Moore filed a motion to conform the pleadings to the evidence, Super.Ct.Dom.Rel.R. 15(b), as well as a motion for award of counsel fees. In the first motion, Mrs. Moore sought to assert a counterclaim for custody, child support, separate maintenance, and counsel fees (in connection with the District of Columbia custody litigation only). In the second motion she asked for the same counsel fees, specified the reasons for requesting them, and itemized the matters and amounts claimed.

By written order of February 28, 1977, the court granted the motion to conform. It awarded to defendant Sidney Moore custody of Jessica, child support of $500 per month, separate maintenance of $500 per month, and counsel fees in the amount requested, $5,916.65. The court granted plaintiff Reuben Moore visitation rights, subject to the continued posting of a $7,500 bond. * * * Plaintiff Reuben Moore now appeals. * * *

Appellant now asserts, as he did at trial, that because appellee requested no affirmative relief in pretrial pleadings the court erred in affording her any relief. It is one thing, he argues, to deny his claim for custody; it is another to award custody to appellee, as well as child support, separate maintenance, and attorneys' fees. He essentially contends, therefore, that the court abused its discretion in permitting the post-trial pleading amendment under Super.Ct.Dom.Rel.R. 15(b), since he was unaware at trial that the matters ultimately stated in appellee's counterclaim were at stake; he was not prepared, nor given an adequate opportunity, to contest them.

Our treatment of this argument must begin with Rule 15(b), which is identical to Fed.R.Civ.Pro. 15(b). Our analysis is accordingly aided by authorities which have interpreted the federal rule. Rule 15(b) is an attempt to favor substance over form, i.e., "to avoid the tyranny of formalism," Rosden v. Leuthold, 107 U.S.App.D.C. 89, 92, 274 F.2d 747, 750 (1960), and thus promote the resolution of cases on their merits by permitting the amendment of pleadings to reflect the actual litigation which transpired. Wright & Miller, Fed.Prac. & Proc., Civil § 1491. * * * If issues not raised in pleadings are tried by express consent of the parties, there can be no question about the propriety of permitting amendment. The difficult issue arises when, as in most Rule 15(b) cases, "implied consent" is asserted.

Whether parties have impliedly contested a matter—i.e., whether parties recognize that an issue not stated by the pleadings entered the case * * *—is determined by searching the trial record for indications that the party contesting the amendment received actual notice of the injection of the unpleaded matters, as well as an adequate opportunity to litigate such matters and to cure any surprise from their introduction. * * *

The clearest indications of a party's implied consent to try an issue lie in the failure to object to evidence, or in the introduction of evidence which is clearly apposite to the new issue but not to other matters specified in the pleadings. * * * Having in mind the tension between the desire to abandon formalism and, on the other hand, the need to assure fair notice and opportunity to litigate, we turn to the facts to assess whether the trial court's grant of permission to amend and, ultimately, its resolution of the additional issues were within the purview of discretion granted under Rule 15(b).

A. Custody

Although at the time of trial only appellant, and not his wife, had filed an action for custody, we conclude—without difficulty—that appellant was on timely notice that the court would decide not merely whether he was entitled to custody but, more broadly, would determine *who* was entitled to custody. Mrs. Moore asserted in her answer to appellant's complaint that "the best interests of the child" would be served by the child's being in her custody. Moreover, both parties introduced evidence supporting their respective qualifications for custodian. * * *

Appellant accordingly can claim no surprise or lack of notice or opportunity to litigate. The issue of Mrs. Moore's right to permanent custody—even if not raised by the pleadings—clearly was tried by the parties and the court. * * *

B. Child Support

The pretrial pleadings do not include a claim for child support. Our determination, therefore, again must be whether the issue was litigated by implied consent. For two reasons we find that it was.

First, and most germane, we believe that the resolution of child support inheres in a custody battle where the best interests of the child are the focal concern. * * * The trial judge recognized this relationship when she opined that a grant of support was required by the court's duty to afford complete relief. Second, our conclusion is bolstered by appellee's introduction of evidence of the financial needs of the child. As appellee points out, this evidence was not contested on relevance grounds; it served to put appellant on notice. * * *

In light of these two factors, we conclude that appellant received ample notice that the matter of child support would be determined and that he therefore impliedly consented. The trial court accordingly did not abuse its Rule 15(b) discretion in permitting appellee's amendment of the pleadings to raise the issue of child support.

C. Visitation Rights and Bond

Appellant does not dispute that visitation rights are a proper subject for determination as part of the overall custody question. In her Rule 15(b) motion, appellee did not request imposition of a bond covering her husband's visits with Jessica. However, because trial courts are given broad discretion in resolving custody cases, * * * and ought to fashion relief to foster and safeguard a child's best interests, * * * we find no fault with the imposition of a bond upon a parent whose history reflected a capacity for absconding with the child. The judge was acting within the scope of her duties and powers to grant complete relief. Rule 54(c). She did not abuse her discretion.

D. Attorneys' Fees

This court has determined that even though there is no specific statutory authorization for attorneys' fees awards in child custody cases, courts are empowered to award them to a parent who has enlisted legal assistance to protect the interests of the child. * * *

Although counsel fees for the assertion of a minor's interests are not as integral to a custody claim as child support, we believe that, given legal precedent, the prospect of incurring such fees would surely be within the contemplation of an opposing party. We note in this connection that evidence of expenditures for counsel fees to District of Columbia lawyers was admitted without objection. We also recognize that the trial judge initially reserved judgment on the issue, entertained a motion and opposition, and then held a hearing before awarding the fees. On this record we find no prejudicial surprise to appellant. * * *

E.   SEPARATE MAINTENANCE

The grant of spousal support is a different matter. The initial pleadings did not mention a claim for separate maintenance, which is not customarily a part of a child custody suit between parents whose marital relationship had not been—and was not being—litigated. While evidence of Mrs. Moore's financial needs was admitted without objection relatively late in the proceedings, we cannot conclude that this evidence was so uniquely pertinent to her support alone, in contrast with the custody or the child support issues, that it justifies our concluding that appellant had adequate, timely notice of, and an opportunity to contest, a claim by his wife for her own support. We find no other indication of record that appellant impliedly consented to try his wife's support claim, Rule 15(b), nor can we conclude that the award was a proper, supportable element of full relief in the child custody action. Rule 54(b) [sic]. We therefore find an abuse of trial court discretion in permitting amendment of the pleadings to include separate maintenance and, thereafter, in making such an award.

* * *

[Affirmed in part, reversed in part.]

Notes and Questions

1.   Notice the tactical dilemma faced by a party when the opposition seeks to introduce evidence at trial on an issue that clearly is not within the pleadings. The litigant may object and keep the evidence out, but this will induce the other side to request leave to amend, perhaps even to add an issue of which the party seeking amendment previously was not aware. On the other hand, a failure to object may be taken as implied consent to try the issue, thus permitting an amendment to conform to the proof. Whenever a party fails to object in this situation a second dilemma must be faced—whether or not to produce evidence on the point in question.

Even a party who objects to the evidence may face further problems. Suppose the court erroneously holds that the original pleadings encompass the newly introduced issue? In HAYES v. RICHFIELD OIL CORP., 38 Cal.2d 375, 382, 240 P.2d 580, 584 (1952), the court held:

> A variance between the allegations of a pleading and the proof will not be deemed material unless it has actually misled the adverse party to his prejudice * * *. If anything, Richfield's continued insistence [throughout the trial] that the issue was not presented by the pleadings indicates that it was fully aware that the [trial] court's rulings would permit recovery under * * *

[the new] theory. It does not appear that Richfield has been in any way prejudiced by the variance * * *.

See also Louisiana Farm Bureau Mut. Ins. Co. v. Dunn, 484 So.2d 853 (La.App. 1986). But see Concrete Serv. Corp. v. Investors Group, Inc., 79 N.C.App. 678, 340 S.E.2d 755 (1986); Mondell v. Grant AMC/Jeep, Inc., 75 Or.App. 635, 707 P.2d 637 (1985).

2. Should the court in *Moore* have remanded the case for consideration of whether an amendment under the District of Columbia rule was appropriate on the separate maintenance issue? Such an amendment normally would require the court to reopen the case for additional evidence. Of what significance is the fact that *Moore* was not a jury case? What other factors should be considered in deciding whether an amendment after trial is proper?

3. Would serious prejudice to the opposing party—for example, the death of an important witness—automatically preclude the amendment, or should the court balance the alleged prejudice against the interests of the party seeking to amend? See generally Donnici, *The Amendment of Pleadings—A Study of the Operation of Judicial Discretion in the Federal Courts*, 37 S.Cal.L.Rev. 529 (1964).

BEECK v. AQUASLIDE 'N' DIVE CORP.

United States Court of Appeals, Eighth Circuit, 1977.
562 F.2d 537.

BENSON, DISTRICT JUDGE.*

This case is an appeal from the trial court's exercise of discretion on procedural matters in a diversity personal injury action.

Jerry A. Beeck was severely injured on July 15, 1972, while using a water slide. He and his wife, Judy A. Beeck, sued Aquaslide 'N' Dive Corporation (Aquaslide), a Texas corporation, alleging it manufactured the slide involved in the accident, and sought to recover substantial damages on theories of negligence, strict liability and breach of implied warranty.

Aquaslide initially admitted manufacture of the slide, but later moved to amend its answer to deny manufacture; the motion was resisted. The district court granted leave to amend. On motion of the defendant, a separate trial was held on the issue of "whether the defendant designed, manufactured or sold the slide in question." This motion was also resisted by the plaintiffs. The issue was tried to a jury, which returned a verdict for the defendant, after which the trial court entered summary judgment of dismissal of the case. Plaintiffs took this appeal, and stated the issues presented for review to be:

1. Where the manufacturer of the product, a water slide, admitted in its Answer and later in its Answer to Interrogatories both filed prior to the running of the statute of limitations that it designed, manufactured and sold the water slide in question, was it an abuse of the trial court's discretion to grant leave to amend to the manufacturer in order to deny these admissions after the running of the statute of limitations?

* * *

* The Honorable Paul Benson, Chief Judge,   North Dakota, sitting by designation.
United States District Court for the District of

I. Facts

* * *

In 1971 Kimberly Village Home Association of Davenport, Iowa, ordered an Aquaslide product from one George Boldt, who was a local distributor handling defendant's products. The order was forwarded by Boldt to Sentry Pool and Chemical Supply Co. in Rock Island, Illinois, and Sentry forwarded the order to Purity Swimming Pool Supply in Hammond, Indiana. A slide was delivered from a Purity warehouse to Kimberly Village, and was installed by Kimberly employees. On July 15, 1972, Jerry A. Beeck was injured while using the slide at a social gathering sponsored at Kimberly Village by his employer, Harker Wholesale Meats, Inc. Soon after the accident investigations were undertaken by representatives of the separate insurers of Harker and Kimberly Village. On October 31, 1972, Aquaslide first learned of the accident through a letter sent by a representative of Kimberly's insurer to Aquaslide * * *. Aquaslide forwarded this notification to its insurer. Aquaslide's insurance adjuster made an on-site investigation of the slide in May, 1973, and also interviewed persons connected with the ordering and assembly of the slide. An inter-office letter dated September 23, 1973, indicates that Aquaslide's insurer was of the opinion the "Aquaslide in question was definitely manufactured by our insured." The complaint was filed October 15, 1973. Investigators for three different insurance companies, representing Harker, Kimberly and the defendant, had concluded that the slide had been manufactured by Aquaslide, and the defendant, with no information to the contrary, answered the complaint on December 12, 1973, and admitted that it "designed, manufactured, assembled and sold" the slide in question.

The statute of limitations on plaintiff's personal injury claim expired on July 15, 1974. About six and one-half months later Carl Meyer, president and owner of Aquaslide, visited the site of the accident prior to the taking of his deposition by the plaintiff. From his on-site inspection of the slide, he determined it was not a product of the defendant. Thereafter, Aquaslide moved the court for leave to amend its answer to deny manufacture of the slide.

II. Leave to Amend

Amendment of pleadings in civil actions is governed by Rule 15(a) * * *.

In Foman v. Davis, 371 U.S. 178, 83 S.Ct. 227, 9 L.Ed.2d 222 (1962), the Supreme Court had occasion to construe * * * Rule 15(a) * * *:

> Rule 15(a) declares that leave to amend "shall be freely given when justice so requires," this mandate is to be heeded. * * * If the underlying facts or circumstances relied upon by a plaintiff may be a proper subject of relief, he ought to be afforded an opportunity to test his claim on the merits. In the absence of any apparent or declared reason—such as undue delay, bad faith or dilatory motive on the part of the movant, repeated failure to cure deficiencies by amendments previously allowed, undue prejudice to the opposing party by virtue of allowance of the amendment, futility of amendment, etc.—the leave sought should, as the rules require, be "freely given." Of course, the grant or denial of an opportunity to amend is within the discretion of the District Court * * *.

371 U.S. at 182, 83 S.Ct. at 230. * * *

This Court in Hanson v. Hunt Oil Co., 398 F.2d 578, 582 (8th Cir.1968), held that "[p]rejudice *must be shown.*" (Emphasis added). The burden is on the party opposing the amendment to show such prejudice. In ruling on a motion for leave to amend, the trial court must inquire into the issue of prejudice to the opposing party, in light of the particular facts of the case. * * *

Certain principles apply to appellate review of a trial court's grant or denial of a motion to amend pleadings. First, as noted in Foman v. Davis, allowance or denial of leave to amend lies within the sound discretion of the trial court, * * * and is reviewable only for an abuse of discretion. * * * The appellate court must view the case in the posture in which the trial court acted in ruling on the motion to amend. * * *

It is evident from the order of the district court that in the exercise of its discretion in ruling on defendant's motion for leave to amend, it searched the record for evidence of bad faith, prejudice and undue delay which might be sufficient to overbalance the mandate of Rule 15(a) * * * and Foman v. Davis, that leave to amend should be "freely given." Plaintiffs had not at any time conceded that the slide in question had not been manufactured by the defendant, and at the time the motion for leave to amend was at issue, the court had to decide whether the defendant should be permitted to litigate a material factual issue on its merits.

In inquiring into the issue of bad faith, the court noted the fact that the defendant, in initially concluding that it had manufactured the slide, relied upon the conclusions of three different insurance companies, each of which had conducted an investigation into the circumstances surrounding the accident. This reliance upon investigations of three insurance companies, and the fact that "no contention has been made by anyone that the defendant influenced this possibly erroneous conclusion," persuaded the court that "defendant has not acted in such bad faith as to be precluded from contesting the issue of manufacture at trial." The court further found "[t]o the extent that 'blame' is to be spread regarding the original identification, the record indicates that it should be shared equally."

In considering the issue of prejudice that might result to the plaintiffs from the granting of the motion for leave to amend, the trial court held that the facts presented to it did not support plaintiffs' assertion that, because of the running of the two year Iowa statute of limitations on personal injury claims, the allowance of the amendment would sound the "death knell" of the litigation. In order to accept plaintiffs' argument, the court would have had to assume that the defendant would prevail at trial on the factual issue of manufacture of the slide, and further that plaintiffs would be foreclosed, should the amendment be allowed, from proceeding against other parties if they were unsuccessful in pressing their claim against Aquaslide. On the state of the record before it, the trial court was unwilling to make such assumptions, and concluded "[u]nder these circumstances, the Court deems that the possible prejudice to the plaintiffs is an insufficient basis on which to deny the proposed amendment." The court reasoned that the amendment would merely allow the defendant to contest a disputed factual issue at trial, and further that it would be prejudicial to the defendant to deny the amendment.

The court also held that defendant and its insurance carrier, in investigating the circumstances surrounding the accident, had not been so lacking in diligence as to dictate a denial of the right to litigate the factual issue of manufacture of the slide.

On this record we hold that the trial court did not abuse its discretion in allowing the defendant to amend its answer.

Notes and Questions

"Delay, standing alone, is an insufficient basis for denying leave to amend, and this is true no matter how long the delay." Wallace Hardware Co. v. Abrams, 223 F.3d 382, 409 (6th Cir.2000). Does that statement go too far? Even if the opposing party shows no prejudice, are there reasons for denying leave to amend at some point? Is a trial judge obligated to instruct a litigant as to how it may amend its pleading to state a valid claim or defense and then permit it to do so? That was the position of Judge Schwartzer in Bautista v. Los Angeles County, Note 5, p. 519, supra, in which the trial judge had dismissed plaintiffs' second amended complaint with prejudice. Judge O'Scannlain disagreed with Judge Schwartzer on the ground that the parties and their counsel, and not the courts, have the obligation to draft proper pleadings.

WORTHINGTON v. WILSON

United States District Court, Central District of Illinois, 1992.
790 F.Supp. 829.

MIHM, CHIEF JUDGE.

* * *

According to the amended complaint, the Plaintiff Richard Worthington ("Worthington") was arrested on February 25, 1989 by two police officers in the Peoria Heights Police Department. At the time of his arrest, Worthington was nursing an injured left hand and so advised the arresting officer. The officer responded by grabbing and twisting Worthington's injured hand and wrist, which prompted Worthington to shove the officer away and tell him to "take it easy." A second officer arrived on the scene and the two officers wrestled Worthington to the ground and handcuffed him. The officers then hoisted Worthington from the ground by the handcuffs, which caused him to suffer broken bones in his left hand. These allegations are taken as true by this court for purposes of the pending motions.

Exactly two years later, on February 25, 1991, Worthington, by his attorney Gary Morris, filed a complaint in the Circuit Court of Peoria County against the Village of Peoria Heights and "three unknown named police officers." This complaint recited the facts above and claimed that the officers' actions deprived Worthington of his constitutional rights in violation of the Civil Rights Act of 1964, 42 U.S.C. § 1983. * * * The Village removed the action to this court * * *.

* * *

On June 17, 1991, Worthington filed an amended complaint which named as Defendants Dave Wilson and Jeff Wall ("the Defendants"), the two officers who arrested Worthington on February 25, 1989. This amended complaint contains no claim against the Village of Peoria Heights. These Defendants * * * moved to dismiss the amended complaint on the grounds that the statute of limitations had run and that the complaint failed to state a proper claim under § 1983. Worthington responded to this motion and a hearing was held before the Magistrate on October 31, 1991. On December 19, 1991, the Magistrate issued a recommendation that both the motion to dismiss and the motion for sanctions be allowed. Worthington filed an objection to this recommendation * * *. On March 17, 1992, this court held an additional hearing on the pending motions.

I. STATUTE OF LIMITATIONS/RELATION BACK

* * *

A. *Schiavone Notice Requirements*

As an initial matter, there is no doubt that the statute of limitations for a § 1983 action in Illinois is two years. * * * Therefore, as noted by the Magistrate, Worthington's action against the Defendants must have been filed by February 25, 1991. Since the amended complaint was not filed until June 17, 1991, the only way the amended complaint can be found to be timely filed is if it relates back to the filing of the original complaint. * * *

* * *

Until December 1, 1991, Rule 15(c) provided, in relevant part:

> Whenever the claim or defense asserted in the amended pleading arose out of the conduct, transaction, or occurrence set forth or attempted to be set forth in the original pleading, the amendment relates back to the date of the original pleading. An amendment changing the party against whom a claim is asserted relates back if the foregoing provision is satisfied and, within the period provided by law for commencing the action against the party to be brought in by amendment that party (1) has received such notice of the institution of the action that the party will not be prejudiced in maintaining his defense on the merits, and (2) knew or should have known that, but for a mistake concerning the identity of the proper party, the action would have been brought against the party.

In [Schiavone v. Fortune],[a] * * * the Supreme Court interpreted this provision to require that, in addition to the amended complaint arising out of the same conduct set forth in the original complaint, the new party must have received actual notice of the action (and that it was the proper party) before the statute of limitations period expired. * * * As noted by the Magistrate and counsel for the Defendants, it appears that the Defendants did not receive notice of this action against them by February 25, 1991. Thus, under the old

---

a. 477 U.S. 21, 106 S.Ct. 2379, 91 L.Ed.2d 18 (1986). In *Schiavone,* the plaintiffs mistakenly failed to name the correct defendant in the original complaint. The plaintiffs meant to sue the owners of *Fortune* magazine; however, instead of naming "Time, Incorporated," they named "Fortune," which is not a legal entity. The plaintiffs were unable to serve "Fortune," so they amended their complaint to name "Time, Incorporated." Both the amendment and service of process on "Time, Incorporated" took place after the statute of limitations had run.

version of Rule 15(c) and Schiavone, the amended complaint against the officers would not relate back and would thus be untimely filed.

However, as of December 1, 1991, Rule 15(c) reads differently. * * *

* * * [R]elation-back is now governed by a modified standard. An amended complaint which changes the name of the defendant will relate back to the filing of the original complaint if it arises out of the same conduct contained in the original complaint and the new party was aware of the action within 120 days of the filing of the original complaint.

Thus, under the amended version of Rule 15(c), Worthington's amended complaint, which arises out of the very same conduct in its original complaint, would relate back to February 25, 1991 if the Defendants were aware, before June 25, 1991, that they were the officers referred to as "unknown named police officers" in the original complaint. At oral argument on March 12, 1992, counsel for the Defendants conceded that they were aware of the pendency of the action within this period; thus, under the new version of Rule 15(c), the amended complaint would be timely because the Defendants received notice of the action within 120 days of the original filing. * * *

* * *

B. *"Mistake"*

The Defendants also argue that relation back is not permitted here under Rule 15(c) because there was no "mistake" concerning the identity of the proper party. * * *

The Defendants argue that the failure of the original complaint to name Wilson and Wall was not due to a "mistake" but rather was due to a lack of knowledge over the proper defendant. The Defendants argue that while Rule 15(c) permits amendments which change a mistaken name in the original complaint, it does not permit a plaintiff to replace "unknown" parties with actual parties. * * * Wood v. Worachek, 618 F.2d 1225, 1230 (7th Cir.1980) and Rylewicz v. Beaton Services, Ltd., 888 F.2d 1175, 1181 (7th Cir.1989) * * * reflect the Seventh Circuit's view that an amended complaint which replaces fictitious names with actual names due to an initial lack of knowledge concerning the proper defendant does not involve a "mistake" and is therefore not entitled to relation back under Rule 15(c). * * * These holdings would seem to control in this case, since Worthington concedes that he designated the Defendants as "unknown named police officers" in the original complaint because he was unaware of their identities at that time. Moreover, the recent amendment of Rule 15(c) would not seem to undercut the applicability of these holdings, since the language concerning mistake is identical in both versions. Accordingly, the court finds that, pursuant to the Seventh Circuit authority noted above, Worthington's amended complaint is not entitled to relation back.

* * *

C. *State Law*

This brings us to Worthington's only real argument in support of relation-back. Worthington asserts that the issue of relation-back in this case is not governed by Rule 15(c), but rather is governed by § 2–413 of the Illinois Code of Civil Procedure. That section provides, in relevant part:

> Unknown Parties. If in any action there are persons interested therein whose names are unknown, it shall be lawful to make them parties to the action by the name and description of unknown owners, or unknown heirs or legatees of any deceased person, who may have been interested in the subject matter of the action previous to his or her death * * *.

Worthington suggests that this provision would allow the amended complaint to relate back because his inability to discover the names of the arresting officers was not for want of due diligence. This court need not address the question of whether Worthington's efforts would satisfy § 2–413, because it now finds this provision to be inapplicable in this action.

In support of the notion that an Illinois procedural rule would govern the issue of relation back in this action, Worthington cites Cabrales v. County of Los Angeles, 644 F.Supp. 1352 (C.D.Cal.1986), which held that relation-back of an amendment which added a new party was an issue governed by state law. * * * Perhaps even more important is the Ninth Circuit's decision on the appeal of this case. * * * In affirming the trial court's decision, the Ninth Circuit stated:

> * * * "[T]he length of the limitations period, and closely related questions of *tolling and application*, are to be governed by state law." The California relation back doctrine is such a tolling issue that * * * must be decided under state law. Also, as the district court noted, statutes of limitation define the substantive rights of parties. The California pleading practice allows new defendants to be named after the original complaint is filed without violating the statute of limitations is such a substantive state policy that it is applicable in the federal courts.

864 F.2d at 1463–64.

* * * The decision rests on the principle that, because federal courts borrow state statutes of limitation for § 1983 claims, they must also borrow state rules of procedure which increase or decrease those statutes of limitations, such as tolling or relation-back.

This decision seems to be at odds with Seventh Circuit authority.[2] In Lewellen v. Morley, 875 F.2d 118 (7th Cir.1989), Judge Easterbrook agreed with the Ninth Circuit's general proposition that "[w]hen state law supplies the period of limitations, it also supplies associated tolling and extension rules." * * * However, after noting that state law rules which affect the period of limitations are often part of the state law which a federal court borrows for § 1983 cases, Judge Easterbrook noted a bright-line limitation on this principle: "[f]ederal courts absorb state law only when federal law neglects the topic." * * * In other words, even though a state rule may affect the state statute of limitations, a federal court in a civil rights case does not

---

2. Moreover, the decision seems to represent an extension of law on this topic. Courts have struggled with the issue of the applicability of state relation-back doctrines in the context of diversity cases, presumably because of the elusive substance/procedure distinction. * * * But in federal question cases, the issue is much simpler—federal law controls. The only exception to this is that state law at times provides the statute of limitations, as is true in § 1983 cases. Thus, while this court borrows § 13–202 (and presumably state rules which are inextricably entwined with the statute of limitations) from Illinois for § 1983 cases, it does not borrow any and all state procedural rules which may have some impact on the limitations period, particularly where there is a federal rule of procedure directly on point. * * *

borrow that rule unless there is no similar federal provision. In this case, there is a federal rule (Rule 15(c)) which addresses the issue of relation-back of unknown named defendants addressed in § 2–413. * * * To the extent that § 2–413 would dictate a contrary result, it is at odds with federal law. As noted in Lewellen, when there is such a clash between state and federal rules, "[f]ederal law wins these contests every time." * * *

* * *

Notes and Questions

1. Before Rule 15(c) was amended there was disagreement among the circuits about whether relation-back is "substantive" or "procedural." Compare Marshall v. Mulrenin, 508 F.2d 39 (1st Cir.1974), with Davis v. Piper Aircraft Corp., 615 F.2d 606 (4th Cir.), certiorari dismissed 448 U.S. 911, 101 S.Ct. 25, 65 L.Ed.2d 1141 (1980). In SCHIAVONE v. FORTUNE, described at p. 575, n.a, supra, a diversity case, the Supreme Court applied Rule 15(c) instead of New Jersey's more liberal relation-back rule because the plaintiffs had conceded in the District Court that the New Jersey rule governing relation-back was procedural only. The Third Circuit had determined that the District Court's reliance on this concession in applying Rule 15(c) did not constitute reversible error, even though the plaintiffs had changed their position and contended that relation-back is substantive and that under *Erie,* p. 374, supra, and *Walker,* p. 402, supra, the District Court was bound to apply the New Jersey rule. As a result the Supreme Court avoided a collision with *Erie* that might have resolved the conflicting rules among the circuits. Does the subsequent revision of Rule 15 obviate the need for an *Erie* analysis? Does Rule 15(c)(1) incorporate state relation-back law into the Federal Rules?

2. Should the *Worthington* court have discussed Rule 15(c)(1) when it decided not to apply Illinois relation-back law? Cf. Jordan v. Tapper, 143 F.R.D. 567 (D.N.J.1992) (New Jersey relation-back law applied in diversity case pursuant to amended Rule 15(c)(1)).

3. Should a federal court apply Rule 15(c)(1) or Rule 15(c)(3) when it confronts a state relation-back rule that is more restrictive than Rule 15(c)(3)? Would this present an *Erie* problem? Note that subdivisions (c)(1), (c)(2), and (c)(3) are alternative methods of relation-back. Whose rights are impaired if Rule 15(c)(1) is applied? If Rule 15(c)(3) is applied? Whenever state relation-back law is different from Rule 15(c)(3), is it a zero-sum game in terms of abridging state-created rights?

4. How much "notice" is required to satisfy Rule 15(c)(3)(A)? In *Schiavone,* Justice Blackmun had concluded for relation-back law that "[t]he linchpin is notice, and notice within the limitations period." The 1991 amendment allows a plaintiff an additional 120 days to notify a party against whom she has a claim, but does it clarify the meaning of "notice"? See Berndt v. Tennessee, 796 F.2d 879, 884 (6th Cir.1986); Korn v. Royal Caribbean Cruise Line, Inc., 724 F.2d 1397, 1401 (9th Cir.1984); O'Brien v. Grand Rapids, 783 F.Supp. 1034, 1038 (W.D.Mich. 1992); Smith v. TW Services, Inc., 142 F.R.D. 144, 147 (M.D.Tenn.1991).

5. Does the Seventh Circuit interpret too narrowly the "mistake" requirement in Rule 15(c)(3)(B)? If the primary concern is notice to the defendant, why should the plaintiff's state of mind matter? In a section of the *Worthington* opinion that has not been included in this book, the District Court suggested that

plaintiffs can circumvent the Seventh Circuit's bar on replacing fictitious defendants with actual defendants by naming random defendants. Would this be detrimental to the purpose of Rule 15(c)(3)?

6.   In STAGGERS v. OTTO GERDAU CO., 359 F.2d 292, 297 (2d Cir.1966), the original plaintiff, an assignee of the claim, died prior to trial. Subsequently, and after the statute of limitations on the claim had run, an amendment substituted both the original plaintiff's administrator and the assignor of the claim as parties plaintiff. The trial court held that the amendment did not relate back to the time of the original complaint. The Court of Appeals reversed:

> No matter who the plaintiffs are, the "transactions" with which we are concerned are those which led to the establishment and breach of the * * * contracts * * * set forth in the "original pleading." There is no meaningful statute of limitations problem here; the claims of all potential plaintiffs relate back to the date of the original pleading.

Does this language go too far? Are there different considerations with regard to relation back of amendments when it is a plaintiff rather than a defendant who is added? Rules and statutes such as Federal Rule 15(c) usually are oriented solely toward joinder of new defendants. When a new plaintiff is joined after the limitations period has passed, is it significant that the jurisdiction relies on a new-cause-of-action theory rather than a same-transaction-or-occurrence rule in deciding generally whether amendments relate back? See Maxson v. McElhinney, 370 Pa. 622, 88 A.2d 747 (1952) (in wrongful-death action brought by deceased's widow who had no standing to sue, an amendment substituting deceased's personal representative would state a new cause of action and would not relate back). See also Brauer v. Republic Steel Corp., 460 F.2d 801 (10th Cir.1972) (amendment naming additional plaintiffs and adding new negligence claim after limitations period had run held to relate back to original claim for breach of warranty).

In connection with the joinder of new plaintiffs under Rule 15(c), consider the 1966 amendments to Federal Rule 17(a) and the Advisory Committee's comments, which appear in the Supplement. For a thorough discussion of the interrelation between Rule 15(c) and Rule 17(a), see Unilever (Raw Materials) Ltd. v. M/T Stolt Boel, 77 F.R.D. 384 (S.D.N.Y.1977). Cf. Newell v. Harrison, 779 F.Supp. 388 (E.D.La.1991) (rejecting the use of Rule 15(c) for adding plaintiffs).

7.   For commentary on *Schiavone* and relation-back rules, see Bauer, *Schiavone: An Un–Fortune-ate Illustration of the Supreme Court's Role as Interpreter of the Federal Rules of Civil Procedure*, 63 Notre Dame L.Rev. 720 (1988); Brussack, *Outrageous Fortune: The Case for Amending Rule 15(c) Again*, 61 S.Cal.L.Rev. 671 (1988); Epter, *Unfortunate Decision: The Aftermath of the Supreme Court's Eradication of the Relation–Back Doctrine*, 17 Fla.St.U.L.Rev. 713 (1990); Lewis, *The Excessive History of Federal Rule 15(c) and Its Lessons for Civil Rules Revision*, 86 Mich.L.Rev. 1057 (1987).

SECTION E.   SUPPLEMENTAL PLEADINGS

———

Read Federal Rules of Civil Procedure 7(a) and 15(d) in the Supplement.

———

Notes and Questions

1. "The office of a supplemental complaint is to aid the cause of action already averred, not to enable the plaintiff to recover upon a cause of action which has accrued since the action was commenced." HALSTED v. HALSTED, 7 Misc. 23, 27 N.Y.S. 408 (Com.Pl.1894). This passage was quoted with approval in Giglio v. Konold, 5 Ohio App.2d 250, 251, 214 N.E.2d 806, 808 (1965) (plaintiff cannot file supplemental complaint alleging defendants' refusal to obey trial court order pending appeal; proper step is to file new action for contempt). See also Mork v. Waltco Truck Equip. Co., 70 Ohio App.3d 458, 591 N.E.2d 379 (1990); Flood v. Simpson, 45 Cal.App.3d 644, 119 Cal.Rptr. 675 (2d Dist.1975). Cf. Wallace v. Hanover Ins. Co., 164 So.2d 111 (La.App.1964) (defendant cannot raise by supplemental pleading an affirmative defense of fraud when only defense relied upon in original answer was premature filing of claim). What reason, if any, is there for prohibiting a "new cause of action" in a supplemental pleading?

Compare the statement by the revisers of New York's supplemental pleadings statute, N.Y.C.P.L.R. 3025(b), which appears in the Supplement in conjunction with Federal Rule 15(d): "[This new section is] * * * intended to grant the widest possible discretion to the court in granting leave to serve supplemental pleadings and imposing terms, even if the pleader had no cause of action at the time of the original pleading but has subsequently acquired and stated one in a supplemental pleading." N.Y. Advisory Comm. on Practice and Procedure, *First Preliminary Report* 78 (1957). Taking its cue from the revisers' statement, the court in HERZOG v. HERZOG, 43 Misc.2d 1062, 252 N.Y.S.2d 704 (Sup.Ct.1964), permitted a wife suing for separation to add a cause of action for divorce based on alleged evidence that her husband had become an adulterer. The husband protested—unsuccessfully—that the supplemental complaint was being improperly used to obtain divorce jurisdiction over him in a suit that had begun as a simple separation action. Wasn't the court clearly unfair to Mr. Herzog? Does the New York rule go too far? In another New York case, the court denied permission to file a supplemental pleading when (1) it alleged new theories of liability based upon facts not previously alleged; (2) plaintiff permitted three years to elapse, during which discovery proceeded on its original legal theories, before seeking leave to serve supplemental complaint; and (3) plaintiff failed to file an affidavit establishing the merit of the proposed supplemental complaint or a reasonable excuse for its delay in seeking leave to serve it. Hypertronics Inc. v. Digital Equip. Corp., 159 A.D.2d 607, 552 N.Y.S.2d 662 (2d Dep't 1990). The New York provision is further analyzed in 3 Weinstein, Korn & Miller, *New York Civil Practice* ¶¶ 3025.12, 3025.17–.25.

2. In the lower federal courts, there is substantial authority for the proposition that Rule 15(d) permits the bringing of new claims in a supplemental complaint, because it "promote[s] the economical and speedy disposition of the controversy." Keith v. Volpe, 858 F.2d 467, 473 (9th Cir.1988). See Cabrera v. City of Huntington Park, 159 F.3d 374 (9th Cir.1998); Rowe v. United States Fidelity & Guar. Co., 421 F.2d 937 (4th Cir.1970). To reach essentially the same result, the Supreme Court in Griffin v. County School Board of Prince Edward County, 377 U.S. 218, 84 S.Ct. 1226, 12 L.Ed.2d 256 (1964), construed plaintiff's original "cause of action" broadly so that a new claim was considered part of the same old cause of action.

On the other hand, the court in Planned Parenthood of Southern Arizona v. Neely, 130 F.3d 400 (9th Cir.1997), reversed a trial court decision to permit a supplemental complaint that introduced a separate and new cause of action, at least when the initial case had been finally determined on the merits without any need for the trial court to maintain jurisdiction or oversee the implementation of that decision. The original decision held a parental consent abortion statute to be unconstitutional. The supplemental complaint sought to challenge the validity of an amended version of that statute.

Note that Rule 13(e) permits defendants to use a supplemental pleading to assert counterclaims that arise after filing an answer. What policy reasons would justify treating plaintiffs differently than defendants? Why should a plaintiff's right to file a supplemental pleading under Rule 15(d) be narrower than a defendant's right under Rule 13(e)?

3. Suppose, rather than adding supplemental facts setting out a "new cause of action" to an already validly stated claim, a party seeks to add supplemental facts without which the original pleading is defective. Are the considerations relevant to the two situations the same? Federal Rule 15(d) provides that a supplemental pleading *may* be allowed "even though the original pleading is defective in its statement of a claim for relief or defense." Until 1963, when this provision was added, the federal courts were split as to whether curative supplemental pleadings should ever be allowed. Under what circumstances should a court deny leave to supplement a defective pleading? See generally 6A Wright, Miller & Kane *Federal Practice and Procedure: Civil 2d* § 1505 (1990) (2001 Pocket Part).

4. Are supplemental pleadings governed by the same relation-back analysis as amended pleadings? One view is reflected in DAVIS v. PIPER AIRCRAFT CORP., 615 F.2d 606, 609 n. 3 (4th Cir.1980). In that case, the plaintiff moved to amend his complaint pursuant to Rule 15(a) to reflect his new capacity as ancillary administrator of an estate, which allowed him to go forward with a wrongful death action filed nine months earlier. The Court of Appeals noted that:

> Technically this was more properly an attempt to file a supplemental pleading under Fed.R.Civ.P. 15(d) than an amended pleading under Fed.R.Civ.P. 15(a) because the new matter occurred after rather than before the original complaint was filed. For relation back purposes, the technical distinction between the two is not of critical importance, and is frequently simply disregarded by courts, e.g. Rowe v. United States Fidelity & Guar. Co., 421 F.2d 937 (4th Cir.1970). So long as the test of Fed.R.Civ.P. 15(c) is met, a supplemental pleading should ordinarily be given the same relation back effect as an amended pleading. * * * On that basis, our analysis will treat Fed.R. 15(c) as applying to the supplemental pleading actually attempted here. * * *

See Knauer v. Johns–Manville Corp., 638 F.Supp. 1369, 1372 n. 1 (D.Md.1986). Some courts apply relation-back analysis directly to Rule 15(d). See Security Ins. Co. of New Haven v. United States, 338 F.2d 444 (9th Cir.1964). But see Slavenburg v. Boston Ins. Co., 30 F.R.D. 123 (S.D.N.Y.1962). See generally 6A Wright, Miller & Kane, *Federal Practice and Procedure: Civil 2d* § 1508 (1990) (2001 Pocket Part). Note, however, "[o]ne major difference between practice under Rule 15(a) and Rule 15(c) * * * is that certain amendments may be made as a matter of course within stated time periods, whereas all supplemental pleadings require leave of court." 6A Wright, Miller & Kane, *Federal Practice and Procedure: Civil 2d* § 1504 (1990) (2001 Pocket Part).

SECTION F. PROVISIONS TO ENSURE TRUTHFUL ALLEGATIONS

———

Read Federal Rules of Civil Procedure 11 and 23.1 and related materials in the Supplement.

———

SUROWITZ v. HILTON HOTELS CORP.

Supreme Court of the United States, 1966.
383 U.S. 363, 86 S.Ct. 845, 15 L.Ed.2d 807.

Certiorari to the United States Court of Appeals for the Seventh Circuit.

MR. JUSTICE BLACK delivered the opinion of the Court.

Petitioner, Dora Surowitz, a stockholder in Hilton Hotels Corporation, brought this action in a United States District Court on behalf of herself and other stockholders charging that the officers and directors of the corporation had defrauded it of several million dollars by illegal devices and schemes designed to cheat the corporation and enrich the individual defendants. The acts charged, if true, would constitute frauds of the grossest kind against the corporation, and would be in violation of the Securities Act of 1933, the Securities Exchange Act of 1934, and the Delaware General Corporation Law. * * * The [detailed] complaint [containing more than 60 printed pages] was signed by counsel for Mrs. Surowitz in compliance with Rule 11 of the Federal Rules of Civil Procedure which provides that "The signature of an attorney constitutes a certificate by him that he has read the pleading; that to the best of his knowledge, information, and belief there is good ground to support it; and that it is not interposed for delay."[b] Also pursuant to Rule 23(b) [now Rule 23.1] of the Federal Rules, the complaint was verified by Mrs. Surowitz, the petitioner, who stated that some of the allegations in the complaint were true and that she "on information and belief" thought that all the other allegations were true.

So far as the language of the complaint and of Mrs. Surowitz's verification was concerned, both were in strict compliance with the provisions of Rule 23(b) which states that a shareholder's complaint in a secondary action must contain certain averments and be verified by the plaintiff. Notwithstanding the sufficiency of the complaint and verification under Rule 23(b), however, the court, without requiring defendants to file an answer and over petitioner's protest, granted defendants' motion to require Mrs. Surowitz to submit herself to an oral examination by the defendants' counsel. In this examination Mrs. Surowitz showed in her answers to questions that she did not understand the complaint at all, that she could not explain the statements made in the complaint, that she had a very small degree of knowledge as to what the lawsuit was about, that she did not know any of the defendants by name, that

———

b. The quoted language is from Rule 11 prior to its revision in 1983.

she did not know the nature of their alleged misconduct, and in fact that in signing the verification she had merely relied on what her son-in-law had explained to her about the facts in the case. On the basis of this examination, defendants moved to dismiss the complaint, alleging that "1. It is a sham pleading, and 2. Plaintiff, Dora Surowitz, is not a proper party plaintiff. * * * " In response, Mrs. Surowitz's lawyer, in an effort to cure whatever infirmity the court might possibly find in Mrs. Surowitz's verification in light of her deposition, filed two affidavits which shed much additional light on an extensive investigation which had preceded the filing of the complaint. Despite these affidavits the District Judge dismissed the case holding that Mrs. Surowitz's affidavit was "false," that being wholly false it was a nullity, that being a nullity it was as though no affidavit had been made in compliance with Rule 23, that being false the affidavit was a "sham" and Rule 23(b) required that he dismiss her case, and he did so, "with prejudice."

The Court of Appeals affirmed the District Court's dismissal * * * despite the fact that the charges made against the defendants were viewed as very serious and grave charges of fraud and that "many of the material allegations of the complaint are obviously true and cannot be refuted." 342 F.2d, at 607. We cannot agree with either of the courts below and reverse their judgments. * * *

Mrs. Surowitz, the plaintiff and petitioner here, is a Polish immigrant with a very limited English vocabulary and practically no formal education. For many years she has worked as a seamstress in New York where by reason of frugality she saved enough money to buy some thousands of dollars worth of stocks. She was of course not able to select stocks for herself with any degree of assurance of their value. Under these circumstances she had to receive advice and counsel and quite naturally she went to her son-in-law, Irving Brilliant. Mr. Brilliant had graduated from the Harvard Law School, possessed a master's degree in economics from Columbia University, was a professional investment advisor, and in addition to his degrees and his financial acumen, he wore a Phi Beta Kappa key. In 1957, six years before this litigation began, he bought some stock for his mother-in-law in the Hilton Hotels Corporation, paying a little more than $2,000 of her own money for it. * * *

About December 1962, Mrs. Surowitz received through the mails a notice from the Hilton Hotels Corporation announcing its plan to purchase a large amount of its own stock. Because she wanted it explained to her, she took the notice to Mr. Brilliant. Apparently disturbed by it, he straightway set out to make an investigation. Shortly thereafter he went to Chicago, Illinois, where Hilton Hotels has its home office and talked the matter over with Mr. Rockler. Mr. Brilliant and Mr. Rockler had been friends for many years. * * * The two decided to investigate further, and for a number of months both pursued whatever avenues of information that were open to them. By August of 1963 on the basis of their investigation, both of them had reached the conclusion [that defendants were engaged in a fraudulent scheme, and Mr. Brilliant explained this to Mrs. Surowitz.] * * *

* * * When, on the basis of this conversation, Mrs. Surowitz stated that she agreed that suit be filed in her name, Mr. Rockler prepared a formal complaint which he mailed to Mr. Brilliant. Mr. Brilliant then, according to

both his affidavit and Mrs. Surowitz's testimony, read and explained the complaint to his mother-in-law before she verified it. Her limited education and her small knowledge about any of the English language, except the most ordinarily used words, probably is sufficient guarantee that the courts below were right in finding that she did not understand any of the legal relationships or comprehend any of the business transactions described in the complaint. She did know, however, that she had put over $2,000 of her hard-earned money into Hilton Hotels stock, that she was not getting her dividends, and that her son-in-law who had looked into the matter thought that something was wrong. She also knew that her son-in-law was qualified to help her and she trusted him. It is difficult to believe that anyone could be shocked or harmed in any way when, in the light of all these circumstances, Mrs. Surowitz verified the complaint, not on the basis of her own knowledge and understanding, but in the faith that her son-in-law had correctly advised her either that the statements in the complaint were true or to the best of his knowledge he believed them to be true.

* * * Rule 23(b) was not written in order to bar derivative suits. Unquestionably it was originally adopted and has served since in part as a means to discourage "strike suits" by people who might be interested in getting quick dollars by making charges without regard to their truth so as to coerce corporate managers to settle worthless claims in order to get rid of them. * * *

When the record of this case is reviewed in the light of the purpose of Rule 23(b)'s verification requirement, there emerges the plain, inescapable fact that this is not a strike suit or anything akin to it. Mrs. Surowitz was not interested in anything but her own investment made with her own money. Moreover, there is not one iota of evidence that Mr. Brilliant, her son-in-law and counselor, sought to do the corporation any injury in this litigation. In fact his purchases for the benefit of his family of more than $50,000 of securities in the corporation, including a $10,000 debenture, all made years before this suit was brought, manifest confidence in the corporation, not a desire to harm it in any way. The Court of Appeals in affirming the District Court's dismissal, however, indicated that whether Mrs. Surowitz and her counselors acted in good faith and whether the charges they made were truthful were irrelevant once Mrs. Surowitz demonstrated in her oral testimony that she knew nothing about the content of the suit. * * *

We cannot construe Rule 23 or any other one of the Federal Rules as compelling courts to summarily dismiss, without any answer or argument at all, cases like this where grave charges of fraud are shown by the record to be based on reasonable beliefs growing out of careful investigation. The basic purpose of the Federal Rules is to administer justice through fair trials, not through summary dismissals as necessary as they may be on occasion. These rules were designed in large part to get away from some of the old procedural booby traps which common-law pleaders could set to prevent unsophisticated litigants from ever having their day in court. If rules of procedure work as they should in an honest and fair judicial system, they not only permit, but should as nearly as possible guarantee that bona fide complaints be carried to an adjudication on the merits. Rule 23(b), like the other civil rules, was written to further, not defeat the ends of justice. The serious fraud charged here, which of course has not been proven, is clearly in that class of deceitful conduct which the federal securities laws were largely passed to prohibit and protect against. There is, moreover, not one word or one line of actual evidence in this record indicating that there has been any collusive conduct or trickery by those who filed this suit except through intimations and insinuations without any support from anything any witness has said. The dismissal of this case was error. It has now been practically three years since the complaint was filed and as yet none of the defendants have even been compelled to admit or deny the wrongdoings charged. They should be. The cause is reversed and remanded to the District Court for trial on the merits.

Reversed and remanded.

Mr. Justice Harlan, concurring.

Rule 23(b) directs that in a derivative suit "the complaint shall be verified by oath" but nothing dictates that the verification be that of the plaintiff shareholder. * * * In the present circumstances, it seems to me the affidavit of Walter J. Rockler, counsel for Mrs. Surowitz, amounts to an adequate verification by counsel, which I think is permitted by a reasonable interpretation of the Rule at least in cases such as this. On this premise, I agree with the decision of the Court.

Notes and Questions

1. Compare Roussel v. Tidelands Capital Corp., 438 F.Supp. 684, 688 (N.D.Ala.1977), reaffirming the dismissal of an action under Rule 23.1, because, among other things, plaintiff admitted he verified the pleading without reading it, and thus had demonstrated he was not likely to represent the shareholders fairly and adequately. Why is a dismissal ever an appropriate way of enforcing the verification provision of Rule 23.1? Shouldn't plaintiff be prosecuted for the crime of perjury instead? Of what significance is it that any recovery in a suit under Rule 23.1 goes directly to the corporation, not to plaintiff? Suppose the statute of limitations on the claim runs just before the dismissal. What additional problems would this raise?

2. Why does Rule 23.1 require verification? Why doesn't the Rule 11 procedure suffice? In those state courts in which fact pleadings generally do not have to be verified, there are certain exceptions. Some of the typical ones found in state practice are: petitions for divorce (Iowa Code Ann. § 598.7; Kan.Stat.Ann. § 60–1604(a); Okl.Stat.Ann. tit. 43, § 105), petitions brought by the state to enjoin a nuisance (Okl.Stat.Ann. tit. 12, § 1397), and complaints to obtain support of an illegitimate child (Iowa Code Ann. § 600B.13). What makes these actions sufficiently distinctive to require verification?

3. To what extent should a plaintiff or defendant be excused from a verification requirement if an admission of truth might subject him to criminal prosecution? See N.Y.C.P.L.R. § 3020(a) (verification excused for matters concerning which party would be privileged from testifying as a witness). If no excuse is allowed, should the prosecution be barred from using the verified pleading as evidence? See DeCamp v. First Kensington Corp., 83 Cal.App.3d 268, 147 Cal. Rptr. 869 (2d Dist.1978) (prosecution barred from use of pleading and all information obtained as a result of reading it).

Permissive pleading rules such as those embodied in the Federal Rules and comparable state systems provide an opportunity for abuse. For example, is it appropriate for a party to institute a colorable claim with the sole intention of pressuring another party into settling? Or would it be right for a party who has been sued on a legitimate claim to interpose a counterclaim on a questionable legal theory—simply to induce plaintiff to drop the suit?

Rule 11 attempts to curb abuse of the federal pleading rules by imposing affirmative duties on attorneys and by raising the possibility of sanctions for failure to discharge them. As is clear from *Surowitz,* the pre–1983 incarnation of Rule 11 employed a subjective standard to judge attorney conduct—so long as attorneys acted in good faith, they were not subject to sanctions even if it later became clear that their legal theory was faulty or that the facts did not support their claims.

Unfortunately, this pre–1983 version of Rule 11 did not work the way its framers intended—indeed, it was largely ignored, widely perceived as ineffectual, and rarely used. One study reveals that, between 1938 and 1976, there were only twenty-three reported cases in which a party invoked Rule 11 to strike a pleading and only nine cases in which violations were found. Risinger, *Honesty in Pleading and its Enforcement: Some "Striking" Problems with Federal Rule of Civil Procedure 11,* 61 Minn.L.Rev. 1 (1976). Consequently, the Rule was significantly strengthened in 1983.

The 1983 amendments to Rule 11 made several important changes to overcome the reluctance of courts to impose sanctions and to ensure that attorneys would "stop and think" before filing papers. The amended Rule replaced the subjective good faith test with an objective standard of reasonableness; required that attorneys make a reasonable prefiling inquiry into both the facts and the law bearing on the contents of filed papers; made sanctions mandatory for a violation of the Rule; and gave judges discretion to impose different types of sanctions and to sanction clients or attorneys.

Under the 1983 amendments, practice under Rule 11 increased dramatically, creating a "cottage industry" in Rule 11 motions and litigation that exceeded everyone's expectations. By 1991, over 3,000 cases dealing with Rule 11 had been reported. See Vairo, *Rule 11: Where We Are and Where We Are Going,* 60 Fordham L.Rev. 475, 480 (1991). And, as one court recognized, "[t]he large number of reported opinions can only be a fraction of the large number of instances in which sanctions have been imposed under" Rule 11. Zaldivar v. City of Los Angeles, 780 F.2d 823, 829 (9th Cir.1986). Between 1989 and 1992, Rule 11 was the subject of five Supreme Court decisions.

One study of Rule 11 under the 1983 amendments revealed that it had a significant impact on the behavior of attorneys even when no sanctions were awarded. Kritzer, Marshall & Zemans, *Rule 11: Moving Beyond the Cosmic Anecdote,* 75 Judicature 269 (1992). In the twelve months preceding the study, 24.5 percent of lawyers had experienced an in-court reference to Rule 11, and 30.3 percent had experienced out-of-court references to Rule 11. More than one-third of the lawyers surveyed said that a fear of sanctions resulted in "extra pre-filing review of pleadings, motions, or other documents subject to Rule 11," lending credence to the notion that it was encouraging lawyers to "stop and think" before acting.

An irony of practice under the 1983 amendments was that Rule 11 itself became a source of tactical litigation. According to some, it was used as a "hardball" technique to intimidate and harass opponents by many of the very attorneys whose abusive behavior Rule 11 was meant to control. See Gaiardo v. Ethyl Corp., 835 F.2d 479, 484–85 (3d Cir.1987); Cole, *Rule 11 Now,* 17 Litigation, Spring 1991, at 10. Other practices included "bloated requests" for attorney's fees. See Frantz v. United States Powerlifting Fed'n, 836 F.2d 1063, 1066 (7th Cir.1987).

In response to the explosion of Rule 11 litigation, which many felt was counterproductive, the Advisory Committee on the Federal Rules of Civil Procedure gathered comments on the 1983 amendments and proposed another set of amendments, which the Supreme Court adopted. The changes became effective in 1993. Although these amendments preserved the "stop and think" objective of the 1983 Rule, the Advisory Committee tried to achieve it without the "chilling effect" the 1983 amendments may have had on counsel advancing novel legal theories. The amendments also eliminated the fee-shifting character that Rule 11 had acquired as a result of courts almost routinely imposing monetary sanctions for violations of the Rule.

The new Rule is simpler, allows more court discretion in the imposition of monetary sanctions, and has added a twenty-one day "safe harbor" during which the filing party may withdraw the challenged paper without censure. Furthermore, the 1993 amendments change the requirement that an attorney must have a "good faith" motive for bringing a claim to a requirement that the claim must be nonfrivolous. This replaces a subjective standard with one that is more objective and, it is hoped, will allow attorneys leeway to advance novel arguments. The new Rule also has a wider scope of application than the 1983 amendment, however, in that it applies to all representations to the court and requires the filing party to monitor the continuing validity of the contents of every signed paper as the case proceeds. Finally, present Rule 11 also allows sanctions against the law firms or parties responsible for violations as well as the individual attorney who actually signed the document.

HADGES v. YONKERS RACING CORP.

United States Court of Appeals, Second Circuit, 1995.
48 F.3d 1320, 30 Fed.R.Serv.3d 1165.

[Hadges, a harness racehorse driver, trainer, and owner had been licensed by the New York State Racing Board in 1972. The license was suspended and revoked in 1974, reissued in 1976, and suspended for a six-month period in 1989.

Hadges was denied the ability to work at a number of racetracks following the 1989 reinstatement of his license. He sued Yonkers Racing Corporation ("YRC") in both state and federal court for barring him from working at Yonkers Raceway. The federal claim, based on a denial of due process, was dismissed because the court found no state action; the court noted however, that had other tracks (including the Meadowlands in New Jersey) "followed YRC's decision" state action could have been established. (Based partially on an affidavit that so asserted, it was the court's understanding that Hadges could work at other tracks in the region.) In his state action, which alleged that he had been blackballed by New York State tracks, the state court ruled against Hadges on all claims.

In 1992 Hadges brought suit in federal district court against the Meadowlands Raceway (a state agency) based on the same claim as in the YRC case. The case settled; before the settlement, however, the Meadowlands' General Manager submitted an affidavit that, pursuant to a 1992 resolution, the YRC ban would provide a basis for a Meadowlands ban.

Hadges appealed the New York state court decision, and filed a Rule 60(b) motion in the New York federal action requesting that the original decision against him be vacated because the affidavit which had claimed he could work at other tracks was fraudulent. With the Rule 60(b) motion, Hadges and his attorney, William Kunstler, signed statements saying that Hadges had not worked in over four years; neither mentioned the state appeal.

In reply to the Rule 60(b) motion, YRC presented evidence that showed Hadges had raced at Monticello five times in 1991 and seven times in 1993. YRC moved for dismissal and requested that the court impose sanctions on Hadges and possibly Kunstler "for misrepresentation and for failing to disclose the state court action to the district court." Hadges admitted that he had raced at Monticello but offered the excuse that he had only made a total of $100 from the 12 races together. Hadges also submitted a "scratch" sheet that he claimed documented the fact that the New York State Racing Board scratched him (barred him) from a race in 1989 following the re-issuance of his license. YRC later demonstrated, however, that the sheet was from a November 1987 race.

The district court denied the Rule 60(b) motion, but found that it was "not so frivolous as to warrant Rule 11 sanctions." The court did ask, however, that Hadges and Kunstler submit papers arguing against the imposition of sanctions for misrepresentation of Hadges's racing history. Hadges claimed that the erroneous submission of the sheet was a mistake, and that the 1989 scratching incident was a separate one for which he submitted proof in the form of an affidavit. Kunstler claimed that he did not know that the sheet was from 1987, but that the date was irrelevant because the sheet was useful as evidence anyway.]

* * *

Thereafter, in the second ruling on appeal to us, the judge imposed a Rule 11 sanction of $2,000 on Hadges as an appropriate sanction for his misrepresentations. The judge also censured Kunstler under Rule 11 for failing to make adequate inquiry as to the truth of Hadges's affidavits and for failing to inform the court of the pending state court litigation. In the course of his opinion, the judge stated:

> Mr. Kunstler is apparently one of those attorneys who believes that his sole obligation is to his client and that he has no obligations to the court or to the processes of justice. Unfortunately, he is not alone in this approach to the practice of law, which may be one reason why the legal profession is held in such low esteem by the public at this time.

Kunstler responded in a letter to the court, in which he argued that the court erred in sanctioning his client $2,000 and in censuring him. In particular, he objected to the court's characterization of him as an attorney "who believes that his sole obligation is to his client," and he objected to the court's charge that his approach to law practice was in part responsible for the low public esteem for the legal profession. Kunstler went on to state his opinion that the court's comment was "generated by an animus toward activist practitioners who, like myself, have, over the years, vigorously represented clients wholly disfavored by the establishment."

The court treated the letter as an application to reargue the sanction issues. Its order denying the application is the third ruling on appeal to us. In that order, the court quoted at length from a recent New York state court opinion criticizing Kunstler's law partner, Ronald L. Kuby in an entirely unrelated case. * * * The judge's order further reprimanded Kunstler stating:

> Finally, Mr. Kunstler claims that he is entitled to "consideration" because of his representation of unpopular clients. Undoubtedly an attorney who assumes or is assigned the defense of an unpopular case or client and does so at risk to his practice or standing in the community (such as the fictional attorney Atticus Finch in Harper Lee's "To Kill a Mockingbird") is entitled to some consideration. However, an attorney who aggressively and repeatedly seeks to represent unpopular causes or questionable clients for personal reasons of his own is not deserving of any particular consideration. And an attorney who places himself and his causes above the interests of justice is entitled to none.

This appeal from the judgment for YRC in the Rule 60(b) action and from the two April 1994 rulings on sanctions followed.

II. DISCUSSION

* * *

[In Part A the court upheld the district court's denial of Rule 60(b) relief.]

* * *

B. Rule 11 sanctions

As we have already noted, not only did the district court rule against Hadges regarding his claims of fraud on the court in *Hadges I*, but it went on to impose Rule 11 sanctions on both Hadges and Kunstler for their own misrepresentations and omissions. This determination was based on two principal grounds: (1) misstatement of the date of the alleged "scratching" incident and (2) misstatement regarding Hadges's lack of work in the years since the YRC ban. In addition, the court based Kunstler's censure on his failure to inform the court of the state court action. * * *

As noted above, an amended version of Fed.R.Civ.P. 11 came into effect on December 1, 1993, five days before Hadges filed his complaint in the Rule 60(b) action in the district court.

* * *

1. Hadges's sanction

Hadges argues that the district court abused its discretion in imposing sanctions on him. YRC argues that the sanctions were justified. We believe that Hadges is correct.

In imposing sanctions, the district court apparently did not take into account YRC's failure to comply with the revised procedural requirements of Rule 11. In this case, YRC did not submit the sanction request separately from all other requests, and there is no evidence in the record indicating that YRC served Hadges with the request for sanctions 21 days before presenting it to the court. Thus, YRC denied Hadges the "safe-harbor" period that the current version of the Rule specifically mandates. * * *

If Hadges had received the benefit of the safe-harbor period, the record indicates that he would have "withdrawn or appropriately corrected" his misstatements, thus avoiding sanctions altogether. Hadges did in fact correct one of his misstatements by admitting in an affidavit, sworn to on December 28, 1993, just 12 days after YRC asked for sanctions, that he had raced at Monticello in 1991 and 1993. Thus, this misstatement is not sanctionable.

Hadges also explained and corrected his misstatement about the 1989 date of the first scratching incident and described another scratching incident in 1989 involving another horse (Dazzling GT). This correction was supported by his own affidavit sworn to on March 17, 1994, and the affidavit of Erik Schulman, sworn to on March 16, 1994. Both were filed with the district court on March 21, 1994, just one week after the court issued its order stating that it was considering imposition of sanctions. Apparently, YRC had not previously requested sanctions on the basis of the scratching incident. Although YRC subsequently questioned whether the Dazzling GT incident described by Hadges and Schulman had taken place, the district court did not rely on this as a basis for imposing sanctions. We note that Kunstler also filed an affidavit making similar retractions.

* * *

Rule 11 also provides that a court may impose sanctions on its own initiative. * * * If a court wishes to exercise its discretion to impose sanctions sua sponte, it must "enter an order describing the specific conduct that appears to violate subdivision (b) and directing an attorney, law firm, or party to show cause why it has not violated subdivision (b) with respect thereto." * * * In this case, the court indicated that it was imposing sanctions in response to YRC's request and did not state that it was imposing sanctions on Hadges sua sponte. We doubt that sua sponte sanctions would have been justified here. The advisory committee note on the 1993 amendment specifically states that such sanctions "will ordinarily be [imposed] only in situations that are akin to a contempt of court." Hadges's conduct did not rise to that level.

Thus, under all the circumstances, particularly the failure to afford Hadges the 21–day safe-harbor period provided by revised Rule 11, we believe that the sanction of Hadges should be reversed.

2. *Kunstler's censure*

Like Hadges, Kunstler did not receive the benefit of the safe-harbor period. The district court imposed sanctions on Kunstler for failing to adequately investigate the truth of Hadges's representations prior to submitting them to the court and for failing to disclose that Hadges had brought an action against YRC in New York state court. Kunstler argues that the court's censure of him was an abuse of discretion because the court was motivated by a personal or political animus against him and because his conduct was not sufficiently egregious to justify imposition of sanctions.

In our decisions concerning the former version of Rule 11 we have had occasion to address the reasonableness of an attorney's reliance on information provided by a client. In *Kamen v. American Tel. & Tel. Co.,* 791 F.2d 1006 (2d Cir.1986), the plaintiff brought suit against her employer and supervisors under the Rehabilitation Act of 1973 and state law. Employers are not liable under the Rehabilitation Act unless they receive "[f]ederal financial assistance." 29 U.S.C. § 794. The employer sent letters to the plaintiff's attorney asserting that it did not receive federal financial assistance, but her attorney persisted in prosecuting the Rehabilitation Act suit. The district court agreed with the employer and dismissed the claims. Although plaintiff's attorney had submitted an affirmation stating that his client had advised him that the employer received federal grants, the district court imposed sanctions. We found that the district court abused its discretion because the attorney's reliance on his client's statements was reasonable. * * *

A few years later, we relied on *Kamen* in holding that "[a]n attorney is entitled to rely on his or her client's statements as to factual claims when those statements are objectively reasonable." *Calloway v. Marvel Entertainment Group,* 854 F.2d 1452, 1470 (2d Cir.1988), rev'd in part on other grounds sub nom. *Pavelic & LeFlore v. Marvel Entertainment Group,* 493 U.S. 120, 110 S.Ct. 456, 107 L.Ed.2d 438 (1989). This interpretation is in keeping with the advisory committee notes on former Rule 11, which indicates that the reasonableness of an inquiry depends upon the surrounding circumstances, including

> such factors as how much time for investigation was available to the signer; whether he had to rely on a client for information as to the facts underlying the pleading ...; or whether he depended on forwarding counsel or another member of the bar.

Advisory committee note on 1983 amendment to Fed.R.Civ.P. 11.

In *Calloway,* at least one of the plaintiff's claims "was never supported by any evidence at any stage of the proceeding," and we affirmed the district court's imposition of sanctions. * * * However, we went on to set forth a procedure for district courts to follow in analyzing whether an attorney has conducted a reasonable inquiry into the facts underlying a party's position.

> In considering sanctions regarding a factual claim, the initial focus of the district court should be on whether an objectively reasonable evidentiary basis for the claim was demonstrated in pretrial proceedings or at trial. Where such a basis was shown, no inquiry into the adequacy of the attorney's pre-filing investigation is necessary.

* * *

The new version of Rule 11 makes it even clearer that an attorney is entitled to rely on the objectively reasonable representations of the client. No longer are attorneys required to certify that their representations are "well grounded in fact." * * * The current version of the Rule requires only that an attorney conduct "an inquiry reasonable under the circumstances" into whether "factual contentions have evidentiary support." * * * Thus, the new version of Rule 11 is in keeping with the emphasis in *Calloway* on looking to the record before imposing sanctions.

In its first sanction decision in April 1994, the district court here stated:

> With respect to plaintiff's counsel, William M. Kunstler, the situation is not quite as clear. There is nothing to indicate that, on the serious factual misrepresentations made in plaintiff's papers, Mr. Kunstler had independent knowledge of their falsity. However, it is equally clear that he made no attempt to verify the truth of the plaintiff's representations prior to submitting them to the court.

Apparently, the district court did not focus, as Rule 11 now requires, on whether the pretrial proceedings provided "evidentiary support" for the factual misrepresentations with which the court was concerned.

It is clear that the record before the district court contained evidentiary support for Kunstler's incorrect statements. As to the scratching incident, the record included a sworn statement by Hadges describing an October 1989 incident in which he claimed to have been scratched from driving the horse "Me Gotta Bret." A scratch sheet, which did not reveal the year in which it was made out, was also part of the record. Kunstler later submitted an affidavit admitting the error and stating that he had no idea that the 1989 date was wrong. He further maintained that regardless of its date, the scratch sheet was relevant to show collaboration between the Racing Board and YRC in 1987, which would subject the latter to § 1983 liability. Moreover, it appears to be undisputed that most of the evidence YRC produced to persuade the court that the event had taken place in 1987 was within its possession, not Hadges's. See *Kamen*, 791 F.2d at 1012 (noting reasonableness of relying on client representations where "the relevant information [is] largely in the control of the defendants").

We also believe that the record contained evidentiary support for the claim that Hadges had not worked for four years. At the time the district court granted YRC summary judgment in Hadges's Rule 60(b) action, it had before it Hadges's affidavit asserting that he had written to racetrack General Managers asking for driving privileges and had not received any replies. The record also contained attorney Faraldo's affidavit asserting that Hadges had followed his advice in writing these letters. Moreover, Kunstler represented Hadges in the Meadowlands suit in which Meadowlands admitted banning Hadges based upon the YRC ban. We believe that in light of his familiarity with the Meadowlands litigation and the sworn statements of his client and another attorney, Kunstler had sufficient evidence to support a belief that Hadges had not participated in harness horseracing in New York since the YRC ban. * * *

The district court also believed that censure of Kunstler was justified because "he had to be aware of the recent state court litigation, still on appeal, but made no mention of it in his initial papers." Kunstler concedes that he was aware of this litigation but maintains that he did not believe that it was necessary to bring the proceedings to the court's attention because the New York Supreme Court had not ruled on the merits of the state law blackballing claim. As noted above, we agree with the view that the state court opinion was not a decision on the merits of that issue. Even if it were, there would be no tactical advantage in not mentioning the state court ruling to the district court since YRC was a party to both actions (indeed, it was represented by the same law firm and the same attorney in both actions) and could be expected to inform the district court of the state court action if it were helpful.

Moreover, the portion of the court's opinion in the Rule 60(b) action that listed the possible bases for imposition of sanctions omitted any reference to Kunstler's nondisclosure of the state court action. Rule 11 specifically requires that those facing sanctions receive adequate notice and the opportunity to respond. * * * Although YRC had requested sanctions on this ground, as discussed above, that request was procedurally improper. Thus, although Kunstler would have been wiser to alert the court to the state court proceedings, the nondisclosure was not a proper ground for sanctioning him.

* * *

Finally, the remarks of the district court, which we have quoted in substantial part above, contribute to our conclusion that the sanction of Kunstler was unjustified. These remarks have the appearance of a personal attack against Kunstler, and perhaps more broadly, against activist attorneys who represent unpopular clients or causes. We find the court's criticism of Kunstler's law partner, Ronald L. Kuby, for his activities in *another* case, especially unwarranted. For all these reasons, we reverse the imposition of the sanction of censure on Kunstler.

* * *

Notes and Questions

1.   Compare the *Hadges* court's definition of what is reasonable to that of the Supreme Court (before the 1993 amendment) in BUSINESS GUIDES, INC. v. CHROMATIC COMMUNICATIONS ENTERPRISES, INC., 498 U.S. 533, 111 S.Ct. 922, 112 L.Ed.2d 1140 (1991). Business Guides, Inc. sought a temporary restraining order, through its law firm against the publication of a directory by Chromatic Communications Enterprises, Inc., on the ground that Chromatic had copied the listings from the Business Guides, Inc. guide. Business Guides claimed to know of the copying because Chromatic had "reprinted" ten seeded listings, i.e. listings that were deliberately printed incorrectly in order to be able to prove such copying. When the judge's law clerk asked to check the listings, however, Business Guides retracted their claim that three of the ten listings were seeds. The clerk, after calling the numbers, discovered that nine of the ten supposedly incorrect listings were actually valid numbers and thus were not valid proof of copying. Although Chromatic did not in the end pursue sanctions against the law firm because the firm had become insolvent, a magistrate recommended that both Business Guides and the law firm be sanctioned (the firm for not investigating further when the first three listings were retracted by Business Guides) and the Supreme Court upheld the sanctions imposed against Business Guides. The Court equated the standards applicable to attorneys and represented parties and wrote that "*any party* who signs a pleading, motion or other paper * * * [has] an affirmative duty to conduct a reasonable inquiry into the facts and the law before filing." (emphasis added)

2.   Could Kunstler have easily checked the facts of Hadges's work history? What about Hadges? In *Business Guides, Inc.,* the court specifically did not hold

the law firm responsible for the first presentation of the 10 listings because of the rushed nature of a TRO filing. How much effect should outside factors, like shortage of time, have on the imposition of sanctions?

3. If Business Guides had been able to withdraw its application without penalty upon the discovery by the District Court that the listings were valid, or if sanctions had been thrown out for lack of a safe-harbor period, would justice have been better served? In dissenting from the adoption of the 1993 amendment Justice Scalia wrote:

> The proposed revision would render the Rule toothless, by allowing judges to dispense with sanction, by disfavoring compensation for litigation expenses, and by providing a 21–day "safe harbor". * * * The Rules should be solicitous of the abused (the courts and the opposing party), and not of the abuser. Under the revised Rule, parties will be able to file thoughtless, reckless, and harassing pleadings, secure in the knowledge that they have nothing to lose: If objection is raised, they can retreat without penalty. The proposed revision contradicts what this court said only three years ago: "Baseless filing puts the machinery of justice in motion, burdening courts and individuals alike with needless expense and delay." Cooter & Gell v. Hartmarx Corp., 496 U.S. 384, 398 (1990).

Order of the Supreme Court Amending the Federal Rules of Civil Procedure (April 22, 1993), reprinted in 146 F.R.D. 404, 507 (1993) (Scalia, J., dissenting). Do you agree?

4. Prior to the 1993 amendments, the Supreme Court ruled that Rule 11 did not permit sanctions to be imposed on an individual attorney's law firm on whose behalf he signed the papers. PAVELIC & LeFLORE v. MARVEL ENTERTAINMENT GROUP, 493 U.S. 120, 110 S.Ct. 456, 107 L.Ed.2d 438 (1989). Writing for the majority, Justice Scalia argued that such sanctions would not further deterrence. Justice Marshall in a lone dissent claimed it was "unwise" to limit the trial judge's options. Since the amendment generally lessened the sanctions imposed for violations, why do you think Rule 11 was broadened to include the law firms of the signing lawyers?

5. In *Business Guides,* the District Court raised Rule 11 *sua sponte.* May a nonparty seek sanctions under Rule 11? A nonparty witness was permitted to make a Rule 11 motion in Port Drum Co. v. Umphrey, 852 F.2d 148, 150–51 & nn. 2–3 (5th Cir.1988). Under what circumstances is this appropriate? What if a party and his counsel make false allegations about a nonparty? In New York News, Inc. v. Kheel, 972 F.2d 482 (2d Cir.1992), the Court of Appeals ruled that "Kheel as a non-party and a non-participant could not move for sanctions unless he satisfied the intervention requirements of Rule 24." Should a person be allowed to intervene to protect his reputation or the integrity of the judicial process?

6. The 1993 amendment limited the sanctions imposed by a court "to what is sufficient to deter repetition of such conduct or comparable conduct by others similarly situated. * * * [A]ction[s] may consist of, or include, directives of a nonmonetary nature, an order to pay penalty into court, or, * * * if warranted for effective deterrence, an order directing payment to the movant of some or all of the reasonable attorney's fees and other expenses incurred as a direct result of the violation." Rule 11(c)(2). This language was meant to change the presumption of monetary damages that had come to exist under the 1983 rule: "[t]he court, upon motion or upon its own initiative, shall impose * * * an appropriate sanction, which may include an order to pay to the other party or parties the amount of the

reasonable expenses incurred because of the filing of the pleading, motion, or other paper, including a reasonable attorney's fee." The distinction, and change in philosophy, is discussed if not explicitly acted upon in Kirk Capital Corp. v. Bailey, 16 F.3d 1485 (8th Cir.1994). Courts have imposed non-monetary sanctions, including requiring the errant attorney to circulate the court's opinion finding him in violation of Rule 11 to every member of his firm; suspension or disbarment from practice; judicial reprimands in open court or through publication of a critical opinion; or requiring him to take continuing legal education courses.

7.   How extensive an inquiry into the law underlying a cause of action must an attorney undertake to satisfy the Rule's requirement that the claim is "warranted by existing law"? The District Court in GOLDEN EAGLE DISTRIBUTING CORP. v. BURROUGHS CORP., 103 F.R.D. 124 (N.D.Cal.1984), reversed 801 F.2d 1531 (9th Cir.1986), rehearing denied with a dissenting opinion 809 F.2d 584 (9th Cir.1987), examined the Model Rules of Professional Conduct and explained that:

> A court has a right to expect that counsel will state the controlling law fairly and fully; indeed, unless that is done the court cannot perform its task properly. A lawyer must not misstate the law, fail to disclose adverse authority (not disclosed by his opponent), or omit facts critical to the application of the rule of law relied on.

Id. at 127.

In *Golden Eagle,* the plaintiff's counsel had cited a 1965 California Supreme Court case supporting its argument and had not cited a 1979 California Supreme Court opinion that was inconsistent with the 1965 case. Counsel distinguished the later case in its reply brief after it had been cited by the opposition, arguing that the 1965 case had not been overruled. Counsel did not address two intermediate court opinions that discussed the effect of the 1979 opinion on the 1965 opinion.

The District Court held that Rule 11 sanctions were appropriate for failure to cite adverse authority. The court noted that "as early as February 1984, Shepard lists [one of the intermediate court cases] under [the 1965 case] as 'distinguished'" and suggested that therefore counsel should have been aware of the case and should have cited it as adverse authority.

On appeal, the Ninth Circuit unanimously reversed. The court conceded that Rule 11 was designed to create an affirmative duty of investigation, both as to law and as to fact, before motions are filed. But the court went on to say that, in order to avoid chilling creativity in advocacy, courts should be careful not to hold lawyers to a standard measured by what the judge later decides. Rather, courts should measure the lawyer's performance by an objective standard, applied as of the time the lawyer was making the decision in question.

The Ninth Circuit panel opined that the objective inquiry authorized by Rule 11 does not empower district courts to assess the manner in which motions are presented. The appellate court did not quarrel with the District Court's "salutary admonitions against misstatements of the law, failure to disclose directly adverse authority, or omission of critical facts." 801 F.2d at 1539. But it concluded that Rule 11 does not envision an evaluation under ethical standards of the accuracy of a lawyer's arguments.

8.   In the *Hadges* decision the court noted that Kunstler was not liable for sanctions for not mentioning a connected case because "YRC * * * could be expected to inform the district court of the state court action if it were helpful." Is this too lenient a standard, or is the court's attitude justified in the name of the

adversary system? If the latter, can a lawyer excuse himself for not disclosing possibly relevant facts during discovery by claiming it was the other side's responsibility to find them out?

9. The Private Securities Litigation Reform Act, see Note 4, p. 534, supra, creates sanctions for actions within the ambit of the statute that are similar to the 1983 version of Rule 11. Does it make sense to have tougher sanction rules in certain substantive contexts?

10. For more information on the evolution and effect of Rule 11, see Armour, *Practice Makes Perfect: Judicial Discretion and the 1993 Amendments to Rule 11,* 24 Hofstra L.Rev. 677 (1996); Burbank, *The Transformation of American Civil Procedure: The Example of Rule 11,* 137 U.Pa.L.Rev. 1925 (1989). See generally 5A Wright & Miller, *Federal Practice and Procedure: Civil 2d* §§ 1331–39 (1990) (2001 Pocket Part).

11. Rule 11 is not the only sanctioning provision available to the federal courts. The most notable other provision is 28 U.S.C. § 1927, which gives courts authority to impose excess costs against attorneys who have "unreasonably and vexatiously" increased the costs of litigation by "multipl[ying] the proceeding." However, because the statute requires a determination of bad faith, it rarely is invoked. See Salovaara v. Eckert, 222 F.3d 19, 35 (2d Cir.2000). Other statutes authorize courts in specific kinds of actions to award attorney's fees to a prevailing defendant if the plaintiff's claim is frivolous, unreasonable, or ground-less. See, e.g., § 706(k) of Title VII of the Civil Rights Act of 1964, 42 U.S.C. § 2000e–5(k) (1988) (employment discrimination actions).

Courts also have an "inherent power" to sanction parties. In CHAMBERS v. NASCO, INC., 501 U.S. 32, 111 S.Ct. 2123, 115 L.Ed.2d 27 (1991), the Supreme Court held, 5–4, in an opinion by Justice White, that the District Court had properly used its "inherent power" to sanction a party's bad-faith conduct. Justice White explained that federal courts have an "inherent power" to punish conduct that abuses the judicial process and have discretion in fashioning an appropriate sanction. He reasoned that neither Section 1927, Rule 11, nor other Federal Rules displace a court's inherent power to impose attorney's fees as a sanction for bad-faith conduct. The plaintiff Chambers had engaged in bad-faith conduct that violated Rule 11, but much of his bad-faith conduct was outside the scope of Rule 11 because it did not involve filing papers with the court. Section 1927 was inappropriate because it only applies to attorneys. Thus, it was proper for the District Court to use its inherent power to sanction all of Chamber's conduct, because to apply Rule 11 and the other rules separately would "foster extensive and needless satellite litigation." Justice Kennedy dissented and severely criticized the ruling: "Upon a finding of bad faith, courts may now ignore any and all textual limitations on sanctioning power. By inviting district courts to rely on inherent authority as a substitute for attention to the careful distinctions con-tained in the rules and statutes, today's decision will render these sources of authority superfluous in many instances." Id. at 67, 111 S.Ct. at 2144, 115 L.Ed.2d at 59.

Chapter 9

JOINDER OF CLAIMS AND PARTIES: EXPANDING THE SCOPE OF THE CIVIL ACTION

In the simplest paradigm form of a lawsuit, a single plaintiff asserts a single cause of action against a single defendant. Although the equity courts were more flexible, the common-law courts, with their emphasis on the unitary civil action, rarely deviated from this model and developed rules relating to joinder along strict and formalistic lines. See generally Blume, *A Rational Theory for Joinder of Causes of Action and Defences, and for the Use of Counterclaims*, 26 Mich.L.Rev. 1 (1927); Sunderland, *Joinder of Actions*, 18 Mich.L.Rev. 571 (1920). As the complexity of society increased and more intricate disputes were generated, the need for obviating piecemeal litigation became widely recognized. The most obvious method of accomplishing this objective was by expanding the scope of civil actions by permitting the joinder of claims and parties. This Chapter will explore the various forms that this expansion has taken.

SECTION A. JOINDER OF CLAIMS

HARRIS v. AVERY

Supreme Court of Kansas, 1869.
5 Kan. 146.

VALENTINE, J. This action was brought in the court below by Avery * * *. The petition states two causes of action,—false imprisonment and slander,— and alleges that both arose out of the same transaction. Harris demurred to this petition, on the ground "that it appears on the face of the petition that several causes of action are improperly joined." The district court overruled the demurrer, and this ruling is assigned as error. The petition shows that the two causes of action are founded upon the following facts: Harris met Avery in the city of Fort Scott, and, in the presence of several other persons, called Avery a thief; said he had a stolen horse; took the horse from Avery, and kept the horse for four or five days; arrested Avery, and confined him in the county jail with felons four or five days. We think these facts, as detailed in the petition, constitute only one transaction, * * * and whether they constitute more than one cause of action, under our Code practice, may be questionable.

* * * But as we have not been asked to decide the latter question, we will pass it over and treat the case as though the facts stated constitute two causes of action.

Section 89 of the Code (Comp.Laws, 138,) provides "that the plaintiff may unite several causes of action in the same petition, whether they be such as have heretofore been denominated legal or equitable, or both, when they are included in either one of the following classes: First, *the same transaction* or transactions connected with the same subject of action." This differs in many respects from the common-law rule. At common law, "where the same form of action may be adopted for several distinct injuries, the plaintiff may, in general, proceed for all in one action, though the several rights affected were derived from different titles," (1 Chit.Pl. 201; Tidd, Pr. 11;) and different forms of action may be united, "where the same plea may be pleaded and the same judgment given on all the counts of the declaration, or whenever the counts are of the same nature, and the same judgment is to be given on them, although the pleas be different." 1 Chit.Pl. 200.

In the action at bar, if Harris had arrested Avery on a warrant, which Harris had maliciously and without probable cause obtained from a court of competent jurisdiction, and had also converted the horse to his own use, then at common law Avery would have had three distinct causes of action, which he could unite in one suit: *First,* an action for the false imprisonment or malicious prosecution; *second,* an action of slander for the words spoken; and, *third,* an action of trover for the conversion of the horse. These may all be united in an action on the case, * * * trover being a species of case. Avery might, also, at common law unite with these causes of action as many other causes of action as he might have, for malicious prosecution, slander, trover, criminal conversation, nuisance, and other causes of action which may be sued in an action on the case, and although they each may have arisen out of a different transaction, and at a different time, and in a different place. But if Harris arrested Avery without any process—which was the fact in this case— and in an entirely irregular manner, then the two causes of action for false imprisonment and slander could not at common law be united, as the first would have to be sued in an action of trespass and the second in an action on the case, and it would make no difference whether they both arose out of the same transaction or not. Our Code has abolished all the common-law forms of action * * *. It follows the rules of equity more closely than it does those of the common law, one object seeming to be to avoid the multiplicity of suits, and to settle in one action, as equity did, as far as practicable, the whole subject-matter of a controversy. * * * It is probably true that the two causes of action for false imprisonment and slander cannot, under our Code, be united, unless both arise out of the same transaction, one being an injury to the person and the other being an injury to the character; but we do not know of any reason why they should not be united when both do arise out of the same transaction. * * *

The order of the district court overruling the demurrer to the petition is affirmed.

Notes and Questions

1. The typical code provision authorized joinder of claims when they fell within one of several statutory classes, which generally included the following:

(a) Contracts, express or implied;

(b) Injuries to the person;

(c) Injuries to character;

(d) Injuries to property;

(e) Actions to recover real property, with or without damages;

(f) Actions to recover chattels, with or without damages; and

(g) Actions arising out of the same transaction or transactions connected with the same subject of the action.

In what ways do these categories differ from the use of the common-law forms of action as guidelines for the joinder of claims? What is the logic of each of these classes? Is the code approach to joinder of claims as described in *Harris* any less formalistic than the common-law theory? Joinder at common law and under the codes is discussed in Clark, *Code Pleading* §§ 68–70 (2d ed. 1947); Blume, *A Rational Theory for Joinder of Causes of Action and Defences, and for the Use of Counterclaims*, 26 Mich.L.Rev. 1 (1927).

2. Read Federal Rule 18. Note that it removes all obstacles to joinder of claims and permits the joinder of both legal and equitable actions; the only restriction on the claims that may be joined is imposed by subject-matter jurisdiction requirements. What are the advantages of permitting liberal joinder of claims? Are there any disadvantages? In SPORN v. HUDSON TRANSIT LINES, 265 App.Div. 360, 38 N.Y.S.2d 512 (1st Dep't 1942), the court had before it an attempt to join five causes of action for negligence resulting in personal injuries with one cause of action for malicious prosecution. It stated:

> The causes of action for negligence and for malicious prosecution are essentially different in nature; each type involves different rules of law; each requires different testimony to establish a case and each carries a different measure of damages. If a single jury were to try both types of action at the one time, there is a strong likelihood that confusion would exist in the minds of the jurors as to the rules of law to be applied to the respective actions and they would undoubtedly entertain much difficulty in applying the various parts of testimony introduced to the appropriate cause of action. There is nothing in common to be found in the two types of action.

> Moreover, it is clear that if these actions were tried together jurors might, quite naturally, engender a prejudice against the appellant in the negligence actions if the proof adduced in the malicious prosecution action were to show that, in causing the arrest of one of the respondents for reckless driving, there was, as alleged in the complaint, malice and want of probable cause. In such a situation it might well be that a jury would be unduly liberal in assessing damages under the causes of action in negligence and that they might visit upon appellant in those actions damages which were punitive rather than compensatory.

> In the interest of justice, we think there should be a severance. * * * The avoidance of a multiplicity of suits is much to be desired, but where, as here,

the enforcement of such a rule might entail prejudice to appellant's substantial rights and would tend to confuse the jury, the divergent causes of action should be severed.

Id. at 361–62, 38 N.Y.S.2d at 514. Would the result in *Sporn* have been different if the action had been brought in a federal court? Read Federal Rule 42. Does the availability of severance of claims eliminate all of the objections to permitting unrestricted joinder of claims as an initial matter? To what extent does the court's power to sever claims prevent the system from achieving the objectives of a liberal joinder rule?

3. Note that Federal Rule 18 only describes the claims that a plaintiff may assert against defendant; it does not require plaintiff to join all claims in a single action. Should there be compulsory joinder of all related claims existing between the litigants? See Friedenthal, *Joinder of Claims, Counterclaims and Cross–Complaints: Suggested Revision of the California Provisions*, 23 Stan.L.Rev. 1, 11–17 (1970). Michigan's joinder provision, Michigan Court Rule 2.203(A), which is in the Supplement following Federal Rule 18, is unusual in that it provides for the compulsory joinder of certain claims. See generally Honigman & Hawkins, *Michigan Court Rules Annotated*, Rule 203, Author's Comment; Meisenholder, *Joinder of Claims and Parties—The New Michigan Pre–Trial Procedural Rules—Models For Other States?*, 61 Mich.L.Rev. 1389, 1417 (1963).

4. Even though the joinder of claims by plaintiffs in the federal courts is permissive, the principles of res judicata, which prohibit the splitting of a cause of action into two or more lawsuits, often have the effect of compelling plaintiff to join all related claims. See generally Blume, *Required Joinder of Claims*, 45 Mich.L.Rev. 797 (1947). Thus, for example, if A and B are involved in an automobile accident in which A suffers both bodily injury and damage to her automobile, the risk of res judicata typically will lead A to join both claims in one action, although Federal Rule 18 does not require her to do so. See pp. 1225–31, infra.

SECTION B. ADDITION OF CLAIMS

1. COUNTERCLAIMS

The counterclaim in its present form did not exist at common law, although it has well-recognized precursors in set-off and recoupment and in equity practice. The philosophy underlying set-off and recoupment was the common sense view that someone should not be compelled to pay one moment what he will be entitled to recover back the next. Judge Clark outlined the development and theory of set-off and recoupment as follows:

> * * * At first * * * [recoupment] was limited to a showing of payment, or of former recovery. Later, recoupment was developed so as to allow a defendant to show for the purpose of reducing the plaintiff's recovery any facts arising out of the transaction sued upon or connected with the subject thereof, which facts might have founded an independent action in favor of the defendant against the plaintiff. * * * It was not necessary that the opposing claims be liquidated, or that they be of the same character; i.e., a claim in "tort" could be set off against one in "contract." It was essential, however, that the claims of both plaintiff and defendant involve the same "subject-matter," or arise out of the "same transaction" * * *.

But where the defendant's claims arose out of a transaction different from that sued upon, the common-law recoupment was unavailable. The defendant, therefore, was compelled to bring a separate suit in order to satisfy his claim against the plaintiff. Equity, at an early date, relieved the defendant of this hardship by allowing a set-off of claims [growing out of a transaction different from the plaintiff's claim] * * *.

Under the set-off * * *, it was necessary that the demands either be liquidated, or arise out of contract or judgment. It was necessary, also, that the demands be due the defendant in his own right against the plaintiff, or his assignor, and be not already barred by the statute of limitations * * *.

Clark, *Code Pleading* § 100, at 634–36 (2d ed. 1947). See also Waterman, *Set-Off, Recoupment and Counterclaim* §§ 302–03 (2d ed. 1872). The utility of the common-law recoupment and set-off practice was limited because in the former situation defendant was not permitted to recover affirmative relief; the claim could be used only to reduce or "net out" plaintiff's recovery. In the case of set-off the claim had to be for a liquidated amount.

The movement for procedural reform in the mid-nineteenth century gave passing attention to the problem of defendant's claims against plaintiff; the original New York Field Code of 1848 made no provision for counterclaims. Amendments in 1852 corrected this omission and permitted as a counterclaim:

1. A cause of action arising out of the contract or transaction set forth in the complaint, as the foundation of the plaintiff's claim, or connected with the subject of the action; and

2. In an action arising on contract, any other cause of action arising on contract, and existing at the commencement of the action.

See Blume, *A Rational Theory for Joinder of Causes of Action and Defences, and for the Use of Counterclaims,* 26 Mich.L.Rev. 1, 48 (1927).

The English Judicature Act of 1873 eliminated the historic limitations on defendant's ability to assert claims against plaintiff. Then, at the beginning of this century, a number of states amended their codes to adopt the English practice. Note that the text of Federal Rule 13(a) goes beyond the English and code practice by *requiring* defendant to assert certain claims. Is this step desirable? Why? See generally Kennedy, *Counterclaims Under Federal Rule 13,* 11 Houston L.Rev. 255 (1974).

———

Read Federal Rules of Civil Procedure 13(a)–(f) and the accompanying material in the Supplement.

———

UNITED STATES v. HEYWARD–ROBINSON CO.

United States Court of Appeals, Second Circuit, 1970.
430 F.2d 1077.

FREDERICK VAN PELT BRYAN, DISTRICT JUDGE.*

This is an appeal from a judgment for the plaintiff entered in the United States District Court for the District of Connecticut * * *.

The action involves two subcontracts for excavation work between D'Agostino Excavators, Inc. (D'Agostino) and The Heyward–Robinson Company, Inc. (Heyward) as prime contractor on two construction jobs in Connecticut. One of the prime contracts, for the construction of barracks at the Naval Submarine Base in New London, Groton, was with the federal government (the Navy job). The other, a non-federal job, was for the construction of a plant for Stelma, Inc. at Stamford (the Stelma job).

D'Agostino brought this action against Heyward and its surety, Maryland Casualty Company (Maryland) under the Miller Act * * * to recover payments alleged to be due on the Navy job. Heyward answered, denying liability on the Navy job and counterclaiming for alleged overpayments and extra costs of completing both the Navy job and the Stelma job. In reply, D'Agostino denied liability on the Heyward counterclaims and interposed a reply counterclaim to recover from Heyward monies alleged to be due on the Stelma job.

At the trial, the two subcontracts in suit were treated together. D'Agostino claimed that Heyward had breached both subcontracts by failing to make progress payments as required and that substantial sums were owing to it from Heyward on both jobs. Heyward claimed that D'Agostino had breached both subcontracts by permitting its compensation and employee liability insurance to lapse; that, as a result, Heyward on October 19, 1965 had terminated both; and that D'Agostino was liable for overpayments and costs of completion on both.

The issue as to whether Heyward had breached the subcontracts prior to October 19, 1965, when Heyward claimed to have terminated them, was submitted to the jury as a special question. The jury found that Heyward had breached the subcontracts prior to that date.

After amendment of the complaint by D'Agostino to allege a claim in quantum meruit for the work performed on both jobs, special questions then were submitted to the jury as to the reasonable value of the work performed by D'Agostino on each project and the net amount owed by Heyward to D'Agostino on both. The jury found, in answer to these questions, that the net amount owed by Heyward to D'Agostino on both jobs was $63,988.36. Judgment against Heyward was rendered accordingly. Under a formula agreed to by the parties, it was determined that the amount due to D'Agostino on the Navy job was $40,771.46 and judgment was entered against Maryland in that sum.

* * *

I.

Appellants' initial contention is that the District Court had no jurisdiction over the counterclaims on the Stelma job. They therefore contend that

_____
* Of the Southern District of New York, sitting by designation.

the Stelma claims must be dismissed and that since D'Agostino's claims on the Navy and Stelma jobs were presented to the jury as inseparable, the judgment below must be reversed.

Appellants urge that the Stelma counterclaims are not compulsory counterclaims over which the federal court acquired jurisdiction ancillary to the jurisdiction which it had over D'Agostino's Miller Act claim stated in the complaint. They say that these are permissive counterclaims over which the court had no ancillary jurisdiction and which lacked the required independent basis of federal jurisdiction.

This jurisdictional issue is raised for the first time in this Court. In the Court below appellants affirmatively urged that the Stelma counterclaims were compulsory. Nevertheless, it is well settled that lack of federal jurisdiction may be raised for the first time on appeal, even by a party who originally asserted that jurisdiction existed or by the court sua sponte. * * * We turn, then, to the jurisdictional issue.

It is apparent from the record that there is no independent basis of federal jurisdiction over the Stelma counterclaims. Both D'Agostino and Heyward are New York corporations with offices in New York. There is thus no diversity jurisdiction. Clearly there is no jurisdiction under the Miller Act over these counterclaims since the Stelma contract did not involve public work for the federal government.

The question is whether the Stelma counterclaims are compulsory or are permissive. Under the rule in this circuit, if they are permissive there is no Federal jurisdiction over them unless they rest on independent jurisdictional grounds. * * * On the other hand, if they are compulsory counterclaims, they are ancillary to the claim asserted in the complaint and no independent basis of Federal jurisdiction is required * * *.

Under Rule 13(a) Fed.R.Civ.P. a counterclaim is compulsory "if it arises out of the transaction or occurrence that is the subject matter of the opposing party's claim." In United Artists Corp. v. Masterpiece Productions, Inc., 221 F.2d 213 (2d Cir.1955) * * *, Chief Judge Clark said:

> In practice this criterion has been broadly interpreted to require not an absolute identity of factual backgrounds for the two claims, but only a logical relationship between them. Lesnik v. Public Industrials Corp., 2 Cir., 144 F.2d 968, 975, citing and quoting, inter alia, Moore v. New York Cotton Exchange, 270 U.S. 593, 610, 46 S.Ct. 367, 371, 70 L.Ed. 750, thus: " 'Transaction' is a word of flexible meaning. It may comprehend a series of many occurrences, depending not so much upon the immediateness of their connection as upon their logical relationship." * * *

Thus " * * * courts should give the phrase 'transaction or occurrence that is the subject matter' of the suit a broad realistic interpretation in the interest of avoiding a multiplicity of suits." * * * As the Supreme Court [has] said * * *:

> The requirement that counterclaims arising out of the same transaction or occurrence as the opposing party's claim "shall" be stated in the pleadings was designed to prevent multiplicity of actions and to achieve

resolution in a single lawsuit of all disputes arising out of common matters. * * *

In the case at bar the counterclaims were compulsory within the meaning of Rule 13(a). There was such a close and logical relationship between the claims on the Navy and Stelma jobs that the Stelma counterclaims arose out of the same "transaction or occurrence" as those terms are now broadly defined. Both subcontracts were entered into by the same parties for the same type of work and carried on during substantially the same period. Heyward had the right to terminate both subcontracts in the event of a breach by D'Agostino of either. Heyward also had the right to withhold monies due on one to apply against any damages suffered on the other. Progress payments made by Heyward were not allocated as between jobs and were made on a lump sum basis for both as though for a single account.

A single insurance policy covered both jobs. The letters of Heyward to D'Agostino of October 8 and 19, 1965 threatening termination and terminating both jobs, allegedly because of the cancellation by D'Agostino of this joint insurance coverage and failure to properly man both projects, treated both jobs together. These letters formed the basis of one of Heyward's major claims at the trial.

The controversy between the parties which gave rise to this litigation was with respect to both jobs and arose from occurrences affecting both. Indeed, it would seem to have been impossible for Heyward to have fully litigated the claims against it on the Navy job without including the Stelma job, because the payments it made to D'Agostino could not be allocated between the two jobs.

As the appellants themselves point out in their brief, the "Stelma and Navy claims were so interwoven at the trial that they are now absolutely incapable of separation." The proof as to payments and alleged defaults in payments was made without any differentiation between the two claims and neither of the parties was able to offer any evidence of apportionment. Finally, the evidence as to the breaches of contract claimed by the respective parties related in the main to both contracts rather than to one or the other.

The jurisdictional question so belatedly raised by the appellants must be viewed in light of the record as a whole. So viewed, it is plain that the Stelma counterclaims bare [sic] a logical and immediate relationship to the claims on the Navy job. Thus they arose out of the "transaction or occurrence which is the subject matter" of the suit instituted by D'Agostino on the Navy job and are compulsory counterclaims under Rule 13(a). The Stelma counterclaims were thus ancillary to the claims asserted in the complaint over which the Federal Court had acquired jurisdiction under the Miller Act, and there is jurisdiction over them. * * * To require that the closely related Navy and Stelma claims must be litigated separately would result in fragmentation of litigation and multiplicity of suits contrary to one of the major purposes of Rule 13(a). * * *

* * *

The judgment below is affirmed.

FRIENDLY, CIRCUIT JUDGE (concurring).

I cannot agree that, as maintained in Part I of the majority opinion, the counterclaim relating to the Stelma job was compulsory under F.R.Civ.P. 13(a). Of course, it is tempting to stretch a point when a jurisdictional objection is so belatedly raised by the very party who clamored for the exercise of jurisdiction until the decision went against it. But we must consider the question as if Heyward had not pleaded the Stelma counterclaim and proceeded to sue D'Agostino in some other court for failure to perform that subcontract, and D'Agostino then claimed that Heyward's failure to bring the Stelma transaction into this Miller Act suit barred the later action. Despite the desirability of requiring that all claims which in fact arise "out of the transaction or occurrence that is the subject of the opposing party's claim" be litigated in a single action, courts must be wary of extending these words in a way that could cause unexpectedly harsh results.

Even on a liberal notion of "logical relation," * * * I am unable to perceive how Heyward's claim for breach of the Stelma subcontract arose "out of the transaction or occurrence" to wit, the Navy subcontract, that was the subject matter of D'Agostino's Miller Act claim. Whatever historical interest there may be in the circumstances that the two subcontracts were entered into between the same parties for the same type of work and were carried on during substantially the same period, these facts seem to me to be lacking in legal significance. So likewise do D'Agostino's having furnished a single insurance policy to cover both jobs and Heyward's having cancelled the subcontracts in one letter rather than two. The boiler-plate in each subcontract, whereby "if one or more other contracts, now or hereafter, exist between the parties," a breach of any such contract by D'Agostino might, at Heyward's option be considered a breach of the contract at issue and Heyward might terminate any or all contracts so breached and withhold moneys due on any contract and apply these to damages on any other, might meet the test if Heyward had availed itself of these rights, but it did not.

All that is left is that, as the trial proceeded, it turned out that some of Heyward's payments were not earmarked as between the two subcontracts. However, the determination whether a counterclaim is compulsory must be made at the pleading stage. The complaint was specific on how much Heyward owed on the Navy subcontract, and the counterclaims were equally so on how much D'Agostino owed for failure to complete this and how much it owed for failure to complete the Stelma subcontract. To say that the failure to earmark some payments made it impossible to try the claims separately ignores the law on application of payments. If Heyward did not specify the application of its payments, as it could, and D'Agostino had not made an application of them, as it could in default of specification by Heyward, the court would do this. * * *

* * *

[Although Judge Friendly disagreed with the majority's holding that the counterclaims were compulsory, he nevertheless argued that they should not be dismissed on the ground that permissive counterclaims need not have an independent jurisdictional basis.]

GREAT LAKES RUBBER CORP.
v. HERBERT COOPER CO.

United States Court of Appeals, Third Circuit, 1961.
286 F.2d 631.

BIGGS, CHIEF JUDGE. This is an appeal from an order of the court below dismissing a counterclaim of Great Lakes Rubber Corporation (Great Lakes), made against Herbert Cooper Co., Inc. (Cooper), on the ground that the court lacked jurisdiction of the subject matter of the counterclaim. * * *

On May 12, 1959, Great Lakes filed an amended complaint naming Cooper as defendant. Jurisdiction was allegedly based on diversity. The allegations fall roughly into three groups. First, it was alleged that Howard Cooper and Joseph Herbert had been employed by Great Lakes * * * and that they left Great Lakes' employ taking with them certain information relating to the flexible rubber tubing manufactured by Great Lakes, and lists disclosing Great Lakes' customers; that shortly thereafter they, with others, founded Cooper; that Cooper competed for and obtained customers that were, until then, customers of Great Lakes; and, that Cooper's "offering to sell, and manufacturing and selling flexible tubing made and offered for sale with utilization of knowledge and information acquired while these men [Cooper and Herbert] were in a fiduciary relationship with plaintiff" constituted "acts of unfair competition and unfair business practices."

* * * [The second allegation was that Cooper had obtained government contracts for tubing of a type that would infringe on patents licensed to Great Lakes, and that Cooper had been able to submit the lowest bid for these contracts because it was not paying patent royalties. Great Lakes claimed that Cooper "is and has been in an unfair competitive position" because of its operations as an "unlicensed infringer."]

Third, it was alleged that Cooper implied to customers of Great Lakes that the quality of the tubing manufactured by Great Lakes was inferior; that Cooper represented to the United States Air Force that no validly patented ideas, processes or inventions held by others would be utilized in fulfilling its contracts for flexible tubing, that their representations were false; and, that these acts have damaged and imminently threaten Great Lakes' business operations.

Great Lakes referred to various contracts with the United States Army and Air Force which it alleged it had failed to obtain but which Cooper did obtain, and further specified an Air Force contract on which it was then being underbid by Cooper and which it would not obtain if Cooper's acts of "unfair competition" were not enjoined. Great Lakes asked for relief in the form of an injunction, an accounting for profits and an award of damages.

On June 23, 1959, Cooper filed an answer to the amended complaint and a counterclaim which asserted that Great Lakes, Fred T. and Robert E. Roberts, * * * and various * * * companies and individuals "have been and still are * * * conspiring together and attempting both individually and in concert to restrain and monopolize interstate commerce" in violation of Sections 1 and 2 of the Sherman Act, 15 U.S.C.A. §§ 1 and 2. The conspiracy was alleged to include, without limitation, the making of false representations to certain of Cooper's material suppliers that they were guilty of contributory infringement when the conspirators knew that the supplied items were staple articles of commerce and could not be the basis of such liability.

The counterclaim also alleged, and this is of prime importance in the instant case, "the bringing of a series of unjustified lawsuits by the conspirators in bad faith and without color of right with the sole object of harassing and preventing defendant from competing in the manufacture and sale of flexible hose and thus eliminating defendant as a competitor, including this action [i.e., the action brought by the filing of the amended complaint by Great Lakes] * * *." The counterclaim asked treble damages, costs and attorneys' fees.

On July 2, 1959, Cooper moved to dismiss Great Lakes' amended complaint on the ground that there was no diversity of citizenship between the parties. By order dated December 9, 1959, the court granted Cooper's motion to dismiss. Jurisdiction of Cooper's counterclaim was retained on the ground that it had an independent basis of jurisdiction in that it asserted a claim arising under the laws of the United States. No appeal was taken from that order. * * *

On December 28, 1959, Great Lakes filed an answer and a counterclaim to Cooper's counterclaim. Great Lakes' counterclaim repeated in substance the allegations of its amended complaint. The counterclaim is distinguishable from the amended complaint only in that it is more specific and in that it * * * [contained further allegations of misconduct by Cooper].

On January 6, 1960, Cooper moved to dismiss the Great Lakes counterclaim on the ground that the court below lacked jurisdiction of the subject matter. In opposition to this motion Great Lakes contended that the court had ancillary jurisdiction of its counterclaim as a compulsory counterclaim arising out of the same transaction and occurrences that were the subject matter of Cooper's claim arising under the Federal antitrust laws. On May 5, 1960, the court granted Cooper's motion to dismiss on the ground that Great Lakes' counterclaim was not a compulsory counterclaim. This appeal followed.

A federal court has ancillary jurisdiction of the subject matter of a counterclaim if it arises out of the transaction or occurrence that is the subject matter of an opposing party's claim of which the court has jurisdiction. * * * Similarly, a counterclaim that arises out of the transaction or occurrence that is the subject matter of an opposing party's claim is a "compulsory counterclaim" within the meaning of Rule 13(a) of the Federal Rules of Civil Procedure. It is stated frequently that the determination of ancillary jurisdiction of a counterclaim in a federal court must turn on whether the counterclaim is compulsory within the meaning of Rule 13(a). Such a statement of the law relating to ancillary jurisdiction of counterclaims is not intended to suggest that Rule 13(a) extends the jurisdiction of the federal courts to entertain counterclaims for the Federal Rules of Civil Procedure cannot expand the jurisdiction of the United States courts. What is meant is that the issue of the existence of ancillary jurisdiction and the issue as to whether a counterclaim is compulsory are to be answered by the same test. It is not a coincidence that the same considerations that determine whether a counterclaim is compulsory decide also whether the court has ancillary jurisdiction to adjudicate it. The tests are the same because Rule

13(a) and the doctrine of ancillary jurisdiction are designed to abolish the same evil, viz, piecemeal litigation in the federal courts.

We have indicated that a counterclaim is compulsory if it bears a "logical relationship" to an opposing party's claim. Zion v. Sentry Safety Control Corp., 3 Cir., 1958, 258 F.2d 31. * * * The phrase "logical relationship" is given meaning by the purpose of the rule which it was designed to implement. Thus, a counterclaim is logically related to the opposing party's claim where separate trials on each of their respective claims would involve a substantial duplication of effort and time by the parties and the courts. Where multiple claims involve many of the same factual issues, or the same factual and legal issues, or where they are offshoots of the same basic controversy between the parties, fairness and considerations of convenience and of economy require that the counterclaimant be permitted to maintain his cause of action. Indeed the doctrine of *res judicata* compels the counterclaimant to assert his claim in the same suit for it would be barred if asserted separately, subsequently.

Cooper alleges that the claims originally asserted in Great Lakes' amended complaint, reiterated in substance in its counterclaim, are "unjustified" and were brought in "bad faith and without color of right with the sole object of harassing and preventing defendant [Cooper] from competing in the manufacture and sale of flexible hose." These are the only allegations set out by Cooper's counterclaim which demonstrate a relationship within the purview of Rule 13(a) to Great Lakes' amended complaint or counterclaim. But that they do demonstrate a relationship is unquestionable. It is clear that a determination that Cooper's claims that the claims asserted in Great Lakes' amended complaint and reiterated in substance in its counterclaim are harassing will entail an extensive airing of the facts and the law relating to Great Lakes' counterclaim. It follows that the court below was in error in dismissing Great Lakes' counterclaim on the ground that it was permissive. We hold that Great Lakes' counterclaim was a compulsory one within the meaning of Rule 13(a).

* * *

The judgment will be reversed * * *.

Notes and Questions

1. In the years following the adoption of the Federal Rules, there was considerable disagreement as to the wisdom of the compulsory counterclaim. Consider the following arguments:

> Compulsory counterclaim rules may at first blush appear harsh. On their face they are opposed to the dominant trend in procedure today which is to get away from penalizing a party's procedural errors by an adverse judgment against an otherwise meritorious claim. Yet such rules are an important part of the movement to end a multiplicity of litigation, and thus are in the interest of both litigants and the public. Since there is never any need for a party to incur the penalty for failure to counterclaim, and since there are ample remedies for the party who has so acted through inadvertence, the actual working of the rules has not been harsh. Their salutary effect has been had with comparatively little injustice * * *.

Wright, *Estoppel by Rule: The Compulsory Counterclaim Under Modern Pleading,* 38 Minn.L.Rev. 423, 465 (1954).

* * * Certainly a rule of compulsion extended to every allowable counterclaim cannot be regarded as defensible. If a compulsory rule is ever justifiable it is only when the counterclaim operates by way of defense to the principal claim. Just as a defendant may not with impunity withdraw a defense, so we may without violence to the traditional maxim deny him the right to withdraw a counterclaim if this in whole or part is of a defensive nature. * * *

Millar, *Civil Procedure of the Trial Court in Historical Perspective* 138 (1952). Is Professor Millar arguing for a return to common-law recoupment? Are there any strong arguments for going further than he suggests by not making counterclaims compulsory under any circumstances?

2. Section 1367(a) provides for supplemental jurisdiction over claims that are part of "the same case or controversy under Art. III of the Constitution" as the plaintiff's claim. See pp. 308–20, supra. Is "the same case or controversy" a broader definition of relatedness than "transaction and occurrence" under Rule 13(a) and (b)? If it is broader, does Section 1367(a) provide a jurisdictional base for some permissive counterclaims? See Unique Concepts, Inc. v. Manuel, 930 F.2d 573 (7th Cir.1991). See also Solow v. Jenkins, 2000 WL 489667, at *1 (S.D.N.Y. 2000). Section 1367(b) places a limit on plaintiff's seeking supplemental jurisdiction for a claim when subject-matter jurisdiction is based on diversity. Should this limit also apply to a defendant's compulsory counterclaim?

3. In applying Federal Rule 13(a), the critical question is: What constitutes a "transaction or occurrence"? Four tests have been suggested:

(a) Are the issues of fact and law raised by the claim and counterclaim largely the same?

(b) Would res judicata bar a subsequent suit on defendant's claim absent the compulsory counterclaim rule?

(c) Will substantially the same evidence support or refute plaintiff's claim as well as defendant's counterclaim?

(d) Is there any logical relation between the claim and the counterclaim?

The fourth of these tests has been called "the one compelling test of compulsoriness." Do you agree? What are the strengths and weaknesses of each of these tests? See 6 Wright, Miller & Kane, *Federal Practice and Procedure: Civil 2d* § 1410 (1990). For a detailed discussion of the myriad meanings of "transaction," see Kane, *Original Sin and the Transaction in Federal Civil Procedure,* 76 Texas L.Rev. 1723 (1998).

4. The classic definition of "transaction" is found in MOORE v. NEW YORK COTTON EXCHANGE, 270 U.S. 593, 46 S.Ct. 367, 70 L.Ed. 750 (1926). Plaintiff, Moore, sought to compel defendant to install a price quotation ticker in plaintiff's place of business. Defendant counterclaimed for damages, alleging that although plaintiff had been denied permission to use quotations from defendant's exchange, plaintiff "was purloining them and giving them out." In the course of holding defendant's counterclaim compulsory under former Equity Rule 30, the Court said:

* * * "Transaction" is a word of flexible meaning. It may comprehend a series of many occurrences, depending not so much upon the immediateness of their connection as upon their logical relationship. The refusal to furnish the quotations is one of the links in the chain which constitutes the transaction upon which appellant here bases its cause of action. It is an important part of the transaction constituting the subject-matter of the counterclaim. It is the one circumstance without which neither party would have found it necessary to seek relief. Essential facts alleged by appellant enter into and constitute in part the cause of action set forth in the counterclaim. That they are not precisely identical, or that the counterclaim embraces additional allegations, as, for example, that appellant is unlawfully getting the quotations, does not matter. To hold otherwise would be to rob this branch of the rule of all serviceable meaning, since the facts relied upon by the plaintiff rarely, if ever, are in all particulars, the same as those constituting the defendant's counterclaim. * * *

Id. at 610, 46 S.Ct. at 371, 70 L.Ed. at 757.

5. Consider the application of the transaction-or-occurrence test in the following cases. In INTERNATIONAL UNION, UNITED AUTOMOBILE, AIRCRAFT & AGRICULTURAL IMPLEMENT WORKERS v. PIASECKI AIRCRAFT CORP., 241 F.Supp. 385 (D.Del.1965), the union brought suit against an employer for violation of a collective-bargaining agreement. Defendant counterclaimed for damages resulting from a strike by the union. The court said:

* * * Thus, the complaint charges damages resulting to employees by reason of (1) Piasecki's alleged default in making contributions to the insurance program, (2) for the violation of seniority provisions of the contract, (3) lost wages, (4) lost union dues and (5) lost vacation benefits. On the other hand, the subject matter of the counterclaim is a common law tort action for damages * * *.

While * * * there is a broad relationship between the two, nevertheless, the questions of fact relevant to alleged violence on the picket line are not common to the subject matter of the complaint and the two claims do not represent the "same basic controversy."

Id. at 389. Is the court's application of the test correct?

In GLOBE INDEM. CO. v. TEIXEIRA, 230 F.Supp. 444 (D.Haw.1963), plaintiff insurance company joined the insured and the injured parties in a declaratory-judgment action. Plaintiff disclaimed liability under the policy because at the time of the accident the insured was driving a car without the permission of the owner. The injured defendants cross-and counterclaimed for damages. The court held that the counterclaims did not arise from the same transaction or occurrence and were not compulsory because "the subject matter of the complaint herein is the liability or non-liability of plaintiff on the insurance policy," whereas "the subject matter of the counterclaims is the negligence or non-negligence of defendant." Would the result have been any different under any of the tests set forth in Note 3?

In *Globe*, defendants' counterclaims were not even permitted to stand as permissive because the insurance policy prohibited suits against the insurer until the amount of the insured's liability had been established. Can the court refuse to entertain a permissive counterclaim if there are independent jurisdictional grounds supporting it? When might the court wish to do so and what alternative does the court have to dismissing the counterclaim?

6. In ZELTZER v. CARTE BLANCHE CORP., 414 F.Supp. 1221 (W.D.Pa. 1976), the holder of a credit card brought an action against the issuer for alleged violations of the Truth in Lending Act. The court held that although the plaintiff's claim against the credit card company and the latter's debt collection counterclaim

both arose out of a single occurrence, the plaintiff's purchase of airline tickets through the use of his credit card, there was not the same basic controversy between the parties but rather mere transactional identity, and the debt-collection counterclaim, rooted in state law, was not compulsory, but permissive. The court stated:

> Plaintiff brings this action exclusively under a federal statute, the Truth in Lending Act. At issue is whether Carte Blanche complied with the technical requirements of the Act, and the regulations promulgated thereunder, in terms of disclosure of required credit information in its periodic billings to plaintiff. The outcome would seem to turn upon an interpretation of federal law, as well as upon the resolution of disputed factual issues regarding the disclosures.

> Defendant's counterclaim, however, bears no relationship to these matters, but is, rather, a debt collection suit rooted in and governed by state contract law. While the two claims stem from the same underlying business transaction, they involve entirely distinct legal issues: plaintiff's claim concerns the application of the * * * Act; the counterclaim does not concern the * * * Act or any other federal law. Moreover, the factual issues are distinct. Plaintiff's claim entails proof of a limited set of facts relating to the nature of the disclosures made by defendant. The counterclaim involves proof of a contract, its validity, the record of payments and plaintiff's default. In these circumstances * * * I find that the respective claims are "offshoots" of the same basic transaction, but not the "same basic controversy between the parties," and that separate trials on each distinct claim will not involve a "substantial duplication of effort and time by the parties and the courts." The two claims are thus not logically related * * *.

Id. at 1223–24. Is the court correct? Of what significance is Congress' desire to create, by passing the Truth in Lending Act, an incentive for private attorneys general to police consumer credit practices? Should factors like this affect the application of the transaction-or-occurrence test of Federal Rule 13(a)?

7. The states have widely divergent attitudes toward compulsory counterclaims. The Minnesota compulsory-counterclaim rule, for example, is virtually identical to Federal Rule 13(a), except that the reference to "occurrence" is omitted from the Rule, which has led that state's courts to read the Rule restrictively. In HOUSE v. HANSON, 245 Minn. 466, 72 N.W.2d 874 (1955), the Minnesota Supreme Court held that "Rule 13.01 was approved by this court with the express understanding and intent that the omission therefrom of the word 'occurrence' would insure that tort counterclaims would not be compulsory."

Consequences of Failing to Plead a Counterclaim

Rule 13(a) is silent as to the consequences of a failure to raise a compulsory counterclaim. It seems clear that an unasserted compulsory counterclaim cannot be raised in a subsequent suit in a federal court, see, e.g., Twin Disc, Inc. v. Lowell, 69 F.R.D. 64 (E.D.Wis.1975), although the courts differ as to the proper theory for reaching this conclusion. Some apply a res judicata principle, others use waiver; and yet another group relies on estoppel. See Scott, *Collateral Estoppel by Judgment*, 56 Harv.L.Rev. 1 (1942) (res judicata theory); Wright, *Estoppel by Rule: The Compulsory Counterclaim Under Modern Pleading*, 38 Minn.L.Rev. 423 (1954) (estoppel). Does it make any difference which theory is used?

Under what circumstances should the liberal amendment policy of Federal Rule 13(f) be used to permit the tardy assertion of a compulsory counterclaim? See Safeway Trails, Inc. v. Allentown & Reading Transit Co., 185 F.2d 918 (4th Cir.1950), in which leave to amend was granted when the excuse for failing to plead an omitted counterclaim was that defendant's lawyer had not read the Federal Rules! For a strict application of the barring effect of a failure to assert a compulsory counterclaim, see Schneeberger v. Hoette Concrete Constr. Co., 680 S.W.2d 301 (Mo.App.1984). If the statute of limitations has run on a counterclaim between the filing of the original action and defendant's motion under Rule 13(f), so that the claim would be barred if asserted independently, does the filing of the counterclaim relate back to the filing of the original action under Rule 15(c)? Should the result depend on whether the counterclaim is compulsory or permissive?

Hypothesize an action in a federal court in which defendant fails to raise a compulsory counterclaim. Does the failure to bring the claim in federal court prevent defendant from raising it in a subsequent state-court action? What if defendant brings suit on the unasserted claim in a state court before the federal action is terminated? Should the state court hearing the alleged counterclaim grant a motion to dismiss based on the assertion that Federal Rule 13(a) barred the state action? What other action might it take? Should the federal court hearing plaintiff's suit restrain further proceedings in the state court?

The answer * * * depends upon a determination of whether or not Congress intended in adopting Rule 13(a) to create another statutory exception to its policy of Federal Courts' non-interference with State Court actions. [See 28 U.S.C. § 2283.] Insofar as the effect of a party's failure to plead a compulsory counterclaim * * * in a Federal action is concerned the Congressional intent is clear—said party is thereafter barred from pleading same on the ground that it is res judicata. However, insofar as the effect of such failure on a State Court action is concerned the Congressional intent is not so clear; thus, in the absence of a clearer expression than is contained in Rule 13(a) we are unwilling to say that Congress * * * intended to grant Federal Courts the authority to enjoin State Court actions * * *.

FANTECCHI v. GROSS, 158 F.Supp. 684, 687 (E.D.Pa.1957), appeal dismissed 255 F.2d 299 (3d Cir.1958).

Are the considerations any different when the situation is reversed and the first action is brought in a state court in which a compulsory-counterclaim rule is in effect and the second case is in a federal court? Can plaintiff in the state proceeding ask the state court to enjoin the parties to a federal court action from litigating what should have been a compulsory counterclaim in the state court? Should the federal court grant a motion to dismiss? Cf. Donovan v. City of Dallas, 377 U.S. 408, 84 S.Ct. 1579, 12 L.Ed.2d 409 (1964). Should one state be required to give full faith and credit to another state's compulsory-counterclaim rule?

Notes and Questions

1. In SOUTHERN CONSTRUCTION CO. v. PICKARD, 371 U.S. 57, 83 S.Ct. 108, 9 L.Ed.2d 31 (1962), the Southern Construction Company was the prime contractor on contracts with the United States for the rehabilitation of certain barracks at Fort Campbell, Tennessee, and Fort Benning, Georgia. The plumbing and heating subcontractor on both projects was the respondent Samuel J. Pickard, doing business as Pickard Engineering Company. Pickard's primary supplier on both projects was the Atlas Supply Company.

Pickard filed suit against Southern in district courts in both Georgia and Tennessee under the Miller Act for amounts due on the contracts. Defendant elected to assert its counterclaim for the amount paid in settlement to Atlas in the Tennessee suit, the second of the two suits commenced. Pickard answered that the counterclaim was barred for failure to raise it in the first suit as a compulsory counterclaim.

The Supreme Court accepted the District Court's ruling that the $35,000 settlement had not been allocated as between the Tennessee and Georgia projects and that it therefore could have been asserted in either action. It stated, however, that Rule 13(a) does not operate to prohibit its use in the later Tennessee action. The Court found the policy of preventing multiplicity of actions and achieving resolution in a single lawsuit of all disputes arising out of common matters to be inapplicable in these circumstances:

> * * * The Rule was particularly directed against one who failed to assert a counterclaim in one action and then instituted a second action in which that counterclaim became the basis of the complaint. * * *

> It is readily apparent that this policy has no application here. In this instance, the plaintiff-respondent, who originally sought to combine all his claims in a single suit, correctly concluded that he was required by statute to split those claims and to bring two separate actions in two different districts. The fragmentation of these claims, therefore, was compelled by federal law, and the primary defendant in both actions was thus for the first time confronted with the choice of which of the two pending suits should be resorted to for the assertion of a counterclaim common to both. Under these circumstances, we hold that Rule 13(a) did not compel this counterclaim to be made in whichever of the two suits the first responsive pleading was filed. Its assertion in the later suit, to which Southern, not without reason, considered it more appurtenant * * * by no means involved the circuity of action that Rule 13(a) was aimed at preventing. * * *

Should the "common-law" exception to Rule 13(a) the Supreme Court invoked in *Pickard* be limited to the situation in which the governing substantive law requires plaintiff to bring related claims in separate districts?

2. Several exceptions to the compulsory-counterclaim rule are set out in the text of Rule 13(a) itself. Consider their relevance to the following situations.

(a) In UNION PAVING CO. v. DOWNER CORP., 276 F.2d 468 (9th Cir. 1960), the court discussed the passage in Rule 13(a) providing that waiver will not result from the failure to assert a counterclaim that already is the subject of litigation pending in another court:

> * * * The purpose of this exception is seemingly to prevent one party from compelling another to try his cause of action in a court not of the latter's

choosing when the same cause of action is already the subject of pending litigation in another forum, one which was probably chosen by the owner of the cause of action concerned. The language of the exception clause in Rule 13(a)—"such a claim *need not* be so stated (as a counterclaim) if at the time the action was commenced the claim was the subject of another pending action"—seems clearly permissive. [Emphasis added.] * * * It does not preclude him from electing instead to counterclaim his cause of action in the instant case.

This conclusion is reinforced by the fact that under Rule 13(b) pending litigation on the same cause of action has no effect on the ability to plead a permissive counterclaim. Thus, under the district court's theory, a cause of action which did *not* arise out of the same transaction or occurrence as the main claim could be pleaded as a counterclaim under Rule 13(b) even though the counterclaim was the subject of another pending action; but a claim so closely connected with the main action that it would otherwise be a compulsory counterclaim subject to waiver under Rule 13(a) cannot be pleaded at all if it is the subject of another pending action. Such a result is wholly unreasonable. * * *

Id. at 470–71.

(b) If defendant has a claim that arises out of the same transaction or occurrence as plaintiff's claim but it can be brought only against plaintiff and a third person who is "indispensable" and over whom defendant cannot obtain jurisdiction, is assertion of the claim mandatory?

(c) If five days after defendant serves her answer she becomes the assignee of a claim against plaintiff and if the assigned claim arose out of the same transaction or occurrence as plaintiff's claim against defendant, must defendant amend her answer and assert it? Cf. Federal Rule 13(e). What if the counterclaim is acquired during the trial?

(d) If defendant is sued in one capacity (e.g., as an administrator in an action based on the negligence of an intestate) and has a counterclaim in another capacity (e.g., as a beneficiary in a wrongful-death action) that arises out of the same transaction or occurrence, is it compulsory? See Newton v. Mitchell, 42 So.2d 53 (Fla.1949).

3.   Assume plaintiff commences an action within the appropriate statute of limitations and defendant has a compulsory counterclaim that would be barred by the statute of limitations if asserted in an independent action. Should the claim be permitted? Compare Minex Resources, Inc. v. Morland, 467 N.W.2d 691 (N.D. 1991), with Imbesi v. Carpenter Realty Corp., 357 Md. 375, 744 A.2d 549 (2000). Does it make any difference if defendant's claim was not time-barred when plaintiff commenced the suit but became so before defendant was required to answer? Assuming that the claim would be barred if asserted as a counterclaim, should it be permitted if it otherwise qualifies as a common-law recoupment or set-off? See American Law Institute, *Study of the Division of Jurisdiction Between State and Federal Courts* 258 (1969).

4.   If defendant's answer contains a counterclaim, must plaintiff assert a compulsory counterclaim to defendant's counterclaim? Does it matter whether defendant's counterclaim is compulsory or permissive? Is a counterclaim to a counterclaim likely to be so confusing that it will prevent the orderly disposition of the case? Would it make any difference if plaintiff amended the complaint to

include the claim rather than asserting it as a counterclaim? See Millar, *Counterclaim Against Counterclaim*, 48 Nw.U.L.Rev. 671, 690 (1954).

2. CROSS–CLAIMS

———

Read Federal Rules of Civil Procedure 13(g) and (h) and the accompanying material in the Supplement.

———

LASA PER L'INDUSTRIA DEL MARMO SOCIETA PER AZIONI v. ALEXANDER

United States Court of Appeals, Sixth Circuit, 1969.
414 F.2d 143.

[This controversy arose out of the construction of the Memphis, Tennessee City Hall. Southern Builders, a Tennessee corporation, was retained by the City as the principal contractor. Southern Builders' performance was secured by a bond, with Continental Casualty as surety. Southern Builders subcontracted with Alexander Marble and Tile Co., a partnership comprised of Tennessee residents, and Marble International, Inc., a Texas corporation, to supply and install some marble in the new City Hall. Alexander then contracted with LASA, an Italian corporation, to supply it with marble.

LASA alleged that it had fully performed its contract with Alexander and that Alexander owed it $127,240.80 out of the $468,641.26 contract price. It sued Alexander, Marble International, Southern Builders, Continental Casualty, and the City for the balance due.

Alexander filed an answer and counterclaim in which it alleged that LASA had breached the contract by not shipping the marble on time, by shipping marble of the wrong type, by shipping damaged marble, and by failing to ship all the marble it was obligated to ship. Alexander further alleged that the contract price was only $265,050.00. It sought restitution of the amount it overpaid LASA plus damages resulting from LASA's breach of contract.

Southern Builders filed an answer and counterclaim. In its counterclaim, Southern Builders alleged that LASA failed to ship marble as agreed to Alexander, and claimed damages resulting from that breach by LASA.

Alexander filed a cross-claim against Southern Builders, Continental Casualty, and the City for money alleged to be due on its contract with Southern Builders. Southern Builders and Continental Casualty filed answers and Southern Builders filed a cross-claim against Alexander for breach of contract.

Alexander filed third-party complaints against A.L. Aydelott and Associates, Inc. and against Aydelott individually alleging that they, as architects on the project, negligently supervised the project, wrongfully required Alexander to install marble in inclement weather, wrongfully directed Southern Builders to terminate its contract with Alexander, willfully refused to approve Alexander's estimates for work done, and wrongfully and maliciously injured Alexander's business reputation. Alexander sought unliquidated actual and punitive damages as well as treble damages, under a Tennessee statute, for inducing Southern Builders to breach the subcontract.

Alexander also sued Southern Builders for actual and punitive damages resulting from the wrongful termination of its contract and for injury to the business reputation of Alexander.]

PHILLIPS, CIRCUIT JUDGE.

* * * The confusion in pleadings that can arise out of cross-claims, counterclaims and a third-party complaint, all involving the same construction project, is demonstrated by the present appeal.

* * *

Among the pleadings were a cross-claim filed by the defendant subcontractor, Alexander, against the prime contractor, its surety and the City of Memphis; a counterclaim filed by the prime contractor against Alexander; and a third-party complaint filed by Alexander against the architect. The third-party complaint was treated by the District Court as a cross-claim against the architect as was the counterclaim of the prime contractor against Alexander.

Construing Rules 13(g) and 13(h) * * *, the District Court dismissed the two cross-claims and the third-party complaint, holding that they do not arise out of the same transaction or occurrence that is the subject matter of the original action or of a counterclaim therein.

We reverse.

* * *

Under the Federal Rules of Civil Procedure the rights of all parties generally should be adjudicated in one action. Rules 13 and 14 are remedial and are construed liberally. Both Rules 13 and 14 are "intended to avoid circuity of action and to dispose of the entire subject matter arising from one set of facts in one action, thus administering complete and evenhanded justice expeditiously and economically." Blair v. Cleveland Twist Drill Co., 197 F.2d 842, 845 (7th Cir.). The aim of these rules "is facilitation not frustration of decisions on the merits." Frommeyer v. L. & R. Construction Co., 139 F.Supp. 579, 585 (D.N.J.).

A decision involving jurisdiction over cross-claims in litigation growing out of a construction project similar in some respects to the issues presented on this appeal is Glens Falls Indemnity Co. v. United States, 229 F.2d 370 (9th Cir.). In that case the Court said:

> It is well settled that a grant of jurisdiction over particular subject matter includes the power to adjudicate all matters ancillary to the particular subject matter. * * * Therefore, if either a cross-claim under Rule 13 or a third-party claim under Rule 14 does arise out of the subject matter of the original action and involves the same persons and issues, the claim is ancillary to the original action. In such cases, if the court has jurisdiction to entertain the original action, no independent basis of

jurisdiction for the cross-claim or third-party claim need be alleged or proved. 229 F.2d at 373–374.

* * *

The District Court held that no part of Alexander's cross-claim against the prime contractor, his third-party complaint against the architect or of the prime contractor's cross-claim against Alexander for breach of contract arose out of the transaction or occurrence that is the subject matter of the original action or the two counterclaims. With deference to the well-written opinion of the District Judge, we disagree.

* * *

The words "transaction or occurrence" are given a broad and liberal interpretation in order to avoid a multiplicity of suits. * * *

Our reading of the pleadings in this case convinces us that there is a "logical relationship" between the cross-claims (including the third party complaint against the architect) and the "transaction or occurrence" that is the subject matter of the complaint and the two pending counterclaims. Although different subcontracts are involved, along with the prime contract and specifications, all relate to the same project and to problems arising out of the marble used in the erection of the Memphis City Hall. The recurring question presented by the various pleadings is directed to the principal issue of who is responsible for the marble problems which arose on this job. Blame is sought to be placed upon plaintiff as furnisher of the marble, upon Alexander as subcontractor, upon the prime contractor and upon the architect. Many of the same or closely related factual and legal issues necessarily will be presented under the complaint, counterclaims and cross-claims in the resolution of these issues. It seems apparent that some of the same evidence will be required in the hearing on the cross-claims and in the hearing or hearings with respect to the complaint and the two pending counterclaims.

We understand it to be the purpose of Rule 13 and the related rules that all such matters may be tried and determined in one action and to make it possible for the parties to avoid multiplicity of litigation. The intent of the rules is that all issues be resolved in one action, with all parties before one court, complex though the action may be.

In support of the decision of the District Court it is argued that, since a jury trial has been demanded, the complications and confusions of the cross-claims are such that it would be impossible to try the numerous issues before the jury in an orderly manner. The short answer to this contention is that the District Judge is authorized by Rule 42(b) to order separate trials on any cross-claim, counterclaim, other claim or issues. If on the trial of this case the District Court concludes that separate trials on one or more of the counterclaims, cross-claims or issues would be conducive to expedition and economy, Rule 42(b) provides a practical solution to this problem.

Reversed and remanded for further proceedings not inconsistent with this opinion.

McAllister, Senior Circuit Judge (dissenting).

* * *

The questions of fact or law involved in the original suit filed by LASA, and the counterclaim for overpayment filed by Alexander, are totally different from Alexander's claim against Southern Builders, claiming damages on the ground that Southern Builders wrongfully prevented and obstructed Alexander from performing its duties; wrongfully forced Alexander off the job; wrongfully brought in an outside subcontractor to complete the job at a highly inflated price, all of which was wrongfully and illegally charged to the account of Alexander—as well as Alexander's allegation in its same cross-claim against Southern Builders charging that Southern Builders and Aydelott entered upon a course of action wrongfully injuring the business reputation of Alexander for which it claimed $250,000 in punitive damages.

Alexander's cross-claim against Aydelott for treble damages in the amount of $750,000 for wrongfully and maliciously damaging Alexander's business reputation by abuse, harassment and public blame, and wrongfully and illegally inducing and procuring by inducement, persuasion or insistence, the breach and violation of Alexander's contract with Southern Builders, was an action in tort.

* * *

* * * Alexander's cross-claim against Aydelott does not arise out of the transaction or occurrence that is the subject matter of the original action—it does not arise out of the transaction or occurrence upon which LASA's suit is based. Nor does it arise out of "a counter-claim *therein*"—that is, out of a counterclaim in LASA's suit.

* * *

* * * [W]e are of the opinion that the cross-claims are not related to the original claim and the counterclaims, and that there is no identity of the many factual issues involved in the original claim and counterclaims, and in the cross-claims.

The proofs in LASA's suit and in Alexander's and Southern Builders' counterclaims against LASA would be entirely different from the proofs in Alexander's cross-claim against Southern Builders and its cross-claim against Aydelott.

* * *

The only claims in this case that arise out of the transaction or occurrence that is the subject matter of the original action *for balance due on a contract* are the counterclaims filed against LASA by Alexander and Southern Builders, *claiming breach of that contract*—not Alexander's two cross-claims against Southern Builders and Aydelott for their claimed deliberately malicious, tortious, and damaging conduct, for which Alexander claimed damages of several hundred thousand dollars.

In accordance with the foregoing, in my opinion, the judgments of the District Court should be affirmed in accordance with the opinion of Chief Judge Bailey Brown.

Notes and Questions

1. Is the reasoning of the majority or dissenting opinion more persuasive? Should the fact that different subcontracts were involved, which arguably meant that different transactions were before the court, be determinative? What ways other than dismissal could be employed to deal with the complexity of the litigation or to avoid confusion?

2. Should transactionally related cross-claims be compulsory? Generally speaking, cross-claims are permissive, and failure to raise them does not bar suit in a subsequent action. Why should this be so? Doesn't this lead to a multiplicity of suits? Isn't judicial economy fostered by hearing all transactionally related claims in one suit? Or, is it unfair to force defendants to file cross-claims in a forum not of their own choosing merely because of the actions of the plaintiff?

3. Some states have adopted a narrow definition of a transaction for cross-claim purposes. In LIEBHAUSER v. MILWAUKEE ELEC. RY. & LIGHT CO., 180 Wis. 468, 193 N.W. 522 (1923), plaintiff-passenger sued to recover for personal injuries allegedly sustained while a passenger on one of defendant-railway company's street cars when it collided with an automobile owned and driven by defendant Kroscher. Kroscher cross-claimed against the railway company alleging that the collision was due solely to the negligence of the company and seeking $150 for damages to his automobile. The Wisconsin cross-claim provision in effect at the time stated that "A defendant * * * may have affirmative relief against a codefendant * * * but in all such cases such relief must involve or in some manner affect the contract, transaction or property, which is the subject-matter of the action." The court, construing that statute, dismissed the cross-claim, saying:

> Whether or not the defendant Kroscher may set up by way of cross-complaint a cause of action and demand affirmative relief against his codefendant depends upon whether or not the relief which Kroscher asks involves the transaction which constitutes the subject-matter of plaintiff's action. * * * The subject-matter of the action, then, in this case is the plaintiff's right to have the defendants exercise the required degree of care in respect to her. Manifestly, the relief demanded by Kroscher in his cross-complaint against the company in no way involves or affects the plaintiff's main primary right. Kroscher's cause of action, if any he has, arose by reason of the failure of the company to exercise the required degree of care in respect to him, and it was entirely complete before plaintiff's cause of action arose. It cannot, therefore, be said logically that the relief demanded by Kroscher in his cross-complaint involves in any respect the transaction which is the subject-matter of the plaintiff's action or her main primary right.
>
> The mere fact that the two occurrences were nearly contemporaneous in time in no manner affects the question. * * *
>
> A careful study of the matter * * * convinces us that the revisers intended to limit the cases where cross-complaints might be filed to those where the rights of the plaintiff were necessarily involved. Underlying this is a sound public policy. Plaintiff should have a right to bring her action and obtain an adjudication of her rights without being compelled to become a mere observer in a contest between two defendants which in no way whatever concerns her. In the present case it is conceivable that the plaintiff might establish without difficulty a right of recovery against both defendants, and be entitled to receive compensation for the injuries complained of, and yet the

determination of her right might be compelled to await the issue of long litigation between the defendants, in which she was in no way concerned, and in which the act by which her main primary right was invaded was in no way involved. * * * To make the plaintiff's right to judgment dependent upon final adjudication of an independent controversy existing between the defendants is in effect to grant her the right to appeal to the courts upon a condition. This should not be. * * *

Id. at 473–74, 475–76, 481–82, 193 N.W. at 524–25, 525. Compare the reasoning of the *Liebhauser* case with Section 3019(b) of the New York Civil Practice Rules, which is in the Supplement following Rule 13. In what ways do the two provisions differ? The New York statute is discussed in 3 Weinstein, Korn & Miller, *New York Civil Practice* ¶ 3019.14.

4. In EARLE M. JORGENSON CO. v. T.I. UNITED STATES, LTD., 133 F.R.D. 472 (E.D.Pa.1991), plaintiff filed suit to recover cleanup costs and other damages arising from environmental contamination of real property. T.I. United States, one of seven defendants, impleaded a third-party defendant, Tosti. Another one of the original defendants, Reed, then cross-claimed against Tosti for indemnity and contribution. Tosti moved to dismiss, arguing that he as a third-party defendant and Reed as an original defendant were not "coparties" under Rule 13(g). The court found that Reed and Tosti were coparties, not opposing parties, and thus, the original defendant could cross claim against Tosti for indemnity and contribution.

> The approach taken by [Georgia Ports Authority v. Construzioni Meccaniche, 119 F.R.D. 693 (S.D.Ga.1988)] is realistic and sensible. Facing an identical procedural constellation, the court "construe[d] 'co-party' to mean any party that is not an opposing party." * * *

>> This comports with the structure of the federal rules, which envision three types of claims that may be asserted by defendants: counterclaims, third-party claims, and cross-claims. Rule 13(a) provides that a counterclaim may be brought against any "opposing party." Rule 14(a) provides that a third-party complaint may be brought against "a person not a party." Finally, Rule 13(g) provides for cross-claims against "co-parties." Certainly, the relationship between an original defendant and a third-party defendant fits somewhere into this framework. Characterizing the relationship as that of "co-parties" appears to be the logical choice.

> *Georgia Port Authority,* 119 F.R.D. at 695.

> "Any party asserting a claim, whether an original claim, counterclaim, cross-claim or third-party claim, becomes an opposing party to the party sued." [Greenbaum, *Jacks or Better to Open: Procedural Limitations on Co–Party and Third–Party Claims*, 74 Minn.L.Rev. 507, 551 (1990)] "Opposing parties," therefore, are parties that formally oppose each other on a pleaded claim, such as plaintiffs and original defendants, or third-party plaintiffs and the third-party defendants they have joined. Inasmuch as defendant Leonard Reed and third-party defendant Tosti are not such opposing parties, Reed's cross-claim is proper under Rule 13(g). The motion to dismiss will be denied.

Id. at 474–75. But see Murray v. Haverford Hosp. Corp., 278 F.Supp. 5, 6 (E.D.Pa.1968) (defining coparties as "parties having like status, such as, co-defendants").

Was there another way to preserve Reed's claim against Tosti? In a footnote, the District Court suggested that it could sever plaintiff's claim against Reed under Rule 21. "This would enable Reed to implead Tosti because Tosti would not be a party to the severed action. Fed.R.Civ.P. 14(a). Then the two actions could be consolidated. Fed.R.Civ.P. 42. However, this approach evades the real issue and is not a 'just, speedy, and inexpensive determination' of the action. Fed.R.Civ.P. 1." For further discussion of this issue, see the Greenbaum article cited by the court in the *Jorgenson* case and Note, *Defining "Co–Party" Within Federal Rule of Civil Procedure 13(g): Are Cross–Claims Between Original Defendants and Third Party Defendants Allowable?*, 66 Ind.L.J. 549 (1991).

5. Can a party plaintiff cross-claim against a coplaintiff? If so, under what circumstances? In DANNER v. ANSKIS, 256 F.2d 123 (3d Cir.1958), the driver and passenger of one car sued the driver of a second car for damages arising out of a two-car collision. The passenger-plaintiff also attempted to cross-claim for her injuries against the driver-plaintiff. The trial court's dismissal of the cross-claim was affirmed:

> The purpose of Rule 13(g) is to permit a defendant to state as a cross-claim a claim against a co-defendant growing out of the same transaction or occurrence that is the subject matter of the original action * * *, and to permit a plaintiff against whom a defendant has filed a counterclaim to state as a cross-claim against a co-plaintiff a claim growing out of the transaction or occurrence that is the subject matter of the counterclaim. * * * This, we think, is the clear intent of the language of the rule. In other words, a cross-claim is intended to state a claim which is ancillary to a claim stated in a complaint or counterclaim which has previously been filed against the party stating the cross-claim. * * * Unless so limited the rule could have the effect of extending the jurisdiction of the district court to controversies not within the federal judicial power. * * * Accordingly, Rule 13(g) does not authorize a plaintiff to state as a cross-claim against a co-plaintiff a claim arising out of the transaction or occurrence which is also the subject matter of their common complaint against the defendant. * * *

Id. at 124. Is the court's approach to the question of cross-claims between coplaintiffs sound? How is the *Danner* court defining "transaction"? Harrison v. M.S. Carriers, Inc., 1999 WL 195539, at *1 (E.D.La.1999) disagreed with the Third Circuit's analysis and allowed such a cross-claim.

6. Rule 13(h) is used to add parties not already in the suit. In order to invoke Rule 13(h), a party must be asserting a Rule 13(a), 13(b), or 13(g) claim against someone who already is a party. Note that this differs from claims under Rule 14. In *LASA*, Alexander's claim against the architect, Aydelott, originally was pleaded as a Rule 14 claim. The District Court and the Sixth Circuit treated it as if it were a motion to bring in an additional cross-defendant under Rule 13(h); the courts thus viewed Aydelott as a codefendant on the cross-claims against Southern Builders and the others. Isn't it true, therefore, that Rule 14 claims can be transformed into Rule 13(h) motions whenever defendant can assert a cross-claim against a party? Is there any tactical advantage in doing so? Are the additional party's rights different if it is brought in under Rule 13(h) rather than Rule 14? See the discussion of Rule 14 at pp. 649–56, infra.

7. May a court assert supplemental jurisdiction over Rule 13(h) parties joined to a compulsory counterclaim? After the Supreme Court's decision in Finley v. United States, 490 U.S. 545, 109 S.Ct. 2003, 104 L.Ed.2d 593 (1989), p. 306, supra, there was uncertainty over whether courts could assert jurisdiction over these parties. This matter was resolved when Congress enacted 28 U.S.C. § 1367 in 1990, creating supplemental jurisdiction. Supplemental jurisdiction is available

for all related claims that form part of the same case or controversy as the original claims. Section 1367(a) expressly provides that "such supplemental jurisdiction shall include claims that involve the joinder or intervention of additional parties." Review pp. 298–320, supra.

SECTION C. IDENTIFYING PARTIES WHO MAY SUE AND BE SUED

———

Read Federal Rule of Civil Procedure 17 in the Supplement.

———

ELLIS CANNING CO. v. INTERNATIONAL HARVESTER CO.

Supreme Court of Kansas, 1953.
174 Kan. 357, 255 P.2d 658.

PARKER, JUSTICE. * * *

In its petition plaintiff alleged that in furnishing service on its tractor defendant negligently started a fire in that vehicle resulting in damage amounting to $479.79; that plaintiff was insured in The Potomac Insurance Company against the loss, under a policy containing a subrogation clause; that it had been paid in full for the amount of its loss; and that it had commenced and was maintaining the action to recover such amount in its own name for the use and benefit of the insurance company.

Defendant's amended answer denied *seriatim* all acts of negligence * * *; admitted all allegations of that pleading respecting insurance, the amount of the loss, and the fact such loss had been fully paid by the insurance company; and then, in the third paragraph thereof, * * * alleged and charged, that since plaintiff was seeking to recover the amount paid to it by the insurer as full compensation for the loss of the tractor, the insurance company was the real party in interest and plaintiff had no legal right to maintain the action.

Plaintiff's motion to strike paragraph three of the answer and its demurrer to the same paragraph of that pleading * * * were overruled by the trial court. This appeal followed.

The appellant insists, the appellee concedes, and we agree, the sole question involved is whether the insured (appellant), after having been paid the full amount of its loss, is a real party in interest and legally entitled to maintain this action, for the use and benefit of the insurer, to recover such loss from the party (appellee), whose negligence is alleged to be responsible therefor. The question thus raised is not new in this jurisdiction and we frankly concede is one on which there is apparent conflict in our decisions.

Subject to certain exceptions, not here involved, our statute, G.S.1949, 60–401, requires that "Every action must be prosecuted in the name of the real party in interest." Given its common and accepted meaning, particularly where—as here—it must be conceded the appellant is no longer directly interested in the subject matter of the litigation, it would seem that, in and of itself, language of the statute would compel a negative answer to the question now under consideration. * * *

Notwithstanding, earlier decisions * * * holding that in the situation disclosed by the pleadings in the case at bar, the insurer is the real and only party in interest and must undertake the maintenance of the action for his reimbursement, it must and should be frankly admitted that in * * * [two decisions], as appellant contends, we held the insured might maintain the action in his own name for the use and benefit of the insurer. Be that as it may it must be conceded, that fully aware of the rule announced in those cases, we have repudiated what was there said and held with respect to such rule and now recognize and adhere to the doctrine that under the facts and circumstances disclosed by such pleadings an insured who has been fully paid for his loss is not the real party in interest * * * and hence cannot maintain an action to recover the amount of such loss in his own name for the use and benefit of the insurer. Conversely stated, the rule now recognized and applied is, that under the confronting conditions and circumstances the right of action against the alleged wrongdoer vests wholly in the insurer who * * * may, and indeed must, bring the action as the real and only party in interest if one is to be maintained. * * *

The judgment is affirmed.

Notes and Questions

1. A person is injured due to the negligence of another. She receives payment from an insurance company. The insurance company persuades the insured to sue the negligent party in her name in state court rather than the insurance company pursuing the action itself. Why would the insurance company wish to do this? Consider the following reasons:

(a) The insurance company thinks that a jury might be more sympathetic to an injured individual than to a large company.

(b) The injured party and the negligent party are not diverse. Had the insurance company pursued the action, the parties would have been diverse and the defendant (if not a citizen of the forum state) could have removed the action to federal court. The insurance company wanted the action to remain in state court, where it thought it could get a higher award.

2. Can there be more than one real party in interest to a suit? Suppose, for example, that an injured party is only partly covered by insurance. Can she sue the negligent party? Can the insurance company? Or, must the two sue jointly? In PINEWOOD GIN CO. v. CAROLINA POWER & LIGHT CO., 41 F.R.D. 221 (D.S.C.1966) the court held that the parties should be made to sue jointly, but that each had an interest in the outcome. The court, however, indicated that the result might be different if joinder of the parties would destroy diversity.

3. Is the real party in interest to be determined using a federal standard, or would a federal court adjudicating a state-based claim be bound by the rule of the state in which it sits? In R.J. REYNOLDS TOBACCO CO. v. LANEY & DUKE STORAGE WAREHOUSE CO., 39 F.R.D. 607 (M.D.Fla.1966), the court held that a Florida rule allowing only the insured to enforce a claim against a tortfeasor, even after payment by an insurer, was procedural and not substantive. Since it did not feel bound to follow Florida law on the matter, the court felt comfortable

holding that under Rule 17(a) the insurer and not the insured was the real party in interest. The court distinguished this state procedural rule, however, from a rule that determined whether a subrogee had a right to receive the proceeds of a recovery in a tort action. According to the court, this latter rule was substantive, and thus the state rule had to be applied.

4. Generally, courts have held that diversity of citizenship is to be determined by the citizenship of the real party in interest. Does this invite maneuvers designed to create or destroy diversity jurisdiction? Suppose, for example, that a nondiverse party wishes to sue in federal court. Can she assign her claim to another party so that complete diversity would exist? Alternatively, can a party assign a claim so as to defeat diversity?

When assignments or appointments are used to create diversity, 28 U.S.C. § 1359, see Note 7, p. 269, supra, appears to be relevant. Federal courts generally have permitted assignments or appointments to destroy diversity—in large part because of the absence of a statute like Section 1359 treating the destruction of diversity. See generally Case Note, *"Root, Root, Root for the Home Team": Pete Rose, Nominal Parties and Diversity Jurisdiction,* 66 N.Y.U.L.Rev. 148 (1991).

5. If the party designated in the original complaint is not the real party in interest, should a substitution of the proper party be given retroactive effect to the date of the original complaint for statute-of-limitations purposes? Should a motion for substitution be made under the provisions of Federal Rule 25(c), or does Rule 15(c)(2) adequately cover the situation? See Link Aviation, Inc. v. Downs, 117 U.S.App.D.C. 40, 325 F.2d 613 (D.C.Cir.1963). Federal Rule 17(a) was amended in 1966 to add the provision that no action shall be dismissed because it was not prosecuted in the name of the real party in interest until a reasonable time has been allowed for substitution. The Advisory Committee's Notes, which appear in the Supplement, specifically limit the application of this passage to cases in which the proper party to sue is difficult to ascertain or when an excusable mistake has been made. Does the court have any discretion to refuse substitution? For example, if a suit originally is brought by John Doe against an airline for personal injuries arising out of an airline crash, should the court later allow the names of all the victims of the disaster to be substituted as the real parties in interest?

6. Various authorities have advocated the abolition of the real-party-in-interest concept. Even New York, the originator of the real-party-in-interest rule, has abolished it. According to 2 Weinstein, Korn & Miller, *New York Civil Practice* ¶ 1004.01:

> * * * [I]t was unnecessary because (1) the law would be the same without any express rule, (2) it was an inept statement of an obvious principle of substantive law, (3) it misleadingly seemed to say that the action must be brought by the party to be benefited, and (4) the second part of [the former New York rule (which was similar to the second sentence of Federal Rule 17(a))] * * * was not an exception to the first part even though it was cast in the form of an exception.
>
> The question of who has a substantive right and whether that right has been violated to the extent that an action for redress may be brought is a matter of substantive not procedural law. Where a claim is, for example, assigned before the action is commenced, the assignor lacks any substantive right against the debtor which can be enforced. Analysis is impeded by attempting to treat the problem in terms of "real party in interest."

See also Entman, *More Reasons for Abolishing Federal Rule of Civil Procedure 17(a): The Problem of the Proper Plaintiff and Insurance Subrogation*, 68 N.C.L.Rev. 893 (1990).

7.   In addition to the rules on real party in interest, two other concepts are relevant to determining who may sue or be sued—"capacity" and "standing." Capacity refers to the ability of an individual or corporation to enforce rights or to be sued by others. Many states, for example, have special rules to deal with suits by or against minors and mental incompetents. See Federal Rules 17(b) and 17(c).

Standing is a concept, most relevant in the federal courts, used to ensure that the parties before the court will vigorously argue the legal claims at issue. Federal standing rules, which are derived primarily from Article III, are treated in detail in Federal Courts and Constitutional Law courses. Only summary treatment may be given here. Present doctrine requires that the litigant suffer an injury, that the injury arise out of or relate to the litigation, and that the litigant have a personal stake in the outcome of the suit. See 13 & 13A Wright, Miller & Cooper, *Federal Practice and Procedure: Jurisdiction and Related Matters 2d* §§ 3531, 3531.16 (1984).

8.   It is useful to contrast the three issues of capacity, real party in interest, and standing to show how they operate together. Capacity rules are designed to protect a party by ensuring that she is represented adequately. So, a representative will be appointed to advance the interests of a minor or a mental incompetent, who might not be able to understand fully the nature of the issues involved in the lawsuit.

Real-party-in-interest rules serve to protect the opposing party's interests by ensuring that only the litigant who has a true stake in the outcome can sue or be sued. This prevents situations in which a person first might be sued by the person who holds the nominal title to a claim, and after successfully defending that claim, is subjected to a second action by the real party in interest. Puerto Rico v. Cordeco Dev. Corp., 534 F.Supp. 612, 614 (D.Puerto Rico 1982).

Standing rules protect the judicial system (and persons not parties to the suit) more than the individual litigants involved in the case. These rules ensure that only bona fide disputes between adverse parties come before the courts.

It is possible, therefore, to have a case in which a real party in interest (the beneficiary of a will, for example) lacks capacity to sue (perhaps because he is a minor). Moreover, even if this hypothetical beneficiary had capacity to sue, he might not have standing to raise particular claims. So, for example, the beneficiary of the will might not be able to bring an action against the government on the ground that the estate tax is used for illegal purposes by the government since the injury suffered is of a general nature, not particular to the litigant, and hence the beneficiary lacks standing to sue.

SECTION D.   CLAIMS INVOLVING MULTIPLE PARTIES

1.   PERMISSIVE JOINDER OF PARTIES

Joinder of parties at common law was controlled by the substantive rules of law, often as reflected in the forms of action, rather than by notions of judicial economy and trial convenience. Plaintiffs who were asserting joint rights were compelled by these principles to join their respective claims in a single action; permissive joinder of plaintiffs, in the sense of plaintiffs having an option to join their claims when they were not joint, did not exist. The common-law rules governing joinder of defendants were slightly more flexible: joint tortfeasors and defendants whose contract obligations were both joint and several could be joined at the plaintiff's option.

The equity courts adopted a more flexible approach to permissive joinder of parties than prevailed in the common-law courts. They allowed all persons having an interest in the subject matter of the action or in the relief demanded to join in a single proceeding.

The early codes adopted the equity rule as a general provision governing joinder of parties. Many state courts read this language as imposing a two-part requirement for joinder of plaintiffs, however. As a result, joinder of plaintiffs was restricted to those cases in which all plaintiffs were interested in both the subject matter of the action and all the relief demanded. Joinder of defendants was even more restricted by code provisions relating to joinder of causes of action, which typically required all parties to be interested in each of the joined causes.

For a history of American joinder rules, see 7 Wright, Miller & Kane, *Federal Practice and Procedure: Civil 3d* § 1651 (2001); Blume, *Free Joinder of Parties, Claims, and Counterclaims,* 2 F.R.D. 250 (1943); Legislation, *Recent Trends in Joinder of Parties, Causes, and Counterclaims,* 37 Colum.L.Rev. 462 (1937). For a comparative view, see Millar, *The Joinder of Actions in Continental Civil Procedure,* 28 Ill.L.Rev. 26, 177 (1933).

————

Read Federal Rules of Civil Procedure 20, 21, and 42(a) in the Supplement.

————

RYDER v. JEFFERSON HOTEL CO.

Supreme Court of South Carolina, 1922.
121 S.C. 72, 113 S.E. 474.

MARION, J. The complaint in this action * * * alleges in substance that the plaintiff Charles A. Ryder and the plaintiff Edith C. Ryder are husband and wife; that [they] * * * became guests of the defendant Jefferson Hotel Company * * *; that thereafter, during the night * * *, the defendant S.J. Bickley, acting as the servant and agent of the defendant Jefferson Hotel Company, roused the plaintiffs by rapping upon their room door, and in a rude and angry manner insulted the plaintiff Edith C. Ryder; that as a result of the insults * * * the plaintiffs were compelled to give up the accommodations due them and leave the said hotel, and were forced at midnight and at great inconvenience and uncertainty to seek another lodging place; that by reason of such high-handed, malicious, and willful conduct, on the part of the said hotel and its servant and agent, the plaintiffs were greatly injured in their reputations, credit, and business, and that the plaintiff Charles A. Ryder has suffered great loss of custom and has been deprived of great gains and profits * * *; and that * * * the plaintiffs have been damaged in the sum of $10,000.

Defendants separately demurred to the complaint upon the ground that it appeared upon the face thereof that several causes of action had been improperly united therein, for the reason that the several causes of action united do not affect all the parties to the action. From an order overruling the demurrer, defendants appeal.

The sole question for determination is: Does the complaint contain two causes of action which may be joined in the same complaint? It is apparent, as appellants suggest, that the complaint alleges a cause of action by Charles A. Ryder against the defendants for a personal tort—that is, for a breach of duty growing out of the relationship existing between the parties, to wit, innkeeper and guest—and also a cause of action by Edith C. Ryder against the defendants for a tortious breach of duty growing out of the same relationship. It is also apparent that both of these alleged causes of action arose out of the same transaction, in the sense that the injury to each of the plaintiffs was caused by the same delict. But appellants contend that it is equally apparent from the allegations of the complaint that the rights invaded and the injuries sustained are necessarily several, and that plaintiffs cannot maintain a joint action and recover joint damages therefor. We think that contention must be sustained.

Section 218 of the Code of Procedure (1912), classifying the various causes of action which may be united in the same complaint, contains this proviso:

> But the causes of action, so united, must all belong to one of these classes, and, except in actions for the foreclosure of mortgages, must affect all the parties to the action, and not require different places of trial, and must be separately stated.

The rule applicable is thus stated by Judge Pomeroy in his work on Code Remedies (4th Ed.) p. 215:

> When a tort of a personal nature * * * is committed upon two or more, the right of action must, except in a very few special cases, be several. In order that a joint action may be possible, there must be some prior bond of legal union between the persons injured—such as partnership relation—of such a nature that the tort interferes with it, *and by virtue of that very interference* produces a wrong and consequent damage common to all. It is not every prior existing legal relation between the parties that will impress a joint character upon the injury and damage. Thus, if a husband and wife be libeled, or slandered, or beaten, although there is a close legal relation between the parties, it is not one which can be affected by such a wrong, and no joint cause of action will arise. * * *

That the rights infringed and the injuries suffered by the two plaintiffs in the case at bar are several, and not joint, would not seem open to question. To illustrate: If the two plaintiffs, husband and wife, occupying the same berth in a sleeping car, had both been physically injured in a wreck of the train, it would scarcely be contended that they could properly bring a joint action for the damages sustained by each on account of the carrier's delict. The complaint here does not state a cause of action for injuries to the wife alone * * *. Neither is the husband's alleged cause of action based upon loss of consortium and expenses incurred on behalf of the wife. The wife's cause of action as alleged does not "affect" the husband, and the husband's cause of action does not "affect" the wife, in the sense that the Code of Procedure (section 218) requires that the causes of action joined in the same complaint "must affect all parties to the action." Neither has a legal interest in the pecuniary recovery of the other, and in contemplation of law there can be no joint and common damage to both resulting from a wrong which gives rise to separate and distinct rights personal to each. * * *

At common law it seems that even the husband's cause of action for the loss of the wife's services and companionship and expenses incurred by him on account of injury to the wife could not be joined with the cause of action for injuries personal to the wife. * * * In the case at bar not only are the parties plaintiff different, and the potential elements of damage recoverable by the parties different, but neither party has the right to sue for the benefit of the other * * *.

The order of the circuit court is reversed.

GARY, C.J., and COTHRAN, J., concur.

FRASER, J. (dissenting). * * * The plaintiffs * * * were expelled from the hotel, under the allegation that they were not husband and wife. It was a denial of the joint relationship that caused the trouble.

It seems to me that the illustrations used are not appropriate to the case. When a husband and wife are injured in one railroad accident, the injuries are individual, and not joint. It seems to me that the case is somewhat like an injury to a copartnership. I do not think that it will be doubted that the copartnership can bring an action for injury to the copartnership, although the injury to the two copartners may not be the same. * * * In the joint action the other copartner may not be able to recover for the injury peculiar to himself; but the injury to the copartnership is a joint injury, and for this injury it may recover. Here the offense was against the husband and wife and affected their relation as husband and wife. This is manifestly a joint injury. * * *

For these reasons I dissent.

Notes and Questions

1. Doesn't *Ryder* emasculate the concept of permissive joinder by allowing joinder only when the parties are "united in interest" and presumably would be *compelled* to join? In this connection consider the court's reliance on Pomeroy's statement that "although there is a close legal relation between the parties, it is not one which can be *affected* by such a wrong, and no joint cause of action will arise." (Emphasis added.) If the injury *affected* a relationship, wouldn't the parties to that relationship be classified as necessary or indispensable parties and be required to join? Is the joint-interest standard consistent with the objectives of permissive joinder? Reconsider these questions after completing the material on necessary joinder, pp. 633–49, infra. The *Ryder* approach has been rejected in a substantial number of jurisdictions. See, e.g., Peters v. Bigelow, 137 Cal.App. 135, 30 P.2d 450 (3d Dist.1934).

2. How would *Ryder* have been decided by a federal court? What are the factors that should be weighed under Rule 20 in deciding a permissive-joinder

question? Consider the following cases. In REKEWEG v. FEDERAL MUT. INS. CO., 27 F.R.D. 431 (N.D.Ind.1961), judgment on merits affirmed 324 F.2d 150 (7th Cir.1963), certiorari denied 376 U.S. 943, 84 S.Ct. 798, 11 L.Ed.2d 767 (1964), the court permitted an injured plaintiff to join a claim against an insurance company and its agent for fraudulently inducing plaintiff's attorney to delay the filing of a personal-injury claim until after the statute of limitations had run with a claim against plaintiff's attorney for negligent delay in bringing a timely action. But in SUN–X GLASS TINTING OF MID–WISCONSIN, INC. v. SUN–X INT'L, INC., 227 F.Supp. 365 (W.D.Wis.1964), an action for fraud in which eight distributors sought to join as plaintiffs against the company for which they agreed to act as distributors, the court found that there was no single transaction or occurrence since the solicitation, negotiation, and execution of each distributor's contract was unrelated to any of the other contracts. Can these two cases be reconciled?

3.   In AKELY v. KINNICUTT, 238 N.Y. 466, 144 N.E. 682 (1924), one hundred ninety-three plaintiffs joined in an action alleging that they were induced to purchase shares of stock in a corporation by defendant's prospectus. The question of fraud was common to all but separate questions relating to individual plaintiffs also were certain to arise—e.g., whether each plaintiff justifiably relied on the prospectus. Defendant objected to joinder on the grounds that (1) the presence of separate questions outweighed the advantages of joinder and (2) the claims did not arise out of the same transaction. The court upheld joinder because the fraud issue was fundamental and would involve more dispute and elicit more evidence than any other issue. The court also held that there was but one transaction, stating:

> * * * The transaction in respect of or out of which the cause of action arises is the purchase by plaintiff of his stock * * * and such purchases conducted by one plaintiff after another respectively plainly constitute a series of transactions within the meaning of the statute. The purchase by plaintiff of his stock is not robbed of its character as a "transaction" because * * * the transaction was not a dual one occurring between the plaintiff and the defendants, and the many purchases by plaintiffs respectively do not lose their character as a series of transactions because they occurred at different places and times extending through many months.

Id. at 474, 144 N.E. at 684. Compare Goodman v. H. Hentz & Co., 265 F.Supp. 440 (N.D.Ill.1967). Could plaintiffs in *Akely* have brought a class action under Federal Rule 23? See pp. 701–08, infra.

4.   In LUCAS v. CITY OF JUNEAU, 15 Alaska 413, 127 F.Supp. 730 (1955), and STATE EX REL. SMITH v. WEINSTEIN, 398 S.W.2d 41 (Mo.App.1965), plaintiff's injuries were sustained through the negligence of A and were aggravated by the subsequent negligence of B, an ambulance driver, while taking plaintiff to the hospital. In *Lucas*, the ambulance accident occurred eighteen days after the original injury to plaintiff. In both cases, the court concluded that the ambulance trips were necessitated by the original accidents and permitted joinder.

In WATTS v. SMITH, 375 Mich. 120, 134 N.W.2d 194 (1965), plaintiff was a passenger in a car that was struck from the rear twice in one day—once when plaintiff and his driver were en route to work in the morning and again when they were returning home in the afternoon. Plaintiff attempted to join the drivers of both cars which struck him in a single lawsuit. Michigan Court Rule 2.206(A) allows persons to be joined in one action as defendants (1) if there is asserted against them jointly, severally, or in the alternative, any right to relief in respect of or arising out of the same transaction, occurrence or series of transactions or occurrences, and if any question of law or fact common to all of them will arise in the action; or (2) if it appears that their presence in the action will promote the convenient administration of justice. Relying on the second provision, the Michigan court allowed joinder because separation of the causes would permit each defendant to argue that it was uncertain what injuries plaintiff sustained from each accident. Do you perceive any problems in permitting joinder in this case? See Note, *The Challenge of the Mass Trial*, 68 Harv.L.Rev. 1046 (1955).

5. Many of the tactical factors that must be considered before attempting to join multiple defendants are discussed in Friedenthal, *Whom to Sue—Multiple Defendants*, in 5 *Am.Jur. Trials* 1–25 (1966).

TANBRO FABRICS CORP. v. BEAUNIT MILLS, INC.

Supreme Court of New York, Appellate Division, First Department, 1957.
4 A.D.2d 519, 167 N.Y.S.2d 387.

Breitel, Justice. * * *

The underlying business dispute spawned three lawsuits. In the first action * * *, the seller, Beaunit, sought to recover the purchase price of goods sold and delivered to Tanbro. The buyer, Tanbro, counterclaimed for breach of warranty for improper manufacture, as a result of which the goods were subject to "yarn slippage." The seller replied to the counterclaim by denying that the slippage was due to improper manufacture. A portion of the goods still being in the hands of the processor, Tanbro initiated another action * * *, in replevin, to recover these goods. The processor, Amity, counterclaimed for its charges and asserted its claim to the goods under an artisan's lien. In the exchanges that preceded and attended the bringing of these lawsuits, the buyer Tanbro received Beaunit's assertion that the yarn slippage was caused by the processor's improper handling, while with equal force the processor charged the same defect to Beaunit as a consequence of its improper manufacture.

At this juncture, Tanbro, the buyer, brought the third lawsuit * * * against Beaunit and Amity, charging the goods were defective because of yarn slippage and that such slippage was caused by either the seller, Beaunit, or alternatively the processor, Amity, or both. This is the main action before the court.

At Special Term, the buyer Tanbro moved to consolidate the three actions. Beaunit and Amity separately cross-moved to dismiss the complaint in the buyer's main action on the ground that there were prior actions pending between the parties with respect to the same cause of action. The motion to consolidate was denied and Beaunit's cross-motion to dismiss the complaint as against it was granted.

* * *

Both the seller and the processor resist consolidation. They do so on the ground that each had a separate and different relationship to the buyer, and that each was involved in a separate and independent contract. Therefore, they say, there is not involved the "same transaction or occurrence," nor any common question of law or fact to sustain either a joinder of parties or a consolidation of the actions. They stress that the buyer Tanbro wishes to pit against each other the seller and the processor on the issue of responsibility for the alleged defect, while the buyer sits back free from the obligation to prove a full case, as it would otherwise have to do in separate actions against the seller and the processor. The buyer, on the other hand, argues that what is identical to the cases are the goods and the defect, with the common question of who is responsible for the defect. The buyer concedes that it would have to prove the defect, and also prove that the defect must have been caused by either the seller or the processor or both of them; that, therefore, this involves a single transaction or occurrence and involves a common question of fact.

The controlling statute is Section 212 of the Civil Practice Act. * * * The portion pertinent to the joinder of defendants reads as follows:

> 2.   All persons may be joined in one action as defendants if there is asserted against them jointly, severally, or in the alternative, any right to relief in respect of or arising out of the same transaction, occurrence, or series of transactions or occurrences and if any question of law or fact common to all of them would arise in the action. * * *

A reading of the section by itself would suggest little or no difficulty in permitting a joinder of parties in the buyer's main action or a consolidation of the three actions. However, the section has a history, which has created some confusion as to the meaning and application of the section.

The seller and the processor rely heavily on Ader v. Blau, 241 N.Y. 7, 148 N.E. 771, 41 A.L.R. 1216. The case arose under the predecessor statute permitting joinder * * *. In that case the plaintiff sought to join in one death action the person charged with having caused the accident resulting in the injuries ending in death and a treating physician who, it was charged, by his incompetence, was the cause of the decedent's death. The Court of Appeals * * * [held] that Section 258 of the Civil Practice Act, since repealed, albeit a restriction on joinder of causes of action in pleading, was a limiting factor in permitting joinder of parties. Applying the statute, it held the joinder impermissible.

In reaction to this decision * * * Section 258 was repealed in favor of a broad pleading section * * *. In making the recommendation, the Judicial Council referred to the *Ader* case, supra, and the fact that the court had regarded the area of joinder of parties limited by the pleading restrictions of Section 258. It added, "Complete freedom should be allowed in the joinder of causes of action as in the joinder of parties, and it is submitted that the correct approach to the joinder both of parties and of causes of action is the English one: May the matters conveniently be tried together? The problem is to combine as many matters as possible to avoid multiplicity and at the same time not unduly complicate the litigation for the jury."

The full effect of the repealer of old Section 258 has, however, not been left to speculation. The Court of Appeals, in Great Northern Telegraph Company v. Yokohama Specie Bank, 297 N.Y. 135, 76 N.E.2d 117, discussed the question frontally. It held that the *Ader* case, supra, was a result of the pleading limitation contained in the old, and now repealed, Section 258. * * * And in the *Great Northern* case, itself, joinder was allowed plaintiff against the Superintendent of Banks for payments due plaintiff, on which claim the Superintendent was asserting as a bar a time limitation provided by statute, and a correspondent Bank, which plaintiff asserted owed a duty to plaintiff to file the claim promptly with the Superintendent of Banks, in the event that it should be held that the claim was barred by lapse of time.

Notably, in the *Great Northern Telegraph* case, and in the English cases relied upon therein, there were joined, as defendants, parties that owed to plaintiff obligations under independent and separate contracts and in independent and separate relationships. In none of the cases was the "same transaction or occurrence" construed to require an identity of duty and relationship. * * *

This then is the background for the present section 212 of the Civil Practice Act. It should be beyond argument, by now, that it is no longer a bar to joinder, and, by parallel reasoning, *a fortiori,* to consolidation, that there is not an identity of duty or contract upon which to assert alternative liability. It is still necessary, of course, that there be a finding that the alternative liability arises out of a common transaction or occurrence involving common questions of fact and law. But this is not a rigid test. It is to be applied with judgment and discretion, in the balancing of convenience and justice between the parties involved * * *. Indeed, the buyer's situation prompted Special Term to comment that the buyer, Tanbro, "is in the unenviable position of not knowing possibly which of its contracting parties is responsible and in separate actions may find itself confronted with defeat in each event though the product as finally delivered may be defective."

* * *

The right of joinder and the privilege to obtain consolidation is always counterbalanced, of course, by the power of the court to grant a severance, or to deny a consolidation, if prejudice or injustice appear. In this case, the danger of separate trials, leading, perhaps, to an unjust and illogical result, is a possibility well worth avoiding. The buyer is entitled to a less hazardous adjudication of his dispute, so long as he is able to make out a prima facie case of alternative liability.

Accordingly, the order of Special Term insofar as it granted the cross motion to dismiss the complaint in the first described action as against the defendant Beaunit and denied the buyer Tanbro's motion to consolidate the three actions should be modified to deny the cross motion and to grant the motion to consolidate, and otherwise should be affirmed * * *.

All concur.

Notes and Questions

1. Where one of two persons are [sic] liable but the plaintiff is not certain he can make out a case against either, the opportunity to join them as defendants is of great tactical importance. The court should not dismiss after the close of plaintiff's case merely because the plaintiff has not shown which of the two defendants is responsible if he has shown that one of them must have been. It is not unfair to require each of the defendants to assume the risk of a failure to show that he was not responsible. Some attorneys sometimes fail to recognize that evidence supplied by one co-defendant may be used against another to support the plaintiff's case. * * * Even if the court

might feel that a prima facie case has not been made out against one of the co-defendants, it should at least reserve decision on the motion to dismiss until after the defendants rest.

2 Weinstein, Korn & Miller, *New York Civil Practice* ¶ 1002.08. See also 7 Wright, Miller & Kane, *Federal Practice and Procedure: Civil 3d* § 1654 (2001).

In *Tanbro,* the buyer's motion was for consolidation. The court's opinion might convey the impression that the court assumed the New York standard for consolidation was identical to that for joinder. In fact, however, the New York consolidation provision is much broader than the New York joinder provision. The text of both have been set out in the Supplement—the former under Federal Rule 42(a) and the latter under Federal Rule 20. In comparing the Federal Rules with the New York provisions note that the Federal Rules also differentiate between joinder and consolidation. Can a discrepancy between the availability of joinder and consolidation be justified?

2. For a history of American joinder rules, see Blume, *Free Joinder of Parties, Claims, and Counterclaims,* 2 F.R.D. 250 (1943), and Legislation, *Recent Trends in Joinder of Parties, Causes, and Counterclaims,* 37 Colum.L.Rev. 462 (1937). For a comparative view, see Millar, *The Joinder of Actions in Continental Civil Procedure,* 28 Ill.L.Rev. 26, 177 (1933).

2. JOINDER OF PERSONS NEEDED FOR A JUST ADJUDICATION—NECESSARY AND INDISPENSABLE PARTIES

BANK OF CALIFORNIA NAT. ASS'N v. SUPERIOR COURT

Supreme Court of California, 1940.
16 Cal.2d 516, 106 P.2d 879.

GIBSON, CHIEF JUSTICE. * * *

Sara M. Boyd * * * died testate in June, 1937, leaving an estate valued at about $225,000. On July 8, 1937, * * * her will was admitted to probate, and petitioner, Bank of California, was appointed executor. The will left individual legacies and bequests amounting to $60,000 to a large number of legatees, * * * some residing in other states and in foreign countries. Petitioner, St. Luke's Hospital, was named residuary legatee and devisee, and thereby received the bulk of the estate.

On October 14, 1937, Bertha M. Smedley, a niece and legatee, brought an action to enforce the provisions of an alleged contract by which decedent agreed to leave her entire estate to the plaintiff. The complaint named as parties defendant the executor and all of the beneficiaries under the will, and prayed for a decree adjudging that plaintiff is, by virtue of the agreement, the owner of the entire estate of the decedent after payment of debts and expenses. It was further prayed that plaintiff's title to the property be quieted * * *.

Summons was served only upon petitioners, the executor and the residuary legatee. No other defendants were served, and none appeared. * * * [At trial] petitioners made a motion * * * for an order to bring in the other defendants, and to have summons issued and served upon them. The motion was made on the ground that all of the other defendants were "necessary and indispensable parties" to the action, and that the court could not proceed without them. The motion was denied by respondent court. Petitioners then applied for a writ of prohibition to restrain the trial until these other parties should be brought in.

In support of their application, petitioners point out that the complaint challenges the right of every legatee and devisee to share in the estate, and prays for an award of the entire property to plaintiff. It is contended that a trial and judgment without the absent defendants would adversely affect the rights of such parties, would result in a multiplicity of suits, and would subject the petitioning executor to inconvenience, expense and the burden of future litigation.

* * * [T]he precise issue is * * * whether the absent defendants are not only proper parties but "indispensable parties" in the sense that service upon them or their appearance is essential to the jurisdiction of the court to proceed in the action. * * *

At common law, joinder of plaintiffs was compulsory where the parties under the substantive law, were possessed of joint rights. * * * Equity courts developed another theory of compulsory joinder, to carry out the policy of avoiding piecemeal litigation and multiplicity of suits. Those persons necessary to a complete settlement of the controversy were usually required to be joined, in order that the entire matter might be concluded by a single suit. Obviously, this theory of joinder covered many situations where the substantive rights were not joint, and accordingly joinder would not have been required in an action at law. * * * Generally speaking, the modern rule under the codes carries out the established equity doctrine. Thus, section 389 of the Code of Civil Procedure states: "The court may determine any controversy between parties before it, when it can be done without prejudice to the rights of others, or by saving their rights; but when a complete determination of the controversy cannot be had without the presence of other parties, the court must then order them to be brought in * * *." * * *

But the equity doctrine as developed by the courts is loose and ambiguous in its expression and uncertain in its application. Sometimes it is stated as a mandatory rule, and at other times as a matter of discretion, designed to reach an equitable result if it is practicable to do so. * * * Bearing in mind the fundamental purpose of the doctrine, we should, in dealing with "necessary" and "indispensable" parties, be careful to avoid converting a discretionary power or a rule of fairness in procedure into an arbitrary and burdensome requirement which may thwart rather than accomplish justice. These two terms have frequently been coupled together as if they have the same meaning; but there appears to be a sound distinction, both in theory and practice, between parties deemed "indispensable" and those considered merely "necessary." * * * " * * * While necessary parties are so interested in the controversy that they should normally be made parties in order to enable the court to do complete justice, yet if their interests are separable from the rest and particularly where their presence in the suit cannot be obtained, they are not indispensable parties. The latter are those without whom the court cannot proceed." Clark[,] Code Pleading, p. 245, note 21. * * *

First, then, what parties are indispensable? There may be some persons whose interests, rights, or duties will inevitably be affected by any decree which can be rendered in the action. Typical are the situations where a number of persons have undetermined interests in the same property, or in a particular trust fund, and one of them seeks, in an action, to recover the whole, to fix his share, or to recover a portion claimed by him. The other persons with similar interests are indispensable parties. The reason is that a judgment in favor of one claimant for part of the property or fund would necessarily determine the amount or extent which remains available to the others. Hence, any judgment in the action would inevitably affect their rights. Thus, in an action by one creditor against assignees for the benefit of creditors, seeking an accounting and payment of his share of the assets, the other creditors were held indispensable * * *. * * * Where, also, the plaintiff seeks some other type of affirmative relief which, if granted, would injure or affect the interests of a third person not joined that third person is an indispensable party. Thus, in an action by a lessor against a sublessee to forfeit a parent lease because of acts of the sublessee, the sublessors (original lessees) were indispensable parties, since a decree of forfeiture would deprive them of their lease. * * *

All of these persons are, of course, "necessary" parties, but the decisions show that they come within a special classification of necessary parties, to which the term "indispensable" seems appropriate. An attempt to adjudicate their rights without joinder is futile. Many cases go so far as to say that the court would have no jurisdiction to proceed without them, and that its purported judgment would be void and subject to collateral attack. The objection being so fundamental, it need not be raised by the parties themselves; the court may, of its own motion, dismiss the proceedings, or refuse to proceed, until these indispensable parties are brought in. * * *

The other classification includes persons who are interested in the sense that they might possibly be affected by the decision, or whose interests in the subject matter or transaction are such that it cannot be finally and completely settled without them; but nevertheless their interests are so separable that a decree may be rendered between the parties before the court without affecting those others. These latter may perhaps be "necessary" parties to a complete settlement of the entire controversy or transaction, but are not "indispensable" to any valid judgment in the particular case. They should normally be joined, and the court, following the equity rule, will usually require them to be joined, in order to carry out the policy of complete determination and avoidance of multiplicity of suits. But, since the rule itself is one of equity, it is limited and qualified by considerations of fairness, convenience, and practicability. Where, for example, it is impossible to find these other persons or impracticable to bring them in, the action may proceed as to those parties who are present.

* * *

The action in these cases is against the distributee personally, and not against the estate; and it is independent of the will and the probate proceeding. Each distributee is individually held as a constructive trustee solely of the property which came to him, and none is interested in the granting or denial of similar relief as to any other. Where there are a number of legatees and devisees, they would all appear to be "necessary" parties in the sense that the main issue, the validity of the testamentary disposition of the property of decedent, affects their property interests, and the entire matter, the disposition of all of the decedent's property, cannot be finally settled without a binding adjudication for or against every legatee or devisee. Hence, the court will usually order them served and brought in unless there is some good reason for not doing so. But the absent defendants in such a case are not indispensable parties. Unlike the situations discussed above, in which any judgment would necessarily affect the rights of the absent persons, the case here is one where plaintiff may litigate her claim against the appearing defendants alone and obtain a decree which binds them alone. The absent defendants, not being before the court, will not be bound by the judgment, whether favorable or unfavorable, and their property interests will not be affected.

* * *

Only brief mention need be made of the contention that the prosecution of the action against less than all of the distributees will cause inconvenience and multiplicity of suits to the injury of the executor. These are all matters within the discretion of the court to consider in connection with its policy to settle the entire controversy in one proceeding, if possible. * * *

We have refrained from discussing the question whether the lower court's denial of the motion to bring in the absent defendants was, under the circumstances, an abuse of discretion. If they were readily available and could have been brought in without serious difficulty, it may well be that the motion should have been granted. On the other hand, if, as is asserted by respondents, many reside outside the state or the country, great difficulty might be encountered in any attempt to bring them in, and the trial might be indefinitely delayed, to the detriment of the present parties. The fact that the interests of the absent defendants are trivial as compared with that of the residuary legatee, which received over seventy-five percent of the estate, is perhaps some indication of the reason why plaintiff chose to go to trial against the latter alone. All these considerations, however, were for the trial court in the first instance, and its determination, though reviewable in the proper manner, cannot be attacked on an application for writ of prohibition.

The alternative writ, heretofore issued, is discharged, and the peremptory writ is denied.

Notes and Questions

1. SHIELDS v. BARROW, 58 U.S. (17 How.) 130, 15 L.Ed. 158 (1854), established the notion that parties could be classified as necessary or indispensable depending on the nature of their substantive rights ("joint" or "severable"). The consequences of this classification were extremely important. If an absent party who was not subject to the jurisdiction of the court or whose joinder would destroy the pre-existing diversity of citizenship was labelled indispensable, the entire action had to be dismissed. On the other hand, if the absentee merely was necessary, the court might exercise its discretion in determining whether or not to continue without that person. Because a plaintiff might have been deprived of any remedy if a party was found to be indispensable, courts often strained to avoid that conclusion. As might be suspected, this method had a debilitating effect on the standard for classification.

2. WARNER v. PACIFIC TEL. & TEL. CO., 121 Cal.App.2d 497, 263 P.2d 465 (2d Dist.1953), involved the following three successive telephone book listings:

(1) Warner, Caryl atty, 639 S Spring—TUkr 9171 Woodland Hills Office, 21042 Rios—DIamnd 85761; (2) Warner, Caryl Mrs. 1600 Westrly Ter—NOrmndy 22011; and (3) Warner, Caryl Mrs. Warner Caryl atty 21042 Rios Wdlnd Hills—DIamnd 85761. The "Mrs. Caryl Warner" in the second listing was the first wife of Caryl Warner; the "Mrs. Caryl Warner" in the third listing was Caryl Warner's wife at the time of the lawsuit. After the telephone company refused to delete or change the second listing, the present Mrs. Warner brought suit against the company for damages on the ground that the existing listings injured her reputation in the community and caused her "emotional distress, humiliation, fear, vexation, annoyance, scorn and ridicule as to her marital status, rendering her sick, with recurrent asthma attacks, to her damage." Plaintiff also asserted that she owned the title "Mrs. Caryl Warner," that the name has acquired a secondary meaning by reason of the professional and social standing of Caryl Warner, that her prestige and dignity were being depreciated, that the telephone listings constitute an invasion of privacy because they depict plaintiff as a party to a bigamous marriage, and that the telephone company knew or should have known that its maintenance of the listings would cause damage to plaintiff. The telephone company demurred to plaintiff's third amended and supplemental complaint on the ground, *inter alia,* that plaintiff had failed to join an indispensable party—the first Mrs. Caryl Warner. In light of the *Bank of California* case, should the California Court of Appeals affirm or reverse the lower court's grant of the demurrer? Why?

3. Is the failure to join an indispensable party really a jurisdictional defect as the *Bank of California* case suggests? See Hazard, *Indispensable Party: The Historical Origin of a Procedural Phantom,* 61 Colum.L.Rev. 1254, 1255–56 (1961).

4. If the indispensable-party rule cannot be justified on the ground that the absentee's rights will be prejudiced by a judgment, are there other considerations that might induce a court to refrain from adjudicating an action when an interested party is not present? Consider MAHR v. NORWICH UNION FIRE INS. SOC'Y, 127 N.Y. 452, 28 N.E. 391 (1891), in which plaintiff brought an action to restrain an insurance company from indemnifying the insured or his assignee. The policy had been issued to Bartlett and although delivered to plaintiff as collateral for a loan, it never was formally assigned. Thereafter Bartlett assigned the policy to Kelly, an Iowa resident, who had not been made a party to the action and could not be joined because he was beyond the jurisdiction of the New York courts. The insurance company moved to dismiss, claiming that Kelly was an indispensable party, but the trial court denied the motion. The Court of Appeals reversed, expressing the fear that "payment or performance may be exacted as many times as there are separate claimants." In fact, Kelly had brought suit against the insurance company in an Iowa court. Even if the threat of an inconsistent decision is remote, shouldn't the threat of multiplicity be sufficient to excuse defendant from defending the action? See Petrogradsky M.K. Bank v. National City Bank, 253 N.Y. 23, 170 N.E. 479, certiorari denied 282 U.S. 878, 51 S.Ct. 82, 75 L.Ed. 775 (1930). Is prejudice to defendant and the possibility of inconsistent adjudications only a factor to be weighed as part of a balancing of competing interests or should the threat of multiple liability be elevated to a constitutional level?

Isn't nationwide service of process, as is now available under the Federal Interpleader Act, 28 U.S.C. § 2361, see pp. 665–77, infra, the most efficacious solution to the joinder-of-parties problem? Notice that a federal court can acquire jurisdiction over an absentee not within the state pursuant to any state long-arm statute, Rule 4(e), and that it also can serve persons brought in under Rule 19 if they are within 100 miles from the place where the action is commenced, whether or not the place of service is within the state in which the action is pending, Rule 4(f). Should the remaining territorial barriers be broken down?

5.   PETTENGILL v. UNITED STATES, 253 F.Supp. 321 (N.D.Ill.1966), which was decided prior to the effective date of the 1966 amendment to Federal Rule 19, involved three separate tax-refund actions, one brought by the administratrix and two by heirs of the deceased, to recover taxes erroneously collected from the decedent's estate. A third heir brought an individual refund action in a Florida District Court. The United States argued that all the heirs were required to join as indispensable parties in a single action. Plaintiffs had commenced separate actions because venue barred them from bringing suit in a single court and because there is no trial by jury in the Court of Claims, an alternative forum. If the court dismissed for lack of an indispensable party, a subsequent action would have been barred by the statute of limitations; if it did not, the government would be put to the expense of defending separate actions. What factors should the court weigh in reaching its result and what should that result be?

6.   Reconsider the hypothetical concerning partial subrogation in Note 1, p. 623, supra. In that context are the insured and the insurer necessary or indispensable parties? If one of the two refuses to join in an action, is there any way to make her a party? In INDEPENDENT WIRELESS TEL. CO. v. RADIO CORP. OF AMERICA, 269 U.S. 459, 46 S.Ct. 166, 70 L.Ed. 357 (1926), the owner of a patent refused to join with plaintiff, an exclusive licensee, in a suit to enjoin further infringement by defendant. The owner was not amenable to process and could not be made a party defendant. The court held that it was proper to treat the recalcitrant absentee as an "involuntary plaintiff" to secure "justice." The involuntary-plaintiff rule is not generally available unless the absent party had a duty to allow the plaintiff to bring suit. What are the advantages of the technique employed in the *Independent Wireless* case? Its disadvantages? In DR. FRED HATFIELD'S SPORTSTRENGTH TRAINING EQUIP. CO. v. BALIK, 174 F.R.D. 496 (M.D.Fla.1997), the court distinguishes *Independent Wireless* because in the case before it, the patent owner himself was bringing the action, and the court saw no reason to find a licensee to be an indispensable party. Does this distinction make sense? Also consider EIKEL v. STATES MARINE LINES, INC., 473 F.2d 959 (5th Cir.1973), in which the absent plaintiff was amenable to the court's process and could be treated as a defendant. The court joined him as a defendant but realigned him as a plaintiff for diversity purposes only. Was this correct?

7.   In KROESE v. GENERAL STEEL CASTINGS CORP., 179 F.2d 760 (3d Cir.), certiorari denied 339 U.S. 983, 70 S.Ct. 1026, 94 L.Ed. 1386 (1950), suit was brought by a shareholder for the declaration of a dividend. Plaintiff did not serve a majority of the members of the board of directors of the corporation. Defendants argued that joinder of a majority was indispensable to the suit since in order to make the court's decree effective, if it decided that a dividend should be declared, the directors would have to be forced to act and this could be done only by binding them to the decree as parties. The court rejected this argument, stating:

> But how can the chancellor's action be made effective? To doubt its effectiveness is to doubt the power of a court wielded by a chancellor with legal imagination. It is certainly true that he cannot do anything to directors who are not subject to his jurisdiction. But he can do a great deal to the property of the corporate group which is within his jurisdiction. The Pennsyl-

vania courts know how to sequester assets of foreign corporations when the case is such that this form of relief is appropriate and the federal courts are equally potent in this respect. If the formal act by the board of directors is necessary under the Delaware General Corporation Law to regularize the dividends to which shareholders are entitled, we cannot think that a receivership or sequestration of a foreign corporation's property will not produce the result. Equity courts have known for a long time how to impose onerous alternatives at home to the performance of affirmative acts abroad as a means of getting those affirmative acts accomplished. In other words, if there is a corporate defendant properly subject to suit within the state and the plaintiff makes out a legal right against the corporation and the corporation has property within the state * * *, the chancellor can accomplish the result the plaintiff is entitled to have accomplished.

Id. at 764–65. Does this holding have any application outside the immediate context of forcing the payment of dividends? Is it indeed any different from simply ordering the corporation to pay dividends, and ignoring the directors? Can a court control the conduct of persons not subject to its personal jurisdiction by seizing control of property they own within its jurisdiction? See Shaffer v. Heitner, p. 154, supra.

———

Read Federal Rule of Civil Procedure 19 and the accompanying material in the Supplement.

———

PROVIDENT TRADESMENS BANK & TRUST CO. v. PATTERSON

United States Supreme Court, 1968.
390 U.S. 102, 88 S.Ct. 733, 19 L.Ed.2d 936.

Certiorari to the Circuit Court of Appeals for the Third Circuit.

MR. JUSTICE HARLAN delivered the opinion of the Court.

This controversy, involving in its present posture the dismissal of a declaratory judgment action for nonjoinder of an "indispensable" party, began nearly 10 years ago with a traffic accident. An automobile owned by Edward Dutcher, who was not present when the accident occurred, was being driven by Donald Cionci, to whom Dutcher had given the keys. John Lynch and John Harris were passengers. The automobile crossed the median strip of the highway and collided with a truck being driven by Thomas Smith. Cionci, Lynch, and Smith were killed and Harris was severely injured.

Three tort actions were brought. Provident Tradesmens Bank, the administrator of the estate of passenger Lynch and petitioner here, sued the estate of the driver, Cionci, in a diversity action. Smith's administratrix, and Harris in person, each brought a state-court action against the estate of Cionci, Dutcher, the owner, and the estate of Lynch. These Smith and Harris actions, for unknown reasons, have never gone to trial and are still pending. The Lynch action against Cionci's estate was settled for $50,000, which the estate of Cionci, being penniless, has never paid.

Dutcher, the owner of the automobile and a defendant in the as yet untried tort actions, had an automobile liability insurance policy with Lumbermens Mutual Casualty Company, a respondent here. That policy had an upper limit of $100,000 for all claims arising out of a single accident. This fund was potentially subject to two different sorts of claims by the tort plaintiffs. First, Dutcher himself might be held vicariously liable as Cionci's "principal"; the likelihood of such a judgment against Dutcher is a matter of considerable doubt and dispute. Second, the policy by its terms covered the direct liability of any person driving Dutcher's car with Dutcher's "permission."

The insurance company had declined, after notice, to defend in the tort action brought by Lynch's estate against the estate of Cionci, believing that Cionci had not had permission and hence was not covered by the policy. The facts allegedly were that Dutcher had entrusted his car to Cionci, but that Cionci had made a detour from the errand for which Dutcher allowed his car to be taken. The estate of Lynch, armed with its $50,000 liquidated claim against the estate of Cionci, brought the present diversity action for a declaration that Cionci's use of the car had been "with permission" of Dutcher. The only named defendants were the company and the estate of Cionci. The other two tort plaintiffs were joined as plaintiffs. Dutcher, a resident of the State of Pennsylvania as were all the plaintiffs, was not joined either as plaintiff or defendant. The failure to join him was not adverted to at the trial level.

The major question of law contested at trial was a state-law question. * * * The District Court * * * directed verdicts in favor of the two estates. * * * The jury * * * found that Cionci had had permission, and hence awarded a verdict to Harris also.

Lumbermens appealed the judgment to the Court of Appeals for the Third Circuit, raising various state-law questions.[1] The Court of Appeals did not reach any of these issues. Instead, after reargument *en banc,* it decided, 5–2, to reverse on two alternative grounds neither of which had been raised in the District Court or by the appellant.

The first of these grounds was that Dutcher was an indispensable party. The court held that the "adverse interests" that had rendered Dutcher incompetent to testify under the Pennsylvania Dead Man Rule also required him to be made a party. The court did not consider whether the fact that a verdict had already been rendered, without objection to the nonjoinder of Dutcher, affected the matter. Nor did it follow the provision of Rule 19 of the Federal Rules of Civil Procedure that findings of "indispensability" must be based on stated pragmatic considerations. It held, to the contrary, that the right of a person who "may be affected" by the judgment to be joined is a "substantive" right, unaffected by the federal rules; that a trial court "may not proceed" in the absence of such a person; and that since Dutcher could not be joined as a defendant without destroying diversity jurisdiction the action had to be dismissed.

---

1. Appellants challenged the District Court's ruling on the Dead Man issue that Dutcher was incompetent to testify under Pennsylvania law against an estate if he had an adverse interest to that of the estate, the fairness of submitting the question as to Harris to a jury that had been directed to find in favor of the two estates whose position was factually indistinguishable, and certain instructions.

* * * Concluding that the inflexible approach adopted by the Court of Appeals in this case exemplifies the kind of reasoning that the Rule was designed to avoid, we reverse.

I.

* * *

We may assume, at the outset, that Dutcher falls within the category of persons who, under [Rule 19] (a), should be "joined if feasible." The action was for an adjudication of the validity of certain claims against a fund. Dutcher, faced with the possibility of judgments against him, had an interest in having the fund preserved to cover that potential liability. Hence there existed, when this case went to trial, at least the possibility that a judgment might impede Dutcher's ability to protect his interest, or lead to later relitigation by him.

The optimum solution, an adjudication of the permission question that would be binding on all interested persons, was not "feasible," however, for Dutcher could not be made a defendant without destroying diversity. Hence the problem was the one to which Rule 19(b) appears to address itself: in the absence of a person who "should be joined if feasible," should the court dismiss the action or proceed without him? Since this problem emerged for the first time in the Court of Appeals, there were also two subsidiary questions. First, what was the effect, if any, of the failure of the defendants to raise the matter in the District Court? Second, what was the importance, if any, of the fact that a judgment, binding on the parties although not binding on Dutcher, had already been reached after extensive litigation? The three questions prove, on examination, to be interwoven.

We conclude, upon consideration of the record and applying the "equity and good conscience" test of Rule 19(b), that the Court of Appeals erred in not allowing the judgment to stand.

Rule 19(b) suggests four "interests" that must be examined in each case to determine whether, in equity and good conscience, the court should proceed without a party whose absence from the litigation is compelled. Each of these interests must, in this case, be viewed entirely from an appellate perspective since the matter of joinder was not considered in the trial court. First, the plaintiff has an interest in having a forum. Before the trial, the strength of this interest obviously depends upon whether a satisfactory alternative forum exists. On appeal, if the plaintiff has won, he has a strong additional interest in preserving his judgment. Second, the defendant may properly wish to avoid multiple litigation, or inconsistent relief, or sole responsibility for a liability he shares with another. After trial, however, if the defendant has failed to assert this interest, it is quite proper to consider it foreclosed.

Third, there is the interest of the outsider whom it would have been desirable to join. Of course, since the outsider is not before the court, he cannot be bound by the judgment rendered. This means, however, only that a judgment is not *res judicata* as to, or legally enforceable against, a nonparty. It obviously does not mean either (a) that a court may never issue a judgment that, in practice, affects a nonparty or (b) that (to the contrary) a court may always proceed without considering the potential effect on nonparties simply because they are not "bound" in the technical sense. Instead, as Rule 19(a) expresses it, the court must consider the extent to which the judgment may "as a practical matter impair or impede his ability to protect" his interest in the subject matter. When a case has reached the appeal stage the matter is more complex. The judgment appealed from may not in fact affect the interest of any outsider even though there existed, before trial, a possibility that a judgment affecting his interest would be rendered. When necessary, however, a court of appeals should, on its own initiative, take steps to protect the absent party, who of course had no opportunity to plead and prove his interest below.

Fourth, there remains the interest of the courts and the public in complete, consistent, and efficient settlement of controversies. We read the Rule's third criterion, whether the judgment issued in the absence of the nonjoined person will be "adequate," to refer to this public stake in settling disputes by wholes, whenever possible, for clearly the plaintiff, who himself chose both the forum and the parties defendant, will not be heard to complain about the sufficiency of the relief obtainable against them. After trial, considerations of efficiency of course include the fact that the time and expense of a trial have already been spent.

Rule 19(b) also directs a district court to consider the possibility of shaping relief to accommodate these four interests. Commentators had argued that greater attention should be paid to this potential solution to a joinder stymie, and the Rule now makes it explicit that a court should consider modification of a judgment as an alternative to dismissal. Needless to say, a court of appeals may also properly require suitable modification as a condition of affirmance.

Had the Court of Appeals applied Rule 19's criteria to the facts of the present case, it could hardly have reached the conclusion it did. We begin with the plaintiffs' viewpoint. It is difficult to decide at this stage whether they would have had an "adequate" remedy had the action been dismissed before trial for nonjoinder: we cannot here determine whether the plaintiffs could have brought the same action, against the same parties plus Dutcher, in a state court. After trial, however, the "adequacy" of this hypothetical alternative, from the plaintiffs' point of view, was obviously greatly diminished. Their interest in preserving a fully litigated judgment should be overborne only by rather greater opposing considerations than would be required at an earlier stage when the plaintiffs' only concern was for a federal rather than a state forum.

Opposing considerations in this case are hard to find. The defendants had no stake, either asserted or real, in the joinder of Dutcher. They showed no interest in joinder until the Court of Appeals took the matter into its own hands. This properly forecloses any interest of theirs, but for purposes of clarity we note that the insurance company, whose liability was limited to $100,000, had or will have full opportunity to litigate each claim on that fund against the claimant involved. Its only concern with the absence of Dutcher was and is to obtain a windfall escape from its defeat at trial.

The interest of the outsider, Dutcher, is more difficult to reckon. The Court of Appeals, concluding that it should not follow Rule 19's command to determine whether, as a practical matter, the judgment impaired the nonparty's ability to protect his rights, simply quoted the District Court's reasoning on the Dead Man issue as proof that Dutcher had a "right" to be joined:

> The subject matter of this suit is the coverage of Lumbermens' policy issued to Dutcher. Depending upon the outcome of this trial, Dutcher may have the policy all to himself or he may have to share its coverage with the Cionci Estate, thereby extending the availability of the proceeds of the policy to satisfy verdicts and judgments in favor of the two Estate plaintiffs. Sharing the coverage of a policy of insurance with finite limits with another, and thereby making that policy available to claimants against that other person is immediately worth less than having the coverage of such policy available to Dutcher alone. By the outcome in the instant case, to the extent that the two Estate plaintiffs will have the proceeds of the policy available to them in their claims against Cionci's estate, Dutcher will lose a measure of protection. Conversely, to the extent that the proceeds of this policy are not available to the two Estate plaintiffs Dutcher will gain. * * * It is sufficient for the purpose of determining adversity [of interest] that it appears clearly that the measure of Dutcher's protection under this policy of insurance is dependent upon the outcome of this suit. That being so, Dutcher's interest in these proceedings is adverse to the interest of the two Estate plaintiffs, the parties who represent, on this record, the interests of the deceased persons in the matter in controversy.[11]

There is a logical error in the Court of Appeals' appropriation of this reasoning for its own quite different purposes: Dutcher had an "adverse" interest (sufficient to invoke the Dead Man Rule) because he would have been *benefited* by a ruling *in favor of* the insurance company; the question before the Court of Appeals, however, was whether Dutcher was *harmed* by the judgment *against* the insurance company.

The two questions are not the same. If the three plaintiffs had lost to the insurance company on the permission issue, that loss would have ended the matter favorably to Dutcher. If, as has happened, the three plaintiffs obtain a judgment against the insurance company on the permission issue, Dutcher may still claim that as a nonparty he is not estopped by that judgment from relitigating the issue. At that point it might be argued that Dutcher should be bound by the previous decision because, although technically a nonparty, he had purposely bypassed an adequate opportunity to intervene. We do not now decide whether such an argument would be correct under the circumstances of this case. If, however, Dutcher is properly foreclosed by his failure to intervene in the present litigation, then the joinder issue considered in the Court of Appeals vanishes, for any rights of Dutcher's have been lost by his own inaction.

If Dutcher is not foreclosed by his failure to intervene below, then he is not "bound" by the judgment in favor of the insurance company and, in theory, he has not been harmed. There remains, however, the practical question whether Dutcher is likely to have any need, and if so will have any opportunity, to relitigate. The only possible threat to him is that if the fund is used to pay judgments against Cionci the money may in fact have disappeared

11. 218 F.Supp. 802, 805–806, quoted at 365 F.2d, at 805.

before Dutcher has an opportunity to assert his interest. Upon examination, we find this supposed threat neither large nor unavoidable.

The state-court actions against Dutcher had lain dormant for years at the pleading stage by the time the Court of Appeals acted. Petitioner asserts here that under the applicable Pennsylvania vicarious liability law there is virtually no chance of recovery against Dutcher. We do not accept this assertion as fact, but the matter could have been explored below. Furthermore, even in the event of tort judgments against Dutcher, it is unlikely that he will be prejudiced by the outcome here. The potential claimants against Dutcher himself are identical with the potential claimants against Cionci's estate. Should the claimants seek to collect from Dutcher personally, he may be able to raise the permission issue defensively, making it irrelevant that the actual monies paid from the fund may have disappeared: Dutcher can assert that Cionci did not have his permission and that therefore the payments made on Cionci's behalf out of Dutcher's insurance policy should properly be credited against Dutcher's own liability. Of course, when Dutcher raises this defense he may lose, either on the merits of the permission issue or on the ground that the issue is foreclosed by Dutcher's failure to intervene in the present case, but Dutcher will not have been prejudiced by the failure of the District Court here to order him joined.

If the Court of Appeals was unconvinced that the threat to Dutcher was trivial, it could nevertheless have avoided all difficulties by proper phrasing of the decree. The District Court, for unspecified reasons, had refused to order immediate payment on the Cionci judgment. Payment could have been withheld pending the suits against Dutcher and relitigation (if that became necessary) by him. In this Court, furthermore, counsel for petitioners represented orally that they, the tort plaintiffs, would accept a limitation of all claims to the amount of the insurance policy. Obviously such a compromise could have been reached below had the Court of Appeals been willing to abandon its rigid approach and seek ways to preserve what was, as to the parties, subject to the appellants' other contentions, a perfectly valid judgment.

The suggestion of potential relitigation of the question of "permission" raises the fourth "interest" at stake in joinder cases—efficiency. It might have been preferable, at the trial level, if there were a forum available in which both the company and Dutcher could have been made defendants, to dismiss the action and force the plaintiffs to go elsewhere. Even this preference would have been highly problematical, however, for the actual threat of relitigation by Dutcher depended on there being judgments against him and on the amount of the fund, which was not revealed to the District Court. By the time the case reached the Court of Appeals, however, the problematical preference on efficiency grounds had entirely disappeared: there was no reason then to throw away a valid judgment just because it did not theoretically settle the whole controversy.

II.

Application of Rule 19(b)'s "equity and good conscience" test for determining whether to proceed or dismiss would doubtless have led to a contrary result below. The Court of Appeals' reasons for disregarding the Rule remain to be examined. The majority of the court concluded that the Rule was inapplicable because "substantive" rights are involved, and substantive rights are not affected by the Federal Rules. Although the court did not articulate exactly what the substantive rights are, or what law determines them, we take it to have been making the following argument: (1) there is a category of persons called "indispensable parties"; (2) that category is defined by substantive law and the definition cannot be modified by rule; (3) the right of a person falling within that category to participate in the lawsuit in question is also a substantive matter, and is absolute.

With this we may contrast the position that is reflected in Rule 19. Whether a person is "indispensable," that is, whether a particular lawsuit must be dismissed in the absence of that person, can only be determined in the context of particular litigation. There is a large category, whose limits are not presently in question, of persons who, in the Rule's terminology, should be "joined if feasible," and who, in the older terminology, were called either necessary or indispensable parties. Assuming the existence of a person who should be joined if feasible, the only further question arises when joinder is not possible and the court must decide whether to dismiss or to proceed without him. To use the familiar but confusing terminology, the decision to proceed is a decision that the absent person is merely "necessary" while the decision to dismiss is a decision that he is "indispensable." The decision whether to dismiss (i.e., the decision whether the person missing is "indispensable") must be based on factors varying with the different cases, some such factors being substantive, some procedural, some compelling by themselves, and some subject to balancing against opposing interests. Rule 19 does not prevent the assertion of compelling substantive interests; it merely commands the courts to examine each controversy to make certain that the interests really exist. To say that a court "must" dismiss in the absence of an indispensable party and that it "cannot proceed" without him puts the matter the wrong way around: a court does not know whether a particular person is "indispensable" until it has examined the situation to determine whether it can proceed without him.

The Court of Appeals concluded, although it was the first court to hold, that the 19th century joinder cases in this Court created a federal, common-law, substantive right in a certain class of persons to be joined in the corresponding lawsuits. At the least, that was not the way the matter started. The joinder problem first arose in equity and in the earliest case giving rise to extended discussion the problem was the relatively simple one of the inefficiency of litigation involving only some of the interested persons. [E]lmendorf v. Taylor, 23 U.S. (10 Wheat.) 152, 6 L.Ed. 289 (1825).] * * *

Following this case there arose three cases, also in equity, that the Court of Appeals here held to have declared a "substantive" right to be joined. It is true that these cases involved what would now be called "substantive" rights. This substantive involvement of the absent person with the controversy before the Court was, however, in each case simply an inescapable fact of the situation presented to the Court for adjudication. The Court in each case left the outsider with no more "rights" than it had already found belonged to him. The question in each case was simply whether, given the substantive involvement of the outsider, it was proper to proceed to adjudicate as between the parties.

* * *

The most influential of the cases in which this Court considered the question whether to proceed or dismiss in the absence of an interested but not joinable outsider is Shields v. Barrow, 17 How. 130, 15 L.Ed. 158, referred to in the opinion below. There the Court attempted, perhaps unfortunately, to stage general definitions of those persons without whom litigation could or could not proceed. In the former category were placed

> Persons having an interest in the controversy, and who ought to be made parties, in order that the court may act on that rule which requires it to decide on, and finally determine the entire controversy, and do complete justice, by adjusting all the rights involved in it. These persons are commonly termed necessary parties; but if their interests are separable from those of the parties before the court, so that the court can proceed to a decree, and do complete and final justice, without affecting other persons not before the court, the latter are not indispensable parties.

The persons in the latter category were

> Persons who not only have an interest in the controversy, but an interest of such a nature that a final decree cannot be made without either affecting that interest, or leaving the controversy in such a condition that its final termination may be wholly inconsistent with equity and good conscience.

These generalizations are still valid today, and they are consistent with the requirements of Rule 19, but they are not a substitute for the analysis required by that Rule. Indeed, the second *Shields* definition states, in rather different fashion, the criteria for decision announced in Rule 19(b). One basis for dismissal is prejudice to the rights of an absent party that *"cannot"* be avoided in issuance of a final decree. Alternatively, if the decree can be so written that it protects the interests of the absent persons, but as so written it leaves the controversy so situated that the outcome may be inconsistent with "equity and good conscience," the suit should be dismissed.

The majority of the Court of Appeals read Shields v. Barrow to say that a person whose interests "may be affected" by the decree of the court is an indispensable party, and that all indispensable parties have a "substantive right" to have suits dismissed in their absence. We are unable to read *Shields* as saying either. It dealt only with persons whose interests must, unavoidably, be affected by a decree and it said nothing about substantive rights. Rule 19(b), which the Court of Appeals dismissed as an ineffective attempt to change the substantive rights stated in *Shields,* is, on the contrary, a valid statement of the criteria for determining whether to proceed or dismiss in the forced absence of an interested person. It takes, for aught that now appears, adequate account of the very real, very substantive claims to fairness on the part of outsiders that may arise in some cases. This, however, simply is not such a case.

* * *

The judgment is vacated and the case is remanded to the Court of Appeals * * *.

Notes and Questions

1. *Provident Tradesmens* interprets the amended version of Federal Rule 19, which was promulgated in 1966. Examine the Advisory Committee's Note to Rule 19, which is set out in the Supplement. What impact does the amendment have on the distinction between necessary and indispensable parties? Given the amendment, what is the purpose of Rule 12(b)(7)? For a negative appraisal of the amended text, see Fink, *Indispensable Parties and the Proposed Amendment to Federal Rule 19,* 74 Yale L.J. 403 (1965).

2. What was the basis of the Court's finding in *Provident Tradesmens* with regard to prejudice for purposes of Rule 19(b) if Dutcher was not joined? Consider the following comments in an article written shortly after the Third Circuit decision dismissing the action and before the Supreme Court's decision.

> * * * How has Dutcher been affected? The judgment declaring that Cionci was driving with permission does not bind Dutcher legally, since he was not a party. Dutcher is free to contest the point with all, including the insurer. Be it noted that although he testified in the action, Dutcher made no attempt to intervene; as the minority suggests, he might have reasonably preferred to stay out of the action. Whereas a judgment declaring Cionci to be an insured did not bind Dutcher, a judgment the other way would very likely have inured to Dutcher's benefit * * *.

Kaplan, *Continuing Work of the Civil Committee: 1966 Amendments of the Federal Rules of Civil Procedure (I),* 81 Harv.L.Rev. 356, 373 (1967).

In what ways might the court shape relief in order to lessen any prejudice? Is the court free simply to grant a remedy other than the one originally requested—for example, by awarding money damages when specific performance might have a detrimental impact on the absentee? Of what importance is the availability of another forum in determining whether the action must be dismissed in the absence of someone whose joinder is not feasible? For a case in which the court determined that it was impossible to shape the relief so as to avoid prejudice to absent parties, see Wichita & Affiliated Tribes of Oklahoma v. Hodel, 788 F.2d 765, 776 (D.C.Cir.1986).

3. What weight should be given to the various factors listed in Rule 19? Because there is no precise formula for determining whether a particular nonparty must be joined under Rule 19(a), the decision has to be made in light of the general policies of the Rule. Can you articulate what those policies are? For example, what is the difference between the Rule 19(a)(1) standard that in the absence of the nonparty "complete relief cannot be accorded among those already parties," and the third factor listed in Rule 19(b), "whether a judgment rendered in the person's absence will be adequate"? The second test set out in Rule 19(a) focuses on the prejudicial effect of not joining the absentee. What type of prejudice must be shown to meet this requirement? See generally Tobias, *Rule 19 and the Public Rights Exception to Party Joinder,* 65 N.C.L.Rev. 745 (1987). For applications of Rule 19(a), see Makah Indian Tribe v. Verity, 910 F.2d 555 (9th Cir.1990); Swerhun v. General Motors Corp., 141 F.R.D. 342 (M.D.Fla.1992).

4. Should a court dismiss an action because of the plaintiff's failure to join an indispensable party plaintiff, even though the defendant can join the missing

party as a Rule 13(h) party to a compulsory counterclaim? In ASSOCIATED DRY GOODS CORP. v. TOWERS FINANCIAL CORP., 920 F.2d 1121, 1124 (2d Cir.1990), the defendant, a commercial subtenant, sought to dismiss the tenant's action for payment of rent because the tenant had failed to join the building's owner, 417 Fifth, as an indispensable party plaintiff. The plaintiff did not join the building owner because he was nondiverse, which would strip the court of subject matter jurisdiction. The District Court dismissed the action pursuant to Rule 19(b). The Second Circuit reversed:

> The drafters of Rule 19(b) did not assign relative weight to each of the factors enumerated in the Rule. Instead, the Rule allows courts themselves to determine the emphasis to be placed on each consideration according to "the facts of [the] given case and in light of the governing equity-and-good-conscience test." * * * In this case, we view as dispositive Towers' ability to avoid all prejudice to itself by asserting a compulsory counterclaim against Associated pursuant to Rule 13(a) and adding 417 Fifth as a party to the counterclaim under Rule 13(h). * * *

5. What should the result be when plaintiff, a citizen of Texas, sues defendant, a citizen of Arkansas, in a federal district court in Arkansas, and, on defendant's motion, the court requires that X, a citizen of Texas, be joined as a defendant in the action?

In SCHUTTEN v. SHELL OIL CO., 421 F.2d 869 (5th Cir.1970), the plaintiff filed suit seeking to evict Shell Oil Company and for an accounting for the removal of oil, gas, and other minerals from land in Plaquemines Parish, Louisiana, claiming ownership of the land. The defendant filed a motion to dismiss on the ground that its lessor, the Board of Commissioners of the Orleans Levee District, who also claimed title to the land in question, was an "indispensable party" who could not be joined since such action would destroy the District Court's diversity jurisdiction. The District Court granted the defendant's motion and dismissed the case.

After concluding that the Levee Board was a party "to be joined if feasible," the Fifth Circuit stated:

> * * * Since it is not feasible to join the Levee Board we must now consider what alternatives are available under the "equity and good conscience" standard. To do this we must apply the pragmatic criteria of subdivision (b) of Rule 19.
>
> The first factor that must be considered is the extent to which a judgment might prejudice the unjoined Levee Board or those already parties. * * * It is clear that courts should not proceed simply because the unjoined party is not "bound" in the technical sense. * * * Furthermore, one of the purposes, though not the sole purpose, of Rule 19 is the avoidance of multiple litigation of essentially the same issues.
>
> The possibility of prejudice to the Levee Board is most certainly not superficial. First, if Shell is ousted the Levee Board's royalty interest would cease in practically the same manner as if the court had decreed a cancellation of the lease. This would happen despite the fact that the Levee Board's claim of ownership would be technically unimpaired by the judgment in the sense that it would not be bound by the judgment.
>
> Second, though not technically bound a judgment would most assuredly create a cloud on the Levee Board's title and greatly diminish the value of the property. This result would be adverse to both appellants and the Board and

would require yet more litigation. A judgment in favor of the appellants would in effect adjudicate the Levee Board's claim of ownership without giving them the right to present their defense and assert their own claim on its merits. While Shell does have a substantial interest in the Levee Board's claim this "interest" would not justify placing the burden of proving the Levee Board's ownership on Shell.

Third, a judgment might result in inconsistent obligations for the defendant Shell Oil Company. * * * Again all of this could come about without affording the Levee Board the opportunity to defend its interests even though the Board would not be bound by the judgment.

A conclusion that as a practical matter the Levee Board would be prejudiced by a judgment rendered in their absence leads us to consider the second and third "factors" of Rule 19: "the extent to which, by protective provisions in the judgment, by the shaping of relief, or other measures, the prejudice can be lessened or avoided", and whether a judgment rendered in the Levee Board's absence will be adequate. Appellants have suggested no way in which these objectives could be accomplished and we are unable to discover any ourselves. Since the litigation revolved around the conflicting claims of ownership, we are unable to envision a decree which would effectively settle any controversy between the appellants and the present defendant, Shell, without doing substantial practical injury to the Levee Board's unassertable claims. Any attempt to fashion a judgment which would lessen this harm would result in a meaningless decree.

* * * [Last we must] consider the fourth and final criteria of Rule 19: whether the appellant has an adequate remedy elsewhere. The answer to this question is that appellants will by no means be prejudiced themselves if forced to pursue their remedy in the courts of the State of Louisiana. Both the Levee Board and Shell are amenable to process in Louisiana. This litigation concerns land situated in Louisiana, is governed by Louisiana law and involves a claim of ownership asserted by an agency of the State of Louisiana. * * * There is, however, an even more compelling reason for appellants to seek relief in the Louisiana courts. * * * By dismissing the case now and directing the appellants to proceed in the Louisiana courts most if not all issues can be settled in one bout of litigation. As noted above, the expeditious and effective disposition of litigation is desirable if not always obtainable. In the present case it is not only desirable but obtainable and is indeed made necessary under the circumstances.

Id. at 874–75.

SECTION E.   IMPLEADER

———

Read Federal Rule of Civil Procedure 14 and the material accompanying it in the Supplement.

———

JEUB v. B/G FOODS, INC.

United States District Court, District of Minnesota, 1942.
2 F.R.D. 238.

NORDBYE, DISTRICT JUDGE. The facts are briefly these: The complainants seek to recover damages from the defendant, B/G Foods, Inc., on the grounds that, in one of the restaurants operated by this defendant, they were served with certain ham which was contaminated, unwholesome, and deleterious to the health, causing complainants to become sick and distressed to their damage. * * * Prior to the service of the answer, on application of the defendant, an ex parte order was obtained, making Swift and Company a third-party defendant. The third-party complaint set forth that the ham served was canned "Swift Premium Ham", a product of Swift and Company, and purchased in a sealed can by B/G Foods the day preceding the serving of the ham to the complainants. It is asserted that B/G Foods was entirely free from any blame or negligence in connection therewith. It is further alleged in the third-party complaint that "if any of said ham was unwholesome, poisonous, deleterious or otherwise in any way unfit for human consumption, such condition was caused solely and entirely by negligence and carelessness and unlawful conduct on the part of Swift and Company." Further, that "Swift and Company is liable to indemnify and reimburse B/G Foods, Inc., for the whole amount of any recovery made by plaintiff, * * * against B/G Foods, Inc., on account of said ham being served to her in its food shop. * * *" Judgment is prayed that any recovery be against Swift and Company and not B/G Foods, Inc., and that B/G Foods, Inc., have judgment against Swift and Company for any and all sums which may be adjudged against B/G Foods, Inc., in favor of the plaintiff.

The motion to vacate the order is based on the showing that plaintiffs have not amended, and have refused to amend, their complaints to state any cause of action against Swift and Company. It is therefore the position of the third-party defendant that no relief can be granted against it in this proceeding; that [Federal] Rule 14 * * * is merely procedural and does not create any substantive rights; that no right of contribution or indemnity exists under the Minnesota law merely because a suit has been commenced; and that the party must have suffered some loss or paid more than his share of the loss before any rights will inure. It is pointed out that, as yet, the B/G Foods has suffered no loss and has made no payment growing out of the incident in question.

That the rights over and against Swift and Company, which B/G Foods may have by reason of any loss sustained by it, must be governed by the substantive laws of this State is entirely clear. The invoking of the third-party procedural practice must not do violence to the substantive rights of the parties. However, an acceleration or an expedition of the presentation of such rights does not conflict with any Minnesota law. [Federal] Rule 14 * * * permits the impleader of a party "who is or may be liable." The fact that an independent action for money recovery could not be brought at this time does not militate against B/G Foods' right to invoke a procedure which will determine rights of the parties concurrently with that of the basic proceeding, and if and when any loss has been sustained as to which Swift and Company is liable over, the laws of this State in regard thereto may be made effective.

* * * Rule 14 is not restricted to the rights of indemnity or contribution which are presently enforcible [sic] * * *.

The apparent purpose of Rule 14 is to provide suitable machinery whereby the rights of all parties may be determined in one proceeding. Manifestly if Swift and Company is liable over to B/G Foods, Inc., for any or all damages sustained by reason of the tortious act alleged, no cogent reason is suggested why the original defendant should not avail itself of this rule. Otherwise, B/G Foods, Inc., would be required to await the outcome of the present suit, and then if plaintiffs recover, to institute an independent action for contribution or indemnity. The rule under consideration was promulgated to avoid this very circuity of proceeding. Neither is any good reason suggested why the determination of the entire controversy in one proceeding will prejudice the rights of any of the parties. Certainly, plaintiffs cannot complain. They have not availed themselves of the opportunity to join Swift and Company as a party defendant. To require the same jury to determine the controversy between the third-party plaintiff and third-party defendant will not harm or jeopardize their rights or position before these triers of fact. The rights of Swift and Company are likewise not prejudiced by being made a third-party defendant. If it is liable over, it is concerned with the payment by B/G Foods, Inc., of any loss or damage obtained by these plaintiffs. However, the recognition or preservation of that right presents no particular difficulty. Any judgment against it by way of contribution or indemnity may be stayed until the judgment in the original proceeding against the B/G Foods, Inc., is paid or satisfied. One jury impaneled to determine the entire controversy may not only save time and expense, but it is fair to assume that the ends of justice will be served by disposition of the entire matter through the facilities of one jury. * * *

The motion, therefore, to vacate the order making Swift and Company a third-party defendant in each of the above-entitled cases, is denied. * * *

Notes and Questions

1. In a diversity case in a state that adheres to the common-law rule prohibiting contribution among joint tortfeasors, must a federal court deny impleader of a joint tortfeasor? Note that in *Jeub* the applicable state law recognized a substantive right of action but merely failed to provide a procedural device for the acceleration or concurrent determination of the liability as part of the principal lawsuit. How might the court shape the relief on an accelerated or contingent claim to reflect the limitations of substantive state law?

2. What factors should the court consider in determining whether to allow a third-party defendant to be impleaded? May a defendant-insured in a negligence action implead the liability insurer under Rule 14 when the insurance policy contains either a "no action" clause or a provision to the effect that "nothing contained in this policy shall give any person or organization any right to join the company as a codefendant in any action against the insured to determine the latter's liability"?

3. In MISKELL v. W.T. COWN, INC., 10 F.R.D. 617 (E.D.Pa.1950), defendant moved to bring in a third party. Plaintiff opposed the motion on the ground that the third party was a sailor who might be unavailable at the time of trial or

exempted from appearing under the Soldiers' and Sailors' Civil Relief Act. The court rejected plaintiff's arguments, stating:

> The plaintiff's concern is, I believe, premature. For even though the motion to implead be granted, this Court has, under the Federal Rules, ample discretion to protect the plaintiff from prejudice and inconvenience. If, at the time of trial, the third party is not required to answer, the Court may order a separate trial between plaintiff and defendant under Rule 42(b) and, under Rule 54(b) enter a separate judgment. In this manner, not only may the plaintiff be protected but the defendant may also be protected against the necessity of filing a separate suit should the situation not require it. * * *

Id. at 618.

———

In GOODHART v. UNITED STATES LINES CO., 26 F.R.D. 163 (S.D.N.Y.1960), plaintiff sued for personal injuries caused by defendant's employee. The court denied a motion to implead the employee:

> I feel safe in taking judicial notice of the fact that the operator of a hi-lo [defendant's employee] will not be financially able to indemnify defendant to any substantial extent. Defendant must have some other reason or reasons for seeking impleader. One of those reasons is that jurors will likely render a smaller verdict if they are required to find that an individual employee of defendant is ultimately responsible for its payment. Another is that the interest of the hi-lo operator in a verdict for his employer will be heightened. * * *
>
> In seeking the first result defendant, in effect, asks me to give it the advantage of the chance that the jury will proceed upon a false supposition that the hi-lo operator will pay the judgment. In seeking the second result defendant, in effect, asks me to help him threaten the hi-lo operator with the necessity of going through bankruptcy unless he testifies favorably to defendant. Neither of these pleas recommends itself to the court as a subject for exercise of the court's discretion. Such legitimate claim as defendant may have against the hi-lo operator is amply protected by defendant's right to bring a separate suit.

Id. at 164.

Notes and Questions

1. Would permitting impleader but granting a motion for separate trials under Rule 42(b), as suggested in *Miskell,* have adequately protected plaintiff from possible prejudice? Are there any advantages to this procedure?

2. Rule 14 does not allow a defendant to implead an existing defendant. See Horton v. Continental Can Co., 19 F.R.D. 429 (D.Neb.1956). But there are at least two other possible procedures for a defendant to assert its claims against an existing defendant. What are they? What difference does it make if a defendant's claim is brought under Rule 14 or some "other appropriate procedure"? What is the logic of Rule 13(a), (b), and (g) permitting or requiring counterclaims and cross-claims to be asserted against persons who already are parties and Rule 14(a) denying impleader in that context?

3. * * * This practice [impleader] has its roots in the common-law procedure of "vouching to warranty," whereby a person whose title to land has been attacked could notify his vendor of the attack if the latter had warranted the title. The vendor, whether or not he chose to participate, would then be bound by the prior determination in a subsequent suit by his vendee.

Developments in the Law—Multiparty Litigation in the Federal Courts, 71 Harv. L.Rev. 874, 907 (1958). In what ways does third-party practice under Federal Rule 14 differ from the common-law procedure of vouching to warranty? See Note 4 on p. 1282, infra. For a discussion of the "vouching-in" procedure, see Degnan & Barton, *Vouching to Quality Warranty: Case Law and Commercial Code,* 51 Calif.L.Rev. 471 (1963).

4. The states take a variety of different approaches to third-party practice. Indeed, the practice in a number of states is very different from that under Federal Rule 14. Many of the reasons for this difference in practice are described in Friedenthal, *The Expansion of Joinder in Cross–Complaints by the Erroneous Interpretation of Section 442 of the California Code of Civil Procedure,* 51 Calif.L.Rev. 494 (1963).

———

REVERE COPPER & BRASS, INC. v. AETNA CAS. & SUR. CO., 426 F.2d 709, 715–17 (5th Cir.1970). Revere sued Aetna on a surety bond executed in connection with a construction contract, alleging that Fuller, the builder, had breached express and implied warranties and specific contract provisions, had been negligent, had made false representations, and had failed to complete its work within the prescribed time. It sought damages of $2,045,000. Aetna impleaded Fuller under Rule 14(a), claiming that the builder had agreed to indemnify Aetna for all losses sustained as a result of the suretyship. Fuller asserted a "counterclaim" against Revere seeking $1,328,880 based on the breach of certain express and implied warranties and for wanton and willful misconduct. Revere moved to dismiss Fuller's claim on the ground that there was no diversity of citizenship between Revere and Fuller; the District Court held the claim to be within its ancillary jurisdiction. On appeal, the Fifth Circuit, after discussing the six reported district court decisions dealing with the question, affirmed, holding that the claim clearly fell within the core of aggregate facts upon which the original claim rested and thus was within the court's ancillary jurisdiction. Judge Morgan, speaking for the court, stated:

It is easily seen that Fuller's claim arises out of the aggregate of operative facts which forms the basis of Revere's claim in such a way to put their logical relationship beyond doubt. The two claims are but two sides of the same coin. The construction was not completed before the time provided in the two contracts. If Revere is not responsible for the delay, as Fuller alleges, Fuller must at least be guilty of breach of contract, not to mention the other allegations of fault in Revere's complaint. To paraphrase the Supreme Court in Moore v. New York Cotton Exchange * * * [Note 4, p. 609, supra]: so close is the connection between the case sought to be stated in Revere's complaint and that set up in Fuller's Rule 14(a) counterclaim that it only needs the failure of the former to establish the foundation for the latter.

Not only is the parallel between a Rule 14(a) counterclaim and a compulsory counterclaim under Rule 13(a) so close as to be persuasive on the question of ancillarity, the parallel between the instant case and cases dealing with the ability of an intervenor of right under Rule 24(a) to counterclaim against the original plaintiff without an independent basis of federal jurisdiction removes any substantial doubt. It is well established that a contractor who has agreed to indemnify his surety on a performance bond can intervene as a party defendant as of right in a suit on the performance bond against the surety and then assert his counterclaim against the plaintiff, even in the absence of an independent ground of federal jurisdiction. * * * It would be anomalous to hold that Fuller could have asserted its counterclaim against Revere free of any jurisdictional impediment if it had taken the initiative of intervening, and yet hold that since Fuller was brought into this action involuntarily as a third-party defendant, its counterclaim must satisfy the requirements of strict diversity and thus fail.

* * * Revere argues that since there must be an independent ground of jurisdiction to support the original plaintiff's claim against a third-party defendant, the same requirement must be met by the third-party defendant in asserting a counterclaim against the original plaintiff. Suffice it to say that the two situations are the converse of each other only superficially and that there are differences which militate against identical treatment. First of all, the plaintiff has the option of selecting the forum where he believes he can most effectively assert his claims, he has not been involuntarily brought to a forum, faced with the prospect of defending himself as best he can under the rules that forum provides, or defending himself not at all. Since a plaintiff could not initially join a non-diverse defendant, it is arguable he should not be allowed to do so indirectly by way of a fortuitous impleader. Moreover, there is the possibility, whether real or fanciful, of collusion between the plaintiff and an overly cooperative defendant impleading just the right third party. Whatever the merit or demerit of these reasons, they point to a sufficient difference to require that the application of ancillary jurisdiction to each type of claim must be decided separately. Consequently, this decision is to be strictly limited to the precise question decided.

Notes and Questions

1. The *Revere* case is discussed in 59 Ky.L.J. 506 (1970); 1970 Wash.U.L.Q. 511; and 49 N.C.L.Rev. 503 (1971). In Owen Equipment & Erection Co. v. Kroger, p. 305, supra, the Supreme Court validated the conclusion in *Revere* that a claim by the original plaintiff against the third-party defendant arising out of the transaction or occurrence that is the subject matter of plaintiff's claim against the original defendant may be interposed only if it meets independent jurisdictional requirements. Does a rereading of *Kroger* reveal any reason to doubt the conclusion in *Revere* that a claim by a third-party defendant against the original plaintiff is within the ancillary jurisdiction of the federal courts?

2. Before Congress enacted 28 U.S.C. § 1367, the effect of Finley v. United States, p. 306, supra, on a District Court's ability to assert ancillary jurisdiction over an impleader claim between the third-party plaintiff and the third-party

defendant was unclear. Section 1367 now provides for supplemental jurisdiction over additional claims so long as they are part of the same case or controversy as the action over which the court has original jurisdiction. This standard encompasses impleader claims and additional related claims asserted by the third-party plaintiff against the third-party defendant. See Washington Hosp. Center Nat'l Rehabilitation Hosp. v. Collier, 947 F.2d 1498, 1501 (D.C.Cir.1991). However, when a federal court's subject matter jurisdiction is based solely on diversity, Section 1367(b) withholds supplemental jurisdiction from plaintiffs who bring claims against parties joined pursuant to Rule 14. This provision codifies the Supreme Court's ruling in Owen Equipment & Erection Co. v. Kroger, p. 305, supra.

How would *Revere* be decided under Section 1367? See generally Freer, *Compounding Confusion and Hampering Diversity: Life After Finley and the Supplemental Jurisdiction Statute,* 40 Emory L.J. 445 (1991); Oakley, *Recent Statutory Changes in the Law of Federal Jurisdiction and Venue: The Judicial Improvement Acts of 1988 and 1990,* 24 U.C.Davis L.Rev. 735 (1991).

3.   According to the existing case law, the statutory venue limitations have no application to Rule 14 claims even if they would require the third-party proceeding to be heard in another district had it been brought as an independent action. However, should jurisdiction and venue be treated the same or differently in the context of a claim by the third-party defendant against the original plaintiff? See generally 6 Wright, Miller & Kane, *Federal Practice and Procedure: Civil 2d* § 1445 (1990).

4.   Are there any limitations on the third-party defendant's ability to assert a claim against the third-party plaintiff? Against the original plaintiff? In HEINTZ & CO. v. PROVIDENT TRADESMENS BANK & TRUST CO. v. KERR, 30 F.R.D. 171 (E.D.Pa.1962), plaintiff alleged that defendant negligently permitted Kerr to open a bank account in plaintiff's name and to draw checks without plaintiff's permission. Defendant impleaded Kerr. Kerr then filed a claim against plaintiff for services rendered and materials furnished to plaintiff in connection with the establishment of a branch office managed by Kerr. The court found Kerr's claim within Rule 14 because it arose out of the same transaction as the original suit.

> * * * The only distinction between a counterclaim under Rule 13(a) and the sort of claim we have before us under Rule 14 is that defendant "must" plead his counterclaim under Rule 13(a) if it grows out of the same transaction or occurrence, whereas under Rule 14, the third party "may" plead his claim for relief. But this, we think, is a distinction without a difference. The ancillary nature of the claim is not to be determined by whether the pleader "must" or "may" assert it, but by its relation to the transaction that is the subject of the main suit.

Id. at 174. If the original plaintiff has a counterclaim arising out of the same transaction as the claim asserted by the third-party defendant, is it compulsory? Can the original plaintiff assert a permissive counterclaim against the third-party defendant?

Another problem in third-party practice is exemplified by NOLAND CO. v. GRAVER TANK & MFG. CO., 301 F.2d 43 (4th Cir.1962), which grew out of a suit originally brought by Ruscon Construction Company, a general contractor, against Noland, a subcontractor, for the difference between the cost of a water tank and the subcontractor's bid price. Noland's bid was based on estimates given to it by Graver, a water tank supplier. Noland impleaded Graver not only to obtain indemnity for his liability to Ruscon but also to recover $4,000 in contemplated profits. The District Court allowed Noland only the indemnity. The Fourth Circuit framed the issue as

> * * * whether, under Rule 14, a third-party defendant, *once made a party to an action,* can be proceeded against by the third-party plaintiff upon a claim closely related to, yet different from and for an amount in excess of, the original plaintiff's claim asserted in the primary action. * * *

Id. at 49. The court then held:

> * * * In view of the ease with which disposition of all claims herein could be made in this one action, we conclude that Rule 14 should be construed to be sufficiently broad and flexible so as to permit the District Court, in the exercise of its sound discretion, to make such disposition.

Id. at 50. In a more recent Third Circuit opinion, SCHWAB v. ERIE LACKAWANNA R. CO., 438 F.2d 62 (3d Cir.1971), the court held that although it would be improper to allow the third-party plaintiff to bring an additional claim against the third-party defendant under Rule 14, the claim was proper under Rule 18 and came within the ancillary jurisdiction of the court. Does it make any difference under which rule the claim is asserted? Does it make any difference if the third-party plaintiff's additional claim does not have a close nexus with the ancillary claim under Rule 14? See United States v. United Pacific Ins. Co., 472 F.2d 792 (9th Cir.1973).

SECTION F.   INTERPLEADER

Read Federal Rule of Civil Procedure 22, 28 U.S.C. §§ 1335, 1397, and 2361, and the accompanying material in the Supplement.

Interpleader is a device designed to enable a party who might be exposed to multiple claims to money or property under her control to settle the controversy in a single proceeding. For example, if two people claim that each is the sole beneficiary of a life insurance policy, the insurance company, in the absence of a joinder device such as interpleader, would be required to defend against both in two actions. Not only would the company be forced to incur the expense of additional litigation, but it would be faced with the possibility that, in separate lawsuits, *both* claimants might win.

1.   HISTORICAL LIMITATIONS ON THE USE OF INTERPLEADER

HANCOCK OIL CO. v. INDEPENDENT DISTRIBUTING CO.

Supreme Court of California, 1944.
24 Cal.2d 497, 150 P.2d 463.

EDMONDS, JUSTICE. * * *

According to the complaint [filed by two corporate lessees of certain real property], in 1936 W.L. Hopkins and Gertrude Ann Hopkins, his wife, leased certain real property to Hancock Oil Company of California and R.R. Bush Oil Company. Landowner's royalties of approximately $1,500. have accrued. It is also alleged that in 1941, Independent Distributing Co., a copartnership composed of Merritt Bloxom, Eugene E. Olwell and Murray M. Olwell, brought an action asserting that W.L. Hopkins, Gertrude Ann Hopkins, and two persons sued by fictitious names, hold the real property described in the lease in trust for them. The relief sought in the suit of Independent Distributing Co. was an accounting of the rents of the land.

The copartnership and the copartners, together with W.L. Hopkins and Gertrude Ann Hopkins, H. James Hopkins and W.L. Hopkins, trustees of Wilbur T. Hopkins Trust, and H. James Hopkins and W.L. Hopkins, trustees of the H. James Hopkins Trust, are named as the defendants in the present suit, the charge of the complaint being that the copartnership and the copartners claim to be the owners of the land described in the lease and entitled to all of the landowner's royalties accrued and to accrue under that agreement. A further assertion of the complaint is that the defendants other than the copartnership and the copartners also claim the same royalties and by reason of these conflicting claims the lessees cannot safely determine to whom the rent should be paid. * * *

To this complaint Merritt Bloxom, Eugene E. Olwell, Murray M. Olwell and Independent Distributing Co. filed an answer alleging that they are the owners of the property and entitled to all of the rents and profits from it. They also assert that the defendants named Hopkins are holding title to the property in trust for them. The defendants other than the copartners and the copartnership interposed a general demurrer and a special demurrer upon the ground of uncertainty. Each demurrer was sustained without leave to amend and the corporations' appeal is from the judgment which followed that order.

From an opinion of the trial judge, it appears that the demurrers were sustained upon the sole ground that a tenant may not question the title of his landlord at the date of the lease; accordingly, a suit by a tenant to interplead his landlord and one who claims the rent agreed to be paid in accordance with the terms of the lease by which he holds possession of the real property is in violation of this fundamental principle. The appellants assert that a suit in interpleader does not constitute a denial of the landlord's title but is simply a means by which the tenant may discharge his obligation to pay rent under the lease without becoming involved in the conflict between different claimants to the amount due and unpaid. * * *

The common law bill of interpleader had four essential elements: (1) The same thing, debt, or duty must be claimed by both or all the parties against whom the relief is demanded; (2) all of the adverse titles or claims must be dependent, or be derived from a common source; (3) the one seeking the relief must not have nor claim any interest in the subject matter; and (4) he must have incurred no independent liability to either of the claimants. See 4 Pomeroy's Equity Jurisprudence, 5th Ed.1941, § 1322, p. 906.

These requirements have been termed historical limitations upon this otherwise expeditious equitable proceeding * * *, and in 1881 section 386 of the Code of Civil Procedure was amended to broaden the remedy. The statute * * * declares * * * : "And whenever conflicting claims are or may be made upon a person for or relating to personal property, or the performance of an obligation, or any portion thereof, such person may bring an action against the conflicting claimants to compel them to interplead and litigate their several claims among themselves. The order of substitution may be made and the action of interpleader may be maintained, and the applicant or plaintiff be discharged from liability to all or any of the conflicting claimants, although their titles or claims have not a common origin, or are not identical, but are adverse to and independent of one another." The provision of this enactment, that interpleader lies "although their titles or claims have not a common origin * * * but are adverse to and independent of one another," directly abrogates the common law requirement that all the adverse titles or claims must be dependent or be derived from a common source, and it is therefore clear that privity between the conflicting claimants need not be shown to invoke the remedy under the code. * * *

Early in the history of interpleader, it was held that one who sought to maintain such a suit must show outstanding claims, identical in every respect and without the slightest degree of variation, to the same thing, debt or duty. In the case of conflicting claims to specific personal property, this rigid formalism did not seriously interfere with the effectiveness of the proceeding. But where, as is generally the situation modernly, the subject matter of the conflicting claims was an obligation, a debt or a duty, the requirement as to the identity of the defendant's demands very often prevented a stakeholder from using interpleader where he was doubly vexed with respect to one liability. For example, under the narrow rule of the common law, if one person claimed all of the fund held by a bank and another person asserted the right to only a portion of that fund, the bank could not secure a determination of its liability by means of the equitable proceeding. The Legislature has removed this restriction, yet the very rationale of interpleader compels the conclusion that the amendment does not allow the remedy where each of the claimants asserts the right to a different debt, claim or duty. If the conflicting claims are mutually exclusive, interpleader cannot be maintained, but the fact that an identical right is not asserted by each of the claimants does not preclude the use of the remedy. * * *

In the present case, the plaintiffs have alleged that each of the two groups against whom interpleader is sought claims the right to receive the rents and royalties reserved in the lease. If Independent Distributing Co. and the members of that copartnership should assert that they are entitled to the reasonable value of the use and occupation of the land leased to the plaintiffs, together with the mesne profits or damages for waste, the trial court would be required to deny the plaintiffs the right to interplead those parties with their lessors. Under such circumstances the claims of the parties would not relate to the same obligation. But as the appellants' complaint pleads that there are conflicting claims concerning their obligation to pay the rents and royalties reserved by the lease, the lessors and the third parties must answer and, if each of them agrees that his claim concerns the right to those rents and royalties, the lessees should be discharged from liability upon payment of their obligations under the lease.

As to the remaining common law principles governing a suit of interpleader, the appellants' complaint conforms with the requirement that the plaintiff in such a proceeding must stand in the position of a disinterested stakeholder. However, much of the present controversy centers about the last element which is specified as essential. Although the complaint discloses no obligation of the appellants other than under the lease, the respondents assert that the obligation to pay rent constitutes an independent liability and bars the remedy of interpleader.

* * * The rule concerning independent liability is stated in Corpus Juris as follows: "Interpleader will not lie if the stakeholder has incurred some personal obligation to either of the claimants, independent of the title or the right to possession, because such claimant would in that event have a claim against him which could not be settled in a litigation with the other claimant." 33 C.J. 439. * * * The Supreme Court of Maine put the matter most convincingly when it said: "The mere fact that a contractual relation exists between plaintiff and one of the defendants, under which the fund is required to be paid to such claimant, does not of itself defeat the right of interpleader. * * * If such were the law, it would be difficult to conceive of any set of facts which would enable a bank, a trustee, or other custodian of funds, or even a bailee, to maintain interpleader. The obligation referred to in the rule must be independent of the title or right of possession of the fund or property in question. * * * " First National Bank v. Reynolds, 127 Me. 340, 143 A. 266, 268, 60 A.L.R. 712. * * *

Although Professor Pomeroy declares that an independent liability "arises from the very nature of the original relation subsisting between" the landlord and tenant, he states that such a suit is proper whenever there is some privity between the claimant and the lessor, as, for example, when the relation of trustee and *cestui que trust* has been created between them. It seems, therefore, that the reason why the author asserts that the relationship of the landlord and tenant precludes interpleader by the tenant is not that, under the lease, there is an independent liability but because there is no privity between the landlord and the one joined with him as a defendant. * * *

From what has been said, then, it is clear that, in the present case, as according to the facts alleged in the complaint, the relations inter se of the respondents and the copartners are such that the decision will determine the liability of the lessees to each of them, there is no independent liability which will bar the remedy of interpleader; accordingly the appellants' complaint is sufficient with respect to those of the four common law requirements for interpleader not abolished or modified by the amendment in 1881 to section 386 of the Code of Civil Procedure. * * *

[The court went on to consider the effect of the common-law rule that a tenant may not dispute the title of his landlord at the time of the commencement of the relation.]

Notwithstanding the strict common law limitation on interpleader in landlord-tenant cases which is justified by an ancient rule of real property, the code provision concerning the remedy must be liberally construed. A remedial statute, its purpose is to avoid a multiplicity of suits and prevent vexatious litigation. * * *

* * * [I]n the absence of the right to interplead the landlord and the adverse claimant to the rent, the tenant is faced with the unfortunate alternative of forfeiting his lease or possibly paying twice. * * * And there is no action at law adequate to shield him from vexation by multiple litigation over the obligation for rent, against the risk of double liability upon the same obligation, and against insecurity of tenancy.

Furthermore, interpleader is not only of importance to the tenant; it is also of advantage to the third party claimant. If the tenant may not interplead his landlord and another under the common law rule, the third party must establish his right to rent in a separate action. During the progress of this litigation the tenant would pay the rents to the landlord. It is entirely conceivable that before judgment was rendered the tenant might become insolvent, leaving the third party without recourse, or because of financial difficulties overtaking the landlord, the tenant would be required to pay his obligation twice.

Unquestionably the landlord may suffer some disadvantage in being forced to defend a suit in interpleader. While the litigation continues the rent is withheld from him without interest. But the tenant may not maintain such a suit upon the mere pretext or suspicion of double vexation; he must allege facts showing a reasonable probability of double vexation. Without accurately appraising the rationale of interpleader, by some decisions this court has mentioned as an additional requirement that the plaintiff must allege facts showing a doubt as to which claimant he can safely pay. * * * However, to demand from a plaintiff that he express a doubt as to which adverse claimant he is liable is an admission that the basis upon which the right to interpleader rests is the avoidance of double liability. "The right to the remedy by interpleader is founded, however, not on the consideration that a man may be subjected to double liability, but on the fact that he is threatened with double vexation in respect to one liability." Pfister v. Wade, * * * 56 Cal. at page 47 * * *.

The complaint therefore states a cause of action against a general demurrer and denial of leave to amend was an abuse of discretion even if the special demurrer was well taken. * * *

The judgment is reversed.

[The dissenting opinion of JUSTICE CARTER has been omitted.]

Notes and Questions

1. Does the fact that modern interpleader is a remodeling by the equity courts of the common-law writ of interpleader explain why its availability was limited prior to statutory modification?

2. The California Supreme Court states in *Hancock* that interpleader would have been denied if Independent Oil Company had asserted a claim for profits and damages. In such a situation, the court reasoned, "the claims of the parties [Independent and Hopkins] would not relate to the same obligation." What does the court mean by "the same obligation"? Consider the probable content of the allegations if Independent had asserted a claim for profits and damages and Hopkins had asserted a claim for the rents; would the claims have been mutually exclusive?

3. The typical interpleader suit has two stages. The first determines whether interpleader is proper; in it, the controversy is between the stakeholder on one side and all the claimants on the other. If interpleader is granted, the first stage ends with a decree allowing the stakeholder to withdraw from the case and

enjoining the claimants from taking any further proceedings against the stake-holder. Before retiring, however, the stakeholder is required to deposit the money or property involved in the dispute with the court, generally less court costs and attorney's fees. In the second stage, the contest is among the claimants to determine their respective rights to the property or fund deposited in court. See McClintock, *Equity* § 188 (2d ed. 1948); 4 Pomeroy, *Equity Jurisprudence* § 1320 (5th ed. 1941).

4. The third requirement for interpleader mentioned in the *Hancock* case is that the party seeking interpleader must neither have nor claim any interest in the subject matter. The first case in which the requirement appeared, Mitchell v. Hayne, 2 Simons & Stuart 63, 57 Eng.Rep. 268 (Ch.1824), cites no authority and gives no reasons for its adoption. Nevertheless, the requirement has been accepted by most American jurisdictions. See, e.g., Texas v. Florida, 306 U.S. 398, 406–07, 59 S.Ct. 563, 568, 83 L.Ed. 817, 825 (1939); Maxim v. Shotwell, 209 Mich. 79, 176 N.W. 414 (1920). For this requirement's early history, see Hazard & Moskovitz, *An Historical and Critical Analysis of Interpleader,* 52 Calif.L.Rev. 706, 744–47 (1964). At the time the *Hancock* case was decided, this requirement was still in full force in California. However, in 1951, Section 386 of California's Code of Civil Procedure, which is set out in the Supplement under Federal Rule 22, was amended to permit a defendant to interpose a claim to a portion of the property or money in dispute. Is there any reason why the right of an interested stakeholder to interplead apparently exists under the California statute only in favor of a defendant stakeholder? Can Section 386 be construed to give the same right to the plaintiff? See Note, *1951 Amendment to California Code of Civil Procedure Section 386,* 39 Calif.L.Rev. 591, 594 (1951). For a sharp attack on the no-interest-in-the-subject-matter requirement, see Chafee, *Modernizing Interpleader,* 30 Yale L.J. 814, 840–42 (1921).

5. The fourth historical requirement—that the stakeholder must not have incurred any independent liability with regard to the stake to either of the claimants—derived from the principle that the stakeholder should retire from the case once interpleader was allowed. By way of illustration, assume that a bailee who is subject to conflicting claims to the bailed article has expressly acknowl-edged the title of one of the claimants to it. Interpleader could not be granted because a decision awarding ownership to the other claimant might not terminate the controversy concerning the bailed item; the losing claimant still might have a cause of action against the stakeholder based on the latter's acknowledgment of title, and the stakeholder could not withdraw from the litigation at the end of the first stage of the suit. What underlies the principle that the stakeholder must be neutral, disinterested, and withdraw permanently from the suit when interpleader is allowed?

EX PARTE MERSEY DOCKS & HARBOUR BOARD, [1899] 1 Q.B. 546 (C.A.), involved a situation similar to the hypothetical above. The court permitted interpleader and concluded that if the claimant with an independent cause of action regarding the stake lost as against the other claimant, he would be allowed to assert it against the bailee in a third stage of the same suit. Compare the hardship to the claimant of two contests, first with another claimant and then with the bailee, with the hardship to the bailee of two actions and a possible double recovery. Is the solution adopted in the *Mersey* case desirable? The status of this requirement in the federal courts is discussed in Note, *The Independent Liability Rule as a Bar to Interpleader in the Federal Courts,* 65 Yale L.J. 715 (1956).

2. JURISDICTIONAL PROBLEMS

The historic territorial approach to jurisdiction over the person has raised a number of peculiar problems in the interpleader context. Occasionally, the stakeholder will not be able to obtain in personam jurisdiction over all of the claimants in any one state because of the limitations imposed by the Due Process Clause of the Fourteenth Amendment. To overcome this difficulty, courts often have characterized interpleader as an in rem or quasi-in-rem proceeding and predicated jurisdiction on the presence of the stake within the territorial reach of the court. Assuming that this is a sound approach, should it make any difference that the stake is a debt rather than a chattel or a trust fund? In the case that follows, the Supreme Court was faced with the question of whether to treat a debt as an in rem or quasi-in-rem base for interpleader. Before proceeding, it might be advisable to review the materials in Chapter 2 on jurisdiction over the person and jurisdiction over property. In particular, reread Shaffer v. Heitner, p. 154, supra.

NEW YORK LIFE INS. CO. v. DUNLEVY

Supreme Court of the United States, 1916.
241 U.S. 518, 36 S.Ct. 613, 60 L.Ed. 1140.

Certiorari to the Circuit Court of Appeals for the Ninth Circuit.

MR. JUSTICE McREYNOLDS delivered the opinion of the court:

Respondent, Effie J. Gould Dunlevy, instituted this suit in the Superior Court, Marin county, California, January 14, 1910, against petitioner and Joseph W. Gould, her father, to recover $2,479.70, the surrender value of a policy on his life which she claimed had been assigned to her in 1893, and both were duly served with process while in that state. It was removed to the United States District Court, February 16, 1910, and there tried by the judge in May, 1912, a jury having been expressly waived. Judgment for amount claimed was affirmed by the Circuit Court of Appeals. * * *

The insurance company by an amended answer filed December 7, 1911, set up in defense * * * that Mrs. Dunlevy was concluded by certain judicial proceedings in Pennsylvania wherein it had been garnished and the policy had been adjudged to be the property of Gould. * * *

In 1907 Boggs & Buhl recovered a valid personal judgment by default, after domiciliary service, against Mrs. Dunlevy, in the Common Pleas Court at Pittsburgh, where she then resided. During 1909, "the tontine dividend period" of the life policy having expired, the insurance company became liable for $2,479.70, and this sum was claimed both by Gould, a citizen of Pennsylvania, and his daughter, who had removed to California. In November, 1909, Boggs & Buhl caused issue of an execution attachment on their judgment, and both the insurance company and Gould were summoned as garnishees. He appeared, denied assignment of the policy, and claimed the full amount due thereon. On February 5, 1910,—after this suit was begun in California,—the company answered, admitted its indebtedness, set up the conflicting claims to the fund, and prayed to be advised as to its rights. At the same time it filed a petition asking for a rule upon the claimants to show cause why they should not interplead and thereby ascertain who was lawfully entitled to the proceeds, and, further, that it might be allowed to pay amount due into court for benefit of proper party. An order granted the requested rule, and directed that notice be given to Mrs. Dunlevy in California. This was done, but she made no answer and did not appear. Later the insurance company filed a second petition, and, upon leave obtained thereunder, paid $2,479.70 into court, March 21, 1910. All parties except Mrs. Dunlevy having appeared, a feigned issue was framed and tried to determine validity of alleged transfer of the policy. The jury found, October 1, 1910, there was no valid assignment, and thereupon, under an order of court, the fund was paid over to Gould.

Beyond doubt, without the necessity of further personal service of process upon Mrs. Dunlevy, the Court of Common Pleas at Pittsburgh had ample power through garnishment proceedings to inquire whether she held a valid claim against the insurance company, and, if found to exist, then to condemn and appropriate it so far as necessary to discharge the original judgment. Although herself outside the limits of the state, such disposition of the property would have been binding on her. * * * But the interpleader initiated by the company was an altogether different matter. This was an attempt to bring about a final and conclusive adjudication of her personal rights, not merely to discover property and apply it to debts. And unless in contemplation of law she was before the court, and required to respond to that issue, its orders and judgments in respect thereto were not binding on her. Pennoyer v. Neff * * *.

Counsel maintain that having been duly summoned in the original suit instituted by Boggs & Buhl in 1907, and notwithstanding entry of final judgment therein, "Mrs. Dunlevy was in the Pennsylvania court and was bound by every order that court made, whether she remained within the jurisdiction of that court after it got jurisdiction over her person or not;" and hence, the argument is, "When the company paid the money into court where she was, it was just the same in legal effect as if it had paid it to her." This position is supposed to be supported by our opinion in Michigan Trust Co. v. Ferry, 228 U.S. 346, 57 L.Ed. 867, 33 S.Ct. 550, where it is said: "If a judicial proceeding is begun with jurisdiction over the person of the party concerned, it is within the power of a state to bind him by every subsequent order in the cause. * * * This is true not only of ordinary actions, but of proceedings like the present. It is within the power of a state to make the whole administration of the estate a single proceeding, to provide that one who has undertaken it within the jurisdiction shall be subject to the order of the court in the matter until the administration is closed by distribution, and, on the same principle, that he shall be required to account for and distribute all that he receives, by the order of the probate court."

Of course the language quoted had reference to the existing circumstances, and must be construed accordingly. The judgment under consideration was fairly within the reasonable anticipation of the executor when he submitted himself to the probate court. But a wholly different and intolerable condition would result from acceptance of the theory that, after final judgment, a defendant remains in court and subject to whatsoever orders may be entered under title of the cause. * * * The interpleader proceedings were not essential concomitants of the original action by Boggs & Buhl against Dunlevy, but plainly collateral; and, when summoned to respond in that action, she was not required to anticipate them. * * *

The established general rule is that any personal judgment which a state court may render against one who did not voluntarily submit to its jurisdiction, and who is not a citizen of the state, nor served with process within its borders, no matter what the mode of service, is void, because the court had no jurisdiction over his person. * * *

We are of opinion that the proceedings in the Pennsylvania court constituted no bar to the action in California, and the judgment below is accordingly affirmed.

Notes and Questions

1. Partially in response to the *Dunlevy* decision, Congress passed the Federal Interpleader Act in 1917. The statute was successively broadened in 1926 and 1936 and was reconstituted in 1948 as part of the United States Judicial Code. It now appears as 28 U.S.C. §§ 1335, 1397, 2361. The present Interpleader Act manifests a congressional intent to avoid a repetition of the *Dunlevy* decision in an action arising in a federal court. For example, Section 1397 permits venue to be laid in any judicial district in which one or more of the claimants reside and Section 2361 permits nationwide service of process in order to reach all of the claimants. Further recognition of the interstate quality of interpleader and the need for the exercise of federal judicial power in this context is the provision in Section 1335 permitting the federal courts to assert jurisdiction when the stake is worth as little as $500. In light of the principles of federal jurisdiction explored in Chapters Two and Three, can the Federal Interpleader Act be challenged on constitutional grounds? The Federal Interpleader Acts are analyzed in a series of articles by their principal proponent, the late Professor Chafee: *Interstate Interpleader*, 33 Yale L.J. 685 (1924); *Interpleader in the United States Courts*, 41 Yale L.J. 1134 (1932), 42 Yale L.J. 41 (1932); *The Federal Interpleader Act of 1936*, 45 Yale L.J. 963, 1161 (1936); *Federal Interpleader Since the Act of 1936*, 49 Yale L.J. 377 (1940).

2. Interpleader under the Federal Interpleader Act is referred to as "statutory interpleader." Interpleader under Federal Rule 22, known as "rule interpleader," is somewhat different. Although the fourfold requirements of the old equitable remedy are not necessary, the usual jurisdictional, venue, and process limitations still apply. Statutory and rule interpleader are further discussed on pp. 665–77, *infra*.

3. Is *Dunlevy* consistent with Shaffer v. Heitner, p. 154, *supra*? For a case reaching the same result as *Dunlevy*, see Hanna v. Stedman, 230 N.Y. 326, 130 N.E. 566 (1921). In view of the extent to which state judicial power over nonresidents has been extended since the *Dunlevy* decision, would the Supreme Court limit the state's power over interpleader today as it did in *Dunlevy*? Which of the cases in Chapter 2 are relevant to this question? Do the "long-arm" or "single-act" statutes render the *Dunlevy* problem moot or is there still some area in which federal interpleader can profitably function? Does the presence of the Federal Interpleader Act make it easier or harder for the Supreme Court to eliminate the *Dunlevy* limitation on state jurisdictional power? See von Mehren & Trautman, *Jurisdiction to Adjudicate: A Suggested Analysis*, 79 Harv.L.Rev. 1121, 1156–59 (1966). For a modern approach to *Dunlevy*, see *Developments in the Law—Multiparty Litigation in the Federal Courts*, 71 Harv.L.Rev. 874, 914–18 (1958).

4. Section 216 of the New York Civil Practice Law and Rules permits a stakeholder who has been sued by one claimant to apply to the court for permission to send notice of the action's pendency to another claimant who is not subject to the court's personal jurisdiction. The proceeding is then suspended and the nonresident may intervene within a year and ten days after the date the notice is sent. If the nonresident claimant does not appear within that period, the claim is barred in New York. The claim also may be barred in those states having "borrowing statutes" under which another jurisdiction's statutes of limitations are applied in certain situations rather than those of the forum. However, the stakeholder is not protected if the nonresident claimant asserts a right to the property in another jurisdiction before the statutory period has elapsed or in a jurisdiction that will not "borrow" New York's statute. Because of these risks, the New York Court of Appeals has held that the defendant stakeholder can challenge the claim of the resident claimants by asserting that title is held by a nonresident claimant. Solicitor v. Bankers Trust Co., 304 N.Y. 282, 107 N.E.2d 448 (1952). Are there any constitutional objections to the New York statute? See also 1 Weinstein, Korn & Miller, *New York Civil Practice* ¶ ¶ 216.01–.03.

5. In WESTERN UNION TEL. CO. v. PENNSYLVANIA, 368 U.S. 71, 82 S.Ct. 199, 7 L.Ed.2d 139 (1961), a case brought by the state to obtain wired funds that were never claimed, the Supreme Court stated:

> * * * [W]hen a state court's jurisdiction purports to be based, as here, on the presence of property within the State, the holder of such property is deprived of due process of law if he is compelled to relinquish it without assurance that he will not be held liable again in another jurisdiction or in a suit brought by a claimant who is not bound by the first judgment. * * *

Id. at 75, 82 S.Ct. at 201, 7 L.Ed.2d at 142. If this statement is applicable to individual claims, as well as to a claim by the state to a particular fund, a court would have to dismiss a suit by a resident claimant against the stakeholder when there are potential nonresident claimants who cannot be brought within the jurisdiction of the court. Does this make it unwise to extend the *Western Union* doctrine to include private claims?

6. Can a stakeholder create in rem jurisdiction by depositing a stake with the court? N.Y.C.P.L.R. § 1006(g) permits a party to pay a sum of money into court when the money is "payable in the state pursuant to a contract or claimed as damages for unlawful retention of specific real or personal property in the state." It then states: "Upon compliance with a court order permitting such deposit or retention, the sum of money shall be deemed specific property within the state * * *." Doesn't this rule confer unlimited personal jurisdiction in interpleader actions in the New York courts?

3. INTERPLEADER IN THE FEDERAL COURTS

Reread 28 U.S.C. §§ 1335, 1397, 2361 and Federal Rule of Civil Procedure 22.

PAN AMERICAN FIRE & CAS. CO. v. REVERE

United States District Court, Eastern District of Louisiana, 1960.
188 F.Supp. 474.

WRIGHT, DISTRICT JUDGE. On February 3, 1960, a * * * large tractor and trailer collided head-on with a bus carrying school children. The bus driver and three of the children were killed and 23 others were injured, some very seriously. A few moments later, compounding the disaster, another collision occurred between two cars following the bus. * * *

Alleging that three suits against it have already been filed and that numerous other claims have been made, the tractor's liability insurer has instituted this interpleader action, citing all potential claimants. It asks that they be enjoined from initiating legal proceedings elsewhere or further prosecuting the actions already filed and that they be directed to assert their claims in the present suit. Plaintiff has deposited a bond in the full amount of its policy limits, $100,000, and avers that "it has no interest" in these insurance proceeds, being merely "a disinterested stakeholder." On the other hand, the Company denies liability toward any and all claimants. This apparently contradictory position is explained by the statement of its counsel, incorporated in the record as an amendment to the complaint, that plaintiff "has no further claim" on the sum deposited with the court, but cannot technically admit "liability" since that would amount to a concession that its assured was negligent and expose him to a deficiency judgment.

The only question presented at this stage of the proceeding is whether, under the circumstances outlined, the remedy of interpleader is available to the insurer. * * *

1. *Jurisdiction.* * * *

[The court concluded that the jurisdictional amount and diversity requirements of the Interpleader Act and Federal Rule 22 had been satisfied.]

2. *Strict Interpleader or Bill in the Nature of Interpleader.* Apparently of the opinion that the answer may affect the availability of the remedy sought here, the parties have debated the question whether this is a case for "true," "strict," or "pure" interpleader or whether the present facts support only an action "in the nature of interpleader." The difference between the two is that in strict interpleader the plaintiff is a disinterested stakeholder while in the action in the nature of interpleader he is himself a claimant, whether directly or by denying the validity of some or all of the other claims. * * * Thus, if the casualty insurer had brought in the claimants and said to them: "Gentlemen, I put before you the full amount of the policy which those of you who prove your claims must divide between you, but I deny that any of you is entitled to any portion of the fund and pray that all your demands be rejected and that the deposit be returned to me in due course," clearly this would not be a true interpleader but an action in the nature of interpleader. The problem here is whether the allegation of disinterestedness already noted changes the character of the action to one of strict interpleader. * * *

But does it matter how the action is characterized? It would seem to make no difference since both Rule 22 and the Interpleader Act expressly provide for actions in the nature of interpleader as well as strict bills, the drafters in each case voicing their intent to erase the distinction. But before so concluding, we must dispose of an old rule of equity that gave importance to the difference between "pure" and "impure" bills of interpleader.

3. *Special Equitable Ground for Bill in the Nature of Interpleader.* Though apparently known to the early common law, modern interpleader developed in the chancery courts and is today considered an equitable remedy. Hence, in theory at least, the resort to equity must be justified by the absence of an adequate remedy at law. One might suppose that exposure to unnecessary vexation by a multiplicity of suits on the same obligation were a sufficient ground for equitable relief. And so it is if the conditions of strict interpleader are met. But, for reasons that no one bothered to explain, the rule was otherwise when the plaintiff was not a mere stakeholder. It was laid down that a bill in the nature of interpleader would not lie unless supported by some special equity besides double vexation. Thus, a suit like this one which has no independent equitable basis could not be maintained unless it could be characterized as a true bill of interpleader.

Though it was perhaps more honored in the breach than the observance, such was the rule. But, inherently weak, it could not long survive the liberalizing force of the Interpleader Act of 1936 and the Rules of Civil Procedure promulgated in 1938. Indeed, once the difference between strict bills and bills in the nature of interpleader was eliminated, there remained no basis for distinguishing the requirements and demanding special equities for the action in the nature of interpleader. Henceforth, it could be assumed that the prerequisites of interpleader were the same whether the plaintiff were interested or not, and that these conditions were spelled out in the written provisions. The point was forcibly made by Judge Chesnut whose celebrated opinion in John Hancock Mut. Life Ins. Co. v. Kegan, * * * [22 F.Supp. 326 (D.Md.1938)], noted the absurdity of distinguishing between the equities required for "pure" and "impure" interpleader and held that exposure to undue harassment by a multiplicity of suits was a sufficient ground to maintain a bill in the nature of interpleader. * * *

The present law, then, is that the only equitable ground necessary for interpleader, whether the plaintiff is a disinterested stakeholder or not, is exposure to double or multiple vexation. But, of course, this does not mean that every person threatened with a multiplicity of suits is entitled to interplead. The function of interpleader is to rescue a debtor from *undue* harassment when there are several claims made against the *same fund*. It is because the aggregate demands exceed the insurer's contractual obligation that the condition is here satisfied.

4. *Exposure to Multiple Liability.* Though the Interpleader Act makes no such requirement, Rule 22 apparently permits interpleader only if the claims "are such that the plaintiff is or may be exposed to double or multiple *liability*." (Emphasis added.) In theory at least, this is not necessarily the same thing as exposure to double or multiple *vexation* on a single obligation. There may be situations in which the debtor, though harassed by many suits on account of one transaction, is never in danger of being compelled to pay the same debt twice. Indeed, here, the argument is advanced that because it has fixed the limits of its liability in its policy, the insurer is not exposed to

multiple liability no matter how many claims are filed, and, therefore, is not entitled to maintain interpleader, at least under the Rule.

But the requirement is not a strict one. * * * The key to the clause requiring exposure to "double or multiple liability" is in the words "may be." The danger need not be immediate; any possibility of having to pay more than is justly due, no matter how improbable or remote, will suffice. At least, it is settled that an insurer with limited contractual liability who faces claims in excess of his policy limits is "exposed" within the intendment of Rule 22, and we need go no further to find the requirement satisfied here.

5. *Adversity of Claimants.* In a somewhat overlapping objection, it is said that the present claims are not characterized by that "adversity" to one another which is a prerequisite of interpleader. It is of course true that they are identical neither in origin nor in amount and that they are, in some degree at least, independent demands. But, despite the objection of purists who would retain the old doctrine of complete "mutual exclusiveness," both Rule 22 and the Interpleader Act now expressly provide that this is no bar to the remedy. On the other hand, there remains a requirement that the claimants be "adverse" in some way. The question is whether that requirement is met when, as here, the claimants, though in theory indifferent toward each other, are in fact competing for a fund which is not large enough to satisfy them all. The answer is clear. As Judge Thompson said in Fidelity & Deposit Co. of Maryland v. A.S. Reid & Co., D.C.E.D.Pa., 16 F.2d 502, 504: "In that situation it is to the interest of its claimant to reduce or defeat altogether the claim of every other claimant. * * *"

6. *Fault of Plaintiff.* * * *

[The court here held that the plaintiff was not guilty of "unclean hands," which would have barred equitable relief.]

7. *Unliquidated Tort Claims as Justifying Interpleader.* Over and above the technical objections already disposed of, the argument is advanced that interpleader is not an appropriate method of adjudicating unliquidated tort claims. Such a bald proposition might be rejected summarily were it not for the startling fact that there appears to be no precedent in the federal courts for granting interpleader in the present situation. * * *

At the outset, it seems clear that interpleader will lie when there are several tort claimants who have obtained judgments which aggregate more than the amount of the policy. Indeed, in that case it can make no difference whether the claims originated in tort or contract. Moreover, it is settled that interpleader is available to an insurer whose policy is insufficient to satisfy contract claims, though they have not been reduced to judgment. Why, then, should the remedy be denied to a blameless insurer faced with excessive tort claims? Three reasons have been suggested: (1) As to quantum, at least, tort claims are more conjectural than contract claims; (2) since it is not directly liable to the claimants, the insurer's exposure as to tort claims is "remote" until they have been reduced to judgment; and (3) tort claims "are peculiarly appropriate for jury trial," which would have to be denied under the equitable practice of interpleader.

The effect of the first objection is only this: that it is more difficult in the case of tort claims to determine whether the aggregate will exceed the policy limits so as to render the claimants "adverse" and expose the insurer to "multiple liability." It may be that there are few cases in which this result can be reasonably anticipated, but, clearly, this is one of them.

The second objection, though it forms the basis of the only reported decision denying interpleader to an automobile liability insurer,[36] is no better. Indeed, under the "may be exposed" clause of Rule 22 and the "may claim" clause of the Interpleader Act, it would not seem to matter how remote the danger might be. But, in any event, prematurity is no defense under the peculiar Louisiana law which allows a direct action against the automobile liability insurer.

8. *Jury Trial.* On the theory that the resort to equity defeats the right of trial by jury, it has been said that once interpleader is granted all issues in the case must be tried to the judge alone. There is, however, eminent authority to the contrary, including Judge Learned Hand, Professor Chafee, and Professor Moore, who hold that legal issues arising in an interpleader action can be tried before a jury. Whatever may be the right solution in another case, here it seems clear that the questions of liability and damages ought to be put to a jury. * * * Nothing in Rule 22 or the Interpleader Act opposes such a procedure. Indeed, the provision of the Federal Rules which permits separate trial of distinct issues invites this solution. * * * Each claimant can be given a full opportunity to prove his case before a jury, reserving to the court only the task of apportioning the fund between those who are successful if the aggregate of the verdicts exceeds the amount of the insurance proceeds.

9. *Enjoining of Other Proceedings.* Usually interpleader will not be really effective unless all claimants are brought before the same court in one proceeding and restricted to that single forum in the assertion of their claims. * * * Immediately, the question arises whether Section 2283 of Title 28 of the Code presents an obstacle to enjoining state court proceedings.

As amended in 1948, that section prohibits a federal court from interfering with a pending state court action except in three situations: (1) Where such a course is "expressly authorized by Act of Congress"; (2) where the issuance of an injunction by the federal court is "necessary in aid of its jurisdiction"; and (3) where the court's action is required "to protect or effectuate its judgments." Clearly, the first exception is applicable to a suit brought under the Interpleader Act since that statute expressly empowers the court to enjoin the claimants "from instituting or prosecuting any proceeding in any State or United States court affecting the property, instrument or obligation involved in the interpleader action * * *." But the exception does not apply to an action under Rule 22, for the quoted provision authorizing stay orders is restricted to statutory interpleader. If state court proceedings can be enjoined when interpleader is brought under the Rule it must be by virtue of the second exception in Section 2283.

The question whether the court entertaining a non-statutory interpleader suit may enjoin state court proceedings on the same issues on the theory that it is "necessary in aid of its jurisdiction" is not free from doubt. * * * But * * * every indication is that, regardless of the Interpleader Act, the power of

36. American Indemnity Co. v. Hale, D.C.W.D.Mo., 71 F.Supp. 529, 533–534.

a federal court to enjoin pending state court proceedings in a case like this one will be sustained. Certainly that result is desirable, if not indispensable. * * *

10. *Venue and Service of Process.* * * * [T]here are two procedural limitations on actions under the Rule which become important whenever the claimants are not all within the territorial jurisdiction of the district court. The first is that the only proper venue for the suit when the defendants do not all reside in the same state is the residence of the plaintiff; the second, that process cannot run beyond the boundaries of the state in which the court sits. These restrictions are of course waivable, but if objection is raised by the affected defendant, they usually form an absolute bar to the action. Thus, here, if Rule 22 alone were applicable, absent a waiver of venue by Wells [a passenger in one of the cars following the bus], the suit would have to be instituted at the plaintiff's domicile in Texas, and none of the defendants could be validly served unless they were found in that state.

But the situation is different when jurisdiction exists under the statute, for the Interpleader Act specially provides that the action may be commenced in any district where one defendant resides and that process will run throughout the United States. Unfortunately, these exceptional rules apply only to statutory interpleader. The present suit, then, is maintainable only under the Interpleader Act unless the Wisconsin defendant waives venue and voluntarily appears or is found in Louisiana.

11. *Conclusion.* * * * [T]he prayer for interpleader will be granted, without, however, discharging the plaintiff who is contractually bound to resist the demands. Injunctions will issue restraining all parties from further prosecuting any pending suits against plaintiff or its assured on account of the accident described, or from instituting like proceedings before this or any other court. All defendants will be required to enter their claims by way of answer in this action within thirty days from notice of this judgment. Thereafter, upon timely demand by any one of the parties, the court will order a joint jury trial of all the claims upon the issues of liability and damages. In the event the aggregate of the verdicts should exceed the amount of plaintiff's liability, the court reserves unto itself the task of apportioning the insurance proceeds in such manner as it deems just.

The motion to dismiss will be denied.

Notes and Questions

1. If an insurance company faced with the *Pan American* situation pays the full amount of the policy to certain claimants, either by way of settlement or in satisfaction of a judgment, can it defend later actions by unpaid claimants by arguing that it has already exhausted the policy? To what extent is the answer to this question relevant in determining whether interpleader should be granted?

2. STEPHENSON v. BURDETT, 56 W.Va. 109, 117–18, 48 S.E. 846, 850 (1904):

> * * * The only material difference between the two kinds of bills, pointed out by the courts and the law writers is that, in a bill in the nature of a bill of interpleader, the plaintiff may show that he has an interest in the subject matter of the controversy between the defendants. * * * There is no suggestion * * * that there is any further departure from the principles governing a

pure bill of interpleader. Must not the defendants claim the same thing from the plaintiff, according to the requirement in a pure bill of interpleader? Must not a relation of privity exist between the defendants? Can a tenant require his landlord to interplead with a third person claiming under a strange and hostile title? If the plaintiff show by his bill that he is in the attitude of a wrongdoer toward one of the defendants, may he require an interpleader? The language of a definition of a bill in the nature of a bill of interpleader, found in the books, does not answer any of these questions in the affirmative, or indicate that the principles governing a pure bill of interpleader are relaxed in any of these particulars. Nor do any of the decided cases countenance such a proposition.

3. In addition to the articles by Professor Chafee cited following the *Dunlevy* case, a useful discussion of federal interpleader is found in 7 Wright, Miller & Kane, *Federal Practice and Procedure: Civil 2d* §§ 1701–21 (1986). See also *Developments in the Law—Multiparty Litigation in the Federal Courts*, 71 Harv. L.Rev. 874, 913–28 (1958).

STATE FARM FIRE & CAS. CO. v. TASHIRE

Supreme Court of the United States, 1967.
386 U.S. 523, 87 S.Ct. 1199, 18 L.Ed.2d 270.

[This case arose out of a collision between a Greyhound bus and a pickup truck in Shasta County, California in September, 1964. Two of the bus passengers were killed and 33 others were injured, as were the bus driver, the driver of the truck, and its passenger. One of the dead and 10 of the injured passengers were Canadians; the rest of the individuals were citizens of five American states.

Four of the injured passengers filed suit in California state courts seeking damages in excess of $1,000,000 and naming as defendants: Greyhound Lines, Inc.; Nauta, the bus driver; Clark, the driver of the truck; and Glasgow, the truck passenger who apparently was its owner. Each of the individual defendants was a citizen of Oregon; Greyhound was a California corporation. Before the California cases came to trial and before any other suits were filed, petitioner, State Farm Fire & Casualty Company, an Illinois corporation, brought this action in the nature of interpleader in the United States District Court for the District of Oregon.

State Farm asserted that at the time of the collision it had in force an insurance policy covering Clark, the driver of the truck, for bodily injury liability up to $10,000 per person and $20,000 per occurrence. State Farm further asserted that the aggregate damages sought in actions already filed in California and other anticipated actions far exceeded the amount of its maximum liability under the policy. Accordingly, it paid into court the sum of $20,000 and asked the court (1) to require all claimants to establish their claims against Clark and his insurer in the Oregon proceeding and in no other action, and (2) to discharge State Farm from all further obligations under its policy. Alternatively, State Farm requested a decree that the insurer owed no duty to Clark and was not liable on the policy, and asked the court to refund the $20,000 deposit. State Farm joined as defendants Clark, Glasgow, Nauta, Greyhound, and each of the prospective claimants. Jurisdiction was predicated both upon the Federal Interpleader Act and general diversity of citizenship.

Personal service was effected on each of the American defendants and registered mail was employed to give notice to the 11 Canadian claimants.

The Oregon District Court issued an order requiring each of the defendants to show cause why he should not be restrained from filing or prosecuting any proceeding affecting the property or obligation involved in the interpleader action. In response, several of the defendants contended that the policy did cover the accident and advanced various arguments for the position that interpleader was inappropriate.

When a temporary injunction along the lines sought by State Farm issued, the respondents moved to dismiss and, in the alternative, sought a change of venue to the district in which the collision had occurred. After a hearing, the District Court declined to dissolve the temporary injunction but continued the motion for a change of venue. Later, the temporary injunction was broadened so that all suits against Clark, State Farm, Greyhound, and Nauta had to be prosecuted in the interpleader proceeding.

On interlocutory appeal, the Ninth Circuit reversed on the ground that in states, such as Oregon, that do not permit a "direct action" against an insurance company until a judgment is obtained against the insured, State Farm could not invoke federal interpleader until the claims against the insured had been reduced to judgment. The Court of Appeals held that prior to that time claimants with unliquidated tort claims are not "claimants" within the meaning of Section 1335 of Title 28 and are not "persons having claims against the plaintiff" within the meaning of Federal Rule 22. The Ninth Circuit directed that the temporary injunction be dissolved and the action be dismissed. The Supreme Court granted certiorari.]

Certiorari to the United States Court of Appeals for the Ninth Circuit.

Mr. Justice Fortas delivered the opinion of the Court.

* * *

I.

Before considering the issues presented by the petition for certiorari, we find it necessary to dispose of a question neither raised by the parties nor passed upon by the courts below. Since the matter concerns our jurisdiction, we raise it on our own motion. * * * The interpleader statute * * * has been uniformly construed to require only "minimal diversity," that is, diversity of citizenship between two or more claimants, without regard to the circumstance that other rival claimants may be co-citizens. The language of the statute, the legislative purpose broadly to remedy the problems posed by multiple claimants to a single fund, and the consistent judicial interpretation tacitly accepted by Congress, persuade us that the statute requires no more. There remains, however, the question whether such a statutory construction is consistent with Article III of our Constitution * * *. In Strawbridge v. Curtiss, 3 Cranch 267, 2 L.Ed. 435 (1806), this Court held that the diversity of citizenship statute required "complete diversity": where co-citizens appeared on both sides of a dispute, jurisdiction was lost. But Chief Justice Marshall there purported to construe only "The words of the act of Congress," not the Constitution itself. And in a variety of contexts this Court and the lower courts have concluded that Article III poses no obstacle to the legislative extension of federal jurisdiction, founded on diversity, so long as any two adverse parties are not co-citizens. Accordingly, we conclude that the present case is properly in the federal courts.

II.

We do not agree with the Court of Appeals that, in the absence of a state law or contractual provision for "direct action" suits against the insurance company, the company must wait until persons asserting claims against its insured have reduced those claims to judgment before seeking to invoke the benefits of federal interpleader. That may have been a tenable position under the 1926[8] and 1936 interpleader statutes.[9] These statutes did not carry forward the language in the 1917 Act authorizing interpleader where adverse claimants "may claim" benefits as well as where they "are claiming" them.[10] In 1948, however, in the revision of the Judicial Code, the "may claim" language was restored.[11] Until the decision below, every court confronted by the question has concluded that the 1948 revision removed whatever requirement there might previously have been that the insurance company wait until at least two claimants reduced their claims to judgments. The commentators are in accord.

Considerations of judicial administration demonstrate the soundness of this view which, in any event, seems compelled by the language of the present statute, which is remedial and to be liberally construed. Were an insurance company required to await reduction of claims to judgment, the first claimant to obtain such a judgment or to negotiate a settlement might appropriate all or a disproportionate slice of the fund before his fellow claimants were able to establish their claims. The difficulties such a race to judgment pose for the insurer, and the unfairness which may result to some claimants, were among the principal evils the interpleader device was intended to remedy.

III.

The fact that State Farm had properly invoked the interpleader jurisdiction under § 1335 did not, however, entitle it to an order both enjoining prosecution of suits against it outside the confines of the interpleader proceeding and also extending such protection to its insured, the alleged tortfeasor. Still less was Greyhound Lines entitled to have that order expanded so as to protect itself and its driver, also alleged to be tortfeasors, from suits brought by its passengers in various state or federal courts. Here, the scope of the litigation, in terms of parties and claims, was vastly more extensive than the confines of the "fund," the deposited proceeds of the insurance policy. In

---

8. 44 Stat. 416 (1926), which added casualty companies to the enumerated categories of plaintiffs able to bring interpleader, and provided for the enjoining of proceedings in other courts.

9. 49 Stat. 1096 (1936), which authorized "bill[s] in the nature of interpleader," meaning those in which the plaintiff is not wholly disinterested with respect to the fund he has deposited in court. * * *

10. 39 Stat. 929 (1917). See Klaber v. Maryland Cas. Co., 69 F.2d 934, 938–939, 106

A.L.R. 617 (C.A.8th Cir.1934), which held that the omission in the 1926 Act of the earlier statute's "may claim" language required the denial of interpleader in the face of unliquidated claims (alternative holding).

11. * * * [I]t was widely assumed that restoration of the "may claim" language would have the effect of overruling the holding in *Klaber,* supra, that one may not invoke interpleader to protect against unliquidated claims. * * *

these circumstances, the mere existence of such a fund cannot, by use of interpleader, be employed to accomplish purposes that exceed the needs of orderly contest with respect to the fund.

There are situations, of a type not present here, where the effect of interpleader is to confine the total litigation to a single forum and proceeding. One such case is where a stakeholder, faced with rival claims to the fund itself, acknowledges—or denies—his liability to one or the other of the claimants. In this situation, the fund itself is the target of the claimants. It marks the outer limits of the controversy. It is, therefore, reasonable and sensible that interpleader, in discharge of its office to protect the fund, should also protect the stakeholder from vexatious and multiple litigation. In this context, the suits sought to be enjoined are squarely within the language of 28 U.S.C. § 2361 * * *.

But the present case is another matter. Here, an accident has happened. Thirty-five passengers or their representatives have claims which they wish to press against a variety of defendants: the bus company, its driver, the owner of the truck, and the truck driver. The circumstance that one of the prospective defendants happens to have an insurance policy is a fortuitous event which should not of itself shape the nature of the ensuing litigation. * * * [A]n insurance company whose maximum interest in the case cannot exceed $20,000 and who in fact asserts that it has no interest at all, should not be allowed to determine that dozens of tort plaintiffs must be compelled to press their claims—even those claims which are not against the insured and which in no event could be satisfied out of the meager insurance fund—in a single forum of the insurance company's choosing. There is nothing in the statutory scheme, and very little in the judicial and academic commentary upon that scheme, which requires that the tail be allowed to wag the dog in this fashion.

State Farm's interest in this case * * * receives full vindication when the court restrains claimants from seeking to enforce against the insurance company any judgment obtained against its insured, except in the interpleader proceeding itself. To the extent that the District Court sought to control claimants' lawsuits against the insured and other alleged tortfeasors, it exceeded the powers granted to it by the statutory scheme.

We recognize, of course, that our view of interpleader means that it cannot be used to solve all the vexing problems of multiparty litigation arising out of a mass tort. But interpleader was never intended to perform such a function, to be an all-purpose "bill of peace." Had it been so intended, careful provision would necessarily have been made to insure that a party with little or no interest in the outcome of a complex controversy should not strip truly interested parties of substantial rights—such as the right to choose the forum in which to establish their claims, subject to generally applicable rules of jurisdiction, venue, service of process, removal, and change of venue. None of the legislative and academic sponsors of a modern federal interpleader device viewed their accomplishment as a "bill of peace," capable of sweeping dozens of lawsuits out of the various state and federal courts in which they were brought and into a single interpleader proceeding. And only in two reported instances has a federal interpleader court sought to control the underlying litigation against alleged tortfeasors as opposed to the allocation of a fund among successful tort plaintiffs. See Commercial Union Ins. Co. of New York

v. Adams, 231 F.Supp. 860 (D.C.S.D.Ind.1964) (where there was virtually no objection and where all of the basic tort suits would in any event have been prosecuted in the forum state), and Pan American Fire & Cas. Co. v. Revere * * *.

In light of the evidence that federal interpleader was not intended to serve the function of a "bill of peace" in the context of multiparty litigation arising out of a mass tort, of the anomalous power which such a construction of the statute would give the stakeholder, and of the thrust of the statute and the purpose it was intended to serve, we hold that the interpleader statute did not authorize the injunction entered in the present case. Upon remand, the injunction is to be modified consistently with this opinion.

IV.

The judgment of the Court of Appeals is reversed * * *.

[JUSTICE DOUGLAS dissented on the ground that the litigants were not "claimants" to the fund as required by the Federal Interpleader Act. He pointed out that the insurance policy specifically provided that no action could be brought against the company until the insured's obligation was determined. Furthermore, he argued, both California and Oregon law did not permit a direct action against the insurer until after final judgment against the insured. The Justice also took issue with the majority's construction of the words "may claim" in the Federal Interpleader Act.]

Notes and Questions

1. In TREINIES v. SUNSHINE MINING CO., 308 U.S. 66, 60 S.Ct. 44, 84 L.Ed. 85 (1939), the Supreme Court held that a federal court could constitutionally assert jurisdiction under the Federal Interpleader Act despite the cocitizenship of the stakeholder and one of the claimants. In arriving at this conclusion, the Court said that the stakeholder's "disinterestedness as between the claimants and as to the property in dispute" was demonstrated by his deposit of the fund in court and his discharge, which left the dispute to be ironed out between the adverse claimants. Id. at 72, 60 S.Ct. at 48, 84 L.Ed. at 90. Was it realistic for the Court to regard the disinterested stakeholder as a nominal party for diversity purposes? Can you reconcile the Court's conclusion with the fact that under Federal Rule 22(1) jurisdiction is proper if there is diversity between the stakeholder and the claimants, even though there is no diversity between the claimants? But what if the stakeholder in *Treinies* had asserted a claim to the money? Would the requisite diversity have existed? In other words, should the Court's reasoning also extend to bills in the nature of a bill of interpleader? See Bierman v. Marcus, 140 F.Supp. 66, 70 (D.N.J.1956), reversed on other grounds 246 F.2d 200 (3d Cir.1957). But cf. Boice v. Boice, 135 F.2d 919, 920 (3d Cir.1943). Does *State Farm* answer this question?

2. Note that in the principal case, the stakeholder was a citizen of Illinois and defendants were citizens of California, Oregon, several other states, and Canada. A number of claimants were citizens either of the same state or Canada. Since *Treinies* only dealt with cocitizenship as between the stakeholder and a claimant, on what basis does the Supreme Court in *State Farm* cavalierly decide that cocitizenship between adverse claimants does not destroy diversity jurisdiction since there was diversity between two or more of the claimants to the fund

and between State Farm and all of the named defendants? Would the result have been different in *State Farm* if there had not been diversity between State Farm and the named defendants as well as an absence of "complete diversity" among all of the claimants?

Perhaps the leading case on the subject of diversity in statutory interpleader actions prior to *State Farm* was HAYNES v. FELDER, 239 F.2d 868 (5th Cir.1957), which involved a Texas stakeholder who brought interpleader against two rival sets of claimants consisting of a citizen of Texas on one side opposed by four joint claimants of whom three were citizens of Texas and one was a citizen of Tennessee. In an exhaustive and illuminating opinion, the Fifth Circuit held that sufficient diversity existed for purposes of the Federal Interpleader Act and seemingly adopted a test of "minimal diversity." In what ways is *State Farm* distinguishable from *Haynes*? These two cases and the subject of minimal diversity in statutory interpleader actions are discussed in 14 Wright, Miller & Cooper, *Federal Practice and Procedure: Jurisdiction and Related Matters 3d* § 3636 (1998).

3.   When an action has been brought against a stakeholder in a federal court, there is some authority permitting a stakeholder to file a bill of interpleader or a bill in the nature of a bill of interpleader against plaintiff and one or more of the claimants, regardless of the citizenship of the added claimants. If the resulting interpleader suit is considered ancillary to the suit against the stakeholder, it is immaterial that the stakeholder is a cocitizen with any of the added claimants or that these claimants are themselves cocitizens. See Sherman Nat. Bank v. Shubert Theatrical Co., 238 F. 225 (S.D.N.Y.1916), affirmed 247 F. 256 (2d Cir.1917). For a discussion of ancillary jurisdiction and interpleader, see Chafee, *Interpleader in United States Courts*, 41 Yale L.J. 1134, 1145–60 (1931).

4.   Consider the following situation. Decedent was a stockholder in both A and B Corporations. His stock certificates in these two corporations are in the hands of C–2, a broker, who contends that she bought the stock from decedent. C–1, decedent's executrix, says that decedent merely entrusted the stock certificates to C–2 for safekeeping. Each claimant requests that A Corporation recognize her as the owner of the stock. The corporation interpleads. In addition to responding to the interpleader, C–1's answer demands that C–2 hand over the stock in B Corporation. Ownership of both sets of certificates turns on precisely the same facts. If the interpleader suit is brought under the Federal Interpleader Act, should the court adjudicate the ownership of both the A and B stock? For an argument that an interpleader suit should permit litigation of claims between the claimants in an interpleader suit other than claims for the disputed fund, see Chafee, *Broadening the Second Stage of Interpleader*, 56 Harv.L.Rev. 541, 929 (1943).

But consider the statement in *Tashire* that "our view of interpleader means that it cannot be used to solve all the vexing problems of multiparty litigation arising out of a mass tort." 386 U.S. at 535, 87 S.Ct. at 1206, 18 L.Ed.2d at 278. Does this prohibit cross-claims between interpleader claimants, the assertion of an unrelated claim by a disinterested stakeholder against a claimant, and a counter-claim by a claimant against the stakeholder? See generally 7 Wright, Miller & Kane, *Federal Practice and Procedure: Civil 3d* § 1715 (2001).

Assume that the interpleader suit concerning the A stock is brought in New York and that C–1 is a citizen of New York and C–2 is a citizen of Illinois and was personally served in that state under the Interpleader Act. If C–1 had started a separate action for the B stock, she would have had to travel to Illinois to try the suit because she could not have served C–2 with process in New York. Can the nationwide service of process permitted by the Interpleader Act be used to assert jurisdiction over the claims to the B stock by C–1 and C–2 in the suit involving the A stock? Cf. Moreno v. United States, 120 F.2d 128 (1st Cir.1941). See also Hagan v. Central Ave. Dairy, Inc., 180 F.2d 502 (9th Cir.1950). What if C–2 had been the first party to demand the B stock in her answer in the interpleader suit?

Applicable Law in Federal Interpleader Cases

In GRIFFIN v. McCOACH, 313 U.S. 498, 61 S.Ct. 1023, 85 L.Ed. 1481 (1941), the Supreme Court held that in a statutory interpleader suit based on diversity jurisdiction a federal court is bound by the *Erie* doctrine to apply the conflict-of-law rules of the state in which it sits. The case was decided on the same day as Klaxon Co. v. Stentor Elec. Mfg. Co., p. 423, supra. Yet, in certain statutory interpleader actions, the courts of the forum state might never have been able to hear a comparable case due to Fourteenth Amendment limitations on their personal jurisdiction. For a compelling argument that federal courts should develop their own conflicts rules when a federal act extends service of process beyond what is permitted a state by the Constitution, see *Developments in the Law—Multiparty Litigation in the Federal Courts,* 71 Harv.L.Rev. 874, 924–26 (1958). Are there any other arguments to suggest the inapplicability of *Erie* and *Klaxon* in statutory interpleader cases? The *Griffin* decision has been criticized in Cook, *The Federal Courts and the Conflict of Laws,* 36 Ill.L.Rev. 493, 507–15 (1942). Can a federal court grant interpleader under Federal Rule 22 when the state courts would deny interpleader because the stakeholder alleges a personal interest in the outcome of the case?

SECTION G.   INTERVENTION

As discussed earlier in this chapter, through devices such as Federal Rules 19 and 20, the parties may add additional parties to the lawsuit under certain circumstances. These Rules, however, are devices at the disposal of parties already in the lawsuit. But suppose a person learns of a lawsuit, the result of which might affect her. Should she be allowed to enter it as an additional party?

Read Federal Rule of Civil Procedure 24 in the Supplement.

BRUNE v. McDONALD
Supreme Court of Oregon, 1938.
158 Or. 364, 75 P.2d 10.

KELLY, JUSTICE. * * *

It appears from the original complaint of plaintiff that on the 16th day of August defendant was driving his automobile, with plaintiff as his guest therein, * * * on the Mount Hood Loop Road, toward Hood river, and that, when in the vicinity of Van Horn, defendant drove his automobile off the highway, along the edge thereof, across a culvert, through a fence and into a tree, causing injuries to plaintiff.

To support the charge of gross negligence on defendant's part, plaintiff specifically alleged in her original complaint that defendant operated his automobile at an excessive rate of speed, failed to keep his automobile under control, failed to maintain a proper lookout, and failed and neglected to heed plaintiff's remonstrance against defendant's maintenance of such excessive speed. In said original complaint plaintiff also alleged that prior to said accident defendant had imbibed alcoholic liquor, and, in the face of plaintiff's positive opposition thereto, drank excessively of alcohol.

On the 19th day of December, 1936, an amended complaint was filed from which reference to defendant's use of alcohol was omitted.

On the 9th day of January, 1937, said Pacific Indemnity Company procured an order granting said company leave to file a complaint in intervention herein.

On the 15th day of January, 1937, said Pacific Indemnity Company filed its complaint in intervention, in which said company alleged * * * it insured defendant against loss by reason of the liability imposed by law upon him for damages on account of bodily injuries suffered or alleged to have been suffered by any person other than his employees as a result of the ownership, maintenance, or use for pleasure purposes of the automobile referred to in the amended complaint herein, subject to a limitation to the sum of $5,000 for bodily injuries sustained by any one person.

* * *

The intervener, in its complaint in intervention, alleges:

* * *

"V. That prior to the trip during which said accident occurred plaintiff and defendant were and had been for a long time intimate friends and associates, frequently in the company of each other, and on frequent parties together, at which intoxicating liquors were consumed, and in the consumption of which both participated, and that plaintiff was well aware of the habits of defendant with respect to the use of intoxicating liquor.

"VI. That on the afternoon of Sunday, August 16, 1936, plaintiff and defendant embarked upon a pleasure trip around the Mount Hood Loop Highway, taking with them a bottle of intoxicating liquor for consumption during the trip, and they did from time to time during said trip jointly participate in drinking said intoxicating liquor and at Government Camp on said highway jointly engaged in drinking other intoxicating liquor with other persons.

"VII. That after said accident defendant gave to this intervenor several conflicting stories about the occurrences leading up to said accident, at first alleging that, while he was operating his automobile carefully and at a moderate speed, it was forced from the highway by another automobile, and then later that both plaintiff and defendant had consumed a considerable quantity of intoxicating liquor on the trip and that the accident occurred because of a momentary lapse of attention on his part while the automobile was being operated at a moderate speed; later plaintiff and defendant learned that there could be no recovery under said policy on such allegations and then connived and conspired with each other to mulct this intervenor of damages under said insurance policy and to that end jointly agreed that plaintiff should file an action against defendant for damages on account of her personal injuries and should allege that at the time of the accident defendant was grossly intoxicated and operating his automobile at a grossly high rate of speed and that defendant should represent to this intervenor that such charges were true and should deny to this intervenor that plaintiff participated in any of the drinking done on the trip, or knew that defendant was or was becoming intoxicated, thereby presenting an appearance of liability on the part of the defendant to plaintiff where none in truth and in fact existed, and with the intent of defrauding this intervenor of a substantial part of the face of said insurance policy.

"VIII. That in pursuance of said conspiracy plaintiff caused a complaint to be filed in this cause wherein she made the charges heretofore referred to against defendant and defendant thereupon represented to intervenor that said charges were all true, and further represented that the plaintiff did not participate in the drinking of any liquor on said trip, that plaintiff was not aware that he was or was becoming intoxicated and was not aware of his habits respecting intoxicating liquor because of his peculiar ability and capacity to imbibe large quantities of intoxicating liquor without other persons being aware of the fact, all of which representations made by the defendant were false and known by him and by plaintiff to be false and were made in accordance with their joint agreement to deceive and defraud this intervenor.

"IX. That by reason of the matters aforesaid said policy of insurance is void as to the accident in which plaintiff was injured and neither plaintiff nor defendant should be permitted to look to said policy in equity and in good conscience for any reimbursement or damages growing out of said accident; that plaintiff and defendant are planning to procure the entry of a judgment in favor of plaintiff and against defendant for a sum equal to the face of said policy but have agreed that plaintiff will look solely to this intervenor for the payment of said judgment and will make no attempt to collect any part of said judgment from defendant; that plaintiff will, unless restrained by this Court, procure a judgment to be entered against defendant and will then delay action on said policy of insurance until just prior to the expiration of the period of limitation applicable thereto, by which time the witnesses to establish the facts concerning said accident and said conspiracy of plaintiff and defendant, and the fraud perpetrated on defendant will have scattered and be unavailable. * * * "

* * *

The question here is whether said complaint in intervention states facts sufficient to warrant the court in granting the relief sought by the intervener, which is an injunction restraining the prosecution of plaintiff's cause of action until it can be determined whether defendant has breached the terms and conditions of said policy of insurance, as alleged by intervener.

The view usually expressed by the courts is that originally, in jurisdictions in which the common law prevailed, intervention was unknown except that it was in use to some extent in the ecclesiastical courts, and that apparently it is derived from the civil law. Therefore, in common-law jurisdictions intervention is usually regarded as of purely statutory origin. * * *

The generally accepted rule is that the right or interest which will authorize a third person to intervene must be of such a direct and immediate character that the intervener will either gain or lose by the direct legal operation of the judgment. * * *

It is obvious that the direct legal operation of the judgment in the case at bar would not cause intervener either to gain or lose anything.

It is equally apparent that the complaint in intervention herein tenders an entirely new and different issue from those of the complaint.

* * *

It will be noted that the intervener does not seek to interpose an answer to the complaint of plaintiff upon the merits of her alleged claim at law. Tested by a demurrer, the clause, "thereby presenting an appearance of liability on the part of the defendant to plaintiff where none in truth and in fact existed," does not constitute a statement of any defense to plaintiff's legal demand against defendant.

The relief sought by intervener is equitable. Intervener prays for an injunction restraining the further prosecution of plaintiff's action against defendant, until it can be determined whether the intervener would be liable to defendant upon its policy of insurance in case plaintiff should secure a judgment against defendant herein.

The reason assigned for seeking this relief is that by the time the judgment, if any, is procured by plaintiff against defendant, and proceedings are instituted to recover on intervener's policy, the intervener's witnesses to the alleged conspiracy will have become scattered and difficult, if not impossible, to procure, and that intervener will be confronted by a woman claimant whose femininity will render it much harder for intervener than if the same issue should be tried before plaintiff's claim against defendant has been adjudicated.

No case has been cited wherein such a procedure as intervener seeks to establish has been approved. The cases cited by intervener deal with sureties and with parties in interest who have been omitted in the original proceeding.

The policy of the courts generally has been to deal with the insurer in such a case as this as not being a party in interest and on the trial to guard against any willful reference to such insurer or to the fact that defendant is insured.

* * *

In giving effect to the allegations of the complaint in intervention we must assume that in case plaintiff prevails against defendant, the intervener will not be liable to defendant in any sum on that account. No liability on intervener's part could result in case defendant prevailed. We think that the supposed embarrassment which intervener alleges it will suffer by reason of the lapse of time necessary to determine this action at law, before the question of the validity or nonvalidity of intervener's policy of insurance can be presented, is not such an interest as * * * [permits intervention].

* * *

The controversy before the court, when the complaint in intervention was filed, was based upon a charge by plaintiff against defendant of gross negligence constituting the proximate cause of personal injury to plaintiff whereby plaintiff suffered damages in the amount demanded. It is obvious that this controversy may be completely determined without any reference, to intervener's policy of insurance. Certainly an invalid, void policy of insurance could not in any way affect the issues tendered in plaintiff's complaint.

* * *

We hold that no error was committed by the circuit court in sustaining plaintiff's demurrer to the complaint in intervention.

The judgment of the circuit court is affirmed.

___

KNAPP v. HANKINS, 106 F.Supp. 43, 47–48 (E.D.Ill.1952):

It is argued that the [insurance] Company may sit idly by and let the defendant employ counsel of his own choosing to defend the action. Under the terms of the policy defendant is obligated only to cooperate with the Company in defense of the suit. It would be unfair to require defendant to defend the case at his own expense if the policy is valid, even though he might subsequently recover such expenses from the Company; it would be equally unfair to require the Company to defend Hankins if the policy is void. * * *

Lastly, the plaintiffs and the defendant contend that the intervention by the Company will introduce new issues in the controversy between plaintiffs and defendant and that the plaintiffs are not interested in the controversy between the Company and the defendant.

* * * The allowance of intervention in the suit will not change the issues between the plaintiffs and the defendant one iota, but before these issues are tried the Company and the defendant will be permitted to determine the validity of the policy. A separate trial will no doubt be had on the issues raised by the intervening petition.

___

WHARFF v. WHARFF, 244 Iowa 496, 502–03, 56 N.W.2d 1, 4–5 (1952). Plaintiff-husband brought a divorce action against defendant-wife. In his complaint plaintiff described certain real estate held under a tenancy in common by the parties and asked that each party be declared to have certain rights of ownership therein. In her answer, defendant alleged that the real estate had been purchased in part with money she held in trust for her children by a previous marriage. The children petitioned to intervene, claiming the existence of a trust agreement under which their mother, defendant, held the sum of $21,500 for them, part of which had been invested in the real estate in question. The intervention petition prayed for a trust to be impressed for the benefit of the children. The denial of plaintiff's motion to strike the petition of intervention was affirmed by the Supreme Court of Iowa, which said:

> * * * It is true that persons not parties to the litigation would not be bound by its result and might bring a separate action. But we think the rule that a multiplicity of suits will be avoided wherever possible has a direct application. It might also happen that if the plaintiff and defendant here should try out their action first, and intervenors be relegated to a separate suit, different and contradictory results would be reached. A division of the property of the original parties without the benefit of such evidence as the intervenors might produce could very well be inequitable, resulting, at the best, in an action to modify the divorce decree by the litigant whose rights were adversely affected by a later trial of the separate action to enforce a trust. * * * There seems every reason in policy why, if there are third parties claiming an interest in either the real or personal property, the entire matter should be decided at once. Such a course will do away with a multiplicity of suits and will enable the court to make orders concerning property rights and allowances with a full knowledge of the exact extent of the interests of the litigants. In the case at bar, if the court is not to be permitted to know the real interest of the plaintiff and defendant in the realty and personalty now owned by them, if this must be left to determination in a future and separate suit brought by the proposed intervenors, it will be greatly hampered in making a fair order. * * *

Notes and Questions

1. As *Brune* notes, intervention is a relatively new development and largely statutory in nature. By allowing a third person to interject himself into a lawsuit, it undercuts the traditional notion that a plaintiff is allowed to control his suit. See 7C Wright, Miller & Kane, *Federal Practice and Procedure: Civil 2d* § 1901 (1986).

2. Is the statement in *Brune* that "the direct legal operation of the judgment * * * would not cause intervenor either to gain or lose anything" accurate? Does it mean that a party will be allowed to intervene only if the judgment will bind that party by principles of res judicata or collateral estoppel? Would the intervenors in *Wharff* have been affected by these doctrines had they not been allowed to intervene?

3. How might the *Brune* court have decided the intervention issue in *Wharff*? Can the difference in outcome in the two cases be explained by the *Wharff* court's willingness to consider the forum's interest in efficient adjudication of claims?

4. Should an insurance company be allowed to intervene in an action in which the policyholder is potentially liable for $12.5 million in damages under state and federal environmental clean-up statutes? In TRAVELERS INDEMNITY CO. v. DINGWELL, 884 F.2d 629 (1st Cir.1989), the insurer had issued a general liability policy to the company, but during the pendency of an indemnification action against the company, it was reserving the right to deny coverage. The court denied the insurer's Rule 24(a)(2) motion to intervene because the insurer's interest, although direct, nevertheless was contingent. The court found strong

policy reasons to support its decision. Intervention would interfere with the company's right to control its defense, and it would allow the insurer "a double bite at escaping liability." See generally Tobias, *Standing to Intervene,* 1991 Wis.L.Rev. 415.

SMUCK v. HOBSON

United States Court of Appeals, District of Columbia Circuit, 1969.
132 U.S.App.D.C. 372, 408 F.2d 175.

[In Hobson v. Hansen, 269 F.Supp. 401 (D.D.C.1967), a class action brought on behalf of Black and poor children, the court found that the plaintiffs were being denied their constitutional rights to equal educational opportunities because the District of Columbia schools were being operated on a basis that was racially and economically discriminatory. The Board of Education voted not to appeal and ordered Dr. Carl Hansen, the Superintendent of Schools, not to appeal. Nonetheless, Dr. Hansen and Carl Smuck, one of the dissenting Board members, filed notices of appeal. In addition, motions to intervene were made in the District Court and in the Court of Appeals by Dr. Hansen and twenty parents who said they "dissent from" the court's decision. The Court of Appeals decided to hold the direct appeals in abeyance and remanded the intervention motions for a hearing. The District Court granted the motions to intervene, even though neither Hansen nor the parents had shown a substantial interest that could be protected only through intervention, "in order to give the Court of Appeals an opportunity to pass on the intervention questions raised here, and the questions to be raised by the appeal on the merits * * *." Hobson v. Hansen, 44 F.R.D. 18, 33 (D.D.C. 1968). The Court of Appeals then considered the matter *en banc.*]

BAZELON, CHIEF JUDGE * * *. These appeals challenge the findings of the trial court that the Board of Education has in a variety of ways violated the Constitution in administering the District of Columbia schools. Among the facts that distinguish this case from the normal grist of appellate courts is the absence of the Board of Education as an appellant. Instead, the would-be appellants are Dr. Carl F. Hansen, the resigned superintendent of District schools, who appeals in his former official capacity and as an individual; Carl C. Smuck, a member of the Board of Education, who appeals in that capacity; and the parents of certain school children who have attempted to intervene in order to register on appeal their "dissent" from the order below.

* * * Whatever standing he might have possessed to appeal as a named defendant in the original suit * * * disappeared when Dr. Hansen left his official position. Presumably because he was aware of this, he subsequently moved to intervene under Rule 24(a) of the Rules of Civil Procedure in order to appeal as an individual. * * * He does not claim that a reversal or modification of the order by this Court would make his return to office likely. Consequently, the supposed impact of the decision upon his tenure is irrelevant insofar as an appeal is concerned, since a reversal would have no effect. Dr. Hansen thus has no "interest relating to the property or transaction which is the subject of the action" sufficient for Rule 24(a), and intervention is therefore unwarranted.

We also find that Mr. Smuck has no appealable interest as a member of the Board of Education. While he was in that capacity a named defendant, the

Board of Education was undeniably the principal figure and could have been sued alone as a collective entity. Appellant Smuck had a fair opportunity to participate in its defense, and in the decision not to appeal. Having done so, he has no separate interest as an individual in the litigation. The order directs the board to take certain actions. But since its decisions are made by vote as a collective whole, there is no apparent way in which Smuck as an individual could violate the decree and thereby become subject to enforcement proceedings.

The motion to intervene by the parents presents a more difficult problem requiring a correspondingly more detailed examination of the requirements for intervention of right.

* * *

The phrasing of Rule 24(a)(2) as amended parallels that of Rule 19(a)(2) concerning joinder. But the fact that the two rules are entwined does not imply that an "interest" for the purpose of one is precisely the same as for the other. The occasions upon which a petitioner should be allowed to intervene under Rule 24 are not necessarily limited to those situations when the trial court should compel him to become a party under Rule 19. And while the division of Rule 24(a) and (b) into "Intervention of Right" and "Permissible Intervention" might superficially suggest that only the latter involves an exercise of discretion by the court, the contrary is clearly the case.

The effort to extract substance from the conclusory phrase "interest" or "legally protectable interest" is of limited promise. Parents unquestionably have a sufficient "interest" in the education of their children to justify the initiation of a lawsuit in appropriate circumstances, as indeed was the case for the plaintiff-appellee parents here. But in the context of intervention the question is not whether a lawsuit should be begun, but whether already initiated litigation should be extended to include additional parties. The 1966 amendments to Rule 24(a) have facilitated this, the true inquiry, by eliminating the temptation or need for tangential expeditions in search of "property" or someone "bound by a judgment." It would be unfortunate to allow the inquiry to be led once again astray by a myopic fixation upon "interest." Rather, as Judge Leventhal recently concluded for this Court, "[A] more instructive approach is to let our construction be guided by the policies behind the 'interest' requirement. * * * [T]he 'interest' test is primarily a practical guide to disposing of lawsuits by involving as many apparently concerned persons as is compatible with efficiency and due process."[12]

The decision whether intervention of right is warranted thus involves an accommodation between two potentially conflicting goals: to achieve judicial economies of scale by resolving related issues in a single lawsuit, and to prevent the single lawsuit from becoming fruitlessly complex or unending. Since this task will depend upon the contours of the particular controversy, general rules and past decisions cannot provide uniformly dependable guides. The Supreme Court, in its only full-dress examination of Rule 24(a) since the 1966 amendments, found that a gas distributor was entitled to intervention of right although its only "interest" was the economic harm it claimed would follow from an allegedly inadequate plan for divestiture approved by the

---

12. Nuesse v. Camp, 128 U.S.App.D.C. 172,   385 F.2d 694, 700 (1967).

Government in an antitrust proceeding.[14] While conceding that the Court's opinion granting intervention in Cascade Natural Gas Corp. v. El Paso Natural Gas Co. "is certainly susceptible of a very broad reading," the trial judge here would distinguish the decision on the ground that the petitioner "did show a strong direct economic interest, for the new company [to be created by divestiture] would be its sole supplier." Yet while it is undoubtedly true that "*Cascade* should not be read as a carte blanche for intervention by anyone at any time," there is no apparent reason why an "economic interest" should always be necessary to justify intervention. The goal of "disposing of lawsuits by involving as many apparently concerned persons as is compatible with efficiency and due process" may in certain circumstances be met by allowing parents whose only "interest" is the education of their children to intervene. In determining whether such circumstances are present, the first requirement of Rule 24(a)(2), that of an "interest" in the transaction, may be a less useful point of departure than the second and third requirements, that the applicant may be impeded in protecting his interest by the action and that his interest is not adequately represented by others.

This does not imply that the need for an "interest" in the controversy should or can be read out of the rule. But the requirement should be viewed as a prerequisite rather than relied upon as a determinative criterion for intervention. If barriers are needed to limit extension of the right to intervene, the criteria of practical harm to the applicant and the adequacy of representation by others are better suited to the task. If those requirements are met, the nature of his "interest" may play a role in determining the sort of intervention which should be allowed—whether, for example, he should be permitted to contest all issues, and whether he should enjoy all the prerogatives of a party litigant.

Both courts and legislatures have recognized as appropriate the concern for their children's welfare which the parents here seek to protect by intervention. While the artificiality of an appeal without the Board of Education cannot be ignored, neither can the importance of the constitutional issues decided below. The relevance of substantial and unsettled questions of law has been recognized in allowing intervention to perfect an appeal. And this Court has noted repeatedly, "obviously tailored to fit ordinary civil litigation, [the provisions of Rule 24] require other than literal application in atypical cases."[20] We conclude that the interests asserted by the intervenors are sufficient to justify an examination of whether the two remaining requirements for intervention are met.

* * *

[The court then determined that the disposition of the action might impair the applicants' ability to protect their interests if they were not allowed to intervene.]

14. Cascade Natural Gas Corp. v. El Paso Natural Gas Co., 386 U.S. 129, 132–136, 87 S.Ct. 932, 17 L.Ed.2d 814 (1967).

20. Textile Workers Union, etc. v. Allendale Co., 96 U.S.App.D.C. 401, 403, 226 F.2d 765, 767 (1955) (en banc), cert. denied, Allendale Co. v. Mitchell, 351 U.S. 909, 76 S.Ct. 699, 100 L.Ed. 1444 (1956), cited in Nuesse v. Camp, 128 U.S.App.D.C. 172, 385 F.2d 694, 700 (1967).

The remaining requirement for intervention is that the applicant not be adequately represented by others. No question is raised here but that the Board of Education adequately represented the intervenors at the trial below; the issue rather is whether the parents were adequately represented by the school board's decision not to appeal. The presumed good faith of the board in reaching this decision is not conclusive. * * * As the conditional wording of Rule 24(a)(2) suggests in permitting intervention "unless the applicant's interest is adequately represented by existing parties," "the burden [is] on those opposing intervention to show the adequacy of the existing representation." In this case, the interests of the parents who wish to intervene in order to appeal do not coincide with those of the Board of Education. The school board represents all parents within the District. The intervening appellants may have more parochial interests centering upon the education of their own children. While they cannot of course ask the Board to favor their children unconstitutionally at the expense of others, they like other parents can seek the adoption of policies beneficial to their own children. Moreover, considerations of publicity, cost, and delay may not have the same weight for the parents as for the school board in the context of a decision to appeal. And the Board of Education, buffeted as it like other school boards is by conflicting public demands, may possibly have less interest in preserving its own untrammeled discretion than do the parents. It is not necessary to accuse the board of bad faith in deciding not to appeal or of a lack of vigor in defending the suit below in order to recognize that a restrictive court order may be a not wholly unwelcome haven.

* * *

Our holding that the appellants would be practically disadvantaged by a decision without appeal in this case and that they are not otherwise adequately represented necessitates a closer scrutiny of the precise nature of their interest and the scope of intervention that should accordingly be granted. The parents who seek to appeal do not come before this court to protect the good name of the Board of Education. Their interest is not to protect the board, or Dr. Hansen, from an unfair finding. Their asserted interest is rather the freedom of the school board—and particularly the new school board recently elected—to exercise the broadest discretion constitutionally permissible in deciding upon educational policies. Since this is so, their interest extends only to those parts of the order which can fairly be said to impose restraints upon the Board of Education. And because the school board is not a party to this appeal, review should be limited to those features of the order which limit the discretion of the old or new board.

* * *

[A partial concurring opinion by JUDGE McGOWAN and dissenting opinions by JUDGES DANAHER and BURGER are omitted.]

Notes and Questions

1. In addition to the reasons offered in *Smuck*, typical grounds for the assertion of inadequacy of representation for purposes of intervening as of right under Rule 24(a)(2) are: the applicant's interests are not represented at all,

Purnell v. City of Akron, 925 F.2d 941 (6th Cir.1991); the applicant and the attorney who supposedly represents his interest are antagonistic, United States v. C.M. Lane Lifeboat Co., 25 F.Supp. 410 (E.D.N.Y.1938), but see Stadin v. Union Elec. Co., 309 F.2d 912 (8th Cir.1962), certiorari denied 373 U.S. 915, 83 S.Ct. 1298, 10 L.Ed.2d 415 (1963); and there is collusion between the representative and the adverse parties, Virginia v. Westinghouse Elec. Corp., 542 F.2d 214 (4th Cir.1976). See generally Shapiro, *Some Thoughts on Intervention Before Courts, Agencies and Arbitrators,* 81 Harv.L.Rev. 721 (1968); Note, *Intervention in Government Enforcement Actions,* 89 Harv.L.Rev. 1174 (1976).

It often is held that the United States adequately represents the public interest in antitrust suits and intervention in those cases is denied absent a clear showing to the contrary. Is this approach justifiable? How does the Department of Justice determine what the public interest is?

2. What factors affect the standard for adequate representation? In NATIONAL RESOURCES DEFENSE COUNCIL, INC. v. NEW YORK STATE DEPARTMENT OF ENVIRONMENTAL CONSERVATION, 834 F.2d 60 (2d Cir.1987), the American Petroleum Institute (API) appealed a District Court order denying its motion to intervene in a lawsuit brought by the Natural Resources Defense Council, Inc. and other groups concerned with air pollution against the New York State Department of Environmental Conservation, the United States Environmental Protection Agency, and the administrators of both agencies. The Court of Appeals affirmed:

> This suit is a so-called "citizen suit". It seeks to compel the state defendants to implement four ozone pollution control strategies contained in New York's State Implementation Plan (SIP). * * * One of the ozone control strategies, known as Stage II, requires the use of equipment designed to capture gasoline vapors that escape when automobile fuel tanks are filled at gasoline stations. API, whose members own or supply some 3500 gasoline stations in New York City, asserts an interest in challenging the efficacy of the Stage II strategy * * * [T]he only issues concerning Stage II in this citizen suit are whether New York has unlawfully delayed implementation of Stage II and whether the State has a nondiscretionary duty to implement Stage II forthwith. * * * [T]he District Judge * * * ruled that API had not demonstrated a sufficient interest not already adequately represented by existing parties to the lawsuit.

> * * * API contends that in this suit it too has an interest different from that of New York. API's interest, it urges, is economic, whereas the State's interest is governmental.

> We think API misperceives the concept of an interest "adequately represented" within the meaning of Rule 24. A putative intervenor does not have an interest not adequately represented by a party to a lawsuit simply because it has a motive to litigate that is different from the motive of an existing party. So long as the party has demonstrated sufficient motivation to litigate vigorously and to present all colorable contentions, a district judge does not exceed the bounds of discretion by concluding that the interests of the intervenor are adequately represented. * * *

> In this case API may be motivated to defend the plaintiffs' suit because of economic interests not necessarily shared by the state and federal defendants, but there has been no showing that the nature of those economic interests is related to colorable legal defenses that the public defendants would be less

able to assert. * * * The fact that API wishes to advance contentions the existing defendants apparently believe are unavailing does not require API's intervention where no nexus exists between the interest asserted and the contentions sought to be put forth. * * *

Is this case consistent with *Smuck*? Why do you think the two come out differently?

3. Should there be a different standard for an intervenor to take an appeal than for a party who seeks to intervene in the original action? Should the original party's motive in deciding not to appeal be a relevant consideration? In the Seventh Circuit, "intervention to take an appeal is permissible only if the original parties' decision to discontinue the battle reflects 'gross negligence or bad faith.'" United States v. Chicago, 897 F.2d 243, 244 (7th Cir.1990), citing United States v. South Bend Community School Corp., 692 F.2d 623, 627 (7th Cir.1982).

4. An example of a federal statute that permits intervention is Section 902 of the Civil Rights Act of 1964, 42 U.S.C. § 2000h–2, which gives the United States an unconditional right to intervene in actions seeking relief against a denial of equal protection of the laws under the Fourteenth Amendment on account of race, color, religion, sex, or national origin. See Lemon v. Bossier Parish School Bd., 240 F.Supp. 709 (W.D.La.1965), affirmed 370 F.2d 847 (5th Cir.1967), certiorari denied 388 U.S. 911, 87 S.Ct. 2116, 18 L.Ed.2d 1350 (1967). Perhaps the single most important statutory provision permitting intervention by the United States is Section 2403(a) of the Judicial Code, which applies to actions challenging the constitutionality of an act of Congress. This provision has even enabled the United States to intervene to show that a case should be decided on nonconstitutional grounds. See Smolowe v. Delendo Corp., 36 F.Supp. 790 (S.D.N.Y.1940), affirmed on other grounds 136 F.2d 231 (2d Cir.), certiorari denied 320 U.S. 751, 64 S.Ct. 56, 88 L.Ed. 446 (1943). The government also has used it to show that the suit is collusive and there is no case or controversy before the court. See United States v. Johnson, 319 U.S. 302, 63 S.Ct. 1075, 87 L.Ed. 1413 (1943). See 7C Wright, Miller & Kane, *Federal Practice and Procedure: Civil 2d* § 1906 (1986), for a discussion of other statutes conferring an unconditional right to intervene. 28 U.S.C. § 2403(b) extends the intervention right to states in actions involving the constitutionality of state statutes.

5. Both Rule 24(a) and Rule 24(b) require that an application to intervene be "timely." As the court noted in *Smuck,* intervention after judgment will be allowed only in unique situations. One court has stated:

> The rationale which seems to underlie this general principle * * * is the assumption that allowing intervention after judgment will either (1) prejudice the rights of the existing parties to the litigation or (2) substantially interfere with the orderly processes of the court.

McDONALD v. E.J. LAVINO CO., 430 F.2d 1065, 1072 (5th Cir.1970).

What factors should the court consider when determining whether a motion to intervene is timely? Should a different standard be used for deciding the timeliness of motions to intervene permissively as opposed to motions to intervene as of right? If so, why? Sullivan, *Enforcement of Government Antitrust Decrees by Private Parties: Third Party Beneficiary Rights and Intervenor Status,* 123 U.Pa.L.Rev. 822, 873–92 (1975), explores the possibility of post-judgment intervention in government antitrust suits in order to enforce the judgment.

6. Must an intervenor present an independent basis for subject-matter jurisdiction? Before Congress enacted Section 1367 of the Judicial Improvements Act of 1990, as a general rule, if the applicant had a right to intervene under Rule 24(a), no independent basis for jurisdiction was required. See Lenz v. Wagner, 240 F.2d 666 (5th Cir.1957). An independent basis for jurisdiction was required for permissive actions. See, e.g., Reedsburg Bank v. Apollo, 508 F.2d 995 (7th Cir.1975). When subject-matter jurisdiction for the original action is based on diversity, Section 1367(b) now clearly bars nondiverse plaintiffs seeking to intervene under Rule 24(a). See generally Moore, *The Supplemental Jurisdiction Statute: An Important But Controversial Supplement to Federal Jurisdiction*, 41 Emory L.J. 31 (1992); Perdue, *The New Supplemental Jurisdiction Statute— Flawed But Fixable*, 41 Emory L.J. 69 (1992); Steinman, *Section 1367—Another Party Heard From*, 41 Emory L.J. 69 (1992).

7. Can an intervenor assert additional claims, counterclaims, cross-claims, or third-party claims in the lawsuit? Should your answer depend upon whether the intervention was discretionary or as of right? Does the answer turn on the nature of the claim: compulsory or permissive? See 7C Wright, Miller & Kane, *Federal Practice and Procedure: Civil 2d* § 1917 (1986). What should the result be under Section 1367?

ATLANTIS DEVELOPMENT CORP. v. UNITED STATES

United States Court of Appeals, Fifth Circuit, 1967.
379 F.2d 818.

JOHN R. BROWN, CIRCUIT JUDGE. This case involves a little bit of nearly everything—a little bit of oceanography, a little bit of marine biology, a little bit of the tidelands oil controversy, a little bit of international law, a little bit of latter day Marco Polo exploration. But these do not command our resolution since the little bits are here controlled by the less exciting bigger, if not big, problem of intervention. The District Court declined to permit mandatory intervention as a matter of right or to allow intervention as permissive. As is so often true, a ruling made to avoid delay, complications, or expense turns out to have generated more of its own. With the main case being stayed by the District Court pending this appeal, it is pretty safe to assume that the case would long have been decided on its merits (or lack of them) had intervention of either kind been allowed. And this seems especially unfortunate since it is difficult to believe that the presence of the attempted intervenor would have added much to the litigation. All of this becomes the more ironic, if not unfortunate, since the intervenor[1] and the Government sparring over why intervention ought or ought not to have been allowed, each try to persuade us the one was bound to win, the other lose on the merits which each proceeds to argue as though the parties were before or in the court. Adding to the problem, or perhaps more accurately aiding in the solution of it, are the mid–1966 amendments to the Federal Rules of Civil Procedure including specifically those relating to intervention. We reverse.

What the jousting is all about is the ownership in, or right to control the use, development of and building on a number of coral reefs or islands comprising Pacific Reef, Ajax Reef, Long Reef, an unnamed reef and Triumph

---

1. Atlantis Development Corporation, Ltd., a Bahamian corporation, will be referred to interchangeably as either Atlantis or Intervenor.

Reef which the intervenor has called the "Atlantis Group" because of the name given them by Anderson, its predecessor in interest and the supposed discoverer. * * *

Just how or in what manner these reefs were "discovered" is so far unrevealed. Some time in 1962 William T. Anderson discovered the reefs apparently by conceiving the idea of occupying them through the construction of facilities for fishing club, marina, skin diving club, a hotel, and, perhaps as the chief lure, a gambling casino. Anderson made some sort of claim to it and with facilities unavailable to the adventurous explorers of the long past, he gave public notice of this in the United States and in England by newspaper advertisements in late 1962 and early 1963. These "rights" were acquired by Atlantis Development Corporation, Ltd., the proposed intervenor. Reflecting the desire manifested now by the persistent efforts to intervene to have legal rights ascertained in a peaceful fashion through established tribunals and not by self-help or the initiation of physical activities which would precipitate counter moves, physical or legal, or both, Atlantis (and predecessors) patiently sought permission from all governmental agencies, state and federal—just short of the United Nations—but to no avail. * * * In December 1964 on learning that the defendants in the main case had formally sought a permit from the Engineers, Atlantis notified the Government of its claim to ownership of the islands and the threatened unauthorized actions by the defendants. This precipitated further communications with the Department of Justice with Atlantis importuning, apparently successfully, the Government to initiate the present action.

It was against this background that the litigation commenced. The suit is brought by the United States against the main defendants.[5] The complaint was in two counts seeking injunctive relief. In the first the Government asserted that Triumph and Long Reefs are part of the bed of the Atlantic Ocean included in the Outer Continental Shelf subject to the jurisdiction, control and power of disposition of the United States. The action of the defendants (note 5, supra) in the erection of caissons on the reefs, the dredging of material from the seabed, and the depositing of the dredged material within the caissons without authorization was charged as constituting a trespass on government property. In the second count the Government alleged that the defendants were engaged in the erection of an artificial island or fixed structure on the Outer Continental Shelf in the vicinity of the reefs without a permit from the Secretary of the Army in violation of the Outer Continental Shelf Lands Act, 43 U.S.C.A. § 1333(f) and 33 U.S.C.A. § 403. * * *

Atlantis seeking intervention by proposed answer and cross-claim against the defendants admitted the jurisdiction of the District Court. It asserted that the United States has no territorial jurisdiction, dominion or ownership in or over the reefs and cannot therefore maintain the action for an injunction, and that conversely Atlantis has title to the property by discovery and occupation. In the cross-claim, Atlantis charged the defendants as trespassers against it. Appropriate relief was sought by the prayer.

---

5. Acme General Contractors, Inc., and J.H. Coppedge Company, each Florida corporations, and Louis M. Ray, a resident of Dade County, Florida.

The District Court without opinion declared in the order that intervenor "does not have such an interest in this cause as will justify its intervention, either as a matter of right or permissively." Leave was granted to appear amicus curiae.

We think without a doubt that under former F.R.Civ.P. 24(a), intervention as a matter of right was not compelled under (a)(2). The situation did not present one in which the intervenor "is or may be bound" by a decree rendered in his absence in the sense articulated most recently in *Sam Fox*[9] in terms of res judicata. Although not quite so clear, we also think it did not measure up to the notions loosely reflected in a case-by-case development under which, although res judicata was technically lacking, the decree is considered "binding" since in a very practical sense it would have an immediate operative effect upon the intervenor. In none of these cases was it suggested that if the only effect of the decree in intervenor's absence would be to raise the hurdle of stare decisis, this would amount to the absentee being bound as a practical matter.

This brings us squarely to the effect of the 1966 Amendments and the new F.R.Civ.P. 24(a). * * *

In assaying the new Rule, several things stand out. The first, as the Government acknowledges, is that this amounts to a legislative repeal of the rigid *Sam Fox* * * * res judicata rule. But more important, the revision was a coordinated one to tie more closely together the related situations of joinder * * * and class actions * * * .

As the Advisory Committee's notes reflect, there are competing interests at work in this area. On the one hand, there is the private suitor's interests in having his own lawsuit subject to no one else's direction or meddling. On the other hand, however, is the great public interest, especially in these explosive days of ever-increasing dockets, of having a disposition at a single time of as much of the controversy to as many of the parties as is fairly possible consistent with due process.

In these three Rules the Advisory Committee, unsatisfied with the former Rules which too frequently defined application in terms of rigid legal concepts such as joint, common ownership, res judicata, or the like, as well as court efforts in applying them, deliberately set out on a more pragmatic course. For the purposes of our problem, this course is reflected in the almost, if not quite, uniform language concerning a party who claims an interest relating to the subject of the action and is so situated that the disposition of the action may as a practical matter impair or impede his ability to protect that interest * * *.

Although this is question-begging and is therefore not a real test, this approach shows that the question of whether an intervention as a matter of right exists often turns on the unstated question of whether joinder of the intervenor was called for under new Rule 19. Were this the controlling inquiry, we find ample basis here to answer it in the affirmative. Atlantis— having formally informed the Government in detail of its claim of ownership to the very reefs in suit, that the defendants were trespassing against it, and

---

9. Sam Fox Publishing Co. v. United States, 1961, 366 U.S. 683, 81 S.Ct. 1309, 6 L.Ed.2d 604.

having successfully urged the Government to institute suit against the defendants—seems clearly to occupy the position of a party who ought to have been joined as a defendant under new Rule 19(a)(2)(i) * * *.

This interim conclusion is, of course, a rejection of the Government's approach made for this day, case, and time only that all new Rule 24(a) was to do was to abandon the rigidity of *Sam Fox* and codify the ameliorative exceptions * * * to escape the unfortunate consequences of a rule expressed in terms of the party being "bound," i.e., res judicata. Any such narrow approach is to deprecate the painstaking work of the Advisory Committee especially the deliberate efforts to dovetail F.R.Civ.P. 19, 24 and 23 together with two of them being radically rewritten.

When approached in this light, we think that both from the terms of new Rule 24(a) and its adoption of 19(a)(2)(i) intervention of right is called for here. Of course F.R.Civ.P. 24(a)(2) requires both the existence of an interest which may be impaired as a practical matter and an absence of adequate representation of the intervenor's interest by existing parties. There can be no difficulty here about the lack of representation. On the basis of the pleadings * * * Atlantis is without a friend in this litigation. The Government turns on the defendants and takes the same view both administratively and in its brief here toward Atlantis. The defendants, on the other hand, are claiming ownership in and the right to develop the very islands claimed by Atlantis.

Nor can there be any doubt that Atlantis "claims an interest relating to the property or transaction which is the subject of the action." The object of the suit is to assert the sovereign's exclusive dominion and control over two out of a group of islands publicly claimed by Atlantis. This identity with the very property at stake in the main case and with the particular transaction therein involved (the right to build structures with or without permission of the Corps of Engineers) is of exceptional importance. For 24(a)(2) is in the conjunctive requiring both an interest relating to the property or transaction and the practical harm if the party is absent. This sharply reduces the area in which stare decisis may, as we later discuss, supply the element of practical harm.

This brings us then to the question whether these papers reflect that in the absence of Atlantis, a disposition of the main suit may as a practical matter impair or impede its ability to protect that interest—its claim to ownership and the right to control, use and develop without hindrance from the Government, the Department of Defense, or other agencies. Certain things are clear. Foremost, of course, is the plain proposition that the judgment itself as between Government and defendants cannot have any direct, immediate effect upon the rights of Atlantis, not a party to it.

But in a very real and practical sense is not the trial of this lawsuit the trial of Atlantis' suit as well? Quite apart from the contest of Atlantis' claim of sovereignty vis-a-vis the Government resulting from its "discovery" and occupation of the reefs, there are at least two basic substantial legal questions directly at issue, but not yet resolved in any Court at any time between the Government and the defendants which are inescapably present in the claim of Atlantis against the Government. One is whether these coral reefs built up by accretion of marine biology are "submerged lands" under the Outer Continental Shelf Lands Act, 43 U.S.C.A. § 1331 et seq. The second basic question is whether, assuming both from the standpoint of geographical location and their nature they constitute "lands," does the sovereignty of the United States extend to them with respect to any purposes not included in or done for the protection of the "exploring for, developing, removing, and transporting * * *" natural resources therefrom, 43 U.S.C.A. § 1333(a)(1). Another, closely related, is whether the authority of the Secretary of the Army to prevent obstruction of navigation extended by § 1333(f) to "artificial islands and fixed structures," includes structures other than those "erected thereon for the purpose of exploring for, developing, removing, and transporting" mineral resources therefrom (§ 1333(a)(1) * * *).

The Government would avoid all of these problems by urging us to rule as a matter of law on the face of the moving papers that the intervenors could not possibly win on the trial of the intervention and consequently intervention should be denied. In support it asserts that the claim that the reefs are beyond the jurisdiction of the United States is self-defeating, and under the plain meaning of the Outer Continental Shelf Lands Act and the facts revealed from the Coast and Geodetic Chart of which we must take judicial knowledge as proof of all facts shown.

The first is at least contingently answered by § 1333(b) which invests jurisdiction in the United States District Court of the nearest adjacent state. As to the others, it is, of course, conceivable that there will be some instances in which the total lack of merit is so evident from the face of the moving papers that denial of the right of intervention rests upon a complete lack of a substantial claim. But it hardly comports with good administration, if not due process, to determine the merits of a claim asserted in a pleading seeking an adjudication through an adversary hearing by denying access to the court at all. * * *

If in its claim against the defendants in the main suit these questions are answered favorably to the Government's position, the claim of Atlantis for all practical purposes is worthless. That statement assumes, of course, that such holding is either approved or made by this Court after an appeal to it and thereafter it is either affirmed, or not taken for review, on certiorari. It also assumes that in the subsequent separate trial of the claim of Atlantis against the Government the prior decision would be followed as a matter of stare decisis. Do these assumptions have a realistic basis? Anyone familiar with the history of the Fifth Circuit could have but a single answer to that query. This Court, unlike some of our sister Circuit Courts who occasionally follow a different course, has long tried earnestly to follow the practice in which a decision announced by one panel of the Court is followed by all others until such time as it is reversed, either outright or by intervening decisions of the Supreme Court, or by the Court itself en banc. That means that if the defendants in the main action do not prevail upon these basic contentions which are part and parcel of the claim of Atlantis, the only way by which Atlantis can win is to secure a rehearing en banc with a successful overruling of the prior decision or, failing in either one or both of those efforts, a reversal of the earlier decision by the Supreme Court on certiorari. With the necessarily limited number of en banc hearings in this Circuit and with the small percentage of cases meriting certiorari, it is an understatement to characterize these prospects as formidable.

That is but a way of saying in a very graphic way that the failure to allow Atlantis an opportunity to advance its own theories both of law and fact in the trial (and appeal) of the pending case will if the disposition is favorable to the Government "as a practical matter impair or impede [its] ability to protect [its] interest." That is, to be sure, a determination by us that in the new language of 24(a)(2) stare decisis may now—unlike the former days under 24(a)(2)—supply that practical disadvantage which warrants intervention of right. It bears repeating, however, that this holding does not presage one requiring intervention of right in every conceivable circumstance where under the operation of the Circuit's stare decisis practice, the formidable nature of an en banc rehearing or the successful grant of a writ of certiorari, an earlier decision might afford a substantial obstacle. We are dealing here with a conjunction of a claim to and interest in the very property and the very transaction which is the subject of the main action. When those coincide, the Court before whom the potential parties in the second suit must come must itself take the intellectually straight forward, realistic view that the first decision will in all likelihood be the second and the third and the last one. Even the possibility that the decision might be overturned by en banc ruling or reversal on certiorari does not overcome its practical effect, not just as an obstacle, but as the forerunner of the actual outcome. * * *

Reversed.

Notes and Questions

1. Early commentary on the 1966 amendment to Federal Rule 24 appears in Cohn, *The New Federal Rules of Civil Procedure,* 54 Geo.L.J. 1204, 1229–32 (1966); Kaplan, *Continuing Work of the Civil Committee: 1966 Amendments of the Federal Rules of Civil Procedure (I),* 81 Harv.L.Rev. 356, 400–07 (1967).

2. In what ways other than those described in *Atlantis* does the amended text of Federal Rule 24 have the effect of liberalizing intervention as of right? Prior to 1966, one of the two conditions on intervention of right was a showing that the representation of the intervenor "is or may be inadequate." Under amended Rule 24(a), if the other conditions of that provision are satisfied, intervention is of right unless it is shown that the applicant's interest is adequately represented by existing parties. What is the effect of this change? Intervention classically has been viewed as having three functions: protection of nonparties, trial convenience, and protection of the original parties. In what ways has the balance among these three functions been altered by the 1966 amendments?

3. Why does Rule 24 distinguish between intervention as of right and permissive intervention? In Shreve, *Questioning Intervention of Right—Toward a New Methodology of Decisionmaking,* 74 Nw.U.L.Rev. 894 (1980), the author argues that trial court judges should be allowed to exercise their discretion in all non-statutory intervention cases. He says that intervention as of right has had the effect of adding needless appellate review, resulting in inefficiencies. According to the author, a procedural device designed, in part, to improve the use of court resources has had the opposite effect in many cases.

Chapter 10

CLASS ACTIONS

Read Federal Rule of Civil Procedure 23 and the material accompanying it in the Supplement.

In the last Chapter we saw that the scope of the civil action has expanded dramatically. However, it still often is not feasible for a plaintiff to sue individually or for all of those relevant to a dispute to be joined in a single action. Class action practice has developed to address these situations. But, if a small group of representatives are allowed to advance the claims of a large number of people, concerns about the due process rights of absent class members and proper application of the rules of finality are implicated. Each decision about whether to proceed on a class basis, therefore, obliges a judge to balance the advantages of a single adjudication with notions of fairness to absent people whose claims may be extinguished by the action.

As you read this Chapter, it will become clear that there are two ways of viewing the modern class-action device: It can be viewed simply as another joinder device, or it can be viewed as something different—a representational device that empowers the named class representative to act on behalf of others similarly situated whether or not they could have sued independently, or even wanted to do so. See generally Hutchinson, *Class Actions: Joinder or Representational Device?*, 1984 Sup.Ct.Rev. 459. Although the 1966 amendments to Rule 23 moved in the direction of the representational model, courts (including the Supreme Court) have vacillated between the two views of the class-action device just described. Thus, as you read, be sensitive to this vacillation and ask yourself if the choice between the models produces different results in concrete cases. And, at the close of the Chapter, ask yourself whether the class-action device is only a procedural convenience that goes slightly beyond Rule 20, or whether the device makes possible litigation on the part of absentee class members that they otherwise would be unable to maintain.

One other general issue should engage your attention. The rules governing class actions depart from the traditional notion that individuals can be bound by a court judgment only when they themselves have had a day in court. What justifies this departure? What is there about the procedures that have been developed around the class-action device that makes it possible and fair to bind a party who has not made an appearance in court? As you consider these questions, pay special attention to the connections among the doctrines governing res judicata, notice, and adequate representation.

Today, the class action device continues to be a work in progress. The Advisory Committee on Civil Rules of the United States Judicial Conference has been studying, with the aid of numerous lawyers and academics, whether Rule 23 is in need of revision and, if so, what shape any changes should take. As you progress through this Chapter, put yourself in role as a member of the Committee and consider the changes you would make.

SECTION A. HISTORY AND PHILOSOPHY OF THE CLASS ACTION

The history of the class action can be traced to the English "bill of peace" in the seventeenth century. The "bill" was a procedural device utilized by the Courts of Chancery to allow an action to be brought by or against representative parties when (1) the number of persons involved was too large to permit joinder, (2) all the members of the group possessed a joint interest in the question being adjudicated, and (3) the named parties adequately represented the interests of those who were not present. If these three conditions were met, the judgment that ultimately was entered was binding on all the members of the represented group. An excellent summary of the history of class actions can be found in Yeazell, *From Medieval Group Litigation to the Modern Class Action* (1987).

Although provisions for class actions based upon the English procedure existed in various state codes and the Federal Equity Rules, Federal Rule 23, as originally adopted in 1938, represented the first attempt to provide for class actions in a mature form. Moreover, with the adoption of the Federal Rules the class action became available in both legal and equitable actions in the federal courts.

Originally Rule 23 attempted to describe when a class action was proper in a highly conceptualized way. However, this structure proved to be confusing to apply, see 7A Wright, Miller & Kane, *Federal Practice and Procedure: Civil 2d* § 1752 (1986), which led the Advisory Committee in 1966 to rewrite Rule 23 completely to substitute functional tests for the conceptual categories and to provide some procedural guidance for the courts with regard to handling class actions. The amendments also made clear that a judgment in a class action is binding on all class members, except in those cases in which the right to opt-out under Rule 23(c)(2) applies and has been exercised.

The evolution of the rules governing class actions parallels in part an evolution in society and in society's understanding of the role of courts. As two early commentators on the Federal Rules put it:

> Modern society seems increasingly to expose men to * * * group injuries for which individually they are in a poor position to seek legal redress, either because they do not know enough or because such redress is disproportionately expensive. If each is left to assert his rights alone if and when he can, there will at best be a random and fragmentary enforcement, if there is any at all. This result is not only unfortunate in

the particular case, but it will operate seriously to impair the deterrent effect of the sanctions which underlie much contemporary law. The problem of fashioning an effective and inclusive group remedy is thus a major one.

Kalven & Rosenfield, *The Contemporary Function of a Class Suit,* 8 U.Chi. L.Rev. 684, 686 (1941). This state of affairs remains true today.

———

Since the 1966 amendments, even the utility of class actions has been the subject of much debate. The following excerpt summarizes the extremes of the debate and attempts to characterize and explain the experience with class actions in the years following 1966.

———

MILLER, *OF FRANKENSTEIN MONSTERS AND SHINING KNIGHTS: MYTH, REALITY, AND THE "CLASS ACTION PROBLEM,"* 92 Harv.L.Rev. 664, 665–66, 677–81 (1979):

* * * Opinions regarding the effect of the revision range over an amazing gamut. Class action adherents would have us believe it is a panacea for a myriad of social ills, which deters unlawful conduct and compensates those injured by it. Catch phrases such as "therapeutic" or "prophylactic" and "[taking] care of the smaller guy" are frequently trumpeted. Its opponents have rallied around characterizations of the procedure as a form of "legalized blackmail" or a "Frankenstein Monster." They also have charged widespread abuse of the rule by lawyers and litigants on both sides of the "v.," including unprofessional practices relating to attorneys' fees, "sweetheart" settlement deals, dilatory motion practice, harassing discovery, and misrepresentations to judges. Finally, some have questioned the wisdom of imposing the burdens of class actions on an already overtaxed federal judiciary. They assert that many Rule 23 cases are unmanageable and inordinately protracted by opposing counsel, creating a certain millstone or dinosaur character that diverts federal judges from matters more worthy of their energies.

Yet despite the attention that has been riveted on Rule 23, we have precious little empiric evidence as to how it actually has been functioning, in terms of either its alleged benefits or supposed blasphemies. Even if the negative effects of class actions were assumed, they would have to be balanced against the societal benefits derived from deterring socially proscribed conduct and providing small claim rectification—considerations that thus far have escaped measurement and perhaps always will.

* * *

* * * [T]he past twelve years have been characterized by radical swings in the administration of the amended rule and judicial attitudes toward it. As a result, each class action decision must be considered in terms of when it was rendered and which court issued it. The movement of the decisions has resembled that of a pendulum, and although the arc on the swings has been diminishing, the practice continues to vary. The period since the revision can

be divided into three time frames, each characterized by distinctive attitudes and practices. The divisions are used to provide a generalized description of the periods. Although they may appear arbitrary to some, I offer them only as a device for structuring my impressions gleaned from a perusal of the cases and thinking about our experience under the revision.

During the first period, dating from 1964, when many members of the bench and bar actually began to invoke the new text in anticipation of its promulgation, until approximately 1969, the legal community exhibited considerable euphoria over the rule's potential. Hopes were great that the class action would prove instrumental in dispensing justice to socially or economically disadvantaged groups as well as to small claimants generally. Statements that the rule "should be given a liberal rather than a restrictive interpretation," and that "if there is to be an error made, let it be in favor and not against the maintenance of the class action," were characteristic of this first period. The possibilities for class action litigation seemed limitless.

Unfortunately, during this period of great expectations many lawyers and judges appear not to have paid sufficient attention to the prerequisites for class action treatment prescribed by the rule. Cases often were certified as class actions on the basis of rather conclusory assertions of compliance with Rule 23(a) and (b). Settlements were sometimes approved without an in-depth analysis of the underlying merits of the claim, the economics of the litigation, or the feasibility of distributing the funds to class members. In addition, fee petitions were not scrutinized as carefully as experience now suggests they should have been. Enthusiasm for the class action fed upon itself, and the procedure fell victim to overuse by its champions and misuse by some who sought to exploit it for reasons external to the merits of the case. Mistakes, in most cases honest mistakes of faith, were made. By the end of this first phase, class action practice had been given a very black eye. Unfortunately, many members of the legal community formed negative impressions of the class action during this period that continue to influence them today despite radical changes in the conditions that gave rise to the procedure's unsavory reputation.

Quite naturally a reaction developed. Numerous voices were raised condemning excessive attorneys' fees and decrying the growing burdens of class action litigation. The spotlight was cast on certain cases involving questionable conduct or seemingly inexplicable fee awards, such as the settlement in the Playboy litigation, which reportedly gave club members chits for a small number of drinks and the lawyers a six-figure fee. And, not surprisingly, opposition to class action requests in specific cases stiffened. Defendants began treating the decision under Rule 23(c)(1) as if it were Armageddon and mounted major challenges to class action certification, inevitably producing proliferated precertification discovery and motion practice devoted to the structure of the suit rather than to the substance of the claim.

Accordingly, from 1969 to approximately 1973 or perhaps 1974, antipathy to the class action became palpable. Federal courts were much readier to deny certification; attorneys' fee applications were eviscerated; interlocutory appeals were sought, and many were accepted, to review certification questions. The defense bar developed numerous litigation techniques to make the class action venture as unattractive as possible, including attacking class counsel's professional conduct. It was a very difficult time for the class action practitioner, and the viability of the device itself was in serious doubt. The picture was made all the bleaker by the Supreme Court's restrictive decisions in Snyder v. Harris,[a] Zahn v. International Paper Co.,[b] and Eisen v. Carlisle & Jacquelin.[c]

In my judgment, the pendulum has swung again, and we are now in a third phase, which began in 1973 or 1974 in some courts, more recently in others, and perhaps not at all in still others. We probably will remain in this phase for some time, quite possibly until the end of the generation-long period Professor Kaplan envisioned. It is a period characterized by increasing sophistication, restraint, and stabilization in class action practice. The current phase is marked by great concern within the profession about the excesses of the first two periods. The shock waves sent out by *Snyder, Zahn,* and *Eisen* have encouraged many plaintiffs' lawyers to be much more precise and careful. By defining their classes and describing the scope of their claims realistically, they are acting more responsibly than before. The result is that classes have become more reasonable aggregations of litigants, thus reducing the manageability problems created by sheer class size. In addition, plaintiffs' lawyers are beginning to recognize that there may be good reasons, such as the danger of getting trapped in the morass of giving notice and securing judicial approval of any settlement required under Rule 23, to resist the almost reflexive impulse to seek class action treatment. For their part, judges are now sensitive to the desirability of requiring counsel to make full factual presentations on questions of certification, settlement, and fees. Finally, defendants are becoming somewhat less intransigent in their opposition to requests for class certification, at least in restraining their use of boilerplate arguments against it.

One key to this third phase is that district judges are now exploiting the arsenal of procedural powers set out in subdivisions (c) and (d) of the rule, which largely went unnoticed for a number of years following Rule 23's revision. More judges are aware that there are possibilities other than an across-the-board grant or denial of certification. Instead of wielding a meat axe, courts increasingly are operating with a scalpel. As a result, district judges frequently redefine classes to improve manageability; grant partial certification when appropriate to take advantage of the economics of group adjudication on at least some issues; bifurcate the adjudication of liability from the remedy phase in certain cases to improve efficiency; insist on a high level of legal skill to improve the quality of representation, which serves to reduce the risk of collateral attack; establish subclasses when antagonisms or conflicts exist within the group; and employ efficient management techniques during the precertification period to achieve an early determination of that issue. On a more general level, the growing judicial willingness to control the

a. 394 U.S. 332, 89 S.Ct. 1053, 22 L.Ed.2d 319 (1969) (individual claims of class members cannot be aggregated to meet federal court jurisdictional-amount requirements). See pp. 735–38, infra.

b. 414 U.S. 291, 94 S.Ct. 505, 38 L.Ed.2d 511 (1973)(each claim in a federal class action must independently satisfy the jurisdictional-amount requirement). See pp. 735–38, infra.

c. 417 U.S. 156, 94 S.Ct. 2140, 40 L.Ed.2d 732 (1974) (named class members must bear the costs of individual notice to each class member in a Rule 23(b)(3) class action). See Note 6, p. 724, infra.

discovery process and prevent its overuse is being felt in the class-action context.

———

Eight years after he wrote his *Harvard Law Review* article, Professor Miller served as the Reporter for a study of complex litigation for the American Law Institute. In it, he wrote:

> Class actions have proven to be the most effective legal technique for avoiding piecemeal litigation and preserving legal resources. Nevertheless, the class action suit continues to be eyed with suspicion by many courts. In complex cases, the goals of the class action device have been frustrated by strict adherence to the requirements of Rule 23. Often, complex multiparty, multiforum cases are denied class action treatment. Certification of large scale tort action classes is rare. Courts deny certification based on decisions that the commonality of interest requirement is not satisfied and based on fear that the size of the class would make the litigation unwieldy and inefficient.
>
> Generally, present treatment of class action suits begins with an initial skepticism towards the class. Cases that involve incidents of personal injury occurring in a series of related events that may be separated by time or geography are usually denied certification. In the case of property damage, the class may receive certification but courts are wary that the litigation may degenerate into individual suits over specific pieces of property. Courts are split as to whether mass tort cases should be certified as 23(b)(1)(B) cases. Proponents argue that certification is more beneficial when total damages requested exceeds defendant's net worth. Detractors are concerned that such certification is merely a shortcut around notice and opt-out requirements. * * *
>
> The usefulness of the class action device for future complex litigation raises two issues concerning the suitability of class actions to modern litigation needs. The first issue is whether the scope of the class action should be broadened to include more types of litigation. The second is whether courts should increase the frequency with which they certify mandatory classes. Presently, class actions are used relatively infrequently in many multiparty, multiforum litigation contexts. With some adjustments the class action device could be made a valuable litigation tool.

American Law Institute, *Preliminary Study of Complex Litigation*, Report, 61–70 (1987). The Preliminary Study was followed by a comprehensive exploration of the subject, which led to the American Law Institute's formal approval of *Complex Litigation: Statutory Recommendations and Analysis* (1994).

In 1996, the Research Division of the Federal Judicial Center conducted an empirical study of the use of Rule 23 in four federal districts. Williging, Hooper & Niemic, *An Empirical Analysis of Rule 23 to Address the Rulemaking Challenges*, 71 N.Y.U.L.Rev. 74 (1996). It was a surprise to some that the study found that not all applications of Rule 23 are difficult; indeed, there are significant numbers of "routine" class actions, particularly in securities and civil rights litigation. The findings suggest that these well-established applications might be affected significantly by changes in Rule 23. The study also seemed to demonstrate that attorney's fees were not disproportionate to class recoveries. Moreover, as with most civil litigation, class actions follow the general pattern of settlement in lieu of trial. Although anecdotes abound that the mere instigation of a class action suit or at least its certification coerces settlements even in frivolous cases, the study seemed to belie that notion because the certified cases that settled had survived motions to dismiss or motions for summary judgment.

SECTION B.   OPERATION OF THE CLASS–ACTION DEVICE

1. INTRODUCTION

Because the 1966 amendments to Federal Rule 23 had a significant impact on state class-action procedures, that Rule provides a paradigm that can be used to study the operation of class-action provisions generally. Although there are defendant class actions, the plaintiff class action (which is far more common) will be the model used in this discussion. Most of the observations made about the plaintiff class action are applicable to defendant class actions as well, however.

2. THE INITIATION OF CLASS ACTIONS

Although Rule 23 expressly gives courts power to issue certification orders sua sponte, they normally are issued in response to a motion made by the litigant who ultimately will be named class representative. Frequently, that litigant's initial complaint contains both individual and class allegations, and the motion for certification is filed concurrently with the initial complaint or shortly thereafter; it is not uncommon, however, for a litigant to move for class certification substantially after the initial filing, following an amendment of the complaint to include class allegations.

The individual who wants to initiate a class action need not get the permission of potential class members before moving for certification, and the consent of class members generally is not a prerequisite for a court's certifying a suit as a class action. In fact, potential class members often oppose the class suit, either wishing to bring their own individual suits, or preferring not to have suit brought at all. In many jurisdictions (including the federal system), certain class members are provided an opportunity to "opt out" of the class. In other jurisdictions (several state systems, for example), individuals are not considered members of the class until they have been notified of its existence and have chosen to "opt in" to the class.

In practice, attorneys often play a critical role in causing class suits to be brought. Sometimes, attorneys simply persuade individuals who have a legal problem that the best way to obtain a remedy is by filing a class action embracing the claims of others who are similarly situated. Other times, attorneys actually solicit clients for class suits. For example, in what many think is a modern version of ambulance chasing, a lawyer, upon hearing of a disaster, may contact one of the victims and may offer to serve as counsel in a class action. The Supreme Court has held that this form of solicitation—for the lawyer's personal gain—is prohibited by legal ethical rules. See Ohralik v. Ohio State Bar Association, 436 U.S. 447, 98 S.Ct. 1912, 56 L.Ed.2d 444 (1978). But there are other examples in which the solicitation of clients for class suits is permissible. For instance, during the 1960's and 1970's NAACP lawyers went to the South to inform minorities of their legal rights and to offer themselves as counsel to those who decided to bring suit. The Supreme Court has held that offers of legal services in this context are a form of political expression, and that prohibitions against solicitation are invalid on First Amendment grounds. See In re Primus, 436 U.S. 412, 98 S.Ct. 1893, 56 L.Ed.2d 417 (1978).

3. CERTIFICATION

a. *The Requirements for Certification*

The district judge must make seven affirmative findings before a suit can be certified, and the plaintiff has the burden of establishing all seven prerequisites. Two of them are not expressed in Rule 23 and have been developed by the courts. Four more are enumerated in Rule 23(a). The seventh is that the district judge must find that the case falls within one of the three categories of class actions described in Rule 23(b).

The first requirement is that there be a class. This may sound self-evident, and in most instances the plaintiff will describe an ascertainable group that claims to be injured in a similar fashion—for example, recipients of a particular welfare benefit or employees of a certain company. However, occasionally the plaintiff will offer a very vague description. A class described as "all poor people" is insufficient without providing some objective criteria that determine who is poor for purposes of class membership. Conversely, the plaintiff's description of the class can err by being too specific. In TIJERINA v. HENRY, 48 F.R.D. 274 (D.N.M.1969), the class was characterized as all people with Spanish surnames having Spanish, Mexican, or Indian ancestry who spoke Spanish as a primary or secondary language. It would take enormous effort to ascertain who was in that class because the membership characteristics are so complex. The district court allowed the class description to be amended to include all people with Mexican or Spanish surnames. Although this created a much larger class, the result avoided the managerial and administrative difficulties of ascertaining who satisfied all three original conditions.

The second prerequisite is that the class representative must be a member of the class. This is essentially a standing requirement. Again, the requirement may sound self-evident, but there have been cases in which the named plaintiff turned out not to be a member of the class. For example, if the claims of all named plaintiffs have been satisfied before class certification, the action may be dismissed as moot even though a live controversy remains as to other class members. See Bradley v. Housing Authority, 512 F.2d 626 (8th Cir.1975). However, if the matter at issue (such as pretrial detention without a probable cause hearing) is such that the class representative's individual interest, in the normal course of events, will expire before a ruling can be made on class certification, the class may be certified despite the mootness of the named plaintiff's claim. See Gerstein v. Pugh, 420 U.S. 103,

110–11 n. 11, 95 S.Ct. 854, 861 n. 11, 43 L.Ed.2d 54, 63 n. 11 (1975). See also United States Parole Comm'n v. Geraghty, 445 U.S. 388, 100 S.Ct. 1202, 63 L.Ed.2d 479 (1980) (named plaintiff may appeal denial of class certification even if individual claim has become moot); Sosna v. Iowa, 419 U.S. 393, 95 S.Ct. 553, 42 L.Ed.2d 532 (1975) (class action is not rendered moot if named plaintiff's claim becomes moot *after* class certification).

The first of the four express prerequisites is Rule 23(a)(1), which requires that the class be so numerous that joinder of all members is "impracticable." In most instances this requirement is mechanical. If a class has more than forty members, "numerosity" usually is satisfied; if the class numbers less than twenty-five, "numerosity" usually is lacking. When the class is between twenty-five and forty members, variables such as the geographic dispersion of class members and the size of their individual claims become important. Joinder generally is impracticable if the claims are small, because people are not likely to become involved in litigation if only a small amount of money is at stake. On the other hand, joinder usually is feasible if each individual's stake is relatively large.

The second and third express prerequisites are embodied in Rule 23(a)(2) and Rule 23(a)(3). Neither has created many difficulties for the courts. Rule 23(a)(2), the "commonality" requirement, mandates that the action raise questions of law or fact common to the class. One significant common question is enough. Rule 23(a)(3), the "typicality" prerequisite, requires that the claims of the representative party be typical of those of the class. This provision does not seem to have any independent purpose since any objective it might serve already will be achieved by the commonality requirement and the adequacy requirement of Rule 23(a)(4), discussed below. Few courts focus on typicality, and it tends to be discussed in almost conclusory terms.

The final express prerequisite, Rule 23(a)(4), is that the court find that the representative party will fairly and adequately protect the interests of the class. This is probably the single most important Rule 23(a) requirement, and the one most heavily litigated. It derives its importance from two factors. First, on a philosophical level, Rule 23(a)(4) embodies the due process concerns that animated the Supreme Court's decision in Hansberry v. Lee, 311 U.S. 32, 61 S.Ct. 115, 85 L.Ed. 22 (1940), p. 718, infra. The class action seeks to bind parties who have not *literally* had their "day in court." However, as members of a defined group with similar claims and proper representation, they have had a *figurative* day in court. It is Rule 23(a)(4) that ensures the quality of that representation. Second, on a pragmatic level, a defect in the adequacy of representation in an action might leave the judgment vulnerable to collateral attack. See Gonzales v. Cassidy, Note 3, p. 721, infra. It would be an extremely wasteful expenditure of time and effort to go through the certification process, complete extensive discovery, negotiate and approve a settlement or actually adjudicate the merits of the case, and draft and enter a judgment, only to have everything unravelled years later by someone who does not want to be bound by the result and claims that the adequacy requirement was not met.

What constitutes adequacy of representation? It has three elements. First, the representative parties themselves must be adequate. The court should ascertain whether the named plaintiffs have a substantial stake in the litigation, or if there is any reason to believe that they are motivated by factors unrelated to the case itself, such as greed, vindictiveness, or pursuit of a competitive advantage. The court also should examine the relationship between the representative party and the lawyer. The two should be different people and have no strong family or financial relationship that would undermine the party's independent judgment about matters relating to the conduct of the action.

Second, the court should inquire into the adequacy of the class' lawyer. As with the representative party, much of the inquiry will focus on the lawyer's bona fides, but technical competence also is important. All of the lawyer's resources must be evaluated—professional experience, motivation, support personnel, and other professional commitments. Class actions usually are highly complex, protracted, and technical lawsuits, and the district judge must satisfy himself that the lawyer will be able to meet the challenges they pose.

Third, the court has an affirmative responsibility to examine the class itself, to see if it is beset by any internal antagonism. A conflict within the class that goes to the matter in litigation will defeat the party's claim of representative status. The seminal Supreme Court decision in Hansberry v. Lee, p. 718, infra, illustrates this situation. To alleviate the problem of internal antagonism, the court must divide the class into sub-classes, often aligning a sub-class with the defendant, or separating those issues that merit class-action treatment from those that do not.

After the district judge has determined that the suit satisfies the six prerequisites already discussed, she must decide that it falls within one of the three categories of class actions enumerated in Rule 23(b). The first category, Rule 23(b)(1), which might be referred to as the "prejudice" class action, contains two clauses. Both ask whether individual actions might cause prejudice that can be avoided by using the class-action device. Subdivision (A) looks for prejudice to the non-class party; subdivision (B) inquires into prejudice to members of the class.

Subdivision (A) deals with the risk that individual actions would create "incompatible standards of conduct" for the party opposing the class. It is important to note that the Rule does *not* refer to the situation in which the defendant in a series of actions would have to pay damages to some claimants but not to others. Rather, the Rule applies when different results in individual actions would place the non-class party in a position of total uncertainty, not knowing how to treat the class as a whole. For example, consider a voting rights dispute involving a question of eligibility for registration. If applicants sue individually, some may win and others may lose. The election board then would be in the position of not knowing whether to register all the individuals similarly situated who have not brought suit. If a class action is brought, the judgment will bind all of the class members, and the board can take appropriate action.

Subdivision (B) of Rule (23)(b)(1) requires that individual actions "substantially impair or impede" the ability of class members to protect their interests. The classic example is a case in which there are multiple claimants to a limited fund, such as the proceeds of an insurance policy. If litigants are allowed to proceed individually, there is a risk that those who sue first will deplete the fund and leave nothing for the latecomers; thus, the latter group would "as a practical matter" be prejudiced by individual actions.

The second class-action category includes suits for injunctive or declaratory relief under Rule 23(b)(2). More cases have been brought under this provision than under either of the two other. Its primary application is in injunction suits such as employment discrimination, consumer, or environmental cases. Note that for an action to fall within Rule 23(b)(2), the defendant's conduct need only be "generally applicable" to the class; there is no requirement that the conduct be damaging or offensive to every class member. Thus, a suit to enjoin the enforcement of a school dress code can be instituted under Rule 23(b)(2) even though a majority of the students are not offended by the code and are willing to comply with it, since the school, by trying to enforce the code, acts in a manner generally applicable to the entire student body. It has been held that Rule 23(b)(2) only authorizes certification of a class of plaintiffs, and that actions against a defendant class may not be certified under this provision. Henson v. East Lincoln Township, 814 F.2d 410 (7th Cir.), certiorari granted 484 U.S. 923, 108 S.Ct. 283, 98 L.Ed.2d 244 (1987), certiorari dismissed 506 U.S. 1042, 113 S.Ct. 1035, 122 L.Ed.2d 111 (1993). But see Frederick County Fruit Growers Ass'n v. McLaughlin, 703 F.Supp. 1021, 1031–32 and 709 F.Supp. 242, 244–47 (D.D.C.1989).

Finally, Rule 23(b)(3) describes the "damage" class action, so called because the only tie among the members of the class is that they claim to have been injured in the same way by the defendant. This is the category often used in adjudicating mass torts. Two special prerequisites govern the application of this provision. First, questions of law or fact common to the class members must "predominate" over any questions affecting only individual class members. Second, the court must find that a "class action is superior to other available methods for the fair and efficient adjudication of the controversy." These special requirements are designed to ensure that the efficiency and economy objectives of Rule 23(b)(3) are met.

Although it is easy to state the Rule 23(b)(3) tests, the district courts have not applied them with a great deal of uniformity. Questions of predominance and superiority have become highly individualistic and fact dependent, and since the ruling on the certification question is interlocutory, and until recently not subject to immediate appellate review, we have limited guidelines from the Courts of Appeals. Nevertheless, a reading of Rule 23(b)(3) cases does suggest several recurring problems associated with its application.

The first problem is divining the meaning of "predominance." It is unclear whether the district judge is to count the issues and see whether a majority are common, or to evaluate the issues and see if the most important are common. Furthermore, in some cases common and individual issues seem to be in equilibrium no matter which method of determining predominance is followed. The key to resolving this difficulty lies in ascertaining whether the efficiency and economy of common adjudication outweigh the interest each class member may have in individual adjudication. For example, if the case involves a discriminatory practice in hiring or promotion, there probably is predominance. On the other hand, in a case brought by a group of securities investors who are claiming that a broker has unnecessarily multiplied transactions in their accounts, there probably is no predominance because what constitutes this so-called "churning" of one investor's account may not for another. This is particularly true since people have different investment objectives.

The "superiority" prerequisite obliges the court to compare the class action with other adjudicative possibilities. The most obvious include leaving the disputants to individual actions, administrative proceedings, or an agreement to be bound by the result in a single "test" case.

Rule 23(b)(3) outlines four factors that the court should consider in deciding the superiority and predominance questions. The fourth, difficulties likely to be encountered in the management of a class action, generally is viewed as the key to the two requirements. Matters such as the size or contentiousness of the class, the number of class members who seek to intervene and participate in the action, or the onerousness of the Rule 23(c)(2) notice requirement are to be considered when deciding if the class action is manageable. See Eisen v. Carlisle & Jacquelin, Note 6, p. 724, infra.

b. The Certification Decision

A judge can draw upon several sources in evaluating whether a proposed class meets the requirements for certification. There is the paper record—the complaint, the briefs supporting and opposing class certification, and any other affidavits or papers submitted to the court. In addition, there may be a hearing on the certification motion. If a court chooses to hold a hearing, it must be careful to limit its inquiry to the appropriateness of class certification; the Supreme Court has ruled that courts may not make a preliminary inquiry into the merits of the underlying substantive claim in considering whether to certify a class action. See Eisen v. Carlisle & Jacquelin, Note 6, p. 724, infra. And, finally, there may be discovery to ascertain information about the nature of the class.

Ultimately, a court may certify the class as proposed; may deny the certification motion; or may certify a modified class. It is the last option that is most interesting, because it gives the court great flexibility. In addition, Rule 23(c) gives judges the power to amend certification decisions at any time before a decision on the merits. Some judges, when granting certification, highlight the tentative character of their decisions by certifying classes conditionally.

In issuing a certification order, the judge defines the terms on which the class-action suit will proceed. First, the order approves a particular description of the class—that is, it defines who is included in it. For example, the court might certify a class consisting of all female employees of the Widget Company from 1998 to the present. The court has broad power to divide a proposed class into smaller constituent subclasses, each with its own named representatives. Thus, for example, it could choose to certify several classes, each consisting of female employees of the Widget Company working at separate plants.

Second, the certification order defines the substantive issues the suit will consider. For instance, a class suit might entertain a broad range of issues (such as allegations of company-wide gender discrimination in hiring, promotion, and pay, as well as allegations of sexual harassment by foremen in all of the company's factories), or it might take a more narrow approach (limiting the class issues to allegations of gender discrimination in a single plant's promotion decisions). A judge even may decide to certify a "partial class action"—that is, considering on a class basis only a limited number of factual issues relevant to a larger cause of action. For example, although controversial, in a products liability suit, a judge could create a "partial class action" by certifying only the issue of whether a pharmaceutical manufacturer knew of a drug's potentially lethal side effects before introducing it on the market. In such a case, individual suits, litigated simultaneously or subsequently, would be pursued on the other issues.

Third, and finally, the certification order appoints a class representative. In plaintiff class actions, the parties seeking certification normally will nominate themselves as class representatives. In defendant class actions plaintiff, who would be the party most likely to seek class treatment, nominates particular members of defendant class to serve in the representative capacity. It is important to note, however, that the parties' nominations are not dispositive. Judges have discretion in appointing class representatives, and are free to accept, reject, or modify the parties' suggestions. Judges even may choose to supplement the parties' nominations by appointing as class representatives individuals who are not before the court.

c. The Importance of Certification

Certification is perhaps the most critical stage in the life of a class action. The papers, hearings, and discovery that inevitably are generated force the court to analyze the nature of the parties and the issues involved in the case. The certification process is even more critical from the parties' point of view. Most importantly, the certification decision dictates the relative leverage that the parties can bring to settlement negotiations. The value of settlement leverage cannot be underestimated, because most class suits are settled before trial. Moreover, for the party opposing the class, a certification order means more than a loss of leverage; the threat that a class may be certified may be a danger in itself, because the certification of a class may create unfavorable publicity.

The tactical importance of the certification stage is increased because certification orders, until recently, generally have not been appealable. In the federal system, appeals typically are available only from a final judgment. See 28 U.S.C. § 1291. In the years following the 1966 amendment to Federal Rule 23, some federal Courts of Appeals held that some orders denying class certification were appealable under 28 U.S.C. § 1291 on the theory that they, in effect, were final decisions. These courts felt that, especially when the individual class members' claims were small, the denial of certification signaled the "death knell" of the litigation. In COOPERS & LYBRAND v. LIVESAY, 437 U.S. 463, 98 S.Ct. 2454, 57 L.Ed.2d 351 (1978), the Supreme Court rejected the death-knell doctrine. In so doing, the Court noted that the order granting or denying class status to a group is subject to redetermination by the judge. Thus the decision is not a final order and it does not affect the merits. The holding in *Coopers & Lybrand* did not make it impossible to obtain review of a certification order, however, because the Court noted that in some situations it might be possible to obtain review of a denial of certification under the provisions of 28 U.S.C. § 1292(b), which permits appeals from orders involving a "controlling question of law as to which there is a substantial ground for difference of opinion and [when] an immediate appeal from the order may materially advance the ultimate termination of the litigation." In addition, a number of certification decisions were reviewed on mandamus. See, e.g., Castano v. American Tobacco Co., p. 754, infra, which responded to the view that appellate review was needed to bring some stability and uniformity to class action practice.

The situation changed dramatically in 1998 with the adoption of Rule 23(f), which allows the Courts of Appeal to accept an appeal from an order granting or denying class certification. A wide range of certification issues have since been reviewed by the federal appellate courts on this interlocutory basis. See, e.g., Carter v. West Publishing Co., 225 F.3d 1258 (11th Cir.2000).

For a discussion of individual, class, and systemic concerns that factor into the certification decision, especially in mass accident cases, see Note, *Class Certification in Mass Accident Cases Under Rule 23(b)(1)*, 96 Harv. L.Rev. 1143 (1983). See also *The Supreme Court, 1977 Term*, 92 Harv.L.Rev. 5, 234 (1978).

4. NOTICE

The question of notice to absent class members has tremendous theoretical and practical importance to class actions, and will be considered many times throughout this Chapter. At this point only the mechanical aspects of the notice question will be discussed: who prepares it, what information must be included in the notice, who should receive notice, and who should bear its cost.

a. *Preparation*

Ambiguity in the language of Rule 23 makes it unclear whether the court or the parties should prepare the notice forms. Charging the class representatives with this responsibility introduces the possibility that the notice will be used for improper purposes, such as solicitation for a litigation fund. Yet, because drafting and production can be time-consuming, most courts direct the class representative to draft the notice and permit the opposing party to make objections. This limits the court's role to mediating disputes between the parties and insuring that notice is provided.

b. *The Content of Notice and Who Should Receive Notice*

Rule 23's notice requirement depends on the category of class action involved. There are relatively specific notice requirements for Rule 23(b)(3) class actions. In Rule 23(b)(1) and Rule 23(b)(2) class actions, however, courts have tremendous discretion with regard to notice.

Rule 23(c) dictates who should receive notice in a Rule 23(b)(3) class action. The language of the Rule itself is somewhat unclear as to whether individual notice to each class member is always required. However, the Supreme Court held in Eisen v. Carlisle & Jacquelin, Note 6, p. 724, infra, that Rule 23(c) does require such notice in every Rule 23(b)(3) class action.

Rule 23(c) unambiguously lists the required content of notice for a Rule 23(b)(3) class action. In addition, the notice usually provides the class members with a description of the class claim, as well as any counterclaims that may have been filed against the class. Many courts require the notice to include a disclaimer stating that the notice of the pending action does not indicate that the court believes the class will prevail on the merits.

Rule 23(c) applies only to suits brought under Rule 23(b)(3); the court's power to shape the form of the notice in Rule 23(b)(1) and (b)(2) suits derives from Rule 23(d)—and that Rule contains no specific directives regarding notice. Thus, in many Rule 23(b)(1) and (b)(2) suits, judges decide that no notice is necessary. In other situations, judges may conclude that only general notice is needed, such as notice by publication.

c. Costs

The Supreme Court has held that the costs of providing notice must be borne by the party seeking class treatment. If the class suit is successful, the costs of sending notice may be subtracted from the class recovery, thus making each class member share the costs on a pro-rata basis.

The costs of producing a mailing list often constitute a large part of the overall expense of providing notice. In some class actions defendant's records will be the best, if not the only, source of information from which a list can be constructed. In the past, some litigants sought to use the discovery process to obtain a plaintiff-class mailing list. This shifted to defendant a major portion of the expenses of providing notice, because in federal discovery practice the party that must comply with a discovery request must bear the costs of production. The Supreme Court disapproved this practice in OPPENHEIMER FUND, INC. v. SANDERS, 437 U.S. 340, 98 S.Ct. 2380, 57 L.Ed.2d 253 (1978), in which it emphasized that the costs of class notice must be borne by the class representative. *Oppenheimer* did not prohibit the representative from requesting certain business records of defendant that might aid in preparing the class mailing list; it merely required that the class representative bear the cost of producing such lists.

5. ORDERS REGULATING THE CONDUCT OF PRETRIAL AND TRIAL PROCEEDINGS

In addition to certification and notice orders, various other orders are possible under Rule 23(d). For example, the court may create a timetable for discovery and for the presentation of issues at trial; set time limits on oral presentations made by counsel; establish a committee of counsel (consisting of the attorneys representing various members of the class) to make decisions about the prosecution of the class' case; and, regulate the substantive aspects of discovery (for example, by determining the parties from whom discovery may be sought and the items which may be requested). Frequently, courts will issue these management orders after they have held a pretrial conference.

It is unclear whether nominal parties, those who are part of the class but who do not participate in the management of the suit, can be subject to a discovery order. Complying with a discovery request can be onerous, and failure to respond can result in severe sanctions. For this reason, typically only named parties are required to submit to a discovery request. However, courts sometimes permit discovery from unnamed parties in class-action suits. Compare Brennan v. Midwestern United Life Ins. Co., 450 F.2d 999 (7th

Cir.1971), certiorari denied 405 U.S. 921, 92 S.Ct. 957, 30 L.Ed.2d 792 (1972) (nominal parties must comply with a discovery order), and Dellums v. Powell, 566 F.2d 167 (D.C.Cir.1977) (same), with Wainwright v. Kraftco Corp., 54 F.R.D. 532 (N.D.Ga.1972) (nominal parties need not comply with discovery order). See also Kline v. First Western Government Secs., 1996 WL 122717 (E.D.Pa.1996) (embracing the rationale of *Brennan*, but denying motion to compel discovery on the facts of the case).

It also is unclear how counterclaims against absent class members should be handled, or if they should be handled at all. The majority of federal district courts simply have assumed that such counterclaims are acceptable. Those courts that have considered the question in depth are split on the issue. In rejecting the counterclaim, one court asserted the absent class member's right "passively to await the outcome of the principal suit." See Donson Stores, Inc. v. American Bakeries Co., 58 F.R.D. 485 (S.D.N.Y.1973). Others have refused to entertain counterclaims on the ground that permitting them would encourage members to opt out of the suit. On the other hand, some courts have found persuasive the argument that since the absent members will reap the benefits of the judgment if favorable, they should be subject to its adverse effects. See National Super Spuds, Inc. v. New York Mercantile Exchange, 75 F.R.D. 40 (S.D.N.Y.1977), reversed on other grounds 638 F.2d 283 (2d Cir.1980), affirmed 456 U.S. 353, 102 S.Ct. 1825, 72 L.Ed.2d 182 (1982); Wolfson v. Artisans Savings Bank, 83 F.R.D. 552 (D.Del.1979).

6. PROVING CLASS CLAIMS AND ADMINISTERING CLASS RE-LIEF

The fundamental characteristic of the class-action device is that the class representative serves as a proxy for the absent class members, thus making it possible to adjudicate the claims of the entire class by evaluating the claims of the class representative. A proxy is appropriate because the class-certification decision ensures congruity between the injuries and the interests of the class representative and those of the absent class members. Whether the class representative can serve as a complete proxy for the absent class members, however, depends on the nature of the underlying cause of action. In many situations, it may be necessary to supplement treatment of the class representative's claims with proceedings designed to evaluate some aspect of each class member's individual claims.

The necessity of supplementary proceedings to "individualize" aspects of a class suit may vary with the relief sought. Class suits for injunctive relief closely resemble individual suits for injunctive relief. The problems involved in proving the defendant's liability, of determining the proper relief, and of administering relief are all quite formidable, but are not materially increased by class treatment. In suits for monetary relief, however, courts entertaining class actions inevitably face problems not present in traditional litigation. In these class suits, the court must complete three analytically separate tasks: it must determine if defendant is liable; it must calculate the amount of damages to the class; and, it must distribute the proper share of the award to individual class members. Often, one or more of these tasks demands fragmentation or "individualization" of the class.

Courts have approached the task of individualization in different ways. One approach is to use a single trial to determine both defendant's liability (if any) and the amount of damages. These determinations are based on the representative's individual claims, which in some cases are supplemented by statistics and expert testimony. When liability and the amount of damages are set, the court determines how to distribute the class award among individual class members.

A second approach used by courts to individualize class suits is the bifurcated trial. The first trial considers only the issue of liability, using the same evidence techniques as would be used in an ordinary proceeding. The second trial, which occurs only if defendant is found liable, addresses the amount of damages. This second proceeding may be a highly individualized one (involving, for example, mini-trials on individual damages claims, or administrative proceedings on individual claims), or it may be a general proceeding designed to calculate the damages to the class as a whole.

A third approach to calculating class relief, known as "sampling," was developed by then District Judge Parker in the context of the asbestos litigation. In the "sampling" process, the judge selects some cases at random to adjudicate, and then combines the outcomes of these sample cases statistically to yield results for the larger class population. The sample cases receive their actual awards, but the others all receive the statistically determined sum. This process is explained and criticized in great detail in Bone, *Statistical Adjudication: Rights, Justice, and Utility in a World of Process Scarcity,* 46 Vand.L.Rev. 561 (1993).

In cases in which the costs of identifying and distributing the award exceed the award due each class member, or when the amount of money that can be economically distributed to class members does not exhaust the amount of the defendant's liability as determined at trial, courts sometimes utilize a fourth approach—the "fluid class recovery." In such cases, the class' award is used to provide a general benefit to class members rather than to compensate them individually. For example, in DAAR v. YELLOW CAB CO., 67 Cal.2d 695, 63 Cal.Rptr. 724, 433 P.2d 732 (1967), a class action was brought against a taxi company to recover for alleged overcharges to its customers. Since it was impossible to identify each person who had been overcharged, the court ordered the defendant to lower its prices to all riders for a certain period of time, on the theory that the recovery would go to the next best class.

An award of damages in a class action suit does not end the matter because the court must set a method of distribution. Some class members may not be aware of the suit. Others may not know of its outcome. For whatever reason, various class members may fail to claim damages. The fluid class recovery is often employed in these cases to insure that the damage award is spread evenly and benefits all the members of the class. In some cases the remaining money is given to appropriate charities.

7. SETTLEMENT

Rule 23(e) provides that a class action cannot be dismissed or compromised without court approval and that notice of any proposed dismissal or compromise must be given to all class members. In this regard the Rule is virtually unique in American law, as it is inconsistent with the general principle that litigants are free to settle or terminate a lawsuit as they see fit. Underlying Rule 23(e) is the same philosophy discussed in connection with adequacy of representation. See pp. 703–04, supra. First, due process demands that the absent class members be protected from an unfair settlement made because the representative parties have lost their enthusiasm for the litigation. In addition, the efficiency and economy objectives of Rule 23 would be subverted if the judgment produced by the settlement proves to be vulnerable to collateral attack, a situation that might arise if the settlement does not take proper account of the rights of the absent class members.

In evaluating a settlement proposal a court must consider whether it is fair, reasonable, and in the best interests of the individuals who will be affected by it. Those proposing settlement have the burden of showing that this standard has been met. Whether the class as a whole favors the proposed settlement is an extremely important factor for courts to weigh in deciding whether to approve the settlement. The will of any particular class member, however, is not dispositive. Settlements can be approved over the objections of the class representatives, as well as over the objections of absent class members who received and responded to the notice of settlement. Moreover, these objecting class members are free to appeal the court's decision approving the settlement when a judgment based on it is entered.

Several problems involving class-action settlements have surfaced. Since courts and litigants have recognized the extreme cost, time, and complexity involved in mass tort litigation, the settlement option has become increasingly desirable. However, courts have divided over when the requirements of Rule 23(e) become applicable. For example, what procedures must be followed if the representatives reach a settlement with the defendants before the suit is certified as a proper class action—must there be notice, court approval, formal certification? There has been considerable disagreement over this question.

One school of thought argued that a settlement never should be allowed prior to certification because the district judge does not have sufficient information to discharge his responsibilities under Rule 23(e). Without completing the seven-part certification process, he does not know whether the representation is adequate, whether there are conflicts within the class, or whether the economics of the case dictate the proposed settlement. On the other hand, by going through the certification process, the district judge will be educated and in a better position to assess the bona fides of any settlement that subsequently is proposed.

The other school of thought argued that the judicial system should encourage settlement whenever it is possible to do so. Since the certification question is an extremely difficult one and often takes years to resolve, the litigants should not be inhibited from settling by artificially declaring that the certification process must be completed first. Furthermore, a court may order a hearing on the proposed settlement, at which it can satisfy itself that there has been no abuse of the settlement procedure and that the agreement would not prejudice putative class members. This school of thought emphasized the need to give trial judges discretion, and argued that it is pointless to require a class-certification determination if that process' essential function can be served by less burdensome proceedings.

A lively practice developed of forming settlement classes prior to certification and then applying the Rule 23(e) procedure with varying degrees of intensity. Although the Supreme Court did not reject this practice in Amchem Prods., Inc. v. Windsor, p. 760, infra, it made clear that satisfaction of the class action prerequisites had to be demonstrated in the course of the settlement procedure.

8. THE ROLE OF ATTORNEYS

Two features of the traditional conception of the attorney-client relation are that (1) the attorney gives advice to the client and the client makes final decisions about litigation strategy, and (2) the attorney acts with virtually unmitigated loyalty to the client's best interest. Class-action litigation strains both of these notions. Class-action attorneys exercise significant control over decisions made on behalf of the class, because class representatives generally provide less supervision and guidance than do other types of clients. And, it is difficult to define "loyalty to the client" when it is not clear who the "client" is. Should the attorney give complete loyalty to the interests and wishes of the class representative? To those of each member of the class? To the attorney's conception of the best interests of the class as a whole? These questions are difficult ones, and current ethical rules offer attorneys little help in resolving them. Moreover, the class-action device challenges the traditional notions of the lawyer's role because, frequently, class suits involve a large number of independent lawyers (or legal teams) representing interests that sometimes are in tension. The role of the individual lawyer in this context is not easy to define. See Castano v. American Tobacco Co., p. 754, infra.

Some courts use their authority under Rule 23(d) to issue orders designed to foster orderly interaction among class attorneys and between the class attorneys and the court. For instance, a court may order the counsel representing the various class members to elect a management committee, empowered to make decisions on behalf of the class. These committees usually are governed by majority rule, though the court may provide that dissenting class attorneys can bring significant and material grievances to the attention of the court. Courts creating committees of this type frequently select two attorneys to play a special role in facilitating its operation. One attorney serves the role of "lead counsel," with responsibility for chairing meetings, drafting papers, and making arguments in court. Another serves as "liaison counsel," with responsibility for coordinating the flow of paper among the class attorneys and between the committee of counsel and the members of the class.

These management devices have problems of their own, as is illustrated by IN RE FINE PAPER ANTITRUST LITIGATION, 98 F.R.D. 48 (E.D.Pa. 1983), affirmed in part, reversed in part 751 F.2d 562 (3d Cir.1984). Forty-one law firms submitted fee petitions totalling $21 million, which represented forty percent of the class' total recovery.

In discussing why the attorneys' fees applications were so excessive, Judge McGylnn [sic] describes how the lawyers had established an organizational structure of committees and subcommittees to handle each task in the case, and how that very structure caused mismanagement. "It was inevitable that this type of structure would generate wasted hours on useless tasks, propagate duplication and mask outright padding." One of the worst examples was a charge of approximately fifteen hundred hours by nine law firms for preparing and taking the deposition of one third-party witness.

Kane, *Of Carrots and Sticks: Evaluating the Role of the Class Action Lawyer,* 66 Texas L.Rev. 385, 390 (1987). Professor Kane goes on to describe possible prescriptions:

> Cases like *Fine Paper* finally provoked the judiciary to force lawyers to become more efficient. The 1983 amendments to the Federal Rules provide judicial authority and guidance for pretrial management on an expansive scale. By exercising tight control early in the litigation, courts may be able to compel class action lawyers to stay abreast of these cases, keep fees down, and most importantly, to keep the cases moving along.
>
> * * *
>
> * * * To force litigating attorneys to learn the lessons of ill-managed litigation, courts are encouraging more economical management through their control of attorney fee awards. Courts now often carefully assess attorney fee petitions and disallow fees for work that is duplicative or unproductive.

Id. at 390–92.

Some commentators have argued that in the context of securities class actions market forces, rather than the court, should determine who serves as lead counsel and how he or she is compensated. Since institutional investors are the largest shareholders in publicly held companies, they may be well-situated to monitor the conduct of plaintiffs' attorneys on behalf of all members of the plaintiff class. By shifting this role from the courts to the shareholders themselves, representational costs would be reduced. The Private Securities Litigation Reform Act of 1995, 15 U.S.C. § 78u–4, has adopted this principle by creating a "rebuttable presumption" that the most adequate lead plaintiff will be the party with the largest financial interest in the relief sought by the class. See Weiss & Beckerman, *Let the Money do the Monitoring: How Institutional Investors Can Reduce Agency Costs in Securities Class Actions,* 104 Yale L.J. 2053 (1995). See also Note 4, p. 534, supra.

Since the economics of mass tort litigation leave individual plaintiffs with minimal control over the class attorneys, a few writers have proposed a judicially conducted auction of representation rights to reduce agency costs in class actions. Lawyers would offer their services based on proposals as to their ability to provide beneficial outcomes, personal attention, and other values. The fact that attorneys would be competing for approval of a judge (acting on behalf of the class) might induce attorneys to provide the package that best promotes the plaintiffs' interests at an attractive "price." See Macey & Miller, *The Plaintiffs' Attorney's Role in Class Action and Derivative Litigation: Economic Analysis and Recommendations for Reform,* 58 U.Chi.L.Rev. 1 (1991). However, some critics have suggested that allowing a court to choose the "winning" attorney is unwise because it is impossible for a court to understand a plaintiff's position and needs, particularly at the very outset of a case: "no mechanism exists that reduces the task to a simple equation, and simplifying techniques always entail value judgments." Resnik, Curtis & Hensler, *Individuals Within the Aggregate: Relationships, Representation, and*

Fees, 71 N.Y.U.L.Rev. 296, 389 (1996). Moreover, the process might prove time-consuming, contentious, and raise questions as to the independence of the lawyer selected by the court. Nonetheless, the practice is beginning to find favor with some federal courts.

9. ATTORNEYS' FEES

Although there is no reference in Rule 23 to the power of the court to award attorneys' fees, the attorney for the successful representative parties typically will be awarded a fee. The rationale for this practice is that since his work on behalf of the representatives has conferred a benefit on all the class members, fairness demands that counsel be compensated out of the fund awarded them. In many contexts a "reasonable" fee is awarded pursuant to a specific statutory provision designed to provide an incentive for "private attorneys general." In other contexts, courts award attorneys' fees out of the common fund created by the recovery from defendant. The Supreme Court has rejected the argument that fee awards are prohibited by the traditional American rule that the losing party shall not be forced to bear the winning parties' legal expenses. Boeing Co. v. Van Gemert, 444 U.S. 472, 100 S.Ct. 745, 62 L.Ed.2d 676 (1980).

Traditionally, the factor most relied upon in setting the amount of the attorneys' fees was the amount of benefit that the lawsuit produced. Because this guideline was easily abused, however, many courts turned to a more complicated method for calculating fee awards. Under a formula accepted in many courts, petitioning attorneys must present the trial judge with detailed time records of the hours expended by each lawyer on the case. The records must be broken down to give some indication of the nature of the work that was done (pleading, research, discovery, negotiation, or trial) and the status of each lawyer who worked on the case (senior or junior partner, or senior or junior associate). The time records enable the judge to make a detailed appraisal of precisely what kind of work each attorney did and how long it took to do it. This has several consequences. It virtually eliminates any possibility of misrepresentation concerning the amount of time counsel spent on any facet of the case; it provides the court with an indication of the character and quality of plaintiffs' lawyers; and it offers a benchmark for deciding how efficiently the work was performed.

Once the time records are presented to the judge, a "normal billing rate" is then attributed to each of the lawyers for each of the tasks done. This means differentiating in terms of hourly rates among different lawyers and different tasks requiring various levels of legal skill. With both time and rate figures before the court, the judge then engages in what has been called a "lodestar" computation—multiplying every lawyer's time by the rate for each of the functions performed. This produces the basic working figure for fixing the final fee.

This "lodestar" can then be modified on the basis of two factors by the court. The first permits the amount of the fee to be enlarged or reduced in light of the "contingency" factor. Simply put, how risky was the case? In contexts such as antitrust or securities regulation, was there a prior government prosecution or something else that facilitated plaintiff's class action? Did the plaintiff have to break new substantive or procedural ground to maintain the action? Basically, the contingency factor gives the judge discretion to adjust the fee to compensate lawyers who pursue cases that redress improper conduct or perform some social benefit on a contingent fee basis with no assurance they would be compensated.

However, in PENNSYLVANIA v. DELAWARE VALLEY CITIZENS' COUNCIL, 483 U.S. 711, 107 S.Ct. 3078, 97 L.Ed.2d 585 (1987), the Court curtailed federal judges' ability to award risk multipliers when awarding a fee under a statutory fee provision. The Court stated that risk enhancement is to be discouraged because it was not intended by Congress, is difficult to administer, and the reasonable hourly rate should be adequate to compensate the attorney. And in CITY OF BURLINGTON v. DAGUE, 505 U.S. 557, 112 S.Ct. 2638, 120 L.Ed.2d 449 (1992), the Court held that enhancement of an attorney's fee in light of the "contingency" factor was improper under the fee-shifting statutes at issue in that case and *Delaware Valley*. The Court reasoned that "an enhancement for contingency would likely duplicate in substantial part factors already subsumed in the lodestar," and that it "would make the setting of fees more complex and arbitrary, hence more unpredictable, and hence more litigable." Id. at 562, 566, 112 S.Ct. at 2641, 2643, 120 L.Ed.2d at 456, 459.

The second factor is the "quality" of the lawyers' performance. It focuses on the manner in which each lawyer actually functioned in the particular case. Was she helpful in moving the litigation toward resolution? Was she prepared? Did she do a good job for the client? Did she work efficiently? Again, this factor gives the district judge great discretion in fixing the final fee.

The time-rate computation gives the impression of mathematical precision, but there are several inherent ambiguities making it neither a stable measure nor an easily applied one. First, courts disagree regarding which hours may be included in the fee computation. Can time expended in preparing the fee application itself be included? Compare City of Detroit v. Grinnell Corp., 560 F.2d 1093 (2d Cir.1977), with Miller v. Mackey Int'l, Inc., 70 F.R.D. 533 (S.D.Fla.1976). Second, the notion that there are fixed hourly rates that can be attributed to all lawyers in all situations and used as objective markers of their worth is illusory. For lawyers who ordinarily operate on a contingent fee basis, "normal billing rate" has no meaning. Even in corporate practice the rates generally are not fixed, but depend upon a wide range of variables and geographic locations. And when the lawyers in a large, multiparty case come from many different parts of the country, what normal billing rate should be used? And, third, the lodestar approach does not encourage attorneys to manage their time well, to avoid duplicative work, or to settle the matter at as early a point as possible.

The flaws in the lodestar method have prompted many courts to return to the percentage-of-the-fund approach, particularly in "common fund" cases. The trend in that direction followed the publication of a report by a task force, appointed by the Third Circuit to study the subject. Court Awarded Attorney's Fees, Report of the Third Circuit Task Force, 108 F.R.D. 237 (1985). It concluded that the measure of recovery, rather than the number of actual hours expended, is the best determinant of the reasonableness and quality of the time expended. Thus, many Courts of Appeals have concluded that fees should be computed as a percentage of the common fund recovered for the class. See, e.g., Camden I Condominium Ass'n v. Dunkle, 946 F.2d 768, 774 (11th Cir.1991). However, the lodestar method is still controlling in federal "statutory fee" cases in which a prevailing plaintiff has a statutory right to recover reasonable attorney's fees from the defendant. Moreover, as discussed above, that is the construction given these statutes by the courts. Moreover, in many of the cases there may not be a common fund upon which to base a percentage calculation. See, e.g., id. at 774.

Because of the huge costs incurred in the prosecution of class-action lawsuits, it can be difficult to find attorneys willing to expend the time, money, and resources needed. Inventive methods of financing sometimes have been devised to fund these suits. For example, in one case an agreement was made by members of the Plaintiffs' Management Committee to pay a 300% return to certain attorneys who advanced money to finance the suit. The payment was to be made out of the funds awarded to the attorneys, and would not have reduced the amount received by class members. This agreement was upheld by Chief Judge Weinstein, In re Agent Orange Product Liability Litigation, 611 F.Supp. 1452 (E.D.N.Y.1985), but his decision was reversed 818 F.2d 216 (2d Cir.), certiorari denied 484 U.S. 926, 108 S.Ct. 289, 98 L.Ed.2d 249 (1987). For a discussion of the implications of this case, see Johnson, *Ethical Limitations on Creative Financing of Mass Tort Class Actions*, 54 Brooklyn L.Rev. 539 (1988). Since an attorney often acts as the gatekeeper in determining whether to bring a class suit, the structure of fee payments affects the number of these actions filed. Attorneys may reject certain meritorious cases because they involve too much risk to justify the required investment of resources on a contingent basis. One empirical study found that salaried lawyers undertook more innovative suits than attorneys who were dependent on attorney's fees awards. Garth, Nagel & Plager, *The Institution of the Private Attorney General: Perspectives from an Empirical Study of Class Action Litigation*, 61 S.Cal.L.Rev. 353 (1988).

The Supreme Court has grappled with other questions that affect the availability of attorneys' fees in class-action suits. The first issue involved the availability of statutory attorneys' fees. To encourage suits to redress civil rights deprivations, Congress passed the Civil Rights Attorney's Fees Awards Act, 42 U.S.C. § 1988, which makes it easier for victims to find attorneys by authorizing fee-shifting. In MAREK v. CHESNY, 473 U.S. 1, 105 S.Ct. 3012, 87 L.Ed.2d 1 (1985), the Court held it proper to deny recovery of costs, including attorneys' fees, when plaintiffs rejected a settlement offer higher than that ultimately obtained at trial. The Court reasoned that its holding would encourage plaintiffs to accept reasonable settlement offers, sparing themselves and the system the burden of time-consuming litigation. In so doing, however, the Court has made it more risky for plaintiffs to press claims once any reasonable settlement offer has been made.

In 1986, the Court returned to Section 1988, this time to address the propriety of simultaneous negotiations for the class recovery and attorneys' fees. In EVANS v. JEFF D., 475 U.S. 717, 106 S.Ct. 1531, 89 L.Ed.2d 747 (1986), the Court permitted an attorney to waive his Section 1988 fee in order to obtain a favorable recovery for the class. The dissent argued that permitting this linkage between the class' recovery and attorneys' fees in settlement negotiations would put pressure on class counsel that would shrink the pool of attorneys willing to try civil rights cases.

SECTION C. DUE PROCESS CONSIDERATIONS

HANSBERRY v. LEE

Supreme Court of the United States, 1940.
311 U.S. 32, 61 S.Ct. 115, 85 L.Ed. 22.

[This suit was brought in an Illinois state court on behalf of a class of landowners to enforce a racially restrictive covenant involving land in the City of Chicago. The covenant provided that it was not effective unless signed by the "owners of 95 per centum of the frontage." Plaintiff alleged that Hansberry, a black man, had purchased some of the restricted land from an owner who had signed the agreement and that suit was being brought to enjoin the sale as a breach of the covenant. He further alleged that the binding effect of the covenant had been established in an earlier Illinois state court action holding that 95 percent of all the landowners involved had signed the agreement. In response, defendants pleaded that they were not bound by the res judicata effect of the earlier judgment as they had not been parties to that suit and were not successors in interest or in privity with any of the parties to that action. Thus they argued it would be a denial of due process to hold them to the first decree.

The Illinois Circuit Court held that the issue whether the covenant was valid was res judicata, even though it found that only about 54 percent of the owners actually had signed the agreement and that the previous judgment rested on a "false and fraudulent" stipulation of the parties. The Supreme Court of Illinois affirmed. It found that although the stipulation was untrue it was not fraudulent or collusive. The Illinois court then went on to conclude that the first action had been a "class" or "representative" suit, that as such it was binding on all the class members unless reversed or set aside on direct proceedings, and that Hansberry and the persons who had sold the land to him were members of the class represented in the first action and consequently were bound by the decree in that suit.]

Certiorari to the Supreme Court of the State of Illinois.

MR. JUSTICE STONE delivered the opinion of the Court.

* * *

* * * [W]hen the judgment of a state court, ascribing to the judgment of another court the binding force and effect of *res judicata*, is challenged for want of due process it becomes the duty of this Court to examine the course of procedure in both litigations to ascertain whether the litigant whose rights have thus been adjudicated has been afforded such notice and opportunity to be heard as are requisite to the due process which the Constitution prescribes. * * *

It is a principle of general application in Anglo–American jurisprudence that one is not bound by a judgment *in personam* in a litigation in which he is not designated as a party or to which he has not been made a party by service of process. Pennoyer v. Neff * * * [p. 62, supra]. A judgment rendered in such circumstances is not entitled to the full faith and credit which the Constitution and statute of the United States * * * prescribe * * * and judicial action enforcing it against the person or property of the absent party is not that due process which the Fifth and Fourteenth Amendments requires. * * *

To these general rules there is a recognized exception that, to an extent not precisely defined by judicial opinion, the judgment in a "class" or "representative" suit, to which some members of the class are parties, may bind members of the class or those represented who were not made parties to it. * * *

The class suit was an invention of equity to enable it to proceed to a decree in suits where the number of those interested in the subject of the litigation is so great that their joinder as parties in conformity to the usual rules of procedure is impracticable. Courts are not infrequently called upon to proceed with causes in which the number of those interested in the litigation is so great as to make difficult or impossible the joinder of all because some are not within the jurisdiction or because their whereabouts is unknown or where if all were made parties to the suit its continued abatement by the death of some would prevent or unduly delay a decree. In such cases where the interests of those not joined are of the same class as the interests of those who are, and where it is considered that the latter fairly represent the former in the prosecution of the litigation of the issues in which all have a common interest, the court will proceed to a decree. * * *

It is evident that the considerations which may induce a court thus to proceed, despite a technical defect of parties, may differ from those which must be taken into account in determining whether the absent parties are bound by the decree or, if it is adjudged that they are, in ascertaining whether such an adjudication satisfies the requirements of due process and of full faith and credit. Nevertheless there is scope within the framework of the Constitution for holding in appropriate cases that a judgment rendered in a class suit is *res judicata* as to members of the class who are not formal parties to the suit. * * * With a proper regard for divergent local institutions and interests * * *, this Court is justified in saying that there has been a failure of due process only in those cases where it cannot be said that the procedure adopted, fairly insures the protection of the interests of absent parties who are to be bound by it. * * *

It is familiar doctrine of the federal courts that members of a class not present as parties to the litigation may be bound by the judgment where they are in fact adequately represented by parties who are present, or where they actually participate in the conduct of the litigation in which members of the class are present as parties * * * or where the interest of the members of the class, some of whom are present as parties, is joint, or where for any other reason the relationship between the parties present and those who are absent is such as legally to entitle the former to stand in judgment for the latter. * * *

In all such cases, * * * we may assume for present purposes that such procedure affords a protection to the parties who are represented though absent, which would satisfy the requirements of due process and full faith and credit. * * * Nor do we find it necessary for the decision of this case to say that, when the only circumstance defining the class is that the determination of the rights of its members turns upon a single issue of fact or law, a state could not constitutionally adopt a procedure whereby some of the members of the class could stand in judgment for all, provided that the procedure were so devised and applied as to insure that those present are of the same class as those absent and that the litigation is so conducted as to insure the full and fair consideration of the common issue. * * * We decide only that the procedure and the course of litigation sustained here by the plea of res judicata do not satisfy these requirements.

The restrictive agreement did not purport to create a joint obligation or liability. If valid and effective its promises were the several obligations of the signers and those claiming under them. The promises ran severally to every other signer. It is plain that in such circumstances all those alleged to be bound by the agreement would not constitute a single class in any litigation brought to enforce it. Those who sought to secure its benefits by enforcing it could not be said to be in the same class with or represent those whose interest was in resisting performance, for the agreement by its terms imposes obligations and confers rights on the owner of each plot of land who signs it. If those who thus seek to secure the benefits of the agreement were rightly regarded by the state Supreme Court as constituting a class, it is evident that those signers or their successors who are interested in challenging the validity of the agreement and resisting its performance are not of the same class in the sense that their interests are identical so that any group who had elected to enforce rights conferred by the agreement could be said to be acting in the interest of any others who were free to deny its obligation.

Because of the dual and potentially conflicting interests of those who are putative parties to the agreement in compelling or resisting its performance, it is impossible to say, solely because they are parties to it, that any two of them are of the same class. Nor without more, and with the due regard for the protection of the rights of absent parties which due process exacts, can some be permitted to stand in judgment for all.

It is one thing to say that some members of a class may represent other members in a litigation where the sole and common interest of the class in the litigation, is either to assert a common right or to challenge an asserted obligation. * * * It is quite another to hold that all those who are free alternatively either to assert rights or to challenge them are of a single class, so that any group, merely because it is of the class so constituted, may be deemed adequately to represent any others of the class in litigating their interests in either alternative. Such a selection of representatives for purposes of litigation, whose substantial interests are not necessarily or even probably the same as those whom they are deemed to represent, does not afford that protection to absent parties which due process requires. The doctrine of representation of absent parties in a class suit has not hitherto been thought to go so far. * * * Apart from the opportunities it would afford for the fraudulent and collusive sacrifice of the rights of absent parties, we think that the representation in this case no more satisfies the requirements of due process than a trial by a judicial officer who is in such situation that he may have an interest in the outcome of the litigation in conflict with that of the litigants. * * *

The plaintiffs in the [first] case sought to compel performance of the agreement in behalf of themselves and all others similarly situated. They did not designate the defendants in the suit as a class or seek any injunction or other relief against others than the named defendants, and the decree which was entered did not purport to bind others. In seeking to enforce the agreement the plaintiffs in that suit were not representing the petitioners here whose substantial interest is in resisting performance. The defendants in the first suit were not treated by the pleadings or decree as representing others or as foreclosing by their defense the rights of others, and even though nominal defendants, it does not appear that their interest in defeating the contract outweighed their interest in establishing its validity. For a court in this situation to ascribe to either the plaintiffs or defendants the performance of such functions on behalf of petitioners here, is to attribute to them a power that it cannot be said that they had assumed to exercise, and a responsibility which, in view of their dual interests it does not appear that they could rightly discharge.

Reversed.

Notes and Questions

1. For an account of the history surrounding Hansberry v. Lee, including efforts to desegregate Chicago, and noting that the Hansberrys' daughter is Lorraine Hansberry of *Raisin in the Sun* fame, see Kamp, *The History Behind Hansberry v. Lee*, 20 U.C. Davis L.Rev. 481 (1987).

2. In what way does the Due Process Clause apply in the class-action context? In an earlier Chapter it was seen being applied to require that the defendant be given notice of the lawsuit and an opportunity to be heard. See Mullane v. Central Hanover Bank & Trust Co., p. 191, supra; Fuentes v. Shevin, p. 228, supra. In *Hansberry*, however, the Supreme Court focused on the adequacy of class representation, rather than on the notice provided or the opportunity to be heard. See 7A Wright, Miller & Kane, *Federal Practice and Procedure: Civil 2d* § 1765 (1986).

3. At what point should the adequacy of the representation be judged? The Fifth Circuit allowed a collateral attack upon a class-action judgment in GON-ZALES v. CASSIDY, 474 F.2d 67 (5th Cir.1973). In that case, the original class action had challenged the constitutionality of a Texas statute and sought an injunction against its enforcement. The representative in the original action, an uninsured motorist, had been involved in an accident in Texas. Pursuant to statute, his driver's license and vehicle registration were suspended without a hearing on liability because he did not post security—as required by the statute— for the damages claimed by the other party in the accident. Ultimately the statute was held to be unconstitutional, but the relief asked for was applied retroactively to the representative plaintiff and prospectively to all other class members. The collateral attack in *Gonzales* charged that the original representative was inadequate for failing to appeal on the issue of retroactivity as to the class. The Fifth Circuit outlined a two-part test for reviewing whether the named plaintiff adequately represented the class so as to make the judgment in the suit binding on the absent class members:

> * * * (1) Did the trial court in the first suit correctly determine, initially, that the representative would adequately represent the class? and (2) Does it

appear, after the termination of the suit, that the class representative adequately protected the interest of the class? * * *

Id. at 72. The court held that the original plaintiff's failure to appeal the initial judgment rendered him an inadequate representative of the class, since "he was representing approximately 150,000 persons, who, although having had their licenses and registration receipts suspended without due process, were denied any relief by the * * * [trial] court's prospective * * * application of its decision." Id. at 76. The court remanded the case to the District Court for reconsideration of the retroactivity question.

Implicit in the two prongs of *Gonzales* is the notion that adequacy of representation will be examined more than once: first by the court certifying the class, and second by the court called upon to evaluate the binding effect of the first action. Ultimately, a final determination on the adequacy of representation in a class action can only be made through subsequent challenges to the res judicata effect of the suit—some of which may be collateral attacks. Id. at 74.

4. If the adequacy of representation provided by class representation is important to safeguarding the due process rights of class members, courts must be vigilant in examining potential conflicts of interest among class members. The conflict of interest between the class members in the *Hansberry* case unquestionably was enough to preclude adequate representation. In most cases, however, the conflict of interest among class members is less sharply defined than it was in *Hansberry*.

As will be seen later in this Chapter, this issue arises in some mass tort cases in which conflicts exist between already injured plaintiffs and those plaintiffs who simply have been exposed to the danger and have not yet manifested any symptoms. Although the interests of the two groups of plaintiffs are not necessarily antithetical, their differing factual circumstances may put them at odds with one another.

Some proposed classes might include people who prefer not to sue. For example, although certain employees might favor initiating an employment discrimination suit, others may fear that either management or coworkers will retaliate against them. Or, for another example, some potential class members may feel that the benefits of institutional reform sought in a suit do not outweigh the possibility that the suit will force the institution to close. What if the majority of the class members simply does not care whether suit is brought or not? If that is true, should the judicial system invest the additional resources inherent in adjudicating class disputes?

Proposed class members also might differ on how to remedy a particular wrong. For example, some parents challenging discrimination in public schools may believe that improving the quality of education is the most crucial goal, while other parents might see integration, and its long-term social effects, as the key objective.

How much conflict should courts permit in cases in which the disagreement among class members is not attitudinal (as in the examples just cited) but results from the fact that the class is composed of parties who, by the nature of who they are, find themselves in different, or potentially different, positions with regard to the subject of the litigation? Consider whether, as a trial court judge, you would certify the following proposed classes:

(i) The complaint alleges discrimination in hiring, promotion, and conditions of employment; the proposed class includes current minority employees, minorities whose employment applications were denied, and future minority applicants and employees; the sole class representative is a current employee of the company.

(ii) Would your answer to (i) be any different if there were a second class representative whom the defendant arguably had failed to hire because of discrimination?

(iii) An airline has a practice of discharging stewardesses who become pregnant. A suit for injunctive relief is brought on behalf of female airline cabin attendants, including those stewardesses who still are employed. Reinstatement of the former stewardesses, with no loss of seniority, would leapfrog them over the less senior stewardesses who still are actively employed.

(iv) Members of the proposed class in a products-liability suit reside in all parts of the nation, and there are significant differences in the products-liability laws of the various states. Should the class be certified as a single class? Suppose the injured parties can be divided into two groups for whom the applicable laws are substantially the same? What if four groupings are needed? Sixteen? At what point would this subclassing create intolerable management problems?

5. Theoretically, three entities have responsibility for protecting the interests of the class: the class representative or representatives, the class attorneys, and the court. It is not clear, however, that any of these three has a sufficient combination of incentive and information to guard the interests of absent class members.

Courts attach great importance to selecting a class representative who will adequately represent the interests of a proposed class or subclass. Many class representatives fulfill their duties admirably by actively guiding and closely supervising the conduct of the class counsel. But such supervision can entail a considerable amount of time and effort. Furthermore, surfacing conflicts within a class may threaten some of the advantages that the representative may gain from class treatment (such as the prospect of reduced attorneys' fees). Thus, the likelihood that the class representative will adequately protect absent class members' interests depends in large part on individual conscience. Similarly, practical considerations can encourage class attorneys to overlook the best interests of the class when they make tactical decisions. For instance, the prospect of a generous award of fees may tempt a class attorney to recommend a course of action regarding settlement that arguably is not in the class' interest.

Ultimately, it is the court's duty to ensure that the interests of absent class members are protected during a class suit. Nonetheless, although the court is a disinterested party, practical considerations limit its capacity to discharge this function. First, heavy caseloads diminish the ability and desire of judges to spend the time required to supervise class suits, and the same factors make it unlikely that courts will issue orders that will drastically increase the complexity of the proceedings. Second, in large part judges derive their view of a lawsuit from information provided by the parties; in this sense, their knowledge of class conflicts can be no better than that of the parties, and in most instances it is more limited.

The party opposing the class may be an important source of information about class conflicts, but objections raised by class opponents are looked on with suspicion by courts fearful that class opponents are seeking to achieve tactical delays. Furthermore, if those opposing the class believe they can win on the merits, they will want a broadly defined class so as to achieve maximum res judicata effect; if the class opponents believe they will lose on the merits, they will want to raise all possible class conflicts in hopes of avoiding class certification altogether. And, whatever their motivations, class opponents cannot be relied on to protect the absentees' interests because often they will have little information about the nature of the proposed class.

6. In EISEN v. CARLISLE & JACQUELIN, 417 U.S. 156, 94 S.Ct. 2140, 40 ← L.Ed.2d 732 (1974), the Supreme Court relied upon the language and history of Rule 23 to hold that in a Rule 23(b)(3) class action (but not in class actions brought under other sections of the Rule), individual notice must be sent to all class members. In reaching its conclusion about what the Rule requires, the Court rejected a more general argument based on the representational quality of class actions:

> Petitioner further contends that adequate representation, rather than notice, is the touchstone of due process in a class action and therefore satisfies Rule 23. We think this view has little to commend it. To begin with, Rule 23 speaks to notice as well as to adequacy of representation and requires that both be provided. Moreover, petitioner's argument proves too much, for it quickly leads to the conclusion that no notice at all, published or otherwise, would be required in the present case. This cannot be so, for quite apart from what due process might require, the command of Rule 23 is clearly to the contrary. We therefore conclude that Rule 23(c)(2) requires that individual notice be sent to all class members who can be identified by reasonable effort.

Id. at 176–77, 94 S.Ct. at 2151–52, 40 L.Ed.2d at 748. Is *Eisen* constitutionally mandated or merely the Court's interpretation of Rule 23?

7. In RICHARDS v. JEFFERSON COUNTY, ALABAMA, 517 U.S. 793, 116 S.Ct. 1761, 135 L.Ed.2d 76 (1996), a judgment purporting to bind the petitioners, taxpayers subject to the Jefferson County tax, was reversed because the Director of Finance and the City failed to provide adequate notice to the petitioners. Accepting that *Hansberry* could be read to support the possibility that in some class suits adequate representation may cure a lack of notice, the Court found that the proceedings before it did not ensure that "those present [were] * * * of the same class as those absent" and therefore did not provide adequate representation. The parties to the original judgment "did not sue on behalf of a class; their pleadings did not purport to assert any claim against or on behalf of any nonparties and the judgment they received did not purport to bind any county taxpayers who were nonparties." Id. at 801, 116 S.Ct. at 1767, 135 L.Ed.2d at 86.

8. If notice is to serve its function, it must be intelligible to the person who receives it. Only then can a potential class member make an informed decision about opting out of the class. Is it likely that non-lawyers will understand the notice they receive? Is the possibility that the notice will not be understood likely to be greatest in those cases where class members are most in need of protection? Consider the following responses received to a notice advising members of a class of antibiotics purchasers that they had the right to opt out of antitrust litigation seeking damages from several major drug companies:

Dear Sir:

> I received your pamphlet on drugs, which I think will be of great value to me in the future.

Due to circumstances beyond my control I will not be able to attend this class at the time prescribed on your letter due to the fact that my working hours are from 7:00 until 4:30.

Dear Sir:

Our son is in the Navy, stationed in the Caribbean some place. Please let us know exactly what kind of drugs he is accused of taking.

From a mother who will help if properly informed.

> A worried mother,
>
> Jane Doe

Dear Attorney General:

* * * I received a card from you and I don't understand it, and my husband can't read his. Most of the time all I buy is olive oil for healing oil after praying over it, it is anointed with God's power and ain't nothing like dope.

Rhode, *Class Conflicts in Class Actions*, 34 Stan.L.Rev. 1183, 1235 (1982).

SECTION D. CLASS–ACTION PRACTICE

Class-action rules such as Rule 23 are designed to address many of the due process concerns discussed in the previous section. As you read the cases in this Section, ask which of the requirements embodied in Rule 23 are mandated by the Due Process Clause.

WETZEL v. LIBERTY MUTUAL INSURANCE CO.

United States Court of Appeals, Third Circuit, 1975.
508 F.2d 239, certiorari denied 421 U.S. 1011, 95 S.Ct. 2415, 44 L.Ed.2d 679 (1975).

[Sandra Wetzel and Mari Ross were employed as claims representatives in the Pittsburgh office of the Liberty Mutual Insurance Company. Both wanted to be claims adjusters—a position similar to that of claims representative. Both positions were entry level positions open to college graduates, but claims adjusters were paid more and had greater opportunity for promotion. However, claims adjusters were primarily men; claims representatives were primarily women. When Wetzel and Ross applied for adjusters' positions, the company informed them that the position was not open to women.

Wetzel and Ross filed charges with the Pennsylvania Human Rights Commission (PHRC) and the Equal Employment Opportunity Commission (EEOC). After the charges were filed, the company decided to recruit women as claims adjusters, and reviewed its roster of claims representatives for qualified, interested applicants. Approximately 10% of the women claims representatives were hired as claims adjusters.

Both Wetzel and Ross were offered positions as claims adjusters. They rejected the offers because they believed, partly on the basis of information provided by the PHRC, that the offer included unacceptable conditions. Since the PHRC failed to resolve the claims, the EEOC issued letters to sue. Wetzel and Ross commenced a class action alleging that the company's hiring and promotion policies and its pregnancy-related policies as to the female technical employees in its claims department violated Title VII of the Civil Rights Act of

1964, 42 U.S.C. § 2000e et seq. (1970). They further alleged that the company's policy of paying higher salaries to claims adjusters than to claims representatives violated the Equal Pay Act of 1963, 29 U.S.C. § 206(d) (1970).

In response to Wetzel's and Ross's motions, the District Court certified a Rule 23(b)(2) class, which included "all present and future female technical employees in the defendant's claim department without limitation to territory in the entire geographic location in which the defendant does business." The court later refused to require that notice be sent to the nationwide class. The court's final certification order amended the class to include former, as well as future, female technical employees. Although reaffirming its decision to certify a Rule 23(b)(2) class, it acknowledged that the class was maintainable under Rule 23(b)(3) as well. The court saw no need to order the class-action notice required under Rule 23(b)(3).

In response to a summary-judgment motion, the court held that the pregnancy-related policies of the company violated Title VII. That order was appealed. The District Court later found that the hiring and promotion policies also violated Title VII, but denied injunctive relief because the evidence showed that the defendant had discontinued the discriminatory practices. Liberty Mutual appealed this second ruling as well, asking the Third Circuit to review the District Court's management of the class action and its decision to grant summary judgment against the challenged hiring and promotion policies.

In its opinion on this latter appeal, the Third Circuit considered whether the requirements for Rule 23(a) had been met, and concluded that they had been satisfied. It then went on to consider the application of Rule 23(b).]

ROSENN, CIRCUIT JUDGE.

* * *

III

A. CHARACTERISTICS OF (b)(2) AND (b)(3) ACTIONS

* * *

In the usual class action, the determination of whether the action should proceed as a 23(b)(2) or as a 23(b)(3) action offers little difficulty. In the present case, however, the order of the district court finding injunctive relief unnecessary as to Liberty Mutual's hiring and promotional practices in its claims department, because the Company's practices as to these issues have ceased, presents complications. Whether (b)(2) or not (b)(2) is indeed *the* question.

In the instant case, the district court found that the class could be maintained under either 23(b)(2) or 23(b)(3), but exercising its discretion decided to maintain the class under 23(b)(2). Liberty Mutual vigorously contends that the class could only be maintained under (b)(3), and that the procedural prerequisites for maintaining a (b)(3) suit have not been met. We find no error in the district court's determination * * *.

* * * By its very nature, a (b)(2) class must be cohesive as to those claims tried in the class action. * * * Any resultant unfairness to the members of the class was thought to be outweighed by the purposes behind class actions:

eliminating the possibility of repetitious litigation and providing small claimants with a means of obtaining redress for claims too small to justify individual litigation.

Rule 23(b)(3) permits a class action where the questions of law or fact common to the class predominate over questions only affecting individual members and the "class action is superior to other available methods for the fair and efficient adjudication of the controversy." * * *

[The court then summarized the res judicata effect of pre–1966 federal class actions.]

Binding all members of a (b)(3) class, however, was not thought by the Advisory Committee to be as fair as binding all members of a (b)(2) class. By the very nature of a heterogeneous (b)(3) class, there would be many instances where a particular individual would not want to be included as a member of the class.[16] To respect these individual interests, Rule 23(c)(2) was written to afford an opportunity to every potential member to opt out of the class. * * * For the opt out procedure to be effective, 23(c)(2) also provides for notice to be sent to all potential members prior to the final determination of the class. Eisen v. Carlisle & Jacquelin, [Note 6, p. 724, supra] * * *.

With the potential unfairness to members of the (b)(3) class eliminated by the opt out procedure, 23(c)(3) contemplates that all members of the (b)(3) class, as well as members of the (b)(2) class, will be bound by the res judicata effect of the judgment. * * *

B. APPROPRIATENESS OF (b)(2) FOR THIS ACTION

Liberty Mutual contends that this suit could not have been maintained as a class action under (b)(2) because such class actions are limited to only those suits in which final injunctive relief is found to be appropriate. * * *

The district court, after discovery and extensive briefing, considered whether the action here was properly maintained under (b)(2) three separate times. In its last memorandum order of December 6, 1973, the court indicated that maintenance under (b)(2) was proper because Liberty Mutual had " 'acted or refused to act on grounds generally applicable to the class' and the representative plaintiffs seek among other remedies, 'final injunctive relief or corresponding declaratory relief.' " In his opinion of January 9, 1974, Judge Weber noted:

Because the evidentiary materials show that at certain times subsequent to the filing of the administrative charge or within the Complaint the Defendant has ceased or discontinued the discriminatory practices, injunctive relief is not appropriate as to those practices.

372 F.Supp. at 1163.

The precise issue before us then is whether a district court, having determined that a Title VII suit brought in good faith for injunctive relief may be maintained under (b)(2), is required to redetermine that the suit be

---

16. An excellent example is the situation found in Katz v. Carte Blanche Corp., [496 F.2d 747 (3d Cir.1974)]. Assume, contrary to the decision, that a (b)(3) class was allowed to be maintained. Carte Blanche might have counterclaimed against the members of the class for amounts owing from use of the credit card. A delinquent account debtor might have decided that a judgment for amounts owing would outweigh any benefits he might obtain from a favorable judgment resulting from the Truth in Lending Act violation.

maintained under (b)(3) and comply with its procedural requirements once it concludes on a motion for summary judgment that changed conditions make injunctive relief no longer appropriate. We decline to so hold.

First, a Title VII suit against discriminatory hiring and promotion policies is necessarily a suit to end discrimination because of a common class characteristic, in this case sex. The conduct of the employer is actionable "on grounds generally applicable to the class," and the relief sought is "relief with respect to the class as a whole." The class, all sharing a common characteristic subjected to discrimination, is cohesive as to the claims alleged in the complaint. Thus, a Title VII action is particularly fit for (b)(2) treatment, and the drafters of Rule 23 specifically contemplated that suits against discriminatory hiring and promotion policies would be appropriately maintained under (b)(2). * * * Since a Title VII suit is essentially equitable in nature, it cannot be characterized as one seeking exclusively or predominantly money damages. * * *

The basic nature of a Title VII suit is not altered merely because the employer's change of discriminatory policy prior to the motion for summary judgment has obviated the need for injunctive relief. The conduct of the employer is still answerable "on grounds generally applicable to the class," and the relief sought is still "relief with respect to the class as a whole." The cohesive characteristics of the class are the vital core of a (b)(2) action. Functionally, these characteristics of the class are still intact in the suit. Nothing has changed to require the procedural protections of (b)(3) to determine the presence or absence of liability. The class is still appropriately maintained under (b)(2).

Second, the language of (b)(2) does not support the contention that (b)(2) actions are limited to final injunctive relief or declaratory judgments only. Rather, the language describes the type of conduct by the party opposing the class which is subject to equitable relief by class action under (b)(2). * * * Liberty Mutual's policies at the time these charges were made were such that final injunctive relief was appropriate. This satisfies the language of the rule. The nature of these policies, and the nature of the class opposing these policies, does not change merely because subsequent action by Liberty Mutual eliminates the need for final injunctive relief.

Moreover, although the court found that injunctive relief was unnecessary, it did determine the presence of liability on the part of Liberty Mutual. The court did not preclude the possibility of directing affirmative action, in addition to back pay, to remedy conditions caused by the offensive discriminatory practices. Such affirmative action ultimately would, in effect, constitute final injunctive or declaratory relief. * * *

Courts have held that a (b)(2) class is appropriate in a Title VII suit where both final injunctive and monetary relief are granted. * * * Maintenance of a class action under (b)(2) in a Title VII action has also been held to be appropriate when the actions of the defendant after the complaint had been filed had obviated the need for final injunctive relief. * * *

Additionally, only with the benefit of hindsight do we now know that injunctive relief against the Company's hiring and promotion practices was not necessary in this case. At the (c)(1) hearing, the district court specifically found that the conduct of Liberty Mutual made appropriate final injunctive relief. Requiring the court to reconsider and possibly redetermine the class at the time of the summary judgment application and redirect the course of the litigation with notice and other procedural requirements would inevitably complicate a type of litigation which by its nature is complex at its best. For this court to compel a redetermination of the class at that point probably would require the district court to consider the merits of the case, and ultimately would lead to a practice of holding a preliminary hearing on the merits at the time of the initial (c)(1) class determination. This, of course, the Supreme Court has made clear the district court may not do * * *. Eisen v. Carlisle & Jacquelin, [Note 6, p. 724, supra] * * *. It is at the (c)(1) hearing that the class must be shown to possess the characteristics required by (b)(2). Of course, the district court may amend its determination at a later date. See 23(c)(1). But we decline to hold that a court must reconsider its determination when, at the decision for summary judgment, it finds injunctive relief to be inappropriate.

Finally, we have reviewed the (b)(2) issue on this appeal as if the action in the district court involved only the hiring and promotion policies of Liberty Mutual. Wetzel and Ross, however, also attacked in the district court Liberty Mutual's pregnancy related policies, and its policy of paying higher salaries to claims adjusters than to claims representatives. Due to the piecemeal nature of the appeals from the district court, the only substantive issue before us involves the hiring and promotion policies, but in the absence of the argument by Liberty Mutual that different classes should have been created for different issues, we must consider the propriety of the class determination in the light of all the substantive issues raised in the district court. Liberty Mutual has changed, as a result of the charges brought by Wetzel and Ross, neither its pregnancy related policies, nor its higher salary policy to claims adjusters. In the event these policies are found to be violative of Title VII, final injunctive relief will be necessary as redress. The (b)(2) nature of the class, while visible as to the promotion and hiring issues, becomes translucent when viewed in the light of the multifaceted attack upon Liberty Mutual's policies.

Liberty Mutual also contends that if the requirements of both (b)(2) and (b)(3) are met, the court should certify the class under (b)(3) to provide the procedural protections, namely notice and opting out, which (b)(3) affords members of the class. Virtually every class action meeting the requirements of 23(b)(2) will also meet the less severe requirements of 23(b)(3). * * * If the actions are classified under (b)(3), members of the class could elect to opt out and thereby not be bound by the judgment. This would permit the institution of separate litigation and would defeat the fundamental objective of (b)(2), to bind the members of the class with one conclusive adjudication. * * * As discussed above, the procedural protections of (b)(3), opting out and notice, are necessary because of the heterogeneity of the (b)(3) class. They are unnecessary for the homogeneous (b)(2) class.

The recent Supreme Court decision in Eisen v. Carlisle & Jacquelin, * * * does not support the Company's contention. *Eisen* does not extend the (b)(3) notice requirement to (b)(2) actions, nor to actions maintainable under either (b)(2) or (b)(3). We therefore agree with the * * * principle that an action maintainable under both (b)(2) and (b)(3) should be treated under (b)(2) to enjoy its superior res judicata effect and to eliminate the procedural complications of (b)(3) which serve no useful purpose under (b)(2). This principle has been widely adopted in the federal courts. * * *

* * *

IV

Liberty Mutual contends that if the action is maintainable under (b)(2), we should hold that notice should have been given prior to determination of liability to all members of the class, either under our supervisory powers over the circuit district courts or under the requirements of due process.

Suits brought by private employees are the cutting edge of the Title VII sword which Congress has fashioned to fight a major enemy to continuing progress, strength, and solidarity in our nation, discrimination in employment. * * * The imposition of notice and the ensuing costs often discourage such suits. * * * Therefore, we are reluctant to impose notice requirements under our supervisory power for Title VII (b)(2) actions unless Rule 23 so requires or unfairness will result to the parties.

The due process problem surfaces because the class action judgment binds all members of a (b)(2) class. * * *

The Supreme Court [in Mullane v. Central Hanover Bank & Trust Co., p. 191, supra] plainly stated that it had not committed itself to any formula in achieving a balance between the interests of the State and the interests of the individual parties in the litigation or in "determining when constructive notice may be utilized or what test it must meet. Personal notice has not in all circumstances been regarded as indispensable to the process due to residents, and it has more often been held unnecessary as to nonresidents." * * * Because the Court linked the requirement of notice to the particular circumstances of each case, it is important to note that the situation in *Mullane* is significantly different from the situation in a (b)(2) class action. First, *Mullane* dealt with the established interests of individuals in specific property, a common trust fund. Second, the interests of all the beneficiaries in that fund were not identical; some were entitled to interest income, while others were concerned with capital growth. These interests were represented by different guardians, but the personal interests of the guardians functionally differed from the interests of the beneficiaries. Therefore, a significant possibility existed that they did not adequately represent the beneficiaries in the action. Third, the beneficiaries had a resident fiduciary as a caretaker of their interest in the trust "[b]ut it is their caretaker who in the accounting becomes their adversary." * * * Under these circumstances, the possibility that parties having conflicting interests in specific property could be bound by an action of which they had no actual notice and brought by parties who possibly represented those interests inadequately does violate due process. This possibility could not occur in a (b)(2) action.

The very nature of a (b)(2) class is that it is homogeneous without any conflicting interests between the members of the class. Since the class is cohesive, its members would be bound either by the collateral estoppel or the stare decisis effect of a suit brought by an individual plaintiff. Thus, as long as the representation is adequate and faithful, there is no unfairness in giving res judicata effect to a judgment against all members of the class even if they have not received notice. Adequacy of representation of the class is a mandatory requirement for the maintenance of a class action under Rule 23(a). * * * Of course, there may be circumstances when the court, in its discretion, believes that notice to the absent members of the class is necessary for the fair conduct of the action. Rule 23(d)(2) anticipates such situations and permits the court to then require such notice. * * * We decline, therefore, to hold that due process ineluctably requires notice in all (b)(2) class actions.

* * *

We believe that if there is truly adequate representation, the interests of absent parties to a (b)(2) class are protected. We thus agree with the framers of the rule, several district courts that have expressly considered the question, and several of the commentators that notice to absent members of a (b)(2) class is not an absolute requisite of due process. For the foregoing reasons, we have concluded that there was no denial of due process in this case.

Notes and Questions

1. How hermetic are the three categories of class actions created by Rule 23(b)? It has been argued that courts treat anti-discrimination class actions differently from other suits—that courts are willing to permit backpay awards to be made in suits prosecuted under Rule 23(b)(2), even though backpay awards arguably are outside the scope of injunctive relief authorized by Rule 23(b)(2). Note, *Antidiscrimination Class Actions Under the Federal Rules of Civil Procedure: The Transformation of Rule 23(b)(2)*, 88 Yale L.J. 868 (1979). Is it possible that, by treating anti-discrimination suits differently, courts in fact have created a fourth category of class actions—one combining the characteristics of Rule 23(b)(2) and Rule 23(b)(3) suits? Courts have followed the approach taken in *Wetzel* and allowed combined classes for discrimination actions. For the argument that civil rights class actions should be bifurcated into a subdivision (b)(2) class for injunctive relief and a subdivision (b)(3) class for monetary damages, see Rutherglen, *Notice, Scope and Preclusion in Title VII Class Actions*, 69 Va.L.Rev. 11 (1983).

The Advisory Note to Rule 23 states that "[Rule 23(b)(2)] does not extend to cases in which the appropriate final relief relates exclusively or predominantly to money damages." Is it possible to argue that in anti-discrimination suits backpay awards do not predominate?

2. When evaluating the binding effect of a class-action judgment, should a court review both notice and representation? Should adequate representation ever be allowed to cure inadequate notice? Can adequate notice ever cure inadequate representation? See generally Note, *Collateral Attack on the Binding Effect of Class Action Judgments*, 87 Harv.L.Rev. 589 (1974).

In JOHNSON v. GENERAL MOTORS CORP., 598 F.2d 432 (5th Cir.1979), the plaintiffs alleged claims of racial discrimination. In an earlier racial discrimination class suit involving the same factory, the plaintiffs had sought both injunctive and compensatory relief. The injunction was granted, and damages were awarded to the class representatives, but not to the absent class members. The plaintiff in the subsequent suit, Johnson, claimed that he had not received notice of the first suit, and attempted to prosecute his own suit for damages. The Fifth Circuit panel said:

In light of these developments, we have previously suggested that when both monetary and injunctive relief are sought in an action certified under Rule 23(b)(2), notice may be mandatory if absent class members are to be bound. * * * [But w]hen only equitable relief is sought in an action involving a cohesive plaintiff group such as a class of black employees at an assembly plant, the due process interests of absent members will usually be safeguarded by adequate representation alone. As the Advisory Committee on Rule 23 stated, "[i]n the degree that there is cohesiveness or unity in the class and the representation is effective, the need for notice to the class will tend toward a minimum." * * * Where, however, individual monetary claims are at stake, the balance swings in favor of the provision of some form of notice. It will not always be necessary for the notice in such cases to be equivalent to that required in (b)(3) actions. * * * In some cases it may be proper to delay notice until a more advanced stage of the litigation; for example, until after class-wide liability is proven. * * * Before an absent class member may be forever barred from pursuing an individual damage claim, however, due process requires that he receive some form of notice that the class action is pending and that his damage claims may be adjudicated as part of it.

Id. at 437–38.

Is the class in an employment discrimination class action as homogeneous as Judge Rosenn suggests in *Wetzel*? Consider the following case.

GENERAL TELEPHONE CO. v. FALCON, 457 U.S. 147, 102 S.Ct. 2364, 72 L.Ed.2d 740 (1982). Mariano Falcon was passed over for a promotion to field inspector at the same time several white employees with less seniority were granted promotions. He filed charges with the Equal Employment Opportunity Commission (EEOC), stating his belief that he had been denied promotion because of his national origin and that General Telephone's promotion policy operated against Mexican–Americans as a class. The EEOC issued a right-to-sue letter, and Falcon instituted this action under Title VII of the Civil Rights Act of 1964.

Falcon's complaint alleged that General Telephone maintained a policy of discriminating against Mexican–Americans with respect to compensation and conditions of employment and a policy of subjecting Mexican–Americans to continuous employment discrimination. He claimed that as a result of this policy less qualified whites with lower evaluation scores than him and other Mexican–Americans had been promoted more rapidly. The complaint contained no factual allegations concerning General Telephone's hiring practices.

Falcon moved to certify a class of "all hourly Mexican–American employees who had been employed, were employed, or who were to apply for employment, or who had applied or who would have applied had not petitioner practiced racial discrimination in its employment practices." Without conducting an evidentiary hearing, the court certified a class including Mexican–American employees and Mexican–American applicants who had not been hired in the division of the company in which Falcon was employed. The court denied two decertification motions made by General Telephone.

At trial, the District Court found that General Telephone had not discriminated against Falcon in hiring, but that it did discriminate against him in its promotion practices. As to the class, the court found no discrimination in promotion, but did conclude General Telephone had discriminated against Mexican–Americans in its hiring practices. Relief was ultimately awarded to 13 Mexican–Americans who had applied for employment.

The Fifth Circuit rejected Falcon's claim that the class should be broadened to include employees and job applicants at all of General Telephone's plants. It concurrently rejected General Telephone's claim that the class was too broad. On the merits, the Fifth Circuit upheld Falcon's claim of disparate treatment in promotion, but held that the District Court's findings relating to disparate impact in hiring were insufficient to support recovery on behalf of the class. The Supreme Court reversed the Fifth Circuit's affirmance of the certification order:

> We have repeatedly held that "a class representative must be part of the class and 'possess the same interest and suffer the same injury' as the class members." * * *

> * * * We * * * [recognize] the theory behind the Fifth Circuit's across-the-board rule, noting our awareness "that suits alleging racial or ethnic discrimination are often by their very nature class suits, involving classwide wrongs," and that "[c]ommon questions of law or fact are typically present." * * * In the same breath, however, we reiterated that "careful attention to the requirements of Fed.Rule Civ.Proc. 23 remains nonetheless indispensable" and that the "mere fact that a complaint alleges racial or ethnic discrimination does not in itself ensure that the party who has brought the lawsuit will be an adequate representative of those who may have been the real victims of that discrimination." * * *

> We cannot disagree with the proposition underlying the across-the-board rule—that racial discrimination is by definition class discrimination. But the allegation that such discrimination has occurred neither determines whether a class action may be maintained in accordance with Rule 23 nor defines the class that may be certified. Conceptually, there is a wide gap between (a) an individual's claim that he has been denied a promotion on discriminatory grounds, and his otherwise unsupported allegation that the company has a policy of discrimination, and (b) the existence of a class of persons who have suffered the same injury as that individual, such that the individual's claim and the class claims will share common questions of law or fact and that the individual's claim will be typical of the class claims. For respondent to bridge that gap, he must prove much more than the validity of his own claim. Even though evidence that he was passed over for promotion when several less deserving whites were advanced may support the conclusion that respondent was denied the promotion because of his national origin, such evidence would not necessarily justify the additional inferences (1) that this discriminatory treatment is typical of petitioner's promotion practices, (2) that petitioner's promotion practices are motivated by a policy of ethnic discrimination that pervades petitioner's Irving division, or (3) that this policy of ethnic discrimination is reflected in petitioner's other employment practices, such as hiring, in the same way it is manifested in the promotion practices. These additional inferences demonstrate the tenuous

character of any presumption that the class claims are "fairly encompassed" within respondent's claim.

Respondent's complaint provided an insufficient basis for concluding that the adjudication of his claim of discrimination in promotion would require the decision of any common question concerning the failure of petitioner to hire more Mexican–Americans. Without any specific presentation identifying the questions of law or fact that were common to the claims of respondent and of the members of the class he sought to represent, it was error for the District Court to presume that respondent's claim was typical of other claims against petitioner by Mexican–American employees and applicants.

Id. at 156–59, 102 S.Ct. at 2370–71, 72 L.Ed.2d at 749–51.

Notes and Questions

1. Does *Falcon* overrule *Wetzel*? *Falcon* can be understood as requiring only greater specificity in pleading, and merely holding that the pleadings must show a clear and specific link between the individual and class claims. The Court, after all, did conclude the "[t]he District Court's error in this case, and the error inherent in the across-the-board rule, is the failure to evaluate carefully the legitimacy of the named plaintiff's plea that he is a proper class representative under Rule 23(a)." 457 U.S. at 160, 102 S.Ct. at 2372, 72 L.Ed.2d at 752. On the other hand, *Falcon* can be read as in tension with *Wetzel*'s notion that some differences between class members are permissible. The *Falcon* Court, for instance, did frame the question presented in rather general terms as "whether respondent Falcon, who complained that petitioner did not *promote* him because he is a Mexican–American, was properly permitted to maintain a class action on behalf of Mexican–American applicants for employment whom petitioner did not *hire*." (Emphasis added.) Id. at 149, 102 S.Ct. at 2366, 72 L.Ed.2d at 745. The Court's answer to this question was that their claims were not fairly encompassed within Falcon's claim. This language sounds like a substantive requirement that the class be unified in interest. See Chayes, *Foreword: Public Law Litigation and the Burger Court*, 96 Harv.L.Rev. 4, 38 (1982).

2. *Wetzel* and *Falcon* illustrate that the interests of class members are often not identical. The more tenuous the links that bind the class, the greater the chance that individual members will have conflicting aims. Hence, the suit becomes more difficult to litigate and resolve. See Rhode, *Class Conflicts in Class Actions*, 34 Stan.L.Rev. 1183 (1982).

3. The class-action device places the named parties and the class attorneys in a fiduciary relation to the unnamed class members. Unfortunately, some attorneys have abused this relationship. The *Manual for Complex Litigation* § 1.41, at 27–28 n. 43 (5th ed.1982), catalogues a wide range of abuses, such as: misrepresenting the status, purpose, or effects of the class suit; soliciting agreements to pay expenses or soliciting actual payments from potential or actual class members who are not formal parties to the class suit; contacting class members to encourage them to opt out of a Rule 23(b)(3) class suit; and, serving process that appeared to be issued by a court in order to influence a class member to enter into an attorneys' fees contract, submit to discovery, or opt out of a class suit.

Following the suggestions contained in an early edition of the *Manual*, courts sought to minimize such abuses by issuing "gag" orders that limited and controlled communications with class members. In GULF OIL CO. v. BERNARD, 452 U.S. 89, 101 S.Ct. 2193, 68 L.Ed.2d 693 (1981), however, the Supreme Court struck down the imposition of automatic, blanket restrictions on attorney-class communications as being inconsistent with the general policies embodied in Rule 23. It held that such orders "should be based on a clear record and specific findings that reflect a weighing of the need for a limitation and the potential interference with the rights of the parties." Id. at 101, 101 S.Ct. at 2200, 68 L.Ed.2d at 703. Because it resolved the case through statutory interpretation, the Court did not reach the question of whether the First Amendment prohibited orders restricting attorney-class communications. The subject is discussed in *Manual for Complex Litigation 3d* § 30.24 (Fed. Jud. Center 1995).

SECTION E.   CLASS ACTIONS AND JURISDICTION

1. SUBJECT–MATTER JURISDICTION

A class action based upon a federal question does not raise any special problems of subject-matter jurisdiction. A class action based upon diversity, however, does raise two special questions: first, to which class members should the court look in determining whether there is diversity of citizenship and, second, to which class members should the court look in calculating the jurisdictional-amount requirement? The Supreme Court answered the first of these questions in SUPREME TRIBE OF BEN–HUR v. CAUBLE, 255 U.S. 356, 41 S.Ct. 338, 65 L.Ed. 673 (1921), holding that determinations of diversity of citizenship in class actions should be based on the citizenship of the named parties only. See generally 7A Wright, Miller & Kane, *Federal Practice and Procedure: Civil 2d* § 1755 (1986). The Court addressed the second question—calculating the jurisdictional amount—in SNYDER v. HARRIS, 394 U.S. 332, 89 S.Ct. 1053, 22 L.Ed.2d 319 (1969), and ZAHN v. INTERNATIONAL PAPER CO., 414 U.S. 291, 94 S.Ct. 505, 38 L.Ed.2d 511 (1973).

In *Snyder,* Mrs. Margaret E. Snyder, a shareholder of Missouri Fidelity Union Trust Life Insurance Company, brought suits against members of the company's board of directors alleging that they had sold their shares of the company's stock for an amount far in excess of its fair market value, that this excess represented payment to these particular directors to obtain complete control of the company, and that under Missouri law the excess should properly be distributed among all the shareholders of the company and not merely to a few of them. The suit was brought in the United States District Court for the Eastern District of Missouri, diversity of citizenship being the basis for federal jurisdiction. Since petitioner's allegations showed that she sought for herself only $8,740 in damages, respondent moved to dismiss on the ground that the matter in controversy did not exceed $10,000 (the requisite jurisdictional amount at the time). Petitioner contended, however, that her claim should be aggregated with those of the other members of her class, approximately 4,000 shareholders of the company stock. If all 4,000 potential claims were aggregated, the amount in controversy would be approximately $1,200,000. The Supreme Court held that separate and distinct claims could not be aggregated. It noted that "[a]ggregation has been permitted only (1) in cases in which a single plaintiff seeks to aggregate two or more of his claims against a single defendant and (2) in cases where two or more plaintiffs unite to enforce a single title or right in which they have a common or undivided interest." 394 U.S. at 335, 89 S.Ct. at 1056, 22 L.Ed.2d at 323. The Court noted Rule 82's prohibition against using the Federal Rules to expand district-court jurisdiction. It also noted that Congress recently had reenacted the jurisdictional-amount requirement, and in doing so implicitly had taken the judicial rules on aggregation into account.

Justice Fortas, in a dissent joined by Justice Douglas, wrote: "The fundamental change in the law of class actions requires that prior subsidiary doctrines developed for application to the [old class action procedural rules] be harmonized with the new procedural law." Id. at 350, 89 S.Ct. at 1064, 22 L.Ed.2d at 332. The original Rule 23 had depended on confusing concepts of jural relations such as whether claims were common or joint. The 1966 amendments specifically replaced these conceptual categorizations with more functional ones.

In *Zahn,* the petitioners, asserting that they were owners of property fronting on Lake Champlain in Orwell, Vermont, brought a diversity action in the District Court on behalf of a class consisting of themselves and 200 lakefront property owners and lessees. They sought damages from International Paper Co., a New York corporation, for allegedly having permitted discharges from its pulp and paper-making plant, located in New York, to flow into Ticonderoga Creek and to be carried by that stream into Lake Champlain, thereby polluting the waters of the lake and damaging the value and utility of the surrounding properties. The claims of each of the named plaintiffs were found to satisfy the $10,000 jurisdictional amount, but the District Court was convinced "to a legal certainty" that not every individual owner in the class had suffered pollution damages in excess of $10,000. The Supreme Court held that each plaintiff in a Rule 23(b)(3) class action must satisfy the jurisdictional-amount requirement. The majority opinion rested on the traditional rules that courts had used for aggregating claims. It cited BANK OF TROY v. G.A. WHITEHEAD & CO., 222 U.S. 39, 32 S.Ct. 9, 56 L.Ed. 81 (1911), as the "classic statement" of this traditional rule:

> When two or more plaintiffs, having separate and distinct demands, unite for convenience and economy in a single suit, it is essential that the demand of each be of the requisite jurisdictional amount; but when several plaintiffs unite to enforce a single title or right, in which they have a common and undivided interest, it is enough if their interests collectively equal the jurisdictional amount.

Id. at 40–41, 32 S.Ct. at 9, 56 L.Ed. at 82.

The Court also believed that its holding was compelled by the *Snyder* case, which it characterized as "unmistakably reject[ing] the notion that the 1966 amendments to Rule 23 were intended to effect, or effected, any change in the meaning and application of the jurisdictional-amount requirement insofar as class actions are concerned." 414 U.S. at 299, 94 S.Ct. at 511, 38 L.Ed.2d at 518.

Justice Brennan wrote a dissenting opinion, joined by Justices Douglas and Marshall, pointing out that petitioners * * * [had made] no argument inconsistent with the Court's holding that the theory of "joint" claims or interests will not support jurisdiction over nonappearing members of their class. Their contention is rather that a second theory, ancillary jurisdiction, supports a determination that those claims may be entertained. * * *

* * * [R]ules developed to control the exercise of * * * jurisdiction * * * are * * * accommodations that take into account the impact of the adjudication on parties and third persons, the susceptibility of the dispute or disputes in the case to resolution in a single adjudication, and the structure of the litigation as governed by the Federal Rules of Civil Procedure.

Id. at 305, 94 S.Ct. at 514, 38 L.Ed.2d at 521.

Notes and Questions

1. Many commentators have criticized *Snyder* and *Zahn* as unnecessarily hostile to federal class actions. Upon which of the three kinds of federal class actions—Rule 23(b)(1), (b)(2), or (b)(3)—do you think *Snyder* and *Zahn* have the greatest impact?

2. Are not the Supreme Court holdings on determining diversity of citizenship and on calculating jurisdictional amount in class suits somewhat contradictory? In the former, the status of unnamed class members is irrelevant; a suit can be accorded class treatment even if the citizenship of absent class members would, if considered, have destroyed complete diversity. In calculating jurisdictional amount, on the other hand, the Court instructed lower federal courts to look to the individual claims of each member of the proposed class to see if federal jurisdictional-amount requirements are met; class status is appropriate only when all class members, both the class representatives and the absent class members, individually have satisfied the jurisdictional-amount requirement.

Recent Court of Appeals decisions have further refined *Zahn's* holdings regarding jurisdictional-amount requirements in class action suits. In IN RE ABBOTT LABORATORIES., 51 F.3d 524 (5th Cir.1995), the Fifth Circuit held that it had diversity jurisdiction over the named plaintiffs in a class action even though their individual claims were only $20,000, well-under the then applicable $50,000 amount-in-controversy requirement. Under a Louisiana statute, attorney's fees can be included as part of the amount in controversy. The issue was whether the attorney's fees could be attributed to the class representatives, which would bring each named plaintiff's claim over the $50,000 requirement, or whether these fees had to be apportioned pro rata among the class members. The court held that attributing attorney's fees to the class representatives, rather than to the class as a whole, did not conflict with *Zahn*. The court distinguished *Abbott* from *Zahn* by focusing upon the Louisiana statute, which vests the right to attorney's fees in the named plaintiffs directly, rather than in the class as a whole. *Abbott* also is significant because it held that Section 1367, the supplemental jurisdiction statute, overruled *Zahn* and now permits supplemental jurisdiction to be used in diversity-based class actions. A difference of opinion among the Courts of Appeals has developed on that point. See Note 3, p. 319, supra.

3. Class suits based on diversity but involving unincorporated associations pose unique questions. When unincorporated associations are sued in federal court, the court usually looks to the citizenship of each member of the association

to determine whether there is diversity of citizenship. This has made it difficult for unincorporated associations to sue under diversity jurisdiction in federal courts. Some unincorporated associations have sought to circumvent this rule by using the class-action device—naming only carefully selected association members as class representatives. Should this circumvention be permitted? See Patrician Towers Owners, Inc. v. Fairchild, 513 F.2d 216 (4th Cir.1975) (citizenship of the association's members will be considered when association is named as party but not as the class representative).

2. PERSONAL JURISDICTION

In Hansberry v. Lee, p. 718, supra, the Court said that due process is satisfied and the judgment is binding on all class members when the interests of the class are represented adequately during the suit. *Hansberry* involved a state-court judgment. Should it matter whether it is a state court or a federal court?

But is adequacy of representation all that the Constitution requires? The use of the class-action device raises interesting problems related to personal jurisdiction. For example, must the requirements of International Shoe Co. v. Washington, p. 75, supra, and World–Wide Volkswagen Corp. v. Woodson, p. 97, supra, be satisfied in order for the class-action judgment to bind a particular member of a defendant class? See generally Note, *Personal Jurisdiction and Rule 23 Defendant Class Actions,* 53 Indiana L.J. 841 (1978). Similarly, must the requirements of *International Shoe* and *World-Wide Volkswagen* be met before a court can bind any individual member of a plaintiff class? Do the traditional doctrines of personal jurisdiction apply to non-representative class members who are beyond the court's jurisdiction? The following case addresses that question.

PHILLIPS PETROLEUM CO. v. SHUTTS

Supreme Court of the United States, 1985.
472 U.S. 797, 105 S.Ct. 2965, 86 L.Ed.2d 628.

[During the 1970's, Phillips Petroleum produced or purchased natural gas from leased land located in 11 states. Shutts and several other royalty owners possessing rights to leases from which Phillips Petroleum produced the gas brought a class action against the company in a Kansas state court, seeking to recover interest on royalty payments that had been delayed. The trial court certified a class consisting of 33,000 royalty owners. The class representative provided each class member with a notice by first-class mail describing the action and informing each member that he could appear in person or by counsel, that otherwise he would be represented by the named royalty owners, and that class members would be included in the class and bound by the judgment unless they "opted out" of the action by returning a "request for exclusion." The final class consisted of some 28,100 members, who resided in all 50 states, the District of Columbia, and several foreign countries. Notwithstanding that over 99% of the gas leases in question and some 97% of the plaintiff class members had no apparent connection to Kansas except for the lawsuit, the trial court applied Kansas contract and equity law to every claim and found Phillips Petroleum liable for interest on the suspended royalties to all class members. The Kansas Supreme Court affirmed over the company's contentions that the Due Process Clause of the Fourteenth Amendment prevented Kansas from adjudicating the claims of all the class members, and that the Due Process Clause and the Full Faith and Credit Clause prohibited application of Kansas law to all of the transactions between it and the class members.]

Certiorari to the Supreme Court of Kansas.

JUSTICE REHNQUIST delivered the opinion of the Court.

* * *

I

* * *

* * * As a class-action defendant petitioner is in a unique predicament. If Kansas does not possess jurisdiction over this plaintiff class, petitioner will be bound to 28,100 judgment holders scattered across the globe, but none of these will be bound by the Kansas decree. Petitioner could be subject to numerous later individual suits by these class members because a judgment issued without proper personal jurisdiction over an absent party is not entitled to full faith and credit elsewhere and thus has no res judicata effect as to that party. Whether it wins or loses on the merits, petitioner has a distinct and personal interest in seeing the entire plaintiff class bound by res judicata just as petitioner is bound. The only way a class action defendant like petitioner can assure itself of this binding effect of the judgment is to ascertain that the forum court has jurisdiction over every plaintiff whose claim it seeks to adjudicate, sufficient to support a defense of res judicata in a later suit for damages by class members.

While it is true that a court adjudicating a dispute may not be able to predetermine the res judicata effect of its own judgment, petitioner has alleged that it would be obviously and immediately injured if this class-action judgment against it became final without binding the plaintiff class. We think that such an injury is sufficient to give petitioner standing on its own right to raise the jurisdiction claim in this Court.

* * *

II

Reduced to its essentials, petitioner's argument is that unless out-of-state plaintiffs affirmatively consent, the Kansas courts may not exert jurisdiction over their claims. Petitioner claims that failure to execute and return the "request for exclusion" provided with the class notice cannot constitute consent of the out-of-state plaintiffs; thus Kansas courts may exercise jurisdiction over these plaintiffs only if the plaintiffs possess the sufficient "minimum contacts" with Kansas as that term is used in cases involving personal jurisdiction over out-of-state defendants. * * * Since Kansas had no prelitigation contact with many of the plaintiffs and leases involved, petitioner claims that Kansas has exceeded its jurisdictional reach and thereby violated the due process rights of the absent plaintiffs.

In *International Shoe* we were faced with an out-of-state corporation which sought to avoid the exercise of personal jurisdiction over it as a defendant by Washington state court. We held that the extent of the defendant's due process protection would depend "upon the quality and nature of the activity in relation to the fair and orderly administration of the laws * * *." We noted that the Due Process Clause did not permit a State to make a binding judgment against a person with whom the State had no contacts, ties, or relations. * * * If the defendant possessed certain minimum contacts with the State, so that it was "reasonable and just, according to our traditional conception of fair play and substantial justice" for a State to exercise personal jurisdiction, the State could force the defendant to defend himself in the forum, upon pain of default, and could bind him to a judgment. * * *

The purpose of this test, of course, is to protect a defendant from the travail of defending in a distant forum, unless the defendant's contacts with the forum make it just to force him to defend there. As we explained in *Woodson* * * *, the defendant's contacts should be such that "he should reasonably anticipate being haled" into the forum. * * * In Insurance Corp. of Ireland v. Compagnie des Bauxites de Guinee, * * * we explained that the requirement that a court have personal jurisdiction comes from the Due Process Clause's protection of the defendant's personal liberty interest, and said that the requirement "represents a restriction on judicial power not as a matter of sovereignty, but as a matter of individual liberty." * * *

Although the cases like *Shaffer* and *Woodson* which petitioner relies on for a minimum contacts requirement all dealt with out-of-state defendants or parties in the procedural posture of a defendant, * * * petitioner claims that the same analysis must apply to absent class-action plaintiffs. In this regard petitioner correctly points out that a chose in action is a constitutionally recognized property interest possessed by each of the plaintiffs. * * * An adverse judgment by Kansas courts in this case may extinguish the chose in action forever through res judicata. Such an adverse judgment, petitioner claims, would be every bit as onerous to an absent plaintiff as an adverse judgment on the merits would be to a defendant. Thus, the same due process protections should apply to absent plaintiffs: Kansas should not be able to exert jurisdiction over the plaintiffs' claims unless the plaintiffs have sufficient minimum contacts with Kansas.

We think petitioner's premise is in error. The burdens placed by a State upon an absent class-action plaintiff are not of the same order or magnitude as those it places upon an absent defendant. An out-of-state defendant summoned by a plaintiff is faced with the full powers of the forum State to render judgment *against* it. The defendant must generally hire counsel and travel to the forum to defend itself from the plaintiff's claim, or suffer a default judgment. The defendant may be forced to participate in extended and often costly discovery, and will be forced to respond in damages or to comply with some other form of remedy imposed by the court should it lose the suit. The defendant may also face liability for court costs and attorney's fees. These burdens are substantial, and the minimum contacts requirement of the Due Process Clause prevents the forum State from unfairly imposing them upon the defendant.

A class-action plaintiff, however, is in quite a different posture. The Court noted this difference in Hansberry v. Lee * * *, which explained that a "class" or "representative" suit was an exception to the rule that one could not be bound by judgment *in personam* unless one was made fully a party in the traditional sense. * * * As the Court pointed out in *Hansberry,* the class action was an invention of equity to enable it to proceed to a decree in suits where the number of those interested in the litigation was too great to permit joinder. The absent parties would be bound by the decree so long as the named parties adequately represented the absent class and the prosecution of the litigation was within the common interest. * * *

Modern plaintiff class actions follow the same goals, permitting litigation of a suit involving common questions when there are too many plaintiffs for proper joinder. Class actions also may permit the plaintiffs to pool claims which would be uneconomical to litigate individually. For example, this lawsuit involves claims averaging about $100 per plaintiff; most of the plaintiffs would have no realistic day in court if a class action were not available.

In sharp contrast to the predicament of a defendant haled into an out-of-state forum, the plaintiffs in this suit were not haled anywhere to defend themselves upon pain of a default judgment. As commentators have noted, from the plaintiffs' point of view a class action resembles a "quasi-administrative proceeding, conducted by the judge." * * *

A plaintiff class in Kansas and numerous other jurisdictions cannot first be certified unless the judge, with the aid of the named plaintiffs and defendant, conducts an inquiry into the common nature of the named plaintiffs' and the absent plaintiffs' claims, the adequacy of representation, the jurisdiction possessed over the class, and any other matters that will bear upon proper representation of the absent plaintiffs' interest. * * * Unlike a defendant in a civil suit, a class-action plaintiff is not required to fend for himself. * * * The court and named plaintiffs protect his interests. Indeed, the class-action defendant itself has a great interest in ensuring that the absent plaintiffs' claims are properly before the forum. In this case, for example, the defendant sought to avoid class certification by alleging that the absent plaintiffs would not be adequately represented and were not amenable to jurisdiction. * * *

The concern of the typical class-action rules for the absent plaintiffs is manifested in other ways. Most jurisdictions, including Kansas, require that a class action, once certified, may not be dismissed or compromised without the approval of the court. In many jurisdictions such as Kansas the court may amend the pleadings to ensure that all sections of the class are represented adequately. * * *

Besides this continuing solicitude for their rights, absent plaintiff class members are not subject to other burdens imposed upon defendants. They need not hire counsel or appear. They are almost never subject to counterclaims or cross-claims, or liability for fees or costs. Absent plaintiff class members are not subject to coercive or punitive remedies. Nor will an adverse judgment typically bind an absent plaintiff for any damages, although a valid adverse judgment may extinguish any of the plaintiff's claim which was litigated.

Unlike a defendant in a normal civil suit, an absent class-action plaintiff is not required to do anything. He may sit back and allow the litigation to run its course, content in knowing that there are safeguards provided for his protection. In most class actions an absent plaintiff is provided at least with an opportunity to "opt out" of the class, and if he takes advantage of that opportunity he is removed from the litigation entirely. This was true of the Kansas proceedings in this case. The Kansas procedure provided for the mailing of a notice to each class member by first-class mail. The notice, as we have previously indicated, described the action and informed the class member that he could appear in person or by counsel, in default of which he would be represented by the named plaintiffs and their attorneys. The notice further stated that class members would be included in the class and bound by the judgment unless they "opted out" by executing and returning a "request for exclusion" that was included in the notice.

Petitioner contends, however, that the "opt out" procedure provided by Kansas is not good enough, and that an "opt in" procedure is required to satisfy the Due Process Clause of the Fourteenth Amendment. Insofar as plaintiffs who have no minimum contacts with the forum State are concerned, an "opt in" provision would require that each class member affirmatively consent to his inclusion within the class.

Because States place fewer burdens upon absent class plaintiffs than they do upon absent defendants in nonclass suits, the Due Process Clause need not and does not afford the former as much protection from state-court jurisdiction as it does the latter. The Fourteenth Amendment does protect "persons," not "defendants," however, so absent plaintiffs as well as absent defendants are entitled to some protection from the jurisdiction of a forum State which seeks to adjudicate their claims. In this case we hold that a forum State may exercise jurisdiction over the claim of an absent class-action plaintiff, even though that plaintiff may not possess the minimum contacts with the forum which would support personal jurisdiction over a defendant. If the forum State wishes to bind an absent plaintiff concerning a claim for money damages or similar relief at law,[3] it must provide minimal procedural due process protection. The plaintiff must receive notice plus an opportunity to be heard and participate in the litigation, whether in person or through counsel. The notice must be the best practicable, "reasonably calculated, under all the circumstances, to apprise interested parties of the pendency of the action and afford them an opportunity to present their objections." * * * The notice should describe the action and the plaintiffs' rights in it. Additionally, we hold that due process requires at a minimum that an absent plaintiff be provided with an opportunity to remove himself from the class by executing and returning an "opt out" or "request for exclusion" form to the court. Finally, the Due Process Clause of course requires that the named plaintiff at all times adequately represent the interests of the absent class members. * * *

We reject petitioner's contention that the Due Process Clause of the Fourteenth Amendment requires that absent plaintiffs affirmatively "opt in" to the class, rather than be deemed members of the class if they do not "opt out." We think that such a contention is supported by little, if any precedent, and that it ignores the differences between class action plaintiffs, on the one

---

3. Our holding today is limited to those class actions which seek to bind known plaintiffs concerning claims wholly or predominately for money judgments. We intimate no view concerning other types of class action lawsuits, such as those seeking equitable relief. Nor, of course, does our discussion of personal jurisdiction address class actions where the jurisdiction is asserted against a *defendant* class.

hand, and defendants in non-class civil suits on the other. Any plaintiff may consent to jurisdiction. * * * The essential question, then, is how stringent the requirement for a showing of consent will be.

We think that the procedure followed by Kansas, where a fully descriptive notice is sent first-class mail to each class member, with an explanation of the right to "opt out," satisfies due process. Requiring a plaintiff to affirmatively request inclusion would probably impede the prosecution of those class actions involving an aggregation of small individual claims, where a large number of claims are required to make it economical to bring suit. * * * The plaintiff's claim may be so small, or the plaintiff so unfamiliar with the law, that he would not file suit individually, nor would he affirmatively request inclusion in the class if such a request were required by the Constitution. If, on the other hand, the plaintiff's claim is sufficiently large or important that he wishes to litigate it on his own, he will likely have retained an attorney or have thought about filing suit, and should be fully capable of exercising his right to "opt out."

In this case over 3,400 members of the potential class did "opt out," which belies the contention that "opt out" procedures result in guaranteed jurisdiction by inertia. Another 1,500 were excluded because the notice and "opt out" form was undeliverable. We think that such results show that the "opt out" procedure provided by Kansas is by no means *pro forma*, and that the Constitution does not require more to protect what must be the somewhat rare species of class member who is unwilling to execute an "opt out" form, but whose claim is nonetheless so important that he cannot be presumed to consent to being a member of the class by his failure to do so. Petitioner's "opt in" requirement would require the invalidation of scores of state statutes and of the class-action provision of the Federal Rules of Civil Procedure, and for the reasons stated we do not think that the Constitution requires the State to sacrifice the obvious advantages in judicial efficiency resulting from the "opt out" approach for the protection of the *rara avis* portrayed by petitioner.

We therefore hold that the protection afforded the plaintiff class members by the Kansas statute satisfies the Due Process Clause. The interests of the absent plaintiffs are sufficiently protected by the forum State when those plaintiffs are provided with a request for exclusion that can be returned within a reasonable time to the court. * * * Both the Kansas trial court and the Supreme Court of Kansas held that the class received adequate representation, and no party disputes that conclusion here. We conclude that the Kansas court properly asserted personal jurisdiction over the absent plaintiffs and their claims against petitioner.

III

The Kansas courts applied Kansas contract and Kansas equity law to every claim in this case, notwithstanding that over 99% of the gas leases and some 97% of the plaintiffs in the case had no apparent connection to the State of Kansas except for this lawsuit. Petitioner protested that the Kansas courts should apply the laws of the States where the leases were located, or at least apply Texas and Oklahoma law because so many of the leases came from those States. The Kansas courts disregarded this contention and found petitioner liable for interest on the suspended royalties as a matter of Kansas law, and set the interest rates under Kansas equity principles.

Petitioner contends that total application of Kansas substantive law violated the constitutional limitations on choice of law mandated by the Due Process Clause of the Fourteenth Amendment and the Full Faith and Credit Clause of Article IV, § 1. We must first determine whether Kansas law conflicts in any material way with any other law which could apply. There can be no injury in applying Kansas law if it is not in conflict with that of any other jurisdiction connected to this suit.

Petitioner claims that Kansas law conflicts with that of a number of States connected to this litigation, especially Texas and Oklahoma. These putative conflicts range from the direct to the tangential, and may be addressed by the Supreme Court of Kansas on remand under the correct constitutional standard. * * *

* * *

The conflicts on the applicable interest rates, alone—which we do not think can be labeled "false conflicts" without a more thorough-going treatment than was accorded them by the Supreme Court of Kansas—certainly amounted to millions of dollars in liability. We think that the Supreme Court of Kansas erred in deciding on the basis that it did that the application of its laws to all claims would be constitutional.

Four Terms ago we addressed a similar situation in Allstate Ins. Co. v. Hague * * *. In that case we were confronted with two conflicting rules of state insurance law. Minnesota permitted the "stacking" of separate uninsured motorist policies while Wisconsin did not. Although the decedent lived in Wisconsin, took out insurance policies and was killed there, he was employed in Minnesota and after his death his widow moved to Minnesota for reasons unrelated to the litigation, and was appointed personal representative of his estate. She filed suit in Minnesota courts, which applied the Minnesota stacking rule.

The plurality in *Allstate* noted that a particular set of facts giving rise to litigation could justify, constitutionally, the application of more than one jurisdiction's laws. The plurality recognized, however, that the Due Process Clause and the Full Faith and Credit Clause provided modest restrictions on the application of forum law. These restrictions required "that for a State's substantive law to be selected in a constitutionally permissible manner, that State must have a significant contact or significant aggregation of contacts, creating state interests, such that choice of its law is neither arbitrary nor fundamentally unfair." * * * The dissenting Justices were in substantial agreement with this principle. * * *

The plurality in *Allstate* affirmed the application of Minnesota law because of the forum's significant contacts to the litigation which supported the State's interest in applying its law. * * * Kansas' contacts to this litigation, as explained by the Kansas Supreme Court, can be gleaned from the opinion below.

Petitioner owns property and conducts substantial business in the State, so Kansas certainly has an interest in regulating petitioner's conduct in Kansas. * * * Moreover, oil and gas extraction is an important business to

Kansas, and although only a few leases in issue are located in Kansas, hundreds of Kansas plaintiffs were affected by petitioner's suspension of royalties; thus the court held that the State has a real interest in protecting "the rights of these royalty owners both as individual residents of [Kansas] and as members of this particular class of plaintiffs." * * *

* * *

Kansas must have a "significant contact or aggregation of contacts" to the claims asserted by each member of the plaintiff class, contacts "creating state interests" in order to ensure that the choice of Kansas law is not arbitrary or unfair. * * * Given Kansas' lack of "interest" in claims unrelated to that State, and the substantive conflict with jurisdictions such as Texas, we conclude that application of Kansas law to every claim in this case is sufficiently arbitrary and unfair as to exceed constitutional limits.

When considering fairness in this context, an important element is the expectation of the parties. There is no indication that when the leases involving land and royalty owners outside of Kansas were executed, the parties had any idea that Kansas law would control. Neither the Due Process Clause nor the Full Faith and Credit Clause requires Kansas "to substitute for its own [laws], applicable to persons and events within it, the conflicting statute of another state," * * * but Kansas "may not abrogate the rights of parties beyond its borders having no relation to anything done or to be done within them." * * *

Here the Supreme Court of Kansas took the view that in a nationwide class action where procedural due process guarantees of notice and adequate representation were met, "the laws of the forum should be applied unless compelling reasons exist for applying a different law." * * * Whatever practical reasons may have commended this rule to the Supreme Court of Kansas, for the reasons already stated we do not believe that it is consistent with the decisions of this Court. We make no effort to determine for ourselves which law must apply to the various transactions involved in this lawsuit, and we reaffirm our observation in *Allstate* that in many situations a state court may be free to apply one of several choices of law. But the constitutional limitations laid down in cases such as *Allstate* * * * must be respected even in a nationwide class action.

We therefore affirm the judgment of the Supreme Court of Kansas insofar as it upheld the jurisdiction of the Kansas courts over the plaintiff class members in this case, and reverse its judgment insofar as it held that Kansas law was applicable to all of the transactions which it sought to adjudicate. We remand the case to that court for further proceedings not inconsistent with this opinion.

JUSTICE POWELL took no part in the decision of this case.

[JUSTICE STEVENS wrote an opinion concurring in Parts I & II of the Court's opinion and dissenting from Part III.]

Notes and Questions

1. On remand to the Kansas courts after the Supreme Court's decision in *Shutts*, Phillips Petroleum continued to press the argument that the laws of five

states (Louisiana, New Mexico, Oklahoma, Texas, and Wyoming) differed in important respects from the law of Kansas—in particular on the issue of liability for interest on suspended royalties and on the issue of the applicable interest rate where liability is found. These two issues constituted the heart of the legal controversy in the case, and the five identified states embraced 97% of the leases involved. In addressing this argument, the Kansas Supreme Court first analyzed the Supreme Court's decision in *Shutts*:

> * * * As to the choice of law question, however, it was ruled the application of Kansas law to all of the investors' claims for interest violated the due process and full faith and credit clauses. In its analysis, the Court first noted that if the law of Kansas was not in conflict with any of the other jurisdictions connected to the suit, then there would be no injury in applying the law of Kansas. * * * The Court then cited differences in the laws of Kansas, Texas, and Oklahoma which Phillips *contended* existed. It appears, however, no analysis was made by the Court to determine whether these differences existed in fact. * * *

Shutts v. Phillips Petroleum Co., 240 Kan. 764, 767, 732 P.2d 1286, 1291 (1987), certiorari denied 487 U.S. 1223, 108 S.Ct. 2883, 101 L.Ed.2d 918 (1988) (emphasis in original). The Kansas court then examined the laws of the five states—only to find that *none* of the five was in conflict with the law of Kansas. It therefore entered a new judgment reflecting no change in the original outcome of the case regarding liability and the applicable pre-judgment interest rate. See generally Miller & Crump, *Jurisdiction and Choice of Law in Multistate Class Action After Phillips Petroleum Co. v. Shutts,* 96 Yale L.J. 1 (1986), for a discussion of the implications of *Shutts.*

2. Following *Shutts,* some commentators have argued that choice of law practice should move toward the application of a single substantive law in complex litigation, whether it requires choosing the law of one particular state or developing a body of uniform federal law. See, e.g., Nafziger, *Choice of Law in Air Disaster Cases: Complex Litigation Rules and the Common Law,* 54 La.L.Rev. 1001 (1994). Professor Kramer contends that applying the laws of different states is not unmanageable, and that fairness to the litigants requires the application of different laws. Kramer, *Choice of Law Litigation,* 71 N.Y.U.L.Rev. 547 (1996). See generally American Law Institute, *Complex Litigation: Statutory Recommendations and Analysis,* Chapter 6 (1994).

3. In Shaffer v. Heitner, p. 154, supra, the Supreme Court stated that "all assertions of state-court jurisdiction must be evaluated according to the standards set forth in *International Shoe* and its progeny." Does *Shutts* mean that class plaintiffs are not entitled to this protection? Or is *Shutts* based upon the inference of consent from a class member's failure to opt out of the class? Is this reasoning justified only for plaintiffs with small claims that would not be adjudicated but for the inference of consent through silence? Is the inference of consent equally appropriate when the rights of a large claimant are affected?

4. In formulating the due process requirements, the Court in *Shutts* states that each claimant in a multistate class action "must receive notice." Is the Court imposing a requirement that notice actually be received? Insistence on actual notice would go beyond due process requirements for defendants, who can be held to a judgment in a case initiated upon notice "reasonably calculated" to reach them, even if it is never received.

5. Rule 23 imposes notice and opt-out requirements only in subdivision (b)(3) class actions. Does the concept, articulated in *Shutts,* that the right to opt out is a fundamental due process requirement mean that there is a right to opt out of class suits brought as Rule 23 (b)(1) or (b)(2) class actions? Footnote 3 in the *Shutts* opinion implies that the ruling is not limited to subdivision (b)(3) class actions but applies—at a minimum—to claims "wholly or predominately for monetary judgments." This has caused some confusion about what to do when there is a hybrid class action for both equitable and monetary relief. See Williams v. Lane, 129 F.R.D. 636 (N.D.Ill.1990). The Supreme Court has twice heard arguments on the applicability of *Shutts* to Rule 23(b)(1) and (b)(2) classes, but dismissed both cases on the ground that certiorari had been improperly granted. Ticor Title Insurance Co. v. Brown, 511 U.S. 117, 114 S.Ct. 1359, 128 L.Ed.2d 33 (1994) and Adams v. Robertson, 520 U.S. 83, 117 S.Ct. 1028, 137 L.Ed.2d 203 (1997). For a general discussion, see Mullenix, *Getting to Shutts*, 46 Kansas L. Rev. 727 (1998).

6. Is adequacy of representation enough to extinguish a claim after *Shutts?* For the argument that as a general matter due process entitles a class member to intervene as a full party before her claim is extinguished, see Woolley, *Rethinking the Adequacy of Adequate Representation,* 75 Texas L.Rev. 571 (1997).

3. VENUE

In applying venue rules to class actions, should courts look to the residence of every member of the class, including absent class members? Or should courts look to the residence of the class representatives alone? Courts have adopted the latter approach, thus making class-action venue rules resemble class-action personal-jurisdiction rules. Only the residences of the class representatives are important for purposes of venue; the residences of absent class members and intervenors are irrelevant. See 7A Wright, Miller & Kane, *Federal Practice and Procedure: Civil 2d* § 1757 (1986).

SECTION F. THE PRECLUSIVE EFFECT
OF A CLASS–ACTION JUDGMENT

COOPER v. FEDERAL RESERVE BANK OF RICHMOND

Supreme Court of the United States, 1984.
467 U.S. 867, 104 S.Ct. 2794, 81 L.Ed.2d 718.

Certiorari to the United States Court of Appeals for the Fourth Circuit.

Justice Stevens delivered the opinion of the Court.

The question to be decided is whether a judgment in a class action determining that an employer did not engage in a general pattern or practice of racial discrimination against the certified class of employees precludes a class member from maintaining a subsequent civil action alleging an individual claim of racial discrimination against the employer.

I

On March 22, 1977, the Equal Employment Opportunity Commission commenced a civil action against respondent, the Federal Reserve Bank of Richmond. Respondent operates a branch in Charlotte, N.C. (the Bank), where during the years 1974–1978 it employed about 350–450 employees in several departments. The EEOC complaint alleged that the Bank was violating § 703(a) of Title VII of the Civil Rights Act of 1964 by engaging in "policies and practices" that included "failing and refusing to promote *blacks* because of race." * * *

Six months after the EEOC filed its complaint, four individual employees were allowed to intervene as plaintiffs. * * * In due course, the District Court entered an order conditionally certifying the following class pursuant to Federal Rules of Civil Procedure 23(b)(2) and (3):

> "All black persons who have been employed by the defendant at its Charlotte Branch Office at any time since January 3, 1974 * * * who have been discriminated against in promotion, wages, job assignments and terms and conditions of employment because of their race."

After certifying the class, the District Court ordered that notice be published in the Charlotte newspapers and mailed to each individual member of the class. The notice described the status of the litigation, and plainly stated that members of the class "will be bound by the judgment or other determination" if they did not exclude themselves by sending a written notice to the Clerk. Among the recipients of the notice were Phyllis Baxter and five other individuals employed by the Bank. It is undisputed that these individuals—the Baxter petitioners—are members of the class represented by the intervening plaintiffs and that they made no attempt to exclude themselves from the class.

At the trial the intervening plaintiffs, as well as the Baxter petitioners, testified. The District Court found that the Bank had engaged in a pattern and practice of discrimination from 1974 through 1978 by failing to afford black employees opportunities for advancement and assignment equal to opportunities afforded white employees in pay grades 4 and 5. Except as so specified, however, the District Court found that "there does not appear to be a pattern and practice of discrimination pervasive enough for the court to order relief." * * * Finally, the court somewhat cryptically stated that although it had an opinion about "the entitlement to relief of some of the class members who testified at trial," it would defer decision of such matters to a further proceeding. * * *

Thereafter, on March 24, 1981, the Baxter petitioners moved to intervene, alleging that each had been denied a promotion for discriminatory reasons. * * * The District Court stated: "The court has found no proof of any classwide discrimination above grade 5 and, therefore, they are not entitled to participate in any Stage II proceedings in this case." * * * The court added that it could "see no reason why, if any of the would be intervenors are actively interested in pursuing their claims, they cannot file a Section 1981 suit next week...." * * *

A few days later the Baxter petitioners filed a separate action against the Bank alleging that each of them had been denied a promotion because of their race in violation of 42 U.S.C. § 1981. The Bank moved to dismiss the complaint on the ground that each of them was a member of the class that had been certified in the Cooper litigation, that each was employed in a grade other than 4 or 5, and that they were bound by the determination that there was no proof of any classwide discrimination above grade 5. The District

Court denied the motion to dismiss, but certified its order for interlocutory appeal under 28 U.S.C. § 1292(b). The Bank's interlocutory appeal from the order was then consolidated with the Bank's pending appeal in the Cooper litigation.

The United States Court of Appeals for the Fourth Circuit reversed the District Court's judgment on the merits in the Cooper litigation, concluding that (1) there was insufficient evidence to establish a pattern or practice of racial discrimination in grades 4 and 5, and (2) two of the intervening plaintiffs had not been discriminated against on account of race. EEOC v. Federal Reserve Bank of Richmond, 698 F.2d 633 (4th Cir.1983). The court further held that under the doctrine of res judicata, the judgment in the Cooper class action precluded the Baxter petitioners from maintaining their individual race discrimination claims against the Bank. The court thus reversed the order denying the Bank's motion to dismiss in the Baxter action, and remanded for dismissal of the Baxter complaint. We granted certiorari to review that judgment * * *, and we now reverse.

II

Claims of two types were adjudicated in the Cooper litigation. First, the individual claims of each of the four intervening plaintiffs have been finally decided in the Bank's favor. Those individual decisions do not, of course, foreclose any other individual claims. Second, the class claim that the Bank followed "policies and practices" of discriminating against its employees has also been decided. It is that decision on which the Court of Appeals based its res judicata analysis.

There is of course no dispute that under elementary principles of prior adjudication a judgment in a properly entertained class action is binding on class members in any subsequent litigation. * * * Basic principles of res judicata (merger and bar or claim preclusion) and collateral estoppel (issue preclusion) apply. A judgment in favor of the plaintiff class extinguishes their claim, which merges into the judgment granting relief. A judgment in favor of the defendant extinguishes the claim, barring a subsequent action on that claim. A judgment in favor of either side is conclusive in a subsequent action between them on any issue actually litigated and determined, if its determination was essential to that judgment.

III

* * *

The crucial difference between an individual's claim of discrimination and a class action alleging a general pattern or practice of discrimination is manifest. The inquiry regarding an individual's claim is the reason for a particular employment decision, while "at the liability stage of a pattern-or-practice trial the focus often will not be on individual hiring decisions, but on a pattern of discriminatory decisionmaking." * * *

This distinction was critical to our holding in General Telephone Co. of Southwest v. Falcon [p. 732, supra], that an individual employee's claim that he was denied a promotion on racial grounds did not necessarily make him an adequate representative of a class composed of persons who had allegedly been refused employment for discriminatory reasons. * * *

Falcon thus holds that the existence of a valid individual claim does not necessarily warrant the conclusion that the individual plaintiff may successfully maintain a class action. It is equally clear that a class plaintiff's attempt to prove the existence of a companywide policy, or even a consistent practice within a given department, may fail even though discrimination against one or two individuals has been proved. The facts of this case illustrate the point.

The District Court found that two of the intervening plaintiffs, Cooper and Russell, had both established that they were the victims of racial discrimination but, as the Court of Appeals noted, they were employed in grades higher than grade 5 and therefore their testimony provided no support for the conclusion that there was a practice of discrimination in grades 4 and 5. Given the burden of establishing a prima facie case of a pattern or practice of discrimination, it was entirely consistent for the District Court simultaneously to conclude that Cooper and Russell had valid individual claims even though it had expressly found no proof of any classwide discrimination above grade 5. It could not be more plain that the rejection of a claim of classwide discrimination does not warrant the conclusion that no member of the class could have a valid individual claim. "A racially balanced work force cannot immunize an employer from liability for specific acts of discrimination." Furnco Construction Corp. v. Waters, 438 U.S., at 579, 98 S.Ct., at 2950–2951.

* * *

The Court of Appeals was correct in generally concluding that the Baxter petitioners, as members of the class represented by the intervening plaintiffs in the Cooper litigation, are bound by the adverse judgment in that case. The court erred, however, in the preclusive effect it attached to that prior adjudication. That judgment (1) bars the class members from bringing another class action against the Bank alleging a pattern or practice of discrimination for the relevant time period and (2) precludes the class members in any other litigation with the Bank from relitigating the question whether the Bank engaged in a pattern and practice of discrimination against black employees during the relevant time period. The judgment is not, however, dispositive of the individual claims the Baxter petitioners have alleged in their separate action. Assuming they establish a prima facie case of discrimination * * *, the Bank will be required to articulate a legitimate reason for each of the challenged decisions, and if it meets that burden, the ultimate questions regarding motivation in their individual cases will be resolved by the District Court. Moreover, the prior adjudication may well prove beneficial to the Bank in the Baxter action: the determination in the Cooper action that the Bank had not engaged in a general pattern or practice of discrimination would be relevant on the issue of pretext. * * *

The Bank argues that permitting the Baxter petitioners to bring separate actions would frustrate the purposes of Rule 23. We think the converse is true. The class-action device was intended to establish a procedure for the adjudication of common questions of law or fact. If the Bank's theory were adopted, it would be tantamount to requiring that every member of the class be permitted to intervene to litigate the merits of his individual claim.

* * *

The judgment of the Court of Appeals is reversed, and the case is remanded for further proceedings consistent with this opinion.

It is so ordered.

JUSTICE MARSHALL concurs in the judgment.

JUSTICE POWELL took no part in the decision of this case.

Notes and Questions

1. May a judgment in a class action be given collateral estoppel effect in a later action in favor of a plaintiff who elected to opt out of the class action? If allowed, this would enable the plaintiff indirectly to take advantage of a favorable class-action judgment but not preclude him from bringing a separate action—even as to the very matter determined in the class action itself—if there is an unfavorable judgment. Would this undermine the opt-out procedure? See 7B Wright, Miller & Kane, *Federal Practice and Procedure: Civil 2d* § 1789, at 266–67 (1986); Ratliff, *Offensive Collateral Estoppel and the Option Effect,* 67 Texas L.Rev. 63 (1968).

2. What is the preclusive effect of a state court class action settlement upon a second suit brought by the same parties in federal court raising exclusively federal questions? Although such federal claims cannot be brought in state court, the Supreme Court has held that, in accordance with full faith and credit under 28 U.S.C. § 1738, the state judgment may resolve claims within the exclusive jurisdiction of the federal courts and bar their subsequent litigation in a federal court. MATSUSHITA ELECTRIC INDUSTRIAL CO. v. EPSTEIN, 516 U.S. 367, 116 S.Ct. 873, 134 L.Ed.2d 6 (1996). Writing for the majority, Justice Thomas stated:

> That the [state court] judgment at issue is the result of a class action, rather than a suit brought by an individual, does not undermine the initial applicability of [28 U.S.C.] § 1738. The judgment of a state court in a class action is plainly the product of a "judicial proceeding" within the meaning of 28 U.S.C. § 1738. * * * Further, 28 U.S.C. § 1738 is not irrelevant simply because the judgment in question might work to bar the litigation of exclusively federal claims. * * * *Marrese v. American Academy of Orthopaedic Surgeons,* 470 U.S. 373, 105 S.Ct. 1327, 84 L.Ed.2d 274 (1985). * * *

> When faced with a state court judgment relating to an exclusively federal claim, a federal court must first look to the law of the rendering State to ascertain the effect of the judgment. * * * If state law indicates that the particular claim or issue would be barred from litigation in a court of that state, then the federal court must next consider whether, "as an exception to § 1738," it "should refuse to give preclusive effect to [the] state court judgment." Id. at 383. * * *

> * * * [Delaware case law] indicate[s] that even if, as here, a claim could not have been raised in the court that rendered the settlement judgment in a class action, a Delaware court would still find that the judgment bars subsequent pursuit of the claim. [Therefore,] * * * we proceed to the second step of the Marrese analysis and ask whether § 27 of the [Securities] Exchange Act, which confers exclusive jurisdiction upon the federal courts for suits arising under the Act, partially repealed [28 U.S.C.] § 1738. Section 27

contains no express language regarding its relationship with § 1738 or the preclusive effect of related state court proceedings. * * *

* * *

Nor does § 27 evince any intent to prevent litigants in state court—whether suing as individuals or as part of a class—from voluntarily releasing Exchange Act claims in judicially approved settlements. * * * Thus, the Delaware court never trespassed upon the exclusive territory of the federal courts, but merely approved the settlement of a common-law suit pursuant to state and nonexclusive federal law.

Id. at 373–82, 116 S.Ct. at 877–82, 134 L.Ed.2d at 17–22.

3. As noted earlier, the Supreme Court has not yet clarified the due process requirements associated with Rule 23(b)(1) and (b)(2) class actions. If notice and a right to opt out are required, the preclusive effects of judgments in these actions will be affected. See Zachery v. Texaco Exploration & Production, Inc., 185 F.R.D. 230 (W.D.Tex.1999) (refusing certification of a Rule 23(b)(2) class on these grounds).

SECTION G.   THE PROBLEM OF THE MASS TORT CASE

When the Advisory Committee drafted what became the 1966 amendment of Rule 23, the mass tort phenomenon had not yet developed. Nonetheless, the Committee sounded a note of caution that one accident would affect different parties in different ways raising different factual and legal issues—a feature it saw as incompatible with unitary adjudication. The reasons for this initial attitude have been described as follows:

> When personal injury and death claims are involved, a strong feeling prevails that everyone enmeshed in the dispute should have his own day in court and be represented by a lawyer of his own choice. Thus, the possibility that a class action might be used to adjudicate the claims arising out of a mass tort is particularly unattractive to those who believe the device to be inconsistent with the time-honored practice in personal injury cases and to others who fear that use of this procedure may encourage the unseemly solicitation of legal business. Furthermore, the alleged tortfeasor's defenses may depend on facts peculiar to each plaintiff, creating a risk that they may be submerged by the overall magnitude of the litigation or that individual issues actually may predominate so that a class action really would not be economical or expeditious.

7B Wright, Miller & Kane, *Federal Practice and Procedure: Civil 2d* § 1783, at 71–72 (1986).

Attitudes changed, however, and in recent years mass tort class actions have become relatively common—but they are fraught with controversy. Not surprisingly, many people view mass tort class actions as efficient vehicles for resolving disputes by multiple litigants who have similar claims against the same defendant, particularly when practical considerations make individual lawsuits unlikely or impossible. However, as will be seen below, the use of class actions in this context poses numerous and complex procedural questions that often take years to resolve. In addition, the lack of plaintiff autonomy associated with class treatment raises due process concerns in the mass tort setting. Many commentators have criticized the current situation for resulting in huge legal fees, inflated product prices, and corporate bankruptcies. Others continue to believe that the use of class actions in this context promotes the objectives of access, efficiency and deterrence.

Perhaps the best way to explore the complexities of class action practice in this context is to apply Rule 23 to some concrete examples. To that end, consider the consequences of certifying a class in the following actions. Also, keep in mind procedural possibilities other than class actions, such as using the principles of former adjudication and interpleader.

Dalkon Shield

In 1970, the A.H. Robins Company placed the Dalkon Shield, an intrauterine contraceptive device, on the market. Approximately 2.2 million of these devices were purchased by women in the United States, and many women who used the device developed an infection that caused infertility or sustained other injuries. Some evidence existed that A.H. Robins knew that the device would have these effects. By May 31, 1981, approximately 3,258 actions related to the Dalkon Shield had been filed, and 1,573 suits, in which compensatory damages of well over $500 million and punitive damages in excess of $2.3 billion were claimed, were pending. Against the objections of many of the plaintiffs and all the defendants, a District Court in California certified a nationwide class. The Ninth Circuit reversed on the ground that the prevalence of individual issues outweighed any efficiency the class action device might have brought. Which court was correct? Do the inevitable differences in the plaintiffs' medical and sexual histories affect your decision? How should punitive damages be handled? Should they be awarded to one plaintiff or divided amongst them? See In re Northern District of California, Dalkon Shield IUD Products Liability Litigation, 693 F.2d 847 (9th Cir.1982), certiorari denied 459 U.S. 1171, 103 S.Ct. 817, 74 L.Ed.2d 1015 (1983).

In 1989, in a separate action against the manufacturer's liability insurance company, the Fourth Circuit certified a class that sought recovery against the insurer. See In re A.H. Robins Co., 880 F.2d 709 (4th Cir. 1989). The class was certified under Rule 23(b)(1)(A) on the issue of the insurance company's liability as a joint tortfeasor, because it would pose a substantial burden on the company to have to litigate its liability separately with each plaintiff. The class also was certified under Rule 23(b)(1)(B) with respect to the company's contractual liability under its insurance policy provided to A.H. Robins.

Agent Orange

While fighting the Vietnam War, the United States Army and Marine Corps used a defoliant called Agent Orange to clear the brush in the Vietnamese forests. Later, suspicion grew that Agent Orange caused various illnesses in those who were exposed to the chemical, and caused birth defects in their children. A class-action suit based on negligence and products liability was brought on behalf of a plaintiff class consisting of "all persons who were in the United States, New Zealand or Australian Armed Forces at any time from 1962 to 1971 who were injured in or near Vietnam by exposure to Agent Orange or other phenoxy herbicides, [including] spouses, parents and children of veterans born before January 1, 1984, directly or derivatively injured as a result of the exposure." There were over 15,000 named plaintiffs and nearly 2.5 million potential class members. The plaintiffs sought to press individual damage claims as well as their class claims.

Should a plaintiff class be certified? If so, should it be a subdivision (b)(1) or (b)(2) or (b)(3) class? If it should be a subdivision (b)(3) class, does clause (D) of that provision present problems? Are there other problems in certifying the class? Should the judge consider that the chemical companies may go bankrupt from an extremely large judgment? See In re Agent Orange Product Liability Litigation, 100 F.R.D. 718 (E.D.N.Y.1983), 597 F.Supp. 740, 837–42 (E.D.N.Y.1984), affirmed 818 F.2d 145 (2d Cir.1987), certiorari denied 484 U.S. 1004, 108 S.Ct. 695, 98 L.Ed.2d 648 (1988).

The District Court did certify the class in the *Agent Orange* litigation and his decision was upheld on a petition for mandamus by the Second Circuit. Are the different results in *Dalkon Shield* and *Agent Orange* defensible? The plaintiffs in *Agent Orange* were members of the armed services and therefore subject to common government-immunity defenses by the manufacturers of the defoliant. Should that be determinative?

CASTANO v. AMERICAN TOBACCO CO.

United States Court of Appeals, Fifth Circuit, 1996.
84 F.3d 734.

SMITH, CIRCUIT JUDGE.

In what may be the largest class action ever attempted in federal court, the district court in this case embarked "on a road certainly less traveled, if ever taken at all," * * * and entered a class certification order. The court defined the class as:

(a) All nicotine-dependent persons in the United States ... who have purchased and smoked cigarettes manufactured by the defendants;

(b) the estates, representatives, and administrators of these nicotine-dependent cigarette smokers; and

(c) the spouses, children, relatives and "significant others" of these nicotine-dependent cigarette smokers as their heirs or survivors.

Concluding that the district court abused its discretion in certifying the class, we reverse.

I.

A. The Class Complaint

The plaintiffs filed this class complaint against the defendant tobacco companies and the Tobacco Institute, Inc., seeking compensation solely for the injury of nicotine addiction. The gravamen of their complaint is the novel and wholly untested theory that the defendants fraudulently failed to inform consumers that nicotine is addictive and manipulated the level of nicotine in cigarettes to sustain their addictive nature. * * *

* * *

B.   The Class Certification Order

[T]he district court granted, in part, plaintiffs' motion for class certification, concluding that the prerequisites of FED.R.CIV.P. 23(a) had been met. * * *

The court * * * grant[ed] the plaintiffs' motion to certify the class under FED.R.CIV.P. 23(b)(3), organizing the class action issues into four categories: (1) core liability; (2) injury-in-fact, proximate cause, reliance and affirmative defenses; (3) compensatory damages; and (4) punitive damages. * * * It then analyzed each category to determine whether it met the predominance and superiority requirements of rule 23(b)(3). Using its power to sever issues for certification under FED.R.CIV.P. 23(c)(4), the court certified the class on core liability and punitive damages, and certified the class conditionally pursuant to FED.R.CIV.P. 23(c)(1).

* * *

The district court erred in its analysis in two distinct ways. First, it failed to consider how variations in state law affect predominance and superiority. Second, its predominance inquiry did not include consideration of how a trial on the merits would be conducted.

Each of these defects mandates reversal. Moreover, at this time, while the tort is immature, the class complaint must be dismissed as class certification cannot be found to be a superior method of adjudication.

A.   Variations in State Law

Although rule 23(c)(1) requires that a class should be certified "as soon as practicable" and allows a court to certify a conditional class, it does not follow that the rule's requirements are lessened when the class is conditional. As a sister circuit explained:

> Conditional certification is not a means whereby the District Court can avoid deciding whether, at that time, the requirements of the Rule have been substantially met. The purpose of conditional certification is to preserve the Court's power to revoke certification in those cases wherein the magnitude or complexity of the litigation may eventually reveal problems not theretofore apparent. But in this case the District Court seemed to brush aside one of the requirements of Rule 23(b)(3) by stating that at this time "analysis of the individual versus common questions would be for the Court to act as a seer." However difficult it may have been for the District Court to decide whether common questions predominate over individual questions, it should not have sidestepped this preliminary requirement of the Rule by merely stating that the problem of individual questions "lies far beyond the horizon in the realm of speculation."

In re Hotel Tel. Charges, 500 F.2d 86, 90 (9th Cir. 1974).

* * *

A district court's duty to determine whether the plaintiff has borne its burden on class certification requires that a court consider variations in state law when a class action involves multiple jurisdictions. * * *

* * *

A thorough review of the record demonstrates that, in this case, the district court did not properly consider how variations in state law affect predominance. The court acknowledged as much in its order granting class certification, for, in declining to make a choice of law determination, it noted that "[t]he parties have only briefly addressed the conflict of laws issue in this matter." 160 F.R.D. at 554. * * *

The district court's review of state law variances can hardly be considered extensive; it conducted a cursory review of state law variations and gave short shrift to the defendants' arguments concerning variations.[15]

* * *

The court also failed to perform its duty to determine whether the class action would be manageable in light of state law variations. The court's only discussion of manageability is a citation and the claim that "[w]hile manageability of the liability issues in this case may well prove to be difficult, the Court finds that any such difficulties pale in comparison to the specter of thousands, if not millions, of similar trials of liability proceeding in thousands of courtrooms around the nation." *Id.* at 555–56.

* * *

* * * [W]hether the specter of millions of cases outweighs any manageability problems in this class is uncertain when the scope of any manageability problems is unknown. Absent considered judgment on the manageability of the class, a comparison to millions of individual trials is meaningless.

B. Predominance

The district court's second error was that it failed to consider how the plaintiffs' addiction claims would be tried, individually or on a class basis. * * * The district court, based on *Eisen v. Carlisle & Jacquelin,* [Note 6, p. 724, supra], * * * believed that it could not go past the pleadings for the certification decision. The result was an incomplete and inadequate predominance inquiry.

* * *

A district court certainly may look past the pleadings to determine whether the requirements of rule 23 have been met. Going beyond the

---

15. * * * The *Castano* class suffers from many of the difficulties that the *Georgine,* see [*Amchem,* p. 760, infra] court found dispositive. The class members were exposed to nicotine through different products, for different amounts of time, and over different time periods. Each class member's knowledge about the effects of smoking differs, and each plaintiff began smoking for different reasons. Each of these factual differences impacts the application of legal rules such as causation, reliance, comparative fault, and other affirmative defenses.

Variations in state law magnify the differences. In a fraud claim, some states require justifiable reliance on a misrepresentation.

Despite these overwhelming individual issues, common issues might predominate. We are, however, left to speculate. The point of detailing the alleged differences is to demonstrate the inquiry the district court failed to make.

pleadings is necessary, as a court must understand the claims, defenses, relevant facts, and applicable substantive law in order to make a meaningful determination of the certification issues. * * *

The district court * * * just assumed that because the common issues would play a part in every trial, they must be significant. The court's synthesis of *Jenkins* [*v. Raymark Indus., Inc.*, 782 F.2d 468 (5th Cir.1986)] and *Eisen* would write the predominance requirement out of the rule, and any common issue would predominate if it were common to all the individual trials.[19]

The court's treatment of the fraud claim also demonstrates the error inherent in its approach. * * * [A] fraud class action cannot be certified when individual reliance will be an issue. The district court avoided the reach of this court's decision in *Simon* [*v. Merrill Lynch, Pierce, Fenner & Smith, Inc.*, 482 F.2d 880 (5th Cir.1973)] by an erroneous reading of *Eisen;* the court refused to consider whether reliance would be an issue in individual trials.

The problem with the district court's approach is that after the class trial, it might have decided that reliance must be proven in individual trials. The court then would have been faced with the difficult choice of decertifying the class * * * and wasting judicial resources, or continuing with a class action that would have failed the predominance requirement of rule 23(b)(3).[21]

III.

In addition to the reasons given above, regarding the district court's procedural errors, this class must be decertified because it independently fails the superiority requirement of rule 23(b)(3). In the context of mass tort class actions, certification dramatically affects the stakes for defendants. Class certification magnifies and strengthens the number of unmeritorious claims. * * * Aggregation of claims also makes it more likely that a defendant will be found liable and results in significantly higher damage awards. * * *

In addition to skewing trial outcomes, class certification creates insurmountable pressure on defendants to settle, whereas individual trials would not. * * * The risk of facing an all-or-nothing verdict presents too high a risk, even when the probability of an adverse judgment is low. * * * These settlements have been referred to as judicial blackmail.

It is no surprise then, that historically, certification of mass tort litigation classes has been disfavored. The traditional concern over the rights of defendants in mass tort class actions is magnified in the instant case. Our specific concern is that a mass tort cannot be properly certified without a prior track

---

19. An incorrect predominance finding also implicates the court's superiority analysis: The greater the number of individual issues, the less likely superiority can be established. * * * The relationship between predominance and superiority in mass torts was recognized in the Advisory Committee's note to rule 23(b)(3) * * *.

21. Severing the defendants' conduct from reliance under rule 23(c)(4) does not save the class action. A district court cannot manufacture predominance through the nimble use of subdivision (c)(4). The proper interpretation of

the interaction between subdivisions (b)(3) and (c)(4) is that a cause of action, as a whole, must satisfy the predominance requirement of (b)(3) and that (c)(4) is a housekeeping rule that allows courts to sever the common issues for a class trial. * * * Reading rule 23(c)(4) as allowing a court to sever issues until the remaining common issue predominates over the remaining individual issues would eviscerate the predominance requirement of rule 23(b)(3); the result would be automatic certification in every case where there is a common issue, a result that could not have been intended.

record of trials from which the district court can draw the information necessary to make the predominance and superiority analysis required by rule 23. This is because certification of an immature tort results in a higher than normal risk that the class action may not be superior to individual adjudication.

* * * The court acknowledged the extensive manageability problems with this class. Such problems include difficult choice of law determinations, subclassing of eight claims with variations in state law, *Erie* guesses, notice to millions of class members, further subclassing to take account of transient plaintiffs, and the difficult procedure for determining who is nicotine-dependent. Cases with far fewer manageability problems have given courts pause. * * *

The district court's rationale for certification in spite of such problems— i.e., that a class trial would preserve judicial resources in the millions of inevitable individual trials—is based on pure speculation. * * *

What the district court failed to consider, and what no court can determine at this time, is the very real possibility that the judicial crisis may fail to materialize. The plaintiffs' claims are based on a new theory of liability and the existence of new evidence. Until plaintiffs decide to file individual claims, a court cannot, from the existence of injury, presume that all or even any plaintiffs will pursue legal remedies. * * *

As he stated in the record, plaintiffs' counsel in this case has promised to inundate the courts with individual claims if class certification is denied. Independently of the reliability of this self-serving promise, there is reason to believe that individual suits are feasible. First, individual damage claims are high, and punitive damages are available in most states. The expense of litigation does not necessarily turn this case into a negative value suit, in part because the prevailing party may recover attorneys' fees under many consumer protection statutes. * * *

In a case such as this one, where each plaintiff may receive a large award, and fee shifting often is available, we find Chief Judge Posner's analysis [in *In re Rhone–Poulenc Rorer Inc.*, 51 F.3d 1293 (7th Cir.), certiorari denied 516 U.S. 867, 116 S.Ct. 184, 133 L.Ed.2d 122 (1995)] of superiority to be persuasive:

> * * * Each plaintiff if successful is apt to receive a judgment in the millions. With the aggregate stakes in the tens or hundreds of millions of dollars, or even in the billions, it is not a waste of judicial resources to conduct more than one trial, before more than six jurors, to determine whether a major segment of the international pharmaceutical industry is to follow the asbestos manufacturers into Chapter 11.

* * * So too here, we cannot say that it would be a waste to allow individual trials to proceed, before a district court engages in the complicated predominance and superiority analysis necessary to certify a class.

Fairness may demand that mass torts with few prior verdicts or judgments be litigated first in smaller units—even single-plaintiff, single-defendant trials—until general causation, typical injuries, and levels of damages become established. Thus, "mature" mass torts like asbestos or Dalkon Shield may call for procedures that are not appropriate for incipient mass tort cases, such as those involving injuries arising from new products, chemical substances, or pharmaceuticals.

Manual for Complex Litigation § 33.26.

* * *

The remaining rationale for superiority—judicial efficiency—is also lacking. In the context of an immature tort, any savings in judicial resources is speculative, and any imagined savings would be overwhelmed by the procedural problems that certification of a *sui generis* cause of action brings with it.

* * *

The district court's predominance inquiry, or lack of it, squarely presents the problems associated with certification of immature torts. Determining whether the common issues are a "significant" part of each individual case has an abstract quality to it when no court in this country has ever tried an injury-as-addiction claim. * * *

Yet, an accurate finding on predominance is necessary before the court can certify a class. * * * Premature certification deprives the defendant of the opportunity to present that argument to any court and risks decertification after considerable resources have been expended.

* * *

The plaintiffs' final retort is that individual trials are inadequate because time is running out for many of the plaintiffs. They point out that prior litigation against the tobacco companies has taken up to ten years to wind through the legal system. * * *

* * * [T]he plaintiffs' claim that time is running out ignores the reality of the class action device. In a complicated case involving multiple jurisdictions, the conflict of law question itself could take decades to work its way through the courts. Once that issue has been resolved, discovery, subclassing, and ultimately the class trial would take place. Next would come the appellate process. After the class trial, the individual trials and appeals on comparative negligence and damages would have to take place. The net result could be that the class action device would lengthen, not shorten, the time it takes for the plaintiffs to reach final judgment.

* * *

* * * For the forgoing reasons, we REVERSE and REMAND with instructions that the district court dismiss the class complaint.

Notes and Questions

1.   The Fifth Circuit relies upon the fact that the class alleged an "immature tort." The plaintiffs claimed that the defendants failed to inform consumers of the addictive nature of nicotine and that the defendants manipulated the amount of nicotine in cigarettes to sustain their addiction. The Court asserted that these theories had not been litigated often enough in the context of individual tobacco cases to allow the court to assess the relative superiority of the class device as a means of adjudicating such claims. Is the court's point valid? How long must the

class action be held in abeyance before the plaintiffs' theory is thought "mature" enough? See Walker v. Liggett Group, Inc., 175 F.R.D. 226 (S.D.W.Va.1997) (class of tobacco smokers in a lawsuit against Liggett Group, the smallest of the big five tobacco companies not certified, following the *Castano* rationale).

2. What is "immature" about the notion that a failure to warn of a product's defects or of its injurious character, especially when the defendant allegedly manufactured the product knowing it would have the injurious effect? In *In re Rhone–Poulenc Rorer Inc.*, heavily relied on in *Castano*, Judge Posner used the notion of "immaturity" as one of several reasons for granting a writ of mandamus to decertify a class when each plaintiff had a large individual claim.

3. After the *Castano* class failed and legislative reform of the tobacco industry proved unlikely, over forty states filed lawsuits against tobacco companies for their costs in connection with tobacco-related illnesses. The companies negotiated a settlement with the Attorneys General of these states, and in November 1998, the settlement was accepted by forty-six states, the District of Columbia, and five territories. This settlement included payments to the states totalling $206 billion to be paid over the next twenty-five years. Additional settlement provisions include prohibiting tobacco companies from targeting youth in their advertising, using cartoon characters to sell cigarettes, and giving out free samples of tobacco products except in adult establishments. The tobacco companies also were directed to make available all of their research on tobacco to the public. This settlement did not, however, extinguish the claims of individual smokers against the tobacco companies. The failure of federal nationwide class actions such as *Castano* led some plaintiffs to seek relief in state court, and in fact, a few individual plaintiffs and state-wide classes have been more successful in obtaining favorable decisions against tobacco companies after the settlement. See Ieyoub & Eisenberg, *Class Actions in the Gulf South Symposium*: *State Attorney General Actions, the Tobacco Litigation, and the Doctrine of Parens Patriae*, 74 Tulane L.Rev 1859 (2000) (noting that the tobacco industry had not lost a smoking case prior to the states' litigation, but that settlement was followed by plaintiffs' victories in three states). A jury verdict for almost $150 billion in a Florida state court class action is currently on appeal.

———

Not surprisingly, given the transaction costs of litigating a mass tort class action suit that sometimes involves millions of individual claims, there is a great pressure to settle. But since the settlements bring into the foreground questions as to the actual representativeness of the people who are doing the settling and emphasize the due process concerns generally associated with the class action, settlement presents one of the most controversial issues of the day. Reread pp. 711–13, supra.

AMCHEM PRODUCTS, INC. v. WINDSOR

Supreme Court of the United States, 1997.
521 U.S. 591, 117 S.Ct. 2231, 138 L.Ed.2d 689.

Certiorari to the United States Court of Appeals for the Third Circuit.

JUSTICE GINSBURG delivered the opinion of the Court.

This case concerns the legitimacy under Rule 23 * * * of a class-action certification sought to achieve global settlement of current and future asbestos-related claims. The class proposed for certification potentially encompasses hundreds of thousands, perhaps millions, of individuals tied together by this commonality: Each was, or some day may be, adversely affected by past exposure to asbestos products manufactured by one or more of 20 companies. Those companies, defendants in the lower courts, are petitioners here.

* * *

I

A

[The Panel on Multidistrict Litigation] * * * transferred all asbestos cases then filed, but not yet on trial in federal courts to a single district * * * for pretrial proceedings * * *. The order aggregated pending cases only; no authority resides in the MDL Panel to license for consolidated proceedings claims not yet filed.

B

After the consolidation, attorneys for plaintiffs and defendants formed separate steering committees and began settlement negotiations. [These negotiations included efforts to resolve future as well as pending cases.] * * * Settlement talks thus concentrated on devising an administrative scheme for disposition of asbestos claims not yet in litigation. In these negotiations, counsel for masses of [plaintiffs who had filed suit also] * * * endeavored to represent the interests of the anticipated future claimants, although those lawyers then had no attorney-client relationship with such claimants. * * * [An agreement was then reached with regard to the claims that had been filed and the lawyers then] launched this case, exclusively involving persons outside the MDL Panel's province—plaintiffs without already pending lawsuits.

C

The class action thus instituted was not intended to be litigated. Rather, within the space of a single day, January 15, 1993, the settling parties * * * presented to the District Court a complaint, an answer, a proposed settlement agreement, and a joint motion for conditional class certification.

The complaint identified nine lead plaintiffs, designating them and members of their families as representatives of a class comprising all persons who had not filed an asbestos-related lawsuit against a * * * [member of the defendant group (hereinafter referred to as a CCR defendant)] as of the date the class action commenced, but who (1) had been exposed—occupationally or through the occupational exposure of a spouse or household member—to asbestos or products containing asbestos attributable to a CCR defendant, or (2) whose spouse or family member had been so exposed. Untold numbers of individuals may fall within this description. All named plaintiffs alleged that they or a member of their family had been exposed to asbestos-containing products of CCR defendants. More than half of the named plaintiffs alleged that they or their family members had already suffered various physical injuries as a result of the exposure. The others alleged that they had not yet manifested any asbestos-related condition. The complaint delineated no subclasses; all named plaintiffs were designated as representatives of the class as a whole.

The complaint invoked the District Court's diversity jurisdiction and asserted various state-law claims for relief, including (1) negligent failure to warn, (2) strict liability, (3) breach of express and implied warranty, (4) negligent infliction of emotional distress, (5) enhanced risk of disease, (6) medical monitoring, and (7) civil conspiracy. Each plaintiff requested unspecified damages in excess of $100,000. CCR defendants' answer denied the principal allegations of the complaint and asserted 11 affirmative defenses.

A stipulation of settlement accompanied the pleadings; it proposed to settle, and to preclude nearly all class members from litigating against CCR companies, all claims not filed before January 15, 1993, involving compensation for present and future asbestos-related personal injury or death. An exhaustive document exceeding 100 pages, the stipulation presents in detail an administrative mechanism and a schedule of payments to compensate class members who meet defined asbestos-exposure and medical requirements.
* * *

For each qualifying disease category, the stipulation specifies the range of damages CCR will pay to qualifying claimants. Payments under the settlement are not adjustable for inflation. * * * Compensation above the fixed ranges may be obtained for "extraordinary" claims. But the settlement places both numerical caps and dollar limits on such claims. The settlement also imposes "case flow maximums," which cap the number of claims payable for each disease in a given year.

Class members are to receive no compensation for certain kinds of claims, even if otherwise applicable state law recognizes such claims. Claims that garner no compensation under the settlement include claims by family members of asbestos-exposed individuals for loss of consortium, and claims by so-called "exposure-only" plaintiffs for increased risk of cancer, fear of future asbestos-related injury, and medical monitoring. "Pleural" claims, which might be asserted by persons with asbestos-related plaques on their lungs but no accompanying physical impairment, are also excluded. Although not entitled to present compensation, exposure-only claimants and pleural claimants may qualify for benefits when and if they develop a compensable disease and meet the relevant exposure and medical criteria. Defendants forgo defenses to liability, including statute of limitations pleas.

Class members, in the main, are bound by the settlement in perpetuity, while CCR defendants may choose to withdraw from the settlement after ten years. A small number of class members—only a few per year—may reject the settlement and pursue their claims in court. Those permitted to exercise this option, however, may not assert any punitive damages claim or any claim for increased risk of cancer. Aspects of the administration of the settlement are to be monitored by the AFL–CIO and class counsel. Class counsel are to receive attorneys' fees in an amount to be approved by the District Court.

D

On January 29, 1993, as requested by the settling parties, the District Court conditionally certified, under Federal Rule * * * 23(b)(3), an encompassing opt-out class. The certified class included persons occupationally exposed to defendants' asbestos products, and members of their families, who had not filed suit as of January 15. Judge Weiner appointed * * * class counsel, noting that "[t]he Court may in the future appoint additional counsel if it is deemed necessary and advisable." Record, Doc. 11, p. 3 (Class Certification Order). * * * [The class was never divided into subclasses.] In a separate order, Judge Weiner assigned to Judge Reed, also of the Eastern District of Pennsylvania, "the task of conducting fairness proceedings and of determining whether the proposed settlement is fair to the class." See 157 F.R.D., at 258. Various class members raised objections to the settlement stipulation, and Judge Weiner granted the objectors full rights to participate in the subsequent proceedings. * * *

Objectors raised numerous challenges * * * . They urged that the settlement unfairly disadvantaged those without currently compensable conditions in that it failed to adjust for inflation or to account for changes, over time, in medical understanding. They maintained that compensation levels were intolerably low in comparison to awards available in tort litigation or payments received by the inventory plaintiffs. And they objected to the absence of any compensation for certain claims, for example, medical monitoring, compensable under the tort law of several States. Rejecting these and all other objections, Judge Reed concluded that the settlement terms were fair and had been negotiated without collusion. * * * He also found that adequate notice had been given to class members, and that final class certification under Rule 23(b)(3) was appropriate * * *.

Strenuous objections had been asserted regarding the adequacy of representation, a Rule 23(a)(4) requirement. Objectors maintained that class counsel and class representatives had disqualifying conflicts of interests. In particular, objectors urged, claimants whose injuries had become manifest and claimants without manifest injuries should not have common counsel and should not be aggregated in a single class. Furthermore, objectors argued, lawyers representing inventory plaintiffs should not represent the newly formed class.

Satisfied that class counsel had ably negotiated the settlement in the best interests of all concerned, and that the named parties served as adequate representatives, the District Court rejected these objections. * * * Subclasses were unnecessary, the District Court held, bearing in mind the added cost and confusion they would entail and the ability of class members to exclude themselves from the class during the three-month opt-out period. * * *

E

* * * [The Court of Appeals initially held] that the requirements of Rule 23(a) and (b)(3) must be met "without taking into account the settlement" 83 F.3d, at 626 * * *. [However, the court] in fact closely considered the terms of the settlement as it examined aspects of the case under Rule 23 criteria. * * * The Third Circuit recognized that Rule 23(a)(2)'s "commonality" requirement is subsumed under, or superseded by, the more stringent Rule 23(b)(3) requirement that questions common to the class "predominate over" other questions. The court therefore trained its attention on the "predominance" inquiry. * * * The harmfulness of asbestos exposure was indeed a prime

factor common to the class, the Third Circuit observed. * * * But uncommon questions abounded.

In contrast to mass torts involving a single accident, class members in this case were exposed to different asbestos-containing products, in different ways, over different periods, and for different amounts of time; some suffered no physical injury, others suffered disabling or deadly diseases. * * * "These factual differences," the Third Circuit explained, "translate[d] into significant legal differences." Id., at 627. State law governed and varied widely on such critical issues as "viability of [exposure-only] claims [and] availability of causes of action for medical monitoring, increased risk of cancer, and fear of future injury." * * * "[T]he number of uncommon issues in this humongous class action," the Third Circuit concluded, * * * barred a determination, under existing tort law, that common questions predominated * * *.

The Court of Appeals next found that "serious intra-class conflicts preclude[d] th[e] class from meeting the adequacy of representation requirement" of Rule 23(a)(4). * * * Adverting to, but not resolving charges of attorney conflict of interests, the Third Circuit addressed the question whether the named plaintiffs could adequately advance the interests of all class members. The Court of Appeals acknowledged that the District Court was certainly correct to this extent: " '[T]he members of the class are united in seeking the maximum possible recovery for their asbestos-related claims.' " * * * "But the settlement does more than simply provide a general recovery fund," the Court of Appeals immediately added; "[r]ather, it makes important judgments on how recovery is to be allocated among different kinds of plaintiffs, decisions that necessarily favor some claimants over others." 83 F.3d, at 630.

In the Third Circuit's view, the "most salient" divergence of interests separated plaintiffs already afflicted with an asbestos-related disease from plaintiffs without manifest injury (exposure-only plaintiffs). The latter would rationally want protection against inflation for distant recoveries. * * * They would also seek sturdy back-end opt-out rights and "causation provisions that can keep pace with changing science and medicine, rather than freezing in place the science of 1993." * * * Already injured parties, in contrast, would care little about such provisions and would rationally trade them for higher current payouts. * * * These and other adverse interests, the Court of Appeals carefully explained, strongly suggested that an undivided set of representatives could not adequately protect the discrete interests of both currently afflicted and exposure-only claimants.

The Third Circuit next rejected the District Court's determination that the named plaintiffs were "typical" of the class, noting that this Rule 23(a)(3) inquiry overlaps the adequacy of representation question: "both look to the potential for conflicts in the class." Id., at 632. Evident conflict problems, the court said, led it to hold that "no set of representatives can be 'typical' of this class." Ibid.

The Court of Appeals similarly rejected the District Court's assessment of the superiority of the class action. The Third Circuit initially noted that a class action so large and complex "could not be tried." * * * The court elaborated most particularly, however, on the unfairness of binding exposure-only plaintiffs who might be unaware of the class action or lack sufficient information about their exposure to make a reasoned decision whether to stay in or opt out. * * * "A series of statewide or more narrowly defined adjudications, either through consolidation under Rule 42(a) or as class actions under Rule 23, would seem preferable," the Court of Appeals said. *Id.*, at 634.

The Third Circuit, after intensive review, ultimately ordered decertification of the class and vacation of the District Court's antisuit injunction. * * *

We granted certiorari * * * and now affirm.

* * *

III

In the 1966 class-action amendments, Rule 23(b)(3), the category at issue here, was "the most adventuresome" innovation. See Kaplan, A Prefatory Note, 10 B.C. Ind. & Com. L.Rev. 497, 497 (1969) (hereinafter Kaplan, Prefatory Note). Rule 23(b)(3) added to the complex-litigation arsenal class actions for damages designed to secure judgments binding all class members save those who affirmatively elected to be excluded. See 7A Charles Alan Wright, Arthur R. Miller, & Mary Kay Kane, Federal Practice and Procedure § 1777, p. 517 (2d ed.1986) (hereinafter Wright, Miller, & Kane); * * * Rule 23(b)(3) "opt-out" class actions superseded the former "spurious" class action, so characterized because it generally functioned as a permissive joinder ("opt-in") device. See 7A Wright, Miller, & Kane § 1753, at 28–31, 42–44 * * *.

Framed for situations in which "class-action treatment is not as clearly called for" as it is in Rule 23(b)(1) and (b)(2) situations, Rule 23(b)(3) permits certification where class suit "may nevertheless be convenient and desirable." Adv. Comm. Notes, 28 U.S.C.App., p. 697. * * * In adding "predominance" and "superiority" to the qualification-for-certification list, the Advisory Committee sought to cover cases "in which a class action would achieve economies of time, effort, and expense, and promote ... uniformity of decision as to persons similarly situated, without sacrificing procedural fairness or bringing about other undesirable results." [Those who drafted the provision were] * * * [s]ensitive to the competing tugs of individual autonomy for those who might prefer to go it alone or in a smaller unit, on the one hand, and systemic efficiency on the other * * *.

Rule 23(b)(3) includes a nonexhaustive list of factors pertinent to a court's "close look" at the predominance and superiority criteria * * *.

While the text of Rule 23(b)(3) does not exclude from certification cases in which individual damages run high, the Advisory Committee had dominantly in mind vindication of "the rights of groups of people who individually would be without effective strength to bring their opponents into court at all." Kaplan, Prefatory Note 497. * * *

[To protect the rights of individuals, they must be sent notice of their right to opt out and, if they choose to remain without the class, the action may not be dismissed or compromised without notice to them and subsequent court approval.] * * *

In the decades since the 1966 revision of Rule 23, class-action practice has become ever more "adventuresome" as a means of coping with claims too numerous to secure their "just, speedy, and inexpensive determination" one by one. See Fed. Rule Civ. Proc. 1. The development reflects concerns about the efficient use of court resources and the conservation of funds to compensate claimants who do not line up early in a litigation queue. * * *

IV

We granted review to decide the role settlement may play, under existing Rule 23, in determining the propriety of class certification. The Third Circuit's opinion stated that each of the requirements of Rule 23(a) and (b)(3) "must be satisfied without taking into account the settlement." 83 F.3d, at 626 * * * That statement, petitioners urge, is incorrect.

We agree with petitioners to this limited extent: Settlement is relevant to a class certification. The Third Circuit's opinion bears modification in that respect. But, as we earlier observed, * * * the Court of Appeals in fact did not ignore the settlement; instead, that court homed in on settlement terms in explaining why it found the absentees' interests inadequately represented. * * * The Third Circuit's close inspection of the settlement in that regard was altogether proper.

Confronted with a request for settlement-only class certification, a district court need not inquire whether the case, if tried, would present intractable management problems, see Fed. Rule Civ. Proc. 23(b)(3)(D), for the proposal is that there be no trial. But other specifications of the Rule—those designed to protect absentees by blocking unwarranted or overbroad class definitions—demand undiluted, even heightened, attention in the settlement context. Such attention is of vital importance, for a court asked to certify a settlement class will lack the opportunity, present when a case is litigated, to adjust the class, informed by the proceedings as they unfold. See Rule 23(c), (d).

* * * Subdivisions (a) and (b) focus court attention on whether a proposed class has sufficient unity so that absent members can fairly be bound by decisions of class representatives. That dominant concern persists when settlement, rather than trial, is proposed.

The safeguards provided by the Rule 23(a) and (b) class-qualifying criteria, we emphasize, are not impractical impediments—checks shorn of utility— in the settlement-class context. First, the standards set for the protection of absent class members serve to inhibit appraisals of the chancellor's foot kind—class certifications dependent upon the court's gestalt judgment or overarching impression of the settlement's fairness.

Second, if a fairness inquiry under Rule 23(e) controlled certification, eclipsing Rule 23(a) and (b), and permitting class designation despite the impossibility of litigation, both class counsel and court would be disarmed. Class counsel confined to settlement negotiations could not use the threat of litigation to press for a better offer, see Coffee, Class Wars: The Dilemma of the Mass Tort Class Action, 95 Colum.L.Rev. 1343, 1379–1380 (1995), and the court would face a bargain proffered for its approval without benefit of adversarial investigation, see, e.g., Kamilewicz v. Bank of Boston Corp., 100 F.3d 1348, 1352 (7th Cir.1996) (Easterbrook, J., dissenting from denial of rehearing en banc) (parties "may even put one over on the court, in a staged performance"), cert. denied, 520 U.S. 1204, 117 S.Ct. 1569, 137 L.Ed.2d 714 (1997).

Federal courts, in any case, lack authority to substitute for Rule 23's certification criteria a standard never adopted—that if a settlement is "fair," then certification is proper. Applying to this case criteria the rulemakers set, we conclude that the Third Circuit's appraisal is essentially correct. Although that court should have acknowledged that settlement is a factor in the calculus, a remand is not warranted on that account. The Court of Appeals' opinion amply demonstrates why—with or without a settlement on the table—the sprawling class the District Court certified does not satisfy Rule 23's requirements.

A

We address first the requirement of Rule 23(b)(3) that "[common] questions of law or fact ... predominate over any questions affecting only individual members." The District Court concluded that predominance was satisfied based on two factors: class members' shared experience of asbestos exposure and their common "interest in receiving prompt and fair compensation for their claims, while minimizing the risks and transaction costs inherent in the asbestos litigation process as it occurs presently in the tort system." 157 F.R.D., at 316. The settling parties also contend that the settlement's fairness is a common question, predominating over disparate legal issues that might be pivotal in litigation but become irrelevant under the settlement.

The predominance requirement stated in Rule 23(b)(3), we hold, is not met by the factors on which the District Court relied. The benefits asbestos-exposed persons might gain from the establishment of a grand-scale compensation scheme is a matter fit for legislative consideration, * * * but it is not pertinent to the predominance inquiry. That inquiry trains on the legal or factual questions that qualify each class member's case as a genuine controversy, questions that preexist any settlement.

In this respect, the predominance requirement of Rule 23(b)(3) is similar to the requirement of Rule 23(a)(3) that "claims or defenses" of the named representatives must be "typical of the claims or defenses of the class." The words "claims or defenses" in this context—just as in the context of Rule 24(b)(2) governing permissive intervention—"manifestly refer to the kinds of claims or defenses that can be raised in courts of law as part of an actual or impending law suit." Diamond v. Charles, 476 U.S. 54, 76–77, 106 S.Ct. 1697, 1711, 90 L.Ed.2d 48 (1986) (O'CONNOR, J., concurring in part and concurring in judgment).

The Rule 23(b)(3) predominance inquiry tests whether proposed classes are sufficiently cohesive to warrant adjudication by representation. See 7A Wright, Miller, & Kane 518–519. The inquiry appropriate under Rule 23(e), on the other hand, protects unnamed class members "from unjust or unfair settlements affecting their rights when the representatives become fainthearted before the action is adjudicated or are able to secure satisfaction of their individual claims by a compromise." See 7B Wright, Miller, & Kane § 1797, at 340–341. But it is not the mission of Rule 23(e) to assure the class cohesion that legitimizes representative action in the first place. If a common interest in a fair compromise could satisfy the predominance requirement of Rule

23(b)(3), that vital prescription would be stripped of any meaning in the settlement context.

The District Court also relied upon this commonality: "The members of the class have all been exposed to asbestos products supplied by the defendants. . . . " 157 F.R.D., at 316. Even if Rule 23(a)'s commonality requirement may be satisfied by that shared experience, the predominance criterion is far more demanding. * * * Given the greater number of questions peculiar to the several categories of class members, and to individuals within each category, and the significance of those uncommon questions, any overarching dispute about the health consequences of asbestos exposure cannot satisfy the Rule 23(b)(3) predominance standard. * * *

"The [exposure-only] plaintiffs especially share little in common, either with each other or with the presently injured class members. It is unclear whether they will contract asbestos-related disease and, if so, what disease each will suffer. They will also incur different medical expenses because their monitoring and treatment will depend on singular circumstances and individual medical histories." [83 F.3d at 626.] * * * Differences in state law, the Court of Appeals observed, compound these disparities. * * *

No settlement class called to our attention is as sprawling as this one. * * * Predominance is a test readily met in certain cases alleging consumer or securities fraud or violations of the antitrust laws. * * * Even mass tort cases arising from a common cause or disaster may, depending upon the circumstances, satisfy the predominance requirement. The Advisory Committee for the 1966 revision of Rule 23, it is true, noted that "mass accident" cases are likely to present "significant questions, not only of damages but of liability and defenses of liability, . . . affecting the individuals in different ways." * * * And the Committee advised that such cases are "ordinarily not appropriate" for class treatment. * * * But the text of the Rule does not categorically exclude mass tort cases from class certification, and District Courts, since the late 1970's, have been certifying such cases in increasing number. * * * The Committee's warning, however, continues to call for caution when individual stakes are high and disparities among class members great. As the Third Circuit's opinion makes plain, the certification in this case does not follow the counsel of caution. That certification cannot be upheld, for it rests on a conception of Rule 23(b)(3)'s predominance requirement irreconcilable with the Rule's design.

B

Nor can the class approved by the District Court satisfy Rule 23(a)(4)'s requirement that the named parties "will fairly and adequately protect the interests of the class." The adequacy inquiry under Rule 23(a)(4) serves to uncover conflicts of interest between named parties and the class they seek to represent. * * *

As the Third Circuit pointed out, named parties with diverse medical conditions sought to act on behalf of a single giant class rather than on behalf of discrete subclasses. In significant respects, the interests of those within the single class are not aligned. Most saliently, for the currently injured, the critical goal is generous immediate payments. That goal tugs against the interest of exposure-only plaintiffs in ensuring an ample, inflation-protected fund for the future. * * *

The disparity between the currently injured and exposure-only categories of plaintiffs, and the diversity within each category are not made insignificant by the District Court's finding that petitioners' assets suffice to pay claims under the settlement. * * * Although this is not a "limited fund" case certified under Rule 23(b)(1)(B), the terms of the settlement reflect essential allocation decisions designed to confine compensation and to limit defendants' liability. For example, as earlier described, * * * the settlement includes no adjustment for inflation; only a few claimants per year can opt out at the back end; and loss-of-consortium claims are extinguished with no compensation.

The settling parties, in sum, achieved a global compromise with no structural assurance of fair and adequate representation for the diverse groups and individuals affected. Although the named parties alleged a range of complaints, each served generally as representative for the whole, not for a separate constituency. * * *

The Third Circuit found no assurance here—either in the terms of the settlement or in the structure of the negotiations—that the named plaintiffs operated under a proper understanding of their representational responsibilities. * * * That assessment, we conclude, is on the mark.

* * *

V

The argument is sensibly made that a nationwide administrative claims processing regime would provide the most secure, fair, and efficient means of compensating victims of asbestos exposure. Congress, however, has not adopted such a solution. And Rule 23, which must be interpreted with fidelity to the Rules Enabling Act and applied with the interests of absent class members in close view, cannot carry the large load CCR, class counsel, and the District Court heaped upon it. As this case exemplifies, the rulemakers' prescriptions for class actions may be endangered by "those who embrace [Rule 23] * * * too enthusiastically just as [they are by] those who approach [the Rule] * * * with distaste." C. Wright, Law of Federal Courts 508 (5th ed.1994); cf. 83 F.3d, at 634 (suggesting resort to less bold aggregation techniques, including more narrowly defined class certifications).

* * *

For the reasons stated, the judgment of the Court of Appeals for the Third Circuit is

Affirmed.

JUSTICE O'CONNOR took no part in the consideration or decision of this case.

JUSTICE BREYER, with whom JUSTICE STEVENS joins, concurring in part and dissenting in part.

Although I agree with the Court's basic holding that "[s]ettlement is relevant to a class certification," * * * I find several problems in its approach that lead me to a different conclusion. First, I believe that the need for settlement in this mass tort case, with hundreds of thousands of lawsuits, is greater than the Court's opinion suggests. Second, I would give more weight than would the majority to settlement-related issues for purposes of determining whether common issues predominate. Third, I am uncertain about the Court's determination of adequacy of representation, and do not believe it appropriate for this Court to second-guess the District Court on the matter without first having the Court of Appeals consider it. Fourth, I am uncertain about the tenor of an opinion that seems to suggest the settlement is unfair. And fifth, in the absence of further review by the Court of Appeals, I cannot accept the majority's suggestions that "notice" is inadequate.

These difficulties flow from the majority's review of what are highly fact-based, complex, and difficult matters, matters that are inappropriate for initial review before this Court. The law gives broad leeway to district courts in making class certification decisions, and their judgments are to be reviewed by the court of appeals only for abuse of discretion. * * * Indeed, the District Court's certification decision rests upon more than 300 findings of fact reached after five weeks of comprehensive hearings. Accordingly, I do not believe that we should in effect set aside the findings of the District Court. That court is far more familiar with the issues and litigants than is a court of appeals or are we, and therefore has "broad power and discretion ... with respect to matters involving the certification" of class actions. Reiter v. Sonotone Corp., 442 U.S. 330, 345, 99 S.Ct. 2326, 2334, 60 L.Ed.2d 931 (1979. * * *

I do not believe that we can rely upon the Court of Appeals' review of the District Court record, for that review, and its ultimate conclusions, are infected by a legal error. * * * There is no evidence that the Court of Appeals at any point considered the settlement as something that would help the class meet Rule 23. I find, moreover, the fact-related issues presented here sufficiently close to warrant further detailed appellate court review under the correct legal standard. * * *

I

First, I believe the majority understates the importance of settlement in this case. Between 13 and 21 million workers have been exposed to asbestos in the workplace—over the past 40 or 50 years—but the most severe instances of such exposure probably occurred three or four decades ago. * * * This exposure has led to several hundred thousand lawsuits, about 15% of which involved claims for cancer and about 30% for asbestosis. * * * About half of the suits have involved claims for pleural thickening and plaques—the harmfulness of which is apparently controversial. (One expert below testified that they "don't transform into cancer" and are not "predictor[s] of future disease," App. 781.) Some of those who suffer from the most serious injuries, however, have received little or no compensation. * * * These lawsuits have taken up more than 6% of all federal civil filings in one recent year, and are subject to a delay that is twice that of other civil suits. * * *

Delays, high costs, and a random pattern of noncompensation led the Judicial Conference Ad Hoc Committee on Asbestos Litigation to transfer all federal asbestos personal-injury cases to the Eastern District of Pennsylvania in an effort to bring about a fair and comprehensive settlement. * * *

Although the transfer of the federal asbestos cases did not produce a general settlement, it was intertwined with and led to a lengthy year-long negotiation between the cochairs of the Plaintiff's Multi–District Litigation Steering Committee (elected by the Plaintiff's Committee Members and approved by the District Court) and the 20 asbestos defendants who are before us here. * * * In the end, the negotiations produced a settlement that, the District Court determined based on its detailed review of the process, was "the result of arms-length adversarial negotiations by extraordinarily competent and experienced attorneys." [157 F.R.D.], at 335.

The District Court, when approving the settlement, concluded that it improved the plaintiffs' chances of compensation and reduced total legal fees and other transaction costs by a significant amount. Under the previous system, according to the court, "[t]he sickest of victims often go uncompensated for years while valuable funds go to others who remain unimpaired by their mild asbestos disease." Ibid. The court believed the settlement would create a compensation system that would make more money available for plaintiffs who later develop serious illnesses.

I mention this matter because it suggests that the settlement before us is unusual in terms of its importance, both to many potential plaintiffs and to defendants, and with respect to the time, effort, and expenditure that it reflects. All of which leads me to be reluctant to set aside the District Court's findings without more assurance than I have that they are wrong. I cannot obtain that assurance through comprehensive review of the record because that is properly the job of the Court of Appeals and that court, understandably, but as we now hold, mistakenly, believed that settlement was not a relevant (and, as I would say, important) consideration.

Second, the majority, in reviewing the District Court's determination that common "issues of fact and law predominate," says that the predominance "inquiry trains on the legal or factual questions that qualify each class member's case as a genuine controversy, questions that preexist any settlement." * * * I find it difficult to interpret this sentence in a way that could lead me to the majority's conclusion. If the majority means that these pre-settlement questions are what matters, then how does it reconcile its statement with its basic conclusion that "settlement is relevant" to class certification, or with the numerous lower court authority that says that settlement is not only relevant, but important? * * *

Nor do I understand how one could decide whether common questions "predominate" in the abstract—without looking at what is likely to be at issue in the proceedings that will ensue, namely, the settlement. Every group of human beings, after all, has some features in common, and some that differ. How can a court make a contextual judgment of the sort that Rule 23 requires without looking to what proceedings will follow? * * *

The majority may mean that the District Court gave too much weight to the settlement. But I am not certain how it can reach that conclusion. It cannot rely upon the Court of Appeals, for that court gave no positive weight at all to the settlement. * * * The settlement is relevant because it means that these common features and interests are likely to be important in the proceeding that would ensue—a proceeding that would focus primarily upon whether or not the proposed settlement fairly and properly satisfied the interests class members had in common. That is to say, the settlement underscored the importance of (a) the common fact of exposure, (b) the common interest in receiving some compensation for certain rather than running a strong risk of no compensation, and (c) the common interest in avoiding large legal fees, other transaction costs, and delays. * * *

Of course, as the majority points out, there are also important differences among class members. * * * The relevant question, however, is how much these differences matter in respect to the legal proceedings that lie ahead. Many, if not all, toxic tort class actions involve plaintiffs with such differences. And the differences in state law are of diminished importance in respect to a proposed settlement in which the defendants have waived all defenses and agreed to compensate all those who were injured. * * *

These differences might warrant subclasses * * *. Or these differences may be too serious to permit an effort at group settlement. This kind of determination, as I have said, is one that the law commits to the discretion of the district court—reviewable for abuse of discretion by a court of appeals. I believe that we are far too distant from the litigation itself to reweigh the fact-specific Rule 23 determinations and to find them erroneous without the benefit of the Court of Appeals first having restudied the matter with today's legal standard in mind.

Third, the majority concludes that the "representative parties" will not "fairly and adequately protect the interests of the class." Rule 23(a)(4). It finds a serious conflict between plaintiffs who are now injured and those who may be injured in the future because "for the currently injured, the critical goal is generous immediate payments," a goal that "tugs against the interest of exposure-only plaintiffs in ensuring an ample, inflation-protected fund for the future." * * *

I agree that there is a serious problem, but it is a problem that often exists in toxic tort cases. * * * And it is a problem that potentially exists whenever a single defendant injures several plaintiffs, for a settling plaintiff leaves fewer assets available for the others. With class actions, at least, plaintiffs have the consolation that a district court, thoroughly familiar with the facts, is charged with the responsibility of ensuring that the interests of no class members are sacrificed.

But this Court cannot easily safeguard such interests through review of a cold record. "What constitutes adequate representation is a question of fact that depends on the circumstances of each case." 7A Wright, Miller, & Kane, Federal Practice and Procedure § 1765, at 271. * * * The majority's use of the lack of an inflation adjustment as evidence of inadequacy of representation for future plaintiffs, * * * is one example of this difficulty. An inflation adjustment might not be as valuable as the majority assumes if most plaintiffs are old and not worried about receiving compensation decades from now. There are, of course, strong arguments as to its value. But that disagreement is one that this Court is poorly situated to resolve.

Further, certain details of the settlement that are not discussed in the majority opinion suggest that the settlement may be of greater benefit to future plaintiffs than the majority suggests. The District Court concluded that future plaintiffs receive a "significant value" from the settlement due to a variety of its items that benefit future plaintiffs, such as: (1) tolling the statute of limitations so that class members "will no longer be forced to file premature lawsuits or risk their claims being time-barred"; (2) waiver of defenses to liability; (3) payment of claims, if and when members become sick, pursuant to the settlement's compensation standards, which avoids "the uncertainties, long delays and high transaction costs [including attorney's fees] of the tort system"; (4) "some assurance that there will be funds available if and when they get sick," based on the finding that each defendant "has shown an ability to fund the payment of all qualifying claims" under the settlement; and (5) the right to additional compensation if cancer develops (many settlements for plaintiffs with noncancerous conditions bar such additional claims). 157 F.R.D., at 292. For these reasons, and others, the District Court found that the distinction between present and future plaintiffs was "illusory." Id., at 317–318.

I do not know whether or not the benefits are more or less valuable than an inflation adjustment. But I can certainly recognize an argument that they are. * * * The difficulties inherent in both knowing and understanding the vast number of relevant individual fact-based determinations here counsel heavily in favor of deference to district court decisionmaking in Rule 23 decisions. Or, at the least, making certain that appellate court review has taken place with the correct standard in mind.

Fourth, I am more agnostic than is the majority about the basic fairness of the settlement. * * * The District Court's conclusions rested upon complicated factual findings that are not easily cast aside. It is helpful to consider some of them, such as its determination that the settlement provided "fair compensation ... while reducing the delays and transaction costs endemic to the asbestos litigation process" and that "the proposed class action settlement is superior to other available methods for the fair and efficient resolution of the asbestos-related personal injury claims of class members." 157 F.R.D., at 316 (citation omitted) * * *. Indeed, the settlement has been endorsed as fair and reasonable by the AFL–CIO (and its Building and Construction Trades Department), which represents a " 'substantial percentage' " of class members, 157 F.R.D., at 325, and which has a role in monitoring implementation of the settlement, id., at 285. I do not intend to pass judgment upon the settlement's fairness, but I do believe that these matters would have to be explored in far greater depth before I could reach a conclusion about fairness. And that task, as I have said, is one for the Court of Appeals.

* * *

ORTIZ v. FIBREBOARD CORP.

Supreme Court of the United States, 1999.
527 U.S. 815, 119 S.Ct. 2295, 144 L.Ed.2d 715.

[Fibreboard was and is the subject of many personal injury lawsuits arising from exposure to its asbestos products. It already had settled some 45,000 claims, when, along with its insurers, it decided, with a group of plaintiffs' lawyers, on a plan to effect a "Global Settlement" of the majority of its remaining liability. Basically, Fibreboard and its insurers would put up $1,535 billion for asbestos claimants who would file a Rule 23(b)(1)(B) class action, based on the notion that there was a "limited fund" to pay members of the class.

At the time of the settlement agreement a lawsuit was before a California Court of Appeal to determine to what extent, if any, the insurers were liable for a majority of the plaintiff's damages. Thus, the agreement, if approved, would include settlement of that dispute. A separate agreement, the "Trilateral Settlement Agreement," was reached by which the insurers would put up $2 billion to cover the situation that would exist if the class action was not approved by the federal courts. Suit was then brought in the federal court in the Eastern District of Texas. The plan called upon Fibreboard and its insurers to place the agreed upon amount in a trust. Individual claimants were provided with a process for settling their claims with the trust. If no settlement could be reached, claimants were required to engage in mediation, arbitration, and a mandatory settlement conference. After exhausting that process a claimant could bring a court proceeding against the trust, but there would be a $500,000 limit on recovery and punitive damages and prejudgment interest would be barred. The class did not cover all claimants. Some 45,000 individuals who had settled their claims were excluded along with some 53,000 who had suits pending.

The trial court, after extensive hearings, found that the class action met the requirements of Rule 23(a), and fell within the "limited fund" provision of Rule 23(b)(1)(B). It determined that the plan provided a "fair, adequate, and reasonable" settlement under Rule 23(e). On appeal the Fifth Circuit affirmed both the certification of the class and the adequacy of the settlement. The Supreme Court granted certiorari.]

Certiorari to the United States Court of Appeals for the Fifth Circuit.

JUSTICE SOUTER delivered the opinion of the Court.

* * *

I

Like Amchem Products, Inc. v. Windsor, [p. 760, supra] * * * , this case is a class action prompted by the elephantine mass of asbestos cases, and our discussion in Amchem will suffice to show how this litigation defies customary judicial administration and calls for national legislation.

* * *

III

A

* * *

Rule 23(b)(1)(B) speaks from "a vantage point within the class, [from which the Advisory Committee] spied out situations where lawsuits conducted with individual members of the class would have the practical if not technical effect of concluding the interests of the other members as well, or of impairing the ability of the others to protect their own interests." Kaplan, Continuing Work of the Civil Committee: 1966 Amendments of the Federal Rules of Civil Procedure (I), 81 Harv. L.Rev. 356, 388 (1967) (hereinafter Kaplan, Continuing Work). Thus, the subdivision (read with subdivision (c)(2)) provides for certification of a class whose members have no right to withdraw, when "the prosecution of separate actions ... would create a risk" of "adjudications with respect to individual members of the class which would as a practical matter be dispositive of the interests of the other members not parties to the adjudications or substantially impair or impede their ability to protect their interests." * * * Classic examples of such a risk of impairment may, for example, be found in suits brought to reorganize fraternal-benefit societies * * * ; actions by shareholders to declare a dividend or otherwise to "fix [their] rights" * * * ; and actions charging "a breach of trust by an indenture trustee or other fiduciary similarly affecting the members of a large class" of beneficiaries, requiring an accounting or similar procedure "to restore the subject of the trust" * * *. In each of these categories, the shared character of rights claimed or relief awarded entails that any individual adjudication by a class member disposes of, or substantially affects, the interests of absent class members.

* * * One recurring type of such suits was the limited fund class action, aggregating "claims ... made by numerous persons against a fund insufficient to satisfy all claims." Adv. Comm. Notes 697 * * * . As the advisory committee recognized * * *, equity required absent parties to be represented, joinder being impractical, where individual claims to be satisfied from the one asset would, as a practical matter, prejudice the rights of absent claimants against a fund inadequate to pay them all.

Equity, of course, recognized the same necessity to bind absent claimants to a limited fund when no formal imposition of a constructive trust was entailed. * * *

B

The cases forming this pedigree of the limited fund class action as understood by the drafters of Rule 23 have a number of common characteristics, despite the variety of circumstances from which they arose. The points of resemblance are not necessarily the points of contention resolved in the particular cases, but they show what the Advisory Committee must have assumed would be at least a sufficient set of conditions to justify binding absent members of a class under Rule 23(b)(1)(B), from which no one has the right to secede.

The first and most distinctive characteristic is that the totals of the aggregated liquidated claims and the fund available for satisfying them, set definitely at their maximums, demonstrate the inadequacy of the fund to pay all the claims. The concept driving this type of suit was insufficiency, which alone justified the limit on an early feast to avoid a later famine. * * *

Second, the whole of the inadequate fund was to be devoted to the overwhelming claims. * * * It went without saying that the defendant or estate or constructive trustee with the inadequate assets had no opportunity to benefit himself or claimants of lower priority by holding back on the amount distributed to the class. The limited fund cases thus ensured that the class as a whole was given the best deal; they did not give a defendant a better deal than seriatim litigation would have produced.

Third, the claimants identified by a common theory of recovery were treated equitably among themselves. The cases assume that the class will comprise everyone who might state a claim on a single or repeated set of facts, invoking a common theory of recovery, to be satisfied from the limited fund as the source of payment. * * *

In sum, mandatory class treatment through representative actions on a limited fund theory was justified with reference to a "fund" with a definitely ascertained limit, all of which would be distributed to satisfy all those with liquidated claims based on a common theory of liability, by an equitable, pro rata distribution.

C

The Advisory Committee, and presumably the Congress in approving subdivision (b)(1)(B), must have assumed that an action with these characteristics would satisfy the limited fund rationale cognizable under that subdivision. The question remains how far the same characteristics are necessary for limited fund treatment. While we cannot settle all the details of a subdivision (b)(1)(B) limited fund here (and so cannot decide the ultimate question whether settlements of multitudes of related tort actions are amenable to mandatory class treatment), there are good reasons to treat these characteristics as presumptively necessary, and not merely sufficient, to satisfy the limited fund rationale for a mandatory action. At the least, the burden of justification rests on the proponent of any departure from the traditional norm.

It is true, of course, that the text of Rule 23(b)(1)(B) is on its face open to a more lenient limited fund concept, just as it covers more historical antecedents than the limited fund. But the greater the leniency in departing from the historical limited fund model, the greater the likelihood of abuse in ways that will be apparent when we apply the limited fund criteria to the case before us. The prudent course, therefore, is to presume that when subdivision (b)(1)(B) was devised to cover limited fund actions, the object was to stay close to the historical model. As will be seen, this limiting construction finds support in the Advisory Committee's expressions of understanding, minimizes potential conflict with the Rules Enabling Act, and avoids serious constitutional concerns raised by the mandatory class resolution of individual legal claims, especially where a case seeks to resolve future liability in a settlement-only action.

* * * [I]t is clear that the Advisory Committee did not contemplate that the mandatory class action codified in subdivision (b)(1)(B) would be used to aggregate unliquidated tort claims on a limited fund rationale. * * * None of the examples cited in the Advisory Committee Notes or by Professor Kaplan in explaining Rule 23(b)(1)(B) remotely approach what was then described as a "mass accident" case. While the Advisory Committee focused much attention on the amenability of Rule 23(b)(3) to such cases, the Committee's debates are silent about resolving tort claims under a mandatory limited fund rationale under Rule 23(b)(1)(B). It is simply implausible that the Advisory Committee, so concerned about the potential difficulties posed by dealing with mass tort cases under Rule 23(b)(3), with its provisions for notice and the right to opt out, see Rule 23(c)(2), would have uncritically assumed that mandatory versions of such class actions, lacking such protections, could be certified under Rule 23(b)(1)(B). We do not, it is true, decide the ultimate question whether Rule 23(b)(1)(B) may ever be used to aggregate individual

tort claims * * *. But we do recognize that the Committee would have thought such an application of the Rule surprising, and take this as a good reason to limit any surprise by presuming that the Rule's historical antecedents identify requirements.

The Rules Enabling Act underscores the need for caution. * * * Petitioners argue that the Act has been violated here, asserting that the Global Settlement Agreement's priorities of claims and compromise of full recovery abrogated the state law that must govern this diversity action under 28 U.S.C. § 1652. * * * Although we need not grapple with the difficult choice-of-law and substantive state-law questions raised by petitioners' assertion, we do need to recognize the tension between the limited fund class action's pro rata distribution in equity and the rights of individual tort victims at law. Even if we assume that some such tension is acceptable under the Rules Enabling Act, it is best kept within tolerable limits by keeping limited fund practice under Rule 23(b)(1)(B) close to the practice preceding its adoption.

Finally, if we needed further counsel against adventurous application of Rule 23(b)(1)(B), the Rules Enabling Act and the general doctrine of constitutional avoidance would jointly sound a warning of the serious constitutional concerns that come with any attempt to aggregate individual tort claims on a limited fund rationale. First, the certification of a mandatory class followed by settlement of its action for money damages obviously implicates the Seventh Amendment jury trial rights of absent class members. We noted in Ross v. Bernhard [p. 968, infra] that since the merger of law and equity in 1938, it has become settled among the lower courts that "class action plaintiffs may obtain a jury trial on any legal issues they present." * * * By its nature, however, a mandatory settlement-only class action with legal issues and future claimants compromises their Seventh Amendment rights without their consent.

Second, and no less important, mandatory class actions aggregating damage claims implicate the due process "principle of general application in Anglo–American jurisprudence that one is not bound by a judgment in personam in a litigation in which he is not designated as a party or to which he has not been made a party by service of process," Hansberry v. Lee, [p. 718, supra] * * *.

The inherent tension between representative suits and the day-in-court ideal is only magnified if applied to damage claims gathered in a mandatory class. Unlike Rule 23(b)(3) class members, objectors to the collectivism of a mandatory subdivision (b)(1)(B) action have no inherent right to abstain. The legal rights of absent class members (which in a class like this one would include claimants who by definition may be unidentifiable when the class is certified) are resolved regardless either of their consent, or, in a class with objectors, their express wish to the contrary. And in settlement-only class actions the procedural protections built into the Rule to protect the rights of absent class members during litigation are never invoked in an adversarial setting * * *.

IV

The record on which the District Court rested its certification of the class for the purpose of the global settlement did not support the essential premises of mandatory limited fund actions. It failed to demonstrate that the fund was limited except by the agreement of the parties, and it showed exclusions from the class and allocations of assets at odds with the concept of limited fund treatment and the structural protections of Rule 23(a) explained in Amchem.

A

The defect of certification going to the most characteristic feature of a limited fund action was the uncritical adoption by both the District Court and the Court of Appeals of figures agreed upon by the parties in defining the limits of the fund and demonstrating its inadequacy. When a district court, as here, certifies for class action settlement only, the moment of certification requires "heightene[d] attention," Amchem * * *, to the justifications for binding the class members. * * * Thus, in an action such as this the settling parties must present not only their agreement, but evidence on which the district court may ascertain the limit and the insufficiency of the fund, with support in findings of fact following a proceeding in which the evidence is subject to challenge * * * .

We have already alluded to the difficulties facing limited fund treatment of huge numbers of actions for unliquidated damages arising from mass torts, the first such hurdle being a computation of the total claims. It is simply not a matter of adding up the liquidated amounts, as in the models of limited fund actions. Although we might assume arguendo that prior judicial experience with asbestos claims would allow a court to make a sufficiently reliable determination of the probable total, the District Court here apparently thought otherwise, concluding that "there is no way to predict Fibreboard's future asbestos liability with any certainty." 162 F.R.D., at 528. Nothing turns on this conclusion, however, since there was no adequate demonstration of the second element required for limited fund treatment, the upper limit of the fund itself, without which no showing of insufficiency is possible.

The "fund" in this case comprised both the general assets of Fibreboard and the insurance assets provided by the two policies * * *. As to Fibreboard's assets exclusive of the contested insurance, the District Court and the Fifth Circuit concluded that Fibreboard had a then-current sale value of $235 million that could be devoted to the limited fund. While that estimate may have been conservative, at least the District Court heard evidence and made an independent finding at some point in the proceedings. The same, however, cannot be said for the value of the disputed insurance. * * *

We do not, of course, know exactly what an independent valuation of the limit of the insurance assets would have shown. It might have revealed that even on the assumption that Fibreboard's coverage claim was sound, there would be insufficient assets to pay claims, considered with reference to their probable timing; if Fibreboard's own assets would not have been enough to pay the insurance shortfall plus any claims in excess of policy limits, the projected insolvency of the insurers and Fibreboard would have indicated a truly limited fund. (Nothing in the record, however, suggests that this would have been a supportable finding.) Or an independent valuation might have revealed assets of insufficient value to pay all projected claims if the assets were discounted by the prospects that the insurers would win the coverage cases. Or the Court's independent valuation might have shown, discount or no discount, the probability of enough assets to pay all projected claims, precluding certification of any mandatory class on a limited fund rationale. Throughout this litigation the courts have accepted the assumption that the third possibility was out of the question, and they may have been right. But objecting and unidentified class members alike are entitled to have the issue settled by specific evidentiary findings independent of the agreement of defendants and conflicted class counsel.

B

The explanation of need for independent determination of the fund has necessarily anticipated our application of the requirement of equity among members of the class. There are two issues, the inclusiveness of the class and the fairness of distributions to those within it. On each, this certification for settlement fell short.

The definition of the class excludes myriad claimants with causes of action, or foreseeable causes of action, arising from exposure to Fibreboard asbestos. While the class includes those with present claims never filed, present claims withdrawn without prejudice, and future claimants, it fails to include those who had previously settled with Fibreboard while retaining the right to sue again "upon development of an asbestos related malignancy," plaintiffs with claims pending against Fibreboard at the time of the initial announcement of the Global Settlement Agreement, and the plaintiffs in the "inventory" claims settled as a supposedly necessary step in reaching the global settlement * * * . The number of those outside the class who settled with a reservation of rights may be uncertain, but there is no such uncertainty about the significance of the settlement's exclusion of the 45,000 inventory plaintiffs and the plaintiffs in the unsettled present cases, estimated by the Guardian Ad Litem at more than 53,000 as of August 27, 1993 * * * . It is a fair question how far a natural class may be depleted by prior dispositions of claims and still qualify as a mandatory limited fund class, but there can be no question that such a mandatory settlement class will not qualify when in the very negotiations aimed at a class settlement, class counsel agree to exclude what could turn out to be as much as a third of the claimants that negotiators thought might eventually be involved, a substantial number of whom class counsel represent * * * .

Might such class exclusions be forgiven if it were shown that the class members with present claims and the outsiders ended up with comparable benefits? * * * As for the settled inventory claims, their plaintiffs appeared to have obtained better terms than the class members. They received an immediate payment of 50 percent of a settlement higher than the historical average, and would get the remainder if the global settlement were sustained (or the coverage litigation resolved, as it turned out to be by the Trilateral Settlement Agreement); the class members, by contrast, would be assured of a 3-year payout for claims settled, whereas the unsettled faced a prospect of mediation followed by arbitration as prior conditions of instituting suit, which would even then be subject to a recovery limit, a slower payout and the limitations of the trust's spendthrift protection. * * * Finally, as discussed below, even ostensible parity between settling nonclass plaintiffs and class members would be insufficient to overcome the failure to provide the structural protection of independent representation as for subclasses with conflicting interests.

On the second element of equity within the class, the fairness of the distribution of the fund among class members, the settlement certification is likewise deficient. Fair treatment in the older cases was characteristically assured by straightforward pro rata distribution of the limited fund. * * * While equity in such a simple sense is unattainable in a settlement covering present claims not specifically proven and claims not even due to arise, if at all, until some future time, at the least such a settlement must seek equity by providing for procedures to resolve the difficult issues of treating such differently situated claimants with fairness as among themselves.

First, it is obvious after Amchem that a class divided between holders of present and future claims (some of the latter involving no physical injury and to claimants not yet born) requires division into homogeneous subclasses under Rule 23(c)(4)(B), with separate representation to eliminate conflicting interests of counsel. * * * No such procedure was employed here, and the conflict was as contrary to the equitable obligation entailed by the limited fund rationale as it was to the requirements of structural protection applicable to all class actions under Rule 23(a)(4).

Second, the class included those exposed to Fibreboard's asbestos products both before and after 1959. The date is significant, for that year saw the expiration of Fibreboard's insurance policy with Continental, the one which provided the bulk of the insurance funds for the settlement. Pre–1959 claimants accordingly had more valuable claims than post–1959 claimants, * * * the consequence being a second instance of disparate interests within the certified class. While at some point there must be an end to reclassification with separate counsel, these two instances of conflict are well within the requirement of structural protection recognized in Amchem.

* * * Here, just as in the earlier case, the proponents of the settlement are trying to rewrite Rule 23; each ignores the fact that Rule 23 requires protections under subdivisions (a) and (b) against inequity and potential inequity at the pre-certification stage, quite independently of the required determination at postcertification fairness review under subdivision (e) that any settlement is fair in an overriding sense. A fairness hearing under subdivision (e) can no more swallow the preceding protective requirements of Rule 23 in a subdivision (b)(1)(B) action than in one under subdivision (b) (3).

C

A third contested feature of this settlement certification that departs markedly from the limited fund antecedents is the ultimate provision for a fund smaller than the assets understood by the Court of Appeals to be available for payment of the mandatory class members' claims; most notably, Fibreboard was allowed to retain virtually its entire net worth. Given our treatment of the two preceding deficiencies of the certification, there is of course no need to decide whether this feature of the agreement would alone be fatal to the Global Settlement Agreement. To ignore it entirely, however, would be so misleading that we have decided simply to identify the issue it raises, without purporting to resolve it at this time.

Fibreboard listed its supposed entire net worth as a component of the total (and allegedly inadequate) assets available for claimants, but subsequently retained all but $500,000 of that equity for itself. On the face of it, the arrangement seems irreconcilable with the justification of necessity in denying any opportunity for withdrawal of class members whose jury trial rights will be compromised, whose damages will be capped, and whose payments will be delayed. With Fibreboard retaining nearly all its net worth, it hardly appears that such a regime is the best that can be provided for class members. Given the nature of a limited fund and the need to apply its criteria at the certification stage, it is not enough for a District Court to say that it "need not ensure that a defendant designate a particular source of its assets to satisfy the class' claims; [but only that] the amount recovered by the class [be] fair." 162 F.R.D., at 527.

The District Court in this case seems to have had a further point in mind, however. One great advantage of class action treatment of mass tort cases is the opportunity to save the enormous transaction costs of piecemeal litigation, an advantage to which the settlement's proponents have referred in this case. Although the District Court made no specific finding about the transaction cost saving likely from this class settlement, estimating the amount in the "hundreds of millions," id., at 529, it did conclude that the amount would exceed Fibreboard's net worth as the Court valued it, ibid. (Fibreboard's net worth of $235 million "is considerably less than the likely savings in defense costs under the Global Settlement"). If a settlement thus saves transaction costs that would never have gone into a class member's pocket in the absence of settlement, may a credit for some of the savings be recognized in a mandatory class action as an incentive to settlement? It is at least a legitimate question, which we leave for another day. * * *

VI

* * *

The judgment of the Court of Appeals, accordingly, is reversed, and the case is remanded for further proceedings consistent with this opinion.

It is so ordered.

CHIEF JUSTICE REHNQUIST, with whom JUSTICE SCALIA and JUSTICE KENNEDY join, concurring.

JUSTICE BREYER's dissenting opinion highlights in graphic detail the massive impact of asbestos-related claims on the federal courts. * * * Were I devising a system for handling these claims on a clean slate, I would agree entirely with that dissent, which in turn approves the near-heroic efforts of the District Court in this case to make the best of a bad situation. Under the present regime, transactional costs will surely consume more and more of a relatively static amount of money to pay these claims.

But we are not free to devise an ideal system for adjudicating these claims. Unless and until the Federal Rules of Civil Procedure are revised, the Court's opinion correctly states the existing law, and I join it. But the "elephantine mass of asbestos cases," * * * cries out for a legislative solution.

JUSTICE BREYER, with whom JUSTICE STEVENS joins, dissenting.

* * * The District Court, in approving the settlement, made 446 factual findings, on the basis of which it concluded that the settlement was equitable, that the potential claimants had been well represented, and that the distinctions drawn among different categories of claimants were reasonable. * * *

The Court of Appeals, dividing 2 to 1, held that the settlement was lawful. * * * I would not set aside the Court of Appeals' judgment as the majority does. Accordingly, I dissent.

I

A

Four special background circumstances underlie this settlement and help to explain the reasonableness and consequent lawfulness of the relevant District Court determinations. First, as the majority points out, the settlement comprises part of an "elephantine mass of asbestos cases," which "defies customary judicial administration." * * * In the Eastern District of Texas, for example, one out of every three civil cases filed in 1990 was an asbestos case. * * * In the past decade nearly 80,000 new federal asbestos cases have been filed; more than 10,000 new federal asbestos cases were filed last year. * * *

The Judicial Conference found that asbestos cases on average take almost twice as long as other lawsuits to resolve. * * * Judge Parker, the experienced trial judge who approved this settlement, noted in one 3,000–member asbestos class action over which he presided that 448 of the original class members had died while the litigation was pending. Cimino v. Raymark Industries, Inc., 751 F.Supp. 649, 651 (E.D.Tex.1990). And yet, Judge Parker went on to state, if the district court could close "thirty cases a month, it would [still] take six and one-half years to try these cases and [due to new filings] there would be pending over 5,000 untouched cases" at the end of that time. Id., at 652. * * *

Second, an individual asbestos case is a tort case, of a kind that courts, not legislatures, ordinarily will resolve. It is the number of these cases, not their nature, that creates the special judicial problem. The judiciary cannot treat the problem as entirely one of legislative failure, as if it were caused, say, by a poorly drafted statute. Thus, when "calls for national legislation" go unanswered, * * * judges can and should search aggressively for ways, within the framework of existing law, to avoid delay and expense so great as to bring about a massive denial of justice.

Third, in that search the district courts may take advantage of experience that appellate courts do not have. Judge Parker, for example, has written of "a disparity of appreciation for the magnitude of the problem," growing out of the difference between the trial courts' "daily involvement with asbestos litigation" and the appellate courts' "limited" exposure to such litigation in infrequent appeals. * * *

Fourth, the alternative to class-action settlement is not a fair opportunity for each potential plaintiff to have his or her own day in court. Unusually high litigation costs, unusually long delays, and limitations upon the total amount of resources available for payment, together mean that most potential plaintiffs may not have a realistic alternative. And Federal Rule * * * 23 was designed to address situations in which the historical model of individual actions would not, for practical reasons, work. * * *

B

The case before us involves a class of individuals (and their families) exposed to asbestos manufactured by Fibreboard who, for the most part, had not yet sued or settled with Fibreboard as of August 1993. * * * [T]here is no doubt that a realistic assessment of the value of these claims far exceeds Fibreboard's total net worth.

But, as of 1993, one potentially short-lived additional asset promised potential claimants a greater recovery. That asset consisted of two insurance policies, one issued by Continental Casualty, the other by Pacific Indemnity. If the policies were valid (i.e., if they covered most of the relevant claims), they were worth several billion dollars; but if they were invalid, this asset was worth nothing. At that time, a separate case brought by Fibreboard against the insurance companies in California state court seemed likely to resolve the value of the policies in the near future. That separate litigation had a settlement value for the insurance companies. At the time the parties were negotiating, prior to the California court's decision, the insurance policies were worth, as the majority puts it, the value of "unlimited policy coverage" (i.e., perhaps the insurance companies' entire net worth) "discounted by the risk that Fibreboard would ultimately lose the coverage dispute litigation." * * *

The insurance companies offered to settle with both Fibreboard and those persons with claims against Fibreboard (who might have tried to sue the insurance companies directly). The settlement negotiations came to a head in August 1993, just as a California state appeals court was poised to decide the validity of the insurance policies. This fact meant speed was important, for the California court could well decide that the policies were worth nothing. It also meant that it was important to certify a non opt-out class of Fibreboard plaintiffs. If the class that entered into the settlement were an opt-out class, then members of that class could wait to see what the California court did. If the California court found the policies valid (hence worth many billions of dollars), they would opt out of the class and sue for everything they could get; if the California court found the policies invalid (and worth nothing), they would stick with the settlement. The insurance companies would gain little from that kind of settlement, and they would not agree to it. * * *

After eight days of hearings, the District Court found that the insurance policies plus Fibreboard's net worth amounted to a "limited fund," valued at $1.77 billion (the amount the insurance companies were willing to contribute to the settlement plus Fibreboard's value). * * * The court entered detailed factual findings. * * * It certified a "non opt-out" class. And the court approved the parties' Global Settlement Agreement. The Global Settlement Agreement allows those exposed to asbestos (and their families) to assert their Fibreboard claims against a fund that it creates. It does not limit recoveries for particular types of claims, but allows for individual determinations of damages based on all historically relevant individual factors and circumstances. * * * It contains spendthrift provisions designed to limit the total payouts for any particular year, and a requirement that the claimants with the most serious injuries be paid first in any year in which there is a shortfall. It also permits an individual who wishes to retain his right to bring an ordinary action in court to opt out of the arrangement (albeit after mediation and nonbinding arbitration), but sets a ceiling of $500,000 upon the recovery obtained by any person who does so. * * *

II

* * *

The case falls within the Rule's language as long as there was a significant "risk" that the total assets available to satisfy the claims of the class members would fall well below the likely total value of those claims, for in such circumstances the money would go to those claimants who brought their actions first, thereby "substantially impair[ing]" the "ability" of later claimants "to protect their interests." And the District Court found there was indeed such a "risk." * * *

I need not pursue the conceptual matter further, however, for the majority apparently concedes the conceptual point that a fund's limit may equal its "value discounted by risk." * * * But the majority sets forth three additional conditions, which it says are "sufficient ... to justify binding absent members of a class under Rule 23(b)(1)(B), from which no one has the right to secede." * * *

A

In my view, the first condition is substantially satisfied. No one doubts that the "totals of the aggregated" claims well exceed the value of the assets in the "fund available for satisfying them," at least if the fund totaled about what the District Court said it did, namely, $1.77 billion at most. The District Court said that the limited fund equaled in value "the sum of the value of Fibreboard plus the value of its insurance coverage," or $235 million plus $1.535 billion. * * * The Court of Appeals upheld the finding. * * * And the finding is adequately supported.

The District Court found that the insurance policies were not worth substantially more than $1.535 billion in part because there was a "significant risk" that the insurance policies would soon turn out to be worth nothing at all. 162 F.R.D., at 526. The court wrote that "Fibreboard might lose" its coverage, i.e., that it might lose "on one or more issues in the [California] Coverage Case, or that Fibreboard might lose its insurance coverage as a result of its assignment settlement program." Ibid.

* * *

The District Court arrived at the present value of the policies ($1.535 billion) by looking to a different settlement, the settlement arrived at in the insurance coverage case itself as a result of bargaining between Fibreboard and the insurance companies. * * * That settlement, embodied in the Trilateral Agreement, created a backup fund by taking from the insurance companies $1.535 billion (plus other money used to satisfy claims not here at issue) and simply setting it aside to use for the payment of claims brought against Fibreboard in the ordinary course by members of this class (in the event that the federal courts ultimately failed to approve the Global Settlement Agreement).

The Fifth Circuit approved this method of determining the value of the insurance policies. * * * And the majority itself sees nothing wrong with that method in principle. * * *

The majority rejects the District Court's valuation for a different reason. It says that the settlement negotiation that led to the valuation was not necessarily a fair one. The majority says it cannot make the necessary "arms-length bargaining" assumption because "[c]lass counsel" had a "great incentive to reach any agreement" in light of the fact that "some of the same lawyers ... had also negotiated the separate settlement of 45,000" pending cases, which was partially contingent upon a global settlement or other favorable resolution of the insurance dispute. * * *

The District Court and Court of Appeals, however, did accept the relevant "arms-length" assumption, with good reason. The relevant bargaining (i.e., the bargaining that led to the Trilateral Agreement that set the policies' value) was not between the plaintiffs' class counsel and the insurance companies; it was between Fibreboard and the insurance companies. And there is no reason to believe that that bargaining, engaged in to settle the California coverage dispute, was not "arms-length." That bargaining did not lead to a settlement that would release Fibreboard from potential tort liability. Rather, it led to a potential backup settlement that did not release Fibreboard from anything. It created a fund of insurance money, which, once exhausted, would have left Fibreboard totally exposed to tort claims. Consequently, Fibreboard had every incentive to squeeze as much money as possible out of the insurance companies, thereby creating as large a fund as possible in order to diminish the likelihood that it would eventually have to rely upon its own net worth to satisfy future asbestos plaintiffs.

* * * A perfect valuation, requiring lengthy study by independent experts, is not feasible in the context of such an unusual limited fund, one that comes accompanied with its own witching hour. Within weeks after the parties' settlement agreement, the insurance policies might well have disappeared, leaving most potential plaintiffs with little more than empty claims. The ship was about to sink, the trust fund to evaporate; time was important. * * *

B

I similarly believe that the second condition is satisfied. * * * The District Court found equitable treatment, and the Court of Appeals affirmed. But a majority of this Court now finds significant inequities arising out of class counsel's "egregious" conflict of interest, the settlement's substantive terms, and the District Court's failure to create subclasses. * * *

The District Court made 76 separate findings of fact, for example, in respect to potential conflicts of interest. * * * Of course, class counsel consisted of individual attorneys who represented other asbestos claimants, including many other Fibreboard claimants outside the certified class. Since Fibreboard had been settling cases contingent upon resolution of the insurance dispute for several years, any attorney who had been involved in previous litigation against Fibreboard was likely to suffer from a similar "conflict." So whom should the District Court have appointed to negotiate a settlement that had to be reached soon, if ever? Should it have appointed attorneys unfamiliar with Fibreboard and the history of its asbestos litigation? Where was the District Court to find those competent, knowledgeable, conflict-free attorneys? The District Court said they did not exist. Finding of Fact ¶ 372 says there is "no credible evidence of the existence of other 'conflict-free' counsel who were qualified to negotiate" a settlement within the necessary time. * * * Finding of Fact ¶ 317 adds that the District Court viewed it as "crucial ... to appoint asbestos attorneys who were experienced, knowledgeable, skilled and credible in view of the extremely short window of opportunity to negotiate a global settlement, and the very high risk to future claimants presented by the Coverage Case appeal." * * * Where is the clear error?

* * * In addition, more than 150 findings of fact, made after an 8–day hearing, support the District Court's finding that overall the settlement is "fair, adequate, and reasonable." * * *

The Fifth Circuit found that "[t]he record amply supports" these District Court findings. * * * Does the majority mean to set them aside? If not, does it mean to set forth a rigid principle of law, such as the principle that asbestos lawyers with clients outside a class, who will potentially benefit from a class settlement, can never represent a class in settlement negotiations? And does that principle apply no matter how unusual the circumstances, or no matter how necessary that representation might be? Why should there be such a rule of law? If there is not an absolute rule, however, I do not see how this Court can hold that the case before us is not that unusual situation.

Consider next the claim that "equity" required more subclasses. * * * To determine the "right" number of subclasses, a district court must weigh the advantages and disadvantages of bringing more lawyers into the case. The majority concedes as much when it says "at some point there must be an end to reclassification with separate counsel." * * * The District Court said that if there had "been as many separate attorneys" as the objectors wanted, "there is a significant possibility that a global settlement would not have been reached before the Coverage Case was resolved by the California Court of Appeal." * * * Finding of Fact ¶ 346 lists the shared common interests among subclasses that argue for single representation, including "avoiding the potentially disastrous results of a loss ... in the Coverage Case," "maximizing the total settlement contribution," "reducing transactions costs and delays," "minimizing ... attorney's fees," and "adopting" equitable claims payment "procedures." * * * Surely the District Court was within its discretion to conclude that "the point" to which the majority alludes was reached in this case.

* * * The Fifth Circuit found that the District Court "did not abuse its discretion in finding that the class was adequately represented and that subclasses were not required." 90 F.3d, at 982. This Court should not overturn these highly circumstance-specific judgments.

C

The majority's third condition raises a more difficult question. It says that the "whole of the inadequate fund" must be "devoted to the overwhelming claims." * * * Fibreboard's own assets, in theory, were available to pay tort claims, yet they were not included in the global settlement fund. Is that fact fatal?

I find the answer to this question in the majority's own explanation. It says that the third condition helps to guarantee that those who held the

> "inadequate assets had no opportunity to benefit [themselves] or claim-ants of lower priority by holding back on the amount distributed to the class. The limited fund cases thus ensured that the class as a whole was given the best deal; they did not give a defendant a better deal than seriatim litigation would have produced." * * *

That explanation suggests to me that Rule 23(b)(1)(B) permits a slight relaxation of this absolute requirement, where its basic purpose is met, i.e., where there is no doubt that "the class as a whole was given the best deal," and where there is good reason for allowing the third condition's substantial, rather than its literal, satisfaction.

* * *

There is no doubt in this case that the settlement made far more money available to satisfy asbestos claims than was likely to occur in its absence. And the District Court found that administering the fund would involve transac-tion costs of only 15%. * * * A comparison of that 15% figure with the 61% transaction costs figure applicable to asbestos cases in general suggests hundreds of millions of dollars in savings—an amount greater than Fibre-board's net worth. And, of course, not only is it better for the injured plaintiffs, it is far better for Fibreboard, its employees, its creditors, and the communities where it is located for Fibreboard to remain a working enter-prise, rather than slowly forcing it into bankruptcy while most of its money is spent on asbestos lawyers and expert witnesses. I would consequently find substantial compliance with the majority's third condition.

Because I believe that all three of the majority's conditions are satisfied, and because I see no fatal conceptual difficulty, I would uphold the determina-tion, made by the District Court and affirmed by the Court of Appeals, that the insurance policies (along with Fibreboard's net value) amount to a classic limited fund, within the scope of Rule 23(b)(1)(B). * * *

Notes and Questions

1. Following the decertification of the settlement classes in *Amchem* and *Ortiz*, there was disagreement on the effect of these decisions on future mass tort class action settlements. One commentator suggested that: "The real effect of *Amchem* on the law of class action settlement is * * * not a set of particular rules that settlement class cases must conform to, but rather a limit on the kinds of cases that may be brought as class actions." Weber, *A Consent–Based Approach to Class Action Settlement: Improving* Amchem Products, Inc. v. Windsor, 59 Ohio St.L.Rev. 1155, 1177 (1998). Do the Supreme Court decisions suggest that certain mass tort claims are not appropriate for class action certification, or simply that when a large number of claimants are involved and a settlement extinguishes their causes of action without each individual's express consent, the court should pay particular attention to the circumstances in which the settlement was reached as well as its substantive fairness?

2. Is it possible for the courts to fashion an acceptable asbestos settlement, or does the problem, as Chief Justice Rehnquist insists in his concurring opinion in *Ortiz,* "cr[y] out for a legislative solution"? One prominent plaintiffs' class action attorney has commented that "all of the most sincere and intensive efforts by attorneys general, the plaintiffs' bar, the public health community, children's advocates, and politicians themselves failed to produce a Congressional resolution to tobacco claims," concluding that the likelihood of reaching a legislative solution for the asbestos problem is slim. Cabraser, *Class Action Trends and Developments after* Amchem *and* Ortiz, SE28 ALI–ABA 617, 660 (1999). Should the fact that if a settlement is not approved the plaintiffs will suffer additional delay, and might never receive compensation for their injuries, play a role in evaluating of the settlement? Is Congress the right body to provide recourse for victims of asbestos or any other mass tort? Or is it true, as the author notes, that "[w]hat some may find disturbing [about the decisions in *Amchem* and *Ortiz*] is the Supreme Court majority's apparent retreat from the quintessential judicial power and role of dispensing equity in a difficult situation"? Id.

3. In a recent article, Professor Coffee applies the principles of exit, loyalty, and voice that are central to legitimate democratic representation to the class-action context. Coffee, *Class Action Accountability: Reconciling Exit, Voice, and Loyalty in Representative Litigation,* 100 Colum.L.Rev. 370 (2000). Professor Coffee suggests that one element sometimes may be substituted for another, and in fact may be more appropriate in class action situations. The Supreme Court has focused on loyalty and class cohesion, which will likely result in a "division into warring fiefdoms" of subclasses, and ultimately may weaken the claim that the class action is superior to adjudication of individual claims. On the other hand, increasing voice may not be appropriate for class actions, either, because class representatives actually play a very small role in the development of a large class action. For example, it is often class counsel who finds the client in order to bring the class action and not the other way around. Therefore, the best solution may be enhancement of class members' exit opportunities at all stages of the litigation, which ensures that they may opt out when a settlement is not in their best interests. Is this realistic considering the limited information and understanding that ordinary plaintiffs have regarding the settlement and their other options? How much control should class counsel or the class representatives have over important decisions?

4. One critic has suggested that the focus on opt-out rights places too much emphasis on the procedural concerns associated with due process and not enough on its substantive aspects. As Professor Rutherglen points out, although opt-out procedures are designed to protect the class, they have been invoked most often by defendants to defeat attempts at class certification. Since potential members are required to opt-out so early in the proceedings, they do not receive information when it would be most useful to them—at the settlement point. In contrast, if an opt-out notice were sent at settlement, then it could be used by the class to express their approval or disapproval of the attorney's representation. Rutherglen, *Better Late Than Never: Notice and Opt Out at the Settlement Stage of Class Actions,* 71 N.Y.U.L.Rev. 258 (1996).

5. In decertifying the settlement class in *Ortiz,* the Supreme Court criticized Fibreboard's "constructive bankruptcy" (remember that the defendant is still a solvent corporation) because it allowed the defendant corporation to circumvent state law and procedural requirements by treating it as though it were in bankruptcy proceedings. Fibreboard, like any corporate bankrupt, was able to

create a fund limited to its insurance coverage to satisfy all of its tort creditors. However, since the Bankruptcy Code did not actually apply, the defendant did not have to accord all its creditors equal treatment. The defendant was able to place its shareholders ahead of its tort creditors. Thus, Fibreboard was required only to contribute a small sum ($10 million) in comparison to the insurers' contributions to the fund. Bear in mind that it is the creation of this limited fund that qualified Fibreboard for Rule 23(b)(1) certification, making the class mandatory. The dramatic increase in the company's stock price that followed the announcement of the settlement terms suggests that the gains conferred upon its stockholders were substantial.

A more common practice, however, has been for corporations to use bankruptcy proceedings as a way of avoiding extensive future litigation. See, e.g., In re Johns–Manville Corp., 78 F.3d 764 (2d Cir.1996). Under this approach, the corporation reorganizes its assets to create a trust for which all claimants would compete on equal footing. As a result, the shareholders' claims are satisfied only after the tort creditor's claims and the value of the former's equity interest is likely to drop significantly. However, this approach is not without its problems. Settlement funds often are depleted entirely by present claimants, leaving future claimants without recovery.

6.   Subsequent to *Amchem* and *Ortiz*, a settlement class of individuals who took the diet drugs Fenfluramine and Dexfenfluramine, which were found to cause a heart valve abnormality in some patients, was approved in IN RE DIET DRUGS (PHENTERMINE, FENFLURAMINE, DEXFENFLURAMINE) PRODUCTS LIABILITY LITIGATION, 2000 WL 1222042 (E.D.Pa 2000). There were approximately six million individuals in the United States who had been prescribed one of these drugs between 1995 and 1997. Plaintiffs were divided into subclasses depending on the length of time they took the drugs and the severity of their symptoms, and each subclass was assigned separate counsel. Benefits of the settlement included medical monitoring, reimbursement of the purchase price of the drugs, and additional payments depending on the severity of a class member's symptoms, with annual increases in payments for inflation. Claimants had the opportunity to opt out at four different times during the benefit period, including a back-end opt out for individuals who developed more severe symptoms within fifteen years of the settlement date. There was a matrix for determining the amount of an individual's recovery that included not only severity of illness, but also personal and environmental factors that could have contributed to an individual plaintiff's illness. Does the complexity and the likely difficulty of administering this settlement outweigh any benefits gained by joining all plaintiffs in a single action?

Several class action lawsuits have been filed in recent years on behalf of victims of Nazi persecution during World War II. In one, the Eastern District of New York approved a $1.25 billion settlement for targets of racial persecution and their heirs against two leading Swiss banks. IN RE HOLOCAUST VICTIM ASSETS LITIGATION, 105 F.Supp.2d 139 (E.D.N.Y.2000). The class was made up of an estimated 1.4 million potential class members, who sought to recover deposited assets, looted assets, profits made by Swiss and foreign corporations through slave labor, and damages from denial of entry into Switzerland for refugees who tried to escape the Nazis. The class was divided into five subclasses, and a Special Master was appointed to allocate the settlement proceeds among the subgroups. Identifying and contacting potential class members was problematic, because the events that formed the basis of the claims occurred over sixteen years ago, many of the victims died in the Holocaust or in the years thereafter, and the available documentation is limited. Heirs and even the victims themselves may not necessarily know that they are entitled to recovery under the specific claims alleged. Is it true, as the majority in *Amchem* suggests, that even if the problems of commonality and adequate representation are overcome through the creation of subclasses, it will be impossible to provide adequate notice when all of the potential class members can not even be identified? In certifying the class, the court stated that the concerns about adequate representation that befell *Amchem* and *Ortiz* were not relevant in this case because each subclass had separate counsel and a Special Master was designated to determine the appropriate distribution of funds among the subclasses. Is the distribution of funds likely to be resolved successfully, or is the court only delaying an inevitable conflict among the subclasses over the allocation of the settlement?

The Southern District of New York approved an analogous settlement in a class action against Austrian banks based on a finding that 1) it was produced through arm's length negotiation, 2) the substantive nature of the settlement seemed fair, and 3) there were no objections that indicated to the court that the settlement was unfair or inadequate. *In re Austrian and German Bank Holocaust Litigation,* 80 F.Supp.2d 164 (S.D.N.Y.2000). A counterpart class action against German banks is still pending.

Perhaps the most interesting of these cases were a number of class actions against German (and several American) corporations that had profited during World War II by using uncompensated forced and slave laborers, many of whom were "borrowed" from the concentration camps with the aid of the SS, a volunteer, elite unit of the German army. The suits sought the disgorgement of profits made by the corporations and the value of the work performed by class members. These suits were a great embarrassment to the defendants, some of whom are now very active participants in the United States marketplace. Eventually they were settled, with the intercession of several governments, by the establishment of a charitable foundation to which the defendants paid substantial sums.

Various aspects of the *Diet Drugs* and *Holocaust* cases are on appeal at the time of this writing. These appeals may shed some light on the post-*Amchem/Ortiz* status of class action settlements.

Chapter 11

PRETRIAL DEVICES FOR OBTAINING INFORMATION: DEPOSITIONS AND DISCOVERY

SECTION A. THE GENERAL SCOPE OF AND DISCRETIONARY LIMITS ON DISCOVERY

1. INTRODUCTION

The development of pretrial techniques for obtaining information has roughly paralleled the increasing complexity of litigation. Discovery also has provided a partial response to the call for new procedures to supplant, or at least augment, the pleadings, which have proven increasingly inadequate as a device for defining for the parties and the court the precise issues in controversy. The roots of discovery are found in early English equity practice, but the evolution of modern procedures did not begin until the merger of law and equity in the nineteenth century and progressed slowly until the adoption of the Federal Rules of Civil Procedure in 1938. Federal Rules 26 through 37, which are the basic discovery provisions, not only authorize the use of all the discovery techniques known at the time the rules were promulgated but also increase greatly the scope of permissible inquiry and now provide for mandatory disclosure of certain information. So attractive are these provisions that they have been adopted by a large majority of the states, including a number of states that have rejected the federal pleading rules.

Modern discovery has three major purposes. The first, and least controversial, is the preservation of relevant information that might not be available at trial. Basically, this objective relates to the testimony of witnesses who are aged or ill or who will be out of the jurisdiction at the time the trial commences. See Federal Rules 27 and 32(a). The earliest discovery procedures in the federal courts were designed primarily for this purpose. See *Developments in the Law—Discovery*, 74 Harv.L.Rev. 940, 949 (1961).

The second purpose is to ascertain and isolate those issues that actually are in controversy between the parties. There is little dispute that it is appropriate for one party to ask whether another party contests the existence or nonexistence of a fact that the pleadings formally have put in issue. See Federal Rule 36. However, it is not entirely clear precisely how far the

791

discovery devices may be utilized to force a party to set out in detail his factual and legal contentions when the rules of pleading do not require that this be done. The same arguments for and against detailed pleadings as to the law and facts may be made with regard to the appropriate use and scope of discovery. See pp. 793–802, infra.

The final major purpose of discovery is to find out what testimony and other evidence is available on each of the disputed factual issues. Prior to discovery, a party could ascertain these matters only through private investigation; if, for example, a witness refused to discuss a matter with a party, there was no way to learn the substance of that witness' testimony in advance of trial. As a result, cases often turned on the parties' relative access to the facts and their ability to keep certain facts secret until the trial.

To the extent that the person to be questioned is a known eyewitness to the event in controversy, there is little dispute over the propriety of discovery to ascertain what will be said at trial. But the matter is far more complex if a witness, who may be a party or an attorney, obtains evidence during the investigation of the case in preparation for trial. In this context there is a sharp division between those who favor broad discovery to obviate all traces of surprise and those who allege the need for privacy of investigation and development of evidence. Under one thesis it is argued that broad discovery will eliminate the advantage that a wealthy party enjoys over a poorer opponent; others claim that such discovery will induce a lazy litigant to sit back while the opposing party investigates diligently and then, by simply using discovery, to obtain all the fruits of that investigation.

The argument rages not only as to which witnesses may be questioned before trial, but what questions may be asked. For example, should a witness be interrogated not only as to what she would be permitted to say at trial but also as to other matters such as rumors and the like, which, although inadmissible in themselves, might lead to admissible evidence? In connection with this question, read the language of Federal Rule 26(b)(1)–(2) carefully and compare it with the rules for discovery set out in Kelly v. Nationwide Mut. Ins. Co., the case following this Note.

Even if widespread discovery is assumed to be beneficial, however, a question still remains regarding the extent to which its benefits outweigh the increased expenditure of time and money that results from its use. Some discovery devices generally cost very little, but they are the least likely to produce highly significant information. On the other hand, those devices that are most apt to produce substantial results are costly since they require the participation and close supervision of the attorneys. Furthermore, all of the devices are susceptible of abuse, particularly by a wealthy litigant who may engage a less affluent opponent in so much discovery that it becomes cheaper to concede the case. The typical discovery system contains a number of provisions calling for judicial intercession to avoid abuse, but resort to these methods in itself involves some cost; moreover, the results of judicial involvement are not always satisfactory, since judges are reluctant to find that discovery that would be considered appropriate if both parties were of equal financial strength is somehow improper if one of the parties has more limited resources than the other. Yet, if firm control cannot effectively be exercised, discovery ceases to be a means of promoting justice and becomes a tactical weapon for harassment. Because of the imperfections in discovery, many people believe that the scope of discovery should be curtailed at the outset to eliminate the opportunities for abuse, even though this might result in the loss of substantial benefits in terms of access to information. For an analysis of the status of the rules of discovery today, a comparison with procedures in other countries, and the potential directions of change, see Marcus, *Retooling American Discovery for the Twenty–First Century: Toward a New World Order?*, 7 Tul. J. of Int'l & Comp. L. 153 (1999).

2. THE SCOPE OF DISCOVERY

Read Federal Rules of Civil Procedure 26(a), 26(b), 27(a)(1), and 32(a) and the accompanying materials and Ariz.R.Civ.P. 26.1, in the Supplement.

KELLY v. NATIONWIDE MUT. INS. CO.

Ohio Court of Common Pleas, Ashtabula County, 1963.
23 Ohio Op.2d 29, 188 N.E.2d 445.

PONTIUS, JUDGE. Plaintiff sued to recover damages to a motor vehicle under the terms of a comprehensive insurance policy, claiming that the damages arose because someone put sugar in the fuel tank of plaintiff's truck "during the latter part of April, 1961." The defendant denies that such an insurance policy was in effect on April 19, 1961 and otherwise its answer amounts to a general denial. To defendant's answer was attached a list of forty-two interrogatories directed to plaintiff. Plaintiff answered the interrogatories but defendant moved to require more complete answers by plaintiff.

The issue presented by defendant's motion brings into question the proper use by a defendant of interrogatories under R.C. § 2309.43, which reads as follows:

A party may annex to his pleading, other than a demurrer, interrogatories pertinent to the issue made in the pleadings, which interrogatories, if not demurred to, shall be plainly and fully answered under oath by the party to whom they are propounded, or if such party is a corporation, by the president, secretary, or other officer thereof, as the party propounding requires.

Although the old Common Law Bill in Equity for discovery has been largely supplanted in Ohio by this code section as well as R.C. § 2317.07, the question still remains as to whether some of the equitable principles are still in force. * * *

Defendant's answer sets up no affirmative defense. The defendant therefore has assumed no burden of proof. The issue at first instance, at least, would seem to be narrowed to the question, may a defendant who has pleaded only a general denial attach to his answer and have answered by the plaintiff interrogatories which only pry into the evidence by which the plaintiff may sustain his own case, as distinguished from inquiring for ultimate facts within plaintiff's own knowledge which may be pertinent to the issue. In other words, does the plaintiff have to reveal to the defendant in advance of trial evidence which plaintiff hopes to establish in support of his own case?

In some of the older cases in Ohio, trying to interpret this section (R.C. § 2309.43) there seems to have been established the principle that the general purpose of the discovery procedure was to aid a plaintiff in *establishing his case* or a defendant to *establish his defense.* * * * The proper use of interrogatories did not seem to extend to aiding an adversary to destroy his opponent's case. Ward v. Mutual Trucking Company, Ohio Com.Pl., 1 Ohio Supp. 42. In this case Judge Carpenter pointed out that the Ohio statute, which was passed in 1857, was very similar to the English Procedural Act passed in 1854 and quoted with approval at page 44 from the opinion in Whatley v. Crowder, 119 Rep. 645 as follows:

> I think the interrogatories must be confined to matters which might be discovered by a bill of discovery in equity. I adopt the rule in the very terms used by Sir James Wigram (Wigram on Discovery, 261 (2nd Ed.): 'The right of a plaintiff in equity to the benefit of the defendant's oath, is limited to a discovery of such material facts as relate to the plaintiff's case—and does not extend to a discovery of the manner in which the defendant's case is to be established, or to evidence which relates exclusively to his case.' *You may inquire into all that is material to your own case, though it should be in common with that of your adversary; but you may not inquire into what is exclusively his case.* (Italics supplied.)

* * *

Likewise, it has been held that interrogatories are not proper where the information sought is not within the personal knowledge of the other party and is not pertinent to an issue raised by the pleading of the inquirer. * * * It has been held that interrogatories are not proper where the answer calls for mere opinion of the party, * * * nor where the information sought is not within the personal knowledge of the party interrogated. * * *

In more recent cases it has been held that this statute and likewise its counterpart must be liberally construed and that interrogatories are proper if they are designed to seek information *pertinent to the action* as distinguished from being merely *pertinent to an issue* raised by the *pleading of the inquirer.* See Sloan v. S.S. Kresge Company, Ohio Com.Pl., 97 N.E.2d 238; * * * Feinstein v. Cleveland, 67 Ohio Law Abst. 518, "Interrogatories may seek information relevant to any *issue of the action* and to all sides of the case." (Italics supplied.)

Parenthetically, it also may be observed that this same philosophy is to prevail when the information is sought by way of deposition and the inspection and production of documents is sought under R.C. § 2317.32. * * * Many states have liberalized their statutory procedure, pointing toward, if not actually adopting, the very extreme liberal rules of discovery as provided by rules 26 through 37 of the Federal Rules of Civil Procedure. * * *

Certainly the Ohio statute of 1857, regardless of what interpretation may be put upon it, does not go as far nor is it as liberal as the Federal Rules * * *, at least because two additional factors are present:—one, that the interrogatory must be pertinent to the issue made in the pleadings, and two, if admissible in evidence, the answer may be read by either party. (R.C. § 2309.45).

This Court is inclined to the more liberal and later construction of the Ohio statutes as disclosed by Sloan v. S.S. Kresge, rather than the older rule indicated in such cases as * * * Ward v. Mutual Trucking Company; and this Court holds to the view that interrogatories, whether filed with a pleading under favor of R.C. § 2309.43 or separately under R.C. § 2317.07, are proper when:

1. Relevant to an *issue in the action* as distinguished from merely being relevant to an *issue in the pleading* of the inquirer,

2. They do not seek privileged information,

3. The information sought would also be admissible as evidence in the action.

The rule is limited, however, by the further rule that interrogatories may not seek discovery of the manner whereby the opponent's case is to be established nor evidence which relates exclusively to his case, nor to what his witnesses will testify.

In this Court's opinion, there is a marked distinction between records kept by a party in the regular course of his business operations and those amassed by him only after an incident has arisen out of which his lawsuit or defense arises. The former may be ordered produced, if pertinent to an issue in the action; the latter may not. * * *

With these rules in mind further inquiry directed toward the interrogatories of defendant and answers by plaintiff must be made.

The issue in the case as presented by the petition and the answer as distinguished from issues in only one pleading or the other would seem to be:

1. Did the plaintiff hold a comprehensive insurance policy issued by the defendant, which policy was in force in the latter part of April, 1961?

2. Did the policy cover a 1955 White tractor (owned by plaintiff)?

3. Was sugar placed in the mechanism of this tractor?

4. Was the tractor damaged thereby and if so, to what extent?

Defendant's interrogatory number 2 calls upon plaintiff to state whether she was the sole proprietor of a trucking business or whether same was a partnership or corporation at the time of plaintiff's claim. This interrogatory has a direct bearing on the question of truck ownership and policy coverage. The plaintiff's answer to the interrogatory is equivocal. The plaintiff therefore will be directed to answer the interrogatory fully and completely, stating whether she owned the business as a sole proprietor or as a member of a partnership and if so, the other members thereof, or whether the business was incorporated.

Interrogatory number 6 calls for plaintiff to state where the truck was at the time the sugar allegedly got into the mechanism of the truck. The answer given is "Don't personally know." Bearing in mind that previous interrogatories and answers thereto reveal the fact that the truck in question was under the care and custody of someone else other than plaintiff, it would seem as though plaintiff's answer to this interrogatory is full and complete. The motion with respect to interrogatory and answer number 6 is therefore overruled.

Interrogatories numbers 10, 12, and 15 through 33 all deal with matters arising at the time of or after plaintiff's alleged claim arose. None deal with information or records maintained in the normal operation of plaintiff's business. On the contrary, they call for information as to the manner in which the plaintiff may attempt to establish her cause of action and do not countenance information presumably within plaintiff's own personal knowledge. They call for information which plaintiff may or may not be able to produce through testimony of witnesses upon trial. In other words, they call for hearsay or mere opinion evidence if plaintiff's answer of "Don't personally know" is true. Certainly upon trial if plaintiff were so inquired of and should so answer the same or similar interrogatories, she could not then be called upon to give her opinion or an answer which was obviously mere hearsay.

The same objection is true with interrogatories 36 and 37 and the answers given thereto; and likewise interrogatories 39 through 42 and Plaintiff's answers thereto. An additional objection to interrogatory number 42 exists, namely, assuming that a record of a test was made, it calls for the furnishing of information solely in support of plaintiff's cause of action and obviously arises after the claim arose and in connection with plaintiff's preparation for presentation of her claim and her lawsuit. This last mentioned objection is likewise true with many of the other interrogatories heretofore above covered.

Defendant's motion therefore will be overruled in all respects except with reference to the answer given by plaintiff to interrogatory number 2, and plaintiff is directed to file a complete answer as above indicated.

* * *

Notes and Questions

1. In 1970, seven years after *Kelly* was decided, Ohio adopted a set of discovery regulations with a scope almost identical to that of the Federal Rules. What purposes are served by extensive discovery under Rule 26 that are not served by the decision in *Kelly*? Are any particular groups of litigants, such as insurance companies or plaintiffs in negligence actions, favored or prejudiced by broad discovery? Note the limitations on the scope of discovery in Rule 26(b)(2). Do they make the Rule too restrictive? Are there certain categories or types of information not expressly mentioned in Rule 26 that should be beyond the scope of discovery or certain classes of litigation in which discovery should be prohibited or sharply curtailed?

2. One major reason for permitting widespread discovery of the facts before trial is the elimination of surprise. See Klonoski v. Mahlab, 156 F.3d 255, 271 (1st Cir.1998), condemning "trial by ambush." Does full knowledge by one party of all the evidence to be presented by the opposing party lead to a more accurate result at trial, or can justice sometimes be better served if a litigant is surprised by the evidence presented at trial? Compare Hawkins, *Discovery and Rule 34: What's So Wrong About Surprise?*, 39 A.B.A.J. 1075 (1953), with Holtzoff, *The Elimination of Surprise in Federal Practice*, 7 Vand.L.Rev. 576 (1954). See also DiMichel v. South Buffalo Ry., p. 31, supra. Does discovery actually reduce surprise? See Glaser, *Pretrial Discovery and the Adversary Process* 105–09 (1968).

3. Prior to December 1, 2000, Rule 26(b)(1) permitted discovery, without a court order, "of any matter not privileged, which is relevant to the subject matter

involved in the pending action." A major change in language on that date now limits a request for discovery without a court order to nonprivileged matters "relevant to the claim or defense of any party." However, the court, by order, can expand the scope to permit further discovery "of any matter relevant to the subject matter involved in the action," which returns discovery to its prior scope.

The altered language, forms of which had been suggested for many years, is designed to curb sweeping discovery requests that go beyond what is reasonable and necessary and to give more control to the trial judge. See Committee on Rules of Practice and Procedure of the Judicial Conference of the United States, *Preliminary Draft of Proposed Amendments to the Federal Rules of Civil Procedure and Evidence*, pp. 34–36, August 1998. Will the changed language of the rule likely have a significant effect? Will it actually curb excessive discovery or will it merely require more work for federal trial judges? What kinds of motion do you think will be made? See Brazil, *The Adversary Character of Civil Discovery: A Critique and Proposals for Change*, 31 Vand.L.Rev. 1295, 1332 (1978).

SIMPSON v. TRAUM, 63 A.D.2d 583, 404 N.Y.S.2d 619 (1st Dep't 1978). Petitioner applied for an order for a deposition under New York Civil Practice Law and Rules § 3102(c), providing that pre-suit "disclosure to aid in bringing an action, to preserve information or to aid in arbitration, may be obtained, but only by court order." The trial judge granted the application, but the appellate court reversed, stating:

> Pre-action disclosure under CPLR 3102(c) is not available to determine if a cause of action exists. A prima facie cause of action must be demonstrated * * *. An examination to frame a complaint will not be permitted where what is sought is to ascertain or determine whether facts supporting a cause of action exist * * *, nor where petitioner "possesses sufficient information to frame a complaint without the examination which is sought" (New Rochelle Precision Grinding Corp. v. Marino, 9 A.D.2d 685, 191 N.Y.S.2d 561). Nor is it permitted "to explore the feasibility of framing a complaint" (Cotler v. Retail Credit Co., 18 A.D.2d 898, 237 N.Y.S.2d 781).
>
> Here it is clear [from the affidavits submitted in support of the discovery order] that petitioners have sufficient information to frame a complaint. * * * Moreover, the examination sought here is much broader in scope than the limited deposition contemplated by the statute. What is sought is a full-blown deposition of the type appropriate after commencement of an action. * * *

Notes and Questions

1. Why shouldn't there be a specific provision permitting a prospective plaintiff to discover facts to aid in deciding whether or not a legal action is justified and in ascertaining against whom it should be brought? See generally In re Lewis, 11 N.C.App. 541, 181 S.E.2d 806 (1971); 3 Weinstein, Korn & Miller, *New York Civil Practice* ¶¶ 3102.11–.12.

Does a pre-action discovery provision have any practical effect when given a narrow interpretation, as in the *Simpson* case? Consider KEELY v. PRICE, 27 Cal.App.3d 209, 103 Cal.Rptr. 531 (2d Dist.1972), in which defendant successfully demurred to the complaint on the ground that it failed to state a cause of action. The appellate court upheld the demurrer, but reversed the trial court's denial of leave to amend, ordering that plaintiff be afforded sufficient time and opportunity for discovery to assist in making any amendment. Contra, State v. Braunstein, 66 A.D.2d 885, 411 N.Y.S.2d 673 (2d Dep't 1978).

2.   The only Federal Rule permitting pre-action discovery is Rule 27, which provides that a person, with court approval, may take a deposition of himself or any other person for the purpose of perpetuating testimony for a contemplated action that cannot presently be brought. The court must be satisfied that perpetuating the testimony may prevent a failure or delay of justice. It has been held consistently that Rule 27 cannot be used as a means to determine whether a cause of action exists and, if so, against whom it should be brought. See, e.g., In re Solorio, 192 F.R.D. 709 (D.Utah 2000); In re Boland, 79 F.R.D. 665 (D.D.C.1978). Should the scope of a deposition before action be limited to evidence that would be material and admissible at trial or should its scope be the same as that allowed by Rule 26(b)? See Martin v. Reynolds Metals Corp., 297 F.2d 49 (9th Cir.1961) (court refused to limit discovery to admissible evidence but left open the question whether the full scope of Rule 26(b) applies). For a discussion of Rule 27, see Note, *The Preservation and Discovery of Evidence Under Federal Rule of Civil Procedure 27*, 78 Geo.L.J. 593 (1990).

———

GRANT v. HUFF, 122 Ga.App. 783, 178 S.E.2d 734 (1970). Plaintiff, in a personal injury case, attempted to discover defendant's ability to pay a possible judgment by asking for information as to defendant's income, ownership of property, and the limits of a liability insurance policy. This inquiry was held improper on the ground that the information would not lead to admissible evidence at trial. In addition plaintiff sought discovery of the names and addresses of those witnesses defendant intended to use at the trial. This too was rejected on the ground that although plaintiff was entitled to discover who the eyewitnesses were, she was not entitled to know which witnesses defendant in fact would call to the stand.

Notes and Questions

1.   Rule 26(a)(1)(D) as amended in 1993 provides that without awaiting a discovery request defendant must make its insurance policies available to plaintiff for inspection and copying pursuant to Rule 34. How does this information lead to admissible evidence? What is the justification for the amendment? In what way would the decision in Grant v. Huff have been altered if Federal Rule 26(a)(1)(D) had been controlling?

2.   In RENSHAW v. RAVERT, 82 F.R.D. 361 (E.D.Pa.1979), a suit in which plaintiff sought punitive as well as compensatory damages, the court required defendant to answer an interrogatory seeking information concerning his financial status. Can the decision be distinguished from Grant v. Huff and other cases in which permission to discover defendant's general financial status is refused?

Compare Bryan v. Thos. Best & Sons, Inc., 453 A.2d 107, 108 (Del.Super.Ct.1982), in which the court stayed discovery of defendants' financial status until plaintiff could make a showing that "some factual basis for punitive damages existed."

Suppose under state law "punitive" damages are not permitted to punish a defendant, but only to award greater compensation to plaintiff because aggravating circumstances cause plaintiff to "suffer much beyond what he would suffer from the pecuniary loss?" Should this affect the discovery of defendant's financial condition? See Peisner v. Detroit Free Press, 68 Mich.App. 360, 242 N.W.2d 775 (1976).

3.   In ROY v. MONITOR–PATRIOT CO., 112 N.H. 80, 290 A.2d 207 (1972), plaintiff sued defendant newspaper for libel, due to the publication of an article written by columnist Drew Pearson. Under the applicable law, plaintiff could recover only by proving defendant acted maliciously. Prior to trial, plaintiff was permitted to discover the existence and nature of any agreement by which Pearson had promised to indemnify the paper for defamation actions that might result from publication of his columns. Should the discovery have been allowed? Of what consequence would it be that defendant intended to call Pearson to testify on its behalf? See also Maule Industries, Inc. v. Rountree, 264 So.2d 445 (Fla.App. 1972).

LINDBERGER v. GENERAL MOTORS CORP.

United States District Court, Western District of Wisconsin, 1972.
56 F.R.D. 433.

JAMES E. DOYLE, DISTRICT JUDGE. Plaintiff, Gordon C. Lindberger, a citizen of Wisconsin, filed a complaint against the defendants, General Motors Corporation and a division thereof, which are not citizens of Wisconsin. Plaintiff alleges that he suffered personal injuries proximately caused by the negligence of the defendants in manufacturing and designing a front end loader which was sold to the plaintiff's employer. * * *

Attorneys for the defendants have refused to answer interrogatories 23, 25 and 26, which were propounded by the plaintiffs pursuant to Rule 33 * * *. Plaintiffs have filed a motion to compel discovery.

Interrogatory 23 requests the defendants to state whether any changes have been made, and if so to describe such changes, subsequent to the date when the loader in question was produced, in either the design of the braking system or in the warning system for brake malfunctions. Interrogatory 25 requests the defendants to state how any such changes affect the utility of the loader. Interrogatory 26 requests the names of persons responsible for such design changes.

* * *

[Defendants refused to respond to the questions, arguing that the information sought was "privileged" because evidence of subsequent alterations is inadmissible at trial. The court first held that the term "privilege" in Rule 26(b) embraces only those matters traditionally covered by that term under the law of evidence and thus did not apply to this case.]

The * * * question is whether the subject-matter of the interrogatories falls within the scope of examination permitted under Rule 26(b) * * *. [T]he plaintiff need not, at this stage of the proceedings, establish that the evidence sought would be admissible at trial. * * * It is clear that the information sought in the challenged interrogatories is relevant to the subject-matter of this action. The feasibility of the installation of a better brake system and of more adequate warning systems for brake malfunctions may be significant with respect to * * * [defendants' liability]. Furthermore, the knowledge of the defendants about the adequacy of the design of the loader as well as any information on this subject which may have been passed to the employer of the plaintiff may be relevant on the issues of negligence and contributory negligence.

In conclusion, I find that the defendants' refusal to answer interrogatories 23, 25, and 26, is without justification. Accordingly, on the basis of the entire record herein, it is hereby ordered, pursuant to Rule 37 * * *, that the defendants answer interrogatories 23, 25 and 26, within 30 days from the date of entry of this order.

Note

In CORNET STORES v. SUPERIOR COURT, 108 Ariz. 84, 87, 492 P.2d 1191, 1194 (1972), plaintiff, a former manager of one of defendant's stores, sued for wrongful discharge, alleging that under his contract he could be fired only for misconduct, but that in fact he was fired because the contract called for higher pay than that received by the other managers. Plaintiff sought to discover the amount of pay that the other managers received. Defendant, who wished to keep its employee contracts confidential, objected that the inquiry was irrelevant since defendant was willing to stipulate that plaintiff had been the highest paid manager in its system. The court upheld discovery, stating:

> We think, however, that a party to litigation has the right to prove its case in the fashion it deems most satisfactory and may not be compelled by the court to accept an offer to stipulate, the effect of which may not have the same impact upon a jury as the evidence which establishes the fact.

ZINSKY v. NEW YORK CENT. R. CO., 36 F.R.D. 680 (N.D.Ohio 1964). Plaintiff brought suit under the Federal Employers' Liability Act, alleging that his duties were in furtherance of interstate commerce. Defendant denied all allegations in the complaint. Plaintiff then sent the following interrogatory to defendant:

> At the time of the accident, was the plaintiff engaged in duties which were in furtherance of interstate commerce or which directly and substantially affected interstate commerce?

The court upheld defendant's objection that the question improperly called for "a legal analysis of one of the factual issues" in the case, quoting United States v. Selby, 25 F.R.D. 12, 14 (N.D.Ohio 1960), as follows:

> The assertion and discussion of legal theories, and the classification of facts in support thereof, should be by the lawyers at trial and in whatever pre-trial procedures the court may require.

Notes and Questions

1. The *Zinsky* case was decided prior to the 1970 amendment to Federal Rule 33, which added the second paragraph of what is now Rule 33(c). Would *Zinsky* have been decided any differently under the amended rule? Compare JOSEPH v. NORMAN'S HEALTH CLUB, INC., 336 F.Supp. 307, 319 (E.D.Mo. 1971), in which the court upheld an interrogatory asking whether one defendant had ever assigned any promissory notes to another. In overruling an objection that the interrogatory called for a legal conclusion, the court held:

> The final sentence of Rule [33(c)] * * * added by amendment in 1970 * * * does not authorize interrogatories calling for legal conclusions as such. * * * [T]he only kind of interrogatory that is objectionable without more as a legal conclusion is one that extends to "legal issues unrelated to the facts of the case."

What is a legal conclusion unrelated to the facts of the case? Does it encompass the cases upon which a party intends to rely? See Fishermen & Merchants Bank v. Burin, 11 F.R.D. 142 (S.D.Cal.1951). Consider ROGERS v. TRI–STATE MATERIALS CORP., 51 F.R.D. 234, 246 (N.D.W.Va.1970), in which defendant sought to discover any "presumption of law or fact" upon which plaintiff intended to rely. The court upheld the interrogatory as follows:

> Plaintiff may not be schooled on the meaning of the term "res ipsa loquitur" but counsel, largely responsible for preparation of answers to interrogatories, will be able to explain that a state of facts may speak for itself under certain circumstances.

Compare Estate of May v. Zorman, 5 Wash.App. 368, 487 P.2d 270 (1971) (defendants held not required to answer questions asking whether their conduct was negligent).

2. The 1970 amendments also added a provision to Federal Rule 36(a) extending the scope of requests to admit to matters "that relate to statements or opinions of fact or of the application of law to fact." See the Advisory Committee's Note on Rule 36 in the Supplement. Why should the changes as to conclusions appear only in Rules 33 and 36 and not in Rule 26(b)?

3. To what extent should a party's ability to discover the contentions of an adversary be affected by federal decisions upholding as a sufficient pleading under Rule 8 any statement that possibly can be read to state a valid claim for relief or a defense? See pp. 515–21, supra. For example, in a negligence case in which only general allegations of negligence have been made, is it proper to inquire as to the specific acts or omissions upon which the allegations are based? An inquiry of this type was upheld in Brandenberg v. El Al Israel Airlines, 79 F.R.D. 543 (S.D.N.Y. 1978).

4. For an interesting discussion of the use of discovery to ascertain an adverse party's contentions, see James, *The Revival of Bills of Particulars Under the Federal Rules,* 71 Harv.L.Rev. 1473, 1481–83 (1958). As the author states:

> The real objection to requiring detailed statements of contentions is that they tie a party down in such a way that he may be deprived of his substantive rights. This is so because even astute counsel are unable always to forecast the vicissitudes of litigation. Time and again some evidence, or some combination of evidence, will emerge for the first time on trial, or will

be perceived in its full significance for the first time on trial by the party concerned, or by the tribunal.

* * *

Administrative efficiency will, to be sure, be promoted by the narrowing of issues, at least if they stay narrow. * * * If, however, the pleader has failed to specify some particular contention which would have been within the compass of a generalized pleading and which finds unexpected support or appreciation at trial, then the court is frequently put in a dilemma: It must either refuse to decide the case on the true facts and applicable law, or it must disrupt administrative efficiency to allow a continuance. Either resolution of the dilemma represents an evil.

How does the duty to update discovery under Federal Rule 26(e) affect the argument that a party may be too closely bound by his responses?

3. DISCRETIONARY LIMITS ON THE SCOPE OF DISCOVERY

———

Read Federal Rule of Civil Procedure 26(b)(2) and 26(c) in the Supplement.

———

MARRESE v. AMERICAN ACADEMY OF ORTHOPAEDIC SURGEONS

United States Court of Appeals, Seventh Circuit, 1984 (en banc).
726 F.2d 1150, reversed on other grounds 470 U.S.
373, 105 S.Ct. 1327, 84 L.Ed.2d 274 (1985).

[Two orthopaedic surgeons initially sued in state court alleging that they were refused membership in the Academy without a hearing. Although membership in the Academy is not necessary to practice as an orthopaedic surgeon, it was alleged to confer some degree of professional advantage. Finding membership in the Academy was not an "economic necessity," the state court dismissed the complaint on the ground that no valid state law claim was stated. Plaintiffs then sued in federal court, alleging violations of the antitrust laws. In the course of discovery, plaintiffs demanded production by the Academy of correspondence and other documents relating to denials of membership applications between 1970 and 1980. The court ordered the Academy to produce the documents pursuant to an order protecting their confidentiality. The Academy refused to comply with the order, and was held in criminal contempt and fined $10,000. It appealed.]

POSNER, CIRCUIT JUDGE.

* * *

A motion under Rule 26(c) to limit discovery requires the district judge to compare the hardship to the party against whom discovery is sought, if discovery is allowed, with the hardship to the party seeking discovery if discovery is denied. He must consider the nature of the hardship as well as its magnitude and thus give more weight to interests that have a distinctively social value than to purely private interests; and he must consider the possibility of reconciling the competing interests through a carefully crafted protective order. He must go through the same analysis under Rule 26(d) except that an order merely postponing a particular discovery request obviously should be granted more freely than one denying the request altogether.

* * *

* * * [T]here is in this case, if not a First Amendment right, at least a First Amendment interest, which the discovery sought by the plaintiffs would impair and which differentiates this case from the usual antitrust case, where discovery is sought of invoices or salesmen's reports or the minutes of a board of directors' meeting. * * *

* * * [O]ne does not have to be a student of Aristotle and de Tocqueville to know that voluntary associations are important to many people, Americans in particular, and that voluntary professional associations are important to American professionals (the premise of the plaintiffs' antitrust suit, as it was of their Illinois suits). Since an association would not be genuinely voluntary if the members were not allowed to consider applications for new members in confidence, the involuntary disclosure of deliberations on membership applications cannot but undermine the voluntary character of an association and therefore harm worthy interests, whether or not those interests derive any additional dignity from the First Amendment. The threat to such interests is more than speculative in this case. Dr. Marrese's counsel said at the rehearing en banc that he wants to use the membership files as a source of names of Academy members to depose in an effort to find out the motives behind their opposition to his client's application. It is hard to believe that after members of the Academy find themselves deposed for this purpose they will still be willing to offer candid evaluations of prospective members.

The other side of the coin is that barring the plaintiffs or their counsel from all access to the membership files would probably make it impossible for them to prove their antitrust case. But there were various devices that the district judge could have used to reconcile the parties' competing needs. For example, he could have examined the membership files himself *in camera,* a procedure described by the Supreme Court in a related context as "a relatively costless and eminently worthwhile method to insure that the balance between petitioners' claims of irrelevance and privilege and plaintiffs' asserted need for the documents is correctly struck." Kerr v. United States District Court, 426 U.S. 394, 405, 96 S.Ct. 2119, 2125, 48 L.Ed.2d 725 (1976). We are told the membership files may be voluminous. No doubt the files in *all* cases between 1970 and 1980 where applications for membership in the Academy were refused are voluminous, but the place to start an *in camera* examination would be with the files on Drs. Marrese and Treister. If the judge found no evidence in those files of any anticompetitive purpose attributable to the Academy, he would not have to look at any other files. This is not a class action; the plaintiffs are not suing as the representatives of other orthopaedic surgeons who have been denied membership in the Academy.

Better yet, the judge might have followed the procedure discussed in this court's recent decision in EEOC v. University of Notre Dame Du Lac, 715 F.2d 331, 338–39 (7th Cir.1983). There we ordered the files of faculty tenure deliberations edited ("redacted") to remove the names of the deliberating faculty members and any other information that might enable them to be identified, and we directed that on remand the redaction be reviewed *in camera* by the district judge, who would have the originals before him to compare with (and thereby assure the accuracy of) the redactions. Had the same procedure been followed here, the plaintiffs' counsel would have been able to read the files personally. If the files had turned out to contain evidence or leads to evidence of anticompetitive conduct, the plaintiffs' counsel could then have requested the judge to order names revealed to counsel so that the relevant individuals could be deposed. We do not think that only universities should be entitled to such consideration.

The protective order that the judge did enter ("which draws on each party's submission but parallels neither," in his words) was not well designed to protect the privacy of the Academy's members. It not only allowed the plaintiffs themselves—two disappointed applicants for membership—to read the files on their own applications; it allowed the plaintiffs' counsel "to discuss with plaintiffs the general contents" of all of the other files and to depose anyone whose name they found in the files. The order was not calculated to allay the Academy's justifiable anxiety for the confidentiality of its membership deliberations.

Rule 26(d) (control of the sequence and timing of discovery) provided another method of accommodating the competing interests here with minimal damage to either. If there is other discovery that a plaintiff must complete in order to be able to resist a motion by the defendant for summary judgment, and thus a significant probability that his case will fail regardless of what the internal files he is seeking may show, the district judge has the power under Rule 26(d) to require the plaintiff to complete the other, nonsensitive discovery first. See Wright & Miller, *Federal Practice and Procedure* 2040, 2047. And in an appropriate case he has the duty. "As a threshold matter, the court should be satisfied that a claim is not frivolous, a pretense for using discovery powers in a fishing expedition. In this case, plaintiff should show that it can establish jury issues on the essential elements of its case not the subject of the contested discovery." Bruno & Stillman, Inc. v. Globe Newspaper Co., 633 F.2d 583, 597 (1st Cir.1980). * * *

Of course, if the plaintiffs do not need anything beyond the contents of the Academy's membership files to prove their case, they cannot be asked to do any other discovery before getting access to the files. At oral argument we asked Dr. Marrese's counsel whether his discovery would be complete after he saw the membership files and followed up any leads the files contained. He answered that at that point he would file a motion for summary judgment arguing that the Academy had committed a per se violation of the Sherman Act, but that if the motion was denied he would conduct additional discovery, which he admitted would be necessary to prove a Rule of Reason violation. It is unlikely that the district judge would allow him to proceed in so piecemeal a fashion. The judge probably would tell him to complete discovery before moving for summary judgment. See 10 Wright, Miller & Kane, *Federal Practice and Procedure* § 2717 at p. 666 (1983). Assuming discovery would not be at an end when the files were turned over and any leads contained in them were tracked down, Rule 26(d) could have been used to schedule the sensitive discovery last.

We do not hold that all files of all voluntary associations are sacrosanct; we do not even hold that the membership files of an association of medical professionals are sacrosanct. They are discoverable in appropriate circumstances, subject to appropriate safeguards. But we may not ignore as judges what we know as lawyers—that discovery of sensitive documents is sometimes sought not to gather evidence that will help the party seeking discovery to prevail on the merits of his case but to coerce his opponent to settle regardless of the merits rather than have to produce the documents. * * *

* * * There is at least a hint of predatory discovery in this case in the fact that the plaintiffs did not seek access to the federal court system with its liberal discovery rules till after they had lost their state-court suit, and in the determination expressed by Dr. Marrese's counsel to use the Academy's membership files as the basis for deposing the individuals who voted against his client's membership application.

There are so many ways in which Judge Shadur could have prevented the plaintiffs from abusing the discovery process, without denying them any information essential to developing their case, that we are left with the firm conviction that the discovery order he issued, when he issued it, was erroneous. Our conclusion is consistent with the evolving concept of the district judge's managerial responsibility in complex litigation. Although amended Fed.R.Civ.P. 26(b)(1), which expands that responsibility, did not take effect until August 1, 1983, after the discovery order in issue here was issued, the Advisory Committee's Note indicates that the purpose of the amended rule is in part to remind federal district judges of their broad powers—and, we believe, correlative responsibilities—under Rule 26.

* * *

HARLINGTON WOOD, JR., CIRCUIT JUDGE, with whom CUMMINGS, CHIEF JUDGE, and CUDAHY, CIRCUIT JUDGE, join, dissenting.

* * *

Judge Posner's opinion now finds fault in the district court's failure to incorporate other protective devices for resolving the discovery dispute, such as an in camera inspection of the Academy's files or production of a redacted version of the files. I, too, believe that the trial judge could have improved on his discovery order. First, he could have been well-served by taking a look in camera at the Academy files on plaintiffs to see whether the files contained what plaintiffs claimed to need so badly, and whether the Academy had good reason to fight so desperately to keep the files out of sight.

The Supreme Court has commended an in camera view of documents in a discovery dispute to insure the striking of a proper balance between the interests in confidentiality and disclosure. Kerr v. United States District Court, * * *. Failure to make an in camera inspection, however, is not in itself an abuse of discretion. While the district court did not view the Academy's files, it apparently was aware that the state trial court had conducted an in camera inspection of the files in the earlier state court litigation between the same parties. After viewing the files, the state court ordered production over the Academy's objections. * * * Thus, one judge had viewed these materials and determined that the contents were relevant and disclosure was appropriate. We should not ignore the state court's first-hand determination. Further, the Academy has maintained that an in camera inspection would not improve the discovery order. In the Academy's view, as I understand it, an in camera inspection could lead to a discovery order which, even if including redaction of the files, would be an abuse of discretion at this stage of the litigation.

The propriety of the district court's order to produce the unredacted files also must be considered in light of the surrounding circumstances. In the early stages of this litigation, plaintiffs expressed their willingness to accept a redacted version of the Academy's files, at least as the first phase of discovery. The Academy refused plaintiffs' early offer to enter a redaction agreement, and plaintiffs later rescinded the offer. Both sides submitted proposed protective orders to the district court; apparently neither provided for redaction.

The Academy's participation in later court proceedings suggested its general approval of the protective order as it was developing. However, the Academy meanwhile continued to press its effort to avoid any discovery of its files. At oral argument, counsel for Dr. Treister stated that his client now would accept a redaction order if this would not limit the right to seek sanctions against the Academy. The Academy's position at oral argument was that any disclosure of its files, even after excision of names and other identifying information, would enable plaintiffs to determine the source of comments, thereby chilling participation in the Academy's admissions process. The Academy steadfastly maintained that no modification of the district court's protective order would be acceptable to it, and any forced disclosure of confidential information prior to the establishment of a jury issue on antitrust injury would be an abuse of discretion. Although the Academy's stonewalling now has paid off, I do not find an abuse of discretion in the district court's failure to order redaction under these circumstances.

Judge Posner's opinion suggests that the district court should have used its Rule 26(d) powers to control the sequence of discovery in this case. Discovery usually may proceed in any sequence, but the court upon motion, for the convenience of parties and in the interests of justice, may schedule the order of discovery on different issues. Fed.R.Civ.P. 26(d). Judge Posner's opinion correctly notes that the district court's power to order sequential discovery may rise to a duty in some cases, citing Bruno & Stillman, Inc. v. Globe Newspaper Co., 633 F.2d 583 (1st Cir.1980), a reporter's privilege case. The present case does not begin to fit into the *Bruno & Stillman* mold. The interests in the confidentiality of the Academy's files do not require such delicate treatment as do those involved in the case of a reporter seeking to protect confidential news sources from discovery. The district court considered and rejected the Academy's motion to bifurcate discovery. The court was satisfied that plaintiffs' claim was not frivolous, having withstood a motion to dismiss once, and again upon reconsideration. The Academy's proposal for sequential discovery would have required piecemeal discovery, which the district court found would burden plaintiffs unnecessarily since the Academy's confidentiality interests could be preserved adequately through a protective order. I would hold that the district court did not abuse its discretion by refusing to order sequential discovery.

Judge Posner's opinion discusses the misuse of discovery tools to coerce settlement, and apparently concludes that the district court's discovery order failed to prevent plaintiffs from abusing the discovery process. The opinion finds two "hints" of predatory discovery here: first, that plaintiffs sought access to federal court—and its liberal discovery rules—only after losing in the state court; and further, that plaintiffs planned to use information from the Academy's files as the basis for further discovery. The first hint merely returns us to the res judicata issue in the context of a dual court system. The second hint, plaintiffs' plan to follow up leads found in the files, is one of the conventional purposes of discovery.

Upon questioning at oral argument, counsel for the Academy labeled plaintiffs' suit a "fishing expedition," an attempt to gain access to otherwise unavailable information. Under the circumstances, however, plaintiffs' pursuit of the files and plan to seek further discovery using leads from the files were within the bounds of appropriate discovery. The discovery record in this case evidences not the slightest abuse, harassment, or coercion to pressure a settlement. Judicial concern about discovery abuse is always legitimate, but such arguments are gratuitous in the context of this case. The abuse of discovery here instead is the Academy's obstinate defiance of the trial court, which now is sanctioned by this court.

Although not condemning any one omission as an abuse of discretion, the discovery majority is left with the "firm conviction" that the district court's discovery order was erroneous. I am not. The district court sought and received proposed protective orders from the parties, and mediated negotiations on this issue. Bifurcation of discovery was not mandatory in this case, and the court reasonably provided for the Academy's confidentiality concerns through the protective order. The Academy should not now reap a windfall from reversal of the discovery order because the order did not incorporate certain provisions that the Academy still would refuse to accept. The Academy treated the trial judge's reasonable discovery order with contempt and its contempt should be recognized by this court.

* * *

Although the discovery order could have been improved, the district court's fashioning of the terms was not an abuse of discretion under the circumstances of this case. What the merits of this case would have turned out to be, we now will never know; but we must not let a prejudgment on the merits cloud our review of the discovery order. Plaintiffs * * * deserve the opportunity within reasonable limits to develop their case, and then the opportunity to try it before a judge and jury. I would affirm the district court's contempt holding, but on remand I would direct the court to view the Academy's files in camera and to consider possible redaction before actually enforcing the discovery order. * * *

Notes and Questions

1. In 1993, Rule 26(c) was amended to require that a party seeking a protective order make a good faith effort to resolve the discovery dispute with the other party before resorting to judicial involvement. In addition, Rule 26(d) was amended in 1993, and again in 2000, to require that the various parties confer pursuant to Rule 26(f) before commencing formal discovery. What are these changes designed to achieve? What impact might they have on discovery? Should

the requirement that parties confer and decide on a plan for discovery be strengthened by specifying in detail what the parties must do? See Carrington, *Renovating Discovery*, 49 Ala.L.Rev. 51, 73 (1997).

2.   * * * [The] list of circumstances [in amended Rule 26(b)(2)] invokes cost-benefit principles which contemplate both achieving an optimal level of discovery beyond which additional discovery would not be cost-effective and restricting discovery when the dollar amount or values at stake are low. * * *

A potential difficulty with this approach is in finding principled criteria for differentiating between various types of cases. What values should be used in deciding whether, for example, the plaintiff in a $10,000 personal injury case should be limited in the number of depositions he may take, or the plaintiff seeking reinstatement in an employment discrimination case should be prohibited from discovering documents only tangentially related to the claim, or the defendant in a $10,000,000 product liability case should be allowed to require answers to voluminous interrogatories involving the most searching details of the plaintiff's past life? Where, one may ask, are judges expected to find the criteria and analytical structure for making such judgments?

Sherman & Kinnard, *Federal Court Discovery in the 80's—Making the Rules Work*, 95 F.R.D. 245, 276 (1983).

3.   What weight should a court give to limitations on "the parties' resources" in setting limits on discovery? Is a discovery request that otherwise would be barred as disproportionate to the needs of a case permissible simply because the party from which the discovery is sought has a "deep pocket"? On the other hand, should a relatively wealthy litigant be able to buy additional discovery by offering to pay the expenses of a financially weak litigant? Should relatively wealthy antagonists be permitted to stipulate to unlimited discovery?

4.   The 1993 amendments to the discovery rules place self-executing limits on the extent to which parties can make use of the discovery devices. Thus, Rules 30(a)(2)(A) and (B) and 33(a) provide that, unless the parties agree otherwise, leave of court must be obtained if a party wishes to take more than ten depositions, to take the deposition of a witness more than once, or to serve on any other party more than 25 interrogatories, including all discrete subparts. In addition Rule 26(b)(2) provides that, in determining whether to limit discovery, the court must consider "the importance of the proposed discovery in resolving the issues." See also Rule 30(d)(2), as amended in 2000, regarding the presumptive limits on the length of a deposition.

5.   To what extent should the court's assessment of the likelihood of a party prevailing on the merits enter, if at all, into a decision about the scope of discovery? In CABLE ELECTRIC PRODUCTS, INC. v. GENMARK, INC., 586 F.Supp. 1505 (N.D.Cal.1984), vacated on other grounds 770 F.2d 1015 (Fed.Cir. 1985), the court granted summary judgment to defendant in an unfair-competition action brought by the manufacturer of a light-sensitive "night light." It rejected plaintiff's request that the court not rule on the motion until it had the opportunity to complete discovery concerning actual confusion that may be occurring in the marketplace as a result of alleged similarities in labeling and packaging the products, since the court thought that the probability was "vanishingly small" that plaintiff could uncover such evidence. If Rule 26(b)(2) had been in effect when *Cable Electric Products* was decided, could the decision have been supported on the ground that "the burden and expense of the proposed discovery outweighs its likely benefit"? See generally Note, *Summary Judgment Before the*

Completion of Discovery: A Proposed Revision of Federal Rule of Civil Procedure 56(f), 24 U.Mich.J.L.Ref. 253 (1990).

SEATTLE TIMES CO. v. RHINEHART

Supreme Court of the United States, 1984.
467 U.S. 20, 104 S.Ct. 2199, 81 L.Ed.2d 17.

[Rhinehart and the Aquarian Foundation, a religious group of which he was spiritual leader, brought an action for defamation and invasion of privacy in a Washington state court against the publishers and authors of several critical articles. Pursuant to state discovery rules modeled on the Federal Rules, the trial court issued an order compelling plaintiffs to identify donors and the amounts each contributed, and to produce a list of the foundation's members. However, the court also issued a protective order prohibiting defendants from publishing the information or otherwise using it except as necessary to prepare for and try the case. Plaintiffs had submitted affidavits showing that public release of donor and membership lists would adversely affect foundation membership and subject its members to harassment. Both sides appealed and the Washington Supreme Court affirmed both orders. The state Supreme Court held that the protective order served the interest of the judiciary in protecting the integrity of its discovery processes, an interest sufficient to sustain it against the claim that it infringed on First Amendment rights.]

Certiorari to the Supreme Court of Washington.

JUSTICE POWELL delivered the opinion of the Court.

* * *

* * * The Washington Civil Rules enable parties to litigation to obtain information "relevant to the subject matter involved" that they believe will be helpful in the preparation and trial of the case. Rule 26, however, must be viewed in its entirety. Liberal discovery is provided for the sole purpose of assisting in the preparation and trial, or the settlement, of litigated disputes. Because of the liberality of pretrial discovery permitted by Rule 26(b)(1), it is necessary for the trial court to have the authority to issue protective orders conferred by Rule 26(c). It is clear from experience that pretrial discovery by depositions and interrogatories has a significant potential for abuse. This abuse is not limited to matters of delay and expense; discovery also may seriously implicate privacy interests of litigants and third parties. The Rules do not distinguish between public and private information. Nor do they apply only to parties to the litigation, as relevant information in the hands of third parties may be subject to discovery.

There is an opportunity, therefore, for litigants to obtain—incidentally or purposefully—information that not only is irrelevant but if publicly released could be damaging to reputation and privacy. The government clearly has a substantial interest in preventing this sort of abuse of its processes. * * * The prevention of the abuse that can attend the coerced production of information under a State's discovery rule is sufficient justification for the authorization of protective orders.[22]

---

22. The Supreme Court of Washington   properly emphasized the importance of ensur-

We also find that the provision for protective orders in the Washington Rules requires, in itself, no heightened First Amendment scrutiny. To be sure, Rule 26(c) confers broad discretion on the trial court to decide when a protective order is appropriate and what degree of protection is required. The Legislature of the State of Washington, following the example of the Congress in its approval of the Federal Rules of Civil Procedure, has determined that such discretion is necessary, and we find no reason to disagree. The trial court is in the best position to weigh fairly the competing needs and interests of parties affected by discovery.[23] The unique character of the discovery process requires that the trial court have substantial latitude to fashion protective orders.

The facts in this case illustrate the concerns that justifiably may prompt a court to issue a protective order. As we have noted, the trial court's order allowing discovery was extremely broad. It compelled respondents—among other things—to identify all persons who had made donations over a 5-year period to Rhinehart and the Aquarian Foundation, together with the amounts donated. In effect the order would compel disclosure of membership as well as sources of financial support. The Supreme Court of Washington found that dissemination of this information would "result in annoyance, embarrassment and even oppression." * * * It is sufficient for purposes of our decision that the highest court in the State found no abuse of discretion in the trial court's decision to issue a protective order pursuant to a constitutional state law. We therefore hold that where, as in this case, a protective order is entered on a showing of good cause as required by Rule 26(c), is limited to the context of pretrial civil discovery, and does not restrict the dissemination of the information if gained from other sources, it does not offend the First Amendment.

The judgment accordingly is

Affirmed.

[The concurring opinion of JUSTICE BRENNAN, with whom JUSTICE MARSHALL joined, is omitted.]

Notes and Questions

1.   What is "good cause" for a protective order under Rule 26(c)? The courts generally have required the moving party to demonstrate that "disclosure will work a clearly defined and very serious injury." Citicorp v. Interbank Card Ass'n, 478 F.Supp. 756, 765 (S.D.N.Y.1979). The movant must make a showing by "a particular and specific demonstration of fact, as distinguished from stereotyped and conclusory statements." General Dynamics Corp. v. Selb Mfg. Co., 481 F.2d 1204, 1212 (8th Cir.1973). If the movant sustains its burden, the court then considers the interests of the nonmoving party, of nonparties, and of the public in not restricting disclosure. Does all this suggest that a district judge's decision to

ing that potential litigants have unimpeded access to the courts: "[A]s the trial court rightly observed, rather than expose themselves to unwanted publicity, individuals may well forego the pursuit of their just claims. The judicial system will thus have made the utilization of its remedies so onerous that the people will be reluctant or unwilling to use it, resulting in frustration of a right as valuable as that of speech itself." 654 P.2d, at 689. * * *

23.   In addition, heightened First Amendment scrutiny of each request for a protective order would necessitate burdensome evidentiary findings and could lead to time-consuming interlocutory appeals, as this case illustrates. * * *

grant or deny a protective order is not controlled by legal rules or standards, but is left to the judge's unfettered discretion? Does the degree of discretion left to district judges make the application of the discovery rules unpredictable and uneven? Does it foster discovery disputes, or encourage lawyers to negotiate and settle their disputes?

To what extent is it relevant that a suit is brought chiefly for the purpose of obtaining private information about the defendant for purposes of disclosing it publicly? Suppose a third person, desirous of obtaining such private information, finances plaintiff's suit?

2. Consider the following cases in which it was argued that interests of privacy justified the issuance of a protective order barring the requested discovery:

(a) MUTUAL OF OMAHA INS. CO. v. GARRIGAN, 31 Ohio Misc. 1, 4, 285 N.E.2d 395, 396–97 (Com.Pl.1971). Plaintiff insurance company brought an action against the widow of its insured, asking for a declaration that the insured's death by carbon monoxide poisoning had not been accidental and hence was not covered by the policy. The company sought to discover the corpse, which would have required disinterment. The court refused, stating:

> While liberal discovery rules are to be encouraged and are generally accepted, it is questionable that they should be used to override the long standing common law and statutory limitations on disinterment. Historically, disinterment has been ordered in only rare instances and then only after the insurance company has presented evidence to show it is "reasonably certain that an examination may reveal something that will show fraud or mistake * * *." It is the opinion of this court that the plaintiffs have failed to meet that burden of proof. * * * Absent express statutory authorization, this court is not willing to extend the liberal discovery rules of Ohio into the grave.

(b) WILLIAMS v. THOMAS JEFFERSON UNIVERSITY, 343 F.Supp. 1131, 1132 (E.D.Pa.1972). Plaintiff, in a medical malpractice action involving abortion, sought to discover the names of women who had previously had abortions at defendant hospital. The stated purpose was to gather evidence to impeach testimony expected to be given by defendant doctor. Discovery was denied. The court said:

> * * * In the abstract, abortion is discussed openly and with fervor. Nevertheless, it is an extremely personal thing to each woman who has had an abortion. The consequences of allowing revelation and examination when considered in terms of family relationships and individual friendships could be disastrous to the subjects of an inquiry of the type plaintiff wants to make. A collateral attack for impeachment purposes does not weigh very heavily in a balancing of interests when opposed to such obvious reasons for privacy.

(c) RASMUSSEN v. SOUTH FLORIDA BLOOD SERVICE, INC., 500 So.2d 533 (Fla.1987), and SNYDER v. MEKHJIAN, 125 N.J. 328, 593 A.2d 318 (1991). In both of these cases, persons who claimed to have received an HIV-positive blood transfusion sought discovery from a blood bank as to the identity of the blood donor. The Florida court denied the motion for discovery, stating:

> Disclosure of donor identities in any context involving AIDS could be extremely disruptive and even devastating to the individual donor. * * * The probative value of the discovery sought by Rasmussen is dubious at best. The potential of significant harm to most, if not all, of the fifty-one unsuspecting donors in permitting such a fishing expedition is great and far outweighs the plaintiff's need under the circumstances.

500 So.2d at 537–38. On the other hand, the New Jersey court, relying on statutory authorization for disclosure of an HIV-infected donor's record upon "showing good cause therefor," allowed plaintiffs "limited discovery" of the donor. It was suggested that "either a 'veiled' deposition or one conducted on written interrogatories might provide plaintiffs adequate discovery and also protect the donor's privacy interests." 125 N.J. at 333, 593 A.2d at 320.

(d) A number of cases involve attempts to discover a party's prior sexual history, particularly of a plaintiff who files a sexual harassment suit? How should the court balance defendant's desire for such material with the obvious need for privacy both for plaintiff and those with whom plaintiff was sexually involved? See Comment, *The Conflicting Mandates of FRE 412 and FRCP 26: Should Courts Allow Discovery of Sexual Harassment Plaintiff's Sexual History?*, 1999 U.Chi.Legal F. 519.

3. Should a protective order be fashioned to protect one's right to assert a Fifth Amendment privilege in a criminal proceeding? In SEC v. POWER SECURITIES CORP., 142 F.R.D. 321 (D.Colo.1992), the United States Attorney had begun a grand jury investigation into possible criminal-law violations stemming from the same events that gave rise to the SEC's civil suit. The court granted the motion of one of the defendants for a protective order postponing his deposition in the civil suit. It reasoned that this could possibly avoid having him face the dilemma of deciding whether to testify at a deposition in the civil case—with the possibility that his testimony could lead to the bringing of criminal charges against him—or whether to refuse to testify at the deposition, which could result in an adverse judgment in the civil case.

4. What standard should a court apply if asked to modify an existing protective order limiting the disclosure of sensitive information? In PALMIERI v. NEW YORK, 779 F.2d 861 (2d Cir.1985), the court sustained a magistrate's refusal to grant the State's Attorney General, in connection with an on-going investigation into possible criminal antitrust violations, access to the settlement agreement in a private antitrust suit and to other documents when the magistrate believed that meaningful discovery would not have occurred and the case would not have been settled absent a provision specifically barring the Attorney General from seeing the documents. The court held that a party seeking to modify the order must show that it was granted improvidently or must demonstrate some extraordinary circumstance or compelling need for disclosure of the information. Is this burden too demanding? Does it contravene the commitment to openness embodied in the discovery rules?

5. It has become commonplace in large cases for parties to stipulate to protective orders negotiated by opposing counsel. And judges generally assent to these agreements, in large part to move cases along and avoid controversy. The stipulations typically provide for "umbrella" protection for confidential information, which is defined as any information that is designated "confidential" by the producing party. As Judge Becker observed in ZENITH RADIO CORP. v. MATSUSHITA ELECTRIC INDUSTRIAL CO., 529 F.Supp. 866, 889 (E.D.Pa.1981): "We are unaware of any case in the past half-dozen years of even a modicum of complexity where an umbrella protective order has not been agreed to by the parties and approved by the court." The result of these orders is that virtually all nonpublic documents are designated confidential without any individualized review. Why have these orders become so common? What is the strategic significance for a defendant of a confidentiality order? Does disclosure to third persons open the door to misuse of the court system for blackmail or extortion through the

threat of suits involving sensitive issues? What does a plaintiff's attorney gain by agreeing to a broad protective order? Are these orders consistent with the Supreme Court's analysis in *Seattle Times*? Or is some degree of judicial review necessary? Should umbrella orders be enforced as written? What standard should a court apply if asked to modify an existing protective order to permit the disclosure of discovered material to non-parties? Is it relevant that the matter shielded from public view by the protective order is alleged to impact on the public health and safety? For a discussion of these issues, see Miller, *Confidentiality, Protective Orders, and Public Access to the Courts*, 105 Harv.L.Rev. 428 (1991).

The Publicity in Taking Evidence Act of 1913, 15 U.S.C. § 30, provides that depositions of witnesses in actions by the government in antitrust suits under the Sherman Act "shall be open to the public as freely as are trials in open court." In United States v. Microsoft Corp., 165 F.3d 952 (D.C.Cir.1999), the court held that this provision was consistent with Federal Rule 26(c), justifying the lower court, in its discretion, to order that the news media and members of the public be permitted to attend depositions in the case.

6.   Review the sample protective order governing discovery and the protection and exchange of confidential information that is reproduced in the Supplement. What problems do the provisions of the order attempt to address? Are the solutions satisfactory? Are there other possibilities that might better protect a company's trade secrets and other confidential information?

7.   On protective orders generally, see Dore, *Secrecy by Consent: The Use and Limits of Confidentiality in the Pursuit of Settlement*, 74 Notre Dame L.Rev. 283 (1999); Friedenthal, *Secrecy and Confidentiality in Civil Litigation: Discovery and Party Agreements*, 9 J. of L. & Policy 61 (2000).

SECTION B.   THE MECHANICS OF THE DISCOVERY DEVICES

1.   MANDATORY DISCLOSURE

———

Study Federal Rule of Civil Procedure 26(a) in the Supplement.

———

Under Rule 26(a) as amended in 1993, and again in 2000, the initial step in the discovery process is mandatory disclosure of certain information. The Rule also calls for the automatic disclosure of certain other matters later in the pretrial process.

COMAS v. UNITED TELEPHONE COMPANY OF KANSAS

United States District Court, District of Kansas, 1995.
1995 WL 476691.

RUSHFECT, MAGISTRATE JUDGE. Under consideration is a Motion to Compel Defendant's Rule 26(a)(1) Disclosures. * * * [P]laintiff Craig A. Comas seeks to compel defendant United Telephone Company of Kansas to produce all information encompassed by Rule 26(a)(1). He further seeks his reasonable expenses, including attorney's fees incurred in making this motion. Subsequent to the motion defendant made many of the initial disclosures required by Rule 26(a)(1). Defendant suggests only an issue concerning formal discovery remains, rather than a Rule 26(a)(1) dispute. It suggests that the parties can resolve the issue without court intervention.

Plaintiff contends that defendant should produce personnel files of four individuals whose treatment is at issue. He also seeks production of an internal investigative file prepared by defendant in connection with his previous Equal Employment Opportunity Commission (EEOC) charges. Pursuant to Rule 26(a)(1), plaintiff submits that the parties agreed to voluntarily produce all relevant materials as an alternative to formal discovery. He maintains that the personnel files and the internal EEOC investigative file should be produced in accordance with this agreement.

Defendant concedes that, pursuant to Rule 26(a)(1), the parties agreed to furnish copies of non-privileged documents, rather than describe them. It submits that the parties have also agreed upon an appropriate protective order for the internal investigation file. Thus it has agreed to waive any privilege for the file and to produce copies of it. Defendant contends, however, that personnel files of persons other than plaintiff should not be produced in its initial Rule 26(a)(1) disclosures. It maintains that such production is more appropriate as formal discovery. It nevertheless has agreed to produce redacted copies of the personnel files.

* * *

Initial disclosures may be made by describing or categorizing potentially relevant materials so that the opposing party may "make an informed decision regarding which documents might need to be examined." Fed. R.Civ.P. 26(a)(1) Advisory Committee's Notes (1993 Am.). The rule does not require that either party produce documents at this initial stage. If only a description or categorization is provided, "the other part[y] [is] expected to obtain the documents desired by proceeding under Rule 34 or through informal requests."

Rule 26(a)(1) allows initial disclosures to be made by producing copies of the relevant documents. Parties, therefore, may agree to produce all relevant documents without discovery requests. Production at this stage speeds the discovery process. The parties here agreed to make their Rule 26(a)(1) disclosures by such production. Defendant has agreed, moreover, to produce redacted copies of the personnel files. It has agreed to waive any applicable privilege to the internal EEOC investigative file. The parties proceed as if the personnel files and EEOC investigative file are in the possession, custody, or control of defendant and "are relevant to disputed facts alleged with particularity in the pleadings." Thus such documents are appropriately part of the initial disclosures. See Fed.R.Civ.P. 26(a)(1)(B). Defendant shall produce the redacted personnel files and the EEOC investigation file, if it has not already done so.

In this instance the court will not compel unredacted personnel files. First, plaintiff has not suggested that redacted copies would fail to comply with the duty of defendant. Second, compelled production in this instance rests upon agreements between the parties. Although the court may enforce an unchallenged, unequivocal agreement, it declines to enforce disputed, unclear terms. In this instance, some parts of the agreement appear unclear.

* * *

Rule 37 clearly calls for sanctions, when the party makes disclosure after a motion to compel has been filed with the court. Although, absent stipulation or court order, Rule 26(a)(1) requires parties to produce all relevant materials within ten days of the Rule 26 meeting between the parties, defendant did not produce its initial disclosures until three weeks after plaintiff filed his motion. Even now it is unclear whether defendant has produced the EEOC investigative file or the four redacted personnel files, despite its assurances that it would do so. In accordance with Rule 37, defendant and its counsel shall have 25 days from the date of this order to show why the court should not require one or both of them to pay the reasonable expenses incurred in preparation and defense of this motion. Plaintiff shall have 15 days from the date of this order to serve and file an affidavit of time and expense expended on this motion.

For the foregoing reasons, the court sustains in part, deems moot in part, and defers ruling in part the Motion to Compel Defendant's Rule 26(a)(1) Disclosures. Within twenty days of the date of this order, defendant shall produce redacted personnel files which it agreed to provide as part of its disclosures under Rule 26(a)(1) and the EEOC investigation file, if it has not already done so. * * * After defendant has had its opportunity to be heard in accordance with Fed.R.Civ.P. 37, the court will rule upon the issue of sanctions. * * *

Notes and Questions

1. Mandatory disclosure has been the subject of intense controversy among judges, practitioners, and legal scholars since it was first proposed. For a discussion of the controversy surrounding Rule 26(a)(1), see Sorenson, *Disclosure Under Federal Rule of Civil Procedure 26(a)—'Much Ado About Nothing?'*, 46 Hastings L.J. 679 (1995). Prior to the amendment of Rule 26 in 2000, mandatory disclosure applied to every type of case. The amendment added a new provision, Rule 26(a)(1)(E), excluding eight types of cases in which there is little need for discovery or in which a party is likely to be conducting his or her own case.

2. Before it was altered in 2000, Rule 26(a)(1) expressly permitted a federal district court by local rule to determine not to employ the mandatory disclosure rules in any of its cases. As a result almost one-third of the districts promulgated "opt-out" provisions. See Yamamoto, *Procedural Politics and Federal Rule 26: Opting–Out of "Mandatory" Disclosure,* 16 U.Haw.L.Rev. 167 (1994). The present Rule eliminates the "opt-out" provision, but permits a trial judge to provide that mandatory disclosure will not be required in any specific case. What justification could there be for an "opt-out" rule? Why was it eliminated?

3. Does mandatory disclosure contravene the lawyer's duty to the client and thereby weaken the adversary system? Note that the 2000 amendments to Rule 26(a)(1) require a party only to provide information that will "support its claims and defenses." Previously each party had to provide information "relevant to disputed facts alleged with particularity in the pleadings." What is the likely effect of the altered language? In addition, the change in the Rule exempted from

mandatory disclosure information to be used "solely for impeachment." What is the purpose of the exemption? What type of information is "solely for impeachment?"

2. DEPOSITIONS

―――――――

Study Federal Rules of Civil Procedure 26(d), 30, and 31 in the Supplement.

―――――――

An oral deposition allows an attorney for a party to question any person (the "deponent"), under oath, whether a party or not, regarding the subject matter of the case. One of the most significant features of federal deposition procedure is that it is designed to function by private arrangement among the parties and without need for judicial intervention. Although the rules as to when, how, before whom, and on what notice as to time and place a deposition may be taken are spelled out in detail (see Federal Rules 28, 30, 31, and 32(d) respectively), Rule 29 permits the parties to stipulate in writing to take a deposition "before any person, at any time or place, upon any notice, and in any manner." Invariably, the parties designate as officer the reporter who records the questions, the answers, and any objections made by the parties or by the witness. When the deposition is concluded, the reporter prepares a transcript, which the deponent then is called upon to sign.

Under modern discovery rules, an attorney schedules a deposition merely by serving a notice on the opposing attorney. The notice must include the name and address of the deponent, if known, and the date, time, and place of the deposition. If the deponent is a party, the notice is sufficient to require the party's appearance, and a subpoena is unnecessary. The notice may include a demand that the party produce documents and other items of evidence at the deposition, in which case the procedure of Rule 34 applies (although it is not clear whether the thirty–day period of Rule 34 applies to a demand for production under Rule 30(b)(5)).

If the deponent is not a party, the notice of deposition will not be sufficient to compel the non-party's appearance. There is no requirement that a non-party be subpoenaed to a deposition. However, a non-party is not subject to any sanction if he is not subpoenaed and does not appear, or if he appears but fails to bring requested documents or other items. A person who fails to respond to a subpoena will be subject to a citation for contempt of court. In addition, if a party notices a deposition, but does not subpoena the witness, and, if the witness fails to appear, that party may be ordered to pay the reasonable expenses, including attorneys' fees, of any other party for wasting time appearing at the place where the deposition was to be taken. See Rule 30(g)(2). Thus, unless full cooperation of the non-party witness is certain, the use of a subpoena is advisable.

Under Federal Rule 30(b)(6) an attorney may notice the deposition of a corporation or association, requiring the latter to produce the person or persons having knowledge of the subject matter upon which the deposition is to be taken. Of course, the party seeking the information must detail the issues that are to be explored in order that the organization can ascertain which of its personnel has the relevant knowledge. This form of corporate depositions is useful particularly when the party taking the deposition is unaware of which individual or individuals within a large organization has the information that is needed.

Most commonly, the details as to a deposition are worked out among all of the attorneys in order to accommodate their schedules and that of the person to be deposed. If the parties cannot agree on the time, place, or details of the examination, then a court order may be obtained with respect to the disputed matters.

The usual expectation is that a deposition will proceed without court involvement. The deponent usually will answer even those questions to which counsel object, unless the deponent's counsel instructs him not to answer. Counsel interpose objections at depositions to preserve their right to object to another party's use of the deposition's transcript at trial. Counsel must object at the deposition if the ground for the objection is one that might be corrected at the time. For example, an attorney who is aware that the deposition officer omitted swearing the witness cannot object at trial, because a timely objection at the deposition would have given the officer the opportunity to correct the oversight. Misconduct during pretrial depositions includes "speaking objections," namely, objections made in a manner that intentionally or unintentionally instruct the witness as to the answer to be given or desired by the objecting counsel, as well as blatant coaching during private discussions between the witness and his attorney during the deposition. What tactics might counsel taking the deposition use to prevent or control such abuses? Under Rule 30(d)(1), which was added in 1993, and amended in 2000, a deponent may be instructed not to answer only "to preserve a privilege, to enforce a limitation on evidence directed by the court, or to present a motion under Rule 30(d)(4)" to terminate or limit an examination that is oppressive or conducted in bad faith." According to one commentator:

> Depositions are usually conducted in an adversarial but cooperative atmosphere, and thus it is rarely necessary to involve the court. Most litigators take seriously their duty of good faith in participating in the discovery process. The lawyer tempted to disrupt may be deterred by the prospects of reciprocal treatment from opposing counsel and sanctions from the court.

Suplee, *Depositions: Objectives, Strategies, Tactics, Mechanics and Problems,* 2 Rev.Litigation 255, 282 (1982). Still, problems arise, and some attorneys adopt abusive tactics.

Notes and Questions

1. The most important of the discovery devices is the oral deposition. * * * It is the only significant discovery device that may be directed against any person, and is not confined to parties to the action. It is the only discovery device that permits examination and cross-examination of a live witness by counsel, where there is no opportunity to reflect and carefully shape the information given. Thus, despite its expense, it is the most valuable device if the deponent has important information.

Wright, *Federal Courts* § 84, at 610 (5th ed. 1994).

2. Ever since modern discovery rules first appeared, courts have been faced with the situation in which the parties are vying to take the first deposition, each attempting to pin down the opponent or the opponent's key witness before submitting himself or his own witnesses to the discovery process. Is there really a substantial advantage to deposing first? Does this advantage exist for an honest party as well as for an unscrupulous party who will deliberately color her testimony? See generally *Developments in the Law—Discovery*, 74 Harv.L.Rev. 940, 954–58 (1961).

Prior to amendments to the discovery rules in 1970, the federal courts generally had held that the party who first served a notice of a deposition was entitled to priority as to that deposition. This is still the situation in many states. See, e.g., N.Y.C.P.L.R. 3106. The problem is complicated by the fact that in most of these jurisdictions plaintiff is prohibited, without leave of court, from serving a notice of deposition for a specific period of time in order to permit defendant to learn of the suit and employ counsel. Leave of court normally has been permitted only under exceptional circumstances. Since there is no comparable restriction on defendant, she will receive priority merely by serving notice during the period plaintiff is required to wait. How serious a problem is this? According to the Advisory Committee a comprehensive study revealed that in only 16 per cent of the cases did defendants move for discovery within plaintiff's waiting period and that obviously in some of these cases priority was not a motive.

In 1993, Rule 26(d) was amended to abolish plaintiff's waiting period. As further amended in 2000 it provided that, unless the deponent is expected to depart from the country or leave of court is obtained, neither party may commence any discovery until all the parties have conferred to discuss possible resolution of the case, to arrange for the mandatory disclosures required by Rule 26(a), and to develop a proposed discovery plan. To what extent do you think that this approach will alleviate any bickering between the parties as to priority of discovery?

For extensive discussions of the priority problem see 8 Wright, Miller & Marcus, *Federal Practice and Procedure: Civil 2d* §§ 2045–47 (1994); *Developments in the Law—Discovery*, 74 Harv.L.Rev. 940, 954–58 (1961).

3. In 2000, Rule 30(d)(2) was amended to limit a deposition to one day of seven hours, unless otherwise agreed by the parties and the deponent, or extended by court order. Previously there was no specific time limit, although the court could impose one.

4. The practical problems involved in taking and defending depositions are discussed in Suplee, *Depositions: Objectives, Strategies, Tactics, Mechanics and Problems*, 2 Rev.Litigation 255 (1982). Useful sources on the strategic and tactical uses of the discovery devices generally, including depositions, are Dombroff, *Discovery* (1966); and Haydock, Herr & Stempel, *Fundamentals of Pretrial Discovery* 120–391 (1985).

———

Read Federal Rules of Civil Procedure 37(d) and 45(d)-(e) in the Supplement.

———

LESS v. TABER INSTRUMENT CORP.

United States District Court, Western District of New York, 1971.
53 F.R.D. 645.

CURTIN, DISTRICT JUDGE. Teledyne, Inc., a non-party foreign corporation concededly doing business in this judicial district, was properly served by plaintiff with a subpoena commanding it to appear in this district for examination through "Henry E. Singleton, Chairman and Chief Executive Officer and * * * Edmund M. Kaufman, Assistant Secretary." Kaufman is no longer employed by Teledyne, and plaintiff concedes that his presence may not be compelled. Singleton, who is presently Chairman of Teledyne's Board of Directors and based at its Los Angeles, California, headquarters, was not personally served with a subpoena. The questions before the court are whether Singleton, a non-party director of a non-party corporation, may be required to submit to examination and, if so, shall he be so required and under what conditions.

Under the present discovery provisions of the Federal Rules of Civil Procedure, the deposition of a corporate party may be taken from a director named in the notice given to the corporation. The director need not be personally subpoenaed, and the corporation must produce him or risk the imposition of sanctions under Rule 37(d). * * * Teledyne argues that a different rule should apply to the director of a non-party corporation.

* * *

The Rules do not suggest that a different principle applies to discovery from a party corporation than applies to discovery from a non-party corporation. Rule 30(a), which governs the taking of depositions upon oral examination, does not distinguish between parties and non-parties; it simply provides that "any party may take the testimony of *any person, including a party,* by deposition upon oral examination." Fed.R.Civ.P. 30(a) (emphasis added). The provision that "[t]he attendance of witnesses may be compelled by subpoena as provided in Rule 45," Fed.R.Civ.P. 30(a), also connotes no operative distinction between parties and non-parties. The provision is merely intended to assure that the non-party whose testimony is sought submits to examination. There is no necessity for requiring service of a subpoena upon a party since adequate sanctions are provided in Rule 37 in the event that the party fails to respond to a notice to take a deposition.

* * * [A] non-party witness, even more than a party, must be protected against undue burden and expense. * * * Therefore, the court does not choose to depart from the ordinary rules that a mere witness will not be required to leave his residence and business and travel great distances for the convenience of the parties * * * and that the deposition of a corporation should be taken at its principal place of business. * * *

It is therefore the order of this court that the deposition upon oral examination of Henry E. Singleton be taken at the principal place of business of Teledyne, Inc. * * *.

Notes and Questions

1. Should the court in the *Less* case have discussed Federal Rule 30(b)(6)? Doesn't that provision clearly provide that a corporation has the right to choose who shall testify on its behalf? Are there reasons why the choice should be left to the corporation? See generally the Advisory Committee's Notes on the 1970 amendments to Rule 30, which appear in the Supplement. Even in the absence of a rule comparable to Rule 30(b)(6) some courts have held that the selection is to be made by the corporation, at least until it becomes apparent that the person chosen does not possess all the relevant facts known to the corporation. E.g., Fernandez v. St. John's Episcopal Hospital, 70 A.D.2d 627, 416 N.Y.S.2d 638 (2d Dep't 1979). Compare Atlantic Cape Fisheries v. Hartford Fire Ins. Co., 509 F.2d 577 (1st Cir.1975), which holds that Rule 30(b)(6) does not alter the right of a party who takes the deposition of a corporation that is also a party to designate which officer, managing agent, or director shall appear to answer on behalf of the corporation.

2. What if a corporate party whose deposition is noted under Rule 30(b)(6) deliberately selects as the person to testify someone who appears for the deposition but who lacks information sufficient to respond to the questions asked? Can the court order sanctions under Rule 37(d) without first issuing an order to compel discovery and giving the deponent an opportunity to comply? Courts have split on the question. Read literally, Rule 37(d) applies only if a witness fails to appear. For a discussion of the cases, and a rejection of the literal reading of the Rule, see Black Horse Lane Assoc., L. P. v. Dow Chem. Corp., 228 F.3d 275 (3d Cir.2000) (a lack of knowledge by the selected deponent is tantamount to a failure to appear under Rule 37(d)).

3. As previously noted, the party who gives notice of the taking of a deposition is not required to subpoena even a nonparty witness whose testimony is sought. If no subpoena is issued, however, and the witness fails to attend, Federal Rule 30(g)(2) permits certain sanctions to be imposed upon the party who failed to use a subpoena. What tactical reasons might motivate a party to refrain from serving a subpoena on a witness? Note that under Rule 45(b)(2), if a witness refuses to cooperate, so that she must be subpoenaed, the deposition may have to be held in a district other than the one in which the case has been filed. Suppose the witness disobeys the subpoena. If she appears but refuses to answer questions properly put to her, the parties may seek assistance under Rule 37(a). What is the purpose of this provision? Note that, prior to 1993, if the witness was a party, Rule 37(a)(1) permitted either the court where the action was pending or the one where the deposition was being taken to issue orders relating to the deposition. The existing Rule 37(a)(1), however, requires that applications for an order directed to a party must be made to the court in which the action is pending, while applications to depose a person not a party must be made to the court of the district where the discovery is to be taken. Is there any reason for distinguishing between party and nonparty witnesses?

CARSON v. BURLINGTON NORTHERN INC., 52 F.R.D. 492 (D.Neb. 1971). Plaintiff was injured when a steel press he was operating came down on his hand, allegedly due to defendant's negligence. Defendant moved to take plaintiff's deposition at the scene of the accident using video tape. Plaintiff objected that this procedure could only produce a staged, unnatural recreation. The court granted the motion, holding that the 1970 amendment to Federal Rule 30(b)(4) specifically provided for video taping. The court, however, did hold that plaintiff would not be required to touch or operate the press; he only would be required to use a pointer to show the manner in which he operated the machine on the day of the accident.

Notes and Questions

1. Traditionally, depositions have been recorded by stenographic means only. See Bailey v. Superior Court, 19 Cal.3d 970, 140 Cal.Rptr. 669, 568 P.2d 394 (1977) (in absence of specific statutory provision or agreement among the parties, videotape recording is prohibited). However, the modern trend is to allow sound recordings and videotaping, either in lieu of or in addition to stenographic recording. Indeed, Bailey v. Superior Court was legislatively overruled in 1980. Cal.Civ.Proc.Code § 2025(*l*) now provides that a deposition may be videotaped if the notice of deposition so provides. See also Lester v. Lester, 69 Misc.2d 528, 330 N.Y.S.2d 190 (Sup.Ct.1972); Mich.Ct.Rules 2.315. Rule 30(b)(2) was amended in 1993 to provide that "[u]nless the court orders otherwise, [the testimony at a deposition] may be recorded by sound, sound-and-visual, or stenographic means"—thus making it clear that it no longer would be necessary to supplement a videotaped deposition with a stenographic recording. However, the comments of the Advisory Committee point out that a written transcript will have to be prepared if the deposition is to be offered in evidence.

2. Does the use of tape-recorded depositions raise any special problems? Who should provide and be in charge of the recording equipment? Is there ever a need for more than one recording machine? See Colonial Times, Inc. v. Gasch, 509 F.2d 517 (D.C.Cir.1975); Champagne v. Hygrade Food Products, Inc., 79 F.R.D. 671 (E.D.Wash.1978); Barham v. IDM Corp., 78 F.R.D. 340 (N.D.Ohio 1978).

3. What are the advantages to be gained from audio and video tape-recorded depositions? Does the availability of videotape technology solve any of the practical problems associated with discovery? For example, would a videotape of a deposition aid a court in deciding disputes over the propriety of particular questions or the sufficiency of certain answers? For practical suggestions concerning the conduct of videotape depositions, see Balabanian, *Medium v. Tedium: Video Depositions Come of Age,* 7 Litigation 25, 26–27 (1980).

———

Rule 31 authorizes the taking of depositions upon written questions. In what circumstances might an attorney find a written deposition more useful than an oral one? In what circumstances is a written deposition preferable to Rule 33 interrogatories? See Schmertz, *Written Depositions Under the Federal and State Rules as Cost–Effective Discovery at Home and Abroad,* 16 Villa.L.Rev. 7 (1970).

3. INTERROGATORIES TO PARTIES

———

Read Federal Rule of Civil Procedure 33 in the Supplement.

———

Written interrogatories allow one party to send to another a series of questions to be answered under oath within a specific time. The procedure is extremely simple. No court order is required and no officers need be appointed; the entire exchange is accomplished by mail. If a question is thought to be improper, the responding party may say so rather than answering. The interrogating party then has the option of seeking a court order requiring an answer.

A party has the duty to respond to interrogatories not only on the basis of her own knowledge but also with regard to the knowledge of other persons that reasonably can be obtained through investigation. Thus, a party must consult with her attorney, employees, and other agents who have or might have knowledge.

In addition to the duty to investigate, some jurisdictions require the responding party to state her opinions or contentions as to the facts that are relevant to the subject matter of the action. Under this approach, it would be appropriate to ask a defendant whether he was negligently driving his vehicle at the time of the accident. The defendant would be free to answer the question "No," but he could not refuse to answer on the ground that it was somehow inappropriate.

Special rules have been adopted regarding a party's duty to respond to interrogatories requiring an investigation of its business records. When the answer may be derived from the answering party's business records, and when it would be just as easy for the requesting party to search those records as it would be for the responding party, then the responding party, instead of answering, may specify the records from which the answers may be obtained and give the inquiring party a reasonable opportunity to look at them. This does not mean that the responding party can simply say, "The answer is in our records," and then turn all records over to the inquiring party, knowing full well that the latter never will be able to locate the appropriate documents. The responding party must designate with some specificity just what documents contain the information in order that the inquiring party can find it. Further, if there would be a far greater burden on the inquiring party to ascertain the information than there would be on the responding party, then the latter must ascertain the answer itself.

Interrogatories may not be used to obtain information from a nonparty. Information from a nonparty may be obtained by deposition, however.

Notes and Questions

1. Since interrogatories can be prepared by an attorney in his own office and at his leisure, thereby avoiding the expense of oral depositions and the time consumed therein, they may be very effectively employed where a thoroughgoing deposition is not necessary. * * * Illustrative of this type of use is the situation encountered in reference to an attempt to ascertain the names of persons having knowledge of relevant facts concerning the matter in litiga-

tion. * * * If the "adverse party" is a partnership, association, or corporation, one single interrogatory directed to the group covers the information in the hands of all members, agents, employees, etc. * * * If such information were sought by depositions * * * this would necessitate the taking of numerous depositions and the costs incurred therewith, with no assurance that all persons who might have knowledge would be questioned.

Feirich & Feirich, *Interrogatories to Parties and Demands to Admit,* 1959 U.Ill. L.F. 733, 734. Did the adoption of Federal Rule 30(b)(6) in 1970 or the 1993 changes to Rule 26(a) affect the significance of written interrogatories? In what ways are written interrogatories under Rule 33 less effective than an oral examination under Rule 30? See 8A Wright, Miller & Marcus, *Federal Practice and Procedure: Civil 2d* § 2163 (1994).

2. How extensive should the duty of investigation be under Rule 33? Should a corporate party be charged with the responsibility of finding out what is known by each of its employees regardless of the size and nature of the business? Should the duty extend to information known to employees of subsidiary corporations that are not parties? See Sol. S. Turnoff Drug Distributors Inc. v. N.V. Nederlandsche Combinatie Voor Chemische Industrie, 55 F.R.D. 347 (E.D.Pa.1972). To what extent should the duty include former employees?

Should the first sentence of Rule 33 be construed as not requiring an individual party to make an investigation into matters that are outside that party's personal knowledge? See Hickman v. Taylor, p. 849, infra, in which the Supreme Court said that a party cannot refuse to answer interrogatories merely because an attorney, rather than the party, knows the facts. Should the obligation to inquire extend beyond the party's employees and agents, perhaps to a spouse or other members of the party's immediate family?

3. Prior to 1970, Federal Rule 33 only permitted interrogatories to be served on an adverse party. This requirement, which still exists in some states, was a source of confusion and controversy. Some courts held that parties were adverse only if the pleadings formally established an issue between them; others held that an actual conflict of interest was sufficient. See generally Gorman Rupp Industries, Inc. v. Superior Court, 20 Cal.App.3d 28, 97 Cal.Rptr. 377 (2d Dist.1971); 8A Wright, Miller & Marcus, *Federal Practice and Procedure: Civil 2d* § 2171 (1994).

4. Should Federal Rule 33 be further altered to permit service of interrogatories on nonparty witnesses? See *Developments in the Law—Discovery,* 74 Harv. L.Rev. 940, 1020–22 (1961).

5. Must a party in response to an interrogatory disclose information it has, regardless of its reliability or credibility? In RILEY v. UNITED AIR LINES, INC., 32 F.R.D. 230 (S.D.N.Y.1962), plaintiff served interrogatories, asking defendant to state in detail how the accident occurred. In holding insufficient defendant's response that it had "no knowledge sufficient to answer the interrogatories because all the crew members died in the accident," the court said:

> * * * It is apparent from the opposing affidavit that defendant has already obtained certain information from third persons relating to some of the interrogatories * * *. In this situation, defendant should furnish whatever information it now has, regardless of when or from whom it acquired it. * * *

> Defendant may state in its answers what the source of the information is, if it so desires, [but when] * * * the information has been obtained by

persons under defendant's control solely from [questions addressed to] third persons, defendant is not required to admit its accuracy. * * *

Id. at 233. Assuming the information is disclosed, may a party be required to answer a further interrogatory that asks the party's opinion as to whether the information is true or not? See Shapiro, *Some Problems of Discovery in an Adversary System,* 63 Minn.L.Rev. 1055, 1072–77 (1979).

————

RICH v. MARTIN MARIETTA CORP., 522 F.2d 333, 343–45 (10th Cir.1975). The plaintiffs sued on behalf of themselves and the class of persons allegedly affected by the defendant's discrimination in promotions at its plant in Colorado. The trial court sustained the defendant's objections to 69 interrogatories that requested statistical information as to the numbers of Blacks, Hispanos, and women hired, fired, promoted, and demoted in each department of the plant, and the work records of the employees in these departments. At the conclusion of the trial, the court dismissed the plaintiffs' action for lack of evidence. The Tenth Circuit reversed the judgment and remanded, in part, because of the trial court's order limiting the scope of discovery:

> It is plain that the scope of discovery through interrogatories and requests for production of documents is limited only by relevance and burdensomeness, and in an [equal employment opportunity] case the discovery scope is extensive. This is a factor which the court should balance on the benefit side as against the burden to the defendant in answering the interrogatories. * * * If the information sought promises to be particularly cogent to the case, the defendant must be required to shoulder the burden. There is a remedy, of course, if the effort fizzles. The costs can finally be assessed to the interrogating parties.

* * *

> The plaintiffs' requested information as to hiring, firing, promotion and demotion of blacks, Hispanos and women on a plant-wide basis and within individual departments was relevant in either an individual or class action. Particularly in light of the contention of the defendant and the findings of the court that the circumstantial evidence was ambiguous, it became the more necessary for the plant-wide statistics and facts to be obtained and presented, for they very likely would prove crucial to the establishing or failure to establish a prima facie case.

> In Woods v. North American Rockwell Corp., 480 F.2d 644 (10th Cir.1973), the plaintiff contended that he was given an examination which was irrelevant in relationship to the job he was seeking. The court held that since the plaintiff made no showing that the test itself produced a discriminatory result, plaintiff had failed to establish a prima facie case. The court went on to hold that the plaintiff was required to demonstrate with statistics or otherwise the discriminatory effect of the promotion test. We think it is plain, therefore, that the plaintiffs had a right to the information and statistics from which they could have compiled trends and policies on the numbers of white persons receiving promotions during

the relevant time periods in the departments and throughout the plant opposed to the number of blacks, Hispanos and women who received promotions. If it is true that the immediate evidence and circumstances pertaining to the plaintiffs are not sufficient to constitute a prima facie case, plant-wide statistics and department statistics are of the highest relevance.

If the plaintiffs do establish a prima facie case and if the defendant is able to rebut it by showing a business necessity, such information or statistics would also be relevant to an attempt by the plaintiffs to show that the business necessity was pretextual. * * *

Under the facts and circumstances of this case, taking into account that defendant was allowed to defend with plant-wide statistics, the relevance of the information sought by the plaintiffs both in support of their initial case and for the purpose of rebuttal has a high degree of relevance and cannot be ruled out as burdensome. In all likelihood the defendant already has the figures isolated and computed. If not, it ought to proceed forthwith compiling them or at least compiling information from which the plaintiffs can prepare their evidentiary tables or statistics. The fact that they might have been generally invited to peruse the defendant's documents does not fill the bill. Such an approach does not compel the defendant to come forward with everything demanded as does an interrogatory.

Notes and Questions

1. It has been said that a party ordinarily cannot be forced to prepare his opponent's case. See Kainz v. Anheuser–Busch, Inc., 15 F.R.D. 242, 252 (N.D.Ill. 1954). Consequently, interrogatories that require a party to make extensive investigations, research, compilation, or evaluation of data for the adversary are in many circumstances improper. E.g., Halder v. International Tel. & Tel. Co., 75 F.R.D. 657 (E.D.N.Y.1977). Yet, it also has been held that the fact that answering interrogatories will require a party to expend considerable time, effort, and expense, or may interfere with its business operations, is not reason enough to disallow them if the information sought is relevant. E.g., Roesberg v. Johns–Manville Corp., 85 F.R.D. 292 (E.D.Pa.1980). How can these positions be reconciled?

2. Federal Rule 33(d) addresses the problem of burdensome interrogatories by expressly providing a party the option of producing its business records in lieu of answering. It was adapted from Cal.Code Civ.Proc. § 2030(f)(2), which appears in the Supplement. The Federal Rule differs in that it adds the requirement that "the burden of deriving or ascertaining the answer" must be "substantially the same for the party serving the interrogatory as for the party served." What is the justification for this additional requirement?

An informative discussion of Rule 33(d) is found in IN RE MASTER KEY ANTITRUST LITIGATION, 53 F.R.D. 87 (D.Conn.1971):

   * * * Since a respondent is required to answer proper interrogatories, it is not plausible to assume that a response that an answer may (or may not) be found in its records, accompanied by an offer to permit their inspection is sufficient. This is little more than an offer to play the discredited game of blindman's bluff at the threshold level of discovery. * * *

I conclude that the option afforded by [Rule 33(d)] * * * is not a procedural device for avoiding the duty to give information. It does not shift to the interrogating party the obligation to find out *whether* sought after information is ascertainable from the files tendered, but only permits a shift of the burden to dig it out once the respondents have specified the records from "where the answer" can be derived or ascertained. If the answers lie in the records of the defendants, they should say so; and if, on the other side, they do not, they should say that. * * *

Id. at 90.

3. In 1980, then Rule 33(c) (now Rule 33(d)) was amended to require a party exercising the option to produce its business records to specify the records from which the answer can be found in sufficient detail to permit the interrogating party to locate and to identify them as readily as can the party served. The clarification sought to prevent the party served from directing the interrogating party to a mass of business records or by offering to make all their records available. Just how specific must a party be?

4. Interrogatories had been cited as the most abused of the available discovery devices. In response, many federal district courts adopted local rules providing that, except on leave of court, no party shall serve on any other party more than a fixed number of interrogatories, often 20. For an interesting opinion explaining and defending one such rule, see Crown Center Redevelopment Corp. v. Westinghouse Elec. Corp., 82 F.R.D. 108 (W.D.Mo.1979).

5. In 1993, Rule 33(a) was amended for the first time to impose a presumptive limit on the numbers of interrogatories that a party may serve. It provides that, unless the parties stipulate otherwise or leave of court is obtained, a party may serve on any other party no more than 25 interrogatories, "including all discrete subparts." The original draft proposed by the Advisory Committee established a limit of 15 interrogatories; in response to comments by the bench and bar, the number was increased to 25. The Notes of the Advisory Committee indicate that although parties cannot evade the limitation "through the device of joining as 'subparts' questions that seek information about discrete separate subjects," nevertheless "a question asking about communications of a particular type should be treated as a single interrogatory" even though it asks for a number of specific details regarding the particular communication.

In WILLIAMS v. BOARD OF COUNTY COMMISSIONERS, 192 F.R.D. 698, 701–02 (D.Kan.2000), the court attempted to explain what counts as a single interrogatory as follows:

Extensive use of subparts, whether explicit or implicit, could defeat the purposes of the numerical limit * * *. On the other hand, if all subparts count as separate interrogatories, the use of interrogatories might be unduly restricted or requests for increases in the numerical limit might become automatic. * * * The Advisory Committee addressed this issue and provided some guidance as to when subparts should and should not count as separate interrogatories:

* * * Parties cannot evade * * * [the] presumptive limitation through the device of joining as 'subparts' questions that seek information about discrete separate subjects. However, a question asking about communications of a particular type should be treated as a single interrogatory even though it requests that the time, place, persons present, and contents be separately stated for each such communication."

* * * A respected commentator has elaborated on that statement as follows:

> "[I]t would appear that an interrogatory containing subparts directed at eliciting details concerning the common theme should be considered a single question, although the breadth of an area inquired about may be disputable. On the other hand, an interrogatory with subparts inquiring into discrete areas is more likely to be counted as more than one for purposes of the limitation.

8A Charles A. Wright, Arthur R. Miller & Richard L. Marcus, Federal Practice and Procedure § 2168.1, at 261 (2d ed.1994).

The seven interrogatories currently before the Court contain 117 subparts. Although the Court is not inclined to review in detail each of the 117 subparts * * * a summary review of the interrogatories * * * leads the Court to believe that defendant * * * has exceeded the maximum number of interrogatories allowed * * *.

Is the court's opinion of any help to defendant in reformulating and reducing its interrogatories to be within the limits? Is there a more certain way to define a single interrogatory for purposes of the Rule?

4. DISCOVERY AND PRODUCTION OF PROPERTY

———

Read Federal Rules of Civil Procedure 34 and 45 in the Supplement.

———

Rule 34 and its state counterparts give a party the right to compel an opponent to produce documents and other tangible things for inspection and copying, and to allow the party entry to land or property in the possession or control of the opponent in order to inspect, measure, survey, photograph, test or sample the property, or to observe an operation taking place on the property. A party wanting to inspect documents and things or to enter property first must confer with other parties in accordance with Rule 26(d). Following this conference, a party simply serves a notice on the opponent stating what the party wants to see, and when, where, and how the party would like to see it.

A request must describe the items to be discovered "with reasonable particularity," a flexible standard that varies with circumstances. Most courts allow discovery of general categories of items if the description is easily understood (e.g., all written communications between plaintiff and defendant between July 1 and September 1, 2001). Many attorneys combine Rule 33 interrogatories that ask the opposing party to identify documents with a Rule 34 request that the party produce "all documents identified" in the opposing party's answers to the interrogatories.

A request must specify a reasonable time, place, and manner for the inspection. The time usually is set at least thirty days after service of the request because the opposing party generally has at least thirty days to respond. The place typically designated for production of documents is the office of the requesting party's attorney, unless it is more convenient to examine the documents where they are kept or to have them copied at some other place. The manner depends on the kind of items requested. In practice, attorneys negotiate the time, place, and manner of production.

The party that receives a request serves a written response on the requesting party, as well as any other parties to the lawsuit, within the time specified by the Rule. The response states the responding party's objections, if any, to part or all of the requested production or inspection. Absent objection, the responding party must produce the documents as requested, or admit counsel to its premises for the scheduled inspection.

If the request for production of documents or inspection of premises is addressed to a nonparty, the litigant must serve a subpoena pursuant to Rule 45. Under former Rule 45, it was not possible to make use of a subpoena to obtain documents or inspect property. Rather, the litigant had to take the nonparty's deposition and in connection with the deposition serve a subpoena ordering the nonparty to bring the designated items to the deposition. In the alternative, the litigant could bring a separate action against the nonparty to obtain discovery. The necessity of using these cumbersome procedures was eliminated when Rule 45 was amended in 1991. The amended Rule now provides that an attorney may issue a subpoena commanding any person to give testimony, to produce and permit inspection and copying of designated records or other tangible objects, or to permit inspection of premises.

Notes and Questions

1. Prior to the amendment of Federal Rule 34 in 1970, it provided for document discovery only on motion to the court granted upon a showing of good cause. Most states have adopted the 1970 changes. What justifications are there for a good-cause requirement? What advantages resulted from its elimination? See the Notes of the Advisory Committee accompanying the 1970 amendment to Federal Rule 34, which appear in the Supplement.

2. In BELCHER v. BASSETT FURNITURE INDUSTRIES, INC., 588 F.2d 904 (4th Cir.1978), an employment discrimination case, the Fourth Circuit reversed the District Court's grant of permission to plaintiff's experts to conduct a five-day inspection of a factory, coupled with interviews of workers selected at random. The purported purpose of the inspection was to uncover evidence relating to an allegation that blacks had been relegated to less attractive jobs than had whites. The court found that the inspection had a great potential for disruption of the factory's activities, while the benefits to be derived seemed slight. Is the decision correct? Consider the court's observation that "since entry upon a party's premises may entail greater burdens and risks than mere production of documents, a greater inquiry into the necessity for inspection would seem warranted." Id. at 908. Do you agree?

3. Under Rule 26(a)(1)(B) a party must identify a relevant document, but does not have to turn it over unless the other side asks for it, even if it constitutes a "smoking gun." Not surprisingly, lawyers are tempted to interpret a request narrowly to avoid having to make a damaging disclosure. For example, attorneys for General Motors in a personal injury action involving the design of the fuel storage system on a 1973 Oldsmobile Omega argued that a request for "any report dated between January 1, 1966 and January 13, 1978 which pertains to any alternative fuel system design proposed, suggested, investigated, studied, consid-

ered, analyzed, and/or tested" "for possible incorporation in the 1969 through 1975 X-body series of cars" did not require it to produce reports that did not specifically mention X-body cars. Its interpretation of the request became apparent when GM was forced to explain why it had not disclosed reports of test data referred to in one of the documents it had disclosed:

> From the context of the documents that have been produced by GM, it is apparent that GM was crash testing alternative fuel storage systems in anticipation of the enactment of more stringent government safety standards for fuel system integrity. In other words, GM's goal was general product improvement. It is sophistic for GM to assert that the tests do not fall within plaintiff's document request because they relate to overall product improvement as opposed to the improvement of a particular product, i.e., 1969 through 1975 X-body vehicles. The scope of plaintiffs' document request * * * is manifestly broad and it was unreasonable for GM to construe it so narrowly. The Court is convinced that any modifying language is likely to be interpreted by GM in such a manner so as to result in further disagreement as to the scope of the document request which would in turn involve more judicial involvement in adjudicating the dispute, and so on. Consequently, GM will be ordered to produce within 60 days any report dated between January 1, 1966 and January 13, 1978 which pertains to any fuel system design proposed, suggested, investigated, studied, considered, analyzed, and/or tested by GM.

SELLON v. SMITH, 112 F.R.D. 9, 13–14 (D.Del.1986). The court went on to award attorney's fees against the manufacturer for this and other discovery misconduct. Why would GM's counsel pursue such tactics, given the substantial likelihood of being caught? Was it a situation in which a defendant was willing to risk the imposition of sanctions because the stakes were so high? What are an attorney's professional obligations in such a situation?

4.   Consider the following description of the practice of document discovery under Rule 34, at least in more complex cases:

> * * * The Rule requires that the demand [for documents] be made for "designated documents," but since the party making the demand typically lacks sufficient information to describe the documents with specificity and knows only the subject matters as to which he expects the opposing party's documents to relate, his Rule 34 demand calls for all documents relating to those subject matters. Since he also expects that the opposing party will narrowly construe the language of his demand so as to avoid producing damaging materials, he attempts, in the first instance, to make that language all-encompassing, and considerable time and expense is generally expended in the very drafting of those requests.

> The opposing party customarily objects to the breadth and burden of the demand—again expending great effort in his submission. Lawyers and company personnel are often dispatched to estimate the volume of documents involved and the number of man-days required for file searches and production. Negotiations are then held regarding the objections, and the party seeking production files a Rule 37 motion with a supporting (and, again, typically extensive) memorandum. The opposing party files his papers consisting of an equally long memorandum and affidavits particularizing the burdensomeness of the demands. Hearings are held on the objections—often before a magistrate with appeals to the court. Rulings are finally made and the production goes forward. The demanding party then moves under Rule 37 to

compel the production of documents he believes were improperly withheld; hearings are then held on that motion; possibly depositions in aid of the motion will be taken; and hearings may be required for rulings regarding the propriety of questions asked on such depositions. The opposing party will, of course, serve his own Rule 34 demand, and in a suit between two companies that will double the work involved.

Second Circuit Commission on the Reduction of Burdens and Costs in Civil Litigation (Draft, Sept. 18, 1978).

5.   Rule 34 requires that data be produced in a "reasonably usable form." In KOZLOWSKI v. SEARS, ROEBUCK & CO., 73 F.R.D. 73 (D.Mass.1976), an action for damages for injuries suffered when pajamas manufactured by defendant caught fire, Sears objected to plaintiff's discovery of prior complaints about the flammability of its pajamas; "because of its longstanding practice of indexing claims alphabetically by name of claimant, rather than by type of product, there is no practical way for anyone to determine whether there also have been any complaints similar" to plaintiff's. Id. at 75–76. The court rejected the argument, stating that the fact that compliance with the request would be costly or time-consuming ordinarily is not a valid objection. In the court's view, to permit Sears to "frustrate discovery by creating an inadequate filing system, and then claiming undue burden, would defeat the purposes of the discovery rule." Id. at 76. Rule 34(b) was amended in 1980 to permit the responding party to turn over the documents either in the order that they are kept in the ordinary course of business or in an organized fashion with proper labeling to correspond with the categories set forth in the request. Would *Kozlowski* have to be decided differently today in light of the 1980 amendment to Rule 34(b)?

From time to time a litigant will respond to a request under Rule 34 by producing a large number of unsorted documents, some of which are unrelated to the case. How should the court respond to complaints by the party who sought the discovery? See Rothman v. Emory University, 123 F.3d 446 (7th Cir.1997) (affirming the trial court's imposition of monetary sanctions).

6.   Does a business, having created a document that might be used by an adversary in future litigation, have an obligation to keep the record? How should a court respond to a business that destroys documents in anticipation of litigation, or after litigation has begun but before the adversary has served a discovery request? How should it respond to the destruction of documents pursuant to a written plan that appears neutral on its face, but effectively denies a litigant useful evidence? See Oesterle, *A Private Litigant's Remedies for an Opponent's Inappropriate Destruction of Documents,* 61 Texas L.Rev. 1185 (1983); Fedders & Guttenplan, *Document Retention and Destruction: Practical, Legal and Ethical Considerations,* 56 Notre Dame L.Rev. 5 (1980).

7.   To what extent does a party have a right to obtain e-mail messages from an opposing party's computer? In Playboy Enterprises, Inc. v. Welles, 60 F.Supp.2d 1050 (S.D.Cal.1999), the court went further and ordered disclosure of relevant messages that had been deleted but nevertheless could be retrieved from the responding party's hard drive. The court recognized that it could not simply order a hard drive turned over to the opposing party since it could include privileged messages between a client and attorney as well as other private messages having nothing to do with the case. Moreover, loss of its hard drive for any significant period could seriously disrupt a party's business. How then could the court proceed? For a discussion of the problems raised by the discovery of electronic information, see Scheindlin & Rabkin, *Electronic Discovery in Federal*

Civil Litigation: Is Rule 34 up to the Task?, 41 B.C.L.Rev. 327 (2000). See also Note, *Allocating Discovery Costs in the Computer Age: Deciding Who Should Bear the Costs of Discovery of Electronically Stored Data*, 57 Wash. & Lee L.Rev. 257 (2000).

HART v. WOLFF

Supreme Court of Alaska, 1971.
489 P.2d 114.

CONNOR, JUSTICE. Plaintiff Victor Hart has appealed from the dismissal of his complaint for failure to comply with an order to produce certain documents for defendant's inspection. * * *

On December 12, 1963, Hart filed suit against Wolff alleging that on two occasions Wolff had made statements defaming Hart. The statements concerned an alleged misappropriation of funds by Hart in the formation of Arctic Bowl, Inc., an Alaska corporation which Hart and Wolff, along with others, had organized in 1958 to operate a bowling alley in Fairbanks.

Wolff was vice-president of the corporation from 1958 until September 1959, when Metropolitan Mortgage and Securities Co., Inc., a Washington corporation, purchased a controlling interest in Arctic Bowl, Inc. Following this change in corporate control, Wolff ceased to be vice-president of the corporation. Hart, who had served as president in 1958 and 1959, remained with the corporation as a manager of the bowling alley.

* * *

Hart argues on appeal that the superior court could not properly order the production of records of Arctic Bowl, Inc., under Civil Rule 34, because the records were not in the possession, custody, or control of a party to the pending action. It is true that an order issued pursuant to Civil Rule 34 may be directed only against a party having possession, custody or control of the records. The order in question here was directed against Hart. Thus, the question which faces us is whether Hart had control over the records sought to be produced.

A prima facie case of control is all that need be established to justify issuance of an order under Civil Rule 34. * * * We believe that Wolff made a prima facie showing that Victor Hart had sufficient control over these records to justify the court's order of December 15, 1969.

The record in this case indicates that while Hart was no longer an officer of Arctic Bowl, Inc., at the time the motions to produce were made he was employed by that corporation in a position of authority and trust. Further, he was also employed during the same time by Metropolitan Mortgage, the controlling shareholder in Arctic Bowl, to handle Metropolitan's business affairs in Fairbanks.

This court in the past has favored liberal construction of the civil rules governing discovery. * * * While Rule 34 certainly has proper limits, the concept of "control" should not be given a hypertechnical construction that will undermine the policy favoring liberal pretrial discovery. As the United States Supreme Court stated in Societé Internationale Pour Participations

Industrielles Et Commerciales S.A. v. Rogers, 357 U.S. 197, 206, 78 S.Ct. 1087, 1092, 2 L.Ed.2d 1255 (1958):

> Rule 34 [F.R.Civ.P.] is sufficiently flexible to be adapted to the exigencies of particular litigation. The propriety of the use to which it is put depends upon the circumstances of a given case * * *.

Thus, though Hart may not have had the authority to *force* Metropolitan to produce the records for Wolff's inspection, we believe the nature of Hart's relationships with Arctic Bowl and with Metropolitan Mortgage were such that the court could infer that he had some influence over Metropolitan with respect to Arctic Bowl, Inc., and could have used that influence to produce the records. In fact, following the issuance of the production order, at the hearing on the motion to strike, Hart himself testified that he imagined he did have some influence over Metropolitan.

In opposition to defendant's motions to produce, Hart merely stated that he was not an officer or director of Arctic Bowl, Inc., and that he did not have the records in his possession, custody or control. At no time did he deny that he had a close employee-employer relationship with the corporation and with the corporation's major shareholder. We hold on this record that plaintiff failed to rebut the prima facie showing of control made by Wolff. The order to produce the records was, therefore, proper.

* * *

There is support in the record that plaintiff Victor Hart willfully refused to obey the December 15, 1969, order in that he himself testified that he made no efforts to produce the records of Arctic Bowl during the thirty days following that order. Nor did he make any satisfactory explanation to the court why they had not been produced. * * * In these circumstances, we cannot say that the superior court abused its discretion in dismissing plaintiff's complaint. The order is affirmed.

* * *

RABINOWITZ, JUSTICE (concurring in part, dissenting in part).

* * * I find the record devoid of any factual basis for the majority's conclusion that Wolff made out a prima facie case of Hart's "possession, custody, or control" of Arctic Bowl's records. I cannot perceive any policy considerations, or precedential bases, for the majority's adoption of an "influence" test, either actual or potential, in substitution for the "possession, custody, or control" standards of Civil Rule 34. Nor can I agree that notions of "influence" and of liberal pretrial discovery policies furnish an adequate foundation for the discovery order and subsequent sanction which were entered.

* * *

One further comment. It strikes me as rather unusual that Wolff's battery of attorneys took approximately five years to obtain a decision on the Civil Rule 34 motion to require Hart to produce the records of Arctic Bowl, Inc. Equally extraordinary is the fact that Wolff's counsel never attempted to employ any other available discovery procedures, such as a subpoena duces tecum directed to a nonparty under Civil Rule 45* * *, to obtain the records of Arctic Bowl, Inc.

* * *

Notes and Questions

1. In Societé Internationale v. Rogers, quoted in *Hart*, plaintiff argued that it did not have "control" over documents it had been ordered to produce under Rule 34, because the production of the documents, which were in plaintiff's physical possession in Switzerland, would be in violation of the criminal laws of that country. The Supreme Court rejected the argument, stating that "[p]etitioner is in a most advantageous position to plead with its own sovereign for relaxation of penal laws or for adoption of plans which will at the least achieve a significant measure of compliance with the production order * * *." See generally Note, *Foreign Nondisclosure Laws and Domestic Discovery Orders in Antitrust Litigation,* 88 Yale L.J. 612 (1979).

2. As the dissenting judge in Hart v. Wolff noted, items in the possession or control of a nonparty may be sought pursuant to Rule 45. Why didn't the attorney for the defendant in *Wolff* use Rule 45 to subpoena the documents directly from the corporation? Do you think that the attorney might have taken a different course of action had the 1991 amendment to Rule 45, noted in the supplement following the rule, been in effect at that time?

3. To what extent should a nonparty be able successfully to object to a subpoena ordering it to produce items for discovery? Rule 45(c)(3)(A)(iii) provides that an objection is proper on the ground of privilege, for example, if a lawyer is asked to reveal confidential information received from a client. Another ground for objection to a subpoena by a nonparty (Rule 45(c)(3)(A)(iv)) is that obeying the command of the subpoena would subject the nonparty to "undue burden." But suppose the nonparty wishes to challenge on the ground that the evidence sought is not relevant to the underlying controversy between the parties or desires to protect other nonparties from harm that would result from revelation of nonprivileged material received in confidence? Consider Dade Cty. Medical Ass'n v. Hlis, 372 So.2d 117 (Fla.App.1979), in which the court stated that although a nonparty could not object to discovery as not relevant, it could raise objections based on its own interest in preserving confidentiality or even based on similar interests of "unrepresented strangers" to the action.

COALITION OF BLACK LEADERSHIP v. DOORLEY, 349 F.Supp. 127 (D.R.I.1972). Plaintiffs brought a civil-rights action against the city police department alleging that during the course of an arrest plaintiffs were beaten, kicked, and otherwise subject to harassment. At trial, defendants sought to introduce photographs of plaintiffs taken on the night of the arrest, presumably to show that there were no signs of physical abuse. Plaintiffs objected on the ground that defendants had failed to produce the photographs upon a request under Rule 34 asking for:

> All case records, incident reports, police log book entries and other related documents, memoranda, and reports regarding, involving, or referring to the arrests and jailing of * * * [plaintiffs].

The court held:

Defendants, who had the photographs made pursuant to the arrests * * * attached to case files, produced the files but not the photographs. They argue that plaintiffs did not ask for photographs, so they were under no compulsion to produce them. I note that in Rule 34(a) * * * the term "documents" is expressly stated to include photographs. The photographs were within the scope of the discovery request. The failure to produce them would be sufficient to warrant their exclusion [at trial] under Fed.R.Civ.P. 37 * * *.

Note and Questions

Rule 34(a) permits discovery of any "designated documents." Was the court in *Coalition* too liberal regarding the designation requirement? Why shouldn't the designation be as precise as the circumstances permit? Should the party who seeks production have a duty to utilize other methods of discovery first, in order to learn what items exist, in order that a precise designation can be made? See Rios v. Donovan, 21 A.D.2d 409, 250 N.Y.S.2d 818 (1st Dep't 1964).

5. PHYSICAL AND MENTAL EXAMINATIONS

———

Read Federal Rule of Civil Procedure 35 in the Supplement.

———

In many lawsuits, a party will need to have its own medical professionals physically examine an adverse party whose condition is in controversy. However, a compelled medical examination involves an intrusion on a person's privacy, and some medical tests can entail discomfort and pain.

Rule 35 requires a court order for an examination and imposes strict standards. A court can force a party to submit to examination or to make persons under their legal custody or control available for examination. But the person's physical or mental condition must be in controversy, and the movant must show "good cause" to compel the examination. The determination of good cause involves weighing the pain, danger, or intrusiveness of the examination against the need for, or usefulness of, the information to be gained.

In practice, most physical and mental examinations occur as a result of agreements between attorneys. The primary effect of Rule 35 is to encourage parties to stipulate to examinations. Examinations are routine in personal injury actions, as well as in litigation involving issues of paternity, incompetence, and undue influence. Of course, the Rule is available in those cases in which the parties cannot agree. Stipulations typically address questions concerning the time and place of the examination, and the procedures to be used. Rule 35 gives the examined party the right to a copy of the examiner's report, even if the party submitted to an examination without the compulsion of a court order.

SCHLAGENHAUF v. HOLDER

Supreme Court of the United States, 1964.
379 U.S. 104, 85 S.Ct. 234, 13 L.Ed.2d 152.

Certiorari to the United States Court of Appeals for the Seventh Circuit.

MR. JUSTICE GOLDBERG delivered the opinion of the Court.

This case involves the validity and construction of Rule 35(a) of the Federal Rules of Civil Procedure as applied to the examination of a defendant in a negligence action. * * *

An action based on diversity of citizenship was brought in the District Court seeking damages arising from personal injuries suffered by passengers of a bus which collided with the rear of a tractor-trailer. The named defendants were The Greyhound Corporation, owner of the bus; petitioner, Robert L. Schlagenhauf, the bus driver; Contract Carriers, Inc., owner of the tractor; Joseph L. McCorkhill, driver of the tractor; and National Lead Company, owner of the trailer. Answers were filed by each of the defendants denying negligence.

Greyhound then cross-claimed against Contract Carriers and National Lead for damage to Greyhound's bus, alleging that the collision was due solely to their negligence in that the tractor-trailer was driven at an unreasonably low speed, had not remained in its lane, and was not equipped with proper rear lights. Contract Carriers filed an answer to this cross-claim denying its negligence and asserting "[t]hat the negligence of the driver of the * * * bus [petitioner Schlagenhauf] proximately caused and contributed to * * * Greyhound's damages."

* * *

Contract Carriers and National Lead then petitioned the District Court for an order directing petitioner Schlagenhauf to submit to both mental and physical examinations by one specialist in each of the following fields:

(1) Internal medicine;

(2) Ophthalmology;

(3) Neurology; and

(4) Psychiatry.

For the purpose of offering a choice to the District Court of one specialist in each field, the petition recommended two specialists in internal medicine, ophthalmology, and psychiatry, respectively, and three specialists in neurology—a total of nine physicians. The petition alleged that the mental and physical condition of Schlagenhauf was "in controversy" as it had been raised by Contract Carriers' answer to Greyhound's cross-claim. This was supported by a brief of legal authorities and an affidavit of Contract Carriers' attorney stating that Schlagenhauf had seen red lights 10 to 15 seconds before the accident, that another witness had seen the rear lights of the trailer from a distance of three-quarters to one-half mile, and that Schlagenhauf had been involved in a prior accident.

* * *

While disposition of this petition was pending, National Lead filed its answer to Greyhound's cross-claim and itself "cross-claimed" against Greyhound and Schlagenhauf for damage to its trailer. * * *

The District Court, on the basis of the petition filed by Contract Carriers, and without any hearing, ordered Schlagenhauf to submit to nine examinations—one by each of the recommended specialists—despite the fact that the petition clearly requested a total of only four examinations.

Petitioner applied for a writ of mandamus in the Court of Appeals against the respondent, the District Court Judge, seeking to have set aside the order requiring his mental and physical examinations. The Court of Appeals denied mandamus, one judge dissenting * * *.

We granted certiorari to review undecided questions concerning the validity and construction of Rule 35. * * *

Rule 35 on its face applies to all "parties," which under any normal reading would include a defendant. Petitioner contends, however, that the application of the Rule to a defendant would be an unconstitutional invasion of his privacy, or, at the least, be a modification of substantive rights existing prior to the adoption of the Federal Rules of Civil Procedure and thus beyond the congressional mandate of the Rules Enabling Act.

These same contentions were raised [and rejected] in Sibbach v. Wilson & Co., [p. 399, supra] * * *, by a plaintiff in a negligence action who asserted a physical injury as a basis for recovery. * * * Petitioner does not challenge the holding in *Sibbach* as applied to plaintiffs. He contends, however, that it should not be extended to defendants. We can see no basis * * * for such a distinction. * * * Issues cannot be resolved by a doctrine of favoring one class of litigants over another.

We recognize that, insofar as reported cases show, this type of discovery in federal courts has been applied solely to plaintiffs, and that some early state cases seem to have proceeded on a theory that a plaintiff who seeks redress for injuries in a court of law thereby "waives" his right to claim the inviolability of his person.

* * * [The Court then rejected the "waiver" theory on the basis of language in the *Sibbach* case.] The chain of events leading to an ultimate determination on the merits begins with the injury of the plaintiff, an involuntary act on his part. Seeking court redress is just one step in this chain. If the plaintiff is prevented or deterred from this redress, the loss is thereby forced on him to the same extent as if the defendant were prevented or deterred from defending against the action.

* * *

Petitioner contends that even if Rule 35 is to be applied to defendants, which we have determined it must, nevertheless it should not be applied to him as he was not a party in relation to Contract Carriers and National Lead—the movants for the mental and physical examinations—at the time the examinations were sought. * * * While it is clear that the person to be examined must be a party to the case,[12] we are of the view that * * * Rule 35

---

12. Although petitioner was an agent of Greyhound, he was himself a party to the

action. He is to be distinguished from one who is not a party but is, for example, merely the only requires that the person to be examined be a party to the "action," not that he be an opposing party *vis-à-vis* the movant. There is no doubt that Schlagenhauf was a "party" to this "action" by virtue of the original complaint. * * * Insistence that the movant have filed a pleading against the person to be examined would have the undesirable result of an unnecessary proliferation of cross-claims and counterclaims and would not be in keeping with the aims of a liberal, nontechnical application of the Federal Rules. * * *

While the Court of Appeals held that petitioner was not a party *vis-à-vis* National Lead or Contract Carriers at the time the examinations were first sought, it went on to hold that he had become a party *vis-à-vis* National Lead by the time of a second order entered by the District Court and thus was a party within its rule. This second order, identical in all material respects with the first, was entered on the basis of supplementary petitions filed by National Lead and Contract Carriers. These petitions gave no new basis for the examinations, except for the allegation that petitioner's mental and physical condition had been additionally put in controversy by the National Lead answer and cross-claim, which had been filed subsequent to the first petition for examinations. Although the filing of the petition for mandamus intervened between these two orders, we accept, for purposes of this opinion, the determination of the Court of Appeals that this second order was the one before it and agree that petitioner was clearly a party at this juncture under any test.

Petitioner next contends that his mental or physical condition was not "in controversy" and "good cause" was not shown for the examinations, both as required by the express terms of Rule 35.

* * *

It is notable * * * that in none of the other discovery provisions is there a restriction that the matter be "in controversy," and only in Rule 34 is there Rule 35's requirement that the movant affirmatively demonstrate "good cause."[a]

This additional requirement of "good cause" was reviewed by Chief Judge Sobeloff in Guilford National Bank of Greensboro v. Southern Ry. Co., 297 F.2d 921, 924 (C.A.4th Cir.), in the following words:

> * * * The specific requirement of good cause would be meaningless if good cause could be sufficiently established by merely showing that the desired materials are relevant, for the relevancy standard has already been imposed by Rule 26(b). Thus, by adding the words " * * * good cause * * *," the Rules indicate that there must be greater showing of need under Rules 34 and 35 than under the other discovery rules.

The courts of appeals in other cases have also recognized that Rule 34's good-cause requirement is not a mere formality, but is a plainly expressed limitation on the use of that Rule. This is obviously true as to the "in

agent of a party. * * * It is not now necessary to determine to what extent, if any, the term "party" includes one who is a "real party in interest" although not a named party to the action. Cf. Beach v. Beach, 72 App.D.C. 318, 114 F.2d 479, 131 A.L.R. 804.

a. The "good cause" requirement was eliminated from Rule 34 in 1970. See Note 1, p. 828, supra.

controversy" and "good cause" requirements of Rule 35. They are not met by mere conclusory allegations of the pleadings—nor by mere relevance to the case—but require an affirmative showing by the movant that each condition as to which the examination is sought is really and genuinely in controversy and that good cause exists for ordering each particular examination. Obviously, what may be good cause for one type of examination may not be so for another. The ability of the movant to obtain the desired information by other means is also relevant.

Rule 35, therefore, requires discriminating application by the trial judge, who must decide, as an initial matter in every case, whether the party requesting a mental or physical examination or examinations has adequately demonstrated the existence of the Rule's requirements of "in controversy" and "good cause," which requirements, as the Court of Appeals in this case itself recognized, are necessarily related. 321 F.2d, at 51. * * *

Of course, there are situations where the pleadings alone are sufficient to meet these requirements. A plaintiff in a negligence action who asserts mental or physical injury * * * places that mental or physical injury clearly in controversy and provides the defendant with good cause for an examination to determine the existence and extent of such asserted injury. This * * * applies equally to a defendant who asserts his mental or physical condition as a defense to a claim, such as, for example, where insanity is asserted as a defense to a divorce action. * * *

Here, however, Schlagenhauf did not assert his mental or physical condition either in support of or in defense of a claim. His condition was sought to be placed in issue by other parties. Thus, under the principles discussed above, Rule 35 required that these parties make an affirmative showing that petitioner's mental or physical condition was in controversy and that there was good cause for the examinations requested. This, the record plainly shows, they failed to do.

The only allegations in the pleadings relating to this subject were the general conclusory statement in Contract Carriers' answer to the cross-claim that "Schlagenhauf was not mentally or physically capable of operating" the bus at the time of the accident and the limited allegation in National Lead's cross-claim that, at the time of the accident, "the eyes and vision of * * * Schlagenhauf was [sic] impaired and deficient."

The attorney's affidavit attached to the petition for the examinations provided:

> That * * * Schlagenhauf, in his deposition * * * admitted that he saw red lights for 10 to 15 seconds prior to a collision with a semi-tractor trailer unit and yet drove his vehicle on without reducing speed and without altering the course thereof.

> The only eye-witness to this accident known to this affiant * * * testified that immediately prior to the impact between the bus and truck that he had also been approaching the truck from the rear and that he had clearly seen the lights of the truck for a distance of three-quarters to one-half mile to the rear thereof.

> * * * Schlagenhauf has admitted in his deposition * * * that he was involved in a [prior] similar type rear end collision. * * *

This record cannot support even the corrected order which required one examination in each of the four specialties of internal medicine, ophthalmology, neurology, and psychiatry. Nothing in the pleadings or affidavit would afford a basis for a belief that Schlagenhauf was suffering from a mental or neurological illness warranting wide-ranging psychiatric or neurological examinations. Nor is there anything stated justifying the broad internal medicine examination.

The only specific allegation made in support of the four examinations ordered was that the "eyes and vision" of Schlagenhauf were impaired. Considering this in conjunction with the affidavit, we would be hesitant to set aside a visual examination if it had been the only one ordered. However, as the case must be remanded to the District Court because of the other examinations ordered, it would be appropriate for the District Judge to reconsider also this order in light of the guidelines set forth in this opinion.

* * *

Accordingly, the judgment of the Court of Appeals is vacated and the case remanded to the District Court to reconsider the examination order in light of the guidelines herein formulated and for further proceedings in conformity with this opinion.

Vacated and remanded.

Mr. Justice Black, with whom Mr. Justice Clark joins, concurring in part and dissenting in part.

* * *

In a collision case like this one, evidence concerning very bad eyesight or impaired mental or physical health which may affect the ability to drive is obviously of the highest relevance. It is equally obvious, I think, that when a vehicle continues down an open road and smashes into a truck in front of it although the truck is in plain sight and there is ample time and room to avoid collision, the chances are good that the driver has some physical, mental or moral defect. When such a thing happens twice, one is even more likely to ask, "What is the matter with that driver? Is he blind or crazy?" Plainly the allegations of the other parties were relevant and put the question of Schlagenhauf's health and vision "in controversy." * * *

Mr. Justice Douglas, dissenting in part.

* * * When the defendant's doctors examine plaintiff, they are normally interested only in answering a single question: did plaintiff in fact sustain the specific injuries claimed? But plaintiff's doctors will naturally be inclined to go on a fishing expedition in search of *anything* which will tend to prove that the defendant was unfit to perform the acts which resulted in the plaintiff's injury. And a doctor for a fee can easily discover something wrong with any patient—a condition that in prejudiced medical eyes might have caused the accident. Once defendants are turned over to medical or psychiatric clinics for an analysis of their physical well-being and the condition of their psyche, the effective trial will be held there and not before the jury. There are no lawyers in those clinics to stop the doctor from probing this organ or that one, to halt a further inquiry, to object to a line of questioning. And there is no judge to sit as arbiter. The doctor or the psychiatrist has a holiday in the privacy of his office. The defendant is at the doctor's (or psychiatrist's) mercy; and his report may either overawe or confuse the jury and prevent a fair trial.

* * *

Neither the Court nor Congress up to today has determined that any person whose physical or mental condition is brought into question during some lawsuit must surrender his right to keep his person inviolate. Congress did, according to *Sibbach*, require a plaintiff to choose between his privacy and his purse; but before today it has not been thought that any other "party" had lost this historic immunity. Congress and this Court can authorize such a rule. But a rule suited to purposes of discovery against defendants must be carefully drawn in light of the great potential of blackmail.

* * *

[JUSTICE HARLAN's dissenting opinion is omitted.]

Notes and Questions

1. In CRIDER v. SNEIDER, 243 Ga. 642, 256 S.E.2d 335 (1979), a wrongful-death case arising from an automobile accident, defendant, during discovery, argued that he could not recall any of the events surrounding the accident because of "traumatic amnesia." Plaintiff thereupon moved unsuccessfully to require defendant to submit to a mental and physical examination. The Georgia Supreme Court held that the trial court's refusal to grant the motion was not an abuse of discretion in that plaintiff had failed to show good cause since it appeared that the facts and circumstances of the collision could be established by other sources of evidence. If no other sources had existed, could the court have properly granted the motion?

2. In WINTERS v. TRAVIA, 495 F.2d 839 (2d Cir.1974), the court refused to order plaintiff to submit to a physical or mental examination. Plaintiff was a Christian Scientist seeking damages on the ground that forced medication administered to her during involuntary hospitalization violated her right to freedom of religion. The court ruled that her present condition was not in controversy since plaintiff was willing to abandon any claim that any present or anticipated physical or mental disability or condition was caused by the medical treatment on which the case was based.

3. In 1970, Federal Rule 35(a) was amended to encompass persons "in the custody or under the legal control of a party." "Agents of a party" are not included in the Rule, although this had been recommended by the Advisory Committee in 1955. What reasons are there for not including agents? The 1970 amendment also redefined "physical condition" specifically to include blood type. For a general discussion of the need for the 1970 changes, see Note, *Physical Examination of Non-Parties Under the Federal Rules of Civil Procedure*, 43 Iowa L.Rev. 375 (1958). See also 8A Wright, Miller & Marcus, *Federal Practice and Procedure: Civil 2d* §§ 2231–39 (1994).

4. Rule 35(a) was amended in 1991 to substitute the phrase "by a suitably licensed or certified examiner" for "by a physician or psychologist." The Advisory Committee's Notes explained that the intent of the amendment is to include "other certified or licensed professionals, such as dentists or occupational therapists, * * * who may be well-qualified to give valuable testimony about the physical or mental condition that is the subject of the dispute."

5. N.Y.C.P.L.R. 3121 provides for physical examinations to be taken upon notice without a prior court order or showing of "good cause." Although in 1970, Federal Rule 34 was amended to eliminate the good-cause requirement as to discovery of documents and other items, the good-cause requirement in Rule 35 was retained. Is there more reason for a showing of good cause as a prerequisite when a physical examination is desired than there is when discovery of documents is sought?

6. In ABDULWALI v. WASHINGTON METRO AREA TRANSIT AUTHORITY, 193 F.R.D. 10 (D.D.C.2000), plaintiff sued for negligent infliction of emotional distress resulting from the sight of her child being killed in a subway train accident. Defendant sought a psychiatric examination of plaintiff, who requested the court to permit her attorney to attend the examination and to have the examination recorded. She also requested that she receive any notes made by the psychiatrist during the examination and that the examination be limited to three hours duration. The court rejected all of plaintiff's requests, noting that the greater weight of federal authority favors the exclusion of a party's attorney.

What arguments could each of the parties make to support their positions? Would it make a difference if plaintiff was seeking damages for physical injuries and the examination was not being conducted by a psychiatrist? Suppose plaintiff was seeking to have her own physician present, rather than her lawyer? Should she be able to have her husband or her mother attend? Are there special times when attendance by another person or a recording of the examination should be permitted or not permitted?

BENNING v. PHELPS, 249 F.2d 47 (2d Cir.1957). Prior to suit, plaintiff voluntarily submitted to a physical examination by defendant's physician. Thereafter plaintiff refused to submit to another examination and defendant moved the trial court to order plaintiff to do so. The court granted the motion and ordered defendant to provide plaintiff with a copy of the report of the examining physician. In compliance with the court's order, defendant delivered to plaintiff a copy of the physician's report, and then moved, under Rule 35(b)(1), to require plaintiff to give defendant the reports of plaintiff's doctors. The trial court denied the motion, and the appellate court affirmed as follows:

> * * * [D]efendant is entitled to receive copies of the plaintiff's medical reports only if the plaintiff has previously requested and received copies of medical reports from the defendant. * * * Here the plaintiff received copies of the defendant's reports pursuant to an order of the court, and not pursuant to his own request. Since the trial court might properly have concluded that "good cause" had not been shown, * * * and hence might have refused to compel the plaintiff to submit to the second examination requested by the defendant, we cannot find that it erred in the condition which it placed upon its order.

Id. at 48–49.

In CHASTAIN v. EVENNOU, 35 F.R.D. 350 (D.Utah 1964), plaintiff voluntarily submitted to a physical examination by a physician designated by defendants, and plaintiff received a copy of the report in exchange for copies of certain reports by his own physicians. But plaintiff specifically withheld one physician's report, arguing that Rule 35(b) was inapplicable since no court-ordered examination had ever taken place. The court ordered production of the withheld report on the ground that the spirit of Rule 35 so demanded.

Notes and Questions

1. What means other than Rule 35(b)(1) might the defendant in *Benning* have used to discover the contents of the reports of plaintiff's doctors? Does the availability of other means make Rule 35(b)(1) unnecessary?

2. Rule 35(b)(3) was added in 1970, in recognition of the fact that much discovery takes place by agreement of the parties without resort to court appearances. How far does this new provision go? Would it alter the result in *Benning*?

LEWIN v. JACKSON, 108 Ariz. 27, 492 P.2d 406 (1972). Plaintiff sued for slander, alleging as damages the fact that she had been disinherited by her parents. Defendant sought to take the deposition of plaintiff's father, who had become incompetent and had been placed under the guardianship of plaintiff. Plaintiff objected, asking for a protective order under Rule 26(c) on the ground that her father was not physically or mentally able to give a deposition. The court stayed the deposition but ordered the father to undergo a medical examination for the purpose of determining whether or not he could be deposed. Plaintiff objected on the ground that Arizona Rule 35 (identical to Federal Rule 35) did not permit the examination in question. The court concluded that although the father was a person under the "custody" and "legal control of plaintiff," Rule 35 did not apply because the action had not been brought on his behalf. Nonetheless the court held the examination to be proper as part of the inherent power of a court "to assure itself not only that a witness' testimony will be accurate and lucid, but also that the act of testifying will not endanger the health of the proposed witness."

Questions

1. Is the court in *Lewin* correct in holding that the requested medical examination did not fall within the scope of Rule 35? Could such an examination be justified as part of an order under Rule 26(c) controlling the course of a deposition? Should Rule 35 be considered the exclusive source of power by which a court can require a nonparty to submit to an examination?

2. How far does the inherent power invoked by the *Lewin* court extend? For example, can the court order a person who witnessed an event upon which the suit is based to submit to an eye examination to determine if that person can see well enough to be considered a competent witness at a deposition or at trial? If so, how effective is the limitation of Rule 35 to parties?

6. REQUESTS TO ADMIT

Read Federal Rule of Civil Procedure 36 in the Supplement.

————

Rule 36 authorizes a party to serve on another party written requests to admit the truth of certain matters of fact or of the application of law to fact, or the genuineness of a document or other evidence that may be used at trial. Rule 36 is not a true discovery device since it does not require the responding party to disclose information. Requests for admissions are used to shape information already known into statements that expedite the trial by limiting the issues in dispute and by obviating some of the formalities that control the introduction of evidence at trial. Although responses to other discovery devices are not conclusive proof and may be contradicted at trial, responses to Rule 36 requests constitute conclusive evidence, unless withdrawn, and cannot be contradicted at trial. However, requests for admissions may function as a discovery device if a party uses them early enough in the litigation to help identify the issues not in dispute and to target the remaining issues for discovery.

A request for admission may be served without the necessity of a court order at any time after the parties have conferred in accordance with Rule 26(d), although usually not later than thirty days before a fixed trial date. Rule 36 provides that each matter of admission must be set forth separately, but says nothing else about the format for requests. However, Form 25 appended to the Federal Rules of Civil Procedure, which is reproduced in the Supplement, provides an illustration of a request for admissions.

The party who receives a request to admit must respond under oath and in timely fashion, admitting or denying each matter for which an admission is requested, or providing a detailed explanation why it cannot admit or deny the matter. The responding party may also object to a request because improperly phrased (as "vague," "ambiguous," "a compound sentence," or otherwise defectively drafted), or because it seeks privileged or protected information. The responding party may request a court to extend its time to respond. (Rule 29 provides that counsel may stipulate to extend the time limits set forth in Rule 36 unless the stipulation would "interfere with any time set for completion of discovery, for hearing of a motion, or for trial.")

If the party who receives a request to admit does nothing, the matter in the request is deemed admitted. Rule 36, unlike other discovery rules, is self-executing. Once the time to respond has passed, the requesting party can rely on the matters admitted and take no further discovery on those issues. If a party serves a late response, and the opponent refuses to accept it, a court may excuse the party's failure to respond in a timely manner. Likewise, a court may permit a party to withdraw or modify an admission in a timely response. In either situation, the court's decision turns on the degree of prejudice the requesting party will suffer because of its reliance on the admission. Because courts so frequently granted a responding party's request for relief from its failure to respond, leaving requesting parties uncertain about the validity of the admission, and, hence, the necessity of developing evidence for trial, Rule 36(a) was amended in 1970 to permit a requesting party to move for an order deeming the matter to be admitted. Thus, a litigant takes a serious risk by failing to respond to Requests for Admissions. The court may well find that the failure was not justified, that the admissions have been made, and that, as a result, summary judgment is appropriate. See, e.g., Jones v. Sweeney, 2000 WL 1611129 (N.D.Ind.2000).

Although Rule 36 and its state counterparts can be enormously useful, in practice requests for admissions are the least used of the discovery devices. See Connolly, Holleman & Kuhlman, *Judicial Controls and the Civil Litigation Process: Discovery* 28 (1978). Attorneys tend to think of requests to admit as part of trial preparation, not discovery. They postpone their use to the very end, and frequently fail to file requests before the time fixed by the court to complete discovery runs out. Dombroff, *Discovery* 260 (1986).

Notes and Questions

1. Rule 36 formerly limited requests for admissions to matters of "fact." As amended in 1970, the Rule permits requests for admissions to inquire into matters relating to "statements or opinions of fact or of the application of law to fact, including the genuineness of any document described in the request." Does the amended provision authorize requests for admissions of law unrelated to the facts of the case? See 8A Wright, Miller & Marcus, *Federal Practice and Procedure: Civil 2d* §§ 2254–56 (1994). Although a number of jurisdictions have amended their rules to accord with the current version of Federal Rule 36, see, e.g., Ariz.R.Civ.P. 36; Fla.R.Civ.P. 1.370, other states have not, e.g., N.Y.C.P.L.R. § 3123(a).

Why do some courts appear so wary of requests to admit? Is there any justification for holding improper requests to admit facts that are "in controversy" or that are the ultimate facts in issue? Doesn't it make more sense to permit the request to admit to be made so that the responding party can deny it, if untrue? See Comment, *The Dilemma of Federal Rule 36*, 56 Nw.U.L.Rev. 679, 684–85 (1961).

2. What is a "reasonable inquiry" and when is information not "readily obtainable" by an answering party? In LUMPKIN v. MESKILL, 64 F.R.D. 673 (D.Conn.1974), the court held that the defendants in a school desegregation case were required to admit or deny the accuracy of statistics concerning the racial composition of schools that were derived from the random sampling techniques used by the plaintiff's expert. Note that it is well established under Rule 33 that a party has a duty to investigate to ascertain and disclose information that is not within its personal knowledge but reasonably within its power to obtain. Should the standards for investigation be as extensive under Rule 36?

3. Is a party required to admit a matter he believes to be true? Or only a matter that he reasonably believes, on the basis of the admissible evidence known to him, that the proponent who is seeking the admission can prove at trial? Suppose an individual sues a corporation for injuries sustained in a motor vehicle accident, allegedly caused by the negligent driving of defendant's employee. The employee, apparently the only eyewitness, when asked, states that she unlawfully went through a traffic signal. Must the corporate defendant, if requested to do so, admit the unlawful act, even though it suspects that its employee, motivated by compassion for the victim, might not be telling the truth? Suppose that ten impartial witnesses all tell the same story as the employee. Could defendant legitimately deny the request to admit on the theory that all of them could

possibly be lying or mistaken? See generally Finman, *The Request for Admissions in Federal Civil Procedure*, 71 Yale L.J. 371, 404–09 (1962); Shapiro, *Some Problems of Discovery in an Adversary System*, 63 Minn.L.Rev. 1055, 1078–92 (1979).

4. If a party serves a denial of the matters in the request to admit and at trial the matter is proved by the party requesting the admission, then Rule 37(c) provides that the latter may collect from the other party the reasonable expenses incurred in making the proof. How useful is this sanction? How can a party show that a given matter has been "proved"? See Board of Directors, Water's Edge v. Anden Group, 136 F.R.D. 100 (E.D.Va.1991).

7. THE DUTY TO SUPPLEMENT RESPONSES

———

Read Federal Rule of Civil Procedure 26(e) and the accompanying Advisory Committee's Notes in the Supplement.

———

Rule 26(e), adopted in 1970 and amended in 1993, was designed to eliminate inconsistent decisions regarding the existence and scope of the duty to update discovery answers. Note that the Rule is not all-encompassing. What information obtained subsequent to the original responses is not covered by it?

The 1993 amendments to Rule 26(e) broadened the obligation to supplement discovery responses, requiring that disclosures and responses to interrogatories, requests for production, and requests for admissions be supplemented "if the party learns that in some material respect the information disclosed is incomplete or incorrect" and if the updated information has not otherwise been made known to the other parties.

Why should there be any duty to supplement answers given in the course of discovery? Doesn't this duty constitute an undue burden on a responding party? Why isn't it enough that the discovering party simply can send a later set of interrogatories or engage in discovery immediately before trial if it wants up-to-date replies from another party? Would it be wise to limit the duty to the giving of names of any newly discovered witnesses? See *Developments in the Law—Discovery*, 74 Harv.L.Rev. 940, 961–63 (1961). Should the duty continue until and even during trial? See Everett v. Morrison, 478 S.W.2d 312 (Mo.1972) (party must disclose identity of witness discovered after trial was in progress).

What is the appropriate sanction for a breach of a duty to supplement answers? Most courts merely have prohibited the admission of the undisclosed evidence or prohibited the undisclosed witnesses from giving testimony. Indeed, Rule 37(c)(1) specifically provides that a party may not use any witness or any information not disclosed to the other party or not supplemented as required by Rule 26(e)(1).

As an alternative to imposing sanctions upon the offending party, a court usually has the option of postponing the trial of a case, or granting a continuance or recess, so that the other side may complete discovery and prepare to meet any new testimony. See, e.g., Shelak v. White Motor Co., 581 F.2d 1155, 1159 (5th Cir.1978) (defendant permitted additional time to prepare for trial when interrogatory answers were supplemented three days before trial); Washington Hospital Center v. Cheeks, 129 U.S.App.D.C. 339, 394 F.2d 964 (D.C.Cir.1968) (trial recessed to permit the taking of the deposition of expert witness whose name had not been previously given). Is this procedure ordinarily better than sanctions?

Note that much of the discussion of Rule 26(e) seems to involve situations in which a party seeks to utilize witnesses or evidence at trial that the party failed to disclose as required by the Rule. What happens when the undisclosed information would strongly benefit the opposing party, who, deprived of the information, suffers an adverse judgment? Is there anything the latter can do once he becomes aware of the situation? See the discussion of Federal Rule 60 at pp. 1110–14, supra. What sanctions would be appropriate in such a case?

8. USE OF DISCOVERY AT TRIAL

Read Federal Rules of Civil Procedure 32, 36(b), and 30(e) in the Supplement.

Attorneys can use the discovery devices simply to find out information, but commonly they anticipate using an adversary's or a witness's answers at trial: as admissions, to refresh a witness's recollection, or to provide a basis for cross-examination or impeachment. And sometimes a response to discovery can be used in lieu of or in addition to live testimony. The use of discovery responses at trial is governed by two sets of rules: the rules of procedure and the rules of evidence. As you read the following material, consider how the possibility that discovery responses may be used at trial should affect the conduct of discovery before trial. Are there circumstances in which the objective of obtaining discovery and the objective of using discovery responses at trial conflict?

RICHMOND v. BROOKS
United States Court of Appeals, Second Circuit, 1955.
227 F.2d 490.

CLARK, CHIEF JUDGE. Plaintiff, residing with her present husband in California, brought suit in the New York Supreme Court against defendant, her former husband, now divorced and a resident of New York, to collect loans she had made to him. It also appears—although the court below held it immaterial—that she conducts a business in Beverly Hills, California, in merchandising women's used garments, known as "Gowns of the Stars." Defendant removed the action to the district court below and the case went to trial to a jury some three and a half years later after the taking of various depositions of the defendant in New York and the plaintiff in California, the latter by interrogatories and cross interrogatories. At the trial plaintiff offered her deposition as her proof, but the court refused to receive it and later dismissed her action for failure of proof, refusing to grant her motion for a mistrial and for adjournment. Her appeal challenges these rulings.

In excluding the deposition the trial judge held that the defendant was entitled to require the presence of the plaintiff as a part of her case and the opportunity to cross-examine her before the jury. Certain cases cited to him as differently construing [Federal Rule 32(a)] * * *, the governing rule, he distinguished as applying only to a *defendant's* proof. * * *.

[The Rule] * * * is quite clear in its terms, which apply without exception equally to plaintiffs and defendants. * * *

In * * * Hyam v. American Export Lines, 2 Cir., 213 F.2d 221 * * *, libellant, a resident of Bombay, India, sued in the court below for cargo damage on a shipment carried by respondent from Philadelphia to Bombay; and the parties were at issue preliminarily as to whether libellant's deposition in Bombay should be taken by written interrogatories, as he sought, or by "open commission," with the entire cost thereof paid by him, as sought by the respondent. The district court's solution was to deny the libellant's application and to order him to appear for oral examination in New York. When he failed to comply, his action was dismissed. We reversed, suggesting the "unusually and seriously burdensome" character of the requirement made below and finding error of law on the part of the district judge in failing to exercise discretion to accord the protection invoked by libellant pursuant to [what is now Federal Rule 26(c)] * * * and in proceeding erroneously on the theory that the respondent had the right to have the suing party in New York for oral examination. We said, * * * 213 F.2d 221, 223: "The federal courts are open to foreign suitors as to others, and procedural rules are not to be construed in such fashion as to impose conditions on litigants which in their practical effect amount to a denial of jurisdiction."

Applying this principle as a touchstone, we can find no occasion to add something to the rule which is not there and which effectually distorts its purpose and utility. The tactical burden assumed by the plaintiff in proceeding to trial in her absence, to which the first judge below called attention, is likely to limit frequent resort to this course; but a suitor not able to afford a New York trip should not be denied all remedy here. There is nothing in the general law to demand such a result. * * *

The defendant relies further on the limiting provision of [Rule 32(a)(3)(B)], * * * *viz.,* "unless it appears that the absence of the witness was procured by the party offering the deposition"; and he points out that the plaintiff was in New York City with her husband during the Christmas holidays some two weeks prior to the start of the trial on January 17, 1955. The district court did not consider this issue, rejecting as immaterial plaintiff's business interests in California; and hence we have no finding as to it. But no reason is apparent to justify a requirement that plaintiff must live in New York City—of course expensively, since that is the only mode of life there—awaiting the uncertain call of a case for trial or be penalized for a normal Christmas trip. * * *

It is suggested, as in 4 Moore's Federal Practice 1195–1197 (2d Ed.1950), that the "unless" clause just quoted may present an issue of construction as to whether the "absence" in question is from the territory embraced within the 100–mile radius or is from the trial itself, and that only the former interpretation (which is favored) permits a California resident as such to use his own deposition. Perhaps too much is made of this assumed dichotomy; it is not apparent why in this carefully defined context absence from the trial should not be tested for the validity of the excuse on the same principles as absence from the territory. Be that as it may, the language used, referring to different stages of trial *or hearing,* and obviously pointing back to the defining clause which sets forth the basic reasons for admissibility, makes it quite clear that the former is meant.

* * *

Reversed and remanded.

Notes and Questions

1. The court in COLONIAL REALTY CORP. v. BRUNSWICK CORP., 337 F.Supp. 546 (S.D.N.Y.1971), questioned whether the *Brooks* decision ought to apply automatically to a case in which plaintiff showed no hardship whatever and in which her credibility was a vital factor. Does Rule 32(a) provide the trial court with any discretion in such a case? See Giannetti v. Fenwick, 166 N.J.Super. 491, 400 A.2d 103 (App.Div.1979).

In EFERAKEYA v. TWIN CITY STATE BANK, 245 Kan. 154, 160, 777 P.2d 759, 764 (1989), the court, in interpreting a state rule identical to Federal Rule 32, refused to follow *Brooks,* stating: "We hold that, when the absence of a party is due merely to a preference to use the deposition rather than to testify orally at trial, absence is in effect 'procured' by that party. We construe an absence from trial as a result of an act of will, a voluntary absence, or an unexplained absence as 'procured.'" Does this language go too far? The Kansas court went on to hold that the trial judge has discretion to determine, under all of the circumstances of the case, whether or not a party has procured his or her absence.

2. Suppose plaintiff in *Brooks* had sought to introduce her answers to a set of interrogatories served on her by defendant. In CALLAWAY v. PERDUE, 238 Ark. 652, 658–59, 385 S.W.2d 4, 8–9 (1964), the court stated that the answers were "self-serving declarations," and were inadmissible under the rules of evidence. In what ways do answers to interrogatories differ from the transcript of a deposition for purposes of using them at trial under Federal Rule 32(a)?

Assume that a party, pursuant to its duty to update responses under Federal Rule 26(e), sends a supplementary set of answers much more favorable to itself than the original replies to deposition questions. May the adverse party introduce the original replies at trial? The court in MANGUAL v. PRUDENTIAL LINES, INC., 53 F.R.D. 301 (E.D.Pa.1971), held "yes," in accordance with normal evidence rules, which allow an adverse party to utilize any statement of its opponent. The court in *Mangual* went on to hold, however, that the party who made the responses was entitled to put in its subsequent answers, arguing that this was consistent with the policy of Rule 32(a)(4) providing that if only part of a deposition is introduced, the court, in the interests of justice, may order other portions to be introduced as well. Is the court's analogy a sound one?

3. Rule 36(b) was amended in 1970 to make clear that admissions under that Rule are conclusive for purposes of the pending action unless the court, on motion,

permits the admission to be withdrawn or amended. Prior to the change a few courts had held that an admission was merely an item of evidence that could be rebutted at trial. See generally Finman, *The Request for Admissions in Federal Civil Procedure,* 71 Yale L.J. 371, 421–22 (1962). Should the application of Rule 36(b) be automatic or should it apply only when the party who wishes to rely on an admission offers it into evidence? See National Bank of Georgia v. Hill, 148 Ga.App. 688, 252 S.E.2d 192 (1979) (court will ignore admission not offered into evidence).

4.   Federal Rule 33 contains no provision comparable to Rule 36(b). Should an answer to an interrogatory also be binding at trial? How does Federal Rule 26(e), which deals with the duty to supplement responses, affect your answer?

5.   Florida Rule of Civil Procedure 1.330(a) is almost identical to Federal Rule 32(a). One exception, which is spelled out in Rule 1.390(b), is as follows:

> The testimony of an expert or skilled witness may be taken at any time before the trial in accordance with the rules for taking depositions and may be used at trial, regardless of the place of residence of the witness or whether he is within the distance prescribed by Rule 1.330(a)(3). No special form of notice need be given that the deposition will be used for trial.

What is the purpose of this rule? In the August 1991 draft of the proposed amendments to the Federal Rules, the Advisory Committee suggested Rule 32(a)(3) be amended to provide that the deposition of an expert may be used at trial even if the expert could be made available to testify in person. 137 F.R.D at 119–21. However, this provision encountered "substantial opposition," and in May 1992 the Advisory Committee decided to eliminate this proposed change. Was that wise?

SECTION C. SPECIAL PROBLEMS REGARDING THE SCOPE OF DISCOVERY

1. MATERIALS PREPARED IN ANTICIPATION OF TRIAL

Read Federal Rule of Civil Procedure 26(b)(3) and the related materials in the Supplement.

HICKMAN v. TAYLOR

Supreme Court of the United States, 1947.
329 U.S. 495, 67 S.Ct. 385, 91 L.Ed. 451.

Certiorari to the Circuit Court of Appeals for the Third Circuit.

MR. JUSTICE MURPHY delivered the opinion of the Court.

This case presents an important problem under the Federal Rules * * * as to the extent to which a party may inquire into oral and written statements of witnesses, or other information, secured by an adverse party's counsel in the course of preparation for possible litigation after a claim has arisen.

Examination into a person's files and records, including those resulting from the professional activities of an attorney, must be judged with care. It is not without reason that various safeguards have been established to preclude unwarranted excursions into the privacy of a man's work. At the same time, public policy supports reasonable and necessary inquiries. Properly to balance these competing interests is a delicate and difficult task.

On February 7, 1943, the tug "J.M. Taylor" sank while engaged in helping to tow a car float of the Baltimore & Ohio Railroad across the Delaware River at Philadelphia. The accident was apparently unusual in nature, the cause of it still being unknown. Five of the nine crew members were drowned. Three days later the tug owners and the underwriters employed a law firm, of which respondent Fortenbaugh is a member, to defend them against potential suits by representatives of the deceased crew members and to sue the railroad for damages to the tug.

A public hearing was held on March 4, 1943, before the United States Steamboat Inspectors, at which the four survivors were examined. This testimony was recorded and made available to all interested parties. Shortly thereafter, Fortenbaugh privately interviewed the survivors and took statements from them with an eye toward the anticipated litigation; the survivors signed these statements on March 29. Fortenbaugh also interviewed other persons believed to have some information relating to the accident and in some cases he made memoranda of what they told him. At the time when Fortenbaugh secured the statements of the survivors, representatives of two of the deceased crew members had been in communication with him. Ultimately claims were presented by representatives of all five of the deceased; four of the claims, however, were settled without litigation. The fifth claimant, petitioner herein, brought suit in a federal court under the Jones Act on November 26, 1943, naming as defendants the two tug owners, individually and as partners, and the railroad.

One year later, petitioner filed 39 interrogatories directed to the tug owners. The 38th interrogatory read: "State whether any statements of the members of the crews of the Tugs 'J.M. Taylor' and 'Philadelphia' or of any other vessel were taken in connection with the towing of the car float and the sinking of the Tug 'John M. Taylor'. Attach hereto exact copies of all such statements if in writing, and if oral, set forth in detail the exact provisions of any such oral statements or reports."

Supplemental interrogatories asked whether any oral or written statements, records, reports or other memoranda had been made concerning any matter relative to the towing operation, the sinking of the tug, the salvaging and repair of the tug, and the death of the deceased. If the answer was in the affirmative, the tug owners were then requested to set forth the nature of all such records, reports, statements or other memoranda.

The tug owners, through Fortenbaugh, answered all of the interrogatories except No. 38 and the supplemental ones just described. While admitting that statements of the survivors had been taken, they declined to summarize or set forth the contents. They did so on the ground that such requests called "for privileged matter obtained in preparation for litigation" and constituted "an attempt to obtain indirectly counsel's private files." It was claimed that answering these requests "would involve practically turning over not only the complete files, but also the telephone records and, almost, the thoughts of counsel."

In connection with the hearing on these objections, Fortenbaugh made a written statement and gave an informal oral deposition explaining the circumstances under which he had taken the statements. But he was not expressly asked in the deposition to produce the statements. The District Court for the Eastern District of Pennsylvania, sitting en banc, held that the requested matters were not privileged. 4 F.R.D. 479. The court then decreed that the tug owners and Fortenbaugh, as counsel and agent for the tug owners forthwith "Answer Plaintiff's 38th interrogatory and supplemental interrogatories; produce all written statements of witnesses obtained by Mr. Fortenbaugh, as counsel and agent for Defendants; state in substance any fact concerning this case which Defendants learned through oral statements made by witnesses to Mr. Fortenbaugh whether or not included in his private memoranda and produce Mr. Fortenbaugh's memoranda containing statements of fact by witnesses or to submit these memoranda to the Court for determination of those portions which should be revealed to Plaintiff." Upon their refusal, the court adjudged them in contempt and ordered them imprisoned until they complied.

The Third Circuit Court of Appeals, also sitting en banc, reversed the judgment of the District Court. 153 F.2d 212. It held that the information here sought was part of the "work product of the lawyer" and hence privileged from discovery under the Federal Rules of Civil Procedure. The importance of the problem, which has engendered a great divergence of views among district courts, led us to grant certiorari. * * *

There is an initial question as to which of the deposition-discovery rules is involved in this case. Petitioner, in filing his interrogatories, thought that he was proceeding under Rule 33.

* * * [I]t does not appear from the record that petitioner filed a motion under Rule 34 for a court order directing the production of the documents in question. Indeed, such an order could not have been entered as to Fortenbaugh since Rule 34, like Rule 33, is limited to parties to the proceeding, thereby excluding their counsel or agents.

Thus to the extent that petitioner was seeking the production of the memoranda and statements gathered by Fortenbaugh in the course of his activities as counsel, petitioner misconceived his remedy. Rule 33 did not permit him to obtain such memoranda and statements as adjuncts to the interrogatories addressed to the individual tug owners. A party clearly cannot refuse to answer interrogatories on the ground that the information sought is solely within the knowledge of his attorney. But that is not this case. Here production was sought of documents prepared by a party's attorney after the claim has arisen. Rule 33 does not make provision for such production, even when sought in connection with permissible interrogatories. Moreover, since petitioner was also foreclosed from securing them through an order under Rule 34, his only recourse was to take Fortenbaugh's deposition under Rule 26 and to attempt to force Fortenbaugh to produce the materials by use of a subpoena *duces tecum* in accordance with Rule 45. * * * But despite petitioner's faulty choice of action, the District Court entered an order, apparently under Rule 34, commanding the tug owners and Fortenbaugh, as their agent and counsel, to produce the materials in question. Their refusal led to the anomalous result of holding the tug owners in contempt for failure to produce that which was in the possession of their counsel and of holding Fortenbaugh in contempt for failure to produce that which he could not be compelled to produce under either Rule 33 or Rule 34.

But under the circumstances we deem it unnecessary and unwise to rest our decision upon this procedural irregularity, an irregularity which is not strongly urged upon us and which was disregarded in the two courts below. * * * [T]he basic question at stake is whether any of those devices may be used to inquire into materials collected by an adverse party's counsel in the course of preparation for possible litigation. The fact that the petitioner may have used the wrong method does not destroy the main thrust of his attempt. * * * [I]n the present circumstances, for the purposes of this decision, the procedural irregularity is not material. * * *

In urging that he has a right to inquire into the materials secured and prepared by Fortenbaugh, petitioner emphasizes that the deposition-discovery portions of the Federal Rules of Civil Procedure are designed to enable the parties to discover the true facts and to compel their disclosure wherever they may be found. It is said that inquiry may be made under these rules, epitomized by Rule 26, as to any relevant matter which is not privileged; and since the discovery provisions are to be applied as broadly and liberally as possible, the privilege limitation must be restricted to its narrowest bounds. On the premise that the attorney-client privilege is the one involved in this case, petitioner argues that it must be strictly confined to confidential communications made by a client to his attorney. And since the materials here in issue were secured by Fortenbaugh from third persons rather than from his clients, the tug owners, the conclusion is reached that these materials are proper subjects for discovery under Rule 26.

As additional support for this result, petitioner claims that to prohibit discovery under these circumstances would give a corporate defendant a tremendous advantage in a suit by an individual plaintiff. Thus in a suit by an injured employee against a railroad or in a suit by an insured person against an insurance company the corporate defendant could pull a dark veil of secrecy over all the pertinent facts it can collect after the claim arises merely on the assertion that such facts were gathered by its large staff of attorneys and claim agents. At the same time, the individual plaintiff, who often has direct knowledge of the matter in issue and has no counsel until some time after his claim arises could be compelled to disclose all the intimate details of his case. By endowing with immunity from disclosure all that a lawyer discovers in the course of his duties, it is said, the rights of individual litigants in such cases are drained of vitality and the lawsuit becomes more of a battle of deception than a search for truth.

But framing the problem in terms of assisting individual plaintiffs in their suits against corporate defendants is unsatisfactory. Discovery concededly may work to the disadvantage as well as to the advantage of individual plaintiffs. Discovery, in other words, is not a one-way proposition. It is available in all types of cases at the behest of any party, individual or corporate, plaintiff or defendant. The problem thus far transcends the situation confronting this petitioner. And we must view that problem in light of the limitless situations where the particular kind of discovery sought by petitioner might be used.

We agree, of course, that the deposition-discovery rules are to be accorded a broad and liberal treatment. No longer can the time-honored cry of "fishing expedition" serve to preclude a party from inquiring into the facts underlying his opponent's case. Mutual knowledge of all the relevant facts gathered by both parties is essential to proper litigation. To that end, either party may compel the other to disgorge whatever facts he has in his possession. The deposition-discovery procedure simply advances the stage at which the disclosure can be compelled from the time of trial to the period preceding it, thus reducing the possibility of surprise. But discovery, like all matters of procedure, has ultimate and necessary boundaries. As indicated by Rules 30(b) and (d) and 31(d), limitations inevitably arise when it can be shown that the examination is being conducted in bad faith or in such a manner as to annoy, embarrass or oppress the person subject to the inquiry. And as Rule 26(b) provides, further limitations come into existence when the inquiry touches upon the irrelevant or encroaches upon the recognized domains of privilege.

We also agree that the memoranda, statements and mental impressions in issue in this case fall outside the scope of the attorney-client privilege and hence are not protected from discovery on that basis. * * *

But the impropriety of invoking that privilege does not provide an answer to the problem before us. Petitioner has made more than an ordinary request for relevant, non-privileged facts in the possession of his adversaries or their counsel. He has sought discovery as of right of oral and written statements of witnesses whose identity is well known and whose availability to petitioner appears unimpaired. He has sought production of these matters after making the most searching inquiries of his opponents as to the circumstances surrounding the fatal accident, which inquiries were sworn to have been answered to the best of their information and belief. Interrogatories were directed toward all the events prior to, during and subsequent to the sinking of the tug. Full and honest answers to such broad inquiries would necessarily have included all pertinent information gleaned by Fortenbaugh through his interviews with the witnesses. Petitioner makes no suggestion, and we cannot assume, that the tug owners or Fortenbaugh were incomplete or dishonest in the framing of their answers. In addition, petitioner was free to examine the public testimony of the witnesses taken before the United States Steamboat Inspectors. We are thus dealing with an attempt to secure the production of written statements and mental impressions contained in the files and the mind of the attorney Fortenbaugh without any showing of necessity or any indication or claim that denial of such production would unduly prejudice the preparation of petitioner's case or cause him any hardship or injustice. For aught that appears, the essence of what petitioner seeks either has been revealed to him already through the interrogatories or is readily available to him direct from the witnesses for the asking.

* * *

In our opinion, neither Rule 26 nor any other rule dealing with discovery contemplates production under such circumstances. That is not because the subject matter is privileged or irrelevant, as those concepts are used in these rules. Here is simply an attempt, without purported necessity or justification, to secure written statements, private memoranda and personal recollections prepared or formed by an adverse party's counsel in the course of his legal duties. As such, it falls outside the arena of discovery and contravenes the public policy underlying the orderly prosecution and defense of legal claims. Not even the most liberal of discovery theories can justify unwarranted inquiries into the files and the mental impressions of an attorney.

Historically, a lawyer is an officer of the court and is bound to work for the advancement of justice while faithfully protecting the rightful interests of his clients. In performing his various duties, however, it is essential that a lawyer work with a certain degree of privacy, free from unnecessary intrusion by opposing parties and their counsel. Proper preparation of a client's case demands that he assemble information, sift what he considers to be the relevant from the irrelevant facts, prepare his legal theories and plan his strategy without undue and needless interference. That is the historical and the necessary way in which lawyers act within the framework of our system of jurisprudence to promote justice and to protect their clients' interests. This work is reflected, of course, in interviews, statements, memoranda, correspondence, briefs, mental impressions, personal beliefs, and countless other tangible and intangible ways—aptly though roughly termed by the Circuit Court of Appeals in this case [153 F.2d 212, 223] as the "work product of the lawyer." Were such materials open to opposing counsel on mere demand, much of what is now put down in writing would remain unwritten. An attorney's thoughts, heretofore inviolate, would not be his own. Inefficiency, unfairness and sharp practices would inevitably develop in the giving of legal advice and in the preparation of cases for trial. The effect on the legal profession would be demoralizing. And the interests of the clients and the cause of justice would be poorly served.

We do not mean to say that all written materials obtained or prepared by an adversary's counsel with an eye toward litigation are necessarily free from discovery in all cases. Where relevant and non-privileged facts remain hidden in an attorney's file and where production of those facts is essential to the preparation of one's case, discovery may properly be had. Such written statements and documents might, under certain circumstances, be admissible in evidence or give clues as to the existence or location of relevant facts. Or they might be useful for purposes of impeachment or corroboration. And production might be justified where the witnesses are no longer available or can be reached only with difficulty. Were production of written statements and documents to be precluded under such circumstances, the liberal ideals of the deposition-discovery portions of the Federal Rules * * * would be stripped of much of their meaning. But the general policy against invading the privacy of an attorney's course of preparation is so well recognized and so essential to an orderly working of our system of legal procedure that a burden rests on the one who would invade that privacy to establish adequate reasons to justify production through a subpoena or court order. That burden, we believe, is necessarily implicit in the rules as now constituted.

Rule 30(b), as presently written, gives the trial judge the requisite discretion to make a judgment as to whether discovery should be allowed as to written statements secured from witnesses. But in the instant case there was no room for that discretion to operate in favor of the petitioner. No attempt was made to establish any reason why Fortenbaugh should be forced to produce the written statements. There was only a naked, general demand for these materials as of right and a finding by the District Court that no recognizable privilege was involved. That was insufficient to justify discovery under these circumstances and the court should have sustained the refusal of the tug owners and Fortenbaugh to produce.

But as to oral statements made by witnesses to Fortenbaugh, whether presently in the form of his mental impressions or memoranda, we do not believe that any showing of necessity can be made under the circumstances of this case so as to justify production. Under ordinary conditions, forcing an attorney to repeat or write out all that witnesses have told him and to deliver the account to his adversary gives rise to grave dangers of inaccuracy and untrustworthiness. No legitimate purpose is served by such production. The practice forces the attorney to testify as to what he remembers or what he saw fit to write down regarding witnesses' remarks. Such testimony could not qualify as evidence; and to use it for impeachment or corroborative purposes would make the attorney much less an officer of the court and much more an ordinary witness. The standards of the profession would thereby suffer.

Denial of production of this nature does not mean that any material, nonprivileged facts can be hidden from the petitioner in this case. He need not be unduly hindered in the preparation of his case, in the discovery of facts or in his anticipation of his opponents' position. Searching interrogatories directed to Fortenbaugh and the tug owners, production of written documents and statements upon a proper showing and direct interviews with the witnesses themselves all serve to reveal the facts in Fortenbaugh's possession to the fullest possible extent consistent with public policy. Petitioner's counsel frankly admits that he wants the oral statements only to help prepare himself to examine witnesses and to make sure that he has overlooked nothing. That is insufficient under the circumstances to permit him an exception to the policy underlying the privacy of Fortenbaugh's professional activities. If there should be a rare situation justifying production of these matters, petitioner's case is not of that type.

We fully appreciate the wide-spread controversy among the members of the legal profession over the problem raised by this case. It is a problem that rests on what has been one of the most hazy frontiers of the discovery process. But until some rule or statute definitely prescribes otherwise, we are not justified in permitting discovery in a situation of this nature as a matter of unqualified right. When Rule 26 and the other discovery rules were adopted, this Court and the members of the bar in general certainly did not believe or contemplate that all the files and mental processes of lawyers were thereby opened to the free scrutiny of their adversaries. And we refuse to interpret the rules at this time so as to reach so harsh and unwarranted a result.

We therefore affirm the judgment of the Circuit Court of Appeals.

Affirmed.

Mr. Justice Jackson, concurring.

* * *

To consider first the most extreme aspect of the requirement in litigation here, we find it calls upon counsel, if he has had any conversations with any of the crews of the vessels in question or of any other, to "set forth in detail the exact provision of any such oral statements or reports." Thus the demand is not for the production of a transcript in existence but calls for the creation of a written statement not in being. But the statement by counsel of what a witness told him is not evidence when written. Plaintiff could not introduce it to prove his case. What, then, is the purpose sought to be served by demanding this of adverse counsel?

Counsel for the petitioner candidly said on argument that he wanted this information to help prepare himself to examine witnesses, to make sure he overlooked nothing. He bases his claim to it in his brief on the view that the Rules were to do away with the old situation where a law suit developed into "a battle of wits between counsel." But a common law trial is and always should be an adversary proceeding. Discovery was hardly intended to enable a learned profession to perform its functions either without wits or on wits borrowed from the adversary.

The real purpose and the probable effect of the practice ordered by the district court would be to put trials on a level even lower than a "battle of wits." I can conceive of no practice more demoralizing to the Bar than to require a lawyer to write out and deliver to his adversary an account of what witnesses have told him. Even if his recollection were perfect, the statement would be his language permeated with his inferences. Every one who has tried it knows that it is almost impossible so fairly to record the expressions and emphasis of a witness that when he testifies in the environment of the court and under the influence of the leading question there will not be departures in some respects. Whenever the testimony of the witness would differ from the "exact" statement the lawyer had delivered, the lawyer's statement would be whipped out to impeach the witness. Counsel producing his adversary's "inexact" statement could lose nothing by saying, "Here is a contradiction, gentlemen of the jury. I do not know whether it is my adversary or his witness who is not telling the truth, but one is not." Of course, if this practice were adopted, that scene would be repeated over and over again. The lawyer who delivers such statements often would find himself branded a deceiver afraid to take the stand to support his own version of the witness's conversation with him, or else he will have to go on the stand to defend his own credibility— perhaps against that of his chief witness, or possibly even his client.

Every lawyer dislikes to take the witness stand and will do so only for grave reasons. This is partly because it is not his role; he is almost invariably a poor witness. But he steps out of professional character to do it. He regrets it; the profession discourages it. But the practice advocated here is one which would force him to be a witness, not as to what he has seen or done but as to other witnesses' stories, and not because he wants to do so but in self-defense.

And what is the lawyer to do who has interviewed one whom he believes to be a biased, lying or hostile witness to get his unfavorable statements and know what to meet? He must record and deliver such statements even though he would not vouch for the credibility of the witness by calling him. Perhaps the other side would not want to call him either, but the attorney is open to the charge of suppressing evidence at the trial if he fails to call such a hostile witness even though he never regarded him as reliable or truthful.

Having been supplied the names of the witnesses, petitioner's lawyer gives no reason why he cannot interview them himself. If an employee-witness refuses to tell his story, he, too, may be examined under the Rules. He may be compelled on discovery as fully as on the trial to disclose his version of the facts. But that is his own disclosure—it can be used to impeach him if he contradicts it and such a deposition is not useful to promote an unseemly disagreement between the witness and the counsel in the case.

It is true that the literal language of the Rules would admit of an interpretation that would sustain the district court's order. * * * But all such procedural measures have a background of custom and practice which was assumed by those who wrote and should be by those who apply them. * * * Certainly nothing in the tradition or practice of discovery up to the time of these Rules would have suggested that they would authorize such a practice as here proposed.

The question remains as to signed statements or those written by witnesses. Such statements are not evidence for the defendant. * * * Nor should I think they ordinarily could be evidence for the plaintiff. But such a statement might be useful for impeachment of the witness who signed it, if he is called and if he departs from the statement. There might be circumstances, too, where impossibility or difficulty of access to the witness or his refusal to respond to requests for information or other facts would show that the interests of justice require that such statements be made available. Production of such statements are governed by Rule 34 and on "Showing good cause therefor" the court may order their inspection, copying or photographing. No such application has here been made; the demand is made on the basis of right, not on showing of cause.

I agree to the affirmance of the judgment of the Circuit Court of Appeals which reversed the district court.

Mr. Justice Frankfurter joins in this opinion.

Notes and Questions

1. In 1970, Federal Rule 26(b)(3) was added specifically to deal with the discovery of work product. In what ways does the work-product doctrine in the Rule differ from that stated in *Hickman*? Does *Hickman* survive the codification of the work-product doctrine in the Rule in any way? See Clermont, *Surveying Work Product*, 68 Cornell L.Rev. 755 (1983).

2. Prior to the adoption of Rule 26(b)(3), many of the states that had adopted federal discovery rules already had added special provisions to deal with work-product and related problems. These provisions vary from state to state. See Friedenthal, *Discovery and Use of an Adverse Party's Expert Information,* 14 Stan.L.Rev. 455, 474–79 (1962).

3. Courts have split on the question whether and when Rule 26(b)(3) covers documents containing the results of a party's investigations made prior to hiring an attorney or the initiation of litigation. An example of a case in which discovery was permitted is THOMAS ORGAN CO. v. JADRANSKA SLOBODNA PLOVID-BA, 54 F.R.D. 367 (N.D.Ill.1972), involving a claim for damaged goods. Some seven months prior to the time plaintiff hired an attorney, its insurer conducted an investigation of the facts regarding the loss. The court held that the report of the investigation was made in the ordinary course of business and not for litigation, noting that in the vast majority of situations involving insurance claims,

matters are settled without litigation. But discovery was denied in ALMAGUER v. CHICAGO, R.I. & P. R. CO., 55 F.R.D. 147 (D.Neb.1972), in which a railroad employee brought suit against his employer for injuries incurred on the job. Plaintiff was not allowed to obtain a copy of a statement of an eyewitness taken by defendant's claims agent two months before plaintiff had employed a lawyer. The court said that whenever a railroad employee claims to have been injured on the job "the expectation of litigation * * * is a reasonable assumption."

Should the determination whether a report written prior to any legal action is discoverable be decided in terms of the likelihood that a lawsuit ultimately would be filed? See Abel Investment Co. v. United States, 53 F.R.D. 485, 489 (D.Neb. 1971) (Internal Revenue Service field agent reports regarding plaintiff's tax liabilities held to be routine, and hence discoverable, since only a few such reports result in litigation).

4. Should work-product protection be denied to any material prepared as part of an organization's normal course of business even if the probability of litigation is overwhelming? A New York court apparently so ruled, holding that subdivision (g) of N.Y.C.P.L.R. § 3101, which requires disclosure of "any written report of an accident prepared in the regular course of business operations," supersedes subdivision (d)(2) of that section which protects writings "created * * * in preparation for litigation." Pataki v. Kiseda, 80 A.D.2d 100, 437 N.Y.S.2d 692 (2d Dep't 1981).

Federal courts appear to be split between two different positions. Some appear to provide protection only if the information sought was developed "primarily" to assist in litigation. See, e.g., United States v. El Paso Co., 682 F.2d 530 (5th Cir.1982). Others apply work product even though the information was developed for business purposes if the business issue is the prospect of litigation. Thus if a business engages in an investigation to determine if a certain course of conduct would result in a lawsuit against the business, and litigation is expected, the latter group of courts hold that work product protection is appropriate because the inquiry was "in anticipation of litigation" under Rule 26(b)(3). See, e.g., United States v. Adlman, 134 F.3d 1194 (2d Cir.1998) (providing a comprehensive discussion of the different positions).

5. Rule 26(b)(3) refers only to "discovery of documents and tangible things." May a party ask by way of interrogatory what a specific document says? See PETERSON v. UNITED STATES, 52 F.R.D. 317, 320 (S.D.Ill.1971): "It is clear to this court that discovery of a detailed description of the contents of documents through interrogatories is equivalent to discovery of the documents themselves. The discovery sought by plaintiff through the interrogatories is therefore covered by rule 26(b)(3)." Is the court correct? Suppose plaintiff merely asked a question regarding a relevant fact, the answer to which was known to defendant only through documents uncovered by investigations of his attorney. Would such a question fall within the scope of the Rule? Should it? For a general discussion of the distinction between "documents and tangible things" and facts learned from them, see 8A Wright, Miller & Marcus, *Federal Practice and Procedure: Civil 2d* § 2023, at 330–34 (1994).

6. Rule 26(b)(3) allows discovery of material otherwise protected "only upon a showing that the party seeking discovery has substantial need of the materials in the preparation of the party's case and that the party is unable without undue hardship to obtain the substantial equivalent of the materials by other means." In SNEAD v. AMERICAN EXPORT–ISBRANDTSEN LINES, INC., 59 F.R.D. 148, 151 (E.D.Pa.1973), plaintiff, who had brought suit to recover for personal injuries,

moved for a court order requiring defendant to answer interrogatories as to whether defendant had possession of any secret motion pictures taken of plaintiff that would tend to bear on the scope of plaintiff's injuries. The court held as follows:

> * * * The only time there will be a substantial need to know about surveillance pictures will be in those instances where there would be a major discrepancy between the testimony the plaintiff will give and that which the films would seem to portray. By the same token this would be the only instance where there is a substantial need to withhold that information from plaintiff's counsel. If the discrepancy would be the result of the plaintiff's untruthfulness, the substantial need for his counsel to know of the variance can hardly justify making the information available to him. On the other hand, if the discrepancy would result from misleading photography, the necessary background information should be made available to the plaintiff's attorney so the fraud can be exposed. It goes without saying that the means to impeach should not be the exclusive property of the defense. * * *

> I conclude these purposes can best be achieved by requiring the defense to disclose the existence of surveillance films or be barred from showing them at trial. If the defense has films and decides it wants to use them, they should be exhibited to the plaintiff and his counsel. * * *

> Before any of these disclosures, however, the defense must be given an opportunity to depose the plaintiff fully as to his injuries, their effects, and his present disabilities. Once his testimony is memorialized in deposition, any variation he may make at trial to conform to the surveillance films can be used to impeach his credibility, and his knowledge at deposition that the films may exist should have a salutary effect on any tendency to be expansive. * * *

Isn't it true that whenever a document or other item is to be introduced into evidence by one party, there will be a need for discovery, at least for the purpose of determining whether such an item has been forged, distorted, or altered in some way?

Is the *Snead* court's view as to the relevance of surveillance films too narrow? Shouldn't it have considered the impact of the admission of such evidence on the substantive questions before the court as opposed to mere impeachment? Impeachment is solely for the purpose of casting doubt on the veracity of a witness. But films of a party's physical condition when that condition is at issue goes well beyond "impeachment." It is direct evidence of the condition itself. Rule 26(a)(3) exempts from automatic discovery evidence to be used "solely" for impeachment. Although one might argue that this supports the notion that evidence bearing only on a witness' veracity is work product that need not be revealed on discovery, there seems little doubt that evidence that bears directly on the facts at issue in the case cannot be kept hidden until trial and then held to be admissible. The vast majority of courts permit discovery of such evidence if it is to be used at trial, regardless of its intended purpose. See Gutshall v. New Prime, Inc., 196 F.R.D. 43 (W.D.Va.2000). Suppose in *Snead* the motion pictures strongly supported plaintiff's case and would not have been introduced at trial by defendant. Should they be protected from discovery by plaintiff?

7. Rule 26(b)(3) states that the court shall "protect against disclosure of the mental impressions, conclusions, and opinions of an attorney or other representative of a party." How can this provision be harmonized with Rules 33(c) and 36(a),

which, as amended in 1970, allow interrogatories and requests for admissions involving opinions or contentions that relate to fact or the application of law to fact?

8. Courts are divided on the degree of protection to be given "opinion" work product. In an important case, the Fourth Circuit has held that "no showing of relevance, substantial need or undue hardship should justify compelled disclosure of an attorney's mental impressions, conclusions, opinions or legal theories." DUPLAN CORP. v. MOULINAGE ET RETORDERIE DE CHAVANOZ, 509 F.2d 730, 734 (4th Cir.1974), certiorari denied 420 U.S. 997, 95 S.Ct. 1438, 43 L.Ed.2d 680 (1975). But in XEROX CORP. v. INTERNATIONAL BUSINESS MACHINES CORP., 64 F.R.D. 367 (S.D.N.Y.1974), the court ordered the production of counsel's notes of interviews with defendant's employees who could not recall crucial information at their depositions even if it was not feasible to excise the portions containing the attorney's mental impressions. "A party should not be allowed to conceal critical, non-privileged, discoverable information, which is uniquely within the knowledge of the party and which is not obtainable from any other source, simply by imparting the information to its attorney and then attempting to hide behind the work product doctrine after the party fails to remember the information." Id. at 381–82.

Plaintiffs in SHELTON v. AMERICAN MOTORS CORP., 805 F.2d 1323 (8th Cir.1986), were the parents of a sixteen-year-old who was killed in a "roll-over" accident while driving a Jeep CJ–5 manufactured by the defendant. They brought suit against the manufacturer, A.M.C., alleging negligence, strict liability and failure to warn. Plaintiffs sought and a magistrate allowed them to depose various A.M.C. personnel, including A.M.C.'s in-house litigation counsel, Rita Burns. However, during Burns' deposition, she refused to answer questions concerning the existence or nonexistence of documents, including any list of lawsuits filed against A.M.C. that involved the Jeep CJ–5, records of roll-over propensity tests other than those previously disclosed, any documents, films, prints, or memoranda that had been suppressed for the purposes of previous Jeep overturn cases, documents and videotapes of the Jeep Celebrity Challenge Races, computer modeling data, and several other items. Ms. Burns asserted that disclosure of her knowledge of the existence or nonexistence of any documents would reveal her mental impressions and that therefore the information sought by plaintiffs was protected work product. Should the court have ordered Ms. Burns to answer the questions?

9. Rule 26(b)(3) excludes from protection a party's own prior statement concerning the action. Why? See the Advisory Committee's Note to Rule 26(b)(3) set out in the Supplement. The Rule also permits a nonparty witness to obtain a copy of his statement upon request. Are the reasons for allowing a witness to obtain his own statement the same for a nonparty as they are for a party? Might a court usefully postpone release of the statement of a witness until after she has been deposed?

10. The work-product doctrine has been the subject of a considerable number of comments, debates, and judicial decisions in state as well as federal courts. See generally Cohn, *The Work–Product Doctrine: Protection, Not Privilege,* 71 Geo.L.J. 917 (1983); Taine, *Discovery of Trial Preparations in the Federal Courts,* 50 Colum.L.Rev. 1026 (1950); Tolman, *Discovery Under the Federal Rules: Production of Documents and the Work Products of the Lawyer,* 58 Colum.L.Rev. 498 (1958); Note, *The Work Product Doctrine,* 68 Cornell L.Rev. 760 (1983); *Develop-*

ments in the Law—Discovery, 74 Harv.L.Rev. 940, 1027–46 (1961); Comment, *The Work Product Doctrine in the State Courts,* 62 Mich.L.Rev. 1199 (1964).

2. PRIVILEGES AND WORK PRODUCT–THE EXTENT OF PROTECTION

Rule 26(b)(1) limits discovery to matter that is "not privileged," and the usual view has been that the same rules of privilege apply to discovery as apply at the trial. A privilege rule gives a person a right to refuse to disclose information that he otherwise would be required to provide. It also may give a person the right to prevent someone else from disclosing information, or it may give its possessor a right to refuse to become a witness. A rule of privilege is a counterweight to the general power of courts to compel testimony. Modern pretrial discovery involves an extension of the judicial power to compel disclosure and has been met by the expansion of old privileges and the creation of new ones that will check this power.

One rule of privilege that all American courts recognize is the attorney-client privilege. They also agree on its basic contours. For the privilege to attach to a communication, four elements must be present:

> (1) [T]he asserted holder of the privilege is or sought to be a client; (2) the person to whom the communication was made (a) is a member of the bar of a court, or his subordinate and (b) in connection with this communication is acting as a lawyer; (3) the communication relates to a fact of which the attorney was informed (a) by his client (b) without the presence of strangers (c) for the purpose of securing primarily either (i) an opinion on law or (ii) legal services or (iii) assistance in some legal proceeding, and not (d) for the purpose of committing a crime or tort; and (4) the privilege has been (a) claimed and (b) not waived by the client.

United States v. United Shoe Machinery Corp., 89 F.Supp. 357, 358–59 (D.Mass.1950).

Because the attorney-client privilege results in the suppression of relevant facts, courts tend to construe it narrowly and to resolve doubtful cases against a finding of privilege. One observer has said that "[w]hile often unexpressed, the crucial factor limiting the privilege's availability is not the past law of the privilege but the developing rules of liberal discovery. * * * At least when precedent is not absolutely clear, whether a party can assert the privilege will often depend less on the jurisdiction's law of privilege than on the particular judge's attitude toward liberal discovery." Bartell, "The Attorney–Client Privilege and the Work–Product Doctrine," in *ALI–ABA Civil Procedure and Litigation in Federal and State Courts,* vol. I, at 507 (1987).

UPJOHN CO. v. UNITED STATES

Supreme Court of the United States, 1981.
449 U.S. 383, 101 S.Ct. 677, 66 L.Ed.2d 584.

Certiorari to the United States Court of Appeals for the Sixth Circuit.

JUSTICE REHNQUIST delivered the opinion of the Court.

We granted certiorari in this case to address important questions concerning the scope of the attorney-client privilege in the corporate context and the applicability of the work-product doctrine in proceedings to enforce tax summonses. * * * With respect to the privilege question the parties and various *amici* have described our task as one of choosing between two "tests" which have gained adherents in the courts of appeals. We are acutely aware, however, that we sit to decide concrete cases and not abstract propositions of law. We decline to lay down a broad rule or series of rules to govern all conceivable future questions in this area, even were we able to do so. We can and do, however, conclude that the attorney-client privilege protects the communications involved in this case from compelled disclosure and that the work-product doctrine does apply in tax summons enforcement proceedings.

I

Petitioner Upjohn Co. manufactures and sells pharmaceuticals here and abroad. In January 1976 independent accountants conducting an audit of one of Upjohn's foreign subsidiaries discovered that the subsidiary made payments to or for the benefit of foreign government officials in order to secure government business. The accountants so informed Mr. Gerard Thomas, Upjohn's Vice President, Secretary, and General Counsel. * * * He consulted with outside counsel and R.T. Parfet, Jr., Upjohn's Chairman of the Board. It was decided that the company would conduct an internal investigation of what were termed "questionable payments." As part of this investigation the attorneys prepared a letter containing a questionnaire which was sent to "All Foreign General and Area Managers" over the Chairman's signature. The letter began by noting recent disclosures that several American companies made "possibly illegal" payments to foreign government officials and emphasized that the management needed full information concerning any such payments made by Upjohn. The letter indicated that the Chairman had asked Thomas, identified as "the company's General Counsel," "to conduct an investigation for the purpose of determining the nature and magnitude of any payments made by the Upjohn Company or any of its subsidiaries to any employee or official of a foreign government." The questionnaire sought detailed information concerning such payments. Managers were instructed to treat the investigation as "highly confidential" and not to discuss it with anyone other than Upjohn employees who might be helpful in providing the requested information. Responses were to be sent directly to Thomas. Thomas and outside counsel also interviewed the recipients of the questionnaire and some 33 other Upjohn officers or employees as part of the investigation.

On March 26, 1976, the company voluntarily submitted a preliminary report to the Securities and Exchange Commission on Form 8–K disclosing certain questionable payments. A copy of the report was simultaneously submitted to the Internal Revenue Service, which immediately began an investigation to determine the tax consequences of the payments. Special agents conducting the investigation were given lists by Upjohn of all those interviewed and all who had responded to the questionnaire. On November 23, 1976, the Service issued a summons pursuant to 26 U.S.C. § 7602 demanding production of:

> All files relative to the investigation conducted under the supervision of Gerard Thomas to identify payments to employees of foreign governments and any political contributions made by the Upjohn Company or any of its affiliates since January 1, 1971 and to determine whether any

funds of the Upjohn Company had been improperly accounted for on the corporate books during the same period.

The records should include but not be limited to written questionnaires sent to managers of the Upjohn Company's foreign affiliates, and memoranda or notes of the interviews conducted in the United States and abroad with officers and employees of the Upjohn Company and its subsidiaries. App. 17a–18a.

The company declined to produce the documents specified in the second paragraph on the grounds that they were protected from disclosure by the attorney-client privilege and constituted the work product of attorneys prepared in anticipation of litigation. On August 31, 1977, the United States filed a petition seeking enforcement of the summons under 26 U.S.C. §§ 7402(b) and 7604(a) in the United States District Court for the Western District of Michigan. That court adopted the recommendation of a magistrate who concluded that the summons should be enforced. Petitioners appealed to the Court of Appeals for the Sixth Circuit which rejected the Magistrate's finding of a waiver of the attorney-client privilege, * * * but agreed that the privilege did not apply "[t]o the extent that the communications were made by officers and agents not responsible for directing Upjohn's actions in response to legal advice * * * for the simple reason that the communications were not the 'client's.' " * * * The court reasoned that accepting petitioner's claim for a broader application of the privilege would encourage upper-echelon management to ignore unpleasant facts and create too broad a "zone of silence." Noting that Upjohn's counsel had interviewed officials such as the Chairman and President, the Court of Appeals remanded to the District Court so that a determination of who was within the "control group" could be made. In a concluding footnote the court stated that the work-product doctrine "is not applicable to administrative summonses issued under 26 U.S.C. § 7602."
* * *

II

Federal Rule of Evidence 501 provides that "the privilege of a witness * * * shall be governed by the principles of the common law as they may be interpreted by the courts of the United States in light of reason and experience." The attorney-client privilege is the oldest of the privileges for confidential communications known to the common law. 8 Wigmore, Evidence § 2290 (McNaughton rev. 1961). Its purpose is to encourage full and frank communication between attorneys and their clients and thereby promote broader public interests in the observance of law and administration of justice. The privilege recognizes that sound legal advice or advocacy serves public ends and that such advice or advocacy depends upon the lawyer's being fully informed by the client. * * * Admittedly complications in the application of the privilege arise when the client is a corporation, which in theory is an artificial creature of the law, and not an individual; but this Court has assumed that the privilege applies when the client is a corporation * * *.

The Court of Appeals, however, considered the application of the privilege in the corporate context to present a "different problem," since the client was an inanimate entity and "only the senior management, guiding and integrating the several operations, . . . can be said to possess an identity analogous to the corporation as a whole." * * * Such a view, we think, overlooks the fact that the privilege exists to protect not only the giving of professional advice to those who can act on it but also the giving of information to the lawyer to enable him to give sound and informed advice. * * * The first step in the resolution of any legal problem is ascertaining the factual background and sifting through the facts with an eye to the legally relevant. * * *

In the case of the individual client the provider of information and the person who acts on the lawyer's advice are one and the same. In the corporate context, however, it will frequently be employees beyond the control group as defined by the court below—"officers and agents . . . responsible for directing [the company's] actions in response to legal advice"—who will possess the information needed by the corporation's lawyers. Middle-level—and indeed lower-level—employees can, by actions within the scope of their employment, embroil the corporation in serious legal difficulties, and it is only natural that these employees would have the relevant information needed by corporate counsel if he is adequately to advise the client with respect to such actual or potential difficulties. * * *

The control group test adopted by the court below thus frustrates the very purpose of the privilege by discouraging the communication of relevant information by employees of the client to attorneys seeking to render legal advice to the client corporation. The attorney's advice will also frequently be more significant to noncontrol group members than to those who officially sanction the advice, and the control group test makes it more difficult to convey full and frank legal advice to the employees who will put into effect the client corporation's policy. * * *

The narrow scope given the attorney-client privilege by the court below not only makes it difficult for corporate attorneys to formulate sound advice when their client is faced with a specific legal problem but also threatens to limit the valuable efforts of corporate counsel to ensure their client's compliance with the law. In light of the vast and complicated array of regulatory legislation confronting the modern corporation, corporations, unlike most individuals, "constantly go to lawyers to find out how to obey the law[.]" * * * [I]f the purpose of the attorney-client privilege is to be served, the attorney and client must be able to predict with some degree of certainty whether particular discussions will be protected. An uncertain privilege, or one which purports to be certain but results in widely varying applications by the courts, is little better than no privilege at all. The very terms of the test adopted by the court below suggest the unpredictability of its application. The test restricts the availability of the privilege to those officers who play a "substantial role" in deciding and directing a corporation's legal response. * * *

The communications at issue were made by Upjohn employees to counsel for Upjohn acting as such, at the direction of corporate superiors in order to secure legal advice from counsel. * * * Information, not available from upper-echelon management, was needed to supply a basis for legal advice concerning compliance with securities and tax laws, foreign laws, currency regulations, duties to shareholders, and potential litigation in each of these areas. The communications concerned matters within the scope of the employees' corporate duties, and the employees themselves were sufficiently aware that they were being questioned in order that the corporation could obtain legal advice. The questionnaire identified Thomas as "the company's General Counsel" and referred in its opening sentence to the possible illegality of payments such as the ones on which information was sought. * * * A statement of policy accompanying the questionnaire clearly indicated the legal implications of the investigation. The policy statement was issued "in order that there be no uncertainty in the future as to the policy with respect to the practices which are the subject of this investigation." It began "Upjohn will comply with all laws and regulations," and stated that commissions or payments "will not be used as a subterfuge for bribes or illegal payments" and that all payments must be "proper and legal." Any future agreements with foreign distributors or agents were to be approved "by a company attorney" and any questions concerning the policy were to be referred "to the company's General Counsel." * * * This statement was issued to Upjohn employees worldwide, so that even those interviewees not receiving a questionnaire were aware of the legal implications of the interviews. Pursuant to explicit instructions from the Chairman of the Board, the communications were considered "highly confidential" when made, * * * and have been kept confidential by the company. Consistent with the underlying purposes of the attorney-client privilege, these communications must be protected against compelled disclosure.

The Court of Appeals declined to extend the attorney-client privilege beyond the limits of the control group test for fear that doing so would entail severe burdens on discovery and create a broad "zone of silence" over corporate affairs. Application of the attorney-client privilege to communications such as those involved here, however, puts the adversary in no worse position than if the communications had never taken place. The privilege only protects disclosure of communications; it does not protect disclosure of the underlying facts by those who communicated with the attorney * * *. Here the Government was free to question the employees who communicated with Thomas and outside counsel. Upjohn has provided the IRS with a list of such employees, and the IRS has already interviewed some 25 of them. While it would probably be more convenient for the Government to secure the results of petitioner's internal investigation by simply subpoenaing the questionnaires and notes taken by petitioner's attorneys, such considerations of convenience do not overcome the policies served by the attorney-client privilege. As Justice Jackson noted in his concurring opinion in Hickman v. Taylor * * *: "Discovery was hardly intended to enable a learned profession to perform its functions . . . on wits borrowed from the adversary."

* * *

III

Our decision that the communications by Upjohn employees to counsel are covered by the attorney-client privilege disposes of the case so far as the responses to the questionnaires and any notes reflecting responses to interview questions are concerned. * * * To the extent that the material subject to the summons is not protected by the attorney-client privilege as disclosing communications between an employee and counsel, we must reach the ruling by the Court of Appeals that the work-product doctrine does not apply to summonses issued under 26 U.S.C. § 7602.[6]

The Government concedes, wisely, that the Court of Appeals erred and that the work-product doctrine does apply to IRS summonses. * * * This doctrine was announced by the Court over 30 years ago in Hickman v. Taylor * * *. In that case the Court rejected "an attempt, without purported necessity or justification, to secure written statements, private memoranda and personal recollections prepared or formed by an adverse party's counsel in the course of his legal duties." * * * The Court noted that "it is essential that a lawyer work with a certain degree of privacy" * * *. The "strong public policy" underlying the work-product doctrine * * * has been substantially incorporated in Federal Rule * * * 26(b)(3).

* * * Nothing in the language of the IRS summons provisions or their legislative history suggests an intent on the part of Congress to preclude application of the work-product doctrine. Rule 26(b)(3) codifies the work-product doctrine, and the Federal Rules of Civil Procedure are made applicable to summons enforcement proceedings by Rule 81(a)(3). * * * While conceding the applicability of the work-product doctrine, the Government asserts that it has made a sufficient showing of necessity to overcome its protections. * * * The Government stresses that interviewees are scattered across the globe and that Upjohn has forbidden its employees to answer questions it considers irrelevant. The above-quoted language from *Hickman,* however, did not apply to "oral statements made by witnesses ... whether presently in the form of [the attorney's] mental impressions or memoranda." * * * As to such material the Court did "not believe that any showing of necessity can be made under the circumstances of this case so as to justify production * * *." * * * Forcing an attorney to disclose notes and memoranda of witnesses' oral statements is particularly disfavored because it tends to reveal the attorney's mental processes * * *.

Rule 26 accords special protection to work product revealing the attorney's mental processes. The Rule permits disclosure of documents and tangible things constituting attorney work product upon a showing of substantial need and inability to obtain the equivalent without undue hardship. * * * Rule 26 goes on, however, to state that "[i]n ordering discovery of such materials when the required showing has been made, the court shall protect against disclosure of the mental impressions, conclusions, opinions or legal theories of an attorney or other representative of a party concerning the litigation." Although this language does not specifically refer to memoranda based on oral statements of witnesses, the *Hickman* court stressed the danger that compelled disclosure of such memoranda would reveal the attorney's mental processes. It is clear that this is the sort of material the draftsmen of the Rule had in mind as deserving special protection. * * *

* * * It is clear that the Magistrate applied the wrong standard when he concluded that the Government had made a sufficient showing of necessity to overcome the protections of the work-product doctrine. The Magistrate applied the "substantial need" and "without undue hardship" standard articu-

---

6. The following discussion will also be relevant to counsels' notes and memoranda of interviews with the seven former employees should it be determined that the attorney-client privilege does not apply to them. * * *

lated in the first part of Rule 26(b)(3). The notes and memoranda sought by the Government here, however, are work product based on oral statements. If they reveal communications, they are, in this case, protected by the attorney-client privilege. To the extent they do not reveal communications, they reveal the attorneys' mental processes in evaluating the communications. As Rule 26 and *Hickman* make clear, such work product cannot be disclosed simply on a showing of substantial need and inability to obtain the equivalent without undue hardship.

While we are not prepared at this juncture to say that such material is always protected by the work-product rule, we think a far stronger showing of necessity and unavailability by other means than was made by the Government or applied by the Magistrate in this case would be necessary to compel disclosure. * * *

Accordingly, the judgment of the Court of Appeals is reversed, and the case remanded for further proceedings.

[The concurring opinion of CHIEF JUSTICE BURGER is omitted.]

Notes and Questions

1. In state courts, the attorney-client privilege is a creation of state law (state common law or statute), not of federal law. For state courts, the *Upjohn* decision is not binding authority, and several have not found its reasoning to be persuasive. See, e.g., Consolidation Coal Co. v. Bucyrus–Erie Co., 89 Ill.2d 103, 59 Ill.Dec. 666, 432 N.E.2d 250 (1982) (rejecting *Upjohn* and adopting the "control group" test).

In federal courts, the privilege is solely a matter of federal law, except that Federal Rule of Evidence 501 directs a federal district court sitting in a diversity case to apply the privilege law that would be applied by the courts of the state in which the federal court sits. When federal and state law claims are joined, federal law may govern the attorney-client privilege, Valente v. Pepsico, Inc., 68 F.R.D. 361, 366 n. 10 (D.Del.1975), unless the allegedly privileged communication relates solely to the state law claims.

2. The *Upjohn* opinion did not announce a set of rules controlling the attorney-client privilege. How, then, can a corporation predict whether or not a communication will be found to be privileged? It has been suggested that the following rules underlie the *Upjohn* analysis: 1) the communication must be one that would not have been made but for the contemplation of legal services; 2) the content of the communication must relate to the legal services being rendered; 3) the information-giver must be an employee, agent, or independent contractor with a significant relationship to the corporation and the corporation's involvement in the transaction that is the subject of legal services; 4) the communication must be made in confidence; and 5) the privilege may be asserted either by the corporation or by the information-giver. Sexton, *A Post–Upjohn Consideration of the Corporate Attorney–Client Privilege,* 57 N.Y.U.L.Rev. 443 (1982). Do you agree?

For more on *Upjohn,* see Waldman, *Beyond Upjohn: The Attorney–Client Privilege in the Corporate Context,* 28 Wm. & Mary L.Rev. 473 (1987); Saltzburg, *Corporate and Related Attorney–Client Privilege Claims: A Suggested Approach,* 12 Hofstra L.Rev. 279 (1984); Williams, *The Scope of the Corporate Attorney–Client Privilege in View of Reason and Experience,* 25 Howard L.J. 425 (1982).

3.   Does the employee or the former employee who speaks to the corporation's attorney enjoy the protection of the attorney-client privilege? Suppose, for example, that a corporation conducts an internal investigation concerning its accounting practices and an employee or a former employee, in the course of describing how sloppy the practices are, admits to embezzling funds. Can the employee invoke the attorney-client privilege to prevent disclosure of the admission? Can the corporation authorize its attorney to disclose the admission? In UNITED STATES v. STUCKEY, No. 81 Cr. 35 (S.D.N.Y.1981), affirmed per curiam 671 F.2d 494 (2d Cir.1981), certiorari denied 455 U.S. 1017, 102 S.Ct. 1711, 72 L.Ed.2d 134 (1982), the Second Circuit affirmed the conviction of a corporate manager who revealed incriminating material to special counsel for the corporation during an intra-corporate investigation. The District Court had concluded that the manager failed to demonstrate the existence of an attorney-client relationship between himself and counsel, and the corporation had waived its privilege with respect to the conversation. In this light, how far must a corporation's attorney go to make clear to an employee the nature of their relationship, and to warn the employee of the risks of using counsel for the corporation as the employee's personal counsel?

4.   The attorney-client privilege is waived if a protected communication is disclosed voluntarily to third persons, and once waived, a party can be forced to disclose not only the specific communication but all communications involving the same subject matter. See Duplan Corp. v. Deering Milliken, Inc., 397 F.Supp. 1146 (D.S.C.1974). A party must assert the privilege when information is sought and cannot selectively reveal portions of a communication and maintain the privilege for the remainder. Nguyen v. Excel Corporation, 197 F.3d 200, 206 (5th Cir.1999). The possibility of waiving the attorney-client privilege strongly influences a lawyer's handling of discovery disputes. Any slip in screening materials that are produced in discovery can result in waiver. Disclosure to non-parties can destroy the privilege. Showing privileged materials to a prospective witness or expert in advance of a deposition or of trial can forfeit the privilege's protection. What might be the costs of such broad waiver rules for litigants? For the courts? Are the costs justified by the cases in which the waiver rules result in making evidence available—sometimes critical evidence, that would not otherwise be heard? See Marcus, *The Perils of Privilege: Waiver and the Litigator*, 84 Mich.L.Rev. 1605 (1986). See also *Developments in the Law—Privileged Communications*, 98 Harv. L.Rev. 1450, 1629–65 (1985); Davison & Voth, *Waiver of the Attorney–Client Privilege*, 64 Or.L.Rev. 635 (1986).

5.   Should any voluntary disclosure of work product waive its protection? A majority of courts have held that the disclosure of work product to third persons waives the immunity only if the disclosure substantially increases the opportunity for potential adversaries to obtain the information. See, e.g., GAF Corp. v. Eastman Kodak Co., 85 F.R.D. 46, 51–52 (S.D.N.Y.1979). A majority of courts also have held that a voluntary disclosure of work product to an adversary waives the protection, but the waiver is limited to the material actually disclosed and does not extend to all work-product materials on the same subject matter. See Duplan Corp. v. Deering Milliken, Inc., 540 F.2d 1215, 1222–23 (4th Cir.1976). What accounts for the different waiver rules for work product compared with the attorney-client privilege?

6.   The attorney-client privilege is an example of an "absolute" privilege. If the privilege attaches to a communication, a court cannot compel its disclosure no matter how compelling the adversary's need for the information. Some privileges

are "qualified." How might this difference affect the courts' handling of the two types of privileges?

7.   The attorney-client privilege is just one of the privileges that affect the scope of discovery. The Constitution is the source of several privileges—for example, the Fifth Amendment privilege against self-incrimination. Other privileges are founded on common law and statutes. Among the widely recognized privileges are the privileges for communications between husband and wife, priest and penitent, and physician and patient. Other privileges struggle for recognition—for example, a privilege for communications between accountants and their clients. See generally *Developments in the Law—Privileged Communications*, 98 Harv.L.Rev. 1450 (1985).

8.   The 1993 amendments to the Federal Rules added a new Rule 26(b)(5), which requires that a claim of privilege or work product be made expressly and that the nature of the items withheld be described in a manner that enables other parties to assess the applicability of the privilege. Failure to comply will result in a loss of protection. See McCoo v. Denny's Inc., 192 F.R.D. 675, 690–91 (D.Kan. 2000).

3.   EXPERT INFORMATION

––––––

Read Federal Rule of Civil Procedure 26(a)(2) and 26(b)(4) in the Supplement.

––––––

PERRY v. W.S. DARLEY & CO.

United States District Court, Eastern District of Wisconsin, 1971.
54 F.R.D. 278.

MYRON L. GORDON, DISTRICT JUDGE. The plaintiff Robert Perry, a volunteer fireman, seeks damages for injuries allegedly sustained when he was struck by a fire truck as he attempted to activate a pump manufactured and installed on the truck by the defendant. The defendant has moved for an order compelling disclosure of the names of certain experts who examined the truck and pump shortly after the accident; the refusal to disclose the names occurred during the oral deposition of Ward Johnson, an employee of the workmen's compensation carrier for the fire department for which Mr. Perry works.

Counsel for the plaintiffs objected to disclosure of the experts' names on the basis that such information "constitutes both privileged communication and work product." However, the defendant argues in its brief that the experts are potential witnesses who "have knowledge of relevant facts" and that it is entitled, pursuant to Rule 26(b)(1), to the "identity and location of persons having knowledge of any discoverable matter."

The plaintiffs state that

It should be noted that the [defendant's] question did not seek the disclosure of the identity of experts which plaintiffs expect to call as witnesses upon the trial, which disclosure is explicitly required by the

July 1, 1970, amendment to the Federal Rules. Federal Rule 26(b)(4)(A). However, significantly, no similar requirement is made for the disclosure of identity of experts not retained or specially employed for purposes of testifying at trial. See Rule 26(b)(4)(B).

Some courts recently have refused to adopt the position taken in earlier cases in which discovery of facts known by an expert was allowed but discovery of the expert's opinions and conclusions was refused. In United States v. Meyer, 398 F.2d 66, 73 (9th Cir.1968), the court stated:

> No fact-opinion distinction is found in the discovery rules, Rule 26(b) extends discovery broadly to "any matter, not privileged, which is relevant to the subject matter involved in the pending action." In 1946 the Supreme Court rejected a proposal to amend the rules to restrict discovery of writings reflecting the conclusions of experts. The nearly contemporaneous use of the word "fact" in certain passages in the opinion in Hickman v. Taylor, * * * cannot be taken as an implicit adoption of the rejected limitation.

See also 8 Wright & Miller, *Federal Practice and Procedure: Civil* § 2029, at 247 (1970).

In addition, the Advisory Committee note to Rule 26(b)(4) states, in part:

> It should be noted that the subdivision does not address itself to the expert whose information was not acquired in preparation for trial but rather because he was an actor or viewer with respect to transactions or occurrences that are part of the subject matter of the lawsuit. Such an expert should be treated as an ordinary witness. 48 F.R.D. 487, 503 (1970).

The plaintiffs concede, as stated above, that they have a duty to disclose the identity of any expert whom they expect to call as a witness at the trial. As to experts who have been engaged "in anticipation of litigation or preparation for trial," however, the plaintiffs point to the provisions of Rule 26(b)(4)(B) to the effect that, when such experts are "not expected to be called as * * * [witnesses] * * * at trial," facts known or opinions held by them are discoverable

> * * * only as provided in Rule 35(b) or upon a showing of exceptional circumstances under which it is impracticable for the party seeking discovery to obtain facts or opinions on the same subject by other means.

No means are provided by Rule 26(b) by which it may be determined that an expert is a person whom a party expects to call as a witness at trial. However, Rule 26(e) provides, in part * * * [that a party must supplement its discovery responses with regard to]

> * * * the identity of each person expected to be called as an expert witness at trial, the subject matter on which he is expected to testify, and the substance of his testimony.

Furthermore, the final pretrial order regularly used by this court requires each party to provide the "names and addresses of each side's prospective expert witnesses, together with a narrative statement of each such expert's background and experience."

Rule 26(b)(4)(B) makes no distinction between the identity of an expert and facts known or opinions held by him, although it is stated in 8 Wright & Miller, *Federal Practice and Procedure: Civil* § 2032, at 255 (1970), that, "Apparently one party can find out the names of experts specially retained by another party who are not to be called." However, in an affidavit attached to the defendant's motion, the attorney for the defendant states that, because the experts viewed the fire truck well before the commencement of the present action, "this in and of itself is sufficient cause to require the plaintiff to turn over not only the names of the expert or experts but the reports of said expert or experts."

In my opinion, no showing of "exceptional circumstances" has been made by the defendant in the case at bar, nor is there any evidence to indicate that the experts were actors or viewers "with respect to [the] transactions or occurrences that are part of the subject matter of the lawsuit." Rule 26(b)(4) imposes a more rigorous standard upon the discovery of facts known and opinions held by an expert than is imposed with regard to other witnesses * * *.

Therefore, it is ordered that the defendant's motion for an order compelling answers to certain questions propounded to Ward Johnson be and hereby is denied.

Notes and Questions

1. Is the court in *Perry* correct that the experts who examined the fire truck and pump shortly after the accident were not viewers of the occurrences that gave rise to the lawsuit? And did these experts acquire their information in preparation for trial? One district court, without any special showing, ordered a defendant to disclose the names, reports, notes, and data compilations of outside experts engaged by defendant to assist its post-accident investigation into the sinking of a barge, and of defendant's regular employees who assisted in the investigation. In re Sinking of Barge "Ranger I", 92 F.R.D. 486 (S.D.Tex.1981). Is such a discovery request governed by Rule 26(b)(4)(B)? What factors should a court consider to determine that an expert has been retained or specially employed in anticipation of litigation or preparation for trial?

2. How far does the work-product doctrine go in protecting the facts and opinions of a retained expert who is not expected to testify at trial? What if an expert's conclusions are favorable to the opposing party and a document containing those conclusions is disclosed accidentally? Can the expert be called by the opposing party to testify at trial?

3. Rule 26(b)(4)(B) permits discovery of facts and opinions from an expert employed in anticipation of trial and who will not be called to testify, but only upon a showing of special circumstances. What circumstances justify discovery under this provision? See Disidore v. Mail Contractors of America, Inc., 196 F.R.D. 410, 415–19 (D.Kan.2000). Suppose that special circumstances are not shown for discovering the facts known and opinions of such an expert. Is the expert's identity nonetheless discoverable? Is any special showing required to compel the disclosure of such an expert's identity? AGER v. JANE C. STORMONT HOSPITAL & TRAINING SCHOOL FOR NURSES, 622 F.2d 496 (10th Cir.1980), was an action by a father against a hospital and a doctor for allegedly causing the death of his wife during labor and injuries to his infant daughter that left her

brain damaged and paralyzed. During discovery, the doctor's counsel asked plaintiff, in interrogatories, to disclose the names and addresses of any experts that plaintiff had contacted about the case, but who were not going to testify. Plaintiff's counsel refused to answer the interrogatories. The Court of Appeals held that if these experts had been contacted only informally, plaintiff could not be required to disclose their identity under any circumstances; if they had been retained formally, disclosure of their identity would be required only upon a showing of exceptional circumstances. For a contrary view, see Baki v. B.F. Diamond Constr. Co., 71 F.R.D. 179 (D.Md.1976); Sea Colony, Inc. v. Continental Ins. Co., 63 F.R.D. 113 (D.Del.1974). See generally 8A Wright, Miller & Marcus, *Federal Practice and Procedure: Civil 2d* §§ 2032–33 (1994).

4. Prior to 1993, Federal Rule 26(b)(4)(A)(i) provided for limited discovery regarding information of experts who were to be called to testify. Discovery, which was limited to interrogatories unless the Court otherwise provided, was found to be inadequate and unsatisfactory:

> The results of the survey indicate that the actual practice of discovery of expert witnesses expected to be called at trial varies widely from the two-step procedure of Rule 26(b)(4)(A). The interrogatory overwhelmingly is recognized as a totally unsatisfactory method of providing adequate preparation for cross-examination and rebuttal. In practice, full discovery is the rule, and practitioners use all available means of disclosure including both the discovery of expert's reports and depositions.

Graham, *Discovery of Experts Under Rule 26(b)(4) of the Federal Rules of Civil Procedure: Part Two, An Empirical Study and a Proposal,* 1977 U.Ill.L.F. 169, 172. See also McLaughlin, *Discovery and Admissibility of Expert Testimony,* 63 Notre Dame L.Rev. 760 (1988). Rule 26(a)(2)(B), as amended in 1993, however, requires the disclosure of written reports of any "witness who is retained or specially employed to provide expert testimony." The report must include "a complete statement of all opinions to be expressed and reasons therefor." In addition, Rule 26(b)(4)(A) provides that "[a] party may depose any person who has been identified as an expert whose opinions may be presented at trial." What are the arguments for and against this expanded discovery of the opinions of expert witnesses?

5. May a party obtain discovery of an expert who is not employed by any of the parties to the lawsuit? Richard Snyder, a research scientist, had conducted research and published a report that concluded that "utility vehicles, particularly the Jeep CJ–5, experience a disproportionately high roll over rate in accidents." In several personal injury cases involving utility vehicles, the manufacturer sought to take Snyder's deposition and to compel him to produce all background notes and materials pertaining to his report. Snyder had not been retained by any party to the suit, but other expert witnesses had used Snyder's research report as a basis for their opinions. In each case, Snyder moved to quash the subpoenas. How should the courts have ruled? Compare Buchanan v. American Motors Corp., 697 F.2d 151 (6th Cir.1983), and In re Snyder, 115 F.R.D. 211 (D.Ariz.1987) (quashing the subpoena), with Wright v. Jeep Corp., 547 F.Supp. 871 (E.D.Mich.1982) (enforcing the subpoena but requiring the manufacturer to pay Snyder a reasonable fee, costs, and part of the expenses of the original research). Is the discovery of an expert such as Snyder just a matter of compensation? What other considerations might prompt a court to bar such discovery? See Rule 26(b)(4)(C). See also Deitchman v. E.R. Squibb & Sons, Inc., 740 F.2d 556 (7th Cir.1984).

6. A comprehensive and influential analysis of the discovery of expert information under the Federal Rules is Graham, *Discovery of Experts Under Rule 26(b)(4) of the Federal Rules of Civil Procedure: Part One, An Analytical Study,* and *Part Two, An Empirical Study and a Proposal,* 1976 U.Ill.L.F. 895; 1977 U.Ill.L.F. 169.

7. State provisions regarding the discovery of expert information vary considerably. For example, N.Y.C.P.L.R. 3101(d), which accompanies Rule 26 in the Supplement, is more restrictive than Federal Rules 26(a)(2) and 26(b)(4).

KRISA v. EQUITABLE LIFE ASSURANCE SOCIETY

United States District Court, Middle District of Pennsylvania, 2000.
196 F.R.D. 254.

This case concerns Equitable's decision to deny Krisa's application for disability benefits under insurance policies issued to Krisa by Equitable. * * *

A. The Production of Draft Expert Reports and Written Analyses Prepared by Testifying Experts

Krisa seeks production of preliminary reports and other documents created by Equitable's experts in connection with this litigation. Equitable responds that it need not produce the draft reports and written analyses generated by its experts because such documents are protected by the work product doctrine codified in Rule 26(b)(3) * * * . Equitable's argument disregards the fact that the protection afforded by Rule 26(b)(3) is subject to Rule 26(b)(4), which generally authorizes discovery of testifying expert witnesses. * * * [T]he structure of Rule 26 and the Advisory Committee Notes that accompanied the authorization of expert witness discovery in 1970 suggest the conclusion that documents prepared by expert witnesses are not within the ambit of the work product doctrine. * * * [T]he Rules plainly contemplate discovery of not only the opinions the testifying experts intend to advance at trial, but also preliminary or tentative opinions expressed by the testifying experts that may be in conflict with their final opinions. * * *

The conclusion that draft reports and other documents prepared by Equitable's witnesses in this case are not covered by the work product privilege is consistent with the policy considerations underlying the privilege. The work product privilege is based upon "the general policy against invading the privacy of an attorney's course of preparation." Bogosian v. Gulf Oil Corp., 738 F.2d 587, 592 (3d Cir.1984) * * *. * * * Equitable's representations indicate that counsel's mental processes and opinions are not contained in the expert's draft reports. Thus, requesting production of these documents will not invade the privacy to be accorded Equitable's trial counsel in developing litigation strategies and theories. Moreover, Krisa could be deprived of information that would be material to effective cross-examination of Equitable's experts if deprived of the expression of the evolution of the experts' opinions.

B. Communications From Equitable's Counsel to Testifying Expert Witnesses

There has been a significant split among courts that have addressed whether core attorney work product shared with a party's expert is discoverable. * * * Our Court of Appeals addressed this issue in *Bogosian*, 738 F.2d at 595, and held that core work product generated by an attorney was shielded from discovery even if disclosed to an expert. * * * [That court relied on *Upjohn* for the proposition that special protection is to be accorded an attorney's mental impressions, conclusions, and opinions.]

Although courts have noted that "the reasoning of those cases interpreting the Rule prior to 1993 on this subject is probably obsolete," they have remained divided on whether attorney work product is discoverable when given to an expert. [The 1993 amendments to Rule 26(a)(2) require a party to disclose automatically the expert's opinions, the basis and reasons therefor, and "the data or other information considered by the witness in forming the opinions."]

Several courts have held that the 1993 Amendments to Rule 26(a)(2) were "designed to mandate full disclosure of those materials reviewed by an expert witness, regardless of whether they constitute opinion work product." Karn [v. Ingersoll–Rand Co., 168 F.R.D. 633, 637 (N.D.Ind.1996)]. * * * Those courts that have favored the disclosure of attorney work work product argue that their "bright-line" interpretation "makes good sense on several policy grounds: effective cross-examination of expert witnesses will be enhanced; the policies underlying the work product doctrine will not be violated; and, finally, litigation certainty will be achieved–counsel will know exactly what documents will be subject to disclosure and can react accordingly." Karn, 168 F.R.D. at 639.

However, other courts have rejected the reasoning of Karn [and other cases]. * * * In Haworth, [Inc. v. Herman Miller, Inc., 162 F.R.D. 289 (W.D.Mich.1995)] the court stated that "for the high privilege accorded attorney opinion work product not to apply would require clear and unambiguous language. . . ." Id. at 295. * * *

The policy reason apparently given the most weight by courts in favor of the "bright-line" rule for production of materials disclosed to an expert is that an expert cannot be properly impeached without knowledge of all the relevant materials that shaped the expert's opinion. E.G. Karn, 168 F.R.D. at 639. In Begosian, however, our Court of Appeals noted that "the marginal value on cross-examination that the expert's view may have originated with an attorney's opinion or theory does not warrant overriding the strong policy against disclosure of documents consisting of core attorney's work product." 738 F.2d at 595. The Third Circuit recognized that even where an expert's opinion originated with the attorney, the most effective way to discredit an opposing expert is the presentation of one's own credible expert. * * *

Adoption of a "bright-line" rule in favor of mandating production of attorney work product, while increasing the potential for a party to effectively cross-examine an opponent's expert, abridges the attorney work product privilege without specific authority to do so. * * *

Only one document sent by Equitable's counsel to an expert contains attorney work product, and only one document prepared by an expert witness * * * embodies core work product. * * * Equitable will not be compelled to produce those documents.

Notes and Questions

1. In JOHNSON v. GMEINDER, 191 F.R.D. 638 (D.Kan.2000), the court stated that a large majority of courts and commentators take the position that work product protection does not apply to information supplied to a party's expert. It noted that the Advisory Committee's Notes to the 1993 amendment to Rule 26(a)(2)(B) strongly support that view: "Given this obligation of disclosure, litigants should no longer be able to argue that materials furnished to their experts to be used in forming their opinions—whether or not ultimately relied upon by the expert—are privileged or otherwise protected from disclosure * * *."

2. Should the courts distinguish between those materials not developed by the attorney that fall within the work product definition of Rule 26(b)(3) and those materials that involve an attorney's mental impressions, theories, and opinions?

3. What if materials are developed by an expert who will not testify at trial and thus are protected under Rule 26(b)(4), but are then provided to another expert for the party who will testify? The court in Johnson v. Gmeinder required disclosure. In that case the expert who was to testify at trial argued that although he had read the materials, he did not rely on them for his opinion. Should work product protection apply to those materials that the expert states did not form a basis for his conclusions?

SECTION D.   SANCTIONS AND JUDICIAL SUPERVISION OF DISCOVERY

———

Read Federal Rules of Civil Procedure 26(g) and 37 in the Supplement.

———

CINE FORTY–SECOND STREET THEATRE CORP. v. ALLIED ARTISTS PICTURES CORP.

United States Court of Appeals, Second Circuit, 1979.
602 F.2d 1062.

IRVING R. KAUFMAN, CHIEF JUDGE.

* * *

I

Appellee Cine * * * has operated a movie theater in New York City's Times Square area since July 1974. It alleges that those owning neighboring theaters on West Forty–Second Street * * * entered into a conspiracy with certain motion picture distributors to cut off its access to first-run, quality films. Bringing suit on August 1, 1975, Cine claimed $3,000,000 in treble damages under the antitrust laws, and sought an injunction against the defendants' alleged anticompetitive practices.

On November 6, 1975, the eleven defendants served plaintiff with a set of consolidated interrogatories. Cine thereupon secured its adversaries' consent to defer discovery on the crucial issue of damages until it could retain an expert to review the rival exhibitors' box office receipts. Not until four months after the deadline upon which the parties had agreed, however, did Cine file its first set of answers to the remaining interrogatories. Moreover, even casual scrutiny reveals the patent inadequacy of these responses. Many were bare, ambiguous cross-references to general answers elsewhere in the responses. Highly specific questions concerning the design of Cine's theater were answered with architectural drawings that did not even purport to show the dimensions requested.

Although Cine now complains bitterly that these interrogatories amounted to pure harassment, it never moved to strike them as irrelevant or as harassing. Rather, it filed supplemental answers, which were similarly deficient, and then failed to obey two subsequent orders from Magistrate Gershon compelling discovery. At a hearing in October of 1977, the magistrate found Cine's disobedience to have been willful, and assessed $500 in costs against it. Soon afterwards, she further warned plaintiff that any further noncompliance would result in dismissal.

By the summer of 1978, as this conflict was coming to a head, Cine had still not retained the expert it claimed was necessary to respond to the damages interrogatories. Magistrate Gershon quite reasonably and leniently ordered Cine merely to produce a plan to answer, but this yielded no result. The magistrate then directed Cine to answer the damages interrogatories, admonishing its counsel that future nonfeasance would be viewed in light of past derelictions. Cine did file two sets of answers, one over two months late and both seriously deficient.

* * *

At a formal hearing on October 19, 1978, * * * after noting plaintiff's history of disobedience in the face of her own repeated warnings, the magistrate concluded that Cine's present non-compliance was willful. "[T]he plaintiff," she stated, "has decided when it will be cooperative and when it will not be cooperative, and that it does not have any right to do." She thereupon recommended to the district court that Cine be precluded from introducing evidence with respect to damages. This sanction was, of course, tantamount to a dismissal of Cine's damage claim, but left standing its claim for injunctive relief.

Judge Goettel, the district judge to whom Magistrate Gershon's order was submitted for approval, reacted to Cine's behavior as did Magistrate Gershon. He wrote, "[i]f there were ever a case in which drastic sanctions were justified, this is it." But Judge Goettel could not fully accept the magistrate's finding of willfulness. * * * [He] apparently believed it possible that Cine's counsel, confused as to the precise terms of Magistrate Gershon's oral orders, could have thought in good faith that the answers were not due. Action taken upon that baseless belief, however, was, at the very least, grossly negligent. The district court "regretfully" concluded that under Flaks v. Koegel, 504 F.2d 702 (2d Cir.1974), it lacked the power, absent a finding of willfulness, to impose the extreme sanction recommended by the magistrate. Instead, the court merely assessed costs in the amount of $1,000.[6] But, recognizing that he

6. Defendants estimate that their actual   costs in seeking to compel discovery total at

might have "misperceive[d] the controlling law of this circuit," Judge Goettel certified this interlocutory appeal on his own motion under 28 U.S.C. § 1292(b).

* * *

II

The question before us is whether a grossly negligent failure to obey an order compelling discovery may justify the severest disciplinary measures available under Fed.R.Civ.P. 37. This rule provides a spectrum of sanctions[8] * * * [that] serve a threefold purpose. Preclusionary orders ensure that a party will not be able to profit from its own failure to comply. * * * Rule 37 strictures are also specific deterrents and, like civil contempt, they seek to secure compliance with the particular order at hand. * * * Finally, although the most drastic sanctions may not be imposed as "mere penalties," Hammond Packing Co. v. Arkansas, 212 U.S. 322, 29 S.Ct. 370, 53 L.Ed. 530 (1909) * * *, courts are free to consider the general deterrent effect their orders may have on the instant case and on other litigation, provided that the party on whom they are imposed is, in some sense, at fault. National Hockey League v. Metropolitan Hockey Club, Inc., 427 U.S. 639, 96 S.Ct. 2778, 49 L.Ed.2d 747 (1976) (per curiam); Societé Internationale Pour Participations Industrielles Et Commerciales v. Rogers, 357 U.S. 197, 78 S.Ct. 1087, 2 L.Ed.2d 1255 (1958).

Where the party makes good faith efforts to comply, and is thwarted by circumstances beyond his control—for example, a foreign criminal statute prohibiting disclosure of the documents at issue—an order dismissing the complaint would deprive the party of a property interest without due process of law. See *Societé Internationale, supra*, 357 U.S., at 212, 78 S.Ct. 1087. It would, after all, be unfair and irrational to prevent a party from being heard solely because of a nonculpable failure to meet the terms of a discovery order. * * *

* * * Judge Goettel apparently believed that Cine's counsel simply did not understand the exact requirements of the magistrate's unwritten order compelling discovery. If so, Cine's failure to answer the damages interrogatories might not rise to the level of "willfulness" or "bad faith" for both of these conditions imply a deliberate disregard of the lawful orders of the court. * * * The question, then, is whether gross negligence amounting to a "total dereliction of professional responsibility," but not a conscious disregard of court orders, is properly embraced within the "fault" component of *Societé Internationale's* triple criterion.

Fault, of course, is a broad and amorphous concept, and the Courts of Appeals have had considerable difficulty construing it in this context. Indeed, one court defined "fault" by the apparent oxymoron "intentional negligence." *Bon Air Hotel, Inc.*, * * * 376 F.2d at 120. Thus, commentators have opined that an element of willfulness or conscious disregard of the court's orders is a

least $50,000.

8. Rule 37 was amended in 1970 to permit the imposition of a broader range of sanctions. By deleting the word "wilfully" from subsection (d) of the Rule, the drafters intended "that wilfullness [be] relevant only to the selection of sanctions, if any, to be imposed." Advisory Committee Note * * *.

prerequisite to the harsher categories of Rule 37 sanctions. * * * But the appellate cases commonly cited for this proposition hold only that dismissal is an abuse of discretion where failure to comply was not the result of the fault of any party. * * *

Unless we are to assume that the Court chose its words carelessly, we must accord the term "fault" a meaning of its own within the *Societé Internationale* triad. And plainly, if "fault" has any meaning not subsumed by "willfulness" and "bad faith," it must at least cover gross negligence of the type present in this case. The holding in Edgar v. Slaughter, 548 F.2d 770, 773 (8th Cir.1977), which contains the apparent suggestion that dismissal is appropriate only for actions taken "deliberately or in bad faith," does not conflict with this conclusion. Counsel's action in that case at worst amounted to simple negligence and indeed may have been partially excusable, id. at 773 n. 4. Flagrant negligence of the type involved in the case at bar was simply not at issue.

In the only case that actually presented the question now before us, Affanato v. Merrill Bros., 547 F.2d 138 (1st Cir.1977), the First Circuit implicitly adopted the view we have expressed. There, the district court had entered a default judgment after what the appellant court characterized as "a series of episodes of nonfeasance which amounted, in sum, to a near total dereliction of professional responsibility" on the part of defendant's counsel. Id. at 141. The Court of Appeals affirmed, noting that counsel's failures "went well beyond ordinary negligence"—but without finding willfulness or bad faith. Id.

In the final analysis, however, this question cannot turn solely upon a definition of terms. We believe that our view advances the basic purposes of Rule 37, while respecting the demands of due process. The principal objective of the general deterrent policy of *National Hockey* is strict adherence to the "responsibilities counsel owe to the Court and to their opponents," 427 U.S. at 640, 96 S.Ct. at 2780. Negligent, no less than intentional, wrongs are fit subjects for general deterrence * * *. And gross professional incompetence no less than deliberate tactical intransigence may be responsible for the interminable delays and costs that plague modern complex lawsuits. An undertaking on the scale of the large contemporary suit brooks none of the dilation, posturing, and harassment once expected in litigation. * * * The parties, and particularly their lawyers, must rise to the freedom granted by the Rules and cooperate in good faith both in question and response.

Considerations of fair play may dictate that courts eschew the harshest sanctions provided by Rule 37 where failure to comply is due to a mere oversight of counsel amounting to no more than simple negligence * * *. But where gross professional negligence has been found—that is, where counsel clearly should have understood his duty to the court—the full range of sanctions may be marshalled. Indeed, in this day of burgeoning, costly and protracted litigation courts should not shrink from imposing harsh sanctions where, as in this case, they are clearly warranted.

A litigant chooses counsel at his peril, Link v. Wabash Railroad Co., 370 U.S. 626, 82 S.Ct. 1386, 8 L.Ed.2d 734 (1962), and here, as in countless other contexts, counsel's disregard of his professional responsibilities can lead to extinction of his client's claim. * * *

Plaintiff urges that because it has at last filed answers to the damage interrogatories, it should be permitted to prove its losses at trial. But it forgets that sanctions must be weighed in light of the full record in the case * * *. Furthermore, "[i]f parties are allowed to flout their obligations, choosing to wait to make a response until a trial court has lost patience with them, the effect will be to embroil trial judges in day-to-day supervision of discovery, a result directly contrary to the overall scheme of the federal discovery rules," *Dellums* [v. Powell], * * * 184 U.S.App.D.C. at 343–44, 566 F.2d at 235–36. Moreover, as we have indicated, compulsion of performance in the particular case at hand is not the sole function of Rule 37 sanctions. Under the deterrence principle of *National Hockey,* plaintiff's hopelessly belated compliance should not be accorded great weight. Any other conclusion would encourage dilatory tactics, and compliance with discovery orders would come only when the backs of counsel and the litigants were against the wall.

In light of the fact that plaintiff, through its undeniable fault, has frozen this litigation in the discovery phase for nearly four years, we see no reason to burden the court below with extensive proceedings on remand. Judge Goettel's opinion makes it abundantly clear that but for his misinterpretation of the governing law in this circuit, he would have wholeheartedly adopted Magistrate Gershon's original recommendation. Accordingly, the judge's order declining to adopt the magistrate's recommendation that proof of damages be precluded is reversed.

OAKES, CIRCUIT JUDGE (concurring):

I concur in the result. It may be that the fault for the inexcusable delays in compliance with the discovery requests and orders lay with the client or with the complexity of the interrogatories and requests of opposing counsel. If the latter, remedy lay with an application under Fed.R.Civ.P. 26(c). If the former, then the magistrate's recommendation of preclusion strikes at the proper party. It would be with the greatest reluctance, however, that I would visit upon the client the sins of counsel, absent client's knowledge, condonation, compliance, or causation.

Notes and Questions

1. Discovery disputes get to court in two ways. First, a party confronting a discovery request might seek a protective order under Rule 26(c) or Rule 30(d). Alternatively, a party confronting a discovery request might refuse to comply and the party seeking discovery would have to move, pursuant to Rule 37(a), "for an order compelling [disclosure or] discovery." Is there any reason for a party objecting to a discovery request to shoulder the burden of moving for a protective order, instead of waiting for the other party to move for an order to compel? When are sanctions available under Rule 37 for failing to comply with a discovery request before a court issues an order to compel?

2. Rule 37 was revised in 1993 to reflect the addition of the mandatory disclosure provision in Rule 26(a), by providing a means to compel that disclosure. The revised Rule 37 also provides that a party who fails to disclose information in accordance with Rule 26(a) is precluded from introducing the information as evidence at trial. This measure does not require a motion by the opposing party.

3. Pursuant to the 1993 amendments to Rule 37(a)(2), attorneys must attempt to resolve discovery disputes informally before filing a motion to compel

discovery. Any motion to compel disclosure or discovery "must include a certification that the movant has in good faith conferred or attempted to confer" with the party against whom relief is sought in an effort to obtain the requested information without court action. Prior to the 1993 changes, many local court rules already had included such requirements.

4. Although the Federal Rules went into effect in 1938, until relatively recently judges were extremely reluctant to apply available sanctions to curb violations of the discovery rules. Renfrew, *Discovery Sanctions: A Judicial Perspective,* 67 Calif.L.Rev. 264, 271–78 (1979); Note, *The Emerging Deterrence Orientation in the Imposition of Discovery Sanctions,* 91 Harv.L.Rev. 1033, 1034, 1038–44 (1978).

> The typical pattern of sanctioning that emerges from the reported cases is one in which the delay, obfuscation, contumacy, and lame excuses on the part of litigants and their attorneys are tolerated without any measured remedial action until the court is provoked beyond endurance. At that point the court punishes one side or the other with a swift and final termination of the lawsuit by dismissal or default. This "all or nothing" approach to sanctions results in considerable laxity in the day-to-day application of the rules. Attorneys are well aware that sanctions will be imposed only in the most flagrant situations.

Rodes, Ripple & Mooney, *Sanctions Imposable for Violations of the Federal Rules of Civil Procedure* 85 (Fed.Jud.Center 1981).

In more recent years, however, a notable change has taken place. Spurred in part by the Supreme Court's opinions in NATIONAL HOCKEY LEAGUE v. METROPOLITAN HOCKEY CLUB, INC., 427 U.S. 639, 96 S.Ct. 2778, 49 L.Ed.2d 747 (1976), and ROADWAY EXPRESS, INC. v. PIPER, 447 U.S. 752, 100 S.Ct. 2455, 65 L.Ed.2d 488 (1980), which strongly supported the use of sanctions, judges have applied and upheld sanctions in a much wider variety of situations. See American Bar Association, *Sanctions: Rule 11 and Other Powers* 34–36, 46–48, 61–70, 79–82, 97–101, 115–16, 128–29, 138–42, 158–60, 170, 175–77, 182, 186–87 (2d ed. 1988) (surveying recent decisions). Nonetheless, although the number of reported decisions suggests that sanctions have become routine, there is a lingering sense that many judges remain reluctant to impose sanctions for discovery abuse. What factors might account for this continued reluctance? Does it suggest that there are significant institutional limitations that effectively preclude heavy reliance on sanctions to curb discovery abuses?

5. The most severe sanction that a court can impose is dismissal of plaintiff's complaint or ordering the entry of judgment against defendant. It generally is noted that these sanctions are disfavored because the courts are reluctant to deny a litigant her day in court. An appellate court will scrutinize the decision closely whenever such severe sanctions are imposed to ensure that the determination is within the proper bounds of the trial court's discretion. See Chrysler Corp. v. Carey, 186 F.3d 1016, 1020–22 (8th Cir.1999) (affirming entry of judgment of liability against defendants). It often is stated that a "court must impose the least severe sanction that will be adequate to serve its purposes but the sanction should not be so minimal that it undermines those purposes." See Doe v. Gonzaga University, 99 Wash.App. 338, 361, 992 P.2d 545, 558–59 (2000). Do these pronouncements underscore a reluctance on the part of trial judges to take a firm stand against significant discovery abuse? Is that appropriate?

6. The Supreme Court in *Societé Internationale,* cited in *Cine,* addressed itself to constitutional limitations on discovery sanctions and held that an action could not be dismissed for failure to comply with discovery orders when compliance required the cooperation of a foreign government and when plaintiff appeared to be making a good-faith effort to obtain that cooperation. See generally 8A Wright, Miller & Marcus, *Federal Practice and Procedure: Civil 2d* § 2283 (1994). Do the decisions in *Societé Internationale* and *Cine* render most of the nonmonetary sanctions in Rule 37(b) and (d) unavailable for routine use in curbing discovery abuse?

On the issue of the standard for the imposition of severe sanctions for discovery abuse, see generally Epstein, Corcoran, Krieger & Carr, *An Up–Date on Rule 37 Sanctions After National Hockey League v. Metropolitan Hockey Clubs, Inc.,* 84 F.R.D. 145 (1980); Note, *Federal Rules of Civil Procedure: Defining a Feasible Culpability Threshold for the Imposition of Severe Discovery Sanctions,* 65 Minn.L.Rev. 137 (1980).

7. When the discovery rules were amended in 1970, it was thought that one reason judges were reluctant to impose sanctions was that the sanctions then described in Rule 37 were too drastic. The amended Rule sought to overcome this objection by making more generally available the sanction of requiring a party or his attorney to pay to his opponent the reasonable expenses incurred by the failure to make discovery. Rules 37(a)(4), 37(b), 37(d). Nonetheless, it was found in one survey that "a decided majority of the judges reported that they 'seldom' or 'almost never' award the costs of bringing or opposing a discovery-related motion." Ellington, *A Study of Sanctions for Discovery Abuse* 8 (1979). But see Werner, *Survey of Discovery Sanctions,* 1979 Ariz.St.L.J. 299, 316 (evidence that judges may be less reluctant now to exercise a literal application of Rule 37's expense sanction). Is the appropriate answer to make the award of expenses mandatory? See Shroeder & Frank, *Discovery Reform: Long Road to Nowheresville,* 68 A.B.A.J. 572, 574 (1982).

8. Rule 26(g), which was added in 1983, grants the federal courts authority to impose sanctions to deter both excessive discovery and evasion. The rule imposes on each attorney the duty, before proceeding with respect to any discovery matter, to make a reasonable inquiry and to certify that certain standards have been met, and it mandates sanctions against attorneys, their clients, or both, who violate this duty. What is a "reasonable inquiry" under the Rule.

Does Rule 26(g) impose upon the lawyer an obligation that is inconsistent with his traditional role in the adversary process and the ethical obligation of undivided allegiance to his client? "It is incongruous to require a lawyer to advise his client that, although the information is relevant, material, and may be helpful in formulating his case, the information should not be sought because it would be too burdensome on the other party. It would be equally incongruous to require him to certify that this is not the case." Fishbein, *New Federal Rule 26: A Litigator's Perspective,* 57 St. John's L.Rev. 739, 745–46 (1983). Assuming this is to be the case, is it really a problem?

Note that under Federal Rule 11(d) neither the ethical requirements of Rule 11 nor the protections afforded before sanctions are imposed, are applicable with regard to discovery matters. Instead the latter are governed by Rules 26(g) and 37. Should the obligations of an attorney or party differ between discovery and other matters? Why? Should the discovery rules on sanctions be amended to contain a twenty-one day safe harbor provision comparable to that in Rule 11(c)(1)(A)?

9.   If a court must determine whether an attorney or his client should be sanctioned, doesn't that make the attorney and client adversaries? Would the attorney have to withdraw as counsel in order to avoid the conflict? What if the attorney's defense to the sanction depends on a privileged communication with the client? Or the disclosure of work product? Is the best answer to leave the resolution of the question of who pays the sanction to the attorney and the client?

10.   What procedures must be followed before a sanction for discovery abuse can be imposed? Due process requires at least prior notice and an opportunity to be heard. See Roadway Express, Inc. v. Piper, 447 U.S. 752, 767 & n. 14, 100 S.Ct. 2455, 2464 & n. 14, 65 L.Ed.2d 488, 501–02 & n. 14 (1980). Might an evidentiary hearing also be required? In what circumstances would discovery relating to sanctions issues be appropriate? Could the sanctioning process itself clog the courts with satellite litigation, or become a tool for harassment or abuse? In MIRANDA v. SOUTHERN PACIFIC TRANSPORTATION CO., 710 F.2d 516 (9th Cir.1983), the court held that two attorneys facing court-imposed sanctions for violating local court rules regarding a pretrial conference were entitled to an opportunity to request a hearing and to show cause why the sanctions should not be imposed.

11.   In J.M. CLEMINSHAW CO. v. CITY OF NORWICH, 93 F.R.D. 338 (D.Conn.1981), the court fined defendant's attorney $150 for unnecessary delay in filing his client's answers to discovery requests of plaintiff and of the court. These fines were payable to the court, and were in addition to costs and attorney's fees to the opposing party. The court deemed it necessary to impose the additional penalty because an award of expenses to the opposing party alone was too low adequately to punish the violation. Is the additional sanction authorized by Rule 26(g) or Rule 37? If not, is it authorized by Section 1927 of Title 28 of the United States Code or the inherent power of a court to regulate the conduct of the attorneys who practice before it? See generally Note, *Sanctions Imposed by Courts on Attorneys Who Abuse the Judicial Process,* 44 U.Chi.L.Rev. 619 (1977).

————

SOFAER, SANCTIONING ATTORNEYS FOR DISCOVERY ABUSE UN-DER THE NEW FEDERAL RULES: ON THE LIMITED UTILITY OF PUNISHMENT, 57 St. John's L.Rev. 680, 696–98, 720–29 (1983):

Empirical studies demonstrate that discovery presents no significant problem in most cases in the federal courts. One study, conducted for the Federal Judicial Center (FJC) and based on 3,000 cases from six metropolitan districts, showed that no discovery requests were filed in 50% of all cases, and only 5% of all cases contained 10 or more discovery initiatives. The cases involving 10 or more discovery initiatives, however, had an average of 17.47 requests each, accounting for about 60% of all discovery enforcement motions in the entire sample. Moreover, the average number of enforcement motions per discovery request was twice as high in the cases having high levels of discovery as in all other cases combined. Nine enforcement motions were made in each of the few cases with over 31 discovery requests. Similarly, in Professor Ellington's study on sanctions for discovery abuse, more than 6,000 cases, over 50% of the total studied, involved no discovery activity; and of those cases which did involve discovery activity, over 70% had no recorded discovery problem. As the FJC discovery study concluded, "discovery abuse, to the extent it exists, does not permeate the vast majority of federal filings."

On the other hand, discovery abuse may at least partially explain the intensive discovery activity and disputes that exist in the small proportion of cases involving high levels of discovery. Moreover, subjective evidence of widespread concern over discovery abuse suggests that, although such abuse may be confined to a relatively small proportion of all cases, those cases are so intensively litigated that they have a significant impact on the federal judicial system. * * *

* * *

Attorneys abuse the discovery process by seeking evidence that is unnecessary, or by seeking evidence for an improper purpose, or by imposing unnecessary costs in seeking necessary material. Some familiar examples are the documentary request that calls for every paper that relates to a corporation's policies and activities on safety, hiring, firing, or pricing; the set of interrogatories with multipage introductory definitions, followed by questions that would require thousands of hours to answer, calling for all the evidence relating to each of the respondent's legal positions; and the series of largely if not entirely aimless depositions intended to impose huge costs and pressures upon an opponent.

Failures to make or to cooperate in discovery are, however, at least as prevalent a source of abuse as unnecessary or oppressive demands. Prior to the adoption of the federal rules in 1938, relatively little discovery was possible, and thus virtually all discovery abuse took the form of opposition to discovery, even when it was reasonable and limited. * * * [F]ailures [to cooperate in discovery] * * * remain widespread. Here, also, shocking conduct, though still rare, has become too familiar: documents are purged on concocted claims of privilege, destroyed, secretly withheld, produced in unusable form, or buried in truckloads of irrelevant paper; answers to interrogatories are flatly refused for improper reasons or for no reason at all; deponents are repeatedly instructed not to answer on grounds other than privilege, and depositions are delayed or terminated upon the unilateral decision of a party's attorney.

* * *

Discovery abuse exists because some litigation is itself abusive. An examination of some of the categories of cases that generate the greatest amount of discovery conflict shows that a large proportion are ultimately found to lack merit. Class actions of all kinds, for example, have high rates of dismissal. Even where recoveries are obtained through settlement, as in many securities and antitrust cases, there is often evidence that the costs and risks of litigation, rather than any merit to the claims, prompted the defendant's willingness to settle. Meritless claims or defenses generate controversy in discovery; one side will argue that little or no discovery is necessary, while the other will seek as much discovery and delay as possible.

The present system imposes only nominal costs for the right to sue and to consume the public resources expended in running the federal courts. If a valuable commodity can be obtained at nominal cost, or, as with *in forma pauperis* litigation, for nothing, the commodity will be consumed without the restraint and responsibility that a higher, though still subsidized, cost would encourage. Furthermore, litigation incentives also exist in many cases, because of the low rates of prejudgment interest awarded in the federal courts. A party who owes money, or knows that he will eventually have to satisfy a claim, will consider the cost of contesting the claim as against the cost of paying it. * * * The prejudgment interest rate must be raised to a point that will discourage litigation, not engender it.

Massive discovery also occurs because Congress and the Executive permit the use of the federal courts as the forum for litigating highly complex, political, and social issues. For example, the recent cases of United States v. IBM and United States v. AT & T generated discovery costs equal to the costs generated by hundreds or thousands of ordinary cases. In cases such as these, in which the issues are so vague and conceptually seamless, and the stakes are so high, the parties involved will press to discover every conceivably useful piece of evidence, while at the same time vigorously opposing discovery by their opponents. Large, dynamic corporations do not lightly accept efforts by the government or private persons to subject them to damages that reach the hundreds of millions and threaten their very existence. Controversies touching the public, such as suits to correct the effects of discrimination, or to improve conditions in jails or mental institutions, or to implement school desegregation, are often hard-fought by both sides at all stages.

Discovery is also made costly because of the legal theories on which courts have permitted suits to proceed, and because many standards of law on important issues have been left unsettled by appellate courts for long periods of time. Expanded notions of strict liability, for example, enable plaintiffs to file complaints in which they need do little more than allege an injury that is believed to have resulted from some dangerous instrumentality or activity, and this will generally entitle them to search for an explanation through discovery. Civil rights claims permit persons of any race, sex, or religion, people over 40 years old, handicapped persons, and prisoners, to litigate on mere subjective belief, or on totally unsupported allegations. Once deemed properly commenced, these cases generate substantial costs, including discovery costs, which often fall upon public and quasi-public entities such as universities and hospitals, in addition to private defendants. * * * Further, many statutes and common-law rules turn on state of mind or other subjective evidence; these generate more discovery than those which rest on objective standards. In some very intensely litigated areas, especially under the securities and antitrust laws, it is unclear which of two or more standards will apply, and parties are forced to discover and litigate on all possible theories to make a complete record.

* * *

Perhaps the mightiest catalyst for discovery abuse is the so-called American Rule, under which unsuccessful litigants do not pay their opponent's attorney's fees, even those made necessary by their failure to drop or settle a losing cause. The effect of this rule on discovery is profound: a party can have as much discovery as it wants by paying only the costs of *seeking* that discovery; the costs of compliance are generally borne without recompense by the opposing party. This means that a party can inflict the costs of collecting, organizing, duplicating, and delivering documents simply by asking for them;

or can impose the costs of obtaining answers to burdensome interrogatories simply by asking questions; or can trigger the costs of depositions, simply by demanding the presence of witnesses and examining them. No express authority exists that would enable courts to require parties to pay in advance for the discovery they claim is necessary, although in egregious cases courts occasionally impose such a condition. * * *

The relatively low cost of seeking discovery leads all parties, not just plaintiffs, to engage in excessive discovery. Attorneys may seek unnecessarily broad discovery simply as a means of self-defense against the economic coercion of discovery by opponents. By seeking massive discovery against a party that has already sought extensive discovery, the attorney conveys a message to his opponent that he intends to make the costs of litigating equal, thereby tending to deter broad requests. Alternatively, resistance to discovery may be the most effective means for defending against excessive discovery. A vigorous defense will tend to deter excessive demands, albeit also increasing the costs of reasonable demands. * * *

The economic incentives for discovery abuse have also been increased by hourly billing practices. The incentive for abuse, paradoxically, is greatest in cases in which an attorney has no paying client to whom to answer. For example, the government's only constraints on how much it can spend on discovery are political. Attorneys for plaintiffs in class action suits and in contingency fee situations must often finance discovery, operating as a constraint on the types of cases they will commence. Once a judgment is made that a recovery is likely, however, the incentives for unnecessary discovery in such cases become even greater than usual, since discovery costs are recoverable out of the settlement or award. In fact, unnecessary discovery is encouraged by [an] * * * approach for computing attorney's fees in class actions and other cases [, which] * * * virtually [guarantees that the costs of discovery will be recovered] * * *, at least to the extent that the amount sought falls between 20 and 30% of the total recovery. This approach in effect pays attorneys for all discovery, including as a practical matter most unnecessary attempts to obtain or to resist disclosures.

Nor can we look to defense counsel for protection against abusive practices in such cases, since extensive discovery may also be attractive to them. As Milton Gould recently wrote:

> Many years ago, I heard an eminent defense lawyer compare the lawyers for plaintiffs to the Apaches who harassed the wagon trains in the Old West. But now, the defense lawyers seem to welcome the derivative suit as an opportunity for young partners and associates to sit in endless depositions, while the clock ticks away the golden hours.

Notes and Questions

1. For a comprehensive analysis of the reasons for discovery abuse and the difficulty of ascertaining methods to control it, see Beckerman, *Confronting Civil Discovery's Fatal Flaws*, 84 Minn.L.Rev. 505 (2000).

2. There is lively debate as to the 1993 amendments' impact on discovery abuse. In "Discovery as Abuse" Judge Easterbrook argues that discovery abuse does not stem from deficiencies in the discovery rules and, therefore, that changes

in the rules cannot prevent such abuse. Easterbrook, *Discovery As Abuse,* 69 B.U.L.Rev. 635 (1989). Professor Mullenix disputes the notion that discovery abuse was pervasive prior to the 1993 amendments, claiming that these reforms were unnecessary and merely create further confusion. Mullenix, *Discovery in Disarray: The Pervasive Myth of Pervasive Discovery Abuses,* 46 Stan.L.Rev. 1393 (1994).

3. An important part of the judicial response to discovery abuse is reflected in the series of amendments to Rules 16 and 26 to encourage active judicial supervision of the discovery process. In 1980, Rule 26(f) was adopted to provide for a discovery conference among the parties and the court, but it was not contemplated as a routine procedure. Then, in 1983, Rule 16 was amended to encourage district courts to schedule early pretrial conferences and required them, after consultation with the parties by pretrial conference or otherwise, to issue scheduling orders limiting the time of the parties, among other things, to complete discovery. In 1993, Rule 26(f) was altered and harmonized with Rule 16. Rule 26(f) was amended to require the parties to meet by themselves to arrange for mandatory disclosures under Rule 26(a)(1) and to develop a comprehensive proposed discovery plan that they then present to the court prior to the time the court's scheduling order is due under Rule 16(b). However, courts were free to issue standing orders that exempted all, or certain types of cases, from the Rule 26(f) requirements. In 2000, Rule 26(f) was amended once again. First, it eliminated the need of the parties to "meet," allowing them to "confer" instead to avoid logistical problems that sometimes sent litigants to court for relief. Second, it eliminated standing exemption orders but left intact the power of the court to exempt or alter the requirements for any particular case before it. (The amended rule does exempt those special cases that are exempted from mandatory disclosure under Rule 26(a)(1).) These Rules are designed to counter the procrastination and delay that is natural to busy lawyers and to give the courts ample control over the discovery process. The next Chapter takes up questions concerning the changed role of judges generally in managing the pretrial phase of litigation, including discovery.

4. The courts also have obligations if the discovery process is to work appropriately. For example, the failure of a trial court to take charge of a case and issue timely rulings on matters of substantive law—for example, the proposed dismissal of one of plaintiff's set of allegations that fails to state a claim for relief—can confuse defendant as to its obligations to comply with discovery orders and requests related to the challenged claim. In that situation, if the trial judge imposes severe sanctions on defendant for failure to comply with court ordered discovery, to what extent should the court of appeals become involved? See Chudasama v. Mazda Motor Corp., 123 F.3d 1353 (11th Cir.1997).

Chapter 12

PRETRIAL MANAGEMENT AND THE PRETRIAL CONFERENCE

SECTION A. CASE MANAGEMENT

Read Federal Rule of Civil Procedure 16 and the material accompanying it in the Supplement.

MILLER, THE ADVERSARY SYSTEM: DINOSAUR OR PHOENIX, 69 Minn.L.Rev. 201, 219–21 (1984):

Given the tremendous frustration throughout the legal profession and the public at large with the current state of affairs, one must ask seriously whether the adversary system as we know it has become too costly and inefficient a device for resolving civil disputes. There is a growing feeling that the only means of preserving any substantial portion of the system may be to control the excesses of lawyer hyperactivity through the infusion of active judicial management from institution of a case to its termination. This approach flies in the face of the traditional vision of our system as one in which lawyers conduct cases and judges preside from a neutral distance, stepping in only to decide questions and disputes that are framed by the advocates. There has been understandable reluctance to tinker with, let alone jeopardize or fundamentally alter, the basic tenets of a system so entrenched and venerated.

Fortunately, the mood of the profession seems to be changing, largely because of increased caseloads. * * *

In short, the notion that judges should leave cases to the lawyers has been compromised substantially by the widespread frustration with the present situation and the resulting recognition of the need for effective management. The Federal Judicial Center's 1977 study of district court case management procedures revealed that all the courts visited had procedures designed to manage and control cases starting at their early stages. The differences among the courts studied lay not in their willingness to adopt methods to manage cases, for each court had such procedures, but rather in the means employed, their effectiveness in moving cases along expeditiously, and the number of cases each judge could handle. The impact of case management was dramatic, with courts employing strong management controls having an average disposition time for cases that was approximately half of the average figure for courts using few such controls.

Moreover, the impression that judges are unwilling to depart from their traditional role as passive and detached arbiters appears to be mistaken. To the contrary, there seems to be a strong spirit of willingness among judges to assume the role of active managers and to experiment with procedures designed to enhance their effectiveness in that role, although in some quarters, particularly at the state level, the flesh of experience and training may yet be weak. Significantly, follow-ups to another Federal Judicial Center study found that participating districts whose efficiency had been low already had adopted procedures found to be common in the more efficient courts.

Even attorneys, usually seen as jealous guardians of control over their cases, are not averse to a stronger judicial hand. Ironically, this is due in part to the natural tendency to define abuse as what the opposition is doing to one. Lawyers do not tend to see abusers when they look in the mirror, but rather only when they look across the negotiating table or the courtroom. Given the frustration felt by many litigators about the atmosphere of lawlessness that often bogs down actions through hyperactivity, missed deadlines, and repeated rescheduling, the judge is seen as an ally against a common enemy—the abusive opponent. Thus, the bar may not be a major obstacle to more aggressive management and enforcement of the rules, even at the expense of a measure of its independence and autonomy.

———

RESNIK, MANAGERIAL JUDGES, 96 Harv.L.Rev. 374, 376–85 (1982):

Until recently, the American legal establishment embraced a classical view of the judicial role. Under this view, judges are not supposed to have an involvement or interest in the controversies they adjudicate. Disengagement and dispassion supposedly enable judges to decide cases fairly and impartially. The mythic emblems surrounding the goddess Justice illustrate this vision of the proper judicial attitude. Justice carries scales, reflecting the obligation to balance claims fairly; she possesses a sword, giving her great power to enforce decisions; and she wears a blindfold, protecting her from distractions.

Many federal judges have departed from their earlier attitudes; they have dropped the relatively disinterested pose to adopt a more active, "managerial" stance. In growing numbers, judges are not only adjudicating the merits of issues presented to them by litigants, but also are meeting with parties in chambers to encourage settlement of disputes and to supervise case preparation. Both before and after the trial, judges are playing a critical role in shaping litigation and influencing results.

* * *

* * * Today, federal district judges are assigned a case at the time of its filing and assume responsibility for shepherding the case to completion. Judges have described their new tasks as "case management"—hence my term "managerial judges." As managers, judges learn more about cases much earlier than they did in the past. They negotiate with parties about the course, timing, and scope of both pretrial and posttrial litigation. These managerial responsibilities give judges greater power. Yet the restraints that formerly circumscribed judicial authority are conspicuously absent. Managerial judges frequently work beyond the public view, off the record, with no obligation to provide written, reasoned opinions, and out of reach of appellate review.

This new managerial role has emerged for several reasons. One is the creation of pretrial discovery rights. The 1938 Federal Rules of Civil Procedure embodied contradictory mandates: a discovery system ("give your opponent all information relevant to the litigation") was grafted onto American adversarial norms ("protect your client zealously" and therefore "withhold what you can"). In some cases, parties argued about their obligations under the discovery rules; such disputes generated a need for someone to decide pretrial conflicts. Trial judges accepted the assignment and have become mediators, negotiators, and planners—as well as adjudicators. Moreover, once involved in pretrial discovery, many judges became convinced that their presence at other points in a lawsuit's development would be beneficial; supervision of discovery became a conduit for judicial control over all phases of litigation and thus infused lawsuits with the continual presence of the judge-overseer.

Partly because of their new oversight role and partly because of increasing case loads, many judges have become concerned with the volume of their work. To reduce the pressure, judges have turned to efficiency experts who promise "calendar control." Under the experts' guidance, judges have begun to experiment with schemes for speeding the resolution of cases and for persuading litigants to settle rather than try cases whenever possible. During the past decade, enthusiasm for the "managerial movement" has become widespread; what began as an experiment is likely soon to become obligatory.
* * *

———

As discussed in the following excerpt, Federal Rule 16 was amended in 1983 to enhance judicial pretrial management. In 1993, Rule 16 was further amended, which is discussed in Note 1, below.

MILLER & CULP, THE NEW RULES OF CIVIL PROCEDURE: MANAGING CASES, LIMITING DISCOVERY, Nat.L.J., Dec. 5, 1983, pp. 23–25:

Federal Rule 16 was the first major pretrial conference rule in American procedural history and remained unchanged between 1938 and 1983. But its effectiveness became increasingly limited in recent years.

The original rule called for an eve-of-trial conference designed to organize the evidence, the witnesses and the documents to make the trial as efficient as possible. Unfortunately, Rule 16 missed the heart of today's pretrial problem.

Since more than 90 percent of the civil cases do not reach trial, former Rule 16, at most, spoke to only a small portion of the cases. Of those cases that reach trial, most of them are so simple that they do not need a pretrial conference to facilitate the trial. Many of the remaining cases are so complicated they need more than an eve-of-trial conference—they need management from the outset of the pretrial process.

The advisory committee's explicit goal in revising Rule 16 was to legitimize judicial management and to encourage district judges to recognize it as part of their duties. * * *

* * *

Reducing the time frame from institution to pretrial termination certainly would be socially desirable. Since the cost of a significant amount of litigation is tax deductible, taxpayers end up footing much of the bill. Moreover, every frivolous or unnecessary motion consumes valuable public resources, such as judges and courtrooms, and drains human resources.

Furthermore, many of our most talented young lawyers may spend up to one-fifth of their legal careers on pretrial proceedings in enormous cases that often are competitive wars rather than legitimate legal disputes. By any standard, allowing litigants to play expensive dilatory games in our courts is socially costly. Thus, the advisory committee felt that the expenditure of some judge power to accelerate and improve pretrial proceedings was desirable.

* * *

Perhaps the most critical element, indeed, the most controversial feature, of new Rule 16 is Subdivision (b). It states that unless a lawsuit falls within a category of cases specifically exempted by local rule, a scheduling order "shall" be issued within 120 days of the filing of the complaint. It is anticipated that most districts will exempt cases involving review of administrative decisions, many Social Security matters, forfeitures, prisoner petitions and odometer cases. In many ways, the rule asks for something in the nature of a status conference, which most judges currently require; however, it goes further and demands the issuance of a *scheduling order*.

Many judges dislike the mandatory scheduling order because it affirmatively requires action and because they fear that the obligation will consume considerable time. * * *

The mandated scheduling order should have significant impact in complex, intractible and intransigent cases that have become a heavy millstone on the backs of federal judges during the past two decades. A district judge must intervene and take affirmative action within 120 days in every case on his docket, except those exempted by local rule.

The mandatory scheduling order *must* dictate the time frames for completing such matters as the pleadings, joinder of parties, jurisdictional, class action and joinder motions, and perhaps motions relating to threshold affirmative defenses. Finally, the order should schedule the discovery phase and perhaps pretrial conferences and the trial itself.

* * *

The goal of the advisory committee was to galvanize each judge into action. In a sense the notion is that by showing the flag, judges will energize the lawyers and start the case moving toward adjudication. But Rule 16 does not require that any pretrial conference take place. Only the issuance of a scheduling order is mandated—whether to hold *any* conference is left to the discretion of the judge.

Subdivision (c) of the Rule lists various matters that can be raised at any conference that might be held. * * *

Rule 16(c)(1), for example, suggests that conference participants may consider the formulation and simplification of the issues, including the elimination of frivolous claims or defenses. This passage attempts to address the intense battle that has been raging between the plaintiff and the defense bars for at least 15 years.

The latter contends that too many claims brought against their clients are vague, ill-defined and baseless. [D]efense counsel [argue] that they are left in the dark and subjected to discovery that is imprecise, overly broad, intrusive, disruptive, and expensive, leading them to "pay-off" unjustified claims simply to get rid of them.

The reference to "formulation" in Rule 16(c)(1) is designed to encourage beginning the process of shaping the action and limiting the issues as early as possible to those that are truly litigable. Granted, there are cases in which an attempt to do this at a threshold pretrial conference would be premature. Indeed, the risk of prematurity is greatest in antitrust, stock fraud and technologically complex cases. In these types of actions, a certain amount of discovery is necessary in order to reach the point at which one can begin to think about defining the issues. But even in these cases, the rule serves to remind the judge and the litigants to think about "shaping" the action as soon as practical.

Another recognition of the legitimacy of judicial involvement is the reference in Rule 16(c) to "the possibility of settlement." * * * Although we now treat settlement as an obvious objective of the pretrial conference, that is a relatively modern phenomenon.

Historically, there was considerable resistance to judicial participation in settlement discussions, let alone judicial pressure towards settlement. The judge was viewed as an impartial arbiter sitting on a high bench in a black robe speaking only when spoken to; the case belonged to the lawyers, including whether to settle.

But reality and practicality have changed the thinking of most in the profession. District judges now understand that in many ways they are system managers, administrators, negotiators and mediators. New Rule 16(c) reflects this change in attitude; it instructs judges that promoting settlement is part of their job and that a Rule 16 conference is a good vehicle for pursuing that objective.

* * *

The extent of judicial involvement in settlement is a much debated subject: Where does facilitation end and undue pressure begin? Does it matter if it is a jury or nonjury trial? Should district judges team up, one judge doing the settlement conferencing for a colleague and vice versa? The advisory committee decided that it would be premature to include anything in the Rule suggesting how a judge should or should not behave.

The other agenda items for pretrial conferences listed in Rule 16(c) are relatively straightforward. A number of them are based on the Manual for Complex Litigation. Indeed, since several of the practices described in the manual have proven effective in the crucible of actual practice, there was every reason to incorporate them into Rule 16(c).

Two new provisions in Rule 16(c) are designed to give the pretrial conference process a legitimacy and seriousness of purpose. If there is to be a conference under Rule 16, the lawyers are directed to attend with authority to stipulate and make admissions, although authority to settle is not mandatory.

This passage is the advisory committee's answer to the recurring complaint that many lawyers do not take pretrial conferences seriously and tend to deny they have authority to stipulate, admit or settle. Now, every attorney attending a conference represents that he or she has authority to stipulate and to admit regarding anything one reasonably should anticipate could come up.

A related new requirement is that the final pretrial conference, which assures that there is at least one conference, must be attended on each side by at least one attorney who actually will conduct the trial. This eliminates the problem of one lawyer appearing at the pretrial conference and a different lawyer trying the case, the latter refusing to abide by the trial plan established at the pretrial conference.

Finally, Rule 16(f) provides that an attorney may be sanctioned for various violations of Rule 16. Sanctions are available when an attorney fails to attend a scheduled conference, disobeys a pretrial order, fails to participate in good faith or is substantially unprepared to participate in the conference. The sanctions follow the pattern established under Rules 7 and 11 of leaving the matter to the court's discretion, with cost-shifting likely to become the norm.

* * *

There are three significant apprehensions regarding new Rule 16. The first is * * * if a judge is not disposed to manage, will he or she pay attention to Rule 16? Certainly there are federal judges who do not manage their dockets aggressively; they have various reasons for this attitude, which by and large reflect their own style or conception of judging. But since younger judges seem more in tune with the need for management, the number of reluctant judges is dwindling as new judges are elevated to the bench.

Another concern about Rule 16 is that it says to a heavily burdened district judge, who may be facing a docket of 500 cases, "Judge, Rule 16 asks for a portion of your valuable work time. That is time that you cannot sit in your courtroom and try cases. But, we honestly believe that time expended in scheduling and management will be offset by time economies you will experience later on in these cases."

Once again, we lack empiric evidence on the subject, but the available data indicate that management conducted early in the action will produce efficiencies later in the proceedings.

"Runaway" discovery often results because a judge who knows very little about a case is in no position to limit or terminate the process. Early management forces the judge to acquire a working knowledge of the larger cases on his docket. That can be useful in scheduling, in shaping discovery and in moving the dispute toward trial. The hope is that by robbing Peter to pay Paul in terms of allocating time, there will be a net savings for all concerned.

A third concern is worth mentioning—a somewhat abstract but nonetheless global one. True disciples of the adversary system believe that litigation should be controlled by the parties through their lawyers. The dogma is that each lawyer has carte blanche to do what he or she thinks is in the best interests of the client—to settle or not, to proceed with dispatch or delay, to pursue one procedure or another.

New Rule 16 rejects this conception because it directs the sharing of power in handling the processing of a lawsuit. A case belongs to the system as much as it does to the litigants and their attorneys. Thus, Rule 16 is a potential threat to the adversary system as it has existed for hundreds of years since it formally calls for a significant change in the relationship between judges and lawyers.

Notes and Questions

1. The 1993 amendments to Rule 16 augment the judge's power over discovery and evidentiary matters in the early stages of the litigation process. Among other changes, the amendments enhance the binding effect of pretrial orders and conferences in later stages of the proceeding and expand trial courts' flexibility to manage cases. For a detailed discussion of the 1993 amendments to Rule 16, see Richey, *Rule 16 Revised and Related Rules: Analysis of Recent Developments for the Benefit of Bench and Bar,* 157 F.R.D. 69 (1994). In 1993 and again in 2000, Rule 26(f), which governs the management of pretrial discovery, was altered to harmonize with Rule 16(b) and improve efficiency. See the discussion at p. 886, supra.

2. As presently constituted, Rule 16 creates an elaborate mechanism for case management. Is there a danger that the mechanism is so elaborate that complying with it will lead to inefficiency? See Tiger, *Turbulence in the Federal Rules of Civil Procedure: the 1993 Amendments and Beyond,* 14 Rev. Litigation 137 (1994). Some critics of judicial case management raise due process and fairness concerns and question whether managerial judging adequately remedies the inefficiencies of the adversarial system. See Schaller, *Managerial Judging: A Principled Approach to Complex Cases in State Court,* 68 Conn.B.J. 77 (1994). Other critics question whether managerial judging undermines the system of checks and balances associated with the division of power between judge and jury. Should pretrial management decisions be subject to judicial review? For an examination of possible structural checks on pretrial judicial power, see Tornquist, *The Active Judge in Pre-trial Settlement: Inherent Authority Gone Awry,* 25 Willa.L.Rev. 743 (1989).

3. Some criticize the imposition of time limits as unrealistic, particularly in complex cases. Note that Rule 16(b) empowers district courts to promulgate local rules exempting classes of cases from Rule 16, and some district courts have exempted complex cases from the requirement of a scheduling conference and order. See Local Rule 9, D.Alaska; Rule 1–15, D.D.C.; Rule 2.4.1, N.D. and S.D.Iowa; Order, M.D.Ala. Read the sample scheduling order set out in the Supplement.

What other types of cases might be suitable for exemption? For example, should routine contract disputes or personal-injury cases be excepted from Rule 16? Isn't it the facts of each case, not its subject matter, that determine whether the case is suitable for pretrial management?

4. A judge may employ any of several techniques to "manage" a case. Some, such as the scheduling order and the pretrial order, are mentioned in Rule 16. Others are authorized by Rule 26(a)(3) or local court rules. And still others may be developed by the judge herself as she performs the function of case manager.

For example, some courts require counsel to go beyond the automatic disclosure requirements of Rule 26(a) by asking for a brief description of the expected testimony of each witness who is likely to testify and to anticipate claims of privilege or work-product immunity. For a discussion of the managerial techniques that have been incorporated into local court rules, see generally Note, *Pretrial Conference: A Critical Examination of Local Rules Adopted by Federal Courts*, 64 Va.L.Rev. 467 (1978).

5. Pretrial scheduling orders frequently are modified even though Rule 16(b) provides that a schedule may be modified only on a showing of good cause. These changes can generate additional paperwork and delay, thereby causing inefficiency in the name of efficiency.

What constitutes "good cause" for the modification of a scheduling order under Rule 16(b)? Some courts have taken a rigid view, holding that the failure of a party fairly to meet a deadline without a sound excuse will result in a denial of relief, even though that will preclude consideration of a matter of substantive significance. See, e.g, Martinez v. Baldwin Steel Co.–Chicago Division, 2000 WL 1029228 (N.D.Ill.2000). The court in FRANCOIS v. McDONALD, 2000 WL 1528083 (E.D.La.2000), was faced with a demand from defendant to preclude plaintiff from using any expert testimony at trial because plaintiff's counsel was thirty-one days late in providing its expert witness list. The court listed four factors to be considered in making its determination: the party's reason for missing the deadline, the importance of the evidence sought to be permitted, potential prejudice to the opposing party, and the availability of a continuance or other method to overcome any prejudice. Although the court stated that it had considered the four factors, it appeared to rely only on the fact that plaintiff did not have a valid excuse for being late. The court granted defendant's motion without discussing the other three factors.

On the other hand, in POTOMAC ELECTRIC POWER CO. v. ELECTRIC MOTOR SUPPLY, INC., 190 F.R.D. 372 (D.Md.1999), despite finding that there was no good reason why a party's expert had not been designated on time under the scheduling order, the court refused to hold that the party's expert would not be permitted to testify at trial. The court noted that the expert was vital to the case and there was limited prejudice to the opposing party. The court called the proposed exclusion of the testimony "drastic," and indicated that minor monetary sanctions could properly be imposed instead. See also Long v. Steepro, 213 F.3d 983 (7th Cir.2000).

6. In the late 1960s a committee of federal judges, known as the Coordinating Committee for Multiple Litigation of the United States District Courts, together with legal scholars and representatives of the bar, drafted a manual of suggested procedures for dealing with the so-called "big case." This manual, which has been revised and updated from time to time, and is now the *Manual for Complex Litigation (Third)* (Fed.Jud. Center 1995), suggests a series of four

pretrial conferences: the first to assume control of the case and to handle preliminary matters such as pleading and the joinder of parties and claims; the second to plan discovery; the third to control the discovery process and provide for pretrial briefs; and the last to plan the details of the trial. The *Manual* recognizes that these procedures must be altered to fit the needs of each case.

For an analysis of the successes and problems faced by the courts in cases in which some of the *Manual*'s procedures have been utilized, see Note, *The Judicial Panel and the Conduct of Multidistrict Litigation,* 87 Harv.L.Rev. 1001 (1974).

7. What is it that makes managerial judging effective? Is it the informal character of the communication among the parties, and among the parties and the judge? Or is it the range of evidence made available to the judge? Or is it simply the pressure created by imposing deadlines?

Do judicial attempts to encourage settlement inevitably affect the judge's ability to preside over a trial in that dispute? Does your answer depend on whether the trial is to a jury or to the bench? Because they fear that a judge who participates in settlement talks might be perceived as partial, some courts ask a second judge, magistrate, or master to help the parties negotiate a settlement. For discussions of the proper judicial role in the settlement process, see generally Craig & Christenson, *The Settlement Process,* 59 F.R.D. 252 (1973); Will, Merhige & Rubin, *The Role of the Judge in the Settlement Process,* 75 F.R.D. 203 (1978); Adams, *Let's Make a Deal: Effective Utilization of Judicial Settlement in State and Federal Courts,* 73 Oregon L.Rev. 427 (1993).

8. We must also remind ourselves that encouraging settlements is a policy problem of paramount importance. In a system founded upon the adversary relationship, in which lawyers are trained to fight, not to negotiate, suggestion of settlement is often taken as a sign of weakness. A settlement is in many respects the closest thing to a truly final judgment that can emerge from litigation. A settlement is not normally appealable, and it normally embodies a commitment by the parties to work together in some manner, a stance that may forestall future litigation.

Flanders, *Blind Umpires—A Response to Professor Resnik,* 35 Hastings L.J. 505, 513–14 (1984).

9. State court attitudes toward pretrial management vary tremendously. A useful summary of many state pretrial procedures appears in Note, *Pretrial Conference Procedures,* 26 S.C.L.Rev. 481 (1974).

G. HEILEMAN BREWING CO. v. JOSEPH OAT CORP.

United States Court of Appeals, Seventh Circuit, 1989 (en banc).
871 F.2d 648.

KANNE, CIRCUIT JUDGE.

May a federal district court order litigants—even those represented by counsel—to appear before it in person at a pretrial conference for the purpose of discussing the posture and settlement of the litigants' case? After reviewing the Federal Rules of Civil Procedure and federal district courts' inherent authority to manage and control the litigation before them, we answer this question in the affirmative and conclude that a district court may sanction a litigant for failing to comply with such an order.

I. Background

A federal magistrate ordered Joseph Oat Corporation to send a "corporate representative with authority to settle" to a pretrial conference to discuss disputed factual and legal issues and the possibility of settlement. Although counsel for Oat Corporation appeared, accompanied by another attorney who was authorized to speak on behalf of the principals of the corporation, no principal or corporate representative personally attended the conference. The court determined that the failure of Oat Corporation to send a principal of the corporation to the pretrial conference violated its order. Consequently, the district court imposed a sanction of $5,860.01 upon Oat Corporation pursuant to Federal Rule of Civil Procedure 16(f). This amount represented the costs and attorneys' fees of the opposing parties attending the conference.

II. The Appeal

Oat Corporation appeals, claiming that the district court did not have the authority to order litigants represented by counsel to appear at the pretrial settlement conference. Specifically, Oat Corporation contends that, by negative implication, the language of Rule 16(a)(5) prohibits a district court from directing represented litigants to attend pretrial conferences. That is, because Rule 16 expressly refers to "attorneys for the parties and any unrepresented parties" in introductory paragraph (a), a district court may not go beyond that language to devise procedures which direct the pretrial appearance of parties represented by counsel. Consequently, Oat Corporation concludes that the court lacked the authority to order the pretrial attendance of its corporate representatives and, even if the court possessed such authority, the court abused its discretion to exercise that power in this case. Finally, Oat Corporation argues that the court abused its discretion to enter sanctions.

A. Authority to Order Attendance

First, we must address Oat Corporation's contention that a federal district court lacks the authority to order litigants who are represented by counsel to appear at a pretrial conference. Our analysis requires us to review the Federal Rules of Civil Procedure and district courts' inherent authority to manage the progress of litigation.

Rule 16 addresses the use of pretrial conferences to formulate and narrow issues for trial as well as to discuss means for dispensing with the need for costly and unnecessary litigation. As we stated in Link v. Wabash R.R., 291 F.2d 542, 547 (7th Cir.1961), aff'd, 370 U.S. 626, 82 S.Ct. 1386, 8 L.Ed.2d 734 (1962):

> Pre-trial procedure has become an integrated part of the judicial process on the trial level. Courts must be free to use it and to control and enforce its operation. Otherwise, the orderly administration of justice will be removed from control of the trial court and placed in the hands of counsel. We do not believe such a course is within the contemplation of the law.

The pretrial settlement of litigation has been advocated and used as a means to alleviate overcrowded dockets, and courts have practiced numerous and varied types of pretrial settlement techniques for many years. * * * Since 1983, Rule 16 has expressly provided that settlement of a case is one of several subjects which should be pursued and discussed vigorously during pretrial conferences.

The language of Rule 16 does not give any direction to the district court upon the issue of a court's authority to order litigants who are represented by counsel to appear for pretrial proceedings. Instead, Rule 16 merely refers to the participation of trial advocates—attorneys of record and pro se litigants. However, the Federal Rules of Civil Procedure do not completely describe and limit the power of the federal courts. * * *

The concept that district courts exercise procedural authority outside the explicit language of the rules of civil procedure is not frequently documented, but valid nevertheless. * * * The Supreme Court has acknowledged that the provisions of the Federal Rules of Civil Procedure are not intended to be the exclusive authority for actions to be taken by district courts. Link v. Wabash R.R., 370 U.S. 626, 82 S.Ct. 1386, 8 L.Ed.2d 734 (1962).

In *Link,* the Supreme Court noted that a district court's ability to take action in a procedural context may be grounded in " 'inherent power,' governed not by rule or statute but by the control necessarily vested in courts to manage their own affairs so as to achieve the orderly and expeditious disposition of cases." 370 U.S. at 630–31, 82 S.Ct. at 1389 (footnotes omitted). This authority likewise forms the basis for continued development of procedural techniques designed to make the operation of the court more efficient, to preserve the integrity of the judicial process, and to control courts' dockets. Because the rules form and shape certain aspects of a court's inherent powers, yet allow the continued exercise of that power where discretion should be available, the mere absence of language in the federal rules specifically authorizing or describing a particular judicial procedure should not, and does not, give rise to a negative implication of prohibition. * * *

In this case, we are required to determine whether a court's power to order the pretrial appearance of litigants who are represented by counsel is inconsistent with, or in derogation of, Rule 16. We must remember that Rule 1 states, with unmistakable clarity, that the Federal Rules of Civil Procedure "shall be construed to secure the just, speedy, and inexpensive determination of every action." * * *

"[The] spirit, intent, and purpose [of Rule 16] is ... broadly remedial, allowing courts to actively manage the preparation of cases for trial." In re Baker, 744 F.2d 1438, 1440 (10th Cir.1984) (en banc), cert. denied, 471 U.S. 1014, 105 S.Ct. 2016, 85 L.Ed.2d 299 (1985). Rule 16 is not designed as a device to restrict or limit the authority of the district judge in the conduct of pretrial conferences. As the Tenth Circuit Court of Appeals sitting *en banc* stated in *Baker,* "the spirit and purpose of the amendments to Rule 16 always have been within the inherent power of the courts to manage their affairs as an independent constitutional branch of government." Id. at 1441 (citations omitted).

We agree with this interpretation of Rule 16. The wording of the rule and the accompanying commentary make plain that the entire thrust of the amendment to Rule 16 was to urge judges to make wider use of their powers and to manage actively their dockets from an early stage. We therefore conclude that our interpretation of Rule 16 to allow district courts to order represented parties to appear at pretrial settlement conferences merely represents another application of a district judge's inherent authority to preserve the efficiency, and more importantly the integrity, of the judicial process.

To summarize, we simply hold that the action taken by the district court in this case constituted the proper use of inherent authority to aid in accomplishing the purpose and intent of Rule 16. We reaffirm the notion that the inherent power of a district judge—derived from the very nature and existence of his judicial office—is the broad field over which the Federal Rules of Civil Procedure are applied. Inherent authority remains the means by which district judges deal with circumstances not proscribed or specifically addressed by rule or statute, but which must be addressed to promote the just, speedy, and inexpensive determination of every action.

B. Exercise of Authority to Order Attendance

Having determined that the district court possessed the power and authority to order the represented litigants to appear at the pretrial settlement conference, we now must examine whether the court abused its discretion to issue such an order.

At the outset, it is important to note that a district court cannot coerce settlement. * * * In this case, considerable concern has been generated because the court ordered "corporate representatives with authority to settle" to attend the conference. In our view, "authority to settle," when used in the context of this case, means that the "corporate representative" attending the pretrial conference was required to hold a position within the corporate entity allowing him to speak definitively and to commit the corporation to a particular position in the litigation. We do not view "authority to settle" as a requirement that corporate representatives must come to court willing to settle on someone else's terms, but only that they come to court in order to consider the possibility of settlement.

* * *

If this case represented a situation where Oat Corporation had sent a corporate representative and was sanctioned because that person refused to make an offer to pay money—that is, refused to submit to settlement coercion—we would be faced with a decide[d]ly different issue—a situation we would not countenance.

* * *

As an alternative position, Oat Corporation argues that the court abused its discretion to order corporate representatives of the litigants to attend the pretrial settlement conference. Oat Corporation determined that because its business was a "going concern":

> It would be unreasonable for the magistrate to require the president of that corporation to leave his business [in Camden, New Jersey] to travel to Madison, Wisconsin, to participate in a settlement conference. The expense and burden on the part of Joseph Oat to comply with this order was clearly unreasonable.

Consequently, Oat Corporation believes that the district court abused its authority.

We recognize, as did the district court, that circumstances could arise in which requiring a corporate representative (or any litigant) to appear at a pretrial settlement conference would be so onerous, so clearly unproductive, or so expensive in relation to the size, value, and complexity of the case that it might be an abuse of discretion. Moreover, "[b]ecause inherent powers are shielded from direct democratic controls, they must be exercised with restraint and discretion." * * * However, the facts and circumstances of this case clearly support the court's actions to require the corporate representatives of the litigants to attend the pretrial conference personally.

This litigation involved a claim for $4 million—a claim which turned upon the resolution of complex factual and legal issues. The litigants expected the trial to last from one to three months and all parties stood to incur substantial legal fees and trial expenses. This trial also would have preempted a large segment of judicial time—not an insignificant factor. Thus, because the stakes were high, we do not believe that the burden of requiring a corporate representative to attend a pretrial settlement conference was out of proportion to the benefits to be gained, not only by the litigants but also by the court.

* * *

We thus conclude that the court did not abuse its authority and discretion to order a representative of the Oat Corporation to appear for the pretrial settlement conference on December 19.

* * *

III. Conclusion

We hold that Rule 16 does not limit, but rather is enhanced by, the inherent authority of federal courts to order litigants represented by counsel to attend pretrial conferences for the purpose of discussing settlement. Oat Corporation violated the district court's order requiring it to have a corporate representative attend the pretrial settlement conference on December 19, 1984. Under these circumstances, the district court did not abuse its discretion by imposing sanctions for Oat Corporation's failure to comply with the pretrial order. The judgment of the district court is hereby affirmed.

Posner, Circuit Judge, dissenting.

Rule 16(a) of the Federal Rules of Civil Procedure authorizes a district court to "direct the attorneys for the parties and any *unrepresented* parties to appear before it for a [pretrial] conference." The word I have italicized could be thought to carry the negative implication that no *represented* party may be directed to appear—that was the panel's conclusion—but I hesitate to so conclude in a case that can be decided on a narrower ground.

* * *

The question of the district court's power to summon a represented party to a settlement conference is a difficult one. On the one hand, nothing in Rule 16 or in any other rule or statute confers such a power, and there are obvious dangers in too broad an interpretation of the federal courts' inherent power to regulate their procedure. One danger is that it encourages judicial high-handedness ("power corrupts"); several years ago one of the district judges in this circuit ordered Acting Secretary of Labor Brock to appear before him for settlement discussions on the very day Brock was scheduled to appear before the Senate for his confirmation hearing. The broader concern illustrated by the Brock episode is that in their zeal to settle cases judges may ignore the value of other people's time. One reason people hire lawyers is to economize on their own investment of time in resolving disputes. * * *

On the other hand, *die Not bricht Eisen* ["necessity breaks iron"]. Attorneys often are imperfect agents of their clients, and the workload of our district courts is so heavy that we should hesitate to deprive them of a potentially useful tool for effecting settlement, even if there is some difficulty in finding a legal basis for the tool. * * *

* * * [F]ortunately we need not answer the question in *this* case—so clear is it that the magistrate abused his discretion, which is to say, acted unreasonably, in demanding that Oat Corporation send an executive having "full settlement authority" to the pretrial conference. This demand, which is different from a demand that a party who has not closed the door to settlement send an executive to discuss possible terms, would be defensible only if litigants had a duty to bargain in good faith over settlement before resorting to trial, and neither Rule 16 nor any other rule, statute, or doctrine imposes such a duty on federal litigants. * * * There is no federal judicial power to coerce settlement. Oat had made clear that it was not prepared to settle the case on any terms that required it to pay money. That was its prerogative, which once exercised made the magistrate's continued insistence on Oat's sending an executive to Madison arbitrary, unreasonable, willful, and indeed petulant. * * *

* * * We should reverse the district court without reaching the question whether there are any circumstances in which a district court may compel a party represented by counsel to attend a pretrial conference.

COFFEY, CIRCUIT JUDGE, with whom EASTERBROOK, RIPPLE and MANION, CIRCUIT JUDGES, join, dissenting.

* * * Unlike the majority, I am convinced that Rule 16 does not authorize a trial judge to require a represented party litigant to attend a pretrial conference together with his or her attorney because the rule *mandates in clear and unambiguous terms that only an unrepresented party litigant and attorneys may be ordered to appear.*

* * *

The newly created "inherent authority" to require represented litigants to appear at a pretrial conference is based upon a legal foundation of quicksand. Exercise of this power has posed and will continue to pose a substantial invitation for judicial abuse. * * *

My conclusion that judges lack the inherent authority to require the presence of a represented party litigant at a pretrial conference does not deprive trial judges of the ability to effectively handle their caseloads. Judges remain free to require the attendance of attorneys and unrepresented parties at pretrial conferences. However, if further measures are taken to coercively require the presence and active participation of a represented party at a pretrial conference, it is my considered belief that judges will be no longer worthy of the aura of impartiality for "the guiding consideration is that the administration of justice should reasonably appear to be disinterested as well as be so in fact." * * *

EASTERBROOK, CIRCUIT JUDGE, with whom POSNER, COFFEY and MANION, CIRCUIT JUDGES, join, dissenting.

Our case has three logically separate issues. First, whether a district court may demand the attendance of someone other than the party's counsel of record. Second, whether the court may insist that this additional person be an employee rather than an agent selected for the occasion. Third, whether the court may insist that the representative have "full settlement authority"—meaning the authority to agree to pay cash in settlement (maybe authority without cap, although that was not clear). Even if one resolves the first issue as the majority does, it does not follow that district courts have the second or third powers, or that their exercise here was prudent.

The proposition that a magistrate may require a firm to send an employee rather than a representative is puzzling. Corporate "employees" are simply agents of the firm. Corporations choose their agents and decide what powers to give them. Which agents have which powers is a matter of internal corporate affairs. Joseph Oat Corp. sent to the conference not only its counsel of record but also John Fitzpatrick, who had authority to speak for Oat. Now Mr. Fitzpatrick is an attorney, which raised the magistrate's hackles, but why should this count against him? Because Fitzpatrick is a part-time rather than a full-time agent of the corporation? Why can't the corporation make its own decision about how much of the agent's time to hire? Is Oat being held in contempt because it is too small to have a cadre of legal employees—because its general counsel practices with a law firm rather than being "in house"?

* * *

Notes and Questions

1. The final paragraph of Rule 16(c), as amended in 1993, now makes it clear that the court may order a litigant to be present or available by phone to consider the possibility of settlement.

2. In many cases, a defendant will be represented by an attorney retained by an insurance company, who generally will control the course of the litigation. Although the insurer is not formally a party to the case, it has the greatest economic interest in the litigation, since it will pay any judgment recovered by the plaintiff. Does the court have the power under Rule 16 to order a representative of the insurance company to appear at a pretrial conference? If such an order cannot be directed to the nonparty insurer, can the same result be obtained by an order directed to the defendant himself? Compare In re Novak, 932 F.2d 1397, 1407–08 (11th Cir.1991), with Lockhart v. Patel, 115 F.R.D. 44 (E.D.Ky.1987), and Dvorak v. Shibata, 123 F.R.D. 608 (D.Neb.1988). See Sherman, *Court-Mandated Alternative Dispute Resolution*, 46 S.M.U.L.Rev. 2079 (1993).

3. What if a party and its attorney appear at a settlement conference as ordered, but announce that the client's policy is never to settle a case and refuse to discuss any compromise? What, if any, sanctions are appropriate? See Shedden v. Wal–Mart Stores, Inc., 196 F.R.D. 484 (E.D.Mich.2000).

4. For a discussion of the operation and significance of Rule 16, see Rosenberg, *The Pretrial Conference and Effective Justice* (1964); Flanders, *Blind Um-*

pires—A Response to Professor Resnik, 35 Hastings L.J. 505 (1984); Peckham, *The Federal Judge as Case Manager: The New Role in Guiding a Case from Filing to Disposition,* 69 Calif.L.Rev. 770 (1981); Richey, *Rule 16 Revisited: Reflections for the Benefit of Bench and Bar,* 139 F.R.D. 525 (1991); Richey, *Rule 16: A Survey and Some Considerations for the Bench and Bar,* 126 F.R.D. 599 (1989).

Read the excerpts from the Civil Justice Reform Act of 1990, 28 U.S.C. §§ 471–479, in the Supplement.

MULLENIX, CIVIL JUSTICE REFORM COMES TO THE SOUTHERN DISTRICT OF TEXAS: CREATING AND IMPLEMENTING A COST AND REDUCTION PLAN UNDER THE CIVIL JUSTICE REFORM ACT OF 1990, 11 Rev. Litigation 165, 167–74 (1992):

The Civil Justice Reform Act of 1990 is effectuating a nationwide procedural revolution that is probably unparalleled since the enactment of the Federal Rules of Civil Procedure in 1938. The Act mandates local, grassroots rulemaking by amateur advisory groups—a novel process that essentially circumvents the usual judicial rulemaking committees that accomplish civil rule reform, which also have been in place since 1938. * * *

[T]he Civil Justice Reform Act needs to be understood against a backdrop of civil justice reform efforts that have been simmering for the last few years in all three branches of the federal government. On the legislative side, the Act requires seemingly precipitous and urgent reform, a mandate that indicates Congress's frustration with the glacial pace of procedural reform that is usually accomplished through third-branch deliberative rulemaking. The Civil Justice Reform Act demonstrates that Congress is going to have procedural justice reform, and is going to have it now.

* * *

* * * [I]t is important to focus on the types of reform measures that the legislation requires or strongly recommends. In this regard, the almost-exclusive emphasis of the Act is on tighter managerial control over pretrial proceedings, curbing discovery abuse, and recourse to alternative dispute resolution. These areas of emphasis raise interesting problems relating to party autonomy and control over the conduct of litigation, as well as party access to federal courts and the right to an adjudicatory model of dispute resolution.

* * *

Congress suggested that the federal courts "are suffering today under the scourge of two related and worsening plagues." The first plague—high costs of litigation and delays that contribute to these high costs—limits federal-court access to the wealthy and lessens the ability of American corporations to compete at home and abroad. The second plague—a scarcity of financial resources dedicated to the federal court system—results in a shortage of federal judges. This shortage, in turn, fuels costs and delays, especially in federal courts with congested criminal dockets largely stemming from drug-related cases.

The Civil Justice Reform Act was intended to address these problems in what Congress deemed a "comprehensive and straightforward fashion." Six cornerstone principles animated the legislative program:

> (1) building reform from the "bottom up"; (2) promulgating a national, statutory policy in support of judicial case management; (3) imposing greater controls on the discovery process; (4) establishing differentiated case management systems; (5) improving motions practice and reducing undue delays associated with decisions on motions; and (6) expanding and enacting the use of alternative dispute resolution.

* * *

Congress made two key policy decisions regarding civil justice reform within the federal system. The first was that reform was to be accomplished locally and to be based on the recommendations of district-wide community advisory groups comprised not only of federal court personnel, but also lawyers and clients or "those who must live with the civil justice system on a regular basis." * * *

The second decision, tied to decentralized reform, was to effectuate a national statutory policy in support of judicial case management that is even more extensive than the current federal rules require or even contemplate. This decision was predicated on the conclusion that early and increased judicial supervision over litigation results in more expeditious disposition of civil cases.

The other guiding principles for civil justice reform that undergird the Act flowed from this Congressional directive to formulate a nationwide program of vigorous civil case management. Accordingly, the Act's legislative history stresses the importance of early and ongoing pretrial court involvement; setting early and firm trial dates; enhancing the use of magistrates; imposing greater controls on the discovery process; establishing differentiated case management systems; reforming motions practice; and expanding and enhancing the use of alternative dispute resolution techniques.

Notes and Questions

1. Note that the Civil Justice Reform Act of 1990, 28 U.S.C. § 473(b)(5), provides that the advisory committee established in each federal judicial district must consider a requirement "that, upon notice by the court, representatives of the parties with authority to bind them in settlement discussions be present or available by telephone during any settlement conference." If this statute had been in effect when *Heileman* was decided, would it have definitively settled the question presented in that case?

2. For a discussion of the plans proposed by various District Courts pursuant to the Civil Justice Reform Act of 1990 and the problems which these plans may present, see Tobias, *Judicial Oversight of Civil Justice Reform,* 140 F.R.D. 49 (1992).

3. As is true of Rule 16, the Civil Justice Reform Act reflects the trend away from the traditional concept of the adversarial system. See Lewis, *Legislatively*

Directed Judicial Activism; Some Reflections on the Meaning of the Civil Justice Reform Act, 28 U.Mich.J.L.Ref. 305 (1995).

4. Does the Civil Justice Reform Act compromise the goal of national uniformity underlying the Federal Rules of Civil Procedure? See Robel, *Fractured Procedure: Civil Justice Reform Act of 1990*, 46 Stan.L.Rev. 1447 (1994).

5. For a discussion of the Civil Justice Reform Act's impact on litigants, see Haig & Stone, *Does All This Litigation "Reform" Really Benefit the Client?*, 66–Aug. N.Y.St.B.J. 10 (1994). See also Kakalik, Dunworth, Hill, McCaffrey, Oshiro, Pace & Vaiana, *Just, Speedy, and Inexpensive? An Evaluation of Judicial Case Management Under the Civil Justice Reform Act* (Institute for Civil Justice, RAND 1996).

SECTION B. EXTRAJUDICIAL PERSONNEL: MASTERS AND MAGISTRATES

Read Federal Rules of Civil Procedure 53, 72, and 73, and the material accompanying Rule 53 in the Supplement.

In recent years there has been increasing interest in utilizing extrajudicial personnel to perform a wide variety of judicial functions, including negotiating settlements, monitoring discovery, holding evidentiary hearings, and determining the proper size and allocation of a damage award in cases in which liability has been determined. It is argued that extrajudicial personnel sometimes can perform these tasks more competently and expeditiously than judges. For example, an expert in a particular area can serve the court well in such technically complex fields as antitrust and products liability. And, more generally, extrajudicial personnel often can interact with the parties in a more informal way than some judges—and the frank exchanges that are part of this informality may move the parties towards a resolution of a dispute. In addition, it is easier for a judge to maintain her impartiality if the pretrial conference or settlement conference is referred to a magistrate.

The Anglo–American legal system long has used extrajudicial personnel to help process disputes. See generally Silberman, *Masters and Magistrates, Part I: The English Model*, 50 N.Y.U.L.Rev. 1070 (1975); Silberman, *Masters and Magistrates, Part II: The American Analogue*, 50 N.Y.U.L.Rev. 1297 (1975). Traditionally, however, their use in civil cases was disfavored. Thus, under former Federal Equity Rule 59, resort to masters was noted as the exception, not the rule. It was believed that resort to such personnel merely increased costs and created delays—without producing any measurable improvement in the quality of adjudication. Though some contemporary commentators still question the value of extrajudicial personnel, crowded dockets and complex cases have led to greater willingness to employ them to handle disputes.

Professor Silberman, who in the past argued vigorously for the use of special masters and magistrates, now believes that courts delegate too much to them. She argues that judicial adjuncts have unnecessarily bureaucratized the judiciary and perhaps even expanded the discovery process. Even more troublesome, according to Professor Silberman, is the potentially unconstitutional delegation of authority to magistrates and special masters to make substantive rulings. See Silberman, *Judicial Adjuncts Revisited: The Proliferation of Ad Hoc Procedure,* 137 U.Pa.L.Rev. 2131 (1989).

Notes and Questions

1. What is the difference between a master and a magistrate in the federal system? When a magistrate hears pretrial motions, does she do so in her capacity as a magistrate, a special master, or both?

2. How do Rule 16 and the Civil Justice Reform Act affect the role of federal magistrates? See Breen, *Mediation and the Magistrate Judge,* 26 U.Memphis L.Rev. 1007 (1996); Dessen, *The Role of the Federal Magistrate Judge in Civil Justice Reform,* 67 St. John's L.Rev. 799 (1993).

3. The Federal Magistrates Act of 1968, 28 U.S.C. §§ 631–639, created a system of magistrates. It placed them under the control of district judges and authorized those judges to assign them "duties [that] are not inconsistent with the Constitution and laws of the United States." This language was so vague, however, that it created controversy over the proper scope of the magistrates' authority and over the weight to be given their determinations. Thus, the Act has been amended several times. Under the 1979 amendments, when both parties consent, a magistrate may "conduct any and all proceedings in a jury or non-jury civil matter and order the entry of judgment in the case, when specially designated to exercise such jurisdiction by the district court in which he serves." A 1990 amendment provides that magistrates are to be known as "United States magistrate judges." The 1983 amendments to the Federal Rules established procedures for cases in which magistrates are used. For the most part, these amendments simply traced the relevant portions of the Federal Magistrates Act.

Does the Magistrates Act grant so much power to magistrates as to make it unconstitutional? Article III grants life tenure and salary protections to judges to ensure that those invested with the judicial power of the United States will not be subject to political pressure. Magistrates do not enjoy these protections. Yet magistrates perform many (and, with the consent of the parties, all) of the functions normally reserved for Article III judges. Is this grant of power inconsistent with the mandate of Article III? Congress considered this question at length before passing the magistrates' bill; the consensus of the expert witnesses that appeared was that the legislation was constitutional. See generally McCabe, *The Federal Magistrate Act of 1979,* 16 Harv.J.Legis. 343, 365–79 (1979). Some commentators still believe the grants to be unconstitutional. See Note, *Article III Constraints and the Expanding Jurisdiction of Federal Magistrates: A Dissenting View,* 88 Yale L.J. 1023 (1979); Note, *Article III Limits on Article I Courts: The Constitutionality of the Bankruptcy Court and the 1979 Magistrate Act,* 80 Colum.L.Rev. 560 (1980). But courts repeatedly have upheld the constitutionality of the Magistrates Act. See, e.g., Orsini v. Wallace, 913 F.2d 474, 477–79 (8th Cir.1990), certiorari denied 498 U.S. 1128, 111 S.Ct. 1093, 112 L.Ed.2d 1197 (1991).

4. How can a magistrate's decision be appealed? How do the procedures for appealing a magistrate's decision differ from the procedures for appealing the judgment of a district-court judge? See 12 Wright, Miller & Marcus, *Federal Practice and Procedure: Civil 2d* §§ 3077.1–80 (1997).

5. For an interesting critique of the use of magistrates in the United States District Courts for the Southern and Eastern Districts of New York, see *Report on Magistrates by the Committee on the Federal Courts of the New York County Lawyers' Association,* 140 F.R.D. 193 (1990).

6. General materials relating to special masters and magistrates include: 6 Wright, Miller & Kane, *Federal Practice and Procedure: Civil 2d* §§ 1521–40 (1990); 12 Wright, Miller & Marcus, *Federal Practice and Procedure: Civil 2d* §§ 3076–80 (1997); Kaufman, *Masters in the Federal Courts: Rule 53,* 58 Colum.L.Rev. 452 (1958); McCabe, *The Federal Magistrate Act of 1979,* 16 Harv.J.Legis. 343 (1979); Silberman, *Masters and Magistrates, Part II: The American Analogue,* 50 N.Y.U.L.Rev. 1297 (1975); Note, *The Expanding Influence of the Federal Magistrate,* 14 J.Marshall L.Rev. 465 (1981). A fascinating set of reflections about the use of special masters, based largely on the experience of the AT & T antitrust litigation, can be found in Brazil, Hazard & Rice, *Managing Complex Litigation: A Practical Guide to the Use of Special Masters* (1983).

SECTION C. THE FINAL PRETRIAL ORDER

Read the sample final pretrial order set out in the Supplement.

PAYNE v. S.S. NABOB

United States Court of Appeals, Third Circuit, 1962.
302 F.2d 803.

McLaughlin, Circuit Judge. In this personal injury admiralty action libellant filed a pretrial memorandum stating that he was relying upon the condition of a winch to prove his cause of action. The judge's pretrial report noted that. Sometime later the suit went to trial. Libellant's attorney included in his opening the fact that the loading had been handled improperly as an important element of his proof of unseaworthiness. The impleaded stevedore employer objected as it was outside the scope of the pretrial memorandum and report. The trial court sustained the objection. Two witnesses on behalf of the libellant, not listed in his pretrial memorandum, were not allowed to testify. Libellant's attorney moved for a continuance and this was denied.

* * *

Appellant * * * would have it that the Standing Order [local rule adopting Rule 16] did not furnish any ground for the court's barring of the unseaworthy allegation and of the witnesses not mentioned in the appellant's pretrial memorandum or the court's pretrial report. This seems to be founded on the thought that a pretrial memorandum is merely preparatory to the conference and that the court's pretrial order is the sole proof of the results of the pretrial procedure. In this instance, goes the contention, the function of appellant's memorandum was exhausted at the conference and since no pretrial "order" was made there were no binding results of the pretrial steps.

[Padovani v. Bruchhausen, 293 F.2d 546 (2d Cir.1961)] * * * is cited for this, where it states:

"Nothing in the rule [16] affords basis for clubbing the parties into admissions they do not willingly make; but it is a way of advancing the trial ultimately to be had by setting forth points on which the parties are agreed after a conference directed by a trained judge."

Appellant was not clubbed into admissions he did not willingly make. It was his own voluntary statement of the basis of his claim that was included in the pretrial report of the judge. The report was never objected to as incorrectly outlining appellant's pretrial statement.

The position now taken that the pretrial report of the trial judge because it is not titled as an "order" does not comply with Rule 16 is without merit. Appellant's pretrial memorandum was filed. In accordance with the Standing Order it contained a "brief summary statement of both the facts of this case and counsel's contention as to the liability of defendant." It also contained "The names and addresses of all witnesses (except rebuttal) whom the plaintiff expects to call to testify at the time of trial." The pretrial conference was held in due course and attended by the attorneys for the parties. Based on the pretrial memoranda and the conference, the district judge drew and filed his report. There was no complaint concerning it or any part of it down to and including the trial until libellant's attorney was stopped in his opening as he went beyond his pretrial outline of alleged liability. The pretrial "report"[2] drawn, signed and filed by the pretrial judge properly and fully (having the particular litigation and its requirements in mind) complies with the requirements of Rule 16. It, including its references to the pretrial memoranda, succinctly fulfilled the letter and spirit of pretrial. It reduced the action to essentials, eliminated surplusage, enabled the parties and the court to prepare for a trial of stated issues, named witnesses and contained no hidden charms. The argument to the contrary, depending as it does on a quibble over the word "report", is rootless.

It is asserted on behalf of the appellant that the Standing Order can only be construed as a request to stipulate, that counsel had no intention of stipulating and that no warning or notice was given by the Standing Order that failure to list the requirements ordered would constitute a stipulation or

---

2. "Pre–Trial Report of Judge Van Dusen

Date Pre–Trial Held: 9/21/59 No. on Consolidated List: 2109 303 of 1958 in Admiralty

Case Title: Hosea Payne v. S.S. Nabob & North German Lloyd v. Lavino Shipping Co.

1. Trial Counsel: L—Philip Dorfman, Esq. & Saul C. Waldbaum, Esq.

R—Robert A. Hauslohner, Esq. (T. Mount will try)

IR—F. Hastings Griffin, Jr., Esq. (P. Price will try)

2. Amendments: If IR wishes to amend pretrial memo, notice to be given to undersigned.

3. Discovery: Respondent will answer impleaded respondent's interrogatories (unexecuted copies to be furnished counsel by September 23).

4. L's Claim: Ship unseaworthy due to improper port winch on after side at #2 hatch. Brakes would not hold when set in neutral. Port winch on house-fall did not work from early hours of morning. See pre-trial memo.

5. R's Claim: Sole cause of injuries was L's negligence and that of his fellow workmen. Two men pushed draft into L and 2 other men said nothing was defective in winches. See pre-trial memo. IR's position—see pre-trial memo.

6. Stipulations:

7. Issues:

8. Legal Issues:

9. Trial Time: 6 days

Francis L. Van Dusen, J."

Francis L. Van Dusen, J.

a waiver of all other theories. Rule 16 gives as the first purpose of pretrial "The simplification of issues". Under the Standing Order counsel were asked to furnish "A brief summary of both the facts of the case and counsel's contentions as to the liability of the defendant." That was done. Libellant's contentions as to the liability of the defendant were inserted into the Court's Report with the note "See pre-trial memo". The Report was filed September 28, 1959. The trial did not commence until March 14, 1960, a five and a half months interval during which no effort was made to change the signed and filed contentions of the libellant regarding the liability of the defendant or to add names of witnesses. The facts that the situation was plain on its face and that the practice was well settled by then, (the Standing Order having been in effect since October 23, 1958), set the tone for this contention on behalf of appellant. Krieger v. Ownership Corporation, 270 F.2d 265 (3 Cir.1959), relied upon by appellant is inapposite. We there held that disputed issues of fact *actually raised* at the pretrial stage could not be resolved by the trial court on motion for summary judgment. It has long been the law that attorneys at the pretrial stage "owe a duty to the court and opposing counsel to make a full and fair disclosure of their views as to what the real issues at the trial will be." Cherney v. Holmes, 185 F.2d 718, 721 (7th Cir.1950) * * *. It is through such disclosure at pretrial that trial prejudice can be avoided. The awareness of appellant's attorney to the trial situation is apparent in his request for a continuance when he told the court "I think under the circumstances I would move for a continuance of the case to give *the other side* ample time, because actually this is a question of surprise." (Emphasis supplied).

It is argued also that the court abused its discretion by refusing to permit amendment of the pretrial memorandum. This was not an easy decision for the trial judge. His inclination clearly, as is habitual with judges, was to help. And help he would have if, in his opinion, he could have done so fairly. But he was confronted with the realization that if he granted the request or allowed a continuance of the trial he was repudiating the whole pretrial theory and system as understood and followed in the Eastern District at a crucial period of its existence. Pretrial was finally on a firm foundation there. The judges had all given it generous and complete attention. This, with the gradual realization of the bar that pretrial was here to stay as a vital element of litigation practice and its resultant full cooperation, had made pretrial procedure routine in the Eastern District. One consequence was that directly and indirectly enormous relief was given the badly clogged trial list. It was admittedly vitally important to make sure that pretrial procedure would continue to function properly. One necessary phase of attaining that objective was, as expressed by the trial judge, "We have come to the point of enforcing it very strictly." In the circumstances he considered himself obliged to deny the motions to amend the pretrial memorandum with respect to liability allegations and witnesses. The refusal of appellant's motion for a continuance is in the same category.

Beyond all doubt the judge acted entirely within his discretion. It was difficult for him, it took courage but it was what this sound, experienced judge had to do as he saw it, in accordance with his judicial obligation.

The decree of the district court will be affirmed.

SMITH CONTRACTING CORP. v. TROJAN CONSTRUCTION CO.

United States Court of Appeals, Tenth Circuit, 1951.
192 F.2d 234.

PHILLIPS, CHIEF JUDGE. The Trojan Construction Company, Inc., brought this action against Smith Contracting Corporation to recover damages, in excess of normal wear and tear, to equipment leased by Trojan to Smith, occurring during the use of the equipment by Smith.

The leases were in writing and the two provisions thereof, here material, in each lease, read as follows:

"2. Determination of Rental Charges. * * *.

"(a) *Monthly Rental Rates* shall not be subject to any deductions on account of any non-working time in the month, but the amount of rent payable for any fraction of a month at the beginning or end of the Rental Period shall be the monthly rental rate, prorated according to the number of calendar days in such fraction.

* * *

"8. Damage to Equipment. The Lessee shall indemnify the Lessor against all loss and damage to equipment during the Rental Period and the appraisal of any such loss or damage shall be based on the equipment values shown by the List of Equipment. Any shortage or damage claim of either party shall be made known to the other party within seven (7) days after receipt of equipment, or such claim shall be void."

A pretrial conference was held and the parties agreed that the action was predicated upon a claim that Smith returned the equipment in a damaged condition not resulting from normal wear and tear; that Smith denied there was any damage other than that resulting from normal wear and tear; and that the only question for determination was such issue of fact.

During the introduction of the testimony of the first witness of Trojan the leases were introduced in evidence. Smith then sought to prove that it paid rental for a full month at the end of the rental period, and that the equipment was returned before the end of the last monthly rental period; asserted that it was entitled to a counterclaim under the provisions of paragraph 2(a) of the leases; and asked leave to amend its answer to conform to such proof. The trial court ruled that Smith might make the proof and that it would take under advisement the question of whether the amendment would be permitted.

The trial court found that the equipment suffered damages, resulting other than from ordinary wear and tear during its use by Smith, aggregating $5,208.50. That finding is supported by substantial evidence, is not clearly erroneous, and is, therefore, binding on this court.

Trojan introduced proof that it verbally notified Craig, Superintendent of Smith, in charge of the work where the equipment was being used, of the damages to the equipment shortly before it was returned and that Craig agreed to have the equipment repaired. It will be observed that the leases did not require notice in writing or other formality in the giving of the notice.

They merely provided that any damage claim should be made known to the other party within seven days after receipt of the equipment. The trial court ruled that the verbal notice to Craig was sufficient notice of the damage required by paragraph 8 of the leases. Craig was the agent of Smith in charge of the work where the equipment was being used. We are of the opinion Craig had apparent authority to receive the notice and that the notice was sufficient. Moreover, the agreement at the pretrial conference eliminated the issue of notice.

The trial court refused to permit Smith to amend its answer to set up a counterclaim for overpayment of rental.

The provisions of the leases are plain. The time when the equipment was returned and the amounts of overpayment of rental could have been readily determined. Trojan did not dispute the claim or assert that it was not prepared to meet it. The trial was before the court and if Trojan needed additional time to check the facts, that time could have been granted. On the record, it seems clear that Smith was entitled to a counterclaim for overpayment of rental and that failure of Smith's counsel to assert it earlier resulted in no prejudice to Trojan.

* * *

It will be observed that the clause [in Rule 13(f)] "or when justice requires," is an independent ground upon which the court may grant leave to set up the counterclaim by amendment.

That portion of Rule 15(a) of the Federal Rules * * *, dealing with amendments to pleadings by leave of court provides that "leave shall be freely given when justice so requires."

We are not unmindful that the agreement arrived at during the pretrial conference as to the issues of fact to be presented did not embrace the issues of fact raised by this counterclaim. We are of the opinion, however, that rigid adherence to pretrial conference agreements should not be exacted, especially where so to do will result in injustice to one party and relaxing of such agreement will not cause prejudice to the other party. Requiring rigid adherence to pretrial conference agreements will tend to discourage cooperation of counsel and their willingness to agree at the pretrial conference as to the real and substantial issues to be presented, and will impair the effectiveness of the pretrial conference procedure.

Upon the facts presented on this record, we think justice required the granting of leave to amend the answer to set up the counterclaim and that denial thereof was an abuse of discretion.

* * *

Notes and Questions

1. The finality of pretrial orders is still a hotly debated issue. For example, see Joseph Manufacturing Co. v. Olympic Fire Corp., 986 F.2d 416 (10th Cir. 1993). Compare Harper v. Dismukes, 202 F.3d 273 (7th Cir.1999).

2. Courts normally treat the final pretrial order—the stipulations, agreements, and statements of counsel made at the final pretrial conference—as

binding for purposes of trial. Kona Technology Corp. v. Southern Pacific Transportation Co., 225 F.3d 595, 604 (5th Cir.2000). The final pretrial order supersedes the pleadings. How binding should this order be? Many of the benefits associated with the use of the pretrial order depend upon its binding effect. But given the exigencies that are an inevitable part of litigation, particularly at the trial level, is strict finality reasonable?

3.   Compare the standards for modifying scheduling orders and final pretrial orders found in Rules 16(b) and 16(e). What justifies the difference? Consider briefly the standards for amending pleadings contained in Rule 15. Pay particular attention to which party has the burden of proof. Which Rule is more sympathetic to amendments? Why?

4.   The pretrial order sometimes has been used to widen consideration of issues beyond those listed in the pleadings. In Howard v. Kerr Glass Manufacturing Co., 699 F.2d 330 (6th Cir.1983), the Sixth Circuit ruled that the final pretrial order prevailed over the original pleadings and that the trial judge had erred in refusing to admit evidence on issues included in the final pretrial order but not in the pleadings.

5.   How should courts penalize the failure to cooperate in the pretrial process? Should the failure to abide by a pretrial order ever result in dismissal of the suit, or in summary judgment? Compare Barreto v. Citibank, N.A., 907 F.2d 15 (1st Cir.1990), with John v. Louisiana, 828 F.2d 1129 (5th Cir.1987). Does Rule 41(b) provide an answer to this question? When would a lesser remedy—such as preclusion of an issue or exclusion of evidence—be appropriate? Do you agree that it was appropriate in *Payne*?

Is the remedy (monetary penalties) provided by the new Rule 16 preferable to the relatively drastic remedies discussed above? Does Rule 16 provide a compensatory remedy (designed to deter and to reimburse the opposing party and the court for the cost of any deviations from a pretrial order made by a party)? Or, does the Rule provide a punitive remedy (designed to encourage compliance with the court order)? An analysis of the use of monetary penalties for noncompliance with pretrial orders can be found in Brazil, *Improving Judicial Controls over the Pretrial Development of Civil Actions: Model Rules for Case Management and Sanctions*, 1981 Am.B.Found.Research J. 873, 921–55; Peckham, *The Federal Judge as Case Manager: The New Role of Guiding a Case from Filing to Disposition*, 69 Calif.L.Rev. 770, 800–04 (1981). A more general discussion of penalties for noncompliance with judicial rules and orders can be found in Rodes, Ripple & Mooney, *Sanctions Imposable for Violations of the Federal Rules of Civil Procedure* (Fed.Jud.Center 1981).

6.   What are the differences between Rule 16 sanctions and Rule 11 sanctions?

> [T]he coverage of Rules 11 and 16 are by no means co-extensive. Rule 11 deals with all motions, pleadings and documents signed by an attorney or party in a lawsuit; Rule 16 relates to all aspects of pre-trial management, including numerous procedures and discussions not necessarily memorialized in a writing.

HARRIS v. MARSH, 679 F.Supp. 1204, 1389 n. 278 (E.D.N.C.1987), modified 123 F.R.D. 204 (E.D.N.C.1988). There are other differences. First, the imposition of attorneys' fees as a sanction is discretionary in Rule 11 and mandatory in Rule 16(f). Second, although Rule 11 punishes acts done for an improper purpose, Rule 16 punishes certain acts regardless of purpose.

The two rules are similar in some respects, as well.

* * * If an allegation or contention is offered in a final pre-trial order without a reasonable factual or legal basis, much like Rule 11, it violates Rule 16. A meritless or frivolous claim, asserted with knowledge that opposing counsel will heighten his final preparation for trial of the claim on the basis of its appearance in the final pre-trial order, is not one alleged in good faith. Thus, with respect to final pre-trial orders, there is no reason to suggest the standards for professional responsibility and, therefore, liability under Rule 16 differ from those previously set forth for Rule 11. Improper motive, bad faith, even reckless behavior, is not a prerequisite for finding a violation of the rule.

Id. at 1389.

Chapter 13

ADJUDICATION WITHOUT TRIAL OR BY SPECIAL PROCEEDING

SECTION A.   SUMMARY JUDGMENT

The Burden Of Establishing That No Factual Dispute Exists

Courts are aided in evaluating summary judgment motions by certain widely recognized rules concerning the burdens to be borne by each party. The moving party has the initial burden of presenting information that clearly establishes that there is no factual dispute regarding the matter upon which summary judgment is sought. This is so even if the adverse party would bear the burden of persuasion on that issue at trial.

To meet its burden on a motion for summary judgment, the moving party normally submits outside evidence such as affidavits of witnesses setting forth facts to which they could testify at trial. If the information presented, taken as true, fails to establish that no factual dispute exists, summary judgment will be denied, even if the opposing party has presented no counter-evidence. If, but only if, the moving party produces information that appears to establish that no factual dispute exists, then the responding party normally must come forward with materials to show that there is a genuine issue of fact or summary judgment will be granted. If the responding party does produce information contradicting that of the moving party or otherwise showing that a factual dispute exists, summary judgment must be denied; the matter is then for the trier of fact after a trial on the merits.

Read Federal Rule of Civil Procedure 56 and the accompanying materials in the Supplement.

913

LUNDEEN v. CORDNER

United States Court of Appeals, Eighth Circuit, 1966.
354 F.2d 401.

Gibson, Circuit Judge. * * *

Appellant, plaintiff below, (hereinafter referred to as plaintiff) is a former wife of one Joseph Cordner, deceased. During their marriage two children were born, Maureen Joan Cordner and Michael Joseph Cordner. Prior to the time of his death Joseph Cordner was working in Libya. Mr. Cordner's employer Socony Mobil Oil Company, Inc. (Socony) carried a group life insurance contract with Metropolitan Life Insurance Company, (Metropolitan) under which Mr. Cordner as the insured had in 1956 designated his children, Maureen and Michael, as equal beneficiaries. In 1958 Joseph Cordner, having been divorced by plaintiff, married intervener, France Jeanne Cordner. In April 1960 a child was born of this second marriage. On October 3, 1962 Joseph Cordner died. During all periods above mentioned Mr. Cordner was in the employ of Socony stationed in Libya. The insurance policy and the annuity were in effect and due proof of loss was made. The contest for the proceeds arises between adverse claimants; the original designated beneficiaries, Maureen Joan and Michael Joseph Cordner; and France Jeanne Cordner, the second wife of assured, and Northwestern, as Trustee under the Last Will and Testament of Joseph F. Cordner, deceased.

On November 5, 1963, plaintiff as guardian and on behalf of her two children Maureen and Michael Cordner, the named beneficiaries, sued the insurer, Metropolitan, to recover the proceeds of the policy. Metropolitan answered that there were adverse claims to the policy benefits. Thereafter, Northwestern as the Trustee under the Last Will and Testament of the deceased, Joseph Cordner, was interpleaded as an additional defendant. Appellee, France J. Cordner, then intervened in the action. Both intervener and Northwestern allege that sometime in 1961 the decedent effected a change of beneficiaries [in favor of intervener]. * * *

It is clear that the first two children of decedent, Maureen and Michael, are the named beneficiaries. However, it is asserted that Joseph Cordner did everything within his power to effect a change of beneficiaries as alleged by intervener. Intervener presented affidavits and exhibits in support of her position and moved for summary judgment. The motion was granted and plaintiff contests this ruling on the ground that a summary judgment is not proper at this point in the litigation and that there remains a genuine issue on a material fact. It is now our task to determine if the summary judgment was properly granted.

* * * Plaintiff accepts as controlling the general rule of law that an insured's attempt to change his beneficiary will be given effect if all that remains to be done is a ministerial duty on the part of the insurer. * * *

Therefore, if deceased completed all the necessary steps required of him to change the beneficiary in his policy, intervener would be entitled to judgment. Furthermore, if intervener can demonstrate this fact so clearly that there is no longer a genuine issue of fact, summary judgment may be properly granted under provisions of Rule 56(c)* * * .

We are of the opinion that the affidavits and exhibits introduced by intervener clearly and undeniably indicate that deceased made a change in his policy's beneficiaries. First, it appears that after deceased's marriage in 1958 to intervener he amended his group hospitalization and employee savings plan to include intervener. Furthermore, certain correspondence conclusively indicates that a change in the life insurance was actually made.

Mr. Iten, an employee of Socony in Libya, whose duties included administration of company benefit plans, * * * prepared a letter to the New York office, dated April 19, 1961, stating that Joseph Cordner desired information as to who were his present beneficiaries under the company benefit plans and that Mr. Cordner had married for a second time and was not certain whether he had changed his beneficiary. * * *

Mr. Iten was transferred from Libya shortly thereafter and his duties were assumed by Mr. Burks. Burks by affidavit stated that early in 1961 Mr. Cordner came to him with a request to change his beneficiaries; that Burks issued the necessary forms to Cordner and gave him instructions on how to complete the forms, at which time Cordner produced a copy of his Will made in North Dakota while vacationing from Libya in 1960. They discussed the form of beneficiary designation which might be appropriate under the terms of the Will. Mr. Cordner personally completed the forms, endorsed the beneficiary changes he wished to make on the back of each form, signed the forms in Burks' presence, (the latter acting as a witness to the signature) and then left the completed forms with Burks for transmittal. Since Burks was unfamiliar with the type of beneficiary changes endorsed on the forms he made a thermofax copy of Cordner's Will and sent this reproduction together with the completed change of beneficiary forms to the New York office in a letter dated May 11, 1961, which letter in part reads as follows:

> Please review the enclosed employee change of beneficiary forms and advise us if this designation is acceptable under the plan.

The Home Office responded by stating in a letter dated June 1, 1961:

> We are processing the Change of Beneficiary forms completed by the above employee [J.F. Cordner] and forwarded to us. * * * We see no reason why the designation will not be acceptable.

Mr. Burks in his earlier affidavit of March 30, 1963 states that to the best of his recollection the change of beneficiary requested by Cordner was as follows:

> "One-fourth of the proceeds to my wife France Jeanne Cordner and the balance to the Northwestern National Bank of Minneapolis, Minnesota in trust for the uses and purposes set forth in my Last Will and Testament."

Burks in his second affidavit prepared for the purpose of the summary judgment proceeding confirmed the factual statements in his earlier affidavit and detailed the discussion and the procedures employed in the requested change of beneficiary by Cordner. He further stated that since the New York office had the Certificate for endorsement and since the Home Office stated in its letter of June 1, 1961 that they were processing the change of beneficiary forms he had no reason to believe that the processing of the changes had not proceeded to completion in the normal course. He was in the New York office at the time when a search of the files was made for the change of beneficiary forms, which, of course, they were unable to locate. When he returned to Tripoli, with instructions from the New York office to continue the search and to forward to New York all company papers having to do with Mr. Cordner's employment, he found a copy of a letter addressed to Cordner by his attorney suggesting the form of beneficiary designation required to effect the provisions of his Will. Burks then recalled that Mr. Cordner had referred to this same letter when discussing beneficiary changes in 1961 and that Cordner had used the suggested language in completing his change of beneficiary forms. After stating that he cannot restate from memory the text of the changes, he said that "I can and do reconfirm, upon my own direct knowledge and positive recollection that beneficiary changes so made by Joseph Franklin Cordner were in the form suggested by his attorney's letter and quoted verbatim from that letter in my prior affidavit."

Further correspondence indicates that the change of beneficiary forms were forwarded to the employer's Annuity and Insurance Department. A search of the department, however, never uncovered the form or the exact language used therein. It also appears by affidavit that all of the above related correspondence was properly identified and was prepared, mailed, received and kept as part of the business records of the company.

Plaintiff presents no counter evidence nor in any way indicates that intervener's evidence is not worthy of belief. Therefore, we believe there is no genuine issue of fact on this point. It is clear that Joseph Cordner actually made a change in the beneficiaries of his life insurance policy.

However, to entitle intervener to summary judgment, it must not only be clear that a change was made, but the wording of that change must be shown beyond any reasonable and genuine dispute. This point, too, was well covered in intervener's supporting papers.

* * *

From the affidavit of the attorney concerning the discussion of deceased's desires, from the letter written by the attorney explaining how the beneficiaries should be changed to effectuate these desires, and from the wording of the Last Will and Testament it is clear that Joseph Cordner intended to change the beneficiaries of his insurance policy by giving one-fourth to intervener and the balance to Northwestern in trust. We can presume that this intent remained with Mr. Cordner during the intervening ten months between the Will's execution and the date of the beneficiary change. * * *

However, in addition to this presumption we have the uncontested affidavits of a non-interested third party who was in a position to be aware of the actual wording of the change. The affiant, Mr. Harold Burks, was a fellow employee of Mr. Cordner in Libya, and supervised Mr. Cordner in filling out the required change of beneficiary forms. Mr. Burks is probably the only person that was in a position to be aware of the wording of the document. His affidavits are entitled to considerable weight in determining the merits of a summary judgment motion, especially where there is no indication of any counter-evidence. Moreover, Mr. Burks' assistance in processing the change in beneficiary was done in the regular course of business of Socony, and pursuant to his assigned duties. It has been held that the clear affidavits from the only persons in a position to be aware of a factual situation can well serve as the basis for a summary judgment. Dyer v. MacDougall, 201 F.2d 265 (2 Cir.1952).

* * *

So, in support of intervener's claim there is undisputed proof that Mr. Cordner had manifested an intent to give intervener one-fourth of his insurance proceeds with the balance going into the trust established by his Will. It is likewise clear beyond any shadow of doubt that Mr. Cordner subsequently made a change in his insurance beneficiaries. The logical conclusion is clear. He made the change in accordance with his prior expressed intent. This presumption is supported by the two affidavits of Mr. Burks which recite from direct and positive recollection that the beneficiary changes were copied from Mr. Cordner's letter from his attorney and were in form exactly as alleged by intervener.

In response to the overwhelming documentary evidence supported by affidavits all of which consistently showed that Cordner had requested a change of beneficiary in accordance with his lawyer's letter and his own Last Will and Testament, the plaintiff submitted her own counter-affidavit to the effect that Mr. Cordner was very much interested in the welfare of his first two children (the named beneficiaries) and was aware of the future financial difficulties they would face. No further information was offered. The Court, therefore, was not presented with a situation where it was asked to weigh conflicting affidavits. The problem was only, did the affidavits and exhibits of intervener sustain the necessary burden in order to allow a summary judgment? The trial court felt the burden was sustained, and from the above related facts we agree with the trial court's conclusion. * * *

We are of the opinion that if this information were presented at trial, intervener would be entitled to a directed verdict in her favor, and it has been said that if the information presented entitles one to a directed verdict, a summary judgment is in order. * * * Intervener having made a sufficient showing, it then rests upon the plaintiff to specify at least some evidence which could be produced at trial. * * * Plaintiff apparently is of the opinion that, since she makes a prima facie case by merely introducing the Certificate showing her children as designated beneficiaries, she is entitled to a trial on the issue of (1) whether any change of beneficiary was made, and (2) if so, what changes were actually made. This we do not feel is a correct view of the law.

The counter-affidavit of the plaintiff does not meet the issues raised and supported by the intervener. This leaves no genuine issue as to any material fact, and presents a predicate for a summary judgment under Rule 56(c)* * *.

* * *

The real gravamen of plaintiff's objection is not that there is conflicting evidence but rather that the summary judgment rests upon the affidavits of Harold Burks. His testimony being so vital to intervener's cause, it is asserted that the case should proceed to trial in order that the demeanor of the witness could be observed and his testimony subjected to the test of cross-examination.

In passing on this contention it might be well to make four preliminary observations. First, affiant Burks appears to be an unbiased witness. He has no financial or personal interest in the outcome of this litigation. Second, there is no doubt but what his testimony is competent both in regard to his mental capacity and his being in a position to directly observe the facts related in his affidavits. Third, his participation in the change of beneficiaries was in the regular course of his duties with Socony. Finally, both affidavits are positive, internally consistent, unequivocal, and in full accord with the documentary exhibits. Therefore, even though cross-examination is a trial right which must be carefully protected, in this case, unlike many others there is no obvious advantage to be gained from a cross-examination. If there were, a summary judgment might arguably be improper. But where there is no indication that the affiant was biased, dishonest, mistaken, unaware or unsure of the facts, the cases declaring that cross-examination is necessary when one of the above is present, have no application here. There being no positive showing that this witness's testimony could be impeached or that he might have additional testimony valuable to plaintiff, summary judgment was properly granted. The opposing party cannot as a matter of course force a trial merely in order to cross-examine such an affiant, nor must the Court deny the motion for summary judgment on the basis of a vague supposition that something might turn up at the trial. * * *

There is absolutely no showing that a trial would produce any different or additional evidence. It appears that Burks is now stationed in Singapore, far beyond the subpoena powers of the trial court. Neither party would be able to compel his attendance before the trial court. Since this witness is out of the jurisdiction, any of the parties, on the other hand, would be free to introduce Burks' testimony by use of a deposition. Therefore, in all likelihood Burks would never have to appear in open court. What would plaintiff have to gain by forcing a trial under these circumstances? We feel very little, if anything. A full trial would not give plaintiff an opportunity to cross-examine Burks in open court, nor would it unveil his demeanor to the trier of fact.

In the event of a trial plaintiff would only be free to obtain Burks' sworn testimony by deposition or upon written interrogatories pursuant to Rule 28(b) or Rule 31 * * * and by 28 U.S.C.A. § 1783(a)(1). Plaintiff, however, was free to take this action even prior to the present motion for summary judgment but chose not to do so. When the motion for summary judgment was presented, plaintiff, if she felt Burks had information valuable to her cause, was again free to move for a delay in judgment and secure Burks' deposition. Again plaintiff took no action. Apparently plaintiff felt she had nothing to gain by a deposition, yet under the circumstances of this case that is probably the most she could expect even if this case went to trial. Therefore, we do not feel that plaintiff is in a position at this time to force a trial. A trial would not secure Burks' presence, it would only force the taking of his deposition, a course previously open to plaintiff which she elected not to pursue.

* * *

The position declaring that a party opposed to a summary judgment based upon affidavits must assume some initiative in showing that a factual issue actually exists is perfectly sound in the light of Rule 56 * * *, which specifically allows the use of affidavits in summary judgment proceedings. For if plaintiff's position is correct that an affiant's credibility is always an issue for the trial court, then the granting of a summary judgment would be virtually impossible when it is based in any way upon an affidavit. Rule 56 would be nullified by the prevailing party's use of one affidavit and the bald objection by the opposing party to the affiant's credibility. The reference in this rule to "affidavits" would therefore be of no effect.

This does not mean that an affiant's credibility cannot properly be put in issue by a litigant, but in doing so specific facts must be properly produced. At this point the 1963 amendment to Rule 56(e) comes into play requiring the opposing party to respond or suffer the fate of a summary judgment, if otherwise appropriate. Plaintiff failed to respond to the adequate and substantial showing of intervener, so the trial court properly granted the summary judgment. Keeping in mind that the purpose of the summary judgment is to avoid useless trials, from the circumstances of this case we believe a trial would indeed be a useless waste of time and expense to the parties as well as a needless inconvenience to the Court.

* * *

Judgment affirmed.

Notes and Questions

1. Of what consequence is it that at trial the intervenor would have had the burden of persuading the trier of fact that it was more probable than not that decedent had changed the names of the beneficiaries? Did the appellate court erroneously assume that the burden was on plaintiff to show that the beneficiaries had not been changed? If so, should the decision below have been reversed?

Consider the paragraph in Cal.Code Civ.Proc. § 437c(e), which is set out in the Supplement, dealing with matters of credibility and lack of an opportunity for cross-examination. What is the objective of this paragraph? Should it be added to Federal Rule 56?

2. In DYER v. MacDOUGALL, 201 F.2d 265, 268–69 (2d Cir.1952), plaintiff brought suit for slander; defendant was granted summary judgment on the basis of the affidavits of all the persons present when the slanderous statements allegedly had been made. All of the affidavits denied plaintiff's allegations. The appellate court affirmed:

> * * * [I]f the cause went to trial, the plaintiff would have no witnesses by whom he could prove the slanders alleged * * * except the two defendants, * * * and they would all deny that the slanders had been uttered. On such a showing how could he escape a directed verdict? It is true that the carriage, behavior, bearing, manner and appearance of a witness—in short, his "demeanor"—is a part of the evidence. The words used are by no means all that we rely on in making up our minds about the truth of a question that arises in our ordinary affairs, and it is abundantly settled that a jury is as little confined to them as we are. They may, and indeed they should, take into consideration the whole nexus of sense impressions which they get from a witness. This we have again and again declared, and have rested our affirmance of findings of fact of a judge, or of a jury, on the hypothesis that this part of the evidence may have turned the scale. Moreover, such evidence may satisfy the tribunal, not only that the witness' testimony is not true, but that

the truth is the opposite of his story; for the denial of one, who has a motive to deny, may be uttered with such hesitation, discomfort, arrogance or defiance, as to give assurance that he is fabricating, and that, if he is, there is no alternative but to assume the truth of what he denies.

Nevertheless, although it is therefore true that in strict theory a party having the affirmative might succeed in convincing a jury of the truth of his allegations in spite of the fact that all the witnesses denied them, we think it plain that a verdict would nevertheless have to be directed against him. This is owing to the fact that otherwise in such cases there could not be an effective appeal from the judge's disposition of a motion for a directed verdict. He, who has seen and heard the "demeanor" evidence, may have been right or wrong in thinking that it gave rational support to a verdict; yet, since that evidence has disappeared, it will be impossible for an appellate court to say which he was. Thus, he would become the final arbiter in all cases where the evidence of witnesses present in court might be determinative.

3.   For a discussion of the implementation of summary judgment, see Brunet, Redish & Reiter, *Summary Judgment: Federal Law and Practice* (2d ed.2000); Swand, *Summary Judgment Practice,* 46 Baylor L.Rev. 721 (1994).

CROSS v. UNITED STATES

United States Court of Appeals, Second Circuit, 1964.
336 F.2d 431.

MOORE, CIRCUIT JUDGE: In this income tax refund suit, plaintiffs-appellees claim that they were entitled to a deduction of $1,300 on their joint return for the year 1954 because of expenses incurred by Professor Ephraim Cross in connection with his summer travel to various Mediterranean and European countries. Upon appellees' motion for summary judgment, the district court, whose examination of the facts included the affidavits of several professors tending to indicate the desirability of foreign travel for a teacher of languages as well as the pre-trial deposition of Professor Cross, concluded that there was no genuine issue as to any material fact, and granted appellees' motion. * * * The Government opposed the summary judgment procedure, claiming a right to cross-examine appellees as to the nature of their expenses and the educational benefits allegedly sought and also to cross-examine the affiant professors. On this appeal the only issue is whether there are triable issues of fact which render the award of summary judgment erroneous.

In 1954 Professor Cross was an Assistant Professor at City College in New York where he taught French, Spanish and romance linguistics (described by him as the study of the development of Latin into the romance languages, the study of the various dialects and the historic stages of those dialects). He, his wife and a pet dog sailed from New York on June 30, 1954 aboard a French freighter. The ship put in briefly in Portugal, Morocco, Tangiers, Oran, Algiers, Naples and Genoa and appellees spent a day or so in each place. When the freighter arrived at Marseilles, twenty-one days after leaving New York, appellees separated. Mrs. Cross joined a friend and continued touring while Professor Cross and their pet dog travelled to Paris. Although he did not pursue a formal course of study or engage in research, Professor Cross did visit schools, courts of law, churches, book publishers, theaters, motion pictures, restaurants, cafes and other places of amusement, read newspapers, listen to radio broadcasts, converse with students and teachers and attend political meetings. He rejoined his wife in this country on September 23, 1954 after his return aboard a French passenger liner.

Section 162(a), Int.Rev.Code of 1954 permits a deduction for "all the ordinary and necessary expenses paid or incurred * * * in carrying on any trade or business * * *." The Regulations promulgated under that section * * * state:

Expenses for education—(a) Expenditures made by a taxpayer for his education are deductible if they are for education (including research activities) undertaken primarily for the purpose of:

(1) Maintaining or improving skills required by the taxpayer in his employment or trade or business, * * *

* * *

Whether or not education is of the type referred to in subparagraph (1) of this paragraph shall be determined upon the basis of all the facts of each case. If it is customary for other established members of the taxpayer's trade or business to undertake such education, the taxpayer will ordinarily be considered to have undertaken this education for the purposes described in subparagraph (1) of this paragraph.

* * *

(c) In general, a taxpayer's expenditures for travel (including travel while on sabbatical leave) as a form of education shall be considered as primarily personal in nature and therefore not deductible.

Appellees claim, and the district court held, that all of Professor Cross's expenses are deductible. Professor Cross asserted in his deposition, which was taken for discovery purposes and did not include cross-examination,

My purpose [in making the trip] was to maintain my contacts with my foreign languages for the purpose of maintaining and improving my skill as a linguist and teacher of languages, and to make my general teaching more effective, and to extend my contacts with foreign culture which I have to teach in connection with my teaching of foreign languages per se, and this can be done effectively and properly only by going into a foreign language area.

The Government disputes this explanation. It contends that all or at least part of Professor Cross's travel was a vacation and thus a personal living expense for which a deduction is not allowed under Section 162 * * *. Moreover, the Government challenges the amount of the claimed deduction and questions whether any portion of that sum was expended on behalf of Mrs. Cross.

We believe that summary judgment was improvidently granted and that the Government is entitled to a trial at which all the circumstances may be developed for the consideration of the trier of fact. Rule 56(c)* * * permits summary judgment only where "there is no genuine issue as to any material fact," a state of affairs not normally encountered where the problem is whether expenses are ordinary and necessary in carrying on a taxpayer's trade or business. * * * Before travelling expenses can be allowed as deductible, there must be a factual determination of what parts, if any, are to be attributed to vacation travel or to educational advancement.

The essentially factual character of the issue is particularly apparent here, where the ultimate facts were warmly contested. While there was no dispute that Professor Cross was a teacher of languages and that he travelled abroad, many of the facts remain largely within his own knowledge and the Government should have the opportunity to test his credibility on cross-examination. Summary judgment is particularly inappropriate where "the inferences which the parties seek to have drawn deal with questions of motive, intent and subjective feelings and reactions." Empire Electronics Co. v. United States, 311 F.2d 175, 180 (2d Cir.1962) * * *. " 'A judge may not, on a motion for summary judgment, draw fact inferences. * * * Such inferences may be drawn only on a trial.' " Bragen v. Hudson County News Co., 278 F.2d 615, 618 (3d Cir.1960). While we have recently emphasized that ordinarily the bare allegations of the pleadings, unsupported by specific evidentiary data, will not alone defeat a motion for summary judgment, Dressler v. M/V Sandpiper, 331 F.2d 130 (2d Cir.1964), this principle does not justify summary relief where, as here, the disputed questions of fact turn exclusively on the credibility of movants' witnesses.

To the teacher of modern languages, particularly in a country far removed from the European continent, it is highly important that his linguistic ear be returned as frequently as possible to the ways in which a foreign language is expressed. Moreover, a thorough familiarity with the current social, political and cultural climate of a country properly may be regarded as a prerequisite to effective classroom presentation of its language. * * *

On the other hand, a mere pleasure trip through various countries by a professor who has some fluency with the language of each country might well not fall within the deductible category. * * *

Who can doubt that the alert American trial lawyer as a part of a summer vacation might not profit greatly by spending some time at the Old Bailey listening to British barristers exhibit their skills. The surgeon, too, might be benefitted in his profession by observing some delicate operation conducted by a European surgeon of renown. Yet it is questionable whether such tangible evidences of constant interest in one's profession entitle a taxpayer to deduct all his summer vacation expenses.

In addition to determining whether the trip was devoted in whole or in part to educational advancement, the trier of the facts will have to ascertain such amounts as are to be attributed to such purpose. Were the preliminary twenty-one days prior to the Marseilles landing all part of an educational program? What part, if any, was allocable to Mrs. Cross? What charges were incurred by the dog? Although probably *de minimis,* the Treasury frequently watches every penny and might not be generously inclined even though the dog were a French poodle.

The district court reasoned that summary judgment should be granted because the Government did not adduce facts to refute Professor Cross's claims as to the purpose of his trip, and that the Government had an opportunity to cross-examine when taking his deposition. The "right to use depositions for discovery * * * does not mean that they are to supplant the right to call and examine the adverse party * * * before the jury. * * * '[W]e cannot very well overestimate the importance of having the witness examined and cross-examined in presence of the court and jury.' " Arnstein v. Porter, 154 F.2d 464, 470 (2d Cir.1946). By the same process, Professor Cross will have an opportunity to show with greater particularity that his more modern approach to the problem of linguistic improvement is far superior to the old-fashioned classroom lecture method.

Reversed and remanded for trial.

Notes and Questions

1. Can the *Cross* case be reconciled with *Lundeen*? Didn't the court in *Cross* blatantly ignore the express language of Federal Rule 56(e)? Why wasn't the government at least required to cross-examine Professor Cross at the deposition as to the truth of his assertions?

2. Should evidence of "interested witnesses" be considered in support of a motion for summary judgment? Is the credibility of that evidence inherently questionable? For a discussion whether matters of inference and credibility are questions of fact for summary-judgment purposes, see Sonenshine, *State of Mind and Credibility in the Summary Judgment Context: A Better Approach,* 78 Nw. U.L.Rev. 774 (1978); Louis, *Federal Summary Judgment Doctrine: A Critical Analysis,* 83 Yale L.J. 745, 749 (1974).

3. Some courts take the position that summary judgment is inappropriate whenever a person's state of mind is at issue. See Petro v. McCullough, 179 Ind.App. 438, 385 N.E.2d 1195 (1979). Contra, Vern Walton Motors v. Taylor, 121 Ariz. 463, 591 P.2d 555 (App.1978). Does it ever make sense to permit a moving party to use his own affidavit to establish his own intent?

4. What did the court in *Cross* mean when it stated that the trial judge was not entitled to "draw fact inferences"? Could more than a single inference be drawn from the facts presented by plaintiff through affidavits and deposition? For an interesting discussion as to whether matters of inference and credibility are questions of fact for summary-judgment purposes, see Note, *Summary Judgment Under Federal Rule of Civil Procedure 56—A Need for a Clarifying Amendment,* 48 Iowa L.Rev. 453, 461–63, 468–69 (1963).

ADICKES v. S.H. KRESS & CO., 398 U.S. 144, 90 S.Ct. 1598, 26 L.Ed.2d 142 (1970). Adickes, a white female teacher at a "freedom school" for black children, entered Kress's restaurant with six of her black students. The waitress took the children's orders but refused service to Adickes because she was a white person in the company of blacks. The police then arrested Adickes on a charge of vagrancy.

Adickes sued Kress for damages under 42 U.S.C. § 1983. She charged that Kress's refusal to serve her was a state-enforced "custom of the community" that denied her civil rights and that Kress's act and the arrest, taken together, constituted a conspiracy between Kress and the police to violate her constitutional right to equal protection. On the conspiracy count, the complaint alleged that a police officer had been in the restaurant and had seen Adickes and her group before Adickes was denied service, and that, given the officer's presence in the store, there was circumstantial evidence from which a jury could infer a conspiracy between the Kress employee and the police to "set up" the arrest for vagrancy by denying Adickes service.

Kress moved for summary judgment and supplied affidavits from the store manager, the chief of police, and the arresting officers denying the existence of a pre-arranged scheme. Adickes responded by pressing her circumstantial case. She noted the allegation in the complaint that the policeman who arrested her had earlier been in the store. She adduced her sworn deposition testimony that "one of [her] students saw a policeman come in," and she offered an unsworn statement by a Kress employee (given by Kress to Adickes in discovery) stating that the officer who later arrested Adickes outside the restaurant had been in the store before Adickes was refused service. However, since the statements were hearsay assertions (and probably inadmissible at trial), the District Court ruled that Adickes had failed to allege any fact from which a conspiracy might be inferred. And, the Court of Appeals affirmed unanimously. The Supreme Court reversed:

> * * * [W]e conclude that respondent [Kress] failed to fulfill its initial burden of demonstrating what is a critical element in this aspect of the case—that there was no policeman in the store. If a policeman were present, we think it would be open to a jury, in light of the sequence that followed, to infer from the circumstances that the policeman and a Kress employee had a "meeting of the minds" and thus reached an understanding that petitioner should be refused service. Because "[o]n summary judgment the inferences to be drawn from the underlying facts contained in [the moving party's] materials must be viewed in the light most favorable to the party opposing the motion," * * * we think respondent's failure to show there was no policeman in the store requires reversal.

> * * *

> * * * "[W]here the evidentiary matter in support of the motion does not establish the absence of a genuine issue, summary judgment must be denied *even if no opposing evidentiary matter is presented.*" Because respondent did not meet its initial burden of establishing the absence of a policeman in the store, petitioner here was not required to come forward with suitable opposing affidavits.

> If respondent had met its initial burden by, for example, submitting affidavits from the policemen denying their presence in the store at the time in question, Rule 56(e) would then have required petitioner to have done more than simply rely on the contrary allegation in her complaint. To have avoided conceding this fact for purposes of summary judgment, petitioner would have had to come forward with either (1) the affidavit of someone who saw the policeman in the store or (2) an affidavit under Rule 56(f) explaining why at that time it was impractical to do so. Even though not essential here to defeat respondent's motion, the submission of such an affidavit would have been the preferable course for petitioner's counsel to have followed. * * *

Id. at 158–61, 90 S.Ct. at 1609–10, 26 L.Ed.2d at 155–56.

———

GORDILLO, SUMMARY JUDGMENT AND PROBLEMS IN APPLYING THE CELOTEX TRILOGY STANDARD, 42 Clev.St.L.Rev. 263, 263–64 (1994):

In an effort to provide swift justice while respecting due process, the courts have refined a tool that in theory serves this purpose superbly: summary judgment. Unfortunately, swift justice and due process often create conflicting interests. As a result, the tool that appears effective in theory presents significant difficulties when judges must apply it in practice.

In Federal Rule * * * 56 it is stated that summary judgment "shall be rendered forthwith if * * * there is no genuine issue as to any material fact and * * * the moving party is entitled to judgment as a matter of law." Obstacles that judges confront when determining whether a genuine issue of material fact exists, are the subject of this Note. Stated simply, a material fact is one which will affect the outcome of the case, and a material fact raises a genuine issue if a reasonable jury could reach different conclusions concerning that fact.

During its 1986 term, the Supreme Court announced the Celotex trilogy of decisions, articulating precise standards for determining the existence of a genuine issue of material fact. Nevertheless, judges have found the easily understood standard difficult to apply.

CELOTEX CORP. v. CATRETT

Supreme Court of the United States, 1986.
477 U.S. 317, 106 S.Ct. 2548, 91 L.Ed.2d 265.

Certiorari to the United States Court of Appeals for the District of Columbia Circuit.

Justice Rehnquist delivered the opinion of the Court.

* * *

Respondent commenced this lawsuit in September 1980, alleging that the death in 1979 of her husband, Louis H. Catrett, resulted from his exposure to products containing asbestos manufactured or distributed by 15 named corporations. Respondent's complaint sounded in negligence, breach of warranty, and strict liability.

* * *

Petitioner's summary judgment motion, which was first filed in September 1981, argued that summary judgment was proper because respondent had "failed to produce evidence that any [Celotex] product * * * was the proximate cause of the injuries alleged within the jurisdictional limits of [the District] Court." In particular, petitioner noted that respondent had failed to identify, in answering interrogatories specifically requesting such information, any witnesses who could testify about the decedent's exposure to petitioner's asbestos products. In response to petitioner's summary judgment motion, respondent then produced three documents which she claimed "demonstrate that there is a genuine material factual dispute" as to whether the decedent had ever been exposed to petitioner's asbestos products. The three documents included a transcript of a deposition of the decedent, a letter from an official of one of the decedent's former employers whom petitioner planned to call as a trial witness, and a letter from an insurance company to respondent's attorney, all tending to establish that the decedent had been exposed to petitioner's asbestos products in Chicago during 1970–1971. Petitioner, in turn, argued that the three documents were inadmissible hearsay and thus could not be considered in opposition to the summary judgment motion.

In July 1982, almost two years after the commencement of the lawsuit, the District Court granted [the motion] * * * because "there [was] no showing that the plaintiff was exposed to the defendant Celotex's product in the District of Columbia or elsewhere within the statutory period." * * * Respondent appealed * * *. The majority of the Court of Appeals held that petitioner's summary judgment motion was rendered "fatally defective" by the fact that petitioner "made no effort to adduce *any* evidence, in the form of affidavits or otherwise, to support its motion." * * * According to the majority, Rule 56(e) * * *, and this Court's decision in Adickes v. S.H. Kress & Co., * * * establish that "the party opposing the motion for summary judgment bears the burden of responding *only after* the moving party has met its burden of coming forward with proof of the absence of any genuine issues of material fact." * * * The majority therefore declined to consider petitioner's argument that none of the evidence produced by respondent in opposition to the motion for summary judgment would have been admissible at trial. * * *

We think that the position taken by the majority of the Court of Appeals is inconsistent with the standard for summary judgment set forth in Rule 56(c)* * *. In our view, the plain language of Rule 56(c) mandates the entry of summary judgment, after adequate time for discovery and upon motion, against a party who fails to make a showing sufficient to establish the existence of an element essential to that party's case, and on which that party will bear the burden of proof at trial. * * *

Of course, a party seeking summary judgment always bears the initial responsibility of informing the district court of the basis for its motion, and identifying those portions of "the pleadings, depositions, answers to interrogatories, and admissions on file, together with the affidavits, if any," which it believes demonstrate the absence of a genuine issue of material fact. But unlike the Court of Appeals, we find no express or implied requirement in Rule 56 that the moving party support its motion with affidavits or other similar materials *negating* the opponent's claim. On the contrary, Rule 56(c), which refers to "the affidavits, *if any*" (emphasis added), suggests the absence of such a requirement. And if there were any doubt about the meaning of Rule 56(c) in this regard, such doubt is clearly removed by Rules 56(a) and (b), which provide that claimants and defendants, respectively, may move for summary judgment *"with or without supporting affidavits"* (emphasis added). The import of these subsections is that, regardless of whether the moving party accompanies its summary judgment motion with affidavits, the motion may, and should, be granted so long as whatever is before the district court demonstrates that the standard for the entry of summary judgment, as set forth in Rule 56(c), is satisfied. One of the principal purposes of the summary judgment rule is to isolate and dispose of factually unsupported claims or defenses, and we think it should be interpreted in a way that allows it to accomplish this purpose.

Respondent argues, however, that Rule 56(e), by its terms, places on the nonmoving party the burden of coming forward with rebuttal affidavits, or other specified kinds of materials, only in response to a motion for summary judgment "made and supported as provided in this rule." According to respondent's argument, since petitioner did not "support" its motion with affidavits, summary judgment was improper in this case. But as we have already explained, a motion for summary judgment may be made pursuant to Rule 56 "with or without supporting affidavits." In cases like the instant one, where the nonmoving party will bear the burden of proof at trial on a dispositive issue, a summary judgment motion may properly be made in reliance solely on the "pleadings, depositions, answers to interrogatories, and admissions on file." Such a motion, whether or not accompanied by affidavits, will be "made and supported as provided in this rule," and Rule 56(e) therefore requires the nonmoving party to go beyond the pleadings and by her own affidavits, or by the "depositions, answers to interrogatories, and admissions on file," designate "specific facts showing that there is a genuine issue for trial." * * *

The Court of Appeals in this case felt itself constrained, however, by language in our decision in Adickes v. S.H. Kress & Co. * * *. In the course of its opinion, the *Adickes* Court said that "both the commentary on and the background of the 1963 Amendment conclusively show that it was not intended to modify the burden of the moving party * * * to show initially the absence of a genuine issue concerning any material fact." * * * We think that this statement is accurate in a literal sense, since we fully agree with the *Adickes* Court that the 1963 Amendment to Rule 56(e) was not designed to modify the burden of making the showing generally required by Rule 56(c). It also appears to us that, on the basis of the showing before the Court in *Adickes,* the motion for summary judgment in that case should have been denied. But we do not think the *Adickes* language quoted above should be construed to mean that the burden is on the party moving for summary judgment to produce evidence showing the absence of a genuine issue of material fact, even with respect to an issue on which the nonmoving party bears the burden of proof. Instead, as we have explained, the burden on the moving party may be discharged by "showing"—that is, pointing out to the District Court—that there is an absence of evidence to support the nonmoving party's case.

The last two sentences of Rule 56(e) were added, as this Court indicated in *Adickes,* to disapprove a line of cases allowing a party opposing summary judgment to resist a properly made motion by reference only to its pleadings. While the *Adickes* Court was undoubtedly correct in concluding that these two sentences were not intended to *reduce* the burden of the moving party, it is also obvious that they were not adopted to *add to* that burden. Yet that is exactly the result which the reasoning of the Court of Appeals would produce; in effect, an amendment to Rule 56(e) designed to *facilitate* the granting of motions for summary judgment would be interpreted to make it *more difficult* to grant such motions. Nothing in the two sentences themselves requires this result, for the reasons we have previously indicated, and we now put to rest any inference that they do so.

* * *

Respondent commenced this action in September 1980, and petitioner's motion was filed in September 1981. The parties had conducted discovery, and no serious claim can be made that respondent was in any sense "railroaded" by a premature motion for summary judgment. Any potential problem with such premature motions can be adequately dealt with under Rule 56(f), which allows a summary judgment motion to be denied, or the hearing on the motion to be continued, if the nonmoving party has not had an opportunity to make full discovery.

In this Court, respondent's brief and oral argument have been devoted as much to the proposition that an adequate showing of exposure to petitioner's asbestos products was made as to the proposition that no such showing should have been required. But the Court of Appeals declined to address either the adequacy of the showing made by respondent in opposition to petitioner's motion for summary judgment, or the question whether such a showing, if reduced to admissible evidence, would be sufficient to carry respondent's burden of proof at trial. We think the Court of Appeals with its superior knowledge of local law is better suited than we are to make these determinations in the first instance.

The Federal Rules of Civil Procedure have for more than 50 years authorized motions for summary judgment upon proper showings of the lack of a genuine, triable issue of material fact. Summary judgment procedure is properly regarded not as a disfavored procedural shortcut, but rather as an integral part of the Federal Rules as a whole, which are designed "to secure the just, speedy and inexpensive determination of every action." * * * Before the shift to "notice pleading" accomplished by the Federal Rules, motions to dismiss a complaint or to strike a defense were the principal tools by which factually insufficient claims or defenses could be isolated and prevented from going to trial with the attendant unwarranted consumption of public and private resources. But with the advent of "notice pleading," the motion to dismiss seldom fulfills this function any more, and its place has been taken by the motion for summary judgment. Rule 56 must be construed with due regard not only for the rights of persons asserting claims and defenses that are adequately based in fact to have those claims and defenses tried to a jury, but also for the rights of persons opposing such claims and defenses to demonstrate in the manner provided by the Rule, prior to trial, that the claims and defenses have no factual basis.

The judgment of the Court of Appeals is accordingly reversed, and the case is remanded for further proceedings consistent with this opinion.

It is so ordered.

JUSTICE WHITE, concurring.

I agree that the Court of Appeals was wrong in holding that the moving defendant must always support his motion with evidence or affidavits showing the absence of a genuine dispute about a material fact. I also agree that the movant may rely on depositions, answers to interrogatories and the like to demonstrate that the plaintiff has no evidence to prove his case and hence that there can be no factual dispute. But the movant must discharge the burden the rules place upon him: It is not enough to move for summary judgment without supporting the motion in any way or with a conclusory assertion that the plaintiff has no evidence to prove his case.

* * *

Petitioner Celotex does not dispute that if respondent has named a witness to support her claim, summary judgment should not be granted without Celotex somehow showing that the named witness' possible testimony raises no genuine issue of material fact. * * * It asserts, however, that respondent has failed on request to produce any basis for her case. Respondent, on the other hand, does not contend that she was not obligated to reveal her witnesses and evidence but insists that she has revealed enough to defeat the motion for summary judgment. Because the Court of Appeals found it unnecessary to address this aspect of the case, I agree that the case should be remanded for further proceedings.

JUSTICE BRENNAN, with whom THE CHIEF JUSTICE and JUSTICE BLACKMUN join, dissenting.

This case requires the Court to determine whether Celotex satisfied its initial burden of production in moving for summary judgment on the ground that the plaintiff lacked evidence to establish an essential element of her case at trial. I do not disagree with the Court's legal analysis. The Court clearly rejects the ruling of the Court of Appeals that the defendant must provide affirmative evidence disproving the plaintiff's case. Beyond this, however, the Court has not clearly explained what is required of a moving party seeking summary judgment on the ground that the non-moving party cannot prove its case. This lack of clarity is unfortunate: district courts must routinely decide summary judgment motions, and the Court's opinion will very likely create confusion. For this reason, even if I agreed with the Court's result, I would have written separately to explain more clearly the law in this area. However, because I believe that Celotex did not meet its burden of production under Federal Rule * * * 56, I respectfully dissent from the Court's judgment.

I

* * * The burden of establishing the nonexistence of a "genuine issue" is on the party moving for summary judgment. * * * This burden has two distinct components: an initial burden of production, which shifts to the nonmoving party if satisfied by the moving party; and an ultimate burden of persuasion, which always remains on the moving party. * * * The court need not decide whether the moving party has satisfied its ultimate burden of persuasion unless and until the court finds that the moving party has discharged its initial burden of production.

* * *

The manner in which this showing can be made depends upon which party will bear the burden of persuasion on the challenged claim at trial. If the *moving* party will bear the burden of persuasion at trial that party must support its motion with credible evidence—using any of the material specified in Rule 56(c)—that would entitle it to a directed verdict if not controverted at trial. * * * Such an affirmative showing shifts the burden of production to the party opposing the motion and requires that party either to produce evidentiary materials that demonstrate the existence of a "genuine issue" for trial or to submit an affidavit requesting additional time for discovery. * * *

If the burden of persuasion at trial would be on the *non-moving* party, the party moving for summary judgment may satisfy Rule 56's burden of production in either of two ways. First, the moving party may submit affirmative evidence that negates an essential element of the nonmoving party's claim. Second, the moving party may demonstrate to the Court that the nonmoving party's evidence is insufficient to establish an essential element of the nonmoving party's claim. * * * If the nonmoving party cannot muster sufficient evidence to make out its claim, a trial would be useless and the moving party is entitled to summary judgment as a matter of law. * * *

Where the moving party adopts this second option and seeks summary judgment on the ground that the nonmoving party—who will bear the burden of persuasion at trial—has no evidence, the mechanics of discharging Rule 56's burden of production are somewhat trickier. Plainly, a conclusory assertion that the nonmoving party has no evidence is insufficient. * * * Such a "burden" of production is no burden at all and would simply permit summary judgment procedure to be converted into a tool for harassment. * * * Rather, as the Court confirms, a party who moves for summary judgment on the ground that the nonmoving party has no evidence must affirmatively show the absence of evidence in the record. * * * This may require the moving party to depose the nonmoving party's witnesses or to establish the inadequacy of documentary evidence. If there is literally no evidence in the record, the moving party may demonstrate this by reviewing for the court the admissions, interrogatories and other exchanges between the parties that are in the record. Either way, however, the moving party must affirmatively demonstrate that there is no evidence in the record to support a judgment for the nonmoving party.

If the moving party has not fully discharged this initial burden of production, its motion for summary judgment must be denied, and the Court need not consider whether the moving party has met its ultimate burden of persuasion. Accordingly, the nonmoving party may defeat a motion for summary judgment that asserts that the nonmoving party has no evidence by calling the Court's attention to supporting evidence already in the record that was overlooked or ignored by the moving party.

* * *

II

I do not read the Court's opinion to say anything inconsistent with or different than the preceding discussion. My disagreement with the Court concerns the application of these principles to the facts of this case.

* * *

On these facts, there is simply no question that Celotex failed to discharge its initial burden of production. Having chosen to base its motion on the argument that there was no evidence in the record to support plaintiff's claim, Celotex was not free to ignore supporting evidence that the record clearly contained. Rather, Celotex was required, as an initial matter, to attack the adequacy of this evidence. Celotex' failure to fulfill this simple requirement constituted a failure to discharge its initial burden of production under Rule 56, and thereby rendered summary judgment improper.

* * *

[A dissenting opinion by JUSTICE STEVENS is omitted.]

Notes and Questions

1.   On remand to the Court of Appeals, a divided panel found that the plaintiff had produced sufficient evidence of exposure and, therefore, that summary judgment was still inappropriate. Catrett v. Johns–Manville Sales Corp., 826 F.2d 33 (D.C.Cir.1987), certiorari denied 484 U.S. 1066, 108 S.Ct. 1028, 98 L.Ed.2d 992 (1988). The majority opinion on remand described the three documents on which plaintiff Catrett based her argument—a transcript of Louis Catrett's testimony in a workmen's compensation claim, in which he indicated his exposure to a product called "Firebar" while working for a company named Anning–Johnson; the letter from T.R. Hoff, the Assistant Secretary of Anning–Johnson, to an Aetna insurance agent reporting on Mr. Catrett's employment with Anning–Johnson; and a letter from the Aetna agent to Mrs. Catrett's counsel essentially restating the contents of Hoff's letter. Catrett argued that, since Celotex supplied the asbestos used by Anning–Johnson, all three documents tended to establish exposure to defendant's product. Celotex countered that the three documents were inadmissible hearsay, out-of-court statements that are inadmissible at trial, and thus should not be considered on the summary-judgment motion. Judge Starr, writing for the majority, stated:

> In the circumstances of this case, we believe that the Hoff letter [a potentially damning piece of evidence] should be considered. The inadmissibility of the letter, despite Celotex's contention to the contrary, is by no means obvious (although we need not and do not pass judgment on its admissibility). Mrs. Catrett argues that the letter is admissible * * * as falling within the business records exception to the hearsay rule. See Fed.R.Evid. 803(6). *More importantly, Celotex never objected to the District Court's consideration of the Hoff letter.* * * * Since it is well established that "inadmissible documents may be considered by the court if not challenged [at trial]," * * * we are satisfied that the Hoff letter is properly (at this stage) to be considered in assessing whether a genuine issue of fact exists.

> [Moreover, i]n her supplemental interrogatory responses, Mrs. Catrett listed Hoff as a witness. There can, of course, be no doubt that this response is properly considered in ruling on a summary judgment motion. * * * Taking this response together with the Hoff letter, the record, dispassionately viewed, reflects the existence of a witness who can testify with respect to Mr. Catrett's exposure to Firebar. Thus, even if the Hoff letter itself would not be admissible at trial, Mrs. Catrett has gone on to indicate that the substance of the letter is reducible to admissible evidence in the form of trial testimony. * * *

Id. at 37–38 (emphasis in original).

Judge Bork, in dissent, wrote:

> * * * [P]laintiff has not identified "specific facts" that would indicate such exposure occurred, and I certainly think that plaintiff has not made the

kind of showing necessary to defeat a directed verdict motion. I would therefore grant defendant's motion for summary judgment.

* * * [T]he mere listing of a potential witness, without more, does not constitute setting forth specific facts. Here plaintiff has never claimed that Mr. Hoff has any personal knowledge that her husband was exposed to asbestos during his year of work at this company, and indeed did not specify the grounds of his possible testimony at all, except to say that he would be able to testify about "facts relevant to the subject matter of this lawsuit." * * * On the other hand, plaintiff has failed ever to answer interrogatories served by defendant that asked for a variety of specific items of information she might have about her husband's possible exposure to asbestos on any occasion. * * *

The majority concludes, however, that we should interpret plaintiff's listing of Mr. Hoff as a witness in light of his letter to the insurance company, thereby finding enough evidence to stave off the equivalent of a motion for directed verdict on causation. This conclusion is incorrect for two reasons. First, the sum total of all this "evidence" falls far short of showing, or even suggesting, that anyone has been identified who can testify from personal knowledge about any asbestos exposure. That lack alone requires that defendant's motion for summary judgment be granted.

In addition, and also dispositive, the letter itself is inadmissible as evidence and thus cannot be considered by this court in evaluating the summary judgment motion. * * * It is settled law that the judge may consider only these specific materials or other evidence that would be admissible at trial. Inadmissible evidence is not to be considered unless, like an affidavit, it is "otherwise provided for" in Rule 56.

Id. at 41.

2. Examine the language of Federal Rule 56(e) and Cal.Code Civ.Proc. § 437c(d), which accompanies the text of the Federal Rule in the Supplement, dealing with the character and content of the affidavits required to support or oppose a summary-judgment motion. Should a federal court, in ruling upon a summary-judgment motion, be required to disregard completely all affidavits containing only hearsay or other matters to which the affiant would not be permitted to testify at trial? Compare Joseph F. Trionfo & Sons, Inc. v. Board of Educ., 41 Md.App. 103, 395 A.2d 1207 (1979) (fact "conclusions" must be ignored).

Suppose A and B were killed in an automobile accident, and A's executor brings suit against B's executor alleging wrongful death. Plaintiff moves for summary judgment on the basis of a deposition of an impartial eyewitness who testified that B drove through a red light. Defendant counters with an affidavit of a police officer who avers that at the scene, shortly after the accident, another impartial eyewitness, now deceased, informed the officer that it was A rather than B who had disobeyed the traffic signal. Should any attention be paid to defendant's affidavit? Should a different test be applied to affidavits on a summary-judgment motion in a case that will be tried by a court than in one that will be heard by a jury?

3. For a helpful discussion of *Celotex,* see Kennedy, *Federal Summary Judgment: Reconciling Celotex v. Catrett with Adickes v. Kress and the Evidentiary Problems Under Rule 56,* 6 Rev. Litigation 227 (1987); Nelken, *One Step*

Forward, Two Steps Back: Summary Judgment After Celotex, 40 Hastings L.J. 53 (1988).

———

KALIS v. COLGATE–PALMOLIVE CO., 231 F.3d 1049 (7th Cir.2000). Plaintiff brought suit against Colgate due to injuries received when a container of liquid fondue fuel exploded. The action was filed ten years after the incident occurred. The container had been purchased by plaintiff's mother. In response to interrogatories, plaintiff was unable to provide any evidence that the fuel was manufactured by Colgate. Her mother, on deposition, testified that she could not recall any type of brand name or warnings on the container or other specific facts that would identify its manufacturer and she did not believe that anything could refresh her memory. In addition, plaintiff failed to respond to a set of requests to admit asking her to admit that she had no knowledge of any written representations on the container. The latter were deemed admitted. On the basis of this information Colgate moved for summary judgment. Subsequently, however, after the period for discovery had passed, plaintiff's mother signed an affidavit stating that her memory had been refreshed by photographs of containers of fuel, including a brand name, that she now recognized matched the container that had exploded. The containers of fuel in the photographs apparently had been manufactured by defendant. Along with her mother's affidavit, plaintiff filed amended answers to her interrogatories and provided belated responses to the requests to admit. She also moved to reopen discovery so as to obtain further information.

The trial court struck these submissions, refused further discovery, and granted summary judgment for the defendant. The Court of Appeals affirmed on the basis that the trial court had not abused its discretion. The appeals court held that as a general rule a party cannot create an issue of fact by submitting an affidavit of a witness in direct conflict with that witness' prior sworn testimony. Moreover, with regard to the requests to admit, it upheld the trial court because plaintiff had failed to move under Rule 36(b) to withdraw or amend the admissions. The court also noted that plaintiff had failed to provide any reason why she needed more time for investigation, given that she already had had two and one-half years for discovery.

Notes & Questions

1. Was the decision of the court to ignore the mother's affidavit valid? Why shouldn't a jury determine which version of her statements is true after listening to her testimony on the witness stand? Was the appeals court correct in holding that its standard of review was whether the trial court abused its discretion, or should it have decided de novo whether the evidence was sufficient to avoid summary judgment? Is the decision consistent with the ultimate result in *Celotex?* Compare Bass v. City of Sioux Falls, 232 F.3d 615 (8th Cir.1999).

2. For an analysis of the differences between stated rules regarding the evidence to be considered and evaluated on a motion for summary judgment and what courts in fact consider and do, see Duane, *The Four Greatest Myths About Summary Judgment,* 52 Wash. & Lee L.Rev. 1523 (1996).

ANDERSON v. LIBERTY LOBBY, INC.

Supreme Court of the United States, 1986.
477 U.S. 242, 106 S.Ct. 2505, 91 L.Ed.2d 202.

[Willis Carto, a right-wing publisher, and Liberty Lobby, the organization he headed, filed a libel suit against *The Investigator* magazine, its president and its publisher, columnist Jack Anderson, for articles that portrayed plaintiffs as neo-Nazi, anti-Semitic, racist, and fascist. Following discovery, defendants moved for summary judgment on the ground that plaintiffs could not prove by clear and convincing evidence that defendants acted with actual malice—with knowledge that the statements were false or with reckless disregard of whether they were true or false—the standard required by New York Times Co. v. Sullivan, 376 U.S. 254, 84 S.Ct. 710, 11 L.Ed.2d 686 (1964), and its progeny for libel suits brought by public figures. In support of the motion, defendants submitted an affidavit from Charles Bermant, the employee who had written the allegedly libelous articles, that stated that he had spent a substantial amount of time researching and writing the articles. His affidavit also detailed the sources for each of the statements in the article, and affirmed that he believed the facts he reported to be true. Plaintiffs responded to the motion by pointing to numerous claimed inaccuracies in the articles. On the issue of malice, plaintiffs showed that one of Bermant's sources was a twelve-year-old article published in *Time* magazine that had been the subject of an earlier libel suit by plaintiff, which resulted in a settlement under which *Time* paid Carto a sum of money and published a favorable article about Liberty Lobby, and that one of the co-authors of the *Time* article was an editor of *The Investigator*. Plaintiffs also showed that another source was a free-lance journalist whom Bermant never met and who was not asked to, and never identified, his sources. Finally, they showed that another editor of *The Investigator* had told the magazine's president that the articles were "terrible" and "ridiculous."

The District Court granted the motion for summary judgment. The Court of Appeals reversed as to some of the allegedly defamatory statements, holding that "a jury could reasonably conclude that the * * * allegations were defamatory, false, and made with actual malice." The Court of Appeals ruled that it was irrelevant on a motion for summary judgment that the standard for proving actual malice was clear and convincing evidence, rather than a preponderance of evidence.]

Certiorari to the United States Court of Appeals for the District of Columbia Circuit.

Justice White delivered the opinion of the Court.

* * *

II

A

Our inquiry is whether the Court of Appeals erred in holding that the heightened evidentiary requirements that apply to proof of actual malice in this *New York Times* case need not be considered for the purposes of a motion for summary judgment. * * * By its very terms, [Rule 56(c)] provides that the mere existence of *some* alleged factual dispute between the parties will not defeat an otherwise properly supported motion for summary judgment; the requirement is that there be no *genuine* issue of *material* fact.

As to materiality, the substantive law will identify which facts are material. Only disputes over facts that might affect the outcome of the suit under the governing law will properly preclude the entry of summary judgment. Factual disputes that are irrelevant or unnecessary will not be counted. * * *

More important for present purposes, summary judgment will not lie if the dispute about a material fact is "genuine," that is, if the evidence is such that a reasonable jury could return a verdict for the nonmoving party. * * *

Our prior decisions may not have uniformly recited the same language in describing genuine factual issues under Rule 56, but is clear enough from our recent cases that at the summary judgment stage the judge's function is not himself to weigh the evidence and determine the truth of the matter but to determine whether there is a genuine issue for trial. As [the cases] indicate, there is no issue for trial unless there is sufficient evidence favoring the nonmoving party for a jury to return a verdict for that party. * * * If the evidence is merely colorable, * * * or is not significantly probative, * * * summary judgment may be granted.

That this is the proper focus of the inquiry is strongly suggested by the Rule itself. Rule 56(d) provides that, when a properly supported motion for summary judgment is made, the adverse party "must set forth specific facts showing that there is a genuine issue for trial." And, as we noted above, Rule 56(c) provides that the trial judge shall then grant summary judgment if there is no genuine issue as to any material fact and if the moving party is entitled to judgment as a matter of law. There is no requirement that the trial judge make findings of fact. The inquiry performed is the threshold inquiry of determining whether there is the need for a trial—whether, in other words, there are any genuine factual issues that properly can be resolved only by a finder of fact because they may reasonably be resolved in favor of either party.

The petitioners suggest, and we agree, that this standard mirrors the standard for a directed verdict under Federal Rule * * * 50(a), which is that the trial judge must direct a verdict if, under the governing law, there can be but one reasonable conclusion as to the verdict. * * * If reasonable minds could differ as to the import of the evidence, however, a verdict should not be directed. * * * As the Court long ago said in Improvement Co. v. Munson, 14 Wall. 442, 448, 20 L.Ed. 867 (1872), and has several times repeated:

> Nor are judges any longer required to submit a question to a jury merely because some evidence has been introduced by the party having the burden of proof, unless the evidence be of such a character that it would warrant the jury in finding a verdict in favor of that party. Formerly it was held that if there was what is called a *scintilla* of evidence in support of a case the judge was bound to leave it to the jury, but recent decisions of high authority have established a more reasonable rule, that in every case, before the evidence is left to the jury, there is a preliminary question for the judge, not whether there is literally no evidence, but whether there is any upon which a jury could properly

proceed to find a verdict for the party producing it, upon whom the *onus* of proof is imposed. * * *

* * *

The Court has said that summary judgment should be granted where the evidence is such that it "would require a directed verdict for the moving party." Sartor v. Arkansas Gas Corp., 321 U.S. 620, 624, 64 S.Ct. 724, 727, 88 L.Ed. 967 (1944). And we have noted that the "genuine issue" summary judgment standard is "very close" to the "reasonable jury" directed verdict standard: "The primary difference between the two motions is procedural; summary judgment motions are usually made before trial and decided on documentary evidence, while directed verdict motions are made at trial and decided on the evidence that has been admitted." Bill Johnson's Restaurants, Inc. v. NLRB, 461 U.S. 731, 745, n. 11, 103 S.Ct. 2161, 2171, n. 11, 76 L.Ed.2d 277 (1983). In essence, though, the inquiry under each is the same: whether the evidence presents a sufficient disagreement to require submission to a jury or whether it is so one-sided that one party must prevail as a matter of law.

B

Progressing to the specific issue in this case, we are convinced that the inquiry involved in a ruling on a motion for summary judgment or for a directed verdict necessarily implicates the substantive evidentiary standard of proof that would apply at the trial on the merits. If the defendant in a run-of-the-mill civil case moves for summary judgment or for a directed verdict based on the lack of proof of a material fact, the judge must ask himself not whether he thinks the evidence unmistakably favors one side or the other but whether a fair-minded jury could return a verdict for the plaintiff on the evidence presented. The mere existence of a scintilla of evidence in support of the plaintiff's position will be insufficient; there must be evidence on which the jury could reasonably find for the plaintiff. The judge's inquiry, therefore, unavoidably asks whether reasonable jurors could find by a preponderance of the evidence that the plaintiff is entitled to a verdict—"whether there is [evidence] upon which a jury can properly proceed to find a verdict for the party producing it, upon whom the *onus* of proof is imposed." *Munson,* supra, 14 Wall., at 448.

* * * [W]here the First Amendment mandates a "clear and convincing" standard, the trial judge in disposing of a directed verdict motion should consider whether a reasonable factfinder could conclude, for example, that the plaintiff had shown actual malice with convincing clarity.

* * * [Similarly], it is relevant in ruling on a motion for summary judgment. When determining if a genuine factual issue as to actual malice exists in a libel suit brought by a public figure, a trial judge must bear in mind the actual quantum and quality of proof necessary to support liability under *New York Times.* For example, there is no genuine issue if the evidence presented in the opposing affidavits is of insufficient caliber or quantity to allow a rational finder of fact to find actual malice by clear and convincing evidence.

Thus, in ruling on a motion for summary judgment, the judge must view the evidence presented through the prism of the substantive evidentiary burden. This conclusion is mandated by the nature of this determination. The question here is whether a jury could reasonably find *either* that the plaintiff proved his case by the quality and quantity of evidence required by the governing law *or* that he did not. Whether a jury could reasonably find for either party, however, cannot be defined except by the criteria governing what evidence would enable the jury to find for either the plaintiff or the defendant: It makes no sense to say that a jury could reasonably find for either party without some benchmark as to what standards govern its deliberations and within what boundaries its ultimate decision must fall, and these standards and boundaries are in fact provided by the applicable evidentiary standards.

Our holding that the clear-and-convincing standard of proof should be taken into account in ruling on summary judgment motions does not denigrate the role of the jury. It by no means authorizes trial on affidavits. Credibility determinations, the weighing of the evidence, and the drawing of legitimate inferences from the facts are jury functions, not those of a judge, whether he is ruling on a motion for summary judgment or for a directed verdict. The evidence of the non-movant is to be believed, and all justifiable inferences are to be drawn in his favor. * * * Neither do we suggest that the trial courts should act other than with caution in granting summary judgment or that the trial court may not deny summary judgment in a case where there is reason to believe that the better course would be to proceed to a full trial. * * *

In sum, we conclude that the determination of whether a given factual dispute requires submission to a jury must be guided by the substantive evidentiary standards that apply to the case. This is true at both the directed verdict and summary judgment stages. Consequently, where the *New York Times* "clear and convincing" evidence requirement applies, the trial judge's summary judgment inquiry as to whether a genuine issue exists will be whether the evidence presented is such that a jury applying that evidentiary standard could reasonably find for either the plaintiff or the defendant. Thus, where the factual dispute concerns actual malice, clearly a material issue in a *New York Times* case, the appropriate summary judgment question will be whether the evidence in the record could support a reasonable jury finding either that the plaintiff has shown actual malice by clear and convincing evidence or that the plaintiff has not.

III

Respondents argue, however, that whatever may be true of the applicability of the "clear and convincing" standard at the summary judgment or directed verdict stage, the defendant should seldom if ever be granted summary judgment where his state of mind is at issue and the jury might disbelieve him or his witnesses as to this issue. * * * We do not understand * * *, however, * * * that a plaintiff may defeat a defendant's properly supported motion for summary judgment in a conspiracy or libel case, for example, without offering any concrete evidence from which a reasonable juror could return a verdict in his favor and by merely asserting that the jury might, and legally could, disbelieve the defendant's denial of a conspiracy or of legal malice. The movant has the burden of showing that there is no genuine issue of fact, but the plaintiff is not thereby relieved of his own burden of producing in turn evidence that would support a jury verdict. * * * We repeat, however, that the plaintiff, to survive the defendant's motion, need only present evidence from which a jury might return a verdict in his favor. If he does so, there is a genuine issue of fact that requires a trial.

IV

In sum, a court ruling on a motion for summary judgment must be guided by the *New York Times* "clear and convincing" evidentiary standard in determining whether a genuine issue of actual malice exists—that is, whether the evidence presented is such that a reasonable jury might find that actual malice had been shown with convincing clarity. Because the Court of Appeals did not apply the correct standard in reviewing the District Court's grant of summary judgment, we vacate its decision and remand the case for further proceedings consistent with this opinion.

It is so ordered.

JUSTICE BRENNAN, dissenting.

* * * This case is about a trial court's responsibility when considering a motion for summary judgment, but in my view, the Court, while instructing the trial judge to "consider" heightened evidentiary standards, fails to explain what that means. In other words, how does a judge assess how one-sided evidence is, or what a "fair-minded" jury could "reasonably" decide? The Court provides conflicting clues to these mysteries, which I fear can lead only to increased confusion in the district and appellate courts.

The Court's opinion is replete with boilerplate language to the effect that trial courts are not to weigh evidence when deciding summary judgment motions * * *.

But the Court's opinion is also full of language which could surely be understood as an invitation—if not an instruction—to trial courts to assess and weigh evidence much as a juror would * * *.

I simply cannot square the direction that the judge "is not himself to weigh the evidence" with the direction that the judge also bear in mind the "quantum" of proof required and consider whether the evidence is of sufficient "caliber or quality" to meet that "quantum." I would have thought that a determination of the "caliber and quality," i.e., the importance and value, of the evidence in light of the "quantum," i.e., amount required could *only* be performed by weighing the evidence.

If in fact, this is what the Court would, under today's decision, require of district courts, then I am fearful that this new rule—for this surely would be a brand new procedure—will transform what is meant to provide an expedited "summary" procedure into a full blown paper trial on the merits. It is hard for me to imagine that a responsible counsel, aware that the judge will be assessing the "quantum" of the evidence he is presenting, will risk either moving for or responding to a summary judgment motion without coming forth with *all* of the evidence he can muster in support of his client's case. Moreover, if the judge on motion for summary judgment really is to weigh the evidence, then in my view grave concerns are raised concerning the constitutional right of civil litigants to a jury trial.

It may well be, as JUSTICE REHNQUIST suggests * * *, that the Court's decision today will be of little practical effect. I, for one, cannot imagine a case in which a judge might plausibly hold that the evidence on motion for summary judgment was sufficient to enable a plaintiff bearing a mere preponderance burden to get to the jury—i.e., that a *prima facie* case had been made out—but insufficient for a plaintiff bearing a clear and convincing burden to withstand a defendant's summary judgment motion. Imagine a suit for breach of contract. If, for example, the defendant moves for summary judgment and produces one purported eyewitness who states that he was present at the time the parties discussed the possibility of an agreement, and unequivocally denies that the parties ever agreed to enter into a contract, while the plaintiff produces one purported eyewitness who asserts that the parties did in fact come to terms, presumably that case would go to the jury. But if the defendant produced not one, but 100 eyewitnesses, while the plaintiff stuck with his single witness, would that case, under the Court's holding, still go to the jury? After all, although the plaintiff's burden in this hypothetical contract action is to prove his case by a mere preponderance of the evidence, the judge, so the Court tells us, is to "ask himself * * * whether a fair minded jury could return a verdict for the plaintiff on the evidence presented." * * * Is there, in this hypothetical example, "a sufficient disagreement to require submission to a jury," or is the evidence "so one-sided that one party must prevail as a matter of law"? * * * Would the result change if the plaintiff's one witness were now shown to be a convicted perjurer? Would the result change if, instead of a garden variety contract claim, the plaintiff sued on a fraud theory, thus requiring him to prove his case by clear and convincing evidence? * * *

In my view, if a plaintiff presents evidence which either directly or by permissible inference (and these inferences are a product of the substantive law of the underlying claim) supports all of the elements he needs to prove in order to prevail on his legal claim, the plaintiff has made out a *prima facie* case and a defendant's motion for summary judgment must fail regardless of the burden of proof that the plaintiff must meet. In other words, whether evidence is "clear and convincing," or proves a point by a mere preponderance, is for the factfinder to determine. As I read the case law, this is how it has been, and because of my concern that today's decision may erode the constitutionally enshrined role of the jury, and also undermine the usefulness of summary judgment procedure, this is how I believe it should remain.

JUSTICE REHNQUIST, with whom THE CHIEF JUSTICE joins, dissenting.

* * *

There is a large class of cases in which the higher standard imposed by the court today would seem to have no effect at all * * * if the Court means what it says, when it states: "Credibility determinations * * * are jury functions, not those of a judge, whether he is ruling on a motion for summary judgment or for a directed verdict. The evidence of the nonmovant is to be believed, and all justifiable inferences are to be drawn in his favor." * * *

* * * But if the application of the standards makes no difference in [cases involving credibility determinations], one may fairly ask in what sort of case *does* the difference in standards make a difference in outcome? * * *

Notes and Questions

1. Is *Anderson* consistent with Rule 56 as construed and applied in *Lundeen* and *Cross*?

2. The law distinguishes two types of evidence: direct and indirect. A witness' statement that "I saw the light and it was green" is direct evidence that the light was green. The inferences required to credit the testimony are that the witness is speaking honestly and accurately recalls the incident. A witness' statement that "I saw the car in the next lane go through the intersection without slowing down" is indirect or circumstantial evidence that the light was green, but is also consistent with the conclusion that "the car in the next lane also ran the red light." The inferences required to believe that the light was green depend not only on the assumption that the witness is worthy of belief, but also on some implicit generalizations about how well drivers obey the law and the probability of two drivers simultaneously running a red light. Is it any more or less appropriate for a judge in deciding a summary judgment motion to "weigh" direct evidence than indirect evidence? Does *Anderson* have any application to cases involving conflicts of direct evidence? What kind of evidence is involved in Justice Brennan's breach-of-contract hypothetical?

3. Under a preponderance-of-evidence standard, a jury returns a verdict for plaintiff if it believes that the probability of his claims being true, given the evidence, is above 50%. After *Anderson,* what standard must a judge use in deciding a motion for summary judgment? See Collins, *Summary Judgment and Circumstantial Evidence,* 40 Stan.L.Rev. 491 (1988); Friedenthal, *Cases on Summary Judgment: Has There Been a Material Change in Standards?,* 63 Notre Dame L.Rev. 770 (1988); Risinger, *Another Step in the Counter–Revolution: A Summary Judgment on the Supreme Court's New Approach to Summary Judgment,* 54 Brooklyn L.Rev. 35 (1988).

———

MATSUSHITA ELECTRIC INDUSTRIAL CO. v. ZENITH RADIO CORP., 475 U.S. 574, 106 S.Ct. 1348, 89 L.Ed.2d 538 (1986). Plaintiffs, a group of American television manufacturers, alleged that a group of twenty one Japanese manufacturers and distributors conspired to fix prices in an effort to monopolize the American market. The trial court granted defendant's motion for summary judgment, but the Third Circuit reversed, arguing that certain "direct evidence" of a concert of action among defendants created a "genuine issue for trial." The Supreme Court held that summary judgment was proper:

> * * * The Court of Appeals erred in two respects: (i) the "direct evidence" on which the court relied had little, if any, relevance to the alleged predatory pricing conspiracy; and (ii) the court failed to consider the absence of a plausible motive to engage in predatory pricing.

* * *

* * * [T]he absence of any plausible motive to engage in the conduct charged is highly relevant to whether a "genuine issue for trial" exists within the meaning of Rule 56(e). Lack of motive bears on the range of permissible conclusions that might be drawn from ambiguous evidence: if petitioners had no rational economic motive to conspire, and if their conduct is consistent with other, equally plausible explanations, the conduct does not give rise to an inference of conspiracy. * * * In sum, in light of the absence of any rational motive to conspire, neither petitioner's (respondent's) pricing practices, nor their conduct in the Japanese market, nor their agreements respecting prices and distribution in the American market, suffice to create a "genuine issue for trial." * * *

Id. at 595–96, 106 S.Ct. at 1360–61, 89 L.Ed.2d at 558–59.

———

FRIEDENTHAL, CASES ON SUMMARY JUDGMENT: HAS THERE BEEN A MATERIAL CHANGE IN STANDARDS?, 63 Notre Dame L.Rev. 770, 771, 787 (1988):

* * * [T]hree recent Supreme Court decisions regarding summary judgment * * * appear to signal somewhat of a turn toward greater approval of summary dispositions. However, their ultimate effect is uncertain and could prove to be limited, in part because a number of Justices dissented in each of these cases, and in part because the Court has somewhat of a history of deciding one summary judgment case one way, only to return later with an opinion leaning the other way. * * * It is important to see, whether, in an era of increasing litigation costs and the consequent maneuverings by parties which are more related to their assets than to the strength of their legal arguments, the legal system gives too little credence to a procedural device that has the potential for providing just results in many cases and which could leave judicial resources free to concentrate on those actions for which a trial is required.

* * *

On the whole, courts in the past have been reluctant to analyze sensitive aspects of summary judgment to determine when the granting of a motion is or is not appropriate. The result, in general, has been to deny summary judgment in cases where it should have been granted. The Supreme Court in its opinions in Anderson and Matsushita, as well as in Celotex, has refocussed attention on summary judgment and has made a start on providing a logical framework for deciding how and when it can be used. Unfortunately, none of the decisions are as clear and precise as one would hope; nevertheless, the net effect should be the more widespread granting of summary judgment in those cases in which it is justified.

Notes and Questions

1. Will relaxed standards for summary judgment help to relieve the strain on the judicial system? For a contrary view, see Issacharoff & Loewenstein, *Second Thoughts About Summary Judgment,* 100 Yale L.J. 73 (1990), an economic analysis arguing that summary judgment standards may lead to fewer settlements

prior to litigation, actually increasing the burden on the judicial system. Is it desirable to have more cases disposed of on summary judgment? Issacharoff and Loewenstein think not:

> [S]ummary judgment fundamentally alters the balance of power between plaintiffs and defendants by raising both the costs and risks to plaintiffs in the pretrial phases of litigation while diminishing both for defendants. Even where summary judgment motions are not filed, the potential use of liberalized summary judgment procedures is sufficient to lower the expected value to plaintiffs of settled claims. Therefore, liberalized summary judgment inhibits the filing of otherwise meritorious suits and results in a wealth transfer from plaintiffs as a class to defendants as a class.

Id. at 75.

2.   The distinction between issues of fact, which must be determined by a jury, and issues of law, which may be determined by a judge, also affects a court's determination of a summary judgment motion. See Rosenthal v. Rizzo, 555 F.2d 390 (3d Cir.1977), certiorari denied 434 U.S. 892, 98 S.Ct. 268, 54 L.Ed.2d 178 (1977).

Courts in almost every American jurisdiction adhere to the doctrine that the jury normally decides whether a person's conduct should be characterized as negligence, even when the historic facts are not in dispute. Whether a party has acted as a reasonably prudent person would act under the same or similar circumstances is usually a question of fact for the jury. See, e.g., Gross v. Southern Ry. Co., 414 F.2d 292, 296 (5th Cir.1969). Why is a jury better qualified than a judge to determine whether the conduct in question meets the reasonable person standard? See Weiner, *The Civil Jury Trial and the Law–Fact Distinction*, 54 Calif.L.Rev. 1867 (1966); pp. 1001–08, infra.

3.   Has the Supreme Court departed from the original purpose of Rule 56 in the *Celotex* trilogy and will it ultimately produce less accurate adjudication? See Stempel, *A Distorted Mirror: The Supreme Court's Shimmering View of Summary Judgment, Directed Verdict, and the Adjudication Process*, 49 Ohio St.L.J. 95 (1988).

Partial Summary Judgment

Rules and statutes permitting summary judgment normally provide that in circumstances in which judgment cannot be granted on the entire action, the court at least may withdraw from trial those aspects of the case that are established in the summary-judgment proceeding. See, e.g., Federal Rule 56(d). Furthermore, in a substantial number of jurisdictions the trial court may enter judgment with regard to any single claim that has been fully determined. See, e.g., Federal Rule 54(b). A major question remains, however, whether a party may secure the entry of summary judgment as to part of a claim that has not been fully adjudicated. For example, if plaintiff salesperson alleges that defendant employer owes him five items of back salary, and plaintiff conclusively establishes a right to two of those items, should plaintiff be entitled to a judgment on the amount of the two items in order to collect immediately from defendant? Do Federal Rules 56(a) and 56(b) answer the problem? A number of federal courts have denied relief by reading Rule 56(a) in light of Rule 54(b) or Rule 56(d). What justification, if any, exists for these decisions? See 10B Wright, Miller & Kane, *Federal Practice and Procedure:*

Civil 3d § 2737 (1998); 11 *Moore's Federal Practice* ¶ 56.14 (3d ed.); Comment, *Partial Summary Judgments Under Rule 56(a)*, 32 U.Chi.L.Rev. 816 (1965).

SECTION B. DISMISSAL OF ACTIONS

Read Federal Rule of Civil Procedure 41 and the materials accompanying it in the Supplement.

1. VOLUNTARY DISMISSAL

The voluntary dismissal allows the moving party to extricate himself from the lawsuit without affecting his legal rights before significant judicial and litigant resources are expended. Generally, a voluntary dismissal places the parties in the positions they occupied before the lawsuit began; it does not, in general, have the effect of an adjudication on the merits. Because voluntary dismissal might be used to harass defendants, if a party attempts to dismiss after previously doing so with respect to the same cause of action, the dismissal is granted, but is viewed as being an adjudication on the merits.

McCANTS v. FORD MOTOR CO., 781 F.2d 855 (11th Cir.1986). Johnny McCants, a member of the United States Army Reserve on a two-week active duty training mission, was killed while riding in a military jeep built by Ford. His administratrix commenced a wrongful death suit in federal district court in Alabama. After discovery proceeded for about a year, interrogatories were served and answered, and defendant had moved for summary judgment based on Alabama's one-year general statute of limitations, the plaintiff moved for an order pursuant to Rule 41(a)(2) for voluntary dismissal of the action without prejudice. The plaintiff sought to dismiss the suit so that she could file a new suit in Mississippi, where the controlling statute of limitations had not expired. The District Court granted the motion to dismiss, and simultaneously denied Ford's motion for summary judgment.

Notes and Questions

1. At common law, plaintiff was permitted, at any time prior to judgment, to dismiss a case voluntarily and without prejudice to refiling the action at a later date. Today the right to dismiss voluntarily generally is governed by a rule or statute that typically permits a dismissal before "trial" or "commencement" of trial. These provisions have raised many problems of interpretation regarding the meaning of the words "trial" and "commencement." A few courts have held that "before trial" means at any time prior to submission of the case to the jury or court for decision. See generally Annot., 1 A.L.R.3d 711 (1965). What justification is there for this construction?

2.   In *McCants,* plaintiff moved to dismiss after defendant had made a motion for summary judgment. Could any plaintiff simply move to dismiss before losing such a motion and refile in another, possibly more sympathetic, court? Could plaintiff do this repeatedly?

3.   What effect does a voluntary dismissal have on the statute of limitations? Is the statute tolled while the initial complaint is active? Or does the notion that the dismissal returns the parties to the position they occupied before the action require the court to refuse to consider the previous action for purposes of applying the statute of limitations? See Delong's, Inc. v. Stupp Bros. Bridge & Iron Co., 40 F.R.D. 127 (E.D.Mo.1965).

4.   Under Rule 41(a)(1) any dismissal is with prejudice if plaintiff previously has dismissed the same action. Should this restriction apply as well when the second dismissal is sought under Rule 41(a)(2)? See American Cyanamid Co. v. McGhee, 317 F.2d 295 (5th Cir.1963).

5.   In Esposito v. Piatrowski, 223 F.3d 497 (7th Cir.2000), plaintiff voluntarily dismissed his initial case against defendant. Plaintiff was ordered to reimburse defendant the costs of that proceeding. Subsequently plaintiff sued on the same cause, joining other defendants with the defendant originally sued. Because plaintiff never did comply with the order to pay costs, the trial court, under Rule 41(b), dismissed the second case, not only against the original defendant but against all the defendants. The court of appeals affirmed. Is the decision consistent with the spirit of Rule 41(d)?

2.   DISMISSAL FOR FAILURE TO PROSECUTE

Courts long have been regarded as possessing inherent discretionary power to dismiss an action if plaintiff does not proceed to trial with "due diligence." Exactly when this power should be invoked has been a matter about which judges have disagreed. Should simple delay by plaintiff be sufficient to justify dismissal, or should prejudice to defendant also be required? In MESSENGER v. UNITED STATES, 231 F.2d 328, 331 (2d Cir. 1956), the court said: "The operative condition of the Rule is lack of due diligence on the part of the plaintiff—not a showing by the defendant that it will be prejudiced by denial of its motion. * * * It may well be that the latter factor may be considered by the court, especially in cases of moderate or excusable neglect, in the formulation of its discretionary ruling." Does this standard make sense? Does it have any practical utility as a guide for the trial judge? What is its effect on appellate-court review of the trial court's exercise of discretion?

Some jurisdictions control dismissals for want of prosecution by statute. Thus, California permits dismissal after the passage of three years from the filing of the complaint, but makes dismissal mandatory when five years have elapsed. Cal.Code Civ.Proc. §§ 583.310, 583.420(a)(2)(A). What justification, if any, is there for this statutory arrangement? Is it superior to a system that leaves the decision solely within the court's discretion? Compare Indiana Rule of Trial Procedure 41(E), which permits dismissal "when no action has been taken in a civil case for a period of sixty [60] days." See also N.Y.C.P.L.R. 3216. In view of the fact that, by definition, cases in which there is a failure to prosecute are not consuming judicial time or energy, why is a formal dismissal procedure necessary?

———

LINK v. WABASH R. CO., 370 U.S. 626, 629–30, 633–34, 82 S.Ct. 1386, 1388, 1390–91, 8 L.Ed.2d 734, 737–38, 739–40 (1962). Petitioner appealed a *sua sponte* dismissal of his diversity negligence action after petitioner and his counsel failed to attend a pretrial conference. The trial date had been set some six years after the action had been commenced, during which two other fixed trial dates had been postponed. The Seventh Circuit affirmed, after which the Supreme Court, in an opinion by Justice Harlan, affirmed, holding:

> The authority of a federal trial court to dismiss a plaintiff's action with prejudice because of his failure to prosecute cannot seriously be doubted. The power to invoke this sanction is necessary in order to prevent undue delays in the disposition of pending cases and to avoid congestion in the calendars of the District Courts. The power is of ancient origin, having its roots in judgments of *nonsuit* and *non prosequitur* entered at common law, e.g., 3 Blackstone, Commentaries (1768), 295–296, and dismissals for want of prosecution of bills in equity * * *. It has been expressly recognized in Federal Rule of Civil Procedure 41(b) * * *.

> * * *

> Accordingly, when circumstances make such action appropriate, a District Court may dismiss a complaint for failure to prosecute even without affording notice of its intention to do so or providing an adversary hearing before acting. Whether such an order can stand on appeal depends not on power but on whether it was within the permissible range of the court's discretion.

> On this record we are unable to say that the District Court's dismissal of this action for failure to prosecute, as evidenced only partly by the failure of petitioner's counsel to appear at a duly scheduled pretrial conference, amounted to an abuse of discretion. * * *

> There is certainly no merit to the contention that dismissal of petitioner's claim because of his counsel's unexcused conduct imposes an unjust penalty on the client. Petitioner voluntarily chose this attorney as his representative in the action, and he cannot now avoid the consequences of the acts or omissions of this freely selected agent. Any other notion would be wholly inconsistent with our system of representative litigation, in which each party is deemed bound by the acts of his lawyer-agent and is considered to have "notice of all facts, notice of which can be charged upon the attorney." * * *

> We need not decide whether unexplained absence from a pretrial conference would *alone* justify a dismissal with prejudice if the record showed no other evidence of dilatoriness on the part of the plaintiff. For the District Court in this case relied on *all* the circumstances that were brought to its attention, including the earlier delays.

In his dissent, Justice Black argued that it was unfair to impose such a harsh penalty upon plaintiff for the misconduct of his attorney. The Justice suggested that numerous other sanctions were available in this instance that could have served the purpose of penalizing the attorney without resorting to a dismissal of the action, thus barring forever the plaintiff's right to recovery for his injuries.

Notes and Questions

1. If the court has power under Rule 41(b) to dismiss the action, does it have an implied authority to fashion other, less onerous sanctions? In J.M. CLEMIN-SHAW CO. v. CITY OF NORWICH, 93 F.R.D. 338, 355 (D.Conn.1981), the court said:

> Fines may be imposed upon offending attorneys under Rule 41(b) even though that rule, by its terms, specifically provides only for the sanction of dismissal of the action. Indeed, fines are an appropriate sanction under Rule 41(b) precisely because dismissal is the only sanction specified by that rule. That is, the district courts have been directed to avoid the harsh result of dismissal in cases where the delays or disobedience have been the fault of counsel rather than their clients. In these cases, the courts may draw on their inherent authority to control the course of litigation to impose on counsel the less severe sanction of a fine. * * * Cf. Schwarz v. United States, 384 F.2d 833, 836 (2d Cir.1967) (affirming dismissal pursuant to Rule 41(b); "suggest[ing] that the [district] court keep in mind the possibility, in future cases of inexcusable neglect by counsel, of imposing substantial costs and attorney's fees payable by offending counsel personally to the opposing party, as an alternative to the drastic remedy of dismissal.") * * *.

2. If her claim has been dismissed under Rule 41(b), can plaintiff sue in state court on the same claim? In ADCOX v. SOUTHERN RY. CO., 182 Tenn. 6, 184 S.W.2d 37 (1944), the court held that a state court could hear the action even if it would be barred in federal court. If Rule 41(b) is designed to protect defendant, doesn't the Tennessee result frustrate the operation of Rule 41(b)? Or is it that Rule 41(b) is designed merely to control the use of the resources of a particular court?

3. Lengthy delays do not necessarily lead to a dismissal for failure to prosecute. For example, in GCIU EMPLOYER RETIREMENT FUND v. CHICAGO TRIBUNE, 8 F.3d 1195 (7th Cir.1993), the Court held that a dismissal with prejudice for failure to prosecute was improper, despite a twenty-two month delay between judicial proceedings, because during that period the litigants were actively negotiating.

4. For a discussion of Rule 41(b), see Note, *Dismissal With Prejudice For Failure To Prosecute: Visiting The Sins Of The Attorney Upon The Client*, 22 Ga.L.Rev. 195 (1987). To see how one state has handled these cases, see Note, *Marshall–Wisconsin v. Juneau Square: Damn The Due Process, Dismiss At Will— A New Appellate Standard Of Review For Dismissal For Failure To Prosecute In Wisconsin*, 1989 Wis.L.Rev. 171 (1989).

SECTION C.   DEFAULT JUDGMENT

Read Federal Rule of Civil Procedure 55 and the accompanying materials in the Supplement.

COULAS v. SMITH

Supreme Court of Arizona, 1964.
96 Ariz. 325, 395 P.2d 527.

UDALL, CHIEF JUSTICE. This is an appeal from an order of the Superior Court of Pima County, denying a motion to set aside a judgment entered against the appellant.

* * *

The plaintiff filed a complaint against the defendant and cross-claimant on two counts. The first count was for $669.32 on an open account. The second count was on a promissory note upon which $3,666.67 was alleged to be due. The cross-claimant answered individually by his attorney and denied any liability to the plaintiff on either count and thereafter filed a cross-claim against the defendant in which he sought judgment against the defendant for any sums or amounts which the plaintiff may obtain against him by virtue of the judgment; for the sum of $4,000 on a debt alleged to be owed by the defendant to him, and $500 attorney's fees. The defendant appeared individually by his attorneys and answered the complaint of the plaintiff, answered the cross-claim of the cross-claimant, and counterclaimed against the plaintiff, seeking damages in the sum of $18,000. The plaintiff replied to the defendant's counterclaim.

On July 11, 1958, the lower court made an order setting the case for trial on October 10, 1958. All counsel were notified by the clerk of the court. On October 6, 1958, counsel for the plaintiff and counsel for the cross-claimant stipulated that the trial be set for December 10, 1958. The lower court ordered that the prior trial date be vacated and the case be reset for trial on December 10, 1958. All counsel were regularly notified by the clerk of the new trial setting. The defendant's counsel was not present before the court on October 6, 1958, and did not participate in the stipulation vacating the original trial setting and resetting the case for trial on December 10, 1958. The defendant and defendant's counsel deny ever receiving any notice from the clerk concerning the new trial date.

On December 10, 1958, the new trial date, the case came on regularly to be heard. The defendant did not appear either in person or by counsel. The court made the following minute entry during the course of the trial:

* * *

The plaintiff Smith and the defendant Bray announce ready for trial.

William J. Bray is sworn, cross-examined, and examined.

Plaintiff's Exhibit 1, being a promissory note in the sum of $4,000.00 dated February 14, 1955, is marked for identification and admitted in evidence.

Nicholas Coulas having failed to appear at this time either in person or by counsel, and it further appearing that this case was previously set for trial both as to the issues framed by the complaint and answer thereto of the defendant Nicholas Coulas and as to the cross-claim filed by the defendant William J. Bray, Jr., against the defendant Nicholas Coulas,

IT IS HEREBY ORDERED that the default of the said defendant Nicholas Coulas be entered as to said complaint and as to said cross-claim and the court proceeding to hear evidence pertaining to said complaint and cross-claim and being fully advised in the premises,

IT IS THEREFORE ORDERED that judgment is hereby rendered * * * against the defendant Nicholas Coulas * * *.

The plaintiff obtained judgment against the defendant on both counts and against the cross-claimant as to count two (the promissory note). The cross-claimant obtained judgment against the defendant on the promissory note. The judgment was entered on December 11, 1958.

On October 29, 1960, nearly two years later, the defendant filed a motion to set aside and vacate the judgment. The trial court denied this motion. * * *

The defendant subsequently filed this appeal.

The defendant contends that the "default" judgment entered against him was void, since he did not receive 3 days' notice of the application for judgment by default pursuant to Rule 55(b) of the Arizona Rules of Civil Procedure * * *. The defendant's contention would be valid if the judgment below was a judgment by default. A default judgment obtains when a defendant fails to plead or otherwise defend. Rule 55. If he has made an appearance in the case, he must be given 3 days' notice of application for judgment by default. * * *

However, the defendant's contention is invalid here since the judgment below was not a default judgment. It should be noted that the defendant did plead to the merits. He answered the complaint and filed a counterclaim. He then failed to appear at the trial in person or by counsel. The trial proceeded, evidence was heard, and a judgment on the merits of the plaintiff's and counter-claimant's claims was entered. The judgment was not by default within the meaning of Rule 55. Therefore Rule 55(b) with its 3–day notice requirement is not applicable. In fact, the trial court would have erred if a default was entered, since the case was at issue. Bass v. Hoagland, 172 F.2d 205 (5th Cir.1949), cert. denied, 338 U.S. 816, 70 S.Ct. 57, 94 L.Ed. 494 (1949) * * *.

The following language is from Bass v. Hoagland * * * concerning the applicability of Rule 55:

"Rule 55(a) authorizes the clerk to enter a default 'When a party against whom a judgment for affirmative relief is sought has failed to plead or otherwise defend as provided by these rules.' This does not require that to escape default the defendant must not only file a sufficient answer to the merits, but must also have a lawyer or be present in court when the case is called for a trial. The words 'otherwise defend' refer to attacks on the service, or motions to dismiss, or for better particulars, and the like, which may prevent default without presently pleading to the merits. *When Bass by his attorney filed a denial of the plaintiff's case neither the clerk nor the judge could enter a default against him. The burden of proof was put on the plaintiff in any trial. When neither Bass nor his attorney appeared at the trial, no default was generated;* the case was not confessed. The plaintiff might proceed, but he would have to prove his case." 172 F.2d p. 210 (emphasis added).

And note this language from Klein v. Rappaport, * * * [90 A.2d 834 (D.C.Mun.Ct.1952)]:

A more serious question is whether the trial court could properly enter a judgment by default on the then state of the record. It must be remembered that defendant had not defaulted in pleading. She had filed an answer and a counterclaim. Plaintiff having replied to the counterclaim, the case was at issue not only on the original claim but on the counterclaim as well. With the litigation in that posture and the judge having decided that there should be no further continuance, he should have proceeded to take proof and enter judgment on the merits. It was not proper to enter a judgment by default. *Absence of a defendant when a case is called for trial after it is at issue does not warrant a judgment against him by default*, but a trial or hearing on the issues is necessary and the judgment which follows is based on the proof adduced. * * *

The defendant relies heavily on the case of Phoenix Metals Corporation v. Roth * * * on page 109 of 79 Ariz., on page 647 of 284 P.2d:

Under the provisions of this rule [Rule 55], no judgment by default may be entered against a defendant who has appeared—as by timely filing an answer—unless he is given notice of the application for judgment.

To the extent the above language implies that a default judgment is proper where a defendant has answered to the merits, it is incorrect. The peculiar fact situation in that case made the above language somewhat misleading. * * * [T]he defendant had filed an answer in fact, but through clerical error the answer was attached to the wrong file and thus it appeared that the defendant had failed to answer and upon application to the clerk the default was erroneously entered and judgment granted thereon. This court held that judgment wholly void. It should therefore be stated that once an answer on the merits is filed and the case is at issue, a default judgment is not proper, and if the defendant fails to appear at the trial a judgment on the merits may be entered against him upon proper proof.

* * *

The contention of the defendant that he did not receive notice of the new trial date is not substantiated by the minutes. The record indicates that the clerk of the superior court notified all counsel of all of the orders and judgment pursuant to Rule 77(h) * * *. It is well settled that in the absence of a showing to the contrary a public officer, such as the clerk of the court in this case, is presumed to have performed the duty imposed upon him by law. * * * In addition, if the defendant's counsel did not receive the notice of the change of the trial date to December 10, 1958, he certainly would have learned of the change in the trial date when he appeared for trial on the earlier date, October 10, 1958.

Since the judgment of the lower court is merely voidable, at most, Rule 60(c) * * * prevents the defendant from attacking the judgment more than six months after it was entered. The defendant attempted to attack the judgment nearly two years after it was entered. * * * The lower court properly denied defendant's motion to set aside and vacate the judgment.

Judgment affirmed.

Notes and Questions

1. In BASS v. HOAGLAND, which is relied upon in *Coulas,* a default judgment was rendered in favor of plaintiff after defendant's counsel, who had filed an answer, had withdrawn from the case. The judgment recited that defendant had been informed of the withdrawal. Defendant did not appeal but collaterally attacked the judgment when enforcement was sought against him in another jurisdiction. Defendant claimed that he did not know of the counsel's withdrawal from the case and was not aware that the adverse judgment had been rendered. A majority of the Fifth Circuit held that, since an answer had been filed, defendant was not in default under Rule 55, that the entry of judgment without trial by jury, which had been demanded, was a violation of the Due Process Clause of the Fifth Amendment, and that the judgment was void. The court indicated that even if the case fell within Rule 55, the failure to give notice under Rule 55(b)(2) might render the judgment void, although in that event no jury trial would be required. The dissenting judge took the position that defendant, by not attending trial, was in default, no jury trial was required and therefore the decision was not void and not subject to collateral attack. The case is discussed in 62 Harv.L.Rev. 1400 (1949) and 59 Yale L.J. 345 (1950). Compare Sheepscot Land Corp. v. Gregory, 383 A.2d 16, 22 (Me.1978) (failure of defendant to appear for trial justifies default even though answer was filed).

2. Federal Rule 54(c) provides that plaintiff may recover all the relief to which he is entitled except that plaintiff is limited to the amount prayed for in the case of a default judgment. Suppose at trial in Coulas v. Smith plaintiff's evidence showed that defendant was liable for $10,000, although only $4,000 had been claimed. Would the court have been justified in awarding plaintiff the full amount?

3. What activities of defendant, short of a formal challenge to the jurisdiction or the pleadings, constitute an "appearance" within the meaning of Federal Rule 55(b)(2)? In RHODES v. RHODES, 3 Mich.App. 396, 142 N.W.2d 508 (1966), plaintiff, in a divorce action, obtained a default judgment against defendant without giving the notice required by the then applicable Michigan General Court Rule 520.2(2), which was analogous to Federal Rule 55(b)(2). Defendant claimed that by signing a property settlement agreement and stipulating that it be incorporated in the divorce judgment, he "appeared" in the action. The court held that defendant had not shown that these acts were intended to constitute an "appearance" and refused to set aside the judgment. For differing views as to what constitutes an appearance, see Wilson v. Moore & Associates, Inc., 564 F.2d 366 (9th Cir.1977), and Petty v. Weyerhaeuser Co., 272 S.C. 282, 251 S.E.2d 735 (1979).

4. It is important to recognize that although relief-from-judgment rules, such as Federal Rule 60(b), do not distinguish between default and other judgments, the courts clearly disfavor default judgments, and, in exercising discretion, are far more willing to set aside default judgments in order that cases may be decided on their merits. See, e.g., Lacy v. Sitel Corp., 227 F.3d 290 (5th Cir.2000). This is often the case when the default is due to the carelessness of counsel. See, e.g., Eastman Kodak Co. v. Guasti, 68 Ill.App.3d 484, 25 Ill.Dec. 20, 386 N.E.2d 291 (1st Dist.1979). Why shouldn't the default judgment be left unopened and the losing party be remitted to a negligence action against a careless attorney? To what extent should a client be required to ensure that its attorney is properly handling the client's case? See Mason Tenders District Council Welfare Fund v. M & M Contracting & Consulting, 193 F.R.D. 112 (S.D.N.Y.2000). It is exceedingly rare that an appellate court will find that a trial court has abused its discretion in setting aside a default judgment. Nevertheless such decisions are reached from time to time. See, e.g., Benjamin v. Dalmo Mfg. Co., 31 Cal.2d 523, 190 P.2d 593 (1948). For a general discussion of the power to set aside judgments, see pp. 1109–15, infra.

5. A special type of default judgment is one that is imposed on a party who has appeared and contested the matters at issue but has willfully violated the rules of procedure or disobeyed an order of the court. Such a "penalty" is invoked normally against parties who are defending claims; if the complaining party is guilty of comparable violations, the most typical remedy is to dismiss the case with prejudice. See, e.g., Federal Rule 41(b). The penalty default most frequently is rendered in cases in which a defending party willfully refuses to comply with orders for pretrial discovery. Federal Rules 37(b)(2)(C) and 37(d) and their state counterparts specifically permit default judgments in these situations. Should "penalty" defaults fall within the scope of Federal Rule 55? Compare Wilver v. Fisher, 387 F.2d 66 (10th Cir.1967) (notice provisions of Rule 55(b)(2) apply to default under Rule 37), with Vitale v. Elliott, 120 R.I. 328, 387 A.2d 1379, 1382 (1978) (Rule 55 does not govern defaults under Rule 37). Are "penalty" defaults subject to the limitation on recovery in Federal Rule 54(c)? In TRANS WORLD AIRLINES, INC. v. HUGHES, 32 F.R.D. 604, 607–08 (S.D.N.Y.1963), modified 332 F.2d 602 (2d Cir.1964), certiorari dismissed 380 U.S. 248, 85 S.Ct. 934, 13 L.Ed.2d 817 (1965), the court, after granting plaintiff's motion for entry of a default judgment on the ground of defendant's failure to produce the owner of 100% of its stock for a deposition, held:

> That branch of the [plaintiff's] motion seeking to increase the *ad damnum* clause from $105,000,000 to $135,000,000 is granted. This is not a case where a party has defaulted in appearance. Here issue was joined and adversary proceedings continued in the pretrial stages of this litigation. The damages originally asserted were unliquidated and TWA is entitled to recover for whatever damage it can show it suffered. Furthermore, Toolco [a defendant] will be represented at the hearings necessary to assess damages under rule 55(b)(2).

Compare Fong v. United States, 300 F.2d 400, 412–13 (9th Cir.), certiorari denied 370 U.S. 938, 82 S.Ct. 1584, 8 L.Ed.2d 807 (1962). Suppose TWA's suit had been on a contract and the damages were for a liquidated sum that plaintiff had erroneously understated in its complaint. Would the result have been different?

6. Consider C & H TRANSPORTATION CO. v. WRIGHT, 396 S.W.2d 443 (Tex.Civ.App.1965). Plaintiff brought suit against a former employer, alleging that the latter erroneously had deducted the sum of $470.55 from the amount due

plaintiff upon termination of the employment. Defendant did not answer or appear and a default judgment was entered. Defendant then appealed on the ground that the complaint failed to allege a cause of action. The court reversed, holding that a default judgment must be supported by a statement of a cause of action in the complaint and that plaintiff's complaint was insufficient because it contained mere conclusions of law.

Suppose defendant in *Wright* had not appealed but instead had challenged the judgment collaterally after it had become final. Should relief have been granted? Should it make a difference if the defective complaint clearly cannot be remedied by an amendment? See Comment, *Attacking a Judgment in California on the Grounds that the Complaint Failed to State a Cause of Action,* 1 U.C.L.A.L.Rev. 195 (1954); 36 Texas L.Rev. 243 (1957); 49 Mich.L.Rev. 446 (1951).

7.   In Trans World Airlines, Inc. v. Hughes, Note 5, supra, after the Supreme Court dismissed certiorari, the case was referred by the District Court to a master for a determination of damages. In the hearing on the confirmation of the master's report, defendants sought to establish "as a matter of law that facts essential to establish * * * violations [of the antitrust laws], although alleged in the complaint, are in fact untrue and could not have been proved by TWA at trial." The District Court rejected this effort:

> * * * TWA did not have to present any evidence to support the well-pleaded allegations of the complaint, and defendants may not offer evidence to controvert such allegations. That opportunity was forfeited by defendants as a result of the default.

> Defendants may show, however, that an allegation is not well pleaded, but only in very narrow, exceptional circumstances [as when] allegations * * * are contrary to facts of which the court will take judicial notice.

Trans World Airlines, Inc. v. Hughes, 308 F.Supp. 679, 683 (S.D.N.Y.1969), affirmed 449 F.2d 51 (2d Cir.1971). The Supreme Court reversed on the ground that defendants' actions were immune from the antitrust laws under 49 U.S.C. §§ 1378, 1384, because they were under the regulatory control of the Civil Aeronautics Board; the Court held that it was not precluded from considering this issue by its earlier dismissal of certiorari, because there had been no final judgment at that time. Hughes Tool Co. v. Trans World Airlines, Inc., 409 U.S. 363, 93 S.Ct. 647, 34 L.Ed.2d 577 (1973).

Chapter 14

TRIAL

SECTION A. TRIAL BY JURY

1. THE INSTITUTION OF TRIAL BY JURY

During its formative period the jury was an activist group that not only judged the evidence but acquired much of it through its own investigation. An example of this drawn from twelfth century English history is the "jury" used to compile the famous Domesday Book, which contained an inventory of William the Conqueror's realm. The Domesday "jury" viewed the land and formed its own judgments without using witnesses. Today, of course, the jury is a passive, disinterested body that renders its decisions on the basis of the information placed before it.

The revered status of jury trial at common law is evidenced by Blackstone's statement that the right "has been, and I trust ever will be, looked upon as the glory of the English law * * * and * * * that it is the most transcendent privilege which any subject can enjoy or wish for, that he not be affected either in his property, his liberty, or his person, but by unanimous consent of twelve of his neighbors and equals." 3 Blackstone, *Commentaries* *378. Yet, in modern English practice, the jury is used comparatively infrequently.

In this country the jury system has been eulogized by the United States Supreme Court on many occasions. For example, in SIOUX CITY & P.R. CO. v. STOUT, 84 U.S. (17 Wall.) 657, 664, 21 L.Ed. 745, 749 (1873), the Court commented:

> * * * Twelve men of the average of the community, comprising men of education and men of little education, men of learning and men whose learning consists only in what they have themselves seen and heard, the merchant, the mechanic, the farmer, the laborer; these sit together, consult, apply their separate experience of the affairs of life to the facts proven, and draw a unanimous conclusion. This average judgment thus given it is the great effort of the law to obtain. It is assumed that twelve men know more of the common affairs of life than does one man, that they can draw wiser and safer conclusions from admitted facts thus occurring than can a single judge.

But not everyone supports our jury system. As one commentator has stated, "The American jury has been the target of relentless criticism throughout the nation's 224–year existence. [As a result of a low-key crusade by special interest groups], issues and cases decided by juries only a decade or so ago are now handled by judges or expert arbitrators—or barred completely." Curriden, *Putting the Squeeze on Juries,* 86 A.B.A.J. 52–53 (Aug. 2000). One outspoken critic of jury trial was Jerome N. Frank, a highly respected judge of the Second Circuit. His opinion of the institution is illustrated by the following passage from his book *Law and the Modern Mind* 180–81 (1930):

> The [jurors] * * * are hopelessly incompetent as fact-finders. It is possible, by training, to improve the ability of our judges to pass upon facts more objectively. But no one can be fatuous enough to believe that the entire community can be so educated that a crowd of twelve men chosen at random can do, even moderately well, what painstaking judges now find it difficult to do. * * * The jury makes the orderly administration of justice virtually impossible.

An excellent summary of Judge Frank's views is found in Paul, *Jerome Frank's Views on Trial by Jury,* 22 Mo.L.Rev. 28 (1957). More recently, the jury system has come under increasing attack from commentators claiming that the system is expensive and slow and that juries cannot understand the complex cases that, today, comprise a large part of courts' dockets. Thus, the late Chief Justice Burger listed the following problems associated with jury trials in civil cases:

> *First,* do we really have truly representative juries? Experienced business executives, bankers, professional people, accountants, professors of economics, statisticians, teachers, and others arguably more competent than most to cope with complex economic or scientific questions, rarely survive to sit in the box. Peremptory challenges in the jury selection process eliminate them and more often they are excused for cause, including the cause that they are too busy! We must stop deluding ourselves. The juries actually selected in most protracted cases are rarely true cross-sections, as we are so fond of repeating.

> * * *

> *Second,* the factual issues in protracted cases are often of enormous complexity. The analysis of documents, of expert testimony, of charts, graphs and other visual aids, and the comprehension of such evidence, present problems which often only a sophisticated business executive, an economist, or another expert could grasp; some cases would baffle even them.

> *Third,* the legal issues, which must be explained to jurors by the trial judge, may take not hours, but a whole day or several days, by way of instructions.

> *Fourth,* there is a limit to the capacity of any of us—jurors or judges—to understand and remember the mass of complicated transactions, documents, and legal principles usually described in the course of a long trial.

Fifth, quite apart from these considerations, there is an enormous—and inordinate—impact on the life of each of twelve jurors, and alternate jurors, thrust for months into a totally strange environment, and then confronted with the burden of decisions in areas in which few, if any of them, have any experience.

Burger, *Thinking the Unthinkable,* 31 Loyola L.Rev. 205, 210–11 (1985).

As you study the remainder of this Section try to formulate judgments on the following questions: To what extent is the jury-trial institution an anachronism? Can we reform it to make it work more effectively in the twenty-first century or should we eliminate it entirely? Have the courts been overly concerned with preserving jury trial even though it has been shown to be cumbersome and uneconomical? If we abandon jury trial, what other devices and procedures are available that might provide a more modern but democratic substitute? Why is it that even opponents of the civil jury simply assume that jury trial must be preserved in "serious criminal cases"? Is jury trial less of an anachronism in criminal than in civil cases? Does it serve any function in the criminal-law context that it doesn't on the civil-law side?

Excellent historical material on the jury can be found in 1 Holdsworth, *A History of English Law* 298–350 (7th ed. 1956); 1 Pollock & Maitland, *The History of English Law* 138–49 (2d ed. 1911); 2 *id.* 616–32, 641–59. See also Thayer, *The Jury and Its Development,* 5 Harv.L.Rev. 249, 295, 357 (1892), substantially reprinted in *A Preliminary Treatise on Evidence at the Common Law* 47–182 (1898). For discussions of civil jury trial in other countries, see Devlin, *Trial by Jury* (3d imp. 1966); Smith, *Civil Jury Trial: A Scottish Assessment,* 50 Va.L.Rev. 1076 (1964).

2. THE RIGHT TO A JURY TRIAL

a. Sources of the Right

Examine the Seventh Amendment to the United States Constitution and the state jury-trial guarantees set out in the Supplement. In what ways are they substantively different from each other? What reasons underlie these differences?

The federal Constitution and most state constitutions do not "create" a right to jury trial. Rather, they "preserve" the right as it existed at common law, either in 1791, the date of the Seventh Amendment's ratification, or, in the case of some states, as of the time the state constitution was adopted. Because the Seventh Amendment was assumed to incorporate the jury-trial practice as of 1791, federal judges frequently have been called upon to determine the actual availability of jury trial as of that date.

* * * Inevitably this calls for some historical inquiry. If the issue in the context in which it arises would have been heard at common law in 1791, when the Seventh Amendment was adopted, or, more accurately, in 1938 when law and equity were merged, it is now triable of right to a jury. There is no right to jury trial if viewed historically the issue would have been tried in the courts of equity or if otherwise it would have been tried without a jury.

* * *

[The historical test] * * * proved difficult to apply, particularly for a generation to which the distinctions between law and equity are ancient, and largely unlearned, history. Courts have complained of being held in "historical bondage" and have apologized for an analysis that "may seem to reek unduly of the study." Even if the history were known, it often could shed but dim light as novel kinds of actions were developed and as modern procedure permitted a hybrid form of lawsuit that could never have existed in the ancient days. A vast and controversial literature developed as scholars sought to solve what were essentially insoluble problems.

9 Wright & Miller, *Federal Practice and Procedure: Civil 2d* § 2302 (1995). For an insight into the difficulties posed by the historical test, see the majority and dissenting opinions in Damsky v. Zavatt, 289 F.2d 46 (2d Cir.1961).

Notes and Questions

1. The significance of the Seventh Amendment's reference to "suits at common law" is described in PARSONS v. BEDFORD, 28 U.S. (3 Pet.) 433, 447, 7 L.Ed. 732, 737 (1830), as follows:

> * * * [By "common law," the framers of the Constitution meant] suits in which legal rights were to be ascertained and determined, in contradistinction to those where equitable rights alone were recognized, and equitable remedies were administered; or where, as in the admiralty, a mixture of public law, and of maritime law and equity, was often found in the same suit. Probably, there were few, if any, states in the Union, in which some new legal remedies, differing from the old common-law forms, were not in use; but in which, however, the trial by jury intervened, and the general regulations in other respects were according to the course of the common law. * * * In a just sense, the amendment then may well be construed to embrace all suits, which are not of equity and admiralty jurisdiction, whatever may be the peculiar form which they may assume to settle legal rights. * * *

See Henderson, *The Background of the Seventh Amendment,* 80 Harv.L.Rev. 289 (1966). For a scholarly analysis taking the view that the framers of the Bill of Rights intended that Congress would have complete power to decide what types of matters were to be tried before a jury, and that therefore much of the Supreme Court's subsequent analyses regarding "suits at common law" has been based upon incorrect assumptions, see Krauss, *The Original Understanding of the Seventh Amendment Right to Jury Trial,* 33 U.Rich.L. Rev. 407 (2000). Does the "suits at common law" limitation make any sense now that law and equity have been merged? Consider this question in connection with Beacon Theatres, Inc. v. Westover, p. 959, infra.

Under existing constitutional doctrine, the Seventh Amendment does not generally apply to proceedings in state courts. See Walker v. Sauvinet, 92 U.S. (2 Otto) 90, 23 L.Ed. 678 (1875). Yet the Supreme Court has held that other parts of the Bill of Rights, such as the freedom of speech and expression in the First Amendment, the protection against searches and seizures in the Fourth Amendment, the privilege against self-incrimination in the Fifth Amendment, and the right to a jury in a criminal trial in the Sixth Amendment apply to the states. In what ways does the Seventh Amendment differ from these provisions? Are there arguments for applying the federal jury-trial guarantee to state-court civil actions? Could there be any state-court actions in which a Seventh Amendment or "federal" jury trial is required at the present time?

    2. If "common law" in 1791 was understood by the framers of the seventh amendment as a process, rather than as a set of perpetually static rules, then one must ask whether, with the passage of time, the historical test has caused the amendment to diverge from the original conception. * * * During the centuries of their coexistence, the jurisdiction of the law courts and the chancellor * * * were subject to an unstatic process of accretion and erosion. * * * What remains constant over the history of this process, however, is the tendency toward expansion and enrichment of the remedies provided by the law courts. * * *

    If future development was contemplated—and if it is correct to view that development as largely one of the expansion of the remedies available at "common law"—then it would seem to follow that the "common law" of the seventh amendment was intended to have a changing meaning over time.

Wolfram, *The Constitutional History of the Seventh Amendment,* 57 Minn.L.Rev. 639, 738, 744 (1973). If the framers of the Amendment understood "common law" as a process in which the remedies available in common-law courts would change over time, is it likely that they viewed the right of jury trial as one that would expand or one that would contract?

    3. In APPLICATION OF SMITH, 381 Pa. 223, 230, 112 A.2d 625, 629 (1955), the Pennsylvania Supreme Court upheld the constitutionality of a statute that provided for compulsory arbitration in certain circumstances. The court said that a statute would not contravene the Pennsylvania constitution's provision on the jury trial unless it

    closes the courts to litigants and makes the decision of the arbitrators the final determination of the rights of the parties; therefore there is no denial of the right of trial by jury if the statute preserves that right to each of the parties by the allowance of an appeal from the decision of the arbitrators or other tribunal. * * *

See also Capital Traction Co. v. Hof, 174 U.S. 1, 19 S.Ct. 580, 43 L.Ed. 873 (1899). There are other inhibitions on securing a jury trial that have been held not to violate the constitutional mandate. For example, a party who requests a jury trial can be required to pay jury fees that ultimately are taxable as costs against the party who loses the action. What if the indexing or docketing fee for a jury trial is higher than the comparable fee for a nonjury trial? See Klein, *Jury Fees and Compensation of Jurors in the State Courts,* 26 F.R.D. 539 (1960).

    4. McELRATH v. UNITED STATES, 102 U.S. (12 Otto) 426, 440, 26 L.Ed. 189, 192 (1880), held that suits against the government in the Court of Claims are not controlled by the Seventh Amendment because they are not suits at common law within its true meaning. "The government cannot be sued, except with its own consent. It can declare in what court it may be sued, and prescribe the forms of pleading and the rules of practice to be observed in such suits." Is the conclusion of the Court in *McElrath* consistent with the spirit of the jury-trial guarantee? If McElrath had not sued the government but the government had initiated suit against him, would he then have had a right to jury trial on any legal issues that might have been raised? Absent any provision in the statute authorizing suit against the government as to whether there is a right to jury trial, the legislative history is controlling. See United States v. Pfitsch, 256 U.S. 547, 41

S.Ct. 569, 65 L.Ed. 1084 (1921) (action under Lever and War Risk Insurance Acts held to be part of district court's general jurisdiction over actions at law and trial by jury held an incident thereto).

b.   The Implementation of the Right to a Jury Trial

———

Review the materials on pp. 491–99, supra.

———

Long before merger, equity developed the clean-up doctrine as a partial response to the problems of the bifurcation of law and equity. Under this doctrine, once an equity court obtained jurisdiction of a suit primarily of an equitable character, the court could decide any incidental legal issues that arose in the course of the litigation.

> Sound considerations of policy lay behind * * * [the] "clean-up" rule, considerations which loom large and real against the background of two entirely independent systems of trial courts. The plaintiff entitled to both legal and equitable remedies needed relief from the burden of two days in court. Even worse was the plight of the litigant who had legitimately but vainly sought the chancellor's aid. The statute of limitations threatened him with total loss of remedy on an admittedly valid claim. It was the more dangerous a choice when crowded dockets and cumbersome procedure made the equitable process less than speedy. In any event, the dangers of a wrong choice of forum involved delay and all-consuming expense of litigation.

> Here then was plaintiff's dilemma: to turn first to law might, as a simple matter of res judicata, lose him the more-desired chancellor's remedy; to turn to equity would often invite decision by an unpredictable conscience and perhaps the loss of all remedy. Equities had to be weighed on an imprecise balance and hardships measured by a rule the fine divisions of which were often known only to the chancellor himself. Small wonder then that the clean-up rule, the disposition of incidental questions legal in nature, was often applied even where all equitable relief was denied.

> The cost of this efficiency was, however, substantial, for it involved the denial of trial by jury on all legal issues so adjudicated. In some situations this price was considered too heavy to pay for the trial convenience achieved. In others, where equity viewed a plaintiff's conduct as sufficiently reprehensible, the chancellor was pleased not to afford him aid by rapid disposition of a remaining issue.

Levin, *Equitable Clean-up and the Jury: A Suggested Orientation,* 100 U.Pa. L.Rev. 320, 320–21 (1951).

Although the codes and the Federal Rules abolish the procedural distinctions between law and equity and substitute a single form of action, they do not abrogate the differences between the substantive and remedial rules of the two systems. See pp. 503–04, supra. Undoubtedly the greatest obstacle to complete unification of law and equity has been the presence of a jury-trial right in actions that would have been triable in a law court under the bifurcated system. Indeed, Professor Chafee, in an unpublished lecture, characterized jury trial as "the sword in the bed that prevents the complete fusion of law and equity." In many ways merger actually has complicated the application of the jury-trial right because a party now may enter a single court with both legal and equitable claims. The problem of defining the contours of the right and the significance of the clean-up doctrine in these "mixed" actions, especially when the legal and the equitable claims overlap, has proven to be of considerable complexity. The problem has been further enhanced by new statutes that create new rights of action with innovative remedies. Not surprisingly, it frequently is difficult to classify a new remedy as legal or equitable. The Supreme Court has itself struggled with the problem, as shown by the following line of cases.

(i) Jury Trial in the Federal Courts

BEACON THEATRES, INC. v. WESTOVER

Supreme Court of the United States, 1959.
359 U.S. 500, 79 S.Ct. 948, 3 L.Ed.2d 988.

Certiorari to the United States Court of Appeals for the Ninth Circuit.

MR. JUSTICE BLACK delivered the opinion of the Court.

Petitioner, Beacon Theatres, Inc., sought by mandamus to require a district judge in the Southern District of California to vacate certain orders alleged to deprive it of a jury trial of issues arising in a suit brought against it by Fox West Coast Theatres, Inc. The Court of Appeals for the Ninth Circuit refused the writ, holding that the trial judge had acted within his proper discretion in denying petitioner's request for a jury. * * *

Fox had asked for declaratory relief against Beacon alleging a controversy arising under the Sherman Antitrust Act, 26 Stat. 209, as amended, 15 U.S.C. §§ 1, 2, and under the Clayton Act, 38 Stat. 731, 15 U.S.C. § 15, which authorizes suits for treble damages against Sherman Act violators. According to the complaint Fox operates a movie theatre in San Bernardino, California, and has long been exhibiting films under contracts with movie distributors. These contracts grant it the exclusive right to show "first run" pictures in the "San Bernardino competitive area" and provide for "clearance"—a period of time during which no other theatre can exhibit the same pictures. After building a drive-in theatre about 11 miles from San Bernardino, Beacon notified Fox that it considered contracts barring simultaneous exhibitions of first-run films in the two theatres to be overt acts in violation of the antitrust laws. Fox's complaint alleged that this notification, together with threats of treble damage suits against Fox and its distributors, gave rise to "duress and coercion" which deprived Fox of a valuable property right, the right to negotiate for exclusive first-run contracts. Unless Beacon was restrained, the complaint continued, irreparable harm would result. Accordingly, while its pleading was styled a "Complaint for Declaratory Relief," Fox prayed both for a declaration that a grant of clearance between the Fox and Beacon theatres is reasonable and not in violation of the antitrust laws, and for an injunction, pending final resolution of the litigation, to prevent Beacon from instituting any action under the antitrust laws against Fox and its distributors arising out of the controversy alleged in the complaint. Beacon filed an answer, a counterclaim against Fox, and a cross-claim against an exhibitor who had intervened. These denied the threats and asserted that there was no substantial competition between the two theatres, that the clearances granted were therefore unreasonable, and that a conspiracy existed between Fox and its distributors to manipulate contracts and clearances so as to restrain trade and monopolize first-run pictures in violation of the antitrust laws. Treble damages were asked.

Beacon demanded a jury trial of the factual issues in the case as provided by Federal Rule * * * 38(b). The District Court, however, viewed the issues raised by the "Complaint for Declaratory Relief," including the question of competition between the two theatres, as essentially equitable. Acting under the purported authority of Rules 42(b) and 57, it directed that these issues be tried to the court before jury determination of the validity of the charges of antitrust violations made in the counterclaim and cross-claim. A common issue of the "Complaint for Declaratory Relief," the counterclaim, and the cross-claim was the reasonableness of the clearances granted to Fox, which depended, in part, on the existence of competition between the two theatres. Thus the effect of the action of the District Court could be, as the Court of Appeals believed, "to limit the petitioner's opportunity fully to try to a jury every issue which has a bearing upon its treble damage suit," for determination of the issue of clearances by the judge might "operate either by way of res judicata or collateral estoppel so as to conclude both parties with respect thereto at the subsequent trial of the treble damage claim." * * *

The District Court's finding that the Complaint for Declaratory Relief presented basically equitable issues draws no support from the Declaratory Judgment Act, 28 U.S.C. §§ 2201, 2202; Fed.Rules Civ.Proc. 57. * * * That statute, while allowing prospective defendants to sue to establish their nonliability, specifically preserves the right to jury trial for both parties. It follows that if Beacon would have been entitled to a jury trial in a treble damage suit against Fox it cannot be deprived of that right merely because Fox took advantage of the availability of declaratory relief to sue Beacon first. Since the right to trial by jury applies to treble damage suits under the antitrust laws, and is, in fact, an essential part of the congressional plan for making competition rather than monopoly the rule of trade * * *, the Sherman and Clayton Act issues * * * were essentially jury questions.

Nevertheless the Court of Appeals * * * held that the question of whether a right to jury trial existed was to be judged by Fox's complaint read as a whole. In addition to seeking a declaratory judgment, the court said, Fox's complaint can be read as making out a valid plea for injunctive relief, thus stating a claim traditionally cognizable in equity. A party who is entitled to maintain a suit in equity for an injunction, said the court, may have all the issues in his suit determined by the judge without a jury regardless of whether legal rights are involved. The court then rejected the argument that equitable relief, traditionally available only when legal remedies are inadequate, was rendered unnecessary in this case by the filing of the counterclaim and cross-claim which presented all the issues necessary to a determination of the right to injunctive relief. Relying on American Life Ins. Co. v. Stewart, 300 U.S. 203, 215, 57 S.Ct. 377, 380, 81 L.Ed. 605, decided before the enactment of the Federal Rules * * *, it invoked the principle that a court sitting in equity could retain jurisdiction even though later a legal remedy became available. In such instances the equity court had discretion to enjoin the later lawsuit in order to allow the whole dispute to be determined in one case in one court. Reasoning by analogy, the Court of Appeals held it was not an abuse of discretion for the district judge, acting under Federal Rule * * * 42(b), to try the equitable cause first even though this might, through collateral estoppel, prevent a full jury trial of the counterclaim and cross-claim which were as effectively stopped as by an equity injunction.[6]

Beacon takes issue with the holding of the Court of Appeals that the complaint stated a claim upon which equitable relief could be granted. As initially filed the complaint alleged that threats of lawsuits by petitioner against Fox and its distributors were causing irreparable harm to Fox's business relationships. The prayer for relief, however, made no mention of the threats but asked only that pending litigation of the claim for declaratory judgment, Beacon be enjoined from beginning any lawsuits under the antitrust laws against Fox and its distributors arising out of the controversy alleged in the complaint. Evidently of the opinion that this prayer did not state a good claim for equitable relief, the Court of Appeals construed it to include a request for an injunction against threats of lawsuits. * * * But this fact does not solve our problem. Assuming that the pleadings can be construed to support such a request and assuming additionally that the complaint can be read as alleging the kind of harassment by a multiplicity of lawsuits which would *traditionally* have justified equity to take jurisdiction and settle the case in one suit, we are nevertheless of the opinion that, under the Declaratory Judgment Act and the Federal Rules * * *, neither claim can justify denying Beacon a trial by jury of all the issues in the antitrust controversy.

The basis of injunctive relief in the federal courts has always been irreparable harm and inadequacy of legal remedies. At least as much is required to justify a trial court in using its discretion under the Federal Rules to allow claims of equitable origins to be tried ahead of legal ones, since this has the same effect as an equitable injunction of the legal claims. And it is immaterial, in judging if that discretion is properly employed, that before the Federal Rules and the Declaratory Judgment Act were passed, courts of equity, exercising a jurisdiction separate from courts of law, were, in some cases, allowed to enjoin subsequent legal actions between the same parties involving the same controversy. This was because the subsequent legal action, though providing an opportunity to try the case to a jury, might not protect the right of the equity plaintiff to a fair and orderly adjudication of the controversy. * * * Under such circumstances the legal remedy could quite naturally be deemed inadequate. Inadequacy of remedy and irreparable harm * * * today must be determined, not by precedents decided under discarded procedures, but in the light of the remedies now made available by the Declaratory Judgment Act and the Federal Rules.

---

6. 252 F.2d at page 874. In Ettelson v. Metropolitan Life Ins. Co., 317 U.S. 188, 192, 63 S.Ct. 163, 164, 87 L.Ed. 176, this Court recognized that orders enabling equitable causes to be tried before legal ones had the same effect as injunctions. In City of Morgantown, W.Va. v. Royal Ins. Co., 337 U.S. 254, 69 S.Ct. 1067, 93 L.Ed. 1347, the Court denied at least some such orders the status of injunctions for the purposes of appealability. It did not, of course, imply that when the orders came to be reviewed they would be examined any less strictly than injunctions. * * *

Viewed in this manner, the use of discretion by the trial court under Rule 42(b) to deprive Beacon of a full jury trial on its counterclaim and cross-claim, as well as on Fox's plea for declaratory relief, cannot be justified. Under the Federal Rules the same court may try both legal and equitable causes in the same action. * * *

Thus any defenses, equitable or legal, Fox may have to charges of antitrust violations can be raised either in its suit for declaratory relief or in answer to Beacon's counterclaim. On proper showing, harassment by threats of other suits, or other suits actually brought, involving the issues being tried in this case, could be temporarily enjoined pending the outcome of this litigation. Whatever permanent injunctive relief Fox might be entitled to on the basis of the decision in this case could, of course, be given by the court after the jury renders its verdict. In this way the issues between these parties could be settled in one suit giving Beacon a full jury trial of every antitrust issue. * * * By contrast, the holding of the court below while granting Fox no additional protection unless the avoidance of jury trial be considered as such, would compel Beacon to split his antitrust case, trying part to a judge and part to a jury. Such a result, which involves the postponement and subordination of Fox's own legal claim for declaratory relief as well as of the counterclaim which Beacon was compelled by the Federal Rules to bring, is not permissible.

Our decision is consistent with the plan of the Federal Rules and the Declaratory Judgment Act to effect substantial procedural reform while retaining a distinction between jury and nonjury issues and leaving substantive rights unchanged. Since in the federal courts equity has always acted only when legal remedies were inadequate, the expansion of adequate legal remedies provided by the Declaratory Judgment Act and the Federal Rules necessarily affects the scope of equity. Thus, the justification for equity's deciding legal issues once it obtains jurisdiction, and refusing to dismiss a case, merely because subsequently a legal remedy becomes available, must be re-evaluated in the light of the liberal joinder provisions of the Federal Rules which allow legal and equitable causes to be brought and resolved in one civil action. Similarly the need for, and therefore, the availability of such equitable remedies as Bills of Peace, *Quia Timet* and Injunction must be reconsidered in view of the existence of the Declaratory Judgment Act as well as the liberal joinder provision of the Rules. * * *

If there should be cases where the availability of declaratory judgment or joinder in one suit of legal and equitable causes would not in all respects protect the plaintiff seeking equitable relief from irreparable harm while affording a jury trial in the legal cause, the trial court will necessarily have to use its discretion in deciding whether the legal or equitable cause should be tried first. Since the right to jury trial is a constitutional one, however, while no similar requirement protects trials by the court, that discretion is very narrowly limited and must, wherever possible, be exercised to preserve jury trial. * * * [O]nly under the most imperative circumstances, circumstances which in view of the flexible procedures of the Federal Rules we cannot now anticipate, can the right to a jury trial of legal issues be lost through prior determination of equitable claims. * * *

As we have shown, this is far from being such a case.

* * *

The judgment of the Court of Appeals is reversed.

Reversed.

MR. JUSTICE FRANKFURTER took no part in the consideration or decision of this case.

MR. JUSTICE STEWART, with whom MR. JUSTICE HARLAN and MR. JUSTICE WHITTAKER concur, dissenting.

* * *

I.

The Court suggests that "the expansion of adequate legal remedies provided by the Declaratory Judgment Act * * * necessarily affects the scope of equity." Does the Court mean to say that the mere availability of an action for a declaratory judgment operates to furnish "an adequate remedy at law" so as to deprive a court of equity of the power to act? That novel line of reasoning is at least implied in the Court's opinion. But the Declaratory Judgment Act did not "expand" the substantive law. That Act merely provided a new statutory remedy, neither legal nor equitable, but available in the areas of both equity and law. When declaratory relief is sought, the right to trial by jury depends upon the basic context in which the issues are presented. * * * If the basic issues in an action for declaratory relief are of a kind traditionally cognizable in equity, e.g., a suit for cancellation of a written instrument, the declaratory judgment is not a "remedy at law." If, on the other hand, the issues arise in a context traditionally cognizable at common law, the right to a jury trial of course remains unimpaired, even though the only relief demanded is a declaratory judgment.

Thus, if in this case the complaint had asked merely for a judgment declaring that the plaintiff's specified manner of business dealings with distributors and other exhibitors did not render it liable to Beacon under the antitrust laws, this would have been simply a "juxtaposition of parties" case in which Beacon could have demanded a jury trial. But the complaint * * * presented issues of exclusively equitable cognizance, going well beyond a mere defense to any subsequent action at law. Fox sought from the court protection against Beacon's allegedly unlawful interference with its business relationships—protection which this Court seems to recognize might not have been afforded by a declaratory judgment, unsupplemented by equitable relief. The availability of a declaratory judgment did not, therefore, operate to confer upon Beacon the right to trial by jury with respect to the issues raised by the complaint.

II.

* * * [T]he Court holds, quite apart from its reliance upon the Declaratory Judgment Act, that Beacon by filing its counterclaim and cross-claim acquired a right to trial by jury of issues which otherwise would have been properly triable to the court. Support for this position is found in the principle that, "in the federal courts equity has always acted only when legal remedies were inadequate. * * * " Yet that principle is not employed in its traditional sense as a limitation upon the exercise of power by a court of equity. This is apparent in the Court's recognition that the allegations of the complaint entitled Fox to equitable relief—relief to which Fox would not have been entitled if it had had an adequate remedy at law. Instead, the principle is employed today to mean that because it is possible under the counterclaim to have a jury trial of the factual issue of substantial competition, that issue must be tried by a jury, even though the issue was primarily presented in the original claim for equitable relief. This is a marked departure from long-settled principles.

It has been an established rule "that equitable jurisdiction existing at the filing of a bill is not destroyed because an adequate legal remedy may have become available thereafter." American Life Ins. Co. v. Stewart * * *. It has also been long settled that the District Court in its discretion may order the trial of a suit in equity in advance of an action at law between the same parties, even if there is a factual issue common to both. * * *

III.

The Court today sweeps away these basic principles as "precedents decided under discarded procedures." It suggests that the Federal Rules * * * have somehow worked an "expansion of adequate legal remedies" so as to oust the District Courts of equitable jurisdiction, as well as to deprive them of their traditional power to control their own dockets. But obviously the Federal Rules could not and did not "expand" the substantive law one whit.

Like the Declaratory Judgment Act, the Federal Rules preserve inviolate the right to trial by jury in actions historically cognizable at common law, as under the Constitution they must. They do not create a right of trial by jury where that right "does not exist under the Constitution or statutes of the United States." Rule 39(a). Since Beacon's counterclaim was compulsory under the Rules, see Rule 13(a), it is apparent that by filing it Beacon could not be held to have waived its jury rights. * * * But neither can the counterclaim be held to have transformed Fox's original complaint into an action at law. * * *

The Rules make possible the trial of legal and equitable claims in the same proceeding, but they expressly affirm the power of a trial judge to determine the order in which claims shall be heard. Rule 42(b). Certainly the Federal Rules were not intended to undermine the basic structure of equity jurisprudence, developed over the centuries and explicitly recognized in the United States Constitution.

For these reasons I think the petition for a writ of mandamus should have been dismissed.

Notes and Questions

1. Consider the relevance of *Beacon Theatres* to the jury-trial right in the following situations:

(a) An action in which plaintiff seeks redress for a single wrong but asks for both legal and equitable relief. An example would be a copyright infringement action in which damages for past infringement (legal) and injunctive relief against future infringement (equitable) are sought. See Bruckman v. Hollzer, 152 F.2d 730 (9th Cir.1946). Suppose that the defendant in addition to denying infringement, puts forward a number of affirmative defenses, some of which pertain only to the demand for legal relief. After the presentation of evidence in the case, the jury renders a general verdict for the defendant. Under what circumstances may the trial judge thereafter enter a judgment for plaintiff for equitable relief? See Ag Services of America v. Nielsen, 231 F.3d 737 (10th Cir.2000).

(b) A situation in which plaintiff is entitled to either legal or equitable relief but not both. For example, a breach of contract action in which plaintiff sues for specific performance or damages in the alternative. If plaintiff demands a jury, will the resolution of the question depend on which relief he prefers and on the extent of the common issues? See Ford v. C.E. Wilson & Co., 30 F.Supp. 163 (D.Conn.1939), affirmed 129 F.2d 614 (2d Cir.1942). If defendant demands a jury trial and plaintiff opposes it, does this mean that plaintiff elects equitable relief?

(c) A case in which a legal counterclaim is asserted against a claim for equitable relief or an equitable counterclaim is asserted against a legal claim. Compare Bendix Aviation Corp. v. Glass, 81 F.Supp. 645 (E.D.Pa.1948), with Liberty Oil Co. v. Condon Nat. Bank, 260 U.S. 235, 43 S.Ct. 118, 67 L.Ed. 232 (1922). Should the permissive or compulsory nature of the counterclaim be relevant in determining whether there is a jury-trial right?

(d) A situation in which an issue that was determined without a jury in an equitable proceeding arises in a subsequent action at law under circumstances in which the doctrine of collateral estoppel (or issue preclusion, as it is now called) normally would bar relitigation. See pp. 1243–44, infra. How should the court rule if one of the parties demands a jury trial in the second action? See Parklane Hosiery Co. v. Shore, p. 1291, infra.

For an excellent analysis of many *Beacon Theatres* problems, see McCoid, *Procedural Reform and the Right to Jury Trial,* 116 U.Pa.L.Rev. 1 (1967).

2. Because of the crowded condition of jury dockets in many parts of the country, application of the *Beacon Theatres* decision may delay the adjudication of cases that would progress more rapidly on a nonjury docket. The delay may cause commercial injury to the litigants. For example, in the *Beacon Theatres* context some parties might hesitate to deal with Fox pending the outcome of the litigation, thereby adversely affecting Fox's commercial relationships during a potentially long period. This problem is partially alleviated by Rule 57, which permits the trial court to advance all declaratory-judgment actions on the calendar for speedy determination. Can the procedure in Federal Rule 42(b) be used to mitigate some of the detrimental effects of the litigation on the parties?

3. Think about the crucial role the court's grant of a preliminary injunction might play in many cases. It freezes the status quo during the case without taking the ultimate fact finding role away from the jury. Is it possible that a preliminary injunction would so strongly affect the litigants' behavior that it would be the de facto end of the case?

DAIRY QUEEN, INC. v. WOOD, 369 U.S. 469, 82 S.Ct. 894, 8 L.Ed.2d 44 (1962), arose out of a licensing agreement entered into by respondents, owners of the trademark "DAIRY QUEEN," under which petitioner agreed to pay $150,000 for the exclusive right to use that trademark in certain parts of Pennsylvania. The contract provided for a small initial payment, with the remaining payments to be made at the rate of 50% of all amounts received by petitioner on sales and franchises to deal with the trademark; minimum annual payments were to be made regardless of petitioner's receipts. In August, 1960, respondents wrote petitioner a letter in which they claimed that the latter had committed "a material breach of that contract" by defaulting on the contract's payment provisions and notified petitioner that the contract would be terminated unless the claimed default was remedied immediately. When petitioner continued to deal with the trademark, respondents brought an action for breach of contract praying for: (1) temporary and permanent injunctions to restrain petitioner from any future use of or dealing in the franchise and the trademark; (2) an accounting to determine the exact amount of money owed by petitioner and a judgment for that amount; and (3) an injunction pending an accounting to prevent petitioner from collecting any money from "Dairy Queen" stores in the territory.

The Eastern District of Pennsylvania granted a motion to strike petitioner's demand for a jury trial on the alternative grounds that either the action was "purely equitable" or, if not purely equitable, the legal issues were "incidental" to equitable issues, and, in either case, no right to trial by jury existed. The Third Circuit refused to mandamus the district judge to vacate this order. The Supreme Court reversed.

The Court first disposed of the District Court's conclusion that there is no right to jury trial on legal issues that are "incidental" to equitable issues.

> * * * The holding in *Beacon Theatres* * * * applies whether the trial judge chooses to characterize the legal issues presented as "incidental" to equitable issues or not. Consequently, * * * *Beacon Theatres* requires that any legal issues for which a trial by jury is timely and properly demanded be submitted to a jury. * * *

Id. at 472–73, 82 S.Ct. at 897, 8 L.Ed.2d at 48.

As to the lower court's conclusion that the action was "purely equitable," the Court said:

> * * * The most natural construction of the respondents' claim for a money judgment would seem to be that it is a claim that they are entitled to recover whatever was owed them under the contract as of the date of its purported termination plus damages for infringement of their trademark since that date. * * * As an action on a debt allegedly due under a contract, it would be difficult to conceive of an action of a more traditionally legal character. And as an action for damages based upon a charge of trademark infringement, it would be no less subject to cognizance by a court of law.

> The respondents' contention that this money claim is "purely equitable" is based primarily upon the fact that their complaint is cast in terms of an "accounting," rather than in terms of an action for "debt" or "damages." But the constitutional right to trial by jury cannot be made to depend upon the choice of words used in the pleadings. The necessary prerequisite to the right to maintain a suit for an equitable accounting,

like all other equitable remedies, is, as we pointed out in *Beacon Theatres*, the absence of an adequate remedy at law. Consequently, in order to maintain such a suit on a cause of action cognizable at law, as this one is, the plaintiff must be able to show that the "accounts between the parties" are of such a "complicated nature" that only a court of equity can satisfactorily unravel them. In view of the powers given to District Courts by Federal Rule * * * 53(b) to appoint masters to assist the jury in those exceptional cases where the legal issues are too complicated for the jury adequately to handle alone, the burden of such a showing is considerably increased and it will indeed be a rare case in which it can be met. * * * A jury, under proper instructions from the court, could readily determine the recovery, if any, to be had here, whether the theory finally settled upon is that of breach of contract, that of trademark infringement, or any combination of the two. * * *

Id. at 476–79, 82 S.Ct. at 899–900, 8 L.Ed.2d at 50–52.

KATCHEN v. LANDY, 382 U.S. 323, 86 S.Ct. 467, 15 L.Ed.2d 391 (1966). Petitioner filed two claims in bankruptcy for sums allegedly due him from an insolvent corporation. The trustee in bankruptcy responded by asserting that certain payments from corporate assets to petitioner and others were "voidable preferences" under the Bankruptcy Act and could be recouped by the trustee in summary bankruptcy proceedings. Despite petitioner's objections, judgment was rendered for the trustee on the preferences and it was ordered that petitioner's claims remain unpaid until after the judgment in favor of the trustee had been satisfied. The Tenth Circuit affirmed.

In the Supreme Court, petitioner argued that a creditor who has received a preference can hold the property under a substantial adverse claim without filing a claim in the bankruptcy proceeding, thereby forcing the trustee to recover the preference by a plenary action under Section 60 of the Act, 11 U.S.C. § 96; in such a plenary action the creditor could demand a jury trial. Petitioner also contended that the situation is the same when a creditor files a claim and the trustee not only objects to its allowance but also demands surrender of the preference; petitioner's theory was that the Bankruptcy Act does not give the bankruptcy court summary jurisdiction to order preferences surrendered; petitioner contended that if it did, it would violate the Seventh Amendment.

After an extensive analysis of the "structure and purpose" of the Bankruptcy Act, the Court held that the Act does confer summary jurisdiction to compel a claimant to surrender preferences. As to the jury-trial issue, the Court said:

> * * * [A]lthough petitioner might be entitled to a jury trial on the issue of preference if he presented no claim in the bankruptcy proceeding and awaited a federal plenary action by the trustee * * *, when the same issue arises as part of the process of allowance and disallowance of claims, it is triable in equity. The Bankruptcy Act, * * * converts the creditor's legal claim into an equitable claim to a pro rata share of the *res* * * *, a share which can neither be determined nor allowed until the creditor

disgorges the alleged voidable preference he has already received. * * *
As bankruptcy courts have summary jurisdiction to adjudicate controversies relating to property over which they have actual or constructive possession * * * and as the proceedings of bankruptcy courts are inherently proceedings in equity * * * there is no Seventh Amendment right to a jury trial for determination of objections to claims * * *.

Petitioner's final reliance is on the doctrine of Beacon Theatres v. Westover * * * and Dairy Queen v. Wood * * *.

The argument here is that the same issues—whether the creditor has received a preference and, if so, its amount—may be presented either as equitable issues in the bankruptcy court or as legal issues in a plenary suit and that the bankruptcy court should stay its own proceedings and direct the bankruptcy trustee to commence a plenary suit so as to preserve petitioner's right to a jury trial. * * *

* * * [P]etitioner's argument would require that in every case where a § 57g objection[a] is interposed and a jury trial is demanded the proceedings on allowance of claims must be suspended and a plenary suit initiated, with all the delay and expense that course would entail. Such a result is not consistent with the equitable purposes of the Bankruptcy Act nor with the rule of Beacon Theatres and Dairy Queen * * *. In neither Beacon Theatres nor Dairy Queen was there involved a specific statutory scheme contemplating the prompt trial of a disputed claim without the intervention of a jury. We think Congress intended the trustee's § 57g objection to be summarily determined * * *. Both Beacon Theatres and Dairy Queen recognize that there might be situations in which the Court could proceed to resolve the equitable claim first even though the results might be dispositive of the issues involved in the legal claim. * * *

Id. at 336–40, 86 S.Ct. at 476–78, 15 L.Ed.2d at 401–03. Justice Black and Justice Douglas dissented for the reasons stated in the dissenting opinion of Judge Phillips in the Court of Appeals. 336 F.2d 535, 540 (10th Cir.1964).

Questions

In what ways does Dairy Queen clarify or go beyond the Beacon Theatres decision? Is Katchen a retreat from Beacon Theatres and Dairy Queen? Compare the Supreme Court's decision in FITZGERALD v. UNITED STATES LINES CO., 374 U.S. 16, 83 S.Ct. 1646, 10 L.Ed.2d 720 (1963), discussing a Jones Act claim, which is under the aegis of a statutory jury-trial right, and a maintenance-and-cure claim, which traditionally has been treated as a nonjury admiralty question. The Court held that the two claims, which arose out of a single occurrence, had to be tried together before a jury. Should the Court have reached that result?

ROSS v. BERNHARD, 396 U.S. 531, 90 S.Ct. 733, 24 L.Ed.2d 729 (1970). Plaintiffs brought a derivative suit in federal court against the directors of a

a. Section 57g of the former Bankruptcy Act forbade the allowance of a claim when the creditor received or acquired a preference that was void or voidable under the Act if he did not surrender the preference.

closed-end investment company of which they were shareholders and joined the company's brokers, alleging that the company had been charged excessive brokerage fees. Plaintiffs' demand for jury trial, granted by the trial court but set aside by the Second Circuit, was upheld by the Supreme Court in a five-to-three decision:

> The common law refused * * * to permit stockholders to call corporate managers to account in actions at law. * * * Early in the 19th century, equity provided relief both in this country and in England. * * * The remedy made available in equity was the derivative suit, viewed in this country as a suit to enforce a *corporate* cause of action against officers, directors, and third parties. As elaborated in the cases, one precondition for the suit was a valid claim on which the corporation could have sued; another was that the corporation itself had refused to proceed after suitable demand, unless excused by extraordinary conditions. Thus the dual nature of the stockholder's action: first, the plaintiff's right to sue on behalf of the corporation and, second, the merits of the corporation's claim itself.

> Derivative suits posed no Seventh Amendment problems where the action against the directors and third parties would have been by a bill in equity had the corporation brought the suit. Our concern is with cases based upon a legal claim of the corporation against directors or third parties. Does the trial of such claims at the suit of a stockholder and without a jury violate the Seventh Amendment?

> * * * The heart of the action is the corporate claim. If it presents a legal issue, one entitling the corporation to a jury trial under the Seventh Amendment, the right to a jury is not forfeited merely because the stockholder's right to sue must first be adjudicated as an equitable issue triable to the court. *Beacon* and *Dairy Queen* require no less.

> If under older procedures, now discarded, a court of equity could properly try the legal claims of the corporation presented in a derivative suit, it was because irreparable injury was threatened and no remedy at law existed as long as the stockholder was without standing to sue and the corporation itself refused to pursue its own remedies. * * *

> * * * Actions are no longer brought as actions at law or suits in equity. Under the Rules there is only one action—a "civil action"—in which all claims may be joined and all remedies are available. Purely procedural impediments to the presentation of any issue by any party, based on the difference between law and equity, were destroyed. In a civil action presenting a stockholder's derivative claim, the court after passing upon the plaintiff's right to sue on behalf of the corporation is now able to try the corporate claim for damages with the aid of a jury. * * * The "expansion of adequate legal remedies provided by * * * the Federal Rules necessarily affects the scope of equity." Beacon Theatres, Inc. v. Westover, 359 U.S., at 509.

> Thus, for example, before-merger class actions were largely a device of equity, and there was no right to a jury even on issues that might, under other circumstances, have been tried to a jury. * * * [I]t now

seems settled in the lower federal courts that class action plaintiffs may obtain a jury trial on any legal issues they present. * * *

Justice Stewart, dissenting, responded:

* * * Since, as the Court concedes, a shareholder's derivative suit could be brought only in equity, it would seem to me to follow by the most elementary logic that in such suits there is no constitutional right to trial by jury. * * *

* * * [T]he Court's effort to force the facts of this case into the mold of *Beacon Theatres* and *Dairy Queen* simply does not succeed. Those cases involved a combination of historically separable suits, one in law and one in equity. * * *

But the present case is not one involving traditionally equitable claims by one party, and traditionally legal claims by the other. Nor is it a suit in which the plaintiff is asserting a combination of legal and equitable claims. For, as we have seen, a derivative suit has always been conceived of as a single, unitary, equitable cause of action. It is for this reason, and not because of "procedural impediments," that the courts of equity did not transfer derivative suits to the law side. * * *

If history is to be so cavalierly dismissed, the derivative suit can, of course, be artificially broken down into separable elements. But so then can any traditionally equitable cause of action, and the logic of the Court's position would lead to the virtual elimination of all equity jurisdiction. An equitable suit for an injunction, for instance, often involves issues of fact which, if damages had been sought, would have been triable to a jury. Does this mean that in a suit asking only for injunctive relief these factual issues *must* be tried to the jury, with the judge left to decide only whether, given the jury's findings, an injunction is the appropriate remedy? * * *

Id. at 534–35, 539–41, 544, 549–50, 90 S.Ct. at 736, 738–39, 741, 743–44, 24 L.Ed.2d at 733–34, 736–37, 739, 742.

Notes and Questions

1. A footnote in the majority opinion in *Ross* provides some guidance regarding the categorization of issues as legal or equitable for Seventh Amendment purposes:

As our cases indicate, the "legal" nature of an issue is determined by considering, first, the pre-merger custom with reference to such questions; second, the remedy sought; and, third, the practical abilities and limitations of juries. * * *

396 U.S. at 538 n. 10, 90 S.Ct. at 738 n. 10, 24 L.Ed.2d at 736 n. 10. The significance of the third factor mentioned by the Court—the practical abilities and limitations of juries—is unclear. Should it give the trial judge discretion to limit the jury trial right to issues that are well suited for lay jury determination? Or should it be construed to deny a jury trial on complex issues or whenever there is community bias? Or is it merely a reformulation of the traditional basis for equity jurisdiction—absence of an adequate remedy at law? Kane, *Civil Jury Trial: The*

Case for Reasoned Iconoclasm, 28 Hastings L.J. 1, 11, 34 (1976), offers one interpretation of the Court's cryptic comment:

> * * * The seventh amendment itself makes no mention of factors other than history that should be considered. Policy considerations or practical concerns were never openly considered in prior Supreme Court jury decisions * * *. Thus, assuming this language can be taken seriously, the use of the issue test [for determining the availability of jury trial] (a more vague, and hence more flexible, means of deciding seventh amendment questions) and the injection of policy considerations into this inquiry appear to represent a movement toward a truly functional jury trial test. * * *

> The language and purpose of the seventh amendment does not prevent the Supreme Court from adopting a functional, nonhistorical approach both to expand and to contract the right to a civil jury trial. The right to a civil jury symbolizes, among other things, notions of fair trial. The decision whether an action falls within the language of the constitutional guarantee may depend upon whether jury trial provides an adequate legal remedy. Thus, if the seventh amendment is read as a rigid historical rule, it not only may be dysfunctional, but in some instances it actually may pose a threat to justice.

But compare Redish, *Seventh Amendment Right to Jury Trial: A Study in the Irrationality of Rational Decision Making,* 70 Nw.U.L.Rev. 486 (1975).

2. Some lower federal courts have read the third "consideration" mentioned in the *Ross* footnote as a basis for denying a jury trial in cases in which the number of parties, complexity of the issues, or conceptual sophistication of the evidence and applicable substantive law support a finding that a jury would not be a rational and capable fact-finder. In re Japanese Electronic Prods. Antitrust Litigation, 631 F.2d 1069 (3d Cir.1980), affirmed in part and reversed in part on other grounds following summary judgment 723 F.2d 238, 319 (3d Cir.1983), reversed on other grounds 475 U.S. 574, 106 S.Ct. 1348, 89 L.Ed.2d 538 (1986). Other federal courts have rejected this approach as too great an incursion on the Seventh Amendment. See, e.g., In re United States Financial Secs. Litigation, 609 F.2d 411 (9th Cir.1979), certiorari denied 446 U.S. 929, 100 S.Ct. 1866, 64 L.Ed.2d 281 (1980). This issue arises most frequently in major securities and antitrust suits, which present issues of a technical and esoteric nature arguably outstripping the capacity of even the most intelligent jurors. Further, these suits often consume months or even years in pretrial discovery and weeks or months in trial, and generate thousands of pages of testimony, exhibits, and supporting documents.

The argument for the "complexity exception" is threefold. First, because this exception was recognized at common law at the time of the drafting and adoption of the Seventh Amendment, it is said to be consistent with the Constitution. See Arnold, *A Historical Inquiry into the Right to Trial by Jury in Complex Civil Litigation,* 128 U.Pa.L.Rev. 829 (1980); Campbell, *Complex Cases and Jury Trials: A Reply to Professor Arnold,* 128 U.Pa.L.Rev. 965 (1980); Arnold, *A Modest Replication to a Lengthy Discourse,* 128 U.Pa.L.Rev. 986 (1980). Second, because there are practical limitations on jurors' knowledge, experience, and ability, it is argued that complex and esoteric cases, such as *Japanese Electronic* or *U.S. Financial Securities,* are best entrusted to the fact-finding capacity of an experienced trial judge. Third, it is contended that to submit to a jury issues exceeding its capacity for rational and sound decisionmaking constitutes a denial of the litigants' due process rights.

In *U.S. Financial Securities,* the District Court on its own motion struck the demands for jury trial because of the complexity of the factual and legal issues involved, the daunting bulk of the evidence ("the equivalent of reading the first 90 volumes of the Federal Reporter, 2d Series"), and the expected duration of the trial (two years). On interlocutory appeal, the Ninth Circuit rejected all three proffered justifications for the complexity exception. The court held that the *Ross* footnote was too casual and cursory and lacked sufficient support to serve as the foundation for a major restriction of the Seventh Amendment right. The court also pointed out that, in its Seventh Amendment cases following *Ross,* the Supreme Court never had addressed the issue of the abilities or competence of jurors. Third, the court maintained that litigants are responsible for presenting their legal claims and supporting materials in comprehensible form and that they and the trial judge have available to them numerous procedural remedies to reshape the litigation into a form that can be understood by jurors.

In *Japanese Electronic,* the Third Circuit reversed the District Court's decision to reject the parties' motions to strike demands for jury trial in Zenith Radio Corp. v. Matsushita Elec. Industrial Co., 478 F.Supp. 889 (E.D.Pa.1979). The court rejected the historical justification and the "juror capacity" argument for the complexity exception, although tentatively accepting the due process argument.

> Although no specific precedent exists for a finding [of] a due process violation in the trial of any case to a jury, the principles that define the procedural requirements of due process would seem to impose some limitations on the range of cases that may be submitted to a jury. The primary value promoted by due process in factfinding procedures is "to minimize the risk of erroneous decisions." * * * A jury that cannot understand the evidence and the legal rules to be applied provides no reliable safeguard against erroneous decisions. Moreover, in the context of a completely adversary proceeding, like a civil trial, due process requires that "the decisionmaker's conclusion * * * rest[s] solely on the legal rules and evidence adduced at the hearing." * * * Unless the jury can understand the legal rules and evidence, we cannot realistically expect that the jury will rest its decision on them.

631 F.2d at 1084.

The Third Circuit maintained that if a jury could not rationally reach a verdict because of the complexity of the case, a court should balance the interests protected by the Fifth and Seventh Amendments. A court would then be justified in finding, as the Third Circuit did in this case, that considerations of procedural due process outweigh the constitutional right to a jury trial.

The Third Circuit cautioned that a jury trial should be denied only in exceptional circumstances. Before concluding that a lawsuit is too complex to be understood by a jury, a court should conduct a multi-level inquiry. First, a court should examine the factors contributing to the lawsuit's complexity. Second, a court should explore possible methods of reducing the complexity of the case or of augmenting the jury's abilities to comprehend it. Third, a court should consider the unique advantages offered by presenting a complex lawsuit to jury scrutiny.

Judge Gibbons dissented, pointing out that, even though the case was complex, the "manifestations of complexity are for the most part products of the liberal joinder rules of the Federal Rules of Civil Procedure and of the district court's ruling consolidating two multi-count cases for trial"; none of these rules is constitutionally required. The solution, Judge Gibbons maintained, is to use the provisions of the Federal Rules providing for separate trials to reduce the case to a form that jurors can understand.

Therefore, a plaintiff who requests a jury trial cannot liberally join parties and claims if these actions contribute to the overly complex nature of the case. Similarly, a defendant who demands a jury trial must seek to prevent a plaintiff from joining many separate claims and creating a complex lawsuit.

On the merits, Judge Gibbons criticized the majority's test for determining whether denial of a jury-trial demand is appropriate, maintaining that:

> * * * [Because,] in the end the factors which are identified will permit the exercise of trial court discretion * * * [,] the exercise of that discretion will sometimes be influenced by unarticulated sympathies for or hostilities toward the underlying policies sought to be advanced in the lawsuit. Trial court discretion, moreover, in any practical sense will be completely unreviewable. * * *

Id. at 1093. Judge Gibbons concluded that his difference with the majority was based in part on differing perceptions "of the nature of the judicial process and the role of juries in that process." Id. Because the jury performs a critical role in the legitimizing of the legal system, "any erosion of citizen participation in [that] system is in the long run likely, in my view, to result in a reduction in the moral authority that supports the process."

The court in *Japanese Electronic* suggested the use of "special trial techniques to increase a jury's capabilities"? What techniques might a court employ? Should the trial or appellate court have the most to say about the complexity of a particular case? The capabilities of a particular jury? Would this lead, in complex cases, to trial by a jury of intellectuals, rather than trial by a jury of peers? Is this constitutional?

The Supreme Court has yet to pass on this issue. *Japanese Electronic* and *U.S. Financial Securities* have provoked a spirited debate over the significance of the *Ross* footnote and the relationship between complex litigation and the Seventh Amendment's guarantee of jury trial in suits at common law: Kane, *Suing Foreign Sovereigns*, 34 Stan.L.Rev. 385 (1982); Lempert, *Civil Juries and Complex Cases: Let's Not Rush to Judgment*, 80 Mich.L.Rev. 68 (1981); Loo, *Rationale for an Exception to the Seventh Amendment Right to a Jury Trial: In re Japanese Electronics Products Antitrust Litigation*, 30 Clev.St.L.Rev. 647 (1981). On strategies and procedural devices for easing the jury's confusion and unfamiliarity with the subjects of and concepts at issue in complex litigation, see Cecil, Hans & Wiggins, *Citizen Comprehension of Difficult Issues: Lessons from Civil Jury Trials*, 40 Am.U.L.Rev. 727 (1991); Luneberg & Nordenberg, *Specially Qualified Juries and Expert Nonjury Tribunals: Alternatives for Coping with the Complexities of Modern Civil Litigation*, 67 Va.L.Rev. 887 (1981).

3. Is there a constitutional right to a nonjury trial on issues that historically were considered equitable and therefore were tried by the chancellor? What is the significance of the statement in *Beacon Theatres* that "the right to jury trial is a constitutional one * * * while no similar requirement protects trials by the court." In MICHAELSON v. UNITED STATES ex rel. CHICAGO, ST. P., M. & O. R. CO., 291 Fed. 940, 946 (7th Cir.1923), the court remarked that "Congress cannot constitutionally deprive the parties in an equity court of the right of trial by the chancellor." The Supreme Court reversed on other grounds 266 U.S. 42, 45 S.Ct. 18, 69 L.Ed. 162 (1924), and simply acknowledged the importance of the question.

Courts in a few states have declared that there is a constitutional right to a nonjury trial. The judicial reasoning is described in Van Hecke, *Trial by Jury in Equity Cases,* 31 N.C.L.Rev. 157, 173 (1953), as follows:

> The courts which have asserted that there is a constitutional right in equity cases to a trial of the facts by the judge alone, appear to have been motivated by (a) tradition, (b) respect for the chancellor's professional skill as a trier of facts, (c) a consciousness that the need for a court of equity had arisen in part from the limitation that jury trial had imposed upon the adequacy of various common-law actions, (d) an over-literal application of state constitutional provisions relating to the structure of state courts, (e) unsympathetic reaction to early legislative attempts to fuse the administration of law and equity into one procedural system, and (f) an uninformed fear of how jury trial would work in equity cases.

Are any of these reasons of sufficient magnitude to counter the policy in favor of jury trials apparent in *Ross, Beacon Theatres,* and *Dairy Queen?*

CURTIS v. LOETHER

Supreme Court of the United States, 1974.
415 U.S. 189, 94 S.Ct. 1005, 39 L.Ed.2d 260.

Certiorari to the United States Court of Appeals for the Seventh Circuit.

MR. JUSTICE MARSHALL delivered the opinion of the Court.

Section 812 of the Civil Rights Act of 1968, 82 Stat. 88, 42 U.S.C. § 3612, authorizes private plaintiffs to bring civil actions to redress violations of Title VIII, the fair housing provisions of the Act * * *. The question presented in this case is whether the Civil Rights Act or the Seventh Amendment requires a jury trial upon demand by one of the parties in an action for damages and injunctive relief under this section.

Petitioner, a Negro woman, brought this action under § 812, claiming that respondents, who are white, had refused to rent an apartment to her because of her race * * *. In her complaint she sought only injunctive relief and punitive damages; a claim for compensatory damages was later added. After an evidentiary hearing, the District Court granted preliminary injunctive relief, enjoining the respondents from renting the apartment in question to anyone else pending the trial on the merits. This injunction was dissolved some five months later with the petitioner's consent, after she had finally obtained other housing, and the case went to trial on the issues of actual and punitive damages.

Respondents made a timely demand for jury trial in their answer. The District Court * * * denied the jury request. * * * After trial on the merits, the District Judge found that respondents had in fact discriminated against petitioner on account of her race. Although he found no actual damages, * * * he awarded $250 in punitive damages, denying petitioner's request for attorney's fees and court costs.

The Court of Appeals reversed on the jury trial issue. * * * In view of the importance of the jury trial issue in the administration and enforcement of Title VIII and the diversity of views in the lower courts on the question, we granted certiorari * * *. We affirm.

The legislative history on the jury trial question is sparse, and what little is available is ambiguous. There seems to be some indication that supporters of Title VIII were concerned that the possibility of racial prejudice on juries might reduce the effectiveness of civil rights damages actions. On the other hand, one bit of testimony during committee hearings indicates an awareness that jury trials would have to be afforded in damages actions under Title VIII. Both petitioner and respondents have presented plausible arguments from the wording and construction of § 812. We see no point to giving extended consideration to these arguments, however, for we think it is clear that the Seventh Amendment entitles either party to demand a jury trial in an action for damages in the federal courts under § 812.

* * * Although the thrust of the Amendment was to preserve the right to jury trial as it existed in 1791, it has long been settled that the right extends beyond the common-law forms of action recognized at that time. * * *

Petitioner nevertheless argues that the Amendment is inapplicable to new causes of action created by congressional enactment. As the Court of Appeals observed, however, we have considered the applicability of the constitutional right to jury trial in actions enforcing statutory rights "as a matter too obvious to be doubted." * * * Although the Court has apparently never discussed the issue at any length, we have often found the Seventh Amendment applicable to causes of action based on statutes. * * * Whatever doubt may have existed should now be dispelled. The Seventh Amendment does apply to actions enforcing statutory rights, and requires a jury trial upon demand, if the statute creates legal rights and remedies, enforceable in an action for damages in the ordinary courts of law.

NLRB v. Jones & Laughlin Steel Corp., 301 U.S. 1, 57 S.Ct. 615, 81 L.Ed. 893 (1937), relied on by petitioner, lends no support to her statutory-rights argument. The Court there upheld the award of back pay without jury trial in an NLRB unfair labor practice proceeding, rejecting a Seventh Amendment claim on the ground that the case involved a "statutory proceeding" and "not a suit at common law or in the nature of such a suit." Id., at 48, 57 S.Ct. at 629. *Jones & Laughlin* merely stands for the proposition that the Seventh Amendment is generally inapplicable in administrative proceedings, where jury trials would be incompatible with the whole concept of administrative adjudication and would substantially interfere with the NLRB's role in the statutory scheme. Katchen v. Landy * * *, also relied upon by petitioner, is to like effect. There the Court * * * recognized that a bankruptcy court has been traditionally viewed as a court of equity, and that jury trials would "dismember" the statutory scheme of the Bankruptcy Act. * * * See also Guthrie National Bank v. Guthrie, 173 U.S. 528, 19 S.Ct. 513, 43 L.Ed. 796 (1899). These cases uphold congressional power to entrust enforcement of statutory rights to an administrative process or specialized court of equity free from the strictures of the Seventh Amendment. But when Congress provides for enforcement of statutory rights in an ordinary civil action in the district courts, where there is obviously no functional justification for denying the jury trial right, a jury trial must be available if the action involves rights and remedies of the sort typically enforced in an action at law.

We think it is clear that a damages action under § 812 is an action to enforce "legal rights" within the meaning of our Seventh Amendment deci-

976 TRIAL Ch. 14

sions. See, e.g., Ross v. Bernhard * * *; Dairy Queen, Inc. v. Wood, * * *. A damages action under the statute sounds basically in tort—the statute merely defines a new legal duty, and authorizes the courts to compensate a plaintiff for the injury caused by the defendant's wrongful breach. As the Court of Appeals noted, this cause of action is analogous to a number of tort actions recognized at common law.[10] More important, the relief sought here—actual and punitive damages—is the traditional form of relief offered in the courts of law.

We need not, and do not, go so far as to say that any award of monetary relief must necessarily be "legal" relief. * * * A comparison of Title VIII with Title VII of the Civil Rights Act of 1964, where the courts of appeals have held that jury trial is not required in an action for reinstatement and back pay, is instructive, although we of course express no view on the jury trial issue in that context. In Title VII cases the courts of appeals have characterized back pay as an integral part of an equitable remedy, a form of restitution. But the statutory language on which this characterization is based—

> [T]he court may enjoin the respondent from engaging in such unlawful employment practice, and order such affirmative action as may be appropriate, which may include, but is not limited to, reinstatement or hiring of employees, with or without back pay * * *, or any other equitable relief as the court deems appropriate, 42 U.S.C. § 2000e–5(g) (1970 ed., Supp. II)—

contrasts sharply with § 812's simple authorization of an action for actual and punitive damages. In Title VII cases, also, the courts have relied on the fact that the decision whether to award back pay is committed to the discretion of the trial judge. There is no comparable discretion here: if a plaintiff proves unlawful discrimination and actual damages, he is entitled to judgment for that amount. Nor is there any sense in which the award here can be viewed as requiring the defendant to disgorge funds wrongfully withheld from the plaintiff. Whatever may be the merit of the "equitable" characterization in Title VII cases, there is surely no basis for characterizing the award of compensatory and punitive damages here as equitable relief.

We are not oblivious to the force of petitioner's policy arguments. Jury trials may delay to some extent the disposition of Title VIII damages actions. But Title VIII actions seeking only equitable relief will be unaffected, and preliminary injunctive relief remains available without a jury trial even in damages actions, Dairy Queen, Inc. v. Wood * * *. Moreover, the statutory requirement of expedition of § 812 actions * * * applies equally to jury and nonjury trials. We recognize, too, the possibility that jury prejudice may deprive a victim of discrimination of the verdict to which he or she is entitled. Of course, the trial judge's power to direct a verdict, to grant judgment

---

10. For example, the Court of Appeals recognized that Title VIII could be viewed as an extension of the common-law duty of innkeepers not to refuse temporary lodging to a traveler without justification, a duty enforceable in a damages action triable to a jury, to those who rent apartments on a long-term basis. See 467 F.2d at 1117. An action to redress racial discrimination may also be likened to an action for defamation or intentional infliction of mental distress. Indeed, the contours of the latter tort are still developing, and it has been suggested that "under the logic of the common law development of a law of insult and indignity, racial discrimination might be treated as a dignitary tort." C. Gregory & H. Kalven, Cases and Materials on Torts 961 (2d ed. 1969).

notwithstanding the verdict, or to grant a new trial provides substantial protection against this risk, and respondents' suggestion that jury trials will expose a broader segment of the populace to the example of the federal civil rights laws in operation has some force. More fundamentally, however, these considerations are insufficient to overcome the clear command of the Seventh Amendment. The decision of the Court of Appeals must be affirmed.

Affirmed.

Notes and Questions

1. In a case decided the same term as *Curtis,* PERNELL v. SOUTHALL REALTY, 416 U.S. 363, 94 S.Ct. 1723, 40 L.Ed.2d 198 (1974), the Court, again speaking through Justice Marshall, decided that because a landlord's right to recover possession of real property was a right protected at common law, the Seventh Amendment jury trial guarantee applies in a summary process action for repossession under the District of Columbia Code.

2. The principal case referred to in the opinion as denying jury trial in actions for reinstatement with back pay under Title VII is Johnson v. Georgia Highway Express, Inc., 417 F.2d 1122 (5th Cir.1969). See also cases cited in Ochoa v. American Oil Co., 338 F.Supp. 914, 923 n. 6 (S.D.Tex.1972), a scholarly opinion that quarrels with the ruling of the Fifth Circuit in *Johnson,* although adhering to it.

3. In LYTLE v. HOUSEHOLD MANUFACTURING, INC., 494 U.S. 545, 110 S.Ct. 1331, 108 L.Ed.2d 504 (1990), the Supreme Court held that a claim under 42 U.S.C. § 1981 is a "suit at common law," thus carrying the right to a jury trial. The district judge had erroneously dismissed an employee's Section 1981 claim, and entered judgment against the plaintiff on his Title VII claim. The Court held that the plaintiff was entitled to a jury in his Section 1981 action and the district judge's Title VII ruling could have no preclusive effect on the jury trial. The Court noted that the availability of a jury trial in a Title VII action was not at issue, and remained an open question.

4. In 1991 Congress clarified its view of the question left open in the *Lytle* case by enacting 42 U.S.C. § 1981a(a), (c), covering claims that respondent unlawfully "intentionally" discriminated against the plaintiff (but excluding cases alleging unlawful discrimination based solely on disparate impact). The statute provides for a right to jury trial in cases brought under Section 1981a. It permits assessment of both compensatory and punitive damages, but specifically excludes back pay and "other equitable relief," which can be sought from the court under the prior existing provisions of Title VII.

5. Given the result in *Curtis,* what techniques might be available to Congress to diminish the availability of jury trials?

TULL v. UNITED STATES

Supreme Court of the United States, 1987.
481 U.S. 412, 107 S.Ct. 1831, 95 L.Ed.2d 365.

Certiorari to the United States Court of Appeals for the Fourth Circuit.

JUSTICE BRENNAN delivered the opinion of the Court.

The question for decision is whether the Seventh Amendment guaranteed petitioner a right to a jury trial on both liability and amount of penalty in an action instituted by the Federal Government seeking civil penalties and injunctive relief under the Clean Water Act * * *

I

The Clean Water Act prohibits discharging, without a permit, dredged or fill material into "navigable waters," including the wetlands adjacent to the waters. * * * "Wetlands" are "swamps, marshes, bogs and similar areas." * * * The Government sued the petitioner, a real estate developer, for dumping fill on wetlands on the island of Chincoteague, Virginia. The Government alleged in the original complaint that the petitioner dumped fill on three sites: Ocean Breeze Mobile Homes Sites, Mire Pond Properties, and Eel Creek. The Government later amended the complaint to allege that the petitioner also placed fill in a man-made waterway, named Fowling Gut Extended, on the Ocean Breeze property.

Section 1319 enumerates the remedies available under the Clean Water Act. Subsection (b) authorizes relief in the form of temporary or permanent injunctions. Subsection (d) provides that violators of certain sections of the Act "shall be subject to a civil penalty not to exceed $10,000 per day" during the period of the violation. The Government sought in this case both injunctive relief and civil penalties. When the complaint was filed, however, almost all of the property at issue had been sold by the petitioner to third parties. Injunctive relief was therefore impractical except with regard to a small portion of the land. * * * The Government's complaint demanded the imposition of the maximum civil penalty of $22,890,000 under subsection (d). * * *

Petitioner's timely demand for a trial by jury was denied by the District Court. During the 15-day bench trial, the petitioner did not dispute that he had placed fill at the locations alleged and did not deny his failure to obtain a permit. Petitioner contended, however, that the property in question did not constitute "wetlands." * * * The Government concedes that triable issues of fact were presented by disputes between experts involving the composition and nature of the fillings. * * *

The District Court concluded that the petitioner had illegally filled in wetland areas on all properties in question, but drastically reduced the amount of civil penalties sought by the Government. * * *

The Court of Appeals affirmed over a dissent, rejecting petitioner's argument that, under the Seventh Amendment, he was entitled to a jury trial. * * *

II

* * * The Court has construed [the Seventh Amendment] * * * to require a jury trial on the merits in those actions that are analogous to "Suits at common law." Prior to the Amendment's adoption, a jury trial was customary in suits brought in the English *law* courts. In contrast, those actions that are analogous to 18th-century cases tried in courts of equity or admiralty do not require a jury trial. * * * This analysis applies not only to common law forms of action, but also to causes of action created by congressional enactment. * * *

To determine whether a statutory action is more similar to cases that were tried in courts of law than to suits tried in courts of equity or admiralty, the Court must examine both the nature of the action and of the remedy sought. First, we compare the statutory action to 18th-century actions brought in the courts of England prior to the merger of the courts of law and equity. * * * Second, we examine the remedy sought and determine whether it is legal or equitable in nature. * * *

A

The petitioner analogizes this Government suit under § 1319(d) to an action in debt within the jurisdiction of English courts of law. Prior to the enactment of the Seventh Amendment, English courts had held that a civil penalty suit was a particular species of an action in debt that was within the jurisdiction of the courts of law. * * *

After the adoption of the Seventh Amendment, federal courts followed this English common law in treating the civil penalty suit as a particular type of an action in debt, requiring a jury trial. * * * Actions by the Government to recover civil penalties under statutory provisions historically have been viewed as one type of action in debt requiring trial by jury.

* * *

In the instant case, the Government sought penalties of over 22 million dollars for violation of the Clean Water Act and obtained a judgment in the sum of $325,000. This action is clearly analogous to the 18th-century action in debt, and federal courts have rightly assumed that the Seventh Amendment required a jury trial.

The Government argues, however, that—rather than an action in debt—the closer historical analogue is an action to abate a public nuisance. In 18th-century English law, a public nuisance was "an act or omission 'which obstructs or causes inconvenience or damage to the public in the exercise of rights common to all Her Majesty's subjects.'" * * * The Government argues that the present suit is analogous to two species of public nuisances. One is the suit of the sovereign in the English courts of equity for a "purpresture" to enjoin or order the repair of an enclosure or obstruction of public waterways; the other is the suit of the sovereign to enjoin "offensive trades and manufactures" that polluted the environment. * * *

It is true that the subject matter of this Clean Water Act suit—the placement of fill into navigable waters—resembles these two species of public nuisance. Whether, as the Government argues, a public nuisance action is a better analogy than an action in debt is debatable. But we need not decide the question. * * * [T]he fact that the subject matter of a modern statutory action and an 18th-century English action are close equivalents "is irrelevant for Seventh Amendment purposes," because "that Amendment requires trial by jury in actions unheard of at common law." It suffices that we conclude that both the public nuisance action and the action in debt are appropriate analogies to the instant statutory action.

The essential function of an action to abate a public nuisance was to provide a civil means to redress "a miscellaneous and diversified group of minor criminal offenses, based on some interference with the interests of the community, or the comfort or convenience of the general public." * * * Similarly, the essential function of an action in debt was to recover money owed under a variety of statutes or under the common law. Both of these 18th-century actions, then, could be asserted by the sovereign to seek relief for an injury to the public in numerous contexts.

We need not rest our conclusion on what has been called an "abstruse historical" search for the nearest 18th-century analogue. * * * We reiterate our previously expressed view that characterizing the relief sought is "[m]ore important" than finding a precisely analogous common law cause of action in determining whether the Seventh Amendment guarantees a jury trial. * * *

B

A civil penalty was a type of remedy at common law that could only be enforced in courts of law. Remedies intended to punish culpable individuals, as opposed to those intended simply to extract compensation or restore the status quo, were issued by courts of law, not courts of equity. * * * The action authorized by subsection 1319(d) is of this character. Subsection (d) does not direct that the "civil penalty" imposed be calculated solely on the basis of equitable determinations, such as the profits gained from violations of the statute, but simply imposes a maximum penalty of $10,000 per day of violation. The legislative history of the Act reveals that Congress wanted the district court to consider the need for retribution and deterrence, in addition to restitution, when it imposed civil penalties. * * * A court can require retribution for wrongful conduct based on the seriousness of the violations, the number of prior violations, and the lack of good-faith efforts to comply with the relevant requirements. * * * It may also seek to deter future violations by basing the penalty on its economic impact. * * * Subsection 1319(d)'s authorization of punishment to further retribution and deterrence clearly evidences that this subsection reflects more than a concern to provide equitable relief. In the present case, for instance, the District Court acknowledged that the petitioner received no profits from filling in properties in Mire Pond and Eel Creek, but still imposed a $35,000 fine. * * * Thus, the District Court intended not simply to disgorge profits but also to impose punishment. Because the nature of the relief authorized by subsection 1319(d) was traditionally available only in a court of law, the petitioner in this present action is entitled to a jury trial on demand.

The punitive nature of the relief sought in this present case is made apparent by a comparison with the relief sought in an action to abate a public nuisance. A public nuisance action was a classic example of the kind of suit that relied on the injunctive relief provided by courts in equity. * * * The Government, in fact, concedes that public nuisance cases brought in equity sought injunctive relief, not monetary penalties. * * * Indeed, courts in equity refused to enforce such penalties. * * *

The Government contends, however, that a suit enforcing civil penalties under the Clean Water Act is similar to an action for disgorgement of improper profits, traditionally considered an equitable remedy. It bases this characterization upon evidence that the District Court determined the amount of the penalties by multiplying the number of lots sold by the petitioner by the profit earned per lot. * * * An action for disgorgement of improper profits is, however, a poor analogy. Such an action is a remedy only for restitution—a more limited form of penalty than a civil fine. Restitution is limited to "restoring the status quo and ordering the return of that which rightfully belongs to the purchaser or tenant." * * * As the above discussion indicates, however, subsection 1319(d)'s concerns are by no means limited to restoration of the status quo.

The Government next contends that, even if the civil penalties under subsection 1319(d) are deemed legal in character, a jury trial is not required. A court in equity was empowered to provide monetary awards that were incidental to or intertwined with injunctive relief. The Government therefore argues that its claim under subsection 1319(b), which authorizes injunctive relief, provides jurisdiction for monetary relief in equity. * * * This argument has at least three flaws. First, while a court in equity may award monetary restitution as an adjunct to injunctive relief, it may not enforce civil penalties. * * * Second, the Government was aware when it filed suit that relief would be limited primarily to civil penalties, since the petitioner had already sold most of the properties at issue. App. 110, 119. A potential penalty of $22 million hardly can be considered incidental to the modest equitable relief sought in this case.

Finally, the Government was free to seek an equitable remedy in addition to, or independent of, legal relief. Section 1319 does not intertwine equitable relief with the imposition of civil penalties. Instead each kind of relief is separably authorized in a separate and distinct statutory provision. Subsection (b), providing injunctive relief, is independent of subsection (d), which provides only for civil penalties. In such a situation, if a "legal claim is joined with an equitable claim, the right to jury trial on the legal claim, including all issues common to both claims, remains intact. The right cannot be abridged by characterizing the legal claim as 'incidental' to the equitable relief sought." * * * Thus, the petitioner has a constitutional right to a jury trial to determine his liability on the legal claims.

III

The remaining issue is whether the petitioner additionally has a Seventh Amendment right to a jury assessment of the civil penalties. At the time this case was tried, § 1319(d) did not explicitly state whether juries or trial judges were to fix the civil penalties. The legislative history of the 1977 Amendments to the Clean Water Act shows, however, that Congress intended that trial judges perform the highly discretionary calculations necessary to award civil penalties after liability is found. * * * We must decide therefore whether Congress can, consistent with the Seventh Amendment, authorize judges to assess civil penalties.

The Seventh Amendment is silent on the question whether a jury must determine the remedy in a trial in which it must determine liability.[9] The answer must depend on whether the jury must shoulder this responsibility as necessary to preserve the "substance of the common-law right of trial by

9. Nothing in the Amendment's language suggests that the right to a jury trial extends to the remedy phase of a civil trial. Instead, the language "defines the kind of cases for which jury trial is preserved, namely 'suits at common law.'" Colgrove v. Battin [p. 1016, infra], * * *. Although " '[w]e have almost no direct evidence concerning the intention of the fram- ers of the seventh amendment itself,' the historical setting in which the Seventh Amendment was adopted highlighted a controversy that was generated * * * by fear that the civil jury itself would be abolished." Ibid. * * * We have been presented with no evidence that the Framers meant to extend the right to a jury to the remedy phase of a civil trial.

jury." * * * Is a jury role necessary for that purpose? We do not think so. " 'Only those incidents which are regarded as fundamental, as inherent in and of the essence of the system of trial by jury, are placed beyond the reach of the legislature.' " * * * The assessment of a civil penalty is not one of the "most fundamental elements." Congress' authority to fix the penalty by statute has not been questioned, and it was also the British practice. * * * In the United States, the action to recover civil penalties usually seeks the amount fixed by the Congress. * * * The assessment of civil penalties thus cannot be said to involve the "substance of a common-law right to a trial by jury," nor a "fundamental element of a jury trial."

Congress' assignment of the determination of the amount of civil penalties to trial judges therefore does not infringe on the constitutional right to a jury trial. Since Congress itself may fix the civil penalties, it may delegate that determination to trial judges. In this case, highly discretionary calculations that take into account multiple factors are necessary in order to set civil penalties under the Clean Water Act. These are the kinds of calculations traditionally performed by judges. * * * We therefore hold that a determination of a civil penalty is not an essential function of a jury trial, and that the Seventh Amendment does not require a jury trial for that purpose in a civil action.

IV

We conclude that the Seventh Amendment required that the petitioner's demand for a jury trial be granted to determine his liability, but that the trial court and not the jury should determine the amount of penalty, if any. The judgment of the Court of Appeals is therefore reversed, and the case is remanded for further proceedings consistent with this opinion.

It is so ordered.

JUSTICE SCALIA, with whom JUSTICE STEVENS joins, concurring in part and dissenting in part.

I join the Court's disposition, and Parts I and II of its opinion. I do not join Part III because in my view the right to trial by jury on whether a civil penalty of unspecified amount is assessable also involves a right to trial by jury on what the amount should be. The fact that the legislature could elect to fix the amount of penalty has nothing to do with whether, if it chooses not to do so, that element comes within the jury-trial guarantee. Congress could, I suppose, create a private cause of action by one individual against another for a fixed amount of damages, but it surely does not follow that if it creates such a cause of action *without* prescribing the amount of damages, that issue could be taken from the jury.

While purporting to base its determination (quite correctly) upon historical practice, the Court creates a form of civil adjudication I have never encountered. I can recall no precedent for judgment of civil liability by jury but assessment of amount by the court. Even punitive damages are assessed by the jury when liability is determined in that fashion. One is of course tempted to make an exception in a case like this, where the government is imposing a non-compensatory remedy to enforce direct exercise of its regulatory authority, because there comes immediately to mind the role of the sentencing judge in a criminal proceeding. If criminal trials are to be the model, however, determination of liability by the jury should be on a standard of proof requiring guilt beyond a reasonable doubt. Having chosen to proceed in civil fashion, with the advantages which that mode entails, it seems to me the government must take the bitter with the sweet. Since, as the Court correctly reasons, the proper analogue to a civil-fine action is the common-law action for debt, the government need only prove liability by a preponderance of the evidence; but must, as in any action for debt, accept the amount of award determined not by its own officials but by twelve private citizens. If that tends to discourage the government from proceeding in this fashion, I doubt that the Founding Fathers would be upset.

Notes and Questions

1. Reread Notes 1 and 2, pp. 970–74, supra. Notice that the majority in *Tull* omits the third factor listed in the *Ross* footnote when it identifies the considerations that determine the existence of a right to jury trial. Does that imply the Supreme Court now believes that the complexity of a trial is not a basis for denying the Seventh Amendment right to a jury trial?

2. The majority in *Tull* declares that the relief sought is the most important factor in determining whether the action is legal or equitable in nature. How can the Court hold that one is not entitled to a jury trial on the question of the amount of relief, when the nature of the relief sought is the very factor that renders the action legal rather than equitable? Does *Tull* authorize taking the task of computing damages away from juries? For a discussion of the Supreme Court's decision in *Tull,* see Note, *Tull v. United States: Jury Trial Required in Statutory Civil Penalty Actions,* 1988 Utah L.Rev. 435.

3. In FELTNER v. COLUMBIA PICTURES TELEVISION, INC., 523 U.S. 340, 118 S.Ct. 1279, 140 L.Ed.2d 438 (1998), the Court engaged in an historical analysis to determine that a constitutional right to jury trial exists in a case for copyright infringement when plaintiff opts to seek damages under a federal statute "in a sum not less than $500 or more than $20,000 as the court considers just," rather than actual damages. The Court held that the jury must decide the amount of the damages because they have been consistently determined by juries in copyright cases. It distinguished *Tull* on the ground that there was no evidence in *Tull* that the amount of civil penalties paid to the Government had historically been determined by jurors. Note that in *Feltner* it was the defendant who demanded that a jury determine the amount of damages. Suppose the demand had been made by plaintiff. Could it be argued that by seeking statutory damages "as the court considers just," plaintiff waives any right to jury trial?

4. As *Tull* illustrates, there often is not a clear line between questions of fact and questions of law. See pp. 1001–08, infra. Issues that are a mixture of law and fact generally go to juries, but not always. Develop your own philosophy as to when such issues should go to juries.

———

ATLAS ROOFING CO. v. OCCUPATIONAL SAFETY & HEALTH RE-VIEW COMMISSION, 430 U.S. 442, 97 S.Ct. 1261, 51 L.Ed.2d 464 (1977). Petitioners were cited for violations of the Occupational Safety and Health Act (OSHA) and fines were imposed on them after hearings before administrative law judges of the Occupational Safety and Health Review Commission (OSHRC). Two Courts of Appeals upheld the Commission's orders and rejected the petitioners' claim that the enforcement scheme violated the Seventh Amendment. In an opinion by Justice White, the Supreme Court affirmed:

* * * At least in cases in which "public rights" are being litigated— e.g., cases in which the Government sues in its sovereign capacity to enforce public rights created by statutes within the power of Congress to enact—the Seventh Amendment does not prohibit Congress from assigning the factfinding function and initial adjudication to an administrative forum with which the jury would be incompatible.

* * * [Petitioners also argue] that the right to jury trial was never intended to depend on the identity of the forum to which Congress has chosen to submit a dispute; otherwise, it is said, Congress could utterly destroy the right to a jury trial by always providing for administrative rather than judicial resolution of the vast range of cases that now arise in the courts. The argument is well put, but it overstates the holdings of our prior cases and is in any event unpersuasive. Our prior cases support administrative factfinding in only those situations involving "public rights," e.g., where the Government is involved in its sovereign capacity under an otherwise valid statute creating enforceable public rights. Wholly private tort, contract, and property cases, as well as a vast range of other cases, are not at all implicated.

More to the point, it is apparent from the history of jury trial in civil matters that factfinding, which is the essential function of the jury in civil cases, * * * was never the exclusive province of the jury under either the English or American legal systems at the time of the adoption of the Seventh Amendment; and the question whether a fact would be found by a jury turned to a considerable degree on the nature of the forum in which a litigant found himself. * * * The question whether a particular case was to be tried in a court of equity—without a jury—or a court of law—with a jury—did not depend on whether the suit involved factfinding or on the nature of the facts to be found. * * * Rather, as a general rule, the decision turned on whether courts of law supplied a cause of action and an adequate remedy to the litigant. If it did, then the case would be tried in a court of law before a jury. * * * Thus, suits for damages for breach of contract, for example, were suits at common law with the issues of the making of the contract and its breach to be decided by a jury; but specific performance was a remedy unavailable in a court of law and where such relief was sought the case would be tried in a court of equity with the facts as to making and breach to be ascertained by the court.

The Seventh Amendment was declaratory of the existing law, for it required only that jury trial in suits at common law was to be "preserved." It thus did not purport to require a jury trial where none was required before. Moreover, it did not seek to change the factfinding mode in equity or admiralty or to freeze equity jurisdiction * * * , preventing it from developing new remedies where those available in courts of law were inadequate. Ross v. Bernhard * * * held that a jury trial is required in stockholder derivative suits where * * * a jury trial would have been available to the corporation. It is apparent, however, that prior to the 1938 Federal Rules of Civil Procedure merging the law and equity functions of the federal courts, the very suit involved in *Bernhard* would have been in a court of equity sitting without a jury, not because the underlying issue was any different at all from the issue the corporation would have presented had it sued, but because the stockholder plaintiff who was denied standing in a court of law to sue on the issue was enabled in proper circumstances, starting in the early part of the 19th century, to sue in equity on behalf of the company.

The point is that the Seventh Amendment was never intended to establish the jury as the exclusive mechanism for factfinding in civil cases. It took the existing legal order as it found it, and there is little or no basis for concluding that the Amendment should now be interpreted to provide an impenetrable barrier to administrative factfinding under otherwise valid federal regulatory statutes. We cannot conclude that the Amendment rendered Congress powerless—when it concluded that remedies available in courts of law were inadequate to cope with a problem within Congress' power to regulate—to create new public rights and remedies by statute and commit their enforcement, if it chose, to a tribunal other than a court of law—such as an administrative agency—in which facts are not found by juries. * * *

* * * [H]istory and our cases support the proposition that the right to a jury trial turns not solely on the nature of the issue to be resolved but also on the forum in which it is to be resolved. Congress found the common-law and other existing remedies for work injuries resulting from unsafe working conditions to be inadequate to protect the Nation's working men and women. It created a new cause of action, and remedies therefor, unknown to the common law, and placed their enforcement in a tribunal supplying speedy and expert resolutions of the issues involved. The Seventh Amendment is no bar to the creation of new rights or to their enforcement outside the regular courts of law.

* * *

Id. at 450, 457–61, 97 S.Ct. at 1266, 1270–72, 51 L.Ed.2d at 472, 476–79.

Notes and Questions

1. Could the Court have reached the result in *Atlas* by invoking the doctrine of Katchen v. Landy, p. 967, supra, rather than creating a new "public rights" exception?

2. Does *Atlas* only create a "public rights" exception to the jury-trial guarantee? Justice White relied on a number of prior cases, including Justice Marshall's dicta in *Curtis* and *Pernell* interpreting NLRB v. Jones & Laughlin Steel Corp., 301 U.S. 1, 57 S.Ct. 615, 81 L.Ed. 893 (1937), as support for the proposition that Congress may avoid the jury-trial guarantee by entrusting enforcement of statutory rights to administrative proceedings in which the Seventh Amendment generally is inapplicable. But neither of those cases indicated that there are any limits on Congress' power to replace common-law actions with statutory actions and assign their adjudication to administrative tribunals, as was

done with OSHA and workmen's compensation. Could the legislature provide that ordinary personal-injury actions be decided by such a tribunal? See In re Opinion of the Justices, 87 N.H. 492, 179 A. 344 (1935); Brown, *Administrative Commissions and the Judicial Power,* 19 Minn.L.Rev. 261 (1935).

3. In LEHMAN v. NAKSHIAN, 453 U.S. 156, 101 S.Ct. 2698, 69 L.Ed.2d 548 (1981), the respondent brought suit against the Navy under the Age Discrimination in Employment Act, 29 U.S.C. §§ 621–634 (ADEA). The Act had been amended to permit suits by civilian employees against government agencies such as the Navy, 29 U.S.C. § 633a(a), and the Supreme Court had held in Lorillard v. Pons, 434 U.S. 575, 98 S.Ct. 866, 55 L.Ed.2d 40 (1978), that jury trials were permitted in suits against private employers under Section 626(c) of the ADEA. The respondent maintained that Section 626(c) also permitted jury trials of suits against the government. The Navy moved to strike the respondent's demand for jury trial, but the District Court and Court of Appeals refused to grant its motion.

The Supreme Court reversed, holding that the right to jury trial was not available in suits against the Government under the ADEA. The Court based its ruling on the traditional principles that the United States, as sovereign, is immune from suit except as it consents to be sued and that, even when it consents to be sued, the terms of its consent bind the federal courts. The Court held, further, that the common law in 1791 did not permit jury trials in suits against the sovereign. The Court rejected arguments based on the legislative history of the ADEA and held also that Federal Rule 38(a) "requires an affirmative grant of the right [to jury trial] where, as in this case, the Seventh Amendment does not apply."

Dissenting for himself and Justices Marshall, Blackmun, and Stevens, Justice Brennan contended that when immunity is waived, Congress must act *explicitly* to restrict consents to suit by forbidding them to be tried to a jury. Relying on the legislative history and emphasizing that ADEA suits against the government are to be brought in the district courts, in which jury trial generally is available, rather than the Court of Claims, in which jury trial never is available, Justice Brennan concluded that by fair implication Congress intended to allow jury trials in ADEA suits against the government.

———

GRANFINANCIERA, S.A. v. NORDBERG, 492 U.S. 33, 109 S.Ct. 2782, 106 L.Ed.2d 26 (1989). Nordberg was the bankruptcy trustee for the debtor, Chase & Sanborn Corporation. Nordberg filed a claim against Granfinanciera to recover funds fraudulently transferred to it from the debtor's estate. Granfinanciera's request for a jury trial was denied on the ground that the bankruptcy courts were, like administrative agencies, outside the Seventh Amendment. The Eleventh Circuit affirmed, arguing that the statutes under which the claim was brought, 11 U.S.C. § 548(a)(2) and 28 U.S.C. § 1411, do not provide for jury trials, and that actions to recover fraudulent conveyances are equitable in nature. The Supreme Court disagreed:

> * * * The form of our analysis is familiar. "First, we compare the statutory action to 18th-century actions brought in the courts of England prior to the merger of the courts of law and equity. Second, we examine the remedy sought and determine whether it is legal or equitable in nature." Tull v. United States * * *. The second stage of this analysis is

more important than the first. * * * If, on balance, these two factors indicate that a party is entitled to a jury trial under the Seventh Amendment, we must decide whether Congress may assign and has assigned resolution of the relevant claim to a non-Article III adjudicative body that does not use a jury as factfinder. * * *

Id. at 42, 109 S.Ct. at 2790, 106 L.Ed.2d at 41.

The Court then performed the analysis, and determined that the recovery of a fraudulent conveyance is an action in which a jury trial is available. The Court then considered the "public right" exception:

> * * * In *Atlas Roofing*, we noted that "when Congress creates new statutory 'public rights,' it may assign their adjudication to an administrative agency with which a jury trial would be incompatible, without violating the Seventh Amendment's injunction that jury trial is to be 'preserved' in 'suits at common law.' " We emphasized, however, that Congress' power to block application of the Seventh Amendment to a cause of action has limits. Congress may only deny trials by jury in actions at law, we said, in cases where "public rights" are litigated: "Our prior cases support administrative factfinding in only those situations involving 'public rights,' e.g., where the Government is involved in its sovereign capacity under an otherwise valid statute creating enforceable public rights. Wholly private tort, contract, and property cases, as well as a vast range of other cases, are not at all implicated."

> We adhere to that general teaching. * * * Congress may devise novel causes of action involving public rights free from the strictures of the Seventh Amendment if it assigns their adjudication to tribunals without statutory authority to employ juries as factfinders. But it lacks the power to strip parties contesting matters of private right of their constitutional right to a trial by jury. * * *

> In certain situations, of course, Congress may fashion causes of action that are closely *analogous* to common-law claims and place them beyond the ambit of the Seventh Amendment by assigning their resolution to a forum in which jury trials are unavailable. * * * Congress' power to do so is limited, however, just as its power to place adjudicative authority in non-Article III tribunals is circumscribed.

> * * * If a statutory right is not closely intertwined with a federal regulatory program Congress has power to enact, and if the right neither belongs to nor exists against the Federal Government, then it must be adjudicated by an Article III court. If the right is legal in nature, then it carries with it the Seventh Amendment's guarantee of a jury trial.

The Court then considered the bankruptcy courts in specific:

> Although the issue admits of some debate, a bankruptcy trustee's right to recover a fraudulent conveyance under 11 U.S.C. 548(a)(2) seems to us more accurately characterized as a private rather than a public right as we have used those terms in our Article III decisions. * * * There can be little doubt that fraudulent conveyance actions by bankruptcy trustees * * * are quintessentially suits at common law that more nearly resemble state-law contract claims brought by a bankrupt corporation to augment the bankruptcy estate than they do creditors' hierarchically ordered

claims to a pro rata share of the bankruptcy res. They therefore appear matters of private rather than public right. * * *

* * * It may be that providing jury trials in some fraudulent conveyance actions—if not in this particular case, because respondent's suit was commenced after the bankruptcy court approved the debtor's plan of reorganization—would impede swift resolution of bankruptcy proceedings and increase the expense of Chapter 11 reorganizations. But "these considerations are insufficient to overcome the clear command of the Seventh Amendment." * * *

Id. at 55–63, 109 S.Ct. at 2797–802, 106 L.Ed.2d at 49–54.

Notes and Questions

1. In footnote 4 of the majority opinion in *Granfinanciera*, Justice Brennan commented:

> This quite distinct inquiry into whether Congress has permissibly entrusted the resolution of certain disputes to an administrative agency or specialized court of equity, and whether jury trials would impair the functioning of the legislative scheme, appears to be what the Court contemplated when, in Ross v. Bernhard, * * * it identified "the practical abilities and limitations of juries" as an additional factor to be consulted in determining whether the Seventh Amendment confers a jury trial right. * * *

Justice Brennan seems to be suggesting that the third prong of the test advanced in *Ross,* abandoned by the Court in subsequent decisions, has resurfaced in *Atlas Roofing* as the "public rights" exception. Does this mean that the complexity of the issues in a case only can lead to a denial of the Seventh Amendment right to a jury trial when Congress has created an administrative agency to provide a forum for the resolution of public rights' disputes? How does this affect the Court of Appeals decisions in *Japanese Electronic* and *U.S. Financial Securities?* Reread Note 2, pp. 971–73, supra.

2. Would the plaintiff in Katchen v. Landy, p. 967, supra, be entitled to a jury trial after the more recent Supreme Court decision in *Granfinanciera?*

3. Does the ruling in *Granfinanciera* mean that a bankruptcy judge can empanel a jury and conduct a trial, or does the Seventh Amendment require an Article III judge to administer the proceedings? Contrast Ben Cooper, Inc. v. Insurance Co. of Pennsylvania, 896 F.2d 1394 (2d Cir.1990) (bankruptcy court can conduct a jury trial), with In re United Missouri Bank, 901 F.2d 1449 (8th Cir.1990) (bankruptcy court cannot). See also Cyr, *The Right to Trial by Jury in Bankruptcy: Which Judge Is to Preside?*, 63 Am.Bankr.L.J. 53 (1989).

CHAUFFEURS, TEAMSTERS AND HELPERS LOCAL 391 v. TERRY

Supreme Court of the United States, 1990.
494 U.S. 558, 110 S.Ct. 1339, 108 L.Ed.2d 519.

Certiorari to the United States Court of Appeals for the Fourth Circuit.

JUSTICE MARSHALL delivered the opinion of the Court except as to Part III–A.

This case presents the question whether an employee who seeks relief in the form of backpay for a union's alleged breach of its duty of fair representation has a right to trial by jury. We hold that the Seventh Amendment entitles such a plaintiff to a jury trial.

I

McLean Trucking Company and the Chauffeurs, Teamsters, and Helpers Local Union No. 391 were parties to a collective-bargaining agreement that governed the terms and conditions of employment at McLean's terminals. The 27 respondents were employed by McLean as truckdrivers in bargaining units covered by the agreement, and all were members of the Union.

* * * Claiming a violation of their seniority rights, respondents filed a * * * grievance with the Union, but the Union declined to refer the charges to a grievance committee on the ground that the relevant issues had been determined in * * * prior proceedings.

In July 1983, respondents filed an action in District Court, alleging * * * that the Union had violated its duty of fair representation * * * [and] sought, *inter alia,* compensatory damages for lost wages and health benefits. * * *

Respondents had requested a jury trial in their pleadings. The Union moved to strike the jury demand on the ground that no right to a jury trial exists in a duty of fair representation suit. The District Court denied the motion to strike. After an interlocutory appeal, the Fourth Circuit affirmed the trial court, holding that the Seventh Amendment entitled respondents to a jury trial of their claim for monetary relief. 863 F.2d 334 (1988). We granted the petition for certiorari to resolve a circuit conflict on this issue * * * and now affirm the judgment of the Fourth Circuit.

II

The duty of fair representation is inferred from unions' exclusive authority under the National Labor Relations Act, 49 Stat. 449, 29 U.S.C. § 159(a) (1982 ed.), to represent all employees in a bargaining unit. *Vaca v. Sipes,* 386 U.S. 171, 177, 87 S.Ct. 903, 909–910, 17 L.Ed.2d 842 (1967). The duty requires a union "to serve the interests of all members without hostility or discrimination toward any, to exercise its discretion with complete good faith and honesty, and to avoid arbitrary conduct." *Ibid.* * * *

III

* * *

To determine whether a particular action will resolve legal rights, we examine both the nature of the issues involved and the remedy sought. "First, we compare the statutory action to 18th-century actions brought in the courts of England prior to the merger of the courts of law and equity. Second, we examine the remedy sought and determine whether it is legal or equitable in nature." *Tull* * * *. The second inquiry is the more important in our analysis. *Granfinanciera.*

A

An action for breach of a union's duty of fair representation was unknown in 18th-century England; in fact, collective bargaining was unlawful. * * * We must therefore look for an analogous cause of action that existed in the 18th century to determine whether the nature of this duty of fair representation suit is legal or equitable.

The Union contends that this duty of fair representation action resembles a suit brought to vacate an arbitration award because respondents seek to set aside the result of the grievance process. In the 18th century, an action to set aside an arbitration award was considered equitable. * * *

The arbitration analogy is inapposite, however, to the Seventh Amendment question posed in this case. No grievance committee has considered respondents' claim that the Union violated its duty of fair representation; the grievance process was concerned only with the employer's alleged breach of the collective-bargaining agreement. Thus, respondents' claim against the Union cannot be characterized as an action to vacate an arbitration award * * *.

The Union next argues that respondents' duty of fair representation action is comparable to an action by a trust beneficiary against a trustee for breach of fiduciary duty. Such actions were within the exclusive jurisdiction of courts of equity. * * * This analogy is far more persuasive than the arbitration analogy. Just as a trustee must act in the best interests of the beneficiaries, * * * a union, as the exclusive representative of the workers, must exercise its power to act on behalf of the employees in good faith * * *. Moreover, just as a beneficiary does not directly control the actions of a trustee, * * * an individual employee lacks direct control over a union's actions taken on his behalf * * *.

The trust analogy extends to a union's handling of grievances. In most cases, a trustee has the exclusive authority to sue third parties who injure the beneficiaries' interest in the trust, * * * including any legal claim the trustee holds in trust for the beneficiaries, * * *. The trustee then has the sole responsibility for determining whether to settle, arbitrate, or otherwise dispose of the claim. * * * Similarly, the union typically has broad discretion in its decision whether and how to pursue an employee's grievance against an employer. * * * Just as a trust beneficiary can sue to enforce a contract entered into on his behalf by the trustee only if the trustee "improperly refuses or neglects to bring an action against the third person," * * * so an employee can sue his employer for a breach of the collective-bargaining agreement only if he shows that the union breached its duty of fair representation in its handling of the grievance * * *.

Respondents contend that their duty of fair representation suit is less like a trust action than an attorney malpractice action, which was historically an action at law * * *.

The attorney malpractice analogy is inadequate in several respects. Although an attorney malpractice suit is in some ways similar to a suit alleging a union's breach of its fiduciary duty, the two actions are fundamentally different. The nature of an action is in large part controlled by the nature of the underlying relationship between the parties. Unlike employees represented by a union, a client controls the significant decisions concerning his representation. Moreover, a client can fire his attorney if he is dissatisfied with his attorney's performance. This option is not available to an individual employee who is unhappy with a union's representation, unless a majority of the members of the bargaining unit share his dissatisfaction. * * * Thus, we find the malpractice analogy less convincing than the trust analogy.

Nevertheless, the trust analogy does not persuade us to characterize respondents' claim as wholly equitable. The Union's argument mischaracterizes the nature of our comparison of the action before us to 18th-century forms of action. As we observed in *Ross v. Bernhard,* * * *, "The Seventh Amendment question depends on the nature of the *issue* to be tried rather than the character of the overall action." * * * [T]o recover from the Union here, respondents must prove both that McLean violated § 301 by breaching the collective-bargaining agreement and that the Union breached its duty of fair representation. When viewed in isolation, the duty of fair representation issue is analogous to a claim against a trustee for breach of fiduciary duty. The § 301 issue, however, is comparable to a breach of contract claim—a legal issue.

Respondents' action against the Union thus encompasses both equitable and legal issues. The first part of our Seventh Amendment inquiry, then, leaves us in equipoise as to whether respondents are entitled to a jury trial.

B

Our determination under the first part of the Seventh Amendment analysis is only preliminary. Granfinanciera * * *. In this case, the only remedy sought is a request for compensatory damages representing backpay and benefits. Generally, an action for money damages was "the traditional form of relief offered in the courts of law." Curtis v. Loether * * *. This Court has not, however, held that "any award of monetary relief must *necessarily* be 'legal' relief." *Ibid.* (emphasis added). See also *Granfinanciera* * * * (WHITE, J., dissenting). Nonetheless, because we conclude that the remedy respondents seek has none of the attributes that must be present before we will find an exception to the general rule and characterize damages as equitable, we find that the remedy sought by respondents is legal.

First, we have characterized damages as equitable where they are restitutionary, such as in "action[s] for disgorgement of improper profits," *Tull* * * *. * * * The backpay sought by respondents is not money wrongfully held by the Union, but wages and benefits they would have received from McLean had the Union processed the employees' grievances properly. Such relief is not restitutionary.

Second, a monetary award "incidental to or intertwined with injunctive relief" may be equitable. *Tull* * * *. * * * Because respondents seek only money damages, this characteristic is clearly absent from the case.[8]

8. Both the Union and the dissent argue that the backpay award sought here is equitable because it is closely analogous to damages awarded to beneficiaries for a trustee's breach of trust. * * *. Such damages were available only in courts of equity because those courts had exclusive jurisdiction over actions involving a trustee's breach of his fiduciary duties. * * *

The Union's argument, however, conflates the two parts of our Seventh Amendment inquiry. Under the dissent's approach, if the action at issue were analogous to an 18th-century action within the exclusive jurisdiction of the courts of equity, we would necessarily conclude that the remedy sought was also equitable because it would have been unavailable in a court of law. This view would, in effect, make the first part of our inquiry dispositive. We have clearly held, however, that the second part of the inquiry—the nature of the relief—is more important to the Seventh Amendment determination. * * * The second part of the analysis, therefore, should not replicate the

The Union argues that the backpay relief sought here must nonetheless be considered equitable because this Court has labeled backpay awarded under Title VII, 42 U.S.C. § 2000e *et seq.* (1982 ed.), as equitable. * * *

The Court has never held that a plaintiff seeking backpay under Title VII has a right to a jury trial. See Lorillard v. Pons, 434 U.S. 575, 581–582, 98 S.Ct. 866, 870–871, 55 L.Ed.2d 40 (1978). Assuming, without deciding, that such a Title VII plaintiff has no right to a jury trial, the Union's argument does not persuade us that respondents are not entitled to a jury trial here. Congress specifically characterized backpay under Title VII as a form of "equitable relief." * * * Congress made no similar pronouncement regarding the duty of fair representation. Furthermore, the Court has noted that backpay sought from an employer under Title VII would generally be restitutionary in nature, see Curtis v. Loether * * *, in contrast to the damages sought here from the union. Thus, the remedy sought in this duty of fair representation case is clearly different from backpay sought for violations of Title VII.

* * *

We hold, then, that the remedy of backpay sought in this duty of fair representation action is legal in nature. Considering both parts of the Seventh Amendment inquiry, we find that respondents are entitled to a jury trial on all issues presented in their suit.

IV

On balance, our analysis of the nature of respondents' duty of fair representation action and the remedy they seek convinces us that this action is a legal one. Although the search for an adequate 18th-century analog revealed that the claim includes both legal and equitable issues, the money damages respondents seek are the type of relief traditionally awarded by courts of law. Thus, the Seventh Amendment entitles respondents to a jury trial, and we therefore affirm the judgment of the Court of Appeals.

It is so ordered.

JUSTICE BRENNAN, concurring in part and concurring in the judgment.

I agree with the Court that respondents seek a remedy that is legal in nature and that the Seventh Amendment entitles respondents to a jury trial on their duty of fair representation claims. * * * I do not join that part of the opinion which reprises the particular historical analysis this Court has employed to determine whether a claim is a "Suit at common law" under the Seventh Amendment, * * *, because I believe the historical test can and should be simplified.

The current test, first expounded in Curtis v. Loether * * *, requires a court to compare the right at issue to 18th-century English forms of action to determine whether the historically analogous right was vindicated in an action at law or in equity, and to examine whether the remedy sought is legal or equitable in nature. However, this Court, in expounding the test, has repeatedly discounted the significance of the analogous form of action for deciding where the Seventh Amendment applies. I think it is time we dispense

"abstruse historical" inquiry of the first part, *Ross* * * *, but requires consideration of the general types of relief provided by courts of law and equity.

with it altogether. I would decide Seventh Amendment questions on the basis of the relief sought. If the relief is legal in nature, *i.e.,* if it is the kind of relief that historically was available from courts of law, I would hold that the parties have a constitutional right to a trial by jury—unless Congress has permissibly delegated the particular dispute to a non-Article III decisionmaker and jury trials would frustrate Congress' purposes in enacting a particular statutory scheme.

I believe that our insistence that the jury trial right hinges in part on a comparison of the substantive right at issue to forms of action used in English courts 200 years ago needlessly convolutes our Seventh Amendment jurisprudence. For the past decade and a half, this Court has explained that the two parts of the historical test are not equal in weight, that the nature of the remedy is more important than the nature of the right. * * * Since the existence of a right to jury trial therefore turns on the nature of the remedy, absent congressional delegation to a specialized decisionmaker, there remains little purpose to our rattling through dusty attics of ancient writs. The time has come to borrow William of Occam's razor and sever this portion of our analysis.

We have long acknowledged that, of the factors relevant to the jury trial right, comparison of the claim to ancient forms of action, "requiring extensive and possibly abstruse historical inquiry, is obviously the most difficult to apply." Ross v. Bernhard * * *. Requiring judges, with neither the training nor time necessary for reputable historical scholarship, to root through the tangle of primary and secondary sources to determine which of a hundred or so writs is analogous to the right at issue has embroiled courts in recondite controversies better left to legal historians. * * *

To rest the historical test required by the Seventh Amendment solely on the nature of the relief sought would not, of course, offer the federal courts a rule that is in all cases self-executing. Courts will still be required to ask which remedies were traditionally available at law and which only in equity. But this inquiry involves fewer variables and simpler choices, on the whole, and is far more manageable than the scholasticist debates in which we have been engaged. Moreover, the rule I propose would remain true to the Seventh Amendment, as it is undisputed that, historically, "[j]urisdictional lines [between law and equity] were primarily a matter of remedy." McCoid, Procedural Reform and the Right to Jury Trial: A Study of *Beacon Theaters, Inc. v. Westover,* 116 U.Pa.L.Rev. 1 (1967). * * *

This is not to say that the resulting division between claims entitled to jury trials and claims not so entitled would exactly mirror the division between law and equity in England in 1791. But it is too late in the day for this Court to profess that the Seventh Amendment preserves the right to jury trial only in cases that would have been heard in the British law courts of the 18th century. See, e.g., * * * Ross v. Bernhard * * *.

We can guard * * * [the jury trial] right and save our courts from needless and intractable excursions into increasingly unfamiliar territory simply by retiring that prong of our Seventh Amendment test which we have already cast into a certain doubt. If we are not prepared to accord the nature of the historical analog sufficient weight for this factor to affect the outcome of our inquiry, except in the rarest of hypothetical cases, what reason do we have for insisting that federal judges proceed with this arduous inquiry? It is time we read the writing on the wall, especially as we ourselves put it there.

JUSTICE STEVENS, concurring in part and concurring in the judgment.

Because I believe the Court has made this case unnecessarily difficult by exaggerating the importance of finding a precise common-law analogue to the duty of fair representation, I do not join Part III–A of its opinion. * * *

* * * Duty of fair representation suits are for the most part ordinary civil actions involving the stuff of contract and malpractice disputes. There is accordingly no ground for excluding these actions from the jury right.

In my view, the evolution of this doctrine through suits tried to juries, the useful analogy to common-law malpractice cases, and the well-recognized duty to scrutinize any proposed curtailment of the right to a jury trial "with the utmost care," * * * provide a plainly sufficient basis for the Court's holding today. I therefore join its judgment and all of its opinion except for Part III–A.

JUSTICE KENNEDY, with whom JUSTICE O'CONNOR and JUSTICE SCALIA join, dissenting.

* * * To determine whether rights and remedies in a duty of fair representation action are legal in character, we must compare the action to the 18th-century cases permitted in the law courts of England, and we must examine the nature of the relief sought. * * *

I disagree with the analytic innovation of the Court that identification of the trust action as a model for modern duty of fair representation actions is insufficient to decide the case. The Seventh Amendment requires us to determine whether the duty of fair representation action "is more similar to cases that were tried in courts of law than to suits tried in courts of equity." Tull v. United States. Having made this decision in favor of an equitable action, our inquiry should end. Because the Court disagrees with this proposition, I dissent.

* * *

II

The Court relies on two lines of precedents to overcome the conclusion that the trust action should serve as the controlling model. The first consists of cases in which the Court has considered simplifications in litigation resulting from modern procedural reforms in the federal courts. Justice Marshall asserts that these cases show that the Court must look at the character of individual issues rather than claims as a whole. * * *. The second line addresses the significance of the remedy in determining the equitable or legal nature of an action for the purpose of choosing the most appropriate analogy. Under these cases, the Court decides that the respondents have a right to a jury because they seek money damages. * * * These authorities do not support the Court's holding.

A

In three cases we have found a right to trial by jury where there are legal claims that, for procedural reasons, a plaintiff could have or must have raised in the courts of equity before the systems merged. In Beacon Theatres, Inc. v. Westover, * * * [w]e ruled that, because Beacon would have had a right to a jury trial on its antitrust claims, Fox could not deprive it of a jury merely by taking advantage of modern declaratory procedures to sue first. The result was consistent with the spirit of the Federal Rules * * *, which allow liberal joinder of legal and equitable actions, and the Declaratory Judgment Act * * *, which preserves the right to jury trial to both parties. * * *

In Dairy Queen, Inc. v. Wood * * * we held, in a similar manner, that a plaintiff, by asking in his complaint for an equitable accounting for trademark infringement, could not deprive the defendant of a jury trial on contract claims subsumed within the accounting. Although a court of equity would have heard the contract claims as part of the accounting suit, we found them severable under modern procedure. See *id.* * * *.

In Ross v. Bernhard * * * a shareholder-plaintiff demanded a jury trial in a derivative action asserting a legal claim on behalf of his corporation. The defendant opposed a jury trial. In deciding the case, we recognized that only the courts of equity had procedural devices allowing shareholders to raise a corporation's claims. We nonetheless again ruled that modern procedure allowed trial of the legal claim to a jury. * * *

These three cases responded to the difficulties created by a merged court system. * * * They stand for the proposition that, because distinct courts of equity no longer exist, the possibility or necessity of using former equitable procedures to press a legal claim no longer will determine the right to a jury. Justice Marshall reads these cases to require a jury trial whenever a cause of action contains legal issues and would require a jury trial in this case because the respondents must prove a breach of the collective-bargaining agreement as one element of their claim. * * *

I disagree. The respondents, as shown above, are asserting an equitable claim. Having reached this conclusion, the *Beacon, Dairy Queen,* and *Ross* cases are inapplicable. Although we have divided self-standing legal claims from equitable declaratory, accounting, and derivative procedures, we have never parsed legal elements out of equitable claims absent specific procedural justifications. Actions which, beyond all question, are equitable in nature may involve some predicate inquiry that would be submitted to a jury in other contexts. For example, just as the plaintiff in a duty of fair representation action against his union must show breach of the collective-bargaining agreement as an initial matter, in an action against a trustee for failing to pursue a claim the beneficiary must show that the claim had some merit. * * * But the question of the claim's validity, even if the claim raises contract issues, would not bring the jury right into play in a suit against a trustee.

* * *

B

The Court also rules that, despite the appropriateness of the trust analogy as a whole, the respondents have a right to a jury trial because they seek money damages. * * * The nature of the remedy remains a factor of considerable importance in determining whether a statutory action had a legal or equitable analog in 1791, but we have not adopted a rule that a statutory action permitting damages is by definition more analogous to a legal action than to any equitable suit. In each case, we look to the remedy to determine whether, taken with other factors, it places an action within the definition of "suits at common law."

In *Curtis* * * *, for example, we ruled that the availability of actual and punitive damages made a statutory antidiscrimination action resemble a legal tort action more than any equitable action. We made explicit that we did not "go so far as to say that any award of monetary relief must necessarily be 'legal' relief." * * * Although monetary damages might cause some statutory actions to resemble tort suits, the presence of monetary damages in this duty of fair representation action does not make it more analogous to a legal action than to an equitable action. Indeed, as shown above, the injunctive and monetary remedies available make the duty of fair representation suit less analogous to a malpractice action than to a suit against a trustee.

* * *

III

The Court must adhere to the historical test in determining the right to a jury because the language of the Constitution requires it. The Seventh Amendment "preserves" the right to jury trial in civil cases. We cannot preserve a right existing in 1791 unless we look to history to identify it. * * *

I would hesitate to abandon or curtail the historical test out of concern for the competence of the Court to understand legal history. We do look to history for the answers to constitutional questions. * * * Although opinions will differ on what this history shows, the approach has no less validity in the Seventh Amendment context than elsewhere.

If Congress has not provided for a jury trial, we are confined to the Seventh Amendment to determine whether one is required. Our own views respecting the wisdom of using a jury should be put aside. Like Justice Brennan, I admire the jury process. Other judges have taken the opposite view. * * * But the judgment of our own times is not always preferable to the lessons of history. Our whole constitutional experience teaches that history must inform the judicial inquiry. Our obligation to the Constitution and its Bill of Rights, no less than the compact we have with the generation that wrote them for us, do not permit us to disregard provisions that some may think to be mere matters of historical form.

Notes and Questions

1. In footnote 8 of his opinion in *Terry* does Justice Marshall provide an adequate explanation for continuing to employ a two-prong test that values the second prong more than the first? Or does the historical analysis "needlessly convolute our Seventh Amendment jurisprudence," as Justice Brennan argues? Justices Marshall and Stevens and the dissenters all disagree on the appropriate historical model for a "duty of fair representation" action. Is this disagreement evidence in favor of severing the historical analysis from the Seventh Amendment test, or is it evidence in favor of keeping the analysis as it is?

2. The Supreme Court's analysis of the scope of the right to jury trial under the Seventh Amendment remains ongoing. In CITY OF MONTEREY v. DEL

MONTE DUNES, 526 U.S. 687, 119 S.Ct. 1624, 143 L.Ed.2d 882 (1999), damages were sought under the Civil Rights Acts, 42 U.S.C. § 1983, on the ground that the city had taken defendant's property without just compensation. The Court rendered three opinions, holding by a 5 to 4 majority, that a jury trial was proper. The four dissenting Justices argued that the case was at heart a condemnation action under the Fifth Amendment to the Constitution for which there is no right to trial by jury. Four Justices disagreed, noting that a condemnation action historically is one brought by the government conceding that it owes compensation to the owner of the property and seeking a fair evaluation of its worth. In *Del Monte Dunes*, the property owner initiated the suit, arguing that the actions of the county with regard to zoning deprived the owner of the value of the property. The four Justices held that such a case is akin historically to a tort action for damages, and thus carries the right to a jury trial under the Seventh Amendment. Justice Scalia concurred with them on the ground that Section 1983 itself, when brought to recover damages, provides for a jury trial, regardless of the nature of the underlying cause.

For a comprehensive review of the Supreme Court jury trial cases, including an analysis of just where *Del Monte Dunes* might fit, see Moses, *What the Jury Must Hear: The Supreme Court's Evolving Seventh Amendment Jurisprudence*, 68 Geo. Wash. L.Rev. 183 (2000).

(ii) Jury Trial in the State Courts

In some states there is a right to jury trial in equity cases, which eliminates the problem presented by *Beacon Theatres* and *Dairy Queen*. In most states that have merged law and equity, however, issues similar to those in the federal courts have arisen since the adoption of the codes.

The Commissioners who prepared the original New York Code of Civil Procedure (1848) were aware of the problem presented by abolishing the distinction between law and equity at a time when that state's constitution continued to guarantee "trial by jury in all cases in which it has been heretofore used."[b] But they may have underestimated the difficulty. Not content to leave the issue solely one of constitutional interpretation as it has been in the federal courts, they attempted to solve it by specific provisions:

> § 208.   Whenever, in an action for the recovery of money only, or of specific real or personal property, there shall be an issue of fact, it must be tried by a jury, unless a jury trial be waived * * *.

> § 209.   Every other issue is triable by the court, which, however, may order the whole issue, or any specific question of fact involved therein, to be tried by a jury * * *.

These provisions were copied in a great many states. But "in most jurisdictions * * * the courts, while occasionally giving the statute some weight, have regarded it generally as merely restating the law-equity dichotomy, and have proceeded to make their determination on historical grounds." Note, *The Right to Jury Trial Under Merged Procedures*, 65 Harv.L.Rev. 453,

---

b.   This language appeared in the New York Constitutions of 1777, 1821, 1846, and 1894. Because it was interpreted to mean that each successive constitution guaranteed jury trial in any case to which it had been extended by the legislature since the adoption of the preceding constitution, it was changed in the constitution of 1938 to guarantee jury trial only "in all cases in which it has heretofore been guaranteed by constitutional provision." See 4 Weinstein, Korn & Miller, *New York Civil Practice* ¶¶ 4101.07–.08.

454 (1952). In civil actions in which damages alone are sought, there has been little difficulty in finding that a jury is required, and of course in traditional equity cases, such as those involving trusts or injunctions, no jury has been allowed. In most states, there has been a reluctance to allow a mixed form of trial, with some issues being tried by the court and some by a jury. When there have been "legal" and "equitable" issues in the same case, the tendency has been to find one or the other the "predominant" concern and try the case accordingly. Perhaps most frequently the decision has been to find the case "predominantly" equitable, with jury trial denied on the "legal" issues on the grounds that they are "incidental," or that a jury trial is waived by joining a legal claim in an equitable action. Id. at 454–55.

The Supreme Court's decisions, from *Beacon Theatres* through *Del Monte Dunes*, have not had a broad impact on the state courts and, in the state opinions in which these cases have been discussed, the reception has been mixed. Court opinions that have looked at the *Beacon Theatres* line approvingly include Perilli v. Board of Education Monongalia County, 182 W.Va. 261, 387 S.E.2d 315 (1989); Bendick v. Cambio, 558 A.2d 941 (R.I.1989); Higgins v. Barnes, 310 Md. 532, 530 A.2d 724 (1987); Benson v. City of Nenana, 725 P.2d 490 (Alaska 1986).

HIATT v. YERGIN

Indiana Court of Appeals, Second District, 1972.
152 Ind.App. 497, 284 N.E.2d 834.

[Plaintiffs alleged that they had simultaneously entered into two contracts with defendants. Under the first, plaintiffs agreed to sell their one-half interest in Henry County Beverage Company to defendants; under the second, defendants agreed to resell the interest to plaintiffs under the same terms if plaintiffs were unable to obtain a Federal Basic Permit and state Alcoholic Beverage Commission approval for their operation of another liquor distributorship. Plaintiffs further alleged that they had performed the first contract and the conditions precedent to the second contract, but that defendants had refused their demand for reconveyance of the Henry County Company stock. They claimed $500,000 damages for the withholding of the stock, and also demanded an accounting for the period during which the stock was withheld. Finally they alleged that they would sustain irreparable injury unless defendants were compelled to return the stock.

Plaintiffs demanded "trial by jury of the action herein and the issues formed on the pleadings herein." The trial court denied the motion, and after a trial found that plaintiffs had not used due diligence in seeking the permit for the operation of the second distributorship, and that they had not applied for the necessary permits for the retransfer of the Henry County Company stock. "If the specific performance requested * * * was granted," said the court, "an operating business would be closed, causing irreparable harm to the owner of the other [half-interest]." The trial court entered judgment against plaintiffs.]

BUCHANAN, JUDGE.

* * * It is our opinion that the trial court did not err in overruling Hiatt's request for a trial by jury because Rules TR. 38(A) and (C) deny a

party a jury trial if the cause is of exclusive equitable jurisdiction; the main theory of this cause is equitable.

* * *

Rules TR. 38 and 39 of the Indiana Rules of Trial Procedure respectively govern Jury Trial of Right and Trial by Jury or by the Court. Pertinent parts of each provide:

Trial Rule 38 *Jury trial of right*

(A) *Causes triable by court and by jury. Issues of law and issues of fact in causes* that prior to the eighteenth day of June, 1852, were of exclusive equitable jurisdiction shall be tried by the court; issues of fact *in all other causes* shall be triable as the same are now triable. In case of the *joinder of causes of action* or defenses which, prior to said date, were of exclusive equitable jurisdiction with *causes of action* or defenses which prior to said date were designated as actions at law and triable by jury— the former shall be triable by the court, and the latter by a jury, unless waived; the trial of both may be at the same time or at different times, as the court may direct.

* * *

(C) *Same: Specification of issues.* In his demand a party may specify the *issues* which he wishes so tried; otherwise he shall be deemed to have demanded trial by jury for all *issues* triable as of right by jury. * * *

The emphasis supplied to the above excerpted portions exhibits to us a semantic cloud hovering over the repeated use of the word "issues" in Rules TR. 38(C) and 39(A)(1) and (2). "Issues" do not exist in a vacuum; they result from factual allegations in civil actions consisting of one or more claims which may or may not be triable by jury because they are "of exclusive equitable jurisdiction." While Rule TR. 38(A) concerns itself with issues in "causes" and "causes of action," subsections (B) and (C) and Rule TR. 39(A)(2) speak only of "issues" which a party may demand be tried by jury. At first blush, it appears that it is "issues" rather than "causes" which determine a party's right to a jury trial. This is not our construction of these Rules.

We thus conclude that * * * a party's right to trial by jury depends upon the nature of the claim(s) stated and not upon the issues that may arise within such claim(s). * * *

[O]ur courts have had little difficulty in determining when a party is entitled to a jury trial as a matter of right, if the cause was either exclusively equitable or exclusively legal, or even if there was a joinder of equitable causes of action with legal causes of action. Reichert v. Krass, (1895) 13 Ind.App. 348, 40 N.E. 706 (foreclosure of a mechanic's lien and matters contained in a counterclaim for damages on breach of contract found to be an exclusively equitable proceeding); * * * Towns v. Smith, (1888) 115 Ind. 480, 16 N.E. 811 (creditor's bill to set aside and cancel a fraudulent conveyance with additional relief seeking to recover a personal judgment on a promissory note deemed an exclusively equitable action); * * * Fish v. Prudential Ins. Co., (1947) 225 Ind. 448, 75 N.E.2d 57 (action to rescind and cancel a life insurance policy with a cross-complaint for full recovery on the policy found to be an essentially equitable cause of action).

* * *

We now turn to the Indiana precedents specifically determining the right to jury trial in causes where one or more of the issues of fact are of exclusive equitable jurisdiction and others are not. The cases are confusing. However, the tendency to deny jury trial in these circumstances is a common thread that runs through most of them.

Typical is Towns v. Smith, supra, where the court announced as early as 1888 that *"if any essential part of a cause* is exclusively of equitable cognizance, the *whole* is drawn into equity"* (emphasis supplied) and tried without a jury. * * *

In further support of the proposition that the whole is drawn into equity when any essential part of a cause is exclusively equitable, is this language in Carmichael v. Adams, * * * [91 Ind. 526 (1883)]:

> The court, having acquired jurisdiction of * * * *a suit in equity* * * * *was not bound to dissect the suit into separate members,* and try each separately, one member as a matter of law, and the other as a matter of equity, but had a right to *treat the case as a unity,* and as one of exclusive equitable jurisdiction.

* * *

> It would lead to confusion and injustice to direct separate trials in such cases. Should a jury find there was no right to recover on the [legal cause of action], and the court adjudge that there was a right to recover on the [equitable cause of action], there would then be a conflict not easily overcome. To be sure, the court might set aside the verdict and grant a new trial, but this, after all, would leave the control with the court, and it might just as well be there in the first instance. (Emphasis supplied.)

* * *

The repetitious use of the word "issues" in Rule TR. 38(C) * * * lends credence to holdings of the United States Supreme Court to the effect that the existence of an issue, not of equitable jurisdiction, even though incidental, in a cause that is otherwise equitable in character requires a jury trial of such issue and, further, that the legal issue must be tried first. Beacon Theatres, Inc. v. Westover * * *; Dairy Queen, Inc. v. Wood * * *. When these cases were decided, the Federal Rules of Civil Procedure contained provisions substantially similar to our Rules * * *.

As the Seventh Amendment to the United States Constitution applies only to civil trials in federal courts, the states are free to develop their own body of law concerning the right to trial by jury in civil matters.

The dissent in Beacon Theatres v. Westover, supra, provides [an additional] reason why we should reject the majority holding that as long as there is any incidental issue of fact not equitable in character for which a jury trial has been demanded, it must be submitted to the jury. The three dissenters potently argued that to adopt the majority view was to "undermine the basic structure of equity jurisprudence, developed over the centuries." * * *

The dissenters expressed the prophetic fear that to adopt the majority approach results in clogging of court calendars with frivolous or dilatory demands for jury trials and leads to administrative impasse. Rules of procedure should not oust equity of "Jurisprudence developed over the centuries and explicitly recognized in the U.S. Constitution[.] * * * The court today sweeps away these basic principles * * * " [quoting *Beacon*.]

Hardly an inviting approach for Indiana to adopt.

* * * [W]e turn to Hiatt's one paragraph Complaint to see if he was improperly denied a jury trial.

An overview of the pleadings indicates a blending of issues of fact predominately of equitable jurisdiction with others not of such character so that the cause is in the nature of a bill in equity.

The choice of the pleader was to plead breach of contract and out of that same transaction or set of circumstances, allege substantive facts the primary object of which was equitable relief. The main theory outlined by the facts pleaded is not for damages, but for specific performance of the agreement(s) between Hiatt and Yergin with an attendant accounting and an injunction as to the manner of the future operation of the Henry County Beverage Company * * *.

* * * While the amount of damages sought, i.e., $500,000.00, is not inconsequential, the recovery of damages appears to be incidental to the main theory of the action. We note that Hiatt's last allegation is that the "Plaintiffs [Hiatt] are without an adequate remedy at law."

The decision of the trial court is therefore affirmed.

[A concurring opinion of White, P.J., is omitted.]

3. THE PROVINCE OF JUDGE AND JURY

SLOCUM v. NEW YORK LIFE INSURANCE CO., 228 U.S. 364, 382, 33 S.Ct. 523, 530, 57 L.Ed. 879, 888 (1913), p. 1060, infra:

In the trial by jury * * * both the court and the jury are essential factors. To the former is committed a power of direction and superintendence, and to the latter the ultimate determination of the issues of fact. Only through the cooperation of the two, each acting within its appropriate sphere, can the constitutional right be satisfied. And so, to dispense with either, or to permit one to disregard the province of the other, is to impinge on that right.

JERKE v. DELMONT STATE BANK, 54 S.D. 446, 456–59, 223 N.W. 585, 589–90 (1929):

* * * We frequently see the phrase, "It is for the jury to say what the facts are." Historically speaking, this may have been true in the sixteenth century, but it has long since ceased to be true. The power and right and duty of the jury is not "to *say* what the facts are," but to adjudge and determine what the facts are by the usual and ordinary intellectual processes; that is, by applying the thinking faculties of their minds to the evidence received and the

presumptions existing in the case, if any, and thereby forming an opinion or judgment. * * *

Jurors do not determine all questions of ultimate fact, even in jury cases. They determine the existence or nonexistence of those facts, and those only, with reference to the existence of which the judgment of reasonable men might differ as a result of the application of their intellectual faculties to the evidence. If the proof offered by the party having the burden in support of the existence of ultimate issuable facts is so meager that a reasonable mind could not therefrom arrive at the existence of such ultimate fact, there is nothing for the jury, and the judge not only may, but should, direct a verdict against the party having the burden of proof.[c] * * *

WEINER, THE CIVIL JURY AND THE LAW–FACT DISTINCTION, 54 Calif.L.Rev. 1867, 1867–68 (1966):

The categories of "questions of law" and "questions of fact" have been the traditional touchstones by which courts have purported to allocate decision-making between judge and jury. * * * Many statutes in effect today echo * * * [the] dichotomy, utilizing the law and fact terminology to identify the respective provinces of the judge and the jurors in a civil case. None of these statutes, however, attempts to define what is meant by a question of law or a question of fact. Nor have the courts shown any inclination to fashion definitions which can serve as useful guidelines. Indeed, when faced with a dispute as to whether a specific issue should be resolved by the judge or the jury, the typical appellate opinion today does no more than label the question as one of law or of fact, perhaps citing some authorities which are equally devoid of any more detailed consideration of the point. * * * A question of law or a question of fact is a mere synonym for a judge question or a jury question.

MARKMAN v. WESTVIEW INSTRUMENTS, INC.

Supreme Court of the United States, 1996.
517 U.S. 370, 116 S.Ct. 1384, 134 L.Ed.2d 577.

Certiorari to the United States Court of Appeals for the Federal Circuit

JUSTICE SOUTER delivered the opinion of the Court.

The question here is whether the interpretation of a so-called patent claim, the portion of the patent document that defines the scope of the patentee's rights, is a matter of law reserved entirely for the court, or subject to a Seventh Amendment guarantee that a jury will determine the meaning of any disputed term of art about which expert testimony is offered. We hold that the construction of a patent, including terms of art within its claim, is exclusively within the province of the court.

---

c. There is substantial evidence that during the colonial period and the first part of the nineteenth century the jury determined questions of law in some jurisdictions and that the law-fact dichotomy was a later development. See Scott, *Trial by Jury and the Reform of Civil Procedure*, 31 Harv.L.Rev. 669, 675–78 (1918); Note, *The Changing Role of the Jury in the Nineteenth Century*, 74 Yale L.J. 170 (1964).

[Plaintiff Markman's] * * * patent describes a system that can monitor and report the status, location, and movement of clothing in a dry-cleaning establishment. The Markman system consists of a keyboard and data processor to generate written records for each transaction, including a barcode readable by optical detectors operated by employees, who log the progress of clothing through the dry-cleaning process. Respondent Westview's product also includes a keyboard and processor, and it lists charges for the dry-cleaning services on bar-coded tickets that can be read by portable optical detectors.

Westview [argues] * * * that Markman's patent is not infringed by its [Westview's] system because the latter functions merely to record an inventory of receivables by tracking invoices and transaction totals, rather than to record an inventory of articles of clothing. Part of the dispute hinges upon the meaning of the word "inventory," a term found in Markman's independent claim 1, which states that Markman's product can "maintain an inventory total" and "detect and localize spurious additions to inventory." The case was tried before a jury, which heard, among others, a witness produced by Markman who testified about the meaning of the claim language.

After the jury compared the patent to Westview's device, it found an infringement of Markman's claim 1 * * *. The District Court nevertheless granted Westview's deferred motion for judgment as a matter of law, one of its reasons being that the term "inventory" in Markman's patent encompasses "both cash inventory and the actual physical inventory of articles of clothing." 772 F.Supp. 1535, 1537–1538 (E.D.Pa.1991). Under the trial court's construction of the patent, the production, sale, or use of a tracking system for dry cleaners would not infringe Markman's patent unless the product was capable of tracking articles of clothing throughout the cleaning process and generating reports about their status and location. Since Westview's system cannot do these things, the District Court directed a verdict * * * .

Markman appealed, arguing it was error for the District Court to substitute its construction of the disputed claim term "inventory" for the construction the jury had presumably given it. The United States Court of Appeals for the Federal Circuit affirmed, holding the interpretation of claim terms to be the exclusive province of the court and the Seventh Amendment to be consistent with that conclusion. 52 F.3d 967 (1995). Markman sought our review on each point, and we granted certiorari. * * *

* * * [This cases raises the question] whether a particular issue occurring within a jury trial (here the construction of a patent claim) is itself necessarily a jury issue, the guarantee being essential to preserve the right to a jury's resolution of the ultimate dispute. In some instances the answer to this * * * question may be easy because of clear historical evidence that the very subsidiary question was so regarded under the English practice of leaving the issue for a jury. But when, as here, the old practice provides no clear answer * * * we are forced to make a judgment about the scope of the Seventh Amendment guarantee without the benefit of any foolproof test.

The Court has repeatedly said that the answer to the * * * question "must depend on whether the jury must shoulder this responsibility *as necessary to preserve the 'substance of the common-law right of trial by jury.'* " *Tull v. United States* [quoting Colgrove v. Battin, p. 1016, infra]] * * *.

Since evidence of common law practice at the time of the Framing does not entail application of the Seventh Amendment's jury guarantee to the construction of the claim document, we must look elsewhere to characterize this determination of meaning in order to allocate it as between court or jury. We accordingly consult existing precedent and consider both the relative interpretive skills of judges and juries and the statutory policies that ought to be furthered by the allocation.

A.

* * * [The Court examined the few cases that were alleged to be relevant and found them to be inconclusive. The Court indicated that, if anything, they supported the view that a jury determination of the issue was not required.]

B.

Where history and precedent provide no clear answers, functional considerations also play their part in the choice between judge and jury to define terms of art. We said in *Miller v. Fenton*, 474 U.S. 104, 114, 106 S.Ct. 445, 451, 88 L.Ed.2d 405 (1985), that when an issue "falls somewhere between a pristine legal standard and a simple historical fact, the fact/law distinction at times has turned on a determination that, as a matter of sound administration of justice, one judicial actor is better positioned than another to decide the issue in question." So it turns out here, for judges, not juries, are the better suited to find the acquired meaning of patent terms.

The construction of written instruments is one of those things that judges often do and are likely to do better than jurors unburdened by training in exegesis. Patent construction in particular "is a special occupation, requiring, like all others, special training and practice. The judge, from his training and discipline, is more likely to give a proper interpretation to such instruments than a jury, and he is, therefore, more likely to be right, in performing such a duty, than a jury can be expected to be." *Parker v. Hulme*, 18 F. Cas., at 1140. Such was the understanding nearly a century and a half ago, and there is no reason to weigh the respective strengths of judge and jury differently in relation to the modern claim; quite the contrary, for "the claims of patents have become highly technical in many respects as the result of special doctrines relating to the proper form and scope of claims that have been developed in the courts and the Patent Office." Woodward, Definiteness and Particularity in Patent Claims, 46 Mich. L.Rev. 755, 765 (1948).

Markman would trump these considerations with his argument that a jury should decide a question of meaning peculiar to a trade or profession simply because the question is a subject of testimony requiring credibility determinations, which are the jury's forte. It is, of course, true that credibility judgments have to be made about the experts who testify in patent cases, and in theory there could be a case in which a simple credibility judgment would suffice to choose between experts whose testimony was equally consistent with a patent's internal logic. But our own experience with document construction leaves us doubtful that trial courts will run into many cases like that. In the main, we expect, any credibility determinations will be subsumed within the necessarily sophisticated analysis of the whole document, required by the standard construction rule that a term can be defined only in a way that comports with the instrument as a whole. * * * Thus, in these cases a jury's capabilities to evaluate demeanor, * * * to sense the "mainsprings of human conduct," * * * or to reflect community standards, * * * are much less significant than a trained ability to evaluate the testimony in relation to the overall structure of the patent. The decisionmaker vested with the task of construing the patent is in the better position to ascertain whether an expert's proposed definition fully comports with the specification and claims and so will preserve the patent's internal coherence. We accordingly think there is sufficient reason to treat construction of terms of art like many other responsibilities that we cede to a judge in the normal course of trial, notwithstanding its evidentiary underpinnings.

C

Finally, we see the importance of uniformity in the treatment of a given patent as an independent reason to allocate all issues of construction to the court. As we noted in *General Elec. Co. v. Wabash Appliance Corp.*, 304 U.S. 364, 369, 58 S.Ct. 899, 902, 82 L.Ed. 1402 (1938), "[t]he limits of a patent must be known for the protection of the patentee, the encouragement of the inventive genius of others and the assurance that the subject of the patent will be dedicated ultimately to the public." Otherwise, a "zone of uncertainty which enterprise and experimentation may enter only at the risk of infringement claims would discourage invention only a little less than unequivocal foreclosure of the field," *United Carbon Co. v. Binney & Smith Co.*, 317 U.S. 228, 236, 63 S.Ct. 165, 170, 87 L.Ed. 232 (1942), and "[t]he public [would] be deprived of rights supposed to belong to it, without being clearly told what it is that limits these rights." *Merrill v. Yeomans*, 94 U.S. 568, 573, 24 L.Ed. 235 (1877). * * *

Uniformity would, however, be ill served by submitting issues of document construction to juries. Making them jury issues would not, to be sure, necessarily leave evidentiary questions of meaning wide open in every new court in which a patent might be litigated, for principles of issue preclusion would ordinarily foster uniformity. * * * But whereas issue preclusion could not be asserted against new and independent infringement defendants even within a given jurisdiction, treating interpretive issues as purely legal will promote (though it will not guarantee) intrajurisdictional certainty through the application of stare decisis on those questions not yet subject to interjurisdicitional uniformity under the authority of the single appeals court.

* * *

Accordingly, we hold that the interpretation of the word "inventory" in this case is an issue for the judge, not the jury, and affirm the decision of the Court of Appeals for the Federal Circuit.

It is so ordered.

Notes and Questions

1. In DOBSON v. MASONITE CORP., 359 F.2d 921 (5th Cir.1966), plaintiff brought suit for breach of an oral agreement by which he was to clear timber from defendant's lands, sell it, pay a set amount of the money received to defendant, and retain the rest as compensation for his work. There was no dispute about the

existence of the contract or its terms. The sole question was whether such an oral agreement was enforceable under the state Statute of Frauds. If the contract was interpreted as one for services, it would be enforceable; if it was found to be a contract for the sale of timber, recovery would be barred. The issue was presented to a jury on a special interrogatory. It determined that the contract was for services and rendered a verdict for plaintiff. The trial court rejected this finding, found that as a matter of law the contract was one for the sale of timber and held for defendant. On appeal the decision was reversed, the Fifth Circuit stating:

> The district court, apparently because there was no dispute regarding the existence of the oral contract or its terms, felt that only a legal question, what was the effect of the contract, was involved. But "legal effect" is the result of applying rules of law to the facts; necessarily this determination must await a determination of all the facts. And, as we have stated, deciding what is the meaning of the contract is a question of fact.

Id. at 923–24.

2. Is the decision in *Dobson* incompatible with *Markman*? Can *Markman* be reconciled with the decision in Byrd v. Blue Ridge Rural Electric Cooperative, Inc., p. 386, supra? Recall that in *Byrd*, a diversity-of-citizenship case, the Court upheld the right to trial by jury on the issue whether plaintiff was an employee of defendant under the terms of the state worker's compensation act even though, on that single issue, state court judges, rather than juries, would make that determination.

3. In RANKIN v. FIDELITY INSURANCE, TRUST & SAFE DEPOSIT CO., 189 U.S. 242, 23 S.Ct. 553, 47 L.Ed. 792 (1903), the existence or nonexistence of a contract depended upon the effect given to a series of letters that were contradictory in many respects. The Supreme Court held that the question whether a contract existed was for the jury subject to the court's instruction. In HOLTMAN v. BUTTERFIELD, 51 Cal.App. 89, 196 P. 85 (1st Dist.1921), plaintiff alleged that an undisputed unambiguous letter constituted a contract. The court held that there being no contradictory evidence, the question was for the court. Can the two cases be harmonized? Is either case inconsistent with *Dobson*? In what way is it relevant that in *Dobson* the contract was oral? What difficulties in differentiating questions of law from questions of fact do these cases suggest? See generally 5 Corbin, *Contracts* § 24.30, at 326–27 (1998). Shifting to another context, should the interpretation of the words of an unambiguous contract be left to the jury or to the court? In that connection, re-examine *Dobson*, *Rankin*, and *Holtman*. What about the issue of negligence? Should a court or jury decide whether undisputed conduct was or was not negligent? See the classic discussion in Holmes, *The Common Law* 123–26 (1881). See also Gergen, *The Jury's Role in Deciding Normative Issues in the American Common Law*, 68 Fordham L.Rev. 407 (1999).

4. To what extent should the categorization of a particular issue as one of fact or law depend, as it did in part in *Markman*, on whether the question should be decided with reference to a fixed standard that applies to all members of the community impartially or as an ad hoc matter in particular cases? When an issue is classified as one of "law," the rule binds litigants in subsequent cases. Of course, the crucial question is: When is the need for a precise legal standard sufficient to justify withdrawing the matter from the jury? In many contexts the answer depends on whether the system has accumulated enough experience on the issue to justify announcing a standard that will be binding in future cases. Another basis for differentiation is whether the issue involves a sensitive area that warrants a "popular" or "communal" judgment. Consider, for example, the case

of a prosecution of a publisher for distributing an allegedly obscene book. Shouldn't the decision to give the question of obscenity to a judge or a jury depend on whether the need for certainty on that issue outweighs the desirability of a judgment by the community as reflected by several juries passing on the question in different locales?

5. Juries frequently have been accused of invading the province of the judge by ignoring its instructions, fabricating their own rules of law, and applying them to the facts. E.g., Frank, *Courts on Trial* 110–11 (1949). Consider the following excerpt in terms of whether the jury really is abusing its function:

> Some might view the jury's * * * [ability to ignore the law] as a disadvantage of the jury. However it does ensure that the process of adjudication is democratic and allows for the flexibility from the potentially rigid application of rules of law that do not countenance novel situations or fact patterns. Furthermore the actions of the jury in importing community values into the adjudicatory process are incremental in the sense that a single jury can act only in the case before it based on the facts presented to it. The ability of the jury to import community values into the process of adjudication is also what allows it to function as a "bulwark of liberty" and to resist abusive exercise of governmental power against the citizenry. * * * Finally * * * the juror's responsibility for the outcome and capacity for empathy and sympathy may lead to an increasingly liberal, vital and nonapathetic society.

Smith, *Structural and Functional Aspects of the Jury: Comparative Analysis and Proposals for Reform*, 48 Ala.L.Rev. 441, 473–74 (1997). See also James, *Functions of Judge and Jury in Negligence Cases*, 58 Yale L.J. 667 (1949); Kalven, *The Dignity of the Civil Jury*, 50 Va.L.Rev. 1055, 1062–68 (1964). Does the fact that the law often lags behind social reality justify the jury stepping outside its historical bounds and "taking the law into its own hands"? Isn't the jury's invasion of the court's province and its knocking "off many rough edges of the law" likely to inhibit change in the law by making legislative and judicial innovation "unnecessary"?

6. To what extent does our willingness to permit juries to modify the legal rules described by the judge depend on the particular substantive issues and the parties involved in the case? Should the jury have a different degree of freedom in criminal cases than in civil cases, especially in light of the fact that a verdict of acquittal in a criminal case cannot be set aside? Consider the following passage from Professor Howe's review of Kalven & Zeisel, *The American Jury*, in *Scientific American*, vol. 215, pp. 295, 298, Sept., 1966.

> * * * As the study shows, juries commonly tend to disregard a fundamental axiom of our jurisprudence that the only parties to litigation in the criminal law are the state and the defendant. Thanks to this sloppy indifference, many jurors allow the contributory negligence or the viciousness of the victim of the crime to enter into their weighing of the culpability of the defendant. In other words, the jurors confound the clear distinction between the civil and the criminal law and look on the action charged to the defendant as a tort rather than a crime. "The cases," we are told, "show a bootlegging of tort concepts of contributory negligence and assumption of risk into the criminal law."

> * * * Many will ask the same question James Fenimore Cooper asked more than a century ago: In a society that has been foolish enough to

establish an elective judiciary and wise enough to make judicial tenure subject to good behavior, does a jury serve any more useful purpose than that of a symbol of freedom? On Patriot's Day we celebrate the fortitude of the juries that set William Penn and John Peter Zenger free. On what days shall we celebrate the courage of those solid yeoman who, in our own day, saw fit to let * * * [those accused of killing] Medgar Evers, Mrs. Viola Liuzzo and Jonathan Daniels go free? There are surely occasions on which one is tempted to suggest that the time has come to amend our constitutions so as to allow the abolition of the jury even in criminal cases. * * *

Before that happens, however, I hope that someone will undertake a study no less extensive than the Chicago–Ford jury project to determine whether or not our judges are to be trusted with the power that would be theirs were they to go it alone. I confess *The American Jury* seems infected by an excessive respect for the vision, wisdom and integrity of American judges. I have too often heard practicing lawyers from our large cities insist that the one reason—and that a compelling one—for preserving jury trial is that it is our best safeguard against the corruption of judges.

Doesn't the fact that it is very rare for a jury verdict to be overturned despite certain acts of "misconduct" or even when it appears to be against the weight of the evidence demonstrate that our judicial system is fully prepared to allow, and often encourages, the jury to manipulate the legal standards offered by the trial judge? In this connection, reread Texas Employers' Ins. Ass'n v. Price, p. 46, supra, and Lavender v. Kurn, p. 49, supra; consider this question again in connection with the material on jury misconduct on pp. 1089–95, infra.

4. TACTICAL CONSIDERATIONS IN DECIDING BETWEEN TRIAL BY JUDGE OR BY JURY

As will be discussed later, the right to trial by jury may be waived. Unless the right is invoked properly by one of the parties, the case can be decided by the trial judge sitting alone, as are cases in which the right does not exist. In many jurisdictions the judge has the power in a nonjury case or when a jury-trial right is waived to impanel an advisory jury whose verdict the court has discretion either to embrace or ignore. See, e.g., Federal Rule 39(c).

a. *Institutional Factors*

Even when an attorney feels that a client's chances of winning on the merits are the same whether the case is tried by judge or by jury, there may be a decided tactical advantage in choosing one form of trial over another. Suppose, for example, that plaintiff in a personal-injury action is in serious financial difficulty. Obviously she will want to pursue the fastest litigation route possible in order to obtain a recovery at an early date. In many jurisdictions there is a substantial backlog of cases on the jury-trial calendar and a long wait is inevitable, whereas the judge-trial calendar is practically current and the case may be heard within a few months. If the suit has been brought in a jurisdiction in which this type of imbalance between the jury and nonjury calendars exists, plaintiff probably will waive the jury. On the other hand, a defendant who knows plaintiff's plight will demand a jury trial, hoping to force plaintiff into a quick settlement favorable to defendant.

Similar considerations exist when time may ameliorate the extent of plaintiff's injuries. For example, if a young unmarried girl is seriously injured in an accident so that her physician will testify that there is a chance she may never be able to have children, a substantial verdict is likely. But she will be awarded far less if her case is not heard for a number of years and she has married and had a family in the interim. In cases of serious injury defendant usually has little to lose and much to gain by delay, except when the injuries are of a degenerative nature.

Also significant is the difference in cost between a jury and nonjury trial. On the average, a jury trial takes considerably more time than does a court trial. Jurors must be selected and instructed, more witnesses are called to testify, final arguments are longer, and more recesses are required. The result usually is higher counsel fees, more extensive payments to experts, and increased trial costs in the form of fees for jurors and witnesses. Although the witness fees often ultimately will be paid by the losing party, jury trial increases the financial gamble by a party who is uncertain as to his chances for success.

Still another factor to be considered in an era of extensive scientific development is the complexity of the case and the ability of jurors to digest the evidence to be presented. What steps might be taken to assist a jury in such a situation? See Note, *Pretrial Mediation of Complex Scientific Cases: A Proposal To Reduce Jury and Judicial Confusion*, 75 Chi.–Kent L.Rev. 981 (2000).

b. *Psychological Factors*

When is a jury more likely to give a favorable verdict than a judge? Are there substantial differences between judge and jury attitudes on questions of liability? On measuring damages? Every trial lawyer has a number of personal theories regarding these matters. Only a few empiric studies have been made and they are limited in scope. The available evidence indicates, however, that the similarities between judge and jury cases tend to outweigh the differences. As to the question of liability, statistics indicate that the judge and jury would agree in upwards of 80 percent of the cases. On the other hand, juries do seem to have a greater tendency to find against corporate and government defendants both as to liability and the amount of awards. See Broeder, *The University of Chicago Jury Project*, 38 Neb.L.Rev. 744, 750–51 (1959). But see Bledsoe, *Jury or Nonjury Trial—A Defense Viewpoint*, in 5 Am.Jur. Trials 123, 129, 139 (1966) (amount of jury awards on the average do not exceed awards by judges).

In making the choice between judge and jury, a lawyer has much more to go on in the context of a particular case than these generalized comparisons between judge and jury trials. An attorney will consider the nature of the case, the characteristics of the parties and the witnesses, the passions that may surround the trial, the type of jurors who are likely to be chosen, and the background and predilections of the trial judge, if the judge's identity is known in advance, which often is not the case. Each of these factors is important in deciding whether the judge or the jury is most likely to identify with and be sympathetic to a lawyer's client. For an interesting empirical study regarding jury attitudes toward various types of witnesses, attorneys, and parties, see Sonaike, *The Influence of Jury Deliberation on Juror Perception of Trial, Credibility, and Damage Awards,* 1978 Brigham Young U.L.Rev. 889.

Finally, the decision to demand a jury may depend on counsel's assessment of whether he is more effective in a judge or jury trial. In presenting a case to jurors the attorney must be a a bit of a showman; he must be entertaining or their attention will wander; he must know how to excite their interest so that presentation of crucial testimony appears as a triumphant climax; and he must establish rapport with each and every juror, taking pains not to antagonize any of them by his actions or his appearance. By contrast, a lawyer in a nonjury trial need not concentrate heavily on the form of presentation since the judge will look for and pick out the significant aspects of the testimony even if they are not presented dramatically.

Rarely during the course of a jury case will an attorney have any clear sense of his success or failure in convincing the jury. He only can follow the planned presentation and hope that it was properly conceived. A sudden shift of tactics or a change of emphasis will tend to confuse and alienate the jurors. On the other hand, in a nonjury case, the judge, through statements during conferences, questions from the bench, and rulings on minor points, is constantly supplying the lawyers with clues as to her impressions of the case and the testimony. A sensitive attorney, upon detecting that things are not going well, may be able to salvage the case by changing the focus or direction of the testimony. For an interesting discussion of the different levels of involvement in the trial process as between the judge, sitting as a trier of fact, and the jury, see Wolf, *Trial by Jury: A Sociological Analysis,* 1966 Wis.L.Rev. 820. For an excellent debate on the choice of judge or jury, see Clermont & Eisenberg, *Trial by Jury or Judge: Transcending Empiricism,* 77 Cornell L.Rev. 1124 (1992), and Gross, *Settling for a Judge: A Comment on Clermont & Eisenberg,* 77 Cornell L.Rev. 1178 (1992).

5. DEMAND AND WAIVER OF TRIAL BY JURY

SEGAL v. AMERICAN CAS. CO.

United States District Court, District of Maryland, 1966.
250 F.Supp. 936.

NORTHROP, DISTRICT JUDGE. This case involves defendants' motion to strike plaintiffs' demand for a jury trial. * * *

In essence, plaintiffs claim that they are entitled to a jury trial, notwithstanding the fact that this action was removed from the Circuit Court of Worcester County on April 3, 1963, that the answer was filed on November 25, 1964, and that a demand for a jury trial in this court was not made until June 29, 1965. The demand, urge the plaintiffs, was filed for the sole purpose of informing the court and counsel for the defendants that plaintiffs did not consent to trial without a jury. Thus, they claim that they would be entitled to a jury trial even in the absence of the June 1965 demand.

* * *

It is the contention of plaintiffs that the time limitations of Rule 38(b) are not applicable in this case, inasmuch as Rule 81(c) removes the necessity for a demand when no demand would have been necessary, under state law, in the court from which the case was removed. * * *

I

Plaintiffs claim that "state law" did not require that a demand for jury trial be made in the Circuit Court for Worcester County, and that, therefore, they were not required to demand a jury trial in this court, but were entitled to trial by jury without demand. This claim must be rejected.

Section 2 of Rule VII of the court from which this case was removed reads as follows:

> On the Saturday of the second week preceding each jury term at 10 o'clock A.M., there shall be a preliminary call by the clerk of cases on the civil docket appearing on the trial calendar. As each case is called the litigants, in proper person or by attorneys, will indicate by proper order whether the respective cases will be tried or continued at the first available trial date under these rules, *and if to be tried whether a jury will be required.* * * * The election of a jury at the preliminary call shall be final for the next ensuing jury session of the court unless the parties shall agree and the court consent otherwise, or unless the case shall be settled, continued or removed by order of court. * * * (Emphasis added.)

In the Circuit Court for Worcester County, if a request for a jury trial is not made at the preliminary call of the docket, a jury trial cannot be had. Thus, by rule of the court, if the party seeking trial by jury does not signify this election, his case is not tried before a jury. This procedure in Worcester County is different from that in certain other counties in the state of Maryland; in these other counties, the filing of a case on the law side of the court automatically results in the setting of the case for jury trial, with no further action being required of the litigants. The issue, then, is whether the rule of court in Worcester County is "state law in the court from which the case is removed." This court concludes that it is.

* * *

The rule in the Circuit Court for Worcester County is not contrary to or conflicting with any statute or any rule of the Maryland Court of Appeals. Nor does the rule contravene section 6 of Article XV of the Maryland Constitution, preserving the *right* to jury trial. Rather, the local rule, like the corresponding federal rules, merely states the manner in which the *right* to a jury trial must be *exercised.* The local rule, having the force and effect of law, * * * is "state law" within the meaning of Federal Rule 81(c).

II

* * *

Admittedly, at the time of removal this case was in the early stages. The time for the preliminary call of the docket in the state court, and, therefore, the time at which an election for a jury trial would have to be made, were a long way off. This situation is similar to that in McRae v. Arabian American Oil Co., 34 F.R.D. 513 (S.D.N.Y.1964). There, state law required a demand for a jury trial at a stage in the proceedings subsequent to the stage reached by the time of removal. The plaintiffs in that case claimed that since, at the stage reached by the time of removal, they were not required to make formal demand for a jury trial, Rule 81(c) obviated the necessity for a demand after removal. * * * [T]he court replied:

> * * * The answer to that contention is that the plain language of the amendment does not so provide; it merely obviates the necessity of a demand after removal in the absence of *any* state requirement for a demand. 34 F.R.D. at 515. [Emphasis added.]

This court agrees with the reasoning of the *McRae* case and concludes that under Rule 81(c) a party seeking a jury must, after removal, make a formal demand for a jury trial if, in the court from which the case was removed, he would have had to take some action to exercise his right to a jury trial. This court finds, as did the court in *McRae*, that the necessity for a demand after removal is obviated only where the case automatically would have been set for jury trial in the court from which removed, without the necessity for any action on the part of the party desiring jury trial. * * *

Since the benefits of Rule 81(c) are not available to plaintiffs in this case, the successful exercise of their right to trial by jury depends upon their compliance with the provisions of Rule 38(b). Inasmuch as the demand in the present case was not made until many months after removal and after the answer had been filed, those time limitations have not been met. Plaintiffs, therefore, are not entitled to claim trial by jury as of right.

III

Although this court, in the exercise of its discretion under Rule 39(b), might allow a jury trial notwithstanding the lateness of the demand, it declines to do so.

In Washington County Ins. Co. v. Wilkinson, 19 F.R.D. 177, 178–179 (D.Md.1956), also involving an appeal to the court's discretion where the demand for jury trial had not been timely made, Judge Chesnut remarked:

> In my opinion the determining factor in such cases should be whether, despite the failure to comply with the rule, the nature of the case is such that one or the other of the parties is likely to be really prejudiced by the failure to have a jury trial. Where the issues are predominantly factual rather than legal there is more reason for the liberal exercise of the discretion to grant a jury trial. * * *

> There is still another consideration to be weighed. * * * I think rule 38 providing for the waiver of a jury trial unless specifically demanded within the time mentioned, is an illustration of the general policy of interpretation announced in rule 1. It is a matter of common experience that in civil cases, particularly those of a contractual nature, a nonjury trial can fairly and properly be concluded in substantially less time than is usually required in a jury case. And it should also not be overlooked that, especially where there is a considerable number of cases pending on the docket ready for trial, the time unnecessarily consumed in the trial of a particular case delays the trial of subsequent cases. And it is also to be remembered that needlessly longer trials usually involve more expense to

litigants and to the government which freely provides the courts for the litigants.

On similar grounds, this court declines to exercise its discretion to grant a jury trial:

1. There are ten similar cases pending, each arising from the same storm in Ocean City and each involving a similar clause in the insurance policies.

2. In nine of the ten similar cases, as in this one, the demand for a jury trial was made a number of months after removal and after the filing of the answer.

3. In a case tried earlier, involving the same storm and the same contractual clause, a jury trial consumed two weeks; there is no indication that any of the pending cases would take less time if tried before a jury.

4. The docket of this court is overcrowded, as is the case with most courts today.

5. The expert testimony in each of these cases will be lengthy and complex. * * *

6. The court can see no possible prejudice which would result from a trial before the court without a jury.

7. There will be much less expense for all parties if the cases are tried without a jury.

Therefore, the motion to strike plaintiffs' demand for a jury trial is granted. * * *

Notes and Questions

1. The "discretion" given the district court by Federal Rule 39(b) to permit a jury trial despite the absence of a demand is exercised sparingly. Does the following passage from BECKSTROM v. COASTWISE LINE, 14 Alaska 190, 13 F.R.D. 480, 483 (D.Alaska 1953), explain why?

> * * * For more than two years past, the Court has uniformly denied such requests by reason of the volume of litigation—more than 850 cases a year—coming before this Court for determination. This is more than three times the average number of cases per judge in the 86 * * * District Courts of the United States. The granting of trials by jury in such cases, where demand is not seasonably made, inevitably results in further delay and consequent further "denial of justice" to other litigants, who are presumed to have equally meritorious causes. Until an additional judge is authorized and appointed for this Division the practice will be adhered to. * * *

Is the attitude expressed in *Beckstrom* consistent with this country's commitment to jury trial? Should a constitutional right be used as a pawn in a struggle for more adequately staffed courts?

Contrast the decision in BATTEAST CONSTRUCTION CO. v. HENRY COUNTY BOARD OF COMMISSIONERS, 196 F.R.D. 543 (S.D.Ind.2000):

> In exercising discretion, "the district court ought to approach each application under Rule 39(b) with an open mind * * * rather than with a fixed policy." * * * As a guide to inquiry, other district courts in the Seventh Circuit have

considered five factors * * * (1) whether the issues involved are best tried before a jury; (2) whether the court's schedule or that of the adverse party will be disrupted; (3) the degree of prejudice to the opposing party; (4) the length of the delay; and (5) the reason for the moving party's tardiness in demanding a jury trial.

The *Batteast* court went on to allow a jury trial because (1) the case turned on witness credibility, a matter well suited for juries, (2) the trial was set for nearly a year later and thus no schedules would be disrupted, (3) the opposing party could give no examples of how it would conduct the litigation differently without a jury and why it would be prejudiced, (4) the three-month delay in requesting a jury was not excessive. The court noted that the requesting party had no sound excuse for failing to request a jury on time, but held that was outweighed by the other factors.

2. Are automatic waiver provisions constitutional? In AETNA INSURANCE CO. v. KENNEDY, 301 U.S. 389, 57 S.Ct. 809, 81 L.Ed. 1177 (1937), the Court said that "as the right of jury trial is fundamental, courts indulge every reasonable presumption against waiver." Nonetheless, the constitutionality of waiver provisions has been upheld.

The early code provisions relating to jury trial required an express waiver or a failure to perform certain procedural acts before a party lost his jury-trial right. Practice under these provisions became cumbersome and the affirmative-demand procedure came into vogue, although a few states still require an express waiver. See generally Clark, *Code Pleading* § 17 (2d ed. 1947); 4 Weinstein, Korn & Miller, *New York Civil Practice* ¶ ¶ 4102.01–.22. Courts in many states that have rules patterned after the Federal Rules appear to be more lenient than the federal courts in exercising discretion to relieve a party's failure to make a timely demand. See, e.g., Wood v. Warriner, 62 So.2d 728 (Fla.1953) (jury demand granted even though plaintiff did not request jury until the first day of trial). But see Bloch v. Bentfield, 1 Ariz.App. 412, 403 P.2d 559 (1965) (waiver by failure to appear at trial).

Should a contractual waiver of jury trial be honored? See N.Y. Real Property Law § 259–c. Suppose the waiver is challenged because of fraud or on some other basis; is there a right to jury trial on the issues raised by the challenge?

3. In BERESLAVSKY v. CAFFEY, 161 F.2d 499 (2d Cir.), certiorari denied 332 U.S. 770, 68 S.Ct. 82, 92 L.Ed. 355 (1947), plaintiff sought an injunction against patent infringement. Subsequently he amended the complaint by striking the request for equitable relief and asking for money damages. The court held that plaintiff was entitled to trial by jury even though the Rule 38(b) time period had expired. The court reasoned that although the original complaint carried no right to jury trial, a later amendment changing the claim from equitable to legal relief renewed the right and gave plaintiff an additional ten days to demand a jury. The demand period was not extended in ALCOA S.S. CO. v. RYAN, 211 F.2d 576 (2d Cir.1954), apparently because plaintiff's claim under certain insurance policies remained substantially the same after the amendment, which simply eliminated allegations requesting rescission of an agreement canceling the policies. Does anything turn on whether the party who seeks a jury trial is the same party who amended the pleadings? If plaintiff in *Alcoa* felt that a jury trial on the issues in the amended complaint was tactically important, could it have obtained it by taking a voluntary dismissal under Federal Rule 41, reinstituting the suit, and making a new demand for jury trial? Cf. Noonan v. Cunard S.S. Co., 375 F.2d 69 (2d Cir.1967).

4. In LOCAL 783, ALLIED INDUSTRIAL WORKERS v. GENERAL ELEC-
TRIC CO., 471 F.2d 751 (6th Cir.), certiorari denied 414 U.S. 822, 94 S.Ct. 120, 38
L.Ed.2d 55 (1973), plaintiff, who originally had asked only for injunctive relief,
filed a motion to amend the complaint by adding a legal claim for damages nine
months after the original claim and only eight days before trial. The Court of
Appeals held that the trial judge had erred in permitting the amendment only on
the condition that jury trial be waived.

Should the court consider whether the late request in *Local 783* is being made
for a proper purpose? Given the time required to prepare for a jury trial, late
requests could be an effective means of delaying the trial. What should a court do
when an amendment is sought to change a claim for legal relief, on which jury
trial has been demanded, to a claim for equitable relief? In ruling on the motion to
amend, should the court take into account that a loss of jury trial may be entailed?

6. SELECTION AND COMPOSITION OF THE JURY

a. Size

In PATTON v. UNITED STATES, 281 U.S. 276, 288, 50 S.Ct. 253, 254,
74 L.Ed. 854, 858 (1930), a criminal case, the Court said that the phrase "trial
by jury"

> includes all the essential elements as they were recognized in this country
> and England when the Constitution was adopted * * *. Those elements
> were: (1) That the jury should consist of twelve men, neither more nor
> less; (2) that the trial should be in the presence and under the superin-
> tendence of a judge having power to instruct them as to the law and
> advise them in respect of the facts; and (3) that the verdict should be
> unanimous.

But in WILLIAMS v. FLORIDA, 399 U.S. 78, 90 S.Ct. 1893, 26 L.Ed.2d 446
(1970), the Court held that a state might constitutionally use a jury with six
(or perhaps fewer) members in a criminal case. Because the Court had held in
DUNCAN v. LOUISIANA, 391 U.S. 145, 88 S.Ct. 1444, 20 L.Ed.2d 491 (1968),
that the Sixth Amendment guarantee of jury trial in criminal cases applied to
the states through "incorporation" in the Fourteenth Amendment, the result
in *Williams* required the Court to recognize that such a jury would also satisfy
the constitutional guarantee in federal criminal cases, a recognition it made
explicit.[d]

Seizing upon the holding in *Williams* and transferring its analysis to the
civil-jury guarantee in the Seventh Amendment, numerous federal district
courts in the years following *Williams* used their Rule 83 power to promulgate
local rules to provide that ordinary civil actions shall be tried by six-member
juries.

---

d. Justice Harlan, concurring in *Williams*,
found this kind of after-the-fact rationalization
disturbing: "The decision evinces, I think, a
recognition that the 'incorporationist' view
* * * which underlay *Duncan* * * * must be
tempered to allow the States more elbow room
in ordering their own criminal systems. With
that much I agree. But to accomplish this by
diluting constitutional protections within the
federal system itself is something to which I
cannot possibly subscribe. Tempering the rigor
of *Duncan* should be done forthrightly, by facing up to the fact that at least in this area the
'incorporation' doctrine does not fit well with
our federal structure, and by the same token
that *Duncan* was wrongly decided." 399 U.S. at
118, 90 S.Ct. at 1915, 26 L.Ed.2d at 464.

COLGROVE v. BATTIN, 413 U.S. 149, 93 S.Ct. 2448, 37 L.Ed.2d 522 (1973). Petitioner sought mandamus to compel a federal district judge to impanel a twelve-member jury, notwithstanding Local Rule 13(d)(1) of the District Court for the District of Montana, which provided for a six-member jury in all civil cases. Petitioner argued that the Local Rule violated the Seventh Amendment, the Enabling Act, 28 U.S.C. § 2072, and Federal Rule 48. The Ninth Circuit denied mandamus, and the Supreme Court affirmed, five to four:

> * * * [T]he historical setting in which the Seventh Amendment was adopted highlighted a controversy that was generated not by concern for preservation of jury characteristics at common law but by fear that the civil jury itself would be abolished unless protected in express words. * * *

> * * * We can only conclude, therefore, that by referring to the "common law," the Framers of the Seventh Amendment were concerned with preserving the *right* of trial by jury in civil cases where it existed at common law, rather than the various incidents of trial by jury. In short, what was said in *Williams* with respect to the criminal jury is equally applicable here: constitutional history reveals no intention on the part of the Framers "to equate the constitutional and common-law characteristics of the jury." * * *

> * * * In *Williams,* we rejected the notion that "the reliability of the jury as a factfinder * * * [is] a function of its size," * * * and nothing has been suggested to lead us to alter that conclusion. * * *

> * * * Significantly, our determination that there was "no discernible difference between the results reached by the two different-sized juries" * * * drew largely upon the results of studies of the operations of juries of six in civil cases. * * * Thus, while we express no view as to whether any number less than six would suffice, we conclude that a jury of six satisfies the Seventh Amendment's guarantee of trial by jury in civil cases.

Id. at 152, 155–56, 157, 158–60, 93 S.Ct. at 2450, 2452, 2453–54, 37 L.Ed.2d at 526, 528, 529, 530–31.

The Court further found that the Montana Local Rule did not violate the Enabling Act, since it concluded that the Congress in saying that the rules "shall preserve the right of trial by jury as at common law and as declared by the Seventh Amendment" had not intended to go beyond the Seventh Amendment guarantee itself. Finally, it held that the Local Rule was not in conflict with Federal Rule 48, saying that the latter was only concerned with numbers stipulated by the parties, and was inapplicable when a number was imposed regardless of the parties' consent.

Notes

1. The majority and dissenting opinions in *Colgrove* cite a number of studies of the six-member jury, including Devitt, *The Six–Man Jury in the Federal Court,* 53 F.R.D. 273 (1971), and Zeisel, *And Then There Were None: The Diminution of the Federal Jury,* 38 U.Chi.L.Rev. 710 (1970), which are two excellent presenta-

tions of opposing views. For an interesting critique of the Court's use of empirical data in *Colgrove*, see Zeisel & Diamond, *"Convincing Empirical Evidence" on the Six Member Jury*, 41 U.Chi.L.Rev. 281 (1974). See also Sperlich, * * * *And Then There Were Six: The Decline of the American Jury*, 63 Judicature 262 (1980). Local rules providing for six-member juries in federal civil actions are now common.

2. Note that Federal Rule 48 was amended in 1991 to permit a court to decide the size of the jury so long as it consisted of no fewer than six and no more than twelve members. Prior to the amendment, the Rule merely allowed parties to stipulate that the jury could consist of any number less than twelve. In 1996 the Advisory Committee recommended the restoration of the twelve person jury. The proposal was rejected by the Judicial Conference of the United States.

3. In some states, juries of less than six members are permitted in civil trials. Reread Virginia Code § 8.01–359 in the Supplement, following Federal Rule 48. In Virginia, three person juries are an option if the parties consent, and some Virginia judges consider a three-member jury to be a superior trier of fact. See Painter v. Fred Whitaker Co., 235 Va. 631, 369 S.E.2d 191 (1988).

b. *The Selection of "Favorable" Jurors*

The process of trying to choose people who will make favorable jurors is extremely complex. Not only is it important to assess the way in which each individual juror is likely to view the case, but it also is necessary to analyze what effect each juror may have on the others during the course of deliberations. For example, one study indicates that as to issues involving scientific or technical information, a juror who has some relevant expertise wields considerable influence over the other jurors and often may control the verdict. Broeder, *Occupational Expertise and Bias as Affecting Juror Behavior: A Preliminary Look*, 40 N.Y.U.L.Rev. 1079 (1965). See also Bevan, Albert, Loiseaux, Mayfield & Wright, *Jury Behavior as a Function of the Prestige of the Foreman and the Nature of His Leadership*, 7 J.Pub.L. 419 (1958).

As a general rule a lawyer will seek jurors who will identify and sympathize with his client. Practically speaking, however, the lawyer only can guess at who they are, since he cannot possibly be aware of all of an individual juror's biases and hostilities. But see Suggs & Sales, *Using Communication Clues To Evaluate Prospective Jurors During the Voir Dire*, 20 Ariz.L.Rev. 629 (1978). Consider, for example, a case brought by a young mother for the wrongful death of her husband. One would think that her attorney would be overjoyed if the jury contained a woman who also had been widowed and left with small children to raise. But the lawyer would not be pleased to learn that the juror in question, after a short period of mourning, had happily remarried, since that would greatly affect her attitude as to the proper amount of damages. Even if the juror had not remarried, her presence would be less desirable if her own marriage had been so unhappy that she preferred her present status. See generally Broeder, *Plaintiff's Family Status as Affecting Jury Behavior: Some Tentative Insights*, 14 J.Pub.L. 131 (1965). For an interesting discussion of the potential impact of the age of jurors on verdicts, see Zeigler, *Young Adults as a Cognizable Group in Jury Selection*, 76 Mich.L.Rev. 1045 (1978).

(i) Empaneling the Jury

Jury selection is a two-stage process. First, a list of potential jurors, the venire, is compiled and they are assembled. A number of them, equal to the number who will serve, usually twelve or six, are then selected at random to sit as a tentative jury. Second, these tentative jurors are questioned by the judge and/or by the attorneys to determine whether each of them can fairly and appropriately decide the case. This questioning is called *"voir dire."* If one of them is dismissed, his or her place is taken by another member of the venire, selected at random, who is in turn subject to questioning. This process continues until the final panel is in place.

————

THIEL v. SOUTHERN PACIFIC CO., 328 U.S. 217, 66 S.Ct. 984, 90 L.Ed. 1181 (1946). Plaintiff, in an action for negligence, moved to strike the jury panel on the ground that it had been unfairly selected. The clerk of the court and the jury commissioner testified that they had deliberately and intentionally excluded from the jury lists all persons who work for a daily wage. They noted that in the past, because of the financial hardship imposed by jury service, those workers were inevitably excused by the judge. Workers who were paid by the week or the month, as well as the wives of daily wage earners were included on the jury lists. The Court held that such an exclusion cannot be justified "without doing violence to the democratic nature of the jury system. Were we to sanction an exclusion of this nature * * * we would breathe life into any latent tendencies to establish the jury as an instrument of the economically and socially privileged." Id. at 223–24, 66 S.Ct. at 987, 90 L.Ed. at 1186. Although the judge can excuse individuals for whom jury service would be a financial hardship, that cannot justify the exclusion of all daily wage earners regardless of whether an actual hardship is involved. The dissent noted that the matter was one of judicial administration, and that no constitutional issue was at stake. It took the position that selection of jurors from a jury pool that contained weekly wage earners and wives of daily workers was sufficient to avoid reversal of a judgment otherwise untainted by error.

Notes and Questions

1. Read 28 U.S.C. §§ 1861–66 in the Supplement. The *Report of the Committee on the Operation of the Jury System of the Judicial Conference of the United States,* on which the present federal jury-selection statute is based, appears at 42 F.R.D. 353 (1967).

How representative of the community is a federal jury in view of the substantial classes of people who are exempt or may be exempted under Section 1863(b)(6) or who may be excused under Section 1863(b)(5)? Qualifications for jury service vary from state to state and include such factors as citizenship, local residence, ownership of property, health, and payment of taxes.

To what extent should individuals automatically be excluded from jury duty because of physical handicaps, such as persons who are blind or deaf? In GALLOWAY v. SUPERIOR COURT, 816 F.Supp. 12 (D.D.C.1993), the court held that blind persons cannot automatically be excluded. "[P]laintiff has offered uncontradicted evidence that blind individuals, like cited jurors, weigh the content of the testimony given and examine speech patterns, intonation, and syntax in assessing credibility." Id. at 16. The court went on to note that with reasonable accommodation, a juror who might otherwise not be able to serve in a case may be qualified to do so. "[S]ign language interpreters are provided to deaf individuals serving on Superior Court juries. A similar service could be employed for blind jurors [allowing them] * * * to serve satisfactorily in most cases." Id. at 19. Who should bear the cost of such "reasonable accommodation"?

2. The most common method for creating jury lists is by relying on voter registration records. 28 U.S.C. § 1863(b)(2) requires federal jury lists to be based on these records, with the use of supplemental sources when that is necessary to promote the interests of fair representation, as described in 28 U.S.C. §§ 1861 and 1862. Supplemental sources can include driver's license or public utilities lists, state tax rolls, or telephone lists.

Exclusive reliance on voter registration lists has been much criticized. Because of the under-representation of minority and low income persons in voter registration records, as well as the low percentage of voters overall, many have argued that use of multiple lists should be constitutionally compelled. See Kairys, Kadane & Lehoczky, *Jury Representativeness: A Mandate for Multiple Source Lists*, 65 Calif.L.Rev. 776 (1977); Munsterman & Munsterman, *The Search for Jury Representativeness*, 11 Just.Sys.J. 59 (1986); Note, *Jury Source Representativeness and the Use of Voter Registration Lists*, 65 N.Y.U.L.Rev. 590 (1990).

3. The special or "blue ribbon" jury, which is composed of people who are specially selected because of their above-average intelligence, is an attempt to meet the contention that the ordinary juror is incompetent to deal with the complex problems of modern litigation. In FAY v. NEW YORK, 332 U.S. 261, 67 S.Ct. 1613, 91 L.Ed. 2043 (1947), the Supreme Court upheld the constitutionality of a New York statute that gave the trial court discretion to empanel a "blue ribbon" jury upon application of either party. Would the Supreme Court uphold a federal statute that provided for "blue ribbon" juries in federal courts? Are "blue ribbon" juries consistent with the Seventh Amendment or the idea that a person should be "judged by peers" or by a group that represents a cross-section of society? See Oldham, *Origins of the Special Jury*, 50 U.Chi.L.Rev. 137 (1983).

4. The use of questionnaires, personal interviews, and psychological tests has been suggested for ascertaining the competence of prospective jurors. To what extent is the following passage from Note, *Psychological Tests and Standards of Competence for Selecting Jurors*, 65 Yale L.J. 531, 541 (1956), wishful thinking?

> * * * A more competent jury may force a change in the tactics of advocacy, so that attorneys will put greater emphasis on rational rather than emotional appeals. Parties may also be dissuaded from taking weak cases to court in the hope of achieving an unjustified result. Exclusionary rules of evidence, evolved to protect litigants from inept juries, can be liberalized. Juries held in higher esteem will restore respect for the right of trial by jury, and even, perhaps, for jury duty.

Wouldn't psychological testing of jurors result in the erosion of our traditional views of jury composition? Would they be permissible under *Thiel*?

(ii) Challenging Individual Jurors

Challenges to individual jurors—sometimes called challenges to the polls—are of two kinds: for cause and peremptory. Challenges for cause permit a prospective juror to be rejected when partiality can be shown.

Peremptory challenges permit rejection of jurors without any statement of reason and usually are based on an assumed partiality that may not be susceptible of proof.

FLOWERS v. FLOWERS

Court of Civil Appeals of Texas, 1965.
397 S.W.2d 121.

CHAPMAN, JUSTICE. The subject matter of this suit involves a question of the disqualification of a juror in a child custody contest tried to a jury * * *.

This case was tried in a town and county of very small population where the record shows many members of the jury panel had heard what they referred to as gossip or rumors concerning the case. The parties to the suit are Billie Charlene Flowers, plaintiff below, the mother; and R.A. Flowers, Jr., the father. The victims of the unfortunate broken home are three little girls ranging in ages from two to ten at the time of the filing of divorce by their mother in January 1964.

* * *

The jurors were told on voir dire examination that the evidence would show that plaintiff drank some socially and on one or two occasions had consumed alcoholic beverages to excess. They were questioned as to whether that fact standing alone would prejudice them against her as a fit and proper person to have custody of the children.

The record preserved upon examination of Mrs. Schmidt as a prospective juror shows that she first testified she was well acquainted with the Flowers family, belonged to the same Baptist church they did in the little town of Miami, and that she had no opinion formed in the case at all. Then when counsel said to her the evidence will show "that Billie does drink upon social occasions with the crowd at a dance, or something of that sort, she would have a highball or cocktail, and it will show on one occasion that she had too much, or two times had too much, what is your attitude—," she answered:

A. I am against drinking in any manner, any kind.

Q. Any way or any fashion at all?

A. Any type.

Q. Mrs. Schmidt, that would definitely affect your judgment in the case wouldn't it?

A. If the evidence was true.

Q. Could you enter the—you would take a seat as a juror with a positive feeling that any drinking whatsoever is wrong, and it is bad so far as the mother of these little girls is concerned,—

A. Anybody else.

Q. If the evidence shows Billie has had one drink or two—drinks at a social occasion, you would hold that against her?

A. I don't approve.

The court then took over the examination and asked her a number of questions, one of which was:

Q. Well, are you saying by that, Mrs. Schmidt, that you wouldn't grant either party to this law suit custody of their children if they drank?

A. I am.

The court then turned to leading questions to the juror as to her attitude about passing upon whether the mother was a fit person to have the custody of the girls, saying:

Q. Dependent upon the testimony you hear in a trial; the mere fact that she got drunk a few times and threw a conniption fit or something, you wouldn't hold that against her and think she wasn't—

A. Not especially.

The court then overruled the challenge of the juror for cause.

The record also shows by affidavit of a lady juror panelist who sat next to Mrs. Schmidt during voir dire examination that Mrs. Schmidt stated " * * * she felt sorry for R.A. Flowers, Jr. and that you had to admire a man that would go on to Sunday School and church after what had happened to him." Mrs. Philpot's affidavit also affirmed that Mrs. Schmidt made a statement to one of the other prospective jurors sitting next to her before the jury was selected that Billie Flowers had run off and left R.A. Flowers, Jr. once before and that both of such statements were made before she was selected and sworn to serve as a juror.

At both the motion for mistrial and motion for new trial based partly upon the proceedings just related, the court declined to hear Mrs. Philpot's tendered testimony as a witness in support of her affidavit. Upon the hearing of the motion for new trial Mrs. Flowers' attorney testified there were eleven jurors, including Mrs. Schmidt, who were undesirable to the plaintiff and that if Mrs. Schmidt on voir dire had correctly stated her attitude reflected by Mrs. Philpot's affidavit, they would have exercised a peremptory challenge as to her rather than as to some other juror. * * *

Article 2134, Vernon's Ann.Tex.Civ.St., provides as one of the disqualifications: "Any person who has a bias or prejudice in favor of or against either of the parties."

This disqualification for bias or prejudice extends not only to the parties personally, but also to the subject matter of the litigation. * * * Compton v. Henrie, Tex., 364 S.W.2d 179.

In defining the terms "bias" and "prejudice" as used in Article 2134 our Supreme Court in the HENRIE case just cited has said:

Bias, in its usual meaning, is an inclination toward one side of an issue rather than to the other, but to disqualify, it must appear that the state of mind of the juror leads to the natural inference that he will not or did not act with impartiality. Prejudice is more easily defined for it means pre-judgment, and consequently embraces bias; the converse is not true. * * *

Mrs. Schmidt's statements indicate to us both bias and prejudice factually and such a prejudgment of the case as to indicate she could not have acted with impartiality. If we are correct in this factual conclusion then under the authorities just cited her disqualification is not a matter of discretion with the trial court but a matter of law. * * *

Even if we are in error in our pronouncements in the preceding paragraphs, it cannot be gainsaid that the record shows bias and prejudice on the part of Mrs. Schmidt toward plaintiff and toward her alcoholic consumption her attorney admitted would be shown before the examination of the jury on voir dire. From the viewpoint of this writer, such feelings on the part of Mrs. Schmidt are to her credit even if it did disqualify her as a juror. But even if under the facts of this case bias or prejudice was a fact to be determined by the trial court, those feelings having been clearly established, her answer of "Yes, sir" to a leading question to the effect that she would be able to decide the case on the evidence submitted, should be disregarded. * * * In any event we believe the court abused its discretion in refusing to hold the juror disqualified.

* * *

The judgment of the trial court is reversed and remanded for a new trial.

Notes and Questions

1. An unlimited number of challenges for cause are permitted each party. These challenges are determined by the trial judge, although some states have experimented with so-called "triers"—independent officials who have the responsibility of determining challenges for cause. On what grounds should a juror be challenged for cause? Can the judge disqualify a prospective juror on the court's own motion or must he wait for a motion from one of the parties? May jurors be interrogated as to possible racial, religious, economic, or political prejudice? Is it relevant that the plaintiff or defendant is an individual or an organization espousing an unpopular viewpoint or cause? What if plaintiff or defendant merely happens to be a member of a group of this type? See Casey v. Roman Catholic Archbishop, 217 Md. 595, 143 A.2d 627 (1958).

2. The number of peremptory challenges allowed each side varies among the states. The general range is from two to six. In the federal courts each side is permitted three. See 28 U.S.C. § 1870. Should the number be increased if there are multiple parties on one or both sides? Since the number of peremptory challenges is limited, they usually are carefully husbanded. Can the use of the peremptory challenge be reconciled with the principle that a jury should be composed of a representative sampling of the community?

EDMONSON v. LEESVILLE CONCRETE COMPANY, INC.

Supreme Court of the United States, 1991.
500 U.S. 614, 111 S.Ct. 2077, 114 L.Ed.2d 660.

Certiorari to the United States Court of Appeals for the Fifth Circuit.

MR. JUSTICE KENNEDY delivered the opinion of the Court.

We must decide in the case before us whether a private litigant in a civil case may use peremptory challenges to exclude jurors on account of their race. * * * This civil case originated in a United States District Court, and we apply the equal protection component of the Fifth Amendment's Due Process Clause. * * *

I

Thaddeus Donald Edmonson, a construction worker, was injured in a job-site accident at Fort Polk, Louisiana, a federal enclave. Edmonson sued Leesville Concrete Company for negligence in the United States District Court for the Western District of Louisiana, claiming that a Leesville employee permitted one of the company's trucks to roll backward and pin him against some construction equipment. Edmonson invoked his Seventh Amendment right to a trial by jury.

During voir dire, Leesville used two of its three peremptory challenges authorized by statute to remove black persons from the prospective jury. Citing our decision in Batson v. Kentucky, 476 U.S. 79, 106 S.Ct. 1712, 90 L.Ed.2d 69 (1986), Edmonson, who is himself black, requested that the District Court require Leesville to articulate a race-neutral explanation for striking the two jurors. The District Court denied the request on the ground that Batson does not apply in civil proceedings. As impaneled, the jury included 11 white persons and 1 black person. The jury rendered a verdict for Edmonson, assessing his total damages at $90,000. It also attributed 80% of the fault to Edmonson's contributory negligence, however, and awarded him the sum of $18,000.

Edmonson appealed, and a divided en banc panel affirmed * * *. We granted certiorari, and now reverse the Court of Appeals.

II

A

In Powers v. Ohio, 499 U.S. 400, 111 S.Ct. 1364, 113 L.Ed.2d 411 (1991), we held that a criminal defendant, regardless of his or her race, may object to a prosecutor's race-based exclusion of persons from the petit jury. Our conclusion rested on a two-part analysis. First, following our opinions in *Batson* and in Carter v. Jury Commission of Greene County, 396 U.S. 320, 90 S.Ct. 518, 24 L.Ed.2d 549 (1970), we made clear that a prosecutor's race-based peremptory challenge violates the equal protection rights of those excluded from jury service. * * * Second, we relied on well-established rules of third-party standing to hold that a defendant may raise the excluded jurors' equal protection rights. * * *

That an act violates the Constitution when committed by a government official, however, does not answer the question whether the same act offends constitutional guarantees if committed by a private litigant or his attorney. The Constitution's protections of individual liberty and equal protection apply in general only to action by the government. * * * Racial discrimination, though invidious in all contexts, violates the Constitution only when it may be attributed to state action. * * * Thus, the legality of the exclusion at issue here turns on the extent to which a litigant in a civil case may be subject to the Constitution's restrictions. * * *

The trial judge exercises substantial control over voir dire in the federal system. See Fed.Rule Civ.Proc. 47. The judge determines the range of information that may be discovered about a prospective juror, and so affects the exercise of both challenges for cause and peremptory challenges. In some cases, judges may even conduct the entire voir dire by themselves, a common practice in the District Court where the instant case was tried. See Louisiana Rules of Court, Local Rule W.D.La. 13.02 (1990). The judge oversees the exclusion of jurors for cause, in this way determining which jurors remain eligible for the exercise of peremptory strikes. In cases involving multiple parties, the trial judge decides how peremptory challenges shall be allocated among them. 28 U.S.C. § 1870. When a lawyer exercises a peremptory challenge, the judge advises the juror he or she has been excused. * * *

The principle that the selection of state officials, other than through election by all qualified voters, may constitute state action applies with even greater force in the context of jury selection through the use of peremptory challenges. Though the motive of a peremptory challenge may be to protect a private interest, the objective of jury selection proceedings is to determine representation on a governmental body. Were it not for peremptory challenges, there would be no question that the entire process of determining who will serve on the jury constitutes state action. The fact that the government delegates some portion of this power to private litigants does not change the governmental character of the power exercised. * * *

Here, as in most civil cases, the initial decision whether to sue at all, the selection of counsel, and any number of ensuing tactical choices in the course of discovery and trial may be without the requisite governmental character to be deemed state action. That cannot be said of the exercise of peremptory challenges, however; when private litigants participate in the selection of jurors, they serve an important function within the government and act with its substantial assistance. If peremptory challenges based on race were permitted, persons could be required by summons to be put at risk of open and public discrimination as a condition of their participation in the justice system. The injury to excluded jurors would be the direct result of governmental delegation and participation.

Finally, we note that the injury caused by the discrimination is made more severe because the government permits it to occur within the courthouse itself. Few places are a more real expression of the constitutional authority of the government than a courtroom, where the law itself unfolds. Within the courtroom, the government invokes its laws to determine the rights of those who stand before it. In full view of the public, litigants press their cases, witnesses give testimony, juries render verdicts, and judges act with the utmost care to ensure that justice is done.

Race discrimination within the courtroom raises serious questions as to the fairness of the proceedings conducted there. Racial bias mars the integrity of the judicial system and prevents the idea of democratic government from becoming a reality. * * * In the many times we have addressed the problem of racial bias in our system of justice, we have not "questioned the premise that racial discrimination in the qualification or selection of jurors offends the dignity of persons and the integrity of the courts." Powers * * *. To permit racial exclusion in this official forum compounds the racial insult inherent in judging a citizen by the color of his or her skin. * * *

III

It remains to consider whether a prima facie case of racial discrimination has been established in the case before us, requiring Leesville to offer race-neutral explanations for its peremptory challenges. In *Batson*, we held that determining whether a prima facie case has been established requires consideration of all relevant circumstances, including whether there has been a pattern of strikes against members of a particular race. * * * The same approach applies in the civil context, and we leave it to the trial courts in the first instance to develop evidentiary rules for implementing our decision.

The judgment is reversed, and the case is remanded for further proceedings consistent with our opinion.

It is so ordered.

JUSTICE O'CONNOR, with whom THE CHIEF JUSTICE and JUSTICE SCALIA join, dissenting.

* * * As an initial matter, the judge does not "encourage" the use of a peremptory challenge at all. The decision to strike a juror is entirely up to the litigant, and the reasons for doing so are of no consequence to the judge. It is the attorney who strikes. The judge does little more than acquiesce in this decision by excusing the juror. In point of fact, the government has virtually no role in the use of peremptory challenges. Indeed, there are jurisdictions in which, with the consent of the parties, voir dire and jury selection may take place in the absence of any court personnel. * * *

Whatever reason a private litigant may have for using a peremptory challenge, it is not the government's reason. The government otherwise establishes its requirements for jury service, leaving to the private litigant the unfettered discretion to use the strike for any reason. This is not part of the government's function in establishing the requirements for jury service. * * *

Racism is a terrible thing. It is irrational, destructive, and mean. Arbitrary discrimination based on race is particularly abhorrent when manifest in a courtroom, a forum established by the government for the resolution of disputes through "quiet rationality." * * *. But not every opprobrious and inequitable act is a constitutional violation. The Fifth Amendment's Due Process Clause prohibits only actions for which the Government can be held responsible. The Government is not responsible for everything that occurs in a courtroom. The Government is not responsible for a peremptory challenge by a private litigant. I respectfully dissent.

––––––––

In J.E.B. v. ALABAMA ex rel. T.B., 511 U.S. 127, 114 S.Ct. 1419, 128 L.Ed.2d 89 (1994), the State of Alabama, on behalf of the mother of a minor child, brought suit in a state court against the defendant for paternity and child support. The state used nine of its ten peremptory challenges to remove male jurors, with the result that the jury consisted solely of women. The Alabama courts rejected the defendant's objection that the use of peremptory challenges solely to exclude persons on the basis of gender violated the Fourteenth Amendment's Equal Protection Clause. A divided Supreme Court, noting that both federal and state courts were in disagreement on the matter, reversed. Justice Blackmun, writing for himself and three others, stated:

> Discrimination in jury selection, whether based on race or on gender, causes harm to the litigants, the community and the individual jurors

who are wrongfully excluded from participation in the judicial process. * * *

* * * All persons, when granted the opportunity to serve on a jury, have the right not to be excluded summarily because of discriminatory and stereotypical presumptions that reflect and reinforce patterns of historical discrimination. Striking individual jurors on the assumption that they hold particular views simply because of their gender is "practically a brand upon them, affixed by the law, an assertion of their inferiority." *Strauder v. West Virginia*, 100 U.S. at 308, 25 L.Ed. 6664 (1880).

Our conclusion that litigants may not strike potential jurors solely on the basis of gender does not imply the elimination of all peremptory challenges. * * * Parties still may remove jurors who they feel might be less acceptable than others on the panel; gender simply may not serve as a proxy for bias. * * * Even strikes based on characteristics that are disproportionately associated with one gender [e.g. employment in the military or as nurses] could be appropriate, absent a showing of pretext.

Id. at 140–43, 114 S.Ct. at 1427-29, 128 L.Ed.2d at 104–06.

Justice Kennedy concurred in a separate opinion strongly supporting the notion that sex discrimination in the courts could not be tolerated. Justice O'Connor also concurred in a separate opinion. She wrote:

Today's decision severely limits a litigant's ability to act on * * * intuition, for the import of our holding is that any correlation between a juror's gender and attitudes is irrelevant as a matter of constitutional law. * * * [T]o say that gender makes no difference as a matter of law is not to say that gender makes no difference as a matter of fact. * * * In extending [our holdings on race] * * * to gender we have * * * taken a step closer to eliminating the peremptory challenge, and diminishing the ability of litigants to act on sometimes accurate gender-based assumptions about juror attitudes.

* * *

Accordingly, I adhere to my position that the Equal Protection Clause does not limit the exercise of peremptory challenges by private civil litigants * * *. This case itself presents no state action dilemma for here the State of Alabama itself filed the paternity suit. * * * But what of the next case? Will we, in the name of fighting gender discrimination, hold that the battered wife—on trial for wounding her abusive husband—is a state actor? will we preclude her from using her peremptory challenges to ensure that the jury of her peers contains as many women members as possible? I assume we will, but I hope we will not.

Id. at 149–51, 114 S.Ct. at 1432–33, 128 L.Ed.2d at 109–10.

Justice Scalia, writing for himself and two other Justices, dissented. Essentially he agreed with Justice O'Connor's assessment of the importance of the peremptory challenge system and argued that it did not deny anyone the equal protection of the laws even in the case before the Court.

Notes and Questions

1. Under *Batson* upon which both *Edmonson* and *J.E.B.* are based, once a prima facie case of discrimination has been made out, the judge may require an explanation of the motivation for dismissing the juror in question. If the judge is not satisfied with the lawyer's explanation, the challenge may be disallowed. To what extent do the holdings in these cases seriously undermine the notion of the peremptory challenge as a means of obtaining a fair jury? See Underwood, *Discrimination in Jury Selection: Whose Right Is It Anyway?*, 92 Colum.L.Rev. 725 (1992).

2. In civil cases, the jury-trial guarantee in the Seventh Amendment has not been incorporated into the Fourteenth Amendment's Due Process Clause. The jury in *Edmonson* was a federal jury. The *J.E.B.* case extended the Court's reasoning by using the Equal Protection Clause to encompass state jury trials. Of what consequence is it that, like the situation in *J.E.B.*, the number of preemptory challenges in state courts may exceed the number in federal jury trials?

3. After *Batson*, *Edmonson*, and *J.E.B.*, should it be considered forbidden to exercise peremptory challenges on the basis of religion or political affiliation? In this regard, do religion and politics differ from race and gender?

(iii) Conducting the Voir Dire

Rules concerning the extent to which the judge or the lawyers conduct *voir dire* vary among jurisdictions. Federal Rule 47(a) leaves the entire matter entirely in the district judge's discretion. Some states have held it error not to allow each juror to be examined by counsel prior to the exercise of challenges, e.g. Whitlock v. Salmon, 104 Nev. 24, 752 P.2d 210 (1988). See Babcock, *Voir Dire: Preserving Its Wonderful Power*, 27 Stan.L.Rev. 545 (1975). In *Whitlock* the court argued that trial counsel are likely to know their case better than the judge and therefore are more aware of what areas to probe in order to ascertain a juror's bias or antagonism; and jurors may be less candid in answering questions regarding their biases when asked by the trial judge. Do you agree? See Jones, *Judge-Versus Attorney-Conducted Voir Dire: An Empirical Investigation of Juror Candor*, 11 Law & Human Behav. 131 (1987).

Notes and Questions

1. How far can an attorney go in relating the *voir dire* examination to the lawsuit that the jury will hear? Would it be prejudicial for the lawyer to set out a hypothetical situation based on his view of the facts in the particular case and to ask questions as to how the jurors would react to those facts or how the jurors would apply certain legal principles to those facts?

2. How about questions on *voir dire* regarding the fact that the defendant is insured for the liability the plaintiff seeks to impose? Should the plaintiff's counsel be barred from mentioning insurance? Should either counsel be able to ask whether jurors or relatives work for or own stock in an insurance company? Many defense lawyers ask jurors: "Can you be fair even though you know that a verdict that must be paid by an insurance company ultimately might result in a raise in your own premiums?" See King v. Westlake, 264 Ark. 555, 572 S.W.2d 841 (1978). For a colorful debate on questions about insurance on *voir dire*, read the four opinions in Fossness v, Panagos, 376 Mich. 485, 138 N.W.2d 380 (1965).

SECTION B. THE SCOPE AND ORDER OF TRIAL

1. SETTING THE CASE FOR TRIAL

In theory, a case should be tried once the pleadings are filed, discovery completed, settlement explored and rejected, and all pretrial motions decided. Normally, however, trial will not take place until one of the parties takes affirmative action to have the case placed on the appropriate trial calendar and the court disposes of all the cases previously on that calendar. The wait for the case to be reached by the court can be long, often as much as four or five years when the case is to be tried before a jury.

The technique for placing a case on a waiting list for trial will vary from jurisdiction to jurisdiction. Generally it requires only a simple motion. But how is it possible to set a trial date in advance? Is it possible to know when the previous case assigned to a trial judge will be completed so that he and his courtroom will be available? How can one be certain that the lawyers will be free of other pressing obligations, or that crucial witnesses will not be indisposed? The answer, of course, is that there is no such certainty. Any scheduled trial date is at best tentative and is likely to be postponed a number of times.

The jockeying by the courts and the lawyers to bring a case to trial is an art. When sloppily done, it can lead to last minute alterations and result in unused courtrooms, unreasonable delays, and great logjams of cases waiting for trial. Even with the most careful and conscientious cooperation between court and counsel there may be difficulty. Ideally, if the court finds its own schedule altered so that the originally selected date for trial cannot be adhered to, it will inform the parties as far in advance as possible to enable them to readjust their schedules. Similarly, when a lawyer for one of the parties recognizes that a date for trial conflicts with another and more pressing obligation, that attorney will inform the court in advance to obtain a change in schedule. Adjustment usually is feasible for most lawyers who spend relatively little time in active trial practice. But for an attorney who spends the bulk of his time in litigation, accommodation is most difficult, since a change in the trial date for one case probably will raise a conflict with a trial date for another.

Perhaps courts should require every trial attorney to have a sufficient staff to ensure that some lawyer in the firm will be available to handle a case whenever it is called. Would such a requirement be fair to the attorney or to the clients who have confided in him and relied on his expertise? See Gorman, *Excessive Delay in the Courts*, 21 Clev.St.L.Rev. 118 (1972).

Should modern management techniques and systems theory be applied to rationalize the flow of business through the courts? What risks might there be? Of what assistance might computers be to judicial administration? See Adams, *The Move Toward Modern Data Management in the Courts*, 23 U.Fla.L.Rev. 217 (1971); Nagel, Neef & Munshaw, *Bringing Management Science to the Courts to Reduce Delay*, 62 Judicature 128 (1978).

2. ORDER OF TRIAL

a. Jury Cases

Although the courts invariably have discretion to determine the order of trial, they usually do not deviate from standard practice, which is as follows:

1. Plaintiff's opening statement
2. Defendant's opening statement
3. Plaintiff's presentation of direct evidence
4. Defendant's presentation of direct evidence
5. Plaintiff's presentation of rebuttal evidence
6. Defendant's presentation of rebuttal evidence
7. Opening final argument by plaintiff
8. Defendant's final argument
9. Closing final argument by plaintiff
10. Giving instructions to the jury.

b. Nonjury Cases

Although jury and nonjury cases generally are handled in the same way, there are a number of significant differences in scope. For example, the court often will dispense with the opening statement and the closing argument, and, of course, there is never a need to give instructions. Some jurisdictions provide that an attorney has an absolute right to argue, even in nonjury cases. Rarely will that right be exercised, however, if the judge, as is often the situation, makes clear that she believes an argument to be unnecessary.

3. THE BURDEN OF PROOF

a. Burden of Production

The term "burden of proof" usually refers to two different burdens: the burden of production and the burden of persuasion. The burden of production, sometimes called the burden of going forward, usually is placed on the plaintiff in civil actions. This means that the plaintiff is responsible for "producing" a certain threshold amount of evidence to raise a claim. That threshold is defined as the minimum amount of evidence needed to satisfy the standard or proof and, thus, win the case. Put another way, one has met the burden of production if he has produced enough evidence for a reasonable jury to decide in his favor. Therefore, one can meet the burden of production even if all the evidence produced is refuted by the opposing party.

Meeting the burden of production does not ensure victory—one must still "persuade" the fact finder—but failing to meet it will ensure defeat. If the party charged with the burden of production has failed to adduce enough evidence, a summary judgment motion (prior to trial) or a directed verdict motion (at trial) will be granted. The burden of production must be met for the case to get to the trier of fact.

b. The Burden of Persuasion

If the burden of production is met, the case can move forward to the stage of persuasion. Once there is enough evidence for the plaintiff to win, the defendant will try to cast doubt on the credibility or reliability of that evidence, in addition to bringing forth evidence of his own. Each party will try to persuade the trier of fact that its evidence is more weighty than the other's. If the plaintiff has the burden of persuasion, and does not convince the jury (or judge, in a bench trial) by the standard of proof required, the jury must rule for the defendant. Even if the plaintiff has satisfied the burden of production and the defendant brings forth no evidence of his own, if the jury is not persuaded that the plaintiff's evidence is sufficiently reliable or credible, the defendant must prevail.

c. Standards for Meeting the Burden of Persuasion

The standard for meeting the burden of persuasion represents the quantity and quality of evidence a party must produce at trial to prevail. The three most common standards are (1) preponderance of the evidence, (2) clear and convincing evidence, and (3) beyond a reasonable doubt. These standards usually are not defined any more specifically than their plain meaning suggests, although a "preponderance" is considered to be "more than fifty percent," and the clear and convincing standard lies somewhere between a preponderance and "beyond a reasonable doubt."

In most civil cases, the party bearing the burden of persuasion must prove by a preponderance of the evidence that she is entitled to the relief requested. In some civil actions, such as libel and slander and child custody proceedings, the clear-and-convincing-evidence standard often is used. And in all criminal cases, the prosecution must prove its case beyond a reasonable doubt.

d. Shifting Burdens

The term "burden of proof" usually refers to both production and persuasion, and these burdens usually fall on same party at trial, either plaintiff or defendant. But there are times when the burden of production is placed on one party and the burden of persuasion on the other. In these cases, once the burden of production is satisfied, the burden of persuasion "shifts" to the other party.

One example of a type of action in which the burden shifts is an employment discrimination action under Title VII of the Civil Rights Act of 1964. In proceedings under this statute, the employee must make out a prima facie case (meet the burden of production) that there was discrimination. At that point, the burden of persuasion falls on the employer, who must prove by clear and convincing evidence that the firing was not race related. If the employee fails to meet the burden of production, she will lose the case. But once she meets that burden, it is the employer who must persuade the jury or else lose.

4. TACTICAL CONSIDERATIONS REGARDING THE OPENING STATEMENT

Normally, a case begins with plaintiff's opening statement. In the rare situation in which defendant has the burden of proof on *all* issues, such as when defendant admits plaintiff's allegations and goes to trial solely on his own affirmative defenses, the position of the parties is reversed throughout the trial and defendant has the right to open. Most lawyers regard the right to deliver the opening statement as so important that when they represent plaintiff they include some allegations in the complaint that defendant must deny in order to preserve the right. The reasons for viewing the right to open as substantial are fairly obvious. At the outset of the case the jurors are fresh, attentive, and impressionable. A carefully constructed statement laying out plaintiff's case in a positive, coherent fashion can convince the jurors that plaintiff's version of the facts is the correct one, which will force defendant to fight an uphill battle to offset plaintiff's initial advantage. On experimental studies of the advantages in order of argument and proof, see Walker, Thibaut & Andreoli, *Order of Presentation at Trial,* 82 Yale L.J. 216 (1972). See also Lawson, *Order of Presentation as a Factor in Jury Presentation,* 56 Ky.L.J. 523 (1968).

At common law, defendant did not make his opening statement until plaintiff had presented the affirmative case. Today, in most jurisdictions, however, defendant has the option of making an opening statement immediately after plaintiff has done so. Most trial lawyers recommend that defendant open at the earliest opportunity. If defendant waits, the initial impression created by plaintiff's opening statement may be so fortified by the opening evidence that the case is lost by the time defendant begins presenting the opposing evidence. Defendant may be able to neutralize plaintiff's initial advantage if the former immediately sets out a contrary version of the facts. For an opposite view, see Stramondo & Goodspeed, *Defendant's Presentation,* 57 Mass.L.Q. 179 (1972), in which the authors take the position that defendant's opening argument is more effective when it refutes plaintiff's evidence.

One of the most difficult tactical questions regarding the opening argument is whether or not a party should avoid mentioning an important issue or a dramatic piece of evidence in the hope of gaining an advantage through surprise. With the availability of modern discovery techniques, it has become increasingly difficult to surprise one's opponent; moreover opposing counsel, by raising and disposing of the issue in his own opening argument, will insulate the jury from a dramatic shock. Nevertheless, with some items of evidence the less said about them in advance, the greater their impact. This occurs, for example, in cases in which defendant suddenly displays a movie of plaintiff, allegedly crippled for life as a result of defendant's negligence, playing tennis on the day before trial. However, since most items of evidence are not of such caliber, it generally is considered unsound to keep them secret, because doing so weakens the effectiveness of the opening statement and gives significant advantage to the opposition. For some interesting views on the tactics and style of opening argument, see Colley, *Opening Statement: Structure, Issues, Techniques,* 18 Trial 52 (Nov.1982); Fuchsberg, *Opening Statements—Plaintiff's View,* in 5 Am.Jur. Trials 285 (1966); Stern, *Opening Statements—Defense View,* in 5 Am.Jur. Trials 305 (1966).

Just as an attorney's opening statement may advance a client's cause, it also may reveal fatal flaws in the claim or defense. If this occurs, in most jurisdictions the opposing party may move immediately for the entry of a judgment. The theory of this motion is the same as the philosophy underlying the demurrer and summary judgment—the court is not required to try a case once it becomes clear that one of the parties *must* prevail.

5. THE PRESENTATION OF EVIDENCE

a. *The Problems of Admissibility*

The admissibility of evidence at trial is determined by a large and complex set of rules. Each lawyer must plan carefully and in advance of trial to make certain that the evidence considered to be important will be accepted. Often, if an item of evidence cannot be admitted under one rule, it can come in under another. Moreover, except in rare circumstances, no proffered item of evidence will be excluded unless the opposing party objects to its introduction. As a result, an attorney often will offer otherwise inadmissible evidence in the hope that it will not be challenged. A lawyer must be careful, however, not to do this unsuccessfully too often as it may antagonize the judge or jury. Similarly, in many circumstances the opposing party will be well advised not to challenge inadmissible evidence that is not seriously prejudicial. An attorney who constantly objects may antagonize the jury by appearing to be an obstructionist. Even if the objections are sustained, the jurors may begin to believe something is being hidden from them, and will assume that the answers, had they been permitted, would have been unfavorable to the lawyer's client.

In some situations, even the most diligent attorney is powerless to keep inadmissible, highly prejudicial statements from the jurors. For example, a witness simply may blurt out such a statement voluntarily without having been asked a question pertaining to it. In such cases, the court has a choice. It may admonish the jury not to consider the evidence or it may declare a mistrial. In the latter case the jury is dismissed and the trial must begin anew before an entirely different panel. Obviously such drastic action is taken only when the error is severely prejudicial. Yet, is it realistic to expect jurors to ignore completely something they have heard and are told to forget?

b. *The Technique of Presentation*

Much has been written concerning the way in which evidence should be presented. Most of this commentary can be distilled into one basic observation: the better the preparation before trial, the better the presentation.

Usually most evidence is presented at trial through the examination and cross-examination of witnesses. A party should call witnesses in a logical order so that the jury will know, at every step of the way, what part of the case is being explored. Usually the most important witnesses are called first to put the jurors in a favorable frame of mind. The testimony of less important witnesses will then be understood by the jury as backing and fortifying that party's version of the facts. There are, of course, many factors that interfere with a planned presentation. First, the opposition, through cross-examination, will attempt to upset the pattern not only by raising questions as to the witnesses' accuracy but also by injecting new considerations that tend to confuse the jurors. Second, a party who wishes to stay on the good side of witnesses, particularly experts, may be forced to accommodate their interests by calling them when it is convenient for them to testify rather than at the most logical point in the trial. Finally, no matter how fine the preparation, every trial produces a number of surprises to which the lawyer must react immediately. If, for example, during cross-examination of an opposition witness, the interrogating attorney receives a surprise favorable response, he must press forward on the issue immediately, before the witness and the opposing attorney have the time and opportunity to soften the impact by planning an explanation.

Cross-examination is a potent trial weapon. With it a clever attorney can raise doubts concerning the accuracy of even the most accomplished and prepared witness, let alone an unsophisticated witness who actually is trying to cover up the facts. Consider, for example, the effect on the trier of fact of the following exchange from an actual cross-examination of a woman as reported in *Saturday Review,* August 19, 1967, p. 12, col. 2:

Q: Did you ever stay all night with this man in New York?

A: I refuse to answer that question.

Q: Did you ever stay all night with this man in Chicago?

A: I refuse to answer that question.

Q: Did you ever stay all night with this man in Miami?

A: No.

There are two ways to minimize the effects of cross-examination. The first is to make certain that the witness is clear as to the story and is telling the truth. This requires the attorney and the witness to go over the facts in detail shortly before the trial begins. Even after this precaution the excitement of the trial may so unnerve the witness that he forgets even the most basic facts. Consider the following actual exchange (with the names changed), again as reported in *Saturday Review,* August 19, 1967, p. 12, col. 2:

Q: What is your brother-in-law's name?

A: Borofkin.

Q: What's his first name?

A: I can't remember.

Q: He's been your brother-in-law for forty-five years and you can't remember his first name?

A: No, I tell you I'm too excited! (Rising from the witness chair and pointing to Borofkin.) Nathan, for God's sake tell them your first name!

The second method of limiting the effectiveness of cross-examination is for the attorney on direct examination to raise and dispense with any matter that might cast doubt on a witness' veracity if it were raised for the first time on cross-examination. For example, in most jurisdictions an attorney may impugn the credibility of an opposition witness by introducing evidence showing that the witness previously has been convicted of a felony. If the fact that the witness had once been convicted of a felony is raised at the very beginning of his testimony by the attorney who called him, the jury will tend to think of the witness as a person willing to suffer embarrassment to tell the truth; but if the matter is first raised on cross-examination, the jurors may tend to consider the witness a person who is trying to hide important facts. For a detailed treatment of tactical considerations in the presentation of evidence, see generally Keeton, *Trial Tactics and Methods* (2d ed. 1973).

c.   The Role of the Trial Judge in the Presentation of Evidence

Suppose that an attorney's presentation of a case appears inadequate. To what extent should the trial judge take over the trial by interrogating the witness herself and perhaps by calling new witnesses she believes should be heard? Does it make a difference if the case is before a jury? These questions raise some fundamental considerations regarding the role of the trial judge: Is the court a mere umpire who must stand aloof except when called upon to make decisions or a participant with the right to supervise the conduct of the trial to help ensure a just result?

Although there is general agreement that judges do have some power to call and interrogate witnesses, there is considerable controversy as to the extent of the power. For example, in some jurisdictions it has been held that a case may be reversed if the trial judge frequently interrupts counsel's presentation or engages in extensive examination of the witnesses. See Laub, *Trial and Submission of a Case From a Judge's Standpoint,* 34 Temple L.Q. 1, 5–6 (1960). In other jurisdictions, however, the power apparently is unlimited and the only question is how it is to be exercised. See Gitelson & Gitelson, *A Trial Judge's Credo Must Include His Affirmative Duty to be an Instrumentality of Justice,* 7 Santa Clara Law. 7 (1966).

In recent years judges generally have tended to increase their active participation in the trial process. It even has been suggested that they *must* take a hand when the failure to do so will result in a miscarriage of justice, but as yet judgments have not been reversed on this ground.

d.   The Power of Jurors to Question Witnesses

What if a juror is dissatisfied with the evidence? Should he be permitted to ask a witness questions that were not asked by the attorneys? Would it be feasible, tactically, for an attorney to object to the question if it called for inadmissible evidence? Is there some means by which this latter problem could be avoided?

6.   THE CLOSING ARGUMENT

a.   The Nature of the Argument

Closing argument is important because it is the only time when the attorneys can organize the evidence in the case for the trier of fact in a coherent fashion, without interruption, and when the logical implications of the evidence can be spelled out in detail.

Normally, final argument is in three parts, with plaintiff having the benefit of speaking both first and last. If, however, the only issues in the case are those upon which defendant has the burden of proof, the roles of the parties are reversed and defendant speaks first and last. Often the court will limit the amount of time available to each party. See Annot., 3 A.L.R.3d 1341 (1965). Whether or not such limits are imposed, the arguments should be brief, concise, sincere, and easily understood, and they should emphasize the vital points of the case. See Comment, *Understatement and Overstatement in Closing Arguments,* 51 La.L.Rev. 651 (1991); Bergan, *Thoughts About Closing Argument,* Section of Litigation, American Bar Association (Summer 1986); Sisson, *The Closing Argument,* 57 Mass.L.Q. 319 (1972).

b. *Proper Versus Improper Argument*

A proper argument is one that follows from the facts of the case as supported by the evidence or inferences that properly can be drawn from the evidence. An argument is improper when it is based upon matters not in evidence, appeals to passion or racial or religious prejudice, contains references to the financial ability of the parties or includes remarks as to whether defendant is insured against the claimed liability, requests that the jurors treat the attorney's client as they would wish to be treated were they in the party's position, or distorts the evidence in order to arrive at unjustified inferences. See, e.g., Klein v. Herring, 347 So.2d 681 (Fla.App.1977). In practice, lawyers are permitted considerable leeway in argument, with limitations being imposed only in certain easily defined circumstances. Opposing counsel will be reluctant to challenge an improper argument for fear of appearing weak, particularly if there is any chance that the challenge will not be upheld by the trial judge. At the same time, many courts have been hesitant to interfere on their own motion, unless the argument gets completely out of hand. Is there any justification for such judicial reluctance? Shouldn't judges take a more active role in preventing abuse of the trial process? See Rinehart, *Final Argument,* 28 F.R.D. 235 (1960).

It often is difficult to detect an improper argument that is introduced subtly. Consider, for example, a case in which plaintiff, injured in a hit-and-run auto collision, is attempting to prove that defendant was the driver of the other car. Plaintiff's only evidence is that the accident occurred on Sunday and that the other car involved belonged to a neighbor of defendant who had permitted defendant to borrow it every Sunday for several months prior to the collision. In trying to convince the jury of the importance of this circumstantial evidence, plaintiff's attorney might say: "Suppose I were to tell you that defendant's fresh fingerprints were found on the steering wheel of the car shortly after the accident and that defendant's sweater was found near the accident. Surely there would be no doubt in your minds after that as to who was driving, even though no one saw defendant." Obviously such an argument, though proper on its face, should not be permitted, since members of the jury might well believe that the fingerprints and the sweater were indeed found at the scene, although nothing in the evidence so indicates. For an excellent discussion of this and other similar problems of improper argument, see Levin & Levy, *Persuading the Jury with Facts Not in Evidence: The Fiction–Science Spectrum,* 105 U.Pa.L.Rev. 139 (1956).

SECTION C. TAKING THE CASE FROM THE JURY—MOTIONS FOR JUDGMENT AS A MATTER OF LAW, DIRECTED VERDICTS, AND JUDGMENTS NOTWITHSTANDING THE VERDICT

1. THE CONSTITUTIONAL ISSUES

GALLOWAY v. UNITED STATES

Supreme Court of the United States, 1943.
319 U.S. 372, 63 S.Ct. 1077, 87 L.Ed. 1458.

Certiorari to the United States Circuit Court of Appeals for the Ninth Circuit.

MR. JUSTICE RUTLEDGE delivered the opinion of the Court.

Petitioner seeks benefits for total and permanent disability by reason of insanity he claims existed May 31, 1919. On that day his policy of yearly renewable term insurance lapsed for nonpayment of premium.

* * * At the close of all the evidence the District Court granted the Government's motion for a directed verdict. Judgment was entered accordingly. The Circuit Court of Appeals affirmed. * * * Both courts held the evidence legally insufficient to sustain a verdict for petitioner. He says this was erroneous and, in effect, deprived him of trial by jury, contrary to the Seventh Amendment.

* * *

I.

Certain facts are undisputed. Petitioner worked as a longshoreman in Philadelphia and elsewhere prior to enlistment in the Army November 1, 1917. He became a cook in a machine gun battalion. His unit arrived in France in April, 1918. He served actively until September 24. From then to the following January he was in a hospital with influenza. He then returned to active duty. He came back to the United States, and received honorable discharge April 29, 1919. He enlisted in the Navy January 15, 1920, and was discharged for bad conduct in July. The following December he again enlisted in the Army and served until May, 1922, when he deserted. Thereafter he was carried on the Army records as a deserter.

In 1930 began a series of medical examinations by Veterans' Bureau physicians. On May 19 that year his condition was diagnosed as "Moron, low grade; observation, dementia praecox, simple type." In November, 1931, further examination gave the diagnosis, "Psychosis with other diseases or conditions (organic disease of the central nervous system—type undetermined)." In July, 1934, still another examination was made, with diagnosis: "Psychosis-manic and depressive insanity incompetent * * *."

Petitioner concededly is now totally and permanently disabled by reason of insanity and has been for some time prior to institution of this suit. It is conceded also that he was sound in mind and body until he arrived in France in April, 1918.

The theory of his case is that the strain of active service abroad brought on an immediate change, which was the beginning of a mental breakdown that has grown worse continuously through all the later years. Essential in this is the view it had become a total and permanent disability not later than May 31, 1919.

[Petitioner's evidence was as follows: Two witnesses who had served with him in France testified to conduct on petitioner's part there that evinced a disturbed mind. A boyhood friend, one O'Neill, testified that in 1919 petitioner "was a wreck compared to what he was before he went away; * * * [his] mind was evidently unbalanced." A chaplain testified that he had observed a Private Galloway in an Army mental ward in 1920 who appeared insane; his identification of petitioner, however, was less than positive. Petitioner's naval commanding officer deposed that petitioner had caused trouble by disobedience and absence without leave, and his Army commanding officer in 1921 deposed that he was sometimes "one of the very best soldiers," and at other times undependable, that he had alternate periods of gaiety and depression, talked incoherently at times, but seemed to get along well with other soldiers. A physician who first saw petitioner shortly before trial testified as to his conclusion, based upon his own observation as well as the other testimony and petitioner's documentary medical history, that petitioner was born with an inherent instability, that he had "gone to pieces" in France, and that he was insane at all times subsequent to July 1918.]

II.

* * *

But if the record is taken to show that some form of mental disability existed in 1930, which later became total and permanent, petitioner's problem remains to demonstrate by more than speculative inference that this condition itself began on or before May 31, 1919 and continuously existed or progressed through the intervening years to 1930.

To show origin before the crucial date, he gives evidence of two abnormal incidents occurring while he was in France, one creating the disturbance before he came near the fighting front, the other yelling that the Germans were coming when he was on guard duty at the Marne. There is no other evidence of abnormal behavior during his entire service of more than a year abroad.

* * *

O'Neill's testimony apparently takes no account of petitioner's having spent 101 days in a hospital in France with influenza just before he came home. But, given the utmost credence, as is required, it does no more than show that petitioner was subject to alternating periods of gaiety and depression for some indefinite period after his return, extending perhaps as late as 1922. But because of its vagueness as to time, dates, frequency of opportunity for observation, and specific incident, O'Neill's testimony concerning the period from 1922 to 1925 is hardly more than speculative.

We have then the two incidents in France followed by O'Neill's testimony of petitioner's changed condition in 1919 and its continuance to 1922.[11] There is also the testimony of Commander Platt and Lt. Col. James E. Matthews as to his service in the Navy and the Army, respectively, during 1920–1922. Neither thought petitioner was insane or that his conduct indicated insanity. Then follows a chasm of eight years. * * *

This period was eight years of continuous insanity, according to the inference petitioner would be allowed to have drawn. If so, he should have no need of inference. Insanity so long and continuously sustained does not hide itself from the eyes and ears of witnesses. The assiduity which produced the evidence of two "crazy" incidents during a year and a half in France should produce one during eight years or, for that matter, five years in the United States.

Inference is capable of bridging many gaps. But not, in these circumstances, one so wide and deep as this. Knowledge of petitioner's activities and behavior from 1922 or 1925 to 1930 was peculiarly within his ken and that of his wife, who has litigated this cause in his and presumably, though indirectly, in her own behalf. His was the burden to show continuous disability. What he did in this time, or did not do, was vital to his case. Apart from the mere fact of his marriage, the record is blank for five years and almost blank for eight. For all that appears, he may have worked full time and continuously for five and perhaps for eight, with only a possible single interruption.

No favorable inference can be drawn from the omission. It was not one of oversight or inability to secure proof. That is shown by the thoroughness with which the record was prepared for all other periods, before and after this one, and by the fact petitioner's wife, though she married him during the period and was available, did not testify. The only reasonable conclusion is that petitioner, or those who acted for him, deliberately chose, for reasons no doubt considered sufficient (and which we do not criticize, since such matters including tactical ones, are for the judgment of counsel) to present no evidence or perhaps to withhold evidence readily available concerning this long interval, and to trust to the genius of expert medical inference and judicial laxity to bridge this canyon.

In the circumstances exhibited, the former is not equal to the feat, and the latter will not permit it. No case has been cited and none has been found in which inference, however expert, has been permitted to make so broad a leap and take the place of evidence which, according to all reason, must have been at hand. To allow this would permit the substitution of inference, tenuous at best, not merely for evidence absent because impossible or difficult to secure, but for evidence disclosed to be available and not produced. This would substitute speculation for proof. Furthermore, the inference would be more plausible perhaps if the evidence of insanity as of May, 1919, were

11. Chaplain Mathews' testimony would be highly probative of insanity existing early in 1920, if petitioner were sufficiently identified as its subject. However, the bare inference of identity which might otherwise be drawn from the mere identity of names cannot be made reasonably in view of its overwhelming contradiction by other evidence presented by petitioner and the failure to produce records from Fort MacArthur Hospital or the Army or from persons who knew the fact that petitioner had been there at any time. The omission eloquently testifies in a manner which no inference could overcome that petitioner never was there. The chaplain's testimony therefore should have been stricken, had the case gone to the jury * * *.

stronger than it is, such for instance as Chaplain Mathews' testimony would have furnished if it could be taken as applying to petitioner. But, on this record, the evidence of insanity as of that time is thin at best, if it can be regarded as at all more than speculative.

Beyond this, there is nothing to show totality or permanence. * * *

III.

What has been said disposes of the case as the parties have made it. For that reason perhaps nothing more need be said. But objection has been advanced that, in some manner not wholly clear, the directed verdict practice offends the Seventh Amendment.

It may be noted, first, that the Amendment has no application of its own force to this case. The suit is one to enforce a monetary claim against the United States. It hardly can be maintained that under the common law in 1791 jury trial was a matter of right for persons asserting claims against the sovereign. Whatever force the Amendment has therefore is derived because Congress * * * has made it applicable. Even so, the objection made on the score of its requirements is untenable.

If the intention is to claim generally that the Amendment deprives the federal courts of power to direct a verdict for insufficiency of evidence, the short answer is the contention has been foreclosed by repeated decisions made here consistently for nearly a century. More recently the practice has been approved explicitly in the promulgation of the Federal Rules of Civil Procedure. * * * The objection therefore comes too late.

Furthermore, the argument from history is not convincing. It is not that "the rules of the common law" in 1791 deprived trial courts of power to withdraw cases from the jury, because not made out, or appellate courts of power to review such determinations. The jury was not absolute master of fact in 1791. Then as now courts excluded evidence for irrelevancy and relevant proof for other reasons. The argument concedes they weighed the evidence, not only piecemeal but *in toto* for submission to the jury, by at least two procedures, the demurrer to the evidence and the motion for a new trial. The objection is not therefore to the basic thing, which is the power of the court to withhold cases from the jury or set aside the verdict for insufficiency of the evidence. It is rather to incidental or collateral effects, namely, that the directed verdict as now administered differs from both those procedures because, on the one hand, allegedly higher standards of proof are required and, on the other, different consequences follow as to further maintenance of the litigation. Apart from the standards of proof, the argument appears to urge that in 1791, a litigant could challenge his opponent's evidence, either by the demurrer, which when determined ended the litigation, or by motion for a new trial which, if successful, gave the adversary another chance to prove his case; and therefore the Amendment excluded any challenge to which one or the other of these consequences does not attach.

The Amendment did not bind the federal courts to the exact procedural incidents or details of jury trial according to the common law in 1791, any more than it tied them to the common-law system of pleading or the specific rules of evidence then prevailing. Nor were "the rules of the common law" then prevalent, including those relating to the procedure by which the judge regulated the jury's role on questions of fact, crystalized in a fixed and immutable system. On the contrary, they were constantly changing and developing during the late eighteenth and early nineteenth centuries.[23] In 1791 this process already had resulted in widely divergent common-law rules on procedural matters among the states, and between them and England. * * *

This difficulty, no doubt, accounts for the amorphous character of the objection now advanced, which insists, not that any single one of the features criticized, but that the cumulative total or the alternative effect of all, was embodied in the Amendment. The more logical conclusion, we think, and the one which both history and the previous decisions here support, is that the Amendment was designed to preserve the basic institution of jury trial in only its most fundamental elements, not the great mass of procedural forms and details, varying even then so widely among common-law jurisdictions.

Apart from the uncertainty and the variety of conclusion which follows from an effort at purely historical accuracy, the consequences flowing from the view asserted are sufficient to refute it. It may be doubted that the Amendment requires challenge to an opponent's case to be made without reference to the merits of one's own and at the price of all opportunity to have it considered. On the other hand, there is equal room for disbelieving it compels endless repetition of litigation and unlimited chance, by education gained at the opposing party's expense, for perfecting a case at other trials. The essential inconsistency of these alternatives would seem sufficient to refute that either or both, to the exclusion of all others, received constitutional sanctity by the Amendment's force. The first alternative, drawn from the demurrer to the evidence, attributes to the Amendment the effect of forcing one admission because another and an entirely different one is made,[28] and thereby compels conclusion of the litigation once and for all. The true effect of imposing such a risk would not be to guarantee the plaintiff a jury trial. It would be rather to deprive the defendant (or the plaintiff if he were the challenger) of that right; or, if not that, then of the right to challenge the legal sufficiency of the opposing case. The Amendment was not framed or adopted

23. E.g., during the eighteenth and nineteenth centuries, the nonsuit was being transformed in practice from a device by which a plaintiff voluntarily discontinued his action in order to try again another day into a procedure by which a defendant could put in issue the sufficiency of the plaintiff's evidence to go to the jury, differing from the directed verdict in that respect only in form. * * * The nonsuit, of course, differed in consequence from the directed verdict, for it left the plaintiff free to try again. * * *

Similarly the demurrer to the evidence practice was not static during this period as a comparison of Cocksedge v. Fanshaw, 1779, 1 Doug. 118, with Gibson v. Hunter, 1793, 2 H.Bl. 187, and the American practice on the demurrer to the evidence reveals * * *. Nor was the conception of directing a verdict entirely unknown to the eighteenth century common law. * * * While there is no reason to believe that the notion at that time even approximated in character the present directed verdict, the cases serve further to show the plastic and developing character of these procedural devices during the eighteenth and nineteenth centuries.

28. By conceding the full scope of an opponent's evidence and asserting its insufficiency in law, which is one thing, the challenger must be taken * * * also to admit he has no case, if the other's evidence is found legally sufficient, which is quite another thing. In effect, one must stake his case, not upon its own merit on the facts, but on the chance he may be right in regarding his opponent's as wanting in probative content. If he takes the gamble and loses, he pays with his own case, * * * without opportunity for the jury to consider it. To force this choice and yet deny that afforded by the directed verdict would be to imbed in the Constitution the hypertechnicality of common-law pleading and procedure in their heyday. * * *

to deprive either party of either right. It is impartial in its guaranty of both. To posit assertion of one upon sacrifice of the other would dilute and distort the full protection intended. The admitted validity of the practice on the motion for a new trial goes far to demonstrate this.[29] It negatives any idea that the challenge must be made at such a risk as the demurrer imposed. As for the other alternative, it is not urged that the Amendment guarantees another trial whenever challenge to the sufficiency of evidence is sustained. * * * That argument, in turn, is precluded by the practice on demurrer to the evidence.

Each of the classical modes of challenge, therefore, disproves the notion that the characteristic feature of the other, for effect upon continuing the litigation, became a part of the Seventh Amendment's guaranty to the exclusion of all others. * * * Alternatives so contradictory give room, not for the inference that one or the other is required, but rather for the view that neither is essential.

Finally, the objection appears to be directed generally at the standards of proof judges have required for submission of evidence to the jury. But standards, contrary to the objection's assumption, cannot be framed wholesale for the great variety of situations in respect to which the question arises. * * * The matter is essentially one to be worked out in particular situations and for particular types of cases. Whatever may be the general formulation, the essential requirement is that mere speculation be not allowed to do duty for probative facts, after making due allowance for all reasonably possible inferences favoring the party whose case is attacked. The mere difference in labels used to describe this standard * * * cannot amount to a departure from "the rules of the common law" which the Amendment requires to be followed. * * *

Judged by this requirement, or by any standard other than sheer speculation, we are unable to conclude that one whose burden, by the nature of his claim, is to show continuing and total disability for nearly twenty years supplies the essential proof of continuity when he wholly omits to show his whereabouts, activities or condition for five years, although the record discloses evidence must have been available, and, further, throws no light upon three additional years, except for one vaguely described and dated visit to his former home. * * * The words "total and permanent" are the statute's, not our own. They mean something more than incipient or occasional disability. We hardly need add that we give full credence to all of the testimony. But that cannot cure its inherent vagueness or supply essential elements omitted or withheld.

Accordingly, the judgment is

Affirmed.

---

29. Under that practice the moving party receives the benefit of jury evaluation of his own case and of challenge to his opponent's for insufficiency. If he loses on the challenge, the litigation is ended. But this is not because, in making it, he is forced to admit his own is insufficient. It is rather for the reasons that the court finds the opposite party's evidence is legally sufficient and the jury has found it outweighs his own. There is thus no forced surrender of one right from assertion of another.

On the other hand, if the challenger wins, there is another trial. But this is because he has sought it, not because the Amendment guarantees it.

M<small>R</small>. J<small>USTICE</small> B<small>LACK</small>, with whom M<small>R</small>. J<small>USTICE</small> D<small>OUGLAS</small> and M<small>R</small>. J<small>USTICE</small> M<small>URPHY</small> concur, dissenting.

* * *

The Court here re-examines testimony offered in a common law suit, weighs conflicting evidence, and holds that the litigant may never take this case to a jury. * * * Today's decision marks a continuation of the gradual process of judicial erosion which in one hundred fifty years has slowly worn away a major portion of the essential guarantee of the Seventh Amendment.

I.

Alexander Hamilton in The Federalist emphasized his loyalty to the jury system in civil cases and declared that jury verdicts should be re-examined, if at all, only "by a second jury, either by remanding the cause to the court below for a second trial of the fact, or by directing an issue immediately out of the Supreme Court."

* * * The first Congress expected the Seventh Amendment to meet the objections of men like Patrick Henry to the Constitution itself. Henry, speaking in the Virginia Constitutional Convention, had expressed the general conviction of the people of the Thirteen States when he said, " * * * We are told that we are to part with that trial by jury with which our ancestors secured their lives and property. * * * I hope we shall never be induced, by such arguments, to part with that excellent mode of trial. No appeal can now be made as to fact in common law suits. *The unanimous verdict of impartial men cannot be reversed.*" * * *

In 1789, juries occupied the principal place in the administration of justice. They were frequently in both criminal and civil cases the arbiters not only of fact but of law. Less than three years after the ratification of the Seventh Amendment, this Court called a jury in a civil case brought under our original jurisdiction. There was no disagreement as to the facts of the case. Chief Justice Jay, charging the jury for a unanimous Court, three of whose members had sat in the Constitutional Convention, said: "For as, on the one hand, it is presumed, that juries are the best judges of facts; it is, on the other hand, presumable, that the court[s] are the best judges of law. But still, both objects are lawfully within your power of decision." State of Georgia v. Brailsford, 3 Dall. 1, 4, 1 L.Ed. 483. * * *

The principal method by which judges prevented cases from going to the jury in the Seventeenth and Eighteenth Centuries was by the demurrer to the evidence. * * * This practice fell into disuse in England in 1793, Gibson v. Hunter, 2 H.Bl. 187, and in the United States federal courts in 1826, Fowle v. Alexandria, 11 Wheat. 320, 6 L.Ed. 484. The power of federal judges to comment to the jury on the evidence gave them additional influence. * * * The right of involuntary nonsuit of a plaintiff, which might have been used to expand judicial power at jury expense was at first denied federal courts. * * *

As Hamilton had declared in The Federalist, the basic judicial control of the jury function was in the court's power to order a new trial. In 1830, this Court said: "The only modes known to the common law to re-examine such facts, are the granting of a new trial by the court where the issue was tried, or to which the record was properly returnable; or the award of a venire facias de novo, by an appellate court, for some error of law which intervened in the proceedings." Parsons v. Bedford, * * * 3 Pet. at page 448, 7 L.Ed. 732. * * *

A long step toward the determination of fact by judges instead of by juries was the invention of the directed verdict.[11] In 1850, what seems to have been the first directed verdict case considered by this Court, Parks v. Ross, 11 How. 362, 374, 13 L.Ed. 730, was presented for decision. The Court held that the directed verdict serves the same purpose as the demurrer to the evidence, and that since there was "no evidence whatever" on the critical issue in the case, the directed verdict was approved. The decision was an innovation, a departure from the traditional rule restated only fifteen years before in Greenleaf v. Birth, 1835, 9 Pet. 292, 299, 9 L.Ed. 132, in which this Court had said: "Where there is no evidence tending to prove a particular fact, the court[s] are bound so to instruct the jury, when requested; but they cannot legally give any instruction which shall take from the jury the right of weighing the evidence and determining what effect it shall have."

This new device contained potentialities for judicial control of the jury which had not existed in the demurrer to the evidence. In the first place, demurring to the evidence was risky business, for in so doing the party not only admitted the truth of all the testimony against him but also all reasonable inferences which might be drawn from it; and upon joinder in demurrer the case was withdrawn from the jury while the court proceeded to give final judgment either for or against the demurrant. * * * Imposition of this risk was no mere technicality; for by making withdrawal of a case from the jury dangerous to the moving litigant's cause, the early law went far to assure that facts would never be examined except by a jury. * * * The litigant not only takes no risk by a motion for a directed verdict, but in making such a motion gives himself two opportunities to avoid the jury's decision; for under the federal variant of judgment notwithstanding the verdict, the judge may reserve opinion on the motion for a directed verdict and then give judgment for the moving party after the jury was formally found against him. In the second place, under the directed verdict practice the courts soon abandoned the "admission of all facts and reasonable inferences" standard referred to, and created the so-called "substantial evidence" rule which permitted directed verdicts even though there was far more evidence in the case than a plaintiff would have needed to withstand a demurrer.

The substantial evidence rule did not spring into existence immediately upon the adoption of the directed verdict device. For a few more years federal judges held to the traditional rule that juries might pass finally on facts if there was "any evidence" to support a party's contention. The rule that a case must go to the jury unless there was "no evidence" was completely repudiated in Schuylkill and Dauphin Improvement Co. v. Munson, 1871, 14 Wall. 442, 447, 448, 20 L.Ed. 867, upon which the Court today relies in part. There the

---

11. I do not mean to minimize other forms of judicial control. In a summary of important techniques of judicial domination of the jury, Thayer lists the following: control by the requirement of a "reasonable judgment"—i.e., one satisfactory to the judge; control of the rules of "presumption" * * *; the control of the "definition of language"; the control of rules of practice, and forms of pleading ("It is remarkable how judges and legislatures in this country are unconsciously travelling towards the old result of controlling the jury, by requiring special verdicts and answers to specific questions. * * * "); the control of "mixed questions of law and fact"; the control of factual decisions by appellate courts. Thayer on Evidence (1898 ed.) p. 208 et seq.

Court declared that "some" evidence was not enough—there must be evidence sufficiently persuasive to the judge so that he thinks "a jury can properly proceed." The traditional rule was given an ugly name, "the scintilla rule", to hasten its demise. * * * The same transition from jury supremacy to jury subordination through judicial decisions took place in State courts.

Later cases permitted the development of added judicial control. * * * [J]ury verdicts on disputed facts have been set aside or directed verdicts authorized so regularly as to make the practice commonplace while the motion for directed verdict itself has become routine. * * * Today the Court comes dangerously close to weighing the credibility of a witness and rejecting his testimony because the majority do not believe it.

* * *

The call for the true application of the Seventh Amendment is not to words, but to the spirit of honest desire to see that Constitutional right preserved. Either the judge or the jury must decide facts and to the extent that we take this responsibility, we lessen the jury function. Our duty to preserve this one of the Bill of Rights may be peculiarly difficult, for here it is our own power which we must restrain. * * * As for myself, I believe that a verdict should be directed, if at all, only when, without weighing the credibility of the witnesses, there is in the evidence no room whatever for honest difference of opinion over the factual issue in controversy. * * *

II.

* * * It is undisputed that the petitioner's health was sound in 1918, and it is evidently conceded that he was disabled at least since 1930. When in the intervening period, did the disability take place?

* * * There is substantial testimony from which reasonable men might conclude that the petitioner was insane from the date claimed.

Two witnesses testify as to the petitioner's mental irresponsibility while he was in France. * * * The Court disposes of this testimony, which obviously indicates some degree of mental unbalance, by saying no more than that it "does not prove he was insane." No reason is given, nor can I imagine any, why a jury should not be entitled to consider this evidence and draw its own conclusions.

* * * The Court analyzes O'Neill's testimony for internal consistency, criticizes his failure to remember the details of his association with the petitioner fifteen years before his appearance in this case, and concludes that O'Neill's evidence shows no more than that "petitioner was subject to alternating periods of gaiety and depression for some indefinite period." This extreme emotional instability is an accepted symptom of the disease from which the petitioner suffers. If he exhibited the same symptoms in 1922, it is, at the minimum, probable that the condition has been continuous since an origin during the war. O'Neill's testimony coupled with the petitioner's present condition presents precisely the type of question which a jury should resolve.

* * * The testimony of his Commanding Officer while he was in the Army, Col. Matthews, is that the petitioner had "periods of gaiety and exhilaration" and was then "depressed as if he had had a hangover"; that

petitioner tried to create disturbances and dissatisfy the men; that he suffered from a belief that he was being treated unfairly; and that generally his actions "were not those of a normal man". The Colonel was not a doctor and might well not have recognized insanity had he seen it; as it was, he concluded that the petitioner was an alcoholic and a narcotic addict. However, the officer was unable, upon repeated investigations, to discover any actual use of narcotics. A jury fitting this information into the general pattern of the testimony might well have been driven to the conclusion that the petitioner was insane at the time the Colonel had him under observation.

All of this evidence, if believed, showed a man healthy and normal before he went to the war suffering for several years after he came back from a disease which had the symptoms attributed to schizophrenia and who was insane from 1930 until his trial. Under these circumstances, I think that the physician's testimony of total and permanent disability by reason of continuous insanity from 1918 to 1938 was reasonable. The fact that there was no direct testimony for a period of five years, while it might be the basis of fair argument to the jury by the government, does not, as the Court seems to believe, create a presumption against the petitioner so strong that his case must be excluded from the jury entirely. Even if during these five years the petitioner was spasmodically employed, we could not conclude that he was not totally and permanently disabled. * * * It is not doubted that schizophrenia is permanent even though there may be a momentary appearance of recovery.

* * *

This case graphically illustrates the injustice resulting from permitting judges to direct verdicts instead of requiring them to await a jury decision and then, if necessary, allow a new trial. The chief reason given for approving a directed verdict against this petitioner is that no evidence except expert medical testimony was offered for a five to eight year period. Perhaps, now that the petitioner knows he has insufficient evidence to satisfy a judge even though he may have enough to satisfy a jury, he would be able to fill this time gap to meet any judge's demand. * * * If, as the Court believes, insufficient evidence has been offered to sustain a jury verdict for the petitioner, we should at least authorize a new trial. * * *

Notes and Questions

1. Traditional rules required a party to assume a risk in order to move for a directed verdict. What policy is served by a rule requiring entry of judgment against a party whose motion is denied? Or by a rule to the effect that before moving for a directed verdict at the end of plaintiff's case, defendant must waive the right to produce evidence if the motion fails? Cf. Morley v. Liverpool & London & Globe Ins. Co., 85 Mich. 210, 48 N.W. 502 (1891); Bartholomew v. Impastato, 12 So.2d 700 (La.App.1943). Or by providing that if plaintiff and defendant both move for a directed verdict at the close of the evidence, they waive the right to jury trial in the event that both motions are denied? See Estes v. Hancock Cty. Bank, 259 Ind. 542, 289 N.E.2d 728 (1972); Bunch v. Davidson, 242 Or. 635, 409 P.2d 910 (1966), overruled by Godell v. Johnson, 244 Or. 587, 418 P.2d 505 (1966); Annot., 68 A.L.R.2d 300 (1959). To what extent are the policies underlying such rules dictated by the same considerations that support jury trial?

Are these rules consistent with rules and decisions in other areas of procedure that have reduced the part played by formal requirements and technical errors? How does Federal Rule 50 treat these questions?

2. What do you think of the following argument as addressed to a case such as *Galloway*?

> It seems to me that in this case the strongest argument in favor of submitting the cause to the jury is the widely divergent views among the members of this court, not only as to the conclusions which may properly be drawn from the testimony, but as to the testimony itself. If the judges of this court so differ in the proportion of four to three, can it be said that there is but one inference to be drawn, or that different minds may not honestly draw different conclusions? If the minds of the members of this court may so honestly differ, why may not the minds of jurors just as honestly differ? The logical deduction from the opinion of the court is that minority judges, and jurors generally, either do not have rational minds, or that they may not honestly reach a conclusion differing from the majority.

NUCCI v. COLORADO & S. RY. CO., 63 Colo. 582, 602, 169 P. 273, 281 (1917) (dissenting opinion).

3. Consider the relationship between a motion for summary judgment before trial under Federal Rule 56 and a Federal Rule 50(a) motion for a judgment as a matter of law after all the evidence has been introduced at trial. Think about the respective roles of the judge and the jury and develop your own philosophy as to when the fact-finding power should be taken away from the jury.

NEELY v. MARTIN K. EBY CONSTRUCTION CO., 386 U.S. 317, 87 S.Ct. 1072, 18 L.Ed.2d 75 (1967). Plaintiff brought a wrongful death action against defendant, claiming that defendant's negligent construction, maintenance, and supervision of a missile silo proximately caused the death of plaintiff's father, who died when he fell from a platform while working at the silo. At the close of plaintiff's case and again at the close of all evidence, defendant moved unsuccessfully for a directed verdict. The jury returned a $25,000 verdict for plaintiff, and the trial judge entered judgment for plaintiff after denying defendant's motions for judgment notwithstanding the verdict (j.n.o.v.) or, alternatively, a new trial.

On appeal, the Court of Appeals for the Tenth Circuit found the evidence insufficient to establish negligence or proximate cause, and reversed the District Court's ruling on defendant's j.n.o.v. motion. Plaintiff appealed to the Supreme Court, arguing that she had had no opportunity to raise claims for a new trial, and therefore an appellate court could not dismiss the case without running afoul of the Seventh Amendment right to a trial by jury. Justice White wrote:

> * * * The question here is whether the Court of Appeals, after reversing the denial of a defendant's Rule 50(b) motion for judgment notwithstanding the verdict, may itself order dismissal or direct entry of judgment for defendant. As far as the Seventh Amendment's right to jury trial is concerned, there is no greater restriction on the province of the jury when an appellate court enters judgment n.o.v. than when a trial

court does; consequently, there is no constitutional bar to an appellate court granting judgment n.o.v. * * *

In our view, therefore, Rule 50(d) makes express and adequate provision for the opportunity—which the plaintiff-appellee had without this rule—to present his grounds for a new trial in the event his verdict is set aside by the court of appeals. If he does so in his brief—or in a petition for rehearing if the court of appeals has directed entry of judgment for appellant—the court of appeals may make final disposition of the issues presented, except those which in its informed discretion should be reserved for the trial court. If appellee presents no new trial issues in his brief or in a petition for rehearing, the court of appeals may, in any event, order a new trial on its own motion or refer the question to the district court, based on factors encountered in its own review of the case.

* * *

In the case before us, petitioner won a verdict in the District Court which survived respondent's n.o.v. motion. In the Court of Appeals the issue was the sufficiency of the evidence and that court set aside the verdict. Petitioner, as appellee, suggested no grounds for a new trial in the event her judgment was reversed, nor did she petition for rehearing in the Court of Appeals, even thought that court had directed a dismissal of her case. Neither was it suggested that the record was insufficient to present any new trial issues or that any other reason required a remand to the District Court. Indeed, in her brief in the Court of Appeals, petitioner stated, "this law suit was fairly tried and the jury was properly instructed." It was, of course, incumbent on the Court of Appeals to consider the new trial question in the light of its own experience with the case. But we will not assume that the court ignored its duty in this respect, although it would have been better had its opinion expressly dealt with the new trial question.

2. STANDARDS FOR MOTIONS FOR JUDGMENT AS A MATTER OF LAW (DIRECTED VERDICT AND JUDGMENT NOTWITHSTANDING THE VERDICT)

———

Read Federal Rule of Civil Procedure 50 in the Supplement.

———

In 1991, Rule 50 was amended to change both the terms "directed verdict" and "judgment notwithstanding the verdict" to read "judgment as a matter of law." The Advisory Committee stated that the purpose of the change was to show not only that directed verdicts and judgments notwithstanding the verdict should be governed by identical standards, but that a motion under Rule 56 for summary judgment is to be governed by the same standard as well. The only difference among motions under Rule 50(a), Rule 50(b), and Rule 56 is the time when they are made. The Advisory Committee noted that the standards governing Rule 50(a) and Rule 50(b) motions have not changed as a result of these Amendments.

DENMAN v. SPAIN

Supreme Court of Mississippi, 1961.
242 Miss. 431, 135 So.2d 195.

LEE, PRESIDING JUSTICE. Betty Denman, a minor, * * * sued * * * [the] executrix of the estate of Joseph A. Ross, deceased, to recover damages for personal injuries sustained by her, allegedly resulting from the negligence of the decedent in the operation of an automobile. The issue was submitted to a jury on the evidence for the plaintiff—no evidence being offered for the defendant—and there was a verdict and judgment for the plaintiff in the sum of $5,000. However, on motion of the defendant, a judgment *non obstante veredicto* * * * was sustained and entered. From that action, the plaintiff has appealed.

* * *

The appellant contends that the evidence offered by her, together with the reasonable inferences therefrom, was sufficient to make an issue for the jury as to whether the alleged negligence of the deceased driver, Ross, proximately caused or contributed to the collision and the consequent damage * * *.

A careful scrutiny and analysis of the evidence is therefore necessary:

Sunday, March 23, 1958, was a rainy, foggy day. About six o'clock that afternoon, at dusk, Mrs. Eva B. Denman, accompanied by her granddaughter, Betty, the plaintiff, was driving her Ford car southward on U.S. Highway 49E. At that time, Joseph A. Ross, accompanied by Miss Euna Tanner and Mrs. J.L. Haining, was driving his Plymouth car northward on said highway. Just south of the Town of Sumner, the cars collided. Mrs. Denman, Miss Tanner and Ross were killed. Betty, nearly seven years of age at the time, and Mrs. Haining were injured. Neither had any recollection of what had happened at the time of the collision. * * *

Plaintiff's father, Stuart Denman, who went to the scene shortly after the collision, described the situation substantially as follows: The Ford car was about seven yards off the paved surface on the east side in a bar pit "heading back towards the railroad track, which is in an easterly direction." The engine and transmission were on the opposite side of the road, out of the car and about fifty yards apart. The Plymouth was also on the east side, facing west, about fifteen yards north of the Ford.

No proof was offered as to skid marks, or other evidence to show the point of contact between these two vehicles. Eleven photographs of the damaged Plymouth, taken from various positions, and thirteen pictures of the damaged Ford, also taken from various positions, other than being mute evidence of a terrible tragedy, depict no reasonable or plausible explanation as to why this collision occurred, or who was responsible for it. * * *

Over objection by the defendant, John Barnett testified that he was driving a Dodge pickup north of [sic] highway 49E on his way to Tutwiler; that he was traveling at a speed of fifty or fifty-five miles per hour; that the Plymouth, which was in the wreck, passed him about three-fourths of a mile south of where the collision occurred, going at a speed of about seventy miles per hour; that when it passed, it got back in its lane, and neither wavered nor wobbled thereafter; that he followed and observed it for a distance of forty or fifty yards, and that it stayed in its proper lane as long as he saw it. Although another car was on the road ahead of him, he could have seen as far as the place of the accident except for the rain and fog.

Over objection by the defendant, Hal Buckley * * * testified that he was also traveling north on 49E on his way to Tutwiler at a speed of forty to fifty miles per hour. About two hundred yards south of the place where the collision occurred, a light green Plymouth, which he later saw at the scene of the accident, passed him at a speed of seventy-five or eighty miles an hour. He could see its taillights after it passed, and "he was just steady going; he wasn't doing no slowing up." He saw it until it ran into the other car. On cross-examination, he said that, after this car passed him, it got back on its side of the road, drove straight, and he did not notice that it ever went back over the center. Also on cross-examination, in an effort at impeachment, a part of the transcript in the other trial,[e] containing this question and answer, was read to him as follows: "What do you estimate the speed of that car was when it passed you—the one that was going the same direction that you were?," and the answer was: "Well, I don't have no idea." * * * He then admitted that when the car passed him, it got back on its side and drove straight ahead, and that he could see the accident, but he could not tell anything about it or on which side of the road it happened. He also did not notice the other car, which came from the other direction.

Since Barnett did not see the car any more after it had gone forty or fifty yards beyond him, and his knowledge of speed was based on what he saw about three-fourths of a mile south of the place where the collision occurred, this evidence was inadmissible * * *. On the contrary, since Buckley testified the speed of this car, when it passed him, was seventy-five to eighty miles an hour and that it did not slow down in the remaining distance of two hundred yards before the collision, such evidence was competent and admissible * * *. The attempted impeachment went to its credibility and not its admissibility.

From this evidence, the plaintiff reasons that the jury could, and did, find that the Ross car was being operated, under inclement weather conditions, at an unlawful and negligent rate of speed, and that, if Ross had had his car under adequate and proper control, in all probability the collision could have been avoided. She voices the opinion that the physical facts, including the pictures of the wrecked vehicles, indicated that the Ford car was probably across the highway at an angle of perhaps forty-five degrees at the time of the collision.

But the testimony of Buckley showed only that the Plymouth was being operated at an excessive and negligent rate of speed. It otherwise showed that

e. Plaintiff had separately sued the estate of her grandmother. Trial in that case resulted in a directed verdict for defendant, which was affirmed. Denman v. Denman, 242 Miss. 59, 134 So.2d 457 (1961).

the car was in its proper lane. He did not notice it go over the center at any time, but it was driven straight down the road. No eyewitness claimed to have seen what happened. There was no evidence to indicate the place in the road where the vehicles came in contact with each other. There was no showing as to the speed of the Ford, whether fast or slow; or as to whether it was traveling on the right or wrong side of the road; or as to whether it slid or was suddenly driven to the wrong side of the road into the path of the Plymouth. The cars were so badly damaged that the pictures afford no reasonable explanation as to what person or persons were legally responsible for their condition. In other words, just how and why this grievous tragedy occurred is completely shrouded in mystery.

The burden was on the plaintiff to prove by a preponderance of the evidence, not only that the operator of the Plymouth was guilty of negligence but also that such negligence proximately caused or contributed to the collision and consequent damage. By the use of metaphysical learning, speculation and conjecture, one may reach several possible conclusions as to how the accident occurred. However such conclusions could only be classed as possibilities; and this Court has many times held that verdicts cannot be based on possibilities. At all events, there is no sound or reasonable basis upon which a jury or this Court can say that the plaintiff met that burden.

The judgment must be affirmed.

Affirmed.

Notes and Questions

1. At this point I am going to say something which you may find very shocking. [The judge] * * * is supposed to submit an issue to the jury if, as the judges say, the jury can decide reasonably either way. But to say that I can decide an issue of fact reasonably either way is to say, I submit, that I cannot, by the exercise of reason, decide the question. That means that the issue which we typically submit to juries is an issue which the jury cannot decide by the exercise of its reason.

The decision of an issue of fact in cases of closely balanced probabilities, therefore, must, in the nature of things, be an emotional rather than a rational act * * *.

Michael, *The Basic Rules of Pleading*, 5 Record of N.Y.C.B.A. 175, 199–200 (1950). Do you agree with Professor Michael? What is the relevance of this comment to the opinion in the *Denman* case?

2. Do you believe a jury could properly have found for plaintiff in the *Denman* case? What inferences would have to be drawn from the evidence to reach such a conclusion? How would you support the proposition that these inferences could reasonably be found to be stronger than other inferences that would not lead to a verdict for plaintiff?

3. Is the *Denman* case contrary to Lavender v. Kurn, p. 49, supra? In PLANTERS MANUFACTURING. CO. v. PROTECTION MUTUAL INSURANCE CO., 380 F.2d 869 (5th Cir.1967), the Court of Appeals concluded that the two cases are inconsistent, and thus had to confront squarely the question whether a state standard for directing a verdict is controlling under *Erie*, a question the United States Supreme Court has found unnecessary to answer in two cases that

raised it. Dick v. New York Life Ins. Co., 359 U.S. 437, 79 S.Ct. 921, 3 L.Ed.2d 935 (1959), and Mercer v. Theriot, 377 U.S. 152, 84 S.Ct. 1157, 12 L.Ed.2d 206 (1964). The Courts of Appeals remain split. Compare Boeing v. Shipman, 411 F.2d 365 (5th Cir.1969) (federal law applies), with Boynton v. TRW Inc., 858 F.2d 1178 (6th Cir.1988) (state law applies). To what extent, if any, does Gasperini v. Center for Humanities, Inc., p. 411, supra, help settle the dispute?

4. Cases like *Denman,* which involve head-on vehicular collisions, present a difficult problem with regard to the control of jury verdicts. The circumstances of these collisions ordinarily suggest that at least one driver was negligent but may not indicate which driver it was, and direct evidence often is lacking because all witnesses are dead. See Annot., 77 A.L.R.2d 580 (1961). Can you suggest a solution to the problem?

5. In KIRCHER v. ATCHISON, TOPEKA & SANTA FE RY. CO., 32 Cal.2d 176, 195 P.2d 427 (1948), plaintiff sued for the loss of a hand, which had been run over by defendant's train. A judgment for plaintiff was affirmed. Justice Carter, for the court, said:

> * * * In the light of all the circumstances * * * it cannot be held as a matter of law, that plaintiff's version was such as to contravene the laws of nature, or as to render the jury's acceptance of it unreasonable. * * * Although he stated quite frankly that he was unable to explain with certainty the manner in which his left hand came to be placed on the east rail * * *, the jury had before it evidence indicating that * * * there was a hole in the depot platform * * * and the ultimate fact that defendant's train ran over his hand at the time and place in question. In these circumstances the jury was not compelled to find against him because he could not with certainty relate the exact manner in which his left hand came to be on the east rail. It could reasonably have inferred that his failure to explain this circumstance was due to the fact that in the critical few minutes he was under the train he was unconscious, or substantially so, from the blow on his head as the outcome of stepping into the hole.

Id. at 184, 195 P.2d at 433.

Justice Traynor, dissenting, said:

> It is my opinion that although the accident as described by plaintiff is not outside the realm of possibility, his version, which is that of an interested and impeached witness, involves so extraordinary and improbable a sequence of events that without corroboration it does not warrant belief by a reasonable jury.

Id. at 189, 195 P.2d at 436.

Does the *Kircher* case present the same kind of issue as the *Denman* case? Should a verdict ever be directed for the party having the burden of producing evidence on an issue when the evidence in that party's favor is testimonial rather than documentary? Hearsay evidence sometimes is excluded on objection because it is not regarded as a reliable basis for a jury's decision. If hearsay evidence comes in without objection, and the party against whom that evidence militates subsequently moves for a directed verdict, should the hearsay evidence be taken into account in determining whether there is sufficient evidence to support a jury verdict for the other party? See Note 1, pp. 931–32, supra.

ROGERS v. MISSOURI PACIFIC R. CO.

Supreme Court of the United States, 1957.
352 U.S. 500, 77 S.Ct. 443, 1 L.Ed.2d 493.

Certiorari to the Supreme Court of Missouri.

Mr. Justice Brennan delivered the opinion of the Court.

A jury in the Circuit Court of St. Louis awarded damages to the petitioner in this action under the Federal Employers' Liability Act. The Supreme Court of Missouri reversed upon the ground that the petitioner's evidence did not support the finding of respondent's liability. * * *

Petitioner was a laborer in a section gang, working on July 17, 1951, along a portion of respondent's double-track line which, near Garner, Arkansas, runs generally north and south. The tracks are on ballast topping the surface of a dirt "dump" with sloping sides, and there is a path about a yard wide bordering each side of the surface between the crest of the slope and the edge of the ballast. Weeds and vegetation, killed chemically preparatory to burning them off, covered the paths and slopes. Petitioner's foreman assigned him to burn off the weeds and vegetation—the first time he was given that task in the two months he had worked for the respondent. He testified that it was customary to burn off such vegetation with a flame thrower operated from a car running on the tracks. Railroad witnesses testified, however, that the respondent discontinued the use of flame throwers at least a year earlier because the fires started by them sometimes spread beyond the railroad right of way.

Petitioner was supplied with a crude hand torch and was instructed to burn off the weeds and vegetation along the west path and for two or three feet down the west slope. The events leading to his mishap occurred after he proceeded with the work to a point within thirty to thirty-five yards of a culvert adjoining the path.

Petitioner testified, without contradiction, that the foreman instructed him and other members of the section gang to stop what they were doing when a train passed and to take positions off the tracks and ties to observe the journals of the passing train for hot boxes. The instructions were explicit not to go on either of the tracks or to stand on or near the ends of the ties when a train was passing on a far track. This was a safety precaution because "the sound of one train would deaden the sound of another one that possibly would come from the other way."

On this day, petitioner heard the whistle of a train which was approaching from behind him on the east track. He promptly "quit firing" and ran north to a place on the path near the mentioned culvert. He was standing a few feet from the culvert observing the train for hotboxes when he became enveloped in smoke and flames. The passing train had fanned the flames of the burning vegetation and weeds, carrying the fire to the vegetation around his position. He threw his arm over his face, retreated quickly back on the culvert and slipped and fell from the top of the culvert, suffering the serious injuries for which he sought damages in this suit.

* * *

We think that the evidence was sufficient to support the jury finding for the petitioner. The testimony that the burning off of weeds and vegetation was ordinarily done with flame throwers from cars on the tracks and not, as here, by a workman on foot using a crude hand torch, when that evidence is considered with the uncontradicted testimony that the petitioner was where he was on this narrow path atop the dirt "dump" in furtherance of explicit orders * * *, supplied ample support for a jury finding that respondent's negligence played a part in the petitioner's injury. These were probative facts from which the jury could find that respondent was or should have been aware of conditions which created a likelihood that petitioner, in performing the duties required of him, would suffer just such an injury as he did. Common experience teaches both that a passing train will fan the flames of a fire, and that a person suddenly enveloped in flames and smoke will instinctively react by retreating from the danger and in the process pay scant heed to other dangers which may imperil him. In this view, it was an irrelevant consideration whether the immediate reason for his slipping off the culvert was the presence of gravel negligently allowed by respondent to remain on the surface, or was some cause not identified from the evidence.

The Missouri Supreme Court based its reversal upon its finding of an alleged admission by the petitioner that he knew it was his primary duty to watch the fire. From that premise the Missouri court reasoned that petitioner was inattentive to the fire and that the emergency which confronted him "was an emergency brought about by himself." It said that if, as petitioner testified, the immediate cause of his fall was that loose gravel on the surface of the culvert rolled out from under him, yet it was his inattention to the fire which caused it to spread and obliged petitioner "to move blindly away and fall," and this was "something extraordinary, unrelated to, and disconnected from the incline of the gravel at the culvert."

We interpret the foregoing to mean that the Missouri court found as a matter of law that the petitioner's conduct was the sole cause of his mishap. But when the petitioner agreed that his primary duty was to watch the fire he did not also say that he was relieved of the duty to stop to watch a passing train for hotboxes. Indeed, no witness testified that the instruction was countermanded. At best, uncertainty as to the fact arises from the petitioner's testimony, and in that circumstance not the court, but the jury, was the tribunal to determine the fact.

We may assume that the jury could properly have reached the court's conclusion. But, as the probative facts also supported with reason the verdict favorable to the petitioner, the decision was exclusively for the jury to make. The jury was instructed to return a verdict for the respondent if it was found that negligence of the petitioner was the sole cause of his mishap. We must take it that the verdict was obedient to the trial judge's charge and that the jury found that such was not the case but that petitioner's injury resulted at least in part from the respondent's negligence.

The opinion may also be read as basing the reversal on another ground, namely, that it appeared to the court that the petitioner's conduct was at least as probable a cause for his mishap as any negligence of the respondent, and that in such case there was no case for the jury. But that would mean that there is no jury question in actions under this statute, although the employee's proofs support with reason a verdict in his favor, unless the judge can say that the jury may exclude the idea that his injury was due to causes with which the defendant was not connected, or, stated another way, unless his proofs are so strong that the jury, on grounds of probability, may exclude a conclusion favorable to the defendant. That is not the governing principle defining the proof which requires a submission to the jury in these cases. The Missouri court's opinion implies its view that this is the governing standard by saying that the proofs must show that "the injury would not have occurred but for the negligence" of his employer, and that "[t]he test of whether there is causal connection is that, absent the negligent act the injury would not have occurred." * * *

Under this statute the test of a jury case is simply whether the proofs justify with reason the conclusion that employer negligence played any part, even the slightest, in producing the injury or death for which damages are sought. It does not matter that, from the evidence, the jury may also with reason, on grounds of probability, attribute the result to other causes, including the employee's contributory negligence. Judicial appraisal of the proofs to determine whether a jury question is presented is narrowly limited to the single inquiry whether, with reason, the conclusion may be drawn that negligence of the employer played any part at all in the injury or death. Judges are to fix their sights primarily to make that appraisal and, if that test is met, are bound to find that a case for the jury is made out whether or not the evidence allows the jury a choice of other probabilities. The statute expressly imposes liability upon the employer to pay damages for injury or death due "in whole or *in part*" to its negligence. (Emphasis added.)

* * *

The Congress when adopting the law was particularly concerned that the issues whether there was employer fault and whether that fault played any part in the injury or death of the employee should be decided by the jury whenever fair-minded men could reach these conclusions on the evidence. Originally, judicial administration of the 1908 Act substantially limited the cases in which employees were allowed a jury determination. That was because the courts developed concepts of assumption of risk and of the coverage of the law, which defeated employee claims as a matter of law. Congress corrected this by the 1939 amendments and removed the fetters which hobbled the full play of the basic congressional intention to leave to the fact-finding function of the jury the decision of the primary question raised in these cases—whether employer fault played any part in the employee's mishap. * * *

The judgment is reversed. * * *

MR. JUSTICE BURTON concurs in the result.

MR. JUSTICE REED would affirm the judgment of the Supreme Court of Missouri.

[Dissenting opinions of JUSTICE FRANKFURTER and JUSTICE HARLAN are omitted.]

Notes and Questions

1. Is the nature of the issue that the Court said should have been left to the jury in *Rogers* different from that in *Lavender, Denman,* and *Kircher?* If so, is the difference significant to the formulation of a standard? Might a judgment as a matter of law be more readily sustained on one type of issue than the other?

2. A municipal ordinance permitted an authorized emergency vehicle to proceed past a stop signal or exceed the speed limit "when the driver of such vehicle sounds a siren, bell or exhaust whistle to the extent reasonably necessary." A police car in rush-hour traffic, on call to a robbery then in progress, proceeded at excessive speed through a red light, and struck plaintiff. In LO CICERO v. COLUMBIA CASUALTY CO., 268 F.2d 440 (5th Cir.), certiorari denied 361 U.S. 917, 80 S.Ct. 261, 4 L.Ed.2d 187 (1959), the court held that the jury should have been instructed that the policeman was negligent as a matter of law in failing to sound the siren. Is this distinguishable from directing a verdict on the issue of negligence when no statute is involved?

3. Justice Frankfurter dissented in the *Rogers* case on the ground that certiorari had been "improvidently granted"; the Justice declined to express himself on the merits. The case is one of many in which he argued that the Supreme Court should not take time to review cases in which the only issue was the sufficiency of the evidence to take a case to the jury. See pp. 1218–22, *infra.*

DANIEL J. HARTWIG ASSOCIATES, INC. v. KANNER

United States Court of Appeals, Seventh Circuit, 1990.
913 F.2d 1213.

KANNE, CIRCUIT JUDGE.

Daniel J. Hartwig Associates, Inc., is an environmental consulting firm that rendered consulting and expert witness services to Allan Kanner, an attorney whose practice is limited to environmental and toxic injury litigation. After Kanner failed to pay Hartwig for its services, Hartwig filed a breach of contract suit in federal district court. The district court directed a verdict in favor of Hartwig in the amount of $44,225.04. Kanner appeals on three grounds: (1) he contends that the district court did not have personal jurisdiction over him; (2) he contends that the district court erred in directing a verdict because a material issue of fact existed as to whether he owed Hartwig for its services; and finally, (3) he contends that the district court denied him due process because the court did not grant a continuance to allow additional time for discovery purposes. Having found none of these three grounds persuasive, we affirm the decision of the district court. [The court's discussion of grounds (1) and (2) is omitted.] * * *

DIRECTED VERDICT

Hartwig agreed to perform consulting and expert witness services for Kanner at an hourly rate plus reimbursement for expenses. Hartwig billed Kanner at a rate of $60 per hour for general consulting, field work and investigative work, and $100 per hour (initially $80 per hour) for in-court testimony and deposition work. Hartwig informed Kanner of the fee schedule and the billing rates in writing. As services were rendered, Hartwig prepared and submitted invoices to Kanner. After Kanner failed to pay several invoices, Hartwig and a number of his employees contacted members of Kanner's staff to inquire about past due payments. Kanner's staff explained that Kanner simply did not have the money to pay the bills but that they would be paid as soon as possible.

Ultimately, Hartwig requested Kanner to execute some promissory notes evidencing his obligation to Hartwig. In September, 1986, Kanner executed three promissory notes, one for each lawsuit in which Hartwig had provided services. The promissory notes provided for payment of interest at a rate of 18% per annum if not paid on the dates set forth in the notes. The notes also provided that Kanner would pay Hartwig reasonable attorney fees incurred in collecting payment. After Kanner executed the notes, Hartwig performed additional services for Kanner worth $6,827.78. Kanner never paid Hartwig for his services.

Hartwig brought a breach of contract suit against Kanner to recover payment for services rendered and attorney fees incurred in collecting payment. At the close of all the evidence, the district judge directed a verdict in favor of Hartwig in the amount of $44,225.04—$40,725.04 for consulting services and interest, and $3,500 for attorney fees pursuant to the terms of the promissory notes. Kanner argues that the district court was precluded from granting a directed verdict in favor of Hartwig because there was a material issue of fact as to whether the contract was void due to various misrepresentations Hartwig made to Kanner prior to entering into the contract.

The evidence indicated that the resume Hartwig sent to Kanner stated that Hartwig had received a Bachelor of Science degree in 1971, and a Master of Science degree "ABT." However, Hartwig actually received a Bachelor of Arts degree not a Bachelor of Science degree; in addition, he received the degree in 1975, not 1971. Moreover, Hartwig intended the initials "ABT" to stand for "all but thesis," meaning that Hartwig had not written his thesis and, therefore, did not actually have a masters degree at the time he sent Kanner his resume. When Hartwig testified as an expert witness during Kanner's trial in California—the Aerojet trial—Hartwig expressed uncertainty on the stand as to whether he had a Bachelor of Arts or a Bachelor of Science degree or what year he received his degree. In addition, the fact that Hartwig had not completed his masters degree was also brought out during Hartwig's testimony in Aerojet.

The evidence also indicated that Hartwig was the principal owner of another company, American Environmental Control, which performed asbestos removal jobs for the state of Wisconsin. At one time, Hartwig Associates held a contract with the state of Wisconsin to supervise and inspect asbestos removal being done by American Environmental. Hartwig never told Kanner about these contracts. Although Hartwig Associates eventually backed out before performing the supervision contract, attorneys at the Aerojet trial brought out the fact that Hartwig entered into contracts that created an obvious conflict of interest.

At trial, Hartwig admitted that there were inaccuracies in his resume. However, Hartwig testified that he explained his educational background in detail to Kanner and his associates including the fact that he had not completed a masters degree. Hartwig also testified that he told Kanner about his interest in American Environmental Control but that there was no need to tell Kanner about any potential conflict of interest because Hartwig Associates never intended to perform its supervision contract. Kanner chose not to appear in the district court at Madison, Wisconsin, for the trial of the case now before us. His counsel appeared but in his case in chief, he presented no witnesses and offered only a single document into evidence.

A motion for a directed verdict raises only a question of law; thus, our review is de novo. * * * Because the district court's jurisdiction was based on diversity of citizenship, the test for granting a directed verdict is supplied by the law of the forum state, here Wisconsin. * * * In determining whether a directed verdict should be granted under Wisconsin law, the evidence is viewed in the light most favorable to the party against whom the motion is made. A court should direct a verdict only if there is no credible evidence to sustain a verdict in favor of the party against whom the motion was made. Wis.Stat. § 805.14(1). * * *

Kanner's only defense to Hartwig's contract action is based on a claim that Hartwig misrepresented his educational background in his resume and that Hartwig did not inform Kanner of the conflict of interest between Hartwig's two companies. At trial, Hartwig testified that he told Kanner about inaccuracies in his resume; in addition, Hartwig testified that he told Kanner about the relationship between his two companies and truthfully represented to Kanner that his ownership of both companies did not create a conflict of interest. Kanner presented no evidence at trial to rebut Hartwig's testimony. Nonetheless, Kanner points out that it is the province of the jury to determine the credibility of interested witness testimony. Kanner argues that a jury could have disbelieved Hartwig's testimony that he told Kanner about inaccuracies on his resume and that he told Kanner about the relationship between his companies. Kanner further argues that this credibility determination amounted to a material issue of fact as to whether Hartwig made misrepresentations that voided the contract. We disagree.

Kanner failed to submit the necessary evidence to support a verdict contrary to that sought by Hartwig. Even if the jury disbelieved Hartwig's testimony and found that Hartwig made material misrepresentations to Kanner, Kanner still would not have carried his burden of establishing a defense. Misrepresentation alone does not amount to a defense. Under Wisconsin law, a defendant who seeks to render a contract voidable due to fraudulent misrepresentation must prove the following elements: (1) a material misrepresentation; (2) reliance on the misrepresentation; and (3) injury or damage due to reliance on the misrepresentation. * * * In addition, the party alleging fraud has the burden of proving the elements by clear and convincing evidence. * * *

Kanner failed to present any evidence demonstrating that he relied on Hartwig's misrepresentations. For example, Kanner did not present evidence that Hartwig's educational credentials were critical to his decision to hire Hartwig. More important, Kanner failed to present any evidence that demonstrated how he was damaged by the misrepresentations—Kanner presented no evidence that Hartwig erroneously consulted Kanner and that the erroneous consultation changed the result Kanner would have obtained in litigation;

nor did Kanner present evidence that Hartwig's services were somehow rendered valueless because of Hartwig's misrepresentations. At oral argument, Kanner told us that he lost the Aerojet trial and that Hartwig's poor performance on the witness stand was a contributing factor to this loss. This revelation came too late and was presented to the wrong court. Kanner's oral argument "testimony" would have obviously served him better before the jury rather than before this court.

This was a simple debt collection case. The amount sought to be recovered was not in dispute. Kanner's indebtedness was plainly evidenced by promissory notes executed by Kanner. At trial, Hartwig testified that Kanner never complained about the quality of Hartwig's work or raised any issue of being misled or damaged by Hartwig's credentials. The only reason Kanner ever gave for failing to pay Hartwig was a lack of funds. Kanner had the burden of proving a defense to the contract—a task made nearly impossible by his choice not to appear for trial or present any witnesses. Kanner simply failed to present any evidence of reliance on Hartwig's misrepresentations or of a causal link between the misrepresentations and a loss he suffered. Accordingly, the district court did not err in directing a verdict in favor of Hartwig.

* * *

For the foregoing reasons, the decision of the district court is affirmed.

Notes and Questions

1. *Hartwig Associates* is a case in which a directed verdict is awarded to a plaintiff. Once Kanner asserted the defense of fraudulent misrepresentation, the burden of persuasion fell upon defendant who failed to prove the defense by clear and convincing evidence. Is it possible for plaintiff to obtain a judgment as a matter of law if she has the burden of persuasion "and it" does not shift? Can the defense force a jury deliberation solely by attacking the credibility of plaintiff's evidence, but introducing no evidence of its own?

2. Suppose defendant, Kanner, testifies at trial that the terms of the oral contract with Hartwig released Kanner from the responsibility to pay for services rendered if Hartwig misrepresented his credentials. Could that testimony force a jury deliberation?

———

The Supreme Court denied certiorari in two cases involving the nature of the evidence to be considered when deciding whether a judgment as a matter of law is appropriate. Schwimmer, DBA Supersonic Electronics, Inc. v. Sony Corp., and Venture Technolog, Inc. v. National Fuel Gas Distribution Corp., 459 U.S. 1007, 103 S.Ct. 362, 74 L.Ed. 2d 398 (1982). Justice White dissented from the denial of certiorari as follows:

> [A conflict in the Circuits concerns] * * * the portion of the evidence a court is to consider in ruling upon a motion for judgment notwithstanding the verdict. These cases indicated that it is the Second Circuit's practice to examine all of the evidence in a manner most favorable to the non-moving party. This is also the position of at least the Fifth and

Seventh Circuits. * * * In the Eighth Circuit, however, it appears that only evidence which supports the verdict winner is to be considered. * * * The first and Third Circuits follow a middle ground: the reviewing court may consider uncontradicted, unimpeached evidence from disinterested witnesses. . . . Thus, the Federal Courts of Appeals follow three different approaches to determining whether evidence is sufficient to create a jury issue. [See 9A C. Wright & A. Miller, *Federal Practice and Procedure: Civil 2d* § 2529 (1995).] * * * Because the scope of review will often be influential, if not dispositive of a motion for judgment n.o.v., this disagreement among the Federal courts of Appeals is of far more than academic interest.

Notes & Questions

1. How seriously should we consider Justice White's concern? Which of the views taken by the Courts of Appeals is most appropriate?

2. Suppose that the trial judge erroneously admitted evidence favorable to the party who won the verdict that has been challenged on a motion for judgment as a matter of law. On appeal from the denial of the motion should the Court of Appeals exclude from its consideration the evidence that should not have been admitted? Why? Why not? See Elbert v. Howmedica, Inc., 143 F.3d 1208 (9th Cir.), certiorari denied 525 U.S. 944, 119 S.Ct. 366, 142 L.Ed.2d 302 (1998).

3. RENEWAL OF A MOTION FOR JUDGMENT AS A MATTER OF LAW (J.N.O.V.)

BALTIMORE & CAROLINA LINE, INC. v. REDMAN, 295 U.S. 654, 656, 658–60, 55 S.Ct. 890, 891–93, 79 L.Ed. 1636, 1637–40 (1935) (opinion by Justice Van Devanter):

This was an action in a federal court in New York to recover damages for personal injuries allegedly sustained by the plaintiff through the defendant's negligence. The issues were tried before the court and a jury. At the conclusion of the evidence, the defendant moved for a dismissal of the complaint because the evidence was insufficient to support a verdict for the plaintiff, and also moved for a directed verdict in its favor on the same ground. The court reserved its decision on both motions, submitted the case to the jury subject to its opinion on the questions reserved, and received from the jury a verdict for the plaintiff. No objection was made to the reservation or this mode of proceeding. Thereafter the court held the evidence sufficient and the motions ill grounded, and accordingly entered a judgment for the plaintiff on the verdict.

The defendant appealed to the Circuit Court of Appeals, which held the evidence insufficient and reversed the judgment with a direction for a new trial. The defendant urged that the direction be for a dismissal of the complaint. But the Court of Appeals ruled that under our decision in Slocum v. New York Life Insurance Company [228 U.S. 364, 33 S.Ct. 523, 57 L.Ed. 879] the direction must be for a new trial. * * *

In Slocum * * * a jury trial in a federal court resulted in a general verdict for the plaintiff over the defendant's request that a verdict for it be directed. Judgment was entered on the verdict for the plaintiff and the defendant obtained a review in the court of appeals. That court examined the evidence, concluded that it was insufficient to support the verdict, and on that basis reversed the judgment given to the plaintiff on the verdict, and directed that judgment be entered for the defendant. The question presented to us was whether, in the situation disclosed, the direction for a judgment for the defendant was an infraction of the Seventh Amendment. We held it was and that the direction should be for a new trial.

It therefore is important to have in mind the situation to which our ruling applied. In that case the defendant's request for a directed verdict was denied without any reservation of the question of the sufficiency of the evidence or of any other matter; and the verdict for the plaintiff was taken unconditionally, and not subject to the court's opinion on the sufficiency of the evidence. * * *

A very different situation is disclosed in the present case. The trial court expressly reserved its ruling on the defendant's motions to dismiss and for a directed verdict, both of which were based on the asserted insufficiency of the evidence to support a verdict for the plaintiff. Whether the evidence was sufficient or otherwise was a question of law to be resolved by the court. The verdict for the plaintiff was taken pending the court's rulings on the motions and subject to those rulings. No objection was made to the reservation or this mode of proceeding, and they must be regarded as having the tacit consent of the parties. * * *

At common law there was a well-established practice of reserving questions of law arising during trials by jury and of taking verdicts subject to the ultimate ruling on the questions reserved; and under this practice the reservation carried with it authority to make such ultimate disposition of the case as might be made essential by the ruling under the reservation, such as nonsuiting the plaintiff where he had obtained a verdict, entering a verdict or judgment for one party where the jury had given a verdict to the other, or making other essential adjustments.

Fragmentary references to the origin and basis of the practice indicate that it came to be supported on the theory that it gave better opportunity for considered rulings, made new trials less frequent, and commanded such general approval that parties litigant assented to its application as a matter of course. But whatever may have been its origin or theoretical basis, it undoubtedly was well established when the Seventh Amendment was adopted, and therefore must be regarded as a part of the common-law rules to which resort must be had in testing and measuring the right of trial by jury as preserved and protected by that amendment.

Notes and Questions

1. In SLOCUM v. NEW YORK LIFE INSURANCE CO., 228 U.S. 364, 33 S.Ct. 523, 57 L.Ed. 879 (1913), the Supreme Court held that once the trial court has denied a defendant's directed verdict motion and allowed the case to go to the jury, the court could not order a judgment contrary to the jury verdict, but could order a new trial. In *Redman,* the Court distinguished *Slocum* because the judge had reserved ruling on the directed verdict, so that the jury verdict was taken subject to his decision on the motion. Note that since the adoption of the Federal

Rules, this procedure no longer is necessary. Under Rule 50(b), even if a pre-verdict motion for judgment as a matter of law is denied, there is an automatic reservation of decision by the court.

2. Rule 50(b) permits a motion for judgment as a matter of law after the verdict only if a directed verdict was requested "at the close of all the evidence." How strict should this requirement be? Suppose defendant unsuccessfully moves for a directed verdict after the close of plaintiff's case but fails to renew the motion after her case has been completed? See Taylor Publishing Co. v. Jostens, Inc., 216 F.3d 465 (5th Cir.2000), holding that technical compliance with the terms of the Rule is excused when its purposes are satisfied. What are the purposes of the Rule other than to satisfy the requirements of *Redman*? Suppose a party who has moved for a judgment as a matter of law at the end of all the evidence solely on the ground that one element of the case has not been proven, argues that the evidence was insufficient to establish a different element when the motion is renewed after the jury verdict? Should the new ground be considered? See Sweeney v. Westvaco Co., 926 F.2d 29 (1st Cir.1991); Affiliated FM Ins. Co. v. Neosho Constr. Co., 192 F.R.D. 662, 667–68 (D.Kan.2000).

SECTION D. INSTRUCTIONS AND VERDICTS

1. INSTRUCTIONS TO THE JURY

———

Read Federal Rule of Civil Procedure 51 and the accompanying materials in the Supplement.

———

Before it retires to deliberate and decide, the court instructs the jury as to the law to be applied and the manner in which it is to reach a decision. The most significant legal controversy regarding the proper sequence of this phase of a jury trial is whether the instructions should come *before* or *after* the final arguments by counsel. In most jurisdictions, the courts take the position that the judge, as the impartial umpire in the case, should have the last word in order that partisan appeals by counsel will be tempered by a dispassionate statement of the law to be applied. Those who favor instructions prior to argument ask: "How can any rational argument be made if the jurors have not yet been told about the law they must apply?" Can this question be satisfactorily answered? Note that Federal Rule 51 was amended in 1987 to give the judge the option to instruct the jury before or after closing arguments, or both. It also might be argued that the jury cannot properly understand the opening statements of counsel or evaluate evidence as it is introduced unless they have prior knowledge of the legal significance of the facts presented. Why then are the instructions not given by the court at the beginning rather than at the end of trial? Would it make sense to give two sets of instructions, one at the beginning of trial and the other at the end?

Normally, the court requires the attorneys to submit proposed instructions at some point during the trial, usually after the evidence has been completed. The court then determines which of these instructions to give and which of its own to add. Under the rules of most jurisdictions, a party cannot appeal the failure to give an instruction that he did not request or the giving of an erroneous instruction to which he made no immediate objection. See, e.g., Federal Rule 51. What is the purpose of rules such as these? Why should an instruction be requested or challenged prior to the time the jury commences its deliberations? Review Alexander v. Kramer Bros. Freight Lines, Inc., p. 38, supra.

From a tactical point of view, the drafting of proposed instructions poses a serious dilemma. On the one hand, every attorney wants a set of instructions that is as favorable to his client as possible. On the other hand, the more slanted the instructions proposed, the less likely they are to be given and the more probable the judge will be antagonized by them since they will be of little assistance. Moreover, there is always the danger that the judge will accept an instruction so prejudicial that a judgment based upon it will be reversed on appeal. This not only is against the interests of the client but also harms the reputation of the attorney in the eyes of the trial judge who will hesitate to trust the attorney in future cases. See generally Powers, *Requests for Instructions*, 28 F.R.D. 239 (1960). Even if the instructions are favorable in substance, they will be totally ignored if they are so long and technical that the jurors cannot understand them. Thus an attorney often is wise to seek a simple, favorable instruction on a point, even though a more complex charge might be framed in much more favorable terms.

KENNEDY v. SOUTHERN CALIFORNIA EDISON CO.

United States Court of Appeals for the Ninth Circuit, 2000.
219 F.3d 988.

[Plaintiffs brought a wrongful death action for the death of their wife and mother from a rare form of cancer, allegedly caused by exposure to nuclear radiation from nuclear rods defectively manufactured in defendant's plant referred to as "SONGS." The applicable California law for such cases was established in Rutherford v. Owens–Illinois, Inc., 16 Cal.4th 953, 67 Cal. Rptr.2d 16, 941 P.2d 1203 (1997), which held that a jury must be instructed that "plaintiff may meet the burden of proving that exposure to defendant's product was a substantial factor causing the illness by showing that in reasonable medical probability it was a substantial factor contributing to the plaintiff's or decedent's risk of developing cancer." The trial court did not give this instruction and the jury found for defendant. Plaintiffs appeal.]

HAWKINS, CIRCUIT JUDGE:

* * *

Having held that a *Rutherford* instruction was required, we now turn to the specific instruction proffered by Kennedy. At oral argument, appellees argued that the requested instruction was not a proper *Rutherford* instruction. We agree.

On two occasions, Kennedy proposed the following instruction * * *:

In order to prove that radiation from the nuclear power plant was a substantial factor, Plaintiffs do not need to prove that it actually contributed to the development of Ellen Marie Kennedy's cancer. If exposure to radiation from the nuclear power plant in reasonable medical probability contributed to her risk of developing cancer then such exposure was a substantial factor in causing her cancer.

The proposed instruction leaves out a small, but critical, phrase. It states that radiation from SONGS need only have "contributed" to Mrs. Kennedy's risk of developing cancer. We read *Rutherford* to require more. Kennedy's burden is not to show that exposure to radiation in reasonable medical probability "contributed" to a risk of cancer. Rather, it is to demonstrate that the exposure in reasonable medical probability was *"a substantial factor"* in contributing to the risk of cancer. The omission of this modifier is essential to a proper *Rutherford* instruction.

* * *

That the proposed instructions were not entirely correct under *Rutherford* is insufficient to affirm the district court's refusal to instruct the jury properly. Ordinarily, a district court does not err in refusing to give incorrect or misleading instructions. *See, e.g., Mitchell v. Keith*, 752 F.2d 385, 388 (9th Cir.1985).

A district court, however, may have an obligation to correctly instruct the jury even after being presented with an arguably improper instruction that nonetheless directs its attention to an important issue. While this issue has not been expressly decided in this circuit, several of our sister circuits have held that such an obligation does exist. *See Webster v. Edward D. Jones & Co., L.P.*, 197 F.3d 815, 820 (6th Cir.1999) ("Even if an incorrect proposed instruction is submitted which raises an important issue of law involved in light of proof adduced in the case, it becomes the duty of the trial court to frame a proper instruction on the issue raised . . ."); *Wilson v. Maritime Overseas Corp.*, 150 F.3d 1, 10 (1st Cir.1998) ("If the request directs the court's attention to a point upon which an instruction to the jury would be helpful, the court's error in failing to charge may not be excused by technical defects in the request.") (quoting 9A Charles A. Wright & Arthur R. Miller, Federal Practice and Procedure § 2552 at 395–97 (1995)); *Bueno v. City of Donna*, 714 F.2d 484, 490 (5th Cir.1983) ("So long as an inadequate or improper request is sufficient to direct the court's attention to a legal defense, the court is thereby alerted that a proper instruction is required."); *Brandes v. Burbank*, 613 F.2d 658, 668 (7th Cir.1980) ("Even though the tendered instruction is not entirely perfect, there are situations where the court is not relieved of its duty to give the substance of the requested instruction where it appears that an instruction on the issue is needful to enable the jury to determine intelligently the question"); *Posttape Assocs. v. Eastman Kodak Co.*, 537 F.2d 751, 757 (3d Cir.1976) ("[I]f an important issue is timely called to [a trial judge's] attention, he should instruct the jury on that matter."); *Chavez v. Sears, Roebuck & Co.*, 525 F.2d 827, 830 (10th Cir.1975) ("Since the trial court bears the ultimate responsibility for properly instructing the jury, we agree with those courts that have ruled that where an instruction would be beneficial to the jury's proper determination of the case, the court may not merely refuse a requested instruction, but instead has a duty to frame the instruction properly and give it to the jury."); *Emery v. Northern Pac. R.R. Co.*, 407 F.2d 109, 113 n. 3 (8th Cir.1969) ("If the request directs the court's attention to a point upon which the jury has not been charged but upon which an instruction would be helpful, the court's error in failing to charge may not be excused by technical defects in a request to charge.") (internal quotation omitted).

In *Ursich v. da Rosa*, 328 F.2d 794, 797 (9th Cir.1964), we held that a district court "was under no obligation to redraw" an incorrect, yet otherwise applicable jury instruction for the requesting party. The holding of *Ursich* was limited by its circumstances. We specifically noted that the requested instruction concerned an "old rule," the doctrine of res ipsa loquitor, and that we "expect[ed] counsel to be aware of it and to frame proper instructions...." *Id.* n. 1. The instant case however, presents a much different scenario. Kennedy requested an instruction based on a "new rule" of state law, one that was only a few months old and had yet to be interpreted or applied by any other court.

Moreover, in a case subsequent to *Ursich*, we implicitly recognized that a trial court may have the obligation to correct improperly requested jury instructions. In *Washington State Bowling Proprietors Ass'n v. Pacific Lanes, Inc.*, 356 F.2d 371, 376–77 (9th Cir.1966), we stated that "we do not suggest a trial court is under no obligation to charge on a material issue after requested to do so, even if the instructions as proposed are faulty...."[6]

Today we make explicit what *Pacific Lanes* suggested, and align this circuit with the majority of our sister circuits. We hold that when the district court is presented with an applicable instruction that raises an important issue of law or directs the court's attention to a point upon which an instruction to the jury would be important, it is not relieved from the responsibility of giving a proper instruction simply because the party making the request has proposed an instruction that does not completely comply with the relevant law.

C. HARMLESS ERROR ANALYSIS

Harmless-error review applies to jury instructions in a civil case. *See, e.g., Caballero v. City of Concord*, 956 F.2d 204, 206 (9th Cir.1992) ("An error in instructing the jury in a civil case requires reversal unless the error is more probably than not harmless."). This review is "less stringent" than review for harmless error in a criminal case, but "more stringent" than review for sufficiency of the evidence. * * * In review of civil jury instructions for harmless error, unlike review under sufficiency of the evidence, the "prevailing party is *not* entitled to have disputed factual issues resolved in his favor because the jury's verdict may have resulted from a misapprehension of the law rather than from factual determinations in favor of the prevailing party." *Cabellero*, 956 F.2d at 207 (emphasis added).

We hold the district court's failure to give a proper *Rutherford* instruction was *not* harmless error. "An error in a trial court's jury instructions relating to the parties' respective burdens of proof ordinarily [requires] reversal." *Larez v. Holcomb*, 16 F.3d 1513, 1518 (9th Cir.1994). *But see Mockler v. Multnomah County*, 140 F.3d 808, 812–814 (9th Cir.1998) (improper instruc-

---

6. Our decision to uphold the district court's refusal to give the proffered instructions was based on the fact that the appellants had failed to resubmit the instructions after the trial judge pointed out the errors, and that the evidence did not support the contention that the requested instruction was on a material issue. * * *

tion on plaintiff's burden of proof held harmless when evidence would support verdict for plaintiff in any event).

* * *

The decision of the district court is REVERSED, and the case is REMANDED for a new trial consistent with this opinion.

Notes and Questions

1. Suppose plaintiffs in *Kennedy* had failed to request any *Rutherford* instruction. The standard notion is that a party waives any objections based on the trial court's failure to give an instruction unless the matter was properly raised below. How strict should courts be in that regard? Reread pp. 38–41, supra. See TURNER CONSTRUCTION CO. v. HOULIHAN, 240 F.2d 435, 439 (1st Cir.1957):

> The first sentence of Rule 51 permits, but does not require, the filing of requests for instructions. If none are filed, the court must nevertheless charge the jury on the broad general fundamental rules of law applicable to the principal issues of fact in the case. * * * If, however, counsel want the jury instructed specifically on particular matters, requests for such instructions must be filed.

2. Compare *Kennedy* with ROMANO v. U–HAUL INTERNATIONAL, 233 F.3d 655, 663 (1st Cir.2000), a case in which the trial court failed to give an instruction initially submitted by the plaintiff who did not thereafter object to its absence from either the list of instructions to be given or the instructions that were in fact given, to the jury.

> An awareness by the parties and the district court [of an issue in the case] * * * is not sufficient to excuse appellants obligation to object to the jury instructions under Rule 51. The requirement that the grounds for objecting to a jury instruction must be distinctly stated is treated seriously by this Court. * * * We will not excuse appellant's failure to argue * * * [that the instruction should have been given] based on a purely speculative claim that the district court has some awareness that [such an instruction would have been appropriate].

3. Would it be more sensible to be lenient with an attorney who fails to request a vital instruction than with one who sits back and permits an erroneous instruction to be given? Consider Fisher v. Ford Motor Co., 224 F.3d 570, 576 (6th Cir.2000), in which the court stated that it reviews *de novo* the accuracy of instructions that were given, whereas it reviews a trial court's decision not to give a requested instruction only for an abuse of discretion. Does this distinction make any sense?

Compare *Turner Constr. Co.*, quoted in Note 1, supra, with Crespo v. Fireman's Fund Indem. Co., 318 F.2d 174 (9th Cir.1963) (even "plain error" will not justify an attack on an instruction not challenged at trial). See WIRTZ v. INTERNATIONAL HARVESTER CO., 331 F.2d 462 (5th Cir.), certiorari denied 379 U.S. 845, 85 S.Ct. 36, 13 L.Ed.2d 50 (1964), in which the court reversed a judgment on the ground that a vital instruction, not challenged below, clearly was incorrect. The appellate court stated that *both* parties have a duty to ensure that important instructions are phrased properly, not just the party who would be injured if the improper instruction were to be given.

Reversals on the basis of improper jury instructions without objections by the parties are rare, although more numerous in recent years when "plain error" is found. See Hunt v. Liberty Lobby, 720 F.2d 631 (11th Cir.1983) (faulty instruction on burden of proof for libel of a public figure reversed for plain error); MacEdward v. Northern Elec. Co. Ltd., 595 F.2d 105 (2d Cir.1979) (failure to give instructions on defense of statute of frauds or on law of promissory estoppel in breach of contract action constituted reversible plain error).

4. Why shouldn't instructions be the sole responsibility of the trial judge? Federal Rule 51 and its state counterparts usually are justified on the ground that a court should be told of its errors and omissions in time to correct them in order to avoid the costs and delays of a new trial. Is there some other reason? Note that Rule 51 requires the trial judge to inform the lawyers prior to their closing arguments as to what instructions will be given. Objections are to be made before the jury retires but out of its hearing. What purpose do these provisions serve?

5. Lawyers and judges always will be seriously concerned with the precise wording of jury instructions as long as technical inaccuracies may lead to reversal on appeal. The irony is that many jurors do not even understand the basic aspects of the instructions, let alone the fine distinctions that often are drawn. Part of the problem is due to the manner in which the instructions are given. All too often the judge reads the instructions in disjointed fashion in a nearly inaudible monotone using technical terms without any regard for the fact that the statements are incomprehensible. Much of this evil could be corrected if trial judges made an effort to improve the way in which they deliver the charge. But even then, it is a great deal to ask of a juror, even in a simple case, to grasp the fine points of the applicable law. As already discussed, see Notes 5 and 6, pp. 1007–08, supra, the value of the jury may lie in the fact that it does not, and is not expected to, apply the law in strict fashion. If this is true, would it not be possible to eliminate instructions or at least limit them to a short generalized statement? Is preservation of appellate review of the technical wording of jury instructions necessary to the proper development and growth of the law? See Charrow & Charrow, *Making Legal Language Understandable: A Psycholinguistic Study of Jury Instructions*, 79 Colum.L.Rev. 1306 (1979); Farrell, *Communication in the Courtroom: Jury Instructions*, 85 W.Va.L.Rev. 5 (1982); Steele & Thornburg, *Jury Instructions: A Persistent Failure To Communicate*, 67 N.C.L.Rev. 77 (1988).

6. Are there instructions, correct under the law, that ought not to be given? Consider a situation in which plaintiff demands both compensatory and punitive damages in a case in which there is a legislative cap on the amount of punitive damages that can be awarded. If a jury awards a greater amount, the court must reduce it to the amount of the cap. Should the jury be instructed as to the maximum amount of punitive damages that plaintiff can receive? Why? Why not? See Kang, *Don't Tell Juries About Statutory Damage Caps: The Merits of Nondisclosure*, 66 U.Chi.L.Rev. 469 (1999).

8. In recent years there has been a strong tendency for courts and lawyers to resort to the use of standard or "pattern" instructions. In a number of jurisdictions such instructions have been developed by courts and judges to cover a wide variety of common legal issues. What advantages and disadvantages are there to the use of standard instructions? Should use of such instructions be required? See Ill.Sup.Ct.Rule § 239(a) in the Supplement.

a. *Commenting on the Evidence by Judges*

NUNLEY v. PETTWAY OIL CO., 346 F.2d 95 (6th Cir.1965). Plaintiff brought suit for personal injuries received when a truck fell off a grease rack in a gas station. The jury found plaintiff to be a licensee rather than an invitee at the time of the accident, and, applying the applicable law, the court entered judgment for defendant. On appeal plaintiff contended that the court had improperly commented to the jury on the licensee-invitee question. During their initial deliberations the jurors were unable to agree on this issue. The judge then called them into the courtroom and urged them to try to arrive at a decision as follows:

> Now, the jury of course is the sole and exclusive judge of the facts in this lawsuit. It is appropriate that the Court in an effort to be possibly of some help to the jury may comment upon the evidence. I refrain from doing that and have refrained until this time from doing it in this case. However, in an effort to be of some possible assistance to you I think that I should under these circumstances make some comment upon the evidence upon this issue of invitee-licensee. I want you to understand, however, that in making these comments that you are not in any degree, in any respect, obligated to receive or accept or agree with what I may say. It is your duty to accept what I say with regard to the law in the case, but it is not your duty to accept any comment that I may make or any evaluation that I may make or conclusion that I might reach on the evidence. That is solely your responsibility and solely your duty. *But, with that understanding, it is the opinion of the Court in this case that, from all the evidence upon the issue of invitee or licensee, that the evidence will establish that at the time and place of the accident the plaintiff was a licensee and not an invitee.* Now, I say that just for the purpose, as I say, of possibly being of some help to you, but I want you to understand that in making that comment you are not obligated whatsoever to accept that comment as your comment or as your opinion in the case, because it is your job and your responsibility to resolve that issue. I only make that with the thought and the hope that it may be of some possible assistance to you. At any rate, I want to ask you once again to retire and consider your verdict and see if you cannot come to some agreement, some verdict that will reflect the views of all of the jurors. * * *

Id. at 98. The Court of Appeals reversed, stating:

> We recognize that the right of a District Judge to comment on the evidence is firmly established in the federal system. See Quercia v. United States, 289 U.S. 466, 53 S.Ct. 698, 77 L.Ed. 1321 (1933) * * *.

> Nonetheless, we believe that under the circumstances enumerated, the trial judge's opinion on the licensee-invitee issue was an opinion on an ultimate fact question peculiarly for jury consideration and amounted to an instructed verdict as to defendant Pettway Oil Company.

> In Quercia v. United States, supra, Chief Justice Hughes commented:

>> This privilege of the judge to comment on the facts has its inherent limitations. His discretion is not arbitrary and uncontrolled, but judicial, to be exercised in conformity with the standards governing the judicial office. In commenting upon testimony he may not assume the role of a witness. He may analyze and dissect the

evidence, but he may not either distort it or add to it. His privilege of comment in order to give appropriate assistance to the jury is too important to be left without safeguards against abuses.

* * *

Nor do we think that the error was cured by the statement of the trial judge that his opinion of the evidence was not binding on the jury and that if they did not agree with it they should find the defendant not guilty. His definite and concrete assertion of fact, which he had made with all the persuasiveness of judicial utterance, as to the basis of his opinion, was not withdrawn. * * *

Id. at 98–99.

Notes and Questions

1. In *Quercia,* a *criminal* case, the Supreme Court reversed a conviction because the following charge was given to the jury:

And now I am going to tell you what I think of the defendant's testimony. You may have noticed, Mr. Foreman and gentlemen, that he wiped his hands during his testimony. It is rather a curious thing, but that is almost always an indication of lying. Why it should be so we don't know, but that is the fact. I think that every single word that man said, except when he agreed with the Government's testimony, was a lie.

Now, that opinion is an opinion of evidence and is not binding on you, and if you don't agree with it, it is your duty to find him not guilty.

Is the court in *Nunley* justified in relying on *Quercia?* Aren't there substantial differences between the two cases?

2. In light of the decision in *Nunley,* what is the meaning of the court's statement: "We recognize that the right of a District Judge to comment on the evidence is firmly established in the federal system"? The trial judge's common-law power to comment on the evidence, as retained in a minority of jurisdictions, includes the power to express an opinion regarding both evidentiary issues and the credibility of witnesses.

Those federal decisions that appear to limit the common-law practice are in line with limitations in a majority of states, which take two basic forms: (1) the trial judge is confined to a statement of the applicable law and deprived of power even to mention the evidence (see Colorado Rule of Civil Procedure 51), or (2) the court is limited to presenting an impartial summary of the evidence (see, e.g., Belk v. Schweizer, 268 N.C. 50, 149 S.E.2d 565 (1966)). It has been suggested that the latter approach is not feasible. Wright, *Instructions to the Jury: Summary Without Comment,* 1954 Wash.U.L.Q. 177. Why?

3. The *Nunley* opinion emphasizes that the judge's comment was on an "ultimate fact question." The Fifth Circuit holds that comments are proper on "evidentiary matters," but not on "ultimate factual issues." Travelers Ins. Co. v. Ryan, 416 F.2d 362, 364 (5th Cir.1969). Is there any sound basis for this distinction?

4. What are the arguments for and against allowance of a broad judicial power to comment on the evidence? Professor Wigmore passionately advocated restoration of the broad power, and severely criticized the federal approach

exemplified in *Quercia*. 9 Wigmore on Evidence § 2551, at 669–70 n. 7 (Chadbourn rev. 1981). See also Weinstein, *The Power and Duty of Federal Judges to Marshall and Comment on Evidence in Jury Trials and Some Suggestions on Charging Juries,* 118 F.R.D. 161 (1988) (favoring permissiveness with respect to judicial comments).

5. Jurisdiction in the *Nunley* case was based on diversity of citizenship. Suppose that the law of the state permits the trial judge to express an opinion as to whether the evidence is sufficient to establish the ultimate facts in the case. To what extent is the federal court allowed to follow the state practice? See Byrd v. Blue Ridge Rural Elec. Co–op., Inc., p. 386, supra.

2. PERMITTING INSTRUCTIONS TO BE TAKEN INTO THE JURY ROOM; NOTE–TAKING AND JUROR DISCUSSIONS DURING TRIAL

A substantial number of state and federal courts either require or permit written instructions to be taken into the jury room. See California Law Revision Commission, *Recommendation and Study Relating to Taking Instructions into the Jury Room,* pp. C–15–C–17 (1956) (Tabular Summary of the Law of Other States). The Study speaks about the merits of these provisions as follows:

> Much can be said, it is believed, for giving a copy of the instructions to the jury, either as a matter of routine or upon the request of a party or of the jury. The instructions are intended to guide the jury's deliberations. Yet, even in a relatively simple case they are usually lengthy and complex. It is hardly reasonable to suppose that the jury, composed as it is of persons unfamiliar with either law or legal language and having heard the instructions but once as given orally by the court, will be able to remember them in detail as it ponders the matters committed to it for decision.

Are there any effective arguments against allowing the jury to possess the written instructions during its deliberations? What effect does the possession of written instructions have on the focus of the jury's discussion? Does possession of written instructions tend to affect the amount of influence some jurors have on the rest of the panel?

In many jurisdictions jurors are permitted and even encouraged to take notes throughout the trial for use during the deliberations. See State ex rel. Dep't of Highways v. Lehman, 462 P.2d 649 (Okl.1969). Does this obviate any need for written instructions? Is there any reason why note-taking should not be permitted? Should the complexity of the litigation or the length of the trial affect the rules on taking written instructions or notes into the jury room? See *Developments in the Law–The Civil Jury,* 110 Harv.L.Rev. 1408, 1509–11 (1997).

Jurors are almost always warned that they are not to discuss the case with anyone, even the other jurors until the case is submitted to them at the close of the trial. What dangers do you see if jurors were to be permitted to discuss the case at an earlier stage? Arizona is an exception. It has adopted a rule permitting jurors to discuss the case among themselves during the course of trial. What are the potential advantages of the Arizona rule? For a study of the participants' views of the Arizona experiment, see Hans, Hannaford &

Munsterman, *The Arizona Jury Reform Permitting Civil Jury Trial Discussions: The Views of Trial Participants, Judges, and Jurors*, 32 U.Mich.J.L.F. 349 (1999).

3. VERDICTS

a. *Submission of the Case to the Jury*

After final arguments are completed and the instructions given, the jurors are placed in the custody of a bailiff or similar court official who guards them during deliberations. It is the bailiff's duty to make certain that the jurors remain together and have no contact with other persons except by court order.

In some cases the jurors will find it difficult to agree on a verdict. If this is due to uncertainty as to the content of the instructions, they may ask the court to reread the instructions, and, if necessary, to augment them. See, e.g., Diniero v. United States Lines Co., p. 41, supra. If the major difficulty is due to disagreement as to what one or more of the witnesses said, the jurors may request that the testimony of those witnesses be read to them. See Annot., 50 A.L.R.2d 176 (1956). Whenever the jury reenters the courtroom, whether for further instructions or for the reading of testimony, it is wise to notify both parties and their attorneys in advance. Otherwise the verdict may be subject to reversal on appeal. What is the purpose of a rule requiring notice? How rigidly should it be enforced?

Suppose after lengthy deliberations the jurors still are unable to agree. How long may they be kept in session? At what point does a court abuse its discretion by forcing them to continue their discussions? When a court does order an end to a session, must it then dismiss the jury and order a new trial? If not, must the jurors be locked up, free from all contact with outsiders, or should they be allowed to go home until such time as they are ordered to reassemble? See Kramer v. Kister, p. 1088, infra; Annot., 77 A.L.R.2d 1086 (1961), for a detailed discussion of these matters.

At some point, of course, if the jurors continue to be unable to agree, they will have to be discharged and a mistrial declared. Courts are extremely reluctant to discharge a jury without its having reached a verdict because of the cost and delay of a new trial. Thus, a court often will urge a stalemated jury to make a further attempt to arrive at a verdict. Although some jurisdictions still require the traditional unanimous jury verdict, a substantial number have tried to cut down the number of stalemates by permitting a verdict to be based on something less than unanimity in civil cases. See, e.g., Cal.Code Civ.Proc. § 618 (three-fourths of jurors must agree); Mich.Ct.Rule 2.512(A) (five-sixths of jurors must agree). In Minnesota a less than unanimous verdict is permitted after the jury has deliberated for a certain length of time. Minn.Stat.Ann. § 546.17. Do you see any reason why the requirement of unanimity should be retained? Does a requirement of unanimity promote or deter the quality of deliberations and the accuracy of decisions? What is the likely effect of eliminating unanimity on the views of jurors who are female or members of ethnic minority groups? See Taylor–Thompson, *Empty Votes in Jury Deliberations*, 113 Harv. L.Rev. 1261 (2000).

In some cases the jury is able to arrive at a verdict almost immediately. Indeed, it may be possible for the jurors to agree without even leaving the jury box. Should a verdict in a complex case ever be subject to attack because it was rendered quickly? Invariably, the courts have said "no." See Annot., 91 A.L.R.2d 1220 (1963). Why should this be so?

b.　The Form of the Verdicts

———

Read Federal Rule of Civil Procedure 49 in the Supplement.

———

The traditional form of the jury decision, used almost exclusively in the great majority of courts, is the general verdict. No matter how complex the case and how long and involved the instructions were, all a jury need do to render a general verdict is to announce which party wins, and, if it is plaintiff, the amount that should be recovered. This type of verdict has two major deficiencies. First, there is no way to tell how the jurors decided specific issues, which, in turn, can result in the unnecessary retrial of the entire case. For example, suppose defendant raises a number of defenses, any one of which, if established, would require a verdict for defendant. Then the court, in an otherwise faultless charge, erroneously instructs the jury on one of these defenses in a manner detrimental to plaintiff, after which the jury finds for defendant. On appeal, the court will be required to reverse, since it has no way of telling whether the verdict was based solely on the tainted defense. If, however, the jury had been required to render a verdict on each one of the defenses, the court would know at once the bases of the jury decision and whether the error in the instruction was harmless. See, e.g., Castilleja v. Southern Pacific Co., 445 F.2d 183 (5th Cir.1971). The second major drawback to the general verdict is the fact that there is no way of knowing whether the jury actually focused its attention on every major aspect of the case as required by the instructions, or whether it ignored the instructions altogether and rendered a decision based solely on sentiment, public opinion, bias, or similar emotion.

To avoid these objections, many writers have advocated use of the special verdict, which requires the jury to answer a series of questions regarding each facet of the case but not to enter a verdict stating who wins. For example, in Frank, *Courts on Trial* 141–42 (1950), the following argument is advanced:

> A special verdict would seem to do away with some of the most objectionable features of trial by jury. The division of functions between jury and judge is apparently assured, the one attending to the facts alone, the other to the legal rules alone. The jury seems, by this device, to be shorn of its power to ignore the rules or to make rules to suit itself. As one court said, special verdicts "dispel * * * the darkness visible of general verdicts." The finding of facts, says Sunderland, "is much better done by means of the special verdict. Every advantage which the jury is popularly supposed to have over the [judge] as a trier of facts is retained, with the very great additional advantage that the analysis and separation

of the facts in the case which the court and the attorney must necessarily effect in employing the special verdict, materially reduce the chance of error. It is easy to make mistakes in dealing at large with aggregates of facts. The special verdict compels detailed consideration. But above all it enables the public, the parties and the court to see what the jury has really done * * *. The morale of the jury also is aided by throwing off the cloak of secrecy, for only through publicity is there developed the proper feeling of responsibility in public servants. So far, then, as the facts go, they can be much more effectively, conveniently, and usefully tried by abandoning the general verdict * * *." [Sunderland, *Verdicts General and Special,* 29 Yale L.J. 253 (1920).]

* * * It is suggested, too, that a special verdict "searches the conscience of the individual juror, as a general verdict does not," because "such are the contradictions in human nature that many a man who will unite in a general verdict for a large and unwarranted sum of money will shrink from a specific finding against his judgment of right and wrong." [Clementson, *Special Verdicts and Special Findings by Juries* 15 (1905).]

This view has been strongly opposed on the ground that the special verdict improperly subverts the fundamental nature of the jury decision. See 9A Wright & Miller, *Federal Practice and Procedure, Civil 2d* § 2503, at 156–57 (1995):

Not all would agree that * * * [making jury decisions more scientific and trustworthy] is desirable, even if it were assumed that it is possible. Little is gained by making the law more scientific if, in the process, it becomes harder to achieve substantial justice. Some of the most famous students of the judicial process have argued that one of the purposes of the jury system is to permit the jury to temper strict rules of law by the demands and necessities of substantial justice and changing social conditions, thereby adding a much needed element of flexibility. Those who share this conception of the role of the jury rightly fear that it will be limited or defeated by the restraints imposed by the special verdict practice, and thus oppose widespread use of it.

These very concerns induced Justices Black and Douglas to issue the following statement in connection with the Court's 1963 amendment of Rule 49, at 374 U.S. 865, 867–68, 83 S.Ct. 43, 44–45 (1963):

* * * Rule 49 should be repealed. * * * Such devices are used to impair or wholly take away the power of a jury to render a general verdict. One of the ancient, fundamental reasons for having general jury verdicts was to preserve the right of trial by jury as an indispensable part of a free government. Many of the most famous constitutional controversies in England revolved around litigants' insistence, particularly in seditious libel cases, that a jury had the right to render a general verdict without being compelled to return a number of subsidiary findings to support its general verdict. Some English jurors had to go to jail because they insisted upon their right to render general verdicts over the repeated commands of tyrannical judges not to do so. Rule 49 is but another means utilized by courts to weaken the constitutional power of juries and to vest judges with more power to decide cases according to their own judgments.

Suppose that in every case in which the trial judge orders a special verdict, she is required to instruct the jury as to the legal consequences of its answers to each of the questions that are to be asked. Would that allay the concerns that some people have expressed about the special verdict? Or would it merely undercut the value of the procedure? Isn't it likely that in most situations even without such an instruction from the judge the jurors will easily figure out which party a particular answer will favor? For a comprehensive discussion of this matter and the strengths and weaknesses of the special verdict procedure, see Kotler, *Reappraising the Jury's Role as Finder of Fact*, 20 Ga.L.Rev. 123 (1985).

One reason why judges are reluctant to utilize the special verdict procedure is the fact that it is difficult to form appropriate questions that will cover the significant elements of the case yet avoid ambiguities that can lead to a reversal on appeal. Reread Diniero v. United States Lines Co. and the Notes following it, pp. 41–45, supra. Does it make sense to require the jury to answer questions about particular details as to what occurred (For example: Did defendant fall asleep at the wheel of his vehicle?) (For example: Was defendant negligent in the operation of his vehicle?)?

A third form of verdict, an intermediate approach, is the general verdict with answers to interrogatories, which requires the jury to give a general verdict but also requires it to provide answers to a series of questions that usually are less extensive than those used with the special verdict. Although this form alleviates some of the concerns about the general verdict, problems arise when the answers to the interrogatories are inconsistent with the general verdict or with each other.

NOLLENBERGER v. UNITED AIR LINES, INC.

United States District Court, Southern District of California, 1963.
216 F.Supp. 734, vacated 335 F.2d 379 (9th Cir.), certiorari dismissed
379 U.S. 951, 85 S.Ct. 452, 13 L.Ed.2d 549 (1964).

HALL, CHIEF JUDGE. [This is a wrongful-death action in which the jury, pursuant to Rule 49(b), rendered a general verdict accompanied by interrogatories. The plaintiffs allege that the answers to the interrogatories are inconsistent with the general verdict. They request that the court either submit additional interrogatories to the jury, or calculate the verdict on the basis of the answers to the questions given, or grant a new trial.]

* * *

The first task of the Court is to determine whether or not the Findings of Fact in the answers, given by the jury to the special interrogatories, are consistent with each other and whether one or more, if consistent with each other, are inconsistent with the general verdict fixing the total sum of damages to the plaintiffs resulting from the death of the decedent. And in doing so, Gallick v. Baltimore & Ohio R.R. Co., 372 U.S. 108, 83 S.Ct. 659, 9 L.Ed.2d 618 (1963), "it is the duty of the courts to attempt to harmonize the answers, if it is possible under a fair reading of them * * *."

The text of the special verdict on damages in the Nollenberger case is as follows:

We, the Jury in the above entitled case, unanimously find as follows:

QUESTIONS	ANSWERS

1. Which one of the following named persons, viz.: William Edward Nollenberger, 45 years of age on April 21, 1958; Catherine B. Nollenberger, his widow, age 47 on April 21, 1958; William Edward Nollenberger, Jr., son, age 20 on April 21, 1958; Lawrence P. Nollenberger, son, age 11 on April 21, 1958; had the shortest life expectancy?

Wm. E. Nollenberger
(Name)

2. How many years was that life expectancy on April 21, 1958?

25
(Total number of years)

3. How many years was decedent's work and earning expectancy from and after April 21, 1958?

15 yrs
(Total number of years)

4. From and after April 21, 1958, what total sum of money do you find the decedent would have earned during the period of his work and earning expectancy stated in your answer to No. 3 above?

$235,210
(Total)

5. From and after the end of his work and earning expectancy, and during the remainder of his life, if any such remained, what total sum of money do you find decedent would have received as a result of his government employment?

$100,200
(Total sum)

6. What is the total reasonable value of services susceptible of being furnished by others which you find it was reasonably probable that decedent would have provided under my instructions to you to the plaintiffs during his lifetime?

$25,000
(Total value)

7. What percentage of his annual earnings, had he lived, from and after April 21, 1958, would have been used by decedent for his own personal expenses which were eliminated by his death?

25%
(Percentage of annual earnings)

8. What percentage of his income would be paid as annual income tax had he lived after April 21, 1958?

15%

9. What percentage of the income from the award will be paid by plaintiffs as income tax?

11%

10. In determining the present reasonable value of services as defined in No. 6 above, what annual rate of inflation, if any, do you find should be allowed?

1%

QUESTIONS	ANSWERS

11. What discount rate should be applied in arriving at the total sum of general damages?

4%
_____
(Discount rate)

12. What sum of money do you find plaintiffs' general damages to be which you assess against Defendant United Air Lines?

$114,655.00

DATED: At Los Angeles, California, January 16, 1963.

S/Burford A. Reynold
_____
Foreman

The answers to the Special Interrogatories No. 1 to No. 11 are plainly consistent with each other and are amply supported by the evidence.

But, in repeated efforts to "harmonize" and "reconcile" the answers to the 11 special interrogatories with the general verdict of $114,655.00, I have been unable to do so. And hence I must and do conclude that they are not harmonious or reconcilable.

While Rule 49(b) * * * under such circumstances permits, as one of three alternatives, the Court to re-submit the matter to the jury for further consideration, the plaintiffs desire the Court to go further and to submit additional interrogatories * * *. [H]ad it been the intention to permit *additional interrogatories* to be submitted *after* the general verdict and answers to the special interrogatories submitted with the verdict, the rule would have so provided, and the rule would not have contained the restrictive language of the second sentence of Rule 49(b) that the Court " * * * shall direct the jury both to make written answers and to render a general verdict," or the language in the fourth sentence of Rule 49(b) (applicable here) that the Court, as one alternative, " * * * may return the jury for *further consideration of its answers and verdict.*"

It could be argued from the portion of the rule last quoted that if that procedure were followed the jury could change both its answers and general verdict, or only the answers and not the general verdict. * * * That such action by the jury was not intended by the Rule is evidenced from the citation in the note to Rule 49 by the Advisory Committee of the case of Victor–American Fuel Co. v. Peccarich (C.C.A.1913) 209 F. 568, cert. den. 232 U.S. 727, 34 S.Ct. 603, 58 L.Ed. 817. In that case the Court stated, at page 571: " * * * these special findings must control when they clearly compel a different judgment from that which would follow the general verdict" * * *.

I conclude (1) that the findings of fact of the jury in answer to special interrogatories control over the general verdict; (2) that it is not within the power of the court under F.R.Civ.P. 49(b) to submit additional interrogatories after the jury has returned its verdict answering special interrogatories and at the same time returned a general verdict; (3) that in * * * Nollenberger * * * the answers to the special interrogatories are consistent with each other and inconsistent with and cannot be reconciled or harmonized with the general verdict; (4) that before granting a new trial, it is the duty of the Court to make calculations from the special interrogatories, and enter a judgment thereon. Which latter, I shall now do.

[The court then calculated the damages at $171,702.00 and entered judgment for that amount.]

* * *

Notes and Questions

1. In overturning the *Nollenberger* decision, the Court of Appeals held as follows (335 F.2d at 407–09):

> The district court stated that after repeated efforts, by mathematical calculation, to harmonize and reconcile the answers to the eleven special interrogatories with the general verdict, no harmony resulted. This may be so. But nothing in the law compelled the jury to calculate its damage awards according to a fixed mathematical formula using only the factors contained in the eleven special findings. * * *

> The jury was admonished to award damages in accordance with all the instructions of the court. No party specifies as error the giving of any of the instructions set forth in the margin.[43]

> * * * Suffice it to say that the answers to the eleven special interrogatories do not exhaust all of the factors of damage included within the instructions, and therefore no square conflict exists between the answers and the general verdict. We are not called upon to consider either whether the jury should not have been permitted to consider one or more of the italicized factors or whether the damage awards manifest such passion or prejudice as would render them inadequate. We hold that the court's utilization of the provisions of Rule 49(b) did not render proper its increase of damages in accordance with mathematical computations based upon the special findings.

2. Is the appellate-court decision in *Nollenberger* realistic? If so, what possible justification was there for the trial court's decision to present the jury with special interrogatories? The appellate court gave plaintiff the option of accepting the jury's general verdict or of having the case returned to the trial court for a ruling on plaintiff's motion for a new trial. Should the Court of Appeals itself have decided whether there should be a new trial in the event that plaintiff decided not to accept the jury award?

3. Just how far should a court go in attempting to reconcile a jury's answers to specific interrogatories, either among themselves or with a general verdict? See Wright v. Wilburn, 194 F.R.D. 54, 57–58 (N.D.N.Y.2000) (court must do all it can to reconcile jury responses even if it must strain to do so). In POPHAM v. CITY OF KENNESAW, 820 F.2d 1570 (11th Cir.1987), plaintiff sued to recover for violations of his civil rights alleging that the police used excessive force to arrest

---

43. * * *

"You should award the plaintiffs herein such sum as, *under all of the circumstances of the case, may be fair and just compensation* for the pecuniary loss which the [widow and child(ren)] have suffered by reason of the death of [decedent].

" * * *

"In weighing these matters, you may consider * * * *the disposition of the deceased, whether it was kindly, affectionate or other-* *wise; whether or not he showed an inclination to contribute to the support of the plaintiffs or any of them;* the earning capacity of the deceased; and *such other facts shown by the evidence as throw light upon the pecuniary value of the support, society, care, comfort and protection* other than the loss of consortium between husband and wife, which the plaintiffs reasonably might have expected to receive from the deceased had he lived. * * * " (Emphasis added.)

him, falsely arrested him, and arrested him in order to deprive him of his First Amendment rights. The trial court submitted special interrogatories, including one asking whether the police used excessive force and another asking whether the officers held qualified immunity. The jury answered both in the affirmative, yet awarded damages to plaintiff. The Court of Appeals, in upholding the jury verdict, held that the trial judge had an obligation to interpret apparently conflicting interrogatories so as to sustain the jury's general verdict. Applying the principle to the facts of the case, the court found that the jury's answer about immunity was made only with respect to the false arrest and First Amendment claims, citing the trial judge's instructions as support for its holding.

4. FINDINGS AND CONCLUSIONS IN NONJURY CASES

Read Federal Rule of Civil Procedure 52 in the Supplement.

ROBERTS v. ROSS

United States Court of Appeals, Third Circuit, 1965.
344 F.2d 747.

Maris, Circuit Judge. The plaintiff, Herbert J. Roberts, appeals from a judgment entered in the District Court of the Virgin Islands dismissing his action brought to recover the sum of $3,087.50 which he alleged the defendant Norman M. Ross, Jr. promised to pay him for services rendered in producing a buyer for a dwelling house which the defendant had built in St. Thomas. The defendant answered, denying any such promise and, subsequently, with leave of court, he filed an amended answer in which he interposed the special defense of the Statute of Frauds.

* * *

On December 30, 1963, the trial judge entered an order stating that he had found for the defendant on the issues presented and directing counsel for the defendant within 10 days to file proposed findings of fact, conclusions of law and draft of judgment. Counsel for the plaintiff was given leave within 10 days thereafter to file objections thereto, which he did. On January 14, 1964 the findings of fact, conclusions of law, and judgment prepared and filed by counsel for the defendant were signed by the trial judge without change. It was concluded as a matter of law that "plaintiff has failed to prove by a preponderance of the evidence that the sale of said property by the defendant was procured through the agency of plaintiff," and that "in any event, said alleged promise not being in writing is within the Statute of Frauds." The plaintiff appealed from the judgment entered thereon dismissing his complaint.

* * *

The defendant * * * argues that * * * the plaintiff failed to prove the alleged agreement by a preponderance of the evidence, and the trial judge was accordingly justified in concluding that any discussion relating to compensating plaintiff for alleged sale of the property was at most the offer of a gratuity on the part of the defendant not specifically enforceable for indefiniteness. The fallacy in defendant's argument is that the trial judge failed to make any such findings. There is no finding as to whether the defendant agreed to pay the plaintiff a commission for producing a customer for the sale of the property—a question which was the crucial issue in the case. And there is no support in the record for the conclusion as a matter of law that "plaintiff has failed to prove by a preponderance of the evidence that the sale of said property by the defendant was procured through the agency of plaintiff." For it was undisputed that the plaintiff brought [the buyer] * * * to the property and introduced him to the defendant as a prospective purchaser. Perhaps the term "agency" in the quoted conclusion is intended to mean that the plaintiff, in doing so, did not act as agent for the defendant, thus possibly implying that the defendant did not agree to pay plaintiff a commission if he producd [sic] a buyer for the property. The trial judge's conclusion is, however, so inadequate as to afford this court no indication of the legal standard under which the evidence was considered.

This Court has had occasion to point out that [Federal] Rule 52(a) * * * requires the trier of the facts to find the facts specially and state his conclusions of law thereon with clarity. The findings of fact and conclusions of law must be sufficient to indicate the bases of the trial judge's decision. * * * The findings and conclusions in the present case do not meet this requirement.

Moreover we have observed in this case and in a number of others which have been brought here from the district court for review that the judge of the court has followed the practice of announcing his decision for the plaintiff or the defendant substantially in the form of a general verdict, either in a written order or by communication to counsel, and of thereupon directing counsel for the prevailing party to prepare and submit findings of fact, conclusions of law and a form of judgment. The trial judge's order has not been accompanied by an opinion setting out, even summarily, the facts and legal conclusions which have brought him to his decision. Obviously the judge must have dealt with the questions of fact and law involved in the case in the course of the reasoning by which he has reached his ultimate conclusion, even though his reasoning has not been articulated and put on paper. But counsel who is called upon to articulate and write out the findings and conclusions must do so without any knowledge of the fact findings and reasoning processes through which the judge has actually gone in reaching his decision.

We strongly disapprove this practice. For it not only imposes a well-nigh impossible task upon counsel but also flies in the face of the spirit and purpose, if not the letter, of Rule 52(a). The purpose of that rule is to require the trial judge to formulate and articulate his findings of fact and conclusions of law in the course of his consideration and determination of the case and as a part of his decision making process, so that he himself may be satisfied that he has dealt fully and properly with all the issues in the case before he decides it and so that the parties involved and this court on appeal may be fully informed as to the bases of his decision when it is made. Findings and conclusions prepared ex post facto by counsel, even though signed by the judge, do not serve adequately the function contemplated by the rule. At most they provide the judge with an opportunity to reconsider the bases of his original decision but without affording the parties any information as to what those bases were or which of them are being reconsidered. At worst they are likely to convict the judge of error because, as here, they are inadequate to support his decision or because, as we have observed in other cases, they are loaded down with argumentative over-detailed partisan matter much of which is likely to be of doubtful validity or even wholly without support in the record.

* * * We * * * do not * * * mean to suggest that a trial judge should not have the right to invite counsel for both parties to submit to him proposed findings of fact and conclusions of law, accompanied by briefs if he desires them, to assist him in formulating his own findings and conclusions and reaching his decision. In the process of studying the facts and the law, findings and conclusions formulated and proposed by the parties may be most helpful to the judge in sharpening the issues and may serve a very useful purpose in aiding him in drafting his own findings and conclusions. In most cases it will appear that many of the findings proposed by one or the other of the parties are fully supported by the evidence, are directed to material matters and may be adopted verbatim and it may even be that in some cases the findings and conclusions proposed by a party will be so carefully and objectively prepared that they may all properly be adopted by the trial judge without change. But it should be remembered that findings and conclusions prepared by a party and adopted by the trial judge without change are likely to be looked at by the appellate court more narrowly and given less weight on review than if they are the work product of the judge himself or at least bear evidence that he has given them careful study and revision. For the latter procedure would assure the appellate court, as Judge Wisdom pointed out in Louis Dreyfus & Cie. v. Panama Canal Company, 5 Cir., 1962, 298 F.2d 733, 738, "that the trial judge did indeed consider all the factual questions thoroughly and would guarantee that each word in the finding is impartially chosen." It has been the general practice of the district judges of the Third Circuit in the past under Rule 52(a) to formulate their findings of fact and conclusions of law in the course of and as a part of their decision-making process and to articulate and file them at the time of announcing the decision, either in an opinion if filed at that time or in a separate document. * * * [W]e strongly approve this practice and direct it to be followed * * * by the court below.

* * *

Notes and Questions

1. Roberts v. Ross is discussed in 51 Cornell L.Q. 567 (1966), in which it is noted that on remand, the trial court, without a new hearing, reversed its earlier decision, and entered judgment for the party against whom it ruled initially. Compare HETEROCHEMICAL CORP. v. UNITED STATES RUBBER CO., 368 F.2d 169, 172 (7th Cir.1966):

> After post-trial briefing and oral arguments, the district court invited findings and conclusions from both parties and ordered an exchange of the proposals. * * * The court thereafter adopted the proposals of United States Rubber.

This court has termed the adoption of proposed findings a "practical and wise custom," in view of the obligation of a prevailing party to assist a busy court. * * * This is particularly true in a case where the evidence is highly technical, so long as the trial court's procedure is fair to both parties and the findings reveal insight and understanding of the basic issue. * * * In view of the district court's procedure in adopting findings of fact and conclusions of law, we are not persuaded that they were "mechanically adopted"; nor can we agree that they do not reveal insight and understanding of the basic issue. * * *

See Shlensky v. Dorsey, 574 F.2d 131 (3d Cir.1978) (adoption of a party's predecision proposed findings invites more careful examination on appeal).

2. In LEIGHTON v. ONE WILLIAM STREET FUND, INC., 343 F.2d 565, 567 (2d Cir.1965), the court discussed Federal Rule 52(a) as follows:

The purpose of Rule 52(a), as it is applied to a non-jury case, is usually stated to be three-fold: (1) to aid the appellate court by affording it a clear understanding of the ground or the basis of the decision of the trial court; (2) to make definite just what is decided by the case to enable the application of *res judicata* and estoppel principles to subsequent decisions; and (3) to evoke care on the part of the trial judge in ascertaining the facts.

Which of the listed purposes of Rule 52(a) do you find most important? How detailed must the findings and conclusions be to satisfy these purposes? See Mazzeo v. Lenhart, 167 F.3d 139 (2d Cir.1999).

3. Rule 52(a) states that the findings of fact by a lower court shall not be set aside unless "clearly erroneous." In 1987, Rule 52(a) was amended to include the phrase "whether based on oral or documentary evidence" because there was confusion among the courts concerning whether the same standard of review existed for findings of fact based on credibility evidence and those based on documentary evidence. Why might courts have drawn this distinction?

Anticipating the change in the rule, the Supreme Court addressed the issue in ANDERSON v. CITY OF BESSEMER CITY, 470 U.S. 564, 105 S.Ct. 1504, 84 L.Ed.2d 518 (1985), although the holding is somewhat cloudy. Justice White, speaking for the majority, explains:

[The clearly erroneous standard applies] * * * even when the district court's findings do not rest on credibility determinations, but are based instead on physical or documentary evidence or inferences from other facts. * * * That the rule goes on to emphasize the special deference to be paid credibility determinations does not alter its clear command: Rule 52(a) "does not make exceptions or purport to exclude certain categories of factual findings unless clearly erroneous." * * *

The rationale for deference of the original finder of fact is not limited to the superiority of the trial judge's position to make determinations of credibility. The trial judge's major role is the determination of fact, and with experience in fulfilling that role comes expertise. Duplication of the trial judge's efforts in the court of appeals would very likely contribute only negligibly to the accuracy of fact determination at a huge cost in diversion of judicial resources. In addition, the parties to a case on appeal have already been forced to concentrate their energies and resources on persuading the trial judge that their account of the facts is the correct one; requiring them to persuade three more judges at the appellate level is requiring too much. * * * For these reasons, review of factual findings under the clearly-erroneous standard—with its deference to the trier of fact—is the rule, not the exception.

When findings are based on determinations regarding the credibility of witnesses, Rule 52(a) demands even greater deference to the trial court's findings; for only the trial judge can be aware of the variations in demeanor and tone of voice that bear so heavily on the listener's understanding of and belief in what is said. * * * This is not to suggest that the trial judge may insulate his findings from review by denominating them credibility determinations, for factors other than demeanor and inflection go into the decision whether or not to believe a witness. Documents or objective evidence may contradict the witness' story; or the story itself may be so internally inconsistent or implausible on its face that a reasonable factfinder would not credit it. Where such factors are present, the court of appeals may well find clear error even in a finding purportedly based on a credibility determination. * * * But when a trial judge's finding is based on his decision to credit the testimony of one of two or more witnesses, each of whom has told a coherent and facially plausible story that is not contradicted by extrinsic evidence, that finding, if not internally inconsistent, can virtually never be clear error.

Id. at 574, 105 S.Ct. at 1511–12, 84 L.Ed.2d at 528–30. What standard did the Supreme Court adopt? Does the additional language in the 1987 version of the Rule settle the issue? See Childress, *"Clearly Erroneous": Judicial Review Over District Courts in the Eighth Circuit and Beyond,* 51 Mo.L.Rev. 93 (1986).

Review Hicks v. United States, p. 54, supra. Would the new language of Rule 52(a) have altered the outcome in that case? Would the Court's language in *Anderson* have altered the outcome?

SECTION E. CHALLENGING ERRORS: NEW TRIAL

1. THE NATURE AND THE SCOPE OF THE POWER TO GRANT A NEW TRIAL

———

Read Federal Rules of Civil Procedure 59 and 61 and the accompanying materials in the Supplement. Note particularly the grounds for new trial listed in Minnesota Rule of Civil Procedure 59.01.

———

The Range of the Trial Court's Discretion

1. Errors committed during the course of a trial may be categorized as follows: (i) those that would result in reversal if the case were to be appealed; (ii) those that may have had an impact on the verdict, but do not justify reversal of the case on appeal, and (iii) those that did not significantly affect the outcome. Obviously errors that do not have any impact on the decision are harmless and it would be an abuse of discretion for the trial court to predicate a new trial on them. On the other hand, errors that would justify a reversal

by an appellate court demand remedial measures at the trial level. A judge should not force a litigant to pay the costs of prosecuting an appeal as well as the costs of the new trial to which he is entitled.

2. Theoretically, it is only with regard to errors that affect the result in the case but would not lead to reversal on appeal that the trial court has discretion to decide whether or not a new trial is appropriate. As a practical matter, however, the almost unlimited power of the court with regard to the granting of new trials is far greater than it might otherwise seem to be. First, an aggrieved litigant may decide to stand or fall on the motion for new trial since the case simply may not be worth the added cost of an appeal or the litigant may not have sufficient funds to continue fighting. Second, in many jurisdictions, the grant of a new trial, not being a final judgment, cannot be appealed. Thus the cost of a new trial will have to be absorbed before an appeal is even possible. Third, the very question of what constitutes reversible error on appeal often is affected by the ruling of the trial judge on the motion for new trial. In those jurisdictions in which a motion for a new trial is a prerequisite for appeal, see, e.g., Evans v. Wilkinson, 419 P.2d 275 (Okl.1966), the denial of a new trial certainly will influence the appellate court in deciding whether the error is harmless for purposes of appeal if the effect of the error in question can better be determined by the trial judge. Even when a motion for a new trial is not required, and when, theoretically, the appellate court should not penalize a litigant for having so moved, knowledge that the trial judge has rejected the alleged error as harmless may have an impact on the appellate-court decision. Finally, in some jurisdictions the trial judge may grant a new trial without specifying or without actually relying on any precise grounds. Obviously this narrows the scope of review of such decisions.

GINSBERG v. WILLIAMS, 270 Minn. 474, 135 N.W.2d 213 (1965). Plaintiff brought suit for damages received in an automobile accident. The jury rendered a verdict for defendant and plaintiff moved for a new trial. The court granted the motion "in the interests of justice," giving no other basis for its ruling. Defendant sought a writ of prohibition to restrain enforcement of the ruling, claiming that the trial court is empowered to grant a new trial only for one of the grounds specifically set forth in Rule 59.01 of the Minnesota Rules of Civil Procedure. The Minnesota Supreme Court granted the writ, holding as follows:

> * * * The causes enumerated in Rule 59.01 are so comprehensive that they include every conceivable reason for which a new trial ought to be ordered. Those causes requiring the exercise of discretion, such as 59.01(1) (irregularities depriving the moving party of a fair trial) and 59.01(8) (insufficiency of the evidence), vest the broadest possible discretionary power in the trial court. To permit granting a new trial "in the interests of justice" would invite an arbitrary exercise of power over which appellate review is not now available. Even if it were, it would be difficult to fashion any effective rules to control arbitrary action since the basis for such an order would necessarily be subjective, varying from judge to judge. Further, each of the causes enumerated is designed to promote justice and prevent injustice. It is one thing to order a new trial

"on the ground that on the evidence substantial justice has not been done" or in the interest of justice on the ground that the evidence does not justify the verdict, and quite another thing to order a new trial simply "in the interests of justice." It is difficult to conceive how such a general ground would add anything to the grounds enumerated in our rules unless it is desirable to restore the common-law power of granting a new trial when the judge is personally dissatisfied with the verdict.

Id. at 483–84, 135 N.W.2d at 220.

Notes and Questions

1.   In COPPO v. VAN WIERINGEN, 36 Wash.2d 120, 123–24, 217 P.2d 294, 297 (1950), the court stated:

One of the reasons assigned by the trial judge in the instant cases for granting new trials is that "substantial justice has not been done." The statutes which enumerate the grounds on which new trials may be granted * * * make no mention of such a ground for a new trial; but we have always upheld the right of the trial judge to grant a new trial when he is convinced that substantial justice has not been done, on the theory that it is an exercise of the trial court's inherent power. * * *

Actually, of course, when a trial judge says that "substantial justice has not been done," he is stating a conclusion for which there must be a reason or reasons. * * * The reason we have barred any review of an order granting a new trial based on this conclusion * * * was expressed by the supreme court of Wisconsin in the case of McLimans v. City of Lancaster, 57 Wis. 297, 15 N.W. 194, 195: "The judge before whom the cause was tried heard the testimony, observed the appearance and bearing of the witnesses and their manner of testifying, and was much better qualified to pass upon the credibility and weight of their testimony than this court can be. *There are many comparatively trifling appearances and incidents, lights and shadows, which are not preserved in the record, which may well have affected the mind of the judge as well as the jury in forming opinions of the weight of the evidence, the character and credibility of the witnesses, and of the very right and justice of the case.* These considerations cannot be ignored in determining whether the judge exercised a reasonable discretion or abused his discretion in granting or refusing a motion for a new trial." (Italics ours.)

2.   Suppose a party moves for a new trial based on a number of specific errors, no one of which alone would be sufficiently prejudicial to justify a new trial. May the court under Ginsberg v. Williams grant the motion on the ground that all of the errors, taken together, deprived the losing party of a fair trial? Cf. Walker v. Holiday Lanes, Inc., 196 Kan. 513, 413 P.2d 63 (1966); Miller v. Staton, 64 Wash.2d 837, 394 P.2d 799 (1964).

3.   To what extent does the decision in *Ginsberg* provide significant appellate-court control over the "arbitrary exercise" of power by the trial judge? What more can the exercise of discretion mean than that the trial judge can decide that errors, trivial in appearance, have resulted in manifest injustice to the party seeking a new trial because of "lights and shadows which are not preserved in the record"?

4. Under what circumstances, if any, should errors during trial justify a new trial in a nonjury case? In the much-quoted opinion in BUILDERS STEEL CO. v. COMMISSIONER, 179 F.2d 377, 379 (8th Cir.1950), the court said:

> In the trial of a nonjury case, it is virtually impossible for a trial judge to commit reversible error by receiving incompetent evidence, whether objected to or not. An appellate court will not reverse a judgment in a nonjury case because of the admission of incompetent evidence, unless all of the competent evidence is insufficient to support the judgment or unless it affirmatively appears that the incompetent evidence induced the court to make an essential finding which would not otherwise have been made. * * * On the other hand, a trial judge who, in the trial of a nonjury case, attempts to make strict rulings on the admissibility of evidence, can easily get his decision reversed by excluding evidence which is objected to, but which, on review, the appellate court believes should have been admitted. * * *

Is the attitude of the court proper? To what extent should the court's reasoning apply to errors other than the improper admission of evidence?

2. INCOHERENT JURY VERDICTS

MAGNANI v. TROGI

Appellate Court of Illinois, Second District, 1966.
70 Ill.App.2d 216, 218 N.E.2d 21.

CORYN, PRESIDING JUSTICE. * * *

Plaintiff's complaint states two separate causes of action. In Count I she seeks recovery of $30,000.00, as Administratrix, for the wrongful death of her decedent, pursuant to the Wrongful Death Act (Ill.Rev.Stats., ch. 70, §§ 1 & 2). By the second count of the complaint she seeks reimbursement, in her individual capacity, for medical and funeral expenses necessarily incurred by her as the result of the injury and death to her husband, pursuant to the Family Expense Statute (Ill.Rev.Stats., ch. 68, § 15).

The Wrongful Death Act provides that any recovery thereunder shall be distributed by the court in which the cause was heard to the widow and next of kin of the decedent, in proportion, as determined by the trial court, "that the percentage of dependency of each such person upon the deceased person bears to the sum of the percentages of dependency of all such persons upon the deceased person." Here, any award of the jury, for a wrongful death, would be apportioned by the trial court to the widow and minor son of decedent. There would be no apportionment of any award made under the provisions of the Family Expense Statute.

* * *

In the instant case, there can be no doubt that the recovery sought under each count of plaintiff's complaint was based on separate causes of action, that is, one action for wrongful death, and the other under the Family Expense Statute. Unfortunately, neither party to this suit tendered separate forms of verdict for each of these counts. Rather, a single form of verdict was submitted by the court to the jury without objection from plaintiff or defendant. Using this form the jury returned the following verdict: "We, the jury, find in favor of the plaintiff and against the defendant. We assess the damages in the sum of $19,000.00." The trial judge, in his memorandum of opinion allowing a new trial, properly expressed the dilemma this verdict created for him by stating: "In the case at bar, there were two counts. Does the single verdict all apply to just one count, or to both counts? It might be that the verdict was all for the wrongful death action, and non-liability as to the medical expense cause of action." After making this observation, the trial judge then concluded that the verdict must be set aside and a new trial ordered as to both the liability and damage aspects of the case. Although other points have been raised in this appeal, we believe the determinative issue to be whether the trial judge, when faced with this situation, abused his discretion by granting a new trial.

The purpose of vesting the trial judge with power to grant a new trial is to permit him, before losing jurisdiction of the case, to correct errors that he or the jury might have made during the course of the trial. Courts of review have repeatedly stated that they will not disturb the decision of a trial court on a motion for new trial unless a clear abuse of discretion is affirmatively shown. The reason for this rule is that the trial court has had the opportunity to consider the conduct of the trial as a whole, and therefore is in a superior position to consider the effects of errors which occurred, the fairness of the trial to all parties, and whether substantial justice was accomplished. * * * Greater latitude is allowed a trial court in granting a new trial than in denying a new trial. * * *

Plaintiff argues that defendant has waived his right to complain of the form of verdict because he did not object to the giving of this form to the jury, but raised the issue for the first time in his post-trial motion. In most instances this would be a valid argument. Here, however, because of the single form of verdict, the jury's determination of liability and damages on each of the two causes of action was not made known. It appears that the jury found liability against the defendant on the wrongful death action, but any conclusion about what the jury's verdict was regarding liability on the family expense action is pure conjecture. Also, the language of the verdict returned gives no indication of the jury's determination as to what portion of the total verdict of $19,000.00 it attributed to damages for wrongful death, and what portion, if any, to damages for medical and funeral expenses. The determination of liability and damages, in the first instance, is to be made by the jury.

The jury returned its verdict on December 21, 1962, and the defendant filed his post-trial motion on January 15, 1963, thereby raising this issue for the first time. It was impossible, then, for the court to re-assemble the jury and instruct them to correct the error in the form of verdict. * * * We are not holding, by this opinion, that the failure to submit to the jury separate forms of verdict in cases involving multiple causes of action should, in every instance, result in the granting of a new trial, but rather, that in the situation presented here it was not an abuse of discretion for the trial judge to grant a new trial.

The order of the Circuit Court of Lake County, granting defendant's motion for new trial, vacating and setting aside the verdict and judgment, and denying defendant's motion for judgment notwithstanding the verdict, is affirmed.

Affirmed.

STOUDER, JUSTICE (dissenting). I do not agree with the opinion of the majority. The record before us clearly shows that Plaintiff waived any individual interest in the verdict. The verdict, then being within the range of the evidence and the law, any possible dilemma facing the trial court was thereby solved.

As was succinctly stated in Hall v. Chicago and Northwestern Ry. Company, 349 Ill.App. 175, 110 N.E.2d 654 "We are not unmindful of the rule and cases which hold that the trial judge is allowed broad discretion in granting motions for a new trial, and that his actions will not be reversed on appeal except in cases of clear abuse of such discretion; but this rule, like all others, has its limitations. A judge is not empowered to set aside a verdict in any case simply because he does not agree with it. * * * " In the instant case the trial court's granting of a new trial was based upon a finding that the forms of verdict submitted to the jury were improper. It therefore should be our duty to examine the propriety of this finding in order to determine the limits which were self-imposed upon the discretion of the trial court.

Upon thorough examination of the record before us I am unable to find that Defendant made any objection to the forms of verdict at the conference on instructions or at any time prior to his post-trial motion. * * * Defendant's failure to object to the forms at the proper time as well as his later failure to show that he was in fact prejudiced compels me in the instant case to find that the trial court's finding was erroneous and Defendant's motion for a new trial should have been denied.

* * *

ROBB v. JOHN C. HICKEY, INC.

Circuit Court of New Jersey, Morris County, 1941.
19 N.J.Misc. 455, 20 A.2d 707.

LEYDEN, JUDGE. The issues presented by the pleadings were the negligence of the defendants and the contributory negligence of the plaintiff's decedent. The jury was instructed concerning the applicable principles of law, in the course of which it was pointed out that if contributory negligence upon the part of the plaintiff's decedent had been established, the comparative degrees of the negligence of the parties was immaterial.

The jury returned a verdict in the absence of the judge and it was recorded at the clerk's desk as follows: "The jury finds that there was negligence on the part of both parties involved—The evidence shown is that the defendant was more negligent than the plaintiff—We therefore recommend an award of $2,000.00 to the plaintiff Clyde J. Robb and against the defendants John C. Hickey, Inc., a New Jersey Corporation and Roger W. King."

Both parties are dissatisfied with the verdict; the plaintiff with its substance and the defendants with its form. Plaintiff has a rule to set aside the verdict upon the ground that it is ambiguous, inconsistent, inadequate and contrary to the charge of the court. Defendants, upon notice, move to mould the verdict into one in favor of the defendants and against the plaintiff, urging that it is merely informal and the intent of the jury to find for the defendants is clearly indicated * * *.

It is true that a verdict must be responsive to the issues and recommendations of the jury dehors the issues submitted by the court, such as the suggestion of the equal division of another fund between the parties * * * or the amount claimed in the suit be donated to the American Red Cross * * * or each party (plaintiff being unsuccessful) pay his own cost * * * or of leniency in a criminal case * * * may be treated as surplusage and properly disregarded.

However, such is not the situation in the instant case. Here the verdict finds both parties guilty of negligence, erroneously compares the degrees of their negligence and recommends an award of $2,000 in favor of the plaintiff and against both defendants. What then did the jury agree upon and intend? Did it find in favor of the defendants as is legally indicated by the first sentence, or in favor of plaintiff in the sum of $2,000 as is clearly indicated by the last sentence? The recommendation of an award to the plaintiff is pertinent to the issues, for basically the liability of defendants to plaintiff in damages was in question. It cannot be treated as surplusage and disregarded. Reading the verdict as a whole, it is self-contradictory, inconsistent and ambiguous. One is left to conjecture and surmise as to the real purpose of the jury. It is defective in substance, not merely in form.

The court may, in fact should, mould an informal verdict to render it formal, effective and to coincide with the substance of the verdict as agreed upon and intended by the jury, but this power is only exercised where the real purpose and intent of the jury clearly, sufficiently and convincingly appears. * * * Where, as here, the verdict is uncertain or ambiguous, it cannot be moulded. The court will not substitute its verdict in place thereof. * * *

This leads to the denial of defendants' motion to mould and is also dispositive of the plaintiff's rule. The latter will be made absolute and a new trial granted.

Notes and Questions

1. Why is the verdict in *Robb* different from a verdict that recommends that the amount claimed be donated to the American Red Cross? Can't a strong argument be made in favor of a new trial in the latter situation? See Rusidoff v. DeBolt Transfer, Inc., 251 Pa.Super. 208, 380 A.2d 451 (1977), in which the trial judge's denial of a new trial was reversed when the jury verdict for defendant was rendered "with reservations due to the evidence provided."

2. Suppose plaintiff brings suit for injuries suffered in an accident allegedly due to defendant's negligence. The jury renders a verdict in favor of plaintiff but assesses damages at zero, although it is clear from the evidence that plaintiff has been badly hurt. May the judge enter judgment on the verdict? See Wingerter v. Maryland Cas. Co., 313 F.2d 754 (5th Cir.1963), and Pitcher v. Rogers, 259 F.Supp. 412 (N.D.Miss.1966), in which the courts answered "yes." Can these decisions be reconciled with *Robb*? To what extent does the answer depend upon the nature of the evidence regarding the causation of damages? There are a number of decisions holding that such a verdict cannot stand. See, e.g., Fugitt v. Jones, 549 F.2d 1001 (5th Cir.1977).

3. How far should a trial court go in attempting to ascertain the "true intent" of the jury in order to be able to "mould" a verdict? Should the court be permitted to ask the jurors what they intended? Why shouldn't all but the clearest

cases be returned for a new trial? Compare Hanolt v. Mlakar, 421 Pa. 136, 218 A.2d 750 (1966), with Gilday v. Hauchwit, 91 N.J.Super. 233, 219 A.2d 873 (App.Div.1966), reversed in part on other grounds 48 N.J. 557, 226 A.2d 834 (1967). Is there any way to avoid the costs and delays of a new trial if the verdict cannot be moulded?

————

KRAMER v. KISTER, 187 Pa. 227, 233–36, 40 A. 1008, 1008–10 (1898):

[The jury agreed to a sealed verdict and separated. When the verdict was opened the next morning, one juror dissented from it; the jury was sent out again and returned shortly with the same verdict, which was entered.]

* * * At common law the jury were kept together from the time they were sworn, as is still the general rule in criminal cases involving life. After they had retired to consider their verdict, they were kept without food, drink, fire, or light until they agreed; and Blackstone says, "It has been held that, if the jurors do not agree in their verdict before the judges are about to leave the town, though they are not to be threatened or imprisoned, the judges are not bound to wait for them, but may carry them round the circuit, from town to town, in a cart." 3 Bl.Comm. 376. From the manner of this mention, it is to be inferred that this latter practice was at least unusual in Blackstone's day; and he says expressly that the deprivation of food, fire, and light was subject to the indulgence of the court. * * * With the prolongation of trials in the more complicated issues of modern times, and especially with the amelioration of manners, the treatment of jurors has gradually become less harsh, and changes of practice have been made in their relief. It is no longer the custom to keep them together and secluded during the whole trial, though I apprehend that the judge may do so in any case where public excitement or other exceptional reason may make it advisable, in the interest of the proper administration of justice, to do so * * *. After the retirement of the jury to consider their verdict, this indulgence terminates, and they are kept together and apart from others until verdict rendered. But, if the adjournment of the court is to such time or under such circumstances as seem likely to lead to serious inconvenience to the jurors, the practice of allowing them to seal a verdict grew up. * * * When a juror dissents from a sealed verdict, there is a necessary choice of evils,—a mistrial, or a verdict finally delivered under circumstances that justly subject it to suspicion of coercion or improper influences. * * * If the dissenting juror was honest in his declaration that he had not agreed to the first verdict, except because he thought he was obliged to, then his agreement to the second without having been instructed as to his rights cannot be freed from a well-founded appearance of coercion. If, on the other hand, the second verdict had been for the defendant, contrary to the first, the inference could hardly have been escaped that the change was produced by new evidence, or information illegally acquired by the dissenting juror, or by even more reprehensible means. The only safe way out of such a situation is to treat it as a mistrial, and discharge the jury. * * *

Notes and Questions

1. Note that very few jurisdictions today require jurors to remain together constantly once the case has been submitted to them. See Annot., 77 A.L.R.2d 1086 (1961). Before allowing the jurors to separate, however, the court normally will warn them not to discuss the case with anyone outside the jury room and not to inspect sites referred to in the testimony or otherwise to obtain evidence. See Steckler, *Management of the Jury*, 28 F.R.D. 190, 191 (1960). What effect should the failure to give these cautionary instructions have on the validity of the verdict? Can we really expect jurors not to have some discussions of a case with other jurors or with their families? What should the court do if it learns that discussions have occurred?

2. Do you agree with the reasoning of the court in *Kramer* as to why the resubmission was improper? To what extent does the case turn upon the time at which the resubmission was made? Suppose, for example, that the original verdict had been an oral one, rendered at the end of the deliberations. Would an immediate resubmission have been justifiable? If so, in light of modern practice permitting jurors to separate during their deliberations, isn't *Kramer* outmoded? See Annot., 164 A.L.R. 1265, 1276–79 (1946).

To what extent should the validity of resubmission depend upon whether the jury has been discharged from the case? Suppose the error in the verdict is first noticed after the jurors have been discharged but while they are still present in the courtroom? See generally Annot., 66 A.L.R. 536 (1930).

3. To what extent may a court resubmit a verdict for defects other than the lack of unanimity or a proper majority?

(a) Suppose, for example, the error is one that the court could correct itself by moulding a proper verdict. Wouldn't it be preferable to resubmit the case to the jury? See Gilday v. Hauchwit, 91 N.J.Super. 233, 219 A.2d 873 (App.Div.1966), reversed in part on other grounds 48 N.J. 557, 226 A.2d 834 (1967).

(b) What if the error was similar to that in Robb v. John C. Hickey, Inc., in which the court held that it could not correct the verdict itself. Would a resubmission to the jury have been improper? See Sigel v. Boston & Me. R. Co., 107 N.H. 8, 216 A.2d 794 (1966) (resubmission held appropriate). Isn't resubmission always preferable to a new trial?

3. JURY MISCONDUCT AND THE INTEGRITY OF THE VERDICT

The general rule that jurors' affidavits cannot be utilized to attack the verdict already has been noted. See Note 2, p. 48, supra. The rule's validity has vigorously been challenged. For example in SOPP v. SMITH, 59 Cal.2d 12, 27 Cal.Rptr. 593, 377 P.2d 649 (1963), an auto accident case, a motion for new trial was based on affidavits of several jurors stating that during the trial they had visited the scene of the accident personally to check driver visibility, road conditions, and distances about which testimony had been produced. The California Supreme Court upheld a denial of a new trial on the ground that the affidavits were inadmissible. Justice Peters dissented:

> The majority, following the rule of stare decisis, adhere to a court created doctrine first announced by Judge Mansfield in Vaise v. Delaval, 1

Term R. 11, 99 Eng.Rep. 944 (K.B.1785). That rule is that affidavits of jurors may not be used to impeach their verdict.

* * * At least 12 jurisdictions, by judicial decision, have [followed the lead of Iowa in modifying] * * * the strict Mansfield rule. * * *

The Iowa rule is based upon the distinction between extrinsic or overt acts which may be corroborated or disproved, such as access to improper matter or an illegal method of reaching a verdict, and intrinsic matters which "inhere in the verdict itself" and hence are known only to the individual juror, such as misunderstanding or prejudice. Because matters which "inhere" in the verdict, including the thought processes and motives of the juror in reaching his decision, are not readily capable of being either corroborated or disproved they should be excluded.

* * *

In spite of the fact that the legal scholars in this field are practically unanimous in their opinion that the Iowa rule is sound, it must be conceded that the majority of the states still adhere to the Mansfield rule. The reason for this has been several times noted. Justice Learned Hand stated it as follows: " * * * judges again and again repeat the consecrated rubric which has so confused the subject; it offers an easy escape from embarrassing choices." (Jorgensen v. York Ice Machinery Corp., * * * (2nd Cir.1947) 160 F.2d 432, 435, cert. denied, 332 U.S. 764, 68 S.Ct. 69, 92 L.Ed. 349.) * * *

Generally speaking, * * * the courts cite one or more of the following reasons for continuing to invoke the strict rule of exclusion: (1) The need for stability of verdicts; (2) the need to protect jurors from fraud and harassment by disappointed litigants; (3) the desire to prevent prolonged litigation; (4) the need to prevent verdicts from being set aside because of the subsequent doubts or change of attitude by a juror; (5) the concept of the sanctity of the jury room.

Wigmore has completely demolished these arguments (8 Wigmore on Evidence (McNaughton rev. 1961) § 2353, pp. 697–699). In 47 Colum.L.Rev. 1373, 1375, it is stated * * * "It is anomalous that the best and usually the only evidence of which the case admits should be excluded [citation]. The objection that admission of this evidence would allow undue tampering with jurors is greatly exaggerated; courts in early decisions before the rule was adopted were apparently not troubled by fear of excessive jury corruption [citations]. The argument that uncertainty of jury verdicts would result from a more liberal rule of admissibility is misdirected since the acceptance of jurors' testimony does not mean that any jury irregularity warrants a new trial, but only that such evidence may be considered in determining whether or not a new trial is required [citation]. The real problem, therefore, is substantive rather than procedural; namely, what kind of jury misbehavior should be considered grounds for reversal."

The fear that under the Iowa rule a juror might have doubts about his verdict and subsequently seek to upset it by an affidavit on motion for new trial is unfounded. This is so because a juror's testimony or affidavit is and should be admissible only when it concerns overt acts. Furthermore, admissibility of the evidence does not a fortiori mean reversal—prejudice must be proved. * * *

* * * The trial court held, as a matter of law, that the affidavits of the offending jurors could not be considered by it. Such testimony was obviously the best evidence available on the issue. Had the wife of one of the offending jurors who accompanied him while he made the improper measurements filed the affidavit to the effect that she had observed her husband, such affidavit would admittedly have been admissible. * * * Yet here where it is admitted that misconduct occurred, the majority say that even though such misconduct may have deprived the plaintiff of a fair trial we will not permit him to show that by the affidavit of the very man that committed the overt act that constituted the misconduct. This is logically absurd. * * *

Id. at 15–20, 27 Cal.Rptr. at 595–98, 377 P.2d at 651–54.

Notes and Questions

1.   In 1969 the California Supreme Court in PEOPLE v. HUTCHINSON, 71 Cal.2d 342, 78 Cal.Rptr. 196, 455 P.2d 132 (1969), reversed its prior stance and accepted Justice Peters' position in Sopp v. Smith. For an example of the difficulties that can arise when the court accepts affidavits of dissenting jurors alleging misconduct of the majority (when only a majority verdict is required), see Johns v. City of Los Angeles, 78 Cal.App.3d 983, 144 Cal.Rptr. 629 (2d Dist.1978) (hearing denied by 4–3 vote of the California Supreme Court).

2.   Suppose the jurors agree upon a verdict but through the mistake of the jury foreman, judge, or court clerk a different verdict is entered. Should affidavits of jurors be admissible to correct the error? Is this "impeachment" within the meaning of the common law? If so, would the case fall within the exceptions permitted by the Iowa rule? See FORD MOTOR CREDIT CO. v. AMODT, 29 Wis.2d 441, 139 N.W.2d 6 (1966), in which the court refused to accept affidavits of eight of twelve jurors to the effect that a "No" rather than a "Yes" answer had been improperly reported as to a crucial interrogatory.

May affidavits be used when a verdict for plaintiff was rendered, but the amount of damages found was omitted? See Hodgkins v. Mead, 119 N.Y. 166, 23 N.E. 559 (1890).

3.   Rule 606(b) of the Federal Rules of Evidence provides:

Inquiry into validity of verdict or indictment. Upon an inquiry into the validity of a verdict or indictment, a juror may not testify as to any matter or statement occurring during the course of the jury's deliberations or to the effect of anything upon his or any other juror's mind or emotions as influencing him to assent to or dissent from the verdict or indictment or concerning his mental processes in connection therewith, except that a juror may testify on the question whether extraneous prejudicial information was improperly brought to the jury's attention or whether any outside influence was improperly brought to bear upon any juror. Nor may his affidavit or evidence of any statement by him concerning a matter about which he would be precluded from testifying be received for these purposes.

For a thorough analysis of the problems of impeachment and the role of the Federal Rule, see Mueller, *Juror's Impeachment of Verdicts and Indictments in Federal Court Under Rule 606(b),* 57 Neb.L.Rev. 920 (1978).

HUKLE v. KIMBLE

Supreme Court of Kansas, 1952.
172 Kan. 630, 243 P.2d 225.

SMITH, JUSTICE. This was an action for damages alleged to have been sustained when plaintiff was caught between a truck driven by one of defendants and a pillar in the driveway of an elevator where plaintiff was employed. Judgment was for the plaintiff. Defendants have appealed.

* * *

Defendants * * * argue that the trial court erred in overruling their motion for a new trial. One of the grounds of this motion was misconduct of the jury. On the hearing of the motion for a new trial testimony of various members of the jury was heard on the question of whether the verdict was a quotient verdict. One of the jurors testified as follows:

Q. Without giving any of the other deliberations—in other words, without telling what was in your mind—I would like to ask you how this verdict was arrived at, the amount of this verdict? A. Mr. Brann was the foreman of the jury and he asked that—or suggested that if the—there was a judgment, which he thought there should be, if we would all put down an amount on a piece of paper, which we did, then someone in the group added it up and divided it by 12 and arrived at the $5,208.33, and then Mr. Brann said, 'Is there anyone that feels this is an unfair amount? Is this the amount that all of us wish, if you don't feel that way why speak up now,' and we all agreed that that would be the amount that we felt was right.

Q. And there had been something said before the quotient was taken, before you divided by 12 to do that to arrive at a verdict? A. I think so. I think it was. I think it was agreed that, before we wrote down those amounts that that would be the fair way, if one person said one amount and someone else said something higher and not knowing any better way, we agreed that an average would be right, and we discussed the average after we took it.

The foreman of the jury testified as follows:

Q. You have heard the testimony of these two other jurors? A. Yes, sir.

Q. Is that what occurred there at the time? A. That is correct.

Q. Do you have anything to add to it at all? A. I don't know as there is anything I could add. I thought it was fair and square.

Q. You suggested that you add their respective figures together and then divide the sum by 12 and that that would be adopted as the verdict; is that right? A. Well, yes.

Plaintiff realizes the potency of this evidence and seeks to counteract it by claiming that on cross-examination these jurors testified that they were asked after the quotient had been reached whether they believed the amount to be fair and all the jury members said it was. The fact remains, however, that the evidence is uncontradicted, that the jury members all agreed that the quotient would be the verdict and it was. * * * The result is the trial court erred in overruling the defendant's motion for a new trial.

Notes and Questions

1. As a practical matter does reversal in the *Hukle* case make any sense? Is the quotient verdict really all that evil? Would it be of significance if the jurors had taken a quotient verdict before deliberating the question of liability? What difference, if any, would it have made had the jury, after arriving at the quotient figure, discussed at length its propriety in light of the evidence? In SCHULZ v. CHADWELL, 558 S.W.2d 183, 186 (Ky.App.1977), the jurors used the quotient method to set an amount for each element of the claimed damage. The court rejected the appellant's claim that the verdict was thus an invalid quotient verdict: "The average of the jurors' views was obtained merely as a basis for further deliberation." For an extensive general discussion of the problems of quotient verdicts, see Annot., 8 A.L.R.3d 335 (1966).

2. There are many forms of jury misconduct, some of which were discussed in Chapter One, see pp. 46–49, supra. Often the question is not whether the conduct was improper but whether the error is so serious that the verdict must be overturned. Assuming that a trial court has before it the following sets of facts, what rulings should it make on motions for a new trial?

(a) The jury, after deliberation, was deadlocked seven to five for defendant, but because, during trial, one juror had learned of the death of a son and wished to return home, the jurors agreed to abide by the vote of the majority, and therefore, without further discussion, rendered a verdict for defendant. See Jorgensen v. York Ice Mach. Corp., 160 F.2d 432 (2d Cir.), certiorari denied 332 U.S. 764, 68 S.Ct. 69, 92 L.Ed. 349 (1947). Suppose the jury, although properly instructed, erroneously believed that a majority verdict was all that was necessary? Cf. Hoffman v. French, Ltd., 394 S.W.2d 259, 266 (Tex.Civ.App.1965).

(b) On *voir dire* in a personal-injury action, the prospective jurors had been asked whether they had ever had any claims arising from the alleged negligence of another person. Four members of the panel had asserted such claims, and they had been paid cash settlements without filing suit. Nonetheless they remained silent, believing the question to relate only to actual lawsuits. These four were not challenged and thus sat on the jury that rendered a verdict for plaintiff. Compare Photostat Corp. v. Ball, 338 F.2d 783 (10th Cir.1964) (denial of new trial reversed), with Derr v. St. Louis Pub. Serv. Co., 399 S.W.2d 241 (Mo.App.1965) (denial of new trial affirmed). Suppose the jurors had understood the question but nevertheless concealed the fact of their prior claims. Should the motives of the jurors bear on the question? See Pierce v. Altman, 147 Ga.App. 22, 248 S.E.2d 34 (1978) (denial of new trial reversed).

(c) After the case was submitted to the jury and the jury deliberated for more than an hour without reaching a verdict the bailiff, on instruction of the court, took the jurors to lunch in a local hotel and supplied them with alcoholic beverages in moderate amounts. Shortly thereafter the jurors returned to the court and, after a half hour of deliberation, rendered a verdict. See Kealoha v. Tanaka, 45 Hawaii 457, 370 P.2d 468 (1962) (denial of new trial affirmed by 3–2 decision). What difference would it make if one juror had become intoxicated? See generally Annot., 6 A.L.R.3d 934 (1966).

(d) During a court recess plaintiff entered an elevator containing three jurors on their way to lunch. Plaintiff initiated a friendly conversation with one of the jurors regarding the fact that some of plaintiff's relatives lived in the area where the juror owned and operated a drugstore. The conversation was short and nothing was said about the case. See United States v. Harry Barfield Co., 359 F.2d 120 (5th Cir.1966) (denial of new trial reversed by a 2–to–1 decision).

There are many cases in which jurors have been charged with misconduct for holding unauthorized conversations concerning the case. See Annot., 62 A.L.R.2d 298 (1958) (contact with a party to the case or his attorney); Annot., 52 A.L.R.2d 182 (1957) (contact with witnesses); Annot., 41 A.L.R.2d 288 (1955) (contact with judges, court officials, and attendants); Annot., 64 A.L.R.2d 158 (1959) (contact with outsiders generally). Most of the decisions turn on the nature of the conversation regarding the case and the extent to which the juror might have been influenced in his decision. See, e.g., Adams v. Davis, 578 S.W.2d 899 (Ky.App. 1979). Does it make sense to presume prejudice conclusively in contexts such as United States v. Harry Barfield Co., above? Should every contact between a juror and a party or attorney, or between a juror and a witness, be considered prejudicial? See Printed Terry Finishing Co. v. City of Lebanon, 247 Pa.Super. 277, 299–300, 372 A.2d 460, 469 (1977) (unexplained contact requires new trial). See generally Note, 4 Houston L.Rev. 583 (1966).

In McDONOUGH POWER EQUIPMENT, INC. v. GREENWOOD, 464 U.S. 548, 104 S.Ct. 845, 78 L.Ed.2d 663 (1984), the respondent was injured in an accident involving a power mower manufactured by the petitioner. During the *voir dire* before the empaneling of the six-member jury, the respondents' attorney asked prospective jurors whether they or any member of their immediate family had sustained any severe injury. The jury ultimately found for the petitioner. After judgment was entered for the petitioner, the respondents' attorney questioned the jurors and discovered that the son of the foreman of the jury had been injured some time before by the explosion of a truck tire, sustaining a broken leg. During the post-judgment interview, the foreman said that "having accidents are [sic] a part of life," and that "all his children have been involved in accidents." Id. at 553 n. 3, 104 S.Ct. at 848 n. 3, 78 L.Ed.2d at 669 n. 3. The District Court, which did not have these details before it, refused the respondents' motion for a new trial. The Tenth Circuit held (based in part on the information quoted above but not presented to the District Court) that the juror's failure to respond to the question during the *voir dire* proceeding constituted juror misconduct requiring a new trial. The Supreme Court reversed:

> To invalidate the result of a 3–week trial because of a juror's mistaken, though honest, response to a question, is to insist on something closer to perfection than our judicial system can be expected to give. A trial represents an important investment of private and social resources, and it ill serves the important end of finality to wipe the slate clean simply to recreate the peremptory challenge process because counsel lacked an item of information which objectively he should have obtained from a juror on *voir dire* examination. * * * We hold that to obtain a new trial in such a situation, a party must first demonstrate that a juror failed

to answer honestly a material question on *voir dire,* and then further show that a correct response would have provided a valid basis for a challenge for cause. The motives for concealing information may vary, but only those reasons that affect a juror's impartiality can truly be said to affect the fairness of a trial.

Id. at 555–56, 104 S.Ct. at 849–50, 78 L.Ed.2d at 671.

Justice Blackmun, joined by Justices Stevens and O'Connor, concurred, stressing that the decision should not be understood as "foreclos[ing] the normal avenue of relief available to a party who is asserting that he did not have the benefit of an impartial jury." Id. at 556, 104 S.Ct. at 850, 78 L.Ed.2d at 672. Justice Brennan, joined by Justice Marshall, concurred in the judgment, proposing a different legal standard:

> * * * In my view, the proper focus when ruling on a motion for new trial in this situation should be on the bias of the juror and the resulting prejudice to the litigant. More specifically, to be awarded a new trial, a litigant should be required to demonstrate that the juror incorrectly responded to a material question on *voir dire,* and that, under the facts and circumstances surrounding the particular case, the juror was biased against the moving litigant. * * *

> * * * [F]or a court to determine properly whether bias exists, it must consider at least two questions: are there any facts in the case suggesting that bias should be conclusively presumed; and, if not, is it more probable than not that the juror was actually biased against the litigant. Whether the juror answered a particular question on *voir dire* honestly or dishonestly, or whether an inaccurate answer was inadvertent or intentional, are simply factors to be considered in this latter determination of actual bias. * * *

Id. at 557–58, 104 S.Ct. at 851, 78 L.Ed.2d at 672–73.

Notes and Questions

Suppose that a finance company is a party in a case and its attorney asks each potential juror if he or she has ever applied unsuccessfully for a loan from the company. One juror falsely and deliberately answers "no." At what point must the finance company object to the juror's participation in the case? Should the answer depend upon how easy it would be for the company to ascertain the name of all unsuccessful loan applicants from the company's files? See Tidewater Finance Co. v. Fiserv Solutions, Inc., 192 F.R.D. 516, 519–20 (E.D.Va.2000).

4. NEW TRIAL BECAUSE THE VERDICT IS AGAINST THE WEIGHT OF THE EVIDENCE

AETNA CASUALTY & SURETY CO. v. YEATTS

United States Circuit Court of Appeals, Fourth Circuit, 1941.
122 F.2d 350.

PARKER, CIRCUIT JUDGE. This is the second appeal in a suit originally instituted to obtain a declaratory judgment with respect to the coverage of a policy of indemnity insurance. * * * The company denied liability on the ground that the defendant Yeatts was engaged in the performance of a criminal abortion at the time he incurred the liability for which the recovery was had against him, and that such liability was expressly excluded from the coverage of the policy. The question as to whether the defendant Yeatts was engaged in such criminal conduct was submitted to the jury, and from verdict and judgment in his favor the plaintiff brings this appeal.

There was testimony below from which the jury would have been amply justified in finding in favor of the plaintiff insurance company on the issue submitted; but the defendant himself was examined as a witness and, if his testimony is believed, he was guilty of no criminal act. No motion for directed verdict was made by the plaintiff, nor was the sufficiency of the evidence to sustain a finding in favor of the defendant challenged in any other way before verdict. After verdict, plaintiff moved for judgment non obstante veredicto and also for a new trial, on the ground that the verdict was contrary to the credible evidence in the case; and exceptions directed to denial of these motions constitute the only points presented by the appeal.

Even if a motion for directed verdict had been made by plaintiff, it is clear that same should have been denied as should also, any motion for judgment non obstante veredicto based thereon * * *.

The motion to set aside the verdict and grant a new trial was a matter of federal procedure, governed by Rule * * * 59 and not subject in any way to the rules of state practice. On such a motion it is the duty of the judge to set aside the verdict and grant a new trial, if he is of opinion that the verdict is against the clear weight of the evidence, or is based upon evidence which is false, or will result in a miscarriage of justice, even though there may be substantial evidence which would prevent the direction of a verdict. The exercise of this power is not in derogation of the right of trial by jury but is one of the historic safeguards of that right. * * * The matter was well put by Mr. Justice Mitchell, speaking for the Supreme Court of Pennsylvania in Smith v. Times Publishing Co., * * * [178 Pa. 481, 36 A. 298], as follows: "The authority of the common pleas in the control and revision of excessive verdicts through the means of new trials was firmly settled in England before the foundation of this colony, and has always existed here without challenge under any of our constitutions. It is a power to examine the whole case on the law and the evidence, with a view to securing a result, not merely legal, but also not manifestly against justice,—a power exercised in pursuance of a sound judicial discretion, *without which the jury system would be a capricious and intolerable tyranny,* which no people could long endure. This court has had occasion more than once recently to say that it was *a power the courts ought to exercise unflinchingly.*" (Italics supplied).

In the same case, Mr. Justice Williams, in a concurring opinion, traces the history of the exercise of this power and sums up his conclusion as follows:

* * *

As early * * * as 1665, the courts at Westminster did precisely what we have done in this case, and for the same reason. The right of trial by jury was not then supposed to give to a successful party the right to insist on an advantage due to the mistake or the willful misconduct of the jury, no matter how grossly unjust and oppressive the result might be; but the supervisory control of the court in banc, sitting as a court of review, was promptly exercised to relieve against the miscarriage of justice. The exercise of this power was then thought to be in aid of trial by jury. * * *

* * *

The distinction between the rules to be followed in granting a new trial and directing a verdict were stated by us with some care in Garrison v. United States, 4 Cir., 62 F.2d 41, 42, * * * as follows: "Where there is substantial evidence in support of plaintiff's case, the judge may not direct a verdict against him, even though he may not believe his evidence or may think that the weight of the evidence is on the other side; for, under the constitutional guaranty of trial by jury, it is for the jury to weigh the evidence and pass upon its credibility. He may, however, set aside a verdict supported by substantial evidence where in his opinion it is contrary to the clear weight of the evidence, or is based upon evidence which is false; for, even though the evidence be sufficient to preclude the direction of a verdict, it is still his duty to exercise his power over the proceedings before him to prevent a miscarriage of justice. * * * "

It is equally well settled, however, that the granting or refusing of a new trial is a matter resting in the sound discretion of the trial judge, and that his action thereon is not reviewable upon appeal, save in the most exceptional circumstances. * * * The rule and the reason therefor is thus stated by Mr. Justice Brandeis in Fairmont Glass Works v. Cub Fork Coal Co., * * * [287 U.S. 474, 53 S.Ct. 254, 77 L.Ed. 439]: "The rule that this Court will not review the action of a federal trial court in granting or denying a motion for a new trial for error of fact has been settled by a long and unbroken line of decisions * * *. The rule precludes likewise a review of such action by a Circuit Court of Appeals. Its early formulation by this Court was influenced by the mandate of the Judiciary Act of 1789, which provided in section 22 that there should be 'no reversal in either (circuit or Supreme) court on such writ of error * * * for any error in fact.' Sometimes the rule has been rested on that part of the Seventh Amendment which provides that 'no fact tried by a jury, shall be otherwise reexamined in any court of the United States than according to the rules of the common law'. More frequently the reason given for the denial of review is that the granting or refusing of a motion for a new trial is a matter within the discretion of the trial court."

While an examination of the record has led us to the conclusion that the trial judge might very properly have granted the motion for new trial, we cannot say that his denial of the motion amounted to an abuse of discretion on his part or that there are present any of the special circumstances which would subject his action to review by this court. The judgment appealed from will accordingly be affirmed.

Affirmed.

Notes and Questions

1. In MARSH v. ILLINOIS CENT. R. CO., 175 F.2d 498, 500 (5th Cir.1949), the district judge had granted judgment notwithstanding the verdict, but had denied an alternative motion for new trial, saying: "It is my judgment that the evidence was insufficient to go to the jury, but if I am wrong in that, then I do not

think a new trial should be granted as there were no other errors of law." The Court of Appeals reversed:

> * * * While it is not our function to weigh the evidence, we do agree with the trial judge's first expressed opinion that the weight of the evidence is "overwhelmingly against the plaintiff". But we do not agree that the grant of a judgment notwithstanding the verdict was therefore justified. There was evidence of the appellant, not very explicit or positive, which if believed might authorize a jury to conclude he was hurt in the manner he claims. Because the trial judge does not believe it, because of appellant's own contradictions and conduct and of opposing evidence which seem to overwhelm it, is not ground for a judgment notwithstanding the verdict, and we must reverse that judgment. * * *

> But it is ground for the trial judge to grant a new trial, though the trial was free of other error. He has in strong terms disapproved the verdict as contrary to the evidence * * *. We have reversed the entering of a final judgment, but it is evident that the new trial ought to be granted and would have been except for the misconception that absence of other error prevented it. The full discretion vested in the trial judge not having been exercised, we will remand the case with direction to the judge to grant a new trial * * * if he continues to think the verdict to be against the overwhelming weight of the evidence.

2. In cases such as Lavender v. Kurn, p. 49, supra, and Denman v. Spain, p. 1048, supra, when there is a lack of proof of what happened rather than a conflict of proof, would the grant of a new trial be any more appropriate than the direction of a verdict? See also McClam v. New York Life Ins. Co., 9 F.Supp. 415, 415–16 (E.D.S.C.1935).

3. In DYER v. MacDOUGALL, 201 F.2d 265, 271 (2d Cir.1952), Judge Frank, concurring, said:

> * * * The well-settled rule is that, in passing on a motion for a directed verdict, the trial judge always must utterly disregard his own views of witnesses' credibility, and therefore of their demeanor; that he believes or disbelieves some of the testimony is irrelevant. When asked to direct a verdict for the defendant, the judge must assume that, if he lets the case go to the jury, the jurymen will believe all evidence—including "demeanor evidence"—favorable to the plaintiff. In other words, the judge must not deprive plaintiff of any advantage that plaintiff might derive from having the jury pass upon the oral testimony. Indeed, the important difference between a trial judge's power on a motion for a new trial and on a motion for a directed verdict is precisely that on a new-trial motion he may base his action on his belief or disbelief in some of the witnesses, while on a directed-verdict motion he may not.

Compare BOWDITCH v. BOSTON, 101 U.S. (11 Otto) 16, 18, 25 L.Ed. 980, 980–81 (1879): "It is now a settled rule in the courts of the United States that whenever, in the trial of a civil case, it is clear that the state of the evidence is such as not to warrant a verdict for a party, and that if such a verdict were rendered the other party would be entitled to a new trial, it is the right and duty of the judge to direct the jury to find according to the views of the court." The *Bowditch* case is but one of many with language of this kind. For an excellent discussion of the standards for granting a directed verdict and a new trial on the weight of the evidence, see the scholarly opinion of Judge (later Justice) Lurton, in Mt. Adams & E.P. Inclined Ry. Co. v. Lowery, 74 Fed. 463 (6th Cir.1896).

4. On the unreviewability of orders denying new trials, see Taylor v. Washington Terminal Co., 133 U.S.App.D.C. 110, 409 F.2d 145, 148 (D.C.Cir.), certiorari denied 396 U.S. 835, 90 S.Ct. 93, 24 L.Ed.2d 85 (1969); Wright, *The Doubtful Omniscience of Appellate Courts,* 41 Minn.L.Rev. 751, 758–63 (1957).

5. Suppose a verdict has been set aside and a new trial granted. If the jury in the second trial returns a verdict similar to the one rendered in the first action, may the court again order a new trial on the ground that the verdict is against the weight of the evidence? Compare Palmer v. Miller, 60 F.Supp. 710 (W.D.Mo.1945) (yes), with Mo.Stat. Ann. § 510.330, which appears in the Supplement following Federal Rule 59. See Friedenthal, Kane & Miller, *Civil Procedure* § 12.4, at 574 (3d ed. 1999): "[A] series of new trial orders in jury cases in which the judge's view of the result does not comport with the jury verdicts would be inappropriate. To order repeated new trials could be an intrusion on the institution of jury trial. The right to jury trial would be meaningless if verdicts could stand only if the judge would reach the same result."

DYER v. HASTINGS, 87 Ohio App. 147, 149–50, 94 N.E.2d 213, 215 (1950):

No judgment may be vacated or set aside and new trial granted upon the ground that the verdict is against the weight of the evidence except as a matter of law; and a judgment will not be vacated or set aside and a new trial granted upon such ground where the verdict is supported by competent, substantial and apparently credible evidence which goes to all the essential elements of the case. * * *

In formulating this rule the word, "substantial," modifying the word, "evidence," is used in the sense of "constituting more than a scintilla of," and the word, "apparently," as used to modify the word "credible," is used to indicate that the court does not undertake to judge the credibility of the evidence, but only to judge whether it has the semblance of credibility.

The evidence in the instant case is in direct and sharp conflict on many essential elements of the case and is such that a verdict for either party would be supported by competent, substantial and apparently credible evidence.

In this situation it was the sole function of the jury to determine the credibility of the evidence, which it did by returning a verdict in favor of the defendant.

IN RE GREEN'S ESTATE, 25 Cal.2d 535, 542–43, 154 P.2d 692, 695–96 (1944):

It is next contended by contestant that the court erred in granting proponent's motion for a new trial on the ground "that the evidence as a whole was insufficient as a matter of law to support a verdict for respondents." The rules of law applicable to an appeal from an order of the trial court granting a motion for a new trial on the ground of the insufficiency of the evidence are well settled and, as stated in one of our most recent decisions, are as follows: " * * * When the motion is granted, as here, for insufficiency of the evidence, it is only in rare cases showing abuse of discretion that an appellate court will interfere because the trial judge must weigh all the evidence and determine the just conclusion to be drawn therefrom. * * * It cannot be held that a trial court has abused its discretion where there is a conflict in the evidence or where there is any evidence which would support a judgment in favor of the moving party." Hames v. Rust, 14 Cal.2d 119, 123, 124, 92 P.2d 1010, 1012 (1939).

* * *

We may not agree with the determination reached by the trial judge or with any of his conclusions. That is not the question before us. It is his duty to weigh the evidence and to pass upon any and all conflicts existing therein. * * * If after such an examination of the evidence he concludes that it is insufficient to support the verdict, his duty is to grant the motion and a reviewing court may not set aside his conclusion unless a showing of abuse of discretion is made out by appellant. * * * As we have seen, if there is any substantial evidence in the case supporting the trial court's action, then we should not interfere with its order granting said motion.

Notes and Questions

1. As for equating the test for directing a verdict to that for setting aside a verdict and granting a new trial, the matter is complicated by the wide range among the tests used in different jurisdictions for setting a verdict aside. * * * [T]he equation is more nearly valid in some jurisdictions than it is in others, but the differences are rather because of variations in the new trial test than because of any variation in the directed verdict test. James, *Sufficiency of the Evidence and Jury–Control Devices Available Before Verdict*, 47 Va.L.Rev. 218, 233–34 (1961).

2. It is difficult to ascertain the standard for granting a new trial in a particular jurisdiction and to compare it with the standard applied in another jurisdiction because of peculiarities regarding the appealability, reviewability, and scope of review of a decision on a motion for a new trial. In many jurisdictions the grant of a new trial may be unappealable because it is not a "final order"; even if appealable, a grant or denial of the motion may not be disturbed on appeal except upon a showing of an abuse of discretion by the trial court, which is rarely found. The result is that the new-trial standard actually is formulated and controlled by trial, not appellate courts; inasmuch as the standard is shaped by courts whose opinions are infrequently reported and therefore will not provide a guideline for other courts, or establish a body of precedent, the standard may vary widely from case to case.

In GREEN v. ACACIA MUTUAL LIFE INSURANCE CO., 156 Ohio St. 1, 100 N.E.2d 211 (1951), the Ohio Supreme Court held unconstitutional the statute under which the Ohio Court of Appeals in Dyer v. Hastings had reviewed the grant of a new trial, because it conferred authority on the Ohio Courts of Appeals to review nonfinal judgments. In AID INVESTMENT & DISCOUNT, INC. v. YOUNKIN, 66 Ohio L.Abs. 514, 118 N.E.2d 183 (App.1951), another court of appeals, reviewing a grant of a new trial, held that by reason of *Green* it could reverse only if it found an abuse of discretion, and, that, although it regarded the trial court's order as erroneous, it could not say it was an abuse of discretion. Do

Green and *Younkin* affect the standard for granting a new trial in Ohio announced in Dyer v. Hastings?

3. In In re Green's Estate, is the California Supreme Court discussing a standard for granting the motion for a new trial or a standard for reviewing the grant of the motion?

A trial judge's decision to grant a new trial is much more likely to be upheld on appeal than a decision to deny a new trial. One reason is that appellate courts recognize that the trial judge is in the best position to have seen errors that may have occurred at trial and to gauge whether those errors may have affected the fairness of the first trial. See Magnani v. Trogi, p. 1084, supra.

4. In a diversity-of-citizenship case in federal court, is the judge bound to apply the standard for new trial that would be applied in the courts of the state in which it sits? Review Gasperini v. Center for Humanities, Inc., p. 411, supra.

5. THE POWER TO GRANT CONDITIONAL AND PARTIAL NEW TRIALS

FISCH v. MANGER

Supreme Court of New Jersey, 1957.
24 N.J. 66, 130 A.2d 815.

JACOBS, J. The plaintiff suffered serious injuries in an automobile accident and, after trial, received a jury verdict in the sum of $3,000. He applied for a new trial because of the inadequacy of the verdict but his application was denied when the defendants consented that the damages awarded to the plaintiff be increased to the sum of $7,500. The plaintiff appealed and we thereafter certified on our own motion.

* * *

The plaintiff's actual expenditures to doctors and nurses and for drugs and hospitalization exceeded $2,200. And although he received most of his normal earnings despite his temporary incapacity, there was a loss of wages approximating $620. While the jury's verdict of $3,000 just about took care of the plaintiff's actual monetary losses, it awarded substantially nothing for his suffering and permanent injuries. Its gross inadequacy was recognized by the trial judge who pointed out that "there was no dispute but that the plaintiff suffered excruciating pain, and was rendered totally helpless for a considerable period of time." On June 28, 1956 the trial judge wrote to the parties advising that unless the defendants filed a consent in writing that the verdict be increased from $3,000 to $7,500, "then the verdict heretofore rendered will be set aside and a new trial granted limited to damages only." The consent was filed by the defendants and on June 30, 1956 a formal order was entered dismissing the plaintiff's motion for a new trial. * * *

The first point which he urges in support of his appeal is that once the trial court had concluded that the damages awarded by the verdict were inadequate it had no legal power whatever to condition the grant of a new trial upon the defendants' failure to consent to a prescribed increase in the verdict. * * * Much has appeared in the law reviews in support of the practices of *remittitur* and *additur* as enlightened aids in securing substantial justice between the parties without the burdensome costs, delays and harass-ments of new trials. See Carlin, *"Remittiturs* and *Additurs,"* 49 W.Va.L.Q. 1 (1942); Note, "Correction of Damage Verdicts by *Remittitur* and *Additur,"* 44 Yale L.J. 318 (1934) * * *. The term *remittitur* is used to describe an order denying the defendant's application for new trial on condition that the plaintiff consent to a specified reduction in the jury's award, whereas the term *additur* is used to describe an order denying the plaintiff's application for a new trial on condition that the defendant consent to a specified increase in the jury's award. While it is now recognized that the two practices are logically and realistically indistinguishable, *remittiturs* have been recognized almost everywhere, whereas *additurs* are still outlawed in some, though by no means all, of the states. * * *

The English precedents prior to the American Revolution are somewhat obscure and they are discussed in the majority and minority opinions in Dimick v. Schiedt, 293 U.S. 474, 55 S.Ct. 296, 302, 79 L.Ed. 603 (1935). There Justice Sutherland, speaking for a majority of five (with Justice Stone, joined by Chief Justice Hughes and Justices Brandeis and Cardozo, dissenting) held that although *remittitur* is permissible in the federal courts, *additur* is prohibited by * * * the Seventh Amendment * * *. In Belt v. Lawes (1884), 12 Q.B. 356, the court sustained the denial of a new trial upon the plaintiff's consent to accept a lesser amount than that awarded by the jury; on appeal, Brett, M.R. not only approved the practice followed below but suggested that the court would also have power "to say that the damages given are too small, but that if the defendant will agree to their being increased to such a sum as may be stated, a new trial shall be refused." * * * In the later case of Watt v. Watt (1905), A.C. 115 the court took an opposite position and rejected the view that a court could condition a denial of a new trial on the plaintiff's acceptance of a reduced verdict. * * * However, Justice Sutherland in the Dimick case did not follow the result in the Watt case and declined to upset the *remittitur* practice, first approved by Justice Story in Blunt v. Little, 3 Fed.Cas.760, No. 1,578 (C.C.Mass.1822), and since reaffirmed in many federal decisions. * * *

In his dissenting opinion in the Dimick case, Justice Stone pointed out that the Seventh Amendment was concerned with substance rather than form and that the Supreme Court had often declined to construe it as perpetuating in changeless form the minutiae of trial practice as it existed in the English courts in 1791; he referred to the many jury procedures unknown to the common law but now well established in federal practice; he considered wholly impersuasive the suggested differentiation between the settled *remittitur* practice which the majority continued and the *additur* practice which it rejected; and he concluded with the following remarks * * *:

> To me it seems an indefensible anachronism for the law to reject the like principle of decision, in reviewing on appeal denials of motions for new trial, where the plaintiff has consented to decrease the judgment or the defendant has consented to increase it by the proper amount, or to apply it in the one case and reject it in the other. It is difficult to see upon what principle the denial of a motion for a new trial, which for centuries has been regarded as so much a matter of discretion that it is not disturbed when its only support may be a bad or inadequate reason, may nevertheless be set aside on appeal when it is supported by a good one:

That the defendant has bound himself to pay an increased amount of damages which the court judicially knows is within the limits of a proper verdict.

The majority opinion in Dimick has been the subject of much criticism and it is doubtful whether the Supreme Court would still subscribe to it;[f] in any event, the Seventh Amendment differs somewhat from our constitutional provision and has no application to proceedings in our state courts. * * * We must look primarily to our own history and precedents in ascertaining whether the highly desirable practices of *remittitur* and *additur* may be adhered to in our State * * *.

The *remittitur* practice has been recognized in New Jersey since early days. * * * [In 1917] the Court of Errors and Appeals had occasion to deal with a negligence case in which the practice of *additur* had been invoked. * * * Chancellor Walker, speaking for the entire court, had this to say ([Gaffney v. Illingsworth,] 90 N.J.L. at page 492, 101 A. at page 243):

> The power of the court in granting a new trial upon the ground that the damages are *excessive*, upon terms that a new trial shall be had unless the plaintiff will accept a certain sum named, less than that awarded by a verdict, is too well established to be questioned. It would seem to follow, by parity of reasoning, that when a new trial is granted because the damages are inadequate, the court may impose like terms, that is, terms to the effect that if the defeated party will pay a certain sum, greater than that awarded by the verdict, the rule will be discharged, subject, doubtless, to the power of an appellate court to vacate any such terms when they appear to be an abuse of discretion. * * *

* * *

Shortly after the adoption of the 1947 Constitution our courts had occasion to deal anew with the practices of *remittitur* and *additur*. In Esposito v. Lazar * * * [2 N.J. 257, 66 A.2d 172 (1949)] the jury returned a verdict for plaintiff in the sum of $1,200; the trial court found the damages inadequate and ordered a new trial limited to damages unless the defendant consented to increasing the award to $3,500. The defendant refused and on retrial the jury awarded $3,000. On appeal, this court, in an opinion by Justice Ackerson, approvingly cited Gaffney v. Illingsworth, supra, and expressly recognized that a trial court has discretionary power to deny a new trial upon the plaintiff's consent to accept a reduced amount or upon the defendant's consent to pay a larger amount. See 2 N.J. at page 259, 66 A.2d at page 173. It held, however, that in the case before it the new trial should not have been limited to damages because the original jury verdict appeared to represent a compromise finding on the issue of liability. * * *

In the light of all of the foregoing, we are satisfied that the practices of *remittitur* and *additur* violate none of our constitutional interdictions and, if fairly invoked, serve the laudable purpose of avoiding a further trial where substantial justice may be attained on the basis of the original trial. * * * Accordingly, we reject the first point urged by the plaintiff and come now to his meritorious contention that, in any event, the prescribed increase to $7,500 was "grossly inadequate and should be set aside." * * * In the instant

---

f. But see Novak v. Gramm, 469 F.2d 430   (8th Cir.1972).

matter, we believe that the trial judge had a mistaken notion of the evidence which led to his prescribing the scanty sum of $7,500. He stated that the plaintiff was not entitled to a "great sum, because he certainly did have a back condition before this accident occurred"; but the evidence in the record points to the view that whatever "back condition" the plaintiff had as a result of the 1950 accident had cleared up and had no relation to the very severe injuries resulting from the 1953 accident. Under these highly special circumstances, we believe that the trial court's action should not be permitted to stand and that the interests of justice will best be served by permitting a second jury to pass on the issue of damages. The separable issue of liability was clearly and properly decided against the defendants; under the evidence it could hardly have been determined otherwise and need not be submitted for redetermination. * * *

Reversed, with direction for a new trial on the issue of damages.

HEHER, J. (concurring in result). * * *

As is shown by Justice Sutherland's analysis of the case history in Dimick v. Schiedt * * *, there was no power in the English courts at the time of the adoption of the New Jersey Constitution of 1776 to increase, either absolutely or conditionally, the damages fixed by a jury in a case such as this. * * *

* * * Justice Sutherland concluded, and with unquestionable authority, that "while there was some practice to the contrary in respect of *decreasing* damages, the established practice and the rule of the common law, as it existed in England at the time of the adoption of the Constitution, forbade the court to *increase* the amount of damages awarded by a jury in actions such as that here under consideration." He observed that "this court in a very special sense is charged with the duty of construing and upholding the Constitution; and in the discharge of that important duty, it ever must be alert to see that a doubtful precedent [involving *remittitur*] be not extended by mere analogy to a different case if the result will be to weaken or subvert what it conceives to be a principle of the fundamental law of the land"; and that "the power to conditionally increase the verdict of a jury does not follow as a necessary corollary from the power to conditionally decrease it," since in the case of a conditional *remittitur* "a jury has already awarded a sum in excess of that fixed by the court as a basis for a *remittitur,* which at least finds some support in the early English practice, while in the second case, no jury has ever passed on the increased amount, and the practice has no precedent according to the rules of the common law."

The "controlling distinction between the power of the court and that of the jury," said Justice Sutherland, "is that the former is the power to determine the law and the latter to determine the facts," and while the *remittitur* practice in the case of an excessive verdict "is not without plausible support in the view that what remains is included in the verdict along with the unlawful excess,—in the sense that it has been found by the jury,—and that the *remittitur* has the effect of merely lopping off an excrescence," yet where an inadequate verdict is increased by the court there is a "bald addition of something which in no sense can be said to be included in the verdict," and if that be done with the consent of the defendant alone, the plaintiff is compelled to forego his "constitutional right to the verdict of a jury and accept 'an assessment partly made by a jury which has acted improperly, and partly by a tribunal which has no power to assess.' "

* * *

There can be no doubt that the *additur* practice sanctioned here contravenes the essence of the common-law right of trial by jury at the time of the adoption of the 1776 Constitution, then and ever since a basic right under the law of England; and this is the very substance of our own constitutional guaranty. * * *

———

POWERS v. ALLSTATE INSURANCE CO., 10 Wis.2d 78, 102 N.W.2d 393 (1960). Plaintiff received a jury award for permanent injuries in the amount of $5,000. The award was excessive and called for a remittitur. The question before the state supreme court was what standard should determine the amount to which the damages should be reduced. The court noted that since its decision in Heimlich v. Tabor, 123 Wis. 565, 102 N.W. 10 (1905), Wisconsin judges had been required to set damages at the lowest amount that a reasonable jury could have awarded. This rule was contrary to the practice in most jurisdictions, in which "the courts follow the practice of allowing the plaintiff the option of avoiding a new trial by remission of the excess above an amount which the court considers reasonable." The court went on to point out that the Wisconsin rule tended to limit the effectiveness of the remittitur practice.

* * * We are firmly of the opinion that if the plaintiff were granted the option of accepting a reasonable amount as determined by the trial or appellate court, instead of the least amount that an unprejudiced jury properly instructed might award, the number of instances in which the plaintiff would be likely to refuse such option and elect a new trial would be greatly reduced.

The court then specifically overruled *Heimlich* and adopted the standard rule.

Notes and Questions

1. Should a trial court have discretion to set a reasonable remittitur figure somewhere between the highest and lowest possible verdicts? Would it make more sense to require, as the alternative to a new trial, the highest amount an unprejudiced jury could properly have awarded plaintiff?

2. Suppose the federal courts had adopted the rule in the *Heimlich* case, which was overruled in *Powers*. Would application of an analogous rule to additur have permitted its use without violation of the Seventh Amendment?

3. In an action under the Federal Employers' Liability Act, 45 U.S.C. § 51, the California Supreme Court held that the trial court could order an additur. Jehl v. Southern Pac. Co., 66 Cal.2d 821, 59 Cal.Rptr. 276, 427 P.2d 988 (1967). In light of *Dimick,* is this holding consistent with Dice v. Akron, Canton & Youngstown R. Co., p. 457, supra?

4. If defendant appeals from a judgment for plaintiff, who has consented to a remittitur, may plaintiff cross-appeal on the ground that the verdict should not

have been reduced? See Jangula v. Klocek, 284 Minn. 477, 170 N.W.2d 587 (1969), 54 Minn.L.Rev. 1096 (1970).

DOUTRE v. NIEC

Michigan Court of Appeals, 1965.
2 Mich.App. 88, 138 N.W.2d 501.

T.G. KAVANAGH, JUDGE. Defendants operate a beauty shop in Flint. On April 19, 1962 plaintiff was given a bleach and color treatment by defendants without a pretreatment patch test. Plaintiff received head and facial injuries as a result of the treatment and sued for damages.

During the trial defendants were not allowed to testify as to the standard of care observed by beauty shops in the Flint area when administering such treatment. The jury awarded plaintiff $10,000. Defendants filed a motion for a new trial. Such motion was granted and a new trial ordered but limited to the question of liability.

Both parties appeal.

The plaintiff alleges error in granting the new trial as to liability on the theory that the court was correct in the first place when he ruled at the trial that the proffered testimony on the standard of care was not admissible. The defendants allege the court erred in limiting the new trial to the issue of liability on the theory that the questions of liability and damages are so closely intertwined that they should be tried together.

As to the plaintiff's claim we find little merit. His objection is based on the theory that the defendants could know of the practices of the trade in Flint only by hearsay. This is not supported by the record.

The record shows that one of the defendants had been in the business for 24 years and the other for 14 years; they had attended conventions of beauticians and observed their practices and said they were abreast of the practices of other beauticians in Genesee County.

We agree with the trial court's last ruling that these witnesses should have been allowed to testify and that to exclude their testimony was error requiring a new trial. Such testimony is admissible because no one is held to a higher standard of care than the average in the industry. * * *

The limitation of the trial to the issue of liability only poses a more difficult problem.

It has long been recognized that the questions of liability and damages are so closely intertwined that they may not usually be separated. The only exception the Michigan Supreme Court has so far recognized is in the case wherein "liability is clear" a retrial of the issue of damage alone may be permitted. * * *

In this case the court reiterated its position that despite the court rule authorizing it (GCR 1963, 527.1), limited new trials are not favored.

No compelling reason moves us to extend the rule.

The trial judge's opinion states: "This ruling (on the evidentiary question) may have materially influenced the jury on the liability issue. It could not, however, by any stretch of the imagination have affected the issue of damages." This bespeaks an assurance we do not share.

In the case before us the damages are not liquidated and the liability was determined pursuant to a trial in which an admitted error touching on liability was committed.

Under these circumstances it seems to us that justice requires that the jury which determines the liability or lack of it should have the responsibility for measuring any damages.

The trial court's order for a new trial shall be extended to all of the issues.

Costs are awarded defendants.

Notes and Questions

1. Compare the dissenting opinion of Judge Freedman in HUTTON v. FISHER, 359 F.2d 913, 920 (3d Cir.1966):

> * * * [A]s a matter of practical justice the damage verdict should not be permitted to stand where the question of liability is to be retried. It is the great and saving virtue of the jury system in accident cases that it permits laymen guided by the courts on questions of law to work out in a worldly way an accommodation between the strict requirements of law and their everyday view of justice. That a defendant therefore suffers disadvantage when a trial is limited to damages and liability is conceded is a fact of life, acknowledged everywhere but in courtrooms. * * * The limitation of a new trial by excluding some of the issues decided is exceptional, and the power to grant a partial new trial must be "exercised with caution." Geffen v. Winer, 100 U.S.App.D.C. 286, 244 F.2d 375, 376 (1957). A retrial of liability will be less than the full relief the defendants are entitled to have, for its effect will be insulated from the damage question into which it ordinarily percolates.

See also Vizzini v. Ford Motor Co., 569 F.2d 754, 760 (3d Cir.1977) (reversing decision to limit new trial to amount of damages).

2. In LARIMER v. PLATTE, 243 Iowa 1167, 53 N.W.2d 262 (1952), in which plaintiff's decedent was killed in a motor-vehicle collision, plaintiff sought damages for wrongful death and defendant counterclaimed for damage to his vehicle and the loss of its use during repair. Based on stipulation of the parties, the court instructed the jury that if it found for defendant on the counterclaim, it must find damages for repairs in the amount of $2205.49. In addition the jury was instructed it could find damages for loss of use not to exceed $600. The jury found for defendant and awarded him $600. Plaintiff's motion for a new trial was overruled on the ground that only defendant was prejudiced by the jury verdict. On appeal the court reversed and granted a new trial on the counterclaim. Plaintiff also requested a new trial on his claim for wrongful death. Should the request have been granted?

3. To what extent should the court, in deciding whether to grant a partial new trial, consider the extra cost to the court and the parties of a new trial on all of the issues?

6. TIMELINESS OF REQUESTS FOR NEW TRIAL

HULSON v. ATCHISON, TOPEKA & SANTA FE RY., 289 F.2d 726 (7th Cir.), certiorari denied 368 U.S. 835, 82 S.Ct. 61, 7 L.Ed.2d 36 (1961). On June 7, 1960, the trial court entered judgment for defendant based on a jury verdict. On June 17, 1960, plaintiffs' attorney orally moved the court for an order extending the time in which to file plaintiffs' motions for a judgment n.o.v. or a new trial. Defendant's attorney was present and made no objection to an extension so long as argument would not interfere with his calendar. Later that day the court granted plaintiffs' counsel a ten-day extension. On June 27, 1960, counsel filed the motion. On July 15, 1960, defendant moved to strike the motion because it had not been filed within the 10–day limits prescribed by Rule 50(b) and Rule 59(b), (d), and (e). The motion to strike was granted and plaintiffs' motion for relief under Rule 60(b) was denied. The trial judge stated that if he had had the power to do so, he would have granted the motion for a new trial. The appeals court affirmed, stating as follows:

> Under Rule 6(b) the trial court "may not extend the time for taking any action under rules * * * 50(b), * * * 59(b)[and others] * * *. If the motion for a new trial is untimely, the trial court has no choice but to deny the motion. * * *

> Plaintiffs candidly admit that they were mistaken in understanding the requirements of the rules, but urge that counsel for all parties and the trial judge in good faith believed at the time that granting the extension of time was proper and permissible under the rules. Ignorance of the rules resulting in an agreement for an unauthorized extension of time cannot serve to furnish grounds for relief under Rule 60(b), under the facts before us in this appeal.

Notes and Questions

1. Under Federal Rule 7(b) a motion in the federal courts normally must be in writing and state the grounds on which it is based. Suppose a party files a timely motion for new trial but fails to specify a ground upon which he intends to rely. May he amend his motion subsequent to the ten–day period? Although there is some authority to the contrary, a large majority of cases have held "no." See 12 *Moore's Federal Practice* ¶ 59.16[2] (3d ed.).

2. Rule 59(d) provides that a court may order a new trial on its own initiative, but again, there is a ten–day limit. Suppose a party files a timely motion but fails to include as a ground an error that the court believes should result in a new trial. May the court order a new trial on such a ground subsequent to the ten–day period? Prior to the 1966 amendment to Federal Rule 59(d) the answer was generally held to be "no." The amendment, adding what is now the second sentence of that Rule, was designed specifically to give the trial courts such power. See Steinberg v. Indemnity Ins. Co., 36 F.R.D. 253 (E.D.La.1964). As a practical matter doesn't this amendment take the sting out of the rule that a party cannot amend a motion once the ten–day period has elapsed?

3. Prior to a 1995 amendment, Rule 59(b) provided only that a motion for new trial had to be *served* within ten days. It was unclear just when the motion had to be *filed*. To clear up the confusion Rule 59(b) was altered to provide that the motion had to be filed rather than served within the ten–day period. Time of service is covered by Rules 6(d) and (e), which relate the required time for service to the time that a hearing on a motion has been set and permit the court within its discretion to alter the usual required time for service.

7. THE POWER TO SET ASIDE A JUDGMENT ON GROUNDS DIS-COVERED AFTER IT WAS RENDERED

———

Read Federal Rule of Civil Procedure 60 in the Supplement.

———

a. *Mistake and Excusable Neglect*

BRIONES v. RIVIERA HOTEL & CASINO, 116 F.3d 379 (9th Cir.1997). Plaintiff sued his former employer for unlawful discharge. Defendant filed a motion to dismiss to which plaintiff, who was acting pro se, failed to respond. The court thus granted the motion. Plaintiff moved for relief under Federal Rule 60(b)(1) on the ground that the court never informed him that his case might be dismissed and on the basis the plaintiff failed to notify his translator and typist of the deadline for filing his opposition to the motion to dismiss. The trial court denied the Rule 60(b) motion. At that time case law had seemed to establish as a *per se* rule that a motion under Rule 60(b) could not be utilized to cure a failure to comply with court rules. See, e.g., Hulson v. Atchison, Topeka & Santa Fe Ry., p. 1107, supra. However the appeals court noted the Supreme Court's decision in Pioneer Inv. Servs. Co. v. Brunswick Associates Ltd. Partnership, 507 U.S. 380, 113 S.Ct. 1489, 123 L.Ed.2d 74 (1993), that analyzed the term "excusable neglect" in a number of different contexts, including Rule 60(b). Although the Supreme Court was dealing with a case under the Bankruptcy Act, it referred directly to Rules 6(b) and 60(b) as follows:

> Although inadvertence, ignorance of the rules, or mistakes construing the rules do not usually constitute "excusable" neglect, it is clear the "excusable neglect" under Rule 6(b) is a somewhat "elastic concept" and is not limited strictly to omissions caused by circumstances beyond the control of the movant. * * * [A]t least for purposes of Rule 60(b), "excusable neglect" is understood to encompass situations in which the failure to comply with a filing deadline is attributable to negligence.

The Supreme Court listed four factors to be considered in deciding if neglect was "excusable" in the bankruptcy case: (1) the danger of prejudice to the opposing party, (2) the length of the delay and its potential impact on the judicial proceedings, (3) the reason for the delay, and (4) whether the moving party acted in good faith.

In view of the *Pioneer* opinion, the *Briones* court remanded the case to the trial court to determine whether or not plaintiff's negligence was "excusable" under all the circumstances.

Notes and Questions

1. Even with a more flexible approach to the use of Rule 60(b)(1), cases in which negligence is held to be excusable are likely to be quite rare. Nearly all of the cases in which relief has been granted involve situations in which a party was

prevented from obtaining any trial whatsoever, such as a default judgment, see Rooks v. American Brass Co., 263 F.2d 166 (6th Cir.1959) (defendant's illness prevented a proper defense), an erroneous stipulation by counsel that resulted in a summary judgment against the client, see Griffin v. Kennedy, 344 F.2d 198 (D.C.Cir.1965), or a dismissal for failure of plaintiff to prosecute the action, see Leong v. Railroad Transfer Serv., Inc., 302 F.2d 555 (7th Cir.1962). Should the Rule specifically be limited to such matters of default? That the courts generally disfavor default judgments and readily set them aside is abundantly clear. In such cases it is often said that the errors of counsel should not be attributed to clients. See, e.g., Mieszkowski v. Norville, 61 Ill.App.2d 289, 209 N.E.2d 358 (2d Dist. 1965).

2. The proper scope of Rule 60(b)(6) has been the subject of considerable litigation. It frequently has been stated that the Rule must have been intended to cover only matters outside the scope of Rules 60(b)(1)–(5). E.g., Pioneer Inv. Servs. Co. v. Brunswick Associates Ltd. Partnership, 507 U.S. 380, 393–94, 113 S.Ct. 1489, 123 L.Ed.2d 74 (1993); Costa v. Chapkines, 316 F.2d 541 (2d Cir.1963); Federal Deposit Ins. Corp. v. Alker, 30 F.R.D. 527, 532 (E.D.Pa.1962), affirmed 316 F.2d 236 (3d Cir.), certiorari denied 375 U.S. 880, 84 S.Ct. 150, 11 L.Ed.2d 111 (1963). Otherwise the specific time limits on motions under Rules 60(b)(1), (2), and (3) would be meaningless. But it is the existence of these very limits that have pressured courts, in the interests of justice, to find that errors ostensibly falling within Rules 60(b)(1), (2), or (3) are somehow so special that they come within Rule 60(b)(6) and hence are not subject to a specific time limitation. Can a strained interpretation of Rule 60(b) be justified by the fact that otherwise few if any cases would fall within Rule 60(b)(6)? See United States v. Karahalias, 205 F.2d 331, 333 (2d Cir.1953). For a comprehensive analysis of Rule 60(b)(6), see Kane, *Relief from Federal Judgments: A Morass Unrelieved by a Rule,* 30 Hastings L.J. 41 (1978).

Note that although Rule 60(b)(6) (as well as Rules 60(b)(4) and (5)) has no specific time limitation, the motion still must be made within a reasonable time. Is a motion under Rules 60(b)(1), (2), or (3) always timely as long as it is filed within the one-year period? See Di Vito v. Fidelity & Deposit Co., 361 F.2d 936, 939 (7th Cir.1966) (failure to move within four and one-half months from discovery of fraud held to bar relief); Schildhaus v. Moe, 335 F.2d 529, 531 (2d Cir.1964) (motion filed within 8 months held untimely).

b. *Newly Discovered Evidence; Fraud*

PATRICK v. SEDWICK, 413 P.2d 169 (Alaska 1966). Plaintiff brought an action for medical malpractice, alleging permanent physical injuries. The case was tried in October 1961 without a jury. In February 1962, the trial judge rendered findings on the issues of liability. These findings were subject to a lengthy appeal and it was not until more than two years later that the appellate court directed the trial court to enter findings for plaintiff on all issues of liability and to proceed to determine damages. The trial judge fixed the amount of damages on the basis of the evidence that had been presented at the trial and entered judgment on January 12, 1965. On January 22, 1965, defendant moved for a new trial on the ground that in 1963 a Dr. Robert Lewy had devised a new treatment that would ameliorate plaintiff's injuries and therefore should reduce his damages. The trial court denied the motion. The judge rejected the significance of the new treatment since there was no assurance that any improvement it might bring would be permanent.

The appellate court affirmed the denial of a new trial with the following explanation:

> * * * [A] motion for new trial on the grounds of newly discovered evidence must meet the following requirements before it [can] be granted:
>
> (1) must be such as would probably change the result on a new trial; (2) must have been discovered since the trial; (3) must be of such a nature that it could not have been discovered before trial by due diligence; (4) must be material; (5) must not be merely cumulative or impeaching.
>
> In addition to the foregoing requirements, it is established that for any evidence to come within the category of "newly discovered" such evidence must relate to facts which were in existence at the time of the trial. * * *
>
> We hold, under the authorities referred to, that the trial court did not abuse its discretion in denying appellee's motion for a new trial on the grounds of newly discovered evidence. It is clear from the record that Dr. Lewy's discovery of the Teflon technique did not occur until a considerable period of time had elapsed after the case was tried in October 1961. Thus, the Lewy technique was not in existence at the time the trial took place and under the above authorities would not qualify as newly discovered evidence.

Id. at 177.

Notes and Questions

1.   In SWIFT AGRICULTURAL CHEMICAL CORP. v. USAMEX FERTILIZ-ERS, INC., 27 Fed.R.Serv.2d 930 (E.D.La.1979), the trial court originally held for plaintiff in a patent-infringement suit regarding the manufacture of a chemical compound. The basic issue was the time in which a key reaction took place. It initially appeared that the reaction time for both plaintiff's and defendant's processes was less than one second. Subsequently, defendant moved for relief under Rule 60(b)(2), claiming that new methods of measurement, developed after the judgment was rendered, showed that defendant's process had a far greater reaction time than that of plaintiff's process and hence there was no infringement. Plaintiff argued that relief was unavailable because the evidence had not been in existence at the time of trial. The court rejected this position on the ground that the reaction time had been in existence and only the means of measuring it had not. Does this decision make any sense? Can it be reconciled with Patrick v. Sedwick?

2.   Suppose plaintiff obtains damages based on testimony that her injuries will prevent her from bearing children. Shortly thereafter plaintiff becomes pregnant and delivers a normal, healthy child. Should the trial court grant a motion by defendant to reopen the case? Cf. Anshutz v. Louisville Ry. Co., 152 Ky. 741, 154 S.W. 13 (1913). See generally Annot., 31 A.L.R.2d 1236 (1953).

3.   To what extent, if any, should Rule 60(b) permit a case to be reopened for consideration of a change in the applicable law? In TITLE v. UNITED STATES, 263 F.2d 28, 31 (9th Cir.), certiorari denied 359 U.S. 989, 79 S.Ct. 1118, 3 L.Ed.2d 978 (1959), appellant sought to set aside a judgment of denaturalization on the ground that some two years thereafter the United States Supreme Court, in a

different case, interpreted the immigration act in such a way as to demonstrate that the original decision in *Title* was erroneous. Appellant relied on Rules 60(b)(4) and (5). The trial court denied the motions and the Court of Appeals affirmed: "Rule 60(b) was not intended to provide relief for error on the part of the court or to afford a substitute for appeal. * * * Nor is a change in the judicial view of applicable law after a final judgment sufficient basis for vacating such judgment entered before announcement of the change." See also Carlson v. Hyundai Motor Co., 222 F.3d 1044 (8th Cir.2000). Assume that the change in the law is announced after the trial court has rendered judgment but before the time for appeal has run? Should it be open to a party to seek relief under Rule 60(b) in that case?

What does Rule 60(b)(5) mean when it allows relief from a judgment when "a prior judgment upon which it is based has been reversed or otherwise vacated"? See Jackson v. Jackson, 276 F.2d 501 (D.C.Cir.), certiorari denied 364 U.S. 849, 81 S.Ct. 94, 5 L.Ed.2d 73 (1960).

————

SMITH v. GREAT LAKES AIRLINES, INC., 242 Cal.App.2d 23, 51 Cal.Rptr. 1 (2d Dist.1966). The airline originally brought an action for breach of contract against Smith, the current plaintiff. The airline claimed that it had purchased a plane from Smith; that Smith promised to turn over documents showing that the plane had been overhauled pursuant to the regulations of the Civil Aeronautics Administration; that Smith failed to produce the necessary documents; and that, as a result, the airline was required by the Administration to make a major overhaul. At trial, an official of the agency testified that the required major overhaul had been completed. As a result, the airline was awarded substantial damages.

This action was instituted by Smith to set aside the original decision on the ground of fraud. Smith contended that in fact a major overhaul was neither required nor made. Allegedly, the government official who testified had conspired with the airline to perjure himself. Smith had not challenged the substance of this testimony at the trial, but had relied on the official status of the witness.

The trial judge sustained a demurrer to Smith's complaint and Smith appealed. The appellate court affirmed on the ground that the fraud alleged was "intrinsic," and that an action can be set aside only on the basis of "extrinsic" fraud. Extrinsic fraud was defined as that which prevents a litigant from making a claim or defense, for example, when one party fraudulently induces the opposing party not to file suit until the statute of limitations has become a bar. On the other hand, intrinsic fraud was said to be that which the trial itself is designed to discover, that is, which witnesses are lying. The court held that Smith should have been ready to meet all the issues in the case, and could not set the decision aside because he had not been prepared.

Notes and Questions

1. The current attitude in the federal courts is demonstrated by the opinion in PEACOCK RECORDS, INC. v. CHECKER RECORDS, INC., 365 F.2d 145, 147

(7th Cir.1966), certiorari denied 385 U.S. 1003, 87 S.Ct. 707, 17 L.Ed.2d 542 (1967), in which the court reversed as an abuse of discretion a denial of a Rule 60(b) motion:

> * * * We hold that where it appears that perjured testimony may have played some part in influencing the court to render a judgment, the perjury will not be *weighed,* on a motion to set aside the judgment. This seems self evident. * * * [If the judgment was obtained in part by the use of perjury] then it was clearly the duty of the district court to set aside the judgment, because poison had permeated the fountain of justice.

2. In BROWN v. PENNSYLVANIA R. CO., 282 F.2d 522 (3d Cir.1960), certiorari denied 365 U.S. 818, 81 S.Ct. 690, 5 L.Ed.2d 696 (1961), plaintiff brought suit under the Federal Employers' Liability Act against the railroad, his employer. Plaintiff's doctor testified that plaintiff's condition was such as to make it increasingly difficult if not impossible for him to work in the future. Defendant's medical witnesses testified that plaintiff had fully recovered from any injuries received in the accident. A verdict was rendered for plaintiff, but in an amount less than had been sought. Shortly after the trial, defendant discharged plaintiff, relying on the testimony given by plaintiff's doctor at the trial. Plaintiff moved for a new trial on damages under Rule 60(b)(3). The motion was denied and the appellate court affirmed. Is the decision sound? Is it consistent with the *Peacock Records* case? Compare Rozier v. Ford Motor Co., 573 F.2d 1332 (5th Cir.1978).

3. Note that Rule 60(b) distinguishes between fraud perpetrated by one party on an opponent and fraud on the court. What is the reason for the distinction? What effect does it have? In HAZEL–ATLAS GLASS CO. v. HART-FORD–EMPIRE CO., 322 U.S. 238, 245–46, 64 S.Ct. 997, 1001, 88 L.Ed. 1250, 1255–56 (1944), plaintiff brought an action in the Court of Appeals to set aside a judgment rendered against it some nine years earlier. The first action had turned on the validity of a patent held by defendant. Both the issuance of that patent by the Patent Office and the determination of its validity by the federal Court of Appeals in the prior action had been affected by an article offered by defendant, ostensibly written by a disinterested expert, but actually prepared by defendant's own officials, to the effect that the machine under patent was a "revolutionary device." One of the attorneys who presented defendant's case in the first action also had participated in the scheme to prepare and publish the fraudulent article. The Court of Appeals refused to set aside the judgment; the Supreme Court reversed:

> Every element of the fraud here disclosed demands the exercise of the historic power of equity to set aside fraudulently begotten judgments. This is not simply a case of a judgment obtained with the aid of a witness who, on the basis of after-discovered evidence, is believed possibly to have been guilty of perjury. Here, even if we consider nothing but Hartford's sworn admissions, we find a deliberately planned and carefully executed scheme to defraud not only the Patent Office but the Circuit Court of Appeals. * * *

> The Circuit Court did not hold that Hartford's fraud fell short of that which prompts equitable intervention, but thought Hazel had not exercised proper diligence in uncovering the fraud and that this should stand in the way of its obtaining relief. We cannot easily understand how, under the admitted facts, Hazel should have been expected to do more than it did to uncover the fraud. But even if Hazel did not exercise the highest degree of diligence, Hartford's fraud cannot be condoned for that reason alone. This matter does

not concern only private parties. There are issues of great moment to the public in a patent suit. * * * Furthermore, tampering with the administration of justice in the manner indisputably shown here involves far more than an injury to a single litigant. It is a wrong against the institutions set up to protect and safeguard the public, institutions in which fraud cannot complacently be tolerated consistently with the good order of society. Surely it cannot be that preservation of the integrity of the judicial process must always wait upon the diligence of litigants. The public welfare demands that the agencies of public justice be not so impotent that they must always be mute and helpless victims of deception and fraud.

Does *Hazel-Atlas* stand for the proposition that a court on its own motion may set aside a judgment obtained by fraud on the court? Was it proper for the Court to find that there had been a fraud on the lower court? See Toscano v. Commissioner, 441 F.2d 930 (9th Cir.1971); Hawkins v. Lindsley, 327 F.2d 356, 359 (2d Cir.1964); Lockwood v. Bowles, 46 F.R.D. 625, 632 (D.D.C.1969). If so, wouldn't ordinary perjury also qualify? Should the notion of fraud on the court apply only to situations such as bribery or corruption of a member of the court or jury?

4. Many jurisdictions, including the federal courts under Rule 60(b), permit an independent action in equity to set aside a judgment, which is discussed after these Notes. As seen in Smith v. Great Lakes Airlines, Inc., fraud is one of the substantive grounds upon which relief may be granted in such an action. Can the distinction between extrinsic and intrinsic fraud be justified when the judgment is attacked collaterally in a separate action as opposed to being attacked directly under a Rule 60(b) type motion? See Maschhoff v. International Union, UAW, 23 Fed.R.Serv.2d 1204 (E.D.Mich.1977) (only extrinsic fraud justifies relief in independent action). Did the acts of the defendants in the *Hazel-Atlas* case, Note 3, supra, qualify as extrinsic fraud? The majority did not discuss the issue; Justice Roberts, in a dissenting opinion, stated that the fraud was extrinsic. 322 U.S. at 261 n. 18, 64 S.Ct. at 1009 n. 18, 88 L.Ed. at 1264 n. 18.

Suppose that instead of putting forth false information, a party merely conceals facts of which she has direct knowledge that would have a definite bearing on the outcome of the case. Does this constitute fraud? If so, is it extrinsic? See Buice v. T. & B. Builders, Inc., 219 Ga. 259, 132 S.E.2d 784 (1963); Jennings v. Bridgeford, 218 Tenn. 287, 403 S.W.2d 289 (1966).

c. The Independent Action to Obtain Relief from a Prior Judgment

1. Federal Rule 60(b) expressly preserves the right of the trial court to entertain an independent action to relieve a party from a prior judgment. What conceivable justification is there for retaining this procedure? Shouldn't Rules 60(b)(1)–(6) be read to cover all possible grounds? Can an independent action be anything more than a method of avoiding the time limits set out in Rule 60(b)? See CAPUTO v. GLOBE INDEM. CO., 41 F.R.D. 239 (E.D.Pa. 1966), in which the court held that the denial of relief under Rule 60(b)(1) because the motion was filed more than a year after judgment did not bar an independent action to set the judgment aside on the same grounds that had been alleged on the motion. Compare LOCKLIN v. SWITZER BROTHERS, INC., 335 F.2d 331 (7th Cir.1964), certiorari denied 379 U.S. 962, 85 S.Ct. 652, 13 L.Ed.2d 557 (1965), in which plaintiff filed a separate action in the Northern District of Illinois to set aside a judgment rendered in a federal

court in California. Previously, plaintiff had made a timely but unsuccessful motion in the latter court under Rule 60(b) to set aside its judgment, advancing the same grounds subsequently alleged in the independent action. The Seventh Circuit affirmed a denial of relief on the ground that the prior decision under Rule 60(b) barred relief in an independent action by way of res judicata. It rejected an argument based on California state decisions that a denial of a post-trial motion should not bar a later independent action to set aside the judgment on the same grounds.

2. In the *Locklin* case the independent action was brought in a jurisdiction other than the one in which the judgment was rendered and the court accepted the case, although it denied relief. Is there any argument that would justify refusal by the second court to accept jurisdiction? See LAPIN v. SHULTON, INC., 333 F.2d 169 (9th Cir.), certiorari denied 379 U.S. 904, 85 S.Ct. 193, 13 L.Ed.2d 177 (1964), which "remanded" the parties for relief to the court issuing the initial judgment. Compare Bankers Mortgage Co. v. United States, 423 F.2d 73 (5th Cir.), certiorari denied 399 U.S. 927, 90 S.Ct. 2242, 26 L.Ed.2d 793 (1970). There is ancillary jurisdiction over an independent action brought in the court that entered the initial judgment. Crosby v. Mills, 413 F.2d 1273 (10th Cir.1969).

3. Suppose a party brings an action in a federal court, based on diversity-of-citizenship jurisdiction, to set aside a judgment rendered in a state court. If the state itself would provide a means of challenging the judgment, should the federal court refuse to hear the case? If the federal court does hear the case, what law should it apply in determining whether relief is appropriate?

Chapter 15

SECURING AND ENFORCING JUDGMENTS

The commencement of a lawsuit or, for that matter, even the entry of a judgment, does not necessarily mean that plaintiff actually will secure the objectives of the action. A victorious plaintiff's ability to collect a judgment depends primarily on defendant's capacity and willingness to pay at the time the award is made and secondarily on the effectiveness of the court's judgment-enforcement procedures in the event the judgment debtor is capable of paying but is being recalcitrant. For example, plaintiff's efforts may be frustrated if defendant has become insolvent during the litigation or has secreted his assets or fraudulently conveyed them to third persons. In short, the arduous litigation process often proves to be a preliminary to the equally protracted travail of collecting the award.

The attempts to enforce a libel judgment against a New York Congressman, the late Adam Clayton Powell, illustrate some of the problems that often face a judgment creditor. In the case of Powell, the creditor was Mrs. Ethel James whose efforts to claim her due are a study in the breakdown of the enforcement process. Mrs. James originally was awarded a $46,000 libel judgment in April, 1963 and that judgment was affirmed by the New York Court of Appeals in July, 1964. Employing a number of tactics, including transfers of property to relatives and invocations of congressional immunity from arrest and process, Powell avoided collection for 32 months. His maneuvers frustrated Mrs. James' attempts to discover Powell's assets in New York and Puerto Rico and resulted in her bringing suit against the Congressman again, basing her claim on the little used common-law tort of evasion of a judgment. After Powell failed to appear for examination in the second suit, his answer was stricken and compensatory damages were set at $75,000 and punitive damages were assessed at $500,000. These were reduced to $56,000 and $100,000 respectively in James v. Powell, 26 A.D.2d 525, 270 N.Y.S.2d 789 (1st Dep't 1966). Pursuit of Powell continued into 1967, but so did his appeals and in early March, 1967, the New York Court of Appeals reversed the verdict in the evasion-of-judgment suit because Puerto Rican law should have been applied to the compensatory-damage claim and New York law, which governed the remainder of the claim, apparently did not permit punitive damages under the circumstances of the case. 19 N.Y.2d 249, 279 N.Y.S.2d 10, 225 N.E.2d 741 (1967). Thus, Mrs. James was left with the original libel judgment and a cause of action under Puerto Rican law. See "No Home in the House," *Time,* March 10, 1967.

At one point Powell was paying off Mrs. James' libel judgment through the proceeds from a long-playing album, "Keep the Faith, Baby," part of which was recorded live at his Caribbean island retreat on Bimini. Mrs. James, apparently disillusioned by the entire episode, decided there must be a better way to make a living than collecting judgments. She followed Powell's example and recorded an album of her own. Fittingly, in some eyes at least, one number on that album exclaims:

> There was once a man
> who said that he
> Would like to retire to Bimini,
> But that was before he
> broke the law,
> And now the people are going
> haw-haw-haw.

Who had the last laugh is not clear, but it certainly was not the courts. Other reports of the pursuit of the Congressman include "Hooking a Catfish," *Newsweek,* December 27, 1965; "Man May Come and Man May Go (But Powell Goes on Forever)," *National Review,* June 29, 1965; and "Monstrous Mackerel," *Time,* December 24, 1965.

SECTION A. METHODS OF SECURING THE JUDGMENT—PROVISIONAL REMEDIES

Most states attempt to maximize a plaintiff's chances for collecting the judgment ultimately secured by providing a series of security devices that operate during the action. These so-called "provisional" remedies primarily are creatures of statute and their character and effectiveness vary considerably from state to state. Thus, in a creditor-oriented state, it is not surprising to find that provisional remedies generally are available in almost all actions, whereas in a debtor-oriented jurisdiction they will be restricted to particular types of actions and be subjected to a variety of procedural restrictions. By virtue of Federal Rule 64, a federal court may use the provisional remedies available to the courts of the state in which it is sitting to the extent the state remedies are not inconsistent with any other federal rule or statute.

Articles 60 through 65 of New York's Civil Practice Law and Rules provide a claimant with the remedies of attachment and garnishment of property and debts, injunction, receivership, and notice of pendency.[a] Since New York's provisional-remedies scheme is one of the most fully developed systems in the United States, the description that follows will use it as a model. For a general discussion of provisional remedies, see Millar, *Civil Procedure of the Trial Court in Historical Perspective* 481–515 (1952). Federal practice is described in 11A Wright, Miller & Kane, *Federal Practice and Procedure: Civil 2d* §§ 2931–36, 2941–62 (1995); 12 Wright, Miller & Marcus, *Federal Practice and Procedure: Civil 2d* §§ 2981–86 (1997). On the practice

---

    a. In 1979, New York repealed N.Y.C.P.L.R. Article 61, which had provided for the provisional remedy of civil arrest.

in particular states, see, e.g., 7 & 7A Weinstein, Korn & Miller, *New York Civil Practice* ¶ ¶ 6001.01–6515.07; Brewer, *Illuminating a Gray Area: Prejudgment Attachment in Arkansas After Springdale Farms Inc. v. McIlroy Bank & Trust,* 38 Ark.L.Rev. 881 (1985).

Although the need to provide creditors with expeditious remedies against recalcitrant debtors seems clear, there is no doubt that from time to time some of the provisional remedies have been used as a bludgeon to collect money that occasionally was not actually due plaintiff. In a series of cases that began in 1969 with Sniadach v. Family Finance Corp., p. 237, supra, the United States Supreme Court has significantly modified the availability of pretrial "provisional" remedies. The Court's decisions have been based on the theory that any interference with the property of a defendant prior to an adjudication of the merits of plaintiff's claim is an unconstitutional invasion of defendant's rights, unless certain procedural safeguards are provided. See generally Countryman, *The Bill of Rights and the Bill Collector,* 15 Ariz. L.Rev. 521 (1973). The state courts have been prompted by the Supreme Court's decisions to construe the scope of provisional remedies narrowly, and to be especially wary of ex parte procedures. Accordingly, in considering the material that follows, the reader must constantly be aware of these dramatic shifts in judicial thinking about provisional remedies.

1. ATTACHMENT

The use of attachment for securing jurisdiction in rem or quasi-in-rem when the court cannot acquire jurisdiction over the person of the defendant was examined in Chapter Two. Reread the cases and notes on pp. 150–67, supra. Attachment also is valuable as a provisional remedy because it prevents defendant from selling or otherwise disposing of any real or personal property that has been taken into the custody of the attaching officer. Since attachment deprives defendant of the use and enjoyment of property long before liability is established (and, of course, in many cases no liability will be found), most jurisdictions limit its availability to certain classes of actions. Further limitations on the remedy's availability have resulted from restrictive judicial construction of attachment statutes. See, e.g., Vershbow v. Reiner, 231 Cal.App.3d 879, 282 Cal.Rptr. 684 (2d Dist.1991). How can the remedy of attachment be harmonized with our traditional notion that plaintiff's right to relief depends upon his establishment of the elements of his claim?

The procedure for invoking the remedy of prejudgment garnishment has been significantly affected by the Supreme Court's decision in SNIADACH v. FAMILY FINANCE CORP., p. 237, supra, which held the Wisconsin prejudgment garnishment procedure unconstitutional. Under it, a summons issued at the request of the creditor's lawyer who served the garnishee to freeze the debtor's wages during the period before trial of the main suit without the wage earner having any opportunity to be heard. Initially, the effect of *Sniadach* on other provisional remedies was unclear. However, in FUENTES v. SHEVIN, p. 228, supra, the Court held unconstitutional state statutes providing for the replevin of chattels without a prior opportunity to be heard. State courts applying *Sniadach* also have invalidated prejudgment garnishment of accounts receivable without notice and a statute permitting a prejudgment writ of immediate possession by a landlord pending a hearing on the merits. See generally Clark & Landers, *Sniadach, Fuentes and Beyond: The Creditor Meets the Constitution,* 59 Va.L.Rev. 355 (1973); Note, *Procedural Due Process—The Prior Hearing Rule and the Demise of Ex Parte Remedies,* 53 B.U.L.Rev. 41 (1973).

Uncertainty about the requirements of due process surfaced again after the Court in MITCHELL v. W.T. GRANT CO., p. 238, supra, upheld the Louisiana sequestration statute permitting the creditor to obtain the writ on ex parte application without giving the debtor either notice or a prior opportunity for a hearing. The Court reasoned that the risk of a wrongful taking was minimized by the creditor's interest in the property prior to the lawsuit, the judicial authorization of the writ, and the immediate availability of a post-seizure hearing.

Then, in NORTH GEORGIA FINISHING, INC. v. DI-CHEM, INC., p. 240, supra, the Court relied on *Fuentes* to invalidate the Georgia garnishment statute, which permitted the writ to be issued on the basis of conclusory allegations by the plaintiff without providing the defendant with an opportunity for an "early" hearing "or other safeguard against mistaken repossession." The opinion for the Court stressed the need for statutes to guard against the risk of initial error resulting in irreparable injury to the defendant even when the debt arises in a commercial context between parties of equal bargaining power, two corporations in this case.

Most recently, in CONNECTICUT v. DOEHR, p. 242, supra, the Court invalidated a Connecticut statute pursuant to which a judge could allow the prejudgment attachment of real estate, without prior notice or hearing, merely upon the plaintiff's assertion under oath that there is probable cause to sustain the validity of his claims. The Court indicated that there must be either a preattachment hearing, a showing of some exigent circumstance, or both, before an order of attachment may issue. Four Justices stated that, in their view, due process also requires the plaintiff to post a bond or some other security.

As you proceed through this Chapter, consider whether the various remedies discussed are valid in light of these Supreme Court cases. See generally Alderman, *Default Judgments and Prejudgment Remedies Meet the Constitution: Effectuating Sniadach and Its Progeny,* 65 Geo.L.J. 1 (1976).

New York's attachment statute, N.Y.C.P.L.R. 6201, permits prejudgment attachment (1) when the defendant is a nondomiciliary residing outside the state or an unlicensed foreign corporation, (2) when the defendant is within the state but diligent efforts to personally serve her have failed, or (3) when the defendant's conduct in connection with the property indicates her intent to defraud creditors or frustrate the enforcement of a potentially unfavorable judgment. In contrast to the New York approach, some states provide that attachment is available in all contract actions, whether against residents or nonresidents, and in any action against a nonresident. What is the logic behind the distinction between the treatment accorded residents and nonresidents? See British Int'l Ins. Co. Ltd. v. Seguros La Republica, S.A., 212 F.3d 138, 141–44 (2d Cir.2000).

All nonexempt tangible and intangible property in which defendant has a recognizable interest is subject to attachment for purposes of securing the enforcement of the prospective judgment. New York permits the attachment of income, whether already earned or to be earned in the future, claims under insurance policies, bank accounts, and assignable choses in action and judgments. Certain property is exempt from attachment in order to permit defendant to maintain his standard of living during the pendency of the action. The elaborate, and somewhat archaic, New York exemptions are set out in N.Y.C.P.L.R. 5205–06. See also pp. 1127–34, infra.

When property of or a debt owed to defendant is in the hands of a third person, that person (the garnishee) may be prohibited from selling, assigning, or interfering with any property in which defendant has an interest or from paying or discharging any debt except as directed by the sheriff or a court order. The garnishee also may be ordered to turn the property or proceeds of the debt over to the court at the conclusion of the action for application to the final judgment.

Even if the statutory requirements for attachment are met and even if plaintiff is willing to post a bond to protect defendant, the court still has discretion to deny the remedy if it believes that the harm to defendant outweighs the risk that plaintiff's judgment will be unenforceable. Thus when the value of the property sought to be attached is significantly greater than defendant's potential liability or when the property is part of an ongoing business, the remedy may be denied. See Interpetrol Bermuda Ltd. v. Trinidad & Tobago Oil Co., 135 Misc.2d 160, 167–69, 513 N.Y.S.2d 598, 603–05 (Sup.Ct.1987).

The mechanics of attachment are relatively simple. A writ of attachment is directed to the appropriate law-enforcement officer, usually the sheriff, who serves the writ on defendant and seizes property equal in value to the amount set forth in the writ. The attachment remains in force for a limited period— usually until the action is concluded or for a fixed period long enough to permit the final determination of plaintiff's claim. In cases of hardship or special circumstances, the court may alter the length of time the attachment remains in force. For further information on the remedy of attachment, see Kheel, *New York's Amended Attachment Statute: A Prejudgment Remedy in Need of Further Revision,* 44 Brooklyn L.Rev. 199 (1978); Comment, *Abuse of Process and Attachment: Toward a Balance of Power,* 30 U.C.L.A.L.Rev. 1218 (1983).

2. PRELIMINARY INJUNCTIONS AND TEMPORARY RESTRAINING ORDERS

A preliminary injunction is available when defendant is acting or threatening to act in a manner that would irreparably injure plaintiff or render the judgment in the action ineffectual. Since a preliminary injunction is granted before there has been a trial on the merits and it often has the same effect as the ultimate relief requested by plaintiff, it may have an extremely adverse impact on defendant; as a result, the courts use preliminary injunctions only in the most appealing and necessary circumstances. Rule 65(c) requires that before an injunction may issue, a bond must be posted under which the defendant may recover if a court later determines that he was "wrongfully enjoined." Moreover, because of the "extraordinary" character of the remedy, the moving party traditionally has been required to show that none of the less drastic provisional remedies provides an adequate alternative. For example, in

CRAMOND v. AFL–CIO, 267 Minn. 229, 126 N.W.2d 252 (1964), plaintiff sought equitable relief and damages to correct his wrongful removal from office in a labor union. The court required plaintiff to demonstrate that there was no alternative to a preliminary injunction and that final relief would be ineffective unless a temporary injunction was issued against a scheduled election. According to the court, the grant or denial of a preliminary injunction depends upon a balancing of the relative harm to each party. See also Los Angeles Memorial Coliseum Comm'n v. National Football League, 634 F.2d 1197 (9th Cir.1980). Is this balancing technique objectionable because it amounts to a trial on the merits and thus is wasteful of judicial time? Are there ways of avoiding this duplication? See Federal Rule 65(a). See generally 11A Wright, Miller & Kane, *Federal Practice and Procedure: Civil 2d* §§ 2947–50 (1995); Leubsdorf, *The Standard for Preliminary Injunctions,* 91 Harv.L.Rev. 525 (1978).

When plaintiff believes that immediate relief is essential, most states will entertain an application for a temporary restraining order (TRO), which will issue upon a showing that irreparable harm will occur absent the order. Unlike the preliminary injunction, an application for a restraining order usually is made ex parte, since time considerations do not permit the giving of formal notice. Because of a concern over the potential unfairness of ex parte proceedings, a number of special conditions, such as those set out in Federal Rule 65(b), usually are imposed when notice is not given to all parties. See 11A Wright, Miller & Kane, *Federal Practice and Procedure: Civil 2d* §§ 2951–53 (1995). When an injunction may infringe on fundamental rights guaranteed by the Constitution, issuance of the injunction may be contingent on notice. Carroll v. President & Commissioners of Princess Anne, 393 U.S. 175, 89 S.Ct. 347, 21 L.Ed.2d 325 (1968). Are temporary restraining orders consistent with the *Sniadach* requirements of notice and an opportunity to defend? To what extent does the imposition of special conditions such as those described in Rule 65(b) satisfy due process considerations? A temporary restraining order generally will remain effective only for a relatively brief period or until a hearing is held on plaintiff's request for a preliminary injunction. See generally Note, *Duration of Temporary Restraining Orders in Federal Courts,* 12 U.Balt.L.Rev. 276 (1983).

Despite the judicial hesitancy in issuing preliminary injunctions and temporary restraining orders, these remedies are among the most useful weapons in the procedural arsenal. Injunctions are extremely flexible and can be molded to restrain or compel the performance of a wide variety of acts. Because the primary purpose of these orders is to preserve the status quo pending a full hearing on the merits, they usually will be negative or prohibitory in character and restrain defendant from acting in a particular fashion. On the other hand, when property must be maintained or a course of conduct continued in order to preserve the status quo or prevent irreparable injury, the court will grant a request that defendant undertake or continue certain activities or honor a given standard of care. Such an order generally is referred to as mandatory or affirmative. A classic discussion of mandatory injunctions appears in then-Judge William Howard Taft's opinion in TOLE-DO, A.A. & N.M. RY. v. PENNSYLVANIA CO., 54 Fed. 730, 741 (C.C.N.D.Ohio), appeal dismissed 150 U.S. 393, 14 S.Ct. 123, 37 L.Ed. 1120 (1893):

The office of a preliminary injunction is to preserve the status quo until, upon final hearing, the court may grant full relief. Generally this can be accomplished by an injunction prohibitory in form, but it sometimes happens that the status quo is a condition not of rest, but of action, and the condition of rest is exactly what will inflict the irreparable injury upon complainant, which he appeals to a court of equity to protect him from. In such a case courts of equity issue mandatory writs before the case is heard on its merits. * * *

In addition to the requirement that defendant's conduct violate plaintiff's rights and tend to render the ultimate judgment ineffectual, the act to be restrained must affect the subject matter of the action. Thus, a preliminary injunction or temporary restraining order relating to defendant's conduct is unavailable in an ordinary tort or contract action for money damages, since money is not considered the "subject" of the action. The objective of the action must be the preservation or a change in the status of property or a right. See generally Eastern Rock Products, Inc. v. Natanson, 239 App.Div. 529, 269 N.Y.S. 435 (3d Dep't 1933). Further, the equitable remedy of a preliminary injunction is unavailable when the plaintiff's claim is essentially a claim at law. See Rosen v. Cascade International, 21 F.3d 1520, 1527–29 (11th Cir.1994) (overturning district court's grant of preliminary injunction freezing defendant's assets in securities fraud case since plaintiff's action was one at law). As to the notion that defendant must be endangering the effectiveness of the final judgment, see, e.g., Maine Product Co. v. Alexander, 115 App.Div. 109, 112, 100 N.Y.S. 709, 711 (1st Dep't 1906) (two cases).

Even if a preliminary injunction is warranted, the court may not have the power to issue it. In GRUPO MEXICANO DE DESARROLLO, S.A. v. ALLIANCE BOND FUND, INC., 527 U.S. 308, 119 S.Ct. 1961, 144 L.Ed.2d 319 (1999), a divided Supreme Court held that a district court had exceeded its authority when it entered a preliminary injunction freezing defendants' use of their assets pending adjudication of plaintiff's right to a lien. Writing for the majority, Justice Scalia concluded that an injunction was beyond the equitable powers conferred on federal courts by the Judiciary Act of 1789. According to Justice Scalia, the Court's holding followed the "well-established general rule that a judgment establishing the debt was necessary before a court of equity would interfere with the debtor's use of his property." Id. at 319, 119 S.Ct. at 1968, 144 L.Ed.2d at 332. Would a preliminary injunction be a greater or lesser interference with the debtor's property than an attachment?

Even if plaintiff demonstrates a need for a preliminary injunction or temporary restraining order, the court may choose not to grant it. The court's discretion will be exercised in light of the same principles of equity that influence a judicial determination as to whether a permanent injunction should issue. These factors include the availability of an adequate legal remedy, the difficulties of administering and enforcing the order, whether the injunction will prove effective, the possibility of irreparable harm, and whether the applicant has "unclean hands" or is guilty of laches. See Comment, *Formulating a Theory for Preliminary Injunctions: American Hospital Supply Corp. v. Hospital Products, Ltd.,* 72 Iowa L.Rev. 1157 (1987); Rendleman, *Inadequate Remedy at Law Prerequisite for an Injunction,* 33 U.Fla.L.Rev. 346

(1981); Laycock, *Injunctions and the Irreparable Injury Rule,* 57 Texas L.Rev. 1065 (1979).

Preliminary injunctions and temporary restraining orders usually bind only the parties to the action, their agents and servants, and anyone acting in collusion with or for the benefit of a party. In determining who is bound by the order, a great deal of caution is exercised to insure that anyone affected by the injunction has had a day in court and that the freedom of individual action and the right to voice personal opinions are not impaired simply because that person is a member of a group or unincorporated organization that has been enjoined by the court. Many courts inquire into the association's control over its members as an aid in determining whether or not individual members should be bound by an order issued against the group. See generally Rendleman, *Beyond Contempt: Obligors to Injunctions,* 53 Texas L.Rev. 873 (1975).

A problem that presents a particularly difficult question is whether a preliminary injunction or temporary restraining order should be used to prohibit parties from commencing or continuing an action in another court or from enforcing a judgment issued by another court. The problem becomes bound up with questions of jurisdiction and conflict of laws when a state court is asked to enjoin the parties from proceeding in an action pending in another state or in a federal court. For an illustration, see MERRITT–CHAPMAN & SCOTT CORP. v. MUTUAL BENEFIT LIFE INS. CO., 237 App.Div. 70, 73, 260 N.Y.S. 374, 378 (1st Dep't 1932), in which the court said it would not interfere with an action in another court "unless it has a clear priority of jurisdiction, or exceptional circumstances are shown to exist which require such drastic remedy." See McClintock, *Equity* § 37 (2d ed. 1948); 7A Weinstein, Korn & Miller, *New York Civil Practice* ¶ 6301.27. What factors are relevant to the question whether a federal court should enjoin parties from proceeding in a state court? See Younger v. Harris, 401 U.S. 37, 91 S.Ct. 746, 27 L.Ed.2d 669 (1971); Huffman v. Pursue, Ltd., 420 U.S. 592, 95 S.Ct. 1200, 43 L.Ed.2d 482 (1975); Pennzoil Co. v. Texaco, Inc., 481 U.S. 1, 107 S.Ct. 1519, 95 L.Ed.2d 1 (1987). For an historical survey of the issue, see Moore, *Conflict of Jurisdiction,* 23 La.L.Rev. 29 (1962). Are the considerations different when a state-court order purports to direct the parties not to proceed in a federal court? See Donovan v. City of Dallas, 377 U.S. 408, 84 S.Ct. 1579, 12 L.Ed.2d 409 (1964). Could a federal court enjoin a foreign defendant from prosecuting a similar action in a foreign country? See Kaepa, Inc. v. Achilles Corp., 76 F.3d 624 (5th Cir.1996). See generally 17 & 17A Wright, Miller & Cooper, *Federal Practice and Procedure: Jurisdiction and Related Matters 2d* §§ 4211–12, 4221–26, 4251–55 (1988).

3. RECEIVERSHIP

Because the remedy originated in equity and therefore can be characterized as "extraordinary," a number of courts refuse to appoint a receiver to act as a custodian or manager of disputed property pendente lite whenever the movant is shown to have an adequate remedy at law or an alternative remedy. See, e.g., State ex rel. Larry C. Iverson, Inc. v. District Court, 146 Mont. 362, 406 P.2d 828 (1965). Even today, however, this hesitancy is both understandable and appropriate since in many instances the remedy will deprive defendant of the control and enjoyment of property without a hearing on the merits or will subject him to the high cost of a receivership. Courts sometimes may prefer receivership when the alternative is the potentially more draconian and expensive remedy of civil arrest. See First National State Bank v. Kron, 190 N.J.Super. 510, 464 A.2d 1146 (App.Div.), certification denied 95 N.J. 204, 470 A.2d 424 (1983).

Defendant's actual or potential insolvency is the primary reason for the appointment of a receiver. Another appropriate use of the remedy is to preserve property pending litigation when there is a substantial danger that the property will be removed from the state, lost, materially injured, or destroyed. See, e.g., Cafadaris v. Bulow, 138 Misc. 301, 244 N.Y.S. 600 (Sup.Ct.1930) (receiver appointed when immigration visa of person in possession of property about to expire). See also Gunther v. Gunther, 283 S.W.2d 826 (Tex.Civ.App.1955) (court stated that receivership may be used when it is incidental to an injunction or *lis pendens*).

In most states, only plaintiff can secure the appointment of a receiver and the receivership extends only to property actually involved in the litigation. New York, however, gives its courts the power to appoint a receiver upon the motion of any person having an "apparent interest" in the property. N.Y.C.P.L.R. 6401. What possible justification is there for such a provision? New York practice also requires any person who moves for the appointment of a receiver to be joined as a party, thereby permitting the movant to protect her interest in the property in the previously commenced action; of course, this practice occasionally may prove burdensome to the person seeking the appointment of the receiver. See 7A Weinstein, Korn & Miller, *New York Civil Practice* ¶ 6401.14. Doesn't this unnecessarily complicate and proliferate the litigation?

A temporary receiver must be disinterested and owes primary allegiance to the appointing court and not to the parties or the person who sought the appointment. Because of this status, virtually all of a receiver's official acts are subject to the approval of the appointing court. When the debtor requests the appointment of a receiver, the court will look to see whether the debtor is manipulating the receivership to hinder and delay recovery by the creditors. See Shapiro v. Wilgus, 287 U.S. 348, 53 S.Ct. 142, 77 L.Ed. 355 (1932).

A temporary receiver's powers are found in the statute or rule authorizing the appointment or in the court order naming the receiver. He usually is required to take possession of the property as soon as possible after the appointing order has been entered. In VANDER VORSTE v. NORTHWESTERN NAT. BANK, 81 S.D. 566, 138 N.W.2d 411 (1965), the basic obligation of a receiver is described as the duty of preserving and protecting the property and assets of the estate that have been placed in protective custody. Although the receiver is not given title to the property, he generally is given the responsibility of managing or disposing of the property and the power to take any action necessary to maintain or improve it. See, e.g., Knickerbocker Fed. Sav. & Loan Ass'n v. 531 E. 144th St., Inc., 39 Misc.2d 23, 240 N.Y.S.2d 112 (Sup.Ct.1963).

In order to prevent dereliction in the performance of his duties, a temporary receiver normally is required to execute and file an undertaking before any official duties are initiated. The undertaking protects the integrity of the court and the litigants by guaranteeing that injuries caused by any defalcation by the receiver can be indemnified.

The appointment of receivers in the federal courts is governed by Federal Rule 66. Section 959(b) of Title 28 of the United States Code defines the receiver's substantive rights, duties, and liabilities. See 12 Wright, Miller & Marcus, *Federal Practice and Procedure: Civil 2d* §§ 2981–86 (1997), for a discussion of federal receivers.

4. CIVIL ARREST

The provisional remedy of civil arrest had its genesis in the common-law practice of commencing an action by taking into custody and imprisoning defendant until judgment was rendered or bail was posted. Although incarceration effectively prevented defendant from rendering the potential judgment unenforceable, its Draconian quality made it a frequent source of abuse. The debtor's prison strikingly portrayed by Charles Dickens in the *Pickwick Papers* illustrates the unpleasant consequences of the remedy. Consequently, courts and legislatures have sharply restricted the availability of civil arrest in most jurisdictions. For an historical discussion of the development and use of civil arrest, see Freedman, *Imprisonment for Debt,* 2 Temple L.Q. 330 (1928). See also Morris & Wiener, *Civil Arrest: A Medieval Anachronism,* 43 Brooklyn L.Rev. 383 (1976).

The availability of civil arrest varies widely from state to state. Some state constitutions (Mississippi Const., Art. III, § 30 and Texas Const., Art. 1, § 18) prohibit imprisonment for debt and thus render civil arrest unavailable; a number of states simply have not enacted legislation authorizing civil arrest, although their constitutions would not prohibit use of the remedy. Other states allow civil arrest only in limited types of actions, such as those based on fraud, deceit, or conversion and those in which injunctive relief is sought.[b]

Even when civil arrest has been authorized by statute, certain public policy exemptions generally limit its application. For example, some courts have exempted all public servants from civil arrest. States granting immunity from service of process to nonresident witnesses also generally extend that immunity to cover civil arrest.

A motion for civil arrest is addressed to the court's discretion, which, in view of the severity of the remedy, is exercised with a great degree of caution. This is exemplified by the following statement from SUMMERS v. DISTRICT COURT, 68 Nev. 99, 108, 227 P.2d 201, 205 (1951):

The legislative authorization of such a remedy based upon probability is an extraordinary grant of power to the courts and carries with it extraordinary judicial responsibilities. The extensive discretion so granted as-

b. Civil arrest is available in many states in actions involving extremely violent or cruel batteries and other "malicious torts." See generally Shatz v. Paul, 7 Ill.App.2d 223, 129 N.E.2d 348 (1st Dist.1955), which contains an excellent historical discussion of the use of arrest. Traditionally, women have been exempted from civil arrest in many states. In 1976, New York modified its statute by deleting the word "women" and substituting the language "parent, guardian or other person * * * whose principal responsibility is * * * the daily care and supervision of [a child under sixteen or an incompetent of any age] * * *." After further restricting the availability of civil arrest, the 1978 amendment eliminated the exemption altogether. N.Y.C.P.L.R. 6101. New York abolished the remedy of civil arrest in 1979.

sumes the highest of judicial wisdom and, accordingly, demands the highest degree of consideration in its exercise.

Furthermore, plaintiff usually must file an "undertaking" guaranteeing the payment of any legal costs and damages that defendant may sustain if the arrest proves to have been wrongful. The undertaking protects defendant and insures that those thinking about invoking the remedy will "look before they leap."

An arrested defendant will be released if bail is posted in an amount designated by the court; the bail then serves as security for any judgment plaintiff ultimately may recover. Bail usually is set high enough to cover the prospective judgment, although the court will avoid setting bail at a figure that makes it impossible for defendant to secure his release. See People v. Tweed, 5 Hun 382 (App.Div.), appeal dismissed 63 N.Y. 202 (1875). But for a grievous example of the possible consequences of civil arrest, see In re Harris, 69 Cal.2d 486, 72 Cal.Rptr. 340, 446 P.2d 148 (1968). Since *Harris,* California has severely restricted the use of civil arrest. See Cal.Civ.Proc. Code § 501 (1995) (noting persons may not be imprisoned in a civil action, whether before or after judgment, with a possible exception if one violates a court order).

5. NOTICE OF PENDENCY

Although not strictly a provisional remedy, the notice of pendency is included in this discussion because of its similarity to the four provisional remedies already described. The genesis of the notice of pendency is found in the common-law doctrine of *lis pendens,* which sought to guarantee the effectiveness of a judgment in an action involving specific tangible property by charging any purchaser or encumbrancer of the property with knowledge that an action involving it had been instituted. Thus, at common law a prospective purchaser or encumbrancer not only had to check all of the conveyance records to be certain of the vendor's good title but also had to investigate whether the vendor was involved in any pending litigation that might affect the property—often a practical impossibility. Today, this burdensome aspect of the *lis pendens* doctrine generally has been restricted by statute. See White, *Lis Pendens in the District of Columbia: A Need for Codification,* 35 Cath. U.L.Rev. 703 (1987). See, e.g., Picerne v. Redd, 72 R.I. 4, 47 A.2d 906 (1946). For a history of the common-law procedure, see Bennett, *Lis Pendens* (1887).

The statutory notice of pendency is designed to protect prospective purchasers and encumbrancers by requiring plaintiff to file a notice of the litigation before the protection of constructive notice can be claimed. Thus, if plaintiff fails to file a notice of pendency and properly index it, he will not be protected against a purchaser or encumbrancer who does not have actual knowledge of the litigation involving the property. In some states, such as New York, notice-of-pendency statutes apply only to real property, which may mean that the harsher *lis pendens* doctrine is still applicable to actions involving personalty. More likely, the common-law practice has been eliminated by negative implication.

Statutory notice of pendency differs from other provisional remedies because it usually does not involve judicial discretion; the right to file a notice is absolute in any litigation falling within the classes enumerated in the notice-of-pendency statute. The only question on which the court must exercise its judgment usually is whether the action affects real property. Obviously, however, the court's power over this issue can be used to restrict or contract the availability of the remedy considerably. See the discussion in Braunston v. Anchorage Woods, Inc., 10 N.Y.2d 302, 222 N.Y.S.2d 316, 178 N.E.2d 717 (1961). Why shouldn't the courts be able to handle notice-of-pendency applications on a discretionary basis?

How can the *lis pendens* procedure be justified in light of the cases discussed pp. 1118–19, supra, which invalidated statutes providing for the attachment of a defendant's property without probable cause or a hearing? Is it significant that the notice of pendency does not deprive anyone of the use or enjoyment of property, but merely gives notice to third parties of the pendency of litigation? Compare Kukanskis v. Griffith, 180 Conn. 501, 430 A.2d 21 (1980) (finding Connecticut's *lis pendens* statute violative of due process requirements because it failed to provide for a hearing), with Chrysler Corp. v. Fedders Corp., 670 F.2d 1316 (3d Cir.1982) (upholding New Jersey's *lis pendens* statute).

6. A POSTSCRIPT

Despite their obvious practical importance to the proper functioning of a judicial system, little effort has been devoted to the rationalization of provisional remedies and their integration into the total procedural picture. Indeed many practitioners are ill-informed as to the availability and operation of provisional remedies in their jurisdiction and often miss an opportunity to protect their clients against debilitating and frustrating post-judgment enforcement procedures. What better evidence of the second-class treatment accorded the subject of provisional remedies is there than the cavalier incorporation of state provisional-remedy practice by Federal Rule 64 and the reference to federal receivership practice "heretofore followed" in Rule 66? With the goals and the structure of federal procedure as a background, see if you can formulate a comprehensive provisional-remedies rule for the federal courts; make certain that it will be consistent with contemporary notions of due process as set forth in the United States Supreme Court cases described on pages 1118–19, supra. In what ways are the availability or unavailability of post-judgment enforcement techniques relevant to framing a provisional-remedies rule? Reconsider this question after studying the remaining materials in this Chapter.

SECTION B. METHODS OF COLLECTING AND ENFORCING THE JUDGMENT

1. EXECUTION

GRIGGS v. MILLER

Supreme Court of Missouri, 1963.
374 S.W.2d 119.

WALTER H. BOHLING, SPECIAL COMMISSIONER. Bill Griggs, on January 19, 1961, sued W. A. Brookshire in ejectment for the possession of a 322 acre farm in Boone County, Missouri, and for damages for withholding possession.

Plaintiff had purchased the farm for $20,600 on January 16, 1961, at a public sale under a general execution against defendant. * * * Defendant's answer was a general denial, and his counterclaim sought to set aside the sheriff's execution sale and deed. * * * The cause was considered and treated by the parties and the court "as one of 'equitable cognizance.' " The court found the issues for the plaintiff and against the defendant on plaintiff's petition; for the plaintiff and the third-party defendant [the sheriff] on defendant's counterclaim; and that plaintiff was entitled to $2,483.24 damages by reason of defendant's withholding of possession of said farm from January 18, 1961, to November 15, 1961, the date of said judgment and decree, and that plaintiff recover $250 per month from and after November 15, 1961, for so long as defendant withheld possession from plaintiff. Defendant Brookshire, after filing his notice of appeal, was incarcerated in the Missouri Penitentiary. * * * Miller was appointed trustee of the Estate of W. A. Brookshire, and substituted as a party litigant for said Brookshire.

* * *

Ray Crouch recovered a judgment against W. A. Brookshire, defendant, in the Circuit Court of Henry County, Missouri, on July 15, 1959, for $1,966.69. Said judgment was affirmed on December 5, 1960 * * *. The right to an execution follows immediately upon the rendition of a judgment. * * * No supersedeas bond was given to stay an execution. * * * A general execution was issued on said judgment to the Sheriff of Boone County on December 10, 1960. The Sheriff levied on defendant's 322 acre farm December 14, 1960, filed a notice of his levy in the office of the Recorder of Deeds of Boone County, and advertised and sold said real estate at public sale on January 16, 1961.

Dorothy Contestible, Administratrix of the Estate of Ralph Burton Collings, Deceased, recovered a judgment of $17,000 against William Albert Brookshire, defendant, in a wrongful death action in the Circuit Court of Audrain County, Missouri, on July 29, 1960. A general execution issued on said $17,000 judgment to the Sheriff of Boone County on December 23, 1960. This execution was mailed to Mrs. Contestible's attorneys in Columbia and was delivered to Sheriff Powell January 10, 1961. He levied upon defendant's 322 acres under said execution on January 11, 1961.

Defendant contends it was error to sell his 322 acre farm without attempting to make the judgment debt, interest and costs out of a portion of said farm.

* * * [A] judgment debtor is to be afforded reasonable protection in levying on and selling his property under execution. Civil Rule 76.21 (§ 513.095) provides in effect that if a judgment debtor gives the officer a list of his property sufficient to satisfy the execution, "the officer shall levy upon the property and, no other, if in his opinion it is sufficient; if not, then upon such additional property as shall be sufficient."

Civil Rule 76.24 (§ 513.210) provides: "When an execution shall be levied upon real estate, the officer levying the same shall divide such property, if susceptible of division, and sell so much thereof as will be sufficient to satisfy such execution, unless the debtor in the execution shall desire the whole of any tract or lot of land to be sold together, in which case it shall be sold accordingly."

And Rule 76.25 (§ 513.100) provides: "The person whose goods, chattels and real estate are taken in execution may elect what part thereof shall be first sold; and if he shall deliver to the officer having charge thereof a statement, in writing, of such election, three days before the day appointed for the sale, stating specifically what goods, chattels and real estate he desires to be first sold, and so on, until the execution be satisfied, the officer shall proceed according to such election, until sufficient money shall be made to satisfy the amount in the execution specified and costs."

It is stated in 21 Am.Jur., Execution, § 380, that an execution is not "leviable upon all the debtor's property, but only upon sufficient property owned by the debtor within the jurisdiction to satisfy the debt, interest, and costs"; and, while the officer is left to his own judgment, he "must exercise the care and discretion which a reasonably prudent man would exercise under like conditions and circumstances." And, with respect to the property to be sold when more than enough to satisfy the debt is seized, it is stated in § 384: "The general rule is that the execution officer may make a division of the property, if that is practicable, and sell only so much of it as is necessary to satisfy the debt." * * * A failure to divide real estate and sell only enough to satisfy the execution [has been] considered an abuse of discretion * * * and a constructive fraud * * *.

* * *

Defendant wrote Sheriff Powell under date of January 11, 1961, re the Crouch judgment, levy and sale, stating, among other things, that his land was worth in excess of $100 an acre; and: "I am restricting the amount which you can sell to the northeast 40 acres of said tract of land. This land is clear. There is no mortgage or encumbrance of any kind against it."

Defendant protested the execution sale to those assembled for the sale and stated in effect that the judgment involved had been obtained in Henry County and the case was on appeal and the judgment was not final; that: "After the judgment becomes final it will be paid"; that Crouch had in his possession cattle belonging to defendant worth $10,000 against which there was no lien; that "I have notified the sheriff that this farm is clear of any mortgages whatsoever; that it is worth approximately $50,000.00; that one forty acre sold would be more than adequate. I have pointed out the forty acres * * * to be sold"; that he was certain the $17,000 judgment against him in the Contestible case would be reversed; that a supersedeas bond would be given; that this sale would be illegal and whoever bought the farm would buy a law suit. (The Contestible judgment, however, was affirmed January 8, 1962, in Contestible v. Brookshire, Mo., 355 S.W.2d 36.)

Sheriff Powell, who had been sheriff for about twenty years, admitted 40 acres of defendant's farm "might have been" worth far in excess of $2,000. Asked why he had not told defendant the 40 acres would not be sufficient, he would take 80 acres, Sheriff Powell answered: "I didn't intend to take 80 acres." He testified he had levied on and held three or four execution sales of defendant's 322 acre farm. He stated he did not know it was illegal to sell $50,000 worth of property to satisfy a $2,000 judgment; and there was testimony he had levied on the 322 acres to collect a $13.00 judgment, and to collect a $600 judgment. He stated "I checked the record and there was several thousand dollars" against all of the farm, and that is why "I levied on all of it." He also stated "I never checked the records." He did not levy on personal property because "It was much easier to do it this way." He knew defendant had stocks in various corporations and had more than 200 head of Hereford cattle on the farm; that they might have sold for at least $200 a head on the market and as registered cattle would have brought more, and that 20 head of the cattle "might have" been sufficient to more than pay the Crouch judgment, interest and costs.

Ray Crouch, the judgment creditor, testified he wanted to and asked his attorney to levy on defendant's farm, and that he knew defendant had collateral * * * to take care of the Crouch judgment. Sheriff Powell testified that Crouch had told him defendant had deposited sufficient collateral with the Hartford Insurance Company to take care of the Crouch judgment.

* * *

A sheriff conducting an execution sale is the agent of the property owner and the judgment creditor, and his duty is to protect the interests of both and to see that the property is not sacrificed. * * * Forced sales of property usually do not bring full value.

Sheriff Powell's advertisement of the sale of defendant's 322 acre farm was to "sell all of said real estate or as much thereof as *it* be necessary to pay the judgment of $1,966.69," in the Henry County Circuit Court, which, with interest and costs, amounted to $2,308.16 on the day of sale.

Defendant's farm was never advertised for sale under the Audrain County (Contestible) execution. Defendant first knew of the levy on his farm under the $17,000 Audrain County judgment about 30 minutes before its sale under the Crouch judgment. Sheriff Powell testified that he sold under the Henry County, and not under the Audrain County, execution.

Defendant's 322 acres was not divided for the purpose of selling but was sold as a whole to plaintiff for $20,600.00. The only bidders were Ed Orr, one of the attorneys for Mrs. Contestible, and Ralph Alexander, a bondsman and attorney for the sheriff. Plaintiff Griggs testified he heard the farm would bring enough to satisfy the two judgments about 15 or 20 minutes before the sale; that about 5 or 10 minutes before it was sold he decided to buy it because "it didn't bring any more than it did," and that he asked Mr. Alexander to bid for him. * * *

It is not questioned but that this 322 acre farm, consisting of approximately eight forties, could have been offered for sale in parcels. Rule 76.24 (§ 513.210) contemplates that the officer "divide such property, if susceptible of division, and sell so much thereof as will be sufficient to satisfy such execution." This was not done, and we hold that it should have been so divided. In Brookshire v. Powell, Mo., 335 S.W.2d 176, 181, the disparity between the market value of this farm and a bid of $2,300 was considered so great as to require setting aside that execution sale and sheriff's deed. In the case at bar the Henry County judgment, interest and costs amounted to $2,308.16; and for that amount under said execution and the constructive levy of the Audrain County execution, but without an advertisement for sale under

Rule 76.36, supra, under said Audrain County execution, it is sought to justify this forced sale for $20,600 of property valued at about $46,000. This record calls for the result reached in Brookshire v. Powell * * *.

Defendant is entitled to relief upon doing equity. * * * Accordingly, if defendant will, within thirty days, deposit in this court, for the use and benefit of those entitled thereto, the sum of $20,600 with interest at the rate of 6% per annum from the date of sale until the same is paid, the decree appealed from will be reversed and the cause remanded with directions to cancel the sheriff's sale and the sheriff's deed to plaintiff made pursuant thereto; otherwise the decree will stand affirmed. In either event the costs are assessed against the estate of defendant Brookshire.

PER CURIAM. The foregoing opinion by BOHLING, Special Commissioner, is adopted as the opinion of the court.

All of the Judges concur.

[The court's opinion on a motion to modify and for a rehearing and the court's supplemental opinion are omitted.]

Notes and Questions

1. Execution is the traditional method of enforcing a money judgment. It applies to both personal and real property. In contemplating the effectiveness of the device, consider the following questions. What is the territorial reach of an execution? In what order should various types of property be levied upon and sold by the officer to whom the execution is delivered? How are priorities determined as between competing executions? Use of the execution in particular situations and the interrelationship between execution and other judgment-enforcement devices are discussed in Heiserman, *Procedures Available for Implementation of a Judgment in Iowa,* 42 Iowa L.Rev. 265 (1957); Walker, *The Collection of Debts From Insolvent and Fully–Mortgaged Debtors,* 43 Tenn.L.Rev. 399 (1976). For further information, see Woodward, *Collecting Money Judgments: Priorities and Procedure,* in 9 Eisenberg, *Debtor-Creditor Law,* ch. 37 (1988).

2. Federal Rule 69 provides that the procedures of the state in which the federal court is sitting are to be followed in enforcing federal-court judgments. By way of exception to the use of state practice, Rule 69 provides that "any statute of the United States governs to the extent that it is applicable." For a discussion of whether a federal statute preempts state practice, see In re Davis, 170 F.3d 475 (5th Cir.) certiorari denied 528 U.S. 822, 120 S.Ct. 67, 145 L.Ed.2d 57 (1999). It has been held that the federal court retains jurisdiction to enforce its own judgments even if the applicable state law seems to require that proceedings to enforce judgments be brought in a specified state court. See Duchek v. Jacobi, 646 F.2d 415 (9th Cir.1981). A judgment creditor who wishes to examine the judgment debtor or any other person as to the debtor's assets may proceed under either state supplementary-proceeding practice or under the Federal Rules relating to depositions and discovery. See generally 12 Wright, Miller & Marcus, *Federal Practice and Procedure: Civil 2d* §§ 3011–15 (1997).

3. One form of execution used to attach intangible property is garnishment. The most common subject is wages, although bank accounts also may be garnished. State law generally exempts part of the judgment debtor's income and real and personal property from enforcement procedures such as execution and garnishment. See generally Abrahams & Feldman, *The Exemption of Wages from*

Garnishment: Some Comparisons and Comments, 3 De Paul L.Rev. 153 (1954). The percentage of income exempted from execution varies from little or nothing to a high of ninety percent. What accounts for this disparity? An excellent critique of garnishment appears in Brunn, *Wage Garnishment in California: A Study and Recommendations*, 53 Calif.L.Rev. 1214 (1965). After an analysis of the existing garnishment pattern, the author concludes:

> The time when a family had few, if any, debts except perhaps a home purchase mortgage may be remembered nostalgically, but it has passed. The years following the end of World War II saw the development of what might be called the American way of debt. * * * Consumer credit has become a major industry and consumer debt consumes a major slice of many a family's income. * * *

> Individual debt, not so long ago discouraged and regarded with suspicion, is now encouraged. * * *

> Even with sales managers named Jesse James, one may grant that the contribution of consumer credit to the economy and to the standard of living of many families is substantial. But when personal debt is no longer unusual, no longer a sign of improvidence, when debt has instead become a mass production, hard-sell item that citizens are widely encouraged to "buy," one may doubt the continued appropriateness of a device such as wage garnishment. * * * Today this harsh remedy, humiliating at best, disastrous to the debtor and his family at worst, seems far less justifiable than in an age when personal debt was uncommon and disfavored. It is time that our attitude toward wage garnishment—which is, after all, a drastic form of intervention by government on behalf of creditors—caught up with our attitude toward debt.

* * *

> Collection agencies find wage garnishment a useful tool, not only because of the debtor's earnings actually reached by levies, but because the threat of garnishment encourages the debtor to make payments. Whether one views this effect as persuasive or coercive depends to some extent on one's point of view. In any event, the encouragement is due to the debtor's fear that he will lose his job if there are more garnishments. The fear is real. Discharges because of repeated wage levies are not uncommon. Employers dislike the added work and expense brought by levies and often limit the number of levies they will permit without discharge. Labor organizations have apparently not been able to bargain effectively on this issue.[c]

> The employee who is threatened with discharge, and who cannot pay, sometimes chooses bankruptcy as a means of saving his job. The expansion of consumer credit in the postwar years has been accompanied by a sharp rise in bankruptcies, particularly in nonbusiness bankruptcies. Bankruptcy rates tend to be lower in states that do not permit wage garnishment or that sharply restrict its use. * * *

> Wage garnishment is costly. Its immediate costs include official fees—chargeable to debtors—expense to employers, and the community's subsidy of the garnishment process. There are other costs in terms of distress and

---

[c]. New York has attempted to solve this problem by statute. See N.Y.C.P.L.R. 5252. Since the publication of the article in text, California has enacted a statute preventing an employee from being discharged because his wages have been garnished. See Cal.Labor Code § 2929.

economic hardship when the family whose earnings are garnished spirals into bankruptcy or unemployment. And there are losses to creditors from garnishment-triggered no-asset bankruptcies. Hardship is not limited to bankruptcy and unemployment; a debtor who avoids both is faced with a * * * wage exemption, [in] an amount that in the great bulk of cases is grossly inadequate.

Id. at 1243–47.

A 1970 amendment to the Consumer Credit Protection Act of 1968 establishes a nationwide limit on the amount of an employee's wages that are subject to garnishment and affords an employee some protection against being discharged as a result of garnishment. See 15 U.S.C. §§ 1673–1674 (1988) (establishing that maximum wages subject to garnishment are 25% of weekly disposable earnings, or amount by which weekly disposable income exceeds 30 times the federal minimum wage, whichever is less).

Various types of real and personal property also are exempt from execution. Exempt property typically is defined by dollar amount and type of property, both of which vary greatly from state to state. Perhaps the most important exemption is the homestead exemption, which protects the family house up to a certain dollar amount. The failure to revise these statutes over long periods of time has led to some incredibly outdated provisions. By way of illustration, see the lists of property exempted from execution by Section 5205 (personal) and Section 5206 (real) of New York's Civil Practice Law and Rules. In some instances the result of a failure to revise these statutes is far from amusing. For example, New York exempts from execution a lot of land that is being used as the principal residence, but only up to a value of $10,000. N.Y.C.P.L.R. 5206(a). For many years, the exemption was limited to $2,000. If the purpose of homestead exemptions is to permit the judgment debtor and family to maintain a minimum standard of living, this exemption may be woefully inadequate. See Dean, *Economic Relations Between Husband and Wife in New York,* 41 Cornell L.Q. 175, 213–14 (1956). See generally 6 Weinstein, Korn & Miller, *New York Civil Practice* ¶ ¶ 5205.01–5206.29. For background on the sources of modern homestead laws, see McKnight, *Protection of the Family Home from Seizure by Creditors: The Sources and Evolution of a Legal Principle,* 86 S.W.Hist.L.Q. 364 (1983). For discussion of a recently updated personal property exemption statute, see Note, *Vermont's New Debtor's Exemption Statute,* 13 Vermont L.Rev. 609 (1989).

Since one of the primary purposes of exemption statutes is to protect the judgment debtor's dependents against an overzealous judgment holder, nearly every state provides that the exemptions do not apply when the attaching creditor is the spouse or a dependent of the debtor, who typically sue for alimony or child support payments. See Fischer v. Fischer, 13 N.J. 162, 98 A.2d 568 (1953). In SCHLAEFER v. SCHLAEFER, 112 F.2d 177, 185 (D.C.Cir.1940), the court said:

> * * * [T]he usual purpose of exemptions is to relieve the person exempted from the pressure of claims hostile to his dependents' essential needs as well as his own personal ones, not to relieve him of familial obligations and destroy what may be the family's last and only security, short of public relief. * * *

4. In an attempt to reduce the cost of enforcing a spouse's duty of support, the National Conference of Commissioners on Uniform State Laws adopted in 1950 the Uniform Reciprocal Enforcement of Support Act. The Act, as amended in

1968, is set forth in 9B Uniform Laws Annotated 381 (1987). In a Prefatory Note, the Act's operation is described as follows:

> The Act itself creates no duties of family support but leaves this to the legislatures of the several states. The Act is concerned solely with the enforcement of the already existing duties when the person to whom a duty is owed is in one state and the person owing the duty is in another state (or under the Act as it has been adopted in a few states is in a different county of the same state).

> Over the years many thousands of cases have been brought under the Act and many millions of dollars have been recovered. As a result, the duty of family support is placed where it belongs, on the shoulders of the one who, under state law, owes the duty. The state is thus relieved from keeping on its relief rolls those, often in destitute circumstances, to whom the duty is owed.

> The amendments of 1968, like previous ones, are designed to plug loop holes and cure defects in the enforcement procedure. Machinery for enforcement in many states is efficient. In a few states it is less so. Sometimes local officials have not fulfilled their duties. The present Act seeks to create ways and means of filling this gap (Sections 12, 18 and 29). Improved machinery for finding the obligor has been written into the Act (Section 17). The new Act has guidelines for the conduct of the trial in the responding state (Sections 21 and 23), for cases where paternity is in issue (Section 27) or where there has been interference with visitation rights (Section 23) or where it may be desirable to take an appeal (Section 34). The procedure for registering and enforcing out-of-state support orders has been simplified (Sections 39 and 40).

Would this type of a system cure some of the deficiencies in the existing procedures for collecting a judgment by execution or garnishment? See generally Note, *Constitutional Implications of the Child Support Enforcement Amendments of 1984*, 24 J.Fam.L. 301 (1986).

5. What if a federal-court judgment is rendered in one judicial district, but the defendant's assets are located in another district? Under 28 U.S.C. § 1963, the judgment may be registered in any other district by filing a certified copy with that district. It then may be enforced in the same manner as any judgment of the court in which it is registered. A 1988 amendment to the statute provides for the registration of a judgment even before it becomes final "when ordered by the court that entered the judgment for good cause shown." For a discussion of the meaning of "good cause" in this context, see Associated Business Telephone Systems Corp. v. Greater Capital Corp., 128 F.R.D. 63 (D.N.J.1989).

2. SUPPLEMENTARY PROCEEDINGS

COHEN, COLLECTION OF MONEY JUDGMENTS IN NEW YORK: SUPPLEMENTARY PROCEEDINGS, 35 Colum.L.Rev. 1007, 1012–14, 1030–34 (1935):

* * * [S]upplementary proceedings existed at common law, although under a different trade name. After the return of execution unsatisfied a creditor was empowered to proceed in equity by way of a judgment creditor's bill for two primary purposes: (a) to reach "equitable" assets beyond the scope of legal execution, and (b) to uncover property owned by the judgment debtor but deviously concealed and "transferred."

The judgment creditor's suit fitted itself into a finely grooved routine in its course through the court of chancery. * * *

* * * [T]he net result of the judgment creditor's bill was an examination of the debtor, a disclosure by him of his property, and the assignment thereof under order of the court to a receiver who acted as the agent of the court in converting the judgment debtor's property into currency, rendering it applicable to the payment of the original claim. * * * [T]he creditor's bill finally became a highly formalized procedure * * *. In their labors to provide a new and simpler scheme for judgment collection the [New York] Code Commissioners devised a practice which was expressly intended to be a substitute for the old creditors' bill: the "supplementary proceedings."

There would be an examination of the judgment debtor. This might disclose: (a) debts due to the judgment debtor, (b) tangible personal property of the judgment debtor in his own possession or in the possession of a third party, (c) real property owned by the judgment debtor. Real property could be reached by execution. For third party debtors there was devised the third party order, and for tangible personal property in the hands of the debtor or third persons there was created an order directing such property to be applied in satisfaction of the judgment. * * * In addition, * * * the Code Commissioners provided that the judge could appoint a receiver of the property of the judgment debtor.

* * *

The effectiveness of the remedy granted by way of supplementary proceedings depends in large part upon the efficiency with which the instrument may be used to discover property of the debtor and have it applied upon the judgment. Conceivably the proceeding may be so broad as to permit all issues as to title to be adjudicated therein with finality. That this has not happened in most Code states is one of the prime causes of the ineffectiveness of the modern judgment collection system. Under the [New York] Field–Throop Code, and under the [New York] Civil Practice Act, the examination is not a trial. It merely affords the creditor an opportunity to question the debtor in an attempt to discover assets.

At the outset the creditor is faced with the problem of obtaining personal service of the order on the debtor. In plenary suits jurisdiction may be obtained by substitution upon debtors who evade service, but no similar provision is available in supplementary proceedings, although these constitute a new proceeding and would seem analogous to a plenary suit. Should the judgment debtor desire to dodge service the creditor can do little but spend time and money trying to catch him. * * *

Having obtained service the creditor will find that the court facilities afforded for the examination are quite meagre. The debtor is not examined in the presence of the Court, nor is the testimony officially transcribed. * * * The * * * statute provides that upon the consent of the debtor or his attorney the examination may be taken before a notary public or commissioner of deeds at any place mutually agreeable to the parties. And it also specifies, in what may be a helpful reform, that the Appellate Division may assign official referees to preside at examinations, although it is to be regretted that the statute did not incorporate the reform * * * that the examination be held immediately after the trial and before the justice then presiding.

* * * Where there is no official supervision, constant disputes arise as to the scope of the examination and the accuracy with which it was transcribed. This tends to hamper the investigation and affords evasive debtors opportunities to change their testimony. Thus the absence of satisfactory judicial facilities, at least in New York City, often results in defeating creditors' efforts at collection.

This situation has been aggravated by some judicially evolved rules defining the creditor's rights. After examining the debtor the creditor naturally desires to adjourn the examination so that he may have an opportunity to investigate the debtor's testimony. Prior to the new statute, such adjournments were denied as a matter of right, and rested solely in the consent of the debtor or the discretion of the justice at Special Term. Moreover the creditor was denied the power to investigate the debtor's books and records. He could subpoena them, but he could not examine them; they could be used solely to "refresh" the debtor's recollection.

The current reforms have attempted to remedy some of these difficulties. Reexaminations of the debtor at stated intervals are permitted. In certain cases the creditor may examine witnesses within six months after the debtor's examination has been closed. * * * And finally, perjury is now punishable as a contempt. However, since the statute predicates the applicability of this sanction upon the "materiality" of the testimony in question, the effectiveness of this sanction will rest largely upon what the court feels is "material" evidence.

These, however, are minor matters. As it stands today the examination merely affords the creditor an opportunity to discover that the debtor's assets do not belong to him, but to his wife and kindred, and that they were transferred to pay long standing obligations to the spouse, as to which no records exist. The scope of the examination is not such as to permit a trial of title; whenever a question of title is raised, the dispute may not be settled within the supplementary proceeding. For any real relief the creditor must start a separate action to set aside transfers obviously made to prevent judgment collection.

Notes and Questions

1. New York extensively revised the supplementary procedures described in the quoted passage in 1935. See Cohen, *Collection of Money Judgments: Experimentation with Supplementary Proceedings*, 36 Colum.L.Rev. 1061 (1936), which outlines these changes and comments on the practice in many other states. New York's judgment-collection procedures were revamped again in 1963. Present New York practice is described in Volume Six of Weinstein, Korn & Miller, *New York Civil Practice*. Because modernization of enforcement procedures generally has lagged throughout the country, the excerpt from the Cohen article provides a good statement of the supplementary proceedings presently in force in many states. See also Note, *Supplementary Proceedings in Illinois: The Uncertain Remedy*, 1979 U.Ill.L.F. 241. However, because discovery within the execution process is now more widely available than it once was, judgment creditors have less occasion to

resort to supplementary proceedings. Federal Rule 60 permits broad discovery in aid of execution. Additionally, of the many states that have loosened or eliminated restrictions on pre-execution discovery of assets, most have followed the pattern of Federal Rule 69. See Woodward, *Enforcement of Money Judgments: Objectives and Restrictions,* in 9 Eisenberg, *Debtor-Creditor Law,* ch. 37, ¶ 37.02 (1988).

2. Should supplementary proceedings be treated as a separate action or merely an adjunct to the action in which the judgment was recovered? On this question compare American State Bank v. Stoltz, 345 N.W.2d 365, 367 (N.D.1984) (part of main action), with Nestor v. Dependable Ins. Co., 535 So.2d 710 (Fla.App. 1988) (separate action). What turns on the answer to this question?

3. Suppose A recovers a judgment from B and during supplementary proceedings B claims that C is in possession of property belonging to B. When A attempts to have the property applied to the judgment, C contests B's interest. How is the dispute between B and C as to the ownership of the property to be determined? If the supplementary proceeding is under the control of a judge, can the court determine the dispute between B and C and, if it finds in B's favor, apply the property to the satisfaction of A's judgment? What objections are there to the judge making such a determination? Compare Letz v. Letz, 123 Mont. 494, 215 P.2d 534 (1950), with Exceletech, Inc. v. Williams, 597 So.2d 275 (Fla.1992).

4. When a judgment is reversed on appeal, what is the status of the enforcement proceedings already undertaken? Is the prevailing party liable for damages caused by the attempt to enforce the judgment? In HARP v. BROOK-SHIRE, 197 Ky. 794, 248 S.W. 177 (1923), H sued B for a declaration that he had a right of way over B's farm. H obtained a temporary injunction to prevent B from interfering with the claimed right of way. The trial court held that H had no right of way and dissolved the injunction. During the pendency of H's appeal, B refused to let H cross the land. The lower court's decision ultimately was reversed and H's right of way upheld. In a subsequent suit by H for damages caused by B's excluding him from the land, the court held that although a party generally is not liable for the consequences of acts performed in obedience to a judgment that later is reversed, B would be held liable since the acts were not directly or expressly authorized by the judgment. But didn't the trial court's decision effectively declare B's ownership of the land and give him the right to control access to it? How could B have protected himself pending H's appeal?

3. CONTEMPT AND BODY EXECUTION

REEVES v. CROWNSHIELD
Court of Appeals of New York, 1937.
274 N.Y. 74, 8 N.E.2d 283.

FINCH, JUDGE. The uncollectibility of money judgments has ever been a subject of concern to bench and bar. A large part of the statute law of this state is designed to enable a judgment creditor to obtain satisfaction upon his money judgment. That a large percentage of these money judgments have remained uncollectible has been confirmed by statistical surveys. Johns Hopkins University Institute of Law, Survey of Litigation in New York (1931). Many debtors who were in a position to pay have evaded their legal obligations by unlawful and technical means. Discontent with this situation resulted in agitation for reform in collection procedure. * * * Finally, in 1935, upon the recommendation of the Judicial Council, a law was enacted creating a new mode of enforcing the payment of judgments. * * *

Section 793 of the Civil Practice Act [currently N.Y.C.P.L.R. 5226] now provides that, in addition to the garnishee provisions of the old law, the court may make an order directing a judgment debtor to make payments in installments out of the income which he receives. Such orders must be made upon notice to the judgment debtor and after he has had an opportunity to show inability to pay, and with due regard to the reasonable requirements of the judgment debtor and his family, as well as of payments required to be made by him to other creditors. Section 801 of the Civil Practice Act [now found in N.Y.C.P.L.R. 5251] provides that refusal to pay after such an order of the court is punishable as a contempt. * * *

This new procedure was invoked against the appellant, in an attempt to collect a judgment for approximately $400. The examination in supplementary proceedings disclosed that he was employed by the Federal Government as a steamship inspector at a salary of $230 per month, less a small pension deduction. He has no children, and the whereabouts of his wife are unknown. Aside from $48 a month paid as rent and his living expenses, he has no financial obligations. The court ordered the appellant to pay installments of $20 per month until the judgment was satisfied. Upon his failure to pay, he was held in contempt and fined the sum of $20, commitment being provided for in default of payment.

An appeal was taken directly to this court from the City Court of New York City on the ground that a constitutional question was involved.

* * *

The judgment debtor challenges the constitutionality of section 793 and section 801 on the ground that in effect they provide for imprisonment for debt. It is admitted that neither the State nor the Federal Constitutions contain provisions expressly prohibiting imprisonment for debt, and that the statutory provision forbidding imprisonment for debt found in section 21 of the New York Civil Rights Law excepts cases otherwise specially prescribed by law. It is asserted, however, that imprisonment for debt is barred by the due process clauses of the State and Federal Constitutions (Const.N.Y. art. 1, § 6; Const.U.S. Amend. 14). No cases so holding are cited * * *. Whatever doubt there may exist as to whether imprisonment for debt without regard to ability to pay may be treated as a deprivation of liberty without due process of law * * *, there can be no doubt that imprisonment for failure to obey an order of a court to make payment out of income, which order is made with due regard to the needs of the debtor and his family, is not violative of the due process clause.

* * *

In the case at bar the judgment debtor has not complained that the order directing the payment of $20 per month is unjust, inequitable, or harsh. His position is an arbitrary refusal to pay. It is based upon the ground that the courts are powerless to compel him to pay out of his income an amount fixed after deducting the sum necessary for his reasonable needs.

The Legislature has seen fit to provide a creditor with a direct remedy for the collection of his just debts. A refusal to recognize such an order by the judgment debtor entitles the creditor to move to have him punished for contempt. Without this right, there would be no power in the court to enforce its order. To compel the judgment debtor to obey the order of the court is not imprisonment for debt, but only imprisonment for disobedience of an order with which he is able to comply. His refusal is contumacious conduct, the same as a refusal to obey any other lawful order of the court.

It also is asserted that the application of this law to the appellant is unconstitutional, since it interferes with the operation of a federal instrumentality. To sustain this contention, reference is made to the cases declaring State laws taxing the salaries of federal officers unconstitutional. * * * Analysis shows that these cases are not in point. The true basis for declaring a state tax on the salaries of federal officers unconstitutional is that since the Federal Government presumably finds it necessary to pay its officers a salary based upon the value of their services, the state should not be permitted to tax the salaries thereby reducing the compensation and making it necessary for the Federal Government to increase the salaries paid by it.

* * *

It is true that the wages of a federal employee cannot be garnisheed, but once his wage has been paid to him a state is not prohibited from ordering him to apply a portion of such income towards the payment of his just debts. The moment the salary is received it becomes a part of the general income of the owner. If he should therewith purchase property the property could be taken under execution for the payment of a judgment against the owner. No reason appears for exempting the income while still held as money and not exempting it when it has been converted into property. * * *

* * *

Orders affirmed.

Notes and Questions

1. Compare the principal case with PEOPLE ex rel. SARLAY v. POPE, 230 App.Div. 649, 650, 246 N.Y.S. 414, 416 (3d Dep't 1930), in which the court said that the "imprisonment of the defendants until the payment of a fine in the amount of the judgment recovered in the contract action would be, in effect, imprisonment for a civil debt." In the absence of an express constitutional provision forbidding imprisonment for debt, is there any theory under which it can be held unconstitutional? See Kinsey v. Preeson, 746 P.2d 542 (Colo.1987). If contempt or body execution is aimed at the recalcitrant or dilatory judgment debtor, how is the good faith, but penniless, debtor protected against being caught in the contempt trap? Is it sufficient simply to require that the judgment debtor's failure be "willful" in order to punish for contempt? See generally Note, *Body Attachment and Body Execution: Forgotten But Not Gone,* 17 Wm. & Mary L.Rev. 543 (1976).

2. What are the differences between body execution and contempt? Should courts in jurisdictions that have prohibited or severely limited body execution use contempt proceedings to circumvent the restrictions on body execution? See Note, *Present Status of Execution Against the Body of the Judgment Debtor,* 42 Iowa L.Rev. 306 (1957). See also the distinctions between contempt and body execution drawn in Zeitinger v. Mitchell, 244 S.W.2d 91 (Mo.1951).

3. Doesn't the *Reeves* case suggest that the problems that frequently arise during supplementary proceedings could be cured by an order to disclose all

hidden or undiscovered assets reinforced by the contempt sanction? How would the court determine whether or not the judgment debtor is telling the truth when he claims to have no leviable property? What types of post-judgment defaults other than the one involved in *Reeves* properly are punishable by contempt? See generally 6 Weinstein, Korn & Miller, *New York Civil Practice* ¶ ¶ 5251.10–.21.

4. LIENS AND PRIORITIES

MATTER OF FORNABAI

United States District Court, District of New Jersey, 1964.
227 F.Supp. 928.

SHAW, DISTRICT JUDGE. This matter comes before the Court * * * on Petition for Review of an order by the Referee in Bankruptcy. The order of the Referee in Bankruptcy dated June 4, 1963 determined that two judgment liens were entitled to priority in satisfaction over tax liens of the United States of America out of a real estate fund being administered by the Court.

The pertinent facts may be recited briefly as follows: On May 2, 1962 Nicholas Fornabai individually and doing business as Fornaby Equipment Co. was adjudicated a bankrupt in a Chapter XI proceeding. The realty of the bankrupt was sold and valid liens against the realty transferred to the proceeds of the sale. The amount thereof held by the Trustee in Bankruptcy is insufficient for full satisfaction of all valid liens.

* * * The lien of the United States is for taxes assessed against the bankrupt pursuant to provisions of the Internal Revenue Code of 1954. Truck Equipment Corporation recovered a judgment in the Superior Court of New Jersey against the bankrupt on December 8, 1960. The amount is $13,716.85 plus interest. Pak–Mor Manufacturing Co. recovered its judgment against the bankrupt in the United States District Court for the District of New Jersey on March 10, 1961. The amount of this judgment is $18,199.61 plus interest. Both judgments were docketed as of the dates of recovery thereof. The United States filed notice of tax liens against the bankrupt. * * *

The precise question presented is whether the liens of the two judgment creditors above mentioned were perfected in the sense that they became choate liens on the realty of the bankrupt prior to the date when the United States filed its notice of tax liens. If so, the judgment liens are entitled to priority.

A judgment docketed in the Superior Court of New Jersey is a lien upon all real estate of the judgment debtor located within the State of New Jersey from the date the judgment is docketed. N.J.S.A. 2A:16–1. * * *

By federal statute it is provided with respect to judgments of the United States District Court that:

Every judgment rendered by a district court within a State shall be a lien on the property located in such State in the same manner, to the same extent and under the same conditions as a judgment of a court of general jurisdiction in such State, and shall cease to be a lien in the same manner and time. * * * 28 U.S.C.A. § 1962.

Taxes assessed against a taxpayer pursuant to the provisions of the Internal Revenue Code of 1954 become liens in favor of the United States upon all property and rights to property belonging to the taxpayer. 26 U.S.C.A. § 6321. But the lien for taxes is not valid "as against any mortgagee, pledgee, purchaser, or *judgment creditor* until notice thereof has been filed." (Emphasis supplied.) 26 U.S.C.A. § 6323. As noted above, the earliest date on which the Government filed notice of a tax lien was April 10, 1961.

Federal law determines which secured creditors are judgment creditors for purposes of protection under Section 6323. * * *

In the case of United States v. Gilbert Associates, Inc., [345 U.S. 361, 73 S.Ct. 701, 97 L.Ed. 1071 (1953)] * * * the Supreme Court stated:

* * *

A cardinal principle of Congress in its tax scheme is uniformity, as far as may be. Therefore, a 'judgment creditor' should have the same application in all the states. In this instance, we think Congress used the words 'judgment creditor' in § 3672 [now 26 U.S.C.A. § 6323] in the usual, conventional sense of a judgment of a court of record, since all states have such courts.

The priority of a lien created by state law over a tax lien of the federal government depends on the time it attached to the property in question and became choate. It is perfected to the point of being a choate lien "when the identity of the lienor, the property subject to the lien, and the amount of the lien are established." United States v. Pioneer American Insurance Co., 374 U.S. 84, 88, 89, 83 S.Ct. 1651, 1655, 10 L.Ed.2d 770 (1963).

Each of the judgments here were recovered in a court of record and docketed therein. The identity of each judgment lienor, the property subject to the judgment lien and the amount thereof has been established. Nevertheless, the Government contends that neither of the judgments imposed a choate lien upon realty of the bankrupt because neither of the judgment creditors caused a writ of execution to issue against the real estate of the bankrupt. In support of its argument, the Government cites N.J.S.A. 2A:17–39 * * *. [The cited statute gives the purchaser of real property good title as against a judgment creditor who has not issued an execution against the property.]

The effect and purpose of the above cited statutory provision is misconstrued. A writ of execution on a judgment does not create the lien; it is merely the procedural means by which the judgment creditor obtains satisfaction out of the proceeds of the sale of realty. * * *

It is clear from the language of the statutory provision upon which the Government relies, and the judicial interpretation of it over many years that its provisions were intended to apply only to priority inter se among those holding liens by judgment or recognizance and that it has no effect in the determination of priority of lien holders other than those mentioned. It creates an exception to the Common Law rule of "the first in time is the first in right," in favor of a subsequent judgment creditor who has issued execution on the judgment and the reason for the exception is clearly stated in the statute. In the early case of Clement v. Kaighn, 15 N.J.Eq. 47 (Chancery 1862), the Court stated that a judgment shall bind the lands of a defendant from the time of actual entry of the judgment on the record of the Court, but that the purpose of the statutory exception among judgment creditors was to give a junior judgment creditor whose execution was first sued out the "proper effect and fruits thereof." * * *

It would be manifestly inequitable if a senior judgment creditor were permitted to stand by while a junior judgment creditor incurred the expense in issuance of a writ of execution, levy upon, and sale of lands of a defendant, and then step in to share first in the proceeds. This would deny the junior lien holder who proceeded with diligence "the proper effect and fruits thereof." It was this inequity in procedural enforcement affecting judgment creditors and liens attaching by recognizance that the State Legislature recognized and sought to correct. Application of the provisions of the statute to priority status of liens other than those existing by virtue of judgment or recognizance would rest upon an interpretation which the plain language of the statutory provision does not support and one which finds no sanction by weight of judicial precedent in the state courts.

There is no rational basis upon which the Government can equate its tax lien in this instance with a judgment lien or recognizance for purposes of claiming the benefit of the provisions of N.J.S.A. 2A:17–39. Its position might be analogous to that of a judgment creditor who had issued execution on a judgment, if it had been *first* to take action to enforce the tax lien against realty of the taxpayer pursuant to the provisions of Title 26 U.S.C.A. § 7403. But that is not the case here. The mere filing of its notice of tax lien without further action to subject property of the taxpayer to payment of the tax liability, does not give the Government a status analogous to that of a judgment creditor who has issued a writ of execution to satisfy a judgment. Accordingly, as between the Government holding a tax lien by virtue of assessment and notice filed and a judgment creditor who has not issued a writ of execution, the common law rule of "the first in time is the first in right," is the applicable rule. * * *

Moreover, it might be stated as a matter of practical observation, that if the provisions of 26 U.S.C.A. § 6323 in favor of prior judgment creditors were to have no application until the property in question was in the process of sale to satisfy a judgment, the limited effect thereof on judgment liens generally would render the intended benefits sterile. This indeed would be a narrow interpretation of a remedial statute with emphasis upon local procedures to enforce satisfaction of a lien rather than upon the substantive right created by the lien.

* * * A judgment entered in the Superior Court of New Jersey is a lien upon all real estate within the jurisdiction of the court from the date of entry thereof. * * * The judgment creates the substantive right of lien, not the writ of execution.

Accordingly, the determination by order of the Referee in Bankruptcy that the two judgment creditors have priority of lien over the federal tax liens is affirmed. An appropriate order in accordance herewith will be submitted.

Notes and Questions

1. Lien and priority-of-lien problems are among the most complex in the law of judgment enforcement. The traditional "lien" situation involves the judgment creditor's right to a particular piece of property as against the judgment debtor or

someone claiming under the latter, such as an assignee or purchaser of the property. The judgment creditor's rights against a transferee are based on the purchaser's or assignee's having actual or constructive notice of the creditor's rights in the property. Questions of "priority of liens," as in the *Fornabai* case, involve a dispute between two or more judgment creditors over the debtor's property. As a general rule, the rights of one creditor *vis à vis* another are based on the equitable principle of "diligence," which seeks to prevent a creditor from refraining from enforcing a judgment while maintaining priority of lien. What factors should determine whether one judgment creditor is more "diligent" than another?

Because courts often confuse "priority-of-lien" and "lien" situations, the line between the two has been somewhat obscured. The New York practice is analyzed in 6 Weinstein, Korn & Miller, *New York Civil Practice* ¶ 5202.02. The terminology is further analyzed in Distler & Schubin, *Enforcement Priorities and Liens: The New York Judgment Creditor's Rights in Personal Property,* 60 Colum.L.Rev. 458 (1960). For illustrations of some of the many problems that arise in this context, see Burroughs, *The Choate Lien Doctrine,* 1963 Duke L.J. 449; Comment, *Priorities of Creditors Under Judgment Creditor's Bills,* 42 Yale L.J. 919 (1933).

2. Section 5202 of New York's Civil Practice Law and Rules expressly provides that an execution creditor's rights in the judgment debtor's personal property are superior to those of anyone who acquires an interest after the delivery of an execution to a sheriff except: (1) transferees who acquire the debt or property for fair consideration before levy and (2) transferees who acquire the debt or property, when it is not capable of delivery, for fair consideration after it was levied upon but without knowledge of the levy. What are the purposes of these two exceptions? See 6 Weinstein, Korn & Miller, *New York Civil Practice* ¶ ¶ 5202.11–.12. The judgment creditor's lien remains in effect as long as the execution is in force but once it expires the judgment creditor's lien terminates and the transfer of any property that was not actually levied upon under the execution made while the execution was in force will be effective as against the judgment creditor.

3. An execution creditor can lose her lien or priority of lien if she allows the execution to become "dormant," which permits the rights of a diligent creditor to be advanced over those of a creditor who is not pursuing the enforcement of a claim. A classic definition of dormancy is found in EXCELSIOR NEEDLE CO. v. GLOBE CYCLE WORKS, 48 App.Div. 304, 310, 62 N.Y.S. 538, 541 (4th Dep't 1900):

> The law * * * seems to be settled that any direction by the execution creditor to the sheriff, which suspends the lien or delays the enforcement of the levy, renders the execution dormant against subsequent creditors or *bona fide* purchasers. However veiled may be the direction; however much it may be founded on a humane desire to protect the debtor; if it is tantamount to a mandate or instruction to the sheriff to withhold the execution of his process during the interim that he accedes to this demand, the levy ceases to be effective. That doctrine rests on public policy and is necessary to prevent fraud and it should receive a fairly rigorous enforcement.

What justification is there for the dormancy doctrine? Should a judgment creditor's execution or attachment become dormant when he directs the sheriff not to levy out of a hope that the judgment debtor will become financially stable if the property and business are not disturbed and the latter is not besieged by creditors?

Chapter 16

APPELLATE REVIEW

SECTION A. THE PRINCIPLE OF FINALITY

1. INTRODUCTION: THE HISTORICAL BACKGROUND

CRICK, THE FINAL JUDGMENT AS A BASIS FOR APPEAL, 41 Yale L.J. 539, 541–43, 545–48, 550 (1932):

From very early times in England the method whereby a litigant came into the king's court and attacked a decision rendered in a feudal or manorial court was the complaint of false judgment. It was early decided, however, that the king's courts could not be charged with a false judgment, and the means whereby the King's Bench corrected errors in the other common law courts was by writ of error, the method destined to survive in many jurisdictions to our own day. The common law decisions involving writ of error are clearly the origin of our rule that only final judgments are appealable. The real factors in the establishment of this practice must go back to the very beginning of the history of the writ of error, and it is impossible at this time to give more than an explanation which is merely plausible.

* * * The matter seems to be connected in some way with the "record" by which the proceedings in the lower court are made known to the King's Bench, for counsel in [John de Ralegh's Case, Y.B. 17 Ed. 3 (R.S.) 234 (1343)] * * * says, "You have no warrant to try this record for the record is not fully here, because the case is still pending in another Court. * * * It is impossible that on one and the same original writ there should be two records in different courts." * * *

If we combine with this conception of the record, the fact that a proceeding on a writ of error seems to have been regarded as a new action, and not merely a continuation of the suit in the inferior court, we see how it may have been that the record could not be sent up until the suit below had been completed. Suing out a writ of error before final judgment would result in two actions in different courts, to the procedure of each of which the formal record was essential. To remove it while the case was pending below "would disturb the proceedings" there, while the reviewing court could not proceed until it was informed of what had happened below.

* * *

We see, then, that [in Blackstone's time] there were three types of pronouncements made during the course of a case [in equity]. First, orders, second, interlocutory decrees, and third, final decrees. Unlike the common law, however, which * * * required a case to go to final judgment before the decisions of the court might be questioned, equity gave relief from all three types of pronouncements. * * *

Thus we see that equity practice never knew the rule of the common law that only final judgments were appealable. Not only could interlocutory decrees be taken to the House of Lords, but also those decisions which had not even attained the dignity of decrees, that is, orders. As to the reason for this, we may tentatively assign two factors. First, appeals to the House of Lords from the Lord Chancellor were established comparatively late in legal history. * * * During the intervening centuries, therefore, a given case had its beginning and ending in the same court, and the only method by which a decision could be altered was by rehearing before the chancellor. * * *

When the House of Lords finally asserted appellate jurisdiction over proceedings in chancery, therefore, it found a system whereby the chancellor passed on all decrees issued, as well as on interlocutory orders, and we need not be surprised that appeals were taken to the Lords from interlocutory decrees because in chancery there was no particular magic in a final decree. * * *

Second, when we consider the character of litigation handled in chancery we see how much more convenient it was to review intermediate decisions as the case progressed. * * * [M]uch of its litigation was of a complicated type unsuited to the more simple common law forms of action. There was a much greater use of subordinate officials than in the common law courts, and the requirement of documentation of evidence introduced difficulties unknown to the King's courts. In equity, judgments were not compelled to follow stereotyped forms, and this made possible dealing with the case by as many orders, decrees, and modifications of the same as were necessary in the particular case. Thus, equity had a more elastic procedure, and also required a less rigid practice on appeal to review the many and varied steps taken below.

When we pass to the American scene we are at once confronted with confusion. * * * However, two main trends seem to have characterized the process.

First, there has been a general tendency to take the common law rule that error lay only after final judgment and to apply it to equity procedure. Second, hampered by this restriction in both law and equity, the courts have gone through elaborate logical exercises in order to escape from the strict application of the restriction * * *.

Another factor which may have had some effect was the failure to keep distinct the practice of law and equity, particularly on appeal. Very commonly one appellate court was established to hear appeals in both law and equity, and in some states, at least, the common law writ of error was the method of appeal in equity cases as well as at law. * * *

2. APPLICATION OF THE BASIC CONCEPT

Read 28 U.S.C. §§ 1291 and 1292 in the Supplement.

COOPER, EXTRAORDINARY WRIT PRACTICE IN CRIMINAL CASES: ANALOGIES FOR THE MILITARY COURTS, 98 F.R.D. 593, 594–96 (1983):

A truly final judgment is one that marks the completion of all the events that will occur in a trial court. Nothing more remains to be done, unless it be execution of a judgment against the defendant.

The advantages that may be gained by deferring appeals until entry of a truly final judgment are familiar, and can be summarized in short order. Immediate review of every ruling made by a trial court could not be tolerated. Repeated interruptions and delays could put the trial process beyond any reasonable control, even if appeals were taken only when there was a good faith and reasonable belief that the court was wrong. The opportunities for less honorable delay and harassment of an adversary also would not go entirely unexploited. More limited opportunities for interlocutory review would not be so disastrous, but would carry some part of the same costs. The possible advantages to be set against these costs arise from the opportunity to correct a wrong ruling. These advantages, however, are reduced by the prospects that most trial court rulings are correct; that wrong rulings often are corrected by the trial court; and that uncorrected wrong rulings will not, in the end, taint the final judgment.

The price that is paid for a final judgment rule, however, can be high. An erroneous ruling may taint everything that follows. If appeal must be delayed until final judgment, it may become necessary to repeat the entire trial proceeding. The costs of repeating the trial go beyond the obvious costs of expense and anxiety. The further proceedings will be held later, and may suffer from lapses of memory, inconsequential inconsistencies that are blown into exaggerated importance, and actual loss of evidence. Beyond these defects, the retrial proceedings often will be affected by lessons learned at the first trial. * * * The problem is more than one of boredom; strategies have been revealed and must be revised, opportunities to sustain truth by impeachment are diminished, and so on.

* * *

Beyond the impact on individual cases, loss of the opportunity for interlocutory review means that some areas of law must develop without much opportunity for appellate guidance. Questions of discovery, for example, may confuse and divide trial courts for years without the guidance and uniformity that appeals could provide.

LIBERTY MUTUAL INSURANCE CO. v. WETZEL
Supreme Court of the United States, 1976.
424 U.S. 737, 96 S.Ct. 1202, 47 L.Ed.2d 435.

Certiorari to the United States Court of Appeals for the Third Circuit.

MR. JUSTICE REHNQUIST delivered the opinion of the Court.

Respondents filed a complaint in the United States District Court for the Western District of Pennsylvania in which they asserted that petitioner's employee insurance benefits and maternity leave regulations discriminated against women in violation of Title VII of the Civil Rights Act of 1964 * * *. The District Court ruled in favor of respondents on the issue of petitioner's liability under that Act, and petitioner appealed to the Court of Appeals for the Third Circuit. That court held that it had jurisdiction of petitioner's appeal under 28 U.S.C. § 1291, and proceeded to affirm on the merits the judgment of the District Court. We granted certiorari * * * and heard argument on the merits. Though neither party has questioned the jurisdiction of the Court of Appeals to entertain the appeal, we are obligated to do so on our own motion if a question thereto exists. * * *

Respondents' complaint, after alleging jurisdiction and facts deemed pertinent to their claim, prayed for a judgment against petitioner embodying the following relief:

(a) requiring that defendant establish non-discriminatory hiring, payment, opportunity, and promotional plans and programs;

(b) enjoining the continuance by defendant of the illegal acts and practices alleged herein;

(c) requiring that defendant pay over to plaintiffs and to the members of the class the damages sustained by plaintiffs and the members of the class by reason of defendant's illegal acts and practices, including adjusted backpay, with interest, and an additional equal amount as liquidated damages, and exemplary damages;

(d) requiring that defendant pay to plaintiffs and to the members of the class the costs of this suit and a reasonable attorneys' fee, with interest; and

(e) such other and further relief as the Court deems appropriate. App. 19.

After extensive discovery, respondents moved for partial summary judgment only as to the issue of liability. * * * The District Court * * *, finding no issues of material fact in dispute, entered an order to the effect that petitioner's pregnancy-related policies violated Title VII of the Civil Rights Act of 1964. It also ruled that Liberty Mutual's hiring and promotion policies violated Title VII. Petitioner thereafter filed a motion for reconsideration which was denied by the District Court. * * *

It is obvious from the District Court's order that respondents, although having received a favorable ruling on the issue of petitioner's liability to them, received none of the relief which they expressly prayed for in the portion of their complaint set forth above. They requested an injunction, but did not get one; they requested damages, but were not awarded any; they requested attorneys' fees, but received none.

Counsel for respondents when questioned during oral argument in this Court suggested that at least the District Court's order of February 20 amounted to a declaratory judgment on the issue of liability pursuant to the provisions of 28 U.S.C. § 2201. Had respondents sought *only* a declaratory judgment, and no other form of relief, we would of course have a different case. But even if we accept respondents' contention that the District Court's order was a declaratory judgment on the issue of liability, it nonetheless left unresolved respondents' requests for an injunction, for compensatory and exemplary damages, and for attorneys' fees. It finally disposed of none of respondents' prayers for relief.

The District Court and the Court of Appeals apparently took the view that because the District Court made the recital required by Fed.Rule Civ. Proc. 54(b) that final judgment be entered on the issue of liability, and that there was no just reason for delay, the orders thereby became appealable as a final decision pursuant to 28 U.S.C. § 1291. We cannot agree with this application of the Rule and statute in question.

Rule 54(b) "does not apply to a single claim action * * *. It is limited expressly to multiple claims actions in which 'one or more but less than all' of the multiple claims have been finally decided and are found otherwise to be ready for appeal." Sears, Roebuck & Co. v. Mackey, 351 U.S. 427, 435, 76 S.Ct. 895, 899, 100 L.Ed. 1297, 1306 (1956). Here, however, respondents set forth but a single claim: that petitioner's employee insurance benefits and maternity leave regulations discriminated against its women employees in violation of Title VII of the Civil Rights Act of 1964. They prayed for several different types of relief in the event that they sustained the allegations of their complaint * * *, but their complaint advanced a single legal theory which was applied to only one set of facts. Thus, despite the fact that the District Court undoubtedly made the findings required under the Rule had it been applicable, those findings do not in a case such as this make the order appealable pursuant to 28 U.S.C. § 1291. * * *

We turn to consider whether the District Court's order might have been appealed by petitioner to the Court of Appeals under any other theory. The order, viewed apart from its discussion of Rule 54(b), constitutes a grant of partial summary judgment limited to the issue of petitioner's liability. Such judgments are by their terms interlocutory, see Fed.Rule Civ.Proc. 56(c), and where assessment of damages or awarding of other relief remains to be resolved have never been considered to be "final" within the meaning of 28 U.S.C. § 1291. * * * Thus the only possible authorization for an appeal from the District Court's order would be pursuant to the provisions of 28 U.S.C. § 1292.

If the District Court had granted injunctive relief but had not ruled on respondents' other requests for relief, this interlocutory order would have been appealable under § 1292(a)(1). But, as noted above, the court did not issue an injunction. It might be argued that the order of the District Court, insofar as it failed to include the injunctive relief requested by respondents, is an interlocutory order refusing an injunction within the meaning of § 1292(a)(1). But even if this would have allowed *respondents* to then obtain review in the Court of Appeals, there was no denial of any injunction sought by *petitioner* and it could not avail itself of that grant of jurisdiction.

Nor was this order appealable pursuant to 28 U.S.C. § 1292(b). Although the District Court's findings made with a view to satisfying Rule 54(b) might be viewed as substantial compliance with the certification requirement of that section, there is no showing in this record that petitioner made application to the Court of Appeals within the 10 days therein specified. And that court's holding that its jurisdiction was pursuant to § 1291 makes it clear that it thought itself obliged to consider on the merits petitioner's appeal. There can be no assurance that had the other requirements of § 1292(b) been complied with, the Court of Appeals would have exercised its discretion to entertain the interlocutory appeal.

Were we to sustain the procedure followed here, we would condone a practice whereby a district court in virtually any case before it might render an interlocutory decision on the question of liability of the defendant, and the defendant would thereupon be permitted to appeal to the court of appeals without satisfying any of the requirements that Congress carefully set forth. We believe that Congress, in enacting present §§ 1291 and 1292 of Title 28, has been well aware of the dangers of an overly rigid insistence upon a "final decision" for appeal in every case, and has in those sections made ample provision for appeal of orders which are not "final" so as to alleviate any possible hardship. We would twist the fabric of the statute more than it will bear if we were to agree that the District Court's order of February 20, 1974, was appealable to the Court of Appeals.

The judgment of the Court of Appeals is therefore vacated, and the case is remanded with instructions to dismiss the petitioner's appeal.

It is so ordered.

MR. JUSTICE BLACKMUN took no part in the consideration or decision of this case.

———

JETCO ELECTRONIC INDUSTRIES, INC. v. GARDINER, 473 F.2d 1228 (5th Cir.1973). Plaintiff Jetco filed suit against three defendants, ETL, Gardiner, and Gardiner Electronics. The trial court granted ETL's motion to dismiss for lack of personal jurisdiction and for failure to state a claim for relief, and an appeal was taken from that order. Several months after the order involving ETL, the trial court entered a second order disposing of Jetco's claims against Gardiner and Gardiner Electronics. On ETL's motion to dismiss the appeal, the Court of Appeals held:

> The March order dismissing appellants' suit against ETL * * * said nothing about appellants' rights as against the other two defendants, Gardiner and Gardiner Electronics * * *. That order is thus not a final judgment * * *. Nor was the later order entering an agreed judgment disposing of appellants' claim against Gardiner and Gardiner Electronics a final judgment [since] * * * it did not adjudicate appellants' rights as against ETL. Nevertheless, these two orders, considered together, terminated this litigation just as effectively as would have been the case had the district judge gone through the motions of entering a single order formally reciting the substance of the earlier two orders. Mindful of the Supreme Court's command that practical, not technical, considerations are to govern the application of principles of finality * * * we decline appellee's invitation to exalt form over substance by dismissing this appeal. We hold that the March order dismissing appellants' suit against ETL is, under the circumstances of this case, within our appellate jurisdiction. * * *

Id. at 1231.

Notes and Questions

1. *Liberty Mutual* illustrates the proposition that the question whether a court may hear an appeal—with its constituent issues of finality, timeliness, and mode—is almost without exception viewed as involving "jurisdiction over the subject matter." See also Firestone Tire & Rubber Co. v. Risjord, 449 U.S. 368, 101 S.Ct. 669, 66 L.Ed.2d 571 (1981); Collins v. Miller, 252 U.S. 364, 40 S.Ct. 347, 64 L.Ed. 616 (1920); United States v. Girault, 52 U.S. (11 How.) 22, 13 L.Ed. 587 (1851). All the doctrinal overtones of that concept are present. For example, a lower appellate court's decision will be reversed for lack of appellate jurisdiction and the appeal will be ordered dismissed even though the issue of the propriety of the appeal was not raised in the lower court; the parties may not waive the requirements for an appeal; neither the trial nor appellate court can supply the defects or depart from the rigid rules of law regarding appeals. What are the reasons for this approach? Are the same dangers present when an appellate court conducts a premature review as when a trial court hears a cause that is not within its competence? See 15 Wright, Miller & Cooper, *Federal Practice and Procedure: Jurisdiction and Related Matters 2d* § 3905 (1992).

2. Does the *Jetco* decision represent a departure from the traditional approach discussed in Note 1 above? Would your answer be different if the trial court's second order, dismissing the case against Gardiner and Gardiner Electronics, had been rendered prior to the time Jetco's appeal was filed? Compare Oak Constr. Co. v. Huron Cement Co., 475 F.2d 1220 (6th Cir.1973) (subsequent trial-court action cannot save appeal that was inappropriate at the time it was filed). Should Jetco be free to file a separate appeal challenging the court's second order?

3. THE NEW YORK APPROACH

New York has taken a different approach than that followed by the federal courts, allowing appeals to the state's intermediate appellate court—the Appellate Division—in a great many situations in which no final judgment has been rendered. Read the New York provision, N.Y.C.P.L.R. 5701, which is found in the Supplement following 28 U.S.C. § 1292. What benefits and burdens does the New York system contain that the federal system does not?

In PEART v. PEART, 48 Hun 79 (N.Y.Sup.Ct.1888), the defendant's motion to require plaintiff to make her complaint more definite and certain was denied, and the defendant appealed. A motion to dismiss the appeal was denied:

> The order is appealable. It is definitely settled so far as this court is concerned, that orders made at a Special Term involving questions as to the form of the pleadings and whether they contain irrelevant, redundant or scandalous matter, or are so indefinite and uncertain that the precise meaning or application of an allegation therein is not apparent, may be reviewed by this court on appeal, and if any error has been committed it may be corrected.

KORN, CIVIL JURISDICTION OF THE NEW YORK COURT OF AP-
PEALS AND APPELLATE DIVISIONS, 16 Buffalo L.Rev. 307, 330, 332
(1967):

It is generally recognized that this broad authority for appeal as of right
from almost every kind of intermediate determination is a prime source of
delay and expense in litigation and imposes an undue burden on the Appellate
Divisions. Nevertheless, the proposal of the CPLR revisers to eliminate the
broad catch-all language met with substantial opposition from some segments
of the bar. The result was a compromise limited only to orders on motions to
require a more definite statement or to strike scandalous or prejudicial matter
in a pleading; as to these CPLR 5701(b) now requires permission to appeal.

* * *

Today * * * it is well known that there is hardly a question of practice
that cannot be appealed; and, if a matter is said to be addressed to the court's
discretion or favor, this may mean a more limited scope of review but will
rarely affect appealability. Appeals on practice matters are legion, ranging far
and wide over questions of venue, parties, consolidation and joint trial,
pleading and pre-trial disclosure. The only meaningful method of inquiry as to
the content of the present standards is to examine the types of orders that
have been held *not* to involve some part of the merits or affect a substantial
right.

Notes and Questions

1. What are the advantages of freely allowing appeals from interlocutory
orders? The disadvantages? Is it better to resolve the question of allowing an
interlocutory appeal by weighing these advantages and disadvantages against each
other in the abstract or by considering them as they apply in each case? See
generally Scheffel, Note, *Interlocutory Appeals in New York—Time Has Come for a
More Efficient Approach*, 16 Pace L.Rev. 607 (1996).

2. In refusing to allow an appeal from an interlocutory order, an unnecessary appellate hearing may be avoided; in allowing an appeal, an unnecessary trial
may be avoided, either by disposing of the case at that stage or by correcting in
advance of trial an error that might otherwise require a new trial. Is there any
basis for supposing that the appellate hearing is more likely to prove unnecessary
than the trial? Is it relevant that the trial judge, hopefully, will be correct in his
rulings more often than he is wrong?

Even if it is assumed that a reversal of the trial court's order by the appellate
court is as probable as its affirmance and consideration is taken of the possibility
that trial may demand more time of lawyers and judges than an appeal, does it
follow that interlocutory appeals should be freely allowed? Consider the effect of
the following factors. (1) In the course of a single lawsuit there may be many
interlocutory orders from which one of the parties would like to appeal; thus, if
finality is required, several appeals may be saved for every trial that would be
saved under the other approach. (2) Not every reversal of an interlocutory order
will terminate the case without trial. (3) The number of appellate courts cannot be
increased as readily as can the number of trial courts in order to take care of
heavier calendars. There will be a serious problem as long as it is the function of

appellate courts not only to review trial-court decisions but to establish and maintain a degree of uniformity in the law.

The debate over the relative merits of a final-judgment rule and an interlocutory-appeal system is intertwined with the larger problem of court congestion at the appellate level. See Project, *The Appellate Division of the Supreme Court of New York: An Empirical Study of Its Powers and Functions as an Intermediate State Court,* 47 Fordham L.Rev. 929, 1006–08 (1979). The attention given to crowding at the trial level has obscured the fact that a comparable problem exists in many reviewing courts.

3. Appeals are expensive. See Willcox, Karlen & Roemer, *Justice Lost—By What Appellate Papers Cost,* 33 N.Y.U.L.Rev. 934 (1958); Note, *Cost of Appeal,* 27 Mont.L.Rev. 49 (1965). Preparation of the necessary briefs and records demands a substantial amount of the lawyer's time, and duplication of these documents is costly, although some progress has been made in recent years by reducing the need to reproduce certain parts of the record and by using cheaper processes than printing for duplicating records and briefs. Substantial travelling costs often are involved because an appellate court usually is not as proximate to the attorneys as is the trial court. Because of expense and the delay caused by congestion, the availability of appeal often presents a tactical opportunity to one of the parties. Is there any effective sanction against the use of appeal for purely tactical reasons? See Kamine, *Frivolous Appeals,* 47 Calif.St.B.J. 307 (1972). In what ways might modern communications and duplication technology reduce the cost of appeals?

4. Should the avoidance of extra expense, delay, and needless hearings be the only consideration in deciding whether to permit appeals from interlocutory orders? Is the trial judge's independence and discretion threatened by too frequent a review? Is a party who has been ordered to answer questions in a deposition interested in obtaining immediate review solely in order to save time or money?

4. DEPARTURES FROM THE FINAL–JUDGMENT RULE IN THE FEDERAL COURTS

a. Amelioration of the Basic Concept

(i) Cases Involving Multiple Claims

———

Read Federal Rule of Civil Procedure 54(b) in the Supplement, with the accompanying material.

———

SEARS, ROEBUCK & CO. v. MACKEY, 351 U.S. 427, 76 S.Ct. 895, 100 L.Ed. 1297 (1956). Mackey brought suit for damages against Sears, Roebuck under the Sherman Antitrust Act (Counts I & II) and under common law for unlawfully inducing a breach of contract (Count III) and unfair competition and patent infringement (Count IV). The District Court dismissed only those claims presented in Counts I and II. On appeal to the Court of Appeals for the Seventh Circuit, the court upheld its appellate jurisdiction under 28 U.S.C. § 1291. The Supreme Court affirmed.

The Court noted that before the promulgation of the Federal Rules, no appeal would have been allowed from the final determination of Counts I and II since the District Court's judgment was not a final decision of the whole case. However, with the adoption of the Federal Rules and the subsequent increase in multiple-claim actions, the promulgators recognized the need to ameliorate the standard that *"all* claims had to be finally decided before an appeal could be entertained from a final decision upon any of them." Id. at 434, 76 S.Ct. at 899, 100 L.Ed. at 1305. Consequently, Rule 54(b) was adopted.

* * * [Rule 54(b), as amended in 1946,] does not relax the finality required of each decision, as an individual claim, to render it appealable, but it does provide a practical means of permitting an appeal to be taken from one or more final decisions on individual claims, in multiple claims actions, without waiting for final decisions to be rendered on *all* the claims in the case. * * *

To meet the demonstrated need for flexibility, the District Court is used as a "dispatcher." It is permitted to determine, in the first instance, the appropriate *time when each "final decision"* upon "one or more but less than all" of the claims in a multiple claims action is ready for appeal. This arrangement already has lent welcome certainty to the appellate procedure. Its "negative effect" has met with uniform approval. The effect so referred to is the rule's specific requirement that for "one or more but less than all" multiple claims to become appealable, the District Court must make both "an express determination that there is no just reason for delay" and "an express direction for the entry of judgment." A party adversely affected by a final decision thus knows that his time for appeal will *not* run against him until this certification has been made.

* * *

In the case before us, there is no doubt that each of the claims dismissed is a "claim for relief" within the meaning of Rule 54(b), or that their dismissal constitutes a "final decision" on individual claims. Also, it cannot well be argued that the claims stated in Counts I and II are so inherently inseparable from, or closely related to, those stated in Counts III and IV that the District Court has abused its discretion in certifying that there exists no just reason for delay. They certainly *can* be decided independently of each other.

Petitioner contends that amended Rule 54(b) attempts to make an unauthorized extension of § 1291. We disagree. It could readily be argued here that the claims stated in Counts I and II are sufficiently independent of those stated in Counts III and IV to satisfy the requirements of Rule 54(b) even in its original form. * * *

* * * The District Court *cannot,* in the exercise of its discretion, treat as "final" that which is not "final" within the meaning of § 1291. But the District Court *may,* by the exercise of its discretion in the interest of sound judicial administration, release for appeal final decisions upon one or more, but less than all, claims in multiple claims actions. The timing of such a release is, with good reason, vested by the rule primarily in the discretion of the District Court as the one most likely to be familiar with the case and with any justifiable reasons for delay. * * *

* * * [Rule 54] does not supersede any statute controlling appellate jurisdiction. It scrupulously recognizes the statutory requirement of a "final decision" under § 1291 as a basic requirement for an appeal to the Court of Appeals. It merely administers that requirement in a practical manner in multiple claims actions and does so by rule instead of by judicial decision. By its negative effect, it operates to restrict in a valid manner the number of appeals in multiple claims actions.

We reach a like conclusion as to the validity of the amended rule where the District Court acts affirmatively and thus assists in properly timing the release of final decisions in multiple claims actions. The amended rule adapts the single judicial unit theory so that it better meets the current needs of judicial administration. Just as Rule 54(b), in its original form, resulted in the release of some decisions on claims in multiple claims actions before they otherwise would have been released, so amended Rule 54(b) now makes possible the release of more of such decisions subject to judicial supervision. The amended rule preserves the historic federal policy against piecemeal appeals in many cases more effectively than did the original rule.

Id. at 435–38, 76 S.Ct. at 899–901, 100 L.Ed. at 1306–07 (emphasis in original).

On the same day it decided *Mackey,* the Supreme Court in COLD METAL PROCESS CO. v. UNITED ENGINEERING & FOUNDRY CO., 351 U.S. 445, 76 S.Ct. 904, 100 L.Ed. 1311 (1956), held that an appeal by defendant was appropriate under Section 1291 and Rule 54(b) even though a counterclaim arising out of the same transaction had not yet been decided. Justice Frankfurter, who concurred in *Mackey,* dissented in *Cold Metal:*

The Court does indicate that what has been the core of the doctrine of finality as applied to multiple claims litigation—that only that part of a litigation which is separate from, and independent of, the remainder of the litigation can be appealed before the completion of the entire litigation—is no longer to be applied as a standard, or at least as an exclusive standard, for deciding what is final for purposes of § 1291. The Court does not, however, indicate what standards the district courts and the courts of appeals are now to apply in determining when a decision is final. It leaves this problem in the first instance to the district courts, subject to review by the courts of appeals for an abuse of discretion. In other instances where a district court's ruling can be upset only for an abuse of its discretion, the scope of review is necessarily narrow. Here, in regard to the present problem, what is to come under review is a newly modified requirement of finality. But the requirement continues to be based upon a statute * * * and that statute defines and constricts the jurisdiction of the courts of appeals. Therefore the issue of compliance with this congressional command would, I should suppose, cast upon the courts of appeals a duty of independent judgment broader than is implied by the usual flavor of the phrase "abuse of discretion."

For me, the propositions emerging from analysis of the relationship of Rule 54(b) to 28 U.S.C. § 1291 are clear.

1. 28 U.S.C. § 1291 is left intact by Rule 54(b). * * *

2. 28 U.S.C. § 1291 is not a technical rule in a game. It expresses not only a deeply rooted but a wisely sanctioned principle against piecemeal appeals governing litigation in the federal courts. * * * The great importance of this characteristic feature of the federal judicial system * * * is made luminously manifest by considering the evils where, as in New York, piecemeal reviews are allowed.

3. * * * What have been called exceptions are not exceptions at all in the sense of inroads on the principle. They have not qualified the core, that is, that there should be no premature, intermediate appeal.

* * *

4. The expansion by the Federal Rules of the allowable content of a proceeding and the range of a litigation inevitably enlarged the occasions for severing one aspect or portion of a litigation from what remains under the traditional test of a "final decision." On the basis of prior cases, we held that it was not a departure from the policy against piecemeal appeals to permit an appeal with respect to that part of a multiple claims litigation based on a set of facts separate and independent from the facts on which the remainder of the litigation was based. * * *

The principles which this Court has heretofore enunciated over a long course of decisions under § 1291 furnish ready guides for deciding the appealability of the certified parts of the litigation in the two cases now before the Court. Count II in Sears, Roebuck & Co. v. Mackey * * * is appealable since the transactions and occurrences involved in it do not involve any of those embraced in Counts III and IV. Count I involves at least two transactions which are also the subject matter of Counts III and IV but is appealable under § 1292(1) as an interlocutory order denying an injunction. In *Cold Metal* * * * the counterclaim, even if not compulsory, is based in substantial part on the transactions involved in the main litigation and hence not appealable.

Id. at 439–43, 76 S.Ct. at 902–04, 100 L.Ed. at 1308–10.

Notes and Questions

1. In CURTISS–WRIGHT CORP. v. GENERAL ELECTRIC CO., 446 U.S. 1, 100 S.Ct. 1460, 64 L.Ed.2d 1 (1980), Curtiss–Wright brought a diversity action, seeking damages and reformation with regard to a series of contracts between it and General Electric. General Electric counterclaimed. As to one of Curtiss–Wright's affirmative claims—for $19 million due on the contracts already performed—the District Court granted summary judgment for Curtiss–Wright. When Curtiss–Wright requested certification of this judgment as a final judgment under Rule 54(b), the court granted the motion—after determining, as required by the Rule, that there was "no just reason for delay." The Third Circuit reversed on the ground that the existence of a nonfrivolous counterclaim limited the power of the District Court to enter a final judgment on the original claim. In the view of the Court of Appeals, the District Court had abused its discretion by granting the Rule 54(b) certification.

The Supreme Court agreed with the District Court:

* * * The mere presence of [nonfrivolous counterclaims] * * * does not render a Rule 54(b) certification inappropriate. If it did, Rule 54(b) would lose

1156   APPELLATE REVIEW   Ch. 16

much of its utility. * * * [C]ounterclaims, whether compulsory or permissive, present no special problems for Rule 54(b) determinations; counterclaims are not to be evaluated differently from other claims. * * * Like other claims, their significance for Rule 54(b) purposes turns on their interrelationship with the claims on which certification is sought. Here, the District Judge determined that General Electric's counterclaims were severable from the claims which had been determined in terms of both the factual and the legal issues involved. The Court of Appeals did not conclude otherwise.

What the Court of Appeals found objectionable about the District Judge's exercise of discretion was the assessment of the equities involved. The Court of Appeals concluded that the possibility of a setoff required that the status quo be maintained unless petitioner could show harsh or unusual circumstances; it held that such a showing had not been made in the District Court.

This holding reflects a misinterpretation of the standard of review for Rule 54(b) certifications and a misperception of the appellate function in such cases. * * *

There are thus two aspects to the proper function of a reviewing court in Rule 54(b) cases. The court of appeals must, of course, scrutinize the district court's evaluation of such factors as the interrelationship of the claims so as to prevent piecemeal appeals in cases which should be reviewed only as single units. But once such juridical concerns have been met, the discretionary judgment of the district court should be given substantial deference, for that court is "the one most likely to be familiar with the case and with any justifiable reasons for delay." * * * The reviewing court should disturb the trial court's assessment of the equities only if it can say that the judge's conclusion was clearly unreasonable. Plainly, sound judicial administration does not require that Rule 54(b) requests be granted routinely. That is implicit in commending them to the sound discretion of a district court. Because this discretion "is, with good reason, vested by the rule primarily" in the district courts, * * * and because the number of possible situations is large, we are reluctant either to fix or sanction narrow guidelines for the district courts to follow. We are satisfied, however, that on the record here the District Court's assessment of the equities was reasonable.

Id. at 9–11, 100 S.Ct. at 1465–66, 64 L.Ed.2d at 11–13.

2. Why did the Supreme Court indicate in *Mackey* that Rule 54(b) would be an unauthorized Rule if it extended the scope of 28 U.S.C. § 1291? Reread 28 U.S.C. § 2072 in the Supplement.

3. Is the purpose of Rule 54(b) the same as that underlying 28 U.S.C. § 1292(b), which allows interlocutory appeals at the joint discretion of the district judge and the court of appeals? Will the appeal of separate claims speed up or delay the final resolution of the entire case? See generally Fogarty, *The Finality of Partial Orders in Consolidated Cases Under Rule 54(b)*, 57 Fordham L.Rev. 637 (1989).

4. If the trial judge determines that there is no reason for delay and orders judgment entered on a separate claim, and no immediate appeal is taken from that order, may the judgment on the separate claim be attacked on an appeal from the final judgment on the entire case? May the propriety of entering judgment on the separate claim be challenged at that time?

5. If the trial judge, in accordance with Rule 54(b), directs entry of judgment on a separate claim that "certainly *can* be decided independently," may the court

of appeals nonetheless refuse to hear the appeal? In PANICHELLA v. PENNSYLVANIA RAILROAD CO., 252 F.2d 452 (3d Cir.1958), the court held that the district judge had abused his discretion in directing the separate entry of judgment against defendant on his claim against an impleaded third party, because (1) the whole matter would be moot if defendant prevailed against plaintiff, (2) the legal effect of the same release was in question both on the third-party claim and the principal claim and thus would have to be determined twice by the Court of Appeals if this appeal were allowed, and (3) the claimed advantage of allowing the appeal—that the two claims could be tried together if the appeal were successful—would necessitate delaying the trial of the principal claim. Does the fact that a third-party claim was involved affect the weight to be given the court's third point?

6. Although district court discretion in invoking Rule 54(b) is broad, it is not unlimited. In GERARDI v. PELULLO, 16 F.3d 1363, 1372 (3d Cir.1994), the court held that the district court abused its discretion when it concluded that [the judgments] were ready for appeal pursuant to Rule 54(b). The court expressed the view "that a district court should be conservative in invoking Rule 54(b) to certify a judgment as final because if an aggrieved party appeals following the certification, the district court effectively will be electing to control the docket of a court of appeals."

(ii) Decisions Involving "Collateral Orders"

In COHEN v. BENEFICIAL INDUSTRIAL LOAN CORP., 337 U.S. 541, 69 S.Ct. 1221, 93 L.Ed. 1528 (1949), Cohen brought a shareholder's derivative suit in a New Jersey federal court. The District Court denied Beneficial's motion to require Cohen to post security for costs pursuant to a New Jersey statute, holding the statute inapplicable to an action in a federal court. The Court of Appeals reversed, and the Supreme Court affirmed that decision. The Justices addressed the question of appealability in the following passage:

> * * * Appeal gives the upper court a power of review, not one of intervention. So long as the matter remains open, unfinished or inconclusive, there may be no intrusion by appeal. But the District Court's action upon this application was concluded and closed and its decision final in that sense before the appeal was taken.
>
> Nor does the statute permit appeals, even from fully consummated decisions, where they are but steps towards final judgment in which they will merge. The purpose is to combine in one review all stages of the proceeding that effectively may be reviewed and corrected if and when final judgment results. But this order of the District Court did not make any step toward final disposition of the merits of the case and will not be merged in final judgment. When that time comes, it will be too late effectively to review the present order and the rights conferred by the statute, if it is applicable, will have been lost, probably irreparably. We conclude that the matters embraced in the decision appealed from are not of such an interlocutory nature as to affect, or to be affected by, decision of the merits of this case.
>
> This decision appears to fall in that small class which finally determine claims of right separable from, and collateral to, rights asserted in the action, too important to be denied review and too independent of the

cause itself to require that appellate consideration be deferred until the whole case is adjudicated. The Court has long given this provision of the statute this practical rather than a technical construction. * * *

We hold this order appealable because it is a final disposition of a claimed right which is not an ingredient of the cause of action and does not require consideration with it. * * * Here it is the right to security that presents a serious and unsettled question. If the right were admitted or clear and the order involved only an exercise of discretion as to the amount of security, a matter the statute makes subject to reconsideration from time to time, appealability would present a different question.

Id. at 545, 69 S.Ct. at 1225, 93 L.Ed. at 1536.

Notes and Questions

1. In LAURO LINES S.R.L. v. CHASSER, 490 U.S. 495, 109 S.Ct. 1976, 104 L.Ed.2d 548 (1989), the plaintiffs were passengers or representatives of former passengers aboard the Achille Lauro when it was hijacked by terrorists of the Palestine Liberation Organization. The passengers were held captive and terrorized, and filed consolidated actions to recover damages. Defendant moved to dismiss on several grounds, including that a forum-selection clause in each passenger ticket required plaintiffs to bring suit in Naples, Italy. The District Court denied the motions to dismiss, concluding that the clause on the ticket did not reasonably communicate the importance of the provision: "[I]t does not give fair warning to the American citizen passenger that he or she is renouncing and waiving his or her opportunity to sue in a domestic forum over a contract made and delivered in the United States." District court transcript dated October 21, 1987, at 5. Defendant sought to appeal the District Court's orders. The Second Circuit dismissed the appeal on the ground that the orders were interlocutory and did not fall into the exception for collateral orders established in *Cohen*. The Supreme Court affirmed, pointing out that, to satisfy the *Cohen* exception, an order must conclusively determine the disputed question, resolve an important issue completely separate from the merits of the action, and be effectively unreviewable on appeal from a final judgment. The Court found that the third condition was not satisfied:

> * * * Petitioner's claim that it may be sued only in Naples, while not perfectly secured by appeal after final judgment, is adequately vindicable at that stage—surely as effectively vindicable as a claim that the trial court lacked personal jurisdiction over the defendant—and hence does not fall within the third prong of the collateral order doctrine.

Id. at 501, 109 S.Ct. at 1979, 104 L.Ed.2d at 555.

In VAN CAUWENBERGHE v. BIARD, 486 U.S. 517, 108 S.Ct. 1945, 100 L.Ed.2d 517 (1988), the Supreme Court unanimously held that the denial of a motion to dismiss on the ground that an extradited person is immune from civil process, or on grounds of *forum non conveniens,* is not a collateral order subject to immediate appeal as a final judgment under Section 1291.

If a motion to dismiss is denied in circumstances such as those in *Chasser* and *Biard,* jurisdiction over the person is asserted and the defendant must bear the full costs of trial and wait for final judgment to appeal. Is this fair to the defendant? Does she have any remedy in the event that an appellate court later finds that jurisdiction was not present? Note that it may be in the interest of plaintiff as well as defendant to have such motions decided before a costly, perhaps meaningless, trial takes place. Should the parties be permitted to obtain an immediate appeal if they make a joint request therefor?

2. Although observing that most discovery orders are not "sufficiently separable from the merits of the underlying dispute" to fall within the *Cohen* standard, the First Circuit has said that denials of protective orders may be immediately appealable under *Cohen,* if resolution of the matter turns on whether irreparable harm will result to appellants, "not from the district court order itself, but from a delay in obtaining appellate review of that order." In re San Juan Star Co., 662 F.2d 108, 112 (1st Cir.1981), quoting In re Continental Investment Corp., 637 F.2d 1, 5 (1st Cir.1980). Thus, the court concluded that it could review interlocutory orders prohibiting the attorneys in a civil rights suit arising out of the shooting of two suspected terrorists from disclosing, prior to trial, to the press, to their clients, or to any third party, any evidence obtained through depositions.

3. In UNITED STATES v. RYAN, 402 U.S. 530, 91 S.Ct. 1580, 29 L.Ed.2d 85 (1971), and COBBLEDICK v. UNITED STATES, 309 U.S. 323, 60 S.Ct. 540, 84 L.Ed. 783 (1940), petitioners had moved unsuccessfully in the District Court to quash subpoenas directing them to appear and produce documents before a grand jury. In each case the Supreme Court held that the Court of Appeals was required to dismiss the appeal from the District Court order. According to the Supreme Court, if petitioners disobeyed the order and were found in contempt, their situation would become "so severed from the main proceeding as to permit an appeal." The Court distinguished PERLMAN v. UNITED STATES, 247 U.S. 7, 38 S.Ct. 417, 62 L.Ed. 950 (1918), in which an appeal was allowed from an order denying a motion to prohibit turning over to a grand jury property already in the custody of the court, on the ground that the person making the motion in that case was otherwise "powerless to avert the mischief of the order." Are the cases really distinguishable? Consider the fact that a grand-jury proceeding has no defined litigants and that it renders no "final judgments" in the same sense as does a court.

In UNITED STATES v. NIXON, 418 U.S. 683, 690–92, 94 S.Ct. 3090, 3098–99, 41 L.Ed.2d 1039, 1053–55 (1974), the President of the United States had been ordered to produce certain tape recordings for examination by a federal district judge. The Supreme Court said that an appeal would lie under the doctrine of the *Perlman* case. It explained that "the traditional contempt avenue to immediate appeal is peculiarly inappropriate due to the unique setting in which the question arises. To require a President of the United States to place himself in the posture of disobeying an order of a court merely to trigger the procedural mechanism for review of the ruling would be unseemly, and would present an unnecessary occasion for constitutional confrontation between two branches of the Government."

4. May a person always obtain review of an interlocutory order by disobeying it and being found in contempt? In what type of case might even this Spartan tactic be unavailable? When it is available, is this method of obtaining review an adequate or rational substitute for allowing an appeal from the interlocutory order in the first place? Hickman v. Taylor, p. 849, supra, was a case in which review was obtained of an interlocutory discovery order through disobedience and contempt. In that case, defendants and their lawyer were found in criminal contempt, and an appeal was allowed. Had they been found in civil contempt—that is, if the contempt citation were intended only to coerce compliance with the order and not

to punish their disobedience of it—defendants, and quite possibly the lawyer as well, would not have been able to appeal because an adjudication of civil contempt is not regarded as a final order as to the parties. See Fox v. Capital Co., 299 U.S. 105, 57 S.Ct. 57, 81 L.Ed. 67 (1936). See also Powers v. Chicago Transit Authority, 846 F.2d 1139 (7th Cir.1988).

In UNITED STATES CATHOLIC CONFERENCE v. ABORTION RIGHTS MOBILIZATION, INC., 487 U.S. 72, 108 S.Ct. 2268, 101 L.Ed.2d 69 (1988), Abortion Rights Mobilization, Inc. and others (collectively, ARM) filed suit against government officials and the United States Catholic Conference and the National Conference of Catholic Bishops (collectively, USCC) to revoke the Roman Catholic Church's tax-exempt status on the ground that the Church had violated the anti-electioneering provision of 26 U.S.C. § 501(c)(3). USCC was later dismissed from the suit, and only the government defendants remained. Nevertheless, ARM served subpoenas on USCC in order to obtain evidence to support its claims. USCC refused to comply with the subpoenas and moved to quash the subpoenas on the ground that the District Court lacked subject-matter jurisdiction over the dispute between ARM and the government defendants. The District Court refused to quash the subpoena. Subsequently, USCC was held in civil contempt. The court assessed fines of $50,000 per day for each day of noncompliance.

The Court of Appeals upheld the contempt citations. It held that a nonparty witness can resist discovery by challenging the trial court's subject-matter jurisdiction in defense of a civil contempt citation only if it can show that there is no colorable basis for exercising subject-matter jurisdiction.

The Supreme Court reversed, holding that

a nonparty witness can challenge the court's lack of subject-matter jurisdiction in defense of a civil contempt citation, notwithstanding the absence of a final judgment in the underlying action. * * * [While] a District Court [has] the power to issue subpoenas as to witnesses and documents, * * * the subpoena power of a court cannot be more extensive than its jurisdiction. * * * Therefore, a nonparty witness may attack a civil contempt citation by asserting that the issuing court lacks jurisdiction over the case.

The right of a nonparty to appeal an adjudication of contempt cannot be questioned. The order finding a nonparty witness in contempt is appealable notwithstanding the absence of a final judgment in the underlying action. * * * Once the right to appeal a civil contempt order is acknowledged, arguments in its legitimate support should not be so confined that the power of the issuing court remains untested. * * *

The challenge in this case goes to the subject matter jurisdiction of the court and hence its power to issue the order. The distinction between subject-matter jurisdiction and waivable defenses is not a mere nicety of legal metaphysics. It rests instead on the central principle of a free society that courts have finite bounds of authority, some of constitutional origin, which exist to protect citizens from the very wrong asserted here, the excessive use of judicial power. The courts, no less than the political branches of the government, must respect the limits of their authority.

Id. at 76–77, 108 S.Ct. at 2270–71, 101 L.Ed.2d at 76–77. Allowing a nonparty witness to challenge the jurisdiction of the court presents a risk that a party might try to avoid the prohibition on interlocutory appeals by collusively having the nonparty witness test the court's jurisdiction as her proxy. In *United States Catholic Conference*, the Supreme Court found that there was ample protection against collusive appeals in a Court of Appeals' ability to treat a witness as a party if it found collusion, and in the sanctions available for frivolous appeals or abuse of court processes. Do these measures really provide adequate safeguards against collusive appeals? Are the procedural rules working properly when a nonparty witness, such as USCC, is permitted to take an interlocutory appeal, but a party to the case, such as ARM, must wait for final judgment?

5. Would the orders in *Ryan* and *Cobbledick* have been appealable in New York? Would a discretionary appeal be available under 28 U.S.C. § 1292(b) to test a discovery order in a federal court? See pp. 1174–79, infra.

6. In FORGAY v. CONRAD, 47 U.S. (6 How.) 201, 203, 12 L.Ed. 404, 405 (1848), the trial court, upon finding that a fraudulent conveyance had been made, ordered property delivered to an assignee in bankruptcy and directed an accounting before a master. The order to deliver was held appealable even before the conclusion of the accounting because of the irreparable injury that might be sustained if the property were disposed of by the assignee in bankruptcy while the accounting was in progress. Chief Justice Taney said: "Undoubtedly, [the decree] * * * is not final, in the strict, technical sense of that term. But this court has not heretofore understood the words 'final decrees' in this strict and technical sense, but has given to them a more liberal, and, as we think, a more reasonable construction, and one more consonant to the intention of the legislature."

In BROWN SHOE CO. v. UNITED STATES, 370 U.S. 294, 82 S.Ct. 1502, 8 L.Ed.2d 510 (1962), the District Court found defendant had violated the antitrust laws and directed divestiture of a subsidiary, but it reserved its ruling on a specific plan of divestiture. On a direct appeal by the shoe company under the Expediting Act, 15 U.S.C. § 29, the Supreme Court held the divestiture decree was sufficiently final to be appealable even though a specific plan had not been formulated. Its own past practice, said the Court, had been to hear such appeals in antitrust cases; the substantive aspects of the case had been fully determined and to delay decision on the merits would chill the "careful, and often extended, negotiation and formulation" of the final divestiture order.

Should an appeal from an order such as those in *Cohen, Forgay, and Brown Shoe* be subject to the requirements of Rule 54(b)? See 10 Wright, Miller & Kane, *Federal Practice and Procedure: Civil 2d* § 2658.4 (1998); Annot., 3 A.L.R.2d 342 (1949). Does the *Brown Shoe* decision reflect the operation of the same considerations that Crick found to have been influential in the history of appeals in English equity? See pp. 1144–45, supra.

In which of the cases thus far considered would it be practical for the proceedings in the lower court to continue while the appeal was being determined? Is this factor relevant to the decision whether to allow appeal? See Note, *Appealability in the Federal Courts*, 75 Harv.L.Rev. 351, 365 (1961).

Cohen has been described as an exception to the final decision rule. The Supreme Court has construed *Cohen* and the collateral order doctrine as being best understood "not as an exception to the 'final decision' rule laid down by Congress in Section 1291, but as a 'practical construction' of it." Digital Equipment Corp. v. Desktop Direct, Inc., 511 U.S. 863, 114 S.Ct. 1992, 128 L.Ed.2d 842 (1994). The case that follows, Coopers & Lybrand v. Livesay, considers the limits of "practical construction."

COOPERS & LYBRAND v. LIVESAY

Supreme Court of the United States, 1978.
437 U.S. 463, 98 S.Ct. 2454, 57 L.Ed.2d 351.

Certiorari to the United States Court of Appeals for the Eighth Circuit.

MR. JUSTICE STEVENS delivered the opinion of the Court.

The question in this case is whether a district court's determination that an action may not be maintained as a class action pursuant to Fed.Rule Civ.Proc. 23 is a "final decision" within the meaning of 28 U.S.C. § 1291 and therefore appealable as a matter of right. Because there is a conflict in the Circuits over this issue, we granted certiorari and now hold that such an order is not appealable under § 1291.

Petitioner, Coopers & Lybrand, is an accounting firm that certified the financial statements in a prospectus issued in connection with a 1972 public offering of securities in Punta Gorda Isles for an aggregate price of over $18 million. Respondents purchased securities in reliance on that prospectus. In its next annual report to shareholders, Punta Gorda restated the earnings that had been reported in the prospectus for 1970 and 1971 by writing down its net income for each year by over $1 million. Thereafter, respondents sold their Punta Gorda securities and sustained a loss of $2,650 on their investment.

* * * [Respondents] alleged that petitioner and other defendants had violated various sections of the Securities Act of 1933 and the Securities Exchange Act of 1934. The District Court first certified, and then, after further proceedings, decertified the class.

Respondents did not request the District Court to certify its order for interlocutory review under 28 U.S.C. § 1292(b). Rather, they filed a notice of appeal pursuant to § 1291. The Court of Appeals regarded its appellate jurisdiction as depending on whether the decertification order had sounded the "death knell" of the action. After examining the amount of respondents' claims in relation to their financial resources and the probable cost of the litigation, the court concluded that they would not pursue their claims individually. The Court of Appeals therefore held that it had jurisdiction to hear the appeal and, on the merits, reversed the order decertifying the class. * * *

Federal appellate jurisdiction generally depends on the existence of a decision by the District Court that "ends the litigation on the merits and leaves nothing for the court to do but execute the judgment." * * * An order refusing to certify, or decertifying, a class does not of its own force terminate the entire litigation because the plaintiff is free to proceed on his individual claim. Such an order is appealable, therefore, only if it comes within an appropriate exception to the final-judgment rule. In this case respondents rely on the "collateral order" exception articulated by this Court in Cohen v. Beneficial Industrial Loan Corp., * * * and on the "death knell" doctrine adopted by several Circuits to determine the appealability of orders denying class certification.

I

* * *

To come within the "small class" of decisions excepted from the final-judgment rule by *Cohen,* the order must conclusively determine the disputed question, resolve an important issue completely separate from the merits of the action, and be effectively unreviewable on appeal from a final judgment. * * * An order passing on a request for class certification does not fall in that category. First, such an order is subject to revision in the District Court. Fed.Rule Civ.Proc. 23(c)(1). Second, the class determination generally involves considerations that are "enmeshed in the factual and legal issues comprising the plaintiff's cause of action." * * * Finally, an order denying class certification is subject to effective review after final judgment at the behest of the named plaintiff or intervening class members. United Airlines, Inc. v. McDonald, 432 U.S. 385, 97 S.Ct. 2464, 53 L.Ed.2d 423. For these reasons, as the Courts of Appeals have consistently recognized, the collateral-order doctrine is not applicable to the kind of order involved in this case.

II

Several Circuits, including the Court of Appeals in this case, have held that an order denying class certification is appealable if it is likely to sound the "death knell" of the litigation. The "death knell" doctrine assumes that without the incentive of a possible group recovery the individual plaintiff may find it economically imprudent to pursue his lawsuit to a final judgment and then seek appellate review of an adverse class determination. Without questioning this assumption, we hold that orders relating to class certification are not independently appealable under § 1291 prior to judgment.

* * *

There are special rules relating to class actions and, to that extent, they are a special kind of litigation. Those rules do not, however, contain any unique provisions governing appeals. The appealability of any order entered in a class action is determined by the same standards that govern appealability in other types of litigation. Thus, if the "death knell" doctrine has merit, it would apply equally to the many interlocutory orders in ordinary litigation— rulings on discovery, on venue, on summary judgment—that may have such tactical economic significance that a defeat is tantamount to a "death knell" for the entire case.

Though a refusal to certify a class is inherently interlocutory, it may induce a plaintiff to abandon his individual claim. On the other hand, the litigation will often survive an adverse class determination. What effect the economic disincentives created by an interlocutory order may have on the fate of any litigation will depend on a variety of factors.[15] Under the "death knell" doctrine, appealability turns on the court's perception of that impact in the individual case. Thus, if the court believes that the plaintiff has adequate incentive to continue, the order is considered interlocutory; but if the court concludes that the ruling, as a practical matter, makes further litigation improbable, it is considered an appealable final decision.

* * *

---

15. *E.g.,* the plaintiff's resources; the size of his claim and his subjective willingness to finance prosecution of the claim; the probable cost of the litigation and the possibility of joining others who will share that cost; and the prospect of prevailing on the merits and reversing an order denying class certification.

A threshold inquiry of this kind may, it is true, identify some orders that would truly end the litigation prior to final judgment; allowing an immediate appeal from those orders may enhance the quality of justice afforded a few litigants. But this incremental benefit is outweighed by the impact of such an individualized jurisdictional inquiry on the judicial system's overall capacity to administer justice.

The potential waste of judicial resources is plain. The district court must take evidence, entertain argument, and make findings; and the court of appeals must review that record and those findings simply to determine whether a discretionary class determination is subject to appellate review. And if the record provides an inadequate basis for this determination, a remand for further factual development may be required. Moreover, even if the court makes a "death knell" finding and reviews the class-designation order on the merits, there is no assurance that the trial process will not again be disrupted by interlocutory review. For even if a ruling that the plaintiff does not adequately represent the class is reversed on appeal, the district court may still refuse to certify the class on the ground that, for example, common questions of law or fact do not predominate. Under the "death knell" theory, plaintiff would again be entitled to an appeal as a matter of right pursuant to § 1291. And since other kinds of interlocutory orders may also create the risk of a premature demise, the potential for multiple appeals in every complex case is apparent and serious.

Perhaps the principal vice of the "death knell" doctrine is that it authorizes *indiscriminate* interlocutory review of decisions made by the trial judge. The Interlocutory Appeals Act of 1958 * * * was enacted to meet the recognized need for prompt review of certain nonfinal orders. However, Congress carefully confined the availability of such review. Nonfinal orders could never be appealed as a matter of right. Moreover, the discretionary power to permit an interlocutory appeal is not, in the first instance, vested in the courts of appeals. A party seeking review of a nonfinal order must first obtain the consent of the trial judge. This screening procedure serves the dual purpose of ensuring that such review will be confined to appropriate cases and avoiding time-consuming jurisdictional determinations in the court of appeals. Finally, even if the district judge certifies the order under § 1292(b), the appellant still "has the burden of persuading the court of appeals that exceptional circumstances justify a departure from the basic policy of postponing appellate review until after the entry of a final judgment." * * * The appellate court may deny the appeal for any reason, including docket congestion. By permitting appeals of right from class-designation orders after jurisdictional determinations that turn on questions of fact, the "death knell" doctrine circumvents these restrictions.

Additional considerations reinforce our conclusion that the "death knell" doctrine does not support appellate jurisdiction of prejudgment orders denying class certification. First, the doctrine operates only in favor of plaintiffs even though the class issue—whether to certify, and if so, how large the class should be—will often be of critical importance to defendants as well. Certification of a large class may so increase the defendant's potential damages liability and litigation costs that he may find it economically prudent to settle and to abandon a meritorious defense. Yet the Courts of Appeals have correctly concluded that orders granting class certification are interlocutory.

Whatever similarities or differences there are between plaintiffs and defendants in this context involve questions of policy for Congress. Moreover, allowing appeals of right from nonfinal orders that turn on the facts of a particular case thrusts appellate courts indiscriminately into the trial process and thus defeats one vital purpose of the final-judgment rule—"that of maintaining the appropriate relationship between the respective courts ... This goal, in the absence of most compelling reasons to the contrary, is very much worth preserving."

Accordingly, * * * the judgment of the Court of Appeals is reversed with directions to dismiss the appeal.

It is so ordered.

Notes and Questions

1. In 1998, the Supreme Court promulgated Rule 23(f), which permits plaintiffs or defendants to petition the Court of Appeals to review a grant or denial of class certification. See p. 708, supra. Under what circumstances should such a petition be granted? Why was Rule 23(f) needed? Couldn't the occasional needs for appeal have been met by 28 U.S.C. § 1292(b), enacted in 1958 to allow discretionary appeals from interlocutory orders that raise a "controlling question of law" if both the trial and appellate courts agree? See pp. 1174–79, infra.

2. Do you think the fact that a defendant in a class suit brought by plaintiffs had no right to appeal the grant of class certification at the time of *Coopers & Lybrand* might have influenced the Supreme Court in its decision to find that there was no right to appeal a denial of certification based upon a "death knell" argument? Are the two situations different? See Note, 27 U.Kansas L.Rev. 529, 535–36 (1979). See also Comment, *The Appealability of Orders Denying Motions for Disqualification of Counsel in the Federal Courts*, 45 U.Chi.L.Rev. 450, 464 (1978).

3. In RICHARDSON–MERRELL, INC. v. KOLLER, 472 U.S. 424, 105 S.Ct. 2757, 86 L.Ed.2d 340 (1985), the Supreme Court reaffirmed its position on disqualification motions, stating that orders disqualifying counsel in civil cases, like orders disqualifying counsel in criminal cases and orders denying motions to disqualify in civil cases, are not collateral orders subject to appeal as final orders. The Court explained:

> * * * One purpose of the final judgment rule embodied in § 1291 is to avoid the delay that inherently accompanies time-consuming interlocutory appeals. * * * When an appellate court accepts jurisdiction of an order disqualifying counsel, the practical effect is to delay proceedings on the merits until the appeal is decided. * * *
>
> The delay accompanying an appeal results not only when counsel appeals "injudicious use of disqualification motions," but also when counsel appeals an entirely proper disqualification order. Most pretrial orders of district judges are ultimately affirmed by appellate courts. * * * Given an attorney's personal and financial interest in the disqualification decision, orders disqualifying counsel may be more likely to lead to an interlocutory appeal than other pretrial rulings, whether those rulings are correct or otherwise. To be sure, an order granting disqualification itself leads to delay. Alternate counsel must often be retained. Even in cases like this one where competent alternate counsel had already entered appearances and participated in the litigation, such counsel will need time to gain the knowledge of the disqualified attorneys. But where the disqualification decision of the trial court is correct, this delay is unavoidable. We do not think that the delay resulting from the

occasionally erroneous disqualification outweighs the delay that would result from allowing piecemeal appeal of every order disqualifying counsel.

Id. at 434, 105 S.Ct. at 2762–63, 86 L.Ed.2d at 348–49.

4. When a disqualification order of the type at issue in *Richardson-Merrell* is granted it can cripple the party whose attorney is disqualified—the attorney may have spent months or even years preparing the case, and replacing her in some instances may be a practical impossibility. Consider the parallel problem raised by IN RE CEMENT ANTITRUST LITIGATION, 673 F.2d 1020 (9th Cir.1981), affirmed sub nom. Arizona v. Ash Grove Cement Co., 459 U.S. 1190, 103 S.Ct. 1173, 75 L.Ed.2d 425 (1983). That case, a complex antitrust suit against cement producers brought by a nationwide class of public and private purchasers of cement and cement-containing products and two state-wide classes of governmental purchasers, was assigned by the Judicial Panel on Multi–District Litigation to the chief judge of the District of Arizona. After two years of coordinated pretrial proceedings, the judge certified the litigation to proceed as a class action, after which the plaintiffs filed a master class list of 210,235 entities. Two years later, defendants moved that the judge recuse himself because his wife owned shares of stock in seven of the 210,235 entities, none of which had requested exclusion from the litigation. The judge recused himself under 28 U.S.C. § 455(b)(4). The Ninth Circuit refused to disturb the judge's decision to grant the recusal motion, holding that an order granting a motion to recuse is neither a final decision within the meaning of Section 1291 nor a collateral order fitting within the *Cohen* exception. The Ninth Circuit held, relying on Hampton v. City of Chicago, 643 F.2d 478 (7th Cir.1981), that the erroneous grant of a motion to recuse does not deprive the litigant opposing the motion of any recognizable interest and rejected the appellants' sweeping arguments that allowing the trial judge's order to stand effectively would disqualify any federal district judge from hearing the case:

> * * * There may well be exceptional situations in which the costs of familiarizing a new judge, in terms of delay, will prove to be very great. However, there will also be situations in which, although the original judge's participation greatly exceeds that of the judge in *Hampton*, the effect of recusal on the course of litigation will be nonexistent or insignificant. It is not necessary to create a general rule permitting immediate appeal of all recusal decisions in order to resolve the exceptional situations. * * * Ultimately, if dissatisfied with the district judge's decision and confident that the litigation will be greatly disrupted, a party may seek a writ of mandamus from the court of appeals. It is for just such an exceptional circumstance that the writ was designed. * * * Plaintiffs have done so here and that petition will be reviewed on the merits.

Id. at 1025. Because only five Justices of the Supreme Court were not disqualified from hearing the case, a quorum of the Court did not exist and the Ninth Circuit's decision was summarily affirmed under 28 U.S.C. § 2109. On the mandamus proceeding, see Note 3, p. 1173, infra.

Do you agree with the Ninth Circuit's refusal to formulate a definite, "bright-line" rule for review of recusal motions? Are the costs of losing a judge fully familiar with the record developed in the case and the legal issues involved significant enough to warrant inclusion of review of recusal orders within the *Cohen* exception? Are recusal orders distinguishable from disqualification orders? See generally Moore, *Appellate Review of Judicial Disqualification Decisions in the Federal Courts*, 35 Hastings L.J. 829 (1984).

5. In BUDINICH v. BECTON DICKINSON & CO., 486 U.S. 196, 108 S.Ct. 1717, 100 L.Ed.2d 178 (1988), the Supreme Court addressed the analogous issue of whether a decision on the merits is final when the recoverability or amount of attorney's fees remains to be determined. Citing, among other cases, *Brown Shoe,* Note 6, p. 1161, supra, the Court found that "[a] question remaining to be decided after an order ending the litigation on the merits does not prevent finality if its resolution will not alter the order or moot or revise decisions embodied in the order." Id. at 199, 108 S.Ct. at 1720, 100 L.Ed.2d at 183. In the interest of providing a uniform rule, attorney's fees were held not to be part of the merits:

> We are not inclined to adopt a disposition that requires the merits or nonmerits status of each attorney's fee provision to be clearly established before [finality can be determined]. Courts and litigants are best served by the bright-line rule, which accords with traditional understanding, that a decision on the merits is a "final decision" for purposes of § 1291 whether or not there remains for adjudication a request for attorney's fees attributable to the case.

Id. at 202, 108 S.Ct. at 1722, 100 L.Ed.2d at 185. Does the holding in *Budinich,* that a decision can be final although attorney's fees remain to be determined, confirm the Seventh Circuit's view in Palmer v. City of Chicago, 806 F.2d 1316 (7th Cir. 1986) that such determinations are "collateral" to the decision on the merits? After *Budinich,* are these orders always collateral? Note that the Seventh Circuit required a case-by-case determination of "irreparable harm" for the attorney's fee award to be a collateral order, while the Supreme Court opted for a bright-line rule that attorney's fees never are part of the merits for the purpose of determining finality under Section 1291. What distinction between the two cases justifies the different approaches? In requiring irreparable harm, does *Palmer* confuse the requirements for finality under Section 1291 with the requirements for an injunction, appealable under Section 1292(a)(1)?

The Judicial Improvements Act of 1990 added subdivision (c) to Section 2072, which allows the Supreme Court to define, by rule, "when a ruling of a district court is final for the purposes of appeal under section 1291 * * *." The Federal Courts Study Committee, which was charged with the task of studying the federal courts and making recommendations, explained the need for that authority as follows:

> The state of the law on when a district court ruling is appealable because it is "final," or is an appealable interlocutory action, strikes many observers as unsatisfactory in several respects. The area has produced much purely procedural litigation. Courts of appeals often dismiss appeals as premature. Litigants sometimes face the possibility of waiving their right to appeal when they fail to seek timely review because it is unclear when a decision is "final" and the time for appeal begins to run. Decision doctrines—* * * especially the "collateral order" rule—blur the edges of the finality principle, require repeated attention from the Supreme Court, and may in some circumstances restrict too sharply the opportunity for interlocutory review.

> We propose that Congress consider permitting the rulemaking process to refine and supplement definitions of appellate jurisdiction under the

Rules Enabling Act, 28 U.S.C. § 2072, which, we emphasize, includes the constraint that "[s]uch rules shall not abridge, enlarge or modify any substantive right." * * * Favorable experience under this limited rule-making authority over appellate jurisdiction might later support a broader delegation of power to treat the entire area of appealability from federal district courts by rule rather than statute.

Report of the Federal Courts Study Committee 95–96 (1990).

In 1992, Congress amended Section 1292(e) of the Judicial Code to authorize the Supreme Court to prescribe rules providing for appeals of interlocutory decisions not otherwise covered by that statute. As of this writing, the Supreme Court has promulgated only one new provision, Rule 23(f), under either Section 2072(c) or Section 1292(e). See Note 1, p. 1165, supra.

b. Avoidance or Evasion of the Basic Concept—Mandamus

———

Read 28 U.S.C. § 1651(a) in the Supplement.

———

LA BUY v. HOWES LEATHER CO.

Supreme Court of the United States, 1957.
352 U.S. 249, 77 S.Ct. 309, 1 L.Ed.2d 290.

Certiorari to the United States Court of Appeals for the Seventh Circuit.

MR. JUSTICE CLARK delivered the opinion of the Court.

These two consolidated cases present a question of the power of the Courts of Appeals to issue writs of mandamus to compel a District Judge to vacate his orders entered under Rule 53(b) * * * referring antitrust cases for trial before a master. The petitioner, a United States District Judge * * *, contends that the Courts of Appeals have no such power and that, even if they did, these cases were not appropriate ones for its exercise. The Court of Appeals for the Seventh Circuit has decided unanimously that it has such power and, by a divided court, that the circumstances surrounding the references by the petitioner required it to issue the mandamus about which he complains. * * *

History of the Litigation.—These petitions for mandamus * * * arose from two antitrust actions instituted in the District Court in 1950. Rohlfing involves 87 plaintiffs * * * [and] six named defendants * * *. Shaffer involves six plaintiffs * * * and six defendants * * *.

The record indicates that the cases had been burdensome to the petitioner. In Rohlfing alone, 27 pages of the record are devoted to docket entries reflecting that petitioner had conducted many hearings on preliminary pleas and motions. * * * It is reasonable to conclude that much time would have been saved at the trial had petitioner heard the case because of his familiarity with the litigation.

* * * The cases were called on February 23, 1955, on a motion to reset them for trial. * * * The petitioner announced that "it has taken a long time to get this case at issue. I remember hearing more motions, I think, in this case than any case I have ever sat on in this court." The plaintiffs estimated that the trial would take six weeks, whereupon petitioner stated he did not know when he could try the case "if it is going to take this long." He asked if the parties could agree "to have a Master hear" it. The parties ignored this query and at a conference in chambers the next day petitioner entered the orders of reference *sua sponte*. The orders declared that the court was "confronted with an extremely congested calendar" and that "exception [*sic*] conditions exist for this reason" requiring the references. The cases were referred to the master "to take evidence and to report the same to this Court, together with his findings of fact and conclusions of law." * * *

Upon petitioner's refusal to vacate the references, these mandamus actions were filed in the Court of Appeals seeking the issuance of writs ordering petitioner to do so. These applications were grounded on 28 U.S.C. § 1651(a), the All Writs Act. * * * Declaring that the references amounted to * * * "a refusal on his [petitioner's] part, as a judge, to try the causes in due course," the Court of Appeals concluded that "in view of the extraordinary nature of these causes" the references must be vacated "if we find that the orders were beyond the court's power under the pertinent rule." * * * And, it being so found, the writs issued under the authority of the All Writs Act. * * *

The Power of the Courts of Appeals.—Petitioner contends that the power of the Courts of Appeals does not extend to the issuance of writs of mandamus to review interlocutory orders except in those cases where the review of the case on appeal after final judgment would be frustrated. * * * The question of naked power has long been settled by this Court. As late as Roche v. Evaporated Milk Association, 1943, 319 U.S. 21, 25, 63 S.Ct. 938, 941, 87 L.Ed. 1185, Mr. Chief Justice Stone reviewed the decisions and, in considering the power of Courts of Appeals to issue writs of mandamus, the Court held that "the common-law writs, like equitable remedies, may be granted or withheld in the sound discretion of the court." * * * Since the Court of Appeals could at some stage of the antitrust proceedings entertain appeals in these cases, it has power in proper circumstances, as here, to issue writs of mandamus reaching them. * * *

The Discretionary Use of the Writs.—It appears from the docket entries to which we heretofore referred that the petitioner was well informed as to the nature of the antitrust litigation * * *. Nevertheless, he referred both suits to a master on the general issue. Furthermore, neither the existence of the alleged conspiracy nor the question of liability *vel non* had been determined in either case. These issues, as well as the damages, if any, and the question concerning the issuance of an injunction, were likewise included in the references. Under all of the circumstances, we believe the Court of Appeals was justified in finding the orders of reference were an abuse of the petitioner's power under Rule 53(b). They amounted to little less than an abdication of the judicial function depriving the parties of a trial before the court on the basic issues involved in the litigation.

The use of masters is "to aid judges in the performance of specific judicial duties, as they may arise in the progress of a cause," Ex parte Peterson, 1920, 253 U.S. 300, 312, 40 S.Ct. 543, 547, 64 L.Ed. 919, and not to displace the court. The exceptional circumstances here warrant the use of the extraordinary remedy of mandamus. * * *

It is also contended that the Seventh Circuit has erroneously construed the All Writs Act as "conferring on it a 'roving commission' to supervise interlocutory orders of the District Courts in advance of final decision." Our examination of its opinions in this regard leads us to the conclusion that the Court of Appeals has exercised commendable self-restraint. It is true that mandamus should be resorted to only in extreme cases, since it places trial judges in the anomalous position of being litigants without counsel other than uncompensated volunteers. However, there is an end of patience and it clearly appears that the Court of Appeals has [since 1938] * * * admonished the trial judges of the Seventh Circuit that the practice of making references "does not commend itself" and " * * * should seldom be made, and if at all only when unusual circumstances exist." * * * Still the Court of Appeals did not disturb the reference practice by reversal or mandamus until this case was decided in October 1955. * * * The record does not show to what extent references are made by the full bench of the District Court in the Northern District; however, it does reveal that petitioner has referred 11 cases to masters in the past 6 years. But even "a little cloud may bring a flood's downpour" if we approve the practice here indulged, particularly in the face of presently congested dockets, increased filings, and more extended trials. * * * [B]e that as it may, congestion in itself is not such an exceptional circumstance as to warrant a reference to a master. If such were the test, present congestion would make references the rule rather than the exception. Petitioner realizes this, for in addition to calendar congestion he alleges that the cases referred had unusual complexity of issues of both fact and law. But most litigation in the antitrust field is complex. It does not follow that antitrust litigants are not entitled to a trial before a court. On the contrary, we believe that this is an impelling reason for trial before a regular, experienced trial judge rather than before a temporary substitute appointed on an *ad hoc* basis and ordinarily not experienced in judicial work. * * * We agree that the detailed accounting required in order to determine the damages suffered by each plaintiff might be referred to a master after the court has determined the over-all liability of defendants, provided the circumstances indicate that the use of the court's time is not warranted in receiving the proof and making the tabulation.

* * *

Affirmed.

Mr. Justice Brennan, with whom Mr. Justice Frankfurter, Mr. Justice Burton and Mr. Justice Harlan join, dissenting.

* * * The case before the Court of Appeals was "not a case where a court has exceeded or refused to exercise its jurisdiction * * *." Rule 53(b) * * * vested Judge La Buy with discretionary power to make a reference if he found, and he did, that "some exceptional condition" required the reference. * * * If Judge La Buy erred in finding that there was an "exceptional condition" requiring the reference or did not give proper weight to the caveat of the Rule that a "reference to a master shall be the exception and not the rule," that was mere error "in ruling on matters within [the District Court's] jurisdiction." * * *

But, regrettable as is this Court's approval of what I consider to be a clear departure by the Court of Appeals from the settled principles governing the issuance of the extraordinary writs, what this Court says in reaching its result is reason for particularly grave concern. I think this Court has today seriously undermined the long-standing statutory policy against piecemeal appeals. My brethren say: "Since the Court of Appeals could at some stage of the antitrust proceedings entertain appeals in these cases, it has power in proper circumstances, as here, to issue writs of mandamus reaching them. * * *" I understand this to mean that proper circumstances are present for the issuance of a writ in this case because, if the litigants are not now heard, the Court of Appeals will not have an opportunity to relieve them of the burden of the added expense and delay of decision alleged to be the consequence of the reference. But that bridge was crossed by this Court in *Roche* * * *.

What this Court is saying, therefore, is that the All Writs Act confers an independent appellate power in the Courts of Appeals to review interlocutory orders. I have always understood the law to be precisely to the contrary. * * *

The power of the Courts of Appeals to issue extraordinary writs stems from § 14 of the Judiciary Act of 1789. Chief Judge Magruder, in In re Josephson, 1 Cir., 218 F.2d 174, provides us with an invaluable history of this power and of the judicial development of its scope. He demonstrates most persuasively that "[t]he all writs section does not confer an independent appellate power; the power is strictly of an auxiliary nature, in aid of a jurisdiction granted in some other provision of law * * *."

The focal question posed for a Court of Appeals by a petition for the issuance of a writ is whether the action of the District Court tends to frustrate or impede the ultimate exercise by the Court of Appeals of its appellate jurisdiction granted in some other provision of the law. The answer is clearly in the affirmative where, for example, the order of the District Court transfers a cause to a District Court of another circuit for decision. That was Josephson, where * * * "the effect of the order is that the district judge has declined to proceed with the determination of a case which could eventually come to this court by appeal from a 'final decision'." * * * In contrast, a District Court order denying a transfer would not come under the umbrella of power under the All Writs Act, since retention of the cause by the District Court can hardly thwart or tend to defeat the power of the Court of Appeals to review that order after final decision of the case. * * *

The view now taken by this Court that the All Writs Act confers an independent appellate power, although not so broad as "to authorize the indiscriminate use of prerogative writs as a means of reviewing interlocutory orders," in effect engrafts upon federal appellate procedure a standard of interlocutory review never embraced by the Congress throughout our history, although it is written into the English Judicature Act and is followed in varying degrees in some of the States. That standard allows interlocutory appeals by leave of the appellate court. * * *

Notes and Questions

1.   In SCHLAGENHAUF v. HOLDER, 379 U.S. 104, 85 S.Ct. 234, 13 L.Ed.2d 152 (1964), the substantive aspects of which are set out at p. 835, supra, the Court upheld the use of mandamus to review an order requiring a defendant to submit to a physical and mental examination:

> It is, of course, well settled that the writ is not to be used as a substitute for appeal * * * even though hardship may result from delay and perhaps unnecessary trial * * *. The writ is appropriately issued, however, when there is "usurpation of judicial power" or a clear abuse of discretion * * *.

> [T]he challenged order * * * appears to be the first of its kind in any reported decision in the federal courts under Rule 35 * * *.

> * * * It is thus appropriate for us to determine on the merits the issues presented and to formulate the necessary guidelines in this area. * * *

> This is not to say, however, that following the setting of guidelines in this opinion, any future allegation that the District Court was in error in applying these guidelines to a particular case makes mandamus an appropriate remedy.

Id. at 110–12, 85 S.Ct. at 238–39, 13 L.Ed.2d at 156–60.

Do the decisions in *LaBuy* and *Schlagenhauf* give sufficient guidance as to when mandamus is an appropriate means of review? Note that both cases involve significant problems regarding application of the Federal Rules. It has been suggested that the *LaBuy* holding might "possibly be limited to issues of judicial administration which have broad significance beyond the particular case." Note, *Appealability in the Federal Courts,* 75 Harv.L.Rev. 351, 377 (1961). Compare WILL v. UNITED STATES, 389 U.S. 90, 88 S.Ct. 269, 19 L.Ed.2d 305 (1967), a criminal case in which the government sought mandamus to overturn a District Court order granting discovery for the defendant. The Court of Appeals granted the writ. The Supreme Court reversed, stating that the facts did not reveal an extraordinary situation for which the writs must be reserved. The Court did not discuss the fact that without mandamus the government cannot obtain guidance on discovery matters since it cannot appeal an acquittal.

Relying heavily on *Will,* the Supreme Court in KERR v. UNITED STATES DISTRICT COURT, 426 U.S. 394, 96 S.Ct. 2119, 48 L.Ed.2d 725 (1976), affirmed a denial of mandamus by a court of appeals in a civil case in which the trial judge had ordered defendants, state correction officers, to turn over to plaintiff a number of prisoner personnel files. Defendants argued that such discovery should be compelled only after a determination by the trial judge that plaintiff's need for the information outweighs its confidentiality. In a cogent opinion the Court reiterated the reasons for limiting use of writs to avoid piecemeal appeals and also recognized that restricting the use of writs to matters of "jurisdiction" in the technical sense would be too narrow. The Court "assumed" that the trial judge would now accept its "suggestion" to review each of the personnel files *in camera* to determine if discovery should be permitted, thus making a writ unnecessary. Isn't such an opinion self-defeating in that it encourages litigants to continue to file for mandamus in the hope that even if it is rejected the Court's opinion will effectively order the relief sought?

2.   In LYONS v. WESTINGHOUSE ELECTRIC CORP., 222 F.2d 184 (2d Cir.), certiorari denied 350 U.S. 825, 76 S.Ct. 52, 100 L.Ed. 737 (1955), the district

judge had stayed an antitrust case pending the determination of a related state-court action. The Court of Appeals held that if a state judgment would have a collateral estoppel effect on the federal action, it would not,

> literally speaking, end the jurisdiction of the district court; but it will do so in substance, if it is an estoppel at all, for it will conclude any further consideration of the existence of the conspiracy, and on that all else depends. For this reason, we hold * * * that the question whether a final judgment will be an estoppel so nearly touches the jurisdiction of the district court, as to make it proper for us to entertain the petition for mandamus.

Id. at 186.

In light of the court's holding on the merits that the state-court judgment "can have no effect upon the decision of the action at bar," was the court justified in directing the District Court to vacate the stay? What would the court have directed if it had ruled the other way on the merits? The Court of Appeals did not in fact issue a writ of mandamus. Its order reads: "Writ of mandamus to go thirty days after the filing of this opinion * * * unless [the stay] * * * has been vacated theretofore." Such conditional orders are common in mandamus cases. Why?

3. In IN RE CEMENT ANTITRUST LITIGATION, 688 F.2d 1297 (9th Cir.1982), a later stage of the controversy over the recusal order described at Note 4, p. 1166, supra, the Ninth Circuit refused to issue a writ of mandamus compelling the district judge to revoke his order granting the defendants' motion that he recuse himself:

> In order to confine the use of mandamus to its proper office, we enunciated five general guidelines * * * to assist in the determination of whether mandamus is the appropriate remedy in a particular case. The guidelines are: (1) whether the party seeking the writ has no other adequate means, such as direct appeal, to attain the relief he desires; (2) whether the petitioner will be damaged or prejudiced in a way that is not correctable on appeal; (3) whether the district court's order is clearly erroneous as a matter of law; (4) whether the district court's order is an oft repeated error or manifests persistent disregard for the federal rules; and (5) whether the district court's order raises new and important problems or issues of law of first impression. * * * Related considerations include: whether the injury alleged by petitioners, although not correctable on appeal, is the kind that justifies invocation of our mandamus authority; whether the petition presents an issue of law which may repeatedly evade appellate review; and whether there are other compelling factors relating to the efficient and orderly administration of the district courts.

> * * * The guidelines are not susceptible of mechanical application; they are not meant to supplant reasoned and independent analysis by appellate courts. In sum, the guidelines serve only as a useful starting point, an analytic framework for determinations regarding the propriety of mandamus relief.

Id. at 1301. Although the Ninth Circuit held that the exercise of supervisory mandamus authority was appropriate in this case because the issue raised was an important issue of first impression capable of evading review because of its collateral nature, it also held that the grant of the recusal motion was not erroneous and that, even if erroneous, it was harmless error. Because only five Justices of the Supreme Court were not disqualified from hearing the appeal, a quorum of the Court did not exist and the Ninth Circuit's decision was affirmed summarily under 28 U.S.C. § 2109. Arizona v. United States District Court, 459 U.S. 1191, 103 S.Ct. 1173, 75 L.Ed.2d 425 (1983).

4. In NIXON v. SIRICA, 487 F.2d 700, 707 (D.C.Cir.1973), a district judge ordered the President of the United States to produce certain tape recordings for the judge's inspection prior to a determination whether the recordings were subject to a grand jury subpoena. The President petitioned for a writ of mandamus, and the Court of Appeals, although denying the petition on the merits, held that it was an appropriate mode of review:

> From the viewpoint of mandamus * * * the central question that the President raises—whether the District Court exceeded its authority in ordering an *in camera* inspection of the tapes—is essentially jurisdictional. It is, too, a jurisdictional problem of "first impression" involving a "basic, undecided question." And if indeed the only avenue of direct appellate review open to the President requires that he first disobey the court's order, appeal seems to be "a clearly inadequate remedy." These circumstances * * * warrant the exercise * * * of our review power under the All Writs Act, particularly in light of the great public interest in prompt resolution of the issues * * *.

See also the discussion of the Supreme Court's ruling in this case, United States v. Nixon, Note 3, p. 1159, supra.

c. Displacement of the Basic Concept—Discretionary Appeals

———

Read 28 U.S.C. § 1292(b) in the Supplement.

———

ATLANTIC CITY ELEC. CO. v. GENERAL ELEC. CO.
United States Court of Appeals, Second Circuit, 1964.
337 F.2d 844.

PER CURIAM. The district court has certified pursuant to section 1292(b) * * * that its order, sustaining objections to interrogatories designed to discover whether damages were actually sustained by plaintiffs who may have shifted such damages, if any, to their customers of electricity, involves a controlling question of law in these litigations and that there is substantial ground for differences of opinion. * * *

In sustaining the objections to the interrogatories posed, the district court has, in effect, foreclosed defendants from pre-trial discovery of facts relating to a defense that plaintiffs have "passed-on" to their customers any damages incurred by plaintiffs and hence are not entitled to recover to the extent that defendants can prove such passing-on.

Upon this application for leave to appeal it would not be appropriate to isolate and endeavor to decide before an appeal from any final judgment this particular question of law. Pre-trial leave to appeal applications must be decided against the background of the entire case. Many important questions of law will undoubtedly arise in these cases but the problem now confronting us is the feasibility and advisability of trying to decide this particular question in advance of trial.

If pre-trial discovery were allowed as defendants request it could easily develop into a multitude of full scale rate cases which could dwarf in time and testimony the already extensive pre-trial proceedings. If the district court is in error * * * defendants will have full opportunity in the event of an adverse judgment, if based in whole or in part upon this error, to have it corrected upon appeal together with any other errors which may be urged. It is doubtful that any discoveries or hearings required to establish the extent of any damages, if the passing-on-doctrine applies, would be more burdensome then than now. Since defendants' rights to this defense are not being taken away or prejudiced on any ultimate appeal by denial of the pre-trial appeal now sought, we believe that the ultimate disposition of these cases would be delayed rather than advanced by granting this application.

Application denied.

Notes and Questions

1. In COMMONWEALTH EDISON CO. v. ALLIS–CHALMERS MANUFACTURING CO., 335 F.2d 203 (7th Cir.1964), having accepted an appeal under Section 1292(b) on the same issue involved in the principal case, the Seventh Circuit held that the passing-on defense was not available, and hence affirmed an order sustaining objections to similar interrogatories. Which of the courts of appeals followed the sounder procedure? Should the Second Circuit have ruled differently if the district judge had directed plaintiffs to answer the interrogatories? See generally Note, *The Final Judgment Rule and Appellate Review of Discovery Orders in Nebraska,* 35 Neb.L.Rev. 469 (1956).

Suppose the trial court in *Atlantic City Elec. Co.* had ruled directly on the applicability of the passing-on defense. Would the Court of Appeals have had less justification for rejecting the appeal? Compare Obron v. Union Camp Corp., 477 F.2d 542 (6th Cir.1973) (allowing appeal).

2. Is Section 1292(b) a solution to the type of problem raised in *Ryan* or *Cobbledick,* Note 3, p. 1159, supra? In UNITED STATES v. WOODBURY, 263 F.2d 784 (9th Cir.1959), the court declined to review an order granting discovery even though the District Court had ordered defendant's answer and counterclaim stricken if it did not comply. But in GROOVER, CHRISTIE & MERRITT v. LoBIANCO, 336 F.2d 969, 973–74 (D.C.Cir.1964), a malpractice action, the court allowed an appeal from an order granting discovery of a letter by defendant to an insurer, detailing defendant's investigation of the case. The court then reversed, finding that "good cause" had not been adequately established under Rule 34, and directed the trial judge to make further findings and to consider whether the letter was privileged under Hickman v. Taylor, p. 849, supra. Judge Wright dissented vigorously, stating: "This case is a graphic illustration of the mischief that results when [Section 1292(b)] * * * is misused. * * * And rather than advance the ultimate termination of this litigation, the dilatory tactics * * *, including this interlocutory appeal, have already been the cause of significant delay." Compare Judge Clark, dissenting, in MATTHIES v. SEYMOUR MANUFACTURING CO., 271 F.2d 740 (2d Cir.1959), certiorari denied 361 U.S. 962, 80 S.Ct. 591, 4 L.Ed.2d 544 (1960): "In passing I might note that this seems to me another illustration of the unfortunate tendency of the new interlocutory appeals statute * * * to overemphasize strict pleading and in so doing to throw our procedure out of line with the liberal spirit fostered by the civil rules." Why should Section 1292(b) have this effect?

3. Would Section 1292(b) be a satisfactory device in *LaBuy* or *Lyons*? See Lear Siegler, Inc. v. Adkins, 330 F.2d 595 (9th Cir.1964). Should the court of appeals be given power to hear appeals from orders fulfilling the requirements described in Section 1292(b) without the certificate of the district judge? Compare Leasco Data Processing Equip. Corp. v. Maxwell, 468 F.2d 1326, 1344 (2d Cir.1972) (court of appeals cannot order trial court to issue certificate).

4. The courts of appeals have not been markedly hospitable to interlocutory appeals under Section 1292(b). Decisions during the 1950's placing strong emphasis on the exceptional nature of the relief, e.g., In re Heddendorf, 263 F.2d 887 (1st Cir.1959); Milbert v. Bison Labs., Inc., 260 F.2d 431 (3d Cir.1958), have not lost their precedential force. In the fiscal year 1966, the courts of appeals considered 68 applications and allowed only 36; in subsequent years the figures were 80 and 41 (1967); 122 and 58 (1968); 105 and 64 (1969). In 1970, both figures increased markedly: 290 applications considered, and 225 allowed. Annual Report of the Director of the Administrative Office of the United States Courts, 1966, p. 160; id. 1967, p. 191; id. 1968, p. 185; id. 1969, p. 195; id. 1970, p. 221. More recent reports have not included these figures.

5. In NICKERT v. PUGET SOUND TUG & BARGE CO., 480 F.2d 1039 (9th Cir.1973), a wrongful-death case, one defendant, A, cross-claimed for indemnity against another defendant, B. Prior to trial on the cross-complaint, the trial court granted a "partial summary judgment" for B stating that if at trial it were to be found that A had negligently contributed to the wrongful death, indemnity would not be permitted. The trial judge thereupon issued a certificate under Section 1292(b)(2) allowing A to appeal. The Court of Appeals admitted that the issue was important and controversial, but nevertheless dismissed the appeal, stating:

> * * * The trial court's announcement of its opinion on this question of law * * * is nothing more * * * than an hypothetical, advisory opinion. It is subject to revision or reversal at any time by the trial judge to the point where a definitive action has been taken on the question; for examples, an instruction to the jury, or the adoption of a conclusion of law in a trial to the court. Similarly, an announcement by this Court of its opinion of the trial judge's tentative opinion would be purely advisory * * *.

Id. at 1041. Do you agree with the appellate court's decision? Does it undercut the policy upon which Section 1292(b) is based? Is it consistent with Rule 56(a), which permits partial summary judgment?

6. For a comprehensive analysis of Section 1292(b), see Note, *Interlocutory Appeals in the Federal Courts Under 28 U.S.C. § 1292(b)*, 88 Harv.L.Rev. 607 (1975).

GILLESPIE v. UNITED STATES STEEL CORP.

Supreme Court of the United States, 1964.
379 U.S. 148, 85 S.Ct. 308, 13 L.Ed.2d 199.

Certiorari to the United States Court of Appeals for the Sixth Circuit.

MR. JUSTICE BLACK delivered the opinion of the Court.

The petitioner, administratrix of the estate of her son Daniel Gillespie, brought this action in federal court against the respondent shipowner-employer to recover damages for Gillespie's death, which was alleged to have occurred when he fell and was drowned while working as a seaman on respondent's ship docked in Ohio. She claimed a right to recover for the benefit of herself and of the decedent's dependent brother and sisters under the Jones Act, which subjects employers to liability if by negligence they cause a seaman's injury or death. She also claimed a right of recovery under the Ohio wrongful death statute because the vessel allegedly was not seaworthy as required by the "general maritime law." The complaint in addition sought damages for Gillespie's pain and suffering before he died, based on the Jones Act and the general maritime law, causes of action which petitioner said survived Gillespie's death by force of the Jones Act itself and the Ohio survival statute, respectively. The District Judge, holding that the Jones Act supplied the exclusive remedy, on motion of respondent struck all parts of the complaint which referred to the Ohio statutes or to unseaworthiness. He also struck all reference to recovery for the benefit of the brother and sisters of the decedent, who respondent had argued were not beneficiaries entitled to recovery under the Jones Act while their mother was living.

Petitioner immediately appealed to the Court of Appeals. Respondent moved to dismiss the appeal on the ground that the ruling appealed from was not a "final" decision of the District Court * * *. Thereupon petitioner administratrix, this time joined by the brother and sisters, filed in the Court of Appeals a petition for mandamus or other appropriate writ commanding the District Judge to vacate his original order and enter a new one * * *. Without definitely deciding whether mandamus would have been appropriate in this case or deciding the "close" question of appealability, the Court of Appeals proceeded to determine the controversy "on the merits as though it were submitted on an appeal"; this the court said it felt free to do since its resolution of the merits did not prejudice respondent in any way, because it sustained respondent's contentions by denying the petition for mandamus and affirming the District Court's order. * * *

In this Court respondent joins petitioner in urging us to hold that 28 U.S.C. § 1291 does not require us to dismiss this case * * *. We agree. * * * [A]s this Court often has pointed out, a decision "final" within the meaning of § 1291 does not necessarily mean the last order possible to be made in a case. * * * It is true that the review of this case by the Court of Appeals could be called "piecemeal"; but it does not appear that the inconvenience and cost of trying this case will be greater because the Court of Appeals decided the issues raised instead of compelling the parties to go to trial with them unanswered. * * * And it seems clear now that the case is before us that the eventual costs, as all the parties recognize, will certainly be less if we now pass on the questions presented here rather than send the case back with those issues undecided. Moreover, delay of perhaps a number of years in having the brother's and sisters' rights determined might work a great injustice on them, since the claims for recovery for their benefit have been effectively cut off so long as the District Judge's ruling stands. And while their claims are not formally severable so as to make the court's order unquestionably appealable as to them, * * * there certainly is ample reason to view their claims as severable in deciding the issue of finality, particularly since the brother and sisters were separate parties in the petition for extraordinary relief. * * * Furthermore, in United States v. General Motors Corp., 323 U.S. 373, 377, 65 S.Ct. 357, 359, 89 L.Ed. 311, this Court contrary to its usual practice reviewed a trial court's refusal to permit proof of certain items of damages in a case not yet fully tried, because the ruling was "fundamental to the further conduct of the case." * * * We think that the questions presented here are equally "fundamental to the further conduct of the case." It is true that if the District Judge had certified the case to the Court of Appeals under 28 U.S.C. § 1292(b), the appeal unquestionably would have been proper; in light of the circumstances we believe that the Court of Appeals properly implemented the same policy Congress sought to promote in § 1292(b) by treating this obviously marginal case as final and appealable * * *.

[The opinion of JUSTICE GOLDBERG, concurring in part and dissenting in part, is omitted.]

MR. JUSTICE HARLAN, dissenting.

* * * The Court substantially affirms the judgment of the Court of Appeals and the parties are remanded to a trial on the merits, but only after they have incurred needless delay and expense in consequence of the loose practices sanctioned by the Court of Appeals and in turn by this Court. This case thus presents a striking example of the vice inherent in a system which permits piecemeal litigation of the issues in a lawsuit.

* * * The justifications given by the Court for tolerating the lower court's departure from the requirements of § 1291 are, with all respect, unsatisfactory.

1. The Court relies on the discretionary right of a district court to certify an interlocutory order to the court of appeals under § 1292(b) when the "order involves a controlling question of law," but the District Court in its discretion—and rightly it turns out—did not make such a certification in this case, and the Court of Appeals, equally correctly in my judgment, refused to order it to do so. * * *

2. Cohen v. Beneficial Industrial Loan Corp. * * * does not support a different result. * * * It is clear in this case that had petitioner proceeded to trial and won on her Jones Act claim, her asserted cause of action for unseaworthiness would have merged in the judgment. * * * Conversely, her claim would have been preserved for appeal had she lost on her Jones Act claim. Surely the assertion that petitioner is entitled to submit her unseaworthiness theory to the jury is not collateral to rights asserted in her action * * *.

3. Finally, the Court's suggestion that "it seems clear now that the case is before us that the eventual costs, as all the parties recognize, will certainly be less if we now pass on the questions presented here rather than send the case back with those issues undecided," * * * furnishes no excuse for avoidance of the finality rule. Essentially such a position would justify review here of any case decided by a court of appeals whenever this Court, as it did in this instance, erroneously grants certiorari and permits counsel to brief and argue the case on the merits. That, I believe, is neither good law nor sound judicial administration.

* * *

[A memorandum by JUSTICE STEWART is omitted.]

Notes and Questions

1. Is the majority or Justice Harlan correct on the appealability under Section 1292(b) of the District Court's order in *Gillespie*?

2. Is *Gillespie* still good law after *Coopers & Lybrand,* p. 1162, supra? See Boughton v. Cotter Corp., 10 F.3d 746, 751–52 (10th Cir.1993) (noting that the doctrine of "pragmatic finality" has been the subject of increasing criticism); Utah v. Kennecott Corp., 14 F.3d 1489, 1495–96 (10th Cir.1994) (construing narrowly the "practical rather than technical construction" of Section 1291).

d. *An Historical Footnote to the Basic Concept—Injunctions*

———

Read 28 U.S.C. § 1292(a)(1) and Federal Rules of Civil Procedure 65(a) and (b) in the Supplement.

———

SMITH v. VULCAN IRON WORKS, 165 U.S. 518, 525, 17 S.Ct. 407, 410, 41 L.Ed. 810, 812 (1897):

The manifest intent of this provision, read in the light of the previous practice in the courts of the United States, contrasted with the practice in courts of equity of the highest authority elsewhere, appears to this court to have been, not only to permit the defendant to obtain immediate relief from an injunction, the continuance of which throughout the progress of the cause might seriously affect his interests, but also to save both parties from the expense of further litigation, should the appellate court be of opinion that the plaintiff was not entitled to an injunction because his bill had no equity to support it.

Notes and Questions

1. Is the Supreme Court's ruling that an appeal under the predecessor of Section 1292(a)(1) allows the reviewing court to consider not only the question whether the injunction should have been issued, but the merits of the whole case, supported by the traditional doctrines regarding the character of equitable relief? Review pp. 958–59, 1144–45, supra.

2. What are the reasons for allowing appeals from interlocutory orders granting or refusing injunctions? Do these reasons apply to orders granting or denying preliminary, as opposed to permanent, injunctions? Could these reasons be served as well by relegating the parties to discretionary appeals under Section 1292(b)?

3. Is the grant or denial of a temporary restraining order appealable under Section 1292(a)(1)? See Grant v. United States, 282 F.2d 165 (2d Cir.1960). In close cases it may be difficult to tell the difference between a preliminary injunction and a temporary restraining order. See Connell v. Dulien Steel Products, Inc., 240 F.2d 414 (5th Cir.1957) (28–day temporary restraining order). Are the differences between preliminary injunctions and temporary restraining orders

relevant to the question whether appeal should be permitted in the case of the former and not permitted in the case of the latter?

In UNITED STATES v. WOOD, 295 F.2d 772 (5th Cir.1961), certiorari denied 369 U.S. 850, 82 S.Ct. 933, 8 L.Ed.2d 9 (1962), a black man who was active in voter registration in Mississippi was arrested for disturbing the peace and ordered to trial in fifteen days. Two days before trial, the United States, moving under 42 U.S.C. § 1971 and alleging that the prosecution would intimidate Blacks in the exercise of their voting rights, brought suit to restrain the criminal action. A temporary restraining order was denied and the government appealed. The Court of Appeals held that it had jurisdiction under Section 1291. Inasmuch as the case would quickly become moot if the restraining order was not issued, the court said, its denial was "a final disposition of the * * * claimed right. * * * [T]o call this de facto dismissal a nonappealable interlocutory order is to preclude review altogether."

4. In SAMPSON v. MURRAY, 415 U.S. 61, 94 S.Ct. 937, 39 L.Ed.2d 166 (1974), the respondent, a probationary federal employee, filed an action to enjoin temporarily her dismissal pending her pursuit of an administrative appeal to the Civil Service Commission. The District Court granted the temporary restraining order and, after an adversary hearing, extended the interim relief until the respondent's supervisor testified about the reasons for her dismissal. The United States Court of Appeals for the District of Columbia Circuit affirmed. The Supreme Court reversed, holding that the Court of Appeals had correctly treated the extension order as a preliminary injunction, but that the order in question failed to meet the standards for such injunctions set by Rule 65. In the Court's view, the respondent had failed to demonstrate irreparable harm. Neither the temporary loss of income (ultimately to be recovered) nor the humiliation and damage to the respondent's reputation were sufficient to constitute irreparable injury justifying the granting of a preliminary injunction.

Justices Douglas, Marshall, and Brennan dissented. Justice Douglas agreed with the majority that the extension order at issue was an appealable order; however, he maintained that the order was a valid stay designed to preserve the status quo until the District Court was able to hold a hearing on the issue of whether the respondent had suffered an irreparable injury justifying the issuing of the order as a preliminary injunction. Justices Marshall and Brennan, on the other hand, argued that the order was not appealable. In their view, because the temporary restraining order at issue did not meet any of the requirements for interlocutory injunctions set forth in Rule 52(a), "no valid preliminary injunction was ever issued." Thus, it did not make sense for the Court to review the District Court's order as the grant of a preliminary injunction. They continued:

> * * * Even if the order entered by the District Court is appealable, it should be appealable only for the purposes of holding it invalid for failure to comply with Rule 52(a). * * *

In addition, the Government had other courses it could have taken in this case. In view of the District Court's error in granting a restraining order of unlimited duration without complying with the requirements for a preliminary injunction, the Government could have moved the District Court to dissolve its order indefinitely continuing the temporary restraining order. Rule 65(b) expressly provides for such a motion. Had the Government followed this course, the District Court could have corrected its error and gone on to resolve the issues presented by the application for a preliminary injunction. The end result would have been the grant or denial of a preliminary injunction, with findings of fact and conclusions of law, which we could meaningfully review.

Here, instead, we find the Supreme Court determining that although the District Court had jurisdiction to grant injunctive relief, the equities of Mrs. Murray's case did not support a preliminary injunction, when neither the District Court nor the Court of Appeals has yet confronted the latter issue. I do not believe this makes for sound law.

Id. at 99–100, 94 S.Ct. at 957, 39 L.Ed.2d at 191–92.

GULFSTREAM AEROSPACE CORP.
v. MAYACAMAS CORP.

Supreme Court of the United States, 1988.
485 U.S. 271, 108 S.Ct. 1133, 99 L.Ed.2d 296.

Certiorari to the United States Court of Appeals for the Ninth Circuit.

JUSTICE MARSHALL delivered the opinion of the Court.

The primary issue in this case is whether a district court order denying a motion to stay or dismiss an action when a similar suit is pending in state court is immediately appealable.

* * *

[Gulfstream sued Mayacamas in state court for breach of contract. Mayacamas did not remove the action to federal court, but, one month later, filed a diversity action against petitioner in the Federal District Court for breach of the same contract. The District Court denied Gulfstream's motion to stay or dismiss the action before it, finding that the facts of the case fell short of those necessary to justify the requested discontinuance of the federal-court action under Colorado River Water Conservation Dist. v. United States, 424 U.S. 800, 96 S.Ct. 1236, 47 L.Ed.2d 483 (1976), which held that, in "exceptional" circumstances, a district court may stay or dismiss an action because of the pendency of similar state-court litigation. The Court of Appeals dismissed petitioner's appeal for lack of jurisdiction, holding that neither 28 U.S.C. § 1291 nor 28 U.S.C. § 1292(a)(1) allowed an immediate appeal from the District Court's order. The court also declined to treat petitioner's notice of appeal as an application for a writ of mandamus under the All Writs Act.

The Supreme Court first rejected petitioner's contention that the District Court's order denying the motion to stay or dismiss the federal-court litigation was immediately appealable under Section 1291. The Court reasoned that such an order does not end the litigation but rather ensures that it will continue in the District Court. The Court added that such an order does not fall within the collateral-order exception to Section 1291, since it fails to satisfy the exception's "conclusiveness" requirement in that it is inherently tentative and not made with the expectation that it will be the final word on the subject addressed: "[A] district court usually will expect to revisit and reassess an order denying a stay in light of events occurring in the normal course of litigation."

After disposing of the Section 1291 issue, the Court considered whether such an order constituted an injunction appealable under Section 1292(a)(1).]

* * *

Petitioner argues in the alternative that the District Court's order in this case is immediately appealable under § 1292(a)(1), which gives the courts of appeals jurisdiction of appeals from interlocutory orders granting or denying injunctions. An order by a federal court that relates only to the conduct or progress of litigation before that court ordinarily is not considered an injunction and therefore is not appealable under § 1292(a)(1). * * * Under the *Enelow-Ettelson* doctrine, however, certain orders that stay or refuse to stay judicial proceedings are considered injunctions and therefore are immediately appealable. Petitioner asserts that the order in this case, which denied a motion for a stay of a federal-court action pending the resolution of a concurrent state-court proceeding, is appealable under § 1292(a)(1) pursuant to the *Enelow-Ettelson* doctrine.

The line of cases we must examine to resolve this claim began some fifty years ago, when this Court decided Enelow v. New York Life Ins. Co., 293 U.S. 379, 55 S.Ct. 310, 79 L.Ed. 440 (1935). At the time of that decision, law and equity remained separate jurisprudential systems in the federal courts. The same judges administered both these systems, however, so that a federal district judge was both a chancellor in equity and a judge at law. In *Enelow*, the plaintiff sued at law to recover on a life insurance policy. The insurance company raised the affirmative defense that the policy had been obtained by fraud and moved the District Court to stay the trial of the law action pending resolution of this equitable defense. The District Court granted this motion, and the plaintiff appealed. This Court likened the stay to an injunction issued by an equity court to restrain an action at law. The Court stated:

> [T]he grant or refusal of * * * a stay by a court of equity of proceedings at law is a grant or refusal of an injunction within the meaning of [the statute.] And, in this aspect, it makes no difference that the two cases, the suit in equity for an injunction and the action at law in which proceedings are stayed, are both pending in the same court, in view of the established distinction between "proceedings at law and proceedings in equity in the national courts. * * * "

* * *

> It is thus apparent that when an order or decree is made * * * requiring, or refusing to require, that an equitable defense shall first be tried, the court, exercising what is essentially an equitable jurisdiction, in effect grants or refuses an injunction restraining proceedings at law precisely as if the court had acted upon a bill of complaint in a separate suit for the same purpose. Id., at 382–383, 55 S.Ct., at 311.

The Court thus concluded that the District Court's order was appealable under § 1292(a)(1).

In Ettelson v. Metropolitan Life Ins. Co., 317 U.S. 188, 63 S.Ct. 163, 87 L.Ed. 176 (1942), the Court reaffirmed the rule of *Enelow*, notwithstanding that the Federal Rules of Civil Procedure had fully merged law and equity in the interim. The relevant facts of *Ettelson* were identical to those of *Enelow*, and the Court responded to them in the same fashion. In response to the argument that the fusion of law and equity had destroyed the analogy between the stay ordered in the action and an injunction issued by a chancellor of a separate proceeding at law, the Court stated only that the plaintiffs were "in no different position than if a state equity court had restrained them from proceeding in the law action." * * * Thus, the order granting the stay was held to be immediately appealable as an injunction.

The historical analysis underlying the results in *Enelow* and *Ettelson* has bred a doctrine of curious contours. Under the *Enelow-Ettelson* rule, most recently restated in Baltimore Contractors, Inc. v. Bodinger, 348 U.S. 176, 75 S.Ct. 249, 99 L.Ed. 233 (1955), an order by a federal court staying or refusing to stay its own proceedings is appealable under § 1292(a)(1) as the grant or denial of an injunction if two conditions are met. First, the action in which the order is entered must be an action that, before the merger of law and equity, was by its nature an action at law. Second, the order must arise from or be based on some matter that would then have been considered an equitable defense or counterclaim. If both conditions are satisfied, the historical equivalent of the modern order would have been an injunction, issued by a separate equity court, to restrain proceedings in an action at law. If either condition is not met, however, the historical analogy fails. When the underlying suit is historically equitable and the stay is based on a defense or counterclaim that is historically legal, the analogy fails because a law judge had no power to issue an injunction restraining equitable proceedings. And when both the underlying suit and the defense or counterclaim on which the stay is based are historically equitable, or when both are historically legal, the analogy fails because when a chancellor or a law judge stayed an action in his own court, he was not issuing an injunction, but merely arranging matters on his docket. Thus, unless a stay order is made in a historically legal action on the basis of a historically equitable defense or counterclaim, the order cannot be analogized to a pre-merger injunction and therefore cannot be appealed under § 1292(a)(1) pursuant to the *Enelow-Ettelson* doctrine.

The parties in this case dispute whether the *Enelow-Ettelson* rule makes the District Court's decision to deny a stay immediately appealable under § 1292(a)(1). Both parties agree that an action for breach of contract was an action at law prior to the merger of law and equity. They vigorously contest, however, whether the stay of an action pending the resolution of similar proceedings in a state court is equitable in the requisite sense. * * *

We decline to address the issue of appealability in these terms; indeed, the sterility of the debate between the parties illustrates the need for a more fundamental consideration of the precedents in this area. This Court long has understood that the *Enelow-Ettelson* rule is deficient in utility and sense. In the two cases we have decided since *Ettelson* relating to the rule, we criticized its perpetuation of "outmoded procedural differentiations" and its consequent tendency to produce incongruous results. * * * We refrained then from overruling the *Enelow* and *Ettelson* decisions, but today we take that step. A half century's experience has persuaded us, as it has persuaded an impressive array of judges and commentators, that the rule is unsound in theory, unworkable and arbitrary in practice, and unnecessary to achieve any legitimate goals.

As an initial matter, the *Enelow-Ettelson* doctrine is, in the modern world of litigation, a total fiction. Even when the rule was announced, it was artificial. Although at that time law and equity remained two separate systems, they were administered by the same judges. When a single official was both chancellor and law judge, a stay of an action at law on equitable grounds required nothing more than an order issued by the official regulating the progress of the litigation before him, and the decision to call this order an injunction just because it would have been an injunction in a system with separate law and equity judges had little justification. With the merger of law and equity, which was accomplished by the Federal Rules * * *, the practice of describing these stays as injunctions lost all connection with the reality of the federal courts' procedural system. As Judge Charles Clark, the principal draftsman of the Rules, wrote:

> "[W]e lack any rationale to explain the concept of a judge enjoining himself when he merely decides upon the method he will follow in trying the case. The metamorphosis of a law judge into a hostile chancellor on the other 'side' of the court could not have been overclear to the lay litigant under the divided procedure; but if now without even that fictitious sea change one judge in one form of action may split his judicial self at one instant into two mutually antagonistic parts, the litigant surely will think himself in Alice's Wonderland." Beaunit Mills, Inc. v. Eday Fabric Sales Corp., 124 F.2d 563, 565 (C.A.2 1942).

The *Enelow* rule had presupposed two different systems of justice administered by separate tribunals, even if these tribunals were no more than two "sides" to the same court; with the abandonment of that separation, the premise of the rule disappeared. The doctrine, and the distinctions it drew between equitable and legal actions and defenses, lost all moorings to the actual practice of the federal courts.

* * *

Most important, the *Enelow-Ettelson* doctrine is "divorced from any rational or coherent appeals policy." * * * Under the rule, appellate jurisdiction of orders granting or denying stays depends upon a set of considerations that in no way reflects or relates to the need for interlocutory review. There is no reason to think that appeal of a stay order is more suitable in cases in which the underlying action is at law and the stay is based on equitable grounds than in cases in which one of these conditions is not satisfied. The rule's focus on historical distinctions thus produces arbitrary and anomalous results. * * * Two orders may involve similar issues and produce similar consequences, and yet one will be appealable whereas the other will not.

For these reasons, the lower federal courts repeatedly have lambasted the *Enelow-Ettelson* doctrine. The rule has been called "a remnant from the jurisprudential attic," * * * "an anachronism wrapped up in an atavism," * * * and a "Byzantine peculiarit[y]" * * *. With the exception of the Federal Circuit, which apparently has not yet confronted an *Enelow-Ettelson* appeal, every Circuit is on record with criticism of the doctrine. One Circuit Judge has urged his court to reject the doctrine outright. * * * Although a majority of the panel declined to do so, it agreed that the *Enelow-Ettelson* rule was " 'artificial,' " " 'medieval,' " and " 'outmoded.' " * * * Another Circuit Judge, in a majority opinion, recently wrote an extensive and scholarly critique of the doctrine and concluded only with great reluctance that repudiating the doctrine would be improper. * * *

Commentators have been no less scathing in their evaluations of the *Enelow-Ettelson* rule. Professor Moore and his collaborators have noted the difficulty of applying archaic labels to modern actions and defenses and expressed the wish that "the Supreme Court will accept the first opportunity offered to decide that the reason for the *Enelow-Ettelson* rule having ceased, the rule is no more." * * * Professor Wright and his collaborators have gone further, arguing that the extensive experience that the courts of appeals have had in attempting to rationalize and apply the rule would justify them in rejecting it. * * *

The case against perpetuation of this sterile and antiquated doctrine seems to us conclusive. We therefore overturn the cases establishing the *Enelow-Ettelson* rule and hold that orders granting or denying stays of "legal" proceedings on "equitable" grounds are not automatically appealable under § 1292(a)(1). This holding will not prevent interlocutory review of district court orders when such review is truly needed. Section 1292(a)(1) will, of course, continue to provide appellate jurisdiction over orders that grant or deny injunctions and orders that have the practical effect of granting or denying injunctions and have " 'serious, perhaps irreparable, consequence.' " * * * As for orders that were appealable under § 1292(a)(1) solely by virtue of the *Enelow-Ettelson* doctrine, they may, in appropriate circumstances, be reviewed under the collateral-order doctrine of § 1291 * * *, and the permissive appeal provision of § 1292(b), as well as by application for writ of mandamus. Our holding today merely prevents interlocutory review of district court orders on the basis of historical circumstances that have no relevance to modern litigation. Because we repudiate the *Enelow-Ettelson* doctrine, we reject petitioner's claim that the District Court's order in this case is appealable under § 1292(a)(1) pursuant to that doctrine.

[The Court also rejected petitioner's contention that the Court of Appeals should have issued a writ of mandamus directing the District Court to grant the requested stay or dismissal of the federal-court action.]

* * * Accordingly, the judgment of the Court of Appeals is affirmed.

It is so ordered.

JUSTICE KENNEDY took no part in the consideration or decision of this case.

[A concurring opinion by JUSTICE SCALIA is omitted.]

Notes and Questions

1. Does Section 1292(a)(1) apply to an order denying a motion for summary judgment in an action in which a permanent injunction is sought? This question, which had plagued the courts of appeals for years, was resolved in SWITZER-LAND CHEESE ASSOCIATION, INC. v. E. HORNE'S MARKET, INC., 385 U.S. 23, 25, 87 S.Ct. 193, 195, 17 L.Ed.2d 23, 25 (1966):

> * * * [T]he denial of a motion for summary judgment because of unresolved issues of fact does not settle or even tentatively decide anything about the merits of the claim. It is strictly a pre-trial order that decides only one thing—that the case should go to trial. Orders that in no way touch on the merits of the claim but only relate to pre-trial procedures are not in our view "interlocutory" within the meaning of § 1292(a)(1). We see no other way to protect the integrity of the congressional policy against piecemeal appeals.

2. In CARSON v. AMERICAN BRANDS, INC., 450 U.S. 79, 101 S.Ct. 993, 67 L.Ed.2d 59 (1981), petitioners brought a class action against the respondent employers, charging violations of Title VII of the Civil Rights Act of 1964 and seeking injunctive and declaratory relief and damages. The parties settled and together moved for entry of a proposed consent decree enjoining further discrimination and implementing an affirmative action plan for hiring and seniority preferences. The District Court denied the motion, holding that, since there was no showing of present or past discrimination, the proposed decree illegally granted racial preferences to the petitioner class and also illegally provided relief to all present and future black employees rather than only to the actual victims of the alleged discrimination. The Fourth Circuit dismissed the petitioners' appeal for want of jurisdiction, holding that the District Court's order was not appealable under Section 1292(a)(1). The Supreme Court unanimously reversed, holding that the order, although not explicitly refusing an injunction, had the practical effect of doing so. The Court also found that the petitioners had satisfied the requirement that the order might have "serious, perhaps irreparable consequences" which could be "effectually challenged" only by immediate appeal. If the District Court order were allowed to stand, the petitioners might lose their opportunity to settle on the negotiated terms. Because consent decrees are the product of lengthy and detailed negotiations and are based upon the express or implied desire of the parties to avoid the costs and uncertainties of litigation, a district court's rejection of that agreement might force litigation when neither party wanted it and might have the serious, perhaps irreparable, consequence of denying the parties their right to compromise their dispute on mutually agreeable terms.

3. If an appeal is not taken from an interlocutory order that is made appealable by Section 1292(a)(1), are matters adjudged therein foreclosed on an appeal from the final judgment? See Victor Talking Mach. Co. v. George, 105 F.2d 697 (3d Cir.), certiorari denied 308 U.S. 611, 60 S.Ct. 176, 84 L.Ed. 511 (1939).

SECTION B.   THE TIME TO APPEAL

Read Federal Rule of Civil Procedure 58 and Rules 3, 4, and 5 of the Federal Rules of Appellate Procedure.

The time limit for appeal is treated as a matter of jurisdiction and cannot be altered by consent of the parties. See 16A Wright, Miller & Cooper, *Federal Practice and Procedure: Jurisdiction and Related Matters 2d* §§ 3949–49.6 (1996). It may be extended by the district court only, not by an appellate court, for thirty days upon a showing of "excusable neglect." The time limitation is triggered when the district court clerk enters a judgment conforming to the requirements of Federal Rule 58. The clerk is required to mail notice of entry of judgment to the parties but a party may elect to serve notice formally on his opponent. Federal Rule 77(d).

UNITED STATES v. F. & M. SCHAEFER BREWING CO.

Supreme Court of the United States, 1958.
356 U.S. 227, 78 S.Ct. 674, 2 L.Ed.2d 721.

Certiorari to the United States Court of Appeals for the Second Circuit.

MR. JUSTICE WHITTAKER delivered the opinion of the Court.

* * * Respondent sued the Government for $7,189.57, alleged to have been illegally assessed and collected from it as federal stamp taxes, and for interest thereon from the date of payment. After issue was joined, respondent moved for summary judgment. The district judge, after hearing the motion, filed an opinion on April 14, 1955 * * * in which, after finding that respondent had paid stamp taxes to the Government in the amount of $7,012.50 and interest in the amount of $177.07, but making no finding of the date or dates of payment, he referred to an earlier decision of the same legal question by his colleague * * * and concluded, saying: "I am in agreement with Judge Leibell's analysis and, accordingly, the plaintiff's motion is granted." Thereupon, the clerk made the following notation in the civil docket: "April 14, 1955. Rayfiel, J. Decision rendered on motion for summary judgment. Motion granted. See opinion on file."

Thereafter, on May 24, 1955, counsel for *respondent* presented to the judge, and the latter signed and filed, a formal document captioned "Judgment," which referred to the motion and the hearing of it and to the "opinion" of April 14, and then,

Ordered, adjudged and decreed that the plaintiff, The F. & M. Schaefer Brewing Co., recover of the defendant, United States of America, the sum of $7189.57 and interest thereon from February 19, 1954 in the amount of $542.80, together with costs as taxed by the Clerk of the Court in the sum of $37, aggregating the sum of $7769.37, and that plaintiff have judgment against defendant therefor.

On the same day the clerk stamped the document "Judgment Rendered: Dated: May 24th, 1955," and made the following notation in the civil docket:

May 24, 1955. Rayfiel, J. Judgment filed and docketed against defendant in the sum of $7,189.57 with interest of $542.80 together with costs $37 amounting in all to $7,769.37. Bill of Costs attached to judgment.

On July 21, 1955, the Government filed its notice of appeal from the order "entered in this action on May 25th, 1955 * * *." Thereafter, respondent moved to dismiss the appeal upon the ground that the opinion of April 14 constituted the "judgment," that the clerk's entry of that date constituted "entry of the judgment," and that the appeal was not taken within 60 days from the "entry of the judgment," as required by [former Civil] Rule 73(a). The Court of Appeals, holding that the opinion of April 14 was a "decisive and complete act of adjudication," and that the notation made by the clerk in the civil docket on that date constituted "entry of the judgment" within the meaning of Rule 58 and adequately disclosed the "substance" of the judgment as required by Rule 79(a), sustained the motion and dismissed the appeal as untimely. * * *

At the outset the Government contends that practical considerations—namely, certainty as to what judicial pronouncements are intended to be final judgments in order to avoid both premature and untimely appeals, to render certain the date of judgment liens, and to enable the procurement of writs of execution, transcripts and certified copies of judgments—require that a judgment be contained in a separate document so labeled, and urges us so to hold. Whatever may be the practical needs in these respects, the answer is that no present statute or rule so requires, as the Government concedes, and the decisional law seems settled that "[n]o form of words * * * is necessary to evince [the] rendition [of a judgment]." United States v. Hark, 320 U.S. 531, 534, 64 S.Ct. 359, 361, 88 L.Ed. 290. * * *

While an opinion may embody a *final decision,* the question whether it does so depends upon whether the judge has or has not clearly declared his intention in this respect in his opinion. Therefore, when, as here, the action is for money only * * * it is necessary to determine whether the language of the opinion embodies the essential elements of a judgment for money and clearly evidences the judge's intention that it shall be his final act in the case. If it does so, it constitutes his final judgment and, under Rule 58, it "directs that a party recover [a sum of] money," and, "upon receipt by [the clerk] of the [opinion]," requires him to "enter judgment forthwith" against the party found liable for the amount awarded, which is to be done by making a brief "notation of [the] judgment in the civil docket [showing the substance of the judgment of the court] as provided by Rule 79(a)." When all of these elements clearly appear final judgment has been both pronounced and entered, and the time to appeal starts to run * * *. And as correctly held by the Court of Appeals, the later filing and entry of a more formal judgment could not constitute a second final judgment in the case nor extend the time to appeal. * * *

But, on the other hand, if the opinion leaves doubtful whether the judge intended it to be his final act in the case—and, in an action for money, failure to determine either expressly or by reference the amount to be awarded is strong evidence of such lack of intention—one cannot say that it "directs that a party recover [a sum of] money"; * * * nor can one say that the clerk's "notation * * * in the civil docket"—if it sets forth no more substance than is contained or directed in the opinion, and being only a ministerial act * * * it may do no more—"show[s] * * * the substance of [a] judgment" of the court * * *.

But respondent argues, as the Court of Appeals held, that the opinion stated the amount of money illegally collected from respondent and, therefore, adequately determined the amount awarded, and that inasmuch as the clerk's entry incorporated the opinion by reference, it, too, adequately stated the amount of the judgment. This contention might well be accepted were it not for the fact that the action also sought recovery of interest on the amount paid by respondent from the date of payment to the date of judgment, and for the fact that the opinion does not state the date or dates of payment and, hence, did not state facts necessary to compute the amount of interest to be included in the judgment. * * * In an effort to counter the effect of these omissions, respondent states that a search of the record, which it urges we should make, would show that the Government's answer admitted the date of payment, and thus would furnish the information necessary to compute the amount of interest to be included in the judgment. * * * This argument cannot be accepted under the facts here for the reason that Rule 79(a) expressly requires that the clerk's entry "shall show * * * the substance of [the] judgment of the court * * *." Surely the amount of a judgment for money is a vital part of its substance. To hold that one must search the whole record to determine the amount, or the facts necessary to compute the amount, of a final judgment for money would be to ignore the quoted provision of Rule 79(a).

The actions of all concerned—of the judge in not stating in his opinion the amount, or means for determining the amount, of the judgment; of the clerk in not stating the amount of the judgment in his notation on the civil docket; of counsel for the Government in not appealing from the "opinion"; of counsel for respondent in preparing and presenting to the judge a formal "judgment" on May 24; and, finally, of the judge himself in signing and filing the formal "judgment" on the latter date—clearly show that none of them understood the opinion to be the judge's final act or to constitute his final judgment in the case. * * *

Reversed.

[The dissenting opinions of JUSTICE FRANKFURTER and JUSTICE HARLAN omitted.]

Notes and Questions

1. Read the Advisory Committee's 1963 Note to Rule 58 in the Supplement. Do the changes made in 1963 substantially ameliorate the problem presented by *Schaefer?* In FOILES v. UNITED STATES, 465 F.2d 163, 168 (7th Cir.1972), the Court of Appeals held that "when the jury verdict is clear and unequivocal, setting forth a general verdict with reference to the sole question of liability and where nothing remains to be decided and when no opinion or memorandum is written, as is the situation described in clause (1) of Rule 58, there is no requirement for a separate document to start the time limits for appeal running." The Supreme Court reversed sub nom. United States v. Indrelunas, 411 U.S. 216, 93 S.Ct. 1562, 36 L.Ed.2d 202 (1973). Should the trial judge be required to direct the entry of a judgment expressly? What changes in Rule 58 short of that might be made? In 2001, a proposed revision of Rule 58 was circulated that attempts to reduce the confusion that has existed.

2. In FIRSTIER MORTGAGE CO. v. INVESTORS MORTGAGE INSUR-ANCE CO., 498 U.S. 269, 111 S.Ct. 648, 112 L.Ed.2d 743 (1991), plaintiff Firstier brought suit to recover on a number of insurance policies issued by defendant ("IMI"). IMI claimed that the policies had been obtained by fraud and moved for summary judgment on this ground. On January 26, 1989, immediately after hearing arguments, the trial judge announced from the bench that he was granting IMI's motion. On February 8, 1989, Firstier filed its notice of appeal identifying the January 26 bench ruling as the decision from which it was appealing. On March 3, 1989, the trial court issued findings of fact and conclusions of law and, in a separate document, entered judgment for IMI.

On appeal, the Supreme Court considered the issue of whether a premature notice of appeal could satisfy the requirements of Federal Rule of Appellate Procedure 4(a)(2). IMI argued that allowing notice of appeal from a nonfinal judgment would be an unauthorized enlargement of appellate jurisdiction. The

Court disagreed, holding that the very purpose of Rule 4(a)(2) was to make premature notices effective:

> * * * Under Rule 4(a)(2), a premature notice of appeal does not ripen until judgment is entered. Once judgment is entered, the Rule treats the premature notice of appeal "as filed after such entry." Thus, even if a bench ruling in a given case were not "final" within the meaning of § 1291, Rule 4(a)(2) would not render that ruling appealable in contravention of § 1291. Rather, it permits a premature notice of appeal from that bench ruling to relate forward to judgment and serve as an effective notice of appeal *from the final judgment.*
>
> * * *
>
> This is not to say that Rule 4(a)(2) permits a notice of appeal from a clearly interlocutory decision * * * to serve as a notice of appeal from the final judgment. * * * In our view, Rule 4(a)(2) permits a notice of appeal from a nonfinal decision to operate as a notice of appeal from the final judgment only when a district court announces a decision that would be appealable if immediately followed by the entry of judgment. In these instances, a litigant's confusion is understandable, and permitting the notice of appeal to become effective when judgment is entered does not catch the appellee by surprise.
> * * *

Id. at 275–76, 111 S.Ct. at 652–53, 112 L.Ed.2d at 752–53. See also Comment, *Ad Hoc Relief for Untimely Appeals,* 65 Colum.L.Rev. 97 (1965).

3. Consider how the Federal Rules of Civil Procedure and the Federal Rules of Appellate Procedure function together. Civil Rule 59(e) concerns motions to alter or amend the judgment, and specifies a ten-day period. It is invoked only to support reconsideration of matters properly encompassed in a decision on the merits. Appellate Rule 4(a)(4) provides that if any party files a timely motion under Rule 59, the time for an appeal shall run from the entry of the order granting or denying such a motion. The rule specifically states that a notice of appeal filed before the disposition of such a motion shall have no effect but a new notice of appeal must be filed within the prescribed time.

In BUCHANAN v. STANSHIPS, INC., 485 U.S. 265, 108 S.Ct. 1130, 99 L.Ed.2d 289 (1988), the District Court entered judgment in favor of Stanships on the merits but did not mention costs. Buckanan filed an appeal. Stanships then filed an application for costs, described as a motion to alter or amend the judgment, which was granted by the District Court. Buckanan did not file a second notice of appeal. Stanships moved to dismiss for failure to file a timely notice of appeal. The Supreme Court, in a per curiam decision, held that the postjudgment motion for costs did not imply a change in the judgment but merely sought what was due because of the judgment:

> * * * Assessment of such costs does not involve reconsideration of any aspect of the decision on the merits. Under Rule 54(d), the "prevailing party" automatically is entitled to costs "unless the court otherwise directs." * * * [A] district judge need not take up the issue at all unless the losing party makes a timely motion for judicial review. * * *
>
> * * * [A] motion for costs filed pursuant to Rule 54(d) does not seek to "alter or amend the judgment" within the meaning of Rule 59(e). Instead, such a request for costs raises issues wholly collateral to the judgment in the main cause of action, issues to which Rule 59(e) was not intended to apply. * * * Because respondents' motion, properly viewed, was a Rule 54(d) motion

for costs rather than a Rule 59 motion to alter or amend a judgment, petitioners' notice of appeal was timely under the Federal Rules of Appellate Procedure.

Id. at 268–69, 108 S.Ct. at 1131–32, 99 L.Ed.2d at 294. See also Osterneck v. Ernst & Whinney, 489 U.S. 169, 109 S.Ct. 987, 103 L.Ed.2d 146 (1989) (motion for discretionary prejudgment interest is a motion "to alter or amend the judgment," rendering previously filed notice of appeal void under Rule 4(a)(4)).

4. Jurisdictional questions often arise when a party fails to comply specifically with statutory requirements for appeal. CHATHAS v. SMITH, 848 F.2d 93 (7th Cir.1988), involved a motion by Chathas in a civil rights case to amend a notice of appeal to include the name of one defendant who was unintentionally omitted. Appellate Rule 3(c) prescribes the contents of the notice of appeal and requires the notice to specify the appellant, the judgment appealed from and the court to which the appeal is taken. The rule does not require the appellant to list the appellees. The court noted that the purpose of the rule is to provide notice to the opposing party that an appeal has been taken and to facilitate a determination whether the appeal was timely. Judge Posner found that:

> The notice of appeal notifies the opposite party that the judgment in his favor is being appealed. Ordinarily it does this just by naming the judgment, but where it names all but one of the defendants the omitted defendant may reasonably believe that he is off the hook and need not hire a lawyer to defend the appeal. * * * This is not such a case, since all the defendants are represented by the same counsel at no expense to themselves * * *. * * * The omission of [the party's] name from the notice of appeal was thus a harmless error.

>   * * * [T]he only reason that occurs to us for a motion to amend a notice of appeal is, by dispelling confusion in the appellees' minds * * *, to forestall their arguing that they were misled. If this function could be performed only by such a motion, no doubt we could find jurisdiction under the All–Writs Act, 28 U.S.C. § 1651, to amend what is functionally a part of the appellate process though it is formally a filing in the district court. * * * But the doubt-dispelling function can be performed by a letter to the appellees' counsel. * * *

Id. at 94. Isn't the court, in effect, ordering the relief the appellant requested? If so, why deny the motion?

In TORRES v. OAKLAND SCAVENGER CO., 487 U.S. 312, 108 S.Ct. 2405, 101 L.Ed.2d 285 (1988), the Supreme Court resolved the jurisdictional issue implicated when Federal Appellate Rule 3(c) is not followed specifically. Torres was one of sixteen plaintiffs who intervened in an employment discrimination suit against Oakland Scavenger. The intervenors claimed to act in their own behalf and on behalf of all persons similarly situated. The District Court dismissed the complaint for failure to state a cause of action. A notice of appeal was filed, but the notice and the order of the Court of Appeals failed to name Torres as an appellant. Oakland Scavenger moved for partial summary judgment on the ground that the prior judgment of dismissal was final as to Torres by virtue of his failure to appeal. The District Court granted the motion and the Court of Appeals affirmed on the ground that if the party is not named, the appellate court lacks jurisdiction over him. Rule 4 prescribes the time limits for filing a notice of appeal. The Supreme Court affirmed.

The Court began by noting that because Rules 3 and 4 are jurisdictional in nature, their requirements are a mandatory prerequisite to appellate jurisdiction. Technical variations from those Rules might be permitted, but allowing courts to exercise jurisdiction over unnamed parties after the time for filing a notice of appeal had passed was considered the equivalent of permitting courts to extend the time for filing a notice of appeal, in contravention of Rule 4. Because Torres did not file the "functional equivalent" of a notice of appeal, nor seek leave to amend the notice of appeal within the time requirements of Rule 4, he could not be included in the appeal, and the judgment became final as to him.

In SMITH v. BARRY, 502 U.S. 244, 112 S.Ct. 678, 116 L.Ed.2d 678 (1992), the Court held that an informal brief (a questionnaire used to explain court procedures to, and interpret the litigation position of, pro se litigants) could serve as the functional equivalent of a notice of appeal under Rule 3. The informal brief contained six questions that Smith answered and returned within the time allowed for filing a notice of appeal. The Court of Appeals dismissed his appeal for want of jurisdiction, holding that the informal brief was not the functional equivalent of a notice of appeal under *Torres* because Smith did not intend to file a notice of appeal. The Supreme Court disagreed, holding that although the filing technically was at variance with the letter of Rule 3, the informal brief was the functional equivalent of a notice of appeal under the Rule. The Court also held that the Court of Appeals erred in relying on Smith's intent in filing the informal brief:

> While a notice of appeal must specifically indicate the litigant's intent to seek appellate review, * * * the purpose of this requirement is to ensure that the filing provides sufficient notice to other parties and the courts. * * * Thus, the notice afforded by a document, not the litigant's motivation in filing it, determines the document's sufficiency as a notice of appeal. If a document filed within the time specified by Rule 4 gives the notice required by Rule 3, it is effective as a notice of appeal.

Id. at 248–49, 112 S.Ct. at 682, 116 L.Ed.2d at 685. Does this mean that in every case, regardless of a litigant's intent in filing a document, the court must determine whether the document is the functional equivalent of a notice of appeal? How is an adverse party to know that a particular filing is the functional equivalent of a notice of appeal requiring a response?

5.   The timely filing of certain motions tolls the time clock for an appeal. If a party files a timely motion in a district court for a judgment notwithstanding the verdict under Rule 50(b), to amend or make additional findings under Rule 52(b), to alter or amend the judgment under Rule 59, or for a new trial under Rule 59, any notice of appeal filed before the disposition of any of the above motions will not be given effect. A new notice of appeal must be filed after the motion is decided. Fed.Rule App.P. 4(a)(4). See also Griggs v. Provident Consumer Discount Co., 459 U.S. 56, 103 S.Ct. 400, 74 L.Ed.2d 225 (1982).

6.   In some states separate appeals lie from the judgment and an order denying a motion for new trial. See, e.g., Minn.R.Civ.App.Proc. 103.03, which is in the Supplement following 28 U.S.C. § 1292. The time for each appeal typically is different, and each raises certain issues not raised by the other. See Note, *Scope of Review in Minnesota and its Dependence upon the Form of Appeal Taken,* 41 Minn.L.Rev. 110 (1956). Under provisions of this type, an appeal from either the judgment or the order cannot be treated as an appeal from the other.

SECTION C.   THE AMBIT OF REVIEW

1. ISSUES SUBJECT TO REVIEW

There are a number of well-defined limits on the scope of appellate review. First, the alleged errors must appear in the trial-court record. Thus it is vital during the course of pretrial preparation as well as during trial itself that an attorney make certain that all rulings and evidence that might form the basis for an appeal be formally recorded. Second, an aggrieved party must have promptly objected to the trial court regarding rulings or events that the judge could have corrected or ameliorated. Normally an error is waived unless a proper objection was taken. Third, even if the issue that the appellant seeks to have reviewed has been presented properly below and has not been waived, it must not constitute "harmless error"—that is, it must have affected substantial rights. Finally, an alleged error must be presented to the appellate court in appellant's brief and the relevant portions of the trial-court record must be brought to the appellate court's attention.

J.F. WHITE CONTRACTING CO. v. NEW ENGLAND TANK INDUSTRIES OF NEW HAMPSHIRE, INC.

United States Court of Appeals, First Circuit, 1968.
393 F.2d 449.

COFFIN, CIRCUIT JUDGE. This appeal concerns a contract to build oil tanker dock facilities on the Piscataqua river. Appellant, J.F. White Contracting Co. (White) agreed to build the dock, consisting of four cylindrical metal cells filled with sand and gravel, connected with each other and with the shore by catwalks. Appellee, New England Tank Industries of New Hampshire, Inc. (Tank), owner of the premises, sues for defective workmanship. Unlike the Piscataqua itself, the case meandered interminably for five years before a jury trial was finally reached. From an adverse verdict in the amount of $20,000 White takes this appeal.

* * *

Appellant * * * [contends] that recovery is barred by a contract provision which stipulated that approval of invoices by Tank's engineer was "final, conclusive, and binding on both parties". Without saying what effect we would give to such a provision under the factual circumstances of this case, we merely observe that we cannot consider this issue on appeal since appellant neither pleaded it as an affirmative defense nor had it "raised, considered nor passed upon in the district court." * * *

* * * White argues alternatively that it was error to have allowed the question of one of the cells being "out of round" to go to the jury. This cell had been struck in the process of installation by a ship and knocked "out of round". White undertook to repair it. This damage, being above the waterline, was visible and much less hidden or latent than the underwater ruptures.

Even if the fact that the dented cell was located some four hundred feet from shore constituted enough evidence of latency for the jury, and even if

Tank had received something less than the cylindrical cell it had bargained for, there was no evidence of the extent to which it was damaged. There was no evidence that the utility or longevity of the cell was affected, nor does there seem to have been sufficient evidence regarding the cost of repairing the dent. The underwater inspection report of the diver Howard B. Pratt did mention that cell 3 was "noticeably out of round" and his original estimate of repairs to cell 3 "as per our drawing" was $43,150. This figure might conceivably be considered some evidence of the cost to repair the dented cell. Without more, however, it would seem to be an insufficient basis for the jury to make any rational determination.

While the court's action in submitting the "out-of-roundness" issue to the jury was error, we are not persuaded that there was even a remote possibility that this error affected the verdict or "the substantial rights of the parties". Fed.R.Civ.P. 61 * * *. Nor does appellant assert that it did. Briefs of both sides argue the adequacy of damages issue by reference solely to testimony of cost of repairs and value addressed to the ruptures. Counsel for Tank did not argue the issue at all to the jury while counsel for White made it clear that it ought not be considered. Finally, the court's instructions on damages were proper and emphasized that only evidence of value, which included evidence of cost of repairs, could be considered. There is no reason to suspect that the jury did not follow these instructions.

* * *

Affirmed.

Notes and Questions

1. What justification is there for a rule that a party may not raise an issue on appeal that was not raised in the trial court? Is it fair to penalize the party for what is likely a lawyer's error? Note that under Rule 60(b) a party may ask a district court to reopen a judgment on the basis of newly discovered facts.

2. What underlies a rule that an error, if "harmless," will not provide a basis for reversal? Is it possible for an appellate court to determine what would have affected a jury's determination? Does this rule give the appellate court broad latitude to disregard error below? Or does the rule make it possible for an appellate court to instruct lower courts without needlessly incurring the systemic costs of a new trial?

———

Even when the issues have been preserved properly in the trial court and presented to the appellate court for review, there is another aspect of the scope of appellate review that must be considered—whether, and in what circumstances, an appellate court may entertain an appeal by the party who, at least ostensibly, won below.

ELECTRICAL FITTINGS CORP.
v. THOMAS & BETTS CO.

Supreme Court of the United States, 1939.
307 U.S. 241, 59 S.Ct. 860, 83 L.Ed. 1263.

Certiorari to United States Circuit Court of Appeals for the Second Circuit.

MR. JUSTICE ROBERTS delivered the opinion of the Court.

This was a suit in equity by the respondents for alleged infringement of a patent. The District Court held claim 1 valid but not infringed and claim 2 invalid. Instead of dismissing the bill without more, it entered a decree adjudging claim 1 valid but dismissing the bill for failure to prove infringement.

The respondents did not appeal, but filed in the Patent Office a disclaimer of claim 2. The petitioners appealed to the Circuit Court of Appeals from so much of the decree as adjudicated claim 1 valid. The appeal was dismissed on the ground that the petitioners had been awarded all the relief to which they were entitled, the litigation having finally terminated in their favor. The court was of opinion that the decree would not bind the petitioners in subsequent suits on the issue of the validity of claim 1.

* * * A party may not appeal from a judgment or decree in his favor, for the purpose of obtaining a review of findings he deems erroneous which are not necessary to support the decree. But here the decree itself purports to adjudge the validity of claim 1, and though the adjudication was immaterial to the disposition of the cause, it stands as an adjudication of one of the issues litigated. We think the petitioners were entitled to have this portion of the decree eliminated, and that the Circuit Court of Appeals had jurisdiction * * * to entertain the appeal, not for the purpose of passing on the merits, but to direct the reformation of the decree.

* * *

Reversed and remanded.

Notes and Questions

1. NEW YORK TELEPHONE CO. v. MALTBIE, 291 U.S. 645, 645, 54 S.Ct. 443, 443, 78 L.Ed. 1041, 1042 (1934) (per curiam):

The District Court * * * permanently enjoined, as confiscatory, the enforcement of the rate orders which are the subject of this suit. The injunction is unqualified. Appellant, having obtained this relief, is not entitled to prosecute an appeal from the decree in its favor, for the purpose of reviewing the portions of the decree fixing the value of appellant's property as of the years 1924, 1926, and 1928, and the rate of return to be allowed. The matters set forth in these portions of the decree are not to be regarded as res judicata in relation to subsequent legislative action by the Public Service Commission in fixing rates for the future or in any judicial proceeding relating to such rates.

Id.

2. Would the decree in *Electrical Fittings* have been res judicata of the validity of claim 1 of the patent? Why else might petitioners in that case have been

concerned about the decree? The Declaratory Judgment Act, 28 U.S.C. §§ 2201–2202, was not in force at the time of the *Electrical Fittings* decision. Had it been, might it have been possible to treat the District Court's decree as a declaratory judgment with respect to claim 1 and consider it as having been entered under the authority of Rule 54(c)?

3. In PARTMAR CORP. v. PARAMOUNT PICTURES THEATRES CORP., 347 U.S. 89, 74 S.Ct. 414, 98 L.Ed. 532 (1954), plaintiff leased its theater to, and entered into a franchise agreement with, defendant; the lease was to be terminable at plaintiff's option if the franchise agreement were terminated. Plaintiff sued to regain possession of the theater, alleging that it was entitled to terminate the lease because the franchise agreement was invalid under the antitrust laws; defendant counterclaimed for damages under the antitrust laws. The trial court denied plaintiff's claim, holding that the franchise agreement was not invalid because no conspiracy in violation of the antitrust laws had been established; it also dismissed the counterclaims. Defendant appealed from the dismissal of its counterclaims, and the Supreme Court held that the trial court's finding of no conspiracy on plaintiff's claim operated as collateral estoppel on the issue. See Note 5, p. 1254, infra. Could defendant have appealed from the judgment in its favor on plaintiff's claim? The majority, citing *New York Tel. Co.* and *Electrical Fittings,* held that it could.

> * * * The finding and conclusion of law * * * were essential to the determination of Paramount's claim for possession of the theatre. Paramount's position * * * was that the agreements were invalid under the federal antitrust statutes as the product of an illegal conspiracy. It is only when a finding of law or fact is not necessary for a decree that the prevailing party may not appeal and the finding does not form the basis for collateral estoppel. * * *

Id. at 99 n. 6, 74 S.Ct. at 420 n. 6, 98 L.Ed. at 541 n. 6. Chief Justice Warren, dissenting, argued:

> * * * Petitioner, as the successful party in the eviction suit, could not appeal the District Court's finding that there was no evidence of conspiracy. * * * The adverse finding was not included in the Court's decree, as in *Electrical Fittings Corp.* * * *

> * * * The Court's opinion cites no case, in this Court or any other, holding that a successful party can appeal findings which are not inserted as part of the decree. Indeed, the opinion overlooks the very holdings of this Court on which it relies for support. * * *

Id. at 109 n. 8, 74 S.Ct. at 425 n. 8, 98 L.Ed. at 546 n. 8.

STANDARD ACCIDENT INS. CO. v. ROBERTS

United States Circuit Court of Appeals, Eighth Circuit, 1942.
132 F.2d 794.

STONE, CIRCUIT JUDGE. The Standard Accident Insurance Company issued its liability policy to Herbert Roberts. Thereafter, personal injury judgments were secured against Roberts by Clyde, Pearl, George Willie and Forest Wayne Primm. Thereafter, the Standard filed this action against Roberts and the Primms to obtain a declaratory judgment that it was not liable to them on the above policy. The trial court found that the cause of the injuries to the Primms was not within the coverage of the policy but determined that the

Standard, "with full knowledge of the date, place and circumstances of the injuries" had assumed and retained control of the investigation and defense of the damage suit under such circumstances that it was estopped from denying liability thereon to the detriment and prejudice of Roberts. This is an appeal by the Standard from the judgment dismissing its petition.

Appellant presents three points: (1) that there was no liability under the policy and liability cannot be extended by estoppel; (2) that no estoppel was proven; (3) that insured was not prejudiced by the acts and conduct of Standard.

Appellees contest the above points and, in addition, urge: (1) that the policy should have been reformed to express the intention of the parties thereto; (2) that the court should have allowed reasonable attorney fees and the statutory penalty; (3) that the policy covered the accident causing the injuries to the Primms. Appellant urges that none of these three additional matters presented by appellees is open here because appellees took no cross-appeal. In this situation as to contentions of the parties, it is necessary to determine just what contentions are examinable here.

Since appellees' contentions as to reformation of the policy and as to allowance of attorney fees and penalty seek to change or to add to the relief accorded by the judgment which was in their favor, they can raise here such issues only by a cross-appeal. * * * On the other hand, the contention that the policy covered the accident seeks only to sustain the judgment for a reason presented at the trial and determined adversely to appellees. The recovery is upon the policy; and it is no more than a change of reason for such recovery, whether it be under the terms of the policy or because of an estoppel to question the applicability of the terms. In such situations the rule is that "a respondent or an appellee may urge any matter appearing in the record in support of a judgment". Le Tulle v. Scofield, 308 U.S. 415, 421, 60 S.Ct. 313, 316, 84 L.Ed. 355. * * * Therefore, appellees may, in support of the decree, urge here this ground that the policy covers the accident.

* * *

Notes and Questions

1.   Read Federal Rule of Appellate Procedure 4(a)(3) in the Supplement. Why is a party permitted to file a notice of appeal within 14 days after another party has noticed an appeal?

2.   Plaintiff's decedent was hired by a contractor to work on defendant railroad's roadbed. Plaintiff brought an action for decedent's death against the railroad in a state court, relying on the Federal Employers' Liability Act and on common-law negligence; the railroad brought a third-party claim against the contractor for indemnity. The trial court held that FELA was not applicable because decedent was not a servant of the railroad and also that the contractor was not liable to the railroad; it submitted the case against the railroad to the jury on common-law negligence, and the jury found for the railroad on the ground of contributory negligence, which is not a defense in an FELA action. Plaintiff appealed, posting an appeal bond in favor of both the railroad and the contractor, but the railroad did not perfect an appeal against the contractor. The Texas Court of Civil Appeals affirmed the judgment, but the United States Supreme Court

reversed, holding the FELA applicable. On remand, the Texas Court of Civil Appeals, in BAKER v. TEXAS & PACIFIC RAILWAY CO., 326 S.W.2d 639, 640 (1959), held that because the "liability vel non of [the contractor] on the Railroad's cross-action centers upon the facts, which will be rehashed even in greater detail than before * * * the situation, in our opinion, justif[ies] a reversal of cause in its entirety." Compare Whitehead v. American Sec. & Trust Co., 285 F.2d 282 (D.C.Cir.1960).

3. What is the effect of a reversal upon a party who took no part in an appeal at all? See In re Barnett, 124 F.2d 1005 (2d Cir.1942).

4. Consider California's exception to the general standard of review. In WARD v. TAGGART, 51 Cal.2d 736, 336 P.2d 534 (1959), plaintiff arranged to buy a parcel of real property through defendant Taggart, who falsely had represented himself to be the exclusive real estate agent for the property. Plaintiff brought a tort action for fraud, and was awarded compensatory damages and exemplary damages.

On appeal, the California Supreme Court agreed with defendant's contention that there can be no recovery in fraud absent "out-of-pocket" loss. Plaintiff had suffered no loss. However, the court permitted plaintiff to recover on a theory of quasi-contract:

> Although this theory of recovery was not advanced by plaintiffs in the trial court, it is settled that a change in theory is permitted on appeal when "a question of law only is presented on the facts appearing in the record * * *." Panopulos v. Maderis, 47 Cal.2d 337, 341, 303 P.2d 738, 741 * * *. The general rule confining the parties upon appeal to the theory advanced below is based on the rationale that the opposing party should not be required to defend for the first time on appeal against a new theory that "contemplates a factual situation the consequences of which are open to controversy and were not put in issue or presented at the trial." * * * Such is not the case here. Although the facts pleaded and proved by plaintiffs do not sustain the judgment on the theory of tort, they are sufficient to uphold recovery under the quasi-contractual theory of unjust enrichment since that theory does not contemplate any factual situation different from that established by the evidence in the trial court. Defendants were given ample opportunity to present their version of the transaction involved, and the issue of whether or not their actions constituted fraud was decided adversely to them by the trial court.

Id. at 742, 336 P.2d at 537–38.

If the Supreme Court of California had not found a quasi-contractual remedy available, and plaintiffs had shown evidence, not offered at trial, of facts, not raised at trial, supporting the existence of a fiduciary relationship between Taggart and himself, what result should have been reached by the court? Read Cal.Code Civ.Proc. § 909 in the Supplement. "Probably the most significant practical characteristic of this California exception is its sparing use, especially in situations where the additional evidence aims at reversal of the judgment instead of affirmance." Louisell & Degnan, *Rehearing in American Appellate Courts*, 44 Calif.L.Rev. 627, 629 n.8 (1956).

5. Plaintiff brought an action for payments due on a subscription for two burial crypts. At the close of plaintiff's case, defendant moved for judgment on the ground that plaintiff had not shown that the mausoleum was constructed in accordance with the plans and specifications; the trial court denied plaintiff

permission to reopen the case to supply the missing proof, and granted defendant's motion. On appeal, the Supreme Court of Arizona found that the refusal to permit plaintiff to reopen had been an abuse of discretion. At that point, should defendant have been permitted to raise for the first time plaintiff's failure to allege and prove that he was a licensed real-estate broker as required by law? See Bowman v. Hall, 83 Ariz. 56, 316 P.2d 484 (1957).

2. SCOPE OF REVIEW OF FACTS

CORCORAN v. CITY OF CHICAGO

Supreme Court of Illinois, 1940.
373 Ill. 567, 27 N.E.2d 451.

MURPHY, JUSTICE. John F. Corcoran * * * began a suit * * * against the city of Chicago * * * to recover damages for personal injuries alleged to have been caused by the negligent acts of the defendant. The cause was tried with a jury and resulted in a verdict for the plaintiff for $5,000. A motion for new trial was overruled and judgment entered on the verdict. On appeal, the Appellate Court for the First District reversed the judgment and remanded the cause for another trial. The plaintiff filed a motion in the Appellate Court asking that the remanding part of the order be stricken [in order that on appeal to the state Supreme Court, that court could then order that the initial verdict be reinstated]. * * * The motion was granted * * *.

The negligence charged was that defendant had carelessly and negligently permitted certain streets to be and remain in an unsafe condition for travel * * *. The evidence was conflicting. The Appellate Court found the verdict was against the manifest weight of the evidence and reversed the judgment for that reason.

It is conceded the power which the Appellate Court assumed to exercise in reviewing the evidence and setting aside the verdict is found in section 92(3b) of the Civil Practice Act * * * which provides that Appellate Courts may review "error of fact, in that the judgment, decree or order appealed from is not sustained by the evidence or is against the weight of the evidence." Plaintiff's position is that such provision, as applied to facts found by a jury upon conflicting evidence, as in the instant case, is unconstitutional, in that the findings of the Appellate Court * * * take from him the right to a trial by jury as guaranteed by section 5 of article 2 of the Constitution * * *.

* * *

Prior to 1837, the law of this state was that the granting or refusal of a motion for a new trial rested in the sound discretion of the trial court and the ruling thereon could not be urged as error in the court of review. * * * In 1837, an act was passed which provided "exceptions taken to opinions or decisions of circuit court overruling motions in arrest of judgment, motions for new trials and for continuance of causes shall hereafter be allowed and the party excepting may assign for error any opinion so excepted to, any usage to the contrary notwithstanding." The substance of the act * * * has been the statutory law of this state since 1837.

* * *

The effect of the operation of the statute was considered in Chicago & Rock Island Railroad Co. v. McKean, 40 Ill. 218, a case where the trial court had overruled a motion for new trial and error was assigned on such ruling. Mr. Justice Breese, speaking for the court, said: "An appellate court was, before the passage of that act, judge of the law only * * *. The old and honored maxim once was, 'the judges respond to the law, the jury to the facts,' but now, by this innovation, the judges of an appellate court have as much power over the facts as the jury had in the first instance, for it is undeniable this court may set aside a verdict if the facts fail to satisfy it of its propriety. * * *"

Plaintiff contends that on all questions of fact where the evidence is conflicting the verdict of the jury can not be set aside as being against the weight of the evidence except by the court that tried the case, and asserts that such was the practice at common law. * * *

* * *

From the authorities cited and others which have been examined, we conclude that there was a practice at common law which authorized courts exercising appellate jurisdiction to set aside verdicts on the grounds the findings of fact were not supported by the evidence. * * *

Judgment affirmed.

Notes and Questions

1. In 1957, the late Professor Charles Alan Wright stated "that, so far as I can find, there is not a single case in which a federal appellate court has ever reversed and ordered a new trial on the ground that the trial court did abuse its discretion in denying a motion [for a new trial on the weight of the evidence] * * *." Wright, *The Doubtful Omniscience of Appellate Courts,* 41 Minn.L.Rev. 751, 760 (1957). At the time he was criticizing a dictum of the Court of Appeals for the District of Columbia Circuit claiming the existence of the power to reverse; but, he observed, "today's dictum claiming extended power for appellate courts is frequently the prelude to tomorrow's holding to that effect." Id. at 763.

Subsequently at least one court of appeals has acted as he prophesied. Georgia–Pac. Corp. v. United States, 264 F.2d 161 (5th Cir.1959). Is there a significant difference between an appellate court's reversing a trial court's order denying a new trial and an appellate court's ordering a new trial because the trial court has erroneously denied a motion for a directed verdict as in Slocum v. New York Life Ins. Co., Note 1, p. 1060, supra? Is there really a difference between reversing an order denying a new trial and reversing an order granting a new trial?

2. The power to reverse denials of new trials on the ground that the verdict is excessive or to condition affirmance upon a remittitur is now asserted by most of the courts of appeals, after "seemingly endless controversy," and in spite of the extremely strong doubts thrown on the subject by Justice Brandeis' opinion in FAIRMOUNT GLASS WORKS v. CUB FORK COAL CO., 287 U.S. 474, 53 S.Ct. 252, 77 L.Ed. 439 (1933). See also the exhaustive opinion of Judge Medina in Dagnello v. Long Island R. Co., 289 F.2d 797 (2d Cir.1961). Why should this power be more commonly found than the power discussed in Note 1?

ORVIS v. HIGGINS

United States Court of Appeals, Second Circuit, 1950.
180 F.2d 537.
Certiorari denied 340 U.S. 810, 71 S.Ct. 37, 95 L.Ed. 595.

FRANK, CIRCUIT JUDGE. [This was an action for refund of federal estate taxes. Deceased husband and his wife each had set up a trust in 1934 in which the other received a life interest. If these trusts were set up independently, the husband's estate was not chargeable with any estate tax on the property that was in the trust created by the wife. If the trusts were set up by mutual agreement, however, each trust being in consideration of the other, then the trust set up by the wife would be treated as a trust set up by the husband, and since the deceased received a life income from the trust, the value of that trust would be taxable to the estate. The trial judge had found that the trusts were set up independently.]

In opinions holding that the findings of trial judges were not "clearly erroneous" within the meaning of Rule 52(a), * * * we have often stressed the importance of a trial judge's advantage over us when he saw and heard the witnesses as they testified. We have pointed out our inability to appraise the cogency of demeanor evidence, lost to us because it cannot be captured in the witness' words as recorded on paper. In so holding, we may perhaps, at times, have overlooked distinctions described in United States v. United States Gypsum Co., 333 U.S. 364, 394–396, 68 S.Ct. 525, 542, 92 L.Ed. 746.

There the Court made it clear that Rule 52(a) merely adopted the equity practice then prevailing in the federal courts. The Court said a finding of a trial court, if it be by a judge, "is 'clearly erroneous' when although there is evidence to support it, the reviewing court on the entire evidence is left with the definite and firm conviction that a mistake has been committed." * * *

In the light of the Gypsum case, we may make approximate gradations as follows: We must sustain a general or a special jury verdict when there is some evidence which the jury might have believed, and when a reasonable inference from that evidence will support the verdict, regardless of whether that evidence is oral or by deposition. In the case of findings by an administrative agency, the usual rule is substantially the same as that in the case of a jury, the findings being treated like a special verdict. Where a trial judge sits without a jury, the rule varies with the character of the evidence: (a) If he decides a fact issue on written evidence alone, we are as able as he to determine credibility, and so we may disregard his finding. (b) Where the evidence is partly oral and the balance is written or deals with undisputed facts, then we may ignore the trial judge's finding and substitute our own, (1) if the written evidence or some undisputed fact renders the credibility of the oral testimony extremely doubtful, or (2) if the trial judge's finding must rest exclusively on the written evidence or the undisputed facts, so that his evaluation of credibility has no significance. (c) But where the evidence supporting his finding as to any fact issue is entirely oral testimony, we may disturb that finding only in the most unusual circumstances.

It follows that evidence sufficient to support a jury verdict or an administrative finding may not suffice to support a trial judge's finding. So in the instant case, perhaps, on the record evidence, we might have affirmed a jury's verdict or an administrative agency's finding in plaintiff's favor. That, however, we need not decide. For here the finding is that of a trial judge, and the evidence consists in large part of facts neither side disputes, in circumstances such that the trial judge's evaluation of credibility becomes unimportant. In short, for reasons we shall state, the undisputed facts are such that we have a "definite and firm conviction" that the trial judge was mistaken in finding that Orvis and Mrs. Orvis "each pursued an independent course" in creating the 1934 trusts, and that no reciprocity was intended. We therefore hold that finding "clearly erroneous," and hold, rather, that each of those trusts was made in consideration of the other.

In so holding we assume that, because of the "evanescent factor which cannot come before us"—i.e., the demeanor of the witnesses—the trial judge fully believed everything they said. Even so, there is nothing in the testimony which in any manner offsets what we believe to be the virtually irresistible inference drawn from the undisputed facts. To offset that inference, the trial judge relied on no positive testimony that Mr. and Mrs. Orvis acted independently but relied merely on negative testimony as to the absence of an expressed intention to act reciprocally, i.e., that "no witness even intimated that the decedent acted with Mrs. Orvis' intention in mind or she with his." The only testimony on which the trial judge relied, or could have relied * * *, is that of Mr. Merritt as to the reasons respectively given to him by husband and wife for the creation of their respective trusts. Not only were those respective reasons strikingly similar but none of them sufficed or purported to explain why each of the trusts set up a life estate; nor did the expression of those reasons at all negative the existence of an intent to make the trusts reciprocal. The finding of an absence of such an intention must, then, depend not on an inference drawn from anything positive in the testimony concerning statements of intention made by Mr. and Mrs. Orvis, but on an inference from their conduct. And that inference, in turn, must rest on a belief in the purely chance concurrence of several events, although the coincidental occurrence of those events would ordinarily be highly improbable. Such a belief ought not to be the foundation of a trial judge's finding on a fact issue, in favor of that side having (like plaintiffs here) the burden of proof as to that issue, unless the purely chance character of those events is positively confirmed by clear evidence. There is no such confirmatory evidence here.

* * *

Reversed and remanded.

CHASE, CIRCUIT JUDGE (dissenting). * * *

This is a typical instance for the application of Civil Rule 52(a). Though trial judges may at times be mistaken as to facts, appellate judges are not always omniscient.

I would affirm.

Notes and Questions

1. In 1985 Rule 52(a) was amended to apply the "clearly erroneous" standard to a trial court's findings of fact, even if they were based on documentary evidence. Would *Orvis* and the decisions in the cases that follow in this Section have been affected by the amendment? Prior to the amendment, commentators expressed the following views:

(a) "There is no logical reason for placing the findings of fact of a trial judge upon a substantially lower level of conclusiveness than the fact findings of a jury of laymen, or those of an administrative agency * * *. The existence of any doubt as to whether the trial court or this Court is the ultimate trier of fact issues in nonjury cases is, we think, detrimental to the orderly administration of justice, impairs the confidence of litigants and the public in the decisions of the district courts, and multiplies the number of appeals in such cases." PENDERGRASS v. NEW YORK LIFE INSURANCE CO., 181 F.2d 136, 138 (8th Cir.1950).

(b) "[E]ven where the question is what finding of fact should be made on the basis of documentary evidence, the trial judge has the advantage of having made the initial sifting of the entire record and of having put it into logical sequence, while the appellate court has lawyers before it picking out bits and pieces of the record to attack or defend a particular finding." Wright, *The Doubtful Omniscience of Appellate Courts,* 41 Minn.L.Rev. 751, 782 (1957).

(c) "We are not final because we are infallible, but we are infallible only because we are final." Justice Jackson, concurring, in BROWN v. ALLEN, 344 U.S. 443, 540, 73 S.Ct. 397, 427, 97 L.Ed. 469, 533 (1953).

2. Reread Hicks v. United States, p. 54, supra. Consider the following:

Taking a cautious view of the propriety of directed verdicts in negligence cases tried to juries, appellate courts have warned, "Our ideas as to what would be proper care vary according to temperament, knowledge, and experience. A party should not be held to the peculiar notions of the judge as to what would be ordinary care." Curiously, most courts have failed to apply these observations to the nonjury trial. Using orthodox terminology, it makes sense to label the reasonable man standard a "question of fact" in the jury case, but a "question of law" in the nonjury case. In the nonjury negligence case, the appellate court, not the trial judge, should be analogized to the jury. * * * [O]nce the facts have been found without clear error, the group of judges on the appellate court is better qualified to decide the issue of negligence than is the trial judge acting alone, according to the teaching of jury cases.

Weiner, *The Civil Nonjury Trial and the Law–Fact Distinction,* 55 Calif.L.Rev. 1020, 1033 (1967).

PULLMAN–STANDARD v. SWINT

Supreme Court of the United States, 1982.
456 U.S. 273, 102 S.Ct. 1781, 72 L.Ed.2d 66.

Certiorari to the United States Court of Appeals for the Fifth Circuit.

JUSTICE WHITE delivered the opinion of the Court.

Respondents were black employees at the Bessemer, Alabama plant of petitioner, Pullman–Standard (the "company"), a manufacturer of railway freight cars and parts. They brought suit against the company and the union petitioners * * * alleging violations of Title VII of the Civil Rights Act of 1964 * * *. As they come here, these cases involve only the validity, under Title VII, of a seniority system maintained by the Company and USW [the United Steel Workers of America]. The District Court found "that the differences in terms, conditions or privileges of employment resulting [from the seniority system] are 'not the result of an intention to discriminate' because of race or color," * * * and held, therefore, that the system satisfied the requirements of § 703(h) of the Act. The Court of Appeals for the Fifth Circuit reversed:

> Because we find that the differences in the terms, conditions and standards of employment for black workers and white workers at Pullman–Standard resulted from an intent to discriminate because of race, we hold that the system is not legally valid under section 703(h) of Title VII, 42 U.S.C. 2000e–2(h). * * *

We granted the petitions for certiorari * * * limited to the first question presented in each petition: whether a Court of Appeals is bound by the "clearly erroneous" rule of Fed.Rules Civ.Proc. 52(a) in reviewing a District Court's findings of fact, arrived at after a lengthy trial, as to the motivation of the parties who negotiated a seniority system; and whether the court below applied wrong legal criteria in determining the *bona fides* of the seniority system. We conclude that the Court of Appeals erred in the course of its review and accordingly reverse its judgment and remand for further proceedings.

* * *

In connection with its assertion that it was convinced that a mistake had been made, the Court of Appeals, in a footnote, referred to the clearly erroneous standard of Rule 52(a). * * * It pointed out, however, that if findings "are made under an erroneous view of controlling legal principles, the clearly erroneous rule does not apply, and the findings may not stand." Finally, quoting from East v. Romine, Inc., 518 F.2d 332, 339 (C.A.5 1975), the Court of Appeals repeated the following view of its appellate function in Title VII cases where purposeful discrimination is at issue:

> Although discrimination *vel non* is essentially a question of fact it is, at the same time, the ultimate issue for resolution in this case, being expressly proscribed by 42 U.S.C.A. § 2000e–2(a). As such, a finding of discrimination or nondiscrimination is a finding of ultimate fact. [Cites omitted.] In reviewing the district court's findings, therefore, we will proceed to make an independent determination of appellant's allegations of discrimination, though bound by findings of subsidiary fact which are themselves not clearly erroneous.

* * * Petitioners submit that the Court of Appeals made an independent determination of discriminatory purpose, the "ultimate fact" in this case, and that this was error under Rule 52. We agree with petitioners that if the Court of Appeals followed what seems to be the accepted rule in that circuit, its judgment must be reversed.

Rule 52 broadly requires that findings of fact not be set aside unless clearly erroneous. It does not make exceptions or purport to exclude certain categories of factual findings from the obligation of a Court of Appeals to accept a district court's findings unless clearly erroneous. It does not divide facts into categories; in particular, it does not divide findings of fact into those that deal with "ultimate" and those that deal with "subsidiary" facts.

The rule does not apply to conclusions of law. The Court of Appeals, therefore, was quite right in saying that if a District Court's findings rest on an erroneous view of the law, they may be set aside on that basis. But here the District Court was not faulted for misunderstanding or applying an erroneous definition of intentional discrimination. It was reversed for arriving at what the Court of Appeals thought was an erroneous finding as to whether the differential impact of the seniority system reflected an intent to discriminate on account of race. That question, as we see it, is a pure question of fact, subject to Rule 52's clearly erroneous standard. It is not a question of law and not a mixed question of law and fact.

* * * Rule 52 does not furnish particular guidance with respect to distinguishing law from fact. Nor do we yet know of any other rule or principle that will unerringly distinguish a factual finding from a legal conclusion. For the reasons that follow, however, we have little doubt about the factual nature of § 703(h)'s requirement that a seniority system be free of an intent to discriminate.

* * *

* * * It would make no sense to say that the intent to discriminate required by § 703(h) may be presumed from such an impact. As § 703(h) was construed in * * * [Teamsters v. United States, 431 U.S. 324, 97 S.Ct. 1843, 52 L.Ed.2d 396 (1977)] there must be a finding of actual intent to discriminate on racial grounds on the part of those who negotiated or maintained the system. That finding appears to us to be a pure question of fact.

This is not to say that discriminatory impact is not part of the evidence to be considered by the trial court in reaching a finding on whether there was such a discriminatory intent as a factual matter. We do assert, however, that under § 703(h) discriminatory intent is a finding of fact to be made by the trial court; it is not a question of law and not a mixed question of law and fact of the kind that in some cases may allow an appellate court to review the facts to see if they satisfy some legal concept of discriminatory intent. Discriminatory intent here means actual motive; it is not a legal presumption to be drawn from a factual showing of something less than actual motive. Thus, a court of appeals may only reverse a district court's finding on discriminatory intent if it concludes that the finding is clearly erroneous under Rule 52(a). Insofar as the Fifth Circuit assumed otherwise, it erred.

Appellees do not directly defend the Fifth Circuit rule that a trial court's finding on discriminatory intent is not subject to the clearly erroneous standard of Rule 52. Rather, among other things, they submit that the Court of Appeals recognized and, where appropriate, properly applied Rule 52 in setting aside the findings of the District Court. This position has force, but for two reasons it is not persuasive.

First, although the Court of Appeals acknowledged and correctly stated the controlling standard of Rule 52, the acknowledgement came late in the court's opinion. The court had not expressly referred to or applied Rule 52 in the course of disagreeing with the District Court's resolution of the factual issues * * *. Furthermore, the paragraph in which the court finally concludes that the USW seniority system is unprotected by § 703(h) strongly suggests that the outcome was the product of the court's independent consideration of the totality of the circumstances it found in the record.

Second and more fundamentally, when the court stated that it was convinced that a mistake had been made, it then not only identified the mistake but also the source of that mistake. The mistake of the District Court was that on the record there could be no doubt about the existence of a discriminatory purpose. * * *

When an appellate court discerns that a district court has failed to make a finding because of an erroneous view of the law, the usual rule is that there should be a remand for further proceedings to permit the trial court to make the missing findings * * *. Likewise, where findings are infirm because of an erroneous view of the law, a remand is the proper course unless the record permits only one resolution of the factual issue. All of this is elementary. Yet the Court of Appeals, after holding that the District Court had failed to consider relevant evidence and indicating that the District Court might have come to a different conclusion had it considered that evidence, failed to remand for further proceedings * * *. Instead, the Court of Appeals made its own determination [and findings] * * * and apparently concluded that the foregoing was sufficient to remove the system from the protection of § 703(h).

Proceeding in this manner seems to us incredible unless the Court of Appeals construed its own well-established Circuit rule with respect to its authority to arrive at independent findings on ultimate facts free of the strictures of Rule 52 also to permit it to examine the record and make its own independent findings with respect to those issues on which the district court's findings are set aside for an error of law. As we have previously said, however, the premise for this conclusion is infirm: whether an ultimate fact or not, discriminatory intent under § 703(h) is a factual matter subject to the clearly erroneous standard of Rule 52. It follows that when a district court's finding on such an ultimate fact is set aside for an error of law, the court of appeals is not relieved of the usual requirement of remanding for further proceedings to the tribunal charged with the task of fact-finding in the first instance.

* * *

[JUSTICE STEVENS concurred in part.]

JUSTICE MARSHALL, with whom JUSTICE BLACKMUN joins * * *, dissenting.

* * *

As the majority acknowledges, where findings of fact "are made under an erroneous view of controlling legal principles, the clearly erroneous rule does not apply, and the findings may not stand." * * * Having found that the District Court's findings * * * were made under an erroneous view of controlling legal principles, the Court of Appeals was *compelled* to set aside those findings free of the requirements of the clearly erroneous rule. But once these two findings were set aside, the District Court's conclusion that the departmental system was bona fide within the meaning of § 703(h) also had to be rejected, since that conclusion was based at least in part on its erroneous determinations * * *.

At the very least, therefore, the Court of Appeals was entitled to remand this case to the District Court for the purpose of reexamining the bona fides of the seniority system under proper legal standards. However, as we have often noted, in some cases a remand is inappropriate where the facts on the record are susceptible to only one reasonable interpretation. * * * In such cases, "[e]ffective judicial administration" requires that the Court of Appeals draw the inescapable factual conclusion itself, rather than remand the case to the District Court for further needless proceedings. * * * Such action is particularly appropriate where the court of appeals is in as good a position to evaluate the record evidence as the district court. The major premise behind the deference to trial courts expressed in Rule 52 is that findings of fact "depend peculiarly upon the credit given to witnesses by those who see and hear them." * * *

In the cases before the Court today this usual deference is not required because the District Court's findings of fact were entirely based on documentary evidence. As we noted in United States v. General Motors Corp., supra, 384 U.S., at 141 n. 16, 86 S.Ct., at 1328 n. 16, "the trial court's customary opportunity to evaluate the demeanor and thus the credibility of the witnesses, which is the rationale behind Rule 52(a) * * *, plays only a restricted role [in] a 'paper case.' " * * *

I believe that the Court of Appeals correctly determined that a finding of discriminatory intent was compelled by the documentary record presented to the District Court. * * *

* * * Because I fail to see how the Court of Appeals erred in carrying out its appellate function, I respectfully dissent from the majority's decision to prolong respondents' 11–year quest for the vindication of their rights by requiring yet another trial.

———

INWOOD LABORATORIES, INC. v. IVES LABORATORIES, INC., 456 U.S. 844, 102 S.Ct. 2182, 72 L.Ed.2d 606 (1982). In a patent infringement suit brought by Ives Laboratories against Inwood Laboratories, the District Court entered judgment for Inwood, finding that Ives had not made the necessary factual showings. The Court of Appeals reversed, making its own review of the evidence, and concluding that the District Court did not give enough weight to the evidence offered by Ives. The court held that the evidence was clearly sufficient to establish a Section 32 violation. The Supreme Court reversed:

> In reviewing the factual findings of the District Court, the Court of Appeals was bound by the "clearly erroneous" standard of Rule 52(a). * * * That Rule recognizes and rests upon the unique opportunity afforded the trial court judge to evaluate the credibility of witnesses and to weigh the evidence. * * * Because of the deference due the trial judge, unless an appellate court is left with the "definite and firm conviction that a mistake has been committed," * * * it must accept the trial court's findings.

> * * *

> Each of [the Second Circuit's] conclusions is contrary to the findings of the District Court. An appellate court cannot substitute its interpretation of the evidence for that of the trial court simply because the reviewing court "might give the facts another construction, resolve the

ambiguities differently, and find a more sinister cast to actions which the District Court apparently deemed innocent." * * *

The Court of Appeals erred in setting aside findings of fact that were not clearly erroneous. Accordingly, the judgment of the Court of Appeals that the petitioners violated § 32 of the Lanham Act is reversed.

Id. at 855–59, 102 S.Ct. at 2186–87, 72 L.Ed.2d at 616–18. Justices White and Marshall concurred in the result only, maintaining that the Rule 52(a) issue had not been properly presented to the Court.

———

In ANDERSON v. CITY OF BESSEMER CITY, 470 U.S. 564, 105 S.Ct. 1504, 84 L.Ed.2d 518 (1985), Anderson filed discrimination charges against the City of Bessemer City, alleging that she was overlooked for a position as Recreation Director with the City on the ground of her sex, and that the position was awarded to a less qualified male applicant. When her efforts at the EEOC proved unsuccessful, petitioner obtained a right-to-sue letter and filed an action in the federal district court. The District Court found, as a matter of fact, that petitioner was the most qualified candidate, and issued further findings of fact and conclusions of law. The Court of Appeals for the Fourth Circuit reversed, holding that the District Court's findings were clearly erroneous and that the court had therefore erred in finding that petitioner had been discriminated against on account of sex.

The Supreme Court reversed. Justice White noted that the District Court did not uncritically accept the findings prepared by the prevailing party but provided a framework for its proposed findings in a preliminary memorandum. This document set forth the District Court's essential findings and directed petitioner's counsel to submit a more detailed set of findings consistent with them. Therefore, the Court concluded, there was no reason to doubt that the ultimate findings represented the court's own considered conclusions or to subject those findings to a more stringent appellate review than is called for by the applicable rules. Id. at 572–73, 105 S.Ct. at 1510–11, 84 L.Ed.2d at 527–28.

The Court then considered whether the Court of Appeals engaged in the type of inquiry required by Federal Rule 52(a) governing findings of fact:

* * * Findings of fact shall not be set aside unless clearly erroneous, and due regard shall be given to the opportunity of the trial court to judge of the credibility of the witnesses. * * *

* * * [A] finding is "clearly erroneous" when although there is evidence to support it, the reviewing court on the entire evidence is left with the definite and firm conviction that a mistake has been committed. * * * "In applying the clearly erroneous standard to the findings of a district court sitting without a jury, appellate courts must constantly have in mind that their function is not to decide factual issues *de novo.*" * * * If the district court's account of the evidence is plausible in light of the record viewed in its entirety, the court of appeals may not reverse it even though convinced that had it been sitting as the trier of fact, it would have weighed the evidence differently. Where there are two permissible

views of the evidence, the factfinder's choice between them cannot be clearly erroneous. * * *

This is so even when the district court's findings do not rest on credibility determinations, but are based instead on physical or documentary evidence or inferences from other facts. * * *

The rationale for deference to the original finder of fact is not limited to the superiority of the trial judge's position to make determinations of credibility. The trial judge's major role is the determination of fact, and with experience in fulfilling that role comes expertise. Duplication of the trial judge's efforts in the court of appeals would very likely contribute only negligibly to the accuracy of fact determination at a huge cost in diversion of judicial resources. In addition, the parties to a case on appeal have already been forced to concentrate their energies and resources on persuading the trial judge that their account of the facts is the correct one * * *.

When findings are based on determinations regarding the credibility of witnesses, Rule 52(a) demands even greater deference to the trial court's findings. * * *

* * * [T]he Fourth Circuit improperly conducted what amounted to a *de novo* weighing of the evidence in the record. * * *

* * * When the record is examined in light of the appropriately deferential standard, it is apparent that it contains nothing that mandates a finding that the District Court's conclusion was clearly erroneous.

Id. at 573–77, 105 S.Ct. at 1511–13, 84 L.Ed.2d at 528–30.

BOSE CORP. v. CONSUMERS UNION OF UNITED STATES, INC., 466 U.S. 485, 104 S.Ct. 1949, 80 L.Ed.2d 502 (1984). Bose, a manufacturer of stereo loudspeaker systems, sued Consumers Union for product disparagement based on statements contained in an article evaluating a loudspeaker system manufactured by Bose. The District Court found that Bose was a "public figure" under the standard of New York Times Co. v. Sullivan, 376 U.S. 254, 84 S.Ct. 710, 11 L.Ed.2d 686 (1964), and its progeny, and therefore held that Bose was required to prove by clear and convincing evidence that the respondent made a false disparaging statement with "actual malice." The court found "actual malice," however, and entered judgment for Bose. The Court of Appeals reversed, holding that its review of the "actual malice" determination was not limited by the "clearly erroneous" standard of Rule 52(a) and that it must perform a de novo review of the record to evaluate the District Court's application of the governing constitutional standard.

The Supreme Court affirmed. Writing for the Court, Justice Stevens noted that the Rule's command of deference to findings of fact made by trial courts seems to conflict with the requirement, embodied in the *New York Times* case, that appellate courts conduct a complete examination of the trial record to measure the judgment by the constitutional protection afforded by the First Amendment. He continued, however:

* * * The conflict between the two rules is in some respects more apparent than real. The *New York Times* rule emphasizes the need for an appellate court to make an independent examination of the entire record; Rule 52(a) never forbids such an examination, and indeed our seminal decision on the rule expressly contemplated a review of the entire record, stating that a "finding is 'clearly erroneous' when although there is evidence to support it, the reviewing court *on the entire evidence* is left with the definite and firm conviction that a mistake has been committed." United States v. United States Gypsum Co. * * * (emphasis supplied). Moreover, Rule 52(a) commands that "due regard" shall be given to the trial judge's opportunity to observe the demeanor of the witnesses; the constitutionally-based rule of independent review permits this opportunity to be given its due. * * *

* * * [T]he rule of independent review assigns to judges a constitutional responsibility that cannot be delegated to the trier of fact, whether the factfinding function be performed in the particular case by a jury or by a trial judge.

Rule 52(a) applies to findings of fact, including those described as "ultimate facts" because they may determine the outcome of litigation. See Pullman–Standard v. Swint * * *. But Rule 52(a) does not inhibit an appellate court's power to correct errors of law, including those that may infect a so-called mixed finding of law and fact, or a finding of fact that is predicated on a misunderstanding of the governing rule of law. * * * Nor does Rule 52(a) "furnish particular guidance with respect to distinguishing law from fact." Pullman–Standard v. Swint * * *.

In a consideration of the possible application of the distinction to the issue of "actual malice," at least three characteristics of the rule enunciated in the *New York Times* case are relevant. First, the common law heritage of the rule itself assigns an especially broad role to the judge in applying it to specific factual situations. Second, the content of the rule is not revealed simply by its literal text, but rather is given meaning through the evolutionary process of common law adjudication; though the source of the rule is found in the Constitution, it is nevertheless largely a judge-made rule of law. Finally, the constitutional values protected by the rule make it imperative that judges—and in some cases judges of this Court—make sure that it is correctly applied. * * *

* * *

The requirement of independent appellate review reiterated in New York Times v. Sullivan is a rule of federal constitutional law. It emerged from the exigency of deciding concrete cases; it is law in its purest form under our common law heritage. It reflects a deeply held conviction that judges—and particularly members of this Court—must exercise such review in order to preserve the precious liberties established and ordained by the Constitution. The question whether the evidence in the record in a defamation case is of the convincing clarity required to strip the utterance of First Amendment protection is not merely a question for the trier of fact. * * *

Id. at 510–11, 104 S.Ct. at 1959–65, 80 L.Ed.2d at 515–23.

The Court then conducted its own *de novo* review, and found that, even accepting all of the purely factual findings of the District Court, the record did not contain clear and convincing evidence that the author of the article or his employer prepared the loudspeaker article with knowledge that it contained a false statement, or with reckless disregard of the truth. In an important passage, the Court held:

> * * * We hold that the clearly erroneous standard of Rule 52(a) * * * does not prescribe the standard of review to be applied in reviewing a determination of actual malice in a case governed by New York Times v. Sullivan. Appellate judges in such a case must exercise independent judgment and determine whether the record establishes actual malice with convincing clarity.

Id. at 514, 104 S.Ct. at 1967, 80 L.Ed.2d at 525–26.

Chief Justice Burger concurred in the result. Justice White dissented, arguing that because the District Court found that the defamatory statement was written with actual knowledge of its falsity, the Court of Appeals erred in reversing the District Court based on its *de novo* review. Justices Rehnquist and O'Connor also dissented:

> It is * * * ironic that, in the interest of protecting the First Amendment, the Court rejects the "clearly erroneous" standard of review mandated by Federal Rule * * * 52(a) in favor of a *"de novo"* standard of review for the "constitutional facts" surrounding the "actual malice" determination. But the facts dispositive of that determination—actual knowledge or subjective reckless disregard for truth—involve no more than findings about the mens rea of an author, findings which appellate courts are simply ill-prepared to make in any context, including the First Amendment context. Unless "actual malice" now means something different from the definition given to the term 20 years ago by this Court in *New York Times,* I do not think that the constitutional requirement of "actual malice" properly can bring into play any standard of factual review other than the "clearly erroneous" standard.

> * * *

> I think that the issues of "falsity" and "actual malice" in this case may be close questions, but I am convinced that the District Court, which heard the principal witness for the respondent testify for almost six days during the trial, fully understood both the applicable law and its role as a finder of fact. Because it is not clear to me that the de novo findings of appellate courts, with only bare records before them, are likely to be any more reliable than the findings reached by trial judges, I cannot join the majority's sanctioning of factual second guessing by appellate courts. I believe that the primary result of the Court's holding today will not be greater protection for First Amendment values, but rather only lessened confidence in the judgments of lower courts and more entirely fact-bound appeals.

> I continue to adhere to the view expressed in Pullman–Standard v. Swint * * * that Rule 52(a) "does not make exceptions or purport to exclude certain categories of factual findings from the obligation of a

court of appeals to accept a district court's findings unless clearly erroneous." * * *

Id. at 515–20, 104 S.Ct. at 1968–70, 80 L.Ed.2d at 526–29.

Notes and Questions

1. Is *Bose* consistent with *Pullman-Standard* and *Inwood Labs*? Do you
accept Justice Stevens' identification and resolution of the conflict between the
"independent review" requirement of *New York Times* and the "clearly erroneous" standard embodied in Rule 52(a)? Or is Justice Rehnquist correct in
challenging as an unwarranted extension of *New York Times* the development by
the majority in *Bose* of a special standard for the application of Rule 52(a) in
defamation cases?

2. Can you identify any other constitutional mandates that would conflict
with the "clearly erroneous" standard? What of the argument that the Civil
Rights Act of 1964 is the statutory embodiment of the constitutional commands on
civil rights embodied in the Fourteenth Amendment? Is there a clash between
constitutional requirements and Rule 52(a) that the majority disregarded in
Pullman-Standard?

3. Appellate courts are often not as deferential to trial court findings as the
standards or the case law would indicate. Goettel, *Appellate Fact Finding—and
Other Atrocities*, 13 Litigation 7 (Fall 1986). In fact, Judge Goettel notes that
"[t]rial judges often can barely recognize their cases in appellate opinions, so
convoluted have the facts become. With the facts so extensively revamped,
reversal becomes inevitable." Id. at 7. See generally Sward, *Appellate Review of
Judicial Fact–Finding*, 40 Kansas L.Rev. 1 (1991).

3. ABUSE OF DISCRETION—REVIEW OF FACTS

In ROLAND MACHINERY CO. v. DRESSER INDUSTRIES, INC., 749
F.2d 380 (7th Cir.1984), Roland Machinery, a dealer in construction equipment, sought a preliminary injunction on its claim under the Clayton Act
against Dresser, a domestic equipment manufacturer, which had cancelled
their exclusive distributorship agreement. Roland Machinery also had an
exclusive distributorship contract with a Japanese equipment manufacturer.
The District Court issued a preliminary injunction and Dresser appealed. The
Seventh Circuit reversed, holding that Dresser had a plausible argument that
an exclusive dealer would promote its line more effectively than a nonexclusive dealer, and would improve the overall competition in the market.

Judge Posner and Judge Swygert disagreed on the appropriate standard
of review in preliminary injunction cases. Judge Posner surveyed the different
elements that a plaintiff must prove in order to obtain a preliminary injunction and determined that the following elements must be present in order for
an injunction to issue:

1. In every case in which the plaintiff wants a preliminary injunction he must show that he has "no adequate remedy at law" and (unless
the statute under which he is suing excuses a showing of irreparable
harm) * * * that he will suffer "irreparable harm" if the preliminary
injunction is not granted. * * *

2.   [P]laintiff must show that an award of damages at the end of trial will be inadequate, * * * seriously deficient as a remedy for the harm suffered. * * *

3.   In deciding whether to grant a preliminary injunction, the court must also consider any irreparable harm that the defendant might suffer from the injunction—harm that would not be either cured by the defendant's ultimately prevailing in the trial on the merits or fully compensated by the injunction bond that Rule 65(c) of the Federal Rules of Civil Procedure requires the district court to make the plaintiff post. * * * [S]ince the defendant may suffer irreparable harm from the entry of a preliminary injunction, the court must not only determine that the plaintiff will suffer irreparable harm if the preliminary injunction is denied—a threshold requirement for granting a preliminary injunction—but also weigh that harm against any irreparable harm that the defendant can show he will suffer if the injunction is granted.

4.   * * * [Plaintiff must show] a likelihood of succeeding on the merits. * * *

5.   If the plaintiff does show some likelihood of success, the court must then determine how likely that success is, because this affects the balance of relative harms (point 3 above). * * *

The idea underlying these * * * approaches is * * * for the district judge * * * to minimize errors * * *. The judge must try to avoid the error that is more costly in the circumstances. That cost is a function of the gravity of the error if it occurs and the probability that it will occur. * * *

6.   Sometimes an order granting or denying a preliminary injunction will have consequences beyond the immediate parties. If so, those interests * * * must be reckoned into the weighing process * * *.

7.   The application of the above principles requires the seasoned judgment of the district court—what is usually called the court's "discretion" * * *.

* * * The factors to be considered are few and definite; they are as we have said spread out on a record; and they are to be compared in a particular sequence and in accordance with a specific formula which requires first deciding whether plaintiff has crossed specific thresholds and then weighting the parties' likely harms from the grant and denial of the preliminary judgment, respectively, by the strength of the plaintiff's case.

Although there is a sense in which equitable relief is inherently discretionary because historically, and still to a large extent, there is no absolute right to an equitable remedy * * *, this is a different meaning of discretion, one that actually cuts against a highly deferential standard of review when as in this case the district court *grants* the preliminary injunction. * * * The exercise of a power so far-reaching ought to be subject to effective, and not merely perfunctory, appellate review. * * *

* * * Although, considering the nature of the judge's determination and the stakes to the parties, we do not think the term abuse of

discretion can be limited to cases where the judge can be said to have acted irrationally or fancifully * * *, we also do not think, considering the imponderable character of the balancing process and the judge's superior feel for the issues which a cold transcript may not fully communicate to the reviewing court, that we are entitled to substitute our judgment for the district judge's. * * * The question for us is to determine whether the judge exceeded the bounds of permissible choice in the circumstances, not what we would have done had we been in his shoes.

We need not be any more precise than this about the meaning of "abuse of discretion" in the context of appellate review of orders granting or denying preliminary injunctions in order to decide this case. * * * For as we * * * see, the district judge committed a clear factual error and a legal effort that require us to set aside his conclusion on the balance of harms, and another legal error with respect to the probable success of Roland on the merits of its antitrust claim.

Id. at 385–91.

In an emphatic dissent, Judge Swygert argued that Judge Posner's new standard of review was unsatisfactory:

* * * [P]rinciples of equity jurisprudence require the maintenance of the "abuse of discretion" standard of review. * * *

* * * I endorse the four-part test set forth by the majority for determining the propriety of granting a preliminary injunction. I believe, however, that the formulation of that or any other test cannot replace the role of discretion in the decision to grant or deny a preliminary injunction. I further believe that the discretion must lie with the district court in the first instance.

* * *

* * * Determining a plaintiff's likelihood of success on the merits prior to trial is unique to interlocutory relief. To fulfill its role of softening the harshness of the law and offering relief when a legal remedy is unavailable, the rules for granting preliminary injunctive relief must remain flexible and able to account for a myriad of situations. In sum, the decision whether to grant a preliminary injunction does not lend itself to a rigid legal formulation. * * *

Because the preliminary injunction is an extraordinary remedy that may impose a great burden on defendants and is granted before a full trial or a final determination of liability, the notion of leaving the decision to the unbridled discretion of judges is particularly troublesome. * * * Thus, I endorse the majority formulation of a coherent test to guide both the district courts and the reviewing courts. I believe, however, that within the confines of that test the district court does and must exercise a large degree of discretion. * * *

The discretion that inheres in the decision whether to grant a preliminary injunction cannot rest with the reviewing court but must lie in the district court. First, it must be remembered that the district court has the responsibility for making a final determination on the merits of the case. * * * Second, given the flexibility of the standard for preliminary injunctive relief and the necessity for discretionary judgments, two courts could easily arrive at different although equally viable conclusions. Refusal to defer to the decision of the lower court in the first instance frequently will result in a substitution of the judgment of the reviewing court for that of the district court. This is a poor use of judicial resources. * * * Finally, and most importantly, if discretionary judgments must be made * * * in deciding to grant or deny preliminary injunctive relief, the trial court with its greater knowledge of the case and the parties * * * is in a better position than a reviewing court to make those judgments. * * *

* * * [U]niform treatment historically has not been and should not be a goal in preliminary injunction decisions, without, of course, condoning arbitrary decisionmaking. The decision to grant or deny a preliminary injunction should depend on the unique circumstances of and the parties in each case. I do not believe that uniform treatment is even possible under the test adopted today. The test is flexible, at least in theory. The sliding scale approach by its nature is antithetical to uniformity. Unique facts are certain to exist in each case which must be factored into the test. The decision to grant or deny injunctive relief simply defies mechanical treatment.

Finally, despite the majority's contention that a preliminary injunction hearing produces a record similar to a trial record, a reviewing court does not have the same access to evidence that the district court has or that the reviewing court has after trial. * * * We should encourage trial judges to refrain from making absolute findings that may impede a fair final resolution on the merits and at the same time to determine the appropriateness of preliminary injunctive relief on the basis of all of the evidence then available to them. I fear that the majority's refusal to defer to the judgments of the trial judge will encourage the opposite; judges will be forced either to make their conclusions explicit and absolute or disregard them. * * *

* * * [E]ven assuming that the district court has committed an isolated error of fact or an isolated mistake of law, the court's ultimate decision to grant or deny preliminary injunctive relief should be reversed only if it constitutes an abuse of discretion under the totality of the circumstances. * * *

Id. at 396–99. Who has the better argument, Judge Posner or Judge Swygert? Whose opinion is more consistent with the Supreme Court's decision in *Anderson*?

Notes and Questions

1. For an analysis of Judge Posner's standard of review in preliminary injunction cases, and of Judge Swygert's opposing view, see Silberman, *Injunctions by the Numbers: Less Than the Sum of Its Parts*, 63 Chi.-Kent L.Rev. 279 (1987).

2. The standard of review is different for declaratory judgments. In the declaratory-judgment context, an appellate court may make two inquiries. It may determine whether the trial court abused its discretion by making an arbitrary

choice to hear a claim for declaratory judgment. Wilmington Chemical Corp. v. Celebrezze, 229 F.Supp. 168 (N.D.Ill.1964). Additionally, it may determine that, even if the action is properly a declaratory-judgment action, the lower court's opinion was nevertheless erroneous. National Health Federation v. Weinberger, 518 F.2d 711 (7th Cir.1975). In other words, the appellate court may engage in *de novo* review. What is it about declaratory judgments that permits *de novo* review?

3. ELDER v. HOLLOWAY, 510 U.S. 510, 114 S.Ct. 1019, 127 L.Ed.2d 344 (1994), was a case involving a claim of qualified immunity from a damages suit charging violation of a federal right. The district court found no controlling Idaho or Ninth Circuit case law. On appeal the Ninth Circuit noticed precedent on point that had been missed by the district court. The Court of Appeals believed, however, that the petitioner could not benefit from the precedent as neither he nor the district court had cited it in the court below. In reversing the Court of Appeals, the Supreme Court held that a court engaged in review of a judgment regarding qualified immunity should use its full knowledge as to relevant precedents.

SECTION D. THE VIEW AT THE TOP—COURTS ABOVE APPELLATE COURTS

Read 28 U.S.C. §§ 1251, 1253–54, 1257 in the Supplement and all the accompanying material.

1. REVIEW AS OF RIGHT

In the federal-court system and in the judicial structure of about one-third of the states, intermediate appellate courts are interposed between the trial courts of general jurisdiction and the highest court. The principal purpose in creating intermediate appellate courts has been to relieve the pressure of burgeoning appellate litigation on the highest court, leaving that tribunal free to concentrate on deciding important and novel questions of law and on maintaining uniformity in the law applied by the lower courts. To achieve this purpose fully, two conditions must be met. Most appeals must begin and end in the intermediate appellate courts, but the possibility of review by the highest court must be open in every case.

Both conditions would be satisfied if the intermediate courts heard every appeal in the first instance and the highest court had complete discretion to review the decisions of those courts. But no American system seems to have fully adopted this approach. In every state that has intermediate appellate courts, as well as in the federal courts, some matters are reviewable directly by the highest court, and, in most systems, some matters, decided in the first instance by the intermediate courts, are appealable as of right to the highest court. The systems differ markedly, however, both in the extent to which the intermediate appellate courts are bypassed and in the amount of discretion given to the highest court to choose the cases it hears.

Notes and Questions

1. Compare the provisions for direct appeal to the Supreme Court of California, the Supreme Court of Georgia, and the Court of Appeals of New York that are set out in the Supplement following 28 U.S.C. § 1254. What is the reason for each of these provisions? Which set of state provisions seems most appropriate?

2. Prior to 1988, when it repealed 28 U.S.C. § 1252, Congress had provided for direct appeal to the Supreme Court of the United States from any decision of a federal district court "holding an Act of Congress unconstitutional in any civil action * * * to which the United States or any of its agencies [or employees] * * * is a party." What might have led Congress to repeal this provision? See Brown Shoe Co. v. United States, 370 U.S. 294, 355, 364, 82 S.Ct. 1502, 1541, 1546, 8 L.Ed.2d 510, 557, 562 (1962) (sharp criticisms of direct appeals by Justice Clark and Justice Harlan). Direct appeals are still available under 28 U.S.C. § 1253. What is the justification for such a provision? Note that the Supreme Court can effect a direct appeal in any case in which certiorari would lie by taking up the case as soon as it is docketed in the court of appeals and before that court considers it, but this power has been rarely exercised. See, e.g., United States v. Nixon, [Note 3, p. 1159, supra] * * *. Do the state courts mentioned in Note 1, supra, possess comparable authority?

3. A significant drawback of a provision for direct appeal is the confusion that may exist as to whether a particular case falls within the provision and as to the appropriate disposition of such case if it is appealed to the wrong court. In a case in which a United States district judge erroneously had refused to convene a three-judge district court, does the court of appeals have jurisdiction to remand the case for determination by a three-judge court, or is the only remedy a petition for mandamus in the United States Supreme Court? See Idlewild Bon Voyage Liquor Corp. v. Epstein, 370 U.S. 713, 82 S.Ct. 1294, 8 L.Ed.2d 794 (1962).

4. For many years, Congress had provided in 28 U.S.C. §§ 1254 and 1257 that the Supreme Court was *required* to review certain decisions of the federal courts of appeals and of state courts in situations involving the validity of state laws under the Constitution, treaties or laws of the United States. In fact, the requirement was somewhat illusory because the Court took the position that it had jurisdiction only if the case involved a "substantial federal question." Zucht v. King, 260 U.S. 174, 43 S.Ct. 24, 67 L.Ed. 194 (1922). Many such appeals were therefore dismissed because the issue was considered remote or already well-settled.

In 1988, Congress amended Sections 1254 and 1257 to provide that such decisions receive no special treatment, but shall be reviewed, as most others, only if the Supreme Court, in its discretion, grants a petition for a writ of certiorari. See pp. 1218–21, infra.

5. The most important restriction on Supreme Court review of state-court decisions regarding federal claims is that the judgment necessarily must turn on a federal question and that it not rest upon an independent state ground. Even if the decision is based on alternative grounds, one federal and one state, review will be denied. Zacchini v. Scripps–Howard Broadcasting Co., 433 U.S. 562, 568, 97 S.Ct. 2849, 2853–54, 53 L.Ed.2d 965, 971–72 (1977). Suppose that the highest state court, in deciding how to interpret its own law, feels bound by federal law. In such cases Supreme Court review is permitted. See id. Why?

In most cases a state court's judgment, based upon a state ground, will have the same effect that it would have had if the court had sustained the claim of a federal right. Should it make any difference whether the state ground is substantive or procedural? See Henry v. Mississippi, 379 U.S. 443, 85 S.Ct. 564, 13 L.Ed.2d 408 (1965). Should the Supreme Court's power be different when the effect of the state court's judgment is to defeat the claim of a federal right? See Sandalow, *Henry v. Mississippi and the Adequate State Ground: Proposals for a Revised Doctrine,* 1965 Sup.Ct.Rev. 187. See generally Wright, *Federal Courts* § 107 (5th ed.1994).

6. Appeals from courts of inferior jurisdiction, such as justice-of-the-peace courts, probate courts, and municipal courts, frequently lie to the trial courts of general jurisdiction. The organization of inferior courts differs so widely from state to state that few generalizations can be drawn. Typically, however, the jurisdictional provisions call for a *de novo* hearing in the court of general jurisdiction and, in the case of very small claims, make the determination of the latter court final and unreviewable.

2. DISCRETIONARY REVIEW

Review 28 U.S.C. §§ 1254(1), 1257(a).

DICK v. NEW YORK LIFE INSURANCE CO., 359 U.S. 437, 448–55, 79 S.Ct. 921, 928–31, 3 L.Ed.2d 935, 943–47 (1959). Justice Frankfurter, dissenting:

Establishment of intermediate appellate courts in 1891 was designed by Congress to relieve the overburdened docket of the Court. The Circuit Courts of Appeals were to be equal in dignity to the Supreme Courts of the several States. The essential purpose of the Evarts Act was to enable the Supreme Court to discharge its indispensable functions in our federal system by relieving it of the duty of adjudication in cases that are important only to the litigants. * * * The Act provided, therefore, that in diversity cases "the judgments or decrees of the circuit courts of appeals shall be final." * * * [However], this Court was given the discretionary power to grant certiorari in these cases, to be exercised if some question of general interest, outside the limited scope of an ordinary diversity litigation, was also involved.

* * *

Time and again in the years immediately following the passage of the Evarts Act this Court stated that it was only in cases of "gravity and general importance" or "to secure uniformity of decision" that the certiorari power should be exercised. * * *

These considerations have led the Court in scores of cases to dismiss the writ of certiorari even after oral argument when it became manifest that the writ was granted under a misapprehension of the true issues. * * *

To strengthen further this Court's control over its docket and to avoid review of cases which in the main raise only factual controversies, Congress in 1916 made cases arising under the Federal Employers' Liability Act * * * final in the Courts of Appeals, reviewable by this Court only when required by the guiding standards for exercising its certiorari jurisdiction.

In 1925 Congress enacted the "Judges' Bill," called such because it was drafted by a committee of this Court composed of Van Devanter, McReynolds, and Sutherland, JJ. At the hearings on the bill * * * Mr. Chief Justice Taft said:

> "No litigant is entitled to more than two chances, namely, to the original trial and to a review, and the intermediate courts of review are provided for that purpose. When a case goes beyond that, it is not primarily to preserve the rights of the litigants. The Supreme Court's function is for the purpose of expounding and stabilizing principles of law for the benefit of the people of the country, passing upon constitutional questions and other important questions of law for the public benefit. It is to preserve uniformity of decision among the intermediate courts of appeal."

* * *

Questions of fact have traditionally been deemed to be the kind of questions which ought not to be recanvassed here unless they are entangled in the proper determination of constitutional or other important legal issues. * * * The proper use of the discretionary certiorari jurisdiction was on a later occasion thus expounded by Mr. Chief Justice Hughes:

> "Records are replete with testimony and evidence of facts. But the questions on certiorari are questions of law. * * * It is only when the facts are interwoven with the questions of law which we should review that the evidence must be examined and then only to the extent that it is necessary to decide the questions of law. * * *"

HARRIS v. PENNSYLVANIA R. CO., 361 U.S. 15, 17–19, 80 S.Ct. 22, 24–25, 4 L.Ed.2d 1, 3–4 (1959). Justice Douglas, concurring:

It is suggested that the Court has consumed too much of its time in reviewing these FELA cases. An examination of the 33 cases in which the Court has granted certiorari during the period [1949–1959] * * * reveals that 16 of these cases were summarily reversed without oral argument and without full opinions. Only 17 cases were argued during this period of more than a decade and, of these, 5 were disposed of by brief *per curiam* opinions. Only 12 cases in over 10 years were argued, briefed and disposed of with full opinions by the Court. We have granted certiorari in these cases on an average of less than 3 per year and have given plenary consideration to slightly more than 1 per year. Wastage of our time is therefore a false issue.

The difference between the majority and minority of the Court in our treatment of FELA cases concerns the degree of vigilance we should exercise in safeguarding the jury trial—guaranteed by the Seventh Amendment and part and parcel of the remedy under this Federal Act when suit is brought in state courts. * * * Whether that right has been impaired in a particular instance often produces a contrariety of views. Yet the practice of the Court in allowing four out of nine votes to control the certiorari docket is well established and of long duration. Without it, the vast discretion which Congress allowed us in granting or denying certiorari might not be tolerable. Every member of the Court has known instances where he has strongly protested the action of the minority in bringing a case or type of case here for adjudication. He may then feel that there are more important and pressing matters to which the Court should give its attention. That is, however, a price we pay for keeping our promise to Congress[3] to let the vote of four Justices bring up any case here on certiorari.

Notes and Questions

1. In the early 1970's, the sharp increase in the number of petitions for review filed with the Supreme Court led some commentators to conclude that the Court was being strangled by its workload. Some of these commentators proposed the creation of a new federal appellate court, positioned between the Supreme Court and the present courts of appeals—the so-called National Court of Appeals. See, e.g., *Report of the Study Group on the Caseload of the Supreme Court* (1972), reprinted at 57 F.R.D. 573 (1972); Commission on Revision of the Federal Court Appellate System, *Structure and Internal Procedures: Recommendations for Change* (1975), reprinted in 67 F.R.D. 195 (1975). Finally, in the early 1980's, Chief Justice Burger endorsed these proposals and considerable interest in them was generated. In 1987, the Senate and the House of Representatives conducted hearings on bills that would have created a temporary, experimental National Court of Appeals or Intercircuit Tribunal. The Supreme Court would have referred cases to this new court for resolution, but would have retained power of ultimate review by writ of certiorari. The results of the experiment would have been assessed at the end of five years, at which time the court could be made permanent or abolished. The legislation failed.

Scholars have questioned whether the Supreme Court inevitably is faced with more cases demanding its attention than it can handle and have challenged the premise upon which the case for a national court of appeals is most often made. See Estreicher & Sexton, *The Supreme Court's Case Selection Process and the National Court of Appeals,* 59 N.Y.U.L.Rev. 1 (1985), in which the authors examine the history and the contours of the debate over the Court's "workload problem," offer a theory of the Court's role in the federal judicial system, and present a detailed examination of the case selection process as it operated in the October 1982 Term. Their study concludes that the unfocused nature of the criteria for case selection presented in what was then Supreme Court Rule 17

---

3. The "rule of four" was given as one of the reasons why the Congress thought that the increase of our discretionary jurisdiction was warranted. The House Report stated:

"Lest it should be thought that the increase of discretionary jurisdiction might impair the administration of justice and lead to partial hearings and not secure a decision by the whole court, it is proper to call attention to the very thorough and complete system by which discretionary jurisdiction is exercised. * * * [According to] Mr. Justice Van Devanter * * * :

"* * *

"' * * * We always grant the petition when as many as four think that it should be granted and sometimes when as many as three think that way. We proceed upon the theory that, if that number out of the nine are impressed with the thought that the case is one that ought to be heard and decided by us, the petition should be granted.' "

H.R.Rep. No. 1075, 68th Cong., 2d Sess., p. 3.

caused the Court to "overgrant," thereby creating the illusion of overload. Professors Estreicher and Sexton argue that revision of these criteria and other minor procedural changes would dispose of the need for a new federal appellate court.

2.   Compare United States Supreme Court Rule 10, which replaced Supreme Court Rule 17, with California Appellate Rule 29, both of which are set out in the Supplement following 28 U.S.C. § 1254. What considerations should govern the highest court of a state in deciding whether to hear a case within its discretionary jurisdiction? See 7 Weinstein, Korn & Miller, *New York Civil Practice* ¶ 5602.04; Cuomo, *The New York Court of Appeals: A Practical Perspective*, 34 St. John's L.Rev. 197, 201 (1960); Poulos & Varner, *Review of Intermediate Appellate Court Decisions in California*, 15 Hastings L.J. 11, 15 (1963). Should these considerations be any different from those followed by the Supreme Court of the United States in ruling on a petition for a writ of certiorari?

3.   THE FINAL JUDGMENT REQUIREMENT UNDER SECTION 1257

Section 1257 limits Supreme Court review to "final judgments of the highest state court in which a decision could be had." The question is whether and to what extent determinations as to what is a final judgment under Section 1257 should be influenced by decisions as to what is final under Section 1291. See pp. 1146–50, 1176–79, supra. In COX BROADCASTING CORP. v. COHN, 420 U.S. 469, 95 S.Ct. 1029, 43 L.Ed.2d 328 (1975), plaintiff brought suit for damages in a state court against the owner of a television station, alleging that the station had wrongfully invaded his privacy by revealing that his daughter had been the victim of rape and murder. Defendant claimed the broadcast was privileged under the First and Fourteenth Amendments to the federal Constitution. The trial judge granted partial summary judgment for plaintiff on liability. The state supreme court overturned the summary judgment, but held that the federal Constitution did not necessarily rule out the possibility of liability and returned the case to the trial court for further proceedings. On appeal, the Supreme Court, noting that the requirement of finality under Section 1257 has been applied in a "pragmatic" rather than in a "mechanical fashion," upheld immediate appeal since the state decision was final as to the federal issue, a vital issue that should be decided as soon as possible so that broadcasters would know what they could or could not publish without fear of a lawsuit. The Court cited Gillespie v. United States Steel Corp., set out at p. 1176, supra, accepting its approach even though it had been decided under Section 1291. Justice Rehnquist dissented, arguing that the policies underlying Sections 1257 and 1291 differ substantially.

Notes and Questions

1.   Does the Supreme Court's decision in Coopers & Lybrand v. Livesay, see p. 1162, supra, undermine the *Cox* decision?

2.   Even if the policies behind Sections 1257 and 1291 differ, should that affect the interpretation given to the word "final" in each? Aren't the reasons for avoiding appeals of interlocutory orders applicable under both provisions? Shouldn't it be up to Congress to create exceptions to Section 1257 as it has with regard to Section 1291?

3.   The Court in *Cox* listed four situations in which a technical definition of "final" may give way to "pragmatic" considerations:

(1) When the decision is final from a practical point of view—for example, when the interlocutory decision clearly dictates the final result.

(2) When the federal issue necessarily would survive no matter how the state courts would rule in subsequent proceedings.

(3) When, under state law, subsequent review could be prohibited—for example, in criminal or certain administrative-law cases in which an acquittal or decision against the government would not be appealable.

(4) When important federal rights are involved and when delay would erode federal policy.

How much emphasis should be placed on the last situation? Suppose in *Cox* the state supreme court merely had vacated the summary judgment and returned the case to the trial court with the admonition, "study anew the defenses based on the federal constitution which were originally treated summarily and without adequate briefing from counsel." Should an immediate appeal to the Supreme Court be permitted to avoid leaving local broadcasters uncertain about their rights? For a comprehensive review of *Cox* and of the final-judgment rule under Section 1257, see Note, *The Finality Rule for Supreme Court Review of State Court Orders*, 91 Harv.L.Rev. 1004 (1978). See, e.g., Jefferson v. City of Tarrant, 522 U.S. 75, 118 S.Ct. 481, 139 L.Ed.2d 433 (1997), in which the Supreme Court stated that it lacked jurisdiction to review an interlocutory order of the Alabama Supreme Court based on the principle that "a state-court decision is not final unless and until it has effectively determined the entire litigation." Id. at 84, 118 S.Ct. at 487, 139 L.Ed.2d at 442.

Chapter 17

THE BINDING EFFECT OF PRIOR DECISIONS: RES JUDICATA AND COLLATERAL ESTOPPEL

"Courts can only do their best to determine the truth on the basis of the evidence, and the first lesson one must learn on the subject of res judicata is that judicial findings must not be confused with absolute truth." Currie, *Mutuality of Collateral Estoppel: Limits of the Bernhard Doctrine*, 9 Stan. L.Rev. 281, 315 (1957).

SECTION A. TERMINOLOGY

Although the doctrine of former adjudication is complex, four common sense principles explain it. First, a party, ordinarily, gets only one chance to litigate a "claim;" if a party litigates only a portion of a claim the first time around, she risks losing the chance to litigate the rest. Second, a party ordinarily gets only one chance to litigate a factual or a legal "issue;" once litigated, she cannot ask a second court to decide it differently later. Third, a party is entitled to at least one "full and fair" chance to litigate before being precluded. And fourth, preclusion may be waived unless it is claimed at an early stage of the litigation.

The effects of a former adjudication have been discussed in varying and occasionally conflicting terminology. Although the time has not yet come when courts will use a single vocabulary, substantial progress has been made toward a convention. Judge Rubin has provided a highly useful summary that sets out the major variations in current terminology:

> The rules of *res judicata,* as the term is sometimes sweepingly used, actually comprise two doctrines concerning the preclusive effect of a prior adjudication. The first such doctrine is "claim preclusion," or true *res judicata*. It treats a judgment, once rendered, as the full measure of relief to be accorded between the same parties on the same "claim" or "cause of action." * * * When the plaintiff obtains a judgment in his favor, his claim "merges" in the judgment; he may seek no further relief on that claim in a separate action. Conversely, when a judgment is rendered for a defendant, the plaintiff's claim is extinguished; the judgment then acts as a "bar." * * * Under these rules of claim preclusion, the effect of a

judgment extends to the litigation of all issues relevant to the same claim between the same parties, whether or not raised at trial. * * * The aim of claim preclusion is thus to avoid multiple suits on identical entitlements or obligations between the same parties, accompanied, as they would be, by the redetermination of identical issues of duty and breach.

The second doctrine, collateral estoppel or "issue preclusion," recognizes that suits addressed to particular claims may present issues relevant to suits on other claims. In order to effectuate the public policy in favor of minimizing redundant litigation, issue preclusion bars the relitigation of issues actually adjudicated, and essential to the judgment, in a prior litigation between the same parties. * * * It is insufficient for the invocation of issue preclusion that some question of fact or law in a later suit was relevant to a prior adjudication between the parties; the contested issue must have been litigated and necessary to the judgment earlier rendered.

KASPAR WIRE WORKS, INC. v. LECO ENGINEERING & MACHINE, INC., 575 F.2d 530, 535–36 (5th Cir.1978).

Another useful summary is the following:

Foreclosure of matters that never have been litigated has traditionally been expressed by stating that a single "cause of action" cannot be "split" by advancing one part in a first suit and reserving some other part for a later suit. The entire cause of action was said to "merge" in a judgment for the plaintiff, leaving a new cause of action on the judgment, or to be subject to the "bar" of a judgment for the defendant. There is now a growing tendency * * * to substitute the word "claim" for the cause of action phrase. Here as in other fields of procedure the new word may help to escape uncomfortable historic legacies of thought expressed in cause of action terms. There is an additional advantage that the resulting "claim preclusion" phrase provides a clear contrast to the concept of "issue preclusion." It remains convenient, however, to supplement this phrase with the words of merger and bar.

Foreclosure of matters that have been once litigated has been described by a wide variety of phrases. For many years, the "awkward phrase" of "collateral estoppel" has been used. The estoppel is characterized as collateral because the later litigation commonly involves a different cause of action; purists accordingly have felt obliged to refer to "direct estoppel" whenever a first suit was ended in a manner that did not give rise to claim preclusion, but that did warrant preclusion of a specific issue. The more modern "issue preclusion" phrase encompasses both varieties of estoppel, and warrants the growing acceptance it has found in current federal decisions.

Finally, courts have found it convenient to identify the judgments that warrant preclusive effect as "final" or as "on the merits." Little harm is done by such phrases in themselves, but they may obscure the fundamental proposition that different requirements are appropriate to different preclusive effects. Dismissal of a suit for want of federal subject matter jurisdiction, for example, should not bar an action on the same claim in a court that does have subject matter jurisdiction, but ordinarily should preclude relitigation of the same issue of subject matter jurisdiction in a second federal suit on the same claim.

18 Wright, Miller & Cooper, *Federal Practice and Procedure: Jurisdiction and Related Matters* § 4402, at 8–11 (1981).

SECTION B. CLAIM AND DEFENSE PRECLUSION

1. CLAIM PRECLUSION

Although it is difficult to give a precise definition of the doctrine of claim preclusion, it is possible to sketch its general form. One formulation is: In certain circumstances, when a second suit is brought, the judgment in a prior suit will be considered conclusive, both on the parties to the judgment and on those in privity with them, as to matters that actually were litigated or should have been litigated in the first suit. Justice Field has provided a more detailed formulation of the same basic rule:

> * * * [A] judgment, if rendered upon the merits, constitutes an absolute bar to a subsequent action. It is a finality as to the claim or demand in controversy, concluding parties and those in privity with them, not only as to every matter which was offered and received to sustain or defeat the claim or demand, but as to any other admissible matter which might have been offered for that purpose. Thus, for example, a judgment rendered upon a promissory note is conclusive as to the validity of the instrument and the amount due on it, although it be subsequently alleged that perfect defences actually existed, of which no proof was offered, such as forgery, want of consideration, or payment. * * * The judgment is as conclusive, so far as future proceedings at law are concerned, as though the defences never existed. * * *

CROMWELL v. COUNTY OF SAC, 94 U.S. (4 Otto) 351, 352–53, 24 L.Ed. 195, 197–98 (1876), p. 1244, infra.

For claim preclusion to operate, three elements must be present. First, only judgments that are "final," "valid," and "on the merits" have preclusive effect. Second, the parties in the subsequent action must be identical to those in the first. This requirement is one of the most important distinctions between claim preclusion and its sister doctrine, issue preclusion. And, third, the claim in the second suit must involve matters properly considered included in the first action. Clearly, this last requirement turns on what the first action decided or should have decided.

RUSH v. CITY OF MAPLE HEIGHTS

Supreme Court of Ohio, 1958.
167 Ohio St. 221, 147 N.E.2d 599.
certiorari denied 358 U.S. 814, 79 S.Ct. 21, 3 L.Ed.2d 57.

[Plaintiff was injured in a fall from a motorcycle. She brought an action in the Municipal Court of Cleveland for damage to her personal property; that court found that defendant city was negligent in maintaining its street and that this negligence was the proximate cause of plaintiff's damages, which were fixed at $100. Defendant appealed and the judgment was affirmed by the

Ohio Court of Appeals and Supreme Court. Plaintiff also brought this action in the Court of Common Pleas of Cuyahoga County for personal injuries she incurred in the same accident; her motion to set trial on the issue of damages alone was granted on the ground that the issue of negligence was res judicata because of the Municipal Court action; judgment was entered on a verdict for $12,000, and the Court of Appeals affirmed.]

HERBERT, JUDGE. The eighth error assigned by the defendant is that "the trial and appellate courts committed error in permitting plaintiff to split her cause of action * * *."

In the case of Vasu v. Kohlers, Inc., 145 Ohio St. 321, 61 N.E.2d 707, 709, 166 A.L.R. 855, plaintiff operating an automobile came into collision with defendant's truck, in which collision he suffered personal injuries and also damage to his automobile. At the time of collision, plaintiff had coverage of a $50 deductible collision policy on his automobile. The insurance company paid the plaintiff a sum covering the damage to his automobile, whereupon, in accordance with a provision of the policy, the plaintiff assigned to the insurer his claim for such damage.

In February 1942, the insurance company commenced an action * * * against Kohlers, Inc., * * * to recoup the money paid by it to cover the damage to Vasu's automobile.

In August 1942, Vasu commenced an action in the same court against Kohlers, Inc., to recover for personal injuries which he suffered in the same collision.

In March 1943, in the insurance company's action, a verdict was rendered in favor of the defendant, followed by judgment.

Two months later an amended answer was filed in the Vasu case, setting out as a bar to the action * * * the judgment rendered in favor of defendant in the insurance company case. A motion to strike that defense * * * [was] sustained * * *. A trial of the action resulted in a verdict for plaintiff, upon which judgment was entered.

On appeal to the Court of Appeals the defendant claimed that the Court of Common Pleas erred in sustaining plaintiff's motion to strike from the defendant's answer the defense of *res judicata* claimed to have arisen by reason of the judgment in favor of the defendant in the action by the insurance company.

The Court of Appeals reversed the judgment of the Court of Common Pleas and entered final judgment in favor of defendant.

This court reversed the judgment of the Court of Appeals, holding in the syllabus, in part, as follows:

* * *

4. Injuries to both person and property suffered by the same person as a result of the same wrongful act are infringements of different rights and give rise to distinct causes of action, with the result that the recovery or denial of recovery of compensation for damages to the property is no bar to an action subsequently prosecuted for the personal injury, unless by an adverse judgment in the first action issues are determined against

the plaintiff which operate as an estoppel against him in the second action.

* * *

6. Where an injury to person and to property through a single wrongful act causes a prior contract of indemnity and subrogation as to the injury to property to come into operation for the benefit of the person injured, the indemnitor may prosecute a separate action against the party causing such injury for reimbursement for indemnity monies paid under such contract.

7. Parties in privy, in the sense that they are bound by a judgment, are those who acquired an interest in the subject matter after the beginning of the action or the rendition of the judgment; and if their title or interest attached before that fact, they are not bound unless made parties.

8. A grantor or assignor is not bound, as to third persons, by any judgment which such third persons may obtain against his grantee or assignee adjudicating the title to or claim for the interest transferred unless he participated in the action in such manner as to become, in effect, a party.

* * * The sixth, seventh and eighth paragraphs deal with the factual situation which existed in the Vasu case, i.e., a prior contract of indemnity and subrogation. Although, as discussed infra, it was not actually necessary to the determination of the issue in that case, attention centers on the fourth paragraph.

* * * [Subsequent] cases, distinguishing and explaining the Vasu case, have not changed the rule established in paragraph four of the syllabus * * *.

However, it is contended here that that rule is in conflict with the great weight of authority in this country and has caused vexatious litigation. * * *

Upon examination of decisions of courts of last resort, we find that the majority rule is followed in the following cases in each of which the action was between the person suffering injury and the person committing the tort, and where insurers were not involved, as in the case here. * * * [The court cited cases from 20 states forming the majority and 5 states forming the minority.]

The reasoning behind the majority rule seems to be well stated in the case of Mobile & Ohio Rd. Co. v. Matthews * * * [115 Tenn. 172, 91 S.W. 194 (1906)], as follows:

> The negligent action of the plaintiff in error constituted but one tort. The injuries to the person and property of the defendant in error were the several results and effects of one wrongful act. A single tort can be the basis of but one action. It is not improper to declare in different counts for damages to the person and property when both result from the same tort, and it is the better practice to do so where there is any difference in the measure of damages, and all the damages sustained must be sued for in one suit. This is necessary to prevent multiplicity of suits, burdensome expense, and delays to plaintiffs, and vexatious litigation against defendants. * * *

The minority rule would seem to stem from the English case of Brunsden v. Humphrey (1884), 14 Q.B. 141. The facts in that case are set forth in the opinion in the Vasu case * * * concluding with the statement:

> The Master of the Rolls, in his opinion, stated that the test is "whether the same sort of evidence would prove the plaintiff's case in the two actions," and that, in the action relating to the cab, "it would be necessary to give evidence of the damage done to the plaintiff's vehicle. In the present action it would be necessary to give evidence of the bodily injury occasioned to the plaintiff, and of the sufferings which he has undergone, and for this purpose to call medical witnesses. This one test shows that the causes of action as to the damage done to the plaintiff's cab, and as to the injury occasioned to the plaintiff's person, are distinct."

The fallacy of the reasoning in the English court is best portrayed in the dissenting opinion of Lord Coleridge, as follows:

> * * * [I]t seems to me a subtlety not warranted by law to hold that a man cannot bring two actions, if he is injured in his arm and in his leg, but can bring two, if besides his arm and leg being injured, his trousers which contain his leg, and his coat-sleeve which contains his arm, have been torn.

There appears to be no valid reason in these days of code pleading to adhere to the old English rule as to distinctions between injuries to the person and damages to the person's property resulting from a single tort. It would seem that the minority rule is bottomed on the proposition that the right of bodily security is fundamentally different from the right of security of property and, also, that, in actions predicated upon a negligent act, damages are a necessary element of each independent cause of action and no recovery may be had unless and until actual consequential damages are shown.

Whether or not injuries to both person and property resulting from the same wrongful act are to be treated as injuries to separate rights or as separate items of damage, * * * a plaintiff may maintain only one action to enforce his rights existing at the time such action is commenced.

The decision of the question actually in issue in the Vasu case is found in paragraphs six, seven and eight of the syllabus, as it is quite apparent from the facts there that the first judgment, claimed to be *res judicata* in Vasu's action against the defendant, was rendered against Vasu's insurer in an action initiated by it after having paid Vasu for the damages to his automobile. * * *

Upon further examination of the cases from other jurisdictions, it appears that in those instances where the courts have held to the majority rule, a separation of causes of action is almost universally recognized where an insurer has acquired by an assignment or by subrogation the right to recover for money it has advanced to pay for property damage.

* * *

In the light of the foregoing, it is the view of this court that the so-called majority rule conforms much more properly to modern practice, and that the rule declared in the fourth paragraph of the syllabus in the Vasu case, on a point not actually at issue therein, should not be followed.

* * *

Judgment reversed and final judgment for defendant.

STEWART, JUDGE (concurring). * * * If it had been necessary [in *Vasu*] to decide the question whether a single tort gives rise to two causes of action as to the one injured by such tort, I would be reluctant to disturb that holding. However, neither the discussion in the Vasu case as to whether a single or double cause of action arises from one tort nor the language of the fourth paragraph of the syllabus was necessary to decide the issue presented in the case, and obviously both such language and such paragraph are obiter dicta and, therefore, are not as persuasive an authority as if they had been appropriate to the question presented.

* * *

ZIMMERMAN, JUDGE (dissenting). I am not unalterably opposed to upsetting prior decisions of this court where changing conditions and the lessons of experience clearly indicate the desirability of such course, but, where those considerations do not obtain, established law should remain undisturbed in order to insure a stability on which the lower courts and the legal profession generally may rely with some degree of confidence.

* * *

Notes and Questions

1. The *Rush* case illustrates three ways in which the adjudication in one action may affect a subsequent lawsuit. The first is one with which you are already familiar: *stare decisis*. Although neither party in *Rush* had been a party to Vasu v. Kohler's, Inc., both of the lower Ohio courts as well as the dissenting judge in the Supreme Court of Ohio regarded that case as controlling in *Rush*. Of course, as the *Rush* case itself demonstrates, the binding force of *stare decisis* is not absolute, and the parties to a later action are free to argue that the law announced in an earlier case should be changed. But a court will not lightly depart from precedent even though the parties who are before it were not represented in the case that established the precedent. The second and third ways in which adjudication in one action may affect a subsequent lawsuit involve the doctrines of claim and issue preclusion introduced in Section A. How does *stare decisis* differ from these concepts?

If the Ohio court had not found claim preclusion in *Rush*, what would have been the effect of issue preclusion? Note that both lower courts in *Rush* held that the only issue open in plaintiff's suit for her personal injuries was the amount of her damages, because the issues of negligence, proximate cause, and contributory negligence had all been conclusively determined by her judgment in the earlier action for property damage.

Among the more valuable sources on res judicata are: Moore, *Federal Practice*, ch. 130–34 (3d ed.); 18 Wright, Miller & Cooper, *Federal Practice and Procedure: Jurisdiction and Related Matters* §§ 4401–78 (1981); *Restatement (Second), Judgments* (1982).

2. Although the Supreme Court has cautioned that, " '*stare decisis* is a principle of policy and not a mechanical adherence to the latest decision,* * *' " Boys Markets, Inc. v. Retail Clerks, 398 U.S. 235, 241, 90 S.Ct. 1583, 1587, 26 L.Ed.2d 199 (1970), it is indisputable that *stare decisis* is a basic self-governing principle within the judicial branch, which is entrusted with the sensitive and difficult task of fashioning and preserving a jurisprudential system that is not based upon "an arbitrary discretion." What should be the *stare decisis* effect of a case interpreting the Constitution? A statute? An administrative regulation?

3. Was the critical language in *Vasu* a holding or dictum? Compare UNITED STATES v. TITLE INSURANCE & TRUST CO., 265 U.S. 472, 485–86, 44 S.Ct. 621, 623, 68 L.Ed. 1110, 1114 (1924), in which Justice Van Devanter said, in connection with an attempt to distinguish an earlier case:

> Enough has been said to make it apparent that that case and this are so much alike that what was said and ruled in that should be equally applicable in this. But it is urged that what we have described as ruled there was *obiter dictum* and should be disregarded, because the Court there gave a second ground for its decision which was broad enough to sustain it independently of the first ground. The premise of the contention is right but the conclusion is wrong; for where there are two grounds, upon either of which an appellate court may rest its decision, and it adopts both, "the ruling on neither is *obiter*, but each is the judgment of the court and of equal validity with the other."

4. What reasons might plaintiff in *Rush* have had for wishing to sue first on the claim for property damage and then separately for the personal injuries?

5. The tests for determining the scope of claim preclusion have undergone a significant development since the beginning of the century. The *Restatement (Second) of Judgments* summarizes this transition:

> In defining claim to embrace all the remedial rights of the plaintiff against the defendant growing out of the relevant transaction (or series of connected transactions), [Section 24 of the Restatement] * * * responds to modern procedural ideas which have found expression in the Federal Rules of Civil Procedure and other procedural systems.

> "Claim," in the context of res judicata, has never been broader than the transaction to which it related. But in the days when civil procedure still bore the imprint of the forms of action and the division between law and equity, the courts were prone to associate claim with a single theory of recovery, so that, with respect to one transaction, a plaintiff might have as many claims as there were theories of the substantive law upon which he could seek relief against the defendant. Thus, defeated in an action based on one theory, the plaintiff might be able to maintain another action based on a different theory, even though both actions were grounded upon the defendant's identical act or connected acts forming a single life-situation. In those earlier days there was also some adherence to a view that associated claim with the assertion of a single primary right as accorded by the substantive law, so that, if it appeared that the defendant had invaded a number of primary rights conceived to be held by the plaintiff, the plaintiff had the same number of claims, even though they all sprang from a unitary occurrence. There was difficulty in knowing which rights were primary and what was their extent, but a primary right and the corresponding claim might turn out to be narrow. Thus it was held by some courts that a judgment for or against the plaintiff in an action for personal injuries did not preclude an action by him for property damage

occasioned by the same negligent conduct on the part of the defendant—this deriving from the idea that the right to be free of bodily injury was distinct from the property right. Still another view of claim looked to sameness of evidence; a second action was precluded where the evidence to support it was the same as that needed to support the first. Sometimes this was made the sole test of identity of claim; sometimes it figured as a positive but not as a negative test; that is, in certain situations a second action might be precluded although the evidence material to it varied from that in the first action. Even so, claim was not coterminous with the transaction itself.

The present trend is to see claim in factual terms and to make it coterminous with the transaction regardless of the number of substantive theories, or variant forms of relief flowing from those theories, that may be available to the plaintiff; regardless of the number of primary rights that may have been invaded; and regardless of the variations in the evidence needed to support the theories or rights. The transaction is the basis of the litigative unit or entity which may not be split.

Restatement (Second), Judgments § 24, comment *a* (1982).

Section 24 lists some considerations that determine whether a factual grouping constitutes a single transaction, and suggests evaluation "whether the facts are related in time, space, origin, or motivation, whether they form a convenient trial unit, and whether their treatment as a unit conforms to the parties' expectations or business understanding or usage." Id. Consider how the different *Restatement* definitions of a claim would affect the court's reasoning in the next case.

6. A party may waive the benefits of preclusion by failing to raise it as an affirmative defense in the second suit. Given the systemic interest in preclusion, do you think a court should be able to raise preclusion on its own initiative?

MATHEWS v. NEW YORK RACING ASSOCIATION, INC.

United States District Court, Southern District of New York, 1961.
193 F.Supp. 293.

MacMahon, District Judge. Defendants move for summary judgment, pursuant to Rule 56(b), Federal Rules on [sic] Civil Procedure, on the ground that a judgment in a prior action in this court is res judicata as to the claim alleged in the complaint.

New York Racing Association Inc. is a New York corporation which operates Jamaica Race Track. It employs defendant Thoroughbred Racing Protective Association Inc., a private detective agency, for security purposes.

Plaintiff brings this action against the Association and Thoroughbred alleging that on April 4, 1958, at Jamaica Race Track, he was "assaulted," "kidnaped," "falsely arrested," and "falsely imprisoned" by employees of Thoroughbred. He further alleges that the defendants charged him with disorderly conduct and maliciously caused him to be prosecuted and convicted in the Magistrate's Court of the City of New York on April 10, 1958. He prays for relief in the form of money damages and an injunction restraining the defendants from interfering with his attendance at race tracks, from publication of libelous statements, and from acting as peace officers.

The prior judgment on which defendants rely was entered in this court on June 30, 1960 following a trial before Judge Palmieri sitting without a jury.

The complaint in that action alleged, among other matters, that plaintiff was assaulted by the defendant's private investigators at Jamaica Race Track on April 4, 1958. It also alleged that the employees of the defendants had made libelous statements concerning the plaintiff on several occasions, including plaintiff's trial for disorderly conduct on April 10, 1958. The relief prayed for in that action was also money damages and an injunction from further interference with plaintiff's attendance at race tracks within the United States. The earlier action named three individuals as defendants. The only two properly served were employees of the defendants named in the present suit.

The doctrine of res judicata operates as a bar to subsequent suits involving the same parties, or those in privity with them, based on a claim which has once reached a judgment on the merits. * * * There can be no doubt that the parties in this action are in privity with those in the earlier suit. * * *

The classic situation in which the doctrine of res judicata comes into play is where a second claim between the same parties is based on the same operative facts as the earlier one. The issues tried in the first claim and any other issues which could have been dealt with there are forever barred by the first judgment. * * *

Thus, the question is whether the claim alleged in this complaint is the same as that in the suit concluded earlier. The term "claim" refers to a group of facts limited to a single occurrence or transaction without particular reference to the resulting legal rights. It is the facts surrounding the occurrence which operate to make up the claim, not the legal theory upon which a plaintiff relies. * * *

The facts upon which plaintiff predicates this action occurred on two days, separated by almost a week, but they are so interrelated as to constitute a single claim. The ejection from the race track on April 4, 1958 was the subject of the subsequent trial for disorderly conduct on April 10, 1958.

The facts relevant to the incident at Jamaica Race Track on April 4, 1958, along with three other separate claims based on different facts, were tried to a conclusion in the earlier suit. There, the plaintiff relied on the acts of the agents occurring on April 4, 1958 as the basis of a claim against them on the theory of assault. Now, he asserts these same acts as the basis of a claim against the agents' principals on the theory of false arrest. In the earlier action, plaintiff relied on the statements of the agents made on April 10, 1958 as the basis of a claim against them on the theory of libel. Now, he asserts those same statements as the basis of a claim against their principals on the theory of malicious prosecution. Clearly, any liability of the defendants for the acts or statements of their agents must be predicated upon the familiar principle of respondeat superior. Thus, if the agents committed no actionable wrong against the plaintiff, neither did their principals. * * *

Essentially, therefore, the same facts are the basis for liability in each suit. The testimony of the witnesses who took part in or saw the ejection of the plaintiff on April 4, 1958 is the same under any theory of liability. The evidence that agents of the defendants characterized plaintiff as undesirable is the same in each suit, whether plaintiff claims the words the agents used are actionable under a theory of libel or under a theory of malicious prosecution.

The plaintiff cannot be permitted to splinter his claim into a multiplicity of suits and try them piecemeal at his convenience. * * * "The plaintiff having alleged operative facts which state a cause of action because he tells of defendant's misconduct and his own harm has had his day in court. He does not get another day after the first lawsuit is concluded by giving a different reason than he gave in the first for recovery of damages for the same invasion of his rights. The problem of his rights against the defendant based upon the alleged wrongful acts is fully before the court whether all the reasons for recovery were stated to the court or not." * * *

The issues relating to plaintiff's ejection from Jamaica Race Track on April 4, 1958 and his trial on April 10, 1958 were tried and determined by Judge Palmieri, who found that upon the facts and law plaintiff had shown no right to relief. He specifically found that plaintiff had physically resisted removal from the track, and that the defendants' employees had used no more force than was reasonably necessary to effect his removal. Therefore, plaintiff is estopped, both directly and collaterally, from maintaining this action. * * *

The court is cognizant of the fact that plaintiff appears pro se, but as the law provides a beginning for litigation, it must also provide an end. The doctrine of res judicata is a barrier against needless multiplication of litigation. "Litigation is the means for vindicating rights, but it may also involve unwarranted friction and waste. The doctrine * * * reflects the refusal of law to tolerate needless litigation. Litigation is needless if, by fair process, a controversy has once gone through the courts to conclusion." Angel v. Bullington, supra, 330 U.S. at pages 192–193, 67 S.Ct. at page 662. * * *

Notes and Questions

1. *Rush* and *Mathews* illustrate one of the primary purposes of the claim-preclusion doctrine: to prevent the splitting of a single claim into two separate suits. In *Rush,* the plaintiff won her first suit for property damage, and the court held that any claims she had for personal injuries were "merged"—in other words, extinguished—in the first suit. In *Mathews,* the plaintiff had lost the first suit. Since the basic factual setting of the claim in the second suit was the same as in the first, the court held that the allegations were "barred" by the earlier judgment. By using a different definition of a "claim," could you make an argument that the second suit should not have been precluded?

2. *Rush* and *Mathews* use the transaction approach to determine the scope of the first suit's preclusive effect. One of the greatest advantages of this test is its flexibility. Yet, flexibility comes at a price. Because a court may interpret the claim presented in the first lawsuit more broadly than a litigant does, the litigant unknowingly may forfeit parts of his action by failing to raise them. For this reason litigants will learn "by trial and error in the harsh school of experience" of the need to raise all possibly connected allegations in the first proceeding. Cleary, *Res Judicata Reexamined,* 57 Yale L.J. 339, 340 (1948). This well may mean that they will advance claims that they otherwise might not have brought to court.

3. In the federal system, the rules governing compulsory counterclaims and supplemental jurisdiction also use a form of transaction test. Does the concept of a "transaction" vary in these different contexts? In defining what a transaction is, should it matter whether a judge is using supplemental jurisdiction to open the

court to litigants or invoking compulsory counterclaim and preclusion rules to shut them out of court?

4. One complicated issue regarding the doctrine of claim preclusion arises in toxic exposure cases, because claims arise both from the immediate need for medical monitoring and from the subsequent development of the disease by some of those exposed. Since damages for tort claims generally require a showing of actual or probable physical injury, the doctrine of claim preclusion creates a problem for potential plaintiffs. Either they may bring early claims for increased medical testing and risk preclusion of later claims of disease, or they take a "wait and see" approach and risk being unable to establish damages to recover their medical monitoring expenses. For an interesting discussion of this issue, including a recommendation for a claim-preclusion exception for toxic exposure cases, see Comment, *Medical Monitoring Plaintiffs and Subsequent Claims for Disease*, 66 U.Chi.L.Rev. 969 (1999).

FEDERATED DEPARTMENT STORES, INC. v. MOITIE, 452 U.S. 394, 101 S.Ct. 2424, 69 L.Ed.2d 103 (1981). Respondents Moitie and Brown were two of seven plaintiffs to file separate antitrust actions against petitioner (*Moitie I* and *Brown I*). The actions were consolidated in the District Court after which they were dismissed for failure to allege an "injury" to their "business or property" within the meaning of Section 4 of the Clayton Act. The other five plaintiffs appealed to the Ninth Circuit. Moitie and Brown, however, did not appeal, but, instead, refiled their actions in state court (*Moitie II* and *Brown II*). The actions were removed to federal court and then dismissed on res judicata grounds. Meanwhile, the five appeals cases were reversed and remanded to the District Court to be reconsidered in light of an intervening Supreme Court opinion. When *Moitie II* and *Brown II* reached the Ninth Circuit on appeal, it held that, although a strict application of res judicata would preclude the second action, an exception should be made when the dismissal rested on a case that had been effectively overruled. The Supreme Court disagreed:

> The Court of Appeals * * * rested its opinion in part on what it viewed as "simple justice." But we do not see the grave injustice which would be done by the application of accepted principles of res judicata. "Simple justice" is achieved when a complex body of law developed over a period of years is evenhandedly applied. The doctrine of res judicata serves vital public interests beyond any individual judge's ad hoc determination of the equities in a particular case. There is simply "no principle of law or equity which sanctions the rejection by a federal court of the salutary principle of *res judicata*." * * * The Court of Appeals' reliance on "public policy" is similarly misplaced. This Court has long recognized that "[p]ublic policy dictates that there be an end of litigation; that those who have contested an issue shall be bound by the result of the contest, and that matters once tried shall be considered forever settled as between the parties." Baldwin v. Traveling Men's Association, 283 U.S. 522, 525, 51 S.Ct. 517, 518, 75 L.Ed. 1244 (1931). We have stressed that "[the] doctrine of *res judicata* is not a mere matter of practice or procedure inherited from a more technical time than ours. It is a rule of fundamen-

tal and substantial justice, 'of public policy and of private peace,' which should be cordially regarded and enforced by the courts * * *." Hart Steel Co. v. Railroad Supply Co., 244 U.S. 294, 299, 37 S.Ct. 506, 507, 61 L.Ed. 1148 (1917). * * *

Id. at 401–02, 101 S.Ct. at 2429–30, 69 L.Ed.2d at 110–11.

Notes and Questions

1. In spite of the harsh language of *Moitie,* there are situations in which considerations of justice and fairness dictate that prior judgments not be given preclusive effect. When the prior judgment was obtained by the use of fraud, courts generally will not consider it binding. See, e.g., McCarty v. First of Georgia Ins. Co., 713 F.2d 609 (10th Cir.1983). Similarly, when there was a clear and fundamental jurisdictional defect that should have prevented the first court from hearing the suit, courts often will hold that the judgment has no preclusive effect.

2. What impact should an appeal have on the preclusive effect of a trial court's judgment? See, e.g., Crawford v. Chabot, 1998 U.S. Dist. LEXIS 4192 (W.D. Mich. 1998), affirmed without opinion 229 F.3d 1151 (6th Cir.2000). Federal courts grant preclusion pending appeal of an underlying judgment, but state rules vary. What should be the effect of a remand for retrial on the preclusive effect of the underlying judgment? What if the legal underpinning of the underlying judgment is overruled? See Federal Rule 60(b)(5); 18 Wright, Miller & Cooper, *Federal Practice and Procedure: Jurisdiction and Related Matters* § 4433 (1981).

3. In *Moitie,* the defendants removed the actions to federal court on the basis of federal question jurisdiction, and the cases subsequently were dismissed due to the preclusive effect of the prior judgment. In a similar case, Rivet v. Regions Bank, 522 U.S. 470, 118 S.Ct. 921, 139 L.Ed.2d 912 (1998), the dispute involved only state issues, but the defendants, relying on *Moitie,* sought to remove the case to federal court on the ground that the plaintiff's action was precluded by a prior federal judgment. The United States Supreme Court rejected this interpretation of *Moitie,* holding that claim preclusion does not create an exception to the rule that a defendant cannot remove under Section 1441(b) on the mere basis of a federal defense. On *Moitie,* see generally Miller, *Artful Pleading: A Doctrine in Search of Definition,* Texas L. Rev. 1781 (1998).

JONES v. MORRIS PLAN BANK OF PORTSMOUTH

Supreme Court of Appeals of Virginia, 1937.
168 Va. 284, 191 S.E. 608.

GREGORY, JUSTICE. William B. Jones instituted an action for damages against the Morris Plan Bank of Portsmouth for the conversion of his automobile. * * *

After the plaintiff had introduced all of his evidence and before the defendant had introduced any evidence on its behalf, the latter's counsel moved to strike the evidence of the plaintiff and the court sustained the motion. A verdict for the defendant resulted.

The facts are that the plaintiff purchased from J.A. Parker, a dealer in automobiles, a Plymouth sedan, agreeing to pay therefor $595. He paid a part of the purchase price by the delivery of a used car to Parker of the agreed value of $245 and after crediting that amount on the purchase price and adding a finance charge of $78.40, there remained an unpaid balance due the dealer of $428. This latter amount was payable in 12 monthly installments of $35.70 each and evidenced by one note in the principal sum of $428.40. The note contained this provision: "The whole amount of this note (less any payments made hereon) becomes immediately due and payable in the event of nonpayment at maturity of any installment thereof." The note was secured by the usual conditional sales contract * * * in which it was agreed that the title to the car would be retained by the dealer until the entire purchase price was paid in full. * * * [T]he contract was assigned to the defendant * * * and the note was indorsed by Parker and delivered to the defendant at the same time.

Installment payments due on the note for May and June were not made when payable and for them an action was instituted in the civil and police court of the city of Suffolk. No appearance was made by the defendant (Jones) in that action and judgment was obtained against him for the two payments. Execution issued upon the judgment and it was satisfied * * * by Jones * * *.

Later the defendant instituted another action against Jones in the same court for the July installment which had become due and was unpaid, and to that action Jones filed a plea of res adjudicata, whereupon the * * * [Bank] took a nonsuit.

* * * [T]he defendant * * * took possession of the automobile without the consent of the plaintiff and later sold it and applied the proceeds upon the note.

Afterwards, the plaintiff instituted the present action for conversion to recover damages for the loss of the automobile. His action in the court below was founded upon the theory that when the May and June installments became due and were unpaid, then under the acceleration clause in the note, the entire balance due thereon matured and at once became due and the defendant having elected to sue him for only two installments instead of the entire amount of the note, and having obtained a judgment for the two installments and satisfaction of the execution issued thereon, it waived its right to collect the balance. He also contends that the note was satisfied in the manner narrated and that the conditional sales contract, the sole purpose of which was to secure the payment of the note, served its purpose and ceased to exist, and, therefore, the title to the automobile was no longer retained, but upon the satisfaction of the note, passed to the plaintiff and was his property when the agent of the defendant removed it and converted it to its own use.

The position of the defendant is that * * * the title to the automobile, which was the subject of the alleged conversion, was not vested in the plaintiff at the time of the action, nor since, because the condition in the contract was that the title should be retained by the seller (whose rights were assigned to the defendant) until the entire purchase price was paid, and that the purchase price had never been paid * * *.

The defendant also contends that the note and conditional sales contract were divisible; that successive actions could be brought upon the installments as they matured; and that it was not bound, at the risk of waiving its right to claim the balance, to sue for all installments in one action.

* * *

We decide that under the unconditional acceleration provision in the note involved here and in the absence of the usual optional provision reserved to the holder, the entire amount due upon the note became due and payable when default was made in paying an installment. * * *

Was it essential that the defendant here institute an action for all of the installments then due, or could it institute its action for only two of the installments and later institute another action for other installments? The answer to that question depends upon the nature of the transaction. If a transaction is represented by one single and indivisible contract and the breach gives rise to one single cause of action, it cannot be split into distinct parts and separate actions maintained for each.

On the other hand, if the contract is divisible giving rise to more than one cause of action, each may be proceeded upon separately.

Was the contract here single and indivisible or was it divisible? Our answer is that the note and conditional sales contract constituted one single contract. The sole purpose of the conditional sales contract was to retain the title in the seller until the note was paid. When that condition was performed, the contract ended.

One of the principal tests in determining whether a demand is single and entire, or whether it is several, so as to give rise to more than one cause of action, is the identity of facts necessary to maintain the action. If the same evidence will support both actions, there is but one cause of action.

In the case at bar, all of the installments were due. The evidence essential to support the action on the two installments for which the action was brought would be the identical evidence necessary to maintain an action upon all of the installments. All installments having matured at the time the action was begun, under well-settled principles, those not embraced in that action are now barred.

* * * At the time the defendant lost its right to institute any action for the remaining installments, the title to the automobile passed to the plaintiff. He was the owner at the time the agent of the defendant took possession of it and exposed it to sale.

It follows that the judgment of the court below will be reversed, and the case will be remanded for the sole purpose of determining the quantum of damages.

Reversed and remanded.

Notes and Questions

1. Why did the court remand only for the purpose of determining damages rather than order a new trial?

2. When a debt is secured by a series of notes or when a bond includes a number of interest coupons, an action on one of the notes or coupons, even though others are due, does not bar a subsequent action on those others. *Restatement, Judgments* § 62, comment *i* (1942); *Restatement (Second), Judgments* § 24, comment *d* (1982). Cf. NESBIT v. RIVERSIDE INDEPENDENT DISTRICT, 144 U.S. 610, 619, 12 S.Ct. 746, 748, 36 L.Ed. 562, 565 (1892):

Each matured coupon is a separable promise, and gives rise to a separate cause of action. It may be detached from the bond and sold by itself. Indeed, the title to several matured coupons of the same bond may be in as many different persons, and upon each a distinct and separate action be maintained. So, while the promises of the bond and of the coupons in the first instance are upon the same paper, and the coupons are for interest due upon the bond, yet the promise to pay the coupon is as distinct from that to pay the bond as though the two promises were placed in different instruments, upon different paper.

3. It particularly is difficult to define the scope of a prior judgment in controversies involving continuing or renewed conduct. The *Restatement (Second) of Judgments* lists some considerations relevant to determining whether a factual grouping constitutes a single transaction, and suggests evaluating "whether the facts are related in time, space, origin, or motivation, whether they form a convenient trial unit, and whether their treatment as a unit conforms to the parties' expectations or business understanding or usage." See *Restatement (Second), Judgments* § 24 (1982).

There are some other useful rules of thumb to be used in cases of continuing or renewed conduct. For example, if the conduct that is the subject of the first action continues after judgment in the first action, claim preclusion would not prevent a second suit. Issue preclusion may apply, however, to matters of status or to issues of fact resolved in the first action. When the purpose of the first suit is to establish general rules of legality, such as when the first suit is a declaratory-judgment action, subsequent claims involving the same conduct are precluded.

Nuisance suits commonly involve continuing conduct. Judgments involving "permanent" nuisances are considered to have full preclusive effect; those involving "temporary" nuisances are not considered to preclude later litigation involving the same behavior. Courts are not always consistent in their classification of nuisances. See 18 Wright, Miller & Cooper, *Federal Practice and Procedure: Jurisdiction and Related Matters* § 4425 (1981).

4. Often, the underlying substantive law will affect the definition of the claim for the purposes of preclusion. For example, if one party to a contract commits a material breach that neither is accompanied nor followed by a repudiation, the law of contracts teaches that the other party is free, on the one hand, to treat the contract as binding and sue for the damages or, on the other hand, to treat the contract as ended. If the aggrieved party chooses the former option, and then suffers further material breaches, she will not be barred from suing for damages not sought in the first suit. See *Restatement (Second), Judgments* § 26, comment *g* (1982).

The expectations of the parties also may be decisive in determining the scope of the prior judgment. Imagine that a wholesale distributor regularly ships goods to a retailer on credit. If the parties conceive of their relationship as a series of discrete transactions, a suit by the creditor seeking to recover any one of the payments would not bar subsequent suits for other payments. If, however, the parties believe they have a single running account, a suit by the creditor would have to seek to recover the entire balance then due.

Can you think of other situations in which substantive law might affect the scope of the prior judgment? See generally 18 Wright, Miller & Cooper, *Federal Practice and Procedure: Jurisdiction and Related Matters* § 4409 (1981).

2. DEFENSE PRECLUSION

MITCHELL v. FEDERAL INTERMEDIATE CREDIT BANK

Supreme Court of South Carolina, 1932.
165 S.C. 457, 164 S.E. 136.

[An action for an accounting against defendant bank for proceeds of a crop of potatoes. Plaintiff alleged that in order to obtain loans from defendant he had—at the behest of defendant's agent—sold his potatoes through a growers' association and assigned the proceeds as security for two notes, totalling $9,000, which had been discounted with defendant; that the potatoes had netted $18,000, but that he had never received any of this, and that the proceeds had been received by defendant or an agent of defendant. In a previous action by defendant on the notes, plaintiff had pleaded in the answer the same facts now the basis of an affirmative claim, but had not counter-claimed or asked relief; judgment had been for him in that action. In the present suit, defendant contended that plaintiff's claim was merged in the earlier judgment. This contention was upheld by the trial court.]

STABLER, J. * * *

We now come to the main question presented by the appeal, namely, Was the circuit judge in error in sustaining the plea in bar to plaintiff's action? Turning to appellant's answer in the federal court case * * * we find that the facts there pleaded by him as a defense to the bank's recovery on its notes are the same as those set out by him in his complaint as the basis of his action in the case at bar, it being alleged that the total amount paid to the bank was in excess of all sums advanced to him on the notes or otherwise, and as a result of the transaction the notes sued upon were fully paid and discharged. In addition, we find in the record of the case before us the following statement by appellant as an admission of fact on his part: " * * * The indebtedness of the bank to Mitchell arising from the embezzlement of the proceeds of the crop was used pro tanto as an offset to the claim of the bank in the Federal Court. The case at bar seeks recovery of the surplusage, over the offset, of the proceeds of the same crop lost by the same embezzlement. The appellant, however, is not seeking to recover in this action the same money that has already been used as an offset."

* * *

In support of his position * * * appellant cites certain decisions of this court, which he claims to be conclusive of the issue, relying especially upon Kirven v. Chemical Co., 77 S.C. 493, 58 S.E. 424, 426.

* * * [T]he record shows that Kirven had bought from the Chemical Company $2,228 worth of fertilizers and had given his note for that amount. The company, upon maturity of the note, brought action against him on his obligation. He at first filed an answer setting up three defenses, the third of which was that the fertilizers furnished were deleterious and destructive to the crops, and that there was an entire failure of consideration for the note. Later, he was permitted to file a supplemental answer in which he withdrew the third defense. On trial in the federal court, the jury rendered a verdict for the Chemical Company. Thereafter, Kirven brought an action against the

company * * * alleging that the defendant caused damage to his crop in the sum of $1,995 by reason of the deleterious effect of the fertilizers furnished. The company set up the defense that the issues in this action were or could have been adjudicated in the [first] suit * * *. A verdict was given Kirven in the amount prayed for, and on appeal * * * it was pointed out that the question raised in the state court was not *actually* litigated and determined in the federal action, and it appears that the court, for that reason, took the view that a bar or estoppel did not exist. Mr. Justice Woods, in his concurring opinion, took the view that, as Kirven elected not to use, as a defense, the fact of *worthlessness,* which might have been available in the action of the company against him, "he was not precluded from using the very different facts of deleteriousness and positive injury caused by appellant's alleged negligence in the manufacture of the fertilizer as the basis of an independent cause of action."

We think the facts of the case at bar, however, present a different situation. * * *

O'Connor v. Varney, 10 Gray (Mass.) 231, was an action on contract to recover damages for Varney's failure to build certain additions to a house according to the terms of a written agreement between the parties. The defendant set up as a defense "a judgment recovered by O'Connor in an action brought by Varney against him on that contract to recover the price therein agreed to be paid for the work, in defence of which O'Connor relied on the same nonperformance by Varney, and in which an auditor to whom the case was referred * * * found that Varney was not entitled to recover under the agreement," as the work had been so imperfectly done that it would require a greater sum than the amount sued for to make it correspond with the contract. At the trial of the second action, the trial judge ruled that the judgment in the first suit was a bar, and directed a verdict for the defendant. The plaintiff O'Connor thereupon appealed.

Chief Justice Shaw, who rendered the opinion of the court, said: "The presiding judge rightly ruled that the former judgment was a bar to this action. A party against whom an action is brought on a contract has two modes of defending himself. He may allege specific breaches of the contract declared upon, and rely on them in defence. But if he intends to claim, by way of damages for nonperformance of the contract, more than the amount for which he is sued, he must not rely on the contract in defence, but must bring a cross action, and apply to the court to have the cases continued so that the executions may be set off. He cannot use the same defence, first as a shield, and then as a sword. * * * "

It will be noted that Varney was not entitled to recover in the first suit because his dereliction amounted to more than he sued for. This would seem to be exactly the situation in the case at bar.

* * * When the bank sued * * * [Mitchell] on his two notes, amounting to about $9,000, he had the option to interpose his claim as a defense to that suit or to demand judgment against the bank, by way of counterclaim, for the amount owing him by it. * * * The transaction out of which the case at bar arises is the same transaction that Mitchell pleaded as a defense in the federal suit. He might, therefore, "have recovered in that action, upon the same allegations and proofs which he there made, the judgment which he now

seeks, if he had prayed for it." He did not do this, but attempted to split his cause of action, and to use one portion of it for defense in that suit and to reserve the remainder for offense in a subsequent suit, which, under applicable principles, could not be done. * * *

The judgment of the circuit court is affirmed.

Questions

1. Compulsory-counterclaim rules, such as Federal Rule 13(a), effectively supersede the rules of preclusion in many contexts. Generally, under Rule 13(a) compulsory counterclaims that are not raised may not be raised in subsequent litigation in federal court. In most situations the broad sweep of compulsory-counterclaim preclusion thus makes it unnecessary to consider whether and how defense preclusion might apply. See Annot., 22 A.L.R.2d 621 (1952).

Defense preclusion does apply, however, in those state court systems in which there is no compulsory-counterclaim rule. Moreover, even when there are compulsory-counterclaim rules, they often contain express exceptions. Rule 13(a), for example, does not require parties to include claims that already are pending in another suit. And, some courts have held Rule 13(a) inapplicable in suits in which no responsive pleading was filed because the action was terminated by default, settlement, or dismissal on motion.

2. At common law, would Mitchell's defense in the first action have been in the nature of a recoupment or a set-off? Assuming that the defense would have been one or the other, would this have made a difference as to the right to bring a later suit for the excess? See p. 600–01, supra.

———

LINDERMAN MACHINE CO. v. HILLENBRAND CO., 75 Ind.App. 111, 127 N.E. 813 (1920). L sold H a machine, and subsequently sued to recover the purchase price; H answered that the contract had been obtained by fraudulent representations as to the machine's capacity to do H's work, that the machine did not perform as represented, and that H had notified L to remove the machine. Judgment was rendered against L. Subsequently H sued L to recover damages for fraud, alleging that it had incurred great expense in transporting, installing, attempting to operate, and removing the machine. L answered that the action was barred by the judgment in the first suit. The court held for H:

> It is true that a party, when sued, must interpose all defenses which he has, and as to them, whether pleaded or not, the judgment is conclusive; but it is not conclusive as to an affirmative right or cause of action which he may have against the plaintiff, and of which he could have taken advantage by way of cross-complaint. He is not compelled to file his cross-complaint, and, on his failure to do so, his rights with reference thereto will not be adjudged. * * *

> There was no issue in the action brought by [L] to recover the purchase price * * * as to the right of [H] to recover the expenses which it had been put to in installing the machinery, and without such issue

therein, [L] is not in position now to invoke against [H] the doctrine of res adjudicata.

Id. at 118, 127 N.E. at 815.

Notes and Questions

1. Is *Linderman* consistent with *Mitchell*?

2. Problems with preclusion also may arise when a dispute involves multiple potential defendants. In FIRST ACCEPTANCE CORP. v. KENNEDY, 95 F.Supp. 861 (N.D.Iowa 1951), reversed on other grounds 194 F.2d 819 (8th Cir.1952), defendant purchased an air conditioner for an onion-drying shed under a conditional-sales agreement with a vendor who assigned the contract to plaintiff. In a suit for the balance of the purchase price, the trial court permitted defendant to raise fraud as a total defense to the contract, even though he had not rescinded the contract. The trial judge's opinion reflects the procedural difficulty that claim preclusion poses:

> The defendant claims that the transaction between the United States Air Conditioning Corporation and the plaintiff placed him in a legal dilemma and that he used the defense of fraud in the only manner left open to him. It is the contention of the defendant that rescission was legally impossible for the reason that rescission could not be made with the United States Air Conditioning Corporation because the title to the subject matter of the sale was in the plaintiff; and that rescission could not be had with the plaintiff because the sum of $2,800 paid by him under the contract had been retained by the United States Air Conditioning Corporation and the plaintiff was under no obligation or duty to make refund of the $2,800 upon rescission. The defendant points out that the United States Air Conditioning Corporation was not subject to service of process in Iowa and, therefore, it could not be made a party to this action.

> The defendant further claims that the damages sustained by him because of the fraud practiced upon him * * * are greatly in excess of the amount which the plaintiff seeks to recover herein; and that if he asserted part of his damages as an offset or by way of recoupment against the plaintiff's claim he would be splitting his cause of action and that he then would be unable to recover the balance of his damages from the United States Air Conditioning Corporation.

> It is plain that the defendant in his pleadings very carefully refrained from attempting to use any part of his damages as an offset or by way of recoupment. The position of the defendant is that since rescission was impossible and since he could not use part of his claim as an offset or by way of recoupment without losing the balance of his claim all that he could do was to ask that the contract be not enforced against him because of fraud in its procurement.

Id. at 870–71.

3. Defense preclusion typically is raised in a subsequent action by the original plaintiff when the defendant tries to assert a defense that was not raised in the earlier action. It undoubtedly should apply if the subsequent action is a suit to enforce the first action; in other kinds of suits, however, the role of defense preclusion is more ambiguous. On the one hand, it could be argued that defense preclusion should not apply, as often defendants will have very good reasons for

not raising a particular defense in the first action (for example, it may have been difficult to obtain the necessary evidence or witnesses). On the other hand, permitting a new defense to be raised may destroy the plaintiff's sense of repose.

Consider JACOBSON v. MILLER, 41 Mich. 90, 1 N.W. 1013 (1879). A landlord brought and prevailed on an action to recover unpaid installments of rent. Subsequently, the landlord brought another suit to recover later unpaid installments. Although he had made no mention of a defense in the initial proceeding, the tenant sought to defend the second suit by alleging that he had never executed the lease. Should the court have permitted the defense to be made? Remember that if the defendant had raised this claim in the first action successfully, the landlord could have taken affirmative steps to remedy the problem, and perhaps even could have found a new tenant. See generally 18 Wright, Miller & Cooper, *Federal Practice and Procedure: Jurisdiction and Related Matters* § 4414 (1981); *Restatement (Second), Judgments* § 22 (1982).

4.   Section 20(1) of the *Restatement (Second) of Judgments* sets forth certain valid and final judgments that are not preclusive: (a) dismissal for lack of jurisdiction, dismissal for improper venue, dismissal for nonjoinder or misjoinder of parties; and (b) election or direction of a nonsuit. However, this list is not exhaustive and those dismissals that are not expressly listed may be considered an adjudication on the merits if the "defendant must incur the inconvenience of preparing to meet the merits. * * * " For instance, in RINEHART v. LOCKE, 454 F.2d 313 (7th Cir.1971), the Seventh Circuit, relying on Rule 41(b), concluded that a dismissal for failure to state a claim precluded a subsequent suit on the claim plaintiff apparently "was attempting to state." This conclusion places upon the plaintiff the burden of either persuading the district court to allow an amendment to the complaint or to appeal the district court's judgment. Do you think this is an appropriate rule? For a contrary result, see Costello v. United States, 365 U.S. 265, 81 S.Ct. 534, 5 L.Ed.2d 551 (1961).

SECTION C.   ISSUE PRECLUSION

One of the most frequently quoted descriptions of what once was called collateral estoppel and is now referred to as issue preclusion was provided by the first Justice Harlan in SOUTHERN PACIFIC RAILROAD CO. v. UNITED STATES, 168 U.S. 1, 48–49, 18 S.Ct. 18, 27, 42 L.Ed. 355, 377 (1897):

> The general principle announced in numerous cases is that a right, question, or fact distinctly put in issue and directly determined by a court of competent jurisdiction, as a ground of recovery, cannot be disputed in a subsequent suit between the same parties or their privies; and, even if the second suit is for a different cause of action, the right, question, or fact once so determined must, as between the same parties or their privies, be taken as conclusively established, so long as the judgment in the first suit remains unmodified. This general rule is demanded by the very object for which civil courts have been established, which is to secure the peace and repose of society by the settlement of matters capable of judicial determination. Its enforcement is essential to the maintenance of social order; for the aid of judicial tribunals would not be invoked for the vindication of rights of person and property if, as between parties and their privies, conclusiveness did not attend the judgments of such tribunals in respect of all matters properly put in issue, and actually determined by them.

As this passage reveals, there is a critical difference between claim preclusion and issue preclusion. Under the doctrine of claim preclusion, a claim may be "merged" or "barred" by a party's failure to raise the claim in a prior action. Issue preclusion, however, applies only to matters argued and decided in an earlier lawsuit.

For issue preclusion to exist, a proceeding must involve the same issue as a previous suit. The term "issue," like the term "transaction" in the context of claim preclusion, is ambiguous and subject to manipulation. And, the application *vel non* of doctrines of issue preclusion sometimes will turn on the ability of advocates to manipulate the definition of this crucial term.

To trigger the doctrines of issue preclusion, however, more than a mere duplication of issues is required. It is necessary to examine the nature of the first action and the treatment that the issue received in it. Just as for claim preclusion, the judgment in the first action must have been of a certain "quality"—that is, it must have been valid, final, and on the merits (the "on the merits" requirement does not apply if the issue being precluded is exclusively a procedural issue). Moreover, the issue raised in a second suit actually must have been litigated in the first action, and must have been decided by the first court. And, determination of that issue must have been necessary to the court's judgment.

Some courts require still more before they will allow a party to invoke issue preclusion. For example, some demand that the issue have occupied a high position in the hierarchy of legal rules applied in the first action—that it was important. Others require "mutuality"—that is, that the party invoking preclusion would have been bound by an unfavorable judgment in the first suit. Fewer and fewer courts now impose these latter two conditions, however, and the mutuality requirement in particular is now widely disregarded.

Issue preclusion can be used in a variety of ways. It can be invoked offensively, when the plaintiff in the second action seeks to preclude litigation of an issue that was decided favorably to him in a prior action. Or, it can be used defensively, when the defendant in the second suit seeks to preclude relitigation of an issue that was decided in his favor in a prior suit. Some courts and commentators further distinguish between "direct" and "collateral" preclusion or estoppel—depending upon whether the second proceeding involves the same cause of action as the first. When the two suits involve the same cause of action, issue preclusion sometimes is referred to as direct estoppel. When the second suit involves a new claim or cause of action, issue preclusion sometimes is referred to as collateral estoppel.

1. ACTUALLY LITIGATED

CROMWELL v. COUNTY OF SAC

Supreme Court of the United States, 1876.
94 U.S. (4 Otto) 351, 24 L.Ed. 195.

Error to the Circuit Court of the United States for the District of Iowa.

MR. JUSTICE FIELD delivered the opinion of the court.

This was an action on four bonds * * * each for $1,000, and four coupons for interest, attached to them, each for $100. The bonds were issued in 1860, and were made payable to bearer, in the city of New York, in the years 1868, 1869, 1870, and 1871, respectively, with annual interest at the rate of ten per cent a year.

To defeat this action, the defendant relied upon the estoppel of a judgment rendered in favor of the county in a prior action brought by one Samuel C. Smith upon certain earlier maturing coupons on the same bonds, accompanied with proof that the plaintiff Cromwell was at the time the owner of the coupons in that action, and that the action was prosecuted for his sole use and benefit.

* * *

In considering the operation of this judgment, it should be borne in mind * * * that there is a difference between the effect of a judgment as a bar or estoppel against the prosecution of a second action upon the same claim or demand, and its effect as an estoppel in another action between the same parties upon a different claim or cause of action. In the former case, the judgment, if rendered upon the merits, constitutes an absolute bar to a subsequent action. [The Court's description of claim preclusion appears at p. 1225, supra.] * * * The language * * * which is so often used, that a judgment estops not only as to every ground of recovery or defence actually presented in the action, but also as to every ground which might have been presented, is strictly accurate, when applied to the demand or claim in controversy. * * *

But where the second action between the same parties is upon a different claim or demand, the judgment in the prior action operates as an estoppel only as to those matters in issue or points controverted, upon the determination of which the finding or verdict was rendered. In all cases, therefore, where it is sought to apply the estoppel of a judgment rendered upon one cause of action to matters arising in a suit upon a different cause of action, the inquiry must always be as to the point or question actually litigated and determined in the original action, not what might have been thus litigated and determined. Only upon such matters is the judgment conclusive in another action.

The difference in the operation of a judgment in the two classes of cases mentioned is seen through all the leading adjudications upon the doctrine of estoppel. Thus, in the case of Outram v. Morewood, 3 East, 346, the defendants were held estopped from averring title to a mine, in an action of trespass for digging out coal from it, because, in a previous action for a similar trespass, they had set up the same title, and it had been determined against them. In commenting upon a decision cited in that case, Lord Ellenborough, in his elaborate opinion, said: "It is not the recovery, but the matter alleged by the party, and upon which the recovery proceeds, which creates the estoppel. The recovery of itself in an action of trespass is only a bar to the future recovery of damages for the same injury; but the estoppel precludes parties and privies from contending to the contrary of that point or matter of fact, which, having been once distinctly put in issue by them, or by those to whom they are privy in estate or law, has been, on such issue joined, solemnly found against them."

* * *

Various considerations, other than the actual merits, may govern a party in bringing forward grounds of recovery or defence in one action, which may not exist in another action upon a different demand, such as the smallness of the amount or the value of the property in controversy, the difficulty of obtaining the necessary evidence, the expense of the litigation, and his own situation at the time. A party acting upon considerations like these ought not to be precluded from contesting in a subsequent action other demands arising out of the same transaction. * * *

If, now, we consider the main question presented for our determination * * * its solution will not be difficult. It appears from the findings in the original action of Smith, that the county of Sac, by a vote of its people, authorized the issue of bonds to the amount of $10,000, for the erection of a court-house; that bonds to that amount were issued by the county judge, and delivered to one Meserey, with whom he had made a contract for the erection of the court-house; that immediately upon receipt of the bonds the contractor gave one of them as a gratuity to the county judge; and that the court-house was never constructed by the contractor, or by any other person pursuant to the contract. It also appears that the plaintiff had become, before their maturity, the holder of twenty-five coupons, which had been attached to the bonds, but there was no finding that he had ever given any value for them. * * * The case coming here on writ of error, this court held that the facts disclosed by the findings were sufficient evidence of fraud and illegality in the inception of the bonds to call upon the holder to show that he had given value for the coupons; and, not having done so, the judgment was affirmed. Reading the record of the lower court by the opinion and judgment of this court, it must be considered that the matters adjudged in that case were these: that the bonds were void as against the county in the hands of parties who did not acquire them before maturity and give value for them, and that the plaintiff, not having proved that he gave such value, was not entitled to recover upon the coupons. * * * The finding and judgment upon the invalidity of the bonds, as against the county, must be held to estop the plaintiff here from averring to the contrary. But as the bonds were negotiable instruments * * * they would be held as valid obligations against the county in the hands of a *bona fide* holder taking them for value before maturity * * *. If, therefore, the plaintiff received the bond and coupons in suit before maturity for value, as he offered to prove, he should have been permitted to show that fact. There was nothing adjudged in the former action in the finding that the plaintiff had not made such proof in that case which can preclude the present plaintiff from making such proof here. The fact that a party may not have shown that he gave value for one bond or coupon is not even presumptive, much less conclusive, evidence that he may not have given value for another and different bond or coupon. The exclusion of the evidence offered by the plaintiff was erroneous * * *.

Judgment reversed, and cause remanded for a new trial.

[The dissenting opinion of JUSTICE CLIFFORD is omitted.]

Notes and Questions

1. A physician sues a patient to collect her fee for services rendered. The patient defaults, judgment is entered, and the judgment is satisfied. Later, the

patient sues the physician for malpractice. Does the earlier default judgment establish that the physician's services were of value, and not worthless or harmful? Is the fact that the patient may have had little incentive to litigate the first suit relevant? Would it make a difference if the malpractice claim was not foreseeable at the time of the first action? What if the patient had strong reasons for wanting to litigate the malpractice claim in a different jurisdiction from the one where the first suit was brought? Compare Gwynn v. Wilhelm, 226 Or. 606, 360 P.2d 312 (1961), with Blair v. Bartlett, 75 N.Y. 150 (1878). See Annot., 77 A.L.R.2d 1410 (1999).

2. Professor Allan Vestal criticizes the actually litigated requirement on the ground that the justifications offered on its behalf are unsound:

> * * * [One argument made in favor of the actually litigated requirement is] that an action may involve "so small an amount that litigation of the issue may cost more than the value of the lawsuit." [*Restatement (Second), Judgments* § 27, comment *e* (1982).] * * * This is a rather curious rationale. It does not support the "actually litigated" requirement; rather it supports a rejection of issue preclusion under any circumstances. If there is insufficient incentive to litigate a matter, then there should be no issue preclusion. Litigation in small claims courts or prosecutions for misdemeanors cannot give rise to issue preclusion because often those actions provide litigants with inadequate incentive to litigate. Although the line is not clearly defined, it seems reasonable to conclude that prosecutions for felonies and civil litigation involving substantial amounts will give rise to issue preclusion. The burden properly falls on the presumably precluded party to show why issue preclusion should not apply.

> * * * [A second argument used to justify the actually litigated requirement is] that "the forum may be an inconvenient one in which to produce the necessary evidence or in which to litigate at all." [Id.] If a valid judgment is going to be handed down, then this forum must have jurisdiction over the defendant and it is the forum of choice of the plaintiff. As the forum of choice of the plaintiff, it is proper to hold that the plaintiff should be bound by any adverse decision reached by the court. It is only in the case of the defendant that he might be able to assert that he should not be bound because it is inconvenient.

> In light of (a) the present constitutional limitations on the exercise of jurisdiction over defendants, (b) the fact that the suit by definition involves a substantial interest, and (c) the availability of procedures to get and present the relevant evidence, this justification is not very persuasive. Would it not be better to hold for issue preclusion, and then permit the apparently precluded party to explain why preclusion should not apply?

> The [*Restatement's*] Comment also gives as a reason for the "actually litigated" rule that a rule to the contrary "might serve to discourage compromise, to decrease the likelihood that the issues in an action would be narrowed by stipulation, and thus to intensify litigation." Id. This litigation, where there is the incentive to litigate, must involve substantial interests on the part of the parties. The issue preclusion that may flow from the judgment does not change the suit from unimportant to important. The suit is, by definition, important. If a compromise is going to be discouraged, it probably will be by the size of the present suit. If there is going to be a refusal to stipulate and thus narrow issues, in all probability it will be because of the

importance of the instant suit and not because of the issue preclusion that may flow from the decision.

Vestal, *The Restatement (Second) of Judgments: A Modest Dissent,* 66 Cornell L.Rev. 464, 473–74 (1981).

3. Section 27 of the *Restatement (Second) of Judgments* adopts the actually litigated requirement. Professor Geoffrey Hazard, the *Restatement's* final Reporter, believes that other trends in civil procedure provide powerful arguments against relaxing the requirement:

> A good case can be made for saying that if a matter is distinctly put in issue and formally admitted, the party making the admission should be bound by it in subsequent litigation. This was the old formulation of the rule of "judicial estoppel," as it was then called: "The former verdict is conclusive only as to facts directly and distinctly put in issue * * *." But how can a matter be "directly and distinctly put in issue"? Obviously, by actual litigation. Another way is through pleadings. In a pleading system where matters are "distinctly put in issue," it makes sense to say that if a proposition is clearly asserted, and if a party is called upon solemnly to admit or deny the proposition, and if the stakes are high enough to assure that the party is serious in dealing with the issue, and if the party then admits or fails to deny the proposition, then he ought to be estopped from controverting it on some other occasion, particularly if that other occasion involves essentially the same transaction. The clearest case for such an estoppel is where a defendant pleads guilty to a substantial criminal charge and then seeks in civil litigation concerning the same transaction to assert that he did not commit the criminal act. Particularly galling is the situation where a criminal convicted on his own guilty plea seeks as plaintiff in a subsequent civil action to claim redress based on a repudiation of the confession. The effrontery or, as some might say it, *chutzpah,* is too much to take. There certainly should be an estoppel in such a case.

> The same principle could apply when an issue is put forward and admitted "distinctly"—that is, clearly and solemnly—in a civil case. It is therefore appropriate to impose an estoppel based on a formal admission in a civil case, and the law of evidence does so. A judicial admission is considered in subsequent litigations as prima facie evidence that the admitted matter is true.

* * *

> Professor Vestal says there should be an estoppel because, where there is an incentive to deny, failure to deny constitutes an admission. This turns the notion of incentive to litigate on its head. The "incentive to litigate" formula, as used in most of the cases and in the *Restatement Second,* allows a party who *did* litigate an issue to relitigate it if the party can show that the original litigation was a side show rather than a struggle to the finish. [See *Restatement (Second), Judgments* § 28, comment *j* (1982).] The *Restatement Second* allows a party to rebut the inference naturally drawn from the fact that the issue was actually litigated—the inference that the party had treated the issue with entire seriousness in the first litigation. In Professor Vestal's system, however, "incentive to litigate" allows a court to conjecture that the party probably had reason to litigate the issue in the first action, and to conjecture further that the failure to litigate is an admission of a proposition not litigated. Professor Vestal's "opportunity" theory allows the court to infer

that the issue was important to a party whose behavior indicates he thought the issue was unimportant, and, having done that, to convict the party by his silence. * * *

Hazard, *Revisiting the Second Restatement of Judgments: Issue Preclusion and Related Problems,* 66 Cornell L.Rev. 564, 577–79, 584 (1981).

4.   Should the actually-litigated requirement eliminate the preclusive effect of a guilty plea in a criminal suit? Not surprisingly, Professor Vestal argues that a guilty plea should be given preclusive effect unless the defendant can show that he lacked an adequate opportunity or incentive to litigate. However, the *Restatement* contains no exception from the actually-litigated requirement for guilty pleas and, thus, concludes that issue preclusion is inapplicable. *Restatement (Second), Judgments* § 85, comment *b* (1982); accord Haring v. Prosise, 462 U.S. 306, 103 S.Ct. 2368, 76 L.Ed.2d 595 (1983) (Virginia law does not preclude a subsequent claim for an alleged Fourth Amendment violation that had not been addressed by a previous state court criminal conviction procured by a guilty plea). But see Allen v. McCurry, p. 1320, infra, in which a guilty plea had preclusive effect because the defendant had an evidentiary hearing regarding a motion to suppress. The *Restatement* does note that guilty pleas are admissible into evidence in later civil suits. See, e.g., DiJoseph v. Vuotto, 968 F.Supp. 244 (E.D.Pa.1997) (the operative facts underlying defendant's aggravated assault conviction were properly admitted in a subsequent claim for alleged violations of the Fourth Amendment, even though defendant's guilty plea itself could not be granted issue preclusive effect), affirmed sub nom. DiJoseph v. City of Philadelphia, 156 F.3d 1224 (3d Cir.1998). Despite the *Restatement*'s position, some courts, without always setting forth a clear rationale, have granted preclusive effect to guilty pleas in subsequent suits involving the essential elements of the crime. See Shapiro, *Should a Guilty Plea Have Preclusive Effect?,* 70 Iowa L.Rev. 2449 (1985).

5.   An interesting application of the actually litigated requirement arises in the context of employment litigation. Should an arbitration proceeding pursuant to the terms of a collective bargaining agreement preclude a plaintiff from pursuing her statutory civil rights claim in state court? In BLANCHETTE v. SCHOOL COMMITTEE OF WESTWOOD, 427 Mass. 176, 692 N.E.2d 21 (1998), issue preclusion was found not to apply. The *Blanchette* court reasoned that the arbitration proceeding only determined the contractual obligations of the school committee under the collective bargaining agreement and did not address plaintiff's civil rights claim: "[Plaintiff] is seeking single bites from two separate apples as she looks to enforce two different sets of rights in the respective forums that are available to her. Nothing in the preclusion doctrine prevents this." Id. at 181, 692 N.E.2d at 26.

6.   How should a court go about determining what was decided in a prior litigation? Will the difficulty of this task be affected by whether the case was tried to a judge or to a jury? Are there any procedural rules that can play a role in defining what a suit has decided? Consider, in particular, Rule 49 and Rule 52.

When the prior decision is ambiguous on what it actually decided, doubts should be resolved against the party seeking to assert preclusion. But it sometimes will be necessary to conduct a hearing to determine what was decided. Is it possible to use the record of the prior trial to help ascertain what issues actually were decided? Is it permissible to introduce extrinsic evidence to prove what issues were litigated? There is some authority for permitting both of these methods of proof. For a general discussion of this topic, see 18 Wright, Miller & Cooper

Federal Practice and Procedure: Jurisdiction and Related Matters § 4420 (1981) (2001 Pocket Part).

2. NECESSARILY DECIDED

RUSSELL v. PLACE

Supreme Court of the United States, 1876.
94 U.S. (4 Otto) 606, 24 L.Ed. 214.

Appeal from the Circuit Court of the United States for the Northern District of New York.

Mr. Justice Field delivered the opinion of the court.

This is a suit for an infringement of a patent to the complainant for an alleged new and useful improvement in the preparation of leather * * *.

The bill of complaint sets forth the invention claimed, the issue of a patent for the same, its surrender for alleged defective and insufficient description of the invention, its reissue with an amended specification, and the recovery of judgment against the defendants for damages in an action at law for a violation of the exclusive privileges secured by the patent.

The bill then alleges the subsequent manufacture, use, and sale by the defendants, without the license of the patentee, of the alleged invention and improvement, and prays that they may be decreed to account for the gains and profits thus acquired by them, and be enjoined from further infringement.

The answer admits the issue of the patent, its surrender and reissue, and, as a defence to this suit, sets up in substance the want of novelty in the invention, its use by the public for more than two years prior to the application for the patent, and that the reissue, so far as it differs from the original patent, is not for the same invention. * * *

The action at law was brought * * * in the ordinary form of such actions for infringement of the privileges secured by a patent. The defendants pleaded the general issue, and set up, by special notice under the act of Congress, the want of novelty in the invention, and its use by the public for more than two years prior to the application for a patent. The plaintiff obtained a verdict for damages, upon which the judgment mentioned was entered; and this judgment, it is now insisted, estops the defendants in this suit from insisting upon the want of novelty in the invention patented, and its prior use by the public, and also from insisting upon any ground going to the validity of the patent which might have been availed of as a defence in that action, and, of course, upon the want of identity in the invention covered by the reissue with that of the original patent.

It is undoubtedly settled law that a judgment of a court of competent jurisdiction, upon a question directly involved in one suit, is conclusive as to that question in another suit between the same parties. But to this operation of the judgment it must appear, either upon the face of the record or be shown by extrinsic evidence, that the precise question was raised and determined in the former suit. If there be any uncertainty on this head in the record—as, for example, if it appear that several distinct matters may have been litigated, upon one or more of which the judgment may have passed, without indicating which of them was thus litigated, and upon which the judgment was rendered—the whole subject-matter of the action will be at large, and open to a new contention, unless this uncertainty be removed by extrinsic evidence showing the precise point involved and determined. * * *

Tested by these views, the question presented * * * is of easy solution. The record of that action does not disclose the nature of the infringement for which damages were recovered. The declaration only avers * * * as the infringement complained of, that the defendants have made and used the invention, and have caused others to make and use it. The patent contains two claims: one for the use of fat liquor generally in the treatment of leather, and the other for a process of treating bark tanned lamb or sheep skin by means of a compound composed and applied in a particular manner. Whether the infringement for which the verdict and judgment passed consisted in the simple use of fat liquor in the treatment of leather, or in the use of the process specified, does not appear from the record. A recovery for an infringement of one claim of the patent is not of itself conclusive of an infringement of the other claim, and there was no extrinsic evidence offered to remove the uncertainty upon the record * * *. The verdict may have been for an infringement of the first claim; it may have been for an infringement of the second; it may have been for an infringement of both. The validity of the patent was not necessarily involved, except with respect to the claim which was the basis of the recovery. A patent may be valid as to a single claim and not valid as to the others. The record wants, therefore, that certainty which is essential to its operation as an estoppel, and does not conclude the defendants from contesting the infringement or the validity of the patent in this suit.

The record is not unlike a record in an action for money had and received to the plaintiff's use. It would be impossible to affirm from such a record, with certainty, for what moneys thus received the action was brought, without extrinsic evidence showing the fact; and, of course, without such evidence the verdict and judgment would conclude nothing, except as to the amount of indebtedness established.

* * *

Decree affirmed.

MR. JUSTICE CLIFFORD dissented.

Notes and Questions

1. Plaintiff brings an action against defendant for personal injuries arising out of a collision of their automobiles. Defendant answers, denying negligence and affirmatively pleading contributory negligence. Evidence is presented on both issues, and there is a general verdict for defendant. If defendant subsequently sues plaintiff for his own injuries arising out of the same accident, may defendant rely upon the first judgment as establishing any part of the case? See *Developments in the Law—Res Judicata*, 65 Harv.L.Rev. 818, 845–46 (1952).

2. In KELLEY v. CURTISS, 16 N.J. 265, 273, 108 A.2d 431, 435 (1954), the New Jersey Supreme Court said: "The case against [defendant] having been submitted to the jury with instructions that he was entitled to a verdict of no cause of action if the jury found either that he was not negligent or that [plaintiff]

was guilty of contributory negligence, the general verdict is to be considered as determining both grounds in [defendant's] favor." Is this holding consistent with Russell v. Place? If not, which case advances the better rule?

3. Should the principles embodied in *Russell* call for a different result if the jury in the first action makes specific findings of fact on each of the alternative grounds? What if the first action is a bench trial and the judge specifically discussed her findings on each of the alternative grounds? In MALLOY v. TROMBLEY, 50 N.Y.2d 46, 427 N.Y.S.2d 969, 405 N.E.2d 213 (1980), issue preclusion was allowed, even though the issue had been an alternative ground in the earlier action. The *Malloy* court's holding was based, in part, on the fact that the judge in the earlier action had provided a complete discussion of his holding on each ground. Compare O'Connor v. G & R Packing Co., 53 N.Y.2d 278, 440 N.Y.S.2d 920, 423 N.E.2d 397 (1981).

4. What should be the outcome if an appellate court, faced with alternative determinations by the trial court, affirms on only one ground? If conservation of judicial resources is the ultimate goal, why should anything short of reversal on appeal strip a conclusive determination of its preclusive effect? See generally Lucas, *The Direct and Collateral Estoppel Effects of Alternative Holdings,* 50 U.Chi.L.Rev. 701 (1983).

RIOS v. DAVIS

Court of Civil Appeals of Texas, Eastland, 1963.
373 S.W.2d 386.

COLLINGS, JUSTICE. Juan C. Rios brought this suit against Jessie Hubert Davis in the District Court to recover damages * * * alleged to have been sustained as a result of personal injuries received * * * in an automobile collision. Plaintiff alleged that his injuries were proximately caused by negligence on the part of the defendant. The defendant answered alleging that Rios was guilty of contributory negligence. Also, among other defenses, the defendant urged a plea of res judicata and collateral estoppel based upon the findings and the judgment entered * * * in a suit between the same parties in the County Court at Law of El Paso County. The plea of res judicata was sustained and judgment was entered in favor of the defendant * * *.

It is shown by the record that * * * Popular Dry Goods Company brought suit against appellee Davis * * * seeking to recover for damages to its truck in the sum of $443.97, alleged to have been sustained in the same collision here involved. Davis answered alleging contributory negligence on the part of Popular and joined appellant Juan C. Rios as a third party defendant and sought to recover from Rios $248.50, the alleged amount of damages to his automobile. The jury * * * found that Popular Dry Goods Company and Rios were guilty of negligence proximately causing the collision. However, the jury also found that Davis was guilty of negligence proximately causing the collision, and judgment was entered * * * denying Popular Dry Goods any recovery against Davis and denying Davis any recovery against Rios.

Appellant Rios in his third point contends that the District Court erred in sustaining appellee's plea of res judicata based upon the judgment of the County Court at Law because the findings on the issues regarding appellant's negligence and liability * * * were immaterial because the judgment entered in that case was in favor of appellant. We sustain this point. * * * The sole basis for the judgment * * * as between Rios and Davis was the findings concerning the negligence of Davis. The finding that Rios was negligent was not essential or material to the judgment and the judgment was not based thereon. On the contrary, the finding * * * that Rios was negligent proximately causing the accident would, if it had been controlling, led [sic] to a different result. Since the judgment was in favor of Rios he had no right or opportunity to complain of or to appeal from the finding that he was guilty of such negligence even if such finding had been without any support whatever in the evidence. The right of appeal is from a judgment and not from a finding. * * * In the case of Word v. Colley, Tex.Civ.App., 173 S.W. 629, at page 634 of its opinion (Error Ref.), the court stated as follows:

> It is the judgment, and not the verdict or the conclusions of fact, filed by a trial court which constitutes the estoppel, and a finding of fact by a jury or a court which does not become the basis or one of the grounds of the judgment rendered is not conclusive against either party to the suit.

* * *

The judgment is, therefore, reversed, and the cause is remanded.

Notes and Questions

1. The verdict in the earlier action in *Rios* reflects the consistent practice, utilized in some states, of submitting a case to the jury on "special issues." Does *Rios* suggest a reason why special verdicts should be used more often?

2. In *Russell,* there was no issue preclusion because the jury gave a general verdict. In *Rios,* even though the jury gave a special verdict, certain issues were not given preclusive effect because the outcome did not depend upon those findings. However, multiple findings have been found preclusive when the jury could not have arrived at the same judgment without each of those findings. See, e.g., Patterson v. Saunders, 194 Va. 607, 74 S.E.2d 204 (1953).

3. The court in *Rios* held that the judgment in the earlier case did not estop Rios from denying his own negligence. Should the earlier judgment estop Davis from denying his own negligence?

4. Suppose Davis had not cross-claimed against Rios, merely impleading the latter on a contingent claim for contribution; that Popular had then made a claim against Rios; that at trial Davis and Rios each had argued the other was solely negligent; and that the jury had found for Popular against both of them. In a subsequent suit by Rios against Davis, would the earlier finding that each had been negligent estop Rios from denying negligence? Compare Byrum v. Ames & Webb, Inc., 196 Va. 597, 85 S.E.2d 364 (1955) (no), with Stangle v. Chicago, R.I. & P.R. Co., 295 F.2d 789 (7th Cir.1961) (yes). In both of these cases, the parties in the later action had been named as codefendants by the plaintiff in the earlier action; should it make any difference if one of them had brought the other in by impleader? Should it make any difference if, in the earlier case, the jury had found one of them negligent, and the other not negligent?

Generally, a judgment does not act as collateral estoppel between coparties unless they are adversaries, and they are considered adversaries only if there is a claim for relief by one coparty against the other. The fact that their interests clash and that they are on opposite sides of every issue does not make them adversaries for this purpose in the absence of such a claim. But see Tuz v. Edward M. Chadbourne, Inc., 310 So.2d 8 (Fla.1975); Note 7, p. 1299, infra.

5. The court in *Rios* supports its view by noting that Rios could not appeal the finding of his negligence in the earlier action. See also *Restatement (Second), Judgments* § 28(1) (1982). Should the prevailing party in the earlier action be permitted in a later action to attack a finding that was necessary to the judgment in the earlier action? Such a situation will not be common, but did arise in an interesting case in Missouri. Plaintiff in the first action sued for partition of an alleged tenancy in common, but defendant answered with a general denial, which in effect disclaimed "all interest or title to the land in dispute." The court found on the basis of the evidence and the pleadings that plaintiff owned the land, and ordered that "plaintiff take nothing by his writ." Subsequently plaintiff sued to eject defendant, who revised his earlier position and answered that he had title to the land. In BARTLEY v. BARTLEY, 172 Mo. 208, 72 S.W. 521 (1903), the Supreme Court of Missouri held that the finding in the earlier case could not be attacked.

6. *Rios* should be compared with HOME OWNERS FEDERAL SAVINGS & LOAN ASSOCIATION v. NORTHWESTERN FIRE & MARINE INSURANCE CO., 354 Mass. 448, 238 N.E.2d 55 (1968), in which the majority opinion states, in what may well be dictum, that "certain findings not strictly essential to the final judgment in the prior action * * * may be relied upon if it is clear that the issues underlying them were treated as essential to the prior case by the court and the party to be bound." What advantages does this test have over the *Rios* approach? What disadvantages? Three of the seven justices dissented.

3. DEFINING AND CHARACTERIZING THE ISSUE

UNITED STATES v. MOSER, 266 U.S. 236, 45 S.Ct. 66, 69 L.Ed. 262 (1924). Moser was a captain when he retired from the Navy. In his first action, he won a ruling that service as a Naval Academy cadet during the Civil War constituted service during the war that entitled him to be retired with the rank and three-fourths of the sea pay of the next higher grade. Although the Court of Claims changed its mind about the interpretation of the pension statutes, he won his next two actions for later installments of his pay on the basis of res judicata. In his fourth action for still later installments, the Court of Claims ruled both that its initial interpretation of the statute had been correct and that in any event he was entitled to rely on res judicata. The Supreme Court affirmed solely on the res judicata ground:

> * * * The question expressly and definitely presented in this suit is the same as that definitely and actually litigated and adjudged in favor of the claimant in the three preceding suits, viz. whether he occupied the status of an officer who had served during the Civil War.

> The contention of the government seems to be that the doctrine of res judicata does not apply to questions of law; and, in a sense, that is true. It does not apply to unmixed questions of law. Where, for example, a court in deciding a case has enunciated a rule of law, the parties in a subsequent action upon a different demand are not estopped from insisting that the law is otherwise, merely because the parties are the same in both cases. But a *fact, question* or *right* distinctly adjudged in the original action cannot be disputed in a subsequent action, even though the

determination was reached upon an erroneous view or by an erroneous application of the law. That would be to affirm the principle in respect of the thing adjudged but, at the same time, deny it all efficacy by sustaining a challenge to the grounds upon which the judgment was based. * * *

Id. at 241–42, 45 S.Ct. at 67, 69 L.Ed. at 264.

COMMISSIONER OF INTERNAL REVENUE v. SUNNEN

Supreme Court of the United States, 1948.
333 U.S. 591, 68 S.Ct. 715, 92 L.Ed. 898.

Certiorari to the United States Circuit Court of Appeals for the Eighth Circuit.

Mr. Justice Murphy delivered the opinion of the Court.

[Under a series of agreements, a taxpayer had licensed a corporation, which he controlled, to use his patents in exchange for payment of a 10% royalty. At various times, the taxpayer assigned his interest in these agreements to his wife without consideration. Income from these agreements was reported on her income tax returns, and these taxes were paid. The Commissioner contended that the income was taxable to the taxpayer himself and a deficiency was assessed against him.]

* * * [T]he Tax Court held that, with one exception, all the royalties paid to the wife from 1937 to 1941 were part of the taxable income of the taxpayer. * * * The one exception concerned the royalties of $4,881.35 paid in 1937 under the 1928 agreement. In an earlier proceeding in 1935, the Board of Tax Appeals dealt with the taxpayer's income tax liability for the years 1929–1931; it concluded that he was not taxable on the royalties paid to his wife during those years under the 1928 license agreement. This prior determination by the Board caused the Tax Court to apply the principle of *res judicata* to bar a different result as to the royalties paid pursuant to the same agreement during 1937.

The Tax Court's decision was affirmed in part and reversed in part by the Eighth Circuit Court of Appeals. * * * Approval was given to the Tax Court's application of the *res judicata* doctrine to exclude from the taxpayer's income the $4,881.35 in royalties paid in 1937 under the 1928 agreement. But to the extent that the taxpayer had been held taxable on royalties paid to his wife during the taxable years of 1937–1941, the decision was reversed on the theory that such payments were not income to him. * * *

If the doctrine of *res judicata* is properly applicable so that all the royalty payments made during 1937–1941 are governed by the prior decision of the Board of Tax Appeals, the case may be disposed of without reaching the merits of the controversy. * * *

* * * [The concepts of res judicata and collateral estoppel] are applicable in the federal income tax field. Income taxes are levied on an annual basis. Each year is the origin of a new liability and of a separate cause of action. Thus if a claim of liability or non-liability relating to a particular tax year is litigated, a judgment on the merits is *res judicata* as to any subsequent proceeding involving the same claim and the same tax year. But if the later proceeding is concerned with a similar or unlike claim relating to a different

tax year, the prior judgment acts as a collateral estoppel only as to those matters in the second proceeding which were actually presented and determined in the first suit. Collateral estoppel operates, in other words, to relieve the government and the taxpayer of "redundant litigation of the identical question of the statute's application to the taxpayer's status." Tait v. Western Md. R. Co., 289 U.S. 620, 624, 53 S.Ct. 706, 707, 77 L.Ed. 1405.

But collateral estoppel is a doctrine capable of being applied so as to avoid an undue disparity in the impact of income tax liability. A taxpayer may secure a judicial determination of a particular tax matter, a matter which may recur without substantial variation for some years thereafter. But a subsequent modification of the significant facts or a change or development in the controlling legal principles may make that determination obsolete or erroneous, at least for future purposes. If such a determination is then perpetuated each succeeding year as to the taxpayer involved in the original litigation, he is accorded a tax treatment different from that given to other taxpayers of the same class. As a result, there are inequalities in the administration of the revenue laws, discriminatory distinctions in tax liability, and a fertile basis for litigious confusion. * * * Such consequences, however, are neither necessitated nor justified by the principle of collateral estoppel. That principle is designed to prevent repetitious lawsuits over matters which have once been decided and which have remained substantially static, factually and legally. It is not meant to create vested rights in decisions that have become obsolete or erroneous with time, thereby causing inequities among taxpayers.

And so where two cases involve income taxes in different taxable years, collateral estoppel must be used with its limitations carefully in mind so as to avoid injustice. It must be confined to situations where the matter raised in the second suit is identical in all respects with that decided in the first proceeding and where the controlling facts and applicable legal rules remain unchanged. * * * As demonstrated by Blair v. Commissioner, 300 U.S. 5, 9, 57 S.Ct. 330, 331, 81 L.Ed. 465, a judicial declaration intervening between the two proceedings may so change the legal atmosphere as to render the rule of collateral estoppel inapplicable. But the intervening decision need not necessarily be that of a state court, as it was in the Blair case. While such a state court decision may be considered as having changed the facts for federal tax litigation purposes, a modification or growth in legal principles as enunciated in intervening decisions of this Court may also effect a significant change in the situation. Tax inequality can result as readily from neglecting legal modulations by this Court as from disregarding factual changes wrought by state courts. In either event, the supervening decision cannot justly be ignored by blind reliance upon the rule of collateral estoppel. * * * It naturally follows that an interposed alteration in the pertinent statutory provisions or Treasury regulations can make the use of that rule unwarranted. * * *

Of course, where a question of fact essential to the judgment is actually litigated and determined in the first tax proceeding, the parties are bound by that determination in a subsequent proceeding even though the cause of action is different. * * * And if the very same facts and no others are involved in the second case, a case relating to a different tax year, the prior judgment will be conclusive as to the same legal issues which appear, assuming no intervening doctrinal change. But if the relevant facts in the two cases are separable, even though they be similar or identical, collateral estoppel does not govern the legal issues which recur in the second case. Thus the second proceeding may involve an instrument or transaction identical with, but in a form separable from, the one dealt with in the first proceeding. In that situation, a court is free in the second proceeding to make an independent examination of the legal matters at issue. It may then reach a different result or, if consistency in decision is considered just and desirable, reliance may be placed upon the ordinary rule of *stare decisis.* Before a party can invoke the collateral estoppel doctrine in these circumstances, the legal matter raised in the second proceeding must involve the same set of events or documents and the same bundle of legal principles that contributed to the rendering of the first judgment. * * *

It is readily apparent in this case that the royalty payments growing out of the license contracts which were not involved in the earlier action before the Board of Tax Appeals and which concerned different tax years are free from the effects of the collateral estoppel doctrine. That is true even though those contracts are identical in all important respects with the 1928 contract, the only one that was before the Board, and even though the issue as to those contracts is the same as that raised by the 1928 contract. * * *

A more difficult problem is posed as to the $4,881.35 in royalties paid to the taxpayer's wife in 1937 under the 1928 contract. Here there is complete identity of facts, issues and parties as between the earlier Board proceeding and the instant one. The Commissioner claims, however, that legal principles developed in various intervening decisions of this Court have made plain the error of the Board's conclusion in the earlier proceeding, thus creating a situation like that involved in Blair v. Commissioner, supra. * * *

The principles which have * * * been recognized and developed by * * * [Helvering v. Clifford, 309 U.S. 331, 60 S.Ct. 554, 84 L.Ed. 788 (1940), and Helvering v. Horst, 311 U.S. 112, 61 S.Ct. 144, 85 L.Ed. 75, 131 A.L.R. 655 (1940)] are directly applicable to the transfer of patent license contracts between members of the same family. They are guideposts for those who seek to determine in a particular instance whether such an assignor retains sufficient control over the assigned contracts or over the receipt of income by the assignee to make it fair to impose income tax liability on him.

Moreover, the clarification and growth of these principles through the Clifford–Horst line of cases constitute, in our opinion, a sufficient change in the legal climate to render inapplicable in the instant proceeding, the doctrine of collateral estoppel relative to the assignment of the 1928 contract. True, these cases did not originate the concept that an assignor is taxable if he retains control over the assigned property or power to defeat the receipt of income by the assignee. But they gave much added emphasis and substance to that concept, making it more suited to meet the "attenuated subtleties" created by taxpayers. So substantial was the amplification of this concept as to justify a reconsideration of earlier Tax Court decisions reached without the benefit of the expanded notions, decisions which are now sought to be perpetuated regardless of their present correctness. Thus in the earlier litigation in 1935, the Board of Tax Appeals was unable to bring to bear on the assignment of the 1928 contract the full breadth of the ideas enunciated in the Clifford–Horst series of cases. And, as we shall see, a proper application of the principles as there developed might well have produced a different result, such as was reached by the Tax Court in this case in regard to the assignments of the other contracts. Under those circumstances collateral estoppel should not have been used by the Tax Court in the instant proceeding to perpetuate the 1935 viewpoint of the assignment.

* * *

The judgment below must therefore be reversed and the case remanded for such further proceedings as may be necessary in light of this opinion.

Reversed.

MR. JUSTICE FRANKFURTER and MR. JUSTICE JACKSON believe the judgment of the Tax Court is based on substantial evidence and is consistent with the law, and would affirm that judgment * * *.

Notes and Questions

1. How might you reconcile *Sunnen* and *Moser*? Both opinions, in a sense, seek to determine if the subsequent suit concerns facts that are separable from those of the first suit. What is the proper test for this separability? Is it whether historically distinct facts are at issue? Is it whether the facts in the subsequent suit legally are indistinguishable from those of the earlier suit?

2. Is the outcome in the *Sunnen* case consistent with the underlying goals of res judicata? Doesn't its holding undermine the sense of reliance that judgments should foster? After all, if Sunnen had lost the first litigation, he probably would not have renewed the contract assigning income to his wife.

3. *Moser* held that "unmixed questions of law" are not subject to issue preclusion. More recently, however, the Supreme Court has recognized that "[a]dmittedly the purpose underlying the exception for 'unmixed questions of law' in successive actions on unrelated claims is far from clear." United States v. Stauffer Chem. Co., 464 U.S. 165, 172, 104 S.Ct. 575, 579, 78 L.Ed.2d 388, 394 (1984). Rather than engaging in the virtually impossible task of delineating the boundary between an issue of fact, law, or mixed fact and law, the Court adopted the more pragmatic approach suggested in *Restatement (Second), Judgments* § 28, comment b (1982):

> When the claims in two separate actions between the same parties are the same or are closely related * * * it is not ordinarily necessary to characterize an issue as one of fact or of law for purposes of issue preclusion. * * * In such a case, it is unfair to the winning party and an unnecessary burden on the courts to allow repeated litigation of the same issue in what is essentially the same controversy, even if the issue is regarded as one of "law."

4. As *Sunnen* and *Moser* illustrate, the careful "delineation" of questions of pure law, and their exemption from issue preclusion, may be important especially when the government is a party. "Decisions of law in cases involving [a public agency] generally have significance beyond their immediate impact * * *. [A] 'repeat' litigant, particularly the government, ordinarily should be free to relitigate a legal issue in subsequent litigation that could result in appeal to a higher level of authority in the legal system." Hazard, *Preclusion as to Issues of Law: The Legal System's Interest,* 70 Iowa L.Rev. 81, 92 (1984).

5. How does the preclusion of pure questions of law relate to the doctrine of *stare decisis*? See Buckley, *Issue Preclusion and Issues of Law: A Doctrinal*

Framework Based on Rules of Recognition, Jurisdiction, and Legal History, 24 Houston L.Rev. 875 (1987).

6. When a court makes a determination on a mixed question of law and fact, how should changes in the relevant substantive law influence whether preclusive effect is given to those determinations? The *Sunnen* opinion helps answer this question. When new historic facts are the basis of the second suit and there has been a change in legal regime since the prior suit was adjudicated, the first judgment will not preclude the second litigation. See, e.g., Spradling v. City of Tulsa, 198 F.3d 1219, 1223 (10th Cir.2000); Bingaman v. Department of the Treasury, 127 F.3d 1431, 1438 (Fed.Cir.1997).

In some situations it is easy to determine when this exception is invoked properly. When a new statute or new regulation has been enacted, or when a controlling Supreme Court precedent has been altered, the exception's application is indisputable. In other situations it is not so clear that a change in substantive law should prevent preclusion. Should preclusion be allowed if there is an inconsistent decision by the same court on similar facts?

7. The frequent changes in tax law arguably prevent any individual from developing much of a sense of repose in tax decisions, and there is a particularly urgent need to treat similarly situated taxpayers alike. These factors suggest that a narrow definition of "issue" may be appropriate in cases involving tax law. In tax, as in other areas, however, the policy considerations that underlie substantive law still must be balanced against the strong individual interests in repose and reliance that particular fact patterns may exhibit. See Webster, *The Limits of Collateral Estoppel in Tax Court Litigation,* 8 B.U.J. Tax Law 43 (1990).

SECURITIES EXCHANGE COMMISSION v. MONARCH FUNDING CORPORATION

United States Court of Appeals, Second Circuit, 1999.
192 F.3d 295.

MCLAUGHLIN, CIRCUIT JUDGE.

The question before us on this appeal, one of first impression, is whether findings made in a criminal sentencing proceeding may preclude relitigation of an issue in a subsequent civil case.

* * * The SEC originally filed this civil suit in September 1985 in the Southern District of New York * * * alleg[ing] that Bertoli and others violated Section 10(b) of the 1934 Act, Rule 10b–5, and Section 17(a)(1)-(3) of the 1933 Act in connection with his involvement in the activities of Monarch Funding Corporation ("Monarch"), a securities brokerage firm in New York City. The SEC sought disgorgement of Bertoli's ill-gotten gains and a permanent injunction enjoining Bertoli from future violations of those laws.

The civil action was placed on Judge Sand's suspense calendar pending the outcome of a related criminal prosecution in the United States District Court for the District of New Jersey. * * *

In the criminal action, Bertoli * * * faced a multiple count indictment. Of particular relevance to this appeal are Counts One and Two, charging Bertoli with RICO violations based on a pattern of racketeering activity involving, inter alia, predicate violations of Section 10(b) and Rule 10b–5. Also relevant to this appeal are Count Three, which charged Bertoli with conspiracy to obstruct justice in violation of 18 U.S.C. § 371, based on his attempts to obstruct the various civil, grand jury and criminal proceedings arising from his alleged fraud, and Count Six accusing him of obstructing justice in violation of 18 U.S.C. §§ 1502 and 1503 by moving certain proceeds of his racketeering activities from the Cayman Islands to the principality of Andorra in Europe.

* * * Following a three-month trial, Bertoli was convicted of the obstruction of justice charges contained in Counts Three and Six. He was acquitted, however, on all other charges, including Counts One and Two, which charged the predicate securities fraud violations.

A. The Original Sentencing

Following Bertoli's conviction, the parties engaged in extensive litigation over various post-trial and sentencing issues. On March 28, 1994, Judge Lechner sentenced Bertoli, issuing a 189 page opinion two days later to, inter alia, "clarify and amplify the rulings made during ... sentencing." United States v. Bertoli, 854 F. Supp. 975, 1164 (D.N.J.1994) ("Bertoli I").

* * * Judge Lechner [calculated] Bertoli's sentence, using the 1993 version of the United States Sentencing Guidelines and accompanying Commentary. Specifically, Judge Lechner applied § 2J1.2, the Guideline applicable to obstruction of justice. That provision provides in pertinent part that: "[i]f the offense involved obstructing the investigation or prosecution of a criminal offense, apply § 2X3.1...." Section 2X3.1, in turn, provides that the offense level is to be calculated on the basis of the criminal conduct underlying the investigation obstructed by the defendant. And, according to Judge Lechner, § 2X3.1 applied even if the defendant was not actually convicted of that underlying criminal conduct. See Bertoli I, 854 F. Supp. at 1144–46. * * *

Judge Lechner found that the underlying criminal conduct that Bertoli had attempted to conceal was securities fraud—specifically, Bertoli's orchestration of what Judge Lechner termed the "Stock Manipulation Schemes."

* * * Judge Lechner sentenced Bertoli to two 100–month concurrent prison terms and three years supervised release. Judge Lechner also imposed, without explanation, a special condition of supervised release barring Bertoli from associating with any person involved in the securities industry.

On appeal, the Third Circuit affirmed Bertoli's conviction but vacated his sentence. See United States v. Bertoli, 40 F.3d 1384, 1401–11 (3d Cir.1994) ("Bertoli II"). The Third Circuit determined that by using the 1993 version of the Guidelines and Commentary, Judge Lechner imposed a sentence in excess of what was permissible under the 1989 version applicable to Bertoli's conduct, thereby violating his right against ex post facto punishment. See Bertoli II, 40 F.3d at 1407.

B. The Resentencing

On remand, the government moved for an enhancement of Bertoli's sentence under Guideline § 2J1.2(b)(2), which Judge Lechner had been prevented from applying at the original sentencing because he had chosen to apply the mutually exclusive § 2X3.1 provision. Section 2J1.2(b)(2) allows for a three-level increase for obstruction of justice convictions if the offense "resulted in substantial interference with the administration of justice." After holding a hearing, Judge Lechner issued an opinion expressly incorporating by reference his factual findings from Bertoli I. See United States v. Bertoli, 89 Cr. 218 (D.N.J. March 22, 1995) ("Bertoli III").

In the second opinion, Judge Lechner found that Bertoli moved assets, induced an important witness to evade service of process, filed false affidavits, and shredded documents, all in an effort to interfere with the government's investigation into Monarch's activities. * * * These activities were, according to Judge Lechner, "critical components of Bertoli's eight year conspiracy to cover up and conceal his illegal fraudulent trading schemes." Id. at 19.

Based on these findings, Judge Lechner concluded that Bertoli had substantially interfered with justice. * * * Imposing the § 2J1.2(b)(2) enhancement[s] * * * [he] sentenced Bertoli to 78 months. In addition, Judge Lechner re-imposed, again without explanation, the special condition of supervised release forbidding Bertoli from associating with any person involved in the securities industry.

The Third Circuit affirmed Bertoli's resentencing by summary order.

C. Judge Sand's Summary Judgment Rulings

* * * Following Bertoli's resentencing, the SEC moved for summary judgment in the pending civil action, arguing that Bertoli should be collaterally estopped by virtue of Judge Lechner's sentencing findings from denying that he violated the federal securities laws. * * *

* * * Bertoli responded by arguing that: (1) sentencing findings should never be given preclusive effect in subsequent civil litigation; and (2) even if they could, applying collateral estoppel in this case would be inappropriate.

* * * Judge Sand rejected Bertoli's arguments for a per se rule. See S.E.C. v. Monarch Funding Corp., 983 F. Supp. 442, 448 (S.D.N.Y.1997) ("Monarch II"). The court recognized the "potential dangers underlying the extension of collateral estoppel to sentencing findings." Id. at 447. Judge Sand reasoned, however, that such dangers should not be dispositive so long as, after "close scrutiny" of the sentencing proceeding, it is clear that the "traditional safeguards" of the collateral estoppel doctrine as set forth by the Supreme Court and by this Court have been met. Id. at 446 (citing Parklane Hosiery Co. v. Shore, 439 U.S. 322, 58 L. Ed. 2d 552, 99 S. Ct. 645 (1979), and Gelb v. Royal Globe Ins. Co., 798 F.2d 38 (2d Cir.1986)).

Applying these traditional safeguards, the district court rejected Bertoli's contention that he had been deprived of an adequate opportunity to litigate his securities fraud liability at sentencing. While acknowledging that the typical sentencing proceeding may afford inadequate procedural opportunities for purposes of collateral estoppel, Judge Sand found that the Bertoli sentencing was "anything but a garden-variety sentencing." * * * [983 F. Supp.] at 458. In the nearly two-year period between Bertoli's conviction and his ultimate sentencing, the parties made voluminous submissions and participated in at least two hearings. See id. at 449–50.

* * *

Based on this analysis, Judge Sand reaffirmed his original determination that: (1) Bertoli was collaterally estopped by Judge Lechner's sentencing findings from denying liability under Section 10(b), Rule 10b–5, and Section 17(a) of the securities laws; and (2) the SEC was entitled to a permanent injunction enjoining Bertoli from future violations of those laws. * * * A final judgment was entered and Bertoli now appeals.

DISCUSSION

* * *

A. Application of Collateral Estoppel to Sentencing Findings

As the district court acknowledged, the application of collateral estoppel to sentencing findings presents a novel issue. While a few cases have brushed against the question, they have done so without much elaboration leaving the darkness unobscured. * * *

Not surprisingly, the parties disagree on how this nettlesome issue should be resolved. For its part, the SEC assumes that collateral estoppel should, at the very least, be presumptively available in the sentencing context so long as the traditional safeguards of the doctrine are met. On the other hand, Bertoli and the various amici assert that sentencing findings should never be given preclusive effect. We chart a middle course.

* * *

First, a plenary civil trial affords a defendant procedural opportunities that are unavailable at sentencing and that could command a different result. Unlike a civil litigant, a criminal defendant's opportunities to take discovery may be limited for sentencing purposes. * * * Although whenever a factor important to sentencing is reasonably in dispute, a defendant must be given an adequate opportunity to present information on that factor, see U.S.S.G. § 6A1.3(a), a defendant has no absolute right either to present his own witnesses or to receive a full-blown evidentiary hearing. See United States v. Prescott, 920 F.2d 139, 143 (2d Cir.1990). Moreover, the evidence admissible against a civil litigant must survive challenge under the Federal Rules of Evidence. By contrast, a sentencing judge "is largely unlimited either as to the kind of information [he] may consider, or the source from which it may come," United States v. Sisti, 91 F.3d 305, 312 (2d Cir.1996) (internal quotation marks omitted) (alteration in original), so long as the information has sufficient indicia of reliability to support its probable accuracy, see U.S.S.G. § 6A1.3(a).

Second, the incentive to litigate a sentencing finding is frequently less intense, and certainly more fraught with risk, than it would be for a full-blown civil trial. As Judge Sand acknowledged, a criminal defendant will often choose not to challenge sensitive issues during sentencing for any number of reasons, including a belief, or at least a hope, that the sentencing court will grant a prosecutorial downward departure motion or other recommendation. In addition, sometimes sentencing procedures may deter a defendant from raising certain issues. See Monarch II, 983 F. Supp. at 448. For instance, given that a sentencing judge may make a finding based on evidence inadmissible in a civil trial without even giving the defendant an evidentiary hearing to challenge that evidence, see Prescott, * * * a defendant may choose to let sleeping dogs lie. Finally, a defendant, though uniquely knowledgeable about underlying events, may be reluctant to testify during sentencing. Again, there are a number of reasons for such reticence—not the least of which is that if the defendant is disbelieved, his sentence may be enhanced under Guideline § 3C1.1.

In light of these legitimate concerns over potential unfairness, it is important to reflect upon whether the efficiency rationale for collateral estoppel would be advanced or hindered, were the doctrine to be freely available in the sentencing context. * * * In our view, several considerations suggest that, despite its theoretical economies, applying collateral estoppel in the sentencing context will just as often multiply, rather than reduce, total litigation.

First, where a civil action is pending or just beyond the horizon, allowing sentencing findings to earn collateral estoppel respect may greatly increase the stakes at sentencing, producing more exhaustive litigation over matters of only tangential importance to the criminal case. This risk is exacerbated by the procedural looseness of sentencing litigation. There is virtually no limit on the extent and character of the evidence that the government may seek to introduce at sentencing. See Sisti, 91 F.3d at 312. Even if the sentencing judge is able to fend off all attempts to introduce gratuitous material, the additional burdens that such an approach would impose on our already over-worked district courts would change the essential nature of sentencing pro-ceedings. They are not supposed to be "mini-trials." United States v. Pugliese, 805 F.2d 1117, 1123 (2d Cir.1986) * * *.

Second, while a permissive approach to collateral estoppel will probably lead to sentencing proceedings of mushrooming complexity, ironically, there is no guarantee that subsequent civil actions will be made proportionately simpler. As Judge Sand acknowledged, the concerns of unfairness raised by Bertoli require a more cautious approach in the civil case—in his words a "close scrutiny" and "searching examination"—than would be otherwise necessary. See Monarch II, 983 F. Supp. at 446, 448.

* * *

While extending collateral estoppel effect to sentencing findings may, in a given case, threaten fairness and/or judicial efficiency, these factors do not justify the blanket prohibition urged by Bertoli. Generally speaking, the same concerns of unfairness and inefficiency were considered by the Parklane Court and were rejected as justifications for a total ban on the use of offensive collateral estoppel. See 439 U.S. at 330–31, 99 S.Ct. at 645. Instead, the Court held that "the preferable approach" is to entrust the task of minimizing such dangers to the discretion of our district courts. Id. at 331. * * * So long as the threat to fairness and/or efficiency has been minimized, we see no need to entirely foreclose application of the doctrine. Indeed, precluding relitigation of findings made during sentencing may promote an institutional goal of particu-lar importance to the criminal process, namely, "preserv[ing] the integrity of the judicial system by eliminating inconsistent results." Johnson, 101 F.3d at 795; see 18 Federal Practice and Procedure § 4416, at 139 (1981) ("preclusion prevents the risk of the clearest and most embarrassing inconsistencies"). For these reasons, we reject the per se rule urged by Bertoli and the amici.

On the other hand, we cannot accept the SEC's position that collateral estoppel should presumptively extend to sentencing findings on the same basis as in other contexts. To the contrary, we conclude that precluding relitigation on the basis of such findings should be presumed improper. While we do not foreclose application of the doctrine in all sentencing cases, we caution that it should be applied only in those circumstances where it is clearly fair and efficient to do so. And the burden should be on the plaintiff in the civil case to prove these elements.

B. The Instant Case

In this case, the SEC has failed to show that preclusion was fair, as that concept is refined in Gelb. See 798 F.2d at 44–45. In addition, the record reveals that application of collateral estoppel here was simply not efficient. For these reasons, we conclude that Judge Sand erred in precluding Bertoli from litigating his securities fraud liability afresh.

As noted above, to minimize the potential unfairness caused by applying collateral estoppel to a finding that may be wrong, it is essential that the finding have been "necessary" to the judgment in the first action. See id. As explained by Judge Learned Hand, the necessity requirement "protects" against unfairness, by ensuring that the issue will be "really disputed and that the loser will have put out his best efforts." The Evergreens v. Nunan, 141 F.2d 927, 929 (2d Cir.1944).

We recognize that in other contexts there is authority for relaxing the necessity requirement. * * * However, given the potential for unfairness associated with applying collateral estoppel based on sentencing findings, we hold that only the stricter approach remains appropriate in the sentencing context. Hence, regardless of how carefully considered an issue may have been during the process leading up to decision, and regardless of what may be inferred from that decision, estoppel does not apply to a finding that was not legally necessary to the final sentence. See 18 Charles Alan Wright, Arthur R. Miller & Edward H. Cooper, Federal Practice and Procedure § 4421, at 196 (1981).

* * *

And in this case, it was not legally necessary for Judge Lechner to find that Bertoli committed securities fraud to impose the § 2J1.2(b)(2) enhancement. It is true that in Bertoli I Judge Lechner found that Bertoli committed securities fraud by orchestrating the Stock Manipulation Schemes, and that that finding was expressly incorporated by reference into the Bertoli III decision. It is also true that in Bertoli III, Judge Lechner found that Bertoli "substantially interfered with the administration of justice" under § 2J1.2(b)(2), to "cover up" his securities fraud. This does not mean, however, that it is legally necessary for a defendant to be found guilty of securities fraud to impose the § 2J1.2(b)(2) enhancement. * * *

* * *

To have violated Section 10(b) and Rule 10b–5, Bertoli must have: (1) made a material misrepresentation or a material omission as to which he had a duty to speak, or used a fraudulent device; (2) with scienter; (3) in connection with the purchase or sale of securities. * * * Essentially the same elements are required under Section 17(a)(1)-(3) in connection with the offer or sale of a security, though no showing of scienter is required for the SEC to obtain an injunction under subsections (a)(2) or (a)(3). * * *

While Judge Lechner's findings regarding Bertoli's various obstructive acts may have been necessary to the § 2J1.2(b)(2) enhancement, contrary to Judge Sand's conclusion, none of those findings establish the elements of securities fraud. * * *

We also reject * * * the SEC's contention that the securities fraud findings were necessary to the special condition of Bertoli's release that he not associate with any persons involved in the securities industry.

* * *

For a finding to merit estoppel effect it must not only be necessary to the final judgment, but must also have been actually litigated and actually decided in the initial action. * * * A corollary of the actual litigation and decision requirements is that "[w]hen a court cannot ascertain what was litigated and decided, issue preclusion cannot operate." 18 James W. Moore et al., Moore's Federal Practice, § 132.03[2][g] (3d ed. 1998) * * *.

In light of these principles, we need not address the potentially far reaching issue of whether it was necessary for Judge Lechner to find that Bertoli committed securities fraud before imposing the special condition. Throughout sentencing proceedings, the special condition of supervised release received little attention from either the parties or the court. * * *

Moreover, Judge Lechner never specifically ruled that he was banning Bertoli from the securities industry because Bertoli had violated the securities laws. * * * After all, Bertoli was convicted of obstruction of justice, not securities fraud, and it is possible that Judge Lechner imposed the ban on the basis of the obstruction of justice alone. * * * In light of the fact that Bertoli's conviction for obstruction of justice arose from his interference with investigations focusing on securities fraud, Judge Lechner may have believed that banning him from the securities industry was "reasonably necessary to protect the public," * * * even if Bertoli himself had not committed securities fraud, simply because he had obstructed the government's efforts to police that industry. * * * [I]n the absence of clarity on this issue, applying collateral estoppel on the basis of the special condition would be improper. * * *

In sum, application of collateral estoppel in this case failed to satisfy the prerequisites to preclusion that are designed to ensure fairness.

In addition, we conclude that precluding relitigation in this case failed to promote the primary rationale for collateral estoppel, namely: judicial economy. The sentencing proceedings in the criminal action were exhaustive. * * * [T]here was a high degree of cooperation between the SEC and the New Jersey United States Attorney's Office in the criminal action. Given that cooperation, we cannot say that the criminal action was not complicated by efforts to have express findings made on tangential issues at sentencing in order to give the SEC a chance to invoke collateral estoppel in the subsequent civil action. More importantly, however, collateral estoppel did not do much to simplify the civil action. Even discounting the added complexities associated with the novelty of the issue, the district court's "close scrutiny" and "searching examination" in this case required considerable effort—in all probability more effort than would have been required for a summary adjudication under Federal Rule of Civil Procedure 56(c), or even for a trial. In light of such efforts, it made little sense to bar Bertoli from litigating his securities fraud liability *ab initio*. * * *

We raise this point to make clear that in determining whether to apply collateral estoppel to sentencing findings in the future, district courts should start by making a threshold assessment of whether it will be efficient to do so. Given the potential unfairness associated with extending collateral estoppel to sentencing findings generally, if the court reasonably determines that the doctrine will not promote efficiency, it should feel free to deny preclusion for that reason alone.

* * *

The decision of the district court granting summary judgment based on the doctrine of offensive collateral estoppel is vacated. * * *

THE EVERGREENS DOCTRINE. In addition to limiting collateral estoppel to identical issues, courts sometimes have distinguished between "ultimate" and "mediate" facts when determining whether issues decided in one suit will be viewed as preclusive in a later one. The most influential explanation of this distinction is found in Judge Learned Hand's opinion in THE EVERGREENS v. NUNAN, 141 F.2d 927 (2d Cir.), certiorari denied 323 U.S. 720, 65 S.Ct. 49, 89 L.Ed. 579 (1944). The gist of the doctrine is simple. Imagine a lawsuit as a logical structure resembling a pyramid. At its base are the facts introduced into evidence. From these facts are drawn conclusions that, when combined with other deductions or evidence, lead eventually to "ultimate facts" that establish a legal right, duty, or status. The ultimate facts are the summit of the structure; all that supports them are "mediate data." *The Evergreens* held that only matters constituting ultimate facts in the second action are subject to being precluded by collateral estoppel.

The controversy in *The Evergreens* turned on the value for tax purposes of cemetery lots appropriated by the City of New York. The lots were of two kinds, improved and unimproved. An earlier proceeding had determined the value of the improved lots, and that determination was accepted in the later action without dispute. The earlier proceeding also had fixed the cost of upgrading the unimproved lots to "improved" status. The plaintiff maintained that these two findings taken together should determine the value of the unimproved lots: the uncontested value of the improved lots minus the cost of improving them should be taken as the value of the unimproved lots.

The Second Circuit rejected this argument, relying on the distinction between ultimate and mediate facts. Judge Hand first noted that authorities differed concerning whether mediate facts or only ultimate facts in the first suit are decided conclusively by the judgment. The question presented, however, was whether a determination, either mediate or ultimate in the first suit, could establish a mediate fact in the second suit. On this question, authority was silent; Judge Hand decided that collateral estoppel could not be used.

This determination was based on the notion that the conclusion that would result if estoppel were to apply might be both unintended and unjust because the deductions that may be drawn from a given fact are unpredictable. Restricting the use of collateral estoppel to ultimate issues in the second suit attempts to ensure that the consequences of issues decided by the first judgment plainly are visible when that judgment was entered.

What jural relevance facts may acquire in the future it is often impossible even remotely to anticipate. Were the law to be recast, it would therefore be a pertinent inquiry whether the conclusiveness * * * might not properly be limited to future controversies which could be thought reasonably in prospect when the first suit was tried. That is, of course, not the law as it stands * * *.

Id. at 929.

Notes and Questions

1. The "law as it stands" has changed since the *Evergreens* decision. Many jurisdictions now acknowledge the policies outlined in the opinion, but not necessarily the technical separation of mediate from ultimate facts. Commentators criticize this mediate and ultimate fact terminology as difficult to understand and even more difficult to apply. See Heckman, *Collateral Estoppel as the Answer to Multiple Litigation Problems in Federal Tax Law: Another View of Sunnen and The Evergreens,* 19 Case W.Res.L.Rev. 230 (1967); Polasky, *Collateral Estoppel— Effects of Prior Litigation,* 39 Iowa L.Rev. 217 (1954). Some courts have been considerably more critical, rejecting *The Evergreens'* analysis as inconsistent with the purposes of collateral estoppel:

[Criticism of *The Evergreens* rule] is based primarily upon the difficulty in administering a distinction between ultimate and mediate facts, and the lack of correspondence of such a distinction to any intelligible reasons for limiting preclusion. * * *

[E]ven though a fact may be regarded in theory as less than an ultimate fact, the parties may have expended great effort in proving whether or not that fact existed, and the fact may even have been regarded by everyone involved in the litigation as the key issue in a dispute. In these circumstances, * * * the rule is at odds with the purposes of the doctrine of issue preclusion: the conservation of judicial resources and the fostering of reliance on prior judicial action by minimizing the possibility of inconsistent decisions and by protecting a prevailing party from vexatious litigation. * * *

On this basis, many courts * * * have ignored the *Evergreens* rule, and they have measured the scope of preclusion, not by a distinction between ultimate and mediate facts, but rather by focusing more directly on the quality and extensiveness of litigation in the first action. For that reason too, the *Restatement (Second) of Judgments* § 27 comment j has rejected the distinction between ultimate and evidentiary facts, instead according preclusive effect to determinations that are essential or necessary to the judgment.

* * *

Accordingly, we hold, following the Restatement, that preclusive effect may be accorded to a decision on an issue if that issue was "actually recognized by the parties as important and by the trier of fact as necessary to the first judgment." *Restatement (Second) of Judgments* § 27 comment j.

SYNANON CHURCH v. UNITED STATES, 820 F.2d 421, 426–27 (D.C.Cir.1987).

2. A second part of Judge Hand's analysis in *The Evergreens*—which looks to the role that the issue will play in the second litigation—seems to embody legitimate concerns, but they have been well concealed in Judge Hand's formula-

tion. The following excerpt may help cast some light on the purposes that underlie *The Evergreens* rule:

> The valid core of the Evergreens rule might be preserved by expanding the requirement that the first action afford a full and fair opportunity to litigate the common issue. Substantial changes in the legal context or the consequences of the issue, particularly, could support the conclusion that the initial opportunity was not sufficient to support preclusion. It would be more difficult to consider the need to retry related issues on substantially the same evidence through the full and fair opportunity test. Reliance on the full and fair opportunity test would also work against relitigation because of a common reluctance to challenge directly the adequacy of a prior action. Wise administration of the full and fair opportunity test can go far; it may not go far enough.

> In the end, the question can be simply put. There are strong reasons to adopt a general rule that issue preclusion is defeated by substantial changes in the legal context in which the issue arises, by substantial changes in the consequences it may entail, or by the need to retry related issues. A general rule framed in these terms would force attention to the real sources of concern. It seems likely that such a general rule would not defeat issue preclusion in any substantial portion of the cases that satisfy all of the other requirements. Even when the result is to deny preclusion, there may be little injury to the values generally served by preclusion. Nonetheless, the price might prove too high. Federal courts have not yet spun any such rule out of the Evergreens decision, and any proof of its value must await the effort and the experience.

18 Wright, Miller & Cooper, *Federal Practice and Procedure: Jurisdiction and Related Matters* § 4424, at 242 (1981).

SECTION D. THE REQUIRED QUALITY OF JUDGMENT

Only judgments of a certain quality will give rise to preclusion. For the most part, this Chapter's discussion of preclusion doctrine has assumed that the prior judgment satisfied that requirement. It will now be examined in greater detail.

The traditional words used to describe a judgment of sufficient quality to create preclusion is that the judgment must be valid, final, and on the merits. These terms are not unambiguous, however; indeed, they are somewhat misleading. Courts often enter judgments that are considered "on the merits," despite the fact that the judgment resulted from less than a full adjudicatory proceeding. In addition, courts increasingly are faced with the prior determinations of state or federal administrative agencies that act in a quasi-judicial capacity. This Section is designed to highlight some of the difficult questions the "quality of judgment" requirement raises.

1. JUDGMENTS OF JUDICIAL TRIBUNALS

HANOVER LOGANSPORT, INC. v.
ROBERT C. ANDERSON, INC.

Court of Appeals of Indiana, Third District, 1987.
512 N.E.2d 465.

[Hanover Logansport, Inc. ("Hanover") and Robert C. Anderson, Inc. ("Anderson") entered into a lease agreement pursuant to which Hanover agreed to lease certain property to Anderson for use as a liquor store. Hanover failed to deliver the premises on the agreed upon date, and Anderson filed suit for breach of the lease. Before trial, Hanover offered to deliver the real estate to Anderson, and Anderson accepted with the following reservation: "[T]he offer is only accepted for purposes of mitigation of damages and not in settlement of damages arising to Plaintiff caused by Defendants' breach of contract."

The parties filed a stipulation that "the judgment as stipulated to by the Defendants herein should be recorded of record in the judgment record book of the County of St. Joseph." Anderson took possession of the premises, and, after several months, Hanover filed a motion to dismiss the earlier breach action. The trial court denied the motion, and Hanover appealed, arguing that the prior consent judgment precluded any further litigation based on the same cause of action.]

STATON, JUDGE.

* * *

Hanover makes the following argument:

1. The complaint seeks specific performance of the lease or *in the alternative* money damages for loss of profits *over the term of the lease.*

2. Hanover made an offer of real estate pursuant to [Indiana Trial Rule 68] consistent with one of the alternatives—specific performance—in the complaint.[a]

3. Anderson accepted the offer.

4. Under T.R. 68, the clerk is required to enter judgment.

5. Anderson took possession of the real estate.

6. By accepting the offer of real estate and taking possession of the premises, Anderson chose its remedy and is now barred by law from continuing the litigation.

Anderson argues that (1) an offer of judgment under T.R. 68 may be in part or in whole; and (2) both Hanover and the trial court were on notice that the offer of judgment did not address and dispose of the whole of its claim. Anderson points to the portion of its acceptance which states: " * * * Further, the offer is only accepted for purposes of mitigation of damages and not in settlement of damages arising to Plaintiff caused by Defendants' breach of

a. Indiana Rules of Procedure, Trial Rule 68, is similar to Federal Rule 68, and is set out in the Supplement.

contract." In its brief, Anderson states: "The acceptance of said offer specifically states that the lease between the parties would be as contracted, subject to the conditions in the lease, but that the Plaintiff did not waive damages for breach of contract which arose due to the failure of Defendant to honor its contract *between the date the offer was signed and the date the Court entered an Order approving the settlment [sic] as to possession.'* " (Emphasis added.)

Thus, we address the following issue: Whether, by law, a plaintiff, who accepts an offer of judgment which conforms to one of the alternative prayers for relief contained in his complaint, may then seek additional damages arising from the same cause of action.

* * *

A consent judgment has a dual aspect. It represents an agreement between the parties settling the underlying dispute and providing for the entry of judgment in a pending or contemplated action. See James, Consent Judgments as Collateral Estoppel, 108 U.Pa.L.Rev. 173, 175 (1959). It also represents the entry of such a judgment by a court—with all that this means in the way of committing the force of society to implement the judgment of its courts. Id.

As a result of this dual aspect, some courts and commentators focus on the contractual aspect of a consent judgment, thus determining whatever its preclusive effect may be by ascertaining the intent of the parties—in the same way courts construe other agreements. * * *

Yet, other courts and commentators focus on the entry of a consent judgment by a court and argue that such a judgment possesses the same force with regard to *res judicata* and collateral estoppel as a judgment entered after a trial on the merits. * * *

Proponents of the consent-judgment-as-contract theory argue that if consent judgments are given preclusive effect regardless of the intent of the parties, such a rule would lessen the chance of compromise between them. This, they argue, is true for two reasons. First, in many cases, the application of such a rule (at least in regard to the collateral estoppel aspect of the rule) would be unforeseeable—it would reach into all possible future disputes among the parties, no matter how hard it may be to predict them at the outset of the first litigation. Second, if all issues and claims must be negotiated and dealt with in a consent judgment or foregone forever, parties will be reluctant to enter into such an agreement for fear that they will "miss" something.

But, proponents of the consent-judgment-as-final judgment theory counter that the preclusive effect of a consent judgment serves several objectives. Among them, economy is achieved in the use of judicial resources, the harassment of parties avoided, and the possibility of inconsistent results is eliminated. * * *

* * *

We note that T.R. 68 is intended to encourage settlements, discourage vexatious suits, and avoid protracted litigation. See 12 Wright & Miller, *Federal Practice and Procedure,* § 3001. Therefore, the result we reach should serve those purposes.

Because we agree that if all issues and claims must be negotiated and dealt with in a consent judgment or foregone forever, parties will be reluctant to enter into such agreements, we adopt the consent-judgment-as-contract theory and hold that the preclusive effect of a consent judgment must be measured by the intent of the parties. However, it must be clear that *both* parties have agreed to reserve an issue or claim. *And,* it must be precisely stated what issues or claims are being reserved.

* * *

[I]n order to insure that both parties have agreed to reserve a claim or issue[9] and that the reserved claim or issue is clearly apparent to both parties, we hold that (1) the reservation must be incorporated into the offer of judgment itself and (2) it must be an inherent part of the original complaint. Thus, for example, before a party may reserve an additional cause of action in a consent judgment, that cause of action must have been originally set out on the face of the complaint. Because Anderson did not include a claim for damages for delay in tendering the real estate in its Complaint, it is precluded from reserving such a claim in the consent judgment.[10]

* * *

[T]his rule will avoid protracted litigation, since it requires plaintiffs to reserve a claim or issue both in the complaint and in the consent judgment. If we were to require such a reservation only in the consent judgment (as Anderson asks us to do here), the potential for protracted litigation would be too great. For example, in a situation where A and B have entered a consent judgment and B thinks the controversy has ended, such a rule would allow A: (1) to argue that it had no intention of ending the controversy and (2) to proceed on the alleged balance of its claim. This could potentially allow the litigation to continue on and on through the years.

But, under the rule we have set forth here, A would not be allowed to make such a claim unless it was shown that a reservation was made in A's complaint and in the consent judgment. In this way, courts can be assured it was also B's intention to continue the litigation.

Therefore, we reverse and remand to the trial court, with instructions to enter a judgment on the offer of judgment and to grant Hanover's motion to dismiss.

Reversed and remanded.

9. Here, we are dealing with the reservation of a claim for damages. However, there may be cases where a party desires to reserve an issue or another cause of action. The same rule would apply in those situations.

10. Indiana Rules of Procedure, Trial Rule 12(B) states, in part:

"* * * When a motion to dismiss is sustained for failure to state a claim under subdivision (B)(6) of this rule the pleading may be amended once as of right pursuant to Rule 15(A) within ten [10] days after service of notice of the court's order sustaining the motion and thereafter with permission of the court pursuant to such rule. * * * "

However, Anderson may not take advantage of this rule by amending the complaint, then arguing it has met the requirements set out by this opinion. Obviously, the claim or issue must be in the complaint at the time the parties reach an agreement and enter a consent judgment.

Notes and Questions

1. Should the agreement between Hanover and Anderson be considered a court judgment, or is it more properly characterized as a contract? If it is merely a contract, should the intent of the parties as to its preclusive effect be dispositive? Did the parties require the approval of the court in the form of a judgment to make a new contract?

2. Do you agree that a rule that did not make the intent of the parties dispositive would have the effect of discouraging consent judgments?

3. Most courts agree that consent judgments should be claim preclusive, but they differ on the issue preclusive, effect such judgments should receive. Judge Staton seemed to assume that if a consent judgment was afforded res judicata effect it would also automatically be conclusive as to all facts that were necessarily in issue in the first action. Is this a valid assumption given the "actually litigated" requirement for issue preclusion? Consider the court's comments in AMERICAN MUTUAL LIABILITY INSURANCE CO. v. MICHIGAN MUTUAL LIABILITY CO., 64 Mich.App. 315, 235 N.W.2d 769 (1975):

> [C]ollateral estoppel rules do not require that a consent judgment bind a party to facts which were originally in issue in the action that was settled. A consent judgment reflects primarily the agreement of the parties. * * * The parties have not litigated the matters put in issue, they have settled. The trial judge has not determined the matters put in issue, he has merely put his stamp of approval on the parties' agreement disposing of those matters. But a judgment can be given collateral estoppel effect only as to those issues which were actually and necessarily adjudicated. * * * It follows that because the issues involved in the settled case were not actually adjudicated, one of the prerequisites to giving a judgment collateral estoppel effect is not satisfied.

Id. at 327, 235 N.W.2d at 776.

The *American Mutual* court stated in a footnote that collateral estoppel would apply if the parties' intention to bind themselves on certain issues of fact was reflected in the consent judgment. Compare this with the approach in *Hanover*, which held that collateral estoppel would apply unless the parties made clear their intention *not to be bound*. Which approach better furthers the goals underlying preclusion?

4. Should a final judgment be stripped of its preclusive effect if both parties consent to that result on appeal? A stipulated reversal allows parties seeking to facilitate settlement during the pendency of an appeal to join in asking the appellate court to set aside a trial court judgment, rather than dismissing the appeal, thereby avoiding the preclusive effect of a final judgment. The California Supreme Court had an opportunity to rule on the permissibility of that effect in NEARY v. REGENTS OF UNIVERSITY OF CALIFORNIA, 3 Cal.4th 273, 10 Cal.Rptr.2d 859, 834 P.2d 119 (1992), in which the plaintiff obtained a jury verdict of $7 million against defendants. Both parties appealed, and while the appeals were pending, the parties agreed to settle. The parties then filed a joint application to the California Court of Appeal asking it to reverse the trial court's judgment and remand the case for dismissal with prejudice. The Court of Appeal denied the request, but the California Supreme Court reversed, holding that stipulated reversals are consistent with the policy in favor of peaceful settlements and should be granted absent a showing of extraordinary circumstances warranting an exception to this general rule.

What did the court mean by "extraordinary circumstances" that might justify an exception to a rule allowing peaceful resolution of a dispute between two parties? One concern is that an overly broad policy of allowing stipulated reversals might lead to judicial inefficiency in cases of potential nonmutual collateral estoppel. See pp. 1288–1300, infra. Allowing a losing defendant in such cases to effect a stipulated reversal with the plaintiff upon appeal would allow the defendant potentially to insulate itself from collateral estoppel in later cases, thereby denying subsequent plaintiffs the benefit of having complex liability issues resolved in the initial litigation. The California legislature recognized this possibility and during its 1999–2000 session modified California Code of Civil Procedure § 128(a)(8) to provide that an appellate court shall not permit a stipulated reversal "unless the court finds both of the following: (a) there is no reasonable possibility that the interests of nonparties or the public will be adversely affected by the reversal; and (b) that the reasons of the parties for requesting reversal outweigh the erosion of public trust that may result from the nullification of a judgment and the risk that the availability of stipulated reversal will reduce the incentive for pretrial settlement."

5. Suppose that rather than settling the dispute in *Hanover*, the parties merely stipulated most of the material facts concerning the lease agreement. The case went to trial, further factual findings were made, and a decision was rendered for Hanover against Anderson. Should the admissions in those stipulations be available in a subsequent suit between the parties? What if the suit is between another plaintiff and Hanover, and the complaint is based upon the same alleged breach of the lease? What light does Rule 36 shed on this problem?

6. Even though a consent judgment does not result from a full hearing "on the merits," the bargaining of the parties permits some reliance on the quality of the agreement reached. Modern rules of procedure, however, allow courts to dismiss an action and enter judgment at various stages of a litigation prior to a final verdict. Rule 12, for example, enumerates several situations in which a suit can be dismissed at the outset, and Rule 50 allows parties to obtain a judgment as a matter of law at the close of their opponents' evidence. These dismissals are not based upon the agreement of the parties, and, indeed, usually are opposed vigorously. Should a judgment consented to by the parties be considered more "on the merits" than an involuntary dismissal or judgment? Why?

———

HOUSING AUTHORITY FOR LA SALLE COUNTY v. YOUNG MEN'S CHRISTIAN ASSOCIATION OF OTTAWA, 101 Ill.2d 246, 78 Ill.Dec. 125, 461 N.E.2d 959 (1984). In 1932, the federal government sought to condemn easements over certain property for the purpose of constructing a system of locks and dams on the Illinois River. Seventy parties were summoned to court to adjudicate the title to the property so the government would know who was entitled to compensation as a result of the condemnation. With respect to a certain parcel of land, the government's petition pointed to a conflict over the title between Ella E. Deenis and The First Trust Company of Ottawa, Illinois ("First Trust"). Deenis failed to appear after being served properly with summons, resulting in a default judgment in favor of First Trust. The judgment determined that First Trust owned the property in question, and First Trust was awarded $650 as compensation for the easements.

The second suit arose over fifty years later between the parties' successors in interest to the property. The Housing Authority for La Salle County,

Deenis' successor in interest, sought an injunction prohibiting the Young Men's Christian Association of Ottawa ("YMCA"), First Trust's successor in interest, from constructing a parking lot on the real estate. The YMCA asserted the earlier judgment in the condemnation action as collateral estoppel with respect to the title to the property. The court decided that the case was governed by the principles of *res judicata* rather than collateral estoppel, but nonetheless held that the earlier judgment was conclusive as to the parties' rights:

> * * * When Deenis defaulted and the court entered a judgment finding First Trust to be the fee owner of the property, the title dispute was resolved and the doctrine of *res judicata* applied to bar any relitigation of that claim.

> Although the judgment against Deenis was by default, it is entitled to the same preclusive effect under the doctrine of *res judicata* as any other judgment. Some courts have held that default judgments have limited preclusive effects under the doctrine of collateral estoppel. * * * However, default judgments are always *res judicata* on the ultimate claim or demand presented in the complaint.

* * *

> The housing authority argues that Deenis lacked sufficient incentive to litigate the issue of title in the condemnation proceeding and, therefore, it is inequitable to accord the judgment in that proceeding preclusive effect as having determined the ownership of the disputed parcel. This argument is unpersuasive. Under special circumstances, the absence of an incentive to litigate might be relevant in the application of collateral estoppel (Restatement (Second) of Judgments sec. 28(5)(c) (1982)), but no authority suggests that it is relevant when the doctrine to be applied is *res judicata*.

Id. at 253, 78 Ill.Dec. at 129, 461 N.E.2d at 963.

Notes and Questions

1. Suppose a small Massachusetts computer company contracts with a large California microchip supplier. The computer company refuses to pay for a shipment, alleging that a large percentage of the chips are defective. The supplier files suit in California to recover $2,000, the balance due on the contract. The computer company chooses not to defend the action because the liability isn't large enough to justify the cost of litigation, and a default judgment is entered against it. Subsequently, the computer company is sued for $1,000,000 by a customer whose computer exploded due to a defective chip. The computer company impleads the supplier, seeking indemnification. But the supplier argues that the judgment in the California suit determined that it had delivered chips produced to specifications. Should the default judgment be given preclusive effect in these circumstances? Is the supplier seeking claim or issue preclusion? Should the absence of incentive to litigate be treated differently where issue preclusion, rather than claim preclusion, is sought?

2. How should the dismissal of a prior action on the ground that it was barred by a statute of limitations be treated in a subsequent suit on the same

matter? Suppose a discharged employee brings a sex-discrimination suit against her employer, but the case is dismissed because it was filed after the limitations period had expired. The employee then files a second suit based on breach of contract, a cause of action that would not be barred by the statute of limitations. Is the second action precluded?

Would your answer change if the contract action was brought in a different court system from the one in which the sex-discrimination suit had been lodged? If both jurisdictions apply the same limitations period to sex-discrimination claims, isn't it clear that the result should be the same as it would be if the second suit were brought in the same system? But, what if the second jurisdiction applies a more liberal statute of limitations to sex-discrimination claims—one that would not have barred the first suit? Is it possible in these circumstances that limitations rulings should be held to preclude only specific limitations issues and not the underlying claim?

Read Federal Rule 41(b). Does it answer any of these questions. See also Semtek International Inc. v. Lockheed Martin Corp., p. 1326, infra.

3. How should prior criminal proceedings affect subsequent litigation? Suppose that upon trial in federal court a criminal defendant, who asserted the defense of entrapment, was acquitted of charges of knowingly engaging in the business of dealing in firearms without a license, in violation of federal law. Suppose that the government then instituted an in rem action for forfeiture of the firearms involved pursuant to a federal statute which authorizes forfeitures of any firearms used or intended to be used in violation of federal law. Can the defendant argue that the in-rem proceeding is precluded by the prior acquittal? Remember, acquittal on the criminal charge merely reflected the existence of a reasonable doubt about the defendant's guilt; the jury did not find that it was more probable than not that the defendant did not have possession of the firearms with an intent to violate federal law. See United States v. One Assortment of 89 Firearms, 465 U.S. 354, 104 S.Ct. 1099, 79 L.Ed.2d 361 (1984).

2. JUDGMENTS OF NONJUDICIAL TRIBUNALS

HOLMBERG v. STATE, DIVISION OF RISK MANAGEMENT

Supreme Court of Alaska, 1990.
796 P.2d 823.

MOORE, JUSTICE.

Karen Holmberg asks us to reverse the Alaska Workers' Compensation Board ("AWCB") decision denying her permanent total disability benefits on the ground that a later decision of the Public Employees Retirement Board ("PERB") conclusively determined that she was not physically able to perform her duties as an employee of the State of Alaska. * * *

* * *

I.

Karen Holmberg began working for the State of Alaska, Division of Risk Management ("Risk Management") in 1979. She has a history of back injuries dating to the early 1960s. * * *

* * *

* * * On February 18, 1988, AWCB awarded Holmberg temporary total disability benefits, but denied her claim for permanent total disability benefits. Holmberg appealed AWCB's denial of permanent total disability benefits to the superior court in March 1988.

Holmberg also sought disability benefits from [the Public Employees Retirement System ("PERS")]. The Division of Retirement and Benefits ("Retirement and Benefits"), which administers PERS, awarded her nonoccupational disability benefits. However, the Disability Review Board denied her claim for occupational disability benefits. Holmberg appealed this initial decision to PERB. On April 20, 1988, after AWCB had denied her claim for permanent total disability benefits, PERB found that Holmberg was permanently and totally disabled as a result of accidents at work, and accordingly, awarded her occupational disability benefits.

Holmberg supplemented the record in her appeal from the prior AWCB decision with the new PERB decision. In the proceedings before the superior court, Holmberg argued that the AWCB decision should be reversed because of the preclusive effect of the later PERB decision. The superior court affirmed the AWCB decision and Holmberg appealed.

II.

Holmberg's primary contention is that PERB's factual determination that she was physically unable to perform her duties at Risk Management should be given binding effect in this appeal of the AWCB decision against her. * * *

* * *

The state does not contend that PERB decisions should not be given preclusive effect. Rather, the state argues that preclusive effect should not be given to PERB determinations in AWCB proceedings. We have not addressed the question how res judicata principles apply between different agencies. The Supreme Court has held that litigation conducted before one agency or official is generally binding on another agency or official of the same government because officers of the same government are in privity with each other. *Sunshine Anthracite Coal Co. v. Adkins,* 310 U.S. 381, 402–03, 60 S.Ct. 907, 916–17, 84 L.Ed. 1263 (1940). The Court stated that "[t]he crucial point is whether or not in the earlier litigation the representative of the United States had authority to represent its interests in a final adjudication of the issue in controversy." 310 U.S. at 403, 60 S.Ct. at 917. * * *

The United States Court of Appeals has applied this authority principle in appropriate cases. In *Safir v. Gibson,* 432 F.2d 137 (2d Cir.), *cert. denied,* 400 U.S. 850, 91 S.Ct. 57, 27 L.Ed.2d 88 (1970), the court relied on the authority principle in holding that the Federal Maritime Commission's determination that the rates of a conference of common carriers were unfair and unjustly discriminatory precluded the independent Maritime Administration from relitigating the issue. * * * In *Porter & Dietsch, Inc. v. FTC,* 605 F.2d 294 (7th Cir.1979), *cert. denied,* 445 U.S. 950, 100 S.Ct. 1597, 63 L.Ed.2d 784 (1980), the court refused to give preclusive effect to a Postal Service factual determination concerning the safety of a diet pill in a Federal Trade Commission proceeding. The court found that there was "a clear and convincing need for a new determination of the issue ... because of the potential impact of the determination on the public interest or the interests of persons not themselves parties to the initial action." 605 F.2d at 300.

The court's holding in *Porter & Dietsch* illustrates the principle that preclusion may be defeated by finding such an important difference in the functions of different agencies that one does not have authority to represent the interests of the other. * * *

[The court noted that the disability standards for PERB and AWCB decisions differ, but went on to state] * * * they provide no substantial reason why AWCB should be allowed to relitigate the narrow factual question whether Holmberg is physically able to continue performing her job with Risk Management. * * *

* * *

III.

Having found no substantial reason not to give PERB determinations preclusive effect in AWCB proceedings in general, we next consider whether the necessary elements of collateral estoppel exist in this case. There are three necessary conditions to the application of collateral estoppel:

1. The plea of collateral estoppel must be asserted against a party or one in privity with a party to the first action;

2. The issue to be precluded from relitigation by operation of the doctrine must be identical to that decided in the first action;

3. The issue in the first action must have been resolved by a final judgment on the merits. * * *

* * *

A.

* * * Privity exists between different agencies of the same government unless "there are important differences in the authority of the respective agencies." Briggs v. State, 732 P.2d 1078, 1082 (Alaska 1987). This is the same test that determines whether the decision of one agency binds another agency. In the privity context, however, the question is not whether the forum agencies are in privity, but whether the agencies appearing before them are. * * *

* * * Holmberg * * * argues that Retirement and Benefits is in privity with Risk Management because "the interests of the two agencies are virtually identical for purposes of [her] claims, and Retirement and Benefits had every incentive to vigorously defend the PERS claim."

Holmberg's error is in identifying Retirement and Benefits as the party against which PERB entered judgment. Retirement and Benefits is charged with administrative responsibility for PERS. The significance of this is that when Retirement and Benefits appears before PERB, it represents the interests of PERS, not the interests of the state. Thus, while Retirement and Benefits contested Holmberg's claim before PERB, the state is correct in saying that the party against which PERB entered judgment is the system itself.

* * *

* * * PERS is not a state agency but an independent retirement plan in which public employees are members and in which their employers participate. * * * PERS is funded by contributions from all its employer participants as well as their employees. * * * While an employer's contribution rate depends in part on its compensation experience, Holmberg is wrong in saying that "any award under PERS will ultimately be paid by State funds." To the contrary, PERS awards are made from the trust fund to which all PERS members and PERS participants contribute. While a state agency administers PERS and represents it during appeals, the state as employer is just one participant. The state treasury is affected by a benefit determination only insofar as the state is an employer participant. * * *

* * * The question is not whether PERS is bound by an AWCB decision against one of its members, but whether one of its members is bound by a decision against PERS. The questions are not symmetrical. The PERS constituency is not represented at all in a workers' compensation proceeding. The employer-participant, however, is at least nominally represented in the PERS proceeding to the extent that it has an interest in the PERS fund. At the same time, this nominal representation is not sufficient to assure that the participant has had adequate notice and opportunity to be heard and that its rights and interests have been protected. We therefore hold that the state as a participant in PERS is not in privity with PERS.

B.

Our holding that the state is not in privity with PERS is sufficient to deny affording any preclusive effect to the PERB decision as against the state. However, even if the state and PERS were in privity, the PERB decision would not preclude any issues raised in the earlier AWCB proceeding because the PERB decision was not the first final judgment addressing those issues. Holmberg observes that "[t]his case presents the collateral estoppel issue in a somewhat unusual procedural context." AWCB reached its decision first. While that decision was on appeal, PERB entered a contrary decision which was not appealed. Holmberg argues that the PERB decision was the first final judgment for the res judicata purposes and therefore precludes AWCB's contrary decision because the AWCB decision was appealed.

We disagree. A final judgment retains all of its res judicata effects pending resolution of an appeal of the judgment. * * * This rule respects the principle of repose inherent in the doctrine of res judicata. If a judgment was denied its res judicata effects merely because an appeal was pending, a litigant could refile an identical case in another trial court creating duplicative litigation. This case well illustrates the point. Having lost on the issue whether she was physically able to perform her job duties in the AWCB proceeding, Holmberg appealed the decision and then successfully relitigated the issue before PERB. Retirement and Benefits did not argue that PERB was precluded from relitigating the issue that AWCB already had decided. Now Holmberg asks us to reverse the earlier AWCB determination simply because of the later PERB determination. * * * To reward relitigation of an issue by reversing the original determination is completely at odds with the purpose of collateral estoppel to prevent relitigation of issues that already have been decided.

* * *

In this case, the AWCB decision was the first final judgment even though it was appealed. The later PERB determination that Holmberg was not physically able to perform her duties at Risk Management cannot preclude AWCB's earlier contrary determination. Indeed, if the other requirements of collateral estoppel were satisfied, Retirement and Benefits could have precluded Holmberg from relitigating the issue already decided by AWCB.

* * *

The decision of the superior court is AFFIRMED.

Notes and Questions

1. One of the factors that the *Holmberg* court considered in deciding whether to grant preclusive effect between nonjudicial tribunals was the degree to which the tribunals' functions diverged. In PORTER & DIETSCH, INC. v. FTC, 605 F.2d 294 (7th Cir.1979), certiorari denied 445 U.S. 950, 100 S.Ct. 1597, 63 L.Ed.2d 784 (1980), which was cited in the full opinion of *Holmberg,* the court refused to grant preclusive effect to a factual determination made by the Postal Service in a Federal Trade Commission proceeding concerning the safety of a diet pill despite both agencies' involvement with interstate commerce.

2. In evaluating the effect of the PERB judgment on the AWCB proceeding, the *Holmberg* court examined the procedural safeguards present in order to determine whether the adjudication was sufficiently "judicial" to warrant issue preclusion. The South Carolina Supreme Court disagreed with *Holmberg* in a similar case involving a decision by the state's Employment Security Commission (ESC), holding that the "purposes of the ESC are in conflict with the doctrine of collateral estoppel," since the "legislature intended to minimize procedural hurdles before the ESC so as to enable unemployed claimants to obtain prompt decisions regarding entitlement to unemployment benefits * * * ." See Shelton v. Oscar Mayer Foods Corp., 325 S.C. 248, 481 S.E.2d 706 (1997). The same considerations are present in inter-system preclusion, when a judicial body considers the preclusive effect of a nonjudicial determination. See University of Tennessee v. Elliott, p. 1332, infra.

3. Arbitration proceedings present a policy challenge similar to that posed by administrative determinations—i.e., was the proceeding of sufficient quality that it should carry full preclusive effect? Many courts look to the procedural opportunities afforded to parties in determining what preclusive effect an arbitration award should have. See, e.g., Maidman v. O'Brien, 473 F.Supp. 25 (S.D.N.Y.1979); Clemens v. Apple, 65 N.Y.2d 746, 492 N.Y.S.2d 20, 481 N.E.2d 560 (1985). As Professor Motomura points out, however, arbitration proceedings, by nature, often lack many of the essential elements of adjudication:

As a rule, those who sponsor or conduct arbitration have considerable discretion to adopt procedures that they deem appropriate. While some arbitrations are elaborate, more typically they are less formal than court litigation. As a practical matter, discovery is often limited or unavailable. Arbitrators are not bound by the rules of evidence and indeed may draw on their personal knowledge in making awards. Witnesses need not be required to testify under oath. If a written record of a proceeding exists, it need not be as complete as in litigation. Arbitrators are not required to write decisions that disclose the facts or reasons behind their awards, and in fact are often discouraged from doing so.

Motomura, *Arbitration and Collateral Estoppel: Using Preclusion to Shape Procedural Choices*, 63 Tulane L.Rev. 29, 36 (1988). Do these differences mean that arbitration proceedings will rarely be "judicial" enough to have issue preclusion effect? Or is there a difference between administrative and arbitration proceedings that justifies requiring fewer procedural safeguards in arbitration? See American Ins. Co. v. Messinger, 43 N.Y.2d 184, 191, 401 N.Y.S.2d 36, 40, 371 N.E.2d 798, 803 (1977) ("[V]oluntary choice of the arbitration forum necessarily imports acceptance of the more summary, informal and less structured procedures which characterize arbitration as compared with judicial litigation."). See generally 18 Wright, Miller & Cooper, *Federal Practice and Procedure: Jurisdiction and Related Matters* § 4475 (1981); *Restatement (Second), Judgments* § 84 (1982).

SECTION E.   PERSONS BENEFITTED AND PERSONS BOUND BY PRECLUSION

1.   THE TRADITIONAL MODEL

RALPH WOLFF & SONS v. NEW ZEALAND INS. CO.

Court of Appeals of Kentucky, 1933.
248 Ky. 304, 58 S.W.2d 623.

STANLEY, COMMISSIONER. The opinion of Wolff v. Niagara Fire Insurance Co., 236 Ky. 1, 32 S.W.2d 548, discloses that H.C. Wolff and R.C. Wolff, partners, suffered the partial loss by fire of their candy factory in December, 1924, and that they had twelve insurance policies on the property for a total sum of $19,500. That case was a consolidation of nine suits on as many policies for the aggregate of $14,500. The verdict was for $2,500 in favor of the plaintiffs "to cover the amount of the loss and damage by fire and water." That was construed to be a finding that the total property loss was $2,500. Since the insurance involved in the consolidated action was $^{145}/_{195}$ of the whole coverage, judgment was rendered for that fractional part of the total loss fixed by the jury, that is, for $1,858.90, and that judgment was affirmed.

[Plaintiffs also sued two other insurers, each of whom had insured plaintiffs for $1,000.] * * * Among the several defenses set up in each case was the plea that the policy provided the company should not be liable for a greater proportion of any loss than the amount of the policy bore to the whole insurance covering the property; that in the consolidated cases referred to it had been judicially ascertained and determined that the total loss was $2,500 and by reason thereof the amount of the loss was res judicata and plaintiffs were estopped to assert a greater damage; and that if liable at all it was only for its proportional part, or $^{1000}\!/_{19500}$, to wit $128.20. A demurrer to this plea was overruled * * * and judgment for $128.20 was rendered against each company. * * *

The sole question before us, therefore, is * * * whether the plaintiffs in these suits are bound by the judgment in their cases against the other nine companies.

It is said in Jeter v. Hewitt, 22 How. 352, 364, 16 L.Ed. 345, that "res judicata renders white that which is black, and straight that which is crooked." But all will agree that there are qualifications and that is not true except when there are certain concurring elements, as where one has had a chance, either personally or by representation, to show that black is black and crooked things are crooked. It is conceded, quite naturally, that in order to render a matter res judicata, among other things, there must be identity of parties or their privies; and that is so though the judgment relied upon as a bar involved the same state of facts. * * * The defendants in these actions were not parties to the other one and in no way participated in their defense. There is nothing to show that they even had notice of the pendency of the other suits.

* * * "The fact that persons are interested in the same question or in proving the same facts * * * does not make them privies." Section 438, Freeman on Judgments. * * *

The appellees rest their argument of privity upon what they say is the contractual relation, that is, in effect that as each policy contained the apportionment or contribution clause, they were and are bound together in a common cause. * * * True it is there may be such a contractual relationship that a party becomes bound under certain conditions by the action of another in regard to the matter involved in a suit or by the judgment, such as where he is responsible over, as a warrantor, or as an indemnitor, or as a surety. * * * But we cannot see the application here. The stipulation in the respective contracts of insurance upon the appellants' property was that the company would be liable only for its proportionate share of any loss sustained if other insurance contracts should be made. This, of course, was to avoid duplication of indemnity and to prevent overinsurance. There was no contract nor privity of contract among the insurers. * * * It may be doubted that such would have been claimed had the loss been fixed by the former judgment at what the companies regarded as excessive. To bind the plaintiffs the defendants must also have been bound, for an estoppel is always mutual.

* * *

As further refuting the view that the concurrent or pro rata insurance clauses in the several policies so interlocked the contracts as to make them one in effect * * *, it is held that insurers cannot avail themselves of an adjustment by the insured with another insurer either to defeat recovery or reduce the amount of liability under their contract; and that in ascertaining a company's proportionate share of the loss no regard is to be had to the fact that some of the companies have been settled with for a less sum than they were liable for or have paid more than their share. * * * [T]here can be no difference when the settlement is pursuant to a judicial determination.

* * *

It seems to the court, therefore, that the judgment holding the appellants to be bound by the judgment in the former suit is erroneous. It is accordingly reversed, and the case remanded for consistent proceedings.

Notes and Questions

1. Why should it be true, in the words of the court in the principal case, that "to bind the plaintiffs, the defendants must also have been bound"? Is this principle of mutuality based upon any of the purposes we have seen advanced in support of the doctrine of former adjudication? Might the plaintiff in *Ralph Wolff & Sons* have had anything to gain in trying the actions against the insurers in separate groups instead of all at once? Should the answer to the last question affect the decision whether to follow the rule enunciated by the court? Should there be one rule when plaintiff has proceeded purposefully so as to obtain separate trials and another rule when plaintiff was unable to avoid separate trials?

2. Would there have been any reasonable basis in the principal case for restricting plaintiff's total recovery to $2,500, while not restricting the possible liability of the two defendants to $128.20 each?

3. A street car and a coal wagon collided. The driver of the wagon sued the street-car company for his injuries and won, the jury finding that he had not been guilty of any want of ordinary care. Subsequently, a pedestrian, against whom the wagon had been thrown, sued the street-car company and the coal company for her injuries. Should the earlier judgment in favor of the wagon driver operate as res judicata on the issue of his lack of negligence? If a verdict is returned against both defendants, should the court order that the judgment contain a provision that execution must be first satisfied out of the property of the street-car company? See Ertel v. Milwaukee Elec. Ry. & Light Co., 164 Wis. 380, 160 N.W. 263 (1916).

4. When an action is brought against one who is entitled to be indemnified by another if he should lose, a judgment against the indemnitee will bind the indemnitor on the issue of the indemnitee's liability in the first action, if the indemnitor has been "vouched in," that is, if notified of the first action and offered an opportunity to defend. See, e.g., First Nat. Bank v. City Nat. Bank, 182 Mass. 130, 65 N.E. 24 (1902) (so holding, even though the indemnitor was not subject to personal jurisdiction in the state in which the first action was brought). See Note 3, p. 653, supra.

———

CITY OF ANDERSON v. FLEMING, 160 Ind. 597, 602–03, 67 N.E. 443, 445 (1903). Plaintiff suffered personal injuries by stepping into an excavation in the street. She sued the contractor responsible for the excavation, but judgment went against her. Subsequently, she sued the city for the same injuries, and the city pleaded the judgment in favor of the contractor. The Supreme Court of Indiana held for defendant city:

> * * * The established rule in this state is that when a street of a municipal corporation is rendered unsafe by the wrongful acts or negligence of a third person, and the corporation is compelled to pay for injuries caused by said unsafe street, it has a right of action over against the person who rendered the same unsafe, for the amount so paid, and, if

properly notified of the action, such person is bound and concluded by said judgment recovered against the corporation.

* * * It is clearly established * * * that if appellee was injured, without contributory fault on her part, by reason of said excavations being negligently left open, without proper guards or signals, as alleged, appellant would be entitled to recover from the contractor whatever appellee might recover against it. Such right * * * would rest upon the principles of subrogation. Appellant would be entitled to be subrogated to appellee's right of action against the contractor, but the judgment on the merits in the contractor's favor in appellee's action against him conclusively adjudged that he was not liable to appellee, or any person claiming under her, for the same cause of action. If appellee was not entitled to recover for said injury against the contractor, she is not entitled to recover therefor against appellant.

The contractor had the right, if duly notified by appellant, to appear and set up said former judgment in his favor against appellee in bar of this action against appellant, and appellant has the same right; otherwise the contractor would have to defend the same cause twice on its merits.

Notes and Questions

1. *Fleming* illustrates the traditional "indemnity circle" exception to mutuality. The Indiana court removed the mutuality requirement to prevent the defendant from having to pay damages for personal injuries and then risk losing its suit against the government for indemnification. Consider what would happen if the second court were to find the injured person to have been contributorily negligent?

A, an employee acting within the scope of his employment and driving the employer's, B's, car, collides with a car driven by C. C sues A, and judgment is for A. Subsequently B sues C for damages to the car. What effect should the earlier judgment for A have in B's suit against C? See Good Health Dairy Prods. Corp. v. Emery, 275 N.Y. 14, 9 N.E.2d 758 (1937).

2. Suppose on the facts of Question 1 that C had first sued B, and judgment had been for B, and C had then sued A. What effect should the earlier judgment for B have in C's suit against A? Would your answer be different if the second suit had been by A against C? Compare Emery v. Fowler, 39 Me. 326 (1855), with Elder v. New York & Penn. Motor Express, Inc., 284 N.Y. 350, 31 N.E.2d 188 (1940).

3. Suppose that in the first action, A, a real-estate broker, had sued the seller of property, B, for commissions. The trial court dismissed A's action after trial on the ground that A had not produced the person, C, who ultimately had purchased B's property and therefore was not entitled to a brokerage commission. In the second action A sues C for inducing B to breach the brokerage contract causing a loss of the commission. Can C successfully rely on the decision against A in the first action as a bar to A's action against him? See Israel v. Wood Dolson Co., 1 N.Y.2d 116, 151 N.Y.S.2d 1, 134 N.E.2d 97 (1956). The New York cases on mutuality of estoppel are discussed at length in 5 Weinstein, Korn & Miller, *New York Civil Practice* ¶¶ 5011.32–.42.

4.   When a wrongful-death action for the death of a child has been brought by a personal representative and judgment was for defendant, is the mother estopped by the earlier judgment in an action for her personal injuries arising out of the same accident when she would have been one of the beneficiaries if the first action had been successful? See Smith v. Bishop, 26 Ill.2d 434, 187 N.E.2d 217 (1962).

———

These traditional rules of preclusion have changed dramatically in recent years. As you read the remainder of this Section, consider whether it is appropriate to allow a nonparty to take advantage of a favorable judgment when that nonparty would not have been subject to preclusion if the prior judgment had been unfavorable to him. Courts have shown an increasing willingness to permit preclusion (often referred to as nonmutual estoppel) in such circumstances. Also consider whether it is appropriate to bind nonparties by an unfavorable judgment. A limited number of courts have shown a willingness to permit exceptions to the traditional rule that an individual can be bound by a court decision only when he has had his "day in court."

2.   MUTUALITY

BERNHARD v. BANK OF AMERICA NAT. TRUST & SAV. ASS'N

Supreme Court of California, 1942.
19 Cal.2d 807, 122 P.2d 892.

TRAYNOR, JUSTICE. In June, 1933, Mrs. Clara Sather, an elderly woman, made her home with Mr. and Mrs. Charles O. Cook in San Dimas, California. Because of her failing health, she authorized Mr. Cook and Dr. Joseph Zeiler to make drafts jointly against her commercial account in the Security First National Bank of Los Angeles. On August 24, 1933, Mr. Cook opened a commercial account at the First National Bank of San Dimas in the name of "Clara Sather by Charles O. Cook." * * * Thereafter, a number of checks drawn by Cook and Zeiler on Mrs. Sather's commercial account in Los Angeles were deposited in the San Dimas account * * *.

On October 26, 1933, a teller from the Los Angeles Bank called on Mrs. Sather at her request to assist in transferring her money from the Los Angeles Bank to the San Dimas Bank. In the presence of this teller, the cashier of the San Dimas Bank, Mr. Cook, and her physician, Mrs. Sather signed by mark an authorization directing the Security First National Bank of Los Angeles to transfer the balance of her savings account in the amount of $4,155.68 to the First National Bank of San Dimas * * * "for credit to the account of Mrs. Clara Sather." The order was credited by the San Dimas Bank to the account of "Clara Sather by Charles O. Cook." Cook withdrew the entire balance from that account and opened a new account in the same bank in the name of himself and his wife. * * *

Mrs. Sather died in November, 1933. Cook qualified as executor of the estate and proceeded with its administration. After a lapse of several years he filed an account at the instance of the probate court accompanied by his resignation. The account made no mention of the money transferred by Mrs. Sather to the San Dimas Bank; and Helen Bernhard * * * [and other] beneficiaries under Mrs. Sather's will, filed objections to the account for this reason. After a hearing on the objections the court settled the account, and as part of its order declared that the decedent during her lifetime had made a gift to Charles O. Cook of the amount of the deposit in question.

After Cook's discharge, Helen Bernhard was appointed administratrix with the will annexed. She instituted this action against defendant, the Bank of America, successor to the San Dimas Bank, seeking to recover the deposit on the ground that the bank was indebted to the estate for this amount because Mrs. Sather never authorized its withdrawal. In addition to a general denial, defendant pleaded two affirmative defenses: (1) That the money on deposit was paid out to Charles O. Cook with the consent of Mrs. Sather and (2) that this fact is res judicata by virtue of the finding of the probate court * * *. The trial court * * * gave judgment for defendant on the ground that Cook's ownership of the money was conclusively established by the finding of the probate court. * * *

Plaintiff contends that the doctrine of res judicata does not apply because the defendant who is asserting the plea was not a party to the previous action nor in privity with a party to that action and because there is no mutuality of estoppel.

* * *

Many courts have stated the facile formula that the plea of res judicata is available only when there is privity and mutuality of estoppel. * * * Under the requirement of privity, only parties to the former judgment or their privies may take advantage of or be bound by it. * * * A party in this connection is one who is "directly interested in the subject matter, and had a right to make defense, or to control the proceeding, and to appeal from the judgment." * * * A privy is one who, after rendition of the judgment, has acquired an interest in the subject matter affected by the judgment through or under one of the parties, as by inheritance, succession, or purchase. * * * The estoppel is mutual if the one taking advantage of the earlier adjudication would have been bound by it, had it gone against him. * * *

The criteria for determining who may assert a plea of res judicata differ fundamentally from the criteria for determining against whom a plea of res judicata may be asserted. The requirements of due process of law forbid the assertion of a plea of res judicata against a party unless he was bound by the earlier litigation in which the matter was decided. * * * He is bound by that litigation only if he has been a party thereto or in privity with a party thereto. * * * There is no compelling reason, however, for requiring that the party asserting the plea of res judicata must have been a party, or in privity with a party, to the earlier litigation.

No satisfactory rationalization has been advanced for the requirement of mutuality. Just why a party who was not bound by a previous action should be precluded from asserting it as res judicata against a party who was bound by it is difficult to comprehend. * * * Many courts have abandoned the requirement of mutuality and confined the requirement of privity to the party against whom the plea of res judicata is asserted. * * * The commentators are almost unanimously in accord. * * * The courts of most jurisdictions have in effect accomplished the same result by recognizing a broad exception to the requirements of mutuality and privity, namely, that they are not necessary where the liability of the defendant asserting the plea of res judicata is dependent upon or derived from the liability of one who was exonerated in an earlier suit brought by the same plaintiff upon the same facts. * * * Typical examples of such derivative liability are master and servant, principal and agent, and indemnitor and indemnitee. Thus, if a plaintiff sues a servant for injuries caused by the servant's alleged negligence within the scope of his employment, a judgment against the plaintiff of [sic] the grounds that the servant was not negligent can be pleaded by the master as res judicata if he is subsequently sued by the same plaintiff for the same injuries. Conversely, if the plaintiff first sues the master, a judgment against the plaintiff on the grounds that the servant was not negligent can be pleaded by the servant as res judicata if he is subsequently sued by the plaintiff. In each of these situations the party asserting the plea of res judicata was not a party to the previous action nor in privity with such a party * * *. Likewise, the estoppel is not mutual since the party asserting the plea, not having been a party or in privity with a party to the former action, would not have been bound by it had it been decided the other way. The cases justify this exception on the ground that it would be unjust to permit one who has had his day in court to reopen identical issues by merely switching adversaries.

In determining the validity of a plea of res judicata three questions are pertinent: Was the issue decided in the prior adjudication identical with the one presented in the action in question? Was there a final judgment on the merits? Was the party against whom the plea is asserted a party or in privity with a party to the prior adjudication?

* * * Since the issue as to the ownership of the money is identical with the issue raised in the probate proceeding, and since the order of the probate court settling the executor's account was a final adjudication of this issue on the merits * * *, it remains only to determine whether the plaintiff in the present action was a party or in privity with a party to the earlier proceeding. The plaintiff has brought the present action in the capacity of administratrix of the estate. In this capacity she represents the very same persons and interests that were represented in the earlier hearing on the executor's account. In that proceeding plaintiff and the other legatees who objected to the executor's account represented the estate of the decedent. They were seeking not a personal recovery but, like the plaintiff in the present action, as administratrix, a recovery for the benefit of the legatees and creditors of the estate, all of whom were bound by the order settling the account. * * *

The judgment is affirmed.

Notes and Questions

1. In *Bernhard* Justice Traynor mentions that some courts already had recognized that exceptions to the mutuality requirement arise most often in cases involving vicarious liability. Consider these common examples:

(1) A institutes an action for negligence against B, an employee of C, for conduct occurring while B was acting in the scope of employment. If B

prevails, C will be able to raise the first judgment in a suit by A to recover against C.

(2) X corporation is a general contractor liable for the proper performance of an entire contract in which Y is a subcontractor. Z, the beneficiary of the contract, sues Y for incomplete performance and loses. If Z brings a suit against X that raises the same claim as the earlier suit, X will be able to invoke the preclusive effects of this prior judgment.

These exceptions reflect the duality inherent in the vicarious liability relationship. The *Restatement (Second) of Judgments* has outlined the nature of this duality:

> * * * The injured person's claims against the primary obligor and the person vicariously responsible for his conduct are in important respects separate claims. First, neither of the obligors is ordinarily the representative of the other, so that a judgment against one of them ordinarily is not preclusive against the other. * * * Second, a release of one does not ordinarily release the other. * * * Third, one of the obligors may be immune from suit while the other is not, and different statutes of limitations may be applicable to them. Finally, the claims are separate in the sense that neither the rule against "splitting" a claim nor the usual rules of joinder of parties require that they be maintained in a single action.
>
> In an important sense, however, there is only a single claim. The same loss is involved, usually the same measure of damages, and the same or nearly identical issues of fact and law. The substantive legal basis for vicarious responsibility rests largely on the notion that the injured person should have the additional security for recovery of his loss that is represented in imposition of liability on a person other than the primary obligor. The optional additional security thus afforded by rules of vicarious responsibility should not, however, afford the injured person a further option to litigate successively the issues upon which his claim to redress is founded. He is ordinarily in a position to sue both obligors in the same action and may justly be expected to do so. Beyond this, if he is allowed to sue the second obligor after having lost an action against the first, two anomalous consequences may result. First, he may be given recovery for conduct that has already been determined not to be wrongful. Second, if the first action is unsuccessfully maintained against the primary obligor, and the second successfully maintained against the person vicariously responsible, it could happen that the latter could obtain indemnity from the primary obligor. The result would be that the primary obligor would have to pay indirectly an obligation from which he had been directly exonerated.

Restatement (Second), Judgments § 51, comment *b* (1982).

2. In which of the following situations would preclusion be available under *Bernhard*?

(a) Three cars, driven by A, B, and C, respectively, collide in an intersection in a jurisdiction without a compulsory-joinder statute. Driver A, believing that C does not have enough money to satisfy the judgment, institutes a negligence action against B. At trial B is exonerated, the court holding that A's injuries were solely the result of A's own negligence. A then discovers that C actually does have enough money to make him worth suing, and promptly files suit against him. Can C invoke the judgment in A's prior action against B to preclude recovery by A against him?

(b) Assume the same fact pattern as above. Could C assert the judgment in the prior suit as the basis to recover on a counterclaim against A?

(c) A bus owned and driven by D is in an accident. Passenger P1 sues D, alleging that the accident was caused by D's negligent driving. The trial court finds for P1. Passenger P2 files a claim against D, also alleging damages as a result of D's negligence. Is preclusion available to P2? Can you articulate how this fact pattern differs from that of (b)?

(d) What if, on the facts of (c), the bus driver/owner had prevailed in the first suit? When P2 brought the second litigation, could D then use the first suit's judgment as a defense to the second action?

3. Many of the cases involving mutuality of issue preclusion that have arisen since *Bernhard* are noted and briefly discussed in the appendix to Currie, *Civil Procedure: The Tempest Brews*, 53 Calif.L.Rev. 25, 38–46 (1965). Other useful discussions of mutuality include Currie, *Mutuality of Collateral Estoppel—Limits of the* Bernhard *Doctrine*, 9 Stan.L.Rev. 281 (1957); Moore & Currier, *Mutuality and Conclusiveness of Judgments*, 35 Tulane L.Rev. 301 (1961); Polasky, *Collateral Estoppel—Effects of Prior Litigation*, 39 Iowa L.Rev. 217 (1954); Semmel, *Collateral Estoppel, Mutuality and Joinder of Parties*, 68 Colum.L.Rev. 1457 (1968); Note, *A Probabilistic Analysis of the Doctrine of Mutuality of Collateral Estoppel*, 76 Mich.L.Rev. 612 (1978); Note, *Collateral Estoppel Without Mutuality: Accepting the Bernhard Doctrine*, 35 Vand.L.Rev. 1423 (1982).

BLONDER–TONGUE LABORATORIES, INC. v. UNIVERSITY OF ILLINOIS FOUNDATION, 402 U.S. 313, 91 S.Ct. 1434, 28 L.Ed.2d 788 (1971), was the case in which the Supreme Court first began to abrogate the mutuality requirement for the federal system. The University of Illinois Foundation owned, by assignment, a patent for a radio and television antenna. In an infringement action against an antenna manufacturer, a trial court had held the Foundation's patent invalid. But, in a second infringement action against a different defendant, the patent was held to be valid. In TRIPLETT v. LOWELL, 297 U.S. 638, 56 S.Ct. 645, 80 L.Ed. 949 (1936), a case decided shortly before Justice Traynor's *Bernhard* decision, the United States Supreme Court had reaffirmed the rule that a holding that a patent was invalid did not preclude a patent holder from asserting the validity of the patent in subsequent litigation against different defendants. In *Blonder-Tongue*, the Court specifically requested the parties to discuss the vitality of the *Triplett* rule.

The substance of the Court's opinion in *Blonder-Tongue* begins with a review of the seminal state and lower federal-court opinions that had abandoned the mutuality requirement in certain contexts. The Court then offered its own views on the propriety of nonmutual preclusion:

> The cases and authorities discussed above connect erosion of the mutuality requirement to the goal of limiting relitigation of issues where that can be achieved without compromising fairness in particular cases. The courts have often discarded the rule while commenting on crowded dockets and long delays preceding trial. Authorities differ on whether the public interest in efficient judicial administration is a sufficient ground in

and of itself for abandoning mutuality, but it is clear that more than crowded dockets is involved. The broader question is whether it is any longer tenable to afford a litigant more than one full and fair opportunity for judicial resolution of the same issue. The question in these terms includes as part of the calculus the effect on judicial administration, but it also encompasses the concern exemplified by Bentham's reference to the gaming table in his attack on the principle of mutuality of estoppel. In any lawsuit where a defendant, because of the mutuality principle, is forced to present a complete defense on the merits to a claim which the plaintiff has fully litigated and lost in a prior action, there is an arguable misallocation of resources. To the extent the defendant in the second suit may not win by asserting, without contradiction, that the plaintiff had fully and fairly, but unsuccessfully, litigated the same claim in the prior suit, the defendant's time and money are diverted from alternative uses—productive or otherwise—to relitigation of a decided issue. And, still assuming that the issue was resolved correctly in the first suit, there is reason to be concerned about the plaintiff's allocation of resources. Permitting repeated litigation of the same issue as long as the supply of unrelated defendants holds out reflects either the aura of the gaming table or "a lack of discipline and of disinterestedness on the part of the lower courts, hardly a worthy or wise basis for fashioning rules of procedure." Kerotest Mfg. Co. v. C–O–Two Co., 342 U.S. 180, 185, 72 S.Ct. 219, 222, 96 L.Ed. 200 (1952). Although neither judges, the parties, nor the adversary system performs perfectly in all cases, the requirement of determining whether the party against whom an estoppel is asserted had a full and fair opportunity to litigate is a most significant safeguard.

Some litigants—those who never appeared in a prior action—may not be collaterally estopped without litigating the issue. They have never had a chance to present their evidence and arguments on the claim. Due process prohibits estopping them despite one or more existing adjudications of the identical issue which stand squarely against their position. * * * Also, the authorities have been more willing to permit a defendant in a second suit to invoke an estoppel against a plaintiff who lost on the same claim in an earlier suit than they have been to allow a plaintiff in the second suit to use offensively a judgment obtained by a different plaintiff in a prior suit against the same defendant. But the case before us involves neither due process nor "offensive use" questions. Rather, it depends on the considerations weighing for and against permitting a patent holder to sue on his patent after it has once been held invalid following opportunity for full and fair trial.

Id. at 328–33, 91 S.Ct. at 1442–43, 28 L.Ed.2d at 799–800.

Later in the opinion, the Court focused on two economic consequences of continued adherence to the *Triplett* rule. First, the costs of litigating patent suits was inordinately high. For patentees, the average fee was $50,000; for defendants, the fees often ran into the hundreds of thousands of dollars. Second, the statutory presumption in favor of the validity of patents often forced prospective defendants to settle with the patent holders rather than engage in lengthy and expensive litigation challenging the patent. The Court recognized that overturning the *Triplett* rule might serve as a check on the monopoly power that the patent statute gave to patent holders, and noted other decisions in which it had similarly tried to give inventors sufficient incentives without giving them undue protection from competition.

In the penultimate section of the opinion, the Court once again considered the question of resource allocation:

> As the preceding discussion indicates, although patent trials are only a small portion of the total amount of litigation in the federal courts, they tend to be of disproportionate length. Despite this, respondents urge that the burden on the federal courts from relitigation of patents once held invalid is *de minimis*. They rely on the figures presented in the 1961 Staff Report: during the period 1948–1959, 62 federal suits were terminated which involved relitigation of a patent previously held invalid, a figure constituting about 1% of the patent suits commenced during the same period. The same figures show that these 62 suits involved 27 patents, indicating that some patentees sue more than once after their patent has been invalidated. Respondents also urge that most of these 62 suits were settled without litigation. 1961 Staff Report 19. But, as we have suggested, this fact cuts both ways.

> Even accepting respondents' characterization of these figures as *de minimis*, it is clear that abrogation of *Triplett* will save *some* judicial time if even a few relatively lengthy patent suits may be fairly disposed of on pleas of estoppel. More fundamentally, while the cases do discuss reduction in dockets as an effect of elimination of the mutuality requirement, they do not purport to hold that predictions about the actual amount of judicial time that will be saved under such a holding control decision of that question.

Id. at 348–49, 91 S.Ct. at 1452–53, 28 L.Ed.2d at 810–11.

Ultimately, the Court overruled *Triplett* "to the extent it forecloses a plea of estoppel by one facing a charge of infringement of a patent that has once been declared invalid." Id. at 350, 91 S.Ct. at 1453, 28 L.Ed.2d at 811.

Notes and Questions

1. A close reading of the *Blonder-Tongue* opinion reveals that the holding plausibly could be limited to patent actions. Lower federal courts, however, have freely cited it as authority for nonmutual preclusion in all types of substantive claims. The next principal case makes the propriety of that practice clear.

2. What effect should substantive law have on the scope of preclusion rules? Should it matter whether the issue involved is a constitutional one? Should the nature of the parties' expectations about the scope of the first decision have an effect on the reach of nonmutual estoppel?

3. In both *Bernhard* and *Blonder-Tongue* the party that was precluded in the second action was the party who had instituted the first action. Should this be an important factor in determining whether nonmutual preclusion is appropriate? Or should the only relevant consideration be whether the party against whom preclusion is being asserted had a full and fair opportunity to litigate? See Zdanok v. Glidden Co., 327 F.2d 944 (2d Cir.) (Friendly, J.), certiorari denied 377 U.S. 934, 84 S.Ct. 1338, 12 L.Ed.2d 298 (1964); Teitelbaum Furs, Inc. v. Dominion

Insurance Co., 58 Cal.2d 601, 25 Cal.Rptr. 559, 375 P.2d 439 (1962) (Traynor, J.), certiorari denied 372 U.S. 966, 83 S.Ct. 1091, 10 L.Ed.2d 130 (1963); Currie, *Civil Procedure: The Tempest Brews,* 53 Calif.L.Rev. 25 (1965).

PARKLANE HOSIERY CO. v. SHORE

Supreme Court of the United States, 1979.
439 U.S. 322, 99 S.Ct. 645, 58 L.Ed.2d 552.

Certiorari to the United States Court of Appeals for the Second Circuit.

MR. JUSTICE STEWART delivered the opinion of the Court.

* * *

The respondent brought this stockholder's class action against the petitioners in a federal district court. The complaint alleged that the petitioners * * * had issued a materially false and misleading proxy statement in connection with a merger. * * * The complaint sought damages, rescission of the merger, and recovery of costs.

Before this action came to trial, the SEC filed suit against the same defendants in a federal district court, alleging that the proxy statement that had been issued by Parklane was materially false and misleading in essentially the same respects as those that had been alleged in the respondent's complaint. Injunctive relief was requested. After a four-day trial, the District Court found that the proxy statement was materially false and misleading in the respects alleged, and entered a declaratory judgment to that effect. * * * The Court of Appeals for the Second Circuit affirmed * * *.

The respondent in the present case then moved for partial summary judgment against the petitioners, asserting that the petitioners were collaterally estopped from relitigating the issues that had been resolved against them in the action brought by the SEC. The District Court denied the motion on the ground that such an application of collateral estoppel would deny the petitioners their Seventh Amendment right to a jury trial. The Court of Appeals for the Second Circuit reversed * * *. Because of an intercircuit conflict,[3] we granted certiorari.

I

The threshold question to be considered is whether, quite apart from the right to a jury trial under the Seventh Amendment, the petitioners can be precluded from relitigating facts resolved adversely to them in a prior equitable proceeding with another party under the general law of collateral estoppel. Specifically, we must determine whether a litigant who was not a party to a prior judgment may nevertheless use that judgment "offensively" to prevent a defendant from relitigating issues resolved in the earlier proceeding.[4]

* * *

3. The position of the Court of Appeals for the Second Circuit is in conflict with that taken by the Court of Appeals for the Fifth Circuit in Rachal v. Hill, 435 F.2d 59.

4. In this context, offensive use of collateral estoppel occurs when the plaintiff seeks to foreclose the defendant from litigating an issue the defendant has previously litigated unsuccessfully in an action with another party. Defensive use occurs when a defendant seeks to prevent a plaintiff from asserting a claim the

B

The *Blonder-Tongue* case involved defensive use of collateral estoppel * * *. The present case, by contrast, involves offensive use of collateral estoppel—a plaintiff is seeking to estop a defendant from relitigating the issues which the defendant previously litigated and lost against another plaintiff. In both the offensive and defensive use situations, the party against whom estoppel is asserted has litigated and lost in an earlier action. Nevertheless, several reasons have been advanced why the two situations should be treated differently.

First, offensive use of collateral estoppel does not promote judicial economy in the same manner as defensive use does. Defensive use of collateral estoppel precludes a plaintiff from relitigating identical issues by merely "switching adversaries." * * * Thus defensive collateral estoppel gives a plaintiff a strong incentive to join all potential defendants in the first action if possible. Offensive use of collateral estoppel, on the other hand, creates precisely the opposite incentive. Since a plaintiff will be able to rely on a previous judgment against a defendant but will not be bound by that judgment if the defendant wins, the plaintiff has every incentive to adopt a "wait and see" attitude, in the hope that the first action by another plaintiff will result in a favorable judgment. * * * Thus offensive use of collateral estoppel will likely increase rather than decrease the total amount of litigation, since potential plaintiffs will have everything to gain and nothing to lose by not intervening in the first action.[13]

A second argument against offensive use of collateral estoppel is that it may be unfair to a defendant. If a defendant in the first action is sued for small or nominal damages, he may have little incentive to defend vigorously, particularly if future suits are not foreseeable. * * * Allowing offensive collateral estoppel may also be unfair to a defendant if the judgment relied upon as a basis for the estoppel is itself inconsistent with one or more previous judgments in favor of the defendant. Still another situation where it might be unfair to apply offensive estoppel is where the second action affords the defendant procedural opportunities unavailable in the first action that could readily cause a different result.[15]

C

We have concluded that the preferable approach for dealing with these problems in the federal courts is not to preclude the use of offensive collateral estoppel, but to grant trial courts broad discretion to determine when it

plaintiff has previously litigated and lost against another defendant.

13. The *Restatement (Second) of Judgments* (Tent. Draft No. 2, 1975) § 88(3), provides that application of collateral estoppel may be denied if the party asserting it "could have effected joinder in the first action between himself and his present adversary."

15. If, for example, the defendant in the first action was forced to defend in an inconvenient forum and therefore was unable to engage in full scale discovery or call witnesses, application of offensive collateral estoppel may

be unwarranted. Indeed, differences in available procedures may sometimes justify not allowing a prior judgment to have estoppel effect in a subsequent action even between the same parties, or where defensive estoppel is asserted against a plaintiff who has litigated and lost. The problem of unfairness is particularly acute in cases of offensive estoppel, however, because the defendant against whom estoppel is asserted typically will not have chosen the forum in the first action. See *Restatement (Second) of Judgments* (Tentative Draft No. 2, 1975) § 88(2) and Comment *d*.

should be applied. The general rule should be that in cases where a plaintiff could easily have joined in the earlier action or where, either for the reasons discussed above or for other reasons, the application of offensive estoppel would be unfair to a defendant, a trial judge should not allow the use of offensive collateral estoppel.

In the present case, however, none of the circumstances that might justify reluctance to allow the offensive use of collateral estoppel is present. The application of offensive collateral estoppel will not here reward a private plaintiff who could have joined in the previous action, since the respondent probably could not have joined in the injunctive action brought by the SEC even had he so desired.[17] Similarly, there is no unfairness to the petitioners in applying offensive collateral estoppel in this case. First, in light of the serious allegations made in the SEC's complaint against the petitioners, as well as the foreseeability of subsequent private suits that typically follow a successful government judgment, the petitioners had every incentive to litigate the SEC lawsuit fully and vigorously. Second, the judgment in the Commission action was not inconsistent with any previous decision. Finally, there will in the respondent's action be no procedural opportunities available to the petitioner that were unavailable in the first action of a kind that might be likely to cause a different result.[19]

We conclude, therefore, that none of the considerations that would justify a refusal to allow the use of offensive collateral estoppel is present in this case. Since the petitioners received a "full and fair" opportunity to litigate their claims in the SEC action, the contemporary law of collateral estoppel leads inescapably to the conclusion that the petitioners are collaterally estopped from relitigating the question of whether the proxy statements were materially false and misleading.

II

The question that remains is whether, notwithstanding the law of collateral estoppel, the use of offensive collateral estoppel in this case would violate the petitioners' Seventh Amendment right to a jury trial.

A

* * *

Recognition that an equitable determination could have collateral estoppel effect in a subsequent legal action was the major premise of this Court's decision in Beacon Theatres v. Westover [p. 959, supra] * * *.

It is clear that the Court in the *Beacon Theatres* case thought that if an issue common to both legal and equitable claims was first determined by a

17. SEC v. Everest Management Corp., 475 F.2d 1236, 1240 (CA2) ("[T]he complicating effect of the additional issues and the additional parties outweighs any advantage of a single disposition of the common issues"). Moreover, consolidation of a private action with one brought by the SEC without its consent is prohibited by statute. 15 U.S.C. § 78u(g).

19. It is true, of course, that the petitioners in the present action would be entitled to a jury trial of the issues bearing on whether the proxy statement was materially false and misleading had the SEC action never been brought—a matter to be discussed in Part II of this opinion. But the presence or absence of a jury as factfinder is basically neutral, quite unlike, for example, the necessity of defending the first lawsuit in an inconvenient forum.

judge, relitigation of the issue before a jury might be foreclosed by res judicata or collateral estoppel. * * *

B

* * * The petitioners contend that since the scope of the Amendment must be determined by reference to the common law as it existed in 1791, and since the common law permitted collateral estoppel only where there was mutuality of parties, collateral estoppel cannot constitutionally be applied when such mutuality is absent.

The petitioners have advanced no persuasive reason, however, why the meaning of the Seventh Amendment should depend on whether or not mutuality of parties is present. A litigant who has lost because of adverse factual findings in an equity action is equally deprived of a jury trial whether he is estopped from relitigating the factual issues against the same party or a new party. In either case, the party against whom estoppel is asserted has litigated questions of fact, and has had the facts determined against him in an earlier proceeding. In either case there is no further factfinding function for the jury to perform, since the common factual issues have been resolved in the previous action. * * *

The Seventh Amendment has never been interpreted in the rigid manner advocated by the petitioners. On the contrary, many procedural devices developed since 1791 that have diminished the civil jury's historic domain have been found not to be inconsistent with the Seventh Amendment. * * *

The law of collateral estoppel, like the law in other procedural areas defining the scope of the jury's function, has evolved since 1791. * * * [T]hese developments are not repugnant to the Seventh Amendment simply for the reason that they did not exist in 1791. Thus if, as we have held, the law of collateral estoppel forecloses the petitioners from relitigating the factual issues determined against them in the SEC action, nothing in the Seventh Amendment dictates a different result, even though because of lack of mutuality there would have been no collateral estoppel in 1791.

The judgment of the Court of Appeals is

Affirmed.

MR. JUSTICE REHNQUIST, dissenting.

It is admittedly difficult to be outraged about the treatment accorded by the federal judiciary to petitioners' demand for a jury trial in this lawsuit. Outrage is an emotion all but impossible to generate with respect to a corporate defendant in a securities fraud action, and this case is no exception. But the nagging sense of unfairness as to the way petitioners have been treated, engendered by the *imprimatur* placed by the Court of Appeals on respondent's "heads I win, tails you lose" theory of this litigation, is not dispelled by this Court's antiseptic analysis of the issues in the case. It may be that if this Nation were to adopt a new Constitution today, the Seventh Amendment guaranteeing the right of jury trial in civil cases in federal courts would not be included among its provisions. But any present sentiment to that effect cannot obscure or dilute our obligation to enforce the Seventh Amendment, which *was* included in the Bill of Rights in 1791 and which has not since been repealed in the only manner provided by the Constitution for repeal of its provisions.

* * *

The Seventh Amendment requires that the right of trial by jury be "preserved." Because the Seventh Amendment demands preservation of the jury trial right, our cases have uniformly held that the content of the right must be judged by historical standards. * * * If a jury would have been impaneled in a particular kind of case in 1791, then the Seventh Amendment requires a jury trial today, if either party so desires.

To be sure, it is the substance of the right of jury trial that is preserved, not the incidental or collateral effects of common-law practice in 1791. * * *

To say that the Seventh Amendment does not tie federal courts to the exact procedure of the common law in 1791 does not imply, however, that any nominally "procedural" change can be implemented, regardless of its impact on the functions of the jury. * * *

Judged by the foregoing principles, I think it is clear that petitioners were denied their Seventh Amendment right to a jury trial in this case. Neither respondents nor the Court doubt that at common law as it existed in 1791, petitioners would have been entitled in the private action to have a jury determine whether the proxy statement was false and misleading in the respects alleged. The reason is that at common law in 1791, collateral estoppel was permitted only where the parties in the first action were identical to, or in privity with, the parties to the subsequent action. * * * [D]evelopments in the judge-made doctrine of collateral estoppel, however salutary, cannot, consistent with the Seventh Amendment, contract in any material fashion the right to a jury trial that a defendant would have enjoyed in 1791. * * *

* * * [T]he Court seems to suggest that the offensive use of collateral estoppel in this case is permissible under the limited principle set forth above that a mere procedural change that does not invade the province of the jury and a defendant's right thereto to a greater extent than authorized by the common law is permissible. But the Court's actions today constitute a far greater infringement of the defendant's rights than it ever before has sanctioned. * * * The procedural devices of summary judgment and directed verdict are direct descendants of their common-law antecedents. They accomplish nothing more than could have been done at common law, albeit by a more cumbersome procedure. * * *

By contrast, the development of nonmutual estoppel is a substantial departure from the common law and its use in this case completely deprives petitioners of their right to have a jury determine contested issues of fact. * * *

Even accepting, *arguendo,* the majority's position that there is no violation of the Seventh Amendment here, I nonetheless would not sanction the use of collateral estoppel in this case. * * * In my view, it is "unfair" to apply offensive collateral estoppel where the party who is sought to be estopped has not had an opportunity to have the facts of his case determined by a jury. Since in this case petitioners were not entitled to a jury trial in the Securities and Exchange Commission (SEC) lawsuit, I would not estop them from relitigating the issues determined in the SEC suit before a jury in the private action. I believe that several factors militate in favor of this result.

First, the use of offensive collateral estoppel in this case runs counter to the strong federal policy favoring jury trials, even if it does not, as the majority holds, violate the Seventh Amendment. * * *

Second, I believe that the opportunity for a jury trial in the second action could easily lead to a different result from that obtained in the first action before the court and therefore that it is unfair to estop petitioners from relitigating the issues before a jury. * * *

The ultimate irony of today's decision is that its potential for significantly conserving the resources of either the litigants or the judiciary is doubtful at best. That being the case, I see absolutely no reason to frustrate so cavalierly the important federal policy favoring jury decisions of disputed fact questions. The instant case is an apt example of the minimal savings that will be accomplished by the Court's decision. As the Court admits, even if petitioners are collaterally estopped from relitigating whether the proxy was materially false and misleading they are still entitled to have a jury determine whether respondents were injured by the alleged misstatements and the amount of damages, if any, sustained by respondents. * * * Thus, a jury must be impaneled in this case in any event. The time saved by not trying the issue of whether the proxy was materially false and misleading before the jury is likely to be insubstantial.[24] It is just as probable that today's decision will have the result of coercing defendants to agree to consent orders, or settlements in agency enforcement action in order to preserve their right to jury trial in the private actions. In that event, the Court, for no compelling reason, will have simply added a powerful club to the administrative agencies' arsenals that even Congress was unwilling to provide them.

Notes and Questions

1. How should inconsistent prior adjudications affect the application of issue preclusion? This problem was posed most dramatically in the multiple-claimant anomaly developed by Professor Brainerd Currie after the *Bernhard* decision. See Currie, *Mutuality of Collateral Estoppel: The Limits of the Bernhard Doctrine*, 9 Stan.L.Rev. 281 (1957). A train accident injures fifty passengers, and each of these passengers files a separate negligence action against the railroad. The railroad prevails in the first twenty-five suits to reach judgment, but loses the twenty-sixth. How should the twenty-sixth judgment affect the remaining suits?

How might your answer to this question change if the prior twenty-five cases all had been litigated in a court of limited jurisdiction, such as a small-claims court, and if the twenty-sixth judgment was rendered by a court of general jurisdiction? How does this variation on the hypothetical differ from the issue, discussed in Note 2, p. 1247, supra, of whether a judgment by a court of limited jurisdiction should itself preclude the relitigation of certain issues?

Notice the more fundamental implications that the multiple-claimant anomaly has for nonmutual estoppel. Currie's hypothetical was designed to highlight the

---

24. Much of the delay in jury trials is attributed to the jury selection, *voir dire* and the charge. See H. Zeisel, H. Kalven, & B. Buch-   holtz, Delay in the Court 79 (1959). None of these delaying factors will be avoided by today's decision.

aberrant quality of the twenty-sixth judgment. Yet there is no reason that this "aberrant" result might not have been reached in the first trial rather than the twenty-sixth. If the holding against the railroad had been rendered in the first case, nonmutual estoppel would have been available to the remaining forty-nine passengers. In short, although any single decision may be an anomaly, a single decision can still have preclusive effect. Given these observations, do you believe nonmutual estoppel is desirable? Some judges have declined to extend nonmutual collateral estoppel in the face of the conflicting prior judgments. See, e.g., State Farm Fire & Cas. Co. v. Century Home Components, 275 Or. 97, 550 P.2d 1185 (1976).

2. What if before a case settles it yields a judicial finding that conflicts with a prior adjudication of the same issue? Such a finding may result, for example, when a motion to dismiss is denied before a settlement is reached. Can that finding create sufficient inconsistency to block offensive issue preclusion? In JACK FAUCETT ASSOCIATES v. AMERICAN TELEPHONE & TELEGRAPH CO., 744 F.2d 118 (D.C.Cir.1984), certiorari denied 469 U.S. 1196, 105 S.Ct. 980, 83 L.Ed.2d 982 (1985), Judge Mikva wrote for the court: "*Parklane Hosiery* does not hold that only inconsistent final *judgments* can preclude offensive estoppel." Id. at 130. According to Judge Mikva, the issue is only whether "the inconsistency undermines the court's confidence in the correctness of the prior decision." Id.

In the *Jack Faucett* case, the court found another factor weighing against the application of offensive issue preclusion. The prior decision upon which the party seeking preclusion sought to rely had been affirmed by the Second Circuit. In the course of its affirmance, however, the Circuit Court had held that one of the trial judge's evidentiary rulings had been erroneous, though harmless. The Court of Appeals for the District of Columbia Circuit found that the presence of even "harmless" error in the rulings of the trial court upon whose findings a second court was being urged to rely constituted a "serious obstacle" to offensive issue preclusion. Id. at 128. "[W]e decline to hold that the Second Circuit's conclusion of harmless error mandates * * * that we must ignore that error in our analysis of offensive estoppel." Id. at 129.

3. What preclusive effect should be given to a pretrial ruling when parties settle before the case is heard? In GARCIA v. GENERAL MOTORS CORP., 195 Ariz. 510, 990 P.2d 1069 (Ariz.Ct.App.1999), the plaintiffs attempted to use a prior Idaho ruling that prohibited General Motors from using seatbelt evidence in defending a products liability suit. Id. *Garcia* concerned Arizona residents who were injured in Idaho while going on a church camping trip in a van manufactured by General Motors. The passengers were not wearing seatbelts. One of the injured campers sued immediately in federal court in Idaho and subsequently settled with General Motors and the other defendants before trial. Meanwhile, the rest of the passengers brought a suit regarding the same accident in an Arizona state court. They sought to use the Idaho ruling to preclude General Motors from using their failure to wear seatbelts as a defense. In denying the motion, the Arizona court noted that since the second group of plaintiffs easily could have been joined in the first action, the application of offensive collateral estoppel might be improper since it "unfairly allows a plaintiff to sit on the sidelines of the earlier adjudication and to 'wait and see' how it turns out." Id. at 514. The court also found that the ruling was not essential to the ultimate judgment in the Idaho case; therefore, it was not entitled to preclusive effect. Finally, the Arizona court noted that the *in limine* ruling lacked the requisite finality for preclusive effect.

4. What preclusive effect should be given to a guilty verdict? Obviously, since the plaintiff in a subsequent civil action did not have the opportunity to join in the criminal case, the concern that a plaintiff will bring repetitious litigation is not present. On the other hand, the issues necessary to resolve the civil case might be entirely different from those central to the criminal case; therefore, using the criminal conviction as conclusive of civil liability might be unfair. Furthermore, there might be differences in the range of discovery and other procedural opportunities available to a criminal defendant. Thus, in deciding whether or not to allow the civil plaintiff to employ offensive collateral estoppel, courts consider the incentives the defendant had to litigate the first action vigorously, the procedural opportunities available, and any other factors that weigh on fairness. See, e.g. Doe v. Tobias, 715 N.E.2d 829 (Ind.1999) (allowing plaintiff rape victim to assert offensive collateral estoppel against defendant, who had been convicted of the offense in a prior criminal trial).

5. Some have argued that the application of non-mutual collateral estoppel may effect other substantive rights and distort damage awards. For instance, in products liability cases, when the plaintiff successfully invokes offensive collateral estoppel to preclude relitigation of liability, a jury will be instructed to presume liability and make an award on damages. The argument is that a defendant should have the right to present a comparative negligence or causation case. Without this right, even if the product's defect was only a small portion of the cause of the plaintiff's harm, a jury may inappropriately award the plaintiff the full dollar value of the plaintiff's loss. It also is claimed that the application of offensive nonmutual collateral estoppel can thus also reduce the plaintiff's burden of proof. Is this a valid criticism of the doctrine or does the judicial discretion whether to allow offensive collateral estoppel adequately control these risks? See de Villiers, *Technological Risk and Issue Preclusion: A Legal and Policy Critique*, 9 Cornell J. L. & Pub. Policy 523 (2000), and Kennamer, *Issues Raised by the Potential Application of Non–Mutual Offensive Collateral Estoppel in Texas Products Liabilities Cases*, 30 Texas Tech L. Rev. 1127 (1999).

6. What preclusive effect should be given to a compromise verdict? In TAYLOR v. HAWKINSON, 47 Cal.2d 893, 306 P.2d 797 (1957), the California Supreme Court, in an opinion by Justice Traynor, held that the *Bernhard* rule should not be applied due to evidence of a compromise verdict:

> * * * Regardless of the effectiveness of [compromise verdicts] in extinguishing the causes of action or settling the rights directly involved therein * * *, it does not constitute such a determination of the issues involved as to render them res judicata where distinct rights are sought to be litigated in a separate cause of action. * * *

Id. at 896–97, 306 P.2d at 799.

Just how far should a court go in allowing parties in subsequent litigation to prove that the earlier verdict was a compromise? KATZ v. ELI LILLY & CO., 84 F.R.D. 378 (E.D.N.Y.1979), may represent the extreme. A suit prior to *Katz* had held the defendant liable for the wrongful death of the child of a mother who had taken diethylstilbestrol (DES) during pregnancy. Plaintiff Katz sought to take advantage of this prior verdict. The defendant, noticing signs that the earlier verdict may have been a compromise, subpoenaed two members of the jury in the prior case. The plaintiff moved to quash the subpoenas on the ground that the testimony of jurors may not be used to impeach a verdict. The court denied the motion to quash. Could you justify the court's refusal to quash the subpoenas? Would allowing such testimony truly impeach the verdict of the *prior* case? Are there ways to get the jurors' testimony without impeaching the earlier verdict? Should the potential liability of the defendant if preclusion is permitted be allowed to affect the decision of whether to subpoena the jurors? At what point does the effort involved in evaluating the prior verdict outweigh the effort saved in relitigating the substantive issues at stake in the suit?

Since *Parklane* was decided, courts have moved fairly consistently towards accepting offensive nonmutual collateral estoppel in a triumph of efficiency over due process. However, suits against the federal government represent one important exception to this trend. See United States v. Mendoza, 464 U.S. 154, 104 S.Ct. 568, 78 L.Ed.2d 379 (1984). Consider what policy reasons lie behind this decision. Several questions remain after *Mendoza*. Can the federal government Act invoke offensive nonmutual collateral estoppel against a private party? Is a state government similarly excepted from having offensive nonmutual collateral estoppel applied against it?

What preclusive effect should a court give to a compromise *settlement* that requires dismissal of the action with prejudice? In RICE V. CROW, 97 Cal.Rptr.2d 110, 81 Cal.App.4th 725 (Ct.App.2000), Mr. Rice brought suit against his former business partners on his own behalf and derivatively on behalf of the company. During the pendency of the suit, Rice fired his attorneys because of the way they litigated certain issues and sued them for malpractice. The malpractice suit settled in an agreement reciting that it was a compromise and that the parties relinquished all known and unknown claims against each other. Since the second suit would have decided some issues at issue in the first suit, the defendants in the original suit asserted collateral estoppel. The California Court of Appeals said that the plaintiff was only barred from suing parties to the settlement, not from suing other parties. Furthermore, even though the plaintiff would have been precluded from relitigating any issues that *actually* were litigated in the malpractice suit, since the issues never were brought before the court, the doctrine did not apply.

7. What kind of preclusive effect should arise between coparties to an action? Consider SCHWARTZ v. PUBLIC ADMINISTRATOR, 24 N.Y.2d 65, 298 N.Y.S.2d 955, 246 N.E.2d 725 (1969). A multiple car collision resulted in a number of deaths and serious injuries. A passenger in one of the vehicles instituted an action against all of the drivers, alleging that their negligence made them liable for the injuries the passenger had suffered. The passenger prevailed. The question before the court in *Schwartz* was whether this prior judgment should preclude the drivers, who were codefendants in the first action, in subsequent suits against each other. The New York Court of Appeals held that preclusion was appropriate, even when the parties technically were not in an adversarial posture in the first action:

> [I]n preparing for the trial, each defendant now has full discovery against his codefendant whether or not there is a claim between them (CPLR § 3101; Lombardo v. Pecora, 23 A.D.2d 460, 262 N.Y.S.2d 201). At the trial the codefendants have the same rights of cross-examination with respect to each other's witnesses as they have with respect to the passenger's. In every respect they are antagonists, even to the extent that evidence introduced by one codefendant may be relied upon by the other. (See, e.g., Civ.Prac.Act § 212, subd. 3.) In fact, it may rightly be said that in many cases the battle between the codefendants is more strenuous than is their attack against their supposedly main adversary, the plaintiff. The argument that it is unfair to

apply the earlier judgment in the subsequent action between the codefendants, on the ground that the parties were not true adversaries, is wholly
without merit.

Id. at 71–72, 298 N.Y.S.2d at 960, 246 N.E.2d at 729.

When *Schwartz* was litigated, New York was a contributory-negligence state.
It later adopted comparative negligence. Are the problems of preclusion between
coparties reduced when a comparative negligence rule is in force?

    8. Issue preclusion can interfere with a party's right to a jury trial, as
Parklane demonstrates. The Supreme Court has held consistently that the Seventh Amendment does not guarantee the right to relitigate an issue before a jury
if the issue already has been litigated fully in an equitable action. But what
happens if a party is denied a jury trial because of an erroneous trial court ruling
in the prior action? In LYTLE v. HOUSEHOLD MANUFACTURING, INC., 494
U.S. 545, 110 S.Ct. 1331, 108 L.Ed.2d 504 (1990), plaintiff Lytle filed an employment discrimination suit under both Title VII of the Civil Rights Act of 1964, and
42 U.S.C. § 1981. Lytle was entitled to a jury determination of his Section 1981
claims, but not of his Title VII claims. The District Court held that Title VII
provided the exclusive remedy, dismissed the Section 1981 claims from the suit,
and held a bench trial with respect to the remaining Title VII claims.

    The Court of Appeals noted that the dismissal of the Section 1981 claims was
"apparently erroneous," but nevertheless held that Lytle was collaterally estopped
from litigating his Section 1981 claims because they involved issues identical to
the earlier Title VII suit. The court rejected Lytle's claim that the Seventh
Amendment precluded according collateral estoppel effect to the District Court's
erroneous ruling, holding, instead, that judicial economy overrode Lytle's interest
in a jury trial. Justice Marshall, writing for a unanimous Supreme Court,
disagreed:

> Only the District Court's erroneous dismissal of the § 1981 claims enabled
> that court to resolve issues common to both claims, issues that otherwise
> would have been resolved by a jury. * * * It would be anomalous to hold that
> a district court may not deprive a litigant of his right to a jury trial by
> resolving an equitable claim before a jury hears a legal claim raising common
> issues, but that a court may accomplish the same result by erroneously
> dismissing the legal claim. Such a holding would be particularly unfair here
> because Lytle was required to join his legal and equitable claims to avoid the
> bar of res judicata.

* * *

> Although our holding requires a new trial in this case, we view such litigation
> as essential to vindicating Lytle's Seventh Amendment rights. * * * [R]elit-
> igation is the only mechanism that can completely correct the error of the
> court below. Thus, concern about judicial economy, to the extent that it
> supports respondent's position, remains an insufficient basis for departing
> from our longstanding commitment to preserving a litigant's right to a jury
> trial.

    Id. at 551–54, 110 S.Ct. at 1336–37, 108 L.Ed.2d at 515–16.

3. BINDING NONPARTIES

IN RE MULTIDISTRICT CIVIL ACTIONS INVOLVING THE AIR CRASH DISASTER NEAR DAYTON, OHIO, ON MARCH 9, 1967

United States District Court, Southern District of Ohio, 1972.
350 F.Supp. 757.
Reversed sub nom. Humphreys v. Tann,
487 F.2d 666 (6th Cir.1973), certiorari denied
416 U.S. 956, 94 S.Ct. 1970, 40 L.Ed.2d 307 (1974).

MEMORANDUM OPINION AND ORDER

WEINMAN, CHIEF JUDGE. On March 9, 1967 a DC–9 passenger aircraft owned and operated by Trans World Airlines, Inc. and a Beech Baron aircraft owned and operated by the Tann Company collided in mid-air near Dayton, Ohio. As a result of this air disaster, all occupants of both planes were killed. Numerous civil actions seeking recovery for alleged wrongful death and property damage were filed in this Court, other federal district courts and in various state courts across the country. Six actions pending in other federal district courts were transferred to this Court by the Judicial Panel on Multidistrict Litigation for consolidated and coordinated pretrial proceedings pursuant to Section 1407, Title 28 U.S.C. Among the actions transferred to this Court was a passenger wrongful death action against the Tann Company captioned Humphreys v. Herman Tann, et al. which was originally commenced in the United States District Court for the Eastern District of Michigan, Southern Division.

On July 15, 1970 this Court conducted its first pretrial conference for the purpose of scheduling consolidated discovery with respect to all actions pending before the Court arising from the mid-air collision. Thomas F. Wolcott, attorney for plaintiff Humphreys in Case No. 3834ML(F) was among the attorneys attending this first pretrial conference. On July 22, 1970 this Court issued a pretrial order which among other things set forth a schedule for the completion of consolidated discovery in these multidistrict actions.

In accordance with this Court's first pretrial order consolidated discovery was expeditiously completed in these actions. Counsel for all parties including counsel for plaintiff Humphreys was given a full and ample opportunity to participate in all consolidated discovery proceedings, to ascertain all relevant facts concerning the mid-air disaster near Dayton, Ohio and to frame the issues.

After the completion of consolidated discovery the next pretrial conference was scheduled for December 15, 1970. On November 4, 1970 this Court sent an information order to all attorneys advising them that in view of the completion of discovery all counsel shall make a statement to the Court of what he or they expect to prove and further advising all counsel that the Court was planning an early date for trial and would consider recommendations concerning the joinder of party plaintiffs and whether or not there should be separate trials on liability and damages.

The second pretrial conference was held as scheduled. At this conference Craig Spangenberg, Esq. of the Cleveland, Ohio Bar, an acknowledged specialist in the representation of plaintiffs in air disaster cases delivered a statement of the facts which the passenger plaintiffs would attempt to prove in establishing acts of negligence on the part of both Trans World Airlines and the Tann Company. Plaintiffs' counsel who were present at the pretrial conference concurred in Mr. Spangenberg's statement of facts. It was further determined at this second pretrial conference that the passenger wrongful death action captioned Downey v. Trans World Airlines, Inc. and Tann Company would be the first case to proceed for trial. No objection was voiced to the trial of the Downey case first.

For some unexplained reason, Thomas Wolcott, attorney for plaintiff Humphreys, who had received notice of the scheduled December 15 pretrial conference and this Court's desire for a statement of facts from all parties failed to attend the second pretrial conference.

From March 22, 1971 to April 7, 1971 the wrongful death action brought by Vera Downey against Trans World Airlines and Tann Company, Civil Action No. 3521ML was tried to a jury in this Court. At the trial plaintiff was represented by attorney Craig Spangenberg of the Cleveland, Ohio Bar, an extremely experienced and highly competent plaintiff's lawyer, who has a reputation among the Bar as a specialist in air disaster cases. Mr. Spangenberg who was thoroughly familiar with all the facts surrounding the mid-air disaster presented to the jury in the Downey case all the claimed acts of negligence which were acknowledged by all the plaintiffs as constituting a basis for a finding of liability on the part of the Tann Company. In addition attorney Daniel J. O'Neill, counsel for Trans World Airlines, an equally qualified and competent trial attorney who also possessed a high degree of expertise in the highly technical area of aviation law, presented evidence and vigorously attempted to persuade the jury that the sole proximate cause of the mid-air collision was the negligence of the Tann Company pilot. After receiving all relevant evidence concerning the liability of Tann Company and hearing vigorous and well reasoned arguments attempting to fix the responsibility for the mid-air disaster upon the Tann Company pilot, the jury returned a general verdict in favor of the plaintiff in the amount of $300,000 against Trans World Airlines only and found against plaintiff on her claims against the Tann Company. No appeal was filed by any party and upon the satisfaction of the judgment by defendant Trans World Airlines, the judgment in the Downey case became final.

After the judgment in the Downey case became final, a series of motions were filed in the pending Multidistrict cases against the defendant Trans World Airlines seeking to invoke the doctrine of res judicata or collateral estoppel based on the final judgment in the Downey case. In a memorandum opinion issued January 20, 1972 this Court resolved these pending motions with the exception of the motion filed by the Tann Company for summary judgment on the basis of the doctrine of collateral estoppel in all outstanding passenger actions pending against the Tann Company. * * *

* * *

On May 3, 1972, after the [other passenger] * * * actions against Tann Company were settled, this Court heard oral argument on the pending motion. Counsel for plaintiff Humphreys * * * was present and presented oral argument.

Plaintiff Humphreys was not a party to the Downey case in which the liability or responsibility of the Tann Company for the mid-air disaster was determined. Thus the pending motion for summary judgment in the passenger cases raises the interesting but difficult question of whether the doctrine of res judicata or collateral estoppel can be applied against a person who was not a party to the prior action.

* * *

The Bernhard Doctrine abandoning the requirement of strict mutuality is especially applicable to protracted multiple litigation arising from common disasters where the factual and legal issues concerning the liability of defendants are identical. * * *

* * * Had the jury in the Downey case rendered judgment against the Tann Company this Court on the basis of the judgment in the Downey case would have sustained motions for summary judgment on the issue of liability in favor of plaintiffs in the outstanding passenger cases brought against Tann Company.

Turning to the facts of the present case it is clear that two of the essential elements of the Bernhard Doctrine have been satisfied. A final judgment on the merits has been rendered and the issue of whether the Tann Company pilot was guilty of any act of negligence constituting a proximate cause of the mid-air disaster has been actually litigated. The third essential requirement for the application of the doctrine of collateral estoppel however is lacking—that is—the plaintiff Humphreys against whom the doctrine is invoked has not personally litigated the issue of Tann Company's liability. Thus the Tann Company in its motion asks this Court to carry the Bernhard Doctrine one step further and apply the collateral estoppel doctrine against a stranger to the prior action.

Reasons which are not insubstantial have been advanced for the rule denying the application of collateral estoppel against a stranger. These reasons have been aptly summarized as follows:

> The rule * * * is based upon obvious principles of justice, fairness, and requirements of due process of law. The reason for the rule lies in the fact that a stranger to an action does not have the opportunity, vouchsafed to parties, to prove or ascertain the truth of the questions in issue, and the principle that no man's right should be prejudiced without an opportunity of defending it. Indeed, it is a fundamental doctrine of the law that a party to be affected by a personal judgment must have a day in court and an opportunity to be heard. 46 Am.Jur.2d Judgments § 519, page 671.

The constitutional requirement that each person be afforded his day in court is premised upon the underlying principle that fundamental fairness guaranteed by the due process clause of the Fifth and Fourteenth Amendments dictates that no person shall be deprived of a valuable right or claim without first being afforded the right to appear and be heard.

This Court does not believe that the maxim that each man must be given his day in court is so inexorably fixed that it must mandatorily apply where a careful evaluation of the record of pretrial and trial proceedings in the prior action discloses that the absent party was given full and complete opportunity to ascertain and develop all relevant facts and to frame the issues during discovery and the liability issue was adjudicated at a trial conducted in an atmosphere free from errors in substantive, evidentiary and procedural law or trial strategy which if avoided would have changed the result.

In the limited context of these multidistrict litigation cases the Court does not believe the principles of fundamental fairness guaranteed by due process of law are violated by the application of the doctrine of collateral estoppel against plaintiff Humphreys. The Humphreys case was transferred to this Court by the Judicial Panel on Multidistrict Litigation for coordinated and consolidated pretrial proceedings. Coordinated discovery was conducted at which counsel for plaintiff Humphreys was given the opportunity to ascertain and develop all relevant facts concerning the cause of the mid-air collision. Under the coordinated discovery proceedings Humphreys' counsel received the added advantage of reaping the benefit of facts developed by other attorneys who specialize in this type of litigation. At subsequent pretrial conferences counsel for Humphreys had the opportunity to participate in the framing of issues for trial and in selecting the first case to be tried. At the trial itself all parties were represented by highly competent attorneys who can accurately be designated as specialists in aviation disaster litigation. All tenable claims of negligence on the part of Tann Company were presented not only by plaintiffs' counsel but by the equally competent counsel for Trans World Airlines who attempted to convince the jury that the sole proximate cause of the mid-air collision was the negligence of the Tann Company pilot. Well reasoned opening statements and closing arguments were presented to the jury. The Court deems it extremely significant that counsel for plaintiff Humphreys, either in his brief or during oral argument, did not assert that learned counsel for plaintiff Downey failed to introduce all relevant evidence, neglected to present all claims of negligence on the part of Tann or otherwise made errors of commission or omission with respect to substantive, procedural or evidentiary law or trial strategy which resulted or contributed to the verdict in favor of Tann Company. No errors on the part of this Court in the admission of evidence or the charge to the jury have been raised. Having had the advantage of presiding at the trial of the Downey case, this Court can truly say that the Downey case was one of the most skillfully tried cases this Court has had the pleasure of adjudicating.

Finally, this is not the type of case where there is an appreciable danger that the jury verdict in favor of the Tann Company was a compromise motivated by sympathy. The uncontradicted evidence discloses that the deceased passenger Edward Downey was an outstanding individual in terms of his business endeavors and private life. The decedent was a graduate engineer who was selected by his employer for further advancement. The decedent was active in church and civic affairs and at the time of his death left a wife and three minor children. It was obvious that plaintiff's counsel who represented the heirs of other deceased passengers was litigating his most favorable case in an attempt to test the liability and monetary responsibility of both Trans World Airlines and the Tann Company.

Upon considering all these factors the Court concludes that no principle of fundamental fairness inherent in the concept of due process will be offended by the application of the doctrine against plaintiff Humphreys to bar the relitigation of the issue of the Tann Company's liability for the mid-air disaster. In this Court's opinion unfairness will result and the effective administration of justice will be retarded if plaintiff Humphreys is permitted to relitigate an issue which has been fully and fairly adjudicated.

* * *

The Court realizes that this decision does not conform to the weight of authority and appreciates that there is room for reasonable divergence of opinion as to the validity of the result reached herein. However, in view of the great increase in the number of civil actions commenced in the federal district courts in recent years, the Court believes that the federal trial courts should not hesitate to adopt new approaches designed to terminate needless and futile litigation where identical liability issues have been fairly and truly tried in a prior action. Furthermore, the Court believes that this is a proper case in which to test the power of a transferee court in common disaster multidistrict litigation to bar relitigation in subsequent common disaster actions of identical liability issues which have been actually litigated in a prior action arising from the same incident.

Accordingly, the motion of the Tann Company for summary judgment in its favor * * * hereby is sustained and this action hereby is dismissed.

Notes and Questions

1.   The Sixth Circuit reversed Chief Judge Weinman's ruling in the principal case, saying: "We share the concern of the district court for the crowded dockets of federal courts and the proper utilization of judicial time. However, we do not believe that these considerations can overcome the due process objections * * *." Humphreys v. Tann, 487 F.2d 666, 671 (6th Cir.1973), certiorari denied 416 U.S. 956, 94 S.Ct. 1970, 40 L.Ed.2d 307 (1974).

2.   The District Court seems to base its holding on two intertwined but distinct considerations. What are they? Would either, standing alone, provide a sufficient basis for the court to hold a nonparty precluded?

3.   Often, formal relationships between persons will justify nonparty preclusion. For instance, when a guardian litigates a suit on behalf of a minor, the minor will normally be bound by the suit's outcome. Can you think of other relationships that would justify nonparty preclusion? What if a party assigns her rights to a person who then sues upon them? Suppose the assignee is an insurance company and the assignor the insured?

4.   Sometimes a relationship between parties need not be so formal as that between a guardian and a child in order to justify nonparty preclusion. In MONTANA v. UNITED STATES, 440 U.S. 147, 99 S.Ct. 970, 59 L.Ed.2d 210 (1979), the Supreme Court held that when nonparties assume control over litigation in which they have a direct financial or pecuniary interest, they may be precluded from subsequently relitigating issues that the earlier suit resolved. Montana gave contractors different tax treatment depending on whether they contracted to build public or private projects. A contractor on a federal construction project brought a state-court action challenging the constitutionality of this

practice. The United States directed and financed the litigation for the contractor, but it also brought an action challenging the practice in federal court. After the Montana Supreme Court upheld Montana's system of taxation, the United States continued with its federal action. But Montana argued that the federal government was bound by the state-court judgment. When the case reached the Supreme Court, Justice Marshall, writing for the Court, observed that "although not a party, the United States plainly had a sufficient laboring oar in the conduct of the state-court litigation to actuate principles of estoppel." Id. at 154–55, 99 S.Ct. at 974, 59 L.Ed.2d at 217–18.

The *Montana* case suggests other types of representation that might justify nonparty preclusion. What if individuals agree that a case will serve as a test case? Some courts have held that, when sufficient evidence of an agreement exists, nonparties are precluded from relitigating the claims. See, e.g., Boyd v. Jamaica Plain Co–Operative Bank, 7 Mass.App.Ct. 153, 386 N.E.2d 775 (1979). See generally *Restatement (Second), Judgments* § 40 (1982).

5.   A limited number of courts have been willing to permit nonparty preclusion in a narrow range of circumstances in which "virtual" representation has occurred. The theory underlying preclusion in cases of virtual representation, which is similar to the theory upon which class-action rules are based, is that once an issue has been adjudicated by a court in an adequate adversarial contest, it should be considered settled once and for all—both as to those who participated in the litigation and as to those who did not. Thus, preclusion based on virtual representation is very different from the other forms of preclusion, each of which was based upon the fact that, in some sense, the party against whom preclusion was invoked had enjoyed a day in court. See Cauefield v. Fidelity & Casualty Co., 378 F.2d 876, 879 (5th Cir.), certiorari denied 389 U.S. 1009, 88 S.Ct. 571, 19 L.Ed.2d 606 (1967).

6.   Courts can decline to apply nonparty preclusion for various reasons even if the facts of the two cases seem remarkably similar. Consider Jones v. Bates, 127 F.3d 839 (9th Cir.1997). In 1990, California voters passed Proposition 140, which imposed a lifetime limit on the number of terms an individual could spend in state legislative office. In 1991, a group of petitioners, including members of the California Senate and Assembly and individual constituents, challenged Proposition 140's validity directly in the California Supreme Court in Legislature v. Eu, 54 Cal.3d 492, 286 Cal.Rptr. 283, 816 P.2d 1309 (1991). The California Supreme Court upheld the term limits. In 1995, Tom Bates and a number of his constituents filed suit in federal court challenging Proposition 140. Neither Bates nor his constituents had been parties in Legislature v. Eu. However, their complaint was much the same as that filed in the earlier case. The state asserted that Bates' suit was barred by collateral estoppel. In allowing the suit to go forward, the Ninth Circuit found that although the issues were the same and had been actually and necessarily litigated in *Eu*, Bates' constituents did not have the same interests as the *Eu* petitioners. Furthermore, Bates himself could not have had the expectation at the time of *Eu* that his rights would be foreclosed forever given that *Eu* was not a class action and that Bates had not participated. The court stated that "even assuming that Bates and his constituents were in privity with the *Eu* petitioners * * * even when the formal prerequisites for collateral estoppel are present, the public interest may require that relitigation of certain questions of law not be foreclosed." 127 F.3d at 850. Is this the right result given the values that the application of nonmutual collateral estoppel is supposed to promote?

MARTIN v. WILKS

Supreme Court of the United States, 1989.
490 U.S. 755, 109 S.Ct. 2180, 104 L.Ed.2d 835.

Certiorari to the United States Court of Appeals for the Eleventh Circuit.

[The City of Birmingham, Alabama ("City") and the Jefferson County Personnel Board ("Board") entered into consent judgments with black firefighters setting goals for hiring blacks as firefighters and for promoting them. White firefighters subsequently brought suit against the City and the Board alleging that the Whites were being denied promotions illegally in favor of less qualified Blacks. They argued that the consent decrees required promotions based on race, in violation of federal law. The City and the Board responded that consent decrees entered in the earlier suits brought by Blacks (in which the White firefighters had not participated) mandated the procedures followed and that these consent decrees precluded the current suit. The District Court held that the earlier consent decrees provided a defense to the reverse discrimination suits, and that the only issue was whether the promotions of Blacks were consistent with the terms of the decrees. The Court of Appeals reversed, holding that because the white firefighters or their privies were not parties to the earlier litigation, their independent discrimination claims could not be precluded.]

CHIEF JUSTICE REHNQUIST delivered the opinion of the Court.

* * *

All agree that "[i]t is a principle of general application in anglo-American jurisprudence that one is not bound by a judgment *in personam* in a litigation in which he is not designated as a party or to which he has not been made a party by service of process." * * * This rule is part of our "deep-rooted historic tradition that everyone should have his own day in court." 18 C. Wright, A. Miller, & E. Cooper, Federal Practice and Procedure § 4449, p. 417 (1981). A judgment or decree among parties to a lawsuit resolves issues as among them, but it does not conclude the rights of strangers to those proceedings.[2]

Petitioners argue that, because respondents failed to timely intervene in the initial proceedings, their current challenge to actions taken under the consent decree constitutes an impermissible "collateral attack." They argue that respondents were aware that the underlying suit might affect them and if they chose to pass up an opportunity to intervene, they should not be

---

2. We have recognized an exception to the general rule when, in certain limited circumstances, a person, although not a party, has his interests adequately represented by someone with the same interests who is a party. See Hansberry v. Lee [p. 718, supra] * * * ("class" or "representative" suits); Fed.Rule Civ.Proc. 23 (same); Montana v. United States, 440 U.S. 147, 154–155, 99 S.Ct. 970, 974–975, 59 L.Ed.2d 210 (1979) (control of litigation on behalf of one of the parties in the litigation). Additionally, where a special remedial scheme exists expressly foreclosing successive litigation by nonlitigants, as for example in bankruptcy or probate, legal proceedings may terminate preexisting rights if the scheme is otherwise consistent with due process. See NLRB v. Bildisco & Bildisco, 465 U.S. 513, 529–530, n. 10, 104 S.Ct. 1188, 1198, n. 101, 79 L.Ed.2d 482 (1984) ("proof of claim must be presented to the Bankruptcy Court * * * or be lost"); Tulsa Professional Collection Services, Inc. v. Pope, 485 U.S. 478 (1988) (nonclaim statute terminating unsubmitted claims against the estate). Neither of these exceptions, however, applies in this case.

permitted to later litigate the issues in a new action. The position has sufficient appeal to have commanded the approval of the great majority of the Federal Courts of Appeals, but we agree with the contrary view expressed by the Court of Appeals for the Eleventh Circuit in this case.

We begin with the words of Justice Brandeis in Chase National Bank v. Norwalk, 291 U.S. 431, 54 S.Ct. 475, 78 L.Ed. 894 (1934):

> "The law does not impose upon any person absolutely entitled to a hearing the burden of voluntary intervention in a suit to which he is a stranger. * * * Unless duly summoned to appear in a legal proceeding, a person not a privy may rest assured that a judgment recovered therein will not affect his legal rights." * * *

While these words were written before the adoption of the Federal Rules of Civil Procedure, we think the Rules incorporate the same principle; a party seeking a judgment binding on another cannot obligate that person to intervene; he must be joined. * * * Against the background of permissive intervention set forth in *Chase National Bank,* the drafters cast Rule 24, governing intervention, in permissive terms. * * * They determined that the concern for finality and completeness of judgments would be "better [served] by mandatory joinder procedures." * * * Accordingly, Rule 19(a) provides for mandatory joinder in circumstances where a judgment rendered in the absence of a person may "leave * * * persons already parties subject to a substantial risk of incurring * * * inconsistent obligations. * * * " Rule 19(b) sets forth the factors to be considered by a court in deciding whether to allow an action to proceed in the absence of an interested party.

Joinder as a party, rather than knowledge of a lawsuit and an opportunity to intervene, is the method by which potential parties are subjected to the jurisdiction of the court and bound by a judgment or decree. The parties to a lawsuit presumably know better than anyone else the nature and scope of relief sought in the action, and at whose expense such relief might be granted. It makes sense, therefore, to place on them a burden of bringing in additional parties where such a step is indicated, rather than placing on potential additional parties a duty to intervene when they acquire knowledge of the lawsuit. The linchpin of the "impermissible collateral attack" doctrine—the attribution of preclusive effect to a failure to intervene—is therefore quite inconsistent with Rule 19 and Rule 24.

* * *

Petitioners contend that a different result should be reached because the need to join affected parties will be burdensome and ultimately discouraging to civil rights litigation. Potential adverse claimants may be numerous and difficult to identify; if they are not joined, the possibility for inconsistent judgments exists. Judicial resources will be needlessly consumed in relitigation of the same question.

* * *

The difficulties petitioners foresee in identifying those who could be adversely affected by a decree granting broad remedial relief are undoubtedly present, but they arise from the nature of the relief sought and not because of any choice between mandatory intervention and joinder. Rule 19's provisions for joining interested parties are designed to accommodate the sort of complexities that may arise from a decree affecting numerous people in various ways. We doubt that a mandatory intervention rule would be any less awkward. As mentioned, plaintiffs who seek the aid of the courts to alter existing employment policies, or the employer who might be subject to conflicting decrees, are best able to bear the burden of designating those who would be adversely affected if plaintiffs prevail; these parties will generally have a better understanding of the scope of likely relief than employees who are not named but might be affected. Petitioners' alternative does not eliminate the need for, or difficulty of, identifying persons who, because of their interests, should be included in a lawsuit. It merely shifts that responsibility to less able shoulders.

* * *

* * * A voluntary settlement in the form of a consent decree between one group of employees and their employer cannot possibly "settle," voluntarily or otherwise, the conflicting claims of another group of employees who do not join in the agreement. This is true even if the second group of employees is a party to the litigation:

> "[P]arties who choose to resolve litigation through settlement may not dispose of the claims of a third party * * * without that party's agreement. A court's approval of a consent decree between some of the parties therefore cannot dispose of the valid claims of nonconsenting intervenors." *Firefighters v. Cleveland,* 478 U.S. 501, 529, 106 S.Ct. 3063, 3079, 92 L.Ed.2d 405 (1986).

Insofar as the argument is bottomed on the idea that it may be easier to settle claims among a disparate group of affected persons if they are all before the Court, joinder bids fair to accomplish that result as well as a regime of mandatory intervention.

* * *

Affirmed.

JUSTICE STEVENS, with whom JUSTICE BRENNAN, JUSTICE MARSHALL, and JUSTICE BLACKMUN join, dissenting.

As a matter of law there is a vast difference between persons who are actual parties to litigation and persons who merely have the kind of interest that may as a practical matter be impaired by the outcome of a case. Persons in the first category have a right to participate in a trial and to appeal from an adverse judgment; depending on whether they win or lose, their legal rights may be enhanced or impaired. Persons in the latter category have a right to intervene in the action in a timely fashion, or they may be joined as parties against their will. But if they remain on the sidelines, they may be harmed as a practical matter even though their legal rights are unaffected. One of the disadvantages of sideline-sitting is that the bystander has no right to appeal from a judgment no matter how harmful it may be.

In this case the Court quite rightly concludes that the white firefighters who brought the second series of Title VII cases could not be deprived of their legal rights in the first series of cases because they had neither intervened nor been joined as parties. * * * The consent decrees obviously could not deprive them of any contractual rights, such as seniority, * * * or accrued vacation pay, * * * or of any other legal rights, such as the right to have their employer comply with federal statutes like Title VII, cf. *Firefighters v. Cleveland, supra,* 478 U.S., at 529, 106 S.Ct., at 3079. There is no reason, however, why the consent decrees might not produce changes in conditions at the white firefighters' place of employment that, as a practical matter, may have a serious effect on their opportunities for employment or promotion even though they are not bound by the decrees in any legal sense. The fact that one of the effects of a decree is to curtail the job opportunities of nonparties does not mean that the nonparties have been deprived of legal rights or that they have standing to appeal from that decree without becoming parties.

Persons who have no right to appeal from a final judgment—either because the time to appeal has elapsed or because they never became parties to the case—may nevertheless collaterally attack a judgment on certain narrow grounds. If the court had no jurisdiction over the subject matter, or if the judgment is the product of corruption, duress, fraud, collusion, or mistake, under limited circumstances it may be set aside in an appropriate collateral proceeding. * * * This rule not only applies to parties to the original action, but also allows interested third parties collaterally to attack judgments. In both civil and criminal cases, however, the grounds that may be invoked to support a collateral attack are much more limited than those that may be asserted as error on direct appeal. Thus, a person who can foresee that a lawsuit is likely to have a practical impact on his interests may pay a heavy price if he elects to sit on the sidelines instead of intervening and taking the risk that his legal rights will be impaired.

In this case there is no dispute about the fact that respondents are not parties to the consent decrees. It follows as a matter of course that they are not bound by those decrees. Those judgments could not, and did not, deprive them of any legal rights. The judgments did, however, have a practical impact on respondents' opportunities for advancement in their profession. For that reason, respondents had standing to challenge the validity of the decrees, but the grounds that they may advance in support of a collateral challenge are much more limited than would be allowed if they were parties prosecuting a direct appeal.

* * *

There is nothing unusual about the fact that litigation between adverse parties may, as a practical matter, seriously impair the interests of third persons who elect to sit on the sidelines. Indeed, in complex litigation this Court has squarely held that a sideline-sitter may be bound as firmly as an actual party if he had adequate notice and a fair opportunity to intervene and if the judicial interest in finality is sufficiently strong. * * *

There is no need, however, to go that far in order to agree with the District Court's eminently sensible view that compliance with the terms of a valid decree remedying violations of Title VII cannot itself violate that statute or the Equal Protection Clause. The city of Birmingham, in entering into and complying with this decree, has made a substantial step toward the eradication of the long history of pervasive racial discrimination that has plagued its fire department. The District Court, after conducting a trial and carefully considering respondents' arguments, concluded that this effort is lawful and should go forward. Because respondents have thus already had their day in court and have failed to carry their burden, I would vacate the judgment of the Court of Appeals and remand for further proceedings consistent with this opinion.

Notes and Questions

1.   Does the Supreme Court's decision in *Martin* cast doubt on any of the instances of nonparty preclusion raised in Notes 3 through 6, pp. 1305–06, supra?

2.   Does *Martin* make clear that the Sixth Circuit, and not Judge Weinman, had the better argument in *In re Multidistrict*, p. 1301, supra?

3.   The specific holding of *Martin,* in the Title VII arena, was legislatively overruled by Section 108 of the Civil Rights Act of 1991, Pub.L.No. 102–166, tit. I, § 108, 105 Stat. 1071, 1076. The 1991 Act prohibits challenges to employment consent decrees by individuals who had actual notice and a reasonable opportunity to intervene, or whose interests were adequately represented. Does such expansive nonparty preclusion go beyond the bounds of fairness required by the Constitution? See Blonder–Tongue Labs., Inc. v. University of Illinois Foundation, p. 1288, supra ("Some litigants—those who never appeared in a prior action—may not be collaterally estopped without litigating the issue. They have never had a chance to present their evidence and arguments on their claim. Due process prohibits estopping them despite one or more existing judgments of the identical issue which stand squarely against their position.").

4.   Is requiring parties who are aware of litigation that could potentially affect their interests to intervene the equivalent of giving them their "day in court?" Are there other due process concerns? Suppose, for example, that a party becomes aware of litigation that will affect her interests, but the litigation is taking place in a jurisdiction where she would not be subject to *in personam* jurisdiction. Does requiring the party, under threat of preclusion, to adjudicate her interests in a forum where she would not be subject to personal jurisdiction violate her due process rights? Is it enough to say that her interests were adequately represented? See generally Bone, *Rethinking the "Day in Court" Ideal and Nonparty Preclusion,* 67 N.Y.U.L.Rev. 193 (1992).

5.   Consent decrees are used frequently in institutional reform litigation. Given the broad effect of these judgments and the fact that they operate over extended periods of time, should the parties themselves be allowed to seek modification when they feel a change in the relevant facts or law warrants it? See Rule 60(b); Rufo v. Inmates of Suffolk County Jail, 502 U.S. 367, 112 S.Ct. 748, 116 L.Ed.2d 867 (1992).

6.   The issues addressed in *Martin* have generated much commentary. See, e.g., Catania & Sullivan, *Judging Judgments: The 1991 Civil Rights Act and the Lingering Ghost of* Martin v. Wilks, 57 Brooklyn L.Rev. 995 (1992); Grover, *The Silenced Majority:* Martin v. Wilks *and the Legislative Response,* 1992 U.Ill.L.Rev. 43; Kramer, *Consent Decrees and the Rights of Third Parties,* 87 Mich.L.Rev. 321 (1988); Pielemeier, *Due Process Limitations on the Application of Collateral Estoppel Against Nonparties to Prior Litigation,* 63 B.U.L.Rev. 383 (1983).

SECTION F. INTERSYSTEM PRECLUSION

The preceding discussion of preclusion assumed that both the original and subsequent courts were in the same judicial system. Often, however, questions of preclusion are presented to a court that is part of a judicial system different from the court that rendered the prior judgment. Should this affect the preclusive effect given the prior judgment?

———

Read U.S. Const. Art. IV, § 1 and 28 U.S.C. § 1738 in the Supplement.

———

1. INTERSTATE PRECLUSION

HART v. AMERICAN AIRLINES, INC.

Supreme Court of New York, 1969.
61 Misc.2d 41, 304 N.Y.S.2d 810.

FRANK, JUSTICE.

* * *

The actions all arise out of the crash, in Kentucky on November 8, 1965, of an American Airlines aircraft while the plane was en route from La Guardia Airport, New York to an airport in Covington, Kentucky. The crash resulted in the death of 58 out of the 62 persons aboard and, in addition to the multiple actions pending in this court, comparable actions have been instituted in other States and in various United States District Courts.

Of the various actions instituted as a result of the crash, the first case to be tried to conclusion was that brought in the United States District Court, Northern District of Texas (*Creasy v. American Airlines*), which resulted in a verdict in favor of the plaintiff therein against the defendant American Airlines. * * * [I]t is undisputable from the pleadings and papers herein that the issue of defendant airline's liability in these cases is identical to the issue in that regard determined in the Texas action.

In light of the Texas result which has now been affirmed on appeal, plaintiffs Landano and Kirchstein oppose defendant's motion for a joint trial by cross-moving for summary judgment on the issue of liability which, if granted, would obviate a trial on such issue and necessarily require a denial of defendant's motion.

Plaintiffs contend that while, concededly, they were not parties to the Texas action, nevertheless the determination in that action of defendant's liability for the plane crash of November 8, 1965 is, under the doctrine of collateral estoppel, conclusive on the issue of defendant's liability for such crash in the actions brought by these plaintiffs.

* * * [In order to invoke the doctrine of collateral estoppel:] "There must be an identity of issue which has necessarily been decided in the prior action and is decisive of the present action, and, second, there must have been a full and fair opportunity to contest the decision now said to be controlling."

* * * [S]uch requirements are amply met in the instant cases. As already indicated, the issue of defendant airline's liability for the crash in which plaintiffs' decedents perished is identical to the issue of liability litigated in the Texas action where defendant was similarly charged with responsibility for that same accident. Indeed, in an airplane crash there are absent any of the problems with respect to "identity of issue" on liability which might arise in other types of accidents involving multiple participants such as automobile accident cases. With respect to the second requirement, it is in no way disputed that defendant had a full and fair opportunity to contest the issue of its liability in the course of the 19–day trial in the Texas action, and in order to defeat collateral estoppel on this ground the burden rests on the defendant to show that it had no such opportunity.

* * *

Defendant's reliance on "full faith and credit" to defeat the application of collateral estoppel herein is misplaced. This is not a situation where the judgment, as such, of the Texas court is sought to be enforced. What is here involved is a policy determination by our courts that " 'One who has had his day in court should not be permitted to litigate the question anew' " (*B.R. De Witt, Inc. v. Hall,* 19 N.Y.2d 141, 144, *supra*), and, further, refusal "to tolerate a condition where, on relatively the same set of facts, one fact-finder, be it court or jury" may find a party liable while another exonerates him leading to the "inconsistent results which are always a blemish on a judicial system" (*Schwartz v. Public Administrator,* 24 N.Y.2d 65, 74, *supra*). * * *

Perhaps the strongest argument for applying the New York doctrine of collateral estoppel herein is the nature of the showing by defendant of the supposed "inequity" that would ensue from such application. There is a belabored emphasis on the merits of "mutuality of estoppel" and its favored status in "a majority of jurisdictions". Such of course wholly ignores the fact that our highest court has resoundingly stated in terms leaving no room for doubt that "the 'doctrine of mutuality' is a dead letter" (*B.R. De Witt, Inc. v. Hall,* 19 N.Y.2d 141, 147, *supra*). * * *

Among the reasons submitted by defendant as to why it should have an opportunity to retry the issue of its liability, notwithstanding its failure to prove its freedom therefrom on the trial in Texas, is the argument that such issue was submitted to the jury under the substantive law of Kentucky which is less favorable to defendant than is the New York law. While one is tempted to wonder what the argument would be if the situation were reversed, such contention is in any event wholly without merit since a New York court would also be obliged to submit the case under the substantive law of Kentucky, the place where the crash occurred. * * *

* * *

Even more interesting is the argument raised by defendant which may be paraphrased in Biblical terms as "hear them not for they know not what they do". Defendant seriously suggests that the determination in the Texas action should not be accorded further conclusive effect because that action involved only a single claimant and the jury's decision as to defendant's negligence is somehow impaired because rendered "without any awareness whatsoever by the jury that its verdict would determine the obligation of the defendant to many other persons not before it". It is apparently defendant's contention that the issue as to whether or not it was negligent in the operation of its aircraft is in some manner dependent upon the number of claims which may ultimately be asserted against it.

* * *

Accordingly, plaintiffs' cross motion for summary judgment is granted and defendant's motion for a joint trial is denied. Settle order providing for an assessment of damages.

Notes and Questions

1. Do the statutory and constitutional provisions require that states give a judgment the same preclusive effect—neither more nor less—as would the courts of the rendering state? Or do the provisions establish a minimum preclusive effect that one state must give another's judgment? There has been considerable debate over whether a court can rest non-mutual preclusion on the judgment of a court that itself would require mutuality. The more common view appears to be in favor of employing the rules of the rendering court. This approach allows the first court the power to limit the effect of its own proceedings. See 18 Wright, Miller & Cooper, *Federal Practice and Procedure: Jurisdiction and Related Matters* §§ 4467 n. 54, 4469 n. 33 (1981) (2001 Pocket Part). The issue is left open in *Restatement (Second), Judgments* § 86, comment *g* (1982). Nonetheless, some courts have given nonmutual preclusive effect to a judgment that the rendering state's courts would not have treated as preclusive.

In FINLEY v. KESLING, 105 Ill.App.3d 1, 60 Ill.Dec. 874, 433 N.E.2d 1112 (1982), Finley testified in Indiana divorce proceedings that four of his children owned 40% of the stock in a family corporation, and this testimony was accepted as the basis for the division of property. Thereafter he sued his four children in Illinois for a declaration that he was the beneficial owner of the stock. The Illinois court expressed doubt whether Indiana would cling to its traditional mutuality requirement in these circumstances, but concluded that it could apply collateral estoppel without regard to what Indiana might do. In the Illinois court's view, although a second state cannot reduce the effect of a judgment below the level commanded by the law of the judgment state, it can expand its effect. The court, nonetheless, advanced an alternative ground for decision—that Illinois courts would not permit a party to contradict his sworn testimony in a prior proceeding, and that this is a matter independent of the effect of judgments or full faith and credit requirements.

2. What limits does the Due Process Clause place on expanding the preclusive effect given a state judgment? How should the foreseeability of the expanded preclusive effect figure into this question? See Shreve, *Preclusion and Federal Choice of Law*, 64 Texas L.Rev. 1209, 1251–63 (1986).

3. Often a plaintiff may wish to enforce a judgment in a state other than the one that rendered the judgment. The procedures for enforcing an out-of-state judgment vary from state to state. Sometimes it is possible simply to register the existence of the out-of-state judgment with the clerk of the court in which the judgment is to be enforced. Other times the plaintiff must institute a new suit, which is then subject to abbreviated procedures. What requirements do the

constitutional and statutory provisions regarding full faith and credit place on a state's treatment of enforcement proceedings?

The basic implications of full faith and credit are the same for enforcement proceedings as they are for preclusion. There are, however, some exceptions to this general rule. The Supreme Court recently tackled this issue in BAKER v. GENERAL MOTORS CORP., 522 U.S. 222, 118 S.Ct. 657, 139 L.Ed.2d 580 (1998). The Bakers subpoenaed Elwell, a former GM engineering analyst, to testify in a wrongful-death action brought in Missouri against the automobile company. GM asserted Elwell's testimony was barred by a prior Michigan court settlement and permanent injunction generally prohibiting Elwell from testifying in any litigation involving GM. Reversing the Eighth Circuit, the Supreme Court, in an opinion delivered by Justice Ginsburg, held Elwell may testify "without offense" to the full faith and credit requirement: "Recognition, under full faith and credit, is owed to dispositions Michigan has authority to order. But a Michigan decree cannot command obedience elsewhere on a matter the Michigan court lacks authority to resolve." Id. at 240–41, 118 S.Ct. at 667–68, 139 L.Ed.2d at 597. The Court held that Michigan "lacks authority" to dictate evidentiary issues in courts of other states, in actions brought by strangers to the Michigan litigation. However, the Court noted that this exception is a narrow one: "If the Bakers had been parties to the Michigan proceedings and had actually litigated the privileged character of Elwell's testimony, the Bakers would of course be precluded from relitigating that issue in Missouri." Id. at 239 n. 12, 118 S.Ct. at 667 n. 12, 139 L.Ed.2d at 596 n. 12 (internal citations omitted). See also 18 Wright, Miller & Cooper, *Federal Practice and Procedure: Jurisdiction and Related Matters* § 4467 (1981) (2001 Pocket Part)

Another example of the limits of full faith and credit is that judgments based on limited forms of judicial jurisdiction—in rem and quasi-in-rem judgments—need not be honored in execution proceedings. Or, a state may refuse to entertain an enforcement proceeding on grounds that its statute of limitations for such enforcement proceedings has run, even though the statute of the rendering state would not have run. And, for a final example, state statutes often specify that certain items of personal property, such as social-security payments and the last $200 of a savings account, cannot be used to satisfy court judgments. It is not a violation of full faith and credit for a state to refuse to enforce a judgment because it would require attachment of exempt property, even though that property would not have been considered exempt in the state rendering the judgment. For more general discussions of full faith and credit, see Nadelmann, *Full Faith and Credit to Judgments and Public Acts,* 56 Mich.L.Rev. 33 (1957); Radin, *The Authenticated Full Faith and Credit Clause: Its History,* 39 Ill.L.Rev. 1 (1944).

4. Recall the problem of limited appearances discussed in Chapter Two at pp. 188–90, supra. What implications does the existence of claim and issue preclusion have for limited appearances? Suppose that plaintiff P institutes a quasi-in-rem suit in jurisdiction X, which permits limited appearances. Defendant D makes the limited appearance, contesting the merits of the suit but risking only the value of the attached property. Plaintiff wins, but it turns out that the value of the property does not satisfy the judgment of the underlying claim. Can the plaintiff then institute a second suit on the same cause of action, styled either as another quasi-in-rem suit or, if possible, as an in personam suit, in a different jurisdiction, and then assert preclusion based on the earlier quasi-in-rem judgment? Would both claim and issue preclusion be available to such a plaintiff?

Alternatively, suppose the defendant had prevailed in the first proceeding. Could the defendant assert preclusion defensively in subsequent proceedings?

The dilemma posed is easy to state and difficult to resolve. To allow preclusion in such situations undermines the value, if not the very existence, of limited appearances. Not to allow preclusion would be inconsistent with the principles of preclusion as they normally are applied. The *Restatement (Second) of Judgments* would allow preclusion based on judgments in quasi-in-rem suits; the Reporter's Note concludes that consistency within the law of preclusion is of greater value than the existence of limited appearances. See *Restatement (Second), Judgments* § 32, comment *d* (1982).

The position taken by the *Restatement* has been criticized. See Note, *Limited Appearances and Issue Preclusion: Resetting the Trap?*, 66 Cornell L.Rev. 595 (1981). It has been argued that the rule recommended in the *Restatement* may increase use of judicial resources. If no preclusive effect would attach to quasi-in-rem judgments, a rational defendant making limited appearances would never mount a defense more costly than the value of attached property. The threat of greater preclusive effect may cause these defendants to mount more extensive defenses to quasi-in-rem suits. How do you think that this rule of preclusion will affect use of judicial resources? Do you believe that it will increase use of such resources, or merely fail to decrease their use?

———

The substantive areas of matrimonial and custody law presents special problems for the application of preclusion.

THOMPSON v. THOMPSON

Supreme Court of the United States, 1988.
484 U.S. 174, 108 S.Ct. 513, 98 L.Ed.2d 512.

Certiorari to the United States Court of Appeals for the Ninth Circuit.

JUSTICE MARSHALL delivered the opinion of the Court.

We granted certiorari in this case to determine whether the Parental Kidnaping Prevention Act of 1980, 28 U.S.C. § 1738A, furnishes an implied cause of action in federal court to determine which of two conflicting state custody decisions is valid.

I

The Parental Kidnaping Prevention Act (PKPA or Act) imposes a duty on the States to enforce a child custody determination entered by a court of a sister State if the determination is consistent with the provisions of the Act. In order for a state court's custody decree to be consistent with the provisions of the Act, the State must have jurisdiction under its own local law and one of five conditions set out in § 1738A(c)(2) must be met. Briefly put, these conditions authorize the state court to enter a custody decree if the child's home is or recently has been in the State, if the child has no home State and it would be in the child's best interest for the State to assume jurisdiction, or if the child is present in the State and has been abandoned or abused. Once a

State exercises jurisdiction consistently with the provisions of the Act, no other State may exercise concurrent jurisdiction over the custody dispute, § 1738A(g), even if it would have been empowered to take jurisdiction in the first instance, and all States must accord full faith and credit to the first State's ensuing custody decree.

As the legislative scheme suggests, and as Congress explicitly specified, one of the chief purposes of the PKPA is to "avoid jurisdictional competition and conflict between State courts." Pub.L. 96–611, 94 Stat. 3569, § 7(c)(5), note following 28 U.S.C. § 1738A. This case arises out of a jurisdictional stalemate that came to pass notwithstanding the strictures of the Act. In July 1978, respondent Susan Clay (then Susan Thompson) filed a petition in Los Angeles Superior Court asking the court to dissolve her marriage to petitioner David Thompson and seeking custody of the couple's infant son, Matthew. The court initially awarded the parents joint custody of Matthew, but that arrangement became infeasible when respondent decided to move from California to Louisiana to take a job. The court then entered an order providing that respondent would have sole custody of Matthew once she left for Louisiana. This state of affairs was to remain in effect until the court investigator submitted a report on custody, after which the court intended to make a more studied custody determination. * * *

Respondent and Matthew moved to Louisiana in December 1980. Three months later, respondent filed a petition in Louisiana state court for enforcement of the California custody decree, judgment of custody, and modification of petitioner's visitation privileges. By order dated April 7, 1981, the Louisiana court granted the petition and awarded sole custody of Matthew to respondent. Two months later, however, the California court, having received and reviewed its investigator's report, entered an order awarding sole custody of Matthew to petitioner. Thus arose the current impasse.

In August 1983, petitioner brought this action in the District Court for the Central District of California. Petitioner requested an order declaring the Louisiana decree invalid and the California decree valid, and enjoining the enforcement of the Louisiana decree. Petitioner did not attempt to enforce the California decree in a Louisiana state court before he filed suit in federal court. The District Court granted respondent's motion to dismiss the complaint for lack of subject-matter and personal jurisdiction. * * * The Court of Appeals for the Ninth Circuit affirmed. * * * We granted certiorari * * * and we now affirm.

II

* * *

We examine initially the context of the PKPA with an eye toward determining Congress' perception of the law that it was shaping or reshaping. * * * At the time Congress passed the PKPA, custody orders held a peculiar status under the full faith and credit doctrine, which requires each State to give effect to the judicial proceedings of other States, see U.S. Const., Art. IV, § 1; 28 U.S.C. § 1738. The anomaly traces to the fact that custody orders characteristically are subject to modification as required by the best interests of the child. As a consequence, some courts doubted whether custody orders were sufficiently "final" to trigger full faith and credit requirements, * * * and this Court had declined expressly to settle the question. See *Ford v. Ford,* 371 U.S. 187, 192, 83 S.Ct. 273, 276, 9 L.Ed.2d 240 (1962). Even if custody orders were subject to full faith and credit requirements, the Full Faith and Credit Clause obliges States only to accord the same force to judgments as would be accorded by the courts of the State in which the judgment was entered. Because courts entering custody orders generally retain the power to modify them, courts in other States were no less entitled to change the terms of custody according to their own views of the child's best interest. * * * For these reasons, a parent who lost a custody battle in one State had an incentive to kidnap the child and move to another State to relitigate the issue. This circumstance contributed to widespread jurisdictional deadlocks like this one, and more importantly, to a national epidemic of parental kidnaping. At the time the PKPA was enacted, sponsors of the Act estimated that between 25,000 and 100,000 children were kidnaped by parents who had been unable to obtain custody in a legal forum. See Parental Kidnaping Prevention Act of 1979: Joint Hearing on S. 105 before the Subcommittee on Criminal Justice of the Judiciary Committee and the Subcommittee on Child and Human Development of the Committee on Labor and Human Resources, 96th Cong., 2d Sess., 10 (1980) (hereinafter PKPA Joint Hearing) (statement of Sen. Malcolm Wallop).

A number of States joined in an effort to avoid these jurisdictional conflicts by adopting the Uniform Child Custody Jurisdiction Act (UCCJA), 9 U.L.A. §§ 1–28 (1979). The UCCJA prescribed uniform standards for deciding which State could make a custody determination and obligated enacting States to enforce the determination made by the State with proper jurisdiction. The project foundered, however, because a number of States refused to enact the UCCJA while others enacted it with modifications. In the absence of uniform national standards for allocating and enforcing custody determinations, noncustodial parents still had reason to snatch their children and petition the courts of any of a number of haven States for sole custody.

The context of the PKPA therefore suggests that the principal problem Congress was seeking to remedy was the inapplicability of full faith and credit requirements to custody determinations. Statements made when the Act was introduced in Congress forcefully confirm that suggestion. The sponsors and supporters of the Act continually indicated that the purpose of the PKPA was to provide for nationwide enforcement of custody orders made in accordance with the terms of the UCCJA. As Acting Deputy Attorney General Michel testified:

* * *

"In essence [the PKPA] would impose on States a Federal duty, under enumerated standards derived from the UCCJA, to give full faith and credit to the custody decrees of other States. Such legislation would, in effect, amount to Federal adoption of key provisions of the UCCJA for all States and would eliminate the incentive for one parent to remove a minor child to another jurisdiction." PKPA Joint Hearing 48.

* * * [T]he [Full Faith and Credit Clause] "only prescribes a rule by which courts, Federal and state, are to be guided when a question arises in the progress of a pending suit as to the faith and credit to be given by the

court to the public acts, records, and judicial proceedings of a State other than that in which the court is sitting." [*Minnesota v. Northern Securities Co.,* 194 U.S. 48, 72, 24 S.Ct. 598, 605, 48 L.Ed. 870 (1904)]. Because Congress' chief aim in enacting the PKPA was to extend the requirements of the Full Faith and Credit Clause to custody determinations, the Act is most naturally construed to furnish a rule of decision for courts to use in adjudicating custody disputes and not to create an entirely new cause of action. It thus is not compatible with the purpose and context of the legislative scheme to infer a private cause of action. * * *

The language and placement of the statute reinforce this conclusion. The PKPA, 28 U.S.C. § 1738A, is an addendum to the full faith and credit statute, 28 U.S.C. § 1738. This fact alone is strong proof that the Act is intended to have the same operative effect as the full faith and credit statute.

* * *

In sum, the context, language, and history of the PKPA together make out a conclusive case against inferring a cause of action in federal court to determine which of two conflicting state custody decrees is valid. Against this impressive evidence, petitioner relies primarily on the argument that failure to infer a cause of action would render the PKPA nugatory. We note, as a preliminary response, that ultimate review remains available in this Court for truly intractable jurisdictional deadlocks. In addition, the unspoken presumption in petitioner's argument is that the States are either unable or unwilling to enforce the provisions of the Act. This is a presumption we are not prepared, and more importantly, Congress was not prepared, to indulge. State courts faithfully administer the Full Faith and Credit Clause every day; now that Congress has extended full faith and credit requirements to child custody orders, we can think of no reason why the courts' administration of federal law in custody disputes will be any less vigilant. Should state courts prove as obstinate as petitioner predicts, Congress may choose to revisit the issue. But any more radical approach to the problem will have to await further legislative action; we "will not engraft a remedy on a statute, no matter how salutary, that Congress did not intend to provide." *California v. Sierra Club,* 451 U.S. 287, 297 (1981). The judgment of the Court of Appeals is affirmed.

It is so ordered.

[JUSTICE O'CONNOR concurred in part and concurred in the judgment. JUSTICE SCALIA concurred.]

Notes and Questions

1. *Thompson v. Thompson* raises the peculiar issue of inter-state preclusion when each state retains jurisdiction over a dispute. In the context of custody disputes, a court can always reopen proceedings if it is in the best interests of the child. The ability to reopen the case, then, is actually what is granted preclusive effect.

2. In PARKER v. HOEFER, 2 N.Y.2d 612, 162 N.Y.S.2d 13, 142 N.E.2d 194, certiorari denied 355 U.S. 833, 78 S.Ct. 51, 2 L.Ed.2d 45 (1957), the New York Court of Appeals gave full faith and credit to a Vermont final judgment, notwithstanding that the underlying claim would not be enforceable in New York. In

holding that the plaintiff could initiate an enforcement action in New York, the court said:

> * * * [T]he plaintiff is not attempting to enforce in the courts of New York an action for alienation of affections and criminal conversation, which have been abolished in New York but, rather, to enforce a judgment rendered in Vermont as between these parties, which was final and conclusive on the rights litigated. New York cannot retry the case or review as on appeal the Vermont judgment. * * * The present suit, then, is upon an entirely different cause of action from that merged in the judgment * * * and may not be called a suit on an action abolished in New York. * * *

Id. at 617, 162 N.Y.S.2d at 17, 142 N.E.2d at 197.

2. STATE–FEDERAL PRECLUSION

Although the Full Faith and Credit Clause of the Constitution, it generally is agreed, applies only to state courts, Section 1738 (known as the Full Faith and Credit Statute) imposes the same general principles on the federal courts, requiring them to accord full faith and credit to the judgments of state courts. Because the requirement is statutory and not constitutional, however, it may be supervened. For example, the writ of habeas corpus, 28 U.S.C. §§ 2241–2255, provides a federal forum in which people who have been convicted of crimes in state court may litigate constitutional claims arising out of their prosecutions. Under traditional rules of preclusion, this subsequent action would be prevented.

What other circumstances might justify departing from the usual rules of intersystem preclusion? Consider, for example, cases involving federal issues. Should a federal court give preclusive effect to a state-court determination of federal law? What about circumstances in which the federal claim arises only by way of defense, and thus the original action could not have been removed to federal court? What if that issue was an area, such as copyright, which is within the exclusive jurisdiction of the federal courts?

ALLEN v. McCURRY

Supreme Court of the United States, 1980.
449 U.S. 90, 101 S.Ct. 411, 66 L.Ed.2d 308.

[McCurry was charged with possession of heroin in a state-court proceeding. At a pretrial suppression hearing, the trial judge excluded some of the evidence on the ground that it was the product of an illegal police search, but admitted the drugs and other contraband that the officers had found "in plain view." McCurry was subsequently convicted after a jury trial. McCurry later filed a civil action for damages under 42 U.S.C. § 1983, claiming that Allen and other police officers had unconstitutionally searched his house and seized the property that had been used to convict him. The District Court granted Allen and the other defendants summary judgment, holding that McCurry already had raised the Fourth Amendment issue unsuccessfully in the state-court proceeding. The Court of Appeals reversed, holding that the issue should be allowed to go to trial unencumbered by rules of issue preclusion due to the special role of the federal courts in protecting civil rights.]

Certiorari to the United States Court of Appeals for the Eighth Circuit.

Justice Stewart delivered the opinion of the Court.

* * *

In recent years, this Court has reaffirmed the benefits of collateral estoppel in particular, finding the policies underlying it to apply in contexts not formerly recognized at common law. Thus, the Court has eliminated the requirement of mutuality in applying collateral estoppel to bar relitigation of issues decided earlier in federal-court suits, * * * and has allowed a litigant who was not a party to a federal case to use collateral estoppel "offensively" in a new federal suit against the party who lost on the decided issue in the first case * * *. But one general limitation the Court has repeatedly recognized is that the concept of collateral estoppel cannot apply when the party against whom the earlier decision is asserted did not have a "full and fair opportunity" to litigate that issue in the earlier case. * * *

The federal courts generally have * * * consistently accorded preclusive effect to issues decided by state courts. E.g., Montana v. United States, supra; Angel v. Bullington, 330 U.S. 183, 67 S.Ct. 657, 91 L.Ed. 832. Thus, res judicata and collateral estoppel not only reduce unnecessary litigation and foster reliance on adjudication, but also promote the comity between state and federal courts that has been recognized as a bulwark of the federal system. * * *

Indeed, though the federal courts may look to the common law or to the policies supporting res judicata and collateral estoppel in assessing the preclusive effect of decisions of other federal courts, Congress has specifically required all federal courts to give preclusive effect to state-court judgments whenever the courts of the State from which the judgments emerged would do so * * * [citing 28 U.S.C. § 1738]. It is against this background that we examine the relationship of § 1983 and collateral estoppel, and the decision of the Court of Appeals in this case.

III

This Court has never directly decided whether the rules of res judicata and collateral estoppel are generally applicable to § 1983 actions. But in Preiser v. Rodriguez * * *, the Court noted with implicit approval the view of other federal courts that res judicata principles fully apply to civil rights suits brought under that statute. * * * And the virtually unanimous view of the Courts of Appeals since *Preiser* has been that § 1983 presents no categorical bar to the application of res judicata and collateral estoppel concepts.[10] These federal appellate court decisions have spoken with little explanation or citation in assuming the compatibility of § 1983 and rules of preclusion, but the statute and its legislative history clearly support the courts' decisions.

Because the requirement of mutuality of estoppel was still alive in the federal courts until well into this century, * * * the drafters of the 1871 Civil

---

10. * * * A very few courts have suggested that the normal rules of claim preclusion should not apply in § 1983 suits in one peculiar circumstance: Where a § 1983 plaintiff seeks to litigate in federal court a federal issue which he could have raised but did not raise in an earlier state-court suit against the same adverse party. Graves v. Olgiati, 550 F.2d 1327 (C.A.2 1977); Lombard v. Board of Ed. of New York City, 502 F.2d 631 (C.A.2 1974); Mack v. Florida Bd. of Dentistry, 430 F.2d 862 (C.A.5 1970). These cases present a narrow question not now before us, and we intimate no view as to whether they were correctly decided.

Rights Act, of which § 1983 is a part, may have had less reason to concern themselves with rules of preclusion than a modern Congress would. Nevertheless, in 1871 res judicata and collateral estoppel could certainly have applied in federal suits following state-court litigation between the same parties or their privies, and nothing in the language of § 1983 remotely expresses any congressional intent to contravene the common-law rules of preclusion or to repeal the express statutory requirements of the predecessor of 28 U.S.C. § 1738 * * *. Section 1983 creates a new federal cause of action. It says nothing about the preclusive effect of state-court judgments.

Moreover, the legislative history of § 1983 does not in any clear way suggest that Congress intended to repeal or restrict the traditional doctrines of preclusion. The main goal of the Act was to override the corrupting influence of the Ku Klux Klan and its sympathizers on the governments and law enforcement agencies of the Southern States, see Monroe v. Pape, 365 U.S. 167, 174, 81 S.Ct. 473, 477, 5 L.Ed.2d 492, and of course the debates show that one strong motive behind its enactment was grave congressional concern that the state courts had been deficient in protecting federal rights * * *. But in the context of the legislative history as a whole, this congressional concern lends only the most equivocal support to any argument that, in cases where the state courts have recognized the constitutional claims asserted and provided fair procedures for determining them, Congress intended to override § 1738 or the common-law rules of collateral estoppel and res judicata. Since repeals by implication are disfavored, * * * much clearer support than this would be required to hold that § 1738 and the traditional rules of preclusion are not applicable to § 1983 suits.

As the Court has understood the history of the legislation, Congress realized that in enacting § 1983 it was altering the balance of judicial power between the state and federal courts. * * * But in doing so, Congress was adding to the jurisdiction of the federal courts, not subtracting from that of the state courts. * * * The debates contain several references to the concurrent jurisdiction of the state courts over federal questions, and numerous suggestions that the state courts would retain their established jurisdiction so that they could, when the then current political passions abated, demonstrate a new sensitivity to federal rights.

To the extent that it did intend to change the balance of power over federal questions between the state and federal courts, the 42d Congress was acting in a way thoroughly consistent with the doctrines of preclusion. In reviewing the legislative history of § 1983, * * * the Court inferred that Congress had intended a federal remedy in three circumstances: where state substantive law was facially unconstitutional, where state procedural law was inadequate to allow full litigation of a constitutional claim, and where state procedural law, though adequate in theory, was inadequate in practice. * * * In short, the federal courts could step in where the state courts were unable or unwilling to protect federal rights. * * * This understanding of § 1983 might well support an exception to res judicata and collateral estoppel where state law did not provide fair procedures for the litigation of constitutional claims, or where a state court failed to even acknowledge the existence of the constitutional principle on which a litigant based his claim. Such an exception, however, would be essentially the same as the important general limit on rules of preclusion that already exists: Collateral estoppel does not apply where the party against whom an earlier court decision is asserted did not have a full and fair opportunity to litigate the claim or issue decided by the first court. * * * But the Court's view of § 1983 in *Monroe* lends no strength to any argument that Congress intended to allow relitigation of federal issues decided after a full and fair hearing in a state court simply because the state court's decision may have been erroneous.

* * *

The actual basis of the Court of Appeals' holding appears to be a generally framed principle that every person asserting a federal right is entitled to one unencumbered opportunity to litigate that right in a federal district court, regardless of the legal posture in which the federal claim arises. But the authority for this principle is difficult to discern. It cannot lie in the Constitution, which makes no such guarantee, but leaves the scope of the jurisdiction of the federal district courts to the wisdom of Congress. And no such authority is to be found in § 1983 itself. For reasons already discussed at length, nothing in the language or legislative history of § 1983 proves any congressional intent to deny binding effect to a state-court judgment or decision when the state court, acting within its proper jurisdiction, has given the parties a full and fair opportunity to litigate federal claims, and thereby has shown itself willing and able to protect federal rights. And nothing in the legislative history of § 1983 reveals any purpose to afford less deference to judgments in state criminal proceedings than to those in state civil proceedings. There is, in short, no reason to believe that Congress intended to provide a person claiming a federal right an unrestricted opportunity to relitigate an issue already decided in state court simply because the issue arose in a state proceeding in which he would rather not have been engaged at all.

* * *

The only other conceivable basis for finding a universal right to litigate a federal claim in a federal district court is hardly a legal basis at all, but rather a general distrust of the capacity of the state courts to render correct decisions on constitutional issues. * * *

The Court of Appeals erred in holding that McCurry's inability to obtain federal habeas corpus relief upon his Fourth Amendment claim renders the doctrine of collateral estoppel inapplicable to his § 1983 suit. Accordingly, the judgment is reversed, and the case is remanded to the Court of Appeals for proceedings consistent with this opinion.

It is so ordered.

JUSTICE BLACKMUN, with whom JUSTICE BRENNAN and JUSTICE MARSHALL join, dissenting.

* * *

The following factors persuade me to conclude that this respondent should not be precluded from asserting his claim in federal court. First, at the time § 1983 was passed, a nonparty's ability, as a practical matter, to invoke collateral estoppel was nonexistent. One could not preclude an opponent from relitigating an issue in a new cause of action, though that issue had been determined conclusively in a prior proceeding, unless there was "mutuality." Additionally, the definitions of "cause of action" and "issue" were narrow. As a result, and obviously, no preclusive effect could arise out of a criminal proceeding that would affect subsequent *civil* litigation. Thus, the 42d Congress could not have anticipated or approved that a criminal defendant, tried and convicted in state court, would be precluded from raising against police officers a constitutional claim arising out of his arrest.

Also, the process of deciding in a state criminal trial whether to exclude or admit evidence is not at all the equivalent of a § 1983 proceeding. The remedy sought in the latter is utterly different. In bringing the civil suit the criminal defendant does not seek to challenge his conviction collaterally. At most, he wins damages. In contrast, the exclusion of evidence may prevent a criminal conviction. A trial court, faced with the decision whether to exclude relevant evidence, confronts institutional pressures that may cause it to give a different shape to the Fourth Amendment right from what would result in civil litigation of a damages claim. Also, the issue whether to exclude evidence is subsidiary to the purpose of a criminal trial, which is to determine the guilt or innocence of the defendant, and a trial court, at least subconsciously, must weigh the potential damage to the truth-seeking process caused by excluding relevant evidence. * * *

Notes and Questions

1. The logic of *Allen* was soon extended by the Supreme Court. In MIGRA v. WARREN CITY SCHOOL DISTRICT BOARD OF EDUCATION, 465 U.S. 75, 104 S.Ct. 892, 79 L.Ed.2d 56 (1984), the Court found that a prior state-court adjudication precluded the plaintiff from bringing a subsequent suit in federal court, even though the later proceeding was based on constitutional issues that the plaintiff failed to raise, but could have raised, in the earlier state action. Justice Blackmun, who dissented in *Allen*, wrote for the Court:

> Petitioner suggests that to give state-court judgments full issue preclusive effect but not claim preclusive effect would enable litigants to bring their state claims in state court and their federal claims in federal court, thereby taking advantage of the relative expertise of both forums. Although such a division may seem attractive from a plaintiff's perspective, it is not the system established by § 1738. That statute embodies the view that it is more important to give full faith and credit to state-court judgments than to ensure separate forums for federal and state claims. This reflects a variety of concerns, including notions of comity, the need to prevent vexatious litigation, and a desire to conserve judicial resources.

> In the present litigation, petitioner does not claim that the state court would not have adjudicated her federal claims had she presented them in her original suit in state court. Alternatively, petitioner could have obtained a federal forum for her federal claim by litigating it first in a federal court. Section 1983, however, does not override state preclusion law and guarantee petitioner a right to proceed to judgment in state court on her state claims and then turn to federal court for adjudication of her federal claims. We hold, therefore, that petitioner's state-court judgment in this litigation has the same claim preclusive effect in federal court that the judgment would have in the Ohio state courts.

Id. at 84, 104 S.Ct. at 898, 79 L.Ed.2d at 64.

2. *Allen* and *Migra* held that Section 1983 did not imply an exception to Section 1738. Does a congressional grant of exclusive federal jurisdiction imply such an exception? For example, can an action based upon state antitrust law preclude a later action under the Sherman Antitrust Act, over which federal courts have exclusive jurisdiction? In MARRESE v. AMERICAN ACADEMY OF ORTHOPAEDIC SURGEONS, 470 U.S. 373, 105 S.Ct. 1327, 84 L.Ed.2d 274 (1985), a case arising under the Sherman Act, Justice O'Connor set forth a two-step approach for determining the preclusive effect of a state court judgment in a subsequent suit over which federal courts have exclusive jurisdiction. First, applying the Full Faith and Credit Statute, the federal court must determine whether *state* claim-preclusion law would preclude the federal suit. If not, there is no preclusion. If the state would bar the federal action, then, as a second step, the federal court must determine whether the relevant federal law contains an implied or explicit exception to Section 1738. The *Marrese* Court remanded the case before it for a determination of how Illinois would have treated the second lawsuit, thereby avoiding the issue of whether the Sherman Act creates an exception to Section 1738.

In most cases *Marrese* will prevent preclusion. This is so because virtually every state follows the "prior jurisdictional competency" rule, which prohibits preclusion of a claim beyond the rendering court's jurisdiction. Since state courts cannot hear cases when the federal court's jurisdiction is exclusive, the prior jurisdictional competency rule would prevent a state court from precluding such cases; *Marrese* prohibits federal courts from precluding claims that would not be precluded under state rules.

Marrese does raise the possibility, however, of the application of state issue preclusion rules whenever a congressional grant of exclusive jurisdiction is deemed not to imply an exception to Section 1738. The application of state rules of issue preclusion often will effectively eliminate the federal action. See Murphy v. Gallagher, 761 F.2d 878 (2d Cir.1985) (state rules of issue preclusion apply in later federal securities fraud action, over which federal court has exclusive jurisdiction, even though the result is to dispose of the entire federal action). The Supreme Court has since applied the *Marrese* test to a Delaware state court-settlement judgment in a securities class action suit in MATSUSHITA ELECTRIC INDUS-TRIAL CO. v. EPSTEIN, 516 U.S. 367, 116 S.Ct. 873, 134 L.Ed.2d 6 (1996). Justice Thomas held that under Section 1738, the Delaware settlement was entitled to full faith and credit even though it included claims within the exclusive subject matter jurisdiction of the federal courts. Writing separately, Justice Ginsburg dissented from part of the Court's opinion because of the due process problems in denying the plaintiffs the opportunity to raise exclusively federal issues. For an analysis of *Matsushita's* effects on state court global settlements encompassing exclusively federal claims, see Kahan & Silberman, *Matsushita and Beyond: The Role of State Courts in Class Actions Involving Exclusive Federal Claims*, 6 Sup.Ct.Rev. 219 (1997).

3. In KREMER v. CHEMICAL CONSTRUCTION CORP., 456 U.S. 461, 102 S.Ct. 1883, 72 L.Ed.2d 262 (1982), the Court held that, although the plaintiff could have sued in federal court on an employment-discrimination claim initially, once he opted to appeal a state agency determination in state court, he was subject to the usual rules of preclusion. Having litigated in state court, he could only relitigate the issues in federal court if there was reason to doubt the quality, extensiveness, or fairness of the procedures followed in the state-court action. Justice Blackmun, in dissent, argued that the nature of the state-court review was

different than the review a federal district court would give the action. The standard of review in state court was whether the state agency's determination was arbitrary; a federal court would have engaged in a full adjudication on the merits of the employment-discrimination claim.

3. FEDERAL–STATE PRECLUSION

Must a state court grant preclusive effect to a prior federal-court judgment? The general requirement that federal judgments be given full faith and credit in state courts never has been challenged seriously, even though the Full Faith and Credit Clause does not apply to the situation, and even though most courts agree that Section 1738 is inapplicable as well. Commentators invoke various provisions of the Constitution (including the Supremacy Clause and the "case or controversy" doctrine) to support binding state courts to federal-court judgments. The lack of any express provision may reflect the constitutional compromise that relegated to Congress the decision of whether to establish inferior federal courts.

The conclusion that state courts are obliged to grant preclusive effect to federal court judgments does not determine which rules of preclusion the state should apply. There is almost universal agreement that federal preclusion rules usually apply in a state court when the prior federal-court judgment involved a federal question. But should federal preclusion rules define the effect in a subsequent action of a prior federal judgment deciding state-law claims? Arguably, the *Erie* doctrine requires the court to treat a prior federal determination of the claim in the same way that it would treat a prior state determination of the claim; under Section 1738, that would mean the application of the preclusion rules of the state in which the rendering federal court sits.

For many years a lively debate took place among scholars, who reached different conclusions as to a number of the issues. Among the most prominent writings are Burbank, *Interjurisdictional Preclusion, Full Faith and Credit and Federal Common Law: A General Approach,* 71 Cornell L.Rev. 733 (1986)(arguing that Article III is not a grant of power to federal courts as to all matters relating to the preclusive effect of their judgments), and Degnan, *Federalized Res Judicata,* 85 Yale L.J. 741 (1976)(arguing that federal law should define the preclusive effect of all federal judgments). The *Restatement of Judgments* adopted the position that, although federal law ultimately must control the choice of preclusion rules, federal law should mandate the application of state rules when those rules are important to the effectuation of substantive state policies. *Restatement (Second), Judgments* § 87 (1982). See also 18 Wright, Miller & Cooper, *Federal Practice and Procedure: Jurisdiction and Related Matters* §§ 4468, 4472 (1981)(2001 Pocket Part).

SEMTEK INTERNATIONAL INC. v. LOCKHEED MARTIN CORPORATION

Supreme Court of the United States, 2001.
531 U.S. 497, 121 S.Ct. 1021, 149 L.Ed.2d 32.

[Petitioner sued respondent in California state court, alleging breach of contract and various business torts. After removal to the United States

District Court for the Central District of California on the basis of diversity of citizenship, the action was dismissed "on the merits and with prejudice" because it was barred by California's two-year statute of limitations. The Ninth Circuit affirmed. Petitioner also brought suit against respondent in the Circuit Court for Baltimore City, Maryland, alleging the same causes of action, which were not time barred under Maryland's three-year statute of limitations. Respondent asked the California federal court to enjoin this action; it also removed the Maryland state court action on federal-question grounds (diversity grounds were not available because Lockheed "is a Maryland citizen"). The California federal court denied the requested relief, and the Maryland federal court remanded the case to state court because the federal question arose only by way of defense. The Maryland state court granted Lockheed's motion to dismiss on the ground of res judicata. Petitioner appealed the Maryland trial court's order of dismissal to the Maryland Court of Special Appeals. That court affirmed, holding that, regardless of whether California would have accorded claim-preclusive effect to a statute-of-limitations dismissal by one of its own courts, the dismissal by the California federal court barred the Maryland complaint since the res judicata effect of federal diversity judgments is prescribed by federal law, under which the earlier dismissal was "on the merits" and claim preclusive. The Maryland Court of Appeals declined to review the case.]

Certiorari to the Court of Special Appeals of Maryland.

MR. JUSTICE SCALIA delivered the opinion of the Court

* * *

II

Petitioner contends that the outcome of this case is controlled by *Dupasseur v. Rochereau*, 21 Wall. 130, 135 (1875), which held that the res judicata effect of a federal diversity judgment "is such as would belong to judgments of the State courts rendered under similar circumstances," and may not be accorded any "higher sanctity or effect." Since, petitioner argues, the dismissal of an action on statute-of-limitations grounds by a California state court would not be claim preclusive, it follows that the similar dismissal of this diversity action by the California federal court cannot by claim preclusive. While we agree that this would be the result demanded by *Dupasseur*, the case is not dispositive because it was decided under the Conformity Act of 1872, 17 Stat. 196, which required federal courts to apply the procedural law of the forum State in nonequity cases.

Respondent, for its part, contends that the outcome of this case is controlled by Federal Rule * * * 41(b), which provides as follows:

> * * * Unless the court in its order for dismissal otherwise specifies, a dismissal under this subdivision and any dismissal not provided for in this rule, other than a dismissal for lack of jurisdiction, for improper venue, or for failure to join a party under Rule 19, operates as an adjudication upon the merits.

Since the dismissal here did not "otherwise specify" (indeed, it specifically stated that it was "on the merits"), and did not pertain to the excepted subjects of jurisdiction, venue, or joinder, it follows, respondent contends, that the dismissal "is entitled to claim preclusive effect." * * *

Implicit in this reasoning is the unstated minor premise that all judgments denominated "on the merits" are entitled to claim-preclusive effect. That premise is not necessarily valid. The original connotation of an "on the merits" adjudication is one that actually "pass[es] directly on the substance of [a particular] claim" before the court. Restatement § 19, Comment *a*, at 161. That connotation remains common to every jurisdiction of which we are aware. See *ibid*. * * * And it is, we think, the meaning intended in those many statements to the effect that a judgment "on the merits" triggers the doctrine of res judicata or claim preclusion. * * *

But over the years the meaning of the term "judgment on the merits" "has gradually undergone change," R. Marcus, M. Redish, & E. Sherman, Civil Procedure: A Modern Approach 1140-1141 (3d ed. 2000), and it has come to be applied to some judgments (such as the one involved here) that do *not* pass upon the substantive merits of a claim and hence do *not* (in many jurisdictions) entail claim-preclusive effect. * * * That is why the Restatement of Judgments has abandoned the use of the term—"because of its possibly misleading connotations," Restatement § 19, Comment *a*, at 161.

In short, it is no longer true that a judgment "on the merits" is necessarily a judgment entitled to claim-preclusive effect; and there are a number of reasons for believing that the phrase "adjudication upon the merits" does not bear that meaning in Rule 41(b). To begin with, Rule 41(b) sets forth nothing more than a default rule for determining the import of a dismissal (a dismissal is "upon the merits," with the three stated exceptions, unless the court "otherwise specifies"). This would be a highly peculiar context in which to announce a federally prescribed rule on the complex question of claim preclusion, saying in effect, "All federal dismissals (with three specified exceptions) preclude suit elsewhere, unless the court otherwise specifies."

And even apart from the purely default character of Rule 41(b), it would be peculiar to find a rule governing the effect that must be accorded federal judgments by other courts ensconced in rules governing the internal procedures of the rendering court itself. Indeed, such a rule would arguable violate the jurisdictional limitation of the Rules Enabling Act: that the Rules "shall not abridge, enlarge or modify any substantive right" * * *. In the present case, for example, if California law left petitioner free to sue on this claim in Maryland even after the California statute of limitations had expired, the federal court's extinguishment of that right (through Rule 41(b)'s mandated claim-preclusive effect of its judgment) would seem to violate this limitation.

Moreover, as so interpreted, the rule would in many cases violate the federalism principle of *Erie R. Co. v. Tompkins*, [p. 374, supra] * * * by engendering " 'substantial' variations [in outcomes] between state and federal litigation" which would "likely . . . influence the choice of a forum," *Hanna v. Plummer*, [p. 392, supra] * * *. With regard to the claim-preclusion issue involved in the present case, for example, the traditional rule is that expiration of the applicable statute of limitations merely bars the remedy and does not extinguish the substantive right, so that dismissal on that ground does not have claim-preclusive effect in other jurisdictions with longer, unexpired limitation periods. * * * Out-of-state defendants sued on stale claims in California and in other States adhering to this traditional rule would systematically remove state-law suits brought against them to federal court—where, unless otherwise specified, a statute-of-limitations dismissal would bar suit everywhere.

Finally, if rule 41(b) did mean what respondent suggests, we would surely have relied upon it in our cases recognizing the claim-preclusive effect of federal judgments in federal-question cases. Yet for over half a century since the promulgation of Rule 41(b), we have not once done so. * * *

We think the key to a more reasonable interpretation of the meaning of "operates as an adjudication upon the merits" in Rule 41(b) is to be found in Rule 41(a), which, in discussing the effect of voluntary dismissal by the plaintiff, makes clear than an "adjudication upon the merits" is the opposite of a "dismissal without prejudice" * * *. * * * The primary meaning of "dismissal without prejudice," we think, is dismissal without barring the defendant from returning later, to the same court, with the same underlying claim. That will also ordinarily (though not always) have the consequence of not barring the claim from *other* courts, but its primary meaning relates to the dismissing court itself. Thus, Black's Law Dictionary(7th ed. 1999) defines "dismissed without prejudice" as "removed from the court's docket in such a way that the plaintiff may refile the same suit on the same claim," * * * and defines "dismissal without prejudice" as "[a] dismissal that does not bar the plaintiff from refiling the lawsuit within the applicable limitations period," *ibid.*

We think, then, that the effect of the "adjudication upon the merits" default provision of Rule 41(b)—and, presumably, of the explicit order in the present case that used the language of that default provision—is simply that, unlike a dismissal "without prejudice," the dismissal in the present case barred refiling of the same claim in the United States District Court for the Central District of California. That is undoubtedly a necessary condition, but it is not a sufficient one, for claim-preclusive effect in other courts.

III

Having concluded that the claim-preclusive effect, in Maryland, of this California federal diversity judgment is dictated neither by *Dupasseur v. Rochereau*, as petitioner contends, nor by Rule 41(b), as respondent contends, we turn to consideration of what determines the issue. Neither the Full Faith and Credit Clause * * * And no other federal textual provision, neither of the Constitution nor of any statute, addresses the claim-preclusive effect of a judgment in a federal diversity action.

It is also true, however, that no federal textual provision addresses the claim-preclusive effect of a federal-court judgment in a federal-question case, yet we have long held that States cannot give those judgments merely whatever effect they would give their own judgments, but must accord them the effect that this Court prescribes. * * * The reasoning of that line of cases suggests, moreover, that even when States are allowed to give federal judgments * * * no more than the effect accorded to state judgments, that disposition is by direction of *this* Court, which has the last word on the claim-preclusive effect of *all* federal judgments * * *. In other words, in *Dupasseur* the State was allowed (indeed, required) to give a federal diversity judgment no more effect than it would accord one of its own judgments only because reference to state law was the *federal rule that this Court deemed appropriate.* In short, federal common law governs the claim-preclusive effect of a dismissal by a federal court sitting in diversity. * * *

It is left to us, then, to determine the appropriate federal rule. And despite the sea change that has occurred in the background law since *Dupasseur* was decided * * * we think the result decreed by *Dupasseur* continues to be correct for diversity cases. Since state, rather than federal, substantive law is at issue there is no need for a uniform federal rule. And indeed, nationwide uniformity in the substance of the matter is better served by having the same claim-preclusive rule (the state rule) apply whether the dismissal has been ordered by a state or a federal court. This is, it seems to us, a classic case for adopting, as the federally prescribed rule of decision, the law that would be applied by state courts in the State in which the federal diversity court sits. * * * As we have alluded to above, any other rule would produce the sort of "forum-shopping ... and ... inequitable administration of the laws" that *Erie* seeks to avoid * * * since filing in, or removing to, federal court would be encouraged by the divergent effects that the litigants would anticipate from likely grounds of dismissal. * * *

This federal reference to state law will not obtain, of course, in situations in which the state law is incompatible with federal interests. * * * No such conflict with potential federal interests exists in the present case. Dismissal of this state cause of action was decreed by the California federal court only because the California statute of limitations so required; and there is no conceivable federal interest in giving that time bar more effect in other courts than the California courts themselves would impose.

* * *

Because the claim-preclusive effect of the California federal court's dismissal "upon the merits" of petitioner's action on statute-of-limitations grounds is governed by a federal rule that in turn incorporates California's law of claim preclusion (the content of which we do not pass upon today), the Maryland Court of Special Appeals erred in holding that the dismissal necessarily precluded the bringing of this action in the Maryland courts. The judgment is reversed * * *.

It is so ordered.

Notes and Questions

1. Do you agree with the Court's conclusions regarding the relevance of *Erie* and *Hanna*, the Rules Enabling Act, and federal common law (all subjects you have encountered in Chapter 6)? Does the Court's treatment of Federal Rule 41(b) affect your judgment about the questions raised in Note 2, p. 1274, supra?

2. The rule in *Semtek* requires courts to apply the law of the forum state of the prior action to determine the preclusive effect of prior diversity actions. Will this rule, as Justice Scalia claims, really reduce forum shopping? The *Semtek* decision, of course, is completely consistent with the principles espoused in *Erie* and *Klaxon.* Although preclusion doctrines vary from state to state, and state preclusion rules are part and parcel of each state's law, note that if the California preclusion rules had been applied by the Maryland court, that court's dismissal on

res judicata grounds might well have been sustained. Did the Maryland court's failure to do so justify reversal?

3. Will there be situations in which the Supreme Court might conclude that a federal interest would be "incompatible" with the application of a state standard? What would they be? When could a federal court craft its own rule of federal common law of claim preclusion?

4. What happens if a state court, in attempting to apply federal preclusion rules to a prior federal judgment, makes a mistake? If the parties subsequently return to federal court to correct the error, is the federal court bound under Section 1738 to give preclusive effect to the state court's prior decision on the issue of preclusion?

In PARSONS STEEL, INC. v. FIRST ALABAMA BANK, 474 U.S. 518, 106 S.Ct. 768, 88 L.Ed.2d 877 (1986), the Supreme Court held that a state court's rejection of a claim that an earlier federal judgment precludes the state action is itself res judicata in a later federal action to enjoin the enforcement of the state-court judgment.

5. What rules of preclusion should a diversity court apply to the judgment of a prior diversity court from another state? Again, Professor Degnan argues that federal law should govern the effect of the prior federal judgment, whether or not the prior federal judgment involved a federal question. Degnan, *Federalized Res Judicata*, 85 Yale L.J. 741 (1976). Other commentators argue that rules of preclusion are substantive, since they materially affect the outcome of a case, and that *Erie* therefore mandates the application of the rules the state court would apply. As discussed above, however, Note 2, supra, state courts themselves are undecided as to the proper rules of preclusion to apply to a prior diversity judgment. See Note, *Erie and the Preclusive Effect of Federal Diversity Judgments*, 85 Colum.L.Rev. 1505 (1985).

6. If a plaintiff properly brings an action in federal court and fails to include certain related state claims that may have been heard under pendent jurisdiction, should that plaintiff be permitted to litigate those claims in a subsequent state action? The *Restatement (Second) of Judgments* recommends that preclusion result if the federal court would have exercised jurisdiction over the claims. See *Restatement (Second), Judgments* § 25, comment *e* (1982). Yet even assuming that answer, difficult questions remain. How is a court considering such preclusion going to determine whether the first court would have exercised pendent jurisdiction?

One commentator has suggested that whether the federal court would have invoked pendent jurisdiction can be determined by looking at (1) whether there was a common nucleus of operative fact between the federal and state claims, thus ensuring that the federal court would have had the power to exercise pendent jurisdiction, and (2) looking at how the prior court disposed of the federal claim. Assuming the existence of a common nucleus of operative fact, the court should determine which one of four possible ways the prior court disposed of the federal claim. When the federal claim is decided after a full trial on the merits, or when it is decided by default judgment, the state claims should be precluded from subsequent litigation. When the federal claim is dismissed for lack of jurisdiction, improper venue, or failure to join an indispensable party, preclusion should not attach. Similarly, when the federal claim is dismissed for failure to state a claim on which relief can be granted, the plaintiff should not be precluded from subsequently filing a state suit asserting the state claims. See Note, *The Res Judicata Implications of Pendent Jurisdiction*, 66 Cornell L.Rev. 608 (1981).

4. INTERSYSTEM ADMINISTRATIVE PRECLUSION

The Supreme Court has held that Section 1738 is limited in scope to the judgments of courts, and does not apply to the decisions of administrative agencies. Recall the discussion, pp. 1275–80, supra, regarding the quality of administrative determinations and the preclusive effect accorded to factual and legal decisions of administrative agencies. More and more, states are moving toward giving preclusive effect *within the state court system* to the decisions of state administrative agencies. But what preclusive effect should a federal court give to the determination of a state administrative agency?

The door to administrative preclusion in federal courts was opened by the Supreme Court in UNITED STATES v. UTAH CONSTRUCTION & MINING CO., 384 U.S. 394, 86 S.Ct. 1545, 16 L.Ed.2d 642 (1966), in which the Court said: "When an administrative agency is acting in a judicial capacity and resolves disputed issues of fact properly before it which the parties have had an adequate opportunity to litigate, the courts have not hesitated to apply *res judicata* * * *." Id. at 422, 86 S.Ct. at 1560, 16 L.Ed.2d at 661. What factors should determine when an agency is acting in a "judicial capacity"? *Restatement (Second), Judgments* § 83(2) (1982) suggests the following:

> (2) An adjudicative determination by an administrative tribunal is conclusive under the rules of res judicata only insofar as the proceeding resulting in the determination entailed the essential elements of adjudication, including:
>
>> (a) Adequate notice to persons who are to be bound by the adjudication * * *;
>>
>> (b) The right on behalf of a party to present evidence and legal argument in support of the party's contentions and fair opportunity to rebut evidence and argument by opposing parties;
>>
>> (c) A formulation of issues of law and fact in terms of the application of rules with respect to specified parties concerning a specific transaction, situation, or status, or a specific series thereof;
>>
>> (d) A rule of finality, specifying a point in the proceeding when presentations are terminated and a final decision is rendered; and
>>
>> (e) Such other procedural elements as may be necessary to constitute the proceeding a sufficient means of conclusively determining the matter in question, having regard for the magnitude and complexity of the matter in question, the urgency with which the matter must be resolved, and the opportunity of the parties to obtain evidence and formulate legal contentions.

In UNIVERSITY OF TENNESSEE v. ELLIOTT, 478 U.S. 788, 106 S.Ct. 3220, 92 L.Ed.2d 635 (1986), plaintiff was discharged as an employee of the university. He commenced an action in federal court alleging that his racially motivated discharge violated Title VII of the Civil Rights Act of 1964 and 42 U.S.C. § 1983. While the federal lawsuit was pending, a state administrative law judge found that the discharge was not racially motivated, and the University moved for summary judgment in the federal action on the grounds of issue preclusion. The Sixth Circuit denied preclusion on both the Title VII and the Section 1983 claims. The Supreme Court affirmed the Court of

Appeals' ruling that the agency's decision did not preclude the Title VII claim, citing a specific congressional intent that state agency findings *not* preclude later Title VII actions on the same facts. However, reversing in part, the Supreme Court found that the agency's ruling did preclude the Section 1983 claim. The Court reasoned that Congress had not expressed a desire that state-agency decisions not preclude Section 1983 claims; therefore, the general principles of Section 1738 applied. The Court conceded that Section 1738 itself did not require preclusion, because it applies only to court judgments. The Justices felt free, however, to promulgate a common-law rule of preclusion requiring federal courts to give preclusive effect to the decisions of state administrative agencies in circumstances in which the courts of the agency's state would give the decision preclusive effect in a subsequent action.

Notes and Questions

1. Once the Supreme Court found, based on legislative intent, that certain claims could not be precluded by state agency findings of fact (Title VII claims) but that others could be precluded (Section 1983 claims), the federal courts were left to decide which federal statutes fell into each category. In ASTORIA FEDERAL SAVINGS & LOAN ASS'N v. SOLIMINO, 501 U.S. 104, 111 S.Ct. 2166, 115 L.Ed.2d 96 (1991), the Supreme Court provided some guidance as to what level of congressional intent is required to defeat the presumption in favor of administrative preclusion. The Court rejected a test that would have required a "clear statement" by Congress, and held that the presumption would apply unless "administrative preclusion would be inconsistent with Congress' intent in enacting the particular statute." The "clear statement" test would have provided more certainty to lower courts trying to determine when administrative preclusion should apply. Why then did the Court reject the "clear statement" test in favor of a less certain test that requires congressional intent to be discerned by inference?

2. *Elliott* addressed the issue preclusive effect accorded to unreviewed state administrative determinations under federal common law. Does it also require a federal court to give the same *claim* preclusive effect to a state administrative agency as would a court of the rendering state? The court addressed this issue in GJELLUM v. CITY OF BIRMINGHAM, 829 F.2d 1056 (11th Cir.1987). Although *Migra*, Note 1, p. 1324, supra, had held that Section 1983 did not create an exception to state claim preclusion laws under the full faith and credit statute, the court in *Gjellum* saw different interests at stake when the administrative determination was not subject to judicial review:

> With respect to the claim preclusive effect of unreviewed state agency rulings, we conclude that the importance of the federal rights at issue, the desirability of avoiding the forcing of litigants to file suit initially in federal court rather than seek relief in an unreviewed administrative proceeding, and the limitations of state agencies as adjudicators of federal rights override the lessened federalism concerns implicated outside the contours of the full faith and credit statute. In addition, claim preclusion, unlike issue preclusion, does not create a risk of inconsistent results in this context after *Elliott* because claim preclusion seeks to prevent litigation of issues that were not adjudicated before the state agency. We hold therefore that, at least in the context of section 1983 suits, the federal common law of preclusion does not require application of state claim preclusion rules to unreviewed state administrative decisions.

Id. at 1064–65.

Chapter 18

ALTERNATIVE DISPUTE RESOLUTION

SECTION A. INTRODUCTION

1. THE NEED FOR ALTERNATIVE DISPUTE RESOLUTION

The preceding Chapters focused on the procedures associated with one dispute-resolution mechanism: civil litigation. Courts are highly structured institutions in which technically trained representatives (lawyers) present arguments on behalf of their clients before a fact-finding body (judge and/or jury). And, of course, a court's decisions are enforced by the state. But the formality characteristic of courts has a number of disadvantages, which have led some to conclude that in many instances courts are not the best dispute resolution forum. This Chapter will explore some of the major complementary mechanisms grouped under the rubric of "alternative dispute resolution" or "ADR." First, however, some of the predominant complaints lodged against the traditional adjudicative process should be catalogued.

The primary criticisms of litigation are that it takes too long and costs too much. As is well known, it sometimes takes years for a case to work its way through the process. This is partly because of the dramatic increase in the number of cases filed in recent years. However, it also is attributable to the complex set of rules—regarding procedure, evidence, and appellate review—that govern formal public adjudication. These factors combine to create serious administrative costs and problems. In the past several decades, judicial administrators have noted with concern the court system's declining ability to manage the growing caseload with which it is burdened.

Moreover, delays and costs create substantial access barriers for certain classes of litigants. Delays can contribute to serious injustice—both directly, because justice delayed often is justice denied, and indirectly, because the threat of delay may create an artificial pressure on one of the litigants to settle on less than fair terms. Given the cost of litigation, many claims are too small to pursue, and there are times when some citizens cannot afford to pursue even major claims. Not only the poor, but also many middle-income people, cannot afford legal services. Even when they can afford them, people often find themselves "outlitigated" by an opponent with greater resources and experience.

In addition to these administrative and access problems with the litigation system, many commentators have offered more fundamental criticisms regarding the desirability of adversarial adjudication as a means of resolving disputes. One criticism is the removal of parties from direct control over the dispute-resolution process and the crafting of solutions. Lawyers dominate the framing of issues and discussion, and judges impose remedies within strictly defined legal parameters. Moreover, instead of providing for maximal disclosure of relevant facts, the litigation process provides adversaries with incentives that often hide those facts. Finally, litigation tends to polarize the parties, decreasing opportunities for future cooperation and straining the social fabric. This is particularly problematic when disputants have an ongoing relationship, as in the case of neighbors or family members. All of these factors can combine to obstruct disputants from reaching optimal outcomes.

Consider, for example, the following excerpt from Menkel–Meadow, *The Lawyer as Problem Solver and Third–Party Neutral: Creativity and Non–Partisanship in Lawyering*, 72 Temple L. Rev. 785, 788–91 (1999) (footnotes omitted):

The "culture of adversarialism" and the rules that enforce this culture often (not always) distort how we think about legal and human problem solving by assuming there are only two sides to an issue or question, that "truth" about either what happened factually or what is correct legally can best be resolved by vigorous contestations between two fully armed advocates and decided by a third-party judge who is separate from the parties and appointed by the state. Formal rules of discourse and process (evidence) control the rules of debate and contest and are universally recognized as a vast improvement on the historical forms of trial by ordeal or combat. Yet parties are still limited to a stylized form of conversation in which they cannot speak directly to each other. Often, what is most important to parties may be excluded from consideration, as irrelevant or inadmissible, according to our well-worn legal principles, which may protect other important interests (like privileges, trade secrets, bias and prejudice, or constitutional rights).

Once they are locked in legal combat, it is rare to see either party acknowledge much that is right or understandable from the other party's perspective. This phenomenon is what social and cognitive psychologists tell us is "reactive devaluation"—our inability to process accurately, if at all, any information, legitimate objectives, or desires of those who are oppositional to us. So the oppositional discourse of the adversary system may cut us all off from useful information, whether facts, needs, interests, preferences, or values. Similarly, this system of thought can deprive us of * * * "settlement facts"—those crucial (and often confidential) bits of information that really motivate people to resolve disputes or plan transactions (financial information, product or human resource plans, real business, or human needs and interests). Both parties may have incentives to "hide" facts in traditional adversarial settings, and our ethical rules allow much deception (e.g., the presence of witnesses or adverse facts that would help the other side need not be disclosed), and there is no affirmative duty to disclose all that might be important in resolving a dispute. * * *

Most problematic is that practitioners of the adversarial model see its actual and practical goals not as truth seeking (perhaps as "rights" protecting), but as client maximization or "winning," outcomes which, at least after full adversarial hearings, are often binary, on/off decisions about wrong and right, guilt or innocence, and liabilities. The adversarial model, however, may not reflect a more complex world of multiple causes, multiple-party responsibilities, and conflicting, but equally legitimate rights. * * * Litigation approaches all to often focus on what happened in the past, rather than what might happen in the future. Courts, restricted by constitutional, statutory, and common law requirements, have jurisdictional and remedially "limited imaginations." Solutions, except in some class action and institutional reform suits, can do little to "reorient the parties to each other" and structure future on-going relations.

* * *

In response to the litigation deficiencies discussed above a movement arose in the 1970s to provide alternative forums and mechanisms for dispute resolution. This movement has matured and diversified considerably, and "ADR" is now a common element of most lawyers' practices. ADR includes familiar processes such as negotiation, mediation, and arbitration, as well as lesser-known mechanisms, such as early neutral evaluation and summary jury trials. All of these will be discussed at greater length below. These mechanisms are employed both within the formal adjudication system—court-annexed mediation and arbitration—and in private forums.

Some ADR mechanisms are non-adjudicative, meaning that no binding external decision is made to resolve the dispute (as in neutral factfinding, negotiation, mediation, mini-trials, summary jury trials, and early neutral evaluation); other processes more closely mirror the adjudicative function of a court (binding arbitration, private judging). What these mechanisms have in common is a diminished formality of procedural and evidentiary rules. This is often accompanied by a less rigid adherence to the law as the standard of decision, or the substitution of alternate equitable standards. This decreased formality often corresponds to a diminished need for professional representation, but not always. Some of the mechanisms (notably mediation) go even further, attempting to substitute a cooperative "problem-solving" paradigm for the adversarial paradigm.

The purported benefits of ADR mechanisms correspond, roughly, to the criticisms of the litigation system. By decreasing procedural formality (and, in some cases, the corresponding reliance on professional attorneys' services), ADR mechanisms are alleged to save considerable time and money in resolving disputes. Most ADR mechanisms (with the exception of binding arbitration and some forms of private judging) are consensual. This means that parties maintain control over the ability to craft and agree to a flexible remedy, rather than having a result imposed by a binding third-party judgment within more rigidly defined legal parameters. In addition, some non-adversarial forms of ADR, such as mediation and so-called "principled" negotiation, may offer greater opportunities for disclosing "settlement facts." In principle, this should increase the possibility of crafting an appropriate and equitable agreement, as well as providing the basis for future relations between the parties.

Notes and Questions

In response to the pressures exerted on the court system by growing caseloads, Congress has acted to increase the use of ADR in the federal courts. In 1990, the Civil Justice Reform Act was enacted, requiring federal courts to consider ADR mechanisms as a means of reducing expense and delay in litigation. 28 U.S.C. § § 471 *et seq.* In 1998, this "invitation" was upgraded to a requirement that federal courts implement ADR programs under the Alternative Dispute Resolution Act, 28 U.S.C. § 651. For information on the implementation of ADR programs in the federal courts, see Plapinger & Stienstra, *ADR and Settlement in the Federal District Courts* (1996). Many state court systems are, likewise, developing ADR programs. The Executive Branch of the federal government also has begun large-scale ADR programs, a development required by Congress through the enactment of the 1996 Administrative Dispute Resolution Act, 5 U.S.C. §§ 571–583 (1994). The use of ADR in the private sector has increased dramatically as well, with corporations and professional associations institutionalizing mediation and arbitration procedures for the resolution of both internal and external disputes. See, e.g., Cronin–Harris, *Mainstreaming: Systematizing Corporate Use of ADR*, 59 Albany L. Rev. 847 (1996). Some have suggested that such "mainstreaming," particularly in the context of court-annexed ADR, has subverted many of the ADR movement's fundamental goals through a detrimental "co-optation." See Menkel–Meadow, *Pursuing Settlement in an Adversary Culture: A Tale of Innovation Co-opted or "The Law of ADR,"* 19 Fla.St.U. L. Rev. 1 (1990).

Is the United States really as excessively litigious as its critics claim? For an assessment of this question, see Galanter, *Reading the Landscape of Disputes: What We Know and Don't Know (And Think We Know) About Our Allegedly Contentious and Litigious Society*, 31 U.C.L.A. L. Rev. 4 (1983). Isn't it possible that the availability of other dispute-resolution mechanisms, by providing procedures for the resolution of disputes that are now simply "lived with," might increase rather than decrease litigiousness?

Does ADR deliver the benefits it promises? Is it really less costly and faster? The limited data available shows mixed results at best. A Rand Institute for Civil Justice study, undertaken in 1996, found widely varying results depending on the design and implementation of the program. See Kakalik, Dunworth, Hill, McCaffrey, Oshiro, Pace & Vaiana, *An Evaluation of Mediation and Early Neutral Evaluation Under the Civil Justice Reform Act* (1996). Nonetheless, there is at least some evidence of increased disputant satisfaction and savings of time and money using certain ADR techniques in some jurisdictions. See, for example, Rosenberg & Folberg, *Alternative Dispute Resolution: An Empirical Analysis*, 46 Stan. L. Rev. 1487 (1994); Federal Judicial Center, *Report to the Judicial Conference Committee on Court Administration and Case Management: A Study of the Five Demonstration Programs Established Under the Civil Justice Reform Act of 1990*, at 8–10 (1997).

The goals of increasing speed, economy, access, and disputant control as well as reducing problems associated with the adversarial system conflict in significant ways. For example, isn't reducing access the easiest way to increase speed? If few disputants could employ a dispute-resolution system, couldn't the system resolve the disputes brought to it rather quickly? Moreover, is there a danger that by reducing professionalism, formality, and legalism, reform could make access meaningless by removing the protections that come with formal representation governed by norms of law? For a critical assessment of alternative dispute resolution, see Brunet, *Questioning the Quality of Alternative Dispute Resolution*, 62 Tulane L.Rev. 1 (1987).

2. DESIGNING AND IMPLEMENTING ADR MECHANISMS

Few would argue that ADR mechanisms should completely replace traditional adjudication. Rather, ADR offers a complementary means of resolving certain disputes and provides disputants and judicial administrators with a broader palette of options. In order to match the resolution mechanism to the dispute, we must explore the defining elements of the various mechanisms. Methods of dispute resolution can be defined, in part, by the answers they provide to the following four questions: (a) Who resolves the dispute?; (b) What is the source of the standard for resolution?; (c) How are the disputants represented?; and (d) What is the nature and extent of fact-finding and standard-finding? Each of the dispute-resolution mechanisms answers these questions in a particular way

(a) Who resolves the dispute?

Possibilities include:

— a judge, an officer of the state with professional education in the law

— a lawyer with similar professional training

— an expert in the field in which the dispute arose with no legal training at all

— a representative of the community

— the disputants with the help of a neutral third party

— the disputants themselves

In all categories except the last, the disputants invoke the assistance of a neutral third party to play a role in resolving the dispute. These will be referred to collectively as "third-party methods."

(b) What is the source of the standard for resolution?

Possibilities include:

— rules established by legislatures and courts ("law")

— the prior practice of those similarly situated

— community values

— the disputants themselves, determined either before or after the dispute arose

(c) How are the disputants represented?

Possibilities include:

— lawyers

— persons without professional legal training

— the disputants themselves

(d) What is the nature and extent of fact-finding and standard-finding?

Possibilities include:

— the disputants or their representatives could be responsible for the research and

— presentation of evidence to establish facts and arguments to establish the standard for resolution

— the dispute resolver could aid the disputants in performing some or all of these tasks

— the dispute resolver could be responsible for these tasks

By combining answers to these four questions in various ways, a wide array of dispute-resolution mechanisms can be generated. Depending on the nature of the dispute, one mechanism or another would be the most appropriate way to resolve the dispute. Moreover, the appropriate perspective from which to evaluate the mechanisms is in their entirety, as an interconnected system of dealing with disputes. The following list is offered to provide a sense of the wide variety of alternative dispute-resolution mechanisms that are available, but without attempting to be exhaustive.

NEUTRAL FACTFINDING AND OMBUDSPERSONS

Neutral fact-finding is a generic term for the use of a third party to gather information relevant to the settlement of a dispute. One of the most common institutional instances of a neutral factfinder is the ombudsperson. An ombudsperson is a third party who receives and investigates complaints aimed at an institution by its constituents, clients, or employees. She may take actions such as bringing an apparent injustice to the attention of high-level officials, advising the complainant of available options and resources, proposing a settlement of the dispute, or proposing systemic changes in the institution. A neutral factfinder often is employed by the institution against which the complaint is made. In government, an ombudsperson can serve the important function of steering a complaint through a tangled bureaucracy.

Ombudspersons are most likely to be hired in closely regulated institutions, those in which customer satisfaction is critical, and institutions concerned with resolving disputes internally. Universities frequently use ombudspersons to enforce a set of university rules that may be different than those applicable to people generally. Some independent ombudspersons are employed by local media and use publicity as their major tool. The disputants are responsible for resolving the dispute, although the ombudsperson can pressure them to settle. The source of the standard for resolution is either internal policy or commonly shared values. The ombudsperson acts as representative of the complainant, investigating and presenting the facts for her as well as reminding the high-level officials of the policies they have set or the community's shared values.

NEGOTIATION

In a negotiated settlement, the disputants themselves resolve the conflict under whatever standards they choose. Although in the early stages the disputants typically represent themselves, once lawyers become involved they tend to handle the negotiations as well. There is no need for fact-finding or standard-finding as such, since the only facts and standards that matter are those that the disputants choose to recognize. Negotiation is perhaps the most familiar form of dispute resolution and will be discussed in more detail in Section B, pp. 1346–56, infra.

MEDIATION

Mediation is a process in which a neutral third party, who is often but not always a human-relations professional, assists the disputants in reaching a negotiated settlement of their differences. The mediator is not empowered to render a decision. Thus the decision-makers are the disputants themselves. Since mediation ultimately seeks agreement between the disputants, a mediator does not evaluate the strengths and weaknesses of each side's evidence and arguments. Instead, she seeks common ground between the disputants concerning facts and standards. There are, however, different forms of mediation, and mediators have differing conceptions of their proper role. Some mediators are simply communication facilitators. Others are more active, suggesting possible grounds for settlement and attempting to persuade the disputants to do so. Mediators of the former type are more likely to conduct all sessions with both disputants present; mediators of the latter type are more likely to conduct both joint sessions and private sessions with each disputant.

Although the source of the resolution standard is the disputants, when a mediator attempts persuasion, other values, such as those of the mediator or the community, also come into play. Disputants often but not always represent themselves; some mediators actively discourage the presence of lawyers and witnesses. Mediation is most appropriate when the disputants have equal bargaining power. This ordinarily occurs when the conflict is between individuals, rather than a conflict between an individual and a private institution or government. If successful, mediation results in a signed agreement that defines the parties' future behavior. This agreement may be an enforceable contract. Mediation often is used when the disputants have a continuing relationship that is important to preserve. Rather than attempting to assess blame for past conduct, mediation focuses the disputants' attention on the future and the desirability of maintaining an amicable relationship. Disputes between neighbors or family members often are considered particularly suited to mediation. Divorce mediation is considered in greater detail in Section C(1), pp. 1357–63, infra.

Court-annexed mediation builds upon the model of mediation described above but the disputants have not necessarily agreed to mediate their dispute. Instead, certain disputes, usually those involving family matters or small claims, must be referred to a mediator before the court will hear them. Lawyers are likely to be present. If the disputants do not reach an agreement, or refuse to participate in the mediation process, the case goes to trial. In some jurisdictions the mediator makes a recommendation to the court.

EARLY NEUTRAL EVALUATION

It has been observed that parties often do not settle at an early stage in the litigation process because they fail to evaluate the case adequately until the trial process requires them to do so. Early neutral evaluation (ENE) is a mechanism designed to respond to this problem. ENE involves the factual and legal presentation of a dispute to a neutral selected by the parties or a court.

On the basis of this presentation the neutral, often an experienced lawyer, arbitrator, or former judge, provides the parties with an open assessment of their respective positions. This can have the effect of encouraging settlement, but at the very least should help to focus the issues for the litigation process and assist in its efficient management.

MINI-TRIALS

Similar to ENE, but procedurally more complex, the mini-trial is a privately developed method of helping to bring about a negotiated settlement in lieu of protracted corporate litigation. The procedural contours of mini-trials are tailored individually in accordance with the desires of the disputants. A typical mini-trial is a confidential process that entails a period of limited discovery after which attorneys for each side present an abbreviated version of the case before a panel consisting of managers with authority to settle and a neutral advisor. The neutral advisor is often a retired judge or respected lawyer. The managers then enter settlement negotiations.

Thus the parties resolve the dispute aided by the assessment of the neutral advisor as to the likely outcome should the matter go to court. The advisor's impartial appraisal of the conflict encourages the parties to adopt more realistic goals in negotiating a settlement. The source of the resolution standard is the disputants, despite the presence of the neutral legal advisor. Both sides are represented by lawyers, but the key to the process is that the managers see the other side's best case directly, in addition to the filtered version provided by their own lawyer. Facts and standards are researched and presented by the disputants' lawyers, although in an abbreviated way. Mini-trials have been used successfully in disputes that were bogged down in discovery and motion practice by reconverting what had become a lawyer's problem back into a business problem. See *Recent Developments in Alternative Forms of Dispute Resolution,* 100 F.R.D. 512 (1984).

SUMMARY JURY TRIAL

A summary jury trial is similar in some respects to a mini-trial, but is used for cases ready to be tried before a jury. Instead of presenting a formal case before a full jury panel, the lawyers for the parties present an abbreviated case before a panel of six jurors. The presentations usually last less than a week, and the resulting "verdict"—although not binding on the parties— provides a basis for settlement. The summary jury trial has proven to be helpful when each party has a very different view regarding the likely outcome of the case, and prior settlement attempts have been unsuccessful. See Lambros, *The Summary Jury Trial and Other Alternative Methods of Dispute Resolution: Some Cautionary Observations,* 53 U.Chi.L.Rev. 366 (1986).

ARBITRATION

Arbitration is designed to be a less formal, less complex, and quicker means of resolving disputes than court proceedings. Typically, the parties agree before a dispute has arisen to submit all disputes that do arise to an arbitrator, a neutral third party who may or may not be a person with legal training who is empowered by the disputants to render a final and binding decision. Sometimes they agree to arbitrate after the dispute has arisen.

Similarly, the parties may name the arbitrator either before or after the dispute arises. The arbitrator often is selected because of her expertise in the field involved in the dispute. The agreement that defines the arbitrator's powers is generally the source of the standard for resolution, although practices of the relevant industry and general legal principles come into play as well.

Lawyers often represent the disputants, and are responsible for gathering and presenting evidence and arguments. Less time need be spent on these tasks, however, given the arbitrator's experience and expertise in the field and the relaxed rules of evidence. Because it can take place outside of the court structure and because of the shortened fact-finding process, arbitration can be much faster than adjudication. Arbitration has been used extensively in labor-management and commercial disputes since speed is important in both contexts. Arbitration also is used in these situations since it minimizes the disruption to the disputants' continuing relationship and avoids the adversarial setting of adjudication. In fields such as commercial contracts in which trade practices are an important component in determining the governing standard, the fact that an arbitrator with knowledge of the trade is the neutral, rather than a judge or jury, is also a factor.

In addition to standard arbitration, there are several other forms, including final-offer and one-way arbitration. Final-offer arbitration is much like standard arbitration but is used typically to set the terms of contracts (such as the salaries of major league baseball players and some public employees) rather than to interpret and apply contractual provisions. Each party proposes a final offer of settlement, and the neutral must choose between the two. This process encourages parties to be reasonable in the positions they advocate and is designed to encourage serious negotiation in contexts in which it is important that the disputants' dealings not be interrupted. Fact-finding can be more limited because the arbitrator need only choose between two positions rather than find and justify one particular result out of many that are possible. In one-way arbitration only one party agrees to be bound. Some corporations use this technique in response to consumer complaints. The corporation promises to abide by the arbitrator's decision, while the consumer is free to pursue other legal remedies if dissatisfied with the decision.

Court-annexed arbitration builds upon the standard model of arbitration described above except that the parties have not agreed to arbitrate their dispute. Instead, certain disputes, usually those in which the amount in controversy is less than a certain dollar figure, must be referred to an arbitrator before the court will hear them. The arbitrator thus is less likely to have expertise in the subject area in which the conflict arose. Moreover, since the source of the standard for resolution is the law, the arbitrator typically will be a lawyer. The nature and extent of fact-finding and standard-finding are not substantially different from adjudication, although discovery may be limited and the rules of evidence may be relaxed. If dissatisfied with the arbitrator's decision, a disputant can demand a trial *de novo*, but if the disputant fails to obtain a better result at trial, he may be required to pay the costs of the opposing party. Arbitration is considered in more detail in Section C(2), pp. 1363–76, infra.

PRIVATE JUDGING

Disputants who can afford it may utilize private judging in order to avoid the delays of the court system. The disputants agree, after the dispute has arisen and been filed in court, to hire a private judge, often one who is retired, to resolve the dispute. The court then refers the case to that judge.

The source of the standard for resolution is the law and the proceedings are conducted in much the same manner as a bench trial, although in an expedited and simplified manner. Unlike an arbitrator's award, the decision can be appealed as if the court referring it to the private judge had made the decision itself. Thus the disputants can ensure that the resolution will be in accordance with the law, while bypassing the backlog in the trial courts.

———

Given the wide variety of dispute resolution mechanisms available, how are disputes to be "matched" to mechanisms? Consider the following early proposal on how to address this question:

The idea that different types of disputes may be particularly amenable to particular forms of dispute resolution has led to the notion of a multifaceted Dispute Resolution Center. Such a Center, instead of having just one "door" leading to the courtroom, would have many doors directing disputants to the most appropriate dispute-resolution process. Among the doors in such a *multidoor courthouse* might be ones labelled "arbitration," "mediation," and "ombudsman." Provision might also be made for channeling disputes into existing specialized tribunals such as medical malpractice screening boards, small claims courts, or juvenile courts.

The key feature of the multidoor courthouse is the intake screening. Here disputes would be analyzed according to various criteria to determine what mechanism would be best suited for the resolution of the particular controversy. Take, for example, a case involving a minor assault by one neighbor against another growing out of increasing anger over a trespassing dog. Presently such a dispute would probably wind up in criminal court because that is the tag society has placed on this type of conflict. But since the parties really want help in resolving this interpersonal problem, not a determination of whether A struck B, the case might well be sent to mediation, at least in the first instance. Similar treatment might be accorded to a landlord-tenant dispute over the adequacy of the services provided by the landlord. But if the landlord sought to raise questions about the constitutionality of the rent-control law, then obviously that case would have to be sent to the regular court. * * * [The same is true with respect to all cases involving major crimes.

The notion thus is that a sophisticated intake officer would analyze the dispute and refer it to that process, or sequence of processes, most likely to resolve it effectively. The potential benefits of such a multifaceted mechanism are increased efficiency, possible time and cost savings, and the legitimization of various alternative dispute-resolution processes, thus decreasing citizens' frustration in attempting to locate the most appropriate mechanism. An additional benefit is that it would help us to gain a better understanding of the peculiar advantages and disadvantages of particular dispute-resolution processes for specific types of disputes. Perhaps the intake official could also refer disputants' associated nonlegal problems to appropriate social service agencies.

Sander, *The Multidoor Courthouse,* National Forum, Vol. LXIII, No. 4, Fall 1983.

Notes and Questions

1. Proposals for a multidoor courthouse system of dispute resolution have begun to take shape at the state level. See Agnes, *A Reform Agenda for Court–Connected Dispute Resolution in Massachusetts,* 40 Boston B.J. 4 (1996) (advocating public funding for a state alternative dispute-resolution system that uses a referral system and mandatory screening). Doesn't the multidoor courthouse concept put enormous strain on the role of the intake specialist? Is such a concentration of power acceptable? How should the intake specialist be selected, trained, and held accountable? Should his referral be subject to appeal? For a contemporary critique and proposed improvement of the multi-door courthouse concept, see Stempel, *Reflections on Judicial ADR and the Multi–Door Courthouse at Twenty: Fait Accompli, Failed Overture, or Fledgling Adulthood?,* 11 Ohio St. J. on Disp. Resol. 297 (1996).

2. Each forum for dispute resolution has its own strengths and weaknesses. Mediation provides an excellent forum for dealing with disputes involving an ongoing relationship, but often proves useless in a setting characterized by acute antagonism. Arbitration provides a quick and inexpensive method of resolving simple disputes, but frequently is inappropriate in complex multi-party disputes. Litigation is well-equipped to deal with complex issues requiring public adjudication, but is adversarial in nature. What principles should guide an attorney or an intake specialist in choosing the best process for resolving a dispute? Although little has been written on the subject, two commentators suggest a two-fold inquiry to guide decision makers. See Sander & Goldberg, *Fitting the Forum to the Fuss: A User–Friendly Guide to Selection and ADR Procedure,* Negotiations J., Jan. 1994, at 49, 66. First, one must identify the disputants' goals in making a forum choice. For example, does the client simply want to resolve the issue with the least disruption, or is the client angry and seeking someone who will pronounce him "right"? Should the public's interest be a factor in this analysis? Second, if the disputants are amenable to settlement, in what forum might any obstacles to settlement be overcome? For example, if constituency pressures could block an acceptable settlement, which forum would overcome those pressures?

3. Should disputants be compelled to use the alternative mechanisms instead of litigation? For example, should the government require or encourage corporations involved in complicated disputes to have a privately funded mini-trial before proceeding to a full, publicly funded court trial? Is it proper to offer disputants incentives designed to make it attractive for them to use the appropriate mechanism? Who decides which mechanism is appropriate in a particular case and what incentive to offer? The intake specialist? What about alternative dispute-resolution mechanisms such as mini-trials, that are now purely private and voluntary?

Consider the following argument:

Family law issues—domestic violence, equitable distribution, custody, the award and enforcement of spousal and child support—are the principal issues that bring women into the courts. They are also the issues our legal system has never valued highly and that our courts would like to be rid of. * * * Today, across the country, women pursuing family law claims are being pushed out of the courts and into mediation, where there is no record and no accountability. After decades of struggling to make the courts treat seriously the issues generated by the domestic sphere, women are once again seeing these issues privatized. Mediation can be a valuable tool, but it works best for parties equal in power. Women in these cases are often vulnerable. Fearful of violent husbands, less worldly, lacking the economic resources to press their cases in a difficult forum, these women may be easily pressured into compromises which make the mediator feel successful, but which the women come to regret.

Schafran, Women in the Courts Today: How Much Has Changed? [Paper given at Marymount College, "Women and the U.S. Constitution Program," New York, N.Y., Nov. 16, 1987]. See also Grillo, *The Mediation Alternative: Process Dangers for Women,* 100 Yale L.J. 1545 (1991).

4. Some commentators believe that minorities do not fare well in alternative dispute resolution forums, since people who hold prejudicial attitudes tend to show these attitudes more in informal, rather than formal, settings. See Delgado, Dunn, Brown, Lee & Hubbert, *Fairness and Formality: Minimizing the Risk of Prejudice in Alternative Dispute Resolution,* 1985 Wis.L.Rev. 1359. However, a study of 400 law review articles on alternative dispute resolution from 1992 to 1995 revealed that scant attention has been paid to race and gender critiques of alternative dispute resolution. In Yamamoto, *ADR: Where Have the Critics Gone?,* 36 Santa Clara L.Rev. 1055, 1062–66 (1996), the author asks whether "amid mainstream ADR proselytizing by Congress, courts, scholars, and practitioners, a master narrative had emerged that the ADR 'train had already left the station' and whether that narrative has undermined critical legal discourse on the subject."

5. How different are the various ADR mechanisms from litigation? As ADR techniques have developed and become more "mainstream," it has been necessary to develop procedural and evidentiary devices and rules that are highly analogous to those usually employed in litigation. These include notice requirements, "information exchanges" (discovery), party submissions to neutrals (briefs, motions), induced attendance of persons and production of things (subpoenas), consolidation, interim relief, and a number of others. For a discussion of these analogies, see Sabatino, *ADR as "Litigation Lite": Procedural and Evidentiary Norms Embedded Within Alternative Dispute Resolution,* 47 Emory L.J. 1289 (1998).

6. Doesn't an effective channeling system threaten to distance the judiciary from certain disputes and disputants? Might this not only leave some litigants with a form of second-class justice but also reduce judicial exposure to facts and ideas that influence the direction of legal doctrine? For a development of this critique and an argument that ADR programs should not be utilized in cases involving public law or constitutional issues, see Edwards, *Alternative Dispute Resolution: Panacea or Anathema?,* 99 Harv. L. Rev. 668 (1986).

7. Should ADR constitute a parallel "private" system of dispute-resolution, or an integrated element of the public civil dispute-resolution system overseen by the courts? Are ADR mechanisms qualitatively different from litigation, or merely different instances on a spectrum of binding civil dispute-resolution? To the extent

that ADR programs represent instances of state-sponsored dispute resolution, should they be subject to constitutional guarantees of due process? For a consideration of these questions in the context of a proposed "unitary" conception of dispute resolution, see Reuben, *Constitutional Gravity: A Unitary Theory of Alternative Dispute Resolution and Public Civil Justice*, 47 U.C.L.A. L. Rev. 949 (2000).

SECTION B. NEGOTIATED SETTLEMENT

Many of the alternative dispute-resolution mechanisms described in Section A are designed to encourage and facilitate negotiated settlements. Indeed, negotiated settlement is one of the most common forms of alternative dispute resolution. The most historically prevalent negotiation recognized by United States courts is the "plea bargain" system used in criminal courts. These non-trial actions now account for 80–90% or more of criminal dispositions in almost every American jurisdiction. See Galanter, *Reading the Landscape of Disputes: What We Know and Don't Know (And Think We Know) About Our Allegedly Contentious and Litigious Society*, 31 U.C.L.A. L. Rev. 4, 27 (1983). In civil litigation, negotiated settlements account for more than 90% of resolutions nationwide, and more than 95% percent of all federal lawsuits are resolved before trial, most through some type of negotiated settlement. See Thompson, *International Dispute Resolution in the United States and Mexico: A Practical Guide to Terms, Arbitration Clauses, and the Enforcement of Judgment and Arbitral Awards*, 24 Syracuse J. Int'l L. & Com. 1, 17 (1997).

1. THE NATURE OF NEGOTIATIONS AND THE DESIRABILITY OF ENCOURAGING SETTLEMENT

EISENBERG, PRIVATE ORDERING THROUGH NEGOTIATION: DISPUTE–SETTLEMENT AND RULEMAKING, 89 Harv.L.Rev. 637, 638, 644–45, 647–49 (1976):

* * * Adjudication is conventionally perceived as a norm-bound process centered on the establishment of facts and the determination and application of principles, rules, and precedents. Negotiation, on the other hand, is conventionally perceived as a relatively norm-free process centered on the transmutation of underlying bargaining strength into agreement by the exercise of power, horse-trading, threat, and bluff. * * *

* * *

In adjudication (or, at least, that style of adjudication prevalent in complex Western cultures) the universe and operation of norms is highly stylized and tightly controlled. Where norms conflict, a court will characteristically treat one norm as not only subordinate but totally invalid—so that a court which adopts the doctrine of contributory negligence will deny the validity of comparative negligence. Where norms collide, a court will characteristically select one as determinative of the outcome of the case and reject the other as inapplicable—so that in a case to which the norms of privacy and free speech might be applicable, a court will typically hold that the outcome is controlled by one or the other, but not both. Finally, courts tend to treat person-oriented norms as either invalid or irrelevant—so that in the United

States the socially recognized principle that brothers owe each other special obligations will typically give rise to neither a cause of action nor a defense.

In contrast, the universe and operation of norms in dispute-negotiation is typically open-ended. Thus it is characteristic of dispute-negotiation that when norms collide account is taken of both, although the eventual settlement may reflect an adjustment for relative applicability and weight. Similarly, the parties in dispute-negotiation may accord partial or even full recognition to a norm that is generally deemed subordinate or even legally invalid, so that a negligent plaintiff who has no "right" to prevail in a tort action because of the doctrine of contributory negligence may nevertheless make a favorable settlement by reason of the legally invalid but socially real principle of comparative negligence. Finally, parties to dispute-negotiation can and frequently do take person-oriented norms into account as freely as act-oriented norms.

* * *

[Dispute-settlement processes, like adjudication, should be regarded as principled decision-making. This point, as well as the element of reconciliation possible in negotiation, is illustrated by a case reported by the political scientist Daniel Lev.]

[*T's Case*] In late 1960 I [Lev] agreed to accompany an American visitor on a trip across Java. In Jogjakarta we registered at the city's largest hotel * * *.

After registering, T and I went to our room. T went to the bathroom, where the toilet was an old-fashioned one with a wall tank and cord. When T pulled the cord the cover of the tank and the whole mechanism inside came down (though no water), nearly hit him and crashed onto the toilet bowl, knocking a huge chunk out of it. * * * [A] servant came to the room and handed me a note which informed us that the hotel expected Rp. 5,000 for replacement of the toilet. I was astonished at this and without thinking everything over went directly to the hotel office and asked to see the manager. * * * For half an hour or more he and I argued about the bill. I told him that it was not T's fault the tank's insides had come down and that had T been hit by the falling metal, clearly the hotel would have been responsible for damages. * * * The manager would not accept this reasoning and said that T had not been hit by the metal and, since such a thing had never happened before, T must be responsible for the damage * * *. Finally I told him that we would not pay the bill, that it was best to take the matter to court, and that I would ask Judge S [a friend] * * * to talk the problem over * * *.

[In the course of the next several hours the manager and I met at various times to establish our relative power positions by indicating which influential officials we knew, a game often played in this kind of conflict and one that involves a good deal of bluffing. As it happened, a new element was introduced into the affair when a friend from Djakarta stopped at the hotel and mentioned that not long ago another toilet tank had fallen from the wall in the hotel. When the manager was reminded of this, the situation changed somewhat.]

I finally called up Judge S, fully intending to take the case to court or at least to scare the manager into withdrawing his claim * * *. Judge S's reactions left me momentarily speechless. He agreed the civil code was on our side. Then he said, "Well, but of course you are willing to pay part of the expenses for replacing the toilet, aren't you? Offer the manager some money in payment of the damages, to show good will, and then come to a settlement somewhere between his demand and your offer." * * * Only if the manager demands full Rp. 5,000 and refuses the offer to *damai* [compromise] should you take the case to court."

Later * * * accepting Judge S's advice * * * we offered the manager a thousand rupiah. He carried on a bit but finally accepted without demanding more, we had some tea and small talk together, and the issue was never raised again.

* * *

* * * There are * * * at least two other possible interpretations of *T's Case* * * * which [are] * * * consistent with the norm-centered model of dispute-negotiation. First, the outcome may have simply reflected an accommodation of conflicting facts and norms. After all, it could not be unequivocally established that *T* was not at fault—perhaps he pulled too hard on the cord. Furthermore, even if *T* was not at fault, he was nevertheless a cause-in-fact of damage to hotel property. Although modern legal systems have adopted the principle that liability for property damage should normally be predicated on fault, the social sphere continues to recognize a subordinate principle that one is responsible for any property damage that one has caused in fact, regardless of fault. Thus the compromise settlement in *T's Case* may have reflected the likelihood that *T* was at fault and the strength, in this context, of the causation-in-fact principle.

Assume, however, that (as was probably the case) the settlement was not based on the accommodation of conflicting norms and facts * * *. The case can still be interpreted as one in which the outcome turned heavily on principle. Even if it was clear to Lev that *T* was not liable on the basis of the relevant legal rules—that is, even if Lev gave no recognition to any counter-norm or alternative facts—the manager may nevertheless have *believed in good faith* that *T* was liable. On that assumption, if Lev, as *T*'s stand-in, had refused to pay anything, he and the manager would have been left in a state of permanent opposition: The case would have been one in which a claimant had put forth a claim of right, founded, he believed, in justice, and the respondent had answered by denying that the claimant had any right whatsoever on his side—surely a slap in the face that would have made a continued relationship between the parties extremely difficult. On the other hand, if in such a case the respondent makes a payment in satisfaction of the claim, he tacitly admits that the claimant has some degree of right; while the claimant, by accepting, indicates that the books are now closed on the matter. In *T's Case* the hotel manager did not get the full amount he claimed. He was not, however, placed in a position where his claim of right was rejected out of hand. Instead his claim was accepted, but with the modification that a colliding defense was also accepted. The claim and defense were mutually accommodated, and an amicable relationship between the parties could and did continue.

Notes and Questions

1. For another articulation of the argument that the dichotomy between norm-based and normless methods of resolving disputes is too strong, see Fischer & Ury, *Getting to Yes* (1981) (advocating "principled" negotiation). Doesn't the idea of principled negotiation assume that the disputants share certain values? Is this a reasonable assumption?

2. Implicit in the attempts to encourage and facilitate settlements is an assumption that negotiated settlements are desirable. Professor Fiss, on the other hand, argues that "when the parties settle, society gets less than what appears, and for a price it does not know it is paying." He claims:

> The advocates of ADR [alternative dispute resolution] are led to support such measures and to exalt the idea of settlement more generally because they view adjudication as a process to resolve disputes. They act as though courts arose to resolve quarrels between neighbors who had reached an impasse and turned to a stranger for help. Courts are seen as an institutionalization of the stranger and adjudication is viewed as the process by which the stranger exercises power. The very fact that the neighbors have turned to someone else to resolve their dispute signifies a breakdown in their social relations; the advocates of ADR acknowledge this, but nonetheless hope that the neighbors will be able to reach agreement before the stranger renders judgment. Settlement is that agreement. It is a truce more than a true reconciliation, but it seems preferable to judgment because it rests on the consent of both parties and avoids the cost of a lengthy trial.

> In my view, however, this account of adjudication and the case for settlement rest on questionable premises. I do not believe that settlement as a generic practice is preferable to judgment or should be institutionalized on a wholesale and indiscriminate basis. It should be treated instead as a highly problematic technique for streamlining dockets. Settlement is for me the civil analogue of plea bargaining: Consent is often coerced; the bargain may be struck by someone without authority; the absence of a trial and judgment renders subsequent judicial involvement troublesome; and although dockets are trimmed, justice may not be done. Like plea bargaining, settlement is a capitulation to the conditions of mass society and should be neither encouraged nor praised.

* * *

> * * * I * * * see adjudication in more public terms: Civil litigation is an institutional arrangement for using state power to bring a recalcitrant reality closer to our chosen ideals. We turn to the courts because we need to, not because of some quirk in our personalities. We train our students in the tougher arts so that they may help secure all that the law promises, not because we want them to become gladiators or because we take a special pleasure in combat.

Fiss, *Against Settlement*, 93 Yale L.J. 1073, 1075, 1089 (1984). For a response to the critique of settlements presented by Professor Fiss and others, see Menkel-Meadow, *Whose Dispute Is It Anyway?: A Philosophical and Democratic Defense of Settlement (In Some Cases)*, 83 Geo. L.J. 2663 (1995).

3. One of the virtues of negotiated settlements is the privacy they afford. Although this may be desirable for the parties, is it desirable for society as a

whole? Or is this, in Fiss' analysis, part of the price that the public pays when the parties settle? Does the public have a stake in every dispute? See Macklin, *Promoting Settlement, Foregoing the Facts,* 14 N.Y.U.Rev.L. & Soc. Change 579 (1986) (stressing the value of judicial fact-finding as "a source of tested facts" for use in public policy discussion and planning).

4. Others look at negotiated settlements not as an alternative to litigation but rather as a variation of the litigation framework.

> On the contemporary American legal scene the negotiation of disputes is not an alternative to litigation. It is only a slight exaggeration to say that it is litigation. These are not two distinct processes, negotiation and litigation: there is a single process of disputing in the vicinity of official tribunals that we might call "litigation"; that is, the strategic pursuit of a settlement through mobilizing the court process. Full-blown adjudication of the dispute—running the whole course—might be though of as an infrequently pursued alternative to the ordinary course of litigation.

Galanter, *Using Negotiation to Teach About Legal Process,* 34 J.Leg.Educ. 268 (1984). Viewed in this light, legal rules—both substantive and procedural—are simply one set of many "bargaining chips" for the parties to use in litigation. See also Mnookin & Kornhauser, *Bargaining in the Shadow of the Law: The Case of Divorce,* 88 Yale L.J. 950 (1979).

Mark Lazerson has published a case study of the use of procedures as bargaining chips in New York City Landlord–Tenant Court. He argues that the strategy adopted by the South Bronx Legal Services Corporation of using "every available procedural technicality and objection as a defense against tenant eviction proceedings" was quite successful until the Landlord–Tenant Court was replaced by a new court, denominated the Housing Court. It began in 1973, and sought informality, conciliation, and compromise. The author concludes:

> A legal system that encourages conciliation between landlords and tenants—two parties with vastly unequal resources—by curtailing the procedural rights of the weaker can only succeed in amplifying that inequality. Procedural formality recognizes inequality and attempts to compensate for it by making both parties conform to the same standards. Once formality is withdrawn the courts are transformed into collection agencies operating with the seal of the state of New York.

Lazerson, *In the Halls of Justice, the Only Justice is in the Halls,* in Abel, *The Politics of Informal Justice,* vol. I, The American Experience (1982).

2. MECHANISMS FOR ENCOURAGING AND FACILITATING NEGOTIATED SETTLEMENT

Negotiated settlements are not only favored by advocates of alternative forms of dispute resolution, but the procedural rules of most court systems are designed to foster negotiated settlements.

———

Read Federal Rules of Civil Procedure 54(a), 54(d), and 68, and 28 U.S.C. § 1920 in the Supplement.

———

DELTA AIR LINES, INC. v. AUGUST, 450 U.S. 346, 101 S.Ct. 1146, 67 L.Ed.2d 287 (1981). Rosemary August filed suit against Delta Air Lines seeking $20,000 in back pay for violation of Title VII of the Civil Rights Act of 1964. Delta made a formal settlement offer of $450, which August rejected. At trial, judgment was for Delta and the District Court directed that each party bear its own costs. The court held that Federal Rule 68, which directs that a plaintiff who rejects a formal settlement offer must pay post-offer costs if the "judgment finally obtained by the offeree is not more favorable than the offer," was not applicable since Delta's offer of $450 was not a reasonable, good-faith attempt to settle the case. The Court of Appeals for the Seventh Circuit affirmed on the same grounds.

The Supreme Court affirmed the result, although it rejected the reasoning of the lower courts. In an opinion written by Justice Stevens, the Court held that "the plain language, the purpose, and the history of Rule 68" made clear that the words "judgment * * * obtained by the offeree" do not encompass a judgment against the offeree:

> Our interpretation of the Rule is consistent with its purpose. The purpose of Rule 68 is to encourage the settlement of litigation. In all litigation, the adverse consequences of potential defeat provide both parties with an incentive to settle in advance of trial. Rule 68 provides an additional inducement to settle in those cases in which there is a strong probability that the plaintiff will obtain a judgment but the amount of recovery is uncertain. Because prevailing plaintiffs presumptively will obtain costs under Rule 54(d), Rule 68 imposes a special burden on the plaintiff to whom a formal settlement offer is made. If a plaintiff rejects a Rule 68 settlement offer, he will lose some of the benefits of victory if his recovery is less than the offer. Because costs are usually assessed against the losing party, liability for costs is a normal incident of defeat. Therefore, a nonsettling plaintiff does not run the risk of suffering additional burdens that do not ordinarily attend a defeat, and Rule 68 would provide little, if any, additional incentive if it were applied when the plaintiff loses.

> Defendant argues that Rule 68 does provide such an incentive, because it operates to deprive the district judge of the discretion vested in him by Rule 54(d). According to this reasoning, Rule 68 is mandatory, and a district judge must assess costs against a plaintiff who rejects a settlement offer and then either fails to obtain a judgment or recovers less than the offer. * * *

> * * * If, as defendant argues, Rule 68 applies to defeated plaintiffs, any settlement offer, no matter how small, would apparently trigger the operation of the Rule. Thus any defendant, by performing the meaningless act of making a nominal settlement offer, could eliminate the trial judge's discretion under Rule 54(d). We cannot reasonably conclude that the drafters of the Federal Rules intended on the one hand affirmatively to grant the district judge discretion to deny costs to the prevailing party under Rule 54(d) and then on the other hand to give defendants—and only defendants—the power to take away that discretion by performing a token act. Moreover, if the Rule operated as defendant argues, we cannot conceive of a reason why the drafters would have given only defendants,

and not plaintiffs, the power to divest the judge of his Rule 54(d) discretion. * * * When Rule 68 is read literally, however, it is evenhanded in its operation. As we have already noted, it does not apply to judgments in favor of the defendant or to judgments in favor of the plaintiff for an amount greater than the settlement offer. In both of those extreme situations the trial judge retains his Rule 54(d) discretion. * * * Thus unless we assume that the Federal Rules were intended to be biased in favor of defendants, we can conceive of no reason why defendants—and not plaintiffs—should be given an entirely risk-free method of denying trial judges the discretion that Rule 54(d) confers regardless of the outcome of the litigation.

The Court of Appeals, perceiving the anomaly of allowing defendants to control the discretion of district judges by making sham offers, resolved the problem by holding that only reasonable offers trigger the operation of Rule 68. But the plain language of the Rule makes it unnecessary to read a reasonableness requirement into the Rule. * * *

Id. at 352–55, 101 S.Ct. at 1150–52, 67 L.Ed.2d at 292–95.

Justice Rehnquist, joined by Chief Justice Burger and Stewart, dissented:

* * * [T]he Court criticizes the Court of Appeals for its failure to confront "the threshold question whether Rule 68 has any application to a case in which judgment is entered against the plaintiff-offeree and in favor of the defendant-offeror." * * * The Court's resolution of the case turns on that threshold question and it finds that the answer "is dictated by the plain language, the purpose, and the history of Rule 68." * * *

Though the ultimate result reached by the Court is the same as that of the Court of Appeals, the difference in approach of the two opinions could not be more striking. * * * To the Court of Appeals, the mandatory language of Rule 68, at least in a Title VII case, is only discretionary where the offer is not "reasonable" and in "good faith" (neither of which qualifications are found in Rule 68). But to this Court, the Court of Appeals was entirely in error in even reaching that question because Rule 68 has no applicability to a case in which a judgment is entered *against* the plaintiff-offeree and *in favor of* the defendant-offeror. Totally ignoring the common-sense maxim that the greater includes the lesser, the Court concludes that its answer is "dictated by the plain language, the purpose, and the history of Rule 68."

* * *

In my view, there is also no basis for reading into Rule 68 any additional conditions for bringing the Rule into play other than those which are specifically contained in the provisions of the Rule itself. I assume that the Court would agree with this approach in view of its fondness for the "plain meaning" canon of statutory construction. Therefore, the best and shortest response to the Court of Appeals' suggestion that a Rule 68 offer must be "reasonable" and made in "good faith" is that Rule 68 simply does not incorporate any such requirement; it deprives a district court of its traditional discretion under Rule 54 to disallow costs to the prevailing party in the strongest verb of its type known to the English language—"must" * * *. Over a half century ago the Court of Appeals for the Sixth Circuit said "the word 'must' is so imperative in its meaning that no case has been called to our attention where that word has been read 'may.' " Berg v. Merchant, 15 F.2d 990 (1926), cert. denied, 274 U.S. 738, 47 S.Ct. 575, 71 L.Ed. 1317 (1927). To import into the mandatory language of Rule 68 a requirement that the tender of judgment must be "reasonable" or made in "good faith" not only rewrites Rule 68, but also puts a district court in the impossible position of having to evaluate such uncertain and nebulous concepts in the context of an "offer of judgment" that in many cases may have been made years past.

* * *

I read both the "plain language" of the Rule and its history quite differently than does the Court. According to it, a plaintiff—"offeree" under the terms of Rule 68—must *win* in the trial court in order to "obtain" a "judgment" within the meaning of that Rule. But we may call upon the various canons of statutory construction to pass before us in review as many times as we choose without being reduced to this anomalous conclusion.

The term "judgment" is defined in Rule 54(a) * * * to mean a "decree and any order from which an appeal lies." Unquestionably, respondent "obtained" an "order from which an appeal lies" when the District Court entered its judgment in this case. Certainly, respondent did not subscribe to the Court's reasoning because she immediately sought review in the Court of Appeals of the "judgment" which had been entered against her. Rule 68, when construed to include a traditional "take nothing" judgment, * * * as well as a judgment in favor of the plaintiff but less than the amount of the offer, thus fits with the remaining parts of the Federal Rules of Civil Procedure pertaining to judgments and orders in a manner in which the drafters of the Rule surely must have intended. * * *

Obviously, the event that "triggered" the operation of the original Rule 68 was the failure of the plaintiff to obtain a judgment more favorable than that offered. Just as obviously, the plaintiff in this case did not meet her burden of obtaining a judgment more favorable than the $450 she was offered. The operation of Rule 68 was not intended to change when this part of the Rule was amended in 1948 to its present form. * * *

* * * I do think it appropriate to note that no policy argument will convince me that a plaintiff who has refused an offer under Rule 68 and then has a "take nothing" judgment entered against her should be in a better position than a similar plaintiff who has refused an offer under Rule 68 but obtained a judgment in her favor, although in a lesser amount than that which was offered pursuant to Rule 68. The construction of Rule 68 urged by the Court would place in a better position a defendant who tendered $10,000 to a plaintiff under Rule 68 in a case where the plaintiff was awarded $5,000 than where the same tender was made and the plaintiff was awarded nothing.

* * *

Id. at 367–72, 101 S.Ct. at 1157–60, 67 L.Ed.2d at 302–07.

MAREK v. CHESNY, 473 U.S. 1, 105 S.Ct. 3012, 87 L.Ed.2d 1 (1985). Three police officers, in answering a call on a domestic disturbance, shot and killed Alfred Chesny's son. Chesny, on his own behalf and as administrator of his son's estate, filed suit against the officers in federal district court under 42 U.S.C. § 1983 and state tort law. Prior to trial, the police officers made a timely offer of settlement of $100,000, expressly including accrued costs and attorney's fees, but Chesny did not accept the offer. The case went to trial and Chesny was awarded $5,000 on the state-law claim, $52,000 for the Section 1983 violation, and $3,000 in punitive damages. Chesny then filed a request for attorney's fees under 42 U.S.C. § 1983, which provides that a prevailing party in a Section 1983 action may be awarded attorney's fees "as part of the costs." The claimed attorney's fees included fees for work performed subsequent to the settlement offer. The District Court declined to award these latter fees pursuant to Rule 68. The Court of Appeals reversed, but the Supreme Court agreed with the District Court.

The Court held first that the officers' offer was valid under Rule 68. As the Court read it, the Rule does not require that a defendant's offer itemize the respective amounts being tendered for settlement of the underlying substantive claim and for costs. In reaching this result, Chief Justice Burger (who wrote for the majority) asserted that the drafters' concern was not so much with the particular components of offers, but with the judgments to be allowed against defendants. Whether or not the offer recites that costs are included or specifies an amount for costs, the offer allows judgment to be entered against the defendant both for damages caused by the challenged conduct and for costs. In Chief Justice Burger's view, this construction of Rule 68 furthers its objective of encouraging settlements.

Chief Justice Burger next noted that the drafters of the Rule 68 were aware of the various federal statutes that, as an exception to the "American Rule," authorize an award of attorney's fees to prevailing parties as part of the costs in particular cases. From this, he concluded that the term "costs" in the Rule was intended to refer to all costs properly awardable under the relevant substantive statute. Thus, when the underlying statute defines "costs" to include attorney's fees, the fees are to be included as costs for purposes of Rule 68. Since Section 1983 expressly includes attorney's fees as "costs" available to a prevailing plaintiff in a suit under the statute, those fees are subject to the cost-shifting provision of Rule 68. As Chief Justice Burger saw it, rather than "cutting against the grain" of Section 1983, applying Rule 68 in the context of a Section 1983 action is consistent with Section 1988's policies and objectives of encouraging plaintiffs to bring meritorious civil rights suits; Rule 68 simply encourages settlements.

Justice Brennan filed a vigorous dissent for himself and Justices Marshall and Blackmun:

> The question presented by this case is whether the term "costs" as it is used in Rule 68 of the Federal Rules of Civil Procedure and elsewhere throughout the Rules refers simply to those taxable costs defined in 28

U.S.C. § 1920 and traditionally understood as "costs"—court fees, printing expenses, and the like—or instead includes attorney's fees when an underlying fees-award statute happens to refer to fees "as part of" the awardable costs. * * *

The Court's reasoning is wholly inconsistent with the history and structure of the Federal Rules, and its application to the over 100 attorney's fees statutes enacted by Congress will produce absurd variations in Rule 68's operation based on nothing more than picayune differences in statutory phraseology. Neither Congress nor the drafters of the Rules could possibly have intended such inexplicable variations in settlement incentives. Moreover, the Court's interpretation will "seriously undermine the purposes behind the attorney's fees provisions" of the civil rights laws. * * *

Notes and Questions

1. Since the *Marek* decision, a significant amount of federal litigation has addressed whether attorneys' fees are included as part of Rule 68 costs. The *Marek* Court's reliance on statutory interpretation created a situation in which minor variations in the language of attorneys' fee statutes have led to opposing results. See, e.g., U.S. v. Trident Seafoods Corp., 92 F.3d 855 (9th Cir.1996), certiorari denied 519 U.S. 1109, 117 S.Ct. 944, 136 L.Ed.2d 833 (1997) ("costs" under the Clean Air Act only include attorneys' fees for Rule 68 purposes for "unreasonable" actions); Sheppard v. Riverview Nursing Center, Inc., 88 F.3d 1332, 1337 (4th Cir.), certiorari denied 519 U.S. 993, 117 S.Ct. 483, 136 L.Ed.2d 377 (1996) (attorneys' fees are not part of costs for Rule 68 purposes under the Civil Rights Act of 1991, 42 U.S.C. § 2000e–5(g)(2)(B)(i)); Thomas v. Peterson, 841 F.2d 332, 334 (9th Cir.1988) (costs do not include attorneys' fees for Rule 68 purposes under the Equal Access to Justice Act, 28 U.S.C. § 2412).

2. Most litigators agree that post-offer costs excluding attorney's fees (the most significant item of litigation expense) are too small to make a significant difference in deciding whether to settle or go to trial. See Simon, *The Riddle of Rule 68,* 54 Geo.Wash.L.Rev. 1, 55–61 (1985). The allowable items of costs set forth in 28 U.S.C. § 1920 is a short list, and the Supreme Court has cautioned that Rule 54(d) does not give district judges "unrestrained discretion to tax costs to reimburse a winning litigant for every expense he has seen fit to incur in the conduct of his case." In particular, the Court instructed, "the discretion given district judges to tax costs should be sparingly exercised with reference to expenses not specifically allowed by statute." Farmer v. Arabian American Oil Co., 379 U.S. 227, 235, 85 S.Ct. 411, 416, 13 L.Ed.2d 248, 254 (1964). See generally Bartell, *Taxation of Costs and Awards of Expenses in Federal Court,* 101 F.R.D. 553 (1984). Thus, not surprisingly, Rule 68 was rarely used before the late 1970's when defense attorneys turned to the rule as a possible device to undercut the effect of a growing number of statutes, such as 42 U.S.C. § 1988, that altered the usual American rule in favor of prevailing plaintiffs recovering their attorney's fees. But see Crawford Fitting Co. v. J.T. Gibbons, Inc., 482 U.S. 437, 107 S.Ct. 2494, 96 L.Ed.2d 385 (1987).

3. The majority in *Marek* argues that the effect of Rule 68 is neutral because settlements serve the interest of plaintiffs as well as defendants. But does Rule 68 actually encourage settlements? Or is its primary effect to force plaintiffs to accept less in settlement of cases that would settle in the absence of the rule, but on

terms more favorable to plaintiffs? See Miller, *An Economic Analysis of Rule 68,* 15 J.Legal Studies 93 (1986); Rowe, *Predicting the Effects of Attorney Fee Shifting,* 47 Law & Contemp.Prob. 139 (1984).

4. The 1990 Civil Justice Reform Act and the 1998 Alternative Dispute Resolution Act discussed in Section A, p. 1357, supra, have resulted in the implementation of ADR programs in district courts throughout the federal system. What implications do these new statutes have for the use of settlements in civil trials? Do they encourage or discourage the use of negotiated settlements?

5. The majority in *Marek* did not answer the question whether a prevailing civil rights plaintiff also must pay the losing defendant's post-offer attorney's fees if the plaintiff obtains a judgment that is not more favorable than the Rule 68 offer. How will this question be resolved in light of the Court's decision in *Marek*? Does it matter that there is authority to the effect that a prevailing civil rights defendant may not recover attorney's fees under Section 1988 unless the trial court determines that the plaintiff's action was frivolous, unreasonable, or without foundation? See Crossman v. Marcoccio, 806 F.2d 329 (1st Cir.1986), certiorari denied 481 U.S. 1029, 107 S.Ct. 1955, 95 L.Ed.2d 527 (1987).

6. What legal authority authorizes the lower federal courts to set up and require litigants to use alternative dispute-resolution techniques? In STRANDELL v. JACKSON COUNTY, 838 F.2d 884 (7th Cir.1987), the Court of Appeals held that a district court may not require litigants to participate in a non-binding summary jury trial. The court observed that, "in those areas of trial practice where the Supreme Court and the Congress, acting together, have addressed the appropriate balance between the needs for judicial efficiency and the rights of the individual litigant, innovation by the individual judicial officer must conform to that balance." Id. at 886–87. The court found nothing in Rule 16(c)(7) or (11) that authorized a mandatory summary jury trial. It also observed that a mandatory summary jury trial as a pretrial settlement device have a serious effect on the well-established rules concerning discovery and work-product privilege.

By contrast, in FEDERAL RESERVE BANK OF MINNEAPOLIS v. CAREY–CANADA, INC., 123 F.R.D. 603 (D.Minn.1988), the court found that it had the power to compel the parties to attend and participate in a non-binding summary jury trial. The court based its decision on Rules 1 and 16, and reasoned that the summary jury trial procedure, "even if it does not lead to settlement, will be of substantial benefit * * * by clarifying issues for trial, both for the parties and for the court." Id. at 607.

7. Given that the vast majority of civil cases are settled, what role should judges play in negotiated settlements? See Floyd, *Can the Judge Do That?–The Need for a Clearer Judicial Role in Settlement,* 26 Ariz. St. L.J. 45 (1994). The Federal Rules Advisory Committee has considered judges' participation in settlement, but the Committee has not included any suggestions in the rules themselves.

8. Remember that negotiated settlements can trigger claim and/or issue preclusion, thereby affecting subsequent actions between the parties who entered into the nontrial agreement. See generally Chapter 17, supra. To what extent should either party consider the possibility of future disputes when contemplating settlement?

SECTION C.   ALTERNATIVE SYSTEMS OF DISPUTE RESOLUTION

This Section examines several third-party methods of alternative-dispute resolution (ADR). Keep two points in mind as you study them:

First, no matter how informal a dispute-resolution system may be, it requires some procedural structure to enable the participants to conduct themselves and settle their disagreements in an orderly and predictable manner. To what extent are the goals of a nonadjudicative system of dispute resolution in conflict with the need for procedural safeguards?

Second, some proponents of alternative dispute resolution assume, either explicitly or implicitly, that those who choose to work out their disputes by means other than litigation *consent* to be bound by the result. But one party may decide that she does not like the result and may refuse to be bound by it. What provision can be made to bind those who refuse to abide by the results that an ADR system produces? What provision should be made for persons who are not parties to a given dispute but who will be affected by the result produced by the proceeding? To the extent that an alternative dispute-resolution system is able to function only if those who bring disputes to it can agree beforehand to abide by the result, is its practical utility severely limited? To the extent that an alternative dispute-resolution system is endowed with coercive powers to enforce the results it produces, is it merely a variant of a traditional court system?

1. RESOLVING DISPUTES WITHOUT ADVERSARINESS: ALTERNATIVES TO ADJUDICATION

Mediation is a method of alternative dispute resolution commonly used to resolve commercial disputes, medical malpractice claims, and family law issues. The following material focuses on divorce mediation, but the issues and concerns discussed are similar to those that must be addressed in all mediation processes, regardless of the subject matter of the dispute.

———

WINKS, DIVORCE MEDIATION: A NONADVERSARY PROCEDURE FOR THE NO–FAULT DIVORCE, 19 J.Fam.L. 615, 616–25, 634–40 (1981):

II. HISTORICAL BACKGROUND

A. Adversary Law, Adversary Procedures

* * *

The law [historically] reflected society's disapproval of divorce by setting up a succession of legal impediments which could be overcome only by the very rich or the very tenacious. As soon as the marriage institution was threatened by dissolution, the law intervened with clumsy inefficiency. As one court noted, "in every divorce suit the state is a third party whose interests take precedence over the private interests of the spouses." The desire to manage one's private affairs without the intrusion of this third party doubtless contributed to the high incidence of informal divorce: desertion, separation and the "Enoch Arden" divorce [permitting remarriage following a spouse's disappearance].

A divorce was granted only after exhaustive judicial inquiry into the appropriate grounds, which were narrowly defined. The process required that there be one party desirous of divorce, the other in opposition. * * *

* * *

Even scrupulous lawyers were placed in the difficult position of having to evade the law in order to help their clients. The tawdry machinations which were often necessary to provide adequate justification for divorce—the staged raid on a hotel room to prove adultery, the perjured testimony—contributed to the poor image of the family lawyer. Frustration and anger were displaced from the law to the lawyer, who was forced to demand the public disclosure of private affairs in an adversary legal setting.

* * *

B.   Nonadversary Law, Adversary Procedures

No-fault divorce was designed to preserve the privacy of the parties by eliminating the need for public recrimination. Wrongs no longer had to be spelled out in embarrassing personal detail. Legal vocabulary was changed: divorce became dissolution, plaintiff and defendant became petitioner and respondent. But the removal of fault from the pleadings was not accompanied by the removal of fault from the procedures. * * *

Where there are adversary procedures, there are secrets to be disclosed. The secrets ferreted out by the divorce lawyer are now secrets of the checking account rather than secrets of the bedroom. But when custody is in dispute, defects of character and lapses in behavior continue to be brought before the court to demonstrate parental unfitness.

Ideally, adversary procedures facilitate disclosure. In theory, each side tells its own truth and uncovers the truth concealed by the other. All too often, however, the truth is suppressed, or at least distorted. Each side presents self-serving information and strives mightily to keep the other side ignorant. Attorneys have little opportunity to counteract this distortion because of the ground rules for divorce. Clients provide a picture of their marriage which lawyers cannot revise because they have no contact with the other spouse. Such contact is enjoined by the profession * * *.

Clients are often directed not to talk with the other spouse. * * * Like the child's game of "telephone," messages must be transmitted from husband to his attorney to her attorney to wife, with inevitable distortion.

Adversary lawyers may reinforce the conflict between the parties and create obstacles to settlement. * * * The assumption that divorce lawyers will escalate the hostility has led some arbitrators and attorneys to suggest that the settlement be concluded before the lawyer steps in.

An adversary family lawyer of many years' experience has identified the two crucial determinants of the divorce outcome: the opposing counsel and the presiding judge. The comment reflects perhaps the gravest defect of the adversary process—the lack of direct involvement of the divorcing parties. The removal of the parties from the sphere of controversy is regarded as a means of promoting objectivity in resolving differences. The lawyer is the client's "affiliate." * * * Unfortunately, affiliates are not always so evenly matched. The competent lawyer pitted against an irresponsible fighter will be limited in strategy and options, and the client will be the worse for it.

Where the differences between the parties cannot be resolved through the negotiation of their attorneys, classic divorce strategy calls for each attorney to threaten to go all the way to trial, set a court date and then tell the judge more time is needed to settle. The ensuing hallway negotiations and a few minutes of the court's time decide the future of the couple. Because judges seldom question settlements, this hasty decisionmaking bears the stamp of finality. As a consequence, the parties may accede to open-court stipulations that they do not understand until they sign the agreement weeks later. Unfortunately, motions to set aside such agreements seldom succeed.

If the attorneys cannot reach agreement, the judge assumes an active role. A common bench tactic is to invite opposing counsel into chambers. The judge gives a cursory first look at the file when counsel walk in. The attorneys interrupt each other as each nervously urges acceptance of his client's position. On the basis of this truncated version of the issues, the judge tells them what (s)he would do. The attorneys return to their clients with the easy excuse that they made concessions in order to avoid the risk of an imposed settlement.

Another judicial ploy is the crowded calendar. At the time scheduled for trial, the parties are advised that no room is available. Because it may be months before a new date can be set, the parties are pressured to reach agreement to avoid the uncertainty of delay.

Often attorneys settle not out of reluctance to litigate but out of familiarity with the judge's rulings. * * * Domestic relations judges in the San Francisco Bay area have coauthored a booklet of guidelines that make protracted litigation foolhardy and impractical. Such guidelines encourage settlement and save the divorcing parties from the expense and emotion of the contested divorce. But implicit in the guidelines as well as in the other procedures used to arrive at agreement is the assumption that the judges and the attorneys know what the divorcing parties want or what they ought to want.

* * *

III. AN ALTERNATIVE NONADVERSARY PROCEDURE: DIVORCE MEDIATION

* * * The mediator represents neither party in a divorce action. He is what Louis Brandeis called "counsel for the situation." The mediator's task is to provide the information which will enable the parties to arrive at a fair settlement; he is counselor and advisor, but not decisionmaker.

Perhaps little real difference exists between representing both parties and representing neither party, but the distinction, however cosmetic, is perceived as important by the legal profession. The role of disinterested advisor is regarded as more consonant with the attorney's traditional function than the role of representative of two parties with clearly differing interests.

* * *

A. *How Divorce Mediation Works*

Communication with both parties may begin even before the first interview. When a client calls for an appointment, one mediator asks that the other spouse call to confirm. Because mediation is so uncommon, couples often have little notion of what is involved. The two telephone conversations serve to emphasize the procedure's mutuality.

The constraints of the mediation process are carefully explained at the initial interview. The couple are made aware of the necessity for full consent and disclosure, the attorney's inability to represent either party in litigation and confidentiality of all attorney-client communications. Failure to warn leaves the attorney open to the charge of legal malpractice. The parties are told that they may consult outside attorneys at any time. Both sign a consent form which explains their rights and responsibilities. They are reminded that the mediator "is not acting as attorney for either party nor as attorney for both parties." Clients are alerted to their differing interests. * * *

* * *

The attorney proceeds with special care at the initial interview. Neutral, open-ended questions elicit responses that enable the interviewer to observe the dynamics of the marital relationship. Traditional legal skills of definition, clarification and summarization come into play. By summarizing what each party has said, the lawyer enables them to hear themselves more clearly and to identify problems with some detachment.

After the initial interview, the lawyer may see each client separately, then together again. * * * Some spouses may unburden themselves more freely in a separate interview. The mediator learns which areas each considers important, and where concessions can be made. Then when the parties are together, negotiations can proceed more swiftly.

* * *

A single attorney must avoid being co-opted by one party, and needs to monitor his or her own reactions in order to maintain strict impartiality. This does not mean that the mediator does not take sides. In the give and take of negotiation the skilled mediator will know when and how to alter the balance. When a stalemate occurs the mediator may shift the topic of negotiation, then reopen the issue when it provides an area for compromise.

If there are children, most lawyers deal with child support, custody and visitation first. Resolution of these issues shows the couple that cooperation will be possible in other areas as well. Custodial arrangements necessarily involve financial planning. * * * Shared responsibility for the resolution of the custodial issue makes resolution of other issues easier.

In helping the couple draft an agreement, the lawyer uses the therapeutic tool of having each clarify goals and objectives. Do both parties expect their children to go to college? How will this expense be taken care of? Do both expect to be self-supporting? Will one spouse need or want vocational training? * * *

The mediator does not naively assume that parties will willingly disclose financial or other secrets. Self-protection is both inevitable and desirable. The motivation for full and fair disclosure is realistic awareness that if the parties cannot agree, the courts will make the agreement for them. They are dependent on each other's cooperation and must bargain in good faith.

Just as the personal injury lawyer "cools the client out," or prepares the client to accept less than the anticipated windfall, so the family lawyer prepares both spouses to accept a realistic division of assets. Each party must adjust expectations. They cannot merely discard the detritus (the inconveniently present spouse and sometimes the community debts) and hold on to the fruits of the marriage. The client who dreams of "winning big" may need to be reminded that even in adversary proceedings no one wins big any more. Additionally, it does little good to be awarded a whopping settlement if the other spouse, understandably resentful and antagonistic, will not abide by the provisions. The statistics on alimony, child support and visitation are a sad indicator of the minimal enforcement of settlement provisions. An agreement that reflects realistic expectations may well prevent future litigation.

* * *

The mediator may accompany the clients to court and appear as a friend of the court, or stay away entirely. One attorney pointed out that his presence is not needed, and his absence saves the clients money. The parties' appearance in court on their own behalf serves to underscore their autonomy and responsibility for the agreement.

Notes and Questions

1. What issues should be discussed in a divorce mediation? Should the disputants determine the "subject-matter jurisdiction" of the mediator? Or should a mediator decide, for example, that custody is inseparable from child support and refuse to mediate one without the other?

2. Divorce mediation raises significant questions of professional responsibility. Should a lawyer engage in divorce mediation at all? If so, who is the client? Doesn't representation of both spouses involve a serious conflict of interest? Is it a sufficient response to this problem simply to decide that the lawyer-mediator does not represent either disputant? Or should a lawyer only become involved in the process as a drafter of the agreement that the disputants have reached with the help of a nonlawyer mediator? On the other hand, is a nonlawyer who mediates a divorce dispute engaged in the unauthorized practice of law? See, e.g., Silberman, *Professional Responsibility Problems in Divorce Mediation,* 16 Fam.L.Q. 107 (1981); Crouch, *Divorce Mediation and Legal Ethics,* 16 Fam.L.Q. 219 (1982).

3. What role should a mediator play in the resolution of a dispute? Should he facilitate the discussion or merely evaluate the information the parties present? What action should a mediator take if she believes one party could be harmed by the resolution process? See Riskin, *Understanding Mediators' Orientations, Strategies, and Techniques: A Grid for the Perplexed,* 1 Harv. Negot. L. Rev. 7 (1996).

4. The mediator's impartiality is of obvious concern. How do we guarantee that one party's interests are not overlooked? Must disputants have independent counsel in order to protect their interests in the mediation process? What problems might that cause?

5. The fate of children is often central in divorce mediation. Should children be allowed to participate in the mediation? Should they have separate representation? Who should determine what is in the best interests of the children in the

context of divorce mediation? For further discussion, see Guggenheim, *The Right to be Represented but Not Heard: Reflections on Legal Representation for Children*, 59 N.Y.U.L. Rev. 76 (1984); Spencer & Zammit, *Mediation—Arbitration: A Proposal for Private Resolution of Disputes Between Divorced or Separated Parents*, 1976 Duke L.J. 911 (1976).

6. Should all the information revealed in the mediation process be made known to the court if the parties cannot produce an agreement and proceed to litigation? Can a mediator be called to testify or to give a recommendation based on the mediation proceedings? If a child is involved and a trial judge subsequently has to review what action would be in the best interests of that child, shouldn't all relevant information, including anything that was disclosed in the mediation, be made known to the judge?

7. Parties in mediation do not have a discovery mechanism to force the opposing side to reveal information (such as financial or mental health information) that may be critical to a full and fair evaluation of the dispute. How does a mediator insure that all relevant information is made available? Should a mental-health professional be retained to undertake independent fact-finding to learn information that otherwise might not be revealed? How can mediation prevent a party from hiding assets?

8. When should a court enforce a mediated agreement? Should a court be more willing to enforce an agreement if the disputants each had counsel? What should a court do if it feels the mediator was biased or if there is evidence of incomplete disclosure by one party?

9. Consider the following:

The unequal financial and social power of men and women makes mediation an unfair means of resolving family-related disputes. Women do not have equal bargaining power and cannot assert equal power in an informal setting unrepresented by counsel. In families where domestic violence and child sexual abuse is present, the lack of legal protection offered by mediation can be life threatening for abused family members. Mediation is inappropriate with respect to any issue (be it related to violence or not) if there has been any act or threat of violence against the women or children, since the threat of violence coerces involuntary compromise.

Lefcourt, *Women, Mediation and Family Law*, Clearinghouse Rev. 266, 269 (July 1984). For another discussion of the view that mediation of family-related disputes often results in unfair treatment of women, see Grillo, *The Mediation Alternative: Process Dangers for Women*, 100 Yale L.J. 1545 (1991). See also Bryan, *Killing Us Softly: Divorce Mediation and the Politics of Power*, 40 Buffalo L. Rev. 441 (1992).

10. Race, ethnicity, and cultural values significantly affect family dispute resolution. How should a mediator evaluate cultural values or practices that differ from what is considered to be the norm? For an enlightening discussion on how race, ethnicity, and culture may impact family dispute mediation, see Mabry, *African Americans "Are Not Carbon Copies" of White Americans, The Role of African American Culture in Mediation of Family Disputes*, 13 Ohio St. J. on Disp. Resol. 405 (1998). See also Delgado, Dunn, Brown, Lee & Hubbert, *Fairness and Formality: Minimizing the Risk of Prejudice in Alternative Dispute Resolution*, 1985 Wis. L. Rev. 1359.

11. Some jurisdictions have implemented mandatory mediation programs to resolve family law disputes. Under these programs, disputants cannot be heard in court until they have attempted mediation. Do mandatory divorce mediation

programs violate due process? See King, *Burdening Access to Justice: The Cost of Divorce Mediation on the Cheap*, 73 St. John's L. Rev. 375 (1999).

2. THE ADVERSARY PROCESS WITHOUT LAW: ARBITRATION

a. *Introduction*

Arbitration is probably the most common third-party method of alternative dispute resolution. The parties select an arbitrator or arbitrators, who conduct hearings and then reach a decision. The arbitration hearing is an adversary proceeding, in which each of the parties presents its case, with full opportunity for cross-examination and rebuttal. Frequently, the decision of the arbitrator, called an "award," is then entered in court, much as a judgment in a formally adjudicated case is entered. In each case, both parties are bound to abide by the award, even though in certain limited circumstances, discussed below, either or both parties may seek to challenge, modify, or even vacate the award.

Arbitration is the method of alternative dispute resolution with which the American legal system has had the longest experience; not surprisingly, therefore, it also is the third-party method that has adapted itself most closely to work with the legal system. Arbitration developed in the commercial and the labor-management contexts. Commercial arbitration was the first to develop. Labor arbitration first appeared during the latter half of the nineteenth century in response to repeated outbreaks of labor unrest, but did not achieve widespread acceptance until after World War II. More recently, arbitration has become a tool for resolving disputes in a variety of contexts, including banking and medicine:

> * * * For several decades now, many practitioners and their clients have preferred arbitration over litigation as a means of resolving disputes. In some practice areas (labor, banking, securities, construction and medical malpractice), the use of arbitration is so wide-spread that it is rapidly becoming the standard practice for certain types of disputes. In California, for example, the trend is pervasive in both the medical malpractice field and banking industry, where an agreement to arbitrate is a common prerequisite for patients of many hospitals and doctors and for the deposit and bankcard customers of many banks.

Adler & Roth, *Legal Overview*, in *The Alternative Dispute Resolution Practice Guide* 2–1, 2–3–2–4 (Roth, Wulff & Cooper eds. 1999).

As a general matter, arbitration (whether commercial, labor, or otherwise) is contractual: either the parties must have agreed in writing before the dispute in question to submit disagreements to arbitration, or they must have entered into an agreement to submit an existing dispute to arbitration.

In addition to the arbitration agreement, both federal and state statutes play a significant role in shaping the context in which arbitration occurs. The federal statute, the Federal Arbitration Act, 9 U.S.C. §§ 1 et seq., and the major state arbitration statutes were enacted in the 1920s. The Federal Arbitration Act and Article 75 of New York's Civil Practice Law and Rules are the most notable statutes of this type, and both have served as models for other states' arbitration statutes.

b. *How Arbitration Works*

The parties may select an arbitrator in their agreement to arbitrate, or they may authorize a neutral party, such as the American Arbitration Association, to select arbitrators. In circumstances in which the agreement does not designate an arbitrator or a method to select an arbitrator, both the federal Act and the New York statute, for example, provide that an arbitrator may be named by a court on application of one or all of the parties. 9 U.S.C. § 5; N.Y.C.P.L.R. § 7504.

Arbitration can take place before a single arbitrator or before a panel of arbitrators (most often consisting of three members). Usually, the agreement will specify the number. It is common, for example, for an agreement to provide for a panel of three arbitrators—one appointed by each party and a third appointed by the American Arbitration Association. When the agreement specifies the number of arbitrators it governs; when it does not, both the Federal Arbitration Act and the New York statute provide that the arbitration hearing shall be conducted by a single arbitrator.

Although arbitration is a form of adversary adjudication, its procedural structure depends largely on the pre-dispositions of the arbitrator or arbitrators conducting a given hearing. The arbitrator is relatively free to shape the hearing as he sees fit. The arbitrator has three broad areas of responsibility: (1) the pre-hearing phase; (2) the hearing; and (3) the award and the opinion (if an opinion is thought necessary).

The pre-hearing phase is the least structured and thus is the most governed by individual preference. For example, it is frequently the case that the parties, represented by counsel, submit briefs (often indistinguishable from those that would be submitted in a formal adjudication) and argue their case at a hearing. In other arbitrations, the parties may choose to submit their respective cases in documentary form and waive hearings entirely. And in still other arbitrations, the parties may, but are not required to (and often do not), submit written statements, presentations, and even briefs to arbitrators. Patterns of practice tend to become associated with particular types of arbitration. For example, commercial arbitrators receive written briefs frequently. By contrast, labor arbitrators tend to discourage them.

Pre-hearing discovery is often limited to what the parties voluntarily disclose. However, arbitrators are empowered at the request of either party to subpoena documents, as well as persons, for the hearing, and counsel generally can agree on a procedure to review the subpoenaed documents in advance of the hearing. Further, arbitration fora in the securities industry offer formalized discovery proceedings in the pre-hearing phase that permit the parties themselves to serve written requests for information or documents on other parties to the arbitration. See NASD Code of Arbitration Procedure § 32. See also NYSE Arbitration Rule 619.

The hearing phase is somewhat more structured than the pre-hearing phase. The hearing itself is an adversary proceeding; its conduct is best described by Rule 29 of the Association's Commercial Arbitration Rules:

> The Arbitrator may, at the beginning of the hearing, ask for statements clarifying the issues involved.

The complaining party shall then present its claim and proofs and its witnesses, who shall submit to questions or other examination. The defending party shall then present its defense and proofs and its witnesses, who shall submit to questions or other examination. The Arbitrator has discretion to vary this procedure but shall afford full and equal opportunity to all parties for the presentation of any material or relevant proofs.

Exhibits, when offered by either party, may be received in evidence by the Arbitrator.

Although the arbitrator is the sole judge of the relevance and materiality of evidence offered and need not conform to the legal rules of evidence, some arbitrators believe that at least some compliance with traditional rules of evidence is both necessary and beneficial:

You do not have to call them the rules of evidence, but you have to have a way of sorting out information and evaluating what is happening. It cannot be denied that a large part of what goes on in hearings is people getting things off their chests, and this, of course, bears on your attitude toward evidentiary problems as they arise. The arbitrator's basic problem is to find out as much as possible about what really happened.

Jones, *Problems of Procedure and Evidence,* in *Arbitration in Practice* 48, 52 (Zack ed. 1984).

Because the arbitrator has such broad discretion to choose to admit or exclude evidence or to hear or refuse to hear witnesses (although arbitrators that have spoken to the issue counsel their colleagues to err on the side of inclusiveness), his or her power to find facts and decide questions of law virtually is unlimited.

Occasionally, although both parties may consent to submit their dispute to arbitration, one party does not appear at the hearing. Although the arbitrator is not permitted either to abandon the hearing on the ground that one party is not present, he is not permitted to rule automatically in favor of the appearing party. The New York statute pertaining to evidence at arbitration hearings, N.Y.C.P.L.R. § 7506(c), as well as common arbitration practice dictate that the appearing party be permitted to put in its statements and evidence and that the arbitrator consider this material in reaching his or her decision on the issue submitted.

The final phase of an arbitration produces the award. The arbitrator's award of a dispute need not contain anything more than a statement of the rights and obligations of the parties to that dispute, and their associations discourage them from giving reasons for a decision. See Coulson, *Business Arbitration—What You Need to Know* 29 (3d ed. 1986) ("Written opinions can be dangerous because they identify targets for the losing party to attack."). However, if the parties request a written statement of decision before the arbitrator is appointed, the American Arbitration Association requires that the arbitrators render a reasoned award. R–44 of the AAA Commercial Arbitration Rules. In addition, if the arbitration agreement between the parties requires that the arbitrators make findings of fact and conclusions of law, they are bound to do so. Even in the absence of requests or agreements to render a written award, arbitrators frequently prepare opinions setting forth their reasoning:

> The Supreme Court in [United Steelworkers of America v. Enterprise Wheel & Car Corp., 363 U.S. 593, 80 S.Ct. 1358, 4 L.Ed.2d 1424 (1960)] * * * said that while arbitrators do not owe the Court an explanation of their decisions, "a well reasoned opinion tends to engender confidence in the integrity of the process and aids in clarifying the underlying agreement." * * * Although the parties may of course waive an opinion, except in the small minority of cases involving bench decisions, there is no demand for awards without opinions. The parties almost always want something in writing, something that will explain why we awarded as we did. * * * The parties are interested in principles and guidelines for the future. For their future guidance, they are entitled to the arbitrator's findings of fact, his or her view of the evidence, understanding of the respective contentions of the parties, and finally, the relevant interpretation and application of the parties' agreement.

Rehmus, *Writing the Opinion,* in *Arbitration in Practice* 209, 209–10 (Zack ed. 1984).

Both issues of arbitrability—whether the issues submitted properly are before the arbitrator and whether the arbitration procedures have been followed correctly—and issues on the merits usually are addressed in opinions. Often, the arbitrator finds himself under the obligation to write not only for the parties (the company and the union) but also for the NLRB, other employers and unions (for opinions frequently are circulated throughout the industry), and occasionally for the courts (to ensure that, if the award is challenged in the courts, the reviewing court understands the reasoning and conclusions underlying the award).

Notes and Questions

1. Consider the following:

> * * * Arbitration provides not only a speedier form of adjudication, but its very nature lends itself to the accurate projection of reasonable, budgeted legal costs. Another singular feature offered by arbitration is the experience and expertise brought to the adjudication process by arbitrators who invariably have familiarity with the nature of the industry in which the parties to the dispute conduct business. Typically, neither the trial judge assigned to a calendar matter nor the jury has this type of in-depth background. The speed with which arbitration proceeds also encourages a timely assessment of the settlement value of a case, and concomitantly, its eventual settlement. In short, the practitioner can properly expect increasing resort to arbitration as an alternative means of dispute resolution.

DiBenedetto, *Practical Guide: An Outline for Arbitration Under the Civil Practice Law and Rules,* 48 Albany L.Rev. 763, 777–78 (1984).

2. Advocates of arbitration maintain that it is a flexible device capable of resolving more complex disputes than conventional two-party disputes, but the various structures and rules for arbitration presuppose that the dispute in question will be a two-party dispute. Are the arbitration procedures described in this section as adaptable to multi-party disputes as proponents of arbitration

contend? What difficulties would an arbitrator face in adjudicating a multi-party dispute?

3.   Although at first it may appear that issues of notice and service of process do not arise in the context of arbitration, arbitration proceedings may take place *ex parte* if one side doesn't appear. See p. 1365, supra. If a party proves that she had no notice of the arbitration, should she be allowed to challenge the award arrived at by the arbitration in the *ex parte* proceeding? See N.Y.C.P.L.R. § 7511(b)(2).

4.   Most often, the parties themselves bring matters to arbitration. This is not always the case, however. Under both the federal and the New York statutes, a defendant in a civil suit may move to halt the suit pending arbitration on the basis that the parties previously had entered into an agreement to arbitrate. 9 U.S.C. § 3; N.Y.C.P.L.R. § 7503(a). Conversely, when a party to an arbitration agreement refuses to submit a dispute to arbitration, the other party may move in court to compel the dispute's submission to arbitration. 9 U.S.C. § 4; N.Y.C.P.L.R. § 7503(a).

c.   *The Extent to Which the Dispute Is Subject to Arbitration*

Initially, the judicial system viewed arbitration with distrust. For example, in Wilko v. Swan, 346 U.S. 427, 74 S.Ct. 182, 98 L.Ed. 168 (1953), the Supreme Court ruled that claims arising under Section 12(2) of the Securities Act of 1933 were not subject to compulsory arbitration. In recent years, however, we have witnessed a dramatic shift from distrust of and reluctance to enforce arbitration agreements to a strong presumption in favor of arbitration as a sound, acceptable method of resolving disputes without litigation.

One step in this shift was SOUTHLAND CORP. v. KEATING, 465 U.S. 1, 104 S.Ct. 852, 79 L.Ed.2d 1 (1984). In *Southland,* the appellant, the owner and franchisor of 7–Eleven convenience stores, entered into franchise agreements with over 800 franchisees located in the state of California. Between September 1975 and May 1977, a class of these franchisees as well as several individual appellees sued the appellant for breach of contract, fraud, misrepresentation, breach of fiduciary duty, and violations of the California Franchise Investment Law. The California courts consolidated the various actions. Pursuant to the terms of the franchise agreements, the appellant sought arbitration of all the claims. However, the California Supreme Court held that the appellees' claims under the Franchise Investment Law were not arbitrable under the arbitration clauses, interpreting the California Investment Law to require judicial consideration of claims brought under that statute and concluding that the California statute did not contravene Section 2 of the Federal Arbitration Act, which provides that an arbitration provision relating to a transaction involving commerce "shall be valid, irrevocable, and enforceable, save upon such grounds as exist at law or in equity for the revocation of any contract."

The Supreme Court reversed, holding that "in enacting Section 2 of the federal Act, Congress declared a national policy favoring arbitration and withdrew the power of the states to require a judicial forum for the resolution of claims which the contracting parties agreed to resolve by arbitration. * * * Congress has thus mandated the enforcement of arbitration agreements." The Court rejected the argument advanced in dissent by Justices O'Connor and

Rehnquist that Congress intended the Act only to be a procedural restraint on federal courts; writing for the Court, Chief Justice Burger maintained that the possibility of forum-shopping by litigants militated in favor of reading the statute as a source of substantive law binding both federal and state courts.

In a series of more recent cases, the Court has further expanded the reach of the Federal Arbitration Act. In SHEARSON/AMERICAN EXPRESS, INC. v. McMAHON, 482 U.S. 220, 107 S.Ct. 2332, 96 L.Ed.2d 185 (1987), the Court upheld the compulsory arbitration of claims under Section 10(b) of the Securities Exchange Act of 1934 and under the Racketeer Influenced and Corrupt Organizations Act (RICO). Although a section of the Securities Exchange Act provided that "[t]he district courts of the United States * * * shall have exclusive jurisdiction" of violations of the Act, and another section declared void any agreement "to waive compliance with any provision" of the Act, the Court interpreted these provisions as to prohibit only a waiver of compliance with the substantive provisions of the Act. Noting that the arbitration procedures of the various stock exchanges had been specifically approved by the Securities and Exchange Commission, the Court reasoned that arbitration tribunals are "fully capable of handling" claims of Securities Exchange Act violations. Id. at 232–34, 107 S.Ct. at 2341, 96 L.Ed.2d at 198–99. Similarly, the Court rejected the arguments that RICO claims are "too complex to be subject to arbitration," that "the 'overlap' between RICO's civil and criminal provisions" precluded arbitration even of civil RICO claims, and that "the public interest in the enforcement of RICO precludes its submission to arbitration." Id. at 239–40, 107 S.Ct. at 2344, 96 L.Ed.2d at 202.

Two years later, in RODRIGUEZ de QUIJAS v. SHEARSON/AMERICAN EXPRESS, 490 U.S. 477, 109 S.Ct. 1917, 104 L.Ed.2d 526 (1989), the Court held that a predispute agreement to arbitrate claims arising under the Securities Act of 1933 was enforceable. Going one step beyond its decision in the *McMahon* case, the Court concluded "that *Wilko* was incorrectly decided and is inconsistent with the prevailing uniform construction of other federal statutes governing arbitration agreements in the setting of business transactions." Id. at 484, 109 S.Ct. at 1921, 104 L.Ed.2d at 536. In both *McMahon* and *Rodriguez,* Justices Stevens, Brennan, Marshall, and Blackmun dissented, asserting that the policy arguments presented were not sufficient to "overturn an interpretation of an Act of Congress that has been settled for many years." Id. at 487, 109 S.Ct. at 1923, 104 L.Ed.2d at 539.

In GILMER v. INTERSTATE/JOHNSON LANE CORP., 500 U.S. 20, 111 S.Ct. 1647, 114 L.Ed.2d 26 (1991), the Court held that claims arising under the Age Discrimination in Employment Act (ADEA) are subject to compulsory arbitration. The Court explained that the purpose of the Federal Arbitration Act "was to reverse the longstanding judicial hostility to arbitration agreements that had existed at English common law and had been adopted by American courts, and to place arbitration agreements upon the same footing as other contracts." Id. at 24, 111 S.Ct. at 1651, 114 L.Ed.2d at 36. It went on to reject the arguments that arbitration would fail to address the "important social policies" embodied in ADEA and would "undermine the role of the EEOC in enforcing the ADEA." After dismissing a number of arguments directed against the fairness of arbitration proceedings, the Court found that the arbitration agreement in *Gilmer* did not result from "unequal bargaining power between employers and employees." It reasoned that there was no indication "that Gilmer, an experienced businessman, was coerced or defrauded into agreeing to the arbitration clause." Id. at 29–30, 111 S.Ct. at 1656, 114 L.Ed.2d at 41–42.

Justices Stevens and Marshall dissented. They pointed to a provision contained in Section 1 of the Federal Arbitration Act: "Nothing herein contained shall apply to contracts of employment of * * * any * * * class of workers engaged in foreign or interstate commerce." This exclusion, they argued, "should be interpreted to cover any agreements by the employee to arbitrate disputes with the employer arising out of the employment relationship" even where—as was the situation in *Gilmer*—the arbitration agreement was not a part of the contract of employment. Id. at 32, 111 S.Ct. at 1659, 114 L.Ed.2d at 46. The dissenters also contended that compulsory arbitration "conflicts with the statutory purpose animating the ADEA." Id. at 33, 111 S.Ct. at 1660, 114 L.Ed.2d at 47.

In ALLIED–BRUCE TERMINIX COS. v. DOBSON, 513 U.S. 265, 115 S.Ct. 834, 130 L.Ed.2d 753 (1995), the Court held that a pre-dispute agreement to arbitrate trumped a state statute invalidating such agreements. The Court explained that the Federal Arbitration Act's grant of enforcement of written arbitration provisions in contracts "evidencing a transaction involving commerce" extends the Act's federal supremacy to the limits of Congress' Commerce Clause power. Id. at 270–72, 115 S.Ct. at 837–38, 130 L.Ed.2d at 756–57. The Court acknowledged that the statute's basic purpose, to put arbitration provisions on the same footing as a contract's other terms, was consistent with that broad interpretation of the Act's language. Id. at 272–274, 115 S.Ct. at 838–39, 130 L.Ed.2d at 758. Justices Thomas and Scalia dissented, reiterating the view advanced by Justices O'Connor and Rehnquist in dissent in *Southland* that Congress intended that the Act only be a procedural restraint in federal court.

———

PRIMA PAINT CORP. v. FLOOD & CONKLIN MANUFACTURING CO., 388 U.S. 395, 87 S.Ct. 1801, 18 L.Ed.2d 1270 (1967). Prima purchased Flood & Conklin's paint business and entered into an agreement with F & C pursuant to which the latter agreed to provide Prima with consulting services for a period of six years. The agreement contained a broad arbitration clause. Prima soon determined that F & C was insolvent, and it sued in federal District Court for rescission of the consulting agreement, alleging that it was fraudulently induced to enter into the agreement. F & C moved to stay the court action pending arbitration, contending that the issue presented—whether there was fraud in the inducement of the consulting agreement—was a question for the arbitrators and not for the District Court. The Supreme Court ruled that the issue was arbitrable:

> [W]e think that Congress has provided an explicit answer. That answer is to be found in § 4 of the [United States Arbitration] Act, which provides a remedy to a party seeking to compel compliance with an arbitration agreement. Under § 4, with respect to a matter within the jurisdiction of the federal courts save for the existence of an arbitration clause, the

federal court is instructed to order arbitration to proceed once it is satisfied that "the making of the agreement for arbitration or the failure to comply [with the arbitration agreement] is not in issue." Accordingly, if the claim is fraud in the inducement of the arbitration clause itself—an issue which goes to the "making" of the agreement to arbitrate—the federal court may proceed to adjudicate it. But the statutory language does not permit the federal court to consider claims of fraud in the inducement of the contract generally. * * * We hold, therefore, that in passing upon a § 3 application for a stay while the parties arbitrate, a federal court may consider only issues relating to the making and performance of the agreement to arbitrate. In so concluding, we not only honor the plain meaning of the statute but also the unmistakably clear congressional purpose that the arbitration procedure, when selected by the parties to a contract, be speedy and not subject to delay and obstruction in the courts.

* * *

In the present case no claim has been advanced by Prima Paint that F & C fraudulently induced it to enter into the agreement to arbitrate "[a]ny controversy or claim arising out of or relating to this Agreement, or the breach thereof." This contractual language is easily broad enough to encompass Prima Paint's claim that both execution and acceleration of the consulting agreement itself were procured by fraud. Indeed, no claim is made that Prima Paint ever intended that "legal" issues relating to the contract be excluded from arbitration, or that it was not entirely free so to contract. Federal courts are bound to apply rules enacted by Congress with respect to matters—here, a contract involving commerce—over which it has legislative power. The question which Prima Paint requested the District Court to adjudicate preliminarily to allowing arbitration to proceed is one not intended by Congress to delay the granting of a § 3 stay.

Id. at 403–07, 87 S.Ct. at 1806-07, 18 L.Ed.2d at 1277–79.

Notes and Questions

1. Different presumptions govern arbitrations in the commercial and labor-management contexts. In labor arbitrations, it is presumed that unless a matter specifically is excluded from the coverage of the arbitration clause, the parties are obligated to arbitrate their dispute under that provision. See United Steelworkers of America v. American Manufacturing Co., 363 U.S. 564, 80 S.Ct. 1343, 4 L.Ed.2d 1403 (1960); United Steelworkers of America v. Warrior & Gulf Nav. Co., 363 U.S. 574, 80 S.Ct. 1347, 4 L.Ed.2d 1409 (1960); and United Steelworkers of America v. Enterprise Wheel & Car Corp., 363 U.S. 593, 80 S.Ct. 1358, 4 L.Ed.2d 1424 (1960) (the *Steelworker Trilogy* cases). By contrast, in disputes arising under commercial contracts that do not contain a blanket provision, the clause is held not to apply unless it clearly covers the issue. See, e.g., Perkins & Will Partnership v. Syska Hennessy, 41 N.Y.2d 1045, 396 N.Y.S.2d 167, 364 N.E.2d 832 (1977). It should be noted that the source of the federal courts' authority to enforce labor arbitration awards is Section 301 of the Labor–Management Relations Act of 1947, 29 U.S.C. § 185, rather than the Federal Arbitration Act.

Why should there be a difference between labor arbitrations and commercial arbitrations concerning the presumption of arbitrability? Is it a sound reason for the presumption of arbitrability in labor arbitration to say that it is essential to preserve the vital continuing relationships between labor and management? Is the presumption of arbitrability in the labor field a modification of the conventional common-law principle that parties should be understood to waive causes of action in a lawsuit arising out of a given dispute unless they specifically reserve them? Why, then, should there be a presumption against arbitrability in the commercial context? Does the latter presumption manifest the system's willingness to preserve the parties' right to adjudicate disputes absent a specific agreement to the contrary? Conversely, is the presumption of arbitrability in the labor context a complement to the "no-strike" clause found in many collective-bargaining agreements?

2.   Do arbitrators have the power to award punitive damages? In FAHNESTOCK & CO. v. WALTMAN, 935 F.2d 512 (2d Cir.1991), the court vacated the punitive-damages portion of an arbitration award. Since the *Fahnestock* case was brought to the federal court as a diversity case, the court found that state law governed the propriety of a punitive-damage award by arbitrators, and the New York Court of Appeals has held that arbitrators have no power to award punitive damages, even if agreed upon by the parties. Moreover, the court found that the arbitration in *Fahnestock* was conducted pursuant to the rules of the New York Stock Exchange which, unlike those of the AAA, "have no provisions relating to remedy or relief." Judge Mahoney dissented, reasoning that "a state law which limits freedom of contract with respect to arbitration agreements covered by the FAA [Federal Arbitration Act] conflicts with the FAA and is preempted by it." Id. at 520.

In MASTROBUONO v. SHEARSON LEHMAN HUTTON, INC., 514 U.S. 52, 115 S.Ct. 1212, 131 L.Ed.2d 76 (1995), the Supreme Court upheld an arbitrator's award of $400,000 in punitive damages against Shearson Lehman Hutton, Inc. The parties had signed a securities agreement that stated the agreement was governed by New York law, and that any controversy arising out of the transaction be settled by arbitration pursuant to National Association of Securities Dealers (NASD) rules. New York law does not authorize arbitrators to award punitive damages, see Garrity v. Lyle Stuart, Inc., 40 N.Y.2d 354, 386 N.Y.S.2d 831, 353 N.E.2d 793 (1976), but the NASD rules appeared broad enough to contemplate a punitive damages remedy.

In upholding the award, the Court reasoned that, at most, the New York choice-of-law clause introduced "an ambiguity into an arbitration agreement that would otherwise allow punitive damage awards." Id. at 64, 115 S.Ct. at 1218, 131 L.Ed.2d at 82. The Court also added that, in interpreting an arbitration agreement covered by the FAA, courts should regard the federal policy favoring arbitration, and should construe ambiguous language against the party that drafted it (Shearson Lehman Hutton in this case).

Does *Mastrobuono* overrule *Fahnestock?* Does it matter that *Fahnestock* does not involve a choice of law provision? In its opinion in *Mastrobuono,* the Court acknowledged differing views at the circuit court level on whether choice-of-law provisions preclude arbitral awards of damages. Does *Mastrobuono* resolve this? See Dean Witter Reynolds v. Trimble, 166 Misc.2d 40, 631 N.Y.S.2d 215 (Sup.Ct. 1995) (stating that *Mastrobuono* only involved interpretation of an arbitration agreement, and state courts are not bound to follow the Supreme Court's interpretation).

3. Some have read the *Gilmer* decision as expanding the role of arbitration in deciding statutory discrimination claims. It is not clear, however, that the decision moves toward allowing binding arbitration in Title VII claims and other statutory discrimination claims not arising under the ADEA. The issue is further complicated by the Civil Rights Act of 1991, which promotes the use of binding arbitration in some contexts, but whose legislative history seems to suggest the Act precludes compulsory arbitration of Title VII claims. For further discussion, see, e.g., Adams, *Compulsory Arbitration of Discrimination Claims and the Civil Rights Act of 1991: Encouraged or Proscribed?*, 44 Wayne L. Rev. 1619 (1999); McMillian, *Collective Bargaining Agreements, Mandatory Arbitration and Title VII: Varner v. National Super Markets, Inc.*, 32 Ga. L. Rev. 287 (1997); Sternlight, *Panacea or Corporate Tool?: Debunking the Supreme Court's Preference for Binding Arbitration*, 74 Wash. U. L.Q. 637 (1996).

4. The expansion of international trade and commercial transactions in the past fifty years has created a need for private international commercial dispute resolution. Many commercial parties are uncomfortable adjudicating disputes in foreign court systems because they are unfamiliar with the procedures and law of foreign forums and fear favoritism to nationals. The demand for mechanisms for private commercial dispute resolution has led to the development of international commercial arbitration rules (such as the International Chamber of Commerce (ICC) Rules). These are applied in international arbitration centers around the world. Using these accepted rules and forums, private parties are able to arbitrate and resolve their commercial disputes without submitting the dispute to a foreign forum. Given these resources, why might parties still prefer to resolve their dispute in court? Should an international commercial arbitration decision be enforceable in any forum in the world?

d. Enforcement

As a general rule, once the arbitrator has issued his award and decision, the parties have a period of time during which they can apply to modify or correct the award. Under the New York statute, for example, the parties have twenty days in which to apply to the arbitrator to modify or correct the award. N.Y.C.P.L.R. § 7509. And, under both the Federal Arbitration Act and the New York statute, the parties have three months in which to apply to a court to modify or to correct or even to vacate the award. 9 U.S.C. § 12; N.Y.C.P.L.R. § 7511(a).

Once the award has been issued (and assuming it is not modified, corrected, or vacated), it may be submitted to the relevant court for confirmation and entry as if it were a judgment of that court. 9 U.S.C. § 9; N.Y.C.P.L.R. § 7510. Under both the federal and New York statutes, the award must be submitted within one year after its delivery by the arbitrator to the applying party. The nonapplying party may choose either to accept the award (and, thus, not to challenge the application) or to challenge the application. In New York, a failure to move to vacate or modify the award within the three months prescribed for that procedure does not deprive the nonapplying party of any recognized ground to oppose a motion to confirm the award. See State Farm Mutual Automobile Ins. Co. v. Fireman's Fund Ins. Co., 121 A.D.2d 529, 504 N.Y.S.2d 24 (2d Dep't 1986).

Both statutes give judges the discretion to order re-opening of the arbitration, although the New York statute, N.Y.C.P.L.R. § 7511(d), also permits the judge to order an entirely new arbitration proceeding.

———

SPRINZEN v. NOMBERG, 46 N.Y.2d 623, 415 N.Y.S.2d 974, 389 N.E.2d 456 (1979). Respondent was employed as a business agent by the petitioner, a labor organization, for service in New Jersey, Connecticut, and Pennsylvania. The respondent agreed to a restrictive covenant providing that, for five years after the termination of his employment with the petitioner, he would refrain from organizing workers within New York, New Jersey, Pennsylvania, and Connecticut. The respondent also agreed to submit all complaints and disputes whatsoever of whatever kind or nature to arbitration.

After three years, the respondent changed jobs and accepted a position with another union as its business representative for an area including Manhattan and Staten Island. The petitioner demanded arbitration, seeking to enjoin the respondent from continuing his new employment. The respondent initially submitted to arbitration but, after unsuccessfully challenging the partiality of the arbitrator (who had been named by the original agreement), the respondent refused to participate in the proceedings. The arbitrator heard the petitioner's evidence and ruled for the petitioner. The New York Supreme Court, Special Term, affirmed the award, and the respondent appealed. The Appellate Division reversed, holding that the "arbitration award under the circumstances of this case [is] in contravention of public policy." The New York Court of Appeals, reversing the Appellate Division and reinstating the award, discussed the evolving nature of public policy:

> In furtherance of the laudable purposes served by permitting consenting parties to submit controversies to arbitration, the law has adopted a policy of noninterference, with few exceptions, in this mode of dispute resolution. Quite simply, it can be said that the arbitrator is not bound to abide by, absent a contrary provision in the arbitration agreement, those principles of substantive law or rules of procedure which govern the traditional litigation process. * * * An arbitrator's paramount responsibility is to reach an equitable result, and the courts will not assume the role of overseers to mold the award to conform to their sense of justice. Thus, an arbitrator's award will not be vacated for errors of law and fact committed by the arbitrator * * * and "[e]ven where the arbitrator states an intention to apply a law, and then misapplies it, the award will not be set aside" * * *.

> Despite this policy of according an arbitrator seemingly unfettered discretion in matters submitted to him by the consent of the parties, it is the established law in this State that an award which is violative of public policy will not be permitted to stand. * * * The courts, however, must exercise due restraint in this regard, for the preservation of the arbitration process and the policy of allowing parties to choose a nonjudicial forum, embedded in freedom to contract principles, must not be disturbed by courts, acting under the guise of public policy, wishing to decide the dispute on its merits, for arguably every controversy has at its core some

issue requiring the application, or weighing, of policy considerations. Thus, there are now but a few matters of concern which have been recognized as so intertwined with overriding public policy considerations as to either place them beyond the bounds of the arbitration process itself or mandate the vacatur of awards which do violence to the principles upon which such matters rest. * * *

* * *

While it is true that considerations of public policy militate against the enforcement of restrictive covenants of future employment * * *, these covenants are not per se unenforceable as being null and void. * * * Each case turns upon its own distinct facts. If the restrictive covenant is found, under all the circumstances, to be "reasonable in time and area, necessary to protect the employer's legitimate interests, not harmful to the general public and not unreasonably burdensome to the employee," it will be subject to specific enforcement. * * *

Here, the parties, by reason of a broad arbitration clause contained in their signed agreement, submitted the issue of the enforceability of the restrictive covenant to arbitration, clearly a proper forum for the resolution of their dispute in this private matter. By so doing, the parties placed upon the arbitrator, not the courts, the responsibility of passing upon the merits of their controversy with the expectation that a just, yet practical, result would be reached. While there may be some doubt whether we would have enforced the restrictive covenant now before us had this dispute been adjudicated in the courts, such consideration is irrelevant to the disposition of this case, for courts will not second-guess the factual findings or the legal conclusions of the arbitrator. The utility of the arbitration process itself is derived from its autonomy, and courts must honor the choice of the parties to have their controversy decided within this framework. Insofar as public policy considerations do not absolutely preclude the enforcement of restrictive covenants of future employment for a reasonable period of time or related business concerns, we conclude that the arbitrator had the power to pass upon the issue of both the reasonableness and the necessity of the restrictions imposed upon the employee. Having thus concluded, and acknowledging the wide latitude afforded arbitrators in formulating just relief, the award rendered should not now be disturbed.

Id. at 629–32, 415 N.Y.S.2d at 976–79, 389 N.E.2d at 458–60.

Notes and Questions

1. Arbitrators do not receive any in-depth professional training or briefing on their task:

> * * * The result is a dearth of written material for training new arbitrators, upgrading the skills of practicing arbitrators, or showing the parties how arbitrators think. Experienced arbitrators may reflect on how their individual cases fit into the larger patterns of conflict resolution. Unfortunately, too few take the time, or are willing to make the time, to share these thoughts with others. Some have written papers or volumes on labor relations subjects, often

intended for a broader audience than those who actually participate in arbitrations. Few arbitrators have had any opportunity to write informally for other arbitrators or for practitioners on the substantive or procedural issues one confronts in daily practice.

Zack, *Preface*, in *Arbitration in Practice* v–vi (Zack ed. 1984). Given that arbitrators are afforded such broad discretion and that, as arbitrator Edgar A. Jones, Jr., has pointed out, "[t]he number of arbitrator's awards challenged in court is less than two hundred out of more than twenty-five thousand (perhaps as many as forty thousand) awards issued each year," Jones, *Problems of Procedure and Evidence*, in *Arbitration in Practice* 49 (Zack ed. 1984), is it not troubling that arbitrators' awards can be challenged only on the relatively narrow grounds set forth in *Sprinzen?*

2. Courts will rule certain contracts void as against public policy and refuse to enforce them. Is the *Sprinzen* court saying that courts will rule certain arbitration awards void as against public policy and refuse to enforce them? Does this opinion imply that parties may order their own affairs except in the narrowly defined context in which the legislature has determined that they cannot or should not determine their affairs? How is this legislative power limited in the arbitration context? Is it merely a matter of substantive contract law?

3. In reaching her decision, the arbitrator is not required to apply rules of decision derived from federal or state statutes, common-law rules, or even rules derived from the decisions of other arbitrators, although she may draw on such sources for guidance in reaching a decision. It has become common practice for parties to arbitration proceedings to circulate arbitration awards and decisions. Considering the legal system's reluctance to disturb arbitration awards and decisions except in certain narrowly defined circumstances, is this use of arbitration awards and decisions as nonbinding precedent sound? Should later arbitrators depend on awards and decisions that may have been flawed but whose flaws were not of sufficient dimension or significance to support a challenge in court?

4. How much preclusive effect should be given to an arbitrator's award in subsequent litigation? As to claim preclusion, it seems safe to infer that most agreements to submit disputes to arbitration contemplate that the award will merge or bar all of the claims and defenses involved. Unless the express terms of the agreement or the peculiar custom of a trade dictate otherwise therefore, subsequent judicial proceedings on the same claim or defenses ordinarily should be precluded. But see Wolf v. Gruntal & Co., 45 F.3d 524 (1st Cir.1995) (holding arbitration decision does not preclude claims over which that arbitrator has no jurisdiction). Special statutory schemes may provide judicial remedies that are intended to supplement arbitration without regard to the intent of the parties. Thus, the Supreme Court has ruled that grievance arbitration under a collective-bargaining contract does not preclude an employment-discrimination claim under Title VII of the Civil Rights Act of 1964; at most, the findings of the arbitrator can be admitted in evidence with such weight as the court may find appropriate. Alexander v. Gardner–Denver Co., 415 U.S. 36, 94 S.Ct. 1011, 39 L.Ed.2d 147 (1974). Recall the questions the *Gilmer* decision raised in the context of statutory discrimination claims. Could overriding public policies make some disputes unfit for arbitration? Should the courts or the legislature decide what these public policies might be?

As to issue preclusion, one commentator has concluded that most courts "accord collateral estoppel to arbitral findings on a case-by-case basis, depending on the magnitude of the differences between the litigation and a given arbitration." Motomura, *Arbitration and Collateral Estoppel: Using Preclusion to Shape Procedural Choices*, 63 Tulane L. Rev. 29 (1988). What considerations might shape a decision to grant issue-preclusive effect to arbitral awards and decisions? What about the fact that many arbitral awards are unwritten? To what extent might issue preclusion be necessary to support the values of stability, repose, and reliance generated by an arbitrator's award?

Many courts have given issue-preclusive effect to an arbitrator's award. See, e.g., Greenblatt v. Drexel Burnham Lambert, Inc., 763 F.2d 1352 (11th Cir.1985); Falgren v. State Board of Teaching, 545 N.W.2d 901 (Minn.1996). On the other hand, in McDonald v. City of West Branch, 466 U.S. 284, 104 S.Ct. 1799, 80 L.Ed.2d 302 (1984), the Supreme Court held that, in light of the important federal statutory and constitutional rights that a 42 U.S.C. § 1983 action is designed to safeguard, a federal court could not bar a civil-rights action brought under that statute by affording res judicata or collateral estoppel effect to an award in an arbitration proceeding brought pursuant to the terms of a collective-bargaining agreement.

Index

References are to pages

†